THE BRITISH ANTIQUE DEALERS' ASSOCIATION

BADA's Rutland Gate headquarters will provide a variety of information to collectors and enthusiasts. These include:
- Guidelines on buying and selling antiques
- Advice on BADA experts to consult
- The BADA Guarantee and Arbitration Service
- The BADA Assessment Service
- How to become a Friend of the BADA Trust (double membership £25; single membership £15)
- Lists of antiques fairs to visit

A list of members is sent free on request to:
The British Antique Dealers' Association, 20 Rutland Gate, London SW7 1BD
Telephone: 071-589 4128; Fax: 071-581 9083

P. A. Oxley
Antique Clocks & Barometers

The leading U.K. dealer in quality restored antique longcase clocks

Very large selection always available

Prices from £2,000 to £30,000

For further details see page 551

THE OLD RECTORY • CHERHILL • NR. CALNE • WILTSHIRE SN11 8UX
TEL: 0249 812742 FAX: 0249 821285

guide to THE ANTIQUE SHOPS of BRITAIN
1994

1994 Edition

compiled by Carol Adams

FRONT COVER: *A pair of ebony elephants, a nest of ebony/ivory inlaid tables and real red roses.*

© Copyright 1993
Antique Collectors' Club Ltd.
World Copyright reserved
ISBN 1 85149 167 8

British Library CIP Data
Guide to the antique shops of Britain.
- 1994
  (June 1993-June 1994)
  1. Great Britain. Antiques trades:
  Directories - Serials
  I. Antique Collectors' Club
  380.1'457451'02541

No part of this publication may be reproduced, stored in a retrieval system, or transmitted in any form or by any means, electronic, mechanical, photocopying, recording or otherwise plagiarised without the prior written permission of the Antique Collectors' Club Ltd., of 5 Church Street, Woodbridge, Suffolk, England.

While every reasonable care has been exercised in compilation of information contained in this Guide, neither the Editors nor The Antique Collectors' Club Ltd., or any servants of the Company accept any liability for loss, damage or expense incurred by reliance placed on the information contained in this book or through omissions or incorrect entries howsoever incurred.

Printed in England by Antique Collectors' Club Ltd., Woodbridge, Suffolk.
Telephone: (0394) 385501

IONA ANTIQUES

19th Century English Animal Paintings

A prize middle white sow, signed and dated J. Dalby 1844.
Oil on canvas. 19in. x 24in., 48cm x 61cm

Illustrated Catalogue available

IONA ANTIQUES
PO BOX 285 LONDON W8 6HZ ENGLAND

TEL: 071-602 1193   FAX: 071-371 2843

LAPADA

LONDON AND PROVINCIAL ANTIQUE DEALERS' ASSOCIATION

The sign of commitment to a strict Code of Practice

The golden LAPADA chandelier symbol in a dealer's window indicates membership of an internationally recognised association with demanding requirements in respect of knowledge and integrity. All members have signed a commitment to a strict Code of Practice drawn up in consultation with the Office of Fair Trading, and the LAPADA Antique Buyers' Charter offers independently scrutinised conciliation should a dispute arise with a member.

With hundreds of member dealers throughout the UK, including specialists in virtually every period and style from antiquities to art deco, as well as those with a general stock of antiques, quantity shipping goods, restorers and specialist fine art shippers, LAPADA is the largest UK trade association in the field.

Whatever your requirements, LAPADA's free computerised information service is available to put you in touch with appropriate members in your part of the country.

Leaflet, lists of members and further information available free from:

**The London and Provincial Antique Dealers' Association
Suite 2.14,
535 Kings Road
Chelsea, London SW10 0SZ**

**Telephone: 071-823 3511
Facsimile: 071-823 3522**

Our only rival.

Gander & White have only one rival. The walnut. Nature has created in the walnut, the perfect model for individual high-quality packaging. Each walnut shell provides tailor-made protection for its contents; in the same way we create unique individual packing for every work of art entrusted to our care.

Specialised packing and shipping of antiques and works of art

Groupage container services by air and sea to and from North America

Weekly door-to-door road groupage services to major European cities

Household removals • High security storage

Export and Import Custom Services including MIBS

LONDON – NEW YORK – PARIS

PACKERS & SHIPPERS

Gander & White Shipping Ltd., 21 Lillie Road, London SW6 1UE.
Tel: 071 381 0571. Fax: 071 381 5428

New Pound, Wisborough Green, Billingshurst, West Sussex RH14 0AY
Tel: 0403 700044 Fax: 0403 700814

Gander & White Inc., 33-31 Greenpoint Avenue, Long Island City, N.Y. 11101
Tel: 718 784 8444 Fax: 718 784 9337

Gander & White Shipping Sarl, 24 Rue Licien Sampaix 75010, Paris
Tel: 331 4202 1892 Fax: 331 4206 3331

HAMILTON ANTIQUES

5 Church Street
Woodbridge
Suffolk
telephone
(0394) 387222

Always a good selection of
18th, 19th and 20th century good
quality furniture at reasonable prices

See editorial for opening hours

¾ hour from Harwich
½ hour from Felixstowe

COTSWOLD ANTIQUE DEALERS' ASSOCIATION

A wealth of Antiques in the heart of England

from a Brass in Northleach Church

Please write to the Secretary
for a free brochure.

FOR ASSISTANCE WITH BUYING, SHIPPING, ACCOMMODATION DURING YOUR VISIT, WRITE TO:

Secretary, CADA,
Barcheston Manor,
Shipston-on-Stour, Warwickshire CV36 5AY
Telephone (0608) 661268

Thames Valley Antique Dealers Association

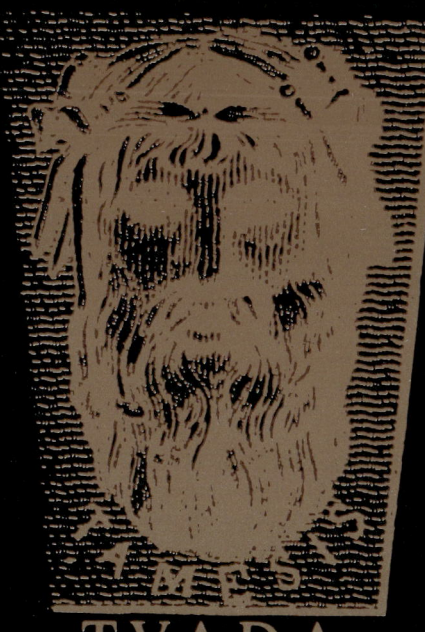

T.V.A.D.A.

Over 30 Dealers with wide ranging stocks

For further details, please contact:
The Secretary,
6, High Street,
Wallingford,
Oxon, OX10 0BP
Tel: (0491) 834393

Travel to the States with a Sophisticated Companion

" . . . the ultimate American guide to antique shops."
Maine Antique Digest

*S*loan's Green Guide leads you straight to 2500 of the best antiques shops in six New England states - enabling you to buy good antiques at good prices. With details for five antiques shopping tours, a twelve month antiques show calendar, a geographic list of over 200 multiple dealer shops, profiles of 30 outstanding collections on public view and QuickCodes giving dealer specialties, it's the Collector's Choice.

$25 p.p. by air $20 by sea -
MasterCard/VISA - Ring (617) 723-3001

The Antique Press, 9 Brimmer Street,
Boston MA 02108-1001 USA

H.W. KEIL LTD

Telephone
BROADWAY
0386 852408

TUDOR HOUSE
BROADWAY
WORCESTERSHIRE

Member of the
British Antique
Dealers'
Association

17th & 18th Century Furniture · Works of Art

Showing interesting pieces from our various rooms where can be seen a wide selection of 17th, 18th and early 19th century periods

Originators of the well known Keil's dark and light wax polish, available in 10 oz and 2 lb sizes

In association with H.W. Keil (Cheltenham) Ltd., 129-131 The Promenade, Cheltenham.

JACQUELINE OOSTHUIZEN

Mon to Fri 10-6
23 Cale Street
(Chelsea Green)
off Sydney Street
London SW3

Wed & Sat 8-4
1st Floor - Upstairs
Georgian Village
Camden Passage
London N1

Superb Selection STAFFORDSHIRE
Figures, Animals, Cottages, Toby Jugs
also ANTIQUE & ESTATE JEWELLERY

Weekends by appointment

Phones: 071-352 6071   071-376 3852   071-226 5393
Answering Service 081-528 9001   pager No. 806930

Ripley Antiques
HEATHER DENHAM

Specialising in 18th and 19th Century Furniture and Decorative Items for Trade and Export

67 High Street, Ripley, Surrey. Telephone Guildford (0483) 224981
2 mins. from Junction 10 on the M25 and 30 mins. from London on the A3

RANDOLPH

97-99 HIGH STREET
HADLEIGH, SUFFOLK IP7 5EJ
TEL: (0473) 823789

Dealers in Antique Furniture & Accessories

ESTABLISHED IN 1921

A small Queen Anne walnut kneehole desk with pull-out centre cupboard and retaining the original handles. English. Circa 1710.
Height 28 $^{3}/_{4}$" Width 30 $^{3}/_{4}$" Depth 19 $^{3}/_{4}$"

PICTON HOUSE

ANTIQUES • WORKS OF ART • INTERIOR DESIGN

Picton House has been associated with Antiques and Fine Art for over 30 years

OPEN DAILY 9.30AM-5.30PM
OR BY APPOINTMENT
CLOSED SUNDAYS

A fine George III mahogany library breakfront secretaire bookcase
height 8' 7" x width 8' 3" x depth 2' 0"

High Street, Broadway, Worcestershire WR12 7DT Tel. (0386) 853807 Fax. (0386) 858199

Witney Antiques

L.S.A. & C.J. Jarrett

96-100 CORN STREET, WITNEY, OXFORDSHIRE
Tel: 0993 703902. Fax: 0993 779852

An outstanding stock of 17th, 18th and early 19th century furniture, clocks and works of art.

Derek Roberts

25 Shipbourne Road, Tonbridge, Kent. TN10 3DN
Tel. (0732) 358986. Fax (0732) 770637

We have one of the finest and most extensive stocks of clocks available anywhere. Why not come and see us? We are 30 miles South of London, 40 minutes by train from Charing Cross. Gatwick is $\frac{1}{2}$ hr. and Heathrow 1 hr. Alternatively please phone and see if we have what you are seeking. If not we will try and find it for you. Items stocked include longase, bracket, wall, skeleton, musical, mystery and novelty clocks, regulators, chronometers, music boxes and barometers.

Books written by and available from us: British Skeleton Clocks, £39.50; Continental and American Skeleton Clocks, £60; British Longcase Clocks, £75; Collectors Guide to Clocks, £12.95. p. & p. UK £4. Overseas £5.

APOLLO ANTIQUES LTD

ANTIQUE &
DECORATIVE
ENGLISH &
CONTINENTAL
FURNITURE
SUITABLE FOR
MOST MARKETS

*The Saltisford
Warwick, CV34 4TD
Tel: 0926 494746
Fax: 0926 401477*

ARTHUR BRETT AND SONS LIMITED

Dealers in Antique Furniture
42 St. Giles Street, NORWICH, NR2 1LW
Telephone: Norwich 628171 (STD 0603) Fax: 0603 630245

**Open Monday-Friday 9.30-5.00
Saturday 10.00-4.00**

*Rare George II walnut veneered Admiral's
kneehole desk. Circa 1750.
Height 41 1/2", Width 43", Depth 28"*

The Antique Print Shop

Fine Watercolours, Old Prints and Maps

**11 Middle Row • East Grinstead
West Sussex RH19 3AX
Telephone: (0342) 410501
Facsimile 0342 322149**

Open: Mondays to Saturdays 9.30-6

A very wide selection of antique prints:

Topography, Flowers, Animals, Birds, Marine, Military, Architectural, Sporting, Sports, Childrens, Caricatures, etc.

English County and Foreign Maps a Speciality

Rare Maps for the collector. Decorative Prints.

Early English Watercolours & Drawings.

Full Framing and Restoration Service immediately available.

An Antique Collectors' Club Title

The Dictionary of Worcester Porcelain Volume I 1751-1851
by John Sandon

With 600+ dictionary entries, an historical survey, an illustrated section on marks, detailed information on recent excavations at the Worcester factory, contemporary accounts of visits to factories and an extensive bibliography, this is the definitive work. The author is director of ceramics at Phillips auctioneers, London, and regularly appears on the *Antiques Roadshow*.

**ISBN 1 85149 156 2
400pp, 450 b & w illus, 100 colour
£45.00**

Available from:
Antique Collectors' Club
5 Church Street, Woodbridge
Suffolk IP12 1DS
Tel: (0394) 385501 Fax: (0394) 384434

or Market Street Industrial Park
Wappingers' Falls, New York 12590, USA
Tel: 914 297 0003 Fax: 914 297 0068

Time moves on ...

With our rare combination of up-to-the minute techniques and traditional craftsmanship, you can trust Trans Euro to deliver the most delicate items safely and on time. Many of Britain's major antique and fine art dealers already do.

However far the destination, or how fragile the shipment, contact Trans Euro and we'll make sure everything goes like clockwork.

DRURY WAY, BRENT PARK, LONDON NW10 0JN. TEL: 081-784 0100

PARIS   LONDON   ABERDEEN

J. Green & Son
Antiques

1 Coppice Lane,
Queniborough, Leicester
Telephone Leicester 606682

Antique Collectors' Club Titles

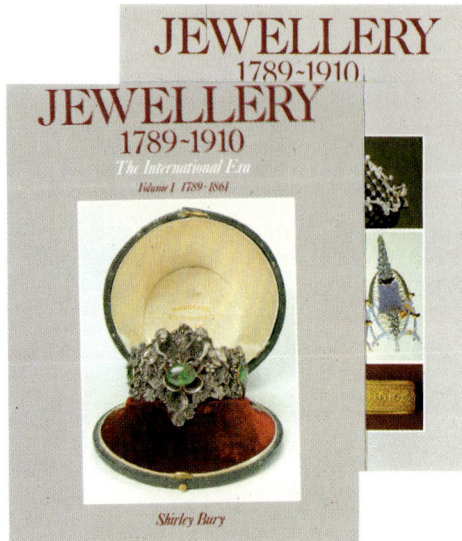

**Jewellery 1780-1910
The International Era - 2 vols**
by Shirley Bury F.S.A.
A detailed and beautifully illustrated work by the former Keeper of Metalwork at the Victoria and Albert Museum. The book details the design, manufacture, fashion and history of every kind of jewellery. Covers the development of fashions, materials and techniques of 19th century jewellery. The historical background of this important era is examined, from popular everyday jewellery to that worn by Royalty and the nobility.
**Vol. I 1789-1861, 472pp, 231 b & w illus, 104 col, ISBN 1 85149 148 1
Vol.II 1862-1910, 424pp, 191 b & w illus, 110 col, ISBN 1 85149 149 X
£47.50 per volume £95.00 the set**

The Price Guide to Jewellery 3000BC-1950AD
by Michael Poynder
Describes and illustrates hundreds of examples of the type of jewellery that is popular with buyers world-wide. The prices are constantly being updated so that the book is an essential guide to those anxious to buy.
**388pp, 340 b & w illus, 44 col
ISBN 0 902028 50 2, £29.95**

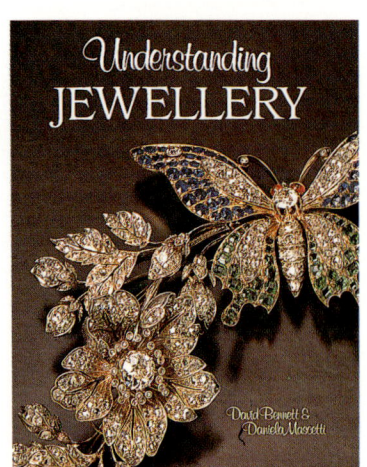

Understanding Jewellery *by David Bennett and Daniela Mascetti*
Written by two leading Sotheby's experts, a practical book covering the jewellery of the last 200 years for those interested in buying. Fashions in jewellery are described with examples of a range of fakes, alterations, repairs and comparisons of varying degrees of quality. Features a concise guide to gem stones.
**388pp, 30 b & w illus, 738 col illus,
ISBN 1 85149 075 2, £35.00**

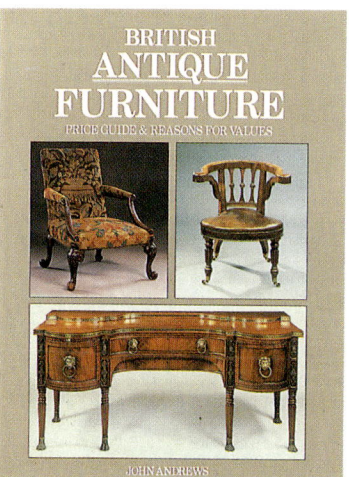

Victorian and Edwardian Furniture Price Guide and Reasons for Values
by John Andrews
In this major revision of his highly acclaimed Price Guide to Victorian, Edwardian and 1920s Furniture, John Andrews has written a thorough, logical and easily understandable guide to what is the most popular period in British antique furniture today.
**ISBN 1 85149 118 X, 300pp
1,000 b & w illus, 100 col illus, £29.95**

British Antique Furniture: Price Guide and Reasons for Values
by John Andrews
For the last twenty years this book has in its various editions outsold all other books on British antique furniture simply because it is unique in explaining what to look for when assessing the value of antique pieces. This classic guide consists of some 1,200 photographs specially selected by the experienced author to show just how and why values vary. In this third edition, the colour plates have been added to illustrate the huge financial importance of patination and colour, something which has never before been explained and illustrated.
**ISBN 1 85149 090 6, 392pp
1,150 b & w illus, 106 col illus, £35.00**

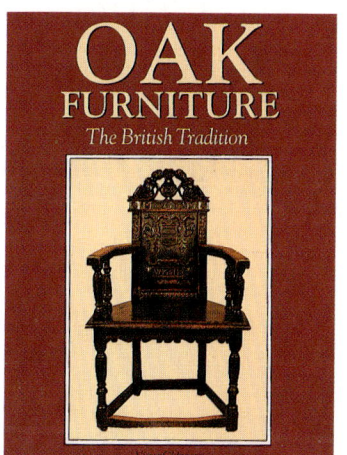

Available from:
Antique Collectors' Club, 5 Church Street
Woodbridge, Suffolk IP12 1DS
Tel: (0394) 385501 Fax: (0394) 384434

or Market Street Industrial Park
Wappingers' Falls, New York 12590, USA
Tel: 914 297 0003 Fax: 914 297 0068

Oak Furniture - The British Tradition *by Victor Chinnery*
The only serious book on oak in print, this important and deeply researched work examines regional influences on furniture design, construction and other methods of dating, and has a useful pictorial index arranged chronologically. **ISBN 1 85149 013 2, 620pp, 2,000 b & w illus, 22 col illus, £49.50**

Christopher Bangs

Early metalware and metalwork and works of art

By Appointment Only
P.O. Box 662, London SW11 3DG
Telephone: 071-223 5676 Fax: 071-223 4933 Mobile: 0836 333532

Contents

	Page
Introduction	24
Some Questions and Answers about this Book	25
How to use this Guide	26
Abbreviations in entries	27
London	30
Avon - Yorkshire	140
Channel Islands	592
Northern Ireland	596
Scotland	600
Wales	630
Packers and Shippers	644
Auctioneers	658
Services	676
Town and Village alphabetical list	686
Dealers, Shops and Galleries index	695
Antiques Centres and Markets Dealers' index	758
Specialist Dealers	767
Stop Press	816

Acknowledgements

Our main sources of information are still trade magazines, papers, catalogues and so on, but we would like to thank the increasing number of antique dealers, private collectors and members of the Antique Collectors' Club who provide much of our information about new shops and passing on comments which go to make our information complete. Without this assistance our job would be more difficult.

We would also like to thank dealers who supported us with advertising and those who sent in information about their own, as well as other, establishments. Each year we include a form at the end of the Guide which dealers can use to update details about their own business. In anticipation of next year's Guide, we are grateful to those dealers who make use of this form.

Finally, thanks must go to the editorial team of The Guide to the Antique Shops of Britain, which carries out the mammoth task of compiling and indexing the entries.

C.A.

Editor **Carol Adams**
Advertisement Sales **Jean Johnson**
Editorial Team **Judith Neal Diana Dutson**

Introduction

This is the 22nd edition of the **Guide to the Antique Shops of Britain** which is universally accepted as *the* guide for anybody who wishes to buy antiques in Britain.

This year we have listed nearly 7,000 establishments, plus the last minute entries included in the Stop Press section. Each of the entries is checked annually, which as the reader will readily understand is a colossal task. Increasingly, serious dealers recognise the importance of the Guide and send us very detailed information without having to be reminded that it is due. At the other end of the scale we send hundreds of reminders and make telephone calls, together costing thousands of pounds, to make sure that shops are still there. It is indicative of the high regard in which the Guide is held that dealers are kind enough to tell us about the shops that have opened or closed in their locality and we are most grateful for this unsolicited help.

For the price of a few gallons of petrol, the risk of visiting non-existent shops is dramatically reduced but perhaps more importantly, time spent in fruitless journeys may be saved. The provision of motorways is very poor by international standards and many foreign visitors tend to underestimate how long it will take to make a visit.

We would stress that quantity of entries is meaningless without detail and here we pride ourselves that the range of information is more detailed and up-to-date than has been available elsewhere. Indeed, much of it is unique giving not only obvious facts - name of proprietor, address, telephone number, opening hours, stock, but also an indication of size of showrooms and price ranges. It is felt that these, although only general, give an indication of the quantity and quality of stock likely to be seen, facts which may well influence a prospective buyer's decision whether to visit a shop or not - in fact a time saver.

Additional information gives details of dealers' trade association memberships, the date the shop was established, and location and parking guidance plus street maps for those towns with over 25 entries. None of these points are necessarily decisive in themselves but, in conjunction with other details, valuable aids which build up a useful picture of the sort of establishment you are likely to find should you decide to visit. However, we strongly recommend that if you know the sort of pieces you want to buy, telephone first and plan the trip accordingly. Dealers questioned this way are normally very honest about their stock.

We start preparing the next Guide in early 1994 and so we should be grateful if dealers would let us know of any changes in their businesses - alterations in type of stock, price range, opening hours are especially important; to assist with this a form appears at the back of the Guide. Notes of changes to other establishments in the area would also be an enormous help.

We are always interested to receive your views about the Guide. How it can be improved or changes that you feel can be made. So please write if you feel that you have something to contribute.

Some Questions and Answers about this Book

You claim that this Guide is far and away the best. Why?
At the time of going to press the Guide lists more antique shops, galleries, warehouses and other antique businesses than are listed in any other publication. The individual entries are detailed, listing items such as stock - often in considerable depth, how to find the shop - which is often not easy, hours of business, and other information not normally available.

But surely any directory must contain some out-of-date entries?
Yes, but to make sure entries are as up to date as possible, each one is checked every year as near publication as possible. And because the Guide to the Antique Shops of Britain is accepted by dealers and collectors alike as *the* directory, over 75 per cent of dealers up date or confirm their annual entry. Where there is an element of doubt, the editorial team check, if need be, by telephone. We have a four figure editorial telephone bill!

Normally a £14.50 book only has 150 to 200 pages. This one has over 900; why is it so cheap?
Dealers like the Guide and, realising that buyers find it essential, give their active support by advertising. Without advertising revenue each copy would cost £30.00.

I bought a copy last year; do I really need to buy this new edition?
Obviously some businesses stay exactly as they are each year. But, perhaps surprisingly, well over half the entries in this edition have been changed in some respect since the last edition. Some dealers go into different types of antiques, often because they cannot get enough of the items in which they previously specialised. Others, approaching retirement, curtail their business hours. Locations and proprietors change. All this is in addition to those who set up new businesses, while others give up or retire. It is a constantly changing scene.

How to use this Guide

The Guide is set out under six main headings: London, England, Channel Islands, Northern Ireland, Scotland and Wales. Counties are listed alphabetically (with the exception of Scotland); within counties there is a listing of towns and within the towns an index of shops, or galleries. London is divided into postal districts. In Scotland, as the majority of shops are concentrated in the central part and some counties have very few, we felt it would be easier for users of the Guide if towns were listed in alphabetical order rather than separated into their respective counties.

To make route planning easier, there is a map at the beginning of each county, coded to show the number of antique shops in any one town, city or village. The roads indicated on the map are only a broad intimation of the routes available and it is advisable to use an up-to-date road map showing the latest improvements in the road system.

Apart from the six main headings mentioned above, there are further helpful lists; an alphabetical list of towns indicating the counties in which they appear for those not familiar with the location of towns within counties, e.g. Woodbridge is shown in the county of Suffolk. One therefore turns to the Suffolk section to look up Woodbridge. This listing is a valuable aid to the overseas visitor. The second is particularly important to British collectors and dealers, giving an alphabetical list of the name of every shop, proprietor and company director known to be connected with the antique shop or gallery. Thus, if A. Bloggs and B. Brown own an antique shop called Castle Antiques, there will be entries included under Bloggs, A., Brown, B. and Castle Antiques. Listings of specialist dealers, auctioneers, and shippers and packers are also included.

One point that collectors and dealers alike constantly seem to miss is that use of the telephone offers great savings of time and money. Nearly all dealers have to make unscheduled calls during opening hours and the 'back in 5 minutes' notice which has been in the window of a small shop for 20 minutes is a cause of great irritation to the potential buyer. If you have to be a hundred miles along the road in two hours, but there is something in the back of the shop which looks interesting, then the decision to wait or not to wait is even more agonising. A telephone call in advance can forestall such frustrations. When you telephone, it is usually quite acceptable to describe what you are looking for in terms of Antique Collectors' Club books. Increasingly one sees advertisements referring to page numbers. Most dealers have at least some of the books and use them as a basis for communicating information.

All but a handful of dealers are factual and reasonably accurate in describing their stock to us, but there are probably one or two who insist on listing their stock on the basis of what they would like to have, rather than as it is. Information on such dealers from those who use the Guide is greatly appreciated as are any suggestions and ideas; indeed it has been the kindness of so many collectors and dealers who take the trouble to drop us a postcard or telephone (0394) 385501 and tell us about misleading entries or closures that has helped us to ensure that the Guide has become Britain's premier listing of antique shops and galleries.

Abbreviations in entries

In order to cut the bulk of this book as much as possible without curtailing the amount of information, we have made some very simple contractions in the entries.

BADA and LAPADA: Members are indicated by using a bold type face.

EST: Shows the year in which the shop was established or the number of years the dealer or firm has been trading.

CL: Days when the business is normally closed. It follows the hours of opening. In some small businesses these may prove erratic, as it is often necessary for the dealer to go out at short notice. Unless otherwise stated shops are closed on Sundays. If making a long journey, it is advisable to telephone and make an appointment.

SIZE: A guide to the size of the showrooms is given to indicate the quantity of stock likely to be seen. Small is under 600 sq. ft. (60 sq. metres), medium between 600 and 1,500 sq. ft. (60 and 150 sq. metres) and large over 1,500 sq. ft. (150 sq. metres).

STOCK: Dealers are asked to list their stock in order of importance, so that the items listed can be expected to comprise a significant part of the stock. The price range is of very general application and is designed to give some idea to prospective buyers of the type of items to be seen. In an age of inflation the price levels quoted will often be too low, but nevertheless it is felt that they act as a useful general indication of the level of quality. Not stocked items are indicated after those which are stocked. The items listed are not normally to be found in this shop. Advertisements often give extra information on the size of showrooms, etc.

LOC: Location of shop. This is a description given by the owner designed to help the would-be caller. Road numbers in the entries are not necessarily shown on the county maps of the Guide, which are merely general aids to direction.

PARK: This indicates how easy it is for a car to park for 15 minutes outside the shop. Where parking is not easy, alternative suggestions for parking are often given.

TEL: In additon to their business numbers some dealers have listed their home telephone numbers, so customers can ring for an appointment outside business hours. Clearly callers should use discretion and only make out-of-business calls where they are seriously interested and in any event not late at night or early in the morning.

SER: Additional services which the dealer offers. Where 'buys at auction' is shown in this section, it indicates that if an auction is one which a dealer might normally attend, he may be approached to act as bidder on behalf of someone else. Check the cost of this service, and any others offered, beforehand.

VAT: Indicates which of the VAT schemes, standard or special, are operated. In some cases both schemes are in operation and some very small shops are not registered.

London

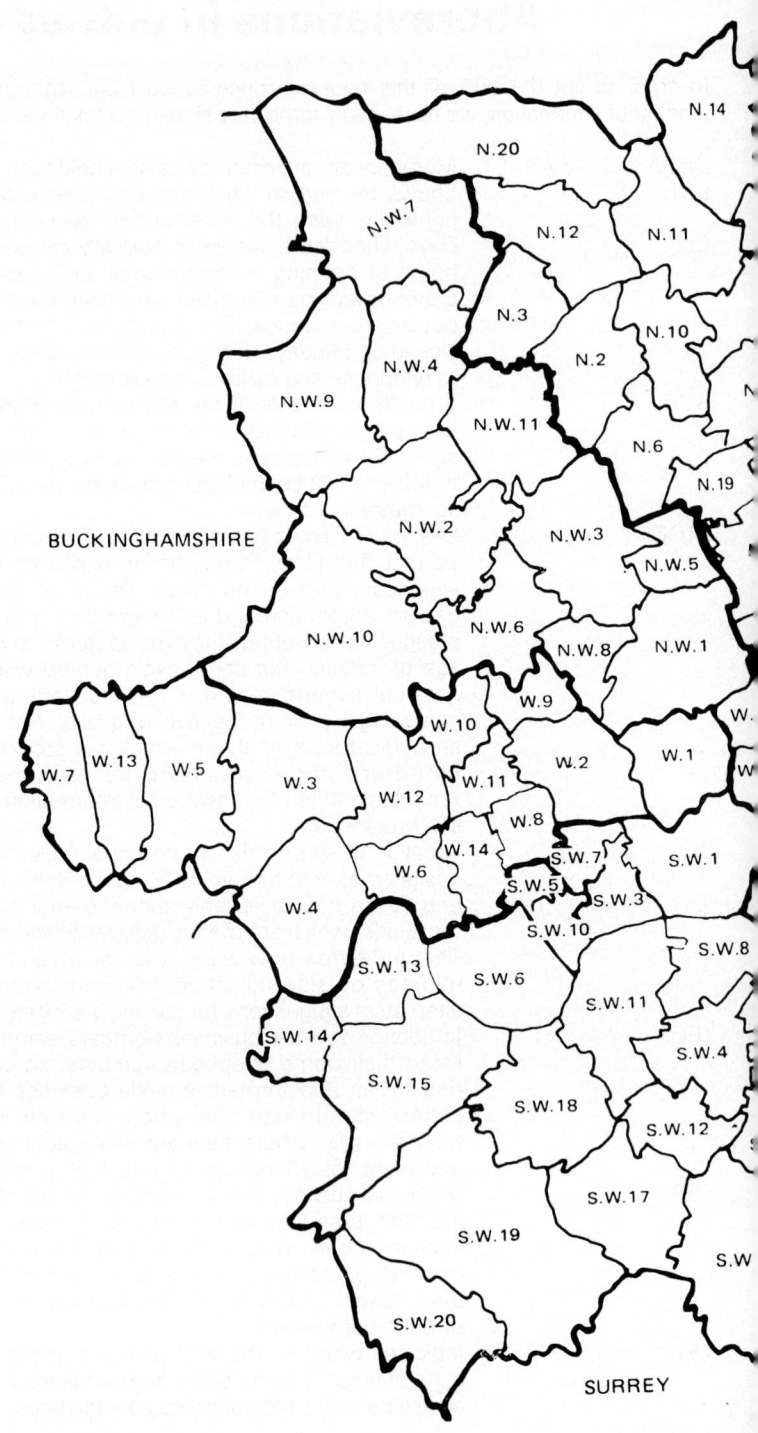

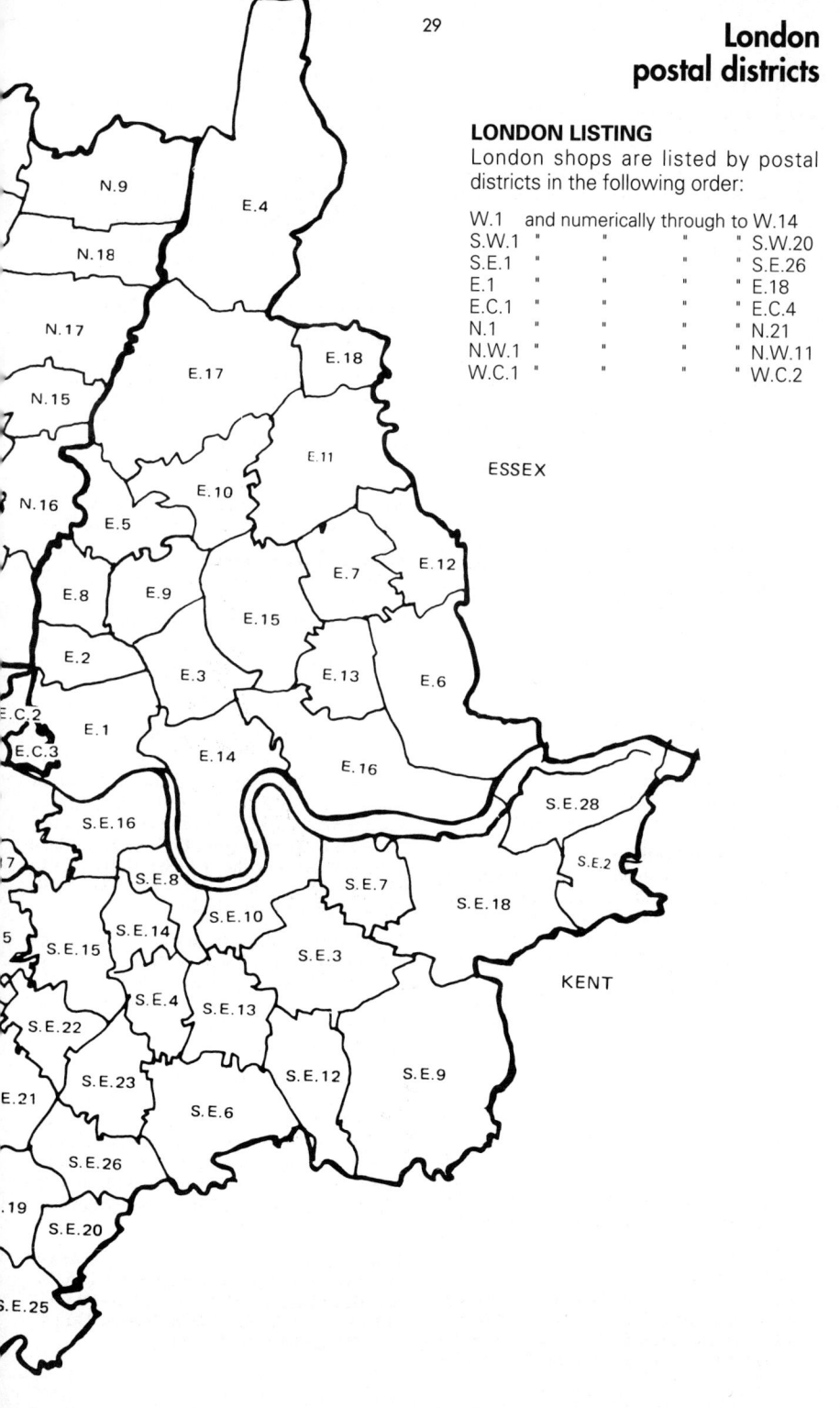

LONDON W.1

A.D.C. Heritage Ltd   BADA LAPADA
(F. and T. Raeymaekers and E. Bellord). Open by appointment only. *STOCK: Silver, old Sheffield plate.* TEL: 081 995 3066; fax - 081 747 4794. SER: Valuations; restorations; buys at auction.

Aaron Gallery
34 Bruton St. (M. and D. Aaron). Est. 1910. Open 10-6, Sat. by appointment. *STOCK: Islamic and ancient art, Oriental carpets.* TEL: 071 499 9434/5; fax - 071 499 0072.

Agnew's   BADA
43 Old Bond St, and 3 Albemarle St. SLAD. Est. 1817. Open 9.30-5.30, Thurs. 9.30-6.30. CL: Sat. SIZE: Large. *STOCK: Paintings, drawings, watercolours, engravings and sculptures of all schools.* TEL: 071 629 6176; fax - 071 629 4359. VAT: Spec.

Adrian Alan Ltd.
66/67 South Audley St. Est. 1963. Open 10-6. CL: Sat. SIZE: Large. *STOCK: English and continental furniture, especially fine 19th C; sculpture and works of art.* TEL: 071 495 2324; fax - 071 495 0204. VAT: Stan/Spec.

Alexander and Berendt Ltd
1A Davies St. Open 9.30-5.30. CL: Sat. SIZE: Large. *STOCK: Fine 17th-18th C French and other continental furniture and works of art.* PARK: Meters. TEL: 071 499 4775. VAT: Spec.

Philip Antrobus Ltd
11 New Bond St. Est. 1815. *STOCK: Jewellery.* TEL: 071 493 4557; fax - 071 495 2120.

Argyll Etkin Gallery
48 Conduit St, New Bond St. (Argyll Etkin Ltd). Est. 1954. Open 9-5.30. CL: Sat. SIZE: Medium. *STOCK: Classic postage stamps, postal history and covers, historical documents and antique letters, 1400-1950, £50-£25,000; stamp boxes and associated writing equipment, 1700-1930, £50-£500.* LOC: Near Oxford Circus. PARK: Savile Row. TEL: 071 437 7800 (6 lines). SER: Valuations; collections purchased. FAIRS: Major stamp exhibitions worldwide. VAT: Stan.

Armour-Winston Ltd
43 Burlington Arcade. Est. 1952. Open 9-5. Sat. 9.30-2. SIZE: Small. *STOCK: Jewellery, especially Victorian; gentlemen's cufflinks.* LOC: Off Piccadilly. Between Green Park and Piccadilly tube stations. PARK: Savile Row. TEL: 071 493 8937. SER: Valuations; restorations. VAT: Stan/Spec.

Sean Arnold
Sogo Store, Criterion Building Place, Piccadilly Circus. Open 10-7. SIZE: Small. *STOCK: Golf clubs, 1840-1915, £50-£100+; golf art, 17th-18th C, to £1,000+; collectibles, 18th C, £100-£500.*

W.1 continued

PARK: Nearby. TEL: 071 333 9000. SER: Valuations; buys at auction (golfing items). VAT: Stan.

Asprey plc   BADA
165-169 New Bond St. Est. 1781. Open 9-5.30. CL: Sat. pm. SIZE: Large. *STOCK: Furniture, works of art, clocks, silver, jewellery, Fabergé and objets de vertu, glass.* PARK: Albemarle St., entrance No.22. TEL: 071 493 6767; fax - 071 491 0384. SER: Valuations; restorations (furniture, jewellery, clocks, silver). VAT: Stan/Spec.

Astarte Gallery
Shop 5, Britannia Hotel, Grosvenor Sq. (A.G. Davies). Est. 1956. Open daily, Sat. and Sun. by appointment. SIZE: Medium. *STOCK: Roman, Greek and Egyptian art and artifacts, necklaces and other jewellery, £5-£15,000; medallions, some ancient coins, general antiques; books relating to stock.* PARK: Easy. TEL: 071 409 1875; fax - same; hotel - 071 629 9400, ext. 7002. SER: Buys at auction (antiquities). VAT: Stan/Spec.

Atlantic Bay Carpets
7 Sedley Place. (W. Grodzinski and Z. Golebiowski). Est. 1945. Open 9-5, Sat. 9-1. SIZE: Medium. *STOCK: Oriental and European carpets and textiles.* LOC: Near Bond/Oxford St. PARK: Easy. TEL: 071 355 3301; fax - 071 355 3760. SER: Valuations; restorations; buys at auction (as stock). VAT: Stan/Spec.

Gregg Baker Oriental Art
   BADA LAPADA
34 Brook St. Est. 1985. Open 10-6, weekends by appointment. SIZE: Small. *STOCK: Japanese and Chinese works of art and screens, mainly 18th-19th C, £100-£10,000.* LOC: Close to Bond St./Brook St. junction. PARK: Meters. TEL: 071 629 7926; fax - 071 495 3872. SER: Valuations. VAT: Stan/Spec.

John and Arthur Beare   BADA
7 Broadwick St. (J. and A. Beare Ltd). Est. 1892. Open 9-12.15 and 1.30-5. CL: Sat. *STOCK: Violins, violas, cellos, bows and accessories.* TEL: 071 437 1449. SER: Valuations. VAT: Stan/Spec.

Benardout and Benardout   BADA
18 Grosvenor St, Mayfair. (R. and L. Benardout). Est. 1961. Open 10-5, Sat. and Sun. by appointment. SIZE: Large. *STOCK: Carpets and rugs, 19th-20th C; tapestries, 16th-19th C.* LOC: New Bond Street. TEL: 071 355 4531; fax - 071 491 9710. SER: Valuations; restorations; buys at auction.

Paul Bennett   LAPADA
48A George St. (M. Dubiner). Open 9.15-6. CL: Sat. SIZE: Large. *STOCK: Silver, 1740-1963, £10-£10,000; Sheffield plate.* PARK: Meters. TEL: 071 935 1555/486 8836. VAT: Stan/Spec.

LONDON

Asprey

165-169 New Bond Street
London W1Y 0AR
Telephone 071 493 6767
Facsimile 071 491 0384

725 Fifth Avenue
New York, NY 10022
Telephone (212) 688 1811
Facsimile (212) 826 3746

A George III teaset by
John Emes, 1805, 71 1/2ozs

W.1 continued

Bentley & Co Ltd   LAPADA
8 New Bond St, and 19 Burlington Arcade. Open 10-5. STOCK: Jewellery, Fabergé, objets d'art. PARK: Meters. TEL: 071 629 0651/495 3783. SER: Valuations. VAT: Stan/Spec.

Bernheimer Fine Arts Ltd   BADA
32 St. George St. (K.O. Bernheimer). CINOA. Est. 1985. Open 10-5.30, weekends by appointment. SIZE: Large. STOCK: European furniture, 17th-19th C, £2,000-£500,000; Oriental porcelain, 16th-18th C, £1,500-£100,000. LOC: Parallel to Bond St. PARK: Hanover Sq. TEL: 071 499 0293. SER: Valuations; buys at auction. FAIRS: Grosvenor House. VAT: Spec.

Peter Biddulph
35 St George St. Open 9.30-6.30. CL: Sat. STOCK: Violins, violas and cellos. TEL: 071 491 8621.

H. Blairman and Sons Ltd.   BADA
119 Mount St. (G.J., M.P.,W.Y. Levy and L.G. Hannen). Est. 1884. Open daily. CL: Sat. SIZE: Medium. STOCK: English and French antiques, mid-18th to early 19th C; works of art, mounted porcelain, Chinese mirror pictures; architect designed furniture, 19th C. TEL: 071 493 0444; fax - 071 495 0766. FAIRS: Grosvenor House. VAT: Spec.

W.1 continued

Anne Bloom Fine Jewellery
10a New Bond St. Est. 1960. Open 9.30-6. STOCK: Fine jewellery, 1850-1992; period silver frames and mirrors. TEL: 071 491 1213; fax - 071 409 0777. SER: Valuations and repairs. VAT: Stan/Spec.

N. Bloom & Son (Antiques) Ltd
LAPADA
40/41 Conduit St. (I. Harris). Est. 1912. Open 10-6. CL: Sat. SIZE: Medium. STOCK: Silver, 16th C to second-hand; jewellery, including art deco paste items, 18th-20th C, £100-£50,000. Not stocked: Furniture, glass, china. LOC: Next to Westbury Hotel. TEL: 071 629 5060; fax - 071 437 5026. SER: Valuations; restorations, repairs; buys at auction. VAT: Stan/Spec.

Blunderbuss Antiques
29 Thayer St. (T. Greenaway). Open 9.30-4.30. STOCK: Arms and armour, militaria. TEL: 071 486 2444.

Bond Street Antiques Centre
124 New Bond St. (Atlantic Antique Centres Ltd). Est. 1970. Open 10-5.45. CL: Sat. SIZE: Large - 30 dealers. STOCK: Wide range of general antiques especially jewellery. LOC: Bond St. or Green Park tube stations. TEL: Enquiries -

LONDON

W.1 continued
071 351 5353; fax - 071 351 5350. Below are listed some of the dealers at this market.

Emmy Abe
Stand 33. *Jewellery.* TEL: 071 629 1826.

Eli Abramov LAPADA
Stand 2. (Morelle Davidson). *Jewellery, silver and objets d'art.* TEL: 071 629 4764/408 0066.

Accurate Trading Co
Stand 1C & 21. (E. Fahimian). *Jewellery.* TEL: 071 629 0277.

Clayre Armitage
Stand 14. *Jewellery and objects.* TEL: 071 493 5830.

Bond Street Watches
Stand 12. (Abdalah Mahfoot). *Watches and clocks.* TEL: 071 495 8801/495 8992.

Adele de Havilland
Stand 18. *Oriental porcelain, netsuke, jade.* TEL: 071 499 7127.

David Duggan LAPADA
Stands 1A, 1B. *Vintage watches.* TEL: 071 408 0134; fax - 071 408 1727.

Elisabeth's Antiques LAPADA
Stands 42/43. (Mrs E. Hage). *Jewellery.* TEL: 071 491 1723.

Anthony Green Antiques
Stand 39. *Watches and objects.* TEL: 071 409 2854; fax - 071 408 0010.

Joanna Hoffman BADA
Stand 16. *Clocks.* TEL: 071 419 2327. SER: Valuations; restorations.

Inchwood
Stand 17. (Mrs D. Feldman). *Miniature portraiture.* TEL: 071 495 4116.

Myra Antiques and JLA Ltd
Stands 29/30. (Mrs M. Sampson, Messrs Lack and Sampson). *Jewellery and objects.* TEL: 071 408 1508/499 1681.

Sadi Nasser
Stand 34. (Mrs S. Noorani). *Jewellery.* TEL: 071 491 2081.

Nonesuch Antiques LAPADA
Stand 3. (Mrs E. Michelson). *Jewellery and objects.* TEL: 071 629 6783.

P.M.R. Antiques
Stand 15. (Peter Rosen). *Jewellery.* TEL: 071 495 4406.

Place Vendome
Stand 38. (D. Shenny). *Silver, jewellery and objects.* TEL: 071 629 3008.

Anita Ray
Stand 40. *Jewellery.* TEL: 071 409 2107.

W.1 continued
Vinci Antiques
Stands 7/8/9. (A. Vinci). *Silver, jewellery, objets d'art.* TEL: 071 499 1041.

Xelana Antiques
Stand 32. (Mrs A.M. Sanchez-Martin). *Clocks and ivory.* TEL: 071 629 9415.

Bond Street Silver Galleries
111-112 New Bond St. Open 9-5.30. CL: Sat. PARK: Meters. TEL: 071 493 6180. Below are listed the dealers at these galleries. *Mainly trade.*

Brian Beet
Silver and works of art. TEL: 071 437 4975; fax - 071 495 8635.

A. and B. Bloomstein Ltd
BADA LAPADA
Silver, Sheffield plate. TEL: 071 493 6180; fax -071 495 3493. SER: Valuations; restorations.

Peter Cameron
Silver and old Sheffield plate. TEL: 071 499 0330.

Phillip Cull
Silver and Sheffield plate. TEL: 071 493 2047.

O. Frydman
Silver, Sheffield and Victorian plate. TEL: 071 493 4895. VAT: Stan/Spec.

P. Greenhalgh
Silver and old Sheffield plate, books on silver. TEL: 071 491 9178.

Hollis and Hollis
Antique silver, jewellery and works of art. TEL: 071 499 8599; fax - 071 408 0819.

A. Pash & Son LAPADA
Silver and old Sheffield plate. TEL: 071 493 5176.

Julian Pawle Ltd LAPADA
(J. Pawle, N.R. Shaw). *Antique and second-hand silver and Sheffield plate, £100-£10,000.* TEL: 071 499 8442; fax - 071 408 0819.

M. Sedler
Silver and plate. TEL: 071 839 3131.

Michael Smith
Silver and old Sheffield plate. TEL: 071 499 2558.

E. Swonnell (Silverware) Ltd LAPADA
Silver, Sheffield plate. TEL: 071 629 9649. VAT: Stan/Spec.

Howard White
Silver and Sheffield plate. TEL: 071 495 1144.

Henry Willis
Silver and Sheffield plate. TEL: 071 491 8949.

W.1 continued

Browse and Darby Ltd
19 Cork St. SLAD. Est. 1977. *STOCK: French and British paintings, drawings and sculpture, 19th-20th C.* TEL: 071 734 7984. VAT: Spec.

Bruford and Heming Ltd   BADA
28 Conduit St. NAG. Open 9-5.30. CL: Sat. *STOCK: Domestic silverware especially flatware, jewellery.* PARK: Meters. TEL: 071 499 7644/629 4289; fax - 071 493 5879. SER: Valuations; restorations. VAT: Stan/Spec.

John Bull (Antiques) Ltd   LAPADA
139A New Bond St. Open 9-4.30. *STOCK: Silver and plate.* TEL: 071 629 1251; fax - 071 495 3001. VAT: Stan/Spec.

Burlington Gallery Ltd
10 Burlington Gardens. (A.S. Lloyd, N.C. Potter and W.M. Lloyd). Est. 1980. Open 9.30-5.30, Sat. 10-5. SIZE: Large. *STOCK: Sporting and decorative prints, 1700 to present day, and works by Cecil Aldin.* LOC: Between Bond St. and Regent St. PARK: Old Burlington St. TEL: 071 734 9228; fax - 071 494 3770. SER: Valuations; buys at auction. VAT: Stan/Spec.

Burlington Paintings Ltd
12 Burlington Gardens. (A. Lloyd and M. Day). Est. 1981. Open 9.30-5.30, Sat. 10-5. SIZE: Small. *STOCK: English and continental oil paintings and watercolours, 19th to early 20th C, from £1,000.* LOC: Between Old Bond St. and Regent St., facing Savile Row. PARK: APCOA Old Burlington St. TEL: 071 734 9984. SER: Valuations; restorations (lining, cleaning, reframing oils and watercolours); buys at auction (pictures). VAT: Stan/Spec.

The Button Queen
19 Marylebone Lane. (T. and M. Frith). Est. 1953. Open 10-6, Sat. 10-1.30. SIZE: Large. *STOCK: Buttons, antique to modern horn and blazer buttons; buckles, mainly 19th C and Edwardian.* LOC: Off Wigmore St. TEL: 071 935 1505. VAT: Stan.

Carrington and Co. Ltd
170 Regent St. Open 9.30-5.30. *STOCK: Regimental jewellery and silver, trophies, watches, clocks.* TEL: 071 734 3727/8.

Lumley Cazalet Ltd
24 Davies St. SLAD. Est. 1967. Open 10-6. CL:Sat. *STOCK: Late 19th and 20th C original prints including Braque, Chagall, Miro, Matisse, Picasso; also drawings by Matisse.* TEL: 071 491 4767.

Antoine Cheneviere Fine Arts   BADA
94 Mount St. Open 9.30-6. CL: Sat. *STOCK: 18th-19th C furniture and paintings, objets d'art from Russia, Italy, Austria, Sweden and Germany.* TEL: 071 491 1007.

W.1 continued

J. Christie   BADA LAPADA
26 Burlington Arcade. (P.S. Christie). CINOA, ADS. Est. 1947. Open 9.30-5.30, Sat. by appointment. *STOCK: Animalier and figurative bronze sculpture, 19th-20th C; jewellery and silver; objets d'art.* PARK: Meters, car park. TEL: 071 629 3070/409 0111; fax - 071 409 0631. VAT: Stan/Spec.

Colefax and Fowler
39 Brook St. Est. 1933. Open 9.30-1 and 2-5.30. CL: Sat. SIZE: Large. *STOCK: Decorative furniture, pictures, lamps and carpets, 18th-19th C.* PARK: Meters. TEL: 071 493 2231. VAT: Stan/Spec.

Collingwood & Company Ltd
171 New Bond St. Est. 1817. Open 10-5.30. *STOCK: Jewellery, silver, objets d'art and clocks.* PARK: Meters. TEL: 071 734 2656; fax - 071 629 5418. SER: Valuations; design and production. VAT: Stan/Spec.

P. and D. Colnaghi & Co Ltd   BADA
14 Old Bond St. Est. 1760. Open 9.30-6. SIZE: Large. *STOCK: Master paintings and drawings, 14th-19th C; English paintings, European sculpture.* TEL: 071 491 7408. SER: Valuations. VAT: Spec.

Connaught Brown plc
2 Albemarle St. (A. Brown). SLAD. Est. 1980. Open 10-6, Sat. 10-12.30. SIZE: Medium. *STOCK: Post Impressionist and modern works, from £5,000+; contemporary, from £500+.* LOC: Off Piccadilly and parallel to Bond St. PARK: Berkeley Sq. TEL: 071 408 0362. SER: Valuations; restorations (paintings, drawings, watercolours and sculpture). FAIRS: Chicago International Art Exposition. VAT: Stan/Spec.

Sandra Cronan Ltd   LAPADA
18 Burlington Arcade. Est. 1975. Open 10-5.30. *STOCK: Unusual jewellery, especially horse and polo related, 18th C to 1940's, £800-£15,000.* LOC: Off Bond St. TEL: 071 491 4851; fax - 071 493 2758. SER: Valuations; design commissions. FAIRS: International Silver and Jewellery; Olympia. VAT: Stan/Spec.

A. B. Davies Ltd
18 Brook St, (Corner of New Bond St). Est. 1920. Open 10-5. CL: Sat. *STOCK: Antique and secondhand jewellery, small silver items and objets d'art.* TEL: 071 629 1053; 071 242 7357 (ansaphone). SER: Valuations; repairs (jewellery and silver). VAT: Stan/Spec.

Barry Davies Oriental Art   BADA
1 Davies St. Open 10-6. CL: Sat. *STOCK: Japanese works of art, netsuke, lacquer and bronzes.* TEL: 071 408 0207.

LONDON

W.1 continued

Richard Day Ltd
173 New Bond St. SLAD. Open 10-5. CL: Sat. STOCK: Old Master prints and drawings. TEL: 071 629 2991; fax - 071 493 7569. VAT: Stan.

Jehanne de Biolley Oriental Art
1st Floor, 29 Conduit St. Est. 1990. Open by appointment only. STOCK: Chinese, Korean and Japanese works of art and porcelain; robin's egg blue glazed Chinese porcelain. LOC: Opposite Westbury Hotel, off New Bond St. TEL: 071 495 4257. SER: Valuations; restorations.

Demas
31 Burlington Arcade. (Mrs E. Paul). Est. 1953. Open 10-5. CL: Sat. pm. STOCK: Georgian, Victorian and art deco jewellery. TEL: 071 493 9496. VAT: Stan.

Anthony D'Offay
9, 21 and 23 Dering St, New Bond St. SLAD. Est. 1965. Open 10-5.30; Sat. 10-1. SIZE: Large. STOCK: Contemporary international paintings, sculpture and drawings. LOC: Near Oxford Circus and Bond St. tube stations. PARK: Meters in Hanover Sq. TEL: 071 499 4100; fax - 071 493 4443. VAT: Stan/Spec.

A. Douch
28 Conduit St. Open by appointment only. STOCK: Jewellery, silver and glass. TEL: 071 493 9413. SER: Valuations. VAT: Stan/Spec.

Charles Ede Ltd
20 Brook St. Est. 1970. Open 12.30-4.30 or by appointment. CL: Mon and Sat. STOCK: Greek, Roman and Egyptian antiquities, £50-£25,000. PARK: Meters. TEL: 071 493 4944. SER: Valuations; buys at auction. VAT: Spec.

Editions Graphiques Gallery
3 Clifford St. (V. Arwas). Est. 1966. Open 10-6, Sat. 10-2. SIZE: Large. STOCK: Art nouveau and art deco, glass, ceramics, bronzes, sculpture, furniture, jewellery, silver, pewter, books and posters 1880-1940, £25-£50,000; paintings, watercolours and drawings, 1880 to date, £100-£20,000; original graphics, lithographs, etchings, woodcuts, 1890 to date, £5-£10,000. LOC: Between New Bond St and Savile Row. PARK: 50yds. TEL: 071 734 3944. SER: Valuations; buys at auction. VAT: Stan/Spec.

D.H. Edmonds Ltd
27 Burlington Arcade, Piccadilly. Open 10-5.30. STOCK: Jewellery, silver, objets d'art, watches, £50-£20,000. TEL: 071 495 3127.

Andrew Edmunds
44 Lexington St. Open 10-6. CL: Sat. STOCK: 18th and early 19th C caricature and decorative prints and drawings. TEL: 071 437 8594; fax - 071 439 2551. VAT: Stan/Spec.

W.1 continued

Emanouel Antiques Ltd LAPADA
64 & 64a South Audley St. (E. Naghi). Est. 1974. Open 10-6, Sat. by appointment. STOCK: Important antiques and fine works of art, 18th-19th C; Islamic works of art. TEL: 071 493 4350; fax - 071 629 3125. VAT: Stan/Spec.

Ermitage Ltd
14 Hay Hill. Est. 1985. Open 10-5. CL: Sat. SIZE: Medium. STOCK: Fabergé objects, £2,000-£60,000+; continental silver, 17th-18th C, £1,000-£50,000+; Russian art, 17th-20th C, £800-£25,000+. LOC: Mayfair area, between Bond St. and Berkeley Sq. PARK: Berkeley Sq. TEL: 071 499 5459; fax - same. SER: Valuations. FAIRS: London Silver and Jewellery; The Orangerie, Berlin; Maastricht. VAT: Stan/Spec.

Eskenazi Ltd BADA
10 Clifford St. (J.E. Eskenazi, L. Bandini and P. Constantinidi). Est. 1960. Open 9.30-6, Sat. by appointment. SIZE: Large. STOCK: Early Chinese ceramics; bronzes, sculpture, works of art; Japanese netsuke and lacquer. TEL: 071 493 5464; fax - 071 499 3136. VAT: Spec.

Essie Carpets
62 Piccadilly. (E. Sakhai). Est. 1766. Open 9.30-6.30, Sun. 10.30-6.30. CL: Sat. SIZE: Large. STOCK: Persian and Oriental carpets and rugs. LOC: Opposite St. James St. and Ritz Hotel. PARK: Easy. TEL: 071 493 7766; home - 071 586 3388. SER: Valuations; restorations; commissions undertaken. VAT: Stan/Spec.

Brian Fielden BADA
3 New Cavendish St. Open 9.30-1 and 2-5.30, Sat. 9.30-1. SIZE: Medium. STOCK: English walnut and mahogany furniture, 18th to early 19th C; mirrors and barometers. LOC: 5 minutes walk north of Bond St. PARK: Meters. TEL: 071 935 6912. VAT: Spec.

The Fine Art Society plc BADA
148 New Bond St. SLAD. Est. 1876. Open 9.30-5.30, Sat. 10-1. SIZE: Large. STOCK: British art, paintings, watercolours, drawings, sculpture, decorative arts, 19th to early 20th C. PARK: 300yds. TEL: 071 629 5116. SER: Buys at auction. VAT: Stan/Spec.

Sam Fogg
14 Old Bond St. Est. 1971. Open by appointment. STOCK: Rare books, manuscripts, all periods. TEL: 071 495 2333. SER: Valuations; buys at auction.

Fortnum and Mason plc
Piccadilly. Open 9.30-6. SIZE: Medium. STOCK: English furniture, 18th C. PARK: Meters. TEL: 071 734 8040.

J.A. Fredericks and Son BADA
Correspondence only to: 99 Hercies Rd., Hillingdon, Middlesex. (J.A. and C.J.

W.1 continued

Fredericks). Est. 1938. Open by appointment. STOCK: *English furniture.* TEL: 0895 255462. VAT: Spec. *Trade Only.*

H. Fritz-Denneville Fine Arts Ltd
31 New Bond St. SLAD. Open 9.30-6, Sat. by appointment. STOCK: *Paintings, drawings and prints, especially German Romantics, Nazarenes and Expressionists.* TEL: 071 629 2466; fax - 071 408 0604. SER: Valuations; restorations; buys at auction.

Frost and Reed Ltd   BADA
16 Old Bond St. SLAD. Est. 1808. Open 9-5.30. CL: Sat. STOCK: *Fine 19th C British and continental paintings, marine and sporting pictures, Impressionist drawings and watercolours; works by Marcel Dyf.* PARK: Meters. TEL: 071 629 2457; fax - 071 499 0299. VAT: Stan/Spec.

Deborah Gage (Works of Art) Ltd
38 Old Bond St. Est. 1982. Open 9.30-5.30. CL: Sat. STOCK: *European decorative arts and paintings, 17th-18th C; French and British pictures, late 19th to early 20th C, from £5,000.* TEL: 071 493 3249; fax - 071 495 1352. SER: Valuations; cataloguing; buys at auction. VAT: Stan/Spec.

Garrard & Co. Ltd
(The Crown Jewellers)   BADA
112 Regent St. (Richard Jarvis). Est. 1735. Open 9-5.30, Sat. 9.30-1. SIZE: Large. STOCK: *Silver, clocks, jewellery, from £100.* TEL: 071 734 7020. SER: Restorations (antique silver and clocks). FAIRS: Grosvenor House and Burlington House. VAT: Stan.

Christopher Gibbs Ltd
8 Vigo St. Est. 1960. Open 9.30-5.30. CL: Sat. SIZE: Large. STOCK: *Pictures of the major painters of all periods; furniture, works of art, garden statuary.* TEL: 071 439 4557. VAT: Spec.

Thomas Gibson Fine Art Ltd
44 Old Bond St. SLAD. Open 10-5. CL: Sat. STOCK: *19th-20th C Masters and selected Old Masters.* TEL: 071 499 8572; fax - 071 495 1924.

Thomas Goode and Co (London) Ltd
19 South Audley St. Est. 1827. Open 9.30-5.30. SIZE: Large. STOCK: *China, glass, tableware, ornamental.* TEL: 071 499 2823. SER: Restorations. VAT: Spec.

Gillian Gould
at Captain O.M. Watts, 49 Albemarle St., Piccadilly. Open 9-6, Thurs. 9-8, Sat. 9.30-5. SIZE: Small. STOCK: *Nautical antiques and collectables, £30-£1,000.* LOC: Near Bond St. PARK: Meters. TEL: 071 493 4633; home - 081 905 5180. SER: Restorations (scientific instruments); buys at auction (nautical and scientific instruments); hire. VAT: Stan.

W.1 continued

Graus Antiques   LAPADA
39-42 New Bond St. (E. and H. Graus). Est. 1948. Open 9.30-5.30. CL: Sat. SIZE: Medium. STOCK: *Watches, jewellery, enamels, objets d'art.* PARK: Meters. TEL: 071 629 6680; fax - 071 629 3361. VAT: Stan/Spec.

Grays Antique Market
58 Davies St. Open 10-6. CL: Sat. TEL: 071 629 7034. Below are listed the dealers at this market.

Abacus Antiques
Stand 313. *Jewellery and objects.* TEL: 071 629 9681.

AG Antiques
Stand 154. *Jewellery.* TEL: 071 493 7564.

Antique Medical Instruments
Stand 123. *Medical.* TEL: 071 499 5334.

Arca
Stand 351. *Objets, ivory, treen, tortoiseshell and walking sticks.* TEL: 071 629 2729.

Arenski
Stand 107. *Furniture and majolica.* TEL: 071 499 6824.

Armada Antiques
Stand 122. *Weapons and militaria.* TEL: 071 499 1087.

Sean Arnold
Stand 316. *Sporting items including golf.* TEL: 071 409 7358.

Aurum
Stand 372. *Jewellery.* TEL: 071 355 3165.

Osman Aytac
Stand 331. *Pens and watches.* TEL: 071 629 7380.

Robert Badir
Stand 144. *Jewellery and objets d'art.* TEL: 071 629 6467.

Jill Barnes
Stand 363. *Jewellery.* TEL: 071 409 2743.

Rosemary Barnes
Stand 152. *Jewellery.* TEL: 071 408 0909.

Peter Benjamin
Stand 127. *Oriental items.* TEL: 071 493 2180.

Barbara Berg
Stand 333. *Jewellery.* TEL: 071 499 0560.

David Bowden
Stand 321. *Oriental items.* TEL: 071 495 1773.

Patrick Boyd-Carpenter
Stand 128. *Paintings and prints.* TEL: 071 491 7623.

LONDON

W.1 continued

Britannia
Stand 101. *Porcelain and pottery.* TEL: 071 629 6772.

Christopher Cavey
Stand 177. *Gems* TEL: 071 495 1743.

Cekay
Stand 172. *Walking sticks, objects.* TEL: 071 629 5130.

Jan Church
Stand 162. *Jewellery.* TEL: 071 499 7936.

Collection
Stand 329. *Jewellery.* TEL: 071 493 2654.

Olivia Collins
Stand 327. *Jewellery.* TEL: 071 499 5478.

Joy Continuum
Stand 124. *Oriental items.* TEL: 071 493 4909.

Phil and Lindy Conynham-Hynes
Stand 324. *Jewellery.* TEL: 071 493 0624.

Cozy World
Stand 385. *Glass and porcelain.* TEL: 071 409 0269.

Croesus
Stand 324. *Jewellery and silver.* TEL: 071 493 0624.

Guy De Rooy
Stand 152. *Jewellery.* TEL: 071 629 6502.

Victoria Delaney
Stand 362. *Jewellery and silver.*

Ronald Falloon
Stand 303. *Silver.* TEL: 071 499 0158.

Jack First
Stand 310. *Silver.* TEL: 071 409 2722.

Sylvana Francis
Stand 342. *Silver.*

Nicola Franks
Stand 344. *Jewellery.* TEL: 071 408 1129.

French Decorative Antiques
Stand 367. *Glass.* TEL: 071 491 0407.

Peter Gaunt
Stand 120. *Antique silver.* TEL: 071 629 1072.

The Gilded Lily LAPADA
Stand 131. *Jewellery.* TEL: 071 499 6260.

Gordon Grahame
Stand 112. *Prints.* TEL: 071 629 3223.

Anita Gray LAPADA
Stand 307. *Oriental items.* TEL: 071 408 1638.

W.1 continued

Sarah Groombridge LAPADA
Stand 335. *Jewellery.* TEL: 071 629 0225.

Hallmark
Stand 359. *Silver.* TEL: 071 409 2937.

Diana Harby
Stand 148. *Lace.* TEL: 071 629 5130.

Brian Harkins
Stand 126. *Chinese and Japanese items.* TEL: 071 409 2530.

Declan Harvey LAPADA
Stand 168. *Jewellery.* TEL: 071 493 0224.

Satoe Hattrell
Stand 156. *Jewellery.* TEL: 071 629 4296.

Hoffman Antiques
Stand 379. *Silver.* TEL: 071 499 4340.

David Hogg
Stand 109. *Tools, instruments and gadgets.* TEL: 071 493 0208.

Lynn and Brian Holmes LAPADA
Stand 304. *Jewellery.* TEL: 071 629 7327.

Iwona
Stand 338. *Silver.* TEL: 071 499 4340.

Katie Jones
Stand 126. *Oriental items..* TEL: 071 409 2530.

John Joseph LAPADA
Stand 345. *Jewellery.* TEL: 071 629 1140.

K. & M. Antiques
Stand 340. *General antiques.* TEL: 071 491 4310.

Margaret Kaye
Stand 374. *Porcelain miniatures.* TEL: 071 499 4340.

Kikuchi Antiques LAPADA
Stand 357. *Objets, jewellery and watches.* TEL: 071 629 6808.

Barbara Lankester
Stand 339. *Jewellery.* TEL: 071 493 0123.

Lazarell
Stand 325. *Jewellery and objets.* TEL: 071 408 0154.

Pat Lennard
Stand 149. *English glass.* TEL: 071 629 5130.

Sue Lewis
Stand 139. *Jewellery.* TEL: 071 409 1350.

Gerald Licht
Stand 158. *Jewellery.* TEL: 071 493 7497.

Monty Lo
Stand 370. *Porcelain and glass.* TEL: 071 493 9457.

W.1 continued

London Antique Print Room
Stand 384. *Prints.* TEL: 071 495 8745.

Gillian Lynch
Stand 339. *Jewellery.* TEL: 071 493 0123.

Peggy Malone
Stand 322. *Jewellery, objets.* TEL: 071 493 7621.

Alison Massey
Stand 376. *Jet.* TEL: 071 493 1634.

Merlin Antiques
Stand 352. *Jewellery.*

Marsha Myers
Stand 386. *Silver.* TEL: 071 493 0768.

Pillows of Bond Street
Stand 301. *Tapestries.* TEL: 071 495 8853.

Podlewski Antiques
Stand 319. *Silver.*

Puzzle House Antiques LAPADA
Stand 108. *General antiques.* TEL: **071 409 2447.**

RBR Group
Stand 175. *Jewellery.* TEL: 071 629 4769.

Wendy Robinson
Stand 152. *Jewellery.* TEL: 071 408 0909.

Charlotte Sayers
Stand 327. *Jewellery.* TEL: 071 499 5478.

Second Time Around
Stand 384. *Watches.* TEL: 071 499 7442.

Second Time Around
Stand 364. *Watches.* TEL: 071 499 7442.

Pat and Alan Shapiro
Stand 161. *Jewellery and objets.* TEL: 071 409 7456.

Sheldon Shapiro
Stand 380. TEL: 071 491 2710.

Spa Antiques
Stand 127. *Oriental items.* TEL: 071 493 2180.

Spectrum
Stand 372. *Jewellery.* TEL: 071 355 3165.

Trianon Antiques
(Bruce Rowley). *Jewellery and objets d'art.* TEL: 071 491 2764; fax - same.

Thimble Society
Stand 134. *Thimbles.* TEL: 071 493 0560.

Michael Ventura-Pauly
Stand 354. *Jewellery, objets.* TEL: 071 495 6868.

The Watch Department
Stand 356. *Watches.* TEL: 071 499 0564.

W.1 continued

Mary Wellard
Stand 164. *General antiques.* TEL: 071 629 5130.

Westminster Group LAPADA
Stand 150. *Jewellery.* **TEL: 071 493 8672.**

David and Linda Wheatley LAPADA
Stand 106. *Oriental.* **TEL: 071 629 1352.**

Wimpole Antiques LAPADA
Stand 348. *Jewellery.* **TEL: 071 499 2889.**

Craig Wyncoll
Stand 125. *Prints.* TEL: 071 409 1498.

Grays Mews
1-7 Davies Mews. Open 10-6. CL: Sat. TEL: 071 629 7034. Below are listed some of the dealers at this market.

Patricia Angeli
Stand L16. *Jewellery.* TEL: 071 493 3098.

The Antique Connoisseur plc
Stand M17. *Watches, Judaica and silver.* TEL: 071 629 3272.

Arms and Armour
Stand G12. *Militaria.* TEL: 071 629 2851.

Elias Assad
Stand A16. *Middle Eastern art.* TEL: 071 499 4778.

Colin Baddiel
Stand B24. *Toys.* TEL: 071 408 1239.

Sarah Fabian Baddiel
Stand B10. *Golfiana including books on golf.* TEL: 071 408 1239.

David Baker
Stand H22. *Oriental.* TEL: 071 629 3788.

Linda Bee
Stand M20. *Art deco.* TEL: 071 629 5921.

Jonathan Broido
Stand K16. *General antiques.* TEL: 071 629 1184.

Sue Brown
Stand M14. *Jewellery.* TEL: 071 491 4287.

Canonball
Stand B24. *Toys.* TEL: 071 499 0482.

Theresa Clayton
Stand L24. *Scent bottles.* TEL: 071 629 1184.

Douglas Clifton-Brown
Stand J26. *Prints and paintings.* TEL: 071 491 1056.

Cloudheath LAPADA
Stand K22. *Jewellery.* **TEL: 071 629 3832.**

Stuart Cropper
Stand C26. *Toys and games.* TEL: 071 629 7036.

LONDON

W.1 continued

Alan Darer
Stand A22. *Oriental.* TEL: 071 629 3644.

Sandys Dickinson
Stand A18. *Chess.* TEL: 071 629 3644.

Donohoe BADA LAPADA
Stand L25. *Jewellery and objets.* TEL: 071 629 5633.

Rosemary Ebrich
Stand C26. *General.* TEL: 071 629 2526.

David Eisler
Stand C24. *Prints and maps.* TEL: 071 629 2526.

Esther and Leslie
Stand M13. *Jewellery and silver.* TEL: 071 629 3596.

Marion Fielding
Stand H10. *Costume jewellery.*

Trevor Gilbert LAPADA
Stand G10. *Silver.* TEL: 071 408 0028.

Gmur and Ouji
Stand K22. *Jewellery.* TEL: 071 629 1184.

Ora Gordon
Stand J27. *Porcelain and boxes.* TEL: 071 499 1319.

Patrick Gould LAPADA
Stand L17. *Lalique.* TEL: 071 408 0129.

Anthony Gray
Stand H26. *Oriental works of art.* TEL: 071 408 1252.

Alice Guillesarian
Stand J16. *General.* TEL: 071 629 3788.

Ronnie Harounoff
Stand K20. *Paintings.* TEL: 071 408 0803.

Ali Jazi
Stand A30. *Islamic works.* TEL: 071 629 2813.

Andre and Minoo Kaae LAPADA
Stand G22. *Jewellery.* TEL: 071 629 1200.

Iraj Lak
Stand G19. *General.* TEL: 071 499 7399.

Lennox Galleries
Stand K10. *Coins.* TEL: 071 629 9119.

Pete McAskie
Stand A12. *Toys.* TEL: 071 629 2813.

Stephen Naegel
Stand B23. *Toys.* TEL: 071 491 3066.

Namdar
Stand B21. *General.* TEL: 071 629 1183.

Notaras Antiques
Stand K37. *Antiquities.* TEL: 071 499 3248.

W.1 continued

Orion
Stand K24. *Oriental.* TEL: 071 629 5476.

Pars Antiques
Stand A14. *Antiquities.* TEL: 071 629 3644.

Madeleine Popper LAPADA
Stand L12. *Jewellery.* TEL: 071 493 2996.

Samiramis LAPADA
Stand E18. *Antiquities.* TEL: 071 629 1161.

Adam Samuels
Stand K33. *Watches.* TEL: 071 495 3998.

Scribes Engraving
Stand C32. *Engraving.* TEL: 071 408 1880.

Shahdad Antiques
Stand B14. *Antiquities including Islamic.* TEL: 071 499 0572.

Peter Sloane
Stand E12. *Antiquities.* TEL: 071 408 1043.

Boris Sosna
Stand K32. *Jewellery.* TEL: 071 629 2371.

Southwell Antiques
Stand A25. *Paintings.* TEL: 071 629 7036.

Ian and Mandy Stanley
Stand L18. *Jewellery.* TEL: 071 629 4038.

Trio
Stand L24. *Scent bottles.* TEL: 071 629 1184.

Trotter and Parsons
Stand L22. *Antiquities.* TEL: 071 408 0463.

Aura Williamson
Stand L10. *Tibetan.* TEL: 071 495 6083.

Oral Yauuz
Stand K28. *Antiquities.* TEL: 071 499 3248.

Helen Zokagg
Stand A20. *Islamic.* TEL: 071 491 2562.

Richard Green BADA
44 and 39 Dover St, and 4 and 33 New Bond St. SLAD. Open 9.30-5.30, Sat. 10-12.30. STOCK: Paintings - Old Master and British; French impressionist and modern British; Victorian sporting and British marine. PARK: Meters. TEL: 071 493 3939; fax - 071 629 2609. VAT: Stan/Spec.

Simon Griffin Antiques Ltd
3 Royal Arcade, 28 Old Bond St. (S.J. Griffin). Est. 1979. Open 10-5, Sat. 10-5.30. STOCK: Silver, old Sheffield plate. TEL: 071 491 7367. VAT: Stan/Spec.

Hadji Baba Ancient Art
34a Davies St. (R.R. Soleimani). Est. 1939. Open 9.30-6, Sat. and Sun. by appointment. SIZE: Medium. STOCK: Ancient and Islamic art, carpets and rugs. LOC: Next to Claridges Hotel. PARK: Meters. TEL: 071 499 9363/9384. SER: Valuations.

HALCYON DAYS

By appointment to Her Majesty The Queen Suppliers of Objets d'Art
By appointment to H.R.H. The Duke of Edinburgh Suppliers of Objet d'Art
By appointment to H.M. Queen Elizabeth, The Queen Mother Suppliers of Objets d'Art
By appointment to H.R.H. The Prince of Wales Suppliers of Objets d'Art

English antiques: 18th-century enamels, Chelsea porcelain miniatures, objects of vertu, Staffordshire figurines, papier mâché, tôle peinte, tea caddies and decorative prints.

14 Brook St., London W1Y 1AA
Telephone: 071 629 8811 Fax: 071 409 0280
4 Royal Exchange, Cornhill, London EC3V 3LL

W.1 continued

Hadleigh Jewellers
30A Marylebone High St. Open 9.30-5.30. STOCK: Jewellery, some silver. TEL: 071 935 4074. SER: Valuations; repairs; hand-made jewellery. VAT: Stan/Spec.

Hahn and Son Fine Art Dealers
47 Albemarle St. (P. Hahn). Est. 1870. Open 9.45-5.30. CL: Sat. STOCK: *English oil paintings, 18th-19th C.* TEL: 071 493 9196. VAT: Stan.

Halcyon Days BADA
14 Brook St. (S. Benjamin). Est. 1950. 9.15-5.30, Sat. 9.30-5.30. STOCK: *18th to early 19th C enamels, papier mâché, tôle, objects of vertu, treen, Staffordshire pottery figures, prints, small unusual Georgian furniture.* LOC: Hanover Sq. end of Brook St. PARK: Meters and in Hanover Sq. TEL: 071 629 8811; fax - 071 409 0280. FAIRS: Grosvenor House. VAT: Stan/Spec.

Hancocks and Co BADA
In association with Young & Stephen Ltd, 1 Burlington Gardens, New Bond St. Est. 1849. Open 9.30-5, Sat. 10.30-4. SIZE: Medium. STOCK: *Jewellery, fine quality, signed pieces, 1800-1950's, £250-£250,000; silver, 17th-20th C, £50-£50,000, especially Omar Ramsden.* LOC: Opposite top of Burlington Arcade.

W.1 continued

TEL: 071 493 8904; fax - 071 493 8905. SER: Valuations; restorations; buys at auction. FAIRS: Fine Art and Antiques, Olympia; International Fine Art and Antiques, Harrods; IAD, New York. VAT: Stan/Spec.

Harcourt Antiques
5 Harcourt Street. (J. Christophe). Est. 1961. Open by appointment only. STOCK: *English, continental and Oriental porcelain, pre-1830.* PARK: Easy. TEL: 071 723 5919/727 6936. VAT: Stan. *Trade Only.*

David Harrington Gallery
27 Berkeley Sq. Open 10-6, Sat. 10-1 or by appointment. STOCK: *Russian and Soviet paintings, 19th-20th C.* TEL: 071 495 3194; fax - 071 409 3175. SER: Valuations. VAT: Stan.

S.H. Harris and Son (London) Ltd
17-18 Old Bond St. (B.C. and R.H. Harris). Est. 1885. Open 9-5. CL: Sat. SIZE: Small. STOCK: *Jewellery and silver.* LOC: 50yds from Piccadilly. PARK: Burlington St. TEL: 071 499 0352. SER: Valuations. VAT: Stan/Spec. *Trade Only.*

Harvey and Gore BADA
4 Burlington Gardens. (B.E. Norman). Est. 1723. Open 9.30-5. CL: Sat. SIZE: Small. STOCK: *Jewellery, £150-£50,000; silver, £50-£15,000; old Sheffield plate, £65-£6,000; antique*

LONDON

W.1 continued

paste. LOC: Near top of Burlington Arcade, off Piccadilly. PARK: 100yds. New Burlington St. TEL: 071 493 2714; fax - 071 493 0324. SER: Valuations; restorations (jewellery and silver); buys at auction. VAT: Stan/Spec.

W.R Harvey & Co (Antiques) Ltd   BADA
5 Old Bond St. (W.R. and A.D. Harvey). Est. 1952. Open 10-5.30. SIZE: Large. *STOCK: Fine English furniture, clocks, barometers, mirrors, paintings, framed engravings and objets d'art, 1675-1830.* LOC: 50yds from Piccadilly. TEL: 071 499 8385; fax - 071 495 0209. SER: Valuations; restorations; buys on commission. FAIRS: Park Lane. VAT: Stan/Spec.

Brian Haughton Antiques
3B Burlington Gardens, Old Bond St. Est. 1965. Open 10-5.30. SIZE: Large. *STOCK: British and European ceramics, porcelain and pottery, 18th-19th C, £100-£50,000.* PARK: Nearby, Savile Row N.C.P. TEL: 071 734 5491. SER: Buys at auction (porcelain and pottery). FAIRS: Organiser - International Ceramics, Park Lane Hotel; International Art and Antiques, Harrods and IAD, New York. VAT: Spec.

Hennell of Bond Street Ltd. Founded 1736 (incorporating Frazer and Haws (1868) and E. Lloyd Lawrence (1830))
12 New Bond St. Open 9-5.30, Sat. 10-4. SIZE: Medium. *STOCK: Fine jewellery, silver and watches.* PARK: Meters. TEL: 071 629 6888. SER: Valuations; restorations (silver, jewellery). VAT: Stan/Spec.

G. Heywood Hill Ltd
10 Curzon St. (J. Saumarez Smith). Open 9-5.30, Sat. 9-12.30. *STOCK: Books, Victorian illustrated, children's and natural history.* TEL: 071 629 0647; fax - 071 408 0286.

Claire Hobson Antiques
at Thomas Goode and Co. Ltd, 19 South Audley St. Open 9.30-5.30. *STOCK: English and continental porcelain and pottery, late 18th to 19th C, £50-£10,000.* TEL: 071 499 2343.

Holland and Holland Ltd
31 and 33 Bruton St. Est. 1835. Open 9.30-5.30, Sat. 10-4. CL: Sat. Jan.-July (No.33 only). SIZE: Medium. *STOCK: Modern and antique guns, rifles, weapons and associated items; sporting prints and pictures; field sports and wildlife books.* PARK: Meters at Berkeley Sq. TEL: 071 499 4411. SER: Valuations. VAT: Stan/Spec.

Holmes Ltd   BADA
29 Old Bond St, and 24 Burlington Arcade. (A.N., B.J. and I.J. Neale). Open 9-5.30. CL: Sat. pm. *STOCK: Jewels and silver.* TEL: 071 493 1396/629 8380. SER: Valuations; restorations. VAT: Stan.

W.1 continued

Dennis Hotz Fine Art Ltd
1st Floor, 9 Cork St. SLAD. Open 10-6, Sat. by appointment. *STOCK: 19th-20th C works of art and sculpture.* TEL: 071 287 8324; fax - 071 287 9713.

How of Edinburgh
1st Floor, 28 Albemarle St. (Mrs G.E.P. How). Est. 1930. Open 9.45-5.30. CL: Fri. and Sat. *STOCK: Silver, to 1800.* PARK: Easy. TEL: 071 408 1867. VAT: Stan/Spec.

Howard Antiques
8 Davies St, Berkeley Sq. Est. 1955. Open 10-6, Sat. by appointment. SIZE: Medium. *STOCK: English and continental furniture, objects.* PARK: N.C.P. nearby. TEL: 071 629 2628. SER: Valuations. VAT: Stan/Spec.

John Jaffa (Antiques) Ltd
13 The Royal Arcade, 28 Old Bond Street. Est. 1972. Open 10-5.30. SIZE: Small. *STOCK: Enamel snuff boxes, 18th C, £300-£2,000; objets de vertu, 18th-19th C, £250-£5,000; silver, 18th-20th C, £100-£5,000.* PARK: Easy. TEL: 071 499 4228. SER: Buys at auction. FAIRS: Florida, Olympia, Rome, Barbican. VAT: Stan/Spec.

C. John (Rare Rugs) Ltd
70 South Audley St, Mayfair. Est. 1947. Open 9-5. CL: Sat. *STOCK: Textiles, pre-1800, carpets, tapestries, embroideries.* TEL: 071 493 5288; fax - 071 409 7030. VAT: Stan/Spec.

Johnson Walker & Tolhurst Ltd   BADA
64 Burlington Arcade. Est. 1849. Open 9.30-5.30. *STOCK: Antique and secondhand jewellery, objets d'art, silver.* TEL: 071 629 2615. SER: Restorations (jewellery, pearl-stringing). VAT: Stan/Spec.

E. Joseph, Booksellers   BADA
1 Vere St. ABA. Est. 1876. Open 9.30-5.30 or by appointment. CL: Sat. *STOCK: Rare and fine books specialising in English literature, colour plate, illustrated and press books, fine bindings, Churchilliana, library sets in leather and original cloth.* LOC: Opposite New Bond St., north side of Oxford St. TEL: 071 493 8353/4/5; fax - 071 629 2579. SER: Valuations. VAT: Stan/Spec.

Alexander Juran and Co   BADA
74 New Bond St. Est. 1951. Open 9.15-5.30. CL: Sat. *STOCK: Caucasian rugs, nomadic and tribal; carpets, rugs, textiles.* TEL: 071 629 2550/493 4484. SER: Valuations; repairs. VAT: Stan/Spec.

Robin Kennedy
29 New Bond St. Open 10-6 or by appointment. CL: Sat. *STOCK: Japanese prints and paintings, £50-£5,000.* TEL: 071 408 1238; home - 081 940 3281.

C. John

BY APPOINTMENT TO
HER MAJESTY QUEEN ELIZABETH II
SUPPLIER OF CARPETS
C. JOHN (RARE RUGS) LTD.

70, SOUTH AUDLEY STREET, MAYFAIR, LONDON W1Y 5FE
TELEPHONE 071-493 5288 FACSIMILE 071-409 7030

Rare and Decorative Carpets, Rugs and Tapestries

Rare 18th century English needlework rug Dimensions 8' 3" x 6' 9"

W.1 continued

Kennedy Carpets and Kelims
LAPADA
9A Vigo St. (M. Kennedy). Est. 1974. Open 9.30-6. SIZE: Large. STOCK: *Decorative carpets, collectable rugs and kelims, mid-19th to early 20th C, £200-£50,000.* LOC: Off Regent St., up Sackville St. from Piccadilly, left into Vigo St., shop on left-hand side. PARK: Sackville Street. TEL: 071 439 8873; fax - 071 437 1201. SER: Valuations; restorations and cleaning (carpets and kelims). VAT: Stan.

Richard Kruml
P.O. Box 4ER. Est. 1966. Open by appointment. STOCK: *Japanese prints, paintings and books, £25-£50,000.* TEL: 071 499 0790; fax - 071 499 0746. VAT: Stan.

La Cloche Freres
LAPADA
8 Blenheim St. Open 10-6, Sat. and Sun. am. by appointment. SIZE: Medium. STOCK: *Fine jewellery, silver, rare wrist and pocket watches, clocks, bronzes, glass, art nouveau and art deco.* LOC: Off Bond St. TEL: 071 355 3471; fax - 071 355 3473. SER: Valuations; restorations. VAT: Stan/Spec.

The Lady Newborough
1 Whitehorse St, Shepherd's Market. (R.D. Rush). Est. 1946. Open 10-6. STOCK: *Jewellery,*

W.1 continued

silverware, objets d'art, Staffordshire ware, objects vertu, British and continental porcelain, paintings and prints. TEL: 071 493 3954. VAT: Stan.

Lane Fine Art Ltd
BADA
123 New Bond St. (C. Foley and A. Nelson). Open 10-6, Sat. 10-1. STOCK: *Oil paintings, 1500-1850 especially English portraits and sporting paintings, landscapes and marines 18th C, £5,000-£500,000.* TEL: 071 499 5020. VAT: Stan/Spec.

D.S. Lavender (Antiques) Ltd
BADA
16b Grafton St. Est. 1945. Open 9.30-5. CL: Sat. STOCK: *Jewels, miniatures, works of art.* PARK: Meters. TEL: 071 629 1782. SER: Valuations. VAT: Stan/Spec.

Ronald A. Lee (Fine Arts) Ltd
BADA
1-9 Bruton Place. (R.A. and C.B. Lee). Est. 1930. Open 10-5. CL: Sat. SIZE: Large. STOCK: *Clocks, furniture, pictures, works of art.* PARK: Meters. TEL: 071 629 5600/499 6266. VAT: Spec.

Lefevre Gallery
30 Bruton St. (Alex Reid and Lefevre Ltd). SLAD. Est. 1871. Open 10-5. CL: Sat. SIZE: Medium. STOCK: *Impressionist paintings, 19th-20th C.* LOC: Between Berkeley Sq. and Bond St. PARK: Meters, Berkeley Sq. TEL: 071 493 2107. SER: Valuations. VAT: Spec.

W.1 continued

The Leger Galleries Ltd BADA
13 Old Bond St. (D.W. Posnett and L.J. Libson). SLAD. Est. 1892. Open 9-5.30, Sat. by appointment. SIZE: Large. STOCK: *Old Masters, English paintings, early English watercolours.* PARK: Meters. TEL: 071 629 3538. SER: Valuations; restorations.

Liberty
Regent St. Est. 1875. Open 9.30-6, Thurs. till 7.30. SIZE: Large. STOCK: *British furniture and metalware, 1860-1930, Gothic Revival, Aesthetic Movement and Arts & Crafts; some Victorian and Edwardian furniture.* LOC: Regent St. joins Piccadilly and Oxford Circus. PARK: Meters and underground in Cavendish Sq. TEL: 071 734 1234. VAT: Stan.

M. and L. Silver Co Ltd
2 Woodstock St. (C. Lasher). Est. 1952. Open 9-5, weekends by appointment. STOCK: *Silver, plate, 1750-1900, £100-£25,000.* LOC: 100yds. from Bond St. Station. TEL: 071 499 5392/5170.

Maas Gallery
15a Clifford St, New Bond St. (J.S. Maas). SLAD. Est. 1960. Open 10-5. CL: Sat. SIZE: Medium. STOCK: *Victorian paintings, drawings, watercolours, illustrations.* LOC: Between New Bond St. and Cork St. PARK: Easy. TEL: 071 734 2302; fax - 071 287 4836. SER: Valuations; buys at auction. VAT: Spec.

MacConnal-Mason Gallery
15 Burlington Arcade, Piccadilly. Est. 1893. Open 9-5.30. SIZE: Medium. STOCK: *Pictures, 19th-20th C.* PARK: Meters. TEL: 071 499 6991. SER: Valuations; restorations. VAT: Spec.

Maggs Bros Ltd BADA
50 Berkeley Sq. (J.F., B.D. and E.F. Maggs, P. Harcourt, R. Harding, H. Bett and J. Collins). ABA. Est. 1853. Open 9.30-5. CL: Sat. SIZE: Large. STOCK: *Rare books, manuscripts, autograph letters, and western miniatures.* PARK: Meters. TEL: 071 493 7160 (4 lines); fax - 071 499 2007. VAT: Stan/Spec.

Mahboubian Gallery
65 Grosvenor St. (H. Mahboubian). TEL: 071 493 9112.

Mallett and Son (Antiques) Ltd BADA
141 New Bond St. Est. 1865. Open 9.15-5.15. CL: Sat. SIZE: Large. STOCK: *English furniture, 1690-1835; clocks, 17th-18th C; china, needlework, decorative pictures, objects and glass.* PARK: Meters in Berkeley Sq. TEL: 071 499 7411; fax - 071 495 3179.

Mallett at Bourdon House Ltd
2 Davies St, Berkeley Sq. Open 9.30-5.30. CL: Sat. SIZE: Large. STOCK: *Continental furniture, clocks, objets d'art; garden statuary and ornaments.*

W.1 continued

PARK: Meters, Berkeley Sq. TEL: 071 629 2444; fax - 071 499 2670. VAT: Stan/Spec.

Mansour Gallery
46-48 Davies St. (M. Mokhtarzadeh). Open 9.30-5.30, Sat. by appointment. STOCK: *Islamic works of art, miniatures; ancient glass and glazed wares; Greek, Roman and Egyptian antiquities.* TEL: 071 491 7444/499 0510. VAT: Stan.

Marks Antiques Ltd LAPADA
49 Curzon St. (A. Marks). Est. 1945. Open 9.30-6 including bank holidays. SIZE: Large. STOCK: *Silver, Sheffield plate.* LOC: Green Park tube, opposite Washington Hotel. PARK: Meters. TEL: 071 499 1788. SER: Valuations; buys at auction. VAT: Stan/Spec.

Marlborough Fine Art (London) Ltd
6 Albemarle St. SLAD. Est. 1946. Open 10-5.30, Sat. 10-12.30. STOCK: *Masters, 19th-20th C.* PARK: Meters or near Cork St. TEL: 071 629 5161.

Marlborough Rare Books Ltd
144 New Bond St. Est. 1946. Open 9.30-5.30. CL: Sat. SIZE: Small. STOCK: *Illustrated books of all periods; rare books on fine and applied arts; English literature.* PARK: Meters. TEL: 071 493 6993. SER: Buys at auction.

Massada Antiques LAPADA
45 New Bond St. (B. and C. Yacobi). Est. 1970. Open 10-5.30, Thurs. 10-6.30. CL: Sat. SIZE: Large. STOCK: *Jewellery, 18th to early 20th C, £50-£25,000; decorative silver £30-£2,500.* LOC: Near Sotheby's. PARK: Grosvenor Garage. TEL: 071 493 4792/493 5610. SER: Valuations; restorations (jewellery). VAT: Stan/Spec.

Mayfair Carpet Gallery Ltd
41 New Bond St. STOCK: *Persian, Oriental rugs and carpets.* TEL: 071 493 0126.

Mayfair Gallery
36 Davies St. (M. Sinai). Open 10-6, Sat. by appointment. STOCK: *19th-20th C antique and decorative art; Gallé, Daum and Lalique glass; Mucha lithographs.* TEL: 071 491 3435; fax - 071 491 3537.

Melton's
27 Bruton Place. (C. Neal). Open 9.30-5.30. CL: Sat. STOCK: *Small antiques and decorative accessories: lamps, prints, textiles, English and Continental.* TEL: 071 409 2938.

Roy Miles Gallery
29 Bruton St. Open 9-6. STOCK: *Major art from China and Russia.* TEL: 071 495 4747.

Nigel Milne Ltd
16c Grafton St. Est. 1979. Open 9.30-5.30, Sat. by appointment. SIZE: Small. STOCK: *Jewellery, Victorian to 1950's, £200-£100,000; silver*

LONDON

W.1 continued

frames. LOC: Corner Grafton St. and Albemarle St., off New Bond St. PARK: Easy. TEL: 071 493 9646/491 2504. SER: Valuations; buys at auction. VAT: Stan/Spec.

John Mitchell and Son BADA
160 New Bond St (1st Floor). SLAD. Est. 1931. Open 9.30-5. CL: Sat. SIZE: Small. *STOCK: Old Master paintings, drawings and watercolours, especially flower paintings, 17th C Dutch, 18th C English and 19th C French.* LOC: Nearest tube Green Park. PARK: Meters. TEL: 071 493 7567. SER: Valuations; restorations (pictures); buys at auction.

Paul Mitchell Ltd BADA
99 New Bond St. Open 9.30-5.30. CL: Sat. SIZE: Large. *STOCK: Picture frames.* PARK: Meters. TEL: 071 493 8732/0860. VAT: Stan/Spec.

Bashir Mohamed Ltd
46 Montagu Sq. Open 10-5 by appointment only. CL: Sat. *STOCK: Islamic art, Indian, Moghul and south east Asian manuscripts and objects.* TEL: 071 723 1844. VAT: Spec.

Moira
22-23 New Bond St. Open 9-6. *STOCK: Fine antique and art deco jewellery.* TEL: 071 629 0160. SER: Valuations.

Sydney L. Moss Ltd BADA
51 Brook St. (P.G. and E.M. Moss). Est. 1910. Open 10-5. CL: Sat. SIZE: Large. *STOCK: Chinese and Japanese paintings and works of art, ceramics, 1500BC-1950; Japanese netsuke, 18th-20th C; reference books (as stock).* LOC: From Grosvenor Sq., up Brook St. to Claridges. PARK: Meters. TEL: 071 629 4670/493 7374; fax - 071 491 9278. SER: Valuations and advice; buys at auction. FAIRS: Grosvenor House. VAT: Spec.

Anthony Mould Ltd
1st Floor, 173 New Bond St. SLAD. Open by appointment. *STOCK: Historic portraits, Old Master and English paintings.* TEL: 071 491 4627.

Paul Nels Ltd LAPADA
6-8 Sedley Place. (P.J. Nels). Open 8.30-5.30. CL: Sat. pm. *STOCK: Rugs, carpets, tapestries and textiles.* TEL: 071 629 1909.

Noortman
40-41 Old Bond St. SLAD. Open 9.30-5.30. *STOCK: Old Masters, French 19th-20th C.* TEL: 071 491 7284.

Richard Ogden Ltd BADA
28 and 29 Burlington Arcade, Piccadilly. Est. 1948. Open 9.30-5.15, Sat. 9.30-4. SIZE: Medium. *STOCK: Antique jewellery, rings.*

W.1 continued

LOC: Near Piccadilly Circus. PARK: Meters. TEL: 071 493 9136/7. SER: Valuations; repairs. VAT: Spec.

The Oriental Art Gallery Ltd.
4 Davies St., St. James's. (Roger Keverne, Ben Janssens, Gerard Hawthorn and Miranda Clarke). Open 9.30-6 and some Sat. *STOCK: Oriental art - Chinese ceramics, porcelain and pottery; cloisonne and painted enamels, jade, lacquer, bronzes, silver and gold; hardstones, paintings, ivory, works of art including Tibetan and Japanese. 2000 BC to 1916.* LOC: Near Mount St. PARK: Easy. TEL: 071 499 7009; home - 081 883 0344 and 081 444 8843. SER: Valuations; restorations; buys at auction. FAIRS: Grosvenor House; Maastricht, New York and Singapore.

Oriental Bronzes Ltd BADA
96 Mount St. Open 10-5.30. CL: Sat. SIZE: Medium. *STOCK: Chinese archaeology, Neolithic to Ming.* LOC: Between Park Lane and Berkeley Sq. PARK: Easy. TEL: 071 493 0309; fax - 071 629 2665.

Partridge Fine Arts plc
144-146 New Bond St. SLAD. Est. 1911. Open 9-5.30. CL: Sat. SIZE: Large. *STOCK: English and French furniture, objets d'art and silver, 18th-19th C ; English, French and Italian paintings, 18th C.* LOC: North of Bruton St., opposite Sotheby's. PARK: Meters. TEL: 071 629 0834; fax - 071 495 6266. SER: Buys at auction. VAT: Spec.

W.H. Patterson Fine Arts Ltd BADA
19 Albemarle St. (W.H. and Mrs. P.M. Patterson and J. White). SLAD. Open 9.30-6. SIZE: Large. *STOCK: 19th C and regular exhibitions for contemporary artists, the New English Art Club, Andrew Coates, Willem Dolphyn and Andrew Flint-Shipman.* LOC: Near Green Park tube station. PARK: Meters. TEL: 071 629 4119. SER: Valuations; restorations. VAT: Spec.

Pelham Galleries BADA
24/25 Mount Street, Mayfair. (A. and L.J. Rubin). Est. 1928. *STOCK: Furniture, English and continental; tapestries, decorative works of art and musical instruments.* TEL: 071 629 0905; fax - 071 485 4511. VAT: Spec.

Ronald Phillips Ltd BADA
26 Bruton St. Est. 1952. *STOCK: English furniture and objets d'art.* TEL: 071 493 2341; fax - 071 495 0843. VAT: Mainly Spec.

S.J. Phillips Ltd BADA
139 New Bond St. (M.S., N.E.L., J.P. and F.E. Norton). Est. 1869. Open 10-5. CL: Sat. SIZE: Large. *STOCK: Silver, jewellery, gold boxes, miniatures.* LOC: Near Bond St. tube station. PARK: Meters. TEL: 071 629 6261; fax - 071 495 6180. SER: Valuations; restorations; buys at auction. FAIRS: Grosvenor House. VAT: Stan/Spec.

W.1 continued

Piccadilly Gallery
16 Cork St. SLAD. Est. 1952. Open 10-5.30, Sat. 10-12.30. CL: Sat. (Aug. and Sept). *STOCK: Symbolist and art nouveau works, 20th C; drawings and watercolours.* PARK: Meters. TEL: 071 629 2875; fax - 071 499 0431. VAT: Spec.

Nicholas S. Pitcher Oriental Art
1st Floor, 29 New Bond St. Open 10.30-5 by appointment. CL: Sat. except by appointment. SIZE: Small. *STOCK: Chinese and Japanese ceramics and works of art, early pottery, to 18th C, £200-£5,000.* LOC: Four doors from Sotheby's, above Gordon Scott shoe shop. PARK: Nearby. TEL: 071 499 6621; home - 071 731 1975. SER: Valuations; buys at auction. VAT: Spec.

Portal Gallery
16a Grafton St/Bond St. (Lionel Levy and Jess Wilder). Est. 1959. Open 10-5.30, Sat. 10-1. SIZE: Medium. *STOCK: Curios, bygones, artefacts, country pieces and objects of virtue, 19th C, £50-£1,000; contemporary British idiosyncratic paintings.* LOC: Junction of New and Old Bond St. PARK: Easy. TEL: 071 493 0706; fax - 071 629 3506. SER: Restorations (paintings including cleaning).

Jonathan Potter Ltd BADA LAPADA
125 New Bond Street. ABA. Est. 1975. Open 10-6, Sat. by appointment. SIZE: Medium. *STOCK: Maps, 16th-19th C, £15-£10,000; prints of London, 18th-19th C, £5-£1,000; atlases and travel books, 16th-19th C, £50-£10,000.* PARK: Meters nearby. TEL: 071 491 3520; fax - 071 491 9754. SER: Valuations; restorations; colouring, framing; buys at auction (maps and prints); catalogue available. VAT: Stan.

Bernard Quaritch Ltd (Booksellers)
5-8 Lower John St, Golden Sq. Est. 1847. Open 9.30-5.30. CL: Sat. SIZE: Large. *STOCK: Antiquarian books.* PARK: Meters, 50yds. TEL: 071 734 2983; fax - 071 437 0967. SER: Buys at auction. VAT: Stan.

Rabi Gallery Ltd
94 Mount St, Mayfair. (R. and V. Soleymani). Est. 1978. Open 10-6. CL: Sat. *STOCK: Ancient and Islamic works of art, carpets and rugs.* TEL: 071 499 8886/7; home - 071 580 9064.

William Redford BADA
99 Mount St. Open 10-5. CL: Sat. SIZE: Small. *STOCK: French furniture, works of art, bronzes, some porcelain.* TEL: 071 629 1165.

David Richards and Sons LAPADA
12 New Cavendish St. (M., H. and E. Richards). Open 9.30-5.30. CL: Sat. SIZE: Large. *STOCK: Silver and plate.* LOC: Off Harley St., at corner of Marylebone High St. PARK: Easy. TEL: 071 935 3206/0322; fax - 071 224 4423. SER: Valuations; restorations. VAT: Stan/Spec.

W.1 continued

The Richmond Gallery
8 Cork St. SLAD. Open 10-6. CL: Sat. *STOCK: Continental paintings, contemporary British artists, 19th-20th C.* TEL: 071 437 9422; fax - 071 734 7018

Jonathan Robinson
1st Floor, 29 New Bond Street. Est. 1984. Open by appointment. SIZE: Small. *STOCK: Chinese porcelain and works of art, from B.C. to 19th C, £200-£5,000.* LOC: Four doors from Sothebys. PARK: Meters. TEL: 071 493 0592. SER: Valuations; consultancy; buys at auction (Oriental items). FAIRS: International Ceramics, Park Lane Hotel. VAT: Spec.

Michael Rose - Source of the Unusual
3 Burlington Arcade, Piccadilly. *STOCK: Victorian, antique and period diamonds, jewellery, watches and Fabergé.* TEL: 071 493 0714.

Russell Rare Books
18 Queen St, Mayfair. (C. Russell). Open 10-5.30. *STOCK: Antiquarian books.* TEL: 071 629 0532; fax - 071 499 2983.

Rutland Gallery
32a St. George St. SLAD. Open 10-5. CL: Sat. and Mon. *STOCK: British primitive paintings and watercolours, 18th-19th C.* TEL: 071 499 5636.

Frank T. Sabin Ltd BADA
5 Royal Arcade, Old Bond St. (John Sabin). Open 9.30-5.30, Sat. 9.30-1. *STOCK: English sporting and decorative prints, 18th-19th C.* TEL: 071 493 3288; fax - 071 499 3593.

Robert G. Sawers
PO Box 4QA. Open by appointment. *STOCK: Books on the Orient, Japanese prints, screens, paintings.* TEL: 071 409 0863; fax - 071 409 0817.

Scarisbrick and Bate Ltd
111 Mount St. (A.C. Bate). Est. 1958. Open 9.30-5.30. CL: Sat. SIZE: Medium. *STOCK: Furniture, decorative items, mid-18th C to early 19th C.* Not stocked: Glass and china. LOC: By Connaught Hotel (off Park Lane). PARK: Meters. TEL: 071 499 2043/4/5; fax - 071 499 2897. SER: Restorations (furniture); buys at auction. VAT: Stan.

Thomas E. Schuster
14 Maddox St. Est. 1973. Open by appointment only. *STOCK: Fine and rare colour plate books and atlases, 1490-1900, £300-£20,000.* TEL: 071 491 2208; fax - 071 491 9872. FAIRS: ABA, Park Lane.

The Schuster Gallery
14 Maddox St. Open 10-5.30, Sat. 10-2. *STOCK: Decorative and rare prints, maps, 1500-1880; medieval manuscripts, £30-£3,000.* LOC: Near Regent St. TEL: 071 491 2208; fax - 071 491 9872. FAIRS: London, New York, Tokyo, San Francisco, Los Angeles.

An Antique Collectors' Club Title

George Chinnery 1774-1852
Artist of India and the China Coast
by Patrick Conner
This book represents the first thorough study of Chinnery's life and work; making use of much hitherto unpublished material, it is both comprehensive and highly readable. It also presents a vivid picture of life in the remote outposts of European empires - Madras, Calcutta, Serampore, Canton, Macau and Hong Kong. Chinnery's career is observed within the context of the all-powerful East India Company, family and social pressures upon expatriates, and relations between different races and classes. The hookah and the opium pipe, the bungalow and the palanquin, the ayah and the tanka boatwoman are elements in the extraordinary society which Chinnery enjoyed and so compellingly portrayed.
ISBN 1 85149 160 0, 320pp
189 b & w illus, 113 col, £45.00

Available from:
Antique Collectors' Club, 5 Church Street, Woodbridge, Suffolk IP12 1DS
Tel: (0394) 385501 Fax: (0394) 384434

or Market Street Industrial Park, Wappingers' Falls, New York 12590, USA
Tel: 914 297 0003 Fax: 914 297 0068

W.1 continued

The Scripophily Shop
Georgian Arcade, Britannia Hotel, Grosvenor Sq. (K. Hollender). Est. 1979. Open 10-5, Sat. and Sun. by appointment. SIZE: Large. *STOCK: Old bonds and shares, 1800-1950, £5-£2,000.* TEL: 071 495 0580. SER: Valuations. VAT: Stan/Spec.

B.A. Seaby Ltd
7 Davies St. Est. 1926. Open 9.30-5, Sat. by appointment. SIZE: Medium. *STOCK: Antiquities, ancient coins; books on coins, archaeology and history.* LOC: Just north of Berkeley Sq., near Green Park and Bond St. underground. TEL: 071 495 2590; fax - 071 491 1595. SER: Valuations; buys at auction. VAT: Stan/Spec.

Shaikh and Son (Oriental Rugs) Ltd
16 Brook St. (M. Shaikh). Open 10-6. CL: Sat. pm. *STOCK: Persian carpets, rugs, £100-£10,000.* TEL: 071 629 3430. SER: Repairing and cleaning.

Sheppard and Cooper Ltd   BADA
11 St George St. Open 10-5.30. CL: Sat. *STOCK: Ancient and antique glass.* **TEL: 071 629 6489; fax - 071 495 2905.**

Michael Simpson Ltd
11 Savile Row. SLAD. Open 9.30-5.30. CL: Sat. *STOCK: Old Master paintings.* TEL: 071 437 5414; fax - 071 287 5967. VAT: Spec.

W.1 continued

W. Sitch and Co. Ltd.
48 Berwick St. (R. Sitch). Est. 1776. Open 8-5, Sat. 8-1. SIZE: Large. *STOCK: Edwardian and Victorian lighting fixtures and floor standards.* LOC: Off Oxford St. TEL: 071 437 3776. SER: Valuations; restorations; repairs. VAT: Stan.

The Sladmore Gallery
32 Bruton Place, Berkeley Sq. (E.F. Horswell and J.A. Hazandras). Open 10-6. CL: Sat. SIZE: Large. *STOCK: Bronze sculptures, 19th C - Mene, Barye, Fremiet, Bonheur; Impressionist, Bugatti, Troubetskoy, Pompon; contemporary, Geoffrey Dashwood birds, wildlife; Gill Parker, sporting, polo.* TEL: 071 499 0365. SER: Valuations; restorations. VAT: Stan/Spec.

Stephen Somerville Ltd
32 St George St. SLAD. Est. 1987. Open 10-5, Sat. and Sun. by appointment. SIZE: Small. *STOCK: Old Master prints and drawings; English paintings, watercolours, prints and drawings, 17th-20th C, £50-£50,000.* LOC: Off Hanover Sq., parallel to New Bond St. TEL: 071 493 8363; home - 071 289 0363. SER: Buys at auction (as stock). FAIRS: World of Watercolours. VAT: Spec.

Henry Sotheran Ltd
2/5 Sackville St, Piccadilly. Est. 1761. Open 9.30-6, Sat. 10-4. *STOCK: Antiquarian books and*

LONDON

W.1 continued

prints, including John Gould prints. TEL: 071 439 6151. SER: Restorations and binding (books, prints); buys at auction. VAT: Stan.

South Audley Antiques LAPADA
36 South Audley St. (F. and A. Ghassemi and R.S Idenden). Open 10-6, Sat. 10-2. STOCK: Fine Victorian and European paintings, continental and English furniture, porcelain, bronzes, glass, K.P.M. plaques; enamels, Persian carpets. TEL: 071 499 3178/3195; fax - 071 355 3548. SER: Interior design. VAT: Spec.

Alfred Speelman BADA
129 Mount St. Est. 1931. Open 10-5. SIZE: Large. STOCK: Chinese and Japanese works of art, Shang era to 19th C. TEL: 071 499 5126. SER: Valuations; buys at auction. VAT: Spec.

Edward Speelman Ltd
175 Piccadilly. SLAD. Est. 1931. Open 10-1 and 2-5. CL: Sat. SIZE: Medium. STOCK: Old Master paintings. PARK: Meters. TEL: 071 493 0657. SER: Valuations; restorations. VAT: Spec.

Stair and Company Ltd BADA
14 Mount St. CINOA. Est. 1911. Open 9.30-5.30. CL: Sat. SIZE: Large. STOCK: 18th C English furniture, works of art, mirrors, chandeliers, barometers, needlework, lamps, clocks, prints. LOC: Past Connaught Hotel, towards South Audley St. PARK: Meters, and Adam's Row. TEL: 071 499 1784/5; fax - 071 629 1050. SER: Restorations; buys at auction. VAT: Spec.

Stoppenbach and Delestre Ltd
25 Cork St. SLAD. Open 10-5.30, Sat. 10-1. STOCK: French paintings, drawings and sculpture, 19th-20th C. TEL: 071 734 3534.

The Taylor Gallery
4 Royal Arcade, Old Bond St. (J. Taylor). Est. 1986. Open 10-5. CL: Sat. SIZE: Large. STOCK: Irish paintings, 20th C; British Impressionists and R.A. artists - Spear, Weight. TEL: 071 493 4111. SER: Restorations; buys at auction (paintings).

F. Teltscher Ltd
17 Crawford St. Est. 1956. Open 11-5. CL: Sat. STOCK: Pictures, wood carvings, works of art. PARK: Meters. TEL: 071 935 0525. SER: Valuations; restorations. VAT: Spec.

Tessiers Ltd BADA
26 New Bond St. (T.P.C. Watkins). Open 9.30-5, Sat. 9.30-3. STOCK: Silver, jewellery, objets d'art. TEL: 071 629 0458; fax - same. SER: Valuations; restorations. VAT: Spec.

William Thuillier
180 New Bond Street. Open by appointment only. STOCK: Old Master paintings and drawings. TEL: 071 499 0106.

W.1 continued

Toynbee-Clarke Interiors Ltd
95 Mount St. (G. and D. Toynbee-Clarke). Est. 1953. Open 9-5.30. CL: Sat. SIZE: Medium. STOCK: Decorative English and continental furniture and objects, 17th-18th C; Chinese hand painted wallpapers, 18th C; French scenic wallpapers, early 19th C; Chinese and Japanese paintings and screens, 17th-19th C. LOC: Between north-west corner of Berkeley Sq. and Park Lane. PARK: Meters. TEL: 071 499 4472; fax - 071 495 1204. SER: Buys at auction. VAT: Stan/Spec.

Tradition - Military Antiques
5a Shepherd St, Mayfair. (R. Belmont-Maitland). Open 9-6. CL: Sat. STOCK: Military uniforms, arms, model soldiers. TEL: 071 493 7452/491 7077. VAT: Stan/Spec.

M. Turpin Ltd LAPADA
27 Bruton St. Open 10-5 or by appointment. CL: Sat. SIZE: Large. STOCK: English and continental furniture, mirrors, chandeliers and objets d'art, 18th C. LOC: Between Berkeley Sq. and Bond St. PARK: Limited and meters. TEL: 071 493 3275/736 3417; fax - 071 244 6254/408 1869.

Under Two Flags
4 St Christopher's Place. (A.C. Coutts). Est. 1973. Open 10-5. CL: Mon. SIZE: Small. STOCK: Toy soldiers, old and new military prints, books, finely detailed painted models of all periods. LOC: Off Wigmore St. TEL: 071 935 6934.

Jan van Beers Oriental Art BADA
34 Davies St. Est. 1978. Open 10-6. CL: Sat. SIZE: Medium. STOCK: Chinese and Japanese ceramics and works of art, 200BC to 1800 AD; Eastern Javanese stone and terracotta sculptures, 12th-14th C. LOC: Between Berkeley Sq. and Oxford St. PARK: Easy. TEL: 071 408 0434. SER: Valuations. FAIRS: Cologne. VAT: Spec.

Venners Antiques
7 New Cavendish St. (Mrs S. Davis). Open 10.15-4.15, Sat. 10-1. CL: Mon. STOCK: 18th-19th C English porcelain and pottery. PARK: Meters. TEL: 071 935 0184. SER: Valuations; buys at auction. VAT: Spec.

Vigo Carpet Gallery LAPADA
6a Vigo St. Open 9-5.30, Fri. 9-5. CL: Sat. STOCK: Oriental and European rugs and carpets, tapestries and needlework. TEL: 071 439 6971; fax - 071 439 2353. SER: Design.

Vigo-Sternberg Galleries BADA LAPADA
37 South Audley St. Est. 1920. Open 9-5. CL: Sat. STOCK: European tapestries, 15th C to contemporary; Oriental and European rugs, 1650-1850. PARK: Meters. TEL: 071 629 8307; fax - 071 629 9591. VAT: Stan/Spec.

STAIR
& COMPANY   ESTABLISHED 1911

A beautifully modelled marble carving by Joseph Gott depicting an Italian greyhound and pups.
English, circa 1825. 57cms wide 29cms deep 36cms high

Joseph Gott (1785-1860) worked for many years in Rome and completed several versions of this subject, all of varying sizes. He exhibited regularly at the Royal Academy from 1820-1848 and works can be seen in the Soane Museum, London as well as in Washington, New York and a large collection is in Angers, France.

We are now in new galleries at

14 MOUNT STREET, LONDON W1Y 5RA
TELEPHONE (071) 499-1784 FACSIMILE (071) 629-1050
also at: 942 MADISON AVENUE, NEW YORK, NY 10021, U.S.A.

LONDON

W.1 continued

Angela Gräfin von Wallwitz   BADA
32 St. George St. Open 10-5. CL: Sat. SIZE: Large. *STOCK: Fine and rare continental pottery, porcelain and works of art, 15th to early 19th C.* LOC: Parallel to Bond St., opposite Sotheby's rear entrance. TEL: 071 499 6453; fax - 071 370 5110. SER: Valuations; buys at auction. FAIRS: Grosvenor House; Basle; Maastricht. VAT: Spec.

Walpole Gallery
38 Dover St. SLAD. Open 9.30-5.30. CL: Sat. except when exhibitions held. *STOCK: Italian Old Master paintings.* TEL: 071 499 6626.

Wartski Ltd   BADA
14 Grafton St. Est. 1865. Open 9.30-5. CL: Sat. SIZE: Medium. *STOCK: Jewellery, 18th C gold boxes, Fabergé, Russian works of art, silver.* PARK: Meters. TEL: 071 493 1141. SER: Restorations; buys at auction. FAIRS: Grosvenor House, International Silver and Jewellery. VAT: Stan/Spec.

Waterhouse and Dodd
1st Floor, 110 New Bond St. (R. Waterhouse and J. Dodd). Est. 1975. Open 10-6, Sat. and Sun. by appointment. SIZE: Medium. *STOCK: British and European oil paintings, watercolours and drawings, 1850-1950, £2,000-£50,000.* LOC: Corner of Brook St. and Bond St. - entrance on Brook St. TEL: 071 491 9293. SER: Valuations; restorations; buys at auction (paintings). FAIRS: City of London Antiques and Fine Art; Olympia. VAT: Spec.

The Weiss Gallery
1B Albemarle St. Open 10-6. CL: Sat. *STOCK: Elizabethan, Jacobean and early European portraits.* TEL: 071 409 0035. SER: Valuations; restorations.

The Welbeck Gallery
18 Thayer St. (D. and S. Spellman). Est. 1975. Open 10-5, Sat. 10.30-12.30. *STOCK: Prints - topographical, natural history, military, birds, 17th-20th C; etchings, engraving, lithographs.* PARK: Meters. TEL: 071 935 4825; home - 071 340 7130. SER: Framing. VAT: Stan.

William Weston Gallery
7 Royal Arcade, Albemarle St. SLAD. Est. 1964. Open 9.30-5.30. CL: Sat. SIZE: Small. *STOCK: Etchings, lithographs, drawings, 1800-1970.* LOC: Off Piccadilly. TEL: 071 493 0722; fax - 071 491 9240. VAT: Spec.

Wildenstein and Co Ltd
147 New Bond St. SLAD. Est. 1934. Open 10-5.30. CL: Sat. SIZE: Large. *STOCK: Impressionist and Old Master paintings and drawings.* PARK: Meters. TEL: 071 629 0602; fax - 071 493 3924.

W.1 continued

Wilkins and Wilkins
1 Barrett St, St Christophers Pl. (M. Wilkins). Est. 1981. Open 11-5. CL: Sat. SIZE: Small. *STOCK: English 18th C portraits and decorative paintings, £700-£20,000.* LOC: Near Selfridges. TEL: 071 935 9613. SER: Restorations; framing. VAT: Stan/Spec.

Wilkinson plc
1 Grafton St. Est. 1947. Open 9.30-5. CL: Sat. *STOCK: Glass, especially chandeliers, 18th C and reproduction; art metal work.* LOC: Nearest underground - Green Park. TEL: 071 495 2477. SER: Restorations and repairs (glass and metalwork).

Williams and Son
2 Grafton St. (J.R. Williams). Est. 1931. Open 9.30-6. CL: Sat. SIZE: Large. *STOCK: British and European paintings, 19th C.* LOC: Between Bond St. and Berkeley Sq. TEL: 071 493 4985/5751; fax - 071 409 7363. VAT: Stan/Spec.

The Christopher Wood Gallery   BADA
141 New Bond Street. SLAD. Est. 1977. Open 9-5.30. CL: Sat. *STOCK: Victorian, Edwardian and pre-Raphaelite paintings, drawings, watercolours, sculpture, studio pottery, Gothic furniture.* TEL: 071 499 7411; fax - 071 495 3179. VAT: Spec.

Linda Wrigglesworth   LAPADA
Ground Floor Suite, 34 Brook St. Est. 1978. Open 9.30-5.30. CL: Sat. SIZE: Small. *STOCK: Chinese costume and textiles of the Qing dynasty, 1644-1911, £200+.* LOC: Corner of South Molton St. PARK: Grosvenor Square. TEL: 071 408 0177. SER: Valuations; restorations; mounting, framing; buys on commission (Oriental). FAIRS: Maastricht, Australia, IAD New York. VAT: Stan/Spec. *Trade only.*

Young and Stephen Ltd   LAPADA
1 Burlington Gardens, New Bond St. (Mr and Mrs S. Burton). Est. 1975. Open 9.30-5.45, Sat. 10.30-3.30. *STOCK: Fine Edwardian, art nouveau and art deco jewellery.* TEL: 071 499 7927; fax - 071 493 8905.

Zadah Gallery
29 Conduit St. Est. 1976. Open 9.30-6. *STOCK: Oriental and European carpets, rugs, tapestries and textiles.* TEL: 071 493 2622/2673.

LONDON W.2

Albion Art (UK) Ltd   LAPADA
(Mr and Mrs G. Jefferson). Open by appointment only. *STOCK: Jewellery, 18th to early 20th C; oil paintings, 18th-19th C, prints, pre-18th to early 20th C.* TEL: 071 258 1949; fax - 071 724 7428. *Trade Only.*

W.2 continued

Bayswater Books
27a Craven Terrace, Lancaster Gate. Est. 1984. Open 11-7. SIZE: Small. STOCK: Antiquarian books, maps and prints, £5-£500; secondhand books, photographica, ephemera, £1-£500. LOC: One-way street running south from Craven Rd. to Bayswater Rd. PARK: Meters or NCP 200 metres. TEL: 071 402 7398. SER: Book search and mail order.

John Bonham, Murray Feely Fine Art
46 Porchester Rd. (Murray Feely). Est. 1983. Open 10.30-12.30 and 2.30-5.30. CL: Mon. SIZE: Small. STOCK: Oils and watercolours, mainly 20th C; sculpture, 18th-19th C; all £150-£5,000. LOC: 50 yards from Royal Oak tube station. PARK: Meters. TEL: 071 221 7208. SER: Valuations. FAIRS: 20th C Art; Hong Kong International Art. VAT: Spec.

Claude Bornoff BADA
20 Chepstow Corner, Pembridge Villas. Est. 1949. Open 9.30-5.30. CL: Sat. SIZE: Medium. STOCK: English and continental furniture, china, metalware and unusual items. PARK: Meters. TEL: 071 229 8947. VAT: Stan/Spec.

Ruby Buckle (Antique Fireplaces)
18 Chepstow Corner, Pembridge Villas. Open 10-6. STOCK: Fireplaces. TEL: 071 229 8843; fax - 071 229 8864.

Connaught Galleries
44 Connaught St. (M. Hollamby). Est. 1966. Open 10-6.30, Sat. 10-1. SIZE: Medium. STOCK: Antique and reproduction sporting, historical, geographical and decorative prints. LOC: Near Marble Arch. PARK: Meters. TEL: 071 723 1660. SER: Picture framing. VAT: Spec.

Craven Gallery
30 Craven Terrace. (C. and A. Quaradeghini). Est. 1974. Open 11-6, Sat. 3-7, other times by appointment. SIZE: Large and warehouse. STOCK: Silver and plate, 19th-20th C; furniture, china and glass, Victorian. LOC: Off Bayswater Rd. PARK: Easy. TEL: 071 402 2802; home - 081 998 0769. VAT: Stan. Trade Only.

Hosains Books and Antiques
25 Connaught St. Est. 1979. Open 11-5. CL: Sat. and Mon. STOCK: Scarce books, manuscripts, miniatures and prints on Islamic world, Tibet, Central Asia and India. TEL: 071 262 7900.

Manya Igel Fine Arts Ltd LAPADA
21/22 Peters Court, Porchester Rd. (M. Igel and B.S. Prydal). Est. 1977. Open 10-5 by appointment only. SIZE: Large. STOCK: Mainly Modern and Contemporary British works, £250-£25,000. LOC: Off Queensway. PARK: Nearby. TEL: 071 229 1669/8429; fax - 071 229 6770. VAT: Spec.

W.2 continued

Ian Lieber
The Shop, 29 Craven Terrace, Lancaster Gate. Est. 1965. Open by appointment. SIZE: Medium. STOCK: Furniture, early 19th C and decorative; porcelain, objets d'art, paintings, costume jewellery. LOC: Near Bayswater Rd. TEL: 071 262 5505. SER: Buys at auction. FAIRS: Olympia. VAT: Stan/Spec.

Daniel Mankowitz
16 Pembridge Sq. Est. 1970. Open by appointment only. SIZE: Medium. STOCK: Furniture, English and continental, 16th-18th C, £100-£10,000; works of art, English and continental, 15th-19th C, £50-£5,000; tapestries, 16th-18th C, £200-£3,000. LOC: Between Kensington Church St. and Westbourne Grove. PARK: Easy. TEL: 071 229 9270; home - same; fax - 071 792 2141. FAIRS: Olympia. VAT: Spec. Trade Only.

William C. Mansell
24 Connaught St. STOCK: Gold, silver, clocks, watches and jewellery. TEL: 071 723 4154. SER: Restorations; repairs.

The Mark Gallery BADA
9 Porchester Place, Marble Arch. (H. Mark). CINOA. Est. 1969. Open 10-1 and 2-6, Sat. 11-1. SIZE: Medium. STOCK: Russian icons, 16th-19th C; modern graphics - French school. LOC: Near Marble Arch. TEL: 071 262 4906; fax - 071 224 9416. SER: Valuations; restorations; buys at auction. VAT: Stan/Spec.

M. McAleer
(M.J. McAleer and Mrs M. McAleer). Est. 1969. Open by appointment. SIZE: Small. STOCK: Small collectable and Irish and Scottish provincial silver. LOC: Near Whiteleys, Bayswater. TEL: 071 727 7979. SER: Buys at auction (silver). VAT: Stan/Spec.

Whitford and Hughes
(Adrian Mibus). Open by appointment only. STOCK: Oil paintings and sculpture, late 19th to 20th C. TEL: 071 221 8097; fax - 071 229 3265.

LONDON W.3

Z.J. Okolski
14 Princes Ave. Est. 1973. Open any time by appointment. SIZE: Medium. STOCK: Oil paintings, 1750-1950. LOC: 1/2 mile from Chiswick flyover, off North Circular Rd; 1/4 mile from Acton Town underground (Piccadilly line). PARK: Easy TEL: 081 992 7032; home - same. SER: Valuations. VAT: Spec.

LONDON W.4

Antiques 132
132 Chiswick High Rd. Est. 1974. Open 10.30-6. SIZE: Small. STOCK: Furniture - aesthetic movement, arts and crafts, art nouveau, art deco;

W.4 continued

related artefacts and ceramics, £10-£3,000. LOC: 1 mile from end of M4. PARK: Easy. TEL: 081 995 0969. SER: Valuations; buys at auction. VAT: Stan/Spec.

The Chiswick Fireplace Co.
68 Southfield Rd, Chiswick. (Mr Bee). Open 9.30-5.30. SIZE: Medium. *STOCK: Original cast iron fireplaces, late Victorian to early 1900's, £200-£1,000.* LOC: 8 minutes walk from Turnham Green underground. PARK: Easy. TEL: 081 995 4011. SER: Restorations. VAT: Stan.

Dick Coats
32 Grantham Rd, Chiswick. Open by appointment. *STOCK: 19th-20th C sculpture and paintings.* TEL: 081 995 9733.

Adrian Hornsey Ltd
The Old Cinema, 160 Chiswick High Rd. Open daily. *STOCK: General antiques and decorative accessories.* TEL: 081 995 4166. SER: Courier.

Moss Galleries - Rachel Moss
LAPADA
2 Prebend Gardens. Est. 1970. Open by appointment only. SIZE: Small. *STOCK: English and Scottish watercolours, 18th-20th C.* LOC: Near Stamford Brook Tube Station. TEL: 081 994 2099. SER: Valuations; restorations; buys at auction. FAIRS: Olympia; World of Watercolours; Twentieth Century. VAT: Spec.

The Old Cinema Antique Department Store
LAPADA
160 Chiswick High Rd. Est. 1977. Open 10-6, Sun. 12-5. SIZE: Large - 15 dealers. *STOCK: General antiques including furniture, gardenalia, decorative and architectural items, 1800-1940, £100-£6,000.* PARK: Easy. TEL: 081 995 4166. SER: Restorations. VAT: Stan/Spec.

The Old Dairy
164 Thames Rd, Strand-on-the-Green, Chiswick. (N.J. Quinn). Est. 1980. Open Tues.-Sun. 10.30-6 and by appointment. SIZE: Medium. *STOCK: 19th C furniture and decorative items including pine, painted and fruitwood armoires, sleighbeds and dressers, £25-£950.* LOC: North side of Thames, east of Kew Bridge, near junction of north and south circulars. PARK: Easy. TEL: 081 994 3140; home - same.

Strand Antiques
166 Thames Rd., Strand-on-the-Green, Chiswick. Est. 1977. Open 12-5 including Sun. or by appointment. SIZE: Large. *STOCK: Books, kitchen items, glass, furniture, jewellery, paintings, prints, fabrics, china, silver, clothes, and collectors' items, £1-£500.* LOC: Behind Bull's Head Public House, about 400yds. from Kew Bridge. PARK: Easy. TEL: 081 994 1912.

W.4 continued

Terry Antiques
The Old Cinema, 160 Chiswick High Rd. (T.H. Murphy). Open 10-6, Sun. 12-5. *STOCK: Furniture - mahogany, walnut, rosewood, some oak, mid 18th to mid 19th C, £100-£3,000; objets d'art, grandfather clocks.* TEL: 081 995 4166; home - 081 889 9781. VAT: Stan.

LONDON W.5

Aberdeen House Antiques
LAPADA
75 St. Mary's Rd. (N. Schwartz). Est. 1971. Open 10-5.30. SIZE: Medium. *STOCK: Furniture and pictures, £50-£2,000; decorative items and textiles, £25-£2,000; china, glass and silver, £25-£1,000; all 18th-20th C.* LOC: On B455 1 mile north of A4. PARK: Easy and at rear. TEL: 081 567 1223/5194. SER: Valuations. FAIRS: Olympia and Barbican. VAT: Stan.

The Badger
12 St. Mary's Rd. (M. and E. Aalders). Est. 1967. Open 9.30-6. SIZE: Medium. *STOCK: Furniture, £100-£2,000; clocks, £1,000-£3,000; both 18th-19th C; ceramics, 19th C, £50-£1,000.* PARK: Easy. TEL: 081 567 5601. SER: Valuations; restorations (furniture and clocks); buys at auction (clocks and watches). VAT: Stan/Spec.

S. Bensiglio Ltd
LAPADA
41 The Ridings. (Mr and Mrs S. Bensiglio). Open by appointment. *STOCK: Rugs and carpets.* TEL: 081 997 2140.

Ealing Gallery
78 St. Mary's Rd, Ealing. (Mrs N. Lane). Open 10.30-5.30. CL: Mon. *STOCK: Oil paintings, £100-£5,000; watercolours, £50-£3,000; both 19th to early 20th C; contemporary paintings, £30-£250.* PARK: Nearby. TEL: 081 840 7883. SER: Valuations; restorations (oils and watercolours); framing. VAT: Spec.

Harold's Place
148 South Ealing Rd. (H. Bowman). Est. 1977. Open 10-6. CL: Wed. SIZE: Medium. *STOCK: Wall plates, commemoratives, porcelain, 19th to early 20th C, £5-£100.* LOC: 1/2 mile north of A4/M4 at Ealing. TEL: 081 579 4825.

The Old Pine Shop
80 St. Mary's Rd, Ealing. (L. A. and K. Denwood). Est. 1971. Open 10-5.30. CL: Mon. SIZE: Medium. *STOCK: Victorian and Edwardian pine furniture, £50-£1,000.* LOC: Midway between Ealing Broadway and A4, on B455, opposite St. Mary's church. PARK: Easy and opposite. TEL: 081 567 7951. SER: Valuations. VAT: Stan.

Terrace Antiques
10 South Ealing Rd. (N. Schwartz). Est. 1971. Open 10-5.30. SIZE: Medium. *STOCK: Victorian furniture and pine, 1850-1920, £50-£500; china,*

W.5 continued

glass and pictures, silver and plate, 1850-1950, £10-£200. LOC: 1 mile north of A4 on B455. PARK: Easy and opposite. TEL: 081 567 5194/ 1223. SER: Valuations. FAIRS: Olympia and Barbican. VAT: Stan.

LONDON W.6

Architectural Antiques
351 King St. (G.P.A. Duc). Est. 1985. Open 9-5, Sat. 10-4. SIZE: Medium. *STOCK: Marble chimney pieces, 18th-19th C, £500-£5,000; French furniture, 19th C, £500-£1,000.* PARK: Easy and Black Lion Lane. TEL: 081 741 7883; fax - 081 741 1109. SER: Valuations; cleaning and polishing (marble chimney pieces on site); repair. VAT: Stan. *Trade Only.*

N. Davighi
117 Shepherd's Bush Rd. Est. 1950. Open 9.30-5. SIZE: Medium. *STOCK: Chandeliers, light fittings, general antiques, Georgian and Victorian.* PARK: Easy. TEL: 071 603 5357. SER: Valuations; restorations (ormolu, chandeliers and brass).

M.L. Waroujian
110-112 Hammersmith Rd. Est. 1959. *STOCK: Antique Oriental carpets and rugs.* TEL: 081 748 7509. SER: Cleaning, repairs (Persian and Oriental carpets). VAT: Spec.

LONDON W8

Al Mashreq Galleries LAPADA
110 Kensington Church St. (J.H. Mantoura). Est. 1983. Open 10-6. SIZE: Medium. *STOCK: Islamic decorative art and antiques.* PARK: Meters. TEL: 071 229 5453. VAT: Spec.

The Antique Home BADA
104A Kensington Church St. (M. Priestley and B.T.W. Rolleston). Est. 1950. Open 10-1 and 2.30-6. CL: Sat. pm. SIZE: Large. *STOCK: English furniture, 18th C, £1,500-£50,000.* PARK: Easy. TEL: 071 229 5892. VAT: Spec.

Valerie Arieta
97b Kensington Church St. Open Mon.-Fri. 10.30-5.30 or by appointment. *STOCK: American, English, continental antiques and American Indian art.* TEL: 071 243 1074/794 7613.

Garry Atkins
107 Kensington Church St. (Garry and Julie Atkins). Est. 1986. Open 10-5.30, Mon. 11-5.30, Sat. am. by appointment. SIZE: Small. *STOCK: English and continental pottery, to 18th C, £50-£5,000; small furniture, to 19th C, £300-£3,000.* LOC: Between Kensington High St. and Notting Hill Gate. PARK: Meters. TEL: 071 727 8737; fax - 071 792 9010. SER: Valuations; buys at auction (English and continental pottery). FAIRS: International Ceramic; Barbican. VAT: Spec.

THE OLD PINE SHOP

80 St Marys Road • Ealing • London W5 5EX
081-567 7951

WE SELL
ENGLISH AND CONTINENTAL
STRIPPED ANTIQUE PINE
FURNITURE
FULLY RESTORED TO A
HIGH STANDARD

200 varied pieces always in stock

We do not specialise, however we do tend to favour wardrobes (usually 20-25 in stock)

W.8 continued

Eddy Bardawil BADA
106 Kensington Church St. (E.S. Bardawil). Est. 1979. Open 10-1 and 2-5.30, Sat. 10-1.30. SIZE: Medium. *STOCK: English furniture - mahogany, satinwood, walnut; mirrors, brass-ware, tea-caddies, all pre-1830, £300-£20,000; prints, 18th C.* LOC: Corner premises, Berkeley Gardens/Church St. PARK: Easy. TEL: 071 221 3967; fax - 071 221 5124. SER: Valuations; restorations (furniture); polishing. VAT: Stan/ Spec.

Barnet Antiques BADA
79 Kensington Church St. *STOCK: 18th to early 19th C English furniture.* TEL: 071 376 2817.

Baumkotter Gallery LAPADA
63a Kensington Church St. (Mrs L. Baumkotter). Est. 1968. Open 9.30-6. CL: Sat. SIZE: Large. *STOCK: 17th-19th C oil paintings.* TEL: 071 937 5171. VAT: Spec.

Bonrose Antiques
207-211 Kensington Church St. *STOCK: French clocks; furniture, porcelain and silver.* TEL: 071 221 3139/727 6597.

LONDON

W.8 continued

David Brower Antiques
113 Kensington Church St. Est. 1965. Open 10-6. CL: Sat. SIZE: Medium. *STOCK: Oriental and continental decorative porcelain, £100-£5,000; French and Oriental furniture, bronzes and clocks.* PARK: Meters nearby. TEL: 071 221 4155. SER: Buys at auction. VAT: Stan/Spec.

The Cameo Gallery   LAPADA
38 Kensington Church St. (M. Levy). Est. 1974. Open 10-5.30, Sun. by appointment. *STOCK: Art nouveau, art deco glass, furniture and bronzes, 1870-1940, £300-£50,000.* LOC: Off Kensington High St. PARK: Nearby. TEL: 071 938 4114; fax - 071 376 0686. SER: Valuations; buys at auction (as stock). VAT: Stan/Spec.

The Lucy B. Campbell Gallery
123 Kensington Church St. Est. 1983. Open 10-6, Sat. 10-4. SIZE: Medium. *STOCK: Fine decorative prints, 17th-19th C; contemporary originals.* Not stocked: Maps and sporting prints. PARK: Meters. TEL: 071 727 2205. SER: Framing. VAT: Stan.

Coats Oriental Carpets
4 Kensington Church Walk, (off Holland St). (A. Coats). Est. 1973. Open 11-5, Sat. 11-3 or by appointment. SIZE: Medium. *STOCK: Oriental carpets and rugs, kelims, £50-£2,000; Oriental textiles and embroideries, £10-£100; all 19th C.* LOC: Small pedestrian alleyway just off Holland St., off south end of Kensington Church St. PARK: Easy. TEL: 071 937 0983; home - 071 370 2355. SER: Valuations; restorations (re-weaving); buys at auction. VAT: Stan/Spec.

Garrick D. Coleman
5 Kensington Court. (G.D. and G.E. Coleman). Est. 1944. Open by appointmentSIZE: Medium. *STOCK: Furniture, 1680-1900, £150-£12,000; chess sets, 1750-1880, £100-£4,000; decorative items, £50-£2,000; glass paperweights, £200-£3,000; conjuring and magic items.* PARK: Easy. TEL: 071 937 5524. VAT: Stan/Spec.

Mary Cooke Antiques Ltd
BADA LAPADA
121A Kensington Church St. Open 9.30-5.30, Sat. am. by appointment. *STOCK: Silver.* TEL: 071 792 8077. SER: Valuations; restorations; buys at auction. FAIRS: Chelsea Spring and Autumn. VAT: Stan/Spec.

Belinda Coote Tapestries
29 Holland St. Resident. Est. 1970. Open 10-6, Sat. 10-1. *STOCK: Reproduction tapestry wall hangings, cushions, fabrics, borders, paisleys; painted furniture.* Not stocked: Glass, enamel, metalwork. LOC: 1st left off Kensington Church St. from Kensington High St. TEL: 071 937 3924. VAT: Stan.

W.8 continued

Mrs. M.E. Crick
166 Kensington Church St. Est. 1897. CL: Sat. *STOCK: Chandeliers, 18th C to modern English and continental, crystal, cut glass and ormolu.* PARK: Meters. TEL: 071 229 1338; fax - 071 792 1073. VAT: Stan.

George Dare
9 Launceston Place, Kensington. Est. 1980. Open anytime by appointment. SIZE: Medium. *STOCK: English watercolours and oil paintings, mainly 18th-19th C, £100-£2,500.* LOC: Turn left off London bound section of Cromwell Rd., opposite the Forum Hotel. PARK: Easy. TEL: 071 937 7072; home - same. SER: Restorations; framing; buys at auction (as stock). VAT: Stan.

Davies Antiques   LAPADA
44A Kensington Church St. (H.Q.V. Davies). Est. 1976. Open 10-5.30, Sat. 10-3. *STOCK: Continental porcelain especially Meissen, 1710-1930.* TEL: 071 937 9216; fax - 071 938 2032.

Richard Dennis
144 Kensington Church St. Est. 1967. Open 10-6, Sat. 10-2. SIZE: Medium. *STOCK: English studio pottery especially Moorcroft, Martin, Doulton, Pilkington and Parian, 1870-1950.* LOC: Near Notting Hill Gate tube. TEL: 071 727 2061. VAT: Stan/Spec.

Denton Antiques
156 Kensington Church St. (M.T. and M.E. Denton). Open 9.30-5.30. CL: Sat. *STOCK: Cut glass including decorative, and objects, mainly 19th C.* TEL: 071 229 5866; fax - 071 792 1073.

Kay Desmonde
17 Kensington Church Walk. Est. 1964. Open Sat 11-3. *STOCK: Dolls, dolls' houses, dolls' house furniture and accessories.* Not stocked: Modern reproductionsTEL: 071 937 2602; home - 04606 3280.

H. and W. Deutsch Antiques   LAPADA
111 Kensington Church St. Est. 1897. Open 10-5. CL: Tues., Wed. and Sat. SIZE: Large. *STOCK: 18th-19th C continental and English porcelain and glassware; silver, plate and enamel ware, miniature portraits; Oriental porcelain, cloisonne, bronzes, £20-£3,000.* TEL: 071 727 5984. VAT: Stan/Spec.

Michael C. German   BADA LAPADA
38B Kensington Church St. Est. 1954. Open 10-5, Sat. 10-3. *STOCK: European and Oriental arms and armour; specialist in walking sticks.* TEL: 071 937 2771.

Geoffrey Godden
at Klaber and Klaber, 2A Bedford Gdns, Kensington Church St. Est. 1900. Open 10-1 and 2-5, Sat. 10.30-4. *STOCK: English ceramics, 19th C.* PARK: Meters. TEL: 071 727 4573.

W.8 continued

A. and F. Gordon BADA
c/o 52c Brunswick Gardens. Est. 1935. Open by appointment only. SIZE: Medium. STOCK: 18th-19th C English and continental furniture; 17th-20th C paintings; decorative arts. SER: Valuations. VAT: Stan/Spec.

Graham and Oxley (Antiques) Ltd BADA
101 Kensington Church St. Open 10-5.30. STOCK: Porcelain, prints and decorative accessories, 18th-19th C. TEL: 071 229 1850.

Green's Antique Galleries
117 Kensington Church St. (S. Green). Open 9-5. SIZE: Medium. STOCK: Jewellery, 18th C to date; pre-1930 clothes and lace; dolls, china, silver, furniture, paintings, masonic and crocodile and leather items. PARK: Easy. TEL: 071 229 9618/9. VAT: Stan/Spec.

Grosvenor Antiques Ltd BADA
27 Holland St, Kensington. (S.C. and E. Lorie). Est. 1950. STOCK: English and continental porcelain and works of art. TEL: 071 937 8649. VAT: Spec.

Robert Hales Antiques Ltd
131 Kensington Church St. Est. 1967. Open 9.30-5.30. CL: Mon. and Sat. SIZE: Small. STOCK: Islamic, Oriental and ethnographic arms and armour; oceanic art, 16th-19th C. PARK: Easy. TEL: 071 229 3887. SER: Valuations; buys at auction. VAT: Spec.

Jonathan Harris BADA
54 Kensington Church St. Open 9.30-6. CL: Sat. SIZE: Large. STOCK: English, continental, Oriental furniture; works of art. LOC: Near Kensington High St. tube station. PARK: Meters. TEL: 071 937 3133. VAT: Spec.

Haslam and Whiteway
105 Kensington Church St. (T.M. Whiteway). Est. 1969. Open 10-6, Sat. 10-2. SIZE: Small. STOCK: British furniture, £80-£10,000; British decorative arts, £20-£5,000; continental and American decorative arts, £5-£500; all 1850-1930. Not stocked: Pre-Victorian items. LOC: From Notting Hill Gate tube station, down Kensington Church St. Shop is approx. 300yds. down on right. PARK: Meters. TEL: 071 229 1145. SER: Valuations; buys at auction. VAT: Stan.

Jeanette Hayhurst Fine Glass
32A Kensington Church St. Open 10-5, Sat. 11-4. STOCK: Glass - 18th C English drinking, fine 19th C engraved, table decanters, contemporary art, scent bottles, Roman and continental. TEL: 071 938 1539.

D. Holmes
47c Earls Court Rd, (in Abingdon Villas), Kensington. Est. 1965. Open Fri. 2-7 and Sat. 10-5,

W.8 continued

or by appointment. STOCK: Decorative items and furniture, 18th-19th C. TEL: 071 937 6961 or 020 888 0254. SER: Restorations (furniture). VAT: Stan/Spec.

Hope and Glory
131a Kensington Church St. (E.L. Titmuss). Open 10-5. CL: Sat. pm. and Mon. STOCK: Royal commemorative china and glass. TEL: 071 727 8424.

Jonathan Horne BADA
66b & 66c Kensington Church St. Est. 1968. Open 9.30-5.30. CL: Sat. and Sun. except by appointment. SIZE: Medium. STOCK: Early English pottery, needlework and works of art. TEL: 071 221 5658; fax - 071 792 3090. VAT: Stan/Spec.

Valerie Howard LAPADA
131E Kensington Church St. Open 10-5.30, Sat. 10-4. STOCK: Mason's and English Ironstone china, 1810-1860, £50-£10,000; French faience especially from Quimper and Rouen regions, 1750-1920, £20-£3,000; mirrors, 19th C, £150-£2,000. LOC: Corner of Peel St. TEL: 071 792 9702 (ansaphone at night). SER: Valuations; restorations (ceramics); buys at auction (as stock). FAIRS: Olympia. VAT: Spec.

Valerie Howard

Specialist in Ironstone China, Mason's particularly. And French faïence from Quimper & Rouen regions.

LAPADA

Weekdays 10 – 5.30, Saturday 10 – 4
131e Kensington Church Street
(On corner of Peel St)
W8 7PT
Tel. 071-792-9702

IONA ANTIQUES

19th Century English Animal Paintings

Illustrated Catalogue available

IONA ANTIQUES
PO BOX 285 LONDON W8 6HZ ENGLAND
TEL: 071-602 1193   FAX: 071-371 2843

W.8 continued

Iona Antiques BADA
PO Box 285. Est. 1974. Open by appointment only. SIZE: Large. STOCK: *19th C animal paintings, £1,000-£40,000*. LOC: 3 minutes walk from Odeon Cinema, Kensington High St. PARK: Nearby. TEL: 071 602 1193; fax - 071 371 2843. FAIRS: Grosvenor House, Olympia, Harrods.

Japanese Gallery
66d Kensington Church St. (Mr. and Mrs C.D. Wertheim). Est. 1977. Open 10-6. STOCK: *Japanese wood-cut prints; books, screens, netsuke*. TEL: 071 229 2934. SER: Authentification; exhibitions.

Melvyn Jay Antiques and Objets d'Art
64a Kensington Church St. Est. 1960. Open 9-5.45, Sat. 11-2. SIZE: Medium. STOCK: *Mid-19th C French decorative furniture, clocks; continental porcelain, bronzes and silver, £5-£5,000; English and continental furniture*. LOC: From Marble Arch to Kensington High St. Bus No.73. PARK: Easy. TEL: 071 937 6832. SER: Valuations; buys at auction. VAT: Stan/Spec.

John Jesse
160 Kensington Church St. Open 10-6, Sat. 11-1. STOCK: *Decorative arts, 1880-1950, especially art nouveau and art deco silver, glass, bronzes and jewellery*. TEL: 071 229 0312; fax - 071 229 4732.

W.8 continued

Howard Jones LAPADA
43 Kensington Church St. (H. Howard-Jones). Est. 1971. Open 10-5. SIZE: Small. STOCK: *Silver, porcelain, bronzes, £20-£5,000*. Not stocked: Furniture. PARK: Nearby. TEL: 071 937 4359. VAT: Stan/Spec.

Peter Kemp
170 Kensington Church St. Est. 1975. Open 10-5. CL: Sat. SIZE: Medium. STOCK: *Porcelain - Chinese, 10th-19th C; Japanese, 17th-19th C; continental, 18th C; Oriental works of art and porcelain, 18th-19th C*. LOC: 200yds. from Notting Hill tube station. PARK: Meters nearby. TEL: 071 229 2988. SER: Valuations; restorations (porcelain); buys at auction (Oriental and continental porcelain). VAT: Spec.

Kensington Church Street Antiques Centre
58-60 Kensington Church St. Open 10-6. SIZE: Below are listed some of the dealers at this Centre.

Abstract
Unit 1. *Cameo glass and decorative items, both 20th C*. TEL: 071 376 2652. VAT: Stan/Spec.

Nicolaus Boston
Majolica (Minton, Wedgwood, George Jones). TEL: 071 376 0425; fax - 071 937 3400. VAT: Stan/Spec.

LONDON

W.8 continued

Henry Boxer
Unit 12. *20th C paintings and drawings.*
TEL: 071 948 1633; mobile - 0836 388771.

Paul Carter, Robinson and Zeitgeist
Liberty metalwork, ceramics and furniture.
TEL: 071 938 4817; fax - 071 937 3400.

Didier Antiques
Unit 2. *Jewellery and silver, objets d'art, 1860-1960, £50-£7,000.* TEL: 071 938 2537. VAT: Stan/Spec.

Freeforms
Unit 6. *20th C decorative arts including postwar design.* TEL: 071 376 0425.

J A G
Unit 6. *Art glass, including Loetz, Murano, 1880-1960, pewter, WMF, Liberty; ceramics, bronzes and ivories.* TEL: 071 938 4404; fax - 071 937 3400.

Masquerade
(Lynn Walker). *Vintage design jewellery and accessories.* TEL: 071 937 8974.

Kensington Fine Arts
46 Kensington Church St. (Mrs S. Lowe). Open 10-6, Sat. 10-2. STOCK: *17th-19th C paintings.* TEL: 071 937 5317. SER: Valuations; restorations.

Klaber and Klaber   BADA
2a Bedford Gardens, Kensington Church St. (Mrs B. Klaber and Miss P. Klaber). Est. 1968. Open 10-1 and 2-5, Sat. 10-4, other times by appointment. SIZE: Medium. STOCK: **English and continental porcelain and enamels, 18th-19th C.** LOC: Turning off Kensington Church St. about half way along. PARK: Meters. TEL: 071 727 4573; fax - 071 435 9459. SER: Restorations (porcelain); buys at auction (porcelain, enamels). FAIRS: Grosvenor House. VAT: Spec.

The Lacquer Chest
71 and 75 Kensington Church St. (G. and V. Andersen). Est. 1959. Open 9.30-5.30. CL: Sat. pm. SIZE: Large. STOCK: *Furniture and unusual items.* LOC: Half-way up left-hand side from High St. PARK: Meters. TEL: 071 937 1306. VAT: Stan/Spec.

Lev (Antiques) Ltd
97 Kensington Church St. (Mrs Lev). Est. 1882. Open 10-1 and 2-5. SIZE: Medium. STOCK: *Jewellery, silver, plate, curios.* PARK: Meters. TEL: 071 727 9248. SER: Restorations (pictures); repairs (jewellery, silver).

Lewis and Lloyd   BADA
65 Kensington Church St. Est. 1968. **Open 10.15-5.45, Sat. 10.15-4. SIZE: Medium. STOCK: *Furniture, 18th-19th C, £1,500-£30,000.* PARK: Easy. TEL: 071 938 3323. VAT: Spec.**

Frances Plowden (née Erskine). Pencil and watercolours (Private collection). From *George Chinnery 1774-1852, Artist of India and the China Coast*, by Patrick Conner, published in 1993 by the **Antique Collectors' Club**, £35.00.

W.8 continued

Libra Antiques
131d Kensington Church St. STOCK: *Blue and white pottery, lustre ware.* TEL: 071 727 2990.

Lindsay Antiques Ltd
99 Kensington Church St. (T. Jellinek and L. Shand). Est. 1965. Open 10-1 and 2.15-5.30, Sat. am. by appointment. SIZE: Large. STOCK: *Early English pottery, decorative and unusual objects, 18th-19th C, £100-£10,000.* PARK: Nearby. TEL: 071 727 2333. FAIRS: Olympia Antiques and Olympia Decorative. VAT: Spec.

Eric Lineham and Sons
62 Kensington Church St. Est. 1953. Open 9.30-5.30. CL: Sat. SIZE: Small. STOCK: *English, continental and Oriental porcelain, English and continental glass, objets d'art, clocks and watches, art nouveau, chandeliers, enamels.* LOC: Half way along Kensington Church St. PARK: Meters. TEL: 071 937 9650. VAT: Stan/Spec.

Little Winchester Gallery
36a Kensington Church St. (I. Berge). Est. 1966. Open 11-6. SIZE: Small. STOCK: *French, Dutch and English paintings, 19th-20th C.* PARK: Easy. TEL: 071 937 8444 (24 hr.). VAT: Spec.

C.H. MAJOR
English Antique Furniture

18th and early 19th century furniture in over 3,000ft. of showrooms

154 KENSINGTON CHURCH STREET, LONDON W8 4BN
TEL: 071 229 1162. FAX: 071 221 9676

W.8 continued

C.H. Major (Antiques) Ltd
154 Kensington Church St. (A.H. Major). Est. 1905. Open 10-6. SIZE: Large. STOCK: English mahogany furniture, from 1760, £200-£25,000. Not stocked: China, glass. PARK: Easy. TEL: 071 229 1162; fax - 071 221 9676; home - 081 997 9018. VAT: Stan/Spec.

E. and H. Manners
66a Kensington Church St. Est. 1986. Open 10-5.30, Sat. and Sun. by appointment. STOCK: European and Oriental ceramics, £100-£20,000; Oriental works of art, £100-£4,000; all pre-19th C. TEL: 071 229 5516; fax - same; home - 081 741 7084. SER: Valuations; restorations; buys at auction (ceramics). FAIRS: International Ceramic. VAT: Spec.

S. Marchant and Son   BADA
120 Kensington Church St. (R.P. Marchant). Est. 1925. Open 9.30-5.30. CL: Sat. STOCK: Chinese and Japanese pottery and porcelain, jades, cloisonné, Chinese furniture and paintings. PARK: Easy. TEL: 071 229 5319/3770. SER: Valuations; restorations (porcelain); buys at auction. VAT: Stan/Spec.

J. and J. May   BADA
40 Kensington Church St. Books and articles on commemorative items. Est. 1967. Open 10-1.30

W.8 continued

and 2.30-6. SIZE: Small. STOCK: Commemorative pottery, 1750-1850; commemorative porcelain, enamels, glass pictures, textiles, objets de vertu. LOC: Underground stations: Notting Hill Gate and Kensington High St. PARK: 25yds. Vicarage Gate. TEL: 071 937 3575. SER: Valuations; buys at auction. VAT: Stan/Spec.

D. Mellor and A.L. Baxter
BADA LAPADA
121 Kensington Church St. Open 10-6.30, Sat. 10-4. STOCK: Leather bound literary sets; antiquarian books on history, science, medicine, travel and exploration; 16th-17th C books on literature, history and medieval manuscripts. TEL: 071 229 2033/221 8822; fax - 071 792 0214.

Michael Coins
6 Hillgate St (off Notting Hill Gate). (M. Gouby). Est. 1966. Open 10-5. CL: Sat. SIZE: Small. STOCK: Coins, English and foreign, 1066 A.D. to date; stamps, banknotes and collectors' items. LOC: From Marble Arch to Notting Hill Gate, turn left at corner of Coronet Cinema. PARK: Easy. TEL: 071 727 1518. SER: Valuations; buys at auction. VAT: Stan/Spec.

LONDON

Antique Collectors' Club Titles

Pocket Edition Jackson's Hallmarks *edited by Ian Pickford*
Contains all assay office, Britannia standard, import and date marks plus the 1,000 most important makers' marks, listed alphabetically by mark, for speedy access, together with comments as to rarity, value and speciality of maker.
ISBN 1 85149 128 7
8½ x 4¾in. 172pp
over 1,000 marks, £12.50 hb
£6.95 pb ISBN 1 85149 169 4
'The ideal travelling and buying companion...easy and quick to use'. - Antiques Bulletin

Available from:
Antique Collectors' Club, 5 Church Street, Woodbridge
Suffolk IP12 1DS
Tel: (0394) 385501 Fax: (0394) 384434

or Market Street Industrial Park, Wappingers' Falls
New York 12590, USA
Tel: 914 297 0003 Fax: 914 297 0068

Jackson's Silver and Gold Marks of England, Scotland and Ireland *edited by Ian Pickford*
This major revised edition of what has been the indispensable book on antique silver for over 80 years, essential to dealers, scholars and collectors, contains some 10,000 corrections to the original material aa well as much vital extra information. The text has been extensively updated by a distinguished team of experts. A key reference book, with approximately 15,000 marks illustrated. **ISBN 0 907462 63 4, 766pp, 400 b & w illus, £45.00**

W.8 continued

D.C. Monk and Son
132-134 Kensington Church St. Open 10.30-5. CL: Sat. *STOCK: Oriental porcelain.* TEL: 071 229 3727. VAT: Stan/Spec.

New Century
69 Kensington Church St. (H.S. Lyons). Est. 1988. *STOCK: Arts and crafts, aesthetic and art nouveau furniture, metal and ceramics, 1870-1920, £20-£3,000.* TEL: 071 937 2410. SER: Valuations; restorations; buys at auction. VAT: Stan/Spec.

Oliver-Sutton Antiques   BADA
34c Kensington Church St. (A. Oliver and P. Sutton). Est. 1967. Open 10-5, Sat. 10-2. CL: Aug. *STOCK: Staffordshire, Walton, Sherratt pottery; 19th C portrait figures, animals, cottages.* TEL: 071 937 0633. VAT: Spec.

Henry Phillips   BADA
2 Campden St. Open 9.30-5.30. SIZE: Small. *STOCK: English furniture, 18th to early 19th C.* LOC: Near Kensington Church St. TEL: 071 727 4079; home - 071 937 3448. SER: Buys at auction (English furniture).

The Pruskin Gallery
73 Kensington Church St. *STOCK: Fine art nouveau and art deco glass, bronzes, silver, furniture, ceramics, paintings, posters and prints.* TEL: 071 937 1994; evenings - 071 243 1939.

W.8 continued

Raffety Ltd   BADA LAPADA
34 Kensington Church St. Open 10-5, Sat. by appointment. *STOCK: Fine English longcase and bracket clocks, 17th-18th C; carriage clocks and barometers.* TEL: 071 938 1100; fax - same. SER: Valuations; buys at auction. VAT: Stan/Spec.

Paul Reeves
32B Kensington Church St. Est. 1976. Open 10-6. *STOCK: Architect designed furniture and artifacts, 1860-1960.* TEL: 071 937 1594.

Reindeer Antiques (Reindeer International Ltd.)
81 Kensington Church St. (J.W. Butterworth). Open 9.30-1 and 2-6. *STOCK: Period English and continental furniture and works of art.* PARK: Meters. TEL: 071 937 3754. VAT: Stan/Spec.

Roderick Antique Clocks   LAPADA
23 Vicarage Gate, Kensington. (R. Mee). Est. 1975. Open 10-5.15, Sat. 10-4. *STOCK: Clocks - French decorative and carriage, 19th C, £250-£2,000; English longcase and bracket, 18th-19th C, £2,000-£7,500.* LOC: At junction of Kensington Church St. PARK: Easy. TEL: 071 937 8517. SER: Valuations; restorations (English and French movements and cases). VAT: Spec.

LONDON

JEAN SEWELL
(Antiques) Limited

**3 CAMPDEN STREET
LONDON W.8
071 727 3122**

Large stock of 18th and 19th century porcelain and pottery. Services and collectors' items.

W.8 continued

J. Roger (Antiques) Ltd BADA
17 Uxbridge St. (J. Roger and C. Bayley). Open by appointment. STOCK: Late 18th to early 19th C small elegant pieces furniture, mirrors, prints, porcelain and boxes. TEL: 071 603 7627/381 2884.

Sabin Galleries Ltd BADA
Campden Lodge, 82 Campden Hill Rd. (S.F, E.P. and P.G. Sabin). SLAD. Open by appointment only. STOCK: English paintings and drawings, pre-1830. TEL: 071 937 0471.

Patrick Sandberg Antiques BADA
140-142 Kensington Church St. (P.C.F. Sandberg). Est. 1983. Open 10-6, Sat. 10-4. SIZE: Large. STOCK: 18th to early 19th C English furniture and accessories - candlesticks, tea caddies, clocks and prints, £500-£25,000. TEL: 071 229 0373; fax - 071 792 3467. FAIRS: Café Royal (February); Olympia (June and November). VAT: Spec.

A.V. Santos BADA
1 Campden St. Open 10-1 and 2-6. CL: Sat. STOCK: Chinese porcelain, 17th-18th C. TEL: 071 727 4872; fax - 071 229 4801. VAT: Spec.

Arthur Seager Antiques Ltd LAPADA
25a Holland St, Resident. (A.A. Seager). Est. 1972. Open 10-5.30, Sun. by appointment.

W.8 continued

SIZE: Medium. STOCK: 16th-17th C oak furniture and carvings; treen, metalware and period pottery, £500-£10,000. LOC: Off Kensington Church St. PARK: Easy. TEL: 071 937 3262. SER: Valuations; restorations (furniture); buys at auction (furniture and pottery). VAT: Stan/Spec.

Select Antiques Gallery Ltd
219 Kensington Church St. (M. Vargha and A. Youssefian). Open 10-6, Sat. 10-3. STOCK: French furniture. TEL: 071 727 4783/229 8732.

M. and D. Seligmann BADA
37 Kensington Church St. Est. 1948. Open 10-6, Sat. 11-3, or by appointment. SIZE: Medium. STOCK: 17th-18th C English country furniture, pottery, treen, objets d'art. LOC: Nearest underground Kensington High St. TEL: 071 937 0400; home - 071 722 4315. SER: Valuations; buys at auction. FAIRS: Fine Arts (Olympia) June and November; Chelsea (Spring and Autumn); Café Royal (Spring); Barbican. VAT: Stan/Spec.

Jean Sewell (Antiques) Ltd BADA
3 Campden St. (R. and J. Sewell). Est. 1956. Open 10-5.30. SIZE: Medium. STOCK: Pottery and porcelain, 18th-19th C, £1-£10,000. Not stocked: Silver, furniture and china after 1880. LOC: From Notting Hill Gate down Kensington Church St., fourth street on right at Churchill public house. PARK: Easy. TEL: 071 727 3122. VAT: Stan/Spec.

Sinai Antiques Ltd
221 Kensington Church St. (E. and M. Sinai). Open 9.30-6. CL: Sat. STOCK: Carpets, Oriental arts, silver, fine arts. TEL: 071 229 6190.

Simon Spero
109 Kensington Church St. Author of 'The Price Guide to 18th C English Porcelain'. Est. 1964. Open 10-5, Sat. 10-1. CL: Mon. except by appointment. SIZE: Medium. STOCK: 18th C English ceramics, enamels and watercolours. PARK: Meters. TEL: 071 727 7413. SER: Valuations; buys at auction. VAT: Spec.

A. Spigard
77 Kensington Church Street. Open 9-6. STOCK: General antiques and furniture. TEL: 071 937 2461. SER: Restorations. VAT: Spec.

Constance Stobo
31 Holland St, off Kensington Church St. STOCK: English lustreware, pottery and Staffordshire animals, Wemyss, 18th-19th C. TEL: 071 937 6282.

Stockspring Antiques LAPADA
114 Kensington Church St. (A. Agnew and F. Marno). Open 10-5.30, Sat. 10-1. STOCK: English, European and Oriental pottery and porcelain. TEL: 071 727 7995. VAT: Spec.

LONDON

W.8 continued

Jacob Stodel BADA
116 Kensington Church St. Est. 1949. STOCK: *Continental furniture, objets d'art, ceramics, English furniture.* TEL: 071 221 2652; fax - 071 229 1293. VAT: Spec.

Sukmano Antiques
133 Kensington Church St. Open 10-6. STOCK: *Oriental items.* TEL: 071 229 4323.

Pamela Teignmouth and Son
108 Kensington Church St. (P. Teignmouth and T. Meyer). Est. 1982. Open 10-6, Sat. 10-4. SIZE: Medium. STOCK: *English and continental furniture, 18th-19th C, decorative items, £100-£5,000.* TEL: 071 229 1602. FAIRS: Olympia and Decorators. VAT: Spec.

Murray Thomson Ltd LAPADA
152 Kensington Church St. Est. 1966. Open 10-6. SIZE: Large. STOCK: *English furniture, 18th-19th C.* TEL: 071 727 1727; fax - 071 727 1825. VAT: Stan/Spec.

Through the Looking Glass Ltd
137 Kensington Church St. (J.J.A. and D.A. Pulton). Est. 1958. Open 10-5.30. SIZE: Medium. STOCK: *Mirrors, 19th C, £500-£1,000.* LOC: 200yds. from Notting Hill Gate. PARK: Side roads. TEL: 071 221 4026. SER: Gilding. VAT: Spec.

Toubian Antiques Ltd
180 Kensington Church St. (N. Toubian). Open 10-6. CL: Sat. STOCK: *General antiques.* TEL: 071 221 6476.

Vandekar Antiques
174 Kensington Church St. Est. 1951. Open 10-5.30, Sat. 10-12.30. SIZE: Medium. STOCK: *Oriental porcelain.* LOC: Near Notting Hill Gate tube station. PARK: Meters. TEL: 071 229 7100.

Mary Wise BADA
27 Holland St, Kensington. Est. 1959. STOCK: *English porcelain, Chinese ceramics and jade, works of art, bronzes.* Not stocked: English pottery, jewellery. TEL: **071 937 8649**. SER: Buys at auction (Chinese and English porcelain). VAT: Spec.

LONDON W.9

Fluss and Charlesworth Ltd LAPADA
1 Lauderdale Rd. (E. Fluss and J. Charlesworth). Est. 1970. Open by appointment. STOCK: *18th to early 19th C furniture and works of art.* TEL: 071 286 8339; mobile - 0831 830323. SER: Interior decor. FAIRS: Café Royal; Olympia; LAPADA.

Robert Hall BADA
140 Sutherland Ave. Est. 1976. Open by appointment. STOCK: *Chinese snuff bottles, Ching dynasty; Oriental works of art, jade carvings, 17th-19th C; all £300-£20,000. Chinese contemporary paintings.* PARK: Easy. TEL:

W.9 continued

071 286 0809; fax - 071 289 3287. SER: Valuations; restorations; buys at auction. VAT: Stan/Spec.

Beryl Kendall, The English Watercolour Gallery
2 Warwick Place, Little Venice. Est. 1953. Open 2-6, Sat. by appointment. CL: Mon. STOCK: *English watercolours, 18th-20th C.* TEL: 071 286 9902.

Charles Spencer
24a Ashworth Rd. Open by appointment. STOCK: *Prints, portraits and original designs relating to the history of the theatre from 17th C to date, £50-£10,000.* LOC: Off Elgin Ave., close Maida Vale station. TEL: 071 286 9396. SER: Valuations; buys at auction (theatrical items). VAT: Stan.

Vale Antiques
245 Elgin Ave, Maida Vale. (P. Gooley). STOCK: *General antiques.* TEL: 071 328 4796.

LONDON W.10

Clive Loveless BADA
29 Kelfield Gardens, North Kensington. Resident.Est. 1968.Open by appointment. SIZE: Small. STOCK: *Near Eastern tribal rugs and kilims, 18th-19th C; textiles - 16th-17th C Ottoman and 18th-19th C Central Asian and African.* LOC: Near Ladbroke Grove. PARK: Easy. TEL: 081 969 5831. SER: Valuations; restorations (antique rugs); buys at auction. VAT: Stan/Spec.

Tower Antiques
463 Harrow Rd. (F. Jackson). Open 10-5.30. SIZE: Small. STOCK: *Furniture, pine, paintings and prints.* LOC: Between Gt. Western Rd. and Ladbroke Grove. PARK: Easy. TEL: 081 969 0535. SER: Valuations; restorations (polishing, wood work); buys at auction; shipping; custom built units.

LONDON W.11

Addison Fine Art
57 Addison Avenue. (Mrs. D. Geddes). Est. 1978. Open by appointment. SIZE: Small. STOCK: *British and continental post-impressionist paintings.* TEL: 071 603 2374. SER: Valuations; restorations; buys at auction (paintings). FAIRS: 20th C British Art (Sept.); Olympia (June). VAT: Spec.

Alice's
86 Portobello Rd. (D. Carter). Est. 1960. Open 9-5. SIZE: Large. STOCK: *General antiques and decorative items.* TEL: 071 229 8187; fax - 071 792 2456.

Arbras Gallery
292 Westbourne Grove. (Bob Brass). Est. 1972. Open Fri. 10-5, Sat. 7-5. SIZE: 2 floors. STOCK: *General antiques - silver, boxes, pottery, jewellery, paintings, furniture, books, prints, textiles and watches.* LOC: 50 yards from Portobello Road. TEL: 071 229 6772. VAT: Stan/Spec.

LONDON

W.11 continued

Axia Art Consultants Ltd
121 Ledbury Rd. Est. 1974. *STOCK: Works of art, icons, textiles, metalwork, woodwork and ceramics, Islamic and Byzantine.* TEL: 071 727 9724.

B. and T. Antiques
79 Ledbury Rd. (Mrs B. Lewis). Open 10-6. *STOCK: Furniture, silver, objets d'art, paintings, 18th C to art deco.* TEL: 071 229 7001.

Serge Baillache
189 Westbourne Grove. Est. 1959. Open 9.30-5.30. CL: Sat. SIZE: Medium. *STOCK: English, continental and decorative furniture, 18th-19th C.* PARK: Meters. TEL: 071 229 2270. VAT: Stan/Spec.

Barham Antiques
83 Portobello Rd. Est. 1954. Open 9.30-5, Sat. 7-5. SIZE: Large. *STOCK: Victorian walnut and inlaid continental furniture, writing boxes, tea caddies, inkwells and inkstands, glass epergnes, silver plate, clocks, paintings.* TEL: 071 727 3845. SER: Valuations; buys at auction.

P.R. Barham
111 Portobello Rd. Est. 1951. Open 9-5. SIZE: Large. *STOCK: Victorian, Edwardian, continental furniture, Oriental porcelain, objets d'art, silver, plate and clocks.* TEL: 071 727 3397. SER: Valuations; buys at auction.

Beagle Gallery
303 Westbourne Grove. (A. and J. Beagle). Open 10.30-5. CL: Mon. *STOCK: Indian, Asian and decorative items.* TEL: 071 229 9524.

David Black Oriental Carpets BADA
96 Portland Rd, Holland Park. Est. 1966. Open 11-6. SIZE: Large. *STOCK: Antique and new Oriental room size decorative carpets; tribal rugs, kilims, dhurries, embroideries, £500-£25,000.* LOC: From Notting Hill Gate, second right after Holland Park tube station. PARK: Meters. TEL: 071 727 2566; fax - 071 229 4599. SER: Valuations; restorations; cleaning underfelt. VAT: Spec.

Norman Blackburn
32 Ledbury Road. Est. 1974. Open 10-6, Sat. 10-5. CL: Mon. *STOCK: Framed prints - decorative, stipple and mezzotints, botanical, sporting, marine, portraits and views, pre-1860.* LOC: Two roads east of Portobello. TEL: 071 229 5316. VAT: Spec.

Books & Things
Arbras Gallery, 292 Westbourne Grove. (M. Steenson). ABA, PBFA. Est. 1972. Open Sat. 7-4, Fri. by appointment. SIZE: Small. *STOCK: Antiquarian books, £25-£500; posters, £50-£500; both 20th C.* PARK: Meters. TEL: 071 370 5593 (anytime). SER: Valuations; buys at auction; catalogues issued. FAIRS: PBFA London, Oxford, Bath; ABA, Chelsea.

W.11 continued

F.E.A. Briggs Ltd
73 Ledbury Rd. Est. 1962. Open 8.30-5.30, Sat. and Sun. 10-4. SIZE: 2 shops and warehouse. *STOCK: Furniture and textiles, Victorian, Edwardian and Georgian.* TEL: 071 727 0909/ 221 4950. SER: Valuations. VAT: Stan/Spec.

Britannia Export Antiques
206 Westbourne Grove. (G. Fiumano). Est. 1973. Open 9.30-6, Sat. 10.30-4. SIZE: Large. *STOCK: Silver and ivory, £300-£10,000; furniture, £500-£20,000; all 18th-20th C.* LOC: 200 yards from Portobello Rd. PARK: Meters. TEL: 071 221 2011. SER: Valuations; restorations (silver, porcelain, ivory, furniture and pictures); buys at auction (as restorations). VAT: Stan/Spec.

John Bull (Antiques) Ltd
163 Portobello Rd. Est. 1940. Open Sat. only 7.30-11. *STOCK: Silver including frames, plate, jewellery.* TEL: 071 629 1251. VAT: Stan/Spec.

Butchoff Antiques LAPADA
229 and 233 Westbourne Grove. Est. 1962. Open 10-6, Sat. 10-2. SIZE: Large. *STOCK: Furniture and decorative smalls, paintings, 18th-20th C, £500-£30,000.* TEL: 071 221 8174; fax - 071 792 8923.

Caelt Gallery
182 Westbourne Grove. Est. 1967. Open 9.30-6. SIZE: Large. *STOCK: Oil paintings, 17th-20th C, £200-£10,000.* PARK: Easy. TEL: 071 229 9309. VAT: Spec.

Jack Casimir Ltd BADA LAPADA
The Brass Shop, 23 Pembridge Rd. Est. 1933. Open 10-5.30. SIZE: Medium. *STOCK: Brass, copper, pewter.* Not stocked: Silver, china, jewellery. LOC: 2 mins. walk from Notting Hill Gate station. PARK: 100yds. TEL: 071 727 8643. SER: Exports. VAT: Stan.

Cassio Antiques
68 Ledbury Rd. Est. 1963. Open 10-5.30. SIZE: Large. *STOCK: Furniture.* TEL: 071 727 0678. VAT: Stan/Spec.

Graham Charge Antiques
305 Westbourne Grove. Est. 1975. Open 9.30-5, Sat. 9-5.30. SIZE: Medium. *STOCK: Furniture, 18th-19th C.* LOC: 50yds. off Portobello Rd. PARK: Easy. TEL: 071 229 7907. VAT: Stan/ Spec.

Cohen and Pearce (Oriental Porcelain) BADA
84 Portobello Rd. (M. Cohen). Est. 1974. Open Fri. 10-4, Sat. 8-4 or by appointment. *STOCK: Chinese porcelain, bronzes, works of art; Japanese prints.* TEL: 071 229 9458; fax - 071 229 9653. SER: Valuations; buys at auction. VAT: Spec.

LONDON

W.11 continued

Garrick D. Coleman
Stand 2, Geoffrey Van Arcade, 105 Portobello Rd. Est. 1944. Open Sat. only 8-2. *STOCK: Furniture, 1680-1900, £150-£12,000; chess sets, 1750-1880, £100-£4,000; decorative items, £50-£2,000; glass paperweights, £200-£3,000; conjuring and magic items.* TEL: 071 937 5524. VAT: Stan/Spec.

Collectors' Fine Art at Rostrum
115 Portobello Rd. (Leon Young). Est. 1987. Open 10-6, Sat. 6.30-6, Sun. by appointment. SIZE: Medium. *STOCK: Oils and watercolours, prints and drawings - Masterworks, decorative and fine Victorian, Pre-Raphaelites and 20th C.* PARK: Easy (during week). TEL: 071 243 0420; home - 071 436 1495. SER: Valuations; restorations; research on paintings; buys at auction.

Sheila Cook
13 Addison Avenue, Holland Park. Est. 1970. SIZE: Small. *STOCK: Textiles and period costume, 1800-1960, £50-£5,000.* PARK: Easy. TEL: 071 603 6602. SER: Valuations; buys at auction. VAT: Stan.

The Corner Portobello Antiques Supermarket LAPADA
282, 284, 288, 290 Westbourne Grove. (B. Lipka & Son Ltd.). Open Fri. 12-4, Sat. 7-6. SIZE: 150 dealers. *STOCK: General miniature antiques, silver and jewellery.* TEL: 071 727 2027. SER: Valuations; restorations.

Curá Antiques
34 Ledbury Rd. (G. Antichi). Open 11-6, Sat. 10.30-1. *STOCK: Continental furniture, sculptures, majolica and paintings.* TEL: 071 229 6880.

Daggett Gallery LAPADA
1st and 2nd Floors, 153 Portobello Rd. (Charles and Caroline Daggett). Est. 1977. Open 10-4 (prior telephone call advisable) and Sat. 9-4. SIZE: Medium. *STOCK: British and European pictures, from £100; frames, from £10; both 18th-20th C; painted furniture and needlepoint carpets, 20th C; military medals, 19th-20th C.* LOC: 200 yards from Westbourne Grove towards Elgin Crescent. PARK: Meters. TEL: 071 229 2248. SER: Restorations (pictures and frames); framing; special paint effects; buys at auction (pictures and military medals). FAIRS: Olympia, Barbican and NEC, Birmingham. VAT: Stan/Spec.

Charles Daggett Gallery LAPADA
1st and 2nd Floors, 153 Portobello Rd. (Charles and Caroline Daggett). Est. 1977. Open 10-4, prior telephone call advisable, and Sat. 9-4. SIZE: Medium. *STOCK: 18th-19th C British pictures.* LOC: 200 yards from Westbourne Grove, towards Elgin Crescent. PARK: Meters. TEL: 071 229 2248; fax - 071 229 0193. SER: Restorations (pictures and frames); framing. FAIRS: Olympia, Barbican and NEC, Birmingham. VAT: Stan/Spec.

W.11 continued

John Dale
87 Portobello Rd. Est. 1950. Open 10-4.30, Sat. 8-5. SIZE: Medium. *STOCK: General antiques.* TEL: 071 727 1304. VAT: Stan.

Michael Davidson
52 and 54 Ledbury Rd. Est. 1961. Open 9.45-12.45 and 1.15-5. CL: Sat. pm. in winter. *STOCK: Regency and period furniture, objets d'art.* TEL: 071 229 6088. SER: Valuations. VAT: Stan/Spec.

Delehar
146 Portobello Rd. Est. 1919. Open Sat. 9-4. SIZE: Medium. *STOCK: General antiques, works of art.* Not stocked: Furniture. TEL: 071 727 9860 or 081 450 9998. VAT: Stan/Spec.

Peter Delehar
146 Portobello Rd. Est. 1919. Open Sat. 10-4. SIZE: Medium. *STOCK: Unusual scientific instruments.* TEL: 071 727 9860 or 081 866 8659. FAIRS: International Scientific and Medical Instrument (Organiser). VAT: Stan/Spec.

Demetzy Books
113 Portobello Rd. (P. and M. Hutchinson). ABA, PBFA. Est. 1972. Open Sat. 7.30-3.30. SIZE: Medium. *STOCK: Antiquarian leather bound books, 18th-19th C, £5-£1,000; Dickens' first editions and children's and illustrated books, 18th-20th C, £5-£200.* LOC: 20yds. from junction with Westbourne Grove, opposite Earl of Lonsdale public house. PARK: Meters. TEL: 0993 702209. SER: Valuations; buys at auction (books). FAIRS: ABA Park Lane; PBFA Russell Hotel, London (monthly); Randolph Hotel, Oxford; ABAA New York, Los Angeles, San Francisco.

E. and A. Di Michele Antiques LAPADA
36 Ledbury Rd. Est. 1973. Open 9.30-1 and 2-5, resident so usually available. *STOCK: Continental furniture and Dutch marquetry.* TEL: 071 229 1823.

Dodo
286 Westbourne Grove. (Liz Farrow). Est. 1960. Open Sat. 7-4 or by appointment. *STOCK: English, American and continental posters, enamels, signs and tins; crate, beer, wine, perfume and soap labels; display figures, showcards, packaging.* Not stocked: Furniture, silver, general antiques. LOC: Near Portobello Rd. TEL: 071 229 3132.

Dolphin Arcade
155-157 Portobello Rd. Open Sat. 7-5.30. SIZE: Large - 34 stalls. *STOCK: Jewellery, silver, Oriental porcelain, English pottery, general antiques.* TEL: 071 727 4883. VAT: Stan/Spec.

Elliott and Snowdon Ltd LAPADA
61A Ledbury Rd. Open 10.30-5, Sat. 9.30-12.30. *STOCK: European works of art.* TEL: 071 229 6900.

LONDON

W.11 continued

The Facade
196 Westbourne Grove. Est. 1973. Open 10.30-5.30. *STOCK: Decorative items, 1900-1930 lighting and furniture - mainly French.* PARK: Easy. TEL: 071 727 2159. VAT: Stan.

Jack Fairman (Carpets) Ltd LAPADA
218 Westbourne Grove. (D.R.J. and S.J. Page). Open 9.30-6, Sun. by appointment. *STOCK: Persian and Oriental carpets and rugs; tapestries.* TEL: 071 229 2262; fax - 071 229 2263. SER: Valuations; repairs; cleaning. VAT: Stan.

Fleur de Lys Gallery
227a Westbourne Grove. (H.S. Coronel). Est. 1967. Open 10.30-5. SIZE: Medium. *STOCK: Oil paintings, 19th C, £500-£3,000.* PARK: Easy, but limited. TEL: 071 727 8595; fax - same; home - 0372 467934.

Judy Fox LAPADA
81 Portobello Rd, and 176 Westbourne Grove. Est. 1970. Open 10-5. SIZE: Large. *STOCK: Furniture and decorative items, 18th-20th C; inlaid furniture, mainly 19th C; pottery and porcelain.* TEL: 071 229 8130; fax - 071 229 6998.

J. Freeman LAPADA
85a Portobello Rd. Est. 1962. Open 9.30-1 and 2-5.30, Sat. 9-6. SIZE: Medium. *STOCK: Victorian silver plate, 1830-1870, £10-£150; Sheffield plate, 1790-1830, £20-£100; Victorian and later silver, £5-£200.* LOC: Nearest tube station Notting Hill Gate. PARK: Easy. TEL: 071 221 5076; fax - 071 221 5329. VAT: Stan.

Gallery 287 LAPADA
287 Westbourne Grove. (Richard Peters). Est. 1978. Open Sat. 6-5, other days by appointment. *STOCK: Ceramics and bronzes - 14th-19th C Chinese, 18th-19th C Japanese and European, all £1,000-£5,000.* TEL: 071 727 2817; home - 081 455 3292. SER: Valuations; buys at auction (as stock). FAIRS: Olympia (June). VAT: Stan/Spec.

Philip Garrick Antiques
42 Ledbury Rd. Open 9.30-6. *STOCK: Furniture, bronzes, works of art, 17th-19th C. Not stocked: Shipping goods* TEL: 071 243 0500.

The Good Fairy Open Air Market
100 Portobello Rd. (S. Pardoe). Est. 1978. Open Sat. 5-5. SIZE: Large - 80 dealers. *STOCK: General antiques including jewellery and silver, 18th-20th C, £5-£2,000.* LOC: Enter Portobello Rd. at Chepstow Villas, market 150 metres along on right-hand side. PARK: Nearby. TEL: 071 720 9341; Sat. only - 071 221 8977.

Graham and Green
4 Elgin Cres. (A. Graham and R. Harrison). Est. 1974. Open 10-6, Sat. 9.30-6. SIZE: Medium.

W.11 continued

STOCK: Turkish kelim rugs, pine and other furniture, re-upholstered Victorian chairs and decorative objects. LOC: Near Portobello Rd. PARK: Meters nearby. TEL: 071 727 4594. VAT: Stan.

Gavin Graham Gallery
47 Ledbury Rd. SLAD. Est. 1973. *STOCK: Oil paintings.* TEL: 071 229 4848; fax - 071 792 9697. VAT: Spec.

Graham-Stewart
293a Westbourne Grove. (M. Graham-Stewart). Est. 1980. Open by appointment. SIZE: Small. *STOCK: African, Polynesian, North and South African ethnographica art and artifacts, £500-£5,000; topographical, ethnographical paintings.* LOC: Between Portobello Rd. and Kensington Park Rd. PARK: Easy. TEL: 071 229 6959. SER: Valuations; buys at auction (ethnographia). VAT: Spec.

Grays Portobello
138 Portobello Rd. Open Sat. 7-4. TEL: 071 221 3069; fax - 071 724 0999. Below are listed the dealers at this market.

C. Bailey
Stand 3. *English and Chinese pottery, porcelain and glass.*

David Baker
Stand 18. *Oriental ceramics and works of art.*

R. Bamady
Stand 17. *Oriental and Islamic works of art, carpets and textiles.*

Pat Bedford and Guy Robbins
Stand 19/20. *Fine art, objets de vertu, antiquities and general antiques.*

Charles Carey
Stand 14/15. *Oriental and European ceramics and antiquities.*

R. Chandra
Stand 27-28. *Tibetan and Nepalese artefacts.*

H.P. Cook
Stand 21. *Porcelain, continental and Oriental.*

Mrs Davies
Stand 14. *Oriental art, fine netsukes, snuff-bottles, jade and bronzes.*

Jo de Sousa
Stand 4. *English ceramics.*

B. Donat
Stand 21. *Antiquities and Oriental works of art.*

J. B. Garrard
Stand 24. *Oriental ceramics.*

A.J. Harris
Stand 13. *Chinese and Japanese works of art and porcelain.*

LONDON

W.11 continued

Marguerite Harrison
Stand 22. *Faience, Quimper.*

J. Hill and L. Denney
Stand 11. *Oriental art and textiles, European bronzes.*

Steven Hyder
Stand 8. *Oriental works of art and porcelain.*

D. Ireland
Stand 25/26. *European and Asian items including costume and textiles.*

C. Kobako
Stand 12. *Oriental antiques and works of art.*

Diane Leloup
Stand 10. *Oriental and ethnic art and jewellery.*

Jenny Levine
Stand 23. *English, continental and Oriental antiquities.*

Mrs Liv
Stand 9. *Oriental and general antiques.*

A. Mohammed
Stand 20. *Oriental porcelain.*

One of a Kind
Stand 7. *Oriental ceramics and antiquities.*

Pars Antiques
Stand 5. *Classical antiques - Roman, Egyptian and Islamic glass, bronze and pottery.*

I.M. Row
Stand 6. *Netsuke, Japanese material and art.*

Simpsons Textiles
Stand 29. (R. Simpson). *Cashmere and European paisley shawls, quilts, tribal carpets, textiles.*

Peter Sloane
Stand 16. *Ancient Islamic and Far Eastern art.*

J. Swallow
Stand 1. *Oriental, including Japanese, and Islamic works of art.*

Patricia Harbottle
Stand 16, Geoffrey Van Arcade, 107 Portobello Rd. (Mrs P. Harbottle). Est. 1989. Open Sat. 7-5. SIZE: Small. *STOCK: Glass, corkscrews, wine and drink related items, 18th-20th C, £5-£500.* TEL: Home - 071 731 1972. SER: Valuations; restorations; buys at auction. FAIRS: Norwich, Snape, Bury St. Edmunds, N.E.C.(August), Harlaxton. VAT: Stan/Spec.

Hirst Antiques
59 Pembridge Rd. Est. 1963. Open 10-6. SIZE: Medium. *STOCK: Four poster and half-tester beds; decorative furniture and articles.* LOC: End of Portobello Rd., near Notting Hill Gate tube station. TEL: 071 727 9364. SER: Valuations.

Adrian Hornsey Ltd
220 Westbourne Grove. *STOCK: General antiques, decorative accessories and architectural furniture.* TEL: 071 221 2571; fax - 071 221 2612.

Eric Hudes
142 Portobello Rd. Est. 1946. Open 9-4.15 Sat. only. *STOCK: Oriental ceramics and works of art, 10th-19th C; early English and European pottery, 17th-19th C; all £100-£1,000.* TEL: 071 727 4643; home - 0376 83767. SER: Worldwide postal transactions. FAIRS: Buxton and Harrogate. VAT: Spec.

J. and B. Antiques LAPADA
Chelsea Galleries, 67 Portobello Rd. (J.E. Green and C.A. Finch). Est. 1978. Open Sat. 7-3 or by appointment. SIZE: Medium. *STOCK: Porcelain and pottery, 18th-19th C, £50-£3,000; objets d'art and vertu, 17th-19th C, £55-£5,000.* TEL: 0295 711689; mobile - 0836 684133. SER: Valuations; buys at auction. VAT: Stan/Spec.

Jones Antique Lighting
194 Westbourne Grove. (Judy Jones). Est. 1978. Open 9.30-6 or by appointment. SIZE: Large. *STOCK: Original decorative lighting, 1860-1960.* Not stocked: Reproductions. TEL: 071 229 6866; fax - same. SER: Valuations; repairs; prop hire. VAT: Stan.

W. Jones and Son (Antiques) Ltd
295 Westbourne Grove. (W. Jones). Est. 1889. Open Fri. and Sat. 10-5. SIZE: Large. *STOCK: Victorian and Edwardian furniture, £50-£1,000.* LOC: Near Portobello Rd. PARK: Easy. TEL: 071 727 7051. VAT: Stan.

Peter Kennedy
First Floor, 305 Westbourne Grove. Open by appointment only. *STOCK: Illustrated antiquarian books, prints and maps; natural history, botany, travel, topography, atlases.* LOC: Near Portobello Rd. TEL: 071 243 1416, fax - 071 243 2271.

Kirsch
Units 11-12, Arbras Gallery, 292 Westbourne Grove. (M. Kirsch Ltd). Est. 1959. Open Fri. and Sat. 10-5. *STOCK: Small furniture and objects, late 18th to 19th C, £50-£2,000.* TEL: Home - 071 372 7617 (24 hrs); mobile - 0831 491498. SER: Valuations.

L'Acquaforte
49A Ledbury Rd. (G. and B. Chighine). Est. 1971. Open 9.30-5.30, Sat. by appointment. SIZE: Medium. *STOCK: Continental watercolours and drawings, 18th-19th C, £200-£15,000; natural history, botanical, topographical and other*

MAGUS ANTIQUES
GRAHAM WALPOLE

Dealers in 18th and 19th Century Fine, Decorative and Collectable Antiques from a Thimble to a Bookcase.

187 Westbourne Grove
London. W11 2RS
Tel: 071-229-0267

Early 19th century ivory veneered needlework box from Vizagapatam

W.11 continued

decorative prints, 16th-19th C, £5-£5,000. LOC: Near Westbourne Grove. PARK: Easy. TEL: 071 221 3388. VAT: Stan/Spec.

Lacy Gallery
38 Ledbury Rd, and 203 Westbourne Grove. Est. 1960. Open 10-5.30, Sat. 10-4. SIZE: Large. STOCK: Period frames, 1700-1940; sporting and decorative paintings and decorative art. LOC: Two roads east of Portobello Rd. PARK: Easy. TEL: 071 229 9105/229 6340. VAT: Stan/Spec.

S. Lampard and Son Ltd
32 Notting Hill Gate. (J.P. Barnett). Est. 1847. Open 11-6. CL: Wed. and Sat. SIZE: Medium. STOCK: Jewellery, silver, clocks. TEL: 071 229 5457. SER: Valuations; restorations. VAT: Stan/Spec.

Joan Leigh
153 Portobello Rd. Est. 1959. STOCK: Art nouveau, art deco. TEL: 071 727 6848.

Lewin Antiques and Textile Arts
82D Portobello Rd. (David Lewin). Est. 1988. Open 11-5, Sat. 9-5.30. SIZE: Medium. STOCK: Dutch colonial furniture, 1900-1930; Indonesian ikat, from 1980. PARK: Easy. TEL: 071 229 2023. VAT: Stan.

M. and D. Lewis
1 Lonsdale Rd, 172, 179, 193 and 212 Westbourne Grove, 83 and 85 Ledbury Rd. Est. 1960. Open 9.30-5.30, Sat. 9.30-4. STOCK: Continental and Victorian furniture, porcelain, bronzes. TEL: 071 727 3908. VAT: Stan.

J. Lipitch Ltd   BADA
177 Westbourne Grove. Est. 1955. Open 10-1 and 2-5.30, Sat. 10-1.30. STOCK: English and continental furniture, 17th-18th C; bronze, ormolu and porcelain. TEL: 071 229 0783. VAT: Spec.

W.11 continued

M.C.N. Antiques
183 Westbourne Grove. Open 9.30-6 or by appointment. STOCK: Oriental and Japanese furniture, porcelain, bronzes, jade, ivory, netsuke, lacquer work. LOC: Near Portobello Rd. market. PARK: Easy. TEL: 071 727 3796; fax - 071 229 8839. SER: Buys at auction. VAT: Stan.

Magus Antiques   LAPADA
187 Westbourne Grove. (G.R. Walpole). Est. 1973. Open 10-5.30. SIZE: Medium. STOCK: Metalware including brass, bronze, Vienna bronzes, and ormolu; pictures, folk art, lighting, furniture and collectables, £100-£15,000. LOC: 300 yards off Portobello Rd. PARK: Easy. TEL: 071 229 0267. FAIRS: Olympia; Decorative Antiques and Textiles, Chelsea Harbour. VAT: Stan.

Robin Martin
44 Ledbury Rd. Est. 1972. Open 10-5.30. SIZE: Medium. STOCK: General antiques, furniture, works of art, early metalware, garden furniture, decorative items. LOC: Westbourne Grove area. TEL: 071 727 1301. VAT: Stan.

Mayflower Antiques
117 Portobello Rd. (J.W. Odgers). Open Sat. 7-3. STOCK: Clocks, mechanical music, scientific and marine instruments, furniture and general antiques. TEL: 071 727 0381; mobile - 0860 315101. VAT: Stan/Spec.

Mercury Antiques   BADA
1 Ladbroke Rd. (L. Richards). Est. 1963. Open 10-5.30. SIZE: Medium. STOCK: English porcelain, 1750-1850; English pottery and Delft, 1700-1850; glass, 1780-1850. Not stocked: Jewellery, silver, plate, art nouveau. LOC: Half minute from Notting Hill Gate underground station, turn into Pembridge Rd. and bear left. TEL: 071 727 5106. VAT: Mainly spec.

Metropolitan Stall Markets
141 Portobello Rd. Open Sat. 8-5. SIZE: Large. Over 60 stalls. STOCK: General antiques. TEL: 071 727 5242.

W.11 continued

Milne and Moller
35 Colville Terrace. (Mr and Mrs C. Moller). Est. 1976. Open during exhibitions, other times by appointment. SIZE: Small. STOCK: Water colours, oils and sculpture, 19th C to contemporary, £50-£3,000. LOC: Near junction of Westbourne Grove and Ledbury Rd. PARK: Easy. TEL: 071 727 1679; home - same. SER: Restorations; framing; buys at auction (watercolours). FAIRS: 20th C British Art; Olympia. VAT: Spec.

Terence Morse and Son Ltd
197 and 237 Westbourne Grove. Est. 1947. Open 10-6, Sat. 11-2. SIZE: Large. STOCK: Furniture, 18th-19th C, £1,000+. LOC: 200yds. from Portobello Rd. PARK: Easy. TEL: 071 229 9380/ 229 4059; fax - 071 792 3284. VAT: Stan/Spec.

Myriad Antiques
131 Portland Rd, Holland Park Ave. (S. Nickerson). Est. 1970. Open 11-6. SIZE: Medium. STOCK: Decorative furniture and objects, mainly 19th C, £10-£1,000. LOC: Between Notting Hill Gate and Shepherds Bush roundabout. TEL: 071 229 1709. VAT: Stan.

Nanking Porcelain Co LAPADA
84 Portobello Rd. (M. Hyams and E. Porter). Est. 1967. Open Fri. 10-4, Sat. 8-4, other times by appointment. STOCK: Fine Chinese export porcelain, 18th-19th C, £250-£20,000; Orientalia, 18th-19th C, £100-£5,000. LOC: Near Notting Hill Gate tube station. TEL: 071 229 9458; home - 071 924 2349. SER: Valuations; buys at auction (Orientalia). VAT: Spec.

Pat Nye
Geoffrey Van Arcade, 105 Portobello Rd. Est. 1963. Open Sat. only 7-3.30 or by appointment. SIZE: Small. STOCK: Needlework samplers, 18th-19th C, £80-£350; brass, £15-£200; snuff boxes and pipe tampers, £15-£150; pottery - gaudy Welsh, £10-£200; all 18th to early 19th C. LOC: Near Westbourne Grove. PARK: Powys Sq. TEL: Home - 081 948 4314. FAIRS: West London and Chelsea. VAT: Stan/Spec.

Oakstar Ltd
Clarendon Road. (Mrs P. Bromage). Est. 1982. Open by appointment only. SIZE: Small. STOCK: French and English furniture, 18th-19th C, £200-£10,000; papier mâché trays, £750-£4,000; mirrors, prints and objets d'art, £200-£5,000. TEL: 071 630 1822. SER: Restorations (lacquer). FAIRS: Decorative Antiques and Textiles; Olympia Fine Art and Antiques; City of London Antiques and Fine Art. VAT: Stan/Spec.

W.11 continued

Old Father Time Clock Centre
1st Floor, 101 Portobello Rd. (John Denvir). Open Fri. 9.30-2 by appointment, Sat. 6-4. STOCK: Clocks - all types, specialist electric including Eureka, mystery, skeleton, dial; barometers, books and spares. TEL: 081 546 6299.

The Old Haberdasher
139 Portobello Rd. (L. Lundie and E. Harvey). Est. 1974. Open Sat. 8-4.30. SIZE: Small. STOCK: Antique ribbons, laces and all trimmings; embroideries, tapestries and lace; bridal dresses. LOC: Opposite Collectors Corner. PARK: Meters until 1.30. TEL: 081 907 8684/904 6001.

Ormonde Gallery LAPADA
156 Portobello Rd. (F. Ormonde). Open 11-5, Sat. 7-5 or by apppointment. STOCK: Early Chinese ceramics; Oriental items including textiles, furniture, collectables, porcelain, netsuke, ivory, jade, snuff bottles, ceramics, bronzes, paintings; Middle Eastern items and carpets. TEL: 071 229 9800 /0424 82226. VAT: Stan/ Spec.

Pembridge Art Gallery
57 Pembridge Rd, Notting Hill Gate. (F.R. Hudson). Open 9.30-6. STOCK: Fine furniture, bronzes, decorative art and paintings. TEL: 071 792 2717.

Peter Petrou
195 Westbourne Grove. Est. 1972. Open 10-6. STOCK: Works of art, Vienna bronzes, Blue John, marbles, tribal, ivories, eccentricities, £200-£20,000. LOC: 500 yards from Portobello Rd. PARK: Easy. TEL: 071 229 9575. FAIRS: Olympia. VAT: Stan/Spec.

E.S. Phillips and Sons
99 Portobello Rd. Est. 1962. Open 10-5. STOCK: Architectural antiques, stained glass. TEL: 071 229 2113; fax - 071 229 1963.

Philp BADA
59 Ledbury Rd. (R. Philp). SLAD. Est. 1961. Open 10-6. STOCK: 16th-17th C English portraiture and Old Master paintings, medieval sculpture, early furniture and 20th C drawings, £50-£40,000. PARK: Easy. TEL: 071 727 7915. VAT: Spec.

Eva Pilbrow Antiques
69 Portobello Rd. Est. 1984. Open Sat. 7-3. STOCK: Unusual decorative objects, samplers and textiles, 17th-19th C. PARK: Meters. TEL: Home - 081 659 9518. FAIRS: Royal Horticultural Hall; Little Chelsea; Sandown Park.

LONDON

An Antique Collectors' Club Title

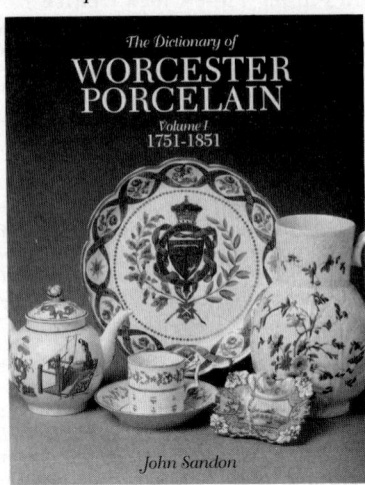

The Dictionary of Worcester Porcelain Volume I 1751-1851
by John Sandon

With 600+ dictionary entries, an historical survey, an illustrated section on marks, detailed information on recent excavations at the Worcester factory, contemporary accounts of visits to factories and an extensive bibliography, this is the definitive work. The author is director of ceramics at Phillips auctioneers, London, and regularly appears on the *Antiques Roadshow*.

ISBN 1 85149 156 2
400pp, 450 b & w illus, 100 colour
£45.00

Available from:
Antique Collectors' Club, 5 Church Street, Woodbridge, Suffolk IP12 1DS
Tel: (0394) 385501 Fax: (0394) 384434

or Market Street Industrial Park, Wappingers' Falls, New York 12590, USA
Tel: 914 297 0003 Fax: 914 297 0068

W.11 continued

Portobello Antique Co
133 Portobello Rd. (L. Meltzer and A. Goldsmith). Open Fri. 11-4.30, Sat. 8-4.30, other times by appointment. STOCK: *Porcelain, small furniture, reproduction silver plate and cutlery.* LOC: Off Westbourne Grove. PARK: Easy. TEL: 071 221 0344; home - 081 958 7373. VAT: Stan/Spec.

Portobello Antique Store
79 Portobello Rd. (J.F. Ewing). Est. 1971. Open 10-4, Sat. 8-4.30. SIZE: Large. STOCK: *Silver and plate, general antiques, £2-£3,000.* LOC: Notting Hill end of Portobello Rd. PARK: Easy weekdays. TEL: 071 221 1994. SER: Export. VAT: Stan.

The Red Lion Market (Portobello Antiques Market)
165/169 Portobello Rd. Est. 1951. Open 5.30-5. SIZE: 200 dealers. STOCK: *General antiques including ethnic antiquities, bronzes, ivory statues, jade, precious metals, dolls, silver and plate, drinking vessels, costumes, Oriental and Western porcelain, furniture, collectables, prints, lace, linen, books, manuscripts, stamps, coins, banknotes, paintings, etchings, sporting memorabilia and curios.* TEL: 071 221 7638. SER: Valuations; shipping.

W.11 continued

Rex Antiques
63 Ledbury Rd. (D. Cura). Open 9-6, Sat. 9-1. STOCK: *Victorian and decorative furniture.* TEL: 071 229 6203.

A. Rezai Persian Carpets
123 Portobello Rd. Open 9-5. STOCK: *Oriental carpets, kilims, tribal rugs and silk embroideries, £70-£1,500.* TEL: 071 221 5012.

Roger's Antiques Gallery
65 Portobello Rd. (Bath Antiques Market Ltd). Open Sat. 7-4.30. SIZE: 65 dealers. STOCK: *Wide range of general antiques and collectables with specialist dealers in most fields, especially jewellery.* TEL: Enquiries - 071 351 5353; fax - 071 351 5350. SER: Valuations.

G. Sarti Antiques Ltd
186 Westbourne Grove. SLAD.Open 9.30-1 and 2-5.30. STOCK: *Cabinets, European and English furniture, marble tables and objects, paintings, 14th-18th C.* TEL: 071 221 7186/727 3493.

Schredds of Portobello   LAPADA
107 Portobello Rd. (H.J. and G.R. Schrager). Est. 1969. Open Sat. 7.30-3.30 or by appointment. SIZE: Small. STOCK: *Collectors' silver, 17th-19th C, £10-£1,000; Delft, 17th-18th C; English porcelain, 18th C.* TEL: 081 348 3314; home - same; fax - 081 341 5971. SER: Valuations; buys

W.11 continued

at auction. FAIRS: West Kensington, Jan. and Aug; City of London, Nov. VAT: Stan/Spec.

Bernard T. Shapero Rare Books BADA
80 Holland Park Avenue. Est. 1979. Open 10-7, Sat. 10-5. SIZE: Large. *STOCK: Antiquarian books - travel, natural history and literature (old and modern).* LOC: Between Shepherds Bush roundabout and Notting Hill Gate. TEL: 071 493 0876. SER: Valuations; restorations (antiquarian books); buys at auction. FAIRS: Book - London, Paris, New York, San Francisco.

Justin Skrebowski
82E Portobello Rd. Est. 1985. Open 1-6.30, Sat. 7.30-6, Sun., Mon. and mornings by appointment. SIZE: Small. *STOCK: Prints, engravings and lithographs, 1700-1850, £50-£500; oil paintings, 1700-1900, £200-£1,500; watercolours, drawings including Old Masters, 1600-1900, £50-£1,000; modern mahogany folio stands and easels.* PARK: Meters. TEL: 071 792 9742; home - 081 871 4295. SER: Valuations. VAT: Stan/Spec.

David Slater
170 Westbourne Grove. Est. 1961. Open 9.30-1 and 2-5.30, Sat. 10-1. SIZE: Large. *STOCK: General antiques, decorative items.* PARK: Easy. TEL: 071 727 3336. VAT: Stan.

Colin Smith and Gerald Robinson Antiques
The Geoffrey Van Arcade, 105 Portobello Rd. Est. 1979. Open Sat., Mon. am. and Fri. by appointment. SIZE: Large. *STOCK: Tortoiseshell, £100-£2,000; silver, ivory and crocodile items.* TEL: 081 994 3783. FAIRS: Olympia. VAT: Stan.

Louis Stanton BADA
299 and 301 Westbourne Grove. (L.R. and S.A. Stanton). CINOA. Est. 1965. Open 9.30-1 and 2-5.30, Sat. 9.30-5.30. SIZE: Medium. *STOCK: Early English oak and walnut furniture, tapestries, sculpture, metalware, objets d'art, pre-1750, £20-£25,000; fine English furniture, clocks and unusual decorative items, 18th to early 19th C.* PARK: Easy. TEL: 071 727 9336; fax - 071 727 5424. SER: Valuations; buys at auction. VAT: Stan/Spec.

Stern Art Dealers LAPADA
46 Ledbury Rd. (M. Stern and Son). Est. 1952. Open 10-6. SIZE: Medium. *STOCK: Oil paintings, 19th-20th C, £200-£5,000.* LOC: Off Westbourne Grove near Portobello. PARK: Easy. TEL: 071 229 6187. SER: Valuations; restorations. VAT: Stan.

Stouts Antiques Market
144 Portobello Rd. Open Sat. only. TEL: 071 727 3649; fax - 0923 897618; mobile - 0850 375501. Below are listed some of the dealers at this market.

W.11 continued

David Beaumont Antiques
Est. 1972. *English and continental silver, from 1600.*

Britannia Export Antiques
Silver, ivory and objets d'art. TEL: 071 221 2011; fax - same.

Eddie Clark
Wrist watches.

James Forbes Fine Art
English and Australian works of art, from 1700.

K. and M. Antiques
(M. G. Harris). *Oriental ceramics, European porcelain, jewellery, all from 1750.* TEL: 071 229 2178; home - 081 907 7488; mobile - 0860 878345.

Kleanthous Antiques LAPADA
(C. and C. Kleanthous). Est. 1969. *Jewellery, watches, clocks, silver and works of art, 1700-1950.* TEL: 071 727 3649; mobile - 0850 375501/375502. VAT: Stan/Spec.

Leon
Clocks and watches, 1700-1950.

S. and G. Antiques
(G. Sirett). *Objets d'art and collectables.* TEL: 071 229 2178; 081 907 7140; mobile - 0860 863360. VAT: Stan.

Sirett Antiques Ltd
(Mrs A. M. Sirett). Est. 1976. *Fine reproduction Chinese porcelain, ivory and objets d'art, £10-£10,000.* TEL: 071 229 2178; home - 081 907 1389/7140. VAT: Stan/Spec. *Trade Only.*

M. and C. Telfer-Smollett
88 Portobello Rd. Est. 1958. Open Thurs., Fri. and Sat. 10-5. SIZE: Medium. *STOCK: Oriental furniture, fabrics, Middle Eastern screens, tables, natural history specimens and tribal art.* TEL: 071 727 0117. VAT: Stan/Spec.

Temple Gallery
6 Clarendon Cross. (R.C.C. Temple). Est. 1959. Open 10-6, weekends and evenings by appointment. SIZE: Large. *STOCK: Icons, Russian and Greek, 12th-16th C, £1,000-£50,000.* PARK: Easy. TEL: 071 727 3809; fax - 071 727 1546. SER: Valuations; restorations; buys at auction (icons). VAT: Spec.

The Textile Company LAPADA
100 Portland Rd., Holland Park. (J. Wentworth and S. Franklyn). Est. 1982. Open Tues., Wed. and Thurs. 10-6 or by appointment. *STOCK: 18th C silks, British and French printed cottons, patchworks, lace, 1600-1850; Paisley and Kashmir shawls, period costume and accessories.* Not stocked: Tapestries, upholstery and cushions.

LONDON

W.11 continued

LOC: From Notting Hill Gate, 2nd right after Holland Park tube station. PARK: Easy. TEL: 071 221 7730; fax - 071 229 8612; home - 071 254 3256. SER: Buys at auction; hire.

Themes and Variations
231 Westbourne Grove. (L. Fawcett). Open 10-1 and 2-6, Sat 10-6. STOCK: Post war and contemporary decorative items, furniture, glass, ceramics, carpets, lamps, jewellery. TEL: 071 727 5531.

Igor Tociapski
39 Ledbury Rd. Est. 1959. Open 10-5.30. CL: Sat and Fri pm. SIZE: Small. STOCK: Clocks, watches, scientific instruments and mechanical music, 1500-1900. Not stocked: Tapestries. PARK: Easy. TEL: 071 229 8317. SER: Restorations (clocks); buys at auction.

Tomkinson Stained Glass
87 Portobello Rd. (S. Tomkinson). Open 10-5, Sat. 7-5. SIZE: Medium. STOCK: Stained glass windows. LOC: 5 minutes from Notting Hill Gate underground. PARK: Easy. TEL: 071 727 1304; 071 267 1669. SER: Valuations; restorations (as stock). VAT: Stan

Christina Truscott
77 Portobello Rd. Est. 1967. Open Sat. 6.30-3.30. STOCK: Chinese export lacquer, small decorative furniture, late 18th to early 19th C, £100-£1000. TEL: 071 727 5263.

Victoriana Dolls   LAPADA
101 Portobello Rd. (Mr and Mrs C. Bond). Open Sat. 8-3 or by appointment. STOCK: Dolls, toys and accessories. TEL: Home - 0737 249525.

Virginia
98 Portland Rd, Holland Park. (V. Bates). Est. 1971. Open 11-6. SIZE: Medium. STOCK: Decorative items, £50-£2,000; textiles, clothes and lace, £25-£500; bathroom fittings, £15-£600; all 19th-20th C. LOC: Holland Park Ave. PARK: Easy. TEL: 071 727 9908. VAT: Stan.

Johnny Von Pflugh Antiques
289 Westbourne Grove. Est. 1985. Open Sat., other times by appointment. SIZE: Small. STOCK: European works of art, Italian oil paintings, gouaches, 17th-19th C, £300-£1,500; fine ironware, 17th-18th C, £300-£800; medical and scientific instruments, 18th-19th C, £200-£1,000. LOC: Off Portobello Rd. PARK: Easy. TEL: 081 740 5306; home - same. SER: Valuations; buys at auction (keys, caskets, medical instruments, Italian oil paintings, and gouaches). FAIRS: Olympia; Little Chelsea (Scientific and Medical). VAT: Spec.

David Wainwright
251 Portobello Rd. Open 10-6, Sat. 9.30-6.30, Sun. 11-4. STOCK: Artefacts from Rajasthan. TEL: 071 792 1988.

W.11 continued

Trude Weaver   LAPADA
71 Portobello Rd. Est. 1968. Open 9.30-5, Sat. 9-5. SIZE: Medium. STOCK: English and continental furniture, decorative objects, textiles. PARK: Easy. TEL: 071 229 8738. SER: Valuations.

A. M. Web   LAPADA
93 Portobello Rd. (J. Donovan). Open Thurs., Fri. and Sat. 11-5. STOCK: Musical boxes, unusual clocks, automata and other mechanical antiques. TEL: 071 727 1485. VAT: Stan.

Wellington Antiques
2-5 Wellington Close. (F.E.A. Briggs Ltd). Open 8.30-5.30, Sat. and Sun.10-4. SIZE: Large. STOCK: Furniture, mainly mahogany, 18th-20th C. LOC: Off Ledbury Rd., near Westbourne Grove. TEL: 071 221 4950. VAT: Stan/Spec.

Westbourne Grove Antique Gallery
174 Westbourne Grove. (M. Worster). Est. 1965. Open 10-6, Sat. 10-5. SIZE: Large - 7 dealers. STOCK: Furniture and decorative items, mainly 18th-19th C, to £4,000. LOC: Off Portobello Road. PARK: Easy. TEL: 071 727 4268; fax - 071 229 5840. SER: Valuations; restorations. VAT: Stan/Spec. Below are listed the dealers at this gallery.

Paul Andretti Antiques
18th-19th C continental furniture.

Canonbury Antiques Ltd.
Furniture, porcelain, bronzes and clocks.

Bryan Hamilton Exports
Individual copies of satinwood and inlaid mahogany pieces of "textbook" furniture.

Barry Joyce Antiques
18th C period furniture.

London Antique Exporters Ltd.
Quality shipping goods, all markets, especially U.S.A.

Linda Reeves
Furniture - period oak, 19th C inlaid and decorative and accessories.

David Wigdor Antiques
18th-19th C furniture and decorative items.

Neil Wibroe Antiques Ltd
185 Westbourne Grove. Est. 1984. Open 9.30-6, Sat. 9.30-5. SIZE: Medium. STOCK: Furniture and works of art, 18th C, £500-£5,000. PARK: Easy. TEL: 071 229 6334; home - same. SER: Valuations; restorations (furniture); buys at auction (furniture). VAT: Stan/Spec.

World Famous Portobello Market
177 Portobello Rd, and 1-3 Elgin Cres. Est. 1951. Open Sat. 5-6. SIZE: 200 dealers. STOCK: General antiques including ethnic antiquities,

W.11 continued

bronzes, ivory statues, jade, precious metals, dolls, silver and plate, drinking vessels and costumes; also specialist golf shop. TEL: 071 221 4964 (24-hour answering service). SER: Valuations; restorations; shipping.

Wynyards Antiques (Lastlodge Ltd.)
5 Ladbroke Rd. Est. 1983. Open 10-5.30, Sat. 10.30-5.30. SIZE: Medium. *STOCK: Treen, £5-£500; small furniture, £35-£2,000; objects of art and interest, £3-£600; all 17th-19th C.* LOC: Near Notting Hill Gate tube station. PARK: Meters. TEL: 071 221 7936. SER: Restorations (furniture); caning; upholstery. FAIRS: Ravenscott at Chelsea Town Hall. VAT: Mainly Spec.

Zebrak
Stand 41, 284 Westbourne Grove. (T. and A. Zebrak). Open Sat., Sun. by appointment. SIZE: Small. *STOCK: Jewellery, silver, watches and objets d'art, 1800-1950, £5-£10,000.* PARK: Nearby. TEL: 0273 202929; mobile - 0860 550668; fax - 0273 321021. SER: Valuations; restorations; import and export. FAIRS: Olympia. VAT: Stan/Spec.

LONDON W.13

Chiswick Antiques
97 Northfield Ave., Ealing. (Mrs D. Rout). Est. 1957. Open 9-5.30. CL: Thurs. SIZE: Medium. *STOCK: Furniture; china, glass and silver, £5-£50; all 18th-19th C.* PARK: Easy. TEL: 081 579 3071/567 4162.

Quest Antiques
90 Northfields Ave., Ealing. (W. A. Turner). Est. 1979. Open 10.30-5, Sat. 9.30-4. CL: Mon. and Wed. SIZE: Small. *STOCK: Furniture, 19th C, to £2,000; objects and bric-a-brac, 19th-20th C, £5-£300.* PARK: Easy. TEL: 081 840 2349; home - same. VAT: Stan.

Rupert's
151 Northfield Ave., Ealing. (R.Loftus Brigham). Open 10-6 or by appointment. CL: Sat. *STOCK: Early wireless equipment.* TEL: 081 567 1368.

W.13 Antiques
10 The Avenue, Ealing. Open Tues., Thurs. and Sat. 10-5 or by appointment. SIZE: Medium. *STOCK: Furniture, china and general antiques, 18th-20th C.* LOC: Off Uxbridge Rd., West Ealing. PARK: Easy. TEL: 081 998 0390. SER: Valuations. VAT: Stan.

LONDON W.14

Andy's All Pine
Olympia Bridge Quay (OBQ), 70 Russell Rd., Kensington. (A. Gibb). Open 9.30-6, weekends by appointment. *STOCK: Pine.* TEL: 071 602 0856; fax - 071 602 8655. SER: Stripping.

W.14 continued

Alyson Burdon
4 Anley Rd. Est. 1975. Open by appointment. SIZE: Small. *STOCK: Decorative items including textiles, costume, £4-£1,000.* LOC: Off Shepherd's Bush Rd. PARK: Easy. TEL: 071 602 1973; home - same. SER: Valuations; buys at auction (textiles and interesting decorative items). FAIRS: Olympia. VAT: Stan.

Charleville Gallery
7 Charleville Rd, West Kensington. (F. King). Est. 1986. Open Wed. 10-7, Thurs. and Fri. 10-6 or by appointment. *STOCK: Textiles, shawls, cushions, bedspreads, linen, £5-£1,000.* LOC: 2 min. walk from West Kensington station or off M4 onto North End Rd. PARK: Easy. TEL: 071 385 3795; home - 071 727 2625.

Stephen Garratt (Fine Paintings)
BADA
60 Addison Rd. Open by appointment only. *STOCK: Oils and watercolours, 18th-20th C.* **TEL: 071 603 0681.**

Heskia
BADA
Est. 1877. Open by appointment only. *STOCK: Oriental carpets, rugs and tapestries.* TEL: 071 373 4489. SER: Valuations; cleaning and repairs.

Richard Joslin
Gordon Mansions, 150 Addison Gardens. Est. 1971. By appointment only. *STOCK: English and continental oils and watercolours, 19th-20th C, £500-£20,000.* LOC: Off Shepherd's Bush Rd., turn into Blythe Rd., 2nd turning on left. PARK: Easy. TEL: 071 603 6435; fax and home - same. SER: Valuations; restorations (oils and watercolours); framing; buys at auction (oils and watercolours, worldwide). VAT: Spec.

D. Parikian
3 Caithness Rd. Open by appointment. *STOCK: Antiquarian books, mythology, iconography, emblemata, continental books pre-1800.* TEL: 071 603 8375; fax - 071 602 1178.

Simpsons - Bespoke Carvings
Blythe Hall, 100 Blythe Rd. (S. Yardy). Open by appointment. *STOCK: Antique and new hand carved mirrors and decorative pieces.* TEL: 071 603 8625.

LONDON S.W.1

Didier Aaron (London) Ltd
BADA
21 Ryder St, St. James's. Open 10-6. CL: Sat. SIZE: Large. *STOCK: French furniture, 18th C, £5,000-£500,000; Old Master and 19th C pictures, £5,000-£500,000; objets d'art, £1,000-£50,000.* **LOC: 20 yds. from Christie's. TEL: 071 839 4716. FAIRS: Paris Biennale; Winter Antiques Show, New York. VAT: Stan/Spec.**

LONDON

S.W.1 continued

Ackermann & Johnson BADA
27 Lowndes St. Est. 1963. Open 9-5.30, Sat. 10-12. SIZE: Medium. *STOCK: English paintings especially sporting, 18th-20th C.* PARK: Meters. TEL: 071 235 6464. SER: Valuations; restorations. VAT: Spec.

Addison-Ross Gallery
40 Eaton Terrace, Belgravia. (T.C.A. and D.A.A. Ross). *STOCK: Paintings and prints especially sporting and natural history.* TEL: 071 730 1536. SER: Interior design (pictures).

Ahuan (UK) Ltd
17 Eccleston St. (O. Hoare). Est. 1975. Open 9.30-5.30. CL: Sat. *STOCK: Early Persian and Islamic works of art.* TEL: 071 730 9382. VAT: Spec.

J. A. Allen & Co. (The Horseman's Bookshop) Ltd.
1 Lower Grosvenor Pl. Est. 1926. Open 9-5.30. CL: Sat. pm. *STOCK: Horse books, from 1600.* PARK: Meters. TEL: 071 834 5606; fax - 071 233 8001. VAT: Stan.

John Allsopp Antiques
26 Pimlico Rd. Open 9.30-6, Sat. 10-1. *STOCK: Decorative furniture and objects, 18th-19th C.* TEL: 071 730 9347.

Verner Åmell Ltd
4 Ryder St, St. James's. Open 10-5.30. CL: Sat. *STOCK: Dutch and Flemish Old Masters, 16th-17th C; 18th C French and 19th C Scandinavian paintings.* TEL: 071 925 2759.

Albert Amor Ltd
37 Bury St, St. James's. Est. 1837. Open 9.30-4.30. CL: Sat. SIZE: Small. *STOCK: 18th C English ceramics, especially first period Worcester and blue and white porçelain.* PARK: Meters. TEL: 071 930 2444; fax - 071 930 9067. SER: Valuations; buys at auction. VAT: Spec.

Anno Domini Antiques BADA
66 Pimlico Rd. (F. Bartman). Est. 1960. Open 10-1 and 2.15-6. CL: Sat. pm. SIZE: Large. *STOCK: Furniture, 17th to early 19th C, £500-£10,000; mirrors, 17th-19th C, £300-£3,000; glass, screens, decorative items and tapestries, £10-£5,000.* Not stocked: Silver, jewellery, arms, carpets, coins. LOC: From Sloane Sq. go down Lower Sloane St., turn left at traffic lights. PARK: Easy. TEL: 071 730 5496; home - 071 352 3084. SER: Buys at auction. VAT: Stan/Spec.

Antiquités
227 Ebury St. (A. De Cacqueray). Open 10-6, Sat. 11-4. *STOCK: French and continental furniture, objets d'art.* TEL: 071 730 5000.

Antiquus
90-92 Pimlico Rd. (E. Amati). Open 9.30-5.30. SIZE: Large. *STOCK: Classical, medieval and Renaissance works of art, paintings, textiles and glass.* LOC: Near Sloane Sq. underground station. PARK: Meters in Holbein Place. TEL: 071 730 8681.

S.W.1 continued

The Armoury of St. James's Military Antiquarians
17 Piccadilly Arcade, Piccadilly. Open 9.30-6. SIZE: Small. *STOCK: British and foreign orders, decorations and medals, 18th C to date, £1-£50,000; militaria; toy and hand-painted collectors model soldiers, £2-£400.* LOC: Between Piccadilly and Jermyn St. TEL: 071 493 5082. SER: Valuations. VAT: Stan/Spec.

Artemis Fine Arts Limited
15 Duke St, St. James's. SLAD. Open 10-5. CL: Sat. *STOCK: Old Master, 19th C and modern drawings and prints.* TEL: 071 930 8733.

Maurice Asprey Ltd
41 Duke St, St. James's. Est. 1956. Open 9.30-5.30, Sat. during Dec. only. SIZE: Small. *STOCK: Antique silver, jewellery, portrait miniatures, objets de vertu and Russian works of art.* LOC: South of Jermyn St. TEL: 071 930 3921; fax - 071 321 0769. SER: Valuations; restorations, repairs, restringing; gold stamping. FAIRS: International Silver and Jewellery (Park Lane Hotel); Grosvenor House; New York International. VAT: Stan/Spec.

Astleys
109 Jermyn St. Est. 1862. CL: Sat. pm. SIZE: Medium. *STOCK: Meerschaum pipes, 19th C, £30-£1,500; pottery, porcelain, primitive and Oriental pipes, £30-£1,500; smoking accessories, cigar boxes, smoking cabinets, tobacco jars, 19th C, £20-£200.* LOC: Near Piccadilly Circus. PARK: Meters. TEL: 071 930 1687. SER: Valuations; restorations (pipes). VAT: Stan.

Chris Beetles Ltd Watercolours and Paintings
10 Ryder St, St. James's. Open 10-5.30, by appointment at weekends. SIZE: Large. *STOCK: English watercolours, 18th-20th C, £500-£50,000.* LOC: 100yds. from Royal Academy. PARK: Meters. TEL: 071 839 7551. SER: Valuations; framing. VAT: Spec.

Belgrave Carpet Gallery Ltd
91 Knightsbridge. (A.H. Khawaja). Open 9.30-6.30. *STOCK: Hand knotted Oriental carpets and rugs.* TEL: 071 235 2541/245 9749.

Belgrave Gallery
22 Mason's Yard, Duke St., St. James's. SLAD. Open 10-6. CL: Sat. *STOCK: 20th C British paintings, watercolours and sculpture.* TEL: 071 930 0294.

Blanchard and Alan Ltd.
86/88 Pimlico Rd. Est. 1990. Open 10-6, Sat. 10-3. SIZE: Medium. *STOCK: English and continental furniture, lighting and objets d'art.* LOC: Near

Anno Domini Antiques

66 Pimlico Road, London S.W.1
071-730 5496

George III mahogany bureau, 37in. x 81in.

LONDON

S.W.1 continued

Sloane Sq. underground station. TEL: 071 823 6310; fax - 071 823 6303. SER: Valuations; restorations; buys at auction. VAT: Stan/Spec.

N. Bloom and Son (Knightsbridge)
at Harrods Ltd., Fine Jewellery Room, Brompton Rd., Knightsbridge. (H. McKeown). Open 10-6. STOCK: Silver, 18th-20th; estate and ancient jewellery, £100-£50,000. TEL: 071 730 1234, ext. 4062/4072. SER: Valuations; restorations; repairs; buys at auction. VAT: Stan/Spec.

John Bly   BADA
27 Bury St, St. James's. (F., N., J. and V. Bly). Est. 1891. Open 9-5.30, Sat. 10-3 and by appointment. STOCK: English furniture, silver, glass, porcelain and pictures, 18th-19th C. TEL: 071 930 1292.

J.H. Bourdon-Smith Ltd   BADA
24 Mason's Yard, Duke St., St. James's. Est. 1954. Open 9.30-6. CL: Sat. SIZE: Medium. STOCK: Silver, 1680-1830, £5. 0-£15,000; Victorian and modern silver, 1830 to date, £25-£10,000 PARK: Meters. TEL: 071 839 4714. SER: Valuations; restorations (silver); buys at auction. FAIRS: Chelsea, British International (Birmingham), Harrogate, Grosvenor House, International Silver and Jewellery, Park Lane, BADA, New York, Harrods. VAT: Stan/Spec.

Brisigotti Antiques Ltd
44 Duke St, St. James's. Open 9.30-1 and 2-5.30. STOCK: European works of art, Old Master paintings. TEL: 071 839 4441/2.

Clive A. Burden Ltd
93 Lower Sloane St. Open 10-5.30, appointment preferred. SIZE: Medium. STOCK: Maps, 1500-1860, antiquarian prints, 1600-1900, both £1-£1,000; antiquarian books, pre-1870, £10-£5,000; Vanity Fair prints. TEL: 071 823 5053. SER: Valuations; buys at auction (maps, prints, books). VAT: Stan.

Camerer Cuss and Co
17 Ryder St, St. James's. (The Cuss Clock Co. Ltd). Est. 1788. Open 9.30-5. CL: Sat. SIZE: Medium. STOCK: Clocks, 1600-1910, £250-£30,000; watches, 1600-1930, £100-£35,000. TEL: 071 930 1941. SER: Valuations; restorations (clocks and watches); buys at auction. VAT: Stan/Spec.

David Carritt Limited
15 Duke St, St. James's. Open 10-5. CL: Sat. STOCK: Old Master, 19th C and modern paintings. TEL: 071 930 8733.

Odile Cavendish
14 Lowndes St. Est. 1971. Open by appointment. SIZE: Large. STOCK: Mainly Oriental furniture, screens, paintings, works of art. PARK: Meters. TEL: 071 243 1668. VAT: Spec.

S.W.1 continued

Chaucer Fine Arts
45 Pimlico Rd. Open 10-6, Sat. 10-1. STOCK: Old Master paintings, sculpture and works of art. TEL: 071 730 2972/5872.

Ciancimino Ltd
99 Pimlico Rd. Open 10-6, Sat. by appointment. STOCK: English and European fine furniture and decorative works of art, early 19th C. TEL: 071 730 9950/9959; fax - 071 730 5365.

Cobra and Bellamy
149 Sloane St. (V. Manussis and T. Hunter). Est. 1976. Open 10.30-6. SIZE: Medium. STOCK: Decorative art and jewellery, 20th C, £50-£1,000. TEL: 071 730 2823. VAT: Stan.

Edward Cohen
40 Duke St, St. James's. STOCK: Paintings. TEL: 071 839 5180. VAT: Spec.

The Connoisseur Gallery
14/15 Halkin Arcade, Motcomb St., Belgravia. (M.Z. Irani). ABA. Est. 1966. Open 10-6. SIZE: Medium. STOCK: Antiquarian books of the Middle East; Arabic manuscripts, Oriental paintings, Islamic works of art, 8th-19th C, £50-£10,000+. LOC: Between Motcomb St. and Lowndes St. PARK: Easy. TEL: 071 245 6431/2. SER: Valuations; restorations; buys at auction. VAT: Spec.

Cornucopia
12 Upper Tachbrook St. Est. 1967. Open 11-6. SIZE: Large. STOCK: Jewellery, 20th C clothing and accessories. PARK: Meters. TEL: 071 828 5752.

Cox and Company
37 Duke St, St. James's. (Mr and Mrs R. Cox). Est. 1972. Open 10-5.30, Sat. by appointment. SIZE: Small. STOCK: European paintings, 19th-20th C, £1,000-£20,000. LOC: Off Piccadilly. TEL: 071 930 1987. SER: Valuations; restorations; buys at auction. VAT: Spec.

Csaky's Antiques
20 Pimlico Rd. Open 10-6. STOCK: Early English and continental oak furniture; carvings, works of art, unusual items. TEL: 071 730 2068.

Peter Dale Ltd   LAPADA
11/12 Royal Opera Arcade, Pall Mall. Est. 1955. Open 9.30-5. CL: Sat. SIZE: Medium. STOCK: Firearms, 16th-19th C; edged weapons, armour, 14th-19th C; militaria. LOC: Arcade behind Her Majesty's Theatre and New Zealand House. PARK: 350yds. Whitcomb St., Public Garage. TEL: 071 930 3695. SER: Valuations; buys at auction. FAIRS: Arms, spring and autumn. VAT: Spec.

Kenneth Davis (Works of Art) Ltd
15 King St, St. James's. Open 9-5. CL: Sat. STOCK: Silver and works of art. TEL: 071 930 0313; fax - 071 976 1306.

S.W.1 continued

Shirley Day Ltd BADA
91b Jermyn St. Est. 1967. *STOCK: Indian, Himalayan and South East Asian sculpture; Japanese screens and paintings.* TEL: 071 839 2804; fax - 071 839 3334. VAT: Spec.

The Delightful Muddle
11 Upper Tachbrook St, Victoria. (M. and J. Storey). Est. 1935. Open Thurs., Fri. and Sat. 11-5. SIZE: Small. *STOCK: China, glass, objets d'art, Victorian and Edwardian, £1-£100; lace, £1-£50; linen, general antiques and bric-a-brac, £3-£65, all to Victorian.* LOC: Near Victoria Station, Upper Tachbrook St. runs into Vauxhall Bridge Rd. at Queen Mother Sports Centre. PARK: Meters.

Guy Dennler Antiques
48A Lower Sloane Street. Open by appointment only. *STOCK: Fine decorative objects, 18th-19th C English furniture, papier mâché, tôle, pictures, porcelain and lamps.* TEL: 071 823 4121.

Douwes Fine Art Ltd
38 Duke St, St. James's. SLAD. Est. 1805. Open 9.30-5.30. CL: Sat. SIZE: Medium. *STOCK: Old Master paintings, drawings, watercolours, prints.* PARK: Meters. TEL: 071 839 5795. VAT: Spec.

Eaton Gallery
34 Duke St., St. James's, and 9 and 12a Princes Arcade, Jermyn St. (D. George). Open 10-5.30. *STOCK: English and European paintings, 19th-20th C and contemporary.* TEL: 071 930 5950; fax - 071 839 8076.

Annamaria Edelstein at Robin Symes
94 Jermyn St. Open 10-5.30. CL: Sat. *STOCK: Old Master drawings.* PARK: Meters. TEL: 071 930 5300.

Christopher Edwards
63 Jermyn St, St. James's. Appointment preferred. *STOCK: English literature, to 1900; early continental books, all subjects.* TEL: 071 495 4263; fax - 071 495 4264.

Christopher Edwards Ltd
62 Pimlico Rd. Open 10-6. *STOCK: 19th C art furniture and applied arts.* TEL: 071 730 4025; fax - 071 823 6873. VAT: Stan/Spec.

Faustus Fine Art Ltd
1st Floor, 90 Jermyn St. Open 9.30-5.30. *STOCK: British and European prints, ancient jewellery, antiquities.* TEL: 071 930 1864. VAT: Spec.

Fernandes and Marche LAPADA
23 Motcomb St. Est. 1956. Open 9.30-5.30. CL: Sat. and Sun. except by appointment. SIZE: Medium. *STOCK: English furniture, giltwood including mirrors and consoles, 18th C.* PARK: Meters. TEL: 071 235 6773; fax - 071 823 2234. VAT: Spec.

S.W.1 continued

N. and I. Franklin
11 Bury St, St. James's. Open 9.30-5.30. CL: Sat. *STOCK: Fine silver and works of art.* TEL: 071 839 3131; fax - 071 839 3132.

J.A.L. Franks
7 Allington St. Est. 1948. *STOCK: Maps and stamps; framed cigarette cards.* LOC: Opposite stage door - Victoria Palace Theatre. TEL: 071 834 8697.

S. Franses Ltd
Jermyn St. at Duke St, St. James's. Est. 1909. Open 9-5. CL: Sat. SIZE: Large. *STOCK: Historic and decorative tapestries, carpets, fabrics and textiles.* TEL: 071 976 1234. SER: Valuations; restorations; cleaning. VAT: Spec.

Victor Franses Gallery BADA
57 Jermyn St, St. James's. Est. 1948. Open 10-5.30, Sat. by appointment. *STOCK: 19th C animalier bronzes, rare carpets and rugs.* TEL: 071 493 6284/629 1144; fax - 071 629 1144. SER: Valuations; restorations.

Galerie Moderne Ltd
10 Halkin Arcade, Motcomb St. Open 9.30-6, Sat. by appointment. *STOCK: René Lalique glass and 20th C Sevres porcelain.* TEL: 071 245 6907.

Gallery '25
4 Halkin Arcade, Motcombe St., Belgravia. (D. Iglesis and R. Lawrence). Est. 1969. Open 9.30-5.30, Sat. 10-2. SIZE: Medium. *STOCK: Art glass, £100-£5,000; signed furniture, £1,000-£10,000; decorative fine art, £500-£5,000; all 1900-1930.* LOC: Arcade between Motcomb St and West Halkin St. PARK: Easy. Cadogan Sq. TEL: 071 235 5178. SER: Valuations; buys at auction (as stock). FAIRS: Park Lane; Olympia. VAT: Stan/Spec.

Gallery Arcticus
First Floor, 176 Sloane St. Open 10-6. CL: Sat. *STOCK: 19th-20th C Scandinavian art, especially Danish Golden Age.* TEL: 071 823 1939; fax - 071 259 6080.

General Trading Co Ltd LAPADA
144 Sloane St. (E. Barlow). Est. 1920. Open 9-5.30. SIZE: Medium. *STOCK: English furniture, £100-£2,000; china, prints, £20-£500; all 18th-19th C.* PARK: 50yds., underground garage (Cadogan Place). TEL: 071 730 0411. VAT: Stan/Spec.

Joss Graham
10 Eccleston St. Open 10-6, Sat. 10-4. *STOCK: Textiles, jewellery and furniture - Indian, Middle Eastern, African and Central Asian including kilims, carpets, embroideries, block-printed cotton bedspreads, cushions, tribal costume, shawls, scarves, necklaces and earrings.* TEL: 071 730 4370.

S.W.1 continued

Martyn Gregory Gallery BADA
34 Bury Street, St. James's. SLAD. Open 10-6. CL: Sat. SIZE: Medium. STOCK: Early English watercolours, 18th-20th C; British paintings, both £500-£100,000; specialists in pictures relating to China. TEL: 071 839 3731. SER: Valuations. VAT: Spec.

Rosemary Hamilton
44 Moreton St. Est. 1985. Open 9.30-5.30. SIZE: Small. STOCK: Small furniture, 1840-1890, £500-£1,000; porcelain and fabrics, £100-£500. LOC: Off Lupus St., Pimlico. PARK: Easy. TEL: 071 828 5018; home - same. SER: Restorations; gilding; polishing. VAT: Stan.

Ross Hamilton Ltd LAPADA
95 Pimlico Rd. (Mark Boyce). Est. 1971. Open 9.30-1 and 2-6, Sat. 11-4. SIZE: Large. STOCK: English and continental furniture, 17th-19th C, £1,000-£100,000; porcelain and objects, 18th-19th C, £1,000-£3,000; paintings, 17th-19th C, £1,000-£10,000+. LOC: 2 minutes walk from Sloane Square. PARK: Side streets. TEL: 071 730 3015. VAT: Stan/Spec.

Han-Shan Tang Ltd
8 Duke Street, St James's. (C. von der Burg). Open 10-6. STOCK: Second-hand and antiquarian books and periodicals on Chinese, Japanese, Korean and central Asian art and culture. TEL: 071 839 6599; fax - 071 976 1832.

Harari and Johns Ltd
12 Duke St, St. James's. SLAD. Open 9.30-6. CL: Sat. STOCK: Old Master paintings. TEL: 071 839 7671; fax - 071 930 0986.

Harrods Ltd
Brompton Rd, Knightsbridge. Open 10-6, Wed., Thurs. and Fri. 10-7. SIZE: Large. STOCK: Fine Victorian, Edwardian and period furniture, paintings, objets d'art. PARK: Own - Brompton Rd. TEL: 071 730 1234, ext. 2759/2808.

Julian Hartnoll
2nd. Floor, 14 Mason's Yard, Duke St., St. James's. SLAD. Est. 1968. Open 2.30-5. STOCK: 19th-20th C British paintings, drawings and prints especially pre-Raphaelite and John Bratby. TEL: 071 839 3842. VAT: Spec.

Hazlitt, Gooden and Fox Ltd
38 Bury St, St. James's. SLAD. Open 9.30-5.30. CL: Sat. SIZE: Large. STOCK: Paintings, drawings and sculpture. PARK: Meters. TEL: 071 930 6422. SER: Valuations; restorations. VAT: Spec.

Thomas Heneage Art Books BADA
42 Duke St, St. James's. Est. 1975. Open 10-6 or by appointment. CL: Sat. STOCK: Art reference books. TEL: 071 930 9223; fax - 071 839 9223.

S.W.1 continued

Heraz (David Hartwright Ltd.)
25 Motcomb St., Belgravia. Est. 1978. Open 10-6, Sat. 10-4. SIZE: Small. STOCK: Cushions, 17th-19th C; antique, Oriental needlework and European carpets and tapestries. PARK: Easy. TEL: 071 245 9497. SER: Valuations; restorations (antique textiles and carpets including cleaning). VAT: Stan.

Hermitage Antiques
97 Pimlico Rd. (B. Vieux-Pernon). Est. 1967. Open 10-6, Sat. 10-4, Sun. by appointment. SIZE: Large. STOCK: Empire and Biedermeier furniture, oil paintings, decorative arts and French provincial furniture. Not stocked: Silver and jewellery. LOC: Off Sloane Square. PARK: Easy. TEL: 071 730 1973; fax - 071 730 6586. VAT: Stan/Spec.

Carlton Hobbs BADA
46 Pimlico Rd. Est. 1975. Open 9-6. STOCK: English and continental furniture, paintings, chandeliers, works of art, £4,000-£850,000. TEL: 071 730 3640/3517; fax - 071 730 6080.

Christopher Hodsoll Ltd
91 Pimlico Rd. Open 9.30-7, Sat. and Sun. by appointment. STOCK: 17th-19th C furniture, pictures, objects and carpets. PARK: Meters. TEL: 071 730 3370. VAT: Stan/Spec.

Hotspur Ltd BADA
14 Lowndes St. (R.A.B. and B.S. Kern). Est. 1924. Open 8.30-6, Sat. 9.30-1. SIZE: Large. STOCK: English furniture, 1690-1800. LOC: Between Belgrave Sq. and Lowndes Sq. PARK: 2 underground within 100yds. TEL: 071 235 1918. VAT: Spec.

Christopher Howe
36 Bourne St. Est. 1982. Open 9.30-7, Sat. 10-4.30, Sun. by appointment. SIZE: Large + additional showroom nearby. STOCK: English furniture, late 18th to 19th C, £500-£20,000; objects and lighting, early 19th C, £100-£10,000. LOC: Near Sloane Sq. and just off Pimlico Rd. PARK: Easy. TEL: 071 730 7987; home - same; fax - 071 730 0157. SER: Valuations; buys at auction (18th-19th C English furniture and accessories). VAT: Stan/Spec.

Christopher Hull Gallery
17 Motcomb St. Open 10-6, Sat. 10-1. STOCK: Modern British paintings. TEL: 071 235 0500.

Sally Hunter Fine Art
11/12 Halkin Arcade, Motcomb St. Open 10-6. CL: Sat. STOCK: Britist art, 1920 to date. TEL: 071 235 0934.

Iconastas
5 Piccadilly Arcade. Open 10-6, Sat. 2-4. STOCK: Russian and Greek icons, Russian works of art, Fabergé, Palekh lacquer, 16th to early 20th C. TEL: 071 629 1433.

ANTIQUES

&

FINE FURNITURE

A large and constantly
changing selection of the finest
quality furniture from the
Victorian and Edwardian eras
is always on display together with
selected objet d'art.
All items are carefully restored
to their original condition
and are available for
immediate delivery.

Antique & Fine Furniture
Department, Third Floor.

Harrods
KNIGHTSBRIDGE

Harrods Limited, Knightsbridge, London SW1X 7XL. Telephone: 071-730 1234

LONDON

S.W.1 continued

Brand Inglis BADA
9 Halkin Arcade, Motcomb St. Open 9-5 or by appointment. CL: Sat. *STOCK: Silver, mainly pre-19th C English.* TEL: 071 235 6604.

David James BADA
3 Halkin Arcade, Motcomb St. (D. and E. James). Est. 1980. Open 11-6, Sat. by appointment. *STOCK: Fine English and continental watercolours.* TEL: 071 235 5552; fax - same.

Jeremy Ltd BADA
29 Lowndes St. (G.M. and J. Hill). Est. 1946. Open 8.30-6. SIZE: Large. *STOCK: English and French furniture, objets d'art, glass chandeliers, 18th to early 19th C.* PARK: Easy. TEL: 071 823 2923. FAIRS: Grosvenor House; IAD New York. VAT: Spec.

The Hugh Johnson Collection
68 St. James's St. Open 9.30-5.30. CL: Sat. *STOCK: Antique and modern wine accessories including decanters, glasses, funnels, port tongs.* TEL: 071 491 4912; fax - 071 493 0602.

R. and J. Jones
6 Bury St, St. James's. Open 9.30-5.30, Sat. by appointment. *STOCK: Dutch, Flemish and Italian paintings, £2,000-£80,000; English and continental ceramics, £200-£30,000; all 17th-18th C.* LOC: Between Jermyn St. and King St. and next to Duke St. TEL: 071 925 2079. SER: Valuations; buys at auction.

Jubilee Antiques
70 Cadogan Place. (Serena Stapleton). Est. 1984. Open 10-5. CL: Sat. and Sun. except by appointment. SIZE: Medium. *STOCK: Fine and decorative furniture,18th-19th C, £50-£5,000.* LOC: Just off Sloane St. PARK: Easy. TEL: 071 823 1034. SER: Valuations; restorations (furniture including lacquer and gilding); buys at auction. FAIRS: Decorative Antiques, Chelsea Harbour; Olympia (June). VAT: Stan/Spec.

Keshishian
73 Pimlico Rd. Est. 1978. Open 9.30-6, Sat. 10-5. SIZE: Medium. *STOCK: European and Oriental carpets, to late 19th C; Aubussons, mid 19th C; European tapestries, 16th-18th C.* LOC: Off Lower Sloane St. PARK: Easy. TEL: 071 730 8810; fax - 071 730 8803. SER: Valuations; restorations. VAT: Stan/Spec.

Dominic King Antique Glass
85 Ebury St, Belgravia. Est. 1986. Open Mon.-Thurs. 10-6. SIZE: Medium. *STOCK: Georgian drinking glasses and decanters; Bristol and Stourbridge coloured glass; Victorian hyacinth and celery glasses; wine related antiques, especially dated and sealed bottles; bells, lacemakers' lamps and unusual items; all £50-£500.* LOC: On foot from Victoria Station via Eccleston St. exit. PARK: Nearby. TEL: 071 824 8319; home - same. FAIRS: N.E.C. and Stourbridge.

S.W.1 continued

King Street Galleries
17 King St, St. James's. (H. O'Nians). Open 9.30-5.30, Sat. 9.30-1. *STOCK: Paintings and watercolours, 19th-20th C.* TEL: 071 930 9392; fax - 071 930 3993.

Knightsbridge Coins
43 Duke St, St. James's. Open 10-6. CL: Sat. *STOCK: Coins - British, American and South African; medals.* TEL: 071 930 7597/930 8215.

Kojis Antique Jewellery
at Harrods Ltd., Brompton Rd., Knightsbridge. Open 10-6. *STOCK: Antique and contemporary jewellery and objects.* TEL: 071 730 1234.

Arthur S. Lewis LAPADA
at Harrods Ltd., Antique Clocks and Musical, Boxes Dept, Brompton Rd., Knightsbridge. Est. 1969. *STOCK: Clocks and musical boxes, 19th C, from £1,000+.* TEL: 071 730 1234, ext. 2360. VAT: Stan/Spec.

M. and D. Lewis
84 Pimlico Rd. Open 10-5, Sat. 10-1. *STOCK: Continental and Victorian furniture, porcelain, bronzes.* TEL: 071 730 1015. VAT: Stan.

Lion, Witch and Lampshade
89 Ebury St. (Mr. and Mrs N. Dixon). Est. 1984. Open 10.30-5.30, Wed. 12.30-5.30, prior telephone call advisable. CL: Sat. *STOCK: Unusual decorative objects, 18th to early 20th C, £5-£150; lamps, wall brackets, chandeliers and candlesticks, £50-£1,000.* PARK: Easy. TEL: 071 730 1774. SER: Restorations (porcelain and glass). VAT: Stan/Spec.

Longmire Ltd (Three Royal Warrants)
12 Bury St, St. James's. Open 9-5, Sat. in Dec. only. *STOCK: Individual antique jewellery, cufflink and dress sets: antique, signed, platinum, gold, gem set, hardstone, pearl, carved crystal or enamel - four vices, fishing, polo, golfing, shooting, big game, ladybird and pigs.* LOC: Coming from Piccadilly, down Duke St., right into King St. past Christies, first right into Bury St. PARK: Easy. TEL: 071 930 8720; fax - 071 930 1898. SER: Custom hand engraving or enamelling in colour - any corporate logo, initials, crest, coats of arms or tartan, any animal (cat, dog etc.), racing silks, sailing burgees, favourite hobbies or own automobiles.

MacConnal-Mason Gallery
14 Duke St, St. James's. Est. 1893. Open 9-6. SIZE: Large. *STOCK: Pictures, 19th-20th C.* PARK: Meters. TEL: 071 839 7693/499 6991. SER: Valuations; restorations. VAT: Spec.

The Mall Galleries
The Mall. Open 10-5 seven days. *STOCK: Paintings.* LOC: Near Trafalgar Sq. TEL: 071 930 6844; fax - 071 839 7830. SER: Contemporary art exhibitions held.

S.W.1 continued

Paul Mason Gallery — BADA
149 Sloane St. Est. 1969. Open 9-6, Wed. 9-7, Sat. 9-1. STOCK: *Marine, sporting and decorative paintings and prints, 18th-19th C; period and old frames, portfolio stands, ship models.* LOC: Sloane Sq. end of Sloane St. PARK: Easy. TEL: 071 730 3683/7359. SER: Valuations; restorations (prints, paintings); buys at auction. FAIRS: England and Europe. VAT: Stan/Spec.

Mathaf Gallery Ltd — LAPADA
24 Motcomb St. SLAD. Est. 1975. Open 9.30-5.30. STOCK: *Paintings, Middle East subjects, 19th C.* TEL: 071 235 0010. SER: Valuations.

Matthiesen Fine Art Ltd. and Matthiesen Works of Art Ltd
7-8 Mason's Yard, Duke St., St. James's. Est. 1978. Open 10-6 or by appointment. CL: Sat. STOCK: *Fine Italian Old Master paintings, 1300-1800; French and Spanish Old Master paintings.* TEL: 071 930 2437; fax - 071 930 1387. SER: Valuations; buys at auction.

Mayorcas Ltd — BADA
38 Jermyn St. (J.D. and L.G. Mayorcas). Est. 1930. Open 9.30-5.30, Sat. 10-1. SIZE: Medium. STOCK: *Tapestries, textiles, embroideries, needlework, church vestments, European carpets and rugs.* TEL: 071 629 4195. SER: Valuations; restorations. VAT: Stan/Spec.

I.J. Mazure and Co. Ltd — BADA
90 Jermyn St. STOCK: *Gold, objets de vertu, Russian works of art including Fabergé.* TEL: 071 839 3101.

Rodd McLennan
24 Holbein Place. Est. 1971. Open 11-1 and 2-5.30. CL: Sat. STOCK: *Biedermeier, Empire, bronze, ormolu, marble accessories.* TEL: 071 730 6330. VAT: Spec.

Christopher Mendez incorporating Craddock and Barnard
58 Jermyn St. Est. 1966. Open 10-5.30. CL: Sat. SIZE: Small. STOCK: *Old Master prints.* TEL: 071 491 0015; fax - 071 495 4949. SER: Valuations; buys at auction. VAT: Stan.

Richard Miles Antiques
8 Holbein Place. Est. 1974. Open 9.30-1 and 2-5.30. CL: Sat. except by appointment. SIZE: Medium. STOCK: *Unusual furniture and works of art, especially Anglo-Indian and Chinese colonial, 18th to early 19th C, £500-£15,000.* LOC: Between Sloane Sq. and Pimlico Rd. PARK: Easy. TEL: 071 730 1957; fax - 071 824 8865. SER: Buys at auction. VAT: Spec.

Lennox Money (Antiques) Ltd
93 Pimlico Rd. (L.B. Money). Est. 1964. Open 9.45-6. CL: Sat. pm. SIZE: Large. STOCK: *Indian colonial and furniture made of unusual woods; chandeliers and textiles.* LOC: 200yds. south of Sloane Sq. TEL: 071 730 3070. VAT: Spec.

Mrs Monro Ltd
16 Motcomb St. Open 9.30-5.30, Fri. 9.30-5. CL: Sat. SIZE: Medium. STOCK: *Small decorative furniture, £500-£1,000+; china, £50-£100; rugs, prints, pictures and general decorative items, from £50; all 18th-19th C.* LOC: Between Lowndes Sq. and Belgrave Sq. PARK: Garage nearby. TEL: 071 235 0326. SER: Restorations (furniture and china). VAT: Stan/Spec.

Moreton Street Gallery
40 Moreton St. (W.M. Pearson-Frasco International Ltd). Est. 1972. Open 9-1 and 2-6. CL: Sat. SIZE: Medium. STOCK: *Contemporary oils, watercolours, limited editions, posters; early engravings - Bunbury, Rowlandson, Hogarth, Gilray and Heath.* LOC: Off Belgrave Rd. PARK: Easy. TEL: 071 834 7773/5 or 7834. SER: Valuations; restorations; buys at auction (originals and engravings). VAT: Stan.

Guy Morrison
91 Jermyn St. SLAD. Open 9.30-5.30. CL: Sat. STOCK: *British paintings from 1900.* TEL: 071 839 1454.

Peter Nahum — LAPADA
5 Ryder St. Open 9.30-5.30. CL: Sat. and Sun. except by appointment. SIZE: Large. STOCK: *British and European paintings, drawings and bronzes, including the. Pre-Raphaelites and Modern British, 19th-20th C, £500-£50,000+.* LOC: 100yds. from Royal Academy. PARK: Meters. TEL: 071 930 6059. SER: Valuations. VAT: Spec.

Ning Ltd
58 Cambridge St. (Mrs P. Grant). Est. 1963. Open 10-6. CL: Sat. STOCK: *Decorative furniture, pre-1860; period pine; Spode, Wedgwood, Davenport and blue and white porcelain; small decorative items.* PARK: Meters. TEL: 071 834 3292. VAT: Spec.

The Old Ephemera and Newspaper Shop
37 Kinnerton St, Belgravia. Est. 1972. Open 11-7, prior telephone call advisable. CL: Mon. SIZE: Large. STOCK: *Ephemera and antiquarian newspapers, from 1642 to 20th C; early photographs and books.* LOC: Kinnerton St. runs from Wilton Place (off Knightsbridge) to Motcomb St. PARK: Underground nearby. TEL: 071 235 7788.

Old London Galleries
4 Royal Opera Arcade, Pall Mall. (Mrs V. Malmed). Open 10.30-5, Sat. 11.30-1.30. STOCK: *18th-19th C hand coloured prints, all subjects, from £5.* LOC: Near the Haymarket. TEL: 071 930 7679. SER: Framing; decorative mount cutting.

S.W.1 continued

Old Maps and Prints
4th Floor, Harrods, Knightsbridge. Est. 1976. STOCK: Maps, 16th C to 1880; prints, watercolours and oils, sporting restrikes; Christie's signed, limited edition graphics. TEL: 071 730 1234, ext. 2124.

Omell Galleries
22 Bury St, St. James's. SLAD. Est. 1949. Open 9.30-5.30. CL: Sat. SIZE: Large. STOCK: English and continental paintings, 19th-20th C, £1,000-£15,000. LOC: From Jermyn St. last street on left hand side (coming from Piccadilly to St. James's St.). PARK: Easy. TEL: 071 839 4274. SER: Restorations. VAT: Stan/Spec.

O'Shea Gallery   BADA
89 Lower Sloane St. ABA. Open 9.30-6, Sat. 9.30-1. STOCK: Maps, topographical, decorative, natural history, sporting and marine prints; rare atlases, illustrated books, 15th-19th C, £5-£25,000. LOC: Near Sloane Sq. TEL: 071 730 0081; fax - 071 730 1386. SER: Decorative framing; restorations. VAT: Stan/Spec.

A. and M. Ossowski
83 Pimlico Rd. Est. 1956. Open 9-6. CL: Sat. pm. SIZE: Medium. STOCK: Carved gilt, 18th C; mirrors, consoles, wood carvings. TEL: 071 730 3256. SER: Valuations; restorations (gilt furniture). VAT: Stan/Spec.

The Parker Gallery   BADA
28 Pimlico Rd. (Thomas H. Parker Ltd). SLAD. Est. 1750. Open 9.30-5.30, Wed. 9.30-8, Sat. by appointment. SIZE: Medium. STOCK: Historical prints, £30-£1,000; English paintings, £450-£15,000; ship models, £70-£20,000; all 1700-1950. LOC: 5 minutes from Sloane Sq. TEL: 071 730 6768; fax - 071 259 9180. SER: Restorations (as stock); mounting; framing. VAT: Stan/Spec.

Michael Parkin Fine Art Ltd
11 Motcomb St. SLAD. Open 10-6, Sat. 10-1. STOCK: British paintings, watercolours, drawings and prints, 1860-1960, £50-£10,000. PARK: Easy. TEL: 071 235 8144/1845; fax - 071 245 9846. VAT: Spec.

Pawsey and Payne   BADA
90 Jermyn St, St. James's. (Hon N.V.B. and L.N.J. Wallop). SLAD. Est. 1910. Open 9.30-5.30. CL: Sat. STOCK: English oils and watercolours, 18th-19th C. PARK: Meters. TEL: 071 930 4221; fax - 071 839 1903. SER: Valuations; restorations. VAT: Spec.

Trevor Philip and Sons Ltd   LAPADA
75a Jermyn St, St. James's. (T. and R. Waterman). Est. 1972. Open 9-6, Sat. 10-4. SIZE: Medium. STOCK: Early medical, scientific and marine instruments; clocks and decorative items, especially globes. PARK: At rear. TEL: 071 930

S.W.1 continued

2954; fax - 071 321 0212. SER: Valuations; restorations (clocks and scientific instruments); buys at auction. VAT: Stan/Spec.

Pickering and Chatto Ltd
Incorporating Dawsons of Pall Mall, 17 Pall Mall. Est. 1820. Open 9.30-5.30. CL: Sat. SIZE: Large. STOCK: English literature, economics, politics, philosophy, science, medicine, manuscripts and autographs. LOC: 300yds. on right from Trafalgar Sq. PARK: Easy. TEL: 071 930 2515; fax - 071 930 8627.

Polak Gallery   BADA
21 King St, St. James's. Est. 1854. Open 9.30-5.30. CL: Sat. SIZE: Medium. STOCK: English and continental oils and watercolours, 19th-20th C. PARK: Meters. TEL: 071 839 2871. SER: Valuations; restorations. VAT: Spec.

Portland Gallery
9 Bury St, St. James's. SLAD. Est. 1985. Open 10-6. CL: Sat. SIZE: Medium. STOCK: Scottish pictures, 20th C, £200-£100,000. TEL: 071 321 0422. SER: Valuations; buys at auction. VAT: Spec.

Michael Priest Antiques
27a Motcomb St, Belgrave Sq. Est. 1979. Open 9.30-5, Sat. by appointment. SIZE: Medium. STOCK: Fine mahogany and walnut, paintings - Old Masters and primitives, late 17th C to mid-19th C, £500-£20,000. TEL: 071 235 7241. SER: Valuations; restorations (English furniture, oil paintings). VAT: Spec.

Pyms Gallery   BADA
13 Motcomb St, Belgravia. (A. and M. Hobart). Est. 1975. Open 10-6. CL: Sat. STOCK: British, Irish and French paintings, 19th-20th C. TEL: 071 235 3050; fax - 071 235 1002. SER: Valuations; restorations; buys at auction. VAT: Spec.

Lesley Rendall Antiques   BADA
69 Pimlico Road. Open 10-6, Sat. 10.30-4.30. STOCK: English furniture and works of art,18th to early 19th C. TEL: 071 730 7206. FAIRS: Olympia. VAT: Stan/Spec.

Geoffrey Rose Ltd   BADA
77 Pimlico Rd. Est. 1961. Open 10.15-1 and 2.15-6 and most Sat. mornings. SIZE: Medium. STOCK: English furniture, late 18th to early 19th C. TEL: 071 730 3004.

Rothman
103-105 Pimlico Rd. (J.A.F. and S.P.J. Rothman). Est. 1981. Open 10-7, Sat. 11-4. SIZE: Large. STOCK: Regency furniture, 1790-1830; giltwood mirrors and furniture, 1750-1830; French clocks and objects, 1780-1830. TEL: 071 730 2558; fax - 071 730 3329; home - 071 730 7200. VAT: Stan/Spec.

THE PARKER GALLERY
(ESTABLISHED 1750)

28, PIMLICO ROAD, LONDON SW1W 8LJ
TEL: 071-730 6768   FAX: 071-259 9180

*Merchantmen and Galliots Becalmed in an Estuary on the Dutch Coast
Oil painting on panel, size 14 1/2 in. x 18 1/2 in., by William Anderson 1801*

*The Leisure Hour. Oil painting on canvas, size 12in. x 18in
by Dean Wolstenholme Jr., 1798-1882*

DEALERS IN PRINTS, PAINTINGS AND WATERCOLOURS OF
THE 18th, 19th & 20th CENTURY, COVERING MARINE,
MILITARY, TOPOGRAPHICAL AND SPORTING SUBJECTS,
MAPS & SHIP MODELS

BADA   SLAD

LONDON

S.W.1 continued

Sainsbury & Mason
145 Ebury St. Est. 1968. Open 10-1 and 2-5.30. *STOCK: Period Oriental and European works of art, especially Chinese and Japanese, bronzes, lacquer, porcelain, glass and pictures.* TEL: 071 730 3393/8331; home - 081 874 4173; fax - 071 730 8334. VAT: Spec.

Saint George's Gallery
8 Duke St, St. James's. Est. 1948. Open 10-6. CL: Sat. *STOCK: Books and catalogues on fine and decorative arts.* PARK: Meters. TEL: 071 930 0935. SER: Catalogues available; postal (worldwide).

The St. James's Art Group
91 Jermyn St. (P. Hook and H. Wyndham). SLAD. Open 10-5. CL: Sat. SIZE: Medium. *STOCK: European pictures, 18th-20th C, £1,000-£1,000,000+.* PARK: Meters. TEL: 071 321 0233. SER: Valuations; buys at auction (European pictures, 18th-20th C).

Sanaiy Carpets
57 Pimlico Rd. (H. Sanaiy). Open 9-6.30. *STOCK: Antique Persian and Oriental carpets and tapestries.* TEL: 071 730 4742; fax - 071 259 9194.

Sarti Gallery Ltd
55 Jermyn St, St. James's. SLAD. Open 10-6. *STOCK: European furniture, marble tables and objects, 14th-18th C paintings.* TEL: 071 491 0449.

Gerald Sattin Ltd BADA
14 King St, St. James's. (G. and M. Sattin). Est. 1966. Open 9-5.30. CL: Sat. pm. SIZE: Medium. *STOCK: English and continental porcelain, 1720-1900; English glass, 1700-1900; both £55-£2,500; English silver, 1680-1920, £55-£5,000.* Not stocked: Oriental and post 1920 items. LOC: Close to Christie's. PARK: Meters. TEL: 071 493 6557; fax - same. SER: Buys at auction. VAT: Stan/Spec.

Seago BADA
22 Pimlico Rd. (T.P. and L.G. Seago). Open Mon.-Fri. 9.30-5.30 or by appointment. *STOCK: Fine 17th-19th C garden sculpture and ornaments in marble, stone, bronze, lead, terracotta, cast and wrought iron.* TEL: 071 730 7502; fax - 071 730 9179.

Julian Simon Fine Art Ltd LAPADA
70 Pimlico Rd. (M. and J. Brookstone). Open 10-6, Sat. 10-4 or by appointment. *STOCK: Fine English and continental pictures, 18th-20th C.* TEL: 071 730 8673; fax - 071 823 6116.

Sims, Reed Ltd
43 Duke Street, St James's. Open 10-6, Sat. by appointment. *STOCK: Rare and out-of-print books on the fine and applied arts; illustrated books.* TEL: 071 493 5660/0952; fax - 071 493 8468.

S.W.1 continued

John Carlton Smith BADA
17 Ryder St, St. James's. Open 9.30-5.30. CL: Sat. *STOCK: Clocks, barometers, chronometers, 17th-19th C.* TEL: 071 930 6622. SER: Valuations. VAT: Spec.

Peta Smyth - Antique Textiles
42 Moreton St, Pimlico. Est. 1977. Open 10-5.30. CL: Sat. *STOCK: European textiles and needlework, 17th-19th C, £10-£1,000; tapestries and cushions.* PARK: Easy. TEL: 071 630 9898. SER: Restorations (needlework, tapestries, textiles etc). FAIRS: Olympia. VAT: Spec.

Somlo Antiques BADA
7 Piccadilly Arcade. (G. and S. Somlo). Est. 1972. Open 10-5.30 or by appointment. CL: Sat. SIZE: Medium. *STOCK: Pocket and wrist watches, from 17th C, from £200.* LOC: Between Piccadilly and Jermyn St. PARK: Meters. TEL: 071 499 6526. SER: Valuations; restorations. VAT: Stan/Spec.

Sotheran's
80 Pimlico Rd. Open 10-6, Sat. 10-4. *STOCK: Architectural, ornamental and topographical prints and drawings.* TEL: 071 730 8756.

Spink and Son Ltd BADA
5-7 King St, St. James's. SLAD. Est. 1666. Open 9.30-5.30. CL: Sat. SIZE: Large. *STOCK: English paintings, watercolours, silver, jewellery; Chinese, Japanese, Indian, South East Asian, Himalayan and Islamic works of art; textiles; Greek and Roman to present day coins, banknotes, bullion, orders, medals and decorations, numismatic books.* PARK: Meters. TEL: 071 930 7888. SER: Valuations; buys at auction; commission sales on behalf of private collectors; coin auctions. VAT: Stan/Spec.

Gerald Spyer and Son (Antiques) Ltd
18 Motcomb St, Belgrave Sq. Est. 1860. Open 10-6. CL: Sat. SIZE: Large. *STOCK: Furniture, mostly English, pre-1830; gilt mirrors, 18th C; bronze and ormolu decorative items, £750-£125,000.* LOC: In area between Sloane Sq., Hyde Park Corner and Knightsbridge. PARK: Easy. TEL: 071 235 3348; fax - 071 823 2234. SER: Buys at auction. VAT: Spec.

Jeremy and Guy Steel
8 Princes Arcade, Jermyn St. Open 10.30-5. CL: Sat. *STOCK: Jewellery.* TEL: 071 287 2528.

Pamela Streather
The Pink House, 4 Studio Place, Kinnerton St. CINOA. Est. 1964. Open by appointment. *STOCK: Works of art, paintings; furniture, 17th-19th C.* TEL: 071 235 3450. VAT: Spec.

Robin Symes Ltd
3 Ormond Yard, Duke of York St., St. James's and 94 Jermyn St. Open 10-5.30. CL: Sat. SIZE: Large. *STOCK: Antiquities, ancient art.* PARK: Meters. TEL: 071 930 9856/7; 071 930 5300.

LONDON

S.W.1 continued

Bill Thomson - Albany Gallery
1 Bury St, St. James's. (W.B. Thomson). SLAD. Open 8.30-6, Sat. by appointment. *STOCK: British drawings, watercolours and paintings, 1700-1850 and some 20th C.* TEL: 071 839 6119.

William Tillman Ltd   BADA
30 St. James's St. Open 9.30-5.30, Sat. by appointment. *STOCK: English furniture, 18th C.* TEL: 071 839 2500.

Peter Tillou Works of Art Ltd   BADA
39 Duke St, St. James's. (S. Rich). Open daily, Sat. by appointment. SIZE: Medium. *STOCK: Master paintings, 16th-19th C; arms and armour, objets d'art, collectors items.* LOC: Just off Piccadilly. PARK: St. James's Sq. TEL: 071 930 9308; fax - 071 930 2088. SER: Valuations; restorations. FAIRS: Maastricht, Holland; Grosvenor House. VAT: Spec. *Trade Only.*

Trafalgar Galleries   BADA
35 Bury St, St. James's. (B. Cohen and Sons). Open 9.30-6. CL: Sat. *STOCK: Old Master and 19th C paintings.* LOC: Just south of Piccadilly. TEL: 071 839 6466/7.

Trove
71 Pimlico Rd. (P.S. Roe and J.P.D. Smith). Est. 1969. Open 10-6. CL: Sat. pm. SIZE: Medium. *STOCK: Furniture, bronzes, sporting paintings and decorative items.* PARK: Easy. TEL: 071 730 6514. SER: Restorations (paintings and furniture); buys at auction. VAT: Spec.

Rafael Valls Ltd   BADA
11 Duke St, St. James's. SLAD. Est. 1976. Open Mon.-Fri. 9.30-6. *STOCK: Old Master, 17th-19th C paintings.* TEL: 071 930 1144; fax - 071 976 1596. VAT: Spec.

Johnny Van Haeften Ltd   BADA
13 Duke St, St. James's. (J. and S. Van Haeften). SLAD. Est. 1978. Open 10-6, Sat. and Sun. by appointment. SIZE: Medium. *STOCK: Dutch and Flemish Old Master paintings, 16th-17th C, £5,000-£500,000.* LOC: Middle of Duke St. TEL: 071 930 3062/3; fax - 071 839 6303. SER: Valuations; restorations (Old Masters); buys at auction (paintings including Old Masters). VAT: Spec.

Edric Van Vredenburgh Ltd
37 Bury St, St. James's. Est. 1961. Open 10-1 and 2-5.30. CL: Sat. SIZE: Small. *STOCK: European decorative arts, 1500-1800; sculpture, early objects; Oriental decorative arts, 18th-19th C.* LOC: Around corner from Christie's. PARK: Easy. TEL: 071 839 5818/9; home - same. SER: Valuations; buys at auction. VAT: Stan/Spec.

Piers Von Westenholz Ltd
76-78 Pimlico Rd. Open 10-6, Sat. by appointment. *STOCK: Furniture, 18th-19th C.* TEL: 071 824 8090.

S.W.1 continued

Rupert Wace Ancient Art Ltd
1st Floor, 107 Jermyn St. Open Mon.-Fri. 10-5. *STOCK: Egyptian, Classical and near Eastern antiquities.* TEL: 071 495 1623.

Waterman Fine Art Ltd
74A Jermyn St, St. James's. Open 9-6, Sat. 10-4. *STOCK: 20th C paintings, watercolours and drawings.* TEL: 071 839 5203; fax - 071 321 0212.

Philip Whyte
32 Bury St, St. James's. Est. 1972. Open Tues., Wed.and Thurs., other times by appointment. SIZE: Medium. *STOCK: Clocks, watches, marine chronometers and other horological items.* LOC: Between Jermyn St. and St. James's St. PARK: Meters. TEL: 071 321 0353; fax - 071 321 0350. VAT: Stan/Spec.

Arnold Wiggins and Sons Ltd   BADA
4 Bury St, St. James's. (M. Gregory). Open 9.30-5. CL: Sat. *STOCK: Picture frames, 16th-19th C.* TEL: 071 925 0195.

Thomas Williams (Fine Art) Ltd
PO Box 909. Open by appointment. *STOCK: Old and modern Master drawings, £300-£150,000.* TEL: 071 930 7818; fax - 071 930 7815. SER: Valuations; buys at auction (paintings and drawings).

LONDON S.W.3

Norman Adams Ltd   BADA
8/10 Hans Rd, Knightsbridge. Est. 1923. Open 9-5.30, Sat. and Sun. by appointment. SIZE: Large. *STOCK: English furniture, 18th C, £650-£250,000; objets d'art (English and French) £500-£50,000; mirrors, glass pictures, 18th C.* LOC: 30yds. off the Brompton Rd. opposite west side entrance to Harrods. TEL: 071 589 5266; fax - 071 589 1968. FAIRS: Grosvenor House. VAT: Spec.

Maria Andipa Icon Gallery   LAPADA
162 Walton St. CINOA. Est. 1968. Open 11-6, Sat. till 2. *STOCK: Icons, Greek, Russian, Byzantine, Coptic, Syrian; country furniture, crosses, crucifixes, embroidery, ethnic jewellery; lacquer eggs and silver icons.* TEL: 071 589 2371. SER: Valuations, restorations; buys at auction. FAIRS: Park Lane Hotel. VAT: Spec.

Antiquarius
131/141 King's Rd. (Atlantic Antiques Centres Ltd). Est. 1970. Open 10-6. LOC: On the corner of King's Rd. and Flood St., next to Chelsea Town Hall. TEL: Enquiries - 071 351 5353; fax - 071 351 5350. Below are listed some of the many specialist dealers at this market.

> #### Nick and Sue Alloway and Sue Norman
> Stand L4. *Blue and white transfer ware.* TEL: 071 352 7217.

We have a large range of interesting collectables including scales, clocks, magazine racks, boxes, fire tools, fenders, and all kinds of wood & brass decorative antiques.

We are exhibiting this year at Chelsea Harbour, and Olympia, London.

Cast iron American Blinking Eye clock circa 1870

**CHELSEA CLOCKS & ANTIQUES
STAND H3, ANTIQUARIUS
135, KINGS RD., LONDON, SW3.
TEL. 071 352 8646**

S.W.3 continued

Nigel Appleby - Jarona Antiques
Stand P1. *General antiques, small silver.* TEL: 071 352 8734.

S. Arena
Stand E5. *General antiques, silver plate.* TEL: 071 352 7989.

S. Aritaka
Stand E3/4. *Watches, pens and lighters, general.* TEL: 071 376 5394.

Bernice Barker
Stand R7/8. *Brass and copper.* TEL: 071 352 8882.

B. Barkoff
Stand R3/4. *General, inkwells, silver including flatware.* TEL: 071 351 5883.

M. Bashir
Stand M11/12. *Jewellery.* TEL: 071 352 7980.

Alexandra Bolla
Stand J1. *Jewellery.* TEL: 071 352 7989.

Stuart Bolster
Stand D1/D2. *Jewellery and objects.* TEL: 071 376 7348.

J. Brady
Stand P13. *Pictures and general.* TEL: 071 372 8882.

S.W.3 continued

William McLeod Brown
Stand L5-7. *Prints especially botanicals, books.* TEL: 071 352 4690.

Miss T. Buchinger
Stand Q3. *Jewellery and silver.* TEL: 071 352 8734.

C. Butterworth
Stand B2/3,C1. *Decorative antiques including lighting.* TEL: 071 352 3583.

Jasmin Cameron
Stand J6. *Antique fountain pens, £55-£1,000; writing materials, £6-£2,000; artist and drawing materials, £35-£1,000; all 18th-19th C.* TEL: 071 351 4154; home - 0474 873875. SER: Valuations; restorations (fountain pens). VAT: Stan.

Mrs V. Carroll
Stand N1. *Jewellery and small items.* TEL: 071 352 8734.

Chelsea Clocks
Stand H3-4, R1-2. (Dixon and Torr). *Clocks and general.* TEL: 071 352 8646.

Eli Cohen
Stand Q2. *General antiques, Oriental art.* TEL: 071 351 7038.

J. Cowan
Stand J2/3. *Jewellery.* TEL: 071 352 1750.

LONDON

S.W.3 continued

Crocodile Shop
Stand Q7/8. (J. Proctor). *Crocodile goods.* TEL: 071 376 5112.

S. Emerson, J. Course and M. Chapman
Stand K1,2,5,6. *General antiques, corkscrews and silver.* TEL: 071 352 7989.

Mrs. P. Evans
Stand N6/7. *Dolls and accessories.* TEL: 071 352 8734.

Flight of Fancy
Stand A9-A11. (Davis and Fawkes). *General antiques.* TEL: 071 352 4314.

French Glasshouse
Stand P14/15/16. (Mr and Mrs M. Bach). *Art deco and art nouveau, glass and china.* TEL: 071 376 5394.

Galya Antiques (Noonstar)
Stand Q4/Q5. (Aytac Osman). *General antiques, china, from 1900.* TEL: 071 352 2099.

S. A. Geris
Stand M2. *Watches.* TEL: 071 351 6607.

C. Gibson
Stand M10. *Silver and plate, general antiques.* TEL: 071 352 4690.

Mrs N. Gold
Stand Q12. *Jewellery, silver and plate.* TEL: 071 352 8734.

Mrs B. Gunn
Stand N13/N14. *Fans, small silver.* TEL: 071 352 4690.

Mrs B. Hamadani
Stand P5. *Gold and silver, general.* TEL: 071 352 8734.

Hayman and Hayman
Stand L2, M14-15. *Frames and watercolours, scent bottles.* TEL: 071 351 6568.

R. Henson
Stand P4. *Coins and medals.* TEL: 071 352 8734.

Messrs. Hickey
Stand D3/D4. *Jewellery and cuff-links.* TEL: 071 352 8201.

Mr Jenner
Stand A1/A2. *General antiques and collectors' items.* TEL: 071 352 7989.

Mrs P. A. Kaskimo
Stand C2. *General antiques, paintings.* TEL: 071 352 7989.

D. Kelly
Stand L3, M13. *Books.* TEL: 071 352 4690.

S.W.3 continued

Robin Lamari
Stand L1,10. *Watches and jewellery.* TEL: 071 351 9256.

H. Lazarov
Stand M21/M16. *Paintings and general.* TEL: 071 351 1972.

Mr and Mrs Lehane
Stand A7/8, B1/6. *Antique travel requisites and sporting memorabilia.* TEL: 071 352 7989.

M. Lexton
Stand N8-11. *Silver.* TEL: 071 351 5980.

Fay Lucas
Stand B4/5. *Jewellery and silver.* TEL: 071 351 6004.

Lynderside Ltd
Stand E6. (Mr and Mrs H. Elkabas). *Silver and jewellery.* TEL: 071 352 3286.

M. Markov
Stand F1/F6. *Decorative arts.* TEL: 071 352 4545.

Mrs. J. Martin
Stand A3. *General antiques.* TEL: 071 352 7989.

G. S. Mathias
Stand R5-6. *Victorian, Edwardian furniture, general, clocks.* TEL: 071 351 0484.

Mrs N. McDonald-Hobley
Stand A4. *Jewellery.* TEL: 071 351 0154.

Mr Mehta
Stand N2/3. *Jewellery.* TEL: 071 351 0697.

M. Michaels
Stand A17. *Watches, 1920's to 1950's.* TEL: 071 352 6217.

Mrs P. Miller
Stand J4/5. *Jewellery.* TEL: 071 352 4690.

Mrs T. Molloy
Stand P2. *Paintings.* TEL: 071 352 8734.

R.S. and S. Necus
Stand A18-19, H1-2. *Silver, plate, objets de vertu.* TEL: 071 352 2405.

H. J. and Miss J. Palmer
Stand M8/9. *Jewellery and silver.* TEL: 071 352 0431.

J. Pierce and M. Mara
Stand A12. *Jewellery, ceramics, commemorative china, general antiques.* TEL: 071 352 8734.

Miss E. Pollock
Stand G1/G4-6. *General antiques, small silver, jewellery and glass.* TEL: 071 352 8734.

LONDON

S.W.3 continued

The Purple Shop
Stand J9-11. (Gardner and Becker). *Antique and period jewellery and art nouveau, art deco.* TEL: 071 352 1127.

K. Reilly
Stand N15/N16. *Art nouveau and art deco.* TEL: 071 352 2366.

Mrs Gwen Riley
Stand D5. *Porcelain and china.* TEL: 071 352 7989.

Joel and Elizabeth Rothman
Stand Q9-10. *Costume jewellery, art deco, beauty and the beast, bronze animals.* TEL: 071 351 5149.

Mrs Michele Rowan
Stand N12. *General and jewellery.* TEL: 071 352 8744.

Scalpay Ltd
Stand K3/K4. (D. Shorn). *Jewellery.* TEL: 071 352 8687.

Miss Jerri Scott
Stand P9-P11. *General antiques and jewellery.* TEL: 071 352 2366/352 9471.

M. Simpson
Stand E1. *Antique ivory.* TEL: 071 352 7989.

Smith
Stand M3/4. *Silver, plate and jewellery.* TEL: 071 351 6497.

K. Spicer
Stand T5/6. *20th C art.* TEL: 071 352 8882.

Mrs Barbara Stone
Stand L8/9. *Antiquarian books.* TEL: 071 351 0963.

Sue Thompson
Stand T1-2. *General, silver.* TEL: 071 352 3494.

S. Thorpe
Stand T3-4. *Silver.* TEL: 071 351 2911.

Brian Tipping
Stand P12. *Antique pipes.* TEL: 071 352 3315.

Mr. Vidich
Stand A14-16. *Prints, etchings and lithographs.* TEL: 071 352 8734.

West Country Jewellery
Stand M6/7. (David Billing). *Jewellery.* TEL: 071 376 8252.

Apter Fredericks Ltd   BADA
265-267 Fulham Rd. (B.and Mrs. C Apter and H. Apter). Open 9.30-6. CL: Sat. *STOCK: English furniture, 17th to early 19th C.* TEL: 071 352 2188; fax - 071 376 5619. VAT: Stan/Spec.

S.W.3 continued

H.C Baxter and Sons   BADA LAPADA
53 Stewarts Grove. (T.J., J. and G.J Baxter). Est. 1928. Open 8.30-5.15. CL: Sat. and Mon. SIZE: Medium. *STOCK: English furniture, 1730-1830, £1,000-£35,000.* LOC: Next to Royal Marsden hospital, South Kensington nearest station. PARK: Meters. TEL: 071 352 9826/0807. VAT: Spec.

Boodle and Dunthorne Ltd
58 Brompton Rd. Open 9-6. *STOCK: Fine English and French jewellery, 19th-20th C, £100-£30,000.* TEL: 071 584 6363.

Joanna Booth   BADA
247 King's Rd, Chelsea. Est. 1963. Open 10-6. SIZE: Medium. *STOCK: Wood carvings, oak furniture, 17th C, £50-£5,000; Old Master drawings, textiles, tapestry.* Not stocked: Silver, glass, pottery, clocks. PARK: Meters. TEL: 071 352 8998; fax - 071 376 7350. SER: Buys at auction. VAT: Spec.

Tony Bunzl   LAPADA
344 King's Rd. Open 10-1 and 2-5.30. SIZE: Medium. *STOCK: European vernacular furniture, 17th-18th C.* PARK: Easy. TEL: 071 352 3697; fax - 071 352 1792. VAT: Stan/Spec.

W.G.T. Burne (Antique Glass) Ltd
BADA
11 Elystan St. (Mrs G., R.V. and A.T.G. Burne). Est. 1936. Open 9-5. CL: Thurs pm. and Sat pm. SIZE: Large. *STOCK: Glass, collectors' pieces, chandeliers, candelabra, cut glass tableware.* PARK: Meters. TEL: 071 589 6074; fax - 081 944 1977. SER: Valuations; renovations and repairs. VAT: Stan/Spec.

Butler and Wilson
189 Fulham Rd. *STOCK: Jewellery, art deco, crocodile and leather accessories.* TEL: 071 352 3045.

John Campbell Picture Frames Ltd
164 Walton St. Open 9.30-5.30. *STOCK: 20th C impressionist and modern British oils and watercolours.* TEL: 071 584 9268; fax - 071 581 3499. SER: Master framing, carving, gilding and restorations.

Century Gallery
100 Fulham Rd, Chelsea. (W. Westley-Richards). Est. 1979. Open 10-6. *STOCK: Oil paintings especially Russian 20th C, from £1,000+.* LOC: Opposite Brompton Hospital. PARK: Easy. TEL: 071 581 1589; fax - 071 589 9468. SER: Valuations; restorations; buys at auction (paintings). VAT: Stan/Spec.

Chelsea Antique Market
245A and 253 King's Rd. Est. 1965. Open 10-6. SIZE: Large - 30 dealers. *STOCK: General antiques, antiquarian books and prints, jewellery.*

S.W.3 continued
LOC: From Sloane Sq. directly along Kings Rd. From South Kensingrton underground along Sidney St. to Kings Rd., turn right. TEL: 071 352 5689/1720; stall-holders - 071 352 1424/5581. VAT: Stan.

Chelsea Rare Books
313 King's Rd. (L.S. Bernard). Est. 1968. Open 10-6. *STOCK: Antiquarian books and prints.* TEL: 071 351 0950. VAT: Stan.

Chenil Galleries
181-183 King's Rd, Chelsea. (Atlantic Antiques Centres Ltd). Est. 1978. Open 10-6. LOC: Next to Chelsea Town Hall. PARK: Sydney St. TEL: 071 351 5353; fax - 071 351 5350. VAT: Stan/Spec. Below are listed some of the many specialist dealers at this market.

G. Accossato
Stand D15. *Small silver, walking sticks and collectables.* TEL: 071 352 2123.

Trevor Allen
Stand E9/10. *Jewellery.* TEL: 071 352 8653.

Baptista Arts   LAPADA
Stand K1/2/10. (John Cox). **Art deco and bronzes. TEL: 071 352 5793.**

Mrs M. Bristow
Stand C6-7. *Silver, frames and flatware.* TEL: 071 352 1285.

A. Brown
Stand M3-4, M6-7. *Staffordshire, imari and blue and white.* TEL: 071 352 7384.

Chelsea Lion
Stand N1,3,9. (Steve Clark). *Dolls, toys, teddy bears.* TEL: 071 351 9338.

A. Coakley
Stand D13-14. *Art deco, art nouveau.* TEL: 071 351 2914.

D. Crowley and Mrs A. Fothergill
Stand D11/12. *Period clothing and textiles.* TEL: 071 351 0011.

G. Dewart
Stand C3. *Prints and paintings.* TEL: 071 352 7384.

Paul Dowling
Stand A6/7. *Decorative prints and frames.* TEL: 071 376 5056.

Mrs Gill Drey
Stand R16/17. *Modern paintings.* TEL: 071 351 2921.

Jerome Eccles
Stand A8-12. *Art deco furniture, accessories and paintings.* TEL: 071 352 5360.

Enigma
Stand Z2. (B. Boycott). *Period clothing.* TEL: 071 352 8581.

S.W.3 continued

Peter Fiell
Stand A1-A4. *Mid century decorative art.* TEL: 071 351 7172.

B. Gordon   LAPADA
Stand C4. **Fine silver and Sheffield plate. TEL: 071 352 5808.**

Mrs S. Hampton
Stand C5. *Decorative items.* TEL: 071 352 7384.

Pamela Haywood
Stand Z3. *Period clothing.* TEL: 071 352 8581.

Il Libro
Stand C8. (G. Toscani). *Books and prints.* TEL: 071 352 9041/823 3248.

Mrs Gwynneth Jones
Stand Z5. *Period clothing.* TEL: 071 352 8581.

Dennis Kingston
Stand R3-4. *Blue and white porcelain.* TEL: 071 352 7384.

Mrs Krell
Stand E5. *General antiques.* TEL: 071 352 8653.

La Verite
Stand R5-8. (Kit and Chizumi Bird). *Jewellery, glass and china.* TEL: 071 351 5999.

Claude and Martine Latreville
Stand B1-2. *Fine silver and jewellery.* TEL: 071 352 5964.

H. Man
Stand P1/2. *Chinese items, art nouveau, art deco.* TEL: 071 376 8037.

McClean
Stand L3-4. *Jewellery, walking sticks, glass, Vienna bronzes.* TEL: 071 351 9526.

Mrs R. Muggleton
Stand G5. *Silver and plate.* TEL: 071 352 2123.

John Pearman
Stand R12. *China, glass, bronzes and objects.* TEL: 071 376 3167.

Maria Perez
Stand A5. *Jewellery.* TEL: 071 351 1986.

Ms O. Pinhas
Stand D1. *Art nouveau, art deco jewellery and objects.* TEL: 071 352 2123.

G. Raffaelli
Stand B7. *Lighters.* TEL: 071 352 8581.

M. Risoli
Stand R13-14. *Furniture and accessories, silver plate.*

LONDON

S.W.3 continued

Rolandi
Stand B3. *Reproduction paintings.*

Salamanca
Stand D5-6. (Mrs D. Martin). *Moorcroft porcelain.* TEL: 071 351 5829.

N. Sonmez
Stand N6-8. *Persian and Oriental carpets.* TEL: 071 351 6611.

S. Tolkien
Stand E1/2. *American designer jewellery.* TEL: 071 376 3660.

C. A. Willcocks
Stand G3-4. *Prints and books.* TEL: 071 352 7384.

Mrs Y. P. Willcocks
Stand K3,4,8,9. *Fans and objects.* TEL: 071 351 6816.

Simon Willis
Stand E4. *Prints and objects.* TEL: 071 352 8653.

Basia Zarzycka
Stand E3. *Couture masks and accessories.* TEL: 071 351 7276.

Richard Courtney Ltd BADA
112-114 Fulham Rd. Est. 1959. Open 9.30-1 and 2-6. CL: Sat. SIZE: Large. *STOCK: English furniture, 18th C, £500-£20,000.* PARK: Easy. TEL: 071 370 4020. VAT: Spec.

Zal Davar LAPADA
344 King's Rd. Est. 1961. Open 10-5. CL: Sat. *STOCK: Furniture, 19th C; decorative items.* TEL: 071 351 5730; fax - 071 352 1792. SER: Buys on commission. VAT: Stan/Spec.

Colin Denny Ltd
18 Cale St. Est. 1968. Open 10-6. *STOCK: Marine works of art, 19th C.* TEL: 071 584 0240. VAT: Stan/Spec.

Robert Dickson Antiques Ltd BADA
263 Fulham Rd. Est. 1969. Open 9.30-5.30, Sat. 10.30-1. SIZE: Medium. *STOCK: Late 18th to early 19th C furniture and works of art, £500-£50,000.* PARK: Easy. TEL: 071 351 0330. VAT: Spec.

Dragons of Walton St. Ltd
23 Walton St. (R. Fisher). *STOCK: Mainly painted and decorated furniture; hand decorated children's furniture, decorative items.* LOC: Close to Harrods. PARK: Hasker St. or First St. TEL: 071 589 3795/0548 /5007; fax - 071 584 4570.

Michael Foster BADA
118 Fulham Rd, Chelsea. Open 9-6, Sat. 9-1. *STOCK: 18th C English furniture and works of art.* TEL: 071 373 3636/3040. SER: Valuations; restorations.

S.W.3 continued

C. Fredericks and Son BADA
92 Fulham Rd. (R.F. Fredericks). Open 9.30-5.30, Sat. by appointment. SIZE: Large. *STOCK: Furniture, 18th C, £500-£15,000.* LOC: Near to South Kensington underground station. PARK: Easy. TEL: 071 589 5847. VAT: Stan/Spec.

Gallery Lingard
Walpole House, 35 Walpole Street. SLAD. Open by appointment only. *STOCK: Architectural drawings and watercolours.* TEL: 071 730 9233.

David Gill LAPADA
60 Fulham Rd. Est. 1986. Open 10-6. SIZE: Medium. *STOCK: Decorative and fine arts, Picasso, Cocteau ceramics and drawings, 1900 to present day.* PARK: Onslow Sq. TEL: 071 589 5946. VAT: Stan.

Godson and Coles Ltd BADA
310 King's Rd. Est. 1978. Open 9.30-6, Sat. 10-4. *STOCK: English furniture, 18th to early 19th C.* TEL: 071 352 8509.

Green and Stone
259 Kings Rd. (R.J.S. Baldwin). Est. 1927. Open 9-5.30, Sat. 9.30-6. *STOCK: Writing and artists' materials, watercolours, 18th-19th C; drawings, 19th C.* LOC: At junction of King's Rd. and Old Church St. PARK: Meters. TEL: 071 352 0837/6521. SER: Restorations (pictures). VAT: Stan.

Robin Greer
30 Sloane Court West. Est. 1965. Open by appointment. *STOCK: Children's and illustrated books, original illustrations.* TEL: 071 730 7392. SER: Catalogues issued.

Grove Antiques
102 Fulham Road. (Mrs W.C.M. Hines and F.J. Van Der Breggen). Est. 1984. Open 10-5 or by appointment. *STOCK: English and continental furniture, £100-£20,000; clocks, decorative metalwork, paintings and architectural items, £50-£5,000.* Not stocked: Silver, gold and jewellery. TEL: 071 581 1589; 081 207 4413; fax - 081 207 4413. VAT: Spec.

Halliday's
28 Beauchamp Place. Est. 1948. Open 10-6. *STOCK: Mantelpieces in carved wood and marble, fire grates, fenders, gas-logs, fireplace accessories.* TEL: 071 589 5534; fax - 071 589 2477. SER: Restorations (fireplace equipment). VAT: Stan/Spec.

James Hardy and Co
235 Brompton Rd. Open 9.30-5.30. *STOCK: Silver including tableware, and jewellery.* PARK: Meters. TEL: 071 589 5050; fax - 071 823 8769. SER: Valuations.

S.W.3 continued

Stephanie Hoppen Ltd BADA
17 Walton St. Est. 1962. Open 9-6, Sat. 11-4. *STOCK: Watercolours, oils and drawings, ancient and modern.* TEL: 071 589 3678.

Malcolm Innes Gallery
172 Walton St. SLAD. Est. 1973. Open 9.30-6 and some Sats. 10-1. *STOCK: Scottish and sporting pictures.* TEL: 071 584 0575/5559; fax - 071 589 1066. SER: Restorations; framing. VAT: Spec.

Anthony James and Son Ltd BADA
88 Fulham Rd. Est. 1949. Open 9.30-5.45, Sat. by appointment. SIZE: Large. *STOCK: Furniture, 1700-1880, £200-£50,000; mirrors, bronzes, ormolu and decorative items, £200-£20,000.* PARK: Easy. TEL: 071 584 1120; fax - 071 823 7618. SER: Valuations; buys at auction. VAT: Spec.

Jazzy Art Deco
181 Kings Rd. (J. Eccles and V. Davies). Open 10-6. *STOCK: Art Deco furniture and decorative items.* TEL: 071 352 5360.

Annabel Jones
52 Beauchamp Place, Knightsbridge. Open 10-5.30. CL: Sat. *STOCK: Jewellery, silver and Sheffield plate.* TEL: 071 589 3215.

Lewis M. Kaplan Associates Ltd
LAPADA
50 Fulham Rd. (L.M. Kaplan and G.D. Watson). Est. 1977. Open 11-6. *STOCK: Art deco and art nouveau glass and furniture, £500-£10,000; signed art deco and art nouveau jewellery especially 1940's 'cocktail', £1,000-£10,000; both 1890-1945.* LOC: At junction with Sydney St. PARK: Sydney St. TEL: 071 589 3108/584 6328. SER: Valuations; buys at auction (art nouveau and art deco). VAT: Stan/Spec.

John Keil Ltd BADA
154 Brompton Rd. Est. 1959. Open 9-6. CL: Sat. except by appointment. SIZE: Large. *STOCK: English furniture, 18th to early 19th C, from £500.* LOC: Near Knightsbridge underground station. PARK: 200yds. TEL: 071 589 6454. SER: Restorations (fine pieces). VAT: Spec.

Stanley Leslie
15 Beauchamp Place. Open 9-5. *STOCK: Silver and Sheffield plate.* PARK: Meters. TEL: 071 589 2333.

Michael Lipitch Ltd
98 Fulham Rd. *STOCK: 18th C to early 19th C English furniture, decoration and works of art.* TEL: 071 589 7327; fax - 071 823 9106.

S.W.3 continued

Peter Lipitch Ltd BADA
120/124 Fulham Rd. Est. 1954. Open 9.30-5.30, Sat. by appointment. SIZE: Large. *STOCK: Fine English furniture and mirrors.* TEL: 071 373 3328; fax - 071 373 8888. VAT: Spec.

Gwyneth Lloyd Antique Textiles
LAPADA
Open by appointment. *STOCK: Antique and decorative embroideries and hangings; some costume and shawls.* TEL: 071 352 4864.

McKenna and Co LAPADA
28 Beauchamp Place. (C. Macmillan and M. McKenna). Est. 1982. Open 10-6. SIZE: Medium. *STOCK: Fine jewellery, Georgian to post war, £50-£10,000; some silver and objects.* Not stocked: Pictures and furniture. LOC: Off Brompton Rd., near Harrods. PARK: Meters. TEL: 071 584 1966; fax - 071 225 2893. SER: Valuations; restorations. FAIRS: Olympia. VAT: Stan/Spec.

The Map House
54 Beauchamp Place. (Hon. C.A. and Mrs. Savile, Lord Mexborough and Countess of Mexborough). Est. 1907. Open 9.45-5.45, Sat. 10.30-5 or by appointment. *STOCK: Antique and rare maps, atlases, engravings and globes.* TEL: 071 589 4325/584 8559; fax - 071 589 1041. VAT: Stan.

Mathon Gallery
38 Cheyne Walk, Chelsea. (Phipps and Co. Ltd). Est. 1980. Open 9.30-5.30 or by appointment, including Sun. SIZE: Medium. *STOCK: British oils, watercolours and sculpture, 19th-20th C, £100-£30,000.* TEL: 071 352 5381; 0684 892242. SER: Valuations; buys at auction (British paintings and sculpture). VAT: Spec.

Merola
178 Walton St. (M. Merola). Open 10-6. *STOCK: Jewellery, handbags, hats and accessories, 1900-1960.* TEL: 071 589 0365; fax - 071 373 4297.

Guy Nevill Fine Paintings Ltd
251A Fulham Rd. Open by appointment 10-5.30. CL: Sat. SIZE: Large. *STOCK: Sporting, country and animal pictures, 18th-20th C, £100-£300,000.* PARK: Easy. TEL: 071 351 4292. VAT: Stan.

Old Church Galleries
320 King's Rd, Chelsea. (Mrs M. Harrington). Open 10-6. *STOCK: Maps and engravings, from 17th C; sporting and decorative prints.* TEL: 071 351 4649. SER: Framing.

JACQUELINE OOSTHUIZEN

Superb Selection STAFFORDSHIRE Figures, Animals, Cottages, Toby Jugs also ANTIQUE & ESTATE JEWELLERY

Mon to Fri 10-6	Wed & Sat 8-4
23 Cale Street	1st Floor-Upstairs
(Chelsea Green)	Georgian Village
off Sydney Street LAPADA MEMBER	Camden Passage
London SW3	London N1

Phones: 071-352 6071   071-376 3852   071-226 5393
Answering Service 081-528 9001 pager No. 806930

S.W.3 continued

Jacqueline Oosthuizen LAPADA
23 Cale St, (Off Sydney St.), Chelsea Green. Est. 1960. Open 10-6, Sat. by chance or appointment, Sun. by appointment. SIZE: Small. *STOCK: Staffordshire figures, animals, cottages and toby jugs, 18th-19th C, £50-£10,000; jewellery, 19th-20th C, £15-£5,000; decorative ceramics including Poole pottery, 19th-20th C, £20-£1,000.* LOC: Near King's Rd. and Fulham Rd. PARK: Easy. TEL: 071 352 6071; answering service - 081 528 9001 (pager no.806930). VAT: Stan/Spec.

Perez
199 Brompton Rd. (Mr Tyran). Est. 1983. Open 10-6. SIZE: Large. *STOCK: Antique carpets, rugs, tapestries and Aubussons.* LOC: 50 yards from Harrods. PARK: Easy. TEL: 071 589 2199 (ansaphone). SER: Valuations; restorations; buys at auction. VAT: Stan/Spec.

David Pettifer Ltd BADA
73 Glebe Place, King's Rd. Est. 1963. Open Tues., Wed. and Thurs. 8.30-6.30, other times by appointment. SIZE: Medium. *STOCK: English furniture and works of art, 18th-19th C.* LOC: From Sloane Sq., 11, 19 or 22 bus. PARK: Easy. TEL: 071 352 3088; fax - same. SER: Buys at auction. VAT: Spec.

S.W.3 continued

Prides of London
15 Paultons House, Paultons Sq. Open by appointment only. *STOCK: Fine furniture, objets d'art.* TEL: 071 586 1227. SER: Interior design.

The Purple Shop •
15 Flood St, Chelsea. (A.J. Gardner and O.M. Becker). Est. 1967. Open 10-6. *STOCK: Antique and period jewellery especially art nouveau and art deco; studio pottery.* LOC: Near Chelsea Town Hall. PARK: Meters and nearby. TEL: 071 352 1127. SER: Valuations. VAT: Stan.

Rogers de Rin LAPADA
76 Royal Hospital Rd, Chelsea. (V. de Rin). Est. 1950. Open 10-5.30. SIZE: Small. *STOCK: Wemyss pottery, objets d'art, decorative furnishings (Regency style), collectors' specialities, 18th-19th C, £50-£10,000.* LOC: Just beyond Royal Hospital, corner of Paradise Walk. PARK: Easy. TEL: 071 352 9007; fax - 071 351 9407. SER: Buys at auction. VAT: Stan/Spec.

Alistair Sampson Antiques Ltd BADA
156 Brompton Rd. (A.H. Sampson, Michael Gillingham and Tobias Jellinek). Open 9.30-5.30. SIZE: Large. *STOCK: English pottery, oak and country furniture, metalwork, needlework, primitive pictures, decorative and interesting items,17th-18th C; Chinese works of art.* PARK: Meters. TEL: 071 589 5272/581 2267; fax - 071 823 8142. VAT: Spec.

Charles Saunders Antiques
255 Fulham Rd. Open 9.30-5.30, Sat. 10-5.30. *STOCK: Decorative furniture, objects and lamps, 18th-19th C.* TEL: 071 351 5242. VAT: Spec.

Christine Schell
15 Cale St. (B. King and C. Davies). Est. 1971. Open 10-5.30, Sat. 10-1. SIZE: Small. *STOCK: Unusual tortoiseshell, silver and enamel objects, late 19th to early 20th C, £150-£2,500.* LOC: North of King's Rd., between Sloane Ave. and Sydney St. PARK: Easy. TEL: 071 352 5563. SER: Valuations; restorations (tortoiseshell, ivory, shagreen, crocodile, leather, enamels, silver and hairbrush re-bristling). FAIRS: Olympia. VAT: Stan/Spec.

Mark Senior
240 Brompton Rd. Est. 1980. Open 10.30-6, Sat. 10-3. SIZE: Medium. *STOCK: English watercolours, 19th C, £100-£3,000.* LOC: Near Victoria and Albert Museum. PARK: Meters. TEL: 071 589 5811. SER: Valuations; restorations; framing; buys at auction (watercolours). VAT: Spec.

Robert Stephenson
1 Elystan Street, Chelsea Green. Open 9.30-5.30, Sat. 10-1. *STOCK: Decorative and Oriental carpets; Oriental and European kilims; needlepoints, kilim-upholstered furniture, cushions and textiles.* TEL: 071 225 2343.

Rogers de Rin Antiques

Specialists in WEMYSS WARE

76 Royal Hospital Road
071 352 9007

London SW3 4HN

OPEN 10am to 5.30pm

We would like to buy collections of Wemyss Ware or individual pieces.

Colour catalogue available on request 071 352 9007

S.W.3 continued

Oliver Swann Galleries
170 Walton St. Est. 1975. Open 10-6, Sat. by appointment. SIZE: Medium. *STOCK: Marine and yachting paintings, 19th-20th C; ships models; all £150-£50,000.* PARK: Easy. TEL: 071 581 4229/584 8684. SER: Valuations; restorations; buys at auction. VAT: Spec.

David Tron Antiques   BADA LAPADA
275 King's Rd. Open 9.30-1 and 2-6. *STOCK: Furniture, 17th-19th C; works of art. (Also trade department).* TEL: 071 352 5918.

Walker-Bagshawe
73 Walton St. (C. Walker and N. Bagshawe). SLAD. Est. 1979. Open 10-6. SIZE: Medium. *STOCK: English and European oils and watercolours, 1870-1930, £2,000-£150,000; arts and crafts furniture, 1900's, £200-£5,000.* LOC: Behind Harrods. PARK: Meters. TEL: 071 589 4582. SER: Valuations; restorations (oils, watercolours, prints); framing; buys at auction (paintings). VAT: Spec.

R. Wearn and Son Ltd
322 King's Rd. Est. 1928. Open 10.30-5, Sat. 10.30-2. *STOCK: General antiques, furniture, 18th-19th C, £200-£4,000.* TEL: 071 352 3918.

S.W.3 continued

David Weston
1 The Portico's, King's Road. (D.A. Weston). Est. 1968. Open by appointment. SIZE: Medium. *STOCK: Globes, scientific and marine items.* TEL: Home - 0424 755624. SER: Valuations. VAT: Stan/Spec.

The 'Bulldog', a popular British mascot, this time wearing goggles, chromium plated. Circa 1935. £40-£60. From ***Automobilia of Europe — Reference and Price Guide***, by Gordon Gardiner and Alistair Morris, published by the **Antique Collectors' Club**, £25.00.

LONDON

O.F. WILSON LTD.

QUEENS ELM PARADE

OLD CHURCH STREET LONDON SW3 6EJ 071-352-9554

English and Continental period decorative furniture, objets d'art; period English & French mantelpieces

Mon. – Fri. 9.30 – 5.30
Sat. 10.30 – 1
Valuations given

Clifford Wright Antiques Ltd.
Antiques and Works of Art

Telephone 071-589 0986
Fax 071-589 3565

104 & 106 Fulham Road,
London SW3 6HT

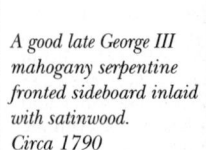

A good late George III mahogany serpentine fronted sideboard inlaid with satinwood. Circa 1790

Height 35" (89cm)
Width 60" (152 1/2 cm)
Depth 27 1/2" (70cm)

S.W.3 continued

O.F. Wilson Ltd   BADA LAPADA
Queens Elm Parade, Old Church St (corner of Fulham Rd.), Chelsea. (P. and V.E. Jackson and M.E. Briscoe-Knight). Est. 1935. Open 9.30-5.30, Sat. 10.30-1. *STOCK: English and French furniture, mantelpieces, objets d'art.* TEL: 071 352 9554. SER: Valuations. VAT: Spec.

Clifford Wright Antiques Ltd   BADA
104-106 Fulham Rd. Est. 1964. Open Mon.-Fri. 9-6 or by appointment. *STOCK: Furniture, period giltwood, looking glasses and consoles, 18th to early 19th C.* TEL: 071 589 0986; fax - 071 589 3565. VAT: Spec.

LONDON S.W.4

Crawley and Asquith Ltd   BADA
5 Crescent Grove. Open by appointment. *STOCK: 18th-19th C paintings, watercolours, prints, books.* TEL: 071 622 2005; fax - 071 622 0005.

HRW Antiques   LAPADA
4a King's Avenue, Clapham. Open 10-5, Sat. 10-1, other times by appointment. SIZE: Large. *STOCK: Furniture and objects of art, 18th-19th C.* TEL: 071 978 1026.

Wingfield Sporting Art
35 Sibella Rd, Clapham. (Mrs M. Wingfield). Open by appointment. *STOCK: Paintings and prints covering over 50 sports.* TEL: 071 622 6301.

LONDON S.W.5

Antique and Modern Furniture Ltd
160 Earls Court Rd. Est. 1941. Open 9.30-1 and 2.30-6. CL: Thurs. *STOCK: Furniture, mainly 18th-19th C.* TEL: 071 373 2935.

Beaver Coin Room
Beaver Hotel, 57 Philbeach Gdns. (J. Lis). Est. 1971. Open by appointment. SIZE: Small. *STOCK: European coins, 10th-18th C, commemorative medals, 15th-20th C; all £5-£5,000.* LOC: 2 mins. walk from Earls Court Rd. PARK: Easy. TEL: 071 373 4553; fax - 071 373 4555. SER: Valuations; buys at auction (coins and medals). FAIRS: London Coin and Coinex. VAT: Stan.

LONDON S.W.6

20th Century Gallery
821 Fulham Rd. (E. Brandl and H. Chapman). Open 10-6, Sat. 10-1. SIZE: Small. *STOCK: Post impressionist and modern British oils and watercolours; original prints.* LOC: Near Munster Rd. junction. PARK: Easy. TEL: 071 731 5888. SER: Restorations (paintings); framing. VAT: Spec.

S.W.6 continued

(55) For Decorative Living
55 New King's Rd, Chelsea. (Mrs J. Rhodes). Open 10.30-5.30. *STOCK: Furniture, lighting and decorative items.* TEL: 071 736 5623. SER: Design.

And So To Bed Limited
638/640 King's Rd. Est. 1970. Open 10-6. SIZE: Large. *STOCK: Brass, lacquered and wooded beds.* LOC: End of King's Rd., towards Fulham. PARK: Easy. TEL: 071 731 3593/4/5. SER: Restorations; spares; interior design. VAT: Stan.

Antique Carpets Gallery
150 Wandsworth Bridge Rd, Fulham. (R. Tyran). Est. 1984. Open 10-6.30, Wed. 10-7.30. SIZE: Large. *STOCK: Carpets, 19th C, £400-£40,000; rugs, 18th-20th C, £300-£3,000; textiles, 19th C, £70-£1,500.* PARK: Easy. TEL: 071 371 9619/9620. SER: Valuations; restorations; buys at auction (Oriental and European carpets, rugs and textiles, tapestries). VAT: Stan/Spec.

Karin Armelin Antiques
592 King's Rd. Open 10-5.30. SIZE: Medium. *STOCK: 18th-19th C English and French furniture, decorative prints.* PARK: Easy. TEL: 071 736 0375. SER: Valuations. VAT: Stan/Spec.

Barclay Samson Ltd
39 Inglethorpe St. Open by appointment only. *STOCK: Pre 1940 original lithographic posters; English and continental watercolours, oil paintings and prints, mainly 19th C.* TEL: 071 381 4341; fax - 071 610 0434. VAT: Spec.

Robert Barley Antiques
48 Fulham High St. (R.A. Barley). Est. 1965. Open 9.30-5.30. CL: Sat. SIZE: Medium. *STOCK: Unusual decorative furniture, objects, lighting.* LOC: Near Putney Bridge. PARK: Easy. TEL: 071 736 4429. VAT: Stan/Spec.

Beresford-Clark
558 King's Rd, Chelsea. Est. 1976. Open 10-5.30, Sat. by appointment. SIZE: Medium. *STOCK: Furniture, decorative paintings, textiles, unusual objects and china.* PARK: Easy. TEL: 071 731 5079.

Big Ben Antique Clocks
5 Broxholme House, New King's Rd. (R. Lascelles). Est. 1978. Open 10-5.30. *STOCK: Clocks especially longcase, from £1,000.* LOC: At junction of Wandsworth Bridge Rd. and New King's Rd. TEL: 071 736 1770; fax - 071 384 1957. SER: Repairs (clocks); buys at auction.

Bishops Park Antiques
53-55 Fulham High St. Open 10-6. *STOCK: Pine especially English and continental, 18th-19th C.* TEL: 071 736 4573.

LONDON

S.W.6 continued

Bookham Galleries
164 Wandsworth Bridge Rd. (J.H. and J. Rowe). Est. 1969. Open 10-5.30. CL: Mon. and Thurs. *STOCK: Furniture, 18th-19th C; Oriental rugs.* TEL: 071 736 5125.

Bowmoore Gallery
77 Peterborough Rd, Fulham. Open by appointment. SIZE: Large. *STOCK: Oil paintings and watercolours, 1850-1950 and selected contemporary artists, £100-£25,000.* LOC: 2 minutes from Parsons Green station or 22 bus. TEL: 071 736 4111. SER: Valuations; restorations (oils and watercolours); re-gilding frames; framing; buys at auction (19th-20th C paintings).

Brandt Oriental Antiques   BADA
(R. Brandt). Est. 1981. Open by appointment. *STOCK: Oriental works of art, £500-£10,000.* TEL: 071 731 6835/1192. VAT: Spec.

Alasdair Brown Antiques
560 King's Rd. Est. 1986. Open 9.30-6, Sat. 10-5. SIZE: Large. *STOCK: Furniture, £500-£10,000;*

---

free!

28 page full colour catalogue of Antique Collectors' Club books.
Over 120 titles included covering a wide range of subjects: furniture, art reference, art history, prints, jewellery, metalwork, glass, horology, ceramics, oriental carpets, collectables, garden history and design, gardening and architecture.

Available free from the
ANTIQUE COLLECTORS' CLUB

5 Church Street
Woodbridge
Suffolk IP12 1DS
Tel: (0394) 385501
Fax: (0394) 384434

S.W.6 continued

decorative items, £100-£5,000; all 18th-19th C; upholstery, 19th C, £350-£5,000. LOC: Just past Lot's Rd. PARK: Easy. TEL: 071 736 8077. SER: Valuations; restorations. FAIRS: Olympia (June and Nov). VAT: Stan/Spec.

I. and J.L. Brown Ltd
632-636 King's Rd. Open 9-5.30. *STOCK: English country and French provincial furniture including tables and country chairs; metalware and decorative items.* TEL: 071 736 4141; fax - 071 736 9164. SER: Restorations.

Rupert Cavendish Antiques   LAPADA
610 King's Rd. Est. 1980. Open 10-6. SIZE: Large. *STOCK: Empire and Biedermeier furniture and oil paintings.* LOC: Just before New King's Rd. PARK: Easy. TEL: 071 731 7041; fax - 071 731 8302. SER: Valuations. VAT: Spec.

Rupert Cavendish Designs   LAPADA
98 Waterford Rd. Open 10-6. *STOCK: Art deco and designed furniture, neo-classical wallpapers and fabrics.* TEL: 071 384 2642; fax - 071 731 8302.

Chanticleer Antiques
6 Tilton St. (S. Wilkinson). Est. 1967. Open by appointment. *STOCK: Decorative and collectors items, 18th-19th C, £100-£2,000; European and Oriental works of art.* TEL: 071 385 0919. VAT: Stan/Spec.

John Clay
263 New King's Rd, Fulham. Est. 1974. Open 8.30-6, Sat. 10-6. SIZE: Medium. *STOCK: Furniture, £50-£5,000; objets d'art and animal objects, silver and clocks, £10-£1,500; all 18th-19th C.* Not stocked: Pine. LOC: Close to Parsons Green, A3. PARK: Easy. TEL: 071 731 5677. SER: Restorations (furniture, objets d'art). VAT: Stan/Spec.

Fergus Cochrane Antiques
570 King's Rd. (F.V. Cochrane). Est. 1981. Open 10-6SIZE: Medium. *STOCK: Decorative lighting, 1700-1930, £100-£2,000.* PARK: Easy. TEL: 071 736 9166. VAT: Stan/Spec.

Peter Collins
92 Waterford Rd. Est. 1971. Open 10-1 and 3-6. CL: Tues. *STOCK: Furniture - country woods or painted, 17th to early 19th C; decorative items.* TEL: 071 736 4149.

The Constant Reader Bookshop
627 Fulham Rd. (S. Ali). Open 10.30-6.30. *STOCK: Books especially art and military.* TEL: 071 731 0218.

Major suppliers of English Country & French Provincial Antique Furniture

I&JL BROWN

636 & 632 Kings Road, Chelsea, London SW6 2DU
Telephone (071) 736 4141

58 Commercial Road, Hereford HR1 2BP
Telephone (0432) 358895 Telefax (0432) 275338

S.W.6 continued

Cooper Fine Arts Ltd
768 Fulham Rd. (J. Hill-Reid). Est. 1976. Open 10-6.30. SIZE: Medium. *STOCK: Oils and watercolours, £200-£5,000; bronzes, £200-£1,000; all 1850-1950.* LOC: Putney Bridge end of Fulham Rd. PARK: Easy. TEL: 071 731 3421; home - same. SER: Valuations; restorations; framing; buys at auction. VAT: Stan/Spec.

J. Crotty and Son Ltd
74 New King's Rd, Parsons Green. Est. 1945. Open 9.30-5. CL: Sat. pm. SIZE: Medium. *STOCK: Fire grates, fenders, 18th-19th C; marble and pine mantelpieces, fire irons and screens, period lighting.* PARK: In adjacent side street. TEL: 071 731 4209. SER: Restorations (antique metal fireplace equipment); buys at auction. VAT: Stan.

Charles Edwards   BADA LAPADA
582 King's Rd. Open 9.30-6. *STOCK: Furniture, 18th-19th C; architectural and decorative items, mirrors, British oil paintings, rugs, carpets, garden furniture and statuary.* TEL: 071 736 8490; fax - 071 371 5436.

Fairfax Fireplaces and Antiques
568 King's Rd. (H. Fairfax). Open 10-5. *STOCK: Fireplaces - cast-iron and pine; railings and balustrades.* TEL: 071 736 5023; fax - same. SER: Restorations; metal polishing; fabricating.

Five Five Six Antiques
556 King's Rd. (Patricia Harvey). Est. 1961. Open 10-6. SIZE: Medium. *STOCK: General decorative items - early and unusual furniture, primitive paintings, watercolours, samplers, needlework cushions, wool and silk works, decorators' accessories.* TEL: 071 731 2016; home - 071 624 5173. SER: Valuations; interior decoration. VAT: Stan.

George Floyd Ltd
592 Fulham Rd. Open 8.30-5.30. SIZE: Large. *STOCK: 18th to early 19th C furniture and accessories.* TEL: 071 736 1649. VAT: Stan/Spec.

Gerald Freedman
Est. 1961. Open by appointment. *STOCK: 17th-18th C Chinese porcelain; European ceramics including Delft, faience and maiolica.* LOC: End of King's Rd, 1 minute from Putney Bridge (District Line station). TEL: 071 736 8666. SER: Valuations.

George d'Epinois
793 Fulham Rd. (A. George). Est. 1979. Open 9.30-5.30. *STOCK: English furniture, 1690-1820, £250-£30,000.* PARK: Easy. TEL: 071 736 2387. SER: Valuations; restorations. FAIRS: Harrogate; Olympia; Brugge, Belgium. VAT: Spec.

Judy Greenwood
657 Fulham Rd. Est. 1978. Open 10-5. *STOCK: Textiles including paisleys, quilts, curtains; decorative furniture.* TEL: 071 736 6037.

S.W.6 continued

Gregory, Bottley and Lloyd
8-12 Rickett St. Est. 1850. SIZE: Medium. *STOCK: Mineral specimens, £1-£5,000; fossils, £5-£500.* LOC: Behind West Brompton underground. PARK: Easy. TEL: 071 381 5522; fax - 071 381 5512. SER: Valuations. VAT: Stan.

Guinevere Antiques
574/580 King's Rd. Open 9.30-6, Sat. 10-6. SIZE: Large. *STOCK: Period and decorative antiques and accessories.* TEL: 071 736 2917; fax - 071 736 8267.

Nicholas Harris   BADA LAPADA
564 King's Rd. Est. 1971. Open 10-6, Sat. 10.30-1.30. *STOCK: Silver and decorative art.* TEL: 071 371 9711; fax - 071 371 9537. SER: Valuations; restorations (silver). VAT: Stan/Spec.

Hollingshead and Co
783 Fulham Rd. (D. Hollingshead). Est. 1946. Open 10-1 and 2-5. CL: Sat. pm. SIZE: Medium. *STOCK: Marble and wood mantelpieces, grates, fenders, fire irons, chandeliers, £50-£20,000.* Not stocked: Furniture. PARK: Easy. TEL: 071 736 6991. SER: Valuations; restorations (marblework and wood mantelpieces). VAT: Stan.

Simon Horn Furniture Ltd
117-121 Wandsworth Bridge Rd. IADDA. Est. 1981. Open 8.30-5.30, Sat. 9.30-5.30, Sun. by appointment. SIZE: Large. *STOCK: Bedframes, chests, £500-£1,000; bedside tables, £150-£350; all 1790-1910.* LOC: South from King's Rd., towards river down Wandsworth Bridge Rd., premises on left at first zebra crossing. PARK: Easy. TEL: 071 731 1279. SER: Restorations (as stock). FAIRS: Delorex, Daily Telegraph Period Home Show. VAT: Stan.

House of Mirrors
597 King's Rd. (Z. Wigek). Est. 1960. Open 10-6. *STOCK: Mirrors.* TEL: 071 736 5885.

Peter Hurford Antiques
618-620 King's Rd. Open 10-5.30. *STOCK: Continental and British decorative objects and furniture, screens and mirrors, 18th-19th C, £100-£10,000.* TEL: 071 731 4655. VAT: Spec.

P.L. James
681 Fulham Rd. Open 7-5. CL: Sat. *STOCK: Gilded mirrors, English and Oriental lacquer, period objects and furniture.* TEL: 071 736 0183. SER: Restorations (painted and lacquer furniture, gilding, carving). VAT: Stan/Spec.

Patrick Jefferson
572 Kings Rd. Est. 1978. Open 9.30-6, Sat. 10-5. SIZE: Medium. *STOCK: Fine 18th-19th C English and continental furniture and works of art.* LOC: Between World's End and Parson's Green. PARK: In side roads. TEL: 071 371 9088. SER: Valuations; buys at auction (furniture and associated items). FAIRS: Olympia (June). VAT: Stan/Spec.

S.W.6 continued

Peter Jeffs at Nicholas Harris
564 King's Rd. Est. 1974. Open daily. SIZE: Medium. *STOCK: Silver and decorative art, 19th-20th C, £100-£10,000.* LOC: On corner King's Rd. and Holmead Rd. PARK: Easy. TEL: 071 371 9711. SER: Restorations (silver); buys at auction (as stock). FAIRS: Olympia. VAT: Stan/Spec.

Just a Second
40-42 Fulham High St. (G. Bastillo). Est. 1973. Open 9.30-1 and 2-6, Sun. 2-6. SIZE: Medium. *STOCK: General antiques.* LOC: Near Putney Bridge. PARK: Easy. TEL: 071 731 1919. SER: Valuations; buys at auction.

Eric King Antiques
11 Crondace Road. Est. 1966. Open by appointment. *STOCK: Decorative furniture and accessories, 18th-20th C.* PARK: Easy. TEL: 071 731 2554.

King's Court Galleries
951/953 Fulham Rd. (Mrs. J. Joel). Open 10-6. *STOCK: Antique maps, engravings, decorative and sporting prints.* TEL: 071 610 6939. SER: Framing.

L. and E. Kreckovic
62 Fulham High St. Open 9.30-5, Sat. 10-5 or by appointment. *STOCK: 19th C furniture especially leather chairs.* TEL: 071 736 0753.

The Lamp Gallery
355 New King's Rd. (G. Jones). Est. 1986. Open 10-6. SIZE: Medium. *STOCK: Interior lighting including art nouveau and art deco lamps, 1860-1960, £10-£1,000+.* LOC: 400yds. from Putney Bridge. PARK: Limited or nearby. TEL: 071 736 6188. SER: Valuations; restorations (metal polishing, electroplating and re-wiring). VAT: Stan.

Lunn Antiques
86 New King's Rd. (S. Lunn). Est. 1975. Open 10-6. *STOCK: Victorian and Edwardian hand worked linens, sheets, bedspreads, pillowcases, tablecloths, Oriental embroidery, pre-war clothing, some early lace and costume.* TEL: 071 736 4638. VAT: Stan.

Magpies
152 Wandsworth Bridge Rd, Fulham. Open 10-6. SIZE: 5 dealers. *STOCK: China, glass, kitchenalia, collectables and furniture.* TEL: 071 736 3738.

Michael Marriott Ltd
588 Fulham Rd. Est. 1979. Open 10-5.30. CL: Sat. pm. and Sun. except by appointment. SIZE: Large. *STOCK: English furniture, 1700-1850, £400-£15,000; leather upholstery, £250-£4,500; framed prints, £45-£800.* LOC: Junction of Fulham Rd. and Parsons Green Lane. PARK: Easy. TEL: 071 736 3110/736 0568. SER: Valuations; restorations. FAIRS: Olympia, Kensington, Kenilworth (Spring and Autumn), London Antique Dealers' (Cafe Royal). VAT: Stan/Spec.

S.W.6 continued

David Martin-Taylor Antiques
LAPADA
56 Fulham High St. Open 9.30-5.30. CL: Sat. SIZE: Medium. *STOCK: Decorative furniture and unusual items, 18th-19th C; early English and American wickers.* LOC: Off Putney Bridge between Fulham Rd. and New King's Rd. PARK: Easy. TEL: 071 731 4135; fax - 071 371 0029. SER: Hire. VAT: Stan/Spec.

Mark Maynard Antiques
651 Fulham Rd. Est. 1977. Open 10-5, Sun. by appointment. SIZE: Medium. *STOCK: Decorative items, £25-£300.* LOC: Near Fulham Broadway underground. PARK: Easy. TEL: 071 731 3533; home - 071 373 4681. VAT: Stan/Spec.

Ian Moggach Antiques
723 Fulham Road. Open 9.30-5.30. CL: Sat. SIZE: Large. *STOCK: 19th C furniture, including desks, writing tables and bookcases, French marble fireplaces, £400-£2,500.* TEL: 071 731 4883.

Sylvia Napier Ltd
LAPADA
554 King's Rd. Est. 1972. Open 10-6. SIZE: Large. *STOCK: Furniture - decorative European, 18th-19th C, £100-£15,000; decorative Oriental, 17th-19th C, £200-£7,000; garden, 19th C, £150-£7,000; objets d'art.* LOC: Near junction with Lots Rd. PARK: Easy. TEL: 071 371 5881. SER: Restorations. VAT: Stan/Spec.

Old Pine
594 King's Rd. (S. and R. Rippingale). Open 10-5.30. *STOCK: Painted and pine furniture.* TEL: 071 736 5999. VAT: Stan.

Old World Trading Co
565 King's Rd. (R.J. Campion). Est. 1970. Open 9.30-6. *STOCK: Fireplaces, chimney pieces and accessories, chandeliers, mirrors, furniture including decorative, works of art.* TEL: 071 731 4708; fax - 071 731 1291.

Paul Orssich
117 Munster Rd, Fulham. Open 10-6, Sat. and other times by appointment. *STOCK: Antiquarian maps and books, especially on Hispanic studies, 16th-19th C, from £25; art deco illustrations, 1898-1935, £15-£500.* TEL: 071 736 3869.

Osterley Antiques Ltd
595 King's Rd. Est. 1960. Open 9.30-5.30. SIZE: Large. *STOCK: Furniture, 18th C.* TEL: 071 731 0334. SER: Valuations; restorations. VAT: Stan/Spec.

M. Pauw Antiques
606 King's Rd. Est. 1985. SIZE: Medium. *STOCK: English and continental furniture, 18th-19th C; decorative items, lighting fixtures, £500-£20,000.* PARK: Easy. TEL: 071 731 4022; fax - 071 731 7356. VAT: Stan/Spec.

S.W.6 continued

The Pine Mine (Crewe-Read Antiques)
100 Wandsworth Bridge Rd, Fulham. (D. Crewe-Read). Est. 1971. Open 9.45-5.45, Sat. till 4.30. SIZE: Large. *STOCK: Georgian and Victorian pine, Welsh dressers, farmhouse tables, chests of drawers, boxes and some architectural items.* LOC: From Sloane Sq., down King's Rd., into New King's Rd., left into Wandsworth Bridge Rd. PARK: Outside. TEL: 071 736 1092. SER: Furniture made from old wood; stripping; export.

Peter Place Antiques
632-636 King's Rd. Usually open 9.30-5.30. *STOCK: 18th-19th C metalware, decorative items, paintings, folk art.* TEL: 071 736 9945.

Powell & Mathers Antiques
571 Kings Road. Open by appointment. *STOCK: 18th-19th C English and continental furniture and decorative objects.* TEL: 071 371 7837.

Antony Preston and Sally Isbell BADA
No.3, 555 King's Road. Est. 1967. Open 10-6. SIZE: Medium. *STOCK: Furniture, 1690-1840, £500-£30,000; bronze and ormolu, candelabra and lamps, 1750-1840, £250-£10,000; upholstery, 1750-1840, £1,000-£15,000.* LOC: Immediately after Stamford Bridge. PARK: Easy. TEL: 071 371 8301. SER: Buys at auction (furniture and works of art). VAT: Stan/Spec.

Richardson and Kailas Icons
BADA LAPADA
65 Rivermead Court, Ranelagh Gardens. (C. Richardson and M. Kailas). Open by appointment. *STOCK: Icons and frescoes.* TEL: 071 371 0491.

Robin Sanders and Sons LAPADA
590 Fulham Rd. Open 10-6, Sat. 10-1. CL: Mon. *STOCK: English furniture, 1650-1800; 19th C Staffordshire pottery; 18th C English glass pictures.* TEL: 071 736 0586.

Sensation Ltd
66 Fulham High St. (M. Fenwick). Est. 1958. Open 9-5, Sat. and Sun. except by appointment. SIZE: Large. *STOCK: English furniture, pottery, porcelain, silver and objets d'art, 17th-19th C; decorative items and painted furniture.* PARK: At rear. TEL: 071 736 4135; fax - 071 371 5486. SER: Valuations; restorations; buys at auction. VAT: Stan/Spec.

David Seyfried Antiques
759 Fulham Rd. Est. 1984. Open 10-5, Sat. by appointment. SIZE: Small. *STOCK: Furniture, 19th C; sofas, stools, Turkish kilims, £250-£400.* Not stocked: Silver. LOC: 130yds. west of Parsons Green Lane. PARK: Easy in side streets. TEL: 071 731 4230; home - 071 736 6730. VAT: Spec.

S.W.6 continued

George Sherlock Antiques
588 King's Rd. Est. 1968. Open 9.30-5.30. SIZE: Large. *STOCK: General antiques, decorative furniture and upholstery, 1650-1900, £20-£15,000.* PARK: Easy. TEL: 071 736 3955; fax - 071 371 5179. VAT: Stan/Spec.

Shield and Allen Ltd
584 and 586 King's Rd. Est. 1968. Open 9.30-5.30. SIZE: Medium. *STOCK: Early furniture, works of art and paintings.* PARK: Easy. TEL: 071 736 7145; fax - 071 736 0029. VAT: Spec.

Spice
2 Wandon Rd, King's Rd. (S. Dix). Resident. Open 9.30-6.30. *STOCK: Early furniture and decorative items.* TEL: 071 736 4619. SER: Export; interior design.

John Spink
14 Darlan Rd, Fulham. Open by appointment. *STOCK: English watercolours, 1720-1920.* TEL: 071 731 8292.

Thornhill Galleries Ltd
76 New King's Rd. Est. 1880. Open 10-5, Sat. 10-3. SIZE: Large. *STOCK: English and French marble, stone and wood chimney-pieces, panelled rooms, architectural features and wood carvings, fire grates and fenders, all 17th-19th C; decorative iron interiors and other fire accessories, 17th-20th C.* LOC: Continuation of King's Rd. Coming from Sloane Sq. shop is on right-hand side. PARK: Easy. TEL: 071 736 5830. SER: Valuations; restorations (architectural items); buys at auction (architectural items). VAT: Stan/Spec.

Through the Looking Glass Ltd
563 King's Rd. (J.J.A. and D.A. Pulton). Est. 1966. Open 10-5.30. SIZE: Large. *STOCK: Mirrors, 18th-19th C.* TEL: 071 736 7799. SER: Restorations. VAT: Spec.

Ferenc Toth
598A King's Rd. (F. and E. Toth). Est. 1978. Open 9.30-5.30. SIZE: Medium. *STOCK: Mirrors, furniture and decorative items, 18th-19th C.* LOC: Fulham end of King's Rd., Chelsea. PARK: Easy. TEL: 071 731 2063; fax - same; home - 071 602 1771. SER: Valuations; buys at auction. VAT: Spec.

Trowbridge Gallery LAPADA
555 King's Road. (M. Trowbridge). Est. 1980. Open 9.30-5.30, Sat 10.30-5. SIZE: Medium. *STOCK: Decorative prints, 17th-19th C, £35-£3,000.* LOC: Near Christopher Wray Lighting. PARK: Easy. TEL: 071 371 8733. SER: Valuations; restorations; buys at auction (antiquarian books and prints); hand-made frames; decorative mounting. FAIRS: Decorative Antiques and Textiles, Olympia, LAPADA, City of London. VAT: Stan.

S.W.6 continued
Tulissio De Beaumont
277 Lillie Road. (David Tulissio and Dominic De Beaumont). Est. 1987. Open 10-6. SIZE: Medium. STOCK: *Chandeliers, wall lights and lamps, 18th-20th C, £100-£1,500; bronzes and sculpture, 19th C, £50-£1,500; general decorative antiques, 18th-20th C, £50-£2,500.* LOC: 10 minutes from New King's Road, next to Fulham Cross. PARK: Easy. TEL: 071 385 0156; mobile - 0831 268218. SER: Restorations (chandeliers). FAIRS: Chelsea Harbour Decorative and Textile. VAT: Stan/Spec.

Francois Valcke
610 King's Rd. Est. 1982. Open 10-6. SIZE: Medium. STOCK: *17th-19th C drawings, prints and oil paintings.* LOC: Past World's End. PARK: Easy. TEL: 071 736 6024; fax - 071 731 8302. SER: Restorations; framing. VAT: Spec.

Vaughan
156-160 Wandsworth Bridge Rd. (M.J. Vaughan and Vaughan Ltd). Est. 1980. Open 10-5. CL: Sat. SIZE: Large. STOCK: *Decorative furniture and objects, 18th-19th C; lamps and light fittings.* PARK: Easy. TEL: 071 731 3133. VAT: Stan/Spec.

Meldrum Walker Gallery
27 Filmer Rd, Fulham. (M. and D. Meldrum Walker). GMC. Open 10-6. STOCK: *19th-20th C oils and watercolours.* TEL: 071 385 2305. SER: Framing.

Leigh Warren Antiques
566 King's Rd. Open 10-5. STOCK: *General antiques and decorative items.* TEL: 071 736 2485.

Whiteway and Waldron Ltd
305 Munster Rd, Fulham. (M. Whiteway and G. Kirkland). Est. 1976. Open 10-6, Sat. 11-4. SIZE: Large. STOCK: *Stained glass, from 1850, £20-£3,000; religious antiques including candlesticks, statuary, gothic and carved church woodwork.* LOC: At junction of Lillie Rd. and Munster Rd. PARK: On forecourt for loading, or Strode Rd. TEL: 071 381 3195. SER: Restorations (stained glass); buys at auction (stained glass and religious items). VAT: Stan.

Christopher Wray's Lighting Emporium
600-606 King's Rd. Est. 1964. Open 10-6. SIZE: Large. STOCK: *Decorative light fittings of 1880s, brass, antiques, decorative objects.* LOC: From Sloane Sq. over Stanley Bridge. PARK: Own. TEL: 071 736 8434; fax - 071 731 3507. VAT: Stan.

LONDON S.W.7
Anglo Persian Carpet Co
6 South Kensington Station Arcade. Est. 1910. Open 9.30-6. STOCK: *Carpets and rugs.* TEL: 071 589 5457. SER: Valuations; restorations (carpets and rugs); cleaning.

S.W.7 continued
Aubrey Brocklehurst BADA
124 Cromwell Rd. Est. 1942. Open 9-1 and 2-5.30 (or later by arrangement), Sat. 10-1. SIZE: Medium. STOCK: *English clocks and barometers.* TEL: 071 373 0319. SER: Valuations; restorations, furniture and clock repairs; buys at auction. VAT: Spec.

Julie Collino
15 Glendower Place, South Kensington. Est. 1971. Open 11-6, Sat. 2-6, Sun. by appointment. STOCK: *Watercolours, oils, etchings, £25-£1,000; china, £25-£500; both 19th-20th C; furniture, £50-£2,000.* LOC: Off Harrington Rd. TEL: 071 584 4733; home - 071 373 5353. FAIRS: Olympia. VAT: Stan/Spec.

Robert Hershkowitz Ltd
Basement, 94 Queens Gate. Est. 1976. Open by appointment only. STOCK: *Fine early British and French photographs.* TEL: 071 373 8994 or 0444 482240.

M.P. Levene Ltd BADA
5 Thurloe Place. Est. 1926. Open 9.30-6. CL: Sat. pm. STOCK: *Silver, old Sheffield plate, various, all prices.* LOC: Few minutes past Harrods near South Kensington Station. PARK: Easy. TEL: 071 589 3755. SER: Valuations; buys at auction. VAT: Stan/Spec.

A. and H. Page
66 Gloucester Rd. Open 9-5.30, Sat. 9-1. STOCK: *Silver, jewellery, objets d'art.* TEL: 071 584 7349. SER: Buys at auction.

Period Brass Lights
9a Thurloe Place, Brompton Rd. (M. Beattie). Est. 1967. STOCK: *Brass reproduction and antique light fittings; suits of armour.* PARK: Meters. TEL: 071 589 8305.

Rêverie
24 Cheval Place, Knightsbridge. (Patricia Johns and Margaret Man). Est. 1983. Open 10.30-5.30, Sat. 10.30-1. SIZE: Small. STOCK: *Small furniture, £100-£1,000; decorative accessories, lighting and textiles, £25-£500; all 18th-19th C.* LOC: 300 yards from Harrods, off Montpellier Sq. PARK: Easy. TEL: 071 589 0133; home - 071 370 3569. FAIRS: Brocante. VAT: Stan/Spec.

The Wyllie Gallery
44 (3) Elvaston Place. (J.G. Wyllie). Open by appointment. STOCK: *19th-20th C marine paintings and etchings, especially works by the Wyllie family.* TEL: 071 584 6024.

LONDON S.W.8
Nicholas Beech
787 and 789 Wandsworth Rd. (N.A. Beech). Est. 1981. Open 10-5.30, Sun. by appointment. SIZE: Medium. STOCK: *Pine furniture, Georgian, Victorian and Edwardian, £20-£1,000; decorative*

LONDON

S.W.8 continued

items, especially kitchen items. LOC: Over Chelsea Bridge (south side), straight over roundabout. At 3rd set of traffic lights turn left, shop 100yds. on right. PARK: Easy. TEL: 071 720 8552. SER: Restorations (pine); buys at auction (pine and decorative items); pine stripping. VAT: Stan.

Capital Clocks
190 Wandsworth Rd. Resident. Est. 1969. Open by appointment only. STOCK: Clocks including longcase, carriage, bracket, mantle and wall; barometers. LOC: 1/2 mile south of Vauxhall Bridge. PARK: Easy. TEL: 071 720 6372 (24hr.). SER: Valuations; restorations (movements and cases). VAT: Spec.

Ed's Trading
763 Wandsworth Rd. Open 9.30-5.30 including Sun. STOCK: Furniture, kitchenalia and collectables, pine doors. TEL: 071 498 2272.

H.W. Newby (A.J. & M.V. Waller) BADA
At C.F.A.S.S. Ltd, 42 Ponton Road. Est. 1949. Open by appointment. SIZE: Large. STOCK: Porcelain, faience, pottery, pre-1830, £50-£5,000; English and continental glass. Not stocked: Silver, jewellery. PARK: Meters. TEL: 081 974 8659; mobile - 0836 294523. SER: Valuations; buys at auction. VAT: Spec.

LONDON S.W.9

Scallywag
224 Clapham Rd, Stockwell. (J.A. Butterworth). Est. 1970. Open 9.30-5.30 including Sun., Thurs. 9.30-7. SIZE: Large. STOCK: Pine, 18th-19th C, £1-£10,000. LOC: 200yds. from Stockwell tube station, on A3 between The Oval and Stockwell. TEL: 071 735 2444; fax - 071 735 0787. SER: Restorations (pine stripping). VAT: Stan/Spec.

LONDON S.W.10

Jonathan Clark Ltd
18 Park Walk, Chelsea. Open 10-6.30, Sat. 11-5. STOCK: Modern British and European paintings and sculpture. TEL: 071 351 3555.

Furniture Cave
533 King's Rd. (R.I.G. Taylor). Est. 1967. Open 10-6. SIZE: Large. STOCK: Furniture, Victorian, pine, oak, country. LOC: Corner of Lots RdPARK: In yard. TEL: 071 352 4229. SER: Shipping; forwarding. VAT: Stan/Spec. There are fifteen dealers some of whom are listed below.

Phillip and R. Allison
Chinese ceramics, kelim and leather seating; reproduction furniture. TEL: 071 351 6423.

Jean Brown
French furniture and objets d'art, mainly 19th C; English furniture especially upholstered, small architectural items and shop fittings. TEL: 071 352 1575.

S.W.10 continued

First Floor
Furniture, art nouveau, art deco, carpets, paintings and prints. TEL: 071 352 2046/351 7232.

N. J. A. Gifford-Mead and Miles d'Agar Antiques LAPADA
Architectural items, sculpture, garden ornaments, fireplaces and unusual items. TEL: 071 352 9904/6143.

Kings Road Gallery
Decorative prints and books.

M.S. M.
Country furniture, especially beds. TEL: 071 352 7305.

Anthony Outred BADA
English and continental furniture, 17th-19th C; decorative items, light fittings and Oriental rugs. TEL: 071 352 8840.

Anthony Redmile Ltd
Unusual decorative objects and antler furniture. TEL: 071 351 3813.

William Handford Antiques
517 King's Rd. Est. 1974. Open 9.30-6. SIZE: Large. STOCK: Period antiques and accessories. LOC: World's End, Chelsea. PARK: Easy. TEL: 071 351 2768. VAT: Stan/Spec.

Hares Antiques
498 King's Rd. (Allan Hare). Est. 1972. Open 10-6, Sat. 10-4. SIZE: Large. STOCK: Furniture especially dining tables and long sets of chairs, 18th to early 19th C, £100-£20,000; upholstery and decorative items. PARK: Easy. TEL: 071 351 1442. SER: Valuations; restorations (upholstery); buys at auction. VAT: Spec.

Hollywood Road Gallery
12 Hollywood Rd, Chelsea. (P. and C. Kennaugh). Open 11-7. STOCK: Oils, watercolours, decorative items, 19th-20th C, £100-£2,000. TEL: 071 351 1973.

Hünersdorff Rare Books and Manuscripts
P.O. Box 582. ABA. Est. 1969. Open by appointment only. STOCK: Continental books in rare editions, early printing, science and medicine, illustrated books, Latin America, horticulture. TEL: 071 373 3899; fax - 071 370 1244.

Langford's Marine Antiques LAPADA
The Plaza, 535 King's Rd. (L.L. Langford). Est. 1941. STOCK: Ships models, antique and marine objects. TEL: 071 351 4881; fax - 071 352 0763. SER: Valuations; restorations. VAT: Stan/Spec.

Stephen Long
348 Fulham Rd. Est. 1966. Open 9-1 and 2.15-5.30. CL: Sat. pm. and Sun. except by appointment. SIZE: Small. STOCK: English pottery,

An Antique Collectors' Club Title

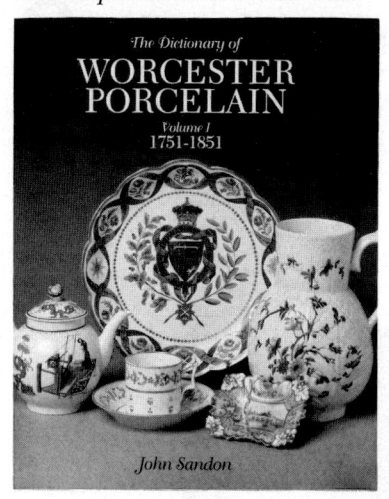

The Dictionary of Worcester Porcelain Volume I 1751-1851
by John Sandon

With 600+ dictionary entries, an historical survey, an illustrated section on marks, detailed information on recent excavations at the Worcester factory, contemporary accounts of visits to factories and an extensive bibliography, this is the definitive work. The author is director of ceramics at Phillips auctioneers, London, and regularly appears on the *Antiques Roadshow*.
ISBN 1 85149 156 2
400pp, 450 b & w illus, 100 colour
£45.00

Available from:
Antique Collectors' Club, 5 Church Street, Woodbridge, Suffolk IP12 1DS
Tel: (0394) 385501 Fax: (0394) 384434

or Market Street Industrial Park, Wappingers' Falls, New York 12590, USA
Tel: 914 297 0003 Fax: 914 297 0068

S.W.10 continued

18th-19th C, to £400; English painted furniture, 18th to early 19th C; toys and games, household and kitchen items, chintz, materials and patchwork, to £500. Not stocked: Stripped pine, large brown furniture, fashionable antiques. LOC: From South Kensington along road on right between Ifield Rd. and Billing Rd. PARK: Easy. TEL: 071 352 8226. VAT: Stan/Spec.

McVeigh and Charpentier
498 King's Rd. Open 10-5.30, other times by appointment. CL: Sat. STOCK: *Furniture and objets d'art, 18th-19th C*. TEL: 071 937 6459.

McWhirter
22 Park Walk. (A.J.K. McWhirter). Open 9.30-6, Sat. 11-2.30. SIZE: Medium. STOCK: *Unusual furniture and works of art, 1680-1930*. LOC: Near St. Stephen's Hospital. PARK: Easy. TEL: 071 351 5399; fax - 071 352 9821. SER: Valuations; buys at auction. VAT: Spec.

Park Walk Gallery
20 Park Walk, Chelsea. (J. Cooper). Est. 1988. Open 10-6.30, Sat. 11-4. SIZE: Medium. STOCK: *Paintings, £250-£100,000; watercolours, £250-£20,000; drawings, £200-£15,000; all 19th-20th C English and Continental*. LOC: Off Fulham Rd. PARK: Easy. TEL: 071 351 0410. SER: Valuations; restorations. FAIRS: 20th C British, Park Lane; The World of Watercolours. VAT: Spec.

S.W.10 continued

H.W. Poulter and Son
279 Fulham Rd. Est. 1946. Open 9.30-5. CL: Sat. pm. SIZE: Large. STOCK: *English and French marble chimney pieces, grates, fenders, fireirons, brass, chandeliers*. PARK: Meters. TEL: 071 352 7268. SER: Restorations (marble work). VAT: Stan/Spec.

Rare Carpets Gallery
496 King's Rd, Chelsea. Est. 1963. Open 10-6. SIZE: Large. STOCK: *European and Oriental decorative carpets, tapestries*. TEL: 071 351 3296; fax - 071 376 4876. SER: Valuations; restorations; cleaning; part exchange. VAT: Stan.

Rendlesham Antiques Ltd
498 King's Rd. Est. 1970. Open 10-6, Sat. 11-2. SIZE: Medium. STOCK: *English and Continental furniture, objets d'art*. TEL: 071 351 1442.

John Thornton
455 Fulham Rd. Open 10-5.30. STOCK: *Antiquarian books especially theology*. TEL: 071 352 8810.

Harriet Wynter Ltd. Arts and Sciences BADA
50 Redcliffe Rd. Est. 1956. Open by appointment. SIZE: Medium. STOCK: *Early scientific instruments and works of art*. TEL: 071 352 6494;

Christopher Bangs

P.O. Box 662, London SW11 3DG
Tel: 071-223 5676. Fax: 071-223 4933. Mobile: 0836 333532

S.W.10 continued
fax - 071 352 9312. SER: Valuations; collection counselling; restorations (globes and instruments); film hire; catalogues. VAT: Stan/Spec.

LONDON S.W.11

Acanthus Art Ltd BADA LAPADA
P.O. Box 211. Open by appointment. *STOCK: English and European ceramics; French printed textiles, 1750-1820; antiquities, ethnographic items, English furniture.* TEL: 071 622 0734. SER: Valuations; restorations; buys at auction (as stock). FAIRS: Grosvenor House, Northern, LAPADA.

Antiques and Things
91 Eccles Rd. (Mrs V. Crowther). Est. 1986. Open 10-5, Sat. 10-6. SIZE: Medium. *STOCK: Decorative curtain furniture and fittings; linen, lace, textiles, Victorian to Edwardian, £1-£500; china, glass, kitchenalia, 18th-19th C, £5-£500; English and French furniture, decorative items, 19th C, £20-£2,000.* LOC: Off Lavender Hill, near Clapham junction. TEL: 071 350 0597; home - 071 622 2081.

Christopher Bangs BADA LAPADA
P.O. Box 662, London, SW11 3DG. CINOA. Est. 1971. Open by appointment only. *STOCK: Domestic metalwork and metalware, works of art and decorative objects.* PARK: Easy. TEL:

S.W.11 continued
071 223 5676 (24hrs); fax - 071 223 4933 (24hrs); mobile - 0836 333532. SER: Valuations; research; commission buys at auction; finder. VAT: Stan/Spec.

Christopher Antiques
173 St. John's Hill, Battersea. (C. Blom and C. Hughes). Est. 1982. Open 10.30-5.30. CL: Wed. SIZE: Small. *STOCK: 16th-19th C country and painted furniture, ironwork and objects.* LOC: Just off South Circular at Wandsworth Common. PARK: EasyTEL: 071 978 5132 (24hrs).

Eccles Road Antiques
60 Eccles Rd, Battersea. (H. Rix). Open 10-5. *STOCK: General antiques, pine furniture and smalls.* TEL: 071 228 1638.

Keith Gretton Old Advertising
Unit 14, Northcote Rd. Antiques Market, 155A Northcote Rd., Battersea. Open 10-6, Sun. 12-5. *STOCK: Advertising, signs, bottles, packaging and display.* LOC: Near Clapham Junction. PARK: Easy. TEL: 071 228 6850; home - 071 228 0741. SER: Valuations.

Just a Second Antiques
27 Battersea Rise. (J. Bastillo). Open by appointment. *STOCK: Furniture, Georgian, Victorian and Edwardian, silver, china, general antiques, £10-£1,500.* TEL: 071 223 5341. VAT: Stan.

S.W.11 continued
Northcote Road Antiques Market
155A Northcote Rd, Battersea. (H. Rix). Open 10-6, Sun. 12-5. SIZE: 30 dealers. STOCK: Art deco, collectables, silver, glass, furniture, lighting, textiles, linen, jewellery, old advertising. TEL: 071 228 6850.

Robert Young Antiques
68 Battersea Bridge Rd. Est. 1974. Open 10-6, Sat. 10-5. CL: Mon. SIZE: Medium. STOCK: English oak and country furniture, 17th-18th C, £500-£10,000; English and European treen and objects of folk art, £20-£10,000; English and European provincial pottery and metalwork, £20-£2,500. LOC: Turn off King's Rd. or Chelsea Embankment into Beaufort St., cross over Battersea Bridge Rd., 9th shop on right. PARK: Opposite in side street. TEL: 071 228 7847; fax - 071 585 0489. SER: Valuations; buys at auction (treen and country furniture). FAIRS: Olympia, Chelsea. VAT: Stan/Spec.

LONDON S.W.12
The Gallery Downstairs   LAPADA
92 Rossiter Road, Balham. (John and Veronica Philllips and Thomas Deans). Resident. Est. 1982. Open by appointment. SIZE: Medium. STOCK: British watercolours and drawings, 1750-1900, £50-£10,000; British prints, 18th-20th C, £50-£150. LOC: South of South Circular Rd. PARK: Easy. TEL: 081 673 5150; home - same. SER: Valuations; restorations (works on paper); buys at auction (as stock). VAT: Spec.

The Kilim Warehouse Ltd
28A Pickets St. (J. Luczyc-Wyhowska). Est. 1982. Open 10-6, Sat. 10-4. SIZE: Medium. STOCK: Kilims from Eastern Europe, Asia Minor and beyond, £50-£8,000. LOC: Near Clapham South tube station and Nightingale Lane. PARK: Easy. TEL: 081 675 3122; fax - 081 675 8494. SER: Restorations; cleaning. VAT: Stan.

Twentieth Century
14 Blandfield Rd, Nightingale Lane. (M. Taylor). Est. 1986. Open Thurs., Fri. and Sat. 11-6, other days by appointment. SIZE: Small. STOCK: Art deco, art nouveau, arts and crafts, decorative items, £50-£100. PARK: Easy. TEL: 081 675 6511. SER: Buys at auction (art deco). FAIRS: Greenwich Art Deco and Kensington Decorative Arts. VAT: Stan.

LONDON S.W.13
Alton Gallery
72 Church Rd, Barnes. Open 10-5. CL: Wed. STOCK: 19th-20th C British art. TEL: 081 748 0606. SER: Framing.

Christine Bridge   LAPADA
78 Castelnau, Barnes. Est. 1972. Open by appointment only. SIZE: Medium. STOCK:

S.W.13 continued
Glass - 18th C collectors and 19th C coloured, engraved and decorative, £50-£6,000; small decorative items - papier mâché, bronzes, needlework, ceramics. LOC: Main road from Hammersmith Bridge. PARK: Easy. TEL: 081 741 5501; fax - same. SER: Valuations; restorations (glass - cutting, polishing, declouding); buys at auction; exports. FAIRS: Olympia; NEC, Birmingham; Decorative, Chelsea Harbour; City of London; West London; LAPADA; Brussels; Tokyo; Melbourne. VAT: Stan/Spec.

Beverley Brook Antiques
29 Grove Rd, Barnes. (N. McCormick). Est. 1976. Open by appointment. SIZE: Medium. STOCK: Glass, china, silver plate. PARK: Side roads. TEL: Home - 081 878 5656. SER: Silver re-plating and cleaning.

Campion
71 White Hart Lane, Barnes. (J. Richards). Est. 1983. Open 10-1 and 2-5.30. SIZE: Small. STOCK: Jewellery, quilts, cushions, carpets, Turkish kilims, prints, small furniture, £5-£250; lamps, candlesticks and Indian coffee tables. LOC: Along river from Barnes High St., turn left at White Hart public house. PARK: Easy. TEL: 081 878 6688; home - same. SER: Framing.

A silver christening bowl, Sheffield, 1932, with a frieze in low relief. Such narrative pieces are typical of some of the best in 20th century christening silver, their design reflecting the illustration in contemporary children's books. Private Collection. From *Yesterday's Children* by Sally Kevill-Davies, published by the **Antique Collectors' Club**, £19.95 pb.

― Kate Dyson ―

THE DINING ROOM SHOP
62-64 White Hart Lane · London SW13 0PZ
Telephone 081-878 1020

Antique tables and sets of chairs, glass, china, cutlery, prints, table linen and lace — all for the dining room.

S.W.13 continued

Simon Coleman Antiques
40 White Hart Lane, Barnes. Est. 1974. SIZE: Large. STOCK: *Country furniture, oak, fruitwood, pine, French and English farm tables, 18th-19th C.* PARK: Easy. TEL: 081 878 5037. VAT: Stan/Spec.

The Dining Room Shop
62/64 White Hart Lane, Barnes. (K. Dyson). Est. 1985. Open 10-5.30, Sun. by appointment. SIZE: Medium. STOCK: *Formal and country dining room furniture, 18th-19th C; glasses, china especially dinner services; cutlery, damask and lace table linen, 19th C; associated small and decorative items.* LOC: Near Barnes railway bridge, turning opposite White Hart public house. PARK: Easy. TEL: 081 878 1020; home - 081 876 5212. SER: Valuations; restorations; finder; interior decorating. VAT: Stan/Spec.

Marilyn Garrow LAPADA
6 The Broadway, White Hart Lane, Barnes. Open 10-5.30. STOCK: *European textiles.* TEL: 081 392 1655; mobile - 0831 861902.

Mark Hancock
45 Melville Rd, Barnes. Open by appointment. STOCK: *19th-20th C paintings.* TEL: 081 748 6272.

S.W.13 continued

Joy McDonald
50 Station Rd, Barnes. Resident. Est. 1966. SIZE: Small. STOCK: *Furniture, 18th-19th C; oak, fruitwood, unusual items, large mirrors.* Not stocked: China, glass. PARK: Easy. TEL: 081 876 6184. SER: Restorations (furniture).

New Grafton Gallery
49 Church Rd, Barnes. (D. Wolfers). Est. 1968. Open 10-5.30. CL: Mon. SIZE: Medium. STOCK: *British paintings and drawings, £150-£3,000.* LOC: Off Castelnau which runs from Hammersmith Bridge. PARK: Easy. TEL: 081 748 8850; home - 081 876 6294. SER: Valuations; restorations; buys at auction. VAT: Stan/Spec.

The Original Remember When
6 and 7 Rocks Lane, Barnes. Est. 1975. Open 9.30-7 including Sun. STOCK: *Pine furniture.* TEL: 081 878 2817.

Randalls Antiques
46/52 Church Rd, Barnes. (E. Appleton). Open 10-5. STOCK: *Furniture, 18th-19th C; jewellery, textiles, decorative arts.* TEL: 081 748 1858; evenings - 081 948 1260.

Jeremy Seale Antiques
56 White Hart Lane, Barnes. Est. 1988. Open 10-1 and 2-5.30, Sat. 10-5. SIZE: Medium. STOCK:

S.W.13 continued

Furniture, 18th-19th C, £300-£6,000; decorative items, 19th C; pictures and prints, 18th-19th C; both £50-£500. LOC: From M3 into London, just off A316 (sign to Mortlake and Barnes), White Hart Lane on right on Barnes approach. PARK: Easy. TEL: 081 876 1041. SER: Finder. VAT: Stan/Spec.

Tobias and The Angel
68 White Hart Lane, Barnes. (A. Hughes). Est. 1985. Open 10-6. SIZE: Large. *STOCK: Quilts, textiles, furniture, country and painted beds, decorative objects, from 1800.* LOC: Parallel to Barnes High St. PARK: Easy. TEL: 081 878 8902; home - 0206 391003. SER: Interior design. VAT: Stan/Spec.

Wren Antiques
49b Church Rd, Barnes. (M.A. Smith). Est. 1980. Open 10-5.30. CL: Mon. SIZE: Small. *STOCK: Georgian and 19th C furniture, £200-£5,000; 18th-19th C clocks, pictures, £200-£3,000; mirrors and overmantels, barometers, boxes, chandeliers.* LOC: Near A3003. PARK: Easy. TEL: 081 741 7841. SER: Valuations; restorations (furniture).

The Wykeham Galleries
51 Church Rd, Barnes. Est. 1989. Open 10-5. CL: Mon. *STOCK: Paintings, sculptures, 20th C, £100-£500.* LOC: From Hammersmith Bridge down Castlenau. PARK: Easy. TEL: 081 741 1277.

LONDON S.W.14

Age of Elegance
61 Sheen Lane, East Sheen. (S. Elliott). Open 11-7, Mon. 10-5, Fri. 10-7, Sat. 11-6 or by appointment. CL: Wed. *STOCK: Linen and lace, china, glass, cutlery and costume jewellery.* TEL: 081 876 0878.

Dixon's Antique Centre
471 Upper Richmond Rd. West, East Sheen. Est. 1981. Open 10-5.30, Sun. 1.30-5.30. CL: Wed. SIZE: Large - 15 dealers. *STOCK: Furniture, porcelain, Doulton, clocks, silver, art deco, Victorian linen and lace, objets d'art.* LOC: South Circular Rd. between Richmond and Putney. PARK: Easy. TEL: 081 878 6788.

John Haines Antiques Ltd
364B Upper Richmond Road West. (J. and S.D. Haines). Est. 1960. Open by appointment. SIZE: Small. *STOCK: Furniture and objects, 17th-18th C, £500-£5,000.* PARK: Easy. TEL: 081 876 4215; home - same. SER: Valuations. FAIRS: Olympia. VAT: Spec. *Trade Only*

Helius Antiques
487-493 Upper Richmond Rd. West. (Mrs M. Rowlands). Est. 1965. Open 10-5, Sat. 10.30-12.45. CL: Sun. and Wed. except by appointment. SIZE: Large. *STOCK: Pedestal desks, bureaux, 18th to early 20th C writing tables, secretaires*

S.W.14 continued

and bookcases; general antiques, decorative furniture. LOC: On South Circular Rd. PARK: Easy. TEL: 081 876 5721. VAT: Stan/Spec.

Sheen Gallery
370 Upper Richmond Rd. West, East Sheen. (M.S. Wardle). Open 10-6. CL: Wed. *STOCK: Watercolours, oil paintings and prints.* TEL: 081 878 1100. SER: Restorations; gilding and framing.

William Sheppee
1a Church Ave. (W. Hiley and A. Cox). Est. 1989. Open 10-6, Sun. by appointment. SIZE: Medium. STOCK: Anglo-*Indian and Indian furniture, 19th C, £500-£6,000; treen, £50-£250.* TEL: 081 392 2379; home - 081 878 9903. SER: Valuations; export. VAT: Stan.

Yesterday's Antiques
315 Upper Richmond Rd. West. (H. Rau). Open 9.30-6, Sun. 9.30-5. *STOCK: Old pine and country furniture.* TEL: 081 876 7536.

LONDON S.W.15

R.A. Barnes Antiques   LAPADA
26 Lower Richmond Rd, Putney. Open 10-5. CL: Sat. SIZE: Large. *STOCK: English, Oriental and continental porcelain, antiques and collectables; Wedgwood, ironstone, china, brass, copper, 19th C; art glass, Regency, Victorian and some 18th C small furniture, primitive paintings.* TEL: 081 789 3371. VAT: Stan/Spec.

The Clock Clinic Ltd   LAPADA
85 Lower Richmond Rd, Putney. (P.M.L. Banks and R.S. Pedler). FBHI. Est. 1971. Open 9-6, Sat. 9-1. CL: Mon. *STOCK: Clocks and barometers.* TEL: 081 788 1407; fax - 081 780 2838. SER: Valuations; restorations (as stock); buys at auction. VAT: Stan/Spec.

Harwood Antiques
24 Lower Richmond Rd, Putney. (G. M. Harwood). Est. 1962. SIZE: Medium. *STOCK: Decorative items and furniture, £150-£2,500; textiles, £150-£500; mirrors, oils, watercolours and prints, £100-£550; all 18th-19th C.* LOC: Continuation of King's Rd., over Putney Bridge. PARK: Nearby. TEL: 081 788 7444.

Jorgen Antiques
40 Lower Richmond Rd, Putney. (A.J. Dolleris). Est. 1960. Open 11-5. CL: Mon. and Sat. SIZE: Large. *STOCK: English and continental furniture, 18th to early 19th C, £50-£5,000.* LOC: Between Putney Bridge and Putney Common. PARK: Easy. TEL: 081 789 7329. VAT: Spec.

Kate House
139 Lower Richmond Rd, Putney. (M. Shamsa). Open 10-5. CL: Mon. *STOCK: Pine, linen, lace, china, bric-a-brac.* TEL: 081 785 9944.

S.W.15 continued
A.V. Marsh and Son
Vale House, Kingston Vale. Est. 1960. Open 9-6. STOCK: Furniture, 18th to early 19th C. TEL: 081 546 5996. VAT: Stan/Spec.

Richard Maude Tools
22 Parkfields, Putney. (R.M.C. Maude). Est. 1977. Open by appointment only. SIZE: Medium. STOCK: Woodworking tools, 18th-19th C, £5-£1,000; ornamental turning lathes, 19th C, £500-£5,000; books and old trade catalogues relating to previous items, 18th-19th C, £5-£250; medical and dental instruments; some early ironwork and keys. LOC: 1/2 mile west of Putney High St., off Upper Richmond Rd. PARK: Easy. TEL: 081 788 2991. SER: Valuations; buys at auction. VAT: Spec.

Michael Phelps Antiquarian Books
19 Chelverton Rd, Putney. Open by appointment. STOCK: Antiquarian books - medicine, science, technology, natural history. TEL: 081 785 6766.

Alan Stone Antiques
3 Wadham Rd, Putney. Open 9-6. STOCK: General antiques. TEL: 081 870 1606/642 6877. SER: Restorations.

Thornhill Galleries Ltd. in association with A. & R. Dockerill Ltd
Rear of 78 Deodar Rd, Putney. Est. 1880. Open 9-5.15, Sat. 10-12.30. SIZE: Large. STOCK: English and French marble, stone and wood chimney-pieces, English and French panelled rooms, architectural features and wood carvings, fire grates and fenders, 17th-19th C; decorative iron interiors and other fire accessories, 17th-20th C. LOC: Off Putney Bridge Rd. PARK: Easy. TEL: 081 874 2101/5669. SER: Valuations; restorations (architectural items); buys at auction (architectural items). VAT: Stan/Spec.

LONDON S.W.16
S. Farrelly
634 Streatham High Rd. Est. 1958. Open 9-5. SIZE: Medium. STOCK: General antiques. PARK: In side roads. TEL: 081 764 4028.

A. and J. Fowle
542 Streatham High Rd. Est. 1962. Open 9.30-7. SIZE: Large. STOCK: General antiques, Victorian and Edwardian furniture. LOC: From London take A23 towards Brighton. PARK: Easy. TEL: 081 764 2896.

Rapscallion Antiques Ltd
25 Shrubbery Rd, Streatham. (Mrs P. Barry). Open 10-5. CL: Mon. and Thurs. STOCK: General antiques and bric-a-brac. TEL: 081 769 8078.

William Reeves Bookseller Ltd
1a Norbury Crescent. Est. 1871. Open by appointment. SIZE: Medium. STOCK: Books about music, 1800-1970, £1-£100. LOC: From station under railway bridge, first left. PARK: Easy. TEL: 081 764 2108.

LONDON S.W.17
Ted Few
97 Drakefield Rd. Resident. Est. 1975. Open by appointment. SIZE: Medium. STOCK: Paintings and sculpture, 1700-1940, £500-£5,000. LOC: 5 mins. walk from Tooting Bec underground station. TEL: 081 767 2314. SER: Valuations; buys at auction. VAT: Spec.

LONDON S.W.18
S.A.G. Art Galleries
589 Garratt Lane, Wandsworth. (S.A. Gaphar). Open 9-5, Sun. 12-5. STOCK: Oils, watercolours, etchings, limited edition prints, 19th-20th C. TEL: 081 944 1404; fax - 081 947 8174.

Mr Wandle's Workshop
202 Garratt Lane, Wandsworth. (S. Zoil). Open 9-5.30. STOCK: Victorian and Edwardian fireplaces and surrounds especially cast iron. TEL: 081 870 5873. SER: Shot-blasting.

Woodentops Country Furniture
537/539 Garratt Lane, Earlsfield. (C. R. Smith). Est. 1987Open 10-7, Sun. 10.30-5. SIZE: Large. STOCK: Pine furniture, mainly reproduction. LOC: Main road between Wandsworth and Tooting. PARK: Easy. TEL: 081 947 6124. SER: Restorations (pine). VAT: Stan.

LONDON S.W.19
Acanthus Antiques
171 Arthur Rd, Wimbledon Park. (I.K. von Lobkowitz and J. Pol). Est. 1983. Open 9.30-1.30 and 2-5.30, Wed. and Sat. 9.30-1.30. CL: Mon. STOCK: Pianos and accessories, 19th C to 1940, £500-£3,000; furniture, 18th-19th C, £50-£2,000; pottery, porcelain and glass, 18th-20th C, £20-£500. LOC: 50yds. from Wimbledon Park tube station. TEL: 081 944 8404. SER: Restorations (pianos). VAT: Stan/Spec.

Adams Room Antiques   LAPADA
18-20 Ridgway, Wimbledon Village. Est. 1971. Open 9.30-5. SIZE: Large. STOCK: 18th-19th C English and French furniture especially dining; decorative Regency chairs, silver. LOC: 4 miles from King's Rd., Chelsea; 1 mile off Kingston by-pass, M3. TEL: 081 946 7047/947 4784. SER: Export orders arranged. VAT: Spec.

The Antique Mews
7 & 8 Merton Abbey Mills, Watermill Way. (Patsy Roy and Chriz Poultney). Est. 1986. Open

LONDON

S.W.19 continued

10.30-3.30, Sat. and Sun. 10-6, Mon. by appointment. SIZE: Small. *STOCK: Victorian pine, £5-£1,200; Victorian country collectables, £5-£150.* LOC: A24 between Colliers Wood and Morden. PARK: Easy. TEL: 081 544 0863; home - 0737 359097. SER: Pine searches undertaken. VAT: Stan/Spec.

Chelsea Bric-a-Brac Shop Ltd
16 Hartfield Rd, Wimbledon. (P. and C. Wirth). Est. 1960. Open 10-6. CL: Wed. SIZE: Medium. *STOCK: Furniture - antique, Victorian, pine, and shipping, 1800-1930, £20-£1,500; brass, copper, steel, £1-£500; bric-a-brac, £1-£250; all from Victorian.* Not stocked: Jewellery, weapons. LOC: Left from Wimbledon station, first turning on right, shop 100yds. on left. PARK: 100yds. TEL: 081 946 6894; home - 081 542 5509. SER: Restorations (wood and upholstery); continental export. VAT: Stan.

Clunes Antiques
9 West Place, Wimbledon Common. Est. 1973. Open 10-4.30. CL: Mon. *STOCK: General small and country antiques, Staffordshire figures, theatrical ephemera.* TEL: 081 946 1643.

Hicks Gallery
2 and 4 Leopold Rd, Wimbledon. (J. Hicks). Open 10-6, Sun. 12.30-5. CL: Mon. *STOCK: British and Continental 18th-20th C oil paintings and watercolours £50-£5,000; modern British and living artists.* LOC: 1/2 mile from Wimbledon station. PARK: Easy. TEL: 081 944 7171. SER: Valuations; restorations; buys at auction; period framing. FAIRS: N.E.C. VAT: Stan/Spec.

The Lighthouse Ltd   LAPADA
75-77 Ridgway, Wimbledon Village. (Mrs E. Kingston). Est. 1969. Open 10-5.30, Sat. 10-6. *STOCK: Oriental and continental table lamps, brass and glass chandeliers and wall lights, furniture, 18th-20th C, £600-£6,000.* PARK: Easy. TEL: 081 946 2050.

Richard Maryan and Daughters
177 Merton Rd. Est. 1966. Open 10-5. CL: Wed. pm. and Mon. SIZE: Large. *STOCK: General antiques.* PARK: Reasonable. TEL: 081 542 5846.

Stefani Antiques
179 Kingston Rd. (K. Stefani). Open 10-6. *STOCK: Furniture, to 1930, £40-£1,000; jewellery, £25-£500; pottery, pictures, silver and plate.* TEL: 081 542 4696.

Mark J. West - Cobb Antiques Ltd
BADA
39B High St, Wimbledon Village. Open 10-6, other times by appointment. SIZE: Medium. *STOCK: Table glass, 18th-19th C, £100-£800;*

S.W.19 continued

decorators' items, glass, ceramics, £50-£1,000; collectors' glass, small furniture, £100-£1,000. PARK: Easy. TEL: **081 946 2811/540 7982.** SER: Valuations; buys at auction. FAIRS: Olympia.

LONDON S.W.20

Hamilton's Corner
407A Kingston Rd. (P. and W Hamilton). Est. 1972. Open 10-5. CL: Wed. SIZE: Medium. *STOCK: Edwardian furniture; stripped pine, shipping goods, £25-£500.* LOC: From A3 at New Malden follow A298 Merton for 1 mile. PARK: Easy. TEL: 081 540 1744. VAT: Stan.

Kensington Sporting Paintings Ltd.
2 The Downs, Wimbledon. (J.S. Bates). Open by appointment only. *STOCK: Oil paintings especially sporting; animalier bronzes, 19th C.* TEL: 081 947 7772. SER: Valuations; restorations.

LONDON S.E.1

Antique Warehouse
175D Bermondsey St, Newhams Row. (Waterloo Trading Co. and Micallef Antiques). Open 8.30-6, Sat. 10-3.30. *STOCK: Georgian, Victorian, Edwardian and shipping furniture.* SER: Robert Boys worldwide shipping.

The Antiques Pavilion
175 Bermondsey Street. (Capital City Investments Ltd). Est. 1966. Open 9.30-6, Fri. 7-6, Sat. 9-2. SIZE: Large. *STOCK: Furniture, Georgian to 1930's, £25-£25,000.* LOC: Near Bermondsey Market, close to Tower Bridge. PARK: Easy. TEL: 071 403 2021. SER: Restorations (re-leathering, French polishing); buys at auction. VAT: Stan.

Sebastiano Barbagallo
Universal House, 294-304 St. James' Rd. Est. 1975. Open 9.30-5.30 by appointment. CL: Sat. SIZE: Large. *STOCK: Early Indian stone sculpture, 2BC to 11th C; early Tibetan art, to 18th C; Asian furniture and architectural fixtures, 18th-19th C; Asian crafts.* LOC: Near Elephant and Castle underground. PARK: Easy. TEL: 071 231 3680; fax - 071 232 1385. FAIRS: Birmingham, NEC; Capital Gift Fair, Top Drawer, IDI, Olympia. *Trade Only.*

Nigel A. Bartlett   BADA
67 St. Thomas St. Open 9.30-5.30. CL: Sat. *STOCK: Marble, pine and stone chimney pieces.* TEL: 071 378 7895/6; fax - 071 378 0388.

Bermondsey Antique Warehouse
173 Bermondsey St. Est. 1974. Open 9.30-5.30. CL: Sat. and Sun. except by appointment. SIZE: Large. TEL: 071 407 2566/403 0022; fax - 071

LONDON

S.E.1 continued
924 3121. Below are listed the dealers at this warehouse.

A. Andrews
General antiques.

Mr Pickwick Antiques LAPADA
(J. Sturton). Est. 1965.*Clocks, shipping goods, general antiques.* TEL: Home - 071 599 6744. VAT: Stan.

G. Viventi
General antiques.

Bermondsey Antiques Hypermarket
Corner of Long Lane and Bermondsey St. (Bath Antiques Market Ltd). Est. 1959. Open Fri. 5 am-2 pm. *STOCK: Wide range of general antiques and collectables including specialist dealers in most fields especially silver.* LOC: Borough, Tower Hill or London Bridge tube stations. TEL: Enquiries - 071 351 5353; fax - 071 351 5350. SER: Valuations; book binding.

Victor Burness Antiques and Scientific Instruments
241 Long Lane, Bermondsey. (V.G. Burness). Est. 1975. Open Fri. 6am-1pm or by appointment. SIZE: Small. *STOCK: Scientific instruments, marine items, 19th C, £20-£1,500.* PARK: Easy. TEL: Home - 0732 454591. SER: Valuations. FAIRS: Portman Hotel.

Euro Antiques Warehouse
Royal Oak Yard, Off Bermondsey St. (Ian Wilson). Est. 1975. Open 10.30-6, Fri. 7-6, Sat. 10.30-3.30. SIZE: Large. *STOCK: Furniture including Victorian, William IV, art deco and period, pre 1840-1930's, £500-£3,000.* PARK: Easy. TEL: 071 403 0765. SER: Valuations; restorations (furniture); buys at auction (furniture). VAT: Stan.

H. M. Fletcher
201 Cardamom Building, 31 Shad Thames. Est. 1905. Open by appointment only. *STOCK: Books, rare and antiquarian.* LOC: 100yds. S.E. of Tower Bridge, next to Butler's Wharf Building. PARK: Easy. TEL: 071 378 1350; fax - 071 403 2044.

Oola Boola Antiques London
166 Tower Bridge Rd. (R. and S. Scales). Est. 1968. Open 9-5.30. Sat.10-5. SIZE: Large. *STOCK: Furniture, £5-£3,000; mahogany, oak, some walnut, Victorian, Edwardian and shipping goods.* TEL: 071 403 0794; home - 081 693 5050; fax - 071 403 8405.

Penny Farthing Antiques
177 Bermondsey St. Est. 1976. Open 10-5. CL: Sat. SIZE: Medium. *STOCK: Furniture, including shipping, £25-£1,000; longcase clocks, £200-£1,000; general small antiques and shipping items, £5-£200.* LOC: 5 mins. from Tower Bridge. PARK: Usually easy. TEL: 071 407 5171. VAT: Stan.

S.E.1 continued

Tower Bridge Antiques LAPADA
159/161 Tower Bridge Rd. Open 9-5, Sat. 9.30-4.30. SIZE: Large. *STOCK: Victorian, Georgian and Edwardian furniture, shipping goods.* TEL: 071 403 3660. VAT: Stan.

George Wissinger and Antonio Mendoza
166 Bermondsey St. Open 9-6. CL: Sat. SIZE: Large. *STOCK: Furniture and paintings.* TEL: 071 407 5795.

LONDON S.E.3

Michael Silverman
PO Box 350. *STOCK: Manuscripts, autograph letters, historical documents.* TEL: 081 319 4452; fax - 081 856 6006. SER: Catalogue available. *Postal Only.*

Vale Stamps and Antiques
21 Tranquil Vale, Blackheath. (H.J. and R.P. Varnham). Est. 1952. Open 10-5.30. CL: Thurs. SIZE: Small. *STOCK: Pottery, 3000 BC-500 AD, and Roman jewellery, £20-£200; bronzes, £50-£350; Georgian and Victorian jewellery, £25-£250.* LOC: Village centre, 100yds. from station. PARK: Nearby. TEL: 081 852 9817. SER: Valuations; buys at auction (antiquities). VAT: Stan/Spec.

Wallace Antiques Ltd
56 Tranquil Vale, Blackheath. Open 9.30-5.30. *STOCK: Furniture including reproduction.* TEL: 081 852 2647.

LONDON S.E.5

Franklin's Camberwell Antiques Market
161 Camberwell Rd. (R. Franklin). Est. 1968. Open 10-6, Sun. 1-6. SIZE: Large - five floors. *STOCK: General antiques, furniture, brass, copper, silver, clocks, pictures, prints, architectural and garden items.* LOC: 1 mile from Elephant and Castle via Walworth Rd. PARK: 50yds. behind building, outside premises on Sunday. TEL: 071 703 8089. VAT: Stan/Spec.

Robert Hirschhorn BADA
Open by appointment. STOCK: English and Continental furniture and works of art, 18th C and earlier. TEL: 071 703 7443; mobile - 0831 405937.

J.H. Joslyn
127a Crofton Road, Camberwell. Open by appointment only. *STOCK: Cloth and metal badges, insignia, etc., worldwide, especially USA, GB, Germany, Italy, 1900-1992.* LOC: From Victoria No.36 bus. PARK: Easy. TEL: 071 703 1856. SER: Film and TV suppliers,1940's re-enactment groups.

S.E.5 continued
Wolseley Fine Arts plc
4 Grove Park, Camberwell. (Rupert Otten). Open by appointment only. *STOCK: British and European 20th C drawings and sculpture, works by David Jones and Eric Gill.* TEL: 071 274 8788; fax - 071 738 4739.

LONDON S.E.6
Wilkinson plc
5 Catford Hill. Est. 1947. Open 9-5. CL: Sat. SIZE: Medium. *STOCK: Glass especially chandeliers, 18th C and reproduction, art metal work.* LOC: Opposite Catford Bridge railway station. Entrance through Wickes D.I.Y. car park. PARK: Easy. TEL: 081 314 1080. SER: Restorations and repairs (glass, metalwork).

LONDON S.E.7
Village Time
43 The Village, Charlton. Open 9-5.30, Sat. 9-5. CL: Thurs. SIZE: Small. *STOCK: Clocks, watches and jewellery.* LOC: B210. PARK: Easy and opposite. TEL: 081 858 2514. SER: Valuations; restorations; repairs (clocks, watches and jewellery). VAT: Stan/Spec.

Ward Antiques
267 Woolwich Rd, Charlton. (T. and M. Ward). Est. 1981. Open 9.30-5.30, Sun. 10-2. SIZE: Medium. *STOCK: Victorian fireplaces, Victorian and Edwardian furniture, £50-£1,000.* LOC: From A102 M take Woolwich/Woolwich ferry turn, 100yds. from roundabout, immediately under railway bridge across the road. PARK: Easy. TEL: 081 305 0963; home - 081 698 0771/ 591 3451; mobile - 0836 231090.

LONDON S.E.8
Antique Warehouse
9-14 Deptford Broadway. Est. 1976. Open 10-6, Sun. 11-4. *STOCK: Furniture, 18th-20th C, £5- £5,000.* LOC: A2. PARK: Limited. TEL: 081 469 0295. VAT: Stan.

LONDON S.E.9
The Fireplace
257 High St., Eltham. (A. Clark). Est. 1978. Open daily. SIZE: Medium. *STOCK: Fireplaces, 19th- 20th C, £100-£1,000.* PARK: Adjacent side streets. TEL: 081 850 4887. SER: Restorations (fireplaces). VAT: Stan.

R.E. Rose FBHI
731 Sidcup Rd, Eltham. Est. 1976. Open 9-5. CL: Thurs. SIZE: Small. *STOCK: Clocks and barometers, 1750-1930, £50-£5,000.* LOC: A20 from London, shop on left just past fiveways traffic lights at Green Lane. PARK: Easy. TEL: 081 859 4754. SER: Restorations (clocks and barometers); spare parts for antique clocks and barometers. VAT: Stan/Spec.

Miniature portrait of Sir James Hadley D'Oyly, 6th Baronet. Pencil and watercolours. (Private collection). From *George Chinnery 1774-1852, Artist of India and the China Coast,* by Patrick Conner, published by the **Antique Collectors' Club** in 1993, £35.00.

LONDON S.E.10
Badgers Antiques
320-322 Creek Rd, Greenwich. (P.D. and J.M. Dempsey). Est. 1979. Open 9-5 including Sun., Wed. and Thurs. by appointment. SIZE: Medium. *STOCK: Victorian and Edwardian furniture, collectables, Pedigree toys, unusual items, £5- £2,000.* LOC: 2 mins. from Cutty Sark, Greenwich Pier. PARK: Nearby. TEL: 081 853 1394; home - same. SER: Valuations; restorations (leather lining, French polishing, cabinet work and upholstery); buys at auction. VAT: Stan.

The Green Parrot
2 Turnpin Lane, Greenwich. (J. Randerson). Est. 1971. *STOCK: Porcelain, bric-a-brac, small furniture, stripped pine chests.* LOC: Off Greenwich Church St. TEL: 081 858 6690. VAT: Stan.

Greenwich Antiques and Ironware Co
14/15 King William Walk, Greenwich. Open 10- 5.30. *STOCK: English and continental furniture; antique and reproduction garden furniture in wrought and cast iron and stone; bric-a-brac and decorative items, £20-£15,000.* LOC: 3/4 mile off A2 towards River Thames. TEL: 081 858 7557; fax - 081 293 4135. SER: Valuations; restorations (furniture and pictures); traditional upholstery; buys at auction.

LAMONT ANTIQUES LTD

TUNNEL AVENUE TRADING ESTATE — THAMES
A102M BLACKWALL TUNNEL APPROACH

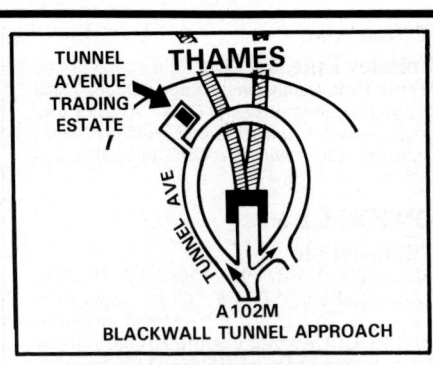

ARCHITECTURAL ITEMS
BARS & FITTINGS
STAINED GLASS ETC
CONTAINER PACKING

Contact Frank Llewellyn or Neil Lamont
Tunnel Avenue Antique Warehouse
Tunnel Avenue Trading Estate
Greenwich
London SE10 0QH
Telephone: 081-305-2230   Fax: 081-305-1805

S.E.10 continued

Greenwich Antiques Market
Greenwich High Rd. Est. 1972. Open Sun. 7.30-4.30, and Sat. (June-Sept.). SIZE: 80 stalls. STOCK: General antiques and bric-a-brac. LOC: Almost opposite railway station. PARK: Adjacent.

The Greenwich Gallery
9 Nevada St. (R.F. Moy). Est. 1965. Open 10-5.30. STOCK: Mainly English oil paintings and watercolours, 18th C to 1950. TEL: 081 305 1666. SER: Restorations; framing; exhibitions. VAT: Spec.

The Junk Shop
9 Greenwich South St. (J.B. and C. Moy). Open 10-6, including Sun. SIZE: Large. STOCK: Period furniture, architectural features, 18th C to 1940. TEL: 081 305 1666. SER: Restorations; polishing.

Lamont Antiques Ltd   LAPADA
Tunnel Avenue Antique Warehouse, Tunnel Avenue Trading Estate, Greenwich. (N. Lamont and F. Llewellyn). Open 9-5.30. CL: Sat. SIZE: Large. STOCK: Architectural fixtures and fittings, bars, stained glass, pub mirrors and signs, shipping furniture, £5-£25,000. PARK: Own. TEL: 081 305 2230; fax - 081 305 1805. SER: Container packing.

S.E.10 continued

Peter Laurie Antiques
28 Greenwich Church St. Open 10-5 including Sun. CL: Fri. am. STOCK: Curiosities, nautical items, weapons, photographic and scientific instruments. TEL: 081 853 5777.

The Warwick Leadlay Gallery
5 Nelson Rd, Greenwich. Est. 1973. Open 9.30-5.30, Sun. and Bank Holidays 11-5.30. SIZE: Large. STOCK: Antiquarian prints, maps and illustrated books, 17th-19th C. LOC: 2 mins. walk from Cutty Sark. PARK: Nearby. TEL: 081 858 0317; home - 081 852 7484. SER: Valuations; restorations, cleaning, colouring; mounting, framing. VAT: Stan.

Main Street Antiques
24 Woolwich Rd. (B. Sessacar). Open 10-6 including Sun. CL: Thurs. STOCK: Victorian pine and fireplaces. TEL: 081 305 1971.

Relcy Antiques
9 Nelson Rd, Greenwich. (R. Challis). Est. 1958. Open 10-6. CL: Sun. except by appointment. SIZE: Large. STOCK: English furniture, especially bureaux and bookcases, £50-£15,000; English and continental pictures, especially marine and sporting, £20-£5,000; instruments and marine items, ships' heads, sextants, telescopes, models, £20-£15,000; all 18th-19th C. Not stocked:

S.E.10 continued
Reproduction and art deco. LOC: 3/4 mile off A2 towards River Thames. TEL: 081 858 2812. SER: Valuations, restorations (furniture and pictures); buys at auction (Georgian and Victorian furniture, pictures). VAT: Stan/Spec.

Rogers Turner Books Ltd
22 Nelson Rd, Greenwich. Est. 1975. Open 10-6. STOCK: Antiquarian books especially on clocks and scientific instruments. TEL: 081 853 5271; Paris - 010 33 13912 1191. SER: Buys at auction (British and European); catalogues available.

South London Book Centre
18-19 Stockwell St, Greenwich. Open 10-6, Sat. and Sun. 9-5. STOCK: Books, records, printed ephemera, contemporary paintings and prints. TEL: 081 853 2151.

Spread Eagle Antiques
8 Nevada St. (R.F. Moy). Est. 1954. Open 10-5.30, including Sun. SIZE: Large. STOCK: Books, period costume, curios, china, bric-a-brac, prints, postcards. Not stocked: FurnitureLOC: A202. From London follow A2, then turn left at Deptford - or follow riverside road from Tower Bridge. PARK: Easy. TEL: 081 305 1666. SER: Valuations; restorations (furniture, china, pictures). VAT: Stan/Spec.

Spread Eagle Antiques
1 Stockwell St. (R.F. Moy). Est. 1954. Open 10-5.30. CL: Thurs. pm. SIZE: Large. STOCK: Furniture, pictures and decorative items, 18th-19th C. PARK: Easy. TEL: 081 305 1666; home - 081 692 1618. SER: Valuations; restorations (pictures, furniture). VAT: Stan/Spec.

Robert Whitfield Antiques   LAPADA
Tunnel Avenue Antique Warehouse, Tunnel Avenue Trading Estate, Greenwich. Open 10-5. CL: Sat. STOCK: Edwardian, Victorian and secondhand furniture, especially bentwood chairs. TEL: 081 305 2230; fax - 081 305 1805. SER: Container packing.

LONDON S.E.13
Robert Morley and Co Ltd   BADA
34 Engate St, Lewisham. Est. 1881. Open 9-5. STOCK: Pianos, harpsichords, clavichords, spinets, virginals. TEL: 081 318 5838; fax - 081 297 0720. SER: Restorations (musical instruments). VAT: Stan.

Whitworth and O'Donnell Ltd
282 Lewisham High St. (A. O'Donnell). Est. 1950. Open 10-5. CL: Thurs. SIZE: Medium. STOCK: Jewellery, £10-£500. TEL: 081 690 1282. SER: Restorations (jewellery). VAT: Stan.

LONDON S.E.15
Peter Allen Antiques Ltd. World Wide Antique Exporters   LAPADA
17-17a Nunhead Green, Peckham. Est. 1966. Open 8-5. CL: Sat. SIZE: Large. STOCK: Fine Victorian furniture. TEL: 071 732 1968.

G. Austin and Sons Ltd
11-23 Peckham Rye. (A., D. and V. Austin). Est. 1870. Open 8.30-5. CL: Thurs. pm. SIZE: Large. STOCK: Furniture, silver, porcelain, pictures, glass, books. PARK: Easy. TEL: 071 639 3163. SER: Free delivery up to 20 miles. VAT: Stan/Spec.

A. Fagiani
30 Wagner St. Est. 1965. Open 8-1 and 2-6, Sat. 8-1. STOCK: Bookcases, pedestal desks. LOC: Off Kent Rd. and Ilderton Rd. TEL: 071 732 7188. SER: Valuations; restorations (furniture); French polishing. VAT: Stan.

LONDON S.E.20
Black Cat
202 High St, Penge. (B. Aust). Open 10-6. CL: Wed. STOCK: Furniture, 19th C; general antiques. LOC: Opposite Kent House Rd., Beckenham. TEL: 081 778 4230/460 0489.

LONDON S.E.21
Acorn Antiques
111 Rosendale Rd, West Dulwich. (Mrs G. Kingham). Open 10-6.30, Sat. 10-5.30. STOCK: Jewellery, china, glass, pictures, silver and plate, some furniture including pine, fire irons and fenders. TEL: 081 761 3349.

LONDON S.E.23
Bygone Bathrooms
39 Honour Oak Park, Brockley. (P. Kelly). Open 9.30-6. STOCK: Victorian and Edwardian bathrooms and fittings. TEL: 081 291 4733.

Oddiquities
61 Waldram Park Rd, and 20 Sunderland Rd., Forest Hill. (Mrs S.A. Butler). Est. 1966. Open 10-6, Sat. 10-4. CL: Sun. except by appointment and Thurs. SIZE: Medium. STOCK: Oil lamps, gas and electric light fitments, 1800-1930; fire furnishings, 1780-1920; all £20-£500; general antiques, 1800-1920, £15-£1,000. Not stocked: Coins, stamps, medals, jewellery. LOC: On South Circular Rd., between Catford and Forest Hill. PARK: Opposite. TEL: 081 699 9574. VAT: Stan.

Reubens
44 Honour Oak Park, Brockley. (R.E. Reubens). Est. 1960. Open 11-6. CL: Sat. SIZE: Medium. STOCK: Tribal weapons, shields and curios, mainly 19th C, £20-£500; electrical items, mechanical bygones, scientific instruments,

LONDON

S.E.23 continued
occasional musical items, 19th C. LOC: 200yds. from Honour Oak station. PARK: Easy. TEL: 081 291 1786; home - same. SER: Finder. FAIRS: Ardingly, Newark, Peterborough. VAT: Stan.

LONDON S.E.24
Under Milkwood
379 Milkwood Rd, Herne Hill. (Nick and Sue Williams). Est. 1988. Open 10-5, Mon. 9-5.30, Sat. 9.30-5.30, Wed. by appointment. SIZE: Small. *STOCK: Victorian and Edwardian fireplaces, £150-£1,000; Victorian pine furniture, £100-£600.* LOC: At rear of Herne Hill station. PARK: Easy. TEL: 071 733 3921; home - 081 761 5357. SER: Valuations; restorations (fireplaces). FAIRS: Ardingly, Newark.

LONDON S.E.25
Engine 'n' Tender
19 Spring Lane, Woodside Green. (Mrs Joyce M. Buttigieg). Est. 1957. Open Thurs. 12-6, Fri. 12-6.30, Sat. 10-6. SIZE: Small. *STOCK: Model railways, mainly pre 1939; Dinky toys, to 1968; old toys, mainly tinplate.* LOC: Near Woodside station. PARK: Easy. TEL: 081 654 0386. SER: Buys at auction (toys and model railways). FAIRS: Local toy.

LONDON S.E.26
Abbott Antiques and Country Pine (formerly Olwen Carthew)
109 Kirkdale. Est. 1972. Open 10-5.30, Thurs. 10-3, Sat. 10-5, Sun. 1-5. *STOCK: Victorian and Edwardian country pine furniture and kitchen items.* LOC: 1/2 mile from South Circular Rd. at Forest Hill. TEL: 081 699 1363. VAT: Stan.

Hillyers
301 Sydenham Rd. Est. 1952. Open 8.30-4, Sat. 8.30-2. CL: Wed. SIZE: Small. *STOCK: Furniture, silver, plate, porcelain, glass, books, bric-a-brac.* PARK: Easy. TEL: 081 778 6361; home - 081 777 2506. SER: Valuations.

Kirkdale Pianos
251 Dartmouth Rd. Open 9.30-6. *STOCK: Pianos.* TEL: 081 699 1928. SER: Export.

Vintage Cameras Ltd
256 Kirkdale, Sydenham. (J. Jenkins). Est. 1968. Open 9-5. SIZE: Large. *STOCK: Vintage cameras, 1840-1950, £50-£5,000; general photographica, 1840-1950, £5-£50.* LOC: Near South Circular Rd. PARK: Nearby. TEL: 081 778 5841/5416. SER: Valuations. VAT: Stan.

LONDON E.2
George Rankin Coin Co. Ltd
325 Bethnal Green Rd. Open 10-5. *STOCK: Coins, medals, medallions and jewellery.* TEL: 071 739 1840/729 1280; fax - 071 729 5023.

E.2 continued
St. Peters Organ Works
St. Peters Close, Warner Pl. (J.P. Mander and I. Bell). Est. 1935. CL: Sat. SIZE: Large. *STOCK: Antique pipe organs.* LOC: Opposite children's hospital, Hackey Rd. PARK: Own. TEL: 071 739 4747. SER: Valuations; restorations. VAT: Stan.

LONDON E.4
Albert and Victoria
Station Approach, Station Rd., Chingford. (S. Salter). Est. 1972. Open Tues. and Wed. 10-4, Fri. and Sat. 10-6. SIZE: Small. *STOCK: General antiques, handworked linen, fashion clothes and accessories, 19th-20th C, £5-£500.* LOC: In forecourt of North Chingford railway station. PARK: Easy. TEL: 081 529 6361.

LONDON E.8
Curious Grannies
2 Middleton Rd, Hackney. (A. and J. O'Kelly). Est. 1974. Open any time by appointment. SIZE: Medium. *STOCK: Boxes - caddies, sewing, writing, snuff, vanity, jewellery and desk, £50-£3,000; musical instruments, plucked string, £250-£1,500; all 18th-19th C.* LOC: Off Kingsland Rd., continuation of Bishopsgate. PARK: Easy. TEL: 071 254 7074; home - same. SER: Valuations; restorations (exceptional instruments only). Registerd with the Conservation Unit of the Museums and Galleries Commission.

LONDON E.11
K.N. and P. Blake - Old Cottage Antiques
8 High St, Wanstead. Est. 1920. Open Thurs. and Fri. 10.30-5.30. SIZE: Medium. *STOCK: Furniture, pre 1840; paintings, 19th and 20th C.* LOC: Near Wanstead station and Snaresbrook. TEL: 081 989 2317/504 9264. SER: Valuations; buys at auction. VAT: Stan/Spec.

LONDON E.14
San Fairy Ann
110 Salmon Lane. (Mr. and Mrs J. McDermott). Est. 1977. SIZE: Small. *STOCK: General antiques, to 1950's, reproduction objets d'art, glass and china.* LOC: Just off Commercial Rd., between Blackwall and Rotherhithe tunnel. PARK: Easy. TEL: 071 987 5771.

LONDON E.17
Antique City
98 Wood St. Est. 1978. Open 9.30-5.00. CL: Thurs. and Sun., except by appointment. SIZE: Large. *STOCK: General antiques, 19th C, £5-£500.* PARK: In side road opposite. TEL: 081 520 4032. *Trade Only.*

E.17 continued
Georgian Village Antiques Market
100 Wood St, Walthamstow. Est. 1972. Open 10-5. CL: Thurs. SIZE: 10 shops. STOCK: *Clocks, barometers, porcelain, postcards, collectables, jewellery, country items, brass, copper, stamps, violins.* LOC: 50yds. from Dukes Head. PARK: Adjacent. TEL: 081 520 6638.

Georgiana's Antiques
134 Palmerston Rd, Walthamstow. (G.P. Webb). Open 10-5. CL: Wed. STOCK: *Victorian and Edwardian furniture and china.* TEL: 081 520 7015.

LONDON E.18
Simply Capital
33 Victoria Rd, South Woodford. Open 10-6. STOCK: *Pine including reproduction, satinwood; Victorian fireplaces, surrounds, smalls.* TEL: 081 530 6229. SER: Installations (fireplaces).

LONDON E.C.1
City Clocks
31 Amwell St. (J. Rosson). FBHI. Est. 1960. Open 9-5, Sat. 9.30-1.30 or by appointment. CL: Mon. SIZE: Medium. STOCK: *Clocks, watches, some furniture, 18th-19th C, £100-£7,000.* PARK: Easy. TEL: 071 278 1154. SER: Valuations; restorations (clocks and watches); buys at auction. VAT: Stan.

Eldridge London
99-101 Farringdon Rd. (B. Eldridge). Est. 1953. Open 10-5, Sat. 10-1. SIZE: Large. STOCK: *Furniture and items of social and historical importance.* PARK: Easy. TEL: 071 837 0379. VAT: Spec.

Jonathan Harris (Jewellery) Ltd
63-66 Hatton Garden (office). (E.C. and D. Harris). Est. 1958. Open 10-5. CL: Sat. STOCK: *Jewellery, £50-£20,000.* PARK: Nearby. TEL: 071 242 9115/242 1558; fax - 071 831 4417. SER: Valuations. FAIRS: Basle, Switzerland and Munich, Germany. VAT: Stan/Spec.

Hirsh Ltd
10 Hatton Garden. (A. Hirsh). Open 10-6 including Sun. STOCK: *Fine jewellery, silver, and objets d'art.* TEL: 071 405 6080/4392. SER: Valuations.

R. Holt and Co. Ltd
98 Hatton Garden. Est. 1948. Open 9.30-5.30. CL: Sat. STOCK: *Chinese artifacts.* TEL: 071 405 0197/405 5286; fax - 071 430 1279. SER: Valuations; restorations (gem stones); gem stone cutting and testing; bead stringing; holistic crystals.

House of Buckingham (Antiques)
113-117 Farringdon Rd. (B.B. White). Est. 1970. Open 9-6. STOCK: *Boxes, clocks, furniture, brass, nautical goods.* TEL: 071 278 2013. VAT: Stan/Spec.

A.R. ULLMANN LTD.
10 HATTON GARDEN
LONDON EC1N 8AH
TEL: 071 405 1877

ANTIQUE AND SECOND HAND JEWELLERY SILVER OBJETS D'ART BOUGHT, SOLD & REPAIRED

Open: Mon – Fri 9am-5pm
Sat 9.30am-5pm

REPAIRS — VALUATIONS

E.C.1 continued
Joseph and Pearce Ltd   LAPADA
63-66 Hatton Garden. Est. 1896. Open by appointment. STOCK: *Jewellery, 1800-1960, £100-£2,500.* LOC: City. TEL: 071 405 4604/7; fax - 071 242 1902. VAT: Stan/Spec. *Trade Only.*

R.I. McKay
88/90 Hatton Garden. Est. 1951. Open by appointment only. SIZE: Small. STOCK: *Jewellery, all periods, from £100.* LOC: Centre of Hatton Garden. PARK: Easy and multi-storey nearby. TEL: 071 405 7544; fax - 071 404 5586. VAT: Stan/Spec. *Trade Only.*

A.R. Ullmann Ltd
10 Hatton Garden. (J.S. Ullmann). Est. 1939. Open 9-5, Sat. 9.30-5. SIZE: Small. STOCK: *Jewellery, gold, silver and diamond; silver and objets d'art.* LOC: Very close to Farringdon and Chancery Lane tube stations. PARK: Multi-storey in St. Cross St. TEL: 071 405 1877; home - 081 346 2546. SER: Valuations; restorations. VAT: Stan/Spec.

LONDON E.C.2
The London Architectural Salvage and Supply Co. Ltd. (LASSCo)
St. Michael's Church, Mark St. (off Paul St.). Est. 1977. Open 10-5. STOCK: *Architectural relics*

LONDON

E.C.2 continued

including doors and door furniture, chimney pieces, flooring, panelled rooms, railings, ironwork, garden and street furniture, glass and ecclesiastical joinery. TEL: 071 739 0448; fax - 071 729 6853

Westland & Company

The former St. Michael's Church, Leonard St. Est. 1986. Open 8.30-6. SIZE: Large. *STOCK: Unusual architectural items including fireplaces, panelling, panelled rooms, shop and light fittings, turret clocks, stone work, ceilings, revolving doors and garden elements; English and Continental furniture and clocks; all £100-£100,000.* LOC: Off Gt. Eastern St. PARK: Easy. TEL: 071 739 8094; fax - 071 729 3620. Correspondence: The Clergy House, Mark St., London, EC2A 4ER

LONDON E.C.3

Ash Rare Books

25 Royal Exchange. (L. Worms). Est. 1946. Open 10-5.30. CL: Sat. SIZE: Small. *STOCK: Books, 1550-1980, £20-£10,000; maps, 1550-1850, £25-£2,000; prints, 1650-1900, £20-£1,000.* LOC: On the Threadneedle St. side of the Royal Exchange, opposite Bank of England. PARK: Nearby. TEL: 071 626 2665; fax - 071 623 9052. SER: Buys at auction (books and maps); picture framing and mount cutting. VAT: Stan

Halcyon Days BADA

4 Royal Exchange. (S. Benjamin). Est. 1950. Open 10-5.30. *STOCK: 18th to early 19th C enamels, papier mâché, tôle, objects of vertu, treen, Staffordshire pottery figures, prints, unusual small Georgian furniture.* TEL: 071 629 8811; fax - 071 409 0280. FAIRS: Grosvenor House. VAT: Stan/Spec

Nanwani and Co

2 Shopping Arcade, Bank Station, Cornhill. Est. 1958. CL: Sat. *STOCK: Precious and semi-precious stones, Oriental items, objets d'art.* TEL: 071 623 8232; fax - 071 283 2548. VAT: Stan

Royal Exchange Art Gallery

14 Royal Exchange. Est. 1974 Open 10.30-5.15. CL: Sat. *STOCK: Oil paintings, watercolours and etchings, especially marine and landscape, 19th-20th C.* TEL: 071 283 4400

Searle and Co Ltd

1 Royal Exchange, Cornhill. Est. 1893. Open 9-5.30. SIZE: Medium. *STOCK: Georgian, Victorian and secondhand silver; Victorian, Edwardian and secondhand jewellery.* LOC: Near Bank underground. PARK: Meters. TEL: 071 626 2456. SER: Valuations; restorations; repairs; engraving. VAT: Stan/Spec

LONDON E.C.4

J. Clarke-Hall Ltd

7 Bride Court, and 22 Bride Lane. ABA. Est. 1934. Open 10.30-6.30. CL: Sat. Bride Lane - open 12-4. SIZE: Small. *STOCK: 18th C English literature, especially Dr. Samuel Johnson, Lewis Carroll and their contemporaries; books on printing; illustrated books and 19th C prints, modern first editions, £3-£2,500.* LOC: Off Bride Lane, which is off bottom of Fleet St., near Ludgate Circus. PARK: Meters. TEL: 071 353 4116/5483. SER: Restorations (book repairs, rebinding); framing. VAT: Stan

LONDON N.1

After Noah

121 Upper St., Islington. (M. Crawford and Z. Candlin). Est. 1990. Open 10-6, Sun. 11-4. SIZE: Medium. *STOCK: Arts and crafts oak and similar furniture, 1880's to 1950's; iron, iron and brass beds; decorative items, bric-a-brac including candlesticks, mirrors, lighting, kitchenalia and jewellery; all £1-£1,000.* PARK: Side streets. TEL: 071 359 4281; fax - same. SER: Restorations. VAT: Stan.

Angel Arcade

116-118 Islington High St, Camden Passage. Open Wed. and Sat. Other days access available to the shops. SIZE: Large. *STOCK: General antiques.*

Annie's Antique Clothes

10 Camden Passage, Islington. (A. Moss). Open 11-5. CL: Mon. TEL: 071 359 0796.

The Antique Trader

357 Upper St, Islington. (D. Rothera and B Thompson). Est. 1968. Open 10-5. SIZE: Large *STOCK: Furniture especially British Arts and Crafts, £150-£10,000.* LOC: Camden Passage Antiques Centre. PARK: Easy. TEL: 071 359 2019; fax - 071 226 9446. VAT: Stan/Spec.

At the Sign of the Chest of Drawers

281 Upper St, Islington. (A. Harms). Open 10-6 including Sun. *STOCK: Pine, country furniture* TEL: 071 359 5909.

Ian Auld

1 Gateway Arcade, Camden Passage, Islington Est. 1968. Open Wed. and Sat. 10-5. SIZE: Small *STOCK: Ethnographic items, African, Oceanic £25-£1,000; antiquities especially pottery, £25 £250; Coptic and pre-Columbian textiles. No stocked: Victoriana.* LOC: Near Angel tube station. PARK: Easy. TEL: 071 359 1440.

Banbury Fayre

6 Pierrepont Arcade, Camden Passage, Islington (N. Steel). Est. 1984. Open Wed., Fri. and Sat SIZE: Small. *STOCK: Collectables, including commemoratives, shipping, Boy Scout movement Boer War, air line travel.* PARK: 200yds. TEL Home - 081 852 5675.

An Antique Collectors' Club Title

The Georgian Bracket Clock 1714-1830
by Richard C.R. Barder

Probably the best single reference on this surprisingly neglected subject. Of the many superior clocks made in England from 1714-1830, the majority were bracket clocks. Superb illustrations complement a text in which the craft of clockmaking and bracket clock design is comprehensively discussed. This book will appeal to the general reader, collector and specialist alike.
ISBN 1 85149 158 9
236pp, 267 b & w illus, 39 colour
£45.00

Available from:
Antique Collectors' Club, 5 Church Street, Woodbridge, Suffolk IP12 1DS
Tel: (0394) 385501 Fax: (0394) 384434

or Market Street Industrial Park, Wappingers' Falls, New York 12590, USA
Tel: 914 297 0003 Fax: 914 297 0068

N.1 continued

William Bedford plc LAPADA
The Merchants Hall, 46 Essex Rd., Islington. (J. Bedford, B. Pass and A. Adam). Est. 1959. Open 9.30-5.30. SIZE: Large. *STOCK: English period furniture and accessories.* **LOC:** 100yds. Camden Passage. **PARK:** Easy. **TEL:** 071 226 9648; fax - 071 226 6225. **VAT:** Stan/Spec.

Boutique Fantasque
13 Pierrepont Row, Camden Passage, Islington. (Mrs M.A.B. Gates). Est. 1962. Open Wed. and Sat. SIZE: Small. *STOCK: Watercolours and prints, general antiques, porcelain, jewellery, small collectors' items.* LOC: From Piccadilly, No.19 bus. Tube to Angel station. PARK: 200yds. TEL: Home - 025 126 2287.

Buck and Payne Antiques LAPADA
5 Camden Passage, Islington. (W.M. Buck and M.H. Payne). Open 10-5, Wed. 8.30-5. *STOCK: French country furniture; unusual and decorative items.* **TEL:** 071 226 4326/354 3603.

Bushwood Antiques LAPADA
317 Upper St, Islington. (A. Bush). Est. 1967. Open 9.30-5.30 or by appointment. SIZE: Large. *STOCK: 18th-19th C furniture, decorators' items, works of art and clocks.* **LOC:** 100yds. from Camden Passage. **PARK:** 50yds. **TEL:** 071 359 2095; fax - 071 704 9578. **VAT:** Stan.

N.1 continued

Camden Passage Antiques Centre
12 Camden Passage. (S. Lemkow). Est. 1960. Open weekdays 10.30-5.30. Also 100 stalls open Wed. 8-3 and Sat. 9-5 - general antiques; Thurs. 9-4 - books. SIZE: 400 shops and boutiques some of which are listed in this section. LOC: Behind the Angel, Islington. TEL: 071 359 0190.

Canonbury Antiques
13 Canonbury Place. (A.C. Holyome). Est. 1965. Open 9-6. CL: Sat. pm. *STOCK: General antiques, upholstered furniture.* TEL: 071 359 2246. SER: Restorations (upholstery).

Patric Capon BADA
350 Upper St, Islington. Est. 1970. Open Wed. and Sat. or by appointment. SIZE: Medium. *STOCK: Unusual carriage clocks, 19th C, £450-£6,000; 8-day and 2-day marine chronometers, 19th C, £850-£4,500; clocks and barometers, 18th-19th C, £400-£6,500.* LOC: Adjacent Camden Passage. PARK: Easy. TEL: 071 354 0487; home - 081 467 5722. SER: Valuations; restorations. FAIRS: Olympia. VAT: Stan/Spec.

Chancery Antiques Ltd
357a Upper St, Islington. (R. and D. Rote). Est. 1950. Open 10.30-5 or by appointment. CL: Mon. and Thurs. SIZE: Medium. *STOCK: Oriental works of art especially Japanese Meiji period.* TEL: 071 359 9035. VAT: Stan/Spec.

N.1 continued

Peter Chapman Antiques LAPADA
10 Theberton St, Islington. (P.J. Chapman). CPTA. Est. 1971. Open 9.30-1 and 2-6. CL: Sun. and public holidays except by appointment. SIZE: Medium. *STOCK: Furniture, 1700-1900, £100-£20,000; paintings, drawings and prints, 17th to early 20th C, £50-£15,000; stained glass and architectural items.* LOC: 5 mins. walk from Camden Passage down Upper St. PARK: Easy. TEL: 071 226 5565; mobile - 0831 913662; fax - 081 348 4846. SER: Valuations; restorations (furniture and period objects); buys at auction. VAT: Stan/Spec.

"Commemoratives"
3 Pierrepont Arcade, Camden Passage, Islington. (F. Annesley). Est. 1971. Open all day Wed. and Sat. and Fri. pm. *STOCK: Commemoratives, especially Royal Torquay, motto ware, eggcups and Art Deco ceramics.* LOC: Northern line underground to Angel. PARK: Meters.

Corrigan Antiques LAPADA
114 Islington High St, Islington. Open 10-4. CL: Thurs. SIZE: Small. *STOCK: Furniture and decorative items, pre-1900. Not stocked: Weapons.* LOC: Near Camden Passage. PARK: Nearby. TEL: 071 704 0678; home - 071 251 8047. VAT: Stan/Spec.

Davidson Brothers
33 Camden Passage, Islington. (S. and C. Davidson). Est. 1981. Open 10-5. SIZE: Medium. *STOCK: Decorative items, £150-£1,000; unusual furniture, £500-£2,500.* LOC: Near Charlton Place. PARK: Meters. TEL: 071 226 7491. FAIRS: Olympia. VAT: Stan/Spec.

Dean's Antiques
52-53 Camden Passage, Islington. Open Wed. and Sat. 9.30-5. *STOCK: Decorative items.* TEL: 071 354 9940.

Dome Antiques (Exports) Ltd
75 Upper St, Islington. (A.D. Woolf). Est. 1961. Open 9.30-5.30. SIZE: Large. *STOCK: English furniture, 1700-1900, £100-£5,000; desks, library and dining tables, sets of chairs.* LOC: Opposite Islington Green. PARK: At rear. TEL: 071 226 7227; mobile - 0831 805888; fax - 071 704 2960. SER: Valuations. VAT: Stan/Spec.

Donay Antiques
35 Camden Passage, Islington. (D.C. Goddard). Est. 1980. Open 9-5.30. SIZE: Large. *STOCK: Games, £30-£1,500; chess sets, £50-£1,500; artists' colour boxes, £400-£800; decorative items, fitted boxes, maps and cards.* LOC: Near Angel tube or bus station. PARK: Nearby. TEL: 071 359 1880.

Feljoy Antiques
Shop 3, Angel Arcade, Camden Passage. Open Wed. and Sat. 8-4. *STOCK: Decorative antiques and textiles.* TEL: 071 354 5336.

N.1 continued

D.J. Ferrant Antiques
21a Camden Passage, Islington. (J. Ferrant). Est. 1963. Open 9.30-4. SIZE: Large. *STOCK: Georgian furniture, clocks, bronzes, general antiques.* PARK: Easy. TEL: 071 359 2597. SER: Buys at auction. VAT: Stan/Spec.

Michael Finney Antique Prints and Books
11 Camden Passage, Islington. Open 10-5. CL: Mon. *STOCK: Prints, 17th-19th C; plate books, watercolours especially David Roberts, Egypt, Holy Land and Spain, £1-£1,000.* PARK: Meters. TEL: 071 226 9280.

"The Fleamarket"
7 Pierrepont Row, Camden Passage, Islington. Open 9.30-6. CL: Mon. SIZE: Large. 26 Standholders. *STOCK: Jewellery, furniture, objets d'art, militaria, guns, swords, pistols, porcelain, coins, medals, stamps, 18th-19th C, £1-£500; antiquarian books, prints, fine art, china, silver, glass and general antiques.* PARK: Easy. TEL: 071 226 8211. SER: Valuations; buys at auction; weapon repairs.

Vincent Freeman
1 Camden Passage, Islington. Est. 1966. Open 10-5. CL: Mon. and Thurs. SIZE: Large. *STOCK: Music boxes, furniture and decorative items, from £100.* TEL: 071 226 6178; fax - 071 226 7231. VAT: Stan/Spec.

Furniture Vault
50 Camden Passage, Islington. Open 9.30-4.30. *STOCK: Furniture, 18th-20th C; decorative bronzes.* TEL: 071 354 1047.

Georgian Village
Islington Green. Open 10-4, Wed. and Sat. 7-5. PARK: Nearby. TEL: 071 226 1571.

"Get Stuffed"
105 Essex Rd., Islington. Est. 1975. Open 10.30-4.30, Thurs. 10.30-1. *STOCK: Stuffed birds, fish, animals, trophy heads; rugs; butterflies, insects.* TEL: 071 226 1364. SER: Restorations; taxidermy; glass domes and cases supplied.

The Graham Gallery LAPADA
104 Islington High St, Camden Passage, Islington. Est. 1973. Open 10-5, Wed. 8-5, Sat. 10-6. CL: Mon. SIZE: Large. *STOCK: Silver, 1750-1930, £100-£15,000; Victorian silver plate, £50-£40,000; Sheffield plate, £100-£5,000; Victorian oil paintings, £2,000-£25,000; Victorian decorative furniture, £1,000-£15,000.* LOC: 2 mins. from Angel Underground. PARK: Easy. TEL: 071 354 2112. VAT: Stan.

Gordon Gridley
41 Camden Passage, Islington. Est. 1968. CL: Mon. SIZE: Large + warehouse nearby. *STOCK: English and continental furniture, paintings,*

ANTIQUE COLLECTING

- **Authoritative articles**
- **Practical buying information**
- **Up-to-date price guides**
- **Annual Investment Issue**
- **Auctions and fairs calendars**
- **Antiques for sale and wanted**

The magazine is published ten times a year and contains pre-publication offers and special Christmas discounts on ACC books

Join NOW and receive your first magazine and our book catalogue FREE
Annual membership: £19.50 UK, £25.00 overseas, US $40 USA, CAN $50 Canada

Antique Collectors' Club
5 Church Street, Woodbridge, Suffolk,
IP12 1DS, England
Tel: (0394) 385501 Fax: (0394) 384434

Market Street Industrial Park, Wappingers' Falls,
New York 12590, USA
Tel: 914 297 0003 Fax: 914 297 0068

For Collectors, By Collectors, About Collecting

LONDON

N.1 continued

decorative objects, metalwork, statuary, scientific instruments, 17th-19th C, £50-£5,000. PARK: Nearby, in Charlton Place. TEL: 071 226 0643. SER: Valuations; restorations. VAT: Stan/Spec.

Linda Gumb   LAPADA
9 Camden Passage, Islington. Est. 1981. Open 9.30-4.30, Wed. 7.30-5, Sat. 9-5. SIZE: Medium. STOCK: Textiles, 18th-19th C; decorative objects, 19th C; all £10-£5,000. PARK: Easy. TEL: 071 354 1184. SER: Buys at auction. FAIRS: Olympia. VAT: Stan.

Rosemary Hart
4 Gateway Arcade, Camden Passage, Islington. Est. 1980. Open 11-4, Wed. and Sat. 9-5. CL: Mon. and Thurs. SIZE: Small. STOCK: Silver and plate, £5-£750. LOC: Near Angel tube station. TEL: 071 359 6839.

Hart and Rosenberg
2 and 3 Gateway Arcade, Camden Passage, Islington. (E. Hart and H. Rosenberg). Est. 1968. Open 10-5, Wed. 9-5. CL: Mon. and Thurs. SIZE: Medium. STOCK: Chinese, Japanese and European porcelain, works of art, decorative items, some furniture, £25-£5,000. LOC: Near Angel tube station. PARK: Nearby. TEL: 071 359 6839. SER: Valuations; buys at auction. VAT: Stan/Spec.

Miriam Haskell
2 Charlton Place. Open 10-5.30. STOCK: Art deco and art nouveau jewellery, fine art; original graphics and sculpture, especially 1920s-1930s. TEL: 071 226 5625.

Sherry Hatcher
5 Gateway Arcade, Camden Passage, Upper St., Islington. Est. 1966. Open 10-5. SIZE: Small. STOCK: Perfume bottles, sugar shakers, silver, boxes and interesting silver items. LOC: Near Angel tube station. PARK: Easy. TEL: 071 226 5679.

Brian Hawkins Antiques   LAPADA
73 Upper St., Islington. Open 9.30-5. STOCK: Furniture, 19th to early 20th C, £50-£1,000+. TEL: 071 359 3957.

Heather Antiques
14 Camden Passage, Islington. Est. 1965. Open 9.30-4.30 or by appointment. CL: Mon. SIZE: Medium. STOCK: Silver and plate. TEL: 071 226 2412. VAT: Stan.

Linda Helm Antiques   LAPADA
Islington. Open by appointment. STOCK: Oak and country furniture; floral watercolours. TEL: 071 609 2716.

Heritage Antiques   LAPADA
112 Islington High St., Camden Passage. (A. Daniel). Est. 1975. Open Wed. 8-4 and Sat. 9.30-5 or by appointment. SIZE: Large. STOCK:

N.1 continued

Metalware, £25-£3,000; some furniture and decorative items. TEL: 071 226 7789 or 0273 26850. VAT: Stan/Spec.

House of Steel Antiques
400 Caledonian Rd. (J. Cole). Est. 1974. Open 10.30-5.30, Sat. by appointment. SIZE: Warehouse. STOCK: Metal items - fireplaces, 18th-19th C, £50-£1,000; spiral staircases, £300-£1,000; balconies, railings, garden furniture, £50-£500; all 19th C. LOC: Near King's Cross. PARK: Own. TEL: 071 607 5889; home - 071 226 5913. SER: Valuations; restorations (welding, polishing, sandblasting); steel furniture manufactured, items made to order. VAT: Stan.

Diana Huntley   LAPADA
8 Camden Passage, Islington. Est. 1970. Open Tues. and Fri. 10-4, Wed. 7.30-5, Thurs. by appointment, Sat. 9-5. STOCK: European porcelain, £50-£2,000; glass objets d'art; all 19th C. TEL: 071 226 4605. SER: Valuations. VAT: Stan/Spec.

Inheritance
8/9/10 Gateway Arcade, Camden Passage, Islington. (A. Pantelli). Est. 1969. Open 10.30-5. CL: Mon. SIZE: Small. STOCK: Jewellery, Oriental and European ceramics, ivories, furniture, cloisonné, clocks, bronzes. TEL: 071 226 8305. SER: Valuations. VAT: Stan/Spec.

Intercol London
Upper Gallery, 11 Camden Passage, Correspondence - 43 Templars Crescent, N3 3QR. (Y. Beresiner). Est. 1977. Open Wed.-Sat. 9-5, other times by appointment. SIZE: Large. STOCK: Playing cards, maps and banknotes and related literature, £5-£1,000+. PARK: Easy. TEL: 081 349 2207; fax - 081 346 9539. SER: Valuations; restorations (maps including colouring); buys at auction (playing cards, maps, banknotes and books). FAIRS: Major specialist European, U.S.A. and Far Eastern. VAT: Stan/Spec.

Islington Antiques
12 and 14 Essex Rd. (R.A. Bent). Open 9-6 STOCK: Pine furniture. TEL: 071 226 6867.

Japanese Gallery
23 Camden Passage, Islington. Open 9.30-4.30 STOCK: Japanese woodcut prints; books porcelain, screens, kimonos, scrolls, furniture general Japanese antiques. TEL: 071 226 3347 SER: Framing.

Jubilee Photographica
10 Pierrepont Row, Camden Passage, Islington (Beryl Vosburgh). Est. 1970. Open Wed. and Sat 10.30-4 or by appointment. SIZE: Small. STOCK Photographica - apparatus, images, daguerreo types, ambrotypes, tintypes, vintage paper prints stereoscopic cards and viewers, magic lantern and slides, topographical and family-albums

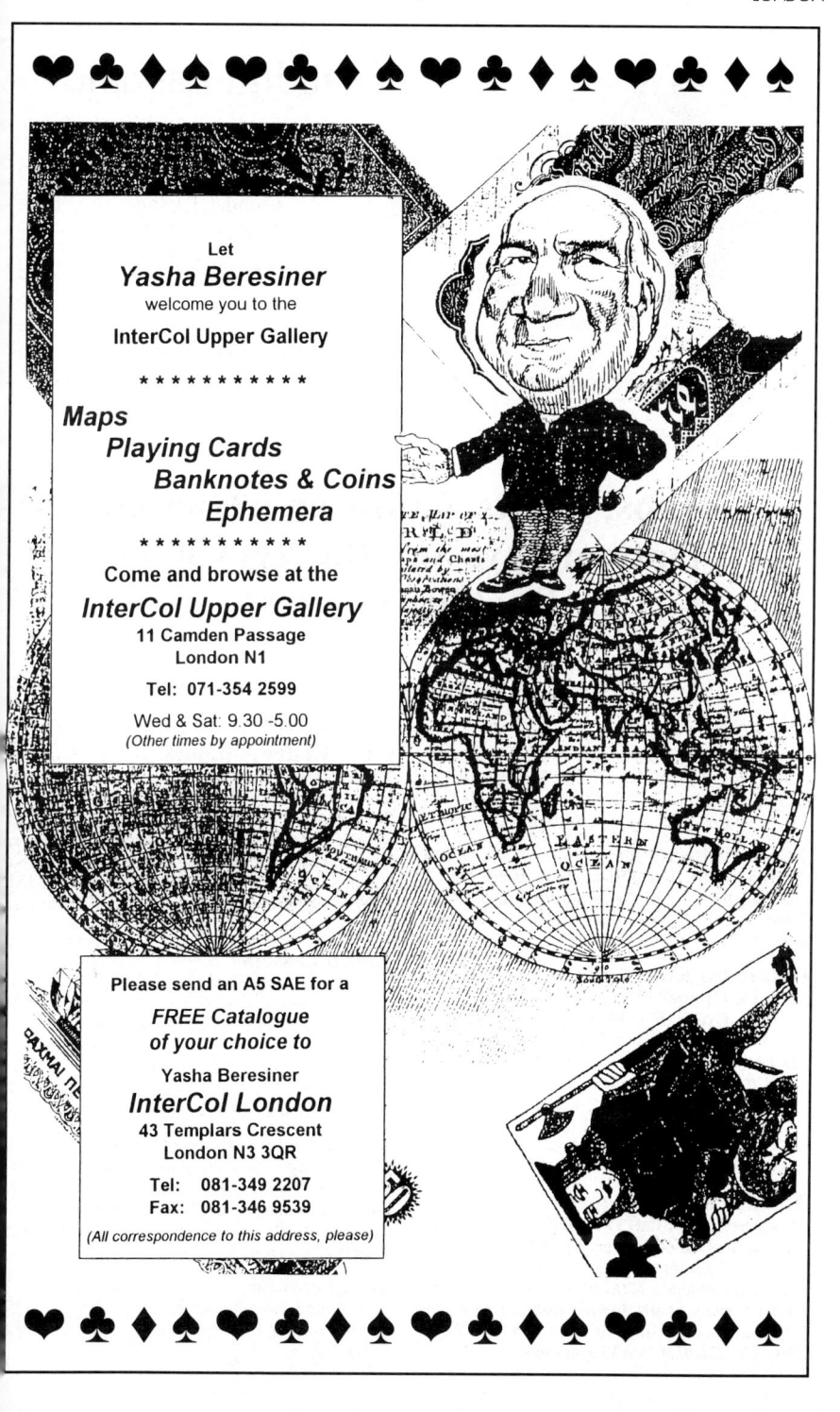

Let
Yasha Beresiner
welcome you to the
InterCol Upper Gallery

* * * * * * * * * *

Maps
   Playing Cards
      Banknotes & Coins
         Ephemera

* * * * * * * * * *

Come and browse at the
InterCol Upper Gallery
11 Camden Passage
London N1

Tel: 071-354 2599

Wed & Sat: 9.30 -5.00
(Other times by appointment)

Please send an A5 SAE for a
*FREE Catalogue
of your choice to*
Yasha Beresiner
InterCol London
43 Templars Crescent
London N3 3QR

Tel: 081-349 2207
Fax: 081-346 9539

(All correspondence to this address, please)

1830 dapple grey rocking horse

Judith Lassalle

ESTABLISHED 1955

7 Pierrepont Arcade,
Camden Passage,
London, N1 8EF
Tel: 071-607 7121

*Open Wed. 7.30-4.00
Sat. 9.30-4.00 or by appointment*

Maps, Prints, Children's Games, Optical Toys and the Very Best Rocking Horses

---

N.1 continued

cabinet cards and cartes de visite, 10p-£1,000. LOC: From Piccadilly Circus, take 19 bus to Angel, Islington. PARK: Meters. TEL: Home - 071 607 5462. SER: Buys at auction.

Julian Antiques LAPADA
54 Duncan St. Est. 1964. Open Wed. 8.30-2 and Sat. 9.30-4 and by appointment. *STOCK: French clocks, fireplaces, bronzes, fenders, mirrors.* TEL: 071 833 0835.

Cassandra Keen Antiques LAPADA
Shop 18, Ground Floor, Georgian Village, 30 Islington Green. Est. 1983. Open Wed. 7.30-4, Sat. 8.30-4, Tues. and Fri. by appointment. SIZE: Small. *STOCK: Decorative items and small English and French furniture, 18th-19th C, from £100-£20,000.* LOC: Part of Camden Passage. PARK: Meters. TEL: 071 226 1571; home - 071 359 6534. SER: Buys at auction (French items). VAT: Stan/Spec.

Thomas Kerr Antiques Ltd LAPADA
11 Theberton St. Est. 1977. Open 10-6, Sat. by appointment. SIZE: Large. *STOCK: English and continental furniture, works of art, paintings and decorative objects, 17th-20th C, £100-£20,000.* LOC: 5 mins. walk down Upper St. towards Highbury and Islington tube. PARK: Easy. TEL: 071 226 0626. VAT: Stan/Spec.

N.1 continued

Carol Ketley Antiques LAPADA
9 Georgian Village, 30/31 Islington Green, Camden Passage. Est. 1979. Open Wed. 8-3, Sat. 10-4, other days by appointment. SIZE: Small. *STOCK: Decanters, drinking glasses, English pottery, 1780-1900, £10-£1,000.* PARK: Nearby. TEL: 071 359 5529; mobile - 0831 827284. FAIRS: Olympia; City of London; Little Chelsea. VAT: Spec.

Judith Lassalle
7 Pierrepont Arcade, Camden Passage, Islington. Est. 1955. Open Wed. 7.30-4, Sat. 9.30-4, other times by appointment. *STOCK: Maps, prints; children's games, optical toys and rocking horses, 17th to early 20th C, £25-£5,000.* PARK: Nearby. TEL: 071 607 7121. SER: Valuations; restorations; buys at auction. FAIRS: Olympia; Ephemera.

John Laurie (Antiques) Ltd LAPADA
351/352 Upper St, Islington. (J. Gewirtz). Est. 1962. Open 9.30-5. SIZE: Large. *STOCK: Silver, Sheffield plate.* TEL: 071 226 0913/6969; fax - 071 226 4599. SER: Restorations; packing; shipping. VAT: Stan.

Sara Lemkow
12 Camden Passage. Open 10-5. *STOCK: Oil lamps, brass, iron, copper, kitchen utensils.* TEL: 071 359 0190.

N.1 continued
Michael Lewis Antiques
16 Essex Rd, Islington. Est. 1977. Open 8-6, Sat. 8-5, Sun. by appointment. SIZE: Large. STOCK: Pine and country furniture, British and Irish, 18th-19th C, £100-£6,500. LOC: 100yds. north of Camden Passage. PARK: Easy. TEL: 071 359 7733. VAT: Stan.

Wan Li
7 Gateway Arcade, 355 Upper St., Camden Passage, Islington. Est. 1969. STOCK: Mainly Chinese works of art, porcelain, some European, fans. VAT: Stan/Spec.

London Militaria Market
Angel Arcade, Camden Passage, Islington. (S. Bosley and M. Warren). Est. 1987. Open Sat. 8-2. SIZE: Large. 35 dealers. STOCK: Militaria, 1800 to date. LOC: Near Angel tube station. PARK: Meters and car parks nearby. TEL: 062882 2503 or 04555 56971.

Heather Lotinga - Dog Box/Cat Box
Stand 4, York Arcade, 80 Islington High St. Open Wed. and Sat. and by appointment. SIZE: Small. STOCK: Decorative and unusual dog and cat items - ceramics, jewellery, pictures and related items. PARK: Nearby. TEL: 071 223 6272; fax - 081 892 4387. SER: Buys at auction; search; shipping and courier. FAIRS: Crufts; National and Supreme Cat Shows. VAT: Stan.

Finbar MacDonnell
17 Camden Passage, Islington. Open 10-6. STOCK: Decorative prints, mainly pre-1850. TEL: 071 226 0537.

The Mall Antiques Arcade
359 Upper St, Islington. (Atlantic Antiques Centres Ltd). Est. 1979. Open 10-5, Wed. 7.30-5, Sat. 9-6. CL: Mon. SIZE: Below are listed the dealers at this Arcade. LOC: 5 mins. from Angel tube station. PARK: Meters. TEL: 071 354 2839; enquiries - 071 351 5353.

S. and J. Afford   LAPADA
Stand G21. *Art nouveau, art deco, glass, ceramics.* TEL: Mobile - **0831 114909.**

Alexandra Alfandary
Stand G9. *Meissen porcelain.* TEL: 071 354 9762.

Alice Springs
Stand G28. (Mrs H. Dumbrell). *Antique jewellery and collectables.*

Alma Antiques
Stand G17. (T. and A. Goldstrom). *Miniatures, objects, watercolours and jewellery.* TEL: 071 359 9045.

N.1 continued
Antique Clocks - Terence Plank   LAPADA
Stand G23. *Clocks - longcase, bracket, wall, regulators, small mantel, carriage, skeleton and lantern; barographs and barometers.* TEL: **071 226 2426;** home - **0689 831431.**

Audley Art Ltd
Stand G20. (A. Singer). *Meissen porcelain and oil paintings.* TEL: 071 704 9507.

Louise Bannister
Stand G27. *Decorative items.* TEL: 071 226 6665.

Sonia Bottrill
Stand G1. *Silver, glass and jewellery.* TEL: 071 354 2839.

Mrs S. Bowen
Stand B6. *Furniture and associated items.* TEL: 071 704 0288.

John Carnie
Stand B5. *Barometers, scientific instruments, related accessories and small furniture.* TEL: 071 226 4992.

P. Collingridge
Stand G6. *Lighting items, brass, furniture.* TEL: 071 354 9189.

D. H. Glass
Stand G2. (Doreen White). *Glass.* TEL: 071 354 3349.

J. Donovan
Stand G10. *Art nouveau and art deco china and objets d'art.* TEL: 071 359 8416; mobile - 0836 277274.

Chris Dunn St. James
Stand G7. *Vintage jewellery.* TEL: 071 704 0127.

Jazy Antiques
Stand G14/15. (Mrs J. Zaziemski). *Porcelain.* TEL: 071 354 2333.

Patricia Kleinman
Stand G3. *English watercolours, 19th to early 20th C.* TEL: 071 704 0798.

Andrew Lineham
Stand G19. *Glass and porcelain.* TEL: 071 704 0195.

Monika
Stand G16. (M. Jartelius). *Fine period costume jewellery and accessories, 1920's-1950's.* TEL: 071 354 3125.

Linda Morgan Antiques
Stand G26. *Antique jewellery.* TEL: 071 359 0654.

D. L. Murphy
Stand G4/5. *Antique silver.* TEL: 071 345 1204.

LONDON

N.1 continued

Nadine Okker
Stand G8. *Porcelain, glass and bronzes.* TEL: 071 359 3541.

Mrs Sylvia Powell
Stand G18. *Decorative arts, art pottery, 1870-1940.* TEL: 071 354 2977.

Piers Rankin
Stand G24/25. *Silver and Sheffield plate.* TEL: 071 354 3349.

Gad Sassower
Stand G13. *Bakelite items, £10-£2,000; radios, early 20th C, £500-£1,000.* TEL: 071 354 4473.

Mike Weedon
Stand G12. *Art nouveau, art deco.* TEL: 071 226 5319.

Michael Young
Stand G22. *Decorative items.* TEL: 071 226 2225.

The Lower Mall

The Clock Studio
Stand B1. (George Riley). *Antique clocks and furniture.* TEL: 071 354 1719.

Peter Lehmann
Stand B8. *Furniture.* TEL: 071 704 0701.

Mrs C. Sidoli
Stand B4. *18th-19th C furniture, paintings and decorative accessories.*

Malcolm D. Stevens
Stand B9/10. *Furniture.* TEL: 071 359 1020.

Graham Woodage
Stand B3/4. *Furniture, clocks and accessories.* TEL: Mobile - 0836 332921.

Laurence Mitchell Antiques Ltd
LAPADA
13 Camden Passage, Islington. (L.P.J. Mitchell). Est. 1972. Open 10-4.30, Wed. 8-5. CL: Mon. except by appointment. STOCK: *European porcelain especially Meissen; English, Oriental and European ceramics, works of art, 18th-20th C.* TEL: **071 359 7579/226 1738.** VAT: Stan/Spec.

Number Nineteen
19 Camden Passage, Islington. (D. Griffiths and J. Wright). Open 10-5. STOCK: *Decorative antiques including bentwood, cane, garden and lacquered bamboo furniture; fairground animals and pub fittings.* TEL: 071 226 1126.

The Old Tool Chest
41 Cross St., Islington. (E.J. Maskell). Open 10-6. STOCK: *Woodworking tools.* TEL: 071 359 9313.

N.1 continued

Jacqueline Oosthuizen
1st Floor, Georgian Village, Camden Passage, Islington. Est. 1960. Open Wed. and Sat. 8-4. SIZE: Small. STOCK: *Staffordshire figures, 18th-19th C, £50-£10,000; jewellery, European and English ceramics, 18th-20th C.* PARK: Nearby. TEL: 071 226 5393/352 6071; answering service - 081 528 9001 (pager no.806930). VAT: Stan/Spec.

Kevin Page Oriental Art
2, 4 and 6 Camden Passage, Islington. Est. 1968. Open 10-4. CL: Mon. SIZE: Large. STOCK: *Oriental porcelain and furniture, cloisonné, bronzes, ivories.* LOC: 1 min. from Angel tube station. PARK: Easy. TEL: 071 226 8558. SER: Valuations. VAT: Stan.

Relic Antiques at Camden Passage
5 Angel Arcade, Camden Passage, Islington. (Malcolm Gliksten). Est. 1968. Open Wed. and Sat. 9-4.30. STOCK: *Näive art, figureheads and trade signs; fairground art; boat and plane models; toys and games, especially Noah's Arks, rocking horses, child's washstands; decorative items, French brocante and country furniture; original tea canisters and period shopfittings, £25-£1,250.* PARK: Meters. TEL: 071 359 9558/387 6039; home - 071 226 5216; fax - 071 388 2691. SER: Valuations; annual auction. VAT: Stan.

Rookery Farm Antiques
12 Camden Passage, Islington. STOCK: *Pine and country furniture.* TEL: 071 359 0190.

Marcus Ross Antiques
14/16 Pierrepont Row, Camden Passage, Islington. Est. 1972. Open 10.30-4.30. CL: Mon. STOCK: *Oriental porcelain, general antiques, Victorian walnut furniture.* TEL: 071 359 8494.

Robin Sims
7 Camden Passage, Islington. Est. 1970. Open Tues. and Fri. 10-4, Wed. and Sat. 8-5. SIZE: Small. STOCK: *General antiques, European and Scandinavian furniture, 1840-1920, £5-£5,000.* Not stocked: Large furniture. LOC: Near Angel underground station. PARK: Easy. TEL: 071 226 2393. VAT: Stan.

Keith Skeel Antique Warehouse
LAPADA
7-9 Elliotts Place. SIZE: Large. STOCK. *Interesting and unusual furniture.* TEL: **071 226 7012.** Trade Only.

Keith Skeel Antiques and Eccentricities
LAPADA
94/98 Islington High St. Est. 1969. Open 9-6 SIZE: Large. STOCK: *Interesting and unusual decorative items.* LOC: 1 min. from the Angel underground station. TEL: **071 359 9894/226 7012.** VAT: Stan. *Trade and Export Only.*

N.1 continued

Style
1 Ground Floor, Georgian Village, Camden Passage. (M. Webb and P. Coakley). Open Wed. 8-3, Sat. 9-4 or by appointment. STOCK: Art nouveau, WMF and Liberty pewter, art deco bronzes, ceramics and glass. TEL: 071 359 7867; home - 081 449 2588; mobile - 0831 229640.

Sugar Antiques
8-9 Pierrepont Arcade, Camden Passage, Islington. (Elayne and Tony Sugarman). Est. 1980. Open Wed. 6.30-4, Sat. 9-4, other times by appointment. SIZE: Medium. STOCK: Wrist and pocket watches, 19th-20th C, £25-£2,000; fountain pens and lighters, early 20th C to 1960's, £15-£1,000; costume jewellery and collectables, 19th-20th C, £5-£500. PARK: Meters. TEL: 071 354 9896 (answerphone). SER: Repairs (as stock); buys at auction (as stock). VAT: Stan.

Swan Fine Art
120 Islington High St., Camden Passage. (P. Child). Open 10-5, Wed. and Sat. 9-5 or by appointment. SIZE: Medium. STOCK: Paintings, fine and decorative sporting and animal, portraits, 17th-19th C, £500-£25,000+. PARK: Easy, except Wed. and Sat. TEL: 071 226 5335; mobile - 0860 795336. VAT: Spec.

Tadema Gallery   LAPADA
10 Charlton Place, Camden Passage, Islington. (S. and D. Newell-Smith). Est. 1978. Open 10-5 and by appointment. CL: Mon. and Thurs. SIZE: Medium. STOCK: Modern British and continental paintings and sculpture; 20th C decorative art including jewellery. PARK: Reasonable. TEL: 071 359 1055 (ansaphone). SER: Valuations. VAT: Stan.

The Textile Company   LAPADA
P.O. Box 2800. (J. Wentworth). Est. 1982. Open by appointment only. STOCK: 18th C silks, British and French printed cottons, patchworks, lace 1600-1850, good Paisley and Kashmir shawls, period costume and accessories. Not stocked: Tapestries, upholstery, cushions. PARK: Easy. TEL: 071 254 3256. SER: Valuations.

Titus Omega
Shop 11, Ground Floor, Georgian Village, Camden Passage. (John Featherstone-Harvey). Est. 1986. Open Wed. 8-4, Sat. 9-4. SIZE: Small. STOCK: Art nouveau, 1890-1910, £700-£3,000. LOC: Islington Green. TEL: 071 226 1571; ansaphone - 071 607 8996. SER: Valuations; buys at auction (art nouveau).

"Turn On" Lighting Ltd
116/118 Islington High St., Camden Passage. Est. 1976. STOCK: Lighting, 1840-1940. TEL: 071 359 7616.

N.1 continued

Leigh Underhill Gallery
100 Islington High St. Est. 1950. Open 9-6. CL: Mon. and Tues. SIZE: Medium. STOCK: Paintings, drawings, sculpture, etchings, works of art. PARK: Meters. TEL: 071 226 5673. VAT: Spec.

Vane House Antiques
15 Camden Passage, Islington. (M. Till and B. Snyder). Est. 1950. Open 10-5. STOCK: 18th to early 19th C furniture. TEL: 071 359 1343. VAT: Stan/Spec.

Mark J. West - Cobb Antiques Ltd
15 Georgian Village, Camden Passage, Islington. Open Wed. and Sat. or by appointment. STOCK: 18th-19th C glasses and decanters; 19th C engraved, cut and coloured glass; decorative antiques. TEL: 071 359 8686; home - 081 540 7982. SER: Valuations. FAIRS: Olympia. VAT: Stan.

Yesterday Child   LAPADA
Angel Arcade, 118 Islington High St. (D. Barrington and G. Wegner). Est. 1970. Open Wed. and Sat. 7.30-3. SIZE: Small. STOCK: Dolls, 1800-1925, £25-£5,000. PARK: Easy. TEL: 071 354 1601; home and fax - 0908 583403. SER: Valuations; restorations. VAT: Stan/Spec.

York Arcade
80 Islington High St., Camden Passage. Open 10-5. CL: Mon. SIZE: 16 dealers. LOC: At top of Camden Passage, 1 min. from Angel tube - Northern Line. PARK: Duncan St. TEL: 071 833 2640. Below are listed some of the dealers at this arcade.

Delmar Art
Unit 8. *Old Masters.*

Dog Box
Unit 6. *Cat and dog items.*

Featherbrain
Unit 4. *Books and related items, pens.*

Fitzgerald
Unit 3. *Jewellery and luggage.*

Inga
Unit 9. *General antiques.*

Inspirations
Unit 11, 12. *Costume jewellery and accessories.*

Terence Parker-Hall
Unit 1. *Art deco, early plastics, radios and 20th C paintings.*

Past and Present
Unit 7. *Ceramics including Clarice Cliff.*

Sarah
Unit 10. *Furniture.*

N.1 continued

John Stroud
Unit 13. *Carpets.*

Almut Wager
Unit 5. *Early jewellery and glass.*

William Wain
Unit 2. *Costume jewellery and accessories.*

LONDON N.2

Amazing Grates
Phoenix House, 61-63 High Rd., East Finchley. (E. Martin). Resident. Est. 1971. Open 10-6. SIZE: Large. *STOCK: Mantelpieces, grates and fireside items, £200-£5,000; Victorian tiling, £2-£20; early ironwork, all 19th C.* LOC: 100yds. north of East Finchley tube station. PARK: Own. TEL: 081 883 9590/6017. SER: Valuations; restorations (ironwork, welding of cast iron and brazing, polishing); installations. VAT: Stan.

The Antique Shop (Valantique)
9 Fortis Green. (Mrs V. Steel). Open 11-6. SIZE: Medium. *STOCK: General antiques especially original lighting and fenders; small furniture, pottery, porcelain, glass, oil paintings, watercolours, prints, mirrors, copper, brass, unusual items, £5-£500.* LOC: 2 mins. from East Finchley tube station. PARK: Side street. TEL: 081 883 7651. SER: Buys at auction.

Martin Henham (Antiques)
218 High Rd, East Finchley. Open 10-6. SIZE: Medium. *STOCK: Furniture, 1710-1920, £5-£1,700; paintings, 1650-1900, £10-£1,000; porcelain, 1750-1920, £5-£1,000.* PARK: Easy. TEL: 081 444 5274. SER: Valuations; restorations (furniture and paintings); buys at auction. VAT: Stan/Spec.

Lauri Stewart - Fine Art
36 Church Lane. Open 10-5. CL: Thurs. *STOCK: Modern British oils and watercolours.* TEL: 081 883 7719. SER: Restorations (oils, watercolours); framing.

LONDON N.3

Park Galleries
20 Hendon Lane, Finchley. Est. 1978. Open 10-6. *STOCK: English watercolours, 18th-20th C; oil paintings and prints.* TEL: 081 346 2176.

LONDON N.4

Marion Gray
33 Crouch Hill. (R.J. Orton). Est. 1955. Open 10-6. CL: Sun. except by appointment. SIZE: Large. *STOCK: Furniture, 17th-19th C, objets d'art.* LOC: Next to Crouch Hill station. TEL: 071 272 0372. SER: Restorations; upholstery. VAT: Stan/Spec.

N.4 continued

Teger Trading and Bushe Antiques
Manor Warehouse, 318 Green Lanes. *STOCK: Antique and reproduction garden statuary, lamps, art deco, art nouveau, animalier, oriental and classical style figures.* TEL: 081 802 0156; fax - 081 802 4110. SER: Restorations; film hire. Trade Only.

LONDON N.5

North London Clock Shop Ltd
72 Highbury Park. (D.S. Tomlin). Est. 1960. Open 9-6. CL: Sat. SIZE: Medium. *STOCK: Clocks, longcase, bracket, carriage, skeleton, 18th-19th C.* LOC: Turn off Seven Sisters Rd. into Blackstock Rd., continue on to Highbury Park. PARK: Easy. TEL: 071 226 1609. SER: Restorations (clocks and barometer); wheel cutting, hand engraving, dial painting, clock reconversions. FAIRS: Olympia. VAT: Stan.

Petherton Antiques
124 Petherton Rd. (V.E. Illingworth). Est. 1987. Open 10.30-6, Thurs. by appointment. CL: Mon. SIZE: Small. *STOCK: Furniture, Georgian to early 20th C, £30-£2,000; boxes, pottery and porcelain, paintings and prints, silver, small decorative items, Victorian and early 20th C, £5-£800.* LOC: Off Balls Pond Rd. PARK: Easy. TEL: 071 226 6597; home - 071 359 5856. SER: Restorations (furniture); buys at auction (furniture).

G.W. Walford
15 Calabria Rd, Highbury Fields. Est. 1951. Open 9.30-5. CL: Sat. *STOCK: Antiquarian books especially illustrated.* TEL: 071 226 5682.

LONDON N.6

John Beer
c/o Richardsons of Highgate, 191-199 Archway Rd., Highgate. Open 9-1 and 2-5. CL: Thurs. *STOCK: Furniture, 1830-1960s especially English arts and crafts, Gothic and art deco.* LOC: 300yds. south Highgate tube station. PARK: Easy. TEL: 0242 576080; mobile - 0860 767194. SER: Valuations; buys at auction. VAT: Stan/Spec.

Centaur Gallery
82 Highgate High St, Highgate Village. (J. and D. Wieliczko). Est. 1960. Open 11-6. *STOCK: 18th to early 19th C oil paintings, watercolours, prints, sculpture, ethnic and folk art, unusual items.* TEL: 081 340 0087.

Fisher and Sperr
46 Highgate High St. (J.R. Sperr). Est. 1945. Open daily 10.30-6. SIZE: Large. *STOCK: Books, 15th C to date.* LOC: From centre of Highgate Village, nearest underground stations Archway (Highgate), Highgate. PARK: Easy. TEL: 081 340 7244. SER: Valuations; restorations (books); buys at auction. VAT: Stan.

Finchley Fine Art Galleries

983 High Road, N. Finchley, London N12 8QR 081-446 4848

200 plus fine 18-20th Century English watercolours and paintings in a constantly changing stock. Four galleries of good quality Georgian, Victorian and Edwardian furniture, pottery, porcelain, smalls, etc.

OPENING TIMES:
TUES, THURS, FRI,
SAT, SUN, 12.30-7.00.
MON,WEDS BY APPOINTMENT

George Cattermole 1800-1868
The Arrest of Charles 1st at Holenby
Watercolour $18^{1}/4 \times 26^{1}/2$

N.6 continued

Betty Gould and Julian Gonnermann Antiques
408-410 Archway Rd, Highgate. Est. 1964. Open 10-5.30, Sat. 9.30-5.30. CL: Thurs. SIZE: Medium. STOCK: Furniture, 18th-20th C, £50-£5,000. LOC: On A1, just below Highgate tube station. PARK: Shepherds Hill. TEL: 081 340 4987. SER: Restorations; French polishing; upholstery.

Home to Home
355c Archway Rd. Open 9.30-6.30. STOCK: Mainly occasional Victorian and Edwardian and some Georgian furniture. TEL: 081 340 8354.

D.M. and P. Manheim (Peter Manheim) Ltd BADA
P.O. Box 1259. (P. Manheim). Est. 1926. Open by appointment only. STOCK: English porcelain, pottery and enamels, 1680-1820. TEL: 081 340 9211. VAT: Spec.

LONDON N.7

Tsar Architectural
487 Liverpool Rd. (A. Purcell and C. Turner). Open 9.30-7. STOCK: Fireplaces and associated items. TEL: 071 609 4238. SER: Restorations.

LONDON N.8

Crouch End Antiques
47 Park Rd, Crouch End. (M.V. Kairis). Est. 1979. Open 10-6. SIZE: Medium. STOCK: Furniture, 19th C, £100-£1,000. LOC: Corner of Shanklin Rd. TEL: 081 348 7652. SER: Valuations; restorations; renovation materials supplied. FAIRS: Alexandra Palace. VAT: Stan/Spec.

Sandra Lummis Fine Art
Flat 7, 17 Haslemere Rd. (Mrs. S. Lummis and Dr T. Lummis). Est. 1985. Viewing by appointment.

N.8 continued

CL: Aug. STOCK: British art (Modernist school), 20th C from Sickert to contemporary, especially Bloomsbury painters, £500-£50,000. LOC: From Highgate Hill, along Hornsey Lane, left at 'T' junction, then 1st right. PARK: Easy. TEL: 081 340 2293; home - same. SER: Commissions; valuations; advice on restoration and framing. VAT: Spec.

LONDON N.10

M.E. Korn
47 Tetherdown, Muswell Hill. (E. Korn). ABA, PBFA. Est. 1971. Open by appointment. STOCK: Books - natural history, medical, science, art and literature, 16th-19th C, £10-£1,000. TEL: 081 883 5251. SER: Valuations; buys at auction (antiquarian books). FAIRS: PBFA, Russell Hotel monthly; York, Oxford, Cambridge; ABAA in California, Boston, New York and Toronto.

LONDON N.12

Finchley Fine Art Galleries
983 High Rd., North Finchley. (S. Greenman). Est. 1972Open 12.30-7 including Sun; Mon. and Wed. by appointment. SIZE: Large. STOCK: 18th-20th C watercolours, paintings, etchings, prints, mostly English, £25-£10,000; Georgian, Victorian, Edwardian furniture, to £4,000; china and porcelain - Moorcroft, Doulton, Worcester, Clarice Cliff, £5-£2,000; musical and scientific instruments, bronzes, early photographic apparatus, fire-arms, shotguns. LOC: Off M25, junction 23, take Barnet road. Gallery on right 3 miles south of Barnet church, opposite Britannia Road. PARK: Easy. TEL: 081 446 4848. SER: Valuations; restorations; framing.

LONDON N.13
Trader Antiques
484 Green Lanes, Palmers Green. (M. Webb). Open 10.30-5. *STOCK: Stripped pine, glass, furniture and general antiques.* TEL: 081 886 9552.

LONDON N.14
C.J. Martin (Coins) Ltd
85 The Vale, Southgate. Open by appointment. *STOCK: Ancient and medieval coins and ancient artefacts.* TEL: 081 882 1509/4359.

LONDON N.16
139 Antiques
139 Green Lanes. (F. Clifton). Open 9-5. CL: Thurs. *STOCK: General antiques mainly tables and chairs.* TEL: 071 354 2466.

W. Forster
83a Stamford Hill. Est. 1952. Open by appointment. *STOCK: Bibliography and books about books.* LOC: Nearest station Manor House (Piccadilly Line) or 253 bus to Stamford Hill Broadway. PARK: Easy. TEL: 081 800 3919.

LONDON N.19
Curios
130c Junction Rd, Archway. Open 12-7 including Sun. *STOCK: Decorative objects especially unusual items; general antiques, pictures, taxidermy and fireplaces.* TEL: 071 272 5603.

LONDON N.20
The Totteridge Gallery
61 Totteridge Lane. Est. 1979. Open daily, Sun. by appointment. SIZE: Small. *STOCK: Oil paintings, £1,000-£25,000; watercolours, £300-£10,000; both 18th to early 20th C. Limited edition Russell Flint prints, 20th C, £500-£3,000.* LOC: Opposite Totteridge and Whetstone tube station. PARK: Easy. TEL: 081 446 7896. SER: Valuations; restorations; frame repairs. VAT: Stan/Spec.

LONDON N.21
Dolly Land
864 Green Lanes, Winchmore Hill. Est. 1977. Open 9.30-4.30. CL: Mon. and Wed. SIZE: Small. *STOCK: Toys including dolls, teddy bears, trains and die-cast, 18th-19th C, £5-£1,000.* PARK: Easy. TEL: 081 360 1053. SER: Valuations; restorations; buys at auction (toys). FAIRS: Doll and Bear.

The Little Curiosity Shop
24 The Green, Winchmore Hill. (Mrs H. Freedman). Est. 1967. Open 10.30-5. CL: Wed. *STOCK: Clocks, porcelain, general antiques, mostly Victorian, bronzes, silver, music boxes, jewellery and diamond items.* LOC: Nearest stations - Winchmore Hill (Eastern Region), and Southgate (Piccadilly Line underground). PARK: Easy. TEL: 081 886 0925. VAT: Stan. *Trade Only.*

N.21 continued
Piermont Antiques Ltd
7 Wades Hill, Winchmore Hill. (G. and K. Pierssene). Est. 1969. Open 10-5, Sat. 10-1 and 2.15-6. CL: Wed. SIZE: Small. *STOCK: Furniture, porcelain, jewellery and silver, linen and collectables, all pre-1939, £1-£700.* PARK: Easy. TEL: 081 886 2486. SER: Valuations.

Winchmore Antiques
14 The Green, Winchmore Hill. (David Hicks and Stewart Christian). Open 10-6. SIZE: Medium. *STOCK: General antiques, £1-£500; architectural brass fittings, vintage lamps and spare parts; all 18th-20th C.* LOC: Junction of 5 roads, at east end of Broad Walk. PARK: Easy. TEL: 081 882 4800. SER: Valuations; restorations (metal polishing, silver plating, oil lamps). VAT: Stan.

LONDON N.W.1
Acquisitions (Fireplaces) Ltd
4-6 Jamestown Road. (K. Kennedy). Est. 1970. Open 9.30-5. SIZE: Medium. *STOCK: Fireplaces, Georgian, Victorian, Edwardian and reproduction, fire-side accessories, £195-£595.* LOC: 3 mins. walk from Camden Town tube station (Camden High St.). PARK: Easy. TEL: 071 485 4955. VAT: Stan.

Adams Antiques
47 Chalk Farm Rd. (Stephen Copsey). Est. 1982. Open 10-6 including Sun. SIZE: Large. *STOCK: Continental pine, 18th C, £150-£2,000.* TEL: 071 267 9241. VAT: Stan.

Art Furniture (London) Ltd
158 Camden St. Open 12-5 including Sun. SIZE: Warehouse. *STOCK: Arts and crafts, art nouveau and art deco furniture, fixtures and fittings, £50-£5,000; bentwood and Lloyd loom.* LOC: Under railway bridge on Camden St. going south. PARK: Easy. TEL: 071 267 4324. SER: Restorations; repolishing. VAT: Stan.

Barkes and Barkes
76 Parkway. (J.N. and P. R. Barkes). Est. 1976. Open Thurs., Fri. and Sat. 12-6. SIZE: Small. *STOCK: Paintings and watercolours, 20th C, £200-£5,000.* LOC: Just north of Regents Park. PARK: Next street. TEL: 071 284 1550. VAT: Spec.

Ian Crispin Antiques
95 Lisson Grove. Est. 1971. Open 10-5. *STOCK: General antiques and shipping goods.* TEL: 071 402 6845. VAT: Stan. *Trade Only.*

East-Asia Co
103 Camden High St. Est. 1972. Open 10-6. *STOCK: Oriental antiquarian books on history and culture; Japanese and Chinese paintings and prints; jade, netsuke, objets d'art; books on Oriental art.* TEL: 071 388 5783; fax - 071 387 5766.

N.W.1 continued
Hearth and Home
13 Chalk Farm Rd. (C. Heath and M.P.W. Smith). Open 10-6 including Sun. *STOCK: Pine furniture, garden statuary and giftware.* LOC: Opposite Camden Lock market. PARK: Easy. TEL: 071 485 9687. SER: Valuations. VAT: Stan/Spec.

Jazzy Art Deco
67 Camden Rd. (J. Eccles and V. Davies). Open 12-6, Sat. 11-6. CL: Mon. *STOCK: Art deco furniture and decorative items.* LOC: Close to Camden Tube Station. TEL: 071 267 3342; home - 081 960 8988.

Richard Kihl (Wine Accessories) Ltd
164 Regents Park Rd, Primrose Hill. Est. 1979. Open 9.30-5, Sat. 11-1 and 2-5. CL: Mon. and Fri. SIZE: Small. *STOCK: Wine related antiques - decanters, claret jugs, coasters, glass, decanting cradles, corkscrews, glass funnels, old bottles, taste vins, 1750-1910, £5-£2,000.* LOC: Close to London Zoo and Primrose Hill. PARK: Easy. TEL: 071 586 5911; fax - 071 586 2960. SER: Restorations (glass). VAT: Stan.

Laurence Corner
62-64 Hampstead Rd. Est. 1967. Open 9.30-6. SIZE: Large. *STOCK: Uniforms - ambassadorial and court dress, swords, helmets, drums; theatrical costumes, props, fancy dress, flags; prints and paintings.* LOC: From Tottenham Court Rd. - Warren St. end - continue into Hampstead Rd., then Drummond St. is first turning on right by traffic lights. PARK: Easy. TEL: 071 388 6811; fax - 071 383 0334. SER: Hire.

McClenaghan-Gilhooly Antiques
125 Camden Mews. (J. McClenaghan). Resident. Open by appointment. SIZE: Medium. *STOCK: Furniture - British country house, Gothic revival and pale oak, £200-£10,000; objects, lighting and works of art, £100-£5,000; all 19th C.* LOC: Parallel to Camden Road. PARK: Easy. TEL: 071 485 7755. VAT: Stan/Spec.

David Miles
Open by appointment. *STOCK: Musical instruments.* TEL: 071 485 1329.

Regent Antiques
9-10 Chester Court, Albany St. (T. Quaradeghini). Est. 1983. Open 10-5.30, Sat. by appointment. SIZE: Large and warehouse. *STOCK: Furniture, 18th C to Edwardian, £50-£5,000+; decorative items and bric-a-brac, 19th-20th C, £10-£1,000.* LOC: 1/4 mile from Gt. Portland St. station towards Camden Town. PARK: Easy. TEL: 071 935 6941; fax - 071 935 7814. SER: Restorations (furniture); gilding. VAT: Stan. *Trade Only.*

Relic Antiques Trade Warehouse
127 Pancras Rd. (M. Gliksten and G. Gower). Est. 1968. Open 10-5.30, Sat. 11-5. *STOCK: Original pond yacht models; ornate French mirrors; small*

N.W.1 continued
decorative items and brocante; näive, advertising and fairground art. PARK: Meters. TEL: 071 387 6039; home - 071 226 5216; fax - 071 388 2691. SER: Valuations. VAT: Stan.

Spatz
4 Castlehaven Rd. (P. Ebbenkhuyson and S. Anchor). Est. 1979. Open Fri. 12-5.30, Sat. and Sun. 11-5.30. SIZE: Small. *STOCK: Victorian lace pillowcases and nightdresses, £19-£40; 1940's dresses, blouses and other daywear, £20-£60.* LOC: At Camden Lock. PARK: NCP nearby. TEL: 071 482 3785. VAT: Stan.

Strike One (Islington) Ltd   BADA
33 Balcombe Street. (J. Mighell). Est. 1968. Open by appointment. SIZE: Medium. *STOCK: Clocks, pre-1870, especially early English wall and Act of Parliament, £2,000-£15,000; English longcase, 1675-1820, £3,000-£40,000; English bracket, lantern, skeleton and French carriage; Vienna regulators; barometers, music boxes, horological books.* PARK: Easy. TEL: 071 224 9719; home - same. SER: Valuations; restorations (clocks, barometers); catalogue available. VAT: Stan/Spec.

This and That (Furniture)
50 and 51 Chalk Farm Rd. (R.P. Schanzer). Est. 1974. Open 10.30-6 including Sun. SIZE: Medium. *STOCK: Country furniture, stripped pine, oak and walnut, 1880-1900.* LOC: Between Roundhouse and Camden Lock. PARK: Easy. TEL: 071 267 5433. VAT: Stan.

Victorian Fireplace Co
53 Camden Lock Place, Chalk Farm Rd., Camden Town. (Geoffrey Moore). Est. 1983. Open 10.30-5, Sun. 10-6. CL Mon. and Tues. SIZE: Small. *STOCK: Fireplaces, £95-£550; fireplace accessories, £10-£125; both 19th C.* LOC: Off junction with Camden High St. PARK: Easy weekdays. TEL: 071 482 2543. SER: Restorations (cast-iron refurbishment, repair and welding). VAT: Stan.

W.E. Walker
277/279 Camden High St. Est. 1930. Open 10-6, weekends by appointment. SIZE: Medium. *STOCK: Furniture, 17th-19th C; modern paintings and ceramics.* PARK: Easy. TEL: 071 485 6210/4433. SER: Valuations; restorations (china). VAT: Spec.

LONDON N.W.2
The Corner Cupboard
679 Finchley Rd. (M. Fry and R. Fischelis). Est. 1950. Open 9.30-5.30. SIZE: Small. *STOCK: Jewellery, 18th-19th C, from £5; silver, china, glass.* LOC: Number 2 or 13 bus from Central London. PARK: Easy. TEL: 071 435 4870. VAT: Stan.

N.W.2 continued

G. and F. Gillingham Ltd LAPADA
62 Menelik Rd. Est. 1960. Open by appointment. STOCK: *19th C English and continental furniture.* TEL: 071 435 5644. *Export Only.*

Gunter Fine Art
4 Randall Ave. (G.A. and A.M. Goodwin). Est. 1977. Open by appointment only. SIZE: Small. STOCK: *Watercolours, 18th-20th C, £150-£3,000; oil paintings, 19th-20th C £200-£3,000.* LOC: North Circular Rd., near Brent Cross shopping centre. PARK: Easy. TEL: 081 452 3997. SER: Buys at auction.

Elizabeth Harvey-Lee
1 Belton Rd. IFPDA. Est. 1986. Open by appointment. STOCK: *Original prints 15th-20th C; artists' etchings, engravings, lithographs, £100-£6,000.* TEL: 081 459 7623. SER: Illustrated stock catalogues to subscribers (£10 p.a.); valuations; collections catalogued. FAIRS: London Original Print - Royal Academy. VAT: Spec.

Soviet Carpet and Art Centre
303-305 Cricklewood Broadway. (S. Rabilizirov). Est. 1983. Open 10.30-5, Sun. 10.30-6. CL: Sat. SIZE: Large. STOCK: *Hand-made rugs, 19th-20th C, £500-£1,000; fine and applied art, 20th C, £100-£500.* LOC: A5. PARK: Side road. TEL: 081 452 2445. SER: Valuations; restorations (hand-made rugs); buys at auction (hand-made rugs, Russian art). VAT: Stan.

"The Stove Shop"
(P. Crabb). Open by appointment. STOCK: *Original Scandinavian, French and English stoves and cooking ranges.* TEL: 081 208 0925. SER: Restorations; installations; hire and consultancy.

LONDON N.W.3

Nan S. Ashcroft
10a Daleham Gardens. Open by appointment. STOCK: *Fine and rare wine related artefacts and glass.* TEL: 071 794 6658.

Patricia Beckman LAPADA
Est. 1968. Open by appointment. STOCK: *Furniture, 18th-19th C.* TEL: 071 435 5050. VAT: Spec.

Tony Bingham LAPADA
11 Pond St. Est. 1964. STOCK: *Musical instruments, books, music, oil paintings, engravings of musical interest.* TEL: 071 794 1596; fax - 071 433 3662. VAT: Stan/Spec.

P.G. de Lotz
20 Downside Cres, Hampstead. ABA. Est. 1967. STOCK: *Antiquarian books on history warfare - naval, military and aviation.* TEL: 071 794 5709; fax - 071 284 3058. SER: Catalogue available; search. *Postal Only.*

N.W.3 continued

Dolphin Coins
2c England's Lane, Hampstead. (R. Ilsley). BNTA. Est. 1966. Open 9.30-5. SIZE: Medium. STOCK: *British and world coins, early and medieval, from 100BC, £20-£50,000.* LOC: Off Haverstock HIll. PARK: Easy. TEL: 071 722 4116; fax - 071 483 2000. SER: Valuations; buys at auction (coins). VAT: Spec.

Stephen Farrelly
152 Fleet Rd. Est. 1948. Open 10-6. CL: Thurs. STOCK: *Pictures, furniture, porcelain, general antiques.* TEL: 071 485 2089.

Keith Fawkes
1-3 Flask Walk, Hampstead. Est. 1970. Open 10-5.30. STOCK: *Antiquarian and general books.* TEL: 071 435 0614.

M. and R. Glendale
Box No 2863. (R. Sands and M.D. Sears). ABA, PBFA. Open by appointment. STOCK: *Books including children's, illustrated and cookery.* TEL: 071 794 4827/431 6170.

Otto Haas (A. and M. Rosenthal)
49 Belsize Park Gardens. Est. 1866. Open 9.30-5 or by appointment. CL: Sat. STOCK: *Manuscripts, printed music, autographs, rare books or music.* TEL: 071 722 1488; fax - 071 722 2364.

Hampstead Antique Emporium
12 Heath St, Hampstead. Est. 1967. Open 10-6 CL: Mon. SIZE: 25 dealers. STOCK: *Jewellery furniture, silver, paintings, prints, metalware glass, lighting, porcelain, collectors' items and objets d'art,18th-19th C.* LOC: 2 mins. walk from Hampstead underground. TEL: 071 794 3297 office - 071 431 0240. SER: Advice (interio decor). The following are a few of the dealers a the Emporium.

Ryba Ala
Jewellery and glass.

Barbara
Tiles, paperweights and collectables.

A. Cheraghzade
Brass figures, china, glass, small furniture.

Sheila Feller
Children's books.

E. Gardner
Furniture, boxes and early prints.

Jackson Antiques
Small furniture, boxes and bronzes.

Lee and Stacey
General antiques, furniture, silver, fine art.

Hammond Leigh
Silver, frames, jewellery.

LONDON

N.W.3 continued

Meadway Books
Children's and illustrated books, modern first editions.

Mount Gallery
18th-20th C pictures.

A. Nassar
Antiquarian travel books.

E. O'Dwyer
Porcelain, glass, small furniture.

Ross Pye
19th C furniture, decorative items, mirrors and small collectables.

D. Quastel
Silver frames and cutlery.

Recollections
Pine furniture and kitchenalia.

Scorpio Antiques
Jewellery and silver.

Shelagh
Small furniture and objets d'art.

Trio
(Miss S. Mendoza). Furniture, porcelain and glass. VAT: Stan.

Platon Hobson
34 Belsize Park Gardens. Est. 1980. Open by appointment. *STOCK: Cushions- 17th C tapestry, 18th C Beauvais tapestries, Aubussons and needleworks, some 19th C, £60-£1,000; decorative objects, furniture and pictures, 18th-19th C, from £100.* LOC: 5 mins. from Belsize Park tube station. PARK: Easy. TEL: 071 722 3703; home - same. SER: Restorations (textiles, some furniture). FAIRS: Decorative. VAT: Stan/Spec. *Trade Only.*

Kendal Antiques LAPADA
91A Heath St, Hampstead. (T.R.G. Brazier). Open 10-6. CL: Mon. SIZE: Small. *STOCK: English Georgian, Victorian and Edwardian furniture, china, porcelain, copper, brass, smalls, oils and watercolours.* LOC: Hampstead Village. PARK: Nearby. TEL: 071 435 4351; workshop - 0480 411 811. SER: Restorations. VAT: Stan/Spec.

Leask Ward LAPADA
Open by appointment only. *STOCK: European and Oriental antiques and paintings.* TEL: 071 435 9781.

John Lyons Gallery
18 South Hill Park, Hampstead. Resident. Est. 1968. Appointment essential. SIZE: Small. *STOCK: Art nouveau, art deco, 20th C paintings, studio ceramics and art glass.* PARK: Easy. TEL: 071 794 3537. SER: Buys at auction.

N.W.3 continued

Duncan R. Miller Fine Arts BADA
17 Flask Walk, Hampstead. SLAD. Open 10-6, Sat. 11-5, Sun. 2-5. SIZE: Small. *STOCK: Modern British and European paintings, drawings and sculpture, especially Scottish Colourist paintings, from £500.* LOC: Off Hampstead High St., near underground station. PARK: Nearby. TEL: 071 435 5462. SER: Valuations; conservation and restoration (oils, works on paper and Oriental rugs); buys at auction. FAIRS: Contemporary Art; Fine Art, Olympia; 20th C British Art; World of Watercolours. VAT: Spec.

Frederick Mulder
83 Belsize Park Gardens. Open by appointment. *STOCK: Old Master and modern original prints; modern illustrated books.* TEL: 071 722 2105; fax - 071 483 4228.

Newhart (Pictures) Ltd
PO Box 1608. (Ann and Bernard Hart). Open by appointment only. *STOCK: Oil paintings and watercolours, 1850-1930, from £500.* TEL: 071 722 2537; fax - 071 722 4335. SER: Valuations; restorations; framing. VAT: Spec.

Osborn Baker Gallery
3 Erskine Rd, Primrose Hill. (L.W. Baker and R.E. Osborn). Est. 1985. Open 10-5. SIZE: Small. *STOCK: Watercolours, 19th C, £100-£500; silver, 18th-19th C, £50-£800; furniture, 17th-19th C, £200-£1,500.* LOC: Off Regents Park Rd. PARK: Easy. TEL: 071 722 1478; home - 081 363 1489. SER: Valuations; restorations (furniture); framing; buys at auction (pictures and furniture). VAT: Stan/Spec

LONDON N.W.4

Talking Machine
30 Watford Way, Hendon. Open 10-5.30, Sat. 11-5. *STOCK: Mechanical music, old gramophones, phonographs, vintage records and 78's, needles and spare parts, early radio, typewriters, sewing machines, juke boxes, early telephones.* TEL: 081 202 3473. SER: Buys at auction. VAT: Stan.

LONDON N.W.5

Y. and B. Bolour
53-79 Highgate Rd. Open 9.30-5.30. CL: Sat. *STOCK: Decorative carpets, rugs and tapestries.* TEL: 071 485 6262; fax - 071 267 7351.

Game Advice
23 Holmes Rd. (S. Elithorn). Est. 1976. Open by appointment only. SIZE: Small. *STOCK: Games, puzzles, jigsaws, cards, educational toys, chess sets; chess, cookery and children's books, £25-£100; ephemera, £5-£50; all 18th-19th C.* LOC: Just off Kentish Town Rd. PARK: Easy. TEL: 071 485 4226. SER: Valuations; restorations; buys at auction. VAT: Stan.

N.W.5 continued
Joseph Lavian
Block 'F', 53-79 Highgate Rd. Est. 1950. Open 9-6. SIZE: Large. STOCK: Oriental carpets, rugs, kelims, tapestries and needlework, Aubusson, Savonnerie and textiles, 17th-19th C. LOC: Kentish Town Station. PARK: Own. TEL: 071 485 7955/482 1234; fax - 071 267 9222. SER: Valuations; restorations.

Barrie Marks Ltd
11 Laurier Rd. ABA. Open by appointment only. STOCK: Antiquarian books - illustrated, private press, colourplate, colour printing; modern first editions. TEL: 071 482 5684; fax - 071 284 3149.

Zoulfaghari
Unit D, 4th Floor, 53-79 Highgate Rd. Est. 1974. Open 9.30-5.30. CL: Sat. SIZE: Large. STOCK: Persian carpets and rugs. LOC: Kentish Town. PARK: Own. TEL: 071 267 5973 (24hrs). SER: Valuations; restorations; buys at auction; cleaning.

LONDON N.W.6
The Barewood Company
58 Mill Lane, West Hampstead. (Arne Kaplan). Open 9-5.30, Sat. 10-4. SIZE: Small. STOCK: Pine furniture including chests of drawers, tables and doors, 19th C, £50-£400+. LOC: Between West End Lane and Kilburn High Rd. PARK: Easy. TEL: 071 435 7244. SER: Valuations; restorations (pine). VAT: Stan.

H. Baron
76 Fortune Green Rd. Open Fri. and Sat. 1-6. STOCK: Antiquarian music, books on music and iconography, autograph music and letters. TEL: 071 794 4041; office and fax - 081 459 2035.

Mr. Temple Brooks
12 Mill Lane, West Hampstead. Resident. Est. 1936. Always available. STOCK: Clocks and watches. TEL: 081 452 9696. VAT: Spec.

John Denham Gallery
50 Mill Lane, West Hampstead. Open 10-5. CL: Sat. STOCK: Paintings, drawings and prints, 17th-20th C, £5-£5,000. TEL: 071 794 2635. SER: Restorations; conservation; re-framing. VAT: Spec.

Gallery Kaleidoscope
66 Willesden Lane. (K. Barrie). Est. 1965. Open 10-6. SIZE: Medium. STOCK: Oils, watercolours, prints, pottery and sculpture, 19th-20th C. LOC: 10 mins. from Marble Arch. PARK: Easy. TEL: 071 328 5833. SER: Restorations; framing. VAT: Stan/Spec.

Scope Antiques
64-66 Willesden Lane. (K. Barrie). Est. 1966. Open 10-6. SIZE: Large. STOCK: Furniture, general antiques, decorative items, silver, bric-a-brac. PARK: Easy. TEL: 071 328 5833. SER: Restorations (silver). VAT: Stan/Spec.

N.W.6 continued
G.T. Siden
69 Compayne Gardens. Open by appointment only. STOCK: 16th-19th C drawings. TEL: 071 624 9045.

LONDON N.W.7
Gerald Clark Antiques
1 High St, Mill Hill Village. (G.J. Clark). Est. 1976. Open by appointment. SIZE: Medium. STOCK: Early English and Victorian Staffordshire pottery, porcelain, small furniture, watercolours and plaques, 18th-19th C. PARK: Easy. TEL: 081 906 0342/958 4295. SER: Valuations; buys at auction. FAIRS: Olympia (June); Kensington (Jan. and Aug.); Barbican (Nov.). VAT: Spec.

LONDON N.W.8
Alfies Antique Market
13-25 Church St. (B. Gray). Open 10-6. CL: Mon. SIZE: 370 stands on 5 floors. TEL: 071 723 6066. Below are listed the dealers at this market.

Accurate Trading Co.
Stand G30. *Jewellery.* TEL: 071 723 1513.

Beth Adams
Stand G43/4. *Art deco.* TEL: 071 723 5613.

Reza Aramesh
Stand F109/111. *Carpets.* TEL: 071 723 1370.

R. S. Benjamin
Stand S121/134. *Paperweights, glass, pottery.* TEL: 071 723 5731.

David Bennett
Stand G124. *General.* TEL: 071 724 0564.

Ursula and Jurgen Berger
Stand G64-5. *Ceramics and glass, jewellery.* TEL: 071 723 0449.

Manley Joseph Black
Stand F59/61. *Unusual and decorative objects, furniture.* TEL: 071 723 0678.

Sophia Blanchard
Stand S41. *Samplers, country furniture.* TEL: 071 723 6105.

Catherine Braithwaite
Stand S7. *Royal Doulton.* TEL: 071 402 0941.

B. Bruno
Stand F10. *Clocks, watches.* TEL: 071 723 1370.

S. Brunswick
Stand G16/17,G20-22. *Furniture, accessories, carpets, textiles and decorative objects.* TEL: 071 723 1513.

Ursula Burnstock
Stand G56/7. *General antiques, furniture.* TEL: 071 723 5613.

N.W.8 continued

David Casolani
Stand F107/8. *Paintings.* TEL: 071 723 1370.

Fred Cheeseman
Stand F116. *General.* TEL: 071 723 1370.

Brenda Klare Gerwat Clark
Stand S1/3. *Dolls and toys, furniture and accessories.* TEL: 071 706 4699.

Ruth Davis
Stand F79/80. *Silver, glass and porcelain.* TEL: 071 723 0429.

S.S. Deacon
Stand G113/4. *Silver and plate.* TEL: 071 723 0564.

Jo del Grosso
Stand F17. *Books.* TEL: 071 724 7231.

Andrew Downs
Stand G82-4. *Collectables and china.* TEL: 071 723 0449.

Drake
Stand G38/9. *Architectural items, brass.* TEL: 071 723 5613.

M. Druks
Stand S46/47. *General antiques.* TEL: 071 723 6105.

East Gates Antiques
Stand G5/6. *Glass, china, cameras.* TEL: 071 724 5650.

Liz Farrow
Stand F73. *Posters.* TEL: 071 706 1545.

Sally Fox
Stands S111/120/2. *Paintings, furniture, accessories.* TEL: 071 723 5731.

Robin Gardiner
Stand G41/2. *Prints and drawings.* TEL: 071 723 0449.

Helen Gardiner Antiques   LAPADA
Stand F3-7,11,12. *Furniture and accessories.*
TEL: 071 723 1370.

William Garraway
Stand G50/51. *Prints, postcards and smalls.* TEL: 071 723 5613.

Genie
Stand S57/8. *General.* TEL: 071 723 6105.

Richard Gibbon
Stand G81. *20th C items.* TEL: 071 723 0449.

Goldsmith and Perris   LAPADA
Stand G53/62/58. *Silver and plate.* TEL: 071 724 7051.

Teresa Gore
Stand S106. *Ceramics and glass; general.* TEL: 071 723 5731.

N.W.8 continued

Marie Gottlieb
Stand B49. *Art deco furniture and artefacts.* TEL: 071 402 1976.

Gramophone Workshop
Stand B9. *Mechanical items.* TEL: 071 724 3437.

Linette Greco
Stand G118. *Jewellery.* TEL: 071 723 0564.

Ena Green Antiques
Stand F74-78. *Furniture and decorative accessories.* TEL: 071 723 0429.

Mary Griffiths
Stand G127. *General.* TEL: 071 723 0564.

J. Hall
Stand F13. *Furniture and accessories.* TEL: 071 723 0678.

Henry Hay
Stand S54. *20th C items.* TEL: 071 723 6105.

M. Heidarieh/A. Bagdhi
Stand G1. *Clocks and watches, general.* TEL: 071 724 5650.

Tina Henning
Stand F14. *18th-19th C oil paintings.* TEL: 071 723 8964.

George Hepburn
Stand B44. *Paintings.* TEL: 071 724 3437.

Peter Herbert
Stand G56/9/61. *Bathroom fittings, lighting.* TEL: 071 724 2200.

E. J. Holden
Stand F130. *Paintings.* TEL: 071 723 1370.

Frances Houlding
Stand G121-4, G95. *Costume jewellery.* TEL: 071 402 2689.

Dudley Howe
Stand S55/56/67. *General antiques, commemoratives.* TEL: 071 723 6105.

Virginia Hoyer-Millar
Stand S105. *Furniture and accessories.* TEL: 071 723 5731.

Incisioni
Stand F40-43. *Original prints, drawings and rare books.* TEL: 071 706 2970.

J. and G. Antiques
Stand B35/6. *General.* TEL: 071 724 3437.

Peter Jacques
Stand S11. *Brass architectural fixtures and fittings.* TEL: 071 723 6105.

Roderick Jones
Stand B30. *Paintings, frames.* TEL: 071 724 3437.

LONDON

N.W.8 continued

Just In Pine
Stand F1-4. *Pine furniture.* TEL: 071 723 1370.

Mary Keays
Stand G119. *Jewellery.* TEL: 071 723 0564.

Mrs Khawaja
Stand G122/3. *Jewellery.* TEL: 071 706 2971.

Kitchen Bygones
Stand B62. *Kitchenalia.* TEL: 071 724 3439.

Simon Kluth
Stand S8. *Furniture and accessories.* TEL: 071 723 6105.

Lamb Silverware
Stand F118/121. *Silver and plate.* TEL: 071 723 2203.

Anthony Lask
Stand F127-9. *Silver and plate.* TEL: 071 723 4648.

Sara Lewis
Stand S16. *Furniture and accessories.* TEL: 071 723 6105.

Joss MacDonald
Stand F23. *Silver.* TEL: 071 723 1370.

Nigel Macdonald
Stand F23. *Furniture and accessories.* TEL: 071 723 1370.

Malcolm
Stand G35. *Furniture and accessories.* TEL: 071 723 0564.

Nigel Martin
Stand S40. *Textiles.* TEL: 071 723 6105.

Francesca Martire
Stand F131-6. *Jewellery, pictures, objects.* TEL: 071 723 1370.

Margaret Miall
Stand G14/15/19. *Light fittings, ceramics and glass.* TEL: 071 723 1513.

George Michaelis
Stand G121. *Jewellery and objects.* TEL: 071 723 0564.

Serge Milan
Stand F46-7. *Paintings.* TEL: 071 723 0678.

Bill Millar
Stand S13. *General and paintings.* TEL: 071 723 6105.

David Miller
Stand B22-5. *Decorative antiques.* TEL: 071 724 3439.

M. Miller
Stand G37. *Decorative items, 1890-1920's and some 1950's.* TEL: 071 723 5613.

N.W.8 continued

M. O. Mohamed
Stand G125/6/133-4. *Period accessories and costume jewellery.* TEL: 071 723 0564.

Nik Oakley Associates
Stand B62. *20th C ceramics.* TEL: 071 724 3439.

Obelisk
Stand F106. *Furniture and accessories.* TEL: 071 723 1370.

The Originals
Stand G49. *Radios; 20th C items.* TEL: 071 723 0449.

Maria Ortola
Stand F105. *General.* TEL: 071 723 1370.

A. J. Partners
Stand G113-14. *Art deco ceramics.* TEL: 071 723 1370.

Michelle Payne
Stand G112 & S53. *Jewellery and general antiques.* TEL: 071 723 1513.

Geoffrey Peake
Stand G82/4. *Art deco items; ceramics especially Susie Cooper.* TEL: 071 723 0449.

Catherine Perman
Stand S112-3. *Furniture and accessories.* TEL: 071 723 5731.

Daniel Perrin
Stand G36. *Art pottery, ceramics and paintings.* TEL: 071 723 5613.

Bob Phillips
Stand B60-1. *Jewellery.* TEL: 071724 3439.

Phoenix
Stand G35. *General, kitchenalia.* TEL: 071 723 5613.

Matteo Picasso
Stand B47-8,50. *Silver and plate, clocks and watches.* TEL: 071 724 3439.

Shoshi Preiss
Stand F48/49/71/72. *Paintings, furniture and accessories.* TEL: 071 723 0678.

Angela Pullan-Wells
Stand G31. *Jewellery.* TEL: 071 723 1513.

Re-Design
Stand S44/5/8/9. *Furniture, accessories.* TEL: 071 723 0678.

Angela Regana
Stand S109. *Carpets, general.* TEL: 071 723 5731.

Celia Reynolds
Stand S42-3. *Furniture and accessories.* TEL: 071 723 6105.

N.W.8 continued

Christina Robinson
Stand G75-78/91/2. *Art deco furniture and accessories.* TEL: 071 723 0449.

Jo Robinson
Stand S108. *Furniture and accessories.* TEL: 071 723 5731.

Albert Rockman
Stand G28/9. *Bric-a-brac, Victoriana, commemoratives, ceramics and glass.* TEL: 071 723 1513.

B. Rockman
Stand G23/24/25. *Victoriana and general antiques, commemoratives, ceramics and glass.* TEL: 071 723 1513.

Alvin Ross
Stand G9-11. *Dolls and toys.* TEL: 071 723 1513.

Dick Salveson
Stand B43-4. *General antiques.* TEL: 071 724 3437.

Samii
Stand S102-3. *Ceramics and glass, general.* TEL: 071 723 5731.

Timothy Saxon
Stand G56-7. *Pictures.* TEL: 071 723 5613.

Patrick Scola
Stand G64-5. *China.* TEL: 071 723 0449.

Jeremy Sewell
Stand G12/13/144/5. *Watercolours, frames and prints.* TEL: 071 723 1513.

F. Shams
Stand G105. *Persian and Oriental art.* TEL: 071 723 0564.

Trudi and Bob Share
Stand F73. *Art deco and later items.* TEL: 071 723 0429.

A. and Z. Shine
Stand G2. *Silver and general.* TEL: 071 724 5640.

Rosemary and Claire Smale
Stand G93/4. *Art deco ceramics.* TEL: 071 723 0449.

Connie Speight
Stand G107-9. *Art deco furniture and accessories.* TEL: 071 723 0564.

Kelvin Spooner
Stand B54. *Prints and drawings.* TEL: 071 724 3439.

SPV Antiques
Stand G35. *General.* TEL: 071 723 5613.

Elsie Taylor
Stand G135. *20th C furniture and accessories.* TEL: 071 723 0564.

N.W.8 continued

Eugene Tiernan
Stand F83-4. *Decorative items.* TEL: 071 723 0429.

David Tilleke
Stand G7/8. *Paintings, prints.* TEL: 071 723 1370.

Tina Art
Stand G40-1. *Furniture, textiles and accessories.*

Vetro
Stand S2/4. *Glass.* TEL: 071 724 0904.

Catherine Wallis
Stand S104. *Furniture and accessories.* TEL: 071 723 5731.

D. Wallis
Stand F15. *Scientific instruments, corkscrews.* TEL: 071 402 1038.

Marie Warner
Stand G136/7/8. *Jewellery, ceramics and glass.* TEL: 071 706 3727.

Steven Watson
Stand G70/4. *20th C glass.* TEL: 071 723 0678.

J. J. White
Stand G66-70/87. *Art deco.* TEL: 071 723 0449.

Norman Wilcocks
Stand G3. *Radios.* TEL: 071 724 5650.

Adu Zatua
Stand S10. *Tribal arts.* TEL: 071 723 6105.

All In One Antiques
1 Church St. (H. Freeman). Open 9.30-5, Mon.10-3. *STOCK: General antiques including upholstered items.* TEL: 071 724 3746. SER: Restorations; upholstery.

Beverley
30 Church St, Marylebone. Open 11-7 or by appointment. *STOCK: Art nouveau, art deco, decorative objects.* TEL: 071 262 1576.

D. and A. Binder
34 Church St. Open 10-6. SIZE: Medium. *STOCK: Traditional shop-fittings, counters, cabinets, vitrines and display stands.* LOC: Near Lisson Grove. TEL: 071 723 0542; fax - 071 724 0837.

Bizarre
24 Church St, Marylebone. (A. Taramasco and V. Conti). Open 10-5. *STOCK: Art deco and art nouveau.* TEL: 071 724 1305; fax - 071 724 1316.

Bobinet Ltd   BADA
P.O. Box 2730. (A. Crisford and S. Whitestone). Est. 1973. Open by appointment only. *STOCK: Watches, clocks and scientific instruments.* TEL: 071 289 1490; fax - 071 289 5119. SER: Valuations; restorations. VAT: Stan/Spec.

LONDON

THE COLLECTOR
9 CHURCH STREET
LONDON NW8 8DT, UK
TEL: 071-706 4586
FAX: 071-706 2948
(Next to Alfies Antiques Market)

OPEN SEVEN DAYS
Mon-Sat 10am-6pm Sunday 10am-2pm

QUALITY COLLECTABLES & LIMITED
EDITIONS INCLUDING.

ROYAL DOULTON, BESWICK, MOORCROFT,
DAVID WINTER, WEDGWOOD,
LILLIPUT LANE, BORDER FINE ART, SPODE,
KEVIN FRANCIS, PENDELFIN, BOSSONS,
ETC...

CREDIT CARDS ACCEPTED
WORLD WIDE MAIL ORDER SERVICE

N.W.8 continued

Camden Art Gallery
22 Church St. (A. Silver, A. Woda and R. Gordon). Est. 1968. Open 10-5. SIZE: Medium. *STOCK: Oil paintings and furniture, 18th-19th C, £300-£10,000.* LOC: Off Edgware Rd. PARK: Easy. TEL: 071 262 3613; fax - 071 723 2333. SER: Valuations; restorations (framing and cleaning). FAIRS: Barbican. VAT: Spec.

Church Street Antiques
8 Church St. (S. Shuster). Est. 1974. Open 10-5.30. SIZE: Medium. *STOCK: Walnut, mahogany and oak furniture, 19th to early 20th C, £50-£2,500; decorative items - bronze, crystal and ormulu.* LOC: Near Lisson Grove. PARK: Easy. TEL: 071 723 7415. VAT: Stan.

The Collector
9 Church St., Marylebone. (Tom Power). Est. 1973. Open 10-6, Sun. 10-2. SIZE: Large. *STOCK: Royal Doulton, from 1900, £50-£200; Beswick, from 1920, £40-£100; Moorcroft, from 1950, £150-£250.* LOC: 500 yards from Edgware Road underground station, 1/2 mile from Marble Arch. PARK: Easy (Not Sat.). TEL: 071 706 4586; fax - 071 706 2948; home - 081 883 0024. SER: Valuations; restorations (ceramics); buys at auction (ceramics). FAIRS: Specialist Decorative Art, mainly Royal Doulton; Alexandra Palace. VAT: Stan.

N.W.8 continued

Nicholas Drummond/Wrawby Moor Art Gallery Ltd
6 St. John's Wood Rd. (J.N. Drummond). Est. 1972. Open by appointment only.
STOCK: English and European oils, £250-£30,000; works on paper. LOC: Pass Lords entrance and next lights, house last bow front on left, facing down Hamilton Terrace. TEL: 071 286 6452; home - same. SER: Valuations; restorations (oils); buys at auction. VAT: Spec.

Robert Franses and Sons
Est. 1969. Open by appointment only. *STOCK: European and Oriental carpets, tapestries, needlework, Turkish village and early Chinese rugs.* TEL: 071 328 0949. SER: Restorations. VAT: Stan/Spec.

Gallery of Antique Costume and Textiles
2 Church St, Marylebone. Open 10-5.30. *STOCK: Curtains, needleworks, paisley shawls, parchment flowers and English quilts, 19th-20th C; tassles, decorative borders, silk panels, velvets and brocades, £5-£20,000.* LOC: 500yds. from Marylebone tube and 1/2 mile from Marble Arch. PARK: Easy. TEL: 071 723 9981 (ansaphone).

The Gallery on Church Street
12 Church St. (E. Phillips). Open 10-5.30. SIZE: Small. *STOCK: Posters, art nouveau and art deco, watercolours, oils and decorative prints.* PARK: Easy. TEL: 071 723 3389; fax - 071 723 3389.

Milne Henderson   BADA
112 Clifton Hill. (S. Milne Henderson). Est. 1970. **Open by appointment.** *STOCK: Japanese, Chinese and Korean paintings and screens.* TEL: 071 328 2171; fax - 071 624 7274. SER: Valuations; buys at auction. VAT: Stan.

Just Desks
20 Church St. (G. Gordon and N. Finch). Est. 1967. Open 9.30-6 or by appointment. *STOCK: Victorian, Edwardian and reproduction desks, writing tables, davenports, bureaux, chairs, filing cabinets and roll tops.* PARK: Meters. TEL: 071 723 7976; fax - 071 402 6416. VAT: Stan.

Nellie Lenson and Roy Smith
11 Church St, Lisson Grove. *STOCK: Decorative items, Vienna bronzes, early brass, animalia, French furniture.* TEL: 071 724 7763.

Magus Antiques
4 Church St. (D.A. Robinson). Est. 1973. Open 10-6. CL: Mon. SIZE: Medium. *STOCK: Porcelain and glass, European and Oriental, £10-£15,000; bronzes, furniture, £100-£15,000.* LOC: Left off Edgware Rd., 200yds. north of Marylebone flyover. PARK: Easy. TEL: 071 724 1278. SER: Valuations; buys at auction. FAIRS: Olympia. VAT: Stan.

JUST DESKS
OFFICE INTERIORS
Showrooms open Monday-Saturday
Brochure available

PERIOD AND REPRODUCTION OFFICE BOARDROOM AND STUDY FURNITURE.

20, Church Street, London, NW8
Tel 071 723 7976
Fax 071 402 6416

N.W.8 continued

Raffles Antiques
40/42 Church St. (D. Greengrass and D. Tupman). Est. 1971. Open 10-6, Sun. by appointment. SIZE: Large. *STOCK: General antiques and decorative art, 18th-20th C, to £10,000.* LOC: Off Lisson Grove. PARK: Easy. TEL: 071 724 6384/706 2497. FAIRS: Olympia. VAT: Stan.

Risky Business
44 Church St. (P.R. John and Mrs C.M. Dobson). Est. 1976. Open 10-6. SIZE: Medium. *STOCK: Decorative furnishings, 1900-1930; vintage sporting paraphernalia, luggage; cane, rattan and club style furniture.* LOC: Near Lisson Grove. PARK: Easy. TEL: 071 724 2194. VAT: Stan.

S. and H. Antiques
7 Church St. (W. Hyde and G. Sinclair). Open 10.30-1 and 2-5.30. *STOCK: Continental porcelain, silver, bronze and decorative items, paintings and works of art, 18th-19th C.* LOC: Near Lisson Grove. PARK: Easy. TEL: 071 724 7118; home - 071 724 5804. SER: Valuations; buys at auction.

Silver Belle
48 Church St. Est. 1986. Open 9.30-5.30, Sun. and Mon. by appointment. SIZE: Medium. *STOCK: Silver and Sheffield plate, china including tea sets.* PARK: Easy. TEL: 071 723 2908; 081 443 0614. SER: Valuations; restorations (re-plating). VAT: Stan/Spec.

Tara Antiques
6 Church St. (G. Robinson). Est. 1971. Open 10-6. CL: Mon. SIZE: Medium. *STOCK: Unusual marble and bronze statuary; Vienna bronzes, silver, furniture, paintings, ivory and tortoiseshell.* PARK: Easy. TEL: 071 724 2405. SER: Buys at auction. VAT: Stan.

Townsends
81 Abbey Rd, St. John's Wood. (M. Townsend). Est. 1972. Open 10-6. SIZE: Large. *STOCK: Fireplaces, £100-£3,000; stained glass, £30-£200; architectural items, £10-£300; all mainly 19th C.* LOC: Corner of Abbey Rd. and Boundary Rd. PARK: Easy. TEL: 071 624 4756. SER: Valuations. VAT: Stan.

WELLINGTON GALLERY
No.1, St. John's Wood, High Street
London NW8 7NG
Tel: 071-586 2620

Antiques, gifts, picture-framing, curtain-making and upholstery

Complete restoration service is available for glass, porcelain, silver, Sheffield plate, oil paintings and furniture.

N.W.8 continued

Simon Tracy Gallery
18 Church St. Est. 1984. Open 10-6, Thurs. 10-8. CL: Mon. *STOCK: British furniture and accessories - arts and crafts, aesthetic movement, architect designed, Gothic revival, art nouveau, 1860-1940, from £100.* TEL: 071 724 5890; fax - 071 262 0275. SER: Valuations; restorations; buys at auction. VAT: Stan/Spec.

Wellington Gallery LAPADA
1 St John's Wood High St. (Mr and Mrs K. Barclay). Open 10-5.30. **STOCK: Fine furniture, 18th-19th C; paintings, Georgian glass, porcelain, silver and Sheffield plate, general antiques. TEL: 071 586 2620.**

Antique Collectors' Club Titles

Art Deco and Other Figures
by Bryan Catley
This sumptuously illustrated book contains the most comprehensive range of art deco figures ever published of the superb sculptures which became fashionable between the wars. The unconventional use of bronze and ivory for many of these sensual and exceptionally high quality figures and their sense of movement and rhythm ensure that large sums are paid by a discriminating international collectors' market. Compiled by the leading specialist dealer in these delightful figures.
**ISBN 0 902028 57 X, 348pp
1,100 b & w illus, 43 col illus, £45.00**

Animals in Bronze
by Christopher Payne
This comprehensive book describes the work of the animalier school, and brings us up to the present day. Practical information to help the collector and dealer.
**ISBN 0 907462 45 6, 424pp
900 b & w illus, 22 col illus, £39.50**

Available from:
Antique Collectors' Club, 5 Church Street
Woodbridge, Suffolk IP12 1DS
Tel: (0394) 385501 Fax: (0394) 384434

or Market Street Industrial Park
Wappingers' Falls, New York 12590, USA
Tel: 914 297 0003 Fax: 914 297 0068

The Barye Bronzes - a catalogue raisonné *by Stuart Pivar* (new edition)
This is a reprint of the author's standard work and is the first modern book on the sculptor Antoine-Louis Barye, the teacher of Rodin and prime mover of the Romantic Movement in art. It contains many improved black and white photographs and additional colour plates. All his known works are illustrated, with many more of Barye's castings of his own work. Barye was a craftsman in bronze almost as much as he was a sculptor; his then new techniques of casting, chiselling and patination are the cornerstone of modern bronze work. **ISBN 1 85149 142 2, 308pp, 300 b & w illus, 20 col, £45.00**

LONDON N.W.9
B.C. Metalcrafts Ltd
69 Tewkesbury Gardens. Est. 1946. Open by appointment only. *STOCK: Lighting, ormolu and marble lamps; Oriental and European vases; clocks, pre-1900, £5-£500.* Not stocked: Silver. TEL: 081 204 2446; fax - 081 206 2871. SER: Restorations and conversions; buys at auction. VAT: Stan/Spec. *Trade Only.*

The Witch Ball
51A Blackbird Hill, Kingsbury. (L.C.M. Drecker). Est. 1941. Open 10-6. SIZE: Medium. *STOCK: Victorian furniture, button chairs.* TEL: 081 200 4937. SER: Restorations; buys at auction.

LONDON N.W.10
David Malik and Son Ltd
5 Metro Centre, Britannia Way, Park Royal. Open 9-5. CL: Sat. *STOCK: Chandeliers, wall lights.* PARK: Easy. TEL: 081 965 4232; fax - 081 965 2401. VAT: Stan.

LONDON N.W.11
Delieb Antiques
31 Woodville Rd. (E. Delieb). Est. 1953. Open by appointment only. CL: Sat. *STOCK: Collectors' silver and rarities.* TEL: 081 458 2083. SER: Valuations. VAT: Spec.

Christopher Eimer
P.O. Box 352. *STOCK: Medals.* TEL: 081 458 9933; fax - 081 455 3535. *Postal Only.*

Hamilton Fine Arts   BADA LAPADA
186 Willifield Way, Hampstead. (V. Hamilton). Open by appointment. *STOCK: 18th-20th C paintings, watercolours and bronzes.* TEL: 081 455 7410. SER: *Restorations; framing.*

LONDON W.C.1
Abbott and Holder
30 Museum St. Est. 1938. Open 9.30-6, Thurs. till 7. *STOCK: Pictures, especially watercolours.* TEL: 071 637 3981 VAT: Spec

Atlantis Bookshop
49a Museum St. Open 10-5.30, Sat. 11-5. *STOCK: Antiquarian books on the occult and paranormal.* TEL: 071 405 2120

Austin/Desmond & Phipps
Pied Bull Yard, 68/69 Great Russell Street. (J. Austin and C. Phipps). SLAD. Open 10.30-6. *STOCK: Modern and contemporary British paintings and prints.* TEL: 071 242 4443; fax - 071 404 4480

Barometer Fair
Pied Bull Yard, Bury Pl., Bloomsbury. (J.M.W. Forster). Open 10-6, Sat. 11-3. SIZE: Medium. *STOCK: Barometers, 1760-1880, £50-£5,000; old Sheffield plate, scientific instruments, prints.*

W.C.1 continued
LOC: Near British Museum. PARK: Nearby. TEL: 071 404 4521/4050. SER: Restorations

Louis W. Bondy
c/o The Avenue Book Shop, 11 Sicilian Avenue. ABA. Est. 1947. Open 11-6, Sat. 11-5.30. SIZE: Small. *STOCK: Rare books.* TEL: 071 405 2733. SER: Valuations. VAT: Stan

Cartographia London
Pied Bull Yard, Bury Pl., Bloomsbury. (J. M.W. Forster). Est. 1976. Open 10-6, Sat. 11-3, other times by appointment. SIZE: Medium. *STOCK: Maps, world-wide, especially British Isles and North America; topographical engravings especially London.* LOC: Near British Museum. PARK: Nearby. TEL: 071 404 4050/4521

Cinema Bookshop
13-14 Great Russell St. (F. Zentner). Est. 1969. Open 10.30-5.30. SIZE: Small. *STOCK: Books, magazines, posters and stills,* LOC: First right off Tottenham Court Rd. PARK: Easy. TEL: 071 637 0206 SER: Mail order. VAT: Stan

Classic Collection
2 Pied Bull Yard, Bury Place. Open 9-5.30. SIZE: Medium. *STOCK: Classic and collectors' cameras, 1850-1960, from £10; daguerreotypes, optical toys and steroscopes.* LOC: Near Great Russell St. and Bloomsbury PARK: Easy. TEL: 071 831 6000; fax - 071 831 5424. SER: Valuations; restorations. FAIRS: Camera Collectors, U.K. and Europe. VAT: Stan

George and Peter Cohn
Unit 21, 21 Wren St. Est. 1947. Open 9-5, Sat. and Fri. pm. by appointment. *STOCK: Decorative lights.* PARK: Forecourt. TEL: 071 278 3749. SER: Restorations (chandeliers and walllights). *Trade Only.*

Sebastian D'Orsai Ltd
39 Theobalds Rd. (A. Brooks). Open 9.30-5. CL: Sat. *STOCK: Framed watercolours.* TEL: 071 405 6663. SER: Restorations (paintings and prints); framing; gilding. VAT: Stan

J.A.L. Franks Ltd
7 New Oxford St. Est. 1947. *STOCK: Stamps, maps, postcards, cigarette cards.* TEL: 071 405 0274; fax - 071 430 1259

Frognal Rare Books
P.O. Box No.20. ABA. *STOCK: Antiquarian books on law, economic and general history, economics, philosophy, French, German, Italian, 1500-1900, £100-£2,000.* TEL: 071 637 7057; fax - 071 637 2650

Jessop Classic Photographica
67 Great Russell St. Open 9-5.30. *STOCK: Classic photographic equipment, cameras and optical toys.* TEL: 071 831 3640; fax - 071 831 3956

LONDON

W.C.1 continued

Marchmont Bookshop
39 Burton St. (D. Holder). Open 11-6.30. CL: Sat. *STOCK: Literature, including modern first editions.* TEL: 071 387 7989

Nortonbury Antiques LAPADA
BCM Box 5345. Open by appointment. *STOCK: Silver, 17th-19th C.* TEL: 0984 31668

I.K. Ong t/a Skoob Two
17 Sicilian Avenue. Open 10.30-6.30. SIZE: Medium. *STOCK: Secondhand and antiquarian books on esoterica, Far Eastern, archaeology, anthropology, classics, theology, sciences and psychology.* TEL: 071 405 0030; fax - 071 404 4398

The Print Room
37 Museum St. (A. Balfour-Lynn and K. Surya). Est. 1984. Open 10-6, Sat. 10-4, other times by appointment. *STOCK: Prints including natural history, views of London, costume plates and caricatures, 1580-1850, £10-£3,000.* LOC: Off Gt. Russell St., opposite British Museum. PARK: N.C.P. Bloomsbury Sq. TEL: 071 430 0159. SER: Valuations; buys at auction (antiquarian books and prints)

Arthur Probsthain
41 Great Russell St. Est. 1902. Open 9-5.30, Sat. 11-4. *STOCK: Books, Oriental and African.* TEL: 071 636 1096. VAT: Stan

S.J. Shrubsole Ltd BADA LAPADA
43 Museum St. (C.J. Shrubsole). Est. 1918. Open 9-5.30. CL: Sat. SIZE: Medium. *STOCK: Silver, late 17th to mid-19th C, £50-£25,000; Sheffield Plate, mid-18th to mid-19th C, £10-£5,000.* LOC: 1 min. from British Museum. PARK: Easy. TEL: 071 405 2712. SER: Valuations; restorations (silver); buys at auction. VAT: Stan/Spec

Skoob Books Ltd
11a-15 Sicilian Ave., Southampton Row, Holborn. Est. 1978. Open 10.30-6.30. SIZE: Large. *STOCK: Books, second-hand literary, technical and scientific.* LOC: In pedestrian arcade, near Holburn Underground. PARK: Easy. TEL: 071 404 3063; fax - 071 404 4398

LONDON W.C.2

Anchor Antiques Ltd
26 Charing Cross Rd. (K.B. Embden and H. Samne). Est. 1964. Open by appointment. *STOCK: Continental and Oriental ceramics, European works of art and objets de vertu.* TEL: 071 836 5686. VAT: Spec*Trade Only.*

Apple Market Stalls
Covent Garden Market. Open every Mon. and first Sun. monthly 7-7. SIZE: 40 stalls. *STOCK: General antiques and collectables.* TEL: 071 836 9136

W.C.2 continued

A.H. Baldwin and Sons Ltd BADA
11 Adelphi Terrace. IAPN, BNTA. Est. 1872. Open 9-5. CL: Sat. SIZE: Medium. *STOCK: Coins, 600 BC to present; commemorative medals, 16th C to present, numismatic literature.* LOC: Off Robert St., near Charing Cross. TEL: 071 930 6879/839 1310; fax - 071 930 9450. SER: Valuations; auction agents for selling and purchasing. VAT: Stan/Spec

Bell, Book and Radmall
4 Cecil Court. Est. 1974. Open 10-5.30, Sat. 10-4.30. *STOCK: First editions of 19th-20th C English and American literature including detective and fantasy fiction.* TEL: 071 240 2161

M. Bord (Gold Coin Exchange)
16 Charing Cross Rd. Est. 1969. Open 9.30-6. SIZE: Small. *STOCK: Gold, silver and copper coins, Roman to Elizabeth II, all prices.* LOC: Near Leicester Sq. underground station. TEL: 071 836 0631/240 0479. SER: Valuations; buys at auction. FAIRS: All major coin. VAT: Stan/Spec

Covent Garden Flea Market
Jubilee Market, Covent Garden. (Sherman and Waterman Associates Ltd). Est. 1975. Open Mon. and Bank Holidays 6.30-5. SIZE: 200 stalls. *STOCK: General antiques.* LOC: South side of piazza, just off The Strand, via Southampton St. PARK: Easy and N.C.P. Drury Lane. TEL: 071 836 2139/240 7405

Ann Creed Books Ltd
22 Cecil Court. Open 10.30-6.30 or by appointment. *STOCK: Antiquarian, fine and applied art books.* TEL: 071 836 7757; fax - 071 240 1439

The Dolls House Toys Ltd
29 The Market, Covent Garden. Open 10-8. *STOCK: Dolls' houses, miniature furniture.* TEL: 071 379 7243. VAT: Stan

W. and G. Foyle Ltd
113-119 Charing Cross Rd. Est. 1904. *STOCK: Antiquarian books.*

Stanley Gibbons
399 Strand. Est. 1856. Open 8.30-7, Sat. 10-4. SIZE: Large. *STOCK: Popular and specialised stamps, postal history, catalogues, albums, accessories.* LOC: Opposite Savoy Hotel. TEL: 071 836 8444; fax - 071 836 7342. SER: Valuations. VAT: Stan/Spec

Grosvenor Prints
28/32 Shelton St, Covent Garden. Est. 1975. Open 10-6, Sat. 11-4. SIZE: Large. *STOCK: Engravings, lithographs, etchings and aquatints especially topographical, dog prints, portraits and decorative.* LOC: Within one-way system near Neal St. PARK: Easy. TEL: 071 836 1979; fax - 071 379 6695. SER: Valuations; restorations; buys at auction. VAT: Stan/Spec

W.C.2 continued

S. and H. Jewell Ltd
26 Parker St. Est. 1830. Open 9-5.30, Sat. by appointment. SIZE: Large. *STOCK: Furniture.* TEL: 071 405 8520. SER: Valuations; restorations. VAT: Stan/Spec

Thomas Kettle Ltd
53a Neal St. (J. King). Resident. Est. 1974. Open 10-7. SIZE: Medium. *STOCK: Wrist watches, 1910-1950, £350-£5,000; contemporary designer jewellery, £40-£2,000.* LOC: Near Covent Garden tube. PARK: Leicester Sq. TEL: 071 379 3579. SER: Valuations; restorations (wrist watches). VAT: Stan

The London Silver Vaults
Chancery House, 53-65 Chancery Lane. Est. 1892. Open 9-5.30. CL: Sat. pm. *STOCK: Silver, plate, jewellery, objets d'art, clocks, watches, collectors' items.* TEL: 071 242 3844. The following are some of the dealers at these vaults

A. M. W. Silverware
Vault 52. TEL: 071 242 3620; fax - 071 831 3923.

Argenteus Ltd
Vault 2. (M. D. Feldman). TEL: 071 831 3637; fax - 071 430 0126. VAT: Stan/Spec.

Benjamin Jewellery Ltd LAPADA
Vault 46. TEL: 071 831 1380; fax - 071 831 4629.

Lawrence Block
Vault 28 and 65. Est. 1959. *Silver especially flatware; jewellery.* TEL: 071 242 0749. SER: Valuations; restorations; buys at auction.

A. Bloom
Vault 27. TEL: 071 242 6189.

Luigi Brian Antiques
Vault 56. TEL: 071 405 2484.

B.L. Collins
Vault 20. TEL: 071 404 0628.

P. Daniel
Vault 51. TEL: 071 430 1327.

B. Douglas
Vault 12/14.

M.J. Dubiner
Vault 38.

R. Feldman Ltd LAPADA
Vault 4/6. TEL: 071 405 6111.

I. Franks LAPADA
Vault 9/11. Est. 1926. TEL: 071 242 4035.

Hamilton
Vault 25.

S. Kalms
Vault 32.

W.C.2 continued

Susan Kyle Antiques
Vault 68. TEL: 071 242 1708. VAT: Stan/Spec.

B. Lampert
Vault 19.

Langfords
Vault 8/10. NAG. Est. 1940. *Silver and plate especially cutlery.* TEL: 071 351 4881; fax - 071 405 6401. SER: Valuations. VAT: Stan/Spec.

Nat Leslie Ltd
Vault 21/22/23. Est. 1940. TEL: 071 242 4787. VAT: Stan/Spec.

Linden and Co. (Antiques) Ltd
Vault 7. (H, F, H.M. and S. C. Linden). TEL: 071 242 4863; fax - 071 405 9946. VAT: Stan/Spec.

C. and T. Mammon
Vault 31 & 64. TEL: 071 405 2397.

J. Mammon Antiques
Vault 30. TEL: 071 242 4704. *Trade Only.*

I.Nagioff (Jewellery)
Vault 63 and 69. (I. and R. Nagioff). Est. 1955. *Jewellery, 18th-20th C, £5-£2,000+; objets d'art, 19th C, to £200.* TEL: 071 405 3766. SER: Valuations; restorations (jewellery). VAT: Stan.

Percy's LAPADA
Vault 16/17. *Candelabra, candlesticks, flatware and collectables.* **TEL: 071 242 3618.**

Rare Art
Vault 15. TEL: 071 405 9968.

Saunders
Vault 60.

David S. Shure and Co
Vault 1. (S. Bulka). Est. 1900. Author. TEL: 071 405 0011. SER: Valuations; restorations. VAT: Stan.

Silstar
Vault 29. (H. Stern). Est. 1955. TEL: 071 242 6740. VAT: Stan/Spec.

B. Silverman BADA
Vault 26/33. (S. and R. Silverman). Est. 1927.TEL: 071 242 3269. SER: Valuations; buys at auction. VAT: Stan/Spec.

Jack Simons (Antiques) Ltd LAPADA
Vault 35 and 37. Est. 1955. TEL: 071 242 3221. VAT: Stan/Spec.

S. and J. Stodel
Vault 24. TEL: 071 405 7009; fax - 071 242 6366.

W.C.2 continued

A. Urbach
Vault 50.

William Walter Antiques Ltd
BADA LAPADA
Vault 3/5. (R.W. Walter). Est. 1927. TEL: 071 242 3248. SER: Valuations; restorations (silver, plate).

A. and G. Weiss
Vault 42/44. TEL: 071 242 7310. VAT: Stan.

Peter K. Weiss
Vault 18. Est. 1955. *Watches, clocks.* TEL: 071 242 8100/7310. VAT: Stan.

Wolfe (Jewellery)
Vault 41. TEL: 071 405 2101. VAT: Stan/Spec.

Arthur Middleton Ltd
12 New Row, Covent Garden. Est. 1968. Open 10-6 or by appointment. SIZE: Small. STOCK: *Scientific instruments - navigation, astronomy, surveying and medical; globes, scales, 18th-19th C, £50-£20,000.* LOC: New Row runs between Leicester Square and Covent Garden. Shop 300yds. east from Leicester Square. TEL: 071 836 7042/836 7062; fax - 071 497 9386. SER: Valuations; buys at auction; prop hire. VAT: Stan

Avril Noble
2 Southampton St, Covent Garden. PBFA. Est. 1964. Open 10-6, Sat. 10-4, Sun. by appointment. SIZE: Large. STOCK: *Maps and engravings of the world, 16th-19th C, £10-£3,000.* LOC: Off the Strand, opposite the Savoy Hotel. PARK: Meters. TEL: 071 240 1970. FAIRS: International Map, London; Bonnington Hotel. VAT: Stan

Pearl Cross Ltd
35 St. Martin's Court. Est. 1897. Open 9.30-4.45. CL: Sat. STOCK: *Jewellery, silver, clocks, watches.* PARK: Meters. TEL: 071 836 2814/240 0795. SER: Valuations; restorations (jewellery, silver). VAT: Stan/Spec

H. Perovetz Ltd
BADA LAPADA
50/52 Chancery Lane. Est. 1945. Open 9-6. SIZE: Large. STOCK: *Silver, Sheffield plate.* TEL: 071 405 8868; fax - 071 242 1211. SER: Valuations. VAT: Stan/Spec

Pleasures of Past Times
11 Cecil Court, Charing Cross Rd. (D.B. Drummond). Est. 1962. Open 11-2.30 and 3.30-5.45 and first Sat. monthly 11-2.30, other times by appointment. SIZE: Medium. STOCK: *Scarce and out-of-print books of the performing arts; early juvenile and illustrated books; vintage postcards, valentines, entertainment ephemera.* Not stocked: Coins, stamps, medals, jewellery, maps, cigarette cards. LOC: In pedestrian court between Charing Cross Rd. and St. Martin's Lane. TEL: 071 836 1142. VAT: Stan

W.C.2 continued

Henry Pordes Books Ltd
58-60 Charing Cross Rd. Open 10-7. STOCK: *Antiquarian books and periodicals, remainders on every subject and most languages.* TEL: 071 836 9031

Reg and Philip Remington
18 Cecil Court, Charing Cross Rd. ABA. Est. 1979. Open 10-5, Sat. by appointment. SIZE: Medium. STOCK: *Voyages and travels, 17th-20th C, £5-£1,000.* LOC: Near Trafalgar Sq. TEL: 071 836 9771. SER: Buys at auction. FAIRS: Edinburgh Book, London Book, Park Lane Hotel. VAT: Stan

Bertram Rota Ltd
9-11 Langley Court. Est. 1923. Open 9.30-5.30. CL: Sat. STOCK: *Antiquarian and secondhand books, especially first editions, private presses, English literature, and literary autographs.* TEL: 071 836 0723

The Silver Mouse Trap
56 Carey St. (A. Woodhouse). Est. 1690. Open 9.30-5.30. CL: Sat. SIZE: Medium. STOCK: *Jewellery, silver.* LOC: South of Lincoln's Inn Fields. TEL: 071 405 2578. SER: Valuations; restorations. VAT: Spec.

Spatz
48 Monmouth St. (P. Ebbinkhuyson and S. Anchor). Est. 1979. Open 11.30-6.30. SIZE: Small. STOCK: *Victorian lace pillowcases and nightdresses, £25-£40; 1940's dresses, blouses and other day wear, £20-£60.* LOC: Near Seven Dials, 2 mins. from Long Acre. PARK: NCP nearby. TEL: 071 379 0703. VAT: Stan

Stage Door Prints
1 Cecil Court, Charing Cross Rd. (A. Reynold). Open 11-6. STOCK: *Prints of performing arts, sports and topographical; signed photographs, maps, Victorian cards, valentines.* TEL: 071 240 1683

Harold T. Storey
3 Cecil Court, Charing Cross Rd. (T. Kingswood). Est. 1929. Open 10-6. STOCK: *Prints, especially naval and military; antiquarian books.* LOC: Between Charing Cross Rd. and St. Martin's Lane. PARK: Trafalgar Square garage. TEL: 071 836 3777

Tooley Adams & Co. Ltd
13 Cecil Court, Charing Cross Rd. (D. Adams and S. Luck). ABA. Est. 1964. Open 9-5. SIZE: Large. STOCK: *Antiquarian maps, atlases, prints; travel and map related reference books.* LOC: Between St. Martin's Lane and Charing Cross Rd. PARK: Gerard St. TEL: 071 240 4406; fax - 071 240 8058. SER: Valuations; restorations; buys at auction. FAIRS: Bonnington Map; Imcos Map. VAT: Stan

LONDON

W.C.2 continued

Trafalgar Square Collectors Centre
7 Whitcomb St. (D.C. Pratchett and R.D. Holdich). Est. 1979. Open 10-5.30, Sat. by appointment only. STOCK: Coins and military items including medals; bonds and banknotes, 18th-20th C, £5-£10,000. LOC: Next to National Gallery. PARK: NCP. TEL: 071 930 1979. SER: Valuations; buys at auction (coins and military medals). VAT: Stan/Spec

Travis and Emery
17 Cecil Court, Charing Cross Rd. (V. Emery). ABA. Est. 1960. Open 10-6. CL: Sat. pm. SIZE: Medium. STOCK: Musical literature, music and prints. LOC: Between Charing Cross Rd. and St. Martin's Lane opposite Odeon. PARK: Meters. TEL: 071 240 2129. VAT: Stan

Watkins Books Ltd
19 & 21 Cecil Court, Charing Cross Rd. Est. 1880. Open 10-6, Wed. 10.30-6. STOCK: Mysticism, occultism, Oriental religions, astrology and contemporary spirituality, new and secondhand books. TEL: 071 836 2182; fax - 071 836 6770

W.C.2 continued

The Witch Ball
2 Cecil Court, Charing Cross Rd. (R. Glassman). Resident. Est. 1969. Open 10.30-6. SIZE: Small. STOCK: Prints relating to the performing arts, from 17th C, topographical prints, 20th C posters. LOC: 2 mins. from Leicester Sq. tube station. PARK: NCP nearby. TEL: 071 836 2922. VAT: Stan

Zeno Booksellers and Publishers
6 Denmark St. Est. 1944. Open 9.30-6, Sat. till 5. SIZE: Medium. STOCK: Antiquarian books on Greece, Cyprus, Turkey, Middle East, and the Balkans. LOC: From Tottenham Court Rd., into Charing Cross Rd., first turning on left. TEL: 071 836 2522

A. Zwemmer Ltd
24 Litchfield St. Est. 1921. Open 9.30-6, Sat. 10-6. SIZE: Large. STOCK: Books on art and fine art; rare and out-of-print catalogue raisonnés. LOC: Just south of Cambridge Circus, Leicester Sq. underground. TEL: 071 379 7886

Antique Collectors' Club Titles

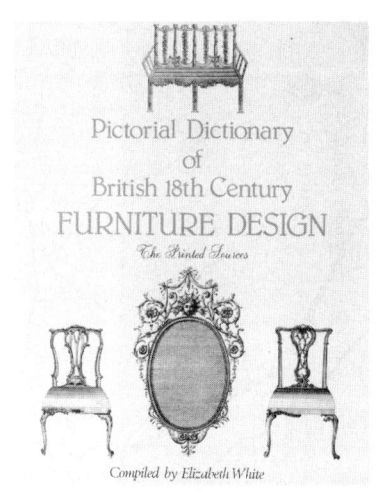

Pictorial Dictionary of British 18th Century Furniture Design
by Elizabeth White
Published designs from 120 sources. The 3,000 named and dated illustrations provide arguably the most important contribution to 18th century furniture studies since Ralph Edwards' **Dictionary of English Furniture**.
ISBN 1 85149 105 8
700pp, 3,500 b & w designs, 24 col £65.00

Pictorial Dictionary of British 19th Century Furniture Design
An A.C.C. Research Project
Compiled from forty-nine key contemporary catalogues from Sheraton to Heal's, including Smith, Tatham, King, Pugin, Morris and Liberty's, it includes an important introduction by the late Edward Joy.
ISBN 0 902028 47 2, 632pp, 6,200 illus, £49.50

Available from:
Antique Collectors' Club, 5 Church Street, Woodbridge, Suffolk IP12 1DS Tel: (0394) 385501 Fax: (0394) 384434

or Market Street Industrial Park, Wappingers' Falls, New York 12590, USA Tel: 914 297 0003 Fax: 914 297 0068

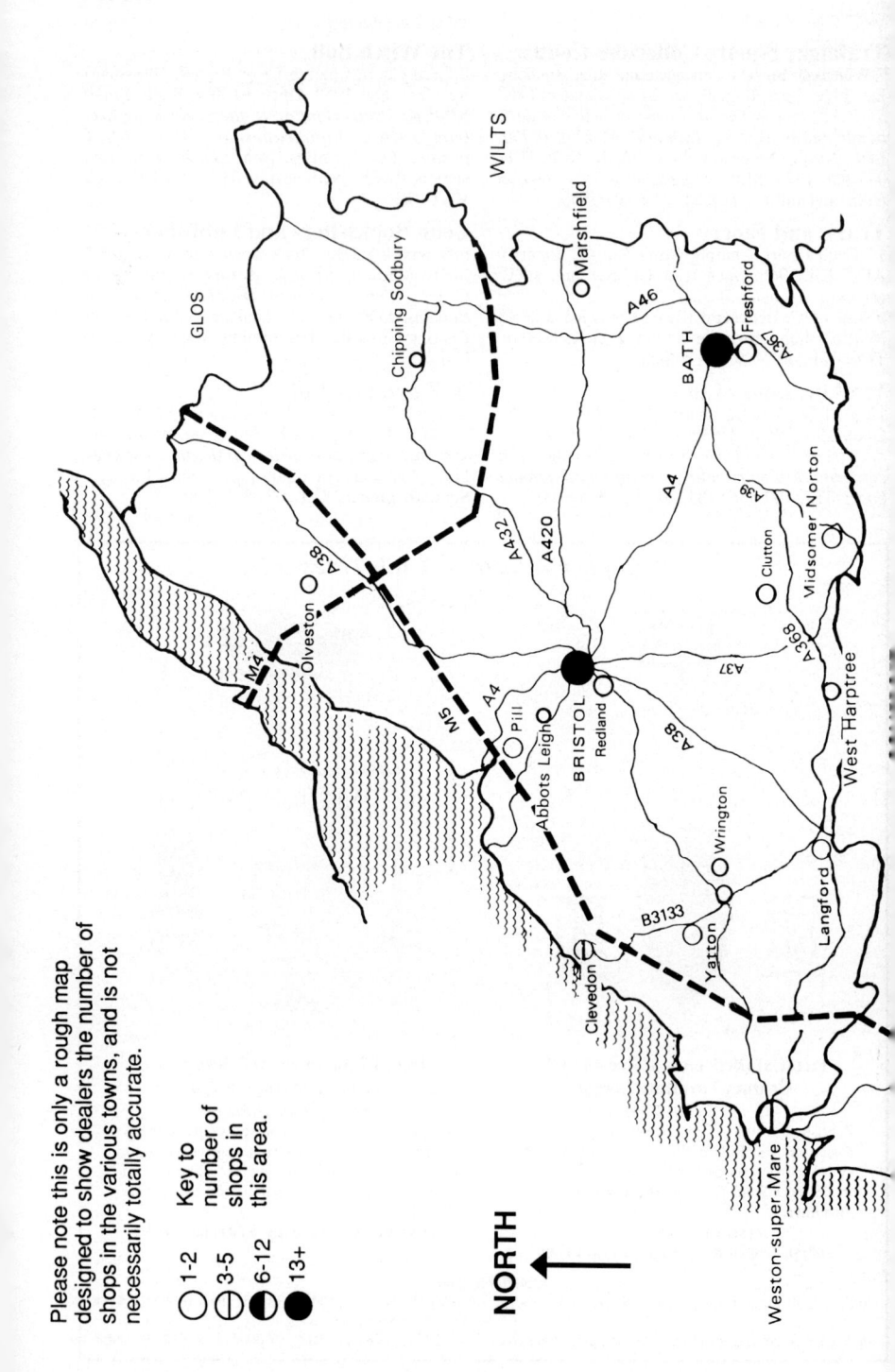

Avon

Avon

Antique Linens & Lace
11 Pulteney Bridge, Bath
Tel. (0225) 465782

Rosalind Mellor, specialist in Fine Antique Linens & Lace including Christening Gowns & Baby Bonnets, Wedding Veils, Table Cloths & Bed Linen, etc.

ABBOTS LEIGH, Nr. Bristol

David March Ceramics LAPADA
Oak Wood Lodge, Stoke Leigh Woods. (D. and S. March). Est. 1981. Open by appointment. STOCK: Interesting and unusual English porcelain including figures, 18th to 19th C; Welsh porcelain, early 19th C. PARK: Easy. TEL: 0275 372422; home - same. SER: Buys at auction (as stock). FAIRS: Wakefield Ceramic; NEC. VAT: Spec.

BATH

'27a' '27b'
27a 27b Belvedere, Lansdown. (P.M. Farnham). Est. 1970. Open 9.30-6, Sun. by appointment. SIZE: Large. STOCK: Rare and interesting furniture and objects. PARK: Easy. TEL: 0225 428256; home - 0272 866597. SER: Buys at auction; interior decoration. Stockists of FBC screens.

4 Miles Buildings
4 Miles Buildings, Off George St. (Nick Kuhn). Est. 1984. Open Wed. and Sat. 10-5. SIZE: Small. STOCK: British fine art, £30-£1,000; popular art - naive art, hooked rugs, country pottery, £10-£500; all 19th-20th C. LOC: City centre, near Bartlett Street Antiques Centres. PARK: Nearby. FAIRS: Bath & Bradford-on-Avon Antique Dealers.

Abbey Galleries
4 Abbey Churchyard. (R. Dickson). Est. 1930. Open 10.30-5.30. STOCK: Jewellery, £50; Oriental, £100; both 18th-19th C; silver, 18th C, £100. Not Stocked: Furniture. TEL: 0225 60565. SER: Valuations; restorations (jewellery and clocks); buys at auction. VAT: Stan.

Adam Gallery
13 John St. (P. and P. Dye). Open 9.30-5.30 or by appointment. STOCK: Late Victorian and Modern British oil paintings and watercolours, especially figurative and landscape, £200-£10,000. TEL: 0225 480406.

Bath continued

Alderson BADA
23 Brock St. (C.J.R. Alderson). Est. 1975. Open 9.30-5.30. STOCK: Furniture, 17th-18th C; period metalwork, glass, silver. LOC: Between the Circus and Royal Crescent. PARK: Easy. TEL: 0225 421652. SER: Valuations. VAT: Spec.

Antique Linens and Lace
11 Pulteney Bridge. (Mrs R. Mellor). Est. 1971. Open 10-5.30 including Sun. SIZE: Small. STOCK: Quality linens and lace, bedspreads, sheets, tablecloths, pillow cases, christening gowns, baby bonnets, collars, veils and shawls, 1850-1920, £10-£600. LOC: City centre. PARK: Great Pulteney St.- 100 yards. TEL: 0225 465782; 0225 754067. VAT: Stan/Spec.

Arkea Antiques
10A Monmouth Place. (G. Harmandian). Est. 1972. STOCK: Furniture, china, silver, clocks. TEL: 0225 429413; home - 0225 835382.

Aspidistra
46 St. James Parade. (J. and J. Waggoner). Est. 1972. Open 11-4. SIZE: Medium. STOCK: Books and prints, music and musical instruments, curiosities, bygones. LOC: 2 mins. walk from Bath Abbey, opposite Technical College. PARK: Limited and multi-storey nearby. TEL: 0225 461948. SER: Valuations.

G.A. Baines of Bath
(G. and J. Baines). By appointment only. STOCK: English furniture, 1740-1840. TEL: 0225 332566. VAT: Spec.

Bartlett Street Antique Centre
5-10 Bartlett St. Open 9.30-5, Wed. 8-5. SIZE: 52+ dealers. STOCK: Wide range of general antiques. TEL: 0225 466689; stallholders - 0225 330267/310457.

Bath Antiques Market
Guinea Lane, Off Lansdown Rd. Est. 1968. Open Wed. only 6.30-2.30. SIZE: 60 dealers. STOCK: General antiques and collectables. LOC: From London A4 across two sets of traffic lights after

AVON

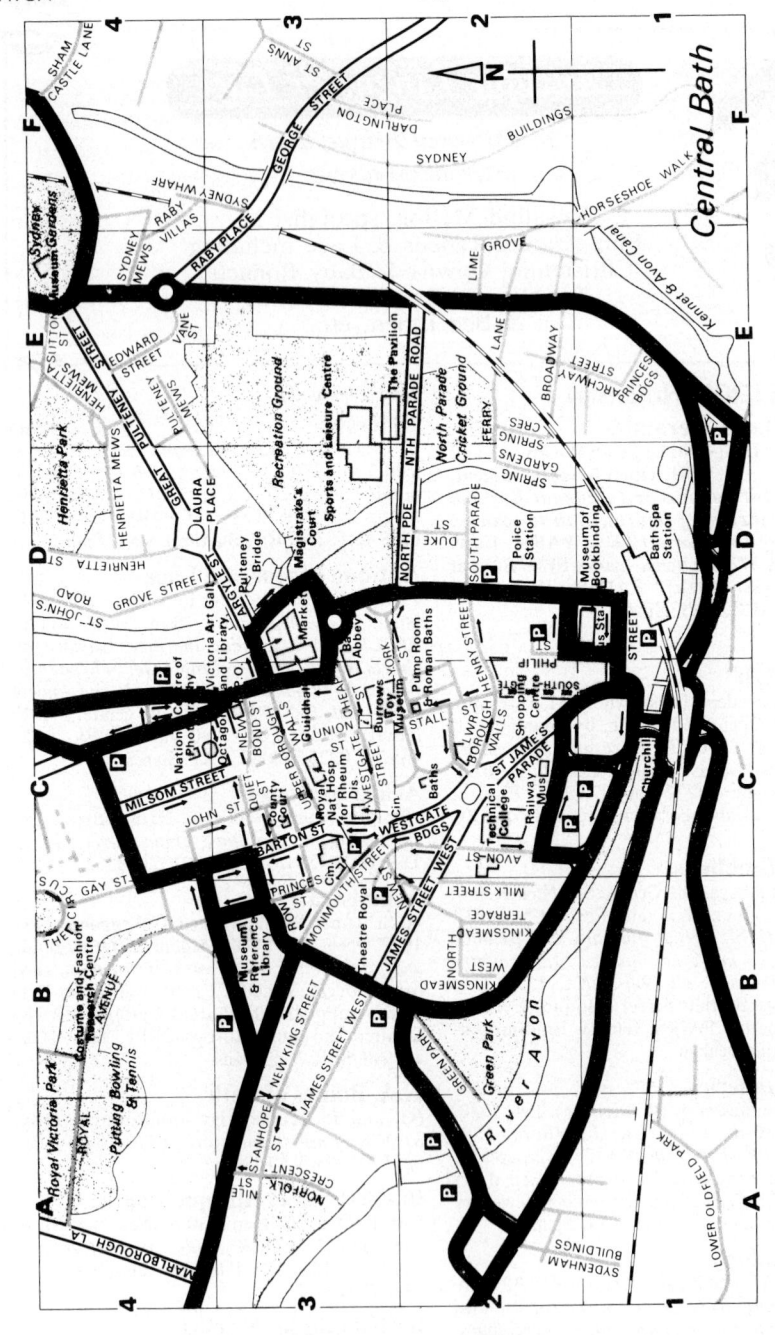

Central Bath

Key to Town Plan

AA Recommended roads	Car Parks
Other roads	Parks and open spaces
Restricted roads	AA Service Centre
Buildings of interest	

© Automobile Association 1988.

Bath continued
entering Bath. Right at third set (Lansdown Rd.) and first right again. PARK: Nearby. TEL: 0225 337638; enquiries - 071 351 5353; fax - 0225 422510. SER: Valuations.

Bath Galleries
33 Broad St. (J. Griffiths). Open 9.30-5. SIZE: Medium. *STOCK: Furniture, paintings, porcelain, jewellery, clocks, barometers, silver.* LOC: 50yds. from Central Post Office. PARK: Walcot St. multi-park, 30yds. TEL: 0225 462946. SER: Valuations; restorations; buys at auction. VAT: Stan/Spec.

Bath Saturday Antiques Market
Walcot St. (A. Whittingham). Est. 1978. Open Sat. 7-5. SIZE: 100 stalls. *STOCK: Wide variety of general antiques, £1-£500.* LOC: Close to Beaufort Hotel. PARK: Multi-storey.

Bath Stamp and Coin Shop
Pulteney Bridge. (H. and A. Swindells). Est. 1946. Open 9.30-5.30. *STOCK: Coins - Roman, hammered, early milled, G.B. gold, silver and copper, some foreign; literature and accessories; banknotes, medals, stamps and postal history.* PARK: Laura Place; Walcott multi-storey. SER: Valuations. VAT: Stan.

George Bayntun
Manvers St. (H.H. Bayntun-Coward). Est. 1829. Open 9-1 and 2-5.30, Sat. 9.30-1. SIZE: Large. *STOCK: Rare books. First or fine editions of English literature, standard sets, illustrated and sporting books, poetry, biography and travel, mainly in new leather bindings; also large stock of antiquarian books in original bindings.* LOC: By railway and bus stations. PARK: 50yds. by station. TEL: 0225 466000; fax - 0225 482122. SER: Restorations (rare books). VAT: Stan.

Beau Nash Antiques
Beau Nash House, Union Passage. Est. 1973. Open 10-5. SIZE: Large. *STOCK: English furniture, 1700-1840, £1,500-£15,000; oil paintings, 1750-1890, £1,000-£10,000; decorative objects, 1760-1890, £150-£1,500.* LOC: 70yds. north of Roman Baths. PARK: Pierrepont St. TEL: 0225 447806. SER: Valuations. VAT: Spec.

Bladud House Antiques
8 Bladud Buildings. (Mrs E. Radosenska). Open 9.30-1 and 2-4.30. CL: Mon. and Thurs. *STOCK: Jewellery and small items.* Not Stocked: Furniture. TEL: 0225 462929.

Blyth Antiques
28 Sydney Buildings. (B. Blyth). Resident. Est. 1971. Open by appointment. *STOCK: Small furniture, samplers, brass and unusual decorative items.* LOC: Off Bathwick Hill. PARK: Easy. TEL: 0225 469766.

Bath continued

Lawrence Brass and Son
93-95 Walcot St. Est. 1973. Open 8-5, Sun. by appointment. SIZE: Small. *STOCK: Furniture, 16th-19th C, £50-£5,000.* Not Stocked: Ceramics, silver, glass. LOC: Main road into town centre. PARK: Easy. TEL: 0225 464057; home - same. SER: Restorations (furniture, clocks and barometers). VAT: Stan/Spec.

Breeze and Behan   LAPADA
6 George St. (R. Behan and G. Breeze). Open 10-5.30. STOCK: Furniture, 18th-20th C. TEL: 0225 466499. VAT: Stan/Spec.

Bryers Antiques
Entrance to the Guildhall Market, High St. (S. Bryers). Est. 1940. *STOCK: Furniture, decorative items, porcelain, glass, silver and Victorian plate.* LOC: Near the bus station. TEL: 0225 466352/460535. VAT: Stan/Spec.

Casemate
12 Bartlett St. (S. Moss). Open 9.30-5, Wed. 8.30-5. SIZE: Small. *STOCK: Antiquities, to 20th C, £10-£10,000.* Not Stocked: Furniture. LOC: Near Gt. Western Antique Centre. PARK: Alfred St. TEL: 0225 465142; fax - same. VAT: Stan/Spec.

Chelsea Interiors
9 Chelsea Rd, Lower Weston. (Christopher Scott-Moody). Est. 1982. Open 10-2 and 3-6, Mon. 12-2 and 3-6. CL: Sat. SIZE: Medium. *STOCK: 18th C English and continental furniture; period and contemporary lighting, porcelain, glass, silver and works of art.* LOC: A4 from city centre, then Newbridge Hill, first left before mini roundabout. PARK: Easy. TEL: 0225 426717; home - 0225 315414. SER: Valuations; restorations; buys at auction (country house furnishings); interior design.

Sheila Cooper t/a Sheila Smith Antiques
Bartlett St. Antique Centre, 7-10 Bartlett St. (S.M. Cooper). Est. 1967. Open 9.30-5. *STOCK: Fans, needlework tools and accessories, Mauchline ware, collectors' items.* LOC: A4 into city. At 3rd set of traffic lights, turn right into Lansdown then 2nd left into Alfred St. TEL: 0225 442730.

Corridor Stamp Shop
7a The Corridor. (G.H. and S.M. Organ). Est. 1970. Open 9.30-5.30. CL: Mon. SIZE: Small. *STOCK: Stamp and postal history, 1700 to date, 5p-£500; albums, reference books; picture postcards, cigarette cards, 1895-1940.* LOC: Within 200yds. of Abbey. PARK: Walcot St. TEL: 0225 463368; home - 0225 316445. SER: Valuations.

Brian and Caroline Craik Ltd
8 Margaret's Buildings. *STOCK: Decorative items, mainly 19th C; metalwork, treen, glass and pewter.* TEL: 0225 337161.

FRANK DUX ANTIQUES

For Georgian glass
and period oak furniture

33, BELVEDERE, BATH BA1 5HR
Tel. and Fax: 0225-312367

Bath continued

John Croft Antiques LAPADA
3 George St. Open 10-5.30. SIZE: Medium. STOCK: Furniture, 17th to early 19th C; clocks, barometers, decorative objects, paintings. LOC: A4, turn left at top of Milsom St., opposite 'Hole in the Wall' restaurant. PARK: Broad St. 100yds. TEL: 0225 466211. VAT: Spec.

Andrew Dando BADA
4 Wood St, Queen Sq. (A.P. and J.M. Dando). Est. 1930. Open 9.30-1 and 2.15-5.30, Sat. 10-1. SIZE: Large. STOCK: English, continental, Oriental porcelain and pottery, 17th to mid-19th C; furniture, 18th to mid-19th C. LOC: 200yds. from bottom of Milsom St. towards Queen Sq. TEL: 0225 422702. SER: Valuations. VAT: Stan/Spec.

D. and B. Dickinson BADA
22 New Bond St. (S.G., D. and N.W. Dickinson and Mrs E.M. Dickinson). Est. 1917. Open 9.30-1 and 2.15-5. CL: Mon. and Sat. p.m. SIZE: Small. STOCK: Jewellery, 1770-1900, £20-£2,000; silver, 1750-1900, £25-£3,000; Sheffield plate, 1770-1845, £50-£1,000. LOC: Next to Post Office. PARK: 100yds. at bottom of street, turn left then right for multi-storey. TEL: 0225 466502. VAT: Stan/Spec.

Bath continued

Martin Dodge Interiors Ltd
15-16 Broad St. (M.J. Dodge). Est. 1969. Open 9.30-5.30. SIZE: Medium. STOCK: Furniture, 18th-19th C; watercolours, oil paintings, decorative items, especially papier mâché, mainly 19th C, £1,000-£10,000. LOC: Main road into city from A4. PARK: Easy, at rear. TEL: 0225 462202.

Dollin and Daines BADA
2 Church St, York St. Est. 1968. Open 10.30-1 and 2-4. CL: Thurs. and Sat. STOCK: Violins, violas, cellos and bows. TEL: 0225 462752. SER: Restorations (as stock).

Peter Dryden Ltd
2 Prince's Buildings, George St. Open 10-5. STOCK: English and continental furniture; works of art. TEL: 0225 423038. VAT: Spec.

Frank Dux Antiques
33 Belvedere, Lansdown Rd. (F. Dux and M. Hopkins). Resident. Open 10-6. SIZE: Medium. STOCK: Georgian and earlier furniture (mainly oak), £250-£5,000; 18th C and later glass, £10-£1,000; unusual decorative items - pottery, pewter, pictures, rugs. LOC: From Broad St. up Lansdown Hill, on right 100yds. past Guinea Lane. PARK: Easy. TEL: 0225 312367; fax - same. SER: Restorations (furniture); replicas made to order; search service. VAT: Spec.

Fiddle Sticks Antiques and Decorative Items
29b Belvedere, Lansdown Hill. (G.L. and V.L. Mason). Est. 1973. Open 11-6, Wed. and Sat. 8.30-5.30. SIZE: Medium. STOCK: Furniture including walnut and mahogany, £75-£5,000; clocks - longcase, bracket and carriage, £60-£4,000; decorative items, pine, £10-£5,000; all 18th-20th C. LOC: 400 yards up Belvedere from Guinea Lane. PARK: Easy. TEL: 0225 318743. SER: Valuations; restorations (furniture, clocks, paintings and prints). FAIRS: Bath. VAT: Stan/Spec.

The Galleon
33 Monmouth St. (D.L. Gwilliam and M.J. Wren). Est. 1972. Open 10-5.30, Sat. 10-6, or by appointment. SIZE: Medium. STOCK: Furniture, jewellery, silver, general collectables and antiques, Georgian to art deco, £5-£1,500. LOC: Near rear of Theatre Royal. PARK: Easy. TEL: 0225 312330. SER: Buys at auction. VAT: Stan/Spec.

George Street Antiques
8 Edgar Buildings, George St. Open 10-5.30. STOCK: Music boxes, clocks, general antiques and unusual collectables. TEL: 0225 444146.

David Gibson BADA LAPADA
4 Wood St, Queen Sq. Est. 1975. Open 10-5.30. CL: Mon. SIZE: Medium. STOCK: Longcase clocks, £2,500-£20,000; barometers and musical boxes. LOC: 200yds. from bottom of Milsom

Bath continued

St. towards Queen Sq., 1st floor above Andrew Dando. PARK: Easy. TEL: 0225 446646. SER: Valuations; restorations. FAIRS: Kenilworth, Olympia, NEC, and Northern (Harrogate). VAT: Spec.

Graylow and Co
George St. Open 10-5. *STOCK: Furniture, especially sets of dining chairs, and decorative accessories, mainly George III.* TEL: 0225 469859; fax - 0272 215405.

Great Western Antique Centre Ltd
Bartlett St. Open 10-5, Wed. 8.30-5. SIZE: 50 stands on the ground floor. There is an additional mkt. every Wed. with 20 stands. LOC: Adjacent to the Assembly Rooms and Museum of Costume. TEL: 0225 424243; stand holders - 0225 310388/428731.

Ancestors
Stand 30. (S. Rosser-Rees). *STOCK: Paintings, small objets d'art and porcelain.*

Antique Linen and Lace
Stands 7 and 8. (M. Adams and J. Watson). *STOCK: Linen and lace.*

Avril Antiques
Stand 25. (A. Brown). *STOCK: Silver, plate and small decorative items.*

Brunel Antiques
Stand 33 and 34. (J. and S. Mildred). *STOCK: Art pottery, arts and crafts, furniture and glass, 1850-1950.*

Churchstoke Booksellers
Stand 39. (B. Howard). *STOCK: Rare books and fine editions.*

Collectable Costume
Stand 42. (M. Adams and K.P. Jones). *STOCK: Antique costume and textiles, pre-1970, and accessories.*

Country Interiors
Stand 10. (L. Macrae-Stewart). *STOCK: Pine furniture.*

Crofton Antiques
Stand 13 and 14. (R. A. Gresham). *STOCK: Pine furniture.*

Deja Vu
Stand 26. (M. P. Nunan). *STOCK: Music boxes, jewellery, Oriental items, silver plate.*

Karen Freegard
Stand 24. *STOCK: Clocks, watches and furniture.*

Jessie's Button Box
Stand 9. (J. Partt). *STOCK: Collectors' and designers' buttons.*

L. B. Antiques
Stand 6. (L. Brine). *STOCK: Scent bottles and smalls.*

Bath continued

Macbeth
Stand 27 and 28. *STOCK: Decorative smalls and silver frames.*

Not Cartier
Stand 48. (G. Tinne). *STOCK: Semi-precious and Venetian glass jewellery.*

Notts Pine
Stand 21. *STOCK: Pine furniture.*

Jeff and Lindy Notts Pine
Stand 38. *STOCK: Pine furniture.*

Off the Rails
Stand 46 and 47. (S. Relph). *STOCK: Antique and period clothes and accessories.*

Ray's
Stand 5. (R. Harris). *STOCK: Jewellery.*

Silk Road Gallery
Stands 36 &37. (A. Lloyd and C. Bale). *STOCK: Antique carpets and rugs; table glass, 18th-19th C.*

Joan Southern
Stand 51. *STOCK: English and continental pine.*

Victoria
Stand 44 and 45. (V. Taylor). *STOCK: Pre 1960's clothes, accessories, textiles and small items.*

Winstone Stamp Co. and S. D. Postcards
Stand 1. (D. Winstone). *STOCK: Postal history, postcards, cigarette cards, collectors' items.* TEL: 0225 445520.

Mike Woodford
Stand 15 and 20. *STOCK: Furniture and general antiques.*

Great Western Antique Centre Ltd. - The Wednesday Market
Bartlett St. Open Wed. 7.30-4. The market has its own separate entrance. SIZE: 20 stands on the lower ground floor Below are listed some of the dealers at this market.

R. B. Crisp
Stand 4. *STOCK: Glass, instruments and general antiques.*

Jill Cullimore
Stand 3. *STOCK: General antiques and automobilia.*

M. Downworth
Stand 6. *STOCK: Dolls and general antiques.*

D. E. Gyles
Stand 12. *STOCK: Furniture and general antiques.*

D. R. and P. E. Martin
Stand 18. *STOCK: Radios, gramophones and 78 rpm records.*

Antique Collectors' Club Titles

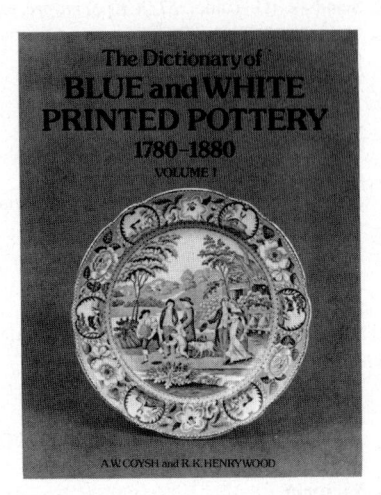

The Dictionary of Blue and White Printed Pottery 1780-1880 Volume I
by A.W. Coysh and R.K. Henrywood
Immediately acclaimed in 1982 as an outstanding reference work, this 1989 edition is reissued in its original form, but now the first of a two volume set. Covers the firms, the craftsmen, the techniques, the wares, the patterns, the titles, and provides a remarkable background to the history of the ceramics industry and the social customs of the day, as well as the personalities and problems involved in the production process. Appendices cover makers' initial marks and a list of source books used by makers of these wares.
ISBN 0 907462 06 5, 424pp, 706 b & w illus, 30 col, £29.95

The Dictionary of Blue and White Printed Pottery Volume II
by A.W. Coysh and R.K. Henrywood
This entirely new second volume includes over 1,000 new or extended entries. These cover many previously unrecorded patterns, recent attributions, newly discovered design sources, and a significant number of additional manufacturers and retailers. Some of the more interesting wares made after the original deadline of 1880 have also been included, with an Appendix illustrating unidentified patterns. An essential acquisition.
ISBN 1 85149 093 0, 240pp, 420 b & w illus, 28 col, £25.00

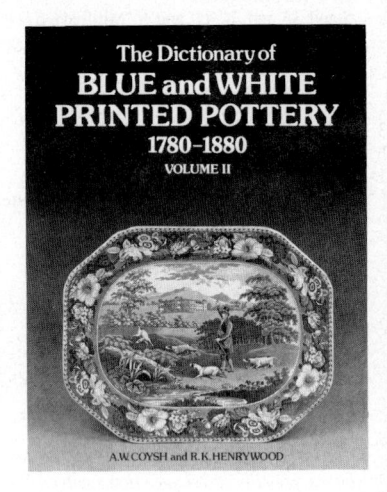

Available from:
Antique Collectors' Club, 5 Church Street, Woodbridge, Suffolk IP12 1DS
Tel: (0394) 385501 Fax: (0394) 384434

or Market Street Industrial Park, Wappingers' Falls, New York 12590, USA
Tel: 914 297 0003 Fax: 914 297 0068

Bath continued

S. Urquhart
Stand 19. STOCK: Decorative and general antiques.

Whittingham
Stand 1. STOCK: Furniture and general antiques.

Sue Boyle
Stand 35. STOCK: Paintings, watercolours and prints.

Gail Hislop
Stand 31 and 32. STOCK: Antique and 20th C jewellery and silver.

George Gregory
Manvers St. (H.H. Bayntun-Coward). Est. 1845. Open 9-1 and 2-5.30, Sat. 9.30-1. SIZE: Large. STOCK: Books, 1600 to date; engravings. LOC: By rail station. PARK: By rail station. TEL: 0225 466055. SER: Restorations (fine books). VAT: Stan.

Haliden Oriental Rug Shop
98 Walcot St. (B.W. Dennis). Est. 1963. Open 10-5. SIZE: Medium. STOCK: Caucasian, Turkish, Persian, Chinese, Afghan and tribal rugs and carpets, 19th C, £50-£3,000; some Oriental textiles - coats, embroideries, wall hangings, 19th C, £50-£750; Chinese porcelain and Oriental works of art, Ming or earlier, £50-£1,500; oil paintings, 19th C, £50-£1,500. LOC: Off main London road into town. PARK: Walcot St. multi-storey. TEL: 0225 469240. SER: Valuations; cleaning; restorations (as stock); buys at auction (as stock).

Helena Hood and Co
3 Margarets Buildings, Brock St. (Mrs L.M. Hood). Est. 1973. Open 9.30-1 and 2.15-5.30, Sat. 10.30-1. CL: Mon. SIZE: Medium. STOCK: Decorative items - furniture, prints, paintings and porcelain, 18th-19th C, £50-£2,500. LOC: Pedestrian walkway running north from Brock St. PARK: Easy. TEL: 0225 424438. SER: Restorations. VAT: Stan/Spec.

Jadis Ltd
The Old Bank, 17 Walcot Buildings, London Rd. (S.H. Creese-Parsons). Est. 1970. Open 9.30-6, Sun. by appointment. SIZE: Medium. STOCK: Furniture, English and European, 18th-19th C; decorative items. LOC: On left hand side of A4 London Rd., entering Bath. PARK: At rear. TEL: 0225 338797; fax - same; mobile - 0836 57245. VAT: Stan/Spec.

Orlando Jones
10b Monmouth Place, Upper Bristol Rd. Open 9.30-5.30. STOCK: Victorian and Edwardian brass bedsteads. TEL: 0225 422750.

Ann King
38 Belvedere, Lansdown Rd. Est. 1977. Open 10-4, Wed. 12-4. SIZE: Small. STOCK: Period clothes, 19th C to 1960; baby clothes, shawls,

Bath continued

bead dresses, linen, lace, curtains, cushions, quilts and textiles. LOC: Around corner from Guinea Lane Antique Market. PARK: Easy. TEL: 0225 336245; home - 0373 864747.

Kingsley Gallery
16 Margarets Buildings, Brock St. (S.M. Walton). Open 10-5.30 or by appointment. SIZE: Medium. STOCK: General antiques and decorative items, 17th-20th C, £30-£20,000. LOC: Off Brock St. between Circus and Royal Crescent. PARK: Nearby. TEL: 0225 448432; home - 0225 833344.

Lansdown Antiques
23 Belvedere, Lansdown Rd. (Chris and Ann Kemp). Open 9-6, Sat. 9-5, Sun. by appointment. STOCK: Painted pine and country furniture, 17th-19th C; metalware, unusual and decorative items. LOC: From A4/A46 junction across 1st set of traffic lights, right at mini roundabout, right at next traffic lights, shop 350yds. on left. PARK: Easy. TEL: 0225 313417; home - same. VAT: Stan/Spec.

Carr Linford
10-11 Walcot Buildings, London Rd. (N., J. and A. Carr Linford). SIZE: Medium. STOCK: Period and decorative furniture, 18th to early 19th C; caddies, small items. LOC: Near pelican crossing. PARK: Opposite. TEL: 0225 317516. FAIRS: Olympia; West London. VAT: Spec.

Looking Glass of Bath
96 Walcot St. (Anthony Reed). Est. 1972. Open 9-6. SIZE: Small. STOCK: Mirrors and picture frames, 18th-19th C; decorative prints, 18th-20th C; all £50-£500. PARK: Easy. TEL: 0225 461969; home - 0275 333595. SER: Valuations; restorations (re-gilding, gesso and compo work, re-silvering and bevelling glass); buys at auction (mirrors and pictures). VAT: Stan.

E.P. Mallory and Son Ltd BADA
1-4 Bridge St, and 5 Old Bond St. Est. 1856. STOCK: Period silver and Sheffield plate, jewellery, objets de vertu, £200-£20,000. TEL: 0225 465885. VAT: Stan/Spec.

Richard and Pamela Nadin
27a Belvedere, Lansdown. Est. 1970. Open 9.30-5.30, Sun. by appointment. SIZE: Small. STOCK: Unusual designer furniture, 19th C, £25-£5,000; some carpets, upholstery. LOC: Near Royal Crescent and Camden Crescent. PARK: Easy. TEL: 0225 428256. SER: Valuations; buys at auction. FAIRS: Olympia and West Kensington. VAT: Stan/Spec.

No.12 Queen Street
12 Queen St. (C. Roberts and K. Stables). Open 9.30-5.30 or by appointment. STOCK: Small furniture; textiles, needlework, samplers, decorative items. TEL: 0225 462363; home - 0225 314846. SER: Interior decorating. VAT: Spec.

Bath continued

Paragon Antiques and Collectors Market
3 Bladud Buildings, The Paragon. (T.J. Clifford and Son Ltd). Est. 1978. Open Wed. 6.30-3.30. SIZE: Large. LOC: Milsom St./Broad St. PARK: 50yds. TEL: 0225 463715.

Patterson Liddle
10 Margaret's Buildings, Brock St. Open 10-5.30. STOCK: Antiquarian books and prints especially British railways, inland waterways and aviation. TEL: 0225 426722. SER: Catalogues issued.

Pennard House Antiques   LAPADA
3/4 Piccadilly, London Rd. (M. and S. Dearden). Est. 1966. Open 9.30-5.30. SIZE: Large. STOCK: Pine, 18th-19th C, £100-£2,000; French provincial furniture, 17th-19th C; £500-£2,500; decorative items, 19th C, £30-£350. LOC: On A4 from east when entering city. PARK: Easy and at rear. TEL: 0225 313791; fax - 0225 448196; home - 074 986 266. SER: Valuations; restorations (furniture). VAT: Stan/Spec. The following dealers are also trading from these premises.

Claire Alderson
STOCK: Country items and decorative smalls.

Robin and Jan Coleman Antiques
STOCK: Interesting and decorative items. VAT: Stan/Spec.

John Davies
STOCK: 18th-19th C furniture especially country and Gothick oak, and decorative smalls. TEL: Home - 0225 852103.

Gene and Sally Foster (Antiques)
STOCK: Decorative and unusal items, 17th-19th C; continental and English painted furniture, paintings, needlework, prints and metalware, £25-£2,500. VAT: Stan/Spec.

Mike Holt
STOCK: 19th C decorative metalware.

Quiet Street Antiques
3 Quiet St. (K. Hastings-Spital). Est. 1985. Open 10-6. SIZE: Large. STOCK: Furniture, 1750-1870, £250-£6,000; objects including bronzes, caddies, boxes, mirrors, £50-£2,000; Royal Worcester porcelain, £30-£2,000; clocks including longcase, wall, bracket and carriage, 1750-1900, £150-£5,000. LOC: 25yds. from Milsom St. PARK: Nearby. TEL: 0225 315727. SER: Buys at auction (furniture and clocks).

P.R. Rainsford
23a Manvers St. Est. 1967. STOCK: Architecture, fine and applied art. TEL: 0225 445107. VAT: Stan.

T.E. Robinson   BADA
3 and 4 Bartlett St. Est. 1957. STOCK: Period furniture, glass, unusual and rare items. TEL: 0225 463982; home - 0225 832307. VAT: Spec.

Bath continued

Michael and Jo Saffell
3 Walcot Buildings, London Rd. Est. 1975. Open 9.30-5, Sat. by appointment. SIZE: Small. STOCK: British tins and other advertising material including showcards and enamels, 1870-1939; decorative items; all £5-£500. LOC: A4 - main road into city from M4. PARK: Side streets opposite. TEL: 0225 315857; home - same.

M. Sainsbury
35 Gay St. Est. 1930. Open by appointment. STOCK: Antiquities, pre 1800. Not Stocked: Fine pictures, silver. TEL: 0225 424808. SER: Valuations. VAT: Spec.

The Saville Row Gallery
1 Saville Row. Est. 1985. Open 9.45-5.00, Sat. 9.45-3, Sun. by appointment. SIZE: Medium. STOCK: Oil paintings and sculpture, 18th-20th C, from £200. LOC: Near London Rd. TEL: 0225 334595. SER: Valuations; restorations (oil paintings and frames). VAT: Stan/Spec.

Scott Antiques
11 London St. Open 10-5.30. STOCK: General antiques, Victoriana, bric-a-brac. TEL: Home - 0225 462423. VAT: Stan/Spec.

Susannah
142/144 Walcot St. (Susan M. Holley). Open 10-5. STOCK: Decorative antiques and textiles. TEL: 0225 445069.

Town and Country Antiques
11 Queen St. (R. Drewett). Open 10.30-5, other times by appointment. STOCK: Fine period and country furniture, metalware, caddies, boxes and period decorative items. PARK: Nearby. TEL: 0225 463176. VAT: Spec.

Trimbridge Galleries
2 Trimbridge. (Mr and Mrs A. Anderson). Est. 1973. SIZE: Medium. STOCK: Watercolours and drawings, £50-£3,000; prints and oil paintings; all 18th to early 20th C. LOC: Just off lower end of Milsom St. PARK: Easy. TEL: 0225 466390.

Walcot Reclamation
108 Walcot St. Est. 1977. Open 8.30-5.30, Sat. 9-5. SIZE: Large. STOCK: Architectural items - chimney pieces, ironwork, doors, fireplaces, garden statuary, period baths and fittings and traditional building materials. PARK: Own and multi-storey nearby. TEL: 0225 444404/335532. SER: Valuations; restorations; brochure available. VAT: Stan.

Glenda Wallis and Gerry Mosdell
6 Chapel Row, Queen Sq. ABA. Est. 1971. Open 10-5.30. SIZE: Large. STOCK: General antiquarian, early and Victorian children's books, illustrated; folklore, Canadiana and prints. LOC: Corner Queen Sq. (city centre). PARK: Easy. TEL: 0225 424677.

ANTIQUES AT PENNARD HOUSE

Now joining Martin Dearden

Five dealers in decorative and country furniture
Robin Coleman, Gene Foster, John Davies, Mike Holt and Claire Alderson

3/4 Piccadilly, London Road, Bath, Avon, BA1 6PL.
Tel: Bath (0225) 313791 Fax: (0225) 448196

**AN ECLECTIC SELECTION OF
THE RARE AND UNUSUAL**

Bath continued

Widcombe Antiques and Pine
9 Claverton Buildings, Widcombe. Est. 1972. SIZE: Medium. *STOCK: Stripped pine.* LOC: A36. PARK: Own at rear. TEL: 0225 428767.

BRISTOL

Alexander Gallery
122 Whiteladies Rd. (J. A. Fardon). Open 9-5.30, Wed. 9-1. *STOCK: 19th-20th C paintings, watercolours and prints.* TEL: 0272 734692; fax - 0272 466991.

Antique Beds
3 Litfield Place. (Mrs V. Dewdney). Est. 1973. Open at all times but appointment advisable. SIZE: Medium. *STOCK: Four-poster beds, 18th-19th C, £995-£5,000.* LOC: Near suspension bridge. PARK: Easy. TEL: 0272 735134; home - same.

Au Temps Perdu
5 Stapleton Rd., Easton. (Peter C. Chapman). Open 10-6. SIZE: Large. *STOCK: Period fireplaces, bathroom ware and doors.* TEL: 0272 555223. LOC: On edge of old market. PARK: Easy.

The Barometer Shop
2 Lower Park Row. (R. Cookson and R. Worthington). Est. 1965. Open 10-5.30 or by appointment. *STOCK: Barometers, clocks and watches, scientific instruments, 18th-19th C; furniture and early metalware.* TEL: 0272 272565. SER: Valuations; restorations; spare parts for barometers and clocks.

Bizarre Antiques
210 Gloucester Rd, Bishopston. (P.J. Parkin). Open 8.15-5. *STOCK: General antiques.* TEL: 0272 427888; home - 0272 503498.

Bristol Antique Market
St. Nicholas Markets, The Exchange, Corn St. (M.R. Harper). Est. 1975. Open Fri. 9-3. SIZE: 12 dealers. *STOCK: Antiques and collectors' items.* TEL: 0272 224014.

Bristol Guild of Applied Art Ltd
68/70 Park St. Est. 1908. Open 9-5.30, Sat. 9-5. *STOCK: Furniture, late 19th-20th C.* TEL: 0272 265548.

Bristol Trade Antiques
192 Cheltenham Rd. (L. Dike). Est. 1970. SIZE: Large and warehouse. *STOCK: General antiques.* TEL: 0272 422790.

Robin Butler   BADA
20 Clifton Rd. Est. 1978. Open 9.30-5.30, Sat. 10-3. SIZE: Medium. *STOCK: Fine furniture, silver, wine antiques, glass and works of art, 1600-1850, from £50.* Not Stocked: Victoriana, weapons, carpets, shipping goods. LOC: Map showing location sent on request. PARK: Easy, in drive to left of shop. TEL: 0272 733017. SER: Valuations. FAIRS: Bath and Olympia. VAT: Spec.

Bristol continued

Carnival Antiques   LAPADA
607 Sixth Avenue, Central Business Park, Hengrove. (A.J. Williams). Est. 1967. Open 9.30-5.30. *STOCK: Glass, china, brass, copper, furniture.* TEL: 0275 892166; home - 0275 835223; fax - 0275 891333. SER: Shipping and packing. VAT: Stan/Spec.

Cleeve Antiques
282 Lodge Causeway, Fishponds. (T. and S.E. Scull). Est. 1978. Open 9.30-5.30. CL: Wed. *STOCK: Furniture and bric-a-brac.* TEL: 0272 658366; home - 0272 567008.

Clifton Antiques Market
26/28 The Mall, Clifton. (Ledwell Ltd.). Est. 1974. Open 10-6. CL: Mon. SIZE: Large - 60 dealers. *STOCK: A wide selection of general antiques and collectors' items, £5-£1,000.* LOC: Near Clifton suspension bridge. PARK: Easy. TEL: 0272 734531. Below are listed some of the dealers at this market.

G. Barnes
STOCK: Jewellery and collectors' items.

Bees and Graves
STOCK: Small items., jewellery, art nouveau art deco.

P. Biggs
STOCK: Silver, general antiques.

J. Brindle
STOCK: Small items, jewellery and clothes.

S. Coles
STOCK: Porcelain, brass and copper, fine furniture.

T. Cox
STOCK: Clocks and watches, pictures and silver plate.

G. Dowling
STOCK: Picture framing and gilding.

Miss S. Foster
STOCK: Unusual diamond and gold jewellery. TEL: 0272 736996; home - 0272 738390. VAT: Stan.

Rachel James
STOCK: Book-binding.

P. Jones
STOCK: Furniture, reproduction and antiques.

R. Jones
STOCK: Clocks, watches. SER: Repairs.

Mrs M. Jubb
STOCK: General antiques, furniture. TEL 0272 734698; home - 0272 738520.

Mrs M. T. Kerridge
STOCK: Silver, jewellery, small items. TEL 0272 738504.

Key to Town Plan

AA Recommended roads	Car Parks
Other roads	Parks and open spaces
Restricted roads	AA Service Centre
Buildings of interest	

© Automobile Association 1988.

AVON

Bristol continued

Mrs R. Littlejohn
STOCK: Jewellery.

Mac-Smith
(P. Mackenzie-Smith). STOCK: Upholstered furniture. TEL: 0272 735678.

Jan Morrison
STOCK: Small items, china, glass, cutlery and linen.

J. Oakes
STOCK: Architectural antiques, copper and brass.

Mrs M. Risdale
STOCK: Silver, gold, jewellery, china. TEL: 0272 734698.

S. Trickey
STOCK: Jewellery. SER: Repairs.

Vincent's
STOCK: Jewellery, old and new.

Cotham Galleries
22 Cotham Hill, Cotham. (D. Jury). Est. 1960. Open 9-5.30. SIZE: Small. STOCK: Furniture, glass, metal. LOC: From city centre up Park St. into Whiteladies Rd. Turn right at Clifton Down station. PARK: Easy. TEL: 0272 736026. SER: Valuations.

Cotham Hill Bookshop
39A Cotham Hill, Cotham. (R. Plant and M. Garbett). Open 9.30-5.30. STOCK: Antiquarian and secondhand books especially fine art; antiquarian prints. TEL: 0272 732344.

David Cross (Fine Art)
7 Boyces Ave, Clifton. Est. 1969. Open 9.30-6. STOCK: British paintings, especially marine, Bristol school; related drawings, prints and watercolours. LOC: Between Victoria Sq. and Regent St. PARK: Easy. TEL: 0272 732614. SER: Valuations; restorations (oils, watercolours, frames); buys at auction; framing. VAT: Spec.

Richard Essex Antiques
Est. 1969. STOCK: General antiques from mid-18th C. TEL: 0272 733949.

Flame and Grate
159 Hotwells Rd., Hotwells. Open 9-5. STOCK: Original cast-iron fireplaces, marble surrounds and fireplace accessories. TEL: 0272 252560/292930. PARK: Easy.

Frocks and Tails
39A Cotham Hill, Cotham. (A.G. Haig-Harrison). Est. 1977. Open 10-5.30. STOCK: Ladies and gentlemens 1920's style evening wear. LOC: Off Whiteladies Rd. PARK: Clifton Down shopping centre or nearby. TEL: 0272 737461. SER: Dinner, tail and morning suit hire.

Bristol continued

Grey-Harris and Co BADA
12 Princess Victoria St, Clifton. Est. 1963. Open 9.30-5.30. STOCK: Jewellery, Victorian; silver, old Sheffield plate. TEL: 0272 737365. SER: Valuations. VAT: Stan/Spec.

Chris Grimes Militaria
13 Lower Park Row. Open 11-5.30. STOCK: Militaria, scientific instruments, nautical items. TEL: 0272 298205.

A.R. Heath
62 Pembroke Rd, Clifton. Open by appointment only. STOCK: Rare books, pamphlets, broadsides, pre-1850. TEL: 0272 741183; fax - 0272 732901.

Kemps
9 Carlton Court, Westbury-on-Trym. (P.M. Kemp). Open 9-5.30. STOCK: Jewellery. TEL 0272 505090.

The Mall Gallery
16 The Mall, Clifton. (C.R.H. Warren). Est. 1971 Open 10-5.30. CL: Mon. and Sat. STOCK: Paintings, £500-£5,000; watercolours, £100-£2,000. TEL: 0272 736263. SER: Buys at auction VAT: Spec.

The Mall Jewellers
4 The Mall, Clifton. STOCK: Jewellery, silver plate. TEL: 0272 733178. VAT: Stan/Spec.

Michael's Antiques
150 Wells Rd. (M. Beese). Resident. TEL: 027. 713943.

Robert Mills Architectural Antiques Ltd
Unit 2 Satellite Business Park, Blackswarth Rd. Redfield. Est. 1969. Open 9.30-5, Sat. 9-12. SIZE Large. STOCK: Architectural items, panelled rooms, shop interiors, Gothic Revival, stained glass, church woodwork, bar and restauran fittings, 1750-1920, £50-£30,000. LOC: A42 from Bristol, turn right at Fire Engine publi house, then left towards Crews Hole, first yard o right. PARK: Easy. TEL: 0272 556542; home 0272 555824; fax - 0272 558146. VAT: Stan.

No. 74 Antiques and Collectables
74 Alma Rd, Clifton. (Mrs S.J. Wilson and Mr M. Skinner). Est. 1989. Open 10.30-5.30. SIZE Medium. STOCK: English walnut and mahogan furniture, 18th-19th C, £100-£4,000+; Englis and continental porcelain, 19th C, £20-£500+ LOC: Turning off Whiteladies Rd., main roa from city centre to M4/M5. PARK: Easy. TEI 0272 733821; home - 0272 730351. SER: Resto ations including upholstery; buys at auctio (furniture). VAT: Stan/Spec.

Rosa Barovier Mentasti
VENETIAN GLASS 1890-1990
This fascinating book traces the historic course of Venetian artistic glassware through the 20th century. The rich illustrated section contains more than 200 colour photographs and gives a close-up and detailed view of this remarkable art. Its historic value is greatly enhanced by the inclusion of many of the rarest pieces from private collections, never before photographed or published.

Both collectors and enthusiasts will find all the necessary information to identify the artisans and styles which have literally made the history of Venetian glass.
ISBN 88 7743 119 9
208pp, 200 colour plates, £45.00

Available from:
Antique Collectors' Club, 5 Church Street, Woodbridge, Suffolk IP12 1DS
Tel: (0394) 385501 Fax: (0394) 384434

or Market Street Industrial Park, Wappingers' Falls, New York 12590, USA
Tel: 914 297 0003 Fax: 914 297 0068

Bristol continued

Oldwoods
1 Colston Yard. (S. Wilcox and S. Duck). Open 10-4, Fri. and Sat. 10-5.30. CL: Mon. *STOCK: Pine and fireplaces.* TEL: 0272 299023. SER: Restorations.

The Oriental Carpet Centre
c/o Maples, 3 Queen's Rd., Clifton. (I. McDonagh). Open 9-5.30. *STOCK: Oriental carpets and rugs.* TEL: 0272 290165.

Period Fireplaces
Unit 17 Enterprise Workshops, Winkworth Place, St. Pauls. (John Ashton and Martyn Roberts). Est. 1987. CL: Sat p.m. SIZE: Small. *STOCK: Fireplaces, 19th C, £250-£350; reproduction fireplaces, £150-£250.* LOC: Just off Ashley Rd. PARK: Easy. TEL: 0272 412258; home - 0272 424091. SER: Valuations; restorations. VAT: Stan.

Potter's Antiques and Coins
60 Colston St. (B.C. Potter). Est. 1965. Open 10.30-5.30. SIZE: Small. *STOCK: Antiquities, 500 B.C. to 1600 A.D., £5-£500; commemoratives, 1770-1953, £4-£300; coins, 500 B.C. to 1967, £1-£100; drinking glass, 1770-1953, £3-£200; small furniture, from 1837, £10-£200.* LOC: Near top of Christmas Steps, close to city centre. PARK: N.C.P. Park Row. TEL: 0272 262551. SER: Valuations; buys at auction. VAT: Stan/Spec.

Bristol continued

Relics - Pine Furniture
109 St. George's Rd, Hotwells. (R. Seville and S. Basey). Est. 1972. Open 10-6. SIZE: Large. *STOCK: Victorian style pine furniture, £25-£700.* LOC: Near cathedral, 1/2 mile from city centre. PARK: Easy. TEL: 0272 268453. VAT: Stan.

John Roberts Bookshop
43 Triangle West, Clifton. (J.T. Roberts). Est. 1955. Open 9.30-5.30. SIZE: Medium. *STOCK: Secondhand and antiquarian books, topographical and other prints.* LOC: Just off Queens Rd. shopping centre. PARK: Nearby, multi-storey. TEL: 0272 268568. SER: Picture framing. VAT: Spec.

R.A. Saunders
162 Raleigh Rd, Bedminster. Open 8-5. *STOCK: Furniture; bric-a-brac.* TEL: 0272 631268; home - 0272 662637. SER: Repairs (clocks and barometers); polishing.

John and Sheila Symes
93 Charleton Mead Drive, Westbury-on-Trym. Open by appointment. *STOCK: Postcards, ephemera and autographs.* TEL: 0272 501074.

The Vintage Wireless Co Ltd
Tudor House, Cossham St., Mangotsfield. (T.G. Rees). Est. 1972. SIZE: Medium. *STOCK: Valve radio receivers, vintage valve hi-fi, 1920-1950;*

Somervale Antiques

Wing Cdr. R.G. Thomas M.B.E. R.A.F. (Ret'd)
6 Radstock Road
Midsomer Norton, Bath, BA3 2AJ
Tel: 0761 412686

Shop open only by appointment. Resident on the premises. 24 hour telephone service. Trains to Bath met by arrangement.

Specialist in 18th and early 19th century English drinking glasses, decanters, cut and coloured, "Bristol" and "Nailsea", glass etc. Also bijouterie; scent bottles.

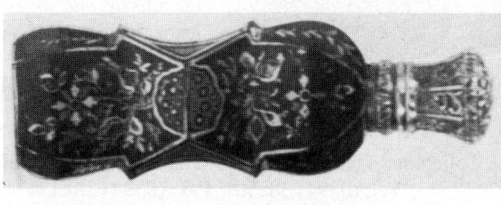

Member of British Antique Dealers' Association
Member of London and Provincial Antique Dealers' Association

Bristol continued

radio components, historical and technical data. LOC: A3174. PARK: Easy. TEL: 0272 565472; fax - 0272 575442. VAT: Stan. *Mail Order Only.*

The Wise Owl Bookshop
26 Upper Maudlin St. Open 10.30-5.30. *STOCK: Antiquarian and secondhand books, all subjects including music and the performing arts; sheet music and records.* TEL: 0272 262738; evenings - 0272 246936.

CHIPPING SODBURY, Nr. Bath

Sodbury Antiques
70 Broad St. (Mrs M. Brown). Est. 1986. CL: Wed. SIZE: Small. *STOCK: Porcelain and china, mainly 18th-19th C, small furniture, £5-£500; secondhand jewellery.* PARK: Easy. TEL: 0454 273369. SER: Buys at auction.

CLEVEDON

Beach Antiques
Adelaide House, 13 The Beach. (D.A. Coles). Open 2-5, Sat. and Sun. 11-5. CL: Mon. and Fri. *STOCK: Jewellery, silver frames, china, brass, glass, mainly small items.* PARK: Easy. TEL: 0275 876881.

Clevedon continued

Clevedon Fine Arts (with Clevedon Books)
14 Woodside Rd. Est. 1972. Open by appointment or post. *STOCK: Maps, charts, prints, books.* TEL: 0275 872304.

John and Carol Hawley Antique Clocks
The Orchard, Clevedon Lane, Clapton Wick. CMBHI. Est. 1972. Open by appointment. *STOCK: Clocks especially longcase, bracket, wall and carriage.* TEL: 0275 852052. SER: Valuations; restorations; repairs.

CLUTTON

Ian and Dianne McCarthy
Arcadian Cottage, 112 Station Rd. Resident. Est. 1958. Open by appointment. SIZE: Medium. *STOCK: Lamps - oil, gas, electric for domestic, industrial, shipping and transport usage; unusual candle lamps; copper and brassware, 17th C to 1920, £5-£500.* PARK: Easy and opposite. TEL: 0761 53188. SER: Valuations; restorations (metalware); cleaning; upholstery; rush seating; spares and lamp-shades. FAIRS: Shepton Mallet. *Trade Only.*

AVON

FRESHFORD, Nr. Bath
Janet Clarke
3 Woodside Cottages. Open by appointment. *STOCK: Antiquarian books on gastronomy, cookery and wine.* TEL: 0225 723186. SER: Catalogue issued.

MARSHFIELD, Nr. Bath
David Bridgwater
112 High St. Open by appointment. *STOCK: Sculptural items, garden ornaments, metalwork, architectural and decorative items.* TEL: 0225 891623.

MIDSOMER NORTON
Somervale Antiques BADA LAPADA
6 Radstock Rd. (Wing Cdr. R.G. Thomas). CINOA. Resident. Open by appointment only. *STOCK: English drinking glasses, decanters, cut and coloured; "Bristol" and "Nailsea"glass; bijouterie; glass scent bottles, 18th to early 19th C.* LOC: On A362 on Radstock side of town. PARK: Easy. TEL: 0761 412686 (24hrs.). SER: Valuations; buys at auction. FAIRS: Chelsea Spring and Autumn; LAPADA, London (Oct.). VAT: Stan/Spec.

OLVESTON, Nr. Bristol
Green Farm Antiques
The Green. (V. Gillespie). Est. 1985. Usually open but prior telephone call advisable. SIZE: Medium. *STOCK: Oak and country furniture, 17th-18th C, £50-£3,000; decorative items.* LOC: 5 mins. from junction 20, M4 or junction 16, M5 or 3 miles from Severn Bridge. PARK: Easy. TEL: 0454 612362; home - same. FAIRS: Reg Cooper.

REDLAND, Nr. Bristol
Something Old, Something New
115 Cold Harbour Rd. (Z. Bouyamourn). Open 10-5.30. *STOCK: General antiques.* TEL: 0272 247479.

WEST HARPTREE, Nr. Bristol
Tilly Manor Antiques
Tilly Manor. (J.D. Scott). Est. 1978. Open 9.30-5.30, Sun. and other times by appointment. SIZE: Large. *STOCK: Town and country furniture, 18th-19th C, £100-£3,000; brass, copper and metalware, 17th-19th C, decorative collectors items, 18th-19th C; all £5-£500.* LOC: Next to church on A368. PARK: Own. TEL: 0761 221888; home - same. SER: Restorations. VAT: Stan/Spec.

WESTON-SUPER-MARE
Bay Tree House Antiques
Stevens Lane, Lympsham. (N.W. and S.M. Adams). Est. 1982. Open 10-5.30 including Sun. SIZE: Warehouse. *STOCK: Stripped pine, satin walnut and mahogany, £25-£2,000.* PARK: Easy. TEL: 0934 750367: home - same.

Weston-Super-Mare continued
D.M. Restorations
3 Laburnum Rd. (D. Pike). Open 9-5. *STOCK: Small mahogany furniture.* PARK: Easy. TEL: 0934 631681.

Harwood West End Antiques LAPADA
13 West St. (A. and D.B.M. Harwood). Est. 1967. Open 9.15-5. *STOCK: General antiques, jewellery, clocks, Victoriana.* TEL: 0934 629874. VAT: Stan/Spec.

Moorland Antiques
134 Moorland Rd. (T. Lim). Open 9-5.30. *STOCK: General antiques.* TEL: 0934 632361.

Sterling Books
43A Locking Rd. Est. 1966. Open 9-6. *STOCK: Books, antiquarian and secondhand, some new; ephemera and prints.* TEL: 0934 625056. SER: Bookbinding and picture framing.

Toby's Antiques
47 Upper Church Rd. (D. White). Open 9-5, Thurs. and Sun. by appointment. *STOCK: Furniture and general antiques.* TEL: 0934 623555.

Winter's Antiques LAPADA
62 Severn Rd. (R.N., E.P. and L.B. Winters). Est. 1967. Open 9-12 and 2-3.30. CL: Sat. p.m. and Thurs. SIZE: Large. *STOCK: Furniture, clocks, smalls and fine art, all periods.* Not Stocked: Coins, stamps. LOC: Off sea front. PARK: Easy. TEL: 0934 620118/623105/81460.

WRINGTON
Sir William Russell Flint Galleries Ltd
The Georgian House, Broad St. Open 9-5, weekends by appointment. SIZE: Small. *STOCK: Prints, £65-£2,000; engravings, £650-£1,000; books, £75-£1,000; watercolours, £1,000-£25,000; all by Sir William and Francis Murray Russell Flint.* LOC: 3 miles south-west of Bristol Airport. PARK: Easy. TEL: 0934 863149. SER: Valuations. FAIRS: British International, Birmingham; Gallery 92. VAT: Stan/Spec.

YATTON, Nr. Bristol
Glenville Antiques LAPADA
120 High St. (Mrs S.E.M. Burgan). Est. 1969. Open 10.30-5. CL: Sun. except by appointment. SIZE: Small. *STOCK: Glass, £5-£750; small furniture, £25-£2,500; pottery and porcelain, £5-£1,500, all mainly 19th C; collectors' items, sewing items.* Not Stocked: Pewter, guns, antique foreign curios, coins, stamps. LOC: On B3133. PARK: Easy. TEL: 0934 832284. VAT: Stan/Spec.

Bedfordshire

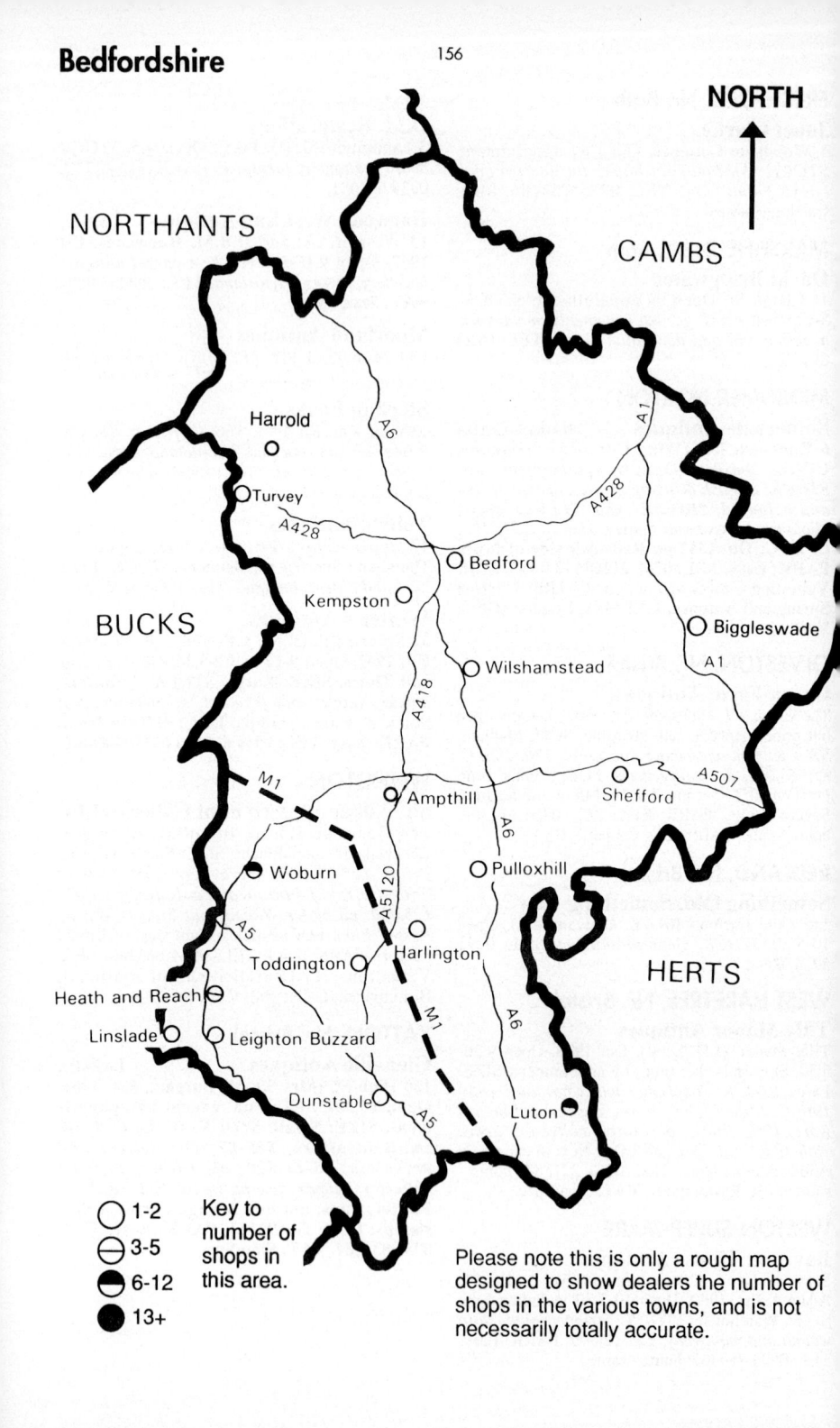

NORTH ↑

NORTHANTS

CAMBS

BUCKS

HERTS

- Harrold
- Turvey
- Bedford
- Kempston
- Biggleswade
- Wilshamstead
- Ampthill
- Shefford
- Woburn
- Pulloxhill
- Toddington
- Harlington
- Heath and Reach
- Linslade
- Leighton Buzzard
- Dunstable
- Luton

Roads: A6, A1, A428, A418, A507, A5120, M1, A5

Key to number of shops in this area.
- ○ 1-2
- ⊖ 3-5
- ⊖ 6-12
- ● 13+

Please note this is only a rough map designed to show dealers the number of shops in the various towns, and is not necessarily totally accurate.

Bedfordshire

AMPTHILL
Ampthill Antiques
Market Square. (A. Olney). Est. 1980. Open 10-5, Sun. 2-5. SIZE: Large. *STOCK: Furniture, collectables, jewellery, watercolours and oil paintings, clocks.* LOC: Town centre. PARK: Easy and at rear. TEL: 0525 403344. SER: Restorations (clocks).

Ampthill Emporium
6 Bedford St. Est. 1978. Open 10-5.30 including Sun. SIZE: Large - 15 dealers. *STOCK: Furniture, mainly 19th C, £50-£5,000; decorative items, £5-£500; books, pine.* LOC: 5 mins. from junction 13, M1. PARK: Easy. TEL: 0525 402131. SER: Restorations (furniture and stripping). VAT: Stan/Spec.

Pat Bently Antiques
7 Kings Arms Yard. Est. 1976. Open 11-5.30 including Sun. CL: Mon. SIZE: Large - 2 shops and showroom. *STOCK: Furniture, beds and decorative items.* PARK: Easy. TEL: 0525 404939. VAT: Stan/Spec.

Robert Harman Antiques   BADA
11 Church St. (R.H. Cannell). Est. 1981. Open 9.30-12.30 and 1.30-5.30, Sun. and evenings by appointment. SIZE: Medium. *STOCK: Furniture and works of art, £500-£30,000; papier mâché, tôle, £200-£5,000; all 18th to early 19th C.* PARK: Easy and opposite. TEL: 0525 402322; home - same. SER: Valuations; restorations (furniture); buys at auction (furniture and works of art). FAIRS: Chelsea Spring & Autumn; Olympia; Café Royal; BADA. VAT: Spec.

The Old Pine Loft
2B Woburn St. Open 10-5, Sat. 10-4. CL: Mon. *STOCK: Victorian fireplaces and doors, old pine.* TEL: 0525 840226. SER: Pine stripping.

The Pine Parlour
82a Dunstable St. (Lynn Barker). Est. 1989. Open 10-5, including Sun. CL: Mon. SIZE: Small. *STOCK: Pine furniture, 19th C, £200-£800; kitchenalia, £5-£60.* PARK: Easy. TEL: 0525 403030; home - same. SER: Valuations.

Ann Roberts Antiques
1 Kings Arms Yard. Est. 1980. Open 11-4.30, Sun. 2-5. CL: Mon. and Tues. SIZE: Medium. *STOCK: Georgian and Victorian fenders, fire irons and wood surrounds; Victorian cast iron fires; brass, copper and iron fire accessories, furniture and clocks.* LOC: Mews off town centre, A507. PARK: 50yds. TEL: 0525 403394.

S. and S. Timms Antiques Ltd   LAPADA
16, 18 and 20 Dunstable St. Est. 1976. Open 9-6, Sat. 10-4, other times by appointment. SIZE: Large. *STOCK: Furniture, 1700-1900, £500-£15,000; copper, brass.* LOC: A5120. PARK:

Ampthill continued

Easy. TEL: 0525 403067; home - 0525 718829; mobile - 0860 482995. FAIRS: Barbican, NEC (August and April), Guildford, Kensington. VAT: Stan/Spec.

BEDFORD
Stapleton's Antiques
51 Ford End Rd. (D.H. Stapleton). Est. 1976. Open 9-5. SIZE: Small and warehouse. *STOCK: General antiques, especially mahogany and oak furniture and clocks, 18th-19th C, £5-£2,000.* LOC: A428. PARK: Easy. TEL: 0234 211087; home - same. SER: Valuations.

BIGGLESWADE
Shortmead Antiques
46 Shortmead St. (S.E. Sinfield). Open 10.30-4. CL: Thurs. SIZE: Small. *STOCK: Furniture, £50-£1,000; boxes, porcelain, silver, bronzes, copper and brass, all pre-1930.* LOC: 1/2 mile from A1. TEL: 0767 601780 (ansaphone).

DUNSTABLE
Castle Coins and Chiltern International Antiques
47a High St. South. Open 9.30-5. *STOCK: Jewellery, coins and medals, general antiques.* TEL: 0582 606751/602778.

HARLINGTON
Willow Farm Pine Centre
Willow Farm. (M. and A. Price). Est. 1974. Open 10-5 every day. SIZE: Large. *STOCK: Country pine.* LOC: Off Barton Rd. PARK: Easy. TEL: 0525 872052; home - same.

HARROLD
Harrold Antique Centre
Chepstow Place, High St. (Geoff and Shirley Knight). Open 10-6 including Sun; Wed. 10-1. SIZE: 20 dealers. *STOCK: Pine and period furniture, linen, clocks, pottery, china and collectables.* TEL: 0234 720666. LOC: Off A428 Bedford-Northampton road. SER: Pine stripping.

HEATH AND REACH, Nr. Leighton Buzzard
"Brindleys"
Woburn Rd. (B. Dawson and Michael Spencer). *STOCK: Pottery and porcelain, £10-£500; paintings and watercolours, 18th-20th C, £100-£1,000; furniture, £100-£1,500; Georgian silver, £20-£1,000.* TEL: 0525 237750; home - 0234 240448.

Charterhouse Gallery Ltd
26 Birds Hill. Open 9.30-5. CL: Fri. *STOCK: 19th to early 20th C watercolours.* PARK: Easy - next door. TEL: 0525 23379.

Antique Collectors' Club Titles

English Earthenware Figures 1740-1840
by Pat Halfpenny
This long awaited volume is an eminently readable account of eighteenth and early nineteenth century production of popular earthenware figures. The leading authority on Staffordshire porcelain and earthenware, the author is Keeper of Ceramics at the City Museum and Art Gallery, Stoke-on-Trent, and is therefore uniquely qualified to write on the subject, for she has at her fingertips the finest collection of English earthenware to be found anywhere in the world, allied with a wealth of archival material.
346pp, 495 b & w illus, 89 col, ISBN 1 85149 114 7, £35.00

Staffordshire Portrait Figures of the Victorian Era
by P.D. Gordon Pugh
A revised edition of the standard work affectionately known as 'Pugh', based on the 1981 revised edition, this book provides what the collector of Staffordshire portait figures has long required: a vast photographic reference to the 1,500 or so portrait figures which encapsulate so much of the history of Victorian England. New colour photographs have been specially taken for this invaluable book.
560pp, 900 b & w illus, 62 col, ISBN 1 85149 010 8, £45.00

English Porcelain Animals *by Dennis G. Rice*
This is the first comprehensive work on the subject of these fascinating and collectable pieces. The fifteen factories that produced them are identified, such as Rockingham, Derby, Minton, Swansea, Copeland, Davenport and Alcock, and potteries such as Charles Bourne, Hilditch & Hopwood, Daniel Edge, and James Dudson.
282pp, 163 b & w illus, 35 col illus, ISBN 1 85149 085 X, £25.00

Available from:
Antique Collectors' Club, 5 Church Street
Woodbridge, Suffolk IP12 1DS
Tel: (0394) 385501 Fax: (0394) 384434

or Market Street Industrial Park
Wappingers' Falls, New York 12590, USA
Tel: 914 297 0003 Fax: 914 297 0068

BEDFORDSHIRE

Heath and Reach continued
Heath Antique Centre
Woburn Rd. Est. 1985. Open 11-5, Sun 1-5. SIZE: Large. LOC: A418 off A5. PARK: Easy. TEL: 0525 237831.

Helton Antiques
Helton House, 28 Birds Hill. (A. H. Cox). Open 10-6. SIZE: Large. STOCK: General antiques, shipping goods, collectable items. TEL: 052 523 474; home - 0525 372887.

KEMPSTON
Queen Adelaide Gallery
79 High St. (W.T. Gibbs). Open 10-6. CL: Mon. STOCK: Oils, watercolours and some prints, 18th-20th C, £50-£7,000. LOC: From Bedford, along Kempston Rd., past South Wing Hospital. PARK: Easy. TEL: 0234 854083; home - same. SER: Valuations; restorations (paintings and frames).

Eva Rogers
Spinney Lodge, The Hoo. Est. 1962. STOCK: General antiques. TEL: 0234 854823; home - same.

LEIGHTON BUZZARD
David Ball Antique and Fine Art   LAPADA
59 North St. (D. and J. Ball). Est. 1968. Open 10-5. SIZE: Large. STOCK: Furniture, general antiques and watercolours, 17th-20th C, £3-£2,000. LOC: A418 to Woburn. PARK: Easy. TEL: 0525 382954; home - 0525 210753. SER: Valuations; restorations. FAIRS: Luton and Dunstable. VAT: Stan/Spec.

LINSLADE, Nr. Leighton Buzzard
Linslade Antiques and Curios
1 New Rd. Est. 1978. Open 9.30-6. STOCK: General antiques, silver, china, furniture, clocks, toys, prints and paintings. LOC: 5 mins. walk from Leighton Buzzard station. TEL: 0525 378348. SER: Courier.

LUTON
Bargain Box
4 & 6a Adelaide St. Open 9-6, Wed. 9-1. STOCK: General antiques. TEL: 0582 423809.

Bernadette's Antiques & Collectables
19a Adelaide St. Open 9-6, Wed. 9-1. STOCK: General antiques. TEL: 0582 21469/423809.

J. Denton (Antiques)
Rear of 440 Dunstable Rd. Est. 1979. Open 10.15-3 or by appointment. CL: Sat. SIZE: Medium. STOCK: Furniture and small items, Victorian and Edwardian; shipping goods, bric-a-brac. LOC: Corner of Arundel Rd. and Dunstable Rd. PARK: Easy. TEL: 0582 582726; home - 0296 661471.

Luton continued
Foye Gallery
15 Stanley St. Est. 1960. Open 9.30-5 or by appointment. STOCK: Engravings, etchings, drawings, watercolours, paintings, maps, books. TEL: 0582 38487. VAT: Stan.

Knight's Gallery
59-61 Guildford St. (J.C. Knight). Est. 1973. Open 9-5, Sat. 10-1. SIZE: Small. STOCK: Watercolours, 19th-20th C, £50-£2,000. LOC: Rear of Guildford St. PARK: Easy. TEL: 0582 36266; home - 0582 604142. SER: Valuations; restorations; framing; buys at auction (watercolours). VAT: Stan.

Leaside Antiques
(T.G. Pepper). Est. 1968. Open by appointment. STOCK: Furniture, to 1910; jewellery, cameras, silver, porcelain, paintings. TEL: 0582 27957. SER: Repairs (jewellery).

PULLOXHILL, Nr. Ampthill
Riches
Unit 2, College Farm. (R.J. Jennings). Open 10-4. CL: Tues. STOCK: General antiques, Victorian furniture. Not Stocked: Jewellery, coins, silver. TEL: 0525 717786. SER: Re-upholstery; re-caning.

SHEFFORD
Secondhand Alley
2-4 High St. Open 9-5.30, Wed. and Sat. 9-5. STOCK: Shipping furniture, bric-a-brac. PARK: Easy. TEL: 0462 814747. VAT: Stan.

TODDINGTON, Nr. Dunstable
Cobblers Hall Antiques
119/121 Leighton Rd. (A.G. and N.E. Huckett). Est. 1974. Open by appointment only. STOCK: English porcelain, mid-18th to mid-19th C, £25-£400. Georgian and early Victorian writing boxes and slopes, treen, Tunbridgeware, period brass and copper. PARK: Easy. TEL: 052 55 2890. FAIRS: Cheltenham, Worcester, Petersfield, Derby, Felbridge, Harrogate, Oatland Park, Ragley Hall and Worksop, NEC.

TURVEY, Nr. Bedford
Fenlan Antiques
Old Working Mens Room, Bamfords Yard, High St. Est. 1982. Open 8-5. CL: Sat. SIZE: Medium. STOCK: Mahogany, rosewood, walnut and oak furniture, 18th to early 20th C, £50-£5,000. LOC: A428. PARK: Easy. TEL: 0234 888916; home - 0234 342775. SER: Restorations; cabinet making; restoration products and sundries; French polishing. FAIRS: Newark. VAT: Stan/Spec.

WILSHAMSTEAD, Nr. Bedford
Manor Antiques
The Manor House, Cottonend Rd. (Mrs S. Bowen). Est. 1976. Open 10-5, Sun. by appointment. SIZE: Large. STOCK: Furniture, 19th C to Edwardian, £50-£4,000; copper and brass, Georgian to Victorian; lighting and oil lamps, Victorian to 1920s; general antiques. LOC: Just off A6, 4 miles south of Bedford. PARK: Own. TEL: 0234 740262; home - same. SER: Restorations (furniture); buys at auction. FAIRS: Luton, NEC, Barbican. VAT: Stan/Spec.

WOBURN
George Large Gallery
13/14 Market Place. Open 10-1 and 2-5.30, Sun. 11-1 and 2-5. STOCK: British art from 1900. TEL: 0525 290658.

Questor
13/14 Market Place. (P. Parkinson-Large). Open 10-1 and 2-5.30, Sun. 11-1 and 2-5. STOCK: Furniture, £50-£1,000; porcelain, jewellery, small antiques. TEL: 0525 290658.

Christopher Sykes Antiques
The Old Parsonage. (C. and M. Sykes). Est. 1949. Open 9-6. SIZE: Large. STOCK: Furniture, 17th to early 19th C, £30-£2,000; scientific instruments, microscopes, sundials, telescopes, sextants, pewter, candlesticks, £20-£2,000; oil paintings (English Schools), porcelain, glass, silver, 19th C, £20-£2,000; pottery, carvings, treen, wine related items and corkscrews, toys, games, metalware. LOC: In main street opposite Post Office on A50. PARK: Easy. TEL: 0525 290259/290467. SER: 130 page illustrated mail order catalogue on corkscrews and wine related antiques available £7 each. VAT: Stan/Spec.

Town Hall Antiques
Market Place. (Elfyn and Elaine Groves). Est. 1978. Open 10-5.30, Sat. 9.30-4.30, Sun. 11-5. CL: Mon. SIZE: Medium. STOCK: Small furniture, £50-£1,000; ceramics, silver and plate, £25-£500; prints and pictures, £5-£1,000; all 19th to early 20th C. LOC: Off A5 and off junction 12 or 13, M1. PARK: Easy. TEL: 0525 290950; home - 0908 371721. SER: Valuations; restorations (pictures, furniture and ceramics). FAIRS: Newark, Ardingly, Shepton Mallet.

The Woburn Abbey Antiques Centre
Est. 1967. Open every day (including Bank Holidays) 11-5 Nov. to Easter; 10-6 Easter to Oct. CL: 4th-5th Sept. and 24th-27th Dec. 1993. LOC: Exits 12 and 13, M1. On A5 follow signs to Woburn Abbey and after entering grounds, follow signs. PARK: Easy. TEL: 0525 290350. Below are listed the dealers at this centre.

Gillian Anderson Antiques
STOCK: Georgian, Victorian and Edwardian furniture, mirrors and decorative items.

Woburn continued
Applecross Antiques
STOCK: Silver, porcelain, pottery especially blue and white transferware, prints, needlework especially samplers.

Armigers
STOCK: Victorian and Edwardian furniture, brass, copper, decorative items.

Mrs Joan Barrington
STOCK: Victorian and Edwardian dolls, juvenalia.

Daniel Bexfield Antiques
STOCK: Georgian, Victorian and Edwardian domestic silver; jewellery.

Ursula Breese
STOCK: Victorian jewellery, glass, lace and decorative items.

Roy Chase
STOCK: 18th-19th C mahogany furniture nautical objects.

John Coleman Antiques
STOCK: Georgian and Victorian mahogany and walnut furniture; mirrors and decorative items.

Collins Antiques
STOCK: 18th-19th C furniture; glass, silver plate, domestic silver.

Cottage Antiques
STOCK: 18th-19th C oak and mahogany furniture; decorative items.

Country Life Interiors
STOCK: Pine furniture, bed and table linen decorative items and engravings.

Dyson-Rook Antiques
STOCK: Georgian, Victorian and Edwardian furniture, glass, domestic silver, decorative items, mirrors.

E. and A. Antiques
STOCK: English and continental porcelain 18th-19th C; watercolours, decorative items.

G. W. Ford & Son Ltd   BADA
STOCK: 18th-19th C furniture; some porcelain, Sheffield plate.

Sylvia Grant
STOCK: Small decorative items, silver and boxes.

Bernard Gulley Antiques   LAPADA
STOCK: Early British oak and associated items.

Hamilton Antiques
STOCK: 18th-19th C mahogany, walnut and rosewood furniture; domestic silver decorative items, prints and porcelain.

Woburn Abbey Antiques Centre

One of the largest Antiques Centres under one roof in Great Britain and the most original — with 40 independent shops and 12 showrooms comprising 50 established dealers, some of whom are members of L.A.P.A.D.A. and B.A.D.A. — is situated in the magnificent South Court of Woburn Abbey.

We are pleased to offer the dealer and private collector a wide range of Antiques: Clocks, Lamps, Porcelain and Glass, Paintings, Prints, Georgian and Victorian Furniture, Jewellery, Georgian Silver, Painted Furniture, Works of Art, etc., at competitive prices.

One of the streets on the ground floor

Within one hour's drive of Oxford, Cambridge, Birmingham and London (via M1, Exit 12 or 13 signposted Woburn Abbey). Trains from St. Pancras to Flitwick or Euston to Bletchley can be met by prior arrangement. Dealers admitted free and their park entrance refunded at the Antiques Centre. Visiting dealers' car park adjacent to the Antiques Centre.

Georgian mahogany tallboy; typical of the stock at the Antiques Centre

**OPEN EVERY DAY OF THE YEAR EXCEPT
4th-5th SEPTEMBER and 24th-27th DECEMBER 1993**

Easter Sunday to October 10-6 p.m. November to Easter 11-5 p.m.

**WOBURN ABBEY ANTIQUES CENTRE, WOBURN ABBEY
BEDFORDSHIRE MK43 0TP**

Telephone Woburn (0525) 290350

Sefton
Antiques for the Country Home

**Woburn Abbey Antiques Centre
Woburn Abbey
Bedfordshire. MK43 0TP
Tel: (0525) 290350 Fax: (0525) 290271**

Woburn continued

Irene Hollings Antiques
STOCK: Furniture and decorative items.

Timothy Jarvis
STOCK: Georgian furniture and decorative items.

Jean Kershaw LAPADA
STOCK: 17th-19th C oak and mahogany furniture, brass, copper ware and country items.

Sue Killinger Antiques
STOCK: Edwardian, Victorian and pine furniture, brass, copper and decorative items.

Marion Langham Ltd
STOCK: Belleek ware, 19th C porcelain and decorative items.

Roger Losa Ltd
STOCK: 18th-19th C oak and mahogany furniture; decorative items, oil paintings and wood carvings.

Elizabeth Maltin
STOCK: 17th-19th C oak, mahogany and walnut furniture; mirrors and decorative items.

Manor Farm Barn Antiques
STOCK: 17th-19th C country furniture, treen, brass, copper and kitchenalia.

Maxim Antiques
STOCK: Decorative items, lamps and mirrors; Georgian furniture.

Mrs Jeanne McPherson
STOCK: Porcelain, decorative items, silver and glass and small 18th and 19th C furniture.

Sybil Mendoza
STOCK: 19th C mahogany furniture, paintings and decorative items.

Tricia Muston-Wise
STOCK: 18th-19th C mahogany, walnut and rosewood furniture; mirrors, light fittings and decorative items; lacquered furniture.

Woburn continued

Bryan Perkins Antiques
STOCK: 18th-19th C mahogany, rosewood and walnut furniture; upholstered furniture, decorative items.

Ron Perry LAPADA
STOCK: Art nouveau, Victoriana and Edwardian furniture, unusual decorative items, light fittings.

Christopher Perry Antiques
STOCK: 18th-19th C oak, mahogany, walnut and rosewood furniture, mirrors, boxes, decorative items.

John Rapley Antiques
STOCK: 17th-19th C oak and mahogany furniture; decorative items.

Susan Rees
STOCK: Commemorative ware pottery.

E. Robertson
STOCK: 18th-19th C English porcelain, mahogany, walnut and rosewood furniture; boxes.

Guy Roe Antiques
STOCK: Georgian furniture, porcelain, decorative items and mirrors.

R. Rynsard
STOCK: Silver.

Terry Scudder
STOCK: 18th-19th C furniture; porcelain, clocks and decorative items.

Sefton Antiques
STOCK: Georgian oak and mahogany furniture; brass and copper, decorative items, papier mâché, treen especially Tunbridgeware.

John Shepherd
STOCK: 18th-19th C furniture; porcelain, mirrors and decorative items.

Sovereign Art
STOCK: Decorative items, porcelain and unusual items, period furniture and silver.

Woburn continued

S. and S. Timms Antiques LAPADA
STOCK: Georgian and Victorian oak and mahogany furniture.

Christina Tooley and Jacqueline Statham
CMBHI. *STOCK: Clocks, barometers, period furniture.*

Paul Treadaway Antiques BADA
STOCK: Georgian mahogany furniture, mirrors, engravings, decorative items.

Underwood Antiques
STOCK: 18th-19th C mahogany furniture; decorative items, mirrors.

Tim Wharton Antiques LAPADA
STOCK: 18th-19th C oak and mahogany furniture; mirrors, brass and copper.

Woburn continued

Margaret Williams
STOCK: 19th C mahogany and walnut furniture, brass ware, silver and plate; boxes, decorative items, mirrors.

Denis Young
STOCK: Pottery - Han, Tang, Sung and Ming dynasties, to 1800.

Woburn Fine Arts
12 Market Place. (Z. Bieganski). Est. 1983. Open 2-5.30, Sat. and Sun. 11-1 and 2-5.30 or by appointment. CL: Thurs. SIZE: Medium. *STOCK: Post-impressionist paintings, 1880-1940; European paintings, 17th-18th C; British paintings, 20th C.* PARK: Easy. TEL: 0525 290624. SER. Restorations (oils and watercolours); framing.

One of a set of Wedgwood tiles showing the month of May from the 'Old English' or 'Calendar' series, produced during the 1880s, and attributed to Helen Jane Arundel Miles. A professional illustrator and artist, she was based at Etruria in the late 1870s, and designed a number of tile series for Wedgwood. The tiles appear in blue, green, brown and polychrome printed versions. Photograph courtesy : Trustees of the Wedgwood Museum, Barlaston, Staffordshire. From *Yesterday's Children* by Sally Kevill-Davies, published by the **Antique Collectors' Club**, £19.95pb.

Berkshire

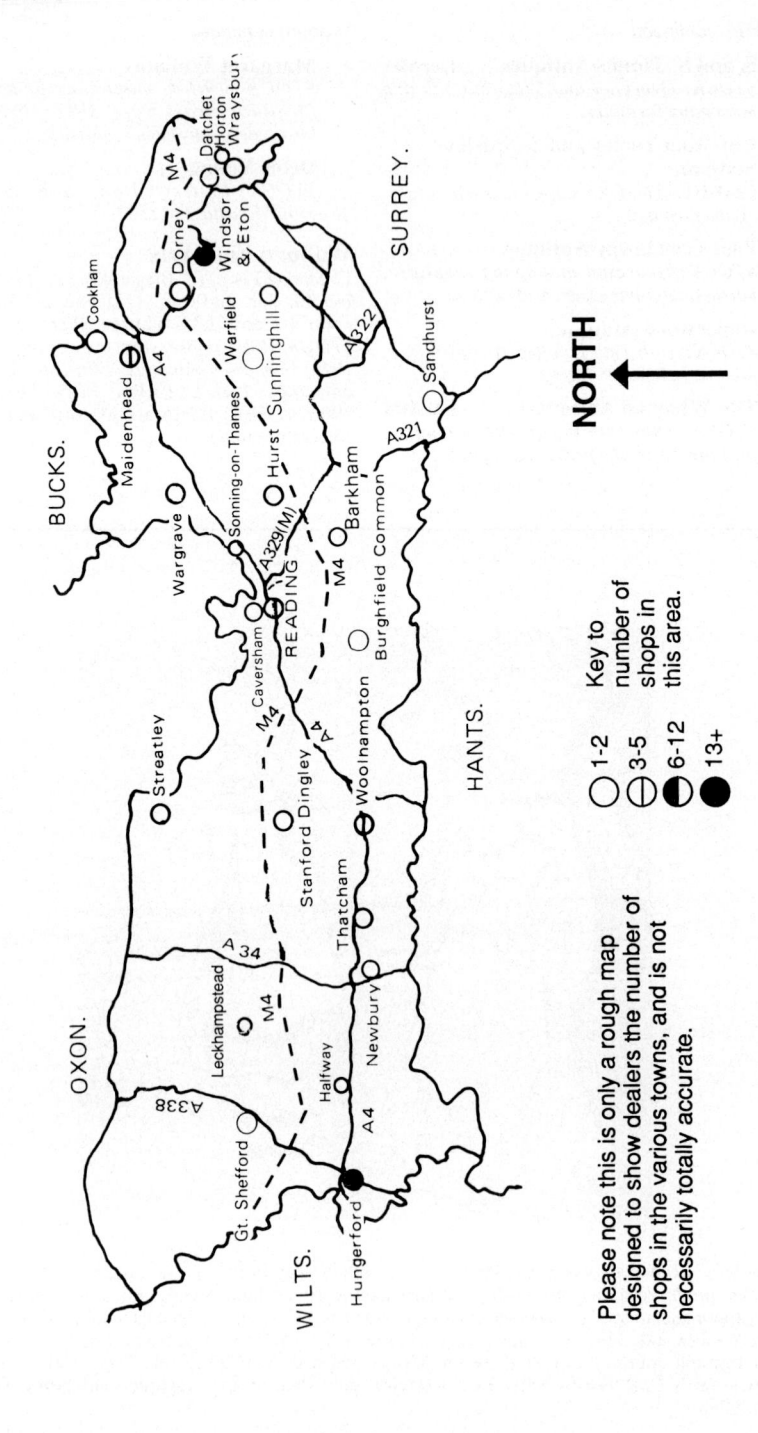

Berkshire

BARKHAM, Nr. Wokingham
Barkham Antique and Craft Centre
Barkham St. (Eileen and Ken Lowes). Open 10.30-5 including Sun. SIZE: Large. *STOCK: Tables, chairs, chests, 18th-20th C, £100-£3,500.* LOC: Off M4 junction 10, A329M to Wokingham, over station crossing to Barkham (B3349), left at Bull public house. PARK: Easy. TEL: 0734 761355; home - 0734 783705. SER: Valuations; restoration (china, French polishing, upholstery, cabinet making, caning); courtesy car from Wokingham station.

John E. Davis Antiques
Edneys Hill Farm, Edneys Hill. Est. 1965. Open every day. SIZE: Large. *STOCK: General antiques.* LOC: M4 junction 10, then A329M to Wokingham, over station crossing to Barkham, left at Barkham sign. PARK: Easy. TEL: 0734 783181; home - same. SER: Valuations; restorations (furniture, clocks and metalwork); buys at auction.

BURGHFIELD COMMON, Nr. Reading
Graham Gallery
Highwoods. (J. Steeds). Est. 1976. Open by appointment at any time. SIZE: Medium. *STOCK: English watercolours, £50-£1,500; English oil paintings, £200-£8,000; English prints, £25-£200; all 19th to early 20th C.* LOC: 4 miles from Reading on Burghfield road. PARK: Easy. TEL: 0734 832320. SER: Valuations; restorations (cleaning, framing).

CAVERSHAM, Nr. Reading
The Clock Workshop
17 Prospect St. (J. M. Yealland). FBHI TVADA. Est. 1980. Open 9.30-5.30, Sat. 10-1. SIZE: Small. *STOCK: Clocks, late 17th to late 19th C, £250-£20,000; barometers, 18th-19th C, £500-£4,000.* LOC: Prospect St. is the beginning of main Reading to Henley road. PARK: North St. TEL: 0734 470741. SER: Valuations; restorations (clocks and barometers); buys at auction. FAIRS: Thames Valley Antique Dealers. VAT: Stan/Spec.

The Collectors Gallery
8 Bridge St, Caversham Bridge. (T.B. and H.J. Snook). TVADA. Open 10-5, Sat. 10-4 or by appointment. SIZE: Large. *STOCK: Watercolours, £60-£4,000; oil paintings, £80-£4,000; collectables, prints and engravings; all 18th-19th C.* TEL: 0734 483663/8. SER: Restorations (paintings); monthly exhibitions.

COOKHAM
Phillips and Sons
The Dower House. Open by appointment. *STOCK: British impressionist paintings by the Staithes group, late 19th to early 20th C, £200-£10,000.* TEL: 0628 529337. SER: Valuations; restorations (pictures); framing. VAT: Spec.

DATCHET
Marian and John Alway Fine Art
BADA LAPADA
Riverside Corner, Windsor Rd. Est. 1978. Open by appointment. *STOCK: Watercolours and oil paintings, 18th to early 20th C, £100-£10,000.* LOC: Junction 5, M4. On corner of Windsor Rd. and Queens Rd. PARK: Easy. TEL: 0753 541163; home - same; fax - 0753 541163. SER: Valuations; restorations (as stock); buys at auction (as stock). VAT: Spec.

DORNEY, Nr. Eton
The Old School Antiques LAPADA
(Lt. Col. V. and Mrs A. Wildish.). Resident. TVADA. Est. 1969. Open 10-5.30 or by appointment. SIZE: Large. *STOCK: Porcelain and English furniture, pre-1850; general antiques. Not Stocked: Items dated post-1850.* LOC: B3026, from M4, junction 7. PARK: Own. TEL: 0628 603247. SER: Valuations; buys at auction. VAT: Spec.

GREAT SHEFFORD, Nr. Hungerford
Ivy House Antiques
Wantage Rd. (J. Hodgson). Est. 1972. Open 10-6. *STOCK: Country and pine furniture, kitchenalia, collectors' items, Victoriana.* LOC: A338, 10 minutes from Hungerford towards Wantage. TEL: 048 839 549.

HALFWAY, Nr. Newbury
Walker and Walker
Halfway Manor. (Alan and Kym Walker). Open by appointment. *STOCK: Fine barometers.* TEL: 0488 58693; mobile - 0831 147480. SER: Restorations.

HORTON, Nr. Windsor
John A. Pearson Antiques BADA
Horton Lodge, Horton Rd. (Mrs J.C.Sinclair Hill). Est. 1902. Open by appointment only. SIZE: Large. *STOCK: English furniture, 1700-1850, £50-£30,000; oil paintings, 17th-19th C, £50-£50,000; decorative objects. Not Stocked: Items after 19th C.* LOC: From London turn off M4, exit 5, past London Airport; from M25 take exit 14. 10 mins from Heathrow. PARK: Easy. TEL: 0753 682136.

HUNGERFORD
Ashley Antiques
129 High St. Est. 1974. Open 10-5, appointment advisable. SIZE: Medium. *STOCK: Furniture and general antiques.* LOC: Main street. PARK: Easy. TEL: 0488 682771. SER: Restorations (furniture).

Below Stairs
103 High St. (S. Hofgartner). Est. 1974. Open 10-6, including Sun. SIZE: Large. *STOCK: Kitchen and decorative garden items, bedroom furniture,*

THE OLD MALTHOUSE
Hungerford, Berks. RG17 0EG
Tel: 0488 682209

Dealer in 18th and 19th Century Furniture, Treen, Brass, Clocks & Barometers

VALUATIONS

ROGER KING ANTIQUES

111 HIGH STREET,
HUNGERFORD, BERKS.
Phone Hungerford 682256

We have a large and varied stock of 18th & 19th century furniture.

Dealers especially welcome.

Hungerford continued
lighting, collectables and interior fittings, mainly 19th C English, £20-£2,500. Not Stocked: Reproductions. LOC: Main street. PARK: Easy. TEL: 0488 682317. SER: Valuations. VAT: Stan.

William Bentley Billiards (Antique Billiard Table Specialist Company)
Standen Manor Farm. Open by appointment every day. SIZE: Large. *STOCK: Billiard tables.* TEL: 0488 681711; 081 940 1152; fax - 0488 685197. SER: Restorations; removals and delivery.

Hungerford continued
Bow House Antiques
3-4 Faulkner Sq, Charnham St. (L.R. Herrington). Open 10-5. CL: Thurs. SIZE: Medium. *STOCK: Small period and Victorian furniture.* LOC: A4. PARK: Easy, own. TEL: 0488 683198; home - 0488 684319. VAT: Spec.

Dolls and Toys of Yesteryear at Bow House Antiques
3-4 Faulkner Sq, Charnham St. (D.M. Herrington). Open 10.30-4. CL: Thurs. SIZE: Medium. *STOCK: Dolls' houses, £150-£3,000; dolls' house furniture and accessories, £1-£300; rocking horses, £500-£1,500; all 19th to early 20th.* PARK: Easy. TEL: 0488 683198; home - 0488 684319. FAIRS: Toy and Doll, Kensington Town Hall; London Victoria International Doll Shows.

The Fire Place (Hungerford) Ltd
Hungerford Old Fire Station, Charnham St. (E.B. and E.M. Smith). Est. 1976. Open 10-1.30 and 2.15-5. SIZE: Large. *STOCK: Fireplace furnishings and metalware especially fenders.* LOC: On A4. PARK: Opposite. TEL: 0488 683420. VAT: Stan/Spec.

Robert and Georgina Hastie   LAPADA
35a High St. Est. 1987. Open 9.30-5, Sun. by appointment. SIZE: Medium. *STOCK: Decorative items, 1750-1920, £50-£6,000; furniture and clocks, 18th-19th C, £200-£6,000; textiles, 19th C, £50-£1,000.* Not Stocked: Silver, porcelain and dolls. LOC: A338. PARK: Easy. TEL: 0488 682873. VAT: Stan/Spec.

Hungerford Arcade
High St. (Wynsave Investments Ltd.). Est. 1972. Open 9.30-5.30, Sun. 10-6. SIZE: Over 70 stallholders. *STOCK: General antiques and period furniture.* PARK: Easy. TEL: 0488 683701.

Roger King Antiques
111 High St. (Mr and Mrs R.F. King). Est. 1974. Open 9.30-5. SIZE: Large. *STOCK: Furniture, 1750-1880, £50-£1,500; china, 19th C; oil paintings.* Not Stocked: Silver, jewellery. LOC: Opposite Hungerford Arcade. PARK: Easy. TEL: 0488 682256. VAT: Spec.

Hungerford continued
Medalcrest Ltd
Charnham House, 29/30 Charnham St. (D.H. Farrow). Est. 1981. Open 9.30-5.30, Sat. 10-6, Sun. by appointment. SIZE: Large. *STOCK: 18th-19th C furniture; barometers, longcase, bracket and carriage clocks, metalware, small items.* TEL: 0488 684157. VAT: Spec.

The Old Malthouse BADA
(P.F. Hunwick). Est. 1963. Open 10-5.30. SIZE: Large. *STOCK: 18th to early 19th C walnut and mahogany furniture; English porcelain; clocks, barometers, glasses, antiquarian books, decorative items, tôleware and brass. Not Stocked: Orientalia.* LOC: A338, left at Bear Hotel, shop is approx. 120yds. on left, just before a bridge. PARK: In front of shop. TEL: 0488 682209. SER: Valuations; buys at auction. FAIRS: Chelsea, Brighton. VAT: Spec.

Riverside Antiques
Charnham St. (M. Stockland). Est. 1976. Open 10-5.30. SIZE: Large. *STOCK: General antiques including furniture and decorative items.* LOC: On A4 just before The Bear Hotel. PARK: Easy. TEL: 0488 682314. VAT: Stan/Spec.

Styles Silver LAPADA
12 Bridge St. (P. and D. Styles). Est. 1974. Open 10-5.30. CL: School holidays. SIZE: Medium. *STOCK: Antique, Victorian and secondhand silver including cutlery.* PARK: Easy. TEL: 0488 683922; home - same. SER: Valuations; repairs; finder. VAT: Stan/Spec.

Victoria's Bedroom
4 Bridge St. (J.A. and M.A. Wallbank-Fox). Open 10-6. CL: Mon. *STOCK: Brass and iron beds.* TEL: 0488 682523.

Youll's Antiques
27 and 28 Charnham St. (B. Youll). Open 10.30-5.30 including Sun. *STOCK: General antiques.*

HURST, Nr. Reading
Peter Shepherd Antiques
Penfold, Lodge Rd. Est. 1962. Open by appointment only. *STOCK: Glass, rarities and books.* TEL: 0734 340755. VAT: Stan/Spec.

LECKHAMPSTEAD, Nr. Newbury
Hill Farm Antiques
Hill Farm, Shop Lane. (Norman Beesley). Open 9-5. *STOCK: 19th C furniture.* TEL: 04882 541/361.

MAIDENHEAD
Jaspers Fine Arts Ltd
36 Queen St. (T.L. Johnson). Open 9-6. *STOCK: Victorian watercolours and paintings; maps and prints.* TEL: 0628 36459. SER: Restorations; framing.

Riverside Antiques Ltd.

18th & 19th century furniture & accessories

Georgian mahogany artist's or writing table (stand later) with double rising top.

Riverside House, Charnham St., Hungerford, Berks. RG17 0EP Exit 14 M4

Margaret Stockland
Telephone: (0488) 682314

BERKSHIRE

Maidenhead continued

Miscellanea
71 St. Marks Rd. (J. Davidson). Open 10-5.30. SIZE: Large. *STOCK: Furniture, books, bric-a-brac, collectors' items.* LOC: 1/2 mile off A4. PARK: Easy. TEL: 0628 23058.

Widmerpool House Antiques
Boulters Lock. Open by appointment only. *STOCK: English furniture, 18th-19th C; oil paintings, watercolours, prints; porcelain, glass, silver, 19th C.* TEL: 0628 23752.

NEWBURY

John Baker Antiques
20 George St, Kingsclere. Est. 1959. Open 9-7, Sat. 10-6. SIZE: Medium. *STOCK: Mahogany, 18th C, £400-£4,000; oak, 17th-18th C, £200-£3,200; desks, Victorian, £480-£1,600.* Not Stocked: Shipping goods. LOC: A339. PARK: Easy (at side). TEL: 0635 298744. SER: Valuations; restorations (furniture); buys at auction. VAT: Stan/Spec.

Griffons Court
Highclere. (Mr and Mrs T.C. Jackson). Est. 1966. Prior telephone call advisable. SIZE: Medium. *STOCK: Fine Georgian furniture, desks, small bookcases, unusual small decorative items, fine paintings.* LOC: 5 miles from Newbury. On A343 at crossroads just inside village boundary. PARK: Easy. TEL: 0635 253247. VAT: Stan/Spec.

READING

Ann Bye Antiques
88 London St. (F.M. and A. Easton). Est. 1968. Open 9-5.30. CL: Wed. p.m. *STOCK: Cottage and pine furniture, country and decorative items.* TEL: 0734 582029.

P.D. Leatherland Antiques
68 London St. TVADA. Est. 1970. Open 9-5. *STOCK: Furniture, 18th C to 1920's; decorative china, clocks, metalware, mirrors and pictures, £5-£4,000.* PARK: Easy. TEL: 0734 581960. VAT: Stan/Spec.

Reading Emporium
1a Merchants Place, (off Friar St). Est. 1972. Open 10-5. SIZE: 11 stalls. *STOCK: General antiques including Victoriana, advertising items, jewellery and bottles.* TEL: 0734 590290.

SANDHURST, Nr. Camberley

Berkshire Metal Finishers Ltd
Swan Lane Trading Estate. (J.A. and Mrs. J. Sturgeon). Est. 1957. Open 8-1 and 2-6, Sat. 8-1 and 2-4, Sun. 9-1. SIZE: Large. *STOCK: Brass, copper and steel metalware; silver plate.* LOC: Off A30 towards Wokingham on A321, after 1.25 miles turn left into Swan Lane, estate 1st turning right, last factory near car park. PARK: Easy. TEL: 0252 873475; fax - 0252 875434. SER: Restorations (metalware polishing and lacquering).

SONNING-ON-THAMES

Csaky's Antiques
Open by appointment only. *STOCK: Early English and continental oak furniture; carvings, works of art, unusual items.* TEL: 0734 697608.

STANFORD DINGLEY, Nr. Reading

Eliot Antiques
(Lady Cathleen Hudson). Est. 1974. Open 10.30-1, Sun. and afternoons by appointment. CL: Mon. SIZE: Small. *STOCK: 18th C English enamels, 18th-19th C objets de vertu, all £150-£3,000.* Not Stocked: Furniture, pictures. PARK: Easy. TEL: 0734 744649; home - 0734 744346. VAT: Spec.

STREATLEY, Nr. Reading

Vine Cottage Antiques
High St. (B.R. and P.A. Wooster). Open 10-5.30. CL: Sun. except by appointment. *STOCK: Furniture and general antiques, 18th-19th C.* TEL: 0491 872425. SER: Restorations; re-upholstery (especially buttoned items). VAT: Spec.

SUNNINGHILL, Nr. Ascot

Antiques of Ascot
3c High St. (K. Price). Open 10-4.45. CL: Wed. *STOCK: General antiques.* PARK: Easy. TEL: 0344 872282.

THATCHAM, Nr. Newbury

Jackdaw Antiques
Bluecoat School. (C. Taylor and C. Heron). Open 10-4.30. CL: Mon. and Tues. *STOCK: General antiques.* PARK: Easy. TEL: 0635 865901.

Richard Kimbell
Country Gardens, Turnpike Rd. (R. and F. Kimbell). Est. 1966. Open 9-6 including Sun. SIZE: Large. *STOCK: Antique pine, £50-£1,000; reproduction pine and country accessories.* PARK: Easy. TEL: 0635 874822.

WARFIELD

Moss End Antique Centre
Moss End Garden Centre. Open 10.30-5. CL: Mon. SIZE: Large - 25 dealers. *STOCK: General antiques.* LOC: A3095. PARK: Own. TEL: 0344 861942.

WARGRAVE

Millgreen Antiques
86 High St. (K. Chate and J. Connell). Open Wed.-Sun. other times by appointment. SIZE: Large - 14 dealers. *STOCK: Furniture, Georgian-Edwardian; small items, china, glass, metal.* PARK: Nearby. TEL: 0734 402955. SER: Restorations (furniture); silver plating; metal polishing.

Wargrave Antiques
66 High St. (John Connell). Open Wed.-Sun. *STOCK: Furniture, Georgian to Edwardian; pine and smalls.* TEL: 0734 402914.

Central Windsor

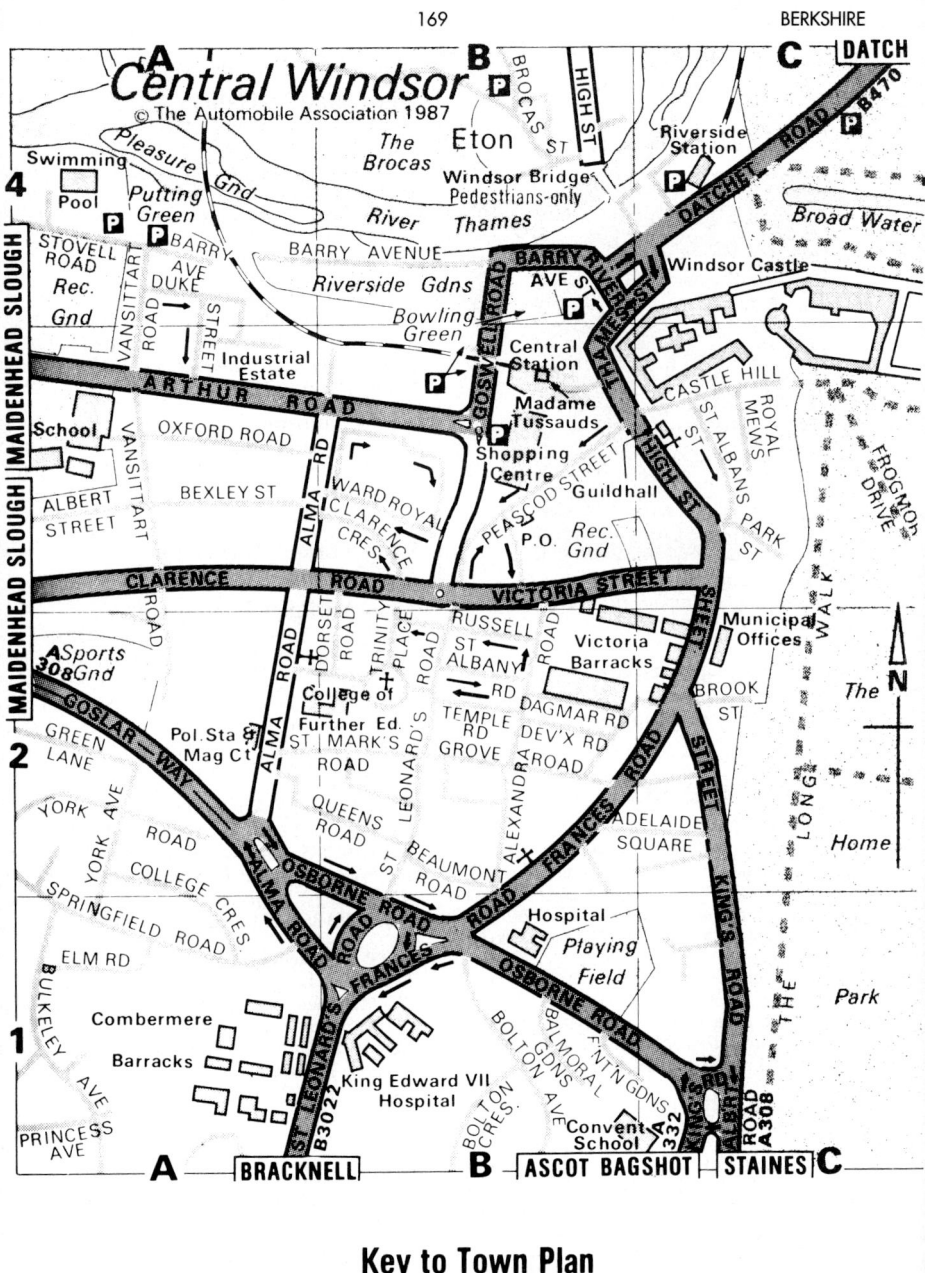

BERKSHIRE

JANET MIDDLEMISS OF
Cavendish Fine Arts

LAPADA MEMBER

TVADA

Specialising in 17th & 18th century fine English furniture and decorative pieces

**127/128 High Street
Eton, Berkshire SL4 6AR
Tel: 0753 860850**

WINDSOR AND ETON

Addrison Bros
25 King's Rd, Windsor. (Mr and Mrs Addrison). Est. 1980. Open 11-6 and occasional Sun. SIZE: Small. STOCK: Furniture, pine, oak, mahogany and walnut, Victorian to 1930, £1-£800. LOC: Close to castle. PARK: Easy. TEL: 0753 863780; home - same.

Antiquus
17 High St, Eton. (Mrs C. Thomas). Open 10-5. STOCK: Furniture, objets d'art, porcelain and textiles. TEL: 0753 831039; home - 840848.

Roger Barnett
91 High St, Eton. Est. 1975. TEL: 0753 867785.

Guy Bousfield   BADA
58 Thames St, Windsor. Est. 1958. Open 8.45-5. CL: Some Mon. and Wed. SIZE: Medium. STOCK: Georgian furniture, 1720-1830, £500-£5,000. LOC: Precinct on castle side of Windsor Bridge. PARK: Easy. TEL: 0753 864575. VAT: Spec.

Cavendish Fine Arts - Janet Middlemiss   LAPADA
127/128 High St, Eton. TVADA. Open 10.30-5. CL: Wed p.m. SIZE: Large. STOCK: Fine Queen Anne and English Georgian furniture, glass and porcelain. TEL: 0734 691904; mobile - 0831 295575. VAT: Stan/Spec.

Windsor and Eton continued

The Compton Gallery
42 Thames St, Windsor. (B.D. Sutton and K.N. Bruendel). Open 10.30-5.30. SIZE: Large. STOCK: General antiques especially china, glassware, Doulton, Gallé pottery and glass, jewellery, cards, furniture, silver, toys and dolls, £5-£15,000. TEL: 0753 830100; mobile - 0836 206361. SER: Valuations.

Country Furniture
79 St. Leonards Rd, Windsor. (Jan Hicks). Open 9.30-6. STOCK: French beds and French provincial furniture, unusual period pine country furniture. TEL: 0753 830154.

Dee's Antiques
89a Grove Rd, Windsor. (D. Johnston). Open 10-6 or by appointment. CL: Mon. SIZE: Small. STOCK: General antiques. TEL: 0753 865627; home - 0753 850926.

Eton Antique Bookshop
88 High St, Eton. TEL: 0753 855534.

Eton Antiques Partnership
80 High St, Eton. (Mark Procter). CMBHI. Est. 1967. Open 10-5.30, Sun. 11-5.30. SIZE: Large. STOCK: Mahogany and rosewood furniture, 18th-19th C. LOC: Slough East exit from M4 westbound. PARK: Nearby. TEL: 0753 860752; home - same. SER: Exporting; interior design consultants. VAT: Stan/Spec.

Eton Gallery Antiques   LAPADA
116 High St, Eton. (V. and J. Smith). TVADA. Open 10.30-5, Sun. by appointment. CL: Mon. and Wed. p.m. STOCK: Furniture, 18th-19th C; oil paintings, longcase clocks and barometers. TEL: 0753 865147/860963. VAT: Spec.

Eyre and Greig Ltd
20 High St, Eton. (Charles Greig and Giles Eyre). CL: Mon. and Wed. afternoons. SIZE: Medium. STOCK: English furniture, pre-1830, £200-£10,000; Anglo-Indian paintings, 1750-1900, £200-£50,000; English glass, 1750-1830, £50-£1,000. PARK: Easy. TEL: 0753 859562. SER: Valuations; buys at auction (paintings and furniture). FAIRS: Olympia Summer and Autumn. VAT: Stan/Spec.

Grove Gallery
89 Grove Rd, Windsor. STOCK: Oils, watercolours, prints. TEL: 0753 865954/853658.

Shirley Hayden Antiques
79 High St, Eton. TVADA. Est. 1980. Open 10-5.30, Sun. 11.30-5. SIZE: Small. STOCK: English mahogany furniture, 18th-19th C, £350-£4,500; decorative items - pictures, mirrors, lamps and porcelain. LOC: First antiques shop on left over the bridge from Windsor, next to The George public house. PARK: Meadow Lane. TEL: 0753 833085; home - 0753 540203. FAIRS: TVADA. VAT: Spec.

BERKSHIRE

Windsor and Eton continued

J. Manley
27 High St, Eton. Est. 1891. Open 9-5. *STOCK: Watercolours, old prints.* TEL: 0753 865647. SER: Restorations; framing, mounting.

Peter J. Martin
40 High St, Eton. TVADA. Est. 1963. Open 9-1 and 2-5. CL: Sun. SIZE: Large and warehouse. *STOCK: Period, Victorian and decorative furniture and furnishings, £50-£5,000; metalware, £10-£500, all from 1800.* LOC: A332. Middle of Eton High St. PARK: 50yds. opposite. TEL: 0753 864901; home - 0753 863987. SER: Restorations; shipping arranged; buys at auction. VAT: Stan/Spec.

Millon Antiques   LAPADA
at Antiquus, 17 High St., Eton. Open 9.30-5. SIZE: Large. *STOCK: English furniture including some walnut, 1700-1850.* TEL: 0753 831039. VAT: Spec.

Morgan Stobbs
61 High St., Eton. (Glenn Morgan). Open 10.30-5.30, Sun. 1-5.30. *STOCK: Furniture and decorative objects.* TEL: 0753 840631.

Mostly Boxes
92 High St, Eton. (G.S. Munday). Est. 1977. Open 9.30-6. SIZE: Small. *STOCK: Mainly wooden boxes, small furniture.* LOC: Centre of High St. PARK: 100yds. TEL: 0753 858470. SER: Restorations (boxes). VAT: Stan.

O'Connor Brothers
Trinity Yard, 59 St. Leonards Rd., Windsor. *STOCK: Furniture and general antiques.* TEL: 0753 866732. VAT: Stan.

Tony L. Oliver
Longclose House, Common Rd., Eton Wick. Est. 1959. Open 9-5 by appointment only. *STOCK: Militaria, medals, badges, insignia especially German 1914-1990; civilian and military vehicles, 1914-1955.* TEL: 0753 862637.

Ulla Stafford Antiques   BADA LAPADA
41 High St, Eton. TVADA. Open daily. SIZE: Large. *STOCK: Georgian and continental furniture, Chinese export porcelain, 18th C; works of art and ceramics, 17th-18th C.* PARK: Easy. TEL: 0753 859625; home - 0734 343208. VAT: Spec.

Studio 101
101 High St, Eton. (Anthony Cove). Est. 1959. Open 10.30-5.30, some Sun. p.m. SIZE: Medium. *STOCK: Mahogany furniture, some 18th C, mainly 19th C, £50-£1,000; brass, silver plate, 19th C, £10-£200.* LOC: Walk over Windsor

Windsor and Eton continued

Bridge from Windsor and Eton Riverside railway station. PARK: Public, at rear of premises. TEL: 0753 863333.

Times Past Antiques Ltd
59 High St, Eton. (P. Jackson). MBHI. Est. 1970. Open 10-6, Sun. 12-5. SIZE: Medium. *STOCK: Clocks and watches, £100-£3,000; furniture, all 18th-19th C; silver, 19th C, £5-£500.* PARK: Reasonable. TEL: 0753 857018; home - same. SER: Valuations; restorations (clocks and watches); buys at auction (clocks). VAT: Stan/Spec.

Turks Head Antiques
98 High St, Eton. Open 10.30-5. CL: Mon. *STOCK: Silver and plate, jewellery, glass and boxes.* TEL: 0753 863939.

WOOLHAMPTON, Nr. Reading
The Bath Chair
Woodbine Cottage, Bath Rd. (J.A. Lewzey). Est. 1980. Open 10-6. CL: Thurs. SIZE: Small. *STOCK: Furniture and general antiques, £5-£5,000.* LOC: A4. PARK: Easy. TEL: 0734 712225. SER: Valuations; buys at auction.

The Old Bakery
Bath Rd. (D.R. Carter). Resident. Est. 1969. *STOCK: Furniture, objets d'art, collectors' items, general antiques.* TEL: 0734 712116.

Old Post House Antiques
Bath Rd. (V. A. Liddiard). Est. 1975. Open 10-6. SIZE: Small. *STOCK: Furniture, 18th-19th C, £50-£300; bric-a-brac and brassware, £2-£100.* LOC: On A4. PARK: Easy. TEL: 0734 712294; home - 0734 713460.

WRAYSBURY
Wyrardisbury Antiques
23 High St. (C. Tuffs). Est. 1978. Open Tues., Wed., Fri. and Sat. 10-5, other times by appointment. SIZE: Small. *STOCK: Clocks, £25-£2,000; small furniture, tea caddies, boxes and watercolours, £10-£500; porcelain, £30-£500.* LOC: A376 from Staines by-pass (A30) or from junction 5 M4/A4 via B470, then B376. PARK: Easy. TEL: 0784 483225. SER: Restorations (clocks).

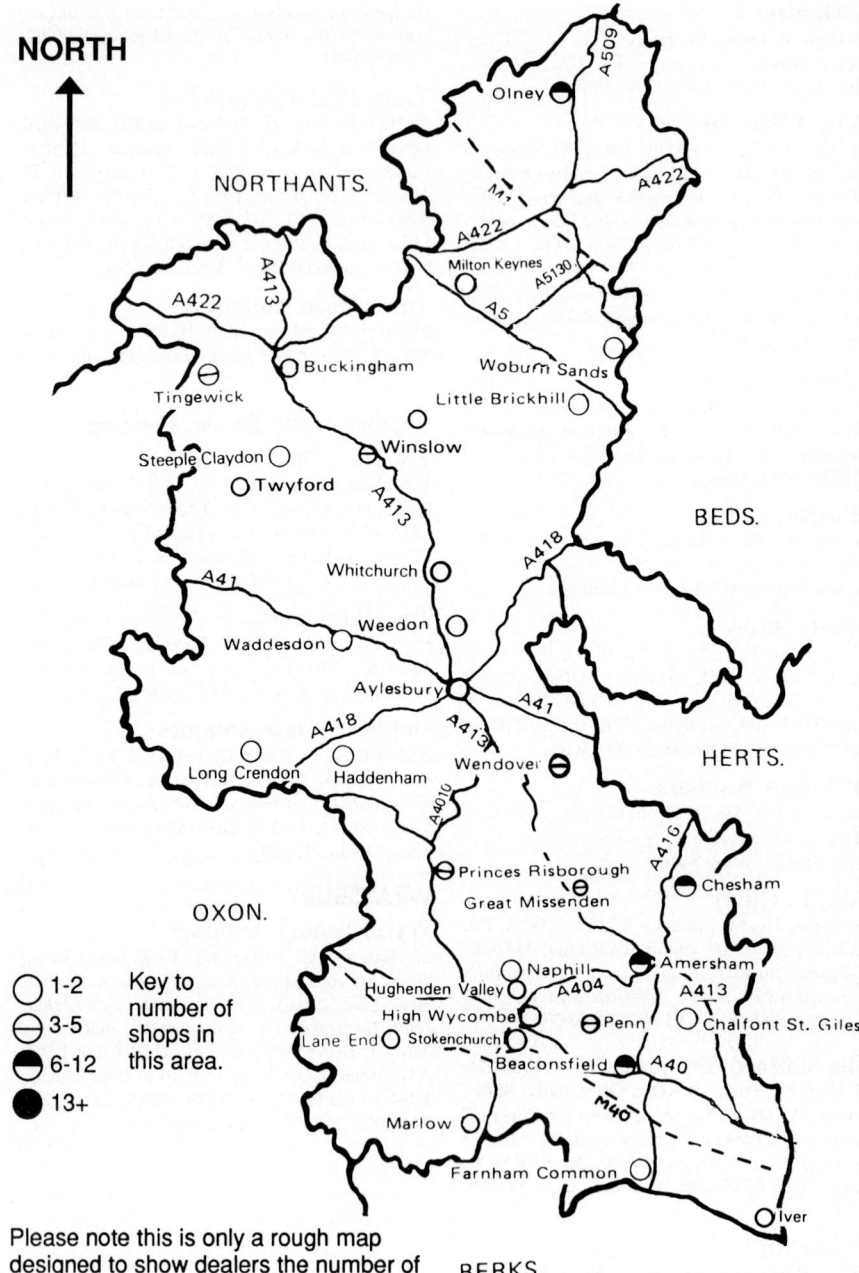

Buckinghamshire

172

NORTH ↑

NORTHANTS.

Olney
A509
A422
M1
A422
Milton Keynes
A5130
A5
A413
A422
Buckingham
Wobum Sands
Tingewick
Little Brickhill
Steeple Claydon
Winslow
Twyford
A413
BEDS.
Whitchurch
A418
Weedon
A41
Waddesdon
Aylesbury
A41
Long Crendon
A418
A413
HERTS.
Haddenham
Wendover
A4010
Princes Risborough
A416
Great Missenden
Chesham
OXON.
Naphill
Amersham
Hughenden Valley
A404
A413
High Wycombe
Penn
Chalfont St. Giles
Lane End
Stokenchurch
Beaconsfield
A40
Marlow
M40
Farnham Common
Iver

Key to number of shops in this area.
○ 1-2
⊖ 3-5
⊖ 6-12
● 13+

BERKS.

Please note this is only a rough map designed to show dealers the number of shops in the various towns, and is not necessarily totally accurate.

Buckinghamshire

AMERSHAM

Amersham Antiques and Collectors Centre
20-22 Whielden St, Old Amersham. Open 9.30-5.30. SIZE: 25-30 dealers. STOCK: Antiques and collectables. TEL: 0494 431282.

The Cupboard Antiques   LAPADA
80 High St, Old Amersham. (N. Lucas). Open 10-5. CL: Fri. STOCK: Georgian, Regency and early Victorian furniture and decorative items. PARK: Easy. TEL: 0494 722882.

"Mon Galerie"
The Old Forge, The Broadway, Old Amersham. (A.R. and D.E. Guy). Est. 1975. STOCK: Watercolours, engravings, 19th-20th c, £20-£500; maps. PARK: Easy. TEL: 0494 721705; workshop - 0296 661884. SER: Valuations; restorations, mounting, framing.

Partridges
67 High St, Old Amersham. (Mrs D. Krolle). Est. 1976. Open 10.30-5.30. CL: Mon. STOCK: Antique and decorative items. PARK: Easy. TEL: 0494 728452.

Michael Quilter
38 High St. Est. 1970. Open 10-5. STOCK: General antiques, stripped pine, copper, brass. PARK: Easy. TEL: 0494 433723. VAT: Stan.

Sundial Antiques   LAPADA
19 Whielden St. (A. and Mrs M. Macdonald). Est. 1970. Open 9.30-5.30. CL: Thurs. SIZE: Small. STOCK: English and European brass, copper, metalware, fireplace furniture, 18th-19th C, £5-£1,500; small period furniture, 1670-1870, £25-£1,500; oil lamps, 1840-1914, £25-£500; decorative items, 1750-1910, £5-£500; weapons, 1600-1860, £25-£1,000; pottery, porcelain, curios, pre-1914, £10-£750. Not Stocked: Jewellery, clocks, coins, oil paintings, stamps, books, silver. LOC: On A404, in Old Town 200yds. from High St. on right; from High Wycombe, 700yds. from hospital on left. PARK: Easy. TEL: 0494 727955. VAT: Stan/Spec.

AYLESBURY

Morton Harvey Antiques
21 Wendover Rd. (J.M. Harvey). Resident. Open 10-5.30. CL: Thurs. STOCK: 18th C and early Victorian furniture, watercolours; general antiques. PARK: Rear of premises. TEL: 0296 84307.

BEACONSFIELD

Christopher Cole (Fine Paintings) Ltd
BADA
4 London End. Est. 1975. Open 9.30-5.30. CL: Mon. STOCK: British oil paintings, 19th-20th C. TEL: 0494 671274.

Beaconsfield continued

June Elsworth - Beaconsfield Ltd
Clover House, 16 London End. (Mrs J. Elsworth). Est. 1983. CL: Mon. SIZE: Small. STOCK: Fine English furniture, 18th-19th C; decorative accessories and silver,19th C. LOC: In old town, on A40. PARK: Easy. TEL: 0494 675611; fax - 0494 671273. VAT: Spec.

Grosvenor House Interiors
51 Wycombe End, Beaconsfield Old Town. (T.I. Marriott). TVADA. Est. 1970. Open 9-1 and 2-5.30. SIZE: Large. STOCK: 18th-19th C furniture, especially upholstered and mid-19th C walnut; fireplaces and accessories. PARK: Easy. TEL: 0494 677498. SER: Interior architectural design, fireplace specialists. VAT: Stan/Spec.

Norton Antiques
56 London End. (T. and N. Hepburn). TVADA. Est. 1966. Open 10-1 and 2-5.30. CL: Wed. SIZE: Medium. STOCK: Furniture 1680-1850, £25-£2,500; oils and watercolours, 19th C, £15-£2,500; clocks, 18th-19th C, £25-£2,000; woodworking and craftsman's hand tools. LOC: On left shortly after entering Beaconsfield Old Town from the east. PARK: Easy. TEL: 0494 673674. SER: Valuations; buys at auction; pine stripping. FAIRS: High Wycombe, TVADA Eton College. VAT: Stan/Spec.

Old Curiosity Shop
47-49 Wycombe End. (D. Barker). Open 9.45-1 and 2.30-5.30. CL: Mon. STOCK: General antiques, small furniture and interesting items. TEL: 0494 674473.

Period Furniture Showrooms
49 London End. (R.E.W. Hearne and S.A. Howells). Est. 1965. Open 9-5.30. SIZE: Large. STOCK: Furniture, 1700-1900, £50-£3,000. LOC: A40 Beaconsfield Old Town. PARK: Own. TEL: 0494 674112. SER: Restorations (furniture). VAT: Stan/Spec.

The Spinning Wheel
86 London End. (Mrs M. Royle). Est. 1945. Open 10-5. CL: Wed. STOCK: English furniture, 18th-19th C, mahogany and oak items, porcelain, glass. TEL: 0494 673055; home - 02407 3294. VAT: Stan/Spec.

BUCKINGHAM

Flappers
2 High St. (M. Goodwin). Open 9.30-1 and 2-5. STOCK: Stripped pine, oak and mahogany furniture; lace, linen; 1920s and 1930s costume. TEL: 0280 813115; evenings - 0604 740234.

CHALFONT ST. GILES

Gallery 23 Antiques
High St. (Mrs A. Vollaro). Est. 1991. Open 10-5. STOCK: Furniture, silver, continental and English porcelain, glass, paintings, prints and watercolours. TEL: 0494 871512.

BUCKINGHAMSHIRE

Chalfont St. Giles continued

Images in Watercolour LAPADA
8 The Lagger. (E. and D. Parkinson). TVADA. Est. 1968. Open by appointment. *STOCK: Watercolours, drawings and some oils, 1800-1930.* LOC: Take road to Seer Green from village centre, on left hand side shortly after passing Milton's Cottage. PARK: Easy. TEL: 0494 875592. SER: Valuations; restorations (oils and watercolours); framing. VAT: Spec.

T. Smith
The Furniture Village, London Rd. Est. 1982. Open 10-5. SIZE: Medium. *STOCK: Furniture, from 1700, £100-£3,000; brass and copper, £20-£500.* LOC: Opposite Pheasant public house. PARK: Easy. TEL: 0494 873031. SER: Valuations; restorations (including upholstery); buys at auction (furniture).

CHESHAM

Albert Bartram
177 Hivings Hill. Est. 1968. Usually open, preferably by appointment. *STOCK: Metalwork, 16th-17th C; pewter, small oak furniture, pottery, £30-£3,000.* LOC: 1 mile from town centre on the Bellingdon road. PARK: Easy. TEL: 0494 783271. VAT: Spec.

Chess Antiques LAPADA
85 Broad St. (M.P. Wilder). Est. 1966. Open 9-5, Sat. 10-5. SIZE: Small. *STOCK: Furniture and clocks.* PARK: Easy. TEL: 0494 783043. SER: Valuations; restorations. VAT: Stan/Spec.

For Pine
340 Berkhampstead Rd. (J. Morgan and D. Hutchin). Open 10-5. CL: Thurs. *STOCK: Pine furniture.* Not Stocked: Reproduction. TEL: 0494 776119.

Omniphil Ltd
Germains Lodge, Fullers Hill. (A.R.T. Muddiman). Est. 1953. Open 9-5.30 or by appointment. CL: Sat. SIZE: Warehouse. *STOCK: Rare prints on all subjects and Illustrated London News from 1842.* TEL: 0494 771851.

Queen Anne House
57 Church St. (Miss A.E. Jackson). Est. 1918. Open Wed., Fri. and Sat. 9.30-5. SIZE: Large. *STOCK: Furniture, decorative and furnishing pieces, porcelain figures, other china, glass, silver plate, copper, brass, Victoriana, Persian rugs.* Not Stocked: Silver, weapons, jewellery. PARK: Easy. TEL: 0494 783811. SER: Buys at auction. VAT: Stan/Spec.

M.V. Tooley, CMBHI
at Chess Antiques, 85 Broad St. Est. 1960. Open 9-6, Sat. 10-5. SIZE: Small. *STOCK: Clocks and barometers.* TEL: 0494 783043. SER: Valuations; restorations; spare parts.

FARNHAM COMMON

A Thing of Beauty
5 The Broadway. (K. and B. Craven). Est. 1973. Open 9.30-1 and 2.30-5, Wed. 9.30-1. SIZE: Medium. *STOCK: English furniture, 1800-1910, £75-£1,000; general antiques, some silver, from 1800, £20-£300; European glassware.* Not Stocked: Maps, books, paintings. LOC: Opposite The Foresters public house in High St. PARK: Easy. TEL: 0753 642099 (24hrs.). SER: Valuations; buys at auction (furniture).

GREAT MISSENDEN

Gemini Antiques
68a High St. (M. Crossley). Open Mon. and Fri. 2-5, Tues. and Thur. 9.30-1, Sat. 9.30-5. CL: Wed. *STOCK: General antiques.* PARK: Opposite. TEL: 024 06 6203.

The Pine Merchants
52 High St. (D.J. Peters). Open 9.30-5.30. CL: Thurs. SIZE: Medium. *STOCK: Stripped pine and Victorian bedsteads.* TEL: 024 06 2002.

Peter Wright Antiques
36b High St. Est. 1974. Open 9-5.30. SIZE: Small. *STOCK: Clocks and small furniture, 18th-19th C, £50-£2,500; curios, £5-£100.* LOC: A413. PARK: Easy. TEL: 024 06 5710 and 0494 891330. SER: Valuations; restorations; buys at auction. VAT: Stan/Spec.

HADDENHAM

H.S. Wellby Ltd
The Malt House, Church End. (C.S. Wellby). Est 1820. Open by appointment 9-6. CL: Sat *STOCK: 18th and 19th C paintings.* TEL: 0844 290036. SER: Restorations. VAT: Spec.

HIGH WYCOMBE

Browns' of West Wycombe
Church Lane, West Wycombe. Est. Pre 1900 Open 8-5.30. CL: Sat. *STOCK: Furniture.* LOC On A40 approximately 3 miles west of High Wycombe on Oxford Rd. PARK: Easy. TEL 0494 524537. SER: Restorations and hand-made copies of period chairs.

Burrell Antiques
Kitchener Works, Kitchener Rd. (G. and P Burrell). Open 8-5.30 (prior telephone cal advisable) and Sat. by appointment. SIZE Medium. *STOCK: Furniture, 1800-1920, £10 £1,000.* LOC: West side of town, nea Desborough Rd. shopping area. PARK: Easy TEL: 0494 523619. SER: Restorations (furniture) VAT: Stan/Spec.

HUGHENDEN VALLEY, Nr. High Wycombe
Pine Reflections
Holly Cottage, Boss Lane. (M. Duda). Est. 1978. By appointment only. *STOCK: Period and continental pine.* TEL: 024 024 3598. SER: Export. Trade Only.

IVER
"Yester-year"
12 High St. (P.J. Frost). Resident. Est. 1969. Open 10.30-6. SIZE: Small. *STOCK: Furniture, porcelain, pottery, glass, metalwork, 18th to early 20th C.* PARK: Easy. TEL: 0753 652072. SER: Valuations; restorations (furniture, pictures); framing; buys at auction.

LANE END, Nr. High Wycombe
Bach Antiques
Essex House, Finings Rd. (C. and Mrs. B. Whitby). Est. 1982. Open 11-5. CL: Mon. SIZE: Small. *STOCK: Furniture including pine, general antiques, pre 1920.* LOC: B482 between Marlow and Stokenchurch, Finings Rd. is extension of High St. PARK: Easy. TEL: 0494 882683. SER: Valuations; restorations (furniture). FAIRS: Lane End monthly.

LITTLE BRICKHILL
Baroq Antiques
(B. Dawson). Est. 1967. Open by appointment only. *STOCK: Pottery and porcelain, £10-£500; paintings and watercolours, 18th-20th C, £100-£1,000; furniture, £100-£1,500.* TEL: 052 523 7750; home - 0234 240448. SER: Buys at auction. VAT: Stan/Spec.

LONG CRENDON
Hollington Antiques
87 Bicester Rd. (J. and V. Asta). Est. 1966. Open all week. SIZE: Medium. *STOCK: Books, china, glass, curios, militaria, prints and drawings.* LOC: B4011. Next to "The Chandos Arms". PARK: Easy. TEL: 0844 208294.

MARLOW
Angela Hone Watercolours   LAPADA
TVADA. Open by appointment only. *STOCK: Watercolours, 1850-1920.* TEL: 0628 484170.

David Messum   BADA
The Studio, Lords Wood. SLAD, TVADA. *STOCK: British Impressionism and fine English paintings.* TEL: 0628 486565. SER: Valuations; restorations; framing. VAT: Stan/Spec.

One of a pair of Flight, Barr and Barr spill vases painted with 'The Cottage Girl', 4 ⅛in. (10.5cm), on turquoise ground, possibly painted by John Pennington, script marks, c.1820. (Phillips). From *The Dictionary of Worcester Porcelain, Vol.I, 1751-1851,* by John Sandon, published in 1993 by the **Antique Collectors' Club**, £45.00.

MILTON KEYNES
Temple Lighting (Jeanne Temple Antiques)
Stockwell House, Wavendon. Est. 1968. SIZE: Medium. *STOCK: Victorian, Edwardian and 1930's light fittings; 19th C furniture; decorative items.* LOC: Just off main Woburn Sands to Newport Pagnell road. TEL: 0908 583597.

NAPHILL, Nr. High Wycombe
A. and E. Foster   BADA
"Little Heysham", Forge Rd. Est. 1972. Open by appointment only. SIZE: Small. *STOCK: English and continental treen, bygones, metalwork, pre-1830. Not Stocked: Silver, glass, porcelain.* LOC: From High Wycombe take the A4128. Take first left after Hughenden Manor; about 2 miles. PARK: Easy. TEL: 0494 562024. FAIRS: Chelsea, Fine Arts Fair, Olympia, Grosvenor House, City of London. VAT: Spec.

OLNEY
Market Square Antiques
(J.D. and H. Vella). Open 10-5.30, Sun. 2-5.30. *STOCK: Furniture, clocks, china, silver, glass, copper, brass, pine.* TEL: 0234 712172. SER: Restorations.

BUCKINGHAMSHIRE

Olney continued

Alan Martin Antiques
Farthing Cottage, Clickers Yard. (A.D. Martin). MBHI. Est. 1978. Open 9-5, Sun. by appointment. SIZE: Small. *STOCK: Clocks, £100-£1,500; watches, £50-£500; lacemaking supplies, 18th-19th C.* PARK: Town Square. TEL: 0234 712446. SER: Restorations (clocks).

Olney Antique Centre
Rose Court. (J.D. and H. Vella). Open 10-5.30, Sun. 12-5.30. *STOCK: China, furniture, jewellery, linen, pine, postcards.* TEL: 0234 712172.

John Overland Antiques
Rose Court, Market Place. Est. 1977. Open 10-5 including Sun. SIZE: Medium. *STOCK: 18th-19th C mahogany and oak furniture, clocks, writing boxes, smalls, brass, copper.* PARK: Market Sq. TEL: 0234 712351. SER: Valuations; restorations (furniture, clocks). VAT: Stan/Spec.

Pine Antiques
10 Market Place. (Allan and Linda Wilkinson). Open 10-5, Sun. 12-5. CL: Wed. *STOCK: Pine furniture.* TEL: 0234 711065; 0908 510226.

Robin Unsworth Antiques
1 Weston Rd. (R. and Z. M. Unsworth). Est. 1971. Open 10-5, Sun. 1-5. SIZE: Small. *STOCK: Longcase and wall clocks, £500-£4,000; period and Victorian furniture, £200-£4,000; objects of art, £50-£1,000.* LOC: 6 miles from junction 14, M1. PARK: Easy. TEL: 0234 711210; home - 0908 617193. SER: Valuations; buys at auction (clocks).

PENN, Nr. High Wycombe

Country Furniture Shop   LAPADA
3 Hazlemere Rd, Potters Cross. (M. and V. Thomas). Est. 1955. Open 9.30-1 and 2-5.30. SIZE: Large. *STOCK: Furniture, Georgian, £100-£5,000; Victoriana, £5-£2,500; large Victorian dining tables, Victorian dining chairs.* LOC: B474. PARK: Easy. TEL: 049 481 2244; home - same. SER: Valuations. VAT: Stan/Spec.

Penn Barn
By the Pond, Elm Rd. (P. J. M. Hunnings). ABA. Est. 1968. Open 9.30-1 and 2-5, Sun. by appointment. SIZE: Medium. *STOCK: Antiquarian books, maps and prints, 19th C, £5-£250; watercolours and oils, 19th-20th C, £50-£500.* LOC: B474. PARK: Easy. TEL: 0494 815691. SER: Restorations; cleaning and repairs. VAT: Stan/Spec.

Francis Wigram
Cottars Barn, Elm Rd. CL: Wed. p.m. *STOCK: General antiques, furniture, English and continental porcelain, works of art, decorative items.* TEL: 049 481 3266.

PRINCES RISBOROUGH

Bell Street Antiques Centre
20/22 Bell St. (J. Booth and J. Blaik). Est. 1985. Open 9.30-5.30, Sun. 12-5. SIZE: Medium. *STOCK: Furniture, 18th-20th C, from £40; glass, china, collectables, copper, brass, mainly 19th C, from £5.* LOC: A4010. TEL: 084 44 3034.

White House Antiques
33 High St. (M. Amor). Est. 1961. Open by appointment. *STOCK: Marble, chandeliers and furniture, £1,000+.* LOC: Town centre. TEL: 084 44 6976; home - same. SER: Valuations.

STEEPLE CLAYDON

Terence H. Porter, Fine Antique European Arms and Armour
"The Beeches". Est. 1963. Open by appointment *STOCK: Pistols, guns and rifles.* TEL: 029 673 8255. SER: Buys at auction; exchange; bi-monthly lists (send large S.A.E.).

STOKENCHURCH

Amend Antiques
Jardinerie Garden Centre, Oxford Rd., Studley Green. (B. Amend). SIZE: Open daily 12-5 *STOCK: General antiques.* PARK: Easy. TEL 0494 482842.

TINGEWICK, Nr. Buckingham

Lennard Antiques   LAPADA
The Laurels, Main St. Est. 1978. Open by appointment. SIZE: Small. *STOCK: Oak and fruitwood country furniture and English delftware 18th to early 19th C.* LOC: On A421 - next door to post office. TEL: 0280 848371. FAIRS: West London; NEC; Kenilworth; Olympia.

Tim Marshall Antiques
Main St. Resident. Open 9.30-6, Sun. 12-6. SIZE Medium. *STOCK: Furniture including pine longcase clocks, copper and brass.* TEL: 0280 848546.

Tingewick Antiques Centre
Main St. (B.J. and R. Smith). Est. 1973. Open 10 5.30, Sun. 11-4.30. CL: Fri. SIZE: Medium *STOCK: Furniture including desks, mainly pin and oak, 19th to early 20th C, £5-£1,000; clocks 18th-19th C, £20-£2,000; collectables, kitchen alia, art deco, pottery, pictures, £1-£1,500.* LOC On A421. TEL: 0280 847922; home - same. SER Valuations; restorations (copper, brass, spelter upholstery; French polishing.

TWYFORD, Nr. Buckingham

Adrian Hornsey Ltd
Three Bridge Mill. Open by appointment. SIZE Large - 25 dealers selling from these premise *STOCK: General antiques, accessories an architectural.* TEL: 0296 738373; fax - 029 738322. SER: Courier.

WADDESDON
Collectors' Corner
106 High St. (Mrs K. Good and Mrs V. Grant). Est. 1967. Open by appointment 10-4. SIZE: Medium. STOCK: Silver, 18th-20th C, £5-£200; porcelain, jewellery, mainly 19th C, £5-£100; general antiques. Not Stocked: Coins, militaria. LOC: A41 opp. entrance to Waddesdon Manor. PARK: Easy. TEL: 0296 651563.

WEEDON, Nr. Aylesbury
Peter Eaton Booksellers Ltd
Lilies. Open 10-5. STOCK: Antiquarian and secondhand books. TEL: 0296 641393. SER: Brochure available.

WENDOVER
Antiques at Wendover
The Old Post Office, 25 High St. (N. Gregory). Open 10-5.30, Sun. 11-5.30. SIZE: Large. 30 dealers. STOCK: General antiques including town and country furniture, flatware, kitchenalia, pottery and porcelain, silver, lamps and lighting, beds and bathroom fittings, decorative and architectural items, glass, metalware, lace, linen, dateline 1930. PARK: Own. TEL: 0296 625335; evenings - 0296 624633.

Bowood Antiques   LAPADA
Bowood Lane. (Miss P. Peyton-Jones). Est. 1960. Open 9-5, Sat. 10-4 (appointment preferred). SIZE: Large. STOCK: Furniture, porcelain, 17th-19th C, £10-£10,000; textiles, prints. LOC: Off A413, signposted Hunts Green, Bowood Lane. PARK: Easy. TEL: 0296 622113; home - same. VAT: Spec.

Sally Turner Antiques   LAPADA
Hogarth House, High St. Open 10-5.30. SIZE: Large. STOCK: Decorative and period furniture, general antiques. PARK: At rear of shop. TEL: 0296 624402.

Wendover Antiques   LAPADA
1 South St. (R. and D. Davies). Est. 1979. Open 9-5.30, prior telephone call advisable. SIZE: Medium. STOCK: Furniture, 17th-19th C; decorative prints, oils; 18th C silk embroideries, silhouettes, miniatures, Georgian decanters, some silver and Sheffield plate; all £50-£5,000. LOC: Near village centre on Wendover-Amersham road. PARK: 100yds. TEL: 0296 622078. VAT: Stan/Spec.

WHITCHURCH
Deerstalker Antiques
28 High St. (R.J. and L.L. Eichler). Open 10-5.30. CL: Mon. SIZE: Medium. STOCK: General antiques. TEL: 0296 641505.

Bowood Antiques

LAPADA MEMBER

Good 17th, 18th and 19th century furniture and other items

Bowood Lane Nr. Wendover Bucks.

(turn off at Hunts Green sign A413 Gt. Missenden-Wendover road)

Tel. Wendover (0296) 622113
Fax. (0296) 696598

WINSLOW
Medina Antiquarian Maps and Prints
8 High St. (P. Williams). Open 9.30-5.30. CL: Thurs. p.m. STOCK: Maps, prints and watercolours. TEL: 0296 712468.

Winslow Antiques Centre
15 Market Sq. Est. 1992. Open 10-5 or by appointment. SIZE: 20 dealers. STOCK: General antiques. LOC: A413. TEL: 0296 714540/714055; fax - 0296 714928.

WOBURN SANDS, Nr. Milton Keynes
Haydon House Antiques   LAPADA
Haydon House, Station Rd. (G. and M. Tyrrell). Est. 1966. Open 10-6, Sat. and Sun. 10-1, other times by appointment. SIZE: Large. STOCK: Furniture and decorators' items, 18th-19th C and Edwardian, £25-£2,000; copper, brass, metalware, bygones, prints, £5-£250. Not Stocked: Coins, silver, jewellery. LOC: 2 miles from exit 13, M1 and 2 miles from Woburn Abbey. PARK: Own. TEL: 0908 582447. VAT: Stan.

Neville's Antiques
50 Station Rd. (N.K.T. Medcalf). Open 10-5. CL: Mon. and Wed. SIZE: Large. STOCK: 18th-19th C furniture, oils, metalwork, £20-£3,000. PARK: Easy. TEL: 0908 584827/583024.

Cambridgeshire

Map of Cambridgeshire showing towns with antique shops, with roads and neighbouring counties (Lincs, Norfolk, Suffolk, Essex, Herts, Beds, Northants) labelled. Towns marked include: Wisbech, Outwell, Wansford, Peterborough, Sawtry, Doddington, Ramsey, Warboys, Little Downham, Ely, Huntingdon, Brampton, St Ives, Chittering, Burwell, Fordham, Chippenham, Landbeach, Swaffham Prior, Southoe, Bottisham, St Neots, Comberton, Cambridge, Orwell, Harston, Pampisford, Little Abington, Fowlmere, Duxford, Melbourn, Ickleton, Bassingbourn.

Please note this is only a rough map designed to show dealers the number of shops in the various towns, and is not necessarily totally accurate.

Key to number of shops in this area:
- ○ 1-2
- ⊖ 3-5
- ⬒ 6-12
- ● 13+

Cambridgeshire

BASSINGBOURN, Nr. Royston
David Bickersteth
4 South End. Est. 1967. Open by appointment. *STOCK: Antiquarian books.* TEL: 0763 245619.

BOTTISHAM, Nr. Cambridge
Cambridge Pine
Hall Farm, Lode Rd. (Mr and Mrs D. Weir). Est. 1980. Open seven days. SIZE: Large. *STOCK: Pine, 18th-19th C; pine and oak reproduction; all £25-£1,400.* LOC: Midway between Bottisham and Lode, near Anglesey Abbey. PARK: Easy. TEL: 0223 811208; home - same. SER: Fitted farmhouse kitchens.

BRAMPTON
Brampton Mill Antiques
87 High St. (D.E. Clark). Est. 1955. Open by appointment only. SIZE: Large. *STOCK: General antiques.* LOC: 1 mile from A1. TEL: 0480 411204/455593; mobile - 0860 340358. VAT: Stan/Spec.

BURWELL
Peter Norman Antiques and Restorations
Sefton House, 57 North St. (P. Norman and A. Marpole). Est. 1975. Open 9-12.30 and 2-5.30. SIZE: Medium. *STOCK: Furniture, clocks, arms and Oriental rugs, 17th-19th C, £250-£10,000.* PARK: Easy. TEL: 0638 742197. SER: Valuations; restorations (furniture, oil paintings, clocks, arms). VAT: Stan/Spec.

CAMBRIDGE
20th Century
169 Histon Rd. (S. Charles). Open 12-6, Sat. 10-5. CL: Mon. *STOCK: Decorative arts, 1880-1980.* TEL: 0223 359482.

Jess Applin Antiques　　BADA
8 Lensfield Rd. Est. 1968. Open 10-5.30. *STOCK: Furniture, 17th-19th C; works of art.* LOC: At junction with Hills Rd., opposite church. PARK: Meters and nearby. TEL: 0223 315168; evenings - 0223 246851. VAT: Spec.

John Beazor and Sons Ltd　　BADA
78-80 Regent St. Est. 1875. Open 9-5. *STOCK: English furniture, late 17th to early 19th C; clocks, barometers and decorative items.* TEL: 0223 355178. SER: Valuations. VAT: Spec.

Benet Gallery
19 Kings Parade, and 26 Long Rd. (G.H. and J. Criddle). Est. 1965. Open 10-5; Long Rd. open by appointment. SIZE: Large. *STOCK: Early maps of Cambridgeshire, engravings of the colleges.* TEL: 0223 353783/248739. VAT: Stan.

Cambridge continued

The Bookroom (Cambridge)
13A St. Eligius St. (E.A. Searle). Est. 1973. Open 9.30-5, Sat. by appointment. SIZE: Small. *STOCK: Science, medicine, natural history, military, naval and marine, English literature, mainly 19th C; some private press, Folio Society publications including out-of-print.* LOC: Trumpington Rd. end of Bateman St. PARK: Panton St. TEL: 0223 69694; home - 0223 354566. SER: Valuations; buys at auction (books). VAT: Stan.

Buckies　　LAPADA
31 Trinity St. (G. McC. and P.R. Buckie). NAG, GMC. Est. 1972. Open 9.45-5. CL: Mon. SIZE: Medium. *STOCK: Jewellery, silver, objets d'art.* PARK: Multi-storey, nearby. TEL: 0223 357910. SER: Valuations; restorations and repairs. VAT: Stan/Spec.

Cambridge Fine Art Ltd　　LAPADA
Priesthouse, 33 Church St., Little Shelford. (R. and J. Lury). Resident. Est. 1972. Open 10-6, Sun. by appointment. SIZE: Large. *STOCK: British and European paintings, 1780-1900; British paintings, 1880-1930; portraits, 1650-1930.* LOC: Next to church. PARK: Easy. TEL: 0223 842866/843537. SER: Valuations; restorations; buys at auction. VAT: Stan/Spec.

Collectors Centre
Hope St. Yard, Hope St. Est. 1970. Open 10-5. CL: Mon. and Tues. SIZE: Medium. *STOCK: Pine, Victoriana, Deco, wind-up gramophones and general items, 19th-20th C.* LOC: Off Mill Rd., Romsey Town. PARK: Own. TEL: 0223 211632. SER: Restorations (pictures); carver and gilder; gramophone repairs.

Collectors' Market
Dales Brewery, Gwydir St (off Mill Rd). (Mrs E.M. Highmoor). Est. 1976. Open 10-5, Sat. 9.30-5.30. SIZE: 8 units. *STOCK: Collectors' items from £1.50-£750, including bygones, prints, pine, bric-a-brac, kitchenalia, art deco, furniture.*

Collins and Clark
14-17 Regent Terrace. (J.G. Collins). Est. 1895. Open by appointment only. *STOCK: English furniture, English and Oriental porcelain, silver, glass.* TEL: 0223 353801. VAT: Spec.

Gabor Cossa Antiques
34 Trumpington St. (M. Edgell and D. Theobaldy). Est. 1948. Open 10-5.30. *STOCK: English ceramics, Delftware, English glass, Oriental ceramics, bijouterie.* LOC: Opposite Fitzwilliam Museum. PARK: 400yds. TEL: 0223 356049. VAT: Spec.

CAMBRIDGESHIRE

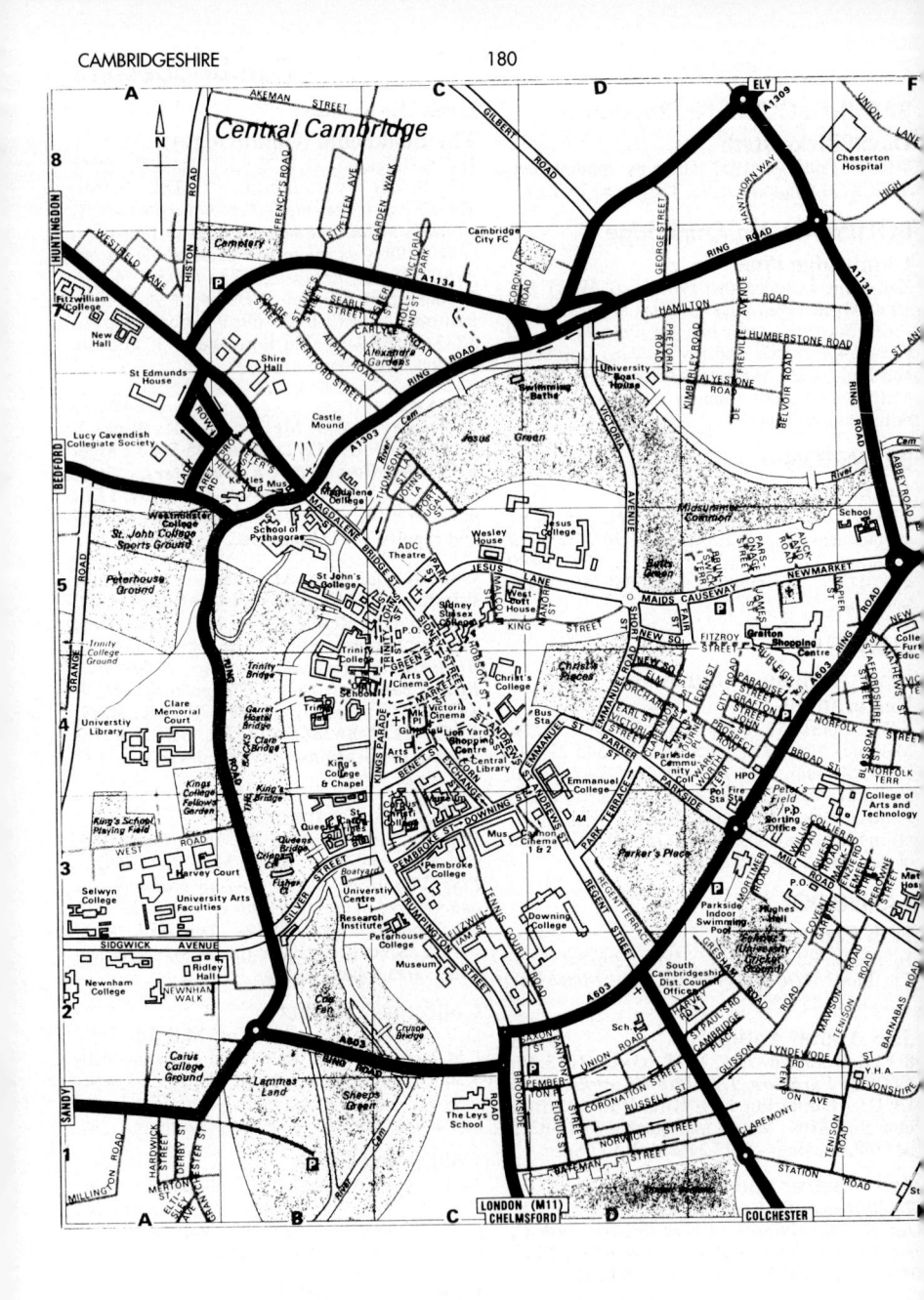

Central Cambridge

Key to Town Plan

- AA Recommended roads
- Other roads
- Restricted roads
- Buildings of interest
- Car Parks
- Parks and open spaces
- AA Service Centre

© Automobile Association 1988.

CAMBRIDGESHIRE

Cambridge continued
Cottage Antiques
16-18 Lensfield Rd. (Mrs A. Owen and Mrs A. Yandell). Est. 1981. Open 10-5.30, Sun. by appointment. SIZE: Medium. *STOCK: 18th-19th C pottery, porcelain, blue and white, Staffordshire figures, glass, country furniture, brass, copper; general antiques and antiquities.* LOC: Opposite Catholic Church. PARK: Nearby. TEL: 0223 316698.

Peter Ian Crabbe
3 Pembroke St. Open 10-4.30. *STOCK: Furniture and porcelain.* TEL: 0223 357117. VAT: Spec.

G. David
3 and 16 St. Edward's Passage. ABA, PBFA. Est. 1896. Open 9.30-5 (No.3). Open 9-5. CL: Thurs. (No.16). *STOCK: Antiquarian books, fine bindings, secondhand and out of print books, selected publishers remainders.* TEL: 0223 354619.

Deighton Bell and Co
13 Trinity St. (Heffers Booksellers). ABA, PBFA. Est. 1700. Open 9-5.30. SIZE: Large. *STOCK: Antiquarian, rare and fine old books, most subjects; also bibliography, typography and illustrated books.* PARK: Multi-storey, 300yds. TEL: 0223 353939. SER: Buys at auction. VAT: Stan.

Galloway and Porter Ltd
30 Sidney St, and 3 Green St. ABA. Est. 1900. *STOCK: Antiquarian and secondhand books.* TEL: 0223 67876.

Derek Gibbons
The Haunted Bookshop, St. Edward's Passage. Est. 1960. Open 9.30-5.30. *STOCK: Antiquarian and illustrated books.* TEL: 0223 312913.

Gwydir Street Antiques Centre
Gwydir St. Open 10-5, Sat. 9.30-5.30. SIZE: 12 dealers. *STOCK: General antiques including furniture, Georgian to 1960's; Victorian sofas and chairs, decorative china and objets d'art, Victorian fireplaces.* LOC: Off Mill Rd. PARK: Opposite.

W. Heffer
Est. 1970. Open by appointment only. *STOCK: General furniture, silver, china, clocks, watches.* TEL: Home - 0223 63634. SER: Valuations; restorations (wood, metalware, silver, china, mother-of-pearl).

Hyde Park Corner Antiques (Antiques Centre)
12 Lensfield Rd. (S.J. Cope-Brown). Open 10-5. SIZE: 8 dealers. *STOCK: Pre-1830 English ceramics; glass, silver, furniture, early metalware, pot-lids and Prattware, treen,*

Cambridge continued
jewellery and early prints. TEL: 0223 353654. SER: Valuations; restorations (pottery, porcelain and furniture).

The Lawson Gallery
7-8 King's Parade. Est. 1967. Open 9.30-5. SIZE: Medium. *STOCK: Local and fine art; reproduction railway posters of '30s, '40s and '50s; prints.* LOC: Opposite King's College. PARK: Lion's Yard. TEL: 0223 313970. VAT: Stan.

Sebastian Pearson Paintings, Prints and Works of Art
3 Free School Lane, Benet St. Est. 1989. Open 10.30-5.30. CL: Mon. SIZE: Medium. *STOCK: Oil paintings and watercolours, £300-£3,500; 20th C British prints (etchings and wood engravings), £60-£600; some Oriental and European works of art.* LOC: City centre. PARK: Nearby. TEL: 0223 323999; home - 0438 871364. SER: Valuations; picture framing. VAT: Spec.

Pembroke Antiques
7 Pembroke St. (K.M. and R.M. Galey). Open 10-5. CL: Mon. SIZE: Small. *STOCK: Silver, 19th C; Victorian jewels; both £50-£500; furniture, 19th C, £500-£1,000.* LOC: 100 yards off Trumpington St., opposite Pembroke College. PARK: 100 yards. TEL: 0223 63246. VAT: Stan/Spec.

Rose Cottage Antiques
Rose Cottage, Brewery Rd., Pampisford. (A. and A. Anness). Open 9-6, Sun. 2-5, other times by appointment. *STOCK: Period furniture, curios; Victorian style solid brass lighting.* PARK: 0223 834631. SER: Restoration (furniture).

Barry Strover
55 Sturton St. Open Mon.-Sat. by chance or by appointment. *STOCK: Mainly pine - primitive country and decorative in original painted condition.* TEL: 0223 66302.

S.J. Webster-Speakman   BADA
79 Regent St. Open 10-5.30. *STOCK: English furniture, clocks, Staffordshire pottery, general antiques.* TEL: 0223 315048; evenings - 0223 354809. VAT: Spec.

CHIPPENHAM, Nr. Ely
Chippenham Antique Centre
La Hogue Farm. (T. Bulmer). Open 10-6 including Sun. and Bank Holidays. STOCK: General antiques. TEL: 0638 751533. LOC: Off A11. PARK: Easy.

CAMBRIDGESHIRE

SIMON & PENNY RUMBLE
Dealers in 17th & 18th Century
oak & country furniture

*At the Old School, Chittering,
Cambridge CB5 9PW (0223) 861831*

OPEN MOST DAYS - PRIOR PHONE CALL ADVISABLE

We are just off the A10 6m north of Cambridge

CHITTERING, Nr. Cambridge
Simon and Penny Rumble Antiques
The Old School. Usually open but prior telephone call advisable. STOCK: Early oak and country furniture, pottery, treen, decorative items. LOC: 6 miles north of Cambridge, off A10. TEL: 0223 861831.

COMBERTON
Comberton Antiques
5a West St. (Mrs M. McEvoy). Est. 1980. Open Mon., Fri. and Sat. 10-5, Sun. 2-5. SIZE: Medium. STOCK: Furniture, 1780-1900, £50-£500; bric-a-brac, 1830-1920, £5-£100; shipping goods. LOC: 6 miles west of Cambridge, 2 miles west of M11. PARK: Easy. TEL: 0223 262674; home - 0223 263457.

DODDINGTON
Doddington House Antiques
2 Benwick Rd. (B.A. Frankland). Est. 1974. STOCK: Furniture, mirrors, clocks, barometers, pictures and interesting items. LOC: At Clocktower. PARK: Easy. TEL: 0354 740755. SER: Restoration (chair caning and rushing, barometers).

DUXFORD
Riro D. Mooney
4 Moorfield Rd. Est. 1946. Open 9-7. SIZE: Medium. STOCK: General antiques, 1780-1920, £5-£1,200. LOC: 1 mile from M11. PARK: Easy. TEL: 0223 832252. VAT: Stan/Spec.

ELY
Mrs Mills Antiques
1a St. Mary's St. (E.T. Mills). FGA. Open 10-1 and 2-5. CL: Tues. STOCK: General small antiques, porcelain and pottery, 18th-19th C; jewellery, small silver items. Not Stocked: Furniture. TEL: 0353 664268. SER: Restorations (porcelain).

Waterside Antiques
The Wharf. (G. Peters). Est. 1986. Open 9.30-5.30, Sun. 1-5.30. SIZE: Large. STOCK: General antiques. LOC: Waterside area. PARK: Easy. TEL: 0353 667066. SER: Valuations.

FORDHAM
Phoenix Antiques
1 Carter St. Est. 1966. Open by appointment. CL: Wed. SIZE: Medium. STOCK: Early European furniture, domestic metalwork, pottery and delft, carpets, scientific instruments, treen and bygones. LOC: Centre of village. PARK: Own. TEL: 0638 720363.

FOWLMERE, Nr. Royston
Mere Antiques
High St. (R.W. Smith). Est. 1979. Open 10-1 and 2-6, including Sun. SIZE: Medium. STOCK: Furniture, porcelain and clocks, 18th-19th C, to £5,000. PARK: Easy. TEL: 0763 208477; home - 0763 208495. SER: Valuations. VAT: Spec.

HARSTON
Antique Clocks
1 High St. (C.J. Stocker). Open every day. LOC: On A10, 5 miles south of Cambridge. PARK: Easy. TEL: 0223 870264.

HUNTINGDON
The Antique Centre
George St. (Stephen Copsey). Est. 1977. Open 10-6, Sun. 12-5. SIZE: Large. STOCK: General antiques, 17th-18th C. LOC: Off Huntingdon ring road. PARK: Easy. TEL: 0480 435100. SER: Valuations; buys at auction. VAT: Stan/Spec.

ICKLETON, Nr. Saffron Walden
Abbey Antiques
18 Abbey St. (K. Wilson). Est. 1974. Open 10-5, Sun. 2-5. SIZE: Large. STOCK: General antiques, 17th-20th C, £1-£1,000. LOC: Turn off at Stumps Cross at Gt. Chesterford, 1 mile to Ickleton, shop is in main street. PARK: Easy. TEL: 0799 30637. SER: Valuations; restorations (furniture); French polishing.

LANDBEACH
P.R. Garner Antiques
104 High St. Est. 1966. Open by appointment only. SIZE: Medium. STOCK: China, glass

CAMBRIDGESHIRE

Landbeach continued
brass, copper, pewter, unrestored furniture, Victorian and earlier; automobilia and collectors cars; shipping goods. LOC: Off A10. PARK: Easy. TEL: 0223 860470. SER: Valuations. VAT: Stan/Spec.

J.V. Pianos and Cambridge Pianola Company
The Limes. (F.T. Poole). Est. 1972. Open by appointment including evenings. SIZE: Medium. STOCK: Pianos. LOC: First building on right in Landbeach from A10. PARK: Easy. TEL: 0223 861348/861507; home - same. SER: Valuations; restorations. FAIRS: City and Classical Music Show (Barbican). VAT: Stan.

LITTLE ABINGTON, Nr. Cambridge
Abington Books
29 Church Lane. (J. Haldane). Est. 1971. By appointment only. SIZE: Small. STOCK: Books on Oriental rugs, from 1877, £1-£5,000; books on classical tapestries, from 17th C, £1-£3,000. PARK: Easy. TEL: 0223 891645; fax - 0223 893724. SER: Valuations; book binding; occasional catalogues; buys at auction (books).

LITTLE DOWNHAM, Nr. Ely
The Old Bishop's Palace Antique Centre
Tower Rd. (Mark Stevens). Est. 1990. Open Fri., Sat. and Sun. and Bank Holidays 10-5.30, other times by appointment. SIZE: 35 dealers. STOCK: General antiques including furniture, paintings and prints, firearms, golf clubs, Asian artefacts, kelims, mainly 18th-19th C, £5-£5,000. LOC: A10 Ely bypass, B1411 to Little Downham, premises opposite The Plough public house. PARK: Own. TEL: 0353 699177; home - same. SER: Valuations; restorations. VAT: Stan/Spec.

MELBOURN, Nr. Royston
P.N. Hardiman
62 High St. (M. and G.A. Hardiman). Est. 1933. Open 8.30-6. CL: Sun. except by appointment. SIZE: Medium. STOCK: English furniture, 18th-19th C; general antiques. LOC: A10 between Royston and Cambridge. PARK: At rear. TEL: 0763 260093. SER: Restorations. VAT: Stan/Spec.

ORWELL
West Farm Antiques   LAPADA
High St. (Mrs J. Kershaw). Est. 1964. Open by appointment only. SIZE: Large. STOCK: Country furniture and general antiques, 17th-19th C, £5-£3,000. Not Stocked: Reproductions, silver, clocks, mechanical objects, jewellery. LOC: 5 miles from exit 12, M11, off A603, 1/2 mile past church on right. PARK: Easy. TEL: 0223 207464. FAIRS: Olympia, British International, Birmingham, Barbican. VAT: Stan/Spec.

OUTWELL, Nr. Wisbech
A.P. and M.A. Haylett
Glen-Royd, 393 Wisbech Rd. Open 9-6 including Sun. STOCK: Country furniture, pottery, treen and metalware, 1750-1900, £5-£500. Not Stocked: Firearms. LOC: A1101. PARK: Easy. TEL: 0945 772427; home - same. SER: Buys at auction. FAIRS: Snape, Bury St. Edmunds.

PAMPISFORD, Nr. Cambridge
Solopark Ltd
Old Railway Station, Station Rd. (R.J. Bird). Open 8-1 and 2-5, Fri. 8-1 and 2-4, Sat. 8-1. STOCK: Reclaimed period architectural items. TEL: 0223 834663.

PETERBOROUGH
Fitzwilliam Antiques Centre
Fitzwilliam St. (Watkins and Stafford Ltd). Open 10-5, Sun. 12-5. SIZE: 50 dealers. STOCK: General antiques. TEL: 0733 65415.

Ivor and Patricia Lewis Antique and Fine Art Dealers   LAPADA
Westfield, 30 Westwood Park Rd. Open by appointment. STOCK: English and French furniture - some signed, porcelain, bronzes. TEL: 0733 344567.

Old Soke Books
68 Burghley Rd. (Peter and Linda Clay). Open 10.30-5.30. CL: Mon. STOCK: Antiquarian and secondhand books, small general antiques including furniture, paintings, prints and postcards. TEL: 0733 64147.

G. Smith and Sons (Peterborough) Ltd
1379 Lincoln Rd, Werrington. (Mike Groucott). Est. 1902. Open 9-5. SIZE: Medium. STOCK: General antiques, furniture and clocks. LOC: Old Lincoln Road, Werrington village. PARK: Easy. TEL: 0733 571630. SER: Upholstery; restorations.

RAMSEY, Nr. Huntingdon
Abbey Antiques
63 Great Whyte. (R. and J. Smith). Est. 1977. Open 10-5 including Sun. CL: Mon. SIZE: Small. STOCK: Furniture including pine, 1850-1930, £50-£500; porcelain, Goss and crested china, 1830-1950, £3-£500; Beswick, Wade and Fen pottery; brass and copper, 1850-1950, £10-£100. PARK: Easy. TEL: 0487 814753. FAIRS: Alexandra Palace, Harrow.

Yesteryear Antiques
79/81 High St. (Mr and Mrs S. Staley Grace). Est. 1977. Open Thurs. - Sun. SIZE: Medium. STOCK: Small items, 19th C, £5-£100; furniture, £100-£300; prints, 19th C watercolours and oils. PARK: Easy. TEL: 0487 815006; home - same. SER: Restorations; picture framing. FAIRS: Clavering.

CAMBRIDGESHIRE

ST. IVES
Broadway Antiques
31 The Broadway. (B.R. Norton). Est. 1980. Open 9.30-4.30. CL: Thurs. SIZE: Small. *STOCK: Furniture, £30-£1,000; metalware, vestas and snuff boxes, treen, corkscrews, £10-£500; all 18th-19th C.* LOC: West end of town, near Norris Museum. PARK: Easy. TEL: 0480 461061; home - 0480 468220. SER: Valuations. FAIRS: Newark, Ardingly, Sandown.

B.R. Knight and Sons
Quay Court, Bull Lane, Bridge St. (M. Knight). Est. 1972. Open 10-4.30. *STOCK: Porcelain, pottery, jewellery, paintings, watercolours, prints, decorative arts.* LOC: Off Bridge St. PARK: Nearby. TEL: 0480 68295.

ST. NEOTS
Peter John
38 St. Mary's St, Eynesbury. (K. Smith). CMG. Open 10-5, but please telephone first. CL: Tues. *STOCK: Jewellery.* PARK: Easy. TEL: 0480 216297. SER: Clockmaker; restorations (clocks); repairs (clocks, jewellery).

Tavistock Antiques
Cross Hall Manor, Eaton Ford. Open by appointment. *STOCK: Period English furniture.* TEL: 0480 472082. *Trade Only.*

SAWTRY
A Barn Full of Brass Beds
Manor Farm, St. Judith's Lane. (Jonathan Tebbs). Open by appointment. *STOCK: Beds - brass and iron.* TEL: 0487 832664.

SOUTHOE, Nr. St. Neots
Midloe Grange Antiques and Design
Midloe Grange, Rectory Lane. (Stephen Copsey). Est. 1977. Open by appointment. SIZE: Large. *STOCK: Eastern European pine and decorative antiques, 18th C, £100-£500.* LOC: Off A1 at Southsoe, 45 minutes from central London to St. Neots station. PARK: Easy. TEL: 0480 407970; home - 0480 404029. VAT: Stan.

SWAFFHAM PRIOR, Nr. Cambridge
Rodney Firmin
Lowfields, Lower End. Est. 1974. Open by appointment only. *STOCK: Clocks - English, French, bracket, longcase and carriage, £500-£20,000.* TEL: 0638 742881. SER: Valuations; restorations; buys at auction. VAT: Spec.

WANSFORD, Nr. Peterborough
Old House Antiques
The Old House, 16 London Rd. (R. Rimes and L. Ayres). Resident. Open 9.30-6. CL: Sun. and Mon. except by appointment. *STOCK: Period*

Wansford continued
lighting, oil lamps, candles, candle tube makers. LOC: On A1 near A47 junction. PARK: Easy. TEL: 0780 783999/783899/783462.

Sydney House Antiques
14 Elton Rd. (G. and R. Hancox). Est. 1972. Open 10-5 including Sun., Mon. 2-5.30, other times by appointment. SIZE: Large. *STOCK: Furniture, including marquetry, 19th-20th C, £150-£2,000; Minton, 1850-1920, £100-£2,000; Doulton and Lambeth, £50-£1,000; Royal Worcester, 1860-1940, £100-£1,500.* PARK: Easy. TEL: 0780 782786. SER: Valuations; buys at auction (Minton, Doulton, Royal Worcester, 19th C furniture).

Wansford Antiques and Oriental Pottery
10 London Rd. (P.E. Hancox). Open 9-5, including Sun. *STOCK: Royal Worcester porcelain; French and inlaid furniture.* TEL: 0780 783253.

WARBOYS
Warboys Antiques
Old Church School, High St. (J. Lambden). Est. 1986. Open 10-5. CL: Mon. SIZE: Medium. *STOCK: Decorative smalls, 18th-20th C; sports equipment, advertising items, 19th-20th C; all £1-£1,500.* LOC: Off A141. PARK: Easy. TEL: 0487 823686. SER: Valuations. FAIRS: Alexandra Palace.

WISBECH
Attic Gallery
88 Elm Rd. (B.G. Ransome). Est. 1980. Open by appointment. SIZE: Small. *STOCK: Georgian and Victorian silver.* PARK: Easy. TEL: 0945 583734.

Country House Interiors
Walpole Antique Centre, Rampart House, Walpole Highway. (Simon Reeve). Resident. Est. 1988. Open 10.30-5 including Sun. SIZE: Large. *STOCK: General antiques - furniture including pine, china and bygones. £1-£1,500.* LOC: A47. PARK: Own. TEL: 0945 881033; home - 0945 880733.

Peter A. Crofts   BADA
Briar Patch, High Rd., Elm. Est. 1949. CL: Sat. *STOCK: General antiques, furniture, porcelain, silver, jewellery.* LOC: A1101. TEL: 0945 584614. VAT: Stan/Spec.

Eric Golding
12 North Brink. Open by appointment only *STOCK: Antiquarian books.* TEL: 0945 582927.

R. Wilding
Lanes End, Gadds Lane, Leverington. *STOCK: Pergolesi pine panelling, pine fireplaces and screens, walnut and mahogany furniture.* TEL 0945 588204. SER: Restorations (re-veneering polishing, conversions and gesso work).

ANTIQUE COLLECTING

- **Authoritative articles**
- **Practical buying information**
- **Up-to-date price guides**
- **Annual Investment Issue**
- **Auctions and fairs calendars**
- **Antiques for sale and wanted**

The magazine is published ten times a year and contains pre-publication offers and special Christmas discounts on ACC books

Join NOW and receive your first magazine and our book catalogue FREE
Annual membership: £19.50 UK, £25.00 overseas, US $40 USA, CAN $50 Canada

Antique Collectors' Club
5 Church Street, Woodbridge, Suffolk,
IP12 1DS, England
Tel: (0394) 385501 Fax: (0394) 384434

Market Street Industrial Park, Wappingers' Falls,
New York 12590, USA
Tel: 914 297 0003 Fax: 914 297 0068

For Collectors, By Collectors, About Collecting

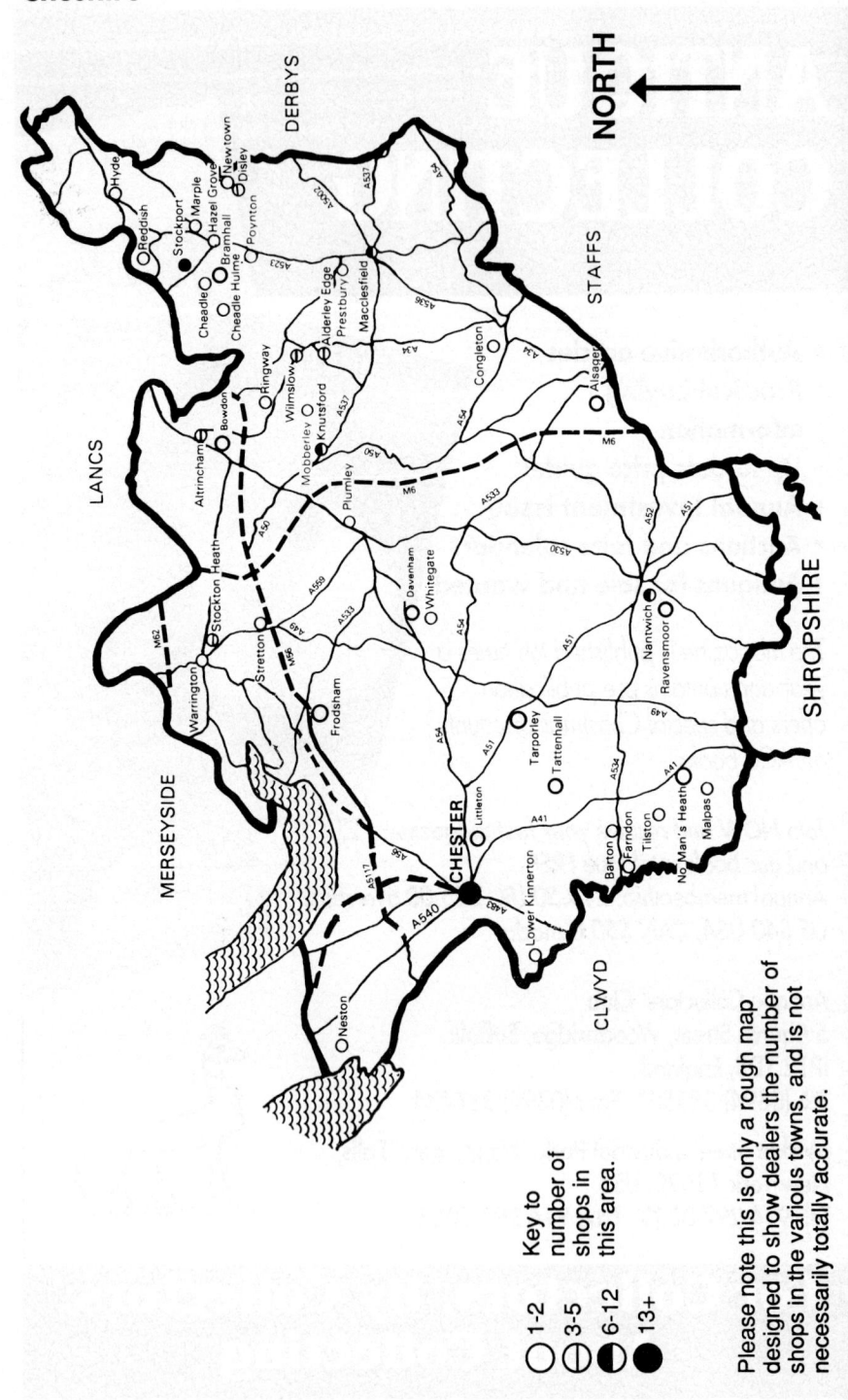

Cheshire

Key to number of shops in this area.

○ 1-2
◐ 3-5
◑ 6-12
● 13+

Please note this is only a rough map designed to show dealers the number of shops in the various towns, and is not necessarily totally accurate.

Cheshire

ALDERLEY EDGE

Alderley Antiques LAPADA
17 London Rd. (G. Bennett and J. Barlow). Est. 1967. Open 10-1 and 2-5. SIZE: Medium. STOCK: Furniture, £300-£20,000; objets d'art, £100-£4,000; paintings, £100-£5,000, all 17th-19th C. LOC: Town centre, near station. PARK: Easy. TEL: 0625 583468; home - 0625 584819. FAIRS: British International, Birmingham; Buxton; Guildford. VAT: Stan/Spec.

Anthony Baker Antiques LAPADA
14 London Rd. (G.D.A. Price). Est. 1974. Open 10-5.30. CL: Mon. SIZE: Medium. STOCK: Furniture and clocks, 17th-19th C, £50-£2,000; glass and pottery. Not Stocked: Jewellery, weapons. LOC: A34, village centre. PARK: Easy. TEL: 0625 582674. VAT: Stan/Spec.

Brook Lane Antiques
93 Brook Lane. (M. Goodwin). Est. 1983. Open Thurs., Fri. and Sat. 11-4. SIZE: Small. STOCK: Stripped Victorian, Edwardian and reproduction pine. TEL: 0625 584896; evenings - 0625 582717. SER: Stencilling; stripping.

The Edge Antiques
8 Trafford Rd. (Vivienne and Andrew Smith). Est. 1977. Open 10-12.30 and 2-4.30, Sat. 10-1, Sun. and Sat. p.m. by appointment. CL: Mon. and Wed. SIZE: Small. STOCK: Victorian light fittings, gas brackets, £100-£500; Victorian pine. LOC: Parallel to London Rd. (A34). PARK: Easy. TEL: 0625 582176; home - 0625 584089.

Sara Frances Antiques
2 West St. (Miss F.S. Broomhead). Est. 1990. Open 10-5.30. CL: Mon. SIZE: Small. STOCK: Furniture, 17th-19th C, £100-£3,500; silver, 19th-20th C, £50-£500; decorative items, 17th-20th C, £100-£2,500. LOC: A34 from Congleton. Off London Rd., shop next to Barclays Bank. PARK: Easy. TEL: 0625 585549; home - 0625 829625. SER: Valuations; restorations (furniture and silver).

D.J. Massey and Son
51a London Rd. Est. 1900. Open 9-5.30, Wed. 9-5. SIZE: Large. STOCK: Gold and diamond jewellery; silver, all periods. LOC: On A34. PARK: Easy. TEL: 0625 583565. VAT: Stan/Spec.

ALSAGER, Nr. Crewe

Trash 'n' Treasure
48 Sandbach Rd. South. (G. and D. Ogden). Est. 1979. Open 10-12 and 1-5, Fri. and Sat. 10-12 and 1-5.30. CL: Wed. SIZE: Medium. STOCK: Ceramics, furniture and pictures, Victorian, Edwardian and 1930's, £5-£1,000. LOC: 10 minutes junction 16, M6. PARK: Nearby. TEL: 0270 872972; 0270 873246. SER: Valuations.

ALTRINCHAM

Altrincham Antiques
39 Hale Rd. and 15 Tipping St. (Michael C. Gilbert). Open every day including Sun. SIZE: Medium. STOCK: General antiques, £5-£6,500. LOC: A538 Hale road. PARK: Own. TEL: 061 941 3554; mobile - 0836 316366. SER: Valuations; buys at auction (large value items only). FAIRS: IACF.

Baron Antiques
64-66 Manchester Rd. Open 10-6. STOCK: General antiques. TEL: 061 928 2943.

Bizarre Decorative Arts North West
116 Manchester Rd. (Malcolm C. and Rebecca Lamb). Resident. Est. 1986. Open 10-6, Sun. by appointment. SIZE: Large. STOCK: Furniture and lighting, £100-£15,000; figurines, bronzes, ceramics including Clarice Cliff, and jewellery, £5-£2,000; all art nouveau and art deco. LOC: A56. PARK: Own. TEL: 061 926 8895; home - same; fax - 061 929 8310. SER: Valuations; restorations (furniture and lighting; silver and chrome plating, pewter polishing); buys at auction (as stock). FAIRS: NEC Aug; Loughborough Art Deco; Kensington Decorative Arts. VAT: Stan/Spec.

Cheyne's
38 Hale Rd. (P.J.L. Cheyne). Est. 1983. Open 10-5.30. SIZE: Medium. STOCK: Furniture, 18th-19th C, £50-£2,000; silver and porcelain, £50-£1,000. LOC: 1.5 miles from junction 6, M56. PARK: Easy. TEL: 061 941 4879; home - 061 980 3094. SER: Valuations; restorations (furniture); buys at auction. VAT: Stan/Spec.

Halo Antiques
97 Hale Rd, and 2a Beech Rd. (P., M. C. and T. Oulton). Est. 1976. Open 10-5. CL: Mon. SIZE: Large. STOCK: Trade items, £5-£5,000; pine. LOC: Exit 6, M56. A538 for 2 miles. PARK: Easy. TEL: 061 941 1800; fax - 061 929 9565. SER: Container packing. VAT: Stan.

New Street Antiques
48 New St. (S. and R. Redford). Open 10-6. CL: Mon. and Wed. STOCK: General antiques, furniture, small silver, porcelain. PARK: Easy. TEL: 061 929 8171; home - 061 928 4827/061 926 8232. SER: Valuations; restorations (furniture, textiles and porcelain); plating and polishing.

Squires Antiques
25 Regent Rd. (V. Phillips). Est. 1977. Open 10-5. CL: Mon. and Wed. SIZE: Medium. STOCK: Small furniture, 1800-1930, £60-£500; small silver, 1850-1970, £20-£400; brass, copper and bric-a-brac, 1850-1940, £10-£400; jewellery, porcelain, fire accessories, light fittings and interior design items. Not Stocked: Large furniture, coins and badges. LOC: Adjacent hospital, and large car park. PARK: Easy. TEL: 061 928 0749. SER: Valuations.

BARTON, Nr. Malpas

Derek Rayment Antiques BADA LAPADA
Orchard House, Barton Rd. (D.J. and K.M. Rayment). Est. 1960. Open by appointment every day. STOCK: *Barometers, 18th-20th C, from £100.* LOC: A534. PARK: Easy. TEL: 0829 270429; home - same. SER: Valuations; restorations (barometers only); buys at auction (barometers). FAIRS: LAPADA; British International, Birmingham; Olympia, West London, Chelsea, Penman; Barbican, Chester, Penman. VAT: Stan/Spec.

BOWDON

Eureka Antiques and Interiors
7a Church Brow. (N. Gibson and A.J. O'Donnell). Est. 1965. Open 10-1 and 2-5, other times by appointment. CL: Mon. and Wed. STOCK: *Furniture, 18th-19th C, £100-£8,000; porcelain, 19th C, £60-£500; collectors' items, tartanware, Scottish jewellery.* LOC: Off M6 towards Manchester, straight on after first traffic lights, turn right after large roundabout. Turn left up hill towards church, shop on left. TEL: 061 926 9722.

BRAMHALL

David H. Dickinson LAPADA
P.O. Box 29. Est. 1976. Open by appointment only. STOCK: *Fine antique furniture and extraordinary works of art.* TEL: 061 440 0688. SER: Valuations.

CHEADLE

Malcolm Frazer Antiques
19 Brooklyn Crescent. Open by appointment. STOCK: *Marine, scientific and decorative antiques.* TEL: 061 428 3781.

Honeypot Antiques
28 Stockport Rd. (Arnold and Betty Preshaw). Est. 1968. Open 9-5, Sun. by appointment. SIZE: Medium. STOCK: *Victorian, art nouveau and art deco china including figures, £10-£1,000; jewellery, Georgian-Victorian, £25-£1,000; general antiques and collectors' items, £5-100.* LOC: Off M63, exit 11, turn right through traffic lights, shop 100 yards on left, next to police station. PARK: Easy - ask at shop. TEL: 061 428 8641. SER: Valuations; restorations (porcelain, china, watches, clocks and jewellery). FAIRS: Park Hall, Charnock; Richards (weekly); Merlin, Shepton Mallet; Ardingly, Newark and Notts.

CHEADLE HULME

Allan's Antiques and Reproductions
10 Ravenoak Rd. (C. Allan). Est. 1979. CL: Wed. STOCK: *Furniture, general antiques, metalware, including silver, especially flatware.* TEL: 061 485 3132.

Cheadle Hulme continued

Recollections
12-14 Mellor Rd. (Angela Smith). Est. 1992 Open Thurs. and Fri.10.30-4.30, Sat. 10.30-4 SIZE: Small. STOCK: *Costume jewellery and accessories, 1930's to 1960's, £5-£25; linen and lace, 1930's, £5-£50; china and cut glass, 19th C to 1960's, £5-£25.* LOC: Above Mellor Lighting 2 miles from railway station. PARK: Easy. TEL 061 485 5182; home - 0625 877831. SER Restorations (Lloyd loom ottomans); costume jewellery repairs; hand-crafted ear-rings from antique beads. FAIRS: Buxton.

CHESTER

Adams Antiques LAPADA
65 Watergate Row. (B. and T. Adams). Est. 1973 Open 10-5. CL: Sun. except by appointment SIZE: Medium. STOCK: *English and continental furniture, £200-£4,000; English and French clocks, £150-£4,000; objets d'art, £10-£1,000; a 18th-19th C.* PARK: Nearby. TEL: 0244 319421 SER: Valuations; restorations (furniture, clocks and oil paintings). VAT: Stan/Spec.

Aldersey Hall Ltd
Town Hall Sq., 47 Northgate St. (Kim Wilding Welton). Est. 1990. Open 8.30-5.30. SIZE: Medium STOCK: *Art deco and general British ceramics, £5 £500; small furniture, £50-£200; all 1880-1940.* LOC: Between library and Odeon cinema. PARK Own 100 yards. TEL: 0244 324885. SER Valuations; buys at auction (art deco ceramics) FAIRS: Alexandra Palace, Loughborough, Ardingly Newark and Birmingham. VAT: Stan/Spec.

Angela Antiques
32 Christleton Rd. (Lionel and Angela Jones). Es 1977. CL: Wed. and Fri. except by appointmen SIZE: Small. STOCK: *Small furniture, pine, chin and collectables, 19th-20th C, £50-£100.* LOC Off A41, 1/2 mile from city centre. PARK Opposite. TEL: 0244 351562; home - 024 329312. SER: Valuations; buys at auction. VAT Stan/Spec.

Antique Exporters of Chester
Open by appointment only. SIZE: Warehouse STOCK: *Furniture.* TEL: 0829 41001; home 0244 570069. SER: Packing. *Export Only.*

The Antique Shop
40 Watergate St. (Peter Thornber). Est. 198. Open 9-5.30, Tues. and Wed. 10-5 (until 6 summer), Sat. 9-6, Sun. (June-Aug.) 11-4. SIZE Small. STOCK: *Metalware including brass pewter, copper and iron, 1700-1900, £50-£250 Doulton character jugs and figures, series war 1890-1960, £50-£250; transfer printed ware, blu and whitre, pot-lids, 1850-1930, £25-£150.* LOC Off Bridge St. PARK: Nearby. TEL: 024 316286; home - 051 327 3853. SER: Restoration (metalwork). FAIRS: Cheshire.

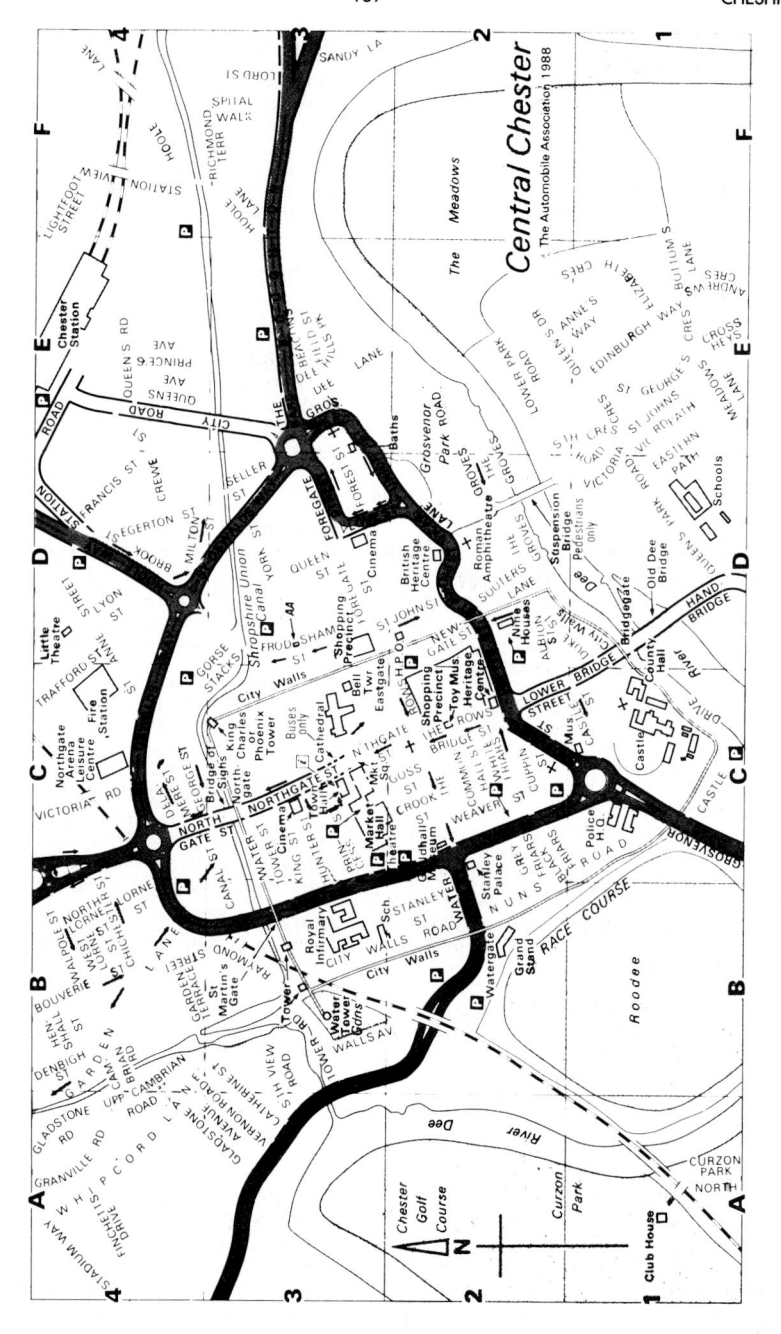

Key to Town Plan

- AA Recommended roads
- Other roads
- Restricted roads
- Buildings of interest
- Car Parks
- Parks and open spaces
- AA Service Centre

© Automobile Association 1988.

Chester continued

Avalon Post Card and Stamp Shop
1 City Walls, Rufus Court, Northgate St. (G.E. Ellis). *STOCK: Postcards, stamps and collectables.* TEL: 0244 318406.

Baron Fine Art
68 Watergate St. (S. and R. Baron). Est. 1984. Open 10-5.15. *STOCK: Watercolours and oils, some etchings, late 19th to early 20th C, some contemporary, £50-£25,000.* PARK: Easy. TEL: 0244 342520/349212. SER: Restorations; framing. FAIRS: Tatton Park; Barbican; LAPADA, January, NEC. VAT: Stan/Spec.

Boodle and Dunthorne Ltd
52 Eastgate St. Est. 1798. Open 9-5.30. SIZE: Large. *STOCK: Jewellery, watches, silver, 18th-19th C, £50-£30,000; clocks and clock sets, mid-19th C, £250-£2,000.* Not Stocked: Furniture. PARK: Multi-storey in Pepper St. TEL: 0244 326666. VAT: Stan/Spec.

Olwyn Boustead Antiques   LAPADA
61 Watergate Row. (Mrs O.L. Boustead). Open 10-5.30. ***STOCK: General antiques including 17th-19th C portraits, town and country furniture, clocks, metalware, lighting and decorative items.*** TEL: 0244 342300.

Chester Furniture Cave
97a Christleton Rd, Boughton. Open 10-5. SIZE: Warehouse. *STOCK: Furniture.* PARK: Easy. TEL: 0244 314798.

City Strippers
121 Brook St. (Brown and Colyer). Est. 1978. Open 9.30-5.30. SIZE: Large. *STOCK: Stripped pine, satin and red walnut, 19th C, £100-£800.* LOC: 1 mile from M56 on Hoole Rd. bridge, around corner from railway station. PARK: Easy. TEL: 0244 349543. SER: Restorations; hand stripping. VAT: Stan/Spec.

Neil Davidson Antiques
26 Christleton Rd. Est. 1990. Open 10-3.30. SIZE: Small. *STOCK: Oak and mahogany furniture, 17th-19th C, £100-£1,000; watercolours and prints, 18th-19th C, £50-£500; Staffordshire pottery, 19th C, £50-£300.* LOC: A41 into city centre. PARK: Opposite. TEL: 0244 312939; home - 0244 371294. SER: Valuations; restorations (furniture and porcelain); buys at auction. VAT: Spec.

Farmhouse Antiques
21-23 Christleton Rd, Boughton. (K. Appleby). Est. 1973. Open 9-5. SIZE: Large. *STOCK: Farmhouse furniture, longcase clocks, Staffordshire pottery, country bygones, mechanical music.* LOC: 1 mile from City centre on A41. PARK: Easy. TEL: 0244 322478; evenings - 0244 318391. SER: Export. VAT: Stan/Spec.

Chester continued

Grosvenor Antiques of Chester
22 Watergate St. (Mrs P.M. Jacobi). Est. 1971 Open 9.30-5.30. SIZE: Medium. *STOCK: Jewellery Georgian and Victorian; furniture, china, porcelain shipping goods, dolls, silver, Oriental carpets and rugs.* Not Stocked: Stamps, coins. PARK: Easy TEL: 0244 315201. SER: Valuations; restorations repairs (jewellery). VAT: Stan/Spec.

Guildhall Fair
Watergate St. Open Thurs. 10-4. SIZE: 20 dealers *STOCK: General antiques.*

Erica and Hugo Harper
27 Watergate Row. Est. 1964. Open 10-4.45. CL Wed. p.m. SIZE: Large. *STOCK: Victoriana, 25p £300; Victorian and Edwardian copper, glass china.* Not Stocked: Jewellery, militaria, coins fine furniture. TEL: 0244 323004; home - 0244 321880.

Jamandic Ltd
22 Bridge St. Row. Est. 1975. Open 9.30-5, Sat 10-1. CL: Sun., except by appointment. SIZE Medium. *STOCK: Decorative furniture, porcelain pictures and prints.* TEL: 0244 312822. SER Interior design; export. VAT: Stan/Spec.

Kayes of Chester
9 St. Michaels Row. (A.M. Austin-Kaye and N.J Kaye). NAG. Est. 1948. Open 9-5.30. SIZE Medium. *STOCK: Diamond rings and jewellery 1850-1950, £20-£15,000; silver and plate, 1700 1930, £20-£8,000; small objects, oils, water colours and ceramics, 19th to early 20th C, £50 £1,000.* PARK: Nearby. TEL: 0244 327149. SER Valuations; restorations (silver, jewellery an plate); buys at auction. VAT: Stan/Spec.

Lowe and Sons
11 Bridge St. Row. Est. 1770. *STOCK: Jeweller and silver, Georgian, Victorian and Edwardian unusual collectors' items.* TEL: 0244 32585♦ VAT: Stan/Spec.

Made of Honour
11 City Walls. (E. Jones). Open 10-5. *STOCK General antiques, Staffordshire figures, Britis ceramics, books, woolworks, samplers, tapestrie beadworks and textiles.* LOC: Next to Eastga clock, wall level. TEL: 0244 314208.

Melody's Antique Galleries   LAPAD♦
30-32 City Rd. (M. Melody). Est. 1977. Ope 10-5.30 or by appointment. SIZE: Larg *STOCK: 17th-19th C oak, mahogany, waln and pine furniture; books, art deco item lighting, silver and plate.* LOC: 400yds. fro station. TEL: 0244 328968. SER: Courie container packing. VAT: Stan/Spec.

Richard A. Nicholson
25 Watergate St. Est. 1961. Open 9.30-1 and 2.1 5. SIZE: Large. *STOCK: Maps, 1540-1840, £*

CHESHIRE

Chester continued

£2,000; prints, 1650-1890, £1-£300; watercolours and drawings, £4-£200. LOC: Town centre 100yds. from The Cross. PARK: 200yds. at bottom of street behind church. TEL: 0244 326818; home - 0244 336004; fax - 0244 336138. SER: Illustrated catalogue issued. VAT: Stan/Spec.

Richmond Galleries
Watergate Building, New Crane St. (Mrs M. Armitage). Est. 1970. Open 10-5.30. SIZE: Large. *STOCK: Pine and country furniture, including Spanish and French; decorative items.* LOC: Direction of Sealand Rd. PARK: Own. TEL: 0244 317602; home - 0244 324275.

St. Peters Art Gallery
St. Peters Churchyard, Northgate St. (D. Hellon). Est. 1984. Open 10-5. SIZE: Medium. *STOCK: Watercolours and oil paintings, 19th to early 20th C, £500-£20,000.* LOC: In city centre off Northgate St. PARK: Nearby. TEL: 0244 345500. VAT: Spec.

Stothert - Antiquarian Books
4 Nicholas St. (T. and E. Stothert). GADAR. Est. 1957. Open 9.30-1 and 2-5.30. SIZE: Medium. *STOCK: Books, 16th-20th C, £2-£1,000.* LOC: At junction with Watergate St. TEL: 0244 340756. VAT: Stan/Spec.

John Titchner & Sons   LAPADA
67 Watergate Row. Open 10-5.30. *STOCK: Furniture, 18th-19th C.* TEL: 0244 326535.

Bernard Walsh Ltd
11 St. Michaels Row. Est. 1950. Open 9-5. SIZE: Large. *STOCK: Silver, bijouterie, objets d'art, porcelain, glass, jewellery.* PARK: Easy. TEL: 0244 326032.

Watergate Antiques
56 Watergate St. (A. Shindler). Est. 1968. Open 9.30-5.30. SIZE: Medium. *STOCK: Silver and plate, porcelain and pottery, furniture, militaria, jewellery.* LOC: From Liverpool first set of traffic lights past Waterfall Roundabout, turn left. PARK: At rear. TEL: 0244 344516; fax - 0244 320350. VAT: Stan.

Joyce and Rod Whitehead
at Made of Honour, 11 City Walls. Open 10-5. *STOCK: Fine art, woolworks, samplers, tapestries, beadwork, textiles and decorative items.* TEL: 0244 314208.

CONGLETON

W. Buckley Antiques Exports
35 Chelford Rd. Open 7 days by appointment. *STOCK: Mainly shipping and Victorian furniture.* TEL: 0260 275299. SER: Shipping.

Congleton Antiques
2 Cross St. (D. Shaw). Open 9.30-4.30. CL: Wed. *STOCK: Furniture and general antiques.* TEL: 0260 298909; home - 0260 275331.

Congleton continued

Little Collectables
8/10 Little St. (L.C. and C. Turner). Est. 1989. CL: Wed. SIZE: Medium. *STOCK: Pottery and glass, Doulton, £5-£1,000.* LOC: Near town centre. PARK: Nearby. TEL: 02650 299098.

Pine Too
8/10 Rood Hill. (Mrs J.P. Tryon). Open 9-5. *STOCK: Pine.* LOC: Just off A34. PARK: Nearby. TEL: 0260 279228.

R. and M. Antiques
7-9 Kinsey St. (Mr and Mrs M.D. Peters). Est. 1973. Open 10-5. CL: Wed. SIZE: Small. *STOCK: General antiques including small furniture, brass, ceramics and silver, mainly 19th C, £10-£600.* LOC: Just off A34, shop adjacent to town hall. PARK: Limited and nearby. TEL: 0260 280404. SER: Valuations; restorations (French polishing, clocks). FAIRS: Grasmere. VAT: Stan/Spec.

CREWE

Steven Blackhurst
102 Edleston Rd. Est. 1988. Open 9.30-5, Sat. 10-5, Sun. by appointment. SIZE: Small. *STOCK: Stripped pine, 19th to early 20th C, £25-£600; satinwood furniture, 1900, £100-£500.* LOC: Turn off Nantwich Rd. (A534), shop 250 yards on left. TEL: 0270 258617; home - 0270 665991.

DAVENHAM, Nr. Northwich

Davenham Antique Centre
461 London Rd. Est. 1985. Open 10-5. CL: Wed. SIZE: 9 dealers. *STOCK: General antiques including furniture, country items, pictures, plated ware, china, brass and copper.* LOC: A533 off A556. TEL: 0606 44350.

Forest Books at Magpie Antiques
4 Church St. (E. Mann). Usually open 11-5, Mon. and Fri. 2-5. CL: Wed. SIZE: Small. *STOCK: Books.* LOC: 1/4 mile off Northwich by-pass, left into Church St. PARK: Easy.

Magpie Antiques
4 Church St. (Mrs E. Bowerman). Est. 1979. Open 11-5, Mon. and Fri. 2-5. CL: Wed. SIZE: Medium. *STOCK: Country items, pictures, books, curios and small furniture, £2-£250.* LOC: 1/4 mile off Northwich by-pass, left into Church St. PARK: Easy. TEL: Home - 0829 260360.

DISLEY

Crescent Antiques
7 Buxton Rd. (J.P. Cooper). Est. 1972. Open 11.30-6.30, Sun. 1.30-6.30. CL: Wed. SIZE: Small. *STOCK: General antiques including furniture, pottery, silver, 19th C, £20-£500.* PARK: Opposite Co-op. TEL: 0663 765677.

CHESHIRE

Sweetbriar Gallery
for
Pictures, Paperweights
& Moorcroft

INTERNATIONAL PAPERWEIGHT DEALER (P.C.A.)

All types
Antique and Modern
£2-£2,000
Dealer packs made up
accurately labelled

***

MOORCROFT OLD AND NEW

***

ETCHINGS
Usual stock includes
Brangwyn and Tunnicliffe and similar

Anne Metcalfe, B.A.

Sweetbriar House,
Robin Hood Lane,
Helsby, Cheshire,   View by Appointment
WA6 9NH   Telephone: 0928 723851

Disley continued

Mill Farm Antiques
50 Market St. (F.E. Berry). Est. 1968. Open every day. SIZE: Medium. STOCK: *Pianos, clocks, shipping goods, general antiques, £50-£5,000.* LOC: A6 7 miles south of Stockport. PARK: Easy. TEL: 0663 764045 (24hrs.). SER: Valuations; restorations (clocks, watches, barometers, music boxes). VAT: Stan/Spec.

FARNDON, Nr. Chester

Stephen Meadowcroft Antiques
65 High St. Open by appointment. STOCK: *Period furniture and decorative objects.* LOC: Take the B5130 from Chester. PARK: Easy. TEL: 0829 270377; mobile - 0860 267591. SER: Valuations; buys at auction. VAT: Stan/Spec.

HAZEL GROVE

Gay's (Hazel Grove) Antiques Ltd
LAPADA
34 London Rd. (G.A. Yeo). Est. 1956. Open by appointment only. STOCK: *18th-19th C furniture.* LOC: On A6. PARK: Easy. TEL: 061 483 5532. VAT: Stan/Spec. *Trade Only.*

Grove Antiques
2 & 3 Lyme St. (Steven J. Bradley). Est. 1981. Open 10-5.30. CL: Wed. SIZE: Small. STOCK:

Hazel Grove continued
General antiques and collectables, £5-£1,000. LOC: Just off A6, Commercial Rd. turning. PARK: Nearby. TEL: 061 483 1003; home - 0260 224204. SER: Valuations. FAIRS: Local.

HELSBY

Sweetbriar Gallery
Robin Hood Lane. (Mrs A. Metcalfe). Est. 1986. Open by appointment only. SIZE: Small. STOCK: *Paperweights, 19th-20th C, £5-£1,500; Moorcroft pottery, 20th C, £15-£1,500; etchings, some watercolours and oils, 19th-20th C, £50-£600.* LOC: Off M56, junction 14. First left at traffic lights, first right after Elf Garage, past three right turns. Premises on hillside with long, low sandstone wall in front. PARK: Easy. TEL: 0928 723851; home - same. SER: Valuations; buys at auction (paperweights and Moorcroft). FAIRS: Glass, Birmingham (April); NEC (Aug.); Bowman, Staffs. County Showground. VAT: Stan/Spec.

HOOLE, Nr. Chester

The Old Butchery
24 Charles St. (Susan P. Moore). Est. 1983. Open 10-4.30, Sat. 10-1. CL: Wed. SIZE: Medium. STOCK: *Brass, copper, fireside items, pine and other small furniture, from 19th C, £5-£500.* LOC: From Hoole road turn into Faulkner St. and left into Charles St. PARK: Easy. TEL: 0244 319394.

HYDE

Peter Bunting Antiques   LAPADA
238 Higham Lane, Werneth Low. Est. 1980. Open by appointment. SIZE: Medium. STOCK: *Early oak and country furniture.* LOC: Off A560 between Hyde and Romily just outside Gee Cross. PARK: Easy. TEL: 061 368 5544. VAT: Stan/Spec.

KNUTSFORD

B.R.M. Coins
3 Minshull St. (Brian Butterworth). Est. 1968. Open 10-5, Sat. 10-1. SIZE: Small. STOCK: *Coins, medals and banknotes, worldwide, BC to date, from 5p; money boxes, scales and weights.* LOC: A50. PARK: Nearby. TEL: 0565 651480; home - 0606 74522. SER: Valuations; buys at auction (as stock).

David Bedale
5-7 Minshull St. Est. 1977. SIZE: Medium. STOCK: *18th -19th C furniture, unusual and decorative items.* PARK: 25 yds. TEL: 0565 653621. VAT: Stan/Spec.

Cranford Clocks
(Mr and Mrs M.E. Uppink). Est. 1988. Open by appointment only. SIZE: Small. STOCK: *Clocks, 1700-1920, £100-£5,000.* LOC: Off M6, junction 19. PARK: Own. TEL: 0565 633331. SER: Valuations; restorations (clock movements).

Knutsford continued
Cranford Galleries
10 King St. (M.R. Bentley). Est. 1964. Open 11-5. CL: Wed. SIZE: Small. *STOCK: Pictures, prints and Victoriana*. Not Stocked: Glass. LOC: Main St. PARK: Easy. TEL: 0565 633646. SER: Framing and mounting. VAT: Stan

Glynn Interiors
92 King St. Est. 1963. Open 9-1 and 2-5. CL: Wed. SIZE: Large. *STOCK: Furniture, 1750-1900, £50-£2,000; Victorian chairs, £50-£650.* Not Stocked: Porcelain. LOC: Ten mins. drive after leaving M6 at Exit 19. PARK: Own. TEL: 0565 634418. SER: Restorations (re-upholstery) and cabinet repairs. VAT: Stan/Spec.

Lion Gallery and Bookshop
15a Minshull St. (R.P. Hepner). GMC. Est. 1964. Open Fri. 10.30-4.30, Sat. 10-4.30. *STOCK: Antiquarian maps, prints and books; watercolours, oils; all 16th-20th C; O.S. maps and early directories.* LOC: King St. 3 mins. M6. PARK: Nearby. TEL: 0565 652915; fax - 0565 750142. SER: Restorations; binding, cleaning, framing and mounting. VAT: Stan.

Tatton Antiques
8 King St. (Sue Halliwell). Est. 1983. Open 10-1 and 2-5, Wed. 10-1, Sat. 10-1 and 2-6, Sun. 2.30-4.30. SIZE: Medium. *STOCK: Furniture, 17th-19th C, £1,000-£1,500; metalware, 17th-19th C, £50-£250; ceramics, 19th C, £50-£100.* PARK: Easy. TEL: 0565 652114. SER: Valuations. VAT: Spec.

Twenty-Two Antiques
22 King St. (T.C. Batley). Est. 1990. Open 10-5, Wed. 10-1.30, Sun. 2-4.30. CL: Mon. SIZE: Small. *STOCK: Small furniture, porcelain, prints and decorative items, £10-£650.* LOC: From junction 19, M6 follow signs to Knutsford town centre towards station. Turn left at traffic lights on to Church Hill and left at bottom into King St., shop on left. PARK: Nearby. TEL: 0565 633655; home - 0565 632801.

LITTLETON, Nr. Chester
John Titchner and Sons   LAPADA
Littleton Old Hall, Little Heath Rd. Open 9-5. CL: Sat. *STOCK: Furniture, 18th-19th C.* TEL: 0244 336986.

LOSTOCK GRALAM, Nr. Northwich
Lostock Antiques
210 Manchester Rd. (Timothy Lawlor and Miss Carol Carter). Est. 1988. Open 10-5.30, Fri. 10.30-6.30, Sun. 11.30-4. CL: Mon. SIZE: Medium. *STOCK: Furniture, 18th-19th C, £150-£1,000; pottery including Clarice Cliff and Wemyss ware, £5-£95; books.* LOC: Off Chester by-pass towards Northwich. PARK: Easy. TEL: 0606 45523. SER: Valuations; restorations (furniture including French polishing); furniture

Lostock Gralam continued
made to order; furniture restoration cream and pure beeswax polish made on premises. FAIRS: Cheshire Show and local. *Trade Only.*

LOWER KINNERTON, Nr. Chester
Brian Edwards Antique Exports
Gell Farm. (B.H. Edwards). Usually open, prior telephone call preferred. SIZE: Warehouse. *STOCK: Georgian, Victorian and Edwardian furniture and some smalls.* LOC: 4.5 miles from Chester. TEL: 0244 660240. SER: Container packing; courier. VAT: Stan/Spec. *Trade Only.*

MACCLESFIELD
Paula Bolton Antiques
83/85 Chestergate. (P. Bolton). Open 9.30-5.30. SIZE: Medium. *STOCK: 19th-20th C silver, jewellery, collectables; some paintings and furniture.* PARK: At rear. TEL: 0625 433033; fax - 0625 430033. VAT: Stan/Spec.

Philip Brooks
6 West Bank Rd, Upton. Est. 1983. Open by appointment. SIZE: Small. *STOCK: Watercolours, oil paintings and prints, 1830-1950, £30-£1,000.* LOC: Off Prestbury Rd., by the Conservative Club. PARK: Easy. TEL: 0625 426275; home - same. SER: Valuations; restorations (cleaning and repairs); buys at auction (watercolours, oils and prints). FAIRS: NEC, Birmingham; Buxton.

Cheshire Antiques
88-90 Chestergate. (D. Knight). Open 11-5.30. CL: Wed. SIZE: Medium. *STOCK: Clocks, from 1650, £500-£1,500; furniture, 18th-19th C, £100-£5,000; porcelain, pottery, glass, all periods.* LOC: From A537, shop is on right in one-way system 100yds. from traffic lights. TEL: 0625 423268. SER: Valuations; restorations (porcelain, clocks). VAT: Stan/Spec.

Robert Copperfield
5-7 Chester Rd. Est. 1960. Open 10-6 or by appointment. *STOCK: 17th-19th C furniture, Oriental rugs, carpets, metalware, textiles, paintings, works of art, ethnographia.* TEL: 0625 511233. VAT: Stan/Spec.

Gatehouse Antiques
72 Chestergate. (W.H. Livesley). Est. 1973. Open 9-1 and 2-5. CL: Sun. except by appointment and Wed. p.m. *STOCK: Small furniture, silver and plate, glass, brass, copper, pewter, jewellery, 1650-1880.* PARK: At rear. TEL: 0625 426476; home - 0625 612841. VAT: Spec.

Hidden Gem
3 Chester Rd. (Mrs P. Tilley). Usually open 9-5 or by appointment. SIZE: Small. *STOCK: Victorian paintings and general antiques.* TEL: Home - 0625 828348.

Macclesfield continued

Hills Antiques
Indoor Market, Grosvenor Centre. (D. Hill). Est. 1968. Open 9.30-5.30. CL: Mon. STOCK: Small furniture, jewellery, collectors' items, stamps, coins, postcards. LOC: Town Centre. PARK: Easy. TEL: 0625 420777/420467.

D.J. Massey and Son
47 Chestergate. Est. 1900. Open 9-5.30. STOCK: Jewellery, gold and diamonds, all periods. TEL: 0625 616133.

Take-a-Seat
18 Jordangate. (Angela and Amy Roberts). Est. 1979. Open 9.30-5, Sat. 10-1. CL: Wed. SIZE: Small. STOCK: Pine furniture including reproduction. LOC: Off A537, turn into Jordangate towards town hall, shop 100 yards on left. PARK: Multi-storey opposite. TEL: 0625 422150; home - same. SER: Restorations (re-rushing and re-caning, stripping).

MALPAS

Stewart Evans
Church St. Est. 1955. Always open. STOCK: General antiques; furniture to 1835. TEL: 0948 860214/860974. SER: Hand-made furniture from old timber; repairs. VAT: Stan/Spec. Trade Only.

MARPLE BRIDGE, Nr. Stockport

The Mulberry Bush
20 Town St. (David M. Brookes). Est. 1983. Open 9.30-4, Wed. 9.30-1, Thurs. 9.30-6, Fri. 9.30-5, Sun. 1-4. SIZE: Small. STOCK: Furniture, 18th-20th C, £50-£1,000; ceramics, collectables, 19th-20th C, £5-£500. LOC: By the river on New Mills road, just off A626. PARK: Easy. TEL: 061 427 8825; home - same. SER: Valuations; buys at auction.

Town House Antiques
50 Town St. (Paul Buxcey). Open 10-6, Sun. 12-5. STOCK: Decorative items including unusual, pine, period furniture, continental beds. TEL: 061 427 1343.

NANTWICH

Adams Antiques   LAPADA
Weaver House, 57 Welsh Row. (S. and N. Summers). Resident. Est. 1975. Open 10-5 or by appointment. SIZE: Medium. STOCK: Oak, mahogany and walnut, mainly 17th-19th C; longcase clocks, desks, chairs, porcelain, lamps, watercolours and paintings and shipping goods, £10-£20,000. LOC: Chester Road out of Nantwich. PARK: Easy. TEL: 0270 625643; home- same. SER: Valuations. VAT: Stan/Spec.

Tim Armitage
99 Welsh Row. (T.J. Armitage). Est. 1967. Open by appointment. SIZE: Small. STOCK: Tin toys, £25-£750; advertising items, £5-£350; both

Nantwich continued
20th C; general antiques, 18th-19th C. LOC: Main road into town from Chester. PARK: Easy. TEL: 0270 626608; home - same. SER: Valuations; buys at auction (toys and models).

Rex Boyer Antiques   LAPADA
Townwell House, 52 Welsh Row. Resident. Est. 1958. Open 9-5.30. SIZE: Large. STOCK: 17th-19th C oak, mahogany and walnut furniture. LOC: Main Nantwich-Chester road. PARK: Easy. TEL: 0270 625953. VAT: Stan/Spec.

Chapel Antiques
47 Hospital St. (Miss D.J. Atkin). Est. 1983. Open 9.30-5.30, Wed. 9.30-1, or by appointment. CL: Mon. SIZE: Medium. STOCK: Oak, mahogany and pine furniture, Georgian and Victorian, £100-£3,000; longcase clocks, pre-1830, £1,000-£3,000; copper, brass, silver, glass, porcelain, pottery and small items, 19th C, £10-£500. LOC: Enter town via Pillory St., turn right into Hospital St. PARK: Easy. TEL: 0270 629508; home - 0270 811437. SER: Valuations; restorations (furniture, clocks).

Stancie Cutler Antique and Collectors Fairs
Nantwich Civic Hall. Est. 1975. Open 1st Thurs. of each month, 12-9, trade from 10 a.m. Bank Holidays and New Year's Day 10-6, trade from 7.30 a.m. SIZE: 75 stands. STOCK: Wide variety of antiques from large furniture to thimbles, mostly pre-1940. Also 3rd Sat. of each month antique collectors' market (70 stands) 9-4, trade from 8. PARK: Easy. TEL: Home - 0270 624288 (ansaphone).

Farthings Antiques
50 Hospital St. (P. and A. Jones). Est. 1964. Open 9-5.30. CL: Wed. p.m. STOCK: Furniture, glass porcelain, silver. TEL: 0270 625117. VAT: Stan/Spec.

Roderick Gibson   LAPADA
2 Chapel Court, Hospital St. Open 9-5 STOCK: Furniture and smalls. TEL: 0270 625301. VAT: Stan/Spec.

Lions and Unicorns
Kiltearn House, 33 Hospital St. (J. Pearson). Open by appointment. SIZE: Large. STOCK: Commemoratives - pottery, porcelain, textiles, glass tins, metals, books and postcards, etc., £5-£350 LOC: Town centre, near church. PARK: Easy. TEL 0270 628892/625678. SER: Catalogue issued and constantly updated. Parcel post worldwide.

Love Lane Antiques
Love Lane. (M. Simon). Open 10-5. CL: Wed SIZE: Small. STOCK: General antiques, 19th 20th C, £5-£500. LOC: Two minutes walk from town square. PARK: Nearby. TEL: 0270 626239.

Nantwich Art Deco and Decorative Arts
87 Welsh Row. (M. J. Poole and P. M. Savill) Est. 1987. Open 10-5. CL: Tues. and Wed. except

CHESHIRE

Nantwich continued
by appointment. SIZE: Small. *STOCK: Art deco and decorative arts, pottery, china, cabinets, £5-£250.* PARK: Easy. TEL: 0270 624876; home - 811541. FAIRS: Loughborough Art Deco; Birmingham 'Wednesday' Rag Market Fair; Alexandra Palace.

Pillory House
18 Pillory St. (D. Roberts). Est. 1968. Open 9-5. CL: Wed. *STOCK: Hand-carved chimney pieces and oak.* TEL: 0270 623524.

Richardson Antiques
89 Hospital St. (Terry Richardson). Est. 1981. Open daily, Sun. by appointment. SIZE: Medium. *STOCK: Furniture, collectables and china.* PARK: Opposite. TEL: 0270 625963; home - 0270 628348. SER: Valuations; restorations (cleaning oil paintings, cabinet making, French polishing, upholstery, clocks). VAT: Spec.

Wyche House Antiques   LAPADA
50 Welsh Row. (J.A. and E.A. Clewlow). Est. 1976. Open 9.30-4.30, Mon. 9.30-1 and 2-4.30. SIZE: Medium. *STOCK: Furniture, silver, china, cranberry glass, brass, copper, 18th-19th C, £25-£5,000.* TEL: 0270 627179. SER: Valuations. FAIRS: Buxton; NEC. VAT: Stan/Spec.

NESTON
Vine House Antiques
Vine House, Parkgate Rd. (P. and M. Prothero). Est. 1969. Open by appointment. SIZE: Medium. *STOCK: Small furniture, mainly 18th-19th C, £20-£400; silver, from late 18th C, £7.50-£500; glass, 18th-19th C, £1-£80; collectors' items. Not Stocked: Clocks, paintings.* LOC: Coming from Chester A540 to West Kirby, 8 miles from Chester turn left to Neston, 50yds. down Parkgate road from village centre. Queen Anne house on right-hand drive in. PARK: Easy. TEL: 051 336 2423. SER: Valuations; buys at auction.

NEWTOWN, Nr. Stockport
Regent House Antiques
8 Buxton Rd. Est. 1961. Open 9-5, Sat. 2-5. *STOCK: English furniture, clocks, Oriental porcelain, oil paintings, watercolours, general antiques.* LOC: A6 near Disley. PARK: Easy. TEL: 0663 742684.

PLUMLEY
Coppelia Antiques
Holford Lodge, Plumley Moor Rd. (V. and R. Clements). Resident. Est. 1970. Open every day by appointment. SIZE: Medium. *STOCK: Over 200 clocks, mainly longcase and wall, £1,000-£12,000; tables - Georgian mahogany, wine, oak gateleg and side; bureaux, desks, chests of drawers, lowboys, coffers, Victorian suites.* LOC: 4 miles junction 19 M6. PARK: Easy. TEL: 0565

Plumley continued
722197. SER: Valuations; restorations (clocks). FAIRS: Kensington, Buxton, Harrogate,Tatton Park, Castle Howard. VAT: Spec.

POYNTON, Nr. Stockport
Harper Fine Paintings
"Overdale", Woodford Rd. (P.R. Harper). Est. 1967. Open by appointment. SIZE: Large. *STOCK: Watercolours, £100-£35,000; oils including European, £250-£60,000; prints, British, £20-£1,000; all mainly 19th-20th C.* LOC: From A523 centre of Poynton lights, turn into Chester Rd., over railway. After 1/4 mile turn right, 1st drive on left after railway bridge. PARK: Easy. TEL: 0625 879105; home - same. SER: Valuations; restorations; buys at auction (as stock). VAT: Stan/Spec.

Jane's Fine Arts
3 and 3a Park Lane. (Jane A. Beeken and Michael Siodmok). Est. 1989. Open 9.30-6, Sun. 11-4.30. SIZE: Medium. *STOCK: Porcelain including Crown Derby, Royal Worcester, Dresden, Limoges and Hammersley, mainly 19th C, £50-£1,000; small furniture, 19th-20th C, £100-£1,000; Vienna wall clocks, 19th C, £500-£1,000.* PARK: Opposite and rear of premises. TEL: 0625 859178; mobile - 0831 274776. SER: Valuations; restorations (furniture and porcelain); buys at auction (porcelain). FAIRS: Buxton, Deanwater, Woodford and Adlington Hall. VAT: Stan/Spec.

PRESTBURY, Nr. Macclesfield
Prestbury Antiques
The Spindle, Rear of The White House, The Village. (P. Ginsberg). Open 10-5 seven days. *STOCK: Furniture, pictures, silver, glass, ceramics, decorative items and collectables, 18th-20th C.* TEL: 0625 827966. VAT: Stan/Spec.

RAVENSMOOR, Nr. Nantwich
Antiques and Curios
Swanley Lane. (Mrs R.A. Booth). Resident. Est. 1971. SIZE: Small. *STOCK: Furniture including country pine and oak; copper, brass, iron and china, 18th-19th C, £50-£10,000.* PARK: Easy. TEL: 0270 624774; home - same. SER: Restorations (pine stripping). FAIRS: Nantwich.

RINGWAY, Nr. Altrincham
Cottage Antiques
Hasty Lane. (J. and J. M. Gholam). Est. 1967. SIZE: Medium. *STOCK: Furniture, metalware, ceramics, glass, early 18th-mid 19th C. Not Stocked: Jewellery, jade and ivory.* LOC: Off junction 6, M56, off A538, very close to airport. PARK: Easy. TEL: 061 980 7961. SER: Valuations.

SIDDINGTON, Nr. Macclesfield
G. Bagshaw Antiques
The Old Smithy, Capesthorne Hall Estate Yard.

CHESHIRE

Siddington continued
Est. 1971. Open 10-5.30. SIZE: Small. *STOCK: General antiques*. LOC: On A34 Congleton Road, near Monks Heath. PARK: Easy. TEL: 0625 860909. SER: Valuations; restorations (ceramics, clock dials re-painted, paintings and prints); framing.

STOCKPORT
Antique Furniture Warehouse
Units 3/4 Royal Oak Buildings, Cooper St. Open 9.30-5.30. SIZE: Large. *STOCK: English and Continental furniture, paintings, bronzes, clocks, shipping goods, art deco, arts and crafts furniture, pottery, porcelain and curios, decorative items, architectural, radios and televisions, silver and silver plate*. LOC: 2 mins. off M56 towards town centre. PARK: Easy. TEL: 061 429 8590. VAT: Stan.

Bright Antiques
6 Portland Grove, Heaton Moor. Est. 1972. Open 9-1 and 2-5, Wed. 9-1, Sat. 9-5. SIZE: Medium. *STOCK: Furniture, pottery, glass and curios, 18th C, £5-£100*. LOC: Off Heaton Moor road near A6. PARK: Easy. TEL: 061 442 9334; home - 061 429 7074. SER: Restorations.

E. R. Antiques Centre
122 Wellington St, off Wellington Rd. South. (E. Warburton). Est. 1979. Open 12-5.30. SIZE: Medium. 6 dealers. *STOCK: Victorian and cut glass, perfume bottles, blue and white china, pottery, curios, jewellery, pictures, linen, £5-£200*. LOC: Turn into Edwards St. by the Town Hall, at 'T' junction turn left, shop 500yds. on left at bollards. PARK: Easy. TEL: 061 429 6646; home - 061 480 5598.

Flintlock Antiques
28 and 30 Bramhall Lane. (F. Tomlinson and Son). Est. 1968. SIZE: Large. *STOCK: Furniture, clocks, pictures, scientific instruments*. TEL: 061 480 9973. VAT: Stan/Spec.

Halcyon Antiques
435 Buxton Rd, Great Moor. (Mrs Jill A. Coppock). Est. 1980. Open 10-5, Sun. by appointment. SIZE: Medium. *STOCK: Porcelain and glass, 1800-1940, £1-£500; furniture, 1750-1940, £50-£1, 000; brass, copper and linen*. LOC: A6, 2 miles south of town. PARK: Easy. TEL: 061 483 5038; home - 061 439 3524. SER: Valuations.

Highland Antiques   LAPADA
65A Wellington Rd. North. (E. Todd). Est. 1970. SIZE: Medium. *STOCK: Chinese and Japanese pottery, porcelain and furniture, 18th-19th C, to £100,000; silver and plate*. LOC: A6. PARK: Easy. **TEL: 061 476 6660; fax - 061 476 6669.** SER: Valuations; restorations; buys at auction. FAIRS: Manchester. VAT: Stan/Spec.

Hole in the Wall Antiques
370 Buxton Rd., Great Moor; warehouses - 1 Lancashire Hill, and Hadfield House, Lancashire Hill. (M. and A. Ledger). Est. 1960. Open 9.30-7, Sun. by appointment. SIZE: Large. *STOCK: Furniture, 18th-20th C, smalls, £50-£1,500*. LOC: A6. PARK: Easy. TEL: 061 483 6603; warehouses - 061 477 3804/061 476 4013. SER: Valuations; restorations; buys at auction.

Imperial Antiques   LAPADA
295 Buxton Rd, Great Moor. (A. Todd). Est. 1972. Open 10-5.30, Sun. by appointment. SIZE: Large. *STOCK: Silver and plate, 19th-20th C; porcelain especially Japanese and Chinese, 18th-19th C; both £10-£1,000*. LOC: A6 Buxton Rd., 1.5 miles south of town centre. PARK: Easy. **TEL: 061 483 3322; home - 061 428 4152.** SER: Buys at auction (as stock). VAT: Stan/Spec.

Limited Editions
35 King St. East. (C.W. Fogg). Est. 1978. Open 9.45-6, Sat. 9.30-5.30. SIZE: Large. *STOCK: Furniture, 19th C, £100-£1,000; arm chairs and couches for re-upholstery*. LOC: Off Warren St., next to Sainsbury's. PARK: Own at rear. TEL: 061 480 1239. SER: Valuations; restorations (furniture). VAT: Stan/Spec.

Nostalgia Architectural Antiques
61 Shaw Heath. (D. and E. Durrant). Est. 1975. Open 10-6, Sat. 10-5. CL: Mon. SIZE: Large. *STOCK: Fireplaces, £200-£15,000; bathroom fittings and architectural items, £50-£2,000; all 18th-19th C*. PARK: At rear. TEL: 061 477 7706. SER: Valuations. VAT: Stan/Spec.

Page Antiques
424 Buxton Rd, Great Moor. Open Mon.-Sat. SIZE: Large. *STOCK: Victorian and Georgian furniture, brass, copper, silver, plate, stripped pine especially for Australian and German markets*. LOC: A6. TEL: 061 483 9202; home - 061 427 2412. VAT: Stan/Spec.

Zippy Antiques
Units 2 and 3 Royal Oak Building, Cooper St. (M. Golding). Est. 1980. Open 9-6, Sun. by appointment. SIZE: Large and warehouse. *STOCK: English ceramics and glass, late 18th C to 1950, £50-£500; furniture, especially inlaid mahogany, Georgian-1950's; arts and crafts items, £10-£5,000*. PARK: Easy. TEL: 061 477 7953; home - same. SER: Valuations. VAT: Stan.

STOCKTON HEATH, Nr. Warrington
Victoriana Antiques
85a Walton Rd. (Mrs J. Taylor). Est. 1976. Open 1-5 or by appointment. CL: Mon. and Thurs. SIZE: Small. *STOCK: Furnishings, to 1930, £50-£1,000 metalware and fireside furniture, to 1910, £30-£800, antique and decorative lighting, to 1930, £15-£500*. LOC: A56 towards Chester, 400yds. from village centre. PARK: Own. TEL: 0925 263263; home - 0925 261035. SER: Valuations; restorations (furniture, metalware). FAIRS: Cumberland Hotel and Deanwater Hotel, Wilmslow (monthly).

CHESHIRE

STRETTON, Nr. Warrington
Antiques Etc.
Shepcroft House, London Rd. (Mr and Mrs M.E. Clare). Est. 1978. Resident, usually available. SIZE: Medium. *STOCK: Furniture, pine, barometers, clocks, instruments and items of interest, £5-£2,000.* LOC: A49, towards Warrington, through Stretton traffic lights, next turning on left. PARK: Easy. TEL: 0925 730431/ 0836 570663.

TARPORLEY
Brenda Arden Antiques   LAPADA
67 High St. Open 10-4. CL: Wed. *STOCK: 18th-19th C oak and mahogany furniture and metalware.* TEL: 0829 733026.

Marie José Burke
The Pavillion, High Street. ADA. Est. 1959. Open 10-5, appointment advisable. CL: Sat. *STOCK: Period English furniture.* VAT: Spec.

TARVIN, Nr. Chester
Antique Fireplaces and Furniture
The Manor House, Church St. (G. O'Toole). Est. 1979. Open 10-5 including Sun. CL: Wed. SIZE: Medium. *STOCK: Fireplaces and ranges, 18th-19th C, £150-£3,000; furniture, 17th-19th C, £30-£2,500.* LOC: At junction of A556 and A51. PARK: Easy. TEL: 0829 40936; home 0606 46717. SER: Valuations; restorations; installations; buys at auction (furniture). VAT: Stan.

TARVIN SANDS, Nr. Chester
Cheshire Brick and Slate Co
Brook House Farm, Salters Bridge. (Malcolm Youde). Est. 1982. Open 8-5.30, Sat. 8-4.30, Sun. 10-4. SIZE: Large. *STOCK: Reclaimed conservation building materials, 16th-20th C; architectural antiques - garden statuary, stonework, lamp posts, gates, fireplaces, bathroom suites, chimney pots and ironwork, 18th-20th C, £50-£1,000; furniture, pews, leaded lights, pottery, 18th-20th C, £5-£1,000.* LOC: Directly off A54 just outside Tarvin. PARK: Own. TEL: 0829 40883; home - same. SER: Valuations; restorations (fireplaces, timber treatment). VAT: Stan.

TATTENHALL, Nr. Chester
The Great Northern Architectural Antique Company Ltd
New Russia Hall, Chester Rd. Open 9.30-4.30 including Sun. SIZE: Large. *STOCK: Period doors, fire surrounds, stained glass, balustrading, bricks, garden statuary, furniture.* LOC: Off A41. PARK: Easy. TEL: 0829 70796; fax - 0829 70971. VAT: Stan.

TILSTON, Nr. Malpas
Well House Antiques
The Well House. (S. French-Greenslade). Est. 1968. Open by appointment only. SIZE: Small. *STOCK: Collectors' items, china, glass, silver.* LOC: From Whitchurch on A41, take B5395 signposted Malpas. PARK: Easy. TEL: 0829 250332.

WARRINGTON
A. Baker and Sons
10 Cairo St. (A.R. Baker). NAG. Est. 1958. Open 9.30-5, Sat. 9.30-4. SIZE: Small. *STOCK: Silver and jewellery, 18th-20th C, from £100.* LOC: Off M6, junction 9, take A50 into town. Cairo St. off Sankey St. between Co-op and Barclays Bank. PARK: Easy. TEL: 0925 33706; fax - same. SER: Valuations; restorations (as stock). VAT: Stan.

The Rocking Chair Antiques
Unit 3, St. Peter's Way. (N., M. and J. Barratt). Est. 1971. Open 9-5.30. SIZE: Large. *STOCK: Furniture and bric-a-brac.* LOC: Off Orford Lane. PARK: Easy. TEL: 0925 52409. SER: Valuations; shipping, packing. VAT: Stan.

WAVERTON
J. Alan Hulme
Antique Maps & Old Prints, 52 Mount Way. Open Mon.-Sat. by appointment. *STOCK: Maps, 16th-19th C; prints, 18th-19th C.* TEL: 0244 336472.

WHITEGATE, Nr. Northwich
The Antiques Shop
Cinder Hill. (T.H. and B.A. Rogerson). Est. 1979. Open 10-5.30, Mon. 2-5.30. CL: Thurs. SIZE: Small. *STOCK: Pottery, porcelain, general antiques, jewellery, silver and plate, £5-£500; furniture, clocks, £100-£2,000; all 18th-19th C; paintings, watercolours, prints, 19th C, £25-£1,000.* LOC: 1.5 miles from A556 (Northwich by-pass) near village post office. PARK: Easy. TEL: 0606 882215; home - same.

WILMSLOW
Peter Bosson Antiques
10B Swan St. Est. 1965. Open 10-1 and 2-5.30, or by appointment. CL: Mon. and Wed. SIZE: Small. *STOCK: Clocks, 1675-1900, £5-£2,000; barometers, unusual items. Not Stocked: Porcelain, silver.* LOC: On A34. PARK: 50yds. away. TEL: 0625 525250; home - 0625 527857. SER: Restorations (clock repair); buys at auction. VAT: Stan/Spec.

Chapel Antiques
59 Chapel Lane. (K. Riley). Est. 1976. Open 9.30-5.30, Wed. 9.30-12.30. SIZE: Medium. *STOCK: Furniture, 17th-20th C, £50-£3,500; porcelain, 19th-20th C, £10-£200; pictures, 19th C, £50-£1,000.* LOC: From Manchester - past town centre on Knutsford road, Chapel Lane second right. PARK: Easy. TEL: 0625 548061; home - 0422 822485. SER: Valuations; buys at auction (furniture). VAT: Spec.

Cleveland

Cleveland

BILLINGHAM
Margaret Bedi Antiques LAPADA
5 Station Rd. Est. 1976. Open by appointment. STOCK: Mainly English period furniture, 1720-1920; oils and watercolours, 19th-20th C. LOC: 300yds. off A19, by village green. PARK: Easy. TEL: 0642 782346; mobile - 0860 577637. VAT: Stan/Spec.

EAGLESCLIFFE, Nr. Stockton-on-Tees
T.B. and R. Jordan (Fine Paintings)
Aslak, Aislaby. Est. 1974. Open by appointment. STOCK: Oil paintings and watercolours, 19th-20th C, £200-£3,000. LOC: Village centre. PARK: Easy. TEL: 0642 782599. SER: Framing; restoration. VAT: Spec.

GUISBOROUGH
Atrium Antiques
12 Chaloner St. (W.L. and M.G. Richardson). Est. 1967. Open 10-1 and 2-5. CL: Sun., Mon. and Wed., except by appointment. STOCK: Furniture, silver, pottery, jewellery, clocks, general items. PARK: Easy. TEL: 0287 632777 anytime.

HARTLEPOOL
Antique Fireplace Centre
15 Mainsforth Terrace. (D.J. Crowther). Open 9-5. CL: Wed. STOCK: Victorian and Edwardian fireplaces, architectural antiques. TEL: 0429 279007.

MARTON, Nr. Middlesbrough
E. and N.R. Charlton Fine Art and Porcelain
69 Cambridge Ave. Resident. Open by appointment. STOCK: Fine porcelain, 18th-19th C; Victorian watercolours and paintings; small Regency furniture. TEL: 0642 319642.

MIDDLESBROUGH
Bradley's Antiques and Jewellery
327 Linthorpe. (P. Bradley). Open 10-5. STOCK: Victorian and shipping items. TEL: 0642 850518.

SALTBURN
Endeavour Antiques
The Hollies, Victoria Terrace. (J. MacAuliffe). Est. 1969. Open by appointment only. SIZE: Small. STOCK: General and interesting antiques, especially 18th-19th C pottery and porcelain; Victorian and Edwardian jewellery. TEL: 0287 622385. VAT: Stan/Spec.

YARM
Ruby Snowden Antiques
20 High St. (R.H. Snowden). Est. 1977. Open 9-5.30, Wed. 9-5, Sun. by appointment. SIZE:

Yarm continued
Medium. STOCK: Furniture, 1700-1930s, £50-£2,000; porcelain and Staffordshire, £5-£200; jewellery, silver, glass, copper and brass. LOC: Opposite library. PARK: Easy. TEL: 0642 785363; home - 0642 597718. SER: Valuations. VAT: Stan/Spec.

An Antique Collectors' Club Title

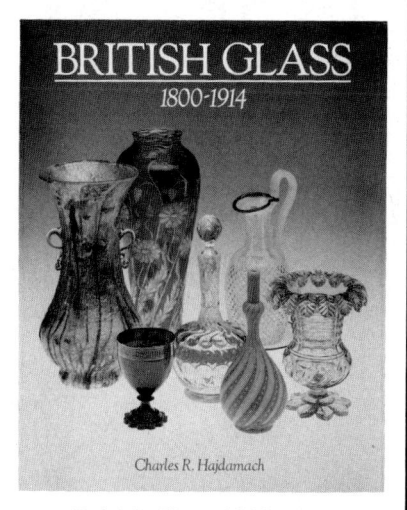

BRITISH GLASS
1800-1914

Charles R. Hajdamach

British Glass 1800-1914
by Charles R. Hajdamach
Details development of glassmaking and decorating techniques and their interaction with changes in fashion. Wide use of contemporary source material facilitates dating of pieces and marks a new high level of scholarship in this important collecting subject.
ISBN 1 85149 141 4
466pp, 430 illus, 50 col, £45.00

Available from:
Antique Collectors' Club
5 Church Street, Woodbridge
Suffolk IP12 1DS
Tel: (0394) 385501 Fax: (0394) 384434

or

Market Street Industrial Park
Wappingers' Falls
New York 12590, USA
Tel: 914 297 0003 Fax: 914 297 0068

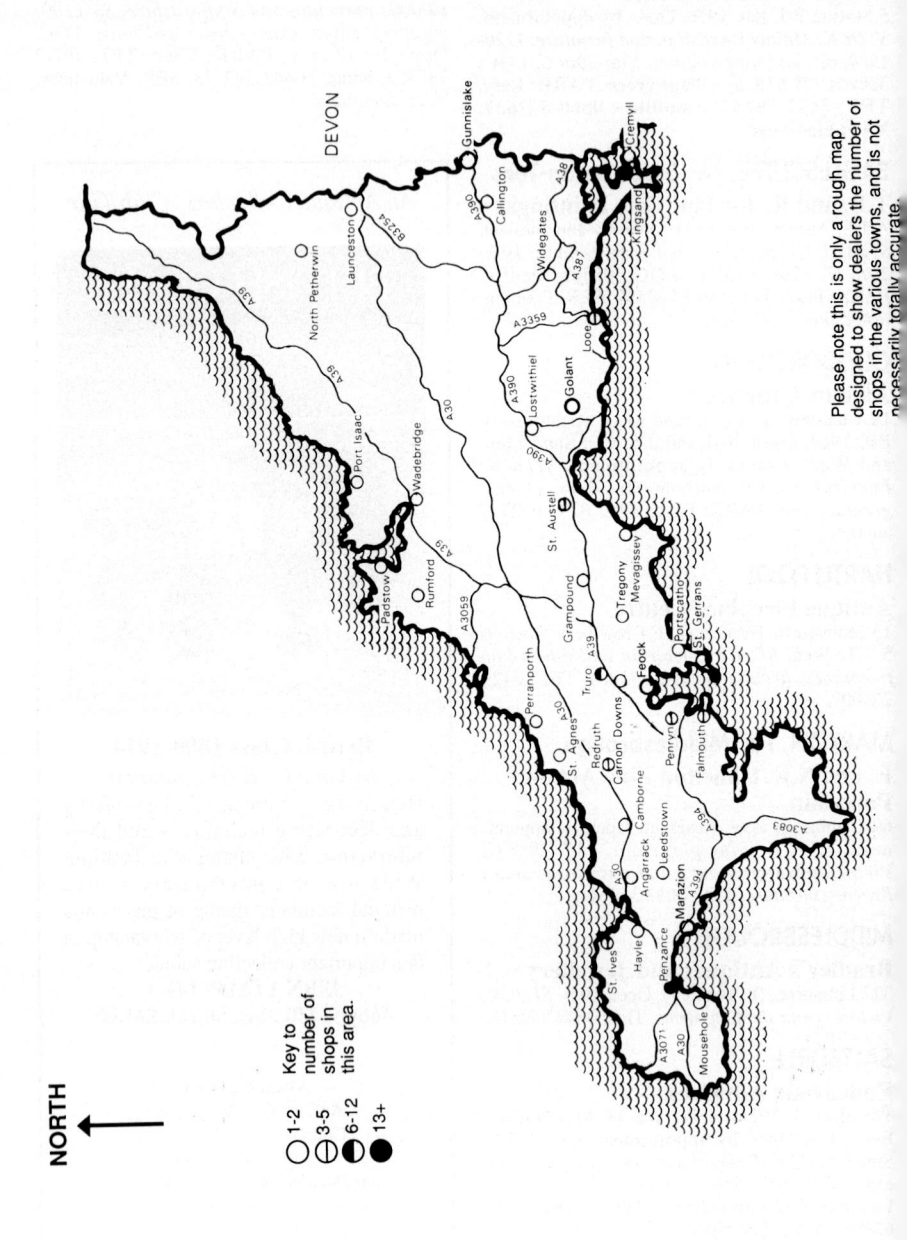

Cornwall

200

Cornwall

ANGARRACK, Nr. Hayle
Paul Jennings Antiques
Millbrook House. Est. 1974. Open by appointment. SIZE: Small. STOCK: *Clocks, furniture, £100-£3,000*. LOC: 1/2 mile from A30. TEL: 0736 754065. VAT: Stan/Spec. *Trade Only.*

BODMIN
Clocks, Art & Antiques
9 St. Nicholas St. (Michael Aitken). Resident. Est. 1972. Open 12-5. CL: Tues. SIZE: Small. STOCK: *Clocks, 18th-19th C, £50-£5,000; art, 19th-20th C, £50-£1,000; general antiques, 18th-20th C, £50-£5,000*. LOC: Lostwithiel road, near P.O. PARK: Nearby. TEL: 0208 74408; home - same. SER: Valuations; restorations (furniture and clocks); buys at auction (furniture and clocks).

BOSCASTLE
Old Pine and Country furniture
The Old Mill. (Frances Wilson). Open 10-5 including Sun. STOCK: *Victorian country pine and Edwardian country furniture*. TEL: 0840 250230.

CAMBORNE
Grate Expectations
West Charles St. (M. Swift). Open 9-5 or by appointment. STOCK: *Fireplaces and surrounds*. LOC: 4th turning on left on Helston road out of Camborne. PARK: Own. TEL: 0209 719898; home - 0736 850505.

Victoria Gallery
28 Cross St. (J.P. Maker). Open 10-5.30, Sat. 10-1. CL: Thurs. STOCK: *Books, pictures, general antiques, furniture, silver and jewellery*. TEL: 0209 719268.

CREMYLL
Cremyll Antiques
The Cottage, Cremyll Beach, Torpoint. STOCK: *Nautical items, small items, jewellery*. TEL: 0752 822934. SER: Repairs (barometers, barographs, watches, clocks, jewellery).

FALMOUTH
E. Cunningham Antiques
5 Webber St. Open 10.30-5.30. STOCK: *General antiques*. TEL: 0326 313207.

John Maggs
54 Church St. (C.C. Nunn). Est. 1900. Open 10-1 and 2-5. SIZE: Medium. STOCK: *Antiquarian prints and maps, to 1850*. Not Stocked: Reproductions. LOC: Main street. PARK: At rear of shop. TEL: 0326 313153. SER: Restorations (prints, bindings); framing.

Rosina's
4 High St. (Mrs R. Gealer). Open 11-4.30.

Falmouth continued
STOCK: *Old dolls, bears and toys, linen and lace, clothes; modern miniatures*. TEL: 0326 311406; home - 0326 317739. SER: Restorations.

Waterfront Antiques Market
1st Floor, 4 Quay St. Open 9-5. SIZE: 12 dealers. STOCK: *Furniture, pottery, porcelain, glass, silver, metalware, kitchenalia, pictures, books, clocks, jewellery, decorative and collectors' items*. TEL: 0326 311491.

FEOCK, Nr. Truro
Strickland and Dorling
Come-to-Good. (P. Strickland and T. Dorling). Usually open. STOCK: *Small furniture, pottery, porcelain, silver, pictures, maps of Cornwall, bijouterie and collectors' items*. TEL: 0872 862394.

GOLANT, Nr. Fowey
Myles Varcoe
Penquite Barn. Est. 1971. Open by appointment only. STOCK: *Pictures, mainly 19th C marine watercolours and oils, £50-£5,000*. LOC: Telephone for instructions. TEL: 0726 833390. VAT: Spec.

GRAMPOUND, Nr. Truro
Pine and Period Furniture
Fore St. (S. Payne). Open 10-5. CL: Sat. STOCK: *Pine and period furniture*. TEL: 0726 883117.

Radnor House
Fore St. (P. Nosworthy). Est. 1972. Open 10-5. SIZE: Medium. STOCK: *Furniture and accessories, pre-1900*. Not Stocked: Jewellery, coins and weapons. LOC: A390. PARK: Easy. TEL: 0726 882921; home - same. SER: Valuations; buys at auction. VAT: Stan/Spec.

HAYLE
Copperhouse Gallery - W. Dyer & Sons
14 Fore St. (A.P. Dyer). Est. 1900. Open 9-1 and 2-5.30, Wed. 9-1. SIZE: Medium. STOCK: *Watercolours, some oils, including Newlyn and St. Ives Schools, 19th to early 20th C, £25-£1,000*. LOC: Main road. PARK: Easy. TEL: 0736 752787; home - 0736 753362. SER: Restorations (watercolours and oils).

LAUNCESTON
Tamar Gallery (Antiques and Fine Art)
5 Church St. (N. and I. Preston). Open 10-1 and 2.30-5, Mon. by appointment. CL: Thurs p.m. SIZE: Medium. STOCK: *Watercolours, 18th-20th C, £30-£2,000; small furniture, 17th-19th C, £100-£1,200; English pottery and porcelain especially 18th-19th C blue and white, £20-£300; Staffordshire, Victorian glass, copper and brass,*

Later King's Head Tavern bottle of Richard Walker dated 1699. In this example the seal has been completely redesigned and, in addition to a new effigy of the king, incorporates the extra letter 'E' for Walker's wife Elizabeth. From ***Understanding Antique Wine Bottles*** by Roger Dumbrell, reprinted in 1992 by the **Antique Collectors' Club**, £14.95.

Launceston continued

objets d'art, decorative items and bygones. LOC: Near St. Mary Magdalene Church. PARK: Near Church. TEL: 0566 774233; home - 0566 82444. SER: Restorations and cleaning (watercolours).

LEEDSTOWN, Nr. Hayle

A.W. Glasby and Son Antiques

(D.E. Glasby). Est. 1936. Open 10.15-12.45 and 2.15-5. CL: Sat. and Mon. SIZE: Large. *STOCK: Furniture, porcelain and clocks, £10-£5,000.* Not Stocked: Coins, medals, scientific instruments. LOC: On main road half-way between Hayle and Helston. PARK: Easy. TEL: 0736 850303. VAT: Stan/Spec.

LOOE

Dowling and Bray

Fore St. Est. 1920. *STOCK: General antiques, furniture, pictures.* TEL: 0503 262797. VAT: Stan.

Tony Martin

Fore St. Est. 1965. Open 9.30-1 and 2-5 appointment advisable. CL: Thurs. p.m. SIZE: Medium. *STOCK: Porcelain, 18th C; silver, 18th-19th C, both £20-£200; glass, furniture, oils and watercolours.* LOC: Main street. TEL: 0503 262734; home - 0503 262228. VAT: Stan/Spec.

Looe continued

West Quay Curios

6 The Quay, West Looe. (C.G. Jay and Miss G. Jones). Est. 1990. Open 10-7, prior telephone call advisable in winter. SIZE: Small. *STOCK: General small antiques and collectors' items, mainly 19th-20th C, 50p to £500.* PARK: Nearby. TEL: 0503 264411. SER: Valuations.

LOSTWITHIEL

John Bragg Antiques

35 Fore St. Open 10-5. *STOCK: Furniture, mainly period mahogany and Victorian.* LOC: 100yds. off A390. TEL: 0208 872827.

Old Palace Antiques

Old Palace, Quay St. (D. Bryant). Open 10-1 and 2-5. CL: Wed. p.m. *STOCK: Pine, general antiques and collectors' items.* TEL: 0208 872909.

MARAZION

Antiques

The Shambles. (Andrew S. Wood). Est. 1988. Open 10-5.30, Sun by appointment. SIZE: Small. *STOCK: General antiques and collectors' items, especially 19th to early 20th C pottery and porcelain including Staffordshire figures; Victorian and early 20th C decorative and pressed glass; art deco ceramics especially*

Marazion continued
Shelley; Goss and crested china, commemorative ware, postcards and bottles. Not Stocked: Weapons and large furniture. LOC: Main street. PARK: Easy. TEL: 0736 711381; home - same.

MEVAGISSEY
J. Barron and Sons
Fore St. TEL: 0726 842172. VAT: Stan.

MOUSEHOLE
Vanity Fayre
Commercial Rd. (J.L. Gillingham MPS, DBA). Est. 1963. Open 10-1 and 2-5. CL: Thurs. SIZE: Medium. STOCK: Small furniture and clocks, 1800-1900, £10-£500; copper, brass, metals, silver, porcelain, 1700-1900, £5-£500; items of interest, bric-a-brac, from 1800, £1-£250; stamps and coins. LOC: Main Penzance road through Newlyn and Mousehole. PARK: Nearby. SER: Buys at auction.

NORTH PETHERWIN, Nr. Launceston
Pine and Country Antiques
Petherwingate. (J. Cooper). Open 10-1 and 2-6. SIZE: Small. STOCK: Furniture, 19th C including restored and stripped pine, £50-£500; general antiques and bygones. PARK: Easy. TEL: 056 685 381. SER: Restorations; stripping.

PADSTOW
Mayflower Antiques
15 Duke St. (Miss C. Hoskin). Est. 1963. Open 10.30-1 and 2.30-5. CL: Afternoons Nov.-Mar. SIZE: Small. STOCK: Jewellery, £5-£150; copper and brass, £2-£50, all 19th to early 20th C; commemorative ware, £5-£90; Victorian and later pottery and china, £5-£50. Not Stocked: Weapons, furniture, clocks. LOC: Centre of Padstow. PARK: On Quay. TEL: Home - 0841 532308.

PENRYN
Broad Street Gallery
9 Broad St. (V. and H. Harris). Est. 1984. Open 10-5, evenings by appointment. CL: Mon. SIZE: Small. STOCK: Watercolours, £50-£1,500; oil paintings, £80-£2,500; some prints, £60-£225; all 19th-20th C. LOC: Main road, Falmouth end of town. PARK: Nearby. TEL: 0326 377216; home - same. SER: Buys at auction (watercolours and oil paintings).

Original Choice
15 Church Rd. (J.M. Gavin). Open 8.30-6. STOCK: General antiques. TEL: 0326 375092.

Leon Robertson Antiques
7 The Praze. Est. 1972. STOCK: Furniture, paintings and general antiques. TEL: 0326 372767.

PENZANCE
Ken Ashbrook Antiques
Leskinnick Place. Est. 1973. Open 10-1 and 2-5, Mon. and Wed. 10-1, Sat. 10.30-1, Tues. and other times by appointment. SIZE: Large. STOCK: Furniture, 18th-20th C, £100-£5,000. LOC: 1 min. from railway station. PARK: Nearby. TEL: 0736 65477; home - same. SER: Valuations; restorations (cabinet work); buys at auction (furniture). VAT: Stan/Spec.

Catherine and Mary Antiques
1/2 Old Brewery Yard, Bread St. (C. Farnes and M. Palmer). Open 10-5, Wed. 10-1. STOCK: Furniture, textiles, linen, lace, smalls and jewellery. TEL: 0736 51053.

Chapel Antiques
10 Chapel St. Open 10-5. CL: Wed p.m. STOCK: Furniture, clocks and smalls. TEL: 0736 63124.

Daphne's Antiques
17 Chapel St. Est. 1976. Open 9-5. SIZE: Medium. STOCK: Early country furniture, Georgian glass, decorative objects, 18th-19th C jewellery. TEL: 0736 61719.

Gallery Tonkin and Gallery Lyonesse
Old Brewery Yard, Bread St. (W.I.J. Fisher). Open 10-5, Wed. 10-1. STOCK: Maps, prints, paintings. TEL: 0736 69855. SER: Restorations.

Brian Humphrys Antiques
1 St. Clare St. Est. 1964. SIZE: Medium. STOCK: Furniture, clocks, silver, jewellery, 18th-19th C, £25-£4,000. PARK: Easy opposite. TEL: 0736 65154. SER: Valuations; buys at auction. VAT: Stan/Spec.

Barbara and David Kirk
Kitts Corner, 51 Chapel St. Est. 1984. Open 10-1 and 2-4.30. CL: Wed. SIZE: Medium. STOCK: Collectors and decorative ceramics and glass, costume jewellery, kitchenalia and prints, 1880-1960, £5-£150. PARK: Easy. TEL: 0736 64507.

Little Jem's
Antron House, 55 Chapel St. (J. Lagden). Open 9.30-5. STOCK: Jewellery, gem stones, costumes, objets d'art, paintings, clocks and watches. TEL: 0736 51400.

New Generation Antiques Market
61/62 Chapel St. Open 10-5. SIZE: 10 dealers. STOCK: Furniture, pottery, porcelain, glass, silver, metalware, kitchenalia, pictures, books, clocks, jewellery, decorative and collectors' items. TEL: 0736 63267.

New Street Books
4 New St. (B.J. Maker). Open 10-5. STOCK: Books and pictures. TEL: 0736 62758.

The Old Posthouse
(incorporating The Bookcellar), 9 Chapel St. (Diana Richards). Open 10-5. STOCK: China,

CORNWALL

Penzance continued

glass, small furniture, curios, decorative items, pictures, jewellery, small silver, objets d'art, antiquarian and secondhand books, cigarette and postcards. TEL: 0736 60320.

Pinewood Studio
46 Market Jew St. (R. Aby). Open 9.30-5.30. STOCK: Pine furniture. Not Stocked: Reproductions. TEL: 0736 68793.

Tony Sanders Penzance Gallery and Antiques
14 Chapel St. Est. 1972. Open 9-5.30 and evenings in summer 7.30-10. SIZE: Medium. STOCK: Oils and watercolours including Newlyn and St. Ives schools, 19th-20th C, £50-£8,000; glass, silver, china and small furniture. TEL: 0736 66620/68461. VAT: Stan.

Vive Antiques
Captain Cutters House, 52 Chapel St. (J. Buchanan). Open 10-5. SIZE: Small. STOCK: Furniture and interesting smalls, 17th-20th C, £10-£1,500. LOC: Town centre. PARK: Easy. TEL: 0736 330100; home - same. SER: Valuations; buys at auction.

PERRANPORTH

St. George's Antiques
33 St. George's Hill. (J. Holmes). Est. 1983. Open Fri. and Sat. 10-1 and 2-5 or by appointment. SIZE: Small. STOCK: 18th-19th C porcelain and pottery, Victorian and Edwardian furniture, glass and paintings, £10-£1,500. LOC: B3285, main coast road. PARK: Nearby. TEL: 0872 572947; home - 0872 573469. FAIRS: NEC (Aug), Westonbirt, Sandown Park, Newark.

PORTSCATHO, Nr. St. Mawes

Curiosity Antiques
(E. and S. Gale). Est. 1965. Open 10-5; by appointment Oct.- Mar. STOCK: General antiques, bric-a-brac. LOC: In main square. PARK: Easy. TEL: 0872 580411.

REDRUTH

Penandrea Gallery
12 Higher Fore St. (W. Dyer and Son). FARG. Est. 1900. Open 9-1 and 2-5. CL: Mon. and Thurs. STOCK: Watercolours, 19th-20th C, £5-£1,000; some oils, prints and Victorian items, £1-£100. LOC: Upper end of main street. PARK: Easy. TEL: 0209 213134. SER: Valuations; restorations; framing (oils and watercolours).

West End Antiques Market
1st Floor, 3 West End. Open 10-5. STOCK: Furniture, brass and copper, silver, glass, porcelain, pictures, prints, linen, specialist and collectors' items. TEL: 0209 217001.

Redruth continued

Richard Winkworth Antiques
Unit 6, Station Rd. Open 9-5.30. SIZE: Large. STOCK: Pine, oak, satin walnut and mahogany furniture; shipping goods, brass, copper, china, glass and smalls. TEL: 0209 216631.

RUMFORD, Nr. Wadebridge

Henley House Antiques
(P. Neale). STOCK: Juvenilia, small antiques, bric-a-brac. TEL: 0841 540322.

ST. AGNES

Ages Ago Antiques
1B Churchtown. (D. and M. Gregson). Open 10-1. STOCK: Furniture and ceramics, from 1800. LOC: Opposite Post Office. TEL: 087 255 3820.

ST. AUSTELL

Ancient and Modern
32-34 Polkyth Rd. (P.J. Watts). Est. 1965. Open 8.30-5. STOCK: General antiques, paintings, clocks, jewellery, bric-a-brac. TEL: 0726 73983. VAT: Stan/Spec.

Mrs. Margaret Chesterton
33 Pentewan Rd. Est. 1965. Open 10-5.30, appointment advisable. CL: Sat. p.m. STOCK: Victoriana, Edwardiana, 1800-1915; some furniture, porcelain, glass, £1-£500; brass, copper, pewter, jewellery, clocks, automata, musical boxes, watercolours. LOC: Coming from Plymouth, travel direct to St. Austell. Keep on main by-pass until roundabout for Mevagissey and Pentewan Rd. House is 100yds. on left down this road. PARK: Easy. TEL: 0726 72926.

The Furniture Store/St. Austell Antiques Centre
37/39 Truro Rd. (R. Nosworthy). Est. 1972. Open 10-4. SIZE: Large - several dealers. STOCK: Wide range of period to 20th C furniture, decorators' items, china, glass, books and metalware. LOC: Town centre, just off A390. PARK: Easy and at rear of warehouse. TEL: 0726 63178; home - 0288 81548. SER: Valuations; restorations (furniture); buys at auction. VAT: Stan/Spec.

ST. GERRANS, Nr. Portscatho

Turnpike Cottage Antiques and Tearooms
The Square. (T. and S. Green). Est. 1988. Open 11-1 and 3-6 including Sun; winter - 3-5.30. SIZE: Medium. STOCK: General antiques, furniture, porcelain, bric-a-brac, £5-£4,000. LOC: Near church. PARK: Easy, at rear. TEL: 0872 580 853; home - same. SER: Valuations; restorations (furniture, watercolours).

CORNWALL

ST. IVES
Mike Read Antique Sciences
"Ayia Napa", Wheal Whidden, Carbis Bay. Est. 1974. Open by appointment. SIZE: Small. *STOCK: Scientific instruments - navigational, surveying, mining, barometers, telescopes and microscopes, medical, 18th-19th C, £10-£5,000.* LOC: Turn right at St. Ives end of Carbis Bay, 100yds. on right. PARK: Easy. TEL: 0736 798219; home - same. SER: Valuations; restorations. VAT: Spec.

TREGONY, Nr. Truro
Clock Tower Antiques
57 Fore St. (The Warne Family). Open 10-6, (extended in summer), evenings and Sun. by appointment. SIZE: Medium. *STOCK: Ceramics, including Doulton stoneware, Mason's Ironstone, 19th C blue and white transferware, £10-£500; paintings and prints, 19th to early 20th C, £50-£1,000; furniture, 18th to early 20th C, £75-£3,000; brass, copper and treen, £10-£300.* Not Stocked: Silver and jewellery. LOC: Village centre, B3287. PARK: Easy. TEL: 087 253 225; home - same.

TRURO
Alan Bennett
24 New Bridge St. Est. 1954. Open 9-5.30. SIZE: Large. *STOCK: Furniture, £50-£5,000; jewellery and porcelain, to 1900, £5-£1,000; paintings and prints, £20-£2,000.* LOC: Eastern side of cathedral. PARK: 100yds. from shop. TEL: 0872 73296. VAT: Stan/Spec.

Blackwater Pine Antiques
Blackwater. (J.S. Terrett). Open 9-6. *STOCK: Pine.* TEL: 0872 560919. SER: Restorations; stripping.

Pydar Antiques and Gallery
Peoples Palace, Pydar St. (D. Severn and J. Poole). Est. 1968. Open 10.30-5 and by appointment. SIZE: Medium. *STOCK: Furniture - English 18th and 19th C, £50-£2,500; Victorian and Edwardian, £50-£2,000; pine, £10-£1,500; silver, plate, porcelain, glass, prints and watercolours, £5-£500.* PARK: Easy. TEL: Home - 0872 510485 or 0637 872034. FAIRS: West Country.

Richard Winkworth Antiques
Calenick St. Open 10-5. SIZE: Large. *STOCK: Georgian and Victorian furniture, brass, copper, china, glass.* TEL: 0872 40901.

WADEBRIDGE
St. Breock Gallery
St. Breock Churchtown. (R.G.G. Haslam-Hopwood). Open 10-5. *STOCK: Watercolours, 19th-20th C; furniture, general antiques and objets d'art.* LOC: Near Royal Cornwall Showground. PARK: Own. TEL: 0208 812543. SER: Restorations; buys at auction.

ALAN BENNETT

18th and 19th century Furniture, Porcelain Silver, Jewellery and Paintings

**NEW BRIDGE HOUSE
NEW BRIDGE STREET
TRURO
CORNWALL
Truro 73296**

Wadebridge continued
Victoria Antiques
21 Molesworth St. (M. and S. Daly). Open Mon.-Sat. SIZE: Large. *STOCK: Furniture, 17th-19th C, £25-£10,000.* LOC: On A39 between Bude and Newquay. PARK: Nearby. TEL: 0208 814160. SER: Valuations; restorations. VAT: Stan/Spec.

WIDEGATES, Nr. Looe
Pink Cottage Antiques
(I. and B. Barrett). Est. 1981. Open 9.30-5, Sun 2-5, longer hours in summer. SIZE: Medium. *STOCK: Furniture, £50-£2,500; brass and copper, £5-£250; china and glass, £2-£300; oil lamps and clocks; all mainly Victorian and Edwardian, some Georgian.* Not Stocked: Clothing, militaria, jewellery, silver. LOC: A387 from Plymouth, 4 miles before Looe. PARK: At rear. TEL: 050 34 258; home - same. SER: Restorations (furniture).

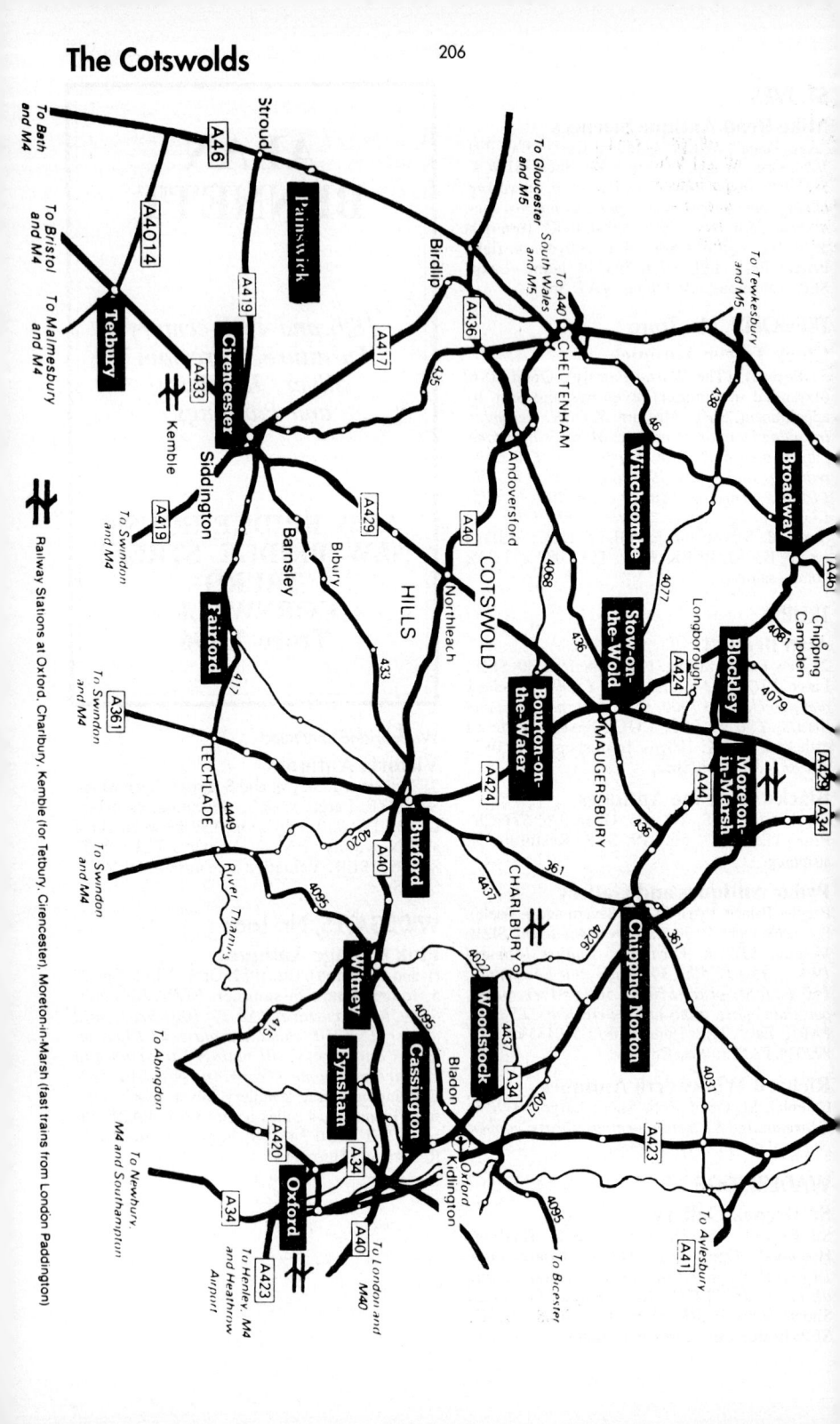

The Cotswolds

THE COTSWOLD ANTIQUE DEALERS' ASSOCIATION

Buy Fine Antiques and Works of Art at provincial prices in England's lovely and historic countryside

The Cotswolds, one of the finest areas of unspoilt countryside in the land, have been called "the essence and the heart of England". The region has a distinctive character created by the use of honey-coloured stone in its buildings and dry stone walls. Within the locality the towns and villages are admirably compact and close to each other and the area is well supplied with good hotels and reasonably priced inns. The Cotswolds are within easy reach of London ($1^1/_2$ hours by road or rail) and several major airports.

Cotswold sheep — which inspired the logo of the Cotswold Antique Dealers' Association — a quatrefoil device with a sheep in its centre — have played an important part in the region's history with much of its wealth created by the woollen industry. As for antiques, shops and warehouses of the CADA offer a selection of period furniture, pictures, porcelain, metalwork, and collectables unrivalled outside London.

With the use of the CADA directory on the following pages, which lists the names of its members, their specialities and opening times, visitors from all over the world can plan their buying visit to the Cotswolds. CADA members will assist all visiting collectors and dealers in locating antiques and works of art. They will give you advice on where to stay in the area, assistance with packing, shipping and insurance and the exchange of foreign currencies. They can advise private customers on what can realistically be bought on their available budgets, and if the first dealer does not have the piece which you are selecting he will know of several other members who will. The CADA welcomes home and overseas buyers in the certain knowledge that there are at least fifty dealers with a good and varied stock, a reputation for fair trading and an annual turnover in excess of £15,000,000.

BARNSLEY

Denzil Verey
Barnsley House. CADA. Resident. Est. 1980. Open 9.30-5.30, Sat. 10.30-5.30, other times by appointment. SIZE: Large. *STOCK: Country furniture, including pine, 18th-19th C; treen, country and kitchen bygones, unusual and decorative items.* LOC: 4 miles from Cirencester on A433 to Burford, 1st large house in village, set back off road on the right. PARK: Easy. TEL: 0285 740402. VAT: Stan/Spec.

BROADWAY

Fenwick and Fisher Antiques
88-90 High St. CADA. Est. 1980. Open 10-6, or by appointment. SIZE: Large. *STOCK: Furniture, oak, mahogany and walnut, 17th to early 19th C; samplers, boxes, treen, Tunbridgeware, delft, decorative items and corkscrews.* TEL: 0386 853227; after hours - 0386 858502.

H.W. Keil Ltd BADA
Tudor House, Broad Close, Eadburgha Hall. (V.M. Keil). CADA. Est. 1925. Open 9-5.30. CL: Thurs. p.m. SIZE: Large. *STOCK: Walnut, oak and mahogany furniture and works of art, 17th-18th C.* TEL: 0386 852408. VAT: Spec.

John Noott Fine Paintings
BADA LAPADA
14 Cotswold Court, The Green. CADA. Est. 1972. Open 9-1 and 2-5.30 or by appointment. SIZE: Large. *STOCK: Paintings and watercolours, 19th-20th C, £50-£50,000.* LOC: Centre of village. PARK: Own. TEL: 0386 852787/ 858969; fax - 0386 858348. SER: Valuations; restorations; framing. VAT: Stan/Spec.

Picton House Antiques
High St. (G.D. Patterson Ltd). CADA. Resident. Est. 1989. Open 9.30-5.30 or by appointment. SIZE: Large. *STOCK: Fine English furniture, works of art.* PARK: Easy. TEL: 0386 853807; home - same. SER: Restorations (furniture); buys at auction. VAT: Spec.

BURFORD

Jonathan Fyson Antiques
50 High St. (J.R. Fyson). CADA. Est. 1972. Open 9.30-1 and 2-5.30. SIZE: Medium. *STOCK: English and continental furniture, decorative brass and steel including lighting and fireplace accessories; papier mâché, tôle, treen, porcelain, glass, jewellery.* LOC: A361. Coming from London on A40 between Oxford and Cheltenham at junction with A361. PARK: Easy. TEL: 0993 823204; home - 036786 223. SER: Valuations. VAT: Spec.

Burford continued

Gateway Antiques
Cotswold Gateway Antiques Centre, Cheltenham Rd., Burford Roundabout. (M.C. Ford and P. Brown). CADA. Est. 1986. Open 10-5.30 and Sun. pm. *STOCK: English and continental furniture, 18th-19th C; decorative accessories.* LOC: On roundabout (A40) Oxford/Cheltenham road. PARK: Easy. TEL: 0993 823678. SER: Valuations. VAT: Stan/Spec.

David Pickup BADA
115 High St. CADA. Est. 1977. Open 9.30-1 and 2-5.30, Sat. 10-1 and 2-4. SIZE: Medium. *STOCK: Fine furniture, from £1,000+; works of art, £500-£10,000; decorative objects, from £100+; all late 17th-19th C.* PARK: Easy. TEL: 0993 822555. FAIRS: New York International. VAT: Spec.

Richard Purdon BADA
158 High St. CADA. Open 9.30-5.30. SIZE: Medium. *STOCK: Antique Eastern carpets, village and tribal rugs and related items.* TEL: 0993 823777; fax - 0993 823719. SER: Valuations; restorations. VAT: Stan/Spec.

Manfred Schotten Antiques
109 High St. (P. Matthey and M. Schotten). CADA. Est. 1957. Open 9.30-5.30 or by appointment. *STOCK: 18th-19th C furniture, antique golf and other sporting collectables.* TEL: 0993 822302; fax - 0993 822055. SER: Restorations.

Robin Shield Antiques BADA LAPADA
134 High St. CADA. Est. 1974. Open 9.30-5.30 or by appointment. SIZE: Medium. *STOCK: Furniture and paintings, £200-£20,000; works of art, £100-£5,000; all 17th-19th C.* LOC: Town centre. PARK: Easy. TEL: 0993 822462; home - 0793 750205. SER: Valuations; buys at auction. VAT: Stan/Spec.

Swan Gallery
High St. (J. and D. Pratt). CADA. Est. 1966. Open 9.30-5.30. SIZE: Large. *STOCK: Country furniture in oak, yew, walnut and fruitwood, 17th-19th C, £300-£9,000; oil paintings, some sculpture, 19th-20th C, £100-£8,000; Staffordshire figures and small decorative items, 18th-20th C, £50-£800.* PARK: Easy. TEL: 0993 822244. SER: Valuations; restorations (furniture). VAT: Mainly Spec.

CHIPPING NORTON

Key Antiques BADA
11 Horse Fair. (D. and M. Robinson). CADA. Resident. Open 9.30-6 or by appointment. SIZE: Medium. *STOCK: Period oak and country furniture, domestic metalware including lighting and downhearth equipment, early*

Chipping Norton continued
carvings, firemarks, keys. LOC: On main road. PARK: Easy. TEL: **0608 643777**. VAT: Spec.

Peter Stroud Antiques
35 New St. CADA. Open 9-5.30. SIZE: Medium. *STOCK: 17th-19th C period furniture, oak, walnut, fruitwood and mahogany including tables, chairs, dressers and bureaux.* LOC: 150yds. from Town Hall down hill on the right. PARK: Own. TEL: 0608 642571. SER: Valuations. VAT: Stan/Spec.

CIRENCESTER

Hares
17-19 Gosditch St. (Allan Hare). CADA. Est. 1972. Open 9.30-5.30, Sun. by appointment. SIZE: Large. *STOCK: Furniture, especially dining tables and long sets of chairs, 18th to early 19th C, £100-£20,000; upholstery and decorative objects.* LOC: Near Market Square. PARK: Easy. TEL: 0285 640077; home - same. SER: Valuations; restorations; traditional upholstery; buys at auction. VAT: Spec.

William H. Stokes BADA
The Cloisters, 6/8 Dollar St. (W.H. Stokes and P.W. Bontoft). CADA. Est. 1968. Open 9.30-5.30, Sat. 9.30-4.30. *STOCK: Early oak furniture, £1,000-£30,000; brassware, £150-£5,000; all 16th-17th C.* TEL: 0285 653907; fax - same. FAIRS: BADA; Grosvenor House. VAT: Spec.

Rankine Taylor Antiques LAPADA
34 Dollar St. (Mrs L. Taylor). CADA. Est. 1969. Open 9-5.30, Sun. by appointment. SIZE: Large. *STOCK: Furniture, 17th-19th C, £100-£20,000; glass, 18th-20th C, £10-£250; silver and decorative items, 17th-20th C, £20-£8,000. Not Stocked: Victoriana, militaria.* LOC: From church, turn right up West Market Place, via Gosditch St. into Dollar St. PARK: Abbey grounds via Spittalgate. TEL: 0285 652529. SER: Valuations; buys at auction (furnishing items). VAT: Spec.

Bernard Weaver Antiques
28 Gloucester St. CADA. Open 9.30-6, Sat. 9.30-1. SIZE: Medium. *STOCK: Furniture, mahogany and oak, 18th-19th C; art nouveau and arts and crafts.* LOC: Continuation of Dollar St. PARK: Easy. TEL: 0285 652055; home - same. SER: Valuations.

FAIRFORD

Blenheim Antiques
Market Place. (N. Hurdle). CADA. Resident. Est. 1972. Open 9.30-6.30. *STOCK: 18th-19th C furniture, clocks.* TEL: 0285 712094. VAT: Stan/Spec.

Fairford continued
Cirencester Antiques Ltd
High St. (Mr and Mrs R.T.G. Chester-Master). CADA. Est. 1959. Open 9-5.30. SIZE: Large. *STOCK: Furniture and works of art, 17th to early 19th C, £50-£50,000.* TEL: 0285 713774.

Gloucester House Antiques Ltd
Market Place. (Mr and Mrs R. Chester-Master). CADA. Est. 1972. Open 9-5.30. SIZE: Large. *STOCK: English and French country furniture in oak, elm, fruitwood, pine; pottery, faïence and decorative items.* PARK: Easy. TEL: 0285 712790; home - 0285 653066; fax - 0285 713324. VAT: Stan/Spec.

MORETON-IN-MARSH

Astley House - Fine Art
Astley House, High St. (D. and N. Glaisyer). CADA. Est. 1974. Open 9-5.30. CL: Wed. SIZE: Medium. *STOCK: Oil paintings and watercolours, 19th-20th C, £200-£10,000.* LOC: Main street. PARK: Easy. TEL: 0608 50601; fax - 0608 51777. SER: Restorations (oils and watercolours); framing; video valuations. VAT: Spec.

Astley House - Fine Art
Astley House, London Rd. (D. and N. Glaisyer). CADA. Est. 1974. Open 10-1 and 2-5.30. CL: Wed. SIZE: Large. *STOCK: Oil paintings, 19th-20th C; large decorative paintings and portraits.* LOC: Town centre. PARK: Easy. TEL: 0608 50601; fax - 0608 51777. SER: Restorations (oils and watercolours); porcelain framing. VAT: Spec.
20th C; some books. TEL: 0451 860519.

Duncan J. Baggott
Woolcomber House, Sheep St. CADA. Est. 1967. Open 9-5.30 or by appointment. SIZE: Large. *STOCK: 17th-19th C. English oak, mahogany, walnut and fruitwood furniture, paintings, prints and needlework, metalware and domestic items, garden statuary.* PARK: Own. TEL: 0451 830662; fax - 0451 832174.

STOW-ON-THE-WOLD

Duncan J. Baggott
Huntsmans Yard, Sheep St. CADA. Est. 1967. Open 9-5, or by appointment. CL: Sat. SIZE: Large. *STOCK: 17th-19th C. English and European furniture, portrait and primitive paintings, architectural items and statuary.* LOC: 200yds. from Fosseway entrance on right hand side through coaching gates. PARK: Own. TEL: 0451 830662; fax - 0451 832174. *Trade Only.*

Baggott Church Street Ltd BADA
Church St. (D.J. and C.M. Baggott). CADA. Est. 1978. Open 9.30-5.30 or by appointment.

Telephone
0451 830476
Fax
0451 830300

The Fosse Way
Stow-on-the-Wold
Gloucestershire
GL54 1JS

Christopher Clarke Antiques

English Furniture and the Decorative Arts

Stow-on-the-Wold continued
SIZE: Large. *STOCK: English furniture, 17th-19th C; portrait paintings, some metalwork, pottery, treen and decorative items.* LOC: South-west corner of market square. PARK: In market square. TEL: 0451 830370; fax - 0451 832174.

Colin Brand Antiques
Tudor House, Sheep St. CADA. Est. 1985. Open 10-1 and 2-5, Sun. by appointment. CL: Wed. SIZE: Medium. *STOCK: Clocks, small furniture, £200-£4,000; porcelain, £30-£600, all pre-1900.* LOC: Opposite Post Office. PARK: Main square. TEL: 0451 831760; home - same. VAT: Spec.

Christopher Clarke Antiques Ltd
BADA
The Fosse Way. (C.J. Clarke). CADA. Est. 1961. Open 9.30-6. SIZE: Medium. *STOCK: Furniture, 17th-19th C, £300-£15,000; walnut, mahogany, metalware, 16th-18th C, £200-£5,000. Not Stocked: Silver, glass, medals, coins, prints.* LOC: Corner of the Fosse Way and Sheep St. PARK: Easy. TEL: 0451 830476; fax - 0451 830300.

Cotswold Galleries
(Richard and Cherry Glaisyer). CADA. Est. 1961. Open 9-5.30 or by appointment. SIZE: Large. *STOCK: Oil paintings, especially 19th-20th C landscape.* TEL: 0451 830586. SER: Restorations; framing.

The Curiosity Shop   BADA LAPADA
The Square. (Antony Preston Antiques Ltd). CADA. Est. 1965. Open 9.30-5.30. SIZE: Large. *STOCK: Furniture, clocks, mirrors, 18th to early 19th C, £500-£10,000.* LOC: Off Fosse Way. PARK: Easy. TEL: 0451 831586. VAT: Stan/Spec.

Fosse Way Antiques
Ross House, The Square. (M. Beeston). CADA. Est. 1969. Open 10-5. SIZE: Large. *STOCK: Furniture and pictures, £150-£5,000; bronzes, porcelain, Sheffield plate, glass and decorative*

Stow-on-the-Wold continued
objects, £50-£1,000; all 18th-19th C. LOC: East side of the Square, behind the Town Hall. PARK: Easy. TEL: 0451 830776. SER: Valuations; buys at auction. VAT: Spec.

Keith Hockin (Antiques) Ltd   BADA
The Square. CADA. Est. 1968. Open 9-6. CL: Sun. except by appointment. SIZE: Medium. *STOCK: Oak furniture, 1600-1750; country furniture in oak, fruitwoods, yew, 1700-1850; pewter, copper, brass, ironwork, all periods. Not Stocked: Mahogany.* PARK: Easy. TEL: 0451 831058. SER: Buys at auction (oak, pewter, metalwork). VAT: Stan/Spec.

Huntington Antiques Ltd   LAPADA
The Old Forge, Church St. (M.F., S.P. and N.M.J. Golding). CADA. Resident. Est. 1974. Open 9.30-5.30 or by appointment. *STOCK: Early period and fine country furniture, metalware, treen and textiles, tapestries and works of art.* TEL: 0451 830842; fax - 0451 832211. SER: Valuations; buys at auction. FAIRS: Maastricht; Madrid; Bruges. VAT: Spec.

Antony Preston Antiques Ltd
BADA LAPADA
The Square. CADA. Est. 1965. Open 9.30-5.30 or by appointment. *STOCK: English and continental furniture and objects, longcase and bracket clocks, barometers, leather upholstery, 18th-19th C.* TEL: 0451 831586. VAT: Stan/Spec.

Samarkand Galleries   LAPADA
2 Brewery Yard, Sheep St. (B. and L. MacDonald). CADA. Est. 1980. Open 10-5.30, Sun. by appointment. SIZE: Medium. *STOCK: Tribal and village rugs and artifacts, 19th C, £100-£10,000; fine decorative carpets, 19th-20th C, £1,000-£10,000+; kelims, 19th-20th C, £200-£2,000.* LOC: Street adjacent to Market Sq. PARK: Easy. TEL: 0451 832322; fax - same; home - 0451 831173. SER: Valuations; restorations; cleaning; exhibitions. VAT: Stan/Spec.

Stow-on-the-Wold continued
Stow Antiques LAPADA
The Square. (Mr and Mrs J. Hutton-Clarke).
CADA. Resident. Est. 1969. Open 10.30-5.30.
SIZE: Large. *STOCK: Furniture, mainly Georgian, £500-£30,000; decorative items, gilded mirrors, £50-£10,000.* PARK: Easy.
TEL: 0451 830377; fax - 0451 870018. SER: Shipping worldwide.

STRETTON-ON-FOSSE

Astley House - Fine Art
The Old School. (D. and N. Glaisyer). CADA. Est. 1974. Open by appointment. SIZE: Large. *STOCK: Large decorative oil paintings, 19th-20th C.* LOC: Village centre. PARK: Easy. TEL: 0608 50601; fax - 0608 51777. SER: Valuations; restorations; framing; exhibitions; mailing list. VAT: Spec.

TADDINGTON

Architectural Heritage
Taddington Manor. CADA. Est. 1978. Open 9.30-5.30, Sat. 10.30-4.30. SIZE: Large. *STOCK: Period panelling, oak, mahogany and pine; chimney pieces in marble, stone, oak and mahogany; garden statuary, fountains, seats and urns; complete shop and pub interiors, ornamental gates, stained, leaded and etched glass; doors, decorative and unusual items.* PARK: Easy. TEL: 038 673 414; fax - 038 673 236. VAT: Stan.

TETBURY

Breakspeare Antiques LAPADA
36 and 57 Long St. (M. and S. Breakspeare). CADA. Resident. Est. 1962. Open 9.30-5.30, if closed ring bell. CL: Some Thurs. p.m. SIZE: Medium. *STOCK: English period furniture, mainly mahogany, 18th to early 19th C, some early walnut, longcase clocks.* PARK: Easy. TEL: 0666 503122; home - same. VAT: Stan/Spec. *Mainly Trade.*

WINCHCOMBE

Prichard Antiques
16 High St. (K.H. and D.Y. Prichard). CADA. Est. 1979. Open 9-6, Sun. by appointment. SIZE: Large. *STOCK: Period furniture, £10-£5,000; treen, £1-£500; metalwork, £5-£500, all 17th-19th C.* LOC: On main Broadway to Cheltenham road. PARK: Easy. TEL: 0242 603566. VAT: Spec.

Witney Antiques
L.S.A. & C.J. Jarrett

*96-100 CORN STREET,
WITNEY, OXFORDSHIRE
Tel: 0993 703902. Fax: 0993 779852*

One of the finest stocks of antique furniture available in the country

WITNEY

Ian Pout Antiques
99 High St. (I. and J. Pout). CADA. Open 10-5.30. *STOCK: 18th-19th C furniture, decorative objects, vintage teddy bears.* TEL: 0993 702616; home - 0869 40205. VAT: Spec.

Witney Antiques BADA
96/100 Corn St. (L.S.A. and C.J. Jarrett). CADA. Est. 1962. Open 9.30-5. SIZE: Large. *STOCK: English furniture, 17th-18th C; bracket and longcase clocks, mahogany, oak and walnut, metalware, needleworks and works of art.* LOC: From Oxford on old A40 through Witney via High St., turn right at T-junction, 400yds. on right. PARK: Easy. TEL: 0993 703902/703887; fax - 0993 779852. SER: Restorations. FAIRS: Park Lane; Grosvenor House. VAT: Spec.

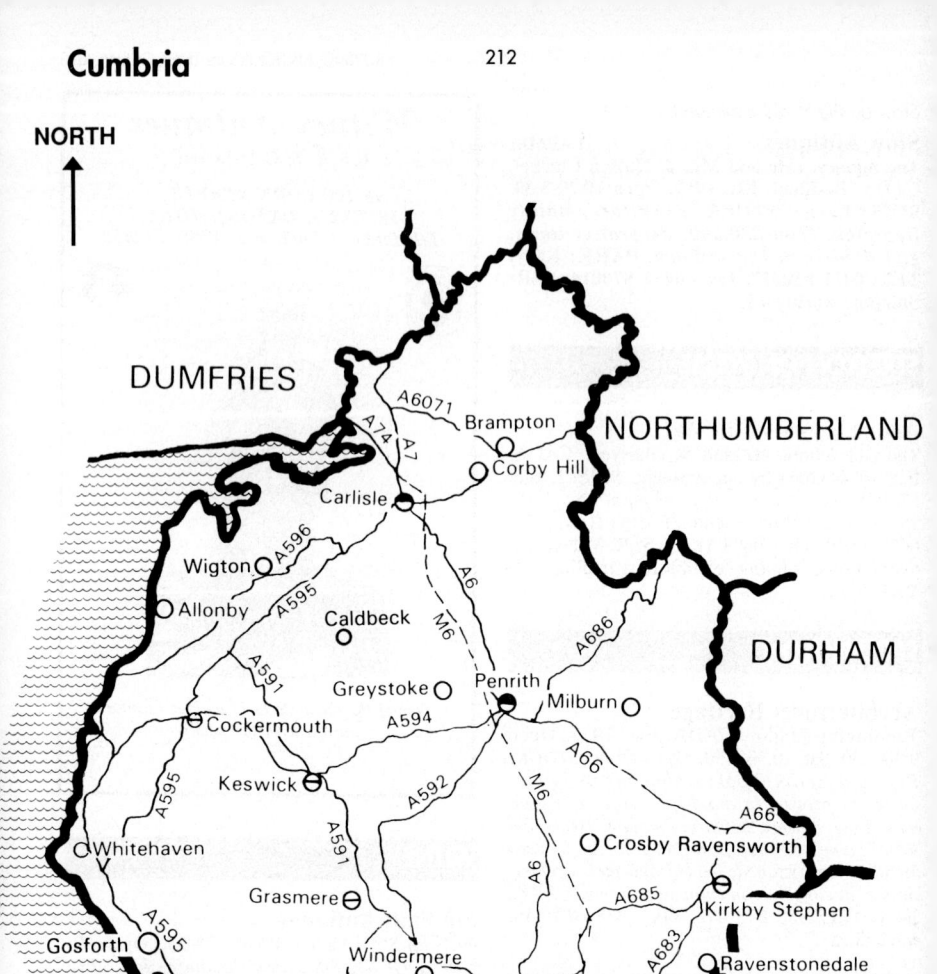

Cumbria

NORTH ↑

DUMFRIES

NORTHUMBERLAND

A6071
Brampton
A74 A7
Corby Hill
Carlisle
Wigton
A596
Allonby
A595
Caldbeck
A6
Greystoke
M6
Penrith
A686
Cockermouth
A594
Milburn
DURHAM
Keswick
A591
A592
A66
Whitehaven
A66
Crosby Ravensworth
Grasmere
A595
A685
Gosforth
Kirkby Stephen
Windermere
A6
A683
Coniston
Ravenstonedale
Bowness-on-Windermere
Kendal
Sedbergh
Newby Bridge
Endmoor
A684
Ulverston
Cartmel
A590
Milnthorpe
NORTH YORKS
Great Urswick
Kirkby Lonsdale
Beetham
Holme
Barrow-in-Furness

LANCS

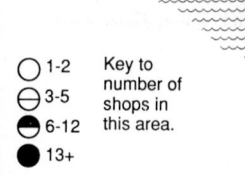

Key to number of shops in this area.
○ 1-2
⊖ 3-5
⊖ 6-12
● 13+

Please note this is only a rough map designed to show dealers the number of shops in the various towns, and is not necessarily totally accurate.

Cumbria

ALLONBY
Cottage Curios
Main St. (B. Pickering). Est. 1965. Open daily from 2 p.m.

ALSTON
Brownside Coach House
(A. and M.J. Graham). Est. 1987. Open 10-6 Easter to end Sept., other times by appointment. CL: Tues. SIZE: Small. *STOCK: Glass, 1780-1920's, to £100.* LOC: 1.5 miles outside Alston on Penrith road. PARK: Easy. TEL: 0434 381263. FAIRS: Grasmere.

BARROW-IN-FURNESS
Antiques
237 Rawlinson St. (H. Vincent). Est. 1965. *STOCK: Jewellery, furniture, paintings, weapons, clocks, brass, copperware, silver, bric-a-brac.* LOC: Off A590 (A6). PARK: Easy. TEL: 0229 823432.

BEETHAM, Nr. Milnthorpe
Peter Haworth
Templebank. Open by appointment. *STOCK: English and Scottish paintings and watercolours, 1850-1950; Moorcroft pottery; all £100-£25,000.* LOC: 1 mile north of Milnthorpe on Lancaster road. PARK: Easy. TEL: 05395 62352; fax - 05395 63438.

BOWNESS-ON-WINDERMERE
J.W. Thornton Antiques Supermarket
North Terrace. SIZE: Large. *STOCK: Fine art, general antiques, furniture, shipping and architectural items, pine, bric-a-brac, paintings, decorators items.* TEL: 05394 42930/45183 or 0229 869745. SER: Valuations; buys at auction. VAT: Stan/Spec.

Unicorn Antiques
1 Longlands. (J. and Mrs M.E. Hughes). Est. 1987. CL: Tues. and Thurs. SIZE: Medium. *STOCK: Bottles, curios and collectables, from 19th C, £1-£100; furniture including country pine, 19th C to 1940, £25-£1,000; country items - iron, copper and stone, 19th C to 1930, £5-£500.* LOC: Main road through village. PARK: Easy. TEL: 05394 88747; home - 05394 45338. VAT: Stan/Spec.

Utopia Antiques Ltd
Lake Rd. (P.J. and Mrs J. Wilkinson). Open 10-5. *STOCK: Pine and country furniture, decorative accessories.* PARK: Easy. TEL: 05394 88464. VAT: Stan.

White Elephant Antiques
66 Quarry Rigg, Lake Rd. (J.C. Moore). Est. 1987. Open 9.30-5.30 including Sun. SIZE: Medium. *STOCK: General antiques, 18th-19th C, £5-£200; reproduction Italian inlaid furniture, £25-£200; Persian, Chinese, Indian and Turkish rugs, £25-*

Bowness-on-Windermere continued
£400. LOC: Far end of Quarry Rigg precinct. PARK: Easy. TEL: 05394 46962; home - 05394 88685. SER: Restorations (rugs); buys at auction.

BRAMPTON
Mary Fell Antiques
Collectors' Corner, 32-34 Main St. Est. 1960. Open Tues., Wed., Fri. and Sat. 11-6, other times by appointment. *STOCK: Sheraton and Victorian furniture, porcelain, china, glass, silver and plate, bric-a-brac, early Victorian oil paintings, pictures, prints, jewellery, pot-lids.* Not Stocked: Coins, armour and swords. LOC: Town centre, beside public car park. PARK: Easy. TEL: Home - 0228 22224. SER: Valuations; restorations (furniture); buys at auction.

CALDBECK
Victoria Park Antiques
Upton. (S.E. McCaw and R. Hefford). Est. 1981. Open Fri., Sat. and Sun. 1-5, other days by appointment. SIZE: Small. *STOCK: Porcelain, 18th to early 19th C, £40-£800; small furniture, late 18th to early 19th C, £100-£1,000; textiles, 19th C, £25-£350.* LOC: Off M6, junction 41. Opposite primary school on B5299. PARK: Easy. TEL: Home - 06998 413. FAIRS: Grasmere May and Oct.

CARLISLE
Carlisle Antique and Craft Centre
Cecil Hall, Cecil St. Open 9.30-5. SIZE: Large plus trade warehouse. LOC: Off Warwick Rd. PARK: Easy. TEL: 0228 21970. Below are listed the dealers at this centre.

Art Deco
STOCK: Clarice Cliff, Susie Cooper, Charlotte Rhead, light fittings and furnishings, furniture.

Fine Pine
STOCK: Stripped pine furniture; mahogany and oak bedroom suites, large furniture, china, quilts.

It's About Time
(B. and W. Mitton). Est. 1985.*STOCK: Longcase, bracket and carriage clocks, watches; Royal Worcester fine porcelain, jewellery, textiles.* TEL: 0228 36910.

Maureen Morland
STOCK: Cane and rush seating. SER: Restorations (as stock).

Mr and Mrs J. Sharp
STOCK: Small Victorian furniture.

Shiners
(B. Lawson). *STOCK: Architectural items including Victorian fireplaces.*

CUMBRIA

The Antique Shop

English antique furniture,
also decorative items

Open 10.00am – 5.00pm
every day including Sunday

CARTMEL, GRANGE-OVER-SANDS,
CUMBRIA, TELEPHONE 05395-36295

Carlisle continued

Warwick Antiques
(J. Wardrope). CMBHI. *STOCK: Period furniture, porcelain, wall and bracket clocks, silver.* SER: Valuations; restorations (clocks).

Yesterday's Pine
STOCK: Pine. SER: Pine stripping.

Charm Antiques
Lonsdale St. (M. Byers). Open 10.30-4. *STOCK: Furniture, Victorian and Edwardian; pine, china, glass and curios.* LOC: Behind bus station. PARK: Easy. TEL: 0228 23035.

James W. Clements
19 Fisher St. Est. 1887. Open 9.30-5. CL: Thurs. *STOCK: Glass, china, silver, Georgian and Victorian; Victorian jewellery.* TEL: 0228 25565. VAT: Stan/Spec.

Maurice Dodd Books
112 Warwick Rd. (R.J. McRoberts). Est. 1945. CL: Sat. p.m. *STOCK: Antiquarian books.* TEL: 0228 22087; fax - same. VAT: Stan/Spec.

A.C. Layne
48 Cecil St. Open by appointment. *STOCK: Clocks and watches.* PARK: Easy. TEL: 0228 45019. SER: Repairs (as stock).

Carlisle continued

Saint Nicholas Galleries (Antiques) Ltd
28 London Rd. (J., C. and F.E. Carruthers). Open 9.30-5. CL: Thurs. SIZE: Medium. *STOCK: General antiques, 18th C, £5-£500.* LOC: City centre. PARK: Nearby. TEL: 0228 34425; home - 0228 22249.

Saint Nicholas Galleries Ltd. (Antiques and Jewellery)
39 Bank St. (C.J. Carruthers). Open 10-5. CL: Mon. SIZE: Medium. *STOCK: Jewellery, silver, plate, Rolex pocket watches, clocks; collectables; Royal Doulton; Dux, Oriental vases; pottery, porcelain; watercolours, oil paintings; pine furniture; brass and copper.* LOC: City centre. PARK: Nearby. TEL: 0228 44459.

Second Sight
4A Mary St. (B. Donowho). Est. 1990. Open 10-5.30 or by aappointment. CL: Thurs. SIZE: Small. *STOCK: Furniture including pine, 17th-20th C; porcelain, silver, glass, paintings, oil lamps, clocks and collectables.* LOC: Off Butchergate. PARK: Easy - adjacent. TEL: 0228 591525; home - 0228 35922. SER: Valuations; restorations; buys at auction (furniture, silver and porcelain).

Souvenir Antiques
Treasury Court, Fisher St. (J. Higham). Open 10-5. SIZE: Small. *STOCK: Porcelain and pottery, Victorian to art deco, £5-£500; coronation ware, crested china, local prints, maps, postcards, Roman and medieval coins, costume jewellery.* Not Stocked: Textiles. LOC: City centre between Fisher St. and Scotch St. PARK: Nearby. TEL: 0228 401281.

CARTMEL

Anthemion - The Antique Shop BADA
(J. and S. Wood). Est. 1982. Open 10-5 seven days. SIZE: Large. *STOCK: English period furniture, 17th to early 19th C, £100-£30,000; decorative items, 17th-19th C, £20-£2, 000.* Not Stocked: Victoriana, bric-a-brac. LOC: Village centre. PARK: Easy. TEL: 053 95 36295; mobile - 0831 860883; home - 053 95 36234. FAIRS: BADA, NEC, Olympia, Northern, Kenilworth, Chester, West London. VAT: Stan/Spec.

Bacchus Antiques -In the Service of Wine
Longlands. (Mrs J.A. Johnson). Est. 1979. Open by appointment only. *STOCK: Fine corkscrews.* TEL: 053 95 36475.

Norman Kerr - Gatehouse Bookshop
The Square. Open by appointment only. *STOCK: Antiquarian books.* TEL: 053 95 36247.

Peter Bain Smith (Bookseller)
Bank Court, Market Sq. In season open every day 10.30-6. CL: Mon. and Tues. from mid Nov. to

Cartmel continued
Easter.Open 1.30-4.30. *STOCK: Books including antiquarian, especially children's and local topography.* LOC: A590 from Levens Bridge, off roundabout at Lindale by-pass through Grange-over-Sands. PARK: Nearby. TEL: 053 95 36369. SER: Valuations.

COCKERMOUTH
Cockermouth Antiques
5 Station St. (E. Bell and G. Davies). Est. 1983. Open 10-5. SIZE: Large. *STOCK: General antiques especially ceramics, furniture, pictures, glass, books, metalware, quilts.* LOC: Just off A66, in town centre opposite Post Office. PARK: Easy. TEL: 0900 826746.

Cockermouth Antiques Market
Courthouse, Main St. Est. 1979. Open 10-5. SIZE: Large - 7 stallholders. *STOCK: Victorian, Edwardian and art deco items, furniture, printed collectables, postcards, books, linen, china, glass, toys, textiles, jewellery and pictures.* LOC: Town centre, just off A66. PARK: 50yds. TEL: 0900 824346. SER: Restorations (furniture); stripping (pine). VAT: Stan/Spec.

Holmes Antiques
1 Market Place. (C. and S. Holmes). Est. 1972. Open 10-5. CL: Thurs. SIZE: Medium. *STOCK: Furniture, paintings, prints, small antiques, collectors' items.* PARK: Rear of premises. TEL: 0900 826114; home - 07687 78364.

CONISTON
The Old Man Antiques
Yewdale Rd. (R. and Y. Williams). Est. 1965. Open daily 9.30-6 Easter-Nov. SIZE: Medium. *STOCK: General antiques especially barometers - 'banjo', from £240 and 'stick' from £450 when available.* LOC: On Ambleside to Ulverston Rd. PARK: Easy. TEL: 053 94 41289. SER: Restorations (barometers, barographs and thermographs).

CORBY HILL, Nr. Carlisle
Langley Antiques
The Forge. (Mrs P. Mather and S. Ginesi). Est. 1976. Open 10.30-5. SIZE: Medium. *STOCK: Country oak, period and Edwardian furniture.* LOC: A69. PARK: Easy. TEL: 0228 560899.

CROSBY RAVENSWORTH, Nr. Penrith
David A. H. Grayling
Lyvennet. Est. 1971. Open by appointment only. *STOCK: Fine and antiquarian books on natural history and all field sports, £5-£2,000.* LOC: Off M6, junction 38 towards Appleby turn left half mile past Orton. PARK: Easy. TEL: 0931 715288; fax - same. SER: Valuations; restorations; fine binding.

Crosby Ravensworth continued
Jennywell Hall Antiques
(Mrs M. Macadie). Est. 1975. Open weekends 12-6, other times by appointment. SIZE: Medium. *STOCK: Oak, mahogany furniture, paintings, small items, 16th-19th C.* LOC: 5 miles from junction 39, M6. PARK: Easy. TEL: 0931 715288; home - same.

ENDMOOR, Nr. Kendal
Calvert Antiques
Sycamore House. (N.A. Hutchinson-Shire). Est. 1986. Open 9.30-5.30, Sun. 10.30-4, other times by appointment. SIZE: Medium. *STOCK: Furniture, 17th to early 19th C; clocks, 17th-19th C.* Not Stocked: China, silver, treen and jewellery. LOC: On A65. Leave M6 at junction 36 on to Skipton/Kirby Lonsdale rd., first exit left to Endmoor. PARK: Easy. TEL: 05395 67597; home - same. SER: Restorations (furniture); replica furniture made to order; upholstery. VAT: Stan/Spec.

GOSFORTH
Archie Miles Bookshop
Beck Place. (Mrs C.M. Linsley). Open 10-5, other times by appointment. CL: Mon. *STOCK: Secondhand, antiquarian and out-of-print books, maps and prints.* TEL: 094 67 25792.

GRASMERE, Nr. Ambleside
Aladdin's Cave
Helm House, Langdale Rd. (J. Harwood). Est. 1975. Open 10-5 including Sun. SIZE: Medium. *STOCK: General and rural antiques, brass and copper, coloured glass, country furniture; local prints; oils and watercolours, 18th-19th C, £5-£500.* LOC: Behind Red Lion Hotel. Turn past garden centre from church, then 1st right. PARK: Easy. TEL: 05394 35774; home - 05394 35449.

Grasmere Galleries
(Neil Gregory). Resident. Est. 1977. Open Sat. and Sun. or by appointment. CL: Mon. SIZE: Small. *STOCK: Period furniture, china, brass, copper and silver, £10-£2,500.* LOC: Opposite Red Lion. TEL: 0539 435631; home - 0946 810862. SER: Valuations. FAIRS: Grasmere.

The Stables
College St. (J.A. and K.M. Saalmans). Est. 1971. Open daily 10-6 Easter-October, other times telephone call advisable. SIZE: Small. *STOCK: Brass and copper items, oil lamps, domestic bygones; pottery, silver, prints, books.* Not Stocked: Weapons, coins. LOC: By the side of Moss Grove Hotel. PARK: Easy. TEL: 05394 35453; home - same.

GREAT URSWICK, Nr. Ulverston
Lilian Wood Antiques
Midtown House. Usually open but prior telephone call advisable. *STOCK: Paintings and decorative items.* LOC: Off A590, Midtown is second house beyond Derby Arms, turning left. PARK: Easy. TEL: 0229 56297.

CUMBRIA 216

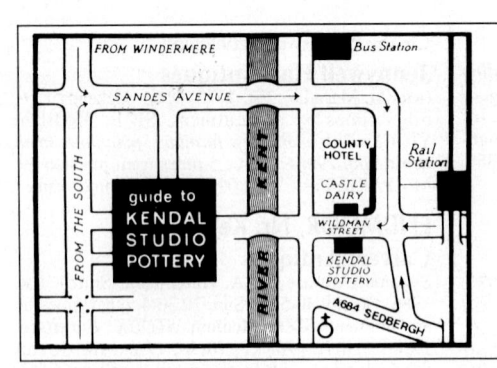

'KENDAL STUDIOS'
ANTIQUES & FINE ART GALLERY
ROBERT & ANDREW O. AINDOW
KENDAL STUDIO POTTERY
2/3 WILDMAN STREET
KENDAL, WESTMORLAND
CUMBRIA LA9 6EN
6 miles from Junction 37 on the M6

Tel. KENDAL (0539) 723291
Open by Appointment
Closed Thursdays & Sundays
Access and Barclaycard, Diners and American Express

GREYSTOKE, Nr. Penrith
Pelican Antiques
Church Rd. (Mrs J. Kirkby). Est. 1897. Open daily but prior telephone call advisable. *STOCK: General small antiques, £5-£300.* PARK: Easy. TEL: 08533 477.

Roadside Antiques
Watsons Farm, Greystoke Gill. (K. and R. Sealby). Resident. Est. 1988. Open every day 10-6. SIZE: Medium. *STOCK: Ceramics, longcase clocks, glass, Staffordshire figures, pot-lids, furniture, small collectables, jewellery, mainly 19th C, £5-£2,000.* LOC: B5288 Penrith/Keswick road to Greystoke, through village, first left then left again, premises second on right. PARK: Easy. TEL: 07684 83279.

HOLME, Nr. Carnforth
JBW Antiques
Green Farm, Duke St. (J. Benson-Wilson). Resident. Est. 1991. Open 9-12.30 and 1-5. SIZE: Small. *STOCK: Pottery, porcelain and glass, silver and plate, mainly 19th C, from £5; costume jewellery, militaria, furniture, mainly small, 18th-19th C.* LOC: A6070 from Carnforth through Burton. Shop opposite public house in village centre. PARK: Easy. TEL: 0524 781377. SER: Valuations; restorations; buys at auction.

KENDAL
Below Stairs
78 Highgate. (S. Ritchie). Open 10-4. *STOCK: Brass, copper, silver, coloured glass, porcelain, collectables.* LOC: Main street under Shakespeare Inn. TEL: 0539 741278.

Brian Blakemore - Dower House Antiques
40 Kirkland. Open 9.15-6, Thurs. 9.15-1. *STOCK: Pottery, porcelain, paintings, furniture.* TEL: 0539 722778.

Cottage Antiques
80 Highgate. (S. Satchell). Est. 1974. Open 11-4.30. CL: Mon. and Thurs. *STOCK: Mainly smalls including pottery, glass, brass, copper,*

Kendal continued
metalware, treen, kitchen items, tool and craft bygones, small silver, some furniture mainly pine. Not Stocked: Coins. LOC: A6. PARK: Nearby. TEL: 0539 722683; home - 05395 68485.

Kendal Studios Antiques
2/3 Wildman St. (R. and A.O. Aindow). Est. 1950. Opening times vary, prior telephone call advisable. CL: Thurs. SIZE: Medium. *STOCK: Ceramics, maps and prints, paintings, oak furniture, art pottery.* LOC: Leave M6 at junction 37, follow one-way system, shop on left. PARK: Nearby. TEL: 0539 723291 (24 hrs. answering service). SER: Restorations; finder; shipping. VAT: Stan/Spec.

The Silver Thimble
39 All Hallows Lane. (V. Ritchie). Est. 1980. Open 10-4. SIZE: Large. *STOCK: Jewellery, silver, glass, linen and lace, porcelain, copper and brass.* LOC: Turn left at second set of traffic lights on main road into Kendal from south, shop 200yds. on right. PARK: Easy. TEL: 0539 731456.

KESWICK
And So To Bed
Lake Rd. (W.I. Raw). Est. 1981. Open 9.30-5. *STOCK: Brass beds, iron and brass beds, mattress and base sets for antique beds, mirrors, linen, quilts, £150-£2,000.* LOC: Top of Main St. TEL: 076 87 74881. VAT: Stan.

John Young and Son (Antiques)
LAPADA
12-14 Main St. Est. 1890. Open 9-5.30. SIZE: Large. **STOCK: General antiques, 18th-19th C.** LOC: Town centre. PARK: At rear. TEL: 076 87 73434. VAT: Stan/Spec.

KIRKBY LONSDALE
Alexander Adamson
Tearnside Hall. (N.J.G., D. and P.A. Adamson). Est. 1863. Open 9.30-5.30. *STOCK: Furniture 17th to early 19th C; glass and porcelain.* PARK: Easy. TEL: 05242 71989. SER: Valuations; restorations (furniture). VAT: Spec.

Haughey Antiques

Antiques and Works of Art

28–30 Market Street
Kirkby Stephen
Cumbria CA17 4QW
Telephone 07683 71302

LAPADA MEMBER

KIRKBY STEPHEN

Haughey Antiques   LAPADA
Market St. (D.M. Haughey). Est. 1969. Open 10-5, Sat. 12-5. SIZE: Large. STOCK: *Furniture, 17th-19th C; garden furniture and statuary.* PARK: Easy. TEL: 076 83 71302. SER: Valuations. VAT: Stan/Spec.

David Hill
36 Market Sq. Est. 1965. Open 9.30-4. SIZE: Medium. STOCK: *Longcase clocks, £350-£1,500; country furniture, £10-£1,000; both 18th-19th C; curios, £5-£50; shipping goods, kitchenalia, iron and brassware.* LOC: On A685. PARK: Easy. TEL: 076 83 71598. VAT: Stan/Spec.

Mortlake Antiques
32-34 Market St. (C.J. and J.A. Bate). Est. 1946. Open Mon., Fri. and Sat. 10-5, other times by appointment. SIZE: Medium. STOCK: *Furniture, period, Victorian, Edwardian and country including stripped pine; treen, kitchenalia, bygones, bric-a-brac and metalware.* Not stocked: Silver, glass, porcelain. LOC: On A685, 2 miles east of junction 38, M6. PARK: Easy. TEL: 076 83 71666 (ansaphone). VAT: Stan/Spec.

LOW NEWTON, Nr. Grange-over-Sands

W.R.S. Architectural Antiques
Yew Tree Barn. (Clive Wilson). Open 10-5, Sun. 1-5 and Bank Holiday Mon. STOCK: *General architectural antiques including fireplaces; period furniture.* TEL: 05395 31498.

MAULDS MEABURN, Nr. Penrith

Cothay Antiques
Meaburn Hall. (V.D. Hodgkiss). Est. 1978. Open Thurs.-Sun. 10.30-6, other times by appointment, trade at any time. SIZE: Large. STOCK: *Early English oak and walnut, 16th-18th C, £400-£20,000; mahogany, 18th-19th C, £500-£20,000; tapestries, 16th-18th C, £200-£20,000; objects, 16th-19th C, £100-£2,000.* LOC: 6 miles from junction 39, M6. PARK: Easy. TEL: 0931 715401; fax - 0931 715306. SER: Valuations; restorations (16th-18th C furniture); buys at auction (as stock). VAT: Spec.

MILBURN, Nr. Penrith

Netherley Cottage Antiques
(J. Heelis). Est. 1970. Usually open 8.30-8 but appointment advisable. SIZE: Small. STOCK: *Country cottage pottery, porcelain and ornaments, 18th-19th C, £1-£70; kitchen and dairy items,*

CUMBRIA

Milburn continued
interesting bygones, brass, watercolours, £1-£85; treen, some Oriental items. Not Stocked: Silver and clocks. TEL: 076 83 61403. SER: Buys at auction.

MILNTHORPE
The Antique Shop
Park Rd. Open Wed. and Fri. 10-4.30. SIZE: Medium. STOCK: General antiques, books, furniture. LOC: From A6, left at traffic lights in village, opposite Post Office. TEL: 05395 62253.

NEWBY BRIDGE
Shire Antiques
The Post House, High Newton, Newton-in-Cartmel. (B. and Mrs J. Shire). Open every day except Tues. SIZE: Medium. STOCK: Early oak furniture, 16th-18th C; Georgian copper, brass, treen. Not Stocked: Silver and jewellery. LOC: On A590 to Barrow, house is 50yds. from main road in village. PARK: Easy. TEL: 053 95 31431; home - same. SER: Valuations; restorations (furniture). VAT: Stan/Spec.

Townhead Antiques   LAPADA
(E.M. and C.P. Townley). Est. 1960. Open 9-5, other times by appointment. SIZE: Large. STOCK: 18th-19th C furniture, silver, porcelain, glass, decorative pieces; clocks, pictures, garden furniture. LOC: A592. 1 mile from Newby Bridge on the Windermere road. PARK: Easy. TEL: 053 95 31321; fax - 053 95 30019. VAT: Stan/Spec.

PENRITH
Antiques of Penrith
4 Corney Sq. (L. Mildwurf and Partners). Est. 1964. Open 10-12 and 1.30-4.45, Sat. 10-12. CL: Wed. SIZE: Large. STOCK: Early oak and mahogany furniture, clocks, brass, copper, glass, china, silver plate, metal, Staffordshire figures, curios. Not Stocked: Jewellery, paintings, rugs. LOC: Near Town Hall. PARK: Easy. TEL: 0768 62801. VAT: Stan.

Arcade Antiques and Jewellery
11 Devonshire Arcade. (P.B. and A.L. Clark). Est. 1981. SIZE: Small. STOCK: Furniture including Edwardian, £20-£1,000; collectable items, £2-£500; jewellery, to £900. LOC: Town centre. PARK: Nearby. TEL: 0768 67754; home - 0768 63635.

Corney House Antiques
Corney House, 1 Corney Place. (Mr and Mrs Mawer). Est. 1983. Open 10-1 and 2-5. CL: Wed. SIZE: Medium. STOCK: Georgian and Victorian furniture and 19th C pine, £100-£3,000; porcelain and pottery, 18th-20th C, £10-£2,000. LOC: Near town hall. PARK: Easy. TEL: 0768 67665. VAT: Stan/Spec.

Penrith continued
The Gallery
54 Castlegate. (K.G. Plant). Est. 1969. Open daily, Wed. and Sun. by appointment. SIZE: Small. STOCK: Paintings and watercolours, 17th-20th C, £50-£20,000. LOC: From town centre towards the railway station. TEL: 0768 65538; home - same. SER: Valuations; buys at auction (paintings). VAT: Stan/Spec.

Hearth and Home
6 Brunswick Rd. Open 9-5. STOCK: Antique and reproduction furniture and decorative accessories, fireplaces and wood burning stoves. TEL: 0768 67200.

Joseph James Antiques
Corney Sq. (G.R. Walker). Est. 1970. Open 9-12.30 and 1.30-5.30. CL: Wed. SIZE: Medium. STOCK: Furniture and upholstery, 18th C and Victorian, £10-£800; porcelain and pottery, £5-£200; silver and plate, pictures, £2-£500; al. 18th-19th C. LOC: On the one-way system in the town, 100yds. from the main shopping area (Middlegate), 50yds. from the town hall. PARK Easy and 100yds. TEL: 0768 62065. SER Restorations; re-upholstery. VAT: Stan.

Penrith Coin and Stamp Centre
37 King St. (Mr and Mrs A. Gray). Resident. Est 1974. Open 9-5.30. CL: Wed. Sept.-May. SIZE Medium. STOCK: Coins, B.C. to date, 1p-£500 jewellery, secondhand, £5-£500; Great Britain and Commonwealth stamps. LOC: Just off town centre. PARK: Behind shop. TEL: 0768 64185 SER: Valuations; jewellery repairs. FAIRS: Many coin. VAT: Stan.

Jane Pollock Antiques
4 Castlegate. Open 9.30-5. CL: Wed. SIZE Medium. STOCK: Georgian and Victorian silver some 20th C small items; Victorian pottery, blue and white lustre; wooden boxes, some smal furniture. LOC: One-way street from town centre towards station. PARK: Easy. TEL: 0768 67211 SER: Valuations; restorations (silver, blue glas. liners); buys at auction (silver, pottery). FAIRS Buxton, Olympia, Kensington, Grasmere, Cheste and Barbican. VAT: Stan/Spec.

RAVENSTONEDALE, Nr. Kirkby Stephen
The Book House
Grey Garth. (C. and M. Irwin). PBFA. Est. 1963 Open every day, appointment preferred. STOCK Books, mainly 19th-20th C, £1-£1,000; some postcards, 20th C, 25p-£10. LOC: Off A685 Square house across road triangle from village school. PARK: Easy. TEL: 05396 23634; home same. SER: Valuations. FAIRS: Northern PBFA VAT: Stan.

SEDBERGH

R. F. G. Hollett and Son
6 Finkle St. (R. F. G. and C. G. Hollett). Est. 1951. Open 10-12 and 1.15-5. SIZE: Medium. *STOCK: Antiquarian books, 15th-20th C, £10-£10,000+; maps, prints and paintings, 17th-19th C, £10-£5,000.* LOC: Town centre. PARK: Nearby. TEL: 05396 20298; fax - 05396 21396. SER: Valuations. VAT: Stan.

Sedbergh Antiques and Collectables
59 Main St. (M.J. Moores). Est. 1976. Open 9.30-12.30 and 2.30-4. SIZE: Small. *STOCK: Porcelain, pottery, small furniture, glass, metalware, jewellery, linen, framed prints.* PARK: Opposite. TEL: 05396 21276.

Stable Antiques
Wheelwright Cottage, 15-16 Back Lane. Est. 1970. Open 10-6. *STOCK: Small furniture, brass, copper, silver, china, prints, small collectors' items, treen.* LOC: 5 miles from exit 37, M6. TEL: 05396 20251.

ULVERSTON

A1A Antiques
59B Market St. (J.W. Thornton). Est. 1960. Open by appointment. SIZE: Large. *STOCK: Bric-a-brac, clocks, furniture, shipping items, pictures, decorators items.* PARK: Easy. TEL: 0229 869745 or 05394 42930/45183. SER: Valuations; restorations; buys at auction. VAT: Stan/Spec.

Elizabeth and Son
Market Hall. (J.R. Bevins). Est. 1960. Open 9-5. CL: Wed. SIZE: Medium. *STOCK: Victorian and Edwardian glass, silver, brass and copper, gold and silver jewellery, books.* LOC: Town centre. PARK: Easy. TEL: 0229 52763.

WHITEHAVEN

Michael Moon
41-43 Roper St. (M. and S. Moon). ABA, PBFA. Est. 1969. Open 9.30-5. SIZE: Large. *STOCK: Antiquarian books including Cumbrian topography.* PARK: Nearby. TEL: 0946 62936. FAIRS: PBFA Northern. VAT: Stan.

WIGTON

S.I. Jackson Antiques
71 High St. Est. 1987. Open by appointment. CL: Thurs. *STOCK: General antiques and decorative items, £10-£500.* PARK: Easy. TEL: 069 73 45034.

WINDERMERE

The Birdcage Antiques
College Rd. (Mrs T.A. Griffiths). Est. 1983. Open Wed., Fri. and Sat. 10-5, or by appointment. SIZE: Small. *STOCK: General antiques, glass, brass and copper, oil lamps, country bygones,*

JANE POLLOCK ANTIQUES
4 CASTLEGATE
PENRITH
CUMBRIA
TEL: (0768) 67211

Open 9.30 – 5.00   Closed Wednesday

A fiddle thread pattern canteen, 6 place setting, mainly Georgian, from our selection of Georgian and Victorian cutlery.

Georgian, Victorian and Twentieth century silver. Nineteenth century pottery, porcelain and wooden boxes.

Windermere continued

Staffordshire, 18th C to 1920; 19th C pottery. LOC: From A591 through village, past end of one-way system, turn right after 50yds. PARK: Nearby. TEL: 05394 45063; home - 05394 43041/43310. VAT: Stan/Spec.

Century Antiques and Victoria Galleries
Victoria Cottage, 13 Victoria St. (D. and R. Hopwood). Est. 1969. Open 9-5.30. CL: Thurs. *STOCK: Furniture, collectors' items, clocks, pictures.* LOC: On main road from station, adjacent to Ellery Hotel. TEL: 05394 44126.

Joseph Thornton Antiques
4 Victoria St. (J.W. Thornton). Est. 1971. Open 10-4.30 or by appointment. SIZE: Large. *STOCK: General antiques, art, architectural and decorators' items, clocks, bric-a-brac.* LOC: 50yds. from railway station. PARK: Easy. TEL: 05394 42930/45183 or 0229 869745. SER: Valuations; buys at auction. VAT: Stan/Spec.

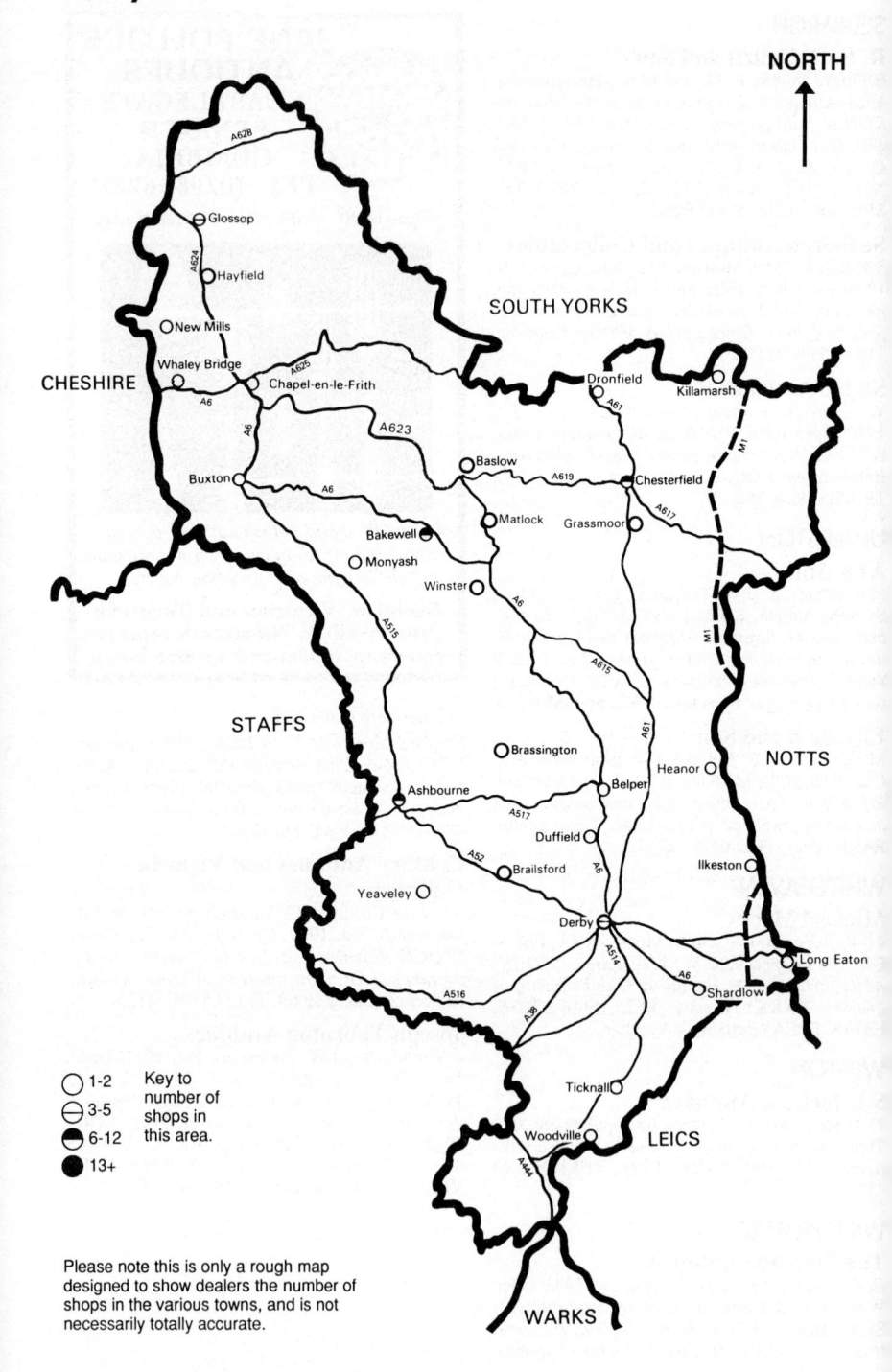

Derbyshire

Derbyshire

ASHBOURNE

Yvonne Adams Antiques
47 Church St. (Mrs Y. S. Adams). Est. 1983. CL: Tues. a.m. and Wed. SIZE: Small. *STOCK: Oak and country furniture, 17th-19th C, £30-£2,000; metalwork, decorative and unusual items.* LOC: A52. PARK: Nearby. TEL: 0335 346466.

Ashbourne Fine Art
Agnes Meadow Farm, Offcote. (S.A. and D.J. Smith). Open by appointment only. *STOCK: 19th-20th C oils, watercolours and dolls.* TEL: 0335 344072.

Cavendish House Gallery
9 Church St. Open 10-5. CL: Wed. *STOCK: Victorian watercolours and oils; watercolours by local artists.* TEL: 0335 344606.

Pamela Elsom - Antiques
5 Church St. Est. 1963. Open 10-5. CL: Wed. p.m. SIZE: Medium. *STOCK: Furniture, £20-£5,000, metalware, both 17th-19th C; period smalls, general antiques, treen, pottery, glass, secondhand books. Not Stocked: Coins, militaria.* LOC: On A52. PARK: Easy. TEL: 0335 343468. SER: Valuations. VAT: Spec.

Manion Antiques
23 Church St. (Mrs V.J. Manion). Est. 1984. Open Thurs., Fri. and Sat. 10-5, other times by appointment. SIZE: Small. *STOCK: Porcelain, silver, jewellery, small furniture, £50-£100+.* PARK: Easy. TEL: 0335 343207; home - same. SER: Valuations.

Out of Time Antiques
21 Church S. (T. Wardle and M. Locke). Est. 1975. Open 10-5.30. CL: Wed. SIZE: Medium. *STOCK: Decorative, collectable and country items, metalware, pottery and textiles; pine, oak and mahogany.* LOC: A52. PARK: Easy. TEL: 0335 342096; home - 0335 342074 and 0538 373838.

Rose Antiques
37 Church St. Est. 1982. Open 10-5. SIZE: Medium. *STOCK: Furniture, silver, porcelain, jewellery, copper, brass and pine.* LOC: A52. PARK: Easy. TEL: 0335 343822; home - 028 375 301.

Spurrier-Smith Antiques   LAPADA
28, 29 and 41 Church St. (I. Spurrier-Smith). Est. 1973. Open 9.30-5.30, Wed. and Sun. by appointment. SIZE: Large (8 showrooms). *STOCK: Furniture, oils, watercolours, porcelain, pottery, metalware, instruments, Oriental bronzes, collectables, pine, decorative items.* TEL: 0335 343669/342198; home - 0629 822502. SER: Valuations. VAT: Stan/Spec.

Kenneth Upchurch
30B Church St. Est. 1972. *STOCK: Oil paintings and watercolours, mainly 19th C; pottery and porcelain.* TEL: 0332 754499.

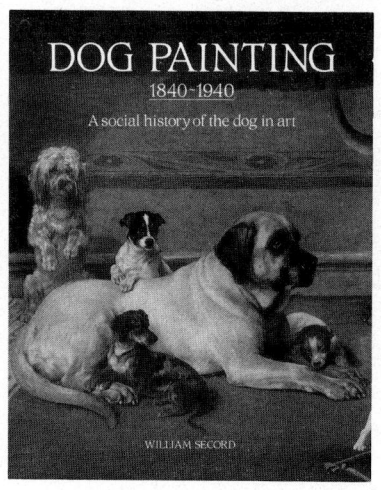

An Antique Collectors' Club Title

Dog Painting 1840-1940
A Social History of the Dog in Art
by William Secord
This fascinating account of the rich inter-relationship between man and dog as recorded in art, charts the changes in breeds in the 19th and 20th centuries.
ISBN 1 85159 139 2, 368pp
317 b & w illus, 150 colour, £35.00

Available from:
Antique Collectors' Club, 5 Church Street, Woodbridge, Suffolk IP12 1DS
Tel: (0394) 385501 Fax: (0394) 384434

or Market Street Industrial Park, Wappingers' Falls, New York 12590, USA
Tel: 914 297 0003 Fax: 914 297 0068

K. Chappell

Antiques & Fine Art
Merchants of Fine Quality Antiques & Objets d'Art
ESTABLISHED OVER HALF A CENTURY

FINE PERIOD FURNITURE & DECORATIVE ACCESSORIES

A fine quality Regency period Mahogany Bookcase of golden colour. Height 50½in., width 33¼in., depth 12in.

KING STREET, BAKEWELL, DERBYSHIRE
Telephone: (0629) 812496
Open 9.30am to 5.30pm Monday to Saturday inclusive

BAKEWELL

Bakewell Antiques and Collectors Centre
King St. Est. 1992. Open 10-5, Sun. 11-5. *STOCK: General antiques and collectables.* TEL: 0629 812496; fax - 0629 814531.

Beedham Antiques Ltd
Holme Hall. (W.H. Beedham). Open by appointment. *STOCK: English oak furniture, 16th-17th C.* LOC: Off A619. TEL: 0629 813285. SER: Valuations; buys at auction. VAT: Spec.

K. Chappell Antiques and Fine Art
BADA
King St. Est. 1940. Open 9.30-5.30. *STOCK: 17th-19th C English furniture, oil paintings, porcelain, pottery, metalwork, clocks and decorative items.* TEL: 0629 812496; fax - 0629 814531. VAT: Stan/Spec.

Michael Goldstone
BADA
Avenel Court. Est. 1927. Open 9-6 or by appointment. SIZE: Large. *STOCK: Oak furniture, 16th-18th C, from £100; walnut furniture, brass, 18th C, from £500.* PARK: Easy. TEL: 0629 812487; home - same. SER: Valuations. VAT: Spec.

Martin and Dorothy Harper Antiques
LAPADA
King St. Open 10-5.30, Sun. by appointment. SIZE: Medium. *STOCK: Furniture, £100-£5,000; metalware, £30-£300; glass, £15-£150; all 17th to late 19th C; needlework, 19th C.* PARK: Easy. TEL: 0629 814757. SER: Valuations; restorations (re-upholstery); buys at auction. VAT: Stan/Spec.

Alan Hill Books
3 Buxton Rd. Est. 1980. Open 10-5.30. *STOCK: Antiquarian books and maps.* TEL: 0629 814841.

Water Lane Antiques
Water Lane. (M. and L. Pembery). Est. 1967. Open 9.30-1 and 1.30-5.30. SIZE: Medium. *STOCK: Furniture, £500-£4,000; metalware, £100-£1,000; objets d'art, £100-£1,500; all 18th-19th C.* LOC: Off Market Sq. PARK: Nearby. TEL: 0629 814161. SER: Valuations; restorations. VAT: Stan/Spec.

BASLOW

Westfield Antiques
(Mrs. D. Pugh). Open by appointment only. *STOCK: Early 19th C porcelain and Chinese embroidery.* TEL: 0246 582386.

BELPER

Belper Antiques Centre
2 Queen St. (R. Briggs). Est. 1973. SIZE: Medium. *STOCK: Pre 1950 smalls and 19th-20th C jewellery, £5-£500; furniture, clocks and pictures, 18th-19th C, £50-£2,000.* LOC: Turn right towards Market Place at Safeway island on A6 north of Derby. PARK: Nearby. TEL: 0773 823002. SER: Valuations; restorations (clocks, gilding, furniture); buys at auction. FAIRS: Newark, Birmingham. VAT: Stan.

Sweetings (Antiques 'n' Things)
1 & 1a The Butts. (K.J. Sweeting and Miss J.L. Bunting). Est. 1971. Open daily. SIZE: Large. *STOCK: Pre 1940's furniture including stripped pine, oak, mahogany, satinwood, £20-£1,000.* LOC: Off A6, near Market Place. PARK: Easy. TEL: 0773 825930/822780. SER: Valuations; restorations (pine and satinwood); shipping. VAT: Stan.

Neil Wayne "The Razor Man"
High Peak Products, Old Baptist Chapel, rear of 'Riflemans Arms', Bridge St. Resident. Est. 1969. Open every day 9.30-6, prior telephone call essential. SIZE: Medium. *STOCK: Razors and shaving items, 18th to early 19th C, £20-£500; knives including fruit, pocket, hunting and cutlery, 17th-19th C, £20-£500; optical and medical items, 17th-20th C, £10-£1,000.* PARK: Easy. TEL: 0773 827910/820566; fax - 0773 825662.

BRAILSFORD

Antique Exporters U.K
The Estate Yard, Post Office Lane. Est. 1977. Open by appointment. SIZE: Large. *STOCK: Special orders only - English furniture, 17th-19th C and reproduction.* LOC: A52 Ashbourne/Derby. PARK: Easy. TEL: 0335 60005; fax - 0335 60121. SER: Restorations; cabinet makers; interior design; packers and shippers. VAT: Stan. *Trade Only.*

BRASSINGTON, Nr. Ashbourne

Knights Antiques
LAPADA
The Old Barn, Middle Lane. Open by appointment. *STOCK: 18th-19th C English furniture, paintings, needlework and decorative items.* TEL: 062 985 317. SER: Valuations.

BUXTON

The Antiques Warehouse
25 Lightwood Rd. (N.F. Thompson). Est. 1983. Open 10.30-4.30 or by appointment. SIZE: Large. *STOCK: Furniture, mainly mahogany, 17th-20th C; paintings, smalls, Victorian brass and iron beds.* LOC: Off A6. PARK: Own. TEL: 0298 72967; home - 0298 871932. SER: Valuations; restorations; buys at auction.

Aquarius Antiques
3A Church St. (I. Sugden and P. Laughton). Est. 1989. Open 9-5. SIZE: Small. *STOCK: Brown furniture and pine, 19th C, £75-£450; bric-a-brac, 50p-£80.* LOC: From market, follow High St, turn

Buxton continued
into Church St., shop next to White Swan. PARK: Limited. TEL: 0298 72209; home - same. SER: Restorations (mainly furniture).

G. and J. Antiques
George St. (G. and J. Claessens). Est. 1964. Open 10-5, Sat. 10-1, Sun. and Sat. p.m. by appointment. SIZE: Large. STOCK: Furniture, Georgian, Victorian and continental, clocks and bronzes, from £500+. LOC: Town centre, on roundabout near Palace Hotel. PARK: Opposite. TEL: 0298 72198; home - 0298 25597. SER: Valuations. VAT: Stan/Spec.

Lewis Antiques
64 Fairfield Rd. (J. and S. Lewis). Resident. Open 10.30-5, other times by appointment. CL: Mon. and Wed. STOCK: General antiques, furniture, smalls, linen, collectables. TEL: 0298 78648.

The Penny Post Antiques
9 Cavendish Circus. (D. and R. Hammond). Est. 1978. Open 10-4.30, Sat. 10-5. CL: Mon. and Wed. SIZE: Small. STOCK: Furniture, 18th to early 20th C, £100-£600; commemoratives and crested china, £5-£75; general antiques. LOC: Town centre, opposite Palace Hotel. PARK: Easy. TEL: Home - 0298 25965.

West End Galleries
8 Cavendish Circus. (A. and A. Needham). Est. 1955. Open 9-5. CL: Sat. SIZE: Large. STOCK: French, Dutch, English furniture; clocks, paintings, works of art, bronzes. LOC: A6. PARK: Easy. TEL: 0298 24546. VAT: Stan/Spec.

What Now Antiques
Cavendish Arcade, The Crescent. (L. Carruthers). Open 10.30-5, Sun. 2-5. STOCK: General antiques and collectables including 19th-20th C pottery, especially Moorcroft and Art Deco; cranberry glass, die-cast toys, jewellery, textiles, watercolours, Victorian and Edwardian furniture, £1-£1,500. TEL: 0298 27178/23417. SER: Valuations.

CHAPEL-EN-LE-FRITH
The Clock House
48 Manchester Rd. (A.W. Thom). MBHI. Resident. Est. 1973. Open 10-6 including Sun. SIZE: Small. STOCK: Clocks, general antiques and jewellery, £5-£5,000. LOC: Turn off A6 at town by-pass. PARK: Easy. TEL: 0298 815174; fax - 0298 816192. SER: Valuations; restorations and repairs (clocks); mail order video cataloguing; producer of instructional horology videos.

CHESTERFIELD
Polly Coleman Antiques
424 Chatsworth Rd, Brampton. Est. 1981. Open Thurs. and Fri. 11-4.30, Sat. 2-5. SIZE: Small. STOCK: Pictures, prints and watercolours, etchings, £50-£350; small furniture, unusual chairs, £150-£250; porcelain, £100-£150; all late 19th C to 1930's. LOC: A619 to Chatsworth House from Chesterfield. PARK: Adjacent, down Old Chapel Lane. TEL: 0246 278146; home - 0246 202225. SER: Valuations; restorations (upholstery); picture framing; buys at auction (pictures and prints).

Anthony D. Goodlad
26 Fairfield Rd, Brockwell. Est. 1974. Open by appointment only. STOCK: General militaria. LOC: Close to town centre. PARK: Easy. TEL: 0246 204004.

Hackney House Antiques
Hackney Lane, Barlow. (Mrs J.M. Gorman). Resident. STOCK: Furniture, 18th-19th C; silver, prints, jewellery, clocks. TEL: 0742 890248. VAT: Stan/Spec.

Ian Morris
479 Chatsworth Rd. Est. 1967. Open 9-5, Sat. 9-1. SIZE: Medium. STOCK: Furniture, 19th to early 20th C, £100-£1,000; pictures, small items. LOC: Main road A619, to Baslow and Chatsworth House. TEL: 0246 235120. SER: Valuations. VAT: Stan/Spec.

Times Past
13 Chatsworth Rd. (Les Lewis). Est. 1977. Open 10-5. CL: Wed. SIZE: Small. STOCK: Furniture, porcelain, clocks, pictures and prints, 18th-19th C, to £2,000. LOC: Town end of Chatsworth Road, opposite B & Q superstore. PARK: Opposite. TEL: 0246 557077. SER: Valuations; restorations (furniture and paintings). VAT: Spec.

Brian Yates Antiques
420 Chatsworth Rd, Brampton. Est. 1977. Open 10-5. SIZE: Medium. STOCK: Country furniture mainly 17th-18th C, £100-£5,000; boxes, £50-£500, porcelain, copper and brass, £10-£300. PARK: Own. TEL: 0246 220395. SER: Restorations (furniture); cane and rush seating; upholstery; handmade reproductions. VAT: Stan/Spec.

DERBY
Abbey House
115 Woods Lane. (Shirley White). Resident. Est 1959. Open by appointment. STOCK: Dolls, teddy bears and all things juvenile. TEL: 0332 31426 fax - same. SER: Repairs (dolls and teddies); restorations (furniture).

Corry's Antiques
52-56 Curzon St. (E.I. Corry). Est. 1954. Open 9-5. CL: Wed. p.m. SIZE: Medium. STOCK: 18th-19th C furniture, fine art, silver and china. TEL 0332 364480. VAT: Spec.

Derby Antique Centre
11 Friargate. (D. Foddy and J. Parkin). Est. 1975 Open 10-5.30, Sun. a.m. by appointment. SIZE

Frederick Miller. Chelsea. Very late red lacquer clock. A silvered dial is unusual with lacquer. Circa 1820. From *The Georgian Bracket Clock, 1714-1830* by Richard C.R. Barder, published in 1993 by the **Antique Collectors' Club**, £45.00.

DERBYSHIRE

Derby continued

Large. STOCK: *Furniture, clocks, porcelain, 18th-19th C, £25-£3,000; silver and jewellery, 19th-20th C, £5-£500; dolls and toys, cameras, linen, pictures, pine, copper and brass.* LOC: Close to city centre and inner ring road. PARK: Restricted and 200yds. TEL: 0332 385002; home - 0332 841331. SER: Restorations (furniture and clocks). VAT: Stan/Spec.

Friargate Pine and Antiques Centre
The Pump House, Friargate Wharf, Stafford St. Entrance. (N. J. Marianski). Open 9-5. STOCK: *Victorian pine and general antiques.* TEL: 0332 41215.

Laura's Bookshop
58 Osmaston Rd. Est. 1969. CL: Mon. and Wed. STOCK: *Antiquarian and secondhand books, antiquarian maps and prints, especially local history and topography.* PARK: Own. TEL: 0332 47094. VAT: Stan.

Tanglewood
142 Ashbourne Rd., and warehouse - Brittania Mills, Markeaton St. (R. Beech). Est. 1979. Open Thurs., Fri. and Sat. 10-5, other times by appointment; warehouse open daily. SIZE: Large. STOCK: *Country pine, from Britain and Eire, 18th-19th C.* LOC: A52. PARK: Easy. TEL: 0332 46005/203851; home - 0335 42663. VAT: Stan.

Charles H. Ward
12 Friar Gate. (M.G. Ward). CL: Wed. p.m. STOCK: *Oil paintings, 19th-20th C; watercolours.* TEL: 0332 42893. SER: Restorations.

DOVERIDGE

Pine Antiques
Bell Farm, Yelt Lane. (M.A. and A. Groves). Open Wed.-Sat. 9-5.30, Sun. 12.30-4.30, other times by appointment. STOCK: *English pine and satinwood furniture, pottery, linen and kitchenalia.* TEL: 0889 564898.

DRONFIELD

Bardwell Antiques
51 Chesterfield Rd. (S. Bardwell). Open 9-5. STOCK: *General antiques.* TEL: 0246 412183.

DUFFIELD, Nr. Derby

Wayside Antiques
62 Town St. (Mrs J. Harding). Est. 1975. STOCK: *Furniture, 18th-19th C, £50-£2,000; porcelain, pictures, boxes and silver.* TEL: 0332 840346. VAT: Stan/Spec.

GLOSSOP

Antiques for All
Old Chapel, 1 Shrewsbury St. (Mrs F. Hickmott). Est. 1980. Open 10-5, Sun. 1-5, other times by appointment. CL: Tues. and Wed. SIZE: Large. STOCK: *Ceramics, glass, furniture, collectors' items, 18th-20th C.* LOC: Take 3rd turning on

Glossop continued

right after traffic lights in town centre, travelling towards Manchester. PARK: Easy. TEL: 0457 866960.

G.L. Dean Antiques
131 High St. West, Glossop. (Graham L. and Joyce C. Dean). Est. 1985. Open Sat. and Fri. and Sun. from 1 p.m, other times by appointment. SIZE: Medium. STOCK: *Decorative and Arts and Crafts furniture, 19th C, £100-£5,000; carved oak furniture, 17th-19th C, £250-£5,000; marble sculptures, lighting, unusual decorative items, 18th-19th C, £25-3,000.* PARK: Easy. TEL: 0457 855694; home - 0457 765562. SER: Valuations. VAT: Stan/Spec.

Derbyshire Clocks
104 High St. West. (J.A. and T.P. Lees). Est. 1975. CL: Tues. STOCK: *Clocks.* TEL: 0457 862677. SER: Restorations (clocks and barometers).

Glossop Antique Centre
Brookfield. (E. and M. Annal). Open Thurs.-Sun. 10-5. SIZE: 14 dealers. STOCK: *General antiques.* LOC: Opposite Ford Garage, on A57. PARK: Easy. TEL: 0457 863904. SER: Valuations; restorations.

Old Cross Gallery
16 Henry St. (Norfolk Square). (Mrs A. Lawson) Est. 1989. Open Wed.-Sat. 10-5, Sun. 2-5, or by appointment. SIZE: Medium. STOCK: *Country furniture, pictures, mirrors, objets d'art, mainly Victorian and Edwardian.* Not Stocked: China silver and jewellery. PARK: Nearby. TEL: 0457 854052.

GRASSMOOR, Nr. Chesterfield

N. and C.A. Haslam
220 Chesterfield Rd. Open by appointment STOCK: *17th-19th C furniture and decorative items.* TEL: 0246 853672 (24 hrs). SER: Buys at auction and on commission. VAT: Stan/Spec.

HAYFIELD, Nr. New Mills

Michael Allcroft Antiques
1 Church St. Open Sat. 12-5, Sun. 11-5, other times by appointment. STOCK: *Pine furniture and decorative items.* TEL: 0663 742684.

HEANOR

Bygones
23c Derby Rd. (Mrs P. Buttifant). Open 10-5. CL Mon. and Wed. STOCK: *Furniture, porcelain objets d'art, paintings and prints.* TEL: 077 768503. SER: Framing.

ILKESTON

Matsell Antiques Ltd
(B. and P. Matsell). Est. 1945. Open by appointment only. STOCK: *English furniture and decorative objects.* LOC: Close to M1, junctio

DERBYSHIRE

Ilkeston continued
25 or 26. TEL: 0602 302446. SER: Specialist photography for antiques/art; buys on commission. FAIRS: British International, Birmingham, Kenilworth, City of London, Buxton, Harrogate, Kensington, Café Royal. VAT: Stan/Spec.

KILLAMARSH
Havenplan's Architectural Emporium
The Old Station, Station Rd. Est. 1972. Open 10-4. CL: Mon. SIZE: Large. *STOCK: Architectural fittings and decorative items, church interiors and furnishings, fireplaces, doors, decorative cast ironwork and masonry, 18th to early 20th C.* LOC: M1, exit 30. Take A616 towards Sheffield, turn right on to B6053, turn right on to B6058 towards Killamarsh, turn right between two railway bridges. PARK: Easy. TEL: 0742 489972; home - 0246 433315. SER: Hire.

LONG EATON
Goodacre Engraving Ltd
Thrumpton Ave, (off Chatsworth Ave.), Meadow Lane. Est. 1948. *STOCK: Longcase and bracket clock movements, parts and castings.* TEL: 0602 734387. SER: Hand engraving, movement repairs, silvering and dial repainting. VAT: Stan.

Miss Elany
2 Salisbury St. (D. and Mrs Mottershead). Est. 1977. Open 9-5. SIZE: Medium. *STOCK: Pianos, 1900 to date, £50-£500; general antiques, Victorian and Edwardian, £25-£200.* PARK: Easy. TEL: 0602 734835. VAT: Stan.

MATLOCK
J.H.S. Antiques
Cavendish Lodge, Wolds Rise. (J.H. Snodin). Resident. Est. 1972. Open by appointment. SIZE: Medium. *STOCK: Furniture, collectables and decorative items, 17th to early 19th C, £40-£2,000.* LOC: 1/4 mile off A632, off Cavendish Rd. PARK: Easy. TEL: 0629 584624; home - same. SER: Valuations. FAIRS: Newark; Bingley Hall, Stafford. VAT: Spec.

MONYASH, Nr. Bakewell
Mrs A. Robinson
Chapel St. Est. 1961. Open Sat., Sun. and Mon. 2-6, or by appointment. *STOCK: Oak, mahogany, porcelain, collectors' items, £1-£1,000.* TEL: 062 981 2926.

NEW MILLS
Regent House Antiques
8 Buxton Rd, New Town. Open 10.30-5, Sat. 2-5, or by appointment. CL: Fri. SIZE: Medium. *STOCK: General antiques, period furniture, clocks; copper, brass, decorative items.* PARK: Easy. TEL: 0663 742684. VAT: Stan/Spec.

SHARDLOW, Nr. Derby
Shardlow Antiques Warehouse
24 The Wharf. Open 10.30-5; viewing Sun. p.m. CL: Fri. SIZE: Large. *STOCK: Furniture, Georgian to shipping.* LOC: Off M1, junction 24. PARK: Own. TEL: 0332 792899/662899.

TICKNALL
Sam Savage Antiques
Hayes Farm, Main St. (S. and M. Savage). Resident. Est. 1969. Open 10.30-5.30. CL: Mon. *STOCK: Early period furniture, 17th-19th C; decorative items, Oriental rugs, paintings.* LOC: Centre of Ticknall, on A514, 4 miles from Ashby-de-la-Zouch, 10 miles west from exit 24, M1 and 6 miles east of Ashby turn-off on M42. PARK: Easy. TEL: 0332 862195. SER: Valuations. VAT: Stan/Spec.

WHALEY BRIDGE
Nimbus Antiques
Chapel Rd. (L.M. and H.C. Brobbin). Est. 1978. Open 9-6, Sun. 2-6. SIZE: Large. *STOCK: Furniture, mainly mahogany, and longcase clocks, 18th-19th C, £500-£2,000.* LOC: A6. PARK: Easy. TEL: 0663 734248; home - 0663 733332. SER: Valuations; restorations. VAT: Stan/Spec.

WINSTER, Nr. Matlock
Winster Arts
Kirby House, Main St. (G. William). Est. 1981. Open 10.30-6 including Sun., Sat. 10-6.30. SIZE: Seven small galleries. *STOCK: General antiques and collectables including ceramics, glass and Oriental, mainly 19th-20th C, £5-£250.* LOC: B5057, 2 miles west of A6 at Darley Dale. PARK: Easy. TEL: 0629 650716; home - same. SER: Restorations (ceramics and furniture). FAIRS: Local.

WOODVILLE
Wooden Box Antiques
32 High St. (Mrs R. Bowler). Est. 1982. Open 10-5 including some Sun. SIZE: Medium. *STOCK: Furniture, Georgian-Edwardian, £75-£400; writing boxes, tea caddies and mirrors, Georgian-Victorian, £50-£150; country pine furniture, Georgian-Edwardian, £30-£450.* LOC: A50, between Ashby de la Zouch and Burton-on-Trent. PARK: Easy. TEL: 0283 212014; home - same. SER: Restorations (furniture); buys at auction (furniture). FAIRS: Some local.

YEAVELEY, Nr. Ashbourne
Gravelly Bank Pine Antiques
(Mr and Mrs Brassington). Open every day including evenings. *STOCK: Pine, 18th-19th C, £50-£500.* PARK: Easy. TEL: 0335 330237; home - same. SER: Valuations; restorations (pine); buys at auction.

Devonshire

NORTH ↑

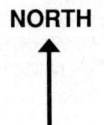

(Map of Devonshire showing towns and roads, bordered by Cornwall to the west and Somerset to the east.)

Towns shown: Lynton, Combe Martin, Woolacombe, Braunton, Barnstaple, Instow, Bideford, South Molton, Bampton, Merton, Chulmleigh, Riddlecombe, Witheridge, Tiverton, Cullompton, Stockland, Kentisbeare, Monkton, Dulford, Honiton, Hatherleigh, Jacobstowe, Morchard Bishop, Holsworthy, Okehampton, Newton St. Cyres, Exeter, Topsham, Woodbury, Sidmouth, East Budleigh, Budleigh Salterton, Bradstone, Lydford, Chagford, Moretonhampstead, Bovey Tracey, Exmouth, Tavistock, Horrabridge, Ashburton, Newton Abbot, Teignmouth, Shaldon, Maidencombe, Torquay, Littlehempston, South Brent, Totnes, Paignton, Brixham, Plymouth, Harbertonford, Modbury, Dartmouth, Kingswear, Kingsbridge, Salcombe.

Key to number of shops in this area.
- ○ 1-2
- ⊖ 3-5
- ⬤ 6-12 (half)
- ● 13+

Please note this is only a rough m[ap]
designed to show dealers the num[ber of]
shops in the various towns, and is [not]
necessarily totally accurate.

Devonshire

ASHBURTON
Ashburton Marbles
Great Hall, North Street. (Adrian Ager). Est. 1976. Open 8-5. CL: Sat. p.m. SIZE: Warehouse and showroom. *STOCK: Marble and wooden fire-surrounds, decorative cast iron interiors; scuttles, fenders, overmantels, 1790-1910; architectural and decorative antiques.* PARK: Easy. TEL: 0364 53189; fax - 0364 54075.

Moor Antiques
19a North St. (T. and Mrs E. Gatland). Est. 1984. CL Wed. p.m. SIZE: Small. *STOCK: Small furniture, 1780-1900, £200-£700; clocks, 1830-1910, £100-£400; silver and china, 1800-1900, £25-£150.* LOC: A38 town centre, 100 yards past town hall. PARK: Nearby. TEL: 0364 53767. SER: Valuations; restorations (clocks, and furniture re-polishing).

The Shambles
22 North St. Est. 1982. Open 10-5, Sat. 10-1. SIZE: 6 dealers. *STOCK: General antiques, 18th C to art deco, £5-£1,000.* LOC: Town centre. PARK: Opposite. TEL: 0364 53848. SER: Valuations. FAIRS: Little Chelsea, Sandown and Kensington Brocante. VAT: Stan/Spec.

AXMINSTER
W.G. Potter and Son
West St. Est. 1863. Open 9-5. CL: Sat. p.m.

Axminster continued
SIZE: Medium. *STOCK: Furniture and clocks, 18th-20th C, £50-£5,000; china, £5-£500.* LOC: In main street (A35) opposite church. PARK: Easy. TEL: 0297 32063. SER: Restorations (furniture); buys at auction. VAT: Stan/Spec.

BAMPTON, Nr. Tiverton
Bampton Antiques
9 Castle St. (V.H. Strange and J.M. Yendell). Est. 1983. Open Thurs., Fri. and Sat. 10.30-5, other days by appointment. SIZE: Medium. *STOCK: Furniture including country, porcelain, glass, collectables, fine art.* LOC: B3227 from Taunton. PARK: Easy. TEL: 0398 331658. SER: Valuations.

Robert Byles
7 Castle St. Est. 1966. Open Mon., Wed. and Fri.2-5, or by knocking or appointment. *STOCK: Early oak, local farmhouse tables and settles, metalwork, pottery, unstripped period pine, architectural items.* TEL: 0398 331515. SER: Restoration materials. VAT: Stan/Spec.

BARNSTAPLE
Artavia Gallery
80 Boutport St. (P.J. Newcombe). Est. 1972. Open 9.30-5. CL: Wed. p.m. SIZE: Medium. *STOCK: Maps, prints, photographs, oils and watercolours, £1-£500.* TEL: 0271 71025. SER: Picture framing, mounting. VAT: Stan.

An Antique Collectors' Club Title

The Antique Collectors' Club has produced this handsome hard cover address book, lavishly illustrated with photographs taken from its bestselling publication **Dog Painting 1840-1940: A Social History of the Dog in Art** by William Secord, an acknowledged expert on the subject of dog painting and former director of The Dog Museum of America.

Each illustration carries details of the breed, artist and date, and the book is interspersed with pertinent and lively phrases and quotations to bring to life the world of dogs. A preface by William Secord puts the genre of dog painting in its true perspective.
**ISBN 1 85149 164 3, 8 ¼ x 5 ⅞ in., 160pp
80 in colour, £9.50 (incl. VAT)**

Available from:
Antique Collectors' Club, 5 Church Street, Woodbridge, Suffolk IP12 1DS
Tel: (0394) 385501 Fax: (0394) 384434

or Market Street Industrial Park, Wappingers' Falls, New York 12590, USA
Tel: 914 297 0003 Fax: 914 297 0068

DEVONSHIRE

Barnstaple continued

Barnstaple Antique Centre
23 Boutport St. Open 10-5. SIZE: Large. *STOCK: Stripped pine, oak and mahogany, 18th-19th C, £75-£2,000.* PARK: Easy. TEL: 0271 327323. VAT: Stan.

Nostalgia
48B Bear St. (A. and C. Pickersgill). Est. 1982. Open 10-4. CL: Wed. SIZE: Small. *STOCK: Clothes and accessories, linen and lace, ceramics including royal and political commemoratives, small furniture, glass and pottery, 19th-20th C, £5-£500.* LOC: Close to junction with Boutport St. PARK: Nearby. TEL: Home - 0271 73751.

Mark Parkhouse Antiques and Jewellery
106 High St. Est. 1976. CL: Wed. *STOCK: Jewellery, furniture, silver, paintings, clocks, glass, porcelain, small collectors' items, 18th-19th C, £100-£10,000.* PARK: Nearby. TEL: 0271 74504. SER: Valuations; buys at auction. VAT: Stan/Spec.

Tudor House
115 Boutport St. (C. and D. Pilon). Est. 1980. Open 9.30-3.30, Wed. 9.30-1. SIZE: Large. *STOCK: Furniture and bric-a-brac, late 18th C and reproduction.* LOC: Off M5, Tiverton link road to town centre. PARK: Easy. TEL: 0271 75370; home - 0271 71750. SER: Valuations; restorations (furniture).

BIDEFORD

Acorn Antiques
11 Rope Walk. (G. Crump). Open 9-5. CL: Wed. p.m. *STOCK: Furniture and collectables.* TEL: 0237 470177. SER: Restorations.

Century Galleries
7 Cooper St. (Thomas Williams Antiques Ltd.). *STOCK: General antiques, jewellery, silverware, china.* TEL: 0237 477245. VAT: Stan/Spec.

J. Collins and Son   LAPADA
The Studio, 63 and 28 High St. (J. and P. Biggs). Est. 1953. Open 9.30-5, trade by appointment. SIZE: Large. *STOCK: Period oak and mahogany furniture; general antiques including framed and restored 19th-20th C oils and watercolours.* LOC: From Bideford Old Bridge turn right, then first left into the High St. PARK: Easy. TEL: 0237 473103; home - 0237 476485; fax - 0237 475658. SER: **Valuations; restorations (period furniture, paintings and watercolours); cleaning and framing; buys at auction.** VAT: Stan/Spec.

Medina Gallery
20 Mill St. (R. Jennings). Est. 1973. Open 9.30-5. CL: Wed. p.m. SIZE: Small. *STOCK: Maps and prints, photographs, oils, watercolours, £1-£500.* PARK: Easy. TEL: 0237 476483. SER: Picture framing, mounting. VAT: Stan.

Bideford continued

Petticombe Manor Antiques
Petticombe Manor, Monkleigh. (O. Wilson). Est. 1971. Open daily until 7 p.m. SIZE: Large. *STOCK: Furniture including dining tables and chairs, desks and bureaux, bookcases and display cabinets, Pembroke and Sutherland tables; china, glass, brass and copper, oils and watercolours, prints and mirrors, hand-stripped pine, mainly 19th to early 20th C.* LOC: Large manor house on A388 Bideford to Holsworthy road. PARK: Own. TEL: 0237 475605; home - same. SER: Restorations (re-upholstery, French polishing, cabinet work). VAT: Stan.

Red House Antiques
25-26 Bridgeland St. (L. Turner). Est. 1983. Open 10-1 and 2-5, Sun. by appointment. CL: Wed. SIZE: Small. *STOCK: Furniture, £100-£1,000; collectables, £5-£100; all 1830-1930.* LOC: Off the quay, shop half way up on left. PARK: Easy. TEL: 0237 470686; home - same. SER: Valuations.

Riverside Antiques
Market Place. (S. Duncan). Open 9-1 and 2-5. CL: Wed. p.m. in winter. *STOCK: General antiques especially porcelain.* TEL: 0237 471043.

Scudders Emporium
Bridge St. (M.B. Chambers). Open 9.30-6. SIZE: Warehouse. *STOCK: General antiques and collectables, to 1940's, £5-£1,500.* PARK: Easy. TEL: 0237 479567; home - 0237 451665. SER: Valuations; restorations; buys at auction.

BOVEY TRACEY

Thomas and James Antiques
St Margaret's House, 6A Station Rd. (Philip Thomas and Anthony J. Mulligan). Est. 1969. Open 10-5, Sat. 10-1, or by appointment. SIZE: Medium. *STOCK: Furniture especially oak, 17th-19th C, to £5,000; English pottery, mainly 18th to early 19th C, to £500; decorative items and works of art, 18th-20th C, to £1,000.* LOC: Off A38 at Drum Bridges exit, across first roundabout, turn right at 2nd, shop 100 yards on left. PARK: Easy. TEL: 0626 835350; home - 0647 40001 and 0404 822146. SER: Valuations; restorations (furniture and ceramics); buys at auction (furniture and ceramics). VAT: Stan/Spec.

BRAUNTON

Eileen Cooper Antiques
Challoners Rd. (Mrs M. Chugg). Est. 1952. Open 10.30-1 and 2-4 or by appointment, but prior telephone call advisable. CL: Usually Wed. p.m. and Mon. SIZE: Small. *STOCK: General antiques and collectable items including silver, jewellery, paintings, prints, lace, fine linen, christening gowns, embroideries, textiles, pottery, furniture. Not Stocked: Coins, medals.* LOC: From Barnstaple

J. Collins and Son
(Established 1953)

ANTIQUES AND FINE PAINTINGS

The Studio • 63 High Street • Bideford
North Devon • EX39 2AN
Tel: Bideford (0237) 473103 • Fax: (0237) 475658
Opening hours - Monday-Saturday 9.30am-5pm
TRADE BY APPOINTMENT PLEASE

LAPADA MEMBER

With the opening of the North Devon Link Road (A361) we are now 40 minutes from the M5 motorway. Take Exit 27 to Bideford Bridge, at roundabout go left, follow road to the quayside, turn right up High Street with National Westminster Bank on the corner, three quarters to the top, parking outside premises for 30 minutes or in long term car park, 3 minutes walk.

Five extensive showrooms specialising in 17th and 18th Century Oak, Georgian and Regency furniture with two galleries of Victorian oil paintings and watercolours. Our entire stock is on photographic record. Colour photographs are available for clients requiring that 'specific item'.

Why not give us a phone call!
Skilled Restoration of Period Furniture Undertaken for Clients both Private and Trade.

NEW GALLERY
PRISCILLA HULL

**Abele Tree House
9 Fore Street
Budleigh Salterton, Devon
Phone Budleigh Salterton
(0395) 443768**

*Fine Art Specialists
Paintings, Watercolours and
Drawings
Maps and Prints
Sculpture and Studio Pottery*

Open Tuesday—Saturday 10—5
and by appointment

*Spring, Summer and Autumn exhibitions
Framing, Valuations*

Braunton continued

across traffic lights at Braunton (6 miles), then 200yds. on right. PARK: Easy. TEL: 0271 813320/816005.

Timothy Coward Fine Silver
Marisco, Saunton. Open by appointment. STOCK: *Antique and early 20th C silver.* TEL: 0271 890466.

BRIXHAM
John Prestige Antiques
1 and 2 Greenswood Court. Est. 1971. Open 8.45-6. CL: Sat. and Sun. except by appointment. SIZE: Large + warehouse. STOCK: *Period and Victorian furniture; shipping goods.* TEL: 0803 856141; home - 0803 853739; fax - 0803 851649. VAT: Stan/Spec.

BUDLEIGH SALTERTON
New Gallery
Abele Tree House, 9 Fore St. (Mrs P. Hull). Est. 1968. Open 10-5 or by appointment. CL: Sun. and Mon. except by appointment. SIZE: Large. STOCK: *Fine art, oil paintings, watercolour drawings, prints from 17th C to modern signed proofs, maps and sculpture.* PARK: Adjacent. TEL: 0395 443768. SER: Valuations; framing.

Budleigh Salterton continued

The Old Antique Shop
15 Fore St. (C. and A. Gosling). Est. 1981. Open 10-12.30 and 1.30-5. CL: Thurs. SIZE: Medium. STOCK: *Furniture, 18th-19th C, £100-£1,300; china, early 19th to early 20th C, £20-£300.* LOC: Sea end of town. PARK: Easy. TEL: 0395 444040; home - 0395 271451. SER: Valuations. FAIRS: Shepton Mallet.

Quinney's
High St. (Miss A. Fearfield). Est. 1947. Open 9.15-12.45, afternoons by appointment. CL: Thurs. STOCK: *Furniture, porcelain, silver, glass.* PARK: Easy. TEL: 0395 442793. SER: Valuations; minor restorations. VAT: Spec.

David J. Thorn
2 High St. Est. 1950. Open Tues. and Fri. 10-1 and 2.15-5.30, Sat. 10-1. SIZE: Small. STOCK: *English, continental and Oriental pottery and porcelain, 1620-1850, £5-£5,000; English furniture, 1680-1870, £20-£5,000; paintings, silver, jewellery, £1-£1,000.* PARK: Easy. TEL: 0395 442448. SER: Valuations. VAT: Stan/Spec.

CHAGFORD
John Meredith
41 New St, and The Square. (J. and A. Meredith). Est. 1979. Open every day 9-1 and 2-5 or by appointment. SIZE: Large. STOCK: *Mahogany, 18th-19th C, £25-£2,000; country oak, 16th-19th C, £5-£1,000; Oriental brass and copper, swords and weapons, large unusual items and large architectural building items.* LOC: 50yds. right of church. PARK: Easy. TEL: 0647 433474; home - 0647 433405. SER: Buys at auction. VAT: Stan/Spec.

Mary Payton Antiques
The Old Market House. (Mrs M. Payton). Est. 1968. Open 10-1 and 2.30-5. CL: Wed. and Mon. SIZE: Small. STOCK: *English pottery and porcelain especially Staffordshire, English glass, 18th-19th C; maps and prints (West Country), 17th-19th C.* Not Stocked: Jewellery, firearms, coins, silver, pewter. LOC: Coming from Whiddon Down (A30) by A382, turn right at Easton Court. Shop in the town square. PARK: Easy. TEL: 0647 432428; home -0647 432388.

Whiddons Antiques and Tearooms
6 High St. (D. Meldrum). Est. 1979. Open 9.30-5.30. SIZE: Medium. STOCK: *General and country items - furniture including pine, clocks, prints, paintings, copper, brass, books and bric-a-brac.* LOC: Opposite church. PARK: Easy. TEL: 0647 433406; home - 0647 433303.

COLYTON
Brookfield Gallery
Market Place. CL: Wed. STOCK: *Furniture, including pine; clocks, prints and pictures.* TEL: 0297 553541.

JOHN PRESTIGE ANTIQUES

1 & 2 GREENSWOOD COURT, GREENSWOOD ROAD
BRIXHAM, DEVON

TEL: 0803 856141
FAX: 0803 851649

∽

We are one of the largest stockists of Period, Victorian and Better Shipping Furniture in the West Country.

∽

We sell furniture suitable for most markets from our two "Trade Only" warehouses — an interesting stock which changes daily.

∽

If you are not already a regular customer — call and see us — you'll soon become one!

Colyton continued
Colyton Antique Centre
Dolphin St. Open 10-5. SIZE: 22 dealers. STOCK: *General antiques and collectables.* PARK: Easy. TEL: 0297 552339.

COMBE MARTIN, Nr. Ilfracombe
Retrospect Antiques
Sunnymede, King St. Est. 1976. Open 9.15-1. STOCK: *General antiques and bric-a-brac.* TEL: 0271 882346.

CULLOMPTON
Cobweb Antiques
The Old Tannery, Exeter Rd. (R. Holmes). Est. 1980. Open 10-5.30. SIZE: Large. STOCK: *Pine and country furniture, painted, decorative and mahogany items, £5-£2,000.* LOC: Half a mile from juction 28, M5. PARK: Easy. TEL: 0884 38207 and 0395 279253. SER: Stripping; restorations; packing; courier. VAT: Stan/Spec.

Cullompton Old Tannery Antiques
Exeter Rd. (Cullompton Antiques Ltd.). Est. 1989. Open 10-5.30, Sat. and Sun. 10-5. SIZE: Large. STOCK: *Pine, oak, mahogany and fruitwood country furniture; china and decorative items.* LOC: Off M5, junction 28, through town centre, premises on right, approximately 1 mile. PARK: Easy. TEL: 0884 38476. VAT: Stan/Spec.

Mills Antiques
The Old Tannery, Exeter Rd. Est. 1979. Open 10-5.30, Sat. and Sun. 10-5. STOCK: *17th C to Edwardian furniture and decorative items.* PARK: Easy. TEL: 0884 32462. VAT: Stan/Spec.

Sunset Country Antiques
The Old Tannery, Exeter Rd. (R.J. and S.E. Reeves). Est. 1981. Open 9.30-5.30. CL: Sat p.m. SIZE: Medium. STOCK: *Furniture - English pine and country especially painted, and decorative items, bric-a-brac and kitchenalia, £10-£2,000.* LOC: M5, junction 28. PARK: Easy. TEL: Home - 0884 32890. SER: Valuations; restorations (stripping and finishing pine).

DARTMOUTH
Chantry Bookshop and Gallery
11 Higher St. (M.P. Merkel). Est. 1969. Open 10.30-5. CL: 15th Jan to 20th Mar. SIZE: Small. STOCK: *Books, 19th-20th C; antiquarian prints, maps, town plans and sea charts; all £5-£1,000.* LOC: Next to 'The Cherub' public house. PARK: Nearby. TEL: 0803 832796; home - 0803 834208.

DREWSTEIGNTON, Nr. Exeter
Peter J. Baldwin Antiques
East Fursham. Resident. Est. 1977. Open by appointment. SIZE: Medium. STOCK: *Furniture - country and pine, 18th-19th C, £50-£2,500; North*

Drewsteignton continued
Devon pottery, 19th-20th C, £2-£250; collectables, 18th-20th C, £5-£500. LOC: Telephone for directions. PARK: Easy. TEL: 064 723 468; home - same. SER: Valuations; restorations (furniture, hand stripping and repair); buys at auction (as stock). *Trade Only.* .

Taylor-Halsey Antiques
Upperton Farm. (M. and R. Halsey). STOCK: *Early oak and country furniture, 17th to early 19th C, £50-£3,000; walnut and other 18th C furniture, £100-£4,000; secondhand and out-of-print books on collecting and vernacular architecture, £1-£200.* TEL: 0647 21691. SER: Valuations; buys at auction. VAT: Stan/Spec.

DULFORD, Nr. Cullompton
G. Mounter
Bakers Farm. Usually open, prior telephone call advisable. STOCK: *Painted country and formal furniture, early and primitive Windsor chairs; unstripped pine.* TEL: 08846 358. *Trade Only.*

EAST BUDLEIGH
Antiques at Budleigh House
Budleigh House. (W. Cook). Est. 1982. Open 10-5, Sat. 10-1. CL: Mon. and Wed. SIZE: Small. STOCK: *18th-19th C small furniture and decorative objects, porcelain, glass, silver and metalware, £5-£1,000.* LOC: Opposite Sir Walter Raleigh public house. PARK: Easy. TEL: 0395 445368; home - same. SER: Valuations; buys at auction.

EXETER
The Antique Centre on the Quay
The Quay. (Mrs P. Crosbie-Smith). Open 10-5 including Sun. SIZE: Several dealers. STOCK: *General antiques and books.* TEL: 0392 214180.

Wm. Bruford and Son Ltd   BADA
1 Bedford St. Est. 1894. Open 9.30-5.30. STOCK: **Jewellery and silver.** Not Stocked: China, glass, furniture, metalware. TEL: 0392 54901. SER: Valuations; restorations (clocks, silver and jewellery). VAT: Stan/Spec.

Coombe Street Galleries
Coombe St. (S. Raybould). Open 10-6 including Sun. SIZE: 9 dealers. STOCK: *Persian carpets and rugs; furniture, collectors' and decorative items, pictures.* TEL: 0392 496464.

Exeter Rare Books
Guildhall Shopping Centre. (R.C. Parry). ABA. Est. 1965. Open 10-1 and 2-5. SIZE: Small. STOCK: *Books, antiquarian, secondhand, out-of-print, 17th-20th C, £5-£500.* LOC: City centre. PARK: Easy. TEL: 0392 436021. SER: Valuations; buys at auction. FAIRS: ABA Chelsea, Bath and Edinburgh.

DEVONSHIRE

Exeter continued
Fagins Antiques
The Old Whiteways Cider Factory, Hele. (C.J. Strong). Open 9.15-5, Sat. 11-5. *STOCK: Furniture, decorative items, architectural and shipping items.* TEL: 0392 882062 and 0395 279660.

Gold and Silver Exchange
Eastgate House, Princesshay. *STOCK: Jewellery, watches including Rolex.* TEL: 0392 217478.

McBains of Exeter   LAPADA
Exeter Airport, Clyst Honiton. *STOCK: Furniture.* LOC: A30, 2 miles from exit 30, M5. Below are listed the dealers who are trading from this address. TEL: 0392 366261; fax - 0392 365572. *Trade Only.*

Ash Brothers Antiques
STOCK: Art deco, unstripped pine, shipping goods. TEL: 0392 364483. VAT: Stan.

Roy Jones & Son
STOCK: Shipping goods, pine, general antiques. TEL: 0392 823968. VAT: Stan.

McBains of Exeter
(I.S., G., R. and M. McBain). Est. 1963. Open 9-6, weekends by appointment. *STOCK: Furniture, period and Victorian; decorative and shipping goods.* TEL: 0392 366261; fax - 0392 365572.

Miscellany Antiques
STOCK: Shipping goods. TEL: 0392 366361.

Leon Robertson Antiques
STOCK: Furniture. TEL: 0392 366361.

Micawber Antiques
New Buildings Lane, 25-26 Gandy St. (Penny Standing). Est. 1984. Open 10-5. CL: Wed. p.m. SIZE: Small. *STOCK: China, pottery and clocks, 1840-1940, £10-£300; oil lamps, metalware, general antiques, £3-£200.* LOC: City centre. PARK: Nearby. TEL: 0392 52200. SER: Valuations; buys at auction (clocks).

Brian Mortimer
87 Queen St. CL: Wed. p.m. *STOCK: General antiques, jewellery, silver, Victoriana.* TEL: 0392 79994. VAT: Stan/Spec.

John Nathan Antiques
153/154 Cowick St, St. Thomas. (I. Doble). Est. 1950. Open 9-5.30. SIZE: Small. *STOCK: Silver and jewellery, £5-£5,000; clocks, including Georgian and Victorian, £25-£3,000.* LOC: From Exeter inner by-pass over new Exe Bridge, take A30 Okehampton Rd. under railway arch, shop on right. PARK: Easy. TEL: 0392 78216. SER: Valuations; restorations (silver and jewellery); buys at auction. VAT: Stan.

Pennies
Pennies Furniture Centre, Unit 2, Wessex Estate, Station Rd., Exwick. (Penelope and Michael

Exeter continued
Clark). Est. 1982. Open 9-6. SIZE: Medium. *STOCK: Furniture, from Victorian; china, glass and bric-a-brac, books.* LOC: Behind St. David's Station, over railway lines. PARK: Easy. TEL: 0392 71928/76532/216238. SER: Valuations. VAT: Stan/Spec.

Pirouette
5 West St. (L. Duriez). Open 10-5. *STOCK: Lace, shawls, babywear, linen, 1920's costume, Victorian and Edwardian bridal wear.* TEL: 0392 432643.

Priory Antiques
19/20 Friernhay St. Est. 1986. Open by appointment only. SIZE: Small. *STOCK: Oak, 17th-18th C; hardwood country furniture.* LOC: Off Fore St. PARK: Adjacent. TEL: 0392 495928.

The Quay Gallery Antiques Emporium
43 The Quay. (A. Nebbett). Est. 1984. Open 10-5. SIZE: Large - 9 dealers. *STOCK: Furniture, marine items, porcelain, silver and plate, decorative items.* LOC: Next to Old Customs House. PARK: Easy. TEL: 0392 213283.

Strip and Wax
Exe St. (David Challice). CL: Thurs. SIZE: Small. *STOCK: Furniture especially Welsh dressers, chests of drawers, tables, all 19th C, £50-£100.* LOC: From St. David's station, follow Bonhay Road to "Mill on the Exe" public house, premises opposite. PARK: Easy. TEL: 0392 52476. SER: Valuations; restorations (veneering, stripping, carcass rebuilding); buys at auction (Victorian pine).

Peter Wadham
5 Cathedral Close. Est. 1967. Open 9-5.30. SIZE: Large. *STOCK: English and decorative furniture, 1650-1850; glass, metalware, pottery and general collectors' items, local prints.* LOC: Centre of city, facing Cathedral, north tower. PARK: Own. TEL: 0392 439741. VAT: Spec.

EXMOUTH
Boase and Vaughan Antiques and Jewellery
5 High St. Est. 1965. Open 10-5. *STOCK: Jewellery, silver and small items for export.* LOC: Town centre. PARK: Easy. TEL: 0395 271528.

Treasures
32-34 Exeter Rd. (L. Treasure). Open 9-5. *STOCK: General antiques.* TEL: 0395 273258.

Wooden Fleece
21 Albion St. (Peter J. Baldwin). Est. 1977. Open 9.30-1 and 2-5.30. CL: Wed. SIZE: Small. *STOCK: Country and pine furniture, 18th-19th C, £50-£2,500; North Devon pottery, 19th-20th C, £5-£250; collectables, 18th-20th C, £5-£500.*

DEVONSHIRE

Exmouth continued
LOC: Town centre. PARK: Easy. TEL: Home - 064 723 468. SER: Valuations; restorations (furniture, hand stripping, repair); buys at auction (as stock).

HATHERLEIGH

Hatherleigh Antiques BADA
15 Bridge St. (S. and M. Dann). Open 9-1 and 2-5, anytime by appointment. CL: Wed. and Thurs. SIZE: Medium. *STOCK: Collectors' furniture and works of art, pre-1700.* PARK: Easy. TEL: 0837 810159; home - 0837 810500. SER: Courses in early furniture. VAT: Spec.

HOLSWORTHY

Victoria Antiques
Victoria Hill. (Bridget and Roger Nosworthy). Usually available but appointment advisable. SIZE: Showroom and warehouse. *STOCK: Furniture including period and decorative, and related items.* PARK: Easy. TEL: 0409 253815; home - 0288 81 548. SER: Valuations; restorations; buys at auction. VAT: Stan/Spec.

HONITON

The Antique Centre Abingdon House
136 High St. (M.V. Melliar-Smith and J.J. Butler). Est. 1985. Open 10-5. SIZE: Large - 15 dealers. *STOCK: General antiques including furniture, porcelain, 19th C watercolours, country and sporting items, luggage and woodworking tools.* LOC: Exeter end of High St. PARK: Nearby. TEL: 0404 42108.

J. Barrymore and Co
73-75 High St. (J. and M. Ogden). Est. 1979. Open 10-5, Thurs. by appointment only. SIZE: Medium. *STOCK: Silver, 17th-20th C, £100-£15,000; Old Sheffield plate, Victorian electroplate, £100-£4,000; jewellery, £150-£5,000; all 19th C to early 20th C.* LOC: Main st. PARK: Easy. TEL: 0404 42244. VAT: Stan/Spec.

Bramble Cross Antiques LAPADA
Exeter Rd. Open 10-5.30. *STOCK: 18th-19th C furniture, clocks and decorative items.* TEL: 0404 47085. VAT: Stan/Spec.

Roderick Butler BADA
Marwood House. Est. 1948. Open 9.30-5.30. SIZE: Large. *STOCK: Furniture, metalwork, works of art (unusual and interesting items), 17th to early 19th C.* LOC: Adjacent to roundabout at eastern end of High St. PARK: In courtyard. TEL: 0404 42169. VAT: Spec.

Christopher J. Button-Stephens Stable Antiques
Plympton House, 59 High St. Open 9.30-1 and 2-5. CL: Sat. p.m. and Thurs. SIZE: Medium. *STOCK: General antiques including copper and brass, from 1800.* LOC: Main St. PARK: Easy. TEL: 0404 42640. VAT: Stan/Spec.

Honiton continued

Fountain Antiques
132 High St. (J. Palmer and G. York). Open 9.30-5.30. *STOCK: General antiques including pictures, books and linen.* TEL: 0404 42074.

Elizabeth Gilmore Antiques LAPADA
126 High St. Open 10-5 or by appointment. SIZE: Large. *STOCK: Period oak, country furniture and paintings.* TEL: 0404 43565; home - 08847 233. SER: Restorations. VAT: Stan/Spec.

Honiton Antique Toys
38 High St. (L. and S. Saunders). Est. 1986. Open 10.30-5. CL: Mon. and Thurs. *STOCK: Toys, dolls and teddies.* PARK: Easy. TEL: 0404 41194.

Honiton Clock Clinic
167 High St. (David Newton). Est. 1992. Open 10-4. SIZE: Small. *STOCK: Clocks and barometers.* LOC: Exeter end of High St. PARK: Nearby. TEL: 0404 47466.

Honiton Fine Art
189 High St. (C.B. and P.R. Greenberg). Est. 1974. Open 9.30-5. SIZE: Medium. *STOCK: English watercolours and oil paintings, 18th-19th C, £300-£5,000; Old Master drawings, Dutch, Italian and French, 16th-18th C, £300-£1,500.* LOC: Town centre. PARK: Easy. TEL: 0404 45942. SER: Valuations; restorations (oil paintings).

Honiton Junction
159 High St. (J. Crackston). Est. 1986. Open 10-5.30. SIZE: Medium. *STOCK: Furniture, smalls.* PARK: Nearby. TEL: 0404 43436.

The Honiton Lace Shop
44 High St. Open 9.30-1 and 2-5. *STOCK: Lace including specialist and collectors; quilts, shawls and other textiles, bobbins and lace making equipment.* TEL: 0404 42416; fax - 0404 47797.

Honiton Old Bookshop
Felix House, 51 High St. (R. Collicott). Est. 1991. Open 10.30-5.30. *STOCK: Books - travel, childrens' illustrated; plate books and bindings; all £50-£500.* LOC: Main street. PARK: Easy. TEL: 0404 47180. SER: Catalogues available (2 annually). FAIRS: London PBFA. VAT: Stan.

House of Antiques
185 and 195 High St. (Kevin Wheeler-Johns and Ian Baum). Est. 1992. Open 10-5. SIZE: Large. *STOCK: Edwardian and Victorian furniture, general antiques.* LOC: Exeter end of High St. PARK: Nearby. TEL: 0404 41648; home - 0752 560711.

L.J. Huggett and Son
Stamps Building, King St. Open 9.30-5, Sat 9.30-1. SIZE: Large. *STOCK: Furniture, 18th-19th C.* TEL: 0404 42043; home - 0404 47117.

Honiton continued
Lombard Antiques
14 High St. (L. Lombard). Est. 1984. Open 10-5.30. SIZE: Small. *STOCK: 18th-19th C English furniture, porcelain and decorative items.* PARK: Easy. TEL: 0404 42140.

Otter Antiques
69 High St. (G.F. Wilkin). Open 9-5.30, Thurs. by appointment only. *STOCK: Silver and plate including cutlery and flatware.* TEL: 0404 42627.

Pilgrim Antiques
145 High St. (G. and J. Mills). Est. 1970. Open 9-5.30. SIZE: Large. *STOCK: Period furniture and longcase clocks.* PARK: Easy. TEL: 0404 41219 or 0404 45316/7. SER: Shipping. VAT: Stan/Spec.

Kenneth Sexton Antiques
"On the Level", 140 High St. Open 9.30-5.30. *STOCK: Country furniture and artefacts.* TEL: 0404 44224.

R. and D. Turner Antiques
122 High St. Est. 1972. Open 10-5. SIZE: Large. *STOCK: Edwardian, Victorian and Georgian furniture; paintings and general antiques.* LOC: Exeter end of High St. PARK: At rear for collection. TEL: 0404 46674; home - 0404 43187.

Upstairs, Downstairs
12 High St. Open 10-5.30. SIZE: Large. *STOCK: 18th-19th C furniture, porcelain, metalware, pictures and clocks.* PARK: Easy. TEL: 0404 44481.

Warehouse Antiques
126A High St. (Christine and Michael Bowyer). Est. 1992. Open 10-5. SIZE: Medium. *STOCK: Country pine and oak furniture; garden statuary.* LOC: Exeter end of High St. PARK: At rear. TEL: 0404 47381.

Wickham Antiques
191 High St. (J. and E. Waymouth). Est. 1986. Open 9.30-5.30. SIZE: Medium. *STOCK: Mahogany and oak country furniture, decorative items.* PARK: Easy. TEL: 0404 44654.

Geoffrey M. Woodhead
53 High St. Est. 1950. Open 9.30-5.30. SIZE: Medium. *STOCK: Books and unusual items.* Not Stocked: Coins, stamps, silver, plate. LOC: A30 opposite largest tree in street. PARK: Easy. TEL: 0404 42969. VAT: Stan/Spec.

HORRABRIDGE
Ye Olde Saddlers Shoppe
(R. Howes). Est. 1970. SIZE: Small. *STOCK: General antiques, furniture, clocks and watches, collectors' items.* LOC: 4 miles from Tavistock on A386. PARK: Easy - opposite or at rear of shop. TEL: 0822 852109.

ILFRACOMBE
Relics
113 High St. (Nicola D. Bradshaw). Resident. Est. 1977. Open 10-1 and 2-5, Thurs. 10-1. SIZE: Small. *STOCK: General antiques and small collectables, Victorian and Edwardian.* LOC: Opposite Post Office. PARK: Nearby. TEL: 0271 865486; home - same. SER: Valuations. VAT: Stan.

INSTOW
Porcupines Bookroom
(S. Lowe). Est. 1963. Open by appointment only. *STOCK: Books, 16th-20th C.* TEL: 0271 861158.

KENTISBEARE, Nr. Cullompton
Sextons
Dulford Cottage. (B.A. and F.B. Ward-Smith). Est. 1979. Open 9-6, Sat. and Sun. by appointment. SIZE: Medium. *STOCK: Country pine and oak, some mahogany, 1720-1900, £50-£2,000; reproduction dressers, £350-£1,200.* LOC: Telephone for directions. PARK: Easy. TEL: 088 46 429; home - same. VAT: Stan. *Trade Only.*

KINGSBRIDGE
Avon House Antiques/Hayward's Antiques
13 Church St. (D.H. and M.S. Hayward). Open 10-1 and 2-5. *STOCK: General antiques.* TEL: 0548 853718.

C. Hawkins Antiques
85 Fore St. Open 9.30-4.30. CL: Thurs. p.m. SIZE: Small. *STOCK: Furniture, art nouveau, general small items, £5-£500.* LOC: On A379 Plymouth-Dartmouth road, in one-way section, main street. PARK: Easy, nearby. TEL: 0548 856829.

Quay Antiques
The Promenade. (D.H. and M.S. Hayward). Open 10-1 and 2-5. *STOCK: General antiques and collectables.* TEL: 0548 856567.

KINGSWEAR, Nr. Dartmouth
David L.H. Southwick Rare Art BADA
Beacon Lodge, Beacon Lane. Open by appointment. *STOCK: Chinese and Japanese works of art.* TEL: **0803 752533;** fax - **0803 752535.**

LYDFORD, Nr. Okehampton
Skeaping Gallery
Townend House. Est. 1972. Open by appointment. *STOCK: Oils and watercolours.* TEL: 082 282 383. VAT: Spec.

LYNTON
Berry's
42 Lee Rd. (Frank Windsor). Est. 1974. Open

DEVONSHIRE

Pugh's Antiques

Pugh's Farm
Monkton
Near Honiton
Devon EX14 9QH
Tel: (0404) 42860 Fax (0404) 47792

FOUR BARNS OF FURNITURE, VICTORIAN, EDWARDIAN, ETC.

Beds and Country Furniture

Fruitwood Farmhouse Tables imported monthly from France

Lynton continued
10.30-12.30 and 2.30-4.30 (winter - Mon., Wed. and Sat. only), prior telephone call advisable. SIZE: Small. *STOCK: 18th to early 20th C furniture, ceramics, glass and metalware, watercolours, oil paintings and prints, books and bindings, all £20-£1,000.* LOC: Main street. PARK: Easy. TEL: 0598 52633. SER: Valuations.

Cantabrian Antiques and Architectural Furnishing
Park St. (I.A. Williamson). Open by appointment only. *STOCK: Architectural antiques, especially early English oak.* TEL: 0598 53282.

Vendy Antiques
29A Lee Rd. (T.W. Vendy and S.P. Phillips). Est. 1964. Open 10-1 and 2-5, Sat. by appointment. *STOCK: General antiques including furniture and smalls, mainly Victorian, £10-£2,000.* PARK: Easy. TEL: 0598 53327; home - 0598 53227.

MAIDENCOMBE, Nr. Torquay
G.A. Whiteway-Wilkinson
Sunsea, Teignmouth Rd. Est. 1943. Open by appointment only. *STOCK: General antiques, fine art and jewellery.* LOC: Approximately halfway out on main Torquay/Teignmouth road. TEL: 0803 329692. VAT: Spec.

MERTON, Nr. Okehampton
Barometer World (Barometers)
Quicksilver Barn. (P.R. Collins). BAFRA. Est. 1979. Open 8-5, Sat. by appointment. SIZE: Medium. *STOCK: Mercurial wheel and stick barometers, 1780-1880, £300-£3,000; aneroid barometers, 1850-1930, £70-£500.* LOC: Between Hatherleigh and Torrington on A386. PARK: Easy. TEL: 08053 443. SER: Valuations; restorations (barometers). VAT: Stan/Spec.

MODBURY, Nr. Ivybridge
Bell Inn Antiques
3 Broad St. (Mr and Mrs E. Christopher-Walsh). Open 10-5 and by appointment. *STOCK: General antiques, pictures, porcelain, chandeliers, silver, jewellery.* TEL: 0548 830715; home - 0548 830238. VAT: Stan.

Fourteen A
14A Broad St. (Bridget Kirke and Marjorie Ridsdill). Est. 1986. Open 10-5. SIZE: Small. *STOCK: Victorian linen, quilts, £1-£250; writing and jewellery boxes, 19th C, £35-£350; china, jewellery, silver, small furniture, tools, luggage, kitchenalia.* LOC: Next to Post Office. PARK: Nearby. TEL: 0548 830732; home - 0548 560055 or 0752 880489. SER: Restorations (boxes and furniture). FAIRS: Ardingly; Shepton Mallet; Sandown Park.

Wild Goose Antiques
34 Church St. (Mr and Mrs E. Christopher-Walsh). Open 10-5 and by appointment. *STOCK: General antiques, pictures, porcelain, chandeliers, silver, jewellery.* TEL: 0548 830715; home - 0548 830238. VAT: Stan.

Ye Little Shoppe
1B Broad St. (Eric W. Ridsdill). Est. 1990. Open 10-5. CL.Wed. SIZE: Small. *STOCK: Tea, writing and jewellery boxes, 19th C, £40-£350; woodworkers and saddlers tools, 19th C to early 20th C, £10-£150; small furniture and china, to £300; oil lamps, 19th-20th C, £18-£300.* LOC: Main street. PARK: Nearby. TEL: 0548 830732. SER: Restorations (writing boxes, including embossed and gilded leathers). FAIRS: Ardingly and Shepton Mallet.

MONKTON, Nr. Honiton
Pugh's Farm Antiques
Pugh's Farm. (G. Garner and C. Cherry). Est. 1974. Open 9.30-5.30, Sun. a.m. by appointment. SIZE: Large. *STOCK: General antiques including Victorian and Edwardian furniture, beds and country farmhouse tables imported from France.* LOC: A30 2 miles from Honiton. PARK: Easy. TEL: 0404 42860; home - same; fax - 0404 47792. VAT: Stan.

MORCHARD BISHOP, Nr. Crediton
Morchard Bishop Antiques
Meadowbank. (J.C. and E.A. Child). Resident. Open by appointment. *STOCK: General antiques, metalwork and treen.* LOC: 8 miles west of Crediton, off A377 at Morchard Rd. PARK: Easy. TEL: 0363 877456.

MORETONHAMPSTEAD
W. Bagnall
Lowton. Est. 1965. Open by appointment. *STOCK: Oak, mahogany and walnut furniture, 17th-18th C.* LOC: 500 yds south of Moretonhampstead off the B3212. PARK: Easy. TEL: 0647 40880; home - same.

The Old Brass Kettle
2-4 Ford St. (H. Clark). Est. 1950. Open 9.30-1 and 2.15-5.30. CL: Sun. except by appointment, and Thurs. SIZE: Medium. *STOCK: Pottery, porcelain and furniture, 19th C.* LOC: A382 from Newton Abbot, B3212 from Exeter. TEL: 0647 40334. SER: Buys at auction. VAT: Spec.

NEWTON ABBOT
The Attic
9 Union St. (G.W. Gillman). Est. 1976. CL: Mon. and Thurs., prior telephone call advisable. SIZE: Medium. *STOCK: General antiques, to £1,000.* LOC: Town centre. PARK: Easy. TEL: 0626 55124. SER: Valuations.

Newton Abbot Antiques Centre
55 East St. (P. and D. Stockman). Est. 1973. Open every Tues. 9-3. LOC: 200yds. from clock tower. PARK: Through arch. TEL: 0626 54074. Below are listed some of the dealers at this market.

Bell Antiques
STOCK: Smalls, china, 19th C.

Biggs Antiques
STOCK: Antiquities, decorative items, decor.

Blockley
STOCK: Decorative objects and furniture.

Robin Brice
STOCK: General antiques, art nouveau, art deco, pictures.

Caunter
STOCK: Victoriana, 19th C china and pottery.

Graham Courtier
STOCK: Furniture, shipping goods and china.

Curio Corner
STOCK: Plate, china, glass, jewellery.

Forster
STOCK: Linen, lace, fabrics.

Newton Abbot continued

Austin Gilmour
STOCK: Oriental china, bronzes and pictures.

Vyvyan Goode
STOCK: Furniture and silver, pictures, objets d'art, glass, plate.

Hendrika
STOCK: General antiques and china.

Jo Hicks - Bolton Galleries
STOCK: Furniture, curios, pictures, silver, jewellery, Staffordshire.

H. Hill
STOCK: Costume, china, fabrics, lace.

B. Hunt
STOCK: Silver and china, furniture, period tools.

Mrs Iredale
STOCK: West Country pottery, Doulton, Staffordshire.

Mr Johnson
STOCK: China, glass, brass and copper, small furniture.

S. Johnson
STOCK: Small items, china, pottery, silver.

John Lawrence
STOCK: Furniture and china, metal toys.

Lewis
STOCK: China, pottery and glass.

Mrs Lock
STOCK: General antiques, china and pottery.

Mr Lovell
STOCK: Period silver.

Mrs Lovell
STOCK: Linen and lace, small china.

Mrs Mathews
STOCK: Furniture, clocks, brass.

M. Morrell
STOCK: Small china, collectables.

G. Mosdell
STOCK: Antiquarian books and prints.

Mr Opie
STOCK: Cast toys and china, small furniture.

P. & D. Antiques
STOCK: Victorian and shipping furniture; Staffordshire, 18th-19th C.

Mrs Peddie
STOCK: Silver, jewellery, furniture, china and pottery including Staffordshire.

Pinchen Antiques
STOCK: Furniture, china.

Newton Abbot continued

B. Pridham
STOCK: Furniture, china, collectors' items, postcards.

N. Pulley
STOCK: Old musical instruments.

Mrs Richards
STOCK: Furniture, bric-a-brac, Victorian and Edwardian.

J. Ruff
STOCK: Crown Derby, Doulton, Royal Worcester.

P. Shearman
STOCK: Furniture, china, brass and copper.

Sherlock
STOCK: Jewellery.

Paul Stockman
STOCK: Pottery and period porcelain, furniture, flat back Staffffordshire.

Village Antiques
STOCK: Silver, china and furniture.

Mrs Vouse
STOCK: Coloured glass, jewellery and china.

Newton Abbot continued

Warham Bursey
STOCK: Porcelain, silver plate, brass and copper, small furniture, glass, objets d'art.

Liz Wheeleker
STOCK: General antiques and decor.

Derick Wilson
STOCK: Jewellery, shipping goods and furniture.

P. Winchester
STOCK: Postcards, china.

Winckworth
STOCK: Clocks, small furniture, jewellery and china, bottles, Goss.

P. Wright
STOCK: General antiques, small items.

Mavis Young
STOCK: Small general antiques.

Old Treasures
126a Queen St. (Mr and Mrs J. F. Gordon). Est. 1971. Open 9.30-4.30, Sat. 9.30-3. CL: Thurs. SIZE: Small. STOCK: Jewellery, £3-£800; glass, porcelain, portrait miniatures. Not Stocked: Large furniture, weapons. LOC: On A380, 100yds. from Queen's Hotel. PARK: Easy. TEL: 0626 67181. FAIRS: British International, Birmingham. VAT: Stan/Spec.

ANTIQUE COLLECTING

- Authoritative articles • Practical buying information
- Up-to-date price guides • Annual Investment Issue
- Auctions and fairs calendars
- Antiques for sale and wanted

The magazine is published ten times a year and contains pre-publication offers and special Christmas discounts on ACC books

Join NOW and receive your first magazine and our book catalogue FREE
Annual membership: £19.50 UK,
£25.00 overseas, US $40 USA, CAN $50 Canada

Antique Collectors' Club
5 Church Street, Woodbridge,
Suffolk, IP12 1DS, England
Tel: (0394) 385501 Fax: (0394) 384434

Market Street Industrial Park, Wappingers' Falls,
New York 12590
USA. Tel: 914 297 0003 Fax: 914 297 0068

DEVONSHIRE

NEWTON ST. CYRES, Nr. Exeter
Gordon Hepworth Gallery
Hayne Farm, Sand Down Lane. (C.G. and I.M. Hepworth). Est. 1990. Open Wed.-Sat. during exhibitions or by appointment. STOCK: Modern British paintings, post-war and contemporary especially West Country - West Cornwall and St. Ives School, £150-£3,000. LOC: A377, 3 miles N.W. of Exeter turn left by village sign, into Sand Down Lane, farm entrance on left, after last white house. PARK: Easy. TEL: 0392 851351; home - same. VAT: Spec.

OKEHAMPTON
Alan Jones Antiques
Fatherford Farm. Est. 1971. Open anytime by appointment. SIZE: Large - warehouse and showroom. STOCK: Furniture - all types, paintings, general antiques. LOC: On A30, one mile from Okehampton. PARK: Easy. TEL: 0837 52970; home - 040 923 428. SER: Valuations. VAT: Stan/Spec.

PLYMOUTH
Annterior Antiques
22 Molesworth Rd, Millbridge. (A. Tregenza and R. Mascaro). Est. 1982. Open 9.30-5.30, Sat. 9.30-5, or by appointment. SIZE: Small. STOCK: Stripped pine, 18th-19th C, £50-£3,000; some painted, mahogany and decorative furniture; brass and iron beds, 19th C, £250-£1,500; decorative small items. LOC: Follow signs to Torpoint Ferry from North Cross roundabout, turn left at junction of Wilton St. and Molesworth Rd. PARK: Easy. TEL: 0752 558277; home - 0752 562774. SER: Buys at auction; finder. VAT: Stan/Spec.

Antique Fireplace Centre
30 Molesworth Rd, Stoke. (B.F. Taylor). Est. 1988. Open 9.30-5.30 or by appointment. STOCK: Fire surrounds - timber, marble, slate, cast iron, £100-£3,500; Georgian and Victorian fire grates, £100-£1,500; accessories including scuttles, coal boxes, fire irons and overmantels, lamps and lanterns. LOC: 50yds. from Victoria Park, map sent on request. PARK: Easy. TEL: 0752 559441/569061. SER: Valuations. VAT: Stan/Spec.

Armada Gallery
19 Citadel Ope, The Barbican. (D.H. and S.J. Donovan). Est. 1986. Open 9-6 including Sun. SIZE: Medium. STOCK: Oils and watercolours, 18th C to date, £50-£1,000. LOC: 1st left off Southside St. PARK: Meters nearby. TEL: 0752 263031; home - 0752 403014. SER: Valuations; restorations; framing. FAIRS: Pavilions, Plymouth. VAT: Stan. Trade Only.

Barbican Antiques Centre
82-84 Vauxhall St, Barbican. (T. Cremer-Price). Open 9.30-5 every day. SIZE: 60+ dealers.

Plymouth continued
STOCK: Silver and plate, art pottery, porcelain, glass, jewellery, coins, stamps, clocks, collectables. PARK: Own. TEL: 0752 266927.

The Barbican Centre
27 New St, The Barbican. (Richard Hills and Partners Ltd). Est. 1980. Open 10-5, Sun. 2-5 summer months only. SIZE: Medium. STOCK: Clocks, silver, jewellery, weapons, general antiques. PARK: Nearby. TEL: 0752 661165; home - 0752 661522. VAT: Stan/Spec.

Alan Jones Antiques
Applethorn Slade Farm, Near Plympton. Resident. Est. 1965. Open by appointment. SIZE: Small. STOCK: Clocks, scientific and marine items, country furniture, primitive and unusual items, 18th-19th C, £5-£500. LOC: Off A38, telephone for directions. PARK: Easy. TEL: 0752 338188. FAIRS: Newton Abbot, Shepton Mallet, Devon County.

M. & A. Antique Exporters
42/44 Breton Side and warehouse -, Unit 18, Recreation Rd. (M. Antonucci). Open 9.30-6; by appointment for export. STOCK: Pine furniture, general antiques and shipping goods. TEL: 0752 665419; fax - 0752 228058. SER: Full container facilities.

Anne-Marie Scott-Masson
Mount Stone House, Devil's Point. Open by appointment only. STOCK: Small period pieces, furnishing fabrics and wallpaper. TEL: 0752 664413. SER: Interior design.

Secondhand Rose
22 Weston Park Rd, Peverell. (Mrs M.R. Kirke). Est. 1978. Open 10-4 Sat. only or by appointment. SIZE: Medium. STOCK: Victorian and Edwardian furniture; pictures, books, ceramics, decorative items, from Victorian. LOC: Main road into city centre. PARK: Easy. TEL: 0752 221715.

Brian Taylor Antiques
24 Molesworth Rd, Stoke. Est. 1975. Open 9-5.30, Sun. by appointment. SIZE: Medium. STOCK: Fireplaces and accessories, country furniture, £50-£2,000; clocks, £50-£2,500, all 18th-19th C; gramophones and phonographs, 1885-1930, £100-£1,000; Oriental items including buddhas and thankas, £50-£2,000. LOC: 50yds. from Victoria Park, map sent on request. PARK: Easy. TEL: 0752 569061; home - same. SER: Valuations; restorations (clocks and gramophones). VAT: Stan/Spec.

Upstairs Downstairs
Camden St, Greenbank. Open 9.30-5.30. STOCK: General antiques especially costume, linen and lace. TEL: 0752 261015.

SALCOMBE, DEVON
A-B Gallery

19th & 20th Century Oils, watercolours and etchings

A.S. Arnold-Brown M.A.
67 Fore Street
(Central, near Whitestrand Car Park)

Open most days especially mornings but appointment advisable by phoning 0548 842764 or 842728

SALCOMBE
A-B Gallery
67 Fore St. (A.S. and J.L. Arnold-Brown). Est. 1966. Usually open, prior 'phone call advisable. SIZE: Medium. *STOCK: Pictures, oils, mid 19th-20th C, £500-£8,000; watercolours, late 19th-20th C, £50-£1,500; etchings and prints, 19th-20th C, £20-£500.* LOC: Central, near Whitestrand car park. TEL: 0548 842764/2728. SER: Valuations. VAT: Spec.

SEATON
Courtyard Antiques and Collectors Centre
8, 10 & 11 Queen St. SIZE: 20 dealers. *STOCK: Small furniture, books and collectors' items.* TEL: 0297 22332.

Etceteras Antiques
Beer Rd. (B. Warren). Est. 1969. Open 10-4 or by appointment. *STOCK: General antiques.* TEL: 0297 21965.

SHALDON, Nr. Teignmouth
Tempus Fugit
16c Fore St. (R.C. Walkley). Est. 1982. Open 10-5, Sat. 10-1, Sun. a.m. by appointment. CL: Thurs. p.m. SIZE: Small. *STOCK: Clocks, 18th-19th C, £25-£6,000; watches, furniture, paintings, jewellery*

Shaldon continued
and porcelain. LOC: From A379 take left turn over bridge to Shaldon. On bend turn left into Fore St., shop on right. PARK: Easy. TEL: 0626 872752. SER: Valuations; restorations (clocks); buys at auction; export facilities. VAT: Stan/Spec.

W. J. Woodhams
25 Fore St. Resident. Est. 1970. Open 10-5.30. SIZE: Small. *STOCK: Furniture, £5-£5,000; silver and porcelain, bric-a-brac, £5-£200; all 18th-19thC.* PARK: Easy. TEL: 0626 872630. SER: Valuations; restorations (furniture); buys at auction (furniture). VAT: Stan/Spec.

SIDMOUTH
Devonshire House Antiques and Collectors Centre
Fore St. SIZE: 20 dealers. *STOCK: Wide selection of china, glass, pictures and books.*

Gainsborough House Antiques
12 Fore St. (K.S. Scratchley). Est. 1937. Open 9-1 and 2-5, Sun. by appointment. CL: Thurs. p.m. (except by appointment) and Sat. p.m. SIZE: Medium. *STOCK: Pottery, porcelain, silver and plate, copper, brass, furniture, Georgian and Victorian, from £10; militaria and medals, 1650 to date, 50p-£500.* LOC: From High St., 100yds. down Fore St. on left. PARK: 75yds. TEL: 0395 514394; home - 0395 515112/513337. SER: Valuations.

Dorothy Hartnell Antiques and Victoriana
At Gallery 21, 21 Fore St. Est. 1974. Open 10-1 and 2-5, Sun. by appointment. CL: Thurs. in winter. SIZE: Medium. *STOCK: Porcelain and pottery, small furniture, brass, pictures, interesting items, £5-£2,500.* LOC: Town centre. TEL: 0395 515291.

The Lantern Shop
4 New St. (Miss J.M. Creeke). Est. 1974. Open 9.45-12.45 and 2.15-4.45. CL: Mon. p.m. and Sat. p.m. SIZE: Medium. *STOCK: Period table lighting, 1750-1950, £45-£1,000; English porcelain, 1800-1915, £5-£1,000; watercolours and oils, 1800-1950, £15-£1,000; small furniture, 1750-1920, £25-£850.* LOC: Town centre, between Market Sq. and Fore St., behind sea front. PARK: Nearby. TEL: 0395 516320. SER: Valuations; restorations (lamps, oil paintings); framing; lamp shade re-covering. VAT: Stan/Spec.

The Lantern Shop Gallery
5 New St. (Miss J.M. Creeke). Est. 1974. Open 10-12.45 and 2.15-4.45. CL: Mon. p.m. and Sat. p.m. SIZE: Medium. *STOCK: Topographical prints, especially East Devon and adjacent counties, 1750-1900, £5-£450; decorative prints and engravings, 1750-1960, £5-£300; maps, especially south-west England, West Midlands and Home Counties, 1600-1850, £10-£400.* LOC:

Antique Collectors' Club Titles

JEWELLERY 1789-1910

Jewellery 1780-1910
The International Era - 2 vols
by Shirley Bury F.S.A.

A detailed and beautifully illustrated work by the former Keeper of Metalwork at the Victoria and Albert Museum. The book details the design, manufacture, fashion and history of every kind of jewellery. Covers the development of fashions, materials and techniques of 19th century jewellery. The historical background of this important era is examined, from popular everyday jewellery to that worn by Royalty and the nobility.

Vol. I 1789-1861, 472pp, 231 b & w illus, 104 col, ISBN 1 85149 148 1
Vol.II 1862-1910, 424pp, 191 b & w illus, 110 col, ISBN 1 85149 149 X
£47.50 per volume £95.00 the set

The Price Guide to Jewellery 3000BC-1950AD
by Michael Poynder

Describes and illustrates hundreds of examples of the type of jewellery that is popular with buyers world-wide. The prices are constantly being updated so that the book is an essential guide to those anxious to buy.
388pp, 340 b & w illus, 44 col, ISBN 0 902028 50 2. £29.95

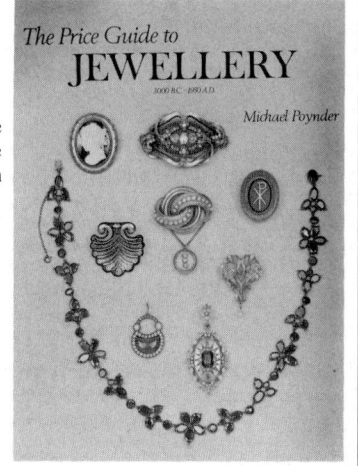

Available from:
Antique Collectors' Club, 5 Church Street
Woodbridge, Suffolk IP12 1DS
Tel: (0394) 385501 Fax: (0394) 384434

or Market Street Industrial Park
Wappingers' Falls, New York 12590, USA
Tel: 914 297 0003 Fax: 914 297 0068

Understanding Jewellery *by David Bennett and Daniela Mascetti*
Written by two leading Sotheby's experts, a practical book covering the jewellery of the last 200 years for those interested in buying. Fashions in jewellery are described with examples of a range of fakes, alterations, repairs and comparisons of varying degrees of quality. Features a concise guide to gem stones.
388pp, 30 b & w illus, 738 col illus, ISBN 1 85149 075 2, £35.00

Sidmouth continued
Town centre between Market Sq. and Fore St., behind the sea front. PARK: Nearby. TEL: 0395 578462. SER: Valuations; restorations (cleaning and re-framing prints). VAT: Stan.

Sidmouth Antique Market
132 High St. (D.G.M. Jones). Est. 1983. Open 9.30-4. CL: Mon. and Thurs. SIZE: Small. STOCK: China, glass, cutlery, costume jewellery, Torquay ware, £1-£250. LOC: Next to Fords. PARK: Nearby. TEL: 0395 577981.

The Vintage Toy and Train Museum
First Floor, Field's Department Store, Market Place. (R.D.N., M.E. and J.W. Salisbury). Open Easter-October inclusive 10-5. STOCK: Hornby Gauge O trains, Hornby-Dublo, Dinky toys, Meccano and other die-cast and tinplate toys of yesteryear, wooden jig-saw puzzles. TEL: 0395 515124, ext. 208; home - 0395 513399.

SOUTH BRENT
Philip Andrade   BADA LAPADA
White Oxen Manor, Rattery. Open 9-6, Sat. 9-1 or by appointment. STOCK: Furniture, 17th to early 19th C, £50-£5,000; English pottery, porcelain, metalware, works of art, 17th to early 19th C. TEL: 0364 72454. SER: Valuations. VAT: Stan/Spec.

P.M. Pollak
Moorview, Plymouth Rd. (Dr. P.M. Pollak). ABA. Est. 1973. Open by appointment. SIZE: Small. STOCK: Antiquarian books especially medicine and science; prints, some instruments, £50-£5,000. LOC: On edge of village, near London Inn. PARK: Own. TEL: 0364 73457; fax - 0364 72918. SER: Valuations; buys at auction; catalogues issued, computer searches.

L.G. Wootton Clocks and Watches
2 Church St. Est. 1948. Open by appointment only. STOCK: Clocks and watches, all periods; small antiques, unusual curios. LOC: Just off A38. PARK: Easy. TEL: 0364 72553. SER: Valuations; repairs and restorations (clocks).

SOUTH MOLTON
Architectural Antiques
West Ley, Alswear Old Rd. (A. Busek). Est. 1978. Open 10-5. CL: Mon. SIZE: Large. STOCK: Architectural fittings, especially panelled rooms, fire surrounds, marble and stonework, stained glass, pub and shop interiors, decorative items. LOC: 1.5 miles from town centre. PARK: Easy. TEL: 0769 573342; fax - 0769 574363. VAT: Stan.

The Furniture Market
14a Barnstaple St. (R.M. Golding). Est. 1971. Open 10-1 and 2-5, Wed 10-1. SIZE: Large - 20 dealers. STOCK: Furniture, collectables, silver

South Molton continued
and glass, to early 20th C, £5-£2,000. LOC: On old A361, 100 yards from town centre. PARK: Nearby. TEL: 0769 573401. SER: Valuations; buys at auction. VAT: Mainly Spec.

Great Western Pine
99 East St. (B. Atwell). Resident. Est. 1987. Open 9-6. SIZE: Medium. STOCK: Stripped pine, 19th C, £75-£300. PARK: Easy. TEL: 0769 572689; home - same. SER: Restorations (pine). VAT: Stan.

The Lace Shop
Bay House, 33 East St. (Fenela Sadler). Est. 1985. STOCK: Lace, 17th-20th C, £5-£1,000; linens, patchwork, bridal veils, head-dresses and dresses, 19th-20th C, £10-£4,000. PARK: Easy. TEL: 0769 573184; home - same. SER: Valuations; restorations (handmade lace and embroidery); bridal gowns to order. VAT: Stan/Spec.

Memory Lane Antiques
100 East St. (D. Mason). Open 9.30-5.30. SIZE: 3 showrooms. STOCK: General antiques including china, glass, silver, jewellery, plate, brass, copper and furniture. TEL: 0769 574288.

Mole Gallery
32 East St. (A. and G. Fry). Est. 1985. Open 9.30-5. SIZE: Large. STOCK: 19th-early 20th C, and contemporary paintings; contemporary prints; artist and framing materials. PARK: Easy. TEL: 0769 573845; home - same. SER: Framing. VAT: Stan/Spec.

South Molton Antiques
103 East St. (D. and W. Nicholl). Est. 1976. Open 9-5. STOCK: Shipping goods, oak, mahogany, Victorian furniture, and pine, £10-£5,000; general antiques. LOC: B3227, east side of town. TEL: 0769 573478. VAT: Stan/Spec.

Treasure Trove
4 East St. (D. Mason). Open 9.30-5.30. SIZE: 2 small showrooms. STOCK: General antiques including china, glass, jewellery, linen, furniture, 1900-1950's. TEL: 0769 574288.

J.R. Tredant
50/50a South St. Usually open. STOCK: General antiques. TEL: 0769 573006; home - 0769 572416. SER: Valuations.

Tredantiques
19 Broad St. (J.C. Tredant). Est. 1982. Open 9.30-5, or by appointment. STOCK: Victorian and Georgian furniture, decorative items, £50-£5,000. LOC: A361. TEL: 0769 573841; home - same. VAT: Stan/Spec.

STOCKLAND, Nr. Honiton
Colystock Antiques
Rising Sun Farm. (D.C. McCollum). Est. 1975. Open seven days. SIZE: Large. STOCK: Pine and

PHILIP ANDRADE

Extensive Stock
Quality Antique Furniture
English & Oriental Porcelain
Works of Art

LAPADA MEMBER

PETER WADHAM

English Decorative Furniture
Glass · Metalware · Pottery
Prints · Collectors Items

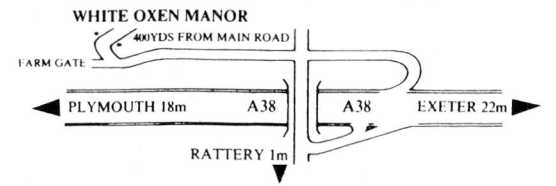

WHITE OXEN MANOR
RATTERY
NEAR SOUTH BRENT, DEVON TQ10 9JX
TELEPHONE 0364 72454

DEVONSHIRE

Stockland continued
oak including English, Irish and Continental, 18th-19th C. TEL: 040 486 271. SER: Container packing and documentation; courier.

TAVISTOCK
King Street Curios
5 King St. (T. and P. Bates). Est. 1979. Open 9-5. SIZE: Medium. STOCK: *Pine furniture, postcards, cigarette cards, china, glass, general collectables, jewellery, to £100.* LOC: Town centre.

Pendar Antiques
8 Drake Rd. (A.R. Martin). Est. 1987. Open 9-5. SIZE: Large. STOCK: *Mahogany, oak and walnut furniture, mainly Victorian to 1920's, £10-£3,000; general antiques and bric-a-brac, granite troughs and fireplaces, 50p-£400.* LOC: Road between Lloyds and Midland Banks. PARK: Nearby. TEL: 0822 617641; home - 0822 617931. SER: Valuations.

TEIGNMOUTH
Charterhouse Antiques
1B Northumberland Place. (A. and S. Webster). Est. 1974. Open 11-1 and 2.15-4.30, Sat. 10-1 and 2-4.30. CL: Mon. and Thurs. SIZE: Small. STOCK: *Pottery and porcelain, especially commemoratives, 18th C to 1930s, £1-£200; Victorian jewellery and small silver, 1800-1930, £5-£400; weapons, small furniture, paintings, 1780-1900, £10-£500.* LOC: If facing sea, turn right at Post Office, third left, shop round corner on left. PARK: Easy and nearby. TEL: 0626 54592.

Extence Antiques
2 Wellington St. (T.E. and L.E. Extence). Est. 1928. Open 9.30-1 and 2-5.30. SIZE: Medium. STOCK: *Furniture, 18th to early 19th C; jewellery, silver, objets d'art, clocks.* PARK: Limited. TEL: 0626 773353. VAT: Stan/Spec.

The Old Passage
13a Bank St. (G. and R.H. Doel). Est. 1981. Open 11-1 and 2.30-4.30. CL: Mon. and Thurs. SIZE: Small. STOCK: *Porcelain, pottery, treen, linen and silver, mainly 19th-20th C, £5-£200.* LOC: Main street. PARK: Nearby. TEL: 0626 772634; home - 0626 776196. SER: Restorations (furniture repair, French polishing). FAIRS: Westpoint, Exeter; Newton Abbot Racecourse; Livestock Market, Exeter.

Timepiece
125 Bitton Park Rd. (Clive and Willow Pople). Est. 1972. Open 10-5.30, Sat. 10-6. CL: Mon. SIZE: Medium. STOCK: *Furniture and clocks, 19th C, £25-£500; kitchenalia and collectables, 19th-20th C, £5-£50.* LOC: On main Newton Abbot road, next to Bitton Park. PARK: Easy. TEL: 0626 770275.

TIVERTON
Antique Architecture and Furniture
5 Twyford Place. (I.M. Hutchings). Resident. Est. 1987. Open by appointment only. SIZE: Small. STOCK: *Antique marble fireplaces and cast iron inserts, £100-£5,000+.* LOC: Off Park Street. PARK: Easy. TEL: 0884 252006; home - same. SER: Restorations; buys at auction (19th C furniture, chimney pieces and decorative inserts).

Bygone Days Antiques
40 Gold St. (N. Park). Open 10-1 and 2-5. CL: Thurs. STOCK: *Furniture, Victorian and Georgian; watercolours and oils.* TEL: 0884 252832; home - 0884 243615.

Chancery Antiques
8-10 Barrington St. Est. 1967. Open 9-5. CL: Sun. and Thurs. except by appointment. SIZE: Large. STOCK: *Furniture, stripped pine, early oak, period mahogany.* PARK: Easy. TEL: 0884 252416; home - 0884 253190. SER: Export facilities; hand-made pine furniture. VAT: Stan/Spec.

TOPSHAM, Nr. Exeter
Allnutt Antiques
13 Fore St. (J. and E. Gage). Est. 1950. Open by appointment. STOCK: *Porcelain, 1800-1890; glass, 1780-1890; silver, from 18th C.* LOC: 1 mile from Countess Weir roundabout (A377) towards Exmouth. PARK: Own. TEL: 0392 874224; home - 0395 32603. SER: Valuations.

TORQUAY
Birbeck Gallery
45 Abbey Rd. Est. 1922. Open 10-5. CL: Sun except by appointment. SIZE: Medium. STOCK *General antiques, Oriental and European paintings, drawings and prints, 19th to early 20th C, to £10,000.* LOC: 200yds. up Abbey Rd. from main street roundabout at Torquay G.P.O. PARK Easy or 200yds. TEL: 0803 297144/214836. SER Valuations; restorations; buys at auction.

The Gold Shop
24 Torwood St. Open 10-5.30. STOCK: *Silver and plate, jewellery.* VAT: Stan.

Perchance Ltd
21 Walnut Rd, Chelston. Resident. Est. 1991 Open 9.30-12.30, afternoons and Sat. by appointment. CL: Wed. SIZE: Small. STOCK *Ceramics, copper, silver, treen and pictures, 19th 20th C, £5-£300.* LOC: Near Torre Abbey and Conference Centre. PARK: Easy. TEL: 080 528506; home - same. SER: Buys at auction (ceramics).

Rocking Horse Pine
3 Laburnum Row. (W. Bone). Open 10-5. CL Mon. STOCK: *Pine, some reproduction; decorative items.* LOC: Off Union St. TEL: 080 296983.

DEVONSHIRE

Torquay continued
Sheraton House
1 Laburnum Row, Torre. (K. Goodman). *STOCK: Period furniture and decorations.* TEL: 0803 293334.

Spencers Antiques
187 Union St, Torre. *STOCK: General antiques.* TEL: 0803 296598.

Colin Stodgell Fine Art   LAPADA
45 Abbey Rd. **Open 10-5. CL: Sat.** *STOCK: Oil paintings, British and continental, 19th C.* **TEL: 0803 292726.** SER: Valuations.

Torre Antique Traders
266 Higher Union St. (P. and Mrs R. Curtis, N. Boulton and I.S. Hutton). Open 10-5. SIZE: Medium. *STOCK: General antiques.* LOC: Continuation of main shopping area (Union St.). PARK: Easy. TEL: 0803 292184.

TOTNES
Bogan House Antiques
43 High St. (C. Mitchell). Est. 1980. Open 10-5, Fri. 9.15-5. CL: Thurs. and Sat. SIZE: Small. *STOCK: Small silver, especially flatware, 18th-19th C; drinking glasses, 18th to early 19th C, both £10-£200; small decorative items, 17th-19th C, £10-£100; Japanese prints.* LOC: Opposite Civic Hall. PARK: Nearby. TEL: 0803 862075. SER: Valuations (silver and drinking glasses, Japanese woodblock prints).

Collards Books
4 Castle St. (B. Collard). Est. 1970. Open 10-5, restricted opening in winter. *STOCK: Antiquarian and secondhand books.* LOC: Opposite castle. PARK: Nearby. TEL: Home - 0548 550246.

Fine Pine Antiques
Woodland Rd, Harbertonford. Est. 1973. Open 9.30-5. *STOCK: Stripped pine and country furniture.* TEL: 0752 892427. SER: Restorations; stripping.

Past and Present
94 High St. (James Sturges). CL: Lunch-times. SIZE: Large. *STOCK: Furniture, £100-£2,000; smalls, bygones, £5-£300; all 18th-20th C.* LOC: A38. PARK: 150 yards. TEL: 0803 866086. FAIRS: Sandown Park.

Beverley J. Pyke - Fine British Watercolours
The Gothic House, Bank Lane. Usually open 10-1 and 2.30-6 but appointment advisable. SIZE: Small. *STOCK: Watercolours, 20th C, £100-£2,000.* LOC: Opposite P.O. in Fore St. PARK: Nearby. TEL: 0803 864219; home - same.

WOODBURY, Nr. Exeter
Woodbury Antiques
Church St. (H. Jarman). Est. 1966. Open 10-5. CL: Wed. in winter. SIZE: Large. *STOCK:*

Woodbury continued
Victorian to Edwardian furniture and items. PARK: Easy. TEL: 0395 32727. VAT: Stan/Spec.

WOOLACOMBE
Woolacombe Bay Antiques
1 Bay Mews, South St. (B.A. and G. Banks). Est. 1963. Open 10.30-1 and 2-5, Tues., Wed. and Thurs. by appointment. SIZE: Medium. *STOCK: Furniture, 18th C to Edwardian, £50-£3,000; clocks, 17th-19th C, £150-£6,000; decorative items, 18th C to Edwardian, £25-£500.* LOC: Town centre. PARK: Easy. TEL: 0271 870167; home - 0271 870774. SER: Valuations; buys at auction (clocks and furniture). VAT: Stan/Spec.

YEALMPTON, Nr. Plymouth
Colin Rhodes Antiques   LAPADA
15 Fore St. Est. 1972. *STOCK: 17th to early 19th C furniture, paintings and objets d'art.* TEL: 0752 881170/862232. SER: Valuations. VAT: Spec.

Yealmantiques
15 Fore St. (Mr. and Mrs E. Christopher-Walsh). Est. 1980. Open 9.30-1 and 2-5, Wed. 9.30-1. CL: Mon. SIZE: Small. *STOCK: Georgian and Victorian furniture, £50-£1,000; china and glass, 19th C, £5-£25.* LOC: A379 Kingsbridge to Plymouth road. PARK: Easy. TEL: 0752 881170; home - 0548 830715/830238. SER: Restorations (furniture including upholstery); buys at auction. VAT: Spec.

---

free!

28 page full colour catalogue of Antique Collectors' Club books. Over 120 titles included covering a wide range of subjects: furniture, art reference, art history, prints, jewellery, metalwork, glass, horology, ceramics, oriental carpets, collectables, garden history and design, gardening and architecture.

Available free from the
ANTIQUE COLLECTORS' CLUB

5 Church Street
Woodbridge
Suffolk IP12 1DS
Tel: (0394) 385501
Fax: (0394) 384434

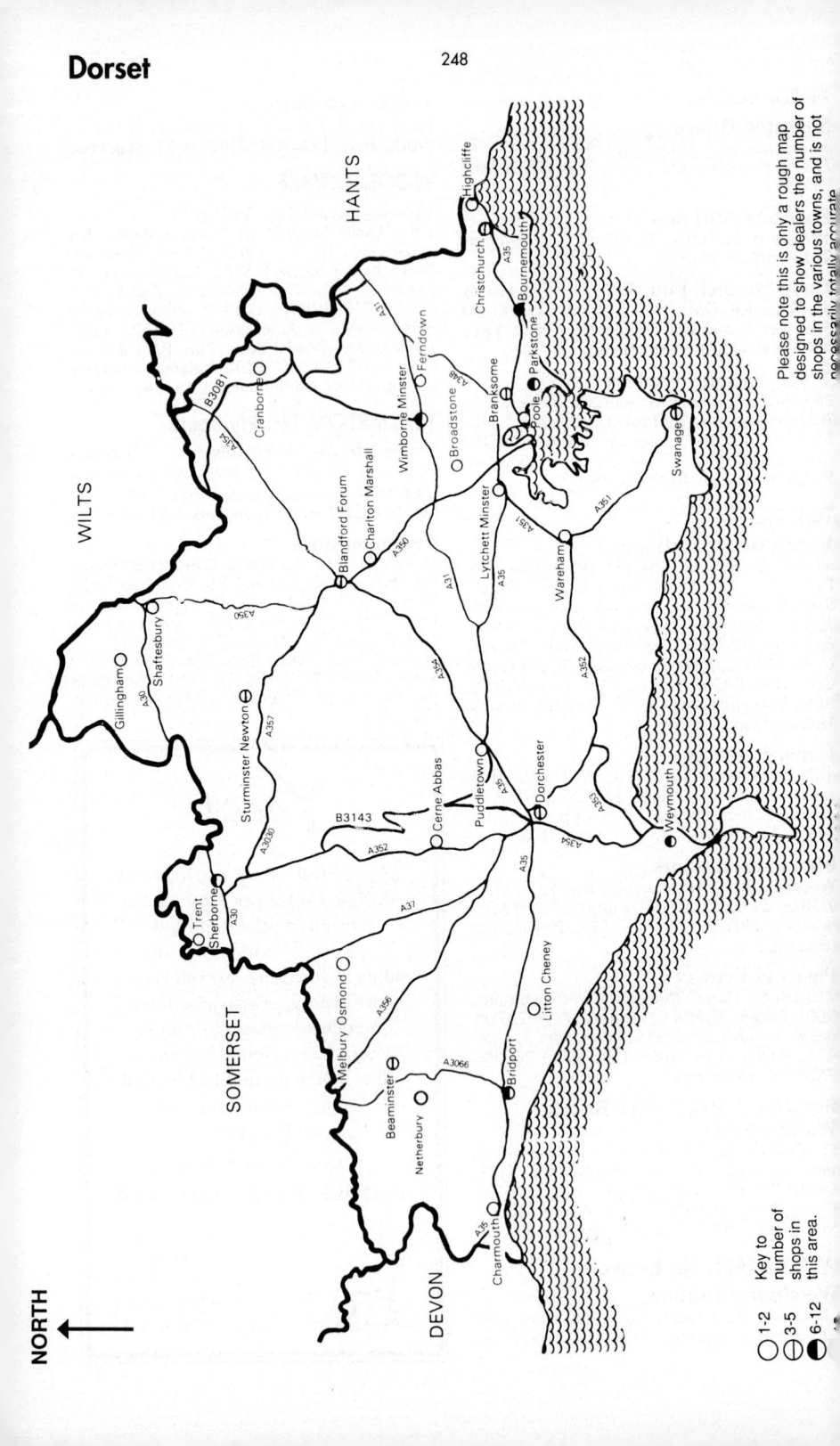

Dorset

Please note this is only a rough map designed to show dealers the number of shops in the various towns, and is not necessarily totally accurate.

Key to number of shops in this area.
○ 1-2
◐ 3-5
● 6-12

Dorset

BEAMINSTER

Beaminster Antiques
4 Church St. (Mrs T.P.F. Frampton). Est. 1982. Open 9.30-5.30. CL: Wed. SIZE: Small. *STOCK: Small furniture, £20-£1,400; silver, £10-£800; jewellery, £5-£1,400, all Georgian to art deco; objets d'art, porcelain, boxes 18th C to art deco, £5-£1,400; brass and pictures, 18th C to 1920s, £1-£1,000. Not Stocked: Coins and medals.* LOC: Just off square. PARK: Easy. TEL: 0308 862591; home - 0935 891395.

Cottage Antiques
17 The Square. Open 10-5.30 or by appointment. CL: Wed. *STOCK: Furniture, paintings, clocks, prints, decorative items.* LOC: A3066. TEL: 0308 862136.

Good Hope Antiques
2 Hogshill St. (D. Beney). Est. 1980. Open 9.30-1 and 2-5. CL: Wed. SIZE: Medium. *STOCK: Clocks especially longcase, bracket and wall, barometers, £500-£5,000; furniture, £200-£2,500; all 18th-19th C.* LOC: Town square. PARK: Easy. TEL: 0308 862119; home - same. SER: Valuations; restorations (clocks, including dials; barometers). VAT: Spec.

Hennessy   LAPADA
Daniels House, Hogshill St. (C. and G.C. Hennessy). Resident. Est. 1977. Open 9.30-6, Sun. and evenings by appointment. SIZE: Medium. *STOCK: Pine, oak country, French provincial, decorative and painted furniture, English and continental, 18th-19th C.* LOC: On A3066, 200yds. north of the Square. PARK: Easy. TEL: 0308 862635. VAT: Stan/Spec.

BLANDFORD FORUM

A & D Antiques
21 East St. (A. and D. Edgington). Est. 1981. Open 10-5, Sun. by appointment. CL: Mon. and Wed. p.m. SIZE: Small. *STOCK: Drinking glasses, 18th C, £50-£1,000; decanters, 19th C, £15-£100; Lalique, £100-£5,000.* LOC: Town centre on main east-west route (one-way system). PARK: Easy. TEL: 0258 455643; home - same. SER: Valuations (glass); buys at auction (18th C drinking glasses and decanters). VAT: Spec.

Ancient and Modern Bookshop (including Garret's Antiques)
34 Salisbury St. (Mrs P. Davey). Open 9.30-12.30 and 1.30-5.30. CL: Wed. *STOCK: Books and small antiques.* TEL: 0258 455276.

Havelin Antiques
(A. Elliot and C. Hesketh). Est. 1977. Open by appointment only. *STOCK: Furniture, 18th-19th C, £200-£2,000; carpets and textiles, 19th C, £30-£1,000; china, 18th-19th C, £25-£1,000; decorative items.* TEL: 0258 452431; fax - 0258 450664. VAT: Stan/Spec.

Blandford Forum continued

Stour Gallery
28 East St. (R. Butler). Est. 1966. Open 10-1 and 2-4, Sun. by appointment. CL: Mon. and Wed. p.m. SIZE: Medium. *STOCK: Watercolours, oils and pastels, early 19th to 20th C, £50-£3,000.* LOC: On right-hand side of High St., on one way system. PARK: Opposite. TEL: 0258 456293; home - 0258 860691. SER: Restorations (oil, watercolours, wash line mounts); framing.

Strowger of Blandford   LAPADA
13 East St. Est. 1962. Open 10.30-1 and 2-5.30, or by appointment. SIZE: Medium. *STOCK: Period furniture.* LOC: A354. PARK: Easy. TEL: 0258 454374/860103.

BOURNEMOUTH

Michael Andrews Antiques
916 Christchurch Rd. Est. 1967. Open 10-5.30. CL: Wed. p.m. SIZE: Medium. *STOCK: Furniture, art nouveau, copper, brass, shipping goods.* PARK: Opposite. TEL: 0202 427615. VAT: Stan.

The Antique Centre
837/839 Christchurch Rd, East Boscombe. (Chris Williams). BDADA. Est. 1981. Open 9.30-5.30. SIZE: Large. *STOCK: Silver plate, old Sheffield to art deco; porcelain and pottery, 18th-20th C; pottery - art deco especially Clarice Cliff and Moorcroft, 1897 to date; bric-a-brac, clothes, Victorian to 1960s; furniture, Georgian to art deco, stripped pine; dolls, Victorian and Edwardian.* PARK: Easy and at rear. TEL: 0202 421052. SER: Restorations (silver and jewellery repairs, replating); buys at auction.

The Antique Shop
646 Wimborne Rd, Winton. Est. 1946. TEL: 0202 527205.

Antiques and Furnishings
339 Charminster Rd. (P. Neath). Open 10-5.30. *STOCK: Furniture including Victorian stripped pine; brass, copper, china, textiles and decorative objects.* TEL: 0202 527976.

The Artist Gallery
1086 Christchurch Rd, Boscombe East. Open 9.30-5. CL: Wed. *STOCK: Limited edition prints - David Shepherd, Sir William Russell Flint, E.R. Sturgeon, Lowry, Gordon King and others.* PARK: Forecourt. TEL: 0202 417066.

Blade and Bayonet
884 Christchurch Rd, Boscombe. (L.M. Martin). Resident. Est. 1982. Open 10-12 and 1-5, Fri. 10-12. SIZE: Medium. *STOCK: Militaria, mid 17th to 20th C, £50-£100.* LOC: Near Pokesdown station. PARK: Easy. TEL: 0202 429891. SER: Valuations; restorations (mainly cleaning weapons). FAIRS: Bournemouth, Southsea, Bovington Tank Museum, Midhurst, Dorking, Farnham.

DORSET 250

Central Bournemouth

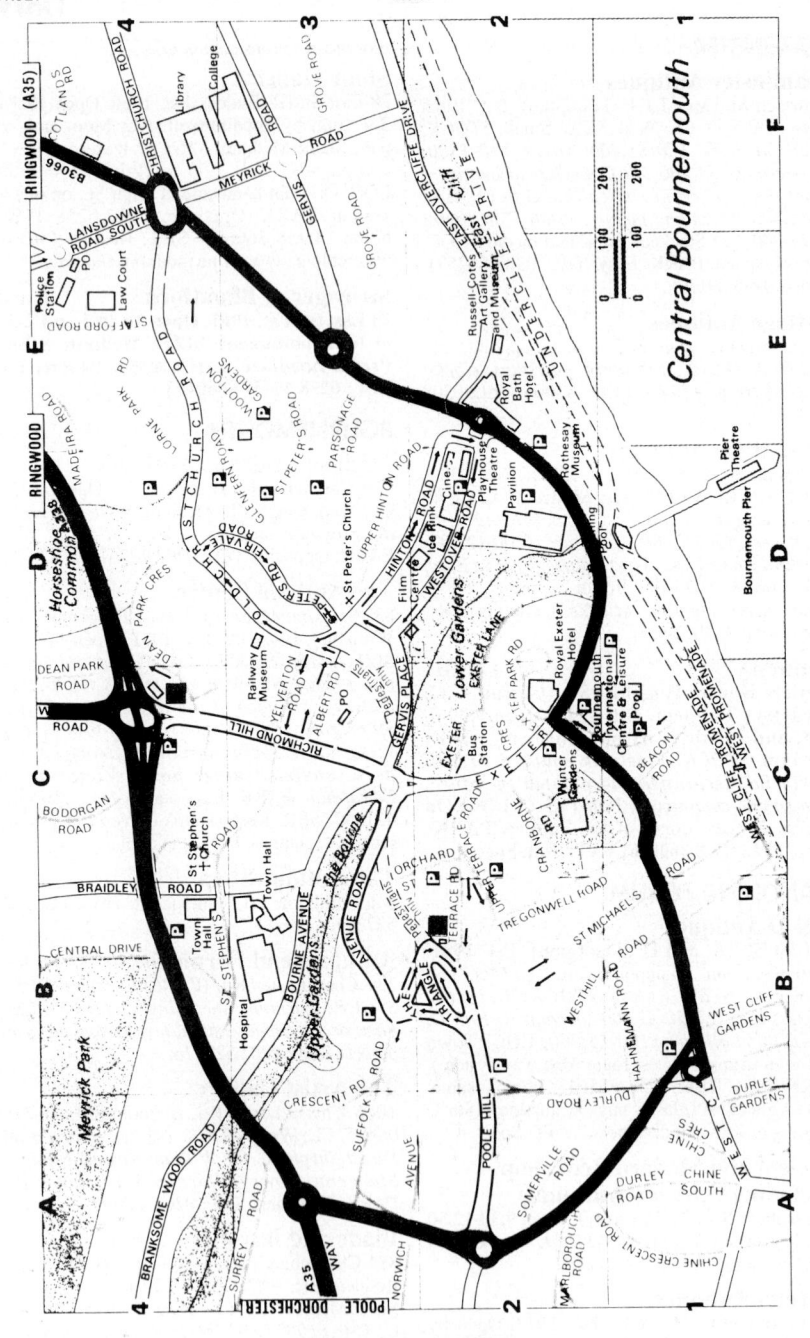

Key to Town Plan

AA Recommended roads
Other roads
Restricted roads
Buildings of interest
Car Parks
Parks and open spaces
AA Service Centre

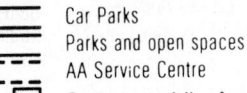

© Automobile Association 1988.

DORSET

BOURNEMOUTH & DISTRICT ANTIQUE DEALERS ASSOCIATION

BOURNEMOUTH

Not just a seaside resort but a good ANTIQUES area with a wide variety of trade calls and goods for both the home and export markets.

90 minutes from LONDON

90 minutes from BRIGHTON

Further information and brochure from:
BOURNEMOUTH & DISTRICT ANTIQUE DEALERS ASSOCIATION
Tel: (0202) 425963 — Fax: (0202) 418456

Bournemouth continued

Boscombe Antiques
731 Christchurch Rd, East Boscombe. (V. Strange and S. Morton). BDADA. Est. 1989. Open 9.30-5, Sat. 9.30-1. SIZE: Large. STOCK: Decorative porcelain, 1860-1900, £30-£1,000; figures, 1860-1900, £100-£1,500; dinner and tea sets, 1850-1920, £50-£2,000. LOC: 200yds. east of shopping precinct, on old A35. PARK: Easy. TEL: 0202 398202; home - 0202 887837/421402. VAT: Spec.

Boscombe Militaria
86 Palmerston Rd, Boscombe. (E.A. Browne). Est. 1981. Open 10-1 and 1.30-5. CL: Wed. SIZE: Small. STOCK: German militaria, £10-£500; British and American militaria, £5-£300, all 1914-1918 and 1939-1945. LOC: Just off Christchurch Rd. PARK: Easy. TEL: 0202 304250; home - same. FAIRS: Winchester, Dorking and major South of England arms.

Boscombe Models and Collectors Shop
802c Christchurch Rd., Boscombe. (Sylvia Hart). Open 10-1 and 2-4.30. CL: Wed. STOCK: Collectors' toys, 19th-20th C, £1-£1,000. TEL: 02902 398884.

Collectors Corner
63 Seabourne Rd, Southbourne. (K. Goodacre). Est. 1988. Open 10-4.30. CL: Wed. SIZE:

Bournemouth continued

Medium. STOCK: Small items, collectables, bottles, furniture, advertyques and Doulton. LOC: 100yds. from Pokesdown station. PARK: Easy. TEL: 0202 420945; home - 0425 620794.

Peter Denver Antiques
36 Calvin Rd, Winton. (P. Denver-White). Est. 1961. Open 10-5. CL: Mon. SIZE: Small. STOCK: Furniture, porcelain, pictures, glass, Georgian-Edwardian, £5-£800. LOC: Off main Wimborne Rd. PARK: Easy. TEL: 0202 532536; home - 0202 513911.

Richard Dunton Antiques
920 Christchurch Rd, Boscombe. (R.D. Dunton). Resident. BDADA. Est. 1980. Open 9-5.30, Sat. and Sun. by appointment. SIZE: Medium. STOCK: English furniture - oak, mahogany and pine, mainly 19th C; Staffordshire blue and white china, glass, brass and copper, £5-£5,000. PARK: Easy. TEL: 0202 425963; fax - 0202 418456. SER: Valuations. VAT: Stan/Spec. Trade Only.

Lionel Geneen Ltd   LAPADA
781 Christchurch Rd, Boscombe. BDADA. Est. 1902. Open 9.15-5, Sat. 9.15-12, other times by appointment. CL: Lunchtimes. SIZE: Large. STOCK: English, continental and Oriental furniture, china and works of art including

DORSET

Bournemouth continued

bronzes, enamels, ivories, jades, art nouveau and art deco, all 17th C to early 20th C. LOC: Main road through Boscombe. PARK: Easy. TEL: 0202 422961; home - 0202 520417. SER: Valuations. VAT: Stan/Spec.

Georgian House Antiques
110-112 Commercial Rd. Est. 1967. Open 9-5.30. CL: Wed. p.m. *STOCK: General antiques, silver, coins, jewellery.* TEL: 0202 554175. VAT: Stan.

The Green Room
796 Christchurch Rd, Boscombe. (P.H. Richards and E. Wright). BDADA. Est. 1974. Open 10-5.30. SIZE: Medium. *STOCK: Table lamps, old electric lighting, 1880-1950, £25-£2,500; decorative items and furnishings, 1780-1930, £30-£3,000.* PARK: Opposite. TEL: 0202 392634. SER: Valuations; restorations (silver and metalware). VAT: Stan/Spec.

H.L.B. Antiques
139 Barrack Rd. (H.L. Blechman). Est. 1969. SIZE: Large. *STOCK: Collectable items.* PARK: Easy. TEL: 0202 429252/482388. VAT: Stan/Spec.

Hampshire Gallery   LAPADA
18 Lansdowne Rd. Est. 1971. *STOCK: Paintings and watercolours, 17th to early 20th C.* TEL: 0202 551211. SER: Valuations; restorations. VAT: Spec.

Hardy's Market
862 Christchurch Rd, Boscombe. (J. Hardy). Open 10-5.30. SIZE: 24 dealers. *STOCK: Art deco, art nouveau, oriental china, glass, Victoriana, architectural brass and collectables.* TEL: 0202 422407/303030.

Moordown Antiques
885 Wimborne Rd. (T.A. Bond). Open Tues. and Thurs. 10-1 and 2.15-5, Sat. 10-1 and 2.15-4. *STOCK: General antiques.* TEL: 0202 513732.

G.B. Mussenden and Son Antiques, Jewellery and Silver
24 Seamoor Rd, Westbourne. Est. 1948. Open 9-5. CL: Wed. SIZE: Medium. *STOCK: Antiques, jewellery, silver.* LOC: Central Westbourne, corner of R.L. Stevenson Ave. PARK: Easy. TEL: 0202 764462. SER: Valuations. VAT: Stan/Spec.

Geo. A. Payne and Son Ltd
742 Christchurch Rd, Boscombe. (H.G. and N.G. Payne). FGA. Est. 1946. Open 9-5.30. SIZE: Small. *STOCK: Jewellery, 19th-20th C, £10-£3,000; silver, 18th-20th C, £30-£1,000; plate, £10-£200.* LOC: Opposite Browning Ave. and Chessel Ave. PARK: Browning Ave. TEL: 0202 394954. SER: Valuations; gemstone testing; restorations (silver, jewellery, clocks, watches). VAT: Stan/Spec.

Bournemouth continued

Pegasus Antiques and Collectables
13 Gladstone Rd. West, Boscombe. (P. Banfield). Est. 1991. Open 9.30-1 and 2-4.30. CL: Wed. SIZE: Small. *STOCK: Textiles - clothes and accessories, embroideries, hand crochet, bed and table lace and linen; bric-a-brac, costume jewellery, boxes, brass and copper, small furniture.* LOC: 1st turning off Palmerston Rd. PARK: Forecourt. TEL: 0202 394493; home - same.

R.E. Porter
2-6 Post Office Rd. Est. 1934. Open 9.30-5. SIZE: Medium. *STOCK: Silver (including early antique spoons up to modern), Georgian, £20-£5,000; jewellery, pot lids, Baxter and Le Blond prints, clocks including second-hand. Not Stocked: Furniture, arms, armour, carpets.* LOC: Coming from the square, take the Old Christchurch Rd. exit from the roundabout, then first turning on left. PARK: 300yds. at top of Richmond Hill. TEL: 0202 554289. SER: Valuations. VAT: Stan/Spec.

Portique
15/16/17 Criterion Arcade. Est. 1971. *STOCK: Silver, jewellery, china, jade, glass including paperweights, cloisonné.* LOC: Coming from the square take the Old Christchurch Rd. from roundabout arcade entrance is between first and second turnings on left. TEL: 0202 552979. VAT: Stan/Spec.

Jonathan L.F. Sainsbury in association with Charles Fox
21 and 22 The Arcade. (Jonathan Sainsbury and Richard and David Snell). Resident. BDADA Open 9-5.30. SIZE: Medium. *STOCK: Furniture 18th-19th C, £300-£10,000; objets d'art, 18th-19th C, £50-£3,000; decorative paintings, 18th-20th C, £200-£5,000.* LOC: 200 yards from Bournemouth Sq. PARK: Nearby. TEL: 0202 557633. SER: Valuations; restorations (cabinet and carving work, polishing); buys at auction (fine furniture and objets d'art - England and America). VAT: Stan/Spec.

Sainsburys of Bournemouth Ltd
LAPADA
23-25 Abbott Rd. Est. 1918. Open 8-1 and 2-6 CL: Sat. p.m. *STOCK: Furniture especially bookcases and dining tables, 18th C, to £15,000* PARK: Own. TEL: 0202 529271; home - 0202 763616; fax - 0202 510028. VAT: Stan/Spec.

St. Andrew's Market
4b Wolverton Rd, Boscombe. Open 9-5.30. SIZE 14 units. *STOCK: 18th-19th C furniture and decorative items.* LOC: Next to R.A. Swift and Sons. TEL: 0202 394470.

Sandy's Antiques
790 Christchurch Rd, Boscombe. BDADA *STOCK: Oriental items, general antiques shipping goods, pre-1930.* TEL: 0202 301190 evenings - 0202 470787. VAT: Stan/Spec.

DORSET

Bournemouth continued
Shickell Antiques
886 Christchurch Rd, Boscombe. (W.J. Shickell). Open 9-5.30. STOCK: *Jewellery, furniture and general antiques.* TEL: 0202 432331; home - 0202 418497.

Shickell Books
869 Christchurch Rd, Boscombe. (W.J. Shickell). Open 10.30-5. CL: Wed. STOCK: *Books, general and antiquarian.* TEL: 0202 418347 (24hr. answerphone).

Shippey's of Boscombe
15-16 Royal Arcade, Boscombe. Est. 1927. Open 9-5. CL: Wed. SIZE: Small. STOCK: *Victorian and later jewellery, objets d'art, silver, china, glass, ivories, £1-£300.* Not Stocked: Pictures. LOC: Centre of Boscombe, at Palmerston Rd. end of Arcade. PARK: Within 200yds. TEL: 0202 396548. SER: Restorations (jewellery). VAT: Spec.

Peter Stebbing
7 Post Office Rd. (P.M. Stebbing). Est. 1960. Open 9.30-5. SIZE: Medium. STOCK: *Furniture, £25-£1,000; glass, silver, £1-£100; metalware, jewellery; all 18th-19th C.* LOC: Next to Head Post Office. PARK: 200yds. TEL: 0202 552587. SER: Valuations.

Sterling Coins and Medals
2 Somerset Rd, Boscombe. (W.V. Henstridge). Est. 1969. Open 9.30-4. CL: Wed. p.m. SIZE: Small. STOCK: *Coins, medals, militaria, World War II German items.* LOC: Next to 806 Christchurch Rd. TEL: 0202 423811. SER: Valuations. VAT: Stan.

D.C. Stuart Antiques
34-40 Poole Hill. Open 9-5.30. STOCK: *General antiques, hand-carved reproduction furniture.* TEL: 0202 555544.

R.A. Swift and Sons   LAPADA
4b Wolverton Rd, Boscombe. BDADA. Est. 1904. Open 9-5.30, Sat. 9-4. SIZE: Large. STOCK: English and continental furniture, 18th-19th C; porcelain, pottery, paintings, silver, Sheffield plate, glass, clocks. TEL: 0202 394470; home - 0202 708321. VAT: Stan/Spec.

M.C. Taylor
995 Christchurch Rd, Boscombe East. (Mark Taylor). CMBHI, BDADA. Est. 1982. SIZE: Small. STOCK: *Clocks, barometers and music boxes, 19th C, £500-£1,000.* LOC: Opposite St. James' School and Kings Park entrance. PARK: Easy. TEL: 0202 429718. SER: Valuations; restorations. VAT: Stan/Spec.

Victorian Chairman
383 Christchurch Rd, Boscombe. (M. Leo). Open 9.30-5.30. STOCK: *Furniture, especially chairs and tables.* TEL: 0202 420996. SER: Upholstery.

Bournemouth continued
Victorian Parlour
874 Christchurch Rd, Boscombe. (D.S. Lloyd). Est. 1984. Open 9.30-5. SIZE: Large. STOCK: *Furniture, Victorian mahogany and pine, to £500; unusual country bygones, Victorian.* PARK: Easy. TEL: 0202 433928. SER: Restorations (cane and rush seating); buys at auction.

Sidney Wright (Booksellers)
12-13 Royal Arcade, Boscombe. Est. 1905. Open 9-5.30. STOCK: *Antiquarian and secondhand books.* TEL: 0202 397153.

Yesterday Tackle and Books
42 Clingan Rd, Boscombe East. (David and Alba Dobbyn). Open by appointment. STOCK: *Fishing tackle and associated items including taxidermy; books.* TEL: 0202 476586. SER: Catalogues issued.

York House Gallery
Queens Park. (Mrs J. Hilliard). Est. 1969. By appointment only. SIZE: Small. STOCK: *Oils and watercolours, Victorian to 20th C, £25-£7,000.* TEL: 0202 394275. SER: Valuations; buys at auction (pictures).

BRANKSOME
Allen's (Branksome) Ltd
447/449 Poole Rd. (D.L and P.J. D'Ardenne). Est. 1948. Open 9-1 and 2.15-6. SIZE: Large. STOCK: *Furniture.* TEL: 0202 763724; fax - 0202 763724. VAT: Stan.

Branksome Antiques
370 Poole Rd. (R.E and L.J. Maskell and B.A. Neal). Est. 1973. Open 10-5. CL: Wed. and Sat. SIZE: Medium. STOCK: *Furniture, 19th-20th C, £50-£200; scientific instruments, 19th C, £100-£300; general antiques and bric-a-brac, £5-£50.* PARK: Easy. TEL: 0202 763324; home - 0258 72296. SER: Buys at auction (as stock). VAT: Stan/Spec.

David Mack Antiques
434-437 Poole Rd, and 43a Langley Rd. Est. 1963. Open 9-5.30 or by appointment. SIZE: Large. STOCK: *18th-19th C tables, chairs, display cabinets, desks, bureaux, bookcases; later furniture and shipping goods.* LOC: 2 doors from Branksome rail station. PARK: Own. TEL: 0202 760005; fax - 0202 765100. SER: Restorations. VAT: Stan/Spec.

BRIDPORT
Batten's Jewellers
26 South St. (R. Batten). Open 9.30-5. STOCK: *Jewellery and silver.* TEL: 0308 56910. SER: Valuations; repairs.

Bridport Antiques Centre
5 West Allington. Open 9-5. SIZE: 10 dealers. STOCK: *Pine and country furniture, lace, linen,*

DORSET

Bridport continued
porcelain, glass, books, prints,watercolours, oils, postcards, jewellery, classical garden ornaments, taxidermy. TEL: 0308 25885.

Cox's Corner
40 St. Michael's Lane. (T.G. Cox). SIZE: Large. *STOCK: Furniture, pictures.* TEL: 0308 23451.

Hobby Horse Antiques
29 West Allington. (J. Rodber). Resident. Est. 1948. Open mornings and all day Fri. and Sat. SIZE: Large. *STOCK: Mechanical antiques, toys, trains, porcelain, brass, copper, bygones, silver, jewellery.* LOC: West Bridport on south side of A35 between Dorchester and Exeter. PARK: Nearby. TEL: 0308 22801.

PIC's Bookshop
11 South St. CL: Thurs. p.m. *STOCK: Books, engravings and prints.*

Tudor House Antiques   LAPADA
88 East St. (P. Knight and D. Burton). Est. 1940. Open 9-1 and 2-5.30, Sun. by appointment. SIZE: Small. *STOCK: General antiques.* LOC: Left hand side of main A35 from Dorchester. PARK: Easy. TEL: 0308 427200; home - same. VAT: Stan/Spec.

Westdale Antiques
4a St. Michael's Trading Estate. (D. Westover and D. Dale). Est. 1981. Open 10-4. CL: Thurs. SIZE: Medium. *STOCK: Restored pine furniture, linen and lace, 19th C, £1-£500.* PARK: Nearby. TEL: 0308 27271 (24 hours). SER: Restorations (ceramics).

BROADSTONE

Galerie Antiques
4/4a Station Approach. (R.M. and G.G. Black). Est. 1905. Open 10-5, Sat. 10-1. CL: Wed. SIZE: Medium. *STOCK: Royal Doulton, stoneware, figurines, character jugs, serieseware, pottery, porcelain, glass, gold, silver and jewellery, 1880 to date, £5-£500; art deco, Clarice Cliff, Shelley, Wade, Carltonware, Poole pottery, 1920 to date, £5-£350.* Not Stocked: Coins and taxidermy. PARK: Easy. TEL: 0202 695428; home - 0202 886735. SER: Valuations; restorations (clocks, watches and jewellery). FAIRS: Ardingly, Alexandra Palace, Doulton and Park Lane Hotel.

CERNE ABBAS

Cerne Antiques
(I. Pulliblank). Est. 1972. Open 10-1 and 2-5, Sun. 2-5. CL: Fri. SIZE: Medium. *STOCK: Silver, porcelain, furniture including unusual items, mainly 19th C, £1-£400.* LOC: A352. PARK: Easy. TEL: 0300 341490; home - same.

CHARLTON MARSHALL, Nr. Blandford

Zona Dawson Antiques
The Old Clubhouse. Est. 1958. Open 10-6. CL: Mon. *STOCK: Mainly furniture, clocks, 18th-19th C.* TEL: 0258 453146.

CHARMOUTH, Nr. Bridport

Charmouth Antique Centre
The Street. (R.G. Dodd). Open 10-5.30. (Jan.and Feb. - open Wed. and Sat. only) CL: Mon. (Oct.-Mar.). SIZE: Medium. 16 dealers. *STOCK: General antiques.* TEL: 0297 60122.

CHRISTCHURCH

J.L. Arditti
88 Bargates. (A. and J.L. Arditti). Est. 1964. Open 9-5.30. CL: Sun. except by appointment. SIZE: Medium. *STOCK: Oriental carpets and rugs, 18th to early 20th C, £500-£8,000.* LOC: From town centre take road towards Hurn airport, left side on corner of Bargates and Twynham Avenue. PARK: Twynham Avenue. TEL: 0202 485414. SER: Valuations; restorations; cleaning (Persian rugs). VAT: Stan/Spec.

Christchurch Carpets
55/57 Bargates. (J. Sheppard). Est. 1963. Open 9-5.30. SIZE: Large. *STOCK: Persian carpets and rugs, 19th-20th C, £100-£1,000.* LOC: Main road. PARK: Adjacent. TEL: 0202 482712. SER: Valuations. VAT: Stan/Spec.

Hamptons
12 Purewell. (G. Hampton). Open 10-6. CL: Sat a.m. SIZE: Large. *STOCK: Furniture, 18th-19th C, general antiques, clocks, china, instruments, metalware, oil paintings, Chinese and Persian carpets and rugs.* PARK: Easy. TEL: 0202 484000.

M. & R. Lankshear Antiques
149 Barrack Rd. (M.I. Lankshear). Open 9.30-6 *STOCK: General antiques, especially militaria and swords; collectables, postcards, cigarette cards, medals and paintings.* PARK: Forecourt TEL: 0202 473091. SER: Valuations.

The Old Stores
West Rd, Bransgore. (W. and Mrs J. Collier) Open Thurs.-Sat. 11-5. *STOCK: General antiques.* TEL: 0425 72616.

CORFE CASTLE

Georgina Ryder   LAPADA
Rempstone Hall. Resident. Est. 1977. Open by appointment only. SIZE: Medium. *STOCK 17th-19th C textiles, tapestries, hangings curtains, cushions and silks; small salon and country French furniture.* LOC: Turn left at Corfe Castle on to Studland Rd., premise

Corfe Castle continued
approximately 2 miles on left. PARK: Easy. TEL: 0929 480382. SER: Valuations; buys at auction (textiles). FAIRS: Olympia; NEC; Decorative, Chelsea Harbour. VAT: Stan/Spec.

CRANBORNE, Nr. Wimborne
Tower Antiques
The Square. (P.W. Kear and P. White). Est. 1975. Open 8.30-5.30. CL: Sat. *STOCK: Georgian and Victorian furniture.* TEL: 072 54 552.

DORCHESTER
Box of Porcelain
51d Icen Way. (R.J. and Mrs. S.Y. Lunn). Est. 1984. Open 10-5. *STOCK: Porcelain including Worcester, Doulton, Belleek.* LOC: Close town centre, near Dinosaur Museum. TEL: 0305 250856. SER: Valuations.

Colliton Antique and Craft Centre
Colliton St, North Sq. Open daily, Sun. by appointment. SIZE: 14 dealers. *STOCK: 18th-20th C furniture, £25-£5,000; brass, bric-a-brac, pictures, china, pine, clocks, jewellery and silver, toys.* LOC: By town clock. PARK: Easy. TEL: 0305 269398/260115. SER: Restorations (cabinet work and metalware). VAT: Stan/Spec.

Dorchester Antiques Market
Hardy Hall. Est. 1979. Open third Wed. each month. SIZE: 30+ stands. *STOCK: General antiques, bygones and collectables.* LOC: Opposite open market. TEL: Enquiries - 0963 62478.

Michael Legg Antiques
15 High East St (Showrooms), and Old Malt House, Bottom-o-Town. (E.M.J. Legg). Open 9-5.30 or any time by appointment. SIZE: Medium. *STOCK: 17th-19th C furniture, porcelain, pictures, silver, glass.* TEL: 0305 264596. VAT: Stan/Spec.

Legg of Dorchester
Regency House, 51 High East St. (W. and H. Legg). Est. 1930. *STOCK: General antiques, Regency and decorative furniture, stripped pine.* TEL: 0305 264964. VAT: Stan/Spec.

John Walker Antiques
52 High West St. Open 9.30-5 or by appointment. SIZE: Small. *STOCK: Early furniture, textiles, metalwork, ceramics, wood carvings, 16th-18th C; British folk art, 16th-19th C.* LOC: Main street. PARK: Easy. TEL: 0305 260324; home - 0305 264000. SER: Valuations; buys at auction. VAT: Spec.

GILLINGHAM
Talisman   LAPADA
The Old Brewery, Wyke. Open 9-6, Sat. 10-5. SIZE: Large. *STOCK: Unusual and decorative items, garden furniture, architectural fittings,*

Gillingham continued
18th-19th C; English and continental furniture. TEL: 0747 824423/824222; fax - 0747 823544. VAT: Stan/Spec.

LITTON CHENEY, Nr. Dorchester
F. Whillock
Court Farm. Open by appointment. *STOCK: Maps and prints.* TEL: 0308 482457. SER: Framing.

LYTCHETT MINSTER
The Old Button Shop
(T. Johns). Est. 1970. Open 2-5, Sat. 11-1. CL: Mon. *STOCK: Small antiques, brass, copper, curios, unusual items, and antique Dorset buttons.* TEL: 0202 622169.

MELBURY OSMOND, Nr. Dorchester
Hardy Country
Holt Mill Farm. Est. 1980. SIZE: Large. *STOCK: Stripped pine country furniture, Edwardian and Victorian, £50-£800.* LOC: Off A37. PARK: Easy. TEL: 0935 873361; home - 0935 83440.

NETHERBURY, Nr. Bridport
Richard Bolton
Ashtree Cottage Workshop, Whitecross. BAFRA. Open by appointment. SIZE: Small. *STOCK: Furniture including country, 18th-19th C, £100-£2,000.* LOC: 250yds. on right past church. PARK: Easy. TEL: 030 888 474; home - same. SER: Valuations; restorations (furniture); buys at auction.

PARKSTONE, Nr. Poole
Ashley Antiques
176 Ashley Rd. (M. Hodson). Open 10-3.30, Sat. 10-4. *STOCK: General antiques.* TEL: 0202 744347.

D.J. Burgess
116-116a Ashley Rd. Open 9.30-5.30. CL: Wed. *STOCK: Clocks, watches, some furniture.* TEL: 0202 730542. SER: Restorations (clocks and watches).

Carlton House Antiques
84 Ashley Rd. Est. 1991. Open 9.30-5.30. SIZE: Medium. *STOCK: Period furniture, silver, paintings, glass.* PARK: Easy. TEL: 0202 744556.

D. J. Jewellery
166-168 Ashley Rd. (D. J. and P. M. O'Sullivan). NAG. Est. 1978. Open 9-5.30. SIZE: Large. *STOCK: Jewellery, £5-£1,000; silver and plate, £5-£600; clocks, watches, objets d'art.* Not Stocked: Furniture. PARK: Easy. TEL: 0202 745148. SER: Valuations (jewellery); restorations (jewellery, clocks, watches); gem testing. VAT: Stan.

Trade supplies
OVERHILL ANTIQUE & Old Pine Warehouse
Wareham Road, Holton Heath, Poole
Dorset BH16 6JW
Tel: 0202 621818. Eves: 0202 665043
I travel in my own truck and unload every other Sunday approx. 8 tons + of good quality old and antique pine from Czechoslovakia and East Germany etc.

One of our large stores
Pine supplied, painted, stripped or finished
Dog carts always in stock

Parkstone continued

Wiffen's Antiques
95/101 Bournemouth Rd. (C. A. Wiffen). Est. 1960. Open 9-5.30. SIZE: Large. *STOCK: Furniture including shipping; porcelain, pictures, silver and plate, clocks, brass and copper, jewellery, statuary and garden items.* TEL: 0202 736567. SER: Valuations; restorations.

Christopher Williams Antiquarian Bookseller
19 Morrison Ave. *STOCK: Books especially antiques, art, bibliography, cookery, wine, topography.* TEL: 0202 743157. *Postal Only.*

POOLE

G.D. and S.T. Antiques
(G.D. and S.T. Brown). Open by appointment. *STOCK: General antiques.* TEL: 0202 676340.

Overhill Antique and Old Pine Warehouse
Wareham Rd., Holton Heath. (Tony Neville). Est. 1975. Open 10-6, Sun. 11-4. SIZE: Large. *STOCK: Continental pine including German and E.European, 1750-1930, £10-£1,500.* LOC: From A35 Bakers Arms roundabout, on to A351 towards Wareham, premises 1 mile. PARK: Own. TEL: 0202 621818; home - 0202 665043. SER: Restorations (pine stripping and finishing).

PUDDLETOWN, Nr. Dorchester

Antique Map and Bookshop
32 High St. (C.D. and H.M. Proctor). Open 9-5. *STOCK: Antiquarian and secondhand books, maps, prints and engravings.* TEL: 0305 848633. SER: Postal.

SHAFTESBURY

The Book in Hand (Christopher Driver)
17 Bell St. CL: Wed p.m. *STOCK: Books including antiquarian; craft pottery.* LOC: Opposite car park. SER: Book searches.

Shaftesbury continued

Gold Hill Antiques and Collectibles
Gold Hill Parade, Gold Hill. *STOCK: Collectibles.*

SHERBORNE

Abbas Antiques
17 Newlands. Open 9-5. *STOCK: Small collectables and furniture.*

Antique Market
Digby Hall. Open one Thurs. each month (dates in local press). SIZE: 40+ dealers. *STOCK: General antiques, bygones and collectables.* TEL: 0258 840224.

Antiques of Sherborne
1 The Green. (C. and L. Greenslade). Open 9.30-5. *STOCK: General antiques, fine furniture, paintings, rugs and collectables.* TEL: 0935 816549; home - 0963 210737. SER: Restorations (furniture, paintings); buys at auction.

Jasper Burton Antiques
23 Cheap St. Est. 1964. Open 9-1 and 2-5. CL: Wed. SIZE: Medium. *STOCK: General antiques, especially furniture.* PARK: Easy. TEL: 0935 814434; home - 0935 812322. VAT: Stan/Spec.

Castleton Country Furniture
Long St. (D. Hamilton). Open 9-5.30, Sun. by appointment. *STOCK: Pine.* TEL: 0935 812195.

Compton Antiques Ltd
2 Church Avenue. (D. Straiton). Est. 1985. Open 10-5.30. SIZE: Medium. *STOCK: English furniture including country, 18th-19th C, £50-£8,000; works of art, porcelain and pictures, £5-£2,500.* LOC: Eastern end of Sherborne abbey. PARK: Nearby. TEL: 0935 817782; home - 0935 815584. SER: Valuations; restorations (furniture and upholstery); buys at auction. VAT: Stan/Spec.

Dodge and Son   LAPADA
28-33 Cheap St. (S. Dodge). Open 9-5.30 SIZE: Large. *STOCK: Period furniture, clocks oils, maps, watercolours, ironwork, statuary, fire accessories including pine mantels.* PARK: At rear. TEL: 0935 815151. VAT: Stan/Spec.

Sherborne continued
Greystoke Antiques
Swan Yard, Off Cheap St. (F.L. and N.E. Butcher). Est. 1970. Open 10-4.30. *STOCK: Silver, Georgian, Victorian and later; some 19th C pottery and porcelain; general antiques.* LOC: Off main street. PARK: Car park adjacent to Swan Yard, or outside shop. TEL: 0935 812833. VAT: Stan/Spec.

Heygate Browne Antiques
South St. (M. and W.Heygate Browne). Open 9.30-5.30. SIZE: Large. *STOCK: 18th-19th C furniture, pottery and porcelain.* LOC: Off Cheap St. towards station. PARK: Easy. TEL: 0935 815487. SER: Valuations; restorations. VAT: Stan/Spec.

The Nook
South St. (B.C. Bruton). *STOCK: General antiques - furniture, china, glass, brass and copper.* TEL: 0935 813987.

Pine on the Green
The Green. (S. Dodge). Open 9-5.30. SIZE: Medium. *STOCK: Restored antique pine furniture, English and continental.* LOC: Off A30, 1st shop on left hand side at the top of the town. PARK: Easy. TEL: 0935 815216.

Sherborne Antique Centre
Mattar Arcade, 17 Newlands. Est. 1965. Open 9-5. SIZE: 5 shops. *STOCK: Fine arts, painting, furniture, rugs, objets d'art, jewellery, gold, silver.* LOC: From A30 via Greenhill. PARK: Easy. TEL: 0935 813464.

The Swan Gallery
51 Cheap St. (S. and Mrs K. Lamb). Est. 1977. Open 9.30-5, Wed. 10-1. SIZE: Large. *STOCK: Watercolours, 18th to early 20th C; prints, maps, antiquarian and secondhand books.* PARK: Easy, at rear. TEL: 0935 814465. SER: Valuations; restorations (paintings, watercolours and prints); framing. VAT: Stan/Spec.

STURMINSTER NEWTON
Quarter Jack Antiques
Bridge St. (A.J. Neilson). Est. 1969. SIZE: Small. *STOCK: 18th-19th C glassware, country oak and mahogany furniture, pictures, walking sticks and horse brasses.* TEL: 0258 72558; home - same. SER: Restorations.

Toll House
Bagber Lane. (R.E. and L.J. Maskell). Est. 1973. Open 9-6 or by appointment. SIZE: Warehouse. *STOCK: Furniture, 19th-20th C, £50-£200; scientific instruments, 19th C, £100-£300; general antiques and bric-a-brac, £5-£50.* PARK: Easy. TEL: 0258 72296. SER: Buys at auction (as stock). VAT: Stan/Spec. *Trade Only.*

COMPTON ANTIQUES

COMPTON ANTIQUES LTD
2 CHURCH AVENUE
SHERBORNE • DORSET • DT9 3BP
TEL: 0935 817782

Sturminster Newton continued
Tom Tribe and Son
Bridge St. CMBHI. Resident. Open 9-5, Sat. 9-1 and by appointment. *STOCK: Longcase and mantle clocks, barometers.* PARK: At side of shop. TEL: 0258 72311. VAT: Stan/Spec.

SWANAGE
Georgian Gems Antique Jewellers
28 High St. (B. Barker). NAG. Est. 1971. Open 9.30-1 and 2.30-5 or by appointment. SIZE: Small. *STOCK: Jewellery, £5-£2,000; silver, £5-£500; both from 1700.* LOC: Town centre. PARK: Nearby. TEL: 0929 424697. SER: Valuations; repairs; gem testing.

The Olde Forge Antiques
273a High St. (D. and J. Ferraris). Est. 1967. Open 10-5. CL: Thurs. SIZE: Small. *STOCK: General antiques, pine and bric-a-brac.* LOC: From town centre just over half a mile up the High St. PARK: Easy. TEL: 0929 423319.

Reference Works
12 Commercial Rd. (B. Lamb). Open by appointment. *STOCK: Reference books on ceramics, all subjects, new and out-of-print, £5-£600; some small British porcelain £10-£400.* TEL: 0929 424423; fax - 0929 422597. SER: Mail order, catalogue available; ceramic research and consultancy. FAIRS: Wakefield Ceramic.

AntiquaTat Antiques

Fully Licensed Restaurant

We have over 7,000 square feet of showrooms and 8,000 square feet of trade warehousing packed with one of the largest displays in Dorset of beautiful furnishing antiques at sensible prices.

Antiquatat Antiques
The Old Civic Centre
Hanham Road
Wimborne Dorset.
Large Car Park

Open 9 a.m. – 4.30 p.m. Mon. – Sat.
Tel: Wimborne (0202) 887396

Export container specialists.

TRENT, Nr. Sherborne

Old Barn Antiques Co
Flamberts. (G.W. Mott). Resident. Est. 1959. Open by appointment. SIZE: Medium. *STOCK: Furniture, 18th-19th C, £300-£3,000.* PARK: Easy. TEL: 0935 850648. SER: Valuations; restorations; upholstery; polishing; cabinet making. VAT: Spec.

WAREHAM

Heirlooms (Antique Jewellers)
21 South St. (M. and Mrs G. Young). FGA, DGA, RJDip. Est. 1986. Open 9-5. CL: Wed. SIZE: Medium. *STOCK: Jewellery, £30-£1,000; silver, £20-£500; both Georgian to Edwardian.* LOC: On main thoroughfare. PARK: At rear. TEL: 0929 554207. SER: Valuations; restorations; gem testing.

WEYMOUTH

Books Afloat
66 Park St. (J. Ritchie). Open 9.30-5.30. *STOCK: Rare and secondhand books especially nautical; maritime ephemera, ship models, paintings, prints.* LOC: Near railway station. PARK: Nearby. TEL: 0305 779774.

Finesse Fine Art
9 Coniston Crescent. (T. Wraight and W. Flint). Open by appointment only. *STOCK: Pre-war*

Weymouth continued

motoring accessories - lamps, badges, metal and Lalique mascots, picnic baskets and other items, from £350-£10,000. TEL: 0305 770463; fax - 0305 761459.

The Nautical Antique Centre
Old Harbour Passage, 3A Hope Square. (D.C. Warwick). Est. 1989. Open 10-1 and 2-5.30, Sat. 10-1, Sun. and Mon., Sat. p.m. by appointment. SIZE: Medium. *STOCK: Mainly maritime, some aeronautical and militaria, 1700 to date, £5-£500.* LOC: Off Brewers Quay, adjacent harbour. PARK: Nearby. TEL: 0305 777838; home - 0305 783180. SER: Buys at auction (nautical items).

North Quay Antique Centre
North Quay. (R.A. Shorey). Open 10-5. CL: Mon. SIZE: 8 dealers. *STOCK: General antiques.* TEL: 0305 779313.

Park Antiquities
Park St. (F. and Mrs J.R. Ballard). *STOCK: General antiques, porcelain, small furniture, treen, advertising items.* LOC: Near railway station. PARK: Nearby. TEL: 0305 787666.

The Treasure Chest
29 East St. (P. Barrett). Open 10-5. CL: Wed. p.m. *STOCK: Maps, prints, general antiques, coins, medals, silver, china.* PARK: Next door. TEL: 0305 772757.

WIMBORNE MINSTER

Antiquatat Antiques LAPADA
The Old Civic Centre, Hanham Rd. (D.W. Schwier). Est. 1973. Open 9-4.30. SIZE: Large. *STOCK: Period furniture, silver, clocks, containers.* PARK: Own. TEL: 0202 887496.

Barnes House Antiques
West Row. Est. 1980. Open 10-5. SIZE: 4 dealers. *STOCK: Mainly furniture, £5-£5,000.* TEL: 0202 886275.

J. Beard
STOCK: Small Edwardian inlaid furniture and jewellery.

Bryan Chew
STOCK: Early oak and country furniture and artefacts.

P. Emptage
STOCK: Edwardian furniture and porcelain.

E. Simpkiss
STOCK: Georgian mahogany furniture and silver.

J.B. Antiques
10A West Row. (J. and Mrs. G. Beckett). Est. 1978. Open 10-4, Fri. and Sat. 9.30-4. CL: Wed.

Wimborne Minster continued

SIZE: Small. *STOCK: Copper, £5-£360; brass, £1-£350; furniture, £30-£1,200; all 18th-20th C.* LOC: 2 mins. from Sq. PARK: Nearby. TEL: Home - 0202 882522. SER: Valuations; restorations (metalware); buys at auction (copper).

T.W. Antiques
12 West Row. (T.E. White). Est. 1988. Open 10-4, Fri. and Sat. 9.30-4. CL: Wed. SIZE: Small. *STOCK: Commemoratives, collectables, Doulton and furniture, £5-£500.* LOC: 2 mins. from Sq. PARK: Nearby. TEL: Home - 0202 888958. SER: Valuations; buys at auction (as stock). FAIRS: Sandown; Alexandra Palace, Wimborne Market.

Victoriana Antiques
3 Leigh Rd. (Mrs P. Hammer). Open Tues., Thurs. and Fri. 10-1 and 2.30-4. *STOCK: General small antiques, glass, jewellery, silver, brass, objets d'art.* PARK: Easy. TEL: 0202 886739.

West Borough Antiques, Fine Art
36 West Borough. (Mrs K. Gale-Yearsley). Open 10-4.30, 10-4 in winter. CL: Wed. *STOCK: General antiques especially porcelain.* TEL: 0202 841167.

One half of a mourning locket ordered from London by Mrs Douglas after the death of her husband and daughter, within ten minutes of each other, from yellow fever in 1800, a few days after the birth of another daughter. The figures were painted by 'An Artist of Merit', with the faces done by Samuel Shelley, 'the first Miniature Painter in London'. The 'platt' of hair is that of Mr Douglas and Betsey. Private Collection. From ***Yesterday's Children*** by Sally Kevill-Davies, published by the **Antique Collectors' Club**, £19.95pb.

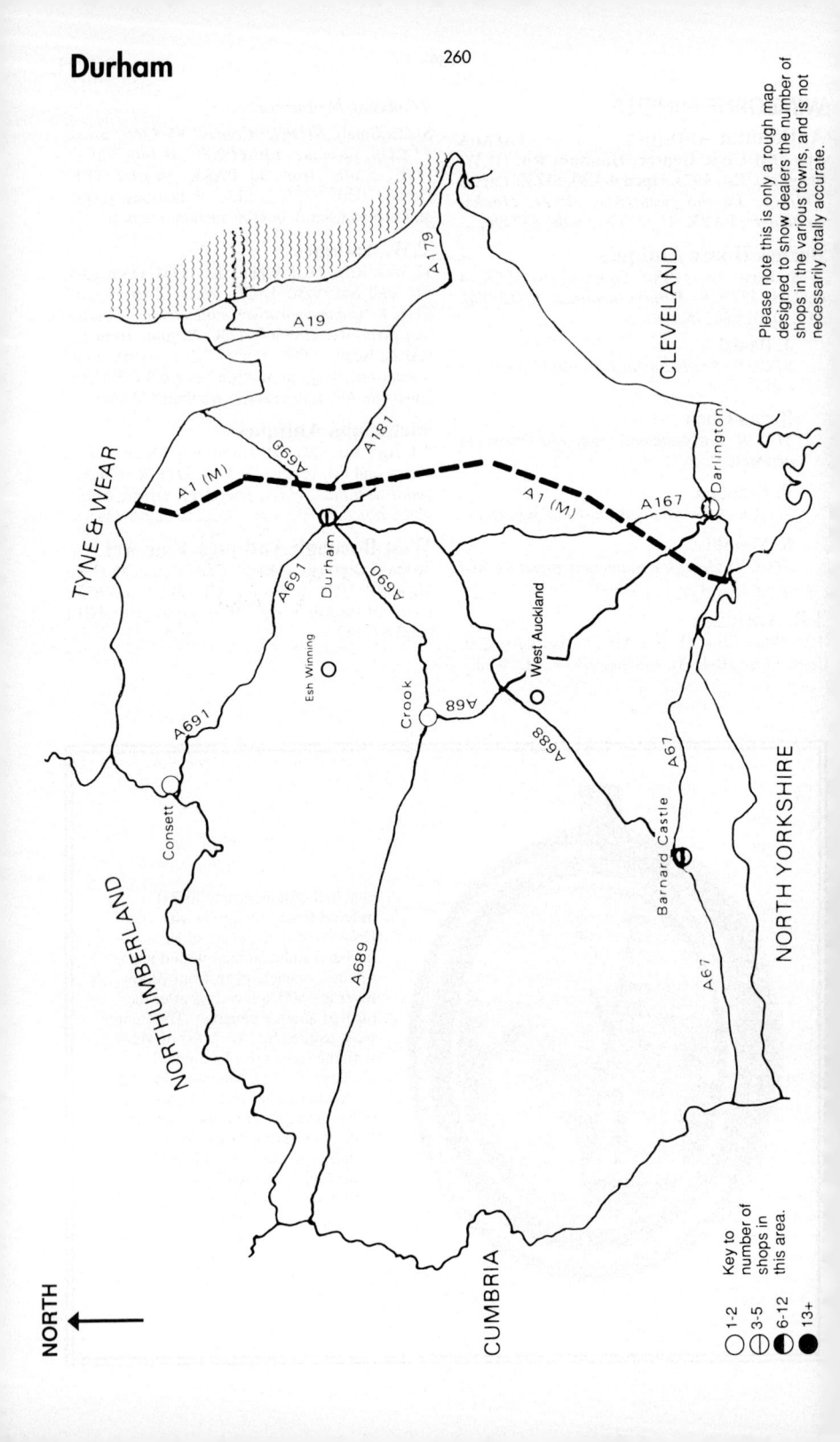

Durham

260

NORTH

Please note this is only a rough map designed to show dealers the number of shops in the various towns, and is not necessarily totally accurate.

Key to number of shops in this area.
○ 1-2
◐ 3-5
◖ 6-12
● 13+

Durham

BARNARD CASTLE

The Ancient Manor House
38 The Bank. (Stephanie Grant). Est. 1977. Open every day 10-5. SIZE: Large. *STOCK: Furniture, pine, pottery and porcelain.* LOC: A67. PARK: Easy. TEL: 0833 37437. SER: Restorations.

The Baliol Gallery
at The Ancient Manor House, 38 The Bank. (Philip Lloyd). Est. 1984. Open 10-5, Sun. 12-4. SIZE: Medium. *STOCK: Paintings, 18th-19th C, £60-£4,500; gilt mirrors, 19th C, £300-£1,200; Georgian and Victorian furniture, 18th-19th C, £3-£800.* LOC: Down The Bank from Market Cross or Bowes Rd. PARK: Easy. TEL: 0833 37437; home - 0833 50696. SER: Valuations, restorations (gilt mirrors, oils and watercolours). FAIRS: Country House; Galloway.

The Collector
Douglas House, The Bank. (R.A. Jordan and P.R. Hunter). Est. !970. Open 10-5. SIZE: Large. *STOCK: Fine oak country furniture, 17th-18th C; period mahogany furniture, 18th-19th C; watercolours, oils, Georgian silver, Persian rugs, pewter, unusual and collectable items.* TEL: 0833 37783. SER: Restorations. VAT: Spec.

Town House Antiques
7 Newgate. (Joan and David White). Est. 1975. Open Wed., Fri. and Sat. *STOCK: Georgian, Victorian and export furniture and decorative items.* LOC: 100yds. from Market Cross on Bowes Museum Rd. TEL: 0833 37021 or 0325 374303. VAT: Stan/Spec.

CONSETT

Harry Raine Antiques
Kelvinside House, Villa Real Rd. Appointment advisable. SIZE: Large. *STOCK: General antiques.* TEL: 0207 503935.

CROOK

Jo Patterson Antiques
Est. 1968. Open by appointment only. SIZE: small. *STOCK: Furniture and smalls, 19th-20th C.* LOC: 6 miles from A68. TEL: 0388 746586.

DARLINGTON

L. Brown and Sons 'The Popular Mart'
6 Hollyhurst Rd. Est. 1976. Open 9.30-5. CL: Wed. p.m. and Sat. p.m., except by appointment. SIZE: Large. *STOCK: General antiques, from late 19th C, £5-£500.* LOC: From town centre, along Woodlands Rd. to Hollyhurst Rd., shop adjacent to Memorial Hospital. PARK: Easy. TEL: 0325 54769; home - 0325 355490. SER: Valuations; buys at auction.

Darlington continued

Bygones
3/5 McMullen Rd. (M. Pitman and A. Walton). Open 10-5.30, Fri. 10-4, Sun. 12-5. CL: Sat. SIZE: Medium. *STOCK: Victorian, Edwardian and period furniture, £100-£3,000; fireplaces, curios, country bygones £5-£500.* LOC: Off Yarm Road. PARK: Easy. TEL: 0325 461399; home - 0325 380884.

Robin Finnegan (Jeweller)
83 Skinnergate. Est. 1974. Open 10-5.30. SIZE: Medium. *STOCK: Jewellery, general antiques, coins and medals, £1-£2,000.* TEL: 0325 489820. SER: Valuations. VAT: Stan.

Nichol and Hill
20 Grange Rd. Open 10-5. *STOCK: Victorian and Edwardian furniture.* TEL: 0325 357431. SER: Restorations, upholstery, interior decoration.

Alan Ramsey Antiques   LAPADA
Unit 10 Dudley Rd, Yarm Road Industrial Estate. Est. 1973. Open Tues., Thurs. and Fri. 10-3. SIZE: Warehouse. *STOCK: Victorian, Edwardian and Georgian furniture.* PARK: Easy. TEL: 0325 361679; home - 0642 711311. VAT: Stan. *Trade Only.*

DURHAM

J. Shotton Antiquarian Books and Prints
89 Elvet Bridge. Est. 1967. Open 9.30-5. CL: Mon. *STOCK: Antiquarian books, coins, prints, maps and paintings.* TEL: 091 386 4597.

ESH WINNING, Nr. Durham

Dunelme Coins and Medals
7 Durham Rd. (P.G. and A.E. Smith). Est. 1982. Open 9-12 and 1-5. CL: Wed. SIZE: Small. *STOCK: Coins, medals and tokens, from ancient Greek to date, £1-£1,000; regimental badges, stamps, gold and silver, banknotes, pre-1920 postcards, autograph letters, curios and small items.* LOC: Main street. PARK: Easy. TEL: 091 373 4446; fax - 091 373 6368. SER: Valuations; coin identification; medal ribbons supplied. VAT: Stan/Spec.

WEST AUCKLAND

Eden House Antiques
10 Staindrop Rd. (Chris and Margaret Metcalfe). Est. 1978. Open daily including Sun. SIZE: Small. *STOCK: Clocks, 18th-19th C, £500-£1,500; furniture, 18th-20th C, £250-£750; bric-a-brac, 19th-20th C, £25-£75.* LOC: A68, approximately 7 mile west of A1M. PARK: Easy. TEL: 0388 833013; home - same. SER: Valuations; restorations (clocks and furniture); buys at auction (clocks and furniture).

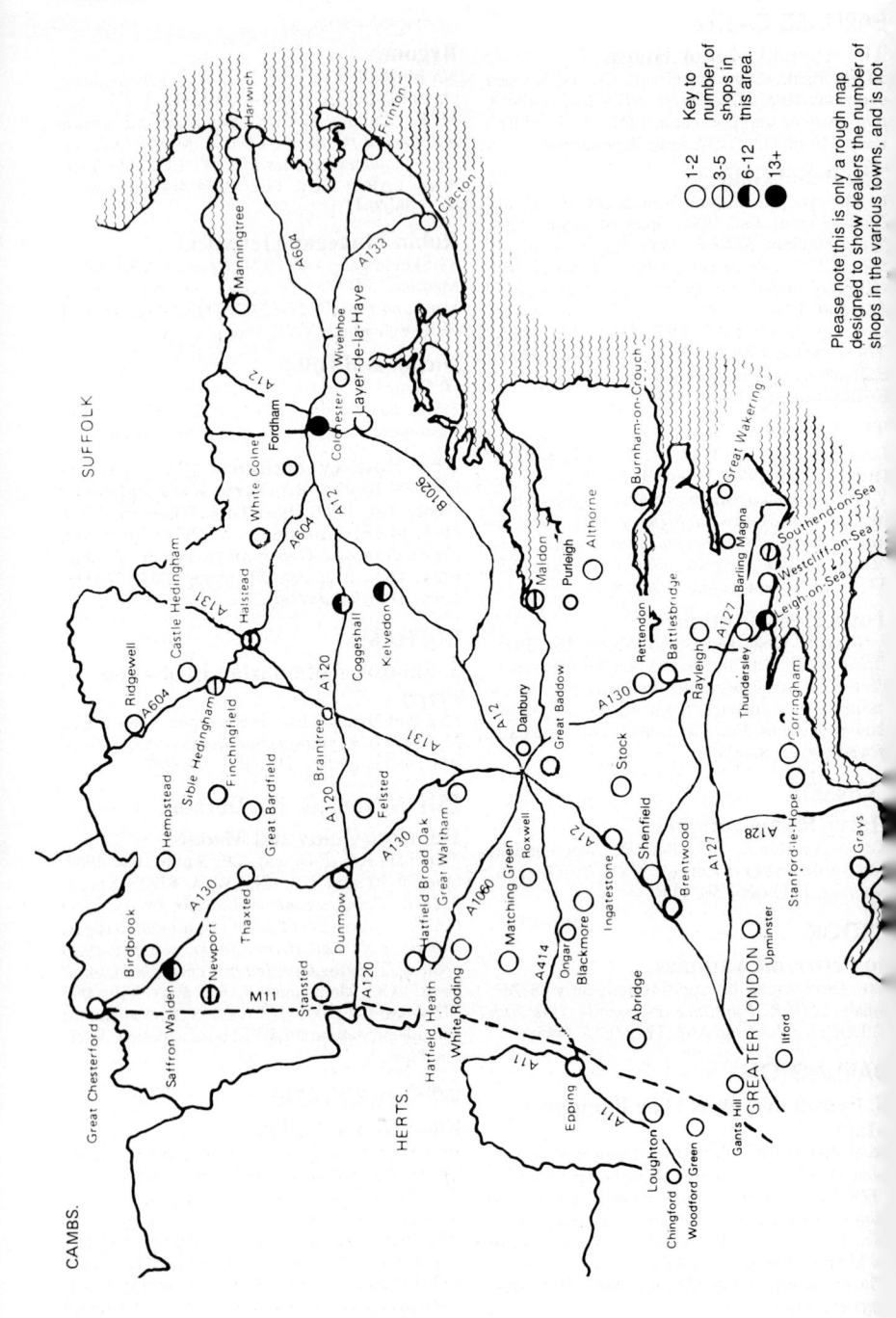

Essex

Essex

ABRIDGE
Abridge Antique Centre
Market Place. (J.S. and F. M. Yewman). Est. 1960. Open 10-5, Thurs. 10-1. SIZE: Large, eleven small shops. STOCK: Clocks, £50-£3,500; furniture, £50-£1,000; both 18th-19th C; small items, china, and porcelain including Doulton, silver, 19th-20th C, £5-£500. LOC: Chigwell-Ongar road opposite The Rodings Restaurant. PARK: Market Sq. TEL: 0992 813113/812107. FAIRS: Local. VAT: Stan/Spec.

ALTHORNE
John Bailey Antique Clocks
5 Austral Way. Open by appointment. STOCK: Longcase clocks, £1,000-£3,500; clocks, £100-£2,000; barometers, Staffordshire ware; books on horology, art and antiques. TEL: 0621 740 279. SER: Restorations and repairs.

BARLING MAGNA
Domino Antiques
Potash Cottage, Barling Road. (S. Parish). Resident. By appointment only. STOCK: Royal Worcester porcelain, £100-£4,000; watercolours, £300-£2,500; English porcelain. TEL: 0702 218691; fax - same. FAIRS: Wakefield Ceramic.

BATTLESBRIDGE
Battlesbridge Antique Centre
SIZE: Over 60 units within adjacent premises (see below). STOCK: Wide range from large furniture to jewellery, all periods with specialist dealers for most items. LOC: A130, mid-way between Chelmsford and Southend. Junction 29, M25, east on A127 to A130, then north for 3 miles. PARK: Own. SER: Restorations (furniture); container facilities.

> **Cromwell House Antique Centre**
> (F. Gallie). TEL: Office - 0268 734005; ground floor dealers - 0268 762612; first floor dealers - 0268 734030.
>
> **Haybarn and Bridgebarn Antique Centres**   LAPADA
> (J. P. Pettitt). TEL: 0268 763500/735884.
>
> **Muggeridge Farm Warehouse**
> (J. F. Gallie). TEL: 0268 769392.
>
> **The Old Granary Antique and Craft Centre**
> (J. F. Gallie). TEL: Office - 0268 769392; workshops - 0268 732166; showrooms - 0268 764197.

BIRDBROOK
. Westrope
The Elms. Est. 1958. Open 9-5, Sat. 10-12, or by appointment. STOCK: Furniture, bric-a-brac, china, dolls, doll's house furniture, garden ornaments. LOC: A604. TEL: 044085 365; evenings - 044085 426.

BLACKMORE, Nr. Ingatestone
Hay Green Antiques
Hay Green Farmhouse. (T. Harding). Open 9.30-5.30. CL: Mon. STOCK: Pine, some mahogany and Victorian furniture. TEL: 0277 821275.

BRAINTREE
Eric Hudes
Paigles, Perry Green, Bradwell. Est. 1946. STOCK: Oriental ceramics and works of art, 10th-19th C; early English and European pottery, 17th-19th C; all £100-£1,000. TEL: 0376 83767. SER: Worldwide postal transactions. FAIRS: Buxton, Harrogate. VAT: Spec. Postal Only.

BRENTWOOD
Brandler Galleries
1 Coptfold Rd. (J. Brandler). Est. 1973. Open 10-5.30, Sun. by appointment. CL: Mon. SIZE: Medium. STOCK: British pictures, 20th C, £100-£10,000. LOC: Near Post Office. PARK: Own at rear. TEL: 0277 222269 (24 hrs); fax - 0277 222786. SER: Valuations (photographs); restorations (picture cleaning, relining, framing); buys at auction (pictures); 2-3 free catalogues annually.

BURNHAM ON CROUCH
Quay Antiques
28 High St. (C. McMullan). Est. 1961. Open 10-5. CL: Wed. STOCK: Paintings, prints, china, glass, Victoriana, jewellery, small furniture. TEL: Home - 0621 782468.

CASTLE HEDINGHAM
Orbell House Gallery
Orbell House. (I. Greene). Resident. Est. 1968. Open by appointment. SIZE: Medium plus gallery. STOCK: Oriental, Persian, Anatolian, Afghan and Caucasian rugs and carpets, £200-£4,000. PARK: Easy. TEL: 0787 60298. SER: Repairing and cleaning (Oriental rugs). FAIRS: Castle Hedingham, Bury St. Edmunds and Snape.

CHINGFORD
Nicholas Salter Antiques
8 Station Approach, Station Rd. Est. 1971. Open 9.30-5, Fri. and Sat. 9.30-6. CL: Thurs. SIZE: Large. STOCK: Furniture, 1850-1930, £150-£500; china and linen, 1870-1950, £30-£150. LOC: Next door to North Chingford station. PARK: Easy. TEL: 081 529 2938.

CLACTON-ON-SEA
L.R. Sharman
80B Rosemary Rd. Est. 1973. Open 9.30-5.15. CL: Wed. SIZE: Small. STOCK: Furniture, 19th C decorative arts, £100-£5,000; jewellery, bronzes, clocks, music boxes, militaria. LOC: Opposite Town and Country Building Society.

ESSEX

Clacton-on-Sea continued
PARK: Own. TEL: 0255 424620. SER: Valuations; restorations (furniture and jewellery). VAT: Stan.

COGGESHALL
Antique Metals
9A East St. (R.M. and S.V. Chaplin). Est. 1959. Open every day 9-6. *STOCK: Brass, copper, polished steel, especially fenders; brass beds.* TEL: 0376 562252.

Antique Pine
63/65 West St. (W.T. Newton). Resident. Open 7 days 10-6. *STOCK: Victorian stripped pine.* TEL: 0376 561972.

Coggeshall Antiques
Doubleday Corner. Open 10-5, Sun. 2-5. SIZE: Large. *STOCK: Furniture, paintings and decorative items, 18th-19th C.* LOC: A120 opposite White Hart Hotel. PARK: At rear. TEL: 0376 562646; home - 0245 256027.

Elkin Mathews
16 Stoneham St. (D.C. Muir). Est. 1887. Open 9.30-1 and 2-4.30, Sat. 10-1 and 2-5. CL: Wed. SIZE: Medium. *STOCK: Antiquarian and secondhand books, 50p-£1,000.* LOC: Just off A120 between Colchester and Braintree. PARK: Own, at rear. TEL: 0376 561730. SER: Valuations; restorations; buys at auction. FAIRS: Major London. VAT: Stan.

Joan Jobson's
5A Church St. (J. Corder). Est. 1974. Open 9.30-5, Sun. 2-5 in summer. SIZE: Medium. *STOCK: Bric-a-brac, Victoriana, general antiques and shipping furniture.* TEL: Home - 0376 561717.

Lindsell Chairs
11 Market Hill. (T.J.L. and A.M. Martin). Est. 1982. Open 10.30-6. CL: Sat. SIZE: Large. *STOCK: Chairs and other seating, some tables, mid-18th C to 1914, £75-£4,000+.* Not Stocked: Windsor, caned, rush seated or commode chairs. LOC: Town centre. PARK: Nearby. TEL: 0376 562766; home - 037 184 222. SER: Restorations. VAT: Stan/Spec.

Mark Marchant (Antiques)
3 Market Sq. Resident. Est. 1960. Open 11-5, Sun. 2.30-5.30. SIZE: Large. *STOCK: Clocks and decorative works, decor furnishings, all periods.* LOC: A120. PARK: Easy. TEL: 0376 561188. SER: Valuations; restorations; buys at auction. VAT: Spec.

COLCHESTER
Badger Antiques
The Old House, The Street, Elmstead Market. (A. Johnson). Resident. Est. 1977. Open 9.30-5.30, Sun. by appointment. SIZE: Medium. *STOCK: Furniture, pine, lace, linen, Victorian underwear,* *clocks, china, glass.* LOC: 4 miles from Colchester on old A133 Clacton road. PARK: Easy. TEL: 0206 822044. SER: Valuations; restorations (furniture and clocks).

Barntiques
Lampitts Farm, Turkeycock Lane, Stanway. (A. Jones and S. Doubleday). Resident. Est. 1978. Open weekends. SIZE: Medium. *STOCK: General antiques and pine.* LOC: Turn left at Eight Ash Green from A604. PARK: Easy. TEL: 0206 210486; home - 0206 21242.

S. Bond and Son
14 North Hill. (M. and R. Bond). Open 9-5.30. CL: Thurs. p.m. SIZE: Large. *STOCK: Furniture, oil paintings, watercolours.* TEL: 0206 572925. SER: Restorations. VAT: Stan/Spec.

Elizabeth Cannon Antiques
85 Crouch St. Open 9.30-5.30. *STOCK: Jewellery, silver, glass, porcelain, collectors' items, period engravings and furniture.* PARK: Easy. TEL: 0206 575817.

Castle Bookshop
37 North hill. (R.J. Green). *STOCK: Antiquarian and secondhand books, maps & prints.* TEL: 0206 577520. VAT: Stan.

Davana Original Interiors
88 Hythe Hill. (D.E. Donnelly). Est. 1963. Open 9.30-5. SIZE: Small. *STOCK: Continental decorative items, French furniture, lighting textiles and curtain accessories, 1800-1930.* PARK: Easy. TEL: 0206 797853. SER: Restorations (metalware); buys at auction (furniture).

Margery Dean Antiques
Mill Farm, Harwich Rd., Gt. Bromley. Est. 1947 Open 9-5, Sun. by appointment. SIZE: Medium *STOCK: Mahogany, country and pine furniture 18th-19th C.* Not Stocked: Reproductions. LOC: (miles from Colchester. 1 1/2 miles off A12 Harwich road, follow signs for Mill Farm camping PARK: Own. TEL: 0206 250485; home - same; fa: - 0206 252040. SER: Valuations. VAT: Spec.

Essex Antiques Centre
Priory St. (Scalpay Securities Ltd). Est. 1969 Open 10-5.30. SIZE: Large - 52 dealers. STOCK *General antiques and collectables.* LOC: Nea town centre, off Queen St. Next to St. Botolph Priory. PARK: Easy. TEL: 0206 871150. SER Restorations (jewellery, furniture, paintings).

Grahams of Colchester
19 Short Wyre St. Open 9-5.30. *STOCK Jewellery and silver.* TEL: 0206 576808. SER Valuations; restorations.

Richard Iles Gallery
10a, 10 and 12 Northgate St. (R. and C. Iles). Es 1970. Open 10-1 and 2-4, Thurs. 10-1. SIZE Small. *STOCK: Watercolours, 19th to early 20*

Antique Collectors' Club Titles

A Collector's History of British Porcelain
by John and Margaret Cushion
This companion volume to our **A Collector's History of English Pottery** is a comprehensive overview of the manufacture of porcelain in Great Britain from mid-18th century to the present.
ISBN 1 85149 155 4
456pp, 641 b & w illus, 130 col, £35.00

A Collector's History of English Pottery
by Griselda Lewis
Now in its fourth edition. *'...this new, revised book must be regarded as the most comprehensive in text and illustrations. In a word, the best.'*
Ceramics Magazine.
**ISBN 1 85149 056 6, 360pp
over 650 b & w illus, 62 col, £35.00**

Available from:
Antique Collectors' Club, 5 Church Street, Woodbridge, Suffolk IP12 1DS
Tel: (0394) 385501 Fax: (0394) 384434

or Market Street Industrial Park, Wappingers' Falls, New York 12590, USA
Tel: 914 297 0003 Fax: 914 297 0068

ESSEX

Colchester continued
C, £75-£700. LOC: Off North Hill. PARK: N.C.P. nearby. TEL: 0206 577877. SER: Valuations; restorations (oils, engravings and watercolours); framing.

Partner and Puxon
7 North Hill. (S.H. and M. Partner). Est. 1937. Open 9-1 and 2.15-5.30. CL: Thurs. p.m. SIZE: Medium. *STOCK: English furniture, 16th to early 19th C, £100-£30,000; porcelain and pottery, 18th-19th C, £10-£2,000; period metalware, £50-£1,500; continental and country furniture, shipping goods, general furnishing items.* LOC: In town centre; North Hill leads from High St. to Railway Station. TEL: 0206 573317. SER: Valuations. VAT: Stan/Spec.

Stock Exchange Antiques
40 Osborne St. (J. Mellish and G. Dean). Open 10-5. *STOCK: General antiques.* TEL: 0206 561997.

Trinity Antiques Centre
7 Trinity St. Est. 1976. Open 9.30-5. SIZE: 8 dealers. *STOCK: General antiques - small furniture, copper, clocks, brass, porcelain, silver, jewellery, collectors' items, Victoriana, maps and prints, linen, pine furniture.* TEL: 0206 577775.

Rita M. Wilkinson Antiques
Heath Farm House, Station Rd., Alresford. Resident. Open by appointment. *STOCK: Mainly 19th C and some selected 20th C furniture especially Victorian dining tables.* LOC: Just off B1027. PARK: Own. TEL: 0206 822805; mobile - 0860 775680.

CORRINGHAM, Nr. Stanford-le-Hope

Bush House
Church Rd. (F. Stephens). Est. 1976. Open by appointment. *STOCK: Staffordshire animals, portrait figures, 1770-1901, £50-£1,000.* LOC: Opposite the church. PARK: Own. TEL: 0375 673463; home - same. SER: Valuations; restorations (pottery and porcelain). FAIRS: Park Lane Hotel; NEC, Birmingham; K.M. Ceramic. VAT: Spec.

DANBURY

Danbury Antiques
(By the Village Green), Eves Corner. (Mrs. Pam Southgate). Open 10-5, Wed. 10-1, Sun. 10.30-1. SIZE: Medium. *STOCK: Jewellery and silver, ceramics, metalware, furniture, 18th to early 20th C, to £400.* PARK: Easy. TEL: 0245 223035. LOC: Off M25, take A12, then A414. SER: Valuations; restorations (jewellery, upholstery, furniture). FAIRS: Furzehill, Margaretting, Billericay. VAT: Stan/Spec.

DUNMOW

Julia Bennet (Antiques)   LAPADA
Flemings Hill Farm, Gt. Easton. Open by appointment. *STOCK: 18th C mahogany, 17th-19th C oak and country furniture, decorative and garden pieces.* TEL: 0279 850279.

Simon Hilton
Flemings Hill Farm, Gt. Easton. Resident. Est. 1937. Open by appointment. *STOCK: Oil paintings, watercolours and drawings, £100-£10,000; fine prints and sculpture, £50-£5,000; all 17th-20th C.* TEL: 0279 850107/850279. SER: Valuations; restorations (oil paintings, watercolours and drawings); buys at auction. VAT: Spec.

EPPING

Epping Galleries
64 - 66 High St. (P. Hellmers). Est. 1972. Open 10-5. CL: Wed. SIZE: Large. *STOCK: Furniture, pine, gramophones, clocks, collectables, linen, 19th-20th C, £5-£300.* LOC: B1393 (A11). PARK: Easy. TEL: 0992 573023. SER: Restorations; framing. VAT: Stan/Spec.

Epping Saturday Market
Rear of 64 - 66 High St. (P. Hellmers). Est. 1977. Open Sat. a.m. SIZE: 60 stalls. *STOCK: General antiques and bric-a-brac.* TEL: 0992 573023.

FELSTED, Nr. Great Dunmow

Argyll House Antiques
Argyll House, Station Rd. (J. Howard and C. Lingham). Est. 1978. CL: Wed. SIZE: Medium. *STOCK: Furniture, Victorian and Edwardian, £25-£1,000; porcelain, 19th C to mid-20th C, £5-£500; collectors' items and ephemera, £1-£250.* LOC: Village centre. PARK: Easy. TEL: 0371 820682; home - same.

FINCHINGFIELD, Nr. Braintree

Andrew Tate
Great Wincey Farm. Est. 1972. Open 9-5, Sat. 9-1 or by appointment. *STOCK: Stripped pine.* TEL: 0371 810004.

FORDHAM

Fordham Antiques
Brook Farm, Halstead Rd. (D. Tyler and P. Hubbard). Est. 1992. Open 10-5, Sun. 12-5. SIZE: Warehouse. *STOCK: Furniture, china and pictures, to 1939, £1-£1,500.* LOC: A604 between Colchester and Halstead. PARK: Own. TEL: 0206 241951. SER: Restorations.

FRINTON-ON-SEA

Dickens Curios
151 Connaught Ave. (Miss M. Wilsher). Est. 1970. Open 9.30-1 and 2.15-5.30; Mon. from 11, Fri. from 10.30; Sat. closed at 5. CL: Wed. p.m. SIZE: Small. *STOCK: Victoriana and earlier*

Frinton-on-Sea continued
items, £5-£200; furniture, 18th-20th C, £5-£300; jewellery, £5-£25; coins and cigarette cards. Not Stocked: Firearms. LOC: From Frinton Station quarter of mile down Connaught Ave., opposite Hammond's Garage. PARK: Easy. TEL: 0255 674134.

Frinton Antiques
(K.J. and Mrs. G.M. Pethick). Est. 1952. Open by appointment. STOCK: Small decorative furniture; fine porcelain, silver, glass and pottery. TEL: 0255 671894. VAT: Stan/Spec.

GANTS HILL
Antique Clock Repair Shoppe
26 Woodford Ave. (K. Ashton). Est. 1971. Open 10-5. STOCK: Clocks, pictures, bric-a-brac. TEL: 081 550 9540.

GRAYS
Grays Collectors Centre
6 London Rd. Open 10-5. SIZE: 25+ dealers. STOCK: Collectables - jewellery, clocks, watches, children's books, toys, silver, de-activated guns, furniture, mirrors, pictures. LOC: Town centre. TEL: 0375 374883. SER: Framing; jewellery workshop.

GREAT BADDOW
Baddow Antique and Craft Centre
The Bringy, Church St. Est. 1969. Open 9-5, Sun. 11-5. SIZE: 22 dealers. STOCK: Furniture, general antiques, Victorian brass bedsteads, bric-a-brac and shipping goods. PARK: Easy. TEL: 0245 76159. SER: Restorations; upholstery.

GREAT BARDFIELD
Golden Sovereign
The Old Police House, High St. (C. and W. Leitch). Est. 1969. Open 10-6. CL: Wed. a.m. and Sat. a.m. SIZE: Small. STOCK: Glass, silver, small furniture, small items, 18th-19th C, from £5. LOC: B1057. From Dunmow, 100yds. beyond Thaxted turning, 2nd shop on left. PARK: Easy. TEL: 0371 810507; home - same.

GREAT CHESTERFORD, Nr. Saffron Walden
C. and J. Mortimer and Son
School St. Est. 1962. Open Thurs., Sat. and Sun. 2.30-5 or by appointment. SIZE: Medium. STOCK: Oak furniture, 16th-18th C, from £400; portrait paintings, 16th-17th C, from £1,500. LOC: From London on B1383. PARK: Easy. TEL: 0799 30261.

GREAT WAKERING
Times Past
195 High St. (M. Sherman and R. Gibson). Est.

Great Wakering continued
1976. Open Tues., Thurs. and Sun. 1.30-5.30. STOCK: Small furniture and decorative items. TEL: 0702 219752.

GREAT WALTHAM, Nr. Chelmsford
The Stores
(M. Webster). Est. 1974. Open 10-5. CL: Sun. and Tues. SIZE: Large. STOCK: Pine furniture. LOC: On A130. PARK: At rear. TEL: 0245 360277; home - 0376 26997. VAT: Stan.

HALSTEAD
Antique Bed Shop
Head St. (V. McGregor). Open Wed.-Sat. 9-6 or by appointment. SIZE: Large. STOCK: Antique wooden beds only. LOC: Leaving town on A131, shop on right. PARK: Own. TEL: 0789 477346.

Halstead Antiques
71 Head St. (P. Earl). Est. 1973. STOCK: Small general antiques, glass, bric-a-brac. TEL: 0787 473265.

Townsford Mill Antiques Centre
The Causeway. (M.T. Stuckey). Open 10-5 including Sun. SIZE: 60 dealers. STOCK: General antiques and collectables. LOC: On A131 Braintree/Sudbury road. TEL: 0787 474451.

HARWICH
Mayflower Antiques
105 High St, Dovercourt. (J.W. Odgers). Est. 1970. Open 10-6. CL: Sat. SIZE: Medium. STOCK: Clocks, mechanical music, scientific and marine instruments, collectors' items. LOC: Main road. PARK: Easy. TEL: 0255 504079; mobile - 0860 315101. VAT: Stan/Spec.

HATFIELD BROAD OAK
Tudor Antiques
(R.M. and P.A. Wood). Est. 1977. Open 9.30-6.30. STOCK: Furniture, porcelain, glass, unusual items. LOC: B183, close to M11 and A120. TEL: 0279 718557.

HATFIELD HEATH, Nr. Bishop's Stortford
Barn Gallery
Parvilles Farm. (H. and M. Scantlebury). Est. 1989. Open Wed. and Sat. 10.30-4 or by appointment. SIZE: Medium. STOCK: Oil paintings and watercolours, 19th-20th C, £250-£5,000; prints, works by living artists. LOC: Turning off A1060 at Hatfield Heath, down Matching Green Rd., opposite Down Hall. PARK: Easy. TEL: 0279 730114; home - 0279 731228. SER: Valuations; restorations. VAT: Stan/Spec.

ESSEX

HEMPSTEAD, Nr. Saffron Walden

Michael Beaumont Antiques
Hempstead Hall. Open 10.30-5. CL: Thurs. and Fri. SIZE: Large. *STOCK: Furniture - oak, mahogany, walnut, rosewood, 17th-19th C, £50-£4,000; Oriental rugs.* LOC: On B1054 between Hempstead and Steeple Bumpstead. PARK: Easy. TEL: 0440 730239. SER: Restorations (furniture). VAT: Stan/Spec.

ILFORD

Belgrave Antiques and Bric-a-Brac
77 Belgrave Rd. (Mrs M.M. Germain). Est. 1969. Open 10-2 and 3.30-6.30. *STOCK: Furniture, paintings, bric-a-brac, books.* TEL: 081 554 8032.

Flowers Antiques
733 High Rd, Seven Kings. (J.C. and A.D. Meeson). Est. 1988. Open 9.30-5.30. CL: Wed. *STOCK: Furniture, Edwardian, Victorian; glass, china.* PARK: Easy. TEL: 081 599 9959.

INGATESTONE

Meyers Gallery LAPADA
66 High St. (Mrs J. Meyers). Est. 1972. Open 10-5. CL: Wed. SIZE: Large. *STOCK: Oil paintings and watercolours, 18th-20th C and living artists, £25-£10,000; small Victorian furniture and decorative items.* PARK: Nearby. TEL: 0277 355335. SER: Restorations; framing. VAT: Stan/Spec.

KELVEDON, Nr. Colchester

Kelvedon Antiques BADA
90 High St. (J. and S.E. Billings). Est. 1965. Open 9.30-5.30. CL: Sun. except by appointment. SIZE: Medium. *STOCK: Furniture, 18th to early 19th C.* LOC: From London on right hand side of main street. PARK: Easy. TEL: 0376 570557. VAT: Stan/Spec.

Kelvedon Antiques Centre
139 High St. (M. Chave). Open 10-5 or by appointment. SIZE: Medium - 6 dealers. *STOCK: Furniture, porcelain, pottery, glass, silver, jewellery, brass, copper, collectors' items, 18th-20th C.* LOC: Off A12 between Chelmsford and Colchester. PARK: Easy. TEL: 0376 570896. FAIRS: Furze Hill, Margaretting.

Kelvedon Art and Antiques
2 High St. (Sarah Mabey). Open 10-5. SIZE: 6 dealers. *STOCK: Furniture, paintings and decorative items, 18th-19th C.* TEL: 0376 573065; home - 0245 256027.

Millers Antiques Kelvedon LAPADA
46 High St. Est. 1920. Open 9-5.30, Sat. 10-4 or by appointment. SIZE: Large. *STOCK: 17th-19th C mahogany, walnut, fruitwood, oak, English and French furniture.* PARK: Own. TEL: 0376 570098; fax - 0376 572186. VAT: Stan/Spec.

Kelvedon continued

G.T. Ratcliff Ltd
Whitebarn, Coggeshall Rd. (W.D. Boyd-Ratcliff and F.D. Campbell). Est. 1935. Open 9-5. CL: Sat. p.m. SIZE: Large. *STOCK: Furniture, mainly 18th-19th C.* LOC: A12. PARK: Easy. TEL: 0376 570234; fax - 0376 571764. VAT: Stan. *Trade Only.*

G.T. Ratcliff Ltd. The Old Antique Shop
Menai House, 41 High St. (Wendy Boyd-Ratcliff and Fiona Campbell). Est. 1938. Open 10-5, Sun. by appointment. SIZE: Large (Trade warehouse). *STOCK: Furniture, smalls and decorative items.* TEL: 0376 570223. VAT: Stan/Spec.

Thomas Sykes Antiques LAPADA
16 High St. (T.W. Sykes and O.P. Folkard). Est. 1983. Open 10-5, Sun. by appointment. SIZE: Large. *STOCK: 18th-19th C furniture and Victorian pictures, £500-£25,000.* LOC: Off A12. PARK: Own. TEL: 0376 571969. SER: Valuations; buys at auction. VAT: Spec.

Templar Antiques
6 Peter's House, High St. (P. Wilson). Est. 1974. Open 10-5. SIZE: Medium. *STOCK: 18th to early 19th C furniture, prints, pictures and glass, including airtwist wineglasses.* LOC: Village centre, off A12. PARK: Own at rear. TEL: 0376 572101.

Times Past
110 High St. (Alan and Victoria Waine). Est. 1979. Open 10-5. CL: Mon. and Wed. SIZE: Small - 4 rooms. *STOCK: Decorative arts - art nouveau, art deco, smalls and furniture, 1890-1940, £5-£1,000.* LOC: B1025. PARK: Easy. TEL: 0376 571858. SER: Valuations. FAIRS: Greenwich Art Deco, Harlow, Hornchurch.

LAYER DE LA HAYE

Pugh's Porcelains LAPADA
Layer Fields House, Field Farm Rd. (J. and J. Pugh). Resident. Open by appointment. SIZE: Medium. *STOCK: English porcelain, late 18th and early 19th C, £20-£2,500.* LOC: Layer Rd. from Colchester, turn left at The Folly. PARK: Easy. TEL: 0206 738170. SER: Buys at auction. FAIRS: Cheltenham, Wakefield Ceramic, Olympia.

LEIGH-ON-SEA

K.S. Buchan
135 The Broadway. Open 10-5. *STOCK: Furniture and general antiques.* TEL: 0702 79440.

Castle Antiques
72 The Broadway. (B.L. Zabell and J.A. Gair). Open 10-5. CL: Wed. *STOCK: 18th-19th C decorative furniture, pottery and porcelain*

ESSEX

Leigh-on-Sea continued
(especially Staffordshire figures and Masons Ironstone); silver, firearms, edged and ethnic weapons, tribal artifacts, antiquities, cased birds and fish. TEL: 0702 75732; mobile - 0860 795354.

Collectors' Paradise
993 London Rd. (H.W. and P.E. Smith). Est. 1967. Open 10-5.30. CL: Fri. SIZE: Small. *STOCK: Clocks, 1870-1930's, from £45; bric-a-brac; postcards, 1900-1930s; cigarette cards, 1889-1939.* LOC: On A13. PARK: Easy. TEL: 0702 73077.

Pall Mall Antiques
104c/104d Elm Rd. (M. Sherman). Open 10-5. *STOCK: Porcelain, copper, brass, glass, general antiques.* TEL: 0702 77235.

Past and Present
81 and 83 Broadway West. (R. Banks). Open 9.30-4.30. CL: Wed. *STOCK: General antiques.* TEL: 0702 79101.

John Stacey and Sons
86-90 Pall Mall. Est. 1946. Open 9-5.30. CL: Sat. p.m. *STOCK: General antiques.* TEL: 0702 77051. SER: Valuations; exporters; auctioneers. VAT: Stan.

J. Streamer Antiques
86 Broadway, and 212 Leigh Rd. Est. 1965. Open 9.30-5.30. CL: Wed. *STOCK: Jewellery, silver, bric-a-brac, small furniture.* TEL: 0702 72895/711633.

Tilly's Antiques
1801 London Rd. (S.T. and R.J. Austen). Est. 1972. Open 10-5. CL: Wed. SIZE: Medium. *STOCK: Furniture, 19th C, £100-£500+; Victorian and Edwardian dolls, £100-£500; general antiques, 19th-20th C, £5-£200.* LOC: A13. PARK: Easy. TEL: 0702 557170. SER: Valuations; restorations (furniture and dolls).

Richard Wrenn Antiques
113/115 Broadway West. Est. 1950. Open 10.30-5.30. CL: Mon., Wed. and Fri. p.m. SIZE: Large. *STOCK: Furniture, £250-£5,000; porcelain, glass, £30-£1,000; jewellery, silver, objets d'art, £40-£2,000; metalware, brass, copper, £20-£500.* LOC: 250yds. west of Leigh church. TEL: 0702 710745. VAT: Stan/Spec.

LOUGHTON
Pearl Morris
Open by appointment. *STOCK: Doulton, Lambeth stoneware and Burslem by major artists.* TEL: 081 508 7117.

MALDON
Abacus Antiques
105 High St. (Mrs J. Davidson). Open 10-4.30. CL: Wed. SIZE: Medium. *STOCK: Jewellery,*

Maldon continued
19th to early 20th C, £10-£500; porcelain, pottery, glass, small silver and collectors' items, 1800-1930, £5-£250; furniture, 19th C and Edwardian, £20-£2,000. Not Stocked: Firearms, coins, stamps, books. LOC: Town centre. PARK: Easy. TEL: 0621 850528; home - same. SER: Valuations.

The Antique Rooms
63D High St. (Mrs E. Hedley). Est. 1966. Open 10-5, Wed. 10-1. SIZE: Medium. *STOCK: Furniture, pottery, porcelain, glass and silver, costume, linen and lace, jewellery, lace-making equipment, collectors' items.* LOC: Just off High St., in courtyard at rear of Maldon bookshop. PARK: Nearby. TEL: 0621 856985.

Clive Beardall Antiques
104B High St. BAFRA. Est. 1982. Open 8-5.30, Sat 8-4.30. SIZE: Small. *STOCK: Furniture, 18th-19thC, £100-£5,000.* LOC: Off High St. in alleyway between Pollards and Peter Foulkes. PARK: Easy. TEL: 0621 857890. SER: Valuations; restorations (furniture). VAT: Stan/Spec.

Beeleigh Abbey Books (W. and G. Foyle Ltd.)
Beeleigh Abbey. Open 9-5, Fri. p.m by appointment. CL: Sat. *STOCK: Rare and antiquarian books.* TEL: 0621 856308; fax - 0621 850064.

Maldon Antiques and Collectors Market
United Reformed Church Hall, Market Hill. Est. 1975. Open first Sat. every month, 9-4.30. SIZE: 20 dealers. PARK: Easy. TEL: 07872 22826.

MANNINGTREE
Forty Nine
High St. (A. Patterson). Open 10-1 and 2-5. *STOCK: General and country antiques.* PARK: Easy. TEL: 0206 396170.

F. Freestone
Kiln Tops, 29 Colchester Rd. Open 9-6, appointment advisable. *STOCK: General antiques, furniture, clocks.* TEL: 0206 392998.

MATCHING GREEN, Nr. Harlow
Stone Hall Antiques
Down Hall Rd. Est. 1971. Open 9-5.30, Sat. and Sun. by appointment. SIZE: Warehouse. *STOCK: Furniture, 17th-19th C, £50-£10,000.* LOC: Turning off A1060 at Hatfield Heath. PARK: Own. TEL: 0279 731440; home - same. VAT: Stan. *Trade & Export Only.*

NEWPORT, Nr. Saffron Walden
Brown House Antiques
High St. (B.E. and J. Hodgkinson). Est. 1978. Open 10-5. SIZE: Medium. *STOCK: Furniture,*

F.G. BRUSCHWEILER (ANTIQUES) LTD.
WHOLESALE & EXPORT
41/67 LOWER LAMBRICKS, RAYLEIGH, ESSEX SS6 7EH

Tel: (STD 0268) 773761 : Private 062 182 8152 : Fax: 0268 773318
We hold over 1,000 pieces of 18th & 19th century furniture in our ever changing stock, as well as other interesting items.
Plus shipping goods.

STOP PRESS! WE HAVE NOW ACQUIRED AN ADDITIONAL WAREHOUSE OF 50,000 SQUARE FEET.

From London Only 35 miles on the A127 or 40 minutes by train from Liverpool Street Station

Member of L.A.P.A.D.A.

Newport continued
from 18th C, £50-£2,500. LOC: B1383, off M11 at Stansted interchange. PARK: Easy. TEL: 0799 40238; home - same. SER: Valuations; restorations; buys at auction (furniture). VAT: Stan/Spec.

Gostick Hall Antiques
Est. 1979. Open by appointment. *STOCK: Victorian and Edwardian jewellery, silver, porcelain, glass.* TEL: 0799 40633.

Newport Gallery
High St. (W. Kemp and E.C. Hitchcock). Open 9.30-5. CL: Mon. *STOCK: Watercolours, prints and oils.* LOC: On B1383, two miles from Saffron Walden. PARK: At rear. TEL: 0799 40623.

ONGAR
Robert Bailey Oriental Rugs
P.O. Box 1110. (R.M. Bailey). Est. 1975. Open by appointment. *STOCK: Persian rugs, 19th-20th C, £500-£3,500; Turkoman and Turkish rugs.* Not Stocked: Chinese, Pakistani and Indian rugs. TEL: 0277 362662. SER: Consultancy; valuations; restorations; cleaning and identification. VAT: Stan/Spec. *Trade Only.*

PURLEIGH, Nr. Chelmsford
David Lloyd Gallery
The Studio, Turnstone, The Street. Open by appointment. *STOCK: 19th-20th C watercolours and oils.* TEL: 0621 828093.

RAYLEIGH
F.G. Bruschweiler (Antiques) Ltd   LAPADA
41-67 Lower Lambricks. Est. 1954. Open 9-5, Sat. by appointment. SIZE: Warehouses. *STOCK: Furniture, 18th-19th C.* LOC: A127 to Weir roundabout through Rayleigh High St. and Hockley Rd., first left past cemetery, then second left, warehouse round corner on left. PARK: Easy. TEL: 0268 773761/773932; home - 062 182 8152; fax - 0268 773318. VAT: Stan. *Trade Only.*

RETTENDON
Antiques Trade Warehouse   LAPADA
Rawlings Farm Buildings, Main Rd. (F.G. Bruschweiler (Antiques) Ltd. and Ian F. Vince). Open 8.30-5.30 or by appointment. CL: Sat. *STOCK: Furniture.* TEL: 0245 400046. LOC: A130.

ESSEX

LITTLEBURY ANTIQUES — LITTLEBURY RESTORATIONS
58/60 FAIRYCROFT ROAD SAFFRON WALDEN ESSEX CB10 1LZ
TELEPHONE & FAX: SAFFRON WALDEN (0799) 527961
Evenings and Weekends: (0279) 771530

Barometers, Marine antiques, fine ship models, Walking sticks, Chess sets and other high quality interesting pieces

Expert restoration by craftsmen; barometers, clocks, all forms of furniture repair, replacement of marquetry, all inlay work carefully matched

*Business hours 9am – 5pm Monday to Friday, Weekend by appointment only
Railway Station: Audley End (1½ miles away) London to Cambridge line*

Rettendon continued

Trading Warehouse
Rawlings Barn, Main Rd. (Ian F. Vince). Open 8.30-5.30. *STOCK: Furniture and smalls, all periods.* LOC: A130. TEL: 0245 400046.

RIDGEWELL, Nr. Halstead
Ridgewell Crafts and Antiques
(A.A. and C.M.J. Godsell and P. Crouch). Est. 1952. Open 10-6.30 including Sun. CL: Wed. SIZE: Medium. *STOCK: Clocks and watches, 19th C, £5-£500; china, brass, copper, some furniture.* LOC: On A604, 6 miles from Haverhill towards Colchester. PARK: Easy. TEL: 044 085 272.

ROXWELL, Nr. Chelmsford
Freeman Antiques
By appointment only. *STOCK: Period oak especially coffers.* TEL: 024 531 286.

SAFFRON WALDEN
Bush Antiques
26-28 Church St. (Mrs. B.E. Bush and Mrs. J.M. Hosford). Est. 1962. Open 10.30-4.30. CL: Thurs. SIZE: Medium. *STOCK: English ceramics including blue and white transfer printed pottery, copper lustre and pink lustre, £25-£250; mahogany and country furnitutre, to £1,000; copper and brass, to £250; all 1800-1860.* LOC: 300 yards north of Market Sq., on crossroads with Museum St. PARK: Nearby. TEL: 0799 523277. FAIRS: Bury St. Edmunds (Spring).

Dolphin Antiques
Kent's Farmhouse, High St., Littlebury. (R.H. Bramwell and L.J. Aldred). Open 9-5.30 but usually available. SIZE: Large. *STOCK: 18th to early 19th C furniture, metalware and glass.* Not Stocked: Jewellery. PARK: Own at rear. TEL: 0799 528067. SER: Valuations. *Resident.*

Lankester Antiques and Books
Old Sun Inn, Church St. and Market Hill. (J. and P. Lankester). Est. 1965. Open 9.30-5.30. SIZE: Large. *STOCK: Furniture, porcelain, pottery, metalwork, general antiques, books, prints and maps.* TEL: 0799 522685. VAT: Stan.

Saffron Walden continued

Littlebury Antiques - Littlebury Restorations Ltd
58/60 Fairycroft Rd. (N.H. D'Oyly). Est. 1962. Open 9-5. CL: Sat. and Sun. except by appointment. SIZE: Medium. *STOCK: Barometers, marine antiques, chess sets, walking sticks and curios.* PARK: Easy. TEL: 0799 527961; fax - same; home - 0279 771530. SER: Valuations; restorations; buys at auction. VAT: Stan/Spec.

Maureen Morris   LAPADA
Open by appointment. *STOCK: Samplers, needleworks, textiles and small country furniture.* TEL: 0799 521338; fax - 0799 522802.

Jane Sumner
9 Market Sq. (Mrs J. Sumner). SIZE: Medium. *STOCK: Early oak, Georgian mahogany, metalware, jewellery.* TEL: 0672 870727. FAIRS: Organiser - London and Kenilworth Antique Dealers.

SHENFIELD
The Chart House
33 Spurgate, Hutton Mount. (C.C. Crouchman). Est. 1974. Open by appointment only. SIZE: Small. *STOCK: Nautical items.* PARK: Easy. TEL: 0277 225012; home - same. SER: Hire of nautical items and equipment; buys at auction. VAT: Stan.

SIBLE HEDINGHAM, Nr. Halstead
Churchgate Antiques
150 Swan St. (B. Wilkinson). Est. 1979. Open 10-5, Sun. by appointment. CL: Mon. SIZE: Large. *STOCK: English and Irish period pine, £75-£1,800.* LOC: A604. PARK: Easy. TEL: 0787 62269; home - 0787 61311. SER: Valuations; restorations (stripping). VAT: Stan.

Hedingham Antiques
100 Swan St. (P. Patterson). Open 10-12.30 and 1.30-5 or by appointment. CL: Wed. p.m. SIZE: Medium and warehouse. *STOCK: Furniture, 1790-1910; china, glass, silver plate, Victorian to*

Sible Hedingham continued
art deco, bric-a-brac. LOC: A604, village centre. PARK: Easy. TEL: 0787 60360; home - same. SER: Restorations.

W.A. Pinn and Sons BADA LAPADA
124 Swan St. (K.H. and W.J. Pinn). Est. 1943. CL: Sun. except by appointment. SIZE: Medium. *STOCK: Furniture, 17th to early 19th C, £100-£5,000; clocks, 18th to early 19th C, £250-£3,500; interesting items, prior to 1830, £10-£1,500.* LOC: On A604 opposite Shell Garage. PARK: On premises. TEL: 0787 61127. FAIRS: Chelsea Spring and Autumn. VAT: Stan/Spec.

SOUTHEND-ON-SEA
Kickshaws
20 Alexandra St. (Mrs A.M. Eddelin). Est. 1974. Open 11-1 and 3-6. CL: Wed. SIZE: Small. *STOCK: General antiques, £5-£500.* LOC: Town centre, 50yds. from High St. PARK: Meters and opposite. TEL: 0702 353630.

Lonsdale Antiques
86 Lonsdale Rd, Southchurch. (H.M. Clark). Open 9-5.30. CL: Wed. *STOCK: Jewellery, pictures, porcelain, general small antiques.* TEL: 0702 462643.

Reddings Art and Antiques
98 London Rd. (F.H. Redding). Resident. Open by appointment only. *STOCK: Oils and watercolours, general antiques.* TEL: 0702 354647.

STANFORD-LE-HOPE
Barton House Antiques
Wharf Rd. (L. and J. Pigney). Est. 1973. Open all times but appointment advisable. SIZE: Medium. *STOCK: 17th-19th C furniture; 18th-19th C English porcelain, including English 18th C blue and white, copper, brass and glass.* LOC: Turn off A13 to centre of town, 200yds. on right hand side. PARK: Easy. TEL: 0375 672494. SER: Valuations; buys at auction. VAT: Spec. *Mainly Trade.*

STANSTED
Linden House Antiques
3 Silver St. (A.W. and K.M. Sargeant). Est. 1961. Open 9-5.30. CL: Sun. except by appointment. SIZE: Large. *STOCK: English furniture, 18th-19th C, £100-£10,000; small decorative items, including library and dining room furniture.* LOC: On A11. TEL: 0279 812372. VAT: Spec.

Valmar Antiques LAPADA
Croft House, High Lane. (John and Marina Orpin). Resident. Est. 1960. Open by appointment. SIZE: Large. *STOCK: Furniture and decorative items, £50-£10,000.* TEL: 0279 813201; fax - 0279 816962. FAIRS: Major British.

STOCK
Sabine Antiques
38 High St. (C.E. Sabine). Est. 1974. Open 10-5 or by appointment. CL: Mon. *STOCK: Furniture from £50; china and glass, from £5.* LOC: Village centre on B1007. PARK: Easy. TEL: 0277 840553. SER: Valuations; restorations (furniture) silver plating; framing.

THAXTED
Thaxted Galleries
1 Newbiggin St. (J.E. Sheppard). Est. 1958. Open 9-5.30. CL: Sun., except by appointment. SIZE: Large. *STOCK: Furniture, £200-£1,000; oak furniture, £250-£1,500; all 17th-18th C; antique lamp bases.* LOC: On B184. PARK: At rear. TEL 0371 830350.

Turpin's Antiques BADA
4 Stoney Lane. (J.F. Braund). SIZE: Large *STOCK: 17th-18th C walnut, oak and mahogany metalware.* TEL: 0371 830495. SER: Restorations; buys at auction. VAT: Spec.

THUNDERSLEY
Bramley Antiques LAPADA
180 Kiln Rd. (S. Grater). Est. 1978. Open 11.30-4.30, Sat. 11.30-6. CL: Mon. and Fri SIZE: Medium. *STOCK: Porcelain and glass £5-£250; furniture, £30-£2,500; linen, silver jewellery, brass, £2.50-£500; all 18th to early 20th C.* LOC: A13. PARK: Easy. TEL: 0702 551800. SER: Valuations; restorations. VAT Stan/Spec.

UPMINSTER
The Old Cottage Antiques
The Old Cottage, Corbets Tey. (R. Edwards). Est 1970. Open 10-5. SIZE: Medium. *STOCK Furniture, shipping goods, porcelain, silver general antiques. Not Stocked: Firearms.* PARK Easy. TEL: 0708 222867.

WESTCLIFF-ON-SEA
David, Jean and John Antiques
Lincoln House Gallery, 587 London Rd. Est 1963. Open 10-5. CL: Wed. SIZE: Large *STOCK: Clocks, furniture, £25-£3,000; porcelain bronzes, weapons, objets d'art, some shipping goods.* LOC: Opposite Jewsons. TEL: 0702 339106; fax - 0268 560536; home - 0268 733330 evenings - 0268 785815. SER: Valuations restorations (clocks, barometers and small furniture). VAT: Stan/Spec.

It's About Time
863 London Rd. (R. and V. Alps). Est. 1980. Open 9-5.30. CL: Wed. SIZE: Medium. *STOCK: Clocks 18th-19th C, £200-£4,000; barometers, Victorian and Edwardian furniture.* LOC: A13. PARK: Easy TEL: 0702 72574; home - 0702 205204.

WHITE COLNE, Nr. Colchester
Compton-Dando (Fine Arts) Limited
Berewyk Hall. (A.C. Compton-Dando). Resident. Open by appointment only. *STOCK: Period English and Continental furniture.* LOC: B1024. At 'King's Head' take left turn marked 'Bures' and make for White Colne parish church. Berewyk Hall lies just beyond, on left. PARK: Easy. TEL: 0787 222200; fax - 0787 222945. SER: Valuations; buys at auction (furniture). VAT: Stan/Spec.

Fox and Pheasant Antique Pine
(J. and J. Kearin). Est. 1978. Open 8-6. SIZE: Large. *STOCK: Stripped pine.* LOC: A604. PARK: Easy. TEL: 0787 223297. SER: Pine stripping; restorations; kitchens.

WHITE RODING
White Roding Antiques
'Ivydene', Chelmsford Rd. (F. and J. Neill). Est. 1971. Open by appointment. SIZE: Medium.

White Roding continued
STOCK: Furniture and shipping goods, 18th-19th C, £10-£1,500. LOC: A1060 between Bishops Stortford and Chelmsford. PARK: Easy. TEL: 0279 876376; home - same. VAT: Stan/Spec.

WOODFORD GREEN
P. and K.N. Blake - Lanehurst Antiques   LAPADA
403 High Rd. Est. 1952. Open by appointment. SIZE: Medium. *STOCK: Furniture, general antiques.* LOC: A11, close to Castle public house. TEL: 081 504 9264. SER: Valuations; buys at auction. VAT: Stan/Spec.

Galerie Lev
1 The Broadway. Open 10-5. *STOCK: Oils, watercolours, collectors' items, silver plate, porcelain.* LOC: Near Woodford underground station. TEL: 081 505 2226. SER: Framing (trade only).

Antique Collectors' Club Titles

Pictorial Dictionary of British 18th Century Furniture Design
by Elizabeth White
Published designs from 120 sources. The 3,000 named and dated illustrations provide arguably the most important contribution to 18th century furniture studies since Ralph Edwards' **Dictionary of English Furniture.**
ISBN 1 85149 105 8
700pp, 3,500 b & w designs, 24 col £65.00

Pictorial Dictionary of British 19th Century Furniture Design
An A.C.C. Research Project
Compiled from forty-nine key contemporary catalogues from Sheraton to Heal's, including Smith, Tatham, King, Pugin, Morris and Liberty's, it includes an important introduction by the late Edward Joy.
ISBN 0 902028 47 2, 632pp, 6,200 illus, £49.50

Available from:
Antique Collectors' Club, 5 Church Street, Woodbridge, Suffolk IP12 1DS Tel: (0394) 385501 Fax: (0394) 384834
or Market Street Industrial Park, Wappingers' Falls, New York 12590, USA Tel: 914 297 0003 Fax: 914 297 0068

Gloucestershire

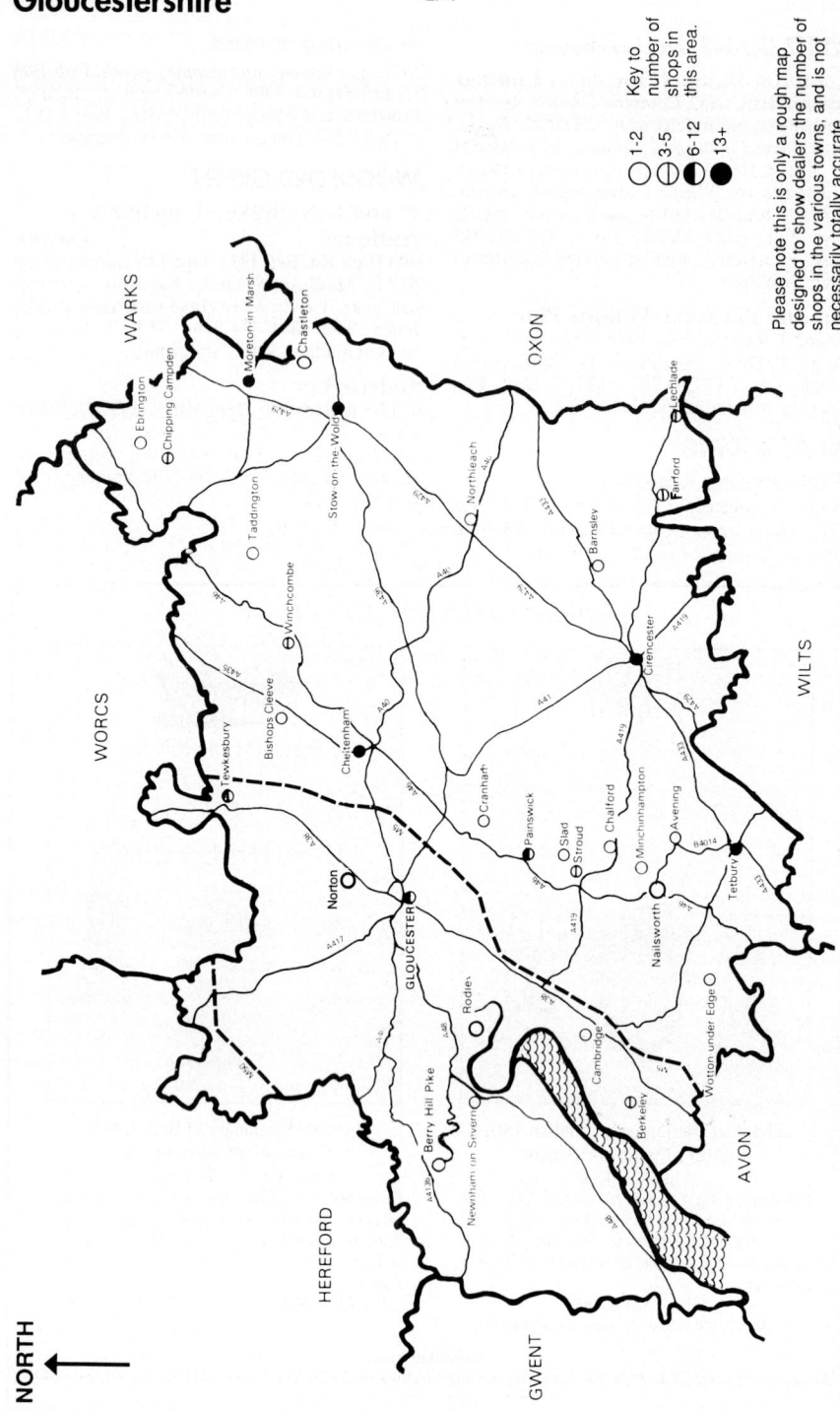

274

Key to number of shops in this area.
○ 1-2
◐ 3-5
◑ 6-12
● 13+

Please note this is only a rough map designed to show dealers the number of shops in the various towns, and is not necessarily totally accurate.

NORTH ←

Gloucestershire

AVENING
Upton Lodge Galleries
Avening House. (J. Grant). Est. 1979. Open by appointment. SIZE: Medium. STOCK: Oils and watercolours, 1880-1950, £100-£5,000. PARK: Easy. TEL: 045 383 4048.

BARNSLEY, Nr. Cirencester
Denzil Verey
Barnsley House. CADA. Resident. Est. 1980. Open 9.30-5.30, Sat. 10.30-5.30, other times by appointment. SIZE: Large. STOCK: Country furniture, including pine, 18th-19th C; treen, country and kitchen bygones, unusual and decorative items. LOC: 4 miles from Cirencester on A433 to Burford, 1st large house in village, set back off road on the right. PARK: Easy. TEL: 0285 740402. VAT: Stan/Spec.

BERKELEY
The Antique Shop
11 High St. (H. Trueman). Resident. Est. 1976. Open Tues., Thurs. and Fri. 9.30-5.30 and Sat.a.m. SIZE: Small. STOCK: Small furniture and decorative items, porcelain, glass, needlework and pictures. LOC: From A38 turn left into High St. past Berkeley Arms Hotel, shop 100yds. on left. PARK: Easy. TEL: 0453 811085.

Berkeley Market
(G. Hawkins and K. Gardiner). Open 9.30-1 and 2-5. CL: Mon. SIZE: Large. STOCK: General antiques, £1-£1,000. LOC: Village centre, just off A38. PARK: Easy. TEL: 0453 511032. VAT: Stan/Spec.

BERRY HILL PIKE, Nr. Coleford
Dean Forest Antiques
The Corner House. (J.R. Turner). Est. 1969. Open 8-8 including Sun. SIZE: Medium. STOCK: Furniture, 18th-20th C, £500-£1,000; porcelain, 18th-20th C, £50-£100; paintings, 19th-20th C, £100-£500. LOC: A4136, Gloucester/Monmouth road. PARK: Easy. TEL: 0594 833211; home - same. SER: Valuations; restorations (caning and French polishing).

BISHOPS CLEEVE, Nr. Cheltenham
Cleeve Picture Framing
Church Rd. (J. Gardner). Open 9-1 and 2-6, Sat. 9-12. STOCK: Prints and pictures. TEL: 0242 672785. SER: Framing, cleaning, restoring (oils, watercolours and prints).

The Priory Gallery
The Priory, Station Rd. (R.M. and E. James). Est. 1977. SIZE: Large. STOCK: British and European watercolours and oils, late 19th-20th C, £1,000-£50,000. LOC: A435. PARK: Easy. TEL: 0242 673226. SER: Valuations; restorations (watercolours, prints and oils); framing; buys at auction (as stock). VAT: Stan/Spec.

Denzil Verey Antiques

Barnsley House,
Near Cirencester,
Gloucestershire. GL7 5EE
Tel: 0285 740 402

18th and 19th century country furniture, pine, treen and unusual items

---

CAMBRIDGE, Nr. Gloucester
Bell House Antiques
Bell House. (G. and J. Hawkins). Resident. Open 10-1 and 2-5. SIZE: Medium. STOCK: General antiques including 19th C pine, £5-£500. LOC: Near Slimbridge, on main A38. PARK: Easy. TEL: 0453 890463. SER: Valuations. VAT: Stan/Spec.

CHALFORD
J. and R. Bateman Antiques
Green Court, High St. Est. !975. Open 9-6 or by appointment. STOCK: Furniture, oak and country, 17th-19th C; decorative items. PARK: Easy. TEL: 0453 883234. SER: Restorations; cabinet making, rushing and caning. VAT: Stan/Spec.

CHASTLETON, Nr. Moreton-in-Marsh
Geoffrey Stead
The Dower House. Est. 1963. Open by appointment only. STOCK: English and continental furniture, decorative objects, paintings. LOC: 4 miles from Moreton-in-Marsh. TEL: 0608 74364; fax - 0608 74533.

CHELTENHAM
Antiques (Cheltenham) LAPADA
(J. Turner). Est. 1950. Open by appointment only. STOCK: General antiques, furniture, porcelain, glass. TEL: 0242 522939. VAT: Stan/Spec.

GLOUCESTERSHIRE 276

Cheltenham continued
Bailey's Quality Antique Lighting and Accessories
16 Suffolk Rd. Open 10-6, Sat. 10.15-6. *STOCK: Antique and pre-war fixtures, fittings, lighting, advertising items.* LOC: Near Bath Rd. shopping area and colleges. PARK: Nearby. TEL: 0242 255897. SER: Spare parts stocked.

David Bannister, F.R.G.S
26 Kings Rd. Est. 1963. Open by appointment only. SIZE: Medium. *STOCK: Early maps and prints, 1480-1850, £5-£5,000; decorative and topographical prints; atlases and colour plate books.* TEL: 0242 514287; fax - 0242 513890. SER: Valuations; restorations; lectures; buys at auction. FAIRS: Organiser - Antique Map and Print (Bonnington Hotel). VAT: Stan.

Bed of Roses
12 Prestbury Rd. (Martin Losh). Est. 1978. Open 10-1 and 2-5, Sat. 9.30-5.30. CL: Mon. SIZE: Large. *STOCK: Fine stripped pine.* LOC: 200 metres on town side of roundabout, B4632, close to Pittville Circus. PARK: Easy. TEL: 0242 231918. VAT: Stan/Spec.

John Beer
23 Priory St. Open by appointment only. SIZE: Large. *STOCK: Furniture and objects especially English arts and crafts, Gothic and art deco, 1830-1960's.* LOC: 200yds. from start of High St. PARK: Easy. TEL: 0242 576080; mobile - 0860 767194. SER: Valuations; buys at auction. VAT: Stan/Spec.

Bottles and Bygones
96 Horsefair St, Charlton Kings. (J. and M. Brown). Est. 1974. Open 10-5.30. CL: Mon. and Tues. *STOCK: Bottles, stoneware, pot-lids, commemorative items, jewellery, enamel signs, crested china, postcards, general antiques, furniture, collectors' items, chimney pots and architectural items.* LOC: 1 mile from Cheltenham off Cirencester road. PARK: Easy. TEL: 0242 236393; home - same.

Edward Bradbury and Son
32 High St. (O. Bradbury). Resident. Est. 1986. Open by appointment. SIZE: Small. *STOCK: Works of art, tribal art, furniture, 18th-19th C; books on art reference, monographs on artists and photographers, manuscripts.* PARK: Nearby. TEL: 0242 221486. SER: Valuations. VAT: Spec.

Butler and Co
111 Promenade. (D.J. Butler). Est. 1968. Open Sat. only. SIZE: Small. *STOCK: English coins, 1st to 20th C; world coins, 19th C; both £5-£25; British campaign medals, 19th-20th C, £50-£100.* PARK: Easy. TEL: 0242 522272; home - 0242 234439. SER: Valuations. FAIRS: Cheltenham.

Cameo Antiques
31 Suffolk Parade. (R.L. Chitty). Est. 1970. Open 10-1 and 2-5. CL: Wed. SIZE: Small. *STOCK:*

Cheltenham continued
General antiques, 19th-20th C, £5-£5,000 furniture, 18th C and decorative; oils an watercolours. Not Stocked: Militaria. PARK Easy. TEL: 0242 236467. VAT: Stan/Spec.

Charlton Kings Antiques Centre
199 London Rd, Charlton Kings. Est. 1984. Oper 9.30-5.30. SIZE: Large - 11 dealers. *STOCK General antiques, including furniture, china glass and pictures, £5-£1,000.* LOC: On A40 PARK: Easy. TEL: 0242 510672.

Cheltenham Antique Market
54 Suffolk Rd. (K.J. Shave). Est. 1970. Oper 9.30-5.30. SIZE: 30 dealers. *STOCK: Genera antiques.* TEL: 0242 529812.

Cocoa
7 Queens Circus. (Cara Wagstaff). Est. 1973 Open 10-5. SIZE: Small. *STOCK: Linens, lace antique wedding dresses and accessories, 19th 20th C., £1-£2,000.* LOC: Rear of Montpellier near Queens Hotel. PARK: Easy. TEL: 024 233588. SER: Re-creations; restorations (perio textiles). VAT: Stan.

Country Life Antiques
8 Rotunda Terr, Montpellier St. Open 10-5 *STOCK: Furniture, scientific instruments, decor ative accessories, pewter, brass and copper* PARK: Easy. TEL: 0242 226919.

Greens of Montpellier
15 Montpellier Walk. Est. 1946. Open 9-5. CL Wed. p.m. SIZE: Medium. *STOCK: Victorian an diamond set jewellery, porcelain, silver, glass fine books and some furniture.* LOC: Conjunctior of Promenade and main shopping centre. PARK Easy. TEL: 0242 512088. SER: Buys at auction VAT: Stan/Spec.

Heydens Antiques and Militaria
420 High St. (R.E.J. Heyden). Open 10-5.30 *STOCK: General antiques and militaria.* TEL 0242 582466.

David Howard
42 Moorend Cres. Est. 1983. Open by appointment *STOCK: Fine oil paintings, watercolours an drawings, 19th-20th C, £500-£5,000.* PARK: Easy TEL: 0242 243379; home - same. SER: Valuations buys at auction; research (pictures). VAT: Spec.

H.W. Keil (Cheltenham) Ltd   BAD/
129-131 Promenade. Est. 1953. SIZE: Large *STOCK: Furniture, paintings, 17th-18th C metalwork, chandeliers.* LOC: Opposite Queen Hotel, at top of Promenade. PARK: Easy. TEL 0242 522509. SER: Upholstery. VAT: Spec.

Kyoto House Japanese Antiques
14 Suffolk Rd. (Mike Smith-Wood). Open 10.30 5.30, Sun. and evenings by appointment. SIZE Medium. *STOCK: Japanese furniture, £100 £6,000; Japanese collectables, £10-£500; a*

GLOUCESTERSHIRE

Cheltenham continued
18th-19th C, Edo and Meiji period. TEL: 0242 262549; home - 0242 519566. SER: Restoration (English and Japanese furniture).

Latchford Antiques
215 London Rd, Charlton Kings. (K. and R. Latchford). Est. 1985. Open 10-5. SIZE: Small. *STOCK: Furniture, china, glass and objets d'art, 18th-19th C, £5-£1,000.* LOC: 2 miles from Cheltenham, on A40 towards London at Sixways Shopping Centre, on right. PARK: Easy. TEL: 0242 226263. VAT: Stan/Spec.

Leckhampton Antiques
215 Bath Rd. (V. Finn). Open 10-4. *STOCK: General antiques.* TEL: 0242 570230.

Manor House Antiques
42 Suffolk Rd. (J.G. Benton). Est. 1972. Open 10-5.30. SIZE: Large. *STOCK: Furniture, general antiques, 19th C and Victorian, £50-£1,500; shipping goods.* Not Stocked: Small items, china and jewellery. LOC: A40. PARK: Nearby. TEL: 0242 232780. VAT: Stan/Spec.

Martin and Co. Ltd   BADA
19 The Promenade. (I.M. and N.C.S. Dimmer). Est. 1890. *STOCK: Silver, Sheffield plate, jewellery, objets d'art.* TEL: 0242 522821/239115. VAT: Stan/Spec.

Montpellier Clocks   BADA
13 Rotunda Terr, Montpellier. (B. Bass). Open 8.30-5.30. *STOCK: Clocks, 17th-19th C; barometers.* LOC: Close to Queens Hotel. PARK: Easy. TEL: 0242 242178. SER: Repairs and restorations.

Elizabeth Niner Antiques
53 Gt. Norwood St. Est. 1972. Open 10-4.30. CL: Wed. SIZE: Medium. *STOCK: Mahogany furniture, 18th-19th C; objets d'art, 1700-1900, £10-£2,000.* LOC: Off Suffolk Rd. PARK: Easy. TEL: 0242 516497. VAT: Stan/Spec.

Patrick Oliver   LAPADA
4 Tivoli St. Est. 1896. SIZE: Large. *STOCK: Furniture and shipping goods.* PARK: Easy. TEL: 0242 513392; home - 0242 519538. VAT: Stan/Spec.

Eric Pride Oriental Rugs
44 Suffolk Rd. GMC. Est. 1980. Open 10-6, Mon. and Sat. by appointment. SIZE: Medium. *STOCK: Rugs and carpets, £100-£4,000; kilims, £300-£2,000; saddle-bags and horse covers, £150-£800; all 19th to early 20th C.* LOC: A40 near Cheltenham College. PARK: Easy. TEL: 0242 580822. SER: Valuations; restorations (cleaning and repairs).

Michael Rayner
11 St. Luke's Rd. Open 10-6, other times by appointment. CL: Mon. and Tues. *STOCK: Books, antiquarian and secondhand.* TEL: 0242 512806.

Cheltenham continued
Scott-Cooper Ltd   BADA
52 The Promenade. Est. 1912. *STOCK: Silver, plate, jewellery, clocks, ivory, enamel, objets de vertu.* TEL: 0242 522580. SER: Restorations and repairs (silver and jewellery). VAT: Stan/Spec.

Tapestry
33 Suffolk Parade. (Mrs G. Hall). Est. 1980. Open 9.30-5.30. SIZE: Medium. *STOCK: Soft furnishings, furniture, stripped pine, late 18th to early 19th C, £50-£1,000.* LOC: 10 mins. walk from The Promenade. PARK: Easy. TEL: 0242 512191; home - 0242 672274. SER: Valuations; restorations (as stock). FAIRS: Shepton Mallet; British International, Birmingham; Ardingly.

John P. Townsend
Ullenwood Park Farm, Ullenwood. Est. 1969. Open 9-5. CL: Sat. SIZE: Medium. *STOCK: Furniture - stripped pine, country and shipping, to 1940's; books.* TEL: 0242 870223. SER: Containers; buys at auction. VAT: Stan/Spec.

Triton Gallery
27 Suffolk Parade. (L. Bianco). Resident. Open 10-5.30, other times by appointment. *STOCK: Furniture including decorative.* TEL: 0242 510477.

Joy Turner Antiques
100 Leckhampton Rd. Open by appointment. *STOCK: General antiques.* TEL: 0242 522939.

Turtle Fine Art
30 Suffolk Parade. (P. Field and W. Forsyth). Est. 1983. Open 9-6.30. SIZE: Medium. *STOCK: Watercolours, oils and prints, 19th-20th C, £30-£3,000.* LOC: Off Suffolk Rd. (A40). PARK: Easy. TEL: 0242 241646; home - same. VAT: Stan/Spec.

CHIPPING CAMPDEN
Antique Heritage
High St. (D.B. Smith). Est. 1981. Open 10.30-5, Sat. 10-5, Sun. 11-5. SIZE: Small. *STOCK: Small items, china, porcelain, tables, boxes, Georgian and Victorian, £15-£400.* LOC: Village centre. PARK: Easy. TEL: 0386 840727. VAT: Stan/Spec.

Campden Country Pine
High St. (Jane and Frank Kennedy). Est. 1988. Open 9-12 and 1-5, Sun. by appointment. SIZE: Small. *STOCK: Victorian pine, £100-£1,000; reproduction pine.* LOC: On village green at Leasebourne end of High St. PARK: Easy. TEL: 0386 840315; home - same. SER: Valuations; restorations (pine); buys at auction (as stock); export.

Pedlars
Lower High St. (A. Yates). Open 10-5. *STOCK: General antiques.* TEL: 0386 840680.

GLOUCESTERSHIRE

Chipping Campden continued

Saxton House Gallery   LAPADA
High St. (S.D. and J. Coy). Open 9-5.30. CL: Thurs. SIZE: Medium. STOCK: *Fine English clocks and barometers, unusual carriage clocks, jewellery, Georgian furniture, paintings and watercolours.* LOC: Village centre. PARK: Easy. TEL: 0386 840278. VAT: Stan/Spec.

School House Antiques   LAPADA
School House, High St. (G. Hammond). Open 9.30-5 including Sun.(June-Sept.). CL: Thurs. (Oct.-May). STOCK: *Clocks, 18th-19th C; furniture including oak and shipping, 17th-19th C; works of art, oils and watercolours.* TEL: 0386 841474; fax - 0386 841367. SER: Restorations.

Stuart House Antiques
High St. (J. Collett). Est. 1985. Open 10-1 and 2-5.30 including Sun. SIZE: Large. STOCK: *China, 19th C; general antiques, from 18th C; all £1-£1,000.* LOC: Opposite market hall. PARK: Easy. TEL: 0386 840995. SER: Valuations; china search; restorations (ceramics).

Swan Antiques
High St. (J. Stocker). Est. 1960. Open 9-5, Thurs. and Sun. by appointment. SIZE: Medium. STOCK: *Jewellery, including Victorian; silver, George II to 1920; porcelain including Royal*

In green, black and white, this Armstrong Siddeley catalogue for the 1935 range includes details of six models with prices from £265 to £1,360. Note pre-selector gear change lever to steering wheel. £10-£15. From ***Automobilia of Europe - Reference and Price Guide***, by Gordon Gardiner and Alistair Morris. Published by the **Antique Collectors' Club**, £25.00.

Chipping Campden continued

Worcester; *decorative items, furniture, 17th C oak to 1860 mahogany.* LOC: Village centre. PARK: Easy. TEL: 0386 840759. SER: Gemmologist; registered valuer. VAT: Stan/Spec.

CIRENCESTER

Jonathan Beech Antique Clocks
Nurses Cottage, Ampney Crucis. Est. 1985. Open 9.30-5.30. SIZE: Medium. STOCK: *Longcase, wall and mantle clocks, 1700-1880, £500-£7,000.* LOC: A417 2 miles from Cirencester, left at The Crown of Crucis, then 300yds. on left. PARK: Easy. TEL: 0285 851495. SER: Restorations (clocks). VAT: Stan/Spec.

Walter Bull and Son (Cirencester) Ltd
10 Dyer St. Est. 1815. Open 9-5. SIZE: Small. STOCK: *Silver, from 1700, £50-£3,000; objets d'art.* LOC: Lower end of Market Place. PARK: At rear. TEL: 0285 653875. VAT: Stan/Spec.

Cirencester Antique Market
Market Place. (Antique Forum Ltd). Open Fri. SIZE: 60 dealers. STOCK: *General antiques.* TEL: 071 233 5786.

Cirencester Antiques Centre
The Waterloo. (Kate Chate and John ff. Downes-Hall). Est. 1991. Open 10-5.30 including Sun. SIZE: Large. STOCK: *Georgian and Edwardian furniture, £50-£2,000; silver and jewellery, from 1700, £10-£2,000; bric-a-brac, 1850-1930, £1-£150.* LOC: Left at traffic lights after Market Pl. or right from London Rd. PARK: Easy. TEL: 0285 644040. SER: Valuations; restorations (furniture, French polishing, silver and jewellery, porcelain and pottery).

Corner Cupboard Curios
2 Church St. (P. Larner). STOCK: *General antiques and gramophonalia.* TEL: 0285 655476.

Forum Antiques
20 West Way, The Forum. (W. Mitchell). Est. 1986. Open 9-5.30, Sat. 9.30-5. SIZE: Medium. STOCK: *Furniture - country oak, fruitwood and yew, 16th-19th C; walnut and mahogany, 17th-18th C, £100-£10,000.* LOC: Left at Police Station in Forum car park, near Market Place. PARK: Easy. TEL: 0285 658406; home - 0453 886783. SER: Valuations; restorations (furniture). VAT: Spec.

Jay Gray Antiques
Syrena House, 1 Cheltenham Rd. (Mrs J. Gray). Est. 1961. Open 9-6 by appointment. STOCK: *English and French furniture; English, continental and Oriental porcelain, 18th-19th C; pictures, silver, glass, collectors' items, objets d'art.* Not Stocked: Uniforms, shawls, Goss china. LOC: Junction of A435 and A417. PARK: Easy. TEL: 0285 652755. SER: Buys at auction. VAT: Spec.

GLOUCESTERSHIRE

RANKINE TAYLOR ANTIQUES
(Mrs. Leslie Taylor)

**34 Dollar Street, Cirencester, Glos. GL7 2AN
Telephone Cirencester 652529**

Interesting collection of Antique Furniture, Silver, Glass and Rare Items.

LAPADA MEMBER

Cirencester continued

Hares
17-19 Gosditch St. (Allan Hare). CADA. Est. 1972. Open 9.30-5.30, Sun. by appointment. SIZE: Large. *STOCK: Furniture, especially dining tables and long sets of chairs, 18th to early 19th C, £100-£20,000; upholstery and decorative objects.* LOC: Near Market Square. PARK: Easy. TEL: 0285 640077; home - same. SER: Valuations; restorations; traditional upholstery; buys at auction. VAT: Spec.

Thomas and Pamela Hudson
At the Sign of the Herald Angel, 19 Park St. Est. 1959. Open 9-5.30. *STOCK: Glass, netsuke, workboxes and needlework tools, needlework, old Sheffield, small objets de vertu.* LOC: From Market Pl., 100yds. beyond Corinium Museum. TEL: 0285 652972. SER: Valuations; buys at auction.

E.C. Legg and Son
3 College Farm Workshops, Tetbury Road. Est. 1902. Open 9-5. CL: Sat. *STOCK: Furniture, 18th-19th C.* PARK: Easy. TEL: 0285 650695. SER: Restorations (furniture, gilt frames); caning; re-leathering.

Robert Mitchell Fine Art
At Forum Antiques, 20 West Way, The Forum. Est. 1986. Open 9-5.30, Sat. 9.30-5. SIZE: Medium. *STOCK: Oil paintings, 19th-20th C, £100-£5,000; watercolours, £100-£1,000; prints, £10-£30; both 20th C.* LOC: 200 yards from bottom of Market Place. PARK: Easy. TEL: 0285 658406. SER: Valuations; restorations (oils and watercolours); buys at auction (oils and watercolours). FAIRS: NEC (Aug). VAT: Spec.

A.J. Ponsford Antiques
51-53 Dollar St. (A.J. and R.L. Ponsford). Est. 1962. Open 8-5.30. CL: Sat. SIZE: Large. *STOCK: Furniture, 1800-1830, £25-£4,000; furniture, 1700-1800, £50-£8,000; copper, brass.* Not Stocked: Silver. LOC: 200yds. from church

Cirencester continued

on left towards Gloucester at junction of Thomas St. and Spitalgate Lane. PARK: 50yds. opposite. TEL: 0285 652355. SER: Valuations; restorations (furniture and oil paintings); rushing, caning, upholstery, picture framing; suppliers of false books; buys at auction. VAT: Stan/Spec.

William H. Stokes   BADA
The Cloisters, 6/8 Dollar St. (W.H. Stokes and P.W. Bontoft). CADA. Est. 1968. Open 9.30-5.30, Sat. 9.30-4.30. *STOCK: Early oak furniture, £1,000-£30,000; brassware, £150-£5,000; all 16th-17th C.* TEL: 0285 653907; fax - same. FAIRS: BADA; Grosvenor House. VAT: Spec.

Rankine Taylor Antiques   LAPADA
34 Dollar St. (Mrs L. Taylor). CADA. Est. 1969. Open 9-5.30, Sun. by appointment. SIZE: Large. *STOCK: Furniture, 17th-19th C, £100-£20,000; glass, 18th-20th C, £10-£250; silver and decorative items, 17th-20th C, £20-£8,000.* Not Stocked: Victoriana, militaria. LOC: From church, turn right up West Market Place, via Gosditch St. into Dollar St. PARK: Abbey grounds via Spittalgate. TEL: 0285 652529. SER: Valuations; buys at auction (furnishing items). VAT: Spec.

P.J. Ward Fine Paintings
11 Gosditch St. Open 9-5. *STOCK: 17th-19th C paintings.* TEL: 0285 658499. SER: Valuations; restorations; framing. VAT: Spec.

Waterloo Antiques
20 The Waterloo. (P.A. Ruttleich and R. Simmonds). Est. 1973. Open 9.30-5.30 including Sun. SIZE: Medium. *STOCK: Georgian furniture, £500-£3,000; English and continental pine, 19th C, £50-£1,000; silver and ceramics, 19th C, £25-£1,000.* LOC: Opposite Waterloo car park. PARK: Opposite. TEL: 0285 644887; home - same. SER: Restorations (furniture stripping); upholstery; buys at auction (furniture and silver).

BERNARD WEAVER ANTIQUES

18th and 19th century Furniture and Objects

Fine serpentine front mahogany chest, c.1785

28 GLOUCESTER STREET
(continuation of Dollar St.)
CIRENCESTER GL7 2DH
Tel: 0285 652055

Cirencester continued

Bernard Weaver Antiques
28 Gloucester St. CADA. Open 9.30-6, Sat. 9.30-1. SIZE: Medium. STOCK: Furniture, mahogany and oak, 18th-19th C; art nouveau and arts and crafts. LOC: Continuation of Dollar St. PARK: Easy. TEL: 0285 652055; home - same. SER: Valuations.

CRANHAM

Heather Newman Gallery
Milidduwa, Mill Lane. Est. 1969. Open every day by appointment. STOCK: British watercolours and drawings, 18th-20th C, £50-£5,000. LOC: Near Prinknash Abbey, just off A46 at Cranham Corner. PARK: Easy. TEL: 0452 812230. SER: Major exhibitions with illustrated catalogues, May and Nov; valuations; buys at auction. FAIRS: World of Watercolours; 20th C British Art. VAT: Spec.

EBRINGTON, Nr. Chipping Campden

John Burton Natural Craft Taxidermy
21 Main St. Est. 1973. Open by appointment. SIZE: Medium. STOCK: Taxidermy - cased and uncased fish, birds and mammals, from Victorian, £40-£2,500; glass domes, sporting trophies. LOC: Village centre. PARK: Easy. TEL: 038678 231; home - same. SER: Valuations; restorations (taxidermy); buys at auction (taxidermy). VAT: Stan.

FAIRFORD

Blenheim Antiques
Market Place. (N. Hurdle). CADA. Resident. Est. 1972. Open 9.30-6.30. STOCK: 18th-19th C furniture, clocks. TEL: 0285 712094. VAT: Stan/Spec.

Cirencester Antiques Ltd
High St. (Mr and Mrs R.T.G. Chester-Master). CADA. Est. 1959. Open 9-5.30. SIZE: Large. STOCK: Furniture and works of art, 17th to early 19th C, £50-£50,000. TEL: 0285 713774.

Columbus
3 High St. (J. Mayo and N. Gammond). Est. 1983. Open 10-6, Sat. and Sun. 10-5. SIZE: Medium. STOCK: General antiques, to £1,000+. LOC: Opposite church on A417. PARK: Easy. TEL: 0285 712841. SER: Valuations; restorations; buys at auction.

Gloucester House Antiques Ltd
Market Place. (Mr and Mrs R. Chester-Master). CADA. Est. 1972. Open 9-5.30. SIZE: Large. STOCK: English and French country furniture in oak, elm, fruitwood, pine; pottery, faïence and decorative items. PARK: Easy. TEL: 0285 712790; home - 0285 653066; fax - 0285 713324. VAT: Stan/Spec.

GLOUCESTERSHIRE

GLOUCESTER

Steven D. Bartrick
The Antique Centre, Severn Rd. Est. 1985. Open 9-5, Sat. 9-4.30, Sun. 1-4.30. *STOCK: Topographical prints and some maps.* LOC: Gloucester dock area. PARK: At side of building. TEL: 0452 529716; home - 0242 231691.

E.J. Cook and Son Antiques
At the Antique Centre, Severn Rd. (E.J. and C.A. Cook). Est. 1949. Open 9.30-5, Sun. 1-5. SIZE: Large. *STOCK: Furniture, clocks, oils and watercolours, small items, 17th-19th C, £50-£6,000.* LOC: On ring road close to dock area. PARK: Easy. TEL: 0452 529716. SER: Restorations (furniture, upholstery and clocks); buys at auction (furniture). VAT: Stan/Spec.

Farr
At the Antique Centre, Severn Rd. (A. and J. Farr). Open 9-5, Sun. 1-4.30. *STOCK: Silver, watches, clocks, furniture, brass and glass.* LOC: Gloucester dock area.

Gloucester Antique Centre
Severn Rd. Open 9.30-5, Sun. 1-5. SIZE: 67 dealers. *STOCK: General antiques.* TEL: 0452 529716; fax - 0452 307161.

Blenheim Antiques
AT FAIRFORD

We Sell Town and Country Furniture, Clocks, Pictures and Decorative Objects.

Market Place, Fairford, Glos.
Telephone: 0285 712094
(Easy parking in the Market Place)

CIRENCESTER ANTIQUES LTD.
HIGH STREET, FAIRFORD, GLOS. GL7 4AB
Telephone: (0285) 713774. Fax: 0285 713324

Fine furniture and works of art from late 17th to early 19th centuries

---

GLOUCESTER HOUSE ANTIQUES LTD.
Market Place, Fairford
Glos. GL7 4AB
Tel: Cirencester 0285 712790
Fax: 0285 713324

We specialise in English and French country furniture, pottery and faïence with a very large selection of armoires and farmhouse tables.

GLOUCESTERSHIRE

Gloucester continued

David Kent Antiques
300 Barton St. Est. 1967. Open 10-4.30, Sat. 10-12.30. STOCK: *Victorian shipping items and books.* LOC: Through town, near ring road, east side. PARK: Easy. TEL: 0452 304396; home - 0452 610976.

Paul Medcalf
Shop 29, Gloucester Antique Centre, Severn Rd. Open 9-5. Sat. 9.30-5, Sun. 1-5. STOCK: *English oils, landscapes and portraits, especially the Birmingham School, £50-£2,000; watercolours, £50-£1,500; etchings, £20-£300.* TEL: 0452 415186.

Military Curios, HQ84
Southgate. (B. Williams). Est. 1964. Open 10-5, including Sun. STOCK: *Blazer badges, medals, worldwide militaria, badges, surplus, gold, silver, miniatures, edged weapons, replicas, air pistols; Jaguar - spares, mascots, posters.* LOC: A38, city centre. PARK: 100 yds (Docks). TEL: 0452 527716; fax - same. SER: Valuations; medal find and mounting; costume hire.

LECHLADE

Antiques Etcetera
High St. (Mrs C.L. Haillay). Est. 1969. Open 10-5, Sun. and evenings by appointment. SIZE: Medium. STOCK: *General antiques, china, copper, glass, country furniture and artifacts, decorators' items.* PARK: Easy. TEL: 0367 252567.

Bell Fine Arts
Cottar's Barn, Downington. (Mrs R.A. Bell). Open by appointment only. STOCK: *Oils, watercolours, Old Master etchings and contemporary items.* TEL: 0367 252255.

Gerard Campbell   BADA
Maple House, Market Pl. (J. and G. Campbell). Est. 1980. Open by appointment. SIZE: Large. STOCK: *Clocks especially Biedermeier Vienna regulators, 18th-19th C, £1,500-£15,000; oils, 20th C, £200-£5,000.* PARK: Easy. TEL: 0367 252267; home - same. SER: Valuations; buys at auction. VAT: Spec.

D'Arcy Antiques
High St. (J.W. and Mrs. M.A. Corbey). Est. 1986. Open 10-5. SIZE: Medium. STOCK: *Furniture, 1800-1940, £50-£1,500; china, 1800-1960, £2-£100; brass, 1780-1960, £2-£100.* LOC: A361, village centre. PARK: Easy. TEL: 0367 252471; home - 0793 852792.

Lechlade Antiques Arcade
5, 6 and 7 High St. (J. Dickson). Open 10-6 including Sun. SIZE: 40+ dealers. STOCK: *General antiques, collectables, books, bric-a-brac.* TEL: 0367 252832. SER: Public commission room.

Lechlade continued

Little Barrow Antiques
High St. (S.J. and M.E. Sheppard). Resident. Open 10.30-6, Sat. and Sun. 11.30-6. SIZE: Small. STOCK: *China and glass, small furniture, collectors' items, 19th-20th C, £5-£500.* PARK: Loading only and nearby. TEL: 0367 253140; home - same. SER: Valuations.

Mark A. Serle (Antiques and Restoration)
6 Burford St. Est. 1978. Open 9.30-5.30, Sun. 1-5.30. SIZE: Small. STOCK: *Collectables, £5-£100; woodworking tools, £5-£50; furniture, £50-£1,000; all 19th C; militaria, £5-£150.* LOC: A361. PARK: Easy. TEL: 0367 253145; home - 0993 851664. SER: Restorations (furniture).

The Swan Antiques and Crafts Centre
Burford St. (Cilla and Ivor Littleton). Est. 1986 Open 10.30-4.30 including Sun. SIZE: 50 dealers. STOCK: *General antiques including furniture collectables, books and pictures, jewellery and ceramics, 19th to early 20th C, £5-£850.* PARK: Own. TEL: 0367 252258; home - 0367 252129. VAT: Stan.

Peter Whitby Antiques
Ashleigh House, High St. Open 10-5.30. STOCK: *Furniture, metalware, porcelain, items of interest* PARK: Easy. TEL: 0367 252347.

MINCHINHAMPTON, Nr. Stroud

J.V. Vosper
20 High St. Est. 1952. STOCK: *Furniture, glass china, silver, brass, plate, bric-a-brac, 18th-20th C.* TEL: 0453 882480. VAT: Stan.

Mick and Fanny Wright
'The Trumpet', West End. Open 10.30-5.30. CL: Mon. and Tues. SIZE: Medium. STOCK: *Watches general antiques, 50p-£1,000.* LOC: Town centre road to the common. PARK: Nearby. TEL: 0453 883027. VAT: Spec.

MORETON-IN-MARSH

Antique Centre
London House, High St. Est. 1979. Open 10-5 including Sun. CL: Tues. SIZE: Large. STOCK: *Furniture, paintings, watercolours, prints domestic artifacts, clocks, silver, jewellery and plate, mainly 17th-19th C, £5-£3,000.* LOC Centre of High St. (A429). PARK: Easy. TEL 0608 51084. VAT: Stan/Spec.

Astley House - Fine Art
Astley House, High St. (D. and N. Glaisyer) CADA. Est. 1974. Open 9-5.30. CL: Wed. SIZE Medium. STOCK: *Oil paintings and watercolours, 19th-20th C, £200-£10,000.* LOC: Mair street. PARK: Easy. TEL: 0608 50601; fax - 0608 51777. SER: Restorations (oils and watercolours) framing; video valuations. VAT: Spec.

Moreton-in-Marsh continued
Astley House - Fine Art
Astley House, London Rd. (D. and N. Glaisyer). CADA. Est. 1974. Open 10-1 and 2-5.30. CL: Wed. SIZE: Large. *STOCK: Oil paintings, 19th-20th C; large decorative paintings and portraits.* LOC: Town centre. PARK: Easy. TEL: 0608 50601; fax - 0608 51777. SER: Restorations (oils and watercolours); porcelain framing. VAT: Spec.

The Avon Gallery
21 Old Market Way. (S. Creaton). Est. 1978. Open 9.30-5. CL: Wed. *STOCK: Prints especially sporting; maps.* TEL: 0608 50614. SER: Picture framing.

Simon Brett   BADA
Creswyke House, High St. Est. 1972. Open 9.30-5.30. *STOCK: English and continental furniture, 17th to early 19th C; works of art, portrait miniatures, old fishing tackle, carved wood fish models.* TEL: 0608 50751; fax - 0608 51791. VAT: Spec.

Chandlers Antiques
High St. (I. Kellam and P. Grout). Open 9.30-1 and 2-5.30. *STOCK: Pottery, porcelain, glass, silver, jewellery, small furniture and general antiques.* TEL: 0608 51347.

Grimes House Antiques
High St. (S. and V. Farnsworth). Est. 1978. Open 9.30-1 and 2-5, other times by appointment. CL: Wed. *STOCK: General antiques, Victorian glass especially cranberry.* TEL: 0608 51029.

Lemington House Antiques
Oxford St. (K.W. and Y.F. Heath). Open 10-6. *STOCK: Furniture, 17th-19th C; porcelain, glass and decorative smalls.* LOC: Close to junction with High St. PARK: Own. TEL: 0608 51443.

Mrs M.K. Nielsen   LAPADA
Seaford House, High St. Est. 1965. Open Thur., Fri. and Sat. 9.30-1 and 2-5 or by appointment. SIZE: Medium. *STOCK: Derby porcelain, £45-£5,000; Worcester, £65-£5,000; furniture, £150-£4,500.* LOC: A429 Fosseway. PARK: Easy. TEL: 0608 50448. VAT: Stan/Spec.

Elizabeth Parker
High St. (P.J. King-Smith). Est. 1975. Open 9-6. SIZE: Large. *STOCK: Furniture, £500-£10,000; English and continental mahogany, satinwood and marquetry, portraits, porcelain, copper and brass; all 18th and 19th C.* LOC: Opposite Manor House Hotel, on Fosseway junction of A44 with Broadway. TEL: 0608 50917. SER: Buys at auction. VAT: Stan/Spec.

Peter Roberts Antiques
High St. Open 10-5.30 or by appointment. SIZE: Large. *STOCK: Decorative furniture, objets d'art, garden furniture, mirrors, beds, 17th-19th C, £50-£10,000.* LOC: Fosseway. PARK: Easy. TEL: 0608 50698. SER: Valuations. VAT: Stan/Spec.

Moreton-in-Marsh continued
Anthony Sampson   BADA
Dale House. Est. 1967. Open 9-1 and 2-5.30, Sun. by appointment. SIZE: Medium. *STOCK: Town and country furniture, to 1830; decorative items.* Not Stocked: Reproductions. LOC: Main street. PARK: Easy. TEL: 0608 50763. VAT: Spec.

Southgate Gallery
Fosse Manor Farm. (J. Constable and N. Collins). Est. 1968. Open by appointment only. *STOCK: Modern British paintings.* TEL: 0608 50051. SER: Restorations (oils).

Windsor House Antiques Centre
High St. Open 10-5.30, Sun. 12-5.30. SIZE: 20-30 dealers. *STOCK: General antiques.* TEL: 0608 50993.

NAILSWORTH
Hand Prints and Watercolours Gallery
3 Bridge St. (J. Hand). Est. 1988. Open 10-1 and 2-5.30. SIZE: Medium. *STOCK: Victorian watercolours and prints, £5-£1,000; decorative prints, £15-£300.* LOC: A46, 4 miles south of Stroud. PARK: Easy. TEL: 045383 4967. SER: Restorations (as stock); buys at auction (as stock). VAT: Stan.

NEWNHAM-ON-SEVERN
Cottonwood
High St. and, The Old House, Lower High St. Open 9.30-1 and 2-5.30. *STOCK: 19th C and Edwardian furniture especially upholstered items, and hand-built reproduction.* PARK: Easy. TEL: 0594 516633; home - 0594 516558. SER: Restorations; re-upholstery.

NORTHLEACH, Nr. Cheltenham
Keith Harding's World of Mechanical Music
The Oak House, High St. (K. Harding, FBHI, C.A. Burnett, CMBHI and E. Harding). Est. 1961. Articles on clocks, musical boxes. Open 10-6 including Sun. *STOCK: Clocks, musical boxes and automata.* TEL: 0451 860181; fax - 0451 861133. SER: Valuations; restorations (musical boxes, clocks); buys at auction. VAT: Stan/Spec.

The Northleach Gallery
The Green. (Sarah and Peter Loveday). Open 9.30-4.30 and Sat. for exhibitions only. *STOCK: Prints and etchings including animal, sporting, topographical and local interest, pre 18th to early 20th C; some books.* TEL: 0451 860519.

NORTON, Nr. Gloucester
Antique Pine
Norton Barn, Wainlodes Lane. (A.P. Jones). Est. 1988. Open 8-5. SIZE: Large. *STOCK: Architectural items including garden ornaments and*

GLOUCESTERSHIRE

Norton continued
architectural effects, £25-£1,000; antique pine, £50-£1,000. LOC: A38 between Gloucester and Tewkesbury. PARK: Easy. TEL: 0452 731236. SER: Buys at auction (garden ornaments and statues). FAIRS: Restorex Period Living, Olympia. VAT: Stan.

PAINSWICK

Craig Carrington Antiques
Brook House. Est. 1970. Open by appointment. STOCK: English and continental furniture and works of art. TEL: 0452 813248. SER: Buys at auction. VAT: Spec.

Country Living
Tibbiwell. (A. and L. Major). Est. 1983. Open 10.30-1 and 2-5. SIZE: Medium. STOCK: Decorative china, £5-£100; pine furniture, £50-£600; both 19th-20th C. LOC: Off A46 at church. PARK: Easy. TEL: 0452 813045; home - same.

Painswick Antique Centre
New St. (R.J.B. Short). Open 10-5, Sat. 9.30-5.30, Sun. 11-5.30. STOCK: General antiques from jewellery to period furniture. LOC: A46, near Painswick church. PARK: Easy. TEL: 0452 812431.

Regent Antiques
Dynevor House, New St. (Mr and Mrs G. Coggins). Est. 1960. Open 10-5.30. SIZE: Medium. STOCK: 17th-18th C oak, walnut and mahogany, £100-£3,000. LOC: Main road opposite church. PARK: Easy. TEL: 0452 812543. VAT: Spec. Trade Only.

Weavers Cottage Antiques
Friday St. Open 10-5. STOCK: Furniture, oak, mahogany, copper, decorative items. TEL: 0452 812609; home - 0452 863291.

RODLEY, Nr. Westbury on Severn

Kelly Antiques
Landeck, Goose Lane. (G. Kelly). Resident. Always open. STOCK: Antique pine. TEL: 0452 760315.

SLAD, Nr. Stroud

Ian Hodgkins and Co. Ltd
Upper Vatch Mill, The Vatch. Open by appointment only. STOCK: Antiquarian books including pre-Raphaelites and associates, the Brontës; 19th C illustrated, children's art and literature books. TEL: 0453 764270.

STOW-ON-THE-WOLD

Acorn Antiques
Sheep St. (M. Masters). Est. 1987. Open 9.30-1 and 2.15-5. Sat. 9.30-1 and 2.30-5. CL: Wed. p.m. SIZE: Medium. STOCK: Ceramics and glass, Victorian, £15-£300; furniture, Georgian,

Stow-on-the-Wold continued
Victorian and Edwardian, £50-£2,000; collectables, 19th-20th C, £1-£50. PARK: Easy. TEL: 0451 831519. SER: Restorations (ceramics).

Ashton Dodkin Antiques
7a Talbot Court. (Robert Ashton and Audrey Dodkin). Est. 1966. Open 10-1 and 2-5.30. SIZE: Large. STOCK: English furniture, silver, china, decorative copper and brass. PARK: Easy. TEL: 0451 870067; home - 0564 777037. VAT: Stan/Spec.

Duncan J. Baggott
Woolcomber House, Sheep St. CADA. Est. 1967. Open 9-5.30 or by appointment. SIZE: Large STOCK: 17th-19th C. English oak, mahogany, walnut and fruitwood furniture, paintings, prints and needlework, metalware and domestic items, garden statuary. PARK: Own. TEL: 0451 830662; fax - 0451 832174.

Duncan J. Baggott
Huntsmans Yard, Sheep St. CADA. Est. 1967. Open 9-5, or by appointment. CL: Sat. SIZE: Large. STOCK: 17th-19th C. English and European furniture, portrait and primitive paintings, architectural items and statuary. LOC: 200yds. from Fosseway entrance on right hand side through coaching gates. PARK: Own. TEL: 0451 830662; fax - 0451 832174. Trade Only.

Baggott Church Street Ltd   BADA
Church St. (D.J. and C.M. Baggott). CADA. Est. 1978. Open 9.30-5.30 or by appointment. SIZE: Large. STOCK: English furniture, 17th-19th C; portrait paintings, some metalwork pottery, treen and decorative items. LOC: Southwest corner of market square. PARK: In market square. TEL: 0451 830370; fax - 0451 832174.

Bow Cottage Antiques
2 Park St. (R. Harvey-Morgan). Open 10-5.30 STOCK: English porcelain, glass, silver paintings, engravings, maps, books, general antiques, small furniture, all 18th-20th C, £5-£150+. TEL: 0451 832311; messages - 0789 292485. VAT: Stan.

Colin Brand Antiques
Tudor House, Sheep St. CADA. Est. 1985. Open 10-1 and 2-5, Sun. by appointment. CL: Wed SIZE: Medium. STOCK: Clocks, small furniture £200-£4,000; porcelain, £30-£600, all pre-1900 LOC: Opposite Post Office. PARK: Main square TEL: 0451 831760; home - same. VAT: Spec.

D. Bryden
Sheep St. Est. 1979. Open 10-12.30 and 2-5. CL Wed. and Thurs. SIZE: Small. STOCK: English silver, 18th-19th C, £50-£7,000; satinwood rosewood and mahogany furniture, Georgian, Victorian and Edwardian, £200-£2,000. LOC: Off A429. PARK: Stow Sq. TEL: 0451 830840. VAT Stan/Spec.

Telephone Cotswold (0451) 831760
COLIN BRAND ANTIQUES
Tudor House, Sheep Street, Stow-on-the-Wold
Gloucestershire GL54 1AA

Stow-on-the-Wold continued

J. and J. Caspall Antiques
Sheep St. Author of "Fire and Light in the Home pre-1820". Est. 1971. Open 9.30-5.30 or by appointment. *STOCK: Period oak, 16th C to 1760; early metalwork, especially lighting and hearth, early woodcarvings, period domestic and decorative items.* PARK: Nearby. TEL: 0451 831160. SER: Valuations. VAT: Spec.

Annarella Clark Antiques
11 Park St. Est. 1968. Open by appointment. SIZE: Medium. *STOCK: Wicker and garden, English and French country and painted furniture, needlework, pottery, quilts and decorative objects.* LOC: Park St. leads from Sheep St., 1st right at lights leading into town. PARK: Easy. TEL: 0451 830535; home - same. VAT: Stan/Spec.

Christopher Clarke Antiques Ltd
BADA
The Fosse Way. (C.J. Clarke). CADA. Est. 1961. Open 9.30-6. SIZE: Medium. *STOCK: Furniture, 17th-19th C, £300-£15,000; walnut, mahogany, metalware, 16th-18th C, £200-£5,000. Not Stocked: Silver, glass, medals, coins, prints.* LOC: Corner of the Fosse Way and Sheep St. PARK: Easy. TEL: 0451 830476; fax - 0451 830300.

Cotswold Antiques Centre
The Square. Open 10-5. PARK: Easy. TEL: 0451 831585. Below are listed some of the dealers at this centre.

Lesley Bellingham
STOCK: Art nouveau, jewellery, Victoriana, decorative items.

John Bunting
STOCK: Post-Impressionist paintings and watercolours.

Nick Clapton
STOCK: 18th-19th C porcelain and pottery.

J. and D. Hall
STOCK: 17th-19th C furniture, porcelain, Staffordshire figures.

Stow-on-the-Wold continued

James Hall
STOCK: Clocks, especially wall, bracket, mantel and longcase.

Pat Johnson
STOCK: Porcelain, pottery, jewellery, silver plate.

Adrienne Lambert
STOCK: 18th-19th C ceramics, small furniture, textiles, decorative items.

Sue London
STOCK: Decorative ceramics, glass, small furniture, silver and plate, linen and lace.

T. Newman
STOCK: Pine and country furniture and artefacts.

M. Nichols
STOCK: Silver, jewellery and ceramics.

Denise Rolfe
STOCK: Masons ironstone, pottery and porcelain, general antiques.

J. Stanley
STOCK: Engravings, 18th-19th C ceramics, glass, furniture, metalware.

Talbot Antiques
STOCK: Porcelain and pottery, especially Welsh.

W. Woodman
STOCK: Roman and medieval artefacts.

Cotswold Galleries
(Richard and Cherry Glaisyer). CADA. Est. 1961. Open 9-5.30 or by appointment. SIZE: Large. *STOCK: Oil paintings, especially 19th-20th C landscape.* TEL: 0451 830586. SER: Restorations; framing.

Country Life Antiques
Grey House, The Square. Open 10-5.30. *STOCK: Furniture, oil paintings, scientific instruments, decorative accessories, pewter, brass, copper.* PARK: Easy. TEL: 0451 831564.

GLOUCESTERSHIRE

Stow-on-the-Wold continued

The Curiosity Shop   BADA LAPADA
The Square. (Antony Preston Antiques Ltd). CADA. Est. 1965. Open 9.30-5.30. SIZE: Large. *STOCK: Furniture, clocks, mirrors, 18th to early 19th C, £500-£10,000.* LOC: Off Fosse Way. PARK: Easy. TEL: 0451 831586. VAT: Stan/Spec.

John Davies Fine Paintings
Church Street Gallery, Church St. Est. 1977. Open 9.30-1 and 2-6. SIZE: Large. *STOCK: British paintings and watercolours, mainly rural, 1890-1950; contemporary exhibitions.* PARK: In square. TEL: 0451 831698; fax - 0451 832477. SER: Restorations (oil paintings, watercolours, pastels, prints and drawings).

Fosse Gallery
The Square. (G. O'Farrell and John Lindsey Fine Art Ltd). Est. 1979. Open 10-5.30. SIZE: Large. *STOCK: British post impressionist paintings and watercolours, £100-£10,000.* LOC: Off Fosseway, A429. PARK: Easy. TEL: 0451 831319. SER: Valuations; buys at auction. VAT: Spec.

Fosse Way Antiques
Ross House, The Square. (M. Beeston). CADA. Est. 1969. Open 10-5. SIZE: Large. *STOCK: Furniture and pictures, £150-£5,000; bronzes, porcelain, Sheffield plate, glass and decorative objects, £50-£1,000; all 18th-19th C.* LOC: East side of the Square, behind the Town Hall. PARK: Easy. TEL: 0451 830776. SER: Valuations; buys at auction. VAT: Spec.

Keith Hockin (Antiques) Ltd   BADA
The Square. CADA. Est. 1968. Open 9-6. CL: Sun. except by appointment. SIZE: Medium. *STOCK: Oak furniture, 1600-1750; country furniture in oak, fruitwoods, yew, 1700-1850; pewter, copper, brass, ironwork, all periods.* Not Stocked: Mahogany. PARK: Easy. TEL: 0451 831058. SER: Buys at auction (oak, pewter, metalwork). VAT: Stan/Spec.

Huntington Antiques Ltd   LAPADA
The Old Forge, Church St. (M.F., S.P. and N.M.J. Golding). CADA. Resident. Est. 1974. Open 9.30-5.30 or by appointment. *STOCK: Early period and fine country furniture, metalware, treen and textiles, tapestries and works of art.* TEL: 0451 830842; fax - 0451 832211. SER: Valuations; buys at auction. FAIRS: Maastricht; Madrid; Bruges. VAT: Spec.

Little Elms Antiques
The Square. (Michael Rowland). Open 10-5. SIZE: Small. *STOCK: Furniture including dressers, ladder and spindle back chairs, gateleg and side tables, 17th-18th C, £100-£5,000.* PARK: Easy. TEL: 0451 870089; home - same. SER: Valuations. VAT: Spec.

Stow-on-the-Wold continued

Martin House Antiques
Sheep St. (G. Finney). Resident. Open 10.30-5.30 CL: Fri. *STOCK: 18th-19th C porcelain and pottery.* TEL: 0451 831217.

No. 2 Park Street Antiques
2/3 Park St. (P.R. Johnson). Open 10-5, Sun. 11-5 SIZE: Large - 22 dealers. *STOCK: General antique including pre-1930 furniture, pictures, brass and copper, china and collectables.* LOC: On main road from town centre towards Chipping Norton. PARK Easy. TEL: 0451 832311. VAT: Stan/Spec.

Peter Norden Antiques
The Little House, Sheep St. Est. 1960. Open 9.30 5.30. SIZE: Medium. *STOCK: Early oak, country period walnut and mahogany furniture, metalware treen, pottery, period firearms especially blunder bussess, armour, 16th to mid 19th C.* Not Stocked Silver, shipping goods. LOC: Off the Fosseway opposite the Post Office. PARK: Easy. TEL: 045 830455; home - 0993 831607. VAT:Spec.

Simon W. Nutter
Wraggs Row, Fosse Way. Open by appointment *STOCK: Furniture, 17th to early 19th C.* TEL 0451 830658.

Oriental Gallery
1 Digbeth St. (Patricia Cater). Open 10-5, Wed 10-1. *STOCK: Chinese and Japanese furnitur and oriental works of art.* TEL: 0451 830944; fa - 0451 870126.

Park House Antiques
Park St. (G. and B. Sutton). Est. 1986. Open 10 5.30, Sun. by appointment only. SIZE: Large *STOCK: Furniture, watercolours and oils, fro 18th C; toys and teddy bears; Victorian liner and lace; porcelain, pottery, glass and collec ables.* PARK: Easy. TEL: 0451 830159; home same. VAT: Stan/Spec.

Antony Preston Antiques Ltd
BADA LAPAD
The Square. CADA. Est. 1965. Open 9.30-5.30 c by appointment. *STOCK: English and continent furniture and objects, longcase and bracket clock barometers, leather upholstery, 18th-19th C.* TE 0451 831586. VAT: Stan/Spec.

Priests Antiques
The Malthouse, Digbeth St. (A.C. Priest). Es 1979. Open 10-5, Sat. 10.30-5. SIZE: Larg *STOCK: Mahogany, 18th to early 19th C; oa walnut, and fruitwood, 17th-18th C; sportir prints and chromolithographs.* PARK: Easy. TE 0451 830592. SER: Valuations. VAT: Spec.

Rosemary Antiques and Paper Moor Books
at No.2 Park Street Antiques, 2-3 Park St. (M R.E. Fletcher.). Est. 1977. Open 10-5, Sun. 11-

Stow-on-the-Wold continued
SIZE: Large. *STOCK: Small furniture, 1880-1930, £50-£300; books, 1800-1940, £5-£100; ceramics, 1880-1920, £5-£150.* LOC: Main road from town centre towards Chipping Norton. PARK: Easy. TEL: 0451 832311; home - 0386 438827.

Ruskin Antiques
5 Talbot Court. (Anne Byrne and William Morris). Est. 1991. Open 9.30-1 and 2-5.30, Sun. 11-1 and 2-4.30. SIZE: Small. *STOCK: Interesting and unusual decorative objects - Arts and Crafts movement and art deco glass and pottery, especially Clarice Cliff, 1700-1930.* LOC: Between The Square and Sheep Street. PARK: Nearby. TEL: 0451 832254; home - 0993 831880. SER: Valuations. FAIRS: NEC; Decorative Arts, Kensington and Loughborough. VAT: Spec.

St. Breock Gallery
Digbeth St. (R.G.G. Haslam-Hopwood). Est. 1979. Open 10-5. SIZE: Medium. *STOCK: Watercolours, 19th-20th C, £50-£3,000; furniture, general antiques and objets d'art.* LOC: Just off Market Sq. PARK: Easy. TEL: 0451 830424; home - 071 229 4918. SER: Restorations; buys at auction. VAT: Spec.

Samarkand Galleries   LAPADA
2 Brewery Yard, Sheep St. (B. and L. MacDonald). CADA. Est. 1980. Open 10-5.30, Sun. by appointment. SIZE: Medium. *STOCK: Tribal and village rugs and artifacts, 19th C, £100-£10,000; fine decorative carpets, 19th-20th C, £1,000-£10,000+; kelims, 19th-20th C, £200-£2,000.* LOC: Street adjacent to Market Sq. PARK: Easy. TEL: 0451 832322; fax - same; home - 0451 831173. SER: Valuations; restorations; cleaning; exhibitions. VAT: Stan/Spec.

Stow Antiques   LAPADA
The Square. (Mr and Mrs J. Hutton-Clarke). CADA. Resident. Est. 1969. Open 10.30-5.30. SIZE: Large. *STOCK: Furniture, mainly Georgian, £500-£30,000; decorative items, gilded mirrors, £50-£10,000.* PARK: Easy. TEL: 0451 830377; fax - 0451 870018. SER: Shipping worldwide.

Talbot Court Galleries
Talbot Court. (J.P. Trevers). Est. 1988. Open 9.30-1 and 2-5.30, Sun. in summer 11-5. SIZE: Medium. *STOCK: Prints and maps, 1600-1900, £5-£500; restrike engravings, £25-£150.* LOC: Behind Talbot Hotel in precinct between the Square and Sheep St. PARK: Nearby. TEL: 0451 832169. SER: Valuations; restorations (cleaning, colouring); framing; buys at auction (engravings). VAT: Stan.

Touchwood International
9 Park St. (K.M. and L.A. Dixon). Resident. Est. 1830. Open 10-5, Sun. by appointment. SIZE: Medium. *STOCK: Oak, walnut, fruitwood, early*

PRIESTS
The Malthouse, Digbeth Street
Stow-on-the-Wold
Gloucestershire
Tel: 0451 30592

George I period walnut chest on chest, c.1720

Stow-on-the-Wold continued
period furniture, medieval to early 18th C, £100-£25,000; treen, metalware and pottery, to 1830; works of art, sculptures, carvings. LOC: On A436 just past junction with Digbeth St. PARK: Easy. TEL: 0451 870800; fax - same. SER: Valuations; restorations (wax polishing, esp. large collections and rare items); upholstery; research - medieval to late 17th C furniture; video service; commissions undertaken; finder. VAT: Stan/Spec.

Vanbrugh House Antiques
Park St. (J. and M.M. Sands). Resident. Est. 1972. Open 10-6 or by appointment. *STOCK: Furniture and decorative items, 17th to early 19th C; early maps, music boxes, square pianos, clocks and barometers.* LOC: Opposite the Bell Inn. PARK: Easy. TEL: 0451 830797. SER: Valuations. VAT: Stan/Spec.

STROUD
Gnome Cottage Antiques
55-57 Middle St. (I.A. McGrane). Est. 1961. Open 9.30-5.30. *STOCK: General antiques, furniture, prints, glass, china.* TEL: 0453 763669.

R.J.D. Fine Arts
12 Wallbridge. (R.J. Dunk). Open 9.30-5. *STOCK: Pictures.* TEL: 0453 764878. SER: Framing.

GLOUCESTERSHIRE

Stroud continued

Shabby Tiger Antiques
18 Nelson St. (S. Krucker). Est. 1975. Open 11-6. STOCK: *19th C furniture, pictures, jewellery, silver and plate, china, glass, metalware, decorative items*. LOC: Nelson St. is adjacent to Parliament St. car park. PARK: Opposite. TEL: 0453 759175.

TADDINGTON, Nr. Cutsdean
Architectural Heritage
Taddington Manor. CADA. Est. 1978. Open 9.30-5.30, Sat. 10.30-4.30. SIZE: Large. STOCK: *Period panelling, oak, mahogany and pine; chimney pieces in marble, stone, oak and mahogany; garden statuary, fountains, seats and urns; complete shop and pub interiors, ornamental gates, stained, leaded and etched glass; doors, decorative and unusual items*. PARK: Easy. TEL: 038 673 414; fax - 038 673 236. VAT: Stan.

TETBURY
Antique Interiors
35 Long St. (Colin Gee). Est. 1971. Open 9-6, Sun. by appointment. SIZE: Medium. STOCK: *English country house furniture, decorative items, plaster busts and sculpture, lacquer, Biedermeier and French Empire furniture, mainly 18th-19th C, £30-£3,000*. PARK: Easy. TEL: 0666 504043; home - same. SER: Valuations; courier. VAT: Stan/Spec.

The Antiques Emporium
The Old Chapel, Long St. (C. and D. Sayers). Est. 1993. Open 10-5, Sun. 1-5. SIZE: Large - 30 dealers. STOCK: *Fruitwood and country furniture, fine oak and mahogany, china, porcelain, treen, clocks and jewellery, £1-£15,000*. Not Stocked: Reproductions. PARK: Nearby. TEL: 0666 505281. SER: Export. VAT: Stan/Spec.

Art-Tique
18 Long St. (George Bristow). Open 9.30-6. CL: Mon. STOCK: *Interiors, textiles, carpets and kelims and objets d'art from the Orient*. TEL: 0666 503597.

Balmuir House Antiques
14 Long St. (P. Whittam). Est. 1969. Open 9.30-5.30, Sun. by appointment. SIZE: Large. STOCK: *Victorian and Edwardian furniture, paintings, mirrors, 19th C, £500-£5,000*. LOC: Town centre. PARK: Easy. TEL: 0666 503822; home - same. SER: Valuations; restorations (furniture, upholstery, paintings). VAT: Spec.

Breakspeare Antiques   LAPADA
36 and 57 Long St. (M. and S. Breakspeare). CADA. Resident. Est. 1962. Open 9.30-5.30, if closed ring bell. CL: Some Thurs. p.m. SIZE: Medium. STOCK: *English period furniture, mainly mahogany, 18th to early 19th C, some early walnut, longcase clocks*. PARK: Easy. TEL: 0666 503122; home - same. VAT: Stan/Spec. *Mainly Trade.*

J. and M. Bristow Antiques
28 Long St. (M.J. and J.A. Bristow). Est. 1964. Open 9.30-1 and 2-5.30, but any time by appointment. CL: Thurs. SIZE: Small. STOCK: *Longcase, bracket and lantern clocks; barometers, 17th-18th C; furniture*. Not Stocked: Victoriana, bric-a-brac. LOC: In main street. PARK: Easy. TEL: 0666 502222. VAT: Spec.

The Chest of Drawers
24 Long St. (A. and P. Bristow). Resident. Est. 1969. Open 9.30-6 or by appointment. CL: Thurs. a.m. SIZE: Medium. STOCK: *Late Georgian, Regency and Victorian furniture; country pieces, 17th-18th C; china and brass*. LOC: On A433. PARK: Easy. TEL: 0666 502105; home - same. VAT: Spec.

Country Homes
61 Long St. (C. and D. Sayers). Est. 1984. Open 9-5.30, Sun. 1-5.30. SIZE: Medium. STOCK: *Pine furniture, 19th C, £100-£1,500; treen*. PARK: Nearby. TEL: 0666 502342. SER: Import/export. VAT: Stan/Spec.

Ann and Roger Day Antiques
5 New Church St. Est. 1975. Open 9-6. SIZE: Medium. STOCK: *Oak and country furniture, early pottery, metalware, treen, some period mahogany*. TEL: 0666 502413. VAT: Stan/Spec.

Dolphin Antiques
48 Long St. (P. and L. Davis). Est. 1986. Open 10-5.30. SIZE: Small. STOCK: *Mainly 19th C decorative porcelain, general antiques, 1750-1930, £20-£2,000*. Not Stocked: Large furniture. PARK: Nearby. TEL: 0666 504242; home - same. VAT: Stan/Spec.

Elgin House Antiques
1 New Church St. (B. Symes). Open every day 10-5.30. STOCK: *18th-19th C oak, mahogany and pine furniture; restored brass and iron beds and accessories; upholstered furniture and decorative items*. TEL: 0666 504068.

Hampton Gallery
10 New Church St. (P. Downey). Resident. Est. 1969. Open by appointment. SIZE: Large. STOCK: *Weapons, arms and armour, 1700-1880, £50-£5,000*. LOC: Off junction 17, M4. PARK: Easy. TEL: 0666 502971. SER: Valuations; buy at auction (arms). FAIRS: All major. VAT: Spec.

Paul Nash Antiques   BADA
Cherington House, Cherington. (P. and A. Gifford Nash). Resident. Est. 1961. Open by appointment only. STOCK: *Fine English furniture, 1680-1840*. LOC: 4 miles from Tetbury. PARK: Own. TEL: 0285 841215. VAT: Spec.

GLOUCESTERSHIRE

Tetbury continued
Old George Antiques and Interiors
3 The Chipping. (Mrs W.M. Wild and J. Tyndall). Est. 1974. Open 10-5.30, Sun. by appointment. SIZE: Medium. *STOCK: Mahogany, decorated and walnut furniture, 17th C to Regency, to £5,000+; decorative items, porcelain, lighting, £500-£1,000+; paintings and rugs, to 20th C, £500-£2,000.* LOC: 100yds. from town centre, turn off main street at Snooty Fox Hotel into The Chipping car park. PARK: Easy. TEL: 0666 503405. SER: Valuations; restorations; interior decor and design; buys at auction. VAT: Stan/Spec.

Old Mill Market Shop
12 Church St. (Mr and Mrs M. Green). Open 10-5.30, Thurs. 10-1. *STOCK: General antiques, collectables and bric-a-brac.* TEL: 0666 503127.

Porch House Antiques
42 Long St. Open 10-5. *STOCK: Furniture, 17th-19th C; paintings, porcelain, pottery and decorative items.* TEL: 0666 502687.

Primrose Antiques
45 Long St. (W.T. and B. Stickland). Est. 1972. Open 9.30-5.30. SIZE: Medium. *STOCK: Oak, mahogany and walnut, brass, copper and pewter, 17th-19th C.* PARK: Easy. TEL: 0666 502440; home - same. VAT: Stan/Spec.

Rudge Antics
46 Long St. (T. and P. Rudge). Open 10-5 or by appointment. *STOCK: Pine furniture.* TEL: 0666 503546.

Upton Lodge Galleries
6 Long St. (J. Grant). Est. 1979. Open 10-6. SIZE: Medium. *STOCK: Oils and watercolours, from 1900, £100-£5,000.* PARK: Easy. TEL: 0666 503416.

Yeo Antiques LAPADA
6 Westonbirt. (B.D. and B.G. Ackrill). **Open by appointment. *STOCK: Furniture, metalware, clocks, porcelain and pottery.* TEL: 0666 880388.** SER: Valuations; restorations. VAT: Stan/Spec.

TEWKESBURY
Abbey Antiques
62 Church St. Est. 1945. CL: Thurs. p.m. *STOCK: General antiques,Victoriana, trade and shipping goods.* TEL: 0684 292378.

Berkeley Antiques and Replay
The Wheatsheaf, 132 High St. (P. Dennis and R. Lane). Open 9.30-5.30. CL: Mon. and Thurs. SIZE: Large. *STOCK: Mahogany, oak, walnut and pine, 17th-19th C, £50-£2,000; brass, copper, silver, china and glass; period clothing, costumes and accessories, fabrics and hangings.* TEL: 0684 292034. SER: Restorations. VAT: Stan/Spec.

Tewkesbury continued
Gainsborough House Antiques
81 Church St. (A. and B. Hilson). Open 9.30-5. *STOCK: Furniture, 18th to early 19th C; glass, porcelain.* TEL: 0684 293072. SER: Restorations; conservation.

F.W. Taylor
71 Church St. Est. 1972. Open 9-5. SIZE: Medium. *STOCK: Furniture,18th-19th C, £150-£3,000; glass, silver, ceramics, prints, copper, brass, decorative and collectable items.* LOC: Close to Abbey. PARK: 100yds. TEL: 0684 295990. SER: Valuations; buys at auction. VAT: Stan/Spec.

Tewkesbury Antique Centre
Tolsey Hall, Tolsey Lane. (J. Preece). Est. 1978. Open 9-5. SIZE: Medium - 10+ units. *STOCK: General antiques.* LOC: Town centre. PARK: Easy. TEL: 0684 294091. SER: Valuations; restorations. VAT: Stan/Spec.

WINCHCOMBE
The Barometer Shop
64 North St. (R. Cookson). *STOCK: Barometers, barographs, clocks, scientific instruments.* TEL: 0242 603256.

Kenulf Fine Arts
5 North St. (E. and J. Ford). Est. 1978. Open 9.30-1 and 2-5.30. *STOCK: 19th to early 20th C oils, watercolours and prints;decorative items and 20th C ceramics; small furniture.* TEL: 0242 603204/602776. SER: Valuations; restorations (oils and watercolours, period framing).

Muriel Lindsay
Queen Anne House. Resident. Est. 1965. Open 9.30-1 and 2-5.30. *STOCK: Staffordshire, metalwork, glass, small items.* TEL: 0242 602319. VAT: Spec.

Prichard Antiques
16 High St. (K.H. and D.Y. Prichard). CADA. Est. 1979. Open 9-6, Sun. by appointment. SIZE: Large. *STOCK: Period furniture, £10-£5,000; treen, £1-£500; metalwork, £5-£500, all 17th-19th C.* LOC: On main Broadway to Cheltenham road. PARK: Easy. TEL: 0242 603566. VAT: Spec.

WOTTON-UNDER-EDGE
Bell Passage Antiques LAPADA
36-38 High St, Wickwar. (Mrs D.V. Brand). Est. 1966. Open 8-5. CL: Mon. and Thurs. SIZE: Large. *STOCK: Furniture, £40-£5,000; glass, £1-£100; porcelain, £1-£800; prints, oils and watercolours, £20-£2,000.* LOC: On B4060. PARK: Easy. TEL: 0454 294251. SER: Valuations; restorations. VAT: Stan/Spec.

Hampshire

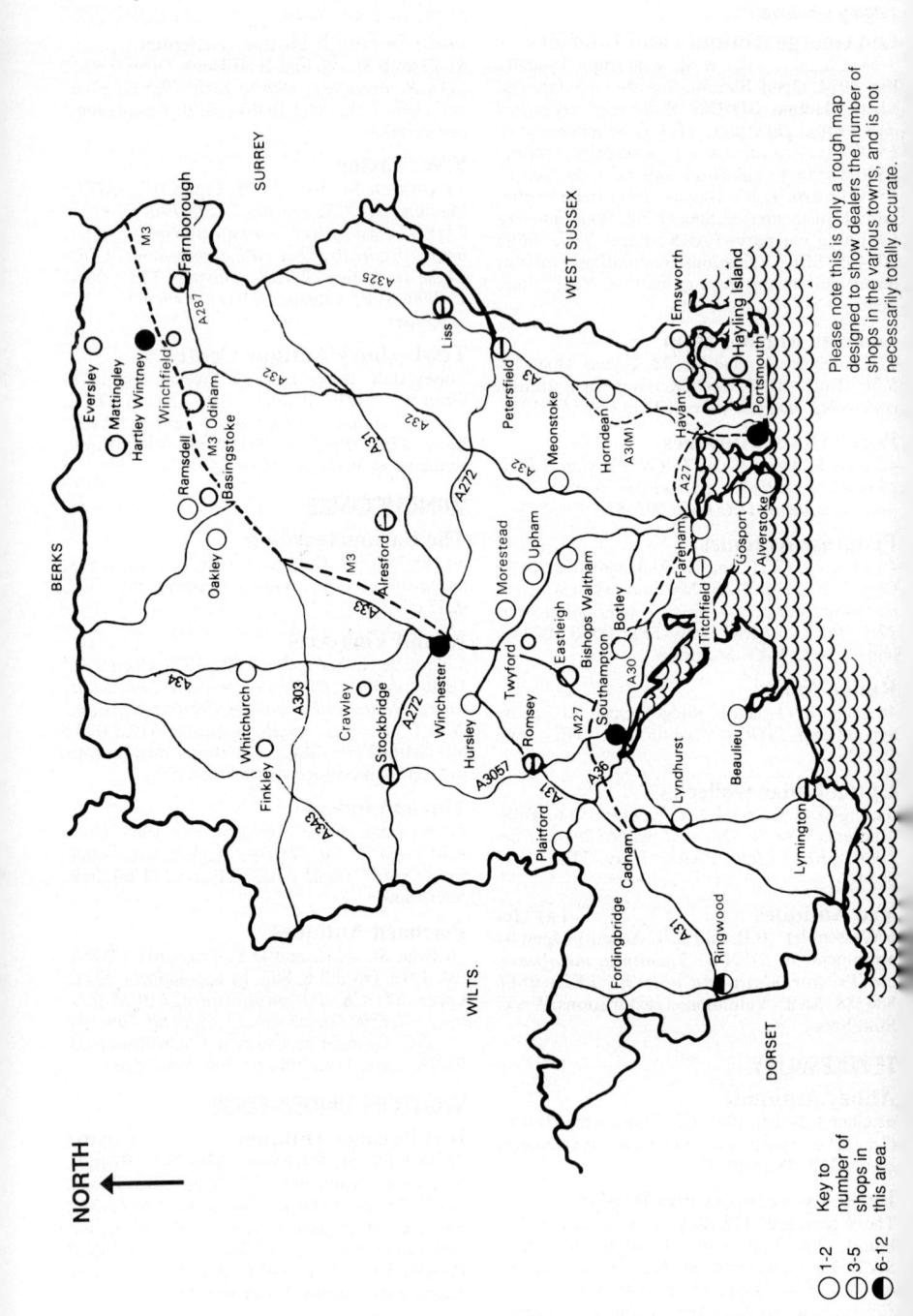

Hampshire

ALRESFORD, Nr. Winchester

Artemesia LAPADA
16 West St. (D.T.L. Wright). Est. 1972. Open 9.30-5. SIZE: Medium. STOCK: Oriental porcelain, works of art, 10th-19th C, £20-£5,000. LOC: A31. PARK: Nearby. TEL: 0962 732277. SER: Valuations. VAT: Spec.

Close Antiques BADA
(C. Baron). Open by appointment only. SIZE: Medium. STOCK: 17th-18th C oak, fruitwood, and walnut country furniture; samplers, Delftware, early brass, copper, iron and treen. LOC: A31 on left entering town from east. PARK: Easy. TEL: 0962 732189. VAT: Spec.

Evans and Evans LAPADA
40 West St. (D. and N. Evans). Est. 1953. Open Fri. and Sat. or by appointment. SIZE: Medium. STOCK: Clocks, watches, 1680-1900, £250-£50,000; musical boxes, 19th C, £500-£12,000; Regency and Victorian barometers, £200-£2,000. Stock only as listed. LOC: A31. Shop on left going north. PARK: Easy. TEL: 0962 732170. SER: Valuations; buys at auction. VAT: Stan/Spec.

Studio Bookshop and Gallery
17 Broad St. (L. Oxley). ABA. Est. 1951. Open 9-5. SIZE: Large. STOCK: Antiquarian books, £5-£2,500; topographical prints, £2-£250; maps, £5-£800. LOC: B3046. PARK: Easy. TEL: 0962 732188. SER: Valuations; restorations (oil paintings, prints); framing. FAIRS: USA, London ABA. VAT: Stan.

ALVERSTOKE, Nr. Gosport

Alverstoke Antiques
47 Village Rd. (Dyer and Follett Ltd). Est. 1960. Open 9-12.45 and 2.15-5.30. SIZE: Small. STOCK: Furniture. PARK: Easy. TEL: 0705 582204. SER: Restorations. VAT: Stan/Spec.

Olive Antiques
2A Church Rd. Est. 1976. Open 8.15-5. SIZE: Medium. STOCK: Gold, silver, diamonds, jewellery, clocks, barometers, mirrors and porcelain, £10-£1,000. LOC: Main road from Fareham to Gosport and then to Alverstoke. PARK: Easy. TEL: 0705 522812. SER: Valuations; gem stone testing.

BASINGSTOKE

Squirrel Collectors Centre
9 New St. (D.P. Stone and Mrs R.A. Austen). Est. 1981. Open 10-5.30. SIZE: Small. STOCK: Jewellery and silver, Victorian and Edwardian, £5-£1,500; books, cigarette and post cards, watches, collectors' and small items. LOC: Near traffic lights at junction with Winchester St. PARK: Nearby. TEL: 0256 464885. SER: Valuations. FAIRS: Farnham Maltings monthly. VAT: Stan.

BEAULIEU

Beaulieu Fine Arts
The Malt House, High St. (Mr and Mrs S.A. Roberts). Est. 1975. Open 9.30-12.30 and 1.30-5.30, Sun. by appointment. SIZE: Medium. STOCK: Watercolours, mainly 19th and early 20th C, from £200; drawings, prints and etchings, from £16; contemporary oils and watercolours. PARK: High St. TEL: 0590 612089. VAT: Stan/Spec.

BISHOPS WALTHAM

Pinecrafts
4 Brook St. (A. Robinson). Open 10-5. SIZE: Large. STOCK: Pine furniture. TEL: 0489 892878. SER: Restorations; stripping. VAT: Stan.

BOTLEY, Nr. Southampton

Jane Burnham-Slipper Antiques
The Tudor House, 8 Winchester St. Est. 1986. Open by appointment. SIZE: Small. STOCK: Glass, 18th-19th C, from £35; silver, Georgian and later, from £50. LOC: 5 minutes from junction 7, M27. PARK: Nearby. TEL: 0489 782354; home - same. FAIRS: Goodwood, Petersfield, Surrey County, Wilton House and other major southern counties. VAT: Stan/Spec.

Butterfly Pine
Old Flour Mills. (K. Shaw). Est. 1986. Open 10-5.30, Thurs. 10-1, Sun. 12-5.30. SIZE: Medium. STOCK: Pine, £500-£1,000; darkwood furniture, £250-£1,500; associated items, porcelain and prints, £50-£500; all 18th-19th C. LOC: Off M27, exit 7. PARK: Easy. TEL: 0489 788194; fax - 0489 790103. SER: Valuations; restorations (clocks, furniture including upholstery, caning and French polishing); buys at auction; finder; furniture made to order from old and new pine. VAT: Stan.

CADNAM

C.W. Buckingham
Twin Firs, Southampton Rd. Resident. Open 9-6 or by appointment. CL: Thurs. STOCK: Mainly pine, some period and Victorian furniture. TEL: 0703 812122.

Hingstons
Minstead Cottage, Romsey Rd. BDADA. Open 9-5 and by appointment. CL: Sat. SIZE: Warehouse. STOCK: General antiques especially furniture, 1830-1930. TEL: 0703 812301; evenings - 0703 812637.

CRAWLEY, Nr. Winchester

Prospect Antiques
Folly Farm. (T.R. Baker and G.M. Marsh). Open 9-5. STOCK: General antiques especially pine. TEL: 0962 776687.

Nicholas Abbott

High Street
Hartley Wintney
Hampshire
Tel: 0252 842365

A good selection of period furniture ranging from 1680 to 1830

EASTLEIGH
Tappers Antiques
186 Southampton Rd. (P.A. Passell). Open 10-5. *STOCK: General collectables and curios.* LOC: 1 mile off M27. TEL: 0703 643105.

EMSWORTH
Tiffins Antiques
12 Queen St. (Mrs P. Hudson). Est. 1987. Open 10-5. SIZE: Small. *STOCK: General antiques, oil lamps and clocks.* TEL: 0243 372497; home - same. SER: Restorations (clocks).

EVERSLEY, Nr. Wokingham
Kingsley Barn Antique Centre
Church Lane. (G. Bazely). Est. 1988. Open 10.30-5. CL: Mon. SIZE: Large. *STOCK: Furniture, china and bric-a-brac.* LOC: 1.5 miles from Blackbush airport. PARK: Easy. TEL: 0734 328518. SER: Restorations (furniture).

FAREHAM
Elizabethans
58 High St. (Mrs E. Keeble). Est. 1961. Open 10-4. *STOCK: Small general antiques, furniture, jewellery.* TEL: 0329 234964 (ansaphone).

FARNBOROUGH
Martin and Parke   LAPADA
97 Lynchford Rd. (J. Martin and J. Warde). Est. 1971. Open 9-5. SIZE: Large. *STOCK: Furniture, shipping goods and books.* TEL: 0252 515311. VAT: Stan.

FINKLEY, Nr. Andover
Parker Fine Art Ltd
Finkley House. (P.A.R. Parker). Open by appointment. *STOCK: Oil paintings, 17th-20th C; frames.* TEL: 0264 352412; fax - 0264 358241; mobile - 0860 323791. SER: Restorations.

FORDINGBRIDGE
Mark Collier   BADA
24 High St. Open by appointment. *STOCK: General decorative antiques. Not Stocked: Coins, medals and stamps.* TEL: 0425 652555; fax - 0425 656886.

Quatrefoil
Burgate. (C.D. and Mrs I. Aston). Resident. Est. 1972. Always open. SIZE: Large. *STOCK: Early oak furniture, 16th-18th C, £50-£15,000; carvings and sculpture, 13th-17th C, £20-£10,000.* LOC: On A338, adjacent Tudor Rose Inn. PARK: Easy. TEL: 0425 653309. VAT: Stan/Spec.

ANDWELLS ANTIQUES LTD

**HIGH STREET
HARTLEY WINTNEY
HANTS**
Tel. Hartley Wintney 842305

18th and early 19th century furniture

GOSPORT

E.T. Cooper
20 Stoke Rd. Est. 1972. Open 9.30-12.30 and 1.30-5. CL: Wed. p.m. SIZE: Medium. *STOCK: Silver, china, glass, furniture, mechanical music, fairground equipment.* LOC: Main road from Lee-on-Solent through Gosport. PARK: In side road. TEL: 0705 585032. SER: Valuations; buys at auction.

Peter Pan's Bazaar
105 Forton Rd. (S.V. Panormo). Est. 1960. CL: Mon., Tues. and Wed. *STOCK: Vintage cameras, early photographica, images, 1850-1950, £5-£1,500.* LOC: Main road into town. PARK: Easy. TEL: 0705 524254. FAIRS: Main south of England.

Peter Pan's of Gosport
105c Forton Rd. (J. McClaren). Est. 1965. CL: Mon., Tues. and Wed. *STOCK: Jewellery, dolls, toys and miniatures.* LOC: Main road into town. PARK: Easy. TEL: 0705 524254. FAIRS: Main south of England.

HARTLEY WINTNEY

Nicholas Abbott
High St. (C. and A. Abbott). Est. 1962. Open 9.30-5.30. SIZE: Large. *STOCK: English furniture, 18th to early 19th C.* LOC: A30. PARK: Easy. TEL: 0252 842365; home - 0734 326269. VAT: Stan/Spec.

Airdale Antiques
at Deva, High St. (E.J. Andreae). Est. 1972. *STOCK: Country furniture, 17th-19th C; polished pine.* TEL: 0252 843538.

Andwells   LAPADA
High St. (P. Heraty). Est. 1967. Open 9-5.30, Sat. 9.30-5.30. SIZE: Large. *STOCK: Georgian and Regency furniture, mainly mahogany.* LOC: Main street. PARK: Easy. TEL: 0252 842305. VAT: Stan/Spec.

Antique House
22 High St. (R.M. Campbell and P. Weaver). Open 9.30-5.30, Sun. by appointment. *STOCK: Georgian and Victorian furniture, watercolours and prints.*

CEDAR ANTIQUES LTD
Derek Green

A wide selection of Country Furniture, Folk Art & Associated Items, always on display

HARTLEY WINTNEY
0252 843252

Hartley Wintney continued

PARK: Easy. TEL: 0252 844499; home - 0276 26412. SER: Restorations (furniture).

Cedar Antiques
High St. (D.S. Green). Est. 1964. Open 9-6, trade any time. SIZE: Large and warehouse. *STOCK: Fine English oak, walnut and country furniture, 17th-18th C, £50-£10,000; French Provincial furniture; longcase clocks, 1680-1780, £800-£5,000; steel and brasswork, £30-£1,000.* Not Stocked: China, glass, silver. LOC: A30. PARK: Opposite. TEL: 0252 843252; fax - 0252 845235. SER: Valuations; restorations (clocks, period furniture). VAT: Stan/Spec.

HAMPSHIRE

Hartley Wintney continued

Bryan Clisby at Andwells Antiques
High St. Est. 1976. Open 9.30-5.30. SIZE: Large. STOCK: *Longcase clocks, 1700-1830, £1,500-£7,000; barometers, 1770-1850, £250-£1,500; bracket, wall and mantel clocks.* LOC: A30 village centre. PARK: Easy. TEL: 0252 716436. SER: Valuations; restorations (clocks and barometers). VAT: Spec.

Deva Antiques
High St. (A. Gratwick). Open 9-5.30. SIZE: Large. STOCK: *18th-19th C English mahogany and walnut furniture.* LOC: Main st. PARK: Easy. TEL: 0252 843538/843656; fax - 0252 842946. VAT: Stan/spec.

Colin Harris Antiques   LAPADA
at Deva, High St. Est. 1966. Open 9-5.30. STOCK: *General antiques, mainly furniture and small decorative items, 18th-19th C, £20-£3,000.* LOC: A30. PARK: Easy. TEL: 0252 843538; home - 0734 732580. FAIRS: British International, Birmingham; Wilton House, Petersfield. VAT: Spec.

Just the Thing   LAPADA
High St. (Sue Carpenter). Est. 1975. Open 9-5 or by appointment. SIZE: Large. STOCK: *Country furniture, Staffordshire figures, brass and copper.* TEL: 0252 843393; home - 0252 842916.

David Lazarus Antiques
High St. Resident. Est. 1973. Open 9.30-5.30; some Sundays, other times by appointment. SIZE: Medium. STOCK: *17th to early 19th C English and continental furniture; objets d'art.* LOC: Main street. PARK: Own. TEL: 0252 842272. VAT: Stan/Spec.

Old Forge Antiques
Old Forge Cottage, The Green. (Mrs M.A.B. Gates). Open 10.30-5, but appointment advisable. CL: Wed. and Sat. except by appointment. SIZE: Medium. STOCK: *General antiques, watercolours, oils, prints.* LOC: A30. PARK: Easy. TEL: 0252 842287.

Phoenix Green Antiques
London Rd. (J. Biles and P.H.M. Hunt). Open 9.30-5.30, Sat. 10-5 or by appointment. SIZE: Large. STOCK: *English and continental country furniture, Georgian mahogany, 18th-19th C.* TEL: 0252 844430.

A.W. Porter and Son
High St. (M.A. Porter). Est. 1844. Open 9-5.30, Sat. 9-5. STOCK: *Clocks, silver, jewellery, glass.* LOC: Opposite Lloyds Bank. TEL: 0252 842676. SER: Restorations (clocks). VAT: Stan/Spec.

Sheila Revell Antiques
at Deva, High St. Open 9-5.30. STOCK: *18th-19th C decorative objects, small furniture and collectors' items.* TEL: 0252 843538.

HAVANT
Antiques and Nice Things
40 North St. (M.T. Davis-Shaw). Est. 1965. Open 10-5. STOCK: *Paintings, prints, porcelain, copper, brass, silver, Sheffield plate, small furniture, maps, clocks, jewellery, glass.* LOC: Near station. PARK: Own. TEL: 0705 484935; home - 0243 372551. SER: Restorations.

HAYLING ISLAND
J. Morton Lee   LAPADA
Cedar House, Bacon Lane. Est. 1984. Open by appointment. STOCK: *Watercolours, 19th-20th C, £50-£10,000.* PARK: Easy. TEL: 0705 464444. SER: Valuations; buys at auction. FAIRS: World of Watercolours, Harrogate, NEC (April/Aug), Buxton, Olympia (June), West London (Aug), Northern, Surrey, Kensington and City. VAT: Stan/Spec.

HORNDEAN
Goss and Crested China Centre
62 Murray Rd. (N.J. Pine). Est. 1968. SIZE: Medium. STOCK: *Goss, 1860-1930, £2-£1,000; other heraldic china, art pottery including Carlton ware, Charlotte Rhead, Chamelion, 1890-1930, £1-£1,000.* PARK: Easy. TEL: 0705 597440. SER: Valuations; buys at auction (Goss). VAT: Stan.

HURSLEY, Nr. Winchester
Hursley Antiques
(S. Thorne). Est. 1980. Open 10-6. STOCK: *Country furniture, brass, copper, metal.* LOC: 2.5 miles from Winchester on Romsey Rd. PARK: Easy. TEL: 0962 775488. SER: Restorations and repairs (metalware).

LISS
J. Du Cros Antiques
Farnham Rd, West Liss. (J. and P. Du Cros). Est. 1982. Open 9.30-5.30, Sun. by appointment. SIZE: Medium. STOCK: *English furniture, 1660-1900, £100-£5,000; treen, metalware.* Not Stocked: Glass and porcelain. LOC: Adjacent Spread Eagle public house on village green A325. PARK: Easy. TEL: 0730 895299. VAT: Stan/Spec.

Pine Collection
71 Station Rd. (Floydmist Ltd - P. Head). Est. 1983. Open 9-1 and 2-5. SIZE: Large. STOCK *Pine furniture, 18th-20th C, £60-£1,500.* LOC: Next to station. PARK: Easy. TEL: 0730 893743 SER: Restorations; stripping, polishing. VAT Stan.

Plestor Barn Antiques
Farnham Rd. Open 9-5. SIZE: Large. STOCK *Furniture, Victorian and Edwardian, shipping goods, pine; china and glass, copper and brass* LOC: A325. TEL: 0730 893922.

HAMPSHIRE

An Antique Collectors' Club Title

The Price Guide to Antique Silver
2nd edition by Peter Waldron
with 1992 prices
One of our most popular titles advises collectors on what to buy and what to avoid. Detailed examination of fakes is an important feature of this classic work.
ISBN 1 85149 165 1, 368pp
1,172 b & w illus, £35.00

Available from:
Antique Collectors' Club, 5 Church Street, Woodbridge, Suffolk IP12 1DS
Tel: (0394) 385501 Fax: (0394) 384634

or Market Street Industrial Park, Wappingers' Falls, New York 12590, USA
Tel: 914 297 0003 Fax: 914 297 0068

LYMINGTON

Captain's Cabin Antiques
1 Quay St. (Mrs D.J. Woon). Est. 1989. Open 9.30-5.30. SIZE: Medium. *STOCK: Furniture and pictures, £50-£5,000; ceramics, £25-£500; marine items, £80-£1,000; all 18th-19th C; silver, objets d'art, £10-£2,000.* PARK: Nearby. TEL: 0590 672912; home - 0590 677130. SER: Valuations; restorations. VAT: Spec.

Corfield Antiques Ltd BADA
120 High St. Open 9.15-5.30. SIZE: Large. **STOCK: *English furniture, porcelain, English School watercolours and oil paintings, 18th to early 19th C; militaria.*** TEL: 0590 673532. SER: Valuations; restorations (furniture, pictures). VAT: Stan/Spec.

Hughes and Smeeth Ltd
1 Gosport St. (P. Hughes and S. Smeeth). ABA. Est. 1976. Open 9.30-5. SIZE: Small. *STOCK: Antiquarian and secondhand books, maps and prints.* LOC: At bottom of High St. PARK: Nearby. TEL: 0590 676324. SER: Valuations; restorations (oil paintings), binding, framing. VAT: Stan.

Lymington Antiques Centre
76 High St. Open 10-5, Sat. 9-5. SIZE: 30 dealers. *STOCK: General antiques and books.* TEL: 0590 670934.

Lymington continued

Barry Papworth
28 St. Thomas St. Est. 1960. Open 9-5. SIZE: Small. *STOCK: Diamond jewellery, £50-£4,000; silver, £25-£1,500; both 18th-19th C. Watches, 19th C, £50-£1,000.* LOC: A337 into town, bay window on left. TEL: 0590 676422. SER: Valuations; restorations. VAT: Stan/Spec.

Robert Perera Fine Art
19 St. Thomas St. (R.J.D. Perera). Open 9.30-1 and 2-5.30, lunch-times and Sun. by appointment. SIZE: Small. *STOCK: British paintings, 19th-20th C, £100-£5,000; occasional ceramics and sculpture, 19th-20th C, £50-£1,500.* LOC: Top (west) end of main shopping area. PARK: Easy. TEL: 0590 678230; home - 0590 673190.

Christopher Williams Antiquarian Bookseller
at Lymington Antiques Centre, 76 High St. Open 10-5, Sat. 9-5. *STOCK: Books especially on antiques, art, bibliography, cookery, wine and topography.* TEL: 0590 670934; home - 0202 743157.

LYNDHURST

Lita Kaye of Lyndhurst BADA
13 High St. (S. and S. Ferder). Est. 1947. Open 9.30-1 and 2.15-5. SIZE: Large. *STOCK:*

HAMPSHIRE

Lyndhurst continued
Furniture, clocks, 1690-1820; decorative porcelain, 19th C. LOC: A35. PARK: 100yds. in High St. TEL: 0703 282337. VAT: Stan/Spec.

MATTINGLEY, Nr. Basingstoke
Anna Hoysted
Goodchilds Farm, Chandlers Green. Open by appointment. STOCK: English watercolours and drawings, 19th-20th C, £50-£1,500. LOC: Near Stratfield Saye Estate between A32 and A33. PARK: Easy. TEL: 0256 882355.

MEONSTOKE
W.D. Trivess
Heathfield House. Est. 1936. Open by appointment only. STOCK: Maps and illustrated topography, 16th-19th C. TEL: 0489 877326. SER: List available. Postal Only.

MORESTEAD, Nr. Winchester
Burgess Farm Antiques
(N. Spencer-Brayn). Est. 1970. Open 9-5. SIZE: Large. STOCK: Furniture, especially pine and country, 18th-19th C, £25-£5,000; architectural items - doors, panelling, fire-places. LOC: 2 miles south of Winchester, off Corehampton road. PARK: Easy. TEL: 0962 777546. SER: Stripping; export. VAT: Stan/Spec.

OAKLEY, Nr. Basingstoke
E.H. Hutchins
48 Pardown, East Oakley. Est. 1933. STOCK: General antiques, Edwardian and later furniture. Not Stocked: China, jewellery, ornaments. LOC: B3400. PARK: Easy. TEL: 0256 780494. VAT: Stan.

ODIHAM
Monaltrie Antiques
76 High St. (Mrs W. Helmore). Est. 1972. Open 10-1 and 2.30-5, Sun. by appointment. CL: Mon. and Wed. p.m. and Sat. p.m. SIZE: Medium. STOCK: Furniture, £250-£1,500; copper and brass, £50-£250; silver and collectables, £50-£300; all 18th-19th C. LOC: 1.5 miles junction 5, M3. PARK: Easy. TEL: 0256 702660; home - same. SER: Valuations; buys at auction. VAT: Spec.

The Odiham Gallery
78 High St. (I. Walker). Open 10-5, Sat. 10-1. STOCK: Decorative and Oriental rugs and carpets. TEL: 0256 703415.

PETERSFIELD
The Barn
Station Rd. (P. Gadsden). Est. 1956. Open 9-5. STOCK: Victoriana, bric-a-brac; also large store of trade and shipping goods. TEL: 0730 262958. VAT: Stan.

Petersfield continued
Cull Antiques   LAPADA
62 Station Rd. (J. Cull). Est. 1978. Open 10-5.30 or by appointment. STOCK: 18th C English furniture and metalwork. TEL: 0730 263670.

Elmore
5 Charles St. (Mr and Mrs L.G. Mortimer). Est. 1969. Open Tues., Fri. and Sat. 9.30-5. STOCK: Small furniture, porcelain, glass, bric-a-brac, pictures and prints. TEL: 0730 262383.

The Petersfield Bookshop   BADA
16a Chapel St. (F. Westwood). ABA. Est. 1918. Open 9-5.30. SIZE: Large. STOCK: Books, old and modern, £1-£500; maps and prints, 1600-1859, £1-£200; oils and watercolours, 19th C, £20-£1,000. LOC: Chapel St. runs from the Square to Station Rd. PARK: Opposite. TEL: 0730 263438. SER: Restorations and rebinding of old leather books; picture-framing and mount-cutting. FAIRS: Northern, Buxton and London ABA. VAT: Stan.

PLAITFORD, Nr. Romsey
Plaitford House Gallery
(W.B. Yeo). Est. 1960. Open most days and any time by appointment. SIZE: Large. STOCK: Oil paintings, watercolours, bronzes, 1800-1950 LOC: 1 mile north of A36 midway between Salisbury and Southampton on the road adjoining Landford and Sherfield English. PARK: Easy TEL: 0794 22221. SER: Valuations; restoration and cleaning (oils and watercolours). VAT: Spec.

PORTSMOUTH
Affordable Antiques
89 Albert Rd, Southsea. (Max Gosling). Est 1987. Open 10.30-3, Sat. 9.30-5.00. SIZE Medium. STOCK: Furniture, Victorian Edwardian and 1930's, £2-£2,000. LOC: Nea Kings Theatre. PARK: Easy. TEL: 070. 293344/230019. SER: Valuations.

Tony Amos Antiques
239 Albert Rd, Southsea. Open 9-5, Sat. 9-12 STOCK: General antiques and shipping goods TEL: 0705 736818.

R.C. Dodson (Exports) Ltd   LAPAD
85/87 Fawcett Rd, Southsea. Open 8.30-5.30 Sat. 9.30-5, other times by appointment STOCK: General antiques. TEL: 0705 829481.

A. Fleming (Southsea) Ltd   BAD.
The Clock Tower, Castle Rd. Est. 1905. Ope 8.30-5. CL: Sat. p.m. SIZE: Large. STOCK Furniture, silver, china, porcelain, genera antiques, jewellery. TEL: 0705 822934. SER Restorations. VAT: Stan/Spec.

Portsmouth continued
The Gallery
11 and 19 Marmion Rd, Southsea. (I. Murphy). Open 10-5. *STOCK: At No.19 - Victorian chairs and chesterfields; at No.11 - furniture, mainly Victorian and Edwardian.* PARK: Nearby. TEL: 0705 822016. VAT: Stan.

Leslie's
107 Fratton Rd. (E. Lord). Est. 1946. Open 9.30-1 and 2-5.30, Sat. until 6. CL: Wed. p.m. SIZE: Small. *STOCK: Victorian and antique rings, brooches, 1850-1920, £10-£350.* Not Stocked: Furniture, pictures. LOC: Fratton railway station, or 4 shops from main Co-op store in Fratton Rd. PARK: Easy. TEL: 0705 825952. SER: Valuations; restorations (antique jewellery). VAT: Stan.

Oldfield Gallery
76 Elm Grove, Southsea. Est. 1970. Open 10-5. SIZE: Medium. *STOCK: Maps and engravings, 16th-19th C, £20-£1,000; decorative prints and some paintings, 19th-20th C, £5-£400.* PARK: Easy. TEL: 0705 838042; fax - 0705 838042. SER: Valuations; restorations (maps and prints); framing. FAIRS: Bonnington Hotel Map (monthly). VAT: Stan.

Portsmouth Stamp Shop
184 Chichester Rd, North End. (G. Coast). Est. 1967. Open 9.15-5.30. *STOCK: Stamps, coins, cigarette cards, postcards, banknotes.* TEL: 0705 663450. VAT: Stan.

Pretty Chairs
189/191 Highland Rd, Southsea. (J. Ruffell). Est. !963. Open 10-5. CL: Wed. p.m. SIZE: Large. *STOCK: Victorian chairs, tables, wood boxes, desks, bureaux, sofas, French style furniture and cabriole-legged chairs.* LOC: Off Eastney Rd. PARK: Easy. TEL: 0705 731411. VAT: Stan/Spec.

Times Past
141 Highland Rd, Southsea. (S. New and S. Hemsworth). Open 10-4, Wed. by appointment. *STOCK: General antiques and shipping goods.* TEL: 0705 822701/0831 418488.

Wessex Medical Antiques
77 Carmarthen Ave. (Dr. D.J. Warren). Est. 1984. Open by appointment. SIZE: Small. *STOCK: Medical items, 18th-19th C, £50-£4,000.* LOC: Off Havant Rd., Drayton. PARK: Easy. TEL: 0705 376518; home - same; fax - 0705 201479. SER: Free catalogue; valuations; buys at auction (as stock). FAIRS: Scientific and Medical, Portman Hotel, London. VAT: Stan.

RINGWOOD
Barbara Davies Antiques
30A Christchurch Rd. Est. 1985. Open Tues. 10-1, Wed. and Fri. 10-3. SIZE: Small. *STOCK: Porcelain, 1760-1935, £5-£100; small furniture, 1900-1935, £20-£100; collectors' items.* LOC:

Ringwood continued
Off A31 into Ringwood, turn off roundabout to Moortown, next roundabout, turn right, shop on left 250yds. PARK: Entrance by chapel just before shop. TEL: Home - 0202 872268. SER: Valuations (pottery and porcelain).

Millers of Chelsea Antiques Ltd
LAPADA
Netherbrook House, 86 Christchurch Rd. BDADA. Est. 1897. Open 9-5.30, Sat. 10-4, other times by appointment. SIZE: Large. *STOCK: Furniture - English and continental country, mahogany and gilt, military, decorative items, treen,18th-19th C, £25-£3,000.* LOC: On B3347 towards Christchurch. PARK: Own. TEL: 0425 472062; fax - 0425 472727. FAIRS: Decorative Antiques, Olympia. VAT: Stan/Spec.

P.E. Palmer Antiques
The Matchbox, 132 Christchurch Rd. Est. 1961. Open 10-4. SIZE: Small. *STOCK: Furniture, collectors' items, 17th-19th C; jewellery, bric-a-brac.* PARK: Easy. TEL: 0425 472640. SER: Valuations.

Pine Company
104 Christchurch Rd. (D.R. and G.B. Smith). Est. 1978. Open 9.30-5.30. SIZE: Large and warehouse. *STOCK: Pine and other wood, 18th-19th C, £30-£1,000; model railways, 19th-20th C, from £5; Chinese furniture.* Not Stocked: Silver, fine china, bric-a-brac. LOC: Almost opposite fire station. PARK: Own. TEL: 0425 476705; home - same; fax - 0425 480467. SER: Restorations. VAT: Stan.

Glen Robinson Interiors and Antiques
82 Christchurch Rd. (Mrs G. Robinson). Est. 1980. Open 10-1 and 2-5. SIZE: Medium. *STOCK: Furniture, £500-£1,000; porcelain, £50-£100; both 19th C; decorative objects.* LOC: Opposite council offices. PARK: Easy. TEL: 0425 480450. SER: Valuations; restorations. VAT: Stan/Spec.

The Tennis Bookshop
West Gate, Moyles Court. (A.P.H. Chalmers). Resident. Est. 1985. Open by appointment. SIZE: Small. *STOCK: Antiques, books and collectable items relating to racket sports.* LOC: Ring for details. PARK: Easy. TEL: 0425 480518. SER: Valuations; buys at auction (as stock); stock lists always available.

ROMSEY
Bell Antiques
8 Bell St. (M. and B.M. Gay). FGA. Est. 1979. Open 9.30-5.30. CL: Wed. p.m. (winter). SIZE: Large. *STOCK: Jewellery and small silver, glass, pottery, porcelain, furniture, prints, mainly 19th-20th C.* LOC: Near market place. PARK: Adjacent. TEL: 0794 514719. VAT: Stan/Spec.

HAMPSHIRE

Romsey continued
Cambridge Antiques
5 Bell St. Open 8.30-5.30. SIZE: Large. *STOCK: Furniture, small china, jewellery, paintings.* LOC: From the West, Romsey by-pass, left into Palmerston St., first left then first right, 100yds. on left. PARK: Nearby. TEL: 0794 512885/ 523089/512069. VAT: Stan/Spec.

Creightons Antique Centre
23-25 Bell St. (K. Creighton). Open 9-6. SIZE: 18 stands. *STOCK: General antiques.* TEL: 0794 522758.

"Old Cottage Things"
Broxmore Park, Sherfield English. (E. Moseley). Est. 1970. *STOCK: Original building, architectural and garden materials; bric-a-brac and furniture.* LOC: A27. TEL: 0794 884538.

Romsey Medal and Collectors Centre
5 Bell St. (T. Cambridge, OMRS). Est. 1980. Open 9-5.30. *STOCK: Medals, badges, militaria, and commemorative china.* LOC: From the west, Romsey by-pass, left into Palmerston St., first left then first right, 100yds. on left. PARK: Nearby. TEL: 0794 512069/512885; fax-830332.

SOUTHAMPTON

Mr. Alfred's "Old Curiosity Shop" and The Morris Gallery (Fine Art Dealer/Valuer)
280 Shirley Rd, Shirley. Est. 1952. Open 9-6. *STOCK: Furniture, 18th-20th C; paintings, porcelain, bronzes, brass, glass, books, silver, jewellery and general antiques.* LOC: On left of main Shirley road, 3/4 mile from Southampton central station. PARK: Outside. TEL: 0703 774772.

Meg Campbell
10 Church Lane, Highfield. Est. 1967. Open by appointment only. *STOCK: English, Scottish and Irish silver, collectors' pieces, old Sheffield plate.* TEL: 0703 557636. SER: Mail order; catalogues available. VAT: Spec.

Cottage Antiques
9 Northam Rd. (K.J. Leslie). Open 9.30-4.30. *STOCK: General antiques, furniture, Victorian, trade goods.* TEL: 0703 221546; home - 0703 452246. VAT: Stan.

Gazelles Art Deco Interiors
31 Northam Rd. (A. Bellamy). Est. 1986. Open 10-4.30. CL: Wed. SIZE: Medium. *STOCK: Art deco ceramics including Clarice Cliff, Susie Cooper, Shelley, Burleigh Ware, Poole, Carlton Ware, Royal Winton; chrome, glass, textiles, furniture, lighting fixtures and fittings.* PARK: Easy. TEL: 0703 235291. FAIRS: Kensington; Greenwich. VAT: Stan.

Southampton continued
H.M. Gilbert and Son
2 1/2 Portland St. (R.C. and A.M. Gilbert). ABA Est. 1859. Open 8.30-5. *STOCK: Antiquarian and secondhand books, £1-£1,000.* PARK: Easy. TEL 0703 226420. SER: Valuations; bookbinding repairs.

R.K. Leslie Antiques
23 Northam Rd. Est. 1961. Open 10-4. CL: Wed p.m. and Sat. *STOCK: Silver, jewellery, curios china, clocks, furniture.* TEL: 0703 224784. VAT Stan.

L. Moody
70 Bedford Place. (J. and A.H. Gubb). Est. 1905 Open 8-5.30. CL: Wed. p.m. SIZE: Large *STOCK: Furniture, 1650-1910; silver, porcelain to 1900.* LOC: Half mile north of Civic Centre PARK: 50yds. in next block. TEL: 0703 333720 SER: Valuations. VAT: Stan/Spec.

Parkhouse and Wyatt Ltd
96 Above Bar. Est. 1794. SIZE: Small. *STOCK Silver, jewellery.* LOC: City centre. PARK Meters. TEL: 0703 226653 ext. 25. SER: Valuations; repairs.

Relics Antiques
54 Northam Rd. (R.M. Simmonds). Open 9-5 *STOCK: General antiques.* TEL: 0703 221635.

Southampton Antiques Centre
at Lodge Road Antiques, 71 Lodge Rd. Open 10-5. CL: Wed. SIZE: Large. *STOCK: Antique and fine old furniture for the home; general small antiques.* LOC: Main road between The Avenue and Portswood Rd. PARK: Easy. TEL: 0703 638086. VAT: Stan/Spec.

Wellington Antiques
109 St Denys Rd. (G.V. Helmer). Open 9-5, Wed 9-1. *STOCK: Clocks, porcelain, small decorative furniture.* TEL: 0703 553022.

STEEPMARSH, Nr. Petersfield
Hugh Evelyn
Unit C4, The Brickyards. Open by appointment *STOCK: Prints, 17th-19th C, £20-£1,000, watercolours, 19th C, £50-£850.* PARK: Easy. TEL: 0730 895655 (24 hours). SER: Restorations (prints, watercolours and pastels).

STOCKBRIDGE
George Hofman Antiques at the Sign of the Black Cat
Brookside, High St. Est. 1973. Open 10-5.30 Wed. 10-4, or by appointment. SIZE: Medium. *STOCK: General antiques, furniture and decorative items.* LOC: A30. PARK: At rear TEL: 0264 810570; home - same. VAT: Stan, Spec.

Stockbridge continued
Lane Antiques
High St. (E.K. Lane). Est. 1981. Open 10-5. CL: Wed. SIZE: Small. *STOCK: English and continental porcelain, 18th-19th C, £50-£100; silver and plate, decorative items, glass, small furniture.* PARK: Easy. TEL: 0264 810435; home - same.

Stockbridge Antiques
High St. (Mrs P. Bradley). Est. 1960. SIZE: Medium. *STOCK: Glass, from 18th C; furniture, 18th-19th C, to £9,000; porcelain, small silver, pictures, rugs.* Not Stocked: Coins, stamps, weapons. LOC: A30. PARK: Easy. TEL: 0264 810829; home - same. VAT: Spec.

Elizabeth Viney   BADA
Jacob's House, High St. (Miss E.A. Viney MBE). Est. 1967. Open 9-5, appointment advisable Mon. and Wed. CL: Sun except by appointment. SIZE: Small. *STOCK: Period furniture - mahogany, walnut, oak and country; treen, brass and copper, especially candlesticks.* Not Stocked: Victoriana. LOC: A30. Opposite old Post Office. PARK: Easy. TEL: **0264 810761**. VAT: Stan/Spec.

TITCHFIELD, Nr. Fareham
Gaylords
75 West St. (D.L. Hebbard). Est. 1970. Open 9.30-5.30. SIZE: Large. *STOCK: Furniture, from*

Titchfield continued
18th C; clocks, shipping goods, £50-£6,000. LOC: Just off M27. PARK: Easy. TEL: 0329 843402; home - 0329 847134. SER: Valuations; buys at auction (furniture). VAT: Stan/Spec.

Pamela Manley Antique Jewellery
6 and 8 South St. Est. 1965. Open Thurs.-Sat. SIZE: Small. *STOCK: Jewellery, 19th to early 20th C, £5-£500; silver and plate, glass, £10-£500; porcelain, bronzes, boxes.* LOC: 1/4 mile from A27. PARK: Easy. TEL: 0329 42794. SER: Valuations; buys at auction.

Titchfield Antiques Ltd
13-15 South St. Open 10-6, Sun. 2-6. CL: Mon. *STOCK: Art nouveau, art deco; silver, glass.* PARK: Easy. TEL: 0329 845968. SER: Restorations (as stock); silver and chrome plating.

TWYFORD, Nr. Winchester
Twyford Antiques
High St. Open 9.30-5.30. SIZE: Large. *STOCK: Clocks, furniture.* TEL: 0962 713484. SER: Valuations; restorations (clocks).

UPHAM, Nr. Southampton
Susanna Fisher
Spencer. Est. 1971. Open by appointment only. *STOCK: Navigational charts and sailing directions, 16th-19th C.* TEL: 048 96 291. SER: Buys at auction; catalogues available. *Mainly Postal.*

An Antique Collectors' Club Title

Starting to Collect Silver
by John Luddington
This is *the* book for the novice collector, which guides the reader through the pitfalls of the silver trade and discusses the pieces to avoid.
**ISBN 0 907462 48 0
228pp, 345 b & w illus, £25.00**

Available from:
Antique Collectors' Club, 5 Church Street, Woodbridge, Suffolk IP12 1DS
Tel: (0394) 385501 Fax: (0394) 384434

or Market Street Industrial Park, Wappingers' Falls, New York 12590, USA
Tel: 914 297 0003 Fax: 914 297 0068

HAMPSHIRE

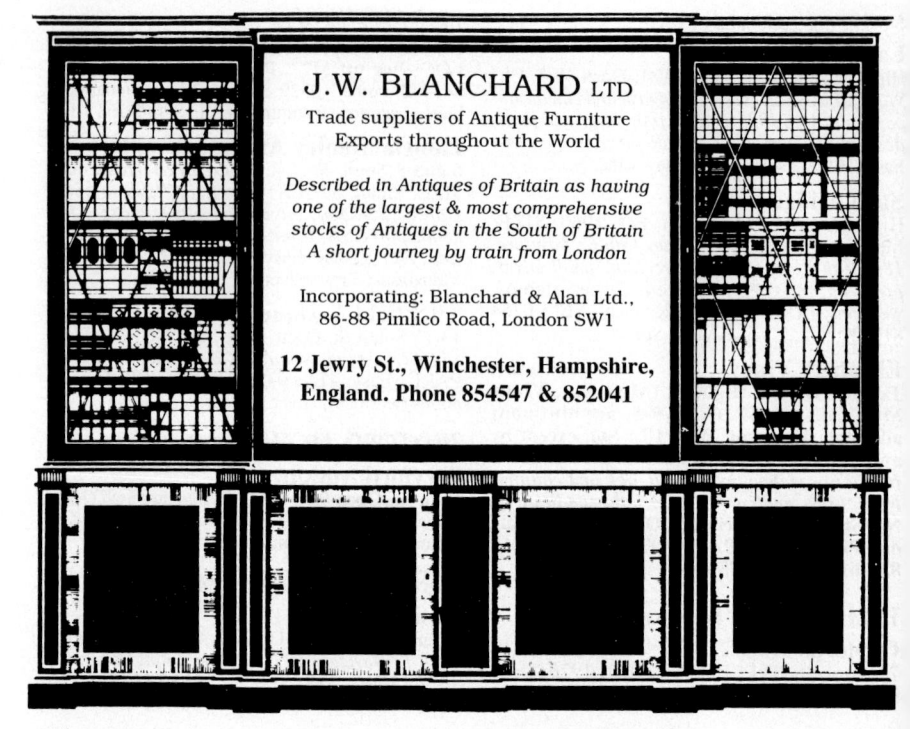

J.W. BLANCHARD LTD
Trade suppliers of Antique Furniture
Exports throughout the World

Described in Antiques of Britain as having one of the largest & most comprehensive stocks of Antiques in the South of Britain A short journey by train from London

Incorporating: Blanchard & Alan Ltd.,
86-88 Pimlico Road, London SW1

12 Jewry St., Winchester, Hampshire, England. Phone 854547 & 852041

Upham continued
Sharbooks
Farthing Cottages. (Mrs H.D. Sharman). Est. 1986. Open by appointment. SIZE: Small. *STOCK: Leather bound books, 18th-20th C, £5-£75.* LOC: 1 mile off B2177. PARK: Easy. TEL: 04896 267; home - same. *Trade Only.*

WHITCHURCH
Regency House Antiques
Regency House, 14 Church St. (J.W.L. Mouat). Resident. Est. 1968. Open by appointment only. SIZE: Medium. *STOCK: 17th-19th C oak and mahogany furniture, longcase clocks; metalwork.* LOC: B3400. On Newbury road, coming from Winchester, take first turning on left at crossroads in Whitchurch. PARK: Opposite. TEL: 0256 892149. SER: Valuations; buys at auction. VAT: Spec.

WINCHESTER
Bell Fine Art
67b Parchment St. (K.E. and B. Bell). Open 9.30-5.30. *STOCK: Victorian watercolours and oils, prints, £5-£5,000.* TEL: 0962 860439; home - 0962 733556. SER: Valuations; restorations (oils and watercolours); buys at auction. VAT: Spec.

Winchester continued
J.W. Blanchard Ltd   LAPADA
12 Jewry St. Est. 1940. Open 9-5. SIZE: Large. *STOCK: General antiques, especially breakfront bookcases.* PARK: Own. TEL: 0962 854547/852041; fax - 0962 842572. VAT: Stan/Spec.

Burns and Graham
4 St. Thomas St. Est. 1971. *STOCK: Furniture, mainly mahogany, 18th to early 19th C, and decorative items.* TEL: 0962 853779. VAT: Stan/Spec.

Peter M. Daly PBFA
Rear of Thompson Antiques, 20a Jewry St. Open Wed., Fri. and Sat. 10-5. *STOCK: Rare and secondhand books.* TEL: Home - 0962 867732.

Polly de Courcy-Ireland   BADA
By appointment only. *STOCK: Early treen, pre-1830 and unusual objects.* **TEL: 0962 865716.**

H.M. Gilbert
19 The Square. (R.C. and A.M. Gilbert). ABA. Open 9-5.30. *STOCK: Antiquarian and second hand books, £1-£1,000.* TEL: 0962 852832. SER: Valuations; repairs; rebinding.

Jewry Street Gallery Ltd
Gallery Corner, St. Thomas St. Open 9-5, Sat. 9-1. SIZE: Medium. *STOCK: Mahogany and giltwood, mainly 18th C and decorative items,*

Winchester continued
some unrestored, £200-£20,000. LOC: Near cathedral. PARK: Easy. TEL: 0962 865039; fax - 0962 840450. SER: Restoration (furniture and giltwood). VAT: Stan/Spec.

Gerald E. Marsh (Antique Clocks)
BADA
32a The Square. Est. 1947. Open 9.30-5. STOCK: *Clocks, English longcase and bracket, £300-£50,000; French and continental, £200-£10,000; early watches and barometers, £150-£7,000; all 1680-1800.* Not Stocked: Other antiques. LOC: Near Cathedral. PARK: Easy. TEL: 0962 844443. SER: Valuations; restorations (clocks); buys at auction. VAT: Spec.

The Pine Cellars
39 Jewry St. (N. Spencer-Brayn). Est. 1970. Open 9-5.30. SIZE: Large and warehouses. STOCK: *Pine and country furniture, 18th-19th C, £10-£2,000; painted furniture, architectural items, panelled rooms.* LOC: One way street, a right turn from top of High St. or St. Georges St., shop 100yds. on right. PARK: Nearby. TEL: 0962 867014/777546. SER: Stripping and export. VAT: Stan/Spec.

Printed Page
2/3 Bridge St. (J. and C. Wright). Est. 1977. CL: Mon. SIZE: Small. STOCK: *Antique maps and prints, 17th-19th C, £1-£1,000.* LOC: Bottom of High St., cross over river and shop is on left. PARK: In Water Lane, adjacent to shop. TEL: 0962 854072; fax - 0962 862995. SER: Valuations; picture framing; restorations (prints, oils and watercolours); mount cutting; buys at auction; postal service. VAT: Stan.

Mary Roofe Antiques   LAPADA
1 Stonemason's Court, 67 Parchment St. (R. and M. Roofe). Est. 1983. Open 10-5, Mon. by appointment. SIZE: Small. STOCK: *18th-19th C furniture, boxes, Tunbridgeware, treen, small collectors' items, £5-£2,500.* LOC: 200yds. from High St. and Buttercross. TEL: 0962 840613; home - 0962 862619.

SPCK Bookshops
24 The Square. Open 9-5.30. STOCK: *Books including antiquarian.* TEL: 0962 866617.

Samuels Spencers Antiques and Decorative Arts Emporium
39 Jewry St. (N. Spencer-Brayn). Open 9-5.30. SIZE: 31 dealers. STOCK: *General antiques.* LOC: One way street, right turn from top of High St. or St. George St., shop 100yds. on right. PARK: Nearby. TEL: 0962 867014/777546.

W.G. Skipwith
5 Parchment St. Est. 1966. CL: Thurs. p.m. SIZE: Small. STOCK: *Prints, some watercolours and oils, 19th-20th C, from £5; some furniture.* LOC:

Winchester continued
Near pedestrian precinct. PARK: Easy. TEL: 0962 852911. SER: Valuations; restorations (oils, watercolours, prints). VAT: Stan/Spec.

Thompson Antiques formerly Ships and Sealing Wax
20a Jewry St. Open 9.30-5. SIZE: Large. STOCK: *Victoriana and later furniture, pine, pictures, decorative items, shipping goods.* TEL: 0962 866633; home - 0962 884504.

Todd and Austin Antiques of Winchester
2 Andover Rd. (W. Todd and G. Austin). Est. 1964. Open 9.30-4.45. SIZE: Medium. STOCK: *Barometers, 19th C; some English and Oriental porcelain, 19th C; English and continental glass, 19th to early 20th C; classic French, English and Bohemian paperweights, mid 19th C; boxes including writing cases, tea caddies, knee desks, 18th and 19th C; objets d'art; visiting card cases, snuff boxes, perfume bottles, miniatures painted on ivory, furniture, cabinets, small decorative items, 19th to early 20th C; decorative silver, clocks, Regency to late 19th C.* LOC: 1 minute from Winchester Station. PARK: Easy. TEL: 0962 869824.

Webb Fine Arts
6 and 8 Romsey Rd. (D.H. Webb). Est. 1955. Open 9-5, Sat. 9-1. SIZE: Large. STOCK: *Oil paintings, Victorian furniture.* LOC: 'The Great Hall' West Gate. PARK: Multi-storey, nearby. TEL: 0962 842273. SER: Valuations; restorations (oil paintings); lining and framing; buys at auction (paintings). VAT: Stan/Spec.

WINCHFIELD, Hartley Wintney
Old Barley Mow Antiques
Sprats Hatch Lane. (Sue Thornton). Resident. Est. 1973. Open 10-6 including Sun., Thurs. 1-6. CL: Mon. SIZE: Medium. STOCK: *Furniture, £25-£2,000; smalls including china and unusual items, £2-£500; pictures, £10-£2,000; all 18th-20th C.* LOC: Off M3, junction 5, 2 miles Fleet side of Hartley Wintney. PARK: Easy. TEL: 0252 816460.

Hereford and Worcester

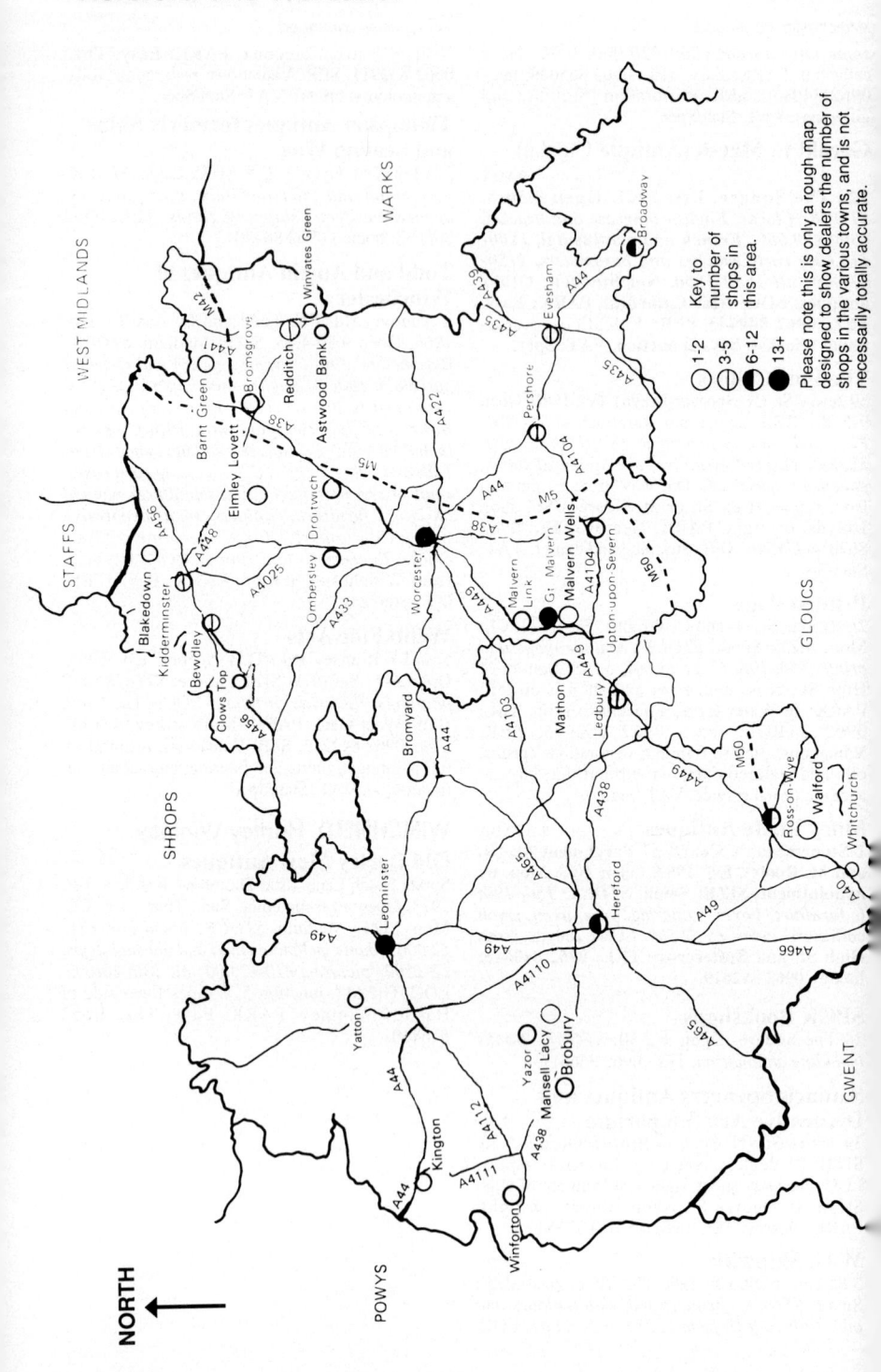

Hereford and Worcester

H.W. KEIL LTD

Telephone
BROADWAY
0386 852408

TUDOR HOUSE
BROADWAY
WORCESTERSHIRE

*Member of the
British Antique
Dealers'
Association*

17th & 18th Century Furniture · Works of Art

An unusual late 18th century mahogany ladies' writing desk on stand, c.1790. Width 2' 8" depth 1' 5 3/4" height 3' 3 1/2"

An excellent small early 19th century mahogany partner desk. Width 4' 7 3/4" depth 3' 0" height 2' 5"

Originators of the well known Keil's dark and light wax polish, available in 10 oz and 2 lb sizes

---

In association with H.W. Keil (Cheltenham) Ltd., 129-131 The Promenade, Cheltenham.

ASTWOOD BANK, Nr. Redditch
Bracebridge Gallery
'Robindale', 49 The Ridgeway. Est. 1987. Open by appointment only. *STOCK: 18th-20th C oil paintings, and rare signed limited edition prints.* TEL: 0527 893557.

Bracebridge Gallery
The Old Bakehouse, Langtree Sq., 1242 Evesham Rd. CL: Sat. *STOCK: Sporting oil paintings, 20th C, £500-£5,000.* LOC: A441. PARK: Easy. TEL: 0527 893557.

BARNT GREEN, Nr. Birmingham
Barnt Green Antiques
93 Hewell Rd. (N. Slater). BAFRA. Est. 1965. Open 9-5.30. SIZE: Medium. *STOCK: Furniture, 17th-19th C, £100-£5,000.* PARK: Easy. TEL: 021 445 4942. SER: Restorations (furniture, gilt frames, clocks, oils). VAT: Stan/Spec.

BEWDLEY
Clent Books
Rose Cottage, Habberley Rd. (I. Simpson). Open by appointment. *STOCK: Antiquarian books, local history, history, topography, £1-£200.* TEL: 0299 401090. SER: Valuations. FAIRS: Waverley Antique and book (Organiser).

Ma's Antiques
89 Welch Gate. (Mrs M. Archer). Est. 1987. Open Thurs.-Sat. 10-1 and 2-5. SIZE: Small. *STOCK: Souvenir ware, Victorian; clocks and pocket watches, 1720-1920, £25-£400; brass and copper, £15-£200.* Not Stocked: Jewellery. LOC: Leave A456 (Bewdley by-pass), enter by town centre sign. PARK: Nearby. TEL: 0299 403845. FAIRS: Cirencester.

BLAKEDOWN, Nr. Kidderminster
Hay Antiques   LAPADA
The Coach House, 20 Birmingham Rd. (J.S. Perks). Est. 1984. Open by appointment. SIZE: Small. *STOCK: Furniture, rosewood and mahogany, mainly 19th C, to £5,000; decorative antiques, to £1,000.* LOC: A456, village centre. PARK: Easy. TEL: 0562 700791; mobile - 0831 517178. SER: Valuations; restorations (furniture); buys at auction. FAIRS: Exhibits country-wide. VAT: Spec.

BROADWAY
Broadway Old Books (formerly Stratford Trevers)
The Long Room, 45 High St. (Mary Jane Grant-Zeid). Open 9.30-1 and 2-5.30, Sun. 11 -1 and 2.30-5.30. SIZE: Large. *STOCK: Antiquarian books, maps and prints.* TEL: 0386 853668. SER: Valuations; restorations; framing; book-binding. VAT: Stan.

Broadway continued

Court Antiques
Unit 5 Cotswold Court, The Green. (E. Taylor). Open 10-5. *STOCK: General Victorian antiques, especially Staffordshire figures and jugs.* TEL: 0386 853472.

Gavina Ewart   BADA
58 High St. (A.J. Ewart). Est. 1964. Open 9.30-1 and 2-5.30. SIZE: Medium. *STOCK: Silver cutlery and dining table silver, Sheffield plate; furniture and porcelain, 18th-19th C.* PARK: Easy. TEL: 0386 853371; fax - 0386 858948. SER: Valuations; restorations (clocks, furniture and barometers). VAT: Stan/Spec.

Fenwick and Fisher Antiques
88-90 High St. CADA. Est. 1980. Open 10-6, or by appointment. SIZE: Large. *STOCK: Furniture, oak, mahogany and walnut, 17th to early 19th C; samplers, boxes, treen, Tunbridgeware, delft, decorative items and corkscrews.* TEL: 0386 853227; after hours - 0386 858502.

J. and S. Gormley Antiques
The Lares, Leamington Rd. Open 10-5 including Sun. CL: Mon. SIZE: Medium. *STOCK: Furniture and related items.* LOC: 400yds. from High St. PARK: Easy. TEL: 0386 853035.

Richard Hagen
Yew Tree House. Open 9.30-5.30, Sun. by appointment. *STOCK: 20th C oils and watercolours.* TEL: 0386 853624/858561; fax - 0386 852172. SER: Valuations; restorations; framing. VAT: Spec.

Hay Loft Gallery
Berry Wormington. (Mrs J.R. Pitt and Miss S.A. Pitt). Resident. Est. 1984. Open 10.30-5.30 or by appointment. SIZE: Medium. *STOCK: Victorian paintings, £250-£15,000; Victorian watercolours £250-£3,000.* LOC: From Broadway, 4 miles on B4632 towards Cheltenham, farm on right hand side. PARK: Easy. TEL: 0242 621202. SER: Restorations. VAT: Spec.

Haynes Fine Art   BADA
The Bindery Galleries, 69 High St. Est. 1972 Open 9-6. SIZE: Large. *STOCK: 16th-20th C British and European paintings, £900-£120,000.* LOC: From Moreton, 50yds. past the Stratford turn off on the left. PARK: Easy. TEL: 0386 852649; home - same; fax - 0386 858187. SER: Valuations; restorations; framing. VAT: Spec.

High Park Antiques
62 High St. Est. 1973. Open 10-5. CL: Mon. SIZE: Large. *STOCK: Furniture, early 19th C silver, china, porcelain, paintings.* LOC: Town centre. PARK: Easy. TEL: 0386 853130; home 0905 772163. SER: Valuations. VAT: Spec.

Howards of Broadway
27a High St. Open 9.30-5.30. SIZE: Small. *STOCK Jewellery, 1700 to modern, £100-£20,000; silver 1700 to modern, £50-£5,000; objects of vertu, 1750*

PICTON HOUSE

ANTIQUES • WORKS OF ART • INTERIOR DESIGN

Picton House has been associated with Antiques and Fine Art for over 30 years

OPEN DAILY 9.30AM-5.30PM
OR BY APPOINTMENT
CLOSED SUNDAYS

A fine George III mahogany library breakfront secretaire bookcase height 8' 7" x width 8' 3" x depth 2' 0"

High Street, Broadway, Worcestershire WR12 7DT Tel. (0386) 853807 Fax. (0386) 858199

Broadway continued

1900, £100-£10,000. PARK: Easy and nearby. TEL: 0386 858924. SER: Valuations; restorations. FAIRS: Kenilworth; Northern; British International; City of London; Chester. VAT: Stan/Spec.

H.W. Keil Ltd   BADA
Tudor House, Broad Close, Eadburgha Hall. (V.M. Keil). CADA. Est. 1925. Open 9-5.30. CL: Thurs. p.m. SIZE: Large. *STOCK: Walnut, oak and mahogany furniture and works of art, 17th-18th C.* TEL: 0386 852408. VAT: Spec.

John Noott Fine Paintings
                              BADA LAPADA
14 Cotswold Court, The Green. CADA. Est. 1972. Open 9-1 and 2-5.30 or by appointment. SIZE: Large. *STOCK: Paintings and watercolours, 19th-20th C, £50-£50,000.* LOC: Centre of village. PARK: Own. TEL: 0386 852787/858969; fax - 0386 858348. SER: Valuations; restorations; framing. VAT: Stan/Spec.

Olive Branch Antiques
80 High St. (P. and S. Riley and Angela). Resident. Est. 1977. Open 9-5.30 including Sun. SIZE: Small. *STOCK: Furniture, to 1900, from £100; clocks, £90-£800; pottery, £5-£150.* LOC: Top end of High St. on A46. PARK: Easy and at rear. TEL: 0386 853831. SER: Restorations (furniture). VAT: Stan/Spec.

Broadway continued

Picton House Antiques
High St. (G.D. Patterson Ltd). CADA. Resident. Est. 1989. Open 9.30-5.30 or by appointment. SIZE: Large. *STOCK: Fine English furniture, works of art.* PARK: Easy. TEL: 0386 853807; home - same. SER: Restorations (furniture); buys at auction. VAT: Spec.

BROBURY, Nr. Hay-on-Wye
Brobury House Gallery
(E. Okarma). Resident. Est. 1972. Open 9-4.30, 9-4 in winter. *STOCK: Old prints, 17th-20th C; watercolours, 19th-20th C.* PARK: Easy. TEL: 09817 229. SER: Restorations (framing). VAT: Stan.

BROMSGROVE
Strand Antiques
22 The Strand. (D.G. Croucher). Est. 1977. Open 9-6. *STOCK: General antiques.* TEL: 0527 72686.

BROMYARD
Lennox Antiques
3 Broad St. (W.A. and E.S. Jones). Est. 1981. Open Thurs.-Sat. 10.30-5. SIZE: Small. *STOCK: Pottery and porcelain, 19th-20th C, £5-£25; glass, £1-£25; small furniture, £10-£200.* LOC:

H. AND B. WOLF ANTIQUES LTD

Specialities
18th and 19th century
porcelain, pottery and glass

**128 WORCESTER ROAD
DROITWICH SPA
HEREFORD & WORCS
TEL (0905) 772320**

*Open Friday & Saturday 9.30am
to 5.30pm
Other days by appointment*

Bromyard continued
Town centre. PARK: Easy. TEL: 0885 483432; home - 0684 575684. SER: Restorations (pottery, porcelain and cloisonné).

CLOWS TOP, Nr. Worcester
Mitchell Hart Antiques
Portland House. (Mr and Mrs M.B. Hart). Est. 1988. Open 9-5.30, Sat. 9.30-6, Sun. by appointment. *STOCK: Furniture, 18th-19th C; glass, pottery, porcelain, paintings, copper and brass.* LOC: On A456/B4202 crossroads. PARK: Easy. TEL: 0299 832239. SER: Restorations; re-upholstery.

DROITWICH
Grant Fine Art
9A Victoria Sq. Est. 1976. Open 9-5 or by appointment. CL: Sat. SIZE: Small. *STOCK: Golfiana, books, prints, pictures, clubs, £5-£1,000.* TEL: 0905 778155; fax - 0905 794507.

H. and B. Wolf Antiques Ltd
128 Worcester Rd. (H.G. and B.J. Wolf). Est. 1948. Open Fri. and Sat. 9.30-5.30 or by appointment. SIZE: Medium. *STOCK: Porcelain, pottery, from 1750, £15-£1,500; glass, from 1725; general antiques.* Not Stocked: Coins, stamps, medals. LOC: A38. PARK: Easy. TEL: 0905 772320; home - same. VAT: Stan/Spec.

ELMLEY LOVETT, Nr. Droitwich
Elmley Heritage
Stone House. (J. Kramer). Est. 1988. Open by appointment. SIZE: Medium. *STOCK: Fireplaces, 18th-19th C, £300-£800; bathroom fittings, Victorian and Edwardian, £100-£300; architectural items.* LOC: Telephone for directions. PARK: Easy. TEL: 029 923 284; home - same. VAT: Stan.

EVESHAM
Magpie Jewellers and Antiques
LAPADA
2 Port St, and 61 High St. (R.J. and E.R. Bunn). Est. 1975. Open 9.30-5.30. SIZE: Large. *STOCK: Silver, jewellery, furniture and general antiques.* TEL: 0386 41631.

Yesterday
79 Port St. (B. Jewell). Est. 1981. Open 10.30-5.30, Sat. 9.30-5.30. SIZE: Medium. *STOCK: Pre-1960 clothes and costume jewellery, £5-£50; pottery, 19th-20th C, £10-£50.* LOC: Opposite Swan Inn. PARK: At rear. TEL: 0386 48068; home - same. SER: Valuations.

GREAT MALVERN
Carlton Antiques
43 Worcester Rd. (T. Guiver). Open 10-5. *STOCK: Edwardian and Victorian furniture.* TEL: 0684 573092. SER: Valuations.

Church Walk Antiques
5 Church Walk. (C. Carmichael). Open 10.30-5. *STOCK: Jewellery, small silver, furniture, decorative items, porcelain and lighting.* TEL: 0684 565192.

Joan Coates of Malvern
26 St. Ann's Rd. Resident. Est. 1969. Open Thurs. and Fri. 10-1 and 2.30-5.30, Sat. 10-1. SIZE: Small. *STOCK: Silver, £10-£250; small furniture, £50-£800; both 18th-20th C; small items.* LOC: From Worcester take A449, in town Foley Arms Hotel on left-hand side, take first right. PARK: Easy. TEL: 0684 575509.

Gray's Antiques of Worcester
Units 24 & 26, Blackmore Park Industrial Estate, Hanley Swan. (D. and M. Gray). Open 8.30-5.30, Sat. and Sun. by appointment. *STOCK: General antiques and shipping goods.* TEL: 0684 560038; fax - 0684 893639. SER: Containers; storage; export.

Great Malvern Antiques
6 Abbey Rd. (R.J. Rice and L. Sutton). Est. 1966. Open 9.30-5.30 or by appointment. CL: Sat. *STOCK: Decorative antiques, furniture, paintings.* LOC: 150yds. from Winter Gardens. PARK: Easy. TEL: 0684 575490; home - same. FAIRS: Olympia; Little Chelsea. VAT: Stan/Spec.

Great Malvern continued
Lismore Gallery
3 Edith Walk. (J. and H. Simmonds). Open 10-6. CL: Wed. *STOCK: Watercolours, 19th to early 20th C; decorative Victorian items.* TEL: 0684 568610.

Malvern Arts
43 Worcester Rd. (S.A. Conein-Veber). Est. 1988. Open 10-5. SIZE: Small. *STOCK: Watercolours, Victorian and Edwardian, £50-£500; oil paintings, 19th-20th C; £80-£1,000+.* LOC: Town centre. PARK: Easy. TEL: 0684 575889. VAT: Stan/Spec.

Malvern Bookshop
7 Abbey Rd. (J.P. and A.M. Gibbs). Est. 1955. Open 9.15-5. CL: Wed. p.m. SIZE: Medium. *STOCK: Antiquarian, secondhand books and remainders.* LOC: Next to Malvern G.P.O. PARK: Easy. TEL: 0684 575915.

Malvern Studios
56 Cowleigh Rd. (L.M. Hall). BAFRA. Open 9-5.15, Fri. and Sat. 9-4.45. *STOCK: Period, Edwardian painted and inlaid furniture, general furnishings.* TEL: 0684 574913. SER: Restorations; woodcarving; polishing; interior design. VAT: Stan/Spec.

Great Malvern continued
Miscellany Antiques
18 and 20 Cowleigh Rd. (R.S. and E.A. Hunaban). Resident. Est. 1974. Open 9-5.30. SIZE: Medium. *STOCK: Walnut, mahogany,17th-19th C, £350-£10,000; porcelain, silver, plate and jewellery.* LOC: B4219 to Bromyard. PARK: Easy. TEL: 0684 566671; fax - 0684 560562. SER: Valuations. VAT: Stan/Spec.

Treasures of Childhood Past - Carrie Tarplett
43 Wyche Rd. Est. 1988. Open every day but prior telephone call advisable. *STOCK: Dolls, doll's house miniatures, teddy bears, and related items.* LOC: Opposite car park, 1 mile from town centre. PARK: Easy, opposite. TEL: 0684 560010.

Whitmore
Teynham Lodge, Chase Rd., Upper Colwall. *STOCK: British and foreign coins, 1700-1950, £1-£500; trade tokens, 1650-1900, £1-£200; commemorative medallions, 1600-1950, £1-£200.* TEL: 0684 40651. *Postal Only.*

Self-portrait sketch. Pen and ink over pencil, dated September 20 1848. Yale Center for British Art. From **George Chinnery, 1774-1852, Artist of India and the China Coast,** published in 1993 by the **Antique Collectors' Club,** £45.00

HEREFORD

I. and J.L. Brown Ltd
58-59 Commercial Rd. Open 8-5.30 but appointment advisable. SIZE: Large. STOCK: Matched sets of period country chairs, £500-£4,000; English country and French provincial furniture, decorative items and brass. LOC: A465, 300 metres from railway station, 100 metres from city ring road. PARK: On premises. TEL: 0432 358895; fax - 0432 275338; home - 0432 840674. SER: Restorations; re-rushing chairs. VAT: Stan/Spec.

Great Brampton House Antiques Ltd
LAPADA
Great Brampton House, Madley. (P.B. Howell). Est. 1969. Open 9-5 or by appointment. SIZE: Large. STOCK: English and French furniture and fine art. TEL: 0981 250244; fax - 0981 251333.

Hereford Antique Centre
128 Widemarsh St. (L. F. Mitchell). Est. 1991. Open 9-5, Sun. 1-5. SIZE: 40 dealers. STOCK: General antiques and collectables. PARK: Easy. TEL: 0432 266242. SER: Restorations; shipping. VAT: Stan.

G.E. Richards and Son Antiques
57 Blueschool St. Est. 1969. Open 9-5. SIZE: Medium. STOCK: General antiques, £2-£2,000. LOC: On ring road by traffic signals. PARK: Nearby, but private loading bay at rear. TEL: 0432 267840; home - 0432 355278 /268827. VAT: Stan/Spec.

Warings of Hereford Antiques
43 St. Owen St. (R. Waring). Open 9-6 including Sun. STOCK: Fine 19th C furniture; gold and silver. TEL: 0432 276241.

KIDDERMINSTER

B.B.M. Jewellery and Antiques
8 and 9 Lion St. (W.V. and A. Crook). Est. 1977. Open 10-5. CL: Tues. SIZE: Medium. STOCK: Jewellery, 19th C, £50-£3,000; coins, £5-£1,000; general antiques, £5-£500. LOC: Adjacent Youth Centre, off ring road. PARK: Easy. TEL: 0562 744118. SER: Valuations; restorations (jewellery, porcelain, silver). VAT: Stan/Spec.

Gorst Hall Restoration
Gorst Hall, Barnetts Lane. (J. R. Callwood). Est. 1984. Open by appointment. SIZE: Medium. STOCK: English furniture, 18th-19th C, £500-£1,000. LOC: Off Kidderminster/Bromsgrove road, just off Comberton rd. PARK: Own. TEL: 0562 515880; home - same; mobile - 0831 634602. SER: Valuations; restorations (French polishing, veneering, carving, wood turning, repairs); buys at auction (furniture). VAT: Stan/Spec.

Kidderminster continued

Hi-Felicity
1 Comberton Rd. (J. Workman). Open 9-5.30. STOCK: Antique pine. TEL: 0562 742549.

LEDBURY

John Nash Antiques and Interiors
1st Floor, Tudor House, 17c High St. (J. Nash and L. Calleja). Est. 1972. Open 10-5.30, Sun. by appointment. CL: Wed. SIZE: Medium. STOCK: Mahogany, oak and walnut furniture, 18th-20th C, £300-£10,000; decorative items, fabrics and wallpapers. TEL: 0531 5714; fax - 0531 5050, home - 0684 40432. SER: Valuations; restorations; buys at auction (furniture, silver). VAT: Stan/Spec.

Serendipity
The Tythings, Preston Court. (Mrs R. Ford). Open 9-5 or by appointment. STOCK: General antiques, 17th-20th C. LOC: Take A449 from Ledbury, turn left on B4215, premises 500yds. or left behind half-timbered house. TEL: 053184 245/380. SER: Restorations (furniture); buys at auction. FAIRS: Kensington; Olympia. VAT Stan/Spec.

Susan Shaw-Cooper
York House, 155 The Homend. Open 9.30-1 and 2-5.30. CL: Wed. STOCK: Georgian, Regency, Victorian and later furniture; silver, plate copper, brass, pewter and glass. LOC: Outskirts of town opposite hospital. PARK: Opposite. TEL 0531 634687.

LEOMINSTER

Barometer Shop
New St. (R. Cookson). Est. 1965. Open 9-5 or by appointment. STOCK: Barometers, barographs clocks, scientific instruments. LOC: Corner of A49 and Broad St. PARK: Easy. TEL: 0568 613652 and 0272 272565. SER: Valuations restorations; barometers and clock spares.

Chapman Antiques
LAPADA
2 Bridge St. (R. Chapman). Est. 1983. Open 10 5 or by appointment. SIZE: Medium. STOCK Fine English mahogany and walnut furniture 17th to early 19th C; clocks; all £300-£15,000+ PARK: Easy. TEL: 0568 615803; mobile - 083 566146. VAT: Stan/Spec.

Coltsfoot Gallery
Hatfield. (Edwin Collins). Est. 1971. SIZE Medium. STOCK: Sporting and wildlife water colours and prints, £20-£2,000. PARK: Easy TEL: 056 882 277; home - same. SER: Restor ations (works of art on paper).

P. and S.N. Eddy
22 Etnam St. Resident. Est. 1951. Open 9-6. CL Sun. except by appointment. SIZE: Small STOCK: Oak and mahogany furniture; saltglaze

Major suppliers of English Country & French Provincial Antique Furniture

I&JL BROWN

58 Commercial Road, Hereford HR1 2BP
Telephone (0432) 358895 Telefax (0432) 275338
636 & 632 Kings Road, Chelsea, London SW6 2DU
Telephone (071) 736 4141

HEREFORD AND WORCESTER

Leominster continued

stoneware, 18th C brass and copper, early metalware, treen and bygones. Not Stocked: Arms, armour, coins, medals, jewellery. LOC: A44. PARK: Easy. TEL: 0568 612813; home - same.

Farmers Gallery
28 Broad St. STOCK: 18th-19th C paintings, prints, maps, needlework and decorative items. LOC: Town centre. PARK: Easy. TEL: 0568 611413.

Jeffery Hammond Antiques   LAPADA
'Shaftesbury House', 38 Broad St. (J. and E. Hammond). Resident. Est. 1970. Open 9-6, Sun. by appointment. SIZE: Medium. STOCK: Furniture and works of art, 18th to early 19th C. LOC: Town centre. PARK: Own. TEL: 0568 614876. SER: Valuations; buys at auction (furniture). VAT: Stan/Spec.

Hubbard Antiques   BADA
The Golden Lion, Bridge St. (D. T. and P. Saunders). Resident. Open 9-5, otherwise ring door bell. STOCK: 16th-18th C oak furniture, especially dressers and coffers; copper, 18th-19th C; patchwork quilts. LOC: North side of town, just off by-pass. PARK: Own. TEL: 0568 614362.

Jennings of Leominster
30 Bridge St. (J.R. Jennings). Est. 1970. Open 9.30-6. SIZE: Medium. STOCK: Furniture, 17th-18th C, £500-£3,000; clocks, £200-£2,000; paintings, £50-£1,000; both 18th-19th C. PARK: Easy. TEL: 0568 612946; home - same. SER: Valuations; restorations (furniture including gilding, clocks). VAT: Spec.

La Barre Ltd
The Place, 116 South St. Est. 1964. Open 8.30-5.30, Sat. 10-4, other times by appointment. SIZE: Large. STOCK: Pine, French fruitwood, mahogany, oak and painted furniture, decorative items, 18th-20th C, £50-£5,000. LOC: On A49 towards Hereford, opp. Community Hospital. PARK: Easy. TEL: 0568 614315; home - 0568 612434 or 0432 58432. VAT: Stan/Spec.

Leominster Antiques   LAPADA
87 Etnam St. (K. and J. Watherington). Resident. Open 9-6, other times by appointment or ring bell. SIZE: Large. STOCK: Furniture, mainly mahogany, 18th-19th C; decorative items, paintings. LOC: A44 Worcester Rd. PARK: Easy. TEL: 0568 613217. VAT: Stan/Spec.

Leominster Antiques Market
14 Broad St. Open 10-5. SIZE: 3 floors. STOCK: General antiques including country and painted furniture, mahogany, oak, treen, Staffordshire figures, pottery, porcelain, textiles, metalware, pictures, jewellery and clocks. TEL: 0568 2189. SER: Restorations (furniture). Below are listed the dealers.

Leominster continued

Architectural Antiques
(S. Breakwell).

Bradshaw and Smith

Miles Bruce

Mrs P. Cox

Mrs O. Dyke

Eardisley Antiques
(W. E. Kinch).

Barbara Ind

M. and J. Phillipson

Michael Stewart Antiques
STOCK: Furniture - period, pine, country, Victorian, some oak and mahogany. TEL: 0568 614946; home - 0568 612197.

Wigmore Interiors

Jeff Wilson and J. Grange

Mayfield House
13 South St. (C.J. Scott-Mayfield). Open by appointment only. STOCK: Furniture, paintings and decorative items. TEL: 0568 612127. SER: Valuations; restorations; upholstery; interior design.

LITTLE MALVERN

St. James Antiques
De Lys Wells Rd. (H. Van Wyngaarden). Open 10-5 or by appointment. STOCK: Pine furniture and lighting. PARK: Easy. TEL: 0684 563404. SER: Restoration. VAT: Stan/Spec.

MALVERN LINK

Kimber and Son
6 Lower Howsell Rd. Est. 1956. Open 9-1 and 2-5, Sat. 9-12.30. STOCK: Furniture, 18th-19th C general antiques. Trade warehouse. TEL: 0684 574339; home - 0684 572000. SER: Restorations. VAT: Stan/Spec.

MALVERN WELLS

Gandolfi House
211-213 Wells Rd. (P. and R. Weller). Open 10-5.30 or by appointment. CL: Mon. STOCK: Paintings, watercolours, prints, 19th-20th C country furniture and smalls. TEL: 0684 569747.

MANSEL LACY

Bernard Gay
The School House. Open Tues.-Sun. 9-6, prior telephone call advisable. STOCK: Pictures and drawings; small fine objects de vertu. TEL: 098122 269.

MATHON, Nr. Malvern
Mathon Gallery
Mathon Court. (Phipps and Co. Ltd). Est. 1980. Open 9.30-5.30 by appointment including Sun. SIZE: Medium. STOCK: *British oils, watercolours and sculpture, 19th-20th C, £100-£30,000.* LOC: Approx. 1 mile west of Malvern, off B4232. TEL: 0684 892242 and 071 352 5381. SER: Valuations; buys at auction (British paintings and sculpture). VAT: Spec.

OMBERSLEY
Stables Antiques
Blacksmiths Cottage, Chatley. (B. Pearce). Est. 1974. Open Sat. 10-5 or by appointment. SIZE: Medium. STOCK: *Furniture especially country, 17th-19th C, £100-£7,000; porcelain and pottery, 18th-19th C, £10-£500; bygones and early metalwares.* LOC: 4 miles north of Worcester on A449. PARK: Easy. TEL: 0905 620353. SER: Valuations; restorations (china); buys at auction. VAT: Spec.

PERSHORE
Hansen Chard Antiques
126 High St. (P.W. Ridler, MBHI). Est. 1983. Open 10-5, Thurs. 10-1 but appointment advisable. CL: Mon. SIZE: Large. STOCK: *Clocks, pre-1940; longcase clocks, pre-1850, £10-£2,000; barometers £50-£1,000.* LOC: On A44. PARK: Easy. TEL: 0386 553423; home - same. SER: Valuations; restorations (as stock); buys at auction (as stock). VAT: Spec.

"The Look In" Antiques
34b High St. Est. 1970. Open 10.15-5.15, other times by appointment. STOCK: *Furniture, bric-a-brac, china, clocks, prints, watercolours, oils, silver, plate, jewellery, glass, metalware, £3-£800.* TEL: 0386 556776; home - 0386 710588.

Penoyre Antiques
9 and 11 Bridge St. Est. 1969. Open 9.30-1 and 2-5.30, Sat. 9.30-5.30, other times by appointment. CL: Thurs. SIZE: Medium. STOCK: *18th-19th C mahogany furniture especially dining; chandeliers, mirrors, paintings, framed prints and engravings, £12-£20,000.* PARK: Easy (in main square or opposite). TEL: 0386 553522; home - 0386 710214. SER: Valuations. VAT: Stan/Spec.

S.W. Antiques
Abbey Showrooms, Newlands. (R.J. Whiteside). Est. 1978. Open 9-5, Sun. 10.30-4. SIZE: Large. STOCK: *19th-20th C furniture including stripped pine, to £3,000.* Not Stocked: Jewellery, small items. LOC: 2 mins. from Abbey. PARK: Own. TEL: 0386 555580; fax - 0386 556205. VAT: Stan/Spec.

ROSS-ON-WYE
Baileys Architectural Antiques
The Engine Shed, Ashburton Industrial Estate. (M. and S. Bailey). Est. 1978. Open 9-5. SIZE: Large. STOCK: *Architectural antiques including stained and etched glass, cast grates, fireplaces, bathroom fittings, street and garden furniture, doors, pews, panelling, bars, overmantels, counters, tiles, brackets, columns, 18th-19th C.* LOC: Gloucester side of town, just off A40. TEL: 0989 63015; fax - 0989 768172.

Barry Cotton Antiques
Flat 1a, Ashfield Lodge, Ashfield Crescent. Open by appointment. STOCK: *Victorian mahogany furniture.* TEL: 0989 62097.

Fritz Fryer Antique Lighting   LAPADA
12 Brookend St. (F. Fryer and J. Graham). Est. 1981. Open 9.30-5.30, Sun. by appointment. SIZE: Large. STOCK: *Decorative lighting, original shades, Georgian to art deco.* TEL: 0989 67416. SER: Restorations; lighting scheme design. FAIRS: Olympia; NEC Birmingham.

Robert Green Antiques
46 High St. Open 10-5. STOCK: *18th-19th C mahogany, oak and decorative furniture, especially dining tables; silver, glass, textiles and ceramics.* TEL: 0989 67504. SER: Valuations.

Robin Lloyd Antiques
23/24 Brookend St. Est. 1970. Open 10-5.30 or any time by appointment. SIZE: Large. STOCK: *Rustic furniture, 17th-19th C, especially Welsh oak, dressers and Windsor chairs, gatelegs, French armoires, farmhouse tables; candlesticks, metalware, sporting memorabilia, unusual items, all £5-£5,000.* LOC: 100yds. downhill from Market Hall. PARK: Nearby. TEL: 0989 62123. VAT: Stan/Spec.

Old Pine Shop
Gloucester Rd. (B. Miller). Est. 1976. Open 10-5.30 or by appointment. SIZE: Large. STOCK: *Pine furniture, especially dressers, chests, tables, desks, blanket boxes, wardrobes, linen presses, 1830-1930; Victorian brass, iron and wooden bedsteads.* LOC: Last shop on main Gloucester road. PARK: Easy and Cantilupe Rd. TEL: 0989 64738; home - 0989 65131. SER: Restorations (pine stripping).

Relics
19 High St. (Mr and Mrs I. Power). Open 10-5. STOCK: *Jewellery, linen, silver, clocks, smalls and furniture.* TEL: 0989 64539. SER: Restorations and repairs (clocks and jewellery).

Ross Old Book and Print Shop
51 and 52 High St. Open 10-1 and 2-5. STOCK: *Antiquarian and secondhand books, prints and maps.* TEL: 0989 67458.

Ross on Wye continued
Trecilla Antiques
36 High St. (Lt. Col. and Mrs I.G. Mathews). Est. 1969. Open 9.30-5. CL: Sun. except by appointment, and Wed. p.m. SIZE: Large. *STOCK: Furniture, longcase clocks, all periods; arms and armoury, £50-£7,500; silver, china, glass, metalware, £10-£3,000; prints, maps, militaria and bygones, £1-£500.* LOC: A40. PARK: Private. TEL: 0989 63010; home - 0981 540274. SER: Valuations; restorations; buys at auction. VAT: Stan/Spec.

SUCKLEY
Holloways
Lower Court. (Edward and Diana Holloway). SIZE: Large. STOCK: Garden statuary, £50-£3,000; garden salvage, £20-£300; architectural antiques, £20-£3,000; all 18th-20th C. TEL: 0886 884665; home - same. LOC: A44 from Worcester towards Leominster, left to village, premises next to church. PARK: Easy. SER: Valuations; restorations; buys at auction. VAT: Stan/Spec.

UPTON-UPON-SEVERN
The Highway Gallery
40 Old St. (J. Daniell). Est. 1969. Open 10.30-5, but appointment advisable. CL: Thurs. and Mon. SIZE: Small. *STOCK: Oils, watercolours, 19th-20th C, £100-£10,000.* Not Stocked: Prints. LOC: 100yds. from crossroads towards Malvern. PARK: Easy. TEL: 0684 592645; home - 0684 592909. SER: Valuations; restorations (reline and clean); buys at auction (pictures). VAT: Spec.

WALFORD, Nr. Ross-on-Wye
Robson Antiques
Little Howle Farm, Howle Hill. (J. Robson). Est. 1982. Open daily including Sun. SIZE: Large. *STOCK: Furniture, from 18th C, £50-£5000.* PARK: Easy. TEL: 0989 768128; home - same. SER: Valuations; buys at auction.

WINFORTON, Nr. Hereford
Gerald and Vera Taylor
Winforton Court. Est. 1965. Open by appointment. SIZE: Medium. *STOCK: Fully restored longcase clocks, 18th to early 19th C; furniture, mainly mahogany, pre-1840.* LOC: Between Hereford and Brecon on A438. PARK: Easy. TEL: 0544 327226. SER: Valuations; buys at auction. VAT: Stan/Spec.

WINYATES GREEN, Nr. Redditch
Lower House Fine Antiques
Lower House, Far Moor Lane. (Mrs J.B. Hudson). Est. 1987. Usually open but prior appointment advisable. SIZE: Small. *STOCK: Furniture, 17th to early 20th C, £100-£4,000; silver and plate, 18th to early 20th C, £10-£1,000; oil lamps, 19th*

Winyates Green continued
C, £50-£500. Not Stocked: Pine furniture. LOC: 3 miles due east Redditch town centre and half a mile from Coventry Highway island, close to A435. PARK: Own. TEL: 0527 25117; home - same. SER: Valuations; restorations.

WORCESTER
Alma Street Warehouse
Alma St. (D. and G. Venn). Open 9.30-1 and 2-4 Sat. 10-3 or by appointment. CL: Mon. p.m. and Thurs. *STOCK: General antiques, stripped pine, satin walnut.* LOC: Off Droitwich Rd. PARK: Easy. TEL: 0905 27493; home - 0905 24943.

Antique Map and Print Gallery
61 Sidbury. (M. Nichols). Open 9-5.30. *STOCK: Antiquarian maps, prints and books.* TEL: 0905 612926. SER: Framing.

Antique Warehouse
Rear of 74 Droitwich Rd, Barbourne. (D. Venn). Open 9-5, Sat. 10-3. *STOCK: General antiques including stripped pine.* TEL: 0905 27493. SER: Stripping pine and walnut.

Antiques and Curios
50 Upper Tything. Open 9.30-5.30. SIZE: dealers. *STOCK: Furniture, especially Victorian and Edwardian desks, dining and bedroom furnishings, mirrors, pictures, curios, jeweller and objets d'art.* TEL: 0905 25412/764547. SER: Restoration; upholstery.

Antiques and Interiors (Victoriana)
41 Upper Tything. Est. 1970. Open 9-5.30. *STOCK: Furniture especially dining tables, desks and Victorian mahogany; jewellery, silver, china, pictures and mirrors.* LOC: A38, extension of Foregate St. TEL: 0905 29014. SER: Restoration (furniture).

Andrew Boyle (Booksellers) Ltd
21 Friar St. Est. 1928. Appointment advisable. CL: Thurs. and Sat. *STOCK: Antiquarian and secondhand books.* TEL: 0905 611700. SER: Buys at auction.

Bygones by the Cathedral   LAPADA
Cathedral Sq. (Gabrielle Doherty Bullock FGA DGA. Est. 1946. Open 9.30-1 and 2-5.30. *STOCK: Furniture, 17th-19th C; silver, Sheffield plate, jewellery, paintings, glass, English and continental pottery and porcelain especially Royal Worcester.* LOC: Adjacent main entrance to Cathedral. TEL: 0905 25388.

Bygones (Worcester)   LAPADA
55 Sidbury. (G.D. Bullock). FGA. Est. 1946. Open 9.30-1 and 2-5.30. *STOCK: Furniture, 17th-19th C; silver, Sheffield plate, jewellery,*

HEREFORD AND WORCESTER

Worcester continued
paintings, glass; *English and continental porcelain and pottery especially Royal Worcester.* LOC: Opposite the public car park in Sidbury and adjacent to the City Walls road junction. TEL: 0905 23132. VAT: Stan/Spec.

John Edwards Antiques
Open by appointment only. *STOCK: English majolica and porcelain.* TEL: 0905 353840; fax - 0905 764370.

Gray's Antiques of Worcester
49 and 50 Upper Tything. (D. and M. Gray). Open 8.30-5.30. *STOCK: General antiques and soft furnishings.* TEL: 0905 724456.

Heirlooms
46 Upper Tything. (W. MacMillan, D. Tarran and L. Rumford). Open 9.30-4.30. *STOCK: General antiques, objets d'art, Royal Worcester porcelain and prints.* TEL: 0905 23332.

Jean Hodge
Peachley Manor, Hallow Lane, Lower Broadheath. Resident. Est. 1969. Open daily including Sun. SIZE: Large. *STOCK: Furniture, 18th-19th C; general antiques, £30-£4,000.* LOC: Off B4204, 3 miles N.W. Worcester. PARK: Easy. TEL: 0905 640255.

Sarah Hodge
Peachley Manor, Hallow Lane, Lower Broadheath. Resident. Est. 1985. Open daily including Sun. SIZE: Large. *STOCK: General antiques, country bygones, pine and kitchenalia.* LOC: Off B4204, 3 miles N.W. Worcester. PARK: Easy. TEL: 0905 640255.

M. Lees and Sons   LAPADA
Tower House, Severn St. Resident. Est. 1955. Open 9.15-5.15, Sat. by appointment. CL: Thurs. p.m. SIZE: Medium. *STOCK: Furniture, 1780-1880; porcelain, 1750-1920.* LOC: At southern end of Worcester Cathedral adjacent to Edgar Tower; near Royal Worcester Porcelain Museum and factory. PARK: Easy. TEL: 0905 26620; home - 0905 427142. VAT: Stan/Spec.

The Original Choice Ltd
56 The Tything. (J. Ellis). Open 10-6, Sun.1-5.30, evenings by appointment. *STOCK: Fireplaces, fenders, tiles, stained glass, mirrors and interior fittings.* TEL: 0905 613330.

St. Georges Antiques
31B Barbourne Rd. Open 10-5.30. TEL: 0905 25915. The following dealers trade from this address.

Collectors World
STOCK: Coins, militaria, cameras and Royal Worcester porcelain.

Worcester continued
Yestertime Antiques
STOCK: Clocks, barometers, furniture and small boxes. SER: Restorations.

Tolley's Galleries
26 College St. (T.M. Tolley). *STOCK: Oriental items especially rugs and Eastern bronzes, 17th-19th C.* PARK: Easy. TEL: 0905 26632. VAT: Stan.

Long Tran Antiques   LAPADA
(L. Tran). Open by appointment only. *STOCK: British and continental fine porcelain.* TEL: 0905 776685; mobile - 0831 400685.

The Tything Antique Market
49 The Tything. (Lawrence's Warehouse Ltd.). Open 10-5. SIZE: Large - 50 units. *STOCK: Wide variety of general antiques.* PARK: Easy. TEL: 0905 610597.

W.H.E.A.P. Antiques
17 Bromyard Rd. (P. Hooper). Open 9-6 or by appointment. *STOCK: General antiques and shipping goods.* TEL: 0905 427796. SER: Restorations; waxing and French polishing.

Worcester Antiques Centre
Reindeer Court, Mealcheapen Street. (Stephen Zacaroli). Est. 1992. Open 10-5. SIZE: Large. *STOCK: Pottery and porcelain, 1750-1940, £10-£2,000; silver, 1750-1940, £10-£3,000; jewellery, 1800-1940, £5-£2,000; furniture, 1650-1930, £50-£5,000.* PARK: Loading only or 50 yards. TEL: 0905 610680/1; fax (after 5 p.m.) - 0905 610681. SER: Valuations; restorations. FAIRS: NEC (April and Aug); East Berkshire (May and Oct). VAT: Stan/Spec.

YATTON, Nr. Leominster
Moreden Prints
(B. Croxton). Open by appointment. *STOCK: Antiquarian and collectable prints and maps.* TEL: 056886 549. SER: Book and print search; mountcutting.

YAZOR
M. and J. Russell
The Old Vicarage. Est. 1969. Usually open Fri. to Mon. and evenings, other times appointment advisable. *STOCK: English period oak and country furniture, some garden antiques.* LOC: 7 miles west of Hereford on A480. TEL: 098 122 674. *Mainly Trade.*

Hertfordshire

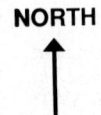

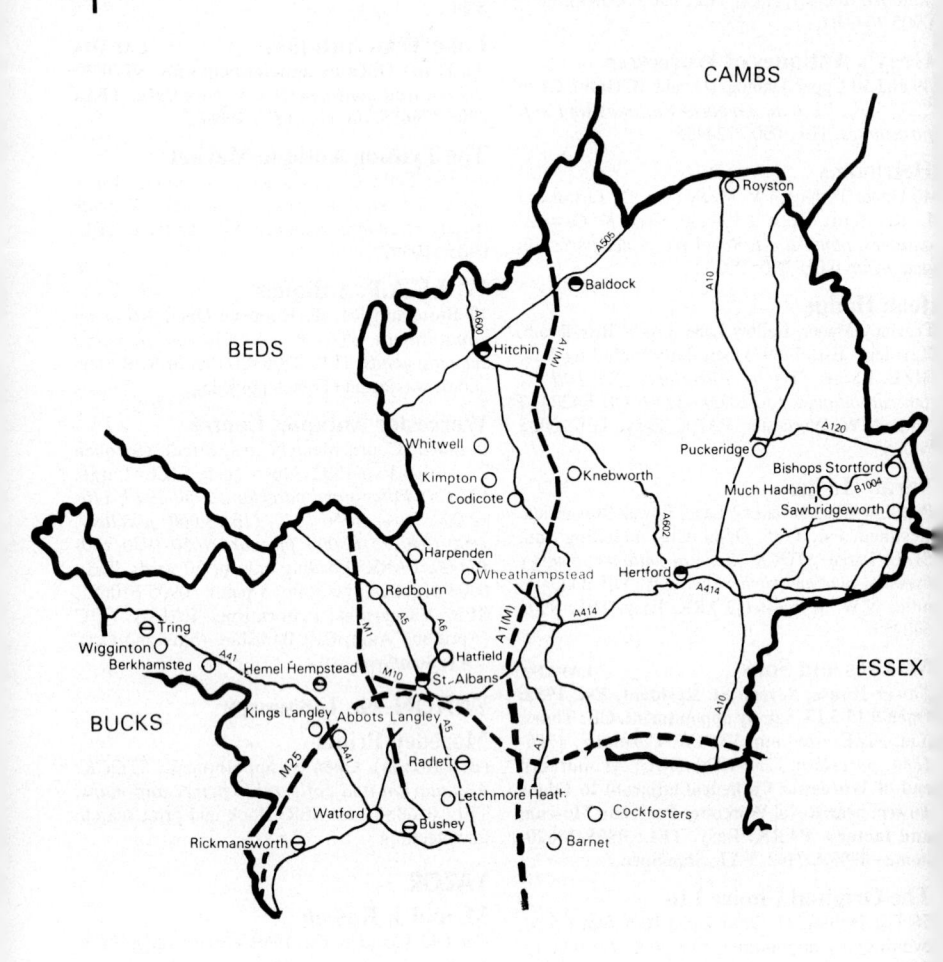

314

NORTH ↑

Key to number of shops in this area.
○ 1-2
⊖ 3-5
◐ 6-12
● 13+

Please note this is only a rough map designed to show dealers the number shops in the various towns, and is not necessarily totally accurate.

Hertfordshire

An Antique Collectors' Club Title

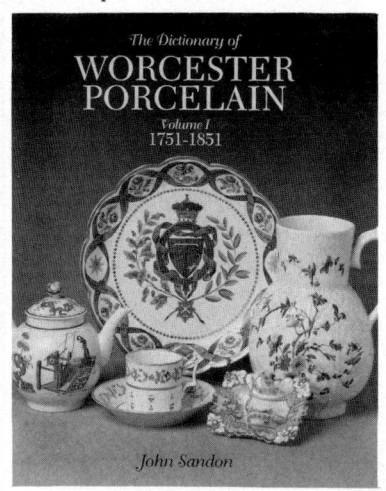

The Dictionary of Worcester Porcelain Volume I 1751-1851
by John Sandon

With 600+ dictionary entries, an historical survey, an illustrated section on marks, detailed information on recent excavations at the Worcester factory, contemporary accounts of visits to factories and an extensive bibliography, this is the definitive work. The author is director of ceramics at Phillips auctioneers, London, and regularly appears on the *Antiques Roadshow*.
ISBN 1 85149 156 2
400pp, 450 b & w illus, 100 colour
£45.00

Available from:
Antique Collectors' Club, 5 Church Street, Woodbridge, Suffolk IP12 1DS
Tel: (0394) 385501 Fax: (0394) 384434

or Market Street Industrial Park, Wappingers' Falls, New York 12590, USA.
Tel: 914 297 0003 Fax: 914 297 0068

ABBOTS LANGLEY, Nr. Watford
Dobson's Antiques
53 High St. Est. 1926. Open 8.30-5.30. CL: Tues. p.m. STOCK: Carved oak, stripped pine, shipping goods, bric-a-brac, £5-£2,000. LOC: 4 miles north of Watford. TEL: 0923 263186. VAT: Stan/Spec.

BALDOCK
The Attic
20 Whitehorse St. (P. Sheppard). Est. 1977. CL: Mon. and Thurs. SIZE: Small. STOCK: Small furniture, china, brass and copper, dolls and teddy bears, £5-£100. LOC: 3 minutes from A1(M). PARK: Easy. TEL: 0462 893880.

Anthony Butt Antiques
7/9 Church St. Resident. Est. 1950. Usually open. STOCK: English furniture, 17th-19th C, £500-£5,000; works of art and objects of interest. Not Stocked: Bric-a-brac, shipping goods. PARK: Easy. TEL: 0462 895272. SER: Valuations. VAT: Spec.

Howards
33 Whitehorse St. (D.N. Howard). Est. 1970. Open 9.30-5.00. CL: Mon. STOCK: Clocks, 18th-19th C, £200-£5,000. PARK: Easy. TEL: 0462 892385. SER: Valuations; restorations and repairs (clocks). VAT: Spec.

Baldock continued

Ralph and Bruce Moss
26 Whitehorse St. (R.A. and B.A. Moss). Est. 1973. Open 9-6. SIZE: Large. STOCK: Furniture, £50-£5,000; general antiques, £5-£5,000. LOC: A505, in town centre. PARK: Own. TEL: 0462 892751. VAT: Stan/Spec.

Arthur Porter
31 Whitehorse St. (A.G.R. Porter). Est. 1969. Open 9-6 seven days. SIZE: Large. STOCK: Pine furniture, 18th-20th C; English, continental and decorative items. LOC: Main street. PARK: Easy. TEL: 0462 895351. SER: Valuations; restorations; stripping; finder. VAT: Stan/Spec.

The Wheelwright
1 Mansfield Rd. (E. and L. Hurst). Resident. Est. 1976. Open 9.30-5.30. CL: Thurs. SIZE: Medium. STOCK: Small porcelain and china, jewellery, small furniture, bric-a-brac, 19th C, £5-£500. LOC: Off A1. PARK: Easy. TEL: 0462 893876.

BARNET
C. Bellinger Antiques
91 Wood St. Est. 1974. Open Thurs., Fri. and Sat. 10-4 or by appointment. SIZE: Medium. STOCK: Furniture, silver and plate, smalls. LOC: Opposite Ravenscroft Park. PARK: Within 100yds. TEL: 081 449 3467. VAT: Stan/Spec.

Park Street Antiques

Mark Shanks
350 High Street · Berkhamsted
Hertfordshire HP4 1HT

Berkhamsted (0442) 864790

A large selection of Fine Furniture, Barometers and Works of Art

---

BERKHAMSTED
Park Street Antiques BADA
350 High St. (Mark Shanks). Est. 1960. Open Tues.-Sat. 9.30-5.30 or by appointment. SIZE: Large. *STOCK: Furniture, £100-£30,000; barometers, £100-£10,000; both 17th-19th C; works of art, £30-£3,000; longcase clocks, rugs and carpets.* Not Stocked: Silver, jewellery, coins. LOC: A41. PARK: At west end of town. TEL: 0442 864790; fax - same; home - 0442 822142. VAT: Stan/Spec.

BISHOP'S STORTFORD
Northgate Antiques
21 Northgate End. (Mrs L.B. Rawsthorne). Est. 1986. Open 9-5, most Sats. 10-12.30. SIZE: Medium. *STOCK: General antiques and collectables.* LOC: 20yds. north of Sworders auction rooms, 2 miles from Junction 8, M11. PARK: Easy. TEL: 0279 656957; home - 0279 722757.

The Windhill Antiquary
4 High St. (G.R. Crozier). Est. 1951. Open 10-1 and 2-4, appointment advisable. CL: Wed. p.m. SIZE: Medium. *STOCK: English furniture, 18th C; carved and gilded wall mirrors, 17th-19th C.* Not Stocked: Shipping goods. LOC: Next to George Hotel. PARK: Up hill - first right. TEL: 0279 651587; home - 0920 821316. VAT: Stan/Spec.

Bishop's Stortford continued

Wiskin Antiques
Glasscocks Business Centre, 14 The Causeway (K. and M. Wiskin). Est. 1973. Open 10.30-5.30 most days. SIZE: Medium. *STOCK: Pine and mahogany; oak, early 20th C; smalls.* LOC: 2 miles from M11, junction 8. PARK: Own. TEL 0279 465503. SER: Restorations (polishing, pine stripping, re-upholstering). VAT: Spec.

BUSHEY, Nr. Watford
Circa Antiques
43 High St, Bushey Village. (K. Wildman). Est 1978. Open 9.30-5.30 or by appointment. SIZE Medium. *STOCK: General antiques, furniture porcelain, silver and clocks.* TEL: 081 950 9233.

Country Life Antiques
33a High St. (Peter Myers). Est. 1981. Open 9-5 SIZE: Large. *STOCK: Victorian and Edwardian furniture, European and Scandinavian pine kitchenalia, watercolours, china and art deco* PARK: Easy. TEL: 081 950 8575. VAT: Stan.

Thwaites and Co
33 Chalk Hill, Oxhey. Est. 1971. Open 9-5, Sat 9.30-12.30. *STOCK: Stringed instruments, from violins to double basses.* TEL: 0923 232412 SER: Restorations.

HERTFORDSHIRE

COCKFOSTERS
H. Pordes Ltd
383 Cockfosters Rd. *STOCK: Antiquarian books including scientific and learned; remainders.* TEL: 081 449 2524; fax - same, but telephone before transmission. *Postal Only.*

CODICOTE
Richard Kimbell
at Country Gardens, High St. Est. 1966. Open 9-6 including Sun. SIZE: Large. *STOCK: Antique pine, 19th C, £50-£1,000.* LOC: Garden centre in village centre. PARK: Easy. TEL: 0438 821616. VAT: Stan.

Wheldon and Wesley Ltd
Lytton Lodge. Est. 1921. Open by appointment only. *STOCK: Antiquarian books on Natural History.* TEL: 0438 820370; fax - 0438 821478. SER: Buys at auction. *Mail Order Only.*

HARPENDEN
Meg Andrews
20 Holly Bush Lane. Est. 1982. Open by appointment. *STOCK: Worldwide collectable, hangable and wearable antique costume and textiles including Chinese embroideries and woven fabrics, robes, shoes, hats, large hangings, Morris and Arts and Crafts embroideries and woven cloths, Paisley shawls, samplers, silkwork pictures; European costumes and textiles.* LOC: Off Junction 10, M1, south on A1081. PARK: Easy. TEL: 0582 460107; home - same. SER: Valuations; advice; buys at auction.

Knights Gallery
38 Station Rd. (J.C. Knights). Open 10-4, Sat. 10-4. CL: Wed. *STOCK: Watercolours, oils and prints.* TEL: 0582 460564. SER: Valuations; restorations; framing; buys at auction.

HATFIELD
Old Cathay Fine Books and Arts
43 Park St, Old Hatfield. (Ian Edwards). Est. 1991. Open 10.30-1 and 2.30-6 including Sun. *STOCK: Edwardian and Victorian colour-plate and colour-picture books and prints, including childrens, especially A. & C. Black Colour Books; antiquarian books, modern first editions, old childrens annuals and old toys.* TEL: 0707 274200/271006. SER: Valuations; restorations.

HEMEL HEMPSTEAD
Abbey Antiques and Fine Art LAPADA
7 High St, Old Town. (L., E., S. and C. Eames). Est. 1962. Open 9.30-5.30. CL: Wed. p.m. SIZE: Medium. *STOCK: Silver, plate, jewellery, £5-£2,000; early English watercolours, £100-£5,000; furniture, 17th-19th C.* LOC: M1, junction 8, A25, junction 20, through main shopping centre to old town. PARK: Easy. TEL: 0442 64667.

Hemel Hempstead continued
SER: Valuations; jewellery design and repair; restorations (as stock). VAT: Stan/Spec.

Antique and Collectors Market
Market Place. (Dacorum Borough Council). Open Wed. 9-2. SIZE: 116 dealers. *STOCK: General antiques.* TEL: 0442 242831.

Cherry Antiques
101-103 High St. (A. and R.S. Cullen). Open 9.30-4.30. CL: Wed. p.m. SIZE: Medium. *STOCK: Victorian, Edwardian, and some period furniture, pine, general antiques, collectors' and decorative items, bric-a-brac, needlework tools, dolls, linens, some silver, plate, jewellery, glass, pottery, porcelain, brass, copper, some shipping items.* PARK: Easy. TEL: 0442 64358. VAT: Stan/Spec.

Georgina Antiques
100 High St. (Roy and Jean Marsh). Est. 1992. Open 10-4. SIZE: Small. *STOCK: Oriental antiquities, £5-£4,000; general antiques and bygones.* LOC: From A41, turn off Two Waters through shopping centre to old town. PARK: Easy. TEL: 0442 256957. SER: Valuations.

HERTFORD
Beckwith and Son
St. Nicholas Hall, St. Andrew St. (A.K. Loveday, FSVA G.C.M. Gray N.P.J. Bunce P. Chappell). Est. 1904. Open 9-1 and 2-5.30. SIZE: Large. *STOCK: General antiques, furniture, silver, pottery, porcelain, prints, weapons, clocks, watches, glass.* Not Stocked: Fabrics. LOC: A602/B158. PARK: Adjacent. TEL: 0992 582079. SER: Valuations; restorations (fine porcelain, furniture, upholstery, silver, clocks). VAT: Stan/Spec.

Robert Horton Antiques
13 Castle St. Est. 1972. Open 9-5. *STOCK: Clocks, barometers, furniture, general antiques.* TEL: 0992 587546. VAT: Stan/Spec.

Pastimes Antiques
5 Old Cross, St. Andrew's St. (J. Crooks and A. Jackson). Est. 1987. Open 9.30-5. SIZE: Medium. *STOCK: Victorian furniture, glass and china, small items.* LOC: On roundabout at junction with Bengeo St. PARK: Nearby. TEL: 0992 581406; home - 0992 558209. SER: Valuations; restorations (upholstery, re-polishing); buys at auction (furniture). FAIRS: Hertford.

Michael Rochford
25 St. Andrew St. Open 10-5. *STOCK: Trade goods including general antiques, furniture.* TEL: 0992 584385.

Village Green Antiques LAPADA
6 and 8 Old Cross. (N. and P. Petre). Est. 1970. Open 10-5.30. CL: Thurs. p.m. SIZE: Large. *STOCK: Furniture, £50-£10,000; porcelain,*

HERTFORDSHIRE

Hertford continued
metalware, works of art, decorative items. LOC: 200 yds. from A414. PARK: At rear. TEL: 0992 587698; home - 0992 586994. VAT: Stan/Spec.

HITCHIN
Bexfield Antiques
13 and 14 Sun St. (A.B. Bexfield). Est. 1962. Open 9.30-5. CL: Wed. STOCK: *Jewellery, silver, porcelain, copper, pewter and furniture.* PARK: Nearby. TEL: 0462 432641.

Countrylife Gallery
41-43 Portmill Lane. (M. Morgan and D.B. Moore). Open by appointment only. SIZE: Small. STOCK: *Watercolours - botanical, flower and natural history, 1780-1930, £50-£500; oils - flowers and natural history, 1850-1930, £500-£5,000.* LOC: Town square. PARK: 50yds. TEL: 0462 433267; home - same. SER: Valuations; restorations; buys at auction (English watercolours and pictures). FAIRS: Royal Horticultural Socy. VAT: Spec.

Michael Gander
10 Bridge St. Est. 1973. Open 9-6. STOCK: *Period furniture, metalware.* TEL: 0462 432678.

Hitchin Antiques Gallery
37 Bridge St. (R.J. Perry). Open 10-5.30. CL: Sun. except by appointment. SIZE: 10 dealers. STOCK: *General antiques including furniture, jewellery, clocks, barometers, paintings, to £5,000.* PARK: Nearby. TEL: 0462 434525; home - 0582 25546. SER: Valuations; restorations (furniture, re-upholstery, clocks and glass). FAIRS: Luton.

Eric T. Moore
24 Bridge St. Open 9.30-1 and 2.15-5.30, Wed. 9-12.30, Sat. 9.30-5.30. STOCK: *Antiquarian books, maps and prints.* TEL: 0462 450497. SER: Picture framing, mount cutting.

R.J. Perry Antiques   LAPADA
38 Bridge St. Open 10-5.30. SIZE: 3 floors. STOCK: *Metalware, interior decorators' pieces, small furniture, general antiques.* TEL: 0462 434525. SER: Valuations; restorations (furniture, upholstery, metalware). FAIRS: Luton.

Phillips of Hitchin (Antiques) Ltd
BADA
The Manor House. (M. and J. Phillips). Est. 1884. Open 9-5.30. SIZE: Large. STOCK: *Furniture, walnut, oak and mahogany, 17th to early 19th C, £500-£20,000.* LOC: In Bancroft, main street of Hitchin. PARK: Easy. TEL: 0462 432067; fax - 0462 441368. SER: Restorations (furniture); books on collecting. FAIRS: Specialist antique exhibitions at the Manor House. VAT: Spec.

KIMPTON
Annick Antiques
28 High St. (R.V. and A.M. Turl). Open seven days 11-5. STOCK: *Victorian, Edwardian and country oak furniture, prints, paintings, general antiques and bric-a-brac.* LOC: Between Wheathampstead and Hitchin. PARK: Easy. TEL: 0438 832491.

KING'S LANGLEY
Frenches Farm Antiques
Tower Hill, Chipperfield. (I. Cross). Est. 1972. Open 2-6 or by appointment. SIZE: Large. STOCK: *Furniture, including pine, £15-£700; porcelain, Victoriana, copper, brass, £3-£100; mainly 18th-19th C.* Not Stocked: Silver, jewellery, firearms, paintings. LOC: From Chipperfield take Bovingdon Rd. On right 500yds. from Royal Oak public house. PARK: Easy. TEL: 0923 265843.

KNEBWORTH
Hamilton and Tucker Billiard Co. Ltd
Park Lane. (H. Hamilton and P. Tucker). Est. 1980. Open 9-5, Sat. 10-4, Sun. by appointment SIZE: Large. STOCK: *Victorian and Edwardian billiard tables, £3,000-£18,000; 19th C convertible billiard/dining tables and accessories, £30-£5,000.* LOC: Near railway station. PARK: Easy TEL: 0438 811995. SER: Valuations; restorations (billiard tables and assorted furniture); buys at auction (as stock). FAIRS: Distinctive Homes at Alexandra Palace; Cologne International Furniture. VAT: Stan.

LETCHMORE HEATH, Nr. Watford
Anne Barlow Antiques
1 Letchmore Cottages. (Mrs Barlow). Est. 1952 Open 2.30-6.30. CL: Mon. SIZE: Small. STOCK *Continental and unusual items especially Quimper pottery, country furniture, faience porcelain, toys clocks, collectors' items, £1-£500.* PARK: Easy TEL: 0923 855270. SER: Valuations.

MUCH HADHAM
Careless Cottage Antiques
High St. (M. Furze). Est. 1979. Open 9.30-5.30 Sun. by appointment. SIZE: Medium. STOCK *General antiques, oak and country furniture 17th-19th C, £100-£2,500; china, glass, small and decorative items.* LOC: On B1004, at north end of village. PARK: Easy. TEL: 027 984 2007.

PUCKERIDGE
St. Ouen Antiques   LAPADA
Vintage Corner, Old Cambridge Rd. (V.C.J. J., J. and S.T. Blake and Mrs P.B. Francis) Est. 1918. Open 10.30-5. SIZE: Large. STOCK *English and continental furniture, decorative items, silver, porcelain, pottery, glass, clocks barometers, paintings.* TEL: 0920 821336. SER Valuations; restorations.

HERTFORDSHIRE

For 100 years and over three generations discerning collectors from all over the world have come to find carefully chosen English period furniture displayed in the period rooms of this Georgian manor house only 30 miles (1 hour by car) from London.

PHILLIPS *of* HITCHIN

(ANTIQUES) LTD.

The Manor House

Hitchin, Herts

SG5 1JW
Members of the British Antique Dealers Association

Telephone: Hitchin 432067 *Cables:* Phillips
STD 0462 Hitchin

HERTFORDSHIRE

RADLETT

Hasel-Britt Ltd
157 Watling St. (Mrs Britton). Est. 1962. Open 10-5.30. CL: Wed. p.m. STOCK: General antiques, 19th C; pottery and porcelain. TEL: 0923 854477.

Old Hat
64 Watling St. (N.G. Rogers). Est. 1972. Open 10-1 and 3-5.30. CL: Wed. p.m. SIZE: Medium. STOCK: General antiques, furniture, Victoriana, £50-£5,000; oils, watercolours, porcelain, bronzes, 18th-19th C, £50-£5,000. LOC: A5. PARK: Easy. TEL: 0923 855753. VAT: Stan/Spec.

REDBOURN, Nr. St. Albans

J.N. Antiques
86 High St. (M. and J. Brunning). Est. 1975. Open 9-6. SIZE: Medium. STOCK: Furniture, 18th-20th C, £5-£3,000; brass and copper, porcelain, 19th C, £5-£100; pictures, 19th-20th C. PARK: 50 yds. TEL: 0582 793603 (24hrs.). SER: Valuations. VAT: Spec.

Tim Wharton Antiques LAPADA
24 High St. Est. 1970. Open 10-5.30, Sat. 10-4. CL: Mon. and usually Thurs. STOCK: Oak and country furniture, 17th-19th C; some mahogany, 18th-early 19th C; copper, brass, ironware and general small antiques. LOC: On left entering village from St. Albans on A5183. PARK: Easy. TEL: 0582 794371. VAT: Stan/Spec.

RICKMANSWORTH

Clive A. Burden
46 Talbot Rd. Est. 1966. Open 9-5, appointment preferred. SIZE; Medium. STOCK: Maps, 1500-1860, £5-£1,500; natural history, botanical and Vanity Fair prints, 1720-1870, £1-£1,000; antiquarian books, pre-1870, £10-£5,000. LOC: In main shopping area. PARK: Nearby. TEL: 0923 778097; fax - 0923 896520; home - 0923 772387. SER: Valuations; buys at auction (as stock). VAT: Stan.

David Harriman Antiques
Open every day by appointment. STOCK: Clocks especially electric - Bulle, Ato, Eureka, Holden, Reclus and Tiffany; 20th C decorative items, bronzes and furniture. TEL: 0923 776919; fax - 0923 773995.

McCrudden Gallery
23 Station Rd. Open 10-5.30. CL: Wed. SIZE: Medium. STOCK: Fine paintings, watercolours, limited editions prints, etching and engravings. LOC: Town centre. PARK: Easy. TEL: 0923 772613. SER: Restorations (pictures and frames); buys at auction.

John Parker - The Whitestocks Collections
Whitestocks Farm, Loudwater Lane. Open Wed.,

Rickmansworth continued
Fri. and Sat. or by appointment. STOCK: Furniture including pine; general antiques. TEL: Mobile - 0831 816688.

ROYSTON

Royston Antiques
29 Kneesworth St. (J. and M. Newnham). Est. 1965. Open 9.30-5. CL: Thurs. SIZE: Medium. STOCK: Furniture, 1750-1930, £50-£2,500; porcelain, books, £5-£500; collectors' items, pine, metalware, bygones. TEL: 0763 243876.

ST. ALBANS

By George! Antiques Centre
23 George St. (D.J. Pyne). Open 10-5. SIZE: Medium. 15 dealers. STOCK: A wide range of general antiques, silver, jewellery and fine arts. LOC: 100yds. from Clock Tower. PARK: Internal courtyard (loading) and nearby. TEL: 0727 53032. SER: Restorations.

The Clock Shop - Philip Setterfield of St. Albans
161 Victoria St. Est. 1974. Open 10.30-6.30, Sat. 10.30-4. CL: Thurs. STOCK: Clocks and watches. LOC: City station bridge. TEL: 0727 56633. SER: Restoration; repairs (clocks, watches, barometers). VAT: Stan/Spec.

Dolphin Antiques LAPADA
Garden Cottage, Dolphin Lodge, Dolphin Yard, off Holywell Hill. (C. Constable). Est. 1967. Open by appointment. SIZE: Small STOCK: Furniture, 18th-19th C, £100-£4,000, porcelain, £20-£1,000; glass, brass and copper £10-£300; pictures, prints, £10-£500. Not Stocked: Coins, medals, weapons. PARK: Nearby. TEL: 0727 863080; home - 0727 861941. VAT: Stan/Spec.

Forget-me-Knot Antiques
at By George! Antiques Centre, 23 George St (Heather Sharp). Est. 1987. Open 10-5, Thurs. 11-5, Sat. 10-5.30, Sun. by appointment. STOCK Jewellery, 19th C to 1930's, £5-£500; china, 19th C to 1960's, £5-£250; collectables, 19th-20th C £1-£200. PARK: Nearby. TEL: 0923 261172 home - 0727 853032. SER: Valuations. FAIRS Ardingly, Redbourne. VAT: Stan.

James of St Albans
11 George St. (S.N. and W. James). Est. 1957 Open 10-5, Thurs. 10-1. STOCK: Furniture including reproduction; smalls, brass and copper topographical maps and prints of Hertfordshire TEL: 0727 56996. VAT: Stan/Spec.

Leaside Antiques
Shop 5, By George Antique Centre, 23 George St (T.G. Pepper). CL: Thurs. STOCK: Edwardian furniture, ceramics, silver, cameras, and collectors items. TEL: 0727 40653; home - 0582 2795 (answerphone). SER: Repairs (jewellery).

HERTFORDSHIRE

St. Alban's continued
Magic Lanterns
at By George! Antiques Centre, 23 George St. (Josie A. Marsden). Est. 1987. Open 10-5, Thurs. 11-5, Sat. 10-5.30, occasional Sun. 1-5. SIZE: Medium. STOCK: *Lighting - candle, gas and early electric, 1800-1940, £50-£600; small furniture, prints, mirrors, china, metalware, fire accessories, 1850-1950, £25-£500.* LOC: Near the abbey. PARK: Multi-storey nearby. TEL: 0727 853032; home - 0727 865680.

Oriental Rug Gallery Ltd
42 Verulam Rd. (R. Mathias and J. Blair). Open 9-6, Sun. 10.30-4. STOCK: *Russian, Afghan, Turkish and Persian carpets, rugs and kelims; Oriental objets d'art.* TEL: 0727 41046.

St. Albans Antique Market
Town Hall, Chequer St. Est. 1978. Open Mon. 9.30 (8.30 trade)-4. CL: Bank Holidays. SIZE: 30 stands. STOCK: *A wide variety of antiques.* TEL: 0727 844957.

Stevens Antiques
41 London Rd. (J.E. Stevens). Est. 1971. Open 10-5.30, Sat. 9.30-5, Sun. by appointment. CL: Thurs. SIZE: Medium. STOCK: *Stripped pine, £25-£500; small antiques - brass, boxes, china, porcelain, £10-£300, all 19th C; Victorian and Edwardian furniture, 19th to early 20th C, £30-£1,000.* LOC: Off Holywell Hill or Chequer St. PARK: Own, at rear. TEL: 0727 57266; home - 0727 50427. VAT: Stan.

Thomas Thorp
9 George St. Est. 1883. CL: Mon. STOCK: *Antiquarian books, prints.* TEL: 0727 865576.

Stuart Wharton
1 George St. FGA DGA. Est. 1967. Open 9.30-5.30. SIZE: Small. STOCK: *Silver, 18th-20th C, £20-£2,000; jewellery, mainly modern, £20-£5,000.* LOC: Near clock tower. PARK: Multi-storey, city centre. TEL: 0727 59489; fax - 0727 55474. SER: Registered valuer (jewellery and silver); goldsmithing, gem testing; buys at auction (silver). VAT: Stan.

SAWBRIDGEWORTH
The Herts and Essex Antique Centre
The Maltings, Station Rd. Est. 1982. Open 10-5, Sat. and Sun. 10.30-6. CL: Mon. SIZE: Large - over 100 dealers. STOCK: *General antiques and collectables, £1-£2,000.* LOC: Town centre opposite B.R. station. PARK: Easy. TEL: 0279 722044. SER: Restorations.

TRING
John Bly   BADA
50 High St. (F., N., J. and V. Bly). Books on furniture and silver. Est. 1891. Open 9-5.30. SIZE: Large. STOCK: *Furniture, antiquities,*

Tring continued
works of art. TEL: 0442 823030. SER: Valuations. VAT: Stan/Spec.

Country Clocks
3 Pendley Bridge Cottages, Tring Station. (T. Cartmell). Resident. Est. 1976. Open daily, prior 'phone call advisable. SIZE: Small. STOCK: *Clocks, 18th-19th C.* LOC: One mile from A41 in village, cottage nearest canal bridge. PARK: Easy. TEL: 0442 825090. SER: Restorations (clocks).

Farrelly Antiques
The Long Barn, 50 High St. (P. Farrelly). Open 9-4. STOCK: *Furniture.* TEL: 0442 891905. SER: Restorations. VAT: Spec.

WARESIDE
Wareside Antiques
(David Broxup). Est. 1983. Open Fri., other days by appointment. SIZE: Medium. STOCK: *Furniture, from 18th C, £100-£2,000.* LOC: On Ware to Much Hadham road. PARK: Easy. TEL: 0920 469434; home - same. SER: Valuations; restorations; buys at auction (furniture).

WATFORD
Copper Kettle Antiques
172 Bushey Mill Lane. (R. and C. Barton). Est. 1970. Open 9.30-4.30. CL: Wed. SIZE: Large. STOCK: *General antiques, Victoriana, paintings, watercolours, books, prints, clocks, furniture.* TEL: 0923 248877. VAT: Stan/Spec.

WHEATHAMPSTEAD
Collins Antiques (F.G. and C. Collins Ltd.)
Corner House. (S.J. and M.C. Collins). Est. 1907. Open 9-1 and 2-5. SIZE: Large. STOCK: *Furniture, mahogany, 1730-1920, £100-£8,000; oak, 1600-1800, £50-£5,000; walnut, 1700-1740, £75-£3,000.* Not Stocked: Silver. LOC: London, A1(M) junction 4 to B653. PARK: Easy. TEL: 058 283 3111. VAT: Stan/Spec.

WHITWELL, Nr. Hitchin
Simon Boosey - Carpets for Country Houses
The Tun House. Est. 1973. Open by appointment. STOCK: *Persian and Oriental carpets and runners, £500-£5,000; fine village and nomad rugs, £250-£2,000; both 1850-1950; small tribal pieces, pre-1950, £75-£500.* LOC: High St. PARK: Easy. TEL: 0438 871563; home - same. SER: Valuations; restorations.

WILSTONE, Nr. Tring
Michael Armson (Antiques) Ltd
34 Tring Rd. Open 9.30-5.30. CL: Wed p.m. SIZE: Large. STOCK: *Furniture, 17th-19th C.* TEL: 0442 890990; mobile - 0860 910034; home - 0296 661141.

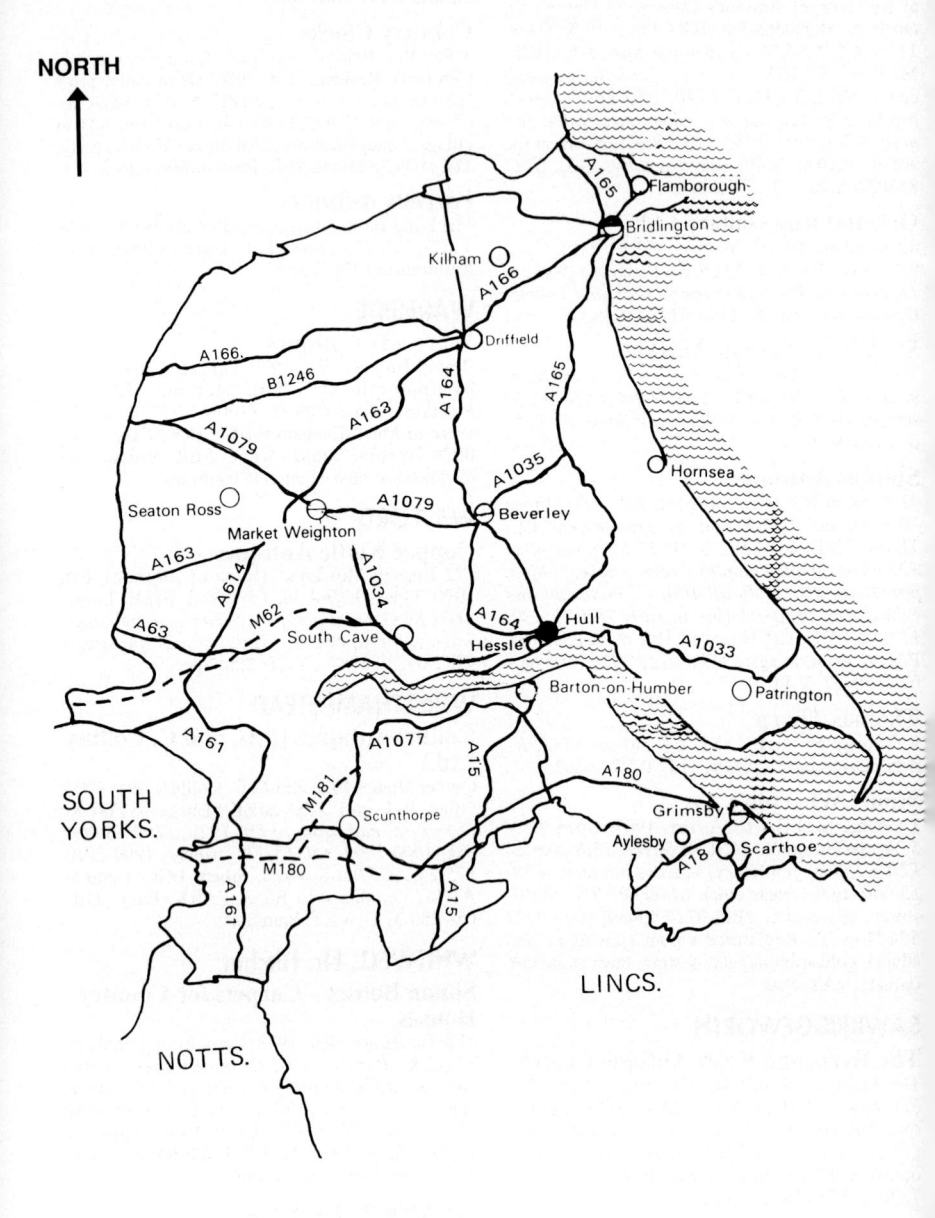

Humberside

Humberside North

BEVERLEY

Hawley Antiques　　　LAPADA
5 North Bar Within. Open 9.30-5. *STOCK: General antiques, furniture, pottery, porcelain, glass, oil paintings, watercolours, silver.* TEL: 0482 868193. SER: Restorations (fine furniture). VAT: Stan/Spec.

Ladygate Antiques
8 Ladygate. (P. and L. Goodman). Est. 1963. Open 9.30-1 and 2-5.30. SIZE: Medium. *STOCK: Furniture, longcase clocks, pottery and porcelain, glass, brass, copper, pewter, jewellery, maritime relics, silver and plate.* Not Stocked: Militaria, coins. PARK: Easy. TEL: 0482 881494; home - 0482 882299/868857.

James H. Starkey Galleries
49 Highgate. Est. 1968. Open 10-5, Sat. 10-1 or by appointment. SIZE: Medium. *STOCK: Oil paintings, 16th-19th C; drawings and watercolours, 17th-19th C.* LOC: Opposite Beverley Minster. PARK: Easy. TEL: 0482 881179; fax - 0482 861644. SER: Valuations; restorations (paintings); buys at auction. VAT: Stan/Spec.

Well Lane Antiques
10 Well Lane. (S. Endley). Est. 1969. Open 11-4, Tues., Wed. and Thurs. 12.30-3.30. SIZE: Small. *STOCK: General antiques, Victorian, Edwardian and art deco, £5-£250.* LOC: Off Butcher Row. TEL: 0482 882868; home - 0482 861599. FAIRS: Local.

BRIDLINGTON

Antique Militaria
2 Princess Terrace. (B. and I. Barker). Open 10-4 in winter, 9-5.30 including Sun. in summer. CL: Tues. and Thurs. *STOCK: Militaria.* TEL: 0262 676846; home - 0262 851118.

C.J. and A.J. Dixon Ltd
1st Floor, 23 Prospect St. Est. 1969. Open 9-5.30. SIZE: Large. *STOCK: War medals and decorations, British and foreign.* LOC: Town centre. PARK: Easy. TEL: 0262 676877/603348; fax - 0262 606600. SER: Valuations; renovations. VAT: Stan/Spec.

Priory Antiques
47-49 High St. (P.R. Rogerson). Est. 1979. Open 10-5. CL: Thurs. *STOCK: Georgian and Victorian furniture.* TEL: 0262 601365.

Sedman Antiques
Carnaby Court, Off Moor Lane, Carnaby. (R.H.S. and M.A. Sedman). Est. 1971. Open 10-5.30, Sun. by appointment. *STOCK: General antiques, period and shipping furniture, Oriental porcelain, Victorian collectors' items.* LOC: Off A165. TEL: 0262 674039. VAT: Stan/Spec.

Sweet's Antiques
24 West St. (John Sweet). Est. 1950. Open 10-6. *STOCK: General antiques, porcelain, glass.* TEL: 0262 677396.

Bridlington continued

G. M. Wheeler Antiques: Style and Design
53 Flamborough Rd. Est. 1987. Open 11-6, Wed. and Sat. 11-5.30, Mon. and Thurs. 12-5.30, Sun. in summer 11-4. SIZE: Small. *STOCK: General antiques including pine, curios and unusual items, 17th-20th C, £5-£1,000.* PARK: Easy. SER: Valuations; restorations; buys at auction (17th-18th C oak, weapons, pictures by local artists).

DRIFFIELD

The Crested China Co
The Station House. (D. Taylor). Est. 1978. Open 9-12.30 and 1.30-5, other times by appointment. *STOCK: Goss and crested china.* TEL: 0377 47042 (24 hr.).

Smith and Smith Designs
58A Middle St. North. (D. A. and C. R. Smith and M.T. Addinall). Est. 1977. Open 9.30-5.30, Sat. 9.30-5, Sun. by appointment. SIZE: Medium + warehouse. *STOCK: Furniture including pine and country, 18th to early 20th C, £50-£2,000; furniture designed and made to order, from £50+.* LOC: Main street. PARK: Easy. TEL: 0377 46321; home - same. SER: Restorations. VAT: Stan/Spec.

FLAMBOROUGH, Nr. Bridlington

Lesley Berry Antiques
The Manor House. (Mrs L. Berry). Resident. Est. 1972. Open 9.30-5.30, other times by appointment. SIZE: Small. *STOCK: Furniture, silver, jewellery, amber, Whitby jet, oils, watercolours, prints, copper, brass, textiles, fountain pens.* Not Stocked: Shipping goods. LOC: On corner of Tower St. and Lighthouse Rd. PARK: Easy. TEL: 0262 850943. SER: Buys at auction.

HESSLE

The Antique Parlour
21 The Weir. (S. Beercock). Est. 1967. CL: Sun. except to trade. *STOCK: General antiques, Victoriana, bric-a-brac, curios.* TEL: 0482 643329.

HORNSEA

Padgetts Antiques, Photographic and Scientific
19 Hull Rd. (G.R. and D.L. Padgett). Est. 1965. Open by appointment. SIZE: Small. *STOCK: Cameras and photographic miscellanea, scientific instruments, clocks.* LOC: Overlooking Hornsea Mere. PARK: Easy. TEL: 0964 534086. FAIRS: London, Newark, Leeds, Manchester.

HULL

Boothferry Antiques
388 Wincolmlee. (P. and J.A. Smith). Est. 1972. Open 8.30-5, Sat. 9-3, other times by appointment. SIZE: Large. *STOCK: Stripped pine, 1800-*

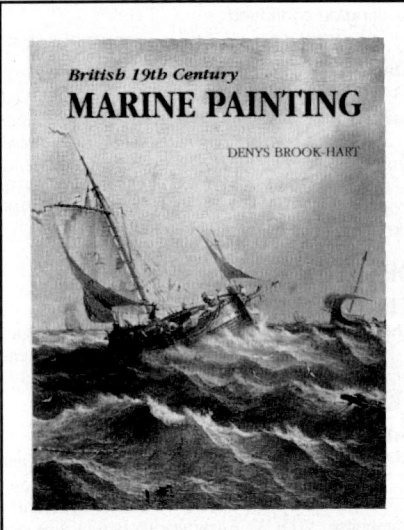

An Antique Collectors' Club Title

British 19th Century Marine Painting

Denis Brook-Hart combined his love of the sea with his professional interests as a fine art consultant to produce this popular volume.
ISBN 0 902028 32 4, 370pp
206 b & w illus, 32 col, £35.00

Available from:
Antique Collectors' Club, 5 Church Street, Woodbridge, Suffolk IP12 1DS
Tel: (0394) 385501 Fax: (0394) 384434

or Market Street Industrial Park, Wappingers' Falls, New York 12590, USA
Tel: 914 297 0003 Fax: 914 297 0068

Hull continued

1930, £20-£2,000; shipping goods, 1870-1940, £10-£1,000; some period furniture. Not Stocked: Jewellery and medals. LOC: Turn left at North Bridge, 1/4 mile on right. PARK: Own (rear). TEL: 0482 225220; home - 0482 666033; fax - 0482 211170. SER: Courier; packing, shipping.

De Grey Antiques
96 De Grey St, Beverley Rd. (G. Dick). Est. 1962. Open 10.30-1 and 2-5.45. SIZE: Medium. STOCK: Furniture, clocks, paintings and watercolours, Victorian; glass, china, pewter, brass, copper and oil lamps. LOC: Off main Beverley Rd., near railway bridge. PARK: Easy. TEL: 0482 442184. SER: Valuations; buys at auction.

Steven Dews Fine Art
66-70 Princes Ave. Open 9-6. CL: Sat. SIZE: Medium. STOCK: Paintings, 19th-20th C. TEL: 0482 42424. SER: Valuations; restorations; framing. VAT: Spec.

Grannie's Parlour
33 Anlaby Rd. (Mrs N. Pye). Open 11-5. STOCK: General antiques, ephemera, Victoriana, dolls, toys, kitchenalia. TEL: 0482 228258; home - 0482 41020.

Hull continued

Grannie's Treasures
1st Floor, 33 Anlaby Rd. (Mrs N. Pye). Open 11-5. SIZE: 4 dealers. STOCK: Advertising items, postcards, tins, bottles, small furniture and pre-1940s clothing. TEL: 0482 228258; home - 0482 41020.

David K. Hakeney Antiques   LAPADA
64 George St. Est. 1971. Open 10-6. SIZE: Medium plus warehouse. STOCK: Georgian, Victorian, Edwardian furniture, smalls, shipping goods. LOC: City centre. TEL: 0482 228190; mobile - 0860 507774. VAT: Stan/Spec.

Imperial Antiques
397 Hessle Rd. (M. Langton). Est. 1982. Open 9-5.30. STOCK: British stripped pine furniture, antique, old and reproduction. TEL: 0482 27439. FAIRS: Newark. VAT: Stan.

Lesley's Antiques
329 Hessle Rd. Est. 1967. Open 10-5.30. SIZE: Medium. STOCK: General antiques, shipping goods; collectors' items, mostly under £25. LOC: On main Hull to Hessle Rd. PARK: Easy. TEL: 0482 23986; home - 0482 646280. SER: Restorations; hire.

HUMBERSIDE NORTH

Hull continued
Geoffrey Mole/Antique Exports
LAPADA
400 Wincolmlee. Est. 1974. Open 9-5, Sat. 9-1. SIZE: Large. STOCK: *Shipping furniture, 1850-1920, £50-£2,000; general antiques, 19th C.* LOC: Half mile east off main Beverley Rd. PARK: Easy. TEL: 0482 27858; fax - 0482 218173. SER: Packing, shipping. VAT: Stan.

Pearson Antiques
The Warehouse, 4 Dalton St. (W.B.T. Grozier). Est. 1972. Open 10-5, Sat. by appointment. SIZE: Large. STOCK: *Furniture, pottery, brass, silver and plate, stuffed birds, stone figures, late 17th C to Edwardian, £50-£1,000.* LOC: Off Cleaveland St. PARK: Easy. TEL: 0482 29647; home - 0482 862927. SER: Valuations. VAT: Spec. *Trade Only.*

Sandringham Antiques
64a Beverley Rd. (P. and P. Allison). Est. 1968. STOCK: *General antiques.* TEL: 0482 847653/20874.

Paul Wilson Ltd
LAPADA
Perth St. West. Open 8-5.30, Sat. 8.30-11.30, other times by appointment. STOCK: *English, Scottish, Irish, Welsh, German, Austrian and Danish pine.* LOC: Near inner ring road, 10 mins. from Humber bridge. Telephone for further details. TEL: 0482 447923/448607; fax - 0482 446055. SER: Export and U.K. delivery; catalogue available. VAT: Stan.

KILHAM, Nr. Driffield
The Old Ropery Antique Clocks,
East St. STOCK: *Clocks - longcase, bracket, carriage and French, Vienna regulator, fusee and wall.* LOC: Village centre, near PO. PARK: Easy. TEL: 0262 420233. SER: Valuations; restorations (furniture and clocks); spares.

MARKET WEIGHTON, Nr. York
C.G. Dyson and Sons
51 Market Place. Est. 1966. Open 9-5.30, Sat. till 5. SIZE: Small. STOCK: *Paintings, prints, maps, clocks, jewellery, silver, £5-£600.* Not Stocked: Porcelain. LOC: On main road in town centre. TEL: 0430 872391. SER: Valuations; restorations.

Grannie's Attic
Kiplingcotes Station. Est. 1964. TEL: 0430 810284.

Houghton Hall Antiques
Cliffe Rd. (M.E. Watson). Est. 1965. Open daily 8-4, Sun. 11-4. SIZE: Large. STOCK: *Furniture, 17th-19th C, £5-£5,000; china, 19th C, £1-£600; paintings and prints, £20-£1,000; objets d'art.* Not Stocked: Coins, guns. LOC: Turn right on

Market Weighton continued
new by-pass from York (left coming from Beverley), 3/4 mile, signposted North Cave - sign on entrance. PARK: Easy. TEL: 0430 873234. SER: Valuations; restorations (furniture); buys at auction. FAIRS: New York (U.S.A.). VAT: Stan/Spec.

Pieter Plantenga
49 Home Rd. Open 9-5. STOCK: *Stripped pine, general furniture.* TEL: 0430 872473.

PATRINGTON
Clyde Antiques
12 Market Place. (S. M. Nettleton). Est. 1978. Open 10-5. CL: Sun., Mon. and Wed. except by appointment. SIZE: Medium. STOCK: *General antiques.* PARK: Easy. TEL: 0964 630650; home - 0964 612471. SER: Valuations. VAT: Stan.

SEATON ROSS, Nr. York
Lewis Hickson CMBHI
Antiquarian Horologist, 'Rosewell'. Est. 1965. Open by appointment only. STOCK: *Longcase, bracket clocks, barometers and instruments.* TEL: 0759 318850. SER: Restorations.

SOUTH CAVE
The Old Copper Shop and Post House Antiques
69 and 75 Market Place. (Mrs E.A. Featherstone). Est. 1986. Open 9.30-4.30. SIZE: Medium. STOCK: *Furniture including pine, 19th-20th C; linen, toys, general antiques and collectors' items.* Not Stocked: Militaria, coins. LOC: A1034. PARK: Easy. TEL: 0430 423988; home - 0482 631110. SER: Valuations.

Penny Farthing Antiques
60 Market Place. (C.E. Dennett). Est. 1987. Open 9.30-4.30, Sun. 12.30-4.30. SIZE: Medium. STOCK: *Furniture, 19th-20th C, £25-£2,000; linen, textiles and samplers, 18th-20th C, £5-£500; general collectables, china and glass, 19th-20th C, £5-£500.* Not Stocked: Militaria and coins. LOC: Main road (A1034). PARK: Easy. TEL: 0430 422958; home - 0430 421575. SER: Valuations; buys at auction. FAIRS: Newark.

Humberside South

AYLESBY, Nr. Grimsby
Robin Fowler (Period Clocks)
Washing Dales, Washing Dales Lane. Open by appointment. SIZE: Large. STOCK: Clocks and barometers, 17th-18th C. TEL: 0472 751335. SER: Restorations (clocks, barometers).

BARTON-ON-HUMBER
Streetwalker Antiques
35 High St. (J.N. Chapman). Open 9.30-1 and 2-5. CL: Thurs. SIZE: Small. STOCK: General antiques, 18th-19th C. LOC: South bank of Humber Bridge, first exit. PARK: Easy. TEL: 0652 33960/660050. SER: Valuations. VAT: Stan.

Streetwalker Antiques Warehouse
Brigg Rd. (J.N. Chapman). Open 9-5.30. SIZE: Large. STOCK: General antiques and shipping furniture, oak and mahogany. TEL: 0652 660050/33960. Trade Only.

GRIMSBY
Bell Antiques
68 Harold St. (V. Hawkey). Est. 1964. Open by appointment, telephone previous evening. SIZE: Large. STOCK: Pine. Not Stocked: Reproduction. PARK: Easy. TEL: 0472 695110; home - same. VAT: Stan. Trade Only.

Goodman Gold
47 Pasture St. (S.N. Goodman). Est. 1978. Open 10.15-5. SIZE: Small. STOCK: Jewellery, £25-£50; smalls, £5-£25; furniture and bric-a-brac,

Grimsby continued
£5-£50; all mainly 19th-20th C. LOC: Town centre just off Victoria St. PARK: Opposite. TEL: 0472 341301; home - 0472 360740. SER: Valuations (jewellery); buys at auction. FAIRS: Memorial Hall, Cleethorpes and local.

Simon Antiques
7 Saunders St. (S.N. Goodman). Open by appointment only. STOCK: Jewellery, smalls, furniture and bric-a-brac, mainly 19th-20th C, £5-£50. TEL: 0472 360740. SER: Valuations (jewellery); buys at auction. FAIRS: Memorial Hall, Cleethorpes and local. Trade Only.

SCARTHOE, Nr. Grimsby
Scarthoe Antiques
38 Louth Rd. (P. Bridges). Est. 1975. Open 10-5. CL: Mon. and Thurs. SIZE: Medium. STOCK: Jewellery, silver, porcelain, collectors' items, maps, prints, linen. LOC: A16. PARK: Easy. TEL: 0472 77394.

SCUNTHORPE
Guns and Tackle
251A Ashby High St. (J.A. Bowden). Open 9-5.30. CL: Wed. STOCK: Guns and militaria. TEL: 0724 865445. SER: Restorations and repairs (guns).

Mill Antiques
249 Ashby High St. (J. and B. Bowden). Open 9-5. CL: Wed. STOCK: Clocks and general antiques. TEL: 0724 865445.

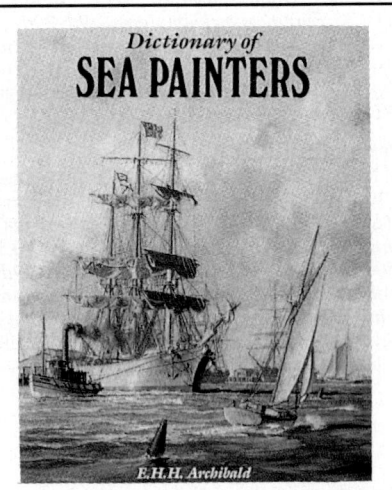

Dictionary of
SEA PAINTERS
E.H.H. Archibald

An Antique Collectors' Club Title

Dictionary of Sea Painters
by E.H.H. Archibald
A new edition of this important work with an enlarged biographical section and many additional illustrations.
**ISBN 1 85149 047 7, 576pp
932 b & w illus, 38 col, £45.00**

Available from:
Antique Collectors' Club, 5 Church Street, Woodbridge, Suffolk IP12 1DS
Tel: (0394) 385501 Fax: (0394) 384434

or Market Street Industrial Park, Wappingers' Falls, New York 12590, USA
Tel: 914 297 0003 Fax: 914 297 0068

The backplate of a timepiece pull-repeating clock by an early provincial maker, Abraham Weston of Lewes, circa 1720, showing the engraving and original backcock apron. From ***The Georgian Bracket Clock 1714-1830*** by Richard C.R. Barder, published in 1993 by the **Antique Collectors' Club, £45.00.**

Isle of Man

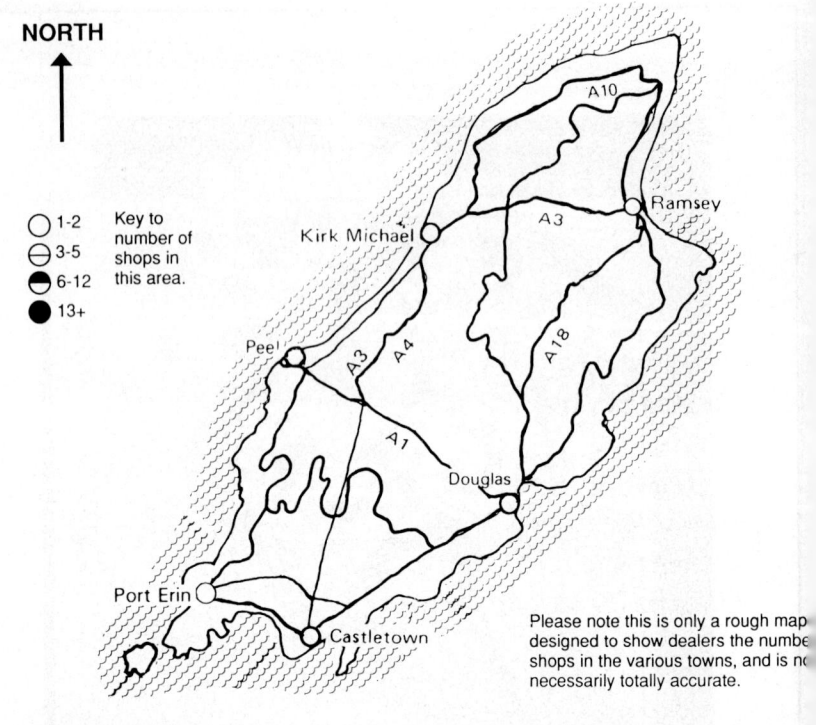

NORTH

Key to number of shops in this area.
- ○ 1-2
- ⊖ 3-5
- ◐ 6-12
- ● 13+

Please note this is only a rough map designed to show dealers the number shops in the various towns, and is no necessarily totally accurate.

CASTLETOWN

J. and H. Bell Antiques
22 Arbory St. Est. 1965. Open 10-5.30. CL: Tues. and Thurs. SIZE: Medium. *STOCK: Jewellery, silver, china, glass, early metalware, furniture, 18th-20th C, £5-£5,000.* PARK: 50yds. TEL: 0624 823132; home - 0624 822414. SER: Valuations. VAT: Stan/Spec.

DOUGLAS

Bacchus
7 North Quay. (P.H. Morrison). Open 11-6. *STOCK: General antiques especially wine related items.* TEL: 0624 663319.

John Corrin Antiques
73 Circular Rd. Est. 1972. Open Sat. 9-5.30 otherwise by appointment. SIZE: Medium. *STOCK: Furniture, 18th-19th C, £100-£6,000; clocks, barometers, 19th C.* LOC: From the promenade, travel up Victoria St., this becomes Prospect Hill and Circular Rd. is on left. PARK: Easy. TEL: 0624 629655; home - 0624 621382. SER: Restorations (barometers, clocks, furniture).

KIRK MICHAEL

Church View House Antiques LAPADA
Main Rd. (P.H. Morrison). Est. 1973. Open by appointment. *STOCK: Furniture, porcelain,*

Kirk Michael continued

pictures, glass, silver, 18th-19th C. LOC: Opposite Parish Church. PARK: Easy. TEL: 0624 878433/663319. SER: Valuations; restorations. VAT: Spec.

PEEL

Dorothea Horn At The Golden Past
18A Michael St. Est. 1982. Open 10.30-4.30. CL: Mon. a.m. and Thurs. Oct.-Mar. SIZE: Medium. *STOCK: Jewellery, porcelain, silver, glass, books, paintings and furniture, 1840-1940, £5-£100.* LOC: Main shopping street. PARK: Easy. TEL: 0624 842170; home - 0624 843839

PORT ERIN

Spinning Wheel
Church Rd. (J.G. and M.B. Craig). Est. 1979. Open 10-5. *STOCK: Silver, plate, china, glass, jewellery, pottery, furniture, linen, brass, bric-a-brac, clocks and watches, flatware.* TEL: 0624 833137/835020. SER: Restorations (furniture); French polishing; caning.

RAMSEY

P.G. Allom and Co. Ltd
1 Parliament St. Est. 1965. *STOCK: Jewellery, silver, some secondhand.* TEL: 0624 812490.

ANTIQUE COLLECTING

- Authoritative articles
- Practical buying information
- Up-to-date price guides
- Annual Investment Issue
- Auctions and fairs calendars
- Antiques for sale and wanted

The magazine is published ten times a year and contains pre-publication offers and special Christmas discounts on ACC books

Join NOW and receive your first magazine and our book catalogue FREE
Annual membership: £19.50 UK, £25.00 overseas,
US $40 USA, CAN $50 Canada

Antique Collectors' Club
5 Church Street, Woodbridge, Suffolk,
IP12 1DS, England
Tel: (0394) 385501   Fax: (0394) 384434

Market Street Industrial Park, Wappingers' Falls,
New York 12590, USA
Tel: 914 297 0003   Fax: 914 297 0068

For Collectors, By Collectors, About Collecting

Isle of Wight

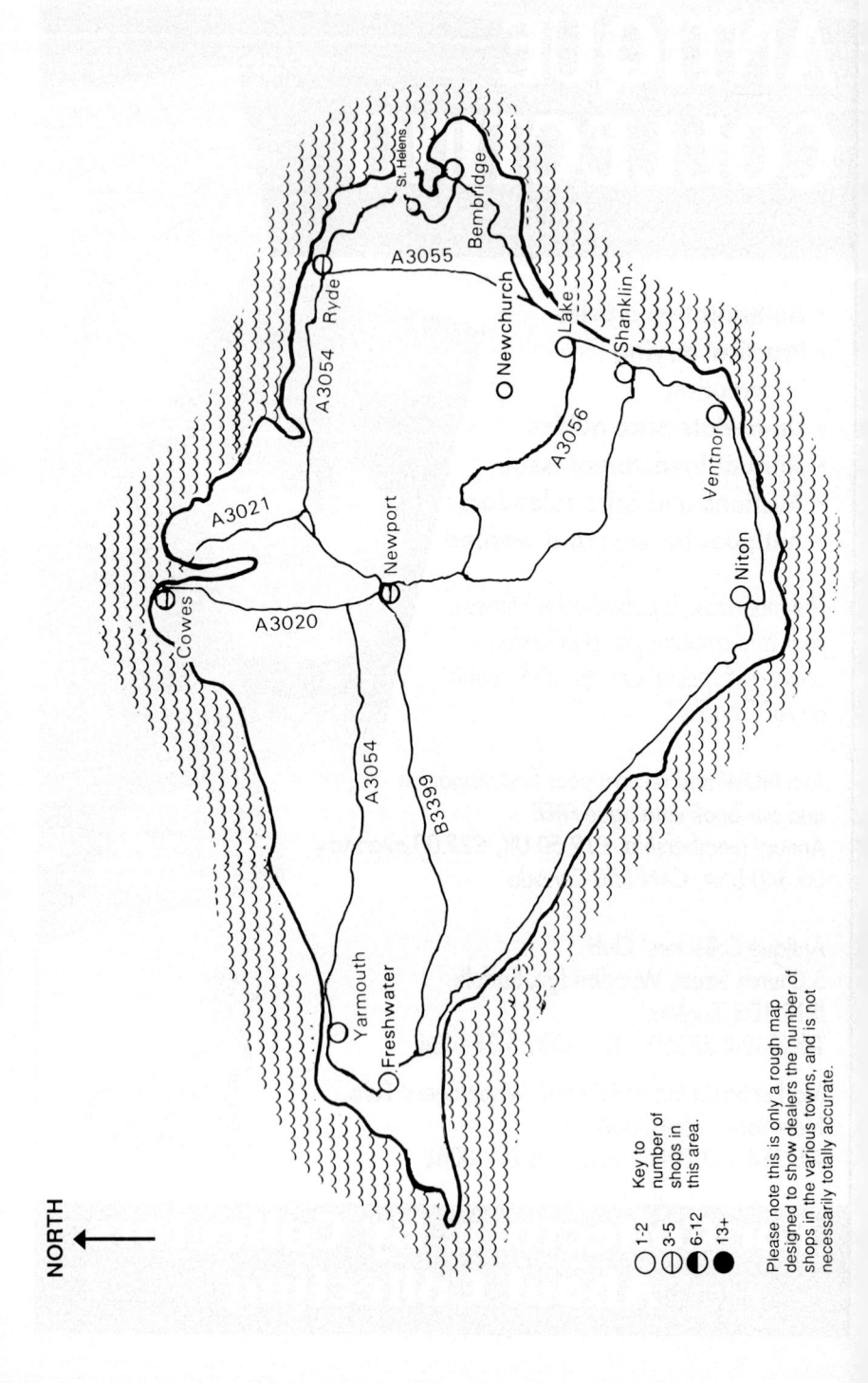

330

Isle of Wight

BEMBRIDGE
Solent Antiques
1 Dennett Rd. (J. and J. Van Daal). Est. 1973. Open 10-4, Sat. 10-5. CL: Thurs. p.m. SIZE: Small. STOCK: Clocks, £200-£3,000; furniture, £200-£1,000; both 19th C. LOC: Off High St. PARK: Easy. TEL: 0983 872107; home - same. SER: Valuations; restorations.

Windmill Antiques   LAPADA
1 Foreland Rd. (E.J. de Kort). Est. 1970. CL: Thurs. p.m. SIZE: Medium. STOCK: Furniture, silver, porcelain, jewellery. TEL: 0983 873666. SER: Valuations; buys at auction. VAT: Stan/Spec.

COWES
Julia Margaret Cameron Gallery
90B High St. (J. Flynn). STOCK: Antiquarian maps and prints especially local. TEL: 0983 290404.

Charles Dickens Bookshop
65 High St. STOCK: Antiquarian and secondhand books, especially 19th C English literature, nautical and children's. TEL: 0983 293598/280586.

Galerias Segui
75 High St. Est. 1976. Open 9.30-5. SIZE: Medium. STOCK: Pine furniture, £60-£600; prints and watercolours, £15-£200; bric-a-brac. LOC: Near Post Office and Red Funnel Pier. PARK: 200yds. TEL: 0983 292148.

The Marine Gallery
1 Bath Rd. Est. 1955. Open 11-1 and 2-5. SIZE: Medium. STOCK: Marine oils, watercolours, prints, models, £50-£20,000. LOC: Continuation of High St. leading to esplanade and sea. PARK: Easy. TEL: 0983 200124; fax - 0983 297282. SER: Valuations; restorations; framing. VAT: Stan/Spec.

FRESHWATER
Aladdin's Cave
147/149 School Green Rd. (Mrs J. Dunn). Est. 1984. Open 9.30-4.30. SIZE: Medium. STOCK: China, collectors' items, glass, linen, furniture, brass, 19th-20th C, £5-£100. PARK: Easy. TEL: 0983 752934; home - 0983 753846.

LAKE
Lake Antiques
Sandown Rd. (P. Burfield). Est. 1982. Open 10-5. CL: Wed. STOCK: General antiques, Victorian and Edwardian furniture, clocks. LOC: On the main Sandown-Shanklin Rd. PARK: On forecourt. TEL: 0983 406888/865005; mobile - 0831 442007.

free!

28 page full colour catalogue of Antique Collectors' Club books. Over 120 titles included covering a wide range of subjects: furniture, art reference, art history, prints, jewellery, metalwork, glass, horology, ceramics, oriental carpets, collectables, garden history and design, gardening and architecture.

Available free from the
ANTIQUE COLLECTORS' CLUB

5 Church Street
Woodbridge
Suffolk IP12 1DS
Tel: (0394) 385501
Fax: (0394) 384834

NEWCHURCH
Vectis Fine Arts
2 Ivy Cottages. (T.R.B. Joyner). Est. 1982. Open by appointment only. STOCK: English watercolours especially marine and Isle of Wight, and etchings, 18th-20th C, £150-£6,000. TEL: 0983 865463. SER: Valuations; restoration; framing; buys at auction (pictures). VAT: Stan/Spec.

NEWPORT
Mike Heath Antiques
3-4 Holyrood St. (M. and B. Heath). Est. 1974. Open 9.30-5. CL: Thurs. SIZE: Medium. STOCK: General antiques and bric-a-brac, 19th-20th C, £5-£500. LOC: Off High St. PARK: Nearby. TEL: 0983 525748; home - same. SER: Restorations (copper and brass). VAT: Stan/Spec.

Marilyn Rose Antiques Centre
87 Pyle St. Est. 1979. Open 10.30-4. STOCK: Silver, porcelain, jewellery, period clothes and effects, small furniture, copper, brass and bric-a-brac. LOC: Opposite R.C. Church. PARK: Easy. TEL: 0983 528850; home - 0983 293846.

Chris Watts Antiques   LAPADA
Heytesbury, Worsley Rd. Open by appointment. STOCK: Furniture, paintings, clocks and metalwork, £50-£3,000; general small items, £50-£500; all 18th-20th C. LOC: Off

HAYTER'S
Dealers in Antique and Victorian Furniture

Trade welcomed

(seven minutes by Hovercraft from Southsea)

**18-20 CROSS STREET, RYDE
ISLE OF WIGHT PO33 2AD TELEPHONE 563795**

Kirk Newport continued
Hunnyhill, old road from town centre towards Cowes. TEL: 0983 298963; mobile - 0860 342558; fax - 0983 290571.

NITON
Startime
The Star, Church St. (R. Tapley). Usually open. STOCK: *Clocks, pocket watches, 1750-1930.* TEL: 0983 730823.

RYDE
Hayter's
18, 19 and 20 Cross St. (R.W. and F.L. Hayter). Est. 1956. Open 9-1 and 2-5.30. CL: Thurs. SIZE: Large. STOCK: *Furniture including Victorian.* LOC: Through main traffic flow from sea front to town centre. TEL: 0983 563795. VAT: Stan/Spec.

Royal Victoria Arcade
Union St. Open 9-5.30; basement market open Thurs., Fri. and Sat. in summer. TEL: 0983 564661. Below are listed some of the dealers in this Arcade.

Crocus
STOCK: *Collectables, art deco to 1950's.*

Echoes
STOCK: *Costume jewellery, militaria and general antiques.*

Helter Skelter Collectables

Mary Jane
STOCK: *General antiques.*

Moonfleet
STOCK: *General antiques.*

Passing Buy
STOCK: *General antiques.*

Treasures
STOCK: *General antiques.*

Uriah's Heap
STOCK: *Jewellery, writing equipment, instruments, china, glass and collectables.*

Ryde continued
Uriah's Heap
9 Royal Victoria Arcade, Union St. (F. Cross). Open 10-5. CL: Tues. and Thurs. STOCK: *Small antiques, china, silver, collectables, linen, lace, fountain pens, jewellery.* TEL: 0983 564661.

ST. HELENS, Nr. Bembridge
St. Helens Antiques
19 Lower Green Rd. Open 10.30-1 and 2.30-5, or by appointment. CL: Mon. and Thurs. STOCK: *General antiques, ceramics, furniture, textiles, glass, Victorian jewellery, prints and violins.* TEL: 0983 874896.

SHANKLIN
The Shanklin Gallery
67 Regent St. Open 9-5. SIZE: Medium. STOCK: *Oils, watercolours, engravings, maps, 18th-20th C, £10-£600.* LOC: Town centre near railway station. PARK: Easy. TEL: 0983 863113. SER: Valuations; restorations (oils, watercolours and prints); framing.

Keith Shotter, Collectors Centre
81 Regent St. Est. 1974. Open 9.30-5. STOCK: *Coins, medals, jewellery, bottles, 50 B.C. to 1930.* LOC: 100yds. from railway station. PARK: Easy. TEL: 0983 862334/853620.

VENTNOR
Ventnor Rare Books
19 Pier St. (N.C.R. and T.A. Traylen). ABA. STOCK: *Antiquarian and secondhand books, prints.* TEL: 0983 853706; fax - 0983 853357.

YARMOUTH
Marlborough House Antiques
St. James Sq. (P.A. Webb). Est. 1972. STOCK: *Local prints and maps, silver, jewellery, pottery, glass, small furniture.* TEL: 0983 760498.

Antique Collectors' Club Titles

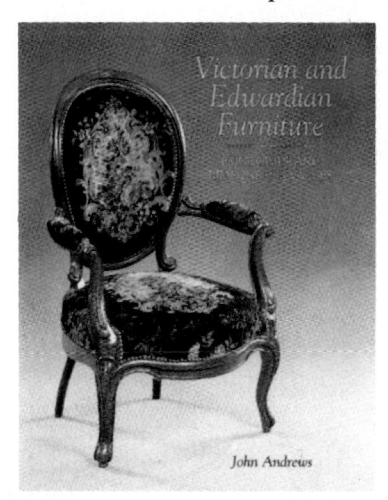

Victorian and Edwardian Furniture Price Guide and Reasons for Values
by John Andrews
In this major revision of his highly acclaimed Price Guide to Victorian, Edwardian and 1920s Furniture, John Andrews has written a thorough, logical and easily understandable guide to what is the most popular period in British antique furniture today.
**ISBN 1 85149 118 X, 300pp
1,000 b & w illus, 100 col illus, £29.95**

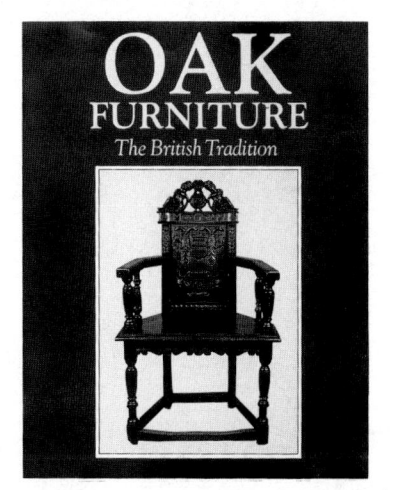

British Antique Furniture: Price Guide and Reasons for Values
by John Andrews
For the last twenty years this book has in its various editions outsold all other books on British antique furniture simply because it is unique in explaining what to look for when assessing the value of antique pieces. This classic guide consists of some 1,200 photographs specially selected by the experienced author to show just how and why values vary. In this third edition, the colour plates have been added to illustrate the huge financial importance of patination and colour, something which has never before been explained and illustrated.
**ISBN 1 85149 090 6, 392pp
1,150 b & w illus, 106 col illus, £35.00**

Available from:
Antique Collectors' Club, 5 Church Street
Woodbridge, Suffolk IP12 1DS
Tel: (0394) 385501 Fax: (0394) 384434

or Market Street Industrial Park
Wappingers' Falls, New York 12590, USA
Tel: 914 297 0003 Fax: 914 297 0068

Oak Furniture - The British Tradition *by Victor Chinnery*
The only serious book on oak in print, this important and deeply researched work examines regional influences on furniture design, construction and other methods of dating, and has a useful pictorial index arranged chronologically. **ISBN 1 85149 013 2, 620pp, 2,000 b & w illus, 22 col illus, £49.50**

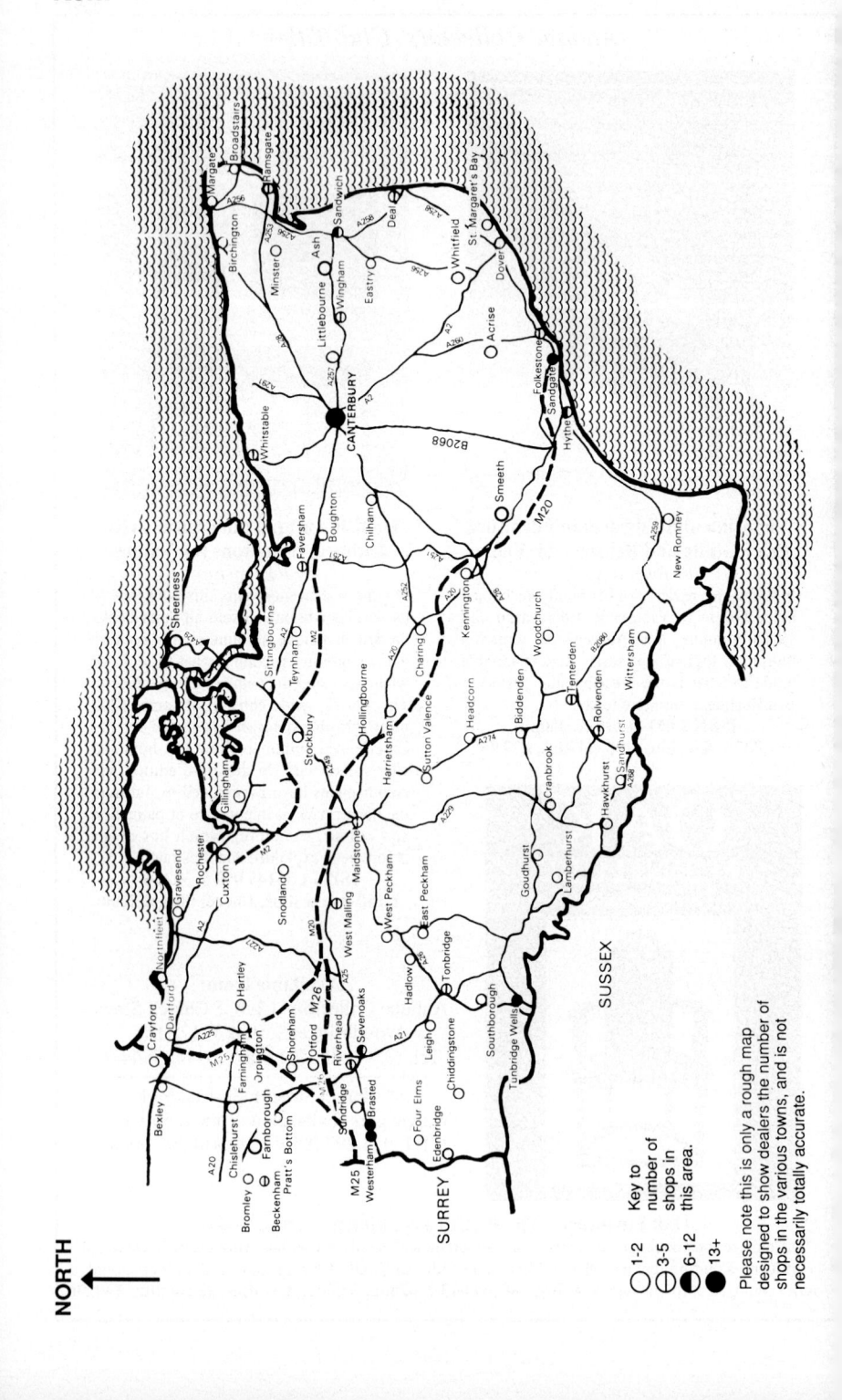

Kent

334

Kent

ACRISE, Nr. Folkestone
R. Kirby Antiques
Caroline Cottage, Ridge Row. Open by appointment only. CL: Mon. STOCK: Early period oak. TEL: 030389 3230.

ASH, Nr. Canterbury
Henry's of Ash
51 The Street. (P.H. Robinson). Est. 1988. Open 10-12.30 and 2-5. CL: Wed. SIZE: Small. STOCK: General antiques, Victorian and art deco, £5-100; small furniture, £50-£500. LOC: Main street. PARK: 50 yards. TEL: 0304 812600. SER: Buys at auction (small items). FAIRS: Ashford, Copthorne, Tunbridge Wells.

ASHFORD
County Antiques
Old Mill Cottage, Kennett Lane, Stanford North. (B. Nilson). Open by appointment. STOCK: General antiques. TEL: 0303 813039.

BECKENHAM
Beckenham Antique Market
Old Council Hall, Bromley Rd. Est. 1979. Open Wed. only 9.30-2. SIZE: 30 stalls. STOCK: General antiques. TEL: 081 777 6300.

Horton's LAPADA
428 Croydon Rd. (D. and R. Horton). FGA. Est. 1978. CL: Mon. and Wed. SIZE: Medium. STOCK: Jewellery and silver, 19th-20th C; furniture, late 18th C to Edwardian; all £500-£1,000; British paintings, early to mid 20th C, £250-£750. LOC: Junction with High St. PARK: Easy. TEL: 081 658 6418. SER: Valuations; restorations (jewellery). VAT: Stan/Spec.

Pepys Antiques
9 Kelsey Park Rd. (S.P. Elton). Est. 1969. Open 10-5.30. CL: Wed. STOCK: Furniture, paintings, clocks, silver, porcelain, copper, brass. LOC: Central Beckenham. TEL: 081 650 0994.

Scallywag
22 High St. (J.A. Butterworth). Est. 1970. Open 9.30-5.30. SIZE: Large. STOCK: Pine, 18th-19th C, £5-£5,000. LOC: 100yds. from Beckenham junction station. PARK: Easy. TEL: 081 658 5633. VAT: Stan/Spec.

Norman Witham
2 High St. Est. 1959. Open Fri. and Sat. STOCK: Porcelain, glass, small furniture, mainly Victorian, £5-£500. TEL: 081 650 9096; evenings 081 650 4651. SER: Valuations.

BEXLEY
Argentum Antiques
18-20 High St. (L.T. Laklia). Est. 1967. Open 9-5. CL: Thurs. p.m. SIZE: Large. STOCK: Silver, plate, clocks, porcelain, jewellery, paintings,

Bexley continued
prints, English and continental furniture. LOC: A210. From London take the A2 to Bexley. PARK: Easy. TEL: 0322 527915. SER: Valuations; restorations; buys at auction. VAT: Stan.

BIDDENDEN, Nr. Ashford
Two Maids Antiques
6 High St. (J. Thornley and R. Norris). Est. 1979. Open 10-5 and by appointment. CL: Mon. and Wed. SIZE: Medium. STOCK: 17th-18th C metalwork, lace bobbins, Victorian picture frames, wood carvings, treen, miniatures and small furniture. LOC: A262. PARK: Opposite. TEL: 0580 291807; home - same.

BIRCHINGTON, Nr. Margate
John Chawner
36 Station Approach. Open 10.30-12.30 and 1.30-5. STOCK: Clocks, barometers, smalls and bureaux. PARK: Easy. TEL: 0843 43309. SER: Repairs (clocks).

BOUGHTON, Nr. Faversham
The Clock Shop Antiques
187 The Street. (S.G. Fowler). MBHI. Resident. Est. 1968. Articles on clocks. Open 10-6. CL: Sun. except by appointment. SIZE: Small. STOCK: Clocks. PARK: Easy. TEL: 0227 751258. SER: Repairs (clocks).

Jean Collyer Antiques
194 The Street. (Mrs J.B. Collyer). Est. 1977. Open Tues. and Fri. 2-5, Sat. 10-5. SIZE: Small. STOCK: Porcelain, glass, furniture, general antiques, 18th to mid-19th C. PARK: Easy. TEL: 0227 751454; home - same. SER: Valuations. VAT: Stan/Spec.

BRASTED, Nr. Westerham
The Attic
The Village House. (R. and J. Brydon). ABA. Resident. Est. 1953. Appointment advisable. STOCK: Antiquarian and out-of-print books. TEL: 0959 563507.

David Barrington
The Antique Shop. Est. 1947. Open 9-6. SIZE: Medium. STOCK: Furniture, 18th C. LOC: A25. PARK: Easy. TEL: 0959 562537. VAT: Stan/Spec.

Brasted Antiques and Interiors
High St. (Mrs R.B. Rowlett). Open 10-5.30. STOCK: Furniture, paintings and bric-a-brac. TEL: 0959 564863. SER: Interior design.

Elizabeth Brooker Antiques at the Village Gallery
High St. Open 10-6. STOCK: Fine decorative Georgian furniture, clocks and objets d'art. TEL: 0959 562503.

KENT

Brasted continued
Courtyard Antiques
High St. (H. La Trobe). Open 10-5.30. *STOCK: General antiques including silver, jewellery, furniture especially extending Victorian dining tables and sets of chairs.* PARK: Easy. TEL: 0959 564483. SER: Valuations; restorations (furniture); French polishing and re-leathering.

Peter Dyke   LAPADA
Kentish House, High St. Est. 1977. Open 10-5, Sat. 1-5. SIZE: Small. *STOCK: Furniture, 18th-19th C, £500-£10,000; paintings, 19th-20th C, £500-£1,000+; decorative objects, 19th C, £150-£1,000.* LOC: A25. PARK: Easy. TEL: 0959 565020; home - 0959 562949. SER: Valuations; buys at auction. VAT: Spec.

Ivy House Antiques
High St. (R. Throp and P. Welsh). Open 10-6. SIZE: Medium. *STOCK: Furniture, porcelain, paintings, decorative items.* LOC: A25. PARK: Easy. TEL: 0959 564581; home - same. VAT: Stan/Spec.

Keymer Son & Co. Ltd
Swaylands Place, The Green. Est. 1977. Open 10-1 and 2.30-5, Sat. 10-5. SIZE: Small. *STOCK: Furniture, £100-£3,000; clocks, £200-£1,000; both 18th-19th C.* LOC: A25. PARK: Easy. TEL: 0959 564203.

Roy Massingham Antiques   LAPADA
The Coach House. Open 9-5 or by appointment. *STOCK: 18th-19th C furniture, pictures and decorative items.* TEL: 0959 562408; mobile - 0860 326825.

Old Bakery Antiques
High St. Open 9.30-5. CL: Mon. *STOCK: Country furniture and decorative items.*

Old Manor House Antiques
The Green, High St. Open daily. *STOCK: Clocks, barometers, bric-a-brac and general antiques.* TEL: 0959 562536.

Rashleigh   LAPADA
High St. (B. Jennings). Open 10-5, Sat. 10.30-5.30. *STOCK: General antiques.* TEL: 0959 563938.

Southdown House Antique Galleries
High St. (R. and D. Thomas). Est. 1978. Open 9.30-5.30. *STOCK: Furniture, porcelain, glass, metalware, tapestries, 18th-19th C; oils and watercolours, 19th C.* TEL: 0959 563522.

Dinah Stoodley
High St. (Mrs D. Stoodley). Est. 1965. Open 9.30-5.30. SIZE: Medium. *STOCK: Oak and country furniture, 1600-1800; pottery, metalware and pewter. Not Stocked: Victoriana, jewellery, silver.* LOC: A25. PARK: Easy. TEL: 0959 563616. VAT: Spec.

Brasted continued
Tilings Antiques
High St. (H. Loveland and P. Fawcett). Est. 1974 Open 10-5.30 or by appointment. SIZE: Medium *STOCK: Furniture, ceramics, decorative items 18th-19th C, £20-£2,000.* LOC: Village centre or A25. PARK: Easy. TEL: 0959 564735. VAT Stan/Spec.

W.W. Warner (Antiques) Ltd   BADA
The Green. (Mrs C.U. Warner). Est. 1957 Open 10-1 and 2-5. SIZE: Medium. *STOCK. English pottery, porcelain, glass and mahogany furniture, 18th-19th C, £100-£1,000. No Stocked: Silver, Victoriana.* LOC: A25. PARK: Easy. TEL: 0959 563698. SER: Buys at Londor auctions. VAT: Spec.

The Weald Gallery
High St. (S.J. and N.V. Turley). Est. 1972. Oper 9.30-5.30. SIZE: Small. *STOCK: Watercolours 1800-1940, £100-£5,000.* LOC: A25. PARK Easy. TEL: 0959 562672. SER: Valuations restorations (watercolours, oil paintings and prints). VAT: Stan/Spec.

BROADSTAIRS
Broadstairs Antiques and Collectables
49 Belvedere Rd. (P. Edwards). Est. 1980. Oper 10.30-4.30 winter, 10-5 summer. CL: Wed *STOCK: General antiques, linen, lace, china and small furniture.* LOC: Opposite Lloyds Bank TEL: 0843 861965.

BROMLEY
Antica
Rear of 35-41 High St. (L. and P. Muccio). Oper 10-5.30. *STOCK: General antiques.* LOC Opposite Debenhams. TEL: 081 464 7661. VAT Stan.

Bromley Antique Market
Widmore Rd. Est. 1968. Open Thursday 7.30-3 SIZE: 70 stalls. *STOCK: General antiques jewellery, books, bric-a-brac, copper, brass and clocks, collectors' items, coins, furs, stamps postcards.* VAT: Stan.

Paraphernalia Antiques and Collectors' Centre
171 Widmore Rd. (Barbara Alaszewski). Est 1982. Open 10-5.30, Sun. 10-2. SIZE: Large - 1 dealers. *STOCK: General antiques, 19th-20th C £5-£100.* LOC: From town centre, take Chislehurst road. PARK: Easy. TEL: 081 31 2997. SER: Valuations.

CANTERBURY
Antique and Design
The Old Oast, Hollow Lane. (Chris Whitfield) Est. 1988. Open 9-6, Sat. 10-6, Sun. by appoint ment. SIZE: Large. *STOCK: Pine furniture*

Canterbury continued
decorative items, 1800-1950, £5-£1,500. LOC: M2 from London, Canterbury exit, straight at first roundabout, right at second and third roundabouts, left at second pedestrian lights, shop 500 yds. TEL: 0227 762871. SER: Restorations; buys at auction. VAT: Stan/Spec.

R. J. Baker
16 Palace St. Est. 1971. Open 9.30-5.30. CL: Thurs. SIZE: Small. *STOCK: Silver and jewellery, 18th-19th C, £500-£2,000; handmade modern silverware, modern jewellery.* LOC: 5 minutes from cathedral, opposite The King's School. PARK: Easy. TEL: 0227 463224. SER: Valuations; restorations; gold and silversmiths; manufacturers. VAT: Stan/Spec.

Burgate Antique Centre
10c Burgate. (Ann and Paul Winterflood). Est. 1986. Open 10-5. SIZE: 12 dealers. *STOCK: Furniture, silver, porcelain, art deco, paintings, militaria, lead soldiers and toys, 19th-20th C.* LOC: City Wall overlooking Cathedral Gardens. TEL: 0227 456500.

The Canterbury Bookshop
37 Northgate. (David Miles). Open 10-5. *STOCK: Antiquarian books, pictures and prints.* TEL: 0227 464773.

Canterbury Weekly Antique Market
Sidney Cooper Centre, St. Peter's St. Open Sat. 8-4.

Chaucer Bookshop
6 Beer Cart Lane. (R. Sherston-Baker). ABA, PBFA. Est. 1977. Open 10-5. SIZE: Medium. *STOCK: Books and prints, 18th-20th C, £5-£150; maps, 18th-19th C, £50-£250.* LOC: 5 minutes walk from cathedral, via Mercery Lane and St. Margaret's St. PARK: Castle St. TEL: 0227 453912. SER: Valuations; restorations (book binding); buys at auction (books, maps and prints). VAT: Stan.

Coach House Antiques
Duck Lane, St. Radigunds, Northgate. Est. 1975. Open daily. SIZE: Large. *STOCK: General antiques, small furniture, ceramics, glass, linen, collectors' items and bygones.* Not Stocked: Jewellery. PARK: Opposite. TEL: 0227 463117.

Conquest House Antiques
17 Palace St. (C.C. Hill and D.A. Magee). Open 10-6. *STOCK: 18th-19th C furniture and decorative items.* TEL: 0227 464587; fax - 0227 451375.

H.S. Greenfield and Son, Gunmakers (Est. 1805)
4/5 Upper Bridge St. (T.S. Greenfield). Est. 1805. *STOCK: English sporting guns, in pairs and singles; continental sporting guns, firearms.* TEL: 0227 456959. SER: Valuations; restorations (antique firearms). VAT: Stan.

Canterbury continued
The Harvey Centre
22/24 Stour St. (B. West and D. Gilbert). Est. 1984. Open 9-5. SIZE: Medium. *STOCK: Furniture, £50-£800; decorative items, £5-£300; both Victorian and Edwardian.* LOC: Off High St. PARK: Nearby. TEL: 0227 452677.

R. and J. L. Henley Antiques
37a Broad St. Open 9-6. *STOCK: General antiques, Victorian brass beds.* TEL: 0227 769055. VAT: Stan/Spec.

Leadenhall Gallery
12 Palace St. (D.L. Greenaway). Open 10-5.30. *STOCK: Prints and maps.* TEL: 0227 457339.

Nan Leith's Brocanterbury
Errol House, 68 Stour St. *STOCK: Art deco, Victoriana, pressed glass, costume jewellery.* LOC: Close to Heritage Museum. TEL: 0227 454519.

Parker-Williams Antiques
22 Palace St. (L. Parker). CL: Sun. a.m. and Thurs. p.m. SIZE: Medium. *STOCK: Furniture 18th-19th C; porcelain, silver, bronzes, pictures, copper, brass, clocks.* TEL: 0227 768341. VAT: Stan/Spec.

Michael Pearson Antiques
2 The Borough, Northgate. Open 10-6. *STOCK: Early oak, clocks, country furniture, wood carvings.* TEL: 0227 459939. SER: Valuations; restorations (clocks).

Pine and Things
Oast Interiors, Wincheap Rd. Est. 1977. Open 9-5.30. SIZE: Large. *STOCK: Pine furniture, 19th C and reproduction, £100-£500; ornaments and collectors' items.* LOC: A28 towards Ashford, 1 mile from city centre. PARK: Easy. TEL: 0227 470283. VAT: Stan.

Rastro Antiques
44a High St. (J. Coppage). Est. 1981. Open 10-5. SIZE: 8 dealers. *STOCK: General antiques and collectors' items, furniture and secondhand books.* LOC: Up narrow lane off High St. PARK: Nearby. TEL: 0227 463537.

The Saracen's Lantern
8-9 The Borough. (W.J. Christophers). Est. 1970. *STOCK: General antiques, silver, jewellery, clocks, watches, Victorian bottles and pot-lids, Georgian, Victorian and Edwardian furniture.* LOC: Near Cathedral opposite King's School. PARK: At rear, by way of Northgate and St. Radigun's St. TEL: 0227 451968.

Stablegate Antiques
19 The Borough, Palace St. (Mrs G. Giuntini). Est. 1989. Open 10-5.30. SIZE: Small. *STOCK: General antiques, furniture and porcelain, Georgian, Victorian and Edwardian, £5-£1,000;*

> **D.R. BRYAN** **C. BRYAN**
>
> # DOUGLAS BRYAN
> ### THE OLD BAKERY
> *Early Oak & Country Furniture*
>
> ST. DAVID'S BRIDGE CRANBROOK KENT TN17 3HN
> TELE. 0580-713103 FAX: 0580 712407
>
> **LAPADA MEMBER**

Canterbury continued
jewellery, glass, objets d'art, collectables. LOC: Between Mint Yard Gate and King's School. PARK: Nearby. TEL: 0227 764086; home - 0227 831639.

Town and Country Furniture
141 Wincheap. (Thomas Moore). Est. 1986. Open 10.30-6.30. SIZE: Medium. *STOCK: Furniture and country collectables, 18th-20th C, £5-£1,000.* LOC: A28 Ashford road. PARK: Nearby. TEL: 0227 762340. SER: Valuations; restorations (furniture and metalware).

Victorian Fireplace
Thanet House, 92 Broad St. (J.J. Griffith). Est. 1980. Open 10-5.30. CL: Mon. SIZE: Medium. *STOCK: Georgian to Victorian fireplaces.* LOC: Town centre. PARK: Nearby. TEL: 0227 767723. SER: Restorations; fitting. VAT: Stan/Spec.

CHARING

Peckwater Antiques and Interiors
13 and 17 The High St. (F.H. and S.M. Tucker). Est. 1983. Open most days 10-5 (prior 'phone call advisable) or by appointment. SIZE: Medium. *STOCK: Furniture, decorative items and soft furnishings.* LOC: Centre village, close to A20. PARK: Easy. TEL: 0233 712592; home - same. SER: Interior design. VAT: Stan/Spec.

CHATHAM

Antiquities
5 Ordnance Mews, The Historic Dockyard. (P. Farmer). Est. 1989. Open daily but prior telephone call advisable. SIZE: Small. *STOCK: Chandeliers and wall lights, mainly 19th C, £100-£5,000; etchings and engravings, mainly 15th-17th C, £2,000-£4,000.* LOC: Follow signs from junction 3, M2. PARK: Easy. TEL: 0634 818866. SER: Restorations (chandeliers); commission manufacture of chandeliers. VAT: Stan.

CHIDDINGSTONE, Nr. Edenbridge

Barbara Lane Antiques
Tudor Cottage. (Mrs E.B. Avery). Est. 1967.

Chiddingstone continued
Open 10-5. *STOCK: General antiques, furniture, silver and plate, porcelain and 20th C collectables.* LOC: Behind Castle Inn. PARK: Easy. TEL: 0892 870577.

CHILHAM, Nr. Canterbury

Peacock Antiques
The Square. (S. Blacklocks). Open 9.30-6, Sat. 10-6, Sun. 2-6. SIZE: Medium. *STOCK: Furniture, 17th-19th C, £200-£4,000; silver, copper and brass, 18th-19th C, £25-£5,000; china, glass, objets d'art, 19th C, £25-£1,000.* LOC: Half a mile off Canterbury to Ashford road and 200yds. off Canterbury to Maidstone road. PARK: Easy. TEL: 0227 730219. VAT: Stan/Spec.

CHISLEHURST

Chislehurst Antiques   LAPADA
7 Royal Parade. (Mrs M. Crawley). Est. 1976. Open 10-1 and 2-5. SIZE: Medium. *STOCK: Furniture, 1760-1900; some porcelain, glass, brass and copper.* LOC: One mile from A20. PARK: Easy. TEL: 081 467 1530. VAT: Stan/Spec.

Michael Sim   LAPADA
1 Royal Parade. Open 9-6 including Sun. SIZE: Medium. *STOCK: English furniture, Georgian and Regency, £500-£50,000; clocks, barometers, globes and scientific instruments, £500-£50,000; Oriental works of art, £50-£5,000; pictures, Victorian, £100-£10,000; portrait miniatures, £300-£5,000; animalier bronzes, £1,000-£10,000.* LOC: 50yds. from War Memorial at junction of Bromley Rd. and Centre Common Rd. PARK: Easy. TEL: 081 467 7040; home - same; fax - 081 467 4352. SER: Valuations; restorations; buys at auction. VAT: Spec.

CRANBROOK

Cranbrook Antique Centre
15 High St. (Mr. and Mrs R. Bisram). Open 10-5. SIZE: 7 dealers. *STOCK: General antiques.* TEL: 0580 712173.

Cranbrook continued
Cranbrook Gallery
21B Stone St. (P.A. Donovan). Open 9.15-5, Sat. 9.15-4. CL: Mon. *STOCK: Watercolours, prints and maps, 18th-19th C.* TEL: 0580 713021.

The Old Bakery Antiques BADA LAPADA
The Old Bakery, St. David's Bridge. (D.R. and C. Bryan). Est. 1971. Open 9.30-5.30, Wed. 9-1 and by appointment. SIZE: Medium. *STOCK: Mainly English oak furniture, 17th-18th C; woodcarvings, some metalware.* LOC: Adjacent Tan Yard car park - off road towards Windmill. PARK: Adjacent. TEL: 0580 713103.

Swan Antiques
Stone St. (R.S. and Mrs A. White). Resident. Est. 1977. Open 10-1 and 2-5.15, Wed., Sun. and other times by appointment. SIZE: Medium. *STOCK: English country furniture, mainly small oak, elm, pine and painted, £15-£4,000; English pottery, treen, pictures and collectables; all pre-1890; decorative items.* LOC: Opposite Barclays Bank. PARK: Nearby. TEL: 0580 712720. SER: Valuations; interiors. FAIRS: Olympia; West London. VAT: Spec.

Wooden Chair Antiques
Waterloo Rd. (Mr and Mrs G. Evans). Open 9.30-5.30. *STOCK: General antiques and pine.* LOC: Opposite Cranbrook Public School. PARK: Easy. TEL: 0580 713671. SER: Restorations (furniture); upholstery.

CRAYFORD
Watling Antiques
139 Crayford Rd. Open 10-6.30. *STOCK: General antiques and shipping goods.* TEL: 0322 523620.

CUXTON, Nr. Rochester
The Country Pine Antiques Co
The Barn, Upper Bush Farm, Upper Bush. (G. Bruce). Open by appointment. *STOCK: English, Irish and continental country stripped pine furniture.* TEL: 0634 717982; fax - same; 0634 844090.

DARTFORD
Dartford Antiques
27 East Hill. (M. Skudder). Est. 1976. Open 10-4. SIZE: Medium. *STOCK: Furniture, 19th-20th C, £25-£100; collectors' items.* LOC: On hill into town from tunnel. PARK: Easy. TEL: 0322 291350. SER: Valuations.

DEAL
Decors
67 Beach St. (N. Loftus-Potter). Est. 1973. Open 9.30-7 including Sun; open in winter Fri.-Mon. or by appointment. *STOCK: Decorative items, general antiques and fabrics (including modern).* PARK: Easy. TEL: 0304 368030; home - same.

Deal continued
José Morales Antiques
138 High St. Open 9.30-5, Sun. by appointment. CL: Thurs. *STOCK: Furniture, early, Victorian and gilt; prints.* TEL: 0304 361461. SER: Gilding.

The Print Room Gallery
95a Beach St. (M. McKenna). Open Mon., Fri. and Sat. 10-1 and 2.30-5.30, other times by appointment. *STOCK: Antiquarian and continental prints and maps.* TEL: 0304 368904.

Quill Antiques
12 Alfred Sq. (A.J. and A.R. Young). Open 9-5.30. *STOCK: General antiques, porcelain, postcards.* TEL: 0304 375958.

Serendipity
168/170 High St. (M. and K. Short). Est. 1976. Open 10-12.30 and 2-4.30, Sat. 9.30-5, or by appointment. CL: Thurs. SIZE: Medium. *STOCK: Staffordshire figures, oil paintings and watercolours, 1780-1940, £35-£1,500; books, postcards, small furniture, collectables.* PARK: Easy. TEL: 0304 369165; home - 0304 366536. SER: Valuations; restorations (ceramics, oil paintings, watercolours, frames).

DOVER
Bonnies
18 Bartholomew St. (P. and R. Janes). Est. 1985. Open 9-5. *STOCK: General antiques.* TEL: 0304 204206/830116. SER: Upholstery; restorations.

W.J. Morrill Ltd
437 Folkestone Rd. (D. Barnes). Est. 1910. Open by appointment. *STOCK: Oil paintings, 18th-20th C, £50-£1,000.* Not Stocked: Watercolours. LOC: 1.5 miles from town centre on main Folkestone road. PARK: Easy. TEL: 0304 201989; home - same. SER: Restorations (paintings); relining and framing. VAT: Stan/Spec. *Trade Only.*

J. and L. Saunders
196/197 London Rd. Est. 1980. Open 9.30-5.30. *STOCK: General antiques.* TEL: 0304 214003.

Stuff
87 London Rd. (R. Bole). Est. 1982. Open 9.30-5.30. CL: Wed. *STOCK: General antiques.* TEL: 0304 215405.

EAST PECKHAM, Nr.Tonbridge
Desmond and Amanda North
The Orchard, Hale St. Est. 1971. Open daily, appointment advisable. SIZE: Medium. *STOCK: Oriental rugs, runners, carpets and cushions, 1800-1939, £60-£3,500.* LOC: On B2015, 150yds. south of junction with B2016. PARK: Easy. TEL: 0622 871353; home - same. SER: Valuations; restorations (reweaving, re-edging, patching, cleaning).

KENT

CHEVERTONS
OF EDENBRIDGE LTD

LAPADA MEMBER

ONE OF THE LARGEST AND MOST VARIED STOCKS OF FURNITURE IN THE SOUTH OF ENGLAND

One hour's drive from London

Car park on premises

Open Monday — Saturday 9 a.m. — 5.30 p.m.

TAYLOUR HOUSE, HIGH STREET, EDENBRIDGE, KENT
Telephone (0732) 863196 and 863358

EDENBRIDGE

Chevertons of Edenbridge Ltd LAPADA
Taylour House, 67-71 High St. (D. Adam). Open 9-5.30. SIZE: Large. *STOCK: Furniture, 17th-19th C, £100-£15,000.* Not Stocked: Silver, oil paintings, porcelain. LOC: From Westerham, on B2026 to Edenbridge. PARK: Easy. TEL: 0732 863196/863358; fax - 0732 864298. VAT: Stan/Spec.

Eden Antiques
73 High St. Open 9-5.30. *STOCK: General antiques and decorative furniture.* TEL: 0732 867346.

ELHAM, Nr. Canterbury

Howard Godfrey Antiques Ltd BADA
The Coach House, The Old Vicarage. Est. 1965. By appointment only. *STOCK: Paintings, furniture, period silver, clocks, porcelain.* TEL: 0303 840462; fax - same. VAT: Stan/Spec.

FARNBOROUGH, Nr. Orpington

Farnborough (Kent) Antiques BADA
10 Church Rd. (J.M. Dewdney). Est. 1970. Open Sat. and by appointment. SIZE: Small. *STOCK: Oak furniture, wood carvings and sculpture, 15th-18th C, £50-£3,000.* Not Stocked: Mahogany and 19th C furniture. LOC: Off A21 near Bromley, 10 mins. M25. PARK: Easy. TEL: 0689 854286/851834. VAT: Spec.

FARNINGHAM

P.T. Beasley
Forge Yard, High St. (P.T. and R. Beasley). Est. 1964. CL: Tues. *STOCK: English furniture, some pewter, brass, Delft, woodcarvings.* LOC: Opposite Social Club. TEL: 0322 862453.

FAVERSHAM

Gunpowder House Antiques
78 Lower West St. (E. Platt). Est. 1967. Open 9-6, Sun. by appointment. *STOCK: General antiques, late 18th-19th C, £10-£1,000.* LOC: From Osprynge, turn left at Alms Houses, then right into West St. PARK: Opposite. TEL: 0795 534208.

Periwinkle Press
119 West St. (A.L. Swain). Est. 1967. *STOCK: Prints, 18th-19th C, £20-£100; maps, watercolours, secondhand books.* TEL: 0795 533086; 0795 426242. SER: Restorations (prints and oils); framing. VAT: Stan.

Squires Antiques (Faversham)
3 Jacob Yard, Preston St. (A. Squires). Est. 1985. Open 10-5. CL: Wed. and Thurs. *STOCK: General antiques.* TEL: 0795 531503.

KENT

FOLKESTONE

Richard Amos
37 Cheriton High St. Open 9.30-12 and 2-5. CL: Wed. p.m. *STOCK: General antiques.* TEL: 0303 275449.

Lawton's Antiques
26 Canterbury Rd. (Ian Lawton). Resident. Open 9-5.30. CL: Wed. SIZE: Small. *STOCK: Paintings, Victorian furniture, silver and china, general antiques.* LOC: Off Dover road. PARK: Easy. TEL: 0303 246418; home - 0303 255431. SER: Valuations; restorations (paintings and furniture); buys at auction. VAT: Stan/Spec.

Alan Lord Antiques
71 Tontine St. (A.G., J.A. and R.G. Lord). Est. 1956. Open 9-1 and 2-4.30. CL: Wed. and Sat. p.m. SIZE: Large. *STOCK: Period and Victorian furniture. Rear warehouse - general goods.* LOC: Road up from harbour. PARK: Easy. TEL: 0303 253674 anytime. VAT: Stan/Spec.

G. and D.I. Marrin and Sons
149 Sandgate Rd. ABA. Est. 1949. Open 9.30-1 and 2.30-5.30. SIZE: Large. *STOCK: Maps, early engravings, topographical and sporting prints, paintings, drawings, books, engravings.* TEL: 0303 253016; fax - 0303 850956. SER: Restorations; framing. VAT: Stan.

Paul and Karen Rennie
Open by appointment only. *STOCK: Decorative arts, 1880-1960, and lithographic posters.* TEL: 0303 242090.

FORDCOMBE, Nr. Tunbridge Wells

John Speed (Maps)
The Long Barn, Ashcombe Priory. Est. 1972. Open by appointment only. *STOCK: Maps, £10-£2,000; atlases, travel and topographical books, £10-£2,000.* TEL: 0892 740688.

FOUR ELMS, Nr. Edenbridge

Treasures
The Cross Roads. (B. Ward-Lee). Open 10-5. *STOCK: Copper, brass, glass, porcelain, silver, jewellery, linen, books, toys, pine, small furniture and collectables.* TEL: 073 270 363.

Yew Tree Antiques
The Cross Roads. (P. Lewis). Est. 1984. Open 9-5. SIZE: Medium. *STOCK: Porcelain and copper, 19th-20th C, £5-£500; glass, jewellery, linen, small furniture and collectables.* LOC: Off A25 - B269. PARK: Easy. TEL: 0732 70 215.

GILLINGHAM

Dickens Antiques
42 Sturdee Ave. (G. Peek). Est. 1979. Open 9-5, Sat. 9-12. CL: Wed. *STOCK: Furniture, jewellery.* TEL: 0634 850950.

GOUDHURST

Old Saddlers Antiques
Church Rd. (S. Curd). Est. 1969. Open 9.30-12.30 and 2.30-5.30. CL: Tues. SIZE: Small. *STOCK: Small furniture, porcelain, small silver items, 1750-1870; pictures, prints, copper, horse brasses, jewellery, 19th C.* Not Stocked: Large furniture. LOC: Opposite Church. PARK: Outside. TEL: 0580 211458. VAT: Spec.

GRAVESEND

Copperfield Antiques
33 Darnley Rd. (Mrs J. Wade and Mrs C. Frid). Est. 1989. Open 10-4.30. CL: Wed. SIZE: Small. *STOCK: Mainly Victoriana, mahogany and satin walnut furniture, some smalls, £5-£500.* LOC: Near railway station. PARK: Nearby. TEL: 0474 535200; home - 0474 569982. SER: Restorations.

Greg Martin Antiques
116 Wrotham Rd. Est. 1982. Open 11-5. CL: Wed. and Sat. *STOCK: General antiques.* TEL: 0474 566067.

HADLOW, Nr. Tonbridge

The Pedlar's Pack
The Square. (Mrs Nina Joy). Est. 1976. Open 10-5.30, Wed. 10-1. CL: Mon. SIZE: Medium. *STOCK: Country furniture, £50-£600; brass, copper, glass and china, £25-£300; all 18th-19th C; small interesting items, 19th-20th C; jewellery, £40-£600.* LOC: On Tonbridge to Maidstone Rd. PARK: Easy. TEL: 0732 851296; home - same.

HARRIETSHAM, Nr. Maidstone

Judith Peppitt
Chegworth Manor Farm, Chegworth. Open by appointment. *STOCK: English watercolours, 19th-20th C.* LOC: 1 mile from Leeds Castle. PARK: Easy. TEL: 0622 859313.

HARTLEY, Nr. Dartford

Hartley Antiques
Yew Cottage, Hartley Green. (Mrs E.E. Lievesley). Est. 1968. Open 9.30-5. CL: Mon. and Wed. SIZE: Small. *STOCK: Silver, plate, jewellery, copper, brass, china, glass, £1-£100.* Not Stocked: Furniture. LOC: .75 mile from Longfield on B260. Between A2 and A20. PARK: Easy. TEL: 0474 702330.

HAWKHURST

Septimus Quayles Emporium
Ockley Rd. (Mrs M.R. Martin). Est. 1971. Open 9.30-5, Sat. 9.30-4. CL: Wed. p.m. *STOCK: General small antiques.* TEL: 0580 752222.

HEADCORN, Nr. Ashford

Penny Lampard
31-33 High St. (Mrs P. Lampard). Est. 1981.

KENT

Headcorn continued
Open 9.30-5.30. SIZE: Large. *STOCK: Stripped pine and dark wood furniture, Art Deco china, clocks and barometers.* PARK: Easy. TEL: 0622 890682. FAIRS: Sutton Valence. VAT: Stan.

HYTHE

The Den of Antiquity
35 Dymchurch Rd. (R. A. Chapman). Est. 1962. Open 9-3 or by appointment. CL: Tues. and Thurs. SIZE: Medium. *STOCK: Jewellery, silver, pottery, porcelain, glass, instruments, objets de vertu and d'art, rare and limited pieces of Royal Doulton.* LOC: A259, main coast road from Folkestone to Hastings. PARK: Easy. TEL: 0303 267162.

Hythe Antique Centre
5 High St. Est. 1973. Open 10-4, Sat. 10-5. CL: Wed. SIZE: Large. *STOCK: Furniture, china, porcelain, paintings, prints and linens.* LOC: 50 yds. from A259 at 1st turning to town centre. PARK: Easy. TEL: 0303 269643.

Kennedy Fine Arts
148 High St. (M. Kennedy). Open by appointment. SIZE: Medium. *STOCK: Oils and watercolours, from 1820, £100-£10,000.* PARK: At rear. TEL: 0303 269323; home - same. SER: Valuations. VAT: Stan/Spec.

Malthouse Arcade
High St. (Mr and Mrs R.M. Maxtone Grahame). Est. 1974. Open Fri. and Sat. 10-6. SIZE: Large - 37 stalls. *STOCK: Furniture, jewellery and collectors' items.* LOC: West end of High St. PARK: 50yds. TEL: 0303 260103; home - 0304 613270.

P.L.B. Enterprises
Open by appointment. *STOCK: Textiles, jewellery, silver and small items.* TEL: 0303 260726.

Radio Vintage
250 Seabrook Rd. (L. Riches). *STOCK: Radios, 1920-1950's.* TEL: 0303 230693. SER: Repairs.

Samovar Antiques
158 High St. (Mrs F. Rignault). Open 9-5, Wed. 9-1. *STOCK: Clocks, Oriental carpets and rugs, general antiques.* TEL: 0303 264339.

Traditional Furniture
248 Seabrook Rd, Seabrook. (M. Hannant). Est. 1977. Open daily. SIZE: Large. *STOCK: Pine, 19th C, £50-£500.* LOC: 1.5 miles from end of M20 on A259. PARK: Easy. TEL: 0303 239931. VAT: Stan.

KENNINGTON, Nr. Ashford

Peter Knight
The Mill House. Est. 1968. Open daily but appointment advisable. *STOCK: General antiques.* LOC: On A28, near The Golden Ball public house. TEL: 0233 623009. VAT: Stan/Spec.

LAMBERHURST

The China Locker
(G. Wilson). Open by appointment only. SIZE: Small. *STOCK: Prints, 18th-19th C, £5-£40.* TEL: 0892 890555. FAIRS: Hilden Manor, Tonbridge; Sacred Heart School, Tunbridge Wells; Penshurst Village Hall.

LEIGH, Nr. Tonbridge

Clive Marsden
Open by appointment only. *STOCK: Furniture and clocks.* TEL: 0732 833794.

Anthony Woodburn   BADA LAPADA
Orchard House, High St. Est. 1975. Open daily, Sun. by appointment. SIZE: Medium. *STOCK: Clocks and barometers, 17th to early 19th C.* LOC: Off A21. PARK: Easy. TEL: 0732 832258; fax - 0732 838023. SER: Valuations; buys at auction (clocks). VAT: Spec.

LITTLEBOURNE, Nr. Canterbury

Jimmy Warren Antiques
Cedar Lodge, 28 The Hill. Est. 1969. Open 9-6 including Sun. *STOCK: Mahogany and oak 1600-1900; decorative garden ornaments.* LOC: A257. PARK: Easy. TEL: 0227 721510. SER: Valuations; restorations. VAT: Stan/Spec.

MAIDSTONE

Charles International Antiques
    LAPADA
3 Market St. (Mr and Mrs C. Bremner). Est. 1968. Open 10-5. *STOCK: Victorian, Edwardian and shipping goods.* TEL: 0622 682882. SER: Valuations; full container and documentation facilities.

Salmagundi
63 Charlton St. (B.C. Shillingford). Est. 1968. Open 11.30-5.30. CL: Wed. and Thurs. SIZE: Small. *STOCK: Victoriana, bric-a-brac, collectable cameras, £5-£200. Not Stocked: Coins, stamps.* LOC: From Maidstone, 1 mile up Tonbridge Rd., turn left at Milton St., then second left. PARK: Easy. TEL: 0622 726859; home same. SER: Valuations.

Sutton Valence Antiques   LAPADA
Unit 4, Haslemere, Parkwood. (T. and N. Mullarkey and M. Marles). Open 9-5.30. SIZE: Large. *STOCK: Shipping furniture.* PARK: Easy. TEL: 0622 675332/843333/843499. Trade Only.

MARGATE

Furniture Mart
Grotto Hill. (R.G. Scott). Est. 1971. CL: Wed. SIZE: Large. *STOCK: General antiques £1-£1,500, shipping goods.* LOC: Corner of Bath Place. TEL: 0843 220653. SER: Restorations; stripping; restoration materials supplied. VAT: Stan.

KENT

Margate continued
Manor House Antiques and Furniture
45/46 Arlington Square. (D. and G.G. Rimington). Open 10-3 in winter, 10-6 in summer including Sun. *STOCK: China, porcelain, small furniture, copper and brass.* LOC: Near railway station. TEL: 0843 295025.

MINSTER, Nr. Ramsgate
Michael Lamb Antiques
The White Horse, 2 Church St. Est. 1967. Open 9.30-6 or by appointment. CL: Sat. SIZE: Small with store. *STOCK: General antiques, some shipping goods, £20-£1,000.* LOC: 3 miles from Sandwich. PARK: Easy. TEL: 0843 821666. SER: Valuations; restorations (furniture). VAT: Stan/Spec.

NEW ROMNEY
Hiscock & Hiscock Antiques
47 High St. (Erna and Paul Hiscock). Resident. Est. 1969. Open 10-1 and 2-5, Wed. and Sun. by appointment. SIZE: Small. *STOCK: Country furniture, samplers and quilts, dolls and teddies, brass and copper, 18th-19th C.* LOC: A259 coast road, town centre, next to traffic lights. PARK: Behind shop. TEL: 0679 64023; home - same. SER: Valuations. FAIRS: NEC Birmingham, Sussex Oak and Country, Ardingly, Newark. VAT: Stan/Spec.

NORTHFLEET
Northfleet Hill Antiques
36 The Hill. (Mrs M. Kilby). Est. 1986. Open Tues., Fri. and Sat. 9.30-5. SIZE: Small. *STOCK: Furniture, 19th to early 20th C, £50-£1,000; collectables, £1-£200.* LOC: A226 near junction with B261 and B2175. PARK: Easy (behind Ye Olde Coach and Horses Inn). TEL: 0474 321521.

ORPINGTON
Antica
48 High St, Green Street Green. Open 10-5.30. *STOCK: General antiques.* TEL: 0689 851181.

OTFORD
Darenth Bookshop
8 High St. Est. 1979. Open 9-5. CL: Wed. *STOCK: Secondhand and antiquarian books; prints, maps and watercolours.* TEL: 0959 522430.

Gossips
11a High St. (A. Brazier). Open 10-5.30, Sun. 11-5.30. SIZE: Medium. *STOCK: Furniture, ceramics, glass, lace and linen, 19th to early 20th C, £5-£500.* LOC: Towards Sevenoaks, 3 miles south of junction 4, M25. PARK: Nearby. TEL: 0959 524322; home - 0622 814145. SER: Valuations; restorations (upholstery, polishing and caning). FAIRS: Gt. Danes Hotel, Maidstone; Donnington Manor Hotel, Sevenoaks; Ravensbourne College, Bromley; Effingham Park, Copthorne, Sussex.

PRATT'S BOTTOM, Nr. Orpington
Celia Jennings   BADA
3 Mount Pleasant Cottages, Rushmore Hill. Open by appointment. *STOCK: Wood carvings and works of art.* TEL: 0689 853250.

RAMSGATE
Ash House
18 Hereson Rd. (P. Wimsett). Est. 1957. Open Fri. and Sat. 11-5, trade by appointment. *STOCK: Stripped pine, general antiques.* TEL: 0843 595480. VAT: Stan.

De Tavener Antiques
24 Addington St. (Mr and Mrs I.E. Gregg). Est. 1983. Open 9.30-5.30, Wed. 9.30-12.30. SIZE: Small. *STOCK: Clocks and barometers, bric-a-brac.* LOC: End of A299, above Sally Line berth. PARK: Easy. TEL: 0843 582213; home - same. SER: Valuations; restorations (clocks and barometers). FAIRS: Great Danes Hotel, Maidstone; Inn on the Lake Hotel, Gravesend.

Granny's Attic
2 Addington St. (Penelope J. Warn). Est. 1987. Open 9.30-5. CL: Thurs. SIZE: Medium. *STOCK: Pre-1940's items, £2-£500.* LOC: Left off harbour approach road or right off Westcliffe Rd. PARK: Easy. TEL: 0843 588955; home - 0843 596288.

Thanet Antiques Trade Centre
45 Albert St. (Mr and Mrs R. Fomison). Est. 1971. Open 9-5, Sun. by appointment. SIZE: Large. *STOCK: Furniture and bric-a-brac, 18th-20th C, £1-£5,000.* LOC: From London Rd. right to seafront. With harbour on right turn first left down Addington St., then last right. PARK: Own. TEL: 0843 597336; home 0843 69950. VAT: Stan.

RIVERHEAD
Amherst Antiques
23 London Rd. (D. Brick). Est. 1985. Open 9.30-5. CL: Wed. SIZE: Small. *STOCK: Furniture, £500-£3,000; porcelain, £50-£2,000; silver, £50-£3,000; Tunbridge ware £50-£1,500.* LOC: A25. PARK: Nearby. TEL: 0732 455047. FAIRS: Buxton, Guildford, Petworth, Stowe, NEC. VAT: Stan/Spec.

Mandarin Gallery
32 London Rd. (J. and Mrs M.C. Liu). Est. 1984. Open 9.30-5. CL: Wed. SIZE: Medium. *STOCK: Chinese rosewood and lacquer furniture, 18th-19th C, £200-£4,000; Oriental porcelain, £35-£3,500; Oriental paintings on silk and paper, £15-£500; both 19th-20th C; jade, stone, ivory and wood carvings.* Not Stocked: Non-Oriental items. LOC: A21. PARK: Easy. TEL: 0732 457399; home - same. SER: Restorations (Chinese furniture); framing.

ROCHESTER
Baggins Book Bazaar
19 High St. Open 10-6 including Sun. *STOCK:*

Rochester continued
Secondhand and antiquarian books. TEL: 0634 811651; fax - 0634 841851.

Cottage Style Antiques
24 Bill Street Rd. (W. Miskimmin). Open 9.30-5.30. CL: Wed. *STOCK: General antiques.* TEL: 0634 717623.

Deo Juvante Antiques
43 High St. (D.M., J.S. and M.D. Rackham). Est. 1989. SIZE: Medium. *STOCK: Furniture, 1650-1930's, £100-£500; smalls, 1800-1950's, £5-£100; gold and silver, 1750-1950's, £20-£100.* LOC: A2 into town, turn right into High St, then first right again. PARK: Limited and nearby. TEL: 0634 840422. SER: Valuations; restorations. VAT: Stan/Spec.

Droods
62 High St. (A.J. Stewart and C. Morgan). Open 10-5.30. *STOCK: General antiques.* TEL: 0634 829000.

Gem Antiques
88 High St. (Jason Hunt). Est. 1980. Open 9-5.30, Sun. 12-6. SIZE: Medium. *STOCK: General antiques including jewellery.* LOC: A20, centre of High St. PARK: Nearby. TEL: 0634 814129. SER: Valuations; restorations(jewellery). FAIRS: Barbican, Olympia, Kenilworth, Goodwood, NEC (Aug), Café Royal. VAT: Stan/Spec.

Francis Iles
Rutland House, La Providence, High St. (The Family Iles). Est. 1960. Open 9.30-5.30. SIZE: Large. *STOCK: Watercolours and oils, mainly 20th C, £50-£10,000.* LOC: Off central High St. PARK: 40yds. TEL: 0634 843081. SER: Restorations (cleaning and relining); framing. VAT: Stan/Spec.

Langley Galleries
155 High St. (K.J. Cook). Est. 1978. Open 9-5.30. *STOCK: Prints, watercolours, oils, 19th-20th C.* TEL: 0634 811802. SER: Restorations and cleaning (watercolours and oils); framing.

Memories
128 High St. (Mrs V.A. Lhermette). Est. 1985. Open 9-5.30. SIZE: Medium. *STOCK: Small furniture, £50-£500; china, £5-£75; both 1900-1950; pictures, late Victorian to Edwardian, £20-£70; collectables, bric-a-brac.* PARK: Opposite. TEL: 0634 811044.

Vines Antiques
18 Crow Lane. (J. Yale and M. Wimble). Est. 1985. Open 9.30-5. SIZE: Small. *STOCK: General antiques including furniture, collectables and ceramics, from 19th C, £1-£500.* LOC: 50 yards off High St. PARK: Nearby. TEL: 0634 815796. FAIRS: Ardingly, Newark and Detling (Kent).

ROLVENDEN, Nr. Cranbrook

Falstaff Antiques
63-67 High St. (C.M. Booth). Est. 1964. Open

Rolvenden continued
9-6. CL: Sun., and Wed. p.m. except by appointment. SIZE: Medium. *STOCK: English furniture £5-£700; china, metal, glass, silver, £1-£200. No Stocked: Paintings.* LOC: On A28, 3 miles from Tenterden, 1st shop on left in village. PARK: Easy. TEL: 0580 241234. SER: Valuations. VAT Stan/Spec.

Kent Cottage Antiques
39 High St. (Mrs R. Amos). Open 9-5.30. *STOCK Porcelain - continental including Meissen, and English; English scent bottles, silver, jewellery and small furniture.* LOC: A28, 3 miles S.E o Tenterden. PARK: Easy. TEL: 0580 241719.

J.D. and R.M. Walters
10 Regent St. GMC. Est. 1977. Open 8-6, Sat p.m. and Sun. by appointment. SIZE: Small *STOCK: Mahogany furniture, 18th-19th C.* LOC A28 turn left in village centre onto B2086, sho on left. PARK: Easy. TEL: 0580 241563; home same. SER: Restorations. VAT: Stan/Spec.

ST. MARGARET'S BAY, Nr. Dover

Impressions and Alexandra's Antiques
1-3 The Droveway. (J. Cox-Freeman). Est. 1979 Open 10-1 and 2.15-4.30, Wed. and Sat. p.m. b appointment only. SIZE: Small. *STOCK Paintings by Victorian and local artists; furniture porcelain and jewellery.* LOC: Between Dove and Deal at top of hill. PARK: Easy. TEL: 030 853102; home - 0304 852682.

SANDGATE, Nr. Folkestone

Antiques Etcetera
93 High St. (H. and M.F. Brown). Est. 1964 Open 11-12.30 and 2.30-5.30, Sun. 11-1. SIZE Small. *STOCK: General antiques - furniture books, bric-a-brac and curios, mainly late 19th t early 20th C, £5-£150.* LOC: A259. PARK: Easy TEL: 0303 249389.

Beaubush House Antiques   LAPAD
95 High St. (J. Winikus). Open 9.30-5, Sat. 10 4. *STOCK: British and Continental porcelai and pottery, 18th to early 19th C.* TEL: 030 249099/251121.

Christopher Buck Antiques   LAPAD
56-60 High St. Est. 1983. Open 10-5. CL: Wec SIZE: Medium. *STOCK: English furniture, 18t C, £500-£30,000; decorative items, 18th-19th C £50-£1,000; local interest prints, 17th-19th C, £25 £1,000.* LOC: 5 mins. from M20. PARK: Easy TEL: 0303 221229. SER: Valuations; restor ations (furniture); upholstery; buys at auction FAIRS: Olympia, Chelsea. VAT: Stan/Spec.

Churchill Galleries
13-15 Sandgate, High St. (Mrs File and Mr Elcombe). Est. 1991. Open 10-6, Sun. 11-6. SIZE Large - 10 dealers. *STOCK: Furniture, porcelai Victoriana, Georgiana, decorator's items.* TEL 0303 249574.

KENT

Sandgate continued

Dench Antiques
Cromwell House, 32 High St. (Mr and Mrs J.W.G. Elcombe). Est. 1980. Open 10-6. SIZE: Medium + warehouse. *STOCK: Continental and English furniture, decorator's items.* PARK: Easy. TEL: 0303 240824. SER: Buys at auction. VAT: Stan/Spec.

Michael Fitch Antiques   LAPADA
99 High St. Open 10-5.30, Sun. by appointment. *STOCK: Georgian, Victorian and Edwardian furniture and clocks.* TEL: 0303 249600; evenings - 0303 230839.

Freeman and Lloyd Antiques
BADA LAPADA
44 High St. (K. Freeman and M.R. Lloyd). Est. 1968. Open 10-5.30. SIZE: Medium. *STOCK: Fine Georgian and Regency English furniture; clocks, paintings and other period items.* LOC: On main coast road between Hythe and Folkestone (A259). PARK: Easy. TEL: 0303 248986 (any time). SER: Valuations. FAIRS: Olympia (Gold Section) June; Olympia (BADA Pavilion) Nov. VAT: Spec.

Robin Homewood Antiques
51/63 High St. (R.A. Homewood). Est. 1984. Open 10-6, Sun. 11-6. *STOCK: General antiques.* TEL: 0303 248987.

Hyron Antiques
86 High St. (R. Welsh). Open 9.30-5.30. *STOCK: General antiques.* TEL: 0303 240698. SER: Buys at auction.

Noble Antiques
59A High St. (F.G. Noble and 4 other dealers). Est. 1976. Open every day. SIZE: Medium. *STOCK: Clocks, furniture, silver, porcelain, jewellery, bric-a-brac, glass and pot-lids, £5-£1,000.* PARK: Easy. TEL: 0303 249466.

Nordens
43/43a High St. Est. 1946. Open 10-5.30 or by appointment. CL: Wed. p.m. *STOCK: General antiques, Victoriana, bric-a-brac.* LOC: Main Folkestone to Hythe Rd. TEL: 0303 248443.

Old English Pine
100 High St. (A. Martin). Open 10-6. *STOCK: Pine furniture and interesting items.* TEL: 0303 248560.

J.T. Rutherford and Son
55 High St. Est. 1963. Open 9-6, Sun. 9-2 or by appointment. SIZE: Medium. *STOCK: Furniture and longcase clocks; weapons - flintlock percussion pistols, muskets, edged weapons, swords including dress.* LOC: A295. PARK: Easy. TEL: 0303 249515; home - 0303 260822. SER: Restorations (furniture); buys at auction. VAT: Stan/Spec.

Sandgate continued

Sandgate Antiques Centre   LAPADA
61-63 High St. (J. Greenwall). Est. 1964. Open 10-6, Sun. 11-6. SIZE: Large. LOC: Folkestone-Brighton road. PARK: Easy. TEL: 0303 248987. SER: Valuations. Below are listed the dealers at this centre.

    David Bracewell Antiques
    Jonathan Greenwall Antiques   LAPADA
    Robin Homewood Antiques
    P. Jennings Antiques
    David Lancefield Antiques
    Annette Mobbs Antiques

SANDHURST
Forge Antiques and Restorations
Rye Rd. (J. Nesfield). Open 9-6. *STOCK: Victoriana, ceramics, glass, furniture including pine, £1-£5,000.* LOC: A268. PARK: Own. TEL: 0580 850308/850665. SER: Restorations (furniture). VAT: Spec.

SANDWICH
Delf Antiques
at King Street Antiques, 18 King St. (Mrs P. Wickens). Est. 1972. CL: Wed p.m. *STOCK: Small furniture and decorative items.* TEL: 0304 612779.

Delf Stream Gallery
14 New St. (N. Rocke). Est. 1985. Open 9-5, Wed. and Sun. by appointment. SIZE: Small. *STOCK: Art pottery, late 19th to 20th C, £50-£200; general antiques, 19th-20th C, £5-£100; pictures and prints, 20th C, £50-£500.* LOC: Main one-way road in town centre, around corner from Market Sq. PARK: Easy. TEL: 0304 617684; home - same. SER: Valuations (art pottery); restorations (as stock); buys at auction. FAIRS: Kensington Decorative Arts; Sandown Park; Dorking Halls and others.

Empire Antiques
Old Council Yard, Gazen Salts, Strand St. (D.A. Magee). Open 8-5, Sat. by appointment. *STOCK: Stripped pine and shipping furniture.* TEL: 0304 614474/612395; fax - 0304 451375. SER: Container; import; export; stripping.

Hythe Galleries
47a Strand St. (Anita Pratt and David Arthy). Est. 1974. Open 10-1 and 2-5. CL: Wed. SIZE: Medium. *STOCK: Victorian jewellery, to £10,000; silver and furniture, to £15,000; antiquarian prints, to £10,000.* LOC: Town centre. PARK: Easy. TEL: 0304 614971; home - 0227 720459. SER: Valuations; restorations (furniture and pictures); buys at auction. FAIRS: Gt. Danes, Ashford.

King Street Antiques
18 King St. (M.J. Boreham). Est. 1988. CL: Wed. p.m. SIZE: Large. *STOCK: Furniture, porcelain*

An Antique Collectors' Club Title

English Domestic Architecture
KENT HOUSES by *Anthony Quiney*
This book explains how Kent came to be the best endowed county in England for its houses which range from the lowliest of smallholder's cottages, to the grandest of magnate's palaces. Chapters on the builders, the materials they used and the historical development of their houses up to the present day are followed by a Gazetteer which puts the buildings into a village-by-village context. Nearly three hundred photographs, many in colour, complete the picture, and over one hundred detailed line drawings and a glossary leave nothing unexplained.
   Kent Houses is a treasure trove for lovers of the county, a first-class work of reference for students and practising architects and a must for architectural historians.
ISBN 1 85149 153 8, 288pp
180 b & w illus, 112 colour plates
126 line drawings, £35.00

Available from:
Antique Collectors' Club, 5 Church Street, Woodbridge, Suffolk IP12 1DS
Tel: (0394) 385501 Fax: (0394) 384434

or Market Street Industrial Park, Wappingers' Falls, New York 12590, USA
Tel: 914 297 0003 Fax: 914 297 0068

Sandwich continued
and bric-a-brac. PARK: Easy. TEL: 0304 65480; home - 0304 611904. VAT: Stan.

Noah's Ark Antique Centre
King St. (Mr and Mrs R.M. Maxtone Graham). Est. 1978. Open 10-5. CL: Wed. SIZE: Medium. STOCK: Staffordshire figures, china, porcelain, antiquarian books, watercolours, oil paintings, prints, small furniture, silver, jewellery, copper and brass. PARK: Guildhall. TEL: 0304 611144; home - 0304 613270. SER: Valuations.

James Porter Antiques
5 Potter St. Est. 1948. Open 9.30-5.30. CL: Wed. STOCK: Period furniture, brass and copper. TEL: 0304 612218.

Nancy Wilson
Monken Quay, Strand St. Open 10-5, other times by appointment. CL: Wed. SIZE: Large. STOCK: Furniture, 1600-1939; clocks, smalls, £50-£3,000. LOC: 100yds. from King's Arms public house. PARK: Easy. TEL: 0304 612345; home - same.

SEVENOAKS

The Antiques Centre
120 London Rd, Tubs Hill. (Ruth Harrison). Est. 1964. Open 9.30-1 and 2-5.30, Sat. 10-5.30, other times by appointment. SIZE: 12 dealers. STOCK: 17th-19th C mahogany, oak, Oriental and pine furniture, clocks, barometers, paintings, porcelain, jewellery, glass, silver, copper and brass, interesting and decorative items; reference books LOC: Near station, on left side of hill. PARK: Opposite or beside. TEL: 0732 452104. VAT: Stan/Spec.

Bradbourne Gallery
4 St. John's Hill. (Jane Ross Antiques and Decoration). Open 9.30-5, Sat. 9-1. SIZE: Several dealers. STOCK: Silver, furniture, ceramics jewellery, glass, prints and paintings, treen, 18th C to Edwardian. LOC: 1 mile from town centre, continuation of High St./Dartford Rd. PARK: Easy. TEL: 0732 460756; fax - same.

Chandlers Antiques
4B St. John's Hill. (C.G. Chandler). Est. 1993.

KENT

Sevenoaks continued
Open 9.30-5, Sat. 9.30-2, Sun. by appointment. SIZE: Medium. *STOCK: Furniture, 18th-19th C, £50-£1,500; glass, ceramics and pictures, 19th-20th C, £10-£500.* PARK: Opposite. TEL: 0732 743680; home - 0732 62154. SER: Valuations; restorations (furniture upholstery). FAIRS: Donnington Manor Hotel, Sevenoaks.

Myola Stead
at The Antiques Centre, 120 London Rd. Open 9 30-1 and 2-5.30, Sat. 10-5.30. SIZE: Small. *STOCK: Furniture, 18th-19th C, £100-£3,000; small decorative items - silver, boxes, glass, pictures, lighting, 19th C, £10-£500; books on antiques and collectables, £5-£100.* PARK: Opposite. TEL: 0732 452104; home - 0732 452040. SER: Book searches undertaken. FAIRS: Newark, Ardingly, Stoneleigh, Sandown Park, Great Danes Hotel, Ashford International Hotel, Copthorne Hotel.

Sheldon Ward Antiques
57 St. Johns Hill. (S.A. Ward). Est. 1966. Open Tues. and Thurs.10-5.30, Fri. 1-5.30, Sat. 10-1. SIZE: Small. *STOCK: Furniture and bric-a-brac, from 19th C, £5-£500.* LOC: Main road to Dartford Tunnel. PARK: Easy. TEL: 0732 455311; home - same. SER: Valuations; restorations (inlay, marquetry, rushing and caning).

SHEERNESS

Times Past
31A St George's Avenue. (Richard Hobbs and Lyn Luxon). Est. 1988. Open 9-4.30. CL: Wed. SIZE: Medium. *STOCK: Shipping furniture, 19th C, £50-£250.* LOC: Just off High St. PARK: Easy. TEL: 0795 660605.

SHOREHAM, Nr. Sevenoaks

The Porcelain Collector
The Old Pony Stable, High St. (D. Porter). Est. 1962. Open by appointment. SIZE: Medium. *STOCK: English and continental porcelain especially Royal Worcester, Royal Doulton, Lambeth, Dresden, Sevres, Royal Vienna, and modern limited editions of military, historical and haute couture subjects; silver, glass, jewellery, metalware, small furniture, toys, clocks, militaria; all from 18th C; art nouveau and art deco.* PARK: Easy. TEL: 0959 523416. SER: Valuations; restorations (porcelain and furniture); buys at auction.

SMEETH, Nr. Ashford

Richard Moate Antiques
Wentworth, Plain Road. Est. 1987. Open by appointment seven days. SIZE: Medium. *STOCK: Pine furniture, £1-£1,000.* LOC: 1 mile from A20. PARK: Easy. TEL: 0303 813241; home - same. VAT: Stan. *Trade Only.*

SNODLAND

Aaron Antiques
90 High St. (R.J. Goodman). Open 10-5 or by appointment. *STOCK: Clocks and pocket watches, paintings and prints, period and shipping furniture, English, continental and Oriental porcelain; antiquarian books, postcards, coins and medals.* TEL: 0634 241748. VAT: Stan.

SOUTHBOROUGH, Nr. Tunbridge Wells

Henry Baines   LAPADA
14 Church Rd. Est. 1968. Open 9.30-5, Sat. 10-4.30. *STOCK: Early oak and country furniture especially sets of chairs; French provincial furniture and decorative items.* PARK: Easy. TEL: 0892 532099. VAT: Stan/Spec.

STOCKBURY

Steppes Hill Farm Antiques   BADA
The Hill Farm, South St. (W.F.A. Buck). Est. 1965. Always open, appointment advisable. SIZE: Medium. *STOCK: English porcelain, pottery, pot-lids, 18th-20th C, £5-£5,000; small silver; caddy spoons, wine labels, silver boxes, 18th-19th C, to £1,000; furniture, 18th-19th C, £10-£5,000.* LOC: 5 mins. from M2 on A249. Enquire in village for Steppes Hill Antiques. PARK: Easy. TEL: 0795 842205. SER:

HENRY BAINES
14 CHURCH ROAD, SOUTHBOROUGH, TUNBRIDGE WELLS, KENT TN4 0RX. TUNBRIDGE WELLS 0892 532099

We offer a varied stock of meticulously restored oak and country furniture, especially dressers, farm tables and matched sets of country chairs.

LAPADA MEMBER

A beautiful wide honey coloured cherrywood drawleaf farm table extending to 11' 9", French c.1800.

Derek Roberts

24-25 Shipbourne Road
Tonbridge, Kent TN10 3DN
Tel: (0732) 358986 Fax: 0732 770637

Fine Antique Clocks

Music Boxes, Barometers
and Tunbridge Ware

*George III mahogany
longcase regulator by
Wyatt of Exeter.
One of six precision
pendulum clocks
currently in stock*

See colour advertisement
at front of book

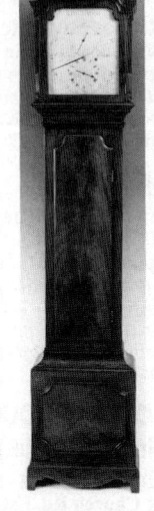

Stockbury continued
Valuations; buys at auction. FAIRS: Chelsea; International Silver and Jewellery; International Ceramics. VAT: Spec.

SUNDRIDGE, Nr. Sevenoaks
Sundridge Gallery
9 Church Rd. (T. and M. Tyrer). Open 10-5.30. STOCK: Watercolours and oils, 19th-20th C; some Oriental rugs. TEL: 0959 564104.

Colin Wilson Antiques
99-103 Main Rd. Open 10-6. STOCK: Victorian mahogany and inlaid Edwardian furniture. TEL: 0959 562043. VAT: Stan/Spec.

SUTTON VALENCE, Nr. Maidstone
Sutton Valence Antiques LAPADA
(T. and N. Mullarkey). Est. 1971. Open 10-5.30. SIZE: Large. STOCK: Furniture, porcelain, clocks, silver, metalware, shipping items, 18th-19th C. LOC: On A274 Maidstone/Tenterden Rd. PARK: Side of shop. TEL: 0622 843333/843499. SER: Valuations. VAT: Stan/Spec.

TENTERDEN
Garden House Antiques
118 High St. (H. Kirkham). Resident. Always open. STOCK: Mainly 18th-19th C furniture, paintings and porcelain; old fishing reels and

Tenterden continued
rods. PARK: Easy. TEL: 0580 763664. SER: Valuations; interior design.

The Lace Basket
1a East Cross and at Garden House, 116 High St. (C. Walls). Open Thur., Fri. and Sat 10-5 (East Cross) Mon.-Sat. (Garden House). STOCK: Textiles, Victorian linen and lace, samplers and quilts. PARK: Opposite. TEL: 0580 763923. SER: Valuations.

John McMaster BADA
5 Sayers Sq, Sayers Lane. Est. 1847. CL: Sun. except by appointment. STOCK: Furniture, engravings, silver, small decorative items. TEL: 0580 762941. SER: Valuations.

Tenterden Antiques Centre
66 High St. (B.M. Jackson). Open 10-5 including Sun. SIZE: 18 dealers. STOCK: Wide range of general antiques. TEL: 0580 765885.

TEYNHAM, Nr. Sittingbourne
Jackson-Grant Antiques
The Old Chapel, 133 London Rd. (D.M. Jackson-Grant). Est. 1966. Open 10-5, Sun. 1-5. SIZE: Large. STOCK: Country furniture, oak, 17th-19th C, £50-£2,000; period walnut, £60-£1,500, mahogany, £100-£1,000; some pine; smalls, 18th C to art deco, £5-£500. LOC: A2 between Faversham and Sittingbourne. PARK: Easy. TEL: 0795 522027; home - same; mobile - 0831 591881. FAIRS: Newark; Ardingly. VAT: Stan/Spec.

TONBRIDGE
Barden House Antiques
1-3 Priory St. (Mrs B.D. Parsons). Open 10-5. SIZE: 5 dealers. STOCK: General antiques and collectables. TEL: 0732 350142; evenings - 0732 355718.

Derek Roberts Fine Antique Clocks, Music Boxes, Barometers BADA
25 Shipbourne Rd. Author of several books on clocks. Est. 1968. Open 9.30-5.30 or by appointment. SIZE: Medium. STOCK: Fine restored clocks, mostly £1,000-£40,000; music boxes; Tunbridge Ware. LOC: A227. From London A21 Tonbridge North turnoff, left 20 yds before first lights, left again and 50 yds up on right. PARK: Easy. TEL: 0732 358986; fax - 0732 770637. SER: Cabinet and clock making. VAT: Spec.

B. Somerset
Stags Head, Stafford Road. Est. 1948. Open 11-6.30. STOCK: Clocks, £500-£5,000. LOC: Off High Street beside castle. TEL: 0732 352017. SER: Valuations; restorations (cabinets, gilt and French polishing); buys at auction (longcase and bracket clocks). VAT: Stan.

Ightham Mote. Conjecturally restored interior perspective of hall, showing the stone arch supporting the central truss of the roof, and a timber arch supporting the truss immediately before the end wall. From **Kent Houses** by Anthony Quiney, published in 1993 by the **Antiques Collectors' Club,** £35.00.

KENT

Free!

28 page full colour catalogue of Antique Collectors' Club books. Over 120 titles included covering a wide range of subjects: furniture, art reference, art history, prints, jewellery, metalwork, glass, horology, ceramics, oriental carpets, collectables, garden history and design, gardening and architecture.

Available free from the
ANTIQUE COLLECTORS' CLUB

5 Church Street
Woodbridge
Suffolk IP12 1DS
Tel: (0394) 385501
Fax: (0394) 384434

TUNBRIDGE WELLS

Aaron Antiques
77 St. Johns Rd. (R.J. Goodman). Open 9-5. STOCK: Clocks and pocket watches, paintings and prints; period and shipping furniture; English, continental and Oriental porcelain; antiquarian books, postcards, coins and medals. TEL: 0634 241748. VAT: Stan/Spec.

Amadeus Antiques
32 Mount Ephraim. (P.A. Davies). Open 10-5, Sun. by appointment. SIZE: Medium. STOCK: Unusual furniture, to art deco, £50-£5,000; china and bric-a-brac, £25-£500. LOC: Near hospital. PARK: Easy. TEL: 0892 544406; 0892 864884. SER: Valuations.

Annexe Antiques
33 The Pantiles. (M. Broad). Est. 1981. Open 9.30-5. CL: Wed. SIZE: Medium. STOCK: 1820-1920 porcelain, Staffordshire, treen, Tunbridge Ware, pictures, books, toys, silver, glass, guns. PARK: Nearby. TEL: 0892 547213.

The Antique Pine Shop
2 Mount Sion. (M. and Mrs M. Erskine-Hill). Open 10-5. CL: Mon. and Wed. STOCK: General antiques, especially pine and porcelain. TEL: 0892 511591.

Tunbridge Wells continued

Baskerville Books
13 Nevill St. (Mike Banwell). Est. 1982. Open 10-5. CL: Wed. SIZE: Small. STOCK: Antiquarian and secondhand books; small collectible antiques and occasional period and shipping furniture. LOC: 50 yards from entrance to Pantiles. PARK: Nearby. TEL: 0892 526776. SER: Valuations.

Chapel Place Antiques
9 Chapel Place. (J. and A. Clare). Open 9.30-6. STOCK: Silver, plate, jewellery, dolls, furniture, some porcelain. TEL: 0892 546561.

Clare Gallery
21 High St. STOCK: Paintings, 19th-20th C. LOC: 200yds. from Central Station. TEL: 0892 538717. SER: Valuations; restorations; framing. VAT: Spec.

Collectables
53 Colebrook Rd. (J.R. Hickmott). Open 9.30-6. STOCK: General antiques and bric-a-brac. TEL: 0892 539085; evenings - 0892 530217.

Corn Exchange Antiques
64 The Pantiles. (B. Henderson). Open 9.30-5. STOCK: Furniture, clocks, books, paintings ceramics and silver. TEL: 0892 539652.

County Antiques
94 High St. (Mrs H. Groves and Mrs I. Hale) Open 10-5, Wed. 10-1. STOCK: Small antiques and decorative items. TEL: 0892 530767.

Cowden Antiques
24 Mount Ephraim Rd. (A. Linstead). Est. 1970 Open 10-5. CL: Wed. SIZE: Medium. STOCK Period oak and mahogany, decorative items and curtains. PARK: Reasonable. TEL: 0892 520752 SER: Interiors. VAT: Stan/Spec.

Franca Antiques
2 Castle St. Est. 1981. Open 9.30-5.30 or by appointment. CL: Mon. and Wed. STOCK Furniture and general antiques, classic maps prints, postal history and stamps. TEL: 0892 525779.

Glassdrumman Antiques
Tunbridge Wells Antique Centre, Union Sq., Th Pantiles. (G. and A.Dyson Rooke). Open 9.30-5 Sat. 9.30-5.30, Sun. 2-5.30. SIZE: Large STOCK: Jewellery, silver, glass, furniture, chin and collectables, 18th-19th C. PARK: Nearby TEL: 0892 533708.

Graham Gallery
1 Castle St. (Joyce Graham). Est. 1987. Open 10.30-5, Sat. 10-5.30. CL: Mon. and Wed STOCK: 19th-20th C watercolours and Moder British paintings, £200-£5,000. LOC: Off High St. PARK: Nearby. TEL: 0892 526695/528005 VAT: Spec.

Tunbridge Wells continued
Hadlow Antiques
P.O Box 134. (M. and L. Adler). Est. 1966. Open by appointment only. SIZE: Small. *STOCK: Clocks, watches, 17th-20th C; dolls and accessories, automata, 18th-20th C; scientific and medical instruments, music boxes, singing birds, gramophones and collectors' items.* TEL: 0825 830368. SER: Valuations; restorations; buys at auction. VAT: Stan/Spec.

Hall's Bookshop
20 Chapel Place. Est. 1898. Open 9.30-5. *STOCK: Antiquarian and secondhand books.* TEL: 0892 527842.

La Trobe and Bigwood Restorations
Motts Farm, Forge Rd., Eridge Green. (H. La Trobe and C. Bigwood). Open 8.30-5.00. CL: Sat. *STOCK: Extending Victorian dining tables, chairs.* TEL: 0892 863840. SER: Restorations; re-leathering; French polishing.

Howard Neville Antiques
21 The Pantiles. (H.C.C. Neville). Est. 1967. Open 9-6. SIZE: Medium. *STOCK: General antiques, furniture, sculpture and works of art, 16th-18th C.* PARK: Easy. TEL: 0892 511461; home - 0435 882409. SER: Valuations; restorations. VAT: Spec.

Pantiles Antiques
31 The Pantiles. (E.M. Blackburn). Est. 1979. Open 10-5.30. CL: Wed. SIZE: Medium. *STOCK: Decorative items, lamps including standard, bronze, copper, brass, furniture, porcelain, pictures.* Not Stocked: Carpets. PARK: Easy. TEL: 0892 531291.

Pantiles Spa Antiques
4-6 Union House, The Pantiles. (J.A. Cowpland). Est. 1985. Open 9.30-5, Sat. 9.30-5.30. SIZE: Large. *STOCK: Furniture, £200-£10,000; pictures, £50-£3,000; clocks, £100-£5,000; pianos, £500-£10,000; porcelain, £50-£2,000; jewellery, £50-£200; silver, £50-£1,000; all 17th-19th C.* PARK: Nearby. TEL: 0892 541377. SER: Restorations (furniture). VAT: Spec.

Phoenix Antiques
51 St. John's Rd. (P. Janes, Miss J. Stott and R. Pilbeam). Est. 1982. Open 10-5.30 or by appointment. SIZE: Medium. *STOCK: Country and mahogany furniture, 18th-19th C, £50-£1,000; decorative furnishings, 18th-19th C, £5-£500.* LOC: On A26 from A21 into town, by St. John's church. PARK: Easy. TEL: 0892 549099. FAIRS: Brocante, Kensington Town Hall; Horticultural Hall, Vincent Sq.

Rare Chairs
37 Quarry Rd. (R. G. Andrews). Open 10-5.30. *STOCK: General antiques especially chairs, Dinky toys and trains.* TEL: 0892 521783. SER: Restorations; upholstery.

ANTIQUE DINING ROOM FURNITURE SPECIALISTS

Extending tables.

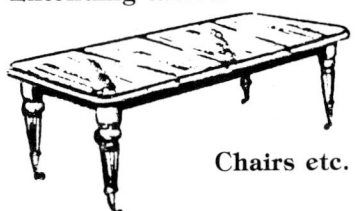

Chairs etc.

● Restoration ● French Polishing & Re-leathering
Sales for
Private ● Trade ● Export Markets

For further details of our showrooms and current stock, please phone.

LA TROBE & BIGWOOD ANTIQUES
0892 863840

Tunbridge Wells continued
Ian Relf Antiques
132/134 Camden Rd. Open 9.30-1.30 and 2.30-5.30. *STOCK: Mainly furniture.* TEL: 0892 538362.

Patricia Russell Antiques
43 Mount Ephraim. Est. 1969. Open 10-5.30 including Sun. *STOCK: Jewellery, silver, glass, porcelain, small furniture.* LOC: Junction of London Rd., and Mount Ephraim, overlooking the common. TEL: 0892 523719; home - 0892 524855.

Graham Stead Antiques Reference Books
Tunbridge Wells Antiques Centre, Union Sq., The Pantiles. Open 9.30-5, Sun. 2-5. *STOCK: Reference books on antiques and collectables, £5-£100; furniture, mainly mahogany, 19th C; £50-£2,000.* PARK: Nearby. TEL: 0892 533708; home - 0732 452040. SER: Book search. FAIRS: Newark, Ardingly, Sandown Park, Ashford, Copthorne Hotel.

Strawsons Antiques
33, 39 and 41 The Pantiles. Est. 1913. Open 9.30-5.30, Wed. 9.30-1. SIZE: Large. *STOCK: Furniture, mahogany, walnut, rosewood, 18th-19th C; silver and plate, Tunbridgeware, boxes, glass.* LOC: Follow directions to Pantiles. PARK: Easy, nearby. TEL: 0892 530607. VAT: Spec.

KENT 352

Tunbridge Wells continued

John Thompson
27 The Pantiles. (J. Macdonald and N. Thompson). Est. 1982. Open 9.30-1 and 2-5.30. SIZE: Medium. *STOCK: Furniture, 17th to early 19th C; porcelain, pottery, glass, decorative items, 18th to early 19th C; paintings, 17th-20th C.* Not Stocked: Jewellery, silver and militaria. PARK: Warwick Park/Lower Walk Pantiles. TEL: 0892 547215. SER: Restorations (furniture). VAT: Spec.

Tunbridge Wells Antique Centre
12 Union Sq, The Pantiles. (N.J. Harding). Est. 1980. Open 9.30-5. SIZE: Large. *STOCK: General antiques, reference books, Staffordshire figures, £2-£4,000.* PARK: Nearby. TEL: 0892 533708. SER: Valuations. VAT: Stan/Spec.

Up Country
The Corn Stores, 68 St. Johns Rd. (G.J. Price and C.M. Springett). Est. 1988. Open 9-5.30. SIZE: Large. *STOCK: British and European country furniture, £50-£5,000; associated decorative and interesting items, £5-£500; all 18th-19th C.* LOC: On main London Rd. to Southborough and A21 trunk road which joins M25 and M26 at Sevenoaks intersection. PARK: Own at rear. TEL: 0892 523341. VAT: Stan.

Alan Wood
at Annexe Antiques, 33 The Pantiles. Open 9.30-5. CL: Wed. *STOCK: Ceramics especially Staffordshire and Royal Doulton figures.* TEL: 0892 547213 (Mon. and Sat.) or 0474 533722.

WEST MALLING

The Old Clock Shop
63 High St. (S.L. Luck). Est. 1970. Open 9-5. SIZE: Large. *STOCK: Grandfather clocks, 17th-19th C; carriage, bracket and wall clocks.* LOC: Half a mile from M20. PARK: Easy. TEL: 0732 843246/840345. VAT: Spec.

Victoria Pataky Antiques and Reproductions
3 The Colonnade, West St. CL: Wed. *STOCK: General antiques, Victoriana.* TEL: 0732 843646.

Scott House Antiques
High St. (M. Smith). Est. 1973. CL: Wed. p.m. *STOCK: General antiques, Victoriana, curios, silver, china, furniture, clocks, prints, £5-£5,000.* LOC: Opposite county library. TEL: 0732 841380/870025.

Andrew Smith Antiques
89 High St. Est. 1978. Open 9.30-5.30, Sun. by appointment. SIZE: Medium. *STOCK: Jewellery, silver, porcelain and clocks; £50-£2,000.* LOC: Off M20, junction 4, A228. PARK: Easy. TEL: 0732 843087; home - same. VAT: Stan/Spec.

WEST PECKHAM, Nr. Maidstone

Langold Antiques
Oxon Hoath. (H.M. Bayne-Powell). Est. 1967 Open 9-1 and 2.15-5.30. CL: Sat. SIZE: Medium *STOCK: English furniture, 18th-19th C.* LOC Coming from A26, turn left at Carpenters Lane or entering Hadlow. Left at T junction, right a crossroads, 400yds. to lodge gates on right Showrooms at rear of mansion. PARK: Easy TEL: 0732 810577. SER: Restorations (furniture) VAT: Spec.

"Persian Rugs"
Vines Farm, Matthews Lane. (R. and G. King) Resident. Est. 1969. Open 9-7, Sun. by appoint ment. SIZE: Large. *STOCK: Persian rugs an carpets, to 1900, £100-£750.* LOC: A26 fron Tonbridge to Maidstone. Just off Hadlow village turn left then right, premises are first on right PARK: Easy. TEL: 0732 850228. SER: Valu ations; restorations (Oriental carpets); buys a auction (Persian carpets). VAT: Stan.

WESTERHAM

Apollo Galleries LAPADA
19 -21 Market Sq. Open 10-5.30. SIZE: Large *STOCK: Oil and watercolour paintings, bronzes 19th to early 20th C; English and continenta furniture, clocks, 18th-19th C; porcelain, glass silver.* TEL: 0959 562200. VAT: Spec.

Brazil Antiques Ltd LAPAD
2 The Green. *STOCK: Furniture, 18th-20th C* TEL: 0959 563048. VAT: Stan/Spec.

Castle Antiques Centre
1 London Rd. (Stewart Ward Properties). Est 1974. Open 10-5. SIZE: Small - 8 dealers *STOCK: General antiques, £5-£500.* LOC: Jus off town centre. PARK: Easy nearby. TEL: 095 562492. SER: Valuations.

Anthony J. Hook
3 The Green. Est. 1948. Open 9-5.30, Sat. 10-4 SIZE: Medium. *STOCK: English furniture, 18th 19th C.* LOC: A25. TEL: 0959 562161. VAT Stan/Spec.

London House Antiques
4 Market Sq. Est. 1977. Open 10-1 and 2.15-5.30 Sun. by appointment. SIZE: Medium. *STOCK Furniture, 18th-19th C; oil paintings, 18th-20t C; both £500-£4,000. Fine and rare books, fin bindings, 17th-20th C; prints and engravings 17th-19th C; all £75-£1,000; small bronzes an sculptures, including modern.* LOC: Off M25 junction 6 on A25 to Westerham. PARK: Easy TEL: 0959 564479; home - same. SER: Restor ations (furniture). VAT: Spec.

Hugh McNair Antiques Centre
1 Fullers Hill. (Stewart Ward). Est. 1991. Ope 10-5, Sun. by appointment. SIZE: Small. *STOCK Furniture and objets de vertu, 19th C, £50-£500*

KENT

Westerham continued
silver, 18th-19th C, £25-£200; dolls, 19th-20th C, £5-£1,000. LOC: Just off A25 in village centre. PARK: Easy. TEL: 0959 562970. SER: Restorations (dolls).

Mistral Galleries
12 Market Sq. (J.N. Hutchinson). Open 9.30-5.30. SIZE: Large. *STOCK: Pictures, 1750-1920, £2,000-£20,000+; furniture, 1700-1910, £2,000-£7,500+; bronze and porcelain, 1800-1900, £1,000-£5,000+.* LOC: A25. PARK: Easy. TEL: 0959 564477. SER: Valuations; restorations (pictures and furniture). FAIRS: Barbican. VAT: Spec.

Old Hall (Sphinx Gallery)   LAPADA
24 Market Sq. (L. Van Den Bussche). Open 10-5.30, other times by appointment. SIZE: Large. *STOCK: Early English and Continental oak furniture, metalware, statues, Delft pottery, decorative items.* PARK: Easy. TEL: 0959 563114.

Regal Antiques
2 Market Square. (E. Lawrence). Open 10-5. CL: Wed. *STOCK: Classic wristwatches, portrait miniatures and jewellery.* TEL: 0959 561778.

Denys Sargeant
21 The Green. Est. 1949. Open 9.30-5.30. *STOCK: Glass, especially chandeliers and candelabras, decanters and lustres.* TEL: 0959 562130. SER: Restorations (chandeliers); cleaning (chandeliers). VAT: Stan/Spec.

Taylor-Smith
4 The Grange, High St. Open 10-5. *STOCK: General antiques, books, furniture, paintings, porcelain, glass and decorative items.* TEL: 0959 563100.

Taylor-Smith
2 High St. Open 10-5; CL: Mon. *STOCK: Books and Sir Winston Churchill items.* TEL: 0959 561561.

WHITSTABLE

Laurens Antiques
2 Harbour St. (G. A. Laurens). Est. 1965. Open 9.30-5.30. SIZE: Medium. *STOCK: Furniture, 18th-19th C, £300-£500+.* LOC: Turn off Thanet Way at Longreach roundabout, straight down to one-way system in High St. PARK: Easy. TEL: 0227 261940; home - same. SER: Valuations; restorations (cabinet work); buys at auction.

Magpie
8 Harbour St. (C. Davies). Est. 1976. Open 9-1 and 2.30-5.30. CL: Sun. and Wed. except by appointment. PARK: In Sydenham St. opposite. TEL: 0227 771666. SER: Restorations; buys at auction. VAT: Stan/Spec.

Tankerton Antiques
136 Tankerton Rd. (W.R. and J. Baker). Est. 1985. Open 10-5, Tues. 10-4, Wed. 10-1. CL:

Whitstable continued
Mon. SIZE: Medium. *STOCK: Furniture, Regency to 1930's, £50-£1,500; china, from 18th C, to £1,500; glass, Regency to 1930's, to £400; postcards and other collectables.* LOC: From A299 Thanet Way take A290/B2205 turn off to Whitstable. Through town and into Tankerton. Shop on right just past roundabout. TEL: 0227 266490. SER: Valuations.

Temple Antiques
139c Tankerton Rd. (B. Von Stackelberg). Open Mon. and Sat. 11-5, other times by appointment. *STOCK: Decorative objects, period antiques, pictures.* TEL: 0227 263677.

WINGHAM, Nr. Canterbury

Bridge Antiques
97 High St. (A. and C. Cripps). Resident. Est. 1968. Open 9-5 or by appointment. CL: Wed. SIZE: Large. *STOCK: English and continental furniture, clocks, dolls and toys, books, shipping goods, bric-a-brac.* TEL: 0227 720445.

Lloyd's Bookshop
27 High St. (Mrs J. Morrison). ABA. Est. 1958. Open daily. SIZE: Large. *STOCK: Antiquarian and secondhand books, prints, watercolours, ephemera, maps, music.* PARK: Easy. TEL: 0227 720774. SER: Valuations. VAT: Stan.

Old College Antiques
31 High St. (Mr and Mrs R. Calvert). Est. 1991. Open 10-5. CL: Wed. SIZE: Medium. *STOCK: Furniture, 17th-19th C, £50-£1,000; general antiques, collectors items, £5-£1,000; paintings, £50-£2,000.* LOC: Main junction in village. PARK: Nearby. TEL: 0227 720783; home - same.

Silvesters   LAPADA
33 High St. (S.N. Hartley and Mr and Mrs G.M.A. Wallis). Est. 1953. Open 9.30-5 by appointment. *STOCK: Furniture, Georgian and Victorian; decorative items, silver, porcelain, glass.* LOC: At main junction in town. **TEL: 0227 720278 and 0843 41524.**

WITTERSHAM

Old Corner House Antiques
6 Poplar Rd. (G., F. and J. Shepherd). Open 10-5. CL: Fri. *STOCK: General antiques, country furniture, samplers; 18th-19th C English pottery including blue and white and creamware; watercolours, 19th to early 20th C.* PARK: Easy. TEL: 0797 270236.

WOODCHURCH, Nr. Ashford

Treasures of Woodchurch
1-3 The Green. (Mrs S. Cottrell). Open 10-5.30. CL: Thurs. SIZE: Medium. *STOCK: Continental and English pine, some dark wood; china, linen, domestic collectables, £1-£500.* LOC: At top of green close to church. TEL: 0233 860249.

Lancashire

354

CUMBRIA

NORTH ↑

NORTH YORKSHIRE

Cowan Bridge
Yealand Conyers
Morecambe
Lancaster
Garstang
Bolton-by-Bowland
Barnoldswick
Clitheroe
Chatburn
Sabden
Colne
Whalley
Brierfield
Trawden
Longridge
Great Harwood
Nelson
Broughton
Samlesbury
Clayton-le-Moors
Padiham
Burnley
Blackpool
Freckleton
Preston
St. Annes-on-Sea
Lytham
Blackburn
Lytham St. Annes
Feniscowles
Accrington
Haslingden
WEST YORKSHIRE
Darwen
Helmshore
Eccleston
Edenfield
Shawforth
Scarisbrick
Chorley
Burscough
Bickerstaffe
Horwich
Bury
Rochdale
Ormskirk
Wigan
Bolton
Whitefield
Atherton
Hollinwood
Saddleworth
Leigh
Swinton
Oldham
Uppermill
Ashton-under-Lyne
Manchester

MERSEYSIDE

CHESHIRE

Key to number of shops in this area.
○ 1-2
⊖ 3-5
◐ 6-12
● 13+

Please note this is only a rough map designed to show dealers the number of shops in the various towns, and is not necessarily totally accurate.

Lancashire

ACCRINGTON

Brittons Jewellers and Antiques
19 Peel St. CL: Wed. STOCK: Jewellery and general small antiques. PARK: Opposite. TEL: 0282 398577/697659.

The Coin and Jewellery Shop
129a Blackburn Rd. Est. 1977. Open 10-5.30. CL: Wed. STOCK: Coins, medals and jewellery. TEL: 0254 384757.

ASHTON-UNDER-LYNE

Kenworthys Ltd   BADA
226 Stamford St. (C.J. and M. Collings). Est. 1880. Open 10-5. CL: Tues. STOCK: Silver and jewellery, all periods, £1-£5,000. PARK: 50yds. away behind shop. TEL: 061 330 3043 (2 lines). SER: Valuations; restorations; buys at auction. FAIRS: Harrogate (N.A.D.F.); Chester; Buxton; Olympia (June and Autumn). VAT: Stan/Spec.

ATHERTON

Victoria's
144/146 Bolton Rd. (J. Stredder). Open 10-5.30. CL: Mon. STOCK: General antiques including pine. TEL: 0942 882311.

BARNOLDSWICK, Nr. Colne

Roy W. Bunn   LAPADA
34/36 Church St. Est. 1986. Open by appointment only. STOCK: Staffordshire figures, 18th-19th C, £45-£2,000. LOC: Main road. PARK: Easy. TEL: 0282 813703; home - same. SER: Valuations; restorations (ceramics); buys at auction. VAT: Spec.

BICKERSTAFFE, Nr. Ormskirk

E.W. Webster   BADA
Wash Farm, Rainford Rd. Est. 1975. Open anytime by appointment. SIZE: Large. STOCK: Furniture, early metal, needlework, treen, decorative items, 1650-1850. Not Stocked: Bric-a-brac. LOC: Exit 3, M58 on to A570, turn left 100yds. PARK: Easy. TEL: 0695 24326. VAT: Spec.

BLACKBURN

Ancient and Modern
56 Bank Top. Est. 1952. Open 9.30-5.30. STOCK: Jewellery, Victorian to date, £20-£2,000. LOC: One mile from town centre. PARK: Easy. TEL: 0254 263256. SER: Valuations; repairs (jewellery, watches); buys at auction (gold, silver, stamps and coins).

Charles Edwards Group
4/8 Lynwood Rd. Open by appointment. SIZE: Large. STOCK: Jewellery. PARK: Easy. TEL: 0254 691748. SER: Valuations; restorations (jewellery). VAT: Stan/Spec.

Blackburn continued

Mitchell's (Lock Antiques)
76 Bolton Rd. (S. Mitchell). Open 9-5. STOCK: General antiques, gold and silver jewellery. TEL: 0254 664663.

Anthony Walmsley
93 Montague St. (A. and F.A. Walmsley). Est. 1968. Open 10-6. CL: Sun. except by appointment. SIZE: Medium. STOCK: General furniture, clocks. Not Stocked: Guns or weapons. LOC: 2 minutes from town centre. Montague St. links Preston New Rd. and Preston Old Rd. PARK: Easy. TEL: 0254 698755 any time. SER: Valuations; restorations; buys at auction; shipping and packing; courier.

BLACKPOOL

Antique Dolls
29a Caunce St. (D. Kavanagh). Open 10-5, appointment advisable. STOCK: Dolls. TEL: 0253 20701.

Arundel Coins Ltd
521 Lytham Rd. Est. 1965. Open 9-5. CL: Sat. SIZE: Large. STOCK: Paintings and furniture, English and ancient coins, gold bullion coins, jewellery and silver, £50-£20,000+. LOC: Lytham Rd. runs from Central Promenade south to Blackpool Airport main gates. Shop is 1/4 mile from airport. PARK: Easy. TEL: 0253 43081. SER: Valuations. VAT: Stan/Spec.

Blackpool Antiques Centre
105-107 Hornby Rd. Open 9-5. CL: Sat. SIZE: Large. STOCK: Irish pine, English hardwood and shipping furniture. TEL: 0253 752514.

Ann and Peter Christian
400/402 Waterloo Rd, Marton. Open 10-5.30. STOCK: Decorative arts and pine furniture. TEL: 0253 763268.

Peter Ireland Ltd
31 Clifton St. Open 9-5. STOCK: Coins, banknotes, war medals and militaria; general antiques, jewellery, pottery, porcelain, commemorative ware, silver. TEL: 0253 21588.

R.H. Latham Antiques
45 Whitegate Drive. Resident. Est. 1958. Open 10-5.30. SIZE: Large. STOCK: Stripped pine, brass, copper and porcelain. TEL: 0253 393950; home - same. SER: Shipping and courier.

Nostalgia
95 Coronation St. (P. Jackson). Est. 1978. Open 10-4, including Sun. in summer. SIZE: Small. STOCK: Commemoratives, 18th-20th C, £3-£1,000. LOC: Town centre, near Winter Gardens. PARK: Easy. TEL: 0253 293251.

Past and Present
126 Harrowside. (A. Boyle). Open 10-5.30. STOCK: General antiques and bric-a-brac. TEL: 0253 42729.

LANCASHIRE

Blackpool continued

The Pine Dresser
1 Ball St, South Shore. (D. Addison). Est. 1978. Open Sat. 10-5, other times by appointment. SIZE: Small. *STOCK: Pine.* LOC: Off Lytham Rd. PARK: Waterloo Rd. TEL: 0253 403862. SER: Restorations; stripping.

BOLTON

Bolton Antique Centre
Central St. (G. Roberts and T. Owen). Open 9.30-5 including Sun. SIZE: 40 dealers. *STOCK: General antiques.* LOC: Behind McDonalds. PARK: Opposite. TEL: 0204 362694.

Corner Cupboard
2 Hawarden St. (Mrs E. Pratt). Open 10-5.30, Sat. 10-2. CL: Mon. and Wed. *STOCK: Bric-a-brac.* TEL: 0204 58948.

Curiosity Shop
832 Bury Rd, Breightmet. (G. Walker). Est. 1983. Open 9-5. SIZE: Small. *STOCK: Shipping goods, £50-£500; bric-a-brac, £1-£100.* LOC: A58, facing Safeways. PARK: Easy. TEL: 0204 21290; home - 0204 31995.

Drop Dial Antiques
Last Drop Village, Hospital Rd., Bromley Cross. (I.W. and I.E. Roberts). Est. 1975. Open every afternoon including Sun. SIZE: Small. *STOCK: Clocks, mainly English and French, 18th-20th C, £100-£4,000; mercury barometers, 19th-20th C, £100-£500; paintings, silver and general antiques, £20-£500.* Not Stocked: Stamps and armour. LOC: Beneath Last Drop Collectors Market. PARK: Easy. TEL: 0204 307186; home - 0257 480995. SER: Valuations; restorations (clocks and barometers). VAT: Stan/Spec.

Last Drop Antique and Collectors Fair
Last Drop Hotel, Bromley Cross. Open Sun. 11-4. SIZE: 40 dealers. *STOCK: General antiques and collectables.*

Memory Lane Antique Centre
Gilnow Lane, Off Deane Rd. (Mrs M. Davies). Open 9-5 including Sun. SIZE: 11 dealers. *STOCK: General antiques.* LOC: Off M61, exit 5. TEL: 0204 380383.

G. Oakes and Son
160-162 Blackburn Rd. Est. 1958. Open 9.30-5. CL: Wed. *STOCK: Furniture and bric-a-brac.* TEL: 0204 26587. SER: Shipping and packing; buys at auction. VAT: Stan.

Park Galleries Antiques, Fine Art and Decor
167 Mayor St. (Mrs S. Hunt). Est. 1964. Open Thurs., Fri. and Sat. 11-5 or by appointment. SIZE: Medium. *STOCK: English and continental furniture, 17th to early 20th C; English and continental pottery and porcelain, miniatures,*

Bolton continued

glass, brass, silver, copper; paintings, 19th C; decorative and collectable items. Not Stocked: Weapons, coins, medals, stamps. LOC: On B6202. PARK: Side and rear. TEL: 0204 29827; home - 061 764 5853. SER: Valuations; restorations (furniture; metalwork replating, pottery and porcelain, paintings; frames regilded; clock movements).

BOLTON-BY-BOWLAND, Nr. Clitheroe

Farmhouse Antiques
23 Main St. (M. Howard). Est. 1980. Open Sat. and Sun. 12-4.30 or by appointment. SIZE: Small. *STOCK: Textiles, linen and quilts, from 1830; beads and jewellery, small Victorian pottery, china, kitchenalia and brasses.* LOC: Off A59, past Clitheroe, through Sawley to village. PARK: Easy. TEL: 02006 244 or 02007 294. FAIRS: Country House events and Bailey in Lancs., Yorks. and Cheshire.

Harrop Fold Clocks (F. Robinson)
Harrop Fold, Lane Ends. Est. 1974. Open by appointment. SIZE: Medium. *STOCK: British clocks, barometers, 18th-19th C, £500-£4,000.* LOC: Through Clitheroe to Chatburn and Grindleton. Take Slaidburn road, turn left after 3 miles. PARK: Own. TEL: 020 07 665; home - same. SER: Valuations; restorations (clocks).

BRIERFIELD, Nr. Nelson

J.H. Blakey and Sons Ltd (Est. 1905)
Church St. and showrooms at, Burnley Rd., Brierfield Centre. Est. 1905. *STOCK: Furniture, brass, copper, pewter, clocks, curios.* TEL: 0282 691655/602493. SER: Restorations. VAT: Stan.

BROUGHTON, Nr. Preston

W.J. Cowell and Sons Architectural Antiques
Church Hill Lodge, D'Urton Lane. Open by appointment only. *STOCK: Coloured leaded windows, doors, telephone kiosks, post boxes, lamp posts, oak timber.* TEL: 0772 864551. SER: Export.

Village Antiques
488 Garstang Rd. (W. and L. Nelson). Open 9.30-5.30 or by appointment. CL: Sat. *STOCK: General antiques, dolls, jewellery and collectors' items, £5-£1,000.* LOC: 1/2 mile from junction 32, M6 on A6. PARK: Easy. TEL: 0772 862648/862066. SER: Valuations.

BURNLEY

Brun Lea Antiques
Dane House Mill, Dane House Rd. Open 8-6. SIZE: Warehouse. *STOCK: Georgian, Victorian, Edwardian and 1930's furniture.* TEL: 0282 413513.

LANCASHIRE

Burnley continued

Brun Lea Antiques (J. Waite Ltd)
3/5 Standish St. Open 9.30-5. SIZE: Warehouse. *STOCK: General antiques and shipping goods.* TEL: 0282 413513.

Mrs S. Falik
Est. 1970. Open by appointment only. SIZE: Medium. *STOCK: Fine 18th to early 19th C porcelain.* PARK: Easy. TEL: 0282 615172. SER: Valuations.

BURSCOUGH, Nr. Ormskirk

West Lancs. Antiques LAPADA
Victoria Mill, Victoria St. (W. and B. Griffiths). Est. 1959. Open 9-5.30, Sat. and Sun.10-5. SIZE: Large. *STOCK: Shipping furniture.* TEL: 0704 894634/893245. SER: Courier; packing and shipping. VAT: Stan.

BURY

Newtons
151 The Rock. (Newtons of Bury). Est. 1931. Open 9-5. SIZE: Small. *STOCK: General antiques, 18th-19th C, £5-£500.* Not Stocked: Continental furniture. LOC: From Manchester through Bury town centre, shop is on left 200yds. before Fire Station. PARK: 50yds. behind shop. TEL: 061 764 1863. SER: Valuations; restorations (furniture). VAT: Stan.

CHATBURN, Nr. Clitheroe

T. Brindle Antiques LAPADA
6 and 8 Sawley Rd. Open 9.30-5.00, Sat. and other times by appointment. *STOCK: Antique and decorative items.* TEL: 0200 40025; fax - 0200 40090.

CHORLEY

Charisma Curios and Antiques
Tall Trees Cottage, 91 Wigan Rd., Euxton. (N. and V.M. Langton). Est. 1977. Open by appointment. *STOCK: General antiques, period furniture.* LOC: A49. PARK: Outside. TEL: 025 72 76845. SER: Restorations (furniture); cane and rush seating.

CLAYTON-LE-MOORS, Nr. Accrington

Edward V. Phillips (Antiques)
238 Whalley Rd. Est. 1980. Open 10-12 and 1-5, Tues. and Fri. 1.30-5, Sat. 10-3, Sun. 12-2. SIZE: Medium. *STOCK: Stripped satin walnut, late 19th C, £100-£500; stripped pine, mid to late 19th C, £100-£500; shipping goods, early 20th C, £50-£1,000.* LOC: 1/2 mile from M65 on A680. PARK: Easy. TEL: 0254 396739; home - 0254 384979. SER: Valuations; restorations (hand stripping, finishing and repairs). VAT: Stan/Spec.

Sparth House Antiques
Sparth House, Whalley Rd. (W. and B. Coleman). Est. 1967. TEL: 0254 872263.

CLITHEROE

Castle Antiques
15 Moor Lane. (J. and B. Tomkinson). Est. 1967. Open 10.30-4.45. CL: Mon. and Wed. SIZE: Large. *STOCK: Shipping goods, stained glass windows, painted pine, Lloyd loom items, clocks, furniture including gateleg tables, large wardrobes and satinwood bedroom suites.* TEL: 0200 26568; home - 0200 41903.

Ethos Gallery
4 York St. (F. and P. Barnes). Est. 1978. Open 9-5, Wed. and Sun. by appointment. SIZE: Medium. *STOCK: Oil paintings and watercolours, 19th-20th C, £100-£5,000; English crystal, 20th C, £5-£100.* LOC: A59 in town centre. PARK: Own. TEL: 0200 27878; home - 0200 22597. SER: Valuations; restorations (oils and watercolours). VAT: Stan.

Lee's Antiques
59 Whalley Rd. (A. Lee). *STOCK: General antiques.* TEL: 0200 24921; home - 0200 25441.

Rebecca Antiques
22 Moor Lane. (B. and A. Donovan). Est. 1967. Open 9-5. CL: Wed. and Sun. except by appointment. SIZE: Medium. *STOCK: Decorative and upholstered items, furniture, £100-£2,000; pictures, brass and objects, £5-£2,000; all 19th-20th C; garden furniture, small architectural items, 18th-20th C, £20-£2,000.* LOC: 15 miles from junction 31, M6, via A59. PARK: Opposite. TEL: 0200 29461; home - 0200 28863. VAT: Stan/Spec.

COLNE

Enloc Antiques
Birchenlee Mill, Lenches Rd. Est. 1978. Open 9-5, Sat. 9-1 or by appointment. SIZE: Warehouse. *STOCK: Pine, 18th-19th C, £5-£1,000; kitchen chairs, 19th C, £25-£45.* TEL: 0282 867101. SER: Restorations (hot stripping, polishing and joinery). VAT: Stan.

COWAN BRIDGE, Via Carnforth

Edward King
Overtown. Est. 1976. Open 9-1 and 2-5.30, lunchtime and Sat. by appointment. SIZE: Small. *STOCK: Drawings, watercolours and oils, 18th-20th C, £500-£5,000.* LOC: 3/4 mile from crossroads in Cowan Bridge on A65, two miles south of Kirkby Lonsdale. PARK: Easy. TEL: 05242 71679. SER: Valuations; restorations (works on paper and oil paintings); buys at auction (as stock). VAT: Stan/Spec.

DARWEN

Cottage Antiques
135 Blackburn Rd. (J. and K. Entwistle). Est. 1983. Open Thurs. and Fri. 3.30-6, Sat. 11.30-4.30, other times by appointment. SIZE: Small.

LANCASHIRE

Darwen continued
STOCK: *Porcelain including Crown Derby and Doulton, £15-£500; small furniture, 19th C, £100-£1,000.* LOC: A666 into Darwen from Blackburn. PARK: Free, opposite by St. Cuthbert's church. TEL: 0254 775891 or 0254 676840 (answerphone).

Darwen Antique Centre
Provident Hall, The Green. (M. Manning and J. Cooney). Est. 1971. Open 9.30-5, Sun 11-5. CL: Tues. SIZE: Large. STOCK: *Pottery, glass, pictures and furniture, £1-£5,000.* LOC: A666, town centre. PARK: Easy. TEL: 0254 760565; home - 0254 776644/776551. SER: Valuations; buys at auction. VAT: Stan/Spec.

K.C. Antiques   LAPADA
538 Bolton Rd. (K. and J. Anderton). Resident. Open 9-6, Sun. 12-5. STOCK: *Georgian, Victorian and Edwardian furniture and decorative items.* LOC: A666. PARK: Easy. TEL: 0254 772252; home - same. SER: Buys at auction. VAT: Stan/Spec.

ECCLESTON

3 L's Antiques
Unit 4 The Arches, Grove Development Centre. (L. Frost). Est. 1989. Open 12-3.30, Sun. 11-5. SIZE: Small. STOCK: *Furniture, 1850-1940, £50-£500; gramophones, 1895-1940, £50-£500; pottery, porcelain and brassware.* LOC: Junction 27, M6, village is 4 miles north via Mossy Lea Rd. Shop situated at Bygone Times Centre. PARK: Easy. TEL: 0257 450290; home - 0942 861105.

Bygone Times Ltd
Grove Mill, The Green. (G. Wilson). Open 8-6 including Sun. SIZE: 150 dealers. STOCK: *General antiques including architectural and North American artifacts.* TEL: 0257 453780.

EDENFIELD, Nr. Bury
The Antique Shop
17 Market St. (J. and J.C. Salisbury). Est. 1964. Open 10-4. SIZE: Large. STOCK: *General antiques, shipping goods, £1-£10,000.* LOC: On A56. PARK: Easy. TEL: 070 682 3107/2351. SER: Valuations. VAT: Stan/Spec.

FENISCOWLES, Nr. Blackburn
Old Smithy
726 Preston Old Rd. (R.C. Lynch). Est. 1967. Open 9-5. SIZE: Large. STOCK: *Period and Victorian fireplaces, pub and architectural items, violins and musical instruments, brass beds, lamps, furniture, shipping items, clothes, Victorian to 1950; jewellery, brass, copper, Victorian lace and linen.* LOC: Opposite Fieldens Arms. PARK: Own or nearby. TEL: 0254 209943; 0254 580874; 0254 249098. SER: Valuations; restorations (wooden items); buys at auction. FAIRS: Park Hall, Charnock Richard.

FRECKLETON, Nr. Preston
L. Booth Antiques and Reproductions
Freckleton Boat Yard, Poolside. Open 10-5 including Sun. STOCK: *Victorian and Edwardian furniture.* TEL: 0772 632439. SER: Restorations.

GARSTANG
Clare's Antiques and Auction Galleries
Wheatsheaf Buildings, Park Hill. (Mrs C.A.L. Campbell-Cameron and Mrs C.L. Allen). Est. 1960. Open 10-4. CL: Mon. and Wed. SIZE: Large. STOCK: *Royal Worcester porcelain, early 20th C, £150-£4,000; Rudelstadt, Meissen, Dresden figures, 19th C, £500-£2,000; silver, jewellery, small furniture.* LOC: Off A6. PARK: Easy. TEL: 0995 605702; home - same. SER: Valuations; restorations (porcelain, jewellery); buys at auction.

GREAT HARWOOD, Nr. Blackburn
Benny Charlesworth's Snuff Box
51 Blackburn Rd. (A. and N. Bartholomew). Est. 1984. Open 10-1 and 2-5, Sat. 10-12. CL: Tues. SIZE: Small. STOCK: *Furniture, china, metal, linen, costume jewellery, prints and paintings.* LOC: 200yds. from town hall clock, off A680. PARK: In front. TEL: 0254 888550. FAIRS: Local.

HASLINGDEN
P.J. Brown Antiques
8 Church St. Open 10-5, Sat. and Sun. by appointment. SIZE: Large and warehouse. STOCK: *General antiques and shipping goods.* LOC: Town centre, off Bury Road, close to M66 and M65. PARK: Easy. TEL: 0706 224888. VAT: Stan.

Clifton House Antiques
Clifton House, 198 Blackburn Rd. (D. Clink). Est. 1958. Open 9-5. SIZE: Medium. STOCK: *General antiques, £5-£500.* PARK: Easy. TEL: 0706 214895.

Fieldings Antiques
176, 178 and 180 Blackburn Rd. Est. 1956. Open 9-4.30, Fri. 9-4. CL: Thurs. SIZE: Large. STOCK: *Longcase clocks, £30-£2,000; wall clocks, sets of chairs, pine, period oak, French furniture, glass shipping goods, toys, steam engines, veteran cars vintage and veteran motor cycles.* PARK: Easy TEL: 0254 63358 or 0706 214254.

P.W. Norgrove - Antique Clocks
38 Bury Rd. Open 9.30-5.30, Sat. 10-5 or by appointment. STOCK: *Longcase and wall clocks* TEL: 0706 211995.

HELMSHORE, Rossendale
Gregory's Antique Pine
Albert Mill. (D. Kennedy). Open 9-5, Sat. 12-5 STOCK: *Pine.* TEL: 0706 220049.

HOLLINWOOD, Nr. Oldham
Fernlea Antiques
305 Manchester Rd. (A.J. and Mrs B. McLaughlin). Open 10-5. *STOCK: General antiques and shipping goods.* TEL: 061 682 0589.

R. J. O'Brien and Son Antiques
291 and 293 Manchester Rd. Est. 1970. Open 9-5, Sat. 9-12 or by appointment. SIZE: Large and trade warehouse. *STOCK: Furniture, Edwardian, Victorian, and 1930's; shipping goods; general antiques and pianos.* LOC: On main Manchester to Oldham rd. PARK: Opposite. TEL: 061 683 4717; home - 061 626 2062.

HORWICH, Nr. Bolton
Alan Butterworth (Horwich)
Unit 6, Union Mill, Albert St. Open by appointment. *STOCK: Continental furniture, 18th-19th C; art nouveau, shipping goods.* TEL: 0204 68094. SER: Export; packing and shipping; courier (GB and Europe).

LANCASTER
Articles Antiques
134/136 Greaves Rd. (J.W. and L.J. Forsyth). Est. 1981. Open 10-5. SIZE: Medium. *STOCK: Furniture, including shipping, £50-£2,000; porcelain, china and glass, £30-£2,000;clocks, £20-£2,000; all 18th-20th C.* LOC: A6 through town from M6, junction 34. PARK: Easy. TEL: 0524 39312; home - 05242 62294. SER: Valuations; repairs (clocks). VAT: Stan/Spec.

The Assembly Rooms Market
King St. Open Thurs., Fri. and Sat. 10-4.30. SIZE: Several dealers. *STOCK: General antiques, jewellery, collectables, period clothing, books and tools, records and stamps.* TEL: Market Superintendent - 0524 66627.

G.B. Antiques Ltd
Lancaster Leisure Park, Wyresdale Rd. (Mrs G. Blackburn). Open 10-5 including Sun. SIZE: Large. 100+ dealers. *STOCK: Porcelain, glass and silver, late 19th to early 20th C; small furniture, Victorian to early 20th C.* LOC: Off M6, junction 33 or 34. PARK: Easy. TEL: 0524 844734; fax - 0524 844735; home - 0772 861593. SER: Valuations; buys at auction. VAT: Stan/Spec.

G.W. Antiques
47 North Rd. and 4 St. Georges Quay Works, St. Georges Quay. (G. Woods). Est. 1978. Open 9-5.30. SIZE: Large and warehouse. *STOCK: Stripped pine, 18th to early 20th C, £30-£1,500; furniture, all periods.* LOC: A6. PARK: 60yds. TEL: 0524 32050/841148. SER: Valuations; restorations (furniture); stripping. VAT: Stan/Spec.

G.B. ANTIQUE CENTRE LANCASTER

Over 100 dealers in 30,000 sq. ft. of space. Showing PORCELAIN, POTTERY, ART DECO, GLASS, BOOKS and LINEN. Also a large selection of MAHOGANY, OAK and PINE FURNITURE.

**OPEN 7 DAYS A WEEK
10.00-5.00**

Plenty of Parking. Cafe and Toilets on site. Come browse and enjoy a tremendous selection of Antiques and Collectables.

G.B. Antiques Ltd.
Lancaster Leisure Park, the former Hornsea Pottery, Wyresdale Rd.,
Lancaster LA1 3LA
Tel: 0524 844734
Fax: 0524 844735

Lancaster continued
Lancaster Leisure Park Antiques Centre
Wyresdale Rd, (on site of former Hornsea Pottery Plant). Open every day 10-5. SIZE: 100 dealers. *STOCK: A wide range of antiques.* LOC: Off M6, junction 33. TEL: 0524 844734.

Lancastrian Antiques
66 Penny St. (S.P. and H.S. Wilkinson). Open 10-4. CL: Wed. *STOCK: General antiques.* TEL: 0524 843764.

W.B. McCormack
6 and 6a Rosemary Lane. Open 10-5. CL: Wed. *STOCK: Rare and secondhand books.* TEL: 0524 36405.

Simon Starkie Antiques
Unit 3, 26 Sun St. Est. 1982. Open 10-4.30. CL: Tues. and Wed. SIZE: Medium. *STOCK: Hand stripped and original painted pine furniture, 18th-19th C, £30-£600; country oak and related items, 17th-19th C, £100-£4,000.* LOC: Town centre, off Church St. PARK: Limited. TEL: Home - 0229 861222. SER: Valuations. FAIRS: Grasmere Spring and Autumn. VAT: Stan/Spec.

Studio Arts Gallery
6 Lower Church St. (T. and I. Dodgson). Open 9-5.30. *STOCK: Oils and watercolours, 19th-20th*

LANCASHIRE

Lancaster continued
C, £50-£25,000; prints, 20th C, £20-£1,000. TEL: 0524 68014; fax - 0524 844422. SER: Valuations; restorations and cleaning (as stock); framing; buys at auction.

Vicary Antiques
18a Brock St. Est. 1974. Open 10-5. CL: Wed. SIZE: Small. STOCK: Paintings, prints, art pottery, works of art, 1850-1950; arts and crafts, furniture, quilts. TEL: 0524 843322. VAT: Stan/Spec.

LEIGH

Leigh Coins, Antiques and Jewellery
4 Queens St. (R. Bibby). Open 9.30-5.30, Wed. 9.30-12.30. STOCK: General antiques and jewellery. TEL: 0942 607947.

LONGRIDGE, Nr. Preston

Charnley Fine Arts
Charnley House, Preston Rd. (R. and J. Crosbie). Est. 1989. Open by appointment. SIZE: Medium. STOCK: Paintings, 19th-20th C, £100-£10,000. LOC: Off M55/M6, north of Preston on B6243. PARK: Easy. TEL: 0772 782800; home - same. SER: Restorations; cleaning.

The Folly
21 Inglewhite Rd. (E. Hamlet). Est. 1982. Open 11-4.30. CL: Wed. SIZE: Medium. STOCK: Furniture, Georgian, Victorian, Edwardian, £20-£600; mirrors, copper and brass. LOC: 6 miles from exit 31, M6. PARK: Easy. TEL: 0772 784786. VAT: Stan.

Joy's Shop
83 Berry Lane. (Miss J. Hamlet). Resident. Est. 1986. Open 9-5. CL: Wed. SIZE: Small. STOCK: Art deco china, jewellery, mirrors, lamps; pine furniture, bedding, chests, dressers, tables. LOC: 6 miles from exit 31, M6. PARK: Nearby. TEL: 0772 782083.

Kitchenalia
'The Old Bakery', 36 Inglewhite Rd. (J. Chilton). STOCK: Kitchenalia, brass, copper ware, pottery, pine and oak country furniture, butchers' blocks, Victorian church pews. TEL: 0772 785411. VAT: Stan/Spec.

LYTHAM

Clifton Antiques
8 Market Sq. (A.P. Allen). Est. 1975. Open 10.30-5. CL: Mon. SIZE: Medium. STOCK: Small pine furniture, silver, jewellery, £5-£500; brass, copper, crochet work. Not Stocked: Weapons, coins. PARK: Easy. TEL: 0253 736356.

LYTHAM ST. ANNES

All Our Yesterdays of Lytham
3 Station Rd. (S. Brickwood and P. Harrison).

Lytham St. Annes continued
Open 11-5. CL: Mon. and Wed. STOCK: General antiques. TEL: 0253 734748.

Snuff Box
5 Market Buildings, Hastings Pl. (Mrs S.C. Tayler). Open 10-5. CL: Wed. STOCK: Silver, jewellery, watches and linen. TEL: 0253 738656.

MANCHESTER

A.S. Antique Galleries
26 Broad St, Salford. (A. Sternshine). Est. 1975. Open 10-5.30. CL: Tues. SIZE: Large. STOCK: Art nouveau and deco bronze and ivory figures, silver, lighting, glass, furniture, jewellery and general antiques. Not Stocked: Weapons. LOC: On A6, one mile from Manchester city centre, next to Salford College of Technology. PARK: Easy. TEL: 061 737 5938 and 0836 368230; fax - 061 737 6626. SER: Valuations; restorations; commission purchasing.

Abstract Antiques
Ginnel Gallery, 16 Lloyd St. (C. Pender). Open 10-5.30, Sat. 11-4. CL: Mon. SIZE: Large. STOCK: Furniture, Gothic, Aesthetic, Arts and Crafts, deco, 1950's, art and studio pottery and glass.

Albion Antiques
643 Stockport Rd, Longsight. (A. Collins). Est. 1971. Open 9-6, Sat. by appointment. SIZE: Medium. STOCK: Furniture, £40-£5,000. LOC: A6. PARK: Easy. TEL: 061 225 4957. SER: Valuations; restorations (furniture and wooden items).

Antique Fireplaces
1090 Stockport Rd, Levenshulme. (D. McMullan). Open 9-6, Sun. 11-5. STOCK: Fireplaces and architectural items. TEL: 061 431 8075.

Antiques Village
Old Town Hall, 965 Stockport Rd., Levenshulme. Est. 1978. Open 9.30-5.30, Sun. 11-4. SIZE: 40+ dealers. STOCK: Mainly furniture. LOC: A6 between Manchester and Stockport. PARK: Own. TEL: 061 224 2410; home - 061 224 2410. SER: Valuations; restorations (re-veneering, upholstery and stripping). FAIRS: Newark. VAT: Stan/Spec.

Authentiques
373 Bury New Rd, Prestwich. (S.G. Rubenstein) Est. 1978. Open by appointment only. STOCK Decorative items - silver, plate, porcelain, glass boxes, Staffordshire, watercolours and prints, small furniture, miniatures, brass, curios, early 19th C to 1920s, £50-£500. LOC: 1/2 mile from junction 17 M62 on A56. PARK: Easy. TEL: 061 773 9606 (ansaphone) and 061 773 0717; fax - 061 725 9579 SER: Valuations; restorations (silver); buys a auction (pictures, silver, furniture). FAIRS: British International, Birmingham.

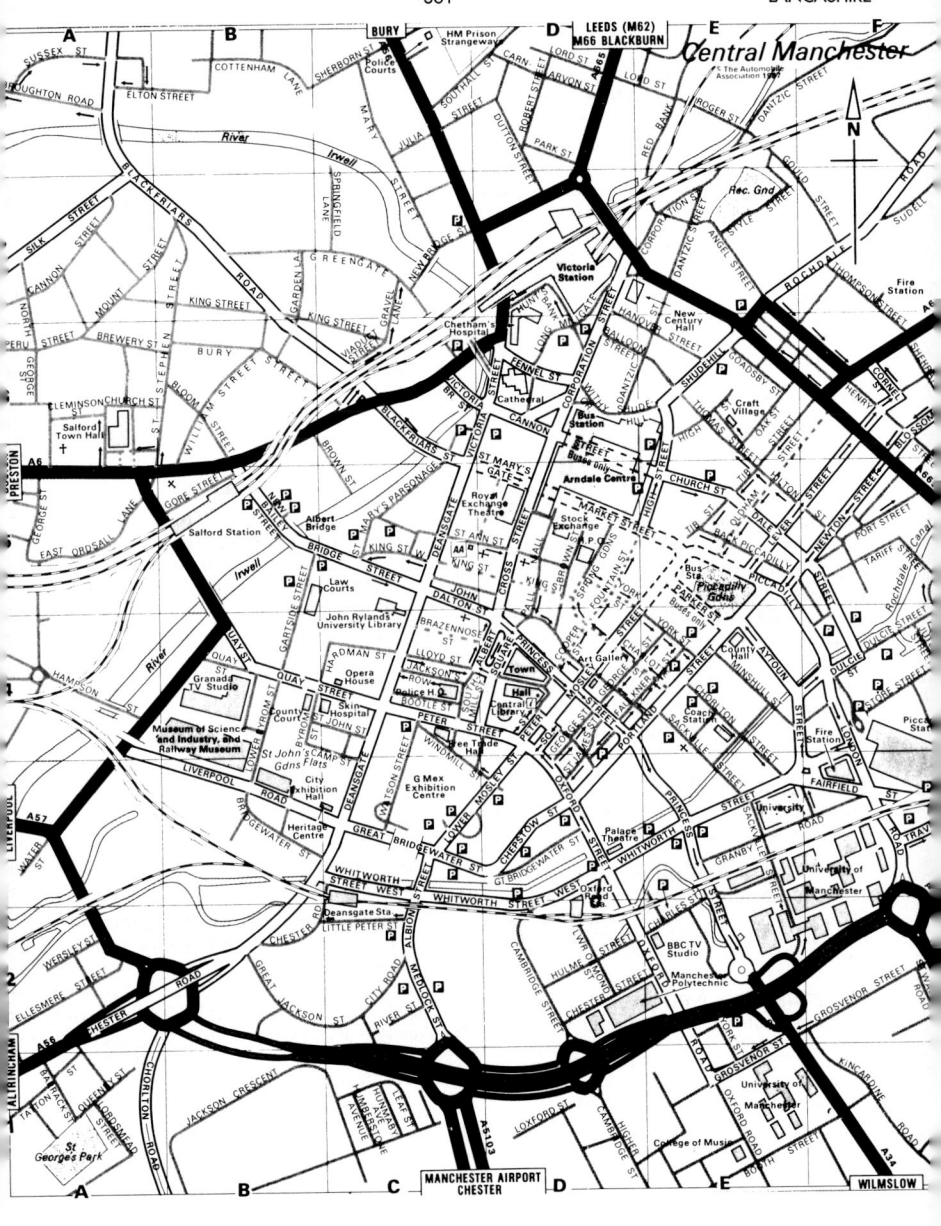

Key to Town Plan

AA Recommended roads	Car Parks	**P**
Other roads	Parks and open spaces	
Restricted roads	AA Service Centre	**AA**
Buildings of interest	© Automobile Association 1988.	

LANCASHIRE

Manchester continued

The Baron Antiques
1 Church Lane, Prestwich. (S. Brunsveld). Open 9.30-6. SIZE: Large. *STOCK: 18th C mahogany and early oak furniture, Victorian walnut, clocks, porcelain, objets d'art, shipping goods.* TEL: 061 773 9929; fax - 061 929 0299. SER: Valuations; restorations.

Boodle and Dunthorne Ltd
1 King St. Est. 1798. Open 9-5.30. SIZE: Large. *STOCK: 18th-19th C silver, Victorian jewellery, £100-£30,000; clocks and clock sets, mid-19th C, £100-£1,000.* Not Stocked: Furniture. TEL: 061 833 9000. VAT: Stan/Spec.

Browzers
14 Warwick St, Prestwich. (A.E. and M. Seddon). Open 10-5. CL: Wed. *STOCK: Secondhand books; prints, maps.* TEL: 061 798 0626/773 2327.

Bulldog Antiques
393 Bury New Rd, Prestwich. (P. Wordsworth). Est. 1971. Open 10.30-6. CL: Sun. except by appointment. SIZE: Large. *STOCK: Georgian, Victorian and Edwardian furniture; clocks especially longcase and wall clock sets, 18th-19th C; militaria, swords, guns, pistols, shotguns, war medals, pottery, prints, pictures, general antiques and shipping goods.* LOC: Exit 17, M62. PARK: At rear. TEL: 061 798 9277; home - 061 790 7153. SER: Restorations (furniture); French polishing, watch and clock repairs. VAT: Stan.

Cathedral Jewellers
26 Cathedral St. Open 10-5, Sat. 10-4. *STOCK: Jewellery.* TEL: 061 832 3042.

Chestergate Antiques
1034 Stockport Rd, Levenshulme. (J.G. Woods). Open 10-5. *STOCK: Clocks, period and Victorian furniture.* TEL: 061 224 7795; home - 061 442 6795.

Christabelle's Antiques
973 Stockport Rd, Levenshulme. Open 10-5.30 including Sun. *STOCK: General antiques, Victorian.* TEL: 061 225 4666.

Didsbury Antiques (Chorlton)
21 Range Rd, Whalley Range. (J. Karczewski-Slowikowski). Est. 1973. Open by appointment. *STOCK: Furniture, pictures, ceramics, 18th-19th C, from £250.* PARK: Easy. TEL: 061 227 9979; home - same. SER: Valuations; buys at auction (furniture, paintings). VAT: Stan.

Family Antiques
405/407 Bury New Rd, Prestwich. (J. and J. Ditondo). Open daily. *STOCK: General antiques.* TEL: 061 798 0036.

Forest Books of Cheshire
in The Ginnell, 16 Lloyd St. (Mrs E. Mann). Open 10-5.30, Wed. 10.30-5.30, Sat. 11-4 (or later) CL:

Manchester continued

Mon. *STOCK: Antiquarian, art, collecting, drama and humanities books and prints.* TEL: 061 833 9037.

Fulda Gallery Ltd
19 Vine St, Salford. (M.J. Fulda). Est. 1969. Open by appointment only. *STOCK: Oil paintings, 1500-1950, £500-£30,000; watercolours, 1800-1930, £350-£10,000.* LOC: Near Salford Police Station off Bury New Rd. TEL: 061 792 1962; mobile - 0836 518313. SER: Valuations; restorations; buys at auction.

Garson and Co. Ltd
47 Houldsworth St, Piccadilly. Open 8-5 (prior telephone call advisable), Sat. by appointment only. *STOCK: Old and modern masters, watercolours, gold carved mirrors, blackamoors, church altars, telescopes.* TEL: 061 236 9393; fax - 061 236 4211. SER: Framing (up to 10in. width); valuations; export.

Gibb's Bookshop Ltd
10 Charlotte St. Est. 1926. *STOCK: Books.* TEL: 061 236 7179.

The Ginnell
16 Lloyd St. (Mr and Mrs J.K. Mottershead). Est. 1973. Open 9.30-5.30, Sat. 11-4. *STOCK: French furniture, art deco, art nouveau, arts and crafts furniture, 1950's pottery and signed glass; antiquarian books.* TEL: 061 833 9037.

M. and N. Haworth Ltd - Antique Gallery
Royal Exchange Building, St Ann's Square. *STOCK: Stamps, cigarette cards, coins, bank notes, medals and memorabilia.* TEL: 061 834 2929; fax - 061 839 4714.

Manchester Antique Company
95 Lapwing Lane, West Didsbury. (J. Long). Est. 1964. Open 9.30-5.30. SIZE: Large. *STOCK: Mainly marquetry walnut and mahogany, some period furniture, silver.* LOC: 3 miles from airport on M56 towards city. PARK: Easy. TEL: 061 434 7752. SER: Valuations; buys at auction (clocks). VAT: Stan.

Eric J. Morten
Warburton St, Didsbury. Est. 1959. Open 10-6. SIZE: Large. *STOCK: Antiquarian books, 16th-20th C, £5-£5,000.* LOC: Off Wilmslow Rd., near traffic lights in Didsbury village. A34. PARK: Easy. TEL: 061 445 7629 and 0265 277959. SER: Valuations; buys at auction (antiquarian books).

Prestwich Antiques Ltd.
371-373 Bury New Rd., Prestwich. (T. Finn). Est. 1973. Open 10.30-6, Sun. 11.30-5. SIZE: Large. *STOCK: Victorian furniture, decorative lighting, to £1,000.* TEL: 061 798 0911; home - 0282 618270. LOC: Off junction 17, M62. PARK: Own at rear. SER: Valuations; restorations (upholstery, polishing and repairs). VAT: Stan/Spec.

ST. JAMES ANTIQUES

Specialists in Antique Jewellery, Silver, Paintings and objets d'art

41 SOUTH KING STREET
ST. JAMES SQUARE MANCHESTER 2

Telephone 061-834 9632 VAT No 147399626

Manchester continued
Paul Quentin
626 Manchester Rd, Bury. (D. and P. Eccleston). Est. 1965. Open 9-6.30. SIZE: Large. *STOCK: General antiques, weapons, copper, brass, pewter, 1650-1920.* Not Stocked: Fine porcelain. LOC: On A56, 2 miles north of junction 17, M62; 1 mile west of junction 3, M66. PARK: Easy. TEL: 061 766 6673.

Royal Exchange Shopping Centre
Antiques Gallery, St. Anne's Sq., Exchange St. Open 9.30-5.30. TEL: 061 834 3731; stallholders - 061 834 1427. Below are listed the dealers at this centre.

Adamas Antiques
STOCK: Jewellery.

Alexander Antiques
STOCK: Jewellery, glass and silver.

Antique and Collectables
STOCK: General antiques.

The Antique Fireplace

M. Bailey
STOCK: Stamps.

Callbox
STOCK: Telephones, pocket watches.

City Jewellers
STOCK: Jewellery and silver.

Coach Gallery (Scorpio)
STOCK: Ethnic art, natural history, unusual items.

M. Davies
STOCK: Jewellery, silver, pottery.

Renee Franks
STOCK: General antiques.

Franks Bookshop
STOCK: Books and ephemera.

Grenville Art Gallery
STOCK: Fine paintings.

Manchester continued
Joan Grupman
STOCK: Stripped pine and jewellery.

M. and N. Haworth Ltd
STOCK: Stamps, coins, post and cigarette cards, medals and memorabilia. TEL: 061 834 2929; fax - 061 839 4714.

Irving Antiques
STOCK: Toys and dolls.

Jenny Jones
STOCK: Jewellery.

Jupiter Antiques
STOCK: General antiques, bric-a-brac, jewellery.

Linen and Lace
STOCK: Table linens and lace.

Manchester Coin and Medal Centre
STOCK: Coins, medals and banknotes.

Phoenix Antiques
STOCK: Jewellery and silverware.

David and Karin Ramsden
STOCK: Furniture, general antiques.

Swan Antiques
STOCK: Jewellery.

St. James Antiques
41 South King St. *STOCK: Jewellery and paintings.* LOC: Off Deansgate, in town centre. TEL: 061 834 9632.

Secondhand and Rare Books
Corner Church St/High St. Open 12-4. *STOCK: Books.* TEL: 061 834 5964 or 0625 861608.

Village Antiques
416 Bury New Rd, Prestwich. (R. Weidenbaum). Est. 1981. Open 10-5, Wed. 10-1. SIZE: Medium. *STOCK: Ornaments and pottery, 19th C, £5-£300; 18th C glass and 18th-19th C porcelain, £50-£500; furniture, 18th to early 20th C, £100-£500.* LOC: Village centre, 2 mins. from M62. PARK: Easy and opposite. TEL: 061 773 3612.

MIDDLETON VILLAGE, Nr. Morecambe

G.G. Exports
25 Middleton Rd. (G. Goulding). Est. 1970. Always available but prior telephone call advisable. SIZE: Large. STOCK: Shipping goods, £30-£500; Victoriana, £50-£3,000; general antiques and pine. LOC: On main road between Morecambe promenade and Middleton village. PARK: Easy. TEL: 0524 851565. SER: 40ft containers weekly to USA. VAT: Stan. Trade Only.

MORECAMBE

Magpies Nest
Unit 4 Plaza Shopping Arcade, Queen St. (B. Byrne). Open 9.30-5. CL: Wed. STOCK: Bric-a-brac, cutlery, china, glass, militaria. TEL: 0524 423328.

Tyson's Antiques
Clark St. (George, Andrew and Shirley Tyson). Est. 1952. Open Sat. 9-12, other times by appointment. SIZE: Large. STOCK: Georgian, Victorian and Edwardian furniture, £10-£10,000. LOC: Opposite fire station. PARK: Easy. TEL: 0524 416763/425235/420098; home - 0524 416763. VAT: Stan/Spec. Trade Only.

Luigino Vescovi
1 and 3 Back Avondale Rd. East. Est. 1970. Open by appointment every day. SIZE: Warehouse. STOCK: Georgian and Victorian items, £50-£5,000. PARK: Easy. TEL: 0524 416732; mobile - 0860 784856. VAT: Stan/Spec.

NELSON

Colin Blakey Fireplaces
115 Manchester Rd. Est. 1906. Open 9.30-5.30, Sat. 9.30-5. STOCK: Fireplaces and hearth furniture, French clock sets, paintings and prints. LOC: Exit 12, M65. PARK: Opposite. TEL: 0282 614941. SER: Manufacturers and suppliers of hand-carved marble fireplaces and hardwood mantels. VAT: Stan.

Brittons Jewellers and Antiques
34 Scotland Rd. Est. 1970. CL: Tues. STOCK: Jewellery and general small antiques. PARK: Opposite. TEL: 0282 697659/398577.

Brooks Antiques
7 Russell St. (D. and S.A. Brooks). Est. 1979. Open 9-5.30, Sun. and Tues. by appointment. SIZE: Medium. STOCK: Furniture, £50-£2,000; smalls, £5-£500; both 1750-1930; postcards, ephemera, early 20th C, to £20. LOC: Town centre, 2 mins. from junction 13, M65. PARK: Easy. TEL: 0282 698148; home - 0282 866234. SER: Valuations. VAT: Stan.

Margaret's Antique Shop
79a Scotland Rd. (M. Owen). Est. 1948. Open 10-6. CL: Tues. SIZE: Small. LOC: Town centre. PARK: Easy.

OLDHAM

Heritage Antiques
123 Milnrow Rd, Shaw. (G. James). Open 2-4. STOCK: General antiques. TEL: 0706 842385; home - 061 633 4961.

Charles Howell Jeweller
2 Lord St. (N.G. Howell). NAG. Est. 1870. Open 9.15-5.15. SIZE: Small. STOCK: Edwardian and Victorian jewellery, £25-£2,000; silver, early to mid 20th C, £40-£1,500; watches, Victorian to mid 20th C, £50-£800. LOC: Town centre, off High St. PARK: Limited or by arrangement. TEL: 061 624 1479. SER: Valuations; restorations (jewellery and watches); buys at auction (jewellery and watches). VAT: Stan/Spec.

H.C. Simpson and Sons Jewellers (Oldham)Ltd
37 High St. Open 9-5.30. STOCK: Clocks, jewellery, watches. TEL: 061 624 7187. SER: Restorations (clocks).

Valley Antiques
Soho St. (R. Byron). Est. 1973. Open 10-6. SIZE: Warehouse. STOCK: General antiques including stripped pine, porcelain, pottery, oak furniture, 19th C, £25-£600. PARK: Easy. TEL: 061 624 5030. SER: Valuations; restorations (pine stripping, upholstery, clocks).

Waterloo Antiques
16 Waterloo St. (B.J. and S. Marks). Est. 1969. Open 9.30-5. SIZE: Medium. STOCK: General antiques, furniture, jewellery. LOC: Town centre. TEL: 061 624 5975; fax - same. SER: Valuations.

ORMSKIRK

Alan Grice Antiques
106 Aughton St. Open 10-6. STOCK: Period furniture. PARK: Easy. TEL: 0695 572007.

Revival Pine Stripping
Beacon View, 181 Southport Rd. (N.F. and M.A. Sumner). Open by appointment. SIZE: Small. STOCK: Pine furniture. TEL: 0695 578308. SER: Stripping.

PADIHAM

C. Crowther
47 Higham Hall Rd, Higham. Open by appointment. STOCK: General antiques. TEL: 0282 774418.

PRESTON

Antique and Reproduction Clocks
73 Friargate. (N.E. Oldfield). FBHI. STOCK: Antique and reproduction clocks. TEL: 0772 58465. VAT: Stan.

The Antique Centre
56 Garstang Rd. (Paul Allison). Open 9-6, Sat. 9.30-5.30, Sun. 10.30-5.30. SIZE: 30 dealers.

Preston continued
STOCK: *Mainly fine art and furniture.* TEL: 0772 882078; fax - 0772 885115. SER: Worldwide shipping; containers.

Barronfield Gallery
47 Friargate. Open 10-5, Thurs. and Sun. by appointment. SIZE: Medium. STOCK: *Victorian and Edwardian watercolours, £100-£10,000.* LOC: Near Ringway on Friargate. PARK: Nearby. TEL: 0772 563465; home - 0772 690512.

Jack Blackburn
41 New Hall Lane. Est. 1968. STOCK: *General antiques.* TEL: 0772 791117. VAT: Stan.

Duckworth's Antiques
45 New Hall Lane. (V.K. and M. Duckworth). Est. 1960. Open 9.30-6. CL: Sun. except by appointment. SIZE: Medium. STOCK: *General antiques.* Not Stocked: Arms, armour, coins, medals. LOC: Main road leading from M6 motorway. PARK: Easy. TEL: 0772 794336; home - 0772 742720.

Peter Guy's Antiques and Fine Furniture
26-30 New Hall Lane. Open 9.30-5.30. STOCK: *English and French furniture.* TEL: 0772 703771; fax - same.

Halewood and Sons
37 Friargate. Est. 1867. CL: Thurs. p.m. STOCK: *Antiquarian books and maps.* TEL: 0772 52603.

Orchard Antiques
22 Woodplumpton Rd, Ashton-on-Ribble. (Mrs P. Dartnell, Mrs J. Davidson, Mrs V. Hadwin and Mrs E. Halsall). Est. 1983. Open 10-5, Sat. 9.30-5.30. SIZE: Small. STOCK: *General antiques, £5-£500.* LOC: Off Lane Ends. PARK: Easy. TEL: 0773 725925. SER: Valuations; restorations (chairs recaned); buys at auction. FAIRS: Newark, Chester, Stafford, Lake District, Mobberley, Harrogate.

Preston Antique Centre
The Mill, New Hall Lane. Open 8.30-5.30, Sat.10-4, Sun. 9-4. SIZE: Large - 40+ dealers. STOCK: *General antiques, Georgian, Victorian and Edwardian; shipping furniture.* TEL: 0772 794498; fax - 0772 651694. SER: Container packing. Below are listed the dealers at this centre.

Aba

Abbey Antiques

Ages Ago Antiques

R. Akeroyd Antiques

D. Aldred

P. Allison

Allsops Antiques

K. Almond

Baron Antiques

Preston continued

J. Blackburn

Bodhouse Antiques

J. Bowler

G. Busato

C. J. and K. Antiques

R. Cooke

Crown Square Antiques

Paul Doran

R. Dunn

Syd and Dave Greenhalgh

Harrington Antiques

N. Hickson

A. Hobrey

B. Hodson

Intergrate

J. Lambert

L. Liberati

Lional of France

K. Long Antiques

M. McDowell

Old Tyme

P. Oracz

Oxford Antiques

J. Patterson

M. Peddler

J. Ralstan

Rocking Chair Antiques

J. Rowley Antiques

Southward Enterprises

T. Sutcliffe

The Trader Antiques

Utopia Antiques Ltd

J. Waite Antiques

Yates Antiques

Preston Book Co
68 Friargate. Est. 1950. Open 9.30-5.30. STOCK: *Antiquarian books.* TEL: 0772 52603. SER: Buys at auction.

Swag
24 Leyland Rd, Penwortham. (M. Fletcher). Est. 1967. Open 9-6. CL: Thurs. p.m. SIZE: Small. STOCK: *Dolls, especially 1830-1920, £5-£250;*

LANCASHIRE

Preston continued
pottery, porcelain, furniture. LOC: 3 miles from exit 29, M6, following St. Anne's signs. PARK: Easy. TEL: 0772 744970. SER: Restorations (dolls).

Frederick Treasure Ltd LAPADA
The Antique Centre, 56 Garstang Rd. (J.F. Treasure). Est. 1908. Open 8-7, Sun. 10-4. SIZE: Large. STOCK: *Furniture, 1650-1900, £20-£10,000.* PARK: Easy. TEL: 0772 882078; office - 0253 736801; mobile - 0860 497850. SER: Valuations. VAT: Stan/Spec.

Ray Wade Antiques
113 New Hall Lane. Est. 1978. Open 10-5.30, Sat. 10.30-4. SIZE: Medium. STOCK: *Decorative items, objets d'art, furniture, paintings, pottery, porcelain, £5-£5,000.* PARK: Easy. TEL: 0772 792950; fax - 0772 651415; mobile - 0836 291336; home - 0253 700715. SER: Valuations; restorations (as stock); buys at auction. VAT: Stan/Spec.

RISHTON, Nr. Blackburn
Speakmans
8 Church St. (P. Speakman). Est. 1856. Open by appointment. SIZE: Small. STOCK: *Pottery, porcelain, glass, clocks, pictures, decorative items.* PARK: Easy. TEL: 0254 885848.

ROCHDALE
S.C. Falk LAPADA
Open by appointment only. STOCK: *Fine English period furniture.* TEL: 0706 44946. VAT: Stan/Spec.

Owen Antiques
191 Oldham Rd. (J.G.T. Owen). Est. 1891. Open 11.30-7, Sun. 2-6. STOCK: *Clocks and paintings, 17th-19th C, £100-£5,000; early oak and walnut, spinning wheels, silver, pewter, pistols, phonographs, wireless sets, coins, model ships, orreries and gothic clocks, nautical items, violins, antiquarian books, early ciné equipment.* LOC: A627 from town centre up hill (Oldham road) for 1/2 mile. Next block to high level pavement on left hand side past railway station. PARK: Limited and nearby. TEL: 0706 48138; home - 0706 353270. SER: Valuations; restorations (clocks and furniture).

SABDEN, Nr. Blackburn
Walter Aspinall Antiques
Pendle Antiques Centre, Union Mill, Watt St. Est. 1964. Open 9-5, Sat. and Sun. 11-4, or by appointment. SIZE: Large. STOCK: *Furniture and bric-a-brac.* LOC: On Pendle Hill between Clitheroe and Padiham. TEL: 0282 776311; fax - 0282 778643. SER: Export; packing; courier; containers.

SADDLEWORTH, Nr. Oldham
Heyday
Huddersfield Rd, Delph. (H.J. Bell). Est. 1972 Open most days including Sun., or by appointment. SIZE: Medium. STOCK: *Furniture and smalls, architectural items, fixtures and fittings £5-£500; art nouveau and art deco items; al 19th-20th C.* LOC: On A62 at road junction tc Rochdale. PARK: Easy. TEL: 0457 875849, home - same.

ST. ANNES-ON-SEA
Pine Antiques
59-61 St. Andrew Rd. South. (R. and G. Shaw) Open 9-5.30. SIZE: Medium. STOCK: *Pine furniture, 19th C £150-£2,500; cast-iron fireplaces, 1890-1930 £200-£500.* PARK: Easy. TEL: 0253 720492 SER: Restorations (pine stripping).

Stamford Antiques
29 The Crescent. (Mrs D. Travis). Est. 1910 Open Mon., Fri. and Sat. 10-6, other times by appointment. SIZE: Medium. STOCK: *Furniture and clocks.* PARK: Easy. TEL: 0253 728385 home - same. SER: Valuations; restorations (clocks). VAT: Stan/Spec.

The Victorian Shop
19 Alexandria Drive. (G.O. Freeman). Open 10-5 STOCK: *General antiques.* TEL: 0253 725700.

SAMLESBURY, Nr. Preston
Samlesbury Hall
Preston New Rd. (Samlesbury Hall Trust). Est 1969. Open 11.30-5 in summer, 11.30-4 in winter CL: Mon. SIZE: Large. STOCK: *General collectable antiques.* LOC: Exit 31, M6 on A677 between Preston and Blackburn. PARK: Easy TEL: 0254 81 2010/2229.

SCARISBRICK
Carrcross Gallery
325 Southport Rd. (G.D. Fairclough). Est. 1985 Open Tues- Sat 10-5, Sun 12-5. SIZE: Medium STOCK: *Victorian fireplaces, £50-£1,000 Victorian brass/steel beds, £150-£500; furniture 18th-19th C, £100-£2,000.* PARK: Easy. TEL 0704 880638; mobile - 0836 371602. SER Valuations; restorations (cast-iron, brass). VAT Stan.

SHAWFORTH, Nr. Rochdale
Shawforth Antiques
193 Market St. (J. and E. Bracewell). Est. 1967 Open 9.30-8, Sun. 9.30-5. SIZE: Small. STOCK *Victoriana, clocks, bric-a-brac.* LOC: Or Rochdale to Bacup Rd. PARK: Easy. TEL: 070 685 3402.

SWINTON
Ambassador House
273 Chorley Rd. (G. White). Open 2-6, prior telephone call advisable. STOCK: General antiques including clocks, silver, paintings, furniture, pottery and porcelain, 17th-18th C. TEL: 061 794 3806. SER: Valuations.

TRAWDEN, Nr. Colne
Jack Moore Antiques and Stained Glass
The Old Rock, Keighley Rd. Open 9-5, Sat. and Sun. 10-4. SIZE: Large. STOCK: Furniture and stained glass. PARK: Easy. TEL: 0282 869478; home - same. SER: Restoration and manufacture of stained glass; container packing; courier. VAT: Stan. *Trade only.*

UPPERMILL
Queen Anne Gallery
High St. (Mrs R. Potts). Open 10.30-5 including Sun. CL: Tues. STOCK: Victorian pine, lace, blue and white. TEL: 0457 874537.

WHALLEY, Nr. Blackburn
The Abbey Antique Shop
43 and 45 King St. (A.D. and E. Austin). Est. 1950. Open 9.30-6. SIZE: Large. STOCK: Furniture, £10-£450; ceramics, £5-£150; both 18th-19th C; pewter, copper and brass, 17th-18th C. Not Stocked: Coins and stamps. LOC: A59. PARK: Easy. TEL: 0254 823139. VAT: Stan/Spec.

Davies Antiques
32 King St. (G., E. and P. Davies). Est. 1971. Open 10-5. SIZE: Small. STOCK: British country furniture and longcase clocks, to £3,000; jewellery, to £500. Not Stocked: Coins, weapons, continental furniture. LOC: A59. PARK: Easy. TEL: 0254 823764. VAT: Stan/Spec.

WHITEFIELD, Nr. Manchester
Henry Donn Gallery
138/142 Bury New Rd. Est. 1954. Open 9.30-5.30. STOCK: Paintings, 19th-20th C, £20-£20,000. LOC: Off M62, junction 17 towards Bury. TEL: 061 766 8819. SER: Valuations; framing; restorations (pictures). VAT: Stan/Spec.

WIGAN
Colin de Rouffignac
57 Wigan Lane. Open 10-5. CL: Wed. STOCK: Furniture, jewellery, oils and watercolours. TEL: 0942 37927.

John Robinson Antiques
172-176 Manchester Rd, Higher Ince. Est. 1965. Open any time. SIZE: Large. STOCK: General antiques. LOC: A577 near Ince Bar. PARK: Easy. TEL: 0942 47773/41671. SER: Export packing. VAT: Stan. *Export and Trade Only.*

Wigan continued
John Roby Antiques
12 Lord St. Open 10-5. CL: Sat. and Wed. STOCK: Furniture, to 1940; bric-a-brac. TEL: 0942 30887.

Whatnot Antiques
90 Wigan Lane. (John Hargraves). Open 9-5. CL: Wed. STOCK: General antiques. TEL: 0942 491880.

YEALAND CONYERS, Nr. Carnforth
M. and I. Finch
15/17 Yealand Rd. Est. 1970. SIZE: Medium. STOCK: Antique and decorative lighting, mirrors, prints, books and furniture. Not Stocked: Jewellery, silver. LOC: 2 miles from M6, exit 35, just off A6. PARK: Easy. TEL: 0524 73 2212. VAT: Stan/Spec.

An Antique Collectors' Club Title

The English Regional Chair
by Bernard D. Cotton
This first study of British regional chairs opens up an entirely new area of collecting. It unearths thousands of names of makers who would otherwise have passed into oblivion and identifies many of their products.
**ISBN 1 85149 023 X, 512pp
over 1,400 b & w illus, 69 col, £49.50**

Available from:
Antique Collectors' Club
5 Church Street, Woodbridge, Suffolk IP12 1DS
Tel: (0394) 385501 Fax: (0394) 384434

or Market Street Industrial Park
Wappingers' Falls, New York 12590, USA
Tel: 914 297 0003 Fax: 914 297 0068

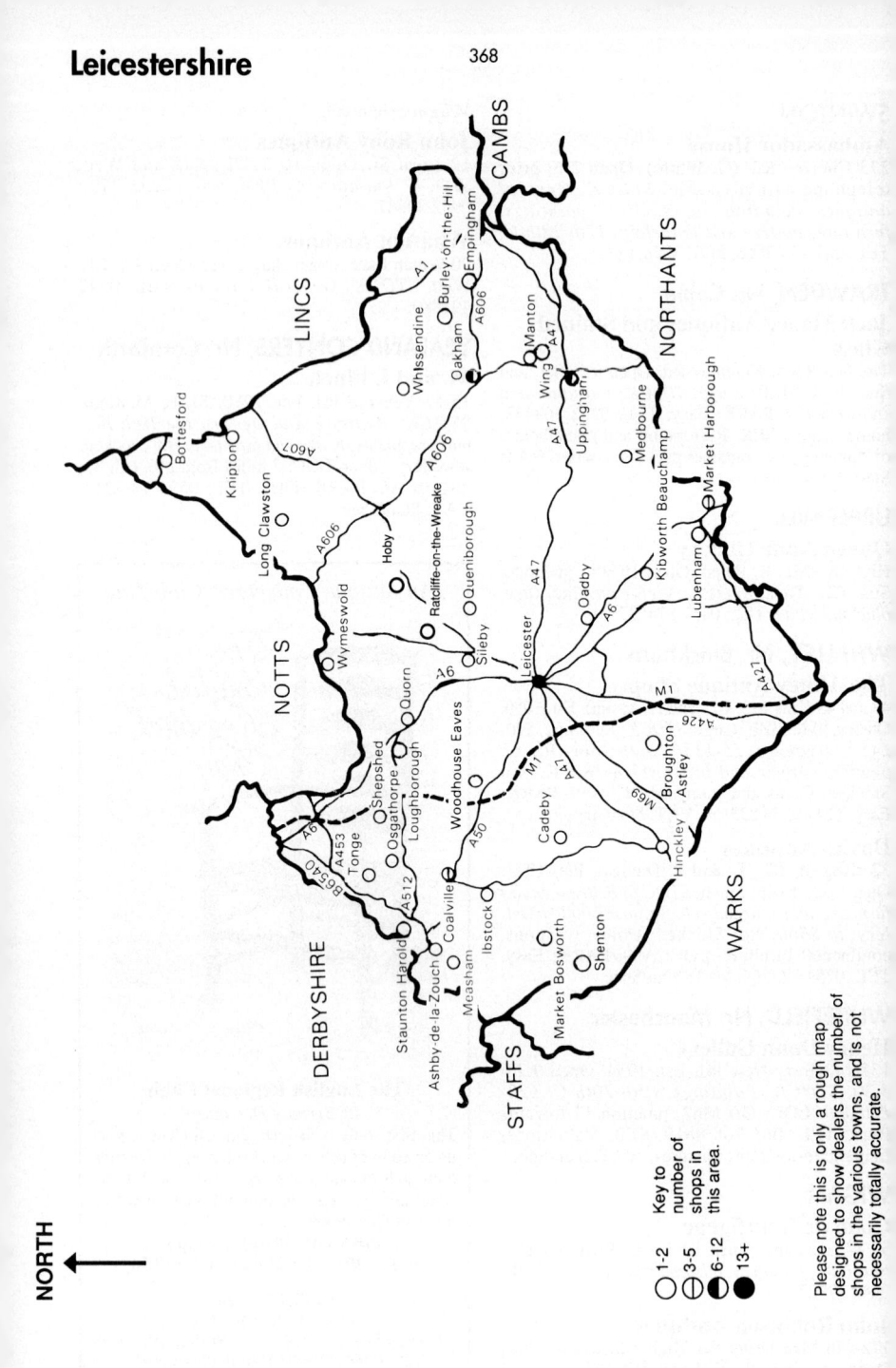

Leicestershire

NORTH ←

Key to number of shops in this area.
○ 1-2
⊕ 3-5
◐ 6-12
● 13+

Please note this is only a rough map designed to show dealers the number of shops in the various towns, and is not necessarily totally accurate.

Leicestershire

"Ivanhoe Antiques"
(JOHN & ANN MANSFIELD)

LAPADA MEMBER

Antique Furniture, Fine Porcelain & Paintings

53, MARKET STREET, ASHBY-DE-LA-ZOUCH, LEICESTERSHIRE.

Tel. Ashby-de-la-Zouch 415424

This dealer has fine quality Georgian furniture, porcelain, oil paintings, prints and some silver

---

ASHBY-DE-LA-ZOUCH

Ivanhoe Antiques LAPADA
53 Market St. (J. and A. Mansfield). Est. 1976. Open 10-5, Sun. by appointment. CL: Wed. SIZE: Medium. *STOCK: Furniture, £25-£3,500, porcelain, Derby, Worcester and Coalport, £10-£1,000, all 19th-20th C; silver and oil paintings, 19th C.* LOC: On A50 in town centre. PARK: Easy. TEL: 0530 415424. VAT: Stan/Spec.

BOTTESFORD

Thomas Keen
51 High St. (T.E. Keen). FRSA. Est. 1970. Appointment advisable. *STOCK: Furniture, 17th-19th C; metalwork, oil paintings, decorative items.* TEL: 0949 42177. SER: Restorations, lectures (furniture).

BROUGHTON ASTLEY, Nr. Leicester

Old Bakehouse Antiques and Gallery
10 Green Rd. (S.R. Needham). Open Thurs.-Sat. 10-6, Sun. 2-5. *STOCK: Period furniture.* PARK: Easy. TEL: 0455 282276.

BURLEY-ON-THE-HILL, Nr. Oakham

Burley Workshop
Home Farm. Est. 1967. Open by appointment. SIZE: Medium. *STOCK: Pine and decorative items, 17th-19th C, £50-£1,000; ironwork, architectural and unusual items.* LOC: On B668, 1/4 mile before village green, on left behind trees, stones mark drive entrance. PARK: Easy. TEL: 0572 757333; home - same. SER: Valuations; restorations (furniture); buys at auction. VAT: Stan/Spec.

CADEBY, Nr. Nuneaton

P. Stanworth (Fine Arts)
The Grange. (Mr and Mrs G. Stanworth). Resident. Est. 1965. Open by appointment. SIZE: Medium. *STOCK: Oil paintings, 18th to early 20th C, £100-£8,000.* LOC: Just off A447. PARK: Easy. TEL: 0455 291023. VAT: Spec.

COALVILLE

Keystone Antiques LAPADA
9 Ashby Rd. (I. and H. McPherson). FGA. Est. 1979. Open 10-5, Sat. 10-4. CL: Wed. SIZE: Medium. *STOCK: Jewellery, Victorian and Georgian, £25-£1,500; silver, 1700-1920, £20-£500; small collectable items, 18th-19th C, £15-£300; oil paintings, furniture, cranberry, needlework tools, Victorian and Georgian table glass.* LOC: A50, town centre. PARK: At rear. TEL: 0530 835966. SER: Valuations (jewellery); gem testing. VAT: Stan/Spec.

Massey's Antiques
26 Hotel St. (Mr and Mrs C.A. Irons). Est. 1969. Open 9-5. CL: Wed. SIZE: Small. *STOCK: Bric-a-brac and bygones, small furniture, 1890-1960.* PARK: Rear. TEL: 0530 832374; home - 0530 832448.

EMPINGHAM, Nr. Oakham

Churchgate Antiques LAPADA
13 Church St. (R. Wheatley). Open Wed., Fri., Sat. and Sun. 10-5, other times by appointment. SIZE: Medium. *STOCK: Furniture, mainly 18th-19th C, £50-£5,000; paintings and prints, £10-£2,000; silver and plate, 19th-20th C, £10-£1,000.* LOC: Opposite church, off A606. PARK: Easy. TEL: 078 086 528.

Old Bakery Antiques
Church St. (Mr and Mrs P.B. Margerison). Open 9.30-5.30, Sun. 10-4.30. CL: Thurs. SIZE: Medium. *STOCK: Furniture, 17th C to 1920, £50-£6,000; china, 1830-1920, £5-£500; copper and brass, 19th C.* Not Stocked: Jewellery. LOC: 4 miles off A1 on A606 towards Oakham. PARK: Easy. TEL: 078 086 243; home - same. SER: Restorations (furniture); buys at auction. VAT: Stan/Spec.

HINCKLEY

House Things Antiques
Trinity Lane, 44 Mansion St. (P.W. Robertson). Est. 1976. Open 10-6. SIZE: Small. *STOCK: Stripped pine, satinwood, oak and walnut, mainly*

LEICESTERSHIRE

Hinckley continued
Victorian and Edwardian, £50-£300; small collectors' items, 1860-1930s, £5-£100; cast iron, fireplaces, brass and iron beds, 1890-1920's, £50-£250. LOC: On inner ring road 200yds. from Leisure Centre. PARK: Easy. TEL: 0455 618518; home - 0455 212797.

HOBY, Nr. Melton Mowbray
Withers of Leicester
The Old Rutland, Church Lane. (S. Frings). Est. 1860. Open 9-5.30. CL: Thurs. p.m. and Sat. SIZE: Medium. STOCK: Furniture, 17th-19th C, £50-£3,000; china, 18th-19th C, £10-£300; oil paintings, 19th C, £5-£500. Not Stocked: Jewellery and coins. PARK: Easy. TEL: 0664 434803. SER: Valuations; restorations (furniture). VAT: Stan/Spec.

IBSTOCK, Nr. Leicester
Mandrake Stephenson Antiques
101 High St. Est. 1979. Open 10-5, Sat. 10-2.30. SIZE: Small. STOCK: Furniture, Georgian-Edwardian, £50-£500; pottery, pictures. PARK: Easy. TEL: 0530 60898; home - 0530 813587. SER: Valuations; restorations (furniture).

KIBWORTH BEAUCHAMP
Vendy Antiques (Kibworth)
17 Fleckney Rd. (D.R. Vendy). Open 10-1 and 2-5, Sat. 11-5. CL: Mon. STOCK: General antiques including furniture and smalls, mainly Victorian, £10-£2,000. TEL: 0533 796133; home - 0533 713025.

KNIPTON, Nr. Grantham
Anthony W. Laywood
ABA. Est. 1967. Open by appointment. SIZE: Medium. STOCK: Antiquarian books, pre-1850, £20-£2,000. LOC: 1.5 miles off the Grantham-Melton Mowbray road. PARK: Easy. TEL: 0476 870224. SER: Valuations; buys at auction.

LEICESTER
The Antiques Complex
St. Nicholas Place. (K.W. Sansom). Open 9.30-5.30. SIZE: Large. STOCK: General antiques including furniture, collectables, clocks, porcelain, glass, jewellery, paintings and decorative items. LOC: Adjacent to High St., near Holiday Inn. PARK: Own. TEL: 0533 533343; fax - 0533 533347. SER: Container packing.

Betty's
9 Knighton Fields Rd. West. (A. Smith). Est. 1968. Open 9.30-5. SIZE: Small. STOCK: Satinwood and pine items, brass and copper, pictures. LOC: Off Saffron Lane. PARK: Easy. TEL: 0533 839048. SER: Valuations; buys at auction.

Leicester continued
Birches Art Deco Shop
18 Francis St, Stoneygate. (C. and H. Birch). Est. 1978. Open 11-5.30, Sun. by appointment. SIZE: Medium. STOCK: Art deco, Victoriana and kitchenalia. LOC: 1 mile south of city centre, off A6. PARK: Easy. TEL: 0533 703235.

Boulevard Antique and Shipping Centre
The Old Dairy, Western Boulevard. Open 10-6, Sun. 12-5 or by appointment. SIZE: 10 dealers. STOCK: Furniture including oak, mahogany, pine and shipping; general antiques and collectables, jewellery, silver and smalls. LOC: 15 minutes junction 21, M1 on to A46. PARK: Own. TEL: 0533 541201/878500. VAT: Stan/Spec.

Britain's Heritage
Shaftesbury Hall, 3 Holy Bones. (Mr and Mrs J. Dennis). Est. 1980. Open daily, Sun. 11-4. SIZE: Large. STOCK: Fireplaces, 18th-20th C, £100-£12,000. LOC: Off Vaughan Way, 70 yards from Holiday Inn. PARK: Easy. TEL: 0533 519592. SER: Valuations; restorations (antique fireplaces). VAT: Stan/Spec.

Corry's   LAPADA
24/26 Francis St., Stoneygate. (Mrs E.I. Corry). Est. 1962. Open 9-5.30. SIZE: Medium. STOCK: Furniture, 18th-19th C, £500-£10,000; paintings, 19th C, £100-£8,000; silver, porcelain and jewellery, 19th-20th C, £5-£5,000. LOC: 3 miles from city centre, south on A6, left into Stoughton Rd., then 2nd left. PARK: Easy. TEL: 0533 703794; home -same. SER: Restorations. FAIRS: NEC (April and Aug.); Barbican, Robert Bailey. VAT: Spec.

Letty's Antiques
6 Rutland St. Est. 1952. STOCK: Silver, jewellery, china and brass. TEL: 0533 626435.

Montague Antiques
60 Montague Rd, Clarendon Park. (A.R. Schlesinger and D.K. Moore). Est. 1987. Open 10-6, Sun. 12-5. CL: Wed. SIZE: Small. STOCK: Furniture, 17th C to 1910, £25-£1,000; ceramics, 18th-20th C; glass, 19th to early 20th C; both £5-£100; silver, plate and general antiques, 19th C. Not Stocked: Weapons and jewellery. LOC: From Welford Rd. (A50) to Victoria Pk. to Queens Rd. then Montague Rd. PARK: Easy. TEL: 0533 706485; home - same. SER: Valuations.

Walter Moores and Son
89 Wellington St. (P. Moores). Est. 1925. Open 8.30-5.30, Sat. 8.30-12.30. CL: Mon. except by appointment. STOCK: Mainly furniture, 1680-1880, £5-£5,000. LOC: From London Rd. railway station go up Waterloo Way, first right, then first left and left again. PARK: Easy. TEL: 0533 551402; home - 0533 707552. VAT: Stan/Spec.

Leicester continued
Oxford Street Antique Centre Ltd
16-26 Oxford St. Open 10-5.30, Sun. 2-5, or by appointment. SIZE: Large trade warehouse. 50 dealers. *STOCK: Period furniture, shipping goods, silver, bric-a-brac and general antiques, 18th to mid-20th C, 50p-£5,000.* LOC: Main ring road. PARK: Own. TEL: 0533 553006; fax - 0533 555863. SER: Container loading facilities; courier. VAT: Stan/Spec.

Hammond Smith
32 West Ave, Clarendon Park. Est. 1981. Open by appointment. SIZE: Small. *STOCK: British watercolours, 1750-1950, £300-£10,000; British etchings, 19th-20th C, £100-£500.* TEL: 0533 709020; home - same. SER: Valuations; restorations (watercolours and prints cleaned, mounted and framed); buys at auction (watercolours). VAT: Spec.

E. Smith (Leicester) Ltd   LAPADA
The Antiques Complex, St. Nicholas Pl. (K.W. Sansom). Est. 1888. Open 9.30-5.30. SIZE: Large. *STOCK: Furniture, 18th-19th C and Edwardian, £100-£5,000; clocks, smalls and paintings.* LOC: Adjacent High St., near Holiday Inn. PARK: Own. TEL: 0533 533343; fax - 0533 533347. SER: Valuations; buys at auction (18th-19th C furniture and paintings); container packing; courier. VAT: Stan/Spec.

LONG CLAWSTON, Nr. Melton Mowbray
Victoriana Architectural
Old Hall Farm, Hose Lane. Open 8.30-5.30. *STOCK: Pine, architectural items.* TEL: 0949 60274. SER: Restorations (oak, mahogany, architectural items, pine stripping); sash windows and ledged doors made from reclaimed pine.

LOUGHBOROUGH
Copperfield Antiques
221a Derby Rd. Est. 1970. Open 10-5. CL: Mon. and Wed. SIZE: Small. *STOCK: Furniture, £50-£1,500; porcelain; £5-£500; both 18th-19th C; brass, copper, china, glass, paintings and boxes, early 19th to early 20th C, £5-£250.* LOC: A6. PARK: Easy. TEL: 0509 232026; home - 0509 239281.

Lowe of Loughborough
37-40 Church Gate. Est. 1846. CL: Sat. SIZE: Large and warehouse. *STOCK: Furniture and period upholstery from early oak, 1600 to Edwardian; mahogany, walnut, oak, £20-£8,000; clocks, bracket and longcase, £95-£2,500; porcelain, pewter, maps, copper and brass.* Not Stocked: Jewellery. LOC: Opposite parish church. PARK: Own. TEL: 0509 212554/217876. SER: Upholstery; restorations; interior design. VAT: Stan/Spec.

LUBENHAM, Nr. Market Harborough
Leicestershire Sporting Gallery and Brown Jack Bookshop
The Old Granary, 62 Main St. (R. and B. Leete). Est. 1958. When closed apply 87 Lubenham Hill. SIZE: Large. *STOCK: Oil paintings, prints including Vanity Fair and sporting; engravings, maps, furniture, including pine, mahogany and oak; antiquarian books, horse brasses, martingales, swingers.* LOC: Centre of village. PARK: Rear of village green opposite. TEL: 0858 465787. VAT: Stan.

Stevens and Son
Old Post Office, 61 Main St. Resident. Open 9-6. *STOCK: General antiques, mainly furniture.* LOC: A427. TEL: 0858 463521. SER: Restorations (furniture).

MANTON
David Smith Antiques
Old Cottage, 20 St. Mary's Rd. Est. 1953. Open 9-5. CL: Sun., except by appointment. *STOCK: Furniture, glass, silver.* PARK: Easy. TEL: 057 285 244. VAT: Stan/Spec.

MARKET BOSWORTH
Corner Cottage Antiques
5 Market Place, The Square. (J. and B. Roberts). Est. 1969. Open 10-5 or by appointment. *STOCK: 18th-20th C furniture, silver, paintings; clocks, porcelain, glass, brass and copper, general antiques.* PARK: Easy. TEL: 0455 290344; home - 0455 282583. VAT: Stan/Spec.

Country Antiques
4 Main St. (M. and A. Boylan). Est. 1980. Open 10-5.30. CL: Tues. SIZE: Medium. *STOCK: Stripped pine.* LOC: Off A447 in market place. PARK: Easy. TEL: 0455 291303; home - same.

MARKET HARBOROUGH
Abbey Antiques
17 Abbey St. (M.A. Muckle). Est. 1977. Open 10.30-5. SIZE: Medium. *STOCK: Furniture, 19th C, £50-£1,000; decorative items, bric-a-brac, £1-£150.* LOC: 100yds. off town centre. PARK: Easy. TEL: 0858 462282; home - 0858 464085. SER: Valuations. VAT: Stan/Spec.

Richard Kimbell Ltd
Riverside Industrial Estate. Est. 1966. Open 9-6, Sat. 9-5, Sun. 1-4. (Trade - Mon.-Fri. only). SIZE: Large warehouse. *STOCK: Pine, 19th C, £50-£1,000.* LOC: Right turn off A427, past railway station towards Corby. TEL: 0858 433444; fax - 0858 467627. SER: Restorations (pine including stripping); shipping and packing; manufacturer. VAT: Stan.

J. Stamp and Sons
The Chestnuts, 15 Kettering Rd. (M. Stamp).

A reeded shape coffee pot in early French style, c.1758-60, 9¼in. (23.5cm), with workmen's marks. (Sotheby's). From **The Dictionary of Worcester Porcelain, Vol.I, 1751-1851** by John Sandon, published in 1993 by the **Antique Collectors' Club**, £45.00.

Market Harborough continued
Resident. Est. 1948. Open 8-5.30, Sat. 9-12.30 or by appointment. SIZE: Medium. STOCK: *Mahogany and oak furniture, 18th-19th C, £500-£5,000; Victorian furniture, £250-£2,500; Edwardian furniture, £100-£1,000.* LOC: On A6. PARK: Easy. TEL: 0858 462524. SER: Valuations (furniture); restorations (furniture). VAT: Stan/Spec.

Duncan Watts Oriental Rugs
64 St. Mary's Rd. Est. 1984. Open 10-5.30. CL: Wed. SIZE: Medium. STOCK: *Oriental rugs, antique and contemporary, £25-£7,500.* LOC: Road from town centre to railway station. PARK: Outside shop. TEL: 0858 432314; home - 0858 462620. SER: Valuations; restorations (rugs). VAT: Stan.

MEASHAM, Nr. Swadlincote
Ashley House Antiques
61 High St. (Mrs P.A. Benton). Est. 1976. Open Thurs., Fri. and Sat. 11-5. SIZE: Small. STOCK: *Wall clocks - Vienna, English and American, £100-£600; Victorian and Edwardian furniture, 19th C, £100-£375; horse brasses, 19th-20th C, £8-£100; Mason's ironstone, £50-£200; Staffordshire figures, £50-£175; ribbon plates, Measham teapots and canalia, £10-£300; oil lamps, £50-£350; brass and copper, £20-£200.* LOC: A453

Measham continued
between Ashby-de-la-Zouch and Tamworth. PARK: Nearby. TEL: 0530 273568; home - 0543 373655.

MEDBOURNE
E. and C. Royall Antiques
10 Waterfall Way. Open 9-6 including Sun. STOCK: *Furniture, pictures, silver, porcelain, glassware, ivories and Oriental bronzes.* TEL: 085 883 744; home - same. SER: Restorations (bronzes, ivories, brassware, metalware, including brass inlay work, woodcarving, upholstery, French polishing).

OADBY
John Hardy Antiques
91 London Rd. Open every day. STOCK: *General antiques.* TEL: 0533 712862. VAT: Stan/Spec.

OAKHAM
Fine Art of Oakham   BADA LAPADA
4 High St. (Dr A.J. Smith). Open 10-5. CL: Mon. STOCK: *Continental oils and watercolours, Victorian and 19th C.* TEL: 0572 755221; fax - 0572 770047.

Gallery Antiques
17 Mill St. (P.W. Jones and G.R. Pickett). Open 9.30-5.30, Sun. 2-5.30. STOCK: *Furniture, £100-£6,000; porcelain, £25-£750; silver, £20-£10,000; all English 18th-19th C.* TEL: 0572 755094; home - 0572 757252. SER: Valuations; restorations (furniture and porcelain). VAT: Stan/Spec.

Grafton Country Pictures
153 Brooke Rd. (F. Ingall). Est. 1967. Open by appointment. STOCK: *Sporting, farming, natural history, decorative prints, 18th and 19th C.* TEL: 0572 757266.

Oakham Antiques
16 Melton Rd. Open 10-3 or by appointment. CL: Tues. and Thurs. STOCK: *Brass, glass, small furniture, postcards, lamps, pictures, prints, silver.* TEL: 066 479 571.

The Old House Gallery
13-15 Market Place. (R.A. Clarke). Est. 1979. Open 9.30-5, Sat. 9.30-4. CL: Thurs. SIZE: Medium. STOCK: *Oil paintings, £50-£3,500; art studio pottery, 1850-1990, £5-£500; watercolours, £25-£2,000; prints and objets d'art, £5-£500; antiquarian county maps, £15-£250.* PARK: Easy. TEL: 0572 755538. SER: Valuations; restorations (oils, watercolours, prints, frames); framing.

Swans Antique Centre
27 Mill St. (P.W. Jones). Est. 1988. Open 9.30-5.30, Sun. 2-5.30. SIZE: Large. 15 dealers. STOCK: *General antiques especially furniture,*

Oakham continued
1600-1900; pine, silver and plate, oils, watercolours, art deco, linen and rugs, prints, jewellery, porcelain, £5-£5,000. LOC: 150yds. from High St. PARK: Easy. TEL: 0572 724364; home - 0572 757252. SER: Valuations; restorations. VAT: Stan/Spec.

Paul Warrington
Mews Cottage, 46 High St. Open by appointment. *STOCK: Period and decorative furniture, architectural items and garden statuary.* TEL: 0572 722414.

OSGATHORPE, Nr. Loughborough
David E. Burrows LAPADA
Manor House Farm. Est. 1973. *STOCK: Pine, oak, mahogany and walnut furniture, clocks, smalls, £50-£20,000.* LOC: Exit 23, M1, turn right off Ashby road, farm next to church. TEL: 0530 222218; mobile - 0863 598664; fax - 0530 223139. VAT: Stan/Spec.

QUENIBOROUGH, Nr. Leicester
J. Green and Son
1 Coppice Lane. (R. Green). Resident. Est. 1932. Appointment advisable. SIZE: Medium. *STOCK: 18th-19th C English and continental furniture.* LOC: Off A607 Leicester-Melton Mowbray Rd. PARK: Easy. TEL: 0533 606682. SER: Valuations; buys at auction. VAT: Stan/Spec.

QUORN
Mill on the Soar Antiques Ltd
1/3 High St. (T.O. and J. York). Open daily, Wed. by appointment. *STOCK: Furniture, 17th-19th C, and associated articles.* LOC: In centre of village, on A6. PARK: Easy. TEL: 0509 414218.

Quorn Pine and Decoratives
The New Mills, Leicester Rd. (S. Yates and S. Parker). Open 9-6, Sat. 9.30-5.30. *STOCK: Pine and country furniture.* TEL: 0509 416031. SER: Stripping and restorations (pine). VAT: Stan/Spec.

RATCLIFFE-ON-THE-WREAKE
Pavilion BADA
Long Gable. (Mrs M. Brown). Est. 1969. Open by appointment. SIZE: Small. *STOCK: English furniture, 18th C.* TEL: 0664 424209. FAIRS: Chelsea.

SHENTON, Nr. Market Bosworth
Whitemoors Antiques and Fine Art
(P. Rixon). Est. 1987. Open 10-5 including Sun. CL: Mon. SIZE: Large. *STOCK: Furniture, £25-£1,000; smalls, £5-£200; prints and pictures, Victorian and early 20th C, £40-£300.* LOC: A5 onto A444 towards Burton-on-Trent, first right then second left. PARK: Easy. TEL: 0455 212250; home - same.

J. Green & Son
Antiques
1 Coppice Lane,
Queniborough, Leicester
Telephone Leicester 606682

SHEPSHED, Nr. Loughborough
G.K. Hadfield
Blackbrook Hill House, Tickow Lane. Resident. Est. 1972. Open Thurs., Fri. and Sat. 9-5, other times by appointment. *STOCK: Clocks, longcase, dial, Act of Parliament, skeleton, Black Forest, American and carriage; secondhand and rare horological books.* LOC: 1.75 miles along the A512 west of M1, exit 23. PARK: Easy. TEL: 0509 503014; fax - 0509 600136. SER: Restoration materials (antique clocks). VAT: Stan/Spec.

SILEBY, Nr. Loughborough
R. A. James Antiques
Ammonite Gallery, 25a High St. *STOCK: Mainly stripped pine, general antiques.* TEL: 050 981 2169.

STAUNTON HAROLD
Ropers Hill Antiques
Ropers Hill Farm. (S. and R. Southworth). Est. 1974. Open 9-5.30 every day or by appointment. SIZE: Small. *STOCK: General antiques, silver and metalware.* LOC: On A453. PARK: Easy. TEL: 0530 413919. SER: Valuations.

TONGE, Nr. Melbourne
The Spindles
(Mrs C. Reynolds). Est. 1972. Resident. Usually

LEICESTERSHIRE

Tonge continued
available but telephone call advisable. SIZE: Large. *STOCK: Clocks, watches, 17th-19th C.* LOC: 3 miles from exit 24 M1. PARK: Easy. TEL: 0332 862609. VAT: Stan.

UPPINGHAM

Bay House Antiques
33 High St. East. Est. 1986. Open 10-5. SIZE: Medium. *STOCK: Pottery, porcelain, glass, brass, copper, pictures, agricultural implements, small Victorian and Edwardian furniture.* LOC: Near Falcon Hotel. PARK: Nearby. TEL: 0572 821045.

Clutter
14 Orange St. (M.C. Sumner). Est. 1982. Open 10-5. CL: Thurs. *STOCK: Victorian linen and lace; textiles including Durham quilts; interesting silver, porcelain, glass, small furniture, kitchenalia, 10p-£1,000.* LOC: Take old A47 from by-pass, shop 25yds. from traffic lights. PARK: Several car parks round corner. TEL: 0572 823745; home - 057 286 243. SER: Valuations; restorations (furniture, brass, copper, silver); hire (christening gowns and Victorian wedding dress and accessories).

John Garner
51-53 High St. East. Est. 1967. Open 9-5.30, Sun. by appointment. SIZE: Large, plus warehouse. *STOCK: Oil paintings, furniture, 18th-19th C; clocks, bronzes, handcoloured sporting, coaching, marine and genre engravings and etchings; garden statuary; decorative pieces.* LOC: Just off A47, close to market place. PARK: Easy. TEL: 0572 823607; fax - 0572 821654. SER: Valuations; restorations (pictures, furniture); framing; courier; export. VAT: Stan/Spec.

Gilberts of Uppingham
Ayston Rd. (M. Gilbert). Open 9.30-1 and 2-5, Wed., Fri. and Sat. 9.30-5. CL: Thurs. *STOCK: General antiques.* TEL: 0572 823486.

Goldmark Books
14 Orange St. (M.M. Goldmark). Open 9.30-5.30 and Sunday afternoons. *STOCK: Antiquarian and secondhand books.* LOC: Between Market Sq. and traffic lights. PARK: Nearby. TEL: 0572 822694.

Marie-Ange Martin Antiques
43 High St. East. Est. 1985. Open 10-5, other times by appointment. CL: Thurs. SIZE: Small. *STOCK: Furniture, 17th to early 19th C; some oil paintings, silver, 18th-19th C; all £500-£5,000.* PARK: Easy. TEL: 0572 821359; home - same.

Not Just Books
Market Place. (R.M. and Mrs F. Waknell). Est. 1988. Open 10-5, Sat. 9.30-5.30. SIZE: Large. *STOCK: Books, especially fiction and theology.* TEL: 0572 821306.

Uppingham continued

T.J. Roberts
39/41 High St. East. Resident. Open 9.30-5.30. *STOCK: Furniture, porcelain and pottery, 18th to 19th C; paintings and prints, 19th to early 20th C.* PARK: Easy. TEL: 0572 821493. VAT: Stan/Spec.

E. and C. Royall Antiques
Printers Yard, High St. East. Open 10-4.30. CL: Thurs. *STOCK: Furniture, pictures, silver, porcelain, glassware, ivories and Oriental bronzes.* TEL: 085 883 744.

Tattersall's
14b Orange St. (J. Tattersall). Est. 1985. Open 9.30-5. CL: Mon. and Thurs. SIZE: Small. *STOCK: Persian rugs, mirrors, sofas, 19th-20th C.* PARK: Easy, 200yds. TEL: 0572 821171. SER: Restorations (rush and cane work, rugs); upholstery.

WHISSENDINE, Nr. Oakham

Old Bakehouse Pine
11 Main St. (E. and W. Stevenson). Open seven days, prior phone call advisable. *STOCK: Stripped pine furniture.* LOC: Off A606, opposite village school. TEL: 066 479 691.

WING, Nr. Oakham

Robert Bingley Antiques
Home Farm, Church St. Open 9-5, Sun. 11-4. SIZE: Large. *STOCK: Furniture, 17th-19th C £50-£5,000; glass, clocks, silver and plate, pictures and porcelain.* LOC: Next to church. PARK: Own. TEL: 057 285 725; home - 057 285 314. SER: Valuations; restorations. VAT: Spec.

WOODHOUSE EAVES, Nr. Leicester

Paddock Antiques
The Old Smithy, Brand Hill. (M., C.A. and T.M Bray). Open Thurs. - Sat. 10-5.30, other times by appointment. *STOCK: Furniture, 1750-1910, to £3,000; porcelain, 1750-1930's, to £2,000; prints glass, copper and brass.* PARK: Outside shop.

WYMESWOLD, Nr. Loughborough

N. Bryan-Peach Antiques
28 Far St. Resident. Open 10-6, Sun. by appointment. SIZE: Medium. *STOCK: Clocks, barometers watches; 18th-19th C furniture, £50-£5,000* PARK: Easy. TEL: 0509 880425. SER: Valuations; restorations; buys at auction. VAT: Spec.

Antique Collectors' Club Titles

The Dictionary of Blue and White Printed Pottery 1780-1880 Volume I
by A.W. Coysh and R.K. Henrywood
Immediately acclaimed in 1982 as an outstanding reference work, this 1989 edition is reissued in its original form, but now the first of a two volume set. Covers the firms, the craftsmen, the techniques, the wares, the patterns, the titles, and provides a remarkable background to the history of the ceramics industry and the social customs of the day, as well as the personalities and problems involved in the production process. Appendices cover makers' initial marks and a list of source books used by makers of these wares.
ISBN 0 907462 06 5, 424pp, 706 b & w illus, 30 col, £29.95

The Dictionary of Blue and White Printed Pottery Volume II
by A.W. Coysh and R.K. Henrywood
This entirely new second volume includes over 1,000 new or extended entries. These cover many previously unrecorded patterns, recent attributions, newly discovered design sources, and a significant number of additional manufacturers and retailers. Some of the more interesting wares made after the original deadline of 1880 have also been included, with an Appendix illustrating unidentified patterns. An essential acquisition.
ISBN 1 85149 093 0, 240pp, 420 b & w illus, 28 col, £25.00

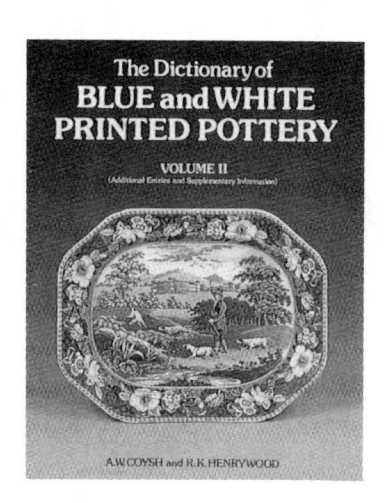

Available from:
Antique Collectors' Club, 5 Church Street, Woodbridge, Suffolk IP12 1DS
Tel: (0394) 385501 Fax: (0394) 384434

or Market Street Industrial Park, Wappingers' Falls, New York 12590, USA
Tel: 914 297 0003 Fax: 914 297 0068

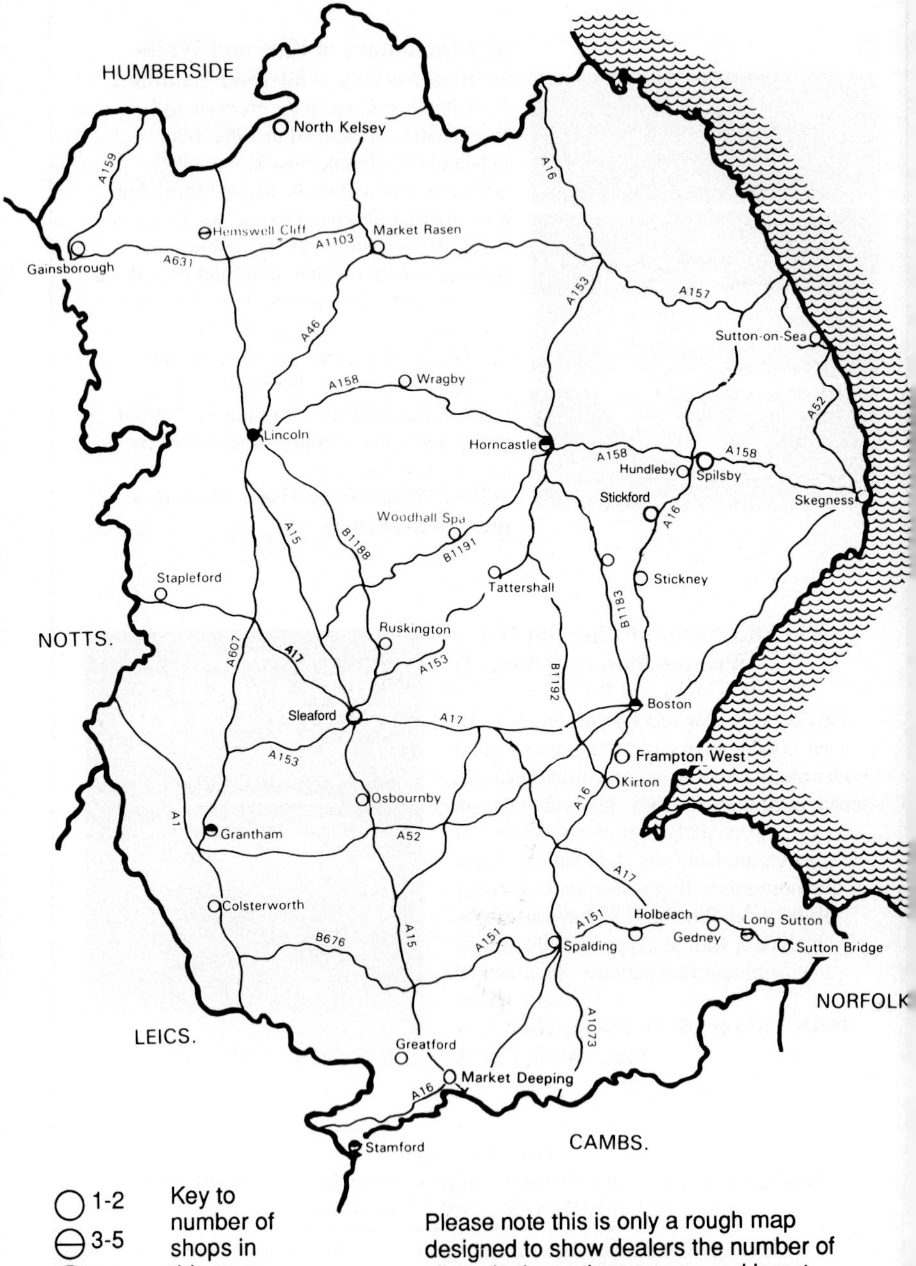
HUMBERSIDE
North Kelsey
A159
Hemswell Cliff
Market Rasen
A1103
Gainsborough
A631
A16
A153
A157
Sutton-on-Sea
A46
A158
Wragby
A52
Lincoln
Horncastle
A158
A158
Hundleby
Spilsby
Stickford
Skegness
A16
Woodhall Spa
A15
B1188
B1191
Tattershall
Stickney
Stapleford
B1183
Ruskington
NOTTS.
A607
A17
A153
B1192
Boston
Sleaford
A17
A153
Frampton West
Kirton
A16
Osbournby
A1
Grantham
A52
A17
Colsterworth
Holbeach
Long Sutton
A151
Gedney
B676
A15
A151
Spalding
Sutton Bridge
NORFOLK
A1073
LEICS.
Greatford
Market Deeping
A16
Stamford
CAMBS.

Symbol	Key to number of shops in this area.
○	1-2
⊖	3-5
◓	6-12
●	13+

Please note this is only a rough map designed to show dealers the number of shops in the various towns, and is not necessarily totally accurate.

Lincolnshire

BOSTON
Boston Antiques Centre
12 West St. (R. Grant). Est. 1978. Open 9-5. CL: Thurs. SIZE: Medium. STOCK: *Jewellery, silver and plate.* LOC: 2 minutes walk from town centre on Spalding side. PARK: 1 mins. walk. TEL: 0205 361510. SER: Valuations; restorations; repairs; export. VAT: Stan.

Tony Coda Antiques
121 High St. Est. 1967. Open 9.30-12.30 and 1.30-5.30. SIZE: Medium. STOCK: *Furniture, 17th-19th C, from £100; paintings, 19th C, to £500; china, silver and clocks, to £200.* LOC: From A16 turn right at roundabout in to London Rd. and then to High St. PARK: Easy. TEL: 0205 352754; home - 0205 722104. SER: Valuations. FAIRS: International Antique and Collectors.

Mary Holland Antiques
7A Red Lion St. (Mrs M. Holland). Est. 1980. Open 10-5, Sun., Mon. and Thurs. by appointment. SIZE: Small. STOCK: *General antiques.* TEL: 0205 363791; home - 0205 353840.

Pen Street Antiques
9A Pen St. (Mrs S.M. Taylor). Est. 1976. Open Wed., Fri. and Sat. 10-1 and 2-4. SIZE: Small. STOCK: *China, glass, silver and plate, jewellery, 1830-1930, £2-£200.* LOC: 40 metres from 'New England' Hotel. PARK: Easy. TEL: 0205 364118; home - same. SER: Buys at auction (bric-a-brac).

Portobellow Row Antiques Centre
93-95 High St. Open 10-4. SIZE: 9 dealers. STOCK: *Furniture, pine, shipping goods, '40's-'60's clothing, kitchenalia, postcards, oil lamps and gramophones.* TEL: 0205 369456. SER: Repairs (oil lamps and gramophones).

That Little Shop
7 Red Lion St. (L.B. Brand). Open Wed. and Fri. 10.30-3.30, Sat. 10.30-4.30. STOCK: *Jewellery and general antiques.* LOC: Behind Woolworths. TEL: Home - 0790 53060.

COLSTERWORTH
Clive Underwood Antiques
46 High St. Est. 1970. Open 9.30-5.30. STOCK: *Furniture, oak, mahogany, 17th-19th C, £45-£10,000; some pictures, glass, porcelain.* LOC: 1/2 mile off A1 between Stamford and Grantham. TEL: 0476 860689. SER: Valuations; restorations; rushing; caning. VAT: Stan/Spec.

FRAMPTON WEST, Nr. Boston
Robert J. Kent Antiques
Pinewood, Ralphs Lane. STOCK: *Pine furniture.* LOC: B1391. TEL: 0205 723739. VAT: Stan.

Gables were again objects of esteem in the 16th and 17th centuries, and consequently decorated; combined ogees and curves appear widely, for instance at Church Cottage, Shuart Lane, St Nicholas at Wade. From **Kent Houses** by Anthony Quiney, published in 1993 by the **Antique Collectors' Club**, £35.00.

GAINSBOROUGH
G. Carrick Antiques
130 Trinity St. Open 8.30-5. STOCK: *General antiques and shipping furniture.* TEL: 0427 611393/810409.

Stanley Hunt Jewellers
22 Church St. (S. and R.S. Hunt). Est. 1952. Open 9-5. CL: Wed. SIZE: Medium. STOCK: *Jewellery, 19th C, £50-£500+.* LOC: Main street from Market Place. PARK: Easy. TEL: 0427 613051; home - same. SER: Valuations; restorations (gold and silver); buys at auction.

Pilgrims Antique Centre
66 Church St. (Michael S. Wallis). Est. 1986. CL: Mon. and Wed. SIZE: Large. STOCK: *Jewellery and silver, £25-£100; pictures, ceramics and textiles, £5-£100; small furniture, £50-£1,000; all 19th-20th C.* LOC: Near Old Hall. PARK: Easy. TEL: 0427 810897. SER: Valuations. FAIRS: Newark and Lincoln Showgrounds; Birmingham.

Mr Van Hefflin
12 High St, Kirton Lindsey. Est. 1820. Open 11-5.30. STOCK: *Jewellery, watches, silver, paintings.* PARK: Easy. TEL: 0652 648044.

LINCOLNSHIRE

PAUL JOHNSTON
Early English Oak

THE OLD RED LION, GEDNEY, SPALDING
LINCOLNSHIRE PE12 0DB. TEL: 0406 362414

GEDNEY
Paul Johnston BADA
Old Red Lion. Resident. Est. 1975. Open 10-6 or by appointment. SIZE: Small. *STOCK: Early English oak and country furniture.* Not Stocked: Mahogany. LOC: Just off A17 on B1359 at Gedney roundabout. PARK: Easy. TEL: 0406 362414.

GRANTHAM
The Attic
84 Westgate. (A. and A. Sharp). Open 8.30-6, Sat. 8.30-5.30, Sun. 10-4. *STOCK: General antiques.* TEL: 0476 64990.

Grantham Clocks
30 Lodge Way. (R. Conder). Resident. Open by appointment. *STOCK: Clocks.* PARK: Easy. TEL: 0476 61784. SER: Restorations.

Grantham Furniture Emporium
4-6 Wharf Rd. (K. and J.E. Hamilton). Est. 1970. Open 10-5, Sun. 11-5. CL: Mon. SIZE: Large. *STOCK: Victorian and Edwardian furniture, £5-£3,000.* LOC: Town centre, near Post Office. PARK: Own at rear. TEL: 0476 62967.

Harold Nadin
109 London Rd. Open 9.30-5. CL: Sat. p.m. *STOCK: Furniture, 17th to early 19th C; general antiques.* TEL: 0476 63562.

Grantham continued

Notions
2a Market Place. (Mrs J. Atterby and Mrs S. Checkley). Est. 1982. Open 10-5, Sat. 9.30-5. CL: Wed. p.m. SIZE: Medium. *STOCK: China and smalls, £5-£100; furniture, £30-£400; all late 19th to 20th C.* LOC: Opposite Angel and Royal Hotel. PARK: Easy. TEL: 0476 63603. FAIRS: Newark.

William Redmile Antiques
15 Elmer St. North. (J.W. Redmile). Est. 1936. Open 9-6. *STOCK: General antiques.* LOC: From London turn right at Angel Hotel. TEL: 0476 64074.

Wilkinson's
The Tyme House, 1 Blue Court. (M. and P. Wilkinson). Est. 1935. Open 9-1 and 2-4, Wed. and Thurs. by appointment. SIZE: Small. *STOCK: Jewellery, watches and silver, 19th C, £50-£1,000.* PARK: Nearby. TEL: 0476 60400 and 0529 413149. SER: Valuations; restorations (including clock and watch movements); buys at auction (rings and watches). VAT: Stan.

GREATFORD, Nr. Stamford
The Complete Automobilist
Dept. GD, The Old Rectory. Est. 1967. Open 9-5. CL: Sat. *STOCK: Hard-to-get parts for older vehicles.* LOC: East of Stamford. PARK: Easy. TEL: 0778 560312; fax - 0778 560738. SER: Catalogue available £1.

HEMSWELL CLIFF, Nr. Gainsborough
The Guardroom Antiques Centre
Old RAF Hemswell. (M. Frith). Open daily including Sun. SIZE: 30 dealers. *STOCK: Wide variey of general antiques including Victorian, Edwardian and continental furniture and smalls.* LOC: Near Caenby Corner Estate. TEL: 0427 668312.

Hemswell Antiques Centres
Caenby Corner Estate. (P.J. and A.R. Miller). Est. 1986. Open 10-5, 7 days a week. SIZE: 270 dealers. *STOCK: Furniture, 17th-19th C; watercolours and oils, 19th C; silver and plate, clocks, porcelain, china, jewellery, dolls, toys, books, prints, clothes.* LOC: A15 from Lincoln then A631 towards Gainsborough, 1 mile from roundabout, follow signs. PARK: Easy. TEL: 0427 668389. SER: Valuations; restorations (oak, mahogany and pine; upholstery); container packing.

Kate
Kate House, Caenby Corner Estate. (Mr Shamsa). Open 10-5 including Sun. *STOCK: Pine including reproduction, general antiques.* TEL: 0427 668724/668904; fax - 0427 668905.

Hemswell Antiques Centres

10 Miles North of Lincoln, 1 Mile from Caenby Corner on the A631 to Gainsborough. Newark 25 Miles

Licensed Restaurant

270 shops in three adjacent buildings selling
Period furniture, shipping furniture, pine furniture, Oriental rugs, longcase clocks, jewellery, prints, books, silver, pictures, ceramics and many collectables.

Tel: Hemswell 668389 (STD 0427)
Open daily 10.00a.m. to 5.00p.m.

Nationwide deliveries arranged. Container, packing service. Single item shipping arranged. Car parking for 400 cars.

Hemswell Antiques Centres, Caenby Corner Estate, Hemswell Cliff, Gainsborough, Lincs. DN21 5TJ

Hemswell Cliff continued

Second Time Around
Hemswell Antique Centre, Caenby Corner Estate. (G.L. Powis and R. Kenyon). Est. 1986. Open 10-5 including Sun. STOCK: *Longcase and bracket clocks, pre 1830, £1,100-£12,000.* LOC: A15 from Lincoln to Caenby Corner roundabout, left towards Gainsborough for 1 mile. (A631). PARK: Easy. TEL: 0427 668389; home - 0522 543167 or 0904 705000. SER: Restorations (clocks).

HOLBEACH, Nr. Spalding

All Our Yesterdays Rural Bygones
North View, Penny Hill. (M.E. and D.C. Pearsey). Resident. Open by appointment. STOCK: *Country tools, ironwork, treen.* LOC: Old A17 next to Bulls Neck public house. TEL: 0406 24636.

P.J. Cassidy (Books)
1B Boston Rd. Est. 1974. Open 10-6. SIZE: Medium. STOCK: *Books, 19th-20th C, £2-£300; maps, prints and engravings, 17th-19th C, £10-£500.* LOC: 1/4 mile from A17. PARK: Nearby. TEL: 0406 26322. SER: Valuations; framing and mount cutting. VAT: Stan.

HORNCASTLE

Clare Boam
22-38 North St. Est. 1977. Open 9-5, Sun 2-4.30.

Horncastle continued

SIZE: Large. STOCK: *Furniture and bric-a-brac, 19th-20th C, to £1,000.* LOC: Louth/Grimsby road out of town. PARK: Easy. TEL: 0507 522381; home - same. VAT: Stan.

Horncastle Antiques
23 North St. (R. Ingram Hill). Est. 1971. Open by appointment only. SIZE: Small. STOCK: *Furniture, 18th-19th C, £50-£500; metalware, 19th C, £50-£200.* LOC: 200yds. from town centre on Louth road. PARK: Easy. TEL: 0507 524415; home - same. VAT: Stan/Spec.

Robert Kitching
9-11 West St. Open 9.30-5. STOCK: *Clocks and general antiques.* TEL: 0507 522120.

The Lincolnshire Antiques Centre
Bridge St. (Karen White). Open 9-5. SIZE: 30+ dealers. STOCK: *General antiques, £5-£5,000.* LOC: To rear of "The Kitchen Range". PARK: Own. TEL: 0507 527794. VAT: Stan/Spec.

The M.C. Trading Co
Stanhope Rd. (M. Clow and M. Chalk). Est. 1968. Open 9-5, Sun. by appointment. SIZE: Large. STOCK: *Furniture -Victorian, Edwardian, inlaid, marquetry, country, European and shipping; silver and plate, boxes, brass and general small items; all £5-£1,000.* PARK: Easy. TEL: 0507 524524; home - 0507 523787. FAIRS: Newark and Ardingly. VAT: Stan/Spec.

Antique Collectors' Club Titles

Art Deco and Other Figures
by Bryan Catley
This sumptuously illustrated book contains the most comprehensive range of art deco figures ever published of the superb sculptures which became fashionable between the wars. The unconventional use of bronze and ivory for many of these sensual and exceptionally high quality figures and their sense of movement and rhythm ensure that large sums are paid by a discriminating international collectors' market. Compiled by the leading specialist dealer in these delightful figures.
ISBN 0 902028 57 X, 348pp
1,100 b & w illus, 43 col illus, £45.00

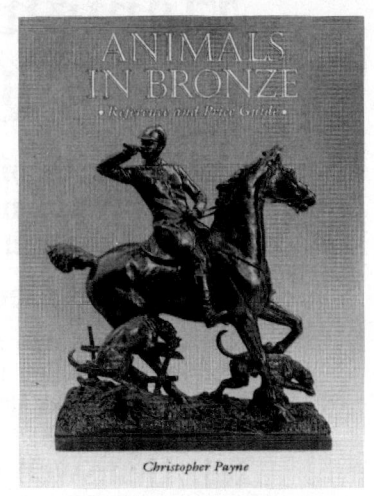

Animals in Bronze
by Christopher Payne
This comprehensive book describes the work of the animalier school, and brings us up to the present day. Practical information to help the collector and dealer.
ISBN 0 907462 45 6, 424pp
900 b & w illus, 22 col illus, £39.50

Available from:
Antique Collectors' Club, 5 Church Street
Woodbridge, Suffolk IP12 1DS
Tel: (0394) 385501 Fax: (0394) 384434

or Market Street Industrial Park
Wappingers' Falls, New York 12590, USA
Tel: 914 297 0003 Fax: 914 297 0068

The Barye Bronzes - a catalogue raisonné *by Stuart Pivar* (new edition)
This is a reprint of the author's standard work and is the first modern book on the sculptor Antoine-Louis Barye, the teacher of Rodin and prime mover of the Romantic Movement in art. It contains many improved black and white photographs and additional colour plates. All his known works are illustrated, with many more of Barye's castings of his own work. Barye was a craftsman in bronze almost as much as he was a sculptor; his then new techniques of casting, chiselling and patination are the cornerstone of modern bronze work. **ISBN 1 85149 142 2, 308pp, 300 b & w illus, 20 col, £45.00**

Horncastle continued
Seaview Antiques
47a East St. (M. Chalk). Open 9-5. SIZE: Large. STOCK: Furniture and smalls, period to shipping, £5-£5,000. LOC: A158. PARK: Easy. TEL: 0507 523287.

Laurence Shaw Antiques
77 East St. Open 8.30-5. SIZE: Large. STOCK: Furniture and general antiques, 17th-20th C, £5-£5,000. TEL: 0507 527638. SER: Transport, delivery and collections. VAT: Stan/Spec.

Staines Antiques
25 Bridge St. (Mrs M.E. Staines). Est. 1991. Open 10-5. CL: Mon. SIZE: Large. STOCK: Furniture, pictures and clocks, £50-£5,000; ceramics, £25-£1,000; all 18th-20th C. LOC: A158 Lincoln to Skegness road, turn off by-pass towards town centre. Shop 200 yards on right, opposite Antiques Centre. PARK: Easy and nearby. TEL: 0507 527976; home - same. SER: Valuations.

Talisman Antiques
51/53 North St. (M.V. Prime). Open 10-5. CL: Mon. SIZE: Large. STOCK: Pine furniture, collectables, satin walnut, model trains. TEL: 0507 526893.

The Warehouse
Bank St. (Mrs M. Brooke and W. Cruickshank). Open 10-5. STOCK: Pine furniture. TEL: 0507 524569; evenings - 0507 527311.

HUNDLEBY, Nr. Spilsby
Alan Lewis Fine Art
The Old Mill House, 35 Main Rd. (A. and M. Lewis). Est. 1987. Open by appointment only. SIZE: Medium. STOCK: Watercolours, £200-£1,500; oils, £500-£5,000; both 1800-1920. LOC: Just off A16. PARK: Easy. TEL: 0790 52817. SER: Valuations; buys at auction (oils and watercolours). FAIRS: Birmingham; Barbican; East Midlands; Arley Hall; some Robert Bailey. VAT: Spec.

KIRTON
Kirton Antiques   LAPADA
3 High St. (A.R. Marshall). Est. 1973. Open 8.30-5, Sat. 8.30-12, or by appointment. SIZE: Warehouse. STOCK: Furniture, shipping goods, bric-a-brac, Georgian, Victorian, Edwardian. TEL: 0205 722595; mobile - 0860 531600; evenings - 0205 722134; fax - 0205 722895. VAT: Stan.

LINCOLN
20th Century Frocks
55 Steep Hill. (Patricia Rowberry). Est. 1986. Open 11-5, Mon. and Wed. by appointment only. SIZE: Small. STOCK: Ladies clothes, hats and accessories, jewellery including costume, mainly '20's and '30's, to 1970, £5-£150; textiles including Canton and paisley shawls, curtains and chenille cloths, £5-£300. LOC: Opposite the Jews House, bottom of Steep Hill. PARK: Danes Terrace. TEL: 0522 545916; home - 0507 533638. SER: Valuations. FAIRS: Newark.

Annette Antiques
77 Bailgate. (Mrs A. Bhalla). Est. 1972. Open 10-12.30 and 1.30-5.30, Sat. 10-5.30. SIZE: Small. STOCK: Porcelain, glass and small silver, 19th-20th C; silver flatware, watercolours, prints and drawings, 18th-20th C; all £10-£150. LOC: 2 minutes from castle and cathedral. PARK: Nearby. TEL: 0522 546838; home - 0205 85219. SER: Restorations (furniture). FAIRS: Alexandra Palace.

Michael Brewer
5 Drury Lane. (M.N. Brewer). Est. 1954. Open by appointment. SIZE: Medium. STOCK: Furniture, oil paintings, silver, porcelain, bronzes, works of art. Not Stocked: Coins. LOC: Close to Cathedral. PARK: 20yds. TEL: 0522 545854. SER: Valuations; buys at auction. VAT: Stan/Spec. Trade Only.

Castle Gallery
61 Steep Hill. (A.R. Buchanan). Est. 1983. Open 10-5.30, Sun. by appointment. SIZE: Large. STOCK: Oil paintings, 18th-19th C and modern British, £150-£8,000; watercolours, 18th-20th C, £50-£3,000; antiquarian maps, mirrors. LOC: 100yds. from Lincoln cathedral. PARK: Easy. TEL: 0522 535078; home - same. SER: Valuations; restorations (oils and watercolours); framing. VAT: Stan/Spec.

Designs on Pine
27 The Strait. Est. 1965. Open 10-5. STOCK: Pine. TEL: 0522 529252.

Doyle Antiques
24 Steep Hill. (A.G. Doyle). Est. 1974. Open 10-5. SIZE: Small. STOCK: Period oak, paintings and clocks. LOC: 100 yds from Cathedral. TEL: 0522 542226. VAT: Spec.

C. and K.E. Dring
111 High St. Open 10-5.30. CL: Wed. STOCK: Victorian and Edwardian inlaid furniture; shipping goods, porcelain, clocks, tin-plated toys, trains and Dinkys, etc. TEL: 0522 540733/792794.

Eastgate Antique Centre
6 Eastgate. (N. Marris, LAPADA). Est. 1970. Open 9.30-5. SIZE: 12 dealers. STOCK: 17th-19th C town and country furniture; oil and water-colour paintings, miniatures, silver, jewellery, brass, copper, pottery, porcelain, clocks, barometers, treen and decorative items. Not Stocked: Bric-a-brac, coins and militaria. LOC: Near Cathedral. PARK: Easy. TEL: 0522 544404.

HARWOOD TATE

**CHURCH MILL CAISTOR ROAD
MARKET RASEN LINCOLNSHIRE Tel: 0673-843579**

Dealer in 18th & 19th century furniture
clocks, pictures & ornamental items

OPEN MONDAY TO FRIDAY 9.30AM TO 5.30PM
SATURDAY 10.00AM TO 1.00PM

Lincoln continued

Golden Goose Books
20 and 21 Steep Hill. (R. West-Skinn and Mrs A. Cockram). Est. 1983. Open 10-5.30. STOCK: *Antiquarian books, bookcases, carpets, decorative items, £1-£5,000.* TEL: 0522 522589; home - 0673 878622.

David J. Hansord and Son   BADA
32 Steep Hill. Est. 1972. Open 9.30-1 and 2-5.30. SIZE: Medium. STOCK: *English and continental furniture, 17th to early 19th C, £100-£10,000; clocks, barometers and scientific instruments, mainly 18th C, from £50.* Not Stocked: Later items. LOC: Few yards from Cathedral. PARK: Easy. TEL: 0522 530044; home - 0522 526983. SER: Valuations; buys at auction. VAT: Stan/Spec.

Harlequin Gallery
22 Steep Hill. (R. West-Skinn). Est. 1962. Open 10-5.30. STOCK: *Antiquarian books, prints, maps, 50p-£15,000.* TEL: 0522 522589; home - 0673 858294.

Dorrian Lambert Antiques
64 Steep Hill. (R. Lambert). Est. 1981. Open 10-5, Wed. and Sun. by appointment. SIZE: Medium. STOCK: *Small furniture, clocks, chairs, pottery, porcelain, jewellery, sporting antiques and collectables, 18th to early 20th C.* PARK:

Lincoln continued

Loading only or nearby. TEL: 0522 545916; home - 042784 686. SER: Valuations; restorations (clocks). FAIRS: Newark Showground.

Lincoln Fine Art
Dernstall House, 33 The Strait. (Mrs D. Glen-Doepel). Est. 1973. Open 10-1 and 2-5.30. STOCK: *Oil paintings including decorative portraits, landscapes, marine, watercolours, abstracts (Dorothy Lee Roberts), miniatures, Old Master paintings, drawings, porcelain and objets d'art, 17th-20th C, £80-£10,000.* LOC: Top of High St., opposite Stadz Café. PARK: Nearby. TEL: 0522 533029. SER: Valuations.

Mansions
5a Eastgate. Open 10-5. STOCK: *Antiques, decorative items, period textiles, linen, etc.* TEL: 0522 513631/560271.

Richard Pullen Jeweller
28 The Strait. Est. 1979. Open 10-4.30. CL: Wed. STOCK: *Jewellery, silver and plate.* LOC: Near Cathedral. PARK: Easy. TEL: 0522 537170. SER: Valuations; repairs (silver, jewellery - including re-threading).

J. and R Ratcliffe
46 Steep Hill. Est. 1954. STOCK: *Furniture, decorative items, 1600-1830.* TEL: 0522 537438.

LINCOLNSHIRE

Lincoln continued
Rowletts of Lincoln
338 High St. (A.H. Rowlett). Open 9-5, Wed. 9-1. STOCK: *Coins and jewellery.* TEL: 0522 524139.

The Strait Antiques
5 The Strait. (F.M. Davies). Est. 1970. Open Thurs. and Fri. 10-4, Sat. 10-4.30. SIZE: Medium. STOCK: *English pottery and porcelain, 18th-19th C, £25-£200; blue and white transfer ware, early 19th C, £5-£50; general antiques and furniture, 19th to early 20th C; dolls.* LOC: At the start of the ascent to the Cathedral from the top of the High St. PARK: Easy, behind shop. TEL: 0522 523130. VAT: Stan/Spec.

James Usher and Son Ltd
6 Silver St. Open 9-5.30. CL: Wed. STOCK: *Silver, jewellery.* TEL: 0522 527547.

LONG SUTTON
E. and J. Northam
15 High St. (Mrs Northam). STOCK: *General antiques, glass, oil lamps, silver.* TEL: 0406 363191.

J.W. Talton
15-19 Market St. (J., W. and J.J. Talton). Resident. Est. 1952. Open 9-5, Wed. 9-12. SIZE: Small. STOCK: *General antiques.* LOC: On old A17. PARK: Easy. TEL: 0406 362147; home - same. SER: Restorations (furniture and cabinet making).

Trade Antiques
7 Market St. (P.E. Poole). Est. 1961. CL: Sat. SIZE: Medium. STOCK: *General shipping goods, clocks and watches.* LOC: A17. PARK: Easy. TEL: 0406 363758. VAT: Stan. *Trade Only.*

MARKET DEEPING
Portland House Antiques
23 Church St. (G.W. Cree and V.E. Bass). Est. 1987. Open Mon.-Sat., or by appointment. SIZE: Medium. STOCK: *Porcelain, glass, furniture, 18th-19th C, £100-£3,000.* PARK: Easy. TEL: 0778 347129; home - same. SER: Buys at auction. FAIRS: Chelsea Harbour Fair. VAT: Stan/Spec.

MARKET RASEN
Carole's Corner
11 Market Place. (Carole Ashley). Est. 1982. Open 10-4. SIZE: Medium. STOCK: *Mainly collectables including militaria, books and china, to £250.* LOC: A631. PARK: Opposite. TEL: 0673 844625; home - 0673 843160.

Harwood Tate
Church Mill, Caistor Rd. (J. Harwood Tate). Open 9.30-5.30, Sat. 10-1. SIZE: Large. STOCK: *Furniture, mahogany, rosewood, oak; clocks, 18th to early 19th C; ornamental items including pictures and prints, 18th-19th C.* Not Stocked:

Market Rasen continued
Shipping goods. LOC: Take A46 from Lincoln, Church Mill is off town centre, north of church. PARK: Easy. TEL: 0673 843579. VAT: Stan/Spec.

NORTH KELSEY MOOR, Nr. Caistor
Sykes Antiques
New Warehouse, Station Yard. SIZE: Large. STOCK: *English and continental pine and French furniture.* PARK: Own. TEL: 0652 678036. SER: Container. VAT: Stan.

OSBOURNBY
Audley House Antiques
North St. (S. Wood). Est. 1948. Open 10-6, Sun. 2-6, or by appointment. STOCK: *Furniture, Georgian, Victorian and some Edwardian; decorative items and treen.* LOC: On A15, 10 miles north of Bourne, turn left into village market place, then right into North St. to far end. PARK: Easy. TEL: 052 95 473/0860 758764. SER: Valuations.

RUSKINGTON
Pinfold Antiques   LAPADA
3 Pinfold Lane. (J. and G.D. Ballinger). Est. 1981. Open by appointment. SIZE: Medium. STOCK: *Longcase clocks, 17th-19th C, £500-£5,000; period English furniture, weapons, £50-£3,000.* PARK: Easy. TEL: 0526 832057. SER: Valuations; restorations (longcase and bracket clocks, period furniture); buys at auction. FAIRS: Olympia, Robert Bailey.

SKEGNESS
G.H. Crowson
50 High St. Open daily 10-6. STOCK: *General antiques, jewellery.* TEL: 0754 764360. *Mostly Trade.*

Romantiques
87 Roman Bank. (P Davis). Open 9.30-5.30. STOCK: *Clocks, furniture, porcelain, smalls and jewellery.* PARK: Easy. TEL: 0754 767879. SER: Restorations (as stock).

SLEAFORD
Victoriana
1 Jermyn St. (Mrs P.C. Pywell). Est. 1970. Open Mon. and Fri. 10.30-5 and usually Sat. 11-5. SIZE: Small. STOCK: *General small antiques, 1820's to 1940's, £5-£250.* LOC: A17. PARK: Nearby. TEL: Home - 0205 722785.

Wilkinson's
The Little Tyme House, 13 Southgate. (M. and P. Wilkinson). Est. 1935. Open 9-1 and 2-4, Wed. and Thurs. by appointment. SIZE: Small. STOCK: *Jewellery, watches and silver, £50-£1,000.* PARK: Nearby. TEL: 0529 413149 and 0476

LINCOLNSHIRE

Sleaford continued
60400. SER: Valuations; restorations (including clock and watch movements); buys at auction (rings and watches). VAT: Stan.

SPALDING
Dean's Antiques
"The Walnuts", Weston St. Mary's. (Mrs B Dean). Est. 1969. Open daily. SIZE: Medium. *STOCK: General antiques, farm and country bygones, £2-£200.* LOC: On Spalding to Holbeach main road A151. PARK: Easy. TEL: 0406 370429.

SPILSBY
Shaw Antiques
39 High St. (Mrs J.M Shaw). CL: Tues. *STOCK: General small antiques and gifts.* TEL: 0790 52317/52297.

Spilsby Antiques
29 Halton Rd. (D. and C Goodland). Est. 1980. Open by appointment. SIZE: Medium. *STOCK: Jewellery, silver.* PARK: Easy. TEL: 0790 52148. VAT: Stan. *Trade Only.*

STAMFORD
Robin Cox Antiques
35-36 St. Peter's St. Est. 1965. Open 9-5, weekends by appointment. *STOCK: English and continental furniture, and works of art, including early oak, mahogany and decorated, wood carvings and sculpture, architectural fittings, garden items, £50-£10,000.* TEL: 0780 64592. VAT: Stan/Spec.

Dawson of Stamford
6 Red Lion Sq. (J Dawson). Open 9-5.30. SIZE: Medium. *STOCK: Jewellery, silver and Georgian furniture.* LOC: Town centre between St. John's church and All Saint's church. TEL: 0780 54166. VAT: Stan/Spec.

St. George's Antiques
1 St. George's Sq. (G.H. Burns). Est. 1974. Open 9-1 and 2-4.30. CL: Sat. SIZE: Small and trade only warehouse. *STOCK: Period and Victorian furniture, some small items.* TEL: 0780 54117; home - 0476 67492. VAT: Stan/Spec.

St. Martin's Antiques and Craft Centre
23a High St., St. Martin's. (P.B. Light). Open 10-5, Sat. and Sun. 10.30-5.30. SIZE: 25 dealers. *STOCK: General antiques including linen.* TEL: 0780 481158.

St. Mary's Galleries
5 St. Mary's Hill. (Mrs O.M. and R.D. Cox). Est. 1961. Open 9-5. SIZE: Medium. *STOCK: Furniture, 1600-1860, £50-£3,000; carvings, treen, wooden and metal implements and tools; jewellery, Victorian and Georgian, £5-£1,000;*

Stamford continued
unusual items, 1600-1900, £5-£200; some textiles oil paintings and watercolours. LOC: On old A south out of Stamford. PARK: Easy, at rear. TEL 0780 64159. VAT: Spec.

John Sinclair
11/12 St. Mary's St. (F.J. Sinclair). Est. 1970 Open 9-5.30. SIZE: Large. *STOCK: Oak country furniture, 18th C, £200-£3,000; Victorian mahogany furniture, £100-£1,000; Edwardian furniture.* LOC: Near A1. PARK: George Hotel car park. TEL: 0780 65421. VAT: Stan/Spec.

Stamford Antiques Centre
The Exchange Hall, Broad St. Open 10-5, Sun 12-5. SIZE: 45 dealers. *STOCK: General antique and collectables, furniture, prints, painting including Old Masters, lace, linen, coins, medals silver, art nouveau and art deco.* LOC: 1 mil from A1. TEL: 0780 62605.

Staniland (Booksellers)
4/5 St. George's St. (M.G. Staniland and B.J Ketchum). Est. 1973. Open 10-5. SIZE: Large *STOCK: Books, mainly 19th-20th C, 50p-£500 postcards, 1890-1930, 10p-£30.* LOC: High S PARK: St. Leonard's St. TEL: 0780 55800; hom - 0780 57615.

Andrew Thomas
Old Granary, 10 North St. Est. 1970. Open 9-6 SIZE: Large. *STOCK: Stripped pine, architectura pine fitments, ironware, oak, mahogany an decorated furniture in original paint.* LOC: From south take old A1 through Stamford. Turn right a second set of traffic lights, warehouse on right PARK: Opposite. TEL: 0780 62236; home - 0780 410627. VAT: Stan.

STAPLEFORD
Allens Antiques
Moor Farm. Open 9-5, Sat. 9-1. *STOCK: Pine* LOC: Off A17 Sleaford Rd. TEL: 0522 788392.

STICKFORD, Nr. Boston
Junktion
The Limes, Fen Road. (J. Rundle). Est. 1981 Open by appointment. SIZE: Medium. *STOCK Early advertising, decorative and architectura items; toys, automobilia, mechanical antiques an bygones; early slot machines, wireless, tele phones, 20th C collectables.* Not Stocked Porcelain and jewellery. LOC: A16 Boston t Spilsby. PARK: Easy. TEL: 0205 480087.

STICKNEY
B. and B Antiques
Main Rd. (B.J. Whittaker and J. Shooter). Ope by appointment. *STOCK: General antiques* PARK: Easy. TEL: 0205 480 204.

SUTTON BRIDGE
Bridge Antiques
30-32 Bridge Rd. (A. Gittins). Est. 1965. Open 8-5 or by appointment. CL: Sat. SIZE: Large. STOCK: Edwardian shipping goods. LOC: A17. PARK: Easy. TEL: 0406 350704.

Old Barn Antiques Warehouse
New Rd. (S. and Mrs T.J. Jackson). Est. 1982. Open 9-5.30 including Sun., other times by appointment. SIZE: Large. STOCK: Furniture - shipping goods, especially Jacobean style barley twist oak, carved oak, mahogany, walnut, pine in the paint. LOC: 1 mile out of village turn by Barclays Bank. PARK: Own. TEL: 0406 350435; home - same. SER: Container packing. *Mainly Trade and Export.*

SUTTON-ON-SEA
Knicks Knacks
41 High St. (Mr and Mrs R.A Nicholson). Est. 1983. Open 10-1 and 2-5, including Sun. CL: Mon. SIZE: Medium + museum. STOCK: Victorian gas lights, brass and iron beds, cast-iron fireplaces, bygones, curios, tools, collectables, pottery, porcelain, art deco, art nouveau, advertising items, furniture and shipping goods, £1-£1,000. LOC: A52. PARK: Easy. TEL: 0507 441916; home - 0507 441657.

TATTERSHALL
Lindum Antiques   LAPADA
Walnut Farm, Tattershall Thorpe. (D.G. and M. Wilby). Est. 1972. Open by appointment only. SIZE: Medium. STOCK: *Pottery, porcelain, and decorative pewter,18th-19th C, £30-£2,000.* TEL: 0526 342454. FAIRS: Most major. VAT: Spec.

Tattershall continued
Wayside Antiques
Market Place. (G Ball). Est. 1969. Open 10-5.30. STOCK: *General antiques.* LOC: On A158. PARK: Easy. TEL: 0526 342436. VAT: Stan/Spec.

WOODHALL SPA
Underwoodhall Antiques
The Broadway Centre, The Broadway. Open 10-5. CL: Wed. SIZE: Medium. STOCK: *Furniture, £10-£1,000; porcelain and china, £5-£500; general antiques, £1-£500; pictures, £5-£500, all 1750 to date.* LOC: B1191. PARK: Easy. TEL: 0526 353815. VAT: Stan/Spec.

V.O.C. Antiques
27 Witham Rd. (D.J. and C.J Leyland). Resident. Est. 1970. Open 9.30-6, Sun. by appointment. SIZE: Medium. STOCK: *17th-19th C furniture, to £5,000; period brass and copper, pottery, porcelain and pictures.* LOC: B1191. PARK: Easy. TEL: 0526 352753; home - same. SER: Valuations. VAT: Stan/Spec.

WRAGBY, Nr. Lincoln
Tealby Pine
Goltho Hall, Goltho. (R.G Chesterton-North). Est. 1965. Open every day but appointment preferred. SIZE: Large. STOCK: *Pine, 18th-19th C, £5-£500.* LOC: From Lincoln on A158. 1 mile before Wragby, take right turn signposted Goltho. PARK: Easy. TEL: 0673 858789; fax - 0673 857023. SER: Restorations (furniture stripping). VAT: Stan/Spec. *Trade Only.*

A scarce A.A. patrolman's brass cap or collar badge. Circa 1920. £6-£10. From *Automobilia of Europe — Reference and Price Guide* by Gordon Gardiner and Alistair Morris, published by the **Antique Collectors' Club,** £25.00

Merseyside

Please note this is only a rough map designed to show dealers the number of shops in the various towns, and is not necessarily totally accurate.

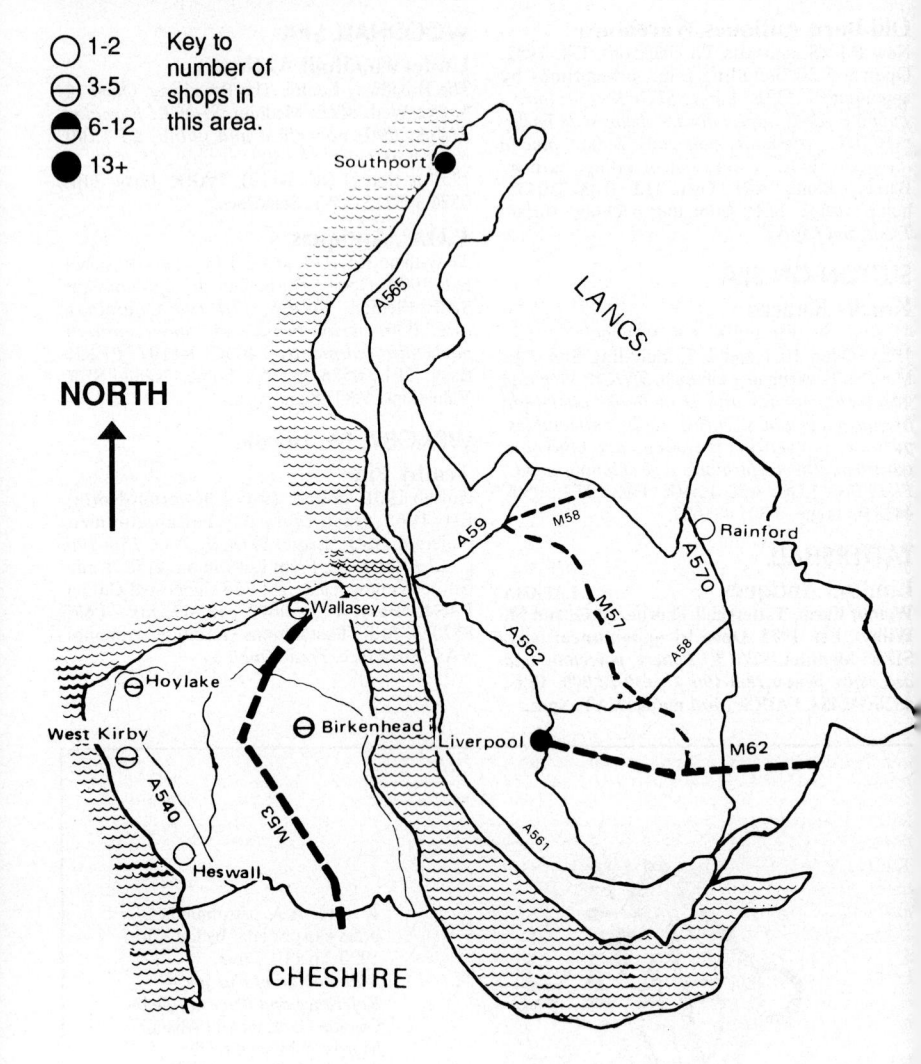

Key to number of shops in this area:
- ○ 1-2
- ⊖ 3-5
- ⊖ 6-12
- ● 13+

NORTH ↑

Southport ●
Rainford ○
Wallasey ⊖
Hoylake ⊖
West Kirby
Birkenhead ⊖
Liverpool ●
Heswall

LANCS.
CHESHIRE

Merseyside

BIRKENHEAD

Bodhouse Antiques
379 New Chester Rd, Rock Ferry. (G. and F.M. Antonini). Open 9-5, Sat. and Sun. by appointment. SIZE: Large. *STOCK: Furniture, 19th C; ceramics, from 19th C; silver plate, 18th-20th C; prints and pictures, 19th C, £25-£1,000+; all £5-£1,000+*. LOC: 1/2 mile from Birkenhead Tunnel, A41 towards Chester. PARK: Easy. TEL: 051 644 9494; home - 051 327 6233. VAT: Stan/Spec.

William Courtney and Sons LAPADA
Tunnel Entrance, Cross/Chester St. Est. 1893. Open daily, Sun. and Thurs. p.m. by appointment. SIZE: Large. *STOCK: General antiques, shipping goods, art glass*. PARK: Easy. TEL: 051 647 8693. VAT: Stan/Spec.

Rose Mount
2 Rose Mount. (A.J. Bampton). Open 10-5. *STOCK: General antiques*. TEL: 051 653 9060.

HESWALL

C. Rosenberg
The Antique Shop, 120-122 Telegraph Rd. Est. 1960. Open 10-5.30. CL: Wed. p.m. *STOCK: Jewellery, silver, porcelain, objets d'art*. TEL: 051 342 1053. VAT: Stan.

HOYLAKE

The Clock Shop
7 The Quadrant. (K. and D. Whay). Est. 1969. Open 10-5. *STOCK: Clocks and jewellery*. PARK: Easy. TEL: 051 632 1888. SER: Restorations (clock and jewellery repairs). VAT: Stan/Spec.

Hoylake Antique Centre
128-130 Market St. Open 9.15-5.30. *STOCK: Furniture, silver, pictures, porcelain, glass and decorative arts*. LOC: A540, in town centre. PARK: At rear. TEL: 051 632 4231.

Market Antiques
80 Market St. (W. Bateman). Est. 1969. Open Thurs. and Fri. 10-1 and 2.15-5, Sat. 10-5, other times by appointment. SIZE: Medium. *STOCK: Furniture, £10-£1,000; trade and shipping goods, silver, glass, china, £2-£250; paintings, prints, £5-£500*. Not Stocked: Weapons, medals, coins. LOC: On main street in town centre A563 or A540. PARK: From Ship Inn forecourt, cars drive in, vans at rear. TEL: 051 632 4059.

LIVERPOOL

Architectural Antiques
60 St. John's Rd, Waterloo. (J. Toole). Est. 1978. Open 10-5, Sat. 10-5.30. SIZE: Medium. *STOCK: Fireplaces, 18th-19th C, £100-£1,000+; doors and sanitary ware, 19th C, from £35*. LOC: Opposite Crosby Rd. (North). PARK: Easy. TEL: 051 949 0819. SER: Valuations; restorations. VAT: Stan.

Liverpool continued

Boodle and Dunthorne Ltd
Boodles House, Lord St. Est. 1798. Open 9-5.30. SIZE: Large. *STOCK: Silver, 18th-19th C, £100-£5,000; clocks and clock-sets, mid-19th C, £200-£4,000; jewellery, Victorian and Georgian, £100-£30,000*. Not Stocked: Furniture. PARK: Paradise St. TEL: 051 227 2525. VAT: Stan/Spec.

Delta Antiques
175/177 Smithdown Rd. (E.P. Jones). Est. 1979. Open 10-12 and 1-5. CL: Sat. a.m and Wed. SIZE: Medium. *STOCK: Stripped pine, 19th C, £50+*. LOC: Ring road, city centre. PARK: Nearby. TEL: 051 734 4277; home - same. SER: Restorations; French polishing.

Edward's Jewellers
45a Whitechapel. (R.A. and E.M. Lewis). FGA. Est. 1967. Open by appointment. CL: Sat. SIZE: Small. *STOCK: Jewellery, silver and plate, 19th-20th C, £50-£400*. LOC: City centre. TEL: 051 236 2909. SER: Valuations. VAT: Stan/Spec.

Halsall Hall Ltd
Halsall Hall, Halsall. (J. Nolan). Est. 1970. Open by appointment 7 days and evenings. SIZE: Large. *STOCK: Export items, from £50; interior design, 17th-19th C*. LOC: On A5147 (old A567). TEL: 0704 841065; home - same. SER: Valuations; restorations; buys at auction. VAT: Stan/Spec. *Trade Only*.

Kensington Tower Antiques Ltd
Christ Church, 170 Kensington. (R. Swainbank). Est. 1960. Open 9-5, Sat. and Sun. by appointment. CL: Mon. SIZE: Large. *STOCK: Shipping goods, general antiques*. LOC: A57. PARK: Easy. TEL: 051 260 9466; fax - 051 260 9130; home - 051 924 6538. VAT: Stan. *Trade Only*.

Liverpool Militaria
48 Manchester St. (Bill Tagg). Open 10.30-5.30. CL: Wed. *STOCK: Militaria especially Japanese swords*. LOC: Next to old tunnel entrance. TEL: 051 236 4404.

Lyver & Boydell Galleries LAPADA
15 Castle St. Est. 1861. Open 10.30-5.30. CL: Sat. SIZE: Medium. *STOCK: Paintings and watercolours, 18th-20th C, £50-£10,000; maps and prints, 16th-19th C, £1-£1,500*. LOC: City centre, opposite Town Hall. PARK: Multi-storey. TEL: 051 236 3256. SER: Valuations; cleaning; framing; restorations; buys at auction. FAIRS: National. VAT: Stan/Spec.

Maggs Antiques Ltd LAPADA
26-28 Fleet St. (G. Webster). Est. 1965. Open daily. *STOCK: General antiques, period and shipping smalls, £1-£1,000*. LOC: In town centre by Central station. PARK: Meters. TEL: 051 708 0221; evenings - 09285 64958. SER: Restorations; container packing, courier.

MERSEYSIDE

Liverpool continued
E. Pryor and Son
110 London Rd. (Mr Wilding). Est. 1876. CL: Wed. *STOCK: General antiques, jewellery, Georgian and Victorian silver, pottery, porcelain, coins, clocks, paintings, ivory and carvings.* TEL: 051 709 1361. VAT: Stan.

Ryan-Wood Antiques
102 Seel St. Est. 1972. Open 9.30-5 or by appointment. *STOCK: Furniture, paintings, china, silver, curios, bric-a-brac, Victoriana, Edwardiana, art deco.* TEL: 051 709 7776; home - 051 709 3203. SER: Restorations. VAT: Stan/Spec.

Stefani Antiques
497 Smithdown Rd. (T. Stefani). Est. 1969. Open 10-1 and 2-5. CL: Wed. SIZE: Medium. *STOCK: Furniture, to 1910, £300-£1,000; jewellery, £25-£500; pottery, silver, old Sheffield plate, porcelain, bronzes.* LOC: On main road. PARK: Easy. TEL: 051 734 1933; home - 051 737 1360. SER: Valuations; restorations.

Swainbanks Ltd
Christchurch, 170 Kensington. Open 9-5 or by appointment. CL: Sat. SIZE: Large. *STOCK: Shipping goods and general antiques.* TEL: 051 260 9466/924 6538; fax - 051 260 9130. SER: Containers. VAT: Stan.

Theta Gallery
29 and 31 Parliament St. (J. Matson). Open by appointment. SIZE: Warehouse. *STOCK: General antiques, especially furniture and clocks.* TEL: 051 708 6375. *Trade Only.*

RAINFORD, Nr. St. Helens
Colin Stock   BADA
8 Mossborough Rd. Est. 1895. Open by appointment. STOCK: Furniture, 18th-19th C. TEL: 074 488 2246.

SOUTHPORT
Andersons
14 Wesley St. Open 9-5. SIZE: Small. *STOCK: Watches and clocks.* LOC: Opposite Morrison's. PARK: Nearby. TEL: 0704 540024. SER: Restorations (as stock); repairs.

Arcadia Antiques   LAPADA
8a Portland St. (Malcolm and Sally Fryer). Est. 1978. Open 10-12.30 and 1.30-5, Sat. until 5.30, Tues. and Sun. by appointment. SIZE: Small. STOCK: English and French furniture, 18th-19th C, £300-£5,000; lighting, 19th to early 20th C, £100-£3,000; decorative items - mirrors, fireplaces, clocks, glass, metalware, textiles, 18th-19th C, £25-£2,000. LOC: Off Lord St., at side of Prince of Wales Hotel. PARK: Easy. TEL: Home - 0704 64441. SER: Valuations; restorations (furniture and lighting); buys at auction (furniture and lighting). FAIRS: Windermere and Grasmere. VAT: Stan/Spec.

Southport continued
C.K. Broadhurst and Co Ltd
5-7 Market St. Est. 1926. Open 9-5.30. *STOCK: Rare books, first editions, coloured plate books, topography.* TEL: 0704 532064/534110; fax - 0704 542009.

Decor Galleries
52 Lord St. (F.D. Glover). CL: Tues. *STOCK: Decorative items, furniture, 18th-19th C.* TEL: 0704 535134. VAT: Stan/Spec.

Fine Pine
19 Market St. (R. and W. Griffiths). Open 10-4.30. CL: Tues. *STOCK: Pine.* TEL: 0704 538056; evenings - 0704 535720. SER: Shipping, packing and courier.

Molloy's Furnishers Ltd
6-8 St. James St. (P. Molloy). Est. 1955. Open daily. SIZE: Large. *STOCK: Mahogany and oak, shipping and Edwardian furniture.* LOC: On A570, Scarisbrick new road. PARK: Easy. TEL: 0704 535204/548101. VAT: Stan.

Neill Gallery
4 Portland St. (E.J. Neill). Est. 1991. Open 10-4.30, Sat. 10-5, Tues. and Sun. by appointment. SIZE: Small. *STOCK: Oil paintings and watercolours, 19th-20th C, £100-£15,000; sculpture, 20th C, £250-£9,000.* LOC: Off Lord St. TEL: 0704 549858. SER: Restorations (oils and watercolours).

Oldfield Cottage Antiques
97 East Bank St. (Mrs R. Potts). Est. 1982. Open 9.30-5.30. *STOCK: Victorian pine, lace, blue and white.* TEL: 061 628 2646.

Osiris Antiques
104 Shakespeare St. (C. and P. Wood). Est. 1983. Open 10.45-4.45, Sat. 11-5.15, Sun. by appointment. CL: Tues. SIZE: Small. *STOCK: Art nouveau and art deco, £10-£1,000; period clothing and accessories, 1850-1950, £5-£200; jewellery, 1880-1960, to £150.* LOC: Just out of town, off main road leading to motorway. PARK: Easy. TEL: 0704 500991; home - 0704 60418. SER: Valuations; buys at auction (art nouveau, art deco); lectures given on Decorative Arts 1895-1930.

Pinocchio
2 & 2A Portland St. Open 9.30-5.30, Sat. 9.30-6, Sun.11-3.30. SIZE: Medium. *STOCK: Antique and reproduction pine, dolls, dolls houses and furnishings, teddy bears and collectables.* LOC: By side entrance of Prince of Wales Hotel, off Lord St. PARK: Nearby. TEL: 0704 535028. SER: Hand carved rocking horses made to order. VAT: Stan/Spec.

The Spinning Wheel
1 Liverpool Rd, Birkdale. (R. Bell). Est. 1966. Open 10-5. CL: Tues. SIZE: Small. *STOCK: General antiques, £5-£1,000+.* TEL: 0704 68245; home - 0704 67613.

Southport continued
Studio 41
340 Liverpool Rd, Birkdale. (B. Sullivan). Open by appointment only. *STOCK: Oils and watercolours, 19th-20th C.* TEL: 0704 579132. SER: Valuations; buys at auction.

Tony and Anne Sutcliffe Antiques
130 Cemetery Rd., and warehouse - 37A Linaker St. Est. 1969. Open 8.30-5 including Sun. or by appointment. SIZE: Large. *STOCK: Shipping goods, Victorian and period furniture.* LOC: Town centre. TEL: 0704 537068; home - 0704 533465. SER: Containers; courier. VAT: Stan/Spec.

H.S. Walne
183 Lord St. Open 10-5. *STOCK: Diamonds, gold, silver, jewellery.* TEL: 0704 532469.

Weldons Jewellers and Antiques
567 Lord St. (H.W. and N.C. Weldon). Est. 1914. Open 9.30-5.30. SIZE: Medium. *STOCK: Furniture, clocks, watches, jewellery, silver, coins. Not Stocked: Militaria.* PARK: Easy. TEL: 0704 532191. SER: Valuations; restorations. VAT: Stan.

The White Elephant
22 Kew Rd. (J. and N. Wajzner). Est. 1967. *STOCK: General antiques, fine art, ethnographica, collectors' items, weapons, medals, coins, books, postcards.* TEL: 0704 60525.

WALLASEY
Arbiter
10 Atherton St, New Brighton. (W.D.L. Scobie and P.D. Ferrett). Resident. Est. 1983. Open 11-5, Sat. 2-5, or by appointment. CL: Mon. *STOCK: Arts and crafts movement and decorative arts, £20-£2,000; Oriental, ethnographic and antiquities, £40-£1,500; original prints and drawings, £80-£500.* LOC: Opposite New Brighton station. PARK: Easy. TEL: 051 639 1159. SER: Valuations; buys at auction; consultant.

Decade Antiques
52 Grove Rd. (A.M. Duffy). Open 10-5. SIZE: Large. *STOCK: General antiques, textiles, decorative items, continental furniture.* LOC: Take A554 via promenade, turn along Harrison Drive, right to Grove Rd. TEL: 051 639 9905/8728 or 051 638 0433.

Victoria Antiques/City Strippers
155-157 Brighton St. (J.M. Colyer). Open 9.30-5.30. CL: Wed. *STOCK: Pre-1930 furniture.* TEL: 051 639 0080.

WEST KIRBY
Helen Horswill Antiques and Decorative Arts
2 Grange Rd. Open 10-5 or by appointment. SIZE: Medium. *STOCK: Furniture, 17th-19th C;*

A late 18th century horn-book. Photograph: Sotheby's. From *Yesterday's Children*, by Sally Kevill-Davies, published by the **Antique Collectors' Club**, £19.95pb.

West Kirby continued
decorative items. LOC: A540. PARK: Easy. TEL: 051 625 8660/625 2803.

Oliver Antiques
62 Grange Rd. (J.O. Horswill). Open 10-5 or by appointment. SIZE: Medium. *STOCK: Decorative items and collectables, 19th-20th C.* LOC: A540. PARK: Easy. TEL: 051 625 2803/8660.

Trentini Antiques   LAPADA
79 Banks Rd. (J. Trentini). Open Tues., Thurs. and Fri. 10.30-4.30 or by appointment. *STOCK: Decorative items and general antiques.* TEL: 051 625 2122.

Victoria Cottage Antiques
6 Village Rd. (Mrs C. Dilger). Est. 1984. Open 10-5. CL: Wed. SIZE: Medium. *STOCK: Staffordshire figures, 1790-1914; pottery and porcelain, 1780-1920; prints and engravings, from 1780; Victorian glass; furniture including small tables, 1800-1920.* LOC: A540 from Chester, turn left into Village Rd. at sandstone monument. PARK: Easy. TEL: 051 625 7517; home - same. SER: Valuations.

Middlesex

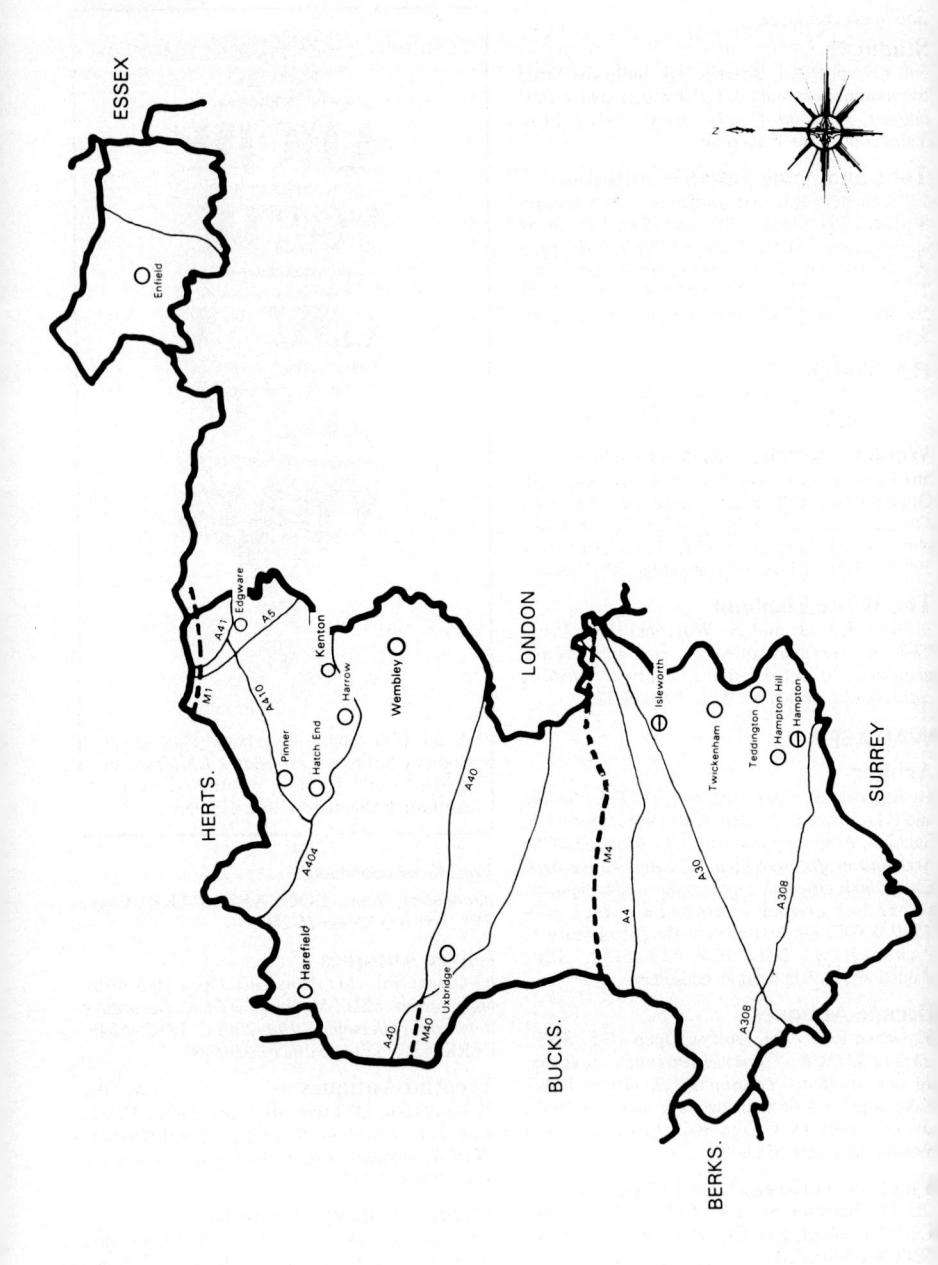

O 1–2
⊖ 3–5
⊖ 6–12
● 13+

Key to number of shops in this area.

Please note this is only a rough map designed to show dealers the number of shops in the various towns, and is not necessarily totally accurate.

Middlesex

EDGWARE
Edgware Antiques
19 Whitchurch Lane. (E. Schloss). Est. 1972. Open Thurs.- Sat. 10-5 or by appointment. SIZE: Medium. STOCK: Furniture, pictures, silver and plate, brass and copper, clocks, bric-a-brac, porcelain and shipping goods. PARK: Easy. TEL: 081 952 1606; home - 081 952 5924.

ENFIELD
Enfield Corner Cupboard
61 Chase Side. Est. 1952. Open 9-5.30, Wed. 9-1. STOCK: Furniture, silver, china. TEL: 081 363 6493.

Richard Kimbell
Country World, Cattlegate Rd., Crews Hill. Est. 1966. Open 9-6 including Sun. SIZE: Large. STOCK: Pine, 19th C, £50-£1,000. LOC: Off junction 24, M25 via A1005 to Enfield, then left into East Lodge Lane. PARK: Easy. TEL: 081 364 6661. VAT: Stan.

La Trouvaille
1A Windmill Hill. (Mrs C.M. Waring). Est. 1982. Open 9.30-5.30. CL: Wed. SIZE: Medium. STOCK: Small general antiques, collectors' items, furniture and prints, 1800-1930. Not Stocked: Weapons. LOC: West of town. PARK: Easy. TEL: 081 367 1080.

R.V. Morgan and Co.
Unit 41, 26-28 The Queensway, Ponders End. Est. 1983. Open by appointment. SIZE: Medium. STOCK: Furniture including continental. TEL: 081 805 0353; home - 081 804 1317. LOC: Off Hertford road, off A10. PARK: At rear. SER: Restorations (furniture - inlays, veneers, turning, carving); furniture made to order. FAIRS: Earls Court. VAT: Stan.

HAMPTON
Hampton Village Antiques Centre
76 Station Rd. (E. Hatvany). Est. 1982. Open 10-5.30. SIZE: Medium - 6 dealers. STOCK: Furniture, clocks, pottery and porcelain, mainly 19th-20th C, £5-£500. LOC: Approx. 1 mile west of Hampton Court Palace. PARK: Easy. TEL: 081 979 5871; home - 081 890 7405. SER: Restorations (metal, porcelain, pottery and clocks); pine furniture made to order. FAIRS: Local.

Peco
72 Station Rd. (C.D. and E.S. Taylor). Est. 1969. Open 9-1 and 2-5.15, Sat. 9-5.15. SIZE: Large. STOCK: Doors, 18th-20th C, £50-£100; fireplaces including marble, 18th-19th C, £100-£500; stoves; French beds. LOC: 1.5 miles from Hampton Court. Turning off Hampton Court/Sunbury Rd. PARK: Own. TEL: 081 979 8310. SER: Restorations (stained glass, cast iron fireplaces, doors); stained glass made to order. VAT: Stan.

Hampton continued
Ian Sheridan's Bookshop Hampton
Thames Villa, 34 Thames St. Est. 1960. Open 10.30-7 including Sun. SIZE: Large. STOCK: Antiquarian and secondhand books. LOC: 1 mile from Hampton Court Palace. TEL: 081 979 1704.

Valtone Pine
78-80 Station Rd. (A.P. Frost). Open 9-6. STOCK: Pine and darkwoods. TEL: 081 979 4060.

HAMPTON HILL
Hampton Hill Gallery
203 and 205 High St. STOCK: Watercolours, drawings, prints, 18th-20th C. TEL: 081 977 1379/5273. SER: Restorations and cleaning (watercolours, prints and paintings); mounting; framing. VAT: Stan/Spec.

Parade Antiques
3 The Parade, Hampton Rd. (Christina Stanhope and Doreen Rogers). Est. 1982. Open 10.30-5.30, Tues. 11.30-5.30. SIZE: Small. STOCK: Furniture, £50-£400; china, to £300; all art nouveau and art deco. LOC: Main road. PARK: Easy. TEL: 081 977 3295.

HAREFIELD
The Jay's Antique Centre
25/29 High St. Open 10-6, Wed. 10-1. SIZE: 15 dealers. STOCK: General antiques, bric-a-brac, gold and silver. TEL: 0895 824738.

HARROW
Kathleen Mann Antiques   LAPADA
49 High St. Est. 1973. Open 9-5 or by appointment. CL: Wed. SIZE: Medium. STOCK: Furniture, 18th-19th C, £25-£3,000; decorative items, £5-£1,000. LOC: Follow Harrow road, or take A40 turning at Greenford roundabout. PARK: Easy. TEL: 081 422 1892. SER: Buys at auction. VAT: Stan/Spec.

Winston Galleries
68 High St, Harrow Hill. (R. and P. Weston). Est. 1970. Open 9.30-5.30, or by appointment. CL: Wed. STOCK: Furniture, porcelain, 18th-19th C; general antiques, silver, plate, clocks. TEL: 081 422 4470. VAT: Stan/Spec.

ISLEWORTH
Crowther of Syon Lodge Ltd
Busch Corner, London Rd. Open 9-5, Sat. and Sun. 11-4. SIZE: Large. STOCK: Period panelled rooms, in pine and oak; chimney-pieces in marble, stone and wood; life-sized classical bronze and marble statues; wrought iron entrance gates, garden temples, vases, seats, fountains and other statues. LOC: Just off the A4, half-way between the West End and London Airport. TEL: 081 560 7978. VAT: Stan/Spec.

MIDDLESEX

Isleworth continued
Yistelworth Antiques
13 Shrewsbury Walk, South St., Old Isleworth. (C.A. Gibbs). Est. 1978. Open 10-5.30, Sun. 11.30-3.30. CL: Wed. SIZE: Medium. *STOCK: Furniture, 19th-20th C, £50-£1,000; china, £5-£200; pictures, £25-£500; both 18th-20th C.* LOC: Off Twickenham Rd. at clock tower, shop in square off rear of Castle public house. PARK: Easy. TEL: 081 847 5429. SER: Valuations.

NORTHWOOD
Northwood Antiques
28 High St. Open by appointment. *STOCK: Victorian and Edwardian furniture, general antiques.* TEL: 0923 824040; workshop - 0895 422467.

PINNER
Artbry's Antiques
44 High St. (A.H. Davies and B.E. Hill). Est. 1969. Open 9-5.30. CL: Wed. p.m. SIZE: Medium. *STOCK: Furniture, £100-£5,000; crystal, £50-£250; both 18th-19th C; clocks, all types, £50-*

Pinner continued
£3,000; paintings, 17th-19th C, £20-£2,000. LOC: From Harrow School through Harrow. PARK: Easy. TEL: 081 868 0834. SER: Valuations; restorations (clocks). VAT: Stan/Spec.

TEDDINGTON
J.W. Crisp Antiques
166 High St. (E. Gould and M. Murren). Open 1-5, Sat. 10-5. CL: Wed. *STOCK: Furniture, porcelain and objets d'art, watercolours and oil paintings.* TEL: 081 977 4309. SER: Restorations; French polishing.

TWICKENHAM
Ailsa Gallery
32 Crown Rd. (C.A. Wiltshire). Open Thurs., Fri. and Sat. 10-5, other times by appointment. SIZE: Small. *STOCK: Paintings, 19th-20th C, £200-£3,000; bronze, decorative arts, small furniture, silver and glass.* LOC: Off St. Margarets Rd., near station. PARK: Easy. TEL: 081 891 2345; home - 081 892 0188. SER: Buys at auction.

Antique Collectors' Club Titles

Pictorial Dictionary of British 18th Century Furniture Design
by Elizabeth White
Published designs from 120 sources. The 3,000 named and dated illustrations provide arguably the most important contribution to 18th century furniture studies since Ralph Edwards' **Dictionary of English Furniture.**
ISBN 1 85149 105 8
700pp, 3,500 b & w designs, 24 col £65.00

Pictorial Dictionary of British 19th Century Furniture Design
An A.C.C. Research Project
Compiled from forty-nine key contemporary catalogues from Sheraton to Heal's, including Smith, Tatham, King, Pugin, Morris and Liberty's, includes an important introduction by the late Edward Joy.
ISBN 0 902028 47 2, 632pp, 6,200 illus, £49.50

Available from:
Antique Collectors' Club, 5 Church Street, Woodbridge, Suffolk IP12 1DS Tel: (0394) 385501 Fax: (0394) 384434

or Market Street Industrial Park, Wappingers' Falls, New York 12590, USA Tel: 914 297 0003 Fax: 914 297 0068

Twickenham continued

Alberts Cigarette Card Specialists
113 London Rd. (J.A. Wooster). Open 10-6, Sat. 10-4. CL: Mon. *STOCK: Original cigarette cards; accessories, film mobilia, Victorian prints, magazines, hand-painted model soldiers, working steam models.* TEL: 081 891 3067. SER: Mail order; shipping; framing; catalogue.

Simon Castle
Est. 1975. Open by appointment. *STOCK: Treen and decorative carvings.* TEL: 081 892 2840.

Anthony C. Hall
30 Staines Rd. Est. 1966. Open 9-5.30. CL: Wed. p.m. and Sat. SIZE: Medium. *STOCK: Antiquarian books.* PARK: Easy. TEL: 081 898 2638.

John Ives Bookseller
5 Normanhurst Drive, St. Margarets. Resident. Est. 1977. Open by appointment at any time. SIZE: Medium. *STOCK: Scarce and out of print books on antiques and collecting, £1-£500.* LOC: Off St. Margarets Rd. near its junction with Chertsey Rd. PARK: Easy. TEL: 081 892 6265. SER: Valuations (as stock).

Marble Hill Gallery
70/72 Richmond Rd. (D. and L. Newson). Est. 1974. Open 10-5.30. *STOCK: Victorian watercolours and fireside furniture, French marble, pine and white Adam style mantels.* PARK: Easy. TEL: 081 892 1488. VAT: Stan/Spec.

David Morley Antiques
371 Richmond Rd. Est. 1968. Open 10-5. CL: Wed. SIZE: Medium. *STOCK: General antiques.* Not Stocked: Large furniture. LOC: Approx. 200yds. from Richmond Bridge. PARK: In side road (adjacent to shop). TEL: 081 892 2986.

Paravent
at Sinclair-Melson, Crane House, Gould Rd. (M. Aldbrook and M. Brittle). Open daily. *STOCK: Screens, 17th-20th C, £500-£10,000.* TEL: 081 893 3492. SER: Restorations. FAIRS: Olympia. VAT: Stan/Spec.

Phelps Antiques　　　　　　　　LAPADA
133-135 St. Margarets Rd. (R.C. Phelps). Est. 1870. Open 9-5.30, Sat. 9-5. SIZE: Large. *STOCK: Victorian and Edwardian furniture and shipping goods.* LOC: Adjacent St. Margaret's station. PARK: Easy. TEL: 081 892 1778/7129; fax - 081 892 3661. SER: Restorations. VAT: Stan/Spec.

Rita Shenton
148 Percy Rd. Est. 1973. Open by appointment only. SIZE: Medium. *STOCK: Clocks, watches, barometers, automata and ornamental turning books, £1-£1,000.* LOC: Continuation of Whitton High St. PARK: Easy. TEL: 081 894 6888; fax - 081 893 8766. SER: Valuations; buys at auction (horological books, clocks); catalogues available. *International postal service.*

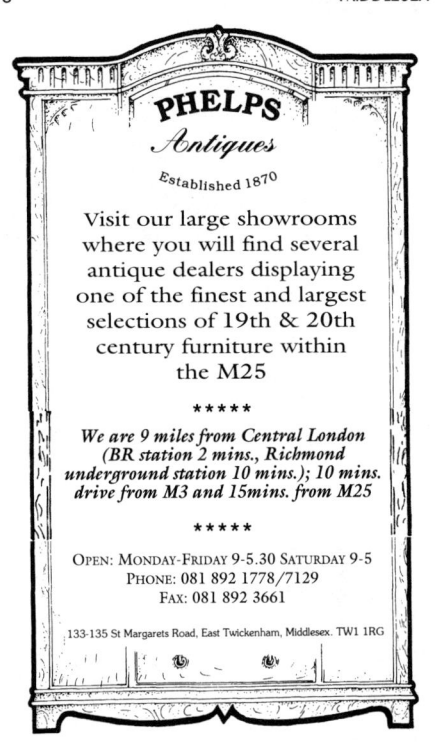

PHELPS
Antiques
Established 1870

Visit our large showrooms where you will find several antique dealers displaying one of the finest and largest selections of 19th & 20th century furniture within the M25

★★★★★

We are 9 miles from Central London (BR station 2 mins., Richmond underground station 10 mins.); 10 mins. drive from M3 and 15mins. from M25

★★★★★

OPEN: MONDAY-FRIDAY 9-5.30 SATURDAY 9-5
PHONE: 081 892 1778/7129
FAX: 081 892 3661

133-135 St Margarets Road, East Twickenham, Middlesex. TW1 1RG

Twickenham continued

Neil Willcox
113 Strawberry Vale. Open by appointment. *STOCK: Wine, apothecary, medical and other bottles, British and continental, 17th to mid 19th C.* TEL: 081 892 5858 (24 hrs). SER: Valuations; mail order, photos supplied; prop hire.

UXBRIDGE

Antiques Warehouse (Uxbridge)
34-36 Rockingham Rd. Est. 1966. Open 10-6. SIZE: Large. *STOCK: General antiques, shipping items, £1-£4,000.* PARK: Easy. TEL: 0895 256963/271012. VAT: Stan.

Thomas Barnard (A.B.A.)
11 Windsor St. Est. 1944. Open 9.30-5. CL: Wed. *STOCK: General antiquarian books; prints, maps, pictures.* TEL: 0895 258054. SER: Bookbinding, framing.

WEMBLEY

L. Kelaty Ltd
Kelaty House, First Way. Est. 1954. Open 8-6, Fri. 8-5. CL: Sat. *STOCK: Rugs and carpets.* TEL: 081 903 9998.

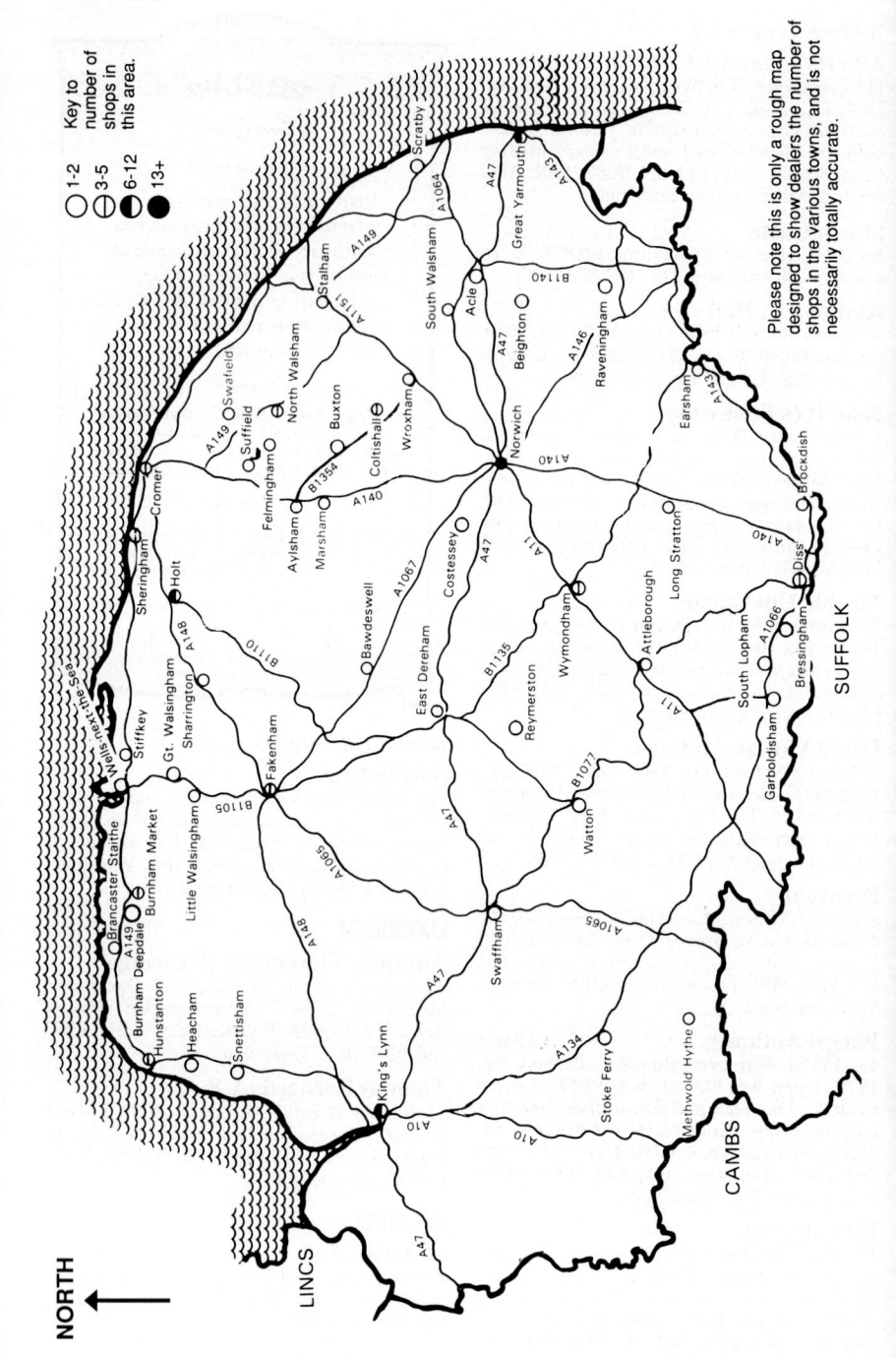

Norfolk

Norfolk

ACLE, Nr. Norwich
Ivy House Antiques
Ivy House, The Street. (N. Pratt). Est. 1970. Open 9-5. SIZE: Small. *STOCK: Furniture, porcelain, pottery, glass, metalware, 18th-20th C, £25-£2,000; pictures, 19th C; garden furniture, 19th-20th C, both £50-£500.* LOC: Village centre. PARK: Easy. TEL: 0493 750682; home - same. SER: Valuations. FAIRS: Norwich. VAT: Stan/Spec.

Lion Antiques
The Old Sale Ring, Cattle Market. (F. Wright). Est. 1947. Open 8.30-5, Sat. by appointment only. *STOCK: Furniture, £25-£250; bric-a-brac, from £5, all Victorian to 1930.* LOC: On A47, opposite church. PARK: Easy. TEL: 0493 751836. SER: Restorations (furniture).

ATTLEBOROUGH
A.E. Bush and Partners
Vineyards Antiques Gallery, Leys Lane. (A.G., M.S. and J.A. Becker). Est. 1940. Open 9-1 and 2-5.30. *STOCK: Walnut and mahogany, 18th-19th C.* LOC: Town outskirts. PARK: Easy. TEL: 0953 454239/452175. SER: Restorations; export and storage; buys at auction. VAT: Stan/Spec.

AYLSHAM
Sheila Hart and John Giles   LAPADA
Open by appointment. *STOCK: Furniture, £200-£5,000; objects, £50-£1,000; all mainly 19th C.* TEL: 0263 768216. SER: Courier. Trade Only.

Pearse Lukies
Bayfield House, White Hart St. Open preferably by appointment. *STOCK: Period oak, sculpture, objects, 18th C furniture.* TEL: 0263 734137. Trade Only.

BAWDESWELL, Nr. East Dereham
Norfolk Polyphon Centre
Wood Farm. (N.B. Vince). Open weekends, week days preferably by appointment. *STOCK: Mechanical music - polyphons, cylinder musical boxes, organs, orchestrions, automata.* LOC: On B1145, 1 mile east of Bawdeswell village and junction with A1067. TEL: 036 288 230. VAT: Stan/Spec.

BRANCASTER STAITHE, Nr. King's Lynn
Brancaster Staithe Antiques
Coast Rd. (M.J. Wilson). Open every day including Sun. *STOCK: Victorian tables, chairs; oak, unusual pine, bookpresses, art deco.* TEL: 0485 210600.

BRESSINGHAM, Nr. Diss
David Bateson Antiques
Lodge Farm. (D. and P. Bateson). Est. 1966. Open by appointment. SIZE: Medium. *STOCK: Country furniture.* LOC: 1.5 miles north of Bressingham off A1066 from Diss. PARK: Easy. TEL: 037 988 629. SER: Valuations.

BROCKDISH, Nr. Diss
Brockdish Antiques
Commerce House. (M. and L.E. Palfrey). Est. 1975. Open 9-5.30. CL: Wed. *STOCK: Mainly 19th C furniture and upholstery.* LOC: A143. TEL: 037 975 498. SER: Restorations; re-upholstery.

BURNHAM DEEPDALE
Steed-Croft Antiques
West End. (J.M. Tate). Est. 1978. Open Mon., Wed., Fri. and Sat. *STOCK: Period furniture, decorative items.* TEL: 0485 210812. SER: Interior design. FAIRS: Major British.

BURNHAM MARKET
M. and A. Cringle
The Old Black Horse. Est. 1965. Open 10-1 and 2-5. CL: Wed. SIZE: Medium. *STOCK: 18th to early 19th C furniture, £50-£2,000; china, glass, pottery, prints, maps, £10-£500.* Not Stocked: Large furniture, Oriental and continental antiques, reproductions. LOC: In village centre. PARK: Easy. TEL: 0328 738456. VAT: Spec.

Anne Hamilton Antiques
North St. (A. Hudson). Open 10-1 and 2-5. CL: Wed. SIZE: Medium. *STOCK: Georgian furniture; longcase clocks, porcelain, decorative items.* LOC: 20yds. from village green towards coast. PARK: Easy. TEL: 0328 738187. VAT: Stan/Spec.

Market House   BADA
(J. Maufe). Resident. Open 10-6 or by appointment. SIZE: Medium. *STOCK: English furniture - walnut, mahogany, rosewood and some oak, late 17th to mid-19th C, £25-£20,000; works of art, mirrors, small decorative items, some porcelain.* Not Stocked: Silver, jewellery. LOC: B1355, large Queen Anne house on green in village centre. PARK: Easy. TEL: 0328 738475. SER: Valuations; buys at auction. VAT: Spec.

BUXTON, Nr. Norwich
As Time Goes By Antique and Tower Clocks
Buxton Mill. (S. Phillips). MBHI. Est. 1981. Open 9.30-5, Sat. and Sun. 10-4. SIZE: Medium. *STOCK: Clocks, £150-£8,000.* LOC: Between Aylsham and Coltishall on B1354. PARK: Easy. TEL: 0603 278080; fax - same; home - 0263 732718; mobile - 0836 753869. SER: Valuations; restorations (clocks). VAT: Stan/Spec.

CLEY

B. and J. Kerridge Antiques
Rocket House, High St. Open 9-5. CL: Thurs. a.m. SIZE: Medium. *STOCK: Period furniture, country house items, smalls.* TEL: 0263 741154.

COLTISHALL

Liz Allport-Lomax
Open by appointment only. *STOCK: Objets de vertu, collectors' items, porcelain, pottery and silver, 18th-19th C; glass, watercolours and oils, all £5-£1,000; copper, brass and furniture, 19th C, £5-£2,000.* TEL: 0603 737631. FAIRS: Langley Park Spring, East Anglian Antique Dealers (organiser).

Eric Bates and Sons
High St. Est. 1973. Open 9-5. SIZE: Large. *STOCK: General antiques, Georgian, Victorian, Edwardian and shipping furniture.* TEL: 0603 738716. SER: Restorations (furniture); upholstery; container packing. VAT: Stan/Spec.

Roger Bradbury Antiques
Church St. Est. 1967. Open by appointment. *STOCK: Fine period furniture, Nanking cargo, objets d'art.* PARK: Easy. TEL: 0603 737444. VAT: Stan.

Coltishall Antiques Centre
High St. (I. Ford). Est. 1980. Open 10-5. SIZE: Large - several specialists. *STOCK: A wide variety of items including porcelain and pottery, silver, jewellery, collectors' items, militaria, glass, Oriental porcelain, plated cutlery, clocks and Georgian, Victorian and Edwardian furniture.* LOC: B1150 on corner of main street. PARK: Easy. TEL: 0603 738306. SER: Valuations; restorations (pottery and porcelain, furniture, objets de vertu, clocks and watches).

Gwendoline Golder
Point House, High St. Est. 1974. Open 11-5. CL: Sun. except by appointment. *STOCK: General antiques and collectors' items.* PARK: Easy. TEL: 0603 738099.

Isabel Neal Cabinet Antiques
Bank House, High St. Est. 1968. Open 9.30-5.30. SIZE: Small. *STOCK: Porcelain, pottery, especially blue and white, 17th-20th C; small furniture, watercolours, copper, brass, pewter, collectors' items.* LOC: B1150 towards North Walsham, shop on right. PARK: Easy. TEL: 0603 737379.

COSTESSEY, Nr. Norwich

The Coach House
Townhouse Rd, Old Costessey. (J. Hines). Resident. Open by appointment. *STOCK: Modern British paintings; drawings, Victorian watercolours and post-war artists; original prints, etchings, engravings; Baxter and Le Blond.* TEL: 0603 742977. SER: Cleaning prints and watercolours; framing.

CROMER

Bond Street Antiques (inc. Jas. J. Briggs Est. 1820)
6 Bond St, and 38 Church St. (M.R.T. and J.A. Jones). NAG, FGA. Est. 1958. Open 9-1 and 2.15-5.30, Sat. 9-6, Sun. by appointment. SIZE: Medium. *STOCK: Jewellery, silver, porcelain, china, glass, small furniture, 18th-20th C, £50-£5,000.* LOC: From Church St. bear right to Post Office, shop on opposite side on street further along. PARK: Easy. TEL: 0263 513134; home - same. SER: Valuations; restorations (watches and jewellery); gem testing and analysis. VAT: Stan.

Benjamin Rust Antiques
3 St. Margaret's Rd. *STOCK: Furniture, 18th-19th C, glass, clocks and decorative items.* LOC: Near Norwich Rd. traffic lights. PARK: Own. TEL: 0263 511452. SER: Restorations.

A.E. Seago
15 Church St. (D.C. Seago). Est. 1937. Open 9-1 and 2-5.15. CL: Sun. and Wed. October to April. SIZE: Small. *STOCK: Furniture, 1790-1910, £25-£2,500.* Not Stocked: Silver, garden furniture, oil paintings. LOC: From Sheringham take main coast road, then New St. into High St. PARK: Easy. 50 yds away around church. TEL: 0263 512733. SER: Valuations.

DISS

Diss Antiques   LAPADA
2 Market Place. Open 9-1 and 2-5, or by appointment. SIZE: Large. *STOCK: Furniture, barometers, clocks, porcelain, copper, brass.* PARK: Nearby. TEL: 0379 642213; home - 0379 651369. SER: Restorations; restoration materials; export facilities. VAT: Stan/Spec.

Gostling's Antique Centre
13 Market Hill. Open 10-5, Thurs. 10-7, Sun. by appointment. LOC: Town centre, next to Barclays Bank. PARK: Easy. TEL: 0379 650360; after hours - 0379 870367. SER: Valuations; restorations (furniture, clocks and musical boxes). VAT: Stan/Spec. The following are some of the dealers at this centre.

John Crawford
STOCK: Books, especially relating to both World Wars.

Steve Doyle
STOCK: Small general antiques and collectors' items.

Michael How
STOCK: Books.

George Norman
STOCK: Watches, 1750-1900.

Raymond Norman
STOCK: Longcase clocks, Victorian and Georgian furniture, music boxes and polyphons.

Diss continued
Liz Randle
STOCK: *China, glass, small antiques.*

EARSHAM, Nr. Bungay
Earsham Hall Pine
Earsham Hall. (R. Derham). Est. 1966. Open 8-5, Sat. and Sun. 10-4. SIZE: Large. STOCK: *Pine furniture.* LOC: On Earsham to Hedenham Rd. PARK: Easy. TEL: 0986 893423; fax - 0986 895656. SER: Container service.

EAST DEREHAM
Dereham Antiques
9 Norwich St. (T. Fanthorpe). Est. 1969. Open 10-5. CL: Mon. and Wed. STOCK: *Jewellery, china, glass, small silver items, paintings, furniture.* PARK: Nearby. TEL: 0362 693200.

EAST RUDHAM
Anne Hamilton Antiques
Mulberry Tree House, The Green. (A. Hudson). Open by appointment. SIZE: Medium. STOCK: *Georgian furniture; longcase clocks, porcelain, decorative items.* LOC: On A148. PARK: Easy, on village green. TEL: 0485 528387. VAT: Stan/Spec.

FAKENHAM
Fakenham Antique Centre
Old Congregational Chapel, 14 Norwich Rd. (Mrs Quainton Allen). Est. 1972. Open 10-4.30, until 5 in summer (Easter onwardds), Thurs. 9-4.30. SIZE: 15 dealers. LOC: Turn off A148 at roundabout to town, turn right at traffic lights, to town centre past Post Office, turn left, centre 50yds. on right. PARK: Easy. TEL: 0328 862941; home - 0328 738131. SER: Restoration (furniture and china); polishing; replacement handles.

Market Place Antiques
28 Upper Market Place. (Jean and Donna Hannent). Open 10-4.30, Wed. 10-1. STOCK: *Victorian jewellery, silver, collectors' items and general antiques.* TEL: 0328 862962.

Sue Rivett Antiques and Bygones
6 Norwich Rd. (Mrs S. Rivett). Est. 1969. Open 10-1. STOCK: *General antiques and bygones.* LOC: On Norwich Rd. into Fakenham. TEL: 0328 862924; home - 0263 860462.

GARBOLDISHAM, Nr.Diss
Swan House Antiques and Crafts
Hopton Rd. (M. Eldridge). Open daily 10-5. STOCK: *General antiques.* PARK: Own. TEL: 095381 8221.

GREAT BIRCHAM, Nr. King's Lynn
Deacon and Blyth Fine Art
The Studio, Moor Farm Stables, Docking Rd.

Great Bircham continued
(Michael R. Deacon and Norman A. Blyth). Est. 1967. Open 10-5 or by appointment. CL: Mon. SIZE: Medium. STOCK: *Oil paintings, 17th-20th C, £200-£6,000; watercolours, 19th C, £250-£3,000.* LOC: A148 from King's Lynn, then B1153 to Gt. Bircham. PARK: Easy. TEL: 048523 779; home - same. SER: Valuations; restorations (as stock); buys at auction (as stock). VAT: Stan/Spec.

GT. WALSINGHAM
Mrs Joan Morton
Est. 1965. Open by appointment. STOCK: *Watercolours, 1880-1960.* TEL: 0328 820855.

GT. YARMOUTH
Barry's Antiques
35 King St. Open 9-5.30. SIZE: Large. STOCK: *Jewellery, porcelain, clocks, glass, pictures.* LOC: In main shopping street. PARK: Opposite. TEL: 0493 842713. VAT: Stan/Spec.

David Ferrow
77 Howard St. South. ABA. Est. 1940. Open 9.30-5.30. CL: Thurs. SIZE: Large. STOCK: *Books, some antiquarian maps, local prints, manuscripts.* LOC: From London, sign before river bridge to The Docks, keep to nearside, turn left and then right to car park. PARK: Easy. TEL: 0493 843800; home - 0493 662247. SER: Valuations; restorations (books and prints). VAT: Stan.

The Ferrow Family Antiques LAPADA
6 and 7 Hall Quay, also 1 George St. Est. 1957. Open 9-5. CL: Thurs. p.m. STOCK: **General antiques, £50-£5,000. Not Stocked: Guns, medals, coins, jewellery.** LOC: **Near Haven Bridge, off A12.** TEL: **0493 855391; home - 0493 663605.** SER: **Valuations; restorations; buys at auction; hire.** VAT: **Stan/Spec.**

Folkes Antiques and Jewellers
74 Victoria Arcade. (Mrs J. Baldry). Est. 1946. Open 10-1 and 2-4.30. STOCK: *General antiques especially jewellery and collectables.* LOC: From A47 into town centre, shop on right. PARK: Easy. TEL: 0493 851354. SER: Valuations. FAIRS: Local collectors.

Gold and Silver Exchange
Theatre Plain. (C. Birch). Open 9.30-5.15. STOCK: *Coins, medals and secondhand jewellery.* TEL: 0493 859430.

The Haven Gallery LAPADA
6/7 Hall Quay. (M. and J. Ferrow). Open 9-5. CL: Thurs. p.m. STOCK: **Watercolours, drawings, prints, oil paintings, 19th C, £10-£6,000.** LOC: **Near Haven Bridge, off A12.** TEL: **0493 855391; home - 0493 663605.** SER: **Valuations; restorations (framing, collections).** VAT: **Stan/Spec.**

NORFOLK

Gt. Yarmouth continued

Peter Howkins
39, 40, 41 and 135 King St. Est. 1946. Open 9-5.30. SIZE: Large. STOCK: *At 135 King St. - jewellery, Victorian to present day, £5-£5,000; silver, George III to present day, £1-£2,000; at 39 and 40 King St. - furniture, upholstery, Georgian to Victorian, £5-£5,000; at 41 King St. - investment antiques.* LOC: From Norwich through town one-way system to road signposted Lowestoft which intersects King St. PARK: Easy. TEL: 0493 844639. SER: Valuations; restorations (jewellery, silver, gold, furniture). FAIRS: Langley.

Wheatleys
16 Northgate St., White Horse Plain, and Fullers Hill. Est. 1971. Open 9.30-5, Thurs. 9.30-1. SIZE: Large. STOCK: *Jewellery and general antiques.* LOC: 2 minutes walk from Market Place. PARK: Easy. TEL: 0493 857219. VAT: Stan.

HEACHAM, Nr. King's Lynn

Peter Robinson
Pear Tree House, 7 Lynn Rd. Est. 1880. Open 9-5. Appointment advisable Mon. and Sat. SIZE: Medium. STOCK: *Furniture, 1600-1900, £10-£5,000; china, 1750-1900, metalwork, 1700-1870; both £2-£1,000.* Not Stocked: Late shipping goods. LOC: Shop on left on entry to village. PARK: Easy. TEL: 0485 70228. SER: Valuations; buys at auction. VAT: Stan/Spec.

HOLT

Collectors Cabin
7 Cromer Rd. (J.M.E. Codling). Est. 1983. Open 10-1 and 2-4.30. CL: Thurs. p.m. SIZE: Small. STOCK: *Bric-a-brac, bygones, toys, 19th C, £5-£25.* LOC: Near Post Office. PARK: Bull St. TEL: 0263 712241.

R.L. Cook
10 Heathfield Rd, High Kelling. Est. 1950. Open by appointment. STOCK: *Antiquarian books.* TEL: 0263 711163.

Simon Gough Books
5 Fish Hill. Est. 1976. Open 9.30-5. STOCK: *Antiquarian and secondhand books; bindings.* TEL: 0263 712650.

In the Picture (The Golf Collection)
16 Chapel Yard. (T. and J. Groves). Open 10-4. SIZE: Medium. STOCK: *Decorative prints, limited editions, maps, sporting (especially golf), £5-£500.* PARK: Easy. TEL: 0263 713720/ 822265/824728; fax - 0263 822097. SER: Framing. VAT: Stan.

Richard Scott Antiques
30 High St. Est. 1967. Open 11-5, Sat. 10-5.30. CL: Thurs. SIZE: Large. STOCK: *Pottery and porcelain, rare and unusual objects.* LOC: On A148. PARK: Easy. TEL: 0263 712479. SER: Valuations; conservation advice. VAT: Stan.

HUNSTANTON

Delawood Antiques
10 Westgate. (Mrs J.E. Woodhouse). Resident. Est. 1975. Open 10-5 Wed., Fri., Sat. and most Sun., other times by chance or appointment. SIZE: Small. STOCK: *General antiques, furniture, jewellery, collectors' items, books, £1-£1,000.* LOC: Near town centre and bus station. PARK: Easy. TEL: 0485 532903; home - same. SER: Valuations, restoration (porcelain and china), advice on security alarms.

Old Bakery Antiques
1 Church St. Est. 1968. Open 11-1 and 2-4. CL: Thurs. and Fri. SIZE: Small. STOCK: *Small items, Victorian and Edwardian; embroideries, Staffordshire figures.* PARK: Easy. TEL: Home - 0485 210396.

R.C. Woodhouse (Antiquarian Horologist)
10 Westgate. MBHI and BWCG. Resident. Est. 1975. Open Wed., Fri, Sat., usually Sun. Other days or eves. by chance or appointment. SIZE: Small. STOCK: *Georgian, Victorian and Edwardian longcase, dial, wall and mantle clocks; some watches and barometers.* LOC: Near town centre and bus station. PARK: Easy. TEL: 0485 532903; home - same. SER: Valuations; restorations (longcase, bracket, chiming, carriage, French, wall clocks, dials, barometers), church and stable clocks locally; advice and fitting of alarms.

KING'S LYNN

Tim Clayton Jewellery
23 Chapel St. Open 9-5. STOCK: *Jewellery, clocks, watches, furniture and pictures, pre 1900.* TEL: 0553 772329. SER: Restorations (silver); bespoke jewellery made to order.

Glenmore Interiors
28 Tower St. (Sid Barber). Open 9-5.30. CL: Wed. SIZE: 15 dealers. STOCK: *General antiques including small items, pine, mahogany and oak furniture, bygones, ornate plasterwork, ceiling roses and Adam style fireplaces.* TEL: 0553 766532.

Norfolk Galleries
Railway Rd. (B. Houchen and G.R. Cumbley). Open 8.30-5.30, Sat. by appointment. STOCK: *Victorian and Edwardian furniture.* PARK: Nearby. TEL: 0553 765060.

Old Curiosity Shop
25 St. James St. (Mrs R.S. Wright). Est. 1980. Open 10.30-5, Sat. 9.30-6. SIZE: Small. STOCK: *General collectable smalls, glass, clothing, linen, jewellery, lighting, art deco and nouveau, furniture, prints, stripped pine and paintings, pre 1930, £1-£500.* LOC: Off Saturday market place towards London Rd. PARK: At rear or nearby. TEL: 0553 766591. FAIRS: Alexandra Palace, Newark and local.

ANTIQUE COLLECTING

- Authoritative articles • Practical buying information
- Up-to-date price guides • Annual Investment Issue
- Auctions and fairs calendars
- Antiques for sale and wanted

The magazine is published ten times a year and contains pre-publication offers and special Christmas discounts on ACC books

Join NOW and receive your first magazine and our book catalogue FREE
Annual membership: £19.50 UK,
£25.00 overseas, US $40 USA, CAN $50 Canada

Antique Collectors' Club
5 Church Street, Woodbridge,
Suffolk, IP12 1DS, England
Tel: (0394) 385501 Fax: (0394) 384434

Market Street Industrial Park, Wappingers' Falls,
New York 12590
USA. Tel: 914 297 0003 Fax: 914 297 0068

King's Lynn continued
The Old Granary Antiques and Collectors Centre
King Staithe Lane, off Queens St. Open 10-5. STOCK: China, glass, books, silver, jewellery, brass, copper, postcards, linen, some furniture, and general antiques. PARK: Easy. TEL: 0553 775509.

Silverton Antiques
23 Chapel St. (Mrs S. Clayton). Open 9-5. STOCK: Glass, porcelain, clocks, furniture and paintings. TEL: 0553 772329. SER: Restorations (clocks and jewellery).

Tower Gallery
Middleton Tower. (T.H. and J. Barclay). Est. 1963. SIZE: Large. STOCK: General antiques including furniture, china, glass, silver, prints, pictures. LOC: One mile off A47. PARK: Easy. TEL: 0553 840203/840581.

LITTLE WALSINGHAM
Howard Fears (Books)
Church Cottage, St. Peter's Rd. Resident. Open by appointment. STOCK: Books especially on church art, architecture, monasticism and literary biography. TEL: 0328 820892.

LONG STRATTON
Old Coach House
Ipswich Rd. Est. 1976. Open 10-1 and 2-5. CL:

Long Stratton continued
Mon. STOCK: General antiques, pine, Victorian and Edwardian export furniture, paintings, copper, brass, china. TEL: 0508 30942.

MARSHAM
L.W. Pead
The Highlands, High St. Est. 1969. Open by appointment. STOCK: General antiques. TEL: 0263 732841; home - 0263 732292.

NORTH WALSHAM
Anglia Antique Exporters
Trade Warehouse, Station Yard, Norwich Rd. (J. Connaughton and P. Keegan). SIZE: Large. STOCK: Victorian, Edwardian, pine and general shipping goods, £10-£1,500. TEL: 0692 406266; home - 026378 568.

Eric Bates and Sons
Melbourne House, Bacton Rd. Est. 1973. Open 8-5.30. SIZE: Large. STOCK: General antiques, Victorian, Edwardian, shipping furniture. TEL: 0692 403221. SER: Restorations (furniture); upholstery; shipping and container packing. VAT: Stan/Spec.

North Walsham Antique Gallery
29 Grammar School Rd. (M.B. and I.F. Hicks). Est. 1970. Open 9-1 and 2-5. CL: Wed. and Sat. p.m. SIZE: Medium. STOCK: China, glass, silver,

ARTHUR BRETT AND SONS LIMITED

Dealers in Antique Furniture
42 St. Giles Street, NORWICH, NR2 1LW
Telephone: Norwich 628171 (STD 0603)
Fax: 0603 630245

Open Mon.-Fri.
9.30-5.00
Sat. 10.00-4.00

George II carved giltwood and gesso mirror. Circa 1735. Height 87" x 47"

North Walsham continued
collectors' items, small furniture. TEL: 0692 405059. SER: Valuations; restorations. VAT: Stan/Spec.

NORWICH

Albrow and Sons
10 All Saints Green. (R. Albrow). NAG. Est. 1868. Open 9.30-5. SIZE: Medium. STOCK: Jewellery, silver, plate, china, glass, antiquarian books. LOC: Opposite Bond's store. PARK: Behind Bond's store. TEL: 0603 622569. SER: Valuations; repairs.

William Allchin Antiques
22-24 St. Benedict St. Est. 1978. Open 10.30-5. STOCK: Victorian and early 20th C lighting; fine English furniture; cast-iron fireplaces, wood and marble surrounds; Victorian brass and iron beds; soft furnishings. LOC: Close to St. Andrew's Hall. PARK: Easy. TEL: 0603 660046; fax - same. SER: Restorations (metalwork, polishing, repairs, re-upholstery, re-wiring). VAT: Stan.

The Bank House Gallery LAPADA
71 Newmarket Rd. (R.S. Mitchell). Resident. Est. 1979. Open by appointment. STOCK: English and continental oil paintings especially Norwich and Suffolk schools, 19th C, £1,000-£50,000. LOC: On A11 between city centre and ring

Norwich continued
road. PARK: Own. TEL: 0603 633380; fax - 0603 633387. SER: Valuations; restorations; buys at auction (paintings). VAT: Stan/Spec.

Arthur Brett and Sons Ltd BADA
40/44 St. Giles St. Est. 1870. Open 9.30-1 and 2.15-5, Sat. 10-4, or by appointment. SIZE: Large. STOCK: Antique furniture, mahogany, walnut and oak, sculpture, metalwork. LOC: Near City Hall. PARK: Easy. TEL: 0603 628171; fax - 0603 630245. FAIRS: Grosvenor House and Harrogate. VAT: Stan/Spec.

Cathedral Gallery
93 Upper St. Giles St. (P. Crowe). Open 10-5.15. STOCK: Antique maps and prints. TEL: 0603 624800.

Cloisters Antiques Fair
St. Andrew's and Blackfriars Hall, St. Andrew's Plain. (Norwich City Council). Est. 1976. Open Wed. only 9.30-3.30. SIZE: 23 dealers. STOCK: Wide variety of general antiques. PARK: Easy. TEL: 0603 628477; fax - 0603 762182; bookings- 0603 425158.

Country and Eastern
8 Redwell St. (J. Millward). Est. 1978. Open daily. STOCK: Oriental rugs, kelims and textiles, late 19th C to early 20th C, £50-£500; primitive and country furniture, 18th-19th C, £25-£500; woolwork pictures, 17th-19th C, £10-£200; bygones, 18th-19th C, £2-£75. LOC: Top of Elm Hill. PARK: Nearby. TEL: 0603 623107. VAT: Stan/Spec.

Crome Gallery and Frame Shop
34 Elm Hill. (J. Willis). Est. 1971. Open 9.30-5. SIZE: Medium. STOCK: Watercolours, £50-£350; oils, £150-£500; prints, £10-£150; mainly 20th C, some 19th C. LOC: Near cathedral. PARK: Easy. TEL: 0603 622827. SER: Valuations; restorations (oils, watercolours, prints). VAT: Stan/Spec.

Peter Crowe, Antiquarian Book Seller
75-77 Upper St. Giles St. Open 9-6. STOCK: Antiquarian books, 17th-18th C, calf, 19th C, cloth and fine bindings, travel, topography and Norfolk; maps and prints. TEL: 0603 624800.

D'Amico Antiques Ltd
20 Highland Rd. (J.E. Wrightson and Mrs P. Mawtus). NAWCC. Resident. Est. 1947. Open by appointment or chance. SIZE: Small. STOCK: Mainly clocks and furniture. LOC: Near Unthank Rd. traffic lights. PARK: Easy. TEL: 0603 52320. VAT: Stan/Spec.

Clive Dennett Coins
66 St. Benedicts St. BNTA. Est. 1970. CL: Thurs. a.m. and lunchtime. SIZE: Small. STOCK: Coins and medals, ancient Greek to date, £5-£5,000; jewellery, 19th-20th C; banknotes, 20th C; both

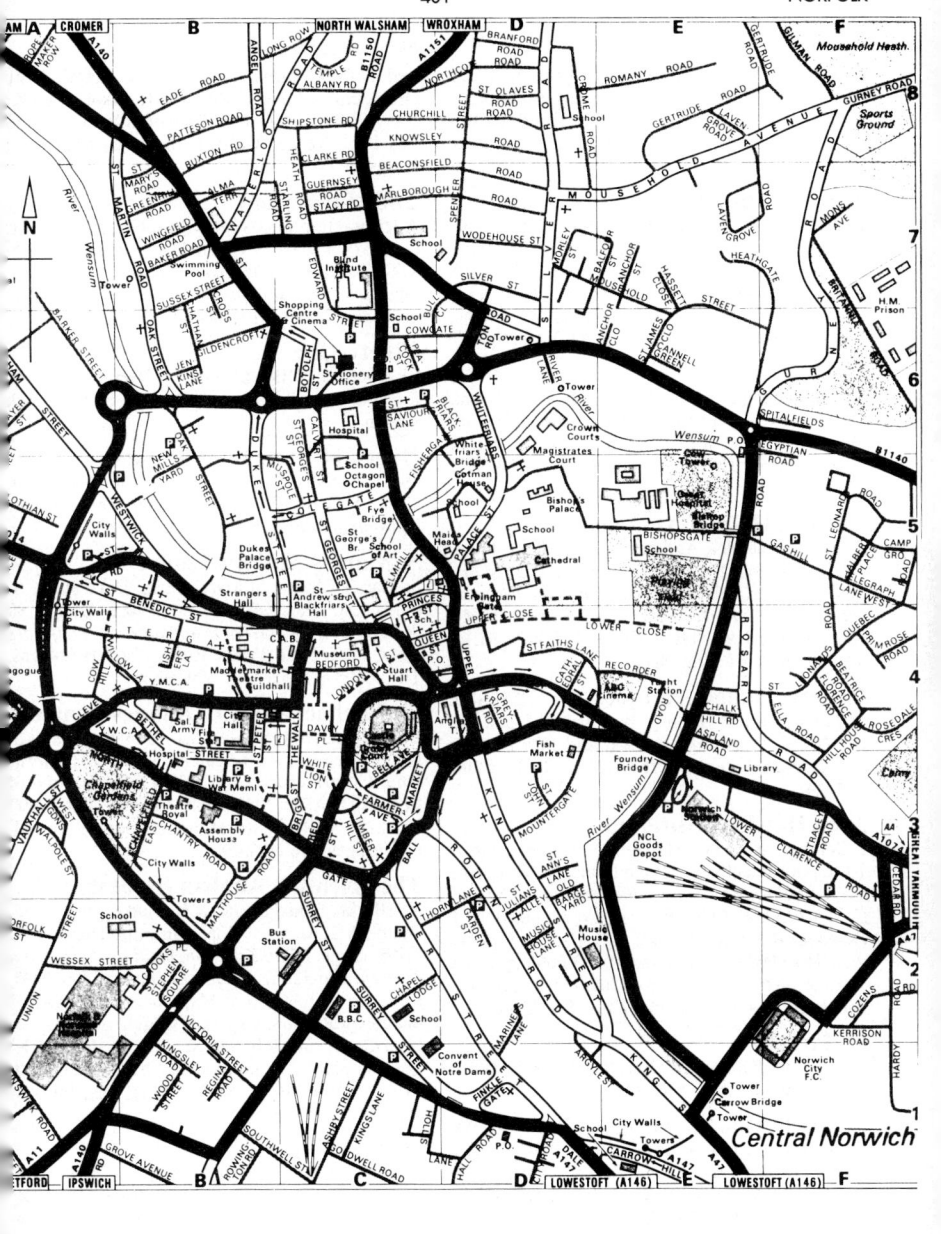

Key to Town Plan

AA Recommended roads
Other roads
Restricted roads
Buildings of interest
Car Parks
Parks and open spaces
AA Service Centre

© Automobile Association 1988.

NORFOLK

Norwich continued

£5-£1,000. PARK: Easy. TEL: 0603 624315. SER: Valuations; buys at auction (as stock). FAIRS: All Simmons; Cumberland Hotel, London; Coinex; Marriott Hotel, London; Tienan, Belgium.

The Fairhurst Gallery
Bedford St. Est. 1951. Open 10-6. SIZE: Large. STOCK: *Oil paintings, £5-£5,000; watercolours, £5-£2,000, both 19th-20th C; frames, 18th-20th C.* LOC: Behind Travel Centre and Travel Australia. TEL: 0603 614214. SER: Valuations; restorations; cleaning; framemakers. VAT: Spec.

Gallery 45
45 St. Benedicts St. (J. Hines). Open 11-3, Sat. 11-4 or by appointment. CL: Mon. STOCK: *Modern British and continental art, British etchings, from 1900.* TEL: 0603 763771/742977. SER: Framing.

Michael Hallam Antiques
St Michael at Plea Antiques Centre, Bank Plain. (M.J. Hallam). Est. 1969. Open 9.30-5. SIZE: Small. STOCK: *Furniture, porcelain, pictures and small items, mainly 19th C, £10-£2,000.* LOC: Near Cathedral. TEL: 0603 413692. SER: Valuations. VAT: Stan/Spec.

Roderic Haugh Antiques   LAPADA
at The Fairhurst Gallery, Bedford St. Open 10-6. STOCK: **Furniture, painted and 18th-19th C; architectural items, gilt mirrors. TEL: 0603 614214.**

John Howkins Antiques
1 Dereham Rd. (J.G. Howkins). Est. 1973. Open 10-5, prior telephone call advisable. SIZE: Large. STOCK: *Furniture and smalls, 18th to early 20th C, £25-£15,000.* LOC: Inner ring road, junction of Dereham Road and Grapes Hill. PARK: Own at rear. TEL: 0603 627832; fax - 0603 666626. SER: Valuations; restorations (furniture, clocks, upholstery); buys at auction. VAT: Stan/Spec.

G. Jarrett
12-14 Old Palace Rd. Est. 1961. TEL: 0603 625847; home - 0603 618244.

Leona Levine Silver Specialist   BADA
35 St. Giles St. Est. 1865. Open 9.30-5. CL: Thurs. STOCK: *Silver and Sheffield plate.* **TEL: 0603 628709.** SER: Valuations; engraving; restorations. VAT: Stan/Spec.

Maddermarket Antiques
18c Lower Goat Lane. Est. 1955. Open 9.30-4.30. STOCK: *Jewellery, silverware.* TEL: 0603 620610.

Mandell's Gallery   BADA
Elm Hill. Est. 1964. Open 9-5.30. SIZE: Large. STOCK: *Oils and watercolours, especially English and Continental works and Norwich*

Norwich continued

and Suffolk painters, 19th-20th C. LOC: Near shopping centre, close to cathedral. PARK: Easy. **TEL: 0603 626892/629180; fax - 0603 767471.** SER: Valuations; restorations; framing. VAT: Spec.

The Movie Shop
Antiquarian and Nostalgia Centre, 11 St. Gregory's Alley. Open 10-5. SIZE: Large. STOCK: *Books, magazines and movie ephemera; furniture, porcelain, pre-1940 clothes and textiles, general antiques.* TEL: 0603 615239.

Ninety-One
91 Upper St. Giles St. Open 9.30-5.30. STOCK: *Furniture including pine and oak.* SER: French spoken.

Queen of Hungary Antiques
49 St. Benedicts St. (V. O'Grady). Resident. Est. 1981. Open 10-5.30. STOCK: *Pine, oak, mahogany and walnut furniture.* TEL: 0603 625082.

St Mary's Antique Centre
St Mary's Church, St Mary's Plain, Duke Street. (I. Ford). Est. 1982. Open 10-4.30. SIZE: Large - 30 dealers. STOCK: *General antiques and collectors items.* LOC: Near HMSO. PARK: Carpark 200 yds. TEL: 0603 612582. SER: Valuations.

St. Michael at Plea Antiques Centre
Bank Plain. (B. Godsafe). Est. 1984. Open 9.30-5. SIZE: Medium - 30 dealers. STOCK: *General antiques, pre-1940, £5-£1,000.* LOC: Near top of Elm Hill. PARK: Multi-storey nearby. **TEL: 0603 619129.** SER: Restorations (furniture, french polishing and re-caning).

The Scientific Anglian (Bookshop)
30-30a St. Benedict St. (N.B. Peake). Est. 1965. Open 10-5.30. CL: Mon. a.m. and Thurs. a.m. SIZE: Large. STOCK: *Secondhand books, old and modern, 30p-£200; antiquarian items, 1500-1900 from £1.* Not Stocked: Maps or prints. LOC: 3 minutes walk from City Hall straight down Upper Goat Lane, turn left into St. Benedict's. PARK: Limited nearby or multi-storey St. Andrew's St. TEL: 0603 624079. SER: Valuations; buys at auction. VAT: Stan.

Oswald Sebley
20 Lower Goat Lane. (P.H. Knights). Est. 1895. Open 9-5.15. CL: Thurs. SIZE: Small. STOCK: *Silver, 18th-20th C, £15-£2,000; jewellery, Victorian, £10-£4,000.* LOC: 150yds. to right of City Hall, down paved street. PARK: Nearby. TEL: 0603 626504. SER: Valuations; restorations (silver and gold jewellery). VAT: Stan/Spec.

This and That
56 Bethel St. (G. Francis). Open 10.30-5.30. STOCK: *General antique and pine furniture.* TEL: 0603 632201.

Norwich continued
James and Ann Tillett
LAPADA
12 and 13 Tombland. Est. 1972. Open 9-6, Sat. 9-1.30. STOCK: *English domestic silver and flatware, from 17th C; mustard pots, collectors' items, barometers, barographs, longcase clocks, jewellery, from 18th C.* LOC: Opposite Erpingham Gate, Norwich Cathedral and Maid's Head Hotel. TEL: 0603 624914. SER: Valuations; restorations (silver); export facilities. VAT: Stan/Spec.

Thomas Tillett & Co
17 St. Giles St. (A. Grigg). Est. 1971. Open daily. SIZE: Medium. STOCK: *Diamond jewellery, 19th-20th C, £50-£2,000; silver, 18th-19th C, £20-£1,000.* PARK: Easy. TEL: 0603 625922. SER: Valuations; restorations (jewellery, silver). VAT: Stan/Spec.

The Tombland Bookshop
8 Tombland. (J.G. and A. Freeman). Open 9.30-5. STOCK: *Antiquarian and secondhand books, maps and prints.* TEL: 0603 760610.

Tooltique
54 Waterloo Rd. (M. Jacobs). Open 9-5.30. CL: Thurs. STOCK: *Woodworking tools including secondhand.* TEL: 0603 414289.

Malcolm Turner
15 St. Giles St. Open 9.30-5. SIZE: Small. STOCK: *Staffordshire, Imari, English and Oriental ceramics, silver, mostly 19th C, £50-£300.* PARK: Nearby. TEL: 0603 627007. SER: Valuations. VAT: Stan/Spec.

Yesteryear
24D Magdalen St. (Mrs E. Watson). Est. 1980. Open 10-5. STOCK: *General antiques, pictures, oils, watercolours, prints, collectors' items, bygones, bric-a-brac, Doulton figures and character jugs, art deco, art nouveau, small furniture.* PARK: Nearby. TEL: 0603 622908 or 0263 721169.

RAVENINGHAM
M.D. Cannell Antiques
Castell Farm. Resident. Open 9-9 including Sun. SIZE: Large. STOCK: *Georgian and Victorian furniture, metalwork, 17th-19th C; garden and decorative items.* LOC: On B1140. PARK: Easy. TEL: 050 846 441. VAT: Stan/Spec.

REEPHAM
The Chimes
Market Place. (D. and H. McDonell). Open 9.30-5.30. CL: Thurs. SIZE: Medium. STOCK: *General antiques, Georgian and Victorian furniture, objets d'art, scientific instruments.* PARK: Easy. TEL: 0603 870480; home - same.

SCRATBY, Nr. Gt. Yarmouth
Keith Lawson Antique Clocks
Scratby Garden Centre, Beach Rd. MBHI. Est. 1979. Open seven days 9-6. SIZE: Large. STOCK: *Clocks and barometers.* LOC: B1159. PARK: Easy. TEL: 0493 730950. SER: Valuations; restorations. VAT: Stan/Spec.

SHARRINGTON, Nr. Holt
Sharrington Antiques
(P. Coke). Est. 1944. Open by chance 9.30-5.00, or by appointment. CL: Jan.-Mar. SIZE: Medium. STOCK: *Small and interesting items, £5-£1,500; china, pictures, embroideries, treen, papier mâché.* LOC: 3 miles west of Holt. PARK: Easy. TEL: 0263 861411; home - 0263 860719.

SHERINGHAM
Rose Denis
20 High St. STOCK: *Jewellery and silver.* TEL: 0263 823699.

Dorothy's Antiques
23 Waterbank Rd. (Mrs D.E. Collier). Est. 1975. STOCK: *Glass, especially cranberry; Royal Worcester, Meissen, Sitzendorf porcelain, commemoratives, Goss china, brass, copper, small furniture, clocks, cased birds, ribbon plates, porcelain shoes, collectors' items.* TEL: 0263 822319; home - 0263 823018.

Parriss
20 Station Rd. (J.H. Parriss). Est. 1947. Open 9-5.30. CL: Wed. SIZE: Medium. STOCK: *Jewellery, £30-£2,500; silver, £40-£2,000; clocks, £100-£3,000.* LOC: A1082, in main street. PARK: Within 150yds. TEL: 0263 822661. SER: Valuations; restorations (jewellery, silver, clocks). VAT: Stan.

The Westcliffe Gallery
2-8 Augusta St. (Parks & Vinsen). Resident. Est. 1979. Open 9.30-1 and 2-5.30, Sat. 9.30-5.30. CL: Wed. SIZE: Medium. STOCK: *Oils, watercolours and drawings, 19th-20th C, £100-£15,000; furniture.* LOC: Town centre. PARK: Easy. TEL: 0263 824320. SER: Valuations; restorations (oils, watercolours, prints); gilding. VAT: Stan/Spec.

SOUTH LOPHAM, Nr. Diss
The Gallery and Things
The Street. (H. and E. Chalk). Open 9.30-5.30 including Bank Holidays. CL: Mon. STOCK: *19th C watercolours, some oils and prints, antiquarian books.* LOC: A1066 Diss/Thetford Rd. TEL: 037 988 761. SER: Framing.

LEO PRATT

OLD CURIOSITY SHOP
SOUTH WALSHAM NORFOLK
Tel: S. Walsham 204

ANTIQUE DEALERS SINCE 1890

Five showrooms of every kind of antique and bygone art. Furniture, porcelain, glass, pictures, enamel, pewter, brass and copper, treen, collectors' items, clocks and watches.
Stock always changing. 1,000 items to choose from.
Closed Sundays. Easy parking.

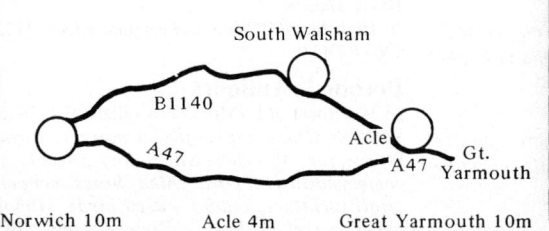

Norwich 10m   Acle 4m   Great Yarmouth 10m

SOUTH WALSHAM

Leo Pratt and Son   LAPADA
Old Curiosity Shop. (R. and E.D. Pratt). Est. 1890. Open 9-1 and 2-5.30. SIZE: Large. *STOCK: Furniture, from 1700; porcelain, glass, pottery, 1830; shipping furniture, metalware.* PARK: Easy. TEL: 060 549 204. SER: Restorations (furniture); buys at auction. FAIRS: Norwich. VAT: Stan/Spec.

STALHAM

Stalham Antique Gallery
High St. (M.B. and I.F. Hicks). Est. 1970. Open 9-1 and 2-5. SIZE: Medium. *STOCK: Furniture, 17th C to 19th C; pictures, china, glass, brass, silver.* Not Stocked: Reproductions. PARK: Easy. TEL: 0692 580636. SER: Valuations; restorations. VAT: Spec.

STIFFKEY

Stiffkey Antiques
The Old Methodist Chapel. Open by arrangement with Stiffkey Lamp Shop. *STOCK: Victorian and Edwardian bathroom fittings; fireplaces, fenders and fire irons, door furniture, books, bric-a-brac, kitchenalia, Japanese and other tinplate toys (many boxed and mint).* PARK: Easy. TEL: 0328 830460; fax - 0328 830005.

Stiffkey continued

The Stiffkey Lamp Shop
Townshend Arms. (R. Belsten and D. Mann). Est. 1976. Open 10.30-6 (winter 10-5), Sun. 11-6. SIZE: Medium. *STOCK: Lamps, gas, electric and oil, 1800-1920, £25-£2,000; rare lamp fittings.* LOC: Coast road near Wells-on-Sea. PARK: Easy. TEL: 0328 830460; fax - 0328 830005. SER: Restorations (lamp fittings). VAT: Stan.

STOKE FERRY, Nr. King's Lynn

Farmhouse Antiques
White's Farmhouse, Barker's Drove. (P. Philpot). Resident. Est. 1969. Open by appointment. *STOCK: General antiques.* TEL: 0366 500588. SER: Restorations; furniture made to order in old timber.

SUFFIELD, Nr. Aylsham

G. and E. Briere
Keepers Cottage. Resident. Est. 1966. Open by appointment. SIZE: Medium. *STOCK: Period furniture, paintings, unusual decorative items.* LOC: First fork left past the garage on Aylsham-North Walsham Rd. TEL: 0263 732651.

SWAFFHAM

Cranglegate Antiques
Market Place. (K.W. Buckie). Resident. Est. 1965. Open Tues., Wed. and Sat. 10-1 and

Swaffham continued
2-5.30. SIZE: Small. *STOCK: General antiques and collectors' items, 17th-20th C, £5-£1,000.* LOC: A47. PARK: In square opposite or in passage at rear. TEL: Home - 0760 721052. FAIRS: Local.

Swaffham Antiques Supplies
66-68 London St. (M. and R. Cross). Est. 1959. Open 10-4. CL: Mon. SIZE: Large. *STOCK: General antiques, 18th-19th C, shipping furniture, £100-£5,000.* LOC: Off A47. PARK: Easy. TEL: 0760 721697; home - same.

SWAFIELD, Nr. North Walsham
Staithe Lodge Gallery
Staithe Lodge. (M.C.A. Foster). Resident. Est. 1976. Open 9-5, Sun. by appointment. CL: Wed. p.m. SIZE: Medium. *STOCK: Watercolours, paintings and prints, 1800-1950, £30-£250.* LOC: On B1145 at the Mundesley end of the North Walsham by-pass. PARK: Easy. TEL: 0692 402669. SER: Restorations; framing; buys at auction (mainly watercolours). VAT: Stan/Spec.

WATTON
Clermont Antiques
Clermont Hall. (P. Jones). Resident. Est. 1983. Open daily. SIZE: Large. *STOCK: Furniture, decorative items, 18th to early 19th C.* LOC: Down farm track, off B1108. PARK: Easy. TEL: 0953 882189. VAT: Spec.

WELLS-NEXT-THE-SEA
Church Street Antiques
2 Church St. (Paula Ford and Lesley Ann Irons). Open 10-4 including Sun., Mon. by appointment. SIZE: Small. *STOCK: Textiles, costume jewellery, general antiques and collectables, £5-£500.* LOC: A149 main coast road, opposite church. PARK: Easy. TEL: 0328 711698.

Wells Antique Centre
The Old Mill, Maryland. Open 10-5 including Sun. SIZE: 13 dealers. *STOCK: General antiques.* PARK: Easy. TEL: 0328 711433.

WROXHAM
T.C.S. Brooke   BADA
The Grange. (M.A., S.T. and L.A.P. Brooke). Est. 1952. Open 9.30-1 and 2.15-5.30. CL: Mon. *STOCK: English porcelain, 18th C; furniture, mainly Georgian; silver, glass, works of art, Oriental rugs.* PARK: Easy. TEL: 0603 782644. SER: Valuations. VAT: Spec.

WYMONDHAM
King
Market Place. (M. King). Est. 1969. Open 9-4. CL: Mon. and Wed., except by appointment. *STOCK: General antiques, furniture, copper, brass, silver, jewellery, porcelain.* PARK: Easy. TEL: 0953 604758; evenings - 0953 602427. VAT: Stan/Spec.

M.E. and J.E. Standley
"Acorns", 23 Norwich Rd, and warehouses at Chandlers Hill. Open Sat. or by appointment. *STOCK: Furniture, 17th-19th C and Victorian.* TEL: 0953 602566.

Turret House
27 Middleton St. (Dr and Mrs D.H. Morgan). PBFA. Resident. Est. 1972. SIZE: Small. *STOCK: Antiquarian books, especially science and medical; scientific instruments.* LOC: Corner of Vicar St., adjacent to War Memorial. TEL: 0953 603462. SER: Buys at auction. FAIRS: London and major provincial PBFA. VAT: Stan/Spec.

Wymondham Antique Centre
No. 1 Town Green. Open 10-5. SIZE: 17 dealers. *STOCK: General antiques and collectables.* TEL: 0953 604817.

Free!

28 page full colour catalogue of Antique Collectors' Club books. Over 120 titles included covering a wide range of subjects: furniture, art reference, art history, prints, jewellery, metalwork, glass, horology, ceramics, oriental carpets, collectables, garden history and design, gardening and architecture.

Available free from the
ANTIQUE COLLECTORS' CLUB

5 Church Street
Woodbridge
Suffolk IP12 1DS
Tel: (0394) 385501
Fax: (0394) 384434

Northamptonshire

NORTH ↑

Key to number of shops in this area.
○ 1-2
⊖ 3-5
⊖ 6-12
● 13+

Please note this is only a rough map designed to show dealers the number of shops in the various towns, and is not necessarily totally accurate.

Northamptonshire

ARTHINGWORTH, Nr. Market Harborough (Leics)
Coughton Galleries Ltd
The Old Manor. (Lady Isabel Throckmorton). Est. 1968. Open Wed., Thurs., Sat. and Sun. 10.30-5, or by appointment. SIZE: Medium. STOCK: Modern British and Irish oil paintings and watercolours. TEL: 085 886 436. VAT: Spec.

BRACKLEY
Brackley Antiques
69 High St. (Mrs B.H. Nutting). Est. 1977. Open 10-6, Wed. 10-12, Sun. by appointment. SIZE: Medium. STOCK: Furniture, especially traditionally upholstered, 19th C, £50-£2,000; ceramics, 18th-20th C, £2-£400; interesting and unusual items. LOC: A43. PARK: Easy. TEL: 0280 703362; home - same. SER: Restorations (furniture and upholstery).

Peter Jackson Antiques
3 Market Place. Open 10.30-1 and 2-5. STOCK: English and continental porcelain and pottery, 18th-19th C; furniture, paintings, silver, jewellery, glass, watercolours and prints. TEL: 0280 703259/0993 882415; mobile - 0860 772860/820028. SER: Valuations; restorations.

Juno's Antiques
4 Bridge St. Open 10-1 and 2-5. CL: Wed. STOCK: General antiques. LOC: Northampton/Oxford road. TEL: 0280 700639.

The Old Hall Bookshop
32 Market Place. (J. and Lady Juliet Townsend). Est. 1977. Open 9.30-1 and 2-5.30. SIZE: Large. STOCK: Antiquarian, secondhand and new books. LOC: Town centre on east side of Market Place. PARK: Easy. TEL: 0280 704146. VAT: Stan.

Right Angle
24 Manor Rd. Open 9.30-5.30, Wed. 9.30-1. STOCK: Watercolours, oils, prints and maps. TEL: 0280 702462. SER: Restorations (frames); gilding and framing.

BRIXWORTH, Nr. Northampton
B.R. Gunnett
128 Northampton Rd. Open by appointment. STOCK: Furniture, bric-a-brac. TEL: 0604 880057.

CASTLE ASHBY
Castle Ashby Gallery
The Old Farmyard. (G.S. Wright - Fine Paintings). Open 10.30-5. CL: Mon. STOCK: Oil paintings - British, 1850-1950, £200-£20,000; continental, £1,500-£10,000; significant contemporary artists. LOC: Adjacent to Castle Ashby House. PARK: Easy. TEL: 0604 696787; fax - same. SER: Valuations; restorations (oils). VAT: Spec.

COSGROVE, Nr. Milton Keynes
Restall Brown and Clennell Ltd
(S. Brown). Est. 1905. Open Mon.-Fri. 8.30-5.30, appointment advisable; other times by appointment. STOCK: English furniture, 17th-19th C. LOC: Off A5, trains can be met at Central Milton Keynes Station. TEL: 0908 565888. VAT: Stan/Spec.

CROUGHTON, Nr. Brackley
Croughton Antiques
29 High St. (L.T. and N. Cross). Est. 1971. Open Wed.-Sun. 10-6 or by appointment. SIZE: Medium. STOCK: General antiques, decorators' items and shipping goods. LOC: B4031. PARK: Easy. TEL: 0869 810203. VAT: Stan/Spec.

FINEDON
Jean Burnett Antiques
37 High St. Est. 1967. Open 10-5, Sun. 2-5. SIZE: Medium- several dealers. STOCK: Needlework tools and accessories, samplers, embroidered pictures and decorative items, 1780-1930, £5-£1,000; general antiques. PARK: Easy. TEL: 0933 681882; home - 0933 680430. SER: Valuations; restorations (furniture, pine stripping and finishing); buys at auction. FAIRS: Stafford, Shepton Mallet, Olympia.

Chancery Antiques
at Finedon Antiques (Antiques Centre), 3 Church St. (R. Andrews). Est. 1973. Open by appointment. STOCK: Furniture and clocks,1780-1900, £10-£500; decorative items, 1850-1930, £10-£100. TEL: 0832 273734.

M.C. Chapman
3 and 3a Church St. Est. 1967. Open 9-5.30. CL: Sat. p.m. SIZE: Large. STOCK: Furniture, 18th-19th C; clocks, 18th-20th C; both £100-£3,000; decorative items, 19th-20th C, £100-£1,000. LOC: On A6. PARK: Easy. TEL: 0933 681260. SER: Valuations; buys at auction. FAIRS: Newark. VAT: Stan/Spec.

Finedon Antiques (Antiques Centre)
3 Church St. (M.C. Chapman). Est. 1973. Open 9.30-5.30, Sun. 2-5. SIZE: Large - 20 dealers. STOCK: Ceramics, glass, paintings, prints and clocks, furniture, silver and plate, mainly 18th to early 20th C. LOC: From roundabout at junction of A6 and A510 take A6 towards Kettering, turn left after 30yds., follow to bottom hill, premises on left. PARK: Easy. TEL: 0933 681260. SER: Export facilities. VAT: Stan/Spec.

Noton Antiques
1 High St. Est. 1978. Open 10-5.30, Sun. 2-5. STOCK: General antiques. TEL: 0933 680973.

Quaker Lodge Antiques
28 Church St. (S. Banks). Resident. STOCK: Period, Victorian and Edwardian furniture and general antiques. TEL: 0933 680371. VAT: Stan/Spec.

Finedon continued
Thorpe Antiques
51 High St. (M.R. Clow). Open 9-5.30, Sat. 2-5, Sun. by appointment. SIZE: Large. *STOCK: Victorian, Edwardian and some period furniture.* PARK: Easy. TEL: 0933 680196. SER: Restorations (furniture); import and export. VAT: Stan/Spec.

FLORE
Christopher Jones at Flore House
Flore House, The Avenue. Est. 1977. Open 10-5, Sat. 11-4.30, Sun. by appointment. SIZE: Large. *STOCK: Decorative and period furnishings, lighting, porcelain, glass and objects, 18th-20th C.* PARK: Easy. TEL: 0327 42165. SER: Valuations; restorations; buys at auction; interior decor advice. FAIRS: Chelsea. VAT: Spec.

V. and C. Madeira
The Huntershields. Est. 1968. Open 9-7, Sun. by appointment. SIZE: Large. *STOCK: Furniture, 17th-19th C, £50-£5,000; decorative items, 19th C, £50-£2,000; metalware, 18th-19th C, £10-£1,000.* LOC: Off M1, junction 16, into Flore, last turning on left, premises on right. PARK: Easy. TEL: 0327 40718; home - same; fax - 0327 349263. VAT: Stan/Spec. *Trade Only.*

GUILSBOROUGH
Nick Goodwin Exports
The Firs, Nortoft Rd. Open every day by appointment. SIZE: Warehouse. *STOCK: Oak, mahogany, walnut, stripped and painted pine, smalls.* TEL: 0280 813115; 0604 740234; fax - same. SER: Restorations; pine stripping, export, shipping and packing; courier.

HARPOLE
Inglenook Antiques
23 High St. (T. and P. Havard). Est. 1971. Open 10-7. CL: Wed. SIZE: Small. *STOCK: Jewellery, £1-£75; stripped pine furniture, £15-£175; general antiques, £1-£200.* LOC: In main street. PARK: Easy. TEL: 0604 830007.

KETTERING
Albion Antiques
36 Duke St. (Shusha Walmsley). Est. 1980. Open Tues. and Fri. 10-6, Sat. 10-1. SIZE: Small. *STOCK: General bric-a-brac and furniture, Georgian-1930s, £5-£100.* LOC: Off Rockingham Rd. PARK: Easy. TEL: 0536 516220; home - same. SER: Caning, rushing and upholstery.

Antiques Warehouse
53-56 Havelock St. (M. Coles). Open 8.30-6. *STOCK: Pine, porcelain, china, shipping goods.* TEL: 0536 411394/510522. SER: Stripping; furniture and kitchens made to order.

Kettering continued
Alexis Brook
74 Lower St. (Mrs A. Brook). Est. 1959. Open from 10 a.m., appointment advisable. CL: Sun. a.m SIZE: Medium. *STOCK: General antiques, £1-£3,000.* LOC: On A6 from Market Harborough House halfway up hill on left before main shopping centre. PARK: At Collingwood Motors, adjacent TEL: 0536 513854.

Dragon Antiques
85 Rockingham Rd. Open 10-4. CL: Thurs *STOCK: Watercolours, oils and Oriental items* TEL: 0536 517017. SER: Framing.

C.W. Ward Antiques
Deene House, 40 Lower St. (Mrs J. Wilson). Est 1912. Open 9-5. SIZE: Medium. *STOCK: Genera antiques, furniture, pottery, porcelain, pewter glass and pictures.* LOC: 25yds. from GPO o A6. PARK: Opposite. TEL: 0536 513537. SER Valuations; restorations (furniture); upholstery and curtain making. VAT: Stan.

KINGSTHORPE, Nr. Northampton
Laila
25 Welford Rd. (L. Gray). Open 9-5.30. *STOCK Pine.* TEL: 0604 715277. SER: Waxing; stripping.

The Old Brigade
10a Harborough Rd. (S.C. Wilson). Est. 1978 Open by appointment. SIZE: Small. *STOCK Military items, 1890's to 1945, £10-£10,000.* LOC: Junction 15, M1. PARK: Easy. TEL: 060 719389; home - same. SER: Valuations; illus catalogue (£3 + SAE). VAT: Stan/Spec.

LONG BUCKBY
Antique Coffee Pot
15 High St. Open 8-5, Sun. 11-2. *STOCK Furniture and bric-a-brac.* TEL: 0327 843849.

R.E. Thompson
17 Church St. Est. 1968. Open 8-5. SIZE: Large *STOCK: Shipping goods, furniture, 19th-20th C stripped pine, clocks, £1-£1,000.* PARK: Easy TEL: 0327 842242/843487. VAT: Stan.

NORTHAMPTON
Adne and Naxos
71-73 Kingsthorpe Rd, Kingsthorpe Hollow. (F Scott). Open 9.30-5.30, Sat. 10-4.30. *STOCK Fine art and furniture.* TEL: 0604 710740.

Buley Antiques
164 Kettering Rd. Est. 1966. Open 10.30-4.45 Thurs. by appointment. SIZE: Medium. *STOCK Victoriana, £5-£200.* PARK: Nearby. TEL: 060 31588; home - 0604 491577. SER: Valuation VAT: Stan.

Cave's OF NORTHAMPTON

111, KETTERING ROAD
Hidden away in our Basement showroom is a large stock full of delightful surprises, mainly 18th and 19th Century Furniture in all woods and in condition worthy of high-class homes.

REGENT HOUSE ROYAL TCE
Gillian Cave's Georgian house furnished with Antiques that are for sale — naturally their condition lives up to her own high standards. Georgian Furniture and a few other items such as pictures and silver.

ANTIQUE DEALERS SHOW CARD AND ASK FOR TRADE FACILITIES
Loop off M1 Exits 15 and 16 or short detour from A5

Northampton continued

F. and C.H. Cave
111 Kettering Rd. Est. 1879. Open 9-5.30. CL: Thurs. SIZE: Large. *STOCK: Furniture - Georgian, Victorian and decorative; general antiques.* LOC: Near town centre, quarter mile outside pedestrianised area. PARK: Adjoining side streets. TEL: 0604 38278. VAT: Stan/Spec.

Michael Jones Jeweller
1 Gold St. Est. 1919. *STOCK: Silver, gold and gem jewellery, French and carriage clocks.* TEL: 0604 32548. VAT: Stan/Spec.

Nostalgia Antiques
190 Kettering Rd. (T.W. Harris). Open 9-5. CL: Thurs. *STOCK: General antiques, clocks, curios.* PARK: Easy. TEL: 0604 33823/713273.

Occultique
73 Kettering Rd. (M.J. Lovett). Est. 1973. Open 10-5. SIZE: Small. *STOCK: Books, 50p-£500.* PARK: Nearby. TEL: 0604 27727. VAT: Stan.

Penny's Antiques
53 Kettering Rd. (Mrs P. Mawby). Est. 1976. Open 11-4, Sat. 10-5. CL: Thurs. SIZE: Small. *STOCK: Shipping goods, kitchen chairs, pictures, army badges, furniture, china, smalls, glass and brass, Victorian to 1940, £5-£100.* LOC: On A43 near town centre. PARK: Easy. TEL: 0604 32429.

Regent House
Royal Terrace. (G. Cave). Est. 1951. Open 10.30-5. CL: Sat. SIZE: Medium. *STOCK: Mainly furniture, 1660-1890, especially Georgian, £100-£18,000.* LOC: Near town centre, just north of Regent Square (road to Leicester); white detached house 100yds. on left hand side (west). PARK: Half-circle drive. TEL: 0604 37992. VAT: Spec.

R.S.J. Savage and Son   LAPADA
Alfred St. (M.J. Savage). Est. 1905. Open 9.30-5.30, Sat. 9-12.30. *STOCK: Oils and water-colours, 18th C to date; antiquarian maps and prints, mirrors, framed pot lids, work by local artists.* LOC: Turn at mini roundabout on Billing Rd., into Alfred St. near hospital.

Northampton continued

Victorian building on left. PARK: Adjoining streets. TEL: 0604 20327. SER: Restorations (paintings); framing; brochure available.

Talent Pastimes Ltd. (Collectors Shop)
85 Kettering Rd. (M.L. Watts). PTS. Est. 1977. Open 9-5, Thurs. 9-2. SIZE: Small. *STOCK: Stamps, from 1840; postal history, from 1600's; covers, from 1840's; all 5p to £500; post and cigarette cards, 20p to £100; toy soldiers and figurines, mainly modern, from £20 a set; accessories.* LOC: A43 near town centre. PARK: Easy. TEL: 0604 36396. VAT: Stan.

Wootton-Billingham
First Floor, 22 St Michael's Rd. (D.J. Veryard). Est. 1897. Open 10.30-4.30. *STOCK: Antiquarian and secondhand books.* TEL: 0604 34531.

OUNDLE, Nr. Peterborough

Quinn Galleries
36 Market Place. (T.P. Quinn). Open 9.30-5.30. *STOCK: Oriental carpets and rugs, furniture, paintings, objets d'art.* TEL: 0832 273744.

PATTISHALL, Nr. Towcester

F. King
Fosters Booth Rd. Open by appointment only. *STOCK: Furniture, English and continental pictures, 18th-19th C.* LOC: Between Towcester and Weedon on A5. TEL: 0327 830326. VAT: Spec.

PAULERSPURY, Nr. Towcester

The Antique Galleries   BADA
Watling St. (M. Cameron). Est. 1948. Open 9-5.30. SIZE: Large. *STOCK: English furniture, 1650-1830; barometers, 1780-1830.* LOC: 3 miles south of Towcester on A5. PARK: Own. TEL: 032 733 238. VAT: Spec.

POTTERSPURY, Nr. Towcester

Reindeer Antiques Ltd   BADA LAPADA
43 Watling St. (J.W. Butterworth). Est. 1959. Open 9-6. SIZE: Large. *STOCK: Period*

NORTHAMPTONSHIRE

Potterspury continued
English furniture, paintings, metal, clocks, garden furniture and statuary. LOC: A5. TEL: 0908 542407/542200; fax - 0908 542121. VAT: Stan/Spec.

RUSHDEN
D.W. Sherwood Antiques Ltd
59 Little St. Est. 1960. *STOCK: General antiques.* TEL: 0933 53265.

Shire Antiques
111 High St. South. (T. Middleton). Open 9.30-5.30, including Sun. CL: Wed. *STOCK: General antiques and shipping goods.* TEL: 0933 315567.

THRAPSTON, Nr. Kettering
John Roe Antiques
Unit 14, Cottingham Way. (Mr and Mrs J. Roe). Est. 1968. Open 9-6, Sat. 10-4. *STOCK: General antiques; continental and American shipping goods; jewellery.* TEL: 0832 732937. VAT: Stan.

TOWCESTER
Clark Galleries
215 Watling St. (A. Clark). Est. 1964. Open 8.30-5.30, Sat. 9.30-4. SIZE: Medium. *STOCK: Landscape paintings, 18th C, £500-£15,000; portraits, 17th-18th C, £500-£5,000.* LOC: M1, junction 15, on A5. PARK: Easy and at rear. TEL: 0327 52957. SER: Valuations; restorations and relining (oil paintings). VAT: Stan/Spec.

Ron Green
209, 227-239 Watling St. West. Est. 1952. Open 9-6 or by appointment. SIZE: Large. *STOCK: English and continental furniture, £30-£30,000; oil paintings, £100-£10,000; decorative items.* TEL: 0327 50387.

John and Jennifer Jones
2 Watling St. Est. 1961. Open 9-6, Sat. 9-5, Sun. by appointment. SIZE: Medium. *STOCK: Furniture, 18th-19th C, £200-£750; shipping goods, 19th C, £25-£200; pictures and china.* LOC: A5. PARK: Easy. TEL: 0327 51898; home - 0327 51675. VAT: Spec.

R. and M. Nicholas
161 Watling St. Open 9.30-6. SIZE: Small. *STOCK: 18th-19th C porcelain, silver and glass.* TEL: 0327 50639.

Shelron Collectors Shop
9 1/2 Brackley Rd. (R. Grosvenor and N. Saunders). PTA. Resident. Est. 1973. Open 10-5. CL: Mon. SIZE: Small. *STOCK: Postcards, from 1890; cigarette and trade cards, from 1880; ephemera, bric-a-brac, books, prints, models, £1-£100.* LOC: Leave M1, junction 15A, 100yds. from A5 traffic lights going west. PARK: Easy. TEL: 0327 50242. SER: Valuations (postcards and cigarette cards). FAIRS: BIPEX, Cheltenham and York Racecourse.

WEEDON
Architectural Heritage of Northants
The Woodyard. Open 9.30-5, Sun. 10-4. CL Mon. *STOCK: Architectural antiques.* LOC: A5 2 miles north of Weedon. TEL: 0327 349249; fax - 0327 349397.

Helios & Co (Antiques)
25/27 High St. (J. Skiba and B. Walters). Open 9 6 including Sun. SIZE: Large. *STOCK: English and continental furniture, especially dining tables; decorative accessories.* PARK: Easy TEL: 0327 40264; evenings - 0525 270247. VAT Spec. SER: Suppliers and restorers to H.M. Govt.

Rococo Antiques and Interiors
5 New St, Lower Weedon. (N.K. Griffiths) Resident. Usually available. *STOCK: Ironwork including brass and iron beds, and architectural items; pine furniture and fireplaces.* LOC: 3 mile junction 16, M1, quarter mile off A5. PARK Easy. TEL: 0327 41288. VAT: Stan/Spec.

Thirty-Eight Antiques Ltd
Building 14, Royal Ordnance Dept. (E.S. and N Saunders). Open 8-5.30, Sat. 8-12, other times b appointment, telephone call advisable. SIZE Large. *STOCK: French decorative and English furniture, mostly light woods, some mahogany pine and mahogany reproductions; panelle rooms, architectural items, stained glass, painte furniture.* TEL: 0327 40766; fax - 0327 4080 SER: Furniture made to order.

The Village Antique Market
62 High St. (E.A. and J.M. Saunders). Est. 196 Open 9.30-5.30, Sun. 10.30-5.30. SIZE: Large 40 dealers. *STOCK: General antiques an interesting items.* LOC: On A45, just off A5 PARK: At side of market. TEL: 0327 42015.

WELLINGBOROUGH
Antiques and Bric-a-Brac Market
Market Sq, Town Centre. Open Tues. 9-4. SIZE 135 stalls. *STOCK: General antiques an collectables.* TEL: 0905 611321.

Park Book Shop
12 Park Rd. (J.A. Foster). Est. 1979. Open 10-5 CL: Thurs. SIZE: Medium. *STOCK: Books, 19 C maps and prints, £5-£75; postcards, 20th C 10p-£5.* PARK: Easy. TEL: 0933 222592. SER Valuations.

Park Gallery
16 Cannon St. (Mrs J. Foster). Est. 1988. Ope 10-5. CL: Thurs. SIZE: Medium. *STOCK: Print maps, 18th-19th C, £5-£50.* LOC: Continuation A510 into town. PARK: Easy. TEL: 093 222592.

Bryan Perkins Antiques
Finedon Rd. (B.H. and J. Perkins). Est. 197 Open 9-5. CL: Sat. p.m. SIZE: Large. *STOCK*

An Antique Collectors' Club Title

George Chinnery 1774-1852
Artist of India and the China Coast
by Patrick Conner

This book represents the first thorough study of Chinnery's life and work; making use of much hitherto unpublished material, it is both comprehensive and highly readable. It also presents a vivid picture of life in the remote outposts of European empires - Madras, Calcutta, Serampore, Canton, Macau and Hong Kong. Chinnery's career is observed within the context of the all-powerful East India Company, family and social pressures upon expatriates, and relations between different races and classes. The hookah and the opium pipe, the bungalow and the palanquin, the ayah and the tanka boatwoman are elements in the extraordinary society which Chinnery enjoyed and so compellingly portrayed.

ISBN 1 85149 160 0, 320pp
189 b & w illus, 113 col, £45.00

Available from:
Antique Collectors' Club, 5 Church Street, Woodbridge, Suffolk IP12 1DS
Tel: (0394) 385501 Fax: (0394) 384434

or Market Street Industrial Park, Wappingers' Falls, New York 12590, USA
Tel: 914 297 0003 Fax: 914 297 0068

Wellingborough continued

Furniture and paintings, 19th C, £200-£2,000; small items. PARK: Easy. TEL: 0933 228812; home - 0536 790259. SER: Valuations; restorations (furniture). VAT: Spec. *Trade Only.*

WEST HADDON
Antiques
9 West End. Est. 1978. Open 10-5.30. CL: Sun., except by appointment. SIZE: Medium. *STOCK: Country furniture, period metalwork, brass and copper, treen and other domestic items.* LOC: A428. PARK: Easy. TEL: 0788 510772; home - 0788 822330. VAT: Spec.

The Country Pine Shop
The Romney Building, Northampton Rd. (H.J. and S.M. Walters). Est. 1985. Open 8 - 5. SIZE: Large. *STOCK: English and continental stripped pine, £30-£1,200.* LOC: A428. TEL: 0788 510430.

Paul Hopwell Antiques   BADA LAPADA
30 High St. Est. 1974. Open 9-6. CL: Sun. except by appointment. SIZE: Large. *STOCK:*

West Haddon continued

17th-18th C oak and walnut country furniture, longcase clocks, metalware: oil paintings and prints mainly sporting and country pursuits. LOC: A428. PARK: Easy. TEL: **0788 510636**. SER: Valuations; restorations (furniture and metalware); buys at auction. VAT: Spec.

WOODFORD HALSE, Nr. Daventry
The Corner Cupboard
14 & 18 Station Rd. (T.R. and Mrs H.M. Stuart). Est. 1980. Open 9-6.30, Sun. 9.30-6.30, Mon., Tues. and Wed. by appointment. SIZE: Medium. *STOCK: English and continental stripped pine, Victorian and Edwardian, £50-£1,000; iron and brass beds, Victorian, £175-£650; sofas, chairs, chesterfields, Victorian, £50-£450.* LOC: Off A361 towards village. After 1 mile turn right up Phipps Rd. to village centre, shops in parade at top of hill. PARK: Easy. TEL: 0327 60725; home - same. SER: Restorations (cabinet, upholstery, contract joinery).

Northumberland

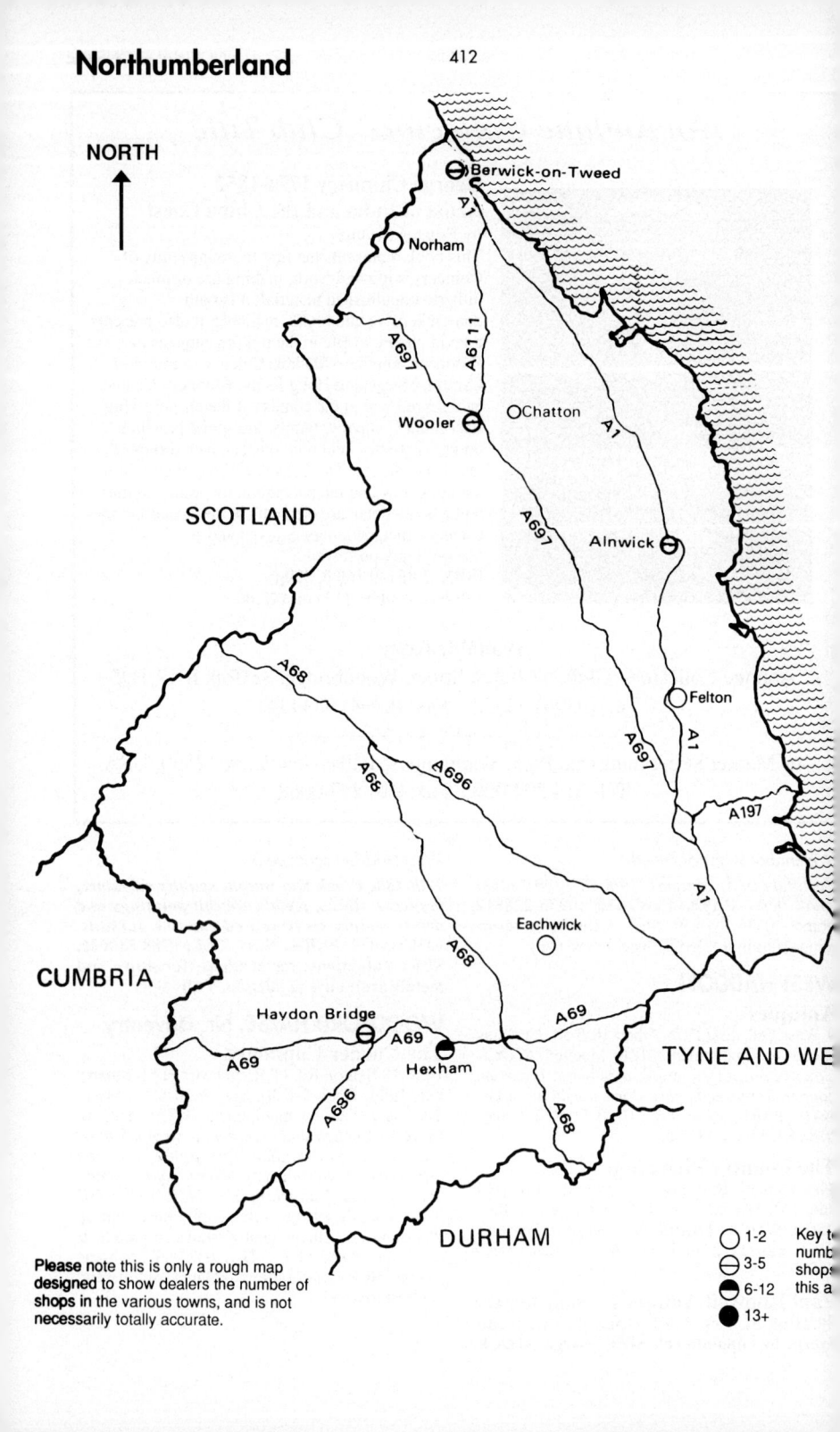

NORTH ↑

- Berwick-on-Tweed
- Norham
- Wooler
- Chatton
- Alnwick
- Felton
- Eachwick
- Haydon Bridge
- Hexham

SCOTLAND

CUMBRIA

TYNE AND WE[AR]

DURHAM

Roads: A1, A6111, A697, A68, A66, A696, A69, A636, A197

Please note this is only a rough map **designed** to show dealers the number of **shops** in the various towns, and is not **necessa**rily totally accurate.

Key to number of shops in this a[rea]:
- ○ 1-2
- ⊖ 3-5
- ⊖ 6-12
- ● 13+

Northumberland

A cast bronze art deco style mascot in the form of a winged female figure, possibly Victory. 7¼ ins.:18.5cm high, circa 1930. £80-£120. From *Automobilia of Europe — Reference and Price Guide,* by Gordon Gardiner and Alistair Morris, published by the **Antique Collectors' Club,** £25.00.

ALNWICK
Country Pine Antiques
2 Bailiffgate. (J. and T. Higson and J. Storey). Est. 1980. Open 10-5. CL: Wed. SIZE: Large. STOCK: Country pine furniture. LOC: Opposite the castle. PARK: Easy. TEL: 0665 603616. SER: Valuations; restorations; buys at auction.

Bottergate Antiques
4 Narrowgate. (Mrs L. Shell). Open 10-5. SIZE: Medium. STOCK: General antiques, £3-£3,000. LOC: Near castle. TEL: 0665 510034; home - 0665 604212. VAT: Stan/Spec.

Ian A. Robertson
Castle Corner, Narrowgate. STOCK: English oak, mahogany furniture, glass, china and brass, 18th-19th C. TEL: 0665 602725.

Tamblyn
2 Bondgate Without. (Mrs S.M. Hirst). Est. 1981. Open 10-4.30. SIZE: Medium. STOCK: General antiques including country furniture, pottery, pictures; antiquities, glass, to 20th C, £5-£450. LOC: Diagonally opposite war memorial at southern entrance to town. PARK: Easy. TEL: 0665 603024; home - same. SER: Valuations.

BERWICK-ON-TWEED
Castlegate Antiques
8 Castlegate. (R. and A. Fairbairn). Est. 1973. Open 9-1 and 2-5 or by appointment. CL: Sat. p.m. SIZE: Medium. STOCK: Clocks, furniture, shipping items, general antiques, Victorian, militaria, £1-£3,000. LOC: Old A1, at junction to Berwick railway station. PARK: Easy. TEL: 0289 306009.

Berwick-on-Tweed continued
Treasure Chest
43 Bridge St. (Y. Scott). Est. 1988. Open 10.30-3, Sat. 10.30-4, CL: Thurs. SIZE: Small. STOCK: China, jewellery, glass, silver plate and small furniture, from 1860, £5-£150. LOC: Approximately 1 mile from A1. PARK: Easy. TEL: Home - 0289 307736. SER: Restorations (china). FAIRS: Local.

CHATTON, Nr. Alnwick
Country Pine Antiques
Church House. (J. Railton). Est. 1980. Open 10-5 or anytime by appointment. SIZE: Warehouse. STOCK: Pine, oak and country furniture, 18th-19th C, £50-£5,000; architectural items. PARK: Easy. TEL: 066 85 323. SER: Valuations; restorations; buys at auction. VAT: Stan/Spec.

EACHWICK
Hazel Cottage Clocks
Hazel Cottage. (E. and M. Charlton). Open 9.30-5.30. SIZE: Medium. STOCK: Clocks, £150-£8,000. LOC: Just off Darras Hall to Stamfordham road, opposite Wylam turn-off. PARK: Easy. TEL: 0661 852415. SER: Restorations and repairs [clocks]. VAT: Spec.

FELTON, Nr. Morpeth
Felton Park Antiques
Felton Park. (D. and A. Burton). Resident. Est. 1973. Open by appointment only. STOCK: Small Georgian furniture, pottery and porcelain - mainly Sunderland lustre, Newhall, blue and

NORTHAMPTONSHIRE 414

Felton continued
white transfer ware. PARK: Easy. TEL: 0670 787319. SER: Valuations; restorations; polishing. VAT: Spec.

HAYDON BRIDGE, Nr. Hexham
Haydon Bridge Antiques
3 Shaftoe St. (J. and J. Smith). Est. 1974. Open 10.30-5 and by appointment. CL: Mon. and Thurs. SIZE: Large. STOCK: *Stripped pine, £5-£500; Victorian and Edwardian oak and mahogany, shipping goods, Victorian oils and watercolours.* PARK: Easy. TEL: 0434 684200; home - 0434 684461. VAT: Stan.

Haydon Gallery
3 Shaftoe St. (J. Smith). Est. 1975. Open 10.30-5.30; Sun., Mon. and Thurs. by appointment. SIZE: Small. STOCK: *Oils and watercolours by North Eastern artists and others, mainly 19th C; some bronzes.* TEL: 0434 684200; home - 0434 684461. SER: Valuations; restorations (oil paintings).

Revival Beds
Oddfellows Workshop, Shaftoe St. (I. Coulson). STOCK: *Fourposters, half testers, traditional wood beds.* PARK: Easy. TEL: 0434 684755.

HEXHAM
Arthur Boaden Antiques   LAPADA
29 and 30 Market Place. (R.J. Boaden). Est. 1948. Open 9-12.30 and 1.30-5. SIZE: Large. STOCK: *Small furniture, antique and Victorian, £100-£3,000; Victorian bric-a-brac, £10-£500; paintings, 19th-20th C, £50-£1,000; Victorian jewellery, from £30.* LOC: Opposite Hexham Abbey, off A69. PARK: Nearby. TEL: 0434 603187. SER: Valuations; jewellery repairs. VAT: Stan/Spec.

Gordon Caris
16 Market Place. Est. 1972. Open 9-5. CL: Thurs. STOCK: *Clocks and watches.* TEL: 0434 602106. SER: Restorations (clocks and watches).

Hallstile Antiques
17 Hallstile Bank. (Mrs P. Neuman). Est. 1982. Open 10-5. CL: Thurs. SIZE: Large. STOCK: *Furniture, 17th to early 19th C, £50-£7,000; paintings and prints, £15-£600; clocks, silver plate, china, porcelain and glass.* LOC: Town centre, just off Market Place. PARK: Nearby. TEL: 0434 602239. SER: Buys at auction.

J.A. and T. Hedley
3 St. Mary's Chare. (D. Hall and W.H. Jewitt). Est. 1819. Open 9-5. CL: Thurs. p.m. SIZE: Medium. STOCK: *17th C to Victorian furniture; 18th C to Edwardian porcelain, silver, glass, china.* LOC: Off Battle Hill (A69). PARK: 400yds. TEL: 0434 602317. SER: Valuations; restorations (furniture); buys at auction (furniture). VAT: Stan/Spec.

Hexham continued
Hexham Antiques (Inc. Hotspur Antiques)
6 Rear Battle Hill. (J. and D. Latham). Est. 1977 Open 10.30-4, Sat. 9.30-4. CL: Wed. and Thurs SIZE: Large. STOCK: *Furniture, clocks, pictures glass, china, boxes and collectors' items, to ar deco.* LOC: Main shopping street, opposit NatWest Bank. PARK: 400 metres. TEL: 043 603851; home - 0434 604813. SER: Valuations buys at auction. VAT: Spec.

Turn of the Century Antiques
8 Market St. (E. Alston). Est. 1975. Open 11-5 CL: MON. and Thurs. STOCK: *Country bygones china, glass, small shipping goods, linen furniture, £1-£400.* PARK: Nearby. TEL: Home 0434 607621.

The Violin Shop
31a Hencotes. (N. Cain). Est. 1970. Open 10-5 o by appointment. STOCK: *Violins, violas, cello and bows.* TEL: 0434 607897.

John Walker Antiques
Stable Buildings, Station Rd. Open 9.30-4.30. Cl Thurs. STOCK: *General antiques, shipping good and architectural items.* TEL: 0434 608520; hom - 0661 842945. VAT: Stan/Spec.

MINISTERACRES
Joyce Adamson Antique Stripped Pine
Ivy Cottage. Est. 1984. Open 10-5, Sun. b appointment. SIZE: Medium. STOCK: *Stripped pine including wardrobes, dressers and boxe 19th C, £25-£550.* LOC: Turn into Ministeracre monastery off A68. PARK: Easy. TEL: 043 682601; home - same. SER: Restorations (pin including stripping); buys at auction.

NORHAM, Nr. Berwick-on-Tweed
J. and D. Stewart
6 and 8 West St. Resident. Est. 1969. SIZI Medium. STOCK: *China, glass, collectors item mainly Victorian.* LOC: 7 miles north of Berwick on-Tweed. PARK: Easy. TEL: 0289 382376.

WOOLER
Border Sporting Gallery
25 High St. (D. and T. Ross). Open 9-5. CL: Sa SIZE: Medium. STOCK: *Sporting oils and prin Snaffles, L. Edwards, Tom Carr, Thorburn, 19 and earlier, £10-£20,000.* LOC: Main St. PAR Easy. TEL: 0668 81872. SER: Valuation restorations. VAT: Stan/Spec.

James Miller Antiques
1-5 Church St. Est. 1947. Open any time by appoi ment. SIZE: Large, and warehouses. STOC *Georgian, Regency and Victorian furniture.* LO A697. PARK: Nearby. TEL: 0668 81500; home 066 87 281. VAT: Stan/Spec. *Trade Only.*

Antique Collectors' Club Titles

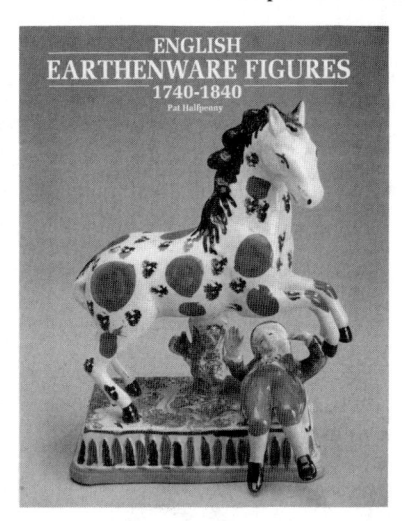

English Earthenware Figures 1740-1840
by Pat Halfpenny
This long awaited volume is an eminently readable account of eighteenth and early nineteenth century production of popular earthenware figures. The leading authority on Staffordshire porcelain and earthenware, the author is Keeper of Ceramics at the City Museum and Art Gallery, Stoke-on-Trent, and is therefore uniquely qualified to write on the subject, for she has at her fingertips the finest collection of English earthenware to be found anywhere in the world, allied with a wealth of archival material.
346pp, 495 b & w illus, 89 col, ISBN 1 85149 114 7, £35.00

Staffordshire Portrait Figures of the Victorian Era
by P.D. Gordon Pugh
A revised edition of the standard work affectionately known as 'Pugh', based on the 1981 revised edition, this book provides what the collector of Staffordshire portait figures has long required: a vast photographic reference to the 1,500 or so portrait figures which encapsulate so much of the history of Victorian England. New colour photographs have been specially taken for this invaluable book.
560pp, 900 b & w illus, 62 col, ISBN 1 85149 010 8, £45.00

English Porcelain Animals *by Dennis G. Rice*
This is the first comprehensive work on the subject of these fascinating and collectable pieces. The fifteen factories that produced them are identified, such as Rockingham, Derby, Minton, Swansea, Copeland, Davenport and Alcock, and potteries such as Charles Bourne, Hilditch & Hopwood, Daniel Edge, and James Dudson.
282pp, 163 b & w illus, 35 col illus, ISBN 1 85149 085 X, £25.00

Available from:
Antique Collectors' Club, 5 Church Street
Woodbridge, Suffolk IP12 1DS
Tel: (0394) 385501 Fax: (0394) 384434

or Market Street Industrial Park
Wappingers' Falls, New York 12590, USA
Tel: 914 297 0003 Fax: 914 297 0068

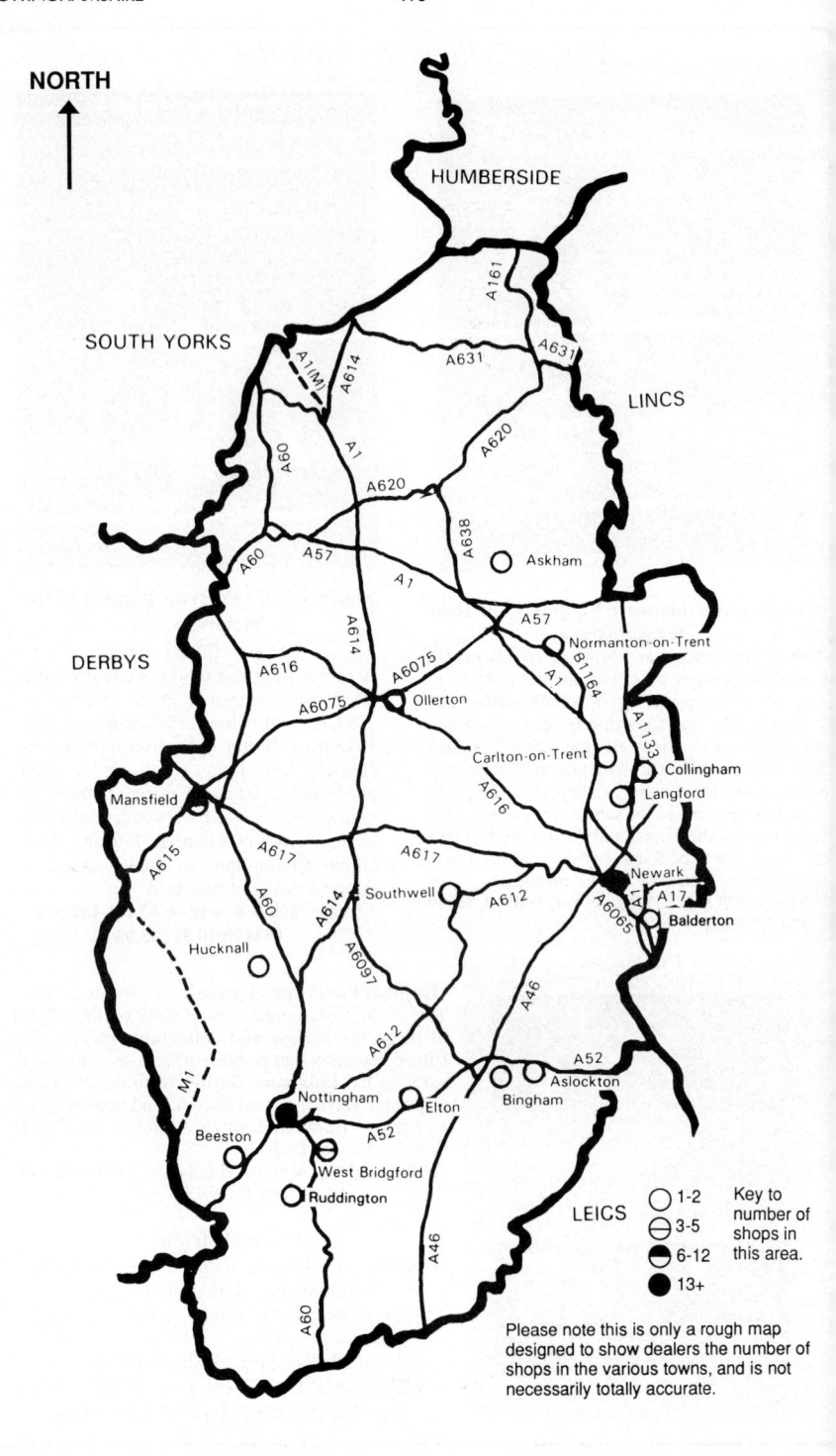

NOTTINGHAMSHIRE

ASKHAM, Nr. Newark
Sally Mitchell Fine Arts
Thornlea. Author of the Dictionary of British Equestrian Artists. FARG. Est. 1967. Appointment advisable. SIZE: Medium. *STOCK: Sporting paintings and prints, mainly 20th C, some 17th-19th C.* LOC: 5 miles from Retford; 5 mins. from Markham Moor roundabout on A1. PARK: Easy. TEL: 077 783 234. SER: Valuations; restorations; framing; lectures; buys at auction.

ASLOCKTON, Nr. Nottingham
Jane Neville Gallery
Elm House, Abbey Lane. (R. Repetto-Wright and J. Neville). Resident. Est. 1979. Open 10-4, Sat., Sun. and Mon. by appointment. SIZE: Medium. *STOCK: Paintings and prints including sporting, 19th-20th C, £50-£5,000.* LOC: A52. PARK: Easy. TEL: 0949 50220. SER: Valuations; restorations; framing; research; print publishers; buys at auction (sporting paintings). VAT: Stan/Spec.

BALDERTON
Blacksmiths Forge
74 Main St. (Mrs J. Sheppard). Est. 1982. Open 12-5, Sat. 9.30-6, Wed. and Sun. by appointment. SIZE: Medium. *STOCK: Pine, beech, satin walnut bedroom furniture, some mahogany and oak, Victorian-Edwardian, £50-£350; smalls, Victorian to 1920, £5-£100; fireplaces, cast-iron and pine surrounds, Georgian to 1920, £20-£350.* LOC: Off A1, follow signs to village, turn right at traffic lights, shop on right next to church. PARK: Easy. TEL: 0636 700008; home - same. SER: Valuations; restorations; stripping; polishing; buys at auction (furniture).

BEESTON
Elizabeth Bailey
33 Chilwell Rd. Est. 1966. Open 10-5.30, Mon. 2-5.30. CL: Thurs. SIZE: Small. *STOCK: Furniture, 18th C to 1930's shipping; general smalls and decorative items, hand-stripped pine.* TEL: 0602 255685; home - 0602 259259. SER: Restorations furniture and longcase clocks).

BINGHAM
E.M. Cheshire   BADA LAPADA
The Manor House, Market Pl. Open 9.30-5.30. CL: Wed. p.m. *STOCK: Furniture, 17th C oak; 18th-19th C mahogany, early metalware.* TEL: 0949 838861. VAT: Stan/Spec.

CARLTON-ON-TRENT, Nr. Newark
Tudor Rose Antiques
D.H. and Mrs C. Rose). Resident. Est. 1984. Open by appointment only. SIZE: Medium. *STOCK: Furniture, 18th-19th C, £50-£2,500; interesting items, 18th-20th C, £10-£500, metalware.* LOC: 1/4 mile from Sutton-on-Trent turning off A1. PARK: Easy. TEL: 0636 821841. FAIRS: Local.

COLLINGHAM, Nr. Newark
The Barn
(J. Richardson). Open by appointment. *STOCK: 18th-19th C furniture and furnishings, treen, textiles, linen and lace, Baxter prints and licencees, Stevengraphs.* TEL: 0636 892884.

Paul Merrill Antiques
The Laurels, High St. Open 9-5, Sun. 10-2. *STOCK: Period and garden furniture.* TEL: 0636 893013.

ELTON, Nr. Nottingham
Rectory Bungalow Workshop
Main Rd. (E.M. and Mrs M.G. Mackie). Est. 1981. Open Sat. 10-5 in summer, 10-12 and 2-3 in winter, other times by appointment. SIZE: Small. *STOCK: Furniture, 17th-19th C; hand-painted, decorative items.* LOC: A52 between Nottingham and Grantham, near Granby/Orston crossroads. PARK: Easy. TEL: 0949 50330/50878; home - same. SER: Restorations (cane and rush seating). VAT: Spec.

HUCKNALL
Curiosity Corner
53a Watnall Rd. (C. Channer). Open 9.15-5, Wed. 9.15-12, Sat. 10.15-2. *STOCK: General antiques.* TEL: 0602 630789.

LANGFORD, Nr. Newark
T. Baker
Langford House Farm. Est. 1966. CL: Sun. except by appointment and Sat. SIZE: Medium. *STOCK: Victoriana, period furniture and oak.* LOC: A1133. PARK: Own. TEL: 0636 704026. *Trade Only.*

MANSFIELD
Antiques Warehouse
375 Chesterfield Rd. North, Pleasley. Est. 1976. Open 9-5, weekends by appointment. SIZE: Large. *STOCK: Victorian and shipping furniture.* LOC: 3 miles off M1, junction 29. PARK: Easy. TEL: 0623 810480. VAT: Stan.

The Book Shelf
7A Albert St. (F.B. and S. Payton). Open 9.30-5. CL: Wed. SIZE: Medium. *STOCK: Antiquarian and secondhand books.* LOC: Town centre. TEL: 0623 648231; home - 0623 640601. SER: Buys at auction (books).

Fair Deal Antiques
138 Chesterfield Rd. North. (D. Lowe). Est. 1972. Open 9.30-5.30. CL: Sat. p.m. and Sun. except by appointment. SIZE: Large. *STOCK: Shipping goods, £50-£100; furniture, mainly mahogany, Victorian, £100-£1,000; period furniture, metalware and small items.* PARK: Easy. TEL: 0623 653768/512419. VAT: Stan. *Trade Only.*

NOTTINGHAMSHIRE

Mansfield continued

Mansfield Antiques
49-51 Ratcliffe Gate. Open 9-5.30 and by appointment. SIZE: Large. STOCK: Furniture. LOC: On A617 Newark Rd. PARK: Easy and adjacent. TEL: 0623 27475; home - 0623 632108. SER: Valuations; buys at auction. VAT: Stan/Spec.

Sheppards Antiques
122-124 Chesterfield Rd. North. (J. and B. Sheppard). Est. 1970. Open 9.30-5.30, Sat. 9.30-1. CL: Wed. STOCK: Furniture, period to shipping, mainly Victorian for Australian and continental markets, £10-£2,500; general small items. LOC: 4 miles from M1, exit 29. PARK: Forecourt. TEL: 0623 631691. VAT: Stan/Spec.

NEWARK

Castle Gate Antiques Centre
55 Castle Gate. Est. 1985. Open 9-5.30. SIZE: Large. LOC: A46 through town, 250yds. from castle. PARK: Easy. TEL: 0636 700076. Below are listed the dealers at this centre.

N. Bryan-Peach Antiques
STOCK: 18th-19th C furniture, clocks and barometers, metalware, £50-£3,000. TEL: Home - 0509 880425. VAT: Stan/Spec.

Evelyn Buckle Antiques
STOCK: Oak and mahogany furniture, 18th-19th C; decorative items. TEL: Home - 0949 42057. VAT: Stan/Spec.

John Dench Antiques
STOCK: 17th-19th C oak, mahogany and walnut furniture; early English pottery. VAT: Stan/Spec.

Dukeries Antiques
STOCK: English oak, mahogany and walnut, 17th-19th C, £100-£5,000. VAT: Stan/Spec.

Leasingham Antiques
STOCK: 18th-19th C mahogany and porcelain.

Parkside Antiques
STOCK: Georgian and Victorian furniture, £100-£3,500. TEL: Home - 0602 609685. VAT: Stan/Spec.

Angelo Perez Antiques   LAPADA
STOCK: 18th-19th C English and continental porcelain, £50-£1,500. TEL: 0606 775090.

Margaret M. Thompson Antiques   LAPADA
STOCK: 19th C oak and mahogany furniture, pictures and decorative items. TEL: Home - 0949 50204. SER: Valuations. VAT: Stan/Spec.

Newark continued

Michael Thompson Antiques
STOCK: 18th-19th C oak and mahogany furniture, decorative items, £50-£2,000. TEL: Home - 0949 50204. VAT: Stan/Spec.

D. and G. Antiques
11 Kings Rd. (Mr and Mrs D. Stutchbury). Est. 1982. Open 9.30-5. CL: Mon. SIZE: Large. STOCK: Furniture, mainly 19th C, £50-£500; porcelain and glass, 19th C, £5-£100; pictures Victorian, £20-£150. LOC: From Market Sq. 500yds., opposite school playing fields. PARK: Easy. TEL: 0636 702782. SER: Restorations buys at auction.

D. and V. Antiques
4A Northgate. (D. and V. Whitehead). Est. 1982 Open 9.30-5. CL: Fri. SIZE: Small. STOCK: Furniture, Victorian and Edwardian, £50+; small items, clocks, oil lamps. LOC: A46 before town centre (Lincoln side). TEL: 0636 71888; home - 0636 76880.

R.R. Limb Antiques
31-35 Northgate. Open 9-6. STOCK: General antiques and pianos. TEL: 0636 74546.

Newark Antique Warehouse
Kelham Rd. Open 8.30-5.30, Sat. 10-4. LOC: Just off A1. PARK: Easy. TEL: 0636 74869. Below are listed the dealers at this warehouse. Trade Only.

A. & J. Antiques
STOCK: 17th-19th C country furniture. VAT Stan/Spec.

A. M. Antiques
STOCK: Period furniture. VAT: Stan/Spec.

B. Benson
STOCK: Furniture and decorative items.

Evelyn Buckle
STOCK: 18th-19th C mahogany. VAT Stan/Spec.

J. Carr
STOCK: 18th-19th C furniture. VAT: Spec.

Michael Chapman
STOCK: General antiques and shipping furniture. VAT: Stan/Spec.

John Dench Antiques
STOCK: 17th-19th C furniture, English pottery, decorative items, longcase clocks £50-£10,000. VAT: Stan/Spec.

Dukeries Antiques
(J. and J. Coupe). STOCK: 17th-19th C furniture; vintage and classic cars. VAT Stan/Spec.

Highfield Antiques
STOCK: 19th C mahogany, walnut and shipping furniture.

NOTTINGHAMSHIRE

Breck Antiques

We have probably the best selection of 18th/19th century porcelain in the area. Stock also includes Derby, Bow, Chelsea and Staffordshire figures, fairings, pot-lids, cranberry, clocks, furniture, etc.

Open Tuesday, Friday and Saturday

726 Mansfield Road, Woodthorpe, Nottingham
Tel: 0602 605263 or 621197

Newark continued

P. R. Straw
STOCK: *Georgian, Victorian and shipping furniture.* VAT: Stan/Spec.

Wickersley Antiques
STOCK: *Mainly Victorian furniture.* VAT: Stan/Spec.

Newark Antiques Centre
Regent House, Lombard St. (Mark Tinsley). Open 9.30-5, Sun. 11-4. SIZE: 55 units and 18 cabinets. STOCK: *Georgian and Victorian furniture, pottery, porcelain, glass, textiles, militaria, clocks, pictures, books, silver, and general antiques.* TEL: 0636 605504.

Portland Antiques
20 Portland St. (C. Duckworth). Est. 1968. Open 9.30-5. CL: Mon. and Thurs. SIZE: Medium. STOCK: *General antiques and smalls, shipping items, pine, collectors' items, £5-£1,000.* LOC: A46, 2 mins. from town centre. PARK: At rear. TEL: 0636 701478; home - 0636 72972. SER: Valuations.

Portland Street Antiques Centre
Portland St. (Sheila Dyson and Barbara Conlon). Est. 1972. Open 10-5. SIZE: 30 dealers. STOCK: *Furniture, silver, glass, ceramics and militaria, mainly 18th-19th C, £5-£1,000.* LOC: A46 200 yards from traffic lights in town centre. PARK: Own at rear. TEL: 0636 74397; home - 0777 870537. SER: Valuations; restorations (upholstery, French polishing, dolls).

Roger Sarsby and Michael Pickering Fine Art
Mill Farm, Kirklington. Open by appointment. STOCK: *British and continental watercolours, 18th-19th C.* TEL: 0636 813394.

Second Time Around
Newark Antiques Centre, Regent House, Lombard St. (G.L. Powis and R. Kenyon). Est. 1985. Open 9.30-5. SIZE: Medium. STOCK: *Clocks, mainly longcase and bracket, to 1830, £1,100-£12,000.* LOC: A46 town centre, opposite

Newark continued

bus station entrance. PARK: Easy. TEL: 0636 605504; home - 0522 543167 or 0904 705000. SER: Restorations (as stock). VAT: Spec.

Jack Spratt Antiques
Unit 5, George St. Open 8-5.30, Sat. 8-4. SIZE: Warehouse. STOCK: *Pine and oak.* PARK: Easy. TEL: 0636 707714/74853; fax - 0636 640595. VAT: Stan.

Wade-Smith and Read
1-3 Castlegate. (A. Wade-Smith and A. Read). Open 9-5. CL: Thur. STOCK: *17th-18th C furniture; decorative items; Eastern rugs.* TEL: 0636 73792.

NOTTINGHAM

Antiques and General Trading Co
145 Lower Parliament St. (C. and M. Drummond-Hoy). Est. 1965. Open 10-5. CL: Thurs. SIZE: Large. STOCK: *Furniture, from 17th C oak to decorative furniture and objects, £50-£5,000.* LOC: A52. PARK: At side. TEL: 0602 585971; home - 0664 62184. SER: Valuations; restorations (furniture). VAT: Stan/Spec.

Breck Antiques
726 Mansfield Rd, Woodthorpe. (P.H.K. Astill). Est. 1969. Open Tues. and Fri. 9-4.30, Sat. 9-5.30 or by appointment. SIZE: Small. STOCK: *18th-19th C porcelain, glass and small Georgian and Victorian furniture.* LOC: Main Mansfield road (A60), 3 miles from city centre. PARK: Easy - large forecourt. TEL: 0602 605263; home - 0602 621197. SER: Valuations; buys at auction (porcelain). VAT: Spec.

N.J. Doris
170 Derby Rd. Open 10-4.30. CL: Thurs. STOCK: *Books, antiquarian and secondhand; postcards and music.* TEL: 0602 781194.

The Golden Cage
99 Derby Rd, Canning Circus. (J. Pearson and J. Paradise). Open 10-5. STOCK: *Clothes including beaded dresses, Victorian, 20's and '70's mens dinner jackets, morning and tweed coats,*

NOTTINGHAMSHIRE

Nottingham continued

waistcoats. TEL: 0602 411600/476478. SER: Hire; clothes made to order.

Granny's Attic
308 Carlton Hill, Carlton. (Mrs A. Pembleton). Open 9-3.30, Sat. 9.30-4. CL: Mon. and Wed. STOCK: *Dolls, miniatures, general antiques and furniture.* TEL: 0602 265204.

Hockley Coins
170 Derby Rd. (D.T. Peake). Open 10-4. CL: Thurs. STOCK: *Coins, medals, badges, postcards, cigarette cards, toys, silver, collectables.* TEL: 0602 790667.

Melville Kemp Ltd   LAPADA
79-81 Derby Rd. Est. 1900. Open 9.30-1 and 2-5.30. CL: Sat. p.m. and Thurs. SIZE: Small. STOCK: *Jewellery, Victorian; silver, Georgian and Victorian, both £5-£10,000; ornate English and continental porcelain, Sheffield plate.* Not Stocked: Furniture. LOC: From Nottingham on main Derby Rd. PARK: Easy. TEL: 0602 417055; fax - 0602 417055. SER: Valuations; restorations (silver, china, jewellery); buys at auction. VAT: Stan/Spec.

Lustre Metal Antiques Nottingham
Cattle Market, Meadow Lane. Est. 1957. Open 9-4.30. STOCK: *Copper, brass, silver, plated and cast iron items, especially fireplaces and beds.* TEL: 0602 863523; evenings - 0602 211046. SER: Restorations; repairs and polishing.

Anthony Mitchell Fine Paintings
                              BADA LAPADA
Sunnymede House, 11 Albemarle Rd., Woodthorpe. (A. and M. Mitchell). Est. 1965. Open by appointment. STOCK: *Oil paintings, £2,000-£100,000; watercolours, £500-£30,000.* LOC: North on Nottingham ring road to junction with Mansfield road, turn right, then 3rd left. PARK: Easy. TEL: 0602 623865; home - same. SER: Valuations; restorations. FAIRS: Olympia, NEC, Harrogate, Cafe Royal. VAT: Spec.

Nottingham Antique Centre
British Rail Goods Yard, London Rd. (P.G. Murdoch). Est. 1969. Open 9-5, Sat. a.m. by appointment. CL: Sat. p.m. SIZE: Large. STOCK: *Shipping furniture, Georgian and Victorian, £50-£200; clocks and pottery, Edwardian, £50-£500; bric-a-brac, Victorian, £5-£25.* LOC: From city centre, head south via Lower Parliament St. to Canal St. island. Carry on to London Rd., turn left at 2nd set of traffic lights. PARK: Easy. TEL: 0602 504504/505548. VAT: Stan.

Pegasus Antiques
62 Derby Rd. (P. and J. Clewer). Open 9.30-5. STOCK: *Fine 18th-19th C furniture, paintings, silver, jewellery, metalware.* TEL: 0602 474220. SER: Liberon restoring products.

Nottingham continued

S. Pembleton
306 Carlton Hill, Carlton. Open 9-5, Sat. 10-5. CL: Mon. and Wed. STOCK: *General antiques.* TEL: 0602 265204.

Mike Pollock
31 Lees Rd, Mapperley. Open 10.30-3.30. STOCK: *General antiques, Victoriana, clocks, mechanical and steam models, toys, bygones.* TEL: 0602 504027 (24 hrs) & 0602 521816; mobile - 0850 262988.

David and Carole Potter Antiques
                                         LAPADA
76 Derby Rd. Est. 1966. Open 10-4. CL: Thurs. SIZE: Medium. STOCK: *Clocks, 18th-19th C, £50-£5,000; period furniture, 17th-19th C; pottery, porcelain and glass, 18th-19th C, £20-£7,000; trade and shipping goods.* LOC: From Nottingham centre, take main Derby Rd., shop on right. PARK: Easy. TEL: 0602 417911; home - 0602 211084. VAT: Stan/Spec.

Val Smith Coins and Antiques
170 Derby Rd. Open 10-4.30. CL: Thurs. STOCK: *Coins, medals, badges, postcards, cigarette cards, toys, jewellery, small collectables.* TEL: 0602 781194.

Station Pine Antiques
103 Carrington St. Open 9.30-5.30. SIZE: Large. STOCK: *Stripped pine and satin walnut furniture.* LOC: Near Midland Station. TEL: 0602 582710.

Top Hat Antiques Centre
66-72 Derby Rd. (Top Hat Exhibitions Ltd). Est. 1978. Open 9.30-5. SIZE: Large. STOCK: *Furniture, Georgian to Edwardian; small porcelain and metal items, to art deco; oils, watercolours and prints, 19th-20th C, £30-£1,000.* LOC: A52 town centre. PARK: Easy. TEL: 0602 419143; home - 0602 258769/678217. VAT: Stan/Spec.

Trident Arms
74 Derby Rd. Est. 1970. Open 9.30-5, Sat. 10-4. SIZE: Large. STOCK: *Arms and armour of all ages and nations.* LOC: From city centre take main Derby Rd., shop on right. PARK: Easy. TEL: 0602 474137; fax - 0602 414199. SER: Valuations. VAT: Stan/Spec.

Vintage Wireless Shop
The Hewarths, Sandiacre. (Mr. Yates). STOCK: *Early wireless and pre-war televisions, crystal sets, horn speakers, valves, books and magazines.* TEL: 0602 393139; fax - 0602 490180; mobile - 0860 362655.

OLLERTON

Hamlyn Lodge
Station Rd. (N., J.S. and M.J. Barrows). Open 10-5, Sun. 12-5. CL: Mon. SIZE: Small. STOCK:

Ollerton continued
General antiques, 18th-19th C, £100-£3,000.
LOC: Off A614. PARK: Easy. TEL: 0623
823600. SER: Restorations (furniture).

RUDDINGTON, Nr. Nottingham
Arthur and Ann Rodgers
7 Church St. Est. 1958. SIZE: Small. *STOCK: Furniture, maps and prints, pottery and china, books.* LOC: Village centre. PARK: Easy. TEL: Home - 0602 216214. SER: Valuations; restorations; framing; buys at auction. VAT: Stan.

SOUTHWELL
Strouds (of Southwell Antiques)
3-7 Church St. (V.N. and J. Stroud). Est. 1972. Open 10-5, Sun. by appointment. SIZE: Large and warehouse. *STOCK: Furniture, clocks, metalware, paintings, 17th-19th C, £10-£10,000.* LOC: Town centre. PARK: Easy. TEL: 0636 815001; home - 0636 814194. VAT: Stan/Spec.

TUXFORD
Sally Mitchell's Gallery
9 Eldon St. FATG. Est. 1966. Open 10-5, Sun. by appointment. SIZE: Medium. *STOCK: Contemporary sporting and animal paintings, £200-£2,500; limited edition sporting and animal*

Tuxford continued
prints, 20th C, £20-£350; sporting paintings, 18th-19th C, £1,500-£6,000. LOC: 1 minute from A1, 14 miles north of Newark. PARK: Easy. TEL: 0777 838 234/655. FAIRS: CLA Game and Burghley Horse Trials. VAT: Stan/Spec.

WEST BRIDGFORD
Bridgford Antiques
2A Rushworth Ave. Open 10-5, Sat. 10-1. SIZE: Small. *STOCK: Furniture and general antiques, pictures, books and postcards.* LOC: Opposite County Hall. TEL: 0602 821835; home - 0602 817161.

Joan Cotton (Antiques)
5 Davies Rd. Est. 1969. Open 9-5. CL: Wed. *STOCK: General antiques, Victoriana, jewellery, silver, china, glass and bygones.* LOC: 1/2 mile along Bridgford Rd. from Trent Bridge, in town centre. PARK: On forecourt. TEL: 0602 813043.

Moulton's Antiques
5 Portland Rd. (J. Moulton). Open 10-5. CL: Mon. *STOCK: General antiques.* TEL: 0602 814354; home - 0602 815973. SER: Restorations (furniture); stripping (pine); pine furniture made to order.

Antique Collectors' Club Titles

Pocket Edition Jackson's Hallmarks *edited by Ian Pickford*
Contains all assay office, Britannia standard, import and date marks plus the 1,000 most important makers' marks, listed alphabetically by mark, for speedy access, together with comments as to rarity, value and speciality of maker.
ISBN 1 85149 128 7
8½ x 4¾in. 172pp
over 1,000 marks, £12.50 hb
£6.95 pb ISBN 1 85149 169 4
'The ideal travelling and buying companion...easy and quick to use'. - Antiques Bulletin

Available from:
Antique Collectors' Club, 5 Church Street, Woodbridge
Suffolk IP12 1DS
Tel: (0394) 385501 Fax: (0394) 384434

or Market Street Industrial Park, Wappingers' Falls
New York 12590, USA
Tel: 914 297 0003 Fax: 914 297 0068

Jackson's Silver and Gold Marks of England, Scotland and Ireland *edited by Ian Pickford*
This major revised edition of what has been the indispensable book on antique silver for over 80 years, essential to dealers, scholars and collectors, contains some 10,000 corrections to the original material aa well as much vital extra information. The text has been extensively updated by a distinguished team of experts. A key reference book, with approximately 15,000 marks illustrated. **ISBN 0 907462 63 4, 766pp, 400 b & w illus, £45.00**

Oxfordshire

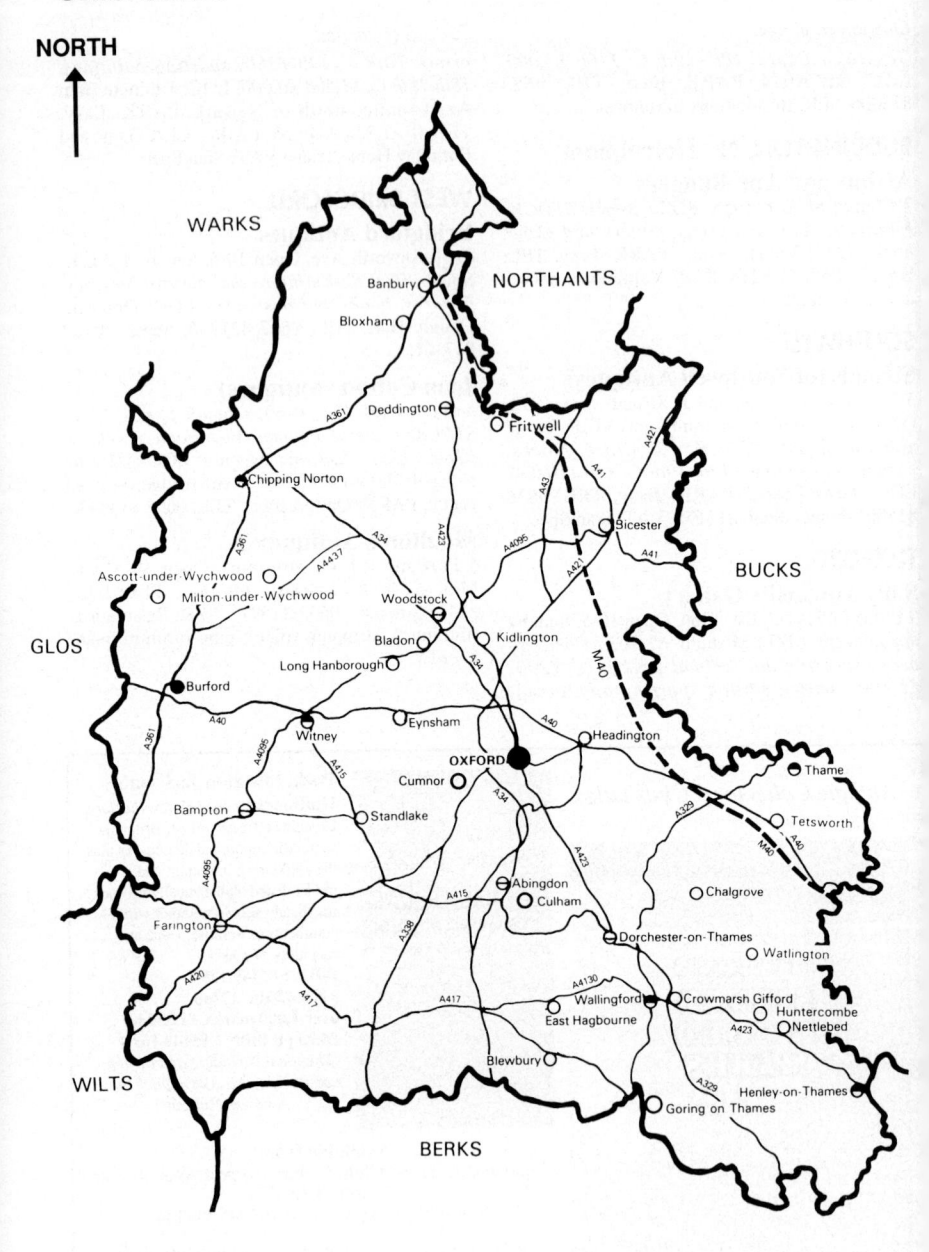

NORTH ↑

422

Map of Oxfordshire showing towns and road network, bordered by Warks, Northants, Bucks, Berks, Wilts, and Glos.

Towns shown:
- Banbury
- Bloxham
- Deddington
- Fritwell
- Chipping Norton
- Bicester
- Ascott-under-Wychwood
- Milton-under-Wychwood
- Woodstock
- Kidlington
- Bladon
- Long Hanborough
- Burford
- Witney
- Eynsham
- Headington
- OXFORD
- Cumnor
- Thame
- Bampton
- Standlake
- Tetsworth
- Abingdon
- Culham
- Chalgrove
- Farington
- Dorchester-on-Thames
- Watlington
- Wallingford
- Crowmarsh Gifford
- East Hagbourne
- Huntercombe
- Nettlebed
- Blewbury
- Goring on Thames
- Henley-on-Thames

Key to number of shops in this area.
- ○ 1-2
- ⊖ 3-5
- ⊜ 6-12
- ● 13+

Please note this is only a rough map designed to show dealers the number of shops in the various towns, and is not necessarily totally accurate.

Oxfordshire

Mark Carter

25, Park Street, Bladon, Nr. Woodstock, Oxford, Oxon. OX20 1RW.
Tel: (0993) 811841. Mobile: 0836 260567

18th and 19th Century Furniture

Opening hours 9.30am - 5.30pm Mon. - Fri.
Saturday by appointment

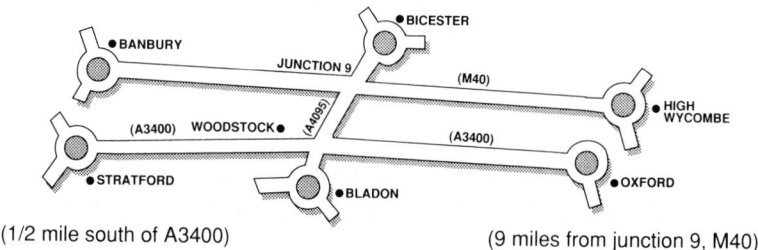

(1/2 mile south of A3400)   (9 miles from junction 9, M40)

ASCOTT-UNDER-WYCHWOOD
Wychwood Antiques
Four Centuries, London Lane. Open by appointment only. *STOCK: English country furniture and decorative items.* TEL: 0993 831571.

BAMPTON
Angela John Antiques
Market Sq. Est. 1975. Open 10-4. SIZE: Medium. *STOCK: Small furniture, 19th C and Edwardian; brass, copper, glass, porcelain, pictures and collectables, £5-£500.* LOC: A4095. PARK: Easy. TEL: 0993 772448.

BANBURY
Judy Vedmore Furniture and Antiques
42 Parson's St. (J. Vedmore and E.J.A. Patterson Co. Ltd). Est. 1978. Open 10-5 by prior appointment. SIZE: Small. *STOCK: Furniture, Georgian to 1930's, £15-£1,000; collectable and unusual items, books, from 1700, £2-£600; silver, jewellery.* LOC: Up from market square. TEL: 0295 269626.

BICESTER
The Barn
Crumps Butts, off Bell Lane. (E. Latimer). Est. 1975. CL: Mon. and Sat. and lunchtimes. SIZE:

Bicester continued
Medium. *STOCK: Furniture, including shipping items, 18th-20th C, £50-£500.* LOC: Town centre. PARK: Easy. TEL: 0869 252958. SER: Restorations; veneering and polishing; buys at auction.

Lisseter of Bicester
3 Kings End. (D. Lisseter). Est. 1945. Open 9-5.30. *STOCK: Furniture, all periods; Victoriana.* PARK: Easy, opposite. TEL: 0869 252402. VAT: Stan/Spec.

BLADON, Nr. Woodstock
Mark Carter Antiques
25 Park St. Est. 1979. Open 9.30-5.30, Sat. by appointment. SIZE: Medium. *STOCK: English mahogany, oak and fruitwood furniture, 17th-19th C, £300-£5,000.* LOC: From Woodstock on A3400, through the village, shop on left. PARK: Opposite. TEL: 0993 811841; home - same. SER: Valuations. VAT: Spec.

Park House Antiques
26 Park St. (H., M. and J. Roseby). Resident. Est. 1978. Open 9-7.30, trade any time. *STOCK: Walnut, mahogany, satinwood and rosewood furniture, early 18th to early 19th C, £200-£7,000; decorative objects, £50-£500.* PARK: Easy. TEL: 0993 812817. VAT: Spec.

GATEWAY ANTIQUES

BURFORD

Over 7,000 sq. ft. of good quality 18th, 19th century and Edwardian furniture — plus a large selection of unusual and decorative items.
Open Monday-Saturday
10am to 5.30pm,
Sundays 2.00pm-5.00pm

**CHELTENHAM ROAD, BURFORD ROUNDABOUT
BURFORD, OXON. OX8 4JA. TEL: (0993) 823678**

BLEWBURY
Blewbury Antiques
London Rd. (S. and E. Richardson). Est. 1973. Open 10-6 including weekends. CL: Tues. *STOCK: General antiques, books, bric-a-brac, country and garden items, oil lamps and oil lamp parts.* PARK: Easy. TEL: 0235 850366.

BLOXHAM, Nr. Banbury
H.C. Dickins
High St. (P. and H.R. Dickins). Open 10-5.30, Sat. 10-1. *STOCK: 19th-20th C British sporting and landscape paintings, watercolours, drawings and prints.* TEL: 0295 721949.

BURFORD
Ashton Gower Antiques   LAPADA
Cotswold Gateway Antiques Centre, Cheltenham Road, Burford Roundabout. (C. Gower). Est. 1987. Open 10-5.30 and Sun. pm. *STOCK: English and continental furniture, mirrors and decorative accessories, 18th-20th C, £25-£5,000.* LOC: On roundabout (A40) Oxford/Cheltenham road. PARK: Easy. TEL: 0993 822450; home - 0993 883279. SER: Valuations; restorations; buys at auction. VAT: Stan/Spec.

The Burford Gallery
Classica House, High St. (B. Etheridge). Est. 1976. Open 9.30-5.30. SIZE: Medium. *STOCK:*

Burford continued

British and continental watercolours, 18th-20th C, £40-£6,000. LOC: 400yds. from A40 roundabout. PARK: Easy. TEL: 0993 822305; home - same. SER: Valuations; framing and mounting; buys at auction (watercolours). VAT: Spec.

Denver House Antiques and Collectables
Denver House, Witney St. (T. and B. Radman). Resident. Est. 1976. Open 10-5.30, Sun. by appointment. SIZE: Medium. *STOCK: Coins and medals, B.C. to date; orders, medals, badges, decorations, military books, police and fire brigade memorabilia, stamps and paper money, 1560 to date; maps, books.* PARK: Easy and nearby. TEL: 0993 822040 (24 hours); fax - 0993 822769. SER: Valuations; restorations (maps and bank notes); buys at auction (coins, stamps, medals, sovereign and stamp cases, maps, covers and tokens). VAT: Stan.

Jonathan Fyson Antiques
50 High St. (J.R. Fyson). CADA. Est. 1972. Open 9.30-1 and 2-5.30. SIZE: Medium. *STOCK: English and continental furniture, decorative brass and steel including lighting and fireplace accessories; papier mâché, tôle, treen, porcelain, glass, jewellery.* LOC: A361. Coming from London on A40 between Oxford and Cheltenham

OXFORDSHIRE

Burford continued

at junction with A361. PARK: Easy. TEL: 0993 823204; home - 036786 223. SER: Valuations. VAT: Spec.

Gateway Antiques
Cotswold Gateway Antiques Centre, Cheltenham Rd., Burford Roundabout. (M.C. Ford and P. Brown). CADA. Est. 1986. Open 10-5.30 and Sun. pm. *STOCK: English and continental furniture, 18th-19th C; decorative accessories.* LOC: On roundabout (A40) Oxford/Cheltenham road. PARK: Easy. TEL: 0993 823678. SER: Valuations. VAT: Stan/Spec.

Horseshoe Antiques and Gallery
97 High St. (B. and Mrs P. Evans). Open 9-5.30. CL: Wed. and Sun. except by appointment. SIZE: Medium. *STOCK: Early oak and country furniture, metalware; 19th-20th C watercolours, oil paintings, longcase clocks.* LOC: East side of High St. PARK: Easy. TEL: 0993 823244; home - 0993 822429. VAT: Spec.

Howards of Burford
51 High St. Open 9.30-5.30. SIZE: Large. *STOCK: Jewellery, 1750-1950, £100-£30,000; silver 1680-1950, £200-£10,000; objects, 1700-1880, £100-£5,000.* PARK: Easy. TEL: 0993 823172.

Lilian Middleton's Antique Doll Shop and Dolls Hospital
54 High St. Est. 1977. Open 9-5, Sun. 10-5. *STOCK: Dolls and accessories, including dolls' house furniture.* SER: Dolls' and teddies' hospital.

Anthony Nielsen Antiques
80 High St. Est. 1977. Open 9.30-1 and 2-5.30. SIZE: Large. *STOCK: Furniture, mahogany, walnut, rosewood, oak, William and Mary to Edwardian, £200-£20,000; copper, brass, £20-£500.* PARK: Easy. TEL: 0993 822014; after hours - 0451 821710.

Old George Inn Antique Galleries
104 High St. (E. and P.R. Johnson). Est. 1992. Open 10-5, usually including Sun. SIZE: Large. *STOCK: General antiques including oak, mahogany, china and treen, early 18th C to 1930's.* LOC: Main road. PARK: Around corner. TEL: 0993 823319.

David Pickup   BADA
115 High St. CADA. Est. 1977. Open 9.30-1 and 2-5.30, Sat. 10-1 and 2-4. SIZE: Medium. *STOCK: Fine furniture, from £1,000+; works of art, £500-£10,000; decorative objects, from £100+; all late 17th-19th C.* PARK: Easy. TEL: 0993 822555. FAIRS: New York International. VAT: Spec.

Burford continued

Richard Purdon   BADA
158 High St. CADA. Open 9.30-5.30. SIZE: Medium. *STOCK: Antique Eastern carpets, village and tribal rugs and related items.* TEL: 0993 823777; fax - 0993 823719. SER: Valuations; restorations. VAT: Stan/Spec.

Manfred Schotten Antiques
109 High St. (P. Matthey and M. Schotten). CADA. Est. 1957. Open 9.30-5.30 or by appointment. *STOCK: 18th-19th C furniture, antique golf and other sporting collectables.* TEL: 0993 822302; fax - 0993 822055. SER: Restorations.

Robin Shield Antiques   BADA LAPADA
134 High St. CADA. Est. 1974. Open 9.30-5.30 or by appointment. SIZE: Medium. *STOCK: Furniture and paintings, £200-£20,000; works of art, £100-£5,000; all 17th-19th C.* LOC: Town centre. PARK: Easy. TEL: 0993 822462; home - 0793 750205. SER: Valuations; buys at auction. VAT: Stan/Spec.

Brian Sinfield Gallery
128 High St. Open 10-5.30. CL: Mon. *STOCK: Early watercolours and paintings, Victorian to contemporary.* TEL: 0993 822603. SER: Valuations; buys at auction.

Swan Gallery
High St. (J. and D. Pratt). CADA. Est. 1966. Open 9.30-5.30. SIZE: Large. *STOCK: Country furniture in oak, yew, walnut and fruitwood, 17th-19th C, £300-£9,000; oil paintings, some sculpture, 19th-20th C, £100-£8,000; Staffordshire figures and small decorative items, 18th-20th C, £50-£800.* PARK: Easy. TEL: 0993 822244. SER: Valuations; restorations (furniture). VAT: Mainly Spec.

Zene Walker, Burford   BADA
The Bull House, High St. (P. Walker). Est. 1954. Open 9-5.30. SIZE: Large. *STOCK: 18th C furniture, English, Welsh, continental and Oriental ceramics and works of art.* TEL: 0993 823284. VAT: Stan/Spec.

Frank Williams
The Old Post Office, High St. Est. 1933. Open 9.30-5.30. SIZE: Large. *STOCK: General antiques, furniture, decorative items.* TEL: 0993 822128. VAT: Spec.

Wren Gallery
4 Bear Court, High St. (S. Hall and G. Mitchell). Est. 1986. Open 10-5.30. SIZE: Medium. *STOCK: 19th-20th C watercolours and drawings.* TEL: 0993 823495. SER: Valuations; restorations (watercolours); buys at auction (watercolours). VAT: Spec.

OXFORDSHIRE

RUPERT HITCHCOX ANTIQUES
At Warpsgrove
Nr. Chalgrove
Oxford

Over 650 items of furniture, mostly mahogany, oak and walnut

Most items in the £100 – £2,000 price bracket

Open Mon. – Sat. 9-5
Sun. 2-5

Tel. Oxford (0865) 890241

4 miles from Watlington (Junction 6 M40)
10 miles from Oxford

CHALGROVE, Nr. Oxford

Rupert Hitchcox Antiques
Warpsgrove. (P. and R. Hitchcox). Est. 1957. Open 9-5, Sun. 2-5 or by appointment. SIZE: Warehouse. *STOCK: Furniture, 1700-1930.* LOC: Halfway between Oxford and Henley, just off the B480, 4 miles M40. TEL: 0865 890241. VAT: Stan/Spec.

CHIPPING NORTON

Bugle Antiques   LAPADA
9 Horsefair. (M. and D. Harding-Hill). Est. 1971. Open 9.30-6. *STOCK: English and French country furniture in oak, elm and fruitwood; Windsor chairs, dressers, bureaux and large tables.* TEL: 0608 643322. VAT: Stan/Spec.

Chipping Norton Antique Centre
Ivy House, 1 Middle Row. (G. Wissinger). Open 10-5 including Sun. SIZE: 20 dealers. *STOCK: A wide variety of smalls and furniture.* PARK: Own. TEL: 0608 644212.

Chipping Norton Books
21 High St. (M.G. Manwaring and Ms E. Kirby). Open 10-5.30. CL: Thurs. in winter. *STOCK: Antiquarian and secondhand books, especially relating to railways.* TEL: 0608 641724.

Chipping Norton continued

The Emporium
26 High St. Open 10-5.30. Collectors Room open 2-5, Sat. 10-5. *STOCK: Bric-a-brac, china, glass, postcards and prints.* TEL: 0608 643103.

Georgian House Antiques
21 West St. Open 9-6. *STOCK: 17th-19th C furniture and paintings.* TEL: 0608 641369.

Jonathan Howard
21 Market Place. (J.G. Howard). Est. 1979. Open by appointment or ring bell. SIZE: Small. *STOCK: Clocks - longcase, wall and carriage, 18th-19th C.* PARK: Easy. TEL: 0608 643065. SER: Valuations; restorations (movement, dials and cases). VAT: Stan/Spec.

Key Antiques   BADA
11 Horse Fair. (D. and M. Robinson). CADA. Resident. Open 9.30-6 or by appointment. SIZE: Medium. *STOCK: Period oak and country furniture, domestic metalware including lighting and downhearth equipment, early carvings, firemarks, keys.* LOC: On main road. PARK: Easy. TEL: 0608 643777. VAT: Spec.

Peter Stroud Antiques
35 New St. CADA. Open 9-5.30. SIZE: Medium. *STOCK: 17th-19th C period furniture, oak, walnut, fruitwood and mahogany including tables, chairs, dressers and bureaux.* LOC: 150yds. from Town Hall down hill on the right. PARK: Own. TEL: 0608 642571. SER: Valuations. VAT: Stan/Spec.

TRADA
21 High St. Open 9-5.30. CL: Thurs. *STOCK: Antiquarian prints, maps and engravings, 1600-1900.* TEL: 0608 644325. SER: Print renovation and colouring; picture frame making.

Peter Wiggins
Raffles Farm, Southcombe. Est. 1969. Usually available. *STOCK: Barometers.* LOC: 1 mile from Chipping Norton on A34. TEL: 0608 642652; home - same. SER: Valuations; restorations (barometers, clocks, automata); clock repairs; buys at auction.

CROWMARSH GIFFORD, Nr. Wallingford

The Pennyfarthing
49 The Street. (Mary Chamberlain). Open Wed.-Sat. 10-5.30. *STOCK: 18th-19th C furniture including pine and kitchenalia; porcelain, silver, brass, copper, linen and decorative items.* PARK: Easy. TEL: 0491 837470.

CULHAM, Nr. Abingdon

Rob Dixon Fine Engravings
Warren Farmhouse, Thame Lane. TVADA. Open by appointment only. *STOCK: Fine and decor-*

Culham continued
ative English and French prints, to 18th C; portraits including fine mezzotints, 16th-19th C; period frames. LOC: Behind European School. TEL: 0235 524676.

CUMNOR, Nr. Oxford
Chris Baylis Country Chairs
TVADA. Open by appointment only. *STOCK: English country chairs in yew, ash and elm - Windsor, wheel-back, rush seated spindle and ladder-back, individual or sets,1780-1900.* TEL: 0865 863566; fax - 0865 864192.

DEDDINGTON
Castle Antiques Ltd   LAPADA
Manor Farm, Clifton. (J. and J. Vaughan). Est. 1968. Open 10-5. SIZE: Large. *STOCK: Furniture, £25-£3,000; silver, metalware, £10-£1,000; pottery, porcelain, £10-£200; kitchenalia.* LOC: B4031 (Aynho Road), 6 miles from junction 10, M40. PARK: Easy. TEL: 0869 38688; evenings - 0869 38294. VAT: Stan/Spec.

The Deddington Antique Centre
Laurel House, Bull Ring, Market Sq. (G. Newark). Est. 1972. Open 10-5. SIZE: Medium - 16 dealers. *STOCK: 18th-19th C furniture, oils, watercolours, porcelain, silver and plate, country furniture and related items, linen, lace and collectors' items.* LOC: Off A4260 Oxford to Banbury road at Deddington traffic lights. PARK: Easy. TEL: 0869 38968. SER: Valuations. FAIRS: Henley and Oxford.

Tuckers Country Store and Art Gallery
Market Place. (R. Gregory). Open daily and Sun. SIZE: Medium. *STOCK: Furniture including country pine, collectors' items, 18th-19th C, £25-£500; oils and watercolours, mainly 19th C, £50-£1,000; clocks, wall and mantel; Victorian linen and costume.* PARK: Outside. TEL: 0869 38215; home - 0869 38397. SER: Valuations; restorations; cleaning (oil paintings). VAT: Stan./Spec.

DORCHESTER-ON-THAMES
Dorchester Galleries
Rotten Row. (D. Knipe). Est. 1978. Open Thurs.-Sat. 10-5. *STOCK: Paintings, £35-£900; prints, £10-£350; both 18th-20th C; glass and china, 19th-20th C, £1-£50; maps, 16th-19th C, £30-£350.* LOC: Off Henley-Oxford road, opposite Dorchester Abbey. PARK: Easy. TEL: 0865 341116. SER: Valuations; restorations; buys at auction (pictures, prints).

Giffengate Antiques
16 High St. (E.M. and S.A. Reily-Collins). Est. 1978. Open 9-5. SIZE: Large. *STOCK: English and continental porcelain, silver, glass, pictures*

Dorchester-on-Thames continued
and furniture, 17th-19th C, £50-£20,000. PARK: Own. TEL: 0865 340028. SER: Valuations. FAIRS: Olympia and Park Lane. VAT: Stan/Spec.

Hallidays Antiques Ltd   LAPADA
The Old College, High St. TVADA. Est. 1950. SIZE: Large. *STOCK: Furniture, 17th-19th C, £100-£20,000; paintings, 18th-19th C, £100-£4,000; decorative and small items, pine and marble mantelpieces, firegrates, fenders, 18th-20th C; room panelling.* PARK: At rear. TEL: 0865 340028. FAIRS: Olympia. VAT: Stan/Spec.

Shambles Antiques
The Barn, 3 High St. (J. and S. Hearnden). TVADA. Est. 1992. Open seven days in summer, winter - Thurs.-Sun. or by appointment. SIZE: Medium. *STOCK: Chairs and decorative country pieces, 18th-19th C.* LOC: Opposite Abbey. PARK: Easy. TEL: 0865 341373; home - 086730 7884 or 071 924 2767. SER: Restorations; upholstery.

EAST HAGBOURNE, Nr. Didcot
E.M. Lawson and Co
Kingsholm. (W.J. and K.M. Lawson). Est. 1921. Usually open 10-5 but appointment preferred. CL: Sat. *STOCK: Antiquarian and rare books, 1500-1900.* PARK: Easy. TEL: 0235 812033. VAT: Stan.

EYNSHAM, Nr. Oxford
John Wilson (Autographs) Ltd
50 Acre End St. ABA. Est. 1967. Open 9-6, Sat. by appointment. SIZE: Large. *STOCK: Autograph letters, historical documents, manuscripts, £10-£50,000.* LOC: From Oxford, off the A40 towards Cheltenham. PARK: Easy. TEL: 0865 880883. SER: Valuations; commissions. FAIRS: ABA London. VAT: Stan/Spec.

FARINGDON
A. and F. Partners   BADA
20 London St. Open by appointment only. SIZE: Medium. *STOCK: English furniture, 17th-19th C, works of art, £100-£20,000. Not Stocked: Victoriana.* LOC: A420. PARK: Easy, within 20yds. TEL: 0367 240078. SER: Valuations. VAT: Spec.

Faringdon Gallery
21 London St. (G.E. Lott). Usually open, appointment preferred. CL: Thurs. *STOCK: Watercolours, oils, etchings and books, 19th-20th C, £50-£6,000.* LOC: A420. PARK: Market Sq. TEL: 0367 242030; home - same. SER: Valuations; restorations (framing and mounting); buys at auction (paintings and prints). VAT: Spec.

La Chaise Antique

Specialists in leather chairs, upholstery and suppliers of loose leather desk tops.

30 London Street, Faringdon, Oxon., SN7 7AA
Tel. Faringdon (0367) 240427. Fax: (0367) 241001 Mobile: (0831) 205002

A very good late Regency D-end dining table with concertina action, in the style of Gillows. The reeded legs all terminating with the original brass castors. Fully extended the table is 4ft wide (122cms) x 13ft. long (397cms). It has 5 interchangeable leaves of which 2 are of the same period but made at a later date. The colour is very good and original. All the leaves are approx. 22in. wide (56cms). Circa 1825.

Faringdon continued

La Chaise Antique
30 London St. (Roger Clark). Est. 1968. Open 10-6. CL: Sun. except by appointment. SIZE: Large. STOCK: Chairs, pre-1860; furniture, 18th-19th C; general antiques, decorators' items. Not Stocked: Silver, porcelain and glass. LOC: A420. PARK: At rear. TEL: 0367 240427; mobile - 0831 205002; fax - 0367 241001. SER: Valuations; restorations; upholstery (leather and fabrics); table top liners. FAIRS: High Wycombe, NEC, Decorative Antiques & Textiles (Chelsea Harbour), Henley (organiser) and City of London (Barbican). VAT: Spec.

HEADINGTON, Nr. Oxford

Ancient & Modern
6 Cherwell Dr. (M.H. Harwood). Est. 1976. Open 9.30-6. SIZE: Medium. STOCK: Furniture and china, £50-£100; collectables, £25-£50, all 19th C. LOC: Near John Radcliffe Hospital. PARK: Easy. TEL: 0865 66408; home - 0865 56643. VAT: Stan.

Barclay Antiques
107 Windmill Rd. (C. Barclay). Est. 1979. Open 10-5.30. CL: Wed. SIZE: Small. STOCK: Porcelain, silver and jewellery, 18th-19th C, £50-£100; period lamps, 20th C, £50-£500. PARK: Easy. TEL: 0865 69551. SER: Valuations. FAIRS: Oxford.

HENLEY-ON-THAMES

Friday Street Antique Centre
2 and 4 Friday St. (J.E. Crocker). Resident. Open 9.30-5.30, Sun. 11-5. SIZE: 15 dealers. STOCK: Art deco, furniture, silver, kitchenalia, curios, objets d'art, memorabilia and automobilia, £3-£500. LOC: First left after Henley bridge, then first right, business on right. PARK: Nearby. TEL: 0491 574104. SER: Valuations; buys at auction.

Henley Antique Centre
Rotherfield Arcade, 2-4 Reading Rd. Open 9.30-6, Sun. 12-6 including Bank Holiday weekends. SIZE: 10 dealers. STOCK: General antiques and bric-a-brac, fine arts, crafts. TEL: 0491 411468.

Henley-on-Thames continued

The Barry M. Keene Gallery
12 Thameside. (B.M. and J.S. Keene). TVADA FATG. Est. 1971. Open 9.30-5.30 and by appointment. STOCK: Watercolours, drawings, paintings, etchings, prints, 18th to early 20th C, contemporary works and sculpture. LOC: Junction 8/9 M4, over bridge, immediate left, 5th building on right. TEL: 0491 577119. SER: Restorations; framing, cleaning, relining, gilding, export. VAT: Stan/Spec.

Richard J. Kingston   BADA LAPADA
95 Bell St. TVADA. Open 9-5 or by appointment. SIZE: Medium. STOCK: Furniture, 17th to early 19th C; silver, porcelain, paintings, antiquarian and secondhand books. LOC: A423 some 1/2 mile from town centre traffic lights. PARK: Easy. TEL: 0491 574535; home - 0491 573133. SER: Restorations. FAIRS: Surrey, Buxton. VAT: Stan/Spec.

Rhino Antiques
20 Market Place. (Sally Shanly). Open 10.15-6, Sun. 12-5. SIZE: 40 dealers. STOCK: General antiques, collectables and bric-a-brac. TEL: 0491 411162; home - 0491 576365.

B.R. Ryland
75 Reading Rd. Est. 1945. Open 9-5. CL: Wed. SIZE: Large. STOCK: Furniture, Victorian and later, £20-£500; copper, brass, clocks, £10-£200; china and glass, all periods, £5-£50. LOC: A4155. From Reading first shop on right on entering Henley. From London M4 turn left after Henley bridge, follow the river past station, then turn left, last shop on the parade. PARK: Opposite. TEL: 0491 573663. VAT: Stan/Spec.

Thames Gallery
Thameside. (S. Came). TVADA. Open 10-5. STOCK: Georgian and Victorian silver; paintings, 19th C. TEL: 0491 572449.

Thames Oriental Rug Co
Thames Carpet Cleaners Ltd, 48/56 Reading Rd. (J. and D. Benardout and C. Aigin). Resident. Est. 1955. Open 9-12.30 and 1.30-5, Sat. 9-12.30. SIZE: Medium. STOCK: Oriental rugs, mid-19th

Henley-on-Thames continued
C to modern. PARK: Easy. TEL: 0491 574676. SER: Valuations; restorations (carpets); cleaning (carpets). VAT: Stan.

HUNTERCOMBE

The Country Seat   BADA LAPADA
Huntercombe Manor Barn. (W. Clegg and H. Ferry). TVADA. Est. 1965. Open 9-5.30, Sun. by appointment. SIZE: Large. *STOCK: Garden statuary, fountains, garden furniture and architectural fittings, panelled rooms and associated furniture, decorative items, 1700-1900; English furniture, 1630-1830; Chinese furniture and artefacts.* LOC: 200 yds down right-hand turn off A423 Nettlebed-Wallingford. PARK: Easy. TEL: 0491 641349; fax - 0491 641533. SER: Valuations; restorations; buys at auction. VAT: Spec.

KIDLINGTON

Handtiques
120 Mill St. (K. Hand). Open 9-5.30. *STOCK: Mainly ceramics, general antiques.* PARK: Easy. TEL: 086 75 6942.

LONG HANBOROUGH

David A. Hallett Antiques (Hanborough Antiques)
125 and 127 Main Rd. Open 10-5, Sun. 2-5. CL: Mon. SIZE: Medium. *STOCK: Furniture, country and period; pottery, porcelain, Victoriana, rural and domestic bygones, brass and copper, collectors' items.* LOC: Going north from Oxford on A34 turn left before Woodstock on to A4095 near Witney. PARK: Easy. TEL: 0993 882767.

MILTON-UNDER-WYCHWOOD

John Jackson   LAPADA
3 The Old School, Church Rd. (J.H. Jackson). Open by appointment. *STOCK: Furniture, 18th-19th C and Oriental; Oriental works of art; watercolours, 19th to early 20th C.* TEL: 0993 831678.

OXFORD

Blackwell's Rare Books
38 Holywell St. Est. 1879. Open 9-6, Tues. 9.30-6. *STOCK: Antiquarian and rare modern books.* TEL: 0865 792792; fax - 0865 248833; telex - 83118. SER: Buys at auction. VAT: Stan/Spec.

Reginald Davis Ltd   BADA
34 High St. Est. 1941. Open 9-5. CL: Thurs. **STOCK: Silver, English and continental, 17th to early 19th C; jewellery, Sheffield plate, Georgian and Victorian. Not Stocked: Glass, china, pewter. LOC: On A40.** PARK: Easy. TEL: 0865 248347. SER: Valuations; restorations (silver, jewellery). VAT: Stan/Spec.

Jeremy's (Oxford Stamp Centre)
98 Cowley Rd. Open 10-12.30 and 2-5. *STOCK:*

Oxford continued
Stamps, postcards and cigarette cards. TEL: 0865 241011.

Christopher Legge Oriental Carpets
25 Oakthorpe Rd, Summertown. (C.T. Legge). Est. 1970. SIZE: Medium. *STOCK: Rugs, various sizes, mainly 19th C, £100-£6,000.* LOC: Near shopping parade. PARK: Easy. TEL: 0865 57572; fax - 0865 54877. SER: Valuations; restorations (re-weaving); courses on rugs and repairing. VAT: Stan.

Laurie Leigh Antiques
36 High St. (L., D. and W. Leigh). Est. 1963. Open 11-6. CL: Thurs. *STOCK: English clocks, keyboard musical instruments.* TEL: 0865 244197. VAT: Stan/Spec.

Roger Little
White Lodge, Osler Rd., Headington. (Dr R. Little). Est. 1988. Open by appointment except Sun. SIZE: Small. *STOCK: English and continental pottery and tiles, £50-£5,000; medieval English pottery, £100-£500; studio pottery, 1850-1960, £50-£500; Islamic pottery and glass, 1500-1850, £50-£1,000. Not Stocked: Anything other than above.* LOC: Near town centre. PARK: Easy. TEL: 0865 62317; home - same. SER: Valuations; restorations (pottery); buys at auction.

Magna Gallery
41 High St. (B. Kentish). Est. 1965. Open 10-5.30. SIZE: Medium. *STOCK: Maps, prints, 1570-1870, 50p-£1,500.* TEL: 0865 245805. SER: Valuations. VAT: Stan.

Niner and Hill Rare Books
43 High St. (P. Hill and M. Niner). Open 10-5.30. *STOCK: Antiquarian and rare books especially on travel and the arts.* TEL: 0865 726105.

Number Ten/Oxford Antiques
10 North Parade. (Mrs P. Clewett). Est. 1979. Open 10-1.30 and some afternoons, prior telephone call advisable. CL: Sun. except by appointment. SIZE: Small. *STOCK: English porcelain and pottery, 1780-1920, £1-£400; small general antiques, including furniture, 1600-1920, £1-£1,500.* LOC: North Parade is second left turning from central Oxford on Banbury road. PARK: 50yds. TEL: 0865 512816; home - same.

The Oxford Antique Trading Co
40/41 Park End St. (D.A. Jones and R.S.J. Howse). TVADA. Open 10-6. SIZE: Large. *STOCK: General antiques, from 18th C to 1930s, £50-£5,000.* LOC: 150yds. from railway station. PARK: Easy. TEL: 0865 793927. SER: Valuations; restorations (furniture, upholstery). VAT: Stan/Spec.

Oxford Antiques Centre
The Jam Factory, 27 Park End St. TVADA. Open 10-5 and 1st Sun. SIZE: 35 dealers. *STOCK: General antiques - 18th-20th C furniture, silver, brass and copper, watercolours and oils, prints, Oriental rugs, period clothes, textiles, luggage,*

THE LAMB ARCADE ANTIQUES CENTRE
THE LARGEST COLLECTION OF ANTIQUES & FINE ARTS IN THE THAMES VALLEY

High Street, Wallingford, Oxon. Tel: (0491) 835166
10-5pm daily 10-4pm Wed. (Sat. till 5.30pm)

Furniture · Silver · Porcelain · Glass · Books · Boxes · Crafts
Jewellery · Brass Bedsteads & Linens · Antique Stringed Instruments
Rugs · Paintings & Engravings · Decorative & Ornamental Items

~ Coffee Shop & Wine Bar ~
A fascinating place to visit

Oxford continued

pens, jewellery, porcelain, ceramics, toys, antiquities, gramophones and radios, books. LOC: Opposite railway station. TEL: 0865 251075. SER: Restorations; repairs (jewellery); silver plating.

Oxford Architectural Antiques
The Old Depot, Nelson St., Jericho. (K.D. Edmonds). Est. 1972. CL: Wed. SIZE: Large. STOCK: Architectural items, especially Victorian fireplaces, bathrooms, ironwork, stained glass, garden ornaments and terraced house items. LOC: 1/2 mile from city centre. PARK: Easy. TEL: 0865 53310. SER: Restorations; fitting undertaken. VAT: Stan.

Payne and Son (Goldsmiths) Ltd   BADA
131 High St. (G.N., E.P. and J.D. Payne). Est. 1790. Open weekdays 9-5. SIZE: Medium. STOCK: British silver, antique, Victorian, modern and secondhand; jewellery, all £50-£10,000+. LOC: Town centre near Carfax traffic lights. PARK: 800yds. TEL: 0865 243787; fax - 0865 793241. SER: Restorations (English silver). VAT: Stan/Spec.

A. Rosenthal Ltd
9-10 Broad St. Est. 1936. Open 9-5.15, Sat. by appointment. STOCK: Continental literature; Judaica; autograph letters; children's books and bibliography. TEL: 0865 243093; fax - 0865 794197. SER: Buys at auction.

Sanders of Oxford Ltd
104 High St. CL: Sat. p.m. SIZE: Large. STOCK: Prints, maps and fans. TEL: 0865 242590; fax - 0865 721748. VAT: Stan/Spec.

A.J. Saywell Ltd. (The Oxford Stamp Shop)
15 Hollybush Row. (I.H. and H.J. Saywell). Est. 1943. Open 10-5.30, Thurs. 10-1. SIZE: Small. STOCK: Stamps, accessories, coins and some medals. LOC: Off Park End St. near railway station. PARK: Easy. TEL: 0865 248889. SER: Valuations. VAT: Stan.

Oxford continued

Thorntons of Oxford Ltd
11 Broad St. Open 9-6. SIZE: Large. STOCK: Antiquarian books. TEL: 0865 242939; fax - 0865 204021.

Titles Old and Rare Books
15/1 Turl St. Est. 1972. Open 9.30-5.30. STOCK: Antiquarian and secondhand books, general subjects, especially literature, fine bird books, natural history, travel and agriculture. TEL: 0865 727928.

Waterfield's
36 Park End St. Open 9.30-5.30. STOCK: Antiquarian and secondhand books, especially academic in the humanities; 17th-18th C English books; philosophy. TEL: 0865 721809.

STANDLAKE, Nr. Witney
Manor Farm Antiques
Manor Farm. (C.W. Leveson-Gower). Est. 1964. Open daily, Sun. by appointment. SIZE: Large. STOCK: Victorian brass and iron beds. PARK: Easy, in Farmyard. TEL: 0865 300303.

TETSWORTH, Nr. Oxford
Tetsworth Antiques
High St. (M. and D. Vine). Open 11-5 including Sun., Sat. 10-5. CL: Mon. and Wed. SIZE: Medium. STOCK: Furniture, china, glass, pine, clocks, £1-£4,000. LOC: A40 between exits 6 and 7, M40. PARK: Easy. TEL: 0844 281636. SER: Valuations; restorations. VAT: Stan/Spec.

THAME
Rosemary and Time
42 Park St. Open 9-6. STOCK: Clocks, watches, barometers. TEL: 084 421 6723. SER: Valuations; restorations; old spare parts. VAT: Stan/Spec.

Thame Antique Galleries
11-12 High St. Open 9-5.30. SIZE: Large. STOCK: Furniture, 18th-19th C; Victorian oil paintings and watercolours. TEL: 084 421 2725.

WALLINGFORD
Michael and Jane de Albuquerque
12 High St. TVADA. Open 10-5. *STOCK: Furniture and decorative items, 18th-19th C.* PARK: At rear. TEL: 0491 832322. SER: Restorations (pictures); framing. VAT: Spec.

The Lamb Arcade
High St. TVADA. Open 10-5, Sat. 10-5.30, Wed. 10-4. TEL: 0491 835048/835166. SER: Restoration (furniture). Below are listed some of the dealers at this centre.

Alicia Antiques
(A. Collins). *STOCK: China, silver and collectors' items.* TEL: 0491 33737; home - 0865 340382.

Antiqus
STOCK: 18th-19th C upholstered furniture, pictures, silver and porcelain figures.

Belcher and Jones
STOCK: Victorian furniture, continental and English pine, lighting.

Anne Brewer Antiques
STOCK: Furniture, china, silver, jewellery and objets d'art. TEL: 0491 38486.

Toby English
STOCK: Antiquarian and secondhand books. TEL: 0491 36389.

Great Expectations
(N. McKie). *STOCK: Victorian brass bedsteads, linens and bedroom furnishings.* TEL: 0491 39909.

Marriott Antiques
STOCK: Victorian furniture, decorative items. TEL: 0491 824433.

Margaret Richmond
STOCK: Small 17th-19th C oak country furniture, accessories and decorative items. TEL: 0491 35166.

Ridgeway Antiques
STOCK: Small interesting furniture, pictures and prints.

Gretel Stone
STOCK: Small furniture, porcelain, silver, pictures and objets d'art.

Julie Strachey
STOCK: Pine. TEL: 0491 35166.

Tags
(T. and A. Green). *STOCK: Collectors' items, curios, jewellery, militaria, scientific instruments and furniture.* TEL: 0491 35048; home - 0491 872962.

Rosemary Toop
STOCK: Boxes, Victorian furniture, collectors' items and lighting. TEL: 0491 35166.

OXFORDSHIRE

Wallingford continued

Waters Violins
STOCK: Old violins, violas and cellos. TEL: 0491 25616. SER: Valuations; restorations.

MGJ Antiques LAPADA
1A St. Martins St. (Mrs M. Jane). Est. 1971. Open 10-4.30, Sat. 10-5. SIZE: Small. *STOCK: Jewellery, Victorian and secondhand, £100-£2,500.* LOC: Town centre. PARK: Nearby. TEL: 0491 834336; home - 0235 848444. SER: Valuations. VAT: Stan/Spec.

An Antique Collectors' Club Title

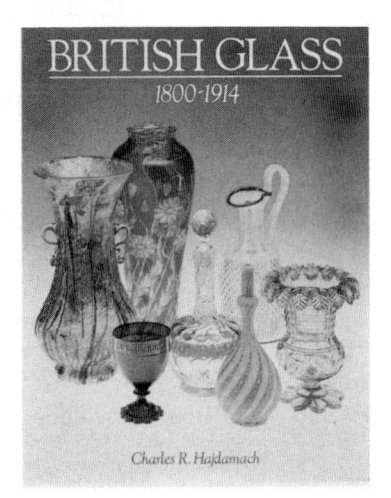

BRITISH GLASS
1800-1914

Charles R. Hajdamach

British Glass 1800-1914
by Charles R. Hajdamach
Details development of glassmaking and decorating techniques and their interaction with changes in fashion. Wide use of contemporary source material facilitates dating of pieces and marks a new high level of scholarship in this important collecting subject.
ISBN 1 85149 141 4
466pp, 430 illus, 50 col, £45.00

Available from:
Antique Collectors' Club
5 Church Street, Woodbridge
Suffolk IP12 1DS
Tel: (0394) 385501 Fax: (0394) 384434

---

or Market Street Industrial Park
Wappingers' Falls
New York 12590, USA
Tel: 914 297 0003 Fax: 914 297 0068

SUMMERS, DAVIS AND SON LIMITED
Calleva House • 6 High Street • Wallingford • Oxfordshire OX10 0BP
Tel: Wall. (0491) 836284 Fax: (0491) 833443

Directoire eterger, c.1795

Specialists in English and Continental Furniture of the 17th-19th Centuries

Wallingford continued

Chris and Lin O'Donnell Antiques
26 High St. Open 10-1 and 2-5. SIZE: Medium. STOCK: Furniture, 18th C to Edwardian, to £1,000; rugs, to £500; small collectables, especially Oriental items; maps. LOC: Into town over Wallingford Bridge, 150yds. along High St. on left-hand side. PARK: Thames St. TEL: 0491 839332.

Mike Ottrey Antiques
16 High St. (M.J. Ottrey). TVADA. Est. 1955. Open 9-5.30. SIZE: Large. STOCK: Furniture, 17th-19th C; oil paintings, copper and brass, decorative and unusual items. LOC: A429. PARK: At rear. TEL: 0491 836429. VAT: Stan/Spec.

Second Time Around Antiques
6 St. Peters St. (C. O'Donnell). Est. 1974. Open 9.30-1 and 2-5. CL: Mon. and Wed. SIZE: Medium. STOCK: Furniture, 18th to early 20th C, to £2,000; clocks, £50-£1,000; small collectors' items - porcelain, silver and brass, £1-£200; some stripped pine. LOC: Into town centre over Wallingford Bridge, turn left into Thames St., then first right. PARK: Easy. TEL: 0491 839345.

Summers, Davis and Son Ltd
BADA LAPADA
Calleva House, 6 High St. (M.S. Baylis and G. Wells). CINOA, TVADA. Est. 1917. Open 8-5.30. SIZE: Large. STOCK: English and continental decorative furniture, 17th-19th C. Not Stocked: Silver, shipping goods. LOC: From London, shop is on left, 50yds. from Thames Bridge. PARK: Opposite, behind castellated gates. TEL: 0491 836284; fax - 0491 833443. VAT: Spec.

WATLINGTON, Nr. Oxford

Cross Antiques
37 High St. (R.A. and I.D. Crawley). TVADA. Est. 1986. Open 10-6, Sun. and Wed. by appointment. SIZE: Small. STOCK: Furniture, £100-£5,000; decorative smalls, clocks and garden items, £50-£2,000; all 1600-1900. LOC: Off B4009 in village centre. PARK: Easy and at rear. TEL: 0491 612324; home - same. SER: Buys at auction.

Stephen Orton Antiques
LAPADA
The Antiques Warehouse, Shirburn Rd. TVADA. Open 9-5, Sat. and other times by appointment. SIZE: Warehouse. STOCK: 18th-19th C furniture, some decorative items. LOC: 2 mins. from exit 6, M40. TEL: 049161 3752; fax - 049161 3875. SER: Valuations; restorations; buying agent. VAT: Stan/Spec.

A white cotton christening robe in full-blown Victorian style, with ruched skirt panels and lace inserts, and edged with pin-tucks and lavish broderie anglaise flounces, used in 1877. Such a dress would have created a fairytale impression far removed from the recent traumas of the baby's birth and first perilous few days of life. Perhaps too, there was a conscious effort on the part of many women to put behind them the ugliness and pain of childbirth. Photograph courtesy Manchester City Art Gallery. From *Yesterday's Children* by Sally Kevill-Davies, published by the **Antique Collectors' Club,** £19.95pb.

Witney Antiques
L.S.A. & C.J. Jarrett

*96-100 CORN STREET,
WITNEY, OXFORDSHIRE OX8 7BU
Tel: 0993 703902. Fax: 0993 779852*

One of the finest stocks of antique furniture available in the country.

WHITCHURCH-ON-THAMES

Nicholas Sibley (Fine Furniture)
at Heron Pictures, High St. Est. 1975. SIZE: Medium. *STOCK: Walnut, mahogany and satinwood furniture, Gothic revival, Arts and Crafts, paintings and works of art, 18th-19th C.* LOC: Off M4, exit 12 towards Newbury. At 2nd roundabout on A4 take Pangbourne road. In Pangbourne turn right at first mini roundabout, turn left at 2nd roundabout, over bridge, premises 800 yards on left. PARK: Easy. TEL: 0734 843286; home - 0734 700379. SER: Valuations; restorations; buys at auction. FAIRS: TVADA. VAT: Stan/Spec.

WITNEY

Country Pine Antiques
14A West End and, 47A High Street. (M.L. Parker and P. Littlewood). Est. 1986. Open 9.30-5.30, Sun. 2-5 or by appointment. SIZE: Medium. *STOCK: Pine, 19th C, £100-£2,000.* LOC: Just off A40 straight over mini roundabout (Oxford Hill), shop on right. PARK: Easy. TEL: 0993 778584/778772. SER: Valuations; restorations (pine). VAT: Stan/Spec.

Colin Greenway Antiques
90 Corn St. Resident. Est. 1975. Open 9.30-6 or by appointment. SIZE: Large. *STOCK: Furniture, 17th-20th C; metalware, decorative and unusual items.* LOC: Along High St. to town centre, turn right, shop 400yds. on right. PARK: Easy. TEL: 0993 705026. VAT: Stan/Spec.

Ian Pout Antiques
99 High St. (I. and J. Pout). CADA. Open 10-5.30. *STOCK: 18th-19th C furniture, decorative objects, vintage teddy bears.* TEL: 0993 702616; home - 0869 40205. VAT: Spec.

Relics
35 Bridge St. (B. Wiles, R. Russell and C. Walker). Est. 1978. Open 9-5.30. SIZE: Large. *STOCK: General antiques and shipping items, 50p-£500.* LOC: Main road. PARK: Easy. TEL: 0993 704611. SER: Restoration products - Liberon and Briwax, brass castors and fittings, upholstery, reproduction paints.

Anthony Scaramanga Antiques BADA
108 & 49 Newland. Est. 1969. Open 10-5, or by appointment. CL: Fri. a.m. and Sun., except by appointment. *STOCK: Samplers, 17th-19th C; needlework pictures, lace, small furniture, Staffordshire figures, blue and white pottery.* LOC: From Oxford on A40, turn off bypass onto A4022, shop on left before coming to A147 and Witney. PARK: Easy. TEL: 0993 703472/700557. VAT: Spec.

Joan Wilkins Antiques
158 Corn St. (Mrs J. Wilkins). Est. 1973. Open 10-5. CL: Tues. *STOCK: Furniture, 18th-19th C, £150-£2,500; 19th C glass, metalware, £10-£500.* LOC: Town centre. PARK: Easy. TEL: 0993 704749. VAT: Spec.

Windrush Antiques
107 High St. (B. Tollett). Resident. Est. 1978. Open 10-5.30. SIZE: Large. *STOCK: Furniture, especially 17th-18th C oak and country chairs; Georgian mahogany, some metalware and porcelain.* LOC: A40, corner of Mill St. and High St. PARK: Private at rear. TEL: 0993 772536.

Witney Antiques BADA
96/100 Corn St. (L.S.A. and C.J. Jarrett). CADA. Est. 1962. Open 9.30-5. SIZE: Large. *STOCK: English furniture, 17th-18th C; bracket and longcase clocks, mahogany, oak and walnut, metalware, needleworks and works of art.* LOC: From Oxford on old A40 through Witney via High St., turn right at T-junction, 400yds. on right. PARK: Easy. TEL: 0993 703902/703887; fax - 0993 779852. SER: Restorations. FAIRS: Park Lane; Grosvenor House. VAT: Spec.

WOODSTOCK

Museum Bookshop
County Museum, Fletcher's House. (Oxfordshire County Council). Est. 1966. Oct.-April. Open Tues.-Fri.10-4, Sat. 10-5, Sun. 2-5. May-Sept.

OXFORDSHIRE

Woodstock continued
Open 10-5, Sat. 10-6, Sun. 2-6. SIZE: Small. STOCK: Books on antiquities, crafts, archaeology and local history. LOC: In town centre, between P.O. and Barclays Bank. PARK: Easy. TEL: 0993 811456. VAT: Stan.

Span Antiques
6 Market Place. Est. 1978. Open 10-1 and 2-5, Sun 1-5. CL: Wed. SIZE: Medium. LOC: Near Town Hall. PARK: Easy. TEL: 0993 811332. SER: Valuations. Below are listed some of the dealers selling from these premises.

Barbara Bibb
STOCK: General antiques.

Doreen Caudwell
STOCK: Table linen and textiles.

Mike and Kate Cowdy
STOCK: Silver.

Andrew Crawforth
STOCK: Kitchen antiques, iron, copper, brass and farming bygones.

Four Seasons Antiques
STOCK: 18th-19th C porcelain and blue and white transfer ware.

Maureen Gough
STOCK: Decorative desk items and small period furniture.

Lis Hall-Bakker
STOCK: Art nouveau and deco.

Jasper Antiques
STOCK: Small silver and objets d'art.

Ilona Johnson-Gibbs
STOCK: Pictures.

Alan Stuart-Mobey
STOCK: Furniture.

Thistle House Antiques
14 Market Place. Open 10-6. STOCK: 18th-19th C furniture, porcelain, pictures. TEL: 0993 811736. SER: Restorations.

Woodstock Antiques   LAPADA
11 Market St. (C. Mason-Pope). TVADA. Est. 1979. Open 9.30-5.30. CL: Sun. and Mon. except by appointment. SIZE: Medium. **STOCK: Staffordshire figures and animals, £150-£6,000; small furniture, £200-£20,000; decorative objects, pictures and prints, £100-£500; all 18th to early 19th C. LOC: Town centre. PARK: Easy. TEL: 0993 811494; home - same. VAT: Stan/Spec.**

An Antique Collectors' Club Title

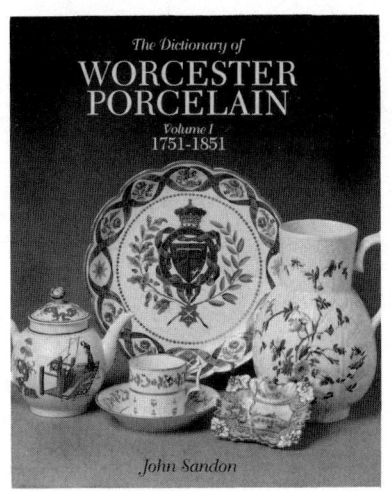

The Dictionary of Worcester Porcelain Volume I 1751-1851
by John Sandon

With 600+ dictionary entries, an historical survey, an illustrated section on marks, detailed information on recent excavations at the Worcester factory, contemporary accounts of visits to factories and an extensive bibliography, this is the definitive work. The author is director of ceramics at Phillips auctioneers, London, and regularly appears on the *Antiques Roadshow*.
ISBN 1 85149 156 2
400pp, 450 b & w illus, 100 colour
£45.00

Available from:
Antique Collectors' Club, 5 Church Street, Woodbridge, Suffolk IP12 1DS
Tel: (0394) 385501 Fax: (0394) 384434

or Market Street Industrial Park, Wappingers' Falls, New York 12590, USA
Tel: 914 297 0003 Fax: 914 297 0068

Shropshire

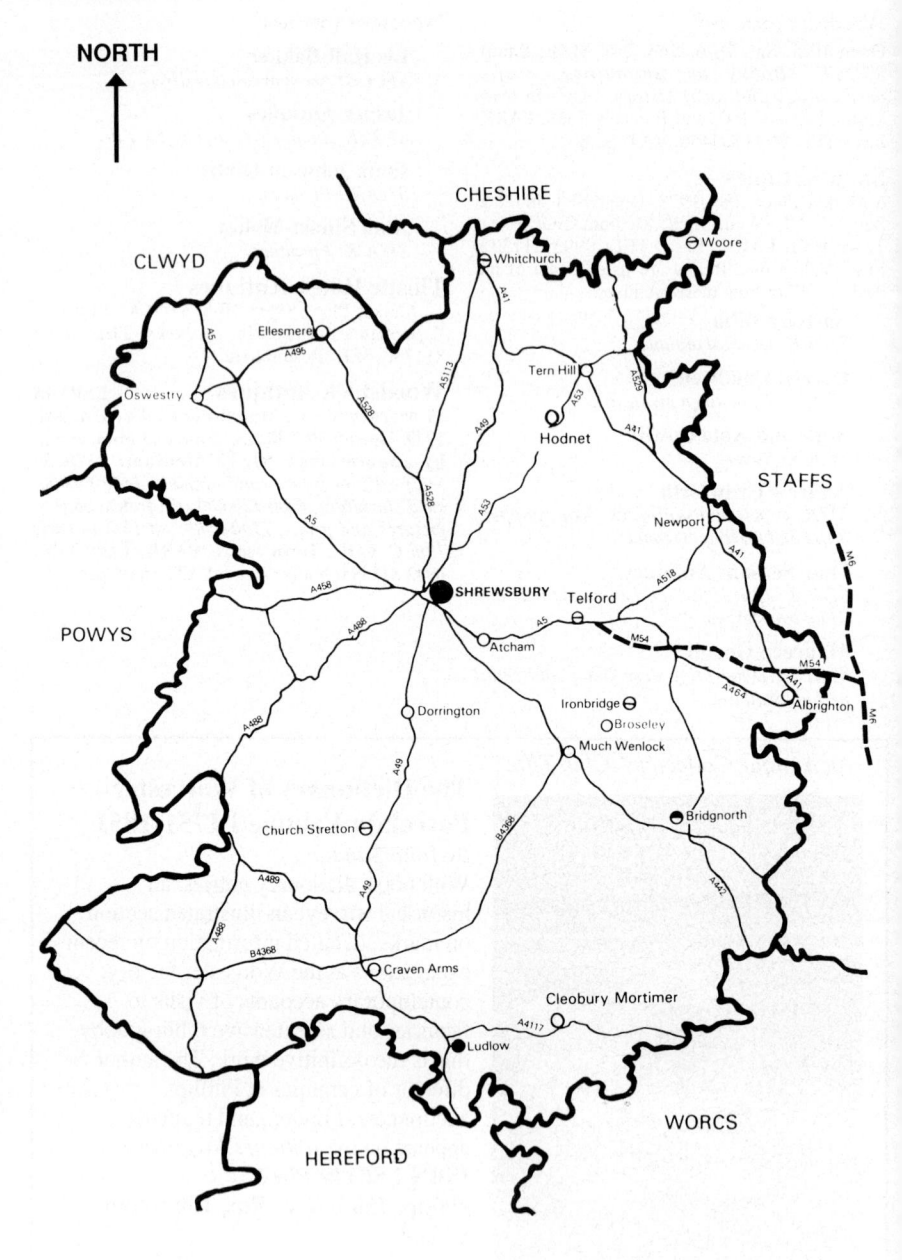

Shropshire

ALBRIGHTON (Neachley)
Doveridge House of Neachley
Long Lane, (alongside RAF Cosford). (Cdr and Mrs H.E.R. Bain). CINOA. Est. 1967. Open 9-6 seven days a week and/or by appointment. SIZE: Large. STOCK: 17th-19th C English and continental furniture, fine art, clocks, decorative artifacts. LOC: From London M1 to M6. Junction 10A via M54 for North and Mid Wales. Leave at Junction 3 (A41) in Wolverhampton/Cosford direction. Half a mile see Neachley signpost, turn immediately right into Long Lane, 4th entrance. From the North, M6 Junction 11, A460 towards Wolverhampton. Join M54 at Junction 1 then as Junction 3 above. PARK: Easy. TEL: 0902 373131/2. SER: Valuations; restorations (furniture and oils); interior design; export.

ATCHAM, Nr. Shrewsbury
Mytton Antiques
Norton Cross Roads. (M.A., E.A. and J.M. Nares). Est. 1972. Open 10-5.30 or by appointment. SIZE: Medium. STOCK: General antiques, especially longcase clocks and reference books. LOC: On B5061 (the old A5) between Shrewsbury and Wellington. PARK: Own. TEL: 0952 86229 (24hrs.). SER: Buys at auction. VAT: Stan/Spec.

BRIDGNORTH
English Heritage
2 Whitburn St, High Town. (P.J. Wainwright). Open 9.30-5. SIZE: Medium. STOCK: Jewellery and general antiques, militaria. LOC: Just off High St. PARK: High St. TEL: 0746 762097. SER: Framing. VAT: Stan/Spec.

Micawber Antiques
64 St. Mary's St. (M. and N. Berthoud). Open 10-5, other days by appointment. CL: Mon. and Thurs. SIZE: Medium. STOCK: English porcelain and pottery, decorative items, £5-£500; small furniture, £100-£1,000. LOC: 100yds. west of town hall in High St. PARK: Easy. TEL: 0746 763254; home - same. SER: Buys at auction (English porcelain).

Pauline Norton Galleries
Bank St. Est. 1963. Open 10.30-1 and 2-5.30 or by appointment. CL: Thurs. SIZE: Medium. STOCK: Oil paintings and watercolours, 19th C, £5-£3,000. LOC: Bank St. is opposite G.P.O. in High St. PARK: Listley St. TEL: 0746 764889. SER: Restorations (paintings); framing. FAIRS: Local. VAT: Spec. *Trade Only.*

Parmenter Antiques
5 Central Court, High St. (J. Parmenter). Open 10-12.30 and 1-5, Sat. 10-5. CL: Wed. and Thurs. SIZE: Medium. STOCK: Furniture, 17th C to Edwardian, £50-£4,000; pictures, objects and silver £3-£800. LOC: Off M6, junction 10 on A454. PARK: Nearby. TEL: 0746 765599; home - 0746 764208. SER: Buys at auction (furniture). FAIRS: NEC Birmingham.

BROSELEY
Gallery 6
6 Church St. (J.A. Boulton). Resident. Est. 1983. Open 9-5, Sun. 2-5. SIZE: Medium. STOCK: Oils, watercolours and prints, late 19th C to contemporary, £100-£2,500. LOC: Junction 4, M54, take A442. PARK: Easy. TEL: 0952 882860. FAIRS: Buxton; NEC Birmingham; Shrewsbury; Edinburgh.

CHURCH STRETTON
Antiques on the Square
2 Sandford Court, Sandford Ave. (Chris Radford). Est. 1985. Open 9.30-5, Sun. by appointment. SIZE: Medium. STOCK: Art nouveau and art deco ceramics, furniture, lighting, glass, 1880-1930, £5-£3,000; collectors items, TV's, radios, £5-£500; decorative items, £5-£1,000; both pre-1939. Not Stocked: Armour, stamps, period furniture. LOC: Off A49. PARK: Easy. TEL: 0694 724111; home - 0694 723072; mobile - 0831 336052. SER: Valuations; restorations (furniture, glass, tapestries, metalware, paintings and ceramics); buys at auction (English furniture pre-1830); research. FAIRS: Nottingham and Greenwich (London) Deco. VAT: Stan/Spec.

Old Barn Antiques   LAPADA
High St. (Lt. Col. and Mrs D.W. Witting). Est. 1980. Open by appointment. SIZE: Medium. STOCK: Furniture, 18th and early 19th C; general antiques, porcelain. Not Stocked: Coins, jewellery, silver, clocks, books and militaria. LOC: Off A49. PARK: At rear. TEL: 0694 723742; home - 0694 722294 (ansaphone). FAIRS: Northern; British International; Buxton; NEC (April and August); Kenilworth (Spring and Autumn); Penman, Chester. VAT: Stan/Spec.

Stretton Antiques
9 High St. (H.A. and J. Davies). Open 10.30-5. STOCK: General antiques. PARK: Easy. TEL: 0694 781330.

Stretton Antiques Market
36 Sandford Ave. (P. and L. Forbes). Est. 1986. Open 9.30-5.30, Sun. and Bank Holidays 10.30-4.30. SIZE: Large - 55 dealers. STOCK: General antiques, shipping items and collectables. LOC: Town centre. PARK: Easy. TEL: 0694 723718. SER: Valuations; buys at auction.

CLEOBURY MORTIMER, Nr. Kidderminster
Cleobury Mortimer Antique Centre
Childe Rd. Open 10-5 including Sun. SIZE: Several dealers. STOCK: Georgian, Victorian, Edwardian and pine furniture, bric-a-brac and architectural items. PARK: Own. TEL: 0299 270513.

JOHN & ANNE CLEGG
12 Old Street, Ludlow

Telephone: Ludlow 873176
Good Country and Other Period Furniture sold

CRAVEN ARMS
I. and S. Antiques
Stokesay, Ludlow Rd. (J. Briscoe). Open 9-5, Sun. 10.30-4.30 in summer. *STOCK: Unstripped pine, shipping goods, treen, country items, bric-a-brac, books, 19th to early 20th C.* TEL: 0588 672263; home - 05884 374.

ELLESMERE
Lynne Davies Antiques
Wharf Rd. Open 10-1 and 2-5.30. SIZE: Medium. *STOCK: Furniture, glass, china, silver, brass and copper.* PARK: Easy. TEL: Home - 0691 623835. SER: Restorations.

White Lion Antiques
Market St. (Mrs D. Wheeldon). Est. 1966. *STOCK: Furniture, clocks, pottery, porcelain, glass.* TEL: 0691 622335.

HODNET, Nr. Market Drayton
Hodnet Antiques
13a and 19a Shrewsbury St. (Mrs J. Scott). Est. 1976. Open Tues. and Fri. 11-3, other days and school holidays by appointment. SIZE: Small. *STOCK: General antiques - china, glass, silver, jewellery, pictures, brass and copper, £1-£500; Victorian and Edwardian furniture, £10-£1,000.* LOC: A53. PARK: Easy. TEL: Home - 0630 638591. SER: Valuations; buys at auction.

IRONBRIDGE
Bill Dickenson
Tudor House Antiques, 11 Tontine Hill. Open 10-5.00. *STOCK: General antiques especially porcelain, including Caughley and Coalport.* LOC: Opposite bridge. TEL: 0952 433783.

Ironbridge Antique Centre
Dale End. (F.G. Cooke). Est. 1968. Open 10-5, Sun. 2-5. SIZE: Large. *STOCK: Porcelain, 1800-1950, £1-£3,000; furniture, pictures, jewellery, general antiques and bric-a-brac, 1700-1930, 50p-£1,000.* PARK: Easy. TEL: 0952 433784. SER: Valuations; restorations (cabinet making); buys at auction.

Peter Whitelaw
Tudor House Antiques, 11 Tontine Hill. Open 10-5.00. *STOCK: General antiques especially porcelain including Caughley and Coalport.* LOC: Opposite bridge. TEL: 0952 433783.

LUDLOW
Antique Corner
12 Old St. (J. and A. Clegg). Resident. Est. 1960. Open 9-5.30. *STOCK: Country and other period furniture, metalware and decorative items.* TEL: 0584 873176.

Architectural Antiques and Interiors
140 Corve St. (R.G. and J. Dickinson). Open

SHROPSHIRE

Ludlow continued
9.30-1 and 2-5. *STOCK: Bathrooms, fireplaces, lighting, doors and other architectural antiques.* TEL: 0584 876207.

D.W. and A.B. Bayliss
22 Old St. Resident. *STOCK: Furniture, 18th-19th C; silver, decorative items.* TEL: 0584 873634. SER: Valuations.

R.G. Cave and Sons Ltd BADA LAPADA
17 Broad St. Resident. Est. 1962. Open 9.30-5.30. *STOCK: Furniture, 1630-1830; clocks, barometers, metalwork, fine art and collectors' items.* PARK: Easy. TEL: 0584 873568. SER: Valuations. VAT: Spec.

The Corve Galleries
12 Corve St. (R. Painter). Open 10-5.30. SIZE: 4 dealers. *STOCK: 19th-20th C paintings, maritime, continental, Newlyn; furniture and general antiques.* TEL: 0584 873420; home - 0584 79301or 0299 400947 (paintings); fax - 0562 825249. SER: Restorations (furniture, pictures, clocks and barometers).

The Curiosity Shop
127 Old St. (J. Luffman). Resident. Open 9.30-5 or by appointment. *STOCK: Longcase, bracket and mantel clocks, music boxes, country furniture, paintings and militaria, £5-£20,000.* TEL: 0584 875927. SER: Valuations; buys at auction (militaria, paintings). VAT: Spec.

G. & D. Ginger
5 Corve St. Resident. Open 9-5. SIZE: Large. *STOCK: Country and mahogany furniture; decorative and associated items.* TEL: 0584 876939.

The Jane Marler Gallery
Dawes Mansion, Church St. Est. 1975. Open 10-5. CL: Thurs. SIZE: Medium. *STOCK: Wildlife, sporting and contemporary paintings and watercolours, £100-£15,000; signed proofs and prints, £5-£1,000; all 19th-20th C.* LOC: Town centre near church. PARK: Nearby. TEL: 0584 874160. SER: Valuations; restorations (oil paintings, watercolours and prints); framing. VAT: Stan/Spec.

Mitre House Antiques
Corve Bridge. (L. Jones). Open 9-5.30. *STOCK: Clocks, pine and general antiques.* TEL: 0584 872138.

Pepper Lane Antique Centre
Pepper Lane. (Mr and Mrs K.L. Morris). Est. 1985. Open 10-5, Sun. by appointment. SIZE: Large. *STOCK: Furniture, £50-£3,000; porcelain, silver, plate, clocks, paintings, jewellery, collectors' items, £5-£1,000; all 18th to early 20th C.* Not Stocked: Linen. LOC: Rear of Boots in King St. PARK: Easy. TEL: 0584 876494; home - 074 632 292. SER: Restorations (furniture, upholstery, clocks).

Ludlow continued
St. Leonards Antiques
Corve St. (A. Smith). Open 9-5. SIZE: 8 dealers. *STOCK: Furniture, silver, jewellery, porcelain, clocks, pictures, Oriental carpets, brass, copper and interesting bygones.* TEL: 0584 875573. SER: Restorations (clocks and furniture).

M. and R. Taylor (Antiques)
53 Broad St. (M. Taylor). Est. 1977. Open from 9 a.m. including evenings. SIZE: Medium. *STOCK: Furniture, mahogany, oak and walnut, Persian rugs, brass and copper, 17th-19th C.* PARK: Nearby. TEL: 0584 874169; home - same. VAT: Stan/Spec.

Teme Valley Antiques
1 The Bull Ring. (C.S. Harvey). Est. 1979. Usually open 10-5.30, Sun. by appointment. SIZE: Medium. *STOCK: English and continental porcelain, 18th to early 20th C, £25-£2,500; furniture, oil and watercolour paintings, £50-£2,500; jewellery, silver, plate, metalware and glass, £10-£3,500; both 17th to early 20th C.* Not Stocked: Militaria, coins and carpets. LOC: Town centre opposite Lunn Poly. PARK: Easy. TEL: 0584 874686. SER: Valuations; buys at auction (porcelain). VAT: Stan/Spec.

MUCH WENLOCK
Cruck House Antiques
23 Barrow St. (Mrs B.Roderick Smith). Est. 1985. Open 9.30-5.30. CL: Wed. SIZE: Small. *STOCK: Silver and watercolours, 19th-20th C, £25-£300; furniture, 19th C, £50-£500; general antiques.* Not Stocked: Weapons and gold. LOC: Near Square. PARK: Easy. TEL: 0952 727165.

Wenlock Fine Art
3 The Square. (J. Redman and P. Cotterill). Est. 1990. Open 10-5 (including Sun. in summer). CL: Mon. and Tues. SIZE: Medium. *STOCK: Modern British paintings, mainly 20th C, some late 19th C, £100-£6,000.* PARK: Nearby. TEL: 0952 728232; home - 0270 629575 or 0584 73270. SER: Valuations; restorations (cleaning); mounting; framing; buys at auction (as stock). VAT: Spec.

NEWPORT
Worth's
34 St. Mary's St. (G.F.E. Worth). Resident. Est. 1932. CL: Thurs. SIZE: Medium. *STOCK: General antiques, 19th C; shipping goods, antiquarian books.* LOC: Opposite church on main A41. PARK: Easy. TEL: 0952 810122. VAT: Stan/Spec.

OSWESTRY
The Antique Shop
King St. Est. 1963. Open 9-5, Sun. by appointment. *STOCK: General antiques and secondhand goods; Victoriana, bric-a-brac.* TEL: 0691 653011.

SHROPSHIRE

Oswestry continued

The Oswald Road Antique and Reproduction Centre
Oswald Rd. (M. and J. Clifford). Open 9.30-5.30. SIZE: Large. *STOCK:* General antiques. TEL: 0691 670690.

SHREWSBURY

David Brown Antiques
20 Castle Gates. (David F.J. Brown). Open 9-5 or by appointment. SIZE: Medium. *STOCK: Furniture, 18th-19th C, £500-£1,000; ceramics, 19th-20th C, £30-£100; brass and copper, 19th C, £25-£200.* TEL: 0743 232073; home - same. LOC: Main road into town, 100 yards from station. PARK: Limited. SER: Valuations; restorations (furniture, brass and copper); buys at auction. VAT: Spec.

Candle Lane Books
28-29 Princess St. (J. Thornhill). Open 9.30-5. *STOCK: Antiquarian and secondhand books.* TEL: 0743 365301.

Juliet Chilton Antiques and Interiors
69 Wyle Cop and, 1 St. Julians Friars. Open 9.30-6. SIZE: Large. *STOCK: Furniture and smalls, mainly 1700's-1920's and some reproduction.* TEL: 0743 358699/366553; fax - 0743 366563. SER: Shipping and packing.

Collectors' Gallery
6-7 Castle Gates. Open 9-6. SIZE: Large. *STOCK: Stamps, coins, postcards, notes, medals and books.* TEL: 0743 272140.

Expressions
17 Princess St. Open 10.30-4.30. CL: Thurs. *STOCK: Art deco originals, ceramics, furniture, jewellery, lighting, mirrors, prints.* TEL: 0743 351731.

Hutton Antiques
18 Princess St. (Mrs P.I. Hutton). Est. 1978. Open 9.30-1 and 2-5. CL: Thurs. SIZE: Medium. *STOCK: Silver, porcelain and glass, 18th-19th C, £50-£500; small furniture, £50-£1,300; Victorian jewellery.* LOC: Off square, near Music Hall. PARK: Easy. TEL: 0743 245810. SER: Valuations.

The Little Gem
18 St. Mary's St. (M.A. Bowdler). Est. 1969. Open 9-5.30. CL: Thurs. (except Dec.). SIZE: Medium. *STOCK: Georgian and Victorian jewellery; unusual gem stones.* Not Stocked: Weapons, coins, medals, furniture. LOC: Opposite St. Mary's Church along from G.P.O. PARK: In side road (St. Mary's Place) opposite shop. TEL: 0743 352085.

F.C. Manser and Son Ltd   LAPADA
53/54 Wyle Cop. (G. Manser and family). Est. 1944. Open 9-5.30. CL: Thurs. p.m. SIZE: Large. *STOCK: Furniture, 17th-20th C,* *£150-£12,000; Oriental items, 15th-20th C, £5-£3,000; silver, plate, copper, 18th-20th C, £5-£6,000; jewellery, 19th-20th C, £50-£6,000.* Not Stocked: Coins, books. LOC: 150yds. town side of English bridge. PARK: Own. TEL: 0743 351120/245730; fax - 0743 271047. SER: Valuations; restorations. VAT: Stan/Spec.

Shrewsbury continued

Raleigh Antiques
23 Belle Vue Rd. (R. and E. Handbury-Madin). GADAR. Est. 1968. Open 10-5. *STOCK: Furniture, pottery, porcelain, glass, jewellery, silver.* PARK: Easy. TEL: 0743 359552. SER: Valuations; restorations (furniture, clocks).

Shrewsbury Antique Centre
15 Princess House, The Square. (J. Langford). Est. 1978. Open 9.30-5.30. SIZE: Large - 37 dealers. *STOCK: General antiques and collectables.* LOC: Town centre just off the Square. PARK: Nearby. TEL: 0743 247704. SER: Valuations; restorations (furniture, pictures and silver).

Shrewsbury Antique Market
Frankwell Quay Warehouse. (J. Langford). Open 9.30-5. SIZE: Large. 45 units. *STOCK: General antiques and collectors' items, £1-£2,000.* LOC: Alongside Frankwell Quay car park. PARK: Easy. TEL: 0743 350916.

Tiffany Antiques
Unit 3 Shrewsbury Antique Centre, 15 Princess House, The Square. (A. Wilcox). Est. 1988. Open 9.30-5.30. SIZE: Small. *STOCK: Silver plate, curios, china, collectables, £10-£600.* LOC: Town centre. PARK: Nearby. TEL: Home - 0270 257425. SER: Buys at auction.

Wyle Cop Antiques and Reproductions
The Old School, Off Wyle Cop. (J. Clifford). Open 10-5.30. *STOCK: Stripped pine, oak, mahogany and satin walnut furniture, late Georgian to Edwardian; wall and grandfather clocks.* TEL: 0743 231180.

STANTON, Nr. Shrewsbury

Marcus Moore Antiques
Booley House, Booley. (M.G.J. and M.P. Moore). Est. 1980. Usually open but prior telephone call advisable. SIZE: Medium. *STOCK: Oak and country furniture, late 17th to 18th C; Georgian mahogany furniture, 18th to early 19th C; all £50-£3,000; associated items.* LOC: Half a mile north of Stanton on right. PARK: Easy. TEL: 0939 200333. SER: Restorations (furniture); polishing. VAT: Stan/Spec.

TELFORD

Haygate Gallery
40 Haygate Rd, Wellington. (Mrs M. Kuznierz). Open 9-5, Sat. 9-1. CL: Wed. *STOCK: Watercolours, oils and general antiques.* LOC: One mile from junction 7, M54. PARK: Easy. TEL: 0952 248553. SER: Framing.

Telford continued
Brian James Antiques
Old Maltings, The Lawns, Wellington. Est. 1985. Open 9-6, Sat. 9.30-12.30, Sun. by appointment. SIZE: Large. *STOCK: Chests of drawers, Georgian to Victorian, £50-£1,500.* LOC: Off M54, junction 6. Follow signs for Telford Hospital then Wellington Centre, turn right at Red Lion. PARK: Easy. TEL: 0952 256592; mobile - 0831 872559; home - 0952 595173. SER: Restorations and conversions. VAT: Stan. *Trade Only.*

Bernie Pugh Antiques
120 High St, Wellington. Resident. Open by appointment only. *STOCK: General antiques.* TEL: 0952 256184; mobile - 0860 219944.

Telford Antiques Centre
High St, Wellington. (J. Langford). Open 10-5, Sun. 2-5. SIZE: 60+ dealers. *STOCK: General antiques.* LOC: 2 mins. from M54. PARK: Easy. TEL: 0952 256450.

TERN HILL, Nr. Market Drayton
L. Onions - White Cottage Antiques
White Cottage, 8 Tern Hill. Est. 1965. Open 9.30-5.30. SIZE: Medium. *STOCK: Furniture, oak and some walnut, brass, 16th-18th C.* LOC: On A41, 200yds. from roundabout at Tern Hill cross roads. PARK: Easy. TEL: 063 083 222. VAT: Stan/Spec.

WHITCHURCH
Civic Antiques
The Dairy Farm, Heath Rd., Prees Heath. (J. Simcox). Resident. Est. 1970. Open 9-5, Sun. and evenings by appointment. SIZE: Large. *STOCK: Pine furniture, from 19th C, £100-£500; continental furniture, £800-£1,000.* LOC: South of Whitchurch A41/A49, southbound lane of dual carriageway. PARK: Easy. TEL: Home - 0948 2626; fax - 0948 3604. SER: Valuations; restorations (pine); buys at auction. VAT: Stan.

Dodington Antiques
15 Dodington, and The Old Music Hall. (G. MacGillivray). Resident. Est. 1978. Always open. SIZE: Large. *STOCK: Oak, fruitwood, walnut country and 18th to early 19th C mahogany furniture, longcase clocks, barometers, £10-£6,000.* LOC: On fringe of town centre. PARK: Easy. TEL: 0948 663399. SER: Buys at auction. VAT: Stan/Spec.

Robert Whitney Antiques
Withinlee, Alport Rd. Open by appointment. SIZE: Medium. *STOCK: Early oak and country furniture, related items.* TEL: 0948 4084.

WOORE, Nr. Crewe
The Mount
12 Nantwich Rd. Est. 1978. Most afternoons and weekends (prior telephone call advisable). *STOCK:*

The front of a scarce R.A.C. full member's badge. Circa 1912. £150-£250. From *Automobilia of Europe — Reference and Price Guide*, by Gordon Gardiner and Alistair Morris, published by the **Antique Collectors' Club**, £25.00.

Woore continued
Watercolours, oils and drawings, Victorian to early 20th C; county maps, prints, engravings and topographical items, from 17th C; all £2-£500. LOC: Junction of A51 and A525. PARK: Easy. TEL: 0630 647274; home - same. SER: Framing; finder (maps and topography).

No. 7 Antiques
7 Nantwich Rd. (D. and J. Belcher). Est. 1983. Open daily, Sun. by appointment. CL: Mon. SIZE: Medium. *STOCK: Kitchenalia and fine country furniture, £25-£5,000; fine ceramics, £5-£500; garden furniture, £50-£500; small items, £50-£200; all 18th to early 20th C.* LOC: Junction A51 and A525. PARK: Easy. TEL: 0630 647118. FAIRS: NEC (Aug.); Bingley Hall, Stafford. VAT: Spec.

Peter Wain   BADA
7 Nantwich Rd. Open 10-5, Sun. by appointment. CL: Mon. SIZE: Medium. *STOCK: European and Oriental ceramics and works of art, 16th-20th C, £50-£5,000.* LOC: A51, opposite church. PARK: Easy. TEL: 0630 647118. SER: Valuations, restorations (ceramics). VAT: Spec.

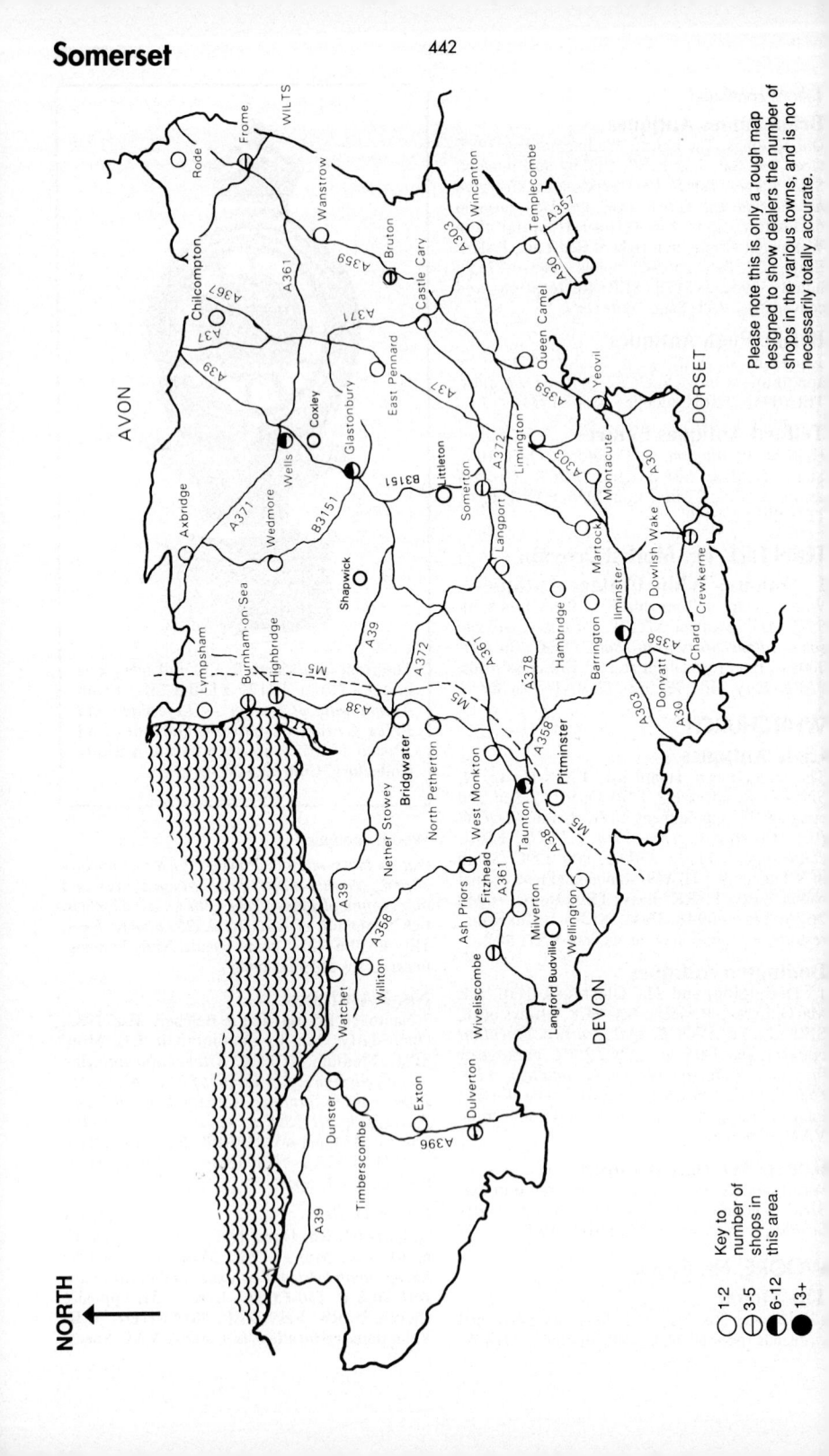

Somerset

Somerset

The Granary Galleries
(RICHARD HALL)

**LARGE STOCK
ENGLISH &
CONTINENTAL
FURNITURE
PORCELAIN
OIL PAINTINGS
SHIPPING GOODS**

**OLD COUNTRY PINE
DRESSERS, TABLES,
etc.**

Court House, Ash Priors, Nr. Bishops Lydeard, Taunton, Somerset
Route A358 out of Taunton on the Minehead Road
Tel. Bishops Lydeard (0823) 432402, private (0823) 432816 after 6.30 pm

ASH PRIORS, Nr. Taunton
The Granary Galleries
Court House. (R. Hall). Est. 1969. Open 8.30-5.30. SIZE: Large. *STOCK: Period items, general antiques, 18th-19th C furniture, some shipping goods.* PARK: Easy. TEL: 0823 432402; home after 6.30 (0823) 432816. VAT: Stan/Spec.

Hall's Antiques
Court House. (A.R. and J.M. Hall). Est. 1945. Open 8.30-5.30. CL: Sun. except by appointment. SIZE: Large. *STOCK: English and continental furniture, 18th-19th C; oil paintings, watercolours, 17th-19th C; all £25-£10,000; shipping goods.* LOC: On A358. PARK: Easy. TEL: 0823 432402; home - same. SER: Valuations; buys at auction. VAT: Stan/Spec.

AXBRIDGE
The Old Post House
Weare, Bridgewater Rd. (R. and M. Seaman). *STOCK: General antiques and country furniture.* TEL: 0934 732372.

BARRINGTON, Nr. Ilminster
Stuart Interiors (Antiques) Ltd
Barrington Court. Open 9-5, Sat. 10-5. SIZE: Large. *STOCK: Oak furniture, £100-£10,000; accessories, £50-£2,500; both pre-1720. Not*

Barrington continued

Stocked: 18th C mahogany. LOC: Between A303 and M5, 5 miles north-east of Ilminster. House is National Trust property, signposted in area. PARK: Easy. TEL: 0460 40349. SER: Valuations; buys at auction (early oak furniture and accessories, interior design and architectural items including oak panelling). VAT: Spec.

BRIDGWATER
Bridgwater Antiques Market
Marycourt Shopping Mall. (C.P. Munro). Est. 1988. Open Fri. and Sat. 9.30-5. SIZE: 20 stalls. *STOCK: Secondhand and antiquarian books, small antiques and bygones.* LOC: Town centre, opposite St. Mary's church. PARK: Nearby. TEL: 0823 451433.

BRUTON
Bruton Gallery
(M. and S. le Marchant). SIZE: Large. *STOCK: 19th-20th C European sculpture and contemporary European paintings.* TEL: 0749 812205. VAT: Stan/Spec.

Gallery 16
16 High St. (Mrs P.S. Wilson). Open 9-5. *STOCK: Oils and watercolours, 19th-20th C.* TEL: 0749 812269.

SOMERSET

Bruton continued

Michael Lewis Gallery
17 High St. Est. 1953. Open 9-6, Sun. by appointment. SIZE: Large. *STOCK: Maps, 1575-1850, £20-£500; prints, 1700-1900, £10-£250.* LOC: A359. PARK: Easy. TEL: 0749 813557; home - same. SER: Picture framing.

M.G.R. Exports
Unit 1 Riverside, Bruton Industrial Estate. Open 8.30-6, Sat. 9-1, and by appointment. SIZE: Large. *STOCK: Georgian, Victorian, Edwardian and shipping items, barley twist oak, Lloyd loom and smalls.* PARK: Easy. TEL: 0749 812460; fax - 0749 812882. SER: Packing and shipping.

BURNHAM-ON-SEA

Adam Antiques
30 Adam St. (R. Coombes). Open 9-5. SIZE: Large. *STOCK: Furniture, clocks, brass, porcelain and shipping goods.* PARK: Easy. TEL: 0278 783193.

Castle Antiques   LAPADA
(T.C. Germain). Open by appointment. *STOCK: Jewellery, silver.* TEL: 0278 785031.

Heape's Antiques
39 Victoria St. (Mrs M.M. Heap). Open 10-1 and 2.30-4.30. *STOCK: Small furniture, fine arts, porcelain, glass, memorabilia.* TEL: 0278 782131.

CASTLE CARY

Cary Antiques Ltd
2 High St. (Mrs J.A. Oldham). Est. 1977. Open 10-5.30. CL: Wed. SIZE: Small. *STOCK: Furniture, Victorian and Edwardian, £30-£500; china, brass and copper, glass, bric-a-brac, pictures, 18th-19th C, £5-£150.* LOC: Town centre, B3152. PARK: Easy. TEL: 0963 50437. SER: Valuations; picture framing; caning and rushing; repairs (china).

John Martin Antiques
High St. Est. 1975. Open 9.30-5. CL: Mon. and Thurs. *STOCK: Clocks, watches, copper and brass, oil lamps, decorative items, jewellery, furniture.* TEL: 0963 50733.

CHARD

Guildhall Antique Market
The Guildhall. Open Thurs. 9-3. SIZE: 26 dealers. *STOCK: General antiques.*

CHILCOMPTON, Nr. Bath

Mendip Pine and Antiques
Knitts Farm, Stockhill Rd. Open Thur., Fri. and Sat. *STOCK: Pine.* TEL: 0761 233282. SER: Restorations; stripping; furniture and kitchens made from reclaimed pine.

COXLEY, Nr. Wells

Wells Reclamation Company
The Old Cider Farm. (H. Davies). Est. 1984. Open 9-5.30. SIZE: Large. *STOCK: Architectural items, 18th-19th C.* LOC: A39 towards Glastonbury from Wells. PARK: Easy. TEL: 0749 677087; home - 0749 677484. SER: Valuations. VAT: Stan.

CREWKERNE

Antique and Country Pine
14 East St. (R.W.H. and M.J. Wheeler). Open 10-5, Sun. 12-4. *STOCK: Country pine.* TEL: 0460 75623.

Julian Armytage
Open by appointment only. *STOCK: Fine sporting, marine and decorative prints, 18th-19th C.* TEL: 0460 73449; fax - same.

Crewkerne Furniture Emporium
Viney Bridge, South St. (A.P. Bucke). Est. 1974. Open 8.30-5.30, Sun. 10-5. *STOCK: Furniture, shipping goods, collectors' items, agricultural bygones.* TEL: 0460 75319.

Oscars - Antique Market
13-15 Market Sq, and North St. (B.J. and H.M. Hall). Est. 1966. Open 10-5.30. SIZE: Large. *STOCK: Victoriana, shipping goods, vintage fishing tackle, china, and books.* LOC: Centre of the square on A30. PARK: Easy. TEL: 0460 72718. VAT: Stan/Spec.

DONYATT, Nr. Ilminster

Something Old
Church Cottage. (Mrs M. Wood). Resident. Est. 1980. Open by appointment. SIZE: Medium. *STOCK: 18th-19th C pottery and porcelain; small furniture.* LOC: 0.75 mile off A303, on A358. PARK: Easy. TEL: 0460 54283.

DOWLISH WAKE, Nr. Ilminster

Dowlish Wake Antiques
(Mrs G. Estling). Est. 1973. Open 10-1 and 2.30-5.30, Sun. by appointment. SIZE: Medium. *STOCK: Ceramics only - English porcelain and pottery, late 18th C to early 20th C.* LOC: Take Ilminster/Crewkerne road and turn off at Kingstone corner, downhill to village. PARK: Easy. TEL: 0460 52784; home - same. VAT: Stan/Spec.

DULVERTON

Acorn Antiques
39 High St. (P. Hounslow). Est. 1988. Open 9.30-5.30. SIZE: Medium. *STOCK: Country furniture, works of art, rugs, textiles, £5-£1000.* LOC: Town centre. PARK: Nearby. TEL: 0398 23286; home - same. SER: Interior design.

DOWLISH WAKE ANTIQUES
(Gillian Estling)
Dowlish Wake, Nr. Ilminster, Somerset
Telephone: 0460 52784

FINE PORCELAIN AND POTTERY

BOW sheep, c.1765

Dulverton continued
Faded Elegance
39 High St. (M. Delbridge). Open 9.30-5.30. STOCK: Textiles and decorative interior design items. TEL: 0398 23286.

Rothwell and Dunworth
2 Bridge St. (Mrs C. Rothwell and M. Dunworth). ABA. Est. 1975. Open 10.30-1 and 2.30-5, Thurs. 10.30-1. SIZE: Medium. STOCK: Antiquarian and secondhand books especially on hunting and horses. LOC: 1st shop in village over River Barle. PARK: 100yds. TEL: 0398 23189. SER: Valuations.

EAST PENNARD, Nr. Shepton Mallet
Pennard House
(M. and S. Dearden). Resident. Est. 1979. Open by appointment. SIZE: Large. STOCK: Pine furniture, 18th-19th C, £100-£2,000; French provincial tables, armoires, buffets, £300-£3,000. LOC: From Shepton Mallet, 4 miles south off A37. PARK: Easy. TEL: 074 986 266; home - same. SER: Valuations; restorations (pine and country furniture). VAT: Stan/Spec. *Trade Only.*

EXTON, Nr. Dulverton
A. Lodge-Mortimer
The Old School House. Open by appointment only. STOCK: Porcelain and pottery, especially

Exton continued
English Delftware and Oriental porcelain, £5-£2,000; objets d'art, £5-£1,000; watercolours. LOC: Just off A396 from Bridgetown on Dunster/Tiverton road. TEL: 064 385 358. SER: Valuations; buys at auction; commissions undertaken; author and lecturer.

FITZHEAD, Nr. Taunton
J.C. White
The Granary. Est. 1960. STOCK: *Country furniture and clocks.* TEL: 0823 400427.

FROME
Frome Antique Centre
The Settle, Cheap St. (M. Vaughan). Open 9-5, Thurs. 9-2. STOCK: *Dolls, china, furniture, brass, medals including masonic, and pictures.* TEL: 0373 465975.

Old Curiosity Shop
15 Catherine Hill. (R. and B. Hackett). Open 10-1 and 2-5. CL: Thurs. STOCK: *Antiquarian books.* TEL: 0373 464482.

Sutton and Sons
15 and 33 Vicarage St. STOCK: *Furniture, 18th-19th C; clocks, pictures, decorative pieces.* TEL: 0373 462062/462526. SER: Restorations and upholstery. VAT: Stan/Spec.

GLASTONBURY
Abbey Antiques
51 High St. (G.E. Browning and Son). Est. 1952. Open 8-5. SIZE: Small. *STOCK: Glass and furniture.* TEL: 0458 831694. VAT: Stan.

Abbots House
4 Benedict St. (Mrs P. Elliott). Est. 1973. *STOCK: Jewellery, silver, china and glass.* TEL: 0458 832123.

Antiques Fair
Glastonbury Abbey Car Park, Market Pl. Est. 1960. Open 9.30-6 (7 days in summer). *STOCK: Unusual and decorative items; furniture, Georgian and Victorian; jewellery.* TEL: 0458 832939.

Antiques Market
Town Hall. Open first Sat. each month. SIZE: 30 stands. *STOCK: Antiques, bygones and collectables.* TEL: 0963 862478.

The Lace & Linen Shop
1 The Monarch, 15 High St. Open daily or by appointment. (Telephone first in winter). SIZE: Large. *STOCK: Textiles, quilts, linen, lace, period clothing, samplers, costume jewellery, smalls, pictures, 50p-£300.* LOC: Off High St., next to Midland Bank. TEL: 0458 210021/834522. SER: Buys at auction. FAIRS: Shepton Mallet.

Monarch Antiques
15 High St. (J.A. Badman). Est. 1970. Open 9.45-5.45. SIZE: Medium. *STOCK: General antiques and collectors' items, religious items including icons; coins, military items, antiquities and weapons, £5-£1,000.* LOC: On A39. PARK: At rear. TEL: 0458 832498. SER: Valuations. VAT: Stan/Spec.

HAMBRIDGE, Nr. Langport
Chalon U.K. Ltd
Old Hambridge Mill. (M. and T. Chalon). Est. 1974. Appointment preferred. SIZE: Large. *STOCK: Painted pine, British and European, 18th-19th C.* TEL: 0458 252374; fax - 0458 251192.

HIGHBRIDGE
C. and R.I. Dyte Antiques   LAPADA
Huntspill Rd. Open 7-6.30 or by appointment. *STOCK: Mahogany, 18th-20th C.* PARK: Easy. TEL: 0278 788590/788605; home - 0278 683761. SER: Packing; transport; documentation.

T.M. Dyte Antiques
1 Huntspill Rd. Open 8.30-5.30. CL: Sat. *STOCK: Shipping goods.* TEL: 0278 786495.

Terence Kelly Antiques
Huntspill Court, West Huntspill. Open by appointment. *STOCK: Furniture, decorative and collectors' items.* TEL: 0278 785052.

Highbridge continued
The Treasure Chest
The Jays, 19 Alstone Lane. (R.J. and V. Rumble). Est. 1964. CL: Sun., except by appointment. SIZE: Medium. *STOCK: General antiques including furniture, 17th-20th C; smalls especially silver plate, metalware glass and musical boxes.* LOC: Off A38 down lane by Royal Artillery public house, 200yds. on left. PARK: Easy. TEL: 0278 787267. SER: Valuations; restorations (pictures); buys at auction. VAT: Stan/Spec. *Trade Only.*

ILMINSTER
Ray Best Antiques   LAPADA
North St. House. (R. and W. Best). Est. 1964. Open 9.30-6, Sat. 11-3. Trade any time by appointment. SIZE: Medium. *STOCK: Furniture, £100-£10,000; clocks, £100-£4,000; metalware, £30-£2,000, all 17th-19th C; porcelain, glass, 18th-19th C, £20-£2,000; silver, country items.* Not Stocked: Coins, stamps, medals. LOC: Town centre, 2nd turning on left down one way street, off Market Sq. next to George Hotel. PARK: Easy. TEL: 0460 52194. SER: Valuations; buys at auction. VAT: Spec.

County Antiques Centre
21-23 West St. (Mrs J.P. Barnard). Resident. Est. 1981. Open 10-5 or by appointment. SIZE: Medium - 8 dealers. *STOCK: 18th-19th C pottery, porcelain, metalwork, furniture and decorative antiques.* LOC: West of town at traffic lights crossing. PARK: At rear. TEL: 0460 54151; home - 0460 52269. SER: Upholstery.

James Hutchison
5 West St. *STOCK: Pictures, frames, china and glass, collectables, furniture.*

Moolham Mill Antiques   BADA
Moolham Mill, Moolham Lane. (R. Cropper). Est. 1966. Open by appointment. SIZE: Medium. *STOCK: Oak furniture, 17th-18th C, mahogany furniture, 18th to early 19th C; Delft pewter, 18th-19th C; metalwork, treen, decorative items, needleworks, samplers.* Not Stocked: Silver, Victorian furniture. LOC: From Ilminster on A303 take A3037 for Chard. One mile from centre of Ilminster take road signposted to Dowlish Wake/Kingstone Premises 300yds. on right. PARK: Easy. TEL: 0460 52834. SER: Valuations; buys at auction. VAT: Spec.

West End House Antiques
34-36 West St. (T.H. Sabine). Est. 1964. Open 9.30-5. SIZE: Large. *STOCK: Furniture, 18th to early 20th C, £50-£700; art deco china including Clarice Cliff, £5-£1,000; pictures, 19th-20th C £10-£500.* LOC: Old A303. PARK: Easy. TEL 0460 52793; home - 0404 42140. SER: Valuations; buys at auction.

ANTIQUE COLLECTING

- **Authoritative articles**
- **Practical buying information**
- **Up-to-date price guides**
- **Annual Investment Issue**
- **Auctions and fairs calendars**
- **Antiques for sale and wanted**

The magazine is published ten times a year and contains pre-publication offers and special Christmas discounts on ACC books

Join NOW and receive your first magazine and our book catalogue FREE
Annual membership: £19.50 UK, £25.00 overseas, US $40 USA, CAN $50 Canada

Antique Collectors' Club
5 Church Street, Woodbridge, Suffolk,
IP12 1DS, England
Tel: (0394) 385501 Fax: (0394) 384434

Market Street Industrial Park, Wappingers' Falls,
New York 12590, USA
Tel: 914 297 0003 Fax: 914 297 0068

For Collectors, By Collectors, About Collecting

SOMERSET

LANGPORT
King's House Antiques
The King's House, Bow St. (Mrs D. Desmond). Est. 1976. Open 9-5, Sat. 9-2, Sun. by appointment. CL: Wed. SIZE: Small. STOCK: Small collectables, £5-£25. LOC: Taunton to Yeovil road. PARK: Easy and nearby. TEL: 0458 250350; home - same. SER: Buys at auction (smalls, pictures). FAIRS: Yeovil.

LIMINGTON, Nr. Yeovil
Genges Farm Antiques
Genges Farm. (R. Gilbert). Resident. Est. 1965. Always available. SIZE: Medium. STOCK: Pine and country furniture especially Irish and period; French provincial furniture and decorative items; period oak and elm. LOC: Off A37. PARK: Easy. TEL: 0935 840464 or 0458 250193.

LITTLETON, Nr. Somerton
Cains Antiques LAPADA
Littleton House. (T. and M.C. Finlay). ADLDA. Est. 1956. Open 10-5, Sun. by appointment. SIZE: Medium. STOCK: Furniture, 18th-19th C, £25-£10,000; Oriental porcelain, ironstone china, designer lamps. LOC: B3151 approximately 1.5 miles north of Somerton. PARK: Easy. TEL: 0458 72341; home - same. SER: Valuations; restorations (furniture and antique lighting fixtures). VAT: Stan/Spec.

Westville House Antiques
Westville House. (D. and M. Stacey). Est. 1986. Open daily, Sun. by appointment. SIZE: Small. STOCK: Furniture - pine, £300-£1,500; satinwood and ash, £200-£1000; all 19th C. LOC: B3151 approximately 1.5 miles north of Somerton. PARK: Easy. TEL: 0458 73376; home - same. SER: Valuations; buys at auction. FAIRS: Bath and West; North Somerset. VAT: Stan/Spec.

LYMPSHAM, Nr. Weston-Super-Mare
Baytree House Antiques
Stevens Lane. (N. and S. Adams). Est. 1982. Open 9-6. SIZE: Large. STOCK: Stripped pine furniture, some smalls. LOC: Off A370 - turn left immediately after first Jeff Brown garage, premises about 3/4 mile on right. PARK: Easy. TEL: 0934 750367. VAT: Stan/Spec.

MEARE, Nr. Glastonbury
Borough Antiques
St. Mary's Rd. (R.C. and L. Tincknell). Resident. Open 10-6 or by appointment. STOCK: Town and country furniture, decorative accessories and 19th C brass. LOC: B3151 between Glastonbury and Wedmore. TEL: 0458 860701.

MILVERTON, Nr. Taunton
Milverton Antiques
Fore St. (A. Waymouth). Est. 1972. Resident,

Milverton continued
open any time. SIZE: Medium. STOCK: Pine and oak country furniture, longcase clocks, interesting china, copper, brass and treen. LOC: 8 miles from Taunton on B3227 Barnstaple road. PARK 50yds. TEL: 0823 400597. VAT: Stan/Spec.

MONTACUTE, Nr. Yeovil
Gerald Lewis BADA
The Old Brewery, The Old Estate Yard. (G. and B. Lewis). Open by appointment. STOCK: 18th to early 19th C furniture and clocks. TEL: 0935 825435.

Montacute Antiques
April Cottage, 12 South St. (E.M. and J.K. Warrick). Open 9-6 including Sun. STOCK: Small furniture, porcelain, glass, pictures, metalware decorative and interesting items. PARK: Easy TEL: 0935 824786.

NETHER STOWEY, Nr. Bridgwater
House of Antiquity
St. Mary St. (M.S. Todd). Est. 1967. Open 10-5 o by appointment. SIZE: Medium. STOCK. Philatelic literature, world topographical, maps handbooks, postcards, ephemera, postal history LOC: A39. PARK: Easy. TEL: 0278 732426 SER: Valuations; buys at auction. VAT: Stan.

NORTH PETHERTON, Nr. Bridgwater
Kathleen's Antiques
60 Fore St. (K. Pocock). Resident. Est. 1971. Oper 9-6.30. SIZE: Medium. STOCK: Furniture, clocks 18th-19th C, £50-£650; oil paintings, watercolours sporting prints, £10-£250; silver, £10-£250; china glass, copper, brass, Victorian, £10-£125. LOC A38. PARK: Easy. TEL: 0278 662535.

PITMINSTER, Nr. Taunton
Pitminster Studio
(Mr and Mrs T. Everett). Open by appointment STOCK: Modern and contemporary British paintings and sculpture, £200-£10,000. LOC: : miles south of Taunton, between pub and church PARK: Easy. TEL: 0823 42710. VAT: Stan/Spec.

QUEEN CAMEL, Nr. Yeovil
R. Bonnett Antiques
High St. Open by appointment. STOCK: Furn iture and smalls, pre-1900. LOC: A359. TEL 0935 850724.

Steven Ferdinando
The Old Vicarage. Open by appointment STOCK: Antiquarian and secondhand books TEL: 0935 850210.

RODE, Nr. Bath
Keyford Antiques
Southfield House, 16 High St. (F. O'Dwyer)

SOMERTON

Large quality stock of Furniture at sensible trade prices
Workshop facilities

JOHN GARDINER ANTIQUES

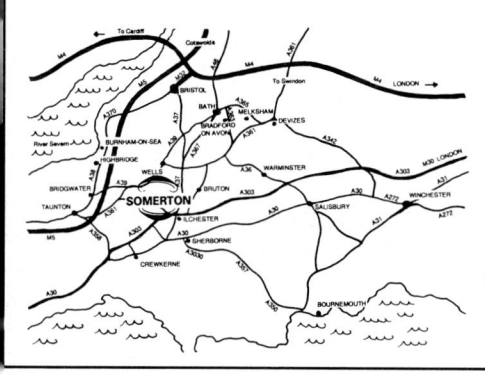

London 2 hours by train
20 minutes from the M5
5 minutes from A303

Monteclefe House
Somerton, Somerset
Tel: 0458 72238/0831 274427
Fax: 0458 74367

Rode continued
Open by appointment. *STOCK:* Georgian and Victorian mahogany and pine furniture, oak and decorative items. TEL: 0373 830531. *Trade Only.*

SHAPWICK, Nr. Bridgwater
King's Farm Antiques
The Old Farmhouse. (D. and G. Rogers). Open by appointment only. SIZE: 2 showrooms. *STOCK: Period oak and country furniture, metalware and treen; linen, lace, textiles, quilts, period clothing, samplers, costume jewellery and smalls.* LOC: Off M5, junction 23, follow A39 for 7 miles. PARK: Own. TEL: 0458 210021. SER: Restorations (furniture).

SOMERTON
John Gardiner Antiques
Monteclefe House. Appointment advisable. *STOCK: General antiques; Edwardian and quality old reproduction furnishings.* LOC: A303. TEL: 0458 72238; mobile - 0831 274327.

The London Cigarette Card Co. Ltd
West St. (I.A. and E.K. Laker, F.C. Doggett and Y. Berktay). Est. 1927. Open daily. SIZE: Medium. *STOCK: Cigarette and trade cards, 1885 to date; sets from £1.50; other cards, from 15p; frames for mounting cards and special*

Somerton continued
albums. PARK: Easy. TEL: 0458 73452. SER: Publishers of catalogues, reference books and monthly magazine; mail order.

Valetta House Antiques
West St. (Mrs J. Gardiner). Open 10-5. CL: Mon. *STOCK: Small general antiques and furniture.* TEL: 0458 74015.

TAUNTON
Philip Barrett Antiques and Prints
Rowford Cottage, Cheddon Fitzpaine. (P. and P. Barrett). Open by appointment. *STOCK: Maps; topographic and sporting prints; Vanity Fair cartoons, country and stripped pine furniture, pottery, porcelain and watercolours.* TEL: 0823 451248.

Joshua Antiques
Paul St. *STOCK: Decorative furnishings.* TEL: 0823 332874.

Rothwell and Dunworth
14 Paul St. (Mrs C. Rothwell and M. Dunworth). ABA. Est. 1975. Open 11-5.30. SIZE: Medium. *STOCK: Antiquarian and secondhand books.* LOC: Off A38, opposite multi-storey car park, behind County Hotel. TEL: 0823 282476. SER: Valuations; book-binding.

SOMERSET

Taunton continued

Selwoods
Queen Anne Cottage, Mary St. Est. 1927. Open 9.30-5. SIZE: Large. STOCK: Furniture, including Victorian and Edwardian. TEL: 0823 272780.

Staplegrove Lodge Antiques
Staplegrove Lodge. (T. Atkins). Est. 1958. Open by appointment only. SIZE: Medium. STOCK: General antiques, furniture, silver, porcelain, pot-lids. LOC: Pink house just off A361 Taunton/Barnstaple road up No Through Road just before the Cross Keys inn. PARK: Own. TEL: 0823 331153; home - same.

Taunton Antiques Market - Silver Street
27/29 Silver St. (Bath Antiques Market Ltd.). Est. 1978. Open Mon. 9-4 including Bank Holidays. SIZE: 130+ dealers. STOCK: General antiques and collectables, including specialists in most fields. LOC: 2 miles from junction 25, M5, toward town centre, 100yds. from Sainsbury Superstore. PARK: Easy. TEL: 0823 289327; enquiries - 071 351 5353; fax - 071 351 5350. SER: Valuations; book binding.

TEMPLECOMBE
Yewtree Antiques
Park House, High St. (B. Hayden). Open 9.30-6. STOCK: General antiques. TEL: 0963 70505.

THORNE ST. MARGARET, Nr. Wellington
Micklem Antiques
Rewe Farm. (C.T., S.E.M. and T.J.M. Micklem). Est. 1962. Open by appointment. STOCK: Early furniture, delft ware, pottery, pewter, needlework and metalware. TEL: 0823 661331.

TIMBERSCOMBE, Nr. Minehead
Zwan Antiques
(M. van Zwanenberg). Open Tues., Thurs. and Sun. p.m. or by appointment. STOCK: Jewellery, 18th-20th C, £1-£2,000; porcelain, 18th-19th C, £5-£1,000; hunting prints and riding items, 19th-20th C, £1-£500; some original sporting pictures, £50-£1,000; small items. LOC: 2 miles out of Dunster on A396. PARK: Outside. TEL: 0643 841608. SER: Valuations; buys at auction.

WANSTROW, Nr. Shepton Mallet
Fred Milton Antiques
Open Sat. and Sun., other times by appointment. SIZE: Large. STOCK: Furniture, Victorian and later. TEL: 074 985 433. VAT: Stan.

WATCHET
Clarence House Antiques
41 Swain St. Est. 1970. Open 10-6.30. CL: Sun. ir winter. SIZE: Medium. STOCK: General antiques pine, brass, copper, bric-a-brac, upholsterec furniture. TEL: 0984 31389. VAT: Stan.

Nick Cotton Antiques and Fine Art
Beechstone House, 47 Swain St. Est. 1970. Oper 10-5.30, Sun. by appointment. SIZE: Medium STOCK: Paintings, 1750-1950; period furniture TEL: 0984 31814 (any time). SER: Restorations framing; research. VAT: Spec.

WEDMORE
Coach House Gallery
Church St. (Mrs V. Davies). Est. 1976. Open 9-6 or by appointment. SIZE: Small. STOCK: Englisa watercolours, 19th and early 20th C; smal furniture, English porcelain; glass and silver 18th C. LOC: Opposite St. Mary's Church. TEL 0934 712718; home - same.

WELLINGTON
Fenwick Billiards
Tonedale Mills. (Nigel Fenwick). Open 9-" including Sun., by appointment only. STOCK Billiard and snooker-dining tables. TEL: 082. 660770; mobile - 0831 833751.

Michael and Amanda Lewis Oriental Carpets and Rugs   LAPADA
8 North St. UKIC. Est. 1982. Open 10-1 and 2 5.30, Mon. and weekends by appointment SIZE: Medium. STOCK: Oriental carpets an rugs, mainly 19th-20th C, £25-£25,000. PARK 100yds. TEL: 0823 667430. SER: Valuations restorations (as stock); repairs and cleaning.

Oxenhams
74 Mantle St. Open 9-9, Sun. by appointment CL: Thurs. p.m. STOCK: General antiques. LOC On A38. PARK: Easy. TEL: 0823 662592.

WELLS
Shelagh Berryman Music Boxes
15 Market Place. Open 10-5.30 or by appoint ment. STOCK: Music boxes, clocks and genera antiques, mainly 19th C. TEL: 0749 676203.

Courtyard Antiques
Palace Courtyard, Priory Rd. (Mr and Mrs M. Mitchell). Est. 1985. Open 9-5, Wed. 9-3, Sa 9.30-5, Sun. by appointment. SIZE: Medium STOCK: Furniture, £100-£300; smalls, £10-£50 both 19th-20th C. LOC: Just off High St., toward Glastonbury. PARK: Easy. TEL: 0749 679533 home - 0749 675028. SER: Valuations; resto ations (upholstery, cane and rush work, china an furniture). FAIRS: Bath and West Showgrounc Shepton Mallet, Newark, Ardingly.

SOMERSET

Wells continued
Bernard G. House (Mitre Antiques)
Market Place. Est. 1963. Open 9.30-5.30. SIZE: Medium. *STOCK: Barometers and scientific instruments, furniture including miniatures and apprentice pieces, 18th-19th C; longcase and bracket clocks, metalware, decorative and architectural items.* PARK: Outside shop. TEL: 0749 672607. SER: Restorations. VAT: Stan/Spec.

Lovejoys
Queen St. (J. Oliver). Est. 1991. Open 10-5 (5.30 May-Sept.), Sat 9.30-5.30. SIZE: Small. *STOCK: Paintings, Edwardian and Victorian furniture, Victorian china.* PARK: Nearby. TEL: 0749 670706; fax - 0275 333302. SER: Restorations. VAT: Stan/Spec.

Edward A. Nowell BADA
12 Market Place. Est. 1952. Open 9-1 and 2-5.30. SIZE: Large. *STOCK: Furniture, clocks, barometers, 17th to early 19th C; jewellery, silver, porcelain, English and continental, all prices. Not Stocked: Victoriana, bric-a-brac, curios, weapons, books.* LOC: From any direction, turn left into Market Place (one-way system). PARK: 20yds. facing shop. TEL: 0749 672415; fax - 0749 670508. SER: Valuations; restorations (furniture, silver, clocks and jewellery); re-upholstery. VAT: Stan/Spec.

Marcus Nowell
21 Market Place. Est. 1973. Open 9.30-5.30. SIZE: Medium. *STOCK: Furniture and decorative items, 18th-19th C, £50-£10,000.* PARK: Easy. TEL: 0749 678051. SER: Valuations; restorations (furniture); buys at auction (furniture). VAT: Stan/Spec.

Jill and David Swale
Sadler Street Gallery, 7a Sadler St. Open 10-6. CL: Mon. *STOCK: Watercolours, old prints.* SER: Framing.

WEST MONKTON, Nr. Taunton
William Morley Antiques
Musgrave's Old Farm. (W.H. Morley). Est. 1970. Open daily, appointment advisable. SIZE: Medium. *STOCK: 17th-18th C oak and country furniture; early brass and metalware; 18th C English drinking glasses.* LOC: From A38 or A361, second house on right on road to village before Monkton Inn. PARK: Easy. TEL: 0823 412751. SER: Valuations; buys at auction; specialist finder.

WILLITON
Edward Venn
52 Long St. Est. 1979. Open 10-5. *STOCK: Furniture, 18th C; clocks.* TEL: 0984 32631 (answer phone). SER: Restorations (furniture, barometers and clocks).

WINCANTON
Barry M. Sainsbury
17 High St. Est. 1958. CL: Thurs. p.m. *STOCK: Oak and mahogany furniture, china, glass, pictures, decorative items.* TEL: 0963 32289. SER: Restorations; cabinet makers. VAT: Stan/Spec.

WIVELISCOMBE
The Carousel Pig
9 High St. (A. McKinley). CL: Thurs p.m. *STOCK: General antiques, country furniture, decorative items, textiles, taxidermy, £5-£2,000.* PARK: Easy. TEL: 0984 24556. SER: Taxidermy; restorations and commissions.

J.C. Giddings
Open by appointment only. SIZE: Large warehouses. *STOCK: Furniture, mostly 18th-19th C.* TEL: 0984 23703. VAT: Stan. *Mainly Trade.*

Heads 'n' Tails
'Bournes House', 41 Church St. (D. McKinley). Resident. Open by appointment. *STOCK: Taxidermy including Victorian cased and uncased birds, mammals and fish, £5-£2,000; decorative items, glass domes.* LOC: Opposite church. PARK: Easy. TEL: 0984 23097; fax - 0984 24445. SER: Taxidermy; restorations; commissions. VAT: Spec.

Peter Lee Antiques
1 Silver St. (P. and A. Lee). Open 9-5. CL: Sat. p.m. *STOCK: Furniture, china, general antiques, fine arts and unsual items.* LOC: B3227, town centre. PARK: Nearby. TEL: 0984 24055.

YEOVIL
Fox and Co
30 Princes St. Est. 1970. *STOCK: Antiquities, coins, medals and militaria, reference books.* PARK: Easy. TEL: 0935 72323. VAT: Stan/Spec.

John Hamblin
Unit 6, 15 Oxford Rd., Penn Mill Trading Estate. (J. and M. A. Hamblin). Est. 1980. Open 8.30-5. CL: Sat. SIZE: Small. *STOCK: Furniture, 1750-1900, £300-£3,000.* PARK: Easy. TEL: 0935 71154; home - 76673. SER: Restorations (furniture); cabinet work. VAT: Stan.

Staffordshire

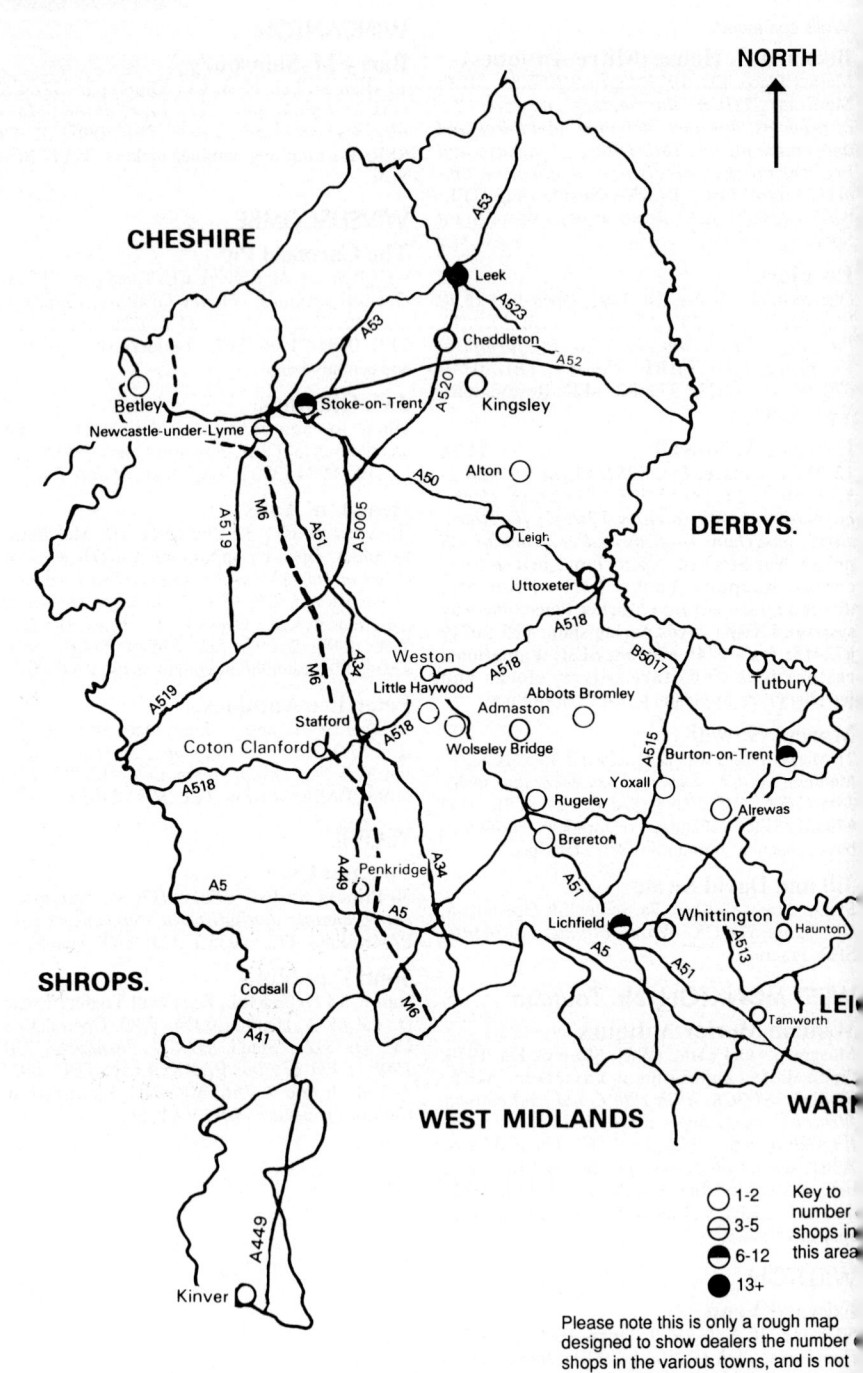

452

NORTH ↑

CHESHIRE

Betley
Newcastle-under-Lyme
Stoke-on-Trent
Cheddleton
Leek
Kingsley
Alton
Leigh
Uttoxeter
Weston
Little Haywood
Stafford
Coton Clanford
Admaston
Abbots Bromley
Wolseley Bridge
Tutbury
Burton-on-Trent
Yoxall
Rugeley
Brereton
Alrewas
Penkridge
Lichfield
Whittington
Haunton
Codsall
Tamworth
Kinver

DERBYS.

SHROPS.

LEI(

WAR

WEST MIDLANDS

Key to number shops in this area

○ 1-2
⊖ 3-5
◐ 6-12
● 13+

Please note this is only a rough map designed to show dealers the number of shops in the various towns, and is not necessarily totally accurate.

Staffordshire

ABBOTS BROMLEY, Nr. Rugeley
Birchwood Antiques
Bromleys, Bagot St. (V. Edwards). Open daily. *STOCK: General antiques, especially blue and white and lace.* TEL: 0283 840288.

ALREWAS, Nr. Burton-on-Trent
Poley Antiques
5 Main St. (D.T. and A.G. Poley). Est. 1977. Open Thurs., Fri. and Sat. 10-5, other times by arrangement. SIZE: Small. *STOCK: General antiques, furniture, silver, china, glass, copper, brass.* Not Stocked: Stamps, coins and militaria. LOC: 20yds. from A38, between Lichfield and Burton. PARK: Own. TEL: 0283 791151; home - same.

BETLEY, Nr. Crewe
Betley Court Gallery
Main Rd. (Prof. G.N. Brown and Dr. F. Brown). Resident. Est. 1980. Open afternoons or by appointment anytime. CL: Mon. SIZE: Large. *STOCK: Oils, watercolours, prints, £20-£5,000; ceramics, specially Doulton Lambeth and Wedgwood, £20-£2,500; both 18th-20th C; furniture, Georgian, Regency, Victorian, £20-£2,500.* Not Stocked: Militaria, clocks. LOC: Village centre. PARK: Easy. TEL: 0270 820652. SER: Buys at auction.

BRERETON, Nr. Rugeley
Rugeley Antique Centre
161/3 Main Rd. Open 9-5, Sun. 12-4.30. SIZE: Large - 28 units. *STOCK: China, glass, pottery, pictures, furniture, pine, treen, linen and shipping goods.* LOC: A51, one mile south of Rugeley town, opposite Cedar Tree Hotel. PARK: Own. TEL: 0889 577166. VAT: Stan/Spec.

BURTON-ON-TRENT
Broadway Studios
27 New St. (F.H. Dyson). Est. 1969. SIZE: Medium. *STOCK: Prints, watercolours, oil paintings, £1-£500.* TEL: 0283 41802. SER: Picture framing and mount cutting. VAT: Stan.

Burton Antiques
1 and 2 Horninglow Rd. (C.H. Arnett). Est. 1977. Open 10-5 every day. SIZE: Large. *STOCK: Shipping and pine furniture.* LOC: A50. PARK: Nearby. TEL: 0283 42331. SER: Valuations; pine stripping; buys at auction.

Derby Street Antique Emporium
38 Derby St. Open 9.30-6, Sun. 11-5. SIZE: Large. *STOCK: General antiques, mainly furniture.* PARK: Large car park. TEL: 0283 45202; fax - 0283 516369. SER: Courier; packing. VAT: Stan.

Austin Pinewood
The Maltings, Wharf Rd. (S. Silvester). Open 9-30. *STOCK: Stripped pine furniture.* TEL: 0283 0860.

Burton-on-Trent continued
C. and R. Scattergood
132 Branston Rd. Open 9-6. *STOCK: Decorative antiques and Wemyss pottery.* TEL: 0283 46695.

CHEDDLETON, Nr. Leek
Jewel Antiques
'Whitegates', 63 Basford Bridge Lane. (B. and D.J. Smith). Est. 1967. Open by appointment. *STOCK: Paintings, prints, jewellery, oil lamps, small furniture and clocks, 18th-19th C, £25-£2,000.* PARK: Easy. TEL: 0538 360744/361247. SER: Buys at auction.

CODSALL
Dam Mill Antiques
Birches Rd. (H. Bassett). Est. 1977. Open 10-1 and 2.30-5.30. CL: Tues. and Thurs. SIZE: Small. *STOCK: General antiques, small furniture, china, glass, copper, brass, silver and jewellery.* PARK: Easy. TEL: 0902 843780.

COTON CLANFORD, Nr. Stafford
C. and J. Mowe
Stokingate Farm. Est. 1970. Open by appointment. *STOCK: General antiques.* TEL: 0785 282799. VAT: Stan/Spec. *Trade Only.*

HAUNTON, Nr. Tamworth
Heart of England Antiques
The Manor Barn. (R. Gilbert and Miss P. Crockett). Est. 1985. Open 10-5.30, Sun. by appointment. SIZE: Large. *STOCK: Furniture, 18th-19th C, £500-£3,000; paintings, £50-£1,000; silver, plate, £5-£200; both 19th C.* LOC: Next to the Manor. PARK: Easy. TEL: Mobile - 0860 434003. SER: Valuations; restorations (furniture, including re-upholstery); buys at auction (furniture and paintings). FAIRS: NEC (Aug.); Stafford; Penns Hall Hotel. VAT: Stan/Spec.

KINGSLEY, Nr. Leek
Country Cottage Interiors
Newhall Farmhouse, Hazels Crossroads. (L. Salmon). Resident. Est. 1972. Open 10-5. SIZE: Medium. *STOCK: Pine, £5-£500; kitchenalia, 25p-£100.* LOC: Off A52. PARK: Own. TEL: 0538 754762.

KINVER
The Antique Centre
128 High St. (R. Harris). Open 10-5.30. SIZE: 10 dealers. *STOCK: Stripped pine, clocks, china, glass, bric-a-brac, furniture, pianos.* TEL: 0384 877441. SER: Stripping.

LEEK
Antiques and Objets d'Art of Leek
70 St. Edwards St. Est. 1955. Open 10-6. CL:

STAFFORDSHIRE

Leek continued
Thurs. STOCK: English and continental furniture; porcelain, silver, glass, oil paintings. TEL: 0538 382587. FAIRS: Buxton. VAT: Spec.

Anvil Antiques
Cross St. Mill, Cross St. (K.L. and J.S. Spooner). Est. 1975. Open 9-6. SIZE: Large. STOCK: Stripped pine, architectural and oak, mahogany, bric-a-brac, decorative items and painted furniture, prints and art. LOC: Ashbourne Rd., from town centre roundabout, turn first left, Victorian mill on right. PARK: Easy. TEL: 0538 371657. VAT: Stan.

Aspleys Antiques and Reproductions Ltd
Compton Mill, Compton. (J. Aspley). Est. 1976. Open 9-6. Sun.10.30-5.30. SIZE: Large. STOCK: General antiques, especially pine, shipping items, bric-a-brac, mainly Victorian and Edwardian. PARK: Own. TEL: 0538 373396. SER: Restorations (mainly pine); shipping and packing; courier service. VAT: Stan.

Sylvia Chapman Antiques
4 St. Edward St. Open 12-5.30. CL: Thurs. STOCK: General small and collectors' items, especially 19th to early 20th C pottery and porcelain, Staffordshire figures and jugs, Victorian coloured glass, treen, copper, brass, kitchenalia. PARK: Opposite. TEL: 0538 399116.

Cyril Cox Antiques
76/78 St. Edward St. Open 10-6. CL: Thurs. SIZE: Medium. STOCK: General antiques including furniture, porcelain, glass, china, gold and silver, pictures, jewellery and linen. LOC: At junction with Brook St. PARK: Nearby. TEL: 0538 399924; home - 0782 511169. SER: Valuations; restorations (furniture and porcelain).

Directmoor Ltd
Albany House, Abbey Green Rd. Open 9-6. SIZE: Large and warehouse. STOCK: English, Irish and continental pine, objets d'art, small and decorative items, oils and watercolours. LOC: A523 Macclesfield Rd. PARK: Easy. TEL: 0538 387474/399876; fax - 0538 371307.

England's Gallery
Ball Haye House, 1 Ball Haye Terr. (F.J. and S. England). Est. 1968. Open 10-5.30. CL: Mon. SIZE: Large. STOCK: Oils and watercolours, 18th-19th C, £500-£10,000; etchings, engravings, lithographs, mezzotints, £50-£4,000. LOC: Towards Ball Haye Green from A523 turn at lights. PARK: Nearby. TEL: 0538 373451; home - 0538 386352. SER: Valuations; restorations (cleaning, relining, regilding); framing, mount cutting; buys at auction (paintings). VAT: Stan.

Gemini Trading
Limes Mill, Abbotts Rd. (T.J. Lancaster and Mrs Y.A. Goldstraw). Est. 1981. Open daily, Sat. and

Leek continued
Sun. by appointment. SIZE: Large. STOCK: Pine, £25-£850; kitchenalia, £5-£35; both 19th C. LOC: Turn off A53 along Abbotts Rd. before town centre. PARK: Easy. TEL: 0538 387834; fax - 0538 399819. VAT: Stan.

Gilligans Antiques
59 St. Edward St. (M.T. Gilligan). Est. 1977. STOCK: Victorian and Edwardian furniture. TEL: 0538 384174.

Grosvenor Antiques
Overton Bank House. Open 9-4.30. STOCK: Clocks, watches and barometers; some furniture. TEL: 0538 385669.

Roger Haynes - Antiques Finder
31 Compton. Open by appointment. STOCK: Pine smalls and decorative items. TEL: 0538 385161.

Johnson's
Park Works, Park Rd. (P. and Mrs J. Johnson). Est. 1976. Open 9-6. SIZE: Medium. STOCK: Pine and country furniture, £50-£1,000; decorative accessories, £50-£500; all 18th-19th C domestic items, 19th C, £5-£50. LOC: Off M6 exit 14 on to A520, just off A523 Macclesfield road. PARK: Easy. TEL: 0538 386745. SER: Restorations (pine). VAT: Stan.

The Leek Antiques Centre
4-6 Brook St. (Barclays House Antiques). Est. 1977. Open 10-5, Sun. by appointment. STOCK: Furniture including sets of chairs and extending dining tables; pottery, oils, watercolours, prints, pine. TEL: 0538 398475; home - 0782 394383/274747. SER: Valuations; restoration (furniture). FAIRS: Bowman's - Staffordshire Showground and NEC. VAT: Stan/Spec.

The Leek Bookshop
4B Victoria Buildings, Broad Street. (R.G Wragg). SIZE: Small. STOCK: Books, 50p-£300. TEL: 0538 373391; evenings - 0538 360044.

Molland Antique Mirrors
40 Compton. (John and Karen Molland). Est 1980. Open 8-7, Sun 10-4. SIZE: Medium. STOCK: Mirrors - gilt, painted and wooden, 19t C, £100-£1,000. LOC: From Stoke-on-Trent, right at 1st traffic lights, shop 200 yards on right. PARK: Easy. TEL: 0538 372553; home - same SER: Delivery; hanging; export packing. FAIRS NEC (Aug). VAT: Stan/Spec.

Odeon Antiques
76-78 St. Edward St. (Steve Ford). Open 10-. STOCK: Lighting, pine and general antique. TEL: 0538 387188/399924. SER: Restoration (lighting).

LEIGH, Nr. Stoke-on-Trent
John Nicholls
Open by appointment only. STOCK: Oa

STAFFORDSHIRE

Leigh continued
furniture and related items, 17th-18th C. LOC: 2 miles from Uttoxeter, just off A50 towards Stoke-on-Trent. SER: 0889 502351; mobile - 0836 244024.

LICHFIELD
Mike Abrahams Books
Cranmere Court, Walsall Rd. PBFA. Est. 1975. Open by appointment. SIZE: Large. *STOCK: Books, especially Midlands topography, 17th C to date, £2-£1,000; documents, ephemera, 17th-20th C, £2-£50.* LOC: On left hand bend of A51 from Rugeley. PARK: Easy. TEL: 0543 256200; home - same. SER: Valuations. FAIRS: Bingley Hall, Stafford and PBFA; Midland Antiquarian Book; Lichfield - Organiser.

The Antique Shop   LAPADA
31 Tamworth St. (Mrs P.M. Rackham). Open 9.30-1.30 and 2.30-5.30. SIZE: Medium. *STOCK: Furniture, pottery, porcelain, silver, prints, paintings, copper and brass, jewellery, glass, £5-£1,000.* PARK: Easy. TEL: 0543 268324.

The Bournemouth Gallery Ltd
P.O Box 23. *STOCK: Limited edition prints.* TEL: 0543 481880. SER: Mail order.

Cordelia and Perdy's Antique Junk Shop
53 Tamworth St. (C.R.J. and P.J. Mellor). *STOCK: General antiques and trade shipping goods.* TEL: 0543 263223.

Images - Peter Stockham
at The Staffs Bookshop, 4 & 6 Dam St. Open 9.30-5.30. *STOCK: Early children's books, art and illustrated books, printed ephemera; antique toys, mainly wooden; games and associated items; fine printing; prints and wood engravings.* TEL: 0543 264093.

James A. Jordan
The Corn Exchange. CMBHI. Open 9-5.30. *STOCK: Clocks especially longcase; watches and barometers.* TEL: 0543 416221; fax - 021 522 2004. SER: Valuations; restorations (clocks and chronometers).

J. Royden Smith
Church View, Farewell Lane, Burntwood. Est. 1972. Open Wed. and Sat. 10.30-5 or by appointment. *STOCK: Antiquarian books, general antiques, bric-a-brac, shipping goods.* TEL: 0543 682217.

The Staffs Bookshop
4 & 6 Dam St. Open 9.30-5.30. *STOCK: Rare, secondhand, antiquarian and collectors books, especially 18th-19th C.* TEL: 0543 264093.

Tudor of Lichfield Antique Centre
Bore St. (Miss S. Burns-Mace). Est. 1992. Open 10-5. SIZE: Small. *STOCK: General antiques*

Lichfield continued
including clocks, glass, jewellery, collectables and toys, from £5. LOC: Off A38. TEL: 0543 263951; home - 0283 790556. SER: Buys at auction.

LITTLE HAYWOOD, Nr. Stafford
Jalna Antiques
Coley Lane. Resident. Est. 1974. Open most times. *STOCK: Furniture, pre-1900. Not Stocked: Shipping goods.* LOC: 1/2 mile off A51, 12 miles north of Lichfield. TEL: 0889 881381. SER: Restorations; re-upholstery. VAT: Spec.

NEWCASTLE-UNDER-LYME
Antique Market
The Stones. (Antique Forum Ltd). Every Tues. 9-4. SIZE: 50+ dealers. *STOCK: General antiques.* TEL: 071 624 4848.

Errington Antiques
63 George St, (corner of George and Albert St.). (G.K. Errington). Open 10-12.30 and 1.30-4.30 CL: Thurs. *STOCK: Oriental items, English furniture, general antiques, lamps.* TEL: 0782 632822.

Hood and Broomfield
Lyme Galleries, 29 Albert St. (J. Hood and G.H. Broomfield). Open 10-5.30, Sat. 10-1. *STOCK: Oils and watercolours, 19th to early 20th C.* TEL: 0782 626859. SER: Restorations; framing. VAT: Spec.

Richard Midwinter Antiques
13 Brunswick St. (Mr and Mrs R. Midwinter). Est. 1987. Open 10-5.30, Thurs. by appointment. SIZE: Medium. *STOCK: Textiles, samplers and embroideries; furniture - oak, walnut, mahogany, 17th-19th C, £50-£10,000; longcase, mantel and wall clocks, £150-£4,000; paintings, £35-£3,000, both 18th-19th C; ceramics and watercolours, 19th C, £15-£1,500. Not Stocked: Pine and ephemera.* LOC: Almost opposite swimming baths. TEL: 0782 712483; home - 0630 872289. SER: Valuations; restorations (framing, clock repair). VAT: Spec.

PENKRIDGE, Nr. Stafford
Golden Oldies
1 and 5 Crown Bridge. (W.A. and M.A. Knowles). Open 10-5.30, Mon. 10-2. PARK: Easy. TEL: 0785 714722. VAT: Stan/Spec.

RUGELEY
Eveline Winter
1 Wolseley Rd. (Mrs E. Winter). Est. 1962. Open 10.30-5. CL: Fri. am, Tues. and Wed. except by appointment. SIZE: Small. *STOCK: Staffordshire figures, pre-Victorian, from £90; Victorian,*

STAFFORDSHIRE

Rugeley continued
£30-£500; copper, brass, glass and general antiques. Not Stocked: Coins and weapons. LOC: Coming from Lichfield or Stafford stay on A51 and avoid town by-pass. PARK: Easy and at side of shop. TEL: 0889 583259.

STAFFORD
The Antique Restoration Studio
1 Newport Rd. (P. Albright). Est. 1989. Open 9-5. SIZE: Small. STOCK: General antiques. TEL: 0785 57999; home - 0785 780424. LOC: Main road. SER: Valuations; restorations. VAT: Stan.

Browse
127 Lichfield Rd. (H. Barnes). Est. 1981. Open 9.30-5. SIZE: Large. STOCK: Furniture, 1860-1940 and reproduction. LOC: Outskirts of town. PARK: Easy. TEL: 0785 41097; home - 660336. SER: Valuations; restorations (caning and rushing).

Windmill Antiques
9 Castle Hill. Open 10-5. SIZE: Medium - several dealers. STOCK: General antiques and decorative items. PARK: Easy. TEL: 0785 228505.

STOKE-ON-TRENT
Ann's Antiques
24 Leek Rd, Stockton Brook. Open 10-5. CL: Thurs. STOCK: Victorian furniture, brass, copper, jewellery, paintings, pottery and unusual items. TEL: 0782 503991. VAT: Stan.

Antiques Workshop and Boulton's Antiques
43-45 Hope St, Hanley. (H. and S. Oakes and J. Rowley). Est. 1974. Open 9.30-5.30, Sun. by appointment. SIZE: Medium. STOCK: Furniture including pine, mahogany and oak; pottery, 18th-20th C; general antiques and bric-a-brac. PARK: Own at rear. TEL: 0782 273645. SER: Valuations; restorations (pine stripping, upholstery, polishing).

Castle Antiques
113 Victoria St, Hartshill. (J. Taylor). Est. 1965. Open 10-5.30. CL: Thurs. SIZE: Medium. STOCK: Edwardian and Victorian furniture and clocks, £100-£1,000. LOC: 300yds. from main road. PARK: 100yds. TEL: 0782 625168. VAT: Stan/Spec.

Five Towns Antiques
17 Broad St, Hanley. (B. and B. Arkinstall). Open 10-5.30. CL: Thurs. SIZE: Small. STOCK: 1930's pottery and porcelain, general antiques. PARK: Nearby. TEL: 0782 272930.

The Potteries Antique Centre
271 Waterloo Rd, Cobridge. (W. and D. Buckley). Est. 1972. Open 9-6 including Sun. SIZE: Large. STOCK: Furniture including pine and shipping, 18th-20th C; pottery and porcelain including Doulton, Moorcroft, Beswick, Wedgewood,

Stoke-on-Trent continued
Coalport, Shelley, 19th-20th C; collectors' items, silver plate, clocks, brass, jewellery, pictures, 18th-20th C; all £1-£5,000. LOC: Off M6, junction 15 or 16 on to A500, follow signs for Festival Park or Potteries Shopping Centre. PARK: Easy. TEL: 0782 201455; home - 0260 281098. SER: Valuations; export facilities - supply and packing; buys at auction (pottery and collectors' items). VAT: Stan/Spec.

W.G. Steele
20 Piccadilly, Hanley. Est. 1770. Open 9-6. STOCK: Victorian and Edwardian jewellery. Not Stocked: Furniture. TEL: 0782 213216.

The Tinder Box
61 Lichfield St, Hanley. (Mr and Mrs G.E Yarwood). Est. 1969. Open 10-5. CL: Sat. SIZE Large. STOCK: Victorian oil lamps and spare parts; early brass and copper, jewellery, furniture and unusual items. PARK: Easy. TEL: 0782 261368/550508. SER: Cleaning (brass and copper).

TAMWORTH
The Tamworth Antique Centre
14 Aldergate. (W.G.V. Turner and J. Smith). Est 1993. Open seven days. SIZE: Large. STOCK English and continental furniture, silver porcelain, clocks, pictures and decorative items 18th to early 20th C, £50-£15,000. LOC: North side of town on A453. 4.5 miles junction 10, M42 via A5 and A51. PARK: Own and opposite. TEL 0827 53031; mobile - 0831 520140; fax - 082 53031. SER: Valuations; buys at auction. FAIRS NEC August.

TUTBURY, Nr. Burton-on-Trent
The Old Chapel Market
High St. (I. Cope). Open 9.30-5.30, Sun. 11-5 STOCK: Victorian, Edwardian and reproduction furniture. PARK: Easy. TEL: 0283 812094.

Town and Country Antiques
40 Monk St. (A.J. Pym). Est. 1985. Open 10-5.3 including Sun. STOCK: Stripped pine, £50-£500 Victorian/Edwardian linen and lace, £5-£150 reproduction pine, £15-£800. TEL: 0283 52055 SER: Valuations. VAT: Stan.

Tutbury Mill Antiques
6 Lower High St. (F.J. and G.J. Allen). Ope seven days 9-5. SIZE: Warehouse. STOCK Georgian, Victorian and Edwardian furniture LOC: A50. Part of Georgian mews. PARK: Ow TEL: 0283 815999; home - 0889 270891.

WESTON, Nr. Stafford
Weston Antique Gallery
Boat Lane. (Mr and Mrs F. Rabone). Est. 197 Open Wed.-Sat. 10-5.30 or by appointment. SIZ

An Antique Collectors' Club Title

The Georgian Bracket Clock 1714-1830
by Richard C.R. Barder

Probably the best single reference on this surprisingly neglected subject. Of the many superior clocks made in England from 1714-1830, the majority were bracket clocks. Superb illustrations complement a text in which the craft of clockmaking and bracket clock design is comprehensively discussed. This book will appeal to the general reader, collector and specialist alike.

ISBN 1 85149 158 9
236pp, 267 b & w illus, 39 colour
£45.00

Available from:
Antique Collectors' Club, 5 Church Street, Woodbridge, Suffolk IP12 1DS
Tel: (0394) 385501 Fax: (0394) 384434

or Market Street Industrial Park, Wappingers' Falls, New York 12590, USA
Tel: 914 297 0003 Fax: 914 297 0068

Weston continued
Small. STOCK: Maps and prints, 17th-19th C, £5-£500; watercolours and etchings, 19th C, £10-£400; Staffordshire pottery and porcelain, small silver and glass, 19th-20th C, £5-£100; small collectable items. LOC: On A518. PARK: Easy. TEL: 0889 270450; home - same. SER: Restorations, framing.

WHITTINGTON, Nr. Lichfield
Milestone Antiques LAPADA
5 Main St. (H. and E. Crawshaw). Resident. Est. 1988. Open Thurs.-Sat. 10-6, Sun. 11-3, other times by appointment. STOCK: Furniture, porcelain, pottery, pictures, brass and copper, 18th-19th C. LOC: A51 Lichfield/Tamworth road, turn north at Whittington Barracks, shop 50yds. past crossroads in village. PARK: Outside. TEL: 0543 432248. VAT: Stan/Spec.

WOLSELEY BRIDGE, Nr. Rugeley
Jalna Antiques
The Old Barn. (G. and D. Hancox). Open 10-5. STOCK: Furniture and smalls. LOC: Junction A51/A513. TEL: 0889 881381.

YOXALL, Nr. Burton-on-Trent
Armson's of Yoxall Antiques LAPADA
The Hollies. (F.R.B. and P.K. Armson). Est. 1955. Open 9-5, Sat. and other times by appointment. SIZE: Large. STOCK: Period furniture and shipping goods. LOC: On A515. TEL: 0543 472352. VAT: Stan/Spec.

H.W. Heron and Son Ltd LAPADA
The Antique Shop, 1 King St. (H.N.M. and J. Heron). Est. 1949. Open 9-6, Sat. 10.30-5.30, Sun. 2-6. SIZE: Medium. STOCK: Furniture, porcelain, glass, pictures, all prices. LOC: On A515 in centre of village, opposite church. PARK: Easy. TEL: 0543 472266; home - same. SER: Valuations. VAT: Stan/Spec.

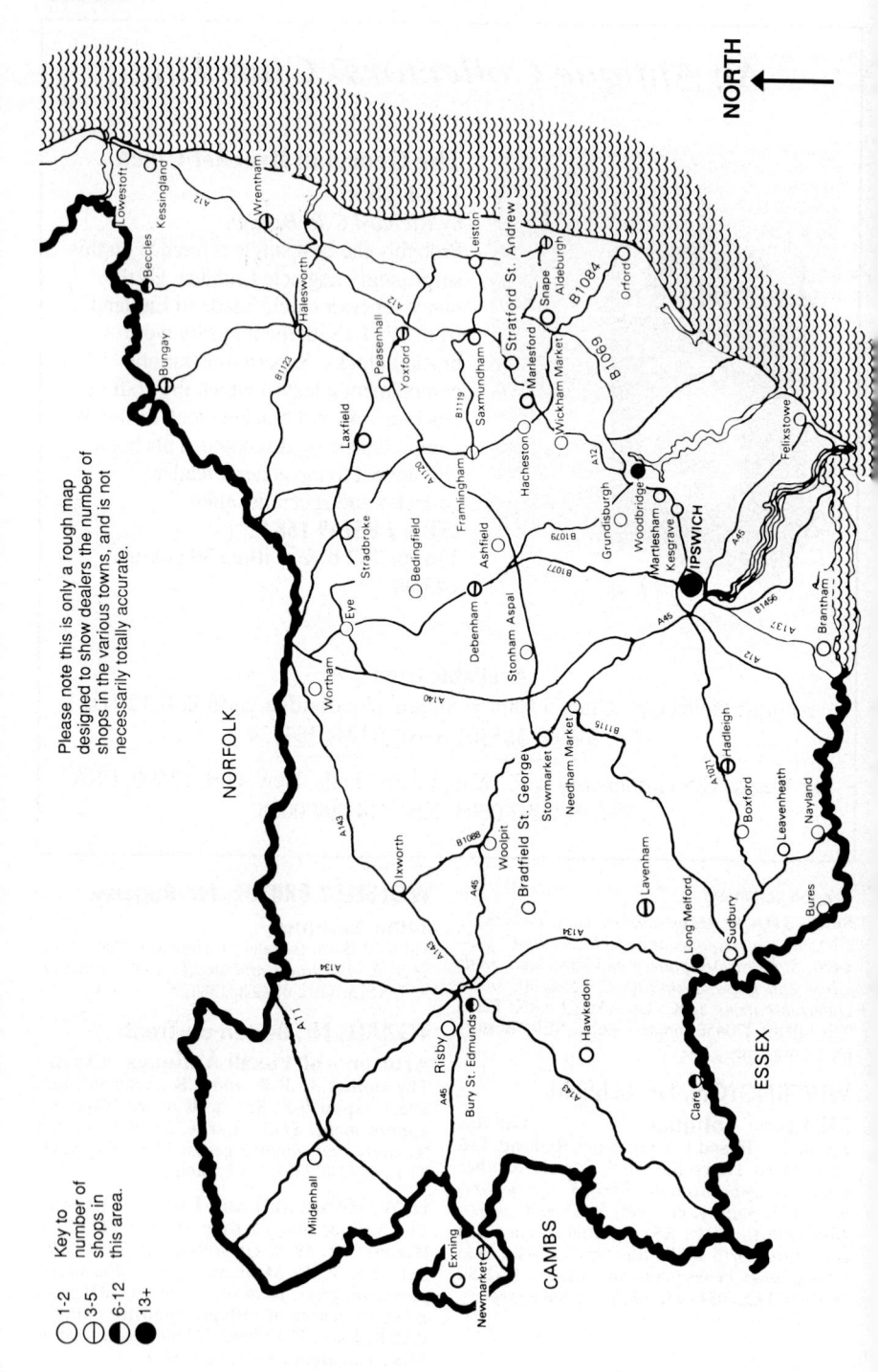

Suffolk

Suffolk

ALDEBURGH

Aldeburgh Galleries
132 High St. (Mr and Mrs W. Dandy and Mr and Mrs S. Haslam). Open 10-5. STOCK: Jewellery, silver, collectables, Steiff bears, general antiques. TEL: 0728 453963. VAT: Spec.

Guillemot
134/136 High St. (L. Weaver). Est. 1973. Open 10-1 and 2-5, Sat. 10-1 and 2-6, Wed. p.m. and Sun. by appointment. SIZE: Medium. STOCK: Pine, elm, oak and fruitwood country furniture, dressers, tables and treen. LOC: Town centre. PARK: Easy. TEL: 0728 453933. VAT: Stan/Spec.

Mole Hall Antiques
102/104 High St. (Peter Weaver). Est. 1976. Open 10-5, Sun. by appointment. SIZE: Small. STOCK: Country furniture, country kitchen items and unusual items. PARK: Easy. TEL: 0728 452361; home - same. VAT: Stan/Spec.

Thompson's Gallery
175 High St. (J. and S. Thompson). Open 10-5 or by appointment. SIZE: Medium. STOCK: Oils and watercolours, 18th-19th C; furniture, 18th to early 20th C; both £300-£10,000. PARK: Easy. TEL: 0728 453743. SER: Valuations; restorations; framing; buys at auction. VAT: Spec.

BECCLES

Besleys Books
4 Blyburgate. (P.A. and P.F. Besley). Est. 1978. Open 9.30-1 and 2-5. CL: Wed. SIZE: Medium. STOCK: Books, 50p-£1,000; prints, £7-£50; maps, £3-£100; all 17th-20th C. LOC: Town centre. PARK: Nearby. TEL: 0502 715762; home - 0502 75649. SER: Valuations; restorations (book binding); buys at auction (books). FAIRS: Various PBFA.

Saltgate Antiques
11 Saltgate. (A.M. Ratcliffe). Resident. Est. 1971. Open 10-5. CL: Wed. p.m. SIZE: Medium. STOCK: Furniture, 17th-19th C, £100-£3,000; clocks, collectors' items, brass, copper, Staffordshire figures, paintings and prints, 19th C bric-a-brac, £5-£300. LOC: Town centre opposite bus station. PARK: Easy. TEL: 0502 712776.

Waveney Antiques Centre
Peddars Lane. Open 10-5.30. SIZE: 26 dealers. STOCK: General antiques, books, furniture, jewellery, silver, clocks and collectors' items. PARK: Easy. TEL: 0502 716147.

BEDINGFIELD, Nr. Eye

The Olde Red Lion
The Street. Est. 1973. Open by appointment. STOCK: Furniture and general antiques. LOC: 3 miles from Eye, 2 miles from Debenham. TEL: 072 876 491. SER: Restorations (furniture, oil paintings, ceramics, snuff boxes, wood carvings).

BLYTHBURGH, Nr. Halesworth

E.T. Webster
Westwood Lodge. Open by appointment. STOCK: Antiquarian books relating to English literature, 16th-20th C; oak for restoration. TEL: 050 270 539.

BOXFORD

The Corner Cupboard
The Old Bakery. Open by appointment only. STOCK: Victoriana, papier mâché, samplers, beadwork and small furniture. PARK: Easy. TEL: 0787 210123.

An Antique Collectors' Club Title

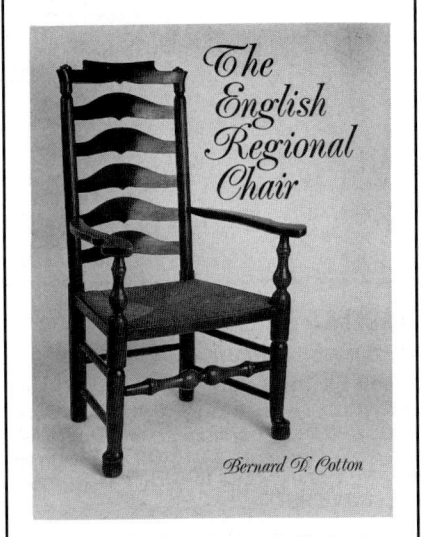

The English Regional Chair
by Bernard D. Cotton
This first study of British regional chairs opens up an entirely new area of collecting. It unearths thousands of names of makers who would otherwise have passed into oblivion and identifies many of their products.
**ISBN 1 85149 023 X, 512pp
over 1,400 b & w illus, 69 col, £49.50**

Available from:
Antique Collectors' Club
5 Church Street, Woodbridge, Suffolk IP12 1DS
Tel: (0394) 385501 Fax: (0394) 384434

or Market Street Industrial Park
Wappingers' Falls, New York 12590, USA
Tel: 914 297 0003 Fax: 914 297 0068

DENZIL GRANT

**HUBBARDS CORNER, BRADFIELD ST. GEORGE,
NR. BURY ST. EDMUNDS, SUFFOLK.
Telephone 0449 736576**

18th century walnut dressing chest

FURNITURE, TAPESTRY, METAL OBJECTS, PAINTINGS

BRADFIELD ST. GEORGE, Nr. Bury St. Edmunds

Denzil Grant Antiques   LAPADA
Hubbards Corner. BAFRA. Est. 1979. Open anytime. *STOCK: Furniture, 16th to early 19th C; tapestry, metalware.* LOC: Off A45 between Bury St. Edmunds and Ipswich. PARK: Easy. TEL: 0449 736576.

BRANTHAM, Nr. Manningtree

Brantham Mill Antiques
(C. Webber). Open Fri.-Sun. *STOCK: Pine, mahogany and country furniture, 18th-19th C, £50-£1,000.* LOC: B1070 off A137. VAT: Stan/Spec.

BUNGAY

Black Dog Antiques
51 Earsham St. (K. Button). Est. 1986. Open daily. *STOCK: General antiques including oak, mahogany and pine, china, linen and collectables, £1-£1000+.* LOC: Opposite Post Office. PARK: Easy. TEL: 0986 895554; home - 0986 894489. SER: Valuations.

Cork Brick Antiques
6 Earsham St. (G. and K. Skipper). Open 10-5.30. *STOCK: Country and decorative antiques; architectural decoration.* PARK: Easy. TEL: 0986 894873; home - 0502 712646.

Bungay continued

Country House Antiques
30 Earsham St. Est. 1979. CL: Mon. and Wed., and Sat. p.m. except by appointment. SIZE: Medium and trade warehouse. *STOCK: Mahogany, inlaid, oak and walnut furniture, 18th-19th C; 19th C porcelain and collectables.* LOC: Near Post Office. PARK: Easy. TEL: 0986 892875; home and warehouse - 0508 58144.

BURY ST. EDMUNDS

Corner Shop Antiques
1 Guildhall St. Open 10-5. *STOCK: Victoriana, porcelain, jewellery, silver, glass and collectors' items.* LOC: Corner of Abbeygate St., opposite Corn Exchange. TEL: 0284 701007.

Guildhall Gallery   LAPADA
1 and 1a Churchgate St. (P.N. Hewes). Est. 1965. Open 10-1 and 2-5.30. CL: Thurs. SIZE: Large. *STOCK: Oil paintings, £100-£5,000; watercolours, £50-£400; sporting prints and others, £10-£250; all 19th C.* PARK: Easy. TEL: 0284 762366. SER: Valuations; restorations; framing. VAT: Stan/Spec.

Guildhall Street Antiques
27 Guildhall St. (Mrs T. Cutting). Est. 1965. Open 9.30-5.30. CL: Mon. a.m. and Thurs. SIZE: Medium. *STOCK: General antiques, bric-a-brac,*

SUFFOLK

Bury St. Edmunds continued
£25-£2,500. LOC: From town centre down Guildhall St. to below Churchgate St. junction. PARK: Easy. TEL: 0284 703060/735278.

Peppers Period Pieces
23 Churchgate St. (M.E. Pepper). Est. 1975. Open 10-5. STOCK: Furniture, oak, elm, yew, fruitwood, mahogany, 16th-19th C; English domestic implements in brass, copper, lead, tin, iron, pewter and treen, 16th to early 20th C; some pottery and porcelain, bygones and collectables, late 19th to early 20th C. Not Stocked: Reproductions. PARK: Easy. TEL: 0284 768786; home - 0359 50606. SER: Valuations; repairs and polishing. VAT: Spec.

Winston Mac (Silversmith)
65 St. John's St. (E.W. McKnight). Est. 1978. Open 9-5. CL: Sun. except by appointment and Sat. SIZE: Small. STOCK: Silver tea services, creamers, salts. PARK: Easy. TEL: 0284 767910. SER: Restorations (silver and plating). VAT: Stan/Spec.

CLARE, Nr. Sudbury
Agnus
41A Nethergate St. (R. and Mrs S. Lamb). Est. 1988. Open 10-1 and 2-5. CL: Wed. SIZE: Small. STOCK: Early oak furniture, 17th to early 18th C; treen and candlesticks, 17th to early 19th C; Victorian and Georgian jewellery. Not Stocked: Pine and 20th C furniture, silver and ceramics. LOC: Village centre, next to post office. PARK: Easy. TEL: 0787 278547. VAT: Spec.

Clare Antique Warehouse
The Mill, Malting Lane. (D. Edwards and J. Tanner). Est. 1974. Open 9.30-5.30. SIZE: Large - over 40 dealers. STOCK: 17th-19th C furniture, textiles, paintings, porcelain, glass, silver, clocks, decorative items, £5-£20,000. LOC: 100yds. from High St. Follow signs for Clare Castle, Country Park. PARK: Easy. TEL: 0787 278449. SER: Valuations; restorations. VAT: Stan/Spec.

The Clare Collector   LAPADA
1 Nethergate St. (J. Verney). Est. 1979. Open 10-1 and 2-5.30. SIZE: Medium. STOCK: English and continental oak, walnut, mahogany and fruitwood furniture, 17th-19th C; pottery and porcelain, prints and watercolours, Oriental and tribal rugs, unusual and decorative items. PARK: Easy. TEL: 0787 277909; home - 0787 277494. VAT: Spec.

Clare Hall Company
The Barns, Clare Hall, Cavendish Rd. Est. 1970. Open any time by appointment. STOCK: Handmade copies of floor standing and table globes. LOC: A1092. PARK: Easy. TEL: Workshop/home - 0787 278445; 0787 277510 (ansaphone). SER: Full cabinet making, especially four-poster beds; restorations; paintwork and upholstery. VAT: Stan/Spec.

THE CLARE COLLECTOR

1 Nethergate Street,
Clare (near Long Melford),
Suffolk.
Telephone: Clare (0787) 277909

17th, 18th and 19th century furniture, pictures, porcelain, works of art and curios at reasonable prices.

Clare continued
Granny's Attic
22 High St. (M. Sadler-Chapman). Est. 1972. Open Sat. only 10.30-5. STOCK: Victorian to 1940's cottage bygones, linens, collectors' items, fashions/accessories. LOC: Off main road, opposite church tower doorway. PARK: Easy.

F.D. Salter Antiques
1-2 Church St. Est. 1959. Open 9-5. CL: Wed. p.m. SIZE: Medium. STOCK: Oak and mahogany furniture, English porcelain, 18th to early 19th C, £10-£2,000. LOC: A1092. PARK: Easy. TEL: 0787 277693. SER: Valuations; restorations (furniture). FAIRS: Bury St. Edmunds and Barbican. VAT: Stan/Spec.

Trinders' Booksellers
Malting Lane. (P. and R. Trinder). Est. 1975. Open Sat. 10-1 and 2-5, Sun. 2-5, weekdays by appointment. SIZE: Medium. STOCK: Books including British Isles topography, architecture, art and antiques reference, Folio Society, true crime, 19th-20th C. PARK: Nearby. TEL: 0787 277130; home - same.

DEBENHAM
Debenham Antique Centre
Foresters Hall, High St. (G. Adams and P. Massey). Open 9.30-5.30, Sun. 2-5. SIZE: Large

RANDOLPH
97-99 HIGH STREET
HADLEIGH, SUFFOLK IP7 5EJ
TEL: (0473) 823789

Dealers in Antique Furniture & Accessories
ESTABLISHED IN 1921

A Suffolk "Mendlesham" armchair in fruitwood with elm seat, the back rails inlaid with boxwood stringing. Circa 1810.

Debenham continued
- several dealers. *STOCK: Furniture and decorative items, 18th-20th C; silver, porcelain and pottery.* PARK: Nearby. TEL: 0728 860777; fax - 0728 860142. SER: Restorations (furniture). VAT: Stan/Spec.

N. Lanchester
21 High St. Open every day. *STOCK: General antiques, 18th-19th C shipping goods and smalls.* TEL: 0728 860756.

EXNING, Nr. Newmarket
Derby Cottage Collectables
Fordham Rd. (V. Cole). Open 9-7 including Sun. SIZE: Medium. *STOCK: Furniture and ceramics, 19th to early 20th C, £5-£1,000; bygones and collectors' items, £1-£100.* LOC: Just off A45 Newmarket by-pass on A142 to Ely. PARK: Easy. TEL: 0638 578422; home - same. VAT: Stan/Spec.

EYE
The Corner Shop
Castle St. (Mrs O.M. Whalley). Est. 1969. CL: Tues. TEL: 0379 870614/870261.

FELIXSTOWE
John McCulloch Antiques
1a Hamilton Rd. Open 9.30-5, Wed. 9.30-1. *STOCK: Furniture, copper, brass, pictures,*

Felixstowe continued
clocks and bric-a-brac. LOC: Main street, sea front end at top of Bent Hill. PARK: Around corner. TEL: 0394 283126; home - 0394 272179.

FRAMLINGHAM
Antiques Warehouse
The Old Station. (David Finbow, Bed Bazaar and Richard Goodbrey). Est. 1992. Open 10-5, Sun. 2-5. CL: Wed. *STOCK: Decorative furniture, pine, Victorian beds,.* PARK: Easy. TEL: 0728 724944. SER: Mattresses made-to-measure.

Bed Bazaar
29 Double St. (B. Goodbrey). Open 9-5.30, appointment advisable. Sun. by appointment only. *STOCK: Victorian brass and iron beds.* LOC: Up Church St. towards Framlingham Castle. Opposite church gates turn right into Double St. PARK: Easy. TEL: 0728 723756; fax - 0728 724626. SER: Restorations (beds); manufacturer of traditional hand-made mattresses, any size to order.

Goodbreys
29 Double St. (R. and M. Goodbrey). Est. 1965. Open Sat. 9-5.30, other times by appointment. SIZE: Large. *STOCK: Decorative items including sleighbeds, upholstery, Biedermeier, simulated bamboo, painted cupboards, lighting, garden furniture, country pieces; pottery, glass, textiles, mirrors, bric-a-brac.* LOC: Up Church St. towards Framlingham Castle. Opposite church gates turn right into Double St. PARK: Easy. TEL: 0728 723756. VAT: Mainly Spec. *Mainly Trade.*

GRUNDISBURGH, Nr. Woodbridge
Bond's Manor Antiques
Bond's Manor. (T.K. and W.E. Hickford). Est. 1983. Open by appointment. SIZE: Small. *STOCK: Furniture and accessories, 17th to early 19th C.* LOC: 1 mile west of village green. PARK: Easy. TEL: 0473 735357; home - same.

The Coach House
(R. and S. Foster-Pegg). Open Thurs.-Sun. 10-5. *STOCK: Fine furniture, porcelain, glass, bric-a-brac and silverware.* TEL: 0473 735569.

HACHESTON, Nr. Wickham Market
Joyce Hardy Pine and Country Furniture
Resident. Open 9.30-5.30. CL: Sun. except by appointment. *STOCK: Pine, especially period dressers and corner cupboards.* LOC: B1116, Framlingham Rd. PARK: Easy. TEL: 0728 746485. SER: Hand-made furniture from old pine.

HADLEIGH, Nr. Ipswich
Randolph   BADA
97 and 99 High St. (B.F. and H.M. Marston). Est. 1921. Open 9.30-5.30, appointment advisable. Sun. by appointment only. SIZE: Medium.

SUFFOLK

ASHLEY ANTIQUES
20a FORE STREET IPSWICH IP4 1JU

SELECTED QUALITY FURNITURE OF THE 18TH & 19TH CENTURY
FINE ANTIQUE RESTORATION & POLISHING UNDERTAKEN
TEL: ASHLEY WARREN 0473 251696. FAX: 0473 233974

Hadleigh continued
STOCK: *Furniture, 1600-1830, £50-£25,000; brass, copper, porcelain, delftware, treen.* Not Stocked: Silver. PARK: Easy. TEL: 0473 823789. SER: Valuations; restorations (furniture). FAIRS: Grosvenor House. VAT: Spec.

Isobel Rhodes
69-73 Angel St. STOCK: *Furniture, oak, country, mahogany; brassware.* TEL: 0473 823754; home - 0473 310409. VAT: Spec.

Gordon Sutcliffe   BADA
11 High St. Est. 1952. Open 9.30-5.30. STOCK: *Furniture, 1620-1820, £100-£10,000; porcelain.* Not Stocked: Victorian furniture, bric-a-brac, reproductions. TEL: 0473 823464. SER: Valuations. FAIRS: Chelsea. VAT: Spec.

Tara's Hall
Victoria House, Market Place. (B. O'Keefe). Est. 1977. Open 10-5. CL: Wed. SIZE: Medium. STOCK: *Textiles and linen, jewellery, art nouveau and art deco, small items.* PARK: Easy. TEL: 0473 824031. SER: Valuations; buys at auction (jewellery, art nouveau objects).

HALESWORTH
Ash Tree Antiques
Ash Tree Farm, Wissett. (P.M. and A.M.F.T. Lambert). Est. 1980. Open Sat. and Sun. 10-5, other times by appointment. SIZE: Medium. STOCK: *Small items and country furniture, 18th C to date, £30-£500; pottery and porcelain, £5-£100.* LOC: 1 mile from Halesworth P.O. on Wissett Rd. PARK: Easy. TEL: 0986 872867; home - same. SER: Buys at auction.

Blyth Bygones
8 Station Rd. Est. 1966. Open 10-5. CL: Thurs. STOCK: *General antiques especially pine.* TEL: 0986 873397. SER: Pine stripping.

Number Six Antiques
Chediston St. (S. Simpkin). Open 10.30-5, Mon. 10.30-3. CL: Thurs. STOCK: *Furniture including pine, small and decorative items, bric-a-brac, china and glass, £5-£500.* PARK: Easy. TEL: 0986 875492.

HAWKEDON, Nr. Bury St. Edmunds
Freya Antiques
at The Old Forge. Usually open but appointment advisable; evenings by appointment. STOCK: *General antiques especially upholstered items.* TEL: 0284 89267; mobile - 0831 651898. SER: Restorations; re-upholstery.

IPSWICH
A. Abbott Antiques
757 Woodbridge Rd. (C. Lillistone). Est. 1965. Open 10.30-5. CL: Wed. SIZE: Medium. STOCK: *Small items, especially clocks and jewellery; Victorian, Edwardian and shipping furniture, £5-£1,000.* PARK: Easy. TEL: 0473 728900; home - same.

Tony Adams Bygones Shop
175 Spring Rd. Open 10-5. CL: Wed. STOCK: *Bygones, especially wireless sets; toy trains, cameras.*

Ashley Antiques
20A Fore St. (A.M. Warren). Open 9-1 and 2-5, Sat. 10-1. SIZE: Small. STOCK: *Furniture, 18th-19th C, £200-£4,000; clocks, 18th-20th C, £200-£3,000; porcelain and glass, 19th C, £20-£200.* Not Stocked: Silver and jewellery. LOC: Off Star Lane. PARK: Easy. TEL: 0473 251696; home - 0473 253041. SER: Restorations (furniture).

Atfield and Daughter
17 St. Stephen's Lane. (D.A. and Miss S.F. Atfield). Est. 1920. Open 9.30-5.30. SIZE: Large. STOCK: *Furniture, clocks, metal, pottery, £5-£500; pistols, swords, guns, militaria, scientific instruments, £10-£800; books on collecting, £5-£15.* LOC: Opposite bus station, Old Cattle Market. PARK: Nearby. TEL: 0473 251518. SER: Valuations; restorations (general cabinet work); buys at auction. VAT: Stan.

Paul Bruce Antiques
Frobisher Rd. Est. 1972. Open by appointment. SIZE: Warehouse. STOCK: *Oak, walnut and mahogany, paintings, general antiques, £20-£6,500.* TEL: 0473 255400/233671; fax - 0473 233656. VAT: Stan/Spec.

Ipswich continued

Sonia Cordell Antiques
13 St. Peters St. Est. 1961. Open 10-4.30. CL: Wed. *STOCK: Small decorative bygones, treen, jewellery, English and foreign silver, needlework tools, ephemera and toys, prints and paintings, especially 20th C British.* PARK: Nearby. TEL: 0473 219508; home - 0394 282254.

Country Bygones and Antiques
13c St. Peters St. (Pat Adams). Open 10-5 usually including Sat. *STOCK: Kitchenalia, country and decorative items, silver, plate, some jewellery, prints, pictures, porcelain and pottery, 18th-20th C.* PARK: In street and nearby. TEL: 0473 253683; home - 03948 392.

Claude Cox at College Gateway Bookshop
3 Silent St. Open 10-5. CL: Wed. SIZE: Medium. *STOCK: Books, from 1470; some local maps and prints.* LOC: Leave inner ring road at Novotel double roundabout, turn into St. Peters St. PARK: Cromwell Square and Buttermarket Centre. TEL: 0473 254776. SER: Valuations; restorations (rebinding); buys at auction; catalogue available.

Croydon and Sons Ltd
50-56 Tavern St. Est. 1865. Open 9-5.30. SIZE: Large. *STOCK: Ceramics, clocks, silver, jewellery, Oriental furniture, £5-£50,000.* LOC: Opposite Great White Horse Hotel. TEL: 0473 256514; fax - 0473 231565. SER: Valuations; restorations. VAT: Stan/Spec.

The Edwardian Shop
556 Spring Rd. *STOCK: 1930's oak furniture.* TEL: 0473 716576; evenings - 0473 712890.

The Fortescue Gallery
27 St. Peter's St. (L. Fortescue). Open 10-4. CL: Mon. except by appointment. *STOCK: 19th C pictures.* PARK: Easy. TEL: 0473 251342.

John Gazeley Associates Fine Art
17 Fonnereau Rd. Est. 1966. Usually open but appointment advisable. SIZE: Small. *STOCK: Decorative oil paintings, watercolours and prints, 18th to early 20th C, £5-£500; topographical engravings of local interest.* LOC: Central Ipswich off Crown St., east side of Christchurch Park. PARK: Easy. TEL: 0473 252420; home - same. SER: Restorations (cleaning, re-lining paintings); framing.

Hubbard Antiques
16 St. Margarets Green. Est. 1964. Open 9-6. SIZE: Large. *STOCK: Furniture and decorative items, 18th-19th C; reproduction period furniture.* PARK: Easy. TEL: 0473 226033/233034; fax - same. SER: Valuations; restorations; export. VAT: Stan/Spec.

Hyland House Antiques
45 Felixstowe Rd. (J. Burton). Open 9.30-5. CL: Wed. and Thurs. SIZE: Large. *STOCK: Pre-war furniture and bric-a-brac.* TEL: 0473 210055/251723/712536.

Majors Galleries
6 St. Helens St. (M. Weiner). Est. 1982. Open 9.30-5.30. SIZE: Medium. *STOCK: Furniture, 19th C; art deco and art nouveau, £1-£1,000; decorative small items including clocks, ornaments, plates and pictures, 19th C.* LOC: Opposite Regent theatre. PARK: Nearby. TEL: 0473 221190.

Orwell Galleries
1 Upper Orwell St. (M. Weiner). Open 9.30-5.30. CL: Wed. SIZE: Medium. *STOCK: Furniture and pine.* TEL: 0473 221190.

Orwell Paint Strippers
Halifax Mill, 427 Wherstead Rd. (M. Weiner). Open 8.30-5.30, Sat. 8.30-5. *STOCK: Pine.* TEL: 0473 680091. SER: Restorations; stripping; pine furniture made to order from old wood.

Tom Smith Antiques
33A St. Peter's St. Est. 1959. *STOCK: Period furniture, accessories, shipping goods, £5-£2,000.* TEL: 0473 210172.

Spring Antiques
436 Spring Rd. (S. Bullard). Est. 1970. Open 9.30-1. CL: Thurs. SIZE: Small. *STOCK: Clocks, brass, silver and plate, china, jewellery.* Not Stocked: Coins, stamps. LOC: From Woodbridge on A1214, bear left at 2nd roundabout for town centre then take left fork at Lattice Barn Inn. Shop opposite Inskil school. PARK: 50yds. in adjacent streets. TEL: 0473 725606.

Thompson's
418 Norwich Rd. (D. and Mrs S. Thompson). Est. 1978. Open 9-5. CL: Sun. except by appointment. SIZE: Medium. *STOCK: Furniture, mainly late Victorian and shipping, 1870 to date, £10-£1,000.* LOC: 1 mile from town centre, on corner at traffic lights next to railway bridge. PARK: Own, at side of premises. TEL: 0473 747793; home - 0473 259199. SER: Valuations; buys at auction (shipping items). VAT: Stan/Spec.

C.A. Wall
11 St. Peter's St. Est. 1972. Open 9.30-5.30. *STOCK: Furniture, £1-£1,200.* LOC: Past Town Hall, down Queen St., St. Nicholas St. to St. Peter's St. PARK: Silent St. TEL: 0473 214366. SER: Restorations. VAT: Stan/Spec.

Gerald Weir Antiques
7-11 Vermont Rd. Open by appointment only. SIZE: Large. *STOCK: Georgian and Victorian furniture.* TEL: 0473 252606/255572.

SUFFOLK

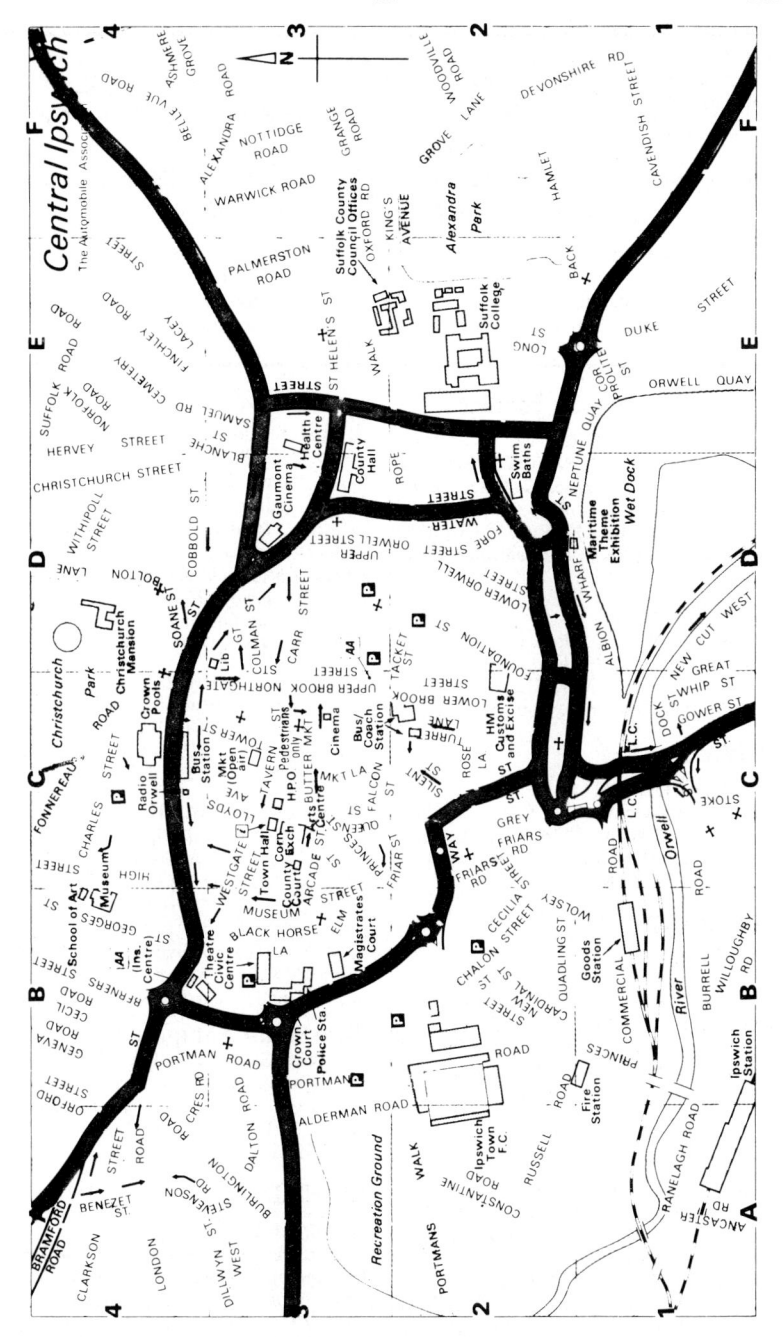

Key to Town Plan

AA Recommended roads	Car Parks
Other roads	Parks and open spaces
Restricted roads	AA Service Centre
Buildings of interest	© Automobile Association 1988.

E.W. Cousins and Son
LAPADA MEMBER

Established since 1910

Main Warehouse, The Old School, Ixworth, Near Bury St. Edmunds, Suffolk

Tel: (0359) 30254 Fax: (0359) 32370

Specialists in Georgian and Victorian furniture
Large selection of clocks and barometers

20,000 sq. ft. of selected furniture
Export Trade welcome
Containers packed
Wholesale and Retail Trade

IXWORTH, Nr. Bury St. Edmunds

E.W. Cousins and Son LAPADA
27 High St, and The Old School. CL: Sat. p.m. SIZE: Large and warehouse. *STOCK: General antiques, 18th-19th C, £50-£6,000; shipping items.* LOC: A143. PARK: Easy. TEL: 0359 30254. SER: Valuations; restorations. VAT: Stan/Spec.

Ixworth Antiques
17 High St. (M. Ginders). Open 10-5. CL: Wed. *STOCK: Victorian and Edwardian furniture, brass and silver plate.* PARK: Easy. TEL: 0359 31691. SER: Polishing (brass); plating (silver).

KESGRAVE

Mainline Furniture
83 Main Rd. (Mr and Mrs R.S. Rust). Est. 1977. Open 9-6. CL: Wed. *STOCK: Furniture, Victorian to 1950's; china and collectables, clocks.* TEL: 0473 623092.

KESSINGLAND

Kessingland Antiques
36A High St. Est. 1976. Open 10-5.30. SIZE: Large. *STOCK: Edwardian, Victorian furniture, general antiques and collectables, watches, clocks, jewellery, shipping goods.* LOC: On A12, 3 miles south of Lowestoft. PARK: On forecourt and own. TEL: 0502 740562. VAT: Stan/Spec.

LAVENHAM, Nr. Sudbury

Antiques
14a High St. (Mrs Cherrie McNeilage). Est. 1975. Open 11-4.30, Wed. 2.30-4.30, Sat. 10.30-5. SIZE: Small. *STOCK: Jewellery, fine linen and lace, textiles and decorative items,1800-1920,£50-£500.* PARK: Easy. TEL: 0787 248524; home - 0206 262105. SER: Valuations; restorations (jewellery). FAIRS: Snape, Bury St. Edmunds. VAT: Stan/Spec.

R.G. Archer
7 Water St. Est. 1970. Open 9-5, Sun. 10-5. *STOCK: Antiquarian and secondhand books.* TEL: 0787 247229.

Lavenham continued

J. and J. Baker
12-14 Water St, and 3a High St. (C.J. and Mrs B.A.J. Baker). Est. 1960. Open 9-1 and 2-5.30. SIZE: Medium. *STOCK: Oak and mahogany furniture, 1600-1870, £100-£10,000; oils and watercolours, 19th C, £150-£5,000; English porcelain and metalware, 18th-19th C, £20-£1,000; collectors' items, £20-£1,000.* LOC: Below Swan Hotel at T junction of A1141 and B1071. PARK: Easy. TEL: 0787 247610. VAT: Stan/Spec.

Lavenham Antiques
74 Water St. (Keith and Margot McCarthy). Open 10-5, Sun. 10-2. CL: Wed. *STOCK: Country furniture, Staffordshire, metalware including brass, and textiles.* TEL: 0787 248348.

Motts of Lavenham
8 Water St. (J.G. and D.M. Mott). Est. 1980. Open 10-4.30, Sun. by appointment. SIZE: Small. *STOCK: Furniture, £20-£1,000; pottery and porcelain, £5-£350; all 19th C; metal toys and diecasts, 20th C, 20p-£100.* LOC: Off High St. by Swan Hotel, shop 200yds. on left. PARK: Easy. TEL: 0449 736637; home - same. SER: Buys at auction (tinplate and diecasts). VAT: Stan.

Tom Smith Antiques
36 Market Place. Est. 1959. SIZE: Large and warehouse. *STOCK: Furniture, early Staffordshire figures, rugs, early maps and decorative prints.* TEL: 0787 247463. SER: Valuations; restorations. VAT: Stan/Spec.

LAXFIELD

Mangate Gallery LAPADA
Old Vicarage. (Mrs S. Beamish). Est. 1968. Open by appointment only. SIZE: Medium. *STOCK: English and continental watercolours and oils, 1800-1960, £150-£10,000.* LOC: Between Framlingham, Stradbroke and Halesworth on the B1117. PARK: Easy. TEL: 0986 798 524. SER: Cleaning and framing. VAT: Spec.

LEAVENHEATH
Clock House
Locks Lane. (A.G. Smeeth). Est. 1983. Open by appointment. SIZE: Small. *STOCK: English clocks, 17th to early 19th C, £1,000-£5,000; French and English clocks, Victorian and Edwardian, £200-£1,000.* PARK: Easy. TEL: 0206 262187; home - same. SER: Valuations; restorations (clocks and furniture); buys at auction (clocks and furniture).

LEISTON
Leiston Furniture Warehouses
High St. (J.R. Warren). Est. 1980. CL: Wed. and Sat. p.m. except by appointment. SIZE: Medium. *STOCK: Furniture, Georgian, Victorian, Edwardian and shipping oak, £20-£2,000.* Not Stocked: Clocks, china, brass and bric-a-brac. LOC: Off High St., driveway beside Geaters Florists. PARK: Easy. TEL: 0728 831414; home - same. SER: Valuations; restorations (furniture). VAT: Stan/Spec.

Leiston Trading Post
13a High St. (A.E. Moore). Est. 1967. Open 10-1 and 2-5, other times by appointment. CL: Wed. pm. *STOCK: Bric-a-brac, Victoriana, Victorian and Edwardian furniture.* PARK: Easy. TEL: 0728 830081; home - 0728 830281. VAT: Stan.

LONG MELFORD
Antique Clocks by Simon Charles
Little St. Mary's Court, Hall St. Est. 1970. Open 9.30-1 and 2-5.30, Sat. 9.30-5, Wed. by appointment. SIZE: Medium. *STOCK: Clocks especially longcase, 17th-19th C, £150-£10,000; barometers, 18th-19th C, £150-£1,000.* LOC: Opposite fire station on main road. PARK: Easy. TEL: 0787 880040; home - 0787 375931. SER: Valuations; restorations (clock movements and cases); buys at auction (clocks). FAIRS: Snape and Bury St. Edmunds. VAT: Stan/Spec.

Ashley Gallery
Belmont House, Hall St. Est. 1965. Open 9.30-5.30 or by appointment. SIZE: Medium. *STOCK: Paintings, watercolour drawings, furniture, porcelain, Oriental rugs.* LOC: A134, opposite Crown Hotel. PARK: Easy. TEL: 0787 375434. VAT: Spec.

Raine Bell
Little St. Marys. Est. 1978. Open 10-1 and 2-5. SIZE: Small. *STOCK: Mahogany furniture, paintings, early 19th C, £500-£1,000.* LOC: Main road opposite fire station. PARK: Easy. TEL: 0787 880040; home - 0787 248298. SER: Restorations. VAT: Spec.

Roger Carling and Tess Sinclair LAPADA
Coconut House, Hall St. Resident. **Usually open 10-1 and 2-5, other times by appointment.** *STOCK: Furniture, mahogany and oak, 18th-19th*

Long Melford continued
C; general antiques, metalware, clocks, barometers, textiles, mirrors, decorative items. TEL: 0787 312012.

Chater-House Gallery
Foundry House, Hall St. (A.D. Chater-House). Open 10-5. SIZE: 14 showrooms. *STOCK: Furniture, Georgian, Victorian and Edwardian; pianos.* TEL: 0787 379831. SER: Valuations; restorations (furniture); upholstery.

Bruno Cooper Antiques
Little St. Marys Court. Est. 1984. Open 10-5.30. SIZE: Medium. *STOCK: Period furniture and works of art, late 17th to early 19th C, £500-£15,000; paintings and bronzes, £500-£15,000.* Not Stocked: Silver, Victoriana and bric-a-brac. LOC: Near Fire Station on main road. PARK: Easy. TEL: 0787 312613; home - 0603 54038. VAT: Spec.

The Enchanted Aviary
63 Hall St. (C.C. Frost). Est. 1970. Open most days, but appointment advisable. SIZE: Medium. *STOCK: Cased and uncased mounted birds, animals, fish, mostly late Victorian, £15-£800.* PARK: Easy. TEL: 0787 378814. VAT: Spec.

---

free!

28 page full colour catalogue of Antique Collectors' Club books. Over 120 titles included covering a wide range of subjects: furniture, art reference, art history, prints, jewellery, metalwork, glass, horology, ceramics, oriental carpets, collectables, garden history and design, gardening and architecture.

Available free from the
ANTIQUE COLLECTORS' CLUB

5 Church Street
Woodbridge
Suffolk IP12 1DS
Tel: (0394) 385501
Fax: (0394) 384434

Long Melford Antiques Centre

NOW BIGGER and BETTER

In addition to the well-known Chapel Maltings premises, we now have the adjacent White Hart extension with its ample parking area, housing many more displays of quality furniture, silver, pictures, clocks, objets d'art, dolls and decorator accessories.

Open Mon-Sat 10am-5.30pm
Chapel Maltings/White Hart, Long Melford
Suffolk. Phone: SUDBURY 0787 79287

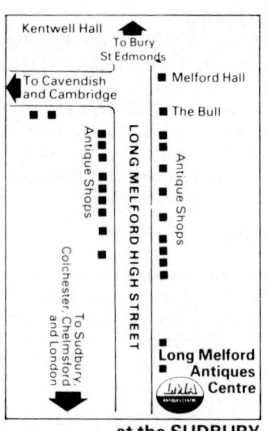

at the SUDBURY end of the town.

Kentwell Hall — To Bury St Edmonds
To Cavendish and Cambridge
Melford Hall
The Bull
LONG MELFORD HIGH STREET
Antique Shops
Colchester, Chelmsford
To Sudbury, Chelmsford and London
Long Melford Antiques Centre

Long Melford continued

Long Melford Antiques Centre
The Chapel Maltings, and the adjacent White Hart Annexe. (Baroness V. von Dahlen). Est. 1984. Open 9.30-5.30 or by appointment. SIZE: Large - 55 dealers. *STOCK: Furniture - early oak, Queen Anne, Georgian, Edwardian and Victorian; silver, china, glass, clocks, dolls, toys and decorators' items, £5-£10,000.* LOC: A134, Sudbury end of village. PARK: Ample, behind White Hart. TEL: 0787 379287/310316. SER: Valuations; restorations (furniture); packing and shipping; buys at auction. VAT: Stan/Spec.

Alexander Lyall Antiques
Belmont House, Hall St. (A.J. Lyall). Est. 1977. Open 9.30-5.30. SIZE: Medium. *STOCK: Furniture, 18th-19th C.* LOC: A134 opposite Crown Hotel. PARK: Easy. TEL: 0787 375434; home - same. SER: Restorations (furniture); buys at auction (English furniture). VAT: Stan/Spec.

Magpie Antiques
Hall St. (Mrs P. Coll). Est. 1985. Open 10.30-1 and 2.15-5, Sat. 10.30-5. CL: Mon. and Wed. SIZE: Small. *STOCK: Smalls including hand-painted china; furniture, Victorian and stripped pine.* LOC: Main street. PARK: Easy. TEL: 0787 310581; home - same.

Long Melford continued

Patrick Marney
The Gate House, Melford Hall. Est. 1964. Open by appointment. SIZE: Small. *STOCK: Fine barometers, 18th-19th C, £1,000-£5,000; pocket aneroids, 19th C, £150-£1,000; scientific instruments, 18th-19th C, £250-£2,000; all fully restored.* LOC: A134. PARK: Easy. TEL: 0787 880533; home - 0787 379193. SER: Valuations; restorations (mercury barometers). VAT: Stan.

Melford Fine Arts
Little St. Mary's. (L. Chambers and D. Keens). Open 10-1 and 2-5.30, Sun. 2-5. CL: Mon. *STOCK: General antiques.* TEL: 0787 312174.

Noel Mercer Antiques
Aurora House, Hall St. Est. 1990. Open 9.30-1 and 2-5.30. SIZE: Medium. *STOCK: Early oak and walnut furniture and works of art, £500-£10,000.* LOC: Centre of Hall St. PARK: Easy. TEL: 0787 311882; home - 0206 323558. SER: Valuations; buys at auction (early oak and walnut). VAT: Spec.

Neptune Antiques   LAPADA
Hall St. (P. and M. Horsman). Est. 1969. Open 10-5.30, Sun. by appointment. SIZE: Large. *STOCK: Furniture, £500-£15,000; objects, £100-£2,000; both 17th-18th C.* LOC: A134 near Bull Hotel. TEL: 0787 375787; home - 0473 251110; fax - 0787 375242. SER:

Long Melford continued

Valuations; restorations (17th-18th C furniture); buys at auction (17th-18th C furniture). FAIRS: Olympia, Barbican, British International, Birmingham. VAT: Spec.

Seabrook Antiques Ltd
Old Maltings Antique Company, Hall St. (D. Edwards and J. Tanner). Open 9.30-5.30. SIZE: Large. *STOCK: Oak country furniture, continental and English mahogany, decorative items, 17th-20th C.* TEL: 0787 379638; fax - 0787 311788; home - same.

Oswald Simpson   BADA LAPADA
Hall St. Est. 1971. Open 9.30-5.30, other times by appointment. *STOCK: Early oak and country furniture, £25-£10,000; brass, copper, pewter and country items, £10-£500; all 17th-19th C; samplers and needlework, 17th-20th C, £25-£1,000.* PARK: Easy. TEL: 0787 377523; home - 0449 740030. SER: Valuations; restorations. VAT: Spec.

Suthburgh Antiques
Red House, Hall St. (R.P. Alston). Est. 1977. Open 12-5. SIZE: Medium. *STOCK: Furniture, 17th C oak, 18th C mahogany, £500-£5,000; Georgian barometers and clocks, £400-£15,000; small collectors' items, boxes, glass, brass, copper, oak carvings and panels, £50-£600.* Not Stocked: Victorian furniture and later items. LOC: Opposite Bull Hotel, A134. PARK: Easy. TEL: 0787 374818; home - same. SER: Valuations; restorations (furniture, barometers); buys at auction. VAT: Stan/Spec.

Tudor Antiques
Little St. Marys. (A.H. Denton-Ford). Est. 1974. Open 9.30-5.30. SIZE: Large. *STOCK: General antiques, £5-£5,000; curios, silver, objets d'art, small furniture, bygones.* LOC: Sudbury end of Long Melford, shop with yellow blind. PARK: Easy. TEL: 0787 375950. SER: Valuations; metal polishing; repairs (metal, clocks, barometers). VAT: Stan/Spec.

Village Clocks
Little St. Mary's. (J.C. Massey). Est. 1975. Open 10-5, Sat. 9.30-5. CL: Wed. SIZE: Small. *STOCK: Clocks - longcase, bracket, wall and mantle, 18th-19th C, £500-£2,500; carriage, 19th C, £500-£1,000.* PARK: Easy. TEL: 0787 375896. SER: Valuations; restorations (as stock); buys at auction (clocks). FAIRS: Uxbridge Horological, Brunel University.

Ward Antiques plc   LAPADA
Hall St. Est. 1982. Open 10-1 and 2-5.30, Sun. by appointment. SIZE: Large. *STOCK: Furniture, 17th to early 19th C, £100-£40,000.* Not Stocked: Silver and glass. LOC: A134. PARK: Easy. TEL: 0787 378265; fax - same; home - 0284 830151. SER: Valuations; restorations; buys at auction (furniture). VAT: Stan/Spec.

LOWESTOFT

Carlton Road Antiques
1 Carlton Rd. (A. and I. Murray). Est. 1983. Open 9.30-5, Sat. 9.30-5.30. SIZE: Large. *STOCK: Stripped pine, £25-£1,000; Victorian furniture, £100-£2,000; china, paintings, mirrors, silver and collectables, £25-£100; all 18th-20th C.* LOC: From A12 into Lowestoft, approximately 2 miles from Bloodmoor Lane roundabout, turn left into Carlton Road. PARK: Easy. TEL: 0502 512946; home - 0502 713896.

Paul Foulger
157 London Road South. Open 9-5. *STOCK: Furniture, paintings and bric-a-brac.* TEL: 0502 573154.

North End Antiques
56-57 High St. (Mr. and Mrs. Fletcher). Open 9-5.30. *STOCK: Victorian furniture and collectables.* TEL: 0502 568535.

W. Taylor Antiques
13 St. Peter's St. (W.D.J. Taylor). Est. 1965. Open Tues., Fri. and Sat. 10-4. SIZE: Small. *STOCK: Furniture, 1840-1910, £5-£250; pictures, 1830-1920, £3-£100; bygones and bric-a-brac, £1-£100.* LOC: Opposite Market Place, High St., A12. PARK: 100yds. opposite. TEL: 0502 573374; home - 0502 730421.

Windsor Gallery
167 London Rd. South. (R.W. Glanfield). Open 9-5. *STOCK: Paintings.* TEL: 0502 512278.

MARLESFORD

Antique Warehouse
Main Rd. Open 9-5. SIZE: Medium. *STOCK: Furniture, period mirrors, decorative lighting and general antiques; hand crafted country furniture.* LOC: A12. PARK: Easy. TEL: 0728 747438; fax - 0728 747426.

MARTLESHAM, Nr. Woodbridge

Martlesham Antiques
The Thatched Roadhouse. (R.F. Frost). Est. 1973. Open daily, Sun. by appointment. SIZE: Large. *STOCK: Furniture and decorative items, 17th-20th C, £25-£3,000.* LOC: A1214 opposite Red Lion public house. PARK: Own. TEL: 0394 386732; fax - 0394 382959.

John Read
29 Lark Rise, Martlesham Heath. Est. 1992. By appointment. SIZE: Small. *STOCK: Staffordshire pottery figures and animals including coloured glaze, underglaze (Pratt) and enamel decoration, 1780-1850, to £2,500.* LOC: A12 Ipswich bypass, opposite B.T. tower. PARK: Easy. TEL: 0473 624897; home - same. SER: Valuations; restorations (as stock); buys at auction.

SUFFOLK

MILDENHALL
Freya Antiques
at Eros Garden Centre, Kenny Hill. Open 10-5. STOCK: General antiques especially upholstered items. PARK: Easy. TEL: 0284 89267; mobile - 0831 651898. SER: Restorations; re-upholstery.

Hunt and Clement
10 North Terrace. Open 10-5.30, Sun. 2-5. STOCK: Pine, Victorian, Edwardian and 1920's shipping goods. TEL: 0638 718025.

NEEDHAM MARKET
Roy Arnold
77 High St. Est. 1974. Open 9.30-5.30 appointment advisable, Sun. by appointment. SIZE: Medium. STOCK: Woodworkers' and craftsmen's tools, scientific instruments and books, including antiquarian, £10-£5,000. LOC: A45, centre of High St. PARK: Easy. TEL: 0449 720110. VAT: Stan/Spec.

The Old Town Hall Antique Centre
High St. (S. and R. Abbott). Open 10-5. SIZE: Several dealers. STOCK: General antiques. TEL: 0449 720773. SER: Repairs (jewellery).

NEWMARKET
Equus Art Gallery
Sun Lane. (L. Eveleigh and T. Minahan). Est. 1989. Open 9.30-5.30. CL: Wed. p.m. SIZE: Medium. STOCK: Equine oils, watercolours and sculpture, 19th-20th C, £300-£1,000; equine prints, 18th-20th C, £50-£2,000. LOC: Off High St. PARK: Nearby. TEL: 0638 560445; home - 0638 666637. VAT: Stan.

Jemima Godfrey
5 Rous Rd. (Miss A. Lanham). Est. 1968. Open Thurs. and Fri. 10-1 and 2-4.30. SIZE: Small. STOCK: Small antiques, jewellery and linen, 19th C. LOC: Just off High St., near clock tower. PARK: Easy. TEL: 0638 663584.

Newmarket Gallery
156 High St. (N.R. Herbert). Resident. Open 9.30-1 and 2-5, Sun. and Wed. by appointment. SIZE: Small. STOCK: Sporting prints, drawings, pictures. LOC: A11 at south end of High St. PARK: Easy. TEL: 0638 661183. SER: Valuations; restorations; buys at auction.

R.E. and G.B. Way
Brettons, Burrough Green. Open 8.30-5.30 appointment advisable. STOCK: Antiquarian and secondhand books on shooting, fishing, horses, racing and hunting and small general section. TEL: 0638 507217.

ORFORD
Castle Antiques
Market Sq. (S. Simpkin). Est. 1969. Open daily

Orford continued
including Sun. 11-4.30. SIZE: Medium. STOCK: Furniture, general small antiques, bric-a-brac glass, china, clocks. TEL: 0394 450100.

PEASENHALL, Nr. Saxmundham
Peasenhall Art and Antiques Gallery
The Street. (A. and M. Wickins). Resident. Est. 1972 Open every day. STOCK: 19th C watercolours and oils; country furniture, all woods; walking sticks TEL: 072 879 224; home - same. SER: Restorations (oils, watercolours, furniture). VAT: Spec.

RISBY, Nr. Bury St. Edmunds
The Risby Barn
(R. and S. Martin). Open 9-5.30, Sun. and Bank Holidays 10-5. SIZE: 24 dealers. STOCK Furniture, porcelain, metalware, tools, pine, ar deco. LOC: Just off A45 west of Bury St Edmunds. TEL: 0284 811126.

SAXMUNDHAM
Antiques and Country Things
The Old Shop, 49 North Entrance, (High St.). (K Veness). Est. 1982. Open 11-5.30. CL: Thurs. p.m SIZE: Large. STOCK: General antiques including small furniture, collectables, bric-a-brac, jewellery 18th-19th C, £1-£1,000. LOC: Opposite bus station near bridge. TEL: 0728 604171.

SNAPE
Snape Antiques and Collectors Centre
Snape Maltings. Est. 1992. Open 7 days 10-6 o until dusk in winter. SIZE: 50 dealers. STOCK General antiques and collectors' items including silver, linen, lace and textiles, country an decorative items. PARK: Easy. TEL: 0728 888038.

SOUTHWOLD
The Emporium Antiques and Collectors Centre
70 High St. (Michael Brown). Est. 1992. Ope 10-5.30, Sun. 12-5. SIZE: Over 30 dealers STOCK: Wide range of general antiques an collectables. PARK: Nearby. TEL: 0502 723909.

SPROUGHTON, Nr. Ipswich
Sproughton Antiques
16/18 Lower St. (L. Pulham). Est. 1992. Open 10 5, Wed. by appointment, Sat. 9-1. SIZE: Small STOCK: Furniture, 17th-19th C, £50-£2,500 objets d'art. TEL: 0473 741661. LOC: Off A12 a Post House on to A1100 to village. Premise opposite Wild Man public house. PARK: Easy SER: Restorations (furniture.)

STOWMARKET
Trench Puzzles
3 Cow Green, Bacton. STOCK: Antique, ol jigsaw and mechanical puzzles. Mail Order Only.

An Antique Collectors' Club Title

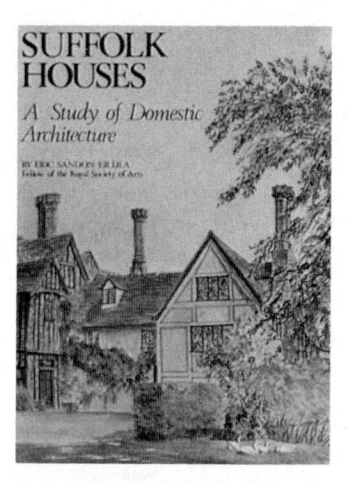

Suffolk Houses
A Study of Domestic Architecture
by Eric Sandon

In the 15th and 16th centuries Suffolk and Norfolk were the most prosperous industrial counties in Britain. Wealth poured into Suffolk, first from the wool staple and then from the cloth trade. Many of the churches were rebuilt and adorned during this period and have been rightly praised. It is strange that, until the publication of this book, so little notice has been taken of Suffolk houses.

The author, Eric Sandon, is a professional architect who has worked for forty years in Suffolk and came to have a deep love of the county and its buildings. As a consequence, this superbly illustrated book gives not only a scholarly and interesting account of the development of house building in the region, but also something of the character of the county itself.

ISBN 0 902028 68 5, 12 x 8 ½ in., 344 pp
389 b & w illus, 94 figs, 10 col, £35.00

Available from:
Antique Collectors' Club, 5 Church Street, Woodbridge, Suffolk IP12 1DS
Tel: (0394) 385501 Fax: (0394) 384434

or Market Street Industrial Park, Wappingers' Falls, New York 12590, USA
Tel: 914 297 0003 Fax: 914 297 0068

SUFFOLK

STRADBROKE, Nr. Eye
Mary Palmer Antiques
The Cottage Farm, New St. (Mrs M.Palmer Stones). Resident. Est. 1980. Open 9-9, Sun. by appointment. SIZE: Small. STOCK: English glass, 1750-1850; furniture, 1700-1900. LOC: B1117. PARK: Easy. TEL: 0379 388100. SER: Valuations; restorations (furniture).

Stubcroft Period Furnishings and Restorations
The Cottage Farm, New St. (G.G. Stones). Est. 1984. Open 9-9 and Sun. pm. SIZE: Small. STOCK: London and country period furniture. LOC: B1117. PARK: Easy. TEL: 0379 388100.

SUDBURY
Antique Clocks by Simon Charles
The Limes, 72 Melford Rd. Est. 1970. Open by appointment only. STOCK: Interesting clocks, especially English longcase, lantern and unusual skeleton clocks,17th-19th C. TEL: 0787 375931. SER: Valuations; free estimates; restorations; repairs.

Napier House Antiques
Church St. Resident. Open 9-5. SIZE: Large. STOCK: Georgian and Victorian furniture. TEL: 0787 375280.

WICKHAM MARKET
Crafers Antiques
The Hill. (Mrs Elizabeth Davies). Est. 1970. Open 9.30-5.30, Tues. and Thurs. 9.30-1 and 2.30-5.30. STOCK: 18th-19th C porcelain and pottery, glass, silver, jewellery, furniture and collectors' items. LOC: Corner of Square, opposite church. PARK: Easy. TEL: 0728 747347 (anytime).

Roy Webb
179 High St. Open Mon., Thurs. and Sat. 10-6 or by appointment. STOCK: Furniture, 18th-19th C; clocks. TEL: 0728 746077; home - 039 43 2697. VAT: Stan.

WOODBRIDGE
Antique Furniture Warehouse
Old Maltings, Crown Pl. (H.T. and R.E. Ferguson). Est. 1976. Usually open 9-5. CL: Sat., Sun. except by appointment. SIZE: Large. STOCK: Furniture, 17th to early 20th C, £200-£10,000; small items. LOC: In centre of town, off Quay St. First warehouse in Crown Place. TEL: 0394 387222. VAT: Stan/Spec. Trade and Export Only.

Bagatelle
40 Market Hill. (N. Lambert). Est. 1990. Open 10.30-5, Wed. and Thur. 10.30-1. SIZE: Medium. STOCK: Orientalia, watercolours, oils and engravings, furniture, china, glass and collectables, 18th-20th C, £10-£2,000. PARK: Nearby. TEL: 0394 380204.

Woodbridge continued
Simon Carter Gallery
23 Market Hill. Est. 1960. Open 9.15-5.30. SIZE: Large. STOCK: English and continental oil paintings, 17th-20th C; English watercolours and drawings, 18th-20th C; furniture, oak and mahogany, 17th-19th C; decorative objects, art deco, studio pottery, some porcelain and prints. Not Stocked: Clocks, silver. PARK: 60yds. behind gallery in Theatre St. TEL: 0394 382242; home - 0394 411894. SER: Three exhibitions held annually. VAT: Spec.

David Gibbins Antiques   BADA
21 Market HIIII. Est. 1964. Open 9.30-5.30, Wed. 9.30-1. STOCK: English furniture, late 16th to early 19th C, £300-£15,000; English pottery and porcelain, metalwork. PARK: Own in Theatre St. TEL: 0394 383531; home - 0394 382685. SER: Valuations; buys at auction. VAT: Spec.

Hamilton Antiques
5 Church St. (H.T. and R.E. Ferguson). Est. 1976. Open 10-5, Wed. 10-1. STOCK: Furniture - mahogany, walnut, oak, fruitwood, 17th-20th C, £200-£10,000. TEL: 0394 387222. VAT: Stan/Spec.

Anthony Hurst Antiques   LAPADA
13 Church St. (C.G.B. Hurst). Est. 1957. Open 9.30-1 and 2-5.30. CL: Wed. p.m. SIZE: Large. STOCK: English furniture, oak, walnut and mahogany, 1600-1900, £100-£5,000. PARK: Easy. TEL: 0394 382500. SER: Valuations; restorations (furniture); buys at auction. VAT: Stan/Spec.

Jenny Jackson Antiques
30 Market Hill. Est. 1960. Open 10.30-1 and 2.30-5 or by appointment. SIZE: Medium. STOCK: General decorative antiques, especially 18th-19th C, including mirrors, rugs, chairs and carvings, £20-£5,000. LOC: Town centre. PARK: Outside shop. TEL: 0394 380667. VAT: Spec.

Lambert's Barn
24A Church St. Open 9.30-1 and 2-5. CL: Wed. p.m. SIZE: Large. STOCK: Mainly Victorian and 20th C furniture, miscellaneous items. PARK: Easy. TEL: 0394 382380.

Edward Manson
8 Market Hill. Open 10-5.30, Wed. 10-1. STOCK: Clocks. TEL: 0394 380235. SER: Restorations (clocks).

Melton Antiques
Kingdom Hall, Melton Rd., Melton. (A. Harvey-Jones). Est. 1975. Open 9.30-5.30. SIZE: Small STOCK: Silver, collector's items, £5-£500, decorative items and furniture, £15-£500; both 18th-19th C; Victoriana and general antiques 19th C, £5-£500. LOC: On right hand-side coming from Woodbridge. PARK: Easy. TEL 0394 386232.

HAMILTON ANTIQUES

5 Church Street
Woodbridge
Suffolk
telephone
(0394) 387222

Always a good selection of
18th, 19th and 20th century good
quality furniture at reasonable prices

See editorial for opening hours

¾ hour from Harwich
½ hour from Felixstowe

SUFFOLK

Suffolk House Antiques
Oak and country furniture
Early pottery and works of art

Suffolk House Antiques
High Street, Yoxford,
Suffolk IP17 3EP.

Telephone Yoxford
(072 877) 8122.

Woodbridge continued

Sarah Meysey-Thompson Antiques
10 Church St. Est. 1962. Open 10-5., Sun. by appointment. SIZE: Medium. STOCK: Small furniture, late 18th to early 19th C; china, glass, decorative items, 19th C; textiles and curtains. PARK: Easy. TEL: 0394 382144; home - 0394 386410. VAT: Spec.

A.G. Voss
24 Market Hill. Est. 1965. Open 10-1 and 2-5. CL: Wed. STOCK: Furniture, 17th to early 19th C, from £65; longcase clocks, 18th C, from £400. PARK: Nearby and at rear. TEL: 0394 385830. SER: Valuations; restorations. VAT: Spec.

WOOLPIT, Nr. Bury St. Edmunds

J.C. Heather
The Old Crown. Est. 1946. Open every day 9-8. SIZE: Large. STOCK: Furniture, 18th-19th C, £20-£1,000. Not Stocked: China. LOC: Near centre of village on right. PARK: Easy. TEL: 0359 40297. VAT: Stan/Spec.

WORTHAM, Nr Eye

The Falcon Gallery
Honeypot Farm. (N. Smith). Resident. Est. 1974. Open by appointment seven days. SIZE: Medium. STOCK: Watercolours and oils, 19th C. LOC: South side of A143 in village centre, overlooking the village green, 4 miles west of Diss. PARK: Easy. TEL: 0379 783312. SER: Annual exhibition in mid-November; valuations; restorations (oils, watercolours); framing. VAT: Stan/Spec.

WRENTHAM, Nr. Beccles

Wren House Antiques
1 High St. (J. and W. Pipe). Open Tues., Thurs. and Sat. 10-5. STOCK: Clocks, china, glass, maps, prints, jewellery. TEL: 0502 75276. SER: Repairs (clocks).

Wrentham Antiques
40-44 High St. (B. Spearing). Always open. SIZE: Large. STOCK: Victorian, Georgian,

Wrentham continued

Edwardian and decorative furniture. LOC: A12. PARK: Easy. TEL: 0502 75583; home - 0502 513633; fax - 0502 75707. SER: Buys at auction. VAT: Stan/Spec.

Wrentham Antiques Centre
The Old Reading Rooms, 7 High Street. Open 10-5.30., Sun. 2-5.30. STOCK: Furniture, china, glass, jewellery, pictures, prints and bric-a-brac. TEL: 0502 75376.

YOXFORD

Red House Antiques
The Red House, Old High Rd. (J. and Mrs M. Trotter). Est. 1987. Open 10-1 and 2-6, Sun. 10-1 and 2-5, Mon. and Wed. by appointment. SIZE: Small. STOCK: Ceramics, 18th-19th C, £5-£1,000; watercolours, 19th-20th C, £100-£800; small furniture, late 18th to early 19th C; objets d'art. Not Stocked: Stamps, arms, silver and clocks. LOC: Off either A1120 or A12, opposite churchyard. PARK: Easy. TEL: 072 877 615; home - same.

Joan Stevens, Bookseller
Rosslyn House, High St. By appointment only. STOCK: Books on literature, poetry, art and women's history. TEL: 0728 77368. SER: Catalogues issued.

Suffolk House Antiques
High St. (A. Singleton). Open 10-1 and 2.15-5.15. CL: Wed. STOCK: 17th-18th C furniture, works of art, paintings, clocks, delftware and metalware. LOC: A1120, just off A12. PARK: Easy. TEL: 072 877 8122.

Gedding Hall — from an engraving in *Excursions through Suffolk,* and a view of the gatehouse. From *Suffolk Houses — A Study of Domestic Architecture* by Eric Sandon, F.R.I.B.A. Reprinted in 1993 by the **Antique Collectors' Club,** £35.00.

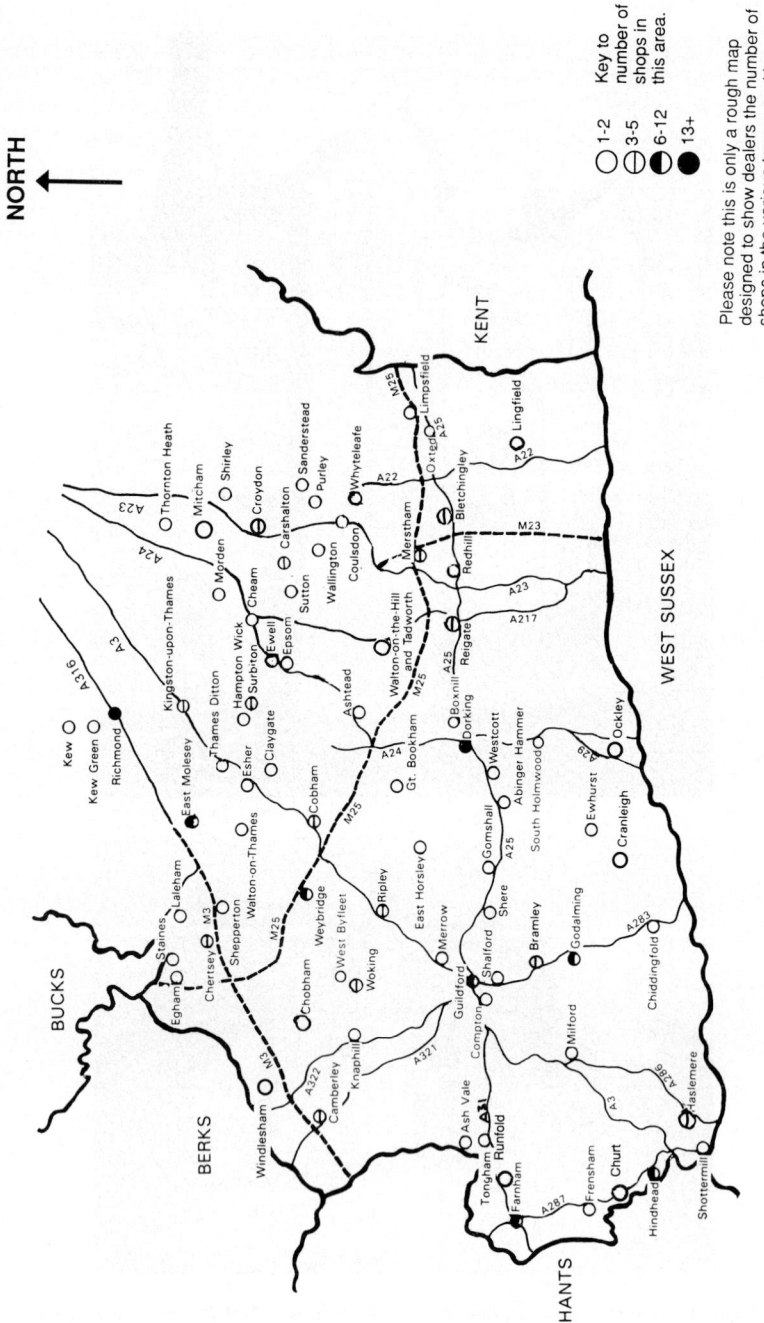

Surrey

Surrey

ABINGER HAMMER

Abinger Bazaar
Guildford Rd. (C. and G. Field). Est. 1978. Open 11.30-5, Thurs., Sat. and Sun. SIZE: Medium. *STOCK: Porcelain, glass, metal, Victorian, Edwardian, 30's and 50's, £1-£300; books, to £50.* LOC: A25 next to trout farm. PARK: Nearby. TEL: 0306 730756.

Stirling Antiques
Aberdeen House. (V.S. Burrell). Est. 1968. Open 9.30-6.30. CL: Thurs. *STOCK: Stained glass, furniture, copper, brass, jewellery, silver, curios, dolls.* PARK: Easy. TEL: 0306 730706. VAT: Stan.

ASH VALE, Nr. Aldershot (Hants)

House of Christian Antiques
5-7 Vale Rd. (A. Bail). Est. 1970. Open 10-5.30. SIZE: Medium. *STOCK: Pine, 19th-20th C, from £30; mahogany and oak furniture, 19th-20th C, £30-£800.* LOC: Take Tongham turning from A31 Hogs Back), right after bridge, over roundabout, left at next roundabout, 1st on left after canal bridge. PARK: Easy. TEL: 0252 314478. SER: Valuations; restorations; stripping.

ASHTEAD

Bumbles
10 The Street. (Bob and Barbara Kay). Open 9.30-5.30. *STOCK: Furniture, lighting, clocks and barometers.* PARK: Easy. TEL: 0372 276219. SER: Restoration and repair (furniture, clocks and barometers); gilding; leathering; polishing.

Memory Lane Antiques
102 The Street. (J. Lock). Est. 1984. Open 10-5. CL: Wed. *STOCK: Toys and general antiques, pre-1920, £5-£1,000.* PARK: Easy. TEL: 0372 273436.

Temptations
8 The Street. (Pauline Watson). FGA, NAG. Open 10-5. *STOCK: Jewellery and silver; reproduction silver frames and earrings.* LOC: Main street. PARK: Easy. TEL: 0372 277713. SER: Valuations; security photography; lecturer. VAT: Stan/Spec.

BLETCHINGLEY

Cider House Galleries Ltd
Corfloh House, 80 High St. (T. Roberts). Est. 1967. Open 9.30-5.30. CL: Sat. p.m. and Sun. except by appointment. SIZE: Large. *STOCK: Paintings, 17th-20th C, from £200.* LOC: A25, behind F.G. Lawrence Auctioneers. PARK: Own. TEL: 0883 742198; fax - 0883 744014. SER: Valuations. VAT: Stan/Spec.

John Anthony Antiques
4 High St. (J.A. and N. Hart). Resident. Open by appointment only. *STOCK: 18th to early 19th C furniture.* TEL: 0883 743197; fax - 0883 742108.

Bletchingley continued

Simon Marsh
The Old Butchers Shop, High St. BAFRA. Est. 1970. Open 10-6. *STOCK: Grandfather clocks; 18th-19th C furniture.* PARK: Easy. TEL: 0883 743350. SER: Restorations (furniture and clocks); upholstery.

Post House Antiques
32 High St. (P. and V. Bradley). Open daily, Sun. by appointment. *STOCK: General antiques especially mirrors, fenders, decorative items and restored lighting.* LOC: A25. PARK: Easy. TEL: 0883 743317. VAT: Stan/Spec.

Quill Antiques
86 High St. (Mrs J. Davies). Est. 1971. Open 10-1 and 2-5.30, other times by appointment. CL: Wed. p.m. *STOCK: General antiques including copper, brass, china, farming bygones, kitchenalia, linen and lace, 50p-£500.* LOC: A25. PARK: Easy. TEL: 0883 743755; home - same.

BRAMLEY, Nr. Guildford

Bramley Antiques
6 High St. (N.J. Drinkwater). Est. 1974. Open 10-1 and 2-5, Sat. 9.30-1 and 2-5.30, Sun. by appointment. CL: Wed. SIZE: Medium. *STOCK: Furniture, £500-£1,000; china, £50-£100; both 18th-19th C. Pictures and prints, 19th C, £5-£25.* LOC: A281 Guildford-Horsham road. PARK: Easy. TEL: 0483 898580. SER: Valuations; restorations (furniture, china and pictures); buys at auction (furniture, china and pictures). FAIRS: Sandown, Dorking Halls. VAT: Stan/Spec.

Drummonds of Bramley Architectural Antiques Ltd
Birtley Farm. Est. 1988. Open 9-6 including Sun. *STOCK: Architectural antiques and salvaged building materials, especially period bathroom equipment, 1800-1950, £30-£8,000.* LOC: 1 mile south of Bramley on A281, on left. PARK: Easy. TEL: 0483 898766; fax - 0483 894393. SER: Restorations (stonework and gates); vitreous re-enamelling of baths. VAT: Stan/Spec.

Memories
High St. (P. Kelsey). Est. 1984. Open 10-5. SIZE: Small - 7 dealers. *STOCK: Victorian and Edwardian furniture, china and glass, silver, linen and lace, collectables and bygones, kitchenalia, stripped pine furniture, art deco.* LOC: South of Guildford on A281. PARK: Easy. TEL: 0483 892205.

CAMBERLEY

235 Antiques
235 London Rd. (R.G. and P.T. Ellis). Est. 1977. Open 10-1 and 2-4. CL: Mon. and Wed. SIZE: Small. *STOCK: Furniture, clocks and silver, 19th-20th C, from £20.* LOC: A30. PARK: Easy. TEL: 0276 24071/32123. SER: Restorations (furniture and clocks).

SURREY

Camberley continued

Antiques - Sheila White
Sandhurst Farmhouse, 207 Yorktown Rd., College Town. *STOCK: General antiques.* LOC: Barn at rear of premises. TEL: 0252 873290.

The Pedlar
231 London Rd. (Z. da Costa). Open 10-5. *STOCK: Georgian and Victorian furniture; general antiques, Chinese porcelain.* TEL: 0276 64750.

CARSHALTON

Antiques
314 Carshalton Rd. (E.M. Marshall). CL: Wed. p.m. *STOCK: General antiques, especially Victorian and Edwardian oil lamps.* TEL: 081 642 2108.

Cambridge Parade Antiques
229-231 Carshalton Rd. Open 10-5. CL: Mon. SIZE: 18 dealers. *STOCK: Wide range of general antiques.* LOC: A232. TEL: 081 643 0014.

Carshalton Antique Galleries
5 High St. (B.A. Gough). Est. 1968. Open 9-5. CL: Wed. SIZE: Large. *STOCK: General antiques, furniture, clocks, glass, china, pictures. Not Stocked: Silver, jewellery, bronze, firearms.* PARK: Nearby. TEL: 081 647 5664; home - 0306 887187. VAT: Stan/Spec.

Cherub Antiques
312 Carshalton Rd. (M. Wisdom). Open 10.30-5.30. CL: Wed. *STOCK: Pine and general antiques.* TEL: 081 643 0028.

CHEAM

Rogers Antiques and Rogers Antique Interiors   LAPADA
22 Ewell Rd, Cheam Village. (M. and C. Rogers). Est. 1971. Open 10-5.30. SIZE: Medium. *STOCK: Furniture, 18th-19th C, £100-£2,000; upholstered and boardroom furniture, Tillman dining tables.* LOC: Village centre, just off Sutton by-pass, A217. PARK: 50yds. TEL: 081 643 8466. SER: Valuations; interior design. VAT: Stan/Spec.

CHERTSEY

Chertsey Antiques
8 Windsor St. (Mrs J. Langmead and Mrs J. Ryan). Open 10-5.30, Wed. 12-5.30. *STOCK: General antiques.* TEL: 0932 563565. SER: Framing.

Mister Sun Antiques
96 Guildford St. (R. Lee). Open 10-5.30. CL: Mon. *STOCK: General antiques.* TEL: 0932 566323.

Surrey Antiques Centre
10 Windsor St. (P.L. Allen). Open 10-5. SIZE: 7 dealers. *STOCK: Furniture, jewellery, glass,*

Chertsey continued

pottery and porcelain, silver, pictures, kitchenalia, books, linen and lace. TEL: 0932 563313 home - 0932 841097.

CHIDDINGFOLD, Nr. Godalming
Manor House Interiors
1 Petworth Rd. (M. Pendleton). *STOCK: Small English collectables, paintings, mirrors, lighting silver, interior design accessories and decorative items; some furniture.* LOC: On A283, near village green. PARK: Easy. TEL: 0428 682727.

CHOBHAM

Greengrass Antiques   LAPADA
Hookstone Farm, Hookstone Lane, West End (D. Greengrass). Open by appointment only *STOCK: Decorative items; furniture, 19th C works of art; shipping goods.* TEL: 027 857582.

The Tarrystone
40-42 High St. (Mrs D. Hanbury). Est. 1960 Open 9-1 and 2-5, Sat. 9-2. *STOCK: Furniture brass, porcelain.* PARK: Easy. TEL: 027 857494.

CHURT, Nr. Farnham
Churt Curiosity Shop
Crossways. (Mark D. Stacey). Est. 1986. Open 10.30-4.30, Sat. 10.30-4. CL: Mon. and Thurs SIZE: Small. *STOCK: Pottery and porcelain small furniture and collectables, 19th-20th C, £5 £400.* LOC: A287 Farnham to Hindhead road PARK: Easy. TEL: 0428 714096; home - 025 764072.

COBHAM

Antics
44 Portsmouth Rd. (K. Needham). Est. 196 Open 9.30-1 and 2-5.30. SIZE: Large. *STOCK Pine furniture, rustic and farmhouse antique: shipping goods.* LOC: A3. PARK: Easy. TEL 0932 865505. VAT: Stan.

Cobham Galleries
65 Portsmouth Rd. (Mrs Jerry Burkard and M T.B. Boyle). Open 10-5, Sun. 11-5. *STOCK Period and country furniture, 19th and early 20, C oils and watercolours, longcase clocks.* LOC South off A3, on second roundabout. PARK Driveway beside shop. TEL: 0932 867909. SER Buys at auction; searches.

COMPTON, Nr. Guildford
The Old Post Office Antiques   LAPAD
The Street. (D. Ford). Open Thurs., Fri. an Sat. 10-5.30. *STOCK: Furniture, Englis, continental and decorative, £100-£3,000 bronzes and porcelain, pictures and decorati items.* LOC: A3 beyond Guildford fro

Compton continued
London, left on to B3000, shop 300yds. on left. PARK: Easy. TEL: 0483 810303; home - same. SER: Valuations. VAT: Stan/Spec.

COULSDON
Decodream
233 Chipstead Valley Rd. Open by appointment only. *STOCK: Pottery - Clarice Cliff, Shorter, Shelley, Foley, F. and C. Rhead and Carlton ware.* PARK: Free. TEL: 081 668 5534.

David Potashnick Antiques
7 The Parade, Stoats Nest Rd. Open 9-5.30, Sat. 9-12 or by appointment. *STOCK: General antiques.* TEL: 081 660 8403. SER: Restorations (furniture).

CRANLEIGH
Pat and Terry Gasson Antiques and Interiors
Open by appointment. *STOCK: Georgian, Victorian and Edwardian furniture, clocks, porcelain and decorative items.* TEL: 0483 277476; mobile - 0860 827651.

Barbara Rubenstein Fine Art
Smithwood House, Smithwood Common. Open by appointment. *STOCK: Watercolours and some oils, 19th-20th C, £250-£7,500.* TEL: 0483 267969; fax - 0483 267535.

CROYDON
Collectors Corner Antiques
43 Brighton Rd, South Croydon. (R. and A. Pope). Est. 1980. CL: Mon. and Wed. *STOCK: Dolls, tin toys, dinkies, lead soldiers and animals, furniture, bric-a-brac.* TEL: 081 680 7511.

G.E. Griffin
43a Brighton Rd, South Croydon. (E.J.H. Robinson). Est. 1896. Open 8-5.30, Sat. 9-5. SIZE: Large. *STOCK: General antiques.* TEL: 081 688 3130. SER: Restorations; upholstery.

Trengove
46 South End. Est. 1890. Open 9-6. SIZE: Large. *STOCK: General antiques, Victoriana; oils, watercolours, 18th-19th C.* LOC: On main road through Croydon. TEL: 081 688 2155. SER: Valuations. VAT: Stan/Spec.

The Whitgift Galleries
77 South End. FATG. Est. 1945. *STOCK: Paintings, 19th-20th C.* TEL: 081 688 0990. SER: Restorations; conservation, framing. VAT: Spec.

DORKING
Antiquaries Antique Centre
56 West St. Open 9.30-5.30. SIZE: Several dealers. *STOCK: Furniture, decorative items, clocks, silver and boxes.* TEL: 0306 743398.

Dorking continued
Tom Burton and Rod Johnston
1st Floor, Dorking Antique Centre, 17/18 West St. Est. 1989. Open 10-5.30. SIZE: Small. *STOCK: Ceramics, mainly British, including ironstone and blue and white; Victoriana including desk sets, 19th C, £50-£300; small furniture, Victorian and Edwardian, £50-£500.* PARK: Nearby. TEL: 0306 740915. FAIRS: Ardingly and Surrey.

Noel Collins
15 West St. Est. 1975. Open 10-5. CL: Wed. *STOCK: Jewellery.*

T. M. Collins
70 High St. Est. 1963. SIZE: Medium. *STOCK: Jewellery, 1800-1900, £25-£3,000.* LOC: Opposite Boots chemist. PARK: Behind shop. TEL: 0306 880790. SER: Valuations; restorations (jewellery). VAT: Stan.

J. and M. Coombes
44 West St. Est. 1965. Open 9-5. *STOCK: General antiques.* TEL: 0306 885479. VAT: Stan.

Dorking Antique Centre
17/18 West St. (Mrs G.D. Emburey). Est. 1989. Open 10-5.30. SIZE: 30 dealers. *STOCK: Period and pine furniture, silver, porcelain, jewellery, copper and brass, pictures and prints, decorative and collectors' items.* LOC: Continuation of High St. into one-way system. PARK: Opposite. TEL: 0306 740915. SER: Restorations.

Dorking Desk Shop   LAPADA
41 West St. (J.G. Elias). Est. 1969. Open 8-1 and 2-5.30, Sat. 10.30-1 and 2-5. SIZE: Large. STOCK: Desks, especially partners, cylinder bureaux, davenports, kneehole and pedestal, 18th to mid-20th C, £100-£10,000. PARK: Nearby. TEL: 0306 883327; evenings - 0306 880535; fax - 0306 875363. VAT: Stan/Spec.

Dorking Emporium Antiques Centre
1A West St. (Mrs S.M. Kenny). Est. 1982. Open 10-5. SIZE: Medium. *STOCK: Furniture, mainly mahogany, 18th-19th C, £100-£5,000; art deco items, including furniture, £15-£700; country bygones, books, collectables.* LOC: A25. PARK: Nearby. TEL: 0306 876646; home - 0883 627270.

Hampshires of Dorking
50-52 West St. (Thorpe and Foster plc). Open 9.30-1 and 2.15-5.30. SIZE: Large. *STOCK: English walnut, mahogany and satinwood furniture, 18th C, £500-£50,000.* PARK: At rear. TEL: 0306 887076/881029 (ansaphone); fax - same. VAT: Spec.

Hebeco
47 West St. Est. 1982. Open 10.30-5. SIZE: Small. *STOCK: Silver and plate, antique and 20th C, £5-£1,000; glass, 18th-20th C, £5-£300; pewter, 17th-19th C; blue and white porcelain, 18th-19th C.* LOC: Off High St. PARK: Nearby.

Dorking continued

TEL: 0306 875396 (answerphone). SER: Valuations. FAIRS: Country Houses. VAT: Stan.

E. Hollander Ltd BADA
The Dutch House, Horsham Rd., South Holmwood. (D.J. and B. Pay). CINOA, BHI. Open by appointment. STOCK: Longcase and bracket clocks, 1675-1860; silver, Sheffield plate, English barometers, 18th-19th C. TEL: 0306 888921. SER: Restorations (clock mechanisms and cases, barometers). FAIRS: Chelsea; Olympia (Summer and Autumn). VAT: Stan/Spec.

Holmwood Antiques
Norfolk Rd, South Holmwood. (R. Dewdney). Open 9-6.30, evenings and weekends by appointment. STOCK: Georgian and Victorian furniture. TEL: 0306 888174/888468.

King's Court Galleries
54 West St. (Mrs J. Joel). Open 9.30-5.30. STOCK: Antique maps, engravings, decorative and sporting prints. TEL: 0306 881757. SER: Framing.

John Lang Antiques
Old King's Head Court, High St. Est. 1985. STOCK: 17th-18th C country oak, brass, copper and decorators' items. TEL: 0306 882203.

Norfolk House Galleries Antique Centre
48 West St. (M. Share). Open 10-5. STOCK: Furniture, especially Georgian and Victorian dining tables and chairs. TEL: 0306 881028; home - 0273 681841.

Nostalgia
1 West St. (Y. Hungerford-Boyle). Open 9.30-5.30, Wed. 9.30-1.30. STOCK: Vintage clothing, textiles, lace, linen, theatrical costume. TEL: 0306 880022; home - 0273 681841. SER: Hire.

Ockley Antiques
43 West St. (P. and A. Atkinson). Est. 1970. Open 9.30-1 and 2-5. SIZE: Large. STOCK: Pine, 17th-20th C, £50-£1,000. LOC: Half way down West St. PARK: Nearby. TEL: 0306 712266/885007; home - 0306 7111271. VAT: Stan.

Oriental Carpets and Decorative Arts
37 West St. (A. and C. Gilchrist and Associates). Open 10.30-6, Wed. by appointment. STOCK: Fine and tribal Oriental carpets and rugs. TEL: 0306 876370. SER: Valuations; repairs and cleaning (rugs and carpets).

The Owl House
4 Lyons Court. (A. Burrill and S. West). Est. 1978. Open 10-5, Wed.10-1, evenings by appointment. SIZE: Small. STOCK: Pine especially large Irish items - dressers, food cupboards, tables, mainly 18th-19th C, £20-

Dorking continued

£1,500; oak, 18th C, £200-£1,000. LOC: Off High St. by Lloyds Bank. PARK: Nearby. TEL: 0306 740239; home - 0372 375864 and 0306 774641. SER: Buys at auction (longcase clocks). FAIRS: Ardingly. VAT: Stan/Spec.

The Quilt Room
20 West St. (P. Lintott and R. Miller). Open 9.30-5. STOCK: Quilts. TEL: 0306 740739.

Elaine Saunderson Antiques
18/18a Church St. (Mrs E.C. Saunderson). Est. 1988. Open 9.30-1 and 2-5.30, Sun. and Wed. by appointment. SIZE: Medium. STOCK: Furniture, late 18th to early 19th C, £50-£10,000; decorative items. Not Stocked: Silver and jewellery. LOC: Turn left into North St. at end of West St. one-way. 100yds. up North St., opposite junction with Church St. PARK: Easy. TEL: 0306 881231/886082; home - same; mobile - 0836 338225. SER: Valuations; restorations (furniture). VAT: Spec.

Michael Schryver Antiques Ltd
The Granary, 10 North St. Est. 1964. Open 8.30-1 and 2-5.30, Sat. 8-12. STOCK: Furniture. LOC: Turn left at top of West St., business at end on right. PARK: Own. TEL: 0306 881110. SER: Valuations; restorations (cabinet work, polishing and upholstery). VAT: Stan/Spec.

Thorpe and Foster plc
49-52 West St. Open 9.30-1 and 2.15-5.30. SIZE: Large. STOCK: English walnut, mahogany and satinwood furniture, 18th C, £500-£50,000. LOC: On A24. PARK: At rear. TEL: 0306 881029/887076; fax - 0306 881029. VAT: Spec.

Victoria and Edward Antiques Centre
61 West St. Est. 1972. Open 9.30-5.30. SIZE: Medium - 28 dealers. STOCK: General antiques. PARK: Nearby. TEL: 0306 889645.

Pauline Watson FGA NAG
Old King's Head Court. Est. 1960. Open 9.30-5. SIZE: Small. STOCK: Jewellery and silver especially Victorian. LOC: In the HIgh Street at the top of West Street. PARK: Behind shop in North St. TEL: 0306 885452. SER: Valuations; lecturer. VAT: Stan/Spec.

West Street Antiques
63 West St. (J.G. Spooner and R. Ratner). Est. 1980. Open 9.30-1 and 2.15-5.30. SIZE: Medium. STOCK: Furniture, 17th to early 20th C, £100-£5,000; arms, 17th-19th C, £100-£10,000; brass, copper, ceramics, collectors' items including fishing tackle. Not Stocked: Jewellery and carpets. LOC: West St. (A25) one-way system. PARK: Nearby. TEL: 0306 883487; home - 0306 730182 and 0372 452877. VAT: Stan/Spec.

Patrick Worth Antiques BADA
11 West St. (B.P. Meyer). Est. 1967. Open 9.30-5.30. CL: Wed. SIZE: Large. STOCK: Period

SURREY

Dorking continued
furniture, decorative items, mainly 18th to early 19th C. **Not Stocked:** Silver, glass and jewellery. **LOC:** A25. **TEL: 0306 884484. VAT:** Spec.

EAST HORSLEY
A.E. Gould and Sons (Antiques) Ltd
Old Rectory Cottage, Ockham Rd. South. (D. and P. Gould). Est. 1949. Open 9.30-5, Sun. by appointment. SIZE: Large. *STOCK: Furniture, 18th C, £200-£5,000; 19th C, £100-£3,000; barometers.* PARK: Easy. TEL: 048 65 3747; home - 081 949 4251. VAT: Stan.

The Old Curiosity Shop
9 Bishopsmead Parade. (A.B. Nasta). Open 10-1 and 2-5, Sat 10-1. CL: Mon. SIZE: Small. *STOCK: Georgian- Edwardian furniture, £100-£800; china.* LOC: On B2038 off A246; Ripley exit off A3. PARK: Easy. TEL: 04865 4994. SER: Restorations.

EAST MOLESEY
Abbott Antiques
75 Bridge Rd. Est. 1970. *STOCK: Clocks.* TEL: 081 941 6398.

The Antiques Arcade
77 Bridge Rd. (J.L. Abbott). Open 10-5. SIZE: 14 dealers. *STOCK: General antiques.* TEL: 081 979 7954.

B.S. Antiques
39 Bridge Rd. (S. Anderman). Est. 1983. Open 10-5. CL: Wed. SIZE: Medium. *STOCK: Clocks, barometers, prints, some furniture.* LOC: Near Hampton Court. PARK: Easy. TEL: 081 941 1812. SER: Valuations; restorations and repairs (clocks and barometers). VAT: Spec.

The Court Gallery
16 Bridge Rd. (J. Clark). Est. 1980. Open 9-5. CL: Mon. SIZE: Small. *STOCK: Oils, watercolours and drawings, 19th-20th C, £50-£1,000; Staffordshire pottery, 19th C, £35-£200.* LOC: From Scilly Isles roundabout turn into Hampton Court Way, Bridge Rd. is on left by Hampton Court Bridge. PARK: Easy. TEL: 081 941 2212. SER: Valuations; restorations (oils and watercolours); framing.

The Gooday Shop and Studio
48-50 Bridge Rd. (R. Gooday). CL: Wed. and mornings. *STOCK: Collectors' items, 1900-1930.* TEL: 081 979 9171.

Hampton Court Antiques
75 Bridge Rd, Hampton Court. (H. Abbott). Open 10-5. *STOCK: General antiques including clocks, furniture, lamps and decorative objects.* TEL: 081 941 6398.

Hampton Court Emporium
52-54 Bridge Rd., Hampton Court (Mr and Mrs

East Molesey continued
A. Smith). Open 10-6, Sun. 10-4. SIZE: Medium. *STOCK: Furniture, to 1930's; porcelain including Doulton; general antiques including jewellery.* PARK: Palace Rd. station. TEL: 081 941 8876. SER: Valuations; restorations. VAT: Stan/Spec.

Howard Hope Phonographs and Gramophones
21 Bridge Rd. Open Fri. and Sat. 10-5 and by appointment. *STOCK: Mechanical and musical items.* LOC: Close by Hampton Court Palace. TEL: 081 941 2472; 081 398 7130. SER: Spare parts.

Nicholas Antiques
31 Bridge Rd. Open 9.30-5. CL: Wed. p.m. *STOCK: Furniture, general antiques and decorative items.* TEL: 081 979 0354. VAT: Stan/Spec.

The Sovereign Antique Centre
53 Bridge Rd. SIZE: 10 dealers. *STOCK: Furniture, pictures and objets d'art.* LOC: Near Hampton Court. TEL: 081 783 0595.

Martin Speed
5 Bridge Rd. Open 10-5, prior telephone call advisable. CL: Sat. *STOCK: General antiques and fine furniture.* LOC: Near Hampton Court Bridge. TEL: 081 979 6690/1087. VAT: Stan/Spec.

EGHAM
Fishers of Surrey
94 High St. (R. and E.S. Fisher). Est. 1972. Open 9-5. CL: Wed. SIZE: Medium. *STOCK: General antiques, Victorian and Edwardian.* LOC: Next to Police Station. PARK: Easy. TEL: 0932 849624. SER: Valuations.

Pastimes (Egham) Ltd
86 Hgh St. (A.S. Carlyon-Gibbs). Est. 1976. Open 10-6. SIZE: Large. *STOCK: Postage stamps - Aden, Bahamas, Barbados, Egypt, Ghana, Hungary, India, Jamaica, Monserrat, Newfoundland, Great Britain, Australia, Papua New Guinea, Mauritius, USA, Eire, Israel, Germany, France, Hong Kong, Gibraltar, Ceylon, Gold Coast, Canada, Austria, Belgium; watercolours, oils and prints, mainly Victorian, £10-£3,000; longcase, bracket, wall, and carriage clocks, watches; furniture, especially chairs, 17th-20th C; porcelain, copper and brass, cloisonné, silver and gold, £5-£500.* PARK: Easy. TEL: 0784 436290; home - 0628 39353. SER: Valuations; restorations (pictures and furniture); framing; clock and watch repairs, French polishing, upholstery; buys at auction.

EPSOM
Fogg Antiques
75 South St. (R. Fogg and M. Hughes). Est. 1982. Open 9-6, Sat. 10-6. SIZE: Medium. *STOCK: English and continental pine, Victorian to 1900s, £50-£1,000.* LOC: A24. TEL: 0372 726931. VAT: Stan.

P. & B. JORDAN
Antiques

90 WEST STREET, FARNHAM GU9 7EN   FARNHAM 716272

Furniture, Porcelain, Oil Paintings, Prints, etc.

Monday-Friday 9.30 a.m. – 1 p.m.   Saturday 9.30 a.m. – 1 p.m. and 2 p.m. – 5.30 p.m.

Epsom continued

Vandeleur Antiquarian Books
6 Seaforth Gdns. (E.H. Bryant). Open by appointment only. STOCK: Antiquarian and secondhand books on all subjects, prints and maps. TEL: 081 393 7752. SER: Valuations; catalogues issued; searches undertaken. VAT: Stan.

ESHER
Jenny Asplund Fine Art
Open by appointment only. STOCK: Fine watercolours and selected oils, 19th-20th C. TEL: 0372 464960.

EWELL
J.W. McKenzie
12 Stoneleigh Park Rd. Est. 1971. Appointment advisable. STOCK: Antiquarian books on cricket. TEL: 081 393 7700.

Token House Antiques   LAPADA
7 Market Parade, High St. (Mrs D. Walker). Est. 1966. Open 11-5. CL: Wed. STOCK: Furniture, 18th-19th C; porcelain, decorative items, metalware and general antiques. LOC: Opposite post office. PARK: At rear. TEL: 081 393 9654. VAT: Stan/Spec.

EWHURST, Nr. Cranleigh
Cranleigh Antiques
Milkhill, The Street. (R. Hoskin). Est. 1976. Open 10-5, Sat. 10-1 and Sun. by appointment. SIZE: Medium. STOCK: Oak and mahogany furniture, 18th-19th C, £5-£1,000; general antiques and bygones. PARK: Easy. TEL: 0483 277318. SER: Valuations. VAT: Stan.

FARNHAM
Annie's Antiques
1 Ridgeway Parade, Frensham Rd. Est. 1972. Open 9.30-5, Fri. 10.30-5. SIZE: Medium. STOCK: Furniture, bric-a-brac, jewellery, 19th to early 20th C, £5-£1,000; general antiques. LOC: 1 mile out of Farnham on A287 towards Hindhead. PARK: Easy. TEL: 0252 713447; home - 0252 723217.

Farnham continued

Bits and Pieces
82 West St. (Mrs C.J. Wickins). CL: Wed. p.m. STOCK: Victoriana, furniture, art nouveau, art deco. TEL: 0252 722355/715043. SER: Costume hire.

Bourne Mill Antiques
Guildford Rd. Est. 1971. Open 10-5.30 every day. SIZE: 75 dealers. STOCK: Furniture in mahogany, walnut, yew, oak and pine, oils and watercolours, linen, porcelain and glass, books, bric-a-brac, collectors' items, tools, rugs and ornaments. TEL: 0252 716663.

Casque and Gauntlet Militaria
55/59 Badshot Lea Rd, Badshot Lea. (R. Colt). Est. 1957. SIZE: Large. STOCK: Militaria, arms, armour. LOC: On Aldershot to Farnham road. PARK: Easy. TEL: 0252 20745, ext. 2. SER: Restorations (metals); re-gilding.

Childhood Memories
27a South St. (Miss M.A. Stanford). STOCK: Teddy bears, dolls, Dinky and Brittain toys, games and childhood collectables.

Christopher's Antiques
Sandford Lodge, 39a West St. (Mr and Mrs C.M. Booth). Resident. Est. 1972. Open 8-1 and 2-5.30, weekends by appointment. SIZE: Large. STOCK: Fruitwood country and mahogany furniture, 18th-19th C; walnut furniture, 17th-18th C. LOC: From Guildford on the A31, turn right at second roundabout. PARK: Easy. TEL: 0252 713794. SER: Valuations; restorations (furniture). VAT: Stan/Spec.

Farnham Antique Centre
27 South St. (Miss M.A. Stanford). Est. 1976. Open 9.30-5. SIZE: Large. 12 dealers. STOCK: General antiques including silver, jewellery, porcelain, brass and copper, clocks, period furniture and collectors' items. LOC: On the one-way system into Farnham, large corner site. PARK: At rear. TEL: 0252 724475.

Heytesbury Antiques   LAPADA
P.O. Box 222. (I. and S. Ingall). Est. 1974.

Farnham continued

Open by appointment only. SIZE: Medium. STOCK: Pre-1830 mahogany, walnut and rosewood furniture, and 19th C decorative furniture, textiles and associated items, £200-£12,000; paintings and bronzes, 19th C, £100-£2,000. TEL: 0252 850893; mobile - 0836 675727. FAIRS: West London, Olympia, Kensington, Decorators and others. VAT: Mainly Spec.

P. and B. Jordan

90 West St. (P.A. and W.E. Jordan). Est. 1962. Open 9.30-1, Sat. 9.30-1 and 2-5.30 or by appointment. SIZE: Medium. STOCK: Furniture and ceramics, from 1750, £50-£500; oil paintings, prints, from 1700, £5-£500; glass, brass fenders, from 1700, £5-£50. Not Stocked: Carpets, tapestries. LOC: On main road through town centre. PARK: Round corner, 'The Hart' Rd. TEL: 0252 716272.

Lion and Lamb Gallery at Biggs of Farnham

West St. (C. and S. Neville). Est. 1975. CL: Wed. STOCK: Landscape, marine, sporting and wildlife pictures, 20th C. TEL: 0252 714154. SER: Restorations (oils and watercolours); framing; mounting.

Maltings Monthly Market

Bridge Sq. Est. 1969. First Sat. monthly. SIZE: 190+ stalls. STOCK: 60% of the dealers sell a wide variety of antiques, bric-a-brac, postcards and collectables. LOC: Follow signs to Wagon Yard car park, Maltings over footbridge. TEL: 0252 726234.

R. and M. Putnam

60 Downing St. Est. 1957. Open 10-1 and 2-5.30; until 5 Sat. CL: Sun. except by appointment. SIZE: Medium. STOCK: Period pine furniture, 18th-19th C; Staffordshire pottery, 19th C; brass, copper, oil and watercolour paintings, oak and mahogany furniture, country items. LOC: Town centre. PARK: Easy. TEL: 0252 715769; home - 0252 715485. SER: Restorations (furniture); buys at auction. VAT: Stan/Spec.

Village Pine

32 West St. (S. McGrath). Est. 1981. Open 10-5. SIZE: Large. STOCK: Pine furniture including dressers, chests of drawers and boxes, unusual and small items, Victorian, £35-£650. LOC: On left past Bishops Table Hotel. PARK: Easy. TEL: 0252 726660.

Karel Weijand Fine Oriental Carpets

LAPADA

Lion and Lamb Courtyard. Est. 1975. Open 9.30-5.30. SIZE: Large. STOCK: Fine antique and contemporary Oriental rugs and carpets, from £150. LOC: Off West St. PARK: Easy. TEL: 0252 726215. SER: Valuations; restorations; cleaning. VAT: Stan/Spec.

Rosa Barovier Mentasti
VENETIAN GLASS
1890-1990

Rosa Barovier Mentasti
VENETIAN GLASS 1890-1990

This fascinating book traces the historic course of Venetian artistic glassware through the 20th century. The rich illustrated section contains more than 200 colour photographs and gives a close-up and detailed view of this remarkable art. Its historic value is greatly enhanced by the inclusion of many of the rarest pieces from private collections, never before photographed or published.

Both collectors and enthusiasts will find all the necessary information to identify the artisans and styles which have literally made the history of Venetian glass.

ISBN 88 7743 119 9
208pp, 200 colour plates, £45.00

Available from:
Antique Collectors' Club
5 Church Street, Woodbridge
Suffolk IP12 1DS
Tel: (0394) 385501 Fax: (0394) 384434

or Market Street Industrial Park
Wappingers' Falls
New York 12590, USA
Tel: 914 297 0003 Fax: 914 297 0068

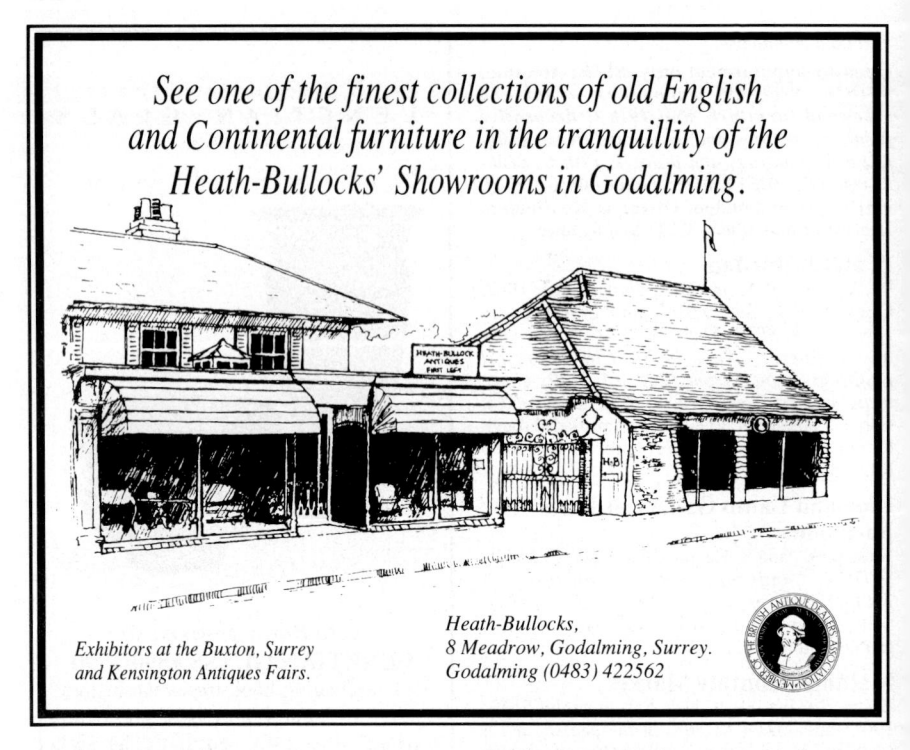

> *See one of the finest collections of old English and Continental furniture in the tranquillity of the Heath-Bullocks' Showrooms in Godalming.*
>
> Exhibitors at the Buxton, Surrey and Kensington Antiques Fairs.
>
> Heath-Bullocks,
> 8 Meadrow, Godalming, Surrey.
> Godalming (0483) 422562

Farnham continued

Wrecclesham Antiques
47 Wrecclesham Rd. (A. Vallis and J. Hudson). Est. 1979. Open daily, Sun. by appointment. SIZE: Medium. STOCK: *Pine, 19th C, £50-£450; clocks, 17th-19th C, £150-£800; Victorian furniture, 19th C, £60-£300.* LOC: A325. PARK: Easy. TEL: 0252 716468; home - same.

FRENSHAM

Douglas Franks
Underhill, Summerfield Lane. Est. 1949. Open by appointment. STOCK: *Furniture and accessories.* TEL: 0252 792996. VAT: Stan/Spec.

GODALMING

Church Street Antiques
15 Church St. (L. Bambridge). Est. 1985. Open 10-5, Wed. 10-1. SIZE: Medium. STOCK: *British ceramics, 1800-1930, £5-£1,000; glass, 1800-1930, £5-£200; silver, 1750-1930, £20-£500.* LOC: Off A3. PARK: Easy and behind shop. TEL: 0483 860894. SER: Valuations; buys at auction (as stock). VAT: Stan/Spec.

Cry for the Moon
31 High St. (J.L. Ackroyd). Est. 1977. Open 9.30-5.30. SIZE: Medium. STOCK: *Mainly jewellery, £50-£10,000; silver and objets d'art.* TEL: 0483 426201; fax - 0483 860117. SER: Valuations;

Godalming continued

repairs (jewellery); jewellery commissions undertaken. VAT: Stan/Spec.

P. and J. Goldthorpe
Bicton Croft, Deanery Rd. Open by appointment only. STOCK: *Paintings, mainly English and Dutch, 17th-18th C.* TEL: 0483 414356.

Heath-Bullocks   BADA
8 Meadrow. (R.J. and M.E. Heath-Bullock). Est. 1926. Open 10-1 and 2-4. SIZE: Large. STOCK: *English and continental furniture, garden ornaments, works of art.* LOC: A3100. From Guildford on the left side approaching Godalming. PARK: Own. TEL: 0483 422562; fax - 0483 426077. SER: Valuations; restorations; upholstery. FAIRS: Exhibitors at and organisers of Buxton, Surrey and Kensington.

Ivelet Books Ltd - Church St. Bookshop
26 Church St. Open 10.30-5.30. STOCK: *Architecture, interiors, fine and applied art, landscape and gardening, natural history.* TEL: 0483 418878; fax - same. SER: Catalogues and lists available.

The Olde Curiosity Shoppe
99 High St. STOCK: *Silver, brass, copper, china, collectables and jewellery.* TEL: 0483 415889.

Godalming continued
Priory Antiques
29 Church St. (P. Rotchell). Open 10-4. CL: Wed. *STOCK: General antiques.* TEL: 0483 421804.

David White Antiques
34 Meadrow. (D. and Y. White). Resident. Est. 1981. Open 9.30-5 and by appointment. CL: Wed. p.m. SIZE: Medium. *STOCK: English country furniture, especially fruitwood and yew, 17th to early 19th C, £50-£5,000; copper, brass and treen, from £20; blue and white printed pottery.* LOC: A3100, opposite Pickfords Depository. PARK: Easy. TEL: 0483 420957. VAT: Stan/Spec.

GREAT BOOKHAM, Nr. Leatherhead
Bookham Galleries
Leatherhead Rd. (J. Rowe). Est. 1969. Open by appointment only. SIZE: Large. *STOCK: Furniture, 18th-19th C.* LOC: A246. PARK: Easy. TEL: 0372 452668. VAT: Stan/Spec.

Roger A. Davis Antiquarian Horologist
19 Dorking Rd. Est. 1971. Open 9.30-12.30 and 2-5.30. CL: Mon. and Wed., Fri. p.m. and Sun. a.m. except by appointment. SIZE: Small. *STOCK: Clocks, 18th-19th C, £100-£4,000.* LOC: From Leatherhead A246 to centre of village, turn left at sign for Polesden Lacey, shop 1/4 mile along Dorking Rd. PARK: Easy. TEL: 0372 457655; home - 0372 453167. SER: Valuations; restorations (mechanical and case work); buys at auction (antique clocks).

GUILDFORD
The Antiques Centre
22 Haydon Place, Corner of Martyr Rd. (Mrs S.D.J. Pullen). Est. 1969. Open 10-4. CL: Mon. and Wed. LOC: Close to Surrey Advertiser. PARK: 100yds. on left from North St. TEL: 0483 67817. The wide variety of goods offered is shown by the principal items of stock which follow the names of some of the dealers listed below.

Peter Bradley
STOCK: Pine, kitchenalia and clocks.
Jennifer Carter
STOCK: China, collectables, bygones.
Elaine Chandler
STOCK: Tom Thumb miniatures, doll's houses and dolls' house miniatures.
Joan Goggin
STOCK: China, collectables, bygones.
Helen McHugh
STOCK: Lace, baby gowns, general antiques, lace cushions.
Sylvia Pullen
STOCK: Silver, jewellery, Devon ware.
Paul Rutterford
STOCK: Post-cards.

Guildford continued
Bijoux Jewellers
12 Epsom Rd. (Mrs N.C. Harper). Est. 1968. Open daily 10-5.30. *STOCK: Jewellery, including secondhand and modern; silver.* LOC: Near Odeon cinema. TEL: 0483 32992. VAT: Stan.

Denning Antiques
1 Chapel St. Open 10-5. *STOCK: Silver, jewellery, lace, linen, and collectors' items.* LOC: Off High St. PARK: Nearby. TEL: 0483 39595.

Peter Goodall
Bull Head Gate, 12b Market St. Est. 1965. Open 10-5, Sat. 10-3. CL: Mon. SIZE: Large. *STOCK: Engravings, etchings, lithographs and aquatints, 17th-20th C, £5-£1,000.* LOC: First right after town clock in High St. into Market St., then first right. PARK: Multi-storey Leapale Rd. (off Market St.). TEL: 0483 36650. SER: Valuations; restorations (prints and watercolours).

Horological Workshops   BADA
204 Worplesdon Rd. (M.D. Tooke). Est. 1968. Open 8.30-5.30, Sat. 9-12.30 or by appointment. *STOCK: Clocks, watches, barometers.* **TEL: 0483 576496.**

Michael Stewart Fine Art Galleries
61 Quarry St. Open 9.30-5.30. CL: Mon. *STOCK: Sir William Russell Flint originals, limited editions, books, engravings and letters.* TEL: 0483 504359.

Thomas Thorp Bookseller
170 High St. Est. 1883. Open 9-5, 5.30 on Sat. SIZE: Large. *STOCK: Books including antiquarian and out-of-print.* LOC: At traffic lights at top of High St. PARK: Road running parallel High St. 200yds. away. TEL: 0483 62770. SER: Valuations; buys at auction (antiquarian books). Private collections bought.

Charles W. Traylen
Castle House, 49/50 Quarry St. Est. 1945. Open 9-1 and 2-5. CL: Mon. SIZE: Large. *STOCK: Fine books and manuscripts, 13th C to date.* PARK: 200yds. TEL: 0483 572424; fax - 0483 450048. SER: Valuations; restorations (bindings); buys at auction. VAT: Stan.

HAMPTON WICK
Hampton Wick Antiques
48 High St. Est. 1957. Open 10-5. *STOCK: Clocks and barometers, general antiques.* TEL: 081 977 3178.

HASLEMERE
Allen Avery Interiors
1 High St. Est. 1971. Open 9-1 and 2.15-5. CL: Sat. p.m. and Wed. *STOCK: English furniture.* TEL: 0428 643883.

SURREY

Haslemere continued

Bow Antiques Ltd
6 Petworth Rd. (R.C. Blandford). Est. 1992. Open 9.30-5, Sat. 10-4. CL: Wed. SIZE: Medium. STOCK: *Furniture, 18th-19th C; prints.* LOC: A286. Left at top of High St. towards Petworth, shop 50 yards on left. PARK: Easy. TEL: 0428 652886; home - 0483 37375. SER: Restorations (furniture including French polishing). VAT: Stan/Spec.

J.K. Glover (Antiques)
Grayswood. LOC: Village Green. TEL: 0428 642184.

Surrey Clock Centre
3 Lower St. (C. Ingrams and S. Haw). Est. 1962. Open 9-1 and 2-5. SIZE: Large. STOCK: *Clocks and barometers.* PARK: Easy. TEL: 0428 651313. SER: Restorations; hand-made parts; shipping orders; clocks made to order. VAT: Stan/Spec.

Wood's Wharf Antiques Bazaar
56 High St. SIZE: 12 dealers. STOCK: *A wide selection of antiques.* LOC: Opposite The Georgian Hotel. TEL: 0428 642125; fax - 0428 725045.

HINDHEAD

Albany Antiques Ltd
8-10 London Rd. (T. Winstanley). Est. 1965. Open 9-6. CL: Sun. except by appointment. STOCK: *Furniture, 17th-18th C, £20-£400; china including Chinese, £5-£400; metalware, £7-£50; both 18th-19th C.* Not Stocked: Silver. LOC: A3. PARK: Easy. TEL: 0428 605528. VAT: Stan/Spec.

M. J. Bowdery   BADA
12 London Rd. Est. 1970. Always available, prior telephone call advisable. STOCK: *Furniture, 18th-19th C.* TEL: 0428 606376; home - 0428 605244. VAT: Stan/Spec.

Oriel Antiques
3 Royal Parade, Tilford Rd. (J. Gear). Est. 1974. Open 9-5.30. CL: Wed. p.m. STOCK: *Furniture and pictures, 18th-19th C.* TEL: 0428 606281.

"Second Hand Rose"
Portsmouth Rd, Bramshott Chase. (S.J. Ridout). Est. 1980. Open 10-5.30 and by appointment. SIZE: Large. STOCK: *Furniture, paintings, bric-a-brac, 18th-20th C.* LOC: On A3, 1 mile S.W. of Hindhead. PARK: Easy. TEL: 0428 604880; home - same. VAT: Stan/Spec.

What Not Antiques
Crossways Rd, Grayshot. (Mrs M. Wylie). Open 9-5.30. STOCK: *General antiques and pine.* TEL: 0428 604871.

KEW

Lloyds of Kew
9 Mortlake Terrace. (D. and E. Lloyd). Open

Kew continued

10-4, Sat. 10-5.30. CL: Wed. STOCK: *Out-of-print books on gardening, botany and some general.* PARK: Easy. TEL: 081 940 2512. SER: Annual catalogues (Oct.).

KEW GREEN

Andrew Davis
6 Mortlake Terrace. Resident. Est. 1969. STOCK: *Decorative and functional items of all periods, including furniture, British ceramics and pictures.* TEL: 081 948 4911. SER: Valuations; framing.

KINGSTON-UPON-THAMES

Glencorse Antiques   LAPADA
321 Richmond Rd, Ham Parade, Ham Common. (M. Igel and B.S. Prydal). Open 10-5.30. STOCK: *18th-19th C furniture; 19th C oils and watercolours.* PARK: Own. TEL: 081 541 0871.

Glydon and Guess Ltd
14 Apple Market. Est. 1940. Open 9.30-5. CL: Wed. STOCK: *Jewellery, small silver, £100-£5,000.* LOC: Town centre. TEL: 081 546 3758. SER: Valuations; restorations. VAT: Stan.

KNAPHILL, Nr. Woking

Knaphill Antiques
38 High St. (P.W. and J. Bethney). Open 8.30-6 CL: Mon. SIZE: Small and warehouse. STOCK: *Barometers, clocks, Georgian, Victorian and Edwardian furniture.* LOC: Off A322 turn righ after the Fox Public House at Bisley toward Knaphill, shop oppposite Crown public house TEL: 0483 473179; home - 0483 811616.

LALEHAM, Nr. Staines

Laleham Antiques
23 Shepperton Rd. (H. and E. Potter). Est. 1970 Open 10-5. SIZE: Medium. STOCK: *Period furniture, pine, porcelain, general and trade antiques.* LOC: B376. PARK: Easy. TEL: 078 450353. VAT: Stan.

LIMPSFIELD

Limpsfield Watercolours
High St. (Mrs C. Reason). FATG. Est. 1985 Open Tues. 11-3, Thurs., Fri. and Sat. 10-3. SIZE Small. STOCK: *Watercolours, £15-£5,000; print and etchings, £5-£200; all 1850-1940 an contemporary.* Not Stocked: Oils. LOC: Fron junction 6, M25 on B269. PARK: Easy. TEL 0883 717010. SER: Valuations; restoration (watercolours, prints and oils); framing includin conservation; cleaning. VAT: Spec.

LINGFIELD

Lingfield Antiques
4 East Grinstead Rd. (A.F. Robertson). Open 9- CL: Wed. p.m. STOCK: *General antiques, furnitur porcelain and silver.* TEL: 0342 834501.

MERROW, Nr. Guildford
The Pine Shop
174 Epsom Rd. (Sheelagh Hamilton). Open 10-6. *STOCK: Pine furniture.* TEL: 0483 572533.

MERSTHAM
The Old Smithy Antique Centre
7 High St. (S.M. Davidson). 10-5. SIZE: 12 dealers. *STOCK: General antiques and collectables.* PARK: Easy. TEL: 0737 642306.

MILFORD, Nr. Godalming
Michael Andrews Antiques
Portsmouth Rd. Est. 1974. Open daily, Thurs. and Sun. by appointment. SIZE: Medium. *STOCK: Furniture, 18th to early 19th C.* LOC: Corner of Cherry Tree Rd. (to Petworth/Haslemere). PARK: Easy. TEL: 0483 420765; home - same. VAT: Stan/Spec.

E. Bailey
Portsmouth Rd. (Eric Bailey). Est. 1979. Open 9-5. CL: Thurs. SIZE: Small. *STOCK: Furniture and tools, from Victorian, £5-£100; china, £5-£25.* LOC: Main road. PARK: Easy. TEL: 0483 422943.

MITCHAM
Cherub Antiques
177 Streatham Rd. (M. Wisdom). Open 10.30-5.30. *STOCK: Pine and general antiques.* TEL: 081 640 7179.

MORDEN
A. Burton-Garbett
35 The Green. Est. 1959. By appointment only. Prospective clients met (at either Morden or Wimbledon tube station) by car. *STOCK: Books on travel, the arts, antiquities of South and Central America, Mexico and the Caribbean, 16th-20th C, £5-£5,000.* TEL: 081 540 2367. SER: Buys at auction (books, pictures, fine arts, ethnographica). VAT: Stan.

OCKLEY
Ockley Antiques
The Green. (P.and A. Atkinson). Open 8.30-5. *STOCK: Pine, 17th-20th C, £50-£1,000.* LOC: Opposite Kings Arms on A29. PARK: Own. TEL: 0306 712266.

OXTED
Antiques Centre
80-84 Station Rd. East. (D. Quigley and Mrs J. Wagstaff). Est. 1992. Open 9-5.30. SIZE: Large. *STOCK: Furniture, Georgian, Victorian and Edwardian, £50-£3,500; rugs and carpets, early to mid 20th C, £50-£2,000; clocks, barometers and watches, 19th C, £50-£4,500; silver and jewellery.* LOC: 3 miles south junction 6, M25;

Oxted continued

off A25. PARK: Easy and at rear. TEL: 0883 712806. SER: Restorations (clocks and upholstery); buys at auction.

Treasures
151 Station Rd. East. Open 10-5. *STOCK: Copper, brass, glass, porcelain, silver, jewellery, linen, books, pine, toys, small furniture and collectables.* TEL: 0883 713301.

PURLEY
Michael Addison Antiques
28-30 Godstone Rd. (M. and N. Addison). Est. 1981. Open 10-5. CL: Wed. p.m. SIZE: Medium. *STOCK: Furniture, 1780-1930, £200-£2,000.* Not Stocked: Bric-a-brac. LOC: A22, 1 mile east of Purley. PARK: Easy. TEL: 081 668 6714. SER: Valuations; restorations; upholstery. VAT: Stan/Spec.

REDHILL
F.G. Lawrence and Sons
89 Brighton Rd. Est. 1891. Open 9-1 and 2-5, Sat. 10-1. CL: Wed. p.m. SIZE: Large. *STOCK: Edwardian, Victorian and Georgian furniture.* LOC: On A23. PARK: Own. TEL: 0737 764196. SER: Valuations; buys at auction. VAT: Stan.

REIGATE
Bourne Gallery Ltd   LAPADA
31/33 Lesbourne Rd. (J. Robertson). Est. 1970. Open 10-1 and 2-5.30. SIZE: Large. *STOCK: 19th-20th C oils and watercolours, £250-£25,000.* PARK: Easy. TEL: 0737 241614. SER: Restorations (oil paintings). VAT: Spec.

Heath Antiques
15 Flanchford Rd. (J. and P. Gibson). Resident. Usually open but prior telephone call advisable. SIZE: Small. *STOCK: Porcelain including Mason's Ironstone and blue and white, 18th-20th C, £5-£250; silver, general antiques, small furniture.* LOC: Reigate Heath, just off A25 main Reigate-Dorking road. PARK: Easy. TEL: 0737 244230; home - same. SER: Valuations.

Bertram Noller (Reigate)
14a London Rd. (A.M. Noller). Est. 1970. Open 9.30-1 and 2-5.30. CL: Tues. and Wed. SIZE: Small. *STOCK: Collectors' items, furniture, grates, fenders, mantels, copper, brass, glass, pewter, £1-£500.* LOC: West side of one-way traffic system. Opposite Upper West St. car park. PARK: Opposite. TEL: 0737 242548. SER: Valuations; restorations (furniture, clocks, bronzes, brass and copper, marble).

Reigate Galleries Ltd
45a Bell St. (J.S. Morrish). Est. 1958. Open 9-5.30, Wed. 9-1. SIZE: Large. *STOCK: Old prints, engravings, antiquarian books.* PARK: Opposite. TEL: 0737 246055. SER: Picture framing. VAT: Stan.

Reigate continued
Showcase
27 Croydon Rd. (L. Blackford and J. Butler). Open 10-4. *STOCK: General antiques.* TEL: 0737 222305.

RICHMOND
Antique Mart
72-74 Hill Rise. (G. and Y. Katz). Open 10-5, Sun. 2-6. CL: Wed. SIZE: Large. *STOCK: Furniture, 18th-19th C.* TEL: 081 940 6942. SER: Buys at auction. VAT: Stan/Spec.

Antiques Arcade
22 Richmond Hill. Est. 1984. Open Thurs., Fri. and Sat. 10.30-5.30. SIZE: Medium. *STOCK: Fine English porcelain and ceramics, 18th-20th C, Staffordshire figures; mahogany, rosewood and walnut furniture, 18th C to Edwardian; children's furniture from 17th C; objets d'art, local prints, collectors items.* PARK: Easy. TEL: 081 940 2035.

Brookville Antiques
222 Sandycombe Rd. (A.K. Khan). Open 10-6. *STOCK: Decorative furniture.* LOC: Near Kew Gardens. TEL: 081 940 6230; home - same.

Country Furniture
6 Onslow Rd. (Jan Hicks and Austin Maude). Open 10-6. *STOCK: French beds and French provincial furniture, unusual period pine country furniture.* TEL: 081 940 7879.

free!

28 page full colour catalogue of Antique Collectors' Club books. Over 120 titles included covering a wide range of subjects: furniture, art reference, art history, prints, jewellery, metalwork, glass, horology, ceramics, oriental carpets, collectables, garden history and design, gardening and architecture.

Available free from the
ANTIQUE COLLECTORS' CLUB

5 Church Street
Woodbridge
Suffolk IP12 1DS
Tel: (0394) 385501
Fax: (0394) 384434

Richmond continued
Court Antiques (Richmond)
12/14 Brewers Lane. (A. and L. Coombs). Est. 1958. Open 9.30-5.30. SIZE: Small. *STOCK: General antiques, jewellery, furniture, silver. Not Stocked: Coins and stamps.* LOC: From Richmond station turn left along the Quadrant into George St., Brewers Lane is on the right. PARK: 30yds. turn left. TEL: 081 940 0515. VAT: Stan.

Dukes Yard Market
1A Duke St. Open 10-5.30. CL: Mon. SIZE: 45 dealers. *STOCK: General antiques, collectables, furnishings.* TEL: 081 332 1051.

Mollie Evans
82 Hill Rise. Est. 1965. Open Thurs.and Sat. 10.30-5.30, Sun. 2.30-5.30 other times by appointment. SIZE: Medium. *STOCK: Early country and painted furniture, pottery, some textiles, interesting bygones, unusual bold decorative items including sculpture, to 1930, £50-£4,000.* LOC: From centre of Richmond, take A307 towards Kingston (Petersham Rd.). Fork left up hill immediately after passing Richmond Bridge on right. PARK: Meters. TEL: 081 948 0182 (ansaphone). SER: Buys at auction. VAT: Spec.

Peter and Debbie Gooday
20 Richmond Hill. Est. 1971. Open Tues., Thurs. and Sat. 11-5.30, Sun. (trade only) 2-5.30, other times by appointment. SIZE: Medium. *STOCK: Decorative items, art nouveau, art deco, arts and crafts including jewellery, pictures and furniture, metalwork especially Liberty pewter, 1880-1950; African and oceanic tribal artefacts; all £20-£3,000.* LOC: 100yds. from Richmond Bridge. PARK: Easy. TEL: 081 940 8652. SER: Buys at auction.

Roland Goslett Gallery
139 Kew Rd. Est. 1974. Open Thurs. and Fri. 10-6, Sat. 10-2, or by appointment. SIZE: Small. *STOCK: English watercolours and oil paintings, 19th to early 20th C, £100-£5,000.* PARK: Easy. TEL: 081 940 4009. SER: Valuations; restorations (oils, watercolours and frames); framing. VAT: Spec.

Hill Rise Antiques LAPADA
26 Hill Rise. (P. Hinde and D. Milewski). Est. 1978. Open 10.30-5.30, Sun. (trade only) 2.30-5.30. CL: Wed. SIZE: Large. *STOCK: 18th-19th C walnut and mahogany furniture and longcase clocks, £100-£10,000; silver and plate, bronzes, mirrors, boxes and glassware.* LOC: 1 mile from A316 (M3). PARK: At rear by arrangement. TEL: 081 332 2941; home - same. FAIRS: Olympia (June), Barbican. VAT: Stan/Spec.

Horton's LAPADA
2 Paved Court, The Green. (D. and R. Horton). FGA. CL: Wed. *STOCK: Jewellery*

Richmond continued
and silver, 18th-20th C, £500-£2,000; British paintings, early to mid-20th C, £250-£750. TEL: 081 332 1775. SER: Valuations.

F. and T. Lawson Antiques
13 Hill Rise. Resident. Est. 1965. Open 10-5.30, Sat. 10-5. CL: Wed. and Sun. a.m. SIZE: Medium. *STOCK: Furniture, 1680-1870; paintings and watercolours; both £30-£1,500; clocks, 1650-1930, £50-£2,000; bric-a-brac, £5 £300.* LOC: Near Richmond Bridge at bottom of Hill Rise on the river side, overlooking river. PARK: Limited and further up Hill Rise. TEL: 081 940 0461. SER: Valuations; buys at auction.

Layton Antiques
1 Paved Court, The Green. (Lady Layton). Est. 1967. Open 10-5. CL: Wed. and Sun. except by appointment. SIZE: Medium. *STOCK: 18th-19th C furniture, silver and decorative items.* LOC: Off The Green at Prince's Head public house. PARK: Easy. TEL: 081 940 2617. VAT: Stan/Spec.

Lion Antiques
16 Brewers Lane. Open 9-5. *STOCK: Silver and jewellery.* TEL: 081 940 8069.

Marryat
88 Sheen Rd. (Marryat (Richmond) Ltd.). Est. 1990. Open 10-5.30. SIZE: Large. *STOCK: English and continental furniture, watercolours and oils, £100-£3,000; ceramics, glass, silver and objets, £10-£500; all 18th-19th C.* LOC: Follow M3/A316 towards Richmond, first left into Church Rd. then left again. PARK: Easy. TEL: 081 332 0262. SER: Valuations; restorations. VAT: Stan/Spec.

Palmer Galleries
10 Paved Court. (C.D. and V.J. Palmer). Est. 1984. Open 10-5. SIZE: Medium. *STOCK: Prints, watercolours and engravings, 19th-20th C, £50-£1,000.* PARK: Richmond Green. TEL: 081 948 2668; home - 081 998 0901. VAT: Stan/Spec.

Piano Nobile Fine Paintings
26 Richmond Hill. (Dr. Robert A. Travers). Est. 1986. Open Thurs.-Sun. SIZE: Medium. *STOCK: Fine 19th C Impressionist and 20th C Post-Impressionist and Modernist British and continental oil paintings and sculpture. Speciality - Les Petits Maitres of the Paris Schools, £500- £50,000.* PARK: Easy. TEL: 081 940 2435; fax - same. SER: Valuations; restorations (paintings and sculpture); framing; buys at auction (19th-20th C oil paintings). FAIRS: Grosvenor. VAT: Stan/Spec.

Richmond Traders
28, 30/32 Hill Rise. Open 10.30-5.30, Sun. 2-5. CL: Wed. SIZE: 16 dealers. *STOCK: General antiques.* TEL: 081 948 4638.

PIANO NOBILE
FINE PAINTINGS

Large stock of 19th/20th C oil paintings and sculpture; several important studio collections represented.

26 RICHMOND HILL
RICHMOND UPON THAMES
SURREY TW10 6QX   TEL/FAX 081-940 2435

Richmond continued

Roderic Antiques
84 Hill Rise. (R. Arnold and E. Gunawardena). Est. 1971. Open 10-5.30, Sun. 2-5.30. CL: Wed. SIZE: Medium. *STOCK: Furniture and decorative items, 18th-19th C, £200-£10,000.* LOC: Hill Rise is road leading to Park from town. PARK: Nearby. TEL: 081 332 6766; home - 081 898 4162. FAIRS: Olympia (June); City of London. VAT: Stan/Spec.

Rowan Antiques
4 Worple Way. Open 10-6. CL: Mon. and Tues. *STOCK: Furniture, Georgian to Victorian; clocks, watercolours.* TEL: 081 332 1167.

RIPLEY

Cedar House Gallery
High St. Resident. Est. 1987. *STOCK: Watercolours and oils, 19th to early 20th C, £500-£10,000.* LOC: 1/2 mile M25/A3 junction. PARK: Easy. TEL: 0483 211221. SER: Restorations.

J. Hartley Antiques Ltd
186 High St. Est. 1949. Open 8.45-5, Sat. 9.45-2.45. *STOCK: Queen Anne and Georgian furniture.* TEL: 0483 224318. VAT: Stan.

Manor House
High St. Est. 1952. SIZE: Medium. *STOCK:*

SURREY

Ripley Antiques
LAPADA MEMBER

HEATHER DENHAM

Specialising in 18th and 19th Century Furniture and Decorative Items for Trade and Export

67 High Street, Ripley, Surrey.
Telephone Guildford (0483) 224981

2 mins. from Junction 10 on the M25 and
30 mins. from London on the A3

Ripley continued

Furniture, 18th C; copper and brass, 18th-19th C; clocks, prints mainly sporting and military; china, glass. LOC: A3. PARK: Easy. TEL: 0483 225350. VAT: Stan/Spec.

Ripley Antiques — LAPADA
67 High St. (H. Denham). Est. 1960. Open 9.30-1 and 2-5.15, Sun. by appointment. SIZE: Large. STOCK: *Furniture, English and French, 18th-19th C; decorative items - mirrors and chandeliers.* LOC: 2 mins. from junction 10 at M25/A3 interchange. PARK: Easy. TEL: 0483 224981/224333. SER: Valuations; restorations. VAT: Stan/Spec.

Sage Antiques and Interiors — LAPADA
The Green Cottage, High St. (H. and C. Sage). GMC. Est. 1971. Open 9.30-1 and 2-5.30, Sat. all day. SIZE: Large. STOCK: *Furniture, mahogany, oak, walnut, 1600-1900, £150-£8,000; oil paintings, £100-£5,000; watercolours, £50-£1,000, china, £2-£500, all 18th-19th C; silver, Sheffield plate, brass, pewter, decorative items, 18th-19th C, £50-£1,000.* LOC: Village centre, on main road. PARK: Easy. TEL: 0483 224396; fax - 0483 211996. SER: Restorations (furniture, pictures); interior furnishing. VAT: Stan.

Anthony Welling Antiques — BADA
Broadway Barn, High St. Est. 1970. Open 9-1 and 2-5.30. Sun. and evenings by appointment.

Ripley continued

SIZE: Large. STOCK: *English oak, 17th-18th C, £250-£8,000; country furniture, 18th C, £200-£6,000; brass, copper, pewter, 18th C, £100-£750.* Not Stocked: Glass, china, silver. LOC: Turn off A3 at Ripley, shop in village centre on service road. PARK: Easy. TEL: 0483 225384. VAT: Spec.

RUNFOLD, Nr. Farnham
The Packhouse
Hewetts Kilns, Tongham Rd. (Mr and Mrs P. Hewett). Est. 1978. Open 10.30-5.30 including Sun. SIZE: Large. STOCK: *Furniture, including period, 1930's, reproduction and country pine; garden statuary, architectural items.* LOC: Turn off A31 (Hogs Back) at Jolly Farmer public house. PARK: Easy. TEL: 0252 783863; home - same. SER: Restorations. FAIRS: Earls Court.

SANDERSTEAD
Shirley Warren — BADA LAPADA
(Mrs S. Warren). ADA. Open by appointment. STOCK: *English and continental glass, antiquity to 19th C, £100-£10,000; reference books.* LOC: 10 mins. from M25, junction 6. PARK: Easy. TEL: 081 657 1751. SER: Valuations. VAT: Spec.

SHEPPERTON
Rickett & Co. Antiques
Church Sq. (A.L. Spencer). Est. 1968. Open 10-5, Wed. 10-1, prior telephone call advisable. STOCK: *Brass and copper, 18th-19th C, £100-£300; fenders and fire tools, oil lamps, inkwells, chandeliers, grandfather clocks.* LOC: 10 mins. from London airport. PARK: Easy. TEL: 0932 243571; home - 0932 222508. SER: Restorations (metal repairs and polishing). VAT: Spec.

SHERE, Nr. Guildford
Shere Antique Centre
Middle St. (J. Watson). Est. 1983. Open 10-5, Sat. 10-5.30, Sun. 11-5.30. SIZE: Large. STOCK: *Victorian and Edwardian items, £5-£500.* LOC: A25. PARK: Easy. TEL: 048 641 2846. VAT: Stan/Spec.

Yesterdays Pine
Gomshall Lane. (J. and V. Stuart). Open 10-5.30. STOCK: *Victorian pine.* TEL: 048 641 3198.

SHIRLEY
Spring Park Jewellers
284 Wickham Rd. (M. McCamley). MGA. Est. 1965. Open 10-5.30. CL: Wed. SIZE: Small. STOCK: *Jewellery, paintings, prints, silver, furniture.* LOC: 2 miles from central Croydon on road to West Wickham. PARK: Easy. TEL: 081 656 2800. SER: Valuations; clock, watch and jewellery repairs; buys at auction.

Anthony Welling

Specialist in C17th and C18th Oak and Country Furniture

*Broadway Barn,
High Street, Ripley,
Surrey, GU23 6AZ
Tel. 0483 225384*

Oak tridarn, c.1750

SHOTTERMILL, Nr. Haslemere
Grannie's Attic
Checkerboards, Hindhead Rd. (A.G.J. Buckland). Open 9.30-6. STOCK: Small general antiques, bric-a-brac and furniture. TEL: 0428 644572.

STAINES
K.W. Dunster Antiques
23 Church St. Open 9.30-5.30. CL: Thurs. SIZE: Medium. STOCK: Clocks, furniture, general antiques, interior decor, jewellery, nautical items. TEL: 0784 453279; home - 0784 483146. VAT: Stan/Spec.

Margaret Melville Watercolours
LAPADA
11 Colnebridge, Market Sq. TVADA. Est. 1980. Open by appointment only. STOCK: English watercolours, 1850-1950, £75-£7,000. TEL: 0784 455395. SER: Valuations; commissions. FAIRS: Eton College (Easter); Guildford (Oct); Bellhouse Hotel, Beaconsfield 2nd. Sun. each month. VAT: Spec.

SURBITON
Cockrell Antiques
278 Ewell Rd. (Sheila and Peter Cockrell). Resident. Est. 1982. Open Thurs., Fri. and Sat. 9-6, other days by appointment. SIZE: Medium.

Surbiton continued
STOCK: Furniture including art deco, from 18th C, £50-£3,000+; decorative items, £50-£500. LOC: Off A3 at Toworth Tower on A240. PARK: Easy. TEL: 081 390 8290; home - same. FAIRS: IACF and Kempton Park. VAT: Stan/Spec.

House of Mallett
77 Brighton Rd. (K. Mallett). Est. 1974. Open Mon., Fri. and Sat. 10-5, Sun. (trade only) 10-1. SIZE: Large. STOCK: Mahogany furniture, general antiques and art pottery, arts and crafts. PARK: Easy. TEL: 081 390 3796.

B. M. Newlove
139-141 Ewell Rd. Est. 1958. Open 9.30-5.30. CL: Wed. SIZE: Medium and store. STOCK: Furniture especially early oak and Georgian mahogany, 17th-19th C, £200-£5,000; china, 18th-19th C, £75-£200; paintings, all periods, £50-£2,000; longcase clocks, Georgian barometers. Not Stocked: Pot-lids, fairings. LOC: Down Kingston by-pass at Tolworth underpass, turn right into Tolworth Broadway, then into Ewell Rd. Shop one mile on. PARK: Easy. TEL: 081 399 8857. VAT: Stan/Spec.

Laurence Tauber Antiques
131 Ewell Rd. Open 9.30-5. CL: Wed. p.m. STOCK: General antiques, especially for Trade. PARK: Easy. TEL: 081 390 0020. VAT: Stan.

SUTTON
S. Warrender and Co
4 and 6 Cheam Rd. (F.R. Warrender). Est. 1953. Open 9-5.30. CL: Wed. SIZE: Medium. *STOCK: Jewellery, 1790 to date, £10-£1,500; silver, 1762 to date, £10-£1,000; carriage clocks, 1860-1900, £115-£800.* TEL: 081 643 4381. SER: Valuations; restorations (jewellery, silver, quality clocks). VAT: Stan.

THAMES DITTON
The David Curzon Gallery
1 High St. Open 10-6. CL: Mon. and Tues. SIZE: Medium. *STOCK: Paintings and watercolours, from 1860, £300-£15,000.* LOC: Between Hampton Court and Surbiton, 5 mins. walk from BR station. PARK: Easy. TEL: 081 398 7860. VAT: Spec.

Clifford and Roger Dade
Boldre House, Weston Green. Open 9.30-6, Sat. and Sun. by appointment. *STOCK: Mahogany furniture, 18th to early 19th C, £200-£3,000.* TEL: 081 398 6293. LOC: On main road from Hampton Court. PARK: On the green. VAT: Spec.

Fern Cottage Antique Centre
28/30 High St. Est. 1960. Open 10-5.30. SIZE: Large. 20 dealers. *STOCK: General antiques, 18th-19th C furniture, maps, prints, porcelain, silver, jewellery.* TEL: 081 398 2281.

Elizabeth Gant
52 High St. ABA. PBFA. Est. 1981. CL: Wed. SIZE: Small. *STOCK: Antiquarian, secondhand and illustrated books, especially childrens; ephemera, toys, 10p-£1,000.* PARK: Nearby. TEL: 081 398 0962; 081 398 5107. SER: Valuations; buys at auction (books). FAIRS: PBFA (London); ABA (Bath and Chelsea).

THORNTON HEATH
Corner Cabinet
446 Whitehorse Rd. (R. Thomas). Est. 1977. Open 10-5. CL: Mon. *STOCK: General antiques and furniture.* LOC: End of Thornton Heath High St., at junction with Whitehorse Lane, opposite parish church. TEL: 081 684 3156.

TONGHAM, Nr. Farnham
The Grange Antiques and Craft Centre
Grange Rd. (G.A. Hooke). Est. 1982. Open 9-5, Sun. 10-3. SIZE: Large. *STOCK: Pre-war furniture, toys and collectables, china and silver, paintings; architectectural items including statues, iron work, doors and flooring, fireplaces and staircases.* LOC: Off A31 between Guildford and Farnham, left at White Hart crossroads, 300 yards on right. PARK: Easy. TEL: 0252 782993/782804. SER: Restorations (furniture). VAT: Stan.

WALLINGTON
Manor Antiques
75A Manor Rd. (M. Webb). Open 10.30-5. CL: Wed. *STOCK: General antiques.* TEL: 081 669 5970.

WALTON-ON-THAMES
Susan Becker
LAPADA
P O Box 160. (S. Becker Fleming). Est. 1959. Open by appointment only. SIZE: Small. *STOCK: Porcelain, English and continental, 18th-20th C, £200-£25,000; glass and fine objects.* LOC: 10 minutes A3, M25, M4. PARK: Easy. TEL: 0932 227820. SER: Valuations. FAIRS: Cumberland Ceramics. VAT: Stan/Spec.

Boathouse Gallery
The Towpath, Manor Rd. (B.E. Clark). CL: Mon. *STOCK: Oil paintings, watercolours, engravings.* TEL: 0932 242718. SER: Picture framing, mounting and restorations. VAT: Stan.

WALTON-ON-THE-HILL AND TADWORTH
Ian Caldwell
LAPADA
9a Tadworth Green, Dorking Rd. Resident. Est. 1978. Open 10-5.30. CL: Wed. SIZE: Medium. *STOCK: Oak, walnut and mahogany furniture especially Georgian.* LOC: 2 miles from M25, 1/4 mile from A217 on B2032 in Dorking direction. PARK: Easy. TEL: 0737 813969. SER: Valuations; restorations. VAT: Stan/Spec.

WEST BYFLEET
Academy Billiard Antiques
5 Camphill Industrial Estate. (R.W. Donnachie). Est. 1975. Open anytime by appointment. SIZE: Large warehouse and showroom. *STOCK: Period and antique billiard/snooker tables, all sizes, 1830-1920; combined billiard/dining tables, period accessories including lighting.* LOC: On A245, 2 miles from M25/A3 junction. PARK: Easy. TEL: 0932 352067; mobile - 0860 523757; fax - 0932 353904. SER: Valuations; restorations; removals; structural advice. VAT: Stan/Spec.

WESTCOTT, Nr. Dorking
Westcott Antiques
The Studio, Parsonage Lane. Est. 1968. Open 9.30-5. CL: Sun. p.m. SIZE: Large. *STOCK: Oak and walnut furniture, 1600-1800; mahogany furniture, 1700-1820.* LOC: A25. Two miles west of Dorking on road to Guildford. PARK: Easy. TEL: 0306 881900. SER: Valuations; restorations (furniture); buys at auction. VAT: Stan/Spec.

The Westcott Gallery
4 Guildford Rd. (Mr and Mrs A. Wakefield). Est. 1989. Open 9-5, Sat. 10-5. SIZE: Medium. *STOCK: Oils and watercolours, 19th-20th C, from £250; contemporary paintings, from £50.* LOC: On A25,

Westcott continued
between Dorking and Guildford. PARK: Opposite. TEL: 0306 876261. SER: Two/three solo exhibitions per year; valuations; restorations (oils, watercolours and frames); framing; fine art insurance, antique dealers scheme.

WEYBRIDGE

Church House Antiques   LAPADA
42 Church St. (M.I. Foster). Est. 1886. Open Thurs., Fri., Sat. 10-5.30. SIZE: Medium. *STOCK: Furniture, 18th-19th C, £95-£7,000; jewellery, 18th-19th C, some modern, £30-£5,000; pictures, silver, plate, decorative items.* Not Stocked: Coins and stamps. PARK: Behind library. TEL: 0932 842190. VAT: Stan/Spec.

The Clock Shop Weybridge
64 Church St. Est. 1970. Open 9.30-6. SIZE: Medium. *STOCK: Clocks, 1685-1900, from £500; French carriage clocks, from £300.* LOC: Opposite Midland Bank on corner. PARK: Easy. TEL: 0932 840407/855503. SER: Valuations; restorations (clocks). VAT: Stan/Spec.

Edward Cross - Fine Paintings
128 Oatlands Drive. Est. 1973. Open Fri. 10-12.30 and 2-4, Sat. 10-12.30. SIZE: Medium. *STOCK: Fine paintings and bronzes, 19th-20th C, £500-£30,000.* LOC: A3050. PARK: Opposite. TEL: 0932 851093. SER: Valuations; restorations (watercolours and oil paintings); buys at auction (pictures). VAT: Spec.

Hatch Antiques   LAPADA
49 Church St. (B.D. Hatch). Est. 1968. Open 10-1 and 2-5.30, Sat. to 5, Wed. p.m. by appointment. CL: Mon. SIZE: Large. *STOCK: Furniture, clocks, general antiques, 17th C to Edwardian.* PARK: Easy. TEL: 0932 846782; home - 0932 849623. SER: Valuations; restorations (furniture and clocks). VAT: Stan/Spec.

Jandora
112 Oatlands Drive, Oatlands Village. (J. Silverstone). Est. 1985. Open 10-5. CL: Wed. SIZE: Medium. *STOCK: China, silver, dolls, prints, collectables, furniture, curios.* PARK: Easy. TEL: 0932 851858; home - 0932 842175. FAIRS: Local and Ardingly.

Not Just Silver
16 York Rd. (Mrs S. Hughes). Est. 1969. Open 9.30-5.30, Sun. by appointment. *STOCK: Silver, from Georgian, £50-£3,500; Old Sheffield plate, £60-£800; English and continental porcelain, 18th-19th C, £30-£800; objets d'art including bronze, to £1,000; furniture, paintings.* LOC: Opposite car park, just off Queens Rd. TEL: 0932 842468; home - 0932 829088. SER: Valuations; restorations (replating, metalwork, glass and porcelain).

R. Saunders
71 Queen's Rd. (J.B. Tonkinson). Est. 1878. Open 9.30-1 and 2.30-5. CL: Wed. SIZE: Medium.

Weybridge continued
STOCK: English mahogany, oak and walnut furniture, wheel and stick barometers, 1650-1830, £50-£5,000; glass, porcelain, silver, watercolours, pewter and brass. Not Stocked: Reproductions. PARK: 150yds. in York Rd. TEL: 0932 842601. SER: Valuations; restorations (furniture). VAT: Spec.

Weybridge Antiques
43 Church St, The Quadrant. (P. Pocock). Est. 1974. Open 9.30-5.30. SIZE: Large. *STOCK: Furniture, oils and watercolours.* LOC: From M25 into town, Church St. is first right. PARK: At rear. TEL: 0932 852503. SER: Valuations; restorations (oil paintings, porcelain, furniture). VAT: Stan/Spec.

WINDLESHAM
Country Antiques
Country Gardens Garden Centre, London Rd. (S. Sommers and C. Martin). Est. 1990. Open 10-5 including Sun. SIZE: Large. *STOCK: Victorian and Edwardian, some Georgian, furniture, £50-£2,000; china and glass, collectables including lace and prints, Victorian to 1930's, £2-£100.* LOC: A30, between Sunningdale and Bagshot; off M3, junction 3. PARK: Easy. TEL: 0344 873404.

WOKING
Keith Baker
42 Arnold Rd. (K.R. Baker). *STOCK: General antiques.* TEL: 0483 767425/761168.

Chattels Antiques
156 High St, Old Woking. (John Kendall). Open by appointment only. SIZE: Small. *STOCK: Clocks, barometers, some small furniture.* LOC: Two miles off A3 at Ripley. PARK: Own. TEL: 0483 771310. SER: Restorations (English clocks, furniture).

Manor Antiques and Restorations
2 New Shops, High St., Old Woking. (A.V. Wellstead). Open 9.30-5, Sat. 10-4. *STOCK: General antiques, pine, china and glass.* TEL: 0483 724666; fax - 0483 750366. SER: Valuations; restorations (furniture, clocks and pictures); picture framing; caning and re-rushing.

The Venture
High St, Old Woking. (D. Wilkins and D. Law). Resident. Est. 1946. Always open. *STOCK: General antiques especially pine, pre-1920.* TEL: 0483 772103.

Wych House Antiques
Aberdeen House, Wych Hill. (A. and C. Perry). Est. 1965. Open 9-6, Sat. 9-1. SIZE: Large and warehouses. *STOCK: Continental and English furniture, pine, decorative items, paintings, kitchenalia.* TEL: 0483 764636. VAT: Stan.

Sussex East

Sussex East

Church of São Domingos, Macau, with street vendors. Pen and ink over pencil. Inscribed in shorthand 'figures correct right size'. Photograph Victoria and Albert Museum. From *George Chinnery, 1774-1852, Artist of India and the China Coast*, published in 1993 by the **Antique Collectors' Club**, £45.00.

ALFRISTON, Nr. Polegate
Alfriston Antiques
The Square. (J. Tourell). Est. 1967. Open 10.30-1 and 2-5.30, appointment advisable during winter months. CL: Mon. and Tues. SIZE: Small. STOCK: Collectors' items, vinaigrettes, snuff boxes, caddy spoons, silver, plate, carriage and other clocks, jewellery, paintings, pot-lids, copper, brass, books. PARK: Easy. TEL: 0323 870498. VAT: Stan/Spec.

Radford Antiques
Twytton House, High Street. Open 10.30-5. SIZE: Medium. STOCK: Metalware, prints, maps, general antiques and jewellery, dolls house kits, miniatures. PARK: Nearby. TEL: 0323 870440.

BATTLE
Magpie Antiques
38 Mount St. (C. and G. Huckvale). *STOCK:*

Battle continued
General antiques, Victoriana, bric-a-brac. TEL: 0424 772194; home - 0424 772341.

BEXHILL-ON-SEA
Barclay Antiques   LAPADA
7 Village Mews, Little Common. (R. and M. Barclay). Est. 1971. Open 10-4.30. CL: Wed. SIZE: Medium. *STOCK: Pottery and porcelain especially Worcester, Derby and Coalport, £200-£600; small furniture including desks and secretaires; watercolours and oils, £500-£2,500; all 18th-19th C; treen including Tunbridgeware, 19th C, £50-£1,800; slag glass, £10-£200.* LOC: Coast road. PARK: Easy. TEL: Home - 0797 222734. SER: Valuations; restorations (furniture and porcelain, exceptional pieces only); buys at auction (porcelain). FAIRS: Kensington; British International, Birmingham; Buxton; Snape; Bath; Guildford; Olympia. VAT: Spec.

Bexhill-on-Sea continued

Bexhill Antique Exporters LAPADA
56 Turkey Rd., and Quakers Mill, Old Town. (H. and K. Abbott). Open 8-5.30. CL: Sat. SIZE: Warehouse. STOCK: Antique and shipping furniture. TEL: 0424 225103/210182; fax - 0424 731430. SER: Container packing.

The Old Mint House LAPADA
45 Turkey Rd. (J.C. and A.J. Nicholson). Est. 1960. Open 9-5.30. CL: Sat. SIZE: Large. STOCK: Oak and mahogany, Victorian, Edwardian and shipping goods, £20-£2,000. PARK: Easy. TEL: 0424 216056; 0323 762337; fax - 0323 762337. SER: Buys at auction; container packing. VAT: Stan.

Springfield Antiques
127 Ninfield Rd., Sidley. (C. and C.J. Georgiou). Open 9-5.30. STOCK: Pine, oak and mahogany furniture; china, pictures, silver and plate, smalls. TEL: 0424 211225.

Stewart Gallery
48 Devonshire Rd. Open 9-5.30. STOCK: Paintings, 19th-20th C; ceramics and glassware. TEL: 0424 223410. SER: Valuations; restorations (paintings and frames). VAT: Stan/Spec.

Village Antiques
17 Village Mews, Little Common. (Mr and Mrs D. Cowpland). Est. 1975. Open 10-5. CL: Wed. SIZE: Medium. STOCK: Furniture. LOC: A259. TEL: 0424 772035. SER: Restorations. VAT: Stan.

BOREHAM STREET, Nr. Hailsham

Camelot Antiques
(Mrs B.C. Chambers). Est. 1968. Open 10-1 and 2.15-5.30. CL: Wed. SIZE: Small. STOCK: Porcelain and pottery, 1800-1930, £5-£300; small furniture, 19th-20th C, £25-£600; silver, copper, brass, glass, Victorian, £5-£300. Not Stocked: Firearms, stamps, medals. PARK: Easy. TEL: 0323 833460. FAIRS: Various county.

BRIGHTLING

John Hunt Galleries
Willingford Lane. (J.A.E. Hunt). Est. 1989. Open by appointment only. SIZE: Medium. STOCK: Oil paintings and watercolours, bronze and marble sculpture, 19th-20th C, £100-£5,000. LOC: South of A265 at Burwash Weald between Burwash and Heathfield. Premises one mile along Willingford Lane. PARK: Easy. TEL: 042 482 239; home - same. VAT: Spec.

BRIGHTON

Alexandria Antiques
3 Hanover Place, Lewes Rd. (A.H. Ahmed). Open 9.30-6, Sat. 9-12. STOCK: Georgian and Victorian furniture; Oriental and European porcelain; oil and watercolour paintings; Oriental carpets, objets d'art. TEL: 0273 688793.

Brighton continued

Antiques and Bedsteads
105 Gloucester Rd. Open 9-6. STOCK: Beds especially iron and brass; decorative, including pine and country, furniture; architectural items, linen and lace; china and glass especially unusual items. TEL: 0273 621434.

Art Deco Etc.
73 Upper Gloucester Rd. (John Clark). Est. 1979. Open 12-5.30, Sun. and other times by appointment. SIZE: Medium. STOCK: Pottery, glass, furniture, lighting, mirrors, pictures and collectors' items, art deco, art nouveau, arts and crafts, 1950's, £5-£2,000. LOC: From Brighton station down Queens Rd., first on right. PARK: Easy. TEL: 0273 329268; home - 0273 202937. SER: Valuations. FAIRS: Decorative Arts, Kensington Town Hall.

Ashton's Antiques
1-3 Clyde Rd, Preston Circus. (R. Ashton). Open 9.30-5, Wed. 9.30-1, Sat. 9.30-4. STOCK: Victorian, Edwardian upholstery and pine; general trade and shipping goods. TEL: 0273 605253. VAT: Stan/Spec.

Attic Antiques
23 Ship St. (F.B. and M.J. Moorhead). Est. 1965. Open 11-1 and 2.15-5, Sat. 12-1, prior telephone call advisable. STOCK: General antiques, 1720-1920, £15-£1,500; English and continental paintings, mainly Victorian and Georgian; clocks, barometers, Oriental antiques, bronzes, English and continental china, tantalus, Victorian oil lamps, copper, brass, pewter; Imari, Canton, Satsuma and Worcester china; Georgian, Victorian, Edwardian and continental furniture. TEL: 0273 326378. VAT: Stan. Mainly Trade.

H. Balchin and Son
18-19 Castle St. (C.B. Balchin). Resident. Est. 1930. Open 9.30-1 and 2.30-5.30. CL: Thurs. and Sat. p.m. SIZE: Large. STOCK: General antiques, 18th-19th C. LOC: From Western Rd., down Preston St., Castle St. is second turning on left. PARK: Loading only. SER: Valuations. VAT: Stan/Spec.

Bears and Friends
32 Meeting House Lane, The Lanes. (P. Goble). Est. 1989. Open 9-5.30, Sat. 9-6, Sun. 10-6 or by appointment. STOCK: Teddy bears and bear related items; antique dolls and miniatures. TEL: 0273 208940; fax - 0273 202736. SER: Valuations; export; mail order catalogue. FAIRS: Major London Teddy Bear and Doll; Stratford-upon-Avon Teddy Bear. VAT: Stan/Spec.

Brighton Antique Wholesalers
39 Upper Gardner St. SIZE: Several dealers. STOCK: 18th-19th C furniture, £50-£5,000. LOC: Off North Rd. PARK: Easy. TEL: 0273 695457.

Bexhill Antique Exporters

Offering one of the largest stocks of antique and shipping furniture in the South East

Bexhill Antique Exporters
56 Turkey Road
Bexhill on Sea, East Sussex
Telephone: 0424 225103/210182
Fax 0424 731430

Bexhill Antique Centre
Quakers Mill, Old Town
Bexhill on Sea, East Sussex
Telephone 0424 210182/225103
Fax 0424 731430

**Open: Monday-Saturday
8.00am-5.30pm
By appointment on Sundays**

After hours 0424 830354

LAPADA MEMBER

Brighton continued

Brighton Architectural Salvage
33-34 Gloucester Rd. (L. F. Moore). Open 9.30-5, Sat. 10-4.30. *STOCK: Restored architectural items including pine furniture; fireplaces and surrounds - marble, pine, mahogany, cast-iron Victorian tiled and cast inserts and over-mantels; doors, stained glass, panelling; cast-iron balcony and street railings, spiral staircases; stonework, lamp posts and light fittings; garden seats and ornaments.* TEL: 0273 681656.

Brighton Flea Market
31A Upper St. James's St. (A. Wilkinson). Est. 1972. Open seven days. SIZE: Large. *STOCK: Bric-a-brac, furniture and collectables, 19th-20th C, £5-£100.* LOC: 50 yards from coast road, Kemp Town. TEL: 0273 624006.

Mary Brown
42 Surrey St. Open 11-5.30. *STOCK: Period clothes, linen and lace, costume jewellery.* LOC: Near station and CAB office. TEL: 0273 721160.

C.A.R.S. (Classic Automobilia & Regalia Specialists)
4-4a Chapel Terrace Mews, Kemp Town. (G. Weiner). SIZE: Small. *STOCK: Collectors' car mascots, badges and associated automobilia, classic pedal and electric children's cars.* TEL: 0273 601960; mobile - 0850 301116; fax - 0273 623846. SER: Catalogue/price list on receipt of SAE.

P. Carmichael
33 Upper North St. (H. Mileham). Est. 1946. Open 9.30-5.30. CL: Sat. p.m. *STOCK: Furniture, 18th-19th C.* TEL: 0273 328072; fax - same. VAT: Stan/Spec.

Sheila Cashin Gallery
40 Upper North St. Est. 1982. Open 10-5, Sat. 10-1, Sun. and evenings by appointment. SIZE: Small. *STOCK: Restored bamboo furniture, especially lacquer tables, £5-£1,000; painted and decorative furniture; tapestry pictures, decorative items especially mirrors, £10-£500.* PARK: Voucher parking nearby. TEL: 0273 326619; home - same.

Circus Antiques
2B Clyde Rd, Preston Circus. Est. 1990. Open 9.30-4, Sat. 10-2. SIZE: Small. *STOCK: Decorative and oak furniture, suites, chairs, mainly late 19th-early 20th C, £50-£1,000; lamps, pictures, porcelain and glass.* LOC: A23 just past Preston Park on one-way system. PARK: London Rd. TEL: 0273 696553; home - 0273 592626.

Connoisseur Antique Gallery
113 Church Rd, Hove. *STOCK: General antiques.* TEL: 0273 777398.

Brighton continued

Christopher G. Cowen Antiques
LAPADA
60 Middle St. (C. and S. Cowen). Open 9.30-5.30, Sat. 10-4. SIZE: Medium. *STOCK: Edwardian, Victorian and Georgian furniture, decorative and Oriental items.* LOC: 2 mins. walk from seafront. PARK: Nearby. TEL: 0273 205757; home - same. SER: Valuations; restorations (furniture); buys at auction. FAIRS: Brighton; Ardingly; Bath. VAT: Stan/Spec.

Graham Deane Antiques
LAPADA
39 Upper North St. Open by appointment. *STOCK: Furniture, china, brass, general antiques.* TEL: 0273 207207.

Graham Deane Antiques
LAPADA
18/19 Marlborough St. Open 9.30-5.30, Sat. 10-1. *STOCK: Furniture, china, brass, general antiques.* TEL: 0273 207207.

Harry Diamond and Son
9 Union St, The Lanes. (R. and H. Diamond). Est. 1937. Open 9-5. *STOCK: Diamond jewellery, antique silver and 19th C French clocks, £50-£20,000.* Not Stocked: Coins, furniture. TEL: 0273 329696. VAT: Stan.

James Doyle Antiques
10 Union St, The Lanes. (J.R. Doyle). Est. 1975. Open 9.30-6. *STOCK: Jewellery, silver.* TEL: 0273 323694; fax - 0273 324330.

D.H. Edmonds Ltd
27 and 28 Meeting House Lane, The Lanes. Est. 1965. Open 10-5.30. SIZE: Large. *STOCK: Jewellery, silver, objets d'art, watches, £50-£20,000.* TEL: 0273 327713/328871. VAT: Stan.

Alan Fitchett Antiques
5-5A Upper Gardner St. Est. 1969. Open 9-5.30. CL: Sat. SIZE: Large. *STOCK: Furniture, 18th-20th C, £50-£10,000; silver plate and works of art.* LOC: Near station. PARK: Easy. TEL: 0273 600894. SER: Valuations; restorations. VAT: Stan.

Paul Goble
44 Meeting House Lane, The Lanes. Est. 1965. Open 9-5.30, Sun. 10-5.30 or by appointment. *STOCK: Jewellery, watches, silver, pictures and prints, teddy bears and dolls.* TEL: 0273 202801; fax - 0273 202736. SER: Trade/export valuation. VAT: Stan/Spec.

The Gold and Silversmiths of Hove
3 Planet House, 1 The Drive, Hove. Open 9-5.30. *STOCK: Jewellery and silver.* TEL: 0273 738489.

Douglas Hall Ltd
23 Meeting House Lane. (A.M. Longthorne). Est. 1968. Open 9.30-5. *STOCK: Silver, jewellery.* TEL: 0273 325323. VAT: Stan.

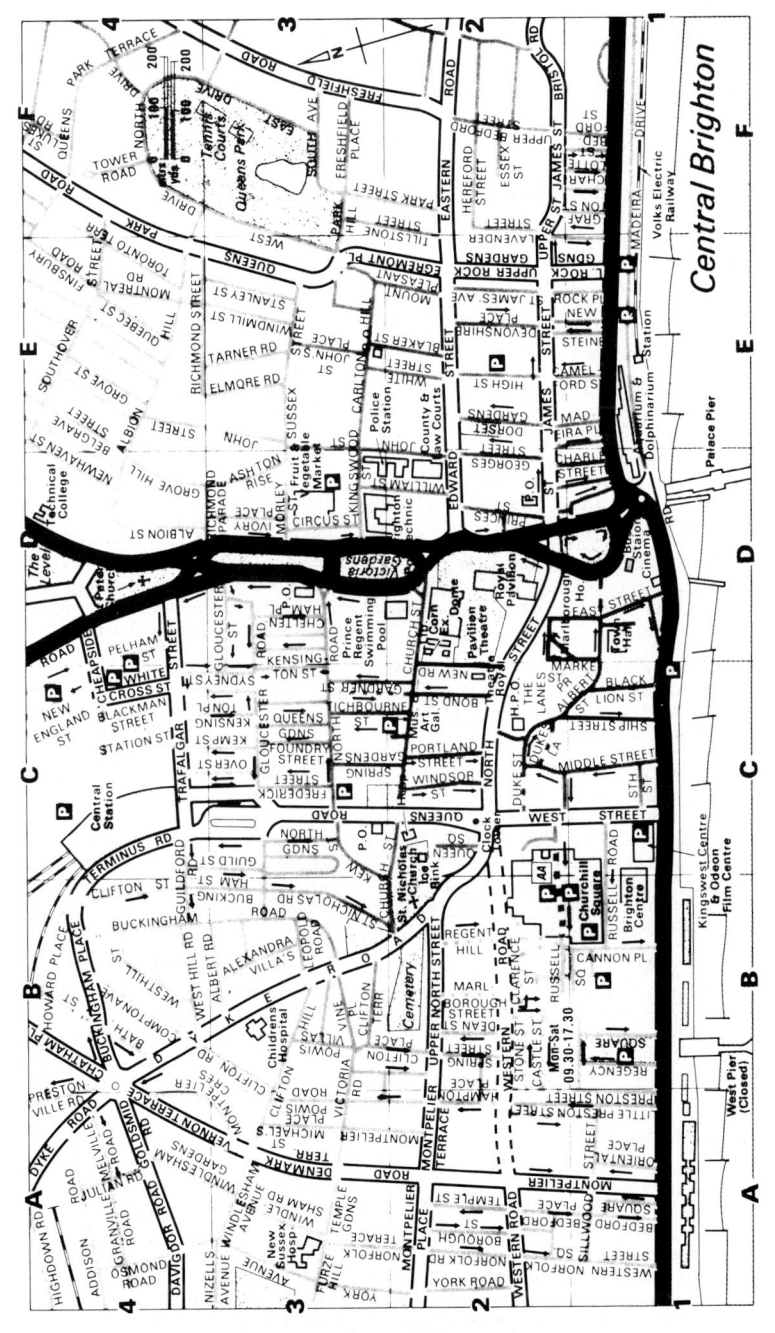

Key to Town Plan

- AA Recommended roads
- Other roads
- Restricted roads
- Buildings of interest
- Car Parks
- Parks and open spaces
- AA Service Centre

© Automobile Association 1988.

Brighton continued

Hallmarks
4 Union St, The Lanes. (J. Hersheson). Est. 1966. Open 9-5. SIZE: Small. *STOCK: Silver and plate, jewellery and clocks, collectables.* TEL: 0273 725477. VAT: Stan/Spec.

Simon Hatchwell Antiques
94 Gloucester Rd. Est. 1961. CL: Sat. SIZE: Large. *STOCK: English and European antiques, paintings, chandeliers, bronzes, carpets, clocks including grandfather, barometers, all 17th-20th C. Not Stocked: Jewellery.* PARK: Own. TEL: 0273 691164. SER: Restorations (barometers and furniture); re-gilding. VAT: Stan/Spec.

Mark and David Hawkins   LAPADA
27 Meeting House Lane, The Lanes. Est. 1958. Open 9-5.30, Sun. by appointment. STOCK: General antiques, arms and armour, £10-£7,500. LOC: Large detached building at south entrance of The Lanes. TEL: 0273 321357. VAT: Stan/Spec.

Holleyman and Treacher Ltd
21a and 22 Duke St. Est. 1937. Open 9-5. *STOCK: Books including antiquarian, music.* TEL: 0273 328007.

The House of Antiques   LAPADA
17 Prince Albert St. (A. Margiotta). Open 10-5.30. STOCK: Jewellery and silver. TEL: 0273 327680/324961. VAT: Stan.

Hove Antique Clocks
68 Western Rd, Hove. (L.W.G. and D.E. Humphrey). Est. 1990. Open 9-5. SIZE: Medium. *STOCK: Clocks - longcase, mantel, bracket, boulle, regulators, wall, skeleton and carriage, 18th-19th C, £50-£2,000.* LOC: Near Floral Clock. PARK: Easy. TEL: 0273 722123; home - 0273 557552/ 561484. SER: Restorations and repairs.

Dudley Hume
46 Upper North St. Est. 1973. CL: Sat. and Sun. except by appointment. SIZE: Medium. *STOCK: Period and Victorian furniture, metal, light fittings.* LOC: Parallel to the Western Rd., one block to the north. TEL: 0273 323461. VAT: Stan/Spec.

Hyndford Antiques
143 Edward St. (Mrs M.C. Skelson). Est. 1968. Open Thurs.-Sat. 11-1 and 2.30-5 or by appointment. SIZE: Small. *STOCK: Bygones, china, collectables, Oriental carvings, £1-£150; prints, ephemera, postcards, 50p-£75; small furniture, £10-£250; all 19th-20th C.* LOC: Edward St. east at right angles to Brighton Pavilion. PARK: Vouchers, near shop. TEL: 0273 679936/602220. FAIRS: Ardingly and Brighton Centre.

Kingsbury Antiques
Hallmarks, 4 Union St. (J.J. Hersheson). Est.

Brighton continued

1966. Open 9-5. *STOCK: Old Sheffield plate, silver, jewellery, glass, clocks, collectables.* TEL: 0273 725477. VAT: Stan/Spec.

Leoframes
70 North Rd. (H. and Mrs A. Schofield and S. Round). Open 9-5.30. *STOCK: Prints and maps.* TEL: 0273 695862. SER: Restorations; framing.

The Leopard
35 Kensington Gdns. (A. and A. Leppard). Est. 1973. Open 9-4, Wed. 9-1, Sat. 9-5. SIZE: Medium. *STOCK: Costume, 19th C, £50-£200; lace, table and bed linen, 19th-20th C, £5-£50; period clothing, early 20th C, £5-£100.* LOC: Pedestrian street at bottom of Gloucester Rd. PARK: Easy. TEL: 0273 695427; home - 0273 507619.

Harry Mason
21A Prince Albert St. Est. 1954. Open 9.30-5.15, Sat. 10-2, Sun. by appointment. SIZE: Large. *STOCK: Silver and plate, 18th-20th C; jewellery, 19th-20th C.* LOC: Adjacent to The Lanes. PARK: Nearby. TEL: 0273 329540/735750. SER: Valuations; restorations (silver and jewellery); buys at auction (as stock); buyers of scrap silver and gold. FAIRS: Sunday London Hotel. VAT: Stan/Spec.

H. Miller Antiques
22a Ship St. Est. 1947. Open 10-5, Sat. 9-1. *STOCK: Silver, jewellery, Sheffield silver, plate.* TEL: 0273 326255. VAT: Stan/Spec.

Patrick Moorhead Antiques
22 Ship St. Open 10-5.30, Sat. 10.30-1.30 or by appointment. SIZE: Shop and large trade warehouse. *STOCK: Furniture, 18th-19th C; general antiques, clocks, paintings, marble, brass; porcelain - English, continental and especially Oriental, Oriental works of art, 18th-19th C.* TEL: 0273 326062.

Michael Norman Antiques Ltd   BADA
15 Ship St. Est. 1965. Open 9-1 and 2-5.30, other times by appointment. STOCK: English furniture. TEL: 0273 329234/5 or 0273 326712; fax - 0273 206556. VAT: Stan/Spec.

Oasis Antiques
39 Kensington Gdns. (I. and A. Stevenson). Est. 1970. Open 10-5, Mon. 11-5, Sat. 8-5. SIZE: Medium. *STOCK: Lighting and furniture, to 1930, £1-£5,000; European and Oriental items including bronzes, art glass, period clothes, linen and lace, gramophones, art nouveau, art deco.* LOC: Off North Road from railway station, centre of north Lanes. PARK: Nearby. TEL: 0273 683885. SER: Restorations (furniture, metals and ceramics); polishing.

Brian Page Antiques
8 Foundry St. Open Sat., and odd times during the week. *STOCK: English and continental decorative arts; art nouveau, arts and crafts furniture,*

Brighton continued
1870-1940; Japanese items including screens, antiques, prints, books and furniture; antique cameras and scientific instruments. TEL: 0273 609310; fax - 0273 620055.

Colin Page Antiquarian Books
36 Duke St. (C.G. Page). Est. 1971. Open 10-5.30. *STOCK: Antiquarian and secondhand books, especially British topography, travel, natural history, illustrated and bindings, 16th-20th C, £1-£5,000.* LOC: Town centre. PARK: Meters or nearby. TEL: 0273 325954; fax - 0273 746246.

Dermot and Jill Palmer Antiques
7-8 Union St, The Lanes. Resident. Est. 1968. Open 9-6, Sun. by appointment. *STOCK: French and English furniture, objects, pictures, mirrors, screens, garden furniture and ornamental pieces, textiles, £50-£5,000.* TEL: 0273 328669 (2 lines); fax - 0273 777641. FAIRS: Olympia, Chelsea Harbour. VAT: Stan/Spec.

Sue Pearson
13 1/2 Prince Albert St. Open 10-4. SIZE: Small. *STOCK: Antique dolls, teddy bears, dolls' house miniatures.* LOC: Lanes area. PARK: N.C.P. TEL: 0273 329247. SER: Valuations; restorations; buys at auction (dolls and bears). FAIRS: Major London Doll and Bear. VAT: Stan/Spec.

Ben Ponting Antiques
53 Upper North St. Open 9.30-5.30, Sat. 10-1. *STOCK: Furniture, 18th-19th C.* TEL: 0273 329409.

Prinny's Gallery
3 Meeting House Lane, The Lanes. Open 9.30-5. SIZE: 26 stands. *STOCK: General antiques, art deco, porcelain, jewellery, collectables, books, maps.* TEL: 0273 204554. SER: Engraving.

Pyramid
9a Kensington Gdns. (C. Slater). Est. 1984. Open 10-5.30, Sat. 9-6. SIZE: Medium. *STOCK: Art deco and 20th C collectors' items; china and glass, £10-£600; furniture and furnishings, £50-£1,500; lighting and pictures, £15-£200.* LOC: Between Gloucester and North roads. PARK: Gloucester Rd., Sydney or Tidy St. TEL: 0273 607791. SER: Valuations; restorations (china).

Recollections
1a Sydney St. (B. Bagley and P. Tooley). Est. 1973. Open 10.30-4.30, Sat. 10.30-5.30. SIZE: Small. *STOCK: Small collectable items, 19th-20th C, £5-£250; brass and copper especially fireplace furniture; Victorian oil lamps.* LOC: From railway station down Trafalgar St. last turning on right. PARK: Opposite in Belmont St. TEL: 0273 681517. SER: Valuations; restorations (metal, china, oil lamps).

Brighton continued
Resners' BADA LAPADA
1 Meeting House Lane. (S. and G.R. Resner). Est. 1918. Open 9.50-5.30. SIZE: Small. *STOCK: Jewellery, £250-£5,000; objets d'art, £250-£1,000; silver, £150-£2,500; all 18th-19th C.* LOC: The Lanes. PARK: Nearby. TEL: 0273 329127; mobile - 0860 704251. SER: Valuations; restorations (jewellery). FAIRS: Kensington, Chelsea, British International, Birmingham; Buxton, Kenilworth, Barbican, Harrogate. VAT: Stan/Spec.

Robinson's Bookshop Ltd
11 Bond St. (Mrs S. Robinson and T.P. and P.M. Brown). Est. 1958. Open 9-5.30. *STOCK: Books on antiques and art; general and technical books.* LOC: North Lanes area. TEL: 0273 329012.

Rodney Arthur Classics
Rear of 64-78 Davigdor Rd, Hove. (R.A. Oliver). Est. 1979. Open 8.15-12.15 or by appointment. SIZE: Medium. *STOCK: Furniture, mainly Victorian and Edwardian shipping, £100-£2,000.* LOC: From Seven Dials, Davigdor Rd. is the exit to the west. PARK: Easy. TEL: 0273 326550. VAT: Stan. *Trade Only.*

Clive Rogers Oriental Rugs
22 Brunswick Rd, Hove. Est. 1974. Open by appointment. SIZE: Medium. *STOCK: Oriental rugs, carpets, textiles; Oriental and Islamic works of art.* LOC: Off Western Rd. PARK: Easy. TEL: 0273 738257; home - same; fax - 0273 738687. SER: Valuations; restorations (as stock); historical analysis commission agents; buys at auction. VAT: Stan/Spec.

Rutland Antiques
48 Upper North St. Open 10.30-5.30, Sun. by appointment. SIZE: Small. *STOCK: Furniture, porcelain, textiles and general antiques.* LOC: North of and parallel to Western Rd. PARK: Reasonable. TEL: 0273 329991.

Shelton Arts
4 Islingword Rd. (G.S. Hodgkison). Est. 1952. Open 9-6. *STOCK: Antiquarian prints, pictures, Rowland Ward wild life prints.* PARK: Easy. TEL: 0273 698345. SER: Framing; mount cutting; dry mounting, heat sealing; restorations (fine art).

Shop of the Yellow Frog
10/11 The Lanes. (J.N. Chalcraft). Est. 1946. Open 9-6, and Sun. during season. SIZE: Small. *STOCK: 19th C jewellery, from £10; 18th-19th C silver, 18th C porcelain, both £5-£500. Not Stocked: Large furniture.* LOC: Near Brighton Pavilion. TEL: 0273 325497. SER: Valuations; restorations (watches, jewellery, furniture); buys at auction.

S.L. Simmons
9 Meeting House Lane, The Lanes. NAG. Est. 1948. Open 9.30-5.30. *STOCK: Jewellery and silver, 19th C.* TEL: 0273 327949. VAT: Stan.

Brighton continued

The Sussex Commemorative Ware Centre
88 Western Rd, Hove. (R. Prior). Est. 1974. Open 9-12, Sat. 9-12 and 2-3, other times by appointment. STOCK: *Antique and modern Royal commemoratives including Doulton and limited editions; Parian.* TEL: 0273 773911. SER: Catalogues (£3, airmail £5).

Tapsell Antiques LAPADA
59 and 59a Middle St. and, 10 Ship St. Gdns. Est. 1948. Open 9-5.30, other times by appointment. SIZE: Large. STOCK: *English and continental furniture, clocks, bronzes, general antiques; Oriental ceramics, lacquer, furniture and bronzes.* TEL: 0273 328341. VAT: Stan/Spec.

Michael Tidey Antiques
87 St. Georges Rd, Kemptown. Resident. STOCK: *English furniture.* TEL: 0273 602389.

Timewarp
6 Sydney St. (Miss J. Whiskin). Est. 1982. Open 10.30-5.45, Sat. 9-6, Sun. by appointment. SIZE: Large. STOCK: *Lamps and shades, art deco to 1960's, £15-£55; Victorian oil lamps and spare parts, to £250; bakelite, furniture, 1930-1940, £2-£300.* LOC: 5 minutes from station, turn right off Trafalgar St. TEL: 0273 607527. SER: Restorations (oil lamps).

Graham Webb
59 Ship St. Est. 1961. Open 10-5. CL: Mon. SIZE: Small. STOCK: *Cylinder and disc musical boxes, all mechanical musical instruments, £650-£45,000.* LOC: Close to the Lanes. PARK: Middle St. TEL: 0273 321803; fax - same; home - 0273 772154. VAT: Stan/Spec.

Stephen and Sonia Welbourne LAPADA
43 Denmark Villas, Hove. Open by appointment. STOCK: *Watercolours and oil paintings, mainly English, some continental, 19th and early 20th C.* LOC: Near Hove station. TEL: 0273 722518. VAT: Spec.

E. and B. White
43-47 Upper North St, and warehouse at 36 Robertson Rd. Est. 1962. Open 9.30-5. CL: Sat. p.m. SIZE: Medium. STOCK: *Oak furniture, £50-£2,000.* LOC: Upper North St. runs parallel to and north of Western Rd. (the main shopping street). TEL: 0273 328706. VAT: Spec.

David Wigdor
30 Trafalgar St. Est. 1968. Open 9.30-5, Sat. and Sun. by appointment. STOCK: *General antiques.* TEL: 0273 677272. VAT: Stan/Spec.

The Witch Ball
48 Meeting House Lane. (Mrs Gina Daniels). Est. 1966. Open 10.30-6. STOCK: *18th-19th C topographical and decorative engravings; 16th-19th C maps.* TEL: 0273 326618. VAT: Stan.

Brighton continued

L. Woolman Antiques
29 Gloucester Rd, North Lanes. Est. 1973. Open 9-5, Sat. 8 a.m.-10 a.m. SIZE: Medium. STOCK: *Continental, Oriental and English porcelain, bronzes, clocks, paintings and decorative furniture, 18th-19th C, £25-£5,000.* LOC: Near station. PARK: Easy. TEL: 0273 609645; home - 0273 779866. SER: Valuations; buys at auction (clocks and watches). VAT: Stan. *Trade Only.*

Yellow Lantern Antiques Ltd LAPADA
34 Holland Rd, Hove. (B.R. and E.A. Higgins). Est. 1950. Open 9-1 and 2.15-5.30, Sat. 9-4. SIZE: Medium. STOCK: *Mainly English furniture, £50-£3,000; French and English clocks; both to 1850; bronzes, 19th C, £100-£1,500; continental porcelain, 1820-1860, £50-£1,000.* Not Stocked: Pottery, oak, 18th C porcelain. LOC: From Brighton seafront to Hove, turn right at Hotel Alexander, shop 100yds. on left past traffic lights (opposite Maples furnishing store.). PARK: Easy. TEL: 0273 771572; home - 0273 455476. SER: Valuations; restorations; buys at auction. FAIRS: Buxton; Harrogate; NEC; Guildford; Bath; Kensington; City of London. VAT: Spec.

Zebrak at Barnes Jewellers
24 Meeting House Lane, The Lanes. (T. and A. Zebrak). Est. 1978. Open daily, Sun. by appointment. SIZE: Small. STOCK: *Jewellery, silver, watches and objets d'art, 1800-1950, £5-£10,000.* PARK: Nearby. TEL: 0273 202929; mobile - 0860 550668; fax - 0273 321021. SER: Valuations; repairs; import/export. FAIRS: Olympia. VAT: Stan/Spec.

BURWASH, Nr. Etchingham

Chateaubriand Antiques Centre
High St. Open 10-5, Sun. 12-5.30. SIZE: 15 dealers. STOCK: *Lace, linen, furniture, country oak, glass, bronzes, paintings, smalls.* LOC: A265. TEL: 0435 882535. SER: Shipping.

Chaunt House
High St. (M. Walsh). Est. 1976. CL: Mon. SIZE: Small. STOCK: *Clocks, 19th C, £50-£1,000; watches and barometers.* LOC: A265. PARK: Easy. TEL: 0435 882221; home - same. SER: Valuations; restorations; buys at auction (as stock). VAT: Stan/Spec.

COODEN

Annies
4 Bixlea Parade, Little Common Rd. (P.A. Rose). Est. 1990. Open 10-5, Wed. and Sun. by appointment. SIZE: Small. STOCK: *China, glass, porcelain and linen, 1800-1930, £5-£500; furniture, from 1880, £50-£750; silver plate, kitchenalia, copper, brass and clocks, from 1800, £5-£150.* LOC: A259 between Bexhill and

Cooden continued
Eastbourne by Little Common roundabout. PARK: Easy. TEL: 0424 846966. SER: Valuations; buys at auction. FAIRS: De La Warr, Bexhill. VAT: Stan/Spec.

DITCHLING
Dycheling Antiques
34 High St. (E.A. Hudson). Est. 1977. Open 10.30-6. SIZE: Large. *STOCK: Georgian, Victorian, Edwardian and country furniture, especially dining chairs, £25-£4,000.* LOC: Off A23 on A273-B2112 north of Brighton. PARK: Easy. TEL: 0273 842929; home - same. VAT: Stan/Spec.

Nona Shaw Antiques
4 and 8 West St. Est. 1954. SIZE: Medium. *STOCK: Porcelain, furniture, glass, copper and brass.* TEL: 0273 843290. VAT: Stan/Spec.

EASTBOURNE
Douglas Barsley Antiques
44 Cornfield Rd. Est. 1966. Open 9-1 and 2-5, Sat. 9-5. *STOCK: Small collectors' items, silver, porcelain, small fine furniture.* TEL: 0323 733666.

Bell Antiques
47 South St. (Mrs M.J. Everett). Open 10-1 and 2-4.30. SIZE: Small. *STOCK: Porcelain and small bijou items, 18th-19th C, £10-£300; furniture, Victorian and Edwardian, £50-£400; paintings and prints, to 1930, £10-£150.* LOC: Road opposite Town Hall. PARK: Easy. TEL: 0323 641339. SER: Valuations.

Wm. Bruford and Son Ltd   BADA
11/13 Cornfield Rd. Est. 1883. Open 9-1 and 2-5.30. SIZE: Medium. *STOCK: Jewellery, Victorian, late Georgian; some silver, clocks (bracket, carriage), watches, from 1750, £50-£1,000. Not Stocked: China, glass, brass, pewter, furniture.* TEL: 0323 725452. SER: Valuations; restorations (clocks and silver). VAT: Stan/Spec.

Bygones
24 Willingdon Rd, Old Town. (J.A. Gearing). Est. 1986. Open 10.30-5. CL: Fri. and Wed. SIZE: Medium. *STOCK: Costume and accessories, 1900 to early 1950's, £5-£150.* LOC: At the end of A22. PARK: Nearby. TEL: 0323 737537; home - 0323 739199. SER: Valuations.

Camilla's Bookshop
57 Grove Rd. (C. Francombe and S. Broad). Est. 1976. Open 10-6. *STOCK: Books including antiquarian and on art, antiques and collectables, and especially naval, military, aviation, technical, needlework, broadcasting.* LOC: Next to police station. TEL: 0323 736001. SER: Valuations.

Eastbourne continued
John Cowderoy Antiques   LAPADA
42 South St. (J.H., R., D.J. and R.A. Cowderoy). GMC. Est. 1972. Open 9.30-1 and 2.30-5. CL: Wed. p.m. and Sat. p.m. SIZE: Large. *STOCK: Clocks, musical boxes, furniture, porcelain, silver and plate, jewellery, copper, brass, paintings.* LOC: 150yds. from Town Hall. PARK: Easy. TEL: 0323 720058. SER: Restorations (clocks, music boxes and furniture). VAT: Stan/Spec.

Crest Collectables
54 Grove Rd. (C. Powell). Open 10-6. *STOCK: General antiques and collectables.* TEL: 0323 721185.

John Day of Eastbourne Fine Art
9 Meads St. Est. 1964. Open 9.30-1 and 2-5. CL: Wed. and Sat. p.m. SIZE: Medium. *STOCK: English, especially East Anglian, and continental paintings and watercolours, 19th C.* LOC: Meads village, west end of Eastbourne. PARK: Easy. TEL: 0323 725634; mobile - 0860 466197. SER: Restorations; framing (oils and watercolours).

Roderick Dew
10 Furness Rd. Est. 1971. *STOCK: Antiquarian books, especially on art and antiques.* TEL: 0323 720239. *Postal Only.*

Eastbourne Antiques Market
80 Seaside. (C. French). Est. 1969. Open 10-5.30. SIZE: Large. 42 stalls. *STOCK: A wide selection of general antiques.* PARK: Easy. TEL: 0323 720128. FAIRS: Eastbourne and others.

Elliott and Scholz Antiques
12 Willingdon Rd. (C.R. Elliott and K.V. Scholz). Est. 1981. Open 9.30-4.30, Wed. and Sat. 9.30-1. SIZE: Small. *STOCK: Small furniture, £500-£1,000; clocks, £100-£300; bric-a-brac, £50-£100; all 19th-20 C.* LOC: A22. PARK: Easy. TEL: 0323 732200. SER: Valuations.

London and Sussex Antiquarian Book and Print Services
Open by appointment. *STOCK: Books including colour plate and literature; prints including Hogarth, 19th to early 20th C.* TEL: 0323 730857.

James Ludby Antiques
34 Church St, Old Town. (G. Ludby). Est. 1967. Open daily; Wed. p.m., Sat. p.m., lunchtimes and Sun. by appointment. SIZE: Small. *STOCK: Furniture, small items, china, glass and brass, unusual interesting items, 18th C to 1930, £5-£500.* PARK: Easy. TEL: 0323 732073. SER: Valuations. FAIRS: Brighton.

The Old Town Antique Centre
52 Ocklynge Rd. (A.D, Stevens). Est. 1990. Open 9.30-5, Sun. 10.30-5. SIZE: Medium. *STOCK: Furniture, £200-£300; china and jewellery, £50-£100; all 19th C.* LOC: East Dean coast road. PARK: Easy. TEL: 0323 416016; home - 0323 645608. FAIRS: Ardingly.

Eastbourne continued

Timothy Partridge Antiques
46 Ocklynge Rd. Open 10-1. *STOCK: Victorian, Edwardian and 1920's furniture.* LOC: In old town, near St. Mary's Church. PARK: Easy. TEL: 0323 638731.

Pharoahs Antiques Centre
28 South St. (W. and J. Pharoah). Est. 1973. Open 10-5. SIZE: Medium. 14 stallholders. *STOCK: A wide range of antiques including jewellery, pine, kitchenalia, china, curios, lace, linen, books, ephemera, Victorian furniture, original light fittings and lamps.* LOC: Near Town Hall. PARK: Easy. TEL: 0323 738655. FAIRS: Ardingly.

Ernest Pickering
44 South St. Est. 1946. Open 9-5. CL: Wed. p.m. and Sat. p.m. *STOCK: Furniture, porcelain, grandfather clocks.* TEL: 0323 730483. VAT: Stan/Spec.

Premier Gallery
24-26 South St. (D. Mazzoli). Est. 1983. Open 10-5.30. SIZE: Large. *STOCK: Antiquarian and second-hand books, including art books; oils and watercolours, 19th-20th C, especially John Bratby R.A, £50-£1,500; prints.* LOC: Near station. PARK: Easy. TEL: 0323 736023. SER: Valuations; restorations (oil paintings and watercolours); buys at auction (modern British paintings). VAT: Stan.

Raymond Smith
30 South St. (J.R. and T. Smith). Resident. Est. 1963. Open 9-5.30. CL: Wed. SIZE: Large. *STOCK: Secondhand and antiquarian books, 16th-20th C, 5p-£1,000; publishers' remainders, 75p-£30; maps and prints, 17th-20th C, 50p-£350.* LOC: 200yds. east of Town Hall. PARK: Easy. TEL: 0323 734128. SER: Valuations. VAT: Stan.

E. Stacy-Marks Ltd   BADA
24 Cornfield Rd. Est. 1889. SIZE: Large. STOCK: Paintings, English, Dutch and continental schools, 18th-20th C. TEL: 0323 720429/732653; fax - 0323 733897. VAT: Stan.

Stewart Gallery
25 Grove Rd. (Gallery Laraine Ltd.). Est. 1970. Open 9-5.30, Sun. 11-5. SIZE: Large. *STOCK: Paintings and ceramics, 19th-20th C, £5-£25,000; onyx and glassware.* LOC: Next to library, 150yds. from station. PARK: Easy. TEL: 0323 729588; fax and home - same. SER: Valuations; restorations (paintings and frames); buys at auction (paintings). VAT: Stan/Spec.

W.H. Weller - Restoration Centre
12 North St. (D. Rothwell). Est. 1892. Open 9.15-5. *STOCK: Metalware, brass, silver, trophies.* TEL: 0323 410972. SER: Restorations; polishing; silver plating; engraving.

Eastbourne continued

Lloyd Williams - Antique Anglo Am Warehouse
2a Beach Rd. Est. 1976. Open 9.30-5, Sat. and Sun. by appointment. SIZE: Large. *STOCK: Shipping furniture, 1850-1920, £50-£3,000, period furniture, pre 1850, £500+; general antiques.* LOC: Off Seaside Rd. PARK: Easy. TEL: 0323 648661; fax - 0323 648658; home - 0892 536627. SER: Restorations; containers. VAT: Stan. Trade Only.

EWHURST GREEN, Nr. Bodiam

Ewhurst Gallery
Court Lodge. (C. Churton). Resident. Open 10-6 including Sun., prior telephone call advisable. *STOCK: 19th-20th C oils, watercolours and drawings.* LOC: 1 mile from Bodiam Castle (N.T.). TEL: 0580 830213.

FLIMWELL

Graham Lower
Stonecrouch Farmhouse. Open by appointment. *STOCK: English and continental 17th-18th C oak furniture.* LOC: A21. TEL: 058 087 535. SER: Valuations. VAT: Spec.

HASTINGS

Abbey Antiques
364 Old London Rd. (A.T. and Y.M. Dennis). Est. 1960. Open 10.30-4.30. CL: Wed. *STOCK: Victorian, Edwardian and shipping furniture, porcelain, brass and copper, glass, linen, lace curios, clocks, barometers, pictures.* LOC: A21 from Dover, 1 mile before Hastings. PARK: Easy. TEL: 0424 429178. VAT: Stan/Spec.

Coach House Antiques
5 George St. (R.J. Luck). Est. 1972. Open 10-5 including Sun. SIZE: Medium. *STOCK: Longcase clocks, 18th-19th C., £1,000+; furniture, 19th C. £100+; collectables including Dinky toys, trains, dolls houses.* PARK: Nearby. TEL: 0580 712930; home - 0622 681719. SER: Valuations; restorations (clocks and furniture); buys at auction (clocks and furniture). VAT: Spec.

George Street Antiques Centre
47 George St. (F. Stanley and P. Heuduk). Est. 1969. Open 9-5, Sun. 11-4. SIZE: Medium - 20 dealers. *STOCK: Small items, 19th-20th C, £5-£500.* LOC: In old town, parallel to seafront. PARK: Seafront. TEL: 0424 429339; home - 0424 813526/713300.

Hallstand
23 Courthouse St. Open 10-5.30. *STOCK: Crested china, jewellery, collectables, small furniture.* LOC: Old Town.

Howes Bookshop
Trinity Hall, Braybrooke Terrace. ABA. Est

Pigeon House Antiques

**52 London Road
Hurst Green
East Sussex TN19 7PN
Tel: (0580) 860474**

18th and 19th century furniture and furnishing pieces.

Hastings continued
1920. Open 9.30-1 and 2.15-5. CL: Sat. p.m. STOCK: *Antiquarian and academic books in literature, history, arts, bibliography.* TEL: 0424 423437. FAIRS: ABA.

Nakota Curios
12 Courthouse St. (D.E. Taylor). Est. 1964. Open 10.30-1 and 2.30-5. CL: Wed. SIZE: Medium. STOCK: *General trade items, decorative china, furniture, Victoriana, jewellery.* Not Stocked: Coins, medals. PARK: Easy. TEL: 0424 438900.

J. Radcliffe
40 Cambridge Rd. Open 10-1 and 2-5. CL: Wed. p.m. STOCK: *General antiques, trade goods.* TEL: 0424 426361.

HERSTMONCEUX
W.F. Bruce Antiques
Gardner St. Est. 1977. Open 10-6 by appointment including Sun. SIZE: Medium. STOCK: *Clocks, early 18th to late 19th C, £100-£5,000; clock movements, early 18th to late 19th C, £100-£2,000; decorative items, mainly 19th C, £100-£1,000.* LOC: A271 towards Battle. PARK: Easy. TEL: 0323 833718; home - same. SER: Buys at auction (clocks, decorative items). VAT: Stan/Spec.

Touchwood
1 The Square. (M.E. Long and S. Miles). Est. 1975. Open 10-4.30, Sun. 10-1. CL: Mon. p.m. and Wed. SIZE: Medium. STOCK: *Victorian pine furniture, £5-£1,000; kitchenalia and bric-a-brac.* LOC: A271 off A23. PARK: Easy. TEL: 0323 832020; home - same; fax - 0323 832525. SER: Stripping. FAIRS: Ardingly. VAT: Stan/Spec.

HORAM, Nr. Heathfield
John Botting Antiques
Winstan House, High St. Open 9.30-5.30. SIZE: Medium. STOCK: *Victorian, Edwardian and some Georgian furniture, mahogany, oak and pine; French furniture; bric-a-brac.* PARK: Easy, on forecourt. TEL: 0435 813553.

HORSEBRIDGE, Nr. Hailsham
Horsebridge Antiques Centre
1 North St. (R. Lane). Resident. Est. 1978. Open 10-1 and 1.30-5. SIZE: Large. STOCK: *General antiques including furniture, silver, glass, pottery, brass and copper.* LOC: A271. PARK: Easy. TEL: 0323 844414. SER: Valuations.

HURST GREEN
Delmas
Little Bernhurst. (P.D. Stimpson). Est. 1973. Open 10-6.30. CL: Wed. STOCK: *English and continental furniture and paintings.* TEL: 0580 860345. VAT: Stan/Spec.

Pigeon House Antiques   LAPADA
52 London Rd. (D.K. and R.M. Wiltshire). Resident. Est. 1974. STOCK: *English and continental furniture, decorative items, mirrors and chandeliers, 18th-19th C.* LOC: On A21, next to the Royal George. PARK: Easy. TEL: 0580 860474. VAT: Stan/Spec.

LEWES
John Bird Antiques
Norton House, Iford. Est. 1970. Open anytime by appointment. STOCK: *Furniture - country pine, oak, fruitwood, painted architectural and garden; paintings, needlework, fabric.* TEL: 0273 483366.

Bow Windows Book Shop
128 High St. (A. and J. Shelley). Open 9-5. SIZE: Large. STOCK: *Books including natural history, English literature, travel, topography.* LOC: Off A27. TEL: 0273 480780. FAIRS: Antiquarian Book.

Lennox Cato   BADA LAPADA
Coombe House Antiques, 121 Malling St. (Mr and Mrs Cato). Resident. Est. 1975. Open 9.30-6, Sat. telephone first and Sun. by appointment. SIZE: Medium. STOCK: *English and continental furniture, decorative mirrors and related items, garden furniture.* LOC: Opposite Esso petrol station on A26. PARK: Private forecourt. TEL: 0273 473862; fax - 0273 479645. SER: Valuations; restorations. VAT: Stan/Spec.

CHARLESTON ANTIQUES

Georgian, Victorian & Edwardian Furniture
4 Lansdown Place, Lewes, East Sussex
Tel: (0273) 477916 or (0273) 483670 evenings
Open Tues-Fri 10am-5pm, Sat 10am-1pm, other times by appointment
U.K. Delivery and shipping arranged

Lewes continued

Charleston Antiques
4 Lansdown Place. (M. and S. Ball). Est. 1980. Open Tues.-Fri. 10-5, Sat. 10-1, other times by appointment. SIZE: Medium. *STOCK: Georgian, Victorian and Edwardian furniture, arts and crafts, £150-£5,000.* LOC: On one-way system towards railway station. PARK: Friars Walk or station. TEL: 0273 477916; home - 0273 483670. VAT: Stan/Spec.

Cliffe Antiques Centre
47 Cliffe High St. (Miss P. Harrison). Est. 1984. Open 9.30-5. SIZE: Medium - 16 dealers. *STOCK: General antiques, £5-£1,000.* LOC: Follow town centre signs, turning left 200 yds. past Safeways. PARK: Easy. TEL: 0273 473266.

Cliffe Gallery Antiques
39 Cliffe High St. (Grimes and Hayward). Open 9.30-5. *STOCK: 18th-20th C furniture including pine, mahogany, oak; china, glass, fabrics and jewellery.* TEL: 0273 471877.

A.J. Cumming
84 High St. Est. 1976. Open 10-5, Sat. 10-5.30. *STOCK: Antiquarian and out of print books.* TEL: 0273 472319. SER: Buys at auction.

H.P. Dennison and Son
22 High St. (D.H. Dennison). Est. 1933. Open 8.30-5. CL: Wed. p.m. SIZE: Medium. *STOCK: Mahogany furniture, early 19th C.* PARK: Easy. TEL: 0273 480655. SER: Valuations; restorations (furniture). VAT: Stan/Spec.

The Drawing Room
53 High St. Open 9.30-5.30. SIZE: Large. *STOCK: Furniture, pictures, objets d'art.* TEL: 0273 478560.

The Emporium Antique Centre
42 Cliffe High St. (A.D. Stevens). Open 9.30-5 including Sun. SIZE: 48 dealers. *STOCK: General antiqus and collectables.* TEL: 0273 486866.

Felix Gallery
Corner of Sun St. and Lancaster St. (W.S.H. and Mrs M.M. Whitehead). Est. 1981. Open 10-6, Sun. 12-6. SIZE: Small. *STOCK: Cats only - pottery, porcelain, bronze and silver, pictures,*

Lewes continued

general objets d'art. English and continental. LOC: 2 mins. from town centre. PARK: Nearby. TEL: 0273 472668; home - same.

Fifteenth Century Bookshop
99 High St. (S. Mirabaud). Est. 1938. Open 10-5.30. *STOCK: Antiquarian and general second-hand books, especially children's and illustrated; prints and teddies.* TEL: 0273 474160.

Renée and Roy Green   BADA
Ashcombe House, Lewes Rd. *STOCK: Furniture and objects, 17th to early 19th C.* **LOC: From Brighton A27, entrance on left-hand side 500yds. before Lewes (A275) turn-off. TEL: 0273 474794.**

Bob Hoare Pine Antiques
Unit Q, Phoenix Place, North St. Open 8-6, Sat. 9-2. *STOCK: Pine.* TEL: 0273 480557; fax - 0273 471298.

Diane Hoskins
11 Friars Walk. Open by appointment. *STOCK: Country furniture, pottery, Georgian glass, some decorative items.* TEL: 0273 475620.

Lewes Antique Centre
20 Cliffe High St. (C. Keen). Est. 1968. Open 9.30-5. SIZE: Large - 42 stallholders. *STOCK: Furniture, china, copper and metalware, glass, clocks.* LOC: A27 from Brighton, 2nd roundabout into Lewes, end of tunnel turn left, then next left, next right into Phoenix car park. 100m. walk to Cliffe High Street. PARK: Easy. TEL: 0273 476148. SER: Shipping.

Pastorale Antiques
15 Malling St. (O. Soucek). Open 10-6 or by appointment. SIZE: Large. *STOCK: Pine and European country furniture, mahogany and decorative items.* TEL: 0273 473259; home - 0435 863044; fax - 0273 473259.

Mary Sautter Pine Furniture
6 Station St. (M. and M. Sautter). Est. 1970. Open 9.30-1 and 2-5. CL: Sat. and Wed. afternoons. SIZE: Large. *STOCK: Pine furniture, 18th-19th C, £150-£1,500; longcase clocks.* LOC:

The Old Mint House

High Street, Pevensey, Near Eastbourne, East Sussex BN24 5LF England
Tel: Eastbourne (0323) 762337. Fax: (0323) 762337

LARGEST ANTIQUE BUSINESS IN THE SOUTH

Vast stock of mahogany, walnut, oak, inlaid and marquetry furniture of all periods, shipping goods and many objet d'art items.
Open daily Monday–Saturday 9.00–17.30, otherwise by appointment
Video available for the larger buyer

Lewes continued
From railway station, in town centre. PARK: Easy, own. TEL: 0273 474842. VAT: Stan.

Southdown Antiques
48 Cliffe High St. (Miss P.I. and K.A. Foster). Est. 1969. Open by appointment. SIZE: Medium. *STOCK: Small antiques, especially 18th-19th C English, continental and Oriental porcelain, objets d'art, works of art, glass, papier mâché trays, silver plate, £50-£350,000; reproduction and interior decor items.* LOC: A27. One-way street north. PARK: Easy. TEL: 0273 472439. VAT: Stan/Spec.

Trevor
Trevor House, 110 High St. Est. 1946. Open by appointment. *STOCK: Furniture, 17th to early 19th C; works of art.* VAT: Spec.

MAYFIELD
Wm. J. Gravener Antiques
High St. (Mr and Mrs Gravener). Resident. Est. 1965. *STOCK: Furniture, longcase clocks.* TEL: 0435 873389. VAT: Spec.

NEWHAVEN
Newhaven Flea Market
28 South Way. (R. Mayne and A. Wilkinson). Est. 1971. Open every day except 25th Dec. 10-5.30. *STOCK: Victoriana, Edwardian, bric-a-brac.* TEL: 0273 517207/516065.

Newhaven continued
Leonard Russell   BADA
21 Kings Ave, Mount Pleasant. Resident. Est. 1981. Open by appointment. SIZE: Small. *STOCK: English pottery figures, groups, animals, busts, lustre, 1720-1840, £80-£1,000; English Toby jugs, 1765-1840, £400-£3,000; Prattware including plaques, Toby and serving jugs, money boxes, animals, cow creamers, £100-£1,000; English commemorative pottery, 1770-1840.* LOC: 500 yards from A259 South Coast Rd., 3/4 mile from town centre. PARK: Easy. TEL: 0273 515153. SER: Valuations; restorations (pottery); buys at auction (pottery).

PEVENSEY
The Old Mint House   LAPADA
(J.C. and A.J. Nicholson). Est. 1901. Open 9-5.30. CL: Sat. SIZE: Large and warehouse. *STOCK: Furniture, Victorian, Edwardian and shipping; porcelain, clocks, 18th-19th C, £20-£10,000.* LOC: A259 coast road. PARK: Easy. TEL: 0323 762337; fax - 0323 762337. SER: Buys at auction. VAT: Stan/Spec.

PEVENSEY BAY
Murray-Brown
Silverbeach, Norman Rd. (G. and J. Murray-Brown). Open by appointment only. *STOCK: Paintings and prints.* TEL: 0323 764298. SER: Valuations; restorations; cleaning; publishing.

ANN LINGARD
Rope Walk Antiques, Rye, Sussex
Telephone: Rye (0797) 223486
10,000 sq. ft. of hand-finished
Antique English Pine Furniture
at reasonable prices
KITCHEN SHOP ★ ANTIQUES
Monday-Saturday 9.00-5.30
SUNDAY by appointment

PLAYDEN, Nr. Rye
Old Post House Antiques
Old Post House. (D. Cooke). Est. 1957. Open any time by appointment. SIZE: Medium. *STOCK: Oil paintings.* LOC: A268, opposite Peace and Plenty public house. PARK: Easy. TEL: 0797 280303. SER: Valuations; restorations; packing and shipping. VAT: Spec.

POLEGATE
Graham Price Antiques Ltd
4 Chaucer Industrial Estate, Dittons Rd. Open 9-6. SIZE: Large. *STOCK: Mainly furniture - pine, country, decorative, French, Irish, European, period and Victorian oak, mahogany and walnut; bric-a-brac and kitchenalia.* LOC: Between Hastings and Brighton on A27. TEL: 0323 487167/485301; fax - 0323 483904. SER: Export, packing, shipping and courier; restorations.

ROBERTSBRIDGE
De Montfort
49 High St. (E.D. and A.A. Sloane). Est. 1961. Open 10.30-5.30. CL: Mon. and Tues. SIZE: Large. *STOCK: English and continental furniture, 1500-1800; Islamic and ancient art; Oriental carpets, kelims, and textiles.* Not Stocked: Any items not included above. LOC: A21. PARK: Easy. TEL: 0580 880698. VAT: Spec.

ROTTINGDEAN
Jupiter Antiques
P.O. Box 609. (B. Dover and D. Szynowski). Est. 1984. By appointment. *STOCK: English porcelain, 18th C, £60-£6,000; signed Royal Worcester and Crown Derby, 19th-20th C, £500-£8,000; decorative English and continental porcelain, 19th C, £50-£2,000.* TEL: 0273 302865/597515. SER: Valuations; buys at auction (British and continental porcelain). FAIRS: Wakefield Ceramic; NEC April and Aug. VAT: Spec.

Trade Wind
Little Crescent. (R. Morley Smith). Est. 1974. Open by appointment only. *STOCK: Small furniture mainly mahogany, 1760-1850; period*

Rottingdean continued
silver caddy spoons, wine labels, sifter spoons, sauce and spice ladles. TEL: 0273 301177.

RYE
Bragge and Sons
Landgate House. (N.H. and J.R. Bragge). Est. 1840. Open 9-5. CL: Tues. p.m. *STOCK: 18th C furniture and works of art.* LOC: Entrance to town - Landgate. TEL: 0797 223358. SER: Valuations; restorations. VAT: Spec.

Curiosity Antiques
16A Landgate. (Patricia Warren). Est. 1986. Open 10.30-5. CL: Mon. and Tues. SIZE: Small. *STOCK: China including tea sets, £5-£500; furniture including cabinets, £50-£500; all 19th-20th C. Linen including Victorian embroidered, and damask tablecloths, £5-£200.* LOC: A259. PARK: Nearby. TEL: 0797 224696.

Herbert Gordon Gasson
The Lion Galleries, Lion St. (T.J. Booth). Est. 1909. Open 9-1 and 2-5.30. CL: Tues. p.m. SIZE: Large. *STOCK: 17th-18th C oak and walnut; Staffordshire and Chinese porcelain.* Not Stocked: Silver and glass. PARK: Easy. TEL: 0797 222208. SER: Restorations. VAT: Stan/Spec.

Landgate Antiques   LAPADA
22 Landgate. (R. and J. Jones). Resident. Est. 1974. Open 9-5.30. *STOCK: Desks, furniture, clocks, decorative 19th C European sculpture.* TEL: 0797 224746.

Ann Lingard - Rope Walk Antiques
LAPADA
18-22 Rope Walk, and 17 Tower St. Est. 1972. Open 9-5.30. SIZE: Large. *STOCK: English pine furniture and accessories; kitchen shop.* Not Stocked: Jewellery, silver and plate. PARK: Own, and public next door. TEL: 0797 223486. VAT: Stan.

Rye Antiques
93 High St. (Mrs D. Turner). Est. 1966. Open 9-6. CL: Sun. except by appointment. SIZE: Small. *STOCK: Small oak, walnut and mahogany furniture, 17th-19th C, £50-£1,000; metalware,*

Rye continued
jewellery, silver and plate, 18th-19th C, £5-£1,000. Not Stocked: Glass, coins, bric-a-brac. PARK: Easy. TEL: 0797 222259. VAT: Stan/Spec.

Wish Ward Antiques
Wish Ward. (E. Proctor). Open 9.30-4.30 including Sun. STOCK: Mainly furniture. TEL: 0797 222383.

ST. LEONARDS-ON-SEA
Aarquebus Antiques
46 Norman Rd. (Mr and Mrs G. Jukes). Resident. Est. 1957. Open 9-6 including Sun. SIZE: Medium. STOCK: Furniture, 18th C, £500-£1,000; shipping goods, Victorian to 1930, £5-£500; glass, gold and silver, 18th-19th C, £5-£1,000. LOC: Take A2100 to St. Leonards-on-Sea, turn right after main P.O. PARK: Easy. TEL: 0424 433267. SER: Valuations; restorations (furniture); pine stripping; buys at auction.

Banner Antiques
56 Norman Rd. (G.M. Schofield). Est. 1972. Open 10-1 and 2.15-5.30. CL: Wed. SIZE: Large. STOCK: Furniture, porcelain, pottery, copper, brass, watercolours. Not Stocked: Jewellery, silver, weapons. PARK: Easy. TEL: 0424 420050.

The Book Jungle
24 North St. (M. Gowen). Est. 1988. Open 10-5. CL: Wed. SIZE: Medium. STOCK: Secondhand books. LOC: Just off seafront. PARK: Nearby. TEL: 0424 421187.

Chapel Antiques
Chapel House, 1 London Rd. (E.R. Alff). Est. 1946. Open 9-5. SIZE: Large. STOCK: Furniture, china, glass and paintings, 17th-19th C, £100-£5,000. PARK: Easy. TEL: 0424 440025. SER: Valuations; restorations (furniture). VAT: Stan/Spec.

Filsham Farmhouse Antiques
111 Harley Shute Rd. (J.H. Yorke). Open 9-5.30. STOCK: Furniture especially oak; brass, copper, clocks and shipping goods. TEL: 0424 433109. VAT: Stan.

Galleon Antiques
70 Sedlescombe Rd. North, and 18 Gensing Rd. Open by appointment. STOCK: Early Chinese and Japanese furniture, carvings, silks, bronzes. TEL: 0424 424145/714981.

Galleria Fine Arts Ltd
77 Norman Rd. Open 10-6. STOCK: Decorative art and furniture, 18th-19th C. TEL: 0424 722317.

The Hastings Antique Centre
59-61 Norman Rd. (R.J. Amstad). Open 10-5.30, Sun. by appointment. TEL: 0424 428561; home - 0424 752922. Below are listed some of the dealers at this centre.

R. J. Amstad
STOCK: Furniture.

St. Leonards-on-Sea continued

R. Armstrong
STOCK: 1930-1950 collectables.

A. Bevan-Jones
STOCK: Decorative items.

Sarah Brixton
STOCK: Lace and linen.

M. Buckton
STOCK: Upholstered furniture. SER: Recovering.

P. Clements
STOCK: Decorative items and textiles.

I. Copeland/S. Longmead
STOCK: Furniture.

T. Cuthbert
STOCK: Period furniture.

S. Dahms
STOCK: Clocks.

W. Dazeley
STOCK: Pine furniture and kitchenalia.

Brenda Fox and Bridget Howett
STOCK: Decorative items.

Eric Freestone
STOCK: Marine pictures, nautical works of art, ship and yacht models.

K. Gumbrell
STOCK: Decorative items.

C. Lonsdale
STOCK: Art deco, art nouveau.

Tony Mathews
STOCK: Tribal art.

G. Mennis
STOCK: Sporting, leather goods.

Neil Slater
STOCK: Decorative French items.

Tiffany Antiques
STOCK: Furniture.

B. Watson
STOCK: Decorative items.

J. Ziebell
STOCK: Tools, kitchenalia, pine.

John Lang Antiques
65 Norman Rd. (J. and C. Lang). Open 10-5, Sat. 10-1. STOCK: General antiques. TEL: 0424 714848.

Monarch Antiques
6 and 19 Grand Parade. (J.H. King). Est. 1983. Open 9-5, Sat. 9-1. SIZE: Medium. STOCK: Furniture, from Victorian, £5-£2,000. LOC: A259. PARK: Easy. TEL: 0424 445841; fax - same; home - 0424 214158. SER: Valuations.

SUSSEX EAST

St. Leonards-on-Sea continued

K. Nunn
at Chapel Antiques, Chapel House, 1 London Rd. Open 9.30-5.30. STOCK: General antiques, weapons and unusual items. TEL: 0424 431093. SER: Buys at auction. VAT: Stan/Spec.

SEAFORD

Molly Alexander
Crouch House, Crouch Lane. Est. 1967. STOCK: Paintings, watercolours and antiquities. LOC: Opposite new Constitutional Club. PARK: Opposite. TEL: 0323 896577.

Richard Alexander
Crouch House, Crouch Lane. Est. 1948. Open by appointment. STOCK: Oriental items, oils and watercolours, £25-£500. PARK: Easy. TEL: 0323 896577.

The Courtyard Antiques Market
13, 15, 17 High St. (Mrs S.E. Barrett). Open 8.30-5.30. SIZE: Medium - 8 dealers. STOCK: General antiques. TEL: 0323 892091.

The Old House
13, 15, 17 High St. (P.R. and S.M. Barrett). Est. 1928. Open 9-5.30. SIZE: Large. STOCK: 18th-19th C furniture, china and glass, £5-£5,000. LOC: Near Railway Station. PARK: Own in South St. TEL: 0323 892091; home - 0323 898364. SER: Valuations; restorations (furniture); shippers. VAT: Stan/Spec.

Seaford's "Barn Collectors' Market" and Studio Bookshop
The Barn, Church Lane. Est. 1967. Open Tues., Thurs. and Sat. 10-4.30. SIZE: Several dealers. STOCK: Collectables including buttons, ephemera, books, post and cigarette cards. LOC: Off High St. TEL: 0323 890010.

Steyne House Antiques
35 Steyne Rd. (J.R. Deakin). Est. 1969. Open 10.30-5, Sat. 10.30-4. CL: Mon. SIZE: Small. STOCK: Victorian Staffordshire figures, pottery and porcelain, copper, brass and decorative items; 18th-19th C, £20-£500+. LOC: Off A259 into Broad St., take 2nd right into High St., then 3rd left. PARK: Easy. TEL: 0323 895088.

SEDLESCOMBE

Holmes House Antiques
The Green. (F.J. Fleischer). Est. 1973. Open 10-12 and 3-6 including Sun. CL: Mon. SIZE: Small. STOCK: Watercolours and oil paintings, £100-£1,000; small silver, £10-£100; both 19th C; furniture, 19th-20th C, £300-£500. PARK: Easy. TEL: 0424 870450.

Mrs C. Kinloch
Bulmer House, The Green. Open Wed.-Sat. 10-5. STOCK: Dolls, teddies and associated items. TEL: 0424 870364.

Sedlescombe continued

Peter and Janet Mew Antiques
The Tithe Barn. Est. 1987. Open 10-6, Sun 10-12.30 and 2.30-5. CL: Mon. SIZE: Medium. STOCK: Oak and mahogany country furniture, £200-£3,000; copper, brass and pewter, £50-£500; blue and white china, £50-£250; all 17th-19th C. LOC: 1 mile off A21. PARK: Easy. TEL: 0424 870159; home - same. SER: Valuations; buys at auction (as stock).

UCKFIELD

Barnes Gallery
8 Church St. (S.J. and A.R. Barnes). Est. 1984. Open 10-5.30. CL: Mon. SIZE: Medium. STOCK: Watercolours and oils, 19th to early 20th, £200-£20,000. PARK: Nearby. TEL: 0825 762066. SER: Restorations; cleaning; framing. VAT: Spec.

Nicholas Bowlby
Owl House, Poundgate. Est. 1981. Open every day by appointment. SIZE: Medium. STOCK: English paintings, watercolours and drawings, 18th-20th C, £50-£20,000. LOC: Just off A26, 1 1/2 miles south of Crowborough. PARK: Easy. TEL: 0892 653722. SER: Valuations; restorations; buys at auction (watercolours and drawings). VAT: Spec.

Ivan R. Deverall
Duval House, The Glen, Cambridge Way. STOCK: Maps. TEL: 0825 762474. SER: Catalogue available; colouring.

Georgian House Antiques
222 High St. (Mr and Mrs P. Hale). Resident. Est. 1976. Open 10-6, Sun. and evenings by appointment. CL: Some Wed. SIZE: Large. STOCK: English domestic oak and country furniture and related decorative items, 1600-1860. Not Stocked Bric-a-brac. LOC: A22. PARK: Nearby. TEL: 0825 765074. SER: Furniture made from 17th C timber. VAT: Spec.

Ringles Cross Antiques
Ringles Cross. (C. and J. Dunford). Est. 1965 Open 9.30-6 or by appointment. STOCK: English furniture, 17th-18th C and accessories; Oriental items. LOC: 1 mile north of Uckfield. PARK: Own. TEL: 0825 762909.

WADHURST

Park View Antiques
High St, Durgates. (B. Ross). Est. 1985. Open 10 5, Sat. 10-5.30, Wed. and Sun. by appointment SIZE: Small. STOCK: Pine, oak and country furniture, 17th-19th C, £100-£1,500; decorative items, 1930's, £25-£150; iron and metalware 17th-19th C, £25-£250. LOC: On B2099 Frant Hurst Green road. PARK: Easy. TEL: 089: 783630; home - 0892 740264. SER: Valuations restorations (furniture).

Antique Collectors' Club Titles

Jewellery 1780-1910
The International Era - 2 vols
by Shirley Bury F.S.A.

A detailed and beautifully illustrated work by the former Keeper of Metalwork at the Victoria and Albert Museum. The book details the design, manufacture, fashion and history of every kind of jewellery. Covers the development of fashions, materials and techniques of 19th century jewellery. The historical background of this important era is examined, from popular everyday jewellery to that worn by Royalty and the nobility.

Vol. I 1789-1861, 472pp, 231 b & w illus, 104 col, ISBN 1 85149 148 1
Vol.II 1862-1910, 424pp, 191 b & w illus, 110 col, ISBN 1 85149 149 X
£47.50 per volume £95.00 the set

The Price Guide to Jewellery 3000BC-1950AD
by Michael Poynder

Describes and illustrates hundreds of examples of the type of jewellery that is popular with buyers world-wide. The prices are constantly being updated so that the book is an essential guide to those anxious to buy.
388pp, 340 b & w illus, 44 col, ISBN 0 902028 50 2. £29.95

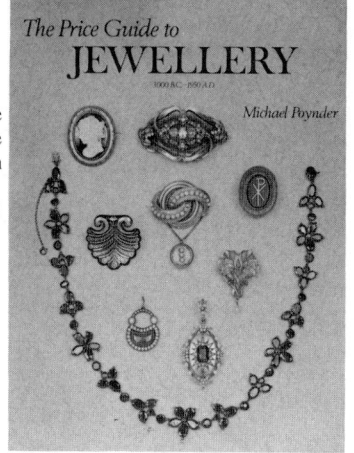

Available from:
Antique Collectors' Club, 5 Church Street
Woodbridge, Suffolk IP12 1DS
Tel: (0394) 385501 Fax: (0394) 384434

or Market Street Industrial Park
Wappingers' Falls, New York 12590, USA
Tel: 914 297 0003 Fax: 914 297 0068

Understanding Jewellery *by David Bennett and Daniela Mascetti*
Written by two leading Sotheby's experts, a practical book covering the jewellery of the last 200 years for those interested in buying. Fashions in jewellery are described with examples of a range of fakes, alterations, repairs and comparisons of varying degrees of quality. Features a concise guide to gem stones.
388pp, 30 b & w illus, 738 col illus, ISBN 1 85149 075 2, £35.00

Sussex West

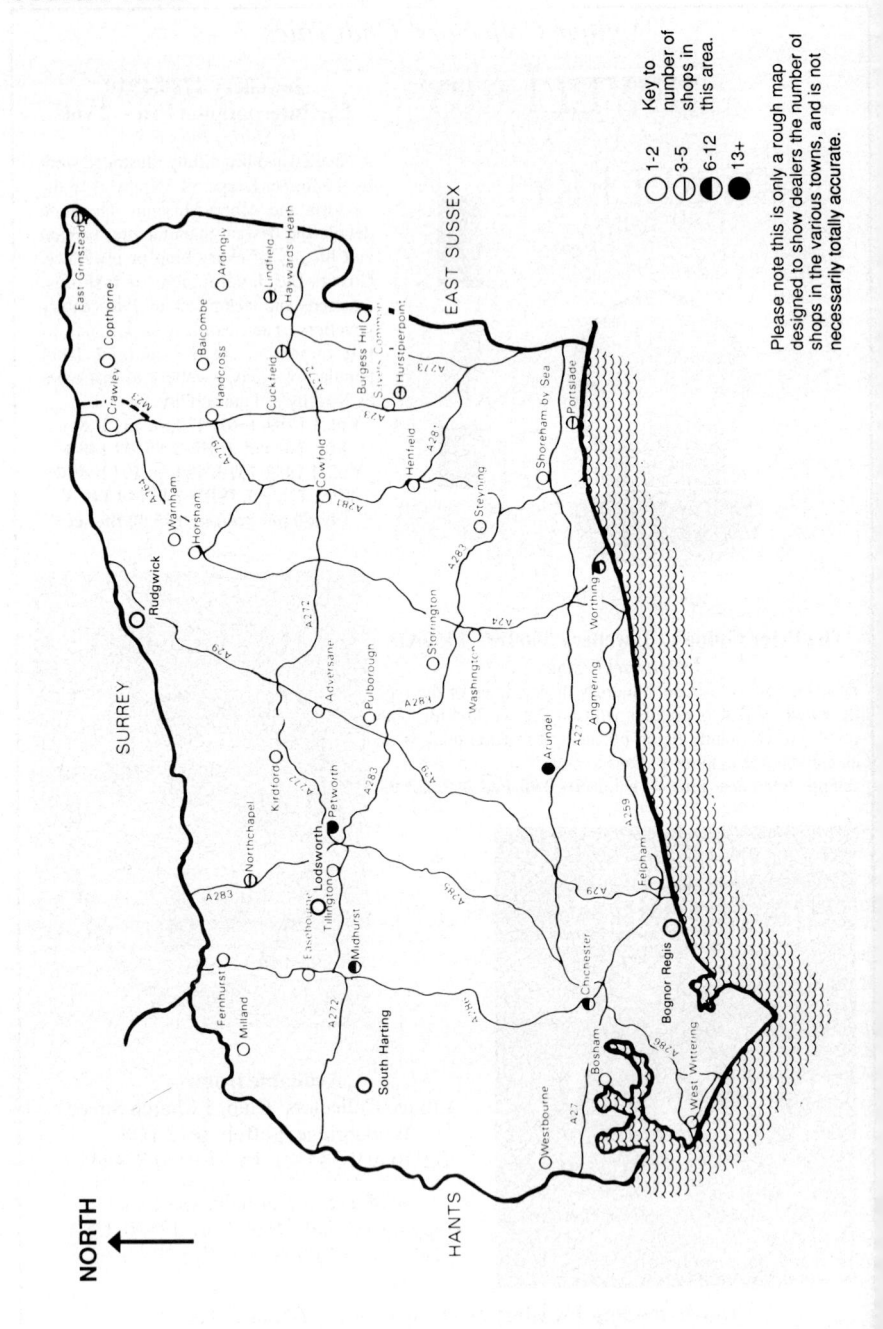

Sussex West

ADVERSANE, Nr. Billingshurst
Antique Centre and Collectors Market
Old House. Open daily including Sun. SIZE: 22 stallholders. *STOCK: General antiques and collectors' items.* PARK: Easy. TEL: 0403 783594/782186.

ANGMERING
Bygones
The Square. (R.A. and Mrs L.R. Whittaker). Est. 1965. Open 10-1 and 2.15-5, Sat. 10-12. CL: Wed. SIZE: Medium. *STOCK: Furniture, £50-£1,000; china, £5-£150; silver, £10-£250; linen, £5-£75; all 1800-1920.* LOC: A280. PARK: Easy. TEL: 0903 786152; home - same. SER: Valuations; buys at auction (furniture).

ARUNDEL
Armstrong-Davis Gallery
The Square. *STOCK: Fine sculptures of all periods; original bronze sculptures by 19th-20th C masters.* TEL: 0903 882752. SER: Commissions accepted for sculpture in relation to architectural, industrial and private projects. Represented in Italy and Switzerland.

Baynton-Williams
37A High St. (R.H. and S.C. Baynton-Williams). Open 10-6. *STOCK: Maps, views, sporting, marine and decorative prints.* TEL: 0903 883588. SER: Valuations; cataloguing.

Country Life by Bursig
1 Tarrant Sq, Tarrant St. (R.H. Bursig). Est. 1978. Open 9.30-5, Sun. 2-5. SIZE: Large. *STOCK: Furniture, oak, mahogany and walnut, 17th-19th C, £50-£2,000; oil paintings and watercolours, £50-£500; porcelain, pewter and brass, £5-£200; all 19th C.* PARK: Easy. TEL: 0903 883456; home - 0243 822045. VAT: Spec.

Richard Davidson Antiques   BADA
Romsey House, 51 Maltravers St. Open by appointment only. *STOCK: Fine furniture, decorative accessories, oil paintings.* TEL: 0903 883141; fax - same. SER: Interior decoration; valuations; restorations. VAT: Spec.

Pat Golding
6 Castle Mews, Tarrant St. Open 10-1 and 2-5. *STOCK: Ceramics and glass, 18th-20th C.*

Phyllis Gordon
Est. 1972. Open anytime by appointment. *STOCK: Georgian and Victorian furniture; button back chairs, porcelain, silver and glass, clocks.* LOC: On B2028. TEL: 0903 883911.

Lasseters
8a High St. Est. 1780. *STOCK: Jewellery, silver.* TEL: 0903 882651. VAT: Stan/Spec.

Mamie's Antiques Centre
5 River Rd. (Mrs M. Eyers). Est. 1966. Open

Arundel continued

Thurs.-Sun. 9-5 or by appointment. SIZE: 30+ dealers. *STOCK: General antiques.* PARK: Easy. TEL: 0903 882012. The following businesses operate from this address.

Phyllis Gordon
Open Sat. 8-4 or by appointment. *STOCK: Small Georgian and Victorian furniture including upholstered chairs, porcelain, glass.* TEL: 0903 883911. SER: Restorations.

The Courtyard
Open Sat. 9-5. *STOCK: Garden statuary.*

The Gallery
Open Sat. 9-5. *STOCK: Period items including fine furniture and porcelain.*

The Studio
Open by appointment. *STOCK: Furniture and general antiques.*

Riverside Gallery and Tearooms
River Rd. (Mrs B. Driver). *STOCK: Paintings, silver, plate, porcelain, glass.* TEL: 0903 882921.

Serendipity Antiques
27 Tarrant St. (A.G. Brown). Est. 1972. Open 9.30-1 and 2-6. CL: Sun. a.m. SIZE: Medium. *STOCK: Victorian prints, watercolours, oils and maps. Not Stocked: China, glass, brass.* LOC: Opposite Norfolk Hotel, turn left for Chichester. PARK: Easy. TEL: 0903 882047. SER: Restorations (oil paintings); colouring (maps and prints). VAT: Stan/Spec.

Sussex Fine Art
7 Castle Mews, Tarrant St. (G.C. and P.A. Miller). Est. 1987. Open Fri. and Sat. 10.30-5.30, Sun. 12-5, other days by appointment. SIZE: Small. *STOCK: English watercolours, 1760-1930, from £100.* LOC: Off High St. PARK: 50yds. TEL: 0903 884055. SER: Framing; buys at auction. VAT: Spec.

Spencer Swaffer   LAPADA
30 High St. Est. 1974. Open 9-6. SIZE: Large. *STOCK: Unusual decorative and traditional items, brass, blue and white, Staffordshire, dinner services, pine, oak dressers, marble tables, bamboo, shop fittings, candlesticks, majolica, French, English, painted and garden furniture.* PARK: Easy. TEL: 0903 882132; fax - 0903 884564. VAT: Stan/Spec.

Tarrant Street Antique Centre
Nineveh House, Tarrant St. (Miss J. Millar and A. Pugh). Open 10-5, Sun. 11-5. SIZE: Large. 14 dealers. *STOCK: Wide range of general antiques including Edwardian and Victorian, country and pine furniture, jewellery and silver, paintings and prints, china and glass, luggage and Oriental rugs.* LOC: Off A27 and A29 into town then second left off High St. PARK: Own forecourt. TEL: 0903 884307. SER: Valuations; restorations.

SUSSEX WEST

Arundel continued
Treasure House Antiques and Collectors Market
31b High St, and Crown Yard car park. Est. 1972. Open 9-5; Crown Yard Sat. 9-5 only. CL: Wed. STOCK: *Victoriana, domestic bygones, porcelain, Goss and crested china models, toys, Royal commemoratives, lace, cameras, lamps, curios, silver, jewellery, clocks, metalware, small furniture.* PARK: Easy. TEL: 0903 507446/883101/882908.

Upstairs Downstairs Antique Centre
29 Tarrant St. Open 10.30-5 including Sun. SIZE: 4 floors. STOCK: *General antiques.* TEL: 0903 883749.

The Walking Stick Shop
Stuart Thompson (Fine Canes), 39 Tarrant St. Est. 1981. Open 8.30-5.30, Wed. 8.30-1, Sun.p.m. by appointment. SIZE: Medium. STOCK: *Walking sticks and canes, 1620 to date, £10-£2,000.* LOC: Off High St. PARK: Easy. TEL: 0903 883796; home - 0903 882713; fax - 0903 884491. SER: Valuations; buys at auction (canes). VAT: Stan.

Whitehouse Antique Interiors
4 Tarrant Square, Tarrant St. (G.G. Cross). Open 10-5. STOCK: *Furniture, porcelain, decorative items.* TEL: 0903 882443.

BALCOMBE
Pine and Design
Haywards Heath Rd. (J.M. Nelson and G. Lindsay-Stewart). Est. 1974. CL: Sun. a.m. SIZE: Medium. STOCK: *Stripped pine furniture, mirrors, sofas, pictures, lace, 18th-19th C, £25-£500.* LOC: B2036. PARK: Easy. TEL: 0444 811700. SER: Restorations and interior design, handmade kitchens and furniture from old pine. VAT: Stan.

Woodall and Emery Ltd
Haywards Heath Rd. Est. 1884. TEL: 0444 811608. VAT: Stan.

BILLINGSHURST
Lannards Gallery
Okehurst Lane. (Mr and Mrs Derek Sims). Open weekends, weekdays by appointment only. STOCK: *Watercolours, oils and furniture, from 1850.* TEL: 0403 782692.

BOGNOR REGIS
Gough Bros. Art Shop and Gallery
71 High St. (S. Neal). Est. 1916. CL: Wed. p.m. SIZE: Medium. STOCK: *Watercolours, £50-£1,000; oils, £100-£1,500; miniatures, £150-£400; all 19th to early 20th C.* LOC: Off High St., behind Unicorn public house. PARK: Nearby. TEL: 0243 823773. SER: Valuations; restorations (oils and watercolours, frames and gilding). VAT: Stan/Spec.

BOSHAM
Bosham Antiques
(L. and M. Lain). Open Wed.-Sat. 10.30-5 or by appointment. STOCK: *Furniture, general antiques.* LOC: A259 at Bosham roundabout. PARK: Own. TEL: 0243 572005. VAT: Stan/Spec.

Mark Chapman Antiques
Open by appointment only. STOCK: *Fine English furniture and decorative items, 17th-19th C.* TEL: 0243 572862. SER: Restorations.

BURGESS HILL
British Antique Exporters Ltd
School Close, Queen Elizabeth Ave. Est. 1963. Open 9-5.30. SIZE: Large. STOCK: *General antiques.* LOC: Off Queen Elizabeth Ave. TEL: 0444 245577. VAT: Stan.

British Antique Replicas
School Close, Queen Elizabeth Ave. Est. 1962. Open 8-5.30, Sat. 9-5.30. SIZE: Large. STOCK: *Furniture, £100-£20,000.* LOC: 3 miles west A23. PARK: Easy. TEL: 0444 245577. SER: Bespoke furniture. VAT: Stan.

CHICHESTER
Almshouses Arcade
19 The Hornet. Est. 1983. Open 9.30-4.30. LOC: 200yds. from Cattle Market at eastern end of city. On one-way system (A286) just before traffic lights at Market Ave. PARK: Easy. Below are listed the dealers at these premises.

Antics
(P. German). STOCK: *General antiques and collectables.*

R.K. Barnett
STOCK: *Antiques and collectables including small furniture.* TEL: 0243 528089.

Overlord
(D. Rowe). STOCK: *Militaria, some general antiques, £5-£100.*

Patty Pearse
STOCK: *General antiques.*

Postcard Corner
STOCK: *Postcards, prints, badges.*

Sheelagh's Cottage
(S. Hughes and P. Fenton). STOCK: *General antiques and collectables.*

Antique Shop
Frensham House, Hunston. (J.M. Riley). Est. 1966. Open 9-6. STOCK: *English furniture - bureaux, chests of drawers, tables, chairs, 1700-1830.* LOC: One mile south of Chichester by-pass on B2145. PARK: Easy. TEL: 0243 782660.

The Canon Gallery   LAPADA
Lane End, Appledram Lane, Dell Quay. (J. Green). Open 9-5.15. STOCK: *19th-20th C*

Chichester continued
watercolours and oils. TEL: 0243 786063. SER: Valuations; restorations; framing.

Gems Antiques
39 West St. (M.L. Hancock). Open 10.30-1 and 2.30-5.30. STOCK: *Period furniture, Staffordshire and porcelain figures, glass and pictures.* TEL: 0243 786173.

Green and Stone of Chichester
1 North House, North St. (R.J.S. Baldwin). Open 9-5.30. STOCK: *Artists' and writing materials, 19th C engravings, watercolours.* TEL: 0243 533953.

Peter Hancock Antiques
40-41 West St. Articles on coins. Est. 1950. Open 10.30-1 and 2.30-5.30. SIZE: Medium. STOCK: *Silver, jewellery, porcelain, furniture, £20-£2,000; pictures, glass, clocks, books, £20-£1,500; all 18th-19th C; enthnographica, art nouveau, art deco, 19th-20th C, £5-£500.* LOC: From Chichester Cross, 17 doors past Cathedral. PARK: Easy. TEL: 0243 786173. SER: Valuations. VAT: Stan/Spec.

Heritage Antiques
77D, 83 and 84 St. Pancras. (D.R. and D.A. Grover). Open 9.30-5.30. STOCK: *Furniture and decorative items.* TEL: 0243 783470/783796.

St. Pancras Antiques
150 St. Pancras. (R.F. and M. Willatt). Est. 1980. Open 9.30-1 and 2-5. CL: Thurs. p.m. SIZE: Small. STOCK: *Militaria, arms and armour, medals, documents, uniforms and maps, 1600-1914, £5-£3,000; china, pottery and ceramics, 1800-1930, £2-£500; small furniture, 18th-19th C, £20-£1,000; coins, ancient to date.* Not Stocked: Silver and carpets. TEL: 0243 787645. SER: Valuations; restorations (arms and armour); buys at auction (militaria).

COCKING, Nr. Midhurst
The Victorian Brass Bedstead Company
Hoe Copse. (David Woolley). Resident. Est. 1970. Open by appointment. SIZE: Large. STOCK: *Victorian and Edwardian brass and iron bedsteads, bases and mattresses, 19th-20th C, £500-£1,000.* LOC: Right behind village Post Office, 3/4 mile left turning to Hoe Copse. PARK: Easy. TEL: 0730 812287. SER: Valuations; restorations (brass and iron bedsteads). VAT: Stan.

COPTHORNE, Nr. Crawley
Copthorne Antiques
Copthorne Bank. (Mrs M. Denman). Open 10-5.30. STOCK: *General antiques including furniture, dolls, china, jewellery, collectables, Victorian watercolours, oils.* LOC: 10 minutes from Gatwick. Off M23, junction 10. TEL: 0342 712802.

COWFOLD
Cowfold Clocks
The Olde House, The Street. (F.M. Henderson). Open 9.30-5.30. CL: Mon. STOCK: *Clocks - English dial, lacquer tavern, bracket, mantel and longcase; stick and wheel barometers, 18th-20th C.* TEL: 0403 864505 (24hr.). SER: Repairs (clocks and barometers); dial painting and restoration.

Squires Pantry Antiques
Station Rd. (L.M. Lasham). Open 10-1 and 2-5. STOCK: *Pine.* TEL: 0403 864869. VAT: Stan/Spec.

CRAWLEY
Jennie Hardman Antiques
Spikemead Farm, Poles Lane, Lowfield Heath. Est. 1971. Open by appointment, including Sun. SIZE: Large. STOCK: *French furniture, country and formal, mainly 19th C, £100-£1,500.* LOC: Off A23 Gatwick. PARK: Easy. TEL: 0293 560294; fax - 0293 539826. SER: Containers. VAT: Stan/Spec. *Trade Only.*

CUCKFIELD
David Foord-Brown Antiques LAPADA
High St. Est. 1988. Open 10-5.30. SIZE: Medium. STOCK: *Furniture, 1780-1880, £300-£5,000; porcelain, 1800-1850, £20-£1,500.* Not Stocked: Country furniture. LOC: A272. PARK: Easy. TEL: 0444 414418. SER: Valuations. VAT: Stan/Spec.

John Hopkins BADA LAPADA
1 The Courtyard, Ockenden Manor. (J., M. and A. Hopkins). Est. 1956. Open by appointment only. STOCK: *English and continental furniture, 17th-19th C, £600-£5,000; watercolours, 19th C, £250-£2,500; glass candelabra, 18th-19th C, £1,800-£5,000.* LOC: Turn off London-Brighton road at Bolney crossroads, towards Cuckfield. PARK: Easy. TEL: 0444 454323/456140. SER: Valuations; buys at auction (English and continental furniture). FAIRS: Most major. VAT: Stan/Spec.

Richard Usher Antiques
23 South St. Est. 1978. Open 10-5.30. CL: Wed. p.m. and Sat. p.m. SIZE: Medium. STOCK: *Furniture, 17th-19th C, £50-£2,000; decorative items.* LOC: A272. PARK: Easy. TEL: 0444 451699. SER: Valuations; restorations.

EASEBOURNE, Nr. Midhurst
Easebourne Antiques
Easebourne Lane. (J. Fynes). Est. 1971. Open daily, Sun. by appointment. SIZE: Medium. STOCK: *General antiques, 19th-20th C, to £500.* LOC: A286. PARK: Easy. TEL: 0730 816240; home - 0798 42353. SER: Valuations.

The Antique Print Shop

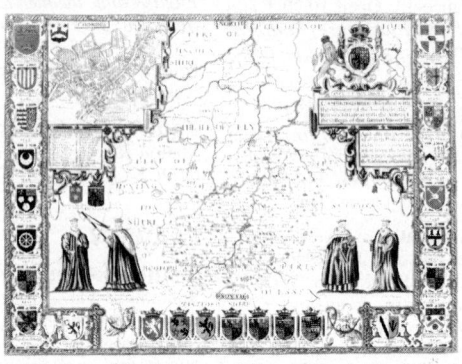

From the 'Theatre of the Empire of Great Britain' by John Speed, published by Bassett and Chiswell 1676

A WIDE SELECTION OF MAPS AND PRINTS
Open Monday to Saturday, 9.30am-6pm

11 Middle Row, East Grinstead, West Sussex, RH19 3AX.
Tel: 0342 410501 Fax: 0342 322149

EAST GRINSTEAD

The Antique Atlas
31A High St. View by appointment. STOCK: Maps, charts, plans and views worldwide. LOC: Entrance Cantelupe Rd. TEL: 0342 315813.

The Antique Print Shop
11 Middle Row. (A.A.W. Daszewski and Mrs A.C. Keddie). Est. 1988. Open 9.30-6. SIZE: Small. STOCK: Prints, pre-1880, £5-£100; maps especially British county, 1500-1870, £10-£1,000; English watercolours and drawings, 1700-1880, £100-£700. LOC: On island in middle High St., opposite St. Swithins church. PARK: Lewes Rd. TEL: 0342 410501; fax - 0342 322149. SER: Restorations; buys at auction (as stock); framing. FAIRS: Monway Fairs, London, City of London Antiques (Barbican).

Keith Atkinson Antiques
Moorhawes, Sandhawes Hill. Open Mon.-Fri. 8-6, other times by appointment. SIZE: Large. STOCK: Furniture, 19th to early 20th C. LOC: A264, close to Dormans Park. PARK: Easy. TEL: 0342 870765; fax - 0342 870767. SER: Packing and shipping. VAT: Stan/Spec.

Hinsdale Antiques
139 West St. Open 10-5, prior telephone call advisable Mon. morning. SIZE: Medium. STOCK: Furniture, 18th to early 20th C; dolls

East Grinstead continued

and related items, late 19th to early 20th C; small items. LOC: Corner of Queen's Rd., near town centre. PARK: Easy. TEL: 0342 303173. SER: Restorations (dolls); interior design.

FELPHAM, Nr. Bognor Regis

Susan and Robert Botting
'Rosedene', 38 Firs Ave. (S.M. and R.M.D. Botting). Est. 1979. Open by appointment. SIZE: Medium. STOCK: Watercolours and oil paintings, 19th C, £500-£20,000. LOC: Off A259. PARK: Easy. TEL: 0243 584515; home - same. SER: Valuations; restorations. FAIRS: City of London; Westminster; Harrogate; Petworth; NEC. VAT: Spec.

FERNHURST, Nr. Haslemere

Sheelagh Hamilton
9b Midhurst Rd. Open 10-5. STOCK: Period pine furniture, pictures. TEL: 0428 653253.

HANDCROSS

Handcross Antiques
High St. Est. 1978. Open 9-4.30. CL: Wed. p.m. and Mon. STOCK: General antiques. TEL: 0444 400784.

Handcross continued
Verralls (Handcross) Ltd
The Old Garage, High St. Open 10-6. *STOCK: Vintage and veteran motor cycles, motor cars.* TEL: 0444 400678. SER: Valuations; buys at auction. VAT: Stan/Spec.

HAYWARDS HEATH
David Burkinshaw
Sugworth Farmhouse, Borde Hill Lane. Open by appointment. *STOCK: Pedestal and partner desks, 1820-1880.* TEL: 0444 459747.

The Doll's House
44 Sussex Rd. (Mrs R.D. Ramm). Open 9.30-5.30. *STOCK: General antiques.* TEL: 0444 451393.

Ramm Antiques
43 Sussex Rd. (R.E. Ramm). *STOCK: Collectables and general antiques.* TEL: 0444 451393.

HENFIELD
Alexander Antiques
Post House, Small Dole. (Mrs J.A. Goodinge). Est. 1971. CL: Sun. except by appointment. SIZE: Medium. *STOCK: Country furniture, brass, copper, pewter, samplers, small collectors' and decorative items, treen.* LOC: A2037. PARK: Easy. TEL: 0273 493121; home - same. VAT: Stan/Spec.

HORSHAM
L.E. Lampard and Sons
23-31 Springfield Rd. Est. 1920. Open 8-1 and 2-5. SIZE: Medium. *STOCK: Mahogany and oak furniture, firebacks, grates.* TEL: 0403 254012/264332. VAT: Stan/Spec.

HURSTPIERPOINT
Chimera Books
17 High St. (R. and J. Lyon). Open by appointment only. SIZE: Large. *STOCK: Antiquarian books especially Oriental art, reference and travel.* TEL: 0273 832255.

The Clock Shop
36 High St. Est. 1974. CL: Wed. p.m. and Mon. *STOCK: Clocks.* TEL: 0273 832081. SER: Restorations (clocks and furniture).

Julian Antiques
124 High St. Est. 1964. Open 9-5. CL: Sat. *STOCK: French clocks, bronzes, art deco, fireplaces, mirrors, furniture.* TEL: 0273 832145.

Michael Miller
The Lamb, 8 Cuckfield Rd. (M. and V. Miller). Est. 1880. Open Sat. 9.30-5, other times appointment advisable. *STOCK: Arms and armour, post-1460, from £5; general antiques.* TEL: 0273 834567. SER: Buys at auction; exporters.

KIRDFORD, Nr. Billingshurst
Sheila Hinde Fine Art   LAPADA
Idolsfold House. **STOCK: Fine paintings and watercolours, animalier bronzes.** TEL: 0403 77576. VAT: Spec.

LINDFIELD
Alma Antiques
79 High St. Est. 1976. Open 10.30-5. CL: Wed. *STOCK: Small collectable items, porcelain, glass, silver, copper, brass, furniture, watercolours and prints.*

Lindfield Galleries - David Adam   BADA
62 High St. Est. 1972. Open 9.30-5.30. *STOCK: Oriental carpets.* TEL: 0444 483817. VAT: Stan/Spec.

LITTLEHAMPTON
The Round Pond
Faux Cottage, 4a Selborne Rd. (John Haynes and Kay Meader). Est. 1962. Open by appointment. SIZE: Small. *STOCK: Vintage model boats especially yachts, 19th C to 1950's, £50-£2,000.* PARK: Easy. TEL: 0903 714261; home - same. SER: Valuations. FAIRS: Chelsea Harbour (Jan). VAT: Stan/Spec.

LODSWORTH
Richard Gardner Antiques
The Stores, The Street. (R. and J.A. Gardner). Resident. Est. 1992. Open 10-5 including Sun. Nov. to Easter - Thurs.-Sun. 10-5. SIZE: Small. *STOCK: Victorian Staffordshire figures, pot-lids, Prattware and Baxter prints, £30-£600; small furniture and general antiques.* LOC: Midway between Petworth and Midhurst. TEL: 07985 513; home - same. SER: Restorations (ceramics). FAIRS: Major southern. VAT: Stan.

MIDHURST
Churchhill Clocks
West St. (W.P. and Dr. E. Tyrrell). Open 9-4.30, Wed. 9-1. *STOCK: Clocks.* TEL: 0730 813891. SER: Restorations; repairs.

Eagle House Antiques Market
Market Sq. (J.H. Brown). Open daily. SIZE: Medium - 15 dealers. *STOCK: General antiques, furniture, silver, porcelain, pictures and glass, £5-£1,000.* PARK: Easy. TEL: 0730 812718.

Foord Antiques   LAPADA
P.O. Box 14. (C.G. and E.S. Foord). Open by appointment. STOCK: Furniture, boxes, treen, metalware, decorative items, 18th to early 19th C. TEL: 079 86 351; mobile - 0836 533655.

Midhurst Antiques Market
Knockhundred Row. (D.M. Brindle-Wood-Williams). Est. 1974. Open 9.30-5. TEL: 0730 814231.

Midhurst continued
Midhurst Walk
West St. Est. 1992. CL: Wed. pm. SIZE: Small - 4 Dealers. *STOCK: Unusual items and decorative arts.* LOC: Near Eagle House Antiques Market. PARK: Easy. TEL: 0730 813207. VAT: Stan/Spec.

West Street Antiques
West St. (A. Goodman). Est. 1984. Open 10-1 and 2-5. CL: Wed. SIZE: Medium. *STOCK: Decorative and country furniture, brass, pottery and porcelain; some oil paintings and early prints, quilts, rugs and jewellery,* £5-£4,000. PARK: Easy. TEL: 0730 815232. SER: Buys at auction.

MILLAND, Nr. Liphook (Hants.)
The Plough
Maysleith. (Mrs I. Morton-Smith). Est. 1980. Open by appointment only. SIZE: Medium. *STOCK: Decorative and collectable agricultural implements, including horsedrawn ploughs, wooden harrows, haysweeps,* £50-£150; *hand tools - saws, hay-knives, wheelwrights, blacksmiths,* £3-£20; *barn and domestic appliances - mangles, cheese presses, butter workers, pulpers, cake crackers,* £50-£150; *all mainly Victorian and Edwardian.* LOC: 1/2 mile off A3 just north of Petersfield, Hants., telephone for directions. PARK: Easy. TEL: 042 876 323; home - same. SER: Buys at auction (agricultural implements). VAT: Stan.

NORTHCHAPEL, Nr. Petworth
D. and A. Callingham Antiques
Est. 1966. CL: Wed. *STOCK: English furniture.* LOC: On A283. TEL: 042 878 379. VAT: Stan/Spec.

N. and S. Callingham Antiques
Est. 1979. Open 9-5.30. CL: Wed. SIZE: Medium. *STOCK: Furniture, 1700-1900,* £10-£10,000. LOC: London Road 5 miles north of Petworth. PARK: Easy. TEL: 042 878 379; home - 0903 724233. SER: Valuations; restorations. VAT: Stan/Spec.

Krüger Smith Fine Art
(M.C. Krüger and H.E. Smith). Est. 1983. Open by appointment. *STOCK: Watercolours, 19th C; oils, 19th-20th C; both* £100-£4,000; *contemporary paintings.* LOC: Just north of Petworth. TEL: 042 878 265 or 0962 771019. SER: Valuations; restorations (watercolours, oils and frames); buys at auction (pictures).

J. Mason Antique Clocks
Rose Villa, London Rd. Est. 1986. Open 9-5.30 or by appointment. SIZE: Medium. *STOCK: Longcase, bracket, English fusee wall dials, barometers, 17th-19th C,* £500-£10,000. LOC: A283, 6 miles north of Petworth. PARK: Easy. TEL: 0428 707500.

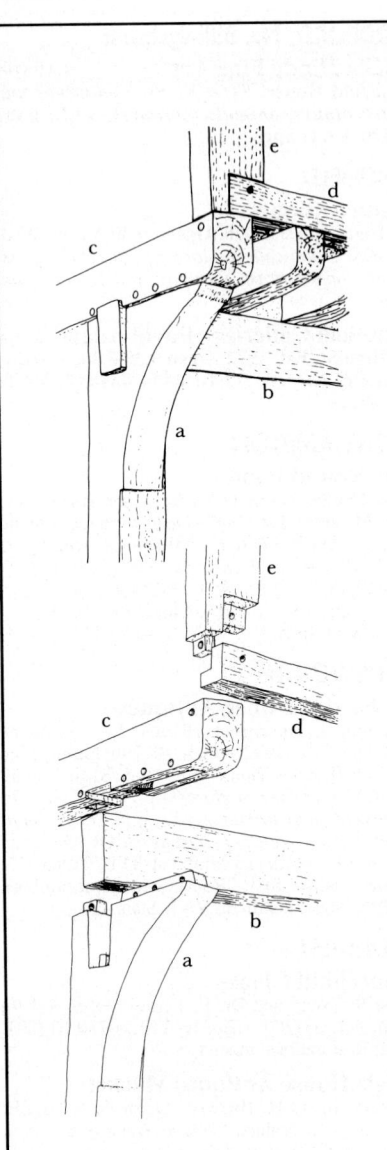

No.1 High Street, Chiddingstone. Jetty: assembled (above) and exploded: (a) lower main-post, swelling into hewn bracket; (b) jetty-plate; (c) end joist (or girding-rail, or mid-rail; (d) bressummer; (e) upper main-post; (f) floor-joist. From **Kent Houses** by Anthony Quiney, published by the **Antique Collectors' Club** in 1993, £35.00.

PETWORTH

Majid Amini - Persian Carpet Gallery LAPADA
Church St. Open 9.30-5. STOCK: Oriental rugs. LOC: A272. PARK: Nearby. TEL: 0798 43344. SER: Valuations; restorations; cleaning.

The Bacchus Gallery
Lombard St. (R. and A. Gillett). Est. 1988. Open 10-1 and 2.15-5.30. SIZE: Small. STOCK: Wine related items. LOC: Cobbled street leading off town square. PARK: Town square. TEL: 0798 42844; fax - 0798 42634. SER: Buys at auction (as stock). VAT: Stan/Spec.

Baskerville Antiques BADA
Saddlers House, Saddlers Row. (A. and B. Baskerville). Est. 1968. Open 9.30-6, Sun. by appointment. SIZE: Medium. STOCK: English clocks, barometers and furniture, £1,000-£15,000; decorative items and instruments, £500-£5,000; all 18th-19th C. LOC: Town centre. PARK: Public, adjoining shop. TEL: 0798 42067; home - same; fax - 0798 43956. VAT: Spec.

Nigel Bassett
Swan House, Market Sq. (N.J. Bassett). Est. 1990. Open 10-1 and 2-5.30. CL: Mon. and Wed. SIZE: Small. STOCK: Dining room antiques, 18th-19th C. PARK: Easy. TEL: 0798 44121. VAT: Stan/Spec.

Lesley Bragge Antiques
Fairfield House, High St. Est. 1974. Open 10-1 and 2-5.30. SIZE: Medium. STOCK: Decorative furniture, 18th-19th C; silver and plate, porcelain, textiles, ormolu, brass, copper, objets d'art, garden furniture. LOC: Off Golden Square. PARK: Nearby. TEL: 0798 42324. SER: Valuations; restorations; upholstery. VAT: Stan/Spec.

Philip Cooper Antiques
The Nook, Golden Sq. (P. Cooper and S. Harrison). Est. 1971. Open by appointment. SIZE: Medium. STOCK: Oak, walnut, fruitwood and mahogany furniture, 17th-18th C, from £500. LOC: Lower end of High St. PARK: Nearby. TEL: 0798 42033. VAT: Spec.

Nigel Cracknell (Antiques) Ltd
Church St, Lombard St. (N.O. Cracknell). Est. 1965. Open 9.30-5, Sat. 10-5.30. SIZE: Large. STOCK: 18th C mahogany and walnut, 19th C rosewood and 17th-18th C oak. PARK: Easy. TEL: 0798 44188; home - 0672 512912. SER: Valuations; restorations. VAT: Stan/Spec.

Frith Antiques
New St. (H.A. and Mrs M.A. Frith). Est. 1974. Open 10-5. SIZE: Small. STOCK: Oak and mahogany country furniture, £50-£3,000; copper, brass, steel and pewter, £10-£500; all 17th-19th C; fishing tackle, 18th-19th C. Not Stocked: Silver. LOC: 50yds. Town Square. PARK: Nearby. TEL: 0798 43155; home - 0798 831606.

Baskerville Antiques

PETWORTH
0798 42067

SUSSEX WEST

Petworth continued

Granville Antiques BADA
High St. (I.E.G. Miller). Est. 1979. Open 10-5.30, Wed. 10-2.30 or by appointment. SIZE: Medium. STOCK: *Period furniture, pre-1840, £50-£15,000; accessories and pictures.* Not Stocked: Militaria and jewellery. LOC: 100yds. from market square. PARK: Nearby. TEL: 0798 43250; home - 0243 542293. SER: Valuations (furniture); restorations (furniture); buys at auction. FAIRS: Olympia. VAT: Spec.

Griffin Antiques
Church St. (R. Wilson and D. Swanson). Est. 1981. Open 10-1 and 2-5.30. SIZE: Medium. STOCK: *Oak and country furniutre, £200-£5,000; metalware, £20-£1,000.* LOC: Town centre. PARK: Easy. TEL: 0798 43306; fax - 0798 42367. VAT: Stan/Spec.

Grove House Antiques
Middle St. (D. Houghton-Connell). Est. 1977. Open 10-1 and 2-5.30, Sun. by appointment. SIZE: Medium. STOCK: *Oak and pine country furniture, unusual decorative items, treen, lace and quilts.* LOC: Between High St. and New St. PARK: Easy. TEL: 0798 43151; home - 0798 42563. SER: Restorations (furniture, paintings). VAT: Stan/Spec.

William Hockley Antiques LAPADA
East St. (D. and V. Thrower). Est. 1974. STOCK: *Fine 18th to early 19th C furniture and decorative items; early English pottery.* TEL: 0798 43172.

John Hopkins BADA LAPADA
Trumpers Corner, East Street. (John, Angela and Mona Hopkins). Est. 1962. Open daily. CL: Wed. p.m. SIZE: Small. STOCK: *Furniture, 17th-19th C; bronzes, glass candelabra, 18th-19th C.* PARK: Nearby. TEL: 0798 43104; 0444 454323. SER: Valuations; buys at auction (as stock). FAIRS: West London; Café Royal (Feb); Westminster; Olympia. VAT: Spec.

Humphry Antiques BADA
North St. (J. and M. Humphry). Open 10-1 and 2-5.30, Sun. by appointment. SIZE: Medium. STOCK: *Early English oak and country furniture, 16th-18th C; wood carvings and sculpture, tapestry, metalwork, unusual and decorative items.* LOC: Opposite St. Mary's Church. PARK: Own. TEL: 0798 43053; home - 0798 42944.

The Madison Gallery
Swan House, Market Sq. (J. and S. Drayson). Open 10-5.30, Sun. by appointment. SIZE: Large. STOCK: *Furniture, including decorative; pictures, accessories.* PARK: Easy. TEL: 0798 43638. SER: Restorations; upholstery. VAT: Stan/Spec.

Petworth continued

John G. Morris BADA
Market Sq. Est. 1962. Open 10-5.30 or by appointment. CL: Wed. p.m. SIZE: Medium. STOCK: *Furniture, English and continental, 1660-1850, from £250; English clocks, 18th-19th C, £2,000-£10,000; English barometers, £800-£4,000; French animalier bronzes, 19th C, £500-£5,000; some porcelain.* Not Stocked: Bric-a-brac, jewellery, Edwardian articles. LOC: On A272. PARK: Easy. TEL: 0798 42305. SER: Valuations; buys at auction. VAT: Stan/Spec.

Petworth Antique Market
East St. (D.M. and P.J. Rayment). Est. 1968. Open 10-5.30. SIZE: Large - 36 dealers. STOCK: *General antiques, books, furniture, brass, copper, pictures, textiles.* LOC: Near church. PARK: Adjoining. TEL: 0798 42073. VAT: Stan/Spec.

Ernest Streeter and Daughter
The Clock House, Lombard St. Est. 1888. CL: Wed. STOCK: *Silver, jewellery.* TEL: 0798 42239. VAT: Stan.

J.C. Tutt Antiques
Angel St. Open 10-5. CL: Some Mon. SIZE: Large. STOCK: *Mahogany and country furniture and accessories.* PARK: Nearby. TEL: 0798 43221.

Michael Wakelin and Helen Linfield
BADA LAPADA
10 New St. Est. 1968. Open 10-5.30. STOCK: *Fine English and continental formal and country furniture - walnut, fruitwoods, faded mahogany and other exotic woods; early brass, bronze, iron and steel; wood carvings, treen, needlework, naïve pictures and lighting.* TEL: 0798 42417. VAT: Spec.

T.G. Wilkinson Antiques Ltd BADA
New St. (T. and S. Wilkinson). Est. 1979. Open 10-5.30. SIZE: Medium. STOCK: *English and continental furniture, paintings and works of art, 17th-19th C, £500-£15,000.* PARK: Town centre. TEL: 0798 44443. VAT: Stan/Spec.

Jeremy Wood Fine Art
East St. Est. 1974. Open 10-1 and 2-5. STOCK: *Oils and watercolours, etchings, 1880-1950, £5-£500; art reference books, illustrated art and travel books, motoring/motor racing art and books, £1-£50.* TEL: 0798 43408. VAT: Spec.

PORTSLADE

Peter Marks Antique Warehouse
1/11 Church Rd. Est. 1965. Open 9.30-6. CL: Sat SIZE: Large. STOCK: *General antiques, shipping goods.* TEL: 0273 415471. VAT: Stan.

J. Powell (Hove) Ltd LAPADA
20 Wellington Rd. Est. 1949. Open 9-6. CL: Sun. and Sat. p.m. except by appointment SIZE: Large. STOCK: *Bookcases, display*

Petworth

West Sussex

Over 20 Antique Shops and Galleries including specialists in Furniture, Pictures, Persian Carpets and Clocks.

The Antiques Centre of the South

Only 1 hour from London, Gatwick and Heathrow

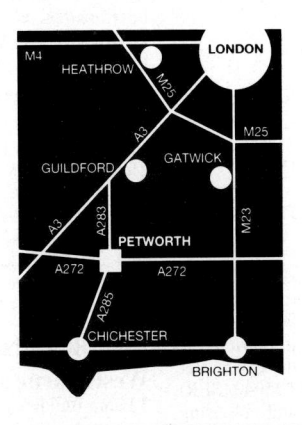

For a free brochure write to:
Petworth Art & Antiques Dealers Association, c/o Fairfield House, High Street Petworth GU28 0AU
Tel (0798) 42324

Portslade continued
cabinets, £110-£1,500; writing tables and desks, £120-£1,200; longcase and bracket clocks, £50-£2,000; general furniture, shipping goods, 18th-20th C, £5-£1,500. Not Stocked: Porcelain, jewellery, silver. LOC: 150yds. west of Boundary Rd., on seafront. PARK: Easy. TEL: 0273 411599; home - 0273 593274. SER: Restorations (furniture). VAT: Stan.

Peter Semus Crafting Antiques
The Warehouse, Gladstone Rd. Open 8-6, Sat. 8-12. STOCK: General antiques, furniture including reproduction. PARK: Easy. TEL: 0273 420154; fax - 0273 430355.

PULBOROUGH
Mulberry House Galleries
Mulberry House, Codmore Hill. Est. 1974. Open 9-6; Wed. p.m., Sat. p.m. and Sun. by appointment. STOCK: Fine art, prints, oil paintings and watercolours. LOC: A29, 1 mile north of Pulborough. PARK: Own. TEL: 0798 872463.

RUDGWICK, Nr. Horsham
Brocante
Clare Cottage Barn, Somersbury Lane, Ellens Green. (J. and M. Hicks). Est. 1984. Open Thurs., Fri. and Sat., other days by appointment. SIZE: Medium. STOCK: Pine, 19th-20th C, £15-£1,500; country and decorative smalls, £5-£100. LOC: Between Horsham and Guildford - telephone for exact details. PARK: Easy. TEL: 0403 822267; home - same. SER: Valuations; buys at auction (clocks).

SAYERS COMMON
Recollect Studios
The Old School, London Rd. (Mr & Mrs J. Jackman). Est. 1970. Open 10-5. CL: Mon. STOCK: Dolls, dolls house miniatures, books, doll restoration materials. LOC: B2118. PARK: Own. TEL: 0273 833314. SER: Restorations (dolls); catalogues available (£2 cash/stamps).

SHOREHAM-BY-SEA
Tudor Cottage Antiques
Upper Shoreham Rd. (Mrs J. Perrett). Resident. Est. 1967. Open daily (also evenings). STOCK: General antiques especially Beswick. LOC: Near Amsterdam Restaurant. TEL: 0273 453554.

SOUTH HARTING, Nr. Petersfield (Hants.)
Julia Holmes Antique Maps and Prints
South Gardens Cottage. By appointment only. SIZE: Medium. STOCK: Maps, 1600-1850, £10-£1,000; prints, especially sporting, all periods, to £500. LOC: End of main street, on the Chichester road. PARK: Opposite. TEL: 0730 825040. SER: Valuations; restorations (cleaning and colouring maps and prints); framing; buys at auction; catalogues. FAIRS: Local and major sporting events. VAT: Stan.

STEYNING
David R. Fileman
Squirrels, Bayards. Open daily. STOCK: Table glass, £20-£1,000; chandeliers, candelabra, £500-£20,000; all 18th-19th C. Collectors' items, 17th-19th C, £25-£2,000; paperweights, 19th C, £50-£5,000. LOC: A283 to north of Steyning village. TEL: 0903 813229. SER: Valuations; restorations (chandeliers and candelabra). VAT: Stan/Spec.

Penfold Gallery and Antiques
30 High St. (Mrs J. Exley-Turner). Open 9.30-4.30. STOCK: Watercolours, oils, prints, etchings and general antiques. TEL: 0903 815595.

STORRINGTON
Thakeham Furniture
Orchardway Stables, Rock Rd. (T.J.G. Chavasse). Est. 1988. Open 8.30-5, Sat. and Sun. by appointment. SIZE: Small. STOCK: Furniture, 1750-1880, £20-£3,000. LOC: Off B2193, one mile north of Storrington. PARK: Easy. TEL: 0903 745474. SER: Restorations (furniture); buys at auction (furniture). VAT: Stan/Spec.

TILLINGTON, Nr. Petworth
Loewenthal Antiques
Tillington Cottage. CL: Wed. STOCK: 18th C furniture and objets d'art. LOC: A272, 1 mile west of Petworth. TEL: 0798 42969.

WASHINGTON, Nr. Pulborough
Chanctonbury Antiques
Clematis Cottage. (G. Troche). Est. 1961. Open 10-5.30. CL: Sun. and Tues. except by appointment. SIZE: Medium. STOCK: Porcelain, needlework, glass, furniture, objets de vertu. LOC: Just off A24. PARK: Easy. TEL: 0903 892233.

Sandhill Barn Antiques (Pine and Country)
Est. 1969. Open by appointment or chance. SIZE: Medium. STOCK: Old painted country furniture, bygones, early iron, brass, copper, treen, kitchen items. Not Stocked: Silver, jewellery, mahogany. LOC: At the Washington roundabout (crossroads of A24 and A283), take the Steyning road and turn left immediately into cul-de-sac. PARK: Easy. TEL: 0903 892210. VAT: Stan. Shipping only.

WESTBOURNE, Nr. Emsworth
Westbourne Antiques
3 Lamb Buildings, The Square. (H.J. and V.J. Lain).

Westbourne continued

Est. 1951. Open Thurs., Fri. and Sat. 9-5. SIZE: Large. STOCK: *Silver, jewellery, collectors' items.* PARK: Nearby. TEL: 0243 373711. SER: Valuations; repairs (jewellery and watches).

WORTHING

A. Biscoe
122 Montague St. (R. Byskou). Open 10-6. STOCK: *Furniture, silver, porcelain, 18th-19th C; jewellery, clocks and objets d'art.* TEL: 0903 202489; home - 0903 782723.

Cheriton Antiques   LAPADA
21 New Broadway, Tarring Rd. (A.C. Biggs and Mrs M.D. Edwardes). Open 9.30-5.30. CL: Wed. STOCK: *Mahogany, walnut and rosewood furniture, 18th-19th C; porcelain, glass, upholstered chairs, couches, lighting.* Not Stocked: Jewellery, silver. LOC: 200yds. east of West Worthing railway station. TEL: 0903 235463 (ansaphone). VAT: Stan/Spec.

Chloe Antiques
61 Brighton Rd. (Mrs D. Peters). Est. 1960. Open 9.30-12.30 and 2-5. SIZE: Small. STOCK: *General antiques, furniture, jewellery, china, glass, bric-a-brac.* LOC: From Brighton, on main rd. just past Beach House Park on corner. PARK: Opposite. TEL: 0903 202697.

Geoffrey Godden Chinaman   BADA
19a Crescent Rd. (G.A. Godden). Est. 1900. Open by appointment. STOCK: *Ceramics, 18th-19th C.* LOC: Town centre. PARK: Easy. TEL: 0903 235958/231901. VAT: Spec.

Worthing continued

Godden of Worthing Ltd   BADA
19 Crescent Rd. (G. and J. Godden). Est. 1900. Open by appointment. STOCK: *Ceramics, 18th-19th C.* PARK: Easy. TEL: 0903 235958/231901. VAT: Spec.

Rathbone Law Antiques
7-9 The Arcade. (R. Law). Open 10-5. CL: Some Wed. STOCK: *Victorian and Edwardian fine jewellery, silver, objets d'art, porcelain dolls.* TEL: 0903 200274.

Rococo Antiques
21 Warwick Rd. (K.P. Jakes). Open 11-5. CL: Fri. STOCK: *General antiques.* TEL: 0903 235896.

Steyne Antique Gallery
29 Brighton Rd. (H.W. and V.I. Melling). Open 9.30-5.30. CL: Mon. STOCK: *Furniture, porcelain, clocks and general antiques.* TEL: 0903 200079.

Robert Warner and Son Ltd
1-13 South Farm Rd. Est. 1940. CL: Wed. p.m. SIZE: Large. STOCK: *Furniture, bric-a-brac.* TEL: 0903 232710; fax - 0903 217515. VAT: Stan.

Wilsons Antiques   LAPADA
57/59 Broadwater Rd. (F. Wilson). Est. 1936. Open 9-5. SIZE: Large. STOCK: *Period furniture, 18th-19th C, £100-£10,000; Edwardian furniture, £50-£4,000; decorative items, 19th C, £10-£750; watercolours and oil paintings, 19th-20th C.* Not Stocked: Pine. PARK: At rear. TEL: 0903 202059. SER: Valuations; restorations (furniture). FAIRS: NEC (April); Olympia (June and Oct.); Barbican. VAT: Stan/Spec.

An Antique Collectors' Club Title

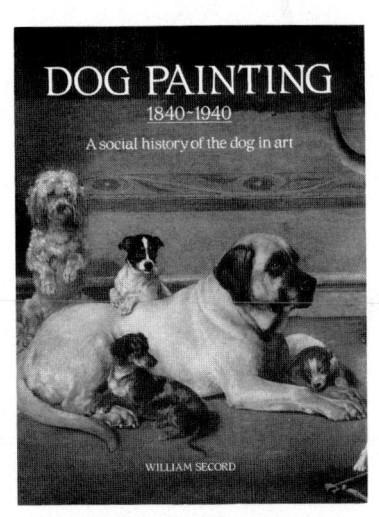

Dog Painting 1840-1940
A Social History of the Dog in Art
by William Secord

This fascinating account of the rich interrelationship between man and dog as recorded in art, charts the changes in breeds in the 19th and 20th centuries.
ISBN 1 85159 139 2, 368pp
317 b & w illus, 150 colour, £35.00

Available from:
Antique Collectors' Club, 5 Church Street,
Woodbridge, Suffolk IP12 1DS
Tel: (0394) 385501 Fax: (0394) 384434

or Market Street Industrial Park, Wappingers'
Falls, New York 12590, USA
Tel: 914 297 0003 Fax: 914 297 0068

Tyne and Wear

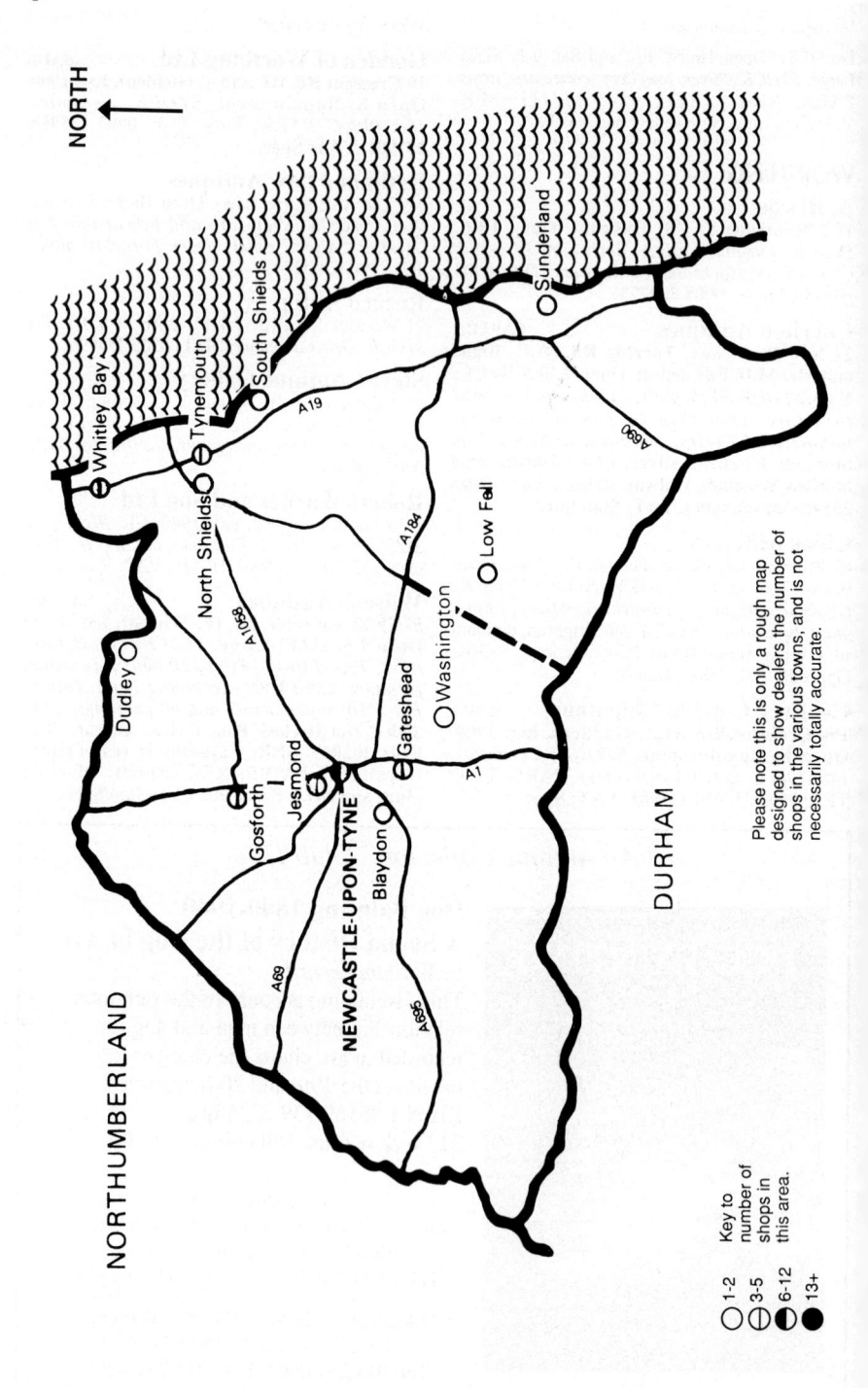

Tyne and Wear

BLAYDON, Nr. Newcastle-upon-Tyne
Blaydon Antique Centre
Bridge House, Bridge St. (Mrs E. Bradshaw). Est. 1978. Open 10-5. SIZE: Large. *STOCK: Furniture including pianos, 18th-20th C, £5-£3,000; china, brass, pictures.* PARK: Easy. TEL: 091 414 3535 (24 hrs.). SER: Valuations. FAIRS: Local.

GATESHEAD
Boadens of Hexham
28 The Boulevard, Antique Village, Metrocentre. (R.J. Boaden). Open 10-8, Thurs. 10-9, Sat. 9-6. *STOCK: Small general antiques, china, glass, silver, paintings, jewellery and reproductions.* TEL: 091 460 0358.

Metro Antiques
31 The Boulevard, Antiques Court, Antique Village, Metrocentre. (R. Welch). Open 10-8, Thurs. 10-9, Sat. 9-6. *STOCK: Furniture, china, jewellery, prints and bric-a-brac, including reproduction.* TEL: 091 460 0340.

Sovereign Antiques
35 The Boulevard, Antique Village, Metrocentre. Open 10-8, Thurs. 10-9, Sat. 9-7. *STOCK: Fine jewellery, diamonds, silver, original prints and maps.* TEL: 091 460 9604.

GOSFORTH, Nr. Newcastle-upon-Tyne
Causey Antique Shop
Causey St. *STOCK: Silver, Victoriana and collectors' items.*

H. and S. Collectables
149 Salters Rd. (H. and Mrs S. Shorrick). Est. 1989. Open 10-5, Sun. by appointment. SIZE: Small. *STOCK: General antiques, china, clocks and collectable items, 1800-1930, £5-£900.* LOC: Off High St, corner of Linden Road. PARK: Easy. TEL: 091 284 6626; home - 091 286 3498.

Anna Harrison Fine Antiques LAPADA
Grange Park, Great North Rd. Est. 1976. Open 10-4.30. SIZE: Large. *STOCK: English furniture, porcelain, oils and watercolours.* LOC: A6125, 3 miles north of city centre, near Regent Centre. PARK: Forecourt. TEL: 091 284 3202; home - 091 236 7652. SER: Valuations; restorations. VAT: Stan/Spec.

MacDonald Fine Art
2 Ashburton Rd. (T. and C. MacDonald). Est. 1976. Open 10-1 and 2.30-5.30. CL: Wed. SIZE: Medium. *STOCK: Watercolours and oils, mainly north-eastern artists, English and Scottish, 18th-20th C.* LOC: 1 mile west of A1. PARK: Easy. TEL: 091 284 4214; home - 091 285 6188. SER: Valuations; restorations (watercolours and oils); framing; buys at auction (watercolours and oils). VAT: Spec.

JESMOND, Nr. Newcastle-upon-Tyne
Geoffrey Hugall
19 Clayton Rd. Est. 1970. Open 10-5 or by appointment. SIZE: Medium. *STOCK: General antiques, furniture, china, period and decorative items.* Not Stocked: Weapons, musical instruments. PARK: Easy. TEL: 091 281 8408. SER: Valuations. VAT: Stan/Spec.

Owen Humble LAPADA
11-12 Clayton Rd. Est. 1958. Open 6 days. SIZE: Large and warehouse. *STOCK: Furniture, general antiques.* PARK: Easy. TEL: 091 281 4602. SER: Restorations. VAT: Stan/Spec.

Osborne Art and Antiques
18c Osborne Rd. (F.T. and S. Jackman). Est. 1974. Open 10-5.15. *STOCK: Victorian oil paintings and watercolours, drawings, topographical engravings and antiquarian maps, etchings, 19th-20th C.* TEL: 091 281 6380. SER: Restorations (pictures); framing. VAT: Stan/Spec.

W. and J. Walker
231 Jesmond Rd. Est. 1976. Open 10-5. CL: Mon. SIZE: Medium. *STOCK: Furniture, clocks, bric-a-brac, 19th C.* LOC: Main road to east coast. PARK: Osborne Ave. - around corner. TEL: 091 281 7286.

LOW FELL, Nr. Gateshead
N. Jewett
639/643 Durham Rd. Est. 1948. Large. *STOCK: Antique and reproduction furniture, glass, china, £5-£5,000.* LOC: On A6127, 3 miles south of Newcastle-upon-Tyne. PARK: On hill opposite. TEL: 091 487 7636. SER: Valuations. VAT: Stan/Spec.

NEWCASTLE-UPON-TYNE
Antiques Centre
8-10 St. Mary's Place East. (B. and G. Punton). Est. 1985. Open 10-5. CL: Mon. SIZE: 18 dealers. *STOCK: General antiques and collectables.* LOC: Opposite Civic Centre. PARK: Nearby. TEL: 091 232 3821/232 9832. SER: Valuations; restorations; metal polishing. FAIRS: York, Leeds, Glasgow. VAT: Stan.

Davidson's The Jewellers Ltd
94 and 96 Grey St. Open 9-5. *STOCK: Jewellery, silver.* TEL: 091 232 2551/232 2895.

The Dean Gallery
42 Dean St. (A.P. Graham). Est. 1970. Open 10-5. CL: Sat. p.m. SIZE: Large. *STOCK: Oils, watercolours, local and national, 18th to early 20th C, £100-£10,000.* LOC: Going north over Tyne Bridge, turn left, and left again. PARK: Easy. TEL: 091 232 1208. SER: Valuations; restorations; framing. VAT: Stan/Spec.

Newcastle-upon-Tyne continued

Intercoin
99 Clayton St. Open 9-4.30. CL: Wed. STOCK: *Coins and items of numismatic interest; jewellery, silver.* LOC: City centre. TEL: 091 232 2064.

Owen's Jewellers
14 Shields Rd, Byker. (D.W. Robertson). Est. 1968. Open 9-5. STOCK: *Jewellery.* TEL: 091 265 4332.

Shiners Architectural Reclamation
123 Jesmond Rd. (B. and A. Lawson). Open 9-5. SIZE: Large. STOCK: *Architectural items including Victorian and Edwardian fireplaces.* LOC: On main road. PARK: Easy. TEL: 091 281 6474. SER: Valuations; metal polishing.

Spicker Jewellers
75 Grainger Market, Alley No.2. STOCK: *Antique, secondhand and Victorian jewellery and silver; Maling china, masonic items, objets d'art, textiles, quilts, tapestries and bric-a-brac.* TEL: 091 232 5057.

R.D. Steedman
9 Grey St. Est. 1907. CL: Sat. p.m. STOCK: *Rare books.* TEL: 091 232 6561.

Warner Fine Art
208 Wingrove Rd, Fenham. (S. and M. Warner). Est. 1989. Open by appointment only. SIZE: Small. STOCK: *Watercolours, £50-£5,000; oils, £500-£5,000; both 19th-20th C; prints and etchings, decorative objects, 18th-20th C, £50-£500; all relating to the north east of England.* LOC: Off A69, Westgate Rd. PARK: Easy. TEL: 091 273 8030 (24 hrs.). SER: Valuations; restorations (watercolours, oils, frames); buys at auction (watercolours, oils, prints, ship models, maritime objects mainly northern).

NORTH SHIELDS

Peter Coulson Antiques
8-10 Queen Alexandra Rd. Est. 1977. Open 10-5. CL: Wed. STOCK: *General antiques; clocks and watches.* TEL: 091 257 9761. SER: Repairs.

Maggie May's
Incorporating Tynemouth Fine Art, 49 Kirton Park Terrace. (Miss M.L. Hayes). Est. 1960. Open 10.30-5.30. CL: Wed. SIZE: Medium. STOCK: *General antiques and collectors' items, art deco, Victorian and Edwardian furniture, china, glass; paintings and watercolours, especially Northumbrian artists, 1800-1950; continental furniture, glassware, porcelain, decorative items, gramophones.* LOC: Opposite The Gunner Inn, near Preston Hospital. TEL: 091 257 0076. SER: Valuations; restorations; framing; French polishing.

SOUTH SHIELDS

The Curiosity Shop
16 Frederick St. Est. 1969. CL: Wed. STOCK: *General antiques, paintings, jewellery, furniture, Royal Doulton.* TEL: 091 456 5560.

SUNDERLAND

Peter Smith Antiques   LAPADA
12-14 Borough Rd. Est. 1968. Open 9.30-4.30, Sat. 9.30-12, other times by appointment. SIZE: Warehouse. STOCK: *Georgian, Victorian, Edwardian longcase clocks, shipping goods, £5-£15,000.* LOC: 10 miles from A1(M); towards docks/Hendon from town centre. PARK: Easy. TEL: 091 567 3537/567 7842; fax - 091 514 2286; home - 091 514 0008. SER: Valuations; restorations; some shipping; containers packed; buys at auction. VAT: Stan/Spec.

TYNEMOUTH

Renaissance Antiques
11 Front St. (E. and N. Moore). Est. 1977. Open Mon., Tues. and Sat. 10.30-1 and 2-4. SIZE: Medium and trade goods store. STOCK: *Furniture, Victorian to art deco, £50-£1,000; china and porcelain, silver, brass and copper, £5-£100; shipping goods.* LOC: Main coast road from Newcastle. PARK: Easy. TEL: 091 259 5555; home - 091 257 4073. SER: Valuations.

Ian Sharp Antiques   LAPADA
23 Front St. Open 10-5.30 or by appointment. STOCK: *Furniture, 18th to early 20th C; British oil paintings, pottery and watercolours; northern pottery, including Maling, Sunderland and Tyneside lustreware, 18th to early 20th C.* TEL: 091 296 0656.

David R. Strain Antiques   LAPADA
66 Front St. Est. 1983. Open 9.30-5. CL: Sat. p.m. SIZE: Medium. STOCK: *Furniture and general antiques, Edwardian, Victorian, Georgian, £5-£2,000.* Not Stocked: Weapons, books, silver and jewellery. LOC: Main coast road from Newcastle, 10 mins. from Tyne tunnel. PARK: Easy. TEL: 091 259 2459; home - 091 259 0300. SER: Valuations; buys at auction (furniture). VAT: Stan/Spec.

WASHINGTON

Harold J. Carr Antiques   LAPADA
Field House, Rickleton. Open by appointment. STOCK: *General antiques and furniture.* TEL: 091 388 6442. SER: Shippers.

Grate Expectations (Fireplaces)
Unit 6, Lee Close, Pattison North Industrial Estate. (Geoffrey Moore). Est. 1983. Open 9-5. SIZE: Large. STOCK: *Fireplaces, £95-£550;*

An Antique Collectors' Club Title

The Antique Collectors' Club has produced this handsome hard cover address book, lavishly illustrated with photographs taken from its bestselling publication **Dog Painting 1840-1940: A Social History of the Dog in Art** by William Secord, an acknowledged expert on the subject of dog painting and former director of The Dog Museum of America.

Each illustration carries details of the breed, artist and date, and the book is interspersed with pertinent and lively phrases and quotations to bring to life the world of dogs. A preface by William Secord puts the genre of dog painting in its true perspective.

**ISBN 1 85149 164 3, 8 1/4 x 5 7/8 in., 160pp
80 in colour, £9.50 (incl. VAT)**

Available from:
Antique Collectors' Club, 5 Church Street, Woodbridge, Suffolk IP12 1DS
Tel: (0394) 385501 Fax: (0394) 384434

or Market Street Industrial Park, Wappingers' Falls, New York 12590, USA
Tel: 914 297 0003 Fax: 914 297 0068

Washington continued
fireplace accessories, £10-£125; both 19th C. LOC: Close to A1 and A19. PARK: Easy. TEL: 091 416 0609. SER: Restorations (cast-iron refurbishment, repair and welding). VAT: Stan.

WHITLEY BAY
The Bric-a-Brac
195 Park View. (C. Rawes). Est. 1953. Open 10-5. SIZE: Medium. *STOCK: General antiques.* TEL: 091 252 6141.

Whitley Bay continued
Northumbria Pine
54 Whitley Rd. (C. and V. Dowland). Est. 1979. Open 9-6. SIZE: Medium. *STOCK: Stripped pine and reproduction items.* LOC: Cullercoats end of Whitley Rd., behind sea front. PARK: Easy. TEL: 091 252 4550. VAT: Stan.

Treasure Chest
2 and 4 Norham Rd. Est. 1974. Open 10.30-1 and 2-4. CL: Wed. and Thurs. SIZE: Small. *STOCK: General antiques.* LOC: Just off main shopping area of Park View, leading to Monkseaton Railway Station. PARK: Easy. TEL: 091 251 2052.

Warwickshire

NORTH ↑

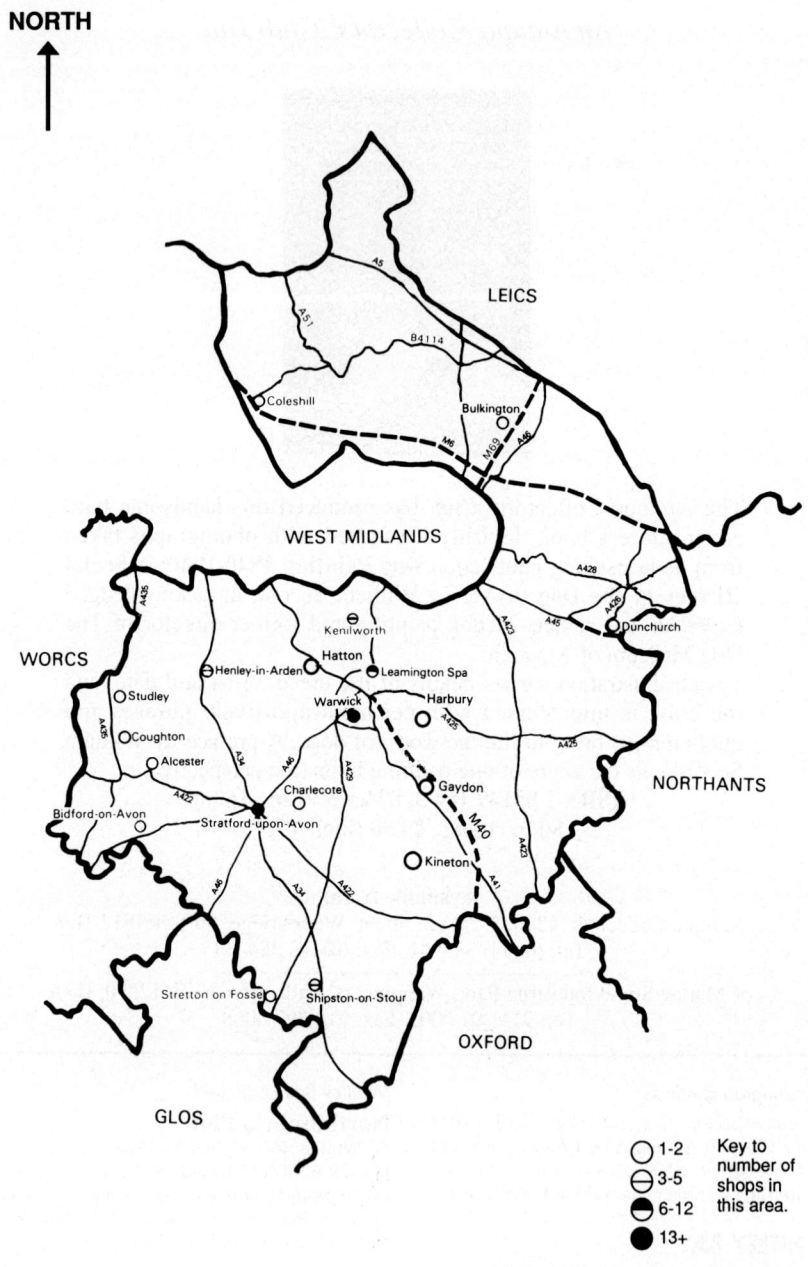

Key to number of shops in this area.
○ 1-2
⊖ 3-5
◐ 6-12
● 13+

Please note this is only a rough map designed to show dealers the number of shops in the various towns, and is not necessarily totally accurate.

Warwickshire

ONE OF THE LARGEST RANGES OF TRADITIONAL WINDSOR CHAIRS

Fauld

TOWN & COUNTRY FURNITURE

58 Commercial Road,
Hereford. HR1 2BP
Telephone: 0432 353183
Telefax: 0432 275338

Ranges of complementary tables & dressers

APPOINTMENT ADVISABLE

ALCESTER
High St. Antiques
11A High St. (B.J. Payne). Est. 1979. Open Tues. 11-1 and 2.30-4.30, Sat. 11-1 and 2.30-5. SIZE: Small. STOCK: Glass and china, 18th-20th C, but mainly 19th C, £5-£200; brass, copper and silver, 19th-20th C, £5-£100+; postcards and art deco china. LOC: On left-hand side near church coming from Stratford-on-Avon road. PARK: Rear of High St. TEL: 0789 764009; home - same. SER: Valuations.

Malthouse Antiques Centre
Market Place. (J. and P. Allcock). Est. 1982. Open 10-5, Sun. 2-5. SIZE: Large. STOCK: Furniture, china, paintings, prints and collectables, 18th-20th C, £5-£2,000. LOC: Off High St. PARK: Easy. TEL: 0789 764032. SER: Restorations.

BIDFORD-ON-AVON
The Antiques Centre
High St. (J.B. Homer). Est. 1983. Open 10-5, Sun. 2-5.30. SIZE: 11 dealers. STOCK: Furniture, china, glass, jewellery, paintings, bygones, clocks. PARK: Easy. TEL: 0789 773680.

Crown Antiques
14 High St. (J. and C. Ford). Resident. Est. 1980. Open 10-5.30, Sat. 10-4.30, Sun. by appointment. CL: Thurs. SIZE: Medium. STOCK: Furniture, 18th-19th C, to £6,000; Edwardian inlaid, £50-£3,000; general antiques. LOC: 100yds. off A439. PARK: Easy. TEL: 0789 772939/772962; mobile - 0831 453794. SER: Valuations; buys at auction (furniture); courier. VAT: Stan/Spec.

BULKINGTON, Nr. Nuneaton
Sport and Country Gallery   LAPADA
Northwood House. (R. and S. Hill). Open any time by appointment. STOCK: 19th-20th C oils and watercolours. TEL: 0203 314335. VAT: Spec.

CHARLECOTE
Country Furniture Antique Centre
Kingsmead Farm. (Mrs J. Seccombe). Resident. Est. 1970. Open 9-5. CL: Mon. SIZE: 6 dealers. STOCK: General antiques, bric-a-brac, pine and country furniture. TEL: 0789 840254.

La-di-da Interior Designs
Kingsmead Farm. (P. Barber). Open 10-4 including Sun. STOCK: General antiques especially upholstered furniture. TEL: 0926 843127.

COLESHILL
Coleshill Antiques and Interiors Ltd
LAPADA
12 and 14 High St. (A.J. Webster). Est. 1958. Open 9.30-5 or by appointment. SIZE: Large.

Coleshill continued
STOCK: Porcelain, furniture, jewellery and silver, £100-£10,000. PARK: Easy. TEL: 0675 462931; 0675 467416. SER: Valuations; restorations; repairs. VAT: Stan/Spec.

Geostran Antiques
Middle Lane, Whitacre Heath. (A. and A.M. Potter). Est. 1983. Open 10-5, Sat., Sun. and other times by appointment. SIZE: Small. STOCK: Small furniture, pre Edwardian, £100+; clocks and collectors' items, 19th C, £20+. LOC: Junction 4, M6, to Coleshill, then B4114, follow signs to Whiteacre Heath. PARK: Easy. TEL: 0675 81483; home - same. SER: Restorations (clocks and small furniture). FAIRS: Birmingham Motor Cycle Museum (April); NEC (August).

DUNCHURCH, Nr. Rugby
Dunchurch Antique Centre
16/16a Daventry Rd. (M. and Mrs G. Vandervelden). Est. 1981. Open 10-5 including Sun. SIZE: Medium - 18 dealers. STOCK: Mainly pre-1930 house furnishings and fitments, collectors' items, toys, antiquities, fireplaces, clocks, shipping goods and pine. LOC: Opposite Guy Fawkes cottage. PARK: Easy. TEL: 0788 817147. VAT: Stan/Spec.

HARBURY, Nr. Leamington Spa
Philip Riman Antiques
4 Honiwell Close. Resident. Est. 1991. Open by appointment. SIZE: Small. STOCK: Fine porcelain; copper, brass and silver; small furniture, country style and mahogany, £100-£1,000; mirrors, especially toilet. LOC: Take "middle road" to Harbury off Fosse Way, then second right into Farm Street and first right, second left and then right at T junction. PARK: Easy. TEL: 0926 612788; home - same. SER: Valuations; restorations (woodwork and longcase clocks); buys at auction. VAT: Stan.

HATTON, Nr. Warwick
Summersons
15 Carthouse Walk, Hatton Country World. (Peter Lightfoot). CMBHI. Open 10-4. STOCK: Clocks and barometers. TEL: 0926 843443. SER: Restorations; horological and barometer materials supplied - free catalogue available.

HENLEY-IN-ARDEN
Arden Gallery
(G.B. Horton). Est. 1963. Open 1-6. CL: Sat. SIZE: Medium. STOCK: Oil paintings, Victorian, £20-£1,000; watercolours, all periods, to £1,500; portrait miniatures. LOC: A3400. PARK: Easy. TEL: 0564 792520. VAT: Spec.

The Chadwick Gallery
Doctors Lane. (R. Barnes). Open 10-5. CL: Mon.

Henley-in-Arden continued
STOCK: *19th to early 20th C watercolours, etchings and engravings; some contemporary works.* TEL: 0564 794820.

Colmore Galleries Ltd   LAPADA
52 High St. Open 11-5.30. STOCK: *Pictures, 19th-20th C.* TEL: 0564 792938. SER: Valuations; restorations; framing.

Lacy Gallery
56 High St. Open Mon. 10-5, Tues., Wed. and Thurs. 10-1. STOCK: *Period frames; sporting and decorative paintings, watercolours and prints, 18th-20th C; art reference books.* TEL: 0564 793073.

Jasper Marsh   BADA
3 High St. (P.R.J. Marsh). Est. 1967. Open 10-5, Sun. p.m. by appointment. STOCK: *English furniture, Georgian, oak and mahogany, 17th to early 19th C; English and Oriental porcelain, Chinoiserie and Oriental art.* TEL: 0564 792088. VAT: Spec.

KENILWORTH

The Allen Gallery
38 Castle Hill. (N.P. Allen). Est. 1990. Open Sat. and Sun. or by appointment. SIZE: Medium. STOCK: *Paintings, watercolours and etchings, 19th-20th C; period frames; carpets and general antiques.* PARK: Easy. TEL: 0926 851435; home - same. SER: Valuations; restorations; framing. FAIRS: Local.

Castle Gallery
1 Thickthorn Mews. (M. and M. Lloyd-Smith). Open by appointment. STOCK: *Watercolours, drawings.* TEL: 0926 58727. SER: Conservation framing.

Janice Paull Antiques   LAPADA
Beehive House, 125 Warwick Rd. Est. 1965. Open Wed., Thurs. and Fri. 10-4, or by appointment. SIZE: Medium. STOCK: *Mason's Ironstone, 1813-1880; pottery and porcelain, 1780-1890; Baxter and Le Blond prints; all from £100.* LOC: Main st. PARK: At rear. TEL: 0926 55253; mobile - 0831 619254. SER: Valuations. FAIRS: NEC (Jan/April/Aug); Olympia (June/Nov); Kenilworth (March/Oct). VAT: Spec.

KINETON

Jeremy Venables
The Old Mill, Mill Lane. Est. 1977. Open 8.30-5.30, Sat. 9.30-1. SIZE: Large. STOCK: *Victorian, Georgian, Edwardian and shipping furniture.* LOC: Junction 12, M40, 2 miles Kineton, past Carpenter's Arms, 1st left. PARK: Easy. TEL: 0926 640971; evenings - 0295 87 8160. SER: Export. VAT: Stan. *Trade only.*

LEAMINGTON SPA

John Goodwin and Sons
Blackdown Mill, Blackdown. Open 9.30-5.30. STOCK: *Victorian and Edwardian furniture; paintings, bric-a-brac and books.* TEL: 0926 450687.

Hague Antiques
2 Regent St. (J. Hague). Est. 1967. Open 2-5. SIZE: Medium. STOCK: *Pine including doors, fireplaces and cupboard fronts.* LOC: One of the main roads which cross the Parade. PARK: Easy. TEL: 0926 337236. VAT: Stan/Spec.

David Hooper Antiques
20 Regent St. Open 9-6. STOCK: *General antiques.* TEL: 0926 429679.

The Incandescent Lighting Company
36 Regent St. (Mrs Patricia Cunningham). Est. 1988. Open 9.30-5.30, Sat. 9-6. SIZE: Medium. STOCK: *Lighting, 19th to early 20th C, £30-£2,500; Victorian, Edwardian and early 20th C glass shades, £25-£100; reproduction period style lighting, shades and components, £2-£1,000.* LOC: Town centre. From Pump Rooms up Parade, turn left, shop 150 yards off Parade on left. PARK: Easy. TEL: 0926 422421. SER: Valuations. VAT: Stan.

Leamington Pine and Antique Centre
20 Regent St. Open 9-6. SIZE: 12 dealers. STOCK: *General antiques.* TEL: 0926 429679.

Olive Green Ltd
12 Station Approach, Avenue Rd. (Colin Heeley). Est. 1987. Open 10-5. CL: Mon. SIZE: Medium. STOCK: *Furniture, £50-£2,000; china, £5-£500, both 18th-19th C; paintings, 19th-20th C, £50-£2,000.* LOC: Opposite library and museum. PARK: Easy. TEL: Mobile - 0860 613610. SER: Valuations.

Spa Antiques
4 Windsor St. (A. Jackson). Open 9.30-6. STOCK: *Oak and country furniture, especially coffers; bible and desk boxes.* TEL: 0926 422927.

Trading Post
39 Chandos St. (B. Morris). Est. 1949. Open 10-12 and 2-4. CL: Thurs. p.m. STOCK: *Small general antiques, Victorian jewellery.* TEL: 0926 421857.

Yesterdays
21 Portland St. (D. and Mrs K. Norbury). Est. 1986. Open Thurs.-Sat. 10-5. SIZE: Small. STOCK: *Furniture, George III to Edwardian, £75-£2,500; china, prints, 1850-1910, £10-£200.* Not Stocked: Pine. LOC: Parallel to The Parade. PARK: Easy. TEL: 0926 450238; home - 0926 316565.

WARWICKSHIRE

SHIPSTON-ON-STOUR

Fine-Lines (Fine Art) LAPADA
The Old Rectory, 31 Sheep St. (L.W. and R.M. Guthrie). Est. 1975. Open seven days by appointment only. SIZE: Medium. STOCK: British and European watercolours, pastels, drawings and selected oils, from 1850, £300-£10,000. LOC: On main one-way street. PARK: Easy. TEL: 0608 662323; home - same. SER: Restorations; cleaning; framing; buys at auction (paintings, watercolours and drawings). VAT: Spec.

The Grandfather Clock Shop
2 Bondgate House, West St., Granville Court. (M.S. Chambers). Est. 1978. Open 9.30-5. CL: Mon. and Thurs. p.m. SIZE: Medium. STOCK: Clocks - longcase, pre-1800, £1,000-£4,000; wall, £250-£1,000; mantle and bracket, 1790-1890, £200-£2,000; barometers, 1790-1860, £350-£1,000; furniture including oak, 17th-18th C. PARK: Easy. TEL: 0608 662144; home - 0926 57487.

Pine and Things
Portobello Farm, Campden Rd. (John Hudson). Est. 1991. Open 9-5. SIZE: Medium. STOCK: Pine, 18th-19th C, £150-£550. LOC: A429. PARK: Easy. TEL: 0608 663849; home - same. VAT: Stan/Spec.

'Time in Hand'
11 Church St. (F.R. Bennett). Open 9-1 and 2-5.30 or by appointment. SIZE: Medium. STOCK: Longcase, carriage and wall clocks, barometers. PARK: Town centre. TEL: 0608 662578. SER: Restorations (clocks, watches, barometers and mechanical instruments).

STRATFORD-UPON-AVON

Abode
Shrieve's House, 40 Sheep St. (Mrs A. and J. Bannister). Est. 1975. Open 9-5.30. SIZE: Large. STOCK: Furniture, pine, interior design items. LOC: Town centre. TEL: 0789 268755. SER: Buys at auction (furniture). FAIRS: Decorex International (Interior Design). VAT: Stan/Spec.

Arbour Antiques Ltd
Poet's Arbour, Sheep St. (R.J. Wigington). Est. 1952. Open 9-5.30, Sat. by appointment. STOCK: Arms, armour. LOC: From town centre towards Theatre and River, behind Lamb's Restaurant through archway at right. PARK: Easy. TEL: 0789 293453. VAT: Spec.

Art Deco Ceramics
Unit 4, The Courtyard, Stratford Antique Centre, Ely St. and Meer St. Antiques Arcade, 10a-11 Meer St. (Howard and Pat Watson). SIZE: Medium. STOCK: Art deco pottery, figurines, face masks and lamps. Not stocked: Militaria, coins and stamps. TEL: 0789 297496/297249; home - 0789 299524. SER: Finder. LOC: 100

Stratford-upon-Avon continued
yards from Shakespeare's birthplace. PARK: Nearby. FAIRS: Loughborough and Warwick Midland Art Deco, Alexandra Palace.

Jean A. Bateman LAPADA
41 Sheep St. NAG. Open 9.30-5. STOCK: Victorian and Georgian jewellery, objets d'art and vertu, including scent bottles. TEL: 0789 298494. SER: Valuations. VAT: Stan/Spec.

Bow Cottage Antiques
at Dolls and Toys Museum, Henley St. (R. Harvey-Morgan). Open 10-5.30. STOCK: English porcelain, glass, silver, paintings, engravings, maps, books; general antiques, small furniture, all 18th-20th C, £5-£150+. TEL: 0789 205883; messages - 0789 292485. VAT: Stan.

Burman Antiques
5 Trinity St. (J. and J. Burman Holtom). Est. 1973. Open by appointment only. STOCK: Ruskin ware, pot-lids, fishing tackle. TEL: 0789 295164. SER: Restorations (clocks).

Tim Harrison Wholesale Exports
Hatton Rock. Est. 1971. CL: Sat. SIZE: Warehouse. STOCK: Shipping goods and large Victorian and Edwardian furniture. PARK: Easy. TEL: 0789 292921. Trade Only.

Howards Jewellers
44a Wood St. (Howards of Stratford Ltd). Est. 1985. Open 9.30-5.30. STOCK: Jewellery, silver, objets d'art, 19th C. LOC: Town centre. PARK: Nearby. TEL: 0789 205404. SER: Valuations; restorations (as stock); buys at auction (as stock). VAT: Stan/Spec.

Jazz
Shop 2, Civic Hall, Rother St. (Mrs S. Hill). Est. 1988. Open 10-6. CL: Mon. SIZE: Small. STOCK: Art deco and art nouveau ceramics, lighting, and furniture, £10-£1,500. LOC: From island in town centre follow Wood St. PARK: Easy. TEL: 0789 298362. SER: Valuations. FAIRS: Decorative Arts, Kensington Town Hall; Art Deco, Loughborough; NEC (Aug).

Lions Den
31 Henley St. (T. and E. Hitchcox and S. Gould). Open 9.30-6 including Sun. STOCK: Moorcroft pottery, porcelain, oil paintings and watercolours. TEL: 0789 415802; fax - 0789 415853.

The Loquens Gallery
The Minories, Rother St. (S. and J. Loquens). Est. 1975. Open 9.15-5, Sun. by appointment. SIZE: Medium. STOCK: English watercolours, some oil paintings, late 18th to early 20th C, to £5,000. LOC: From island in town centre, follow Wood St. to Rother St. junction, entrance to Minories is on right. PARK: Easy. TEL: 0789 297706; home - 0789 750469. SER: Valuations; restorations (cleaning watercolours, relining oils); framing. VAT: Stan/Spec.

The Midlands Most Exciting Antique Arcade

10A/11 Meer Street
Stratford upon Avon CV37 6QB
Telephone: 0789 297249

Only 100 yards from Shakespeare's Birthplace

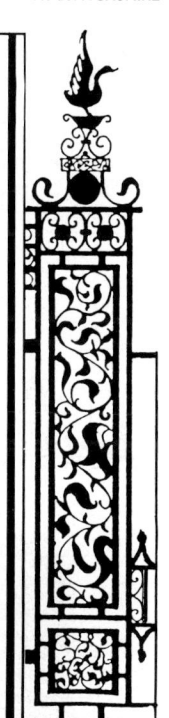

Stratford-upon-Avon continued

Meer Street Antiques Arcade
10A/11 Meer St. (Roger Jones). Open 10-5.30, Sat. 10-6.15. STOCK: Wide range of general antiques. TEL: 0789 297249. LOC: Close to Shakespeare's birthplace.

Rich Designs
11 Union St. (R. Green and D. Jones). Est. 1988. Open Fri. and Sat. 10-5 or by appointment. STOCK: Clarice Cliff pottery, £25-£2,500. PARK: Easy. TEL: 0789 261612.

Stratford Antique Centre
Ely St. (N. Sims). Open 10-5.30 every day. SIZE: 60 dealers. STOCK: General antiques. TEL: 0789 204180.

Robert Vaughan
20 Chapel St. (R. and C.M. Vaughan). ABA. Est. 1953. Open 9.30-6. SIZE: Medium. STOCK: Antiquarian and out-of-print books, maps and prints. LOC: Town centre. PARK: Easy. TEL: 0789 205312. SER: Valuations; buys at auction (books). VAT: Stan.

James Wigington Antiques
'Winchester 73', 276 Alcester Rd. Open by appointment. STOCK: General antiques, arms and armour, cannons, early fishing tackle. TEL: 0789 261418; fax - 0789 261600.

STRETTON-ON-FOSSE, Nr. Moreton-in-Marsh

Astley House - Fine Art
The Old School. (D. and N. Glaisyer). CADA. Est. 1974. Open by appointment. SIZE: Large. STOCK: Large decorative oil paintings, 19th-20th C. LOC: Village centre. PARK: Easy. TEL: 0608 50601; fax - 0608 51777. SER: Valuations; restorations; framing; exhibitions; mailing list. VAT: Spec.

STUDLEY

Prospect Antiques
Chester House, Alcester Rd. (R.T. Felix). Open afternoons and Sat. am. or by appointment. SIZE: Large. STOCK: General furniture, porcelain, glass, bronzes, Oriental items. LOC: A435. PARK: Easy. TEL: 052 785 2494. VAT: Stan/Spec.

WARWICK

Duncan M. Allsop
26 Smith St. ABA. Est. 1965. Open 9.30-5.30. SIZE: Medium. STOCK: Antiquarian and modern books. LOC: 50yds. east of Eastgate. PARK: Nearby. TEL: 0926 493266.

ANTIQUE & DECORATIVE ENGLISH & CONTINENTAL FURNITURE

LAPADA MEMBER

APOLLO ANTIQUES LTD

THE SALTISFORD BIRMINGHAM RD., WARWICK

ALWAYS IN STOCK AT SENSIBLE PRICES...

* FINE PERIOD CONTINENTAL & ENGLISH FURNITURE
* MARQUETRY & INLAID FURNITURE
* VICTORIAN WALNUT & MAHOGANY FURNITURE
* ARTS & CRAFTS & ART NOUVEAU FURNITURE
* ALSO DECORATIVE SMALLS, BRONZES, MARBLE, PICTURES, ETC
* TRADE WAREHOUSE FOR UNRESTORED GOODS

REGULAR DELIVERIES (LONDON TWICE WEEKLY)

TEL. 0926 494746 FAX. 0926 401477

Warwick continued

Apollo Antiques Ltd   LAPADA
The Saltisford, Birmingham Rd. (R.H. Mynott). Est. 1968. Open 9-6, Sat. 9.30-12.30. SIZE: Large and warehouse. *STOCK: Period, decorative English and continental furniture, sculpture, paintings, decorative objects, works of art; Victorian furniture.* PARK: Easy. TEL: 0926 494746; fax - 0926 401477. VAT: Stan/Spec.

John Bolton
Est. 1972. Open by appointment only. *STOCK: Period furniture, longcase clocks.* TEL: 0295 680439.

H.H. Bray Ltd
9 Jury St. (B. and I. Harper). Est. 1929. Open 9.30-5.30. *STOCK: Silver, jewellery, Sheffield plate.* LOC: On main Stratford to Warwick road. PARK: Easy. TEL: 0926 492791. SER: Valuations. VAT: Stan/Spec.

Eastgate Fine Arts
6 Smith St. (K. Pittaway). Open 10-5.30. *STOCK: Original maps, prints, paintings.* TEL: 0926 499777.

John Goodwin and Sons
Unit F and M Budbrooke Industrial Estate, Budbrooke Rd. Open 8.30-5.30, Sat. by appointment. *STOCK: Victorian and Edwardian furniture.* TEL: 0926 491191; fax - same.

Russell Lane Antiques
2-4 High St. (R.G.H. Lane). Open 11-5. *STOCK: Jewellery, silver, porcelain, furniture.* TEL: 0926 494494.

Patrick and Gillian Morley Antiques
LAPADA
62 West St. Est. 1968. Open 9-5.30, Sat. 10-12.30. SIZE: Large. *STOCK: Furniture, 17th to late 19th C; unusual and decorative items, sculpture, carvings and textiles; all £50-£20,000.* LOC: Almost opposite Warwick Castle 2nd car park. PARK: Easy. TEL: 0926 494464; home - 0926 54191; mobile - 0860 562196; fax - 0926 400531. SER: Valuations; buys at auction. VAT: Mainly Spec.

Peggy Nesbitt
Open by appointment. *STOCK: Dolls.* TEL: 0926 491600. SER: Restorations and repairs.

Martin Payne Antiques   LAPADA
30 Brook St. Est. 1971. Open Thurs.-Sat. 10-5.30 or by appointment. *STOCK: Silver including canteens, 18th-19th C, £50-£10,000.* LOC: Between High St. and Market Pl. PARK: Easy. TEL: 0926 494948; home - 0608 661282. SER: Valuations; restorations (silver repairs and replating); buys at auction. FAIRS: Barbican; LAPADA NEC. VAT: Stan/Spec.

Pine Design
33 The Saltisford. (C. Mynott). Open 9.30-5.30.

WARWICKSHIRE

Warwick continued
STOCK: Pine and decorative items. TEL: 0926 494666.

James Reeve
at Quinneys of Warwick, 9 Church St. Est. 1865. Open 9.30-5.30. CL: Sat. p.m. STOCK: Furniture, mahogany, oak, and rosewood, 17th-18th C, £80-£8,000; furniture, 19th C, £50-£3,500; glass, copper, brass, pewter, china. TEL: 0926 498113. VAT: Stan/Spec.

Smith St. Antiques Centre
7 Smith St. (E. Brook and W. Mechilli). Est. 1971. Open 10-5.30. SIZE: Large. LOC: Corner position, Smith St. is an extension of High St. PARK: Easy and at rear. TEL: 0926 497864; home - 0926 882060. VAT: Stan/Spec. Below are listed the dealers at this centre.

Simon Bowler
STOCK: Oriental porcelain, silver and furniture.

Erol Brook
STOCK: Silver and plate, decanters, curios, barometers.

Gary Eames
STOCK: Furniture, clocks, silver, porcelain, jewellery.

Eleanor Antiques
(Mrs E. W. E. Creed). STOCK: Porcelain, 18th to early 20th C, £5-£500; glass, 18th to early 20th C, £2-£75; needlework tools, 19th-20th C, £2-£25. TEL: 0926 400554.

Farfalla
STOCK: Sporting and natural history antiques.

A. Flight
STOCK: Porcelain, glass, silver, small furniture.

Mick Howe
STOCK: Cigarette cards. SER: Framing.

Chris James
STOCK: Military medals, swords, guns.

Walter Mechilli
STOCK: Silver, plate, porcelain, hickory shafted golf clubs.

Jean Stapley
STOCK: Silver, porcelain, Doulton figures, jewellery.

Turtons Antiques
STOCK: Jewellery, silver, gold, pocket watches.

Don Spencer Antiques
36a Market Place. Est. 1963. Open daily. SIZE: Large. STOCK: Desks, 1850-1920, £500-£5,000; dining furniture and bookcases, 1800-1920, £500-£3,000. PARK: Easy. TEL: 0926 499857; home - 0564 775470. VAT: Stan/Spec.

WARWICK

JAMES REEVE

**9 Church Street
Warwick
Tel 0926-498113**

Antique English furniture of the 17th, 18th and early 19th centuries. All items are sold in the finest condition.

Established over 100 years

Warwick continued

Vintage Antiques Centre
36 Market Place. (Peter Sellors). Est. 1977. Open 10-5. SIZE: 15 dealers + cabinets. STOCK: Ceramics, glass, collectables and small furniture, 19th-20th C. PARK: Easy. TEL: 0926 491527.

The Warwick Antique Centre
20-22 High St. Open 6 days a week. SIZE: Approx. 30 dealers. STOCK: General antiques. TEL: 0926 495704.

Warwick Antiques
16-18 High St. (M. Morrison). Est. 1969. Open 9-5, Sat. 10-5. SIZE: Large and warehouses. STOCK: Furniture, mahogany, oak, Chinese; metalware, copper, brass, pewter, glass, china, bygones, curios, statuary, garden furniture, shipping goods. LOC: Midway between E. and W. Gate clock towers. PARK: At rear. TEL: 0926 492482; fax - 0926 493867. SER: Restorations (furniture). VAT: Stan/Spec.

Westgate Antiques LAPADA
28 West St. (D.M. Cunningham). Open 10-5.30, Sat. 10-1. STOCK: Silver - Sheffield and plate; canteens, mahogany furniture, glass, decorative items and boxes, all 18th-19th C. LOC: Near town centre, beyond the West Gate. PARK: Easy. TEL: 0926 494106. SER: Valuations; restorations (silver including re-plating, and furniture). VAT: Stan/Spec.

West Midlands

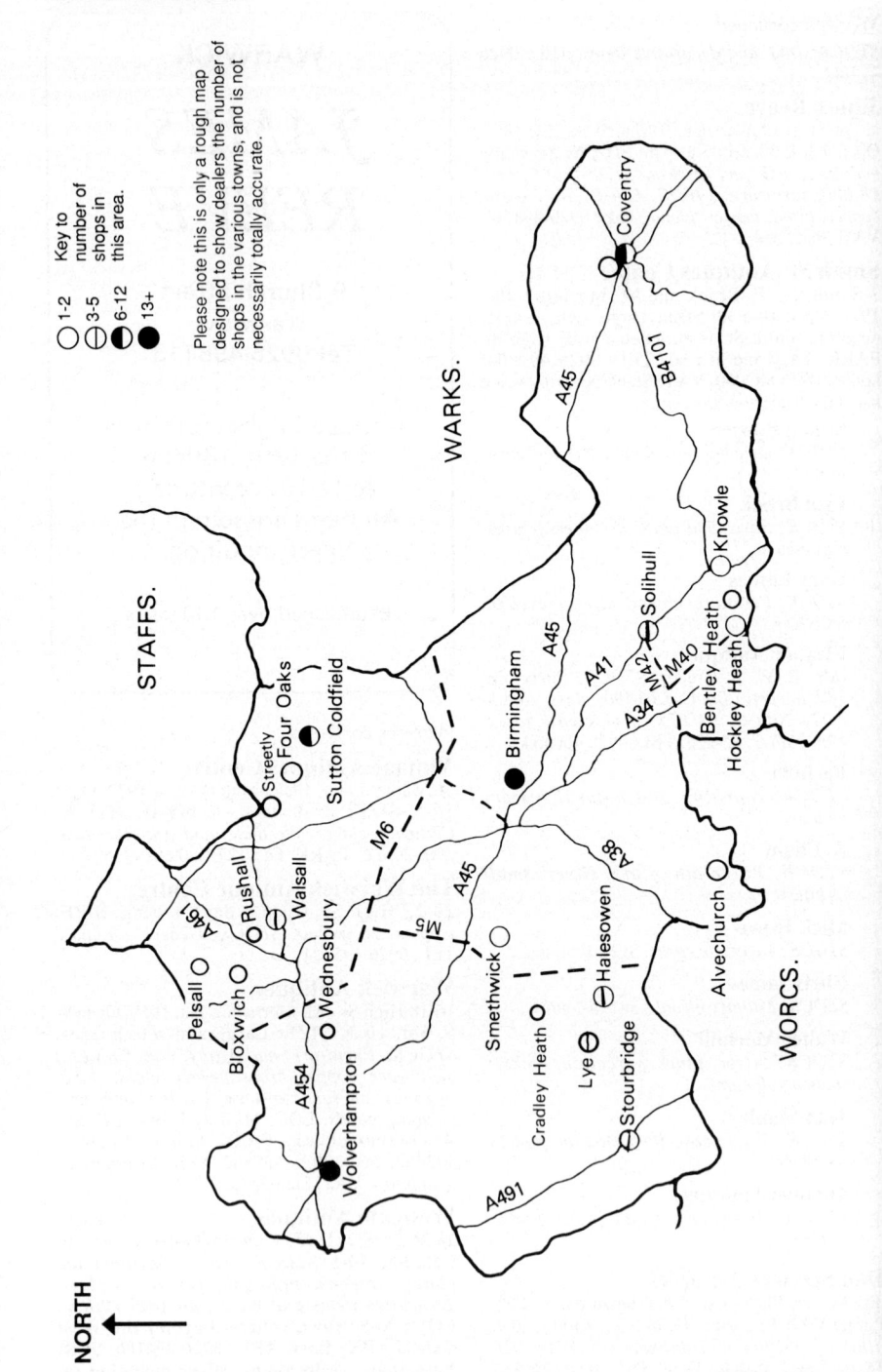

Key to number of shops in this area.

○ 1-2
◐ 3-5
◓ 6-12
● 13+

Please note this is only a rough map designed to show dealers the number of shops in the various towns, and is not necessarily totally accurate.

NORTH ←

STAFFS.
WARKS.
WORCS.

Coventry
Knowle
Bentley Heath
Hockley Heath
Solihull
Birmingham
Four Oaks
Streetly
Sutton Coldfield
Rushall
Walsall
Wednesbury
Pelsall
Bloxwich
Wolverhampton
Smethwick
Cradley Heath
Lye
Halesowen
Stourbridge
Alvechurch

A45, B4101, A41, M42, M40, A34, A38, M6, M5, A454, A461, A491

West Midlands

ALVECHURCH

Woodland Fine Art LAPADA
16 The Square. (C. Haynes). Est. 1971. Open 10-6, Sun. by appointment. SIZE: Medium. STOCK: Oil paintings, fine watercolours, and decorative prints, 19th to early 20th C, £20-£5,000; general antiques. LOC: 1.5 miles from exit 2, M42. PARK: Easy. TEL: 021 445 5886. SER: Valuations; restorations; framing. FAIRS: NEC Birmingham. VAT: Stan/Spec.

BENTLEY HEATH, Nr. Solihull

Roger Widdas Fine Paintings LAPADA
7 Bullivents Close. Open by appointment. STOCK: Drawings, oil paintings and watercolours including British, all 19th to early 20th C. TEL: 0564 773217.

BIRMINGHAM

Always Antiques
285 Vicarage Rd, Kings Heath. (R. and D. Messenger). Open Thurs.-Sat. 9-6, other times by appointment. STOCK: Victorian and Edwardian furniture, dolls, linen, lace and curios. TEL: 021 444 8701.

Architectural Antiques of Moseley
23A St. Mary's Row, Moseley. (R. Stevenson). Open 10-6. SIZE: Large. STOCK: Antique fireplaces and other architectural fixtures and fittings in marble, slate, cast iron and wood, 1800-1930's. PARK: Own. TEL: 021 442 4546. SER: Restorations (as stock); fitting; marble decoration, graining and rag rolling.

Archives
496 Bristol Rd, Selly Oak. (S.D. and I.J. Healey and D. Heywood). Open 9.30-5.30 including Sun. STOCK: Victorian and Edwardian furniture; clocks and upholstery, to 1930. TEL: 021 472 4026.

Peter Asbury Antiques
162 Vicarage Rd, Langley. Open 9-5. CL: Wed. p.m. STOCK: General antiques. TEL: 021 552 1702.

Ashleigh House Antiques
Ashleigh House, 5 Westbourne Rd. (P. and R. Hodgson). Est. 1974. Open by appointment. SIZE: Large. STOCK: Furniture, oils and watercolours, £200-£5,000; clocks, £300-£2,000; objets d'art, £75-£2,000; all 1700-1880. LOC: From Five Ways Edgbaston take Calthorpe Rd. and bear right into Westbourne Rd., premises 150 yards on left. PARK: Easy. TEL: 021 454 6283; home - same. SER: Valuations; restorations (furniture and paintings); buys at auction. FAIRS: Most dateline, Midlands area. VAT: Stan/Spec.

Paul Baxter
Open by appointment only. STOCK: Oriental ceramics and general antiques. TEL: 0564 824920.

Birmingham continued

Birmingham Bookshop
567 Bristol Rd, Selly Oak. STOCK: Out-of-print books, all periods; art books; postcards, prints. TEL: 021 472 8556. VAT: Stan.

Cameo
4 Lonsdale Rd, Harborne. Open 9.30-5.30, Sat. 9.30-4. CL: Mon. and Wed. STOCK: General antiques especially ceramics. TEL: 021 426 6900.

Carleton Gallery
91 Vivian Rd, Harborne. (D. Dunnett). Open 9-5.30, Wed. 9-1. STOCK: Maps and prints. TEL: 021 427 2487.

Chesterfield Antiques
181 Gravelly Lane. (A.I. Beddard). Est. 1977. Open 10-5.30. CL: Wed. STOCK: General antiques. TEL: 021 373 3876.

The City of Birmingham Antique Market
St. Martins Market, Edgbaston St. (Antique Forum (Birmingham) Ltd). Est. 1976. Open Mon 6.30-2. SIZE: Large. Several dealers. STOCK: General antiques, art deco, 5p-£5,000. LOC: Adjacent to Bull Ring. PARK: Multi-storey nearby. TEL: 071 624 4848. SER: Valuations.

Peter Clark Antiques LAPADA
36 St. Mary's Row, Moseley. Open 9-5.30. SIZE: Medium. STOCK: Furniture, mid-17th C to early 20th C, £175-£2,500; silver, early 19th C to early 20th C, £100-£500. LOC: Centre of Moseley. PARK: At rear. TEL: 021 449 8245. SER: Valuations; restorations (furniture). VAT: Stan/Spec.

The Collectors Shop
63 Station St. (J. Cash). Est. 1967. Open 10-4. CL: Wed. p.m. SIZE: Small. STOCK: Coins, militaria, secondhand jewellery, silver, small items. LOC: One minute from New St. Station. PARK: Nearby. TEL: 021 631 2072. SER: Valuations; buys at auction (coins). FAIRS: Most major coin. VAT: Stan/Spec.

R. Collyer
185 New Rd, Rubery. Open 9-5.30. STOCK: Clocks including longcase; watches, barometers, secondhand jewellery. LOC: 1 mile from Lydiate Ash roundabout. TEL: 021 453 2332. SER: Valuations; restorations.

Dolly Mixtures
Open by appointment. STOCK: Dolls and teddies. TEL: 021 422 6959. SER: Restorations.

Eden Coins
P.O. Box 73, Oldbury. (R. Pratt). Est. 1979. Open by appointment. STOCK: Coins, medals and tokens, 18th-20th C, £1-£100. LOC: 1 mile M5, junction 3. TEL: 021 422 5357; home - same. FAIRS: Cumberland Coin.

Birmingham continued

Edgbaston Gallery
42 Islington Row, Five Ways, Edgbaston. (I. Bethell). Est. 1976. Open 12.30-5.30. CL: Sat. and Sun. except by appointment. SIZE: Medium. STOCK: *Oil paintings and watercolours, £50-£1,000; small furniture, clocks, collectors' items; all 19th C.* LOC: Junction of Islington Row and Frederick Rd. PARK: In Frederick Rd. TEL: 021 454 4244; home - 021 459 3568. SER: Valuations; restorations; framing; buys at auction (paintings).

Maurice Fellows
21 Vyse St, Hockley. STOCK: *Objets d'art, jewellery.* TEL: 021 554 0211; fax - 021 507 0807. SER: Valuations; restorations.

Fine Pine
75 Mason Rd, Erdington. (H. Duignan). Open 8.30-5.30. STOCK: *Pine and satin walnut furniture, iron tiled fireplaces and surrounds, general antiques.* TEL: 021 373 6321.

Format of Birmingham Ltd
18 Bennetts Hill. (G. Charman and D. Vice). Open 9.30-5. CL: Sat. STOCK: *Coins, medals.* PARK: New St. station. VAT: Stan/Spec.

Garratt Antiques
35 Stephenson St. Est. 1958. STOCK: *Jewellery, brass, silver, copper, pewter, silver plate, china, crystal, dolls and bric-a-brac.* TEL: 021 643 9507. SER: Valuations; restorations. VAT: Stan/Spec.

The Graves Gallery
3 Augusta St, (Jewellery Quarter). (P. Cassidy). Open 10.30-5. STOCK: *19th-20th C oil paintings and watercolours; general antiques.* TEL: 021 212 1635.

The Halcyon Gallery
59 The Pallasades. (L., P. and R. Green). Open 9-5.30. STOCK: *Modern British oils, watercolours and limited editions - Sir William Russell Flint, David Shepherd, Lowry.* TEL: 021 643 4474.

Bob Harris and Sons, Antiques LAPADA
2071 Coventry Rd, Sheldon. (R.E. Harris). Resident. Est. 1953. Open 9-6. CL: Sun. ßexcept by appointment. STOCK: *18th-19th C furniture and general antiques.* TEL: 021 743 2259. VAT: Stan/Spec.

John Hubbard Antiques LAPADA
224-226 Court Oak Rd, Harborne. Est. 1968. Open 9-6. SIZE: Large. STOCK: *Furniture, 18th-19th C; paintings and watercolours, all £50-£15,000; lighting and decorative items.* LOC: 3 miles from city centre. PARK: Easy. TEL: 021 426 1694. SER: Valuations; restorations; leather linings. VAT: Stan/Spec.

Birmingham continued

Huddington International Antiques Warehouse
73 Western Rd., Hockley. (J. Wilson). Open 9-5, Sat. 9-4. STOCK: *Furniture and shipping goods.* TEL: 021 523 8862; fax - 021 554 1741.

James Antiques - Canalside
Gas St. Basin. (P. and D. James). Est. 1969. Open 12-5 Wed., Sat. and Sun., or by appointment. SIZE: Small. STOCK: *Decorative antiques, small furniture, stained glass, tiles, painted goods, folk art, general, some 18th, mainly 19th C, to £500.* LOC: Central, near NEC. TEL: 021 643 3131; home - 021 444 4628. SER: Valuations; restorations; stained glass repairs; buys at auction.

Tim James Antiques
47 Dogpool Lane, Stirchley. Est. 1990. Open 12-6. CL: Wed. STOCK: *Architectural antiques, fire places and surrounds, furniture, pine, mainly 19th C.* PARK: Easy. TEL: 021 414 0051. SER: Restorations.

Rex Johnson and Sons
28 Lower Temple St. (D. Johnson). Open 9.30-5.30, Sat. 9.30-5. STOCK: *Silver, jewellery, porcelain and glass.* TEL: 021 643 9674.

Rex Johnson and Sons
23 Union St. (R. Johnson). Open 9.30-5.15. STOCK: *Gold, silver, jewellery, porcelain and glass.* TEL: 021 643 7503.

Kestrel House Antiques and Auction Salerooms
72 Gravelly Hill North, Erdington. (E.C. Jones). Est. 1895. Open 10.30-7. SIZE: Large. STOCK: *19th C oil paintings and watercolours.* TEL: 021 373 2375. SER: Fortnightly auctions; restorations; framing; paintings re-lined and cleaned; canvases repaired. VAT: Stan.

March Medals
113 Gravelly Hill North, Erdington. (M.A. March). Est. 1975. Open 10-5, Sat. 10-2. STOCK: *Orders, decorations, campaign medals, militaria and military books.* TEL: 021 384 4901. SER: Catalogues issued. VAT: Stan/Spec.

Maxwells Book Shop
22 Shaftmoor Lane, Acocks Green. (C.M. Prickett). Open 10.30-4.45. CL: Mon. STOCK: *Antiquarian and secondhand books.* TEL: 021 706 8379; 021 744 4671.

F. Meeks & Co
22 Warstone Lane, Hockley. (M.L. and S.R. Durham). Open 9-5, Sat. 9-12. STOCK: *Clocks especially longcase, mantle and wall; scientific instruments, microscopes and sextants, all 18th-19th C; optical instruments, vintage wrist watches and antique pocket watches; £100-£10,000.* TEL: 021 236 9058. SER: Valuations; restorations (clocks); clock and watch parts supplied. VAT: Stan/Spec.

WEST MIDLANDS

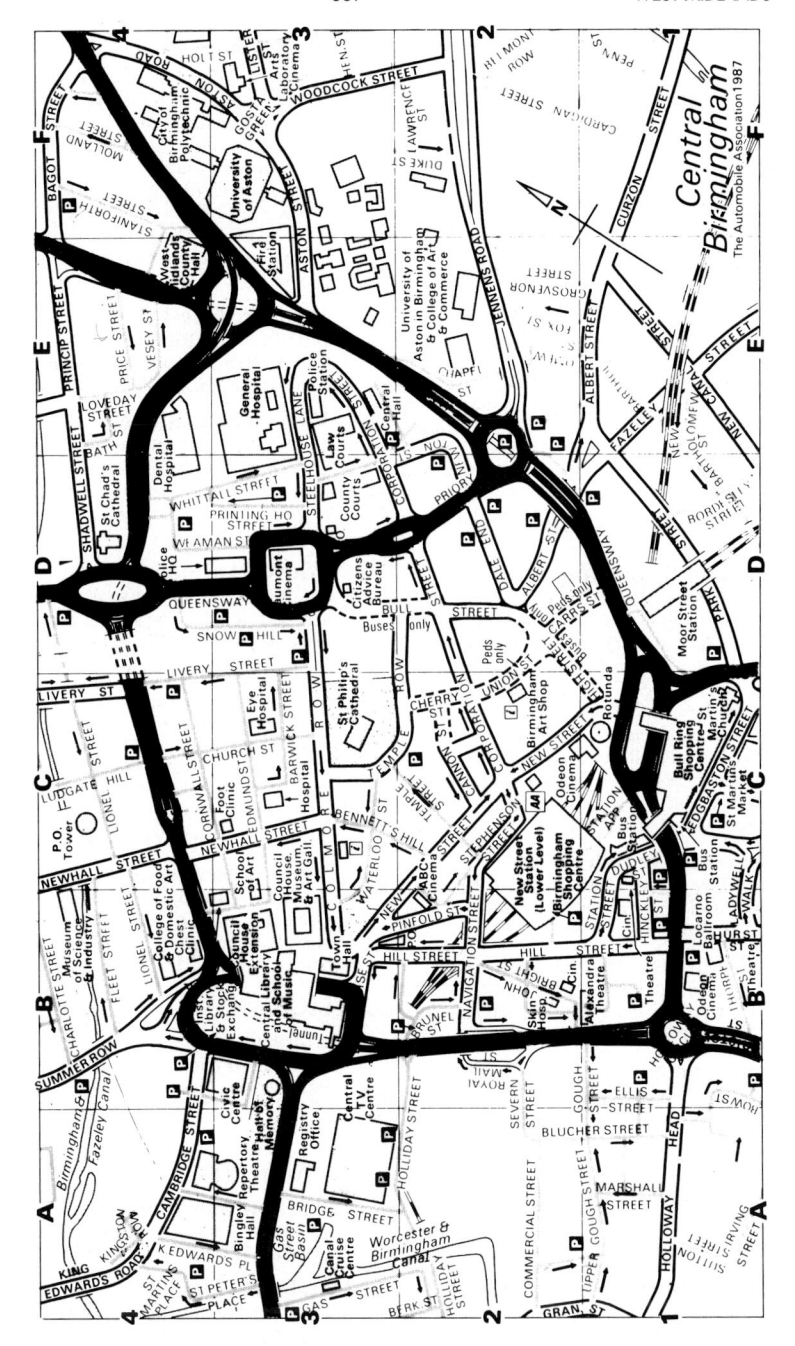

Central Birmingham
The Automobile Association 1987

Key to Town Plan

AA Recommended roads	Car Parks
Other roads	Parks and open spaces
Restricted roads	AA Service Centre
Buildings of interest	© Automobile Association 1988.

Birmingham continued
Moseley Antiques
Unit 5 Woodbridge Rd, Moseley. (Mrs H. Benstead). Est. 1972. Open 10-6. CL: Wed. STOCK: Furniture and clocks. TEL: 021 449 6186.

Moseley Pianos
Unit L, 68 Wyrley Rd., Witton. (Gavin Burrell). Open 10.15-2. CL: Fri. and Sat. except by appointment. SIZE: Warehouse. STOCK: Upright and grand pianos. LOC: 3 minutes from Spaghetti junction (M6, junction 6). PARK: Easy. TEL: 021 327 2701/449 6869; mobile - 0831 560518.

Nathan and Co. (Birmingham) Ltd
31 Corporation St. Est. 1857. Open 9-5. SIZE: Medium. STOCK: Silver and jewellery, £35-£25,000. LOC: A31. PARK: New St. Station. TEL: 021 643 5225. SER: Valuations; restorations (silver and jewellery); buys at auction. FAIRS: British International (Birmingham). VAT: Stan/Spec.

The Old Bakehouse
71 Station Rd, Harborne. (Andrew Brooker-Carey). Est. 1989. Open 10-5.30, Sat. 9.30-5.30. CL: Wed. SIZE: Medium. STOCK: Pine furniture, fireplaces and mirrors, Georgian-Victorian, £50-£1,000; lighting, Victorian to 1920's, £50-£500; garden furniture, from Victorian, £10-£500; Victorian beds, £200-£600; furniture, Georgian to 1920's, £50-£800. LOC: Parallel to High St. PARK: Easy. TEL: 021 428 1928. SER: Valuations; restorations (wood and metal including polishing and painting). VAT: Stan/Spec.

Piccadilly Jewellers
Piccadilly Arcade, New St. (R. and R. Johnson). Open 10-5. STOCK: Jewellery, silver and objects. TEL: 021 643 5791.

S.R. Furnishing and Antiques
18 Stanley Rd, Oldbury. (S. Willder). Est. 1975. STOCK: General antiques and shipping furniture. TEL: 021 422 9788.

Smithsonia
14-16 Piccadilly Arcade, Off New St. (V. Smith and M. Ferguson). Open 10-5.15. STOCK: Jewellery, collectables, prints. TEL: 021 643 8405.

Tatters of Tyseley Ltd
590 Warwick Rd, Tyseley. (N. Smith and G. Jinks). Open 10-5, Fri. 10-7. CL: Mon. STOCK: Victorian and Edwardian fireplaces. TEL: 021 707 4351. SER: Restorations; fitting.

David Temperley Fine and Antiquarian Books
19 Rotton Park Rd, Edgbaston. (D. and R.A. Temperley). Resident. Est. 1967. Open 9.30-5.30 by prior appointment. SIZE: Small. STOCK: Fine antiquarian and rare books especially fine

Birmingham continued
bindings, illustrated and press; fine colour plate books - natural history, costume, travel, topography and atlases, 16th-20th C; early and rare English and European playing cards. LOC: 150 yards off Hagley Rd. (A456) and under 2 miles from city centre. 4 miles junction 3, M5. PARK: Easy. TEL: 021 454 0135; fax - 021 454 1124. SER: Valuations; restorations (book binding and paper); buys at auction (antiquarian books).

Treasure Chest
1407 Pershore Rd, Stirchley. Est. 1960. Open 8.30-6. STOCK: General antiques; trade display cabinets. TEL: 021 458 3705/459 4587.

Victoriana Antiques
287 Bearwood Rd, Bearwood, Warley. Open 10-6. STOCK: Furniture, mahogany, satin and pine, Victorian tiled cast-iron fireplaces and surrounds, costume jewellery, silver, bric-a-brac, textiles TEL: 021 429 8661.

Warley Antique Centre
146 Pottery Rd, Oldbury, Warley. (D.P. Hipkins and A.D. Smith). Open 10-6, Sat. 11-3. STOCK General antiques. TEL: 021 434 383.

The Windmill Gallery
6 Ernest St, Holloway Head. (M. and C. Ashton) Est. 1985. Open 9-5.30, Sat. and Sun. by appointment. SIZE: Medium. STOCK: Watercolours and drawings, 18th-20th C, £100-£3,000+. LOC: City centre. PARK: Easy. TEL: 021 622 3986; fax 021 666 6630. SER: Valuations; restorations mounting, framing. VAT: Spec.

Yesterdays Antiques
125 Pottery Rd, Oldbury, Warley. (D.P. Hipkins) Open 9-6. STOCK: Furniture, clocks, china and porcelain, jewellery, toys. TEL: 021 420 3980 home - 021 429 2287.

BLOXWICH
Cobwebs
639d Bloxwich Rd, Leamore. (Mrs M Hannaway). Open 10.30-4.30. CL: Mon. and Thurs. STOCK: Bric-a-brac. PARK: Easy. TEL 0922 493670.

COVENTRY
The Antique Shop
107 Spon End. (J. Branagh). Open 9-5.30 STOCK: General antiques. TEL: 0203 525915.

Memories Antiques
400A Stoney Stanton Rd. (R.D. Seymour). Est 1964. Open 9.30-5, Sun. 10-2. CL: Wed. STOCK General antiques, Victorian and Edwardian furniture, shipping goods, stripped pine, china gold, silver, paintings and collectors' items Royal Doulton. TEL: 0203 687994/440215.

ANTIQUE COLLECTING

- **Authoritative articles**
- **Practical buying information**
- **Up-to-date price guides**
- **Annual Investment Issue**
- **Auctions and fairs calendars**
- **Antiques for sale and wanted**

The magazine is published ten times a year and contains pre-publication offers and special Christmas discounts on ACC books

Join NOW and receive your first magazine and our book catalogue FREE
Annual membership: £19.50 UK, £25.00 overseas, US $40 USA, CAN $50 Canada

Antique Collectors' Club
5 Church Street, Woodbridge, Suffolk,
IP12 1DS, England
Tel: (0394) 385501   Fax: (0394) 384434

Market Street Industrial Park, Wappingers' Falls,
New York 12590, USA
Tel: 914 297 0003   Fax: 914 297 0068

For Collectors, By Collectors, About Collecting

WEST MIDLANDS 542

Coventry continued
Milton Antiques
93 Dane Rd. (A.P. Ross). Est. 1971. Open by appointment. SIZE: Large. *STOCK: Furniture, shipping goods.* Not Stocked: Glass, china, silver, pictures. LOC: Off A46. PARK: Easy. TEL: 0203 456285. *Trade Only.*

Spon End Antiques
115-116 Spon End. (N. and J. Green). Open 10.30-4.30. *STOCK: Furniture, jewellery, pianos, china, dolls, teddy bears, pre-50's clothes.* TEL: 0203 228379/447628.

Sports Programmes
P.O. Box 74, Chapel St. (A. Stanford). *STOCK: Football programmes.* TEL: 0203 228672. *Postal Only.*

CRADLEY HEATH
Old Hill Auctions
205 Halesowen Rd, Old Hill. (J. Turner). Open 8-5.30 including Sun. *STOCK: Furniture, china, glass, jewellery, 18th to early 20th C.* TEL: 0384 411121.

FOUR OAKS, Nr. Sutton Coldfield
M. Allen Watch and Clockmaker
76A Walsall Rd. (M.A. Allen). Est. 1969. Open 9-5.30, Sun. by appointment. SIZE: Small. *STOCK: Vintage wristwatches - Omega, Longines, Girard, Perregaux and Jaeger le Coultre; clocks - Vienna regulators, 1820-1880, mantle and wall clocks.* LOC: By Sutton Park, close to television mast. PARK: Easy. TEL: 021 308 6117; home - 021 308 8134. SER: Valuations; restorations (clocks and watches). VAT: Stan/Spec.

Robert Taylor
Windy Ridge, Worcester Lane. Est. 1983. Open 9-6 by appointment only, including Sun. *STOCK: Old collectable toys, including Dinky, Corgi, clockwork, tinplate, £5-£1,000.* PARK: Easy. TEL: 021 308 4209. SER: Valuations; buys at auction. FAIRS: NEC, Gloucester, Windsor.

HALESOWEN
Martyn Brown Antiques
130 Hagley Rd, Hayley Green. Open 10-5. CL: Wed. *STOCK: Furniture, clocks, paintings and collectables.* TEL: 021 585 5758.

Clent Books
52 Summer Hill. (I. Simpson). Est. 1978. Open 10-4. CL: Wed. SIZE: Small. *STOCK: Antiquarian books, local history, topography, £1-£200.* LOC: Town centre. PARK: Opposite. TEL: 021 550 0309; home - 0299 401090. SER: Valuations. FAIRS: Waverley Antique and Book (Organiser).

Halesowen Antiques
1-3 Hagley Rd, Hasbury. (C.J. Clarke). Open 9.30-5 or by appointment. *STOCK: Furniture*

Halesowen continued
including shipping; decorative items. LOC: mins from M5 junction 3. PARK: Own. TEL: 02 585 7238. SER: Container packing; courier. VAT Stan/Spec.

Tudor House Antiques
68 Long Lane. (D. Bevan and D. Taylor). Ope 9.30-5.30. *STOCK: Architectural items includin, doors, fireplaces, staircases and pine.* TEL: 02 561 5563.

Robert Withers - Antiques
242 Hagley Rd, Hasbury. Open 9-5.30. CL: Wec and Thurs. *STOCK: Oil paintings and water colours, 19th C; furniture and works of ar* PARK: Easy. TEL: 021 550 4588; evenings - 02 550 9033.

HOCKLEY HEATH, Nr. Solihull
Magpie House
2212 Stratford Rd. (D.P. Fair). Est. 1958. CL: Sa except by appointment. SIZE: Medium. *STOCK Oak and mahogany.* LOC: A34 to Stratford-or Avon, 1 mile from M42, junction 4. PARK: Eas TEL: 0564 782005. VAT: Stan/Spec. *Trade Only*

KNOWLE
Chadwick Antiques
Chadwick End. (Mrs P. Tibenham). Resident. Es 1973. Open 10-5, also some Sun. SIZE: Mediun *STOCK: Furniture, 18th-19th C; collector, items, general antiques.* Not Stocked: O paintings. LOC: A41. PARK: Easy. TEL: 056 782096. SER: Valuations.

LYE, Nr. Stourbridge
The Lye Curios, Inc. Lye Antique Furnishings
181 High St. (Mr and Mrs P. Smith). Est. 197 Open 9-5. SIZE: Medium. *STOCK: Furnitur china, glass, metalware.* PARK: Easy. TEL: 03 897513; home - 0384 62788. SER: Valuations.

Retro Products
Antique Warehouse, The Yard, Star St. (N McHugo). Est. 1980. Open 10-5. CL: Sat. SIZ Large. *STOCK: Furniture - Victorian, Edwardia garden and shipping, £5-£1,000; cast ir metalwork; architectural items.* LOC: O Stourbridge to Birmingham Rd. PARK: Eas TEL: 0384 894042; home - 0384 373332. FAIR Ardingly and Newark. VAT: Stan.

Smithfield Antiques
20 Stourbridge Rd. (R. Harling). Open 9-5.3 other times by appointment. *STOCK: Gener antiques and shipping goods.* TEL: 0384 89782

PELSALL, Nr. Walsall
L.P. Furniture (Mids) Ltd
152 Lime Lane. (P. Farouz). Est. 1982. Op

Pelsall continued
daily, Sun. by appointment. SIZE: Warehouse. STOCK: *Mahogany, Victorian and Edwardian, £50-£750; shipping, to 1950, £25-£750; pine, Victorian and reproduction, £60-£500.* Not Stocked: Smalls, clocks, paintings and carpets. LOC: Junction 12, M6, take A5 towards Cannock, right at second roundabout on B4154, shop 150yds. on left. PARK: Easy. TEL: 0543 370256; home - 0922 495155. SER: Courier, packing, shipping. VAT: Stan.

ROMSLEY, Nr. Halesowen
Kennerley's
2a St. Kenelm's Rd. (G.T. Callwood). Open Tues., Fri. and Sat. 10-5. STOCK: *General antiques.* TEL: 0562 710050. SER: Restorations; stripping.

SMETHWICK, Nr. Warley
Grannies Attic Antiques
437 Bearwood Rd. (B.A. Seymour). Est. 1965. Open 10-6 or by appointment to trade. SIZE: Medium. STOCK: *Dolls, oak, mahogany and walnut furniture, curios, art deco, Victorian and Edwardian clothes, porcelain, books, pictures, fans, toys, records, stuffed animals, brass, copper, jewellery, tools, mirrors, smalls and shipping items, pre-1930, £5-£1,000.* LOC: Off Hagley Rd. PARK: Easy. TEL: 021 429 4180; home - 021 454 7507. SER: Valuations; buys at auction. *Mainly Trade.*

SOLIHULL
Geoffrey Hassall Antiques
20 New Rd. Est. 1972. Open 9.30-1 and 2-5.30. CL: Mon. SIZE: Small. STOCK: *Furniture, 18th-19th C.* Not Stocked: Books, jewellery. PARK: Easy. TEL: 021 705 0068. SER: Restorations (furniture).

Renaissance
18 Marshall Lake Rd, Shirley. (S.K. Macrow). MGMC. Est. 1981. Open 9.30-5.30. SIZE: Small. STOCK: *General antiques.* LOC: Near Stratford Rd. TEL: 021 745 5140. SER: Restorations (repairs, re-upholstery and polishing).

Tilleys Antiques　　　　　　　LAPADA
(S.A. Alpren). **Open by appointment only.** STOCK: *British glass, Oriental pottery, porcelain, shipping goods; silver, 19th C; Worcester.* **TEL: 021 704 1813.** SER: Valuations; restorations (jewellery, silver); repairs (clock, watch).

STOURBRIDGE
Oldswinford Gallery
106 Hagley Rd, Oldswinford. (A.R. Harris). Open 9.30-5. STOCK: *18th-20th C oil paintings, watercolours and prints.* TEL: 0384 395577. SER: Restorations; framing.

A simple solid walnut corner chair with straight legs which belie the earlier date suggested by the shape of the splats, c.1745. When restored £500-£700. From **British Antique Furniture — Price Guide and Reasons for Values** by John Andrews. Third edition published in 1992 by the **Antique Collectors' Club,** £35.00.

Stourbridge continued
S.O.S. Militaria
Curio Corner, 32 Park St. (B.J. Smale). Open 9.30-5. STOCK: *Medals, badges, militaria.* TEL: 0384 379652; evenings - 029 93 5795.

Topaz
32A Market St. (Mr and Mrs B.J. Jones). Est. 1992. Open 9-5, Fri. 9-5.30. SIZE: Small. STOCK: *Collectables, gifts including Royal Doulton figures.* LOC: 1st right off ring road, 1st right into Market St. PARK: Nearby. TEL: 0384 379495. SER: Valuations.

STREETLY, Nr. Sutton Coldfield
Hardwick Antiques
Chester Rd. (P. Chatfield). Open 11-6. CL: Wed. a.m. STOCK: *Jewellery, silver, porcelain, furniture.* LOC: Opposite Ruby Rest. TEL: 021 353 1489.

SUTTON COLDFIELD
Thomas Coulborn and Sons　　BADA
Vesey Manor, 64 Birmingham Rd. (P. Coulborn). Est. 1939. Open 9-5.30. SIZE: Medium. STOCK: ***General antiques, 1600-1830; English furniture, 17th-18th C; paintings and clocks.*** Not Stocked: 19th C bric-a-brac. LOC: 3 miles from Spaghetti Junction. From Birmingham A5127 through Erdington,

WEST MIDLANDS

Sutton Coldfield continued
premises on main road opposite cinema.
PARK: Easy. TEL: 021 354 3974. SER: Valuations; restorations (furniture and paintings); buys at auction. FAIRS: British International, Birmingham (Spring). VAT: Spec.

Stancie Cutler Antique and Collectors Fair
Town Hall. Est. 1981. Open one Wed. monthly 10-6, trade 10-8, prior telephone call advisable. SIZE: 70 stands. *STOCK: General antiques, large furniture to thimbles, mainly pre-1940.* TEL: Home - 0270 624288.

Driffold Gallery
78 Birmingham Rd. (D. Gilbert). Open 10-5.30. CL: Thurs. *STOCK: Oil paintings and watercolours, 19th-20th C.* TEL: 021 355 5433.

Kelford Antiques
14a Birmingham Rd. (E.S. Kelsall). Est. 1968. Open 9-5. CL: Thurs. *STOCK: General antiques, Georgian and Victorian furniture, silver, porcelain, Staffordshire figures, pot-lids, jewellery.* TEL: 021 354 6607. VAT: Stan/Spec.

Osborne Antiques
91 Chester Rd, New Oscott. (C. Osborne). Est. 1976. Open 9-5, Sat. 9-1. CL: Mon. *STOCK: Barometers, clocks and furniture.* TEL: 021 355 6667. SER: Restorations; spares (clocks, barometers).

H. and R.L. Parry Ltd
23 Maney Corner. (H. Parry). Est. 1925. Open 9.30-5.30. SIZE: Medium. *STOCK: Porcelain, silver and jewellery, all periods; metalware, paintings.* LOC: A38 from Birmingham road into Sutton. Cinema on right, on corner of service road in which premises are situated. TEL: 021 354 1178. SER: Valuations. VAT: Stan/Spec.

WALSALL

Jomarc Pianos Ltd.
The Piano Craft Centre, Mill Green Farm, Chester Rd., Aldridge. (P. Hoskinson). Open 9.30-5.30, Sat. 9.30-4. *STOCK: Pianos.* TEL: 0922 743292; 0922 743826.

Nicholls Jewellers and Antiques
57 George St. (R. Nicholls). Open 9-5. *STOCK: Jewellery.* TEL: 0922 641081. SER: Repairs.

Past and Present
66 George St. (G. and Mrs A.J. Ellis). Open 9.30-5. *STOCK: Satin, walnut, mahogany and oak furniture, curios, collectables, linen, ceramics, pottery, porcelain.* LOC: Opposite Sainsbury's car park. TEL: 0922 611151.

Jon and Kate Rutter
The Doghouse, 309 Bloxwich Rd. Open 9-5.30, Sun. by appointment. SIZE: Large. *STOCK: General antiques.* TEL: 0922 30829/24263. VAT: Stan.

Walsall continued
Walsall Antiques Centre
7A The Digbeth Arcade. (J.M. Shaw and S.P. Swaine). Est. 1989. Open 10-5. SIZE: Large - 50 dealers. *STOCK: Porcelain, 1800-1940, £25-£800; furniture, 1800-1930, £50-£2,500; Royal commemoratives, 1820-1937, £10-£1,000.* LOC: In Victorian arcade by the Digbeth St. outdoor market. PARK: Nearby. TEL: 0922 725163/725165; fax after 5pm - 0922 725163. SER: Valuations; buys at auction (Royal commemoratives). FAIRS: Alexandra Palace, NEC (April and Aug), Bingley Hall (Stafford). VAT: Stan/Spec.

WEDNESBURY

Brett Wilkins Antiques
81 Holyhead Rd. Est. 1983. Open Fri. and Sat., other days (including Sun.) by appointment. SIZE: Medium. *STOCK: Shipping items, 1900-1940, £5-£250; Victorian mahogany, 19th C, £100-£500; some pine, 19th-20th C, £100-£500.* LOC: 2 miles off M6, junction 9 on A41. PARK: Easy. TEL: 021 502 0720; mobile - 0860 541260. FAIRS: All major. VAT: Stan.

WOLVERHAMPTON

Antiquities
75-76 Dudley Rd. Est. 1968. Open 10-6. *STOCK: General antiques.* TEL: 0902 459800.

Broad Street Gallery
16 Broad St. (J.E. and J.T. Hill). FATG. Est. 1975. Open 9-5.30. CL: Thurs. p.m. *STOCK: Prints, watercolours, oils, £50-£1,000.* LOC: 3 minutes from St. Peter's Church. PARK: Easy. TEL: 0902 24977. SER: Restorations; framing VAT: Stan.

Collectors' Paradise Ltd
56a Worcester St. (D. Hoppett and R. Butlin). Est 1963. Open 10-5. CL: Thurs. p.m. *STOCK: Arms, armour, militaria, uniforms, bric-a-brac.* TEL: 0902 20315.

Alan M. France
Open by appointment only. *STOCK: Clocks, wris, and pocket watches.* TEL: 0902 731167.

Gemini Antiques
18a Upper Green, Tettenhall. (J. Pettitt). Open 11-4. *STOCK: General antiques.* TEL: 0902 742523 home - 0902 67334.

Ghiberti Antiques and Fine Art
297 Tettenhall Rd., Newbridge. (Miss M Horvath-Toldi). Est. 1986. Open 10-5, Sun. by appointment. SIZE: Small. *STOCK: French furniture, 19th C, £500-£10,000; objets d'art 19th C, £50-£3,000; English furniture, 18th C £500-£3,000.* LOC: 8 miles from junction 10, M6 6 miles from junction 3, M54. PARK: At rear TEL: 0902 750519. SER: Valuations; restorations (furniture including upholstery); buys at auction (furniture and objets d'art). FAIRS: NEC.

An Antique Collectors' Club Title

A Collector's History of British Porcelain
by *John and Margaret Cushion*

This companion volume to our **A Collector's History of English Pottery** is a comprehensive overview of the manufacture of porcelain in Great Britain from mid-18th century to the present.
ISBN 1 85149 155 4
456pp, 641 b & w illus, 130 col, £35.00

Available from:
Antique Collectors' Club, 5 Church Street, Woodbridge, Suffolk IP12 1DS
Tel: (0394) 385501 Fax: (0394) 384434

or Market Street Industrial Park, Wappingers' Falls, New York 12590, USA
Tel: 914 297 0003 Fax: 914 297 0068

Wolverhampton continued

Golden Oldies
5 St. Georges Parade. (W.A. and M.A. Knowles). Open 10-5.30. CL: Mon. *STOCK: Victorian, Edwardian and later furniture, £25-£2,000; paintings, decorative items.* PARK: Easy. TEL: 0902 22397. VAT: Stan/Spec.

Martin-Quick Antiques LAPADA
323 Tettenhall Rd. Est. 1965. Open 9-6, Sat. 9.30-4. SIZE: Large. *STOCK: 18th-19th C furniture, shipping goods, architectural items, stripped pine, silver plate. Not Stocked: Militaria, coins.* LOC: One mile from town centre on A41. PARK: Easy. TEL: 0902 754703; home - 0902 752908; fax - 0902 756889. VAT: Stan/Spec.

Pendeford House Antiques
1 Pendeford Ave, Claregate, Tettenhall. (Mrs B. Tonks). Est. 1980. Open 10.30-5. CL: Thurs. SIZE: Medium. *STOCK: China and porcelain, £5-£500; furniture and clocks, £50-£1,500; oil paintings and watercolours, £50-£500; all 19th-20th C; glass, linen, brass and copper, jewellery and silver.* LOC: From main Tettenhall Rd., turn at traffic lights towards Codsall. At first small traffic island, take 3rd exit, shop next to Jet Garage. PARK: Easy. TEL: 0902 756175; home - same.

The Red Shop
7 Hollybush Lane, Penn. (B. Savage). Open 9.30-5.30. *STOCK: Furniture including pine.* TEL: 0902 342915.

Wolverhampton continued

Second Thoughts
1-3 Coalway Rd, Penn. (Mr and Mrs C.R. Turley). Est. 1977. Open Mon. 9.30-1 and 2-4.30, Thurs. and Sat. 9.30-1, or by appointment. SIZE: Small. *STOCK: Furniture, 18th-19th C; porcelain, glass, watercolours and prints, unsual items.* LOC: A449, 3/4 mile from town centre. PARK: Easy. TEL: 0902 337748/337366. SER: Valuations. VAT: Stan/Spec.

Tatters Decorative Antiques
9 Upper Green, Tettenhall. (Martin and Maureen Logan). Est. 1985. CL: Tues. and Thurs. SIZE: Small. *STOCK: Textiles, tapestries, cushions, rugs and decorative items, 19th to early 20th C, £50-£100; small furniture, £100-£300; Staffordshire pottery, £50-£200; both 19th C.* LOC: Off junction3, M54, A41 towards Wolverhampton. PARK: Easy. TEL: 0902 756500. FAIRS: NEC; Stafford - Bingley Hall.

Wakeman and Taylor Antiques
LAPADA
140b Tettenhall Rd. Est. 1967. Open 8.30-5.30 or by appointment. CL: Sat. SIZE: Large. *STOCK: Furniture, 1700-1900, £100-£10,000.* LOC: One mile from town centre on A41. PARK: Easy. TEL: 0902 751166; home - 0785 284539. VAT: Stan/Spec. *Trade Only.*

Wiltshire

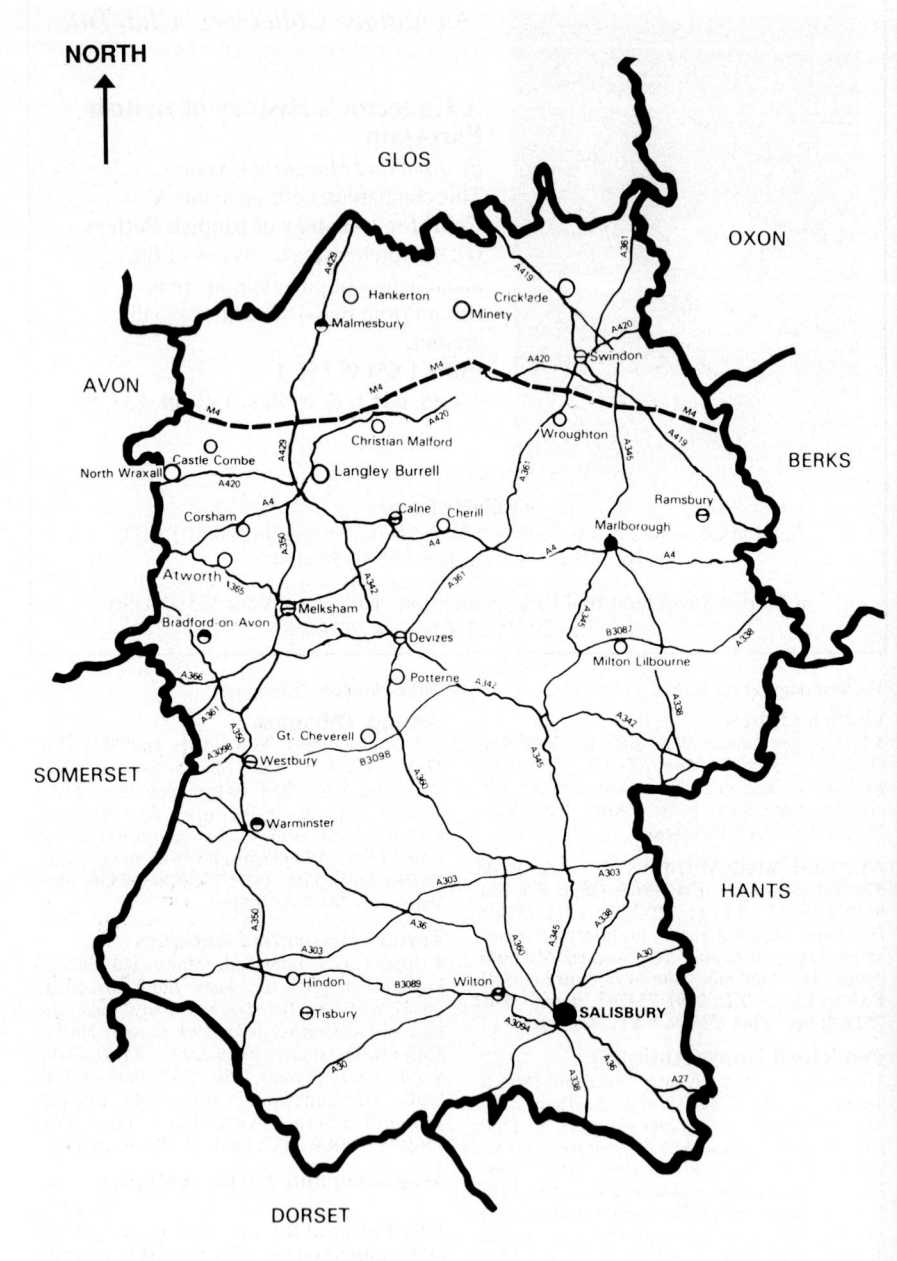

Wiltshire

HARLEY ANTIQUES

LARGEST COLLECTION OF SELECTED ANTIQUES & DECORATIVE OBJECTS IN THE WEST COUNTRY

Full colour brochure sent on request
(Export enquiries only)

THE COMEDY
CHRISTIAN MALFORD
NR. CHIPPENHAM
WILTSHIRE FN15 4BF

TEL: 0249 720112
4 MILES M4 EXIT 17
RESIDENT ON PREMISES

WILTSHIRE

AVON ANTIQUES
25-26-27 MARKET STREET
BRADFORD-ON-AVON
WILTSHIRE BA15 1LL
Tel. (STD 0225) 862052

Eight showrooms of 17th, 18th and early 19th century furniture clocks, barometers, metalwork some textiles, painted and lacquered furniture

Member of the British Antique Dealers Association

ATWORTH, Nr. Melksham
Peter Campbell Antiques
59 Bath Rd. (P.R. Campbell). Est. 1976. Open 10-5, Sun. and Thurs. by appointment. SIZE: Medium. STOCK: *General antiques and decorative items, 18th-19th C.* Not Stocked: Silver and jewellery. LOC: Between Bath and Melksham on A350. PARK: Easy. TEL: 0225 709742; home - same. VAT: Stan/Spec.

BRADFORD-ON-AVON
Avon Antiques   BADA
25,26 and 27 Market St. (V. and A. Jenkins, BA). Est. 1960. Open 9.45-5.30, Sun. by appointment. SIZE: Large. STOCK: *English and some continental furniture, 1600-1880; metalwork, treen, clocks, barometers, some textiles, painted and lacquer furniture.* LOC: A363, main street of town. PARK: Opposite. TEL: 0225 862052. FAIRS: Grosvenor House. VAT: Spec.

Books & Prints
15 Church St. Open 10.30-5, Thurs. 10.30-8. STOCK: *Books.* TEL: 0225 868300.

Harp Antiques   LAPADA
17 Woolley St. (H.A. and J. Roland-Price). Resident. Est. 1973. Open daily 9-6. SIZE: Medium. STOCK: *Georgian and Regency furniture, £100-£8,000; English pottery and porcelain, £30-£3,000; silver, £5-£300.* LOC: B3107, 300yds. from town centre. PARK: Easy. TEL: 0225 865770; home - same. SER: Valuations. VAT: Spec.

Mac Humble Antiques   BADA
7-9 Woolley St. (W. Mc. A. and B.J. Humble). Open 9-6, Sat. 9-5. SIZE: Large. STOCK: *17th-19th C mahogany, fruitwoods, metalware, treen, samplers, silkwork pictures, decorative objects.* TEL: 0225 866329. SER: Valuations; restorations. VAT: Stan/Spec.

Moxhams Antiques   LAPADA
17, 23 and 24 Silver St. (R. and J. Bichard). Est. 1966. Open 9-5.30 or by appointment. SIZE: Large. STOCK: *English and continental furniture, clocks, 1650-1830, £200-£15,000; European and Oriental pottery and porcelain, 1700-1830, £10-£3,000; metals, treen, decorative items, 1600-1900, £5-£5,000.* Not Stocked: Silver, jewellery. PARK: Own, at rear. TEL: 0225 862789; fax - 0225 867844; home - 0380 828557. SER: Valuations. VAT: Stan/Spec.

CALNE
Calne Antiques
2a London Rd. (M. Blackford). Open 9-5 including Sun. STOCK: *Furniture and shipping goods, collectors' items.* LOC: Next to White Hart Hotel. TEL: 0249 816311.

An Antique Collectors' Club Title

A Collector's History of English Pottery
by Griselda Lewis

Now in its fourth edition. *'...this new, revised book must be regarded as the most comprehensive in text and illustrations. In a word, the best.'* Ceramics Magazine.

**ISBN 1 85149 056 6, 360pp
over 650 b & w illus, 62 col, £35.00**

Available from:

Antique Collectors' Club, 5 Church Street, Woodbridge, Suffolk IP12 1DS
Tel: (0394) 385401 Fax: (0394) 384434

or Market Street Industrial Park, Wappingers' Falls, New York 12590, USA
Tel: 914 297 0003 Fax: 914 297 0068

Calne continued

Clive Farahar and Sophie Dupré - Rare Books, Autographs and Manuscripts
14 The Green. Open by appointment. SIZE: Medium. STOCK: *Rare books on voyages and travels, autograph letters and manuscripts, 15th-20th C, £5-£5,000.* LOC: Off A4 in town centre. PARK: Easy. TEL: 0249 821121; fax - 0249 821202. SER: Valuations; buys at auction (as stock). FAIRS: ABA; Universal Autograph Collectors' Club. VAT: Stan.

Hilmarton Manor Press
Hilmarton Manor. (H. Baile de Laperriere). Est. 1967. Book on Silver Auction Records. Open 9-6. SIZE: Medium. STOCK: *New and out-of-print art and photography reference books, some*

Calne continued

antiquarian. LOC: 3 miles from Calne on A3102 towards Swindon. PARK: Easy. TEL: 024 976 208. SER: Buys at auction.

CASTLE COMBE, Nr. Chippenham
Combe Cottage Antiques   BADA
(B. and A. Bishop). Est. 1960. Open 10-1 and 2-6, prior telephone call advisable. SIZE: Medium. STOCK: *Country furniture, £20-£5,000; metalware, £10-£2,000; both 17th to early 19th C; treen, pottery, 18th-19th C, £5-£500; early lighting devices.* Not Stocked: Mahogany furniture, glass, silver, Victoriana. LOC: A420 from Chippenham towards Bristol. After 3 miles bear right on B4039. PARK: 20yds. TEL: 0249 782250. SER: Valuations; specialists in cottage furnishings. VAT: Spec.

CHERHILL, Nr. Calne
P.A. Oxley Antique Clocks and Barometers   LAPADA
The Old Rectory, Main Rd. Est. 1971. Open 9.30-5, other times by appointment. CL: Wed. SIZE: Large. STOCK: *Longcase, bracket, carriage clocks and barometers, 17th-19th C, £500-£30,000.* LOC: A4, not in village. PARK: Easy. TEL: **0249 816227**; fax - **0249 821285**. VAT: Spec.

CHRISTIAN MALFORD, Nr. Chippenham
Harley Antiques   LAPADA
The Comedy. (G.J. Harley). Est. 1959. Open 9-6 including Sun., or later by appointment. SIZE: Large. STOCK: *Furniture, 18th-19th C, £150-£3,000; decorative objects, £30-£1,000.* LOC: B4069, 4 miles off M4, junction 17. PARK: Own. TEL: **0249 720112**; home - same. SER: Colour brochure available (export only). VAT: Stan. *Trade Only.*

CODFORD, Nr. Warminster
Tina's Antiques
75 High St. (T.A. Alder). Open 9-6, Sat. 9-1. STOCK: *General antiques.* TEL: **0985 50828**.

CORSHAM
Matthew Eden
Pickwick End. Resident. Est. 1951. SIZE: Large. STOCK: *Country house furniture and garden items, 17th-19th C.* TEL: **0249 713335**; fax - **0249 713644**. VAT: Spec.

CRICKLADE, Nr. Swindon
Edred A.F Gwilliam
Candletree House, Bath Rd. Est. 1976. Open by appointment. SIZE: Medium. STOCK: *Arms and armour, swords, pistols, long guns, £30-£10,000+.* PARK: Easy. TEL: **0793 750241**. SER: Valuations; buys at auction. FAIRS: Major arms. VAT: Stan/Spec.

DEVIZES
Arena
High St, Potterne. (Bobbie Middleton). Open Wed.-Sat. 10-5, other times by appointment. STOCK: *Furniture and decoration.* LOC: On A360 Devizes to Salisbury, centre of village. TEL: **0380 720584**. VAT: Spec.

Cross Keys Jewellers
The Ginnel, Market Pl. (D. and D. Pullen). Est. 1967. Open 9.30-5.30. STOCK: *Jewellery, silver.* LOC: Alley adjacent Nationwide Building Socy. PARK: Easy. TEL: **0380 726293**. VAT: Stan.

Devizes continued

Sussex House Antiques
1A Bath Rd. (Rita and John Watkins). Est. 1973. Open 10-12.30 and 1.30-5, Sun. and Mon. by appointment. SIZE: Large. STOCK: *Furniture, late 18th to 19th C; pictures and prints, 19th C; smalls.* TEL: **0380 720916**; home - **0380 850018**. LOC: Just outside town at beginning of Bath road (A391). PARK: Own at rear. SER: Valuations; restorations (furniture). VAT: Stan/Spec.

GT. CHEVERELL, Nr. Devizes
Mary Manners Antiques
The Barn, Laurel House, 48 High St. Est. 1976. Open by appointment or by chance. SIZE: Small. STOCK: *Small decorative items, Staffordshire figures, pewter, blue and white transferware, textiles, 18th-19th C, £20-£300.* LOC: Opposite Bell Inn. PARK: Easy. TEL: **0380 812301**; home - same. FAIRS: Chelsea, Shepton Mallet. VAT: Spec.

HINDON, Nr. Salisbury
Monkton Galleries
High St. (J. and B. Dempsey). Resident. Est. 1967. CL: Sat. p.m. SIZE: Medium. STOCK: *Early oak and country furniture; metalware, longcase clocks.* PARK: Easy. TEL: **074 789 235**. SER: Valuations; restorations (metalware, prints and pictures). FAIRS: Buxton; Surrey; NEC. VAT: Spec.

LANGLEY BURRELL, Nr. Chippenham
Harriet Fairfax Fireplaces and General Antiques
Langley Green. Open by appointment only. STOCK: *China, glass, dolls, furniture, fabrics and needlework; architectural items and fittings, brass and iron knobs, knockers; fireplaces, pine and iron, 1780-1950.* TEL: **0249 652030**. SER: Polishing; welding; design consultancy.

MALMESBURY
Antiques - Rene Nicholls
56 High St. (Mrs. R. Nicholls). Est. 1980. Open 10-5.30, Sun. by appointment. SIZE: Small. STOCK: *English pottery and porcelain, 18th to early 19th C, £50-£900; small furniture.* PARK: Opposite. TEL: **0666 823089**; home - same.

Andrew Britten Antiques
48 High St. (T.M. Tyler and T.A. Freeman). Est. 1975. Open 9.30-6, Sun. by appointment. SIZE: Medium. STOCK: *Furniture, 1700-1900, £100-£1,500; decorative brass, wood, glass and porcelain items, £15-£500.* Not Stocked: Jewellery, militaria. PARK: Opposite. TEL: **0666 823376**. VAT: Spec.

P.A. Oxley

Antique Clocks & Barometers

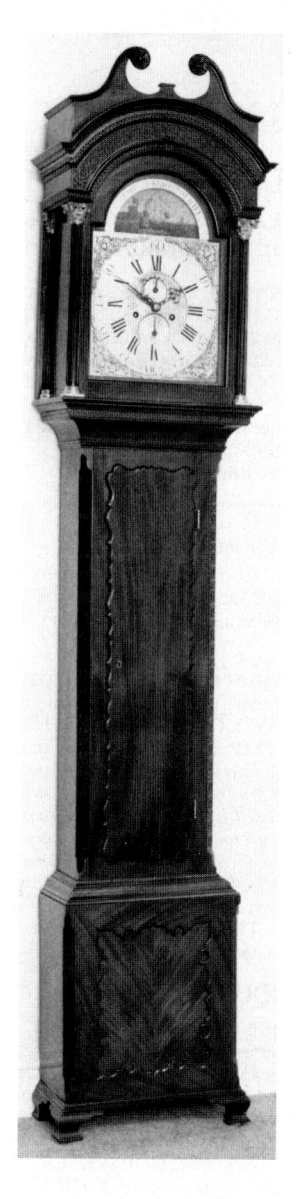

**The Old Rectory · Cherhill · Near Calne
Wiltshire SN11 8UX
Telephone (0249) 816227   Fax (0249) 821285**

P.A. Oxley is one of the longest established and largest quality antique clock and barometer dealers in the U.K. Current stock includes over 40 restored longcase clocks together with bracket clocks, carriage clocks and barometers.

Our extensive stock can be viewed at our large showrooms on the main A4 London to Bath road at Cherhill in Wiltshire just 80 miles from London.

Full shipping facilities are available to any country in the world. U.K. customers are provided with a free delivery and setting up service combined with a twelve month guarantee.

If your desire is for a genuine antique clock or barometer then we will be pleased to see you at Cherhill where you can examine our large stock and discuss your exact requirement. If time is short and you cannot visit us we will send you a selection of colour photographs from which you can buy with confidence.

Hours of opening are 9.30-5.00 every day except Wednesday. Sunday and evening appointments can easily be arranged. We look forward to welcoming you to our establishment.

Michael & Patrica Oxley

Member of The London & Provincial Antique Dealers' Association

WILTSHIRE

THE WILTSHIRE SOURCE FOR FURNITURE 1830 TO 1930

Oak, Mahogany and Pine
Restored and Unrestored

*Over 1/2 our stock is privately purchased
Rapid turnover*

CROSS HAYES ANTIQUES
ANTIQUE WAREHOUSE
19 BRISTOL STREET
MALMESBURY
WILTSHIRE

Open 8.30am to 5pm
Friday, Saturday and Monday
or any time by arrangement

Contact David Brooks
Tel. 0666 824260 Day 0666 822062 Evening
Fax. 0666 823020

RELIC ANTIQUES
AT
BRILLSCOTE FARM

LEA VILLAGE, NR. MALMESBURY,
Tel: 0666-822332 WILTSHIRE Fax: 0666-825598

ARCHITECTURAL ANTIQUES, COUNTRY
FURNITURE, GARDEN ORNAMENTS, PERIOD
SHOP & BAR INTERIORS, FAIRGROUND ART,
VINTAGE ADVERTISING & TRADE SIGNS,
NAÏVE & FOLK ART, DECORATORS' PIECES

(8 miles from M4 Motorway at Exits 16 & 17)
OPEN DAILY 9am-5.30pm
Weekends by appointment

Malmesbury continued

Cross Hayes Antiques   LAPADA
The Antique and Furniture Warehouse, 19 Bristol St. (D. Brooks). Est. 1975. Open Mon., Fri. and Sat. 8.30-5, or by appointment. SIZE: Warehouse. STOCK: Oak, mahogany, walnut and pine furniture, Georgian to 1920's; bric-a-brac. TEL: 0666 824260; home - 0666 822062; fax - 0666 823020. SER: Valuations. VAT: Stan/Spec.

Dovetail Antiques
67/69 High St. (C.R. Perrin). Resident. Est. 1987. Open 10-5.30. SIZE: Small. STOCK: Early oak and country furniture; metalware and treen; mahogany and walnut town furniture, 18th-19th C; Oriental and unusual items, 19th C. Not Stocked: Jewellery and bric-a-brac. PARK: Nearby. TEL: 0666 822191.

J.P. Kadwell
Silver St. Est. 1981. Open 8.15-5.30 including Sun. SIZE: Medium. STOCK: General antiques, £5-£500. PARK: Easy. TEL: 0666 823589; home - same. SER: Restorations (wood); buys at auction.

North Wilts Exporters
The Nurseries, Tetbury Hill. (M. Thornbury). Est. 1972. Open Mon.-Sat. or by appointment. STOCK: American and continental shipping goods, pine, 18th-19th C. LOC: Tetbury road. TEL: 0666 824133; mobile - 0836 260730. SER: Valuations; shipping; import and export. VAT: Stan.

Relic Antiques at Brillscote Farm
Brillscote Farm, Lea. (M. Gliksten and G. Gower). Est. 1975. Open 9-5.30, Sat. and Sun. by appointment. SIZE: Large. STOCK: Old shop and pub fronts and interiors, doors, screens and bars, stained and engraved glass windows and architectural fittings, provincial and country furniture, fairground animals and scenery, 19th C; garden ornaments, nautical and aeronautical models, etc. LOC: Take left turn to Lea off Wootton Bassett Rd., 2nd house on right. PARK: On premises. TEL: 0666 822332. SER: Valuations; buys at auction. VAT: Stan.

MARLBOROUGH

The Antique and Book Collector
Katharine House, The Parade. (C.C. Gange). Est. 1983. Open 9.45-5.30. SIZE: Medium. STOCK: Furniture, 17th-19th C, £200-£2,000; decorative items, £100-£1,000; glass, silver, brass, china, 18th-19th C, £20-£500; paintings and prints, £10-£1,000; books, £5-£500. PARK: Easy. TEL: 0672 514040; home - same. FAIRS: PBFA monthly; Oxfam annually. VAT: Stan/Spec.

Marlborough continued

Cavendish House Antiques
138 High St. (M. Phillips). Open 10-5 including Sun. *STOCK: General antiques and collectors' items.* TEL: 0672 511567.

Cook of Marlborough Fine Art Ltd
LAPADA
High Trees House, Savernake Forest. (W.J. Cook). BAFRA. Est. 1963. Open 10-5, Sat. and Sun. by appointment. SIZE: Medium. *STOCK: Furniture, 18th to early 19th C; objets d'art, 18th-19th C; pictures, 19th-20th C.* LOC: 1.5 miles from Marlborough on A346 towards Burbage. PARK: Easy. TEL: 0672 513017; fax - 0672 514455. SER: Valuations; restorations (furniture including polishing and gilding); buys at auction (furniture). FAIRS: Café Royal; Olympia; Barbican; Harrogate. VAT: Stan/Spec.

Nigel Cracknell (Antiques) Ltd
Cavendish House, 138 High St. Resident. Est. 1965. Trade anytime, appointment advisable. SIZE: Large. *STOCK: 18th and 19th C English furniture, some oak; brass and decorative items.* PARK: Easy. TEL: 0672 512912. VAT: Stan/Spec.

Cross Keys Jewellers
21a High St. (D. and D. Pullen). Est. 1967. Open 9.30-5.30. *STOCK: Jewellery, silver.* LOC: Entrance to Waitrose car park. TEL: 0672 516260. VAT: Stan.

Robert Kime Antiques
Upper Farm, Fosbury. Est. 1968. Open 10-6, Sat. by appointment. *STOCK: Decorative, period furniture.* TEL: 026489 268. VAT: Spec.

Lacewing Fine Art Gallery
124 High St. (N. James). Open 10-5.30. CL: Wed. *STOCK: Paintings and watercolours, 16th-19th C, £200-£10,000.* TEL: 0672 514580.

The Marlborough Parade Antique Centre
The Parade. (T. Page and N. Cannon). Est. 1985. Open 10-5 including Sun. SIZE: 57 dealers. *STOCK: Good quality furniture, paintings, silver, porcelain, glass, clocks, jewellery, copper, brass and pewter, £5-£5,000.* LOC: Adjacent A4 in town centre. PARK: Easy. TEL: 0672 515331. SER: Valuations; restorations (furniture, porcelain, copper, brass); buys at auction. VAT: Stan/Spec.

The Military Parade Bookshop
The Parade. (G. and P. Kent). *STOCK: Military history books especially regimental histories and World Wars 1 and 2.* LOC: Next to The Lamb. TEL: 0672 515470.

Principia Arts and Sciences
5 London Rd. (M. Forrer and N. Acheson). Open 9.30-5.30 and by appointment. *STOCK:*

Marlborough continued

Collectors' items, scientific instruments, small country furniture, treen, pictures, clocks, china, porcelain and books. TEL: 0672 512072; fax - 0672 511551.

Stuart Gallery
4 London Rd. (A.B. Loncraine). Est. 1968. Open Thurs., Fri. and Sat. 9-6.30,. *STOCK: General antiques especially small collectables, watercolours, oils and prints, china, glass, interior design pieces, books, garden items.* PARK: Easy. TEL: 0672 513593.

Annmarie Turner Antiques
22 Salisbury Rd. Est. 1960. Open 9-6, Sat. 9-5, Sun. by appointment. SIZE: Large. *STOCK: Country and Welsh primitive furniture, £50-£1,500; English treen, kitchen, trade and architectural items, £10-£300; paintings and decorative items, £20-£500; all 17th-19th C.* Not Stocked: Jewellery, silver and weapons. LOC: Left side of first roundabout approaching town centre from Hungerford on A4. PARK: Easy and at rear. TEL: 0672 515396; home - same. SER: Valuations. VAT: Spec.

MELKSHAM

Dann Antiques Ltd
Unit 1, Avonside Enterprise Park, New Broughton Rd. Open 9-1 and 2-5 or by appointment. SIZE: Large. *STOCK: 18th-19th C furniture and accessories.* TEL: 0225 707329; fax - 0225 790120; home - 0380 812228.

A deep shell-shaped dish probably used for serving sweetmeats, the decoration in underglaze blue, crescent mark, c.1765-70, 5½in. (14cm). (Phillips). From *The Dictionary of Worcester Porcelain, Vol.I, 1751-1851,* by John Sandon, published in 1993 by the **Antique Collectors' Club,** £45.00.

Rupert Gentle

Dealer in Antiques and
Works of Art

The Manor House,
Milton Lilbourne,
Pewsey, Wiltshire
SN9 5LQ

Telephone (0672) 63344

18th century furniture, needlework and all domestic accessories of the period. Specialising in English and Continental domestic brass, 1600-1800

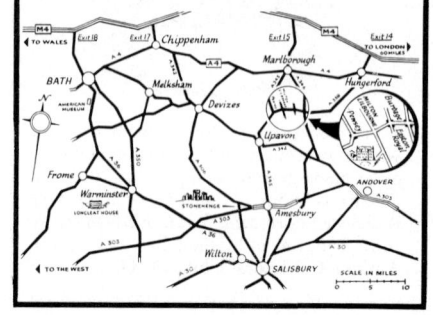

Melksham continued

Alan Jaffray
16 Market Place. Est. 1956. Open 10-1 and 2-5, Sat. by appointment. SIZE: Large. STOCK: Furniture and smalls, 18th-19th C, £50-£2,000. LOC: Main Bath to Devizes Rd. PARK: Easy. TEL: 0225 702269; fax - 0225 790413. VAT: Stan/Spec.

MILTON LILBOURNE, Nr. Pewsey

Rupert Gentle Antiques   BADA
The Manor House. Est. 1954. Open 9.15-6. SIZE: Medium. STOCK: 18th C furniture, needlework, domestic accessories, especially English and continental brass, 1600-1800. LOC: From Hungerford on A4 take A338 for Pewsey. PARK: Easy. TEL: 0672 63344. SER: Valuations; buys at auction. VAT: Stan/Spec.

MINETY, Nr. Malmesbury

Sambourne House Antiques
Sambourne House. (T. Cove). Est. 1984. Open daily, Sun. by appointment. SIZE: Large. STOCK: Pine, 1800-1910, £75-£400; furniture, 20th C, £50-£200; reproduction decorative items, £10-£300. LOC: 10 mins. from M4, junction 16. PARK: Easy. TEL: 0666 860288; home - 0666 822271. SER: Valuations; restorations (pine, renovating, stripping and finishing); kitchens and furniture made from reclaimed pine; buys at auction; export arranged (especially Chicago, U.S.A.). VAT: Stan. *Trade Only.*

NORTH WRAXALL, Nr. Chippenham

Delomosne and Son Ltd   BADA
Court Close. (M.C.F. Mortimer and T.N.M. Osborne). Est. 1905. Articles on chandeliers, glass and porcelain. Open 9.30-5.30; Sat. 9.30-1 (except Bank Holiday weekends). SIZE: Large. STOCK: English and Irish glass, pre-1830, £20-£20,000; glass, chandeliers, English and European porcelain, needlework, papier mâché and treen. LOC: Off A420 between Bath and Chippenham. PARK: Easy. TEL: 0225 891505; fax - 0225 891907. SER: Valuations; buys at auction. FAIRS: International Ceramic. VAT: Spec.

RAMSBURY, Nr. Marlborough

Heraldry Today
Parliament Piece. Est. 1954. Open 9.30-4.30. CL: Sat. STOCK: Heraldic and genealogical books and manuscripts, 50p-£2,000. TEL: 0672 20617; fax - 0672 20163.

Inglenook Antiques
59 High St. (D. White). Est. 1969. Open 10-5. CL: Mon. and Wed. except by appointment. STOCK: Oil lamps, clocks, barometers and spare parts, some furniture. LOC: Off the A4. TEL: 0672 20261. SER: Restorations (longcase clock movements).

SALISBURY

Joan Amos Antiques
7a St. John St. Est. 1983. Open 9.30-1.30 and 2.30-5, Sat. 9.30-1. CL: Wed. SIZE: Small. *STOCK: Porcelain, £20-£200; small furniture, £100-£1,000; both late 19th to early 20th C.* LOC: On right hand side when entering city from south (A354). PARK: Limited. TEL: 0722 330888.

Antique and Collectors Market
37 Catherine St. Open 9-5. SIZE: Large. *STOCK: Silver, plate, china, glass, toys, books, taxidermy, postcards, etc.* TEL: 0722 326033.

The Avonbridge Antiques and Collectors Market
United Reformed Church Hall, Fisherton St. Open Tues. 9-4. SIZE: 15 dealers. *STOCK: General antiques.*

The Barn Book Supply
88 Crane St. (J. and J. Head). Est. 1958. Open 9.30-5. CL: Sat. *STOCK: Antiquarian books on angling, shooting, horses, deerstalking.* TEL: 0722 327767; fax - 0722 339888.

D.M Beach
52 High St. (A. Beach). Est. 1930. Open 9-5.30. SIZE: Large. *STOCK: Antiquarian books, 1500 to date, 5p-£1,000; maps, prints, oils and watercolours, to £1,500.* LOC: From Bournemouth into city, take first possible turn left. Shop is on next corner. PARK: 120yds. down Crane St. TEL: 0722 333801; fax - 0722 333720. SER: Valuations; restorations (leather bindings); buys at auction. FAIRS: U.S.A. and London.

Derek Boston Antiques
223 Wilton Rd, also warehouse at Wilton. Est. 1964. Open 9.30-5. *STOCK: Furniture and majolica.* TEL: 0722 322682; home - 0722 324426. VAT: Stan/Spec.

Robert Bradley
71 Brown St. Est. 1970. Open 9.30-5.30. CL: Sat. p.m. *STOCK: Furniture, 17th-18th C; decorative items.* TEL: 0722 333677. VAT: Spec.

Ronald Carr
6 St. Francis Rd. (R.G. Carr). Est. 1983. Open by appointment. SIZE: Small. *STOCK: Modern British etchings, £5-£1,000.* LOC: 1 mile north of city on A345. PARK: Easy. TEL: 0722 328892; home - same. SER: Buys at auction.

Castle Galleries
81 Castle St. (John C. Lodge). Est. 1971. Open 9.30-5, Sat. 9.30-1. CL: Mon. and Wed. *STOCK: General antiques, coins and medals.* PARK: Easy. TEL: 0722 333734.

Ian G. Hastie   BADA
46 St. Ann St. Est. 1952. *STOCK: English and continental furniture, 17th to early 19th C; works of art, 18th-19th C.* TEL: 0722 322957.

Salisbury continued

Edward Hurst Antiques
Stirling House, Paynes Hill. Est. 1983. Open 9.30-5.30, Sat. 9.30-1.30. SIZE: Medium. *STOCK: Country house furniture and decorative items, 1650-1820.* LOC: Just off St. Anne's St. PARK: Easy. TEL: 0722 320595. VAT: Spec.

The Jerram Gallery
7 St. John St. (Mark Jerram). Open 9.30-5.30, Sat. 10-4. SIZE: Large. STOCK: Oils, watercolours, etchings, sculpture, late 19th C to modern British, £50-£10,000. LOC: St. John St. is an extension of Exeter St., opp. Queen Anne's Gate. PARK: Loading and unloading, car parks nearby. TEL: 0722 412310. SER: Valuations; restorations; framing; finder; buys at auction.

Micawber's
53 Fisherton St. (Mr. and Mrs. E.M. Johnson and others). Est. 1981. Open 9.30-5. CL: Wed. SIZE: 10 stalls. *STOCK: General antiques including jewellery, silver, furniture, clocks, books, porcelain, pine, bottles, glass, lace, linen and clothes.* LOC: 350yds. from railway station towards town centre. PARK: Opposite, behind shops. TEL: 0722 337822. SER: Valuations; restorations (furniture); repairs (watches and jewellery). FAIRS: Local.

T.J. Newsam
St. Martin's House, 49 St. Ann St. Est. 1979. Open by appointment. SIZE: Medium. *STOCK: Longcase and bracket clocks, £500-£15,000.* LOC: Near cathedral. PARK: Easy. TEL: 0722 411059; home - same. SER: Valuations (clocks); buys at auction (English clocks). VAT: Spec.

Chris Wadge Clocks
142 Fisherton St. Open 9-5. CL: Mon. *STOCK: Clocks, movements and spare parts.* TEL: 0722 334467. SER: 400 day specialist.

SEMLEY, Nr. Shaftesbury

May and May Ltd
Whitebridge. Est. 1963. Open by appointment. *STOCK: Antiquarian music and music literature.* TEL: 0747 830034; fax - 0747 830035. SER: Buys at auction.

SWINDON

Antiques and All Pine
11 Newport St, Old Town. (J. and M. Brown). Open 10-5.30. CL: Wed. SIZE: Medium. *STOCK: Pine, china, lace, linen and costume jewellery, general antiques.* LOC: From M4, junction 15 or 16 follow signs to Old Town. PARK: 100yds. TEL: 0793 520259. VAT: Stan/Spec.

Marlborough Sporting Gallery and Bookshop
6 Milton Rd. Est. 1977. Open 9-5, Sat. and Sun. by appointment. SIZE: Medium. *STOCK: Sporting oils, watercolours, £100-£10,000; sporting prints, £20-£5000; all 1800-1975; books,*

Allan Smith
"Amity Cottage", 162 Beechcroft Road
Upper Stratton, Swindon, Wiltshire
(0793) 822977

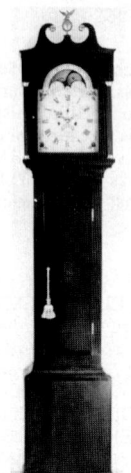

Open any day or evening by appointment

Late 18th century shell inlaid and mahogany crossbanded 8 day oak longcase by Price of Wiveliscombe 7ft. 2in. tall.

I try to maintain stocks which are decorative, unusual, of good quality, proportions and originality. I can usually offer automata, moonphase, painted dial, brass dial, 30 hour, 8 day, London and provincial examples as well as stick and banjo, barometers, wall, bracket and lantern clocks. 20+ longcases usually in stock.

12 Months Written Guarantee
FREE UK DELIVERY & SETTING UP

(Less than 10 minutes from M4 Junction 15)

Swindon continued
1750 to date, £10-£500. LOC: Town Centre. PARK: Easy. TEL: 0793 421458; fax - 0793 421640. SER: Valuations; restorations (oils, watercolours, prints); buys at auction. FAIRS: Major equestrian events. VAT: Spec.

Allan Smith Antique Clocks
162 Beechcroft Rd, Upper Stratton. Est. 1988. Open by appointment. SIZE: Medium. STOCK: Longcase clocks, including automata, moonphase, painted dial, brass dial, 30 hour, 8 day, London and Provincial, £995-£7,950; stick and banjo barometers, mantel, wall, bracket, Vienna and lantern clocks. LOC: Near Baker Arms Inn. PARK: Own. TEL: 0793 822977. SER: Restorations (clocks). VAT: Spec.

Victoria Bookshop
30 Wood St. (S. Austin). Est. 1965. Open 9-5.30. SIZE: Large. STOCK: Books, most subjects, old postcards. LOC: From Marlborough, Chippenham or M4, follow signs to Old Town. PARK: 200yds. reached by pedestrian way. TEL: 0793 527364.

TISBURY

Edward Marnier Antiques
17 High St. (E.F. Marnier). Resident. Est. 1989. Open 10-6, Sun. and Wed. by appointment. STOCK: English and continental furniture, pictures, rugs and interesting decorative objects,

Tisbury continued
17th-20th C, £20-£3,000. PARK: Easy. TEL: 0747 871074. SER: Valuations; buys at auction. VAT: Spec.

Carol Pearson Antiques
2-4 High St. Est. 1984. Open 10-1 and 2-5, Wed. by appointment. SIZE: Large. STOCK: Georgian, Victorian and Edwardian furniture, £25-£3,000; Victorian and Edwardian paintings, £15-£12,000; porcelain, 18th-19th C; decoupage. PARK: Easy. TEL: 0747 870710. SER: Restorations (ceramics and furniture).

WARMINSTER

The Antique Warehouse
61 East St. (P.A. and D. Gale). Open 8.30-5.30, Sat. 9-1, other times by appointment. SIZE: Large. STOCK: General antiques and shipping goods. PARK: Easy. TEL: 0985 219460. SER: Restorations; shipping and packing.

Bishopstrow Antiques
55 East St. (J.M. Stewart Cox). Est. 1974. Open 10-1 and 2-5.30. SIZE: Medium. STOCK: 18th-19th C mahogany, oak and painted furniture; pottery and porcelain, boxes, small silver and decorative items. LOC: On left of old A36 leaving Warminster on Salisbury road, opposite Esso garage. PARK: Easy. TEL: 0985 212683; home - 0985 40877. VAT: Spec.

Britannia Antiques
8a Silver St. (T.A. Goodsman). Open 10-5. STOCK: General antiques. TEL: 0985 217465. SER: Restoration; packing and shipping arranged.

Britannia Antiques Exports
Furlong House, 61 East St. (T.A. Goodsman). Open 8.30-5.30, other times by appointment. SIZE: Large. STOCK: General antiques. TEL: 0985 219360. SER: Restorations; packing; shipping.

Century Antiques
10 Silver St. (N. Giltsoff). Open 10-5.30. STOCK: General antiques. TEL: 0985 217031.

Choice Antiques
4 Silver St. (Avril Bailey). Resident. Open 10-1 and 2-5.30. SIZE: Medium. STOCK: General antiques and decorative items, 18th-19th C, £25-£2,000. PARK: Easy. TEL: 0985 218924. VAT: Stan/Spec.

Edward Fellowes   LAPADA
at Peter Houghton Antiques, 33 Silver St. Est. 1989. Open 10-12.30 and 2-5.30, Sun. by appointment. SIZE: Medium. STOCK: English and continental ceramics, prints, watercolours and oils, 18th-19th C, £50-£1,500. LOC: Bath end of town on A36. PARK: Easy. TEL: 0985 213451; home - 0380 828888. SER: Valuations. FAIRS: NEC, Olympia, most Penman, LAPADA, Harrogate, Surrey. VAT: Spec.

Warminster continued

Peter Houghton Antiques LAPADA
33 Silver St. (P.J. Houghton). Est. 1985. Open 10-12.30 and 2-5.30. SIZE: Medium. *STOCK: English furniture, 18th to early 19th C, £300-£15,000; clocks, watercolours and decorative items.* LOC: West end of town centre at Frome/Bath fork. PARK: Easy. TEL: 0985 213451; home - 0985 216288. SER: Valuations; buys at auction. FAIRS: Olympia, NEC, Westminster, City of London Fine Arts. VAT: Spec.

Emma Hurley Antiques and Textiles
9 Silver St. (Emma and John Hurley). Est. 1970. Open 10-5, Wed. 10-1. SIZE: Medium. *STOCK: Decorative furnishings, 19th C; textiles, 18th-19th C; both £25-£1,000.* LOC: From Bath or Frome road, 200 yards past obelisk monument on right. PARK: Nearby. TEL: 0985 219726; home - 0985 847021. SER: Restorations (china, upholstery). FAIRS: Shepton Mallet, Cheltenham, Bristol, Sandown Park.

Isabella Antiques
16a Silver St. (B.W. Semke). Est. 1990. Open 10-5.30. SIZE: Medium. *STOCK: Furniture, late 18th C to late 19th C, £100-£5,000; boxes and mirrors, 19th C, £50-£500; small clocks, late Victorian, £100-£300.* LOC: Main road. PARK: Easy. TEL: 0985 218933. SER: Buys at auction (furniture). VAT: Spec.

Obelisk Antiques
2 Silver St. (P. Tanswell). Open 10-1 and 2-5.30. SIZE: Large and warehouse. *STOCK: English and continental furniture, 18th-19th C; decorative items, objets d'art.* TEL: 0985 846646; fax - 0985 219901.

K. and A. Welch
1A Church St. Est. 1967. Open 8-6, Sat. 9-1. SIZE: Large. *STOCK: Shipping furniture, 18th-19th C, £10-£2,000.* LOC: A36 west end of town. PARK: Own. TEL: 0985 214687; home - 0985 213433. VAT: Stan/Spec. *Trade Only.*

WEST YATTON, Nr. Chippenham
Heirloom and Howard Ltd
Manor Farm. (D.S. Howard). Est. 1972. Open 9.30-5.30, Sat. 11-5 or by appointment. SIZE: Medium. *STOCK: Porcelain including Chinese armorial, 18th C, £200-£10,000; heraldic items, 18th-19th, £10-£1,000; portrait engravings, 17th-19th C, £10-£50.* LOC: 10 miles from Bath, 1/4 mile off A420 Chippenham/Bristol road. Transport from Chippenham station (4 miles) if required. PARK: Own. TEL: 0249 783038; fax - 0249 783039. SER: Valuations; buys at auction (Chinese porcelain). FAIRS: International Ceramics. VAT: Spec.

WESTBURY
Booth Gallery and Titanic Signals Archive
30 Edenvale Rd. Est. 1970. Open by appointment

Westbury continued

only. *STOCK: Maps and prints.* TEL: 0373 823271; home - same. SER: Valuations; restorations; mounting and framing; print colouring; 350 archive signals on exhibition.

Ray Coggins Antiques
1 Fore St. Open 9-5.30. *STOCK: Period, pine country furniture and decorative, architectural items.* TEL: 0373 826574.

WILTON, Nr. Salisbury
Ian J. Brook, Antiques and Picture Gallery
26 North St. Resident. Est. 1962. Open after hours to trade by appointment. CL: Wed. p.m. *STOCK: Furniture, oil paintings and watercolours, £5-£5,000.* TEL: 0722 743392. VAT: Stan/Spec.

Earle
47 North St. (B. Earle). Est. 1960. Open 9.30-5.30. CL: Wed. SIZE: Small. *STOCK: General antiques.* Not Stocked: Large furniture. LOC: From market place turn directly into North St. PARK: Easy. TEL: 0722 743284.

Pamela Lynch
18 West St. Resident. Open 10-5, Sat. 10-1. CL: Wed. *STOCK: Small furniture, needlework pictures, decorative items, objets de vertu.* TEL: 0722 744113.

A.J. Romain and Sons
The Old House, 11 and 13 North St. *STOCK: Furniture, mainly 17th-18th C; early oak, walnut and marquetry; clocks, copper, brass and miscellanea.* TEL: 0722 743350. VAT: Stan/Spec.

WOOTTON BASSETT, Nr. Swindon
Tubbjoys
118 High St. (Mr and Mrs C.E. Tubb). Est. 1993. Open daily. SIZE: Large. *STOCK: General antiques 1880-1980, £5-£500.* LOC: Off M4, junction 16. PARK: Easy and at rear. TEL: 0793 849499; home - same. SER: Restorations (glass and china, French polishing).

Howard Walwyn Antiques
Est. 1985. Open by appointment only. *STOCK: English oak and country furniture, 17th-18th C, £100-£6,000; English longcase clocks and barometers, £300-£10,000.* TEL: 0793 731089; mobile - 0831 604917. SER: Restorations (barometers, clocks and furniture); buys at auction.

WROUGHTON, Nr. Swindon
Wroughton Antique Centre
23 High St. (H. Sutton). Open 10-5 or by appointment. CL: Wed. SIZE: Medium. *STOCK: Chests, general antiques, bric-a-brac.* LOC: A361. PARK: Easy. TEL: 0793 813232; home - 0793 721235.

Yorkshire North

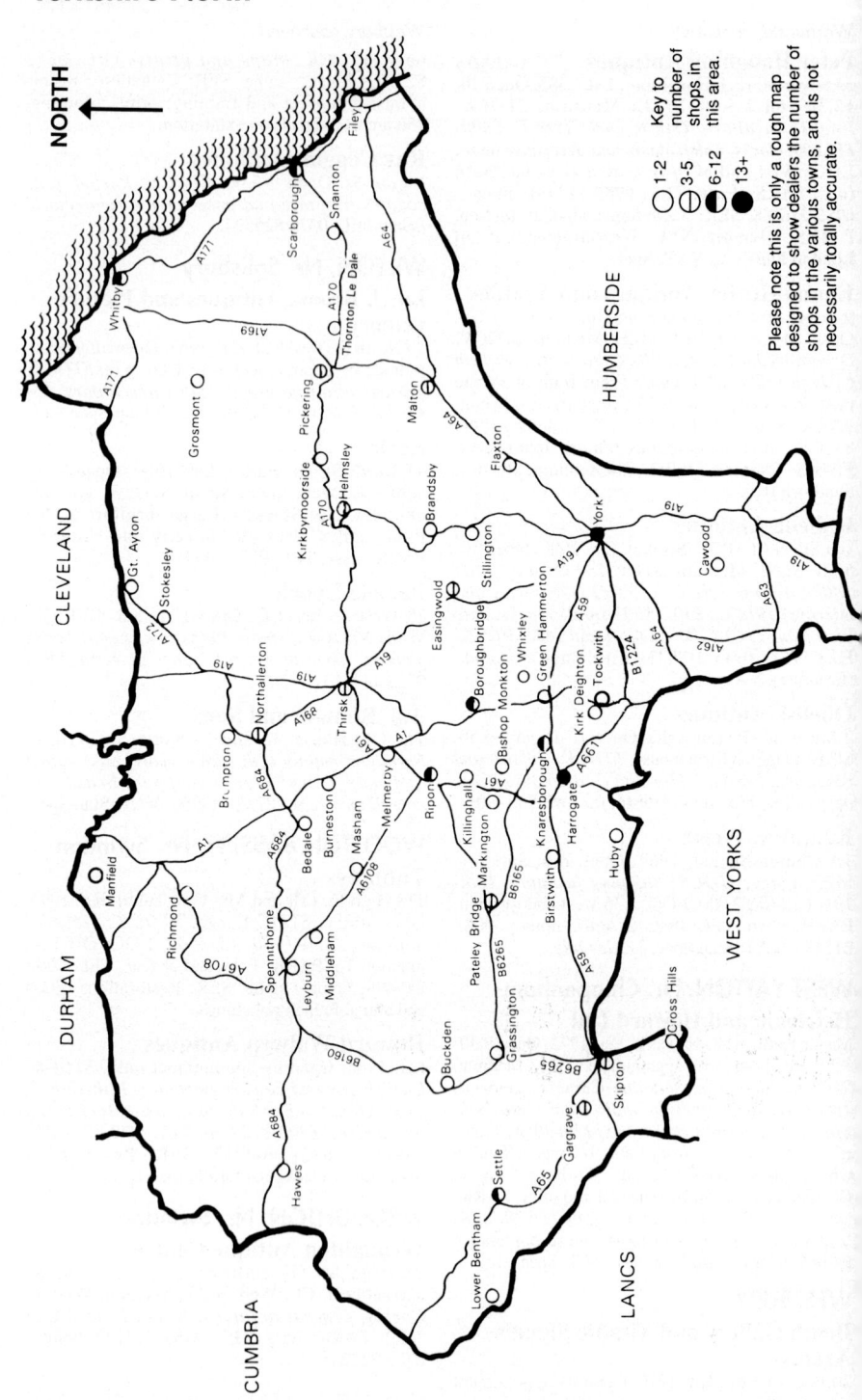

Yorkshire North

BEDALE
Thornton Gallery
Snape. (Mr and Mrs W.H. Turnbull). Est. 1970. Open by appointment. SIZE: Small. *STOCK: Oil paintings, £200-£3,000; watercolours, £50-£1,500; all 19th-20th C.* Not Stocked: Furniture, silver, pewter. LOC: 5 miles from A1 at Leeming Motel. PARK: Easy. TEL: 0677 70318. SER: Valuations. VAT: Spec.

BIRSTWITH, Nr. Harrogate
John Pearson Antique Clock Restoration
Church Cottage. Est. 1978. Open by appointment. *STOCK: Longcase, bracket and wall clocks, 18th C.* LOC: Off A59. PARK: Easy. TEL: 0423 770828; home - same. SER: Restorations (clocks, cases, movements and especially dials).

BOROUGHBRIDGE
Jeffery Bates Antiques
Aberure, Bridge St. Est. 1966. Open 10.30-5. CL: Thurs. SIZE: Medium. *STOCK: Small items and silver including snuff boxes and objets de vertu, £10-£350; pictures, £40-£500; furniture, £150-£1,000; walking sticks, £15-£250; all 18th-19th C.* LOC: 1 mile from A1. PARK: Own. TEL: 0423 324258. SER: Valuations; buys at auction (silver and general antiques). FAIRS: Olympia; Heritage in the West End; Little Chelsea. VAT: Stan/Spec.

Country Antiques
38 High St. (P.W. Raine). Resident. Est. 1969. Open 10-4. CL: Thurs. SIZE: Small. *STOCK: Silver, 17th-20th C, £25-£500; metalware and small furniture, 18th-19th C.* PARK: Easy. TEL: 0423 324017. SER: Buys at auction (silver).

Joan Eyles Antiques   BADA
The Stone Yard, 12 Fishergate. (J.M. and J.C.H. Eyles). Est. 1962. Open 11.30-5. CL: Thurs. *STOCK: Pottery, furniture, general antiques, especially fenders, treen, sewing equipment, textiles.* Not Stocked: Weapons. PARK: Own. TEL: 0423 323357; home - 0423 322487. VAT: Spec.

Galloway Antiques   LAPADA
High St. (Mr and Mrs J.E. Gay). Est. 1977. Open 9.30-5.30, Sun. p.m. by appointment. SIZE: Large. *STOCK: Furniture, 18th-20th C, £50-£3,000; paintings, 19th-20th C, £75-£2,000; decorative items including Wemyss, 18th-20th C, £5-£500.* Not Stocked: Arms and medals. LOC: 1 mile off A1. PARK: Easy. TEL: 0423 324602; home - 0423 506719. SER: Valuations. FAIRS: Castle, NEC.

Anthony Graham Antiques
Aberure, Bridge St. Resident. Est. 1985. Open 11-5. CL: Thurs. SIZE: Medium. *STOCK:*

R.S. WILSON & SONS ANTIQUES

Hall Square
Boroughbridge
N. Yorks YO5 9AN
0423 322417

Good selection of
period furniture and accessories

Est. 1917   B.A.D.A.

Boroughbridge continued
Furniture, 18th-19th C, £50-£2,500; pictures, 19th-20th C, £50-£2,000; general antiques,18th-19th C, from £5. LOC: Off A1. PARK: Easy. TEL: 0423 324258; home - 0423 323952. SER: Valuations.

St. James House Antiques
St. James Sq. (J.D. Wilson). Est. 1989. Open 9-5.30, Thurs.and Sun. by appointment. SIZE: Medium. *STOCK: Furniture, £50-£10,000; brass and copper, £5-£750, all 1750-1920; china, 1740-1900, £5-£1,500.* Not Stocked: Guns. LOC: Town centre. PARK: Own. TEL: 0423 322508; home - same. SER: Valuations; restorations (furniture); upholstery. FAIRS: NEC (Aug); Country House events. VAT: Stan/Spec.

R.S. Wilson and Sons   BADA
Hall Square. Est. 1917. Open 9-5.30. CL: Thurs. p.m. *STOCK: Furniture, 17th-19th C; and accessories.* TEL: 0423 322417; home - 0423 322654. VAT: Stan/Spec.

BRANDSBY
L.L. Ward and Son
Bar House. (R. Ward). Est. 1970. Open 8.30-5. *STOCK: Pine.* TEL: 03475 651.

BROMPTON, Nr. Northallerton
Country Pine Antiques
Unit 45, The Old Mill. (C. Tindler). Open 9-5, Sat. by appointment. *STOCK: Victorian pine.* TEL: 0609 774322.

BUCKDEN, Nr. Skipton
Greystones Antiques
(W. and S. Griffiths). Open by appointment only. *STOCK: Lace-collars, stoles, veils, christening gowns; table and bed linen; prints, collectors' items.* LOC: Centre of Yorkshire Dales National Park. TEL: 0756 760847. SER: Commissions and export.

BURNESTON, Nr. Bedale
Simon Greenwood Antiques
(S. and C. Greenwood). Est. 1976. Open by appointment. *STOCK: Furniture, including upholstered items, 17th-20th C, £5-£1,000; decorative items and textiles.* LOC: 1/4 mile from A1. PARK: Easy. TEL: Home - 0677 422554. SER: Valuations; buys at auction. VAT: Stan/Spec.

W. Greenwood (Fine Art)
Oak Dene, Church Wynd. Est. 1978. Open by appointment. *STOCK: Paintings and watercolours, 19th-20th C, £100-£5,000; frames, £20-£500; mirrors.* LOC: Take B6285 left off A1 northbound, house 1/4 mile on right. PARK: Easy. TEL: 0677 424830; home - 0677 423217. SER: Valuations; restorations (paintings), framing.

CAWOOD, Nr. Selby
Cawood Antiques
Sherburn St. (J.E. Gilham). Open 9-6 including Sun. *STOCK: General antiques, shipping, furniture, copper, brass, porcelain, pictures, collectors' items.* PARK: Easy. TEL: 0757 268533.

CROSS HILLS, Nr. Keighley
Heathcote Antiques
1 Aire St. (M. Webster). Resident. Est. 1979. Open 10-5.30, Sun. 12.30-4. CL: Mon. and Tues. SIZE: Warehouse. *STOCK: Furniture, including pine especially unstripped; smalls.* PARK: Easy. TEL: 0535 635250.

EASINGWOLD
Bow Antiques
94 Long St. (J.W. and R.E. Ager-Harris). Est. 1987. Open 9.30-5. CL: Wed. SIZE: Medium. *STOCK: Furniture, £50-£3,000; glass, £10-£150; both 18th-19th C; porcelain and pottery, 18th-20th C, £15-£300.* Not Stocked: Pictures, jewellery, militaria and gold. LOC: A19. PARK: Easy. TEL: 0347 822596; home - 0347 822478 or 03473 8178.

Easingwold continued

Chapman Medd and Sons
Market Place. Est. 1865. Open 8-12 and 1-5. Open at any time in summer. *STOCK: Country furniture, oak and mahogany.* TEL: 0347 821370.

Old Flame
30 Long St. (D. Lynas and J.J. Thompson). Est. 1988. Open 10-5, Sat. 10-5.30, Sun. 10-4. CL: Mon. SIZE: Medium. *STOCK: Fireplaces, 18th-19th C, £100-£1,000; lighting, 19th C, £25-£250; architectural items, 18th-19th C, £50-£500.* LOC: A19 main street. PARK: Easy. TEL: Home - 0347 888619. SER: Valuations. FAIRS: Newark. VAT: Stan/Spec.

Mrs B.A.S. Reynolds
42 Long St. *STOCK: General antiques, Victorian.* TEL: 0347 821078.

Timothy Summersgill Antiques
Market Place. Open 10-12 and 1.30-4.30, Sat. 10-2. *STOCK: General antiques and collectors' items.* LOC: Above estate agents. TEL: 0347 821366.

White House Farm Antiques
Thirsk Rd. (G. Hood). Resident. Est. 1960. Usually open but prior 'phone call advisable. *STOCK: Rural and domestic bygones, stone troughs, architectural reclamation and garden ornaments.* LOC: Two miles north of Easingwold, on A19. PARK: Easy. TEL: 0347 821479.

FILEY
Cairncross and Sons
31 Bellevue St. (G. Cairncross). Open 9.30-12.45 and 2-4.30. CL: Wed. p.m. *STOCK: Medals, uniforms, insignia, cap badges.* Not Stocked: Weapons. TEL: 0723 513287.

Filey Antiques
1 Belle Vue St. Est. 1970. Open daily 11-4.30; Thurs. to Sat. 11-4 in winter. SIZE: Small. *STOCK: Small furniture, prints, china, bric-a-brac, jewellery.* Not Stocked: Coins, militaria. LOC: Town centre, at corner of Belle Vue St. and West Ave. PARK: Easy. TEL: 0723 513440.

FLAXTON, Nr. York
Elm Tree Antiques
(R. and J. Jackson). Est. 1975. Open 9-5, Sun. 10-5. SIZE: Large. *STOCK: Furniture, 17th C to Edwardian; small items, £5-£5,000.* LOC: 1 mile off A64. PARK: Easy. TEL: 090486 462; home - same. SER: Valuations; restorations (cabinet making, polishing and upholstery).

GARGRAVE, Nr. Skipton
Antiques at Forge Cottage (Inc. Castleberg Antiques) formerly of Settle
22/24 High St. Est. 1989. Open Sat. and

Gargrave continued
afternoons or by appointment. *STOCK: Porcelain, brass, small silver, glass, collectables.* LOC: A65. PARK: Easy.

H. Blackburn
9 East St. Open anytime by appointment. *STOCK: Furniture, pottery, metalware, pictures.* LOC: First left turn off A65 from Skipton after petrol station. TEL: 0756 749796. SER: Valuations; container packing; courier; finder.

Bernard Dickinson
Estate Yard, West St. (H.H. and A.E. Mardall). Resident. Est. 1958. Open 9-5.30 or by appointment. *STOCK: Early English furniture.* LOC: Just off A65 Skipton-Settle road. PARK: Easy. TEL: 0756 748257. VAT: Spec.

Gargrave Gallery
48 High St. (B. Herrington). Appointment advisable. *STOCK: General antiques.* PARK: Easy. TEL: 0756 749641.

Myers Galleries   BADA
Endsleigh House, High St. (R.N. Myers and Son). Est. 1890. Open 9-5.30 or by appointment. SIZE: Medium. *STOCK: Furniture, oak, mahogany, 17th to early 19th C; pottery, porcelain and metalware.* Not Stocked: Victoriana, weapons, coins, jewellery. LOC: A65. Skipton-Settle road. PARK: Behind shop and opposite. TEL: 0756 749587. SER: Valuations. VAT: Spec.

GRASSINGTON, Nr. Skipton
Fairings
Lucy Fold. (D. and M.A. Byrne). Est. 1979. CL: Thurs. SIZE: Small. *STOCK: Georgian and Victorian country antiques including brass, copper, blue and white china, small oak, mahogany and pine furniture, £5-£750.* LOC: Opposite Black Horse Hotel. PARK: Easy. TEL: 0756 752755.

GREAT AYTON
The Great Ayton Bookshop
47 & 53 High St. (M.S. Jones). Est. 1978. Open 10-5.30, Wed. 10-2, Sun. 2-5.30. CL: Mon. SIZE: Medium. *STOCK: Books, rare and secondhand, 50p-£100; postcards, pre-1930, 10p-£20; prints and local maps, 10p-£50.* LOC: 7 miles south of Middlesbrough off Stokesley road. PARK: Easy. TEL: 0642 723358. SER: Valuations. FAIRS: PBFA. VAT: Stan.

GREEN HAMMERTON, Nr. York
The Main Pine Co
Grangewood, The Green. (C. and K.M. Main). Est. 1976. Open 9-5 or by appointment. SIZE: Large. *STOCK: Pine furniture, 18th-19th C, £100-£1,500; architectural pine, 19th-20th C, £50-£1,000; china, linen and bric-a-brac,*

Green Hammerton continued
18th-20th C, £5-£100. LOC: Just off A59. PARK: Easy. TEL: 0423 330451; home - 0423 331078; fax - 0423 331278. SER: Restorations (pine). VAT: Stan.

GROSMONT, Nr. Whitby
Country Connections (Esk House Arts)
Front St. (D.R. and J.M. Stonehouse). Open 10-5 including Sun. *STOCK: Fine art prints and oil paintings.* LOC: Above the Co-op. TEL: 0947 85319; fax - same.

HARROGATE
Ann-tiquities
12 Cheltenham Parade. (Mrs A. Wilkinson). Open 12-4. CL: Wed. *STOCK: Mainly linen.* TEL: 0423 503567.

Antiques and Collectables
37/39 Cheltenham Crescent. (G. Nimmo). Open 9.30-5. *STOCK: Jewellery, silver, furniture, watches, collectors' items.* TEL: 0423 521897.

Armstrong   BADA LAPADA
10-11 Montpellier Parade. (M.A. and C.J. Armstrong). Est. 1976. Open 10-5.30. SIZE: Medium. *STOCK: Fine English furniture, 18th to early 19th C; glasses and works of art, 18th C.* PARK: Easy. TEL: 0423 506843. FAIRS: Olympia (June); Café Royal; Chelsea. VAT: Spec.

Bill Bentley
16 Montpellier Parade. Open 9.30-5.30 or by appointment. SIZE: Large. *STOCK: Oak furniture, 1600-1800; country furniture, 1700-1800; period metalwork and treen.* PARK: Easy. TEL: 0423 564084; home - 0423 564564. VAT: Spec.

Bloomers
41 Cheltenham Crescent. (G.R. and M. Cooper). Est. 1973. Open 11-5. CL: Wed. SIZE: Small. *STOCK: Textiles including quilts, samplers, linen, fans, period clothing and accessories, lace.* LOC: Corner of King's Rd., almost opposite new conference centre. PARK: Nearby. TEL: 0423 569389.

John Daffern Antiques
38 Forest Lane Head, Starbeck. Open 10-5. CL: Tues. and Thurs. SIZE: Small. *STOCK: Mahogany furniture, £250-£5,000; longcase clocks, tea caddies, bronzes, £100-£1,000; pottery and porcelain, £25-£1,000, all 18th-19th C.* LOC: Adjacent to Harrogate Golf Club. PARK: Easy. TEL: 0423 889832; home - 076 586 329. VAT: Stan/Spec.

Derbyshire Antiques Ltd
27 Montpellier Parade. (R.C. and M.T. Derbyshire). Est. 1960. Open 10-5.30. SIZE: Medium. *STOCK: Early oak and walnut, 16th-18th C; Georgian furniture to 1820; decorative items.* TEL: 0423 503115/564242. VAT: Spec.

THE GINNEL
HARROGATE
ANTIQUE CENTRE

Discover in Harrogates Premier Antique Centre, two floors housing 40 shops offering a wide selection of Antiques and a Licensed Restaurant.

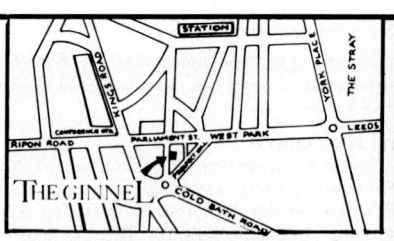

Open 9.30am-5.30pm Mon. to Sat.
The Corn Exchange Building
The Ginnel
Off Parliament Street, Opposite Debenhams
Harrogate HG1 2RB. Tel: 0423 508857

Harrogate continued

Dragon Antiques
10 Dragon Rd. (P.F. Broadbelt). Resident. Est. 1954. Open 11-6. Always available. SIZE: Small. STOCK: *Victorian art glass, £30-£300; art pottery, postcards, G.B. and foreign.* LOC: 5 mins. from town centre, opposite Dragon Road car park. PARK: Easy. TEL: 0423 562037.

Fox's Antique Pine and Country Furniture
83 Knaresborough Rd. (M. and P. Fox). Est. 1958. Open 9-1 and 2.15-6. SIZE: Large. STOCK: *Pine furniture.* LOC: A59. PARK: Easy. TEL: 0423 888116. SER: Stripping (pine and metals).

Garth Antiques   LAPADA
2 Montpellier Mews. (I. Chapman). Open 10-5.30. SIZE: Medium. STOCK: *Furniture, 18th-19th C, £50-£3,000; brass and copper, 19th C, £1-£500; oils and watercolours, £5-£3,000.* LOC: Turn left from Montpellier Parade at Montpellier public house. TEL: 0423 530573. VAT: Stan/Spec.

The Ginnel
Harrogate Antique Centre, The Ginnel. (P. Stephenson). Open 9.30-5.30. SIZE: 30 dealers. STOCK: *All date-lined and vetted - see individual entries.* LOC: Off Parliament St. opposite Debenhams. TEL: 0423 508857. SER: Courier. Below are listed the specialist dealers at this centre.

Abacus
(Julian White). STOCK: *Georgian, Victorian and art nouveau fireplace grates, inserts and surrounds.*

Anglo-Scandinavian
STOCK: *Cutlery, silver plate, inkwells, collectors' and decorative items.*

Fiona Aston
STOCK: *Objets d'art including porcelain and miniatures.*

Andrew Bottomley
STOCK: *Arms, weapons, Oriental items and tribal artifacts.*

Harrogate continued

Bygones
STOCK: *Objets d'art including dolls, small silver, porcelain and jewellery.*

Mia Carter
STOCK: *Oil paintings and watercolours, objets d'art and small furniture.*

Dukeries
STOCK: *Furniture, period and 19th C.*

Felton Park
STOCK: *Pottery.*

Fettes Fine Art
STOCK: *Paintings and ceramics including Parian ware.* TEL: 0904 641344.

Flagship (Paul Richardson)
STOCK: *Marine paintings and artefacts.*

Richard Freeman
STOCK: *British, Oriental and continental ceramics, 18th to early 19th C.* TEL: Mobile - 0860 400535.

Georgian House
STOCK: *Victorian and Edwardian furniture.*

Jeffrey and Pauline Glass
STOCK: *Porcelain and glass, objets d'art, 19th to early 20th C.*

John Hawley
STOCK: *18th-19th C furniture and quality porcelain.*

Helmsley Antiquarian Books
STOCK: *Antiquarian books.*

Sandra James
STOCK: *Jewellery.*

Libra Antiques
STOCK: *Georgian, Victorian and Edwardian furniture and decorative items, including cranberry glass.*

Brian Loomes
STOCK: *Longcase clocks, small period furniture.*

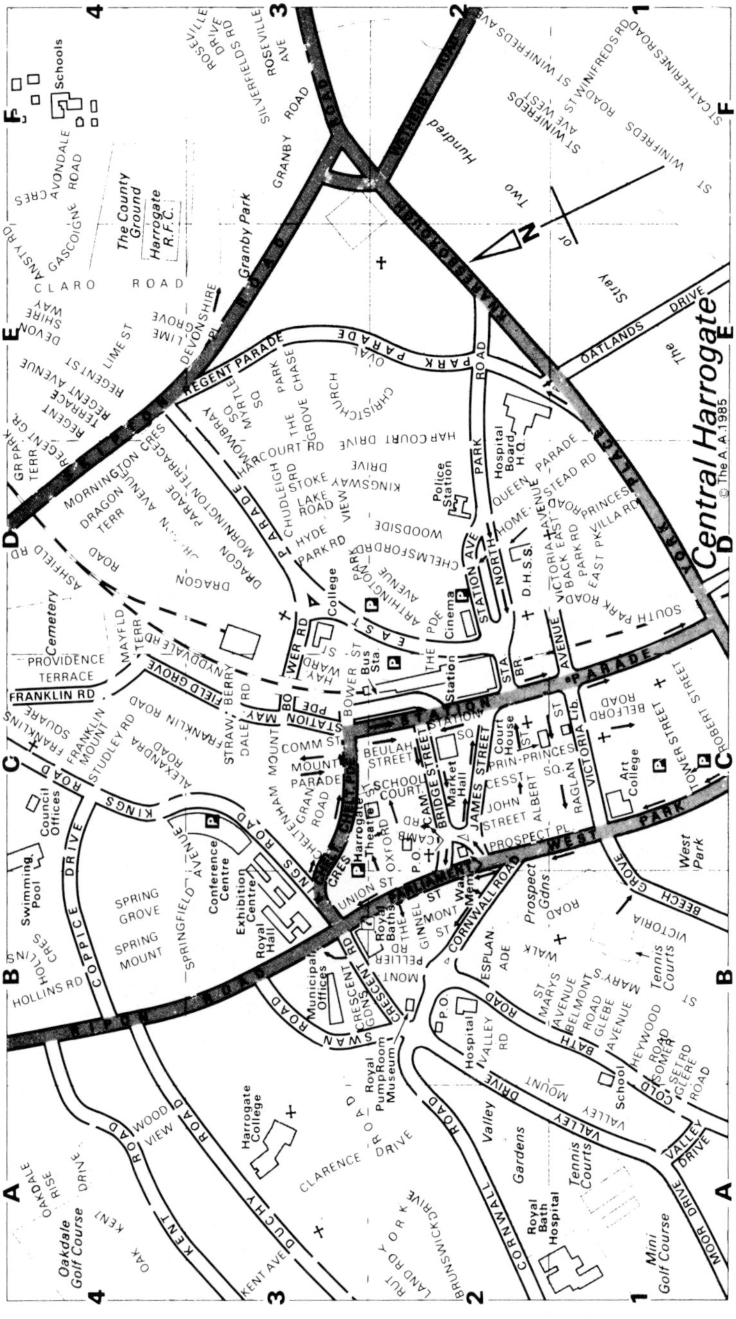

Key to Town Plan

AA Recommended roads	Car Parks
Other roads	Parks and open spaces
Restricted roads	AA Service Centre
Buildings of interest	

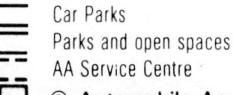

HAWORTH ANTIQUES
JUNE & GLYNN WHITE

We buy and sell longcase, wall, bracket and mantel clocks

Dial and movement restoration services

Furniture and decorative items also stocked

26 Cold Bath Road, Harrogate HG2 0NA
Tel: (0423) 521401
and
Harrogate Road, Huby, Nr. Leeds LS17 0EF
Tel: (0423) 734293
Located on the A658 six miles S.W. of Harrogate

RESIDENT ON PREMISES

BOTH SHOPS ARE OPEN TUES.-SAT.
10am-5pm OR BY APPOINTMENT

Member of British Watch & Clockmakers Guild

Harrogate continued

MBA
STOCK: *Fine antique and later silver.* TEL: Mobile - 0860 710001.

Mark Middleton
STOCK: *19th C furniture and furnishings.*

Brian Naylor
STOCK: *Pottery including Mason's and Staffordshire figures; boxes, small furniture and decorative items; all 18th-19th C.*

Paul Newsome
STOCK: *19th C furniture and collectables.*

P.A. Oxley Antique Clocks and Barometers   LAPADA
STOCK: **Longcase, bracket, carriage clocks and barometers.** TEL: 0423 508566.

Parker Gallery
STOCK: *19th to early 20th C paintings.*

Past Reflections
STOCK: *Victorian and Edwardian furniture, porcelain and silver.*

Prestwich Fine Art
STOCK: *Fine watercolours and oil paintings.*

Graham Reed
STOCK: *19th C porcelain, pictures and small furniture, objets d'art.*

Harrogate continued

Jane Robson
STOCK: *Collectables.*

Rose Fine Art
STOCK: *Botanical and topographical prints, 19th to early 20th C; maps, 18th-19th C.*

J. Shaw & Co
STOCK: *Fine period silver and cutlery.*

Shieling Antiques
STOCK: *Early country furniture, small oak and elm pieces; brass and copper.*

Pauline Stephenson
STOCK: *18th C and Victorian furniture and furnishings.*

H. and M. Suttle
STOCK: *Jewellery and objets d'art.*

Trinity Galleries
STOCK: *Small Victorian silver.*

Whilom
STOCK: *Small Victorian and Edwardian furniture, Victorian watercolours.*

Grove Collectors Centre
Grove Rd. Open 10-4.30. CL: Tues. SIZE: 8 dealers. STOCK: *General antiques including silver, porcelain, cigarette cards, collectables and furniture.* TEL: 0423 561680.

Haworth Antiques
26 Cold Bath Rd. (G. and J. White). Open 10-5 or by appointment. CL: Mon. SIZE: Medium. STOCK: *Clocks, 18th-19th C, £100-£2,000; small furniture, Georgian and Victorian, £50-£1,000.* LOC: 300yds. from Crown Hotel. PARK: Easy. TEL: 0423 521401; home - 0423 734293. SER: Restorations (clocks, dials, re-painted and re-silvered). VAT: Stan/Spec.

R.B. Kendal-Greene
2A Chudleigh Rd. Est. 1964. STOCK: *General antiques.* TEL: 0423 562497; home - 0423 883504. VAT: Stan/Spec. *Trade and Export Only.*

David Lawes
125 Cold Bath Rd. Est. 1962. Open 9-1 and 2.30-5.30. CL: Wed. p.m. and Sat. p.m. SIZE: Small. STOCK: *Philatelic items.* PARK: Easy. TEL: 0423 568428. SER: Valuations.

London House Oriental Rugs and Carpets
9 Montpellier Parade. (N.C. Ries). Est. 1981. Open 10-5.30. SIZE: Medium. STOCK: *Persian, Turkish, Indian, Tibetan, Nepalese, Afghan, Chinese and Rumanian rugs and carpets, 19th-20th C, £25-£5,000; kelims and camel bags, 19th-20th C, £25-£2,000.* LOC: Town centre on The Stray. PARK: Easy. TEL: 0423 567167; home - 0937 845123. SER: Valuations; restorations (handmade rugs). VAT: Stan.

Harrogate continued

David Love BADA LAPADA
10 Royal Parade. (Mr and Mrs D.A. Love). Est. 1969. Open 9-1 and 2-6. SIZE: Large. *STOCK: Furniture, English, 17th-19th C; pottery and porcelain, English and continental; decorative items, all periods.* LOC: Opposite Pump Room Museum. PARK: Easy. TEL: 0423 565797. SER: Valuations; buys at auction. VAT: Stan/Spec.

Charles Lumb and Sons Ltd BADA
2 Montpellier Gardens. (F. and A.R. Lumb). Est. 1920. Open 9-1 and 2-6. SIZE: Medium. *STOCK: Furniture, 17th to early 19th C; metalware, period accessories.* PARK: 20yds. immediately opposite. TEL: 0423 503776; home - 0423 863281; fax - 0423 530074. FAIRS: Harrogate. VAT: Spec.

McTague of Harrogate
17/19 Cheltenham Mount. (P. McTague). Open 9.30-1 and 2-5.30. CL: Mon. SIZE: Medium. *STOCK: Prints, watercolours, some oil paintings, mostly 18th to early 20th C.* LOC: From Conference Centre on Kings Rd., go up Cheltenham Parade and turn first left. PARK: Easy. TEL: 0423 567086. VAT: Stan/Spec.

D. Mason & Son
7/8 Westmoreland St. FGA, NAG. Open 9-5. *STOCK: Victorian, Edwardian and secondhand jewellery; clocks.* TEL: 0423 567305. SER: Repairs (clocks and jewellery).

The Montpellier Gallery
12 Montpellier St. Open 10-5.30. CL: Mon. except by appointment. *STOCK: Fine 20th C paintings, bronzes, furniture and small items.* TEL: 0423 500460; fax - 0423 528400.

Montpellier Mews Antique Market
Montpellier St. Open 10-5.30. SIZE: Various dealers. *STOCK: General antiques - porcelain, jewellery, furniture, paintings, interior decor, linen, glass and silver.* LOC: Behind Weatherells. TEL: 0423 530484.

Ogden of Harrogate Ltd BADA
38 James St. Est. 1893. Open 9-5. SIZE: Large. *STOCK: Jewellery, English silver and plate.* TEL: 0423 504123; fax - 0423 522283. VAT: Stan/Spec.

Omar (Harrogate) Ltd
8 Crescent Rd. (P. McCormick). Est. 1946. Open 9-5.30. SIZE: Medium. *STOCK: Persian, Turkish, Caucasian rugs and carpets, £50-£5,000.* PARK: Easy. TEL: 0423 503675. SER: Valuations; restorations (Oriental carpets); buys at auction. VAT: Stan.

Paraphernalia
38A Cold Bath Rd. (P.F. Hacker). Open 10-5. *STOCK: Postcards, crested china and commemoratives, collectors' items, bric-a-brac.* TEL: Home - 0423 567968.

Harrogate continued

Paul M. Peters Antiques LAPADA
15a Bower Rd. Est. 1967. Open 10-5. CL: Sat. SIZE: Medium. *STOCK: Chinese and Japanese ceramics and works of art, 17th-19th C; European ceramics and glass, 18th-19th C; European metalware, scientific instruments and unusual objects.* LOC: Town centre, at bottom of Station Parade. PARK: Easy. TEL: 0423 560118. SER: Valuations. VAT: Stan/Spec.

Elaine Phillips Antiques Ltd BADA
1 and 2 Royal Parade. Open 9.30-5.30. SIZE: Large. *STOCK: Oak furniture, 1600-1800; country furniture, 1700-1800; some mahogany, 18th to early 19th C; period metalwork and decoration.* LOC: Opposite Crown Hotel. PARK: Easy. TEL: 0423 569745. VAT: Spec.

Pianorama (Harrogate) Ltd
1, 3 and 5 Omega St, Ripon Rd. (M. Sellers). Open 9-5. *STOCK: Period pianos.* TEL: 0423 567573.

Rippon Bookshop
1st Floor, 6 Station Bridge. (Mrs A. Rawson). Est. 1980. Open 10-5. SIZE: Medium. *STOCK: Antiquarian books - local history, £25-£150; local topography and general £5-£25.* LOC: Near railway station and opposite Odeon cinema. PARK: Nearby. TEL: 0423 501835; home - 0765 604848. SER: Valuations; restorations; book-finding.

Shaw Bros
21 Montpellier Parade. (J. and C. Shaw). CL: Wed. p.m. *STOCK: English and continental porcelain, 18th-19th C; silver, jewellery, Meissen, Dresden vases and figures.* TEL: 0423 567466.

Singing Bird Antiques
19 Knaresborough Rd. (A.M. Sagar). Est. 1964. Open 10-4.30. CL: Sat. SIZE: Medium. *STOCK: Furniture, silver, pewter, 18th C; pottery, porcelain.* LOC: On A59, 1 mile out of Harrogate on left, just before pedestrian crossing. PARK: Easy. TEL: 0423 888292; home - 0423 885715.

Smith's (The Rink) Ltd
Dragon Rd. Est. 1906. Open 9-5.30. SIZE: Large. *STOCK: General antiques, 1750-1820, £150; Victoriana, 1830-1900, £50.* LOC: From Leeds, right at Prince of Wales crossing, left at Skipton Rd. and left before railway bridge. PARK: Easy. TEL: 0423 503217. VAT: Stan/Spec.

Sutcliffe Galleries BADA
5 Royal Parade. Est. 1947. Open 10-5. *STOCK: Paintings, 19th C.* LOC: Opposite Crown Hotel. TEL: 0423 562976; fax - 0423 528729. SER: Valuations; restorations; framing.

Thorntons of Harrogate LAPADA
1 Montpellier Gdns. Open 9.30-5.30. *STOCK: 17th-18th C furniture, metalware, clocks, paintings, porcelain, arms and armour, scientific instruments.* TEL: 0423 504118. VAT: Spec.

YORKSHIRE NORTH

Harrogate continued

Traditional Interiors
Library House, Regent Parade. (M. Green). Est. 1976. Open 8.30-5.30, Sat. 8.45-4, Sun. by appointment. SIZE: Medium. STOCK: Pine furniture, Georgian, Victorian, Edwardian, £5-£2,000; treen, kitchenalia and collectors' items. LOC: Overlooking the Stray. PARK: Easy. TEL: 0423 560452. SER: Valuations; restorations; stripping. VAT: Stan/Spec.

Walker Galleries Ltd　　　BADA
6 Montpellier Gdns. Est. 1972. Open 9.30-1 and 2-5.30. SIZE: Medium. STOCK: Oil paintings and watercolours, 18th C furniture. TEL: 0423 567933. SER: Valuations; restorations; framing. FAIRS: Chelsea, Harrogate, NEC, Northern, Barbican. VAT: Spec.

Christopher Warner　　　BADA
15 Princes St. (C.C. Warner, I.P. Legard and G.S.M. Brown). Est. 1770. Open 9.30-5. SIZE: Small. STOCK: Jewellery, 1740-1890; silver, 1720-1840, both £50-£12,000. PARK: Easy. TEL: 0423 503617. SER: Valuations; restorations (silver and jewellery); buys at auction. FAIRS: Harrogate and NEC. VAT: Stan/Spec.

Weatherell's of Harrogate Antiques and Fine Arts　　　LAPADA
29 Montpellier Parade. Open 9-5.30. SIZE: Large. STOCK: Period and fine decorative furniture. TEL: 0423 507810/525004; fax - 0423 520005.

West Park Antiques Pavilion
20 West Park. Open 10-5. CL: Mon. SIZE: Large. TEL: 0423 563658. Below are listed the dealers at this centre.

Aquarius
STOCK: Jewellery and silver.

Shirley Baguley
STOCK: General antiques, small furniture and jewellery.

Jeffrey Bates
STOCK: Fine art, small antiques.

Marcus Burrows
STOCK: Bronzes, paintings, objets d'art, period furniture.

Cavendish Fine Art
STOCK: Paintings and watercolours, 18th-20th C.

Chanticleer Antiques
STOCK: Small antiques, objets d'art.

The Dukeries
STOCK: Period furniture.

Richard Greene Antiques
STOCK: Victorian and period furniture.

Greystones Antiques
STOCK: Lace, linen, veils, collectors' items.

Harrogate continued

Rodney Kent
STOCK: Furniture, oriental porcelain, oil paintings.

L. and P. Antiques
STOCK: Porcelain and furniture.

Jean Lamb
STOCK: Porcelain, furniture and small antiques.

Nicholas Merchant
STOCK: Reference and antiquarian books. TEL: 0423 505370.

Moorlands
STOCK: Furniture. SER: Cabinet makers.

G. Nimmo
STOCK: Silver, plate, objets d'art.

Oakwell Antiques
STOCK: Chandeliers, miniatures, porcelain, objets d'art.

Graham Reed Fine Art
STOCK: 19th C porcelain, pictures and small furniture, objets d'art.

Shieling Antiques
STOCK: Early country furniture, oak and elm, brass and copper.

Steve and Judith Sims
STOCK: Oak and country furniture.

Snodgrass Antiques
STOCK: 19th C and period furniture.

Town and Country
STOCK: Small antiques and jewellery.

Windmill Antiques　　　LAPADA
4 Montpellier Mews, Montpellier St. (B. and J. Tildesley). Est. 1980. Open 10-5.30. SIZE: Small. STOCK: Furniture, £250-£5,000; copper and brass, £20-£500; boxes, inkstands, rocking horses and children's chairs, £50-£2,000; all 18th-19th C. LOC: Behind Montpellier Parade. PARK: Nearby. TEL: 0423 530502; home - 0845 401330. VAT: Spec.

HAWES

Sturman's Antiques
Main St. (A., M.M. and P.J. Sturman). Open 10-5 including Sun. STOCK: Victorian and Edwardian furniture, porcelain, pictures and paintings. TEL: 0969 667742.

HELMSLEY

Rievaulx Books
18 High St. (C. Howard). Est. 1986. Open 10.30-5. CL: Mon. SIZE: Medium. STOCK: Antiquarian books, especially on natural history, field sports, Yorkshire, art and antiques. LOC: From Market Sq., past church, shop 100 yards past Feversham Arms inn. PARK: Easy. TEL: 0439 70912; home - same.

YORKSHIRE NORTH

Helmsley continued
Westway Cottage Restored Pine
Ashdale Rd. and, 28 Bond Gate. (J. and J. Dzierzek). Est. 1986. Open 9-5.30, Sun. 1-5.30, other times by appointment. SIZE: Small. STOCK: *Pine furniture, 19th C, £50-£1,500.* LOC: From A170 from Scarborough, first left into town, then left again at bottom of Ashdale Rd. PARK: Easy. TEL: 0439 70172; home - same. SER: Valuations; restorations (pine).

York Cottage Antiques   LAPADA
7 Church St. (G. and E.M. Thornley and G.E. Cooper). Est. 1976. Open daily April-Dec. 10-4.CL: Wed. Open Fri. and Sat. only Jan.-March, other times by appointment. STOCK: *Early oak and country furniture; 18th-19th C metalware; drinking glasses, pottery and porcelain especially Ironstone, Staffordshire figures, lustre and blue and white; cranberry glass.* LOC: Opposite church. PARK: Adjacent. TEL: 0439 70833; home - same.

HUBY, Nr. Leeds
Haworth Antiques
Harrogate Rd. (G. and J. White). BWCMG. Est. 1969. Open 10-5 or by appointment. CL: Mon. STOCK: *Clocks - wall, longcase and bracket, 18th-20th C, £15-£2,000; small furniture.* Not Stocked: Porcelain, pottery and paintings. LOC: A658. PARK: Own. TEL: 0423 734293. SER: Restorations (clocks and clock dials). VAT: Stan/Spec.

KILLINGHALL, Nr. Harrogate
Norwood House Antiques
88 Ripon Rd. (R.M. Mallaby). Resident. Est. 1981. Open 10-5 or by appointment. CL: Wed. STOCK: *English and continental furniture, 19th C; porcelain, clocks, silver, decorative items.* PARK: Easy. TEL: 0423 506468.

KIRK DEIGHTON, Nr. Wetherby
Elden Antiques
23 Ashdale View. (E. and D. Broadley). Est. 1970. Open 9-11.30 and 12.30-5.30, Sat. 12-5.30. SIZE: Medium. STOCK: *General antiques including small furniture.* LOC: Main road between Wetherby and Knaresborough. PARK: Easy. TEL: 0937 584770; home - same.

KIRKBYMOORSIDE, Nr. Helmsley
Crown Square Antiques
3 Crown Sq. (T. Cooper). Resident. Est. 1988. Open Fri. and Sat., or by appointment. SIZE: Medium. STOCK: *Oak and country furniture, dressers, farmhouse and gateleg tables, spindle and ladderback rush-seated, flat-seated and Windsor chairs, £50-£4,500; associated decorative items, £20-£800; all from 18th C.* LOC: Off Market Pl., behind memorial hall. PARK: Easy. TEL: 0751 33295.

KNARESBOROUGH
Robert Aagaard Ltd
Frogmire House, Stockwell Rd. Est. 1961. Open 9-5, Sat. 10-4. SIZE: Medium. STOCK: *Chimney pieces, marble fire surrounds and interiors.* LOC: Town centre. PARK: Own. TEL: 0423 864805. VAT: Stan.

Bowkett
9 Abbey Rd. (E.S. Starkie). Resident. Est. 1919. Open 9-6. SIZE: Medium. STOCK: *Chairs, small furniture, brass, copper, pot-lids, Goss, books.* LOC: By the river at the lower road bridge. PARK: Easy. TEL: 0423 866112. SER: Restorations (upholstery and small furniture). VAT: Stan/Spec.

Cheapside Antiques
4 Cheapside. (Mrs M.E. Hanson). Open 10-5. CL: Thurs. STOCK: *Furniture, porcelain, metalware and small collectors' items, 1750-1900.* TEL: 0423 867779. VAT: Spec.

The Emporium
Market Flat Lane, Lingerfield. (N. Wadley). Open by appointment. SIZE: Medium and warehouse. STOCK: *Pine and general antiques.* PARK: Easy. TEL: 0423 868539. SER: Packing; shipping; courier. VAT: Stan.

Milton J. Holgate
36 Gracious St. Est. 1972. Open 9-5.30 or by appointment. CL: Thurs. STOCK: *Furniture, longcase clocks and boxes, 18th to early 19th C.* PARK: Easy. TEL: 0423 865219. VAT: Mainly Spec. *Mainly Trade.*

Kellys of Knaresborough
Rear of 96 High St. (D.C. Kelly). Est. 1969. Open Mon., Fri. and Sat. 10-5 or by appointment. SIZE: Large. STOCK: *Chandeliers, wall lights, general lighting, candle sticks, lustres, 19th to early 20th C.* LOC: A59. PARK: Own. TEL: 0423 862041 (24hr. ansaphone). SER: Buys at auction. VAT: Stan/Spec.

The Northern Kilim Centre
24 Finkle St. Open 10.30-5, Sun. 2-5. CL: Thurs. STOCK: *Persian, Turkish, Afghan and Central Asian flat woven rugs and nomadic carpets.* TEL: 0423 866219/866502. SER: Valuations; restorations.

Pictoriana
88 High St. (Mrs A. Goodfellow). Est. 1982. Open 9.30-5.30, Sun. 10.30-4.30. SIZE: Large. STOCK: *Pine including reproduction, £20-£1,000; wood carvings and kitchenalia, £5-£100.* LOC: A59. PARK: Nearby. TEL: 0423 866116; home - 0423 884175. SER: Restorations (pine). VAT: Stan.

The Gordon Reece Gallery
Finkle St. Est. 1981. Open 10.30-5, Sun. 2-5 or by appointment. CL: Thurs. SIZE: Large. STOCK:

YORKSHIRE NORTH

Knaresborough continued
Architectural items, furniture, metalware, carvings and rare textiles, £5-£4,000. LOC: Town centre. PARK: Own. TEL: 0423 866219/866502; home - same. SER: Exhibitions organised and mounted; touring exhibitions. VAT: Stan.

Reflections
23 Waterside. (J. and M.V. McNamara). Resident. Est. 1977. Open Tues.-Sun. 9.30-6, other times by appointment. SIZE: Small. *STOCK: Furniture, 19th C; paintings, 19th to early 20th C, both £50-£1,000; bric-a-brac and brassware; books, 19th to early 20th C, £1-£100.* LOC: Turn off A59 at World's End Inn. PARK: Easy. TEL: 0423 862005.

Charles Shaw
The Old Vicarage, 2 Station Rd. Est. 1981. Open daily including Sun. p.m. SIZE: Medium. *STOCK: Taxidermy, £25-£5,000; country and sporting pictures, £20-£5,000; both 19th-20th C; out-of-print, country and sporting books, £5-£500; small antiques and furniture, 18th-20th C.* LOC: Off High St. A59. PARK: Own. TEL: 0423 867715. SER: Valuations; buys at auction. VAT: Stan/Spec.

Swadforth House   LAPADA
Gracious St. (J. Thompson). Est. 1968. *STOCK: General antiques.* TEL: 0423 864698. VAT: Spec.

LONG PRESTON
Gavèls
3 Station Rd. (Gary K. Blissett). Open by appointment only. *STOCK: 19th-20th C paintings and watercolours.* TEL: 0729 840384.

LOWER BENTHAM
Low Mill Antiques
Mill Lane. (G. Garman). Est. 1987. Open 9.30-5.30 prior telephone call advisable; Sun. by appointment. SIZE: Medium. *STOCK: English, Irish and continental pine, 18th-20th C, £10-£1,000.* LOC: Off M6, junction 34 onto B6480, 15 miles to village, turn right after 2nd bridge. PARK: Own. TEL: 05242 61152; home - 05242 61286. SER: Valuations; restorations; pine stripping. VAT: Stan/Spec.

W.T. and J. Spencer
Arundel House. *STOCK: Stripped pine, oak, mahogany, pottery, porcelain.* LOC: B6480. TEL: 0468 61058.

MALTON
Malton Antique Market
2 Old Maltongate. (Mrs M.A. Cleverly). Est. 1970. Open 9.30-12.30 and 2-5. CL: Thurs. SIZE: Medium. *STOCK: Furniture, Georgian to Victorian, to £1,500; glass, bric-a-brac, porcelain, pottery, copper and brass.* LOC: From York take A64, shop is at main traffic light junction in Malton. PARK: 20yds. further. TEL: 0653 692732. SER: Commission sales.

Malton continued
Matthew Maw Antiques
18 Castlegate. Open 9-5. CL: Thurs. p.m. *STOCK: Furniture including shipping.* LOC: A64. TEL: 0653 694638. VAT: Stan/Spec.

Talents Fine Arts Ltd
7 Market Place. (J. Burrows). Est. 1986. Open daily. SIZE: Medium. *STOCK: Oils, watercolours and prints, 19th C, £20-£500; contemporary local artists.* LOC: A64 near church. PARK: Easy. TEL: 0653 600020. SER: Restorations; framing. VAT: Stan/Spec.

MANFIELD
Trade Antiques - D.D. White
Lucy Cross Cottage. Est. 1975. *STOCK: Georgian, Victorian and export furniture.* LOC: B6275, Scotch Corner to Piercebridge road, on left 3 miles after leaving A1. PARK: Easy. TEL: 0325 374303 or 0833 37021. VAT: Stan/Spec.

MARKINGTON, Nr. Harrogate
Daleside Antiques
Hinks Hall Lane. Est. 1978. Open 8-5, Sat. and Sun. by appointment. *STOCK: Pine furniture, decorative items, architectural features and fittings, 18th-19th C, £50-£3,500; Georgian mahogany furniture; Victorian shop fittings.* TEL: 0765 677888; fax - 0765 677886. SER: Containers; courier; restorations. VAT: Stan.

MASHAM, Nr. Ripon
Aura Antiques
1-3 Silver St. (R. and R. Sutcliffe). Est. 1985. Open 9.15-5.15, Sun. by appointment. SIZE: Medium. *STOCK: Furniture especially mahogany, 18th to mid-19th C, £50-£5,000; metalware - brass and copper, fenders, £5-£250; china, glass, silver and decorative objects, £5-£1,000; all 18th-19th C.* LOC: Corner of Market Sq. PARK: Easy. TEL: 0765 89315; home - 0765 838192. SER: Valuations; buys at auction (mahogany period furniture). VAT: Spec.

MELMERBY, Nr. Ripon
Terry Kindon Antiques Ltd
Unit 23 Melmerby Industrial Estate, Green Lane. Open 9.30-5, other times by appointment. CL: Sat. *STOCK: Mainly furniture and pine.* TEL: 0765 640522. SER: Containers.

MIDDLEHAM, Nr. Leyburn
White Boar Antiques and Books
Kirkgate. (J. and G. Armstrong). Est. 1983. Open 10-5.30. Winter - open 10-4.30 or by appointment CL: Mon. SIZE: Small. *STOCK: Furniture porcelain, 18th-19th C; silver, copper, brass pewter and glass, 19th C, £50-£150; books including antiquarian, 17th-20th C, £1-£450+* LOC: A6108 towards Leyburn. PARK: Opposite TEL: 0969 23901; home - same. SER: Book search.

NORTHALLERTON

The Antique and Art
7 Central Arcade. (Mrs J. Willoughby). Open 10-5. CL: Thurs. *STOCK: Porcelain, pottery, silver, jewellery, glass, prints and paintings.* TEL: 0609 772051; home - 0609 774157.

Collectors Corner
145/6 High St. (J. Wetherill). Est. 1972. Open 10-4, Sat. 10-5, or by appointment. CL:Thurs. *STOCK: General antiques, collectors' items.* LOC: Opposite GPO. TEL: 0609 777623; home - 0609 775199.

PATELEY BRIDGE

Cat in the Window Antiques
22 High St. (Mrs S. Morgan). Est. 1976. Open 2-5 and by appointment. CL: Mon. and Wed. *STOCK: Small furniture, metalware, glass, ceramics, art nouveau, art deco, amber, coral, jet, pictures, sewing items, linen, lace and collectors' items.* PARK: Easy. TEL: 0423 711343.

Brian Loomes
Calf Haugh Farm. Est. 1966. Open 9-5 by appointment. SIZE: Medium. *STOCK: British clocks, especially longcase, wall, bracket and lantern, pre-1840, £500-£10,000. Not Stocked: Foreign clocks.* LOC: From Pateley Bridge, first private lane on left on Grassington Rd. (B6265). PARK: Own. TEL: 0423 711163; home - same. VAT: Spec.

PICKERING

Antiques & Things
South Gate. (J. Whitaker). Open 10-5. CL: Wed. *STOCK: General antiques, dolls, linen.* PARK: At rear. TEL: 0751 76142.

John Hague
18 Hallgarth. Est. 1959. Open by appointment. *STOCK: Furniture, porcelain and general antiques, prints and pictures.* TEL: 0751 72829.

C.H. Reynolds
122 Eastgate. Open 9.30-5.30, Sun. by appointment. *STOCK: General antiques.* TEL: 0751 72785.

RICHMOND

Brown's Antiques   LAPADA
2 New Rd. (G.P. and Mrs J.A. Brown). Open 10-4, Sun. and Wed. by appointment. SIZE: Medium. *STOCK: Furniture, Georgian and Victorian; paintings, porcelain, some silver.* LOC: Top of Market Place, opposite Castle Walk. PARK: Opposite. TEL: 0748 824095; home - 0748 823577. SER: Restorations (furniture). VAT: Stan/Spec.

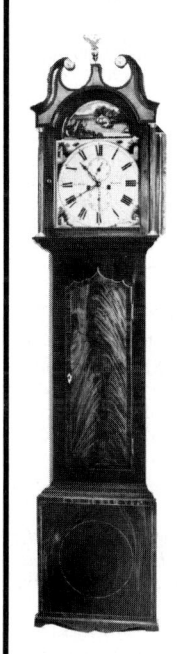

BRIAN LOOMES

Specialist dealer in antique British clocks. Established 26 years. Internationally recognised authority and author of numerous textbooks on antique clocks. We have a large stock of good longcase clocks, mostly 18th century and some early 19th, several wall, bracket and lantern clocks.

Resident on premises. Available 9 to 5 six days a week but telephone appointment essential.

Copies of my current books always in stock.

CALF HAUGH FARMHOUSE, PATELEY BRIDGE, NORTH YORKS.
Tel: **(0423) 711163.**

(On B6265 Pateley-Grassington road.)

RIPON

Balmain Antiques
13 High Skellgate. Open 10-4. *STOCK: Fine furniture, paintings, silver and porcelain.* TEL: 0765 601294.

Pinetree Antiques
44 North St. (M.P. Dunn). Open 9.30-5. *STOCK: Pine furniture.* TEL: 0765 602905.

Rose Fine Art and Antiques
13 Kirkgate. (Mr and Mrs S. Rose). Est. 1984. Open daily, Sun. by appointment. CL: Wed. SIZE: Medium. *STOCK: Pictures, 18th to early 20th C, £5-£2,000; furniture, £50-£1,000; porcelain and glass, £5-£500; both 19th to early 20th C.* LOC: Between Market Place and cathedral. PARK: Nearby. TEL: 0765 690118; home - same. SER: Valuations; restorations (pictures); buys at auction (pictures and prints); framing. VAT: Stan.

Sigma Antiques and Fine Art
Water Skellgate. (D. Thomson). Est. 1963. Open 9.30-5.30. *STOCK: Furniture, 17th-20th C; glass, paintings, 18th-20th C; jewellery, silver, European and Eastern pottery and porcelain; jades, ivories, fine objets d'art, bronzes; continental furniture, ornaments, 18th-20th C; decorators' items.* PARK: Nearby. TEL: 0765 603163; fax - 0765 690933.

Ripon continued
Skellgate Curios
2 Low Skellgate. (J.I. Wain and P.S. Gyte). Est. 1974. Open 11-5. CL: Wed. STOCK: *General antiques, silver, jewellery and curios.* TEL: 0765 601290; home - 0765 635336. VAT: Stan/Spec.

Yesteryear
6 and 7 High Skellgate. (J. Rowlay). Open 10-4.30. CL: Wed. STOCK: *Small furniture, copper, brass, china, jewellery, silver, linen.* TEL: 0765 607801.

SCARBOROUGH
Browns Antiques
6 Seamer Rd. Corner. (Mrs L. Brown). Est. 1973. Open 10-5. SIZE: Medium. STOCK: *Furniture, pictures, porcelain, pottery, objets d'art, Victorian to Georgian, £5-£4,500; art deco, art nouveau.* LOC: At junction of Seamer Rd. and Falsgrave Rd. PARK: Nearby. TEL: 0723 377112. VAT: Stan.

Hanover Antiques
10 Hanover Rd. Est. 1976. Open 10-4. CL: Wed. STOCK: *Militaria, medals, badges and general small items, Dinky toys, 50p-£500.* PARK: Easy. TEL: 0723 374175.

Shuttleworths
7 Victoria Rd. (L.R. Shuttleworth). Open 10-4. CL: Wed. STOCK: *General antiques.* TEL: 0723 366278.

SCARTHINGWELL, Nr. Tadcaster
Scarthingwell Arcades
Scarthingwell Centre, Scarthingwell Farm. (Mrs G. Brier). Est. 1990. Open 10-5 including Sun. SIZE: Large. STOCK: *General antiques - bric-a-brac, pine, small period furniture, from £5.* LOC: Off A162 between Sherburn-in-Elmet and Tadcaster. PARK: Easy. TEL: 0937 557877. SER: Valuations; restorations (furniture); buys at auction.

SETTLE
Folly Antiques
The Folly, Chapel St. (J.A. Yarwood and S. Gannon). Est. 1991. Open 10-5.30. SIZE: Medium. STOCK: *Furniture, mainly oak and mahogany, 1580-1920, £50-£4,900; porcelain and pottery, 1780-1890, £10-£350; jewellery and silver, from 1780, £5-£750; fine art, original paintings, drawings, prints and sculpture, £20-£1,500.* LOC: Town centre. PARK: Easy.

H.I. Milnthorpe
Kirkgate. Est. 1974. Open 9-12.30 and 1.30-5. CL: Wed. SIZE: Medium. STOCK: *English furniture, 17th to early 19th C, £100-£10,000; pottery and porcelain, pre-1850, £20-£1,500.* Not Stocked: Victorian furniture, guns, coins and jewellery. LOC: A65. PARK: Easy. TEL: 0729 823046. SER: Valuations. VAT: Spec.

Settle continued
Mary Milnthorpe and Daughters Antique Shop
Market Place. Est. 1958. Open 9.30-5. CL: Wed. SIZE: Small. STOCK: *Jewellery and silver, 18th-19th C and secondhand.* LOC: Opp. Town Hall. PARK: Easy. TEL: 0729 822331. VAT: Stan/Spec.

Nanbooks
Roundabout, Duke St. (N.M. Midgley). Resident. Est. 1955. Open Tues., Fri. and Sat. 11-12.30 and 2-5.30. SIZE: Small. STOCK: *English pottery, porcelain including Oriental, glass, general small antiques, 17th-19th C, to £150; bric-a-brac, 19th-20th C; some antiquarian books.* Not Stocked: Jewellery. LOC: A65. PARK: Easy. TEL: 0729 823324.

Roy Precious
King William House, High St. Resident. Est. 1972. Open 10-5.30 or by appointment. CL: Wed. SIZE: Medium. STOCK: *Oak and country furniture, some walnut and mahogany, 17th-19th C, £30-£6,000; oil paintings especially portraits, 17th-19th C, £300-£5,000; some pottery and prints.* LOC: Opposite Post Office, on the old High St. PARK: Easy. TEL: 0729 823946. SER: Valuations. VAT: Stan/Spec.

E. Thistlethwaite
The Antique Shop, Market Sq. Est. 1972. Open 9-5. CL: Wed. SIZE: Medium. STOCK: *Country furniture and metalware, 18th-19th C.* LOC: Town centre, A65. PARK: Forecourt. TEL: 0729 822460. VAT: Stan/Spec.

Well Cottage Antiques
Well Cottage, High St. (Mrs J. Lassey). Est. 1987. CL: Mon. and Wed. STOCK: *Porcelain and pottery, pine, 19th-20th C, £5-£100; framed cigarette cards, 20th C, £40-£70.* LOC: Town centre. PARK: Easy. TEL: 0729 823593; home - same. SER: Framing.

SKIPTON
Adamson Armoury
Newmarket St. (J.K. Adamson). Est. 1975. Open 10-4.30. SIZE: Medium. STOCK: *Weapons, 17th 19th C, £10-£1,000.* LOC: A65, 200yds. from town centre. PARK: Rear. TEL: 0756 791355 home - 0756 798859. SER: Valuations. FAIRS: Liverpool, Nottingham, Birmingham, London, Stockport, Chester, Bolton, Warrington, Manchester, Newcastle, Morley, Bedford.

Corn Mill Antiques
High Corn Mill, Chapel Hill. (Mrs M Hawkridge). Est. 1984. Open 10-4. CL: Tues. and Wed. SIZE: Medium. STOCK: *Oak, mahogany and walnut furniture, £100-£2,000; porcelain, silver plate, prints, pictures, brass and copper £5-£500; all Victorian to 1930s.* Not Stocked

19th century print entitled *A Day's Pleasure, The Journey Out*, showing a father pulling his children in a stick wagon. Photograph courtesy Jack Hampshire's Pram Museum. From **Yesterday's Children**, by Sally Kevill-Davies, published by the **Antique Collectors' Club**, £19.95pb.

Skipton continued
Jewellery, gold and silver. LOC: From town centre take Grassington Road, Chapel Hill is first right. PARK: Easy. TEL: 0756 792440; home - 0729 830489. SER: Valuations. VAT: Spec.

Craven Books
23 Newmarket St. (Miss K. Farey and Miss M.G. Fluck). Open 9.30-12.30 and 1.30-5, Sat. 9-12.30 and 1.30-4.30. CL: Tues. and first and last Mon. every month. STOCK: General items. TEL: 0756 792677. SER: Finder (books).

SNAINTON, Nr. Scarborough
Cottage Antiques
19 High St. (Mrs E.A. Shackleton). Resident. Est. 1984. CL: Sat. p.m. SIZE: Small. STOCK: Georgian furniture, pine, clocks, china, glass, jewellery, pictures and unusual cottage items, £1-£1,600. Not Stocked: Weapons and stamps. LOC: A170, equidistant Scarborough and Pickering. PARK: Easy. TEL: 0723 859577. SER: Valuations; restorations (cabinet work).

SPENNITHORNE, Nr. Leyburn
N.J. and C.S. Dodsworth
Thorney Hall. Est. 1973. Open by appointment. SIZE: Medium. STOCK: English furniture and longcase clocks, 18th to early 19th C. LOC: Off A684. TEL: 0969 22177. VAT: Stan/Spec.

STILLINGTON
Pond Cottage Antiques
Brandsby Rd. (C.M. and D. Thurstans). Resident. Est. 1972. STOCK: Pine, kitchenalia, country furniture, treen, metalware, brass, copper. TEL: 0347 810796.

STOKESLEY
Three Tuns Antiques
2 Three Tuns Wynd. (E. and L.C. Payman). Est. 1972. Open 10.30-5. STOCK: Small furniture, jewellery, silver, general small antiques, ceramics, glass. TEL: 0642 711377; home - 0642 724284.

THIRSK
Richard Bennett
18 Kirkgate. Est. 1979. Open by appointment. SIZE: Small. STOCK: Oil paintings, £50-£2,000; watercolours, £50-£500; both 19th to mid-20th C. LOC: Joins Market Place. PARK: Nearby. TEL: 0845 524085; home - same. SER: Restorations (oil paintings); buys at auction; framing.

Cottage Antiques and Curios
1 Market Place. (Mrs E.H. and S.R. Ballard). Est. 1970. Open 9-5. CL: Wed. STOCK: Victorian porcelain and glass, £5-£250; furniture, from 1750, £5-£1,000; brass, copper, silver and plated ware, £3-£300. PARK: Easy. TEL: 0845 522536/523212; home - 0845 577461.

Thirsk continued
B. Ogleby
35, 36 and 37 The Green. Open by appointment only. SIZE: Large. *STOCK: Furniture, 17th-20th C.* TEL: 0845 524120. SER: Shipping and packing. VAT: Stan/Spec. *Trade and Export Only.*

Potterton Books
The Old Rectory, Sessay. (C. Jameson). Open 9-5. SIZE: Large. *STOCK: Classic reference works on art, architecture, interior design, antiques and collecting.* TEL: 0845 401218; fax - 0845 401439. SER: Library accessories; book search; decorative bindings; catalogues issued. FAIRS: London; Germany; USA.

THORNTON LE DALE, Nr. Pickering
Stable Antiques
4 Pickering Rd. (Mrs S. Kitching Walker). Open 2.15-5, mornings by appointment. CL: Mon. SIZE: Small. *STOCK: Porcelain, £5-£500; furniture, £20-£700; silver, glass, brass, plate, copper, collectors' items, £5-£150, all 19th C to 1930's.* LOC: A170. PARK: Easy. TEL: 0751 74435. SER: Valuations. FAIRS: Downe Arms, Wykeham.

TOCKWITH, Nr. York
Raymond Tomlinson (Antiques) Ltd. and Period Furniture Ltd   LAPADA
Moorside. Est. 1971. Open 8-4.30, Sat. 9-4, or by appointment. SIZE: Large. *STOCK: Furniture, £5-£5,000; clocks, £10-£3,000.* LOC: A1 Wetherby take B1224 towards York. After 3 miles turn left on to Rudgate. At end of this road turn left, business 200m on left. PARK: Easy. TEL: 0423 358833; fax - 0423 358188. SER: Export; restorations; container packing. VAT: Stan/Spec. *Trade Only.*

WHITBY
Aird-Gordon Antiques
15 Baxtergate. Open daily. *STOCK: Glass, jewellery, jet, china, small furniture.* TEL: 0947 601515.

The Bazaar
7 Skinner St. (F.A. Doyle). Est. 1970. Open 9.30-5.30. *STOCK: Jewellery, furniture, general antiques, 19th C.* TEL: 0947 602281.

'Bobbins' Wool Craft Antiques
Wesley Hall, Church St. (D. and P. Hoyle). Open 10.30-5 every day February to Christmas. SIZE: Small. *STOCK: General antiques, especially oil lamps, 19th-20th C.* LOC: Between Market Place and steps to Abbey. PARK: Nearby. TEL: 0947 600585. SER: Repairs and spares (oil lamps). VAT: Stan.

Caedmon House
14 Station Sq. (E.M. Stanforth). Est. 1977. Open 10-5. SIZE: Medium. *STOCK: General, mainly small, antiques including jewellery, dolls and china, especially Dresden, to £1,200.* PARK: Easy. TEL: 0947 602120; home - 0947 603930. SER: Valuations; restorations (upholstery and china); repairs (jewellery). VAT: Stan/Spec.

Coach House Antiques
75 Coach Rd, Sleights. (C.J. Rea). Resident. Est. 1973. Open 10-5 (winter months 10.30-4.30). CL: Sun. and Thurs. except by appointment. SIZE: Small. *STOCK: Furniture, especially oak and country; glass, jewellery, linen, metalware, paintings, porcelain, silver, unusual and decorative items.* LOC: On A169, 3 miles south west of Whitby. PARK: Easy, opposite. TEL: 0947 810313.

The Mount Antiques
Khyber Pass. (M. and B. Bottomley). Est. 1973. Open 9.30-5. SIZE: Large. *STOCK: Period mahogany and country oak furniture, dining tables and chairs, pine and kitchenalia, fireplaces and architectural items.* PARK: Own. TEL: 0947 604516. VAT: Stan/Spec.

WHIXLEY
Garth Antiques
The Old School, Franks Lane. (I. Chapman). Est. 1978. Open by appointment. SIZE: Medium. *STOCK: Furniture, 18th-19th C, £50-£3,000; brass and copper, 19th C, £1-£500; oils and watercolours, £5-£3,000.* LOC: A59, turn left at Whixley Hospital, then left opposite The Anchor public house, into old village. PARK: Easy. TEL: 0423 331055. VAT: Stan/Spec.

YORK
Barbican Bookshop
24 Fossgate. Est. 1961. Open 9.15-5.30. *STOCK: Antiquarian books.* TEL: 0904 653643/644878. VAT: Stan.

Barker Court Antiques and Bygones
44 Gillygate. (Mrs D. Yates). Est. 1970. Open 10.30-4.30. CL: Sun. and Wed. except by appointment. SIZE: Small. *STOCK: Pottery and porcelain, glass, plated items, Victorian to 1930, £3-£100.* LOC: 3 mins. walk from York Minster. PARK: Gillygate. TEL: 0904 622611.

Bishopsgate Antiques
23/24 Bishopsgate St. (R. Wetherill). Open 9.15-6. *STOCK: General antiques.* TEL: 0904 623893.

'Bobbins'
31-33 Goodramgate. (D. Hoyle). Open 10-5.30 SIZE: Small. *STOCK: Rush seated country chairs, tools and bygones, small furniture, general antiques, art deco, clocks, oil lamps, 18th-20th C* LOC: Opposite York Minster at junction with Deansgate. PARK: Outside city walls. TEL: 0904 653597. SER: Spares (oil lamps). VAT: Stan.

Raymond Tomlinson Antiques Ltd

Britain's Leading Wholesaler of Antique Furniture Serving Domestic & Overseas Trade.

WE HAVE MOVED
TO LARGER PREMISES

- ♦ New 48,000 sq. ft. Warehouse (4459m^2).
- ♦ 1,000 pieces of furniture arriving every week.
- ♦ Full export services available on site.
- ♦ Trade only Monday to Friday 8.00am-4.30pm.
- ♦ Serving USA, Australia, Japan and all European Markets.
- ♦ 75% of stock sold to UK based dealers.
- ♦ 10 Miles from York, 9 miles from Harrogate, 15 miles from Leeds.

**Specialists in Georgian & Victorian Mahogany Furniture
Full Restoration Facilities**

—— NEW ADDRESS ——

RAYMOND TOMLINSON (ANTIQUES) LTD

MOORSIDE · TOCKWITH · YORK · NORTH YORKSHIRE · ENGLAND YO5 8QG

TELEPHONE: (0423) 358833 (3 LINES) . FAX: (0423) 358188

OPENING HOURS: MON.-FRI. 8.00AM-4.30PM (TRADE ONLY)
SAT. 9.00AM-4.00PM

**LOCATED 4 MILES FROM A1 AT WETHERBY
(TAKE B1224 TOWARDS YORK)**

York continued

Barbara Cattle
45 Stonegate. Open 9-5.30. STOCK: Jewellery and silver, Georgian to date. TEL: 0904 623862.

Coulter Galleries
Open by appointment only. STOCK: Watercolours and oils, pre-1900; frames. TEL: 0904 702101.

Danby Antiques
61 Heworth Rd. (N. and Mrs J. Banks). Resident. Est. 1985. Open seven days (telephone first). SIZE: Small. STOCK: Boxes, 18th-19th C; writing accessories including fountain pens and pencils, unusual collectables, 19th-20th C. LOC: 1 mile from city centre on A1036 (Scarborough Road), turn right signed Heslington (university), 100 yards on left just before traffic lights/church. PARK: Easy. TEL: 0904 415280. SER: Buys at auction. FAIRS: Newark, Stafford, Harrogate, NEC, Chester, Buxton.

Fettes Fine Art
(T. and G. Thornton). Open by appointment. SIZE: Small. STOCK: Pictures - early Victorian, £3,000-£10,000; European schools, 18th C, £3,000-£5,000, 20th C, to £5,000. TEL: 0904 641344. VAT: Stan/Spec.

French Fine Arts
1 Goodramgate. (C.W. Sykes). Open 9-5, other times by appointment. STOCK: Oil paintings. TEL: 0904 654266.

Robert M. Himsworth
28 The Shambles. Est. 1949. Open 9-5. SIZE: Small. STOCK: Antique jewellery. TEL: 0904 625089. VAT: Stan/Spec.

Holgate Antiques
Holgate Rd. (T. Betts). Est. 1980. Open 10-5, Sat. 10-4. STOCK: General antiques, furniture, bric-a-brac. TEL: 0904 30005.

Minster Gate Bookshop
8 Minster Gates. (N. Wallace). Est. 1970. Open 9.30-5.30. SIZE: Large. STOCK: Antiquarian and secondhand books. LOC: Opposite south door of York Minster. PARK: Nearby. TEL: 0904 621812. SER: Valuations; restorations; book finding.

Robert Morrison and Son   BADA
Trentholme House, 131 The Mount. (C. Morrison). Est. 1890. Open 9.30-5, Sat. 9.30-1. SIZE: Large. STOCK: English furniture, 1700-1900; porcelain and clocks. LOC: Near racecourse, one mile from city centre on Leeds Rd. From A1, take A64 to outskirts of York, then take A1036 York west road. PARK: Easy. TEL: 0904 655394. VAT: Stan/Spec.

Newgate Antiques Centre
14 Newgate. (M.S. and D.J. Smith). Est. 1991. Open 9-5.30. SIZE: Small. LOC: Adjacent York market, off Parliament St. PARK: Multi-storey.

York continued

TEL: 0904 679844. VAT: Stan/Spec. Below are listed the dealers at this market.

Danby Antiques
STOCK: Pens, writing instruments, collectables.

Golden Memories of York
STOCK: Antique and secondhand jewellery.

Thacker's Antiques
STOCK: Porcelain, jewellery, glass, silver, £5-£500. TEL: 0904 65805; mobile - 0850 600515.

O'Flynn Antiquarian Booksellers
35 Micklegate. Open 9-6. STOCK: Prints and maps, many hand coloured; antiquarian and secondhand books on history, travel, natural history, sciences, poetry, biographies, literary criticism, general fiction and Scotland. TEL: 0904 641404.

St. John Antiques
26 Lord Mayor's Walk. (R. and J. Bell). Open 10-5. CL: Mon. STOCK: Victorian stripped pine and satinwood furniture. PARK: At rear. TEL: 0904 644263.

Ken Spelman
70 Micklegate. (P. Miller and A. Fothergill). ABA. Est. 1948. SIZE: Large. STOCK: Secondhand and antiquarian books especially fine arts and literature, 50p-£10,000. PARK: Easy. TEL: 0904 624414. SER: Valuations; buys at auction (books); catalogues issued. FAIRS: Bath, Oxford, York, Harrogate and London PBFA and ABA. VAT: Spec.

Taikoo Books Ltd
29 High Petergate. (D. Chilton). Open 10-5.30 by appointment advisable. STOCK: Antiquarian and secondhand books especially on mountaineering, polar, Africiana, Oriental and big game hunting. TEL: 0904 641213.

Thacker's Antiques
42 Fossgate. Open 10-5. SIZE: Large. STOCK: Furniture and bric-a-brac, £5-£5,000. LOC: In city centre, next to Merchant Adventurer's Hall. PARK: Loading only. TEL: 0904 633077; mobile - 0850 600515.

Inez M. P. Yates
5 The Shambles. Est. 1948. Open 10.30-5. CL: Wed. STOCK: Small furniture, porcelain, paintings, jewellery, unusual small collectors items. LOC: City centre, by Kings Sq. TEL: 090 654821.

York Antiques Centre
2 Lendal. Open 9.30-5.30, winter 10-5. SIZE: 2 dealers. STOCK: Antiques and collectable items, 18th-20th C. LOC: Opposite the museum garden. PARK: Easy. TEL: 0904 641445/641582.

YORKSHIRE NORTH

Key to Town Plan

- AA Recommended roads
- Other roads
- Restricted roads
- Buildings of interest
- Car Parks **P**
- Parks and open spaces
- AA Service Centre **AA**

© Automobile Association 1988.

Yorkshire South

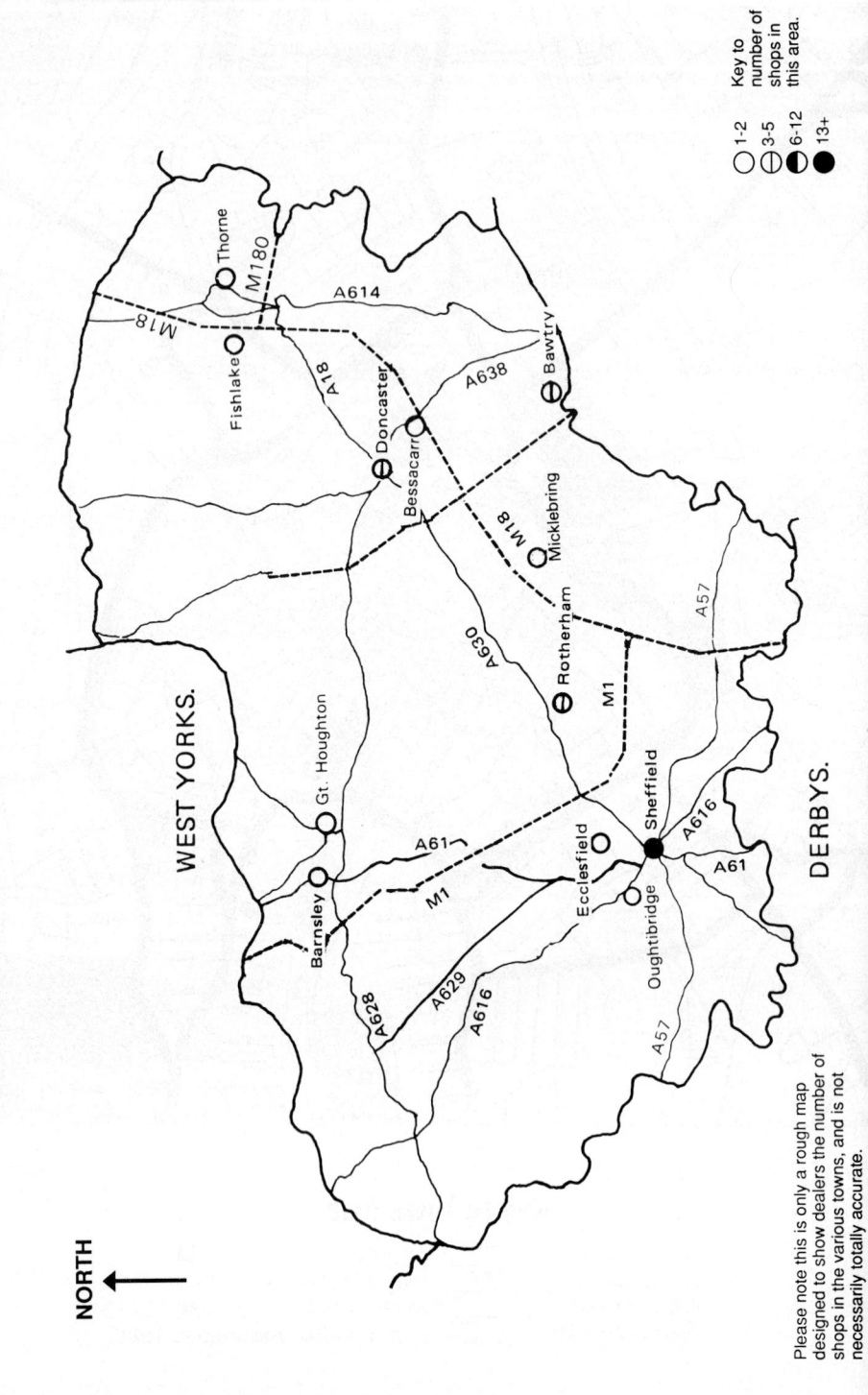

576

Key to number of shops in this area.

○ 1-2
◐ 3-5
◑ 6-12
● 13+

NORTH ←

Please note this is only a rough map designed to show dealers the number of shops in the various towns, and is not necessarily totally accurate.

WEST YORKS.

DERBYS.

- Thorne
- Fishlake
- Doncaster
- Bessacarr
- Bawtry
- Micklebring
- Rotherham
- Gt. Houghton
- Barnsley
- Ecclesfield
- Oughtibridge
- Sheffield

M180, M18, A614, A18, A638, A57, A630, M1, A61, A628, A629, A616

Yorkshire South

BARNSLEY

Charisma Antiques Trade Warehouse
St. Paul's former Methodist Chapel, Market St., Hoyland. (J.C. Simmons). Est. 1980. Open 10-5. SIZE: Large. *STOCK: Furniture, shipping goods, pictures.* LOC: 1.5 miles off M1 exit 36. PARK: Easy. TEL: 0226 747599; home - 0226 790482. VAT: Stan/Spec.

Christine Simmons Antiques
St. Paul's Former Methodist Chapel, Market St., Hoyland. Est. 1976. Open 10-4. SIZE: Medium. *STOCK: Smalls and pictures.* LOC: 1.5 miles from exit 36, M1. PARK: Easy. TEL: 0226 747599/790482.

BAWTRY, Nr. Doncaster

Swan Antiques
2 Swan St. Open 10-5 including Sun. SIZE: Large. *STOCK: Furniture, silver, ceramics, linen, collectables, taxidermy.* PARK: Easy. TEL: 0302 710301.

Treasure House Antiques Centre
4-10 Swan St. Est. 1982. Open 10-5 including Sun. and Bank Holidays. SIZE: Large - various dealers. *STOCK: Silver, porcelain, furniture, carnival glass, postcards, toy trains and general antiques.* PARK: Easy. TEL: 0302 710621.

Timothy D. Wilson   BADA
Grove House, Wharf St. Est. 1926. Open 9-5, appointment advisable, Sun. by appointment only. SIZE: Medium. *STOCK: English oak and country furniture, 17th-18th C; Windsor chairs, metalware, Mason's ironstone, decorative items and textiles.* PARK: Easy. TEL: 0302 710040. VAT: Spec.

BESSACARR, Nr. Doncaster

Keith Stones Grandfather Clocks
5 Ellers Drive. Est. 1988. Open by appointment. SIZE: Small. *STOCK: Grandfather clocks especially painted dial with 30 hour and 8 day movements, Georgian to early 19th C, £750-£2,000.* LOC: Take A638 Bawtry road off racecourse roundabout, through traffic lights after 3/4 mile, take second right into Ellers Rd. then second left. PARK: Easy. TEL: 0302 535258; home - same. SER: Valuations.

DONCASTER

Doncaster Sales and Exchange
20 Copley Rd. Open 9.30-5. CL: Thurs. *STOCK: General small antiques.* TEL: 0302 344857. VAT: Stan.

ECCLESFIELD, Nr. Sheffield

John R. Wrigley
185 The Wheel. Est. 1961. *STOCK: Historic gramophone records; books about records and recordings.* TEL: 0742 460275. SER: Catalogue issued monthly. *Postal Only.*

FISHLAKE

Fishlake Antiques
Pinfold Lane. Resident. Est. 1972. Open by appointment. SIZE: Medium. *STOCK: Rural furniture especially stripped pine; clocks including longcase and wall clocks, Victorian to mid-19th C, £30-£1,000; small Victoriana - writing boxes, lamps, £3-£70; rural collectors' items - cartwheels, ploughs, wheelwright and carpenters' tools, 19th-20th C, £1-£50.* LOC: Off A63. PARK: Own. TEL: 0302 841411.

GREAT HOUGHTON, Nr. Barnsley

Farmhouse Antiques
7 High St. Open 1-5. *STOCK: Period and Victorian furniture, stripped pine; art deco china and ceramics, especially Susie Cooper.* TEL: 0226 754057; home - 0226 753263.

MAPPLEWELL, Nr. Barnsley

A Maze of Pine and Roses
1 Blacker Rd. (Mrs Gioia L. Padgett). Est. 1983. Open 10-5.30, Tues. and Thurs. 10-3, Sat. 10-12, Sun. 12-5.30. CL: Wed. SIZE: Small. *STOCK: Pine, 18th-20th C, £100-£500.* LOC: Off M1, exit 38, head back towards Barnsley, turn into Darton at the church, carry on to Mapplewell, premises on crossroads. PARK: Easy. TEL: 0226 388014; home - 0226 282992 (ansaphone). SER: Valuations; curtains, loose covers, bedspreads made to order from designer fabrics.

MICKLEBRING, Nr. Rotherham

Robert Clark
Sunnyside House. (R.R. Clark). Est. 1955. Open by appointment. *STOCK: Oak and country furniture; silver, English ceramics, metalware and treen.* LOC: From M18, junction 1 turn towards Maltby and Bawtry, left at traffic lights, over crossroads into village, 2nd building on left. PARK: Own. TEL: 0709 812540; mobile - 0831 677571. VAT: Spec.

OUGHTIBRIDGE, Nr. Sheffield

Julie Goddard Antiques
7-9 Langsett Rd. South. (Miss J.P. Goddard). Est. 1982. Open 10-4.30. CL: Wed. SIZE: Large. *STOCK: Furniture - Victorian, Edwardian, £50-£5,000; Georgian, William IV, £100-£3,000. Not Stocked: Jewellery and silver.* LOC: 12 minutes from M1, exit 36 towards Sheffield, shop situated in one-way system (A616). PARK: Easy. TEL: 0742 862261. SER: Restorations (furniture - polishing, veneering, caning and re-rushing); buys at auction (furniture); framing.

ROTHERHAM

Roger Appleyard Ltd   LAPADA
Fitzwilliam Rd, Eastwood Trading Estate. Open 8-6, Sat. 8-1. SIZE: Large. *STOCK:*

Free!

28 page full colour catalogue of Antique Collectors' Club books. Over 120 titles included covering a wide range of subjects: furniture, art reference, art history, prints, jewellery, metalwork, glass, horology, ceramics, oriental carpets, collectables, garden history and design, gardening and architecture.

Available free from the
ANTIQUE COLLECTORS' CLUB

5 Church Street
Woodbridge
Suffolk IP12 1DS
Tel: (0394) 385501
Fax: (0394) 384434

Rotherham continued
General antiques, £5-£1,500. LOC: A630. PARK: Easy. TEL: 0709 367670/377770; fax - 0709 829395. SER: Packing and shipping. VAT: Stan/Spec. *Trade Only.*

John Mason Jewellers Ltd
36 High St. Open 9-5.30. *STOCK: Silver, jewellery.* TEL: 0709 382311. SER: Valuations; repairs. VAT: Spec.

John Shaw Antiques Ltd
The Old Methodist Chapel, Parkgate. Open 9.30-5.30. SIZE: Large. *STOCK: General antiques, £5-£9,000.* TEL: 0709 522340. VAT: Stan.

South Yorkshire Antiques
88-94 Broad St. (A. Swindells). Est. 1955. Open 9.30-4.30. *STOCK: General antiques and shipping furniture.* PARK: Easy. TEL: 0709 526514 or 0709 582688 (24 hr. ansaphone). SER: Valuations; restorations. VAT: Stan.

Philip Turnor Antiques
94a Broad St, Parkgate. Open 9-5, Sat. 10-4. *STOCK: Shipping furniture, 1830-1930.* TEL: 0709 524640.

SHEFFIELD
A. and C. Antiques
239 Abbeydale Rd. (C.E. Maltby). Est. 1984. Open 10.30-5. SIZE: Medium. *STOCK: General*

Sheffield continued
antiques, smalls, jewellery, £30-£500. LOC: Main rd. south of city centre, towards Chesterfield. PARK: Easy. TEL: 0742 589161.

Anita's Holme Antiques
144 Holme Lane, Hillsborough. (A.L. Spalton). Est. 1986. Open 10.30-5.30. SIZE: Medium. *STOCK: General antiques, 19th C, £50-£100.* LOC: A61, turn left at traffic lights opposite Owlerton Sports Stadium, shop 1.5 miles on right. PARK: Easy. TEL: 0742 336698.

Chimney Piece Antique Fires
262 South Rd, Walkley. (J. Young). Open 9.30-5. CL: Wed. *STOCK: Fireplaces.* TEL: 0742 346085.

Cobwebs
208 Whitham Rd, Broomhill. (S.L. Sleath). Est. 1978. Open 10-5. CL: Thurs. and Tues. SIZE: Small. *STOCK: Ceramics, small furniture, jewellery, pictures, 19th C, £5-£300.* LOC: Main road near university. PARK: Nearby. TEL: 0742 681923. SER: Valuations; upholstery.

The Doll's House Antiques
(Mrs S. Gray). Est. 1960. Open by appointment. SIZE: Small. *STOCK: Furniture, small general antiques, 18th to early 20th C, £5-£2,000; dolls, 19th to early 20th C; jewellery, Victorian and Edwardian clothes and accessories, collectors' items; oil paintings and watercolours.* Not Stocked: Stamps, books, coins. TEL: 0742 360061. SER: Restorations (dolls, antique fabrics and garments, porcelain, silver, plate, jewellery, furniture, pictures); buys at auction.

Dronfield Antiques
375-377 Abbeydale Rd. (H.J. Greaves). Est. 1968. Open 10.30-5.30. CL: Thurs. and Sat. except by appointment. SIZE: Large + warehouses. *STOCK: Trade and shipping goods, Victoriana, glass, china.* LOC: A621, 1 mile south of city centre. PARK: Easy. TEL: 0742 550172/581821; home and fax - 0742 556024. VAT: Stan.

Ellis's
144 Whitham Rd. Est. 1943. Open 9-6. *STOCK: Oriental carpets and rugs.* TEL: 0742 662920. VAT: Stan.

Fillibuster and Booth Ltd
749 Ecclesall Rd. Open 10.30-5.30. CL: Thurs. *STOCK: General antiques and collectors' items, oils and watercolours, 1880-1920.* TEL: 0742 682653.

Findley Antiques
314 Langsett Rd. (B. Findley). Est. 1973. Open 9.30-5.30, Sun. by appointment. SIZE: Medium. *STOCK: Shipping items, 1900-1940, £25-£35; bric-a-brac, 1850-1950, £2-£10; general antiques, Victoriana, £100-£150.* LOC: 1 mile from city centre on A616. PARK: Easy. TEL: 0742 346088; home - 0246 435521. VAT: Stan.

Central Sheffield

© The Automobile Association 1987

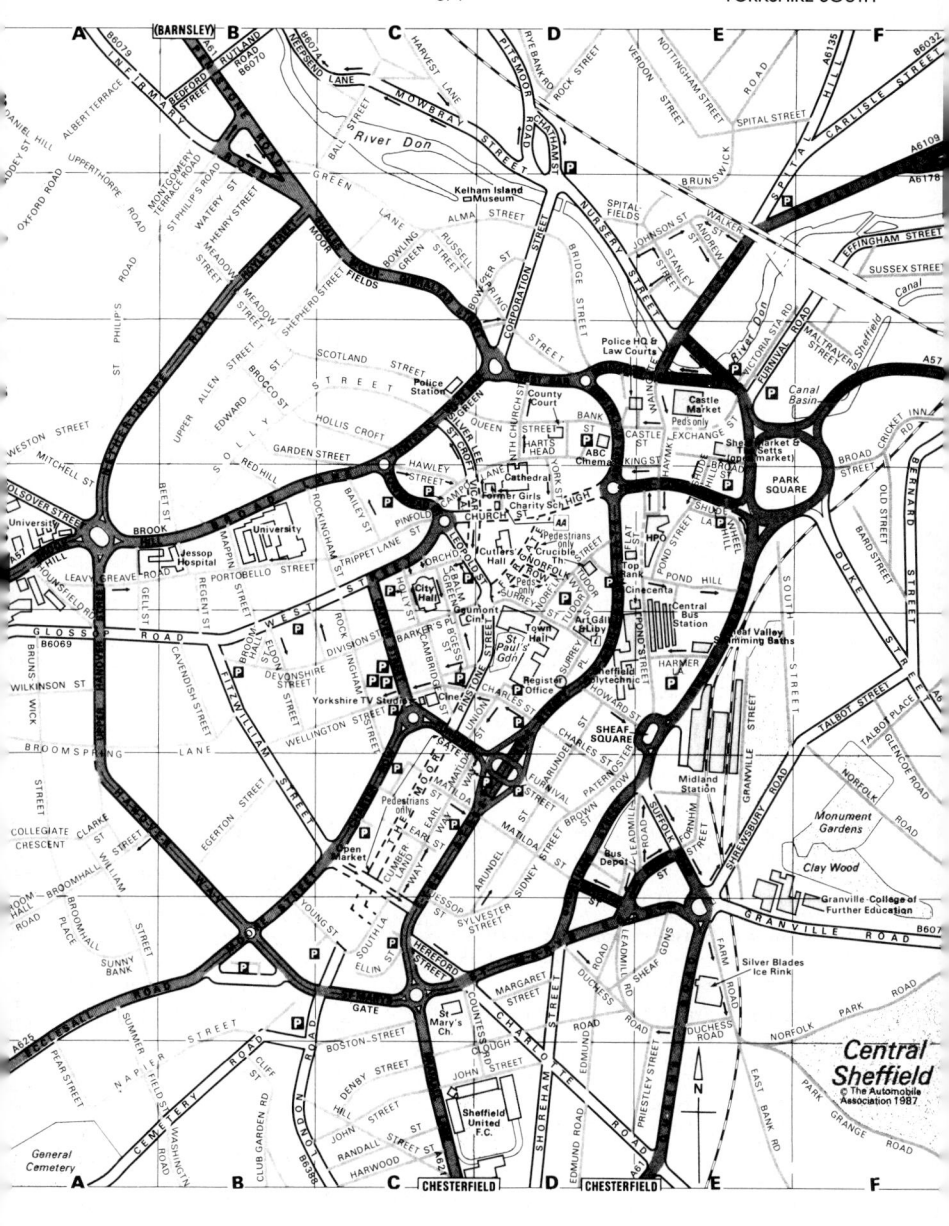

Key to Town Plan

AA Recommended roads	Car Parks
Other roads	Parks and open spaces
Restricted roads	AA Service Centre
Buildings of interest	

© Automobile Association 1988.

Sheffield continued
Fulwood Antiques and The Basement Gallery
7 Brooklands Ave. (Mrs H.J. Wills). Est. 1977. Open Wed. and Fri. 10-5, Sat. 10-1. SIZE: Medium. *STOCK: General small items, fine furniture; oil paintings and watercolours, 19th-20th C, £50-£5,000.* LOC: From city centre towards Broomhill, Fulwood Rd., Nethergreen and straight on for Fulwood. PARK: Easy. TEL: 0742 307387; home - 0742 301346. SER: Valuations; restorations (ceramics, metal and pictures).

Fun Antiques
72 Abbeydale Rd. (B. Harrap). Est. 1978. Open by appointment. SIZE: Medium. *STOCK: Unusual and collectable items including sporting items, toys, advertising, Christmas, arcade and fairground items, 20th C, £5-£1,000.* PARK: Easy. TEL: 0742 553424. SER: Valuations; installations. FAIRS: Harrow, Ardingly, Newark, Stoneleigh. VAT: Stan. *Trade Only.*

Gilbert and Sons
16 Abbeydale Rd. (B. and C. Gilbert). Open 9.30-5. *STOCK: Shipping items.* TEL: 0742 552043.

G.H. Green   LAPADA
334 Abbeydale Rd. Est. 1962. Open 9.30-5. *STOCK: Period and later furniture.* TEL: 0742 550881; home - 0742 309279. VAT: Stan/Spec.

Hibbert Bros. Ltd
117 Norfolk St. (P.A. Greaves). Open 9-5.30. *STOCK: Oils and watercolours.* TEL: 0742 722038.

Alan Hill Books, Sheffield
261 Glossop Rd. Est. 1980. Open 10.30-5.30. *STOCK: Antiquarian books, maps and prints.* TEL: 0742 780594.

Hinson Fine Paintings   BADA
290 Glossop Rd. Open 9-5, Sat. 9-12. *STOCK: Oil paintings, watercolours, fine antiques, 19th C.* TEL: 0742 722082. VAT: Spec.

A.E. Jameson and Co   LAPADA
257 Glossop Rd. (P. Jameson). Est. 1883. Open 9-5.45. SIZE: Large. *STOCK: Furniture, pre-1820, £20-£15,000; glass, china, weapons.* LOC: A57. TEL: 0742 723846; home - 0742 726189. SER: Valuations; restorations (furniture); buys at auction. VAT: Stan/Spec.

The Oriental Rug Shop
763 Abbeydale Rd. (A.A. Hezaveh). Open 10-5. *STOCK: Handmade rugs and carpets.* TEL: 0742 552240/589821; fax - 0742 509088.

Paraphernalia
66/68 Abbeydale Rd. Est. 1972. *STOCK: General antiques, stripped pine, lighting, brass and iron beds.* TEL: 0742 550203. VAT: Stan.

Peter James Antiques
112 and 114 London Rd. (P.J. Conboy). Est. 1980. Open 9.30-5. SIZE: Large. *STOCK:*

Sheffield continued
Furniture - mahogany, walnut, pine, oak and satin walnut, 1800-1920. PARK: Easy. TEL: 0742 700273. SER: Restorations. VAT: Stan.

Porter Prints (Broomhill)
205 Whitham Rd. *STOCK: Maps and prints.* TEL: 0742 685751.

Pot-Pourri
647 Ecclesall Rd, Hunters Bar. (Mrs M. Needham). Est. 1972. Open 10-5.30. *STOCK: Old and antique jewellery, silver, Sheffield plate.* TEL: 0742 669790. VAT: Stan.

N.P. and A. Salt Antiques   LAPADA
Unit 1 and 2, Barmouth Rd. Open 9.30-4.30. CL: Sat. SIZE: Large. *STOCK: Victorian furniture, shipping goods, smalls and toys.* TEL: 0742 582672. SER: Valuations; packing; shipping; courier. *Trade Only.*

Sheffield Pine Centre (inc. Canterbury Place Antiques)
356/358 South Rd. Warehouse - Unit E, Lowfield Cutlery Forge, Guernsey Rd. (P. Coldwell). Open 9-5.30. SIZE: Large. *STOCK: Stripped pine and general antiques.* TEL: 0742 336103/587458.

Tilley's Vintage Magazine Shop
281 Shoreham St. (A.G.J. and A.A.J.C. Tilley). Est. 1979. Open 9-5, other times by appointment. SIZE: Large. *STOCK: Magazines, comics, news-papers, books, postcards, programmes, posters, cigarette cards, prints, ephemera.* LOC: Opposite Sheffield United F.C. PARK: Easy. TEL: 0742 752442. SER: Mail order; valuations.

Turn of the Century
48-50 Barber Rd, Crookesmoor. Open 10-6 (prior telephone call advisable), Sun. and other times by appointment. SIZE: Medium. *STOCK: English furniture, 18th-19th C, £100-£4,000; longcase clocks, 18th to early 19th C, £1,500-£3,500; wall clocks, 19th C, from £500; oil paintings and watercolours, 19th C, from £150; general antiques and collectors items, 18th-19th C, £20-£500.* Not Stocked: Books, coins, militaria. LOC: Follow A57 or inner ring road (Upper Hanover St.-Netherthorpe Rd.) to University roundabout, exit into Bolsover St., continue for 1/2 mile, over traffic lights, shop 150 yards on right. PARK: Easy. TEL: 0742 670947. SER: Repairs and restorations (longcase clocks). VAT: Mainly Spec.

Paul Ward Antiques
Owl House, 8 Burnell Rd., Owlerton. Resident. Est. 1976. Open by appointment. SIZE: Large. *STOCK: Matched sets of Victorian dining and kitchen chairs, country chairs, general antiques.* LOC: 2 miles north of city on A61. TEL: 0742 335980. VAT: Stan/Spec.

THORNE, Nr. Doncaster
Canterbury House
24 Finkle St. Est. 1977. Open 9-5. *STOCK: Jewellery and watches.* TEL: 0405 812102.

Antique Collectors' Club Titles

Victorian and Edwardian Furniture Price Guide and Reasons for Values
by John Andrews
In this major revision of his highly acclaimed Price Guide to Victorian, Edwardian and 1920s Furniture, John Andrews has written a thorough, logical and easily understandable guide to what is the most popular period in British antique furniture today.
**ISBN 1 85149 118 X, 300pp
1,000 b & w illus, 100 col illus, £29.95**

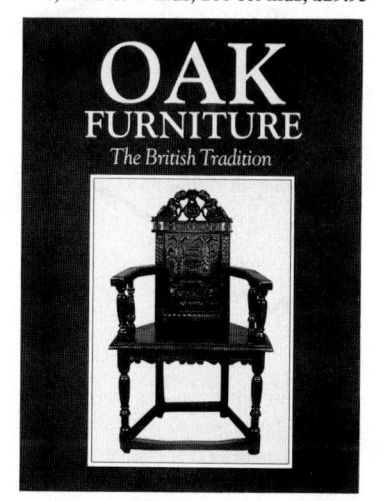

British Antique Furniture: Price Guide and Reasons for Values
by John Andrews
For the last twenty years this book has in its various editions outsold all other books on British antique furniture simply because it is unique in explaining what to look for when assessing the value of antique pieces. This classic guide consists of some 1,200 photographs specially selected by the experienced author to show just how and why values vary. In this third edition, the colour plates have been added to illustrate the huge financial importance of patination and colour, something which has never before been explained and illustrated.
**ISBN 1 85149 090 6, 392pp
1,150 b & w illus, 106 col illus, £35.00**

Available from:
Antique Collectors' Club, 5 Church Street
Woodbridge, Suffolk IP12 1DS
Tel: (0394) 385501 Fax: (0394) 384434

or Market Street Industrial Park
Wappingers' Falls, New York 12590, USA
Tel: 914 297 0003 Fax: 914 297 0068

Oak Furniture - The British Tradition *by Victor Chinnery*
The only serious book on oak in print, this important and deeply researched work examines regional influences on furniture design, construction and other methods of dating, and has a useful pictorial index arranged chronologically. **ISBN 1 85149 013 2, 620pp, 2,000 b & w illus, 22 col illus, £49.50**

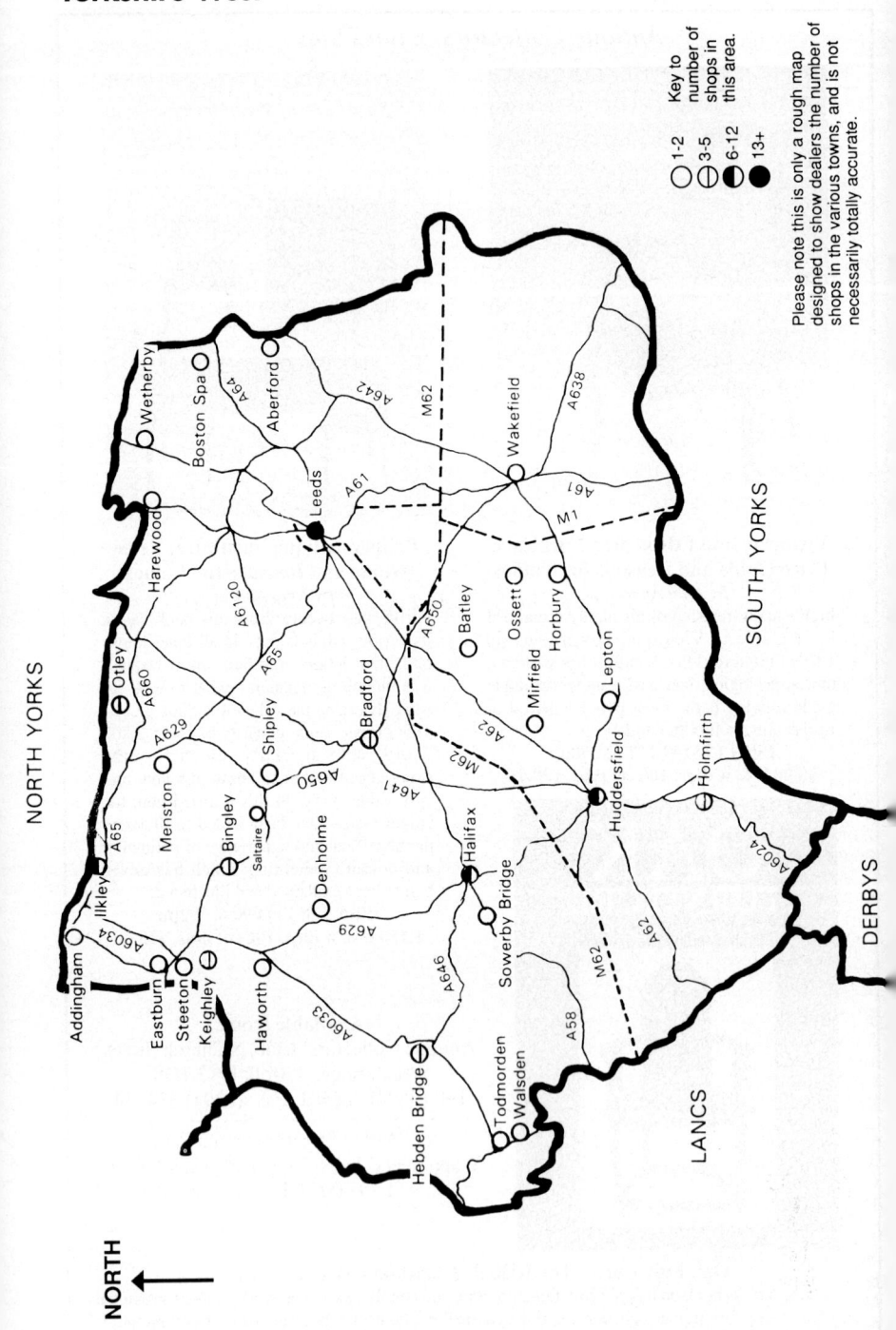

Yorkshire West

582

Yorkshire West

Manor Barn Pine
SPECIALISTS IN ANTIQUE PINE FURNITURE

The most comprehensive range of high quality original antique pine in the North of England. English, Welsh, Irish, Scottish and continental pieces always in stock. Shipping and good quality mahogany pieces also available.

**BURNSIDE MILL, MAIN STREET
ADDINGHAM, ILKLEY, WEST YORKSHIRE
TEL. (0943) 830176**

ABERFORD
Aberford Antiques Ltd
Hicklam House. (J.W.H. Long and C.A. Robinson). Est. 1973. Open 9-5.30, Sundays 10-5.30. SIZE: Large. *STOCK: Stripped pine, Victorian and period, £10-£1,500; Victoriana, £5-£1,000; local prints and maps; Victorian oil paintings.* LOC: Opposite Almshouses at entrance of village. PARK: Easy. TEL: 0532 813209; fax - 0532 813121. SER: Fitted pine kitchens. VAT: Stan/Spec.

ADDINGHAM, Nr. Ilkley
Manor Barn
Burnside Mill, Main St. (Whiteley Wright Ltd). Est. 1972. Open 8-5.30. SIZE: Warehouse. *STOCK: Pine, 17th-19th C and reproduction; oak and shipping goods.* PARK: Easy. TEL: 0943 830176. VAT: Stan/Spec.

BINGLEY
Bingley Antiques Centre
Keighley Rd. (J.B. and J. Poole). Est. 1965. Open 9.30-5, Tues. 10-5, Sun. 2-5. SIZE: Large. *STOCK: Furniture, 18th-19th C; pottery, porcelain, garden furniture. Shipping goods in nearby warehouse.* LOC: On A650, opposite parish church. PARK: Easy. TEL: 0274 567316. SER: Valuations. VAT: Stan/Spec.

E. Carrol
5 Ryshworth Hall, Keighley Rd., Crossflatts. Est. 1970. Open by appointment. SIZE: Small. *STOCK: Oil paintings, watercolours.* LOC: A650. PARK: Easy. TEL: 0274 568800. VAT: Stan.

Curio Cottage
3 Millgate. (Mrs W.J. Windle). Open 2.30-5.30. CL: Tues. and Fri. SIZE: Small. *STOCK: Victoriana, curios and stripped pine.* TEL: Home - 0274 612975.

Victorian House Shop
88 Main St. (J. Foster). Open 11-5, Sun. 2-5. CL: Mon. and Tues. *STOCK: Victorian and reproduction fireplaces, general antiques, bric-a-brac.* TEL: 0274 569278.

BOSTON SPA, by Wetherby
London House Oriental Rugs and Carpets
London House, High St. (M.A. and Mrs I.T.H. Ries). Open 10-5.30 including Sun. CL: Mon. SIZE: Large. *STOCK: Caucasian, Turkish, Afghan and Persian rugs, runners and carpets, £50-£10,000; kelims, tapestries and textiles.* LOC: Off A1, south of Wetherby. PARK: Easy. TEL: 0937 845123; home - same. SER: Valuations; restorations (Oriental carpets and rugs); buys at auction (Oriental carpets and rugs). VAT: Stan.

BRADFORD
Collectors' Corner
5-7 Frizinghall Rd. (C. and G. Douthwaite). Est. 1970. Open 2-7 or by appointment. CL: Mon. and Thurs. *STOCK: Victoriana, bric-a-brac, postcards.* PARK: Easy. TEL: 0274 487098.

The Corner Shop
89 Oak Lane. (Miss Badland). Est. 1961. Open Tues. 2-5.30, Thurs. and Sat. 11-5.30. *STOCK: Pottery, small furniture, clocks and general items.*

Langley's (Jewellers) Ltd
59 Godwin St. TEL: 0274 722280. VAT: Stan.

Low Moor Antiques
233 and 234 Huddersfield Rd, Low Moor. (J.A. Bowler). Est. 1972. Open 9-12 and 2-5. CL: Wed. and Sat. p.m. *STOCK: Shipping furniture, pine, silver plate and general antiques.* TEL: 0274 671047/604835.

EASTBURN, Nr. Keighley
M. Kelly Antiques
41 Main Rd. Est. 1968. Open 9.30-5. SIZE: Medium. *STOCK: English and continental pine, darkwoods and small items, 19th C, to £1,000.* PARK: Easy. TEL: 0535 653002. SER: Restorations (pine stripping). VAT: Stan.

Architectural Salvage
– the largest stock in the UK

A huge mill full of original doors, fire surrounds, pews, stained glass, panelling, shopfittings and bric-a-brac. **PLUS** reproduction lighting, home bars, architectural metalwork, furniture, garden statuary and home decor items.

4 mins from M62 (Junct 24)

Victoria Mills open Mon – Fri 8.30 – 5.30 Sat 8.30 – 5.00

Andy Thornton Architectural Antiques Ltd.
Victoria Mills, Stainland Road, Greetland, Halifax, W Yorks HX4 8AD
Tel: 0422-377314 Fax: 0422-310372

HALIFAX

Ken Balme Antiques
10/12 Keighley Rd, Ovenden. Est. 1986. Open 9-5, Wed. 1-5. *STOCK: General antiques especially Victorian glass and commemorative ware.* TEL: 0422 344193/244830.

Peter Bennion
Open by appointment only. *STOCK: Pottery and porcelain, 18th to early 19th C.* TEL: 0422 824182.

Boulevard Reproductions
369 Skircoat Green Rd. (T. Bright). Open 9.30-7pm, Sun. for viewing. *STOCK: Furniture.* TEL: 0422 368628.

Jean Brear
19 Causeway Head, Burnley Rd. Est. 1955. *STOCK: Antiquarian books; maps, atlases, prints, oils, manuscripts, small antiques.* TEL: 0422 366144.

Collectors Old Toy Shop and Antiques
89 Northgate. (S. Haley). Open 10.30-4.30. *STOCK: Collectors toys, clocks and antiques.* TEL: 0422 360434/822148.

Halifax Antiques Centre
Queens Rd. Est. 1981. Open Tues.-Sat. 10-5. SIZE: Large - 30 dealers. *STOCK: Art deco jewellery, porcelain, linen, costume, mechanical*

Halifax continued
music, pine, oak, mahogany, kitchenalia, decorative collectables. LOC: Follow A58 to Kings Cross, turn at Trafalgar Inn into Queens Rd. corner, 2nd set of lights. PARK: Own. TEL: 0422 366657.

Muir Hewitt Art Deco Originals
Halifax Antiques Centre, Queens Rd. Open 10-5. CL: Mon. *STOCK: Pottery including Susie Cooper, Charlotte Rhead and Clarice Cliff; Shelley ceramics; furniture, lighting and mirrors.* LOC: 1 mile west of town centre on the A58 (A646), turn right into Queens Rd. at Trafalgar Inn traffic lights, centre is at next traffic lights (opp. Lloyds Bank). PARK: Easy. TEL: 0422 366657; home - 0274 882051.

Hillside Antiques
Denholme Gate Rd, Hipperholme. (M. and J. Preston). Est. 1981. Open 10-12.15 and 2-5.15. CL: Wed. SIZE: Small. *STOCK: Pottery, porcelain, small furniture, copper, brass, glass, 1870-1940. Not Stocked: Linen, clothing and gold.* LOC: A644, 150yds. north of Hipperholme crossroads. PARK: Easy. TEL: Home - 0422 202744. FAIRS: Local.

North Bridge Antiques
5 North Bridge. (S. Lester). Open 9-5, Thurs. 9-1. *STOCK: Shipping goods.* TEL: 0422 358474.

Halifax continued
Scott and Varey
10 Prescott St. (W.B. Scott). Est. 1963. Open 9-5.30. SIZE: Large. *STOCK: Furniture, clocks, cast iron, general antiques.* LOC: Town centre near Halifax Building Society. PARK: Easy. TEL: 0422 366928 (24hrs.); fax - 0422 340 277.

Andy Thornton Architectural Antiques Ltd
Victoria Mills, Stainland Rd., Greetland. Est. 1973. Open 8.30-5.30, Sat. 8.30-5. SIZE: Large. *STOCK: Architectural antiques - doors, stained glass, fireplaces, panelling, garden furniture, light fittings, pews and decor items.* PARK: Easy. TEL: 0422 377314; fax - 0422 310372. VAT: Stan.

HAWORTH
Haworth Antiques
Lees Mill, Lees Lane. (R. Smith). Open 8.30-4.30, weekends by appointment. SIZE: Large. *STOCK: General antiques and shipping goods, 1850-1930.* LOC: Main road into Haworth. PARK: Easy. TEL: 0535 643535; home - 0535 644144. SER: Valuations; restorations (furniture). VAT: Stan. *Trade only.*

HEBDEN BRIDGE, Nr. Halifax
Cornucopia Antiques
9 West End. (C. Nassor). Open Thurs., Fri. and Sun. 1-5, Sat. 11-5. *STOCK: Pine, oak and mahogany furniture, art deco, lamps, lighting, pottery, bric-a-brac, kitchenware.* LOC: Town centre behind Pennine Information Centre. PARK: Easy. TEL: 0422 844497.

Larkhall Antiques
39 Market St. (J. Blom). Open 10-5, Sat. 11-5, Sun. 1-5. CL: Tues. *STOCK: General antiques especially furniture.*

HOLMFIRTH, Nr. Huddersfield
Andrew Spencer Bottomley
The Coach House, Huddersfield Rd. Open by appointment. *STOCK: Arms and armour including pistols, swords, daggers, helmets and suits of armour.* TEL: 0484 685234; fax - 0484 681551. SER: Valuations; television and film hire; postal business - catalogues available.

Chapel House Fireplaces
Netherfield House, St. Georges Rd., Scholes. Open strictly by appointment Tues. 9-7, Wed.-Sat. 9-5. *STOCK: Georgian, Victorian and Edwardian grates and mantels; French chimneypieces.* TEL: 0484 682275.

The Toll House Bookshop
32/34 Huddersfield Rd. (E.V. Beardsell). Est. 1978. Open 10-5. *STOCK: Books including antiquarian.* TEL: 0484 686541.

Holmfirth continued
Upperbridge Antiques
9 Huddersfield Rd. (Mrs M. Coop and I. Ridings). Open 1-5, Sun. 2-5. CL: Tues. SIZE: Small. *STOCK: Pottery, linen, metalware, interesting items, Victorian to art deco, £5-£150.* Not Stocked: Jewellery. LOC: A635. PARK: Nearby. TEL: 0484 687200.

HORBURY, Nr. Wakefield
The Old Tithe Barn
16 Tithe Barn St. (J. S. Ingham). Est. 1945. Open daily. CL: Wed. *STOCK: General antiques, especially furniture.* LOC: Between Ossett and Wakefield. PARK: Easy. TEL: 0924 277439; home - same. SER: Restorations (upholstery, French polishing, furniture repairs). VAT: Stan.

HUDDERSFIELD
Beau Monde Antiques
343a Bradford Rd, Fartown. (R.M. Schofield). Est. 1963. Open 9.30-6, Sat. 9.30-5. CL: Wed. pm. SIZE: Medium. *STOCK: Furniture, general antiques, bric-a-brac, £5-£500.* LOC: On A641, 1 mile from town centre. PARK: Easy. TEL: 0484 427565.

Peter Berry Antiques
119 Wakefield Rd, Moldgreen. Open 9.30-5.30, Sat. 9.30-1 and by appointment. *STOCK: Georgian and Victorian furniture; early blue and white porcelain, silver and china.* TEL: 0484 544229(answerphone). SER: Restorations.

Berry Brow Antiques
90/92 Dodds Royd, Woodhead Rd., Berry Brow. (M. Griffiths). Est. 1972. Open 10-2. SIZE: Medium. *STOCK: Victorian and Edwardian furniture, china, bric-a-brac.* LOC: 2 miles from town centre on Holmfirth Rd. PARK: Easy. TEL: 0484 663320.

D.W. Dyson (Antique Weapons)
Wood Lea, Shepley. Est. 1974. Open by appointment only. *STOCK: Antique weapons including cased duelling pistols, armour, miniature arms, rare and unusual items.* LOC: Off A616. PARK: Easy. TEL: 0484 607331; home - same. SER: Valuations; buys at auction (antique weapons); special presentation items made to order in precious metals; advice on restoration; interior design; finder (film props). FAIRS: Dorchester Hotel, London; Dortmund, Stuttgart and other major foreign. VAT: Spec.

Fillans (Antiques) - Geoff Neary Ltd.
2 Market Walk. (G. Neary). NAG FGA. Est. 1852. Open 8.45-5.30. SIZE: Small. *STOCK: English silver, 1700-1980; Sheffield plate, 1760-1840, £10-£500; jewellery, £50-£10,000.* Not Stocked: Other than above. PARK: Town centre multi-storey. TEL: 0484 531609. SER: Valuations; restorations; buys at auction (English silver and jewellery). VAT: Stan/Spec.

Cooper's of Ilkley

Dealers in Fine Antiques and Works of Art for over 80 years.

LAPADA MEMBER

Specialists in walnut, mahogany and oak period furniture, silver, porcelain, paintings, pewter and copper

VALUATIONS

Visit our new extensive showrooms at
**33/35 Church Street
and 50 Leeds Road, ILKLEY, Yorkshire
Tel: Ilkley 608020**

TRADE WELCOMED

Huddersfield continued

Heritage Antiques
10 Byram Arcade, Westgate. (Mrs H. Beaumont and Mrs B. Noble). Open 10-5. CL: Wed. STOCK: General antiques. TEL: 0484 514667.

Huddersfield Antiques
170 Wakefield Rd, Moldgreen. Est. 1971. Open 10.30-4.30 or by appointment. SIZE: Medium. STOCK: Victoriana, bric-a-brac, collectors' items, postcards; warehouse of trade and shipping goods. PARK: Easy. TEL: 0484 539747. SER: Valuations; buys at auction.

"Second Childhood"
26 Byram Arcade, Westgate. Est. 1984. Open 10.30-3.30 or by appointment. CL: Mon. and Wed. SIZE: Small. STOCK: Victorian and Edwardian dolls, dolls' houses, toys, teddy bears, Victorian to 1950s; associated items. LOC: 100 yards from railway and bus stations. TEL: 0484 530117; home - 0484 603854. SER: Valuations; restorations (dolls' hospital and teddy repairs). FAIRS: Major U.K. dolls.

ILKLEY

Burrows and Raper
37 The Grove. (J.B. and L.L. Burrows). Est. 1990. Open 10-5.30. SIZE: Medium. STOCK: Furniture, 18th C, £200-£8,000; silver, 19th C,

Ilkley continued

£30-£400; brass, copper and ceramics; decorative items including tapestry cushions and beeswax candles, 20th C, £1-£100. LOC: West end of The Grove, in main shopping street. PARK: Easy. TEL: 0943 817631. SER: Restorations; buys at auction. VAT: Spec.

J.H. Cooper and Son (Ilkley) Ltd
LAPADA
33-35 Church St, and 50 Leeds Rd. Est. 1910. Open 9-1 and 2-5.30. SIZE: Large. STOCK: English furniture, pre-1830, £100-£10,000; porcelain and silver, pictures. Not Stocked: Post-1880 items. LOC: A65. PARK: Easy. TEL: 0943 608020. SER: Valuations; restorations (furniture); buys at auction. VAT: Stan/Spec.

Keith Richardson Antiques
26 Leeds Rd. Est. 1974. Open 9-5. CL: Wed. SIZE: Medium. STOCK: Jewellery, dolls, glass, furniture, Victoriana, commemorative ware. PARK: Adjacent street. TEL: 0943 600045.

Jack Shaw and Co
The Old Grammar School, Skipton Rd. Est. 1945. Open 9.30-12.45 and 2-5.30. CL: Wed. STOCK: Silver, furniture. TEL: 0943 609467. VAT: Spec.

Simon
25 Church St. (S.G.H. Pratt). SIZE: Medium. STOCK: Furniture and clocks, 17th-19th C,

Ilkley continued
£200-£15,000. Not Stocked: Coins, weapons, jewellery. PARK: Adjacent street. TEL: 0943 602788. SER: Valuations; buys at auction. VAT: Stan/Spec.

KEIGHLEY

Barleycote Hall Antiques   LAPADA
2 Janet St, Crossroads. (R. Hoskins). Resident. Est. 1968. Open most days 11-5. *STOCK: Georgian and Victorian furniture, porcelain, metalwork, paintings, jewellery, Victorian and Edwardian clothing, clocks of all types.* LOC: A629, turn right towards Haworth, 600yds. on right. TEL: 0535 644776. VAT: Stan/Spec.

Keighleys of Keighley
153 East Parade. (B. Keighley and Son). Est. 1939. Open 9-5. CL: Tues. *STOCK: Furniture, jewellery, gold and silver, china.* LOC: Next to the Victoria Hotel. PARK: Easy. TEL: 0535 663439; home - 0535 607180. VAT: Stan.

Real Macoy
2 Janet St. (D. Seal). Open most days 11-5. *STOCK: Quilts, textiles, period clothing.* TEL: 0535 644776.

D. Richardson Antiques
72 Haworth Rd, Crossroads. Open 9-5. CL: Sat. *STOCK: General antiques and shipping goods.* PARK: Easy at rear. TEL: 0535 644982.

LEEDS

Aladdin's Cave
19 Queens Arcade. (P. and S. Isaacs). Est. 1954. CL: Mon. SIZE: Small. *STOCK: Jewellery, £15-£250; collectors' items; all 19th-20th C.* LOC: Town centre. PARK: 100 yards. TEL: 0532 457903; home - 0532 842425. SER: Valuations. VAT: Stan.

The Antique Exchange
400 Kirkstall Rd. (S. Wood). Est. 1976. Open 10.30-3. CL: Tues. and Wed. *STOCK: Furniture including satin walnut and ash, 19th-20th C, £150-£2,000.* LOC: Kirkstall Rd. is 1/2 mile west of Yorkshire Television Studios. PARK: Easy. TEL: 0532 743513. VAT: Stan/Spec.

Batty's Antiques
3 Stanningley Rd. (R.J. Sanderson). Open 10-5. CL: Wed. *STOCK: Period and reproduction oak and pine.* TEL: 0532 639011.

Bishop House Antiques
169 Town St, Rodley. (Mrs J.M. Bishop). Est. 1977. Open Sat. 2-5.30, or by appointment. *STOCK: General antiques, porcelain and glass.* TEL: 0532 563071.

Boston Pine Co.
Globe Mills, Back Row, Holbeck. (Mrs K. Harper and K. Burns). Open 9-4.30. *STOCK:*

An Antique Collectors' Club Title

The Price Guide to Antique Silver
2nd edition by Peter Waldron
with 1992 prices
One of our most popular titles advises collectors on what to buy and what to avoid. Detailed examination of fakes is an important feature of this classic work.
ISBN 1 85149 165 1, 368pp
1,172 b & w illus, £35.00

Available from:
Antique Collectors' Club, 5 Church Street, Woodbridge, Suffolk IP12 1DS
Tel: (0394) 385501 Fax: (0394) 384434

or Market Street Industrial Park, Wappingers' Falls, New York 12590, USA
Tel: 914 297 0003 Fax: 914 297 0068

Leeds continued

Restored pine. TEL: 0532 441650/428007. SER: Hand-built kitches and furniture made from old timber, traditional and painted finishes; restorations; stripping.

Coins International and Antiques International
1 and 2 Melbourne St. (J.M. Harrison). Open 9-5. CL: Sat. *STOCK: Coins, banknotes, medals, silver, gold, general antiques, jewellery, crested china, cigarette cards.* PARK: Easy. TEL: 0532 434230; fax - 0532 345544.

Geary Antiques
114 Richardshaw Lane, Stanningley, Pudsey. (J.A. Geary). Est. 1933. Open 10-5.30. CL: Wed. SIZE: Warehouse. *STOCK: Furniture, Georgian, Victorian and Edwardian; copper and brass.* LOC: 500 yds. from South Leeds Ring Rd. PARK: Easy. TEL: 0532 564122. SER: Restorations (furniture). VAT: Stan/Spec.

William Goldsmith
23 County Arcade. (R.F. Chesterman). Est. 1961. Open 9-5.30. SIZE: Medium. *STOCK: Jewellery, 19th-20th C, £50-£500; clocks, 19th C, £100-£1,000; samplers and prints, 18th-19th C, £25-£100.* LOC: Town centre. PARK: Nearby. TEL: 0532 451345. SER: Valuations; restorations. VAT: Stan.

Kirkstall Antiques
366 Kirkstall Rd. (S.R. and A. Gibson). Est. 1973. Open 10.30-3. CL: Tues. and Wed. SIZE: Medium. *STOCK: Victorian and Edwardian furniture, stripped and painted pine, £5-£500; general small items, £1-£100.* LOC: A65. PARK: Easy. TEL: 0532 757367. VAT: Stan/Spec.

Oakwood Gallery
613 Roundhay Rd, Oakwood. Open 9-6. *STOCK: Fine paintings and prints.* PARK: Easy. TEL: 0532 401348. SER: Framing; restorations; conservation.

Originals
193 Meanwood Rd. Open Thurs.-Sat. 10-3, other times by appointment. *STOCK: Fireplaces; spare parts for Victorian fireplaces.* TEL: 0532 431613.

Parker Gallery
The Grange, 6 Grange Croft, Alwoodly. Open by appointment. *STOCK: Oils, 19th to early 20th C, £200-£5,000.* TEL: 0532 662302; mobile - 0860 253323.

The Piano Shop
39 Holbeck Lane. (M. Besbrode and B. Seals). Open 9-5. *STOCK: Pianos.* TEL: 0532 443685. SER: Restorations; French polishing; hire.

Bryan Smith
26-28 Chapeltown, Pudsey. Open 10-5.30. CL: Sat. *STOCK: Furniture, porcelain, pottery, oils*

Leeds continued

and watercolours, glass and collectable items. PARK: Easy. TEL: 0532 555815; mobile - 0860 393260.

Thirkills Antiques
107 West End Lane, Horsforth. Est. 1963. *STOCK: Paintings, musical, violins, 18th C pottery, porcelain, furniture, smalls.* LOC: 5 mins. south of Leeds-Bradford Airport. TEL: 0532 589160.

Waterloo Antiques Centre
Waterloo House, Crown St. Open 10-5. CL: Mon. SIZE: 45 dealers. *STOCK: General antiques.* LOC: Back of Corn Exchange. TEL: 0532 423194.

Windsor House Antiques (Leeds) Ltd.
LAPADA
18-20 Benson St. (D.K. Smith). Est. 1959. Open 9-5. CL: Sat. SIZE: Large. *STOCK: English furniture, 18th-19th C; paintings, objects.* PARK: Easy. TEL: 0532 444666; fax - 0532 426394. VAT: Stan/Spec.

Year Dot
15 Market St. Arcade. (P. Davis). Open 9.30-5. *STOCK: Oriental pottery and porcelain, paintings, clocks, barometers, glass, copper, brass, bric-a-brac, jewellery, watches.* TEL: 0532 460860.

LEPTON, Nr. Huddersfield

K.L.M. & Co. Antiques
The Antique Shop, Wakefield Rd. (K.L. & J. Millington). Est. 1980. Open 10.30-5, other times by appointment. SIZE: Large and warehouse. *STOCK: Furniture including stripped pine, to 1930s, £25-£1,000; pianos.* LOC: A642 Wakefield road from Huddersfield, shop opposite village church. PARK: Easy and at rear. TEL: 0484 607763; home - 0484 607548. SER: Valuations. VAT: Stan.

MENSTON

Antiques
101 Bradford Rd. (W. and J. Hanlon). Est. 1974. *STOCK: Handworked linen, textiles, pottery, porcelain, art nouveau, art deco, silver, plate, jewellery, small furniture, collectors items, barometers.* PARK: Forecourt. TEL: 0943 877634; home - 0943 463693.

Park Antiques
2 North View, Main St. Resident. Est. 1975. Open 10-6.30, Sun. 10-5.30. CL: Mon. and Tues. SIZE: Medium. *STOCK: Furniture, Georgian to Edwardian, £500-£5,000; decorative items, £100-£1,000, soft furnishings, £500-£2,000.* Not Stocked: Pine, silver. LOC: Opposite the park. PARK: Easy. TEL: 0943 872392. VAT: Stan/Spec.

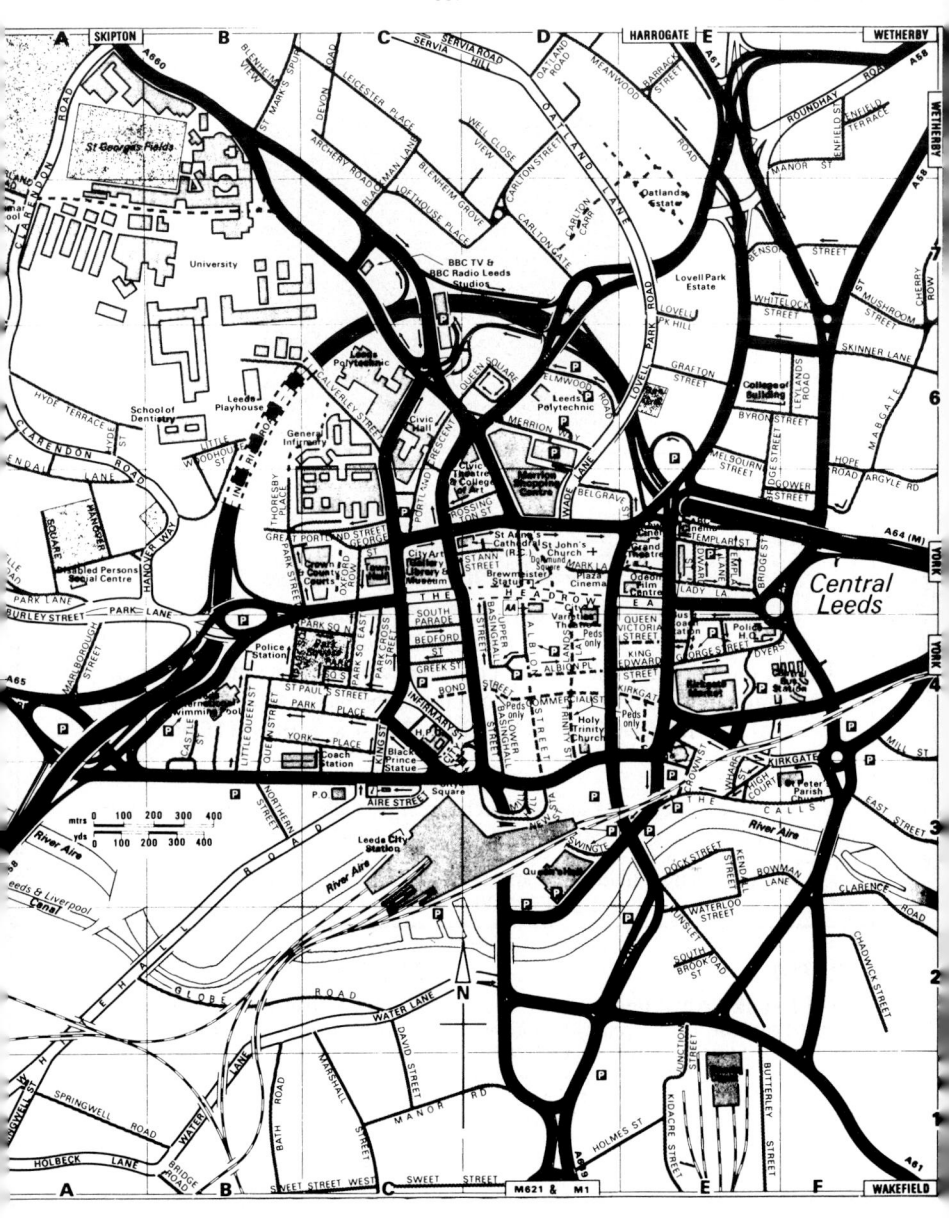

Key to Town Plan

AA Recommended roads
Other roads
Restricted roads
Buildings of interest
Car Parks
Parks and open spaces
AA Service Centre

© Automobile Association 1988.

An Antique Collectors' Club Title

Starting to Collect Silver
by John Luddington

This is *the* book for the novice collector, which guides the reader through the pitfalls of the silver trade and discusses the pieces to avoid.

ISBN 0 907462 48 0. 228pp, 345 b & w illus, £25.00

Available from:
Antique Collectors' Club, 5 Church Street, Woodbridge, Suffolk IP12 1DS
Tel: (0394) 385501 Fax: (0394) 384434

or Market Street Industrial Park, Wappingers' Falls, New York 12590, USA
Tel: 914 297 0003 Fax: 914 297 0068

MIRFIELD

David Brooke Antiques
9A Pratt Lane. Est. 1980. Open by appointment. SIZE: Small. *STOCK: Royal commemoratives, silver plate, 18th-19th C, furniture, general antiques, £5-£1,000.* LOC: Off Lee Green. PARK: Easy. TEL: 0924 492483; home - same. SER: Valuations. FAIRS: Alexandra Palace; Shepton Mallet; Stafford.

Lawn and Lace
5 Knowl Rd. (G.D. Hurst and Mrs N. Gunson). Est. 1988. Open 9.30-5.30, Mon. and Tues. by appointment. SIZE: Small. *STOCK: Textiles including linen and lace, 17th-20th C, £5-£250; dolls and ceramics, £5-£300; small furniture, £15-£500; both 19th-20th C.* LOC: 2 miles east of junction 25, M62. Just off main Huddersfield to Dewsbury road. PARK: Easy. TEL: 0924 491083. SER: Valuations; restorations (textiles and dolls). FAIRS: Newark.

OTLEY, Nr. Leeds

Martin-Clifton Antiques
28 Westgate. (A.S. Ambler and C.M. Rawnsley). Est. 1972. Open 9.30-5.30. SIZE: Medium. *STOCK: Furniture, china, copper and brass, clocks.* LOC: A650. PARK: Easy. TEL: 0943 851117.

SALTAIRE, Nr. Shipley

Carlton Antiques
1 Victoria Rd. (M. Gray and R. Watts). Est. 1989. Open Thurs.,-Sun. 11-5.30. SIZE: Medium. *STOCK: Oak, mahogany and walnut furniture, 17th to late 19th C, £300-£3,000; longcase and mantel clocks, £100-£3,000; oil paintings and watercolours, 19th to early 20th C, £100-£5,000; porcelain and glass, 19th C, £20-£500.* LOC: Off A650. PARK: Nearby. TEL: 0274 530611; home - 0274 545745. SER: Valuations; restorations. VAT: Stan/Spec.

SHIPLEY
R. Bell and Son
37 Briggate. TEL: 0274 582602.
Price-Less Antiques
2 Gaisby Lane. (Mrs P. Lee). Open 10-6. *STOCK: China, bric-a-brac, general antiques.* TEL: 0274 581760.
The Titus Gallery
1 Daisy Place, Saltaire Rd. (C.A. Grice). Est. 1975. Open 10-5.30, Sun. 11-5.30 or by appointment. SIZE: Medium. *STOCK: Oil paintings and watercolours, 18th-20th C, £100-£35,000; occasional furniture, 18th-19th C, £400-£5,000; objets d'art, 18th-20th C, £50-£2,000.* LOC: Near roundabout, at junction of A650 and A657. PARK: Own. TEL: 0274 581894; home - same. SER: Valuations; restorations (oil paintings, watercolours and frames). VAT: Stan/Spec.

SOWERBY BRIDGE, Nr. Halifax
Memory Lane
69 Wakefield Rd. (L. Robinson). Open 10.30-5. SIZE: Warehouse. *STOCK: Pine, oak, dolls and teddies.* TEL: 0422 833223.
Talking Point Antiques
66 West St. (P. and L. Austwick). Open Mon., Thur., Fri., Sat. 10-5.30, other days by appointment. *STOCK: Restored gramophones and phonographs, 78rpm records and sheet music, related items; small furniture; pottery, porcelain and curios.* TEL: 0422 834126.

STEETON
Owls Antiques
1-3 Station Rd. (G.C. Bradley). Open 10-7.30. CL: Tues. *STOCK: Furniture, general antiques, paintings and taxidermy.* TEL: 0535 652614.

TODMORDEN
Echoes
650a Halifax Rd, Eastwood. (P. and R. Oldman). Est. 1980. CL: Tues. SIZE: Medium. *STOCK: Costume, textiles, linen and lace, £5-£500; jewellery, £5-£150; all 19th-20th C.* LOC: A646. PARK: Easy. TEL: 0706 817505; home - same. SER: Valuations; restorations (costume); buys at auction (as stock). VAT: Stan.
Todmorden Fine Art
27 Water St. (Mr Middleton and Mr Gunning). Est. 1981. Usually open but prior telephone call advisable. SIZE: Small. *STOCK: Oil paintings and watercolours, mainly 19th C, £50-£5,000.* LOC: Off M62, junction 20. PARK: Hall St. opposite. TEL: 0706 814723; home - same. SER: Valuations; restorations; framing. VAT: Spec.

WAKEFIELD
Robin Taylor Fine Arts
36 Carter St. Open 9.30-5.30. *STOCK: Oils and watercolours.* TEL: 0924 381809.
D.K. Tuckwell
45 Regent St. Open 10-6 including Sun. *STOCK: General antiques.* PARK: Easy. TEL: 0924 377467.

WALSDEN, Nr. Todmorden
Cottage Antiques (1984) Ltd
788 Rochdale Rd. (G. Slater). Resident. Est. 1978. Open Tues.-Sat. SIZE: Medium. *STOCK: Pine furniture, kitchenalia, 19th C, £5-£1,000; general antiques.* PARK: Easy. TEL: 070 681 3612. SER: Restorations; pine stripping; import and export of continental pine.

WETHERBY
Mitchell-Hill Gallery
2 Church St. (D.G. Mitchell-Hill). Open 9-1 and 2-5, Wed. 9-1. *STOCK: Oils, watercolours and pastels from early 1800.* TEL: 0937 585929.

Raymond Tomlinson Antiques Ltd

Britain's Leading Wholesaler of Antique Furniture

WE HAVE MOVED TO LARGER PREMISES

NEW ADDRESS:

RAYMOND TOMLINSON (ANTIQUES) LTD
MOORSIDE · TOCKWITH · YORK
NORTH YORKSHIRE · ENGLAND YO5 8QG
TEL: (0423) 358833 (3 LINES). FAX: (0423) 358188

Opening Hours:
MON.-FRI. 8.00AM-4.30PM (TRADE ONLY)
SAT. 9.00AM-4.00PM

SEE OUR MAIN ADVERT IN NORTH YORKSHIRE, TOCKWITH SECTION.

Channel Islands
Guernsey

NORTH ↑

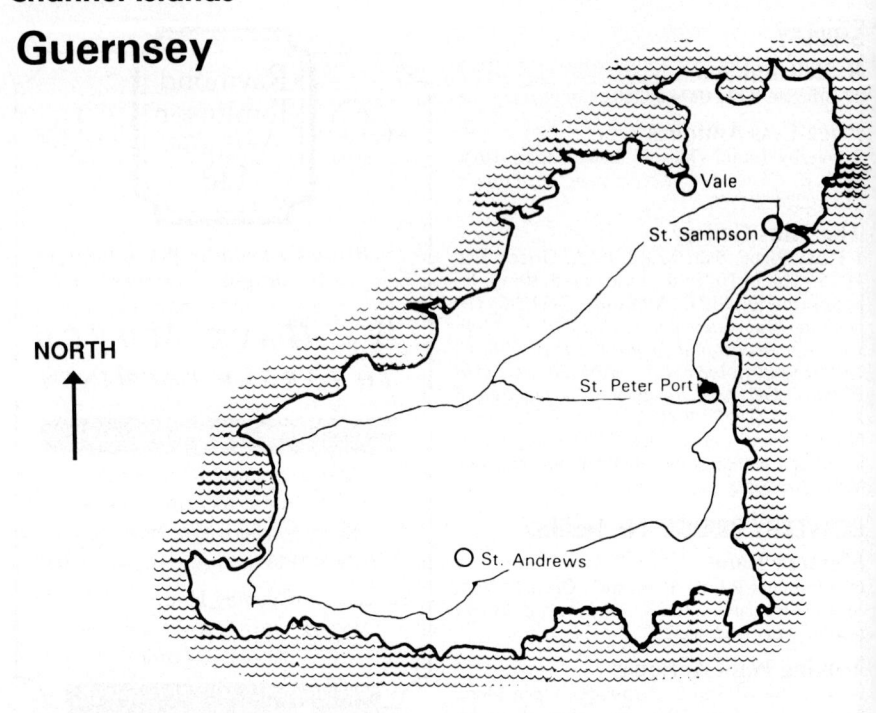

- Vale
- St. Sampson
- St. Peter Port
- St. Andrews

Jersey

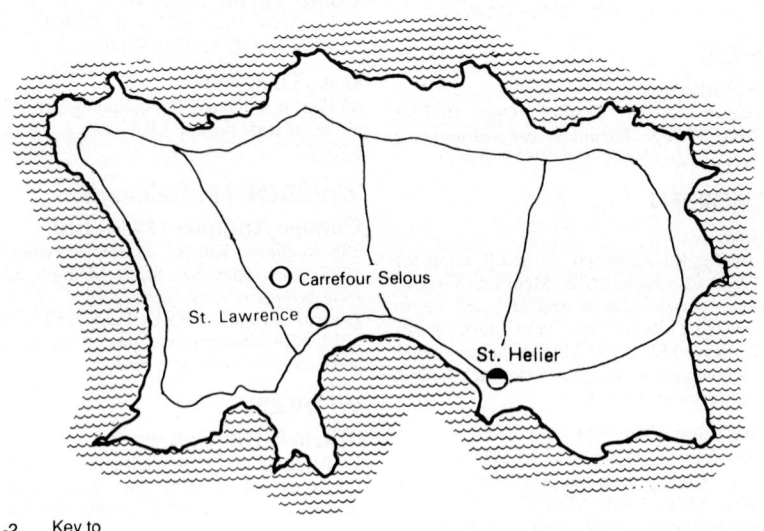

- Carrefour Selous
- St. Lawrence
- St. Helier

Key to number of shops in this area.
- ○ 1-2
- ⊖ 3-5
- ◐ 6-12
- ● 13+

Please note this is only a rough map designed to show dealers the number shops in the various towns, and is not necessarily totally accurate.

Channel Islands

An Antique Collectors' Club Title

George Chinnery 1774-1852
Artist of India and the China Coast
by Patrick Conner
This book represents the first thorough study of Chinnery's life and work; making use of much hitherto unpublished material, it is both comprehensive and highly readable. It also presents a vivid picture of life in the remote outposts of European empires - Madras, Calcutta, Serampore, Canton, Macau and Hong Kong. Chinnery's career is observed within the context of the all-powerful East India Company, family and social pressures upon expatriates, and relations between different races and classes. The hookah and the opium pipe, the bungalow and the palanquin, the ayah and the tanka boatwoman are elements in the extraordinary society which Chinnery enjoyed and so compellingly portrayed.
ISBN 1 85149 160 0, 320pp
189 b & w illus, 113 col, £45.00

Available from:
Antique Collectors' Club, 5 Church Street, Woodbridge, Suffolk IP12 1DS
Tel: (0394) 385501 Fax: (0394) 384434

or Market Street Industrial Park, Wappingers' Falls, New York 12590, USA
Tel: 914 297 0003 Fax: 914 297 0068

Alderney

Victoria Antiques
St. Catherine's, Victoria St. (P.A. Nightingale). Open 10-12.30 and 2.30-4.30. *STOCK: Period and Victorian furniture, glass, silver, china, jewellery, small objets d'art.* TEL: 048 182 3260. SER: Valuations.

Guernsey

ST. MARTIN

Mark Blower Antiques
Briar Cottage, Damouettes Lane. Est. 1978. Open by appointment only. SIZE: Small. *STOCK: English furniture, 18th C, £1,000-£10,000; decorative furnishings, 19th C, to £1,000.* PARK: Easy. TEL: 0481 39098. SER: Valuations; restorations (furniture); buys at auction (furniture).

ST. PETER PORT

Channel Islands Galleries Ltd
Trinity Sq. Centre, Trinity Sq. (G.P. and Mrs C. Gavey). Est. 1967. Open 10-12.30 and 2-5, or by appointment. CL: Thurs. p.m. *STOCK: Antique maps, sea charts and prints of the Channel Islands; oil paintings, watercolours, Channel Islands' books, illustrated, historical, social,*

St. Peter Port continued
geographical and natural history. Not Stocked: General antiques. TEL: 0481 723247; home - 0481 47337.

Grange Antiques
7/8 The Grange. (Mrs K.M. Carré). Est. 1968. Open 9.30-5. CL: Sat. p.m., Thurs. and Sun., except by appointment. SIZE: Medium. *STOCK: Objets d'art, and small furniture, 18th-19th C, £25-£1,000; pottery and porcelain, 18th C to art deco, £5-£500; jewellery, antique and second-hand, £1-£500; linens, silver and plate.* LOC: One of main roads from harbour going inland, shop opposite the Elizabeth College. PARK: 50yds. on right. TEL: 0481 721480. SER: Valuations; buys at auction.

The Pine Collection
17 Mansell St. (P. Head). Est. 1986. Open 9.30-5.30. *STOCK: Pine.* TEL: 0481 726891.

David Proctor Antiques
12 Mansell St. Est. 1973. Open 10-1 and 2-5. CL: Thurs. p.m. SIZE: Small. *STOCK: Period, Victorian and Edwardian furniture, clocks, nautical items, oils, watercolours, silver and plate, items of local interest.* PARK: Nearby. TEL: 0481 726808; home - 0481 46025.

St. James's Gallery Ltd
18-20 The Bordage and 18-20 Smith St. (C.O.

CHANNEL ISLANDS

St. Peter Port continued
Whittam). Est. 1945. CL: Thurs. p.m. and lunch times. SIZE: Large. *STOCK: Furniture, £100-£20,000; porcelain, both 18th-19th C; paintings, 18th-20th C.* TEL: 0481 720070; home - 0481 723999. SER: Valuations; restorations (furniture, upholstery, pictures, framing); buys at auction.

ST. SAMPSON
The Old Curiosity Shop
Commercial Rd. Est. 1978. CL: Mon. and Thurs. *STOCK: Old books, prints, postcards, ephemera, paintings, small furniture, china, glass, silver, brass, £1-£5,000.* TEL: 0481 45324.

VALE
Anne Drury Antiques
Rue de Passeur, L'Ancresse. Est. 1980. Open Wed., Fri. and Sat. or by appointment. SIZE: Medium. *STOCK: Furniture, 18th C to 1920, £50-£6,000; porcelain, 17th C to 1920, £10-£2,000; silver and jewellery, 18th C to 1920, £10-£4,000.* LOC: Off main L'Ancresse Rd. by Copperfields Restaurant. PARK: Easy. TEL: 0481 48386; home - 0481 47814. SER: Valuations. FAIRS: Organiser - St. Pierre Park Hotel.

Geoffrey P. Gavey
Les Clospains, Rue de L'Ecole. Est. 1967. Open by appointment. *STOCK: Maps, sea charts and prints of the Channel Islands; oil and watercolour paintings; Channel Islands books, illustrated, historical, social, geographic and natural history.* Not Stocked: General antiques. TEL: 0481 47337.

Jersey
CARREFOUR SELOUS, ST. LAWRENCE
David Hick Antiques
Alexandra House. Est. 1977. Open Wed., Fri. and Sat. 9.30-5. SIZE: Large and warehouse. *STOCK: Furniture and small items.* TEL: 0534 865965; fax - 0534 865448.

ST. HELIER
John Blench & Son
50 Don St. *STOCK: Fine books, bindings, local maps and prints.* TEL: 0534 25281.

John Cooper Antiques
16 The Market. *STOCK: General antiques.* TEL: 0534 23600.

Grange Gallery and Fine Arts Ltd
39 New St. (G.J. Morris). Est. 1974. Open 9-5.30. CL: Sun., Tues. and Thurs. except by appointment. SIZE: Medium. *STOCK: Oil paintings, 18th-19th C, local prints, 19th C; all £100-£9,000.* LOC: Antique area of St. Helier. PARK: Multi-storey 100yds. TEL: 0534 20077. SER: Valuations; restorations (pictures); buys at auction; framing.

St. Helier continued
Rae Antiques
Savile St. and Clare St. Est. 1947. *STOCK: Clocks, paintings, silver, porcelain, furniture.* TEL: 0534 58071/32171.

Lance and Marcus Rae Antiques
Savile St. Open daily. SIZE: Large. *STOCK: General antiques, furniture, pictures, clocks, silver.* TEL: 0534 32171.

St. Helier Galleries Ltd   BADA
9 James St. (J.H. Appleby). Est. 1953. Open 8.30-5.30. CL: Sat. *STOCK: Paintings, 17th-20th C, all schools; early English watercolours, continental and colonial drawings, from £400+; Channel Island and modern limited edition prints.* LOC: By Minden Place car park. TEL: 0534 67048. SER: Valuations; restorations.

The Selective Eye Gallery
50 Don St. (J. and P. Blench). Est. 1958. Open 9-5. CL: Thurs. and Sat. p.m. SIZE: Medium. *STOCK: Oil paintings, 19th-20th C; maps, prints and antiquarian books, 16th-18th C.* Not Stocked: General antiques. LOC: Town centre. PARK: Multi-storey 100yds. TEL: 0534 25281. SER: Valuations; restorations (pictures). FAIRS: Jersey.

Shepherd's Antiques
4 Wharf St. (J. Shepherd). Est. 1967. Open 11-5, Sat. 9-5. *STOCK: General antiques.* TEL: 0534 601081.

Thesaurus (Jersey) Ltd
3 Burrard St. (I. Creaton). Est. 1973. Open 8.30-6. SIZE: Large. *STOCK: Antiquarian and out of print books, £1-£2,000; maps and prints.* Not Stocked: General antiques. LOC: Town centre. PARK: 100yds. TEL: 0534 37045. SER: Buys at auction. VAT: Spec.

Joan Thomson Antiques
39 Don St. Est. 1967. Open 10-5. SIZE: Medium. *STOCK: Furniture, £200-£3,000; smalls, £10-£500; linen and lace, from £10.* PARK: Nearby. TEL: 0534 80603. SER: Valuations; buys at auction.

Thomson's Furniture Warehouse
4-6 Duhamel Place. Open 10-5. SIZE: Large. *STOCK: General antiques.* TEL: 0534 23673.

Union Street Antique Market
8 Union St. (A.L. Thomson). Est. 1965. Open 10-5. SIZE: Large - several dealers. *STOCK: General antiques.* PARK: 150yds. TEL: 0534 73805; home - 0534 22475. SER: Buys at auction.

ST. LAWRENCE
I.G.A. Old Masters Ltd
5 Kimberley Grove, Rue de Haut. (I.G. and Mrs C.B.V. Appleby). Est. 1953. Open by appointment. *STOCK: Old Master and 19th C paintings.* LOC: Near glass church. PARK: Easy. TEL: 0534 24226; home - same.

Antique Collectors' Club Titles

Art Deco and Other Figures
by Bryan Catley
This sumptuously illustrated book contains the most comprehensive range of art deco figures ever published of the superb sculptures which became fashionable between the wars. The unconventional use of bronze and ivory for many of these sensual and exceptionally high quality figures and their sense of movement and rhythm ensure that large sums are paid by a discriminating international collectors' market. Compiled by the leading specialist dealer in these delightful figures.
**ISBN 0 902028 57 X, 348pp
1,100 b & w illus, 43 col illus, £45.00**

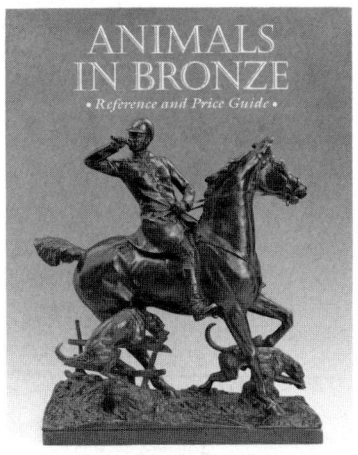

Animals in Bronze
by Christopher Payne
This comprehensive book describes the work of the animalier school, and brings us up to the present day. Practical information to help the collector and dealer.
**ISBN 0 907462 45 6, 424pp
900 b & w illus, 22 col illus, £39.50**

Available from:
Antique Collectors' Club, 5 Church Street
Woodbridge, Suffolk IP12 1DS
Tel: (0394) 385501 Fax: (0394) 384434

or Market Street Industrial Park
Wappingers' Falls, New York 12590, USA
Tel: 914 297 0003 Fax: 914 297 0068

The Barye Bronzes - a catalogue raisonné *by Stuart Pivar* (new edition)
This is a reprint of the author's standard work and is the first modern book on the sculptor Antoine-Louis Barye, the teacher of Rodin and prime mover of the Romantic Movement in art. It contains many improved black and white photographs and additional colour plates. All his known works are illustrated, with many more of Barye's castings of his own work. Barye was a craftsman in bronze almost as much as he was a sculptor; his then new techniques of casting, chiselling and patination are the cornerstone of modern bronze work. **ISBN 1 85149 142 2, 308pp, 300 b & w illus, 20 col, £45.00**

NORTHERN IRELAND

NORTH ↑

Key to number of shops in this area.
- ◯ 1-2
- ⊖ 3-5
- ⬤ 6-12 (half filled)
- ● 13+

Please note this is only a rough map designed to show dealers the number of shops in the various towns, and is not necessarily totally accurate.

NORTHERN IRELAND

BELFAST

The Bell Gallery
13 Adelaide Park. (J.N. Bell). Est. 1964. Open 10-6. SIZE: Medium. *STOCK: British and Irish art, 19th-20th C.* LOC: Off Malone Rd. TEL: 0232 662998. SER: Valuations; restorations (paintings); buys at auction. VAT: Stan/Spec.

Emerald Isle Books
539 Antrim Rd. Est. 1966. Open by appointment. *STOCK: Travel, Ireland, theology.* TEL: 0232 370798; fax - 0232 777288. SER: Catalogues available.

T.H. Kearney & Sons
Treasure House, 123 University St. Resident. *STOCK: Small antiques.* TEL: 0232 231055. SER: Restorations and upholstery. VAT: Stan.

Charlotte and John Lambe
41 Shore Rd. Open 10-5. CL: Sat. *STOCK: English and French furniture, 19th C; pictures and works of art.* TEL: 0232 370761.

Mews Antique Fireplaces and Architectural Salvage
The Gate Lodge, 260 Antrim Rd. (P. O'Flaherty). Open 10.30-5. CL: Mon. *STOCK: Restored Victorian fireplaces and surrounds.* TEL: 0232 751319.

Sinclair's Antique Gallery
19 Arthur St. Est. 1900. Open 9-5.30. CL: Sat. SIZE: Small. *STOCK: Victorian jewellery, china, glass, £10-£1,000; silver, coins.* LOC: 100yds. from city centre. TEL: 0232 322335. VAT: Stan.

County Antrim

ANTRIM

The Country Antiques   LAPADA
219B Lisnevenagh Rd. (David Wolfenden). Open 10-6. SIZE: Large. *STOCK: Furniture, £200-£3,000; jewellery and porcelain, £100-£500, all 19th C.* LOC: Main Antrim-Ballymena line. PARK: Easy. TEL: 08494 29498. SER: Valuations; restoration; buys at auction. VAT: Stan/Spec.

BALLYCLARE

Antique Shop
64a Main St. (T. Heaney). Est. 1971. Open 10-5. *STOCK: 18th-19th C furniture and clocks, £20-£1,000; pottery, glass.* TEL: 096 03 52550. SER: Restorations (clocks and furniture). VAT: Spec.

BUSHMILLS

Dunluce Antiques
33 Ballytober Rd. (Mrs C. Ross). Est. 1978. Open 2-6 or by appointment. CL: Fri. SIZE: Small. *STOCK: Furniture, £50-£1,000; porcelain and glass, £1-£1,000; silver, £5-£5000; all Georgian*

Bushmills continued

to 1930's; paintings, mainly Irish, £50-£10,000. LOC: 1.5 miles off Antrim coast rd. at Dunluce Castle. PARK: Easy. TEL: 02657 31140. SER: Restorations (porcelain).

NEWTOWNABBEY

New Abbey Antiques
Caragh Lodge, Glen Rd., Jordanstown. (A. MacHenry). IADA. Est. 1964. Open 9.30-5.30 or by appointment. SIZE: Medium. *STOCK: General antiques, mostly furniture.* LOC: 6 miles from Belfast to Whiteabbey village, fork left at traffic lights on dual carriageway; turn left into Old Manse Rd. and continue into Glen Rd. PARK: Easy. TEL: 0232 862036. SER: Valuations. FAIRS: Dublin, Belfast and Irish. VAT: Stan/Spec.

PORTBALLINTRAE, Nr. Bushmills

Brian R. Bolt Antiques
88 Ballaghmore Rd. IADA. Open Tues., Thurs. and Sat. 2-6, and by appointment. *STOCK: Silver - small and unusual, objects of vertu, snuff boxes, vesta cases, table, Scottish and Irish provincial; treen, antique and 20th C English and continental glass, studio glass and ceramics, arts and crafts, art nouveau and art deco jewellery, metalwork, vintage fountain pens.* TEL: 02657 31129. SER: Search; catalogues available; postal service.

PORTRUSH

Alexander Antiques
108 Dunluce Rd. (Mrs M. and D. Alexander). Est. 1974. Open 10-6. CL: Sun. except by appointment. SIZE: Large. *STOCK: Furniture, silver, porcelain, fine art, 18th-20th C; oils and watercolours, 19th-20th C.* Not Stocked: Militaria, jewellery, coins. LOC: 1 mile from Portrush on A2 to Bushmills. PARK: Easy. TEL: 0265 822783. SER: Valuations; buys at auction. VAT: Stan/Spec.

County Armagh

ARMAGH

The Hole-in-the-Wall
Market St. (I. Emerson). Est. 1953. *STOCK: General antiques.* LOC: City centre. VAT: Stan/Spec.

FORKHILL

The Half-Door Antique Store
49 Main St. (Tom J. Dooley). Est. 1990. Open 11-1 and 2-6, Sun. 2-6. CL: Mon. SIZE: Small. *STOCK: Belleek porcelain, 1863-1945, £20-£2,000; Victorian and art deco porcelain, £10-£425.* LOC: M1 from Belfast to A1 at Newry. 1 mile south of Newry, turn right for Forkhill (8

NORTHERN IRELAND

Forkhill continued
miles). PARK: Easy. TEL: 0693 888653; home - same. SER: Valuations; buys at auction (Belleek). FAIRS: Castle; Ulster (Culloden Hotel); Killyhevlin Hotel; NEC (Aug.) Newark.

LURGAN
Charles Gardiner Antiques
48 High St. Est. 1968. Open 9-1 and 2-6. CL: Wed. *STOCK: Clocks, furniture and general antiques.* PARK: Own. TEL: 0762 323934.

PORTADOWN
Moyallon Antiques
54 Moyallon Rd. Est. 1975. Usually open. SIZE: Medium. *STOCK: Furniture, 19th C, £50-£1,000; pine and country furniture, 18th-19th C, £50-£500; ceramics and bric-a-brac, £5-£100.* LOC: Portadown - Gilford Rd., 1 mile from Gilford on right-hand side. PARK: Easy. TEL: 0762 831615.

County Down

ANNAHILT
Period Architectural Features and Antiques
263 Ballynahich Rd. (J. Cousans). Open 9.30-5.30. SIZE: Large. *STOCK: Marble chimney pieces, early 18th to late 19th C, £5-£1,000; period panelling and pine pews, stained glass, Victorian bathrooms, decorative architectural items.* TEL: 0846 638091. SER: Valuations; restorations (marble); pine stripping; French polishing; buys at auction. VAT: Stan.

BANBRIDGE
Cameo Antiques
41 Bridge St. (D. and J. Bell). Est. 1966. TEL: 082 06 23241.

DONAGHADEE
Furney Antiques and Interiors
3-4 Shore St. (B. and I. Furney). Est. 1976. Open Wed.-Sat. 9.30-5.30 or by appointment. *STOCK: Period furniture and decorative items.* TEL: 0247 883517/883826; fax - 0247 888729.

GREYABBEY, Nr. Newtownards
The Antique Shop
9 Main St. Est. 1968. *STOCK: General antiques.* TEL: Home - 02477 38333.

Phyllis Arnold Gallery Antiques
Hoops Courtyard. Est. 1968. Open Wed., Fri. and Sat. 11-5. *STOCK: General antiques, small furniture, 19th-20th C watercolours, maps and prints of Ireland.* TEL: 02477 88199; home - 02477 853322. SER: Restorations (maps, prints, watercolours, portrait miniatures); conservation framing. FAIRS: Culloden. VAT: Stan/Spec.

Greyabbey continued
B. B. Antiques
Hoops Courtyard, 5-7 Main St. (B. Beasant). Est. 1989. Open Wed., Fri. and Sat. 11-5. SIZE: Small. *STOCK: Furniture, mahogany and rosewood, 19th C, £200-£1,000; linen, lace and textiles, 19th C to early 20th C, £2-£200.* PARK: Easy. TEL: Home - 0232 654145. FAIRS: Templeton Hotel (Spring); Dunadry Hotel (Spring); Culloden Hotel (Autumn). VAT: Stan.

Old Cross Antiques
3-5 Main St. (C.J. Auld). Resident. Est. 1966. Open 11.30-5.30, other times by appointment. CL: Thurs. SIZE: Medium. *STOCK: Silver, £25-£2,000, porcelain and pottery, £25-£1,200, all 1750-1920; furniture, 1750-1930, £50-£1,500; unusual and interesting bric-a-brac.* Not Stocked: Books, stamps, coins, medals. LOC: Village centre. PARK: Easy. TEL: 02477 88346; home - same.

Priory Antiques
3-5 Main St. (Patty Loane). Est. 1981. Open 11.30-5.30, other times by appointment. CL: Thurs. *STOCK: Jewellery, 1780-1930; silver, 1750-1930; Victorian and Edwardian clothes and linen; small furniture, 1800-1930.* Not Stocked: Books, stamps, coins, medals. LOC: Village centre. PARK: Easy. TEL: 02477 88346.

Timecraft
18 Main St. Est. 1976. Open 11-5.30. CL: Sun. and Thurs., except by appointment. SIZE: Small. *STOCK: Clocks and watches, 19th C, £100-£2,000; jewellery, 19th-20th C, £10-£500.* LOC: Opposite G.P.O. PARK: Easy. TEL: 02477 88416/88252; fax - 02477 88250. SER: Valuations; restorations; buys at auction (clocks and watches).

HOLYWOOD
Herbert Gould and Co.
21-23 Church Rd. (Stephen Gould). Est. 1987. Open 9.15-5.30. SIZE: Medium. *STOCK: Pine, 19th C, £75-£200; collectables, architectural antiques, 19th-20th C, £10-£100.* LOC: 20 yards from maypole in town centre. PARK: Opposite. TEL: 0232 427916. SER: Valuations; pine stripping; buys at auction (as stock). VAT: Stan.

NEWRY
Downshire House Antiques
62 Downshire Rd. (H. and R. McCabe). Open 9-6. *STOCK: General antiques including furniture and porcelain, 18th-19th C, £50-£1,000.* TEL: 0693 66689; home - 0693 5178. SER: Valuations; restorations (furniture). FAIRS: Conway Hotel, Lisburn; Drumkeen Hotel, Belfast. VAT: Stan.

McCabe's Antique Galleries
11-12 St. Mary's St. (H. and R. McCabe). Est. 1910. Open 9.30-1 and 2-5.30, Wed., Sun. and

Newry continued
evenings by appointment. SIZE: Large and warehouse. STOCK: *General antiques including furniture and porcelain, 18th-19th C, £50-£10,000.* PARK: Own. TEL: 0693 62695/66689/69199; home - 0693 5178. SER: Valuations; restorations (furniture). FAIRS: Conway Hotel, Lisburn; Drumkeen Hotel, Belfast. VAT: Stan.

PORTAFERRY
Rock Angus Antiques
2 Ferry St. (D. Dunlop). Open Wed., Fri., Sat. (and Sun. Easter-Sept.) 12-5.30 or by appointment. SIZE: Small. STOCK: *Clocks and furniture, 18th-19th C, £50-£2,500; nautical memorabilia, £50-£500.* LOC: A20 from Newtownards through Greyabbey. PARK: Easy. TEL: 02477 28935; home - same. SER: Valuations; restorations and repairs (clocks); buys at auction (clocks).

WARRENPOINT
Antiques and Fine Art Gallery
3 Charlotte St. (B. Woods). Est. 1991. Open 10.30-1 and 2.30-5.30. CL: Mon. and Wed. SIZE: Medium. STOCK: *Furniture, Georgian to Edwardian, £50-£5,000; paintings, especially Irish, 20th C, £50-£10,000.* LOC: Turn off main road at Newry. PARK: Easy. TEL: 06937 52905. SER: Valuations.

County Londonderry
CLAUDY
K.O. Hagan
'Bensara', 162 Foreglen Rd. STOCK: *Georgian, Victorian and Edwardian furniture, especially pine.* TEL: 0504 338506.

COLERAINE
The Forge Antiques
24 Long Commons. (M.W. Walker). Est. 1977. Open 10-5.30. CL: Thurs. STOCK: *General antiques, silver, clocks, jewellery, porcelain, paintings.* TEL: 0265 51339. VAT: Stan.

PORTSTEWART
The Smithy
Cappagh, 182 Coleraine Rd. (Mrs Bea Macafee). Est. 1967. Open 2-5. SIZE: Medium. STOCK: *Porcelain, jewellery, furniture, silver, bric-a-brac.* LOC: Main road between Coleraine and Portstewart. PARK: Easy. TEL: 0265 832209; home - 0265 52153. VAT: Stan.

County Tyrone
COOKSTOWN
Cookstown Antiques
16 Oldtown St. (T.H. Jebb). Est. 1976. Open Thurs. and Fri. 2-5.30, Sat. 10.30-5.30. SIZE: Small. STOCK: *Jewellery, silver, £10-£1,000; coins, £25-£200; pictures, ceramics and militaria, £5-£1,000; general antiques, all 19th and 20th C.* Not Stocked: Large furniture. LOC: Going north, through both sets of traffic lights, on left at rear of estate agency. PARK: Easy. TEL: 06487 65279; home - 06487 62926. SER: Valuations; buys at auction. FAIRS: All Northern Ireland.

The Saddle Room Antiques
4 Coagh St. (C.J. Leitch). Est. 1968. Open 10-6. CL: Mon. and Wed. STOCK: *China, silver, furniture, glass, jewellery.* TEL: 064 87 62033.

Tea caddies in the shape of fruit attract attention. This super little example is an apple made in applewood. Reproduced late nineteenth century. Late 18th century. £1,500-£2,200. From ***British Antique Furniture — Price Guide and Reasons for Values*** by John Andrews. Third edition published in 1992 by the **Antique Collectors' Club,** £35.00.

SCOTLAND NORTH

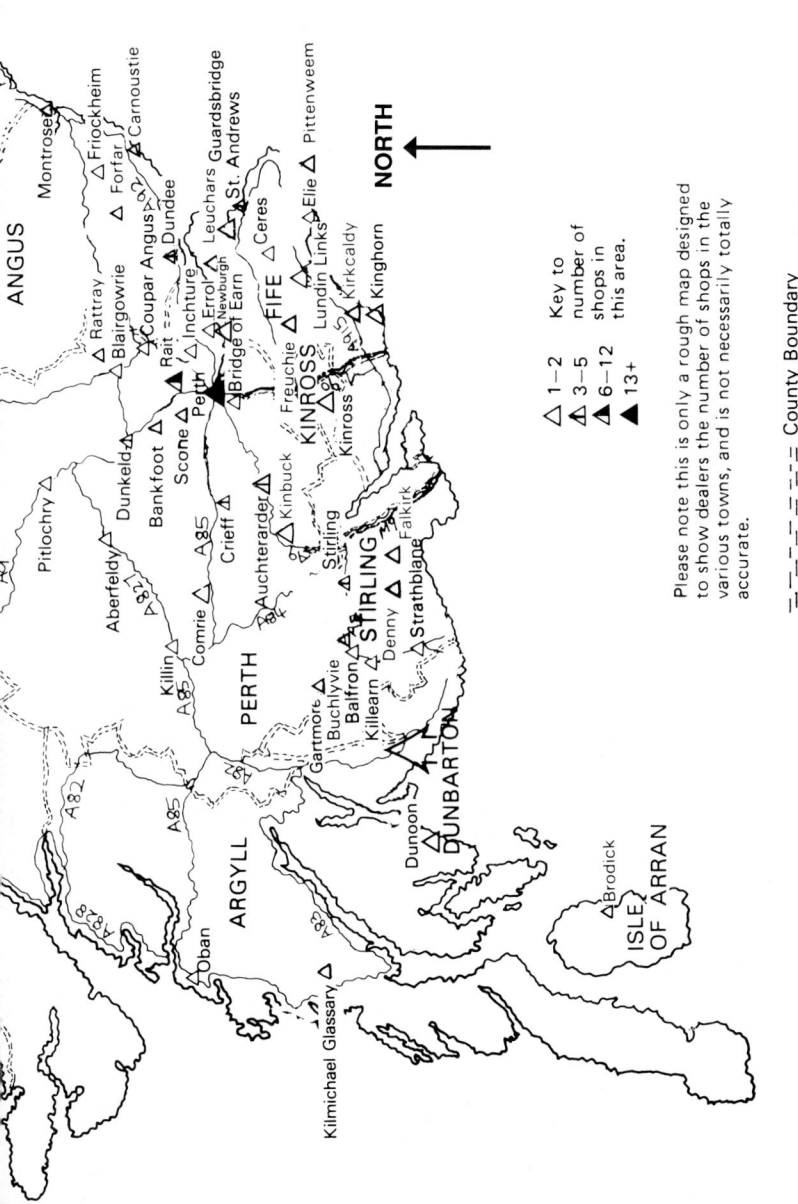

SCOTLAND

SCOTLAND SOUTH

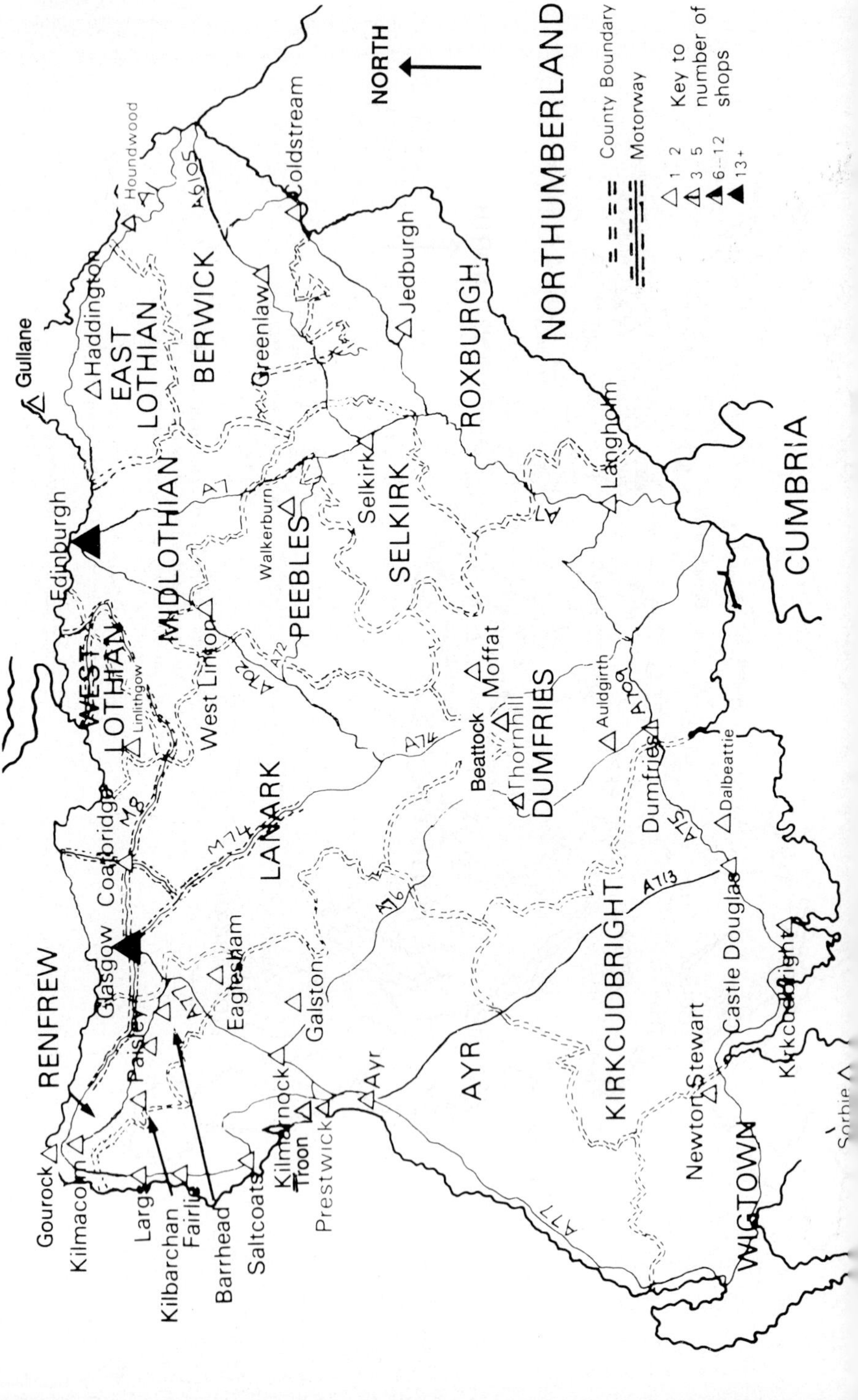

SCOTTISH COUNTY BOUNDARIES

SCOTLAND

THE RENDEZVOUS GALLERY

**ART NOUVEAU
ART DECO**

Also Scottish paintings and watercolours

100 FOREST AVENUE,
ABERDEEN, SCOTLAND
Tel. 0224 323247

ABERDEEN (Aberdeenshire)

Atholl Antiques
322 Great Western Rd. Open 10.30-1 and 2.30-6, or by appointment. *STOCK: Scottish paintings and furniture.* TEL: 0224 593547. VAT: Stan/Spec.

James Benzie
651 George St. Est. 1953. Open 1-4. *STOCK. Small items, glass, china, pottery, copper, brass, silver, pictures.*

Burning Embers
165-167 King St. (J. Bruce). Open 11-5. *STOCK: Fireplaces, bric-a-brac and pine.* TEL: 0224 624664.

Gallery
41 Justice St. (J.H. Wells). Est. 1981. Open 10.30-5.30, Sat. 10.30-4.30. SIZE: Large. *STOCK: Pre-1920 furniture; jewellery, post-1850; curios and Victoriana; paintings and prints, post-1800, from £25.* LOC: Between Castlegate and Beach Boulevard. PARK: Easy. TEL: 0224 625909. SER: Valuations; restorations and repairs (jewellery). VAT: Stan.

McCalls (Aberdeen)
90 King St. (B. McCall). Est. 1948. *STOCK: Jewellery.* PARK: Nearby. TEL: 0224 641916.

Aberdeen continued

McCalls Limited
11 Bridge St. Open 9.30-5.30, Thurs. 9.30-8. *STOCK: Jewellery.* TEL: 0224 584577.

The Rendezvous Gallery
100 Forest Ave. Est. 1973. Open 10-1.30 and 2.30-6. CL: Fri. SIZE: Medium. *STOCK: Art nouveau, art deco, glass, jewellery, bronzes, furniture, £100-£5,000; paintings, watercolours, Scottish School, £200-£5,000.* LOC: Just off Great Western Rd. to Braemar. PARK: Easy. TEL: 0224 323247. VAT: Stan/Spec.

Mr Reynolds
162/164 Skene St. Resident. *STOCK: General antiques.*

Thistle Antiques   LAPADA
28 Esslemont Ave. Est. 1967. TEL: 0224 634692. VAT: Spec.

Elizabeth Watt
69 Thistle St. Est. 1976. Open 10-1 and 2.30-5, Sat. 10-1. SIZE: Small. *STOCK: General antiques.* LOC: Off the west end of Union St. PARK: Nearby. TEL: 0224 647232. SER: Restorations (china, glass).

The Waverley Gallery
18 Victoria St. (G. Wood). Open 9.30-6. *STOCK: Oil paintings and watercolours, £50-£6,000; prints, £20-£2,000; etchings, £40-£400; all 18th-20th C.* LOC: Corner of Waverley Place. TEL: 0224 640633. SER: Valuations; restorations; framing.

Colin Wood (Antiques) Ltd
25 Rose St. Est. 1968. Open 10-12.30 and 2.15-5, Sat. 10-12 and 2.15-4. SIZE: Medium. *STOCK: Furniture, 17th-19th C; works of art, Scottish paintings and silver.* PARK: Multi-storey in Chapel St. TEL: 0224 643019; home - 0224 640640. VAT: Stan/Spec.

William Young Antiques & Fine Art
1 Gaelic Lane, off Belmont St. Est. 1887. Open 9.30-5.30, Sat. 10-4. *STOCK: 17th-19th C furniture, paintings and silver.* TEL: 0224 644757; fax - same.

ABERDOUR (Fife)

Antiques and Gifts
26 High St. (Miss J. Graham). Open Tues.p.m. Wed. p.m. and Thurs., Fri. and Sat. SIZE: Small. *STOCK: General small antiques.* PARK: Station. TEL: 0383 860523.

ABERFELDY (Perthshire)

Denis Young Antiques
Glenlyon. (D.E. and Mrs J.M. Young). Est. 1979 Open by appointment only. *STOCK: Oriental porcelain, 1200-1800; English porcelain and pottery, 1750-1840; English glass, pre-1840 small items. Not Stocked: Silver, jewellery.* TEL 0887 877232. SER: Valuations.

ABERNYTE (Perthshire)
Fine Antique Glass
Smithy Cottage. (S.D. Hole). Open by appointment. SIZE: Small. STOCK: *Decanters and bowls, £40-£1,500; drinking glasses, £20-£1,000; candelabra and chandeliers, £200+; all 1750-1900.* LOC: A85 from Perth, then north on B953. Cottage has stone pillars and is opposite duck pond. TEL: 082886 350.

ALFORD (Aberdeenshire)
R.S. Gordon (Antiques)
Main St. (R. and J. Gordon). Est. 1959. Open 9-5.30. STOCK: *General antiques; clocks, musical boxes, Victoriana, bric-a-brac.* LOC: Between Aberdeen and Huntly on the A944. TEL: 09755 62404. VAT: Stan/Spec.

ARDERSIER (Inverness-shire)
Ardersier Antiques
Ardersier Cottage. (M. and H. Galleitch). Est. 1979. Open 9-6, summer evenings by appointment. SIZE: Small. STOCK: *Paintings, £25-£1,000; toys and dolls, curios, £5-£100; all 19th C.* LOC: A96, near Fort George. PARK: Easy. TEL: 0667 462237; home - same. SER: Valuations; restorations (paintings and furniture stripping); buys at auction.

AUCHTERARDER (Perthshire)
Paul Hayes Gallery
71 High St. PADA. Est. 1962. Open 10-1 and 2-5 or by appointment. CL: Wed. STOCK: *Fine paintings, especially sporting, marine and Scottish post-impressionist, 18th-20th C.* TEL: 0764 662320/663442. VAT: Spec.

Old Abbey Antiques
4 High St. (Gordon M. Cockain). Est. 1982. Open 10.30-5.30. SIZE: Medium. STOCK: *Furniture, Victorian to 1940's, £25-£200; silver and plate, Victorian to 1960's, £10-£100; glass, ceramics, prints and paintings, collectable items and smalls, £3-£250.* LOC: Off Stirling-Perth road, 1.5 miles from Gleneagles Hotel. PARK: Easy. TEL: 0764 664073; home - 0259 42441. VAT: Stan/Spec.

K. Stanley and Son
Regal Buildings, Townhead. (Mr and Mrs Lasiewicz). Est. 1957. Open 10-1 and 2-5. SIZE: Large. STOCK: *Furniture, porcelain, bric-a-brac, shipping goods.* VAT: Stan.

Times Past Antiques
Broadfold Farm. (J.M. Brown). Est. 1970. Open 9-5, weekends 10-4. SIZE: Large. STOCK: *Stripped pine, 19th-20th C, from £50; shipping goods, £5-£500.* LOC: From town centre take Abbey Rd. to flyover A9 at T junction. Turn left, 1st farm on left. PARK: Easy. TEL: 0764 663166; home - same. SER: Restorations (pine); courier; container-packing. VAT: Stan.

WILLIAM YOUNG ANTIQUES

GAELIC LANE
ABERDEEN AB1 1JF
SCOTLAND

GEORGIAN & 19th CENTURY FURNITURE, PAINTINGS, SILVER & GLASS

OPEN MONDAY TO FRIDAY
9.30am to 5.30pm &
SATURDAY 10.00am to 4.00pm

Established 1887

Auchterarder continued

John Whitelaw and Sons Antiques
120 High St. Open 9-5, Sat. 9-2. STOCK: *General antiques; furniture, 17th-19th C.* PARK: Easy. TEL: 0764 662482. VAT: Stan/Spec.

AULDEARN, Nr. Nairn (Nairnshire)
Auldearn Antiques
Dalmore Manse, Lethen Rd. Est. 1980. Open 10-6 including Sun. SIZE: Medium. STOCK: *Victorian linen and lace, kitchenalia, china, furniture, architectural items.* LOC: 1 mile from village. TEL: 0667 53087; home - same.

AULDGIRTH, Nr. Dumfries (Dumfriesshire)
Allanton Antiques
Allanton House. (Mr and Mrs T.L. Burford). Est. 1987. Open 9.30-5.30 including Sun., or by appointment. SIZE: Medium. STOCK: *General antiques and collectors items, linen and lace, kitchenalia, furniture and bric-a-brac, 18th-20th C, 50p-£1,500.* LOC: A76, approximately 7 miles north of Dumfries, 1/4 mile drive to house. PARK: Own. TEL: 038 774 509; home - same. SER: Buys at auction. FAIRS: Edinburgh, Carlisle, Durham, Gateshead, Sunderland, Blackpool.

SCOTLAND

AVOCH (Ross-shire)
Highland Antiques
The Old Post Office. (J. and H. Hesling). HADA, PBFA. Est. 1962. Open 10.30-5. CL: Thurs. STOCK: Furniture, £100-£1,000; paintings, £50-£1,000; both 19th C; general antiques, 18th-19th C, £20-£1,000; antiquarian books especially of Scottish interest. LOC: Village centre. PARK: Easy. TEL: 0381 621000; home - 0463 772250. SER: Valuations; buys at auction. VAT: Stan/Spec.

AYR (Ayrshire)
Antiques
39 New Rd. (T. Rafferty). Est. 1970. Open 10-5. STOCK: General antiques. TEL: 0292 265346.

The Old Curiosity Shop
27 Crown St. (B.D. Kelly). Est. 1970. Open 9-5, Sat. 10-3. SIZE: Medium. STOCK: Furniture and paintings, 19th C, £50-£5,000. LOC: Cross 'Auld Brig' leaving Ayr for Prestwick, 1st left after traffic lights. PARK: Easy. TEL: 0292 280222. SER: Valuations; restorations (French polishing, re-upholstery). VAT: Stan/Spec.

BALFRON (Stirlingshire)
Amphora Galleries
16-20 Buchanan St. (L. Ruglen). Resident. Est. 1961. Open 10-5.30 and by appointment. SIZE: Large. STOCK: General antiques, furniture, decorative items. LOC: On A81. TEL: 0360 40329.

BALLATER (Aberdeenshire)
The McEwan Gallery   LAPADA
Bridge of Gairn. (D. and P. McEwan). Est. 1968. Usually open. SIZE: Medium. STOCK: Oil paintings, watercolours, £50-£50,000; prints, £5-£300; all 18th-20th C; etchings, 17th-19th C, £5-£300; Scottish and natural history books. LOC: First house on the east side of A939 after its junction with A93 outside Ballater. PARK: Easy. TEL: 03397 55429; fax - 03397 55995. SER: Valuations; restorations (framing); buys at auction (paintings, watercolours, books). FAIRS: Buxton, Harrogate, Game, and exhibitions in Canada. VAT: Spec.

BANCHORY (Kincardineshire)
John Bell of Aberdeen Ltd
26 High St. Est. 1899. Open 10-4. CL: Mon. SIZE: Large. STOCK: Georgian furniture. LOC: 12 miles from Aberdeen city centre, towards Balmoral. TEL: 03302 5676. VAT: Stan/Spec.

Bygones
6 Dee St. (V. Watt). Est. 1983. Open 10-1 and 2-5, Sat. 10-5. SIZE: Medium. STOCK: Victoriana, bric-a-brac, small furniture, to £500. LOC: Town centre. PARK: Easy. TEL: 033 02 3095. SER: Valuations. VAT: Stan/Spec.

BANKFOOT (Perthshire)
Antiques & Bygones
Tighvallich, Dunkeld Rd. (W. Wright). Est. 1989. Open by appointment only. SIZE: Small. STOCK: Oil lamps, Victorian and Edwardian, £20-£400. LOC: Off A9 north of Perth. PARK: Easy. TEL: 0738 87452. SER: Restorations (oil lamps).

BANNOCKBURN
Old Mill Antiques (Stirling)
Old Murrayfield, 1A Main St. (G. Dobbie). Open 9-5, Sat. and Sun. 10-4. STOCK: Fireplaces, reproduction mahogany furniture and general antiques. TEL: 0786 817130; fax - 0786 817239.

BARRHEAD, Nr. Glasgow (Renfrewshire)
C.P.R. Antiques and Services
96 Main St. (Mr and Mrs Porterfield). Est. 1965. Open 10-1 and 1.30-5. CL: Tues. SIZE: Medium STOCK: Brass, furniture and curios, 19th-20th C to £5,000. PARK: Easy. TEL: 041 881 5379 SER: Restorations (brass, copper, pewter); spare parts for oil lamps.

BEATTOCK (Dumfriesshire)
T.W. Beaty   LAPADA
Lochhouse Farm. Open 9.30-5; trade - any time by appointment. SIZE: Large and warehouse. STOCK: Furniture, china, glass, brass pictures, 18th-20th C. TEL: 06833 451. VAT Stan/Spec.

BEAULY (Inverness-shire)
Iain Marr Antiques
3 Mid St. (I. and A. Marr). HADA. Est. 1975 Open 10.30-1 and 2-5.30. CL: Thurs. STOCK Silver, jewellery, clocks, porcelain, scientifi instruments, arms, oils, watercolours, smal furniture. LOC: Off Square, on left going north next to Priory stores. TEL: 0463 782372. VAT Stan/Spec.

BLAIRGOWRIE (Perthshire)
Roy Sim Antiques
The Granary Warehouse, Lower Mill St. Es 1977. Open 9-5.30, Sun. 12-5. SIZE: Large STOCK: Furniture, clocks, silver and plate collectables. TEL: 0250 873860.

BRIDGE OF EARN (Perthshire)
Imrie Antiques   LAPAD
Back St. (Mr and Mrs I. Imrie). Est. 196 Open 10-1 and 2-5.30. SIZE: Large. STOCF Victorian and 18th C shipping goods. PARF Easy. TEL: 0738 812784. VAT: Stan.

BRODICK (Isle of Arran)
Village Studio
Kames Cottage, Shore Rd. (C. Mason). Open 10-12.30 and 2-4.30. STOCK: Bric-a-brac, collectables, objets d'art, gold and silver jewellery. TEL: 0770 302213.

BUCHLYVIE (Stirlingshire)
Amphora Galleries
Main St. (L. Ruglen). Est. 1961. Open 10-5.30 or by appointment. SIZE: Large. STOCK: Furniture and decorative items. LOC: On A811 Stirling-Erskine Bridge. TEL: 0360 85203; home - 0360 40329.

CASTLE DOUGLAS (Kirkcudbrightshire)
Bendalls Antiques
221-223 King St. (R.A. Mitchell). Est. 1949. Open 9.30-12.30 and 1.30-5. CL: Thurs. p.m. and Sat. p.m. TEL: 0556 2113. VAT: Stan/Spec.

CERES (Fife)
Ceres Antiques
19 Main St. (Mrs E. Norrie). SIZE: Medium. STOCK: General antiques, china. PARK: Easy. TEL: 033 482 384.

Steeple Antiques
38 Main St. (Mrs Elizabeth Hart). Est. 1980. Open 2-5 including Sun., mornings by appointment. CL: Wed. p.m. SIZE: Medium. STOCK: Porcelain including some Wemyss, 1800-1950, £5-£500; cutlery, silver and plate, £5-£200+; Victorian linen, some furniture, £50-£400. LOC: 3 miles from Cupar. PARK: Easy. TEL: Home - 033 482 553. SER: Valuations; buys at auction (silver, china and furniture).

COATBRIDGE (Lanarkshire)
Michael Stewart Antiques
Hornock Cottages, Gartsherry Rd. Est. 1968. Open by appointment. STOCK: Georgian, Victorian and shipping furniture and smalls. TEL: 0236 422532.

COLDSTREAM (Berwickshire)
Coldstream Antiques
44 High St. (Mr and Mrs J. Trinder). Resident. Open daily. SIZE: Large. STOCK: Furniture, 17th-20th C; general antiques, clocks, silver and shipping goods, 17th-19th C. LOC: A697. TEL: 0890 882552. VAT: Stan/Spec.

Fraser Antiques
65 High St. Est. 1968. Open 10-5. CL: Mon. SIZE: Medium. STOCK: Porcelain, glass, pictures, silver, small furniture, general antiques. SER: Restorations (paintings, clocks, furniture).

COLLESSIE, By Cupar (Fife)
Collessie Antiques
The Glebe. (Mary Malocco). Est. 1977. Open Fri.,

Collessie continued

Sat. and Sun 2-5, other times by appointment. SIZE: Small. STOCK: Porcelain, early 19th C, £5-£100; small furniture, mid 19th C, £50-£350; Paisley shawls and rugs, early 19th C, £100-£600. LOC: Just off A91. PARK: Easy. TEL: 033 781 338; home - same. SER: Restorations (porcelain and furniture). FAIRS: Aberdeen, Edinburgh.

COMRIE (Perthshire)
The Coach House
Dundas St. (Mrs M. Chilcott). Resident. Est. 1972. Open 10.30-12.30 and 2.30-5. CL: Wed. Outside hours and winter months by appointment only. SIZE: Small. STOCK: Pottery and porcelain, from early 19th C, £5-£500; decorative items. LOC: On main road, Crieff to Loch Earn (and Oban). PARK: Easy. TEL: 0764 670765.

COUPAR ANGUS (Perthshire)
Henderson Antiques
35 Lintrose. Est. 1984. STOCK: Furniture. TEL: 0828 27450. VAT: Stan.

CRIEFF (Perthshire)
Antiques and Fine Art
11 Comrie St. (Mrs S. Drysdale). Open 10-1 and 2-5. CL: Wed. p.m. SIZE: Medium. STOCK: Furniture, paintings, silver, general antiques, French paperweights. LOC: A85. PARK: Easy. TEL: 0764 654496; home - 0764 652653. VAT: Spec.

Crieff Antiques
Comrie Rd. (Mrs J. Cormack). Est. 1968. Open 10-12.30 and 2-4.30 and some Sat. CL: Wed. p.m. SIZE: Medium. STOCK: Victorian porcelain, paraffin lamps, £5-£150; music boxes, clocks and small furniture, £10-£500; motor mascots, lamps, badges, collectors advertising items, enamel signs, 20th C, £5-£300. Not Stocked: Large furniture. LOC: On A85 next to Gordon Motors. PARK: Nearby. TEL: 0764 653322/653271.

Strathearn Antiques
2 Comrie St. (R. Torrens). Est. 1977. Open 10-5. SIZE: Medium. STOCK: General antiques, curios, jewellery, coins, medals, books, Royal Doulton items. PARK: Easy. TEL: 0764 654344; home - 0764 653592. SER: Valuations (jewellery). VAT: Stan.

CRUDEN BAY, Nr. Peterhead (Aberdeenshire)
A. Sangster Antiques
7 Main St. (A.H. Sangster). Est. 1982. Open April to end Oct. 1-5, Sat. and Sun. 1-4.30, evenigds and all other times by appointment. SIZE: Small. STOCK: General antiques including furniture, £100-£1,000; porcelain, £100-£500; coins, £100-2,400; pistols, £300-£900; paintings, £200-

SCOTLAND

Cruden Bay continued
£1,000; all 17th to early 20th C. LOC: Aberdeen to Peterhead road (A92) turn right onto A975. PARK: Easy. TEL: 0779 812838; home - same. SER: Valuations; restorations (furniture). FAIRS: Local (winter months). VAT: Stan/Spec.

DALBEATTIE (Kirkcudbrightshire)
Wildman's Antiques
3 Maxwell St. (P. and M. Wildman). Est. 1960. Open 10-12.30 and 1.30-5. SIZE: Medium. STOCK: Jewellery, £50-£500; furniture, £100-£1,500; silver and plate, £50-£1,500; all 19th-20th C. LOC: A711. PARK: Easy. TEL: 0556 610260. SER: Valuations. VAT: Stan/Spec.

DENNY (Stirlingshire)
Century Antiques
Viewfield, 74 Glasgow Rd. (I. Burton). Open by appointment only anytime including Sat., Sun. and evenings. STOCK: Mainly clocks. LOC: From M80, junction 4 or junction 9, M9, on main road through village, corner house opposite fire station. PARK: Easy. TEL: 0324 823333; fax - 0324 825207; mobile - 0860 541917. VAT: Stan/Spec.

DINGWALL (Ross-shire)
Dingwall Antiques
6 Church St. (I. Leslie). Est. 1988. Open 10-5. SIZE: Medium. STOCK: Books, secondhand; china and glass, maps and prints, £1-£200. PARK: Easy. TEL: 0349 65593. VAT: Stan.

DOLLAR (Clackmannanshire)
Hillfoot Antiques
38 Bridge St. (S.A. Milne). Resident. Est. 1984. Open 9-1 and 2-6. CL: Mon. SIZE: Small. STOCK: Furniture including desks, fireplaces, 18th to early 20th C. LOC: Just off Stirling-St. Andrews road. PARK: Easy. TEL: 0259 42495; home - 0259 42228. SER: Restorations (including upholstery); buys at auction (furniture and architectural items). FAIRS: Newark, Harrogate.

DRUMNADROCHIT (Inverness-shire)
Joan Frere Antiques
Drumbuie House. (Mrs J. Frere). Open daily 9-8 May-October, other times by appointment. SIZE: Medium. STOCK: Furniture, especially English oak, pre-1800. Not Stocked: Victoriana, reproductions. LOC: On Loch Ness just before Drumnadrochit village, on A82. PARK: Easy. TEL: 045 62 210; home - same.

DUMFRIES (Dumfriesshire)
I.G. Anderson
Gribton. Open by appointment only. STOCK: Antiquarian and secondhand books. LOC: From Dumfries, take B729 Moniaive road, after 1.25 miles take Newtonairds road. First entry on left. TEL: 0387 721071.

Dumfries continued
The Antiquarian
71 Queensberry St. (H. Mulholland). Est. 1988. Open 10-5. SIZE: Large. STOCK: Furniture, Georgian to Edwardian, £250-£5,000; silver, plate and brass, china and glass, paintings and prints, £25-£1,500. LOC: Town centre. PARK: Easy. TEL: 0387 59970; 0698 264077.

Cairnyard Antiques
Cairnyard House, Beeswing. (B. Farnell). Est. 1971. Open daily or by appointment. SIZE: Medium. STOCK: General antiques, furniture and clocks. LOC: A711, 5 miles S.W. of Dumfries (follow Dalbeattie signs). PARK: Easy. TEL: 0387 73218; home - same.

Dix Antiques
100 English St. (B. and M. Hughes). Est. 1965. Open 10-4.30. CL: Thurs. SIZE: Small and store. STOCK: General antiques, £5-£1,000. LOC: Near cinema. TEL: 0387 64234; home - 0387 65259.

DUNDEE (Angus)
Angus Antiques
4 St. Andrews St. Est. 1964. Open 10-4. CL: Sat. STOCK: Militaria, badges, medals, swords, jewellery, silver, gold, collectors items, art nouveau, art deco, advertising and decorative items, tins, toys, teddy bears. TEL: 0382 22128.

Neil Livingstone
Unit 9 South Grove Works, Brewery Lane. Open 10-4, including Sun. STOCK: Pine, mahogany and oak furniture; decorative items including jewellery. TEL: 0382 21618. Trade Only.

Southgrove Restorations
Unit 4, Southgrove Mill, Lower Pleasance. Open 9-5, Sat. and Sun. 10-4. STOCK: British and continental stripped pine, £40-£3,000. TEL: 0382 29295.

Westport Gallery
3 Old Hawkhill, and 48 Westport. (N. Livingstone). Est. 1976. Open 9-5. SIZE: Medium. STOCK: Decorative items including paintings. LOC: At city centre end of Perth Road, turn into Tay St. and bear left, shop on the right. PARK: Easy. TEL: 0382 21751. SER: Valuations; restorations (furniture, ceramics, paintings); buys at auction (paintings). VAT: Stan/Spec.

DUNFERMLINE (Fife)
Felix Hudson Ltd
2 Queen Anne St. Est. 1950. Open 9-5.15, Wed. 9-12.30. SIZE: Medium. STOCK: China, silver and plate, jewellery, clocks and watches, 18th-20th C, £5-£1,000. PARK: Easy. TEL: 0383 724311; home - 0383 724432. SER: Valuations; restorations; buys at auction. VAT: Stan/Spec.

DUNKELD (Perthshire)
Dunkeld Antiques
Tay Terr. (D. Dytch). Est. 1986. Open 10-5.30, Sun. 12-5.30. SIZE: Large. *STOCK: General antiques especially boxes, office and library furniture, books, 19th-20th C, £1-£1,500.* LOC: Overlooking River Tay, premises are a converted church. PARK: Easy. TEL: 0350 728832; home - same; mobile - 0831 379679. SER: Valuations; buys at auction (clocks and furniture). VAT: Stan/Spec.

Dunkeld Interiors
14 Bridge St. (Mrs B. Cowe). Est. 1984. Open 10-5. CL: Mon. and Thurs. *STOCK: Furniture, 18th-19th C, £500-£6,000; decorative items, 19th-20th C.* LOC: 2 mins. off A9, Perth to Inverness road. PARK: Easy. TEL: 0350 727582; home - same. SER: Finder. VAT: Stan/Spec.

K. Stanley and Son
High St. Est. 1962. *STOCK: General antiques and curios.* VAT: Stan.

DUNOON (Argyllshire)
Fyne Antiques
The Antique Shop, Summerville Place, Sandbank. (M.P. Glenn). Open 10-5. *STOCK: Pine and country items, £5-£200; mahogany and oak furniture, Staffordshire and Scottish pottery.* TEL: 0369 6646; home - 0369 3510. SER: Valuations; restorations (pine).

EAGLESHAM (Renfrewshire)
Eaglesham Antiques Ltd
73 Montgomery St. (M.F. Finlay). Est. 1966. Open 12-5. CL: Mon. *STOCK: Porcelain, silver, glass, objets d'art, paintings, small furniture.* LOC: Original village past Eglington Arms Hotel. PARK: Easy. TEL: 035 53 2814.

EDINBURGH (Midlothian)
Another Time, Another Place
9 East Fountainbridge. (Mrs A. Averbuch). Est. 1984. Open Thurs. and Fri. 1-4.30, Sat. 1-5. SIZE: Small. *STOCK: Period clothing, 19th-20th C, £15-£50; textiles and accessories.* LOC: 3 minutes from Tollcross. PARK: Nearby. TEL: Home - 031 669 3082. SER: Buys at auction (textiles and dolls). FAIRS: Local.

Another World
25 Candlemaker Row. (D. Harrison). Est. 1974. Open Wed., Fri. and Sat. 12-4.30 or by appointment. *STOCK: Netsuke and Oriental art.* TEL: 031 225 1988. VAT: Spec.

Antiques
48 Thistle St. (E. Humphrey). Est. 1946. Open 10-4, Sat. 10-12.30 or by appointment. *STOCK:*

Edinburgh continued
Paintings, glass, china, curios, postcards. TEL: 031 226 3625.

Paddy Barrass
15 The Grassmarket. Est. 1974. Open 12-6, Sat. 10.30-5.30, Sun. in Aug. 2-7. SIZE: Small. *STOCK: Period clothing and household linen, 19th-20th C, £5-£100.* LOC: South side of High St., directly below castle. PARK: Easy. TEL: 031 226 3087. SER: Valuations.

Behar Carpets
12a Howe St. (M. and Mrs P. Slater). Est. 1920. Open 9-5.30. *STOCK: Oriental carpets and rugs, 19th C, from £200.* TEL: 031 225 1069. SER: Valuations; restorations (cleaning and repairs). VAT: Stan.

Berlands of Edinburgh
143 Gilmore Place. (R. Melvin). Open 9-5. *STOCK: Restored antique light fittings.* TEL: 031 228 6760.

Laurance Black Ltd
45 Cumberland St. Est. 1967. Open 10-5, Sat. 10-1. SIZE: Small. *STOCK: Scottish furniture and decorative items, £50-£5,000; pottery and porcelain, £5-£1,000; paintings and prints, £50-£20,000; all 18th-19th C.* PARK: Easy. TEL: 031 557 4545. VAT: Spec.

Joseph Bonnar, Jewellers
72 Thistle St. Open 10.30-5 or by appointment. SIZE: Medium. *STOCK: Antique and period jewellery.* LOC: Parallel with Princes St. PARK: Own. TEL: 031 226 2811. VAT: Stan/Spec.

Bourne Fine Art Ltd
4 Dundas St. (P. Bourne). Est. 1978. Open 10-6, Sat. 10-1. SIZE: Medium. *STOCK: British paintings, 1800-1950.* PARK: Easy. TEL: 031 557 4050. SER: Valuations; restorations; buys at auction; framing. VAT: Stan/Spec.

Cabbies Antiques
10 Randolph Cliff. (Betty Boyd). Est. 1987. Open 1-6, other times by appointment. SIZE: Small. *STOCK: Small furniture, 19th C, £200-£3,000; decorative items including mirrors and textiles, mainly 19th C, £100-£1,000; silver objets de vertu and Scottish provincial, late 18th to 19th C, £25-£1,000; glass, 19th C.* LOC: Beside Dean bridge, west end of city. PARK: Limited and nearby. TEL: 031 225 3289; home - same. SER: Valuations; restorations (furniture, including gilding); buys at auction (19th C furniture). FAIRS: Antiques in Britain, Gt. Northern, Newark and NEC. VAT: Spec.

SCOTLAND

Calton Gallery
EDINBURGH
(Andrew and Sarah Whitfield)

John James Wilson (1818-1875)
Edinburgh and the Port of Leith from
across the Firth of Forth

British and Continental paintings
and watercolours from 1800

10am-6pm Monday to Friday
10am-1pm Saturday

10 Royal Terrace Edinburgh EH7 5AB
Tel: 031-556 1010

Edinburgh continued
Calton Gallery
10 Royal Terr. (A. and S. Whitfield). Est. 1979. Open 10-6, Sat. 10-1. SIZE: Large. *STOCK: Paintings especially marine, and watercolours, £50-£30,000; prints, £10-£1,000; sculpture, to £5,000; all 19th to early 20th C.* PARK: Easy. TEL: 031 556 1010; home - same; fax - 031 558 1150. SER: Valuations; restorations (oils, watercolours, prints); buys at auction (paintings). VAT: Stan/Spec.

Cinders
3 East Trinity Rd. (A. Mutch). Open 10-5, Sat. 10-4. CL: Mon. *STOCK: Fireplaces and furniture.* TEL: 031 552 0491; home - 031 558 3141.

The Carson Clark Gallery. Scotia Maps - Mapsellers
173 Canongate, The Royal Mile. (A.Carson Clark). FRGS. Est. 1971. Open 10.30-5.30. *STOCK: Maps and sea charts.* TEL: 031 556 4710. SER: Valuations.

Collector Centre
63 Viewforth. (Mrs Katharine M. Chalmers). Est. 1973. Open 10-6. CL: Wed. SIZE: Small. *STOCK: General antiques and collectors' items including silver spoons, glass, pottery and porcelain, jewellery, militaria and kitchenalia, from late 17th C, £2-£2,500.* LOC: From King's

Edinburgh continued
Theatre to Gilmore Place, turn left at 1st set of traffic lights, centre 300 yards on right. PARK: Meters (except Sat.). TEL: 031 229 1059. SER: Valuations; advice; research.

The Collectors Shop
49 Cockburn St. (D. Cavanagh). Est. 1960. Open 11-5. *STOCK: Coins, medals, militaria, cigarette and postcards, small collectors' items, jewellery, silver and plate.* Not Stocked: Postage stamps. TEL: 031 226 3391. SER: Buys at auction.

Court Curio Shop
519 Lawnmarket. TEL: 031 225 3972.

Craiglea Clocks
88 Comiston Rd. (Peter and June Carmichael). Est. 1978. Open 10-1 and 2-5.30. CL: Wed. SIZE: Small. *STOCK: Clocks, £40-£1,500; barometers, £50-£300; smalls, £40-£150.* LOC: On Biggar road from Morningside. PARK: Adjacent streets. TEL: 031 452 8568; home - 031 447 6334. SER: Valuations; restorations (clocks and barometers); buys at auction (clocks, barometers and scientific instruments).

Davidson and Begg Antiques Ltd
183-189 Causewayside. (Eric Davidson and Robert Begg). Est. 1967. Open 9-5.30. *STOCK: Furniture - period, continental, Victorian and Edwardian, decorative; silver, bronzes and paintings.* LOC: South side of city, approximately 1 mile from university. PARK: Easy. TEL: 031 662 4221. VAT: Stan/Spec.

Alan Day Antiques   LAPADA
13c Dundas St. Open 1-6, Fri. 12-5. CL: Sat. **STOCK: Furniture, 19th C; general antiques. TEL: 031 557 5220.**

A.F. Drysdale Ltd
20 and 35 North West Circus Place. Est. 1974. Open 10-1 and 2-5, Sat. 10-1. *STOCK: Quality continental reproduction lamps, decorative furniture; antique prints.* TEL: 031 225 4686. VAT: Stan.

George Duff Antiques
254 Leith Walk. Open by appointment. *STOCK: Shipping goods, pre-1940.* TEL: 031 554 8164; home - 031 337 1422. VAT: Stan. *Export Only.*

Dunedin Antiques Ltd
4 North West Circus Place. (D. Ingram and G. Niven). Est. 1973. Open 9.30-1 and 2.30-5.30. SIZE: Large. *STOCK: Furniture, period items, chimney pieces, architectural fittings, 18th-19th C, £100-£15,000.* Not Stocked: Porcelain. LOC: From Princes St. down Frederick St. PARK: Easy. TEL: 031 220 1574; home - 031 556 8140. SER: Valuations; buys at auction (furniture, weapons). VAT: Stan/Spec.

SCOTLAND

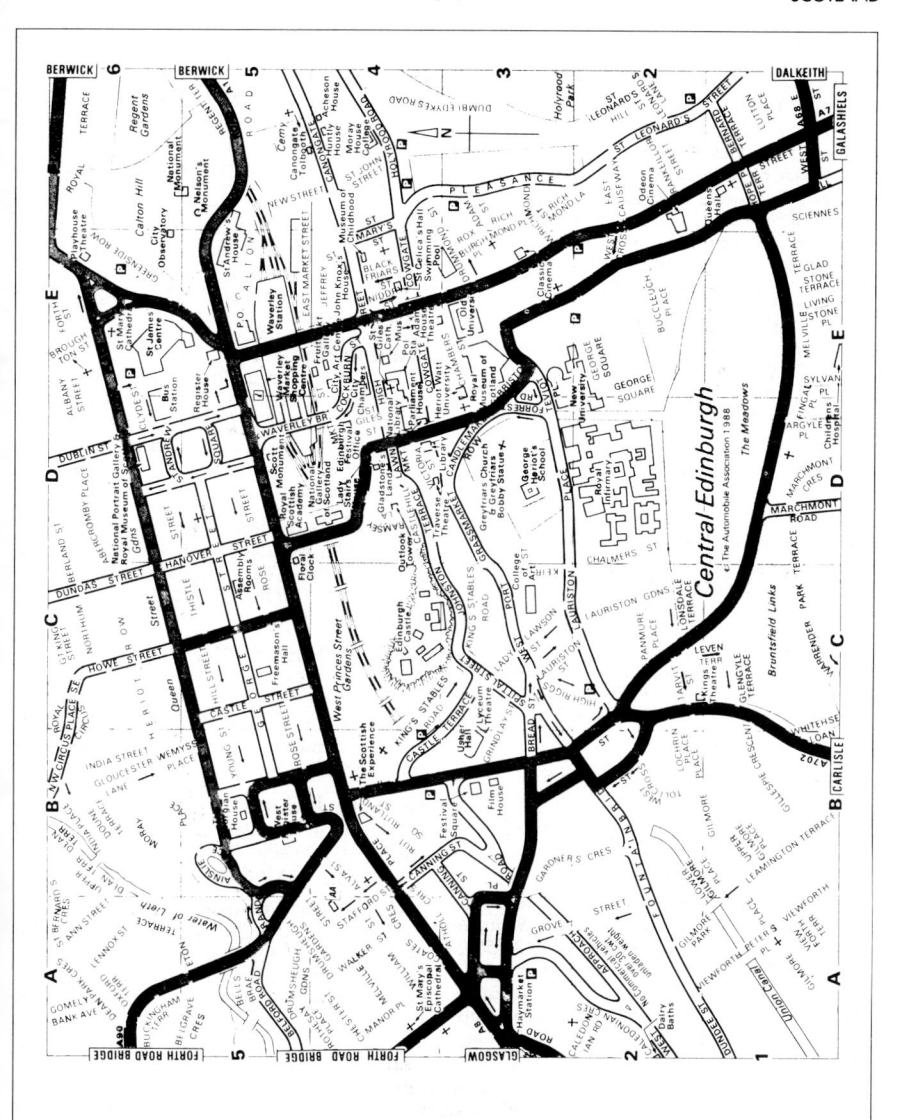

Key to Town Plan

- AA Recommended roads
- Other roads
- Restricted roads
- Buildings of interest
- Car Parks
- Parks and open spaces
- AA Service Centre

© Automobile Association 1988

SCOTLAND

Edinburgh continued

EASY - Edinburgh Architectural Salvage Yard
Unit 6, Couper St., (Off Coburg St.), Leith. (Neil Barrass). Est. 1985. Open 9-5, Sat. 12-5. SIZE: Large. *STOCK: Stripped pine doors, 18th-20th C, £30-£60; fireplaces, 18th-20th C, £40-£2,000; general architectural salvage.* LOC: East from eastern end of Ferry Road into Coburg St., take first left into Couper St. PARK: Easy. TEL: 031 554 7077. SER: Restorations. VAT: Stan.

Edinburgh Coin Shop
2 Polwarth Cres. (T.D. Brown). Open 10-5. CL: Sun. *STOCK: Coins, medals, badges, militaria, postcards, cigarette cards, stamps, jewellery, clocks and watches, general antiques, bullion dealers.* TEL: 031 229 3007/229 2915. VAT: Stan.

Donald Ellis Antiques
7 Bruntsfield Place. (D.G. and C.M. Ellis). Est. 1970. *STOCK: Furniture, clocks, silver, porcelain, copper, brass and collectors items.* LOC: Opposite Links Garage at Bruntsfield Links. PARK: Nearby. TEL: 031 229 4720. SER: Clock repairs.

Tom Fidelo
49 Cumberland St. Open 2-6, Sat. 12-6. *STOCK: Paintings, works of art, 18th-20th C.* LOC: Left at corner of Dundas St. and Cumberland St. PARK: Easy. TEL: 031 557 2444.

E.B. Forrest and Co. Antiques
3 Barclay Terr. *STOCK: Jewellery, plate, cutlery, brass, copper, silver, china, art pottery, glass, linen and lace.* TEL: 031 229 3156.

Forrest McKay
38 Howe St. (M.A. Forrest and S.M. Watt). Est. 1976. Open 10-6, Sat. 10-1. *STOCK: Scottish paintings, £1-£3,000; decorative arts, £2-£500; both 19th-20th C.* LOC: Continuation of Frederick St. which runs from Princes St. PARK: Easy. TEL: 031 226 2589. SER: Valuations; restorations (paintings, watercolours and drawings); framing; buys at auction (paintings, decorative arts). VAT: Spec.

Fyfe's Antiques
41 Thistle St. *STOCK: 18th-19th C furniture, oil paintings, silver, porcelain.* TEL: 031 225 4287. VAT: Stan/Spec.

Georgian Antiques   LAPADA
10 Pattison St, Leith Links. Est. 1976. Open 8.30-5.30, Sat. and other times by appointment. SIZE: Large. *STOCK: Furniture, Georgian, Victorian, inlaid, Edwardian; shipping goods, smalls, £10-£10,000.* LOC: Off Leith Links. PARK: Easy. TEL: 031 553 7286 (24 hrs.); fax - 031 553 6299. SER: Valuations; restorations; buys at auction; packing; shipping; courier. VAT: Stan/Spec.

Edinburgh continued

Gladrags
17 Henderson Row. (K. Cameron). Est. 1977. Open 9.30-6. CL: Mon. *STOCK: Period clothes, linen, lace, beadwork, shawls, costume jewellery, silks and satins, cashmeres and accessories.* TEL: 031 557 1916.

Goodwin's Antiques Ltd
15 and 16 Queensferry St. Est. 1952. Open 9.30-5.30, Sat. 9.30-1. *STOCK: Jewellery, silver.* LOC: Off Princes St., West end. TEL: 031 225 4717. VAT: Stan/Spec.

Hand in Hand
3 North West Circus Place. (Mr and Mrs O. Hand). Est. 1969. Open 10-5.30. CL: Mon. *STOCK: Victorian linen, embroidery, furnishings, lace, Paisley shawls; period costume and accessories including jewellery.* TEL: 031 226 3598. VAT: Stan/Spec.

Herrald Antiques
38 Queen St. Est. 1882. Open 9-5. CL: Sat. p.m. SIZE: Medium. *STOCK: Furniture, Persian rugs.* TEL: 031 225 5939. SER: Restorations. VAT: Stan.

Malcolm Innes Gallery
67 George St. Est. 1981. Open 9.30-6, Sat. 10-1. *STOCK: Scottish landscape, sporting and military pictures.* TEL: 031 226 4151; fax - same. SER: Valuations; restorations; buys at auction; framing. VAT: Spec.

Kenneth Jackson
66 Thistle St. Est. 1969. *STOCK: English and continental furniture, 17th to early 19th C.* TEL: 031 225 9634. VAT: Stan/Spec.

Jacksonville Antiques Warehouse
108A Causewayside. (N.T.C. Clarke). Est. 1974. Open 11-5. SIZE: Warehouse. *STOCK: Furniture, bric-a-brac, shipping goods, 1800-1950, £5-£1,500.* PARK: Easy. TEL: 031 667 0616. SER: Valuations. VAT: Stan.

Kaimes Smithy Antiques
79 Howdenhall Rd. (J. Lynch). Est. 1972. Open 1.30-5.30, Mon. and Thurs. 1.30-5, mornings by appointment. SIZE: Medium. *STOCK: Furniture and clocks, 18th-19th C, £100-£800; porcelain, glass, paintings, prints, copper, brass and curios, 19th C, £20-£300.* LOC: From A720, take A701 (at Straiton junction) into city centre, until 1st set of traffic lights. PARK: Easy. TEL: 031 441 2076; home - same. SER: Valuations; restorations.

David Letham
65 Queen Charlotte St. Est. 1960. Open by appointment. *STOCK: Furniture, decorative objects, collectors' items.* TEL: 031 554 6933. VAT: Spec.

Edinburgh continued

London Road Antiques
15 Earlston Place, London Road. (R. Forrest). Open 12-6. *STOCK: General antiques including stripped pine furniture, decorative items and prints.* TEL: 031 652 2790. SER: Restorations.

William MacAdam BADA
86 Pilrig St. Est. 1976. Open by appointment only. SIZE: Small. *STOCK: Collectors drinking glasses, 17th-19th C, £50-£15,000; coloured glass, 18th-19th C, £25-£5,000; usable, interesting and unusual items, £10-£500.* LOC: Off Leith Walk, halfway down. PARK: Easy. TEL: 031 553 1364. SER: Valuations. FAIRS: Most major. VAT: Spec.

William Macintosh & Co
499 Lawnmarket. (P. and Mrs J. London). Est. 1964. Open 10-6, Sun. 2-5 in summer. SIZE: Large. *STOCK: Brass architectural and light fittings, fenders, pine, panelling, mantelpieces, furniture, Victorian, £5-£100.* LOC: Left at the top of Royal Mile. PARK: Easy. TEL: 031 225 6113. VAT: Stan.

McNaughtan's Bookshop
3a and 4a Haddington Place. Est. 1957. Open 9.30-5.30. CL: Mon. *STOCK: Antiquarian books.* TEL: 031 556 5897.

John Mathieson and Co
48 Frederick St. Open 9-5.30, Sat. 9-4.30. *STOCK: Paintings, watercolours, prints.* TEL: 031 225 6798. SER: Restorations (framing, gilding). VAT: Stan/Spec.

Montresor
35 St. Stephen St. (Pierre De Fresne and Gareth Jones). Est. 1989. Open 10.30-1 and 2-6. CL: Mon. SIZE: Small. *STOCK: Costume and designer jewellery, 1850-1950, £50-£200; art deco and art nouveau lighting, china and glass, £50-£1,000.* LOC: North from Princes St. to Stockbridge. PARK: Easy. TEL: 031 220 6877. SER: Valuations; restorations (paste jewellery). VAT: Stan.

Mulherron Antiques
83 Grassmarket. (F., A. and J. Mulherron). Est. 1970. Open 10-6. SIZE: Large. *STOCK: Furniture, 18th C to Regency, £250-£10,000; Oriental carpets and rugs, £250-£7,500; decorative objects to art deco, £50-£350.* PARK: Easy. TEL: 031 226 5907; home - 031 667 4119. SER: Valuations; restorations (furniture); buys at auction (furniture and Oriental rugs). VAT: Stan/Spec.

T. and J. W. Neilson Ltd
76 Coburg St, Leith. (J. and A. Neilson). Est. 1932. Open 9.30-5. SIZE: Large. *STOCK: Fireplaces, 18th-20th C, £100-£20,000; interiors, fenders, stoves, fenders, fire irons; marble (including French), wood and stone chimney*

Edinburgh continued

pieces. LOC: Continuation of Ferry Rd. PARK: Own. TEL: 031 554 4704; fax - 031 555 2071. SER: Installations (fireplaces). VAT: Stan.

John O. Nelson
22-24 Victoria St. Est. 1957. Open 10-12 and 1.30-5, Sat. 10-1. CL: Tues. *STOCK: Antiquarian maps, prints, watercolours.* LOC: First turning off George IV Bridge on right, past Royal Mile. Victoria St. leads down to Grassmarket. PARK: Castle Terrace, west end. TEL: 031 225 4413; evenings - 031 445 4816. VAT: Stan.

Nest Egg Antiques
5 Grange Rd. (Hugo Laughton). Open 10-6. *STOCK: General antiques especially light fittings, from 1820s.* TEL: 031 667 2328.

Now and Then (Toy Centre)
7 and 9 West Crosscauseway. Open 11-6, Sat. 10-6. *STOCK: Telephones, tin and diecast toys, clockwork and electric model trains, collectable mechanical ephemera, automobilia, juvenalia, clocks, gold and silver watches, small furniture, old advertisements, bric-a-brac.* LOC: City centre off A68. PARK: Nearby. TEL: 031 668 2927; 031 226 2867 (answerphone). SER: Valuations; buys at auction.

Open Eye Gallery Ltd
75/79 Cumberland St. (T. and P. Wilson). Est. 1976. Open 10-6, Sat. 10-4. SIZE: Medium. *STOCK: Early 20th C etchings, contemporary paintings, ceramics and jewellery.* LOC: From Princes St. go east, left into Frederick St. right at bottom of hill. PARK: Easy. TEL: 031 557 1020. SER: Valuations; restorations (paintings and ceramics); buys at auction. VAT: Mainly Spec.

H. Parry
Castle Antiques, 330 Lawnmarket. *STOCK: Silver, porcelain, English and continental furniture, clocks.* TEL: 031 225 7615.

Present Bygones
61 Thistle St. (Pat and Simon McIntyre). Est. 1982. Open 10-5, Sat. 11-4, Sun. by appointment. SIZE: Small. *STOCK: Ceramics, 19th C, £25-£75; textiles, samplers and sewnwork, 18th-19th C, £100-£300; fans, 19th C, £80-£150.* LOC: Between George St. and Queen St. PARK: Meters. TEL: 031 226 7646. SER: Buys at auction (ceramics, paintings and textiles). VAT: Stan/Spec.

Quadrant Antiques
5 North West Circus Place, Stockbridge. (M. Leask). Est. 1965. Open 10-5, Mon. 12-5. SIZE: Medium. *STOCK: Nautical items, general antiques including trade and shipping goods, furniture, clocks, brass beds, 18th-19th C.* PARK: Easy. TEL: 031 226 7282. VAT: Spec.

Edinburgh continued

Alan Rankin
72 Dundas St. Est. 1964. Open by appointment. SIZE: Small. STOCK: Antiquarian books, £5-£500; out-of-print scholarly books from 1850, £1-£40; prints, maps from earliest times to 1860, £1-£200. LOC: From Princes St., down Hanover St. to first block on left past Gt. King St. PARK: Easy. TEL: 031 556 3705; home - same. SER: Valuations; buys at auction.

Royal Mile Curios
363 High St. (L. Bosi and R. Eprile). Open 10.30-5. STOCK: Jewellery and silver. TEL: 031 226 4050.

James Scott
43 Dundas St. Est. 1964. Open 12-1 and 2.30-5.30. CL: Thurs. p.m. STOCK: Curiosities, unusual items, silver, jewellery, small furniture. TEL: 031 556 8260; home - 031 332 0617. VAT: Stan.

The Scottish Gallery
16 Dundas St. (Aitken Dott plc). Est. 1842. Open 10-6, Sat. 10-4 (10-5 during Festival and December). STOCK: 20th C and contemporary Scottish art, crafts, studio ceramics and jewellery. LOC: New Town. TEL: 031 558 1200. VAT: Stan/Spec.

Daniel Shackleton
17 Dundas St. STOCK: Paintings, watercolours, prints. TEL: 031 557 1115. VAT: Spec.

Stockbridge Antiques and Fine Art
8 Deanhaugh St, Stockbridge. Est. 1988. Open 2-5.30. CL: Mon. SIZE: Small. STOCK: Fine French and German dolls, 19th to early 20th C; small furniture and paintings, teddy bears, from 1900; juvenalia, tinplate toys, clockwork trains; costume Victorian whitework including christening robes, dolls clothes; Oriental items, ceramic and glass, all £20-£10,000. Not Stocked: Silver, jewellery and militaria. LOC: 1/2 mile north of Princes St. PARK: Easy. TEL: 031 332 1366. SER: Valuations; buys at auction; restorations (doll and teddy repair and re-costuming).

James Thin (Booksellers)
53-59 South Bridge. Est. 1848. Open Mon.-Sat. STOCK: Antiquarian and secondhand books. TEL: 031 556 6743. SER: Buys at auction.

This and That Antiques and Bric-a-Brac
22 Argyle Place. Open Thurs. to Sat. 2.30-5. STOCK: Porcelain, silver, small furniture, Scottish pottery, bric-a-brac. TEL: 031 229 6069; home - 031 447 1209.

The Thrie Estaits
49 Dundas St. Est. 1970. CL: Sat. STOCK: Pottery, porcelain, glass, unusual and decorative items, some furniture. TEL: 031 556 7384.

Edinburgh continued

The Thursday Shop
5 Clermiston Rd, Corstorphine. (Mrs I.J. Robertson). Est. 1982. Open 10.30-5, Sat. 10-5. CL: Mon. and Wed. SIZE: Small. STOCK: General antiques and bric-a-brac especially unusual items, £5-£500. LOC: Near St. John's Rd. PARK: Nearby. TEL: 031 334 3696. SER: Valuations. FAIRS: Scotfairs, Edinburgh, Ingliston.

Top Brass
77 Dundas St. (Nick Carter and Tom O'Donnell). Est. 1977. Open 10-12.45 and 2-6, Sat. 2-5. SIZE: Small. STOCK: Metal, mainly brass - light fittings, beds, fire accessories, door and window mongery, architectural fittings, 18th to early 20th C, £100-£1,000. LOC: Off Princes St., Hanover St. becomes Dundas St. PARK: Easy. TEL: 031 557 4293. VAT: Stan/Spec.

Unicorn Antiques
65 Dundas St. (N. Duncan). Est. 1967. Usually open 11-6. SIZE: Medium. STOCK: Architectural and domestic brassware, lights, mirrors, glass, china, cutlery and bric-a-brac. Not Stocked: Weapons, coins, jewellery. LOC: From Princes St. turn into Hanover St. Dundas St. is a continuation of Hanover St. TEL: 031 556 7176; home - 031 332 9135.

West Bow Antiques
102 West Bow. Open Tues. to Sat. 11-5. STOCK: Furniture, pottery, porcelain, glass, brass, decorative items. TEL: 031 226 2852.

John Whyte
116b Rose St. Est. 1928. Open 9.30-5.15, Sat 9.30-12.30. STOCK: Jewellery, watches, silver TEL: 031 225 2140. VAT: Stan.

Whytock and Reid
Sunbury House, Belford Mews. (J.C. and D.C Reid). Est. 1807. Open 9-5.30. CL: Sat. p.m. SIZE Large. STOCK: Furniture, English and continenta 18th to early 19th C, £50-£20,000; Eastern rugs carpets, £50-£10,000. Not Stocked: Victoria furniture. LOC: 1/2 mile from West End, of Belford Rd. PARK: Own. TEL: 031 226 4911; fax 031 226 4595. SER: Restorations (furniture, rugs) buys at auction; interiors. VAT: Stan/Spec.

Wild Rose Antiques
15 Henderson Row. (K. and E. Cameron). Ope 9.30-6. CL: Mon. STOCK: General antiques silver, jewellery, glass, pottery and porcelair small furniture, objects, Paisley shawls brassware. TEL: 031 557 1916.

Worthington's Antiques
180-182 Causewayside. (Mrs M. Worthington Est. 1989. Open 12-5. SIZE: Small. STOCK Furniture, Victorian and Georgian, £500-£1,000 blue and white china, 19th C, £50-£450. LOC Main road towards south. PARK: Easy. TEL: 03 662 0438; home - 031 663 8110. VAT: Spec.

Edinburgh continued
Aldric Young
49 Thistle St. *STOCK: General antiques; English and continental furniture, paintings, 18th-19th C.* TEL: 031 226 4101. VAT: Spec.

Young Antiques
36 Bruntsfield Place. (T.C. Young). Est. 1979. Open 10.30-1.30 and from 2.30. CL: Wed. p.m. SIZE: Medium. *STOCK: Victorian and Edwardian furniture, £50-£1,000; ceramics, £20-£2,000; Persian rugs, oils and watercolours, £50-£1,500.* LOC: Near Lothian Rd. PARK: Easy. TEL: 031 229 1361. SER: Valuations; buys at auction (Persian rugs, art pottery).

ELGIN (Morayshire)
West End Antiques
35 High St. (F. Stewart). HADA. Est. 1969. Open daily 9-5.30, Wed. 9-1. *STOCK: Silver, clocks and watches, Victorian jewellery, bric-a-brac.* TEL: 0343 547531; home - 0343 543216. VAT: Stan/Spec.

ELIE (Fife)
Malcolm Antiques
5 Bank St. Est. 1965. *STOCK: Victoriana, collectors' items, curios, clocks.* TEL: 0333 330116.

ERROL (Perthshire)
Errol Antiques
The Cross. (A. Knox). PADA. Est. 1949. Open 8.30-12 and 1-4.30. CL: Sat. and Sun. except by appointment. SIZE: Small. *STOCK: Furniture, 18th-19th C, £50-£5,000; paintings, 17th-20th C, £25-£3,000.* Not Stocked: Porcelain. LOC: 2 miles off A85. PARK: Easy. TEL: 0821 642391. SER: Valuations; restorations (cabinet making); buys at auction (furniture, paintings). VAT: Stan/Spec.

Greycroft Antiques
Greycroft, Station Rd. (D. and Mrs. J. Pickett). Est. 1981. Open 10-5.30 or by appointment. SIZE: Medium. *STOCK: Furniture including desks, bureaux and sofas, to mid-19th C, £500-£8,000; tables, chairs, Oriental porcelain, £50-£1,000; porcelain, brass, copper and bronze, £15-£150.* LOC: A85 between Perth and Dundee. PARK: Easy. TEL: 0821 642221; home - same. SER: Restorations (furniture); buys at auction (furniture). VAT: Stan/Spec.

FAIRLIE (Ayrshire)
Fairlie Antique Shop
86 Main Rd. (E.A. Alvarino). Est. 1976. Open 11-5. CL: Mon. SIZE: Small. *STOCK: Bric-a-brac, £5-£300; small furniture, clocks and silver, £10-£500; jewellery; all Victorian or Edwardian.* LOC: A78. PARK: 25yds. TEL: 0475 568613. SER: Valuations.

FALKIRK (Stirlingshire)
James Finlay
178 Grahams Rd. Est. 1966. Open 9.30-4, Wed. and Sat. 9.30-12. SIZE: Small. *STOCK: Bric-a-brac, 1880-1950; shipping furniture.* LOC: 1/4 mile from town centre. PARK: Easy. TEL: 0324 31505; home - 0324 20264 or 0324 37868.

FOCHABERS (Morayshire)
Antiques and Interior Design
64 High St. (B. Alexander-Forsyth). Open 10-5. *STOCK: Furniture, soft furnishings and Scottish pottery.* TEL: 0343 549313; 0863 671795.

Granny's Kist
Hadlow House, 22 The Sq. (M. Hill). Est. 1985. Open 9-5. SIZE: Medium. *STOCK: Kitchenalia, linen, tools, miscellaneous, £5-£50; furniture, £50-£1,000.* LOC: A96 village centre. PARK: Easy. TEL: 0343 820838; home - 0542 34218. FAIRS: Inverness, Elgin, Aberdeen.

L'Antiquitès
89 High St. (M.L. and J. Holstead). Est. 1983. Open 10-1 and 2-5. SIZE: Medium. *STOCK: General collectables, Oriental, clocks including longcase, glass; furniture, from 18th C oak, to 1930's.* PARK: Easy. TEL: 0343 820238; home - 0343 820572. FAIRS: Drumossie, Inverness, Banchory, Tree Tops.

Pringle Antiques
High St. (G. A. Christie). Est. 1983. Open 9.30-1 and 2-6 every day, closing at 5p.m in winter. SIZE: Medium. *STOCK: Furniture, Victorian, £20-£1,000; general antiques, pictures, brass, pottery, silver and jewellery.* Not Stocked: Books and clothing. LOC: A96, premises are a converted church. PARK: Easy. TEL: 0343 820362; home - 0343 820599. VAT: Stan/Spec.

Marianne Simpson
61/63 High St. (M.R. Simpson). Est. 1990. Open 10-1 and 2-5, or by appointment. SIZE: Small. *STOCK: Books, 19th-20th C, prints, 19th C; ephemera, 19th-20th C; all £1-£100.* LOC: A95. PARK: Easy. TEL: 0343 821192; home - same.

FORRES (Morayshire)
Michael Low Antiques
45 High St. Est. 1967. TEL: 0309 673696. VAT: Stan.

FORTROSE (Ross and Cromarty)
Black Isle Antiques
(Mrs N.J. Stokes and Mrs V. Hourston). HADA. Open by appointment only. SIZE: Small. *STOCK: China.* PARK: Easy. TEL: 0381 20407. SER: Valuations.

SCOTLAND

FREUCHIE (Fife)
Freuchie Antiques
Oxley House, Main St. (C.P. Wakefield). Est. 1980. Sometimes open, prior telephone call advisable. CL: Mainly Fri., Sat. and Sun. SIZE: Medium. STOCK: *Mainly small collectables and postcards, £5-£100.* PARK: Easy. TEL: 0337 57348.

FRIOCKHEIM, Nr. Arbroath (Angus)
M.J. and D. Barclay
29 Gardyne St. Est. 1965. Open 10.30-1 and 2-5.30. CL: Thurs. STOCK: *General antiques including furniture, jewellery, silver, porcelain and clocks.* Not Stocked: Stamps, books, coins. PARK: Easy. TEL: 02412 265. VAT: Stan.

GALSTON (Ayrshire)
Galleries de Fresnes
Cessnock Castle. (The Baron de Fresnes). D.A. (Glas.). Articles on drawings and paintings. Est. 1934. Open 10-6. STOCK: *General antiques, to 1850; silver, glass, oil paintings, 20th C; reproduction pine.* LOC: Approximately 600yds. on Sorn road out of Galston, 6 miles from Kilmarnock. PARK: Easy. TEL: 0563 820314. SER: Valuations; restorations (paintings); buys at auction; courier for overseas traders. *Mainly Trade.*

GARELOCHHEAD (Dumbartonshire)
Dene Hard Antiques
Dene Hard. (Mrs E.B. Ingleby). Est. 1982. Open 10-5, Mon. and Thurs. by appointment. SIZE: Small. STOCK: *Silver, 18th-20th C, £50-£500+; furniture, 19th C, £50-£1,500+; paintings and porcelain, 19th-20th C, £25-£1,800+.* LOC: 1 mile from village on Clynder road. PARK: Easy. TEL: 0436 810669; home - same. SER: Restorations; buys at auction.

GLASGOW (Lanarkshire)
Albany Antiques LAPADA
1347 Argyle St. (P.J. O'Loughlin). Est. 1969. Open 9.30-5.30 or by appointment. CL: Sat. STOCK: *Chinese and Japanese porcelain, Georgian, Victorian and Edwardian furniture, shipping goods.* TEL: 041 339 4267. VAT: Stan/Spec.

All Our Yesterdays
6 Park Rd, Kelvinbridge. (Susie Robinson). Est. 1988. Open 11-5.30, Fri. and Sat. 10-5.30 or by appointment. SIZE: Small. STOCK: *Kitchenalia, mainly 1850-1949, £5-£100; smalls, especially decorative arts, advertising related items, books, etchings and postcards, mechanical items, to £100.* LOC: Near junction of Gt. Western Rd. and Park Rd. and university. PARK: Easy. TEL: 041 334 7788. SER: Valuations; buys at auction; search and hire.

Glasgow continued
Bath Street Antiques Galleries
203 Bath St. Open 10-5, Sat.10-1. SIZE: Large. PARK: Easy. TEL: 041 248 4220. SER: Valuations; restorations (clocks); buys at auction. VAT: Stan/Spec. Below are listed the dealers at this market.

E. A. Alvarino Antiques
STOCK: *Edwardian, Victorian and Georgian furniture and accessories; general antiques, silver, clocks, instruments and paintings.* TEL: 041 221 1888.

Brown's Clocks Ltd
(J. Wilson). CMBHI. STOCK: *Longcase, wall and mantel clocks, £30-£5,000.* TEL: 041 248 6760. SER: Valuations; restorations; buys at auction. VAT: Stan/Spec.

Cooper Hay Rare Books
STOCK: *Antiquarian books and prints.* TEL: 041 226 3074.

Glenburn Antiques
STOCK: *Jewellery, silver, porcelain.*

John Green Fine Art
STOCK: *19th-20th C British and Continental oils, watercolours and etchings.* TEL: 041 221 6025. SER: Restorations; framing.

John Jacks
STOCK: *General antiques.*

Pauline Jamieson
STOCK: *Staffordshire figures, Scottish pottery, general antiques.*

Kilgour Antiques
(Mrs C.G. Kilgour). STOCK: *18th-19th C European and oriental ceramics, jewellery and silver including Scottish; glass, miniatures, samplers and other objects d'art.* TEL: 041 249 4396.

Barclay Lennie Fine Art Ltd LAPADA
STOCK: *Oil paintings, watercolours and sculpture, mainly Scottish, 19th-20th C* TEL: 041 226 5413.

Murray McIlroy
STOCK: *Pottery, porcelain, Scottish paintings furniture and decorative objects 1650-1950* TEL: 041 221 4004.

The Roger Billcliffe Fine Art
134 Blythswood St. Est. 1876. Open 9.30-5.30 Sat. 10-1. SIZE: Large. STOCK: *British paintings watercolours, drawings, sculpture, especiall Scottish, from 1800.* TEL: 041 332 4027. VAT Spec.

Butler's Furniture Galleries Ltd
24-26 Millbrae Rd, Langside. (L. Butler). Ope 9.30-5.30 or by appointment. CL: Sat. STOCK *Furniture, Georgian, Victorian, Edwardian; sma decorative items.* TEL: 041 632 9853/639 339 SER: Valuations.

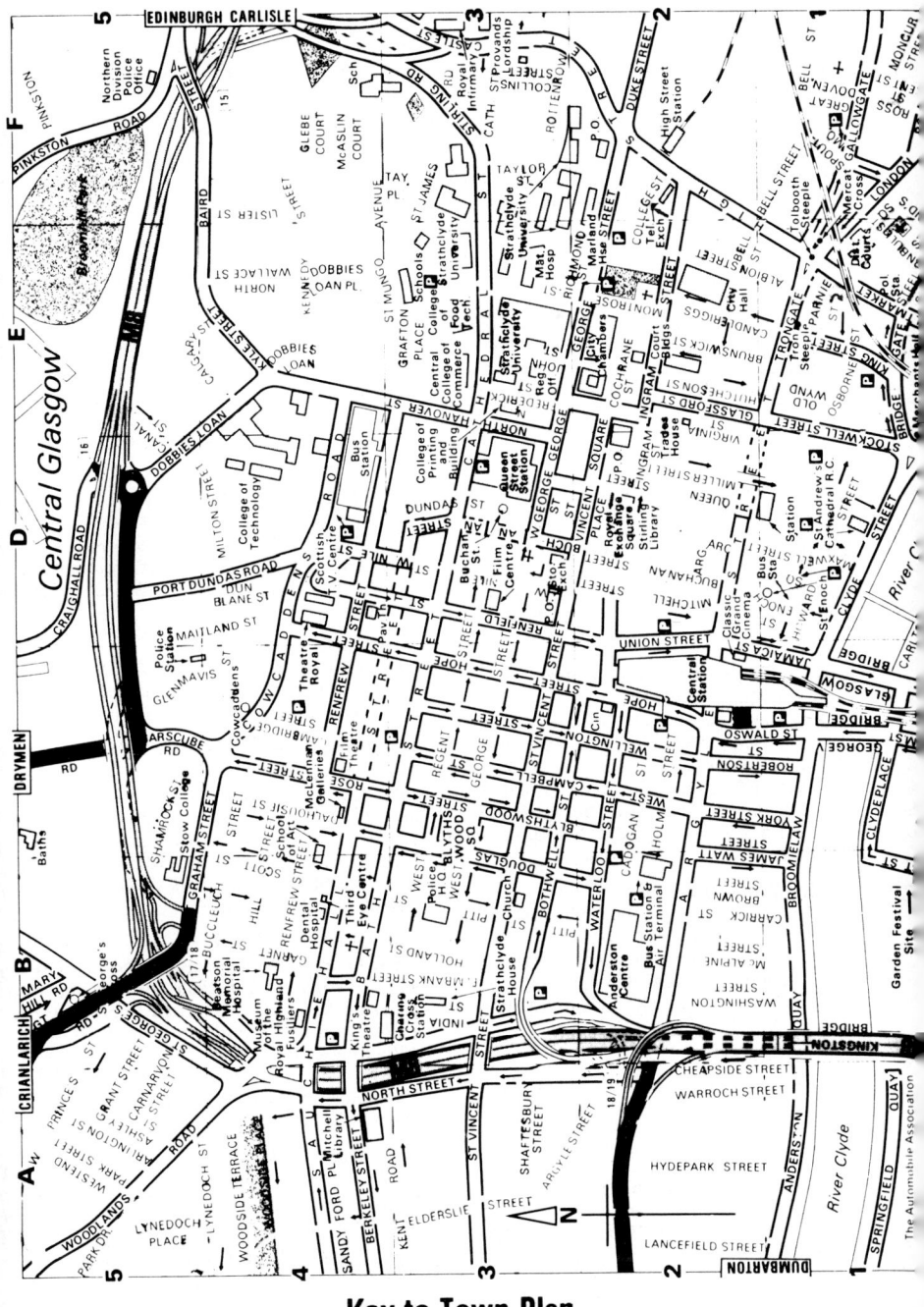

Key to Town Plan

— AA Recommended roads
— Other roads
— Restricted roads
■ Buildings of interest
▦ Car Parks
▦ Parks and open spaces
▦ AA Service Centre

🅿 Car Parks
🅰🅰 AA Service Centre

© Automobile Association 1988.

Glasgow continued

The Den of Antiquity
Langside Lane, 539 Victoria Rd., Queenspark. Est. 1960. Open 10-5 including Sun. STOCK: General antiques. TEL: 041 423 7122; evenings - 041 644 5860. VAT: Stan/Spec.

James Forrest and Co (Jewellers) Ltd
53 West Nile St. Est. 1957. CL: Sat. p.m. STOCK: Silver, jewellery, clocks. LOC: City centre. TEL: 041 221 0494. VAT: Stan.

A.D. Hamilton and Co
7 St. Vincent Place. (Jeffrey Lee Fineman). Est. 1983. Open 9-5.15. SIZE: Small. STOCK: Jewellery and silver, 19th to early 20th C, £100-£500; British coins, medals and banknotes, £10-£150. LOC: City centre, next to George Square. PARK: Meters. TEL: 041 221 5423. SER: Valuations. VAT: Stan/Spec.

Heritage House Antiques
Unit 6a, Yorkhill Quay. Open 9-5. SIZE: 10 dealers. STOCK: General antiques, furnishings, smalls and fine arts. TEL: 041 334 4924.

Caroline Kerr Antiques
103 Niddrie Rd, Queens Park. Open 9.30-5. CL: Sat. STOCK: General antiques. TEL: 041 423 0022; home - 041 946 3787. SER: Buys at auction.

King's Court Antique Centre
Units 1-6, King's Court, King St. (London and Birmingham Properties Ltd). Open 10-5 including Sun. CL: Mon. SIZE: Large - 30+ dealers. STOCK: Furniture, silver and general antiques, pre-1940. LOC: Opposite King St. car park, behind St. Enoch shopping centre. PARK: Easy. TEL: 041 552 7854/7856. SER: Valuations; buys at auction.

Lovatt Antiques Ltd
100 Torrisdale St. Est. 1963. CL: Sat. SIZE: Large. STOCK: General antiques, Victoriana, shipping goods. LOC: Adjacent Queen's Park railway station. TEL: 041 423 6497; home - 041 638 7062/632 4372. SER: Valuations; buys at auction. VAT: Stan/Spec.

Jean Megahy
481 Great Western Rd. (F.G. Halliday). Open 10-5. CL: Sat. p.m. STOCK: Furniture, brass, silver, Oriental items. TEL: 041 334 1315. VAT: Stan/Spec.

Mercat-Hughes Antiques
85 Queen St, 1 Royal Exchange Court. (P. Hughes and C. Forrester). Open 10-5.30 or by appointment. CL: Sat. STOCK: Small furniture, brass, ceramics, clocks, watches, E.P. and silver, jewellery and trade items. TEL: 041 204 0851; home - 041 770 4572.

Muirhead Moffat and Co
182 West Regent St. (D.J. Brewster and J.D

Glasgow continued

Hay). Est. 1896. Open 10-12.30 and 1.30-5. CL: Sat. and Sun. except by appointment. SIZE: Medium. STOCK: Period furniture, barometers and jewellery; clocks, silver, weapons, porcelain, tapestries and pictures. LOC: Off Blythswood Sq. PARK: Easy. TEL: 041 226 4683/226 3406. SER: Valuations; restorations (furniture, clocks, barometers and jewellery); buys at auction. VAT: Stan/Spec.

Ewan Mundy Fine Art Ltd
48 West George St. SLAD. Est. 1981. Open daily. SIZE: Medium. STOCK: Fine Scottish, English and French oils and watercolours, 19th-20th C, from £250; Scottish and English etchings and lithographs, 19th-20th C, from £100; Scottish contemporary paintings, from £50. LOC: City centre. PARK: Nearby. TEL: 041 331 2406. SER: Valuations; restorations arranged; buys at auction (pictures). FAIRS: New York. VAT: Stan/Spec.

Nice Things Old and New
1010 Pollokshaws Rd. (J. and E. Lake). Est. 1961. Open 12-6. STOCK: Interesting and unusual pieces. LOC: Facing Langside Halls and Marlborough House (Shawlands). TEL: 041 649 3826. FAIRS: Organiser.

Nithsdale Antiques
100 Torrisdale St., Queens Park. (W. McDonald). Open 9.30-5.30. STOCK: General antiques. TEL: 041 424 0444/649 7260. SER: Buys at auction.

Pastimes Vintage Toys
140 Maryhill Rd. (Gordon and Anne Brown). Est. 1980. Open 10-5. SIZE: Small. STOCK: Vintage toys, 1910-1980, £1-£300. LOC: From west off junction 17, M8; from east junction 16, M8. PARK: Easy. TEL: 041 331 1008. SER: Valuations. FAIRS: Organisers of Glasgow and Tayside Toy. VAT: Stan.

Pettigrew and Mail LAPADA
7 The Loaning, Whitecraigs, Giffnock. (S. Mail and C. Pettigrew). Est. 1966. Open by appointment only. STOCK: Scottish impressionist, Victorian, English and continental paintings, 19th-20th C, from £500. LOC: Just off A77. PARK: Easy. TEL: 041 639 2989/4592. SER: Valuations; restorations; commissions undertaken. VAT: Spec.

R.L. Rose and Co
19 Waterloo St. Open 9-4. STOCK: Oriental carpets and rugs. TEL: 041 248 3313. SER: Restorations (as stock).

Frank Russell and Son Antiques
Unit 104, 1 Rutherglen Rd. Est. 1972. Open by appointment. SIZE: Large. STOCK: Georgian, Victorian, Edwardian, art deco and bric-a-brac, £5-£5,000. LOC: Near sign for Atlas Express. Close to Shawfield Greyhound Stadium. TEL: 041 647 9608; home - 0236 736785. VAT: Stan.

Glasgow continued
Stenlake and McCourt
1 Overdale St, Langside. Est. 1984. Open 10-5. SIZE: Small. STOCK: *Edwardian postcards; cigarette cards, to 1950; ephemera, 1700-1930; stamps.* LOC: 50yds. from Battlefield monument. PARK: Easy. TEL: 041 632 2304. SER: Valuations (as stock). FAIRS: Bipex; Scottish Philatelic Congress and others. VAT: Stan.

The Victorian Village
53 West Regent St. Open 10-5, Sat. 10-4. LOC: Near Renfield St. PARK: Meters. TEL: 041 332 0808. VAT: Stan/Spec. Below are listed the dealers at these premises.

Anne's Antiques
STOCK: *Bric-a-brac and jewellery.*

Marie Diamond
STOCK: *China, bric-a-brac.*

Ricky Fearon
STOCK: *Antique sport.*

Ian Frame
STOCK: *Militaria.*

Marjory Kerr
STOCK: *Jewellery, china.*

Cathy McLay "Saratoga Trunk"
STOCK: *Textiles, linen and lace, Victorian to 1940's, £2-£500; costume, £5-£500; jewellery, £5-£200; both Victorian to 1950's.* TEL: 041 331 2707.

Putting-on-the-Ritz
STOCK: *20's clothing, jewellery.*

Rosamund Rutherford
STOCK: *Jewellery, Scottish agate, lace.*

Virginia Antique Galleries
31/33 Virginia St, (Off Argyle St.). (M. Robinson). Open 10-5, Sun. 12-5. SIZE: 20 dealers. STOCK: *Furniture, glass, jewellery, silver, porcelain and brass.* TEL: 041 552 2573/8640; office - 041 552 5840.

West of Scotland Antique Centre Ltd
Langside Lane, 539 Victoria Rd., Queens Park. (Wosac Ltd). Est. 1969. Open 9.30-5.30, Sun. 12-5. SIZE: Large - 8 dealers. STOCK: *Pine, Georgian to Edwardian, £50-£3,000.* PARK: Easy. TEL: 041 422 1717. VAT: Stan/Spec.

Woolfsons of James Street Ltd
59/73 James St. Est. 1983. Open 9-5, Sun. 12-5. SIZE: Large. STOCK: *Furniture, £100-£500; porcelain, £25-£500; bric-a-brac, £5-£50; all from 1800.* LOC: 2 minutes from Bridgeton Cross. PARK: Own. TEL: 041 556 7281- check when Jean returns book. SER: Valuations, restorations (French polishing, upholstery, wood); buys at auction. VAT: Stan/Spec.

Glasgow continued
Tim Wright Antiques   LAPADA
147 Bath St. (T. and J. Wright). Est. 1971. Open 9.30-5, Sat. by appointment. STOCK: *Furniture; European and Oriental ceramics and glass, decorative items, silver and plate, brass and copper, mirrors and prints, all £50-£5,000.* LOC: On opposite corner to Christie's, Glasgow. PARK: Multi-storey opposite. TEL: 041 221 0364. VAT: Mainly Spec.

Yesteryear
158 Albert Drive. (I.C. Taylor). Open 11-6. STOCK: *General antiques.* TEL: 041 429 3966.

GOUROCK (Lanarkshire)
Bygones
(R. McPhail). Open 9.30-5.30. STOCK: *General antiques.* TEL: 0475 31114.

GRANTOWN-ON-SPEY (Morayshire)
Strathspey Gallery   LAPADA
40 High St. (Franfam Ltd). Resident. Est. 1971. Open 10-1 and 2-5 (1-2 by appointment), Thurs. 10-1. SIZE: Medium. STOCK: *Furniture inluding early oak; collectors' ceramics and metalware; pictures including wildlife and sporting.* LOC: Town centre. PARK: Easy and behind shop. TEL: 0479 3290; home - same. SER: Valuations. VAT: Mainly Spec.

GREENLAW (Berwickshire)
Greenlaw Antiques
(Mr and Mrs A. Brotherston). Est. 1970. Open Mon. to Fri. and by appointment. SIZE: Large. STOCK: *General antiques, £5-£500.* PARK: Easy. TEL: 036 16 220. VAT: Stan/Spec.

Greenlaw Antiques
The Town Hall. (Mr and Mrs A. Brotherston). Open Sun. and Wed. 2-5. STOCK: *General antiques, £5-£500.*

GUARDBRIDGE, by St. Andrews (Fife)
Circa Antiques
9A Main St. (C. McDonald Craig). Est. 1978. Open 10-5. SIZE: Medium. STOCK: *General antiques, mainly British, 1800-1900, £5-£3,000.* Not Stocked: Postcards, crested china, militaria and weapons. PARK: Rear of premises. TEL: 0334 838896.

GULLANE (East Lothian)
Gullane Antiques
5 Rosebery Place. (E.A. Lindsey). Est. 1981. Open 10.30-1 and 2.30-5. CL: Wed. SIZE: Medium. STOCK: *China and glass, 1850-1930, £5-£100; prints and watercolours, early 20th C, £25-£100; metalwork, 1900's, £5-£50.* LOC: 6 miles north of Haddington, off A1. PARK: Easy. TEL: 0620 842326.

Phone: INCHTURE (0828) 86412

On A85 Perth-Dundee Trunk road

LARGE STOCK OF PERIOD FURNITURE

C.S. MORETON
at
Inchmartine House
INCHTURE · PERTHSHIRE · PH14 9QQ

ALSO ORIENTAL CARPETS and RUGS
—
METALWARE and CERAMICS

Prop. PAUL STEPHENS

HADDINGTON (East Lothian)
Antiques and Things
36 Market St. (T.J. and M.C. Lemon). Est. 1977. Open 10-12.30 and 2-4, Sat. 10-1 and 2-5. CL: Mon. and Wed. SIZE: Small. *STOCK: Furniture and smalls, £2-£1,000.* LOC: 1.5 miles off A1. PARK: Easy. TEL: 062 082 2206.

Elm House Antiques
The Sands, Church St. (Mrs I. MacDonald). Est. 1972. Open daily, appointment advisable, and Sat. 10-1 and 2-5. SIZE: Small. *STOCK: English porcelain and pottery, 18th and 19th C, £20-£600; blue and white earthenware, Scottish pottery, £20-£900; boxes, furniture, £25-£800.* LOC: Off A1, end of High St. PARK: Easy. TEL: 062 082 3413; home - same.

Fine Design
6 Court St. (Mr and Mrs D.J. Nicoll). Est. 1989. Open 10-12.45 and 2.15-5.30, Thurs. 10-12.45. SIZE: Small. *STOCK: Ceramics, 19th-20th C, £5-£1,000; jewellery, Victorian and Edwardian, £10-£600; furniture, 19th C, £50-£2,000.* LOC: 1.5 miles off A1. PARK: Easy. TEL: 062 082 4838; home - 062 082 6168. SER: Valuations; restoration (ceramics); buys at auction (as stock).

Leslie and Leslie
Open 9-1 and 2-5. CL: Sat. *STOCK: General antiques.* TEL: 062 082 2241; fax - same. VAT: Stan.

HOUNDWOOD (Berwickshire)
Houndwood House Antiques LAPADA
Houndwood House. (R. and I. Gourlay). Resident. Est. 1982. Open daily including evenings. SIZE: Large. *STOCK: Furniture, late 18th C to Edwardian, £100-£5,500; paintings, 18th C to 1920, £150-£3,500; smalls, Georgian-Edwardian, £10-£500; decorative items.* LOC: On A1, 13 miles north of Berwick-on-Tweed. PARK: Easy. TEL: 08907 61232. SER: Valuations; restorations (furniture and porcelain especially Wemyss ware); buys at auction. FAIRS: Castle (Scotland, Yorkshire and The South); Antiques in Britain (Scotland). VAT: Spec.

INCHTURE (Perthshire)
C.S. Moreton (Antiques)
Inchmartine House. (P.M. and Mrs M. Stephens). Est. 1922. Open 9-5.30. CL: Sat. *STOCK: Furniture, £50-£10,000; carpets and rugs, £50-£3,000; ceramics, metalware; all 16th C to 1860; old cabinet makers' tools.* LOC: Take A85 Perth/Dundee road, entrance on left at Lodge. PARK: Easy. TEL: 0828 86412; home - same. SER: Valuations; cabinet making and repairs. VAT: Stan/Spec.

INVERNESS (Inverness-shire)
The Attic
Riverside, 17 Huntly St. (P. Gratton). HADA. Est. 1976. Open 10.30-1 and 2-5. CL: Wed. Jan.-Mar. Mon. and Wed. SIZE: Small. *STOCK: Art deco china, jewellery, linen, textiles, period clothes, Victorian to 1940's, from £5.* PARK: The Riverside. TEL: 0463 243117/240324. SER: Valuations. FAIRS: Aberdeen.

Fine Oriental Rugs and Carpets of Inverness
Upper Myrtlefield, Nairnside. (G. MacDonald). Open by appointment only. *STOCK: Persian, Turkoman, Afghanistan, Caucusus, Anatolian rugs and carpets, late 19th C to 1940, £500-£2,000+;.* LOC: From A9 1st left after flyover, 1st left at roundabout, then 2.25 miles on B9006, then 1st right, 1st left. PARK: Easy. TEL: 0463 792198; home - same. SER: Valuations; restorations (cleaning and repair). FAIRS: Aberdeen, Inverness; Hopetown House and Roxburgh Hotel, Edinburgh; Cameron House, Loch Lomond.

JEDBURGH (Roxburghshire)
Mainhill Gallery
Ancrum. (B. and D. Bruce). Est. 1981. Open 10.30-5.30, prior telephone call advisable, or by appointment. SIZE: Medium. *STOCK: Oil paintings, watercolours and etchings, 19th-20th C, some prints, £35-£7,000.* LOC: Just off A68, 3 miles north of Jedburgh, centre of Ancrum. PARK: Easy. TEL: 083 53 518. SER: Valuations; buys at auction. VAT: Spec.

Antique Collectors' Club Titles

British 19th Century Marine Painting
Denis Brook-Hart combined his love of the sea with his professional interests as a fine art consultant to produce this popular volume.
**ISBN 0 902028 32 4, 370pp
206 b & w illus, 32 col, £35.00**

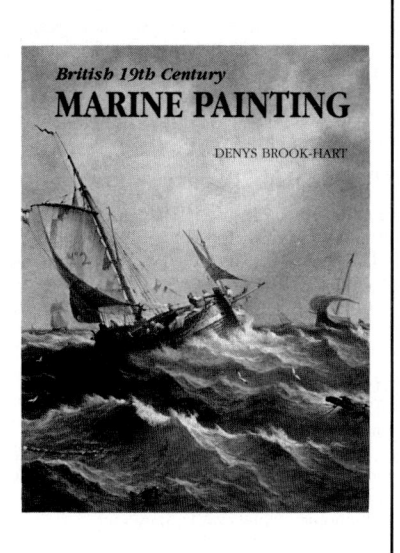

Dictionary of Sea Painters
by E.H.H. Archibald
A new edition of this important work with an enlarged biographical section and many additional illustrations.
**ISBN 1 85149 047 7, 576pp
932 b & w illus, 38 col, £45.00**

Available from:
Antique Collectors' Club, 5 Church Street, Woodbridge, Suffolk IP12 1DS
Tel: (0394) 385501 Fax: (0394) 384434'

or Market Street Industrial Park, Wappingers' Falls, New York 12590, USA
Tel: 914 297 0003 Fax: 914 297 0068

Jedburgh continued
R. and M. Turner
(Antiques and Fine Art) Ltd   LAPADA
34/36 High St. Est. 1965. Open 10-5.30. CL: Sun. except by appointment. SIZE: Large. *STOCK: Furniture, clocks, porcelain, paintings, silver, jewellery, 17th-20th C.* LOC: On A68 to Edinburgh. PARK: Own. TEL: 0835 63445. SER: Valuations; restorations (furniture, pottery, porcelain); packing; shipping; interior design. VAT: Stan/Spec.

KILBARCHAN (Renfrewshire)
Gardner's The Antique Shop   LAPADA
Wardend House, Kibblestone Rd. (G.D. and R.K.F. Gardner). Est. 1950. Open to the trade 7 days a week. Retail 10-1 and 2-6, Sat. 10-1. SIZE: Large. *STOCK: General antiques.* LOC: 12 miles from Glasgow, at far end of Tandlehill Rd. 10 mins. from Glasgow Airport. TEL: 050 57 2292.

Marjorie and Sandy McDougall
10 The Cross. Est. 1968. Open Thurs. to Sun. 1-5, other days by appointment. *STOCK: Textiles, 19th C, £50-£500; furniture, 18th-19th C, £50-£2,000; beds, 19th C, £200-£700+.* LOC: 5 miles on A740 from junction 29, M8. PARK: Easy. TEL: 050 57 2229; home - same. VAT: Stan/Spec.

KILLEARN, Nr. Glasgow (Stirlingshire)
Country Antiques
(Lady J. Edmonstone). Est. 1975. Open Mon.-Sat. SIZE: Small. *STOCK: Small antiques and decorative items, Victoriana and textiles.* LOC: A81. In main st. PARK: Easy. TEL: Home - 0360 70215.

KILLIN (Perthshire)
Maureen H. Gauld
Cameron Buildings, Main St. Est. 1975. Open Mar.-Oct. 10-5.30. SIZE: Small. *STOCK: General antiques, silver and paintings, £5-£2,000.* PARK: Easy. TEL: 0567 820475; home - 0567 820605.

KILMACOLM (Renfrewshire)
Kilmacolm Antiques Ltd
Stewart Place. (H. Maclean). Est. 1973. Open 10-1 and 2.30-5.30. CL: Sun. and Wed. except by appointment. SIZE: Medium. *STOCK: Furniture, 18th-19th C, £100-£8,000; objets d'art, 19th C; jewellery, £5-£5,000; paintings, £100-£5,000.* LOC: First shop on right when travelling from Bridge of Weir. PARK: Easy. TEL: 050 587 3149. SER: Restorations (furniture, silver, jewellery, porcelain). FAIRS: Hopetown House, Perth, Roxburghe, Edinburgh. VAT: Stan/Spec.

KILMARNOCK (Ayrshire)
MacInnes Antiques
5c David Orr St, Bonnington. (Mrs M. MacInnes). Est. 1973. Open by appointment. *STOCK: General antiques.* TEL: 0563 26739.

Kilmarnock continued
QS Antiques
Moorfield Industrial Estate, Troon Road. (J.R. Cunningham and D.A. Johnson). Est. 1980. Open 9-5.30, Sat. 9-5. SIZE: Large. *STOCK: Furniture including stripped pine, 18th-19th C; shipping goods, architectural and collectors' items.* PARK: Easy. TEL: 0292 74377. SER: Restorations (upholstery, stripping). VAT: Stan.

KILMICHAEL GLASSARY, By Lochgilphead (Argyllshire)
Rhudle Mill
(D. Murray). Est. 1979. Open daily, weekends by appointment. SIZE: Medium. *STOCK: Furniture, 18th C to art deco, £30-£3,000; small items and bric-a-brac, £5-£500.* LOC: Signposted 3 miles south of Kilmartin on A816 Oban to Lochgilphead road. PARK: Easy. TEL: 0546 605284; home - same. SER: Restorations (furniture); French polishing; buys at auction.

KILTARLITY, By Beauly (Inverness-shire)
Old Pine Furniture and Jouet
Fuaranbuie, 8 Kinerras. (J. and A. Jeorrett). Open by appointment. *STOCK: Restored pine including Victorian, £25-£600+.* TEL: 046 374 261.

KINCARDINE O'NEIL, Nr. Aboyne (Aberdeenshire)
Amber Antiques
1 Southside, Old Turnpike. (V. Watson). Est. 1982. Open 10.30-6, Sun. 1.30-5. SIZE: Small. *STOCK: Jewellery especially amber, Victorian and Edwardian, £25-£500; silver, Georgian-Edwardian, £10-£500; Oriental objets d'art, £5-£1,000; pictures, 16th-20th C, £25-£500; antiquarian books.* LOC: On North Deeside Rd. PARK: Easy. TEL: 033 984 277; home - 03398 84338. SER: Valuations; buys at auction. FAIRS: Aberdeen, Inverness, Banchory, Newark.

KINGHORN (Fife)
The Pend Antiques
53 High St. Est. 1990. Open 10-5.30; winter - afternoons and Sat. 10-5.30. SIZE: Large. *STOCK: Pre-1930's furniture, prints, china, glass, textiles and general collectables, £1-£750.* PARK: Easy. TEL: 0592 890207; home - 0592 890140. SER: Valuations; restorations; stripping, waxing, small repairs.

KINGSTON-ON-SPEY (Morayshire)
Collectables
Lein Rd. (J. Penman and B. Taylor). Est. 1987. Open daily and last Sun. of month, prior telephone call required. SIZE: Small. *STOCK: Militaria and jewellery, lap desks, china,*

SCOTLAND

LARGE STOCK OF FURNITURE, PORCELAIN, ETC.

GARDNER'S

THE ANTIQUE SHOP

WARDEND HOUSE, KIBBLESTON ROAD
KILBARCHAN, PA10 2PN

20 MINUTES FROM GLASGOW CENTRE
10 MINUTES FROM GLASGOW AIRPORT

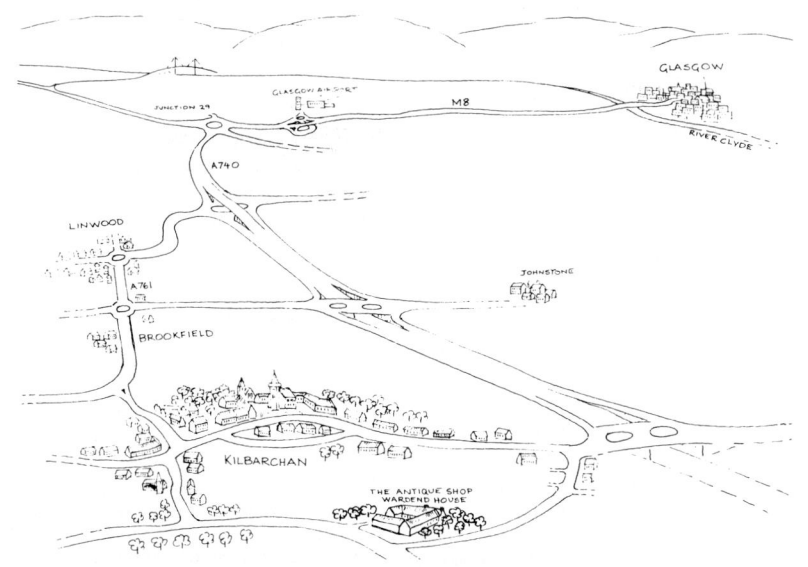

LAPADA
MEMBER

TELEPHONE KILBARCHAN (05057) 2292
ESTABLISHED 1950

SCOTLAND

Kingston-on-Spey continued
collectables, small furniture, £5-£200. LOC: On B9105. PARK: Easy. TEL: 034 387 462; home - same. SER: Valuations. FAIRS: Inverness and Aberdeen.

KINGUSSIE (Inverness-shire)
Mostly Pine
Gynack Cottage, High St. Est. 1980. Open 10-5.30. STOCK: *Stripped pine and country furniture, decorative items, small collectables.* LOC: A9. TEL: 0540 661838. SER: Restorations (pine). VAT: Stan/Spec.

KINROSS (Kinross)
Miles Antiques LAPADA
16 Mill St. (K. and S. Miles). Est. 1979. Open 9-5, weekends by appointment. SIZE: Large. STOCK: *Furniture including decorative, Georgian, Victorian and Edwardian, £100-£5,000; china and pottery, £50-£500.* LOC: Off M90, junction 6. Take right at High St. then second left. PARK: Easy. TEL: 0577 864858; home - 0577 863881. SER: Restorations (upholstery, polishing, small repairs). VAT: Stan/Spec.

Portcullis Antiques
76 High St. (Charles Cranston). Est. 1982. Open 2-5.30, Sat. 11-4.30, Sun. 1-4.30. CL: Mon. and Thurs. SIZE: Small. STOCK: *China and porcelain, 19th-20th C, £50-£100; small furniture, 20th C, £50-£150; brass, silver and plate, 19th-20th C, £5-£300.* LOC: Just off M90. PARK: Opposite in Avenue Rd. TEL: 0577 862276; home - same.

KIRKCUDBRIGHT (Kirkcudbrightshire)
Chapel Antiques
Chapel Farm. (A. Bradley). Est. 1981. Open 9-5 and by appointment. SIZE: Small. STOCK: *China, small and shipping furniture, silver, brass and copper, 18th-20th C, £5-£1,000.* LOC: 200yds. off A75 between Ringford and Twynholm by-passes on A762, 2.5 miles from Kirkcudbright. PARK: Easy. TEL: 055722 281.

Osborne LAPADA
41 Castle St. (R.A. Mitchell). Est. 1948. Open 9-12.30 and 1.30-5. CL: Thurs. p.m and Sat. p.m. TEL: 0557 30441. VAT: Stan/Spec.

LANGHOLM (Dumfriesshire)
The Antique Shop
High St. (R. and V. Baird). Est. 1970. Open 10.30-5.30. CL: Wed. p.m. SIZE: Small. STOCK: *China, glass, pictures, 18th-20th C; jewellery, rugs, 19th-20th C; also Trade Warehouse of furniture, shipping goods and antiquarian books.* LOC: 20 miles north of Carlisle on A7. PARK: 100yds. TEL: 038 73 80238.

LARGS (Ayrshire)
Narducci Antiques
11 Waterside St. (G. Narducci). Open 2.30-5.30 or by appointment. SIZE: Warehouse. STOCK: *General antiques and shipping goods.* TEL: 0475 672612/0294 61687. SER: Packing; export. *Mainly Trade and Export.*

LESLIE BY INSCH (Aberdeenshire)
C.S. Antiques
New Leslie. Open by appointment. SIZE: Medium. STOCK: *Pine, oak and mahogany furniture, 19th C, £50-£500.* LOC: Telephone for directions. PARK: Easy. TEL: 0464 20567; home - same. FAIRS: Tree Tops Hotel, Aberdeen.

LEUCHARS, Nr. St. Andrews (Fife)
Earlshall Castle
(The Baron of Earlshall). Est. 1963. Open by appointment only. SIZE: Small. STOCK: *Arms and armour especially Scottish basket hilted swords and dirks, 16th-19th C, £200-£20,000.* LOC: Signposted on A91 at Guardbridge and in village. PARK: Easy. TEL: 0334 839205; home - same. SER: Valuations; restorations (wood, metal, engraving, chiselling and casting); buys at auction (weapons). VAT: Stan/Spec.

LINLITHGOW (West Lothian)
Heritage Antiques
222 High St. (Mrs A.G. Dunbar). Est. 1980. Open 10-5. CL: Wed. STOCK: *Jewellery, china, glass, silver, small furniture and objects.* PARK: Nearby. TEL: 0506 847460. SER: Valuations; repairs (jewellery).

MOFFAT (Dumfriesshire)
Harthope House Antiques
Church Gate. (Mrs M. Owens). Est. 1979. Open 10-5. CL: Wed. STOCK: *Furniture, general antiques especially Victorian jewellery.* TEL: 0683 20710.

MONTROSE (Angus)
Harper-James
25-27 Baltic St. (D.R. and M.L. James). Resident. Est. 1991. Open 9-5, Sun p.m. and other times by appointment. SIZE: Large. STOCK: *Furniture, clocks, silver and jewellery, 1730-1910, £50-£3,000+; ceramics and pottery, 1800-1945, £10-£650+; general antiques and curios, £2-£750.* LOC: From south turn right at Peel statue, then first left. PARK: Easy. TEL: 0674 671307; home - same. SER: Valuations; restorations (furniture upholstery); buys at auction (furniture); export. FAIRS: Major U.K. VAT: Stan/Spec.

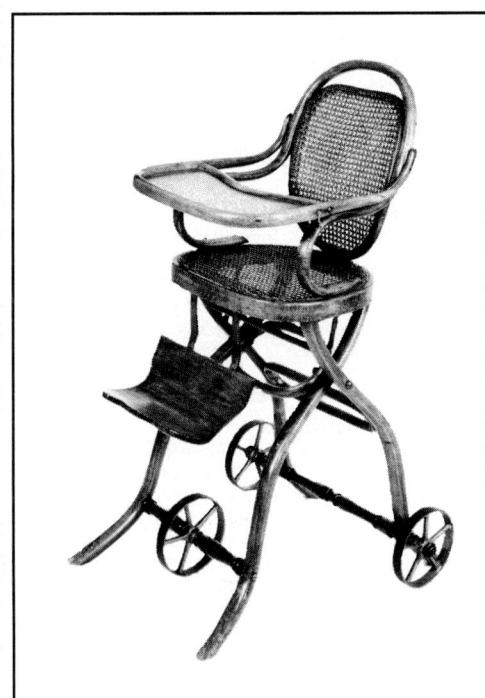

A late 19th century bentwood high chair, with caned back and seat. Designed for comfort and practicality, it has a foot-rest and integral playboard which could be used both at mealtimes and playtime. Its well splayed legs make it extremely stable, an important factor for a piece of furniture designed to hold a sturdy infant. The wheels ensure that it could be wheeled away into a corner when not in use. Photograph: Christie's. From *Yesterday's Children* by Sally Kevill-Davies, published by the **Antique Collectors' Club**, £19.95pb.

NEWBURGH (Fife)
Newburgh Antiques
222 High St. (Miss D.J. Fraser). Est. 1991. Open 10.30-12 and 1.30-5. CL: Mon. SIZE: Small. STOCK: Wemyss ware, 1882-1930, £100-£2,000; Scottish watercolours and oil paintings, 1800-1950's, £100-£1,500; furniture, 1750-1900, £200-£2,000. LOC: A913. PARK: Easy. TEL: 0337 41026; home - 0337 40725. SER: Valuations.

NEWTON STEWART (Wigtownshire)
Pathbrae Antiques
20 Albert St. (R. and D. Williamson and W. and M. Plunkett). Est. 1985. Open 10.30-12.45 and 1.45-5. CL: Wed. p.m. SIZE: Small. STOCK: Porcelain, 19th-20th C, from £5; jewellery, silver and plate. LOC: Main street (A75). PARK: Easy. TEL: 0671 3429. SER: Valuations. VAT: Stan/Spec.

NEWTONMORE (Inverness-shire)
The Antique Shop
Main St. (J. Harrison). Est. 1964. Open 9.30-5.30. SIZE: Medium. STOCK: Small furniture, £20-£500; glass, china, silver, plate, copper, brass, secondhand books. LOC: On A86 opposite Mains Hotel. PARK: Easy. TEL: 0540 673272.

OBAN (Argyllshire)
The McIan Gallery (Campbell-Gibson Fine Arts)
10 Argyll Sq. Est. 1973. Open 9-5.30. STOCK: Victorian and early 20th C watercolours and oil paintings, Scottish and continental, from £200. TEL: 0631 66755/62303. SER: Restorations; framing; valuations; buys at auction.

Oban Antiques
35 Stevenson St. (P. and P. Baker). Est. 1970. Open 9.30-5.30. SIZE: Medium. STOCK: Furniture and general antiques, mainly 19th C; books, collectables, some art deco, £5-£1,500. LOC: Off George (main) St. PARK: Easy. TEL: 0631 66203; home - 0631 77215.

PAISLEY (Renfrewshire)
Heritage Antiques
Walker St. (C.W. Anderson). Est. 1963. Open by appointment. SIZE: Medium. STOCK: Furniture, late 18th-19th C; shipping goods and small items. LOC: Off High St. PARK: Own. TEL: 0506 825579. SER: Valuations. VAT: Stan/Spec.

Paisley Fine Books
17 Corsebar Cres. (Mr and Mrs B. Merrifield). Est. 1985. Open by appointment. SIZE: Small. STOCK: Books on architecture, art, antiques and collecting. TEL: 041 884 2661; home - same. SER: Free book search; catalogues issued.

PERTH (Perthshire)

Ainslie's Antique Warehouse
Unit 3, Gray St. (T.S. and A. Ainslie). Open 9-5, by appointment at weekends. SIZE: Large. STOCK: General antiques. TEL: 0738 36825.

Atholl Antiques
80 Princess St. (M. and L. Gallagher). Open 9.30-1 and 2-5, Sat. 9.30-1. STOCK: General antiques. TEL: 0738 20054.

A.S. Deuchar and Son
10-12 South St. (A.S. and A.W.N. Deuchar). Open 10-1 and 2-5. CL: Sat. SIZE: Large. STOCK: Victorian shipping goods, furniture, 19th C paintings, china, brass, silver and plate. LOC: Glasgow to Aberdeen Rd., near Queen's Bridge. PARK: Easy. TEL: 0738 26297; home - 0738 51452. VAT: Stan/Spec.

Forsyth Antiques
2 St. Paul's Sq. (A.McDonald Forsyth). Est. 1961. Open 10-5. SIZE: Medium. STOCK: Silver, 18th-19th C, £5-£1,000; jewellery, 19th-20th C, £5-£750; Monart glass, 20th C, £5-£500. LOC: Behind St. Paul's Church, junction of High St. and Methven St. PARK: Easy. TEL: 0738 22173. SER: Valuations; buys at auction (silver). VAT: Stan/Spec.

Gallery One
1/2 St. Paul's Sq. (A. McDonald Forsyth). Est. 1990. Open 10-5. STOCK: Scottish pictures, Monart glass, silver, jewellery, furniture. LOC: Junction of High St. and Methven St. PARK: Easy. TEL: 0738 24877. SER: Valuations.

The George Street Gallery
38 George St. (S. Hardie). Open 10-1 and 2-5. CL: Wed. and Sat. p.m. STOCK: Oil paintings, watercolours, prints and etchings by Scottish artists, late 19th to early 20th C. TEL: 0738 38953.

Hardie Antiques
25 St. John St. (T.G. Hardie). PADA. Est. 1980. Open 9.30-5.15, Sat. 10-1. SIZE: Medium. STOCK: Jewellery and silver, 18th-20th C, £5-£5,000. PARK: Nearby. TEL: 0738 33127; home - 0738 51764. SER: Valuations. VAT: Stan/Spec.

Henderson
5 North Methven St. (J.G. Henderson). Est. 1935. Open 9-5.30. CL: Wed. p.m. SIZE: Small. STOCK: Porcelain, glass, 1720-1900, £5-£50; silver, jewellery, 1800-1900, £2-£200; coins, medals and stamps, £1-£100. Not Stocked: Furniture. LOC: On A9. PARK: Easy. TEL: 0738 24836; home - 0738 21923. SER: Valuations. VAT: Stan.

Ian Murray Antique Warehouse
21 Glasgow Rd. Open 9-5, Sat. 10-1. SIZE: Large - 8 dealers. STOCK: General antiques, Victorian, Edwardian and shipping items. PARK: Easy. TEL: 0738 37222. VAT: Stan/Spec.

Perth continued

Robertson and Cox Antiques
60 George St. PADA. Open 10-1 and 2-5. CL: Wed. p.m. and Sat. p.m. SIZE: Medium. STOCK: Furniture, 18th-19th C; paintings, porcelain, Oriental rugs, smalls. TEL: 0738 26300. VAT: Spec.

Tay Street Gallery
70 Tay St. (I.C. Ingram). Est. 1972. Open Tues., Thurs. and Fri. 10-1 and 2-3.30, or by appointment. SIZE: Small. STOCK: Furniture and related items, pictures and prints, 17th-19th C. LOC: Overlooking River Tay. PARK: Easy. TEL: 0738 20604. VAT: Stan/Spec.

PITLOCHRY (Perthshire)

Blair Antiques
14 Bonnethill Rd. (Duncan Huie). PADA. Est. 1976. Open 9-5. CL: Thurs. p.m. STOCK: Period furniture, Scottish oil paintings, silver - some provincial, curios, clocks, pottery and porcelain. LOC: Beside Scotlands Hotel, off A9 to Inverness. TEL: 0796 472624. SER: Valuations; buys at auction. VAT: Stan/Spec.

PITTENWEEM (Fife)

The Little Gallery
20 High St. (Dr. Ursula Ditchburn-Bosch). Est. 1988. Open 10-5, Sun. 2-5. CL: Mon. and Tues. SIZE: Small. STOCK: China, 18th C to 1930's, £5-£100; small furniture, mainly Victorian, £30-£200; rustica, £5-£25; contemporary paintings, £50-£250. LOC: From Market Sq. towards church, on right. PARK: Easy. TEL: 0333 311227; home - same. SER: Valuations.

Pittenweem Antiques and Fine Art
15 East Shore, The Harbour. (K.M. McKillop and D.O. MacNeal). Est. 1974. Open 10-5, Sun. 2-6. SIZE: Medium. STOCK: Fine art and paintings of Scottish school, late 19th C to early 20th C, £500-£1,000; furniture, £500-£1,000, and Scottish pottery, both mid-19th C; small items. PARK: Easy. TEL: 0333 312054. SER: Valuations.

PORTSOY (Aberdeenshire)

Other Times Antiques
13-15 Seafield St. (D. McLean and T. Matheson). Est. 1986. Open 10-5 including Sun. STOCK: General antiques, 1700-1950. TEL: 0261 42866. VAT: Stan/Spec.

PRESTWICK (Ayrshire)

Crossroads Antiques
7 The Cross. (Timothy Okeeffe). Est. 1989. Open 9-5. SIZE: Medium. STOCK: Furniture, 18th-20th C, £5-£1,000+; china and silver, 19th-20th C, £5-£500+. PARK: Nearby. TEL: 0292 74004. SER: Valuations; buys at auction.

Prestwick continued
Yer Granny's Attic
176 Main St. (Mr and Mrs B. Dickson). Est. 1986. Open 10-6, Sun. by appointment. SIZE: Small. STOCK: *General antiques, collectables, bric-a-brac and linen, from Victorian, £1-£100.* LOC: Opposite large sandstone church. PARK: Nearby. TEL: 0292 76312. SER: Restorations; commission work (stained glass).

RAIT (Perthshire)
Rait Village Antiques Centre
LOC: Midway between Perth and Dundee, 1 mile north of A85. PARK: Easy. Below are listed the dealers at this centre:.

The Bothy
(C. McCallum). Est. 1986. STOCK: *Georgian, Victorian, Edwardian pine furniture, small and decorative items, textiles.* TEL: 0821 670205. SER: Buys at auction.

Edward Bowry
TEL: 0821 670318. SER: Restorations (furniture).

Fair Finds
(Lynda Templeman). STOCK: *Furniture including upholstered Victorian chesterfields and armchairs, and pine; smalls and textiles.* TEL: 0821 670379.

Guiscards
Open 10.30-5. CL: Thurs. STOCK: *Textiles especially Paisley shawls and quilts; curtains and pelmets; decorative items including porcelain.* TEL: 0821 670392.

Guiscards Miniatures and Juvenalia
Open 10.30-5. CL: Thurs. STOCK: *Fine miniature furniture and collectables dolls and teddies.* TEL: 0821 670392. SER: Miniature furniture made to order.

Newton Antiques of Edinburgh
TEL: 0821 670205.

Pretty Pictures
(Lynda Templeman). STOCK: *Watercolours and oils, £40-£500.* TEL: 0821 67039.

Templemans
Open 9.30-5. STOCK: *Period and decorative furniture, £200-£20,000.* TEL: 0821 670344; home - 0828 86684. SER: Valuations; museum acquisitions. VAT: Spec.

ST. ANDREWS (Fife)
Bygones
68 South St. (Mrs J. Guest). Open 10-4.30, Sun. 2-4.30. CL: Thurs. STOCK: *Furniture, smalls, silver, bric-a-brac.* LOC: Near town hall. PARK: Easy. TEL: 0334 75849.

Magpie
28 Bell St. (Anne Fraser). Est. 1986. Open 10-1 and 2-5. SIZE: Small. STOCK: *Furniture, £500-£1,000; porcelain, to £1,200; jewellery and*

Free!

28 page full colour catalogue of Antique Collectors' Club books. Over 120 titles included covering a wide range of subjects: furniture, art reference, art history, prints, jewellery, metalwork, glass, horology, ceramics, oriental carpets, collectables, garden history and design, gardening and architecture.

Available free from the
ANTIQUE COLLECTORS' CLUB

5 Church Street
Woodbridge
Suffolk IP12 1DS
Tel: (0394) 385501
Fax: (0394) 384434

St. Andrews continued
silver, to £2,500; all 18th to early 20th C. LOC: Town centre, between South St. and Market St. PARK: Easy. TEL: 0334 74193. SER: Valuations; restorations (furniture, porcelain and jewellery); buys at auction. VAT: Stan/Spec.

A. and F. McIlreavy Rare and Interesting Books
57 South St. (Alan and Fiona McIlreavy). ABA. Est. 1977. Open 9.30-5. SIZE: Medium. STOCK: *Books, 17th-20th C, £5-£1,000.* PARK: Easy. TEL: 0334 72487; home - 0334 870982. SER: Valuations; buys at auction. FAIRS: ABA Edinburgh.

Old St. Andrews Gallery
9 Albany Place. (Mr and Mrs D.R. Brown). Est. 1973. CL: 1-2 daily. SIZE: Medium. STOCK: *Golf memorabilia, 19th C, £100-£20,000; silver, jewellery especially Scottish 19th-20th C, £100-£10,000; general antiques, from 18th C, £50-£5,000.* LOC: Main street. PARK: Easy. TEL: 0334 77840. SER: Valuations; restorations (jewellery, silver); buys at auction (golf memorabilia). VAT: Stan.

Old St. Andrews Gallery
10 Golf Place. Open 10-5.30. STOCK: *Golf memorabilia, art and books, from 18th C, to £10,000.* TEL: 0334 77840.

St. Andrews Fine Art
84a Market St. Open 10-1 and 2-5. STOCK: *Scottish oils, watercolours and drawings, 19th-20th C.* TEL: 0334 74080.

SALTCOATS (Ayrshire)
Narducci Antiques
57 Raise St. (G. Narducci). Est. 1972. Open 10-1 and 2.30-5.30, or by appointment. *STOCK: General antiques and shipping goods.* TEL: 0294 61687/67137. SER: Packing, export, shipping and European haulage. *Mainly Trade and Export.*

SCONE, Nr. Perth (Perthshire)
Robert Ainslie Antiques
80 Perth Rd. Open 9-5, Sat., Sun. and other times by appointment. SIZE: Medium. *STOCK: Georgian, Victorian and Edwardian furnishings and smalls, especially longcase clocks.* TEL: 0738 52438.

SELKIRK (Selkirkshire)
Heatherlie Antiques
6/8 Heatherlie Terr. (A.F.D. Scott). Est. 1979. Open 9-12.30 and 1.30-5. CL: Sat. p.m. SIZE: Medium. *STOCK: Furniture, £50-£1,000; pottery and porcelain, general antiques, brass, bric-a-brac and copper, £5-£250; all 19th-20th C.* LOC: Leave A7 at Selkirk market place and take Moffat/Peebles road for 1/2 mile. PARK: Easy. TEL: 0750 20114. VAT: Stan/Spec.

SORBIE, Nr. Newton Stewart (Wigtownshire)
R.G. Williamson & Co LAPADA
Old Church. Est. 1965. Open 2-4 April-Sept., other times by appointment. SIZE: Large. *STOCK: Furniture, from 1700, from £20; small items, from 18th C, from £5.* LOC: Off A75. PARK: Easy. TEL: 098 885 275; home - same. SER: Valuations; buys at auction. VAT: Stan/Spec.

STIRLING (Stirlingshire)
Abbey Antiques
35 Friars St. (S. Campbell). Resident. Est. 1980. Open 10-5. SIZE: Small. *STOCK: Jewellery, £10-£2,000; furniture including pine, £20-£1,000; paintings, £50-£1,000; bric-a-brac, £1-£100; coins and medals, £1-£1,000; all 18th-20th C.* LOC: Off Murray Pl., part of main thoroughfare. PARK: Nearby. TEL: 0786 447840; home - 0786 470595. SER: Valuations; restorations (china, furniture, jewellery); buys at auction (paintings, furniture, jewellery).

Elizabeth Paterson Antiques LAPADA
Est. 1976. Open by appointment only. SIZE: Large. *STOCK: Furniture including pine; Oriental porcelain.* TEL: 0786 823779. SER: Valuations.

STRACHAN, Nr. Banchory (Kincardineshire)
D'Amico Antiques Ltd
Burn o'Rhoda. (J.E. Wrightson and Mrs P. Mawtus). Est. 1947. Open by appointment. *STOCK: Mainly clocks and furniture.* TEL: 03302 4832.

STRATHBLANE (Stirlingshire)
Whatnots
16 Milngavie Rd. (F. Bruce). Est. 1965. *STOCK: Furniture, paintings, jewellery, silver and plate, clocks, small items, shipping goods, horse drawn and old vehicles.* LOC: 25 miles from Stirling and 10 miles from Glasgow. PARK: Easy. TEL: 0360 70310. VAT: Stan/Spec.

THORNHILL, Nr. Dumfries (Dumfries-shire)
Thornhill Gallery Antique Centre
47-48 Drumlanrig St. (A.S.B. Crawford). Est. 1984. Open 9-5.30 or by appointment. SIZE: Medium - 9 dealers. *STOCK: Furniture, watercolours and oil paintings, glass, porcelain, silver and plate, linen and jewellery.* LOC: A76 in village centre. PARK: Easy. TEL: 0848 30566; home - same.

THURSO (Caithness)
Thurso Antiques
Drill Hall, Sinclair St. (G. and J. Atkinson). HADA. Est. 1971. Open 10-1 and 2-5, Thurs. 10-1. SIZE: Small. *STOCK: Porcelain, 1700-1920, £5-£1,500; jewellery, 1700-1930, £25-£1,000; silver, 1750-1900, £25-£1,000; coins, 1500-1900, £2-£500; paintings, 1750-1920, £25-£1,500; fiddles, 1740-1930, £50-£1,000; medals.* LOC: Near Post Office. PARK: Easy. TEL: 0847 63291. SER: Valuations; restorations; cleaning (paintings); silver, jewellery and fiddle repairs.

TROON (Ayrshire)
Old Troon Sporting Antiques
49 Ayr St. (R.S. Pringle). Est. 1984. CL: Wed. p.m. and Sat. p.m. SIZE: Medium. *STOCK: Golf items, 19th C, to £500+.* LOC: 5 minutes from A77. PARK: Easy. TEL: 0292 311822; home - 0292 313744. SER: Valuations; buys at auction (golf items). VAT: Stan.

UPPER LARGO (Fife)
Waverley Antiques
13 Main St. (D.V. and C.A. St. Clair). Est. 1962. Open 10.30-5.30, Sun. by appointment. SIZE: Small. *STOCK: Furniture, 18th C, £1,200-£3,500; porcelain, 19th C, £300-£350.* LOC: Coast road from Leven to St. Andrews. PARK: Easy. TEL: 033 336 437; home - same. SER: Valuations. VAT: Spec.

WALKERBURN (Peebleshire)
Townhouse Antiques
(B. Brett and J. Juett). Open 10.30-4.30. CL: Wed. *STOCK: Textiles, collectables, china, furniture.* LOC: On A72, 7 miles east of Peebles. TEL: 089 687 694/371.

ANTIQUE COLLECTING

- **Authoritative articles**
- **Practical buying information**
- **Up-to-date price guides**
- **Annual Investment Issue**
- **Auctions and fairs calendars**
- **Antiques for sale and wanted**

The magazine is published ten times a year and contains pre-publication offers and special Christmas discounts on ACC books

Join NOW and receive your first magazine and our book catalogue FREE
Annual membership: £19.50 UK, £25.00 overseas, US $40 USA, CAN $50 Canada

Antique Collectors' Club
5 Church Street, Woodbridge, Suffolk,
IP12 1DS, England
Tel: (0394) 385501 Fax: (0394) 384434

Market Street Industrial Park, Wappingers' Falls,
New York 12590, USA
Tel: 914 297 0003 Fax: 914 297 0068

For Collectors, By Collectors, About Collecting

WALES

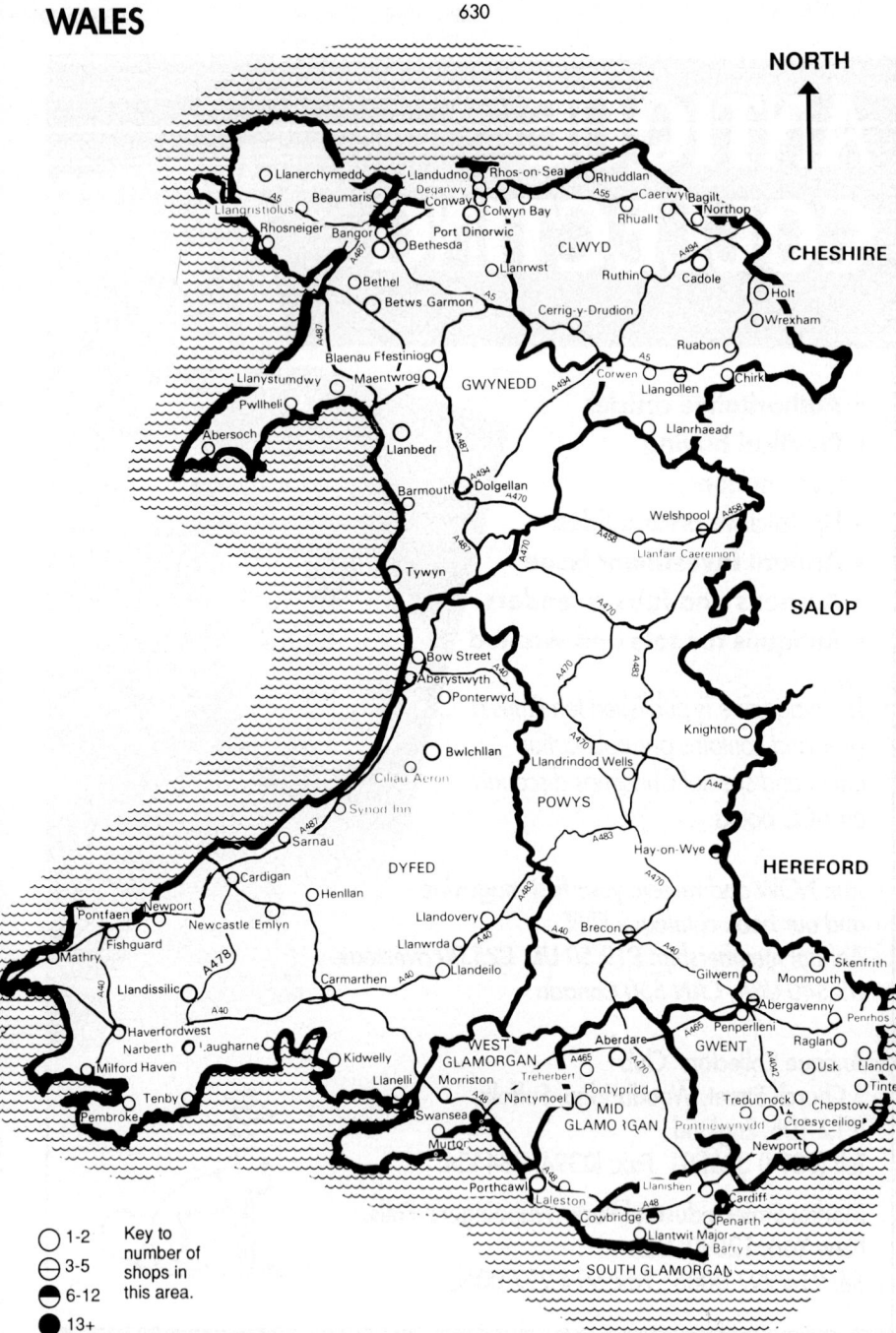

Key to number of shops in this area.
- ○ 1-2
- ⊖ 3-5
- ◐ 6-12
- ● 13+

Please note this is only a rough map designed to show dealers the number of shops in the various towns, and is not necessarily totally accurate.

WALES

Clwyd

BAGILLT
Mayfair Antiques
Green Park House, Green Park, High St. (H. Edwards). Open by appointment. *STOCK: General antiques.* TEL: 0352 711891.

CHIRK
Seventh Heaven
Chirk Mill. (Mr and Mrs J.J. Butler). Est. 1971. Open every day. SIZE: Large. *STOCK: Brass, iron and wooden beds including half-tester, four-poster and canopied, mainly 19th C.* LOC: B5070, below village, off A5 bypass. PARK: Easy. TEL: 0691 777622/773563; fax - 0691 777313. VAT: Stan.

COLWYN BAY
North Wales Antiques - Colwyn Bay
56-58 Abergele Rd. (F. Robinson). Est. 1971. Open 9-5. SIZE: Large warehouse. *STOCK: Shipping items, Victorian, early oak, mahogany and pine.* LOC: On A55. PARK: Easy. TEL: 0492 530521; evenings - 0492 516141. VAT: Stan.

CORWEN
Caxton House Antiques
Bridge St. (M. Holmes Field). Open 10-4.30. CL: Wed. *STOCK: Small furniture, china, pottery, Staffordshire figures, prints, oil lamps, Victorian clothing.* LOC: On A5, 10 miles from Llangollen. TEL: 0490 413276.

HOLT, Nr. Wrexham
Norman Davies
Rock Cottage, Bridge St. Open Sat. and Sun. 10-5, other times by appointment. *STOCK: Furniture, 18th-19th C.* TEL: 0829 270210.

LLANGOLLEN
M. Gallagher (Antiques)
Hall St. Open by appointment. *STOCK: General antiques.* TEL: 0978 860655.

J. and R. Langford
12 Bridge St. (P. and M. Silverston). Est. 1960. CL: Thurs. p.m. and 1-2 daily. SIZE: Medium. *STOCK: Furniture, £100-£3,000; pottery and porcelain, £50-£700; silver, general antiques, clocks, brass and paintings, £20-£2,000; all 18th-19th C.* LOC: Turn right at Royal Hotel, shop on right. PARK: Easy. TEL: 0978 860182; home - 0978 860493. SER: Valuations. VAT: Stan/Spec.

Oak Chest
1 Oak St. Est. 1950. *STOCK: Victorian jewellery and silver.* TEL: 0978 860095. VAT: Stan.

Llangollen continued

Passers Buy (Marie Evans)
Oak St/Chapel St. (Mrs M. Evans). Est. 1970. Open 11-5, Sun. by appointment. SIZE: Medium. *STOCK: Pottery, porcelain, furniture, copper, brass and prints.* LOC: Just off A5. Junction of Chapel St. and Oak St. PARK: Easy. TEL: 0978 860861/757385. FAIRS: Portmeirion Spring and Autumn.

MOLD
Mold Antiques and Interiors
The Old Chapel, 91 Wrexham St. (A. Terry). Est. 1984. CL: Thurs. SIZE: Large. *STOCK: Furniture, 1780-1930, £50-£2,500; pictures and porcelain.* LOC: From Mold Cross into Wrexham St., premises 1/4 mile on right. PARK: Easy. TEL: 0352 752979; home - 0352 750344. FAIRS: Wilmslow Moat House Sunday monthly. VAT: Stan/Spec.

NORTHOP, Nr. Mold
James H. Morris and Co
Old Village School, The Green. Appointment advisable. *STOCK: Furniture, clocks.* LOC: A55. TEL: Home - 035 286 768. SER: Valuations.

RHOS-ON-SEA
Clwyd Coins and Stamps
12 Colwyn Cres. (J.H. Jones). Open by appointment. *STOCK: Coins, stamps and postcards.* TEL: 0492 540610.

Shelagh Hyde
11 Rhos Rd. Est. 1960. Open 10-1 and 2.30-5. CL: Wed. p.m. *STOCK: Trade selection of general antiques; furniture, porcelain, glass.* TEL: 0492 548879.

RHUALLT, Nr. St. Asaph
John Trefor Antiques
Rhuallt Hall Farm. Est. 1967. Open by appointment any time. SIZE: Medium. *STOCK: Oak, walnut and mahogany furniture especially Welsh dressers, longcase clocks, some shipping goods, £5-£6,500. Not Stocked: Jewellery, cards and medals.* LOC: On A55 take Rhuallt turning, B5429, grey stone farmhouse at end of village, close to Smithy Arms. PARK: Easy. TEL: 0745 583604. VAT: Stan/Spec.

RUTHIN
Castell Delmar Antiques
Wrexham Rd. (W.T. Jones). Open by appointment. SIZE: Warehouse. *STOCK: Pre-1930 furniture and shipping goods.* TEL: 0824 704484.

Old Tyme Antiques
21 Clwyd St. (G. and J. Vaughan). Open 10.30-5. CL: Thurs. p.m. in winter. *STOCK: Wall and*

WALES

Ruthin continued
mantel clocks; British, European and Oriental porcelain, Imari ware, Cranberry, Gaudy Welsh china, brass, silver, jewellery, postcards and bric-a-brac. LOC: 100yds. from town square. PARK: Nearby. TEL: Home - 0824 702902. VAT: Stan.

R. and S. M. Percival Antiques
Porth-y-Dwr, 65 Clwyd St. Est. 1979. Open daily, Sun. and Mon. by appointment. SIZE: Medium. STOCK: Pine, mahogany and oak furniture and decorative smalls, 18th-19th C, £100-£1,000+. PARK: Behind shop. TEL: 0824 704454; home - 097 888 370. SER: Valuations; buys at auction (furniture). FAIRS: Newark. VAT: Stan/Spec.

Dyfed

ABERAERON
Colectomania
Corner Shop, Albert St. (K. and J. Whiteland). Est. 1957. Open 10.30-5.30. CL: Thurs. SIZE: Medium. STOCK: Furniture and small items including brass, copper, china, 19th C, £5-£1,000. LOC: Off A487. PARK: Easy. TEL: Home - 0570 470 597. SER: Valuations.

ABERYSTWYTH
The Furniture Cave
33 Cambrian St. (P. David). Est. 1975. Open 9-5, Wed. 9-3, Sat. 10-4. STOCK: Pine, 1700-1930, from £100; general antiques, Victorian and Edwardian, £30-£300; small items, 19th C, £10-£50. LOC: First right off Terrace Rd., at railway station end. PARK: Nearby. TEL: 0970 611234. SER: Restorations.

Howards of Aberystwyth   LAPADA
10 Alexandra Rd. Open 10-5.30. STOCK: Furniture, jewellery, Welsh pottery and copper lustre, gaudy Welsh and early pottery, Staffordshire groups, blue and white, cranberry, glass, silver, prints and maps of Cardiganshire, collectables and decorative items, especially country. TEL: 0970 624973.

Chris Mann Antiques
Westminster Yard, High St. Open by appointment only. STOCK: Clocks especially longcase. TEL: 0970 612127.

AMMANFORD
Amman Antiques
29 Station Rd. (B. Haines). Open by appointment only. STOCK: General antiques. TEL: 0269 592730.

BOW STREET
Garn House Antiques
Garn House. (Mrs M. Hagarty). Est. 1969. Open Mon.-Sat. but to the Trade any time. STOCK:

Bow Street continued
General antiques, furniture, Victoriana, copper, brass, porcelain, glass, collectors' items and Victorian jewellery. TEL: 0970 828562/828885.

BWLCHLLAN, Nr. Lampeter
Jansons Antiques
Aelybryn. (J.C. Jansons). Usually open but prior telephone call advisable. STOCK: Furniture - Welsh oak, original painted pine, primitive Welsh country; brass and iron beds. TEL: 0570 470549.

CARMARTHEN
Cwmgwili Mill
Bronwydd Arms. (M.J. Sandell). Est. 1950. Open 9-1 and 2-6, Sat. 9-1 and 2-6, Sun. by appointment. SIZE: Large. STOCK: Furniture, oak, mahogany and country including dressers, coffers, long tables, and court cupboards, 17th-19th C, £50-£1,000. PARK: Easy. TEL: 0267 231500; home - 0267 237215. VAT: Spec.

Merlins Antiques
Albion Arcade, Blue St. (Mrs J.R. Perry). Open 10.15-4.30. CL: Mon. and Thurs. STOCK: Small items - porcelain, pottery and postcards. TEL: 0267 237728.

CILIAU AERON, Nr. Lampeter
K.W. Finlay Antiques
The Forge, Neuaddlwyd. Est. 1969. Usually open but prior telephone call advisable. SIZE: Medium. STOCK: Furniture, 18th-20th C, £50-£3,000; smalls. Not Stocked: Militaria, jewellery. LOC: A482. PARK: Easy. TEL: 0545 570536; home - same. VAT: Stan/Spec.

FISHGUARD
Hermitage Antiquities
10 West St. (J.B. Thomas). Est. 1976. Open 9.30-1 and 2-5.30. CL: Wed. and Sat. p.m. SIZE: Small. STOCK: Arms, armour and militaria - full suits of armour, 16th-17th C; military long-guns, pistols, swords; cased pistol sets, military headgear, ethnographica, 16th-19th C, £50-£5,000; antiquities, jewellery, objets d'art. LOC: 50yds. on right after leaving Square on Harbour road (West St.). PARK: 300yds. TEL: 0348 873037; home - 0348 872322. SER: Valuations; restorations (arms and armour, inlay work on wheel locks, flintlock parts re-built, woodwork repairs); buys at auction (arms and armour). VAT: Spec.

Manor House Antiques
Main St. (R.E. Davies). Open 9.15-5.30. STOCK: General antiques especially porcelain and pottery. TEL: 0348 873260.

HAVERFORDWEST
Gerald Oliver Antiques
14 Albany Terr, St. Thomas Green. Est. 1957. Open 9.30-1 and 2-5. CL: Thurs. p.m. SIZE:

COUNTRY ANTIQUES
CASTLE MILL, KIDWELLY, DYFED
TEL: (0554) 890534

Pine potboard dresser Carmarthenshire c.1800

Rare yewtree dresser Denbighshire c.1750

LAPADA MEMBER

FIFTEEN SHOWROOMS OF FURNITURE & ACCESSORIES WITH THE EMPHASIS ON ITEMS OF WELSH INTEREST

Haverfordwest continued

Small. STOCK: Furniture, pre-1890, £5-£3,000; ceramics, metalwork, small silver, from 35; unusual, decorative and local interest items. LOC: Via by-pass and up Merlins Hill to St. Thomas Green. PARK: Easy. TEL: 0437 762794. SER: Valuations. VAT: Spec.

Pine Design Workshop and Pine Corner Antiques
19 Bridgend Sq. (B. and J. Palmer). Open 9.30-5, Sat. 10-5. STOCK: Pine. TEL: 0437 765676.

Prendergast Antiques
162-164 Prendergast. (Alan J. Emmins). Est. 1982. Open 10-5. CL: Thurs. SIZE: Medium. STOCK: Furniture, china and decorative items, £5-£500. LOC: From A40 Fishguard road, turn on to B4329 Cardigan road at Withybush Hospital roundabout, premises 2 minutes, next to Jewsons. PARK: Easy. TEL: 0437 765695. SER: Valuations; restorations (furniture). FAIRS: Newark.

HENLLAN, Nr. Newcastle Emlyn
Michael Lloyd
Dolhaidd Garden Cottage. Est. 1987. Open 9-5, prior telephone call advisable. SIZE: Large. STOCK: Country furniture, pine, general antiques. LOC: On A484, 2 miles Newcastle Emlyn. TEL: 0559 370582. VAT: Stan/Spec. Trade Only.

Henllan continued
Tortoiseshell Antiques
Trebedw Guest House. (Mrs P. Taylor). Est. 1972. Open by appointment only. SIZE: Small. STOCK: Carved European ivories, £45-£4,000; jewellery and objects, £35-£1,000; textiles, samplers, needlework tools, £40-£1,000; all 17th to early 19th C. LOC: Off Carmarthen/Cardigan Rd. PARK: Easy. TEL: 0559 370943; home - same. SER: Valuations; restorations (jewellery). FAIRS: Olympia, NEC, West London, Buxton, Kensington, Snape, Tatten Park, Bath, Wilton House and major provincial. VAT: Spec.

KIDWELLY
Country Antiques   LAPADA
Old Castle Mill. (R. and L. Bebb). Open 10-5. CL: Mon. SIZE: Large. STOCK: Welsh country furniture and artefacts; longcase clocks, brass and copper. LOC: Just off A484. PARK: Easy. TEL: 0554 890534. SER: Valuations. VAT: Stan/Spec.

Country Antiques   LAPADA
31 Bridge St. (R. and L. Bebb). Open 10-5. CL: Mon. SIZE: Large. STOCK: Georgian and Victorian furniture and accessories; Persian carpets; collectables. LOC: On A484. PARK: Easy. TEL: 0554 890534/890328. VAT: Stan/Spec.

LAMPETER

Barn Antiques
2 Market St. (N. Megicks). Est. 1980. Open 9-5.30, Wed. 9-1. SIZE: Medium. *STOCK: Pine, oak, mahogany, mainly 19th C, £50-£1,000; reproduction pine and oak.* LOC: Pedestrianised street just off town centre. PARK: Easy. TEL: 0570 423526. SER: Valuations; restorations (reveneering, inlay work, French polishing, pine stripping and finishing). VAT: Stan.

LAUGHARNE

Neil Speed Antiques
The Strand. Est. 1975. Open most days in summer and at least Fri. and Sat. 11-5 in winter, other times by appointment. *STOCK: General antiques, country furniture and associated items.* TEL: 0994 427412.

LLANDEILO

Jim and Pat Ash
The Warehouse, 5 Station Rd. Est. 1977. Open 9.30-5. SIZE: Large. *STOCK: Victorian and antique furniture, Welsh country, oak, pine, mahogany, walnut.* LOC: 50yds. off A40. PARK: Easy. TEL: 0558 823726; home - 0269 850119. SER: Valuations; shipping; courier; buys at auction. VAT: Stan/Spec.

LLANDISSILIO, Nr. Clynderwen

Jeremiah Antiques
The Old Saddlery. (S. and S. Jeremiah). Est. 1980. Open Tues.-Sat. 9.30-5 or by appointment. SIZE: Small. *STOCK: Mahogany furniture, 19th C, £50-£2,500.* LOC: Halfway through village on A478. PARK: Easy. TEL: 0437 563848; home - same. SER: Restorations (furniture, excluding pine); buys at auction.

LLANDOVERY

Dyfri Antiques
11 High St. (B. Leach). Est. 1968. SIZE: Small. *STOCK: Small general antiques, china, pottery, collectors' items, old dolls.* TEL: 0550 20602.

Ovell Antiques
1 Kings Rd. Open 9.30-5. *STOCK: Porcelain including Derby and Worcester; silver, maps and prints.* TEL: 0550 20928.

LLANELLI

Alice's Antiques
24 Upper Park St. (Mrs A. Davies). Est. 1940. Open 10-1 and 2-6. CL: Tues. p.m. SIZE: Small. *STOCK: General antiques, 1850-1950, £5-£50; paintings, silver, Georgian and Victorian, china, metalware.* LOC: On main road in town centre. PARK: At rear. TEL: 0554 773045. SER: Valuations; buys at auction. VAT: Stan.

Llanelli continued

John Carpenter
Resident. Est. 1973. Open by appointment. *STOCK: Musical instruments, furniture, general antiques.* TEL: 0269 831094.

LLANWRDA

Maclean Antiques
Tiradda, Llansadwrn. (D.J. Thorpe). Resident. Est. 1972. Open 9.30-6. SIZE: Large. *STOCK: Period pine, country furniture, brass, period metal.* PARK: Easy. TEL: 0550 777509. VAT: Spec.

MATHRY

Cartrefle Antiques
(M. Hughes and Y. Chesters). Open 10-5.30; in winter Tues.-Sat. 10.30-4, evenings by appointment. *STOCK: General antiques especially jewellery.* PARK: Easy. TEL: 0348 831591.

MILFORD HAVEN

Milford Haven Antiques
Robert St. Est. 1968. Open 10-5. *STOCK: General antiques.* TEL: 0646 692152.

NARBERTH

Barn Court Antiques
12 High St. (A. and M. Evans). Est. 1989. Open 10-5. CL: Mon. SIZE: Medium. *STOCK: Oak, mahogany, walnut and rosewood furniture, Georgian to late Victorian, £100-£5,000; oils and watercolours, £100-£3,000; china and glass, mainly Victorian, £10-£300. Not Stocked: Pine furniture.* LOC: Off A40 on A478. PARK: Easy. TEL: 0834 861421.

NEWCASTLE EMLYN

Castle Antiques
Market Sq. (Mr and Mrs B.G. Houser). Est. 1986. Open 9.30-5.30. SIZE: Small. *STOCK: Furniture, 1700 to 1920s, £500-£2,000; china and glass, Victorian to 1920s; kitchenalia, 18th-19th C; both £5-£200.* LOC: Main road, under clock tower. PARK: Castle St. TEL: 0239 710420; home - same. VAT: Stan/Spec.

PEMBROKE

Pembroke Antique Centre
The Hall, Hamilton Terrace. (M. Davis). Open 10-5. SIZE: 30 dealers. *STOCK: Oak, pine and mahogany furniture, china, porcelain, clocks, prints, collectors' items.* LOC: Old chapel on main street. PARK: Easy. TEL: 0646 687017.

PEMBROKE DOCK

Glyn Jones Antiques
Secondhand Land, 11-13 Bush St. Resident. Open daily. SIZE: Large. *STOCK: Pine, shipping*

Pembroke Dock continued
furniture and smalls. LOC: 1/4 mile from Irish ferry terminal. TEL: 0646 621732. SER: Restorations; pine stripping; container packing.

PONTERWYD, Nr. Aberystwyth
Doggie Hubbard's Bookshop
Ffynnon Cadno. (C.L.B. Hubbard). ABA. Est. 1946. Open 10-5, Sun. by appointment. SIZE: Medium. STOCK: *Rare books on dogs, 16th-19th C, £50-£500; scarce books on dogs, 19th-20th C, £25-£100; other books on dogs, 20th C, £5-£25.* LOC: 1/2 mile form Ponterwyd westwards on A44. PARK: Easy. TEL: 097 085 224; home - same. SER: Valuations; buys at auction (rare dog books). FAIRS: New York and Boston.

SARNAU
Ffynnon Las
(P. and G. Palmer). Est. 1971. Open at any time. SIZE: Small. STOCK: *Decorated furniture in American and European styles, 19th to early 20th C; stripped pine.* LOC: Off A487 9 miles north of Cardigan, down track. PARK: Easy. TEL: 0239 654648; home - same.

SYNOD INN, Nr. Llandysul
Forge Antiques
The Old Forge. (Paul Williams). Est. 1982. Open 10-5 (including Sun. in summer) or by appointment. SIZE: Medium. STOCK: *General antiques, furniture and decorative items, especially Welsh quilts and blankets, 19th-20th C, £5-£2,000.* LOC: 1 mile south of Synod Inn on A487. PARK: Easy. TEL: 0545 580707; home - 0545 580604. VAT: Stan/Spec.

TENBY
Audrey Bull
15 Upper Frog St. Open 9.30-5. STOCK: *Period and Welsh country furniture, general antiques, especially jewellery and silver.* TEL: 0834 843114; home - 0834 813425. VAT: Spec.

Clareston Antiques
Warren St. (K. and Mrs M.J.A. Hunt). Est. 1964. Open 10-5, or by appointment. CL: Wed. SIZE: Small. STOCK: *Georgian and Victorian furniture; English and Welsh porcelain and pottery; silver and models.* LOC: Town centre, near police station. PARK: Easy. TEL: 0834 843350; home - same. SER: Valuations.

Mid Glamorgan

ABERDARE
Market Antiques
Aberdare Market. (J.A. Toms). Open 9-5.30. STOCK: *General antiques.* LOC: Town centre. TEL: 0685 870242.

Welsh Quilts & Blankets

Paul Williams the leading specialist in quilts & blankets at

Forge Antiques

The Old Forge, Synod Inn, Llandysul, Dyfed, SA44 6JX.

Telephone: (0545) 580707 day or (0545) 580604 evening

CAERPHILLY
G.J. Gittins and Son
10 Clive St. Open 9-5, Sat. 10-5. CL: Wed. STOCK: *General antiques, jewellery and shipping goods.* TEL: 0222 868835.

NANTYMOEL, Nr. Bridgend
Quest Antiques
1 Ogwy St. (K. and Mrs L. Bellamy). Est. 1988. Open 9.30-5 including Sun. SIZE: Small. STOCK: *General antiques, Victoriana, bric-a-brac, £5-£100.* Not Stocked: Large furniture. LOC: M4, junction 36 onto A4061. PARK: Easy. TEL: 0656 840403; home - same. FAIRS: Local.

PONTYPRIDD
David Charles
3 Taff-Vale Precinct. (D.C. Newth). Est. 1968. Open 9.30-5.30. SIZE: Large. STOCK: *Victorian oil lamps, £300-£2,000; Victorian glass including epergnes; furniture, 19th-20th C; ceramic figures.* PARK: Under precinct. TEL: 0443 404317; home - 0443 208396. SER: Valuations. VAT: Stan.

Pontypridd Antiques
Old Bakery, Shepherd St., Pwllgwuan. (P. Cooke). Open 9-5, Sat. 9-12. STOCK: *Stripped pine, china, brass and copper, Victorian and Edwardian, £5-£500.* TEL: 0443 407616. Mainly Trade.

PORTHCAWL

Harlequin Antiques
Dock St. (J. Ball). Est. 1974. Open 9-5. *STOCK: General antiques*. TEL: 0656 785910.

TREHERBERT

Steven Evans Antiques
The Warehouse, Abertonllwyd St. Est. 1981. Open by appointment. SIZE: Warehouse. *STOCK: Large furniture - Victorian mahogany, Edwardian inlaid, American shipping, £5-£5,000*. LOC: Junction 34, M4, then A4110. PARK: Own. TEL: 0443 776410/777045; mobiles - 0831 341634/431756. SER: Valuations; restorations; North American specialists; container packing and shipping. VAT: Stan.

TREORCHY

Steven Evans Antiques
Regent St. Open 9-5, Sun. by appointment. SIZE: Warehouse. *STOCK: Victorian mahogany, Edwardian inlaid, American shipping, £5-£5,000.* LOC: Junction 34, M4, then A4110. PARK: Own. TEL: 0443 776410/777045/431756; mobile - 0831 341634. SER: Valuations; restorations; North American specialists; container packing and shipping. VAT: Stan.

South Glamorgan

BARRY

Flame 'n' Grate
99-100 High St. (A. Galsworthy). Open 9-5.30. *STOCK: Antique and reproduction fireplaces and surrounds*. TEL: 0446 744788.

Hawkins Bros. Antiques
5, 21, 22 and 23 Romily Buildings, Woodham Rd., Barry Docks. Open 8-5.30, weekends and other times by appointment. *STOCK: General antiques*. TEL: 0446 746561/721444/749880; evenings - 0446 721393/730878/745205 or 0222 513717.

Irena Art and Antiques
111 Broad St. (Mrs I. Halabuda). Est. 1977. Open daily. SIZE: Small. *STOCK: Furniture, 18th-19th C, £50-£1,000; porcelain and glass, general antiques and art deco, £50-£100*. PARK: Easy. TEL: 0446 747626; home - 0446 732517. SER: Valuations; restorations (cane and rush seating, painted furniture, lacquerware, gold-leafing and gilding); buys at auction (18th C cottage oak furniture, Bergere settees, chairs).

CARDIFF

Alexander Antiques
312 Whitchurch Rd. (J.R. Bradley). Open 10-5.30. *STOCK: Jewellery, clocks and furniture*. TEL: 0222 621824.

Cardiff continued

Back to the Wood
Old Post Office Sorting Office, West Canal Wharf. (I. Cooling). Open 9-5. *STOCK: Pine and fireplaces*. LOC: Next door to Jacobs Antique Centre. TEL: 0222 390939. SER: Restorations (fireplaces); pine stripping.

A. Burge Antiques
54 Crwys Rd. Open 9-5.30. CL: Wed. *STOCK: General antiques including clocks*. TEL: 0222 383268.

Charlotte's Wholesale Antiques
129 Woodville Rd, Cathays. (P.G. Cason). Open 9.30-4. SIZE: Large and warehouse. *STOCK: Shipping goods, general antiques, period furniture*. TEL: 0222 759809/224632.

Cronin Antiques
12 Mackintosh Place, Roath. (J. Cronin). Open 9.30-4.30. *STOCK: General antiques, silver and jewellery*. TEL: 0222 498929.

W.H. Douglas
161 Cowbridge Rd. East. *STOCK: General antiques, Victoriana, trade and shipping goods*. TEL: 0222 224861. *Trade Only*.

Grandma's Goodies
31 Mortimer Rd, Pontcanna. (R. Gronow). Est. 1981. Open Thurs.-Sat. 10-1 and 2-6 or by appointment. SIZE: Medium. *STOCK: Linen, china and bric-a-brac and small furniture, £5-£200*. LOC: 5 minutes by car from town centre to Cathedral Rd. PARK: Easy. TEL: 0222 383142; home - 0222 340901. SER: Prop hire.

Heritage Antiques and Stripped Pine
83 Pontcanna St. (D. Gluck). Est. 1974. Open 9-6. SIZE: Medium. *STOCK: Pine and general antiques, 19th C, £50-£500*. LOC: 1st turning by shops at top end of Cathedral Rd. PARK: Easy. TEL: 0222 390097. SER: Restorations (mainly pine). FAIRS: Sophia Gardens, Cardiff. VAT: Stan.

Jacobs Antique Centre
West Canal Wharf. Open Wed.-Sat. 9.30-5. SIZE: Large - 80 dealers. *STOCK: General antiques, stripped pine and furniture*. LOC: 2 mins. from main railway and bus stations. PARK: 100yds. TEL: Thurs. and Sat. only 0222 390939. SER: Valuations; restorations; buys at auction.

Kings Fireplaces, Antiques and Interiors
163 Cowbridge Rd. East, Canton. (B. Quinn). Est. 1984. SIZE: Medium. *STOCK: Period fireplaces including French marble; Victorian and Edwardian furniture*. LOC: Main road in Canton on west side of city. PARK: Opposite. TEL: 0222 225014. SER: Restorations (furniture and fireplaces); fireplace installations. VAT: Stan.

Cardiff continued
Kings Fireplaces & Architectural Antiques
All Saints Church, Adamsdown Sq., Splott. (B. Quinn). *STOCK: Fireplaces including 19th C French marble, £50-£1,000; furniture including reproduction; Victorian and Edwardian bathroom suites.* TEL: 0222 492439. SER: Restorations (19th C cast iron).

Llanishen Antiques
26 Crwys Rd, Cathays. (Mrs J. Boalch). Open 10.30-4.30. CL: Wed. except by appointment. *STOCK: Furniture, silver, china, glass, bric-a-brac.* TEL: 0222 397244.

Manor House Fine Arts
73 Pontcanna St, Pontcanna. (S.K. Denley-Hill). Est. 1976. Open 10.30-5.30. CL: Mon., Wed. and Sun. except by appointment. SIZE: Medium. *STOCK: Watercolours, oil paintings and prints, £50-£2,000; general antiques and smalls, £10-£1,000; all 1800-1960.* LOC: Pontcanna St. is at north end of Cathedral Rd. PARK: Easy. TEL: 0222 227787. SER: Valuations; restorations; framing and mounting; buys at auction. VAT: Stan/Spec.

Past and Present
242 Whitchurch Rd, Heath. (C. and J. Rowles). Est. 1970. Open Sat. 10.30-5.30. Open to trade all week at rear of shop or by appointment. SIZE: Medium. *STOCK: Clocks, 19th C, £50-£3,000+; furniture, 18th-19th C, £5-£1,000+; china and bric-a-brac, £5-£500.* LOC: From M4 along eastern avenue by-pass, city turn-off by University Hospital, 1st left into Whitchurch Rd. PARK: Nearby. TEL: 0222 621443/759529. SER: Valuations; buys at auction. VAT: Stan.

San Domenico Stringed Instruments
175 Kings Rd, Canton. (H. Morgan). Open 10-1 and 2-5. CL: Sat. p.m. SIZE: Small. *STOCK: Fine violins, violas, cellos and bows, mainly 18th-19th C, £300-£20,000.* LOC: Off Cathedral Rd. or Cowbridge Rd. PARK: Easy. TEL: 0222 235881; home - 0222 777156; fax - 0222 344510. SER: Valuations; restorations; buys at auction. VAT: Stan/Spec.

COWBRIDGE
Bulmer's
42 Eastgate. (Hugh and Louise Bulmer). Est. 1992. Open 10-1 and 2-5.30 (by appointment 1-2), Sat.10-5.30. CL: Mon. SIZE: Small. *STOCK: Furniture, 18th C, £1,000-£2,000; ceramics, 19th C, £50-£200.* PARK: Easy. TEL: 0446 775744; home - 0656 79 721. SER: Valuations; buys at auction. VAT: Stan/Spec.

Cowbridge continued
Cowbridge Antiques
55 Eastgate. (J. and S. Owen). Open 10-5.30, Sat. 10-5. CL: Wed. p.m. *STOCK: Furniture.* TEL: 0446 774774.

Eastgate Antiques
3 The Limes. (L. Herbert). Est. 1984. Open 10-1 and 2-5.30. CL: Wed. SIZE: Medium. *STOCK: Furniture, silver, jewellery, oils and watercolours, 18th C to Edwardian.* LOC: Off A48. PARK: Nearby. TEL: 0446 775111; home - 0446 773505. SER: Buys at auction (furniture). VAT: Stan/Spec.

Havard and Havard
59 Eastgate. (Philip and Christine Havard). Est. 1992. Open 10-1 and 2-5.30, Sat. 10-5.30. CL: Wed p.m. and Mon. SIZE: Small. *STOCK: Oak, mahogany and walnut furniture especially provincial, £100-£5,000; metalware and samplers, £25-£1,000; all 18th-19th C.* LOC: Main street, 500 yards after lights on right. PARK: Easy. TEL: 0446 775021. SER: Valuations. FAIRS: Margam and Duffryn House. VAT: Stan/Spec.

John Owen Gallery
55 Eastgate. (J. and P. Owen). Open 10-5. CL: Wed. p.m. *STOCK: Oils and watercolours.* TEL: 0446 774774. SER: Framing and restorations.

Renaissance Antiques
The Arcade, 49 High St. (R. and J. Barnicott). Est. 1984. Open 10-1 and 2.15-5.30, other times by appointment. CL: Wed. SIZE: Small. *STOCK: Small furniture, Georgian, Victorian and Edwardian, £100-£3,000; brass, copper, plate, decorative ceramics, objets d'art, 18th-20th C, £5-£500.* Not Stocked: Coins, militaria, reproductions. LOC: Main street, in new arcade opposite "Duke of Wellington". PARK: 200 yards. TEL: 0446 773893; home - 0446 774656. SER: Caning.

the Watercolour Gallery
Old Wool Barn, Verity's Court. (P. Allin). Est. 1987. Open from 11. CL: Mon. and Wed. SIZE: Small. *STOCK: Watercolours and etchings, £30-£1,000; occasional oil paintings; all 19th-20th C.* LOC: Off High St. PARK: At rear. TEL: Home - 0446 773324.

LLANISHEN, Nr. Cardiff
Nostalgia Antiques
1 Fidlas Rd. *STOCK: General antiques and collectables.* LOC: 1.25 miles off M4 Pentwyn turn-off, shop at Rhyd-y-Penau roundabout. TEL: 0222 765122; home - 0222 499964 (answerphone).

PENARTH

Corner Cupboard Antiques
4a Station Approach. (Mrs M. Green). Open 10-5. CL: Wed. *STOCK: General antiques.* TEL: 0222 705392.

Stanwells Antiques and Jewellery
36 Windsor Terr. (J. and M. Waters). Open 9.30-1 and 2-5.30. CL: Wed. p.m. *STOCK: China, porcelain, pictures, silver and jewellery.* TEL: 0222 706906.

West Glamorgan

BISHOPSTON, Nr. Swansea

Maybery Antiques
1 Brandy Cove Rd. (W. Maybery). Est. 1969. Open 11-5. *STOCK: Furniture, 18th-19th C; porcelain and pottery, 18th-20th C; paintings, general antiques, 19th-20th C.* TEL: 0792 232550. LOC: .75 of a mile from Murton P.O. PARK: Easy. SER: Valuations.

GORSEINON, Nr. Swansea

Gold and Silver Shop
Cross St. (D. Paine). Open 10-1 and 2-4. *STOCK: Gold and silver, general antiques.* TEL: 0792 891874.

MORRISTON, Nr. Swansea

Aaron Antiques
62-66 Martin St. (A. Davies). Est. 1971. Open 10-5. *STOCK: Furniture, longcase clocks, shipping goods.* TEL: 0792 773271. VAT: Stan.

MURTON, Nr. Swansea

West Wales Antiques LAPADA
18 Manselfield Rd. (W.H. Davies). Est. 1956. Open 10-1 and 2-5. *STOCK: Porcelain, 18th C, £20-£800; Welsh porcelain, 1814-1820, £20-£1,000; dolls, 1880-1920; 18th-19th C furniture, silver, pottery, glass, jewellery and collectors' items.* LOC: M4-A4067-B4436, entrance to Gower Peninsula. TEL: 0792 234318. VAT: Stan/Spec.

SWANSEA

James Allan
22 Park St. (S.J. Allan). Est. 1929. Open 9.30-4.45. SIZE: Small. *STOCK: Jewellery, 1850 to date, £50-£5,000.* LOC: Off Kingsway, round corner from Mothercare. PARK: Nearby. TEL: 0792 652176. SER: Valuations. VAT: Stan.

The Antique Emporium
76 St. Helens Rd. Est. 1977. Open 10-2 and 3-5. SIZE: 7 dealers. *STOCK: Wide range of general antiques.* TEL: 0792 654697.

Swansea continued

Bygone Antiques
Basement of Homeflair, 37-39 St. Helens Rd. (C.A. Oliver). Open 9.30-5. *STOCK: China, furniture, linen and collectors' items.* TEL: 0792 468248.

Keith Chugg Antiques
Gwydr Lane, Uplands. Open 9-5.30, Sat. 9-1. *STOCK: Pianos and general antiques including furniture.* TEL: 0792 472477.

Clydach Antiques
83 High St, Clydach. (R.T. Pulman). Open 10-5, Sat. 10-1. *STOCK: General antiques.* TEL: 0792 843209.

Philip Davies
130 Overland Rd, Mumbles. Open by appointment. *STOCK: British watercolours and oil paintings, 1850-1950, maps and prints, all £25-£10,000.* TEL: Home - 0792 361766 (24hrs). SER: Valuations; restorations (paintings and frames).

Dylan's Bookshop
Salubrious Passage. (J.M. Towns). Open 10-5. *STOCK: Antiquarian books on Welsh history and topography, Anglo/Welsh literature and general books.* TEL: 0792 655255.

Elizabeth Antiques
504 Mumbles Rd. (W. Wickstead). Open 11-5.30. *STOCK: Jewellery and general antiques.* TEL: 0792 361909; home - 0792 798978.

Eynon Hughes Antiques
Henrietta St. (E. and M. Hughes). Est. 1984. Open 10-5. *STOCK: Longcase clocks, £500-£2,500; brass and cast iron beds, £100-£500; furniture, 18th-19th C, £200-£1,000.* PARK: Easy. TEL: 0792 651446; home - 099 427 253. SER: Buys at auction (furniture). *Trade Only.*

Anne and Colin Hulbert (Antiques and Firearms)
17 Approach Rd, Manselton. Est. 1962. CL: Sun. p.m. SIZE: Small. *STOCK: Shipping goods and general antiques.* PARK: Easy. TEL: 0792 653818; home - same. SER: Valuations; buys at auction (furniture). *Trade Only.*

Magpie Antiques
57 St. Helens Rd. (H. Hallesy). Est. 1984. Usually open 10-5. *STOCK: Ceramics including Swansea, Lllanelly and other Welsh potteries; oak and country furniture.* PARK: Easy. TEL: 0792 648522. SER: Valuations; restorations (furniture).

Margaret's Astoria Antiques
High Street Arcade, 10-11 High St. (M Williams). Est. 1979. Open 9-5.30. CL: Mon SIZE: Small. *STOCK: 1920's, 1930's and Victorian jewellery, £25-£500; china, £5-£300 collectables and glass.* LOC: Town centre PARK: Nearby.

Swansea continued

Kim Scurlock
25 Russell St. (A.K. Scurlock). Est. 1982. Open 9.30-5, Mon. 9.30-4.30, Sat. 9.30-1. SIZE: Medium. STOCK: *Victorian pine and country furniture, £25-£1,000; some reproduction pine and mainly Edwardian and Victorian oak and mahogany furniture, £50-£1,000.* LOC: Between Walters Rd. and St. Helens Rd. PARK: Easy. TEL: 0792 643085. SER: Restorations. VAT: Stan.

Swansea Antique Centre
21 Oxford St. Open 10-5 although dealers' times vary. TEL: 0792 466854. Below are listed some of the 18 dealers at this centre.

Aladdin's Cave
STOCK: *General antiques.* TEL: 0792 459576.

Blue Lady
STOCK: *General antiques.*

Catherine Ann Antiques
STOCK: *Bric-a-brac and antiques.*

City Antiques
STOCK: *Jewellery.* SER: Repairs.

Forget-me-Not
STOCK: *China and bric-a-brac.*

Mair's Antiques
STOCK: *Jewellery, glass, china, brass, gold and silver.*

Number Ten
STOCK: *Toys.*

Past Times
(G. Williams). STOCK: *Porcelain, Doulton, militaria and postcards.*

Purdy and Lloyd Antiques
STOCK: *Silver, porcelain, pottery, glass, furniture and collectables.* TEL: 0792 648883; home - 0792 799906.

Bobby Roberts
STOCK: *Furniture and general antiques.*

Allan Treharne
STOCK: *Jewellery.* SER: Repairs.

Winkies
STOCK: *Pre-1950's clothes.*

Thicke Galleries   LAPADA
(T.G. Thicke). Est. 1981. By appointment only. SIZE: Medium. STOCK: *Oils and watercolours, 19th C to early 20th C, to £8,000.* LOC: Coast road to West Swansea. PARK: Easy. TEL: 0792 207515. SER: Valuations; restorations (oils and watercolours). FAIRS: British International, Birmingham; West London; Castle. VAT: Spec.

Gwent

ABERGAVENNY

Henry H. Close
36 Cross St. (Mr and Mrs H. Close). Est. 1968. Open 9-5, and by appointment. STOCK: *18th-19th C furniture, porcelain, pottery, glass, brass, copper, jewellery, silver, prints.* TEL: 0873 853583. VAT: Stan.

H.K. Lockyer
22 Monk St. Open 9.30-5.30. STOCK: *Antiquarian maps, prints and books.* PARK: Opposite. TEL: 0873 855825. VAT: Stan/Spec.

CHEPSTOW

Davies Antiques Centre
12 St. Mary St. (J.F. Davies). Est. 1963. Open 10-5. SIZE: Large - 10+ dealers. STOCK: *Furniture and shipping goods, glass, china, clocks, metalware and collectors items.* PARK: Easy. TEL: 0291 625957; home - 060 083 343. SER: Valuations; buys at auction. VAT: Stan/Spec.

Glance Back Bookshop
17 Upper Church St. Open 10-5.30 including Bank Holidays, and Sun. (Easter to Oct.) - lunchtime to 5.30. SIZE: 8 rooms. STOCK: *Books including antiquarian; stamps, coins, tokens, medals, postcards pre-1930, banknotes, pens, military cap badges, antiquarian maps and prints.* LOC: Town centre. PARK: Easy. SER: Restorations (works on paper, canvas or board); framing and colouring.

Glance Gallery
17a Upper Church St. Open 10-5.30, Sun. in summer 1-5.30. SIZE: Large. STOCK: *Antiquarian prints and maps.* LOC: Town centre. PARK: Easy. SER: Valuations; restorations (canvas, board or paper); framing; hand-colouring.

Plough House Interiors
Upper Church St. (Mr and Mrs P. Jones). Est. 1972. Open 10-5, Sat. 10-4.30, Sun. by appointment. CL: Wed. SIZE: Large. STOCK: *Victorian and Edwardian furniture and shipping goods.* LOC: 2 miles from Severn Bridge and M4. PARK: Easy. TEL: 0291 625200; home - same. SER: Valuations; restorations; buys at auction. VAT: Stan/Spec.

GILWERN, Nr. Abergavenny

Gilwern Antiques
Powell Bros, Main Rd. Est. 1968. CL: Mon. STOCK: *General antiques including furniture, clocks, porcelain, pottery, glass, some silver and jewellery.* LOC: Leave A465 at Aberbaiden Caravan Park roundabout, 1/2 mile along A4077 to top end of Gilwern. PARK: Nearby. TEL: 0873 830276/830584.

WALES

LLANDOGO

Llandogo Antiques
(R. and J. Hall). Resident. Est. 1965. Open 10-1 and 2-5. CL: Tues. SIZE: Small. *STOCK: Ceramics, glass, general antiques and small furniture.* Not Stocked: Large furniture. LOC: Last shop in village going south A466. PARK: 50yds. TEL: 0594 530213.

MONMOUTH

Carol Freeman Antiques
The Gallery, Nailers Lane. Open 10-5. *STOCK: General antiques and secondhand items.* TEL: 0600 772252; home - 0600 712658.

NEWPORT

Antiques of Newport
82 Chepstow Rd. (Mr and Mrs J.M. Duggan). Est. 1953. Open 9.30-5.30. CL: Thurs. *STOCK: Furniture, pottery, porcelain, silver, jewellery, maps, prints, fine art.* TEL: 0633 259935.

Beechwood Antiques
418 Chepstow Rd. (W.J. Samuel). Open 10-12.30 and 2-5.30. *STOCK: General antiques.* TEL: 0633 279192.

PONTNEWYNYDD, Nr. Pontypool

The Pine Barn
Gillingham House, Freeholdland. (L.M. and R.C. Brean). Open 10-5. *STOCK: General antiques and stripped pine furniture.* TEL: 0495 752256; home - same. SER: Restorations; stripping.

TINTERN

Abbey Antiques
(J. Ford). Open 10-5 including Sun. SIZE: Large and warehouse. *STOCK: Country oak, pine and mahogany, shipping furniture, clocks, jewellery, silver, plate, bric-a-brac, china and lace.* LOC: A466, opposite Tintern Abbey. TEL: 0291 689233.

TREDUNNOCK

Betty Williams
Tyr Eglwys. Est. 1975. Open by appointment only. *STOCK: 19th-20th C watercolours.* TEL: 063 349 301.

USK

Castle Antiques
41 Old Market St. (S. Lockyer). Open 12-5 or by appointment. *STOCK: General antiques, especially English and Welsh pottery, porcelain, blue and white transfer ware.* TEL: 0291 672424; home - 049 528 186.

Gwynned

ABERSOCH

Annteaks
Main St. (H. Duke). Est. 1946. Usually open. *STOCK: General antiques especially garden statuary and architectural items.* LOC: Opposite Midland Bank. TEL: 075 881 2353.

BANGOR

Wellfield Antique Centre
Wellfield Court. (T. Andrew). Open Thurs.-Sat. 10-5. SIZE: 20 stands. TEL: 0248 361360.

David Windsor Gallery
201 High St. Est. 1970. Open 10-5. CL: Wed. *STOCK: Oils and watercolours, 18th-20th C; maps, engravings, lithographs.* TEL: 0248 364639. SER: Restorations; framing; mounting. VAT: Stan/Spec.

BARMOUTH

Aspley Antiques and Reproductions Ltd
Llanaber Rd. Open 10.30-5.30 including Sun. SIZE: Large. *STOCK: Oak, mahogany, walnut and pine furniture, mainly 1700's to 1920's.* LOC: In Plas Mynach Castle. TEL: 0341 281057. SER: Shipping; packing; courier; accomodation.

Ron Jones Antiques
(R.W. Jones). *STOCK: General antiques.* TEL: 0341 280691.

BEAUMARIS

Castle Antiques
13 Church St. (J. and S. Jones). Open 9-5.30, Sun. in summer. *STOCK: Country furniture, metalware, prints, brass and collectables.* LOC: Opposite P.O. TEL: 0248 810474.

Museum of Childhood
1 Castle St. *STOCK: Children's toys and memorabilia collectables.* TEL: 0248 712498.

BLAENAU FFESTINIOG

The Antique Shop
74A Manod Rd. (Mrs R. Roberts). Est. 1971. *STOCK: Victoriana, furniture, brass and copper, oil lamps, clocks.* TEL: 0766 830629.

BODORGAN (Anglesey)

Michael Webb Fine Art   LAPADA
Open by appointment only. *STOCK: Victorian and 20th C oil paintings and watercolours.* TEL: 0407 840336. SER: Valuations; restorations; framing. VAT: Spec.

CAENARFON
Revival
Old Market Hall, Palace St. (G. Yorath). Est. 1982. Usually open, prior telephone call advisable. SIZE: Small. *STOCK: Furniture and china, to 1925.* LOC: Coast road. TEL: 0286 85397; home - same. SER: Re-polishing and re-gilding.

CONWAY
Black Lion Antiques
11 Castle St. (M.A. Wilks-Jones). Est. 1957. Open 10-5 and by appointment. SIZE: Small. *STOCK: Small furniture, including stripped pine, china, coloured glass, Victoriana, books, brass, shipping goods, metalware.* LOC: A55. PARK: Easy. TEL: 0492 592470. FAIRS: 3-day dateline.

Char Bazaar
25 Castle St. Open every day Easter to end Sept. *STOCK: Antique, old, rare and novelty teapots. Also permanent display of 1,000+.* TEL: 0492 593429.

Conway Antiques
17 Bangor Rd. (D.E. Calligan). Open 10.30-5. *STOCK: General antiques.* TEL: 0492 592461.

Paul Gibbs Antiques and Decorative Arts
25 Castle St. Open 10-5. *STOCK: Art deco and art nouveau pottery, 1880-1940; Doulton, Moorcroft, unusual teapots.* TEL: 0492 593429.

DEGANWY
Acorn Antiques
Castle Buildings. (K.S. Bowers-Jones). Open 10-5. *STOCK: Ceramics, glass, furniture, pictures, brass and copper, 19th C.* TEL: 0492 584083.

LLANDUDNO
The Antique Shop
24 Vaughan St. (C.G. Lee). Est. 1938. Open 9-5.30. SIZE: Medium. *STOCK: Jewellery, silver, porcelain, glass, ivories, metal goods, from 1700; period furniture, shipping goods.* LOC: Near promenade. PARK: Easy. TEL: 0492 875575.

Collinge Antiques
Wedgewood Building, Gt. Orme's Rd., West Shore. (Nicky Collinge). Est. 1978. Open 9-5.30. SIZE: Large. *STOCK: General antiques including Welsh dressers, dining, drawing and bedroom furniture, clocks, porcelain and pottery, silver, copper and brass, paintings and prints, glass and collectables, mainly Victorian and Edwardian.* LOC: Under half a mile from town centre. PARK: Easy. TEL: 0492 580022/870956. SER: Valuations; restorations including French polishing; buys at auction. VAT: Stan/Spec.

Madoc Antiques and Art Gallery
48 Madoc St. (H. and L. Aldridge). Est. 1975.

Llandudno continued
SIZE: Medium. *STOCK: English watercolours, 18th-20th C, £200-£3,000; furniture, Edwardian, Victorian and Georgian, £250-£6,000; porcelain, silver, pre-1930, £2-£600; longcase clocks, £1,000-£5,500.* PARK: Opposite and at rear. TEL: 0492 879754. SER: Valuations; restorations (clocks). VAT: Stan/Spec.

LLANDUDNO JUNCTION
Collinge Antiques
Old Fyffes Warehouse, Conwy Rd. (Nicky Collinge). Est. 1978. Open 9-5.30. SIZE: Large. *STOCK: General antiques including Welsh dressers, dining, drawing and bedroom furniture, clocks, porcelain and pottery, silver, copper and brass, paintings, prints, glass and collectables, mainly Victorian and Edwardian.* LOC: Just off A55, Conwy exit. PARK: Easy. TEL: 0492 580022/870956. SER: Valuations; restorations including French polishing; buys at auction. VAT: Stan/Spec.

LLANERCHYMEDD
Tony Andrew
8 High St. Est. 1976. Open by appointment only. SIZE: Small + warehouse. *STOCK: Signed limited edition prints by Charles Tunnicliffe; furniture, horse-drawn vehicles.* LOC: Centre of Isle of Anglesey. PARK: Easy. TEL: 0248 470204; home - same; warehouse - 0248 470666. SER: Framing; buys at auction.

LLANRWST
Snowdonia Antiques
(J. Collins). Est. 1961. Open 9-5.30, Sun. by appointment. SIZE: Medium. *STOCK: Period furniture especially longcase clocks.* LOC: Turn off A5 just before Betws-y-Coed on to A496 for 4 miles. PARK: Easy. TEL: 0492 640789. SER: Restorations (furniture); repairs (grandfather clocks).

MAENTWROG
Harvey-Owen Antiques
The Old School. (Mr and Mrs J.L. and L. Harvey). Est. 1972. Open 10-5. *STOCK: General antiques.* TEL: 076 685 310.

PWLLHELI
Rodney Adams Antiques
Hall Place, 10 Penlan St. Resident. Est. 1965. CL: Sun. except by appointment. *STOCK: Period furniture; longcase clocks.* TEL: 0758 613173; evenings - 0758 614337. VAT: Stan/Spec.

RHOSNEIGR
Fan-Fayre Antiques
High St. (S. Richards). Resident. Est. 1976. Open 10-5.30, prior telephone call advisable during

WALES

Rhosneigr continued
winter months. SIZE: Small. *STOCK: Jewellery, porcelain, silver, collectable items, 19th C, £25-£500.* LOC: 5 miles off A5 from the Holyhead Rd., on Anglesey Island. PARK: Easy. TEL: 0407 810580 (24hr. anwer phone). SER: Valuations. FAIRS: St. Martins, Birmingham; Portmeirion, Wales; Newark and Nottinghamshire Showground.

TYWYN
Welsh Art
(Miles K. Wynn Cato). Open by appointment only. *STOCK: Welsh paintings, 1550-1950; Welsh portraits of all periods and historical Welsh material.* TEL: 0654 711715 and 071 736 5002.

Powys
BRECON
Hazel of Brecon
2 Dukes Arcade. (H. Hillman). Est. 1969. Open 10-5. CL: Wed. SIZE: Small. *STOCK: Jewellery, 19th-20th C, £50-£4,000.* LOC: Town centre, just off main square. PARK: Easy. TEL: 0874 625274 (24 hr. answering service). SER: Valuations.

Maps, Prints and Books
7 The Struet. (Mr and Mrs D.G. Evans). Est. 1961. Open 9-1 and 2-5. CL: Wed. SIZE: Large. *STOCK: Books, maps, prints, 17th C, £5-£500.* LOC: A438, near Boots the Chemist. PARK: Opposite. TEL: 0874 622714. VAT: Stan.

Ship Street Galleries
14 Ship St. (Toni and Christine Constantinescu). Est. 1974. Open by appointment only. *STOCK: Continental and English period furniture, pine, shipping goods, 18th-19th C; continental and English glass and porcelain.* TEL: 0874 623926.

Silver Time
2 Dukes Arcade. (L. Hillman). Open 10-5. CL: Wed. SIZE: Small. *STOCK: Silver and gold watches and 19th-20th C silver and plate.* LOC: Town centre, just off main square. PARK: Easy. TEL: 0874 625274 (24 hr. answering service). SER: Repairs; valuations.

CRICKHOWELL
Gallop and Rivers Architectural Antiques
Ty'r Ash, Brecon Rd. (G. P. Gallop and R. A. Rivers). Open 9.30-5.30. *STOCK: Architectural items, pine and country furniture.* TEL: 0873 811084. VAT: Stan.

HAY-ON-WYE
Antiques Market
6 Market St. Open 10-5 including Sun. SIZE: 18 dealers. *STOCK: General antiques and collectables.* LOC: By the Butter Market. TEL: 0497 820175.

Hay-on-Wye continued
Richard Booth's Bookshop
The Limited Bookshop, Five Star Bookshop and Hay Castle Bookshops. Est. 1974. Open 7 days 9.30-5.30, later at weekends and during summer. SIZE: Large. *STOCK: Books, all subjects including American Indians, art, antiques, photography and transport.* LOC: Town centre. TEL: 0497 820322; fax - 0497 821150.

The Corner Shop
5 St. John's Place. (E. Okarma). Open 10-5. *STOCK: Prints, oils and watercolours, 19th-20th C.* TEL: 0497 820045. SER: Framing. VAT: Stan.

Hebbards of Hay
7 Market St. (P.E. Hebbard). Est. 1958. Open 10-5. SIZE: Small. *STOCK: Pottery and porcelain.* LOC: A438, opposite the Post Office. PARK: Own. TEL: 0497 820413.

Tamara Le Bailly Antiques
5 Market St. Open 10.30-5.30. *STOCK: Decorative antiques, lighting and country furniture.* PARK: Nearby. TEL: 0497 821157; home - 0497 820656 (ansaphone).

Mark Westwood Antiquarian Books
High Town. ABA; PBFA. Est. 1976. Open 12.30-5.30, prior telephone call advisable in winter. *STOCK: Antiquarian books especially on science and medicine, 16th-20th C, £50-£500.* TEL: 0497 820068. SER: Valuations; buys at auction (antiquarian books). VAT: Stan.

Wigington Antiques
Chapel Schoolroom, 1 Heolydwr. (B. Wigington). BAFRA. Est. 1961. Open any time by appointment. SIZE: Small. *STOCK: General antiques, mainly furniture, 17th-19th C, to £5,000.* LOC: Corner with Broad St. PARK: Easy. TEL: 0497 820545 (24hr). SER: Valuations; restorations (furniture).

KNIGHTON
Offa's Dyke Antique Centre
4 High St. (M. McAvoy, M. Samuel, I. Watkins and Mrs S.D. Yeomans). Est. 1985. Open 10-1 and 2-5. SIZE: Medium - 16 dealers. *STOCK: Pottery, bijouterie,18th-19th C furniture, £5-£500.* LOC: Near town clock. PARK: Easy. TEL: 0547 528635; evenings - 0547 528940 or 05477 240.

Islwyn Watkins
1 High St. Est. 1978. Open 10-1 and 2.30-5, prior telephone call advisable; Tues. and Wed. by appointment. SIZE: Small. *STOCK: Pottery including studio, 18th-20th C, £25-£350; country and domestic bygones, treen, 18th-20th C, £5-£100; small country furniture, 18th-19th C, £20-£400.* Not Stocked: Jewellery, silver, militaria. LOC: By town clock. PARK: Easy. TEL: 0547 520145; home - 0547 528940. SER: Valuations.

Antique Collectors' Club Titles

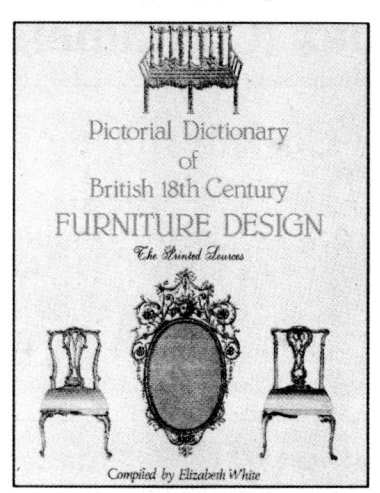

Pictorial Dictionary of British 18th Century Furniture Design
by Elizabeth White
Published designs from 120 sources. The 3,000 named and dated illustrations provide arguably the most important contribution to 18th century furniture studies since Ralph Edwards' **Dictionary of English Furniture.**
ISBN 1 85149 105 8
700pp, 3,500 b & w designs, 24 col £65.00

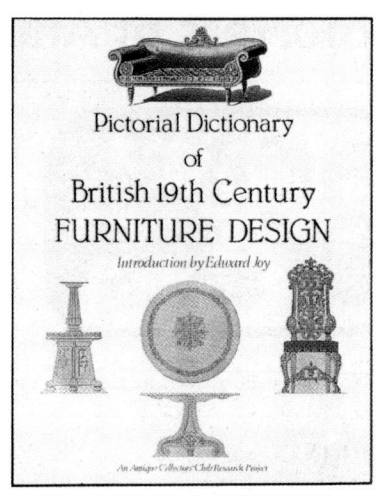

Pictorial Dictionary of British 19th Century Furniture Design
An A.C.C. Research Project
Compiled from forty-nine key contemporary catalogues from Sheraton to Heal's, including Smith, Tatham, King, Pugin, Morris and Liberty's, it includes an important introduction by the late Edward Joy.
ISBN 0 902028 47 2, 632pp, 6,200 illus, £49.50

Available from:
Antique Collectors' Club, 5 Church Street, Woodbridge, Suffolk IP12 1DS Tel: (0394) 385501 Fax: (0394) 384834

or Market Street Industrial Park, Wappingers' Falls, New York 12590, USA Tel: 914 297 0003 Fax: 914 297 0068

LLANFAIR CAEREINION, Nr. Welshpool

Heritage Restorations
Maes y Glydfa. (J. and Mrs F. Gluck). Est. 1970. Open 9-5.30. SIZE: Large. *STOCK:* Pine and country furniture, £50-£2,000; some oak and architectural items, all 18th-19th C. LOC: A458 from Welshpool. Past village, after 2 miles take first left past river bridge and carvan park, then follow signs. PARK: Easy. TEL: 0938 810384; home - same. SER: Restorations (furniture including pine stripping). VAT: Stan/Spec.

WELSHPOOL

F.E. Anderson and Son LAPADA
5-6 High St. (D. and I. Anderson). Open daily. *STOCK: Furniture, 17th-18th C; English and Chinese ceramics, glass, silver, paintings, early metalware.* **TEL: 0938 553340; home - 0938 553324/75509.**

Horley Antiques
19 High St. (C. Darnell). Est. 1970. Open 10-1

Welshpool continued
and 2.15-4, Sat. 10-1. SIZE: Small. *STOCK: Paintings, 19th C, £5-£500; general, mainly small, items.* PARK: Easy. TEL: 0938 552421.

School House Antiques
21 High St. (M.L.G. Robinson). Est. 1977. Open 10.30-1.30 and 2.30-4.30, Thurs. and Sat. 10.30-1.30. SIZE: Medium. *STOCK: Furniture, £250-£7,500; silver and plate, £50-£500; brass and copper, £50-£400; blue and white printed ware, £50-£250; all 18th-19th C; oils and watercolours,19th C, £100-£1,000.* LOC: Town at junction of A458, A483 and A490. PARK: Easy. TEL: 0938 554858; home - 0938 570267. SER: Valuations; restorations (rush and cane seating).

Waterloo Antiques
Salop Rd. (R. and N. Robinson). Est. 1979. SIZE: Medium. *STOCK: Porcelain, furniture, paintings, metalware.* LOC: On A483 on entering town from the east. PARK: Easy. TEL: 0938 553999 (24hr.); home - 0938 555468. VAT: Spec.

Index of Packers and Shippers: Exporters of Antiques (Containers)

AR · GS International Transport Ltd.

SHIPPERS & PACKERS OF ANTIQUES, FINE ART & REMOVALS TO ITALY

Tel: 071 833 3955 or 0444 414667
Fax: 071 837 8672

North London Freight Centre, York Way, Kings Cross, London N1 0BB

LONDON

Anglo Pacific (Fine Art) Ltd   LAPADA
Units 1 and 2, Bush Industrial Estate, Standard Rd., NW10 6DF. Tel: 081 965 0667; fax - 081 965 4954. Packers and shippers of antiques, fine art, household effects and cars. All destinations.

AR. GS International Transport Ltd
North London Freight Centre, York Way, Kings Cross, N1 0BB. Tel: 071 833 3955; fax - 071 837 8672. Fine art and antiques removals by road transport, Europe especially Italy, door-to-door service. Documentation.

London continued

James Bourlet and Sons Ltd.
See entry under Surrey.

Bullens Ltd.
Unit 9 Cranford Way, Tottenham Lane, Hornsey, N8 9DG. Tel: 071 272 6671. Specialist comprehensive removal service.

Davies Turner Worldwide Movers Ltd.
Overseas House, Stewarts Rd., SW8 4UG. Tel: 071 622 4393; fax - 071 720 3897; telex - 2847. Fine art and antiques packers and shippers. Courier and finder service. Full container L.C.L. and groupage service worldwide.

One of a set of three mugs surviving in their original graduated set. Many Worcester mugs were probably sold in this way although few have remained together. These examples all depict George II* along with various nautical subjects printed in black, c.1758-60. (Phillips, Edinburgh). From *The Dictionary of Worcester Porcelain, Vol. I, 1751-1851*, by John Sandon, published in 1993 by the **Antique Collectors' Club**, £45.00

An Antique Collectors' Club Title

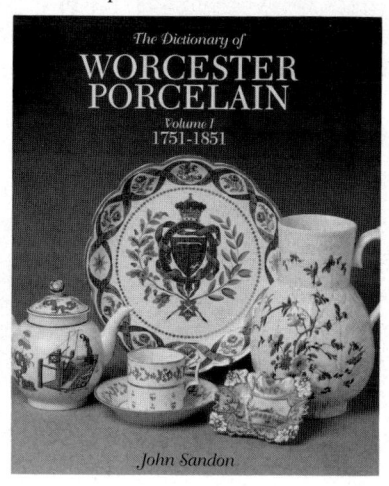

The Dictionary of Worcester Porcelain Volume I 1751-1851
by John Sandon
With 600+ dictionary entries, an historical survey, an illustrated section on marks, detailed information on recent excavations at the Worcester factory, contemporary accounts of visits to factories and an extensive bibliography, this is the definitive work. The author is director of ceramics at Phillips auctioneers, London, and regularly appears on the *Antiques Roadshow*.
ISBN 1 85149 156 2
400pp, 450 b & w illus, 100 colour
£45.00

Available from:
Antique Collectors' Club, 5 Church Street, Woodbridge, Suffolk IP12 1DS
Tel: (0394) 385501 Fax: (0394) 384434

or Market Street Industrial Park, Wappingers' Falls, New York 12590, USA
Tel: 914 297 0003 Fax: 914 297 0068

DAVIES TURNER
Incorporating LOU LEWIS

Art & Antiques Packing & Shipping since 1870

Davies Turner have been skilled packers
and shippers of antiques and fine art since 1870.
Our full and part container services run worldwide,
and we have in-house finders and insurance specialists
to complete the service

Davies Turner Worldwide Movers Limited
Overseas House, Stewarts Road,
London SW8 4UG
Tel: 071-622 4393 Fax: 071-720 3897 Telex: 28471

JAMES BOURLET 1768

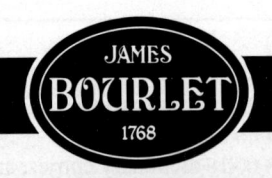

FINE ART PACKERS & SHIPPERS

INSTALLATIONS

STORAGE

HIGH SECURITY

CLIMATE CONTROL VEHICLES

LONDON
06 Beta Way, Thorpe Industrial Park,
Crabtree Road, Egham, Surrey TW20 8RE
Tel: 0784 470000 Telefax: 0784 436252

NEW YORK
21-41 45th Road
Long Island City, New York 11101
Tel: (718) 392-9770 Fax: (718) 392-2470

ANTIQUE & FINE ART SERVICES

FIFTY YEARS' EXPERIENCE OF EXPORT & IMPORT

FINE ART PACKING
By
FENTONS

PERSONAL ATTENTION & SERVICE

COURIER SERVICE · HOTEL RESERVATIONS · DOCUMENTATION
ESTIMATES FREE · CONTAINERISATION · OVERSEAS REMOVALS · INSURANCE

C.R. Fenton, 7 Munton Road, London SE17 1PR
Tel: 071-277 1539 Fax: 071-277 1540 Cable: 8813379 (Fenton G)

Featherston Shipping

LAPADA MEMBER

Fine Art and Antique Packers and Shippers

FOR AN IMMEDIATE QUOTATION FOR SEA AND AIR FREIGHT WORLDWIDE, CALL THE EXPERTS WITH THE PROVEN REPUTATION

**TELEPHONE 071-720 0422 FAX 071-720 6330
24 HAMPTON HOUSE, INGATE PLACE, LONDON SW8 3NS**

London continued

Featherston Shipping Ltd. LAPADA
24 Hampton House, 15-17 Ingate Place, SW8 3NS. Tel: 071 720 0422; fax - 071 720 6330. Antiques and fine art packed and shipped or airfreighted worldwide. Security storage.

London continued

C.R. Fenton and Co. Ltd.
7 Munton Rd., SE17 1PR. Tel: 071 277 1539; fax - 071 277 1540; cable - Fenton G 8813379. Packers and shippers.

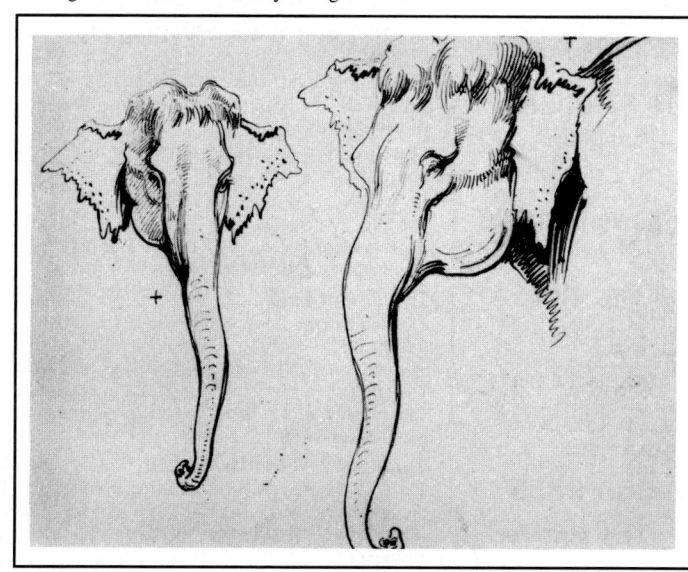

Studies of an elephant. Pen and ink. Photograph courtesy: A. Fairbarns, Esq. From *George Chinnery, 1774-1852, Artist of India and the China Coast*, published in 1993 by the **Antique Collectors' Club**, £45.00.

WORLDWIDE
PACKING, TRANSPORT & DELIVERY 081·965 8733

UNITS 3 & 4, 97 VICTORIA ROAD
LONDON NW10 5ND
FAX 081-965 0249
TELEX 25229 HEDLEY

LOT NO. 13
111 RUE DOCTEUR BAUER
93400 ST. OUEN
FRANCE
TEL 40. 10. 94. 00
FAX 40. 10. 05. 62

30 THOMPSON STREET
NEW YORK
NY 10013. U.S.A.
TEL (212) 219 2877
FAX (212) 219 2826

Hedleys Humpers!

NEW YORK • PARIS • LONDON

INTERPACK
WORLDWIDE LIMITED

ANTIQUES & FINE ART

SEA & AIR FREIGHT
WORLDWIDE

—

Immediate Quotations

—

Personal Service

UNIT 11
HANOVER WEST TRADING ESTATE
161 ACTON LANE, LONDON NW10
ENGLAND, UNITED KINGDOM
FAX 081-453 0544

Tel: 081 – 965 9355

INTERNATIONAL PACKERS & SHIPPERS

London continued

Gander and White Shipping Ltd.
LAPADA
Head Office, 21 Lillie Rd., SW6 1UE. Tel: 071 381 0571; fax - 071 381 5428. Specialist packers and shippers of antiques and works of art.

Gander and White Shipping Ltd.
LAPADA
14 Mason's Yard, Duke St., St. James's, SW1Y 6BU. Tel: 071 930 5383; fax - 071 920 4145; cables - Gandite.

Hedleys Humpers Ltd LAPADA
Units 3 and 4, 97 Victoria Rd., North Acton, NW10 6ND. Tel: 081 965 8733 (10 lines); fax - 081 965 0249; telex - 2522. Weekly deliveries, door-to-door service to Europe, and part load shipments by air and sea to U.S.A.

Interdean Ltd.
3/5 Cumberland Ave., NW10 7RU. Tel: 081 961 4141; telex - 922119; fax - 081 965 4484. Antiques and fine art packed, shipped and airfreighted worldwide. Storage and international removals. Full container L.C.L. and groupage service worldwide.

Interpack Worldwide Ltd
Unit 11, Hanover West Trading Estate, 161 Acton Lane, NW10. Tel: 081 965 9355; fax - 081 453 0544. Worldwide shipping, packing, insurance.

Our only rival.

Gander & White have only one rival. The walnut. Nature has created in the walnut, the perfect model for individual high-quality packaging. Each walnut shell provides tailor-made protection for its contents; in the same way we create unique individual packing for every work of art entrusted to our care.

Specialised packing and shipping of antiques and works of art

---

Groupage container services by air and sea to and from North America

---

Weekly door-to-door road groupage services to major European cities

---

Household removals • High security storage

Export and Import Custom Services including MIBS

LONDON – NEW YORK – PARIS

Gander & White

PACKERS & SHIPPERS

Gander & White Shipping Ltd., 21 Lillie Road, London SW6 1UE.
Tel: 071 381 0571. Fax: 071 381 5428

New Pound, Wisborough Green, Billingshurst, West Sussex RH14 0AY
Tel: 0403 700044 Fax: 0403 700814

Gander & White Inc., 33-31 Greenpoint Avenue, Long Island City, N.Y. 11101
Tel: 718 784 8444 Fax: 718 784 9337

Gander & White Shipping Sarl, 24 Rue Licien Sampaix 75010, Paris
Tel: 331 4202 1892 Fax: 331 4206 3331

LOCKSON SERVICES LTD EST. 50 YEARS

Regular Consolidated Containers

New York • Atlanta • Texas

Full Loads / Part Loads / Single Items

Open for Quotes and Enquiries Saturday 0831 621 428 Sunday

Van at Newark and Ardingly

Insurance • Personal Service • Couriers

• Next Day Parcel Service

Specialist in the Packing & Shipping of Fine Art & Antiques.

To: U.S.A., Japan, South Africa, Far East, Canada, Australia and many more Worldwide Destinations

Phone: 071 - 515 8600
Fax: 071 - 515 4043

29 BROOMFIELD STREET, LONDON E14 6BX

London continued

Kuwahara Ltd. LAPADA
Unit 5 Bittacy Business Centre, Bittacy Hill, NW7 1BA. Tel: 081 346 7744; fax - 081 349 2916. Specialist packers and shippers of antiques and works of art. Regular groupage service to Japan.

Lockson Services Ltd LAPADA
29 Broomfield St., Limehouse, E14 6BX. Tel: 071 515 8600 (6 lines); fax - 071 515 4043; telex - 884222; Specialist packers and shippers of fine art and antiques by air, sea and road to the USA, Japan, Australia, the Far East, Canada, South Africa and many more worldwide destinations. A complete personalised service.

Masterpack Ltd - Fine Art Packers & Shippers
Nationwide Building, Stanley Gardens, The Vale, W3 7SZ. Tel: 071 262 8274; telex - 8813271 Gecoms G. Fine art packers and shippers. Personal service guaranteed.

Momart plc
199-205 Richmond Rd., E8 3NJ. Tel: 081 986 3624; fax - 081 533 0122. Fine art handling including transportation, case making and packing: import/export services, exhibition installation and storage.

Stephen Morris Shipping Ltd.
Barpart House, Kings Cross Freight Terminal, York Way, N1 0UZ. Tel: 071 713 0080; fax - 071 713 0151. Specialist packers and shippers of antiques and fine art worldwide.

Nelson Shipping
7 Glasshouse Walk, Vauxhall, SE11 5ES. Tel: 071 587 0265. Expert export and packing service.

The Packing Shop
Plaza G13, 535 Kings Rd., SW10 0SZ. Tel: 071 352 2021. Fine art and general antiques shipped worldwide, especially United States and Europe.

The Packing Shop
Unit L, London Stone Business Estate, Broughton St., SW8 3QR. Tel: 071 498 3255. Specialised service to overseas antique fairs and exhibitions.

Pitt and Scott Ltd
20/24 Eden Grove, N7 8ED. Tel: 071 607 7321; fax - 071 607 0566; telex - 21857. Packers and shippers of antiques and fine art. Shipping, forwarding and airfreight agents. Comprehensive service provided for visiting antique dealers. Insurance arranged.

L.J. Roberton Ltd LAPADA
Marlborough House, Cooks Rd., Stratford, E15 2PW. Tel: 081 519 2020; fax - 081 519 8571.

Robinsons International LAPADA
24 Somerton Rd., NW2 1SA. Tel: 081 452 5441; fax - 081 452 6664. Specialist packers and shippers of antiques and fine art worldwide. Established over 90 years.

L.J. ROBERTON LTD

EST. 1948

MARLBOROUGH HOUSE,
COOKS RD., STRATFORD, LONDON, E15 2PW

ANTIQUE & FINE ART
PACKERS & SHIPPERS

LAPADA MEMBER

FOR A COMPREHENSIVE AND PERSONAL SERVICE, AT A COMPETITIVE AND REALISTIC COST, OR SIMPLY ADVICE WITHOUT OBLIGATION

FAX	TELEPHONE	TELEX
081-519 8571	081-519 2020	8953984

An Antique Collectors' Club Title

English Domestic Architecture
KENT HOUSES *by Anthony Quiney*

This book explains how Kent came to be the best endowed county in England for its houses which range from the lowliest of smallholder's cottages, to the grandest of magnate's palaces. Chapters on the builders, the materials they used and the historical development of their houses up to the present day are followed by a Gazetteer which puts the buildings into a village-by-village context. Nearly three hundred photographs, many in colour, complete the picture, and over one hundred detailed line drawings and a glossary leave nothing unexplained.

Kent Houses is a treasure trove for lovers of the county, a first-class work of reference for students and practising architects and a must for architectural historians.

ISBN **1 85149 153 8, 288pp**
180 b & w illus, 112 colour plates
126 line drawings, £35.00

Available from:
Antique Collectors' Club, 5 Church Street, Woodbridge, Suffolk IP12 1DS
Tel: (0394) 385501 Fax: (0394) 384434

or Market Street Industrial Park, Wappingers' Falls, New York 12590, USA
Tel: 914 297 0003 Fax: 914 297 0068

PACKERS AND SHIPPERS OF ANTIQUES AND FINE ART

Wingate & Johnston

Established LONDON 1815

With Wingate & Johnston, you can be sure of transport and delivery service of the highest quality. Offering the full range of movement options. Full load container services. Groupage services. And the smaller, one-off consignments. By air, sea or road — worldwide.

In addition, Wingate & Johnston offer a full range of supporting services including – Buyer's Kit and Buyer's Book to record purchases – Buying itineraries — Courier or car hire facilities – Authentification arrangements.

In fact, Wingate & Johnston can take on all the organisational elements of your trip.

* Antiques * Fine Art * Exhibitions *

THE COMPLETE SERVICE.

Wingate & Johnston Ltd.

134 Queens Road
London SE15 2HR

Telephone 071 732 8123
Telex 888310
Fax 071 732 2631

Offices throughout
United Kingdom

Constantine Group

London continued

T. Rogers and Co. (Packers) Ltd
PO Box No. 8, 1A Broughton St., SW8 3QJ. Tel: 071 622 9151; fax - 071 627 3318; telex - 915243. Specialists in storage, packing, removal, shipping and forwarding antiques and works of art. Insurance.

Trans-Euro Fine Art Division LAPADA
Drury Way, Brent Park, NW10 0JN. Tel: 081 784 0100; fax - 081 451 0061; telex - 923368. Specialist packing and worldwide shipping services by air, sea or road. Single items, part loads or full containers. Courier and buyer services.

Wingate and Johnston Ltd LAPADA
134 Queens Road, Peckham, SE15. Tel: 071 732 8123; fax 071 732 2631. Specialists in the international movement of antiques and fine art for over a hundred and fifty years - services incorporate all requirements from case making to documentation and insurance. Freight groupage specialists.

AVON

M. & M. Services
Vale Lane, Hartcliffe Way, Bristol, BS3 5RU. Tel: 0272 666991. Worldwide shippers and packers.

Robinsons International LAPADA
Ashmead Rd., Keynsham, Bristol, BS18 1SX. Tel: 0272 723020; fax - 0272 862723. Specialist packers and shippers of antiques and fine art worldwide. Established over 90 years.

A.J. Williams (Shipping) LAPADA
607 Sixth Ave., Central Business Park, Hengrove, Bristol, BS14 9BZ. Tel: 0275 892166; fax - 0275 891333.

BUCKINGHAMSHIRE

Paget Freight Ltd
Spaceregal Centre, Coln Industrial Estate, Old Bath Rd., Colnbrook, SL3 0NJ. Tel: 0753 682426; fax - 0753 686367. Packing and shipping of antiques and works of art worldwide especially North and South America and Bermuda.

CHESHIRE

The Rocking Chair
Unit 3 St. Peters Way, Warrington. Tel: 0925 52409; fax - 0925 52409. Packers and exporters.

DEVON

Bishop's Blatchpack
Kestrel Way, Sowton Industrial Estate, Exeter, EX2 7PA. Tel: 0392 420404; fax - 0392 423851. International fine art packers and shippers.

PACKERS AND SHIPPERS

trans euro
FINE ART DIVISION

* Worldwide Shipping * Packing
* Insurance * Airfreight * Collections
* Consolidations * Couriers

LAPADA MEMBER

Drury Way, Brent Park
London NW10 0JN
Tel: 081 784 0100 Fax: 081 451 0061

BSI REGISTERED FIRM FS 22227

NATIONAL ACCREDITATION OF CERTIFICATION BODIES

A.J.Williams (Shipping)

Antiques and Fine Art Packers and Shippers

607 SIXTH AVENUE, CENTRAL BUSINESS PARK,
PETHERTON ROAD, HENGROVE, BRISTOL BS14 9BZ
Tel: (0275) 892166 FAX: (0275) 891333

LAPADA MEMBER

Packing & Shipping Worldwide

PACKERS AND SHIPPERS

Alan Franklin Transport

Our door to door weekly service throughout Europe is well known and very reliable
Container services, packing and shipping worldwide.

Unit 8, 27 Black Moor Road
Ebblake Industrial Estate
Verwood, Dorset
England. BH21 6AX
Telephone (0202) 826539
Fax: (0202) 827337

2 Rue Etienne Dolet
93400 St. Ouen
Paris
Telephone 010 33140 115000
Fax: 010 33140 114821

De Klerckstraat 41
B8300 Knokke, Belgium
Telephone and Fax: 010 3250 623579

DORSET

Alan Franklin Transport LAPADA
Unit 8, 27 Blackmoor Rd., Ebblake Industrial Estate, Verwood, BH31 6BE. Tel: 0202 826539; fax - 0202 827337. Container packing and shipping. Weekly door to door European service. Paris Office - 2 Rue Etienne Dolet, 93400 St. Ouen, Paris. Tel: 4011 5000; fax - 4011 4821.

ESSEX

Geo. Copsey and Co. Ltd
Danes Rd., Romford. Tel: 0708 740714 or 081 592 1003. Worldwide packers and shippers.

Scotpac International (U.K.) Ltd
LAPADA
Security House, Abbey Wharf Industrial Estate, Kingsbridge Rd., Barking, IG11 0BT. Tel: 081 591 3388; fax - 081 594 4571; telex - 897325. Packers and shippers - 12 offices throughout U.K.

Spanpak Export Services Ltd
Unit 3, Pacific Wharf, Hertford Rd., Barking, IG11 8BL. Tel: 081 594 4474; fax - 081 594 4475. Antiques and fine art export, packers and shippers worldwide. Fully comprehensive service with all types of packing and casing undertaken by our experienced team. Shipments to all destinations by sea, land and air. Specialised Spanish service.

GLOUCESTERSHIRE

The Removal Company - Barndy & Bendell
7 Wilkinson Rd., Cirencester, GL7 1YT. Tel: 0242 523362. Shipping and packing.

HAMPSHIRE

Cantay Group Ltd
Head Office, Unit D Telford Rd., Houndmills Industrial Estate, Basingstoke, RG21 2YU. Tel: 0256 465533. Specialist packers and shippers.

Cantay Group Ltd
95 Fleet Rd., Fleet, GU13 8PJ. (Correspondence to Basingstoke - address above.)Tel: 0252 811884.Specialist packers and shippers.

Robinsons International LAPADA
Guildford St., Southampton, S09 4UW. Tel: 0703 220069; fax - 0703 331274. Specialist packers and shippers of antiques and fine art worldwide. Established over 90 years.

HUMBERSIDE

Peter Smith t/a Boothferry Antiques
388 Wincolmlee, Hull, HU2 0QL. Tel: 0482 225220/666033. Antiques, shipping goods and stripped pine, single items or container loads. Couriers covering North of England. Full documentation.

CANTAY SHIP ANTIQUES WORLDWIDE
Quotations
Call us Free on
0800 521541
Offices: London · Cotswolds

cantay — The Specialist Shippers

LANCASHIRE

Alan Butterworth (Horwich)
7 Ardley Rd., Horwich, Bolton, BL6 7EG. Tel: 0204 68094. Dealers, export packers and shippers; courier service - UK and continent.

Robinsons International Removers Ltd LAPADA
Unit 1 Egremont Close, Moss Lane Industrial Estate, Whitfield, Manchester, M25 6FH. Tel: 061 766 8414; fax - 061 767 9057. Specialist packers and shippers of antiques and fine art worldwide. Established over 90 years.

Anthony Walmsley Antiques
93 Montagu St., Blackburn, BB2 1EH. Tel: 0254 698755.

LEICESTERSHIRE

Richard Kimbell Ltd
Riverside, Market Harborough, LE16 7PT. Tel: 0858 433444; fax - 0858 467627; telex -32376. Container packers and shippers. Speedy despatch - competitive rates.

MERSEYSIDE

John Mason International Ltd LAPADA
35 Wilson Rd., Huyton, Liverpool, L36 6AE. Tel: 051 449 3038. Specialist packer, full and part container loads, groupage service worldwide, courier and finder service.

MIDDLESEX

Air-Sea Packing Group Ltd
Air-Sea House, Third Cross Rd., Twickenham, TW2 5EB. Tel: 081 893 3303; fax - 081 893 3068. Specialist packers and shippers.

Gander and White Shipping Ltd LAPADA
Unit 1 Skyport Drive, Harmondsworth, UB7 0LB. Tel: 081 897 2772; fax - 081 564 9039. Specialist packers and shippers of antiques and works of art.

Middlesex continued

Vulcan International Services Ltd LAPADA
Unit 8 Ascot Rd., Clockhouse Lane, Feltham, TW14 8QF. Tel: 0784 244152; 0784 248183; telex - 295888. Fine art packers and shippers worldwide.

W.B. Airfreight Ltd
Unit 3 Blackburn Trading Estate, Nathin Close, Stanwell, Staines. Tel: 0784 240666; 0784 248457; telex - 934876. Worldwide by sea and air.

OXFORDSHIRE

Cantay Group Ltd
Unit 1 Oakfield Industrial Estate, Stanton Harcourt Rd., Eynsham, Oxford, OX8 1TN. Tel: 0865 882989; fax - 0865 883310; telex - 837614.

Cotswold Carriers
Unit 9, Worcester Rd. Industrial Estate, Chipping Norton, OX7 5XW. Tel: 0608 642856; fax - 0608 642856. Removals, storage, shipping, door-to-door Continental deliveries.

Robinson International LAPADA
Nuffield Way, Abingdon, OX14 1TN. Tel: 0235 524992; fax - 0235 553573. Specialist packers and shippers of antiques and fine art worldwide. Established over 90 years.

SOMERSET

Colin Dyte Exports Ltd
Huntspill Rd., Highbridge, TA9 3DE. Tel: 0278 788590.

SURREY

James Bourlet and Sons Ltd LAPADA
06 Beta Way, Thorpe Industrial Park, Crabtree Road, Egham, TW20 8RE. Tel: 0784 470000; fax - 0784 436252. Fine art packing, freight forwarding. U.S.A. - 21-41 45th Road, Long Island City, New York 11101. Tel: (718) 392 9770; fax - (718) 392 2470.

PACKERS AND SHIPPERS

Surrey continued

W. Ede & Co
Unit 3, Felmex Trading Estate, 190 London Rd., Wallington, SM6 9RH. Tel: 081 773 9388/9933; fax - 081 773 9011. Worldwide packing and shipping, complete documentation and removals service, container packing.

SUSSEX EAST

Bexhill Antique Exporters
56 Turkey Rd., Bexhill-on-Sea, TN39 5HB. Tel: 0424 225103/210182; fax - 0424 731430. General and shipping furniture. Packing facilities for 20ft. and 40ft. containers, all documentation. Worldwide shipping.

Global Services
West St., Lewes, BN7 2NJ. Tel: 0273 475903. Packers and shippers of antiques, arms, armour and fine works of art.

SUSSEX WEST

Gander and White Shipping Ltd
LAPADA
Newpound, Wisborough Green, Billingshurst, RH14 0AY. Tel: 0403 700044; fax - 0403 700814; telex - 878310. Specialist packers and shippers of fine art and antiques.

Martells International
32 London Rd., East Grinstead, RH19 4DW. Tel: 0342 321303; fax - 0342 317522; telex - 946305. International removers, export packers and shippers.

TYNE AND WEAR

Owen Humble (Packing and Shipping) Ltd
Clayton House, Walbottle Rd., Lemington, Newcastle-upon-Tyne, NE15 9RU. Tel: 091 267 7220. Worldwide service.

WARWICKSHIRE

Scotpac International (U.K.) Ltd
LAPADA
Unit 9 Ratcliffe Road Industrial Estate, Ratcliffe Rd., Atherstone, CV9 1JA. Tel: 0827 714631.

WEST MIDLANDS

Thomas Blakemore Ltd - Shipping U.S.A.
Atlas Works, Sandwell Street, Walsall, WS1 3DR. Tel: 0922 25951/613230; fax - 0922 611330; telex - 338212 G Chacom Blkmr. (U.S.A. - 919 882 6343/919 889 5158; fax - 919 889 3226) Weekly container from Birmingham to High Point, North Carolina, U.S.A. Pick-up and pack, no minimums.

Robinsons International
LAPADA
585 Moseley Rd., Birmingham, B12 9BJ. Tel:

free!

28 page full colour catalogue of Antique Collectors' Club books. Over 120 titles included covering a wide range of subjects: furniture, art reference, art history, prints, jewellery, metalwork, glass, horology, ceramics, oriental carpets, collectables, garden history and design, gardening and architecture.

Available free from the
ANTIQUE COLLECTORS' CLUB

5 Church Street
Woodbridge
Suffolk IP12 1DS
Tel: (0394) 385501
Fax: (0394) 384434

West Midlands continued
021 449 4731; fax - 021 449 9942. Specialist packers and shippers of antiques and fine art worldwide. Established over 90 years.

YORKSHIRE NORTH

H. Blackburn
9 East St., Gargrave, BD23 3RS. Tel: 0756 749796. Export, packers, shippers, courier service.

YORKSHIRE WEST

Turnbulls (Removals) Ltd
287 Roundhay Rd., Leeds. Tel: 0532 495828; fax - 0532 350478. Worldwide service.

SCOTLAND

Scotpac International (U.K.) Ltd
LAPADA
30 Beaverbank Pl., Edinburgh, EH7 4ET. Tel: 031 557 2000. Packers and shippers. Storage.

Scotpac International (U.K.) Ltd
LAPADA
Kilsyth Rd., Kirkintilloch, Glasgow, G66 1TJ. Tel: 041 776 5194; fax - 041 777 6138. Packers and shippers.

WALES

James and Patricia Ash
The Warehouse, Station Rd., Llandeilo, Dyfed SA19 6NG. Tel: 0558 823726. Shipping and container service. Victorian and antique furniture for sale and export.

Left: One of the many grotesque brackets supporting the jetties of Canterbury's houses.

Below: A detail of the gable of Dragon House, Smarden, showing the fascia carved with dragons, and a carved console bracket supporting the end timber of the projecting jetty. From **Kent Houses** by Anthony Quiney, published in 1993 by the **Antique Collectors' Club,** £35.00.

Index of Auctioneers

LONDON

Academy Auctioneers and Valuers
Northcote House, Northcote Avenue, Ealing, W5 3UR. Tel: 081 579 7466/9997. *Monthly sales of antiques, collectables, works of art, furniture, paintings, ceramics, jewellery and silver. Regular general sales. Open 9-5. Valuations.*

Bloomsbury Book Auctions
3 and 4 Hardwick St., EC1R 4RY. Tel: 071 833 2636/7 and 071 636 1945. *Twenty-two sales per year of books, manuscripts and maps and especially disposal of academic libraries. Occasional sales of prints, posters and drawings. Sellers commission 15 % (trade 12.5%); buyers premium 10%.*

Bonhams Chelsea
65-69 Lots Rd., Chelsea, SW10 0RN. Tel: 071 351 7111; fax - 071 351 7754. *Regular sales of watercolours, European and modern pictures, prints, carved frames, furniture, clocks, Oriental and European ceramics, art deco and art nouveau, objects of art, tribal art and antiquities, silver, jewellery, objects of vertu, fountain pens, toys and dolls, textiles, cameras. Annual theme sales to coincide with Chelsea Flower Show - pictures, sculptures and related works of art. Viewing Mon. 8.45-7, Tues.- Fri. 8.45-4.30, Sun. 11-4.*

Bonhams Knightsbridge
Montpelier St., Knightsbridge, SW7 1HH. Tel: 071 584 9161; fax -071 589 4072. *Regular sales of watercolours, Old Masters, European and modern pictures, portrait miniatures, prints, carved frames, furniture, clocks and watches, Lalique, commercial scent bottles, Oriental, European and contemporary ceramics, art deco, art nouveau, objects of art, tribal art and antiquities, silver, jewellery, objects of vertu, books and manuscripts, antique and modern guns, musical instruments, oriental carpets and rugs. Annual theme sales to coincide with Cowes Week, The Boat Show and Crufts - pictures, sculptures and related works of art. Viewing Mon. 8.45-7, Tues.-Fri. 8.45-6 , Sun. 11-4.*

Christie's
8 King St., St.James's, SW1Y 6QT. Tel: 071 839 9060. *Porcelain, pottery, objets d'art and miniatures, pictures including Old Masters, English, Victorian, continental, impressionist, contemporary, prints, drawings, watercolours, art deco, art nouveau; Japanese and Chinese, Islamic and Persian works of art; glass, silver, jewellery, books, modern guns, arms and armour; furniture, carpets, tapestries, clocks and watches, coins and medals, garden statuary, musical instruments, photographs, Russian works of art, sculpture, tribal art, wine, house sales (contents only).*

Christie's South Kensington Ltd
85 Old Brompton Rd., SW7 3LD. Tel: 071 581 7611; fax - 071 584 0431; telex - 922061. *Sales of jewellery, silver, pictures, watercolours, drawings and prints; furniture and carpets, ceramics and works of art, printed books; costume, textiles and embroidery; toys and games, dolls, wines, art nouveau, art deco, cameras. Periodic sales of automata, mechanical music and vintage machines, motoring and aeronautical items including car mascots; Staffordshire portrait figures, pot-lids and Goss; miniatures, antiquities and cigarette and postcards.*

Dowell Lloyd and Co. Ltd
118 Putney Bridge Rd., Putney, SW15 2NQ. Tel: 081 788 7777. *Two sales a week of general antiques and modern items.*

Forrest and Co
79-85 Cobbold Rd., Leytonstone, E11 3NS. Tel: 081 534 2931. *Fortnightly general sales (Thursdays), including antiques and household furniture, china, glassware, carpets, rugs, pictures, prints, etc.*

Stanley Gibbons Auctions Ltd.
399 Strand, WC2R 0LX. Tel: 071 836 8444. *About 12 sales annually of philatelic material in London and overseas venues with Gt.Britain, British Empire and overseas stamps and postal history. Postal bidding and specialist subscription services available - please send for full details and a sample catalogue.*

Glendining and Co
101 New Bond St., W1Y 9LG. Tel: 071 493 2445. *Specialist auctioneers of coins and medals. About 16 sales annually of coins; minimum 4 sales annually of military medals.*

Harmers of London Stamp Auctioneers Ltd.
91 New Bond St., W1A 4EH. Tel: 071 629 0218 fax - 071 495 0260. *Auctions of Great Britain*

AUCTIONEERS

London continued

British Commonwealth, foreign countries, airmail stamps, also postal history and literature, monthly (Sept.-July). Fully illustrated catalogues. Valuations for sale, probate or insurance.

Hornsey Auctions Ltd.
54-56 High St., Hornsey, N8 7NX. Tel: 081 340 5334; fax - same. Sales weekly on Wed. at 6.30. Viewing Tues. 5-8 and Wed. from 10. Open Thurs., Fri. and Mon. 9-6 and Sat. 11-4 to take in for next auction.

Lots Road Galleries
71 Lots Rd., Chelsea, SW10 0RN. Tel: 071 351 7771. Auction sales every Mon. at 3 pm and 6 pm, approximately 500 lots of antique, traditional and decorative furniture, Oriental carpets, curtains, paintings, prints, ceramics, clocks, glass, silver, objets d'art. On view Fri. 10-4, Sat. 10-1, Sun. 10-4 and Mon. 10-6. Items accepted Tues.-Fri. (Settlement 8 days after sale). SAE for catalogue. Valuers, consultants and carriers. VAT registered.

Thomas Moore Auctioneers Ltd.
217-219 High Rd., Greenwich, SE10 8NB. Tel: 081 858 7848. Weekly sales of porcelain, glass, silver, prints and furniture etc., mainly antique items. Periodic sales throughout the year of period antiques and objects - details on application. All sales of Thurs. at 10. Viewing Wed. 2-8 and Thurs. 9-10.

Phillips
101 New Bond St., and Blenstock House, 7 Blenheim St., W1Y 0AS. Tel: 071 629 6602; fax - 071 629 8876; telex - 298855. Two sales a week of furniture, carpets and works of art. Weekly sales of pictures, ceramics, glass and silver. Many specialist sales covering all aspects of art, antiques and collectors' items at frequent intervals, mainly monthly.

Phillips West Two
10 Salem Rd., W2 4DL. Tel: 071 229 9090. Sales of furniture, porcelain and works of art each Mon. with the exception of four pre-arranged dates reserved for pianos. Sales of pictures/paintings alternate with those of collectors' items each Tues. Viewing Thurs. 5.15-7.30pm, Fri. 9-5, Sun. 2-5, morning of sale. Buyers premium 10% plus VAT.

Rippon Boswell and Co.
The Arcade, South Kensington Station, SW7 2NA. Tel: 071 589 4242. International specialist auctioneers of old and antique Oriental carpets. Approximately two auctions annually in London. Also in Germany, Switzerland, U.S.A. and Far East.

Rosebery Fine Art Ltd.
The Old Railway Station, Crystal Palace, Station Road, SE19 2AZ. Tel: 081 778 4024. Sales of

London continued

antique furniture, ceramics, glass, works of art, pictures, silver and jewellery held twice a month on Tues.

Sotheby's
34-35 New Bond St., W1A 2AA. Tel: 071 493 8080. Open for free valuations Mon.-Fri. 9-4.30. Daily sales of paintings, drawings, watercolours, prints, books and manuscripts, European sculpture and works of art, antiquities, silver, ceramics, glass, jewellery, Oriental works of art, furniture, musical instruments, clocks and watches, vintage cars, wine, postage stamps, coins, medals, toys and dolls and other collectors' items.

Southgate Auction Rooms
55 High St., Southgate, N14 6LD. Tel: 081 886 7888. Weekly Mon. sales at 6.30 pm of jewellery, silver, china, porcelain, paintings, furniture. Viewing Sat. 9-12 noon and from 9 on day of sale.

AVON

Aldridges of Bath
The Auction Galleries, 130-132 Walcot St., Bath, BA1 5BG. Tel: 0225 462830; fax - 0225 482811. Weekly (Tues.) sales, broken down into specialist categories:- Antique furniture to include clocks and Oriental carpets; silver and porcelain, glass and metalware; paintings and prints; Victorian and general furniture. Viewing Sat. mornings and Mon. Catalogues available upon annual subscription. Large car park.

Allen & Harris
Bristol Auction Rooms, St. John's Place, Apsley Rd., Clifton, Bristol, BS8 2ST. Tel: 0272 737201. Six-weekly auctions of antique furniture, clocks, rugs, textiles, paintings and prints, glass, pottery, porcelain, books and ephemera, silver, objects of vertu, toys and collectables. View Sat. prior 9.30-1; day prior from 9.30-7, and on day from 9 to sale at 10.30. Fortnightly auctions of Victorian and modern household furniture and effects. View day prior to sale from 12-5 and on day from 9 until sale at 10.30. Specialist auctions and house sales held throughout the year: Catalogue subscription service. Buyers' premium.

Clevedon Salerooms
Herbert Rd., Clevedon, BS21 7ND. Tel: 0275 876699; fax - 0275 343765. Bi-monthly auctions of antique furniture, fine art and collectors' items. Fortnightly sales of Victorian, Edwardian and general furniture and effects. Occasional specialist sales and sales held on vendors' property. Valuations.

Gardiner Houlgate
The Old Malthouse, Comfortable Place, Upper Bristol Rd., Bath, BA1 3AJ. Tel: 0225 447933.

AUCTIONEERS

Avon continued

Regular sales of antique furniture and works of art. Frequent sales of Victorian and later furnishings. Twice monthly jewellery sales, quarterly musical instrument sales. Valuations.

Phillips Auctioneers - Bath
1 Old King St., Bath, BA1 2JT. Tel: 0225 310609. Member of the Phillips Auction Group. Regular fortnightly sales of antiques and Victoriana and bi-monthly sales of antiques and fine art. (All sales include furniture, ceramics, pictures, silver and jewellery).

Taviner's Auction Rooms
Prewett St., Redcliffe, Bristol, BS1 6PB. Tel: 0272 265996. Monthly specialist sales of antique furniture, books, pictures or china, glass, silver, jewellery, metals, objets vertu.

Woodspring Auctions
Churchill Rd., Weston-super-Mare, BS23 3HD. Tel: 0934 628419. Fortnightly sales of Edwardian and general furniture, brass, copper, glass, china and bric-a-brac.

BEDFORDSHIRE

Downer Ross (Auctioneers)
The Old Town Hall, Woburn, MK17 9PZ. Tel: 0525 290502. Sales every four weeks on a Thursday.

Wilson Peacock
The Auction Centre, 26 Newnham St., Bedford, MK40 3JR. Tel: 0234 266366. Antiques sale first Fri. monthly. Viewing Thurs. prior 9-6. General sales every Sat. at 9.30.

BERKSHIRE

Dreweatt - Neate
Donnington Priory, Donnington, Nr. Newbury, RG13 2JE. Tel: 0635 31234; fax - 0635 528195. Sales on the premises mainly on a weekly basis. General furnishing - fortnightly on Tues. Antique furniture - eight annually. Paintings, books, prints, silver and jewellery, ceramics - three of each annually. Members of the SOFAA. Buyers' premium 10%.

Robin Elliott FRICS, IRRV incorporating Chancellors Fine Art
32 High St., Ascot, SL5 7HG. Tel: 0344 872588. Regular sales of antique furniture, porcelain, clocks, glass, silver, plate, oil paintings, watercolours, prints and jewellery.

Martin and Pole
12 Milton Rd., Wokingham, RG11 1DB. Tel: 0734 790460. Sales of antiques and collectables held on third Wed. every month at Wokingham Auction Galleries, Milton Rd.

Berkshire continued

Thimbley and Shorland
31 Great Knollys St., Reading, RG1 7HU. Tel: 0734 508611. Collective sales of antique and modern furniture and effects held monthly on Sat. at Reading Cattle Market. Also four specialist sales of horse-drawn vehicles, harness, horse brasses, driving sundries, whips and lamps, etc.

Duncan Vincent
31 Great Knollys Street, Reading, RG1 7HU. Tel: 0734 594748. About six collective sales annually of antique, Victorian and all good quality modern furniture and effects, approximately 700 lots at Memorial Hall, Shiplake, Nr. Henley-on-Thames.

BUCKINGHAMSHIRE

Pretty & Ellis
Amersham Auction Rooms, 125 Station Rd., Amersham, HP7 0AH. Tel: 0494 729292. Weekly general and monthly selected antique sales held on Thurs. at 10.30.

CAMBRIDGESHIRE

Cheffins, Grain and Comins
The Cambridge Saleroom, 2 Clifton Rd., Cambridge, CB1 4BW. Tel: 0223 213343 (10 lines). Regular weekly and other specialist sales of furniture, clocks, porcelain, silver, pictures, sporting items, wine, rural and domestic bygones.

Cheffins, Grain and Comins
25 Market Place, Ely, CB7 4NP. Tel: 0353 662266. Sales of furniture, china, glass, bric-a-brac at Portley Hill Auction Premises, Littleport, near Ely every Thurs. at 11am.

Grounds and Co.
2 Nene Quay, Wisbech, PE13 1AG. Tel: 0945 585041/2. Two specialist sales annually, each approximately 800 lots.

Phillips
The Golden Rose, 17 Emmanuel Rd., Cambridge, CB1 1JW. Tel: 0223 66523. Regular sales of good furniture, pictures, silver, jewellery, ceramics and Victoriana, enquiries to David Fletcher.

CHESHIRE

Andrew, Hilditch and Son Ltd.
Hanover House, 1A The Square, Sandbach, CW11 0AP. Tel: 0270 767246/762048. Quarterly sales of fine pictures and period furnishings. General and Edwardian furniture sales held weekly.

Cheyne's
38 Hale Rd., Altrincham, WA14 2EX. Tel: 061

AUCTIONEERS

Cheshire continued
941 4879. *Quarterly sales held at All Saints Church Hall, Hale Barns. Viewing day prior 2-4 and 6-8 and sale morning 9-11.*

Robert I. Heyes and Associates
Hatton Buildings, Lightfoot St., Hoole, Chester, CH2 3AL. Tel: 0244 328941. *Sales held first Tues. monthly.*

Frank R. Marshall and Co.
Marshall House, Church Hill, Knutsford, WA16 6DH. Tel: 0565 653284. *Regular sales of antique furniture, objets d'art, silver, pewter, glass, porcelain, pictures, brass and copper. Fortnightly household collective sales including bric-a-brac. Specialised sales in The Knutsford Auction Salerooms.*

Phillips North West
New House, 150 Christleton Rd., Chester, CH3 5TD. Tel: 0244 313936; fax - 0244 340028. *22 salerooms countrywide including Chester.*

Peter Wilson Fine Art Auctioneers
Victoria Gallery, Market St., Nantwich, CW5 5DG. Tel: 0270 623878; fax - 0270 610508. *Bi-monthly sale on Wed. and Thurs. of fine art and antiques, Victorian and Edwardian items; viewing Sun. 2-4, Mon. and Tues. 10-4. Sales of later furnishings and household effects weekly on Thurs. at 11, viewing Wed. 10-4.*

Wright Manley
Beeston Sales Centre, Beeston Castle Smithfield, Tarporley, CW6 0DR. Tel: 0829 260318. *Fortnightly general sales and bi-monthly fine art and furniture sales.*

CORNWALL

Reg Cann
The Auction Rooms, The Parade, Trengrouse Way, Helston, TR13 8ER. Tel: 0872 76611. *Auctions held first Tues. monthly. Office - 29 Coinagehall St., Helston.*

Jefferys
5 Fore St., Lostwithiel, PL22 0BP. Tel: 0208 872245. *Sales alternate Wed. Viewing on Tues. and morning of sale. All sales commence at 10.*

Jefferys
Belmont House, Wadebridge, PL27 7NY. Tel: 0208 812131. *Sales alternate Wed. Viewing Tues. prior and morning of sale. All sales commence at 10.*

Lambrays incorporating R.J. Hamm
Polmorla Walk, Wadebridge, PL27 7AE. Tel: 020 881 3593. *Fortnightly sales of antiques and objets d'art. Illustrated catalogues issued.*

Cornwall continued
W.H. Lane and Son
Fine Art Auctioneers and Valuers, 65 Morrab Rd., Penzance, TR18 2QT and Trafalgar House, Malpas Rd., Truro, TR1 1QH. Tel: 0736 61447/0872 223379; fax - 0736 50097. *Twelve sales annually of antiques and objets d'art. Two specialist book sales annually. Six picture sales annually (specialists in the Newlyn and St. Ives Schools). Two specialist toy sales annually. Frequent house sales.*

David Lay ASVA
The Penzance Auction House, Alverton, Penzance, TR18 4RE. Tel: 0736 61414; fax - 0736 60035. *Sales of fine art, antiques and collectors' items every two weeks.*

M.G.A. Auctions
The Camborne Auction House, West Charles St., Camborne, TR14 8JG. Tel: 0209 711065. *Sales every Thurs. at 6 pm.*

Phillips Cornwall
Cornubia Hall, Par, PL24 2AQ. Tel: 0726 814047. *Monthly sales of antiques, Victorian and later furnishings.*

Pooley and Rogers
Regent Auction Rooms, Abbey St., Penzance. Tel: Office - 0736 63816/7 or 0736 795451; saleroom - 0736 68814. *Bi-monthly sales of antique furniture, objets d'art, silver and jewellery.*

CUMBRIA

Cumbria Auction Rooms
12 Lowther St., Carlisle, CA3 8DA. Tel: 0228 25259. *Weekly sales of Victorian and later furniture and effects. Catalogue sales of antiques and works of art every ten weeks.*

James Thompson
64 Main St., Kirkby Lonsdale, LA6 2AJ. Tel: 05242 71555. *Monthly two day sales of silver, ceramics, general antiques. Special picture sales six times a year.*

Thomson, Roddick and Laurie Ltd.
24 Lowther St., Carlisle, CA3 8DA. Tel: 0228 28939/39636. *Bi-monthly catalogue sales of antiques and collectors' items and regular specialist sales particularly antiquarian books, sporting guns, silver and pictures at Dumfries and Carlisle. Monthly general furniture sales at Wigton and Annan (Dumfriesshire).*

DERBYSHIRE

Neales
The Derby Salerooms, Becket St., Derby, DE1 1HW. Tel: 0332 43286. *Regular sales of antique,*

AUCTIONEERS

Derbyshire continued

Victorian, Edwardian and reproduction furniture and furnishings, pictures, silver, jewellery, ceramics (especially Derbyshire factories), glass, decorative arts and collectors' items.

Noel Wheatcroft
Matlock Auction Gallery, Old English Rd., Off Dale Rd., Matlock, DE4 3LX. Tel: 0629 584591. *Monthly sales of antiques and general items.*

DEVON

Bearne's
Rainbow, Avenue Rd., Torquay, TQ2 5TG. Tel: 0803 296277. *Regular sales of antique furniture, works of art, silver, jewellery, collectors' items, clocks and watches, paintings, ceramics and glass, carpets and rugs. Illustrated catalogues published three weeks prior to sale.*

Bonhams - West Country
Dowell St., Honiton, EX14 8LX. Tel: 0404 41872; fax - 0404 43137. *Regular monthly auctions of furniture, works of art, ceramics, pictures, silver and jewellery, and collectors' items.*

Kingsbridge Auction Sales (J.A.S. Hawkins) inc. Charles Head and Son
85 Fore St., Kingsbridge, TQ7 1AB. Tel: 0548 856829. *Regular sales of antique and general household furniture and effects.*

Lyme-Bay Auction Galleries
28 Harbour Rd., Seaton. Tel: 0297 22453. *General household and antique auctions held every four to six weeks.*

Phillips
Alphin Brook Rd., Alphington, Exeter, EX2 8TH. Tel: 0392 439025; fax - 0392 410361. *Thurs. sales of antique and reproduction furniture and furnishings; oil paintings, watercolours and quality prints; silver and plate, jewellery, porcelain, glass, Victoriana and objets d'art. Book sales held four times a year; annual sporting sale.*

Potburys of Sidmouth
The Auction Rooms, Temple St., Sidmouth, EX10 8LN. Tel: 0395 515555. *Twice monthly sales plus private house sales.*

Rendells
Stone Park, Ashburton, TQ13 7RH. Tel: 0364 53017. *Sales of antique furniture, silver, jewellery, porcelain, glass, clocks, pictures, plate, copper and brass and miscellanea on the last Thursday and Friday of each month.*

Sidmouth Salerooms
Western House, 98-100 High St., Sidmouth,

Devon continued

EX10 8EF. Tel: 0395 513006. *Sales of antiques, silver, pictures, china and objects d'art, third Friday every month. General sales third Saturday.*

John Smale and Co.Ltd.
11 High St., Barnstaple, EX31 1BG. Tel: 0271 42000. *Intermittently throughout the year - private house sales only.*

Taylor's
Honiton Galleries, 205 High St., Honiton, EX14 8LF. Tel: 0404 42404. *Sales of paintings and prints, antiques, silver, books and porcelain every seven weeks.*

Ward and Chowen
1 Church Lane, Tavistock, PL19 8AB. Tel: 0822 612458.

Whitton and Laing
32 Okehampton St., Exeter, EX4 1DY. Tel: 0392 52621. *Monthly auctions of antiques, silver and jewellery. Quarterly book auctions. General auctions weekly.*

DORSET

Cottees, Bullock and Lees
The Market, East St., Wareham, BH20 4NR. Tel: 0929 552826. *Furniture and effects every two weeks.*

Hy. Duke and Son
Fine Art Salerooms, Weymouth Avenue, Dorchester, DT1 1QS. Tel: 0305 265080. *Regular six weekly sales including specialist sections of silver and jewellery, Oriental and English porcelain, English and continental furniture, pictures, books or Oriental rugs.*

Hy. Duke and Son
Weymouth Saleroom, Nicholas St., Weymouth. Tel: 0305 761499. *Bi-weekly general sales.*

House and Son
Lansdowne House, Christchurch Rd., Bournemouth, BH1 3JW. Tel: 0202 556232. *Fortnightly sales of selected furniture, pictures, books, silver, porcelain and glass. Catalogues £1.50 including postage.*

Wm. Morey and Sons
Salerooms, St. Michaels Lane, Bridport, DT6 3RB. Tel: 0308 22078. *Antique and general sales held every three to four weeks.*

Riddetts of Bournemouth
Richmond Hill, Bournemouth Square, Bournemouth, BH2 6EJ. Tel: 0202 555686; fax - 0202 311004. *Fortnightly sales which include fine antiques, jewellery, silver, plate, pictures. Illustrated sale programme free. Catalogue subscription £25 p.a.*

AUCTIONEERS

Dorset continued

Southern Counties Auctioneers
The Livestock Market, Christys Lane, Shaftesbury, SP7 8PH. Tel: 0747 51735. *Regular sales of antique furniture and effects.*

DURHAM

Denis Edkins
Auckland Auction Rooms, 58 Kingsway, Bishop Auckland, DL14 7JF. Tel: 0388 603095. *General and antique sales from time to time.*

G. Tarn Bainbridge and Son
Northern Rock House, High Row, Darlington, DL3 7QN. Tel: 0325 462633/462553. *Three to four collective sales annually and country house sales.*

Thomas Watson and Son
Northumberland St., Darlington, DL3 7HJ. Tel: 0325 462559/5 (two lines). *Regular sales of antiques and good quality house contents.*

ESSEX

Abridge Auction Rooms
Market Place, Abridge, Romford, RM4 1UA. Tel: 0992 813113/812107. *3 sales per month at 7 pm. Bi-monthly sales of jewellery, Victorian and Edwardian furniture and Doulton. (No sale on last Wed. of month).*

Black Horse Agencies - Ambrose
149 High Rd., Loughton, IG10 4LZ. Tel: 081 508 2121 or 081 502 3951. *Sales held on last Thurs. monthly.*

William H. Brown
11-14 East Hill, Colchester, CO1 2QX. Tel: 0206 868070. *Weekly sales of antique and modern furniture, china, glass, silver and decorative items.*

Cooper Hirst Auctions
The Granary Salerooms, Victoria Rd., Chelmsford, CM2 6LH. Tel: 0245 260535. *Regular sales of antiques every 8/9 weeks and weekly Tues. sales of Victoriana, bric-a-brac etc. Catalogue subscription service available.*

Hamptons Fine Art - J.M. Welch and Son
Old Town Hall, Great Dunmow, CM6 1AU. Tel: 0371 872117; fax - 0371 875786. *At the Salerooms, Chequers Lane - selected antique furniture and effects sales every two months. Monthly sales of collectables and household furniture. Catalogue subscription service available.*

Reemans
Head Gate Auction Rooms, 12 Head Gate,

Essex continued

Colchester, CO3 3BT. Tel: 0206 574271/2. *Sales held every Wed. Viewing 9-7 Tues. prior. Evening sale last Tues. monthly.*

Simon H. Rowland
Chelmsford Auction Rooms, 42 Mildmay Rd., Chelmsford, CM2 0DZ. Tel: 0245 354251. *Regular sales by order of the Sheriff of Essex and private vendors.*

Saffron Walden Auctions
1 Market St., Saffron Walden, CB10 1JB. Tel: 0799 513281. *Sales of antique and fine furniture, antique effects and objets d'art held every month.*

John Stacey and Sons
Leigh Auction Rooms, 86-90 Pall Mall, Leigh-on-Sea, SS9 1RG. Tel: 0702 77051. *Monthly sales of furniture, works of art and collectors' items. Catalogue subscription £28 p.a.*

GLOUCESTERSHIRE

Bruton, Knowles
Albion Chambers, 111 Eastgate St., Gloucester, GL1 1PZ. Tel: 0452 521267. *Fine art auctioneers and valuers. House and collective sales held throughout the year. Valuations and inventories prepared.*

Corinium Galleries
25 Gloucester St., Cirencester, GL7 2DJ. Tel: 0285 659057. *Mon. auctions of postcards and small collectables every five weeks.*

Fraser Glennie and Partners
The Old Rectory, Siddington, Cirencester, GL7 6HL. Tel: 0285 659677; fax - 0285 642256. *Monthly sales of antiques, other furniture, collectors' items and musical instruments at the Bingham Hall, Cirencester.*

Mallams Fine Art Auctioneers and Valuers
26 Grosvenor St., Cheltenham, GL52 2SG. Tel: 0242 235712; fax - 0242 241943. Est. 1788. *Regular sales of furniture, ceramics, paintings, textiles, rugs and works of art.*

Moore, Allen and Innocent
33 Castle St., Cirencester, GL7 1QD. Tel: 0285 651831. *Monthly collective sales of over 1,000 lots of antique and other furniture. Bi-annual specialist picture sales and sporting sales. Fri. at 10. Viewing day prior 10.30-8. No buyers premium.*

Short Graham and Co
City Chambers, 4/6 Clarence St., Gloucester, GL1 1DX. Tel: 0452 521177. *Sales of Georgian, Victorian, Edwardian and later furniture,*

AUCTIONEERS

Established 1846

RUSSELL, BALDWIN & BRIGHT

Regular Specialist Sales:
FURNITURE
WORKS of ART
PORCELAIN & POTTERY
SILVER
JEWELLERY
CLOCKS
MUSICAL BOXES
METALWARE
BOOKS and PICTURES

VALUATIONS for all purposes carried out by our qualified staff
SALES by AUCTION of the contents of Town and Country Houses conducted throughout the West Midlands and Wales
Enquiries: The Fine Art Saleroom, Ryelands Road, LEOMINSTER (tel. 0568 611166 fax. 0568 610 519), Herefordshire and at the Portland Room, Malvern, Worcs.

Gloucestershire continued

ceramics, glass, metalwork, silver, plate, jewellery, miscellanea, collectors' items, books, pictures and outside effects every four to six weeks.

Wotton Auction Rooms Ltd
(formerly Sandoe Luce Panes) Tabernacle Rd., Wotton-under-Edge, GL12 7EB. Tel: 0453 844733; fax - 0453 845448. *Monthly catalogued auction; usually 1,000 lots - all categories. House contents sales as instructed.*

HAMPSHIRE

Michael G. Baker FSVA
The Romsey Auction Rooms, 86 The Hundred, Romsey, SO51 8BX. Tel: 0794 513331; fax - 0794 511770. *Monthly sales of antique and period furniture and effects, silver, jewellery and plate.*

Basingstoke Auction Rooms
82-84 Sarum Hill, Basingstoke, RG21 1ST. Tel: 0256 840707. *Regular sales of antiques and fine art and fortnightly general sales. Occasional specialist sales. Catalogues available. Buyers' premium 10%.*

Fox and Sons
5 and 7 Salisbury St., Fordingbridge, SP6 1AD. Tel: 0425 652121; fax - 0425 656690. *Monthly sales of antique and later furniture, silver, plate, metalware, ceramics, pictures etc.*

Hants. and Berks. Auctions
82-84 Sarum Hill, Basingstoke. Tel: 0256 840707. *Monthly sales at Heckfield Village Hall on Sat. 10.30. Viewing previous day 11-9. Sales include antiques, reproduction and household furniture, clocks, porcelain, glass, silver, pictures, etc. Occasional specialist sales. Catalogues available.*

Jacobs and Hunt
Lavant St., Petersfield, GU32 3EF. Tel: 0730 262744. *General antique sales every six to eight weeks on Fri.*

Hampshire continued

May and Son
18 Bridge St., Andover, SP10 1BH. Tel: 0264 323417/363331; fax - 0264 338841. *Monthly sales of antique furniture and effects at Penton Mewsey Village Hall (Lots from private sources only) Private house contents sales.*

D.M. Nesbit and Co.
7 Clarendon Rd., Southsea, Portsmouth, PO5 2ED. Tel: 0705 864321. *Monthly sales of antique furniture, silver, porcelain and pictures.*

Phillips
54 Southampton Rd., Ringwood, BH24 1JD. Tel: 0425 473333. *Regular sales, usually monthly.*

Phillips Fine Art Auctioneers
The Red House, Hyde St., Winchester, SO23 7DX. Tel: 0962 862515; fax - 0962 865166. *Bi-monthly sales of fine furniture, pictures, silver, jewellery, ceramics, metalware, clocks, rugs and works of art. Three-weekly sales of antique, Victorian and Edwardian furniture, ceramics, pictures and objects.*

HEREFORD AND WORCESTER

Griffiths and Co.
57 Foregate St., Worcester, WR1 1DZ. Tel: 0905 26464.

Hamptons Fine Art - Pocock and Lear
The Malvern Sale Room, Barnards Green Rd., Malvern. Tel: 0684 892314/5. *Bi-monthly catalogued antique and fine art auctions. Fortnightly general sales. Specialist sales of Worcester porcelain (single items or collections). Valuations.*

Nationwide Fine Art & Furniture
41-43 High St., Broadway, WR12 7DP. Tel: 0386 852456. *Collective antique and modern furniture sales bi-monthly. Specialist sales of silver and porcelain twice annually.*

Hereford and Worcester continued
Phipps and Pritchard
Bank Buildings, Kidderminster, DY10 1BU. Tel: 0562 822244/5/6 and 822187. *Regular monthly sales of antique furniture, watercolours and oil paintings, copper, brass, glass, china and porcelain, stamps and coins, weapons etc. Private house sales also conducted.*

Russell, Baldwin and Bright
The Fine Art Saleroom, Ryelands Rd., Leominster, HR6 8NZ. Tel: 0568 611166; fax - 0568 610519. *Monthly 2-day sales of antiques and collectors' items (approx. 1,000 lots per sale). Two or three sales per month of antique and household effects.*

Russell, Baldwin and Bright
The Portland Saleroom, Portland Rd., Malvern, WR14 2TA. Tel: 0684 893933. *Monthly sales of antiques and collectors' items.*

HERTFORDSHIRE

Brown and Merry - Tring Market Auctions
Brook Street, Tring, HP23 5EF. Tel: 044282 6446. *Fortnightly Sat. sales of antiques and collectables held at The Market Premises, Brook St., Tring. Fine art sales held on last Fri. of month.*

Pamela and Barry Auctions
Village Hall, Sandridge, St. Albans, AL4 9ST. Tel: 0727 861180. *Antiques and collectors auctions held on the first Tues. monthly. Viewing from 3 pm to start at 7 pm.*

G.E. Sworder and Sons
15 Northgate End, Bishops Stortford, CM23 2ET. Tel: 0279 651388. *Monthly auctions of antique furniture, ceramics, silver, pictures, decorative items. Viewing Sat. prior 9-12 and Mon. prior 10-4. Weekly Thurs. at 11 auction of Victorian, Edwardian and later furniture and collectables. Viewing morning of sale.*

HUMBERSIDE NORTH

Gilbert Baitson
The Edwardian Auction Galleries, Wiltshire Rd, Hull, HU4 6PG. Tel: 0482 500500; after hours - 0482 645241; fax - 0482 500501. *Sales of antique and modern furnishings every Wed. at 10.30. Viewing day prior until 8 pm.*

Dee and Atkinson - Agricultural and Fine Arts
The Exchange Saleroom, Driffield, YO25 7LJ. Tel: 0377 43151; fax - 0377 241041. *Regular bi-monthly sales of antiques, Victorian, Edwardian*

Humberside North continued
and quality furnishings, paintings, silver, jewellery etc. Viewing two days prior. Fortnightly household sales.

H. Evans and Sons
1 St. James's St., Hessle Rd., Hull, HU3 2DH. Tel: 0482 23033; fax - 0482 211954. *Five antiques sales annually, fortnightly general furniture and effects.*

Spencers Auctioneers and Estate Agents
The Imperial and Repository Salerooms, 18 Quay Rd., Bridlington, YO15 2AP. Tel: 0262 676724. *General auctions every Thurs. Regular sales of antiques and fine arts.*

HUMBERSIDE SOUTH

Dickinson, Davy and Markham
DDM Auction Rooms, Old Courts Road, Brigg, DN20 8JJ. Tel: 0652 653666; fax - 0652 650085. *Fine art and antique auctions held every six to eight weeks, also Victorian and household effects every two weeks. Catalogue subscription service available.*

A.E. Dowse and Son
Foresters' Galleries, Falkland Way, Barton-upon-Humber, DN18 5RL. Tel: 0652 32335. *Monthly sales of general antiques and collectors' items.*

Watson Bull & Porter - Auction Rooms
79 Regent St., Shanklin, PO37 7AP. Tel: 0983 863441. *Monthly auctions of antiques and fine arts.*

Ways
The Auction House, Garfield Rd., Ryde, PO33 2PT. Tel: 0983 562255. *Five-weekly sales of antique and modern furniture, silver, copper and brass, oils, watercolours and prints, jewellery, china, clocks, etc.*

KENT

Albert Andrews Auctions and Sales
Maiden Lane, Crayford, Dartford, DA1 4LX. Tel: 0322 528868. *Weekly auctions including antiques, Victorian and Edwardian furniture, bric-a-brac, paintings and clocks, on Wed. at 10. Viewing Tues. 4.30-8.30.*

Auction Centres
Highgate, Hawkhurst, TN18 4EP. Tel: 0580 754545; fax - same. *Weekly sales; sales in country houses, cottages, etc. throughout the south-east. Catalogues by post. Valuations. Storage and delivery.*

Kent continued

Bracketts
27-29 High St., Tunbridge Wells, TN1 1UU. Tel: 0892 533733. *Weekly sales of antiques and general household furniture on Fri. Specialist sales of antiques and sales on the premises.*

The Canterbury Auction Galleries
40 Station Rd. West, Canterbury, CT2 8AN. Tel: 0227 763337; fax - 0227 456770. *Specialist fine art and antiques auctions held bi-monthly on Tues. at 10.30. Quarterly collectors' auctions to include tin and die-cast toys, railway items, studio ceramics, militaria and other items held on Tues. at 11. Viewing for both auctions on Mon. prior. Monthly auctions of Victorian, Edwardian and quality modern furniture and effects held on the first Sat. monthly, commencing at 10. Professional valuations for insurance, probate and family division carried out.*

H. & H. Auctioneers and Valuers
St. Johns St., Off Dover Rd., Folkestone, CT21 3JU. Tel: 0303 269323; Viewing and sale days - 0303 40808. *Monthly antique and fine art sales.*

Halifax Property Services
53 High St., Tenterden, TN30 6BG. Tel: 0580 763200. *Antique and modern furniture and effects usually on first Wed. monthly.*

Hobbs Parker
Romney House, Ashford Market, Ashford, TN23 1PG. Tel: 0233 622222; fax - 0233 46642. *Monthly sales of antiques and household furniture.*

Ibbett, Mosely
125 High St., Sevenoaks, TN13 1UT. Tel: 0732 456731. *Antiques and objets d'art.*

Lambert and Foster
102 High St., Tenterden, TN30 6HT. Tel: 0580 763233. *21 offices throughout Kent and Sussex. Monthly general sales of good quality antique furniture and effects. Special contents sales at private residences in county. Fine art evening sales.*

B.J. Norris
The Quest, West St., Harrietsham. Tel: 0622 859515. *Regular sales at The Agricultural Hall, Maidstone at 10.30. Viewing from 8 on morning prior.*

Phillips
11 Bayle Parade, Folkestone, CT20 1SQ. Tel: 0303 245555; fax - 0303 259178. *Seventeen fine art and Victoriana sales each year.*

Phillips Son and Neale
49 London Rd., Sevenoaks, TN13 1AR. Tel: 0732 740310. *Monthly sales of antiques and collectors' items.*

LANCASHIRE

Acorn Philatelic Auctions
27 Pine Rd., Didsbury, Manchester, M20 0UZ. Tel: 061 434 2580. *Tues. sales, approximately every 5 weeks, held at Unit 6, Block C, Astra Business Centre, Guiness Rd., Trafford Park, Manchester. 10 per year all specialising in paper collectables - postage stamps and history, manuscripts, autographs, picture and cigarette cards, books, prints, drawings and watercolours. Sales commence at 1pm, viewing Mon. previous 10.30-8, and sale morning 9-12.30.*

Capes, Dunn and Co. Fine Art Auctioneers
The Auction Galleries, 38 Charles St., Manchester, M1 7DB. Tel: 061 273 1911; fax - 061 273 3474. Est. 1826. *Catalogues of weekly specialist sales available on request.*

Charles Edwards Group
4/8 Lynwood Rd., Blackburn, BB2 6HP. Tel: 0254 691748. *Quarterly antique, fine art, jewellery auctions. Monthly general sales. Valuations.*

Entwistle Green (Black Horse Agencies)
The Galleries, Kingsway, Ansdell, Lytham St. Annes, FY8 1AB. Tel: 0253 735442. *Sales of antique, reproduction and modern furnishings and appointments held fortnightly on Tues. Approximately 400-600 lots commencing 10. Viewing Sat. morning and Mon. to 3.45. Buyers' premium 10%.*

J.R. Parkinson Son and Hamer Auctions
The Auction Room, Rochdale Rd., Bury. Tel: 061 761 1612/7372. *Specialised auctions of antiques, Victoriana and Edwardiana every six to eight weeks throughout the year.*

LEICESTERSHIRE

William H. Brown
The Warner Auction Rooms, 16/18 Halford St., Leicester, LE1 1JB. Tel: 0533 519777. *Regular sales of antiques, pictures, porcelain, silver etc. Outside sales by arrangement.*

Freckeltons
1 Leicester Rd., Loughborough, LE11 2AE. Tel: 0509 214564. *Monthly sales of general antiques.*

Gilding's Auctioneers and Valuers
Roman Way, Market Harborough, LE16 7PQ. Tel: 0858 410414. *Monthly sales of antiques, weekly sales of Victoriana and collectables.*

Heathcote Ball & Co
Castle Auction Rooms, 78 St. Nicholas Circle, Leicester, LE1 5NW. Tel: 0533 536789; fax - 0533 538517. *Auctions every four to six weeks.*

LINCOLNSHIRE

C.J. Daykin FRICS
69 Northgate, Sleaford, NG34 7BB. Tel: 0529 413954. *General sale Mon. (excluding Bank Holidays) and monthly Thurs. sales.*

James Eley and Son
1 Main Ridge West, Boston, PE21 6QQ. Tel: 0205 361687. *Regular sales at Boston and Skegness.*

Escritt and Barrell
The Saleroom, Dysart Rd., and office - Elmer House, Finkin St., Grantham, NG31 6RD. Tel: 0476 66991. *Three-weekly general shipping and antique sales, Frequent antique sales.*

Thomas Mawer and Son
63 Monks Rd., Lincoln, LN2 5HP. Tel: 0522 524984. *General sales fortnighly. Catalogued antique sales monthly.*

Richardsons
Bourne Auction Rooms, Spalding Rd., Bourne, PE10 9LE. Tel: 0778 422686. *Antiques sales every month. Antique and modern sales every Sat.*

Marilyn Swain
Westgate Hall, Grantham, NG31 6LT. Tel: 0476 68861. *Bi-monthly antique and fine art sales. Occasional specialist and house contents sales. Fortnightly sales of general household furniture and effects.*

MERSEYSIDE

A.J. Cobern
The Grosvenor Salerooms, 93B Eastbank St., Southport, PR8 1DG. Tel: 0704 500515. *Sales of antique, reproduction and modern furnishings held every three to four weeks. Average 600-700 lots commencing at 10. Viewing weekend and two days prior to sale.*

J. Kent (Auctioneers) Ltd.
2/6 Valkyrie Rd., Wallasey, L45 4RQ. Tel: 051 638 3107; fax - same. *Weekly general sale; Monthly antiques and fine art on Wed. at 10. Viewing Tues. 9-6.30.*

Kingsley and Co. Auctioneers
3/4 The Quadrant, Hoylake, Wirral, L47 2EE. Tel: 051 632 5821. *Sales every Tues. of antiques, fine art and general chattels.*

Outhwaite and Litherland
Kingsway Galleries, Fontenoy St., Liverpool, L3 2BE. Tel: 051 236 6561/3. *Victorian, Edwardian and modern furnishings - weekly Tues. General antiques and fine quality reproductions - fortnightly Wed. Fine art sales, including all works illustrative of the fine arts - monthly Wed. Specialist sales of books, wines, stamps etc. periodically. Members of SOFAA.*

NORFOLK

Hugh Beck Auctions
The Cornhall, Cattle Market St., Fakenham, NR21 9AW. Tel: 0328 851557. *Weekly sales of antique and other furniture every Thurs. at 11. Country house sales as instructed.*

Clowes, Nash and Thurgar
6 Tombland, Norwich, NR3 1HE. Tel: 0603 627261. *Antiques and general furniture weekly sales.*

Ewings
Market Place, Reepham, Norwich, NR10 4JJ. Tel: 0603 870473. *Periodic sales of antiques and modern furniture and effects.*

Thos. Wm. Gaze and Son
Diss Auction Rooms, Roydon Rd., Diss, IP22 3LN. Tel: 0379 650306. *Weekly catalogue sales of antiques and cottage furniture on Fri. at 10 am and bi-monthly special catalogue sales.*

Nigel F. Hedge
28B Market Place, North Walsham, NR28 9BS. Tel: 0692 402881. *Fortnightly general and antique sales.*

Hilham's
43 Baker St., Gorleston-on-Sea, NR31 6QT. Tel: 0493 600700. *Art auctions held regularly. Antiques and Victoriana sales held every month.*

James Auctioneers Ltd
PO Box 10, Attleborough, NR17 2AA. Tel: 0953 860888. *Regular sales of collectables. Occasional sales of antiques.*

G.A. Key
Incorporated Auctioneers, 8 Market Place, Aylsham, NR11 6EH. Tel: 0263 733195. *Three weekly sales of period, antique and Victorian furniture, silver, porcelain etc. Bi-monthly picture sales - oils, watercolours and prints etc. Six book and collectors sales annually. Weekly sales of shipping and secondhand furniture.*

NORTHAMPTONSHIRE

Goldsmiths
15 Market Place, Oundle, PE8 4BA. Tel: 0832 272349. *Sales approximately bi-monthly.*

Heathcote Ball & Co
Albion Auction Rooms, Commercial St., Northampton, NN1 1PJ. Tel: 0604 22735 (office); 0604 37263 (auction). *Regular fine art and antique sales, fortnightly general sales, specialist sales. Mailing subscription £15 p.a.*

Southams
Corn Exchange, Thrapston, Kettering, NN14 4JJ. Tel: 0832 734586. *Est. 1900. First Thurs. each*

AUCTIONEERS

Northamptonshire continued

month, viewing Wed. 9.30-8 sales of antiques and superior furniture, silver, plate, copper and brass, fine china, glass, Oriental rugs, oil paintings, watercolours and prints. 10% buyer's premium. Catalogues £2 including postage. Annual subscription £18.

H. Wilford Ltd.
Midland Rd., Wellingborough, NN8 1NB. Tel: 0933 222760/222762. Weekly sales of antique and modern furniture, shipping goods, jewellery etc. every Thursday (over 1200 lots).

NOTTINGHAMSHIRE

Arthur Johnson and Sons (Auctioneers)
The Nottingham Auction Centre, Meadow Lane, Nottingham, NG2 3GY. Tel: 0602 869128; fax - 0602 862139. Approximately 1,000 lots weekly on Sat. at 10 of antique and shipping furniture, silver, gold, porcelain, metalware and collectables.

Neales
192-194 Mansfield Rd., Nottingham, NG1 3HU. Tel: 0602 624141. Specialist sales of paintings, drawings, prints and books; silver, jewellery, bijouterie and watches; European and Oriental ceramics and works of art, glass; furniture and decoration; metalwork, fabrics, needlework, carpets and rugs; collectors' toys and dolls; stamps, coins and medals, post and cigarette cards; autographs and collectors' items. Weekly collective sales (Mon.) of general antique and later furnishings, shipping goods and reproduction furnishings. Period and later ceramics, glass and decorative effects. Sales on the premises of the contents of town and country properties.

Henry Spencer and Sons - Fine Art Auctioneers
20 The Square, Retford, DN22 6BX. Tel: 0777 708633. Specialist sales of furniture, carpets, ornamental items, works of art; paintings, drawings and prints; porcelain and glass, silver, jewellery and bijouterie. Non-specialist sales of furniture and effects held three times a month. Sales on the premises at town and country houses.

Richard Watkinson and Partners
17 Northgate, Newark, NG24 1EX. Tel: 0636 77154. Monthly sales of antique and Victorian furniture, oil paintings, silver etc. Weekly sales of early 20th C and general household furniture.

OXFORDSHIRE

Holloways
49 Parsons St., Banbury, OX16 8PF. Tel: 0295 253197. Sales at least twice monthly.

Oxfordshire continued

Mallams
Fine Art Auctioneers, Bocardo House, 24A St. Michael's St., Oxford, OX1 2EB. Tel: 0865 241358. Frequent sales of furniture, silver, paintings and works of art. House sales arranged on the premises.

Messenger's
Messenger's Salerooms, 27 Sheep St., Bicester, OX6 7JF. Tel: 0869 252901. Antique furniture and effects each month. Specialist sales of carpentry tools, collectors' items and domestic bygones.

Phillips Fine Art Auctioneers
39 Park End St., Oxford, OX1 1JD. Tel: 0865 723524; fax - 0865 791064. Fortnightly sales of Victoriana and general effects. Specialist sales of fine furniture, rugs, works of art, silver, jewellery and ceramics throughout the year.

SHROPSHIRE

Cooper and Green
3 Barker St., Shrewsbury, SY1 1QF. Tel: 0743 232244.

Cooper and Green
The Square, Church Stretton, SY6 6DA. Tel: 0694 722458.

Hall, Wateridge and Owen
Welsh Bridge Salerooms, Shrewsbury, SY3 8LA. Tel: 0743 231212. Regular Victoriana and and household (Fri.). Bi-monthly selected antiques and collectables.

Ludlow Antique Auctions Ltd
29 Corve St., Ludlow, SY8 1DA. Tel: 0584 875157/873496. Specialist fine art and antique auctions every four weeks (Tues.) on the premises.

Perry and Phillips
Newmarket Salerooms, Newmarket Buildings, Listley St., Bridgnorth, WV16 4AW. Tel: 0746 762248. Weekly (Tues.) sales of good quality household furniture and effects. Monthly sales of antique furniture, Victoriana, china, porcelain, pictures etc. Regular specialist and house contents sales.

SOMERSET

Cooper & Tanner Rural Surveyors
Frome Market, Standerwick, Frome, BA11 2PY. Tel: 0373 831010. Weekly sales of antiques and general household chattels 11.15am Wednesdays. Viewing morning of sale. Haulage service.

Greenslade Hunt Fine Art
Magdalene House, Church Square, Taunton, TA1 1SB. Tel: 0823 332525; fax - 0823 323923.

AUCTIONEERS

Somerset continued

Weekly Thurs. sales of Victorian and later furniture and household effects. Monthly, last Thurs., sales of antique furniture, metalwork, ceramics, glass, paintings and prints. Quarterly sales of silver, plate, jewellery and objects of vertu. Viewing 2 days prior, 10-4.

Gribble Booth and Taylor
13 The Parade, Minehead, TA24 5NL. Tel: 0643 702281; saleroom - 0643 703646. *Regular sales every three weeks of antique and other furniture and effects at Mart Road Salerooms, Minehead. Occasional house clearances.*

Lawrence Fine Art Auctioneers Ltd.
South St., Crewkerne, TA18 8AB. Tel: 0460 73041; fax - 0460 74627. *Specialist auctioneers and valuers. Regular sales of antiques and fine art. General sales every Wednesday except first Wednesday of each month.*

The London Cigarette Card Co. Ltd
Sutton Rd., Somerton, TA11 6QP. Tel: 0458 73452. *Suppliers of thousands of different series of cigarette and trade cards and special albums. Publishers of catalogues, reference books and monthly magazine. Regular auctions in London and Somerset. S.A.E. for details. Mail order, open by appointment.*

Richards
The Town Hall, Axbridge, BS26 2AR. Tel: 0934 732969. *Bi-monthly sales of privately entered fine art and selected antiques of all categories. Extra sales conducted on owners' premises when instructed. Valuations; inventories prepared.*

Tamlyn and Son
56 High St., Bridgwater, TA6 3BN. Tel: 0278 458241/2.

Wellington Salerooms
Mantle St., Wellington, TA21 8AR. Tel: 0823 664815. *Six-weekly sales of general antiques. Fortnightly sales of Victorian, Edwardian and shipping goods.*

STAFFORDSHIRE

Armstrong Auctions
Midland Rd., Swadlincote, Burton-on-Trent, DE11 0AH. Tel: 0283 217772. *Weekly general sales and periodic antique sales held in Swadlincote Auction Rooms.*

Bagshaws
The Estate Saleroom, High St., Uttoxeter, ST14 7HP. Tel: 0889 562811, fax - 0889 563795. *Monthly sales of Victorian and general household furniture and effects. Quarterly specialist antique sales.*

Staffordshire continued

John German
The Rotunda, Burton-on-Trent; DE14 1LN. Tel: 0283 42051. *Occasional sales of major house contents; specialist fine art valuation department.*

Hall and Lloyd, Auctioneers
South St., Stafford, ST16 2DZ. Tel: 0785 58176; fax - 0785 228224. Est. 1882. *Regular fortnightly sales of antique and general household furniture and effects. 1,000 or more lots every other Thurs.. Special catalogued sales of antiques held regularly.*

Louis Taylor Fine Art Auctioneers
Britannia House, 10 Town Rd., Hanley, Stoke-on-Trent. Tel: 0782 214111. *Quarterly fine art sales including furniture, pictures, pottery, porcelain, silver and works of art. Specialist Royal Doulton and Beswick auctions. General Victoriana auctions held every two weeks.*

Wintertons
Lichfield Auction Centre, Fradley Park, Fradley, Lichfield, WS13 8NF. Tel: 0543 263256. *Bi-monthly sales of antiques and fine art and sales of Victorian and general furniture every 2-3 weeks.*

SUFFOLK

Abbotts Auction Rooms
Campsea Ashe, Near Woodbridge, IP13 0PS. Tel: 0728 746323. *Monthly sales of Antique Furniture & Effects held on Wednesdays. Viewing two days prior. Sales calendar and catalogues available. Weekly sales of Victoriana & Household Furniture held on Mondays to coincide with livestock market. Viewing Saturday 9-11 am.*

H.A. Adnams
The Auction Room, St. Edmunds Rd. Office - 98 High St., Southwold. Tel: 0502 723292.

Boardman - Fine Art Auctioneers
Station Road Corner, Haverhill, CB9 0EY. Tel: 0440 730414; fax - 0440 730505. *Large sales held bi-monthly specialising in selected fine furniture, clocks and paintings.*

William H. Brown
Olivers Rooms, Burkitts Lane, Sudbury, CO10 6HB. Tel: 0787 880305. *Weekly sales of antique and household furniture and shipping goods. Regular sales of good quality antiques. Enquiries to James Fletcher FRICS, Furniture and Fine Art Department.*

Diamond Mills and Co. Fine Art Auctioneers
117 Hamilton Rd., Felixstowe, IP11 7BL. Tel: 0394 282281 (3 lines). *Quarterly fine art sales. Monthly general sales. Auctions at The Orwell Hall, Orwell Rd., Felixstowe.*

Suffolk continued

Durrant's
10 New Market, Beccles, NR34 9HA. Tel: 0502 712122. *Antique and general furniture auctions every Fri. at Gresham Rd., Beccles.*

Lacy Scott (Fine Art Dept.)
10 Risbygate St., Bury St. Edmunds, IP33 3AA. Tel: 0284 763531; fax - 0284 704713. *Regular sales of fine art including antique and decorative furniture, silver, pictures, ceramics etc. on behalf of executors and private vendors. Regular (every two to three weeks) sales of Victoriana and general household contents. Also regular sales of diecast and tinplate toys (2 of which include working steam scale models) and annual fine wine sales.*

Neal Sons and Fletcher
26 Church St., Woodbridge, IP12 1DP. Tel: 0394 382263. *Two special mixed antiques sales annually. Individual specialised sales and complete house contents sales as required. Household furniture sales on a Wednesday of each month.*

Phillips East Anglia
Dover House, Wolsey St., Ipswich, IP1 1UD. Tel: 0473 255137. *Four two-day specialist sales annually at Bury St. Edmunds. Four book sales in Norwich. Twelve mixed sales in Ipswich.*

SURREY

Chancellors Auctions (formerly Bonsor Penningtons)
74 London Rd., Kingston, KT2 6PX. Tel: 081 541 4139. *Weekly sales on Thurs. One fine art and antiques sale each month. Viewing previous Tues. 2-8 and Wed. 9-5. Sales commence at 10. Three general sales each month, viewing Wed. 2-8 and Thurs. 9-11. Sales start at 11.*

Clarke Gammon Fine Art Auctioneers
The Guildford Auction Rooms, Bedford Rd., Guildford, GU1 4SJ. Tel: 0483 572266/66458.

Croydon Auction Rooms (Rosan and Co.) (incorporating E.Reeves Auctions)
144/150 London Rd., Croydon, CR0 2TD. Tel: 081 688 1123/4/5. *Collective sales every Sat. at 10.*

Hamptons Fine Art
93 High St., Godalming, GU7 1AL. Tel: 0483 423567; fax - 0483 426392. *Regular fine art sales at 93 High Street, specialising in selected fine furniture, rugs, paintings and watercolours, porcelain, glass, jewellery, silver, objets d'art and books. Held on a Wednesday and Thursday. Three sales each month of general and Victorian furniture, shipping goods and household effects, at Queen Street and Bridge Street. Held on*

Surrey continued

Tuesdays and Saturdays. House sales conducted on the premises when instructed. Valuations.

Lawrences' - Auctioneers
Norfolk House, 80 High St., Bletchingley, RH1 4PA. Tel: 0883 743323; fax - 0883 744578. *Six-weekly antique and reproduction furniture and effects.*

Parkins
18 Malden Rd., Cheam, SM3 8SD. Tel: 081 644 6633. *Weekly sales of general household furniture and effects on Mon. at 10 am. Viewing Fri. 2-4pm and Sat. 10am-4pm. Special antique and collectors sales first Mon. monthly. Small antiques and collectors sales third Fri. evening monthly at 7.*

Richmond and Surrey Auctions
Rear of Richmond Station, Kew Road, Richmond, TW9 2NA. Tel: 081 948 6677; fax - 081 948 2021. *Est. 1992. Auctioneers, valuers and consultants.*

Wentworth Auction Galleries
21 Station Approach, Virginia Water, GU25 4DW. Tel: 0344 843711. *Antique and general sales every four to six weeks.*

P.F. Windibank
18-20 Reigate Rd., Dorking, RH4 1SG. Tel: 0306 884556. *Fine art auctions held every four to six weeks throughout the year.*

SUSSEX EAST

Burstow and Hewett
Abbey Auction Galleries, and Granary Sale Rooms, Battle, TN33 0AT. Tel: 0424 772374. *Monthly sales of antique furniture, silver, jewellery, porcelain, brass, rugs etc. at the Abbey Auction Galleries. Also monthly evening sales of fine oil paintings, watercolours, prints, and engravings. At the Granary Sale Rooms - monthly sales of furniture, china, silver, brass, etc.*

Clifford Dann Auction Galleries
Fine Art Auction Galleries, 20-21 High St., Lewes, BN7 2LN. Tel: 0273 480111; fax - 0273 480345. *General sales of period furniture, oil paintings, watercolours, drawings, porcelain, carpets, silver, jewellery, books, toys and other collectors items every six weeks on Tues.*

Fryer's Auction Galleries
Terminus Rd., Bexhill-on-Sea, TN39 3LR. Tel 0424 212994; fax - 0424 224035. *Fortnightly collective sales of household goods including shipping goods and antiques.*

Gorringe's Auction Galleries
15 North St., Lewes, BN7 2PD. Tel: 0273 472503. *Sales approximately every six weeks o*

## Sussex East continued

period furniture, Oriental carpets and rugs, oil paintings, watercolour drawings and prints, decorative china, glass, silver plate. jewellery etc.

Graves, Son and Pilcher Fine Arts
Hove Street, Hove, BN3 2GL. Tel: 0273 735266; fax - 0273 723813. *Monthly sales of fine art including antique furniture, pictures, silver, Oriental carpets and rugs and ornamental items. Specialised sales of primitive art, coins, books and jewellery.*

Edgar Horn's Fine Art Auctioneers
Auction Galleries, 46/50 South St., Eastbourne, BN21 4XB. Tel: 0323 410419. *Approximately ten sales annually, each including antique furniture, porcelain, glass and collectors' items, Oriental rugs and carpets. Specialist sales of silver and jewellery, oil paintings and watercolours, prints etc.*

Raymond P. Inman
The Auction Galleries, 35 and 40 Temple St., Brighton, BN1 3BH. Tel: 0273 774777. *Monthly collective sales, including silver and jewellery.*

Lewes Auction Rooms (Julian Dawson)
56 High St., Lewes, BN7 1XE. Tel: 0273 478221. *Antique furniture and effects every six weeks. General furniture and effects every Mon.*

Wallis and Wallis
West Street Auction Galleries, West St., Lewes, BN7 2NJ. Tel: 0273 480208. *Est. 1928. Nine annual sales of arms and armour, militaria, coins and medals. Specimen catalogue £4.50. Current combined catalogues £7. Die-cast and tin plate toys and models - catalogues £2.75. Commission bids (without charge) accepted. Valuations.*

SUSSEX WEST

R.H. Ellis and Sons
44/46 High St., Worthing, BN11 1LL. Tel: 0903 238999. *Monthly specialist auctions of antique, Victorian and Edwardian furniture and porcelain. Quarterly auctions of silver, watercolours, paintings, Oriental carpets and rugs.*

Garth Denham and Associates
Horsham Auction Galleries, Warnham, RH12 3RZ. Tel: 0403 255699; fax - 0403 253837. *Two day antique sales monthly - good furniture of all periods, silver, jewellery, European and Oriental ceramics and collectors' items, paintings, drawings, prints and bronzes, metalware and Oriental carpets and rugs. Also monthly sales of general antiques, modern and shipping furniture. Periodic sales of books, stamps, coins and medals, arms and armour and specialist collections as advertised.*

Sussex West continued

Nationwide Fine Art and Furniture
Midhurst Auction Rooms, West St., Midhurst, GU29 9NG. Tel: 0730 812456; fax - 0730 814514. *General sales of antique and modern furniture and effects every six weeks.*

Phillips Fine Art Salerooms
Baffins Hall, Baffins Lane, Chichester, PO19 1UA. Tel: 0243 787548. *Sales monthly on Thurs. at 10 am of antique and reproduction furniture, clocks, silver, porcelain, paintings, Persian and other carpets. Viewing day prior.*

Sotheby's Sussex
Summers Place, Billingshurst, RH14 9AD. Tel: 0403 783933; fax - 0403 785153. *Regular sales of paintings, furniture, carpets, clocks, ceramics, glass, silver, jewellery, vertu, sporting guns, toys, dolls, Oriental items and garden statuary.*

Stride and Son
Southdown House, St. John's St., Chichester, PO19 1XQ. Tel: 0243 780207. *Sales last Fri. monthly - antiques and general.*

Sussex Auction Galleries
59 Perrymount Rd., Haywards Heath, RH16 3DR. Tel: 0444 414935. *Auctions of antiques and reproduction furniture and effects including ceramics, silver and jewellery, clocks, Persian rugs and Victoriana. Twice-monthly sales of general household furniture and effects. Also regular sales of lost/found property from Sussex Police Authority and handling agents from Gatwick Airport. Annual catalogue subscription £20. No buyers premium.*

Worthing Auction Galleries
31 Chatsworth Rd., Worthing, BN11 1LY. Tel: 0903 205565. *Fortnightly general antique furniture sales and specialist sales every six to eight weeks. Viewing Sat. prior 9-12 and Mon. 9-1 and 2-4, prior to sale on Tues. and Wed. commencing at 9.30.*

TYNE AND WEAR

Anderson and Garland
Fine Art Salerooms, Marlborough House, Marlborough Crescent, Newcastle-upon-Tyne, NE1 4EE. Tel: 091 232 6278; fax - 091 261 8665. *Regular sales of antique furniture and effects. Fortnightly sales of Victorian and later furniture.*

Boldon Auction Galleries
24a Front St., East Boldon, NE36 0SJ. Tel: 091 537 2630. *Quarterly antique auctions.*

Thomas N. Miller
18-22 Gallowgate, Newcastle-upon-Tyne, NE1 4SN. Tel: 091 232 5617. *Antique auctions every Wednesday.*

WARWICKSHIRE

Bigwood Auctioneers Ltd
The Old School, Tiddington, Stratford-upon-Avon, CV37 7AW. Tel: 0789 269415. *Twice-monthly sales at 11am on Sat. Sales of Fine Furniture and Works of Art held on the last Wed. every month at 11am. Quarterly sales of wine. Catalogue subscription rates available on request. Valuations.*

Black Horse Agencies - Locke and England
18 Guy St., and salerooms -Walton House, 11 The Parade, Leamington Spa, CV32 4RT. Tel: 0926 889100; fax - 0926 470608. *Antique furniture, porcelain, pictures, silver etc. each month. Shipping goods, Victorian and Edwardian furniture, household effects weekly Thurs. at 11. House contents sales. Telephone for further details.*

John Briggs and Parsley
17 Market Street, Atherstone, CV9 1ET. Tel: 0827 718911. *Auctions on clients' instructions.*

Henley-in-Arden Auction Sales Ltd
The Estate Office, Warwick Rd., Henley-in-Arden, B95 5BH. Tel: 0564 793211. *Regular Sat. sales of antique and modern furniture and effects.*

Warwick and Warwick Ltd
Pageant House, Jury St., Warwick, CV34 4EW. Tel: 0926 499031; fax - 0926 491906. *Philatelic auctioneers and private treaty specialists. Auctions normally held on the first Wed. monthly with philatelic material covering the world, also picture postcards, ephemera and cigarette cards.*

WEST MIDLANDS

Biddle & Webb
Ladywood Middleway, Birmingham, B16 0PP. Tel: 021 455 8042. *Fine art sales first Fri. monthly at 11am; antique sales on second Fri. monthly at 11am; silver, jewellery, medals, coins and watches on fourth Fri. monthly at 11am; toys, dolls, model railways and juvenalia sales on Fri. alternate months at 11am. Weekly Tues. sales of Victoriana and collectables at 10.30am.*

Fellows and Sons
Augusta House, 19 Augusta St., Hockley, Birmingham, B18 6JA. Tel: 021 212 2131; fax - 021 212 1249. *Auctioneers and valuers of jewels, silver, fine art, fine wines and spirits.*

James and Lister Lea
42 Bull St., Birmingham, B4 6AF. Tel: 021 200 1100. Est. 1846. *Approximately four sales annually of contents of country and town houses as required. All sale items are from private sources with an emphasis on the more unusual collectors' items. Buyer's premium 8% plus VAT.*

West Midlands continued

Phillips Midlands
The Old House, Station Rd., Knowle, Solihull, B93 0HT. Tel: 0564 776151. *Specialised weekly sales of fine furniture and works of art; silver and jewellery; Victoriana; paintings; collectors' items; ceramics and 19th-20th C decorative arts; books. Free sales programme and subscription on request.*

Walker Barnett and Hill
Waterloo Road Salerooms, Clarence St., Wolverhampton, WV1 4DL. Tel: 0902 773531; fax - 0902 712940. *Victoriana and general household sale once a fortnight on Thurs. at 11. Viewing previous day 10-4. Antique auctions every 6/8 weeks held at Park House Hotel, Shifnal, Shropshire. Viewing previous day 10-8.*

Weller and Dufty Ltd
141 Bromsgrove St., Birmingham, B5 6RQ. Tel: 021 692 1414; fax - 021 622 5605. *Ten sales annually, approximately every five weeks, of antique and modern firearms, edged weapons, militaria etc. Periodic sales of specialist items - books, wine and fine art. Postal bids accepted. Illustrated catalogue available.*

WILTSHIRE

Allen and Harris
The Planks Salerooms, Old Town, Swindon, SN3 1QP. Tel: 0793 615915. *General sales every Saturday at 10am. Quarterly antique sales.*

Hampton Fine Art incorporating Pocock and Lear
20 High St., Marlborough, SN8 1AA. Tel: 0672 516161. *Antique and quality furniture and effects sales first Wed. monthly and general household furniture and effects second Wed. monthly.*

Woolley and Wallis
Salisbury Salerooms, Castle St., Salisbury, SP1 3SU. Tel: 0722 411422; fax - 0722 411426. *Monthly sales of antique furniture, porcelain and pottery, glass and metalwork. Special sales of Eastern carpets and rugs, books and maps, paintings, watercolours and prints, textiles, fans, lace, toys and dolls, musical instruments, Oriental furniture and ceramics, works of art. Quarterly sales of silver and plate, jewellery, watches, objects of art and wines.*

YORKSHIRE NORTH

Boulton and Cooper Ltd
St. Michaels House, Market Place, Malton, YO17 0LR. Tel: 0653 696151. *Members of SOFAA. Alternating monthly antique sales at Malton and York. Fortnightly general sales at Pickering and Seamer.*

AUCTIONEERS

Yorkshire North continued

William H. Brown (Morphets)
4-6 Albert St., Harrogate, HG1 1JL. Tel: 0423 530030. *Sales of antiques and works of art, interspersed with regular sales of general furniture and effects. Catalogue subscription scheme.*

H.C. Chapman and Son
The Auction Mart, North St., Scarborough, YO11 1DL. Tel: 0723 372424; fax - 0723 500697. *Members of SOFAA. Monthly special sales of antiques and fine art held on Tues., viewing Fri. 4-7, Sat. 10-4, Mon. 9-12. Annual catalogue subscription £30. Weekly Mon. sales of Edwardian and later shipping furniture, bric-a-brac and modern furnishings. Viewing Sat. 10-4 and Mon. from 9.*

Hutchinson-Scott
The Grange, Marton-le-Moor, Ripon, HG4 5AT. Tel: 0423 324264. *Periodic general sales plus two or three catalogue sales annually. Specialist in fine antiques and works of art.*

James Johnston
The Square, Boroughbridge, YO5 9AS. Tel: 0423 322382. *Monthly collective auction sales of antique and later furniture and effects at The Village Hall, Whixley, Nr. York and occasional private dispersal sales.*

Nationwide Fine Art
27 Flowergate, Whitby, YO21 3AX. Tel: 0947 603433. *Monthly antiques sales. VAT: Stan. 10% buyers premium.*

Scarthingwell Auction Centre
Scarthingwell, Nr. Tadcaster, LS24 9PG. Tel: 0937 557955. *Evening antique sales held twice a month on a Monday - approx. 500 lots. Viewing on day before sale 12-5pm and from 4pm on day of sale.*

Stephenson and Son
20 Castlegate, York, YO1 1RT. Tel: 0904 625533. *Six sales annually of antique and Victorian furniture, silver and paintings.*

Geoffrey Summersgill ASVA
8 Front St., Acomb, York, YO2 3BZ. Tel: 0904 791131. *Auctions of antiques and household effects and collectors' items.*

Geoffrey Summersgill ASVA
Market Place, Easingwold, YO6 3BJ. Tel: 0347 21366. *Auctions of antiques and household effects and collectors' items.*

Tennants
Harmby Rd., Leyburn, DL8 5SG. Tel: 0969 23780. *Three Saturday sales a month - antiques and modern residual house contents, approximately 1,000 lots. No catalogues. View Fri. On-site parking. Catalogue sales held at Richmond Salerooms.*

YORKSHIRE SOUTH

A.E. Dowse and Son Sheffield
Cornwall Galleries, Scotland St., Sheffield, S3 7DE. Tel: 0742 725858. *Monthly Sat. and quarterly Mon. sales of antiques. Quarterly sales of diecast, tin plate and collectors' toys. Fortnightly sales of modern furniture and shipping goods.*

YORKSHIRE WEST

Armitage, Hewitt and Hellowell
32 Queen St., Huddersfield. Tel: 0484 426118. *Occasional antiques sales.*

Ernest R. de Rome
12 New John St., Westgate, Bradford, BD1 2QY. Tel: 0274 734116/9. *Weekly sales.*

Garside, Waring and Robinson
17 Alexandra St., Halifax, HX1 1BS. Tel: 0422 353527/362138.

Andrew Hartley Fine Arts
Victoria Hall Salerooms, Little Lane, Ilkley, LS29 8EA. Tel: 0943 816363. *Fifty sales annually including six good antique and fine art and other specialist sales.*

Phillips at Hepper House
17a East Parade, Leeds, LS1 2BU. Tel: 0532 448011. *Monthly sales of antique furniture and objects of art and regular speciality sales of pictures, ceramics, silver and jewellery, books etc.*

John H. Raby and Son
Salem Auction Rooms, 21 St. Mary's Rd., Bradford, BD8 7QL. Tel: 0274 491121. *Sales of antique furniture and pictures every four to six weeks.*

CHANNEL ISLANDS

Langlois Auctioneers and Valuers
Westaway Chambers, Don St., St. Helier, Jersey, JE2 4TR. Tel: 0534 22441; fax - 0534 39354. *Periodic antiques sales. Weekly household sales.*

David Procter Auctions
12 Mansell St., The Old Quarter, St. Peter Port, Guernsey. Tel: 0481 726808; home - 0481 46025. *Occasional auctions of property and/or their contents, plus bi-annual catalogue auctions of items of Channel Island interest.*

SCOTLAND

Brown's
Carsluith Hall, Carsluith by Newton Stewart, Wigtownshire. Tel: 0671 3185. *Sales held on last Wed. and Thurs. monthly except Dec.and Jan.*

Scotland continued

Christie's Scotland
164-166 Bath St., Glasgow, Lanarkshire, G2 4TG. Tel: 041 332 8134; fax - 041 332 5759. *Regular specialist sales of jewellery, silver, furniture, paintings, together with sales of particular Scottish interest, including golfing and football memorabilia, whisky, Wemyss Ware.*

Frasers (Auctioneers)
28-30 Church St., Inverness, Inverness-shire, IV1 1EH. Tel: 0463 232395. *Sales every two weeks on Thurs. and Fri.*

William Hardie Ltd
141 West Regent St., Glasgow, Lanarkshire, G2 4TG. Tel: 041 221 6780; fax - 041 248 6237. *Specialist auction sales of Scottish ceramics and decorative arts. Valuations; restorations.*

Leslie and Leslie
Haddington, East Lothian, EH41 3JJ. Tel: 062 082 2241; fax - same. *General auctions every three months.*

Loves Auction Rooms
52-54 Canal St., Perth, Perthshire, PH2 8LF. Tel: 0738 33337. *Regular sales of antique and decorative furniture, jewellery, silver and plate, ceramics, works of art, metalware, glass, pictures, clocks, mirrors, pianos, Eastern carpets and rugs, garden furniture, architectural items. Weekly Fri. sales of Victoriana and household effects at 10.30. Specialist sales of books and collectors' items. Valuations.*

Lyon and Turnball Ltd
51 George St., Edinburgh, Midlothian, EH2 2HT. Tel: 031 225 4627.

McTear's
Royal Exchange Salerooms, Glasgow, Lanarkshire, G1 2DS. Tel: 041 221 4456. *Weekly Fri. sales at 10.30 of antique, reproduction and shipping furniture, jewellery, silver, porcelain and paintings. Viewing prior Thurs. 10-5.*

John Milne
9 North Silver St., Aberdeen, Aberdeenshire, AB1 1RJ. Tel: 0224 639336. *Weekly general sales, regular catalogue sales of antiques, silver, paintings, books, jewellery and collectors' items.*

Robert Paterson and Son
8 Orchard St., Paisley, Renfrewshire, PA1 1UZ. Tel: 041 889 2435. *Sales every second Tues. monthly.*

Phillips Scotland
207 Bath St., Glasgow, Lanarkshire, G2 4HD. Tel: 041 221 8277. *Monthly general sales of Victorian and Edwardian items; specialist sales of jewellery, silver, ceramics, furniture, works of art, books, carpets, 20th C decorative arts and Scottish contemporary art and oil paintings, throughout the year.*

Scotland continued

Phillips Scotland
65 George St., Edinburgh, Midlothian, EH2 2JL. Tel: 031 225 2266. *Monthly sales of oil paintings, furniture, Oriental rugs, works of art, silver. Bi-monthly sales of Continental and Oriental ceramics and works of art, glass, books, watercolours and prints, jewellery, postcards and maps. Two sales annually of dolls and textiles.*

L.S. Smellie and Sons Ltd.
The Furniture Market, Lower Auchingramont Rd., Hamilton, Lanarkshire, ML10 6BE. Tel: 0698 282007. *Fine antiques auctions - third Thurs. in Feb., May, Aug. and Nov.*

Taylor's Auction Rooms
11 Panmure Row, Montrose, Angus, DD10 8HH. Tel: 0674 72775. *Antiques sales held every second Sat.*

Thomson, Roddick and Laurie Ltd.
60 Whitesands, Dumfries, Dumfriesshire, DG1 2RS. Tel: 0387 55366. *Quarterly catalogued antique and collectors' sales; bi-annual shooting and fishing sales.*

Thomson, Roddick and Laurie Ltd.
20 Murray Street, Annan, Dumfriesshire, DG12 6EG. Tel: 0461 202575. *Monthly general house clearance sales; quarterly Victoriana sales.*

WALES

Dodds Property World
Victoria Auction Galleries, Mold, Clwyd, CH7 1EB. Tel: 0352 752552. *Weekly Wed. auctions of general furniture and shipping goods at 10.30am. Bi-monthly auctions of antique furniture, silver, porcelain and pictures etc. at 10.30am on Sats. Catalogues available.*

Peter Francis
Curiosity Salerooms, King St., Carmarthen, Dyfed, SA31 1BH. Tel: 0267 233456/7. *Antiques sales held every six weeks. Household sales at regular intervals.*

Harry Ray and Co.
Lloyds Bank Chambers, Welshpool, Powys, SY21 7RR. Tel: 0938 552555. *Fortnightly country sales.*

Rennies
1 Agincourt St., Monmouth, Gwent, NP5 3DZ. Tel: 0600 712916. *Periodic sales of antique furniture and effects, usually on Thurs.*

Antique Collectors' Club Titles

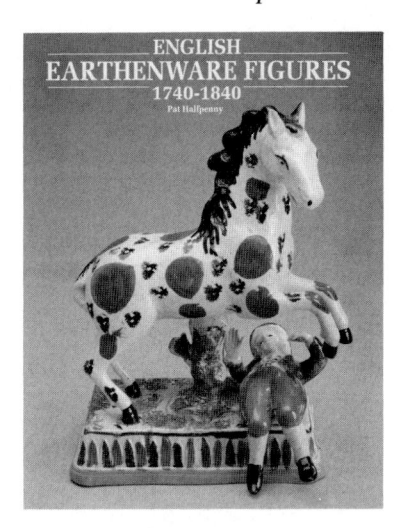

English Earthenware Figures 1740-1840
by Pat Halfpenny

This long awaited volume is an eminently readable account of eighteenth and early nineteenth century production of popular earthenware figures. The leading authority on Staffordshire porcelain and earthenware, the author is Keeper of Ceramics at the City Museum and Art Gallery, Stoke-on-Trent, and is therefore uniquely qualified to write on the subject, for she has at her fingertips the finest collection of English earthenware to be found anywhere in the world, allied with a wealth of archival material.
346pp, 495 b & w illus, 89 col, ISBN 1 85149 114 7, £35.00

Staffordshire Portrait Figures of the Victorian Era
by P.D. Gordon Pugh

A revised edition of the standard work affectionately known as 'Pugh', based on the 1981 revised edition, this book provides what the collector of Staffordshire portait figures has long required: a vast photographic reference to the 1,500 or so portrait figures which encapsulate so much of the history of Victorian England. New colour photographs have been specially taken for this invaluable book.
560pp, 900 b & w illus, 62 col, ISBN 1 85149 010 8, £45.00

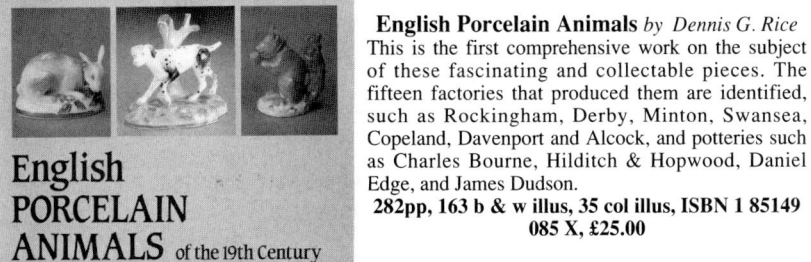

English Porcelain Animals *by Dennis G. Rice*

This is the first comprehensive work on the subject of these fascinating and collectable pieces. The fifteen factories that produced them are identified, such as Rockingham, Derby, Minton, Swansea, Copeland, Davenport and Alcock, and potteries such as Charles Bourne, Hilditch & Hopwood, Daniel Edge, and James Dudson.
282pp, 163 b & w illus, 35 col illus, ISBN 1 85149 085 X, £25.00

Available from:
Antique Collectors' Club, 5 Church Street
Woodbridge, Suffolk IP12 1DS
Tel: (0394) 385501 Fax: (0394) 384434

or Market Street Industrial Park
Wappingers' Falls, New York 12590, USA
Tel: 914 297 0003 Fax: 914 297 0068

SERVICES

This section has been included in the Guide to enable us to list those businesses which do not sell antiques but are in associated trades. The following categories are included:

    Art
    Books
    Carpets and Rugs
    Ceramics
    Clocks and Barometers
    Consultancy
    Courier
    Enamel
    Furniture (including reproduction)
    Glass
    Insurance
    Metalwork (see also Suppliers)
    Reproduction Stonework
    Suppliers
    Toys

We would point out that the majority of dealers also restore and can give advice in this field.

Below are the trade associations mentioned within this section:

    BAFRA - British Antique Furniture Restorers' Association
    GADAR - Guild of Antique Dealers and Restorers
    GMC   - Guild of Master Craftsmen
    MBHI - Member of the British Horological Institute
    UKIC - UK Institute for Conservation
    CGC   - Ceramic and Glass Conservation Group
    BTCM - British Traditional Cabinet Makers
    BFMA - British Furniture Manufacturers Association
    BCFA - British Contract Furniture Association
    ASFI   - Association of Suppliers to Furniture Industry
    GAI   - Guild of Architectural Ironmongers

SERVICES

ART

Terence Howe Fine Art Conservator and Copyist
Studio 109 Highbury Workshops, 22 Highbury Grove, London N5 2EA. Tel: 071 704 1736; fax - 071 359 5016. *Restoration of oil paintings - surface dirt and old varnish removal, lining, wax resin or paste lining; damaged areas or paint losses re-touched using egg tempera and resin glazes. Paintings copied especially Monet and Boudin and other British and French Impressionists, from £1,000 inc. VAT.*

BOOKS

The Manor Bindery Ltd.
Calshot Road, Fawley, Southampton, Hants. SO4 1BB. Tel: 0703 894488; fax - 0703 899418. *Manufacturers of false books, either to use as a display or for cabinet makers to apply to doors and cupboards. Also book tables, decorative objects and accessories, various decorative replica book boxes. leather library shelf edging and range of cabinets with false book doors. Individual items made to order with a book theme.*

CARPETS AND RUGS

Barin Carpets Restoration
57a New Kings Rd., London SW6 4SE. Tel: 071 731 0546. GMC. Conservation Register Museums and Galleries Commission. *Oriental carpets, rugs, European tapestries, Aubussons expertly cleaned, restored and lined. Expert advice, free estimates.*

CERAMICS

China Repairers
64 Charles Lane, London NW8 7SB. Tel: 071 722 8409. (H. Howard and V. Baron.) Est. 1952. *Specialised restorations of all pottery and porcelain; restoration courses held.*

Porcelain Repairs
240 Stockport Rd., Cheadle Heath, Stockport, Cheshire. SK3 0LX. Tel: 061 428 9599; fax - 061 491 4353. CGCG, UKIC. Est. 1970. *Highest standard restorations of European and Oriental ceramics, especially under glaze blue and white, museum repairs, carat gilding and modelling. Cracks and crazing removed without any overpainting or glazing.*

CLOCKS AND BAROMETERS

Timothy Akers
See entry under Furniture

Newcombe and Son
89 Maple Rd., Penge, London SE20 8UL. Tel: 081 778 0816. MBHI, GMC, Conservation

---

ORIENTAL CARPETS, RUGS, EUROPEAN TAPESTRIES, AUBUSSONS EXPERTLY CLEANED, RESTORED AND LINED

Expert Advice and Valuation

BARIN CARPETS RESTORATION
57A NEW KINGS ROAD
LONDON SW6
TEL: 071-731 0546

Clocks and Barometers continued
Register of Museums and Galleries Commission. *Specialist in the making, repair and restoration of fine quality longcase, bracket and wall clocks. Quality clock cases made to order, barometers repaired, silvering and gilding, clock faces (including enamel) restored or repainted, brass and wooden frets, clock hands, all hand cut and finished to order, clocks bought and sold.*

CONSULTANCY

Paul Couts Ltd
The Old Mill House, Milton by Pencaitland, East Lothian, Scotland. Tel: 0875 340669. *Valuations and consultations.*

COURIER

Antique Tours
11 Farleigh Rise, Monkton Farleigh, Nr. Bradford-on-Avon, Wilts. BA15 2QP. Tel: 0225 858527 (24 hr. answerphone); mobile - 0860 598600. (C.J. Veal) Est. 1988. *Private hire chauffeur service; car tours around West Country antiques establishments, up to four persons; service to and from air and sea ports; data and parcel delivery and collection; packing and shipping arranged.*

SERVICES

ENAMEL

Istvan Markovits Ltd.
1-3 Cobbold Mews, London W12 9LB. Tel: 081 749 3000; fax - 081 749 1394. *Badgemakers. Worldwide restorers of enamel antique jewellery. Restorers of clock faces and ceramics.* VAT: Stan.

FURNITURE

Timothy Akers
The Forge, 39 Chancery Lane, Beckenham, Kent. BR3 2NR. Tel: 081 650 9179. BAFRA. *Restorations of 17th-19th C English furniture, longcase and bracket clocks.*

Anthony Allen Antique Restorers
Buxton Rd., New Town, New Mills, Derbys. SK12 3JS. Tel: 0663 745274. BAFRA. *Boulle, marquetry, walnut, oak, veneering restorations and upholstery.*

Alpha (Antique) Restorations
High St., Compton, Berks. RG16 0NL. Tel: 0635 578245; mobile - 0860 575203. BAFRA. *Fine oak, walnut and mahogany. Traditional hand finishes. Veneering and inlaying. Clock cases.*

Guy Bagshaw
The Old Dairy, Plain Farm, East Tisted, Alton, Hants. GU34 3RT. Tel: 0420 58362. BAFRA. *18th to early 19th C English furniture restoration.*

D. Baker
12 Downs Rd., Folkestone, Kent. CT19 5PW. Tel: 0303 255136. Est. 1961. *French polishing, cabinet making and restorations of antique furniture.*

Michael Barrington
The Old Rectory, Warmwell, Dorchester, Dorset. DT2 8HQ. Tel: 0305 852104. BAFRA. *18th-19th C furniture, gilding, upholstery, antique metalwork, organ casework and pipe decoration, mechanical models and toys.*

David Bartram
The Raveningham Centre, Castell Farm, Beccles Rd., Raveningham, Norfolk. NR14 6NU. Tel: 050 846 721. BAFRA. *18th-19th C English furniture, rosewood and walnut, inlay and turning.*

**Batheaston Chairmakers Ltd.
H. Lockhart Ltd.**
Leafield Trading Estate, Corsham, Wilts. SN13 9SW. Tel: 0225 811295; fax - 0225 810501. BFMA. BCFA. *Oak reproduction furniture made from solid kiln dried timbers, antique hand finish. Extensive range of Windsor, ladderback and country Hepplewhite chairs; refectory, gateleg and other extendable tables, Welsh dressers, sideboards and other cabinet models. Trade Only.*

Keith Bawden
Mews Workshop, Montpellier Retreat, Cheltenham, Glos. GL50 2XG. Tel: 0242 230320. BAFRA. *All period furniture restoration, carving, upholstery, chair reproduction.*

Furniture continued

Michael Bennett
100 Market St., Hoylake, Merseyside. L47 3BE. Tel: 051 632 4331. BAFRA. *Invisible repairs, finishing, marquestry and boulle.*

Daniel Berry
Units 210-211, Riverside Business Park, Haldane Place, London SW18 4LZ. Tel: 081 874 2491. BAFRA. *Mahogany and walnut.*

Peter Binnington
65 St. John's Hill, London SW11 1SX. Tel: 071 223 9192. BAFRA. *Decorated surfaces, marquetry, gilding and verré eglomisé, painted and japanned.*

Maxwell Black
Brookhouse Studios, Novington Lane, East Chiltington, Lewes, East Sussex. BN7 3AX. Tel: 0273 890 175. BAFRA.

Martin Body
71 Bower Mount Rd., Maidstone, Kent. ME16 8AS. Tel: 0622 752273. BAFRA. *Gilding - gilt furniture, mirrors and picture frames including carving and gesso repairs.*

David J. Booth
Crows Nest, Edgeley Rd., Barton, Torquay, Devon. TQ2 8ND. Tel: 0803 312091. BAFRA. *Restorations, polishing, upholstery. Barometers, longcase clocks, mahogany and walnut.*

David J. Booth
9 High St., Ewell, Surrey. KT17 1SG. Tel: 081 393 5245. BAFRA. *Restorations and polishing, upholstery. Barometers, longcase clocks, mahogany and walnut.*

Stuart J. Bradbury
The Barn, Hanham Lane, Paulton, Avon. BS18 5PF. Tel: 0761 418910. BAFRA. *All aspects of antique furniture restoration.*

Lawrence Brass & Son
154 Sutherland Avenue, Maida Vale, London W9. Tel: 071 636 3401. BAFRA. *Conservation and restoration of fine antiques, metal work, gilding and upholstery.*

Peter Brazier
Nash Court Farmhouse, Marnhull, Sturminster Newton, Dorset. DT10 1JZ. Tel: 0258 820255. BAFRA. *Comprehensive restoration service.*

Nick Bridges
68 Lower St., Merriott, Somerset. TA16 5NW. Tel: 0460 74672. BAFRA. *Cabinet making, polishing, carving, marquetry, veneering, upholstery, gilding, brass casting.*

Bruton Garden and Conservatory Cast Iron
Station Road Industrial Estate, Bruton, Somerset. BA10 0EH. Tel: 0749 813266; 0860 898869; fax - 0749 813266. *Quality Victorian replica furniture - mahogany, teak, pine, cast iron and Venetian style mirrors. Any item copied in exact detail and exclusive designs catered for.*

THE BRITISH ANTIQUE FURNITURE RESTORERS' ASSOCIATION

As the furniture section of the United Kingdom Institute for Conservation, B.A.F.R.A., founded in 1982, has some ninety accredited members throughout the country. It is the country's only association of highly experienced craftsmen who have undergone a strict procedure of vetting and assessment for their knowledge, skill and integrity.

For further information and a list of members with their specialisms contact:

The Secretary
B.A.F.R.A.
37 Upper Addison Gardens,
Holland Park,
London W14

Tel: 071-371 4586

SERVICES

Furniture continued

James Burrell
Westerfield House, Seavington St. Mary, Ilminster, Somerset. TA19 0QR. Tel: 0460 40610. BAFRA. *18th-19th C furniture, carving, uphostery, marquetry, wax polishing.*

Cane and Able
The Beeches, Bridge Rd., Colby, Norwich, Norfolk. NR11 7EA. Tel: 0263 734792. GMC. *Cane work, rush seating and general furniture restorations.*

Peter G. Casebow
Pilgrims, Mill Lane, Worthing, West Sussex. BN13 3DE. Tel: 0903 264045. BAFRA. *Period furniture, turning, marquetry, inlay, fretwork, polishing.*

Benedict Clegg
Flat C, Madeira Park, Tunbridge Wells, Kent. TN2 5SX. Tel: 0892 548095. BAFRA.

Robert Coleman
The Oasthouse, Three Chimneys, Nr. Ashford, Biddenden, Kent. TN27 8LW. Tel: 0580 291520. BAFRA. *Mahogany and walnut furniture.*

Compton Hall Restoration
Unit A, 133 Riverside Business Centre, Haldane Place, London SW18 4UQ. Tel: 081 874 0762. BAFRA. *Painted furniture, papier-mâché, tôle ware, lacquer and gilding.*

William Cook
167 Battersea High St., London SW11 3JS. Tel: 071 736 5329 or 0672 513017. BAFRA. *18th C and English period furniture.*

Courtlands Restorations
Courtlands, Park Rd., Banstead, Surrey. SM7 3EF. Tel: 0737 352429. BAFRA. *French and wax polishing, cabinet making, turning, carving, veneering, gilding, metal repairs and 18th-19th C furniture.*

Robert H. Crawley
64 Coulson Way, Burham, Bucks. SL1 7PL. Tel: 081 566 5074. BAFRA.

Marie Louise Crawley
39 Woodvale, London SE23 3DS. Tel: 081 299 4121. BAFRA. *Painted furniture, papier-mâché, tôle ware, lacquer and gilding.*

Dan Dent
Stonecourt, Membland, Newton Ferrers, Plymouth, Devon. PL8 1HP. Tel: 0752 872831. BAFRA.

Edward Doulton
22 Waterditchampton, Wilton, Nr. Salisbury, Wilts. SP2 0JA. Tel: 0722 336255. BAFRA.

Reginald W. Dudman Antique Restorations
45 Windmill Rd., Brentford, Middx. TW8 0QQ. Tel: 081 568 5249. BAFRA.

Furniture continued

Michael Durkee
Castle House, 1 Bennetts Field Estate, Wincanton, Somerset. BA9 9DT. Tel: 0963 33884. BAFRA. *All styles of period furniture conservation and finishing. Boulle and inlay work, period finishes.*

English Furniture Manufacturing Associates
4 Northgate Close, Rottingdean, Brighton, Sussex East. BN2 7DZ. Tel: 0273 589744; fax - 0273 589745. Federation of Sussex Industries, IDDA. *English reproduction furniture in burr elm, burr walnut, yew and mahogany. Own/imported Biedermeier pieces in cherry, ebony and olive veneers. Custom work undertaken. All work hand finished. Winner of FSI Export Award 1989.* VAT: Stan. Trade Only.

Everitt and Rogers
Dawsnest Workshop, Grove Rd., Tiptree, Essex. CO5 0JE. Tel: 0621 816508. GADAR. Est. 1953. *Expert antique furniture restoration*

John Farbrother Furniture Restoration
Ivy House, Main St., Shipton-by-Beningbrough, York, North Yorkshire. YO6 1AB. Tel: 0904 470187. GADAR. Est. 1987. *All repairs undertaken, refinishing process from complete strip to reviving existing finish. French polishing, oil, wax and lacquers. Pressurised fluid application woodworm treatment.*

Fauld Town and Country Furniture
Coventry Trading Estate, Siskin Drive, Coventry, West Mids. CV3 4FJ. Tel: 0203 639020; fax - 0203 639134. Est. 1972. *Windsor chairs, £50-£100; farmhouse tables, £200-£1,000; case pieces, £500-£2,000; all traditional reproduction.* VAT: Stan.

Forge Studio Workshops
Stour St., Manningtree, Essex. CO11 1BE. Tel: 0206 396222. BAFRA. *Carving and general restorations.*

G. and R. Fraser-Sinclair & Co
11 Orchard Works, Streeters Lane, Beddington, Surrey. SM6 7ND. Tel: 081 669 5343 or 0883 49467. BAFRA. *18th C furniture.*

Alistair J. Frayling-Cork
2 Mill Lane, Wallingford, Oxon. OX10 0DH. Tel: 0491 26221. BAFRA. *Antique and period furniture, clock cases, ebonising, wood turning and stringed instruments.*

The Furniture Clinic
Vine House, Fair Green, Reach, Cambs. Tel: 0638 741989. *Valuations; restorations, caning, rushing, framing, wood carving and turning, polishing, veneering and upholstery. Design consultant.*

Furniture continued

G.M.S. Restorations
Rear of Bell Passage Antiques, 36-38 High St., Wickwar, Glos. GL12 8MP. Tel: 0454 294251; fax - same. LAPADA, GADAR. Assn. of Master Upholsters. Est. 1986. *Restorers of antique and modern furniture, specialists in French and wax polishing, picture restoration, gilding, inlay and metal work. Chair copying a speciality; traditional and modern upholstery. Work carried out on site in Europe and U.S.A.*

Sebastian Giles Furniture
11 Junction Mews, London W2 1PN. Tel: 081 960 8108. BAFRA.

Melven Glander
Tel: 081 599 7561. GADAR. *Restoration and repair service to furniture, woodwork, clocks and period fixtures and fittings; free estimates and advice. Collection and delivery. Upholstery arranged.*

Glen's Antique Restoration
36 Romola Rd., Tulse Hill, London SE24 9AZ. Tel: 081 671 1880. BAFRA. *Antique restoration, gilding, woodcarving, picture frames, French polishing.*

Mark Griffin
Beard Mill, Stanton Harcourt, Oxford, Oxon. OX8 1AG. Tel: 0865 300919. BAFRA.

John Hartley
The Tankerdale Workshop, Steep Marsh, Petersfield, Hants. GU32 2BH. Tel: 0730 893839; fax - 0730 894523. BAFRA. *Comprehensive restorations including gilding, decorative surfaces and architectural woodwork.*

Philip Hawkins
The Old School Workshop, High St., Maiden Bradley, Nr. Warminster, Wilts. BA12 7JG. Tel: 0985 844752. BAFRA. *16th to early 18th C oak and country furniture restoration.*

Michael Hedgecoe
21 Burrow Hill Green, Chobham, Surrey. GU24 8QS. Tel: 0276 858206. BAFRA. *General restorations, cabinet work, polishing, upholstery, chair making.*

Alan Hessel
The Old Town Workshop, St. George's Close, Moreton-in-Marsh, Glos. GL56 0LP. Tel: 0608 50026. BAFRA. *Comprehensive restoration service. English and continental fine period furniture.*

Richard Higgins (Conservation)
The Old School, Longnor, Nr. Shrewsbury, Shrops. SY5 7PP. Tel: 0743 718162; fax - 0743 718022. BAFRA. Conservation Register Museums and Galleries Commission. *Comprehensive restoration of all fine furniture and clocks, including movements and dials; specialist work to boulle, marquetry, carving, turning and veneer*

Furniture continued

work, lacquer, ormolu, metalwork, casting, glazing, polishing, upholstery, cane and rush seating. Stocks of old timber, veneers, tortoiseshell etc. held to ensure sympathetic restoration.

Stephen Hill
5 Cirencester Workshops, Brewery Court, Cirencester, Glos. GL7 1JH. Tel: 0285 658817 (24 hr). BAFRA. *16th-18th C cabinet making, gilding, carving, upholstery, rush and cane seating.*

Stuart Hobbs Antique Furniture Restoration
Meath Paddock, Meath Green Lane, Horley, Surrey. RH6 8HZ. Tel: 0293 782349. GMC. *Full restoration service for period furniture.*

David Hordern Restorations Ltd.
1A Codrington Mews, Blenheim Crescent, London, W11 2EH. Tel: 071 727 8855. BAFRA. *Boulle, cabinetwork, carving, gilding, lacquer, leather, marble, marquetry, ormolu, upholstery.*

Hunt and Lomas
Village Farm Workshops, Preston Village, Cirencester, Glos. GL7 5PR. Tel: 0285 640111. BAFRA. *17th-19th C oak, mahogany, walnut, satinwood, carving.*

Donald Hunter
The Old School Room, Shipton Oliffe, Cheltenham, Glos. GL54 4JG. Tel: 0242 820755. BAFRA. *Restoration of fine antiques, cabinet making, water gilding, lacquer work, decorative finishes.*

Johnson Antique Restoration
43 High St., Chatteris, Cambs. PE16 6BH. Tel: 0354 692522. GMC, GADAR. *Quality French polishing, caning, basic upholstery, veneering and structural repairs. Restored antique furniture sold at antique fairs.*

Julian Kelly
26a Gopsall St., London N1 5HJ. Tel: 071 739 2949; fax - same. GMC. *Woodcarving to suit all styles. Restorations - leathering, wood turning and metal polishing.*

T. H. Kelsall (Woodcrafts)
82 Main Rd., Slyne with Hest, Lancaster, Lancs. LA2 6AU. Tel: 0524 822347. GMC, GADAR. Est. 1963. *Repair and restoration of fine antique furniture and clocks, barometers and other works. Cabinet making, carving, marquetry, inlays, veneering, turning and polishing. Replica furniture and clock cases made to order.*

Rodney F. Kemble
16 Crag Vale Terrace, Glusburn, Nr. Keighley, West Yorks. BD20 8QU. Tel: 0535 636954. BAFRA. *Cabinet restorations, clock cases, traditional hand finshes and upholstery.*

Kent Traditional Furniture
Moor Lang, Grassington, North Yorks. BD23 5BD. Tel: 0756 753045; fax - 0756 753865. *Specialist in hand made solid oak furniture.*

SERVICES

Furniture continued

Raymond Konyn Antique Restorations
The Old Wheelwright's Shop, Brasted Forge, Brasted, Westerham, Kent. TN16 1JL. Tel: 0959 563863; fax - 0959 561262. BAFRA. *Furniture, traditional upholstery, longcase and bracket clock cases, polishing, brass casting. Antique and Fine Art Disasters Emergency Mobile Unit. Consultancy.*

Roderick Larwood
The Oaks, Station Rd., Larling, Norfolk. NR16 2QS. Tel: 0953 717937. BAFRA. *Brass inlay, 18th to early 19th C furniture.*

Andrew Lelliott
6 Tetbury Hill, Avening, Tetbury, Glos. GL8 8LT. Tel: 0453 835783/832652. BAFRA. *Comprehensive restorations.*

David C. E. Lewry
Wychelms, 66 Gorran Avenue, Rowner, Gosport, Hants. PO13 0NF. Tel: 0329 286901; fax - 0329 289964. BAFRA. *17th to early 19th C furniture.*

Lomas Pigeon & Co. Ltd
The Workshops, Rear of 1 Beehive Lane, Chelmsford, Essex. CM2 9SU. Tel: 0245 353708; fax - 0245 2577. BAFRA. *Period cabinet restoration, French polishing, traditional upholstery, desk linings, rocking horses.*

Timothy J. Long
26 High St., Seal, Sevenoaks, Kent. TN15 0AP. Tel: 0732 62606. BAFRA. *Cabinet restoration, French polishing, upholstery, brass and steel cabinet fittings.*

Bruce Luckhurst
The Little Surrenden Workshops, Ashford Rd., Bethersden, Kent. TN26 3BG. Tel: 0233 820589. BAFRA. *Conservation and restoration training plus comprehensive restoration service.*

David Mitchell
45 St. Michael's Rd., Bedford, Beds. MK40 2LD. Tel: 0234 359976. BAFRA. *Veneering, carving, polishing, problem solving.*

Timothy J. Naylor
Glenwood, Wych Hill Lane, Woking, Surrey. GU22 0AH. Tel: 0483 729244. BAFRA. *Surface decoration.*

M. R. Nelms
Mornmist, Palms Hill, Wem, Shrops. SY4 5PQ. Tel: 0939 233178. GADAR. *Furniture, including fitted antique, restoration and repair, French polishing and heat resistant finishes.*

Nicholas J. Newman
22 Eastcroft Rd., West Ewell, Surrey. KT19 9TX. Tel: 081 393 0538. BAFRA. *Comprehensive including exterior woodwork and locks.*

Nigel Northeast Cabinet Makers
Furniture Workshops, Back Drove, West

Furniture continued

Winterslow, Salisbury, Wilts. SP5 1RY. Tel: 0980 862051; fax - 0980 863986. GADAR. Est. 1982. *Antique restoration and French polishing. New furniture made to order, chairs made to complete sets. Cane and rush seating; fire and flood damage service.* VAT: Stan.

Omri Originals
Kirklea Farm, Badgworth, Somerset. BS26 2QH. Tel: 0934 732323. BAFRA.

Richard P. Owen
805 Christchurch Rd., Boscombe, Bournemouth, Dorset. BH7 6AP. Tel: 0202 434800. BAFRA. *Gilding turning, marquetry, upholstery, metal work, colouring and polishing, cabinet making.*

Simon N. Pallister
Unit D. 33 Albion Rd., Luton, Beds. LU2 0DS. Tel: 0582 453292. BAFRA.

Noel Pepperall
Dairy Lane Cottage, Walberton, Arundel, West Sussex. BN18 0PT. Tel: 0243 551282. BAFRA. *Gilding and painted furniture restoration.*

Charles Perry Restorations Ltd
Praewood Farm, Hemel Hempstead Rd., St. Albans, Herts. AL3 6AA. Tel: 0727 53487. BAFRA.

Terence Petersen
Sunnyvale, Black Dyke Rd., Arnside, Cumbria. LA5 0HJ. Tel: 0524 761975. BAFRA. *Early oak, walnut, boulle, mahogany, marquetry, inlay restorations.*

Timothy L. Phelps Fine Furniture Restorations
8 Mornington Terrace, Harrogate, North Yorkshire. HG1 5DH. Tel: 0423 524604. BAFRA. *All cabinet work including dining tables, large items, architectural woodwork, tooled leathers, polishing and waxed finishes.*

Pinewood Furniture Studio Ltd.
1 Eagle Trading Estate, Stourbridge Rd., Halesowen, West Midlands. B63 3UA. Tel: 021 550 8228; fax - 021 585 5611. *Manufacturers of pine furniture. Special orders undertaken.* VAT: Stan.

Colin J. Piper
Highfield House, The Greens, Leafield, Witney, Oxon. OX8 5NP. Tel: 0993 87593. BAFRA.

Albert Plumb Restoration and Furniture Restoration Supplies
31 Whyke Lane, Chichester, West Sussex. PO19 2JS. Tel: 0243 788468. BAFRA. *Oak, walnut mahogany and country furniture; boulle and marquetry.*

R.M. Restoration
Chaddesden Barn, Morants Court Rd., Dunton,

SERVICES

Furniture continued

Sevenoaks, Kent. TN13 2TR. Tel: 0732 741604. BAFRA. *Period furniture, traditional upholstery, French polishing.*

Nicholas S. Reeve
The Lodge, Ashfield Rd., Framsden, Stowmarket, Suffolk. IP14 6LS. Tel: 0728 860257; fax - same. Est. 1860. *Makers of 16th-18th C oak country style furniture.* VAT:Stan.

Rhodes Restoration
Unit 7 Dongan Rd., Warwick, Warks. CV34 4SW. Tel: 0926 491264. *Antique furniture restorers.*

Godfrey Robertson
Fourwinds, Ablington, Bibury, Cirencester, Glos. GL7 5NX. Tel: 0285 740355; fax - same. BAFRA. *General restorations, willing to work in situ if necessary.*

David R. Solomons and Son
14 Moss Hall Grove, London N12 8PB. Tel: 081 446 1693; works - 081 985 6674; fax - 081 446 9225. British Traditional Cabinet Makers. *Manufacturers of traditional furniture especially in burr/burl elm and burr/burl walnut veneers.* VAT: Stan. *Trade Only.*

Julian Stanley Woodcarving - Furniture
Unit 5 The Sitch, Longborough, Moreton-in-Marsh, Glos. GL56 0QJ. Tel: 0451 831122; fax - same. *Fine quality copies of 16th-19th C antiques - exotic carved furniture, figure carving, portrait busts (especially in lime), mirror frames and architectural pieces of all dimensions. Gilding, upholstery, painting and polishing. Work designed and made to order. No restorations.* VAT: Stan/Spec.

Angus Stewart
Sycamore Barn, Bourton Industrial Park, Bourton-on-the-Water, Cheltenham, Glos. GL54 2HQ. Tel: 0451 21611. BAFRA. *16th-18th C cabinet making, gold leafing, decorative finishes, lacquer, carving, mirrors and glass.*

Roy D. Stratton
Wayside, Main St., Gt. Coxwell, Faringdon, Oxon. SN7 7NB. Tel: 0367 240030. BAFRA. *Georgian, Regency and early Victorian furniture restoration.*

Thakeham Furniture
Rock Rd., Storrington, West Sussex. RH20 3AE. Tel: 0903 745464. BAFRA. *French polishing, veneer repairs, wood turning, marquetry, carving, cabinet work.*

John Tighe
One Oak, Lights Lane, Alderbury, Nr. Salisbury, Wilts. SP5 3AL. Tel: 0722 710231. BAFRA. *18th-19th C furniture restoration.*

Furniture continued

Rodrigo Titian
Unit 4, 326 Kensal Rd., London W10 5BN.Tel: 081 960 6247/969 6126. BAFRA. *Carving, gilding, lacquer, painted furniture, French polishing.*

Tolpuddle Antique Restorers
The Stables, Southover House, Tolpuddle, Dorchester, Dorset. DT2 7HF. Tel: 0305 848739. BAFRA. *Furniture, clocks and barometers, marquetry, veneering and boulle work, lacquer, japaning and gilding.*

Clifford J. Tracy
6-40 Durnford St., London N15 5NQ. Tel: 081 800 4773. BAFRA. *General restorations including boulle, marquetry, leather lining, upholstery.*

Treen Antiques
Treen House, 72 Park Rd., Prestwich, Manchester, Lancs. M25 8FA. Tel: 061 740 1063; fax - 061 720 7244. GADAR, RFS, FHS, UKIC. *Conservation and restoration of all antique furniture (including vernacular) and woodwork, with emphasis on preserving original finish. Research undertaken, housekeeping advice, environmental monitoring and all aspects of conservation. Courses in restoration work held. Listed in Bonham's Directory.*

Neil Trinder
Burrowlee House, Burrowlee Rd., Hillsborough, Sheffield, South Yorks. S62. Tel: 0742 852428/552972. BAFRA. *Boulle, gilding, marquetry, carving, fine furniture.*

Tony Vernon
15 Follett Rd., Topsham, Devon. EX3 0JP. Tel: 0392 874635. BAFRA. *Furniture, cabinet making, upholstery, gilding, veneering, inlay and French polishing.*

Weaver Neave and Daughter
17 Lifford St. Putney, London SW15 1NY. Tel: 081 785 2464. *Recaning and re-rushing of antique furniture in traditional manner with traditional materials.*

Terence Whiffen
2 Butlers Drive, Carterton, Oxon. OX8 3QU. Tel: 0993 845335/850011. BAFRA. *Woodcarving, inlay, turning.*

Robert Williams
Osborn's Farm, 32 Church St., Willingham, Cambs. CB4 5HT. Tel: 0954 60972. BAFRA.

Woods Restorers and Finishers
Castle Buildings, 1 Albion St., Bradford, West Yorks. BD1 2LY. Tel: 0274 736156. GADAR. *Antique furniture restoration - inlay, carving, turning, veneering, French polishing and traditional finishing, cabinet work. Also modern finishing facilities; furniture made to order.*

SERVICES

Furniture continued

Woodside Restoration Services
Beechfield House, Woodside, Frilford Heath, Nr. Abingdon, Oxon. OX13 5DG. Tel: 0865 390588. GADAR. Est. 1968. *All general cabinet repairs and polishing. Full barometer restoration; upholstery. Some mirror repairs and decorative work.*

GLASS

Mill Lane Stained Glass Workshop
Lower House, Mill Lane, Longhope, Glos. GL17 0AA. Tel: 0452 831100. *Design, manufacture and installation of traditional stained glass windows, domestic and secular. Manufacture of traditional leaded lights, including historic and listed buildings. Repair and renovation work undertaken.*

INSURANCE

The Arts and Antiques Service
34 Grantchester Rd., Cambridge, Cambs. CB3 9ED. Tel: 0223 359551; mobile - 0850 932894; fax - 0223 300441. *Professional valuations and insurance for probate, family division. Buying specific items or total refurbishments including architectural - fireplaces, doors. Advice on building up or scaling down collections.*

Minet Ltd.
Fine Arts and Jewellery Division, 66 Prescot St., London E1 8BU. Tel: 071 481 0707; fax - 071 488 9786. *International insurance brokers, specialising in fine arts and jewellery.*

Sneath, Kent and Stuart Ltd.
Stuart House, 53-55 Scrutton St., London EC2A 4QQ. Tel: 071 739 5646; fax - 071 739 6467. Lloyds Insurance Brokers; FATG, IDDA. *Insurance brokers to the antique and fine art trade and to antique collectors. Insurance brokers to LAPADA.*

METALWORK

See also Suppliers

Burgess & Co.
49 St. Mary's Works, Duke St., Norwich, Norfolk. NR3 3AF. Tel: 0603 762280; fax - 0603 760571. *Quality hand-made brass and copper by master coppersmiths trained in traditional techniques including antique restoration, shop fronts and fittings, copper roofs, finials and minarets, canopies, catering equipment. Tinning and re-tinning.*

Alan Reeling Metal Restoration
42 Hodge Bower, Ironbridge, Shrops. TF8 7QL. Tel: 0952 433031. GADAR. *Restoration and refurbishment of metal items including cleaning, repair and polishing.*

REPRODUCTION STONEWORK

Hampshire Gardencraft
Rake Industries, Rake, Nr. Petersfield, Hants. Tel: 0730 895182; fax - 0730 893216. *Manufacturers of antiqued garden ornaments, troughs and pots in reconstituted stone in an old Cotswold stone finish. Many designs, catalogue available.*

SUPPLIERS

C. and A.J. Barmby
140 Lavender Hill, Tonbridge, Kent. TA9 2NJ. Tel: 0732 771590; home - 0732 356479. Est. 1980. *Suppliers of display stands in wire, acrylic and wood; reference books and catalogues; lamps and magnifers. Exhibitor at Alexandra Palace, Harrow, Picketts Lock and all IACF fairs.* VAT: Stan.

Marshall Brass
Long Ground Cottage, Keeling Hall Rd., Foulsham, Norfolk. NR20 5PR. Tel: 036 284 4105; fax - 036 284 4280. GMC. *Suppliers of quality period replica furniture fittings.*

Martin and Co. Ltd
119 Camden St., Birmingham, West Midlands. B1 3DJ. Tel: 021 233 2111; fax - 021 236 0488. ASFI, GAI. *Cabinet hardware supplied - handles, locks, hinges, castors etc.*

J. Shiner and Sons Ltd.
8 Windmill St. , London W1P 1HF. Tel: 071 636 0740; fax - 071 580 0740. *Suppliers of brass handles, castors, locks brass grills and leathers.*

Suffolk Brass
Thurston, Bury St. Edmunds, Suffolk. IP31 3SN Tel: 0359 30888; 0379 898670. *Period replica cabinet fittings in brass and iron. One-off castings in lost wax or sand. Catalogue available. Trade Only.*

The Victorian Ring Box Company
North Lodge, Ardpeaton, Cove, Dunbartonshire, Scotland. G84 0NY. Tel: 0436 850261; fax - same. LAPADA. *International designers, manufacturers and distributors of high quality antique style presentation boxes.*

TOYS

Michael Barrington
See entry under Furniture

Robert Mullis Rocking Horse Maker
55 Berkeley Rd., Wroughton, Swindon, Wilts SN4 9BN. Tel: 0793 813583; fax - same. British Toymakers Guild. *Full or partial restorations of antique horses, some wooden toy restoration. Traditional methods and materials used Collection and delivery. New rocking horses made in five sizes, commissions undertaken.*

ANTIQUED REPRODUCTION

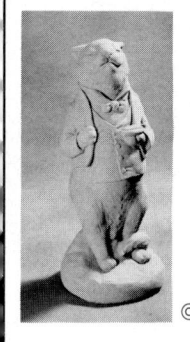

GARDEN ORNAMENTS

MANUFACTURED IN RECONSTITUTED STONE
IN AN OLD COTSWOLD STONE FINISH

100'S OF
DESIGNS
TO
CHOOSE
FROM

IDEAL FOR
SHIPPERS
AND THE
ANTIQUE
TRADE

FOR MORE INFORMATION AND CATALOGUE

PLEASE CONTACT

HAMPSHIRE GARDENCRAFT

RAKE INDUSTRIES
RAKE
Nr. PETERSFIELD
HANTS
PHONE 0730 895182
FAX 0730 893216

ALPHABETICAL LIST OF TOWNS AND VILLAGES WITH THE COUNTIES UNDER WHICH THEY APPEAR IN THIS GUIDE

A

Abbots Bromley, Staffs..
Abbots Langley, Herts.
Abbots Leigh, Avon.
Aberaeron, Dyfed, Wales.
Aberdare, Mid. Glam., Wales.
Aberdeen, Scotland.
Aberdour, Scotland.
Aberfeldy, Scotland.
Aberford, Yorks. West.
Abergavenny, Gwent, Wales.
Abernyte, Scotland.
Abersoch, Gwynedd, Wales.
Aberystwyth, Dyfed, Wales.
Abinger Hammer, Surrey.
Abridge, Essex.
Accrington, Lancs.
Acle, Norfolk.
Acrise, Kent.
Addingham, Yorks. West.
Adversane, Sussex West.
Albrighton, Shrops.
Alcester, Warks.
Aldeburgh, Suffolk.
Alderley Edge, Cheshire.
Alderney, Alderney, C.I.
Alford, Scotland.
Alfriston, Sussex East.
Allonby, Cumbria.
Alnwick, Northumbs.
Alresford, Hants.
Alrewas, Staffs.
Alsager, Cheshire.
Alston, Cumbria.
Althorne, Essex.
Altrincham, Cheshire.
Alvechurch, West Mids.
Alverstoke, Hants.
Amersham, Bucks.
Ammanford, Dyfed, Wales.
Ampthill, Beds.
Angarrack, Cornwall.
Angmering, Sussex West.
Annahilt, Co. Down, N.Ireland.
Antrim, Co. Antrim, N.Ireland.
Ardersier, Scotland.
Armagh, Co. Armagh, N.Ireland.
Arthingworth, Northants.
Arundel, Sussex West.
Ascott-under-Wychwood, Oxon.
Ash, Kent.
Ash Priors, Somerset.
Ash Vale, Surrey.
Ashbourne, Derbys.
Ashburton, Devon.
Ashby-de-la-Zouch, Leics.
Ashford, Kent.
Ashtead, Surrey.
Ashton-under-Lyne, Lancs.
Askham, Notts.
Aslockton, Notts.
Astwood Bank, Herefs & Worcs.
Atcham, Shrops.
Atherton, Lancs.
Attleborough, Norfolk.
Atworth, Wilts.
Auchterarder, Scotland.
Auldearn, Scotland.
Auldgirth, Scotland.
Avening, Glos.
Avoch, Scotland.
Axbridge, Somerset.
Axminster, Devon.
Aylesbury, Bucks.
Aylesby, Humberside South.
Aylsham, Norfolk.
Ayr, Scotland.

B

Bagillt, Clwyd, Wales.
Bakewell, Derbys.
Balcombe, Sussex West.
Balderton, Notts.
Baldock, Herts.
Balfron, Scotland.
Ballater, Scotland.
Ballyclare, Co. Antrim, N.Ireland.
Bampton, Devon.
Bampton, Oxon.
Banbridge, Co. Down, N.Ireland.
Banbury, Oxon.
Banchory, Scotland.
Bangor, Gwynedd, Wales.
Bankfoot, Scotland.
Bannockburn, Scotland.
Barkham, Berks.
Barling Magna, Essex.
Barmouth, Gwynedd, Wales.
Barnard Castle, Durham.
Barnet, Herts.
Barnoldswick, Lancs.
Barnsley, Glos.
Barnsley, Yorks. South.
Barnstaple, Devon.
Barnt Green, Herefs & Worcs.
Barrhead, Scotland.
Barrington, Somerset.
Barrow-in-Furness, Cumbria.
Barry, South Glam., Wales.
Barton, Cheshire.
Barton-on-Humber, Humberside South.
Basingstoke, Hants.
Baslow, Derbys.
Bassingbourn, Cambs.
Bath, Avon.
Battle, Sussex East.
Battlesbridge, Essex.
Bawdeswell, Norfolk.
Bawtry, Yorks. South.
Beaconsfield, Bucks.
Beaminster, Dorset.
Beattock, Scotland.
Beaulieu, Hants.
Beauly, Scotland.
Beaumaris, Gwynedd, Wales.
Beccles, Suffolk.
Beckenham, Kent.
Bedale, Yorks. North.
Bedford, Beds.
Bedingfield, Suffolk.
Beeston, Notts.
Beetham, Cumbria.
Belfast, N.Ireland.
Belper, Derbys.
Bembridge, I. of Wight.
Bentley Heath, West Mids.
Berkeley, Glos.
Berkhamsted, Herts.
Berry Hill Pike, Glos.
Berwick-on-Tweed, Northumbs.
Bessacarr, Yorks. South.
Betley, Staffs.
Beverley, Humberside North.
Bewdley, Herefs & Worcs.
Bexhill-on-Sea, Sussex East.
Bexley, Kent.
Bicester, Oxon.
Bickerstaffe, Lancs.
Biddenden, Kent.
Bideford, Devon.
Bidford-on-Avon, Warks.
Biggleswade, Beds.
Billingham, Cleveland.
Billingshurst, Sussex West.
Bingham, Notts.
Bingley, Yorks. West.
Birchington, Kent.
Birdbrook, Essex.
Birkenhead, Merseyside.
Birmingham, West Mids.
Birstwith, Yorks. North.
Bishop's Stortford, Herts.
Bishops Cleeve, Glos.
Bishops Waltham, Hants.
Blackburn, Lancs.
Blackmore, Essex.
Blackpool, Lancs.
Bladon, Oxon.
Blaenau Ffestiniog, Gwynedd Wales.
Blairgowrie, Scotland.

TOWNS AND VILLAGES

Blakedown, Herefs & Worcs.
Blandford Forum, Dorset.
Blaydon, Tyne & Wear.
Bletchingley, Surrey.
Blewbury, Oxon.
Bloxham, Oxon.
Bloxwich, West Mids.
Blythburgh, Suffolk.
Bodmin, Cornwall.
Bodorgan, (Anglesey), Gwynedd, Wales.
Bognor Regis, Sussex West.
Bolton, Lancs.
Bolton-by-Bowland, Lancs.
Boreham Street, Sussex East.
Boroughbridge, Yorks. North.
Bosham, Sussex West.
Boston, Lincs.
Boston Spa, Yorks. West.
Botley, Hants.
Bottesford, Leics.
Bottisham, Cambs.
Boughton, Kent.
Bournemouth, Dorset.
Bovey Tracey, Devon.
Bow Street, Dyfed, Wales.
Bowdon, Cheshire.
Bowness-on-Windermere, Cumbria.
Boxford, Suffolk.
Brackley, Northants.
Bradfield St. George, Suffolk.
Bradford, Yorks. West.
Bradford-on-Avon, Wilts.
Bradley, Yorks. North.
Brailsford, Derbys.
Braintree, Essex.
Bramhall, Cheshire.
Bramley, Surrey.
Brampton, Cambs.
Brampton, Cumbria.
Brancaster Staithe, Norfolk.
Brandsby, Yorks. North.
Branksome, Dorset.
Brantham, Suffolk.
Brassington, Derbys.
Brasted, Kent.
Braunton, Devon.
Brecon, Powys, Wales.
Brentwood, Essex.
Brereton, Staffs.
Bressingham, Norfolk.
Bridge of Earn, Scotland.
Bridgnorth, Shrops.
Bridgwater, Somerset.
Bridlington, Humberside North.
Bridport, Dorset.
Brierfield, Lancs.
Brightling, Sussex East.
Brighton, Sussex East.
Bristol, Avon.
Brixham, Devon.
Brixworth, Northants.
Broadstairs, Kent.
Broadstone, Dorset.
Broadway, Herefs & Worcs.

Brobury, Herefs & Worcs.
Brockdish, Norfolk.
Brodick, Scotland.
Bromley, Kent.
Brompton, Yorks. North.
Bromsgrove, Herefs & Worcs.
Bromyard, Herefs & Worcs.
Broseley, Shrops.
Broughton, Lancs.
Broughton Astley, Leics.
Bruton, Somerset.
Buchlyvie, Scotland.
Buckden, Yorks. North.
Buckingham, Bucks.
Budleigh Salterton, Devon.
Bulkington, Warks.
Bungay, Suffolk.
Burford, Oxon.
Burgess Hill, Sussex West.
Burghfield Common, Berks.
Burley-on-the-Hill, Leics.
Burneston, Yorks. North.
Burnham Deepdale, Norfolk.
Burnham Market, Norfolk.
Burnham on Crouch, Essex.
Burnham-on-Sea, Somerset.
Burnley, Lancs.
Burscough, Lancs.
Burton-on-Trent, Staffs.
Burwash, Sussex East.
Burwell, Cambs.
Bury, Lancs.
Bury St. Edmunds, Suffolk.
Bushey, Herts.
Bushmills, Co. Antrim , N.Ireland.
Buxton, Derbys.
Buxton, Norfolk.
Bwchllan, Dyfed, Wales.

C

Cadeby, Leics.
Cadnam, Hants.
Caenarfon, Gwynedd, Wales.
Caerphilly, Mid.Glam., Wales.
Calbeck, Cumbria.
Calne, Wilts.
Camberley, Surrey.
Camborne, Cornwall..
Cambridge, Cambs.
Cambridge, Glos.
Canterbury, Kent.
Cardiff, South Glam., Wales.
Carlisle, Cumbria.
Carlton-on-Trent, Notts.
Carmarthen, Dyfed, Wales.
Carrefour Selous, St. Lawrence, Jersey, C.I.
Carshalton, Surrey.
Cartmel, Cumbria.
Castle Ashby, Northants.
Castle Cary, Somerset.
Castle Combe, Wilts.
Castle Douglas, Scotland.
Castle Hedingham, Essex.
Castletown, I. of Man.

Caversham, Berks.
Cawood, Yorks. North.
Ceres, Scotland.
Cerne Abbas, Dorset.
Chagford, Devon.
Chalfont St. Giles, Bucks.
Chalford, Glos.
Chalgrove, Oxon.
Chapel-en-le-Frith, Derbys.
Chard, Somerset.
Charing, Kent.
Charlecote, Warks.
Charlton Marshall, Dorset.
Charmouth, Dorset.
Chastleton, Glos.
Chatburn, Lancs.
Chatham, Kent.
Chatton, Northumbs.
Cheadle, Cheshire.
Cheadle Hulme, Cheshire.
Cheam, Surrey.
Cheddleton, Staffs.
Cheltenham, Glos.
Chepstow, Gwent, Wales.
Cherhill, Wilts.
Chertsey, Surrey.
Chesham, Bucks.
Chester, Cheshire.
Chesterfield, Derbys.
Chichester, Sussex West.
Chiddingfold, Surrey.
Chiddingstone, Kent.
Chilcompton, Somerset.
Chilham, Kent.
Chingford, Essex.
Chipping Campden, Glos.
Chipping Norton, Oxon.
Chipping Sodbury, Avon.
Chirk, Clwyd, Wales.
Chislehurst, Kent.
Chittering, Cambs.
Chobham, Surrey.
Chorley, Lancs.
Christchurch, Dorset.
Christian Malford, Wilts.
Church Stretton, Shrops.
Churt, Surrey.
Ciliau Aeron, Dyfed, Wales.
Cirencester, Glos.
Clacton-on-Sea, Essex.
Clare, Suffolk.
Claudy, Co. Londonderry, N.Ireland.
Clayton-le-Moors, Lancs.
Cleobury Mortimer, Shrops.
Clevedon, Avon.
Cley, Norfolk.
Clitheroe, Lancs.
Clows Top, Herefs & Worcs.
Clutton, Avon.
Coalville, Leics.
Coatbridge, Scotland.
Cobham, Surrey.
Cockermouth, Cumbria.
Cockfosters, Herts.
Cocking, Sussex West.
Codford, Wilts.

TOWNS AND VILLAGES

Codicote, Herts.
Codsall, Staffs.
Coggeshall, Essex.
Colchester, Essex.
Coldstream, Scotland.
Coleraine, Co. Londonderry, N.Ireland.
Coleshill, Warks.
Collessie, Scotland.
Collingham, Notts.
Colne, Lancs.
Colsterworth, Lincs.
Coltishall, Norfolk.
Colwyn Bay, Clwyd, Wales.
Colyton, Devon.
Combe Martin, Devon.
Comberton, Cambs.
Compton, Surrey.
Comrie, Scotland.
Congleton, Cheshire.
Coniston, Cumbria.
Consett, Durham.
Conway, Gwynedd, Wales
Cooden, Sussex East.
Cookham, Berks.
Cookstown, Co. Tyrone, N.Ireland.
Copthorne, Sussex West.
Corby Hill, Cumbria.
Corfe Castle, Dorset.
Corringham, Essex.
Corsham, Wilts.
Corwen, Clwyd, Wales.
Cosgrove, Northants.
Costessey, Norfolk.
Coton Clanford, Staffs.
Coulsdon, Surrey.
Coupar Angus, Scotland.
Coventry, West Mids.
Cowan Bridge, Lancs.
Cowbridge, South Glam., Wales.
Cowes, I. of Wight.
Cowfold, Sussex West.
Coxley, Somerset.
Cradley Heath, West Mids.
Cranborne, Dorset.
Cranbrook, Kent.
Cranham, Glos.
Cranleigh, Surrey.
Craven Arms, Shrops.
Crawley, Hants.
Crawley, Sussex West.
Crayford, Kent.
Cremyll, Cornwall.
Crewe, Cheshire.
Crewkerne, Somerset.
Crickhowell, Powys, Wales.
Cricklade, Wilts.
Crieff, Scotland.
Cromer, Norfolk.
Crook, Durham.
Crosby Ravensworth, Cumbria.
Cross Hills, Yorks. North.
Croughton, Northants.
Crowmarsh Gifford, Oxon.

Croydon, Surrey.
Cruden Bay, Scotland.
Cuckfield, Sussex West.
Culham, Oxon.
Cullompton, Devon.
Cumnor, Oxon.
Cuxton, Kent.

D

Dalbeattie, Scotland.
Danbury, Essex.
Darlington, Durham.
Dartford, Kent.
Dartmouth, Devon.
Darwen, Lancs.
Datchet, Berks.
Davenham, Cheshire.
Deal, Kent.
Debenham, Suffolk.
Deddington, Oxon.
Deganwy, Gwynedd, Wales.
Denny, Scotland.
Derby, Derbys.
Devizes, Wilts.
Dingwall, Scotland.
Disley, Cheshire.
Diss, Norfolk.
Ditchling, Sussex East.
Doddington, Cambs.
Dollar, Scotland.
Donaghadee, Co. Down, N.Ireland.
Doncaster, Yorks. South.
Donyatt, Somerset.
Dorchester, Dorset.
Dorchester-on-Thames, Oxon.
Dorking, Surrey.
Dorney, Berks.
Douglas, I. of Man.
Dover, Kent.
Dowlish Wake, Somerset.
Drewsteignton, Devon.
Driffield, Humberside North.
Droitwich, Herefs & Worcs.
Dronfield, Derbys.
Drumnadrochit, Scotland.
Duffield, Derbys.
Dulford, Devon.
Dulverton, Somerset.
Dumfries, Scotland.
Dunchurch, Warks.
Dundee, Scotland.
Dunfermline, Scotland.
Dunkeld, Scotland.
Dunmow, Essex.
Dunoon, Scotland.
Dunstable, Beds.
Durham, Durham.
Duxford, Cambs.

E

Eachwick, Northumbs.
Eaglescliffe, Cleveland.
Eaglesham, Scotland.
Earsham, Norfolk.

Easebourne, Sussex West.
Easingwold, Yorks. North.
East Budleigh, Devon.
East Dereham, Norfolk.
East Grinstead, Sussex West.
East Hagbourne, Oxon.
East Horsley, Surrey.
East Molesey, Surrey.
East Peckham, Kent.
East Pennard, Somerset.
East Rudham, Norfolk.
Eastbourne, Sussex East.
Eastburn, Yorks. West.
Eastleigh, Hants.
Eastry, Kent.
Ebrington, Glos.
Ecclesfield, Yorks. South.
Eccleston, Lancs.
Edenbridge, Kent.
Edenfield, Lancs.
Edgware, Middx.
Edinburgh, Scotland.
Egham, Surrey.
Elgin, Scotland.
Elham, Kent.
Elie, Scotland.
Ellesmere, Shrops.
Elmley Lovett, Herefs & Worcs.
Elton, Notts.
Ely, Cambs.
Empingham, Leics.
Emsworth, Hants.
Endmoor, Cumbria.
Enfield, Middx.
Epping, Essex.
Epsom, Surrey.
Errol, Scotland.
Esh Winning, Durham.
Esher, Surrey.
Eversley, Hants.
Evesham, Herefs & Worcs.
Ewell, Surrey.
Ewhurst, Surrey.
Ewhurst Green, Sussex East.
Exeter, Devon.
Exmouth, Devon.
Exning, Suffolk.
Exton, Somerset.
Exwick, Devon.
Eye, Suffolk.
Eynsham, Oxon.

F

Fairford, Glos.
Fairlie, Scotland.
Fakenham, Norfolk.
Falkirk, Scotland.
Falmouth, Cornwall.
Fareham, Hants.
Faringdon, Oxon.
Farnborough, Hants.
Farnborough, Kent.
Farndon, Cheshire.
Farnham, Surrey.
Farnham Common, Bucks.

TOWNS AND VILLAGES

Farningham, Kent.
Faversham, Kent.
Felixstowe, Suffolk.
Felpham, Sussex West.
Felsted, Essex.
Felton, Northumbs.
Feniscowles, Lancs.
Feock, Cornwall.
Fernhurst, Sussex West.
Filey, Yorks. North.
Finchingfield, Essex.
Finedon, Northants.
Finkley, Hants.
Fishguard, Dyfed, Wales.
Fishlake, Yorks. South.
Fitzhead, Somerset.
Flamborough, Humberside North.
Flaxton, Yorks. North.
Flimwell, Sussex East.
Flore, Northants.
Fochabers, Scotland.
Folkestone, Kent.
Fordcombe, Kent.
Fordham, Cambs.
Fordham, Essex.
Fordingbridge, Hants.
Forkhill, Co. Armagh , , N.Ireland.
Forres, Scotland.
Fortrose, Scotland.
Four Elms, Kent.
Four Oaks, West Mids.
Fowlmere, Cambs.
Framlingham, Suffolk.
Frampton West, Lincs.
Freckleton, Lancs.
Frensham, Surrey.
Freshford, Avon.
Freshwater, I. of Wight.
Freuchie, Scotland.
Frinton-on-Sea, Essex.
Friockheim, Scotland.
Frome, Somerset.

G

Gainsborough, Lincs.
Galston, Scotland.
Gants Hill, Essex.
Garboldisham, Norfolk.
Garelochhead, Scotland.
Gargrave, Yorks. North.
Garstang, Lancs.
Gateshead, Tyne & Wear.
Gedney, Lincs.
Gillingham, Dorset.
Gillingham, Kent.
Gilwern, Gwent, Wales
Glasgow, Scotland.
Glastonbury, Somerset.
Glossop, Derbys.
Gloucester, Glos.
Godalming, Surrey.
Golant, Cornwall.
Gorseinon, West Glam., Wales.

Gosforth, Cumbria.
Gosport, Hants.
Goudhurst, Kent.
Gourock, Scotland.
Grampound, Cornwall.
Grantham, Lincs.
Grantown-on-Spey, Scotland.
Grasmere, Cumbria.
Grassington, Yorks. North.
Grassmoor, Derbys.
Gravesend, Kent.
Grays, Essex.
Great Ayton, Yorks. North.
Great Baddow, Essex.
Great Bardfield, Essex.
Great Bircham, , Norfolk.
Great Bookham, Surrey.
Great Chesterford, Essex.
Great Harwood, Lancs.
Great Houghton, Yorks. South.
Great Malvern, Herefs & Worcs.
Great Missenden, Bucks.
Great Shefford, Berks.
Great Urswick, Cumbria.
Great Wakering, Essex.
Great Waltham, Essex.
Greatford, Lincs.
Green Hammerton, Yorks. North.
Greenlaw, Scotland.
Greyabbey, Co. Down, N.Ireland.
Greystoke, Cumbria.
Grimsby, Humberside South.
Grosmont, Yorks. North.
Grundisburgh, Suffolk.
Gt. Cheverell, Wilts.
Gt. Walsingham, Norfolk.
Gt. Yarmouth, Norfolk.
Guardbridge, Scotland.
Guildford, Surrey.
Guilsborough, Northants.
Guisborough, Cleveland.
Gullane, Scotland.

H

Hacheston, Suffolk.
Haddenham, Bucks.
Haddington, Scotland.
Hadleigh, Suffolk.
Hadlow, Kent.
Halesowen, West Mids.
Halesworth, Suffolk.
Halfway, Berks.
Halifax, Yorks. West.
Halstead, Essex.
Hambridge, Somerset.
Hampton, Middx.
Hampton Court, Surrey.
Hampton Hill, Middx.
Hampton Wick, Surrey.
Handcross, Sussex West.
Harbury, Warks.
Harefield, Middx.

Harlington, Beds.
Harpenden, Herts.
Harpole, Northants.
Harrietsham, Kent.
Harrogate, Yorks. North.
Harrow, Middx.
Harston, Cambs.
Hartley, Kent.
Hartley Wintney, Hants.
Harwich, Essex.
Haslemere, Surrey.
Haslingden, Lancs.
Hastings, Sussex East.
Hatfield, Herts.
Hatfield Broad Oak, Essex.
Hatfield Heath, Essex.
Hatherleigh, Devon.
Hatton, Warks.
Haunton, Staffs.
Havant, Hants.
Haverfordwest, Dyfed, Wales.
Hawes, Yorks. North.
Hawkedon, Suffolk.
Hawkhurst, Kent.
Haworth , Yorks. West.
Hay-on-Wye, Powys, Wales.
Haydon Bridge, Northumbs.
Hayfield, Derbys.
Hayle, Cornwall.
Hayling Island, Hants.
Haywards Heath, Sussex West.
Hazel Grove, Cheshire.
Heacham, Norfolk.
Headcorn, Kent.
Headington, Oxon.
Heanor, Derbys.
Heath and Reach, Beds.
Hebden Bridge, Yorks. West.
Helmshore, Lancs.
Helmsley, Yorks. North.
Helsby, Cheshire.
Hemel Hempstead, Herts.
Hempstead, Essex.
Hemswell Cliff, Lincs.
Henfield, Sussex West.
Henley-in-Arden, Warks.
Henley-on-Thames, Oxon.
Henllan, Dyfed, Wales.
Hereford, Herefs & Worcs.
Herstmonceux, Sussex East.
Hertford, Herts.
Hessle, Humberside North.
Heswall, Merseyside.
Hexham, Northumbs.
High Wycombe, Bucks.
Highbridge, Somerset.
Hinckley, Leics.
Hindhead, Surrey.
Hindon, Wilts.
Hitchin, Herts.
Hoby, Leics.
Hockley Heath, West Mids.
Hodnet, Shrops.
Holbeach, Lincs.
Hollinwood, Lancs.
Holme, Cumbria.

TOWNS AND VILLAGES

Holmfirth, Yorks. West.
Holsworthy, Devon.
Holt, Clwyd, Wales.
Holt, Norfolk.
Holywood, Co. Down, N.Ireland.
Honiton, Devon.
Hoole, Cheshire.
Horam, Sussex East.
Horbury, Yorks. West.
Horncastle, Lincs.
Horndean, Hants.
Hornsea, Humberside North.
Horrabridge, Devon.
Horsebridge, Sussex East.
Horsham, Sussex West.
Horton, Berks.
Horwich, Lancs.
Houndwood, Scotland.
Hoylake, Merseyside.
Huby, Yorks. North.
Hucknall, Notts.
Huddersfield, Yorks. West.
Hughenden Valley, Bucks.
Hull, Humberside North.
Hundleby, Lincs.
Hungerford, Berks.
Hunstanton, Norfolk.
Huntercombe, Oxon.
Huntingdon, Cambs.
Hursley, Hants.
Hurst, Berks.
Hurst Green, Sussex East.
Hurstpierpoint, Sussex West.
Hyde, Cheshire.
Hythe, Kent.

I

Ibstock, Leics.
Ickleton , Cambs.
Ilford, Essex.
Ilfracombe, Devon.
Ilkeston, Derbys.
Ilkley, Yorks. West.
Ilminster, Somerset.
Inchture, Scotland.
Ingatestone, Essex.
Instow, Devon.
Inverness, Scotland.
Ipswich, Suffolk.
Ironbridge, Shrops.
Isleworth, Middx.
Iver, Bucks.
Ixworth, Suffolk.

J

Jedburgh, Scotland.
Jesmond, Tyne & Wear.

K

Keighley, Yorks. West.
Kelvedon, Essex.
Kempston, Beds.
Kendal, Cumbria.
Kenilworth, Warks.

Kennington, Kent.
Kentisbeare, Devon.
Kesgrave, Suffolk.
Kessingland, Suffolk.
Keswick, Cumbria.
Kettering, Northants.
Kew, Surrey.
Kew Green, Surrey.
Kibworth Beauchamp, Leics.
Kidderminster, Herefs & Worcs.
Kidlington, Oxon.
Kidwelly, Dyfed, Wales.
Kilbarchan, Scotland.
Kilham, Humberside North.
Killamarsh, Derbys.
Killearn, Scotland.
Killin, Scotland.
Killinghall, Yorks. North.
Kilmacolm, Scotland.
Kilmarnock, Scotland.
Kilmichael Glassary, Scotland.
Kiltarlity, Scotland.
Kimpton, Herts.
Kincardine O'Neil, Scotland.
Kineton, Warks.
King's Langley, Herts.
King's Lynn, Norfolk.
Kinghorn, Scotland.
Kingsbridge, Devon.
Kingsley, Staffs.
Kingsthorpe, Northants.
Kingston-on-Spey, Scotland.
Kingston-upon-Thames, Surrey.
Kingswear, Devon.
Kingussie, Scotland.
Kinross, Scotland.
Kinver, Staffs.
Kirdford, Sussex West.
Kirk Deighton, Yorks. North.
Kirk Michael, I. of Man.
Kirkby Lonsdale, Cumbria.
Kirkby Stephen, Cumbria.
Kirkbymoorside, Yorks. North.
Kirkcudbright, Scotland.
Kirton, Lincs.
Knaphill, Surrey.
Knaresborough, Yorks. North.
Knebworth, Herts.
Knighton, Powys, Wales.
Knipton, Leics.
Knowle, West Mids.
Knutsford, Cheshire.

L

Lake, I. of Wight.
Laleham, Surrey.
Lamberhurst, Kent.
Lampeter, Dyfed, Wales.
Lancaster, Lancs.
Landbeach, Cambs.
Lane End, Bucks.
Langford, Notts.
Langholm, Scotland.
Langley Burrell, Wilts.

Langport, Somerset.
Largs, Scotland.
Laugharne, Dyfed, Wales.
Launceston, Cornwall.
Lavenham, Suffolk.
Laxfield, Suffolk.
Layer de la Haye, Essex.
Leamington Spa, Warks.
Leavenheath, Suffolk.
Lechlade, Glos.
Ledbury, Herefs & Worcs.
Leeds, Yorks. West.
Leedstown, Cornwall.
Leek, Staffs.
Leicester, Leics.
Leigh, Kent.
Leigh, Lancs.
Leigh, Staffs.
Leigh-on-Sea, Essex.
Leighton Buzzard, Beds.
Leiston, Suffolk.
Leominster, Herefs & Worcs.
Lepton, Yorks. West.
Leslie By Insch, Scotland.
Letchmore Heath, Herts.
Leuchars, Scotland.
Lewes, Sussex East.
Lichfield, Staffs.
Limington, Somerset.
Limpsfield, Surrey.
Lincoln, Lincs.
Lindfield, Sussex West.
Lingfield, Surrey.
Linlithgow, Scotland.
Linslade, Beds.
Liss, Hants.
Little Abington, Cambs.
Little Brickhill, Bucks.
Little Downham, Cambs.
Little Haywood, Staffs.
Little Malvern, Herefs & Worcs.
Little Walsingham, Norfolk.
Littlebourne, Kent.
Littlehampton, Sussex West.
Littleton, Cheshire.
Littleton, Somerset.
Litton Cheney, Dorset.
Liverpool, Merseyside.
Llandeilo, Dyfed, Wales.
Llandissilio, Dyfed, Wales.
Llandogo, Gwent, Wales.
Llandovery, Dyfed, Wales.
Llandudno, Gwynedd, Wales.
Llandudno Junction, Gwynedd, Wales.
Llanelli, Dyfed, Wales.
Llanerchymedd, Gwynedd, Wales.
Llanfair Caereinion, Powys, Wales.
Llangollen, Clwyd, Wales.
Llanishen, South Glam., Wales.
Llanrwst, Gwynedd, Wales.
Llantwit Major, South Glam., Wales.

TOWNS AND VILLAGES

Llanwrda, Dyfed, Wales.
Lodsworth, Sussex West.
Long Buckby, Northants.
Long Clawston, Leics.
Long Crendon, Bucks.
Long Eaton, Derbys.
Long Hanborough, Oxon.
Long Melford, Suffolk.
Long Preston, Yorks. North.
Long Stratton, Norfolk.
Long Sutton, Lincs.
Longridge, Lancs.
Looe, Cornwall.
Lostock Gralam, Cheshire.
Lostwithiel, Cornwall.
Loughborough, Leics.
Loughton, Essex.
Low Fell, Tyne & Wear.
Lower Bentham, Yorks. North.
Lower Kinnerton, Cheshire.
Lowestoft, Suffolk.
Lubenham, Leics.
Ludlow, Shrops.
Lurgan, Co. Armagh , N.Ireland.
Luton, Beds.
Lydford, Devon.
Lye, West Mids.
Lymington, Hants.
Lympsham, Somerset.
Lyndhurst, Hants.
Lynton, Devon.
Lytchett Minster, Dorset.
Lytham, Lancs.
Lytham St. Annes, Lancs.

M

Macclesfield, Cheshire.
Maentwrog, Gwynedd, Wales.
Maidencombe, Devon.
Maidenhead, Berks.
Maidstone, Kent.
Maldon, Essex.
Malmesbury, Wilts.
Malpas, Cheshire.
Malton, Yorks. North.
Malvern Link, Herefs & Worcs.
Malvern Wells, Herefs & Worcs.
Manchester, Lancs.
Manfield, Yorks. North.
Manningtree, Essex.
Mansel Lacy, Herefs & Worcs.
Mansfield, Notts.
Manton, Leics.
Mapplewell, Yorks. South.
Marazion, Cornwall.
Margate, Kent.
Market Bosworth, Leics.
Market Deeping, Lincs.
Market Harborough, Leics.
Market Rasen, Lincs.
Market Weighton, Humberside North.
Markington, Yorks. North.

Marlborough, Wilts.
Marlesford, Suffolk.
Marlow, Bucks.
Marple Bridge, Cheshire.
Marsham, Norfolk.
Marshfield, Avon.
Martlesham, Suffolk.
Marton, Cleveland.
Masham, Yorks. North.
Matching Green, Essex.
Mathon, Herefs & Worcs.
Mathry, Dyfed, Wales.
Matlock, Derbys.
Mattingley, Hants.
Maulds Meaburn, Cumbria.
Mayfield, Sussex East.
Meare, Somerset.
Measham, Leics.
Medbourne, Leics.
Melbourn, Cambs.
Melbury Osmond, Dorset.
Melksham, Wilts.
Melmerby, Yorks. North.
Menston, Yorks. West.
Meonstoke, Hants.
Merrow, Surrey.
Merstham, Surrey.
Merton, Devon.
Mevagissey, Cornwall.
Micklebring, Yorks. South.
Middleham, Yorks. North.
Middlesbrough, Cleveland.
Middleton Village, Lancs.
Midhurst, Sussex West.
Midsomer Norton, Avon.
Milburn, Cumbria.
Mildenhall, Suffolk.
Milford, Surrey.
Milford Haven, Dyfed, Wales.
Milland, Sussex West.
Milnthorpe, Cumbria.
Milton Keynes, Bucks.
Milton Lilbourne, Wilts.
Milton-under-Wychwood, Oxon.
Milverton, Somerset.
Minchinhampton, Glos.
Minety, Wilts.
Ministeracres, Northumbs.
Minster, Kent.
Mirfield, Yorks. West.
Mitcham, Surrey.
Modbury, Devon.
Moffat, Scotland.
Mold, Clwyd, Wales.
Monkton, Devon.
Monmouth, Gwent, Wales.
Montacute, Somerset.
Montgomery, Powys, Wales.
Montrose, Scotland.
Monyash, Derbys.
Morchard Bishop, Devon.
Morden, Surrey.
Morecambe, Lancs.
Morestead, Hants.
Moreton-in-Marsh, Glos.
Moretonhampstead, Devon.

Morriston, West Glam., Wales.
Mossley, Lancs.
Mousehole, Cornwall.
Much Hadham, Herts.
Much Wenlock, Shrops.
Murton, West Glam., Wales.

N

Nailsworth, Glos.
Nantwich, Cheshire.
Nantymoel, Mid. Glam., Wales.
Naphill, Bucks.
Narberth, Dyfed, Wales.
Needham Market, Suffolk.
Nelson, Lancs.
Neston, Cheshire.
Nether Stowey, Somerset.
Netherbury, Dorset.
New Mills, Derbys.
New Romney, Kent.
Newark, Notts.
Newburgh, Scotland.
Newbury, Berks.
Newby Bridge, Cumbria.
Newcastle Emlyn, Dyfed, Wales.
Newcastle-under-Lyme, Staffs.
Newcastle-upon-Tyne, Tyne & Wear.
Newchurch, I. of Wight.
Newhaven, Sussex East.
Newmarket, Suffolk.
Newnham-on-Severn, Glos.
Newport, Essex.
Newport, Gwent, Wales.
Newport, I. of Wight.
Newport, Shrops.
Newry, Co. Down, N.Ireland.
Newton Abbot, Devon.
Newton St. Cyres, Devon.
Newton Stewart, Scotland.
Newtonmore, Scotland.
Newtown, Cheshire.
Newtownabbey, Co. Antrim, N.Ireland.
Niton, I. of Wight.
Norham, Northumbs.
North Kelsey Moor, Lincs.
North Petherton, Somerset.
North Petherwin, Cornwall.
North Shields, Tyne & Wear.
North Walsham, Norfolk.
North Wraxall, Wilts.
Northallerton, Yorks. North.
Northampton, Northants.
Northchapel, Sussex West.
Northfleet, Kent.
Northleach, Glos.
Northop, Clwyd, Wales.
Northwood, Middx.
Norton, Glos.
Norwich, Norfolk.
Nottingham, Notts.

TOWNS AND VILLAGES

O

Oadby, Leics.
Oakham, Leics.
Oakley, Hants.
Oban, Scotland.
Ockley, Surrey.
Odiham, Hants.
Okehampton, Devon.
Oldham, Lancs.
Ollerton, Notts.
Olney, Bucks.
Olveston, Avon.
Ombersley, Herefs & Worcs.
Ongar, Essex.
Orford, Suffolk.
Ormskirk, Lancs.
Orpington, Kent.
Orwell, Cambs.
Osbournby, Lincs.
Osgathorpe, Leics.
Oswestry, Shrops.
Otford, Kent.
Otley, Yorks. West.
Oughtibridge, Yorks. South.
Oundle, Northants.
Outwell, Cambs.
Oxford, Oxon.
Oxted, Surrey.

P

Padiham, Lancs.
Padstow, Cornwall.
Painswick, Glos.
Paisley, Scotland.
Parkstone, Dorset.
Pateley Bridge, Yorks. North.
Patrington, Humberside North.
Pattishall, Northants.
Paulerspury, Northants.
Peasenhall, Suffolk.
Peel, I. of Man.
Pelsall, West Mids.
Pembroke, Dyfed, Wales.
Pembroke Dock, Dyfed, Wales.
Penarth, South Glam., Wales.
Penkridge, Staffs.
Penn, Bucks.
Penrhos, Gwent, Wales.
Penrith, Cumbria.
Penryn, Cornwall.
Penzance, Cornwall.
Perranporth, Cornwall.
Pershore, Herefs & Worcs.
Perth, Scotland.
Peterborough, Cambs.
Petersfield, Hants.
Petworth, Sussex West.
Pevensey, Sussex East.
Pevensey Bay, Sussex East.
Pickering, Yorks. North.
Pinner, Middx.
Pitlochry, Scotland.
Pitminster, Somerset.
Pittenweem, Scotland.
Plaitford, Hants.

Playden, Sussex East.
Plumley, Cheshire.
Plymouth, Devon.
Polegate, Sussex East.
Ponterwyd, Dyfed, Wales.
Pontnewynydd, Gwent, Wales.
Pontypridd, Mid. Glam., Wales.
Poole, Dorset.
Port Erin, I. of Man.
Portadown, Co. Armagh, N.Ireland.
Portaferry, Co. Down, N.Ireland.
Portballintrae, Co. Antrim, N.Ireland.
Porthcawl, Mid. Glam., Wales.
Portrush, Co. Antrim, N.Ireland.
Portscatho, Cornwall.
Portslade, Sussex West.
Portsmouth, Hants.
Portsoy, Scotland.
Portstewart, Co. Londonderry, N.Ireland.
Potterspury, Northants.
Poynton, Cheshire.
Pratt's Bottom, Kent.
Prestbury, Cheshire.
Preston, Lancs.
Prestwick, Scotland.
Princes Risborough, Bucks.
Puckeridge, Herts.
Puddletown, Dorset.
Pulborough, Sussex West.
Pulloxhill, Beds.
Purley, Surrey.
Pwllheli, Gwynedd, Wales.

Q

Queen Camel, Somerset.
Queniborough, Leics.
Quorn, Leics.

R

Radlett, Herts.
Rainford, Merseyside.
Rait, Scotland.
Ramsbury, Wilts.
Ramsey, Cambs.
Ramsey, I. of Man.
Ramsgate, Kent.
Ratcliffe-on-the-Wreake, Leics.
Raveningham, Norfolk.
Ravensmoor, Cheshire.
Ravenstonedale, Cumbria.
Rayleigh, Essex.
Reading, Berks.
Redbourn, Herts.
Redditch, Herefs & Worcs.
Redhill, Surrey.
Redland, Avon.
Redruth, Cornwall.
Reepham, Norfolk.
Reigate, Surrey.
Rettendon, Essex.

Reymerston, Norfolk.
Rhos-on-Sea, Clwyd, Wales.
Rhosneigr, Gwynedd, Wales.
Rhuallt, Clwyd, Wales.
Richmond, Surrey.
Richmond, Yorks. North.
Rickmansworth, Herts.
Ridgewell, Essex.
Ringway, Cheshire.
Ringwood, Hants.
Ripley, Surrey.
Ripon, Yorks. North.
Risby, Suffolk.
Rishton, Lancs.
Riverhead, Kent.
Robertsbridge, Sussex East.
Rochdale, Lancs.
Rochester, Kent.
Rode, Somerset.
Rodley, Glos.
Rolvenden, Kent.
Romsey, Hants.
Romsley, West Mids.
Ross-on-Wye, Herefs & Worcs.
Rotherham, Yorks. South.
Rottingdean, Sussex East.
Roxwell, Essex.
Royston, Herts.
Ruddington, Notts.
Rudgwick, Sussex West.
Rugeley, Staffs.
Rumford, Cornwall.
Runfold, Surrey.
Rushden, Northants.
Ruskington, Lincs.
Ruthin, Clwyd, Wales.
Ryde, I. of Wight.
Rye, Sussex East.

S

Sabden, Lancs.
Saddleworth, Lancs.
Saffron Walden, Essex.
Salcombe, Devon.
Salisbury, Wilts.
Saltaire, Yorks. West.
Saltburn, Cleveland.
Saltcoats, Scotland.
Samlesbury, Lancs.
Sanderstead, Surrey.
Sandgate, Kent.
Sandhurst, Berks.
Sandhurst, Kent.
Sandwich, Kent.
Sarnau, Dyfed, Wales.
Sawbridgeworth, Herts.
Saxmundham, Suffolk.
Sayers Common, Sussex West.
Scarborough, Yorks. North.
Scarisbrick, Lancs.
Scarthingwell, Yorks. North.
Scarthoe, Humberside South.
Scone, Scotland.
Scratby, Norfolk.
Scunthorpe, Humberside South.
Seaford, Sussex East.

693   TOWNS AND VILLAGES

Seaton, Devon.
Seaton Ross, Humberside North.
Sedbergh, Cumbria.
Sedlescombe, Sussex East.
Selkirk, Scotland.
Semley, Wilts.
Settle, Yorks. North.
Sevenoaks, Kent.
Shaftesbury, Dorset.
Shaldon, Devon.
Shanklin, I. of Wight.
Shapwick, Somerset.
Shardlow, Derbys.
Sharrington, Norfolk.
Shawforth, Lancs.
Sheerness, Kent.
Sheffield, Yorks. South.
Shefford, Beds.
Shenfield, Essex.
Shenton, Leics.
Shepperton, Surrey.
Shepshed, Leics.
Sherborne, Dorset.
Shere, Surrey.
Sheringham, Norfolk.
Shipley, Yorks. West.
Shipston-on-Stour, Warks.
Shirley, Surrey.
Shoreham, Kent.
Shoreham-by-Sea, Sussex West.
Shottermill, Surrey.
Shrewsbury, Shrops.
Sible Hedingham, Essex.
Siddington, Cheshire.
Sidmouth, Devon.
Sileby, Leics.
Skegness, Lincs.
Skipton, Yorks. North.
Slad, Glos.
Sleaford, Lincs.
Smeeth, Kent.
Smethwick, West Mids.
Snainton, Yorks. North.
Snape, Suffolk.
Snodland, Kent.
Solihull, West Mids.
Somerton, Somerset.
Sonning-on-Thames, Berks.
Sorbie, Scotland.
South Brent, Devon.
South Cave, Humberside North.
South Harting, Sussex West.
South Lopham, Norfolk.
South Molton, Devon.
South Shields, Tyne & Wear.
South Walsham, Norfolk.
Southampton, Hants.
Southborough, Kent.
Southend-on-Sea, Essex.
Southoe, Cambs.
Southport, Merseyside.
Southwell, Notts.
Southwold, Suffolk.
Sowerby Bridge, Yorks. West.
Spalding, Lincs.

Spennithorne, Yorks. North.
Spilsby, Lincs.
St. Agnes, Cornwall.
St. Albans, Herts.
St. Andrews, Scotland.
St. Annes-on-Sea, Lancs.
St. Austell, Cornwall.
St. Gerrans, Cornwall.
St. Helens, I. of Wight.
St. Helier, Jersey, C.I.
St. Ives, Cambs.
St. Ives, Cornwall.
St. Lawrence, Jersey, C.I.
St. Leonards-on-Sea, Sussex East.
St. Margaret's Bay, Kent.
St. Martin, Guernsey, C.I.
St. Neots, Cambs.
St. Peter Port, Guernsey, C.I.
St. Sampson, Guernsey, C.I.
Stafford, Staffs.
Staines, Surrey.
Stalham, Norfolk.
Stamford, Lincs.
Standlake, Oxon.
Stanford Dingley, Berks.
Stanford-le-Hope, Essex.
Stansted, Essex.
Stanton, Shrops.
Stapleford, Lincs.
Staunton Harold, Leics.
Steeple Claydon, Bucks.
Steepmarsh, Hants.
Steeton, Yorks. West.
Steyning, Sussex West.
Stickford, Lincs.
Stickney, Lincs.
Stiffkey, Norfolk.
Stillington, Yorks. North.
Stirling, Scotland.
Stock, Essex.
Stockbridge, Hants.
Stockbury, Kent.
Stockland, Devon.
Stockport, Cheshire.
Stockton Heath, Cheshire.
Stoke Ferry, Norfolk.
Stoke-on-Trent, Staffs.
Stokenchurch, Bucks.
Stokesley, Yorks. North.
Storrington, Sussex West.
Stourbridge, West Mids.
Stow-on-the-Wold, Glos.
Stowmarket, Suffolk.
Strachan, Scotland.
Stradbroke, Suffolk.
Stratford-upon-Avon, Warks.
Strathblane, Scotland.
Streatley, Berks.
Streetly, West Mids.
Stretton, Cheshire.
Stretton-on-Fosse, Warks.
Stroud, Glos.
Studley, Warks.
Sturminster Newton, Dorset.
Suckley, Herefs. and Worcs.
Sudbury, Suffolk.
Suffield, Norfolk.

Sunderland, Tyne & Wear.
Sundridge, Kent.
Sunninghill, Berks.
Surbiton, Surrey.
Sutton, Surrey.
Sutton Bridge, Lincs.
Sutton Coldfield, West Mids.
Sutton Valence, Kent.
Sutton-on-Sea, Lincs.
Swaffham, Norfolk.
Swaffham Prior, Cambs.
Swafield, Norfolk.
Swanage, Dorset.
Swansea, Mid-Glam., Wales.
Swindon, Wilts.
Swinton, Lancs.
Synod Inn, Dyfed, Wales.

T

Taddington, Glos.
Tamworth, Staffs.
Tarporley, Cheshire.
Tarvin, Cheshire.
Tarvin Sands, Cheshire.
Tattenhall, Cheshire.
Tattershall, Lincs.
Taunton, Somerset.
Tavistock, Devon.
Teddington, Middx.
Teignmouth, Devon.
Telford, Shrops.
Templecombe, Somerset.
Tenby, Dyfed, Wales.
Tenterden, Kent.
Tern Hill, Shrops.
Tetbury, Glos.
Tewkesbury, Glos.
Teynham, Kent.
Thame, Oxon.
Thames Ditton, Surrey.
Thatcham, Berks.
Thaxted, Essex.
Thirsk, Yorks. North.
Thorne, Yorks. South.
Thorne St. Margaret, Somerset.
Thornhill, Scotland.
Thornton Heath, Surrey.
Thornton le Dale, Yorks. North.
Thrapston, Northants.
Thundersley, Essex.
Thurso, Scotland.
Ticknall, Derbys.
Tillington, Sussex West.
Tilston, Cheshire.
Timberscombe, Somerset.
Tingewick, Bucks.
Tintern, Gwent, Wales.
Tisbury, Wilts.
Titchfield, Hants.
Tiverton, Devon.
Tockwith, Yorks. North.
Toddington, Beds.
Todmorden, Yorks. West.
Tonbridge, Kent.
Tonge, Leics.

TOWNS AND VILLAGES

Tongham, Surrey.
Topsham, Devon.
Torquay, Devon.
Totnes, Devon.
Towcester, Northants.
Trawden, Lancs.
Tredunnock, Gwent, Wales.
Tregony, Cornwall.
Treherbert, Mid. Glam., Wales.
Trent, Dorset.
Treorchy, Mid. Glam., Wales.
Tring, Herts.
Troon, Scotland.
Truro, Cornwall.
Tunbridge Wells, Kent.
Turvey, Beds.
Tutbury, Staffs.
Tuxford, Notts.
Twickenham, Middx.
Twyford, Bucks.
Twyford, Hants.
Tynemouth, Tyne & Wear.
Tywyn, Gwynedd, Wales.

U

Uckfield, Sussex East.
Ulverston, Cumbria.
Upham, Hants.
Upminster, Essex.
Upper Largo, Scotland.
Uppermill, Lancs.
Uppingham, Leics.
Upton-upon-Severn, Herefs & Worcs.
Usk, Gwent, Wales
Uttoxeter, Staffs.
Uxbridge, Middx.

V

Vale, Guernsey, C.I.
Ventnor, I. of Wight.

W

Waddesdon, Bucks.
Wadebridge, Cornwall.
Wadhurst, Sussex East.
Wakefield, Yorks. West.
Walford, Herefs & Worcs.
Walkerburn, Scotland.
Wallasey, Merseyside.
Wallingford, Oxon.
Wallington, Surrey.
Walsall, West Mids.
Walsden, Yorks. West.
Walton-on-Thames, Surrey.
Walton-on-the-Hill and Tadworth, Surrey.
Wansford, Cambs.
Wanstrow, Somerset.
Warboys, Cambs.
Wareham, Dorset.
Wareside, Herts.
Warfield, Berks.
Wargrave, Berks.
Warminster, Wilts.
Warrenpoint, Co. Down, N.Ireland.

Warrington, Cheshire.
Warwick, Warks.
Washington, Sussex West.
Washington, Tyne & Wear.
Watchet, Somerset.
Watford, Herts.
Watlington, Oxon.
Watton, Norfolk.
Waverton, Cheshire.
Wedmore, Somerset.
Wednesbury, West Mids.
Weedon, Bucks.
Weedon, Northants.
Wellingborough, Northants.
Wellington, Somerset.
Wells, Somerset.
Wells-next-the-Sea, Norfolk.
Welshpool, Powys, Wales.
Wembley, Middx.
Wendover, Bucks.
West Auckland, Durham.
West Bridgford, Notts.
West Byfleet, Surrey.
West Haddon, Northants.
West Harptree, Avon.
West Kirby, Merseyside.
West Malling, Kent.
West Monkton, Somerset.
West Peckham, Kent.
West Wittering, Sussex West.
West Yatton, Wilts.
Westbourne, Sussex West.
Westbury, Wilts.
Westcliff-on-Sea, Essex.
Westcott, Surrey.
Westerham, Kent.
Weston, Staffs.
Weston-Super-Mare, Avon.
Wetherby, Yorks. West.
Weybridge, Surrey.
Weymouth, Dorset.
Whaley Bridge, Derbys.
Whalley, Lancs.
Wheathampstead, Herts.
Whissendine, Leics.
Whitby, Yorks. North.
Whitchurch, Bucks.
Whitchurch, Hants.
Whitchurch, Shrops.
Whitchurch-on-Thames, Oxon.
White Colne, Essex.
White Roding, Essex.
Whitefield, Lancs.
Whitegate, Cheshire.
Whitehaven, Cumbria.
Whitley Bay, Tyne & Wear.
Whitstable, Kent.
Whittington, Staffs.
Whitwell, Herts.
Whitwick, Leics.
Whixley, Yorks. North.
Wickham Market, Suffolk.
Widegates, Cornwall.
Wigan, Lancs.
Wigton, Cumbria.
Williton, Somerset.
Wilmslow, Cheshire.
Wilshamstead, Beds.

Wilstone, Herts.
Wilton, Wilts.
Wimborne Minster, Dorset.
Wincanton, Somerset.
Winchcombe, Glos.
Winchester, Hants.
Winchfield, Hants.
Windermere, Cumbria.
Windlesham, Surrey.
Windsor and Eton, Berks.
Winforton, Herefs & Worcs.
Wing, Leics.
Wingham, Kent.
Winslow, Bucks.
Winster, Derbys.
Winyates Green, Herefs & Worcs.
Wisbech, Cambs.
Witney, Oxon.
Wittersham, Kent.
Wiveliscombe, Somerset.
Woburn, Beds.
Woburn Sands, Bucks.
Woking, Surrey.
Wolseley Bridge, Staffs.
Wolverhampton, West Mids.
Woodbridge, Suffolk.
Woodbury, Devon.
Woodchurch, Kent.
Woodford Green, Essex.
Woodford Halse, Northants.
Woodhall Spa, Lincs.
Woodhouse Eaves, Leics.
Woodstock, Oxon.
Woodville, Derbys.
Woolacombe, Devon.
Wooler, Northumbs.
Woolhampton, Berks.
Woolpit, Suffolk.
Woore, Shrops.
Wootton Bassett, Wilts.
Worcester, Herefs & Worcs.
Wortham, Suffolk.
Worthing, Sussex West.
Wotton-under-Edge, Glos.
Wragby, Lincs.
Wraysbury, Berks.
Wrentham, Suffolk.
Wrington, Avon.
Wroughton, Wilts.
Wroxham, Norfolk.
Wymeswold, Leics.
Wymondham, Norfolk.

Y

Yarm, Cleveland.
Yarmouth, I. of Wight.
Yatton, Avon.
Yatton, Herefs & Worcs.
Yazor, Herefs & Worcs.
Yealand Conyers, Lancs.
Yealmpton, Devon.
Yeaveley, Derbys.
Yeovil, Somerset.
York, Yorks. North.
Yoxall, Staffs.
Yoxford, Suffolk.

DEALERS' INDEX

ALPHABETICAL LIST OF SHOPS AND DEALERS AND THE NAME OF THE TOWN AND COUNTY UNDER WHICH THEY APPEAR

In order to facilitate reference to dealers both the names of the dealers and their trade names are indexed separately, i.e. the name of their shop or business, as well as the towns and counties under which they are to be found. Thus A.E. Jones and C. Smith of High Street Antiques will be indexed under

Jones, A.E., Town, County
Smith, C., Town, County
and High Street Antiques, Town, County

There is a separate index to dealers who trade from markets and antiques centres and these are listed within this section, after the main index.

A

20th Century, Cambridge, Cambs.
20th Century Frocks, Lincoln, Lincs.
20th Century Gallery, London, SW6.
"27a" "27b", Bath, Avon.
3 L's Antiques, Eccleston, Lancs.
4 Miles Buildings, Bath, Avon.
(55) For Decorative Living, London, SW6.
139 Antiques, London, N16.
235 Antiques, Camberley, Surrey.
A. and C. Antiques, Sheffield, Yorks. South.
A.D.C. Heritage Ltd, London, W1.
A & D Antiques, Blandford Forum, Dorset.
A. and F. Partners, Faringdon, Oxon.
A.S. Antique Galleries, Manchester, Lancs.
A Thing of Beauty, Farnham Common, Bucks.
A-B Gallery, Salcombe, Devon.
A1A Antiques, Ulverston, Cumbria.
Aagaard Ltd, Robert, Knaresborough, Yorks. North.
Aalders, M. and E., London, W5.
Aaron Antiques, Morriston, West Glam., Wales.
Aaron Antiques, Snodland, Kent.
Aaron Antiques, Tunbridge Wells, Kent.
Aaron Gallery, London, W1.
Aaron (London)Ltd, Didier, London, SW1.
Aaron, M. and D., London, W1.
Aarquebus Antiques, St. Leonards-on-Sea, Sussex East.
Abacus Antiques, Maldon, Essex.
Abbas Antiques, Sherborne, Dorset.
Abbey Antique Shop, The, Whalley, Lancs.
Abbey Antiques, Glastonbury, Somerset.
Abbey Antiques, Hastings, Sussex East.
Abbey Antiques, Ickleton, Cambs.
Abbey Antiques, Market Harborough, Leics.
Abbey Antiques, Ramsey, Cambs.
Abbey Antiques, Stirling, Scotland.
Abbey Antiques, Tewkesbury, Glos.
Abbey Antiques, Tintern, Gwent, Wales.
Abbey Antiques and Fine Art, Hemel Hempstead, Herts.
Abbey Galleries, Bath, Avon.
Abbey House, Derby, Derbys.
Abbots House, Glastonbury, Somerset.
Abbott Antiques, East Molesey, Surrey.
Abbott Antiques, A., Ipswich, Suffolk.
Abbott Antiques and Country Pine (formerly Olwen Carthew), London, SE26.
Abbott, C. and A., Hartley Wintney, Hants.
Abbott, H., East Molesey, Surrey.
Abbott, H. and K., Bexhill-on-Sea, Sussex East.
Abbott and Holder, London, WC1.
Abbott, J.L., East Molesey, Surrey.
Abbott, Nicholas, Hartley Wintney, Hants.
Abbott, S. and R., Needham Market, Suffolk.
Aberdeen House Antiques, London, W5.
Aberford Antiques Ltd, Aberford, Yorks. West.
Abinger Bazaar, Abinger Hammer, Surrey.
Abington Books, Little Abington, Cambs.
Abode, Stratford-upon-Avon, Warks.
Abrahams Books, Mike, Lichfield, Staffs.
Abridge Antique Centre, Abridge, Essex.
Abstract Antiques, Manchester, Lancs.

Aby, R., Penzance, Cornwall.
Academy Billiard Antiques, West Byfleet, Surrey.
Acanthus Antiques, London, SW19.
Acanthus Art Ltd, London, SW11.
Acheson, N., Marlborough, Wilts.
Ackermann & Johnson , London, SW1.
Ackrill, B.D. and B.G., Tetbury, Glos.
Ackroyd, J.L., Godalming, Surrey.
Acorn Antiques, Bideford, Devon.
Acorn Antiques, Deganwy, Gwynedd, Wales.
Acorn Antiques, Dulverton, Somerset.
Acorn Antiques, London, SE21.
Acorn Antiques, Stow-on-the-Wold, Glos.
Acquisitions (Fireplaces) Ltd, London, NW1.
Adam, A., London, N1.
Adam Antiques, Burnham-on-Sea, Somerset.
Adams Antiques, Chester, Cheshire.
Adams Antiques, London, NW1.
Adams Antiques, Nantwich, Cheshire.
Adams, B. and T., Chester, Cheshire.
Adams, D., London, WC2.
Adam, D., Edenbridge, Kent.
Adams, G., Debenham, Suffolk.
Adam Gallery, Bath, Avon.
Adams Ltd, Norman, London, SW3.
Adams, N. and S., Lympsham, Somerset.
Adams, N.W. and S.M., Weston-Super-Mare, Avon.
Adams, Pat, Ipswich, Suffolk.
Adams Antiques, Rodney, Pwllheli, Gwynedd, Wales.
Adams Room Antiques, London, SW19.
Adams Bygones Shop, Tony, Ipswich, Suffolk.
Adams Antiques, Yvonne, Ashbourne, Derbys.
Adams, Mrs Y. S., Ashbourne, Derbys.
Adamson, Alexander, Kirkby Lonsdale, Cumbria.
Adamson Antique Stripped Pine, Joyce, Ministeracres, Northumbs.
Adamson Armoury, Skipton, Yorks. North.
Adamson, J.K., Skipton, Yorks. North.
Adamson, N.J.G., D. and P.A., Kirkby Lonsdale, Cumbria.
Addinall, M.T., Driffield, Humbers North.
Addison, D., Blackpool, Lancs.
Addison Fine Art, London, W11.
Addison Antiques, Michael, Purley, Surrey.
Addison, M. and N., Purley, Surrey.
Addison-Ross Gallery, London, SW1.
Addrison Bros, Windsor and Eton, Berks.
Addrison, Mr and Mrs, Windsor and Eton, Berks.
Adler, M. and L., Tunbridge Wells, Kent.
Adne and Naxos, Northampton, Northants.
Affordable Antiques, Portsmouth, Hants.
After Noah, London, N1.
Age of Elegance, London, SW14.
Ager, Adrian, Ashburton, Devon.
Ager-Harris, J.W. and R.E., Easingwold, Yorks. North.
Ages Ago Antiques, St. Agnes, Cornwall.
Agnew, A., London, W8.
Agnew's, London, W1.
Agnus, Clare, Suffolk.
Ahmed, A.H., Brighton, Sussex East.
Ahuan (UK) Ltd, London, SW1.
Aigin, C., Henley-on-Thames, Oxon.
Ailsa Gallery, Twickenham, Middx.

DEALERS' INDEX

Aindow, R. and A.O., Kendal, Cumbria.
Ainslie Antiques, Robert, Scone, Scotland.
Ainslie, T.S. and A., Perth, Scotland.
Ainslie's Antique Warehouse, Perth, Scotland.
Airdale Antiques, Hartley Wintney, Hants.
Aird-Gordon Antiques, Whitby, Yorks. North.
Aitken, Michael, Bodmin, Cornwall.
Aitken Dott plc,, Edinburgh, Scotland.
Al Mashreq Galleries, London, W8.
Aladdin's Cave, Freshwater, I. of Wight.
Aladdin's Cave, Grasmere, Cumbria.
Aladdin's Cave, Leeds, Yorks. West.
Alan Ltd, Adrian, London, W1.
Alaszewski, Barbara, Bromley, Kent.
Albany Antiques, Glasgow, Scotland.
Albany Antiques Ltd, Hindhead, Surrey.
Albert and Victoria, London, E4.
Alberts Cigarette Card Specialists, Twickenham, Middx.
Albion Antiques, Kettering, Northants.
Albion Antiques, Manchester, Lancs.
Albion Art (UK) Ltd, London, W2.
Albright, P., Stafford, Staffs.
Albrow, R., Norwich, Norfolk.
Albrow and Sons, Norwich, Norfolk.
Aldbrook, M., Twickenham, Middx.
Aldeburgh Galleries, Aldeburgh, Suffolk.
Alder, T.A., Codford, Wilts.
Alderley Antiques, Alderley Edge, Cheshire.
Aldersey Hall Ltd, Chester, Cheshire.
Alderson, Bath, Avon.
Alderson, C.J.R., Bath, Avon.
Aldred, L.J., Saffron Walden, Essex.
Aldridge, H. and L., Llandudno, Gwynedd, Wales.
Alexander Antiques, Cardiff, South Glam., Wales.
Alexander Antiques, Henfield, Sussex West.
Alexander Antiques, Portrush, Co. Antrim, N. Ireland.
Alexander and Berendt Ltd, London, W1.
Alexander Gallery, Bristol, Avon.
Alexander, Molly, Seaford, Sussex East.
Alexander, Mrs M. and D., Portrush, Co. Antrim, N. Ireland.
Alexander, Richard, Seaford, Sussex East.
Alexander-Forsyth, B., Fochabers, Scotland.
Alexandria Antiques, Brighton, Sussex East.
Alff, E.R., St. Leonards-on-Sea, Sussex East.
Alfies Antique Market, London, NW8.
Alfred's "Old Curiosity Shop" and The Morris Gallery (Fine Art Dealer/Valuer), Mr., Southampton, Hants.
Alfriston Antiques, Alfriston, Sussex East.
Ali, S., London, SW6.
Alice's, London, W11.
Alice's Antiques, Llanelli, Dyfed, Wales.
All In One Antiques, London, NW8.
All Our Yesterdays, Glasgow, Scotland.
All Our Yesterdays of Lytham, Lytham St. Annes, Lancs.
All Our Yesterdays Rural Bygones, Holbeach, Lincs.
Allan, C., Cheadle Hulme, Cheshire.
Allan, James, Swansea, West Glam., Wales.
Allan, S.J., Swansea, West Glam., Wales.
Allan's Antiques and Reproductions, Cheadle Hulme, Cheshire.
Allanton Antiques, Auldgirth, Scotland.
Allchin Antiques, William, Norwich, Norfolk.
Allcock, J. and P., Alcester, Warks.
Allen Antiques Ltd. World Wide Antique Exporters, Peter, London, SE15.
Allen, A.P., Lytham, Lancs.
Allen & Co. (The Horseman's Bookshop) Ltd., J. A., London, SW1.
Allen, F.J. and G.J., Tutbury, Staffs.
Allen Watch and Clockmaker, M., Four Oaks, West Mids.
Allcroft Antiques, Michael, Hayfield, Derbys.
Allen Gallery, The, Kenilworth, Warks.
Allen, Mrs C.L., Garstang, Lancs.
Allen, M.A., Four Oaks, West Mids.
Allen, N.P., Kenilworth, Warks.
Allen, P.L., Chertsey, Surrey.
Allens Antiques, Stapleford, Lincs.
Allen's (Branksome) Ltd, Branksome, Dorset.
Allin, P., Cowbridge, South Glam., Wales.
Allison, P. and P., Hull, N. Humbs.
Allison, Paul, Preston, Lancs.
Allnutt Antiques, Topsham, Devon.

Allom and Co. Ltd, P.G., Ramsey, I. of Man.
Allport-Lomax, Liz, Coltishall, Norfolk.
Allsop, Duncan M., Warwick, Warks.
Allsopp Antiques, John, London, SW1.
Alma Antiques, Lindfield, Sussex West.
Alma Street Warehouse, Worcester, Herefs. & Worcs.
Almshouses Arcade, Chichester, Sussex West.
Alpren, S.A., Solihull, West Mids.
Alps, R. and V., Westcliff-on-Sea, Essex.
Alston, E., Hexham, Northumbs.
Alston, R.P., Long Melford, Suffolk.
Alton Gallery, London, SW13.
Altrincham Antiques, Altrincham, Cheshire.
Alvarino, E.A., Fairlie, Scotland.
Alverstoke Antiques, Alverstoke, Hants.
Alway Fine Art, Marian and John, Datchet, Berks.
Always Antiques, Birmingham, West Mids.
Amadeus Antiques, Tunbridge Wells, Kent.
Amati, E., London, SW1.
Amazing Grates, London, N2.
Ambassador House, Swinton, Lancs.
Amber Antiques, Kincardine O'Neil, Scotland.
Ambler, A.S., Otley, Yorks. West.
Amell Ltd, Verner, London, SW1.
Amend Antiques, Stokenchurch, Bucks.
Amend, B., Stokenchurch, Bucks.
Amersham Antiques and Collectors Centre, Amersham, Bucks.
Amherst Antiques, Riverhead, Kent.
Amini - Persian Carpet Gallery, Majid, Petworth, Sussex West.
Amman Antiques, Ammanford, Dyfed, Wales.
Amor Ltd, Albert, London, SW1.
Amor, M., Princes Risborough, Bucks.
Amos Antiques, Joan, Salisbury, Wilts.
Amos, Mrs R., Rolvenden, Kent.
Amos, Richard, Folkestone, Kent.
Amos Antiques, Tony, Portsmouth, Hants.
Amphora Galleries, Balfron, Scotland.
Amphora Galleries, Buchlyvie, Scotland.
Ampthill Antiques, Ampthill, Beds.
Ampthill Emporium, Ampthill, Beds.
Amstad, R.J., St. Leonards-on-Sea, Sussex East.
Anchor Antiques Ltd, London, WC2.
Anchor, S., London, NW1.
Anchor, S., London, WC2.
Ancient and Modern, Blackburn, Lancs.
Ancient & Modern, Headington, Oxon.
Ancient and Modern, St. Austell, Cornwall.
Ancient and Modern Bookshop (including Garret's Antiques), Blandford Forum, Dorset.
Ancient Manor House, The, Barnard Castle, Durham.
And So To Bed, Keswick, Cumbria.
And So To Bed Limited, London, SW6.
Anderman, S., East Molesey, Surrey.
Andersen, G. and V., London, W8.
Anderson, K, Mr and Mrs A., Bath, Avon.
Anderson, C.W., Paisley, Scotland.
Anderson, D. and I., Welshpool, Powys, Wales.
Anderson and Son, F.E., Welshpool, Powys, Wales.
Anderson, I.G., Dumfries, Scotland.
Andersons, Southport, Merseyside.
Anderton, K. and J., Darwen, Lancs.
Andipa Icon Gallery, Maria, London, SW3.
Andrade, Philip, South Brent, Devon.
Andreae, E.J., Hartley Wintney, Hants.
Andrew, T., Bangor, Gwynedd, Wales.
Andrew, Tony, Llanerchymedd, Gwynedd, Wales.
Andrews Antiques, Michael, Bournemouth, Dorset.
Andrews Antiques, Michael, Milford, Surrey.
Andrews, Meg, Harpenden, Herts.
Andrews, R., Finedon, Northants.
Andrews, R. G., Tunbridge Wells, Kent.
Andwells, Hartley Wintney, Hants.
Andy's All Pine, London, W14.
Angel Arcade, London, N1.
Angela Antiques, Chester, Cheshire.
Anglia Antique Exporters, North Walsham, Norfolk.
Anglo Persian Carpet Co, London, SW7.
Angus Antiques, Dundee, Scotland.
Anita's Holme Antiques, Sheffield, Yorks. South.
Annal, E. and M., Glossop, Derbys.

DEALERS' INDEX

Annesley, F., London, N1.
Anness, A. and A., Cambridge, Cambs.
Annette Antiques, Lincoln, Lincs.
Annexe Antiques, Tunbridge Wells, Kent.
Annick Antiques, Kimpton, Herts.
Annie's Antique Clothes, London, N1.
Anno Domini Antiques, London, SW1.
Ann's Antiques, Stoke-on-Trent, Staffs.
Annie's Antiques, Farnham, Surrey.
Annies, Cooden, Sussex East.
Annterior Antiques, Plymouth, Devon.
Ann-tiquities, Harrogate, Yorks. North.
Annteaks, Abersoch, Gwynedd, Wales.
Another Time, Another Place, Edinburgh, Scotland.
Another World, Edinburgh, Scotland.
Anthemion - The Antique Shop, Cartmel, Cumbria.
Antica, Bromley, Kent.
Antica, Orpington, Kent.
Antichi, G., London, W11.
Antics, Cobham, Surrey.
Antiquarian, The, Dumfries, Scotland.
Antiquaries Antique Centre, Dorking, Surrey.
Antiquarius, London, SW3.
Antiquatat Antiques, Wimborne Minster, Dorset.
Antique Architecture and Furniture, Tiverton, Devon.
Antique and Art, The, Northallerton, Yorks. North.
Antique Atlas, The, East Grinstead, Sussex West.
Antique Bed Shop, Halstead, Essex.
Antique Beds, Bristol, Avon.
Antique and Book Collector, The, Marlborough, Wilts.
Antique Carpets Gallery, London, SW6.
Antique Centre, The, Kinver, Staffs.
Antique Centre, Moreton-in-Marsh, Glos.
Antique Centre, The, Preston, Lancs.
Antique Centre, The, Bournemouth, Dorset.
Antique Centre, The, Huntingdon, Cambs.
Antique Centre Abingdon House, The, Honiton, Devon.
Antique Centre and Collectors Market, Adversane, Sussex West.
Antique Centre on the Quay, The, Exeter, Devon.
Antique City, London, E17.
Antique and Collectors Market, Hemel Hempstead, Herts.
Antique Clock Repair Shoppe, Gants Hill, Essex.
Antique Clocks, Harston, Cambs.
Antique Clocks by Simon Charles, Long Melford, Suffolk.
Antique Clocks by Simon Charles, Sudbury, Suffolk.
Antique Coffee Pot, Long Buckby, Northants.
Antique and Collectors Market, Salisbury, Wilts.
Antique Corner, Ludlow, Shrops.
Antique and Country Pine, Crewkerne, Somerset.
Antique and Design, Canterbury, Kent.
Antique Dolls, Blackpool, Lancs.
Antique Emporium, The, Swansea, West Glam., Wales.
Antique Exchange, The, Leeds, Yorks. West.
Antique Exporters of Chester, Chester, Cheshire.
Antique Exporters U.K, Brailsford, Derbys.
Antique Fireplace Centre, Hartlepool, Cleveland.
Antique Fireplace Centre, Plymouth, Devon.
Antique Fireplaces, Manchester, Lancs.
Antique Fireplaces and Furniture, Tarvin, Cheshire.
Antique Forum Ltd, Cirencester, Glos.
Antique Forum Ltd, Newcastle-under-Lyme, Staffs.
Antique Forum (Birmingham) Ltd,, Birmingham, West Mids.
Antique Furniture Warehouse, Stockport, Cheshire.
Antique Furniture Warehouse, Woodbridge, Suffolk.
Antique Galleries, The, Paulerspury, Northants.
Antique Heritage, Chipping Campden, Glos.
Antique Home, The, London, W8.
Antique House, Hartley Wintney, Hants.
Antique Interiors, Tetbury, Glos.
Antique Linens and Lace, Bath, Avon.
Antique Map and Bookshop, Puddletown, Dorset.
Antique Map and Print Gallery, Worcester, Herefs. and Worcs.
Antique Market, Newcastle-under-Lyme, Staffs.
Antique Market, Sherborne, Dorset.
Antique Mart, Richmond, Surrey.
Antique Metals, Coggeshall, Essex.
Antique Mews, The, London, SW19.
Antique Militaria, Bridlington, N. Humbs.
Antique and Modern Furniture Ltd, London, SW5.
Antique Parlour, The, Hessle, N. Humbs.

Antique Pine, Coggeshall, Essex.
Antique Pine, Norton, Glos.
Antique Pine Shop, The, Tunbridge Wells, Kent.
Antique Print Shop, The, East Grinstead, Sussex West.
Antique and Reproduction Clocks, Preston, Lancs.
Antique Restoration Studio, The, Stafford, Staffs.
Antique Rooms, The, Maldon, Essex.
Antique Shop, Ballyclare, Co. Antrim, N. Ireland.
Antique Shop, The, Berkeley, Glos.
Antique Shop, The, Blaenau Ffestiniog, Gwynedd, Wales.
Antique Shop, The, Bournemouth, Dorset.
Antique Shop, The, Chester, Cheshire.
Antique Shop, Chichester, Sussex West.
Antique Shop, The, Coventry, West Mids.
Antique Shop, The, Edenfield, Lancs.
Antique Shop, The, Greyabbey, Co. Down, N. Ireland.
Antique Shop, The, Langholm, Scotland.
Antique Shop, The, Lichfield, Staffs.
Antique Shop, The, Llandudno, Gwynedd, Wales.
Antique Shop, The, Milnthorpe, Cumbria.
Antique Shop, The, Newtonmore, Scotland.
Antique Shop, The, Oswestry, Shrops.
Antique Shop (Valantique), The, London, N2.
Antique Trader, The, London, N1.
Antique Warehouse, London, SE1.
Antique Warehouse, London, SE8.
Antique Warehouse, Marlesford, Suffolk.
Antique Warehouse, The, Warminster, Wilts.
Antique Warehouse, Worcester, Herefs. & Worcs.
Antiques, Barrow-in-Furness, Cumbria.
Antiques, Ayr, Scotland.
Antiques, Carshalton, Surrey.
Antiques, Edinburgh, Scotland.
Antiques, Lavenham, Suffolk.
Antiques, Marazion, Cornwall.
Antiques, Menston, Yorks. West.
Antiques, West Haddon, Northants.
Antiques 132, London, W4.
Antiques and All Pine, Swindon, Wilts.
Antiques Arcade, Richmond, Surrey.
Antiques Arcade, The, East Molesey, Surrey.
Antiques at Budleigh House, East Budleigh, Devon.
Antiques at Forge Cottage (Inc. Castleberg Antiques) formerly of Settle, Gargrave, Yorks. North.
Antiques at Wendover, Wendover, Bucks.
Antiques and Bedsteads, Brighton, Sussex East.
Antiques and Bric-a-Brac Market, Wellingborough, Northants.
Antiques & Bygones, Bankfoot, Scotland.
Antiques Centre, The, Bidford-on-Avon, Warks.
Antiques Centre, The, Guildford, Surrey.
Antiques Centre, Newcastle-upon-Tyne, Tyne and Wear.
Antiques Centre, Oxted, Surrey.
Antiques Centre, The, Sevenoaks, Kent.
Antiques (Cheltenham), Cheltenham, Glos.
Antiques and Collectables, Harrogate, Yorks. North.
Antiques Complex, The, Leicester, Leics.
Antiques and Country Things, Saxmundham, Suffolk.
Antiques and Curios, Ravensmoor, Cheshire.
Antiques and Curios, Worcester, Herefs. & Worcs.
Antiques and Furnishings, Bournemouth, Dorset.
Antiques Emporium, The, Tetbury, Glos.
Antiques Etc., Stretton, Cheshire.
Antiques Etcetera, Lechlade, Glos.
Antiques Etcetera, Sandgate, Kent.
Antiques Fair, Glastonbury, Somerset.
Antiques and Fine Art, Crieff, Scotland.
Antiques and Fine Art Gallery, Warrenpoint, Co. Down, N. Ireland.
Antiques for All, Glossop, Derbys.
Antiques and General Trading Co, Nottingham, Notts.
Antiques and Gifts, Aberdour, Scotland.
Antiques and Interior Design, Fochabers, Scotland.
Antiques and Interiors (Victoriana), Worcester, Herefs. and Worcs.
Antiques Market, Glastonbury, Somerset.
Antiques Market, Hay-on-Wye, Powys, Wales.
Antiques and Nice Things, Havant, Hants.
Antiques and Objets d'Art of Leek, Leek, Staffs.
Antiques of Ascot, Sunninghill, Berks.
Antiques of Newport, Newport, Gwent, Wales.
Antiques of Penrith, Penrith, Cumbria.

DEALERS' INDEX

Antiques of Sherborne, Sherborne, Dorset.
Antiques on the Square, Church Stretton, Shrops.
Antiques Pavilion, The, London, SE1.
Antiques - Rene Nicholls, Malmesbury, Wilts.
Antiques - Sheila White, Camberley, Surrey.
Antiques Shop, The, Whitegate, Cheshire.
Antiques and Things, Haddington, Scotland.
Antiques and Things, London, SW11.
Antiques & Things, Pickering, Yorks. North.
Antiques Trade Warehouse, Rettendon, Essex.
Antiques Village, Manchester, Lancs.
Antiques Warehouse, The, Buxton, Derbys.
Antiques Warehouse, Framlingham, Suffolk.
Antiques Warehouse, Kettering, Northants.
Antiques Warehouse, Mansfield, Notts.
Antiques Warehouse (Uxbridge), Uxbridge, Middx.
Antiques Workshop and Boulton's Antiques, Stoke-on-Trent, Staffs.
Antiquités, London, SW1.
Antiquities, Chatham, Kent.
Antiquities, Wolverhampton, West Mids.
Antiquus, London, SW1.
Antiquus, Windsor and Eton, Berks.
Antonini, G. and F.M., Birkenhead, Merseyside.
Antonucci, M., Plymouth, Devon.
Antrobus Ltd, Philip, London, W1.
Anvil Antiques, Leek, Staffs.
Apple Market Stalls, London, WC2.
Appleby, I.G. and Mrs C.B.V., St. Lawrence, Jersey, C.I.
Appleby, J.H., St. Helier, Jersey, C.I.
Appleby, K., Chester, Cheshire.
Appleton, E., London, SW13.
Appleyard Ltd, Roger, Rotherham, Yorks. South.
Applin Antiques, Jess, Cambridge, Cambs.
Apollo Antiques Ltd, Warwick, Warks.
Apollo Galleries, Westerham, Kent.
Apter, B.and Mrs. C, London, SW3.
Apter Fredericks Ltd, London, SW3.
Apter, H., London, SW3.
Aquarius Antiques, Buxton, Derbys.
Arbiter, Wallasey, Merseyside.
Arbour Antiques Ltd, Stratford-upon-Avon, Warks.
Arbras Gallery, London, W11.
Arcade Antiques and Jewellery, Penrith, Cumbria.
Arcadia Antiques, Southport, Merseyside.
Archer, Mrs M., Bewdley, Herefs. and Worcs.
Archer, R.G., Lavenham, Suffolk.
Architectural Antiques, Liverpool, Merseyside.
Architectural Antiques, London, W6.
Architectural Antiques, South Molton, Devon.
Architectural Antiques and Interiors, Ludlow, Shrops.
Architectural Antiques of Moseley, Birmingham, West Mids.
Architectural Heritage, Taddington, Glos.
Architectural Heritage of Northants, Weedon, Northants.
Archives, Birmingham, West Mids.
Arden Antiques, Brenda, Tarporley, Cheshire.
Arden Gallery, Henley-in-Arden, Warks.
Ardersier Antiques, Ardersier, Scotland.
Arditti, A. and J.L., Christchurch, Dorset.
Arditti, J.L., Christchurch, Dorset.
Arena, Devizes, Wilts.
Argentum Antiques, Bexley, Kent.
Argyll Etkin Gallery, London, W1.
Argyll Etkin Ltd, London, W1.
Argyll House Antiques, Felsted, Essex.
Arieta, Valerie, London, W8.
Arkea Antiques, Bath, Avon.
Arkinstall, B. and B., Stoke-on-Trent, Staffs.
Armada Gallery, Plymouth, Devon.
Armelin Antiques, Karin, London, SW6.
Armett, C.H., Burton-on-Trent, Staffs.
Armitage, Mrs M., Chester, Cheshire.
Armitage, Tim, Nantwich, Cheshire.
Armitage, T.J., Nantwich, Cheshire.
Armour-Winston Ltd, London, W1.
Armoury of St. James's Military Antiquarians, The, London, SW1.
Armson, F.R.B. and P.K., Yoxall, Staffs.
Armson (Antiques) Ltd, Michael, Wilstone, Herts.
Armson's of Yoxall Antiques, Yoxall, Staffs.
Armstrong, Harrogate, Yorks. North.
Armstrong, J. and G., Middleham, Yorks. North.

Armstrong, M.A. and C.J., Harrogate, Yorks. North.
Armstrong-Davis Gallery, Arundel, Sussex West.
Armytage, Julian, Crewkerne, Somerset.
Arnold Gallery Antiques, Phyllis, Greyabbey, Co. Down, N. Ireland.
Arnold, Roy, Needham Market, Suffolk.
Arnold, R., Richmond, Surrey.
Arnold, Sean, London, W1.
Arnold-Brown, A.S. and J.L., Salcombe, Devon.
Art Deco Ceramics, Stratford-upon-Avon, Warks.
Art Deco Etc., Brighton, Sussex East.
Art Furniture (London) Ltd, London, NW1.
Artavia Gallery, Barnstaple, Devon.
Artbry's Antiques, Pinner, Middx.
Artemesia, Alresford, Hants.
Artemis Fine Arts Limited, London, SW1.
Arthy, David, Sandwich, Kent.
Articles Antiques, Lancaster, Lancs.
Artist Gallery, The, Bournemouth, Dorset.
Arundel Coins Ltd, Blackpool, Lancs.
Arwas, V., London, W1.
As Time Goes By Antique and Tower Clocks, Buxton, Norfolk.
Asbury Antiques, Peter, Birmingham, West Mids.
Ash House, Ramsgate, Kent.
Ash Rare Books, London, EC3.
Ash Tree Antiques, Halesworth, Suffolk.
Ash, Jim and Pat, Llandeilo, Dyfed, Wales.
Ashbourne Fine Art, Ashbourne, Derbys.
Ashbrook Antiques, Ken, Penzance, Cornwall.
Ashburton Marbles, Ashburton, Devon.
Ashcroft, Nan S., London, NW3.
Ashleigh House Antiques, Birmingham, West Mids.
Ashley Antiques, Hungerford, Berks.
Ashley Antiques, Ipswich, Suffolk.
Ashley Antiques, Parkstone, Dorset.
Ashley, Carole, Market Rasen, Lincs.
Ashley Gallery, Long Melford, Suffolk.
Ashley House Antiques, Measham, Leics.
Ashton Dodkin Antiques, Stow-on-the-Wold, Glos.
Ashton Gower Antiques, Burford, Oxon.
Ashton, John, Bristol, Avon.
Ashton, K., Gants Hill, Essex.
Ashton, M. and C., Birmingham, West Mids.
Ashton, R., Brighton, Sussex East.
Ashton, Robert, Stow-on-the-Wold, Glos.
Ashton's Antiques, Brighton, Sussex East.
Aspidistra, Bath, Avon.
Aspinall Antiques, Walter, Sabden, Lancs.
Aspley, J., Leek, Staffs.
Aspley Antiques and Reproductions Ltd., Barmouth, Gwynedd, Wales.
Aspleys Antiques and Reproductions Ltd, Leek, Staffs.
Asplund Fine Art, Jenny, Esher, Surrey.
Asprey Ltd, Maurice, London, SW1.
Asprey plc, London, W1.
Assembly Rooms Market, The, Lancaster, Lancs.
Asta, J. and V., Long Crendon, Bucks.
Astarte Gallery, London, W1.
Astill, P.H.K., Nottingham, Notts.
Astley House - Fine Art, Moreton-in-Marsh, Glos.
Astley House - Fine Art, Stretton-on-Fosse, Warks.
Astleys, London, W1.
Aston, C.D. and Mrs I., Fordingbridge, Hants.
At the Sign of the Chest of Drawers, London, N1.
Atfield, D.A. and Miss S.F., Ipswich, Suffolk.
Atfield and Daughter, Ipswich, Suffolk.
Atholl Antiques, Aberdeen, Scotland.
Atholl Antiques, Perth, Scotland.
Atkin, Miss D.J., Nantwich, Cheshire.
Atkins, Garry, London, W8.
Atkins, Garry and Julie, London, W8.
Atkins, T., Taunton, Somerset.
Atkinson, G. and J., Thurso, Scotland.
Atkinson Antiques, Keith, East Grinstead, Sussex West.
Atkinson, P. and A., Dorking, Surrey.
Atkinson, P.and A., Ockley, Surrey.
Atlantic Antiques Centres Ltd, London, W1.
Atlantic Antiques Centres Ltd, London, N1.
Atlantic Antiques Centres Ltd, London, SW3.
Atlantic Bay Carpets, London, W1.
Atlantis Bookshop, London, WC1.

DEALERS' INDEX

Atrium Antiques, Guisborough, Cleveland.
Atterby, Mrs J., Grantham, Lincs.
Attic, The, Baldock, Herts.
Attic, The, Brasted, Kent.
Attic, The, Grantham, Lincs.
Attic, The, Inverness, Scotland.
Attic, The, Newton Abbot, Devon.
Attic Antiques, Brighton, Sussex East.
Attic Gallery, Wisbech, Cambs.
Atwell, B., South Molton, Devon.
Au Temps Perdu, Bristol, Avon.
Audley House Antiques, Osbournby, Lincs.
Auld, C.J., Greyabbey, Co. Down, N. Ireland.
Auld, Ian, London, N1.
Auldearn Antiques, Auldearn, Scotland.
Aura Antiques, Masham, Yorks. North.
Aust, B., London, SE20.
Austen, Mrs R.A., Basingstoke, Hants.
Austen, S.T. and R.J., Leigh-on-Sea, Essex.
Austin, A.D. and E., Whalley, Lancs.
Austin, A., D. and V., London, SE15.
Austin, G., Winchester, Hants.
Austin and Sons Ltd, G., London, SE15.
Austin, J., London, WC1.
Austin, S., Swindon, Wilts.
Austin/Desmond & Phipps, London, WC1.
Austin-Kaye, A.M., Chester, Cheshire.
Austwick, P. and L., Sowerby Bridge, Yorks. West.
Authentiques, Manchester, Lancs.
Avalon Post Card and Stamp Shop, Chester, Cheshire.
Averbuch, Mrs A., Edinburgh, Scotland.
Avery Interiors, Allen, Haslemere, Surrey.
Avery, Mrs E.B., Chiddingstone, Kent.
Avon Antiques, Bradford-on-Avon, Wilts.
Avon Gallery, The, Moreton-in-Marsh, Glos.
Avon House Antiques/Hayward's Antiques, Kingsbridge, Devon.
Avonbridge Antiques and Collectors Market, The, Salisbury, Wilts.
Axia Art Consultants Ltd, London, W11.
Ayres, L., Wansford, Cambs.

B

B. B. Antiques, Greyabbey, Co. Down, N. Ireland.
B. and B Antiques, Stickney, Lincs.
B.B.M. Jewellery and Antiques, Kidderminster, Herefs. and Worcs.
B.R.M. Coins, Knutsford, Cheshire.
B.S. Antiques, East Molesey, Surrey.
B. and T. Antiques, London, W11.
Bacchus, Douglas, I. of Man.
Bacchus Antiques -In the Service of Wine, Cartmel, Cumbria.
Bacchus Gallery, The, Petworth, Sussex West.
Bach Antiques, Lane End, Bucks.
Back to the Wood, Cardiff, South Glam., Wales.
Baddow Antique and Craft Centre, Great Baddow, Essex.
Badger, The, London, W5.
Badger Antiques, Colchester, Essex.
Badgers Antiques, London, SE10.
Badland, Miss, Bradford, Yorks. West.
Badman, J.A., Glastonbury, Somerset.
Bagatelle, Woodbridge, Suffolk.
Baggins Book Bazaar, Rochester, Kent.
Baggott Church Street Ltd, Stow-on-the-Wold, Glos.
Baggott, Duncan J., Stow-on-the-Wold, Glos.
Baggott, D.J. and C.M., Stow-on-the-Wold, Glos.
Bagley, B., Brighton, Sussex East.
Bagnall, W., Moretonhampstead, Devon.
Bagshaw Antiques, G., Siddington, Cheshire.
Bagshawe, N., London, SW3.
Bail, A., Ash Vale, Surrey.
Baile de Laperriere, H., Calne, Wilts.
Bailey, Avril, Warminster, Wilts.
Bailey, E., Milford, Surrey.
Bailey, Elizabeth, Beeston, Notts.
Bailey, Eric, Milford, Surrey.
Bailey Antique Clocks, John, Althorne, Essex.
Bailey, M. and S., Ross-on-Wye, Herefs. and Worcs.
Bailey, R.M., Ongar, Essex.
Bailey Oriental Rugs, Robert, Ongar, Essex.
Bailey's Quality Antique Lighting and Accessories, Cheltenham, Glos.

Baileys Architectural Antiques, Ross-on-Wye, Herefs. & Worcs.
Baillache, Serge, London, W11.
Bain, Cdr and Mrs H.E.R., Albrighton, Shrops.
Baines, G. and J., Bath, Avon.
Baines, Henry, Southborough, Kent.
Baines of Bath, G.A., Bath, Avon.
Baird, R. and V., Langholm, Scotland.
Baker Antiques, Anthony, Alderley Edge, Cheshire.
Baker, A.R., Warrington, Cheshire.
Baker and Sons, A., Warrington, Cheshire.
Baker, C.J. and Mrs B.A.J., Lavenham,, Suffolk.
Baker Oriental Art, Gregg, London, W1.
Baker Antiques, John, Newbury, Berks.
Baker, J. and J., Lavenham, Suffolk.
Baker, Keith, Woking, Surrey.
Baker, K.R., Woking, Surrey.
Baker, L.W., London, NW3.
Baker, P. and P., Oban, Scotland.
Baker, R. J., Canterbury, Kent.
Baker, T., Langford, Notts.
Baker, T.R., Crawley, Hants.
Baker, W.R. and J., Whitstable, Kent.
Bakewell Antiques and Collectors Centre, Bakewell, Derbys.
Balchin, C.B., Brighton, Sussex East.
Balchin and Son, H., Brighton, Sussex East.
Baldry, Mrs J., Gt. Yarmouth, Norfolk.
Baldwin and Sons Ltd, A.H., London, WC2.
Baldwin, Peter J., Exmouth, Devon.
Baldwin Antiques, Peter J., Drewsteignton, Devon.
Baldwin, R.J.S., Chichester, Sussex West.
Baldwin, R.J.S., London, SW3.
Balfour-Lynn, A., London, WC1.
Baliol Gallery, The, Barnard Castle, Durham.
Ball Antique and Fine Art, David, Leighton Buzzard, Beds.
Ball, D. and J., Leighton Buzzard, Beds.
Ball, G, Tattershall, Lincs.
Ball, J., Porthcawl, Mid. Glam., Wales.
Ball, M. and S., Lewes, Sussex East.
Ballard, Mrs E.H. and S.R., Thirsk, Yorks. North.
Ballard, F. and Mrs . J.R., Weymouth, Dorset.
Ballinger, J. and G.D., Ruskington, Lincs.
Balmain Antiques, Ripon, Yorks. North.
Balme Antiques, Ken, Halifax, Yorks. West.
Balmuir House Antiques, Tetbury, Glos.
Bambridge, L., Godalming, Surrey.
Bampton, A.J., Birkenhead, Merseyside.
Bampton Antiques, Bampton, Devon.
Banbury Fayre, London, N1.
Bandini, L., London, W1.
Banfield, P., Bournemouth, Dorset.
Bangs, Christopher, London, SW11.
Bank House Gallery, The, Norwich, Norfolk.
Banks, B.A. and G., Woolacombe, Devon.
Banks, N. and Mrs J., York, Yorks. North.
Banks, P.M.L., London, SW15.
Banks, R., Leigh-on-Sea, Essex.
Banks, S., Finedon, Northants.
Banner Antiques, St. Leonards-on-Sea, Sussex East.
Bannister, Mrs A. and J., Stratford-upon-Avon, Warks.
Bannister, F.R.G.S, David, Cheltenham, Glos.
Banwell, Mike, Tunbridge Wells, Kent.
Barbagallo, Sebastiano, London, SE1.
Barber, P., Charlecote, Warks.
Barber, Sid, King's Lynn, Norfolk.
Barbican Antiques Centre, Plymouth, Devon.
Barbican Bookshop, York, Yorks. North.
Barbican Centre, The, Plymouth, Devon.
Barclay Antiques, Bexhill-on-Sea, Sussex East.
Barclay Antiques, Headington, Oxon.
Barclay, C., Headington, Oxon.
Barclay, Mr and Mrs K., London, NW2.
Barclay, M.J. and D., Friockheim, Scotland.
Barclay, R. and M., Bexhill-on-Sea, Sussex East.
Barclay Samson Ltd, London, SW6.
Barclay, T.H. and J., King's Lynn, Norfolk.
Barclays House Antiques, Leek, Staffs.
Bardawil, Eddy, London, W8.
Bardawil, E.S., London, W8.
Barden House Antiques, Tonbridge, Kent.
Bardwell Antiques, Dronfield, Derbys.
Bardwell, S., Dronfield, Derbys.

DEALERS' INDEX

Barewood Company, The, London, NW6.
Bargain Box, Luton, Beds.
Barham Antiques, London, W11.
Barham, P.R., London, W11.
Barker, B., Swanage, Dorset.
Barker, B. and I., Bridlington, N. Humbs.
Barker Court Antiques and Bygones, York, Yorks. North.
Barker, D., Beaconsfield, Bucks.
Barker, Lynn, Ampthill, Beds.
Barkes and Barkes, London, NW1.
Barkes, J. N. and P. R., London, NW1.
Barkham Antique and Craft Centre, Barkham, Berks.
Barley, R.A., London, SW6.
Barley Antiques, Robert, London, SW6.
Barleycote Hall Antiques, Keighley, Yorks. West.
Barlow Antiques, Anne, Letchmore Heath, Herts.
Barlow, Mrs, Letchmore Heath,, Herts.
Barlow, E., London, SW1.
Barlow, J., Alderley Edge, Cheshire.
Barn, The, Bicester, Oxon.
Barn, The, Collingham, Notts.
Barn, The, Petersfield, Hants.
Barn Antiques, Lampeter, Dyfed, Wales.
Barn Book Supply, The, Salisbury, Wilts.
Barn Court Antiques, Narberth, Dyfed, Wales.
Barn Full of Brass Beds, A, Sawtry, Cambs.
Barn Gallery, Hatfield Heath, Essex.
Barnard, Mrs J.P., Ilminster, Somerset.
Barnard (A.B.A.), Thomas, Uxbridge, Middx.
Barnes, D., Dover, Kent.
Barnes, F. and P., Clitheroe, Lancs.
Barnes Gallery, Uckfield, Sussex East.
Barnes, H., Stafford, Staffs.
Barnes House Antiques, Wimborne Minster, Dorset.
Barnes, R., Henley-in-Arden, Warks.
Barnes Antiques, R.A., London, SW15.
Barnes, S.J. and A.R., Uckfield, Sussex East.
Barnet Antiques, London, W8.
Barnett, J.P., London, W11.
Barnett, Roger, Windsor and Eton, Berks.
Barnicott, R. and J., Cowbridge, South Glam., Wales.
Barnstaple Antique Centre, Barnstaple, Devon.
Barnt Green Antiques, Barnt Green, Herefs. & Worcs.
Barntiques, Colchester, Essex.
Barometer Fair, London, WC1.
Barometer Shop, The, Bristol, Avon.
Barometer Shop, Leominster, Herefs. & Worcs.
Barometer Shop, The, Winchcombe, Glos.
Barometer World (Barometers), Merton, Devon.
Baron Antiques, Altrincham, Cheshire.
Baron Antiques, The, Manchester, Lancs.
Baron, C., Alresford, Hants.
Baron Fine Art, Chester, Cheshire.
Baron, H., London, NW6.
Baron, S. and R., Chester, Cheshire.
Baroq Antiques, Little Brickhill, Bucks.
Barrass, Neil, Edinburgh, Scotland.
Barrass, Paddy, Edinburgh, Scotland.
Barratt, N., M. and J., Warrington, Cheshire.
Barrett, I. and B., Widegates, Cornwall.
Barrett, P., Weymouth, Dorset.
Barrett Antiques and Prints, Philip, Taunton, Somerset.
Barrett, P. and P., Taunton, Somerset.
Barrett, P.R. and S.M., Seaford, Sussex East.
Barrett, Mrs S.E., Seaford, Sussex East.
Barrie, K., London, NW6.
Barrington, D., London, N1.
Barrington, David, Brasted, Kent.
Barron and Sons, J. , Mevagissey, Cornwall.
Barronfield Gallery, Preston, Lancs.
Barrows, N., J.S. and M.J., Ollerton, Notts.
Barry, Mrs P., London, SW16.
Barrymore and Co, J. , Honiton, Devon.
Barry's Antiques, Gt. Yarmouth, Norfolk.
Barsley Antiques, Douglas, Eastbourne, Sussex East.
Bartholomew, A. and N., Great Harwood, Lancs.
Bartlett, Nigel A., London, SE1.
Bartlett Street Antique Centre, Bath, Avon.
Bartman, F., London, SW1.
Barton House Antiques, Stanford-le-Hope, Essex.
Barton, R. and C., Watford, Herts.
Bartram, Albert, Chesham, Bucks.

Bartrick, Steven D., Gloucester, Glos.
Basey, S., Bristol, Avon.
Baskerville Antiques, Petworth, Sussex West.
Baskerville, A. and B., Petworth, Sussex West.
Baskerville Books, Tunbridge Wells, Kent.
Bass, B., Cheltenham, Glos.
Bass, V.E., Market Deeping, Lincs.
Bassett, H., Codsall, Staffs.
Bassett, Nigel, Petworth, Sussex West.
Bassett, N.J., Petworth, Sussex West.
Bastillo, G., London, SW6.
Bastillo, J., London, SW11.
Bate, A.C., London, W1.
Bate, C.J. and J.A., Kirkby Stephen, Cumbria.
Bateman, Jean A., Stratford-upon-Avon, Warks.
Bateman Antiques, J. and R., Chalford, Glos.
Bateman, W., Hoylake, Merseyside.
Bates and Sons, Eric, Coltishall, Norfolk.
Bates and Sons, Eric, North Walsham, Norfolk.
Bates Antiques, Jeffery, Boroughbridge, Yorks. North.
Bates, J.S., London, SW20.
Bates, T. and P., Tavistock, Devon.
Bates, V., London, W11.
Bateson Antiques, David, Bressingham, Norfolk.
Bateson, D. and P., Bressingham, Norfolk.
Bath Antiques Market, Bath, Avon.
Bath Antiques Market Ltd, London, SE1.
Bath Antiques Market Ltd, London, W11.
Bath Antiques Market Ltd., Taunton, Somerset.
Bath Chair, The, Woolhampton, Berks.
Bath Galleries, Bath, Avon.
Bath Saturday Antiques Market, Bath, Avon.
Bath Stamp and Coin Shop, Bath, Avon.
Bath Street Antiques Galleries, Glasgow, Scotland.
Batley, T.C., Knutsford, Cheshire.
Batten, R., Bridport, Dorset.
Batten's Jewellers, Bridport, Dorset.
Battlesbridge Antique Centre, Battlesbridge, Essex.
Batty's Antiques, Leeds, Yorks. West.
Baum, Ian, Honiton, Devon.
Baumkotter, Mrs L., London, W8.
Baumkotter Gallery, London, W8.
Baxter and Sons, H.C, London, SW3.
Baxter, Paul, Birmingham, West Mids.
Baxter, T.J., J. and G.J, London, SW3.
Bay House Antiques, Uppingham, Leics.
Bay Tree House Antiques, Weston-Super-Mare, Avon.
Bayley, C., London, W8.
Baylis Country Chairs, Chris, Cumnor, Oxon.
Baylis, M.S., Wallingford, Oxon.
Bayliss, D.W. and A.B., Ludlow, Shrops.
Bayne-Powell, H.M., West Peckham, Kent.
Baynton-Williams, Arundel, Sussex West.
Baynton-Williams, R.H. and S.C., Arundel, Sussex West.
Bayntun, George, Bath, Avon.
Bayntun-Coward, H.H., Bath, Avon.
Bayswater Books , London, W2.
Baytree House Antiques, Lympsham, Somerset.
Bazaar, The, Whitby, Yorks. North.
Bazely, G., Eversley, Hants.
Beach, A., Salisbury, Wilts.
Beach Antiques, Clevedon, Avon.
Beach, D.M, Salisbury, Wilts.
Beagle, A. and J., London, W11.
Beagle Gallery, London, W11.
Beaminster Antiques, Beaminster, Dorset.
Beamish, Mrs S., Laxfield, Suffolk.
Beardall Antiques, Clive, Maldon, Essex.
Beardsell, E.V., Holmfirth, Yorks. West.
Beare, John and Arthur, London, W1.
Beare Ltd, J. and A., London, W1.
Bears and Friends, Brighton, Sussex East .
Beasant, B., Greyabbey, Co. Down, N. Ireland.
Beasley, P.T., Farningham, Kent.
Beasley, P.T. and R., Farningham, Kent.
Beattie, M., London, SW7.
Beaty, T.W., Beattock, Scotland.
Beau Monde Antiques, Huddersfield, Yorks. West.
Beau Nash Antiques, Bath, Avon.
Beaubush House Antiques, Sandgate , Kent.
Beaulieu Fine Arts, Beaulieu, Hants.
Beaumont, Mrs H., Huddersfield, Yorks. West.

DEALERS' INDEX

Beaumont Antiques, Michael, Hempstead, Essex.
Beaver Coin Room, London, SW5.
Beazor and Sons Ltd, John, Cambridge, Cambs.
Bebb, R. and L., Kidwelly, Dyfed, Wales.
Beckenham Antique Market, Beckenham, Kent.
Becker, A.G., M.S. and J.A., Attleborough, Norfolk.
Becker, O.M., London, SW3.
Becker, Susan, Walton-on-Thames, Surrey.
Beckett, J. and Mrs . G., Wimborne Minster, Dorset.
Beckman, Patricia, London, NW3.
Beckwith and Son, Hertford, Herts.
Bed Bazaar, Framlingham, Suffolk.
Bed of Roses, Cheltenham, Glos.
Bedale, David, Knutsford, Cheshire.
Beddard, A.I., Birmingham, West Mids.
Bedford, J., London, N1.
Bedford plc, William, London, N1.
Bedi Antiques, Margaret , Billingham, Cleveland.
Bee, Mr, London, W4.
Beech Antique Clocks, Jonathan, Cirencester, Glos.
Beech, Nicholas, London, SW8.
Beech, N.A., London, SW8.
Beech, R., Derby, Derbys.
Beechwood Antiques, Newport, Gwent, Wales.
Beedham Antiques Ltd, Bakewell, Derbys.
Beedham, W.H., Bakewell, Derbys.
Beeken, Jane A., Poynton, Cheshire.
Beeleigh Abbey Books (W. and G. Foyle Ltd.), Maldon, Essex.
Beer, John, Cheltenham, Glos.
Beer, John, London, N6.
Beercock, S., Hessle, N. Humbs.
Beese, M., Bristol, Avon.
Beesley, Norman, Leckhampstead, Berks.
Beeston, M., Stow-on-the-Wold, Glos.
Beetles Ltd Watercolours and Paintings, Chris, London, SW1.
Begg, Robert , Edinburgh, Scotland.
Behan, R., Bath, Avon.
Behar Carpets, Edinburgh, Scotland.
Belcher, D. and J., Woore, Shrops.
Belgrave Antiques and Bric-a-Brac, Ilford, Essex.
Belgrave Carpet Gallery Ltd, London, SW1.
Belgrave Gallery, London, SW1.
Bell Antiques, Eastbourne, Sussex East.
Bell Antiques, Grimsby, S. Humbs.
Bell Antiques, Romsey, Hants.
Bell, Book and Radmall, London, WC2.
Bell, D. and J., Banbridge, Co. Down, N. Ireland.
Bell, E., Cockermouth, Cumbria.
Bell Fine Art, Winchester, Hants.
Bell Fine Arts, Lechlade, Glos.
Bell Gallery, The, Belfast, N. Ireland.
Bell, H.J., Saddleworth, Lancs.
Bell House Antiques, Cambridge, Glos.
Bell, I., London, E2.
Bell Inn Antiques, Modbury, Devon.
Bell Antiques, J. and H., Castletown, I. of Man.
Bell, J.N., Belfast, N. Ireland.
Bell, K.E. and B., Winchester, Hants.
Bell of Aberdeen Ltd, John, Banchory, Scotland.
Bell Passage Antiques, Wotton-under-Edge, Glos.
Bell, Raine, Long Melford, Suffolk.
Bell, R., Southport, Merseyside.
Bell, Mrs R.A., Lechlade, Glos.
Bell, R. and J., York, Yorks. North.
Bell and Son, R., Shipley, Yorks. West.
Bell Street Antiques Centre, Princes Risborough, Bucks.
Bellamy, A., Southampton, Hants.
Bellamy, K. and Mrs L., Nantymoel, Mid. Glam., Wales.
Bellinger Antiques, C., Barnet, Herts.
Bellord, E., London, W1.
Belmont-Maitland, R., London, W1.
Below Stairs, Hungerford, Berks.
Below Stairs, Kendal, Cumbria.
Belper Antiques Centre, Belper, Derbys.
Belsten, R., Stiffkey, Norfolk.
Benardout and Benardout, London, W1.
Benardout, J. and D., Henley-on-Thames, Oxon.
Benardout, R. and L., London, W1.
Bendalls Antiques, Castle Douglas, Scotland.
Benet Gallery, Cambridge, Cambs.
Beney, D., Beaminster, Dorset.
Benjamin, S., London, EC3.

Benjamin, S., London, W1.
Bennet (Antiques), Julia, Dunmow, Essex.
Bennett, Alan , Truro, Cornwall.
Bennett, F.R., Shipston-on-Stour, Warks.
Bennett, G., Alderley Edge, Cheshire.
Bennett, Paul, London, W1.
Bennett, Richard, Thirsk, Yorks. North.
Bennion, Peter, Halifax, Yorks. West.
Bensiglio Ltd, S., London, W5.
Bensiglio, Mr and Mrs S., London, W5.
Benson-Wilson, J., Holme, Cumbria.
Benstead, Mrs H., Birmingham, West Mids.
Bent, R.A., London, N1.
Bentley, Bill, Harrogate, Yorks. North.
Bentley & Co Ltd, London, W1.
Bentley, M.R., Knutsford, Cheshire.
Bently Antiques, Pat, Ampthill, Beds.
Bentley Billiards (Antique Billiard Table Specialist Company), William, Hungerford, Berks.
Benton, J.G., Cheltenham, Glos.
Benton, Mrs P.A., Measham, Leics.
Benzie, James, Aberdeen, Scotland.
Beresford-Clark, London, SW6.
Beresiner, Y., London, N1.
Berge, I., London, W8.
Berkeley Antiques and Replay, Tewkesbury, Glos.
Berkeley Market, Berkeley, Glos.
Berkshire Metal Finishers Ltd, Sandhurst, Berks.
Berktay, Y., Somerton, Somerset
Berlands of Edinburgh, Edinburgh, Scotland.
Bermondsey Antique Warehouse, London, SE1.
Bermondsey Antiques Hypermarket, London, SE1.
Bernadette's Antiques & Collectables, Luton, Beds.
Bernard, L.S., London, SW3.
Bernheimer Fine Arts Ltd, London, W1.
Bernheimer, K.O., London, W1.
Berry Brow Antiques, Huddersfield, Yorks. West.
Berry, F.E., Disley, Cheshire.
Berry, Mrs L., Flamborough, N. Humbs.
Berry Antiques, Lesley, Flamborough, N. Humbs.
Berry Antiques, Peter , Huddersfield, Yorks. West.
Berrymam Music Boxes, Shelagh, Wells, Somerset.
Berry's, Lynton, Devon.
Berthoud, M. and N., Bridgnorth, Shrops.
Besbrode, M., Leeds, Yorks. West.
Besley, P.A. and P.F., Beccles, Suffolk.
Besleys Books, Beccles, Suffolk.
Best Antiques, Ray, Ilminster, Somerset.
Best, R. and W., Ilminster, Somerset.
Bethell, I., Birmingham, West Mids.
Bethney, P.W. and J., Knaphill, Surrey.
Betley Court Gallery, Betley, Staffs.
Bett, H., London, W1.
Betts, T., York, Yorks. North.
Betty's, Leicester, Leics.
Bevan, D., Halesowen, West Mids.
Beverley, London, NW8.
Bevins, J.R., Ulverston, Cumbria.
Bexfield, A.B., Hitchin, Herts.
Bexfield Antiques, Hitchin, Herts.
Bexhill Antique Exporters, Bexhill-on-Sea, Sussex East.
Bhalla, Mrs A., Lincoln, Lincs.
Bianco, L., Cheltenham, Glos.
Bibby, R., Leigh, Lancs.
Bichard, R. and J., Bradford-on-Avon, Wilts.
Bickersteth, David, Bassingbourn, Cambs.
Biddulph, Peter, London, W1.
Bieganski, Z., Woburn, Beds.
Big Ben Antique Clocks, London, SW6.
Biggs, A.C., Worthing, Sussex West.
Biggs, J. and P., Bideford, Devon.
Bigwood, C., Tunbridge Wells, Kent.
Bijoux Jewellers, Guildford, Surrey.
Biles, J., Hartley Wintney, Hants.
Billcliffe Fine Art, The Roger, Glasgow, Scotland.
Billings, J. and S.E., Kelvedon, Essex.
Binder, D. and A., London, NW8.
Bingham, Tony, London, NW3.
Bingley Antiques Centre, Bingley, Yorks. West.
Bingley Antiques, Robert, Wing, Leics.
Birbeck Gallery, Torquay, Devon.
Birch, C., Gt. Yarmouth, Norfolk.

DEALERS' INDEX

Birch, C. and H., Leicester, Leics.
Birches Art Deco Shop, Leicester, Leics.
Birchwood Antiques, Abbots Bromley, Staffs.
Bird Antiques, John, Lewes, Sussex East.
Bird, R.J., Pampisford, Cambs.
Birdcage Antiques, The, Windermere, Cumbria.
Birmingham Bookshop, Birmingham, West Mids.
Biscoe, A., Worthing, Sussex West.
Bishop, B. and A., Castle Combe, Wilts.
Bishop House Antiques, Leeds, Yorks. West.
Bishop, Mrs J.M., Leeds, Yorks. West.
Bishops Park Antiques, London, SW6.
Bishopsgate Antiques, York, Yorks. North.
Bishopstrow Antiques, Warminster, Wilts.
Bisram, Mr. and Mrs R., Cranbrook, Kent.
Bits and Pieces, Farnham, Surrey.
Bizarre, London, NW8.
Bizarre Antiques, Bristol, Avon.
Bizarre Decorative Arts North West, Altrincham, Cheshire.
Black Cat, London, SE20.
Black Oriental Carpets, David, London, W11.
Black Dog Antiques, Bungay, Suffolk.
Black Isle Antiques, Fortrose, Scotland.
Black Lion Antiques, Conway, Gwynedd, Wales.
Black Ltd, Laurance, Edinburgh, Scotland.
Black, R.M. and G.G., Broadstone, Dorset.
Blackburn, E.M., Tunbridge Wells, Kent.
Blackburn, Mrs G., Lancaster, Lancs.
Blackburn, H., Gargrave, Yorks. North.
Blackburn, Jack, Preston, Lancs.
Blackburn, Norman, London, W11.
Blackford, L., Reigate, Surrey.
Blackford, M., Calne, Wilts.
Blackhurst, Steven, Crewe, Cheshire.
Blacklocks, S., Chilham, Kent.
Blackpool Antiques Centre, Blackpool, Lancs.
Blacksmiths Forge, Balderton, Notts.
Blackwater Pine Antiques, Truro, Cornwall.
Blackwell's Rare Books, Oxford, Oxon.
Blade and Bayonet, Bournemouth, Dorset.
Bladud House Antiques, Bath, Avon.
Blaik, J., Princes Risborough, Bucks.
Blair Antiques, Pitlochry, Scotland.
Blair, J., St. Albans, Herts.
Blairman and Sons Ltd., H., London, W1.
Blake - Lanehurst Antiques, P. and K.N., Woodford Green, Essex.
Blake - Old Cottage Antiques, K.N. and P., London, E11.
Blake, V.C.J., J., J. and S.T., Puckeridge, Herts.
Blakemore - Dower House Antiques, Brian, Kendal, Cumbria.
Blakey and Sons Ltd (Est. 1905), J.H., Brierfield, Lancs.
Blakey Fireplaces, Colin, Nelson, Lancs.
Blanchard and Alan Ltd., London, SW1.
Blanchard Ltd, J.W., Winchester, Hants.
Blandford, R.C., Haslemere, Surrey.
Blaydon Antique Centre, Blaydon, Tyne and Wear.
Blechman, H.L., Bournemouth, Dorset.
Blench & Son, John, St. Helier, Jersey, C.I.
Blench, J. and P., St. Helier, Jersey, C.I.
Blenheim Antiques, Fairford, Glos.
Blewbury Antiques, Blewbury, Oxon.
Blissett, Gary K., Long Preston, Yorks. North.
Blom, C., London, SW11.
Blom, J., Hebden Bridge, Yorks. West.
Bloom Fine Jewellery, Anne, London, W1.
Bloom and Son (Knightsbridge), N., London, SW1.
Bloom & Son (Antiques) Ltd, N., London, W1.
Bloomers, Harrogate, Yorks. North.
Blower Antiques, Mark, St. Martin, Guernsey, C.I.
Blunderbuss Antiques, London, W1.
Bly, F., N., J. and V., London, SW1.
Bly, F., N., J. and V., Tring, Herts.
Bly, John, London, SW1.
Bly, John, Tring, Herts.
Blyth Antiques, Bath, Avon.
Blyth, B., Bath, Avon.
Blyth Bygones, Halesworth, Suffolk.
Blyth, Norman A., Great Bircham, Norfolk.
Boaden Antiques, Arthur, Hexham, Northumbs.
Boadens of Hexham, Gateshead, Tyne and Wear.
Boaden, R.J., Gateshead, Tyne and Wear.
Boaden, R.J., Hexham, Northumbs.

Boalch, Mrs J., Cardiff, South Glam., Wales.
Boam, Clare, Horncastle, Lincs.
Boase and Vaughan Antiques and Jewellery, Exmouth, Devon.
Boathouse Gallery, Walton-on-Thames, Surrey.
Bobbins, York, Yorks. North.
Bobbins Wool Craft Antiques, Whitby, Yorks. North.
Bobinet Ltd, London, NW8.
Bodhouse Antiques, Birkenhead, Merseyside.
Bogan Antiques, Totnes, Devon.
Bole, R., Dover, Kent.
Bolour, Y. and B., London, NW5.
Bolt Antiques, Brian R., Portballintrae, Co. Antrim, N. Ireland.
Bolton Antique Centre, Bolton, Lancs.
Bolton Antiques, Paula, Macclesfield, Cheshire.
Bolton, John, Warwick, Warks.
Bolton, P., Macclesfield, Cheshire.
Bolton, Richard, Netherbury, Dorset.
Bond, Mr and Mrs C., London, W11.
Bond, M. and R., Colchester, Essex.
Bond and Son, S., Colchester, Essex.
Bond Street Antiques Centre, London, W1.
Bond Street Antiques (inc. Jas. J. Briggs Est. 1820), Cromer, Norfolk.
Bond Street Silver Galleries, London, W1.
Bond, T.A., Bournemouth, Dorset.
Bond's Manor Antiques, Grundisburgh, Suffolk.
Bondy, Louis W., London, WC1.
Bone, W., Torquay, Devon.
Bonham, Murray Feely Fine Art, John, London, W2.
Bonnar, Jewellers, Joseph, Edinburgh, Scotland.
Bonnett Antiques, R., Queen Camel, Somerset.
Bonnies, Dover, Kent.
Bonrose Antiques, London, W8.
Bontoft, P.W., Cirencester, Glos.
Boodle and Dunthorne Ltd, Chester, Cheshire.
Boodle and Dunthorne Ltd, Liverpool, Merseyside.
Boodle and Dunthorne Ltd, London, SW3.
Boodle and Dunthorne Ltd, Manchester, Lancs.
Book House, The, Ravenstonedale, Cumbria.
Book in Hand (Christopher Driver), The, Shaftesbury, Dorset.
Book Jungle, The, St. Leonards-on-Sea, Sussex East.
Book Shelf, The, Mansfield, Notts.
Bookham Galleries, Great Bookham, Surrey.
Bookham Galleries, London, SW6.
Bookroom (Cambridge), The, Cambridge, Cambs.
Books Afloat, Weymouth, Dorset.
Books & Prints, Bradford-on-Avon, Wilts.
Books & Things, London, W1.
Boosey - Carpets for Country Houses, Simon, Whitwell Herts.
Booth, Mr and Mrs C.M., Farnham, Surrey.
Booth, C.M., Rolvenden, Kent.
Booth, J., Princes Risborough, Bucks.
Booth, Joanna, London, SW3.
Booth Antiques and Reproductions, L., Freckleton, Lancs.
Booth Gallery and Titanic Signals Archive, Westbury, Wilts.
Booth, Mrs R.A., Ravensmoor, Cheshire.
Booth, T.J., Rye, Sussex East.
Boothferry Antiques, Hull, N. Humbs.
Booth's Bookshop, Richard, Hay-on-Wye, Powys, Wales.
Bord (Gold Coin Exchange), M., London, WC2.
Border Sporting Gallery, Wooler, Northumbs.
Boreham, M.J., Sandwich, Kent.
Bornoff, Claude, London, W2.
Borough Antiques, Meare, Somerset.
Boscombe Antiques, Bournemouth, Dorset.
Boscombe Militaria, Bournemouth, Dorset.
Boscombe Models and Collectors Shop, Bournemouth, Dorset.
Bosham Antiques, Bosham, Sussex West.
Bosi, L., Edinburgh, Scotland.
Bosley, S., London, N1.
Bosson Antiques, Peter, Wilmslow, Cheshire.
Boston Antiques Centre, Boston, Lincs.
Boston Antiques, Derek, Salisbury, Wilts.
Boston Pine Co., Leeds, Yorks. West.
Botting Antiques, John, Horam, Sussex East.
Botting, Susan and Robert, Felpham, Sussex West.
Botting, S.M. and R.M.D., Felpham, Sussex West.
Bottles and Bygones, Cheltenham, Glos.
Bottomley, Andrew Spencer, Holmfirth, Yorks. West.

DEALERS' INDEX

Bottomley, M. and B., Whitby, Yorks. North.
Boulevard Antique and Shipping Centre, Leicester, Leics.
Boulevard Reproductions, Halifax, Yorks. West.
Boulton, J.A., Broseley, Shrops.
Boulton, N., Torquay, Devon.
Bourdon-Smith Ltd, J.H., London, SW1.
Bourne Fine Art Ltd, Edinburgh, Scotland.
Bourne Gallery Ltd, Reigate, Surrey.
Bourne Mill Antiques, Farnham, Surrey.
Bourne, P., Edinburgh, Scotland.
Bournemouth Gallery Ltd, The, Lichfield, Staffs.
Bousfield, Guy, Windsor and Eton, Berks.
Boustead Antiques, Olwyn, Chester, Cheshire.
Boustead, Mrs O.L., Chester, Cheshire.
Boutique Fantasque, London, N1.
Bouyamourn, Z., Redland, Avon.
Bow Antiques, Easingwold, Yorks. North.
Bow Antiques Ltd, Haslemere, Surrey.
Bow Cottage Antiques, Stow-on-the-Wold, Glos.
Bow Cottage Antiques, Stratford-upon-Avon, Warks.
Bow House Antiques, Hungerford, Berks.
Bow Windows Book Shop, Lewes, Sussex East.
Bowden, J.A., Scunthorpe, S. Humbs.
Bowden, J. and B., Scunthorpe, S. Humbs.
Bowdery, M. J., Hindhead, Surrey.
Bowdler, M.A., Shrewsbury, Shrops.
Bowen, Mrs S., Wilshamstead, Beds.
Bowerman, Mrs E., Davenham, Cheshire.
Bowers-Jones, K.S., Deganwy, Gwynedd, Wales.
Bowkett, Knaresborough, Yorks. North.
Bowlby, Nicholas, Uckfield, Sussex East.
Bowler, J.A., Bradford, Yorks. West.
Bowler, Mrs R., Woodville, Derbys.
Bowman, H., London, W5.
Bowmoore Gallery, London, SW6.
Bowood Antiques, Wendover, Bucks.
Bowyer, Christine and Michael, Honiton, Devon.
Box of Porcelain, Dorchester, Dorset.
Boyce, Mark, London, SW1.
Boyd, Betty, Edinburgh, Scotland.
Boyd-Ratcliff, W.D., Kelvedon, Essex.
Boyd-Ratcliff, Wendy, Kelvedon, Essex.
Boyer Antiques, Rex, Nantwich, Cheshire.
Boylan, M. and A., Market Bosworth, Leics.
Boyle, A., Blackpool, Lancs.
Boyle (Booksellers) Ltd, Andrew, Worcester, Herefs.& Worcs.
Boyle, Mrs T.B., Cobham, Surrey.
Bracebridge Gallery, Astwood Bank, Herefs. & Worcs.
Bracewell, J. and E., Shawforth, Lancs.
Brackley Antiques, Brackley, Northants.
Bradbourne Gallery, Sevenoaks, Kent.
Bradbury and Son, Edward, Cheltenham, Glos.
Bradbury, O., Cheltenham, Glos.
Bradbury Antiques, Roger, Coltishall, Norfolk.
Bradley, A., Kirkcudbright, Scotland.
Bradley, G.C., Steeton, Yorks. West.
Bradley, J.R., Cardiff, South Glam., Wales.
Bradley, P., Middlesbrough, Cleveland.
Bradley, Mrs P., Stockbridge, Hants.
Bradley, P. and V., Bletchingley, Surrey.
Bradley, Robert, Salisbury, Wilts.
Bradley, Steven J., Hazel Grove, Cheshire.
Bradshaw, Mrs E., Blaydon, Tyne and Wear.
Bradshaw, Nicola D., Ilfracombe, Devon.
Bradley's Antiques and Jewellery, Middlesbrough, Cleveland.
Bragg Antiques, John, Lostwithiel, Cornwall.
Bragge Antiques, Lesley, Petworth, Sussex West.
Bragge, N.H. and J.R., Rye, Sussex East.
Bragge and Sons, Rye, Sussex East.
Bramble Cross Antiques, Honiton, Devon.
Bramley Antiques, Bramley, Surrey.
Bramley Antiques, Thundersley, Essex.
Brampton Mill Antiques, Brampton, Cambs.
Bramwell, R.H., Saffron Walden, Essex.
Branagh, J., Coventry, West Mids.
Brancaster Staithe Antiques, Brancaster Staithe, Norfolk.
Brand Antiques, Colin, Stow-on-the-Wold, Glos.
Brand, Mrs D.V., Wotton-under-Edge, Glos.
Brand, L.B., Boston, Lincs.
Brandl, L., London, SW6.
Brandler Galleries, Brentwood, Essex.
Brandler, J., Brentwood, Essex.

Brandt Oriental Antiques, London, SW6.
Brandt, R., London, SW6.
Branksome Antiques, Branksome, Dorset.
Brantham Mill Antiques, Brantham, Suffolk.
Brass, Bob, London, W11.
Brass and Son, Lawrence, Bath, Avon.
Brassington, Mr and Mrs, Yeaveley, Derbys.
Brasted Antiques and Interiors, Brasted, Kent.
Braund, J.F., Thaxted, Essex.
Bray Ltd, H.H., Warwick, Warks.
Bray, M., C.A. and T.M., Woodhouse Eaves, Leics.
Brazier, A., Otford, Kent.
Brazier, T.R.G., London, NW3.
Brazil Antiques Ltd, Westerham, Kent.
Breakspeare Antiques, Tetbury, Glos.
Breakspeare, M. and S., Tetbury, Glos.
Brean, L.M. and R.C., Pontnewynydd, Gwent, Wales.
Brear, Jean, Halifax, Yorks. West.
Breck Antiques, Nottingham, Notts.
Breeze and Behan, Bath, Avon.
Breeze, G., Bath, Avon.
Bremner, Mr and Mrs C., Maidstone, Kent.
Brett and Sons Ltd, Arthur, Norwich, Norfolk.
Brett, B., Walkerburn, Scotland.
Brett, Simon, Moreton-in-Marsh, Glos.
Brewer, Michael, Lincoln, Lincs.
Brewer, M.N., Lincoln, Lincs.
Brewster, D.J., Glasgow, Scotland.
Bric-a-Brac, The, Whitley Bay, Tyne and Wear.
Brick, D., Riverhead, Kent.
Brickwood, S., Lytham St. Annes, Lancs.
Bridge Antiques, Sutton Bridge, Lincs.
Bridge Antiques, Wingham, Kent.
Bridge, Christine, London, SW13.
Bridges, P., Scarthoe, S. Humbs.
Bridgford Antiques, West Bridgford, Notts.
Bridgwater Antiques Market, Bridgwater, Somerset.
Bridgwater, David, Marshfield, Avon.
Bridport Antiques Centre, Bridport, Dorset.
Brier, Mrs G., Scarthingwell, Yorks. North.
Briere, G. and E., Suffield, Norfolk.
Briggs Ltd, F.E.A., London, W11.
Briggs, R., Belper, Derbys.
Brigham, R.Loftus, London, W13.
Bright Antiques, Stockport, Cheshire.
Bright, T., Halifax, Yorks. West.
Brighton Antique Wholesalers, Brighton, Sussex East.
Brighton Architectural Salvage, Brighton, Sussex East.
Brighton Flea Market, Brighton, Sussex East.
Brindle Antiques, T., Chatburn, Lancs.
Brindle-Wood-Williams, D.M., Midhurst, Sussex West.
Brindleys, Heath and Reach, Beds.
Briscoe, J., Craven Arms, Shrops.
Briscoe-Knight, M.E., London, SW3.
Brisigotti Antiques Ltd, London, SW1.
Bristol Antique Market, Bristol, Avon.
Bristol Guild of Applied Art Ltd, Bristol, Avon.
Bristol Trade Antiques, Bristol, Avon.
Bristow, A. and P., Tetbury, Glos.
Bristow, George, Tetbury, Glos.
Bristow Antiques, J. and M., Tetbury, Glos.
Bristow, M.J. and J.A., Tetbury, Glos.
Britain's Heritage, Leicester, Leics.
Britannia Antiques, Warminster, Wilts.
Britannia Antiques Exports, Warminster, Wilts.
Britannia Export Antiques, London, W11.
British Antique Exporters Ltd, Burgess Hill, Sussex West.
British Antique Replicas, Burgess Hill, Sussex West.
Britten Antiques, Andrew, Malmesbury, Wilts.
Brittle, M., Twickenham, Middx.
Britton, Mrs, Radlett, Herts.
Brittons Jewellers and Antiques, Accrington, Lancs.
Brittons Jewellers and Antiques, Nelson, Lancs.
Broad, M., Tunbridge Wells, Kent.
Broad, S., Eastbourne, Sussex East.
Broad Street Gallery, Penryn, Cornwall.
Broad Street Gallery, Wolverhampton, West Mids.
Broadbelt, P.F., Harrogate, Yorks. North.
Broadhurst and Co Ltd, C.K., Southport, Merseyside.
Broadley, E. and D., Kirk Deighton, Yorks. North.
Broadstairs Antiques and Collectables, Broadstairs, Kent.
Broadway Antiques, St. Ives, Cambs.

DEALERS' INDEX

Broadway Old Books (formerly Stratford Trevers), Broadway, Herefs. & Worcs.
Broadway Studios, Burton-on-Trent, Staffs.
Brobbin, L.M. and H.C., Whaley Bridge, Derbys.
Brobury House Gallery, Brobury, Herefs. & Worcs.
Brocante, Rudgwick, Sussex West.
Brockdish Antiques, Brockdish, Norfolk.
Brocklehurst, Aubrey, London, SW7.
Bromage, Mrs P., London, W11.
Bromley Antique Market, Bromley, Kent.
Brook, Alexis, Kettering, Northants.
Brook, Mrs A., Kettering, Northants.
Brook Antiques, Beverley, London, SW13.
Brook, E., Warwick, Warks.
Brook, Antiques and Picture Gallery, Ian J., Wilton, Wilts.
Brook Lane Antiques, Alderley Edge, Cheshire.
Brooke Antiques, David, Mirfield, Yorks. West.
Brooke, Mrs M., Horncastle, Lincs.
Brooke, M.A., S.T. and L.A.P., Wroxham, Norfolk.
Brooke, T.C.S., Wroxham, Norfolk.
Brooker Antiques at the Village Gallery, Elizabeth, Brasted, Kent.
Brooker-Carey, Andrew, Birmingham, West Mids.
Brookes, David M., Marple Bridge, Cheshire.
Brookfield Gallery, Colyton, Devon.
Brooks Antiques, Nelson, Lancs.
Brooks, A., London, WC1.
Brooks, D., Malmesbury, Wilts.
Brooks, D. and S.A., Nelson, Lancs.
Brooks, Philip, Macclesfield, Cheshire.
Brooks, Mr. Temple, London, NW6.
Brookstone, M. and J., London, SW1.
Brookville Antiques, Richmond, Surrey.
Broomfield, G.H., Newcastle-under-Lyme, Staffs.
Broomhead, Miss F.S., Alderley Edge, Cheshire.
Brotherston, Mr and Mrs A., Greenlaw, Scotland.
Brower Antiques, David, London, W8.
Brown, A., London, W1.
Brown Antiques, Alasdair, London, SW6.
Brown, A.G., Arundel, Sussex West.
Brown and Colyer, Chester, Cheshire.
Brown Antiques, David, Shrewsbury, Shrops.
Brown, David F.J., Shrewsbury, Shrops.
Brown, Mr and Mrs D.R., St. Andrews, Scotland.
Brown, Dr. F., Betley, Staffs.
Brown, G.D. and S.T., Poole, Dorset.
Brown, Prof. G.N., Betley, Staffs.
Brown, G.P. and Mrs J.A., Richmond, Yorks. North.
Brown, Gordon and Anne, Glasgow, Scotland.
Brown, G.S.M., Harrogate, Yorks. North.
Brown, H. and M.F., Sandgate, Kent.
Brown House Antiques, Newport, Essex.
Brown Ltd, I. and J.L., Hereford, Herefs. & Worcs.
Brown Ltd, I. and J.L., London, SW6.
Brown, J.H., Midhurst, Sussex West.
Brown, J.M., Auchterarder, Scotland.
Brown, J. and M., Cheltenham, Glos.
Brown, J. and M., Swindon, Wilts.
Brown, Mrs L., Scarborough, Yorks. North.
Brown, Mary, Brighton, Sussex East.
Brown, Mrs M., Chipping Sodbury,, Avon.
Brown, Mrs M., Ratcliffe-on-the-Wreake, Leics.
Brown, Michael, Southwold, Suffolk.
Brown Antiques, Martyn, Halesowen, West Mids.
Brown, P., Burford, Oxon.
Brown Antiques, P.J., Haslingden, Lancs.
Brown, S., Cosgrove, Northants.
Brown and Sons 'The Popular Mart', S., Darlington, Durham.
Brown, T.D., Edinburgh, Scotland.
Brown, T.P. and P.M., Brighton, Sussex East.
Browne, E.A., Bournemouth, Dorset.
Browne, M. and W.Heygate, Sherborne, Dorset.
Browning and Son, G.E., Glastonbury, Somerset.
Brown's Antiques, Richmond, Yorks. North.
Browns Antiques, Scarborough, Yorks. North.
Browns' of West Wycombe, High Wycombe, Bucks.
Brownside Coach House, Alston, Cumbria.
Browse, Stafford, Staffs.
Browse and Darby Ltd, London, W1.
Browzers, Manchester, Lancs.
Broxup, David, Wareside, Herts.
Bruce, B. and D., Jedburgh, Scotland.

Bruce, F., Strathblane, Scotland.
Bruce, G., Cuxton, Kent.
Bruce, J., Aberdeen, Scotland.
Bruce Antiques, Paul, Ipswich, Suffolk.
Bruce Antiques, W.F., Herstmonceux, Sussex East.
Bruendel, K.N., Windsor and Eton, Berks.
Bruford and Heming Ltd, London, W1.
Bruford and Son Ltd, Wm., Eastbourne, Sussex East.
Bruford and Son Ltd, Wm., Exeter, Devon.
Brun Lea Antiques, Burnley, Lancs.
Brun Lea Antiques (J. Waite Ltd), Burnley, Lancs.
Brunning, M. and J., Redbourn, Herts.
Bruschweiler (Antiques) Ltd, F.G., Rayleigh, Essex.
Bruschweiler (Antiques) Ltd, F.G., Rettendon, Essex.
Brunsveld, S., Manchester, Lancs.
Bruton, B.C., Sherborne, Dorset.
Bruton Gallery, Bruton, Somerset.
Bryan, D.R. and C., Cranbrook, Kent.
Bryan-Peach Antiques, N., Wymeswold, Leics.
Bryant, D., Lostwithiel, Cornwall.
Bryant, E.H., Epsom, Surrey.
Bryden, D., Stow-on-the-Wold, Glos.
Brydon, R. and J., Brasted, Kent.
Bryers Antiques, Bath, Avon.
Bryers, S., Bath, Avon.
Buchan, K.S., Leigh-on-Sea, Essex.
Buchanan, A.R., Lincoln, Lincs.
Buchanan, J., Penzance, Cornwall.
Buck Antiques, Christopher, Sandgate, Kent.
Buck and Payne Antiques, London, N1.
Buck, W.F.A., Stockbury, Kent.
Buck, W.M., London, N1.
Bucke, A.P., Crewkerne, Somerset.
Buckie, G. McC. and P.R., Cambridge, Cambs.
Buckie, K.W., Swaffham, Norfolk.
Buckies, Cambridge, Cambs.
Buckingham, C.W., Cadnam, Hants.
Buckland, A.G.J., Shottermill, Surrey.
Buckle (Antique Fireplaces), Ruby, London, W2.
Buckley Antiques Exports, W., Congleton, Cheshire.
Buckley, W. and D., Stoke-on-Trent, Staffs.
Bugle Antiques, Chipping Norton, Oxon.
Buley Antiques, Northampton, Northants.
Bull, Audrey, Tenby, Dyfed, Wales.
Bull (Antiques) Ltd, John, London, W1.
Bull (Antiques) Ltd, John, London, W11.
Bull and Son (Cirencester) Ltd, Walter, Cirencester, Glos.
Bullard, S., Ipswich, Suffolk.
Bulldog Antiques, Manchester, Lancs.
Bullock, G.D., Worcester, Herefs. and Worcs.
Bullock, Gabrielle Doherty, Worcester, Herefs. and Worcs.
Bulmer, Hugh and Louise, Cowbridge, South Glam., Wales.
Bulmer, T., Chippenham, Cambs.
Bulmer's, Cowbridge, South Glam., Wales.
Bumbles, Ashtead, Surrey.
Bunce, N.P.J., Hereford, Herefs. and Worcs.
Bunn, R.J. and E.R., Evesham, Herefs. and Worcs.
Bunn, Roy W., Barnoldswick, Lancs.
Bunting Antiques, Peter, Hyde, Cheshire.
Bunting, Miss J.L., Belper, Derbys.
Bunzl, Tony, London, SW3.
Burden Ltd, Clive A., London, SW1.
Burden, Clive A., Rickmansworth, Herts.
Burdon, Alyson, London, W14.
Burfield, P., Lake, I. of Wight.
Burford Gallery, The, Burford, Oxon.
Burford, Mr and Mrs T.L., Auldgirth, Scotland.
Burgan, Mrs S.E.M., Yatton, Avon.
Burgate Antique Centre, Canterbury, Kent.
Burge Antiques, A., Cardiff, South Glam., Wales.
Burgess, D.J., Parkstone, Dorset.
Burgess Farm Antiques, Morestead, Hants.
Burkard, Mrs Jerry, Cobham, Surrey.
Burke, Marie José, Tarporley, Cheshire.
Burkinshaw, David, Haywards Heath, Sussex West.
Burley Workshop, Burley-on-the-Hill, Leics.
Burlington Gallery Ltd, London, W1.
Burlington Paintings Ltd, London, W1.
Burman Antiques, Stratford-upon-Avon, Warks.
Burman Holtom, J. and J., Stratford-upon-Avon, Warks.
Burne (Antique Glass) Ltd, W.G.T., London, SW3.
Burne, Mrs G., R.V. and A.T.G., London, SW3.

DEALERS' INDEX

Burness Antiques and Scientific Instruments, Victor, London, SE1.
Burness, V.G., London, SE1.
Burnett Antiques, Jean, Finedon, Northants.
Burnett, CMBHI, C.A., Northleach, Glos.
Burnham-Slipper Antiques, Jane, Botley, Hants.
Burning Embers, Aberdeen, Scotland.
Burns and Graham, Winchester, Hants.
Burns, G.H., Stamford, Lincs.
Burns, K., Leeds, Yorks. West.
Burns-Mace, Miss S., Lichfield, Staffs.
Burrell Antiques, High Wycombe, Bucks.
Burrell, G. and P., High Wycombe, Bucks.
Burrell, Gavin, Birmingham, West Mids.
Burrell, V.S., Abinger Hammer, Surrey.
Burrill, A., Dorking, Surrey.
Burrows, David E., Osgathorpe, Leics.
Burrows, J., Malton, Yorks. North.
Burrows, J.B. and L.L., Ilkley, Yorks. West.
Burrows and Raper, Ilkley, Yorks. West.
Bursig, R.H., Arundel, Sussex West.
Burton Antiques, Burton-on-Trent, Staffs.
Burton, D., Bridport, Dorset.
Burton, D. and A., Felton, Northumbs.
Burton, I., Denny, Scotland.
Burton, J., Ipswich, Suffolk.
Burton Antiques, Jasper, Sherborne, Dorset.
Burton Natural Craft Taxidermy, John, Ebrington, Glos.
Burton, Mr and Mrs S., London, W1.
Burton and Rod Johnston, Tom, Dorking, Surrey.
Burton-Garbett, A., Morden, Surrey.
Busek, A., South Molton, Devon.
Bush Antiques, Saffron Walden, Essex.
Bush, A., London, N1.
Bush and Partners, A.E., Attleborough, Norfolk.
Bush, Mrs .B.E., Saffron Walden, Essex.
Bush House, Corringham, Essex.
Bushwood Antiques, London, N1.
Butcher, F.L. and N.E., Sherborne, Dorset.
Butchoff Antiques, London, W11.
Butler and Co, Cheltenham, Glos.
Butler, D.J., Cheltenham, Glos.
Butler, J., Reigate, Surrey.
Butler, J.J., Honiton, Devon.
Butler, Mr and Mrs J.J., Chirk, Clwyd, Wales.
Butler, L., Glasgow, Scotland.
Butler, Robin, Bristol, Avon.
Butler, R., Blandford Forum, Dorset.
Butler, Roderick, Honiton, Devon.
Butler, Mrs S.A., London, SE23.
Butler and Wilson, London, SW3.
Butler's Furniture Galleries Ltd, Glasgow, Scotland.
Butlin, R., Wolverhampton, West Mids.
Butt Antiques, Anthony, Baldock, Herts.
Butterfly Pine, Botley, Hants.
Butterworth, Brian, Knutsford, Cheshire.
Butterworth (Horwich), Alan, Horwich, Lancs.
Butterworth, J.A., Beckenham, Kent.
Butterworth, J.A., London, SW9.
Butterworth, J.W., London, W8.
Butterworth, J.W., Potterspury, Northants.
Buttifant, Mrs P., Heanor, Derbys.
Buttigieg, Mrs Joyce M. , London, SE25.
Button, K., Bungay, Suffolk.
Button Queen, The, London, W1.
Button-Stephens Stable Antiques, Christopher J., Honiton, Devon.
Buxcey, Paul, Marple Bridge, Cheshire.
By George! Antiques Centre, St. Albans, Herts.
Bye Antiques, Ann, Reading, Berks.
Byers, M., Carlisle, Cumbria.
Bygone Antiques, Swansea, West Glam., Wales.
Bygone Bathrooms, London, SE23.
Bygone Days Antiques, Tiverton, Devon.
Bygone Times Ltd, Eccleston, Lancs.
Bygones, Angmering, Sussex West.
Bygones, Banchory, Scotland.
Bygones, Darlington, Durham.
Bygones, Eastbourne, Sussex East.
Bygones, Gourock, Scotland.
Bygones, Heanor, Derbys.
Bygones, St. Andrews, Scotland.
Bygones by the Cathedral, Worcester, Herefs. & Worcs.
Bygones (Worcester), Worcester, Herefs. & Worcs.
Byles, Robert , Bampton, Devon.
Byrne, Anne, Stow-on-the-Wold, Glos.
Byrne, B., Morecambe, Lancs.
Byrne, D. and M.A., Grassington, Yorks. North.
Byron, R., Oldham, Lancs.
Byskou, N., Worthing, Sussex West.

C

C.A.R.S. (Classic Automobilia & Regalia Specialists). Brighton, Sussex East.
C.P.R. Antiques and Services, Barrhead, Scotland.
C.S. Antiques, Leslie By Insch, Scotland.
Cabbies Antiques, Edinburgh, Scotland.
Caedmon House, Whitby, Yorks. North.
Caelt Gallery, London, W11.
Cain, N., Hexham, Northumbs.
Cains Antiques, Littleton, Somerset.
Cairncross and Sons, Filey, Yorks. North.
Cairncross, G., Filey, Yorks. North.
Cairnyard Antiques, Dumfries, Scotland.
Caldwell, Ian, Walton-on-the-Hill and Tadworth, Surrey.
Calleja, L., Ledbury, Herefs. and Worcs.
Calligan, D.E., Conway, Gwynedd, Wales.
Callingham Antiques, D. and A., Northchapel, Sussex West.
Callingham Antiques, N. and S., Northchapel, Sussex West.
Callwood, G.T., Romsley, West Mids.
Callwood, J. R., Kidderminster, Herefs. and Worcs.
Calne Antiques, Calne, Wilts.
Calton Gallery, Edinburgh, Scotland.
Calvert Antiques, Endmoor, Cumbria.
Calvert, Mr and Mrs R., Wingham, Kent.
Cambridge Antiques, Romsey, Hants.
Cambridge Fine Art Ltd, Cambridge, Cambs.
Cambridge Parade Antiques, Carshalton, Surrey.
Cambridge Pine, Bottisham, Cambs.
Cambridge, OMRS, T., Romsey, Hants.
Camden Art Gallery, London, NW8.
Camden Passage Antiques Centre, London, N1.
Came, S., Henley-on-Thames, Oxon.
Camelot Antiques, Boreham Street, Sussex East.
Cameo, Birmingham, West Mids.
Cameo Antiques, Banbridge, Co. Down, N. Ireland.
Cameo Antiques, Cheltenham, Glos.
Cameo Gallery, The, London, W8.
Camerer Cuss and Co, London, SW1.
Cameron Gallery, Julia Margaret, Cowes, I. of Wight.
Cameron, K., Edinburgh, Scotland.
Cameron, K. and E., Edinburgh, Scotland.
Cameron, M., Paulerspury, Northants.
Camilla's Bookshop, Eastbourne, Sussex East.
Campbell, F.D., Kelvedon, Essex.
Campbell, Fiona, Kelvedon, Essex.
Campbell, Gerard, Lechlade, Glos.
Campbell, J. and G., Lechlade, Glos.
Campbell Gallery, The Lucy B., London, W8.
Campbell Picture Frames Ltd, John, London, SW3.
Campbell, Meg, Southampton, Hants.
Campbell Antiques, Peter, Atworth, Wilts.
Campbell, P.R., Atworth, Wilts.
Campbell, R.M., Hartley Wintney, Hants.
Campbell, S., Stirling, Scotland.
Campbell-Cameron, Mrs C.A.L., Garstang, Lancs.
Campden Country Pine, Chipping Campden, Glos.
Campion, London, SW13.
Campion, R.J., London, SW6.
Candin, Z., London, N1.
Candle Lane Books, Shrewsbury, Shrops.
Cannell Antiques, M.D., Raveningham, Norfolk.
Cannell, R.H., Ampthill, Beds.
Cannon Antiques, Elizabeth, Colchester, Essex.
Cannon, N., Marlborough, Wilts.
Canon Gallery, The, Chichester, Sussex West.
Canonbury Antiques, London, N1.
Cantabrian Antiques and Architectural Furnishing, Lynton, Devon.
Canterbury Bookshop, The, Canterbury, Kent.
Canterbury House, Thorne, Yorks. South.
Canterbury Weekly Antique Market, Canterbury, Kent.
Captain's Cabin Antiques, Lymington, Hants.

DEALERS' INDEX

Capital Clocks, London, SW8.
Capital City Investments Ltd, London, SE1.
Capon, Patric, London, N1.
Careless Cottage Antiques, Much Hadham, Herts.
Caris, Gordon, Hexham, Northumbs.
Carleton Gallery, Birmingham, West Mids.
Carling and Tess Sinclair, Roger, Long Melford, Suffolk.
Carlisle Antique and Craft Centre, Carlisle, Cumbria.
Carlton Antiques, Great Malvern, Herefs. & Worcs.
Carlton Antiques, Saltaire, Yorks. West.
Carlton House Antiques, Parkstone, Dorset.
Carlton Road Antiques, Lowestoft, Suffolk.
Carlyon-Gibbs, A.S., Egham, Surrey.
Carmichael, C., Great Malvern, Herefs. and Worcs.
Carmichael, P., Brighton, Sussex East.
Carmichael, Peter and June, Edinburgh, Scotland.
Carnival Antiques, Bristol, Avon.
Carole's Corner, Market Rasen, Lincs.
Carousel Pig, The, Wiveliscombe, Somerset.
Carpenter, John, Llanelli, Dyfed, Wales.
Carpenter, Sue, Hartley Wintney, Hants.
Carr Antiques, Harold J., Washington, Tyne and Wear.
Carr, Ronald, Salisbury, Wilts.
Carr, R.G., Salisbury, Wilts.
Carrcross Gallery, Scarisbrick, Lancs.
Carré, Mrs K.M., St. Peter Port, Guernsey, C.I.
Carrick Antiques, G., Gainsborough, Lincs.
Carrington Antiques, Craig, Painswick, Glos.
Carrington and Co. Ltd, London, W1.
Carritt Limited, David, London, SW1.
Carrol, E., Bingley, Yorks. West.
Carruthers, C.J., Carlisle, Cumbria.
Carruthers, J., C. and F.E., Carlisle, Cumbria.
Carruthers, L., Buxton, Derbys.
Carshalton Antique Galleries, Carshalton, Surrey.
Carter, Miss Carol, Lostock Gralam, Cheshire.
Carter, D., London, W11.
Carter, D.R., Woolhampton,, Berks.
Carter Antiques, Mark, Bladon, Oxon.
Carter, Nick, Edinburgh, Scotland.
Carter Gallery, Simon, Woodbridge, Suffolk.
Cartmell, T., Tring, Herts.
Cartographia London, London, WC1.
Cartrefle Antiques, Mathry, Dyfed, Wales.
Cary Antiques Ltd, Castle Cary, Somerset.
Casemate, Bath, Avon.
Cash, J., Birmingham, West Mids.
Cashin Gallery, Sheila, Brighton, Sussex East.
Casimir Ltd, Jack, London, W11.
Cason, P.G., Cardiff, South Glam., Wales.
Caspall Antiques, J. and J., Stow-on-the-Wold, Glos.
Casque and Gauntlet Militaria, Farnham, Surrey.
Cassidy, P., Birmingham, West Mids.
Cassidy (Books), P.J., Holbeach, Lincs.
Cassio Antiques, London, W11.
Castell Delmar Antiques, Ruthin, Clwyd, Wales.
Castle Antiques, Beaumaris, Gwynedd, Wales.
Castle Antiques, Burnham-on-Sea, Somerset.
Castle Antiques, Clitheroe, Lancs.
Castle Antiques, Leigh-on-Sea, Essex.
Castle Antiques, Newcastle Emlyn, Dyfed, Wales.
Castle Antiques, Orford, Suffolk.
Castle Antiques, Stoke-on-Trent, Staffs.
Castle Antiques, Usk, Gwent, Wales.
Castle Antiques Centre, Westerham, Kent.
Castle Antiques Ltd, Deddington, Oxon.
Castle Ashby Gallery, Castle Ashby, Northants.
Castle Bookshop, Colchester, Essex.
Castle Coins and Chiltern International Antiques, Dunstable, Beds.
Castle Galleries, Salisbury, Wilts.
Castle Gallery, Kenilworth, Warks.
Castle Gallery, Lincoln, Lincs.
Castle Gate Antiques Centre, Newark, Notts.
Castle, Simon, Twickenham, Middx.
Castlegate Antiques, Berwick-on-Tweed, Northumbs.
Castleton Country Furniture, Sherborne, Dorset.
Cat in the Window Antiques, Pateley Bridge, Yorks. North.
Cater, Patricia, Stow-on-the-Wold, Glos.
Cathedral Gallery, Norwich, Norfolk.
Cathedral Jewellers, Manchester, Lancs.
Catherine and Mary Antiques, Penzance, Cornwall.

Cato, Lennox, Lewes, Sussex East.
Cato, Mr and Mrs, Lewes, Sussex East.
Cato, Miles K. Wynn, Tywyn, Gwynedd, Wales.
Cattle, Barbara, York, Yorks. North.
Causey Antique Shop, Gosforth, Tyne and Wear.
Cavanagh, D., Edinburgh, Scotland.
Cave, F. and C.H., Northampton, Northants.
Cave, G., Northampton, Northants.
Cave and Sons Ltd, R.G., Ludlow, Shrops.
Cavendish Fine Arts - Janet Middlemiss, Windsor and Eton, Berks.
Cavendish House Antiques, Marlborough, Wilts.
Cavendish House Gallery, Ashbourne, Derbys.
Cavendish, Odile, London, SW1.
Cavendish Antiques, Rupert, London, SW6.
Cavendish Designs, Rupert, London, SW6.
Cawood Antiques, Cawood, Yorks. North.
Caxton House Antiques, Corwen, Clwyd, Wales.
Cazalet Ltd, Lumley, London, W1.
Cedar Antiques, Hartley Wintney, Hants.
Cedar House Gallery, Ripley, Surrey.
Centaur Gallery, London, N6.
Century Antiques, Denny, Scotland.
Century Antiques, Warminster, Wilts.
Century Antiques and Victoria Galleries, Windermere, Cumbria.
Century Galleries, Bideford, Devon.
Century Gallery, London, SW3.
Ceres Antiques, Ceres, Scotland.
Cerne Antiques, Cerne Abbas, Dorset.
Chadwick Antiques, Knowle, West Mids.
Chadwick Gallery, The, Henley-in-Arden, Warks.
Chalcraft, J.N., Brighton, Sussex East.
Chalk, H. and E., South Lopham, Norfolk.
Chalk, M., Horncastle, Lincs.
Challice, David, Exeter, Devon.
Challis, R., London, SE10.
Chalmers, A.P.H., Ringwood, Hants.
Chalmers, Mrs Katharine M., Edinburgh, Scotland.
Chalon, M. and T., Hambridge, Somerset.
Chalon U.K. Ltd, Hambridge, Somerset.
Chamberlain, Mary, Crowmarsh Gifford, Oxon.
Chambers, Mrs B.C., Boreham Street, Sussex East.
Chambers, L., Long Melford, Suffolk.
Chambers, M.B., Bideford, Devon.
Chambers, M.S., Shipston-on-Stour, Warks.
Chancery Antiques, Finedon, Northants.
Chancery Antiques, Tiverton, Devon.
Chancery Antiques Ltd, London, N1.
Chanticleer Antiques, London, SW6.
Chanctonbury Antiques, Washington, Sussex West.
Chandler, C.G., Sevenoaks, Kent.
Chandlers Antiques, Moreton-in-Marsh, Glos.
Chandlers Antiques, Sevenoaks, Kent.
Channel Islands Galleries Ltd, St. Peter Port, Guernsey, C.I.
Channer, C., Hucknall, Notts.
Chantry Bookshop and Gallery, Dartmouth, Devon.
Chapel Antiques, Kirkcudbright, Scotland.
Chapel Antiques, Nantwich, Cheshire.
Chapel Antiques, Penzance, Cornwall.
Chapel Antiques, St. Leonards-on-Sea, Sussex East.
Chapel Antiques, Wilmslow, Cheshire.
Chapel House Fireplaces, Holmfirth, Yorks. West.
Chapel Place Antiques, Tunbridge Wells, Kent.
Chaplin, R.M. and S.V., Coggeshall, Essex.
Chapman, H., London, SW6.
Chapman, I., Harrogate, Yorks. North.
Chapman, I., Whixley, Yorks. North.
Chapman, J.N., Barton-on-Humber, S. Humbs.
Chapman Antiques, Mark, Bosham, Sussex West.
Chapman, M.C., Finedon, Northants.
Chapman Medd and Sons, Easingwold, Yorks. North.
Chapman, Peter C., Bristol, Avon.
Chapman, P.J., London, N1.
Chapman Antiques, Peter, London, N1.
Chapman, R., Leominster, Herefs. and Worcs.
Chapman, R. A., Hythe, Kent.
Chapman Antiques, Sylvia, Leek, Staffs.
Chappell Antiques and Fine Art, K. , Bakewell, Derbys.
Chappell, P., Hertford, Herts.
Char Bazaar, Conwy, Gwynedd, Wales.

DEALERS' INDEX

Charge Antiques, Graham, London, W11.
Charisma Antiques Trade Warehouse, Barnsley, Yorks. South.
Charisma Curios and Antiques, Chorley, Lancs.
Charles International Antiques, Maidstone, Kent.
Charles, S., Cambridge, Cambs.
Charleston Antiques, Lewes, Sussex East.
Charlesworth, J., London, W9.
Charlesworth's Snuff Box, Benny, Great Harwood, Lancs.
Charleville Gallery, London, W14.
Charlotte's Wholesale Antiques, Cardiff, South Glam., Wales.
Charlton, E. and M., Eachwick, Northumbs.
Charlton Fine Art and Porcelain, E. and N.R., Marton, Cleveland.
Charlton Kings Antiques Centre, Cheltenham, Glos.
Charm Antiques, Carlisle, Cumbria.
Charman, G., Birmingham, West Mids.
Charmouth Antique Centre, Charmouth, Dorset.
Charnley Fine Arts, Longridge, Lancs.
Chart House, The, Shenfield, Essex.
Charterhouse Antiques, Teignmouth, Devon.
Charterhouse Gallery Ltd, Heath and Reach, Beds.
Chate, K., Wargrave, Berks.
Chate, Kate, Cirencester, Glos.
Chater-House, A.D., Long Melford, Suffolk.
Chateaubriand Antiques Centre, Burwash, Sussex East.
Chater-House Gallery, Long Melford, Suffolk.
Chatfield, P., Streetly, West Mids.
Chattels Antiques, Woking, Surrey.
Chaucer Bookshop, Canterbury, Kent.
Chaucer Fine Arts, London, SW1.
Chaunt House, Burwash, Sussex East.
Chavasse, T.J.G., Storrington, Sussex West.
Chave, M., Kelvedon, Essex.
Chawner, John, Birchington, Kent.
Cheapside Antiques, Knaresborough, Yorks. North.
Checkley, Mrs S., Grantham, Lincs.
Chelsea Antique Market, London, SW3.
Chelsea Bric-a-Brac Shop Ltd, London, SW19.
Chelsea Interiors, Bath, Avon.
Chelsea Rare Books, London, SW3.
Cheltenham Antique Market, Cheltenham, Glos.
Cheriton Antiques, Worthing, Sussex West.
Cheneviere Fine Arts, Antoine, London, W1.
Chenil Galleries, London, SW3.
Cherry Antiques, Hemel Hempstead, Herts.
Cherry, C., Monkton, Devon.
Chertsey Antiques, Chertsey, Surrey.
Cherub Antiques, Carshalton, Surrey.
Cherub Antiques, Mitcham, Surrey.
Cheshire Antiques, Macclesfield, Cheshire.
Cheshire Brick and Slate Co, Tarvin Sands, Cheshire.
Cheshire, E.M., Bingham, Notts.
Chess Antiques, Chesham, Bucks.
Chest of Drawers, The, Tetbury, Glos.
Chester Furniture Cave, Chester, Cheshire.
Chesterfield Antiques, Birmingham, West Mids.
Chestergate Antiques, Manchester, Lancs.
Chester-Master, Mr and Mrs R., Fairford, Glos.
Chester-Master, Mr and Mrs R.T.G., Fairford, Glos.
Chesterman, R.F., Leeds, Yorks. West.
Chesters, Y., Mathry, Dyfed, Wales.
Chesterton, Mrs. Margaret , St. Austell, Cornwall.
Chesterton-North, R.G, Wragby, Lincs.
Chevertons of Edenbridge Ltd, Edenbridge, Kent.
Cheyne, P.J.L., Altrincham, Cheshire.
Cheyne's, Altrincham, Cheshire.
Chighine, G. and B., London, W11.
Chilcott, Mrs M., Comrie, Scotland.
Child, J.C. and E.A., Morchard Bishop, Devon.
Child, P., London, N1.
Childhood Memories, Farnham, Surrey.
Chilton Antiques and Interiors, Juliet, Shrewsbury, Shrops.
Chilton, D., York, Yorks. North.
Chilton, J., Longridge, Lancs.
Chimera Books, Hurstpierpoint, Sussex West.
Chimes, The, Reepham, Norfolk.
Chimney Piece Antique Fires, Sheffield, Yorks. South.
China Locker, The, Lamberhurst, Kent.
Chippenham Antique Centre, Chippenham, Cambs.
Chipping Norton Antique Centre, Chipping Norton, Oxon.
Chipping Norton Books, Chipping Norton, Oxon.

Chislehurst Antiques, Chislehurst, Kent.
Chiswick Antiques, London, W13.
Chiswick Fireplace Co., The, London, W4.
Chitty, R.L., Cheltenham, Glos.
Chloe Antiques, Worthing, Sussex West.
Choice Antiques, Warminster, Wilts.
Christabelle's Antiques, Manchester, Lancs.
Christchurch Carpets, Christchurch, Dorset.
Christian, Ann and Peter, Blackpool, Lancs.
Christian, Stewart, London, N21.
Christie, G. A., Fochabers, Scotland.
Christie, J., London, W1.
Christie, P.S., London, W1.
Christophe, J., London, W1.
Christopher Antiques, London, SW11.
Christopher-Walsh, Mr and Mrs E., Modbury, Devon.
Christopher-Walsh, Mr. and Mrs E., Yealmpton, Devon.
Christopher's Antiques, Farnham, Surrey.
Christophers, W.J., Canterbury, Kent.
Chugg Antiques, Keith, Swansea, West Glam., Wales.
Chugg, Mrs M., Braunton, Devon.
Church House Antiques, Weybridge, Surrey.
Church Street Antiques, Godalming, Surrey.
Church Street Antiques, London, NW8.
Church Street Antiques, Wells-next-the-Sea, Norfolk.
Church View House Antiques, Kirk Michael, I. of Man.
Church Walk Antiques, Great Malvern, Herefs. & Worcs.
Churchgate Antiques, Empingham, Leics.
Churchgate Antiques, Sible Hedingham, Essex.
Churchhill Clocks, Midhurst, Sussex West.
Churchill Galleries, Sandgate, Kent.
Churt Curiosity Shop, Churt, Surrey.
Churton, C., Ewhurst Green, Sussex East.
Ciancimino Ltd, London, SW1.
Cider House Galleries Ltd, Bletchingley, Surrey.
Cinders, Edinburgh, Scotland.
Cinema Bookshop, London, WC1.
Circa Antiques, Bushey, Herts.
Circa Antiques, Guardbridge, Scotland.
Circus Antiques, Brighton, Sussex East.
Cirencester Antique Market, Cirencester, Glos.
Cirencester Antiques Centre, Cirencester, Glos.
Cirencester Antiques Ltd, Fairford, Glos.
City Clocks, London, EC1.
City of Birmingham Antique Market, The, Birmingham, West Mids.
City Strippers, Chester, Cheshire.
Civic Antiques, Whitchurch, Shrops.
Claessens, G. and J., Buxton, Derbys.
Clare Antique Warehouse, Clare, Suffolk.
Clare Collector, The, Clare, Suffolk.
Clare Gallery, Tunbridge Wells, Kent.
Clare Hall Company, Clare, Suffolk.
Clare, J. and A., Tunbridge Wells, Kent.
Clare, Mr and Mrs M.E., Stretton, Cheshire.
Clarence House Antiques, Watchet, Somerset.
Clare's Antiques and Auction Galleries, Garstang, Lancs.
Clareston Antiques, Tenby, Dyfed, Wales.
Clark, A., London, SE9.
Clark, A., Towcester, Northants.
Clark Antiques, Annarella, Stow-on-the-Wold, Glos.
Clark, A.Carson, Edinburgh, Scotland.
Clark, B.E., Walton-on-Thames, Surrey.
Clark, D.E., Brampton, Cambs.
Clark Galleries, Towcester, Northants.
Clark Antiques, Gerald, London, NW7.
Clark, G.J., London, NW7.
Clark Gallery. Scotia Maps - Mapsellers, The Carson, Edinburgh, Scotland.
Clark, H., Moretonhampstead, Devon.
Clark, H.M., Southend-on-Sea, Essex.
Clark, J., East Molesey, Surrey.
Clark, John, Brighton, Sussex East.
Clark Ltd, Jonathan, London, SW10.
Clark Antiques, Peter, Birmingham, West Mids.
Clark, P.B. and A.L., Penrith, Cumbria.
Clark, Penelope and Michael, Exwick, Devon.
Clark, Robert, Micklebring, Yorks. South.
Clark, R.R., Micklebring, Yorks. South.
Clark, Roger, Faringdon, Oxon.
Clarke Antiques Ltd, Christopher, Stow-on-the-Wold, Glos.
Clarke, C.J., Halesowen, West Mids.

DEALERS' INDEX

Clarke, C.J., Stow-on-the-Wold, Glos.
Clarke, Janet, Freshford, Avon.
Clarke, Miranda , London, W1.
Clarke, N.T.C., Edinburgh, Scotland.
Clarke, R.A., Oakham, Leics.
Clarke-Hall Ltd, J., London, EC4.
Classic Collection, London, WC1.
Clay, John, London, SW6.
Clay, Peter and Linda, Peterborough, Cambs.
Clayton, Mrs S., King's Lynn, Norfolk.
Clayton Jewellery, Tim, King's Lynn, Norfolk.
Cleeve Antiques, Bristol, Avon.
Cleeve Picture Framing, Bishops Cleeve, Glos.
Clegg, J. and A., Ludlow, Shrops.
Clegg, W., Huntercombe, Oxon.
Clements, James W., Carlisle, Cumbria.
Clements, V. and R., Plumley, Cheshire.
Clent Books, Bewdley, Herefs. & Worcs.
Clent Books, Halesowen, West Mids.
Cleobury Mortimer Antique Centre, Cleobury Mortimer, Shrops.
Clermont Antiques, Watton, Norfolk.
Clevedon Fine Arts (with Clevedon Books), Clevedon, Avon.
Cleverly, Mrs M.A., Malton, Yorks. North.
Clewer, P. and J., Nottingham, Notts.
Clewett, Mrs P., Oxford, Oxon.
Clewlow, J.A. and E.A., Nantwich, Cheshire.
Cliffe Antiques Centre, Lewes, Sussex East.
Cliffe Gallery Antiques , Lewes, Sussex East.
Clifford, J., Shrewsbury, Shrops.
Clifford, M. and J., Oswestry, Shrops.
Clifford and Son Ltd, T.J., Bath, Avon.
Clifton Antiques, Lytham, Lancs.
Clifton Antiques Market, Bristol, Avon.
Clifton, F., London, N16.
Clifton House Antiques, Haslingden, Lancs.
Clisby at Andwells Antiques, Bryan, Hartley Wintney, Hants.
Clock Clinic Ltd, The, London, SW15.
Clock House, The, Chapel-en-le-Frith, Derbys.
Clock House, Leavenheath, Suffolk.
Clock Shop, The, Hoylake, Merseyside.
Clock Shop, The, Hurstpierpoint, Sussex West.
Clock Shop Antiques, The, Boughton , Kent.
Clock Shop - Philip Setterfield of St. Albans, The, St. Albans, Herts.
Clock Shop Weybridge, The, Weybridge, Surrey.
Clock Tower Antiques, Tregony, Cornwall.
Clock Workshop, The, Caversham, Berks.
Clocks, Art & Antiques, Bodmin, Cornwall.
Cloisters Antiques Fair, Norwich, Norfolk.
Close Antiques, Alresford, Hants.
Close, Henry H., Abergavenny, Gwent, Wales.
Close, Mr and Mrs H., Abergavenny, Gwent, Wales.
Clow, M., Horncastle, Lincs.
Clow, M.R., Finedon, Northants.
Clunes Antiques, London, SW19.
Clutter, Uppingham, Leics.
Clwyd Coins and Stamps, Rhos-on-Sea, Clwyd, Wales.
Clydach Antiques, Swansea, West Glam., Wales.
Clyde Antiques, Patrington, N. Humbs.
Coach House, The, Comrie, Scotland.
Coach House, The, Costessey, Norfolk.
Coach House, The, Grundisburgh, Suffolk.
Coach House Antiques, Canterbury, Kent.
Coach House Antiques, Hastings, Sussex East.
Coach House Antiques, Whitby, Yorks. North.
Coach House Gallery, Wedmore, Somerset.
Coakley, P., London, N1.
Coast, G., Portsmouth, Hants.
Coats, A., London, W8.
Coats, Dick, London, W4.
Coats Oriental Carpets, London, W8.
Coates of Malvern, Joan, Great Malvern, Herefs. & Worcs.
Cobblers Hall Antiques, Toddington, Beds.
Cobham Galleries, Cobham, Surrey.
Cobra and Bellamy, London, SW1.
Cobweb Antiques, Cullompton, Devon.
Cobwebs, Bloxham, West Mids.
Cobwebs, Sheffield, Yorks. South.
Cochrane Antiques, Fergus, London, SW6.
Cochrane, F.V., London, SW6.
Cockain, Gordon M., Auchterarder, Scotland.

Cockram, Mrs A., Lincoln, Lincs.
Cockrell Antiques, Surbiton, Surrey.
Cockrell, Sheila and Peter, Surbiton, Surrey.
Cocoa, Cheltenham, Glos.
Cockermouth Antiques, Cockermouth, Cumbria.
Cockermouth Antiques Market, Cockermouth, Cumbria.
Coda Antiques, Tony, Boston, Lincs.
Codling, J.M.E., Holt, Norfolk.
Coggins, Mr and Mrs G., Painswick, Glos.
Coggeshall Antiques, Coggeshall, Essex.
Coggins Antiques, Ray, Westbury, Wilts.
Cohen, Edward, London, SW1.
Cohen, M., London, W11.
Cohen and Sons, B., London, SW1.
Cohen and Pearce (Oriental Porcelain), London, W11.
Cohn, George and Peter, London, WC1.
Coins International and Antiques International, Leeds, Yorks. West.
Coin and Jewellery Shop, The, Accrington, Lancs.
Coke, P., Sharrington, Norfolk.
Coldstream Antiques, Coldstream, Scotland.
Coldwell, P., Sheffield, Yorks. South.
Cole (Fine Paintings) Ltd, Christopher, Beaconsfield, Bucks.
Cole, J., London, N1.
Cole, V., Exning, Suffolk.
Colectomania, Aberaeron, Dyfed, Wales.
Colefax and Fowler, London, W1.
Coleman, Garrick D., London, W11.
Coleman, Garrick D., London, W8.
Coleman, G.D. and G.E., London, W8.
Coleman Antiques, Polly , Chesterfield, Derbys.
Coleman Antiques, Simon, London, SW13.
Coleman, W. and B., Clayton-le-Moors, Lancs.
Coles, D.A., Clevedon, Avon.
Coles, M., Kettering, Northants.
Coleshill Antiques and Interiors Ltd, Coleshill, Warks.
Coll, Mrs P., Long Melford, Suffolk.
Collard, B., Totnes, Devon.
Collards Books, Totnes, Devon.
Collectables, Kingston-on-Spey, Scotland.
Collectables, Tunbridge Wells, Kent.
Collector, The, Barnard Castle, Durham.
Collector, The, London, NW8.
Collectors Cabin, Holt, Norfolk.
Collectors Centre, Cambridge, Cambs.
Collector Centre, Edinburgh, Scotland.
Collectors Corner, Bournemouth, Dorset.
Collectors' Corner, Bradford, Yorks. West.
Collectors Corner, Northallerton, Yorks. North.
Collectors Corner, Waddesdon, Bucks.
Collectors Corner Antiques, Croydon, Surrey.
Collectors' Fine Art at Rostrum, London, W11.
Collectors Gallery, The, Caversham, Berks.
Collectors' Gallery, Shrewsbury, Shrops.
Collectors' Market, Cambridge, Cambs.
Collectors Old Toy Shop and Antiques, Halifax, Yorks. West.
Collectors' Paradise, Leigh-on-Sea, Essex.
Collectors' Paradise Ltd, Wolverhampton, West Mids.
Collectors Shop, The, Birmingham, West Mids.
Collectors Shop, The, Edinburgh, Scotland.
Collessie Antiques, Collessie, Scotland.
Collett, J., Chipping Campden, Glos.
Collicott, R., Honiton, Devon.
Collier, Mrs D.E., Sheringham, Norfolk.
Collier, Mark, Fordingbridge, Hants.
Collier, W. and Mrs J., Christchurch, Dorset.
Collinge Antiques, Llandudno, Gwynedd, Wales.
Collinge Antiques, Llandudno Junction, Gwynedd, Wales.
Collinge, Nicky, Llandudno, Gwynedd, Wales.
Collinge, Nicky, Llandudno Junction, Gwynedd, Wales.
Collings, C.J. and M., Ashton-under-Lyne, Lancs.
Collingwood & Company Ltd, London, W1.
Collins, A., Manchester, Lancs.
Collins Antiques (F.G. and C. Collins Ltd.), Wheathampstead, Herts.
Collins and Clark, Cambridge, Cambs.
Collins, Edwin, Leominster, Herefs. and Worcs.
Collins, J., Llanrwst, Gwynedd, Wales.
Collino, Julie, London, SW7.
Collins, J., London W1.
Collins and Son, J., Bideford, Devon.
Collins, J.G., Cambridge, Cambs.

DEALERS' INDEX

Collins, Peter, London, SW6.
Collins, P.R., Merton, Devon.
Collins, Noel, Dorking, Surrey.
Collins, N., Moreton-in-Marsh, Glos.
Collins, S.J. and M.C., Wheathampstead, Herts.
Collins, T. M., Dorking, Surrey.
Colliton Antique and Craft Centre, Dorchester, Dorset.
Collyer Antiques, Jean, Boughton, Kent.
Collyer, Mrs J.B., Boughton, Kent.
Collyer, R., Birmingham, West Mids.
Colmore Galleries Ltd, Henley-in-Arden, Warks.
Colnaghi & Co Ltd, P. and D., London, W1.
Colt, R., Farnham, Surrey.
Coltishall Antiques Centre, Coltishall, Norfolk.
Coltsfoot Gallery, Leominster, Herefs. & Worcs.
Columbus, Fairford, Glos.
Colyer, J.M., Wallasey, Merseyside.
Colystock Antiques, Stockland, Devon.
Colyton Antique Centre, Colyton, Devon.
Combe Cottage Antiques, Castle Combe, Wilts.
Comberton Antiques, Comberton, Cambs.
Commemoratives, London, N1.
Complete Automobilist, The, Greatford, Lincs.
Compton Antiques Ltd, Sherborne, Dorset.
Compton Gallery, The, Windsor and Eton, Berks.
Compton-Dando, A.C., White Colne, Essex.
Compton-Dando (Fine Arts) Limited, White Colne, Essex.
Conboy, P.J., Sheffield, Yorks. South.
Conder, R., Grantham, Lincs.
Conein-Veber, S.A., Great Malvern, Herefs. and Worcs.
Congleton Antiques, Congleton, Cheshire.
Conlon, Barbara, Newark, Notts.
Connaught Brown plc, London, W1.
Connaught Galleries, London, W2.
Connaughton, J., North Walsham, Norfolk.
Connell, John, Wargrave, Berks.
Connoisseur Antique Gallery, Brighton, Sussex East.
Connoisseur Gallery, The, London, SW1.
Conquest House Antiques, Canterbury, Kent.
Constable, C., St. Albans, Herts.
Constable, J., Moreton-in-Marsh, Glos.
Constant Reader Bookshop, The, London, SW6.
Constantinescu, Toni and Christine, Brecon, Powys, Wales.
Constantinidi, P., London, W1.
Conti, V., London, NW8.
Conway Antiques, Conway, Gwynedd, Wales.
Cook, E.J. and C.A., Gloucester, Glos.
Cook and Son Antiques, E.J., Gloucester, Glos.
Cook, K.J., Rochester, Kent.
Cook of Marlborough Fine Art Ltd, Marlborough, Wilts.
Cook, R.L., Holt, Norfolk.
Cook, Sheila, London, W11.
Cook, W., East Budleigh, Devon.
Cook, W.J., Marlborough, Wilts.
Cooke, D., Playden, Sussex East.
Cooke, F.G., Ironbridge, Shrops.
Cooke Antiques Ltd, Mary, London, W8.
Cooke, P., Pontypridd, Mid. Glam., Wales.
Cookson, R., Bristol, Avon.
Cookson, R., Leominster, Herefs. and Worcs.
Cookson, R., Winchcombe, Glos.
Cookstown Antiques, Cookstown, Co. Tyrone, N. Ireland.
Cooling, I., Cardiff, South Glam., Wales.
Coombe Street Galleries, Exeter, Devon.
Coombes, J. and M., Dorking, Surrey.
Coombes, R., Burnham-on-Sea, Somerset.
Coombs, A. and L., Richmond, Surrey.
Cooney, J. , Darwen, Lancs.
Coop, Mrs M., Holmfirth, Yorks. West.
Cooper Antiques, Bruno, Long Melford, Suffolk.
Cooper Antiques, Eileen, Braunton, Devon.
Cooper, E.T., Gosport, Hants.
Cooper Fine Arts Ltd, London, SW6.
Cooper, G.E., Helmsley, Yorks. North.
Cooper, G.R. and M., Harrogate, Yorks. North.
Cooper, J., North Petherwin, Cornwall.
Cooper, J., London, SW10.
Cooper Antiques, John, St. Helier, Jersey, C.I.
Cooper and Son (Ilkley) Ltd, J.H., Ilkley, Yorks. West.
Cooper, J.P., Disley, Cheshire.
Cooper, P., Petworth, Sussex West.
Cooper Antiques, Philip, Petworth, Sussex West.
Cooper, S.M., Bath, Avon.
Cooper, T., Kirkbymoorside, Yorks. North.
Cooper t/a Sheila Smith Antiques, Sheila, Bath, Avon.
Coote Tapestries, Belinda, London, W8.
Cope, I., Tutbury, Staffs.
Cope-Brown, S.J., Cambridge, Cambs.
Coppage, J., Canterbury, Kent.
Coppelia Antiques, Plumley, Cheshire.
Copper Kettle Antiques, Watford, Herts.
Copperfield Antiques, Gravesend, Kent.
Copperfield Antiques, Loughborough, Leics.
Copperfield, Robert, Macclesfield, Cheshire.
Copperhouse Gallery - W. Dyer & Sons, Hayle, Cornwall.
Coppock, Mrs Jill A., Stockport, Cheshire.
Copsey, Stephen, Huntingdon, Cambs.
Copsey, Stephen, London, NW1.
Copsey, Stephen, Southoe, Cambs.
Copthorne Antiques, Copthorne, Sussex West.
Corbey, J.W. and Mrs . M.A., Lechlade, Glos.
Cordelia and Perdy's Antique Junk Shop, Lichfield, Staffs.
Cordell Antiques, Sonia, Ipswich, Suffolk.
Corder, J., Coggeshall, Essex.
Corfield Antiques Ltd, Lymington, Hants.
Cork Brick Antiques, Bungay, Suffolk.
Cormack, Mrs J., Crieff, Scotland.
Corn Exchange Antiques, Tunbridge Wells, Kent.
Corn Mill Antiques, Skipton, Yorks. North.
Corner Cabinet, Thornton Heath, Surrey.
Corner Cottage Antiques, Market Bosworth, Leics.
Corner Cupboard, Bolton, Lancs.
Corner Cupboard, The, Boxford, Suffolk.
Corner Cupboard, The, London, NW2.
Corner Cupboard, The, Woodford Halse, Northants.
Corner Cupboard Antiques, Penarth, South Glam., Wales.
Corner Cupboard Curios, Cirencester, Glos.
Corner Portobello Antiques Supermarket, The, London, W11.
Corner Shop, The, Bradford, Yorks. West.
Corner Shop, The, Eye, Suffolk.
Corner Shop, The, Hay-on-Wye, Powys, Wales.
Corner Shop Antiques, Bury St. Edmunds, Suffolk.
Cornucopia, London, SW1.
Cornucopia Antiques, Hebden Bridge, Yorks. West.
Corridor Stamp Shop, Bath, Avon.
Corney House Antiques, Penrith, Cumbria.
Coronel, H.S., London, W11.
Corrigan Antiques, London, N1.
Corrin Antiques, John, Douglas, I. of Man.
Corry, E.I., Derby, Derbys.
Corry, Mrs E.I., Leicester, Leics.
Corry's, Leicester, Leics.
Corry's Antiques, Derby, Derbys.
Corve Galleries, The, Ludlow, Shrops.
Cossa Antiques, Gabor, Cambridge, Cambs.
Cotham Galleries, Bristol, Avon.
Cotham Hill Bookshop, Bristol, Avon.
Cothay Antiques, Maulds Meaburn, Cumbria.
Cotswold Antiques Centre, Stow-on-the-Wold, Glos.
Cotswold Galleries, Stow-on-the-Wold, Glos.
Cottage Antiques, Beaminster, Dorset.
Cottage Antiques, Cambridge, Cambs.
Cottage Antiques, Darwen, Lancs.
Cottage Antiques, Kendal, Cumbria.
Cottage Antiques, Ringway, Cheshire.
Cottage Antiques, Snainton, Yorks. North.
Cottage Antiques, Southampton, Hants.
Cottage Antiques (1984) Ltd, Walsden, Yorks. West.
Cottage Antiques and Curios, Thirsk, Yorks. North.
Cottage Curios, Allonby, Cumbria.
Cottage Style Antiques, Rochester, Kent.
Cotterill, P., Much Wenlock, Shrops.
Cotton Antiques, Barry, Ross-on-Wye, Herefs. & Worcs.
Cotton (Antiques), Joan, West Bridgford, Notts.
Cotton Antiques and Fine Art, Nick, Watchet, Somerset.
Cottonwood, Newnham-on-Severn, Glos.
Cottrell, Mrs S., Woodchurch, Kent.
Coughton Galleries Ltd, Arthingworth, Northants.
Coulborn, P., Sutton Coldfield, West Mids.
Coulborn and Sons, Thomas, Sutton Coldfield, West Mids.
Coulson, I., Haydon Bridge, Northumbs.
Coulson Antiques, Peter, North Shields, Tyne and Wear.
Coulter Galleries, York, Yorks. North.
Country Antiques, The, Antrim, Co. Antrim, N. Ireland.

DEALERS' INDEX

Country Antiques, Boroughbridge, Yorks. North.
Country Antiques, Kidwelly, Dyfed, Wales.
Country Antiques, Killearn, Scotland.
Country Antiques, Market Bosworth, Leics.
Country Antiques, Windlesham, Surrey.
Country Bygones and Antiques, Ipswich, Suffolk.
Country Clocks, Tring, Herts.
Country Connections (Esk House Arts), Grosmont, Yorks. North.
Country Cottage Interiors, Kingsley, Staffs.
Country and Eastern, Norwich, Norfolk.
Country Furniture, Richmond, Surrey.
Country Furniture, Windsor and Eton, Berks.
Country Furniture Antique Centre, Charlecote, Warks.
Country Furniture Shop, Penn, Bucks.
Country Homes, Tetbury, Glos.
Country House Antiques, Bungay, Suffolk.
Country House Interiors, Wisbech, Cambs.
Country Life Antiques, Bushey, Herts.
Country Life Antiques, Cheltenham, Glos.
Country Life Antiques, Stow-on-the-Wold, Glos.
Country Life by Bursig, Arundel, Sussex West.
Country Living, Painswick, Glos.
Country Pine Antiques, Alnwick, Northumbs.
Country Pine Antiques, Brompton, Yorks. North.
Country Pine Antiques, Chatton, Northumbs.
Country Pine Antiques, Witney, Oxon.
Country Pine Antiques Co, The, Cuxton, Kent.
Country Pine Shop, The, West Haddon, Northants.
Country Seat, The, Huntercombe, Oxon.
Countrylife Gallery, Hitchin, Herts.
County Antiques, Ashford, Kent.
County Antiques, Tunbridge Wells, Kent.
County Antiques Centre, Ilminster, Somerset.
Court Antiques, Broadway, Herefs. & Worcs.
Court Antiques (Richmond), Richmond, Surrey.
Court Curio Shop, Edinburgh, Scotland.
Court Gallery, The, East Molesey, Surrey.
Courtney Ltd, Richard, London, SW3.
Courtney and Sons, William, Birkenhead, Merseyside.
Courtyard Antiques, Brasted, Kent.
Courtyard Antiques, Wells, Somerset.
Courtyard Antiques and Collectors Centre, Seaton, Devon.
Courtyard Antiques Market, The, Seaford, Sussex East.
Cousans, J., Annahilt, Co. Down, N. Ireland.
Cousins and Son, E.W., Ixworth, Suffolk.
Coutts, A.C., London, W1.
Cove, Anthony, Windsor and Eton, Berks.
Cove, T., Minety, Wilts.
Covent Garden Flea Market, London, WC2.
Coward Fine Silver, Timothy, Braunton, Devon.
Cowbridge Antiques, Cowbridge, South Glam., Wales.
Cowden Antiques, Tunbridge Wells, Kent.
Cowderoy Antiques, John, Eastbourne, Sussex East.
Cowderoy, J.H., R., D.J. and R.A., Eastbourne, Sussex East.
Cowe, Mrs B., Dunkeld, Scotland.
Cowell and Sons Architectural Antiques, W.J., Broughton, Lancs.
Cowen Antiques, Christopher G., Brighton, Sussex East.
Cowen, C. and S., Brighton, Sussex East.
Cowfold Clocks, Cowfold, Sussex West.
Cowpland, Mr and Mrs D., Bexhill-on-Sea, Sussex East.
Cowpland, J.A., Tunbridge Wells, Kent.
Cox, A., London, SW14.
Cox, A. H., Heath and Reach, Beds.
Cox and Company, London, SW1.
Cox Antiques, Cyril, Leek, Staffs.
Cox at College Gateway Bookshop, Claude, Ipswich, Suffolk.
Cox, Mrs O.M. and R.D., Stamford, Lincs.
Cox, Mr and Mrs R., London, SW1.
Cox Antiques, Robin, Stamford, Lincs.
Cox, T.G., Bridport, Dorset.
Cox-Freeman, J., St. Margaret's Bay, Kent.
Cox's Corner, Bridport, Dorset.
Coy, S.D. and J., Chipping Campden, Glos.
Crabb, P., London, NW2.
Crabbe, Peter Ian, Cambridge, Cambs.
Cracknell (Antiques) Ltd, Nigel, Marlborough, Wilts.
Cracknell (Antiques) Ltd, Nigel, Petworth, Sussex West.
Cracknell, N.O., Petworth, Sussex West.
Crackston, J., Honiton, Devon.
Crafers Antiques, Wickham Market, Suffolk.

Craig, J.G. and M.B., Port Erin, I. of Man.
Craiglea Clocks, Edinburgh, Scotland.
Craik Ltd, Brian and Caroline, Bath, Avon.
Cranbrook Antique Centre, Cranbrook, Kent.
Cranbrook Gallery, Cranbrook, Kent.
Cranford Clocks, Knutsford, Cheshire.
Cranford Galleries, Knutsford, Cheshire.
Cranglegate Antiques, Swaffham, Norfolk.
Cranleigh Antiques, Ewhurst, Surrey.
Cranston, Charles, Kinross, Scotland.
Craven Books, Skipton, Yorks. North.
Craven Gallery, London, W2.
Craven, K. and B., Farnham Common, Bucks.
Crawford, A.S.B., Thornhill, Scotland.
Crawford, M., London, N1.
Crawley and Asquith Ltd, London, SW4.
Crawley, Mrs M., Chislehurst, Kent.
Crawley, R.A. and I.D., Watlington, Oxon.
Crawshaw, H. and E., Whittington, Staffs.
Creaton, I., St. Helier, Jersey, C.I.
Creaton, S., Moreton-in-Marsh, Glos.
Cree, G.W., Market Deeping, Lincs.
Creed Books Ltd, Ann, London, WC2.
Creeke, Miss J.M., Sidmouth, Devon.
Creeke, Miss J.M., Sidmouth, Devon.
Creese-Parsons, S.H., Bath, Avon.
Creighton, K., Romsey, Hants.
Creightons Antique Centre, Romsey, Hants.
Cremer-Price, T., Plymouth, Devon.
Cremyll Antiques, Cremyll, Cornwall.
Crescent Antiques, Disley, Cheshire.
Crest Collectables, Eastbourne, Sussex East.
Crested China Co, The, Driffield, N. Humbs.
Crewe-Read, D., London, SW6.
Crewkerne Furniture Emporium, Crewkerne, Somerset.
Crick, Mrs M.E., London, W8.
Criddle, G.H. and J., Cambridge, Cambs.
Crieff Antiques, Crieff, Scotland.
Cringle, M. and A., Burnham Market, Norfolk.
Cripps, A. and C., Wingham, Kent.
Crisford, A., London, NW8.
Crisp Antiques, J.W., Teddington, Middx.
Crispin Antiques, Ian, London, NW1.
Crocker, J.E., Henley-on-Thames, Oxon.
Crockett, Miss P., Haunton, Staffs.
Croft Antiques, John, Bath, Avon.
Crofts, Peter A., Wisbech, Cambs.
Crome Gallery and Frame Shop, Norwich, Norfolk.
Cronan Ltd, Sandra, London, W1.
Cronin Antiques, Cardiff, South Glam., Wales.
Cronin, J., Cardiff, South Glam., Wales.
Crook, W.V. and A., Kidderminster, Herefs. and Worcs.
Crooks, J., Hertford, Herts.
Cropper, R., Ilminster, Somerset.
Crosbie, R. and J., Longridge, Lancs.
Crosbie-Smith, Mrs P., Exeter, Devon.
Cross Antiques, Watlington, Oxon.
Cross (Fine Art), David, Bristol, Avon.
Cross - Fine Paintings, Edward, Weybridge, Surrey.
Cross, F., Ryde, I. of Wight.
Cross, G.G., Arundel, Sussex West.
Cross Hayes Antiques, Malmesbury, Wilts.
Cross, I., King's Langley, Herts.
Cross Keys Jewellers, Devizes, Wilts.
Cross Keys Jewellers, Marlborough, Wilts.
Cross, L.T. and N., Croughton, Northants.
Cross, M. and R., Swaffham, Norfolk.
Crossley, M., Great Missenden, Bucks.
Crossroads Antiques, Prestwick, Scotland.
Crotty and Son Ltd, J., London, SW6.
Crouch End Antiques, London, N8.
Crouch, P., Ridgewell, Essex.
Croucher, D.G., Bromsgrove, Herefs. and Worcs.
Crouchman, C.C., Shenfield, Essex.
Croughton Antiques, Croughton, Northants.
Crowe, P., Norwich, Norfolk.
Crowe, Antiquarian Book Seller, Peter, Norwich, Norfolk.
Crown Antiques, Bidford-on-Avon, Warks.
Crown Square Antiques, Kirkbymoorside, Yorks. North.
Crowson, G.H., Skegness, Lincs.
Crowther, C., Padiham, Lancs.
Crowther, D.J., Hartlepool, Cleveland.

DEALERS' INDEX

Crowther of Syon Lodge Ltd, Isleworth, Middx.
Crowther, Mrs V., London, SW11.
Croxton, B., Yatton, Herefs. and Worcs.
Croydon and Sons Ltd, Ipswich, Suffolk.
Crozier, G.R., Bishop's Stortford, Herts.
Cruck House Antiques, Much Wenlock, Shrops.
Cruickshank, W., Horncastle, Lincs.
Crump, G., Bideford, Devon.
Cry for the Moon, Godalming, Surrey.
Csaky's Antiques, London, SW1.
Csaky's Antiques, Sonning-on-Thames, Berks.
Cull Antiques, Petersfield, Hants.
Cull, J., Petersfield, Hants.
Cullen, A. and R.S., Hemel Hempstead, Herts.
Cullompton Antiques Ltd., Cullompton, Devon.
Cullompton Old Tannery Antiques, Cullompton, Devon.
Cumbley, G.R., King's Lynn, Norfolk.
Cumming, A.J., Lewes, Sussex East.
Cunningham, D.M., Warwick, Warks.
Cunningham Antiques, E., Falmouth, Cornwall.
Cunningham, J.R., Kilmarnock, Scotland.
Cunningham, Mrs Patricia, Leamington Spa, Warks.
Cupboard Antiques, The, Amersham, Bucks.
Curá Antiques, London, W11.
Cura, D., London, W11.
Curd, S., Goudhurst, Kent.
Curio Cottage, Bingley, Yorks. West.
Curios, London, N19.
Curious Grannies, London, E8.
Curiosity Antiques, Portscatho, Cornwall.
Curiosity Antiques, Rye, Sussex East.
Curiosity Corner, Hucknall, Notts.
Curiosity Shop, Bolton, Lancs.
Curiosity Shop, The, Ludlow, Shrops.
Curiosity Shop, The, South Shields, Tyne and Wear.
Curiosity Shop, The, Stow-on-the-Wold, Glos.
Curtis, P. and Mrs R., Torquay, Devon.
Curzon Gallery, The David, Thames Ditton, Surrey.
Cuss Clock Co. Ltd, The, London, SW1.
Cutler Antique and Collectors Fairs, Stancie, Nantwich, Cheshire.
Cutler Antique and Collectors Fair, Stancie, Sutton Coldfield, West Mids.
Cutting, Mrs T., Bury St. Edmunds, Suffolk.
Cwmgwili Mill, Carmarthen, Dyfed, Wales.

D

D. and G. Antiques, Newark, Notts.
D. J. Jewellery, Parkstone, Dorset.
D. and V. Antiques, Newark, Notts.
D. M. Restorations, Weston-Super-Mare, Avon.
D'Amico Antiques Ltd, Norwich, Norfolk.
D'Amico Antiques Ltd, Strachan, Scotland.
D'Arcy Antiques, Lechlade, Glos.
D'Ardenne, D.L and P.J., Branksome, Dorset.
D'Offay, Anthony, London, W1.
D'Orsai Ltd, Sebastian, London, WC1.
D'Oyly, N.H., Saffron Walden, Essex.
da Costa, Z., Camberley, Surrey.
Dacorum Borough Council, Hemel Hempstead, Herts.
Dade, Clifford and Roger, Thames Ditton, Surrey.
Daffern Antiques, John, Harrogate, Yorks. North.
Daggett, Charles and Caroline , London , W11.
Daggett Gallery, London, W11.
Daggett Gallery, Charles, London, W11
Dale, D., Bridport, Dorset.
Dale, John, London, W11.
Dale Ltd, Peter, London, SW1.
Daleside Antiques, Markington, Yorks. North.
Daly, M. and S., Wadebridge, Cornwall.
Daly PBFA, Peter M., Winchester, Hants.
Dam Mill Antiques, Codsall, Staffs.
Danbury Antiques, Danbury, Essex.
Danby Antiques, York, Yorks. North.
Dando, Andrew, Bath, Avon.
Dando, A.P. and J.M., Bath, Avon.
Dandy, Mr and Mrs W., Aldeburgh, Suffolk.
Daniel, A., London, N1.
Daniell, J., Upton-upon-Severn, Herefs. and Worcs.
Daniels, Mrs Gina, Brighton, Sussex East.
Dann Antiques Ltd, Melksham, Wilts.

Dann, S. and M., Hatherleigh, Devon.
Daphne's Antiques, Penzance, Cornwall.
Dare, George, London, W8.
Darenth Bookshop, Otford, Kent.
Darnell, C., Welshpool, Powys, Wales.
Dartford Antiques, Dartford, Kent.
Dartnell, Mrs P., Preston, Lancs.
Darwen Antique Centre, Darwen, Lancs.
Daszewski, A.A.W., East Grinstead, Sussex West.
Davana Original Interiors, Colchester, Essex.
Davar, Zal, London, SW3.
Davenham Antique Centre, Davenham, Cheshire.
Davey, Mrs P., Blandford Forum, Dorset.
David Charles, Pontypridd, Mid-Glam, Wales.
David, G., Cambridge, Cambs.
David, Jean and John Antiques, Westcliff-on-Sea, Essex.
David, P., Aberystwyth, Dyfed, Wales.
Davidson and Begg Antiques Ltd, Edinburgh, Scotland.
Davidson Brothers, London, N1.
Davidson, Eric, Edinburgh, Scotland.
Davidson, J., Maidenhead, Berks.
Davidson, Mrs J., Maldon, Essex.
Davidson, Mrs J., Preston, Lancs.
Davidson, Michael, London, W11.
Davidson Antiques, Neil, Chester, Cheshire.
Davidson Antiques, Richard, Arundel, Sussex West.
Davidson, S. and C., London, N1.
Davidson, S.M., Merstham, Surrey.
Davidson's The Jewellers Ltd, Newcastle-upon-Tyne, Tyne and Wear.
Davies Antiques, London, W8.
Davies Antiques, Whalley, Lancs.
Davies, Mrs A., Llanelli, Dyfed, Wales.
Davies, A., Morriston, West Glam., Wales.
Davies Ltd, A. B., London, W1.
Davies Antiques Centre, Chepstow, Gwent, Wales.
Davies, A.G., London, W1.
Davies, A.H., Pinner, Middx.
Davies Antiques, Barbara, Ringwood, Hants.
Davies Oriental Art, Barry, London, W1.
Davies, C., London, SW3.
Davies, C., Whitstable, Kent.
Davies, Mrs Elizabeth, Wickham Market, Suffolk.
Davies, F.M., Lincoln, Lincs.
Davies, G., Cockermouth, Cumbria.
Davies, G., E. and P., Whalley, Lancs.
Davies, H., Coxley, Somerset.
Davies, H.A. and J., Church Stretton, Shrops.
Davies, H.Q.V., London, W8.
Davies, Mrs J., Bletchingley, Surrey.
Davies Fine Paintings, John, Stow-on-the-Wold, Glos.
Davies, J.F., Chepstow, Gwent, Wales.
Davies Antiques, Lynne, Ellesmere, Shrops.
Davies, Mrs M., Bolton, Lancs.
Davies, Norman, Holt, Clwyd, Wales.
Davies, Philip, Swansea, West Glam., Wales.
Davies, P.A., Tunbridge Wells, Kent.
Davies, R. and D., Wendover, Bucks.
Davies, R.E., Fishguard, Dyfed, Wales.
Davies, V., London, NW1.
Davies, V., London, SW3.
Davies, Mrs V., Wedmore, Somerset.
Davies, W.H., Murton, West Glam., Wales.
Davighi, N., London, W6.
Davis, Andrew, Kew Green, Surrey.
Davis (Works of Art) Ltd, Kenneth, London, SW1.
Davis Antiques, John E., Barkham, Berks.
Davis, M., Pembroke, Dyfed, Wales.
Davis, P., Leeds, Yorks. West.
Davis, P, Skegness, Lincs.
Davis, P. and L., Tetbury, Glos.
Davis Antiquarian Horologist, Roger A., Great Bookham, Surrey.
Davis Ltd, Reginald, Oxford, Oxon.
Davis, Mrs S., London, W1.
Davis-Shaw, M.T., Havant, Hants.
Dawson, B., Heath and Reach, Beds.
Dawson, B., Little Brickhill, Bucks.
Dawson, J., Stamford, Lincs.
Dawson of Stamford, Stamford, Lincs.
Dawson Antiques, Zona, Charlton Marshall, Dorset.
Day Antiques, Alan, Edinburgh, Scotland.

DEALERS' INDEX

Day Antiques, Ann and Roger, Tetbury, Glos.
Day of Eastbourne Fine Art, John, Eastbourne, Sussex East.
Day, M., London, W1.
Day Ltd, Richard, London, W1.
Day Ltd, Shirley, London, SW1.
de Albuquerque, Michael and Jane, Wallingford, Oxon.
De Beaumont, Dominic, London, SW6.
de Biolley Oriental Art, Jehanne, London, W1.
De Cacqueray, A., London, SW1.
de Courcy-Ireland, Polly, Winchester, Hants.
De Fresne, Pierre, Edinburgh, Scotland.
de Fresnes, The Baron, Galston, Scotland.
De Grey Antiques, Hull, N. Humbs.
de Kort, E.J., Bembridge, I. of Wight.
de Lotz, P.G., London, NW3.
De Montfort, Robertsbridge, Sussex East.
de Rin, V., London, SW3.
de Rouffignac, Colin, Wigan, Lancs.
De Tavener Antiques, Ramsgate, Kent.
Deacon and Blyth Fine Art, Great Bircham, Norfolk.
Deacon, Michael R., Great Bircham,, Norfolk.
Deakin, J.R., Seaford, Sussex East.
Dean, Mrs B, Spalding, Lincs.
Dean, G., Colchester, Essex.
Dean Antiques, G.L., Glossop, Derbys.
Dean, Graham L. and Joyce C., Glossop, Derbys.
Dean Antiques, Margery, Colchester, Essex.
Dean Forest Antiques, Berry Hill Pike, Glos.
Dean Gallery, The, Newcastle-upon-Tyne, Tyne and Wear.
Deane Antiques, Graham, Brighton, Sussex East.
Deane Antiques, Graham, Brighton, Sussex East.
Dean's Antiques, London, N1.
Dean's Antiques, Spalding, Lincs.
Deans, Thomas, London, SW12.
Dearden, M. and S., Bath, Avon.
Dearden, M. and S., East Pennard, Somerset.
Debenham Antique Centre, Debenham, Suffolk.
Decade Antiques, Wallasey, Merseyside.
Decodream, Coulsdon, Surrey.
Decor Galleries, Southport, Merseyside.
Decors, Deal, Kent.
Deddington Antique Centre, The, Deddington, Oxon.
Dee's Antiques, Windsor and Eton, Berks.
Deerstalker Antiques, Whitchurch, Bucks.
Deighton Bell and Co, Cambridge, Cambs.
Delawood Antiques, Hunstanton, Norfolk.
Delbridge, M., Dulverton, Somerset.
Delehar, London, W11.
Delehar, Peter, London, W11.
Delf Antiques, Sandwich, Kent.
Delf Stream Gallery, Sandwich, Kent.
Delieb Antiques , London, NW11.
Delieb, E., London, NW11.
Delightful Muddle, The, London, SW1.
Delmas, Hurst Green, Sussex East.
Delomosne and Son Ltd, North Wraxall, Wilts.
Delta Antiques, Liverpool, Merseyside.
Demas, London, W1.
Demetzy Books, London, W11.
Dempsey, J. and B., Hindon, Wilts.
Dempsey, P.D. and J.M., London, SE10.
Den of Antiquity, The, Glasgow, Scotland.
Den of Antiquity, The, Hythe, Kent.
Dench Antiques, Sandgate , Kent.
Dene Hard Antiques, Garelochhead, Scotland.
Denham, H., Ripley, Surrey.
Denham Gallery, John, London, NW6.
Denis, Rose, Sheringham, Norfolk.
Denley-Hill, S.K., Cardiff, South Glam., Wales.
Denman, Mrs M., Copthorne, Sussex West.
Dennett Coins, Clive, Norwich, Norfolk.
Dennett, C.E., South Cave, N. Humbs.
Denning Antiques, Guildford, Surrey.
Dennis, A.T. and Y.M., Hastings, Sussex East.
Dennis, B.W., Bath, Avon.
Dennis, Mr and Mrs J., Leicester, Leics.
Dennis, P., Tewkesbury, Glos.
Dennis, Richard, London, W8.
Dennison, D.H., Lewes, Sussex East.
Dennison and Son, H.P., Lewes, Sussex East.
Dennler Antiques, Guy, London, SW1.
Denny Ltd, Colin, London, SW3.

Denton Antiques, London, W8.
Denton (Antiques), J., Luton, Beds.
Denton, M.T. and M.E., London, W8.
Denton-Ford, A.H., Long Melford, Suffolk.
Denver Antiques, Peter, Bournemouth, Dorset.
Denver House Antiques and Collectables, Burford, Oxon.
Denver-White, P., Bournemouth, Dorset.
Denvir, John, London, W11.
Denwood, L. A. and K., London, W5.
Deo Juvante Antiques, Rochester, Kent.
Derby Antique Centre, Derby, Derbys.
Derby Cottage Collectables, Exning, Suffolk.
Derby Street Antique Emporium, Burton-on-Trent, Staffs.
Derbys, R.C. and M.T., Harrogate, Yorks. North.
Derbyshire Antiques Ltd, Harrogate, Yorks. North.
Derbyshire Clocks, Glossop, Derbys.
Dereham Antiques, East Dereham, Norfolk.
Derham, R., Earsham, Norfolk.
Designs on Pine, Lincoln, Lincs.
Desmond, Mrs D., Langport, Somerset.
Desmonde, Kay, London, W8.
Deuchar, A.S. and A.W.N., Perth, Scotland.
Deuchar and Son, A.S., Perth, Scotland.
Deutsch Antiques, H. and W., London, W8.
Deva Antiques, Hartley Wintney, Hants.
Deverall, Ivan R., Uckfield, Sussex East.
Devonshire House Antiques and Collectors Centre, Sidmouth, Devon.
Dew, Roderick, Eastbourne, Sussex East.
Dewdney, J.M., Farnborough, Kent.
Dewdney, R., Dorking, Surrey.
Dewdney, Mrs V., Bristol, Avon.
Dews Fine Art, Steven, Hull, N. Humbs.
Di Michele Antiques, E. and A., London, W11.
Diamond and Son, Harry, Brighton, Sussex East.
Diamond, R. and H., Brighton, Sussex East.
Dick, G., Hull, N. Humbs.
Dickens Antiques, Gillingham, Kent.
Dickens Bookshop, Charles, Cowes, I. of Wight.
Dickens Curios, Frinton-on-Sea, Essex.
Dickenson, Bill, Ironbridge, Shrops.
Dickins, H.C., Bloxham, Oxon.
Dickins, P. and H.R., Bloxham, Oxon.
Dickinson, Bernard, Gargrave, Yorks. North.
Dickinson, D. and B., Bath, Avon.
Dickinson, David H., Bramhall, Cheshire.
Dickinson, Mrs E.M., Bath, Avon.
Dickinson, R.G. and J., Ludlow, Shrops.
Dickinson, S.G., D. and N.W., Bath, Avon.
Dickson, Mr and Mrs B., Prestwick, Scotland.
Dickson, J., Lechlade, Glos.
Dickson, R., Bath, Avon.
Dickson Antiques Ltd, Robert, London, SW3.
Didsbury Antiques (Chorlton), Manchester, Lancs.
Dike, L., Bristol, Avon.
Dilger, Mrs C., West Kirby, Merseyside.
Dimmer, I.M. and N.C.S., Cheltenham, Glos.
Dingwall Antiques, Dingwall, Scotland.
Dining Room Shop, The, London, SW13.
Directmoor Ltd, Leek, Staffs.
Diss Antiques, Diss, Norfolk.
Ditchburn-Bosch, Dr.Ursula, Pittenweem, Scotland.
Ditondo, J. and J., Manchester, Lancs.
Dix Antiques, Dumfries, Scotland.
Dix, S., London, SW6.
Dixon Ltd, C.J. and A.J., Bridlington, N. Humbs.
Dixon, K.M. and L.A., Stow-on-the-Wold, Glos.
Dixon, Mr. and Mrs N., London, SW1.
Dixon Fine Engravings, Rob, Culham, Oxon.
Dixon's Antique Centre, London, SW14.
Dobbie, G., Bannockburn, Scotland.
Dobbyn, David and Alba, Bournemouth, Dorset.
Doble, I., Exeter, Devon.
Dobson, Mrs C.M., London, NW8.
Dobson's Antiques, Abbots Langley, Herts.
Dodd, J., London, W1.
Dodd Books, Maurice , Carlisle, Cumbria.
Dodd, R.G., Charmouth, Dorset.
Doddington House Antiques, Doddington, Cambs.
Dodge Interiors Ltd, Martin, Bath, Avon.
Dodge, M.J., Bath, Avon.
Dodge, S., Sherborne, Dorset.

DEALERS' INDEX

Dodge and Son, Sherborne, Dorset.
Dodgson, T. and I., Lancaster, Lancs.
Dodington Antiques, Whitchurch, Shrops.
Dodkin, Audrey , Stow-on-the-Wold, Glos.
Dodo, London, W11.
Dodson (Exports) Ltd, R.C., Portsmouth, Hants.
Dodsworth, N.J. and C.S., Spennithorne, Yorks. North.
Doel, G. and R.H. , Teignmouth, Devon.
Doggett, F.C., Somerton, Somerset.
Dolleris, A.J., London, SW15.
Dollin and Daines, Bath, Avon.
Doll's House, The, Haywards Heath, Sussex West.
Doll's House Antiques, The, Sheffield, Yorks. South.
Dolls House Toys Ltd, The, London, WC2.
Dolls and Toys of Yesteryear at Bow House Antiques, Hungerford, Berks.
Dolly Land, London, N21 .
Dolly Mixtures, Birmingham, West Mids.
Dolphin Antiques, Saffron Walden, Essex.
Dolphin Antiques, St. Albans, Herts.
Dolphin Antiques, Tetbury, Glos.
Dolphin Arcade, London, W11.Dolphin Coins, London, NW3.
Dome Antiques (Exports) Ltd, London, N1.
Domino Antiques, Barling Magna, Essex.
Donay Antiques, London, N1.
Doncaster Sales and Exchange, Doncaster, Yorks. South.
Donn Gallery, Henry, Whitefield, Lancs.
Donnachie, R.W., West Byfleet, Surrey.
Donnelly, D.E., Colchester, Essex.
Donovan, B. and A., Clitheroe, Lancs.
Donovan, D.H. and S.J., Plymouth, Devon.
Donovan, J., London, W11.
Donovan, P.A., Cranbrook, Kent.
Donowho, B., Carlisle, Cumbria.
Dooley, Tom J., Forkhill, Co. Armagh, N. Ireland.
Dorchester Antiques Market, Dorchester, Dorset.
Dorchester Galleries, Dorchester-on-Thames, Oxon.
Dorking Antique Centre, Dorking, Surrey.
Dorking Desk Shop, Dorking, Surrey.
Dorking Emporium Antiques Centre, Dorking, Surrey.
Doris, N.J., Nottingham, Notts.
Dorling, T., Feock, Cornwall.
Dorothy's Antiques, Sheringham, Norfolk.
Doubleday, S., Colchester, Essex.
Douch, A., London, W1.
Douglas, W.H., Cardiff, South Glam., Wales.
Douthwaite, C. and G., Bradford, Yorks. West.
Douwes Fine Art Ltd, London, SW1.
Dover, B., Rottingdean, Sussex East.
Dovetail Antiques, Malmesbury, Wilts.
Doveridge House of Neachley, Albrighton, Shrops.
Dowland, C. and V., Whitley Bay, Tyne and Wear.
Dowling and Bray, Looe, Cornwall.
Dowlish Wake Antiques, Dowlish Wake, Somerset.
Downes-Hall, John ff., Cirencester, Gloucs.
Downey, P., Tetbury, Glos.
Downshire House Antiques, Newry, Co. Down, N. Ireland.
Doyle Antiques, Lincoln, Lincs.
Doyle, A.G., Lincoln, Lincs.
Doyle, F.A., Whitby, Yorks. North.
Doyle Antiques, James, Brighton, Sussex East.
Doyle, J.R., Brighton, Sussex East.
Dragon Antiques, Harrogate, Yorks. North.
Dragon Antiques, Kettering, Northants.
Dragons of Walton St. Ltd, London, SW3.
Drawing Room, The, Lewes, Sussex East.
Drayson, J. and S., Petworth, Sussex West.
Drecker, L.C.M., London, NW9.
Drewett, R., Bath, Avon.
Driffold Gallery, Sutton Coldfield, West Mids.
Dring, C. and K.E., Lincoln, Lincs.
Drinkwater, N.J., Bramley, Surrey.
Driver, Mrs B., Arundel, Sussex West.
Dronfield Antiques, Sheffield, Yorks. South.
Droods, Rochester, Kent.
Drop Dial Antiques, Bolton, Lancs.
Drummond, D.B., London, WC2.
Drummond, J.N., London, NW8.
Drummond/Wrawby Moor Art Gallery Ltd, Nicholas, London, NW8.
Drummond-Hoy, C. and M., Nottingham, Notts.
Drummonds of Bramley Architectural Antiques Ltd, Bramley, Surrey.

Drury Antiques, Anne, Vale, Guernsey, C.I.
Dryden Ltd, Peter, Bath, Avon.
Drysdale Ltd, A.F., Edinburgh, Scotland.
Drysdale, Mrs S., Crieff, Scotland.
Du Cros Antiques, J., Liss, Hants.
Du Cros, J. and P., Liss, Hants.
Dubiner, M., London, W1.
Duc, G.P.A., London, W6.
Duck, S., Bristol, Avon.
Duckworth, C., Newark, Notts.
Duckworth, V.K. and M., Preston, Lancs.
Duckworth's Antiques, Preston, Lancs.
Duda, M., Hughenden Valley, Bucks.
Duff Antiques, George, Edinburgh, Scotland.
Duffy, A.M., Wallasey, Merseyside.
Duggan, Mr and Mrs J.M., Newport, Gwent, Wales.
Duignan, H., Birmingham, West Mids.
Duke, H., Abersoch, Gwynedd, Wales.
Dukes Yard Market, Richmond, Surrey.
Dunbar, Mrs A.G., Linlithgow, Scotland.
Duncan, N., Edinburgh, Scotland.
Duncan, S., Bideford, Devon.
Dunchurch Antique Centre, Dunchurch, Warks.
Dunedin Antiques Ltd, Edinburgh, Scotland.
Dunelme Coins and Medals, Esh Winning, Durham.
Dunford, C. and J., Uckfield, Sussex East.
Dunk, R.J., Stroud, Glos.
Dunkeld Interiors, Dunkeld, Scotland.
Dunlop, D., Portaferry, Co. Down, N. Ireland.
Dunluce Antiques, Bushmills, Co. Antrim, N. Ireland.
Dunn, Mrs J., Freshwater, I. of Wight.
Dunn, M.P., Ripon, Yorks. North.
Dunnett, D., Birmingham, West Mids.
Dunster Antiques, K.W., Staines, Surrey.
Dunton Antiques, Richard, Bournemouth, Dorset.
Dunton, R.D., Bournemouth, Dorset.
Dunworth, M., Dulverton, Somerset.
Dunworth, M., Taunton, Somerset.
Durham, M.L. and S.R., Birmingham, West Mids.
Duriez, L., Exeter, Devon.
Durrant, D. and E., Stockport, Cheshire.
Dux Antiques, Frank, Bath, Avon.
Dux, F., Bath, Avon.
Dye, P. and P., Bath, Avon.
Dyer, A.P., Hayle, Cornwall.
Dyer and Follett Ltd,, Alverstoke, Hants.
Dyer and Son, W., Redruth, Cornwall.
Dycheling Antiques, Ditchling, Sussex East.
Dyfri Antiques, Llandovery, Dyfed, Wales.
Dyke, Peter, Brasted, Kent.
Dylan's Bookshop, Swansea, West Glam., Wales.
Dyson (Antique Weapons), D.W., Huddersfield, Yorks. West.
Dyson and Sons, C.G., Market Weighton, N. Humbs.
Dyson, F.H., Burton-on-Trent, Staffs.
Dyson, K., London, SW13.
Dyson, Sheila, Newark, Notts.
Dytch, D., Dunkeld, Scotland.
Dyte Antiques, C. and R.I., Highbridge, Somerset.
Dyte Antiques, T.M., Highbridge, Somerset.
Dzierzek, J. and J., Helmsley, Yorks. North.

E

E. R. Antiques Centre, Stockport, Cheshire.
Eagle House Antiques Market, Midhurst, Sussex West.
Eaglesham Antiques Ltd, Eaglesham, Scotland.
Earle, Wilton, Wilts.
Ealing Gallery, London, W5.
Earlshall Castle, Leuchars, Scotland.
Eames, L., E., S. and C., Hemel Hempstead, Herts.
Earl, P., Halstead, Essex.
Earle, B., Wilton, Wilts.
Earshall, The Baron of, Leuchars, Scotland.
Earsham Hall Pine, Earsham, Norfolk.
Easebourne Antiques, Easebourne, Sussex West.
East-Asia Co, London, NW1.
Eastbourne Antiques Market, Eastbourne, Sussex East.
Eastgate Antique Centre, Lincoln, Lincs.
Eastgate Fine Arts, Warwick, Warks.
Eastgate Antiques, Cowbridge, South Glam., Wales.
Easton, F.M. and A., Reading, Berks.
EASY - Edinburgh Architectural Salvage Yard, Edinburgh, Scotland.

DEALERS' INDEX

Eaton Booksellers Ltd, Peter, Weedon, Bucks.
Eaton Gallery, London, SW1.
Ebbinkhuyson, P., London, NW1.
Ebbinkhuyson, P., London, WC2.
Eccles, J., London, NW1.
Eccles, J., London, SW3.
Eccles Road Antiques, London, SW11.
Eccleston, D. and P., Manchester, Lancs.
Echoes, Todmorden, Yorks. West.
Ed's Trading, London, SW8.
Eddelin, Mrs A.M., Southend-on-Sea, Essex.
Eddy, P. and S.N., Leominster, Herefs. & Worcs.
Ede Ltd, Charles, London, W1.
Edelstein at Robin Symes, Annamaria, London, SW1.
Eden, Matthew, Corsham, Wilts.
Eden Antiques, Edenbridge, Kent.
Eden Coins, Birmingham, West Mids.
Eden House Antiques, West Auckland, Durham.
Edgbaston Gallery, Birmingham, West Mids.
Edge Antiques, The, Alderley Edge, Cheshire.
Edgell, M., Cambridge, Cambs.
Edgington, A. and D., Blandford Forum, Dorset.
Edgware Antiques, Edgware, Middx.
Edinburgh Coin Shop, Edinburgh, Scotland.
Editions Graphiques Gallery, London, W1.
Edmonds Ltd, D.H., Brighton, Sussex East.
Edmonds Ltd, D.H., London, W1.
Edmonds, K.D., Oxford, Oxon.
Edmonstone, Lady J., Killearn, Scotland.
Edmunds, Andrew, London, W1.
Edwardes, Mrs M.D., Worthing, Sussex West.
Edwardian Shop, The, Ipswich, Suffolk.
Edwards Antique Exports, Brian, Lower Kinnerton, Cheshire.
Edwards, B.H., Lower Kinnerton, Cheshire.
Edwards, Charles, London, SW6.
Edwards, Christopher, London, SW1.
Edwards Ltd, Christopher, London, SW1.
Edwards Group, Charles, Blackburn, Lancs.
Edwards, D., Clare, Suffolk.
Edwards, D., Long Melford, Suffolk.
Edwards, H., Bagillt, Clwyd, Wales.
Edwards, Ian, Hatfield, Herts.
Edward's Jewellers, Liverpool, Merseyside.
Edwards Antiques, John, Worcester, Herefs. & Worcs.
Edwards, P., Broadstairs, Kent.
Edwards, R., Upminster, Essex.
Edwards, V., Abbots Bromley, Staffs.
Eichler, R.J. and L.L., Whitchurch, Bucks.
Eimer, Christopher, London, NW11.
Elcombe, Mrs, Sandgate, Kent.
Elcombe, Mr and Mrs J.W.G., Sandgate, Kent.
Elden Antiques, Kirk Deighton, Yorks. North.
Eldridge London, London, EC1.
Eldridge, B., London, EC1.
Eldridge, M., Garboldisham, Norfolk.
Elgin House Antiques, Tetbury, Glos.
Elias, J.G., Dorking, Surrey.
Eliot Antiques, Stanford Dingley, Berks.
Elithorn, S., London, NW5.
Elizabeth Antiques, Swansea, West Glam., Wales.
Elizabeth and Son, Ulverston, Cumbria.
Elizabethans, Fareham, Hants.
Elkin Mathews, Coggeshall, Essex.
Elliot, A., Blandford Forum, Dorset.
Elliott, C.R., Eastbourne, Sussex East.
Elliott, Mrs P., Glastonbury, Somerset.
Elliott, S., London, SW14.
Elliott and Scholz Antiques, Eastbourne, Sussex East.
Elliott and Snowdon Ltd, London, W11.
Ellis Antiques, Donald, Edinburgh, Scotland.
Ellis, D.G. and C.M., Edinburgh, Scotland.
Ellis, G. and Mrs A.J., Walsall, West Mids.
Ellis, G.E., Chester, Cheshire.
Ellis, J., Worcester, Herefs. and Worcs.
Ellis, R.G. and P.T., Camberley, Surrey.
Ellis's, Sheffield, Yorks. South.
Elm House Antiques, Haddington, Scotland.
Elm Tree Antiques, Flaxton, Yorks. North.
Elmley Heritage, Elmley Lovett, Herefs. & Worcs.
Elmore, Petersfield, Hants.
Elsom - Antiques, Pamela , Ashbourne, Derbys.

Elsworth, Mrs J., Beaconsfield, Bucks.
Elsworth - Beaconsfield Ltd, June, Beaconsfield, Bucks.
Elton, S.P., Beckenham, Kent.
Emanouel Antiques Ltd, London, W1.
Embden, K.B., London, WC2.
Emburey, Mrs G.D., Dorking, Surrey.
Emerald Isle Books, Belfast, N. Ireland.
Emerson, I., Armagh, Co. Armagh, N. Ireland.
Emery, V., London, WC2.
Emmins, Alan J., Haverfordwest, Dyfed, Wales.
Empire Antiques, Sandwich, Kent.
Emporium, The, Chipping Norton, Oxon.
Emporium, The, Knaresborough, Yorks. North.
Emporium Antique Centre, The, Lewes, Sussex East.
Emporium Antiques and Collectors Centre, The, Southwold, Suffolk.
Enchanted Aviary, The, Long Melford, Suffolk.
Endeavour Antiques, Saltburn, Cleveland.
Endley, S., Beverley, N. Humbs.
Enfield Corner Cupboard, Enfield, Middx.
Engine 'n' Tender, London, SE25.
England, F.J. and S., Leek, Staffs.
England's Gallery, Leek, Staffs.
English Heritage, Bridgnorth, Shrops.
Enloc Antiques, Colne, Lancs.
Entwistle, J. and K., Darwen, Lancs.
Epping Galleries, Epping, Essex.
Epping Saturday Market, Epping, Essex.
Eprile, R., Edinburgh, Scotland.
Equus Art Gallery, Newmarket, Suffolk.
Ermitage Ltd, London, W1.
Errington Antiques, Newcastle-under-Lyme, Staffs.
Errington, G.K., Newcastle-under-Lyme, Staffs.
Errol Antiques, Errol, Scotland.
Erskine-Hill, M. and Mrs M., Tunbridge Wells, Kent.
Eskenazi Ltd, London, W1.
Eskenazi, J.E., London, W1.
Essex Antiques Centre, Colchester, Essex.
Essex Antiques, Richard, Bristol, Avon.
Essie Carpets, London, W1.
Estling, Mrs G., Dowlish Wake, Somerset.
Etceteras Antiques, Seaton, Devon.
Etheridge, B., Burford, Oxon.
Ethos Gallery, Clitheroe, Lancs.
Eton Antique Bookshop, Windsor and Eton, Berks.
Eton Antiques Partnership, Windsor and Eton, Berks.
Eton Gallery Antiques, Windsor and Eton, Berks.
Eureka Antiques and Interiors, Bowdon, Cheshire.
Euro Antiques Warehouse, London, SE1.
Evans, A. and M., Narberth, Dyfed, Wales.
Evans, B. and Mrs P., Burford, Oxon.
Evans, D. and N., Alresford, Hants.
Evans, Mr and Mrs D.G., Brecon, Powys, Wales.
Evans and Evans, Alresford, Hants.
Evans, Mr and Mrs G., Cranbrook, Kent.
Evans, Mrs M., Llangollen, Clwyd, Wales.
Evans, Mollie, Richmond, Surrey.
Evans Antiques, Steven, Treherbert, Mid. Glam., Wales.
Evans Antiques, Steven, Treorchy, Mid. Glam., Wales.
Evans, Stewart, Malpas, Cheshire.
Eveleigh, L., Newmarket, Suffolk.
Evelyn, Hugh , Steepmarsh, Hants.
Everett, Mrs M.J., Eastbourne, Sussex East.
Everett, Mr and Mrs T., Pitminster, Somerset.
Ewart, A.J., Broadway, Herefs. and Worcs.
Ewart, Gavina, Broadway, Herefs. & Worcs.
Ewhurst Gallery, Ewhurst Green, Sussex East.
Ewing, J.F., London, W11.
Exeter Rare Books, Exeter, Devon.
Exley-Turner, Mrs J., Steyning, Sussex West.
Exports, G.G., Middleton Village, Lancs.
Expressions, Shrewsbury, Shrops.
Extence Antiques, Teignmouth, Devon.
Extence, T.E. and L.E., Teignmouth, Devon.
Eyers, Mrs M., Arundel, Sussex West.
Eyles Antiques, Joan, Boroughbridge, Yorks. North.
Eyles, J.M. and J.C.H., Boroughbridge, Yorks. North.
Eyre, Giles, Windsor and Eton, Berks.
Eyre and Greig Ltd, Windsor and Eton, Berks.

F

Facade, The, London, W11.
Faded Elegance, Dulverton, Somerset.

DEALERS' INDEX

Fagiani, A., London, SE15.
Fagins Antiques, Exeter, Devon.
Fair Deal Antiques, Mansfield, Notts.
Fair, D.P., Hockley Heath, West Mids.
Fairbairn, R. and A., Berwick-on-Tweed, Northumbs.
Fairclough, G.D., Scarisbrick, Lancs.
Fairfax Fireplaces and Antiques, London, SW6.
Fairfax, H., London, SW6.
Fairfax Fireplaces and General Antiques, Harriet, Langley Burrell, Wilts.
Fairhurst Gallery, The, Norwich, Norfolk.
Fairings, Grassington, Yorks. North.
Fairlie Antique Shop, Fairlie, Scotland.
Fairman (Carpets) Ltd, Jack, London, W11.
Fakenham Antique Centre, Fakenham, Norfolk.
Falcon Gallery, The, Wortham, Suffolk.
Falik, Mrs S., Burnley, Lancs.
Falk, S.C., Rochdale, Lancs.
Falstaff Antiques, Rolvenden, Kent.
Family Antiques, Manchester, Lancs.
Fan-Fayre Antiques, Rhosneigr, Gwynedd, Wales.
Fanthorpe, T., East Dereham, Norfolk.
Farahar and Sophie Dupré - Rare Books, Autographs and Manuscripts, Clive, Calne, Wilts.
Fardon, J. A., Bristol, Avon.
Farey, MissK., Skipton, Yorks. North.
Faringdon Gallery, Faringdon, Oxon.
Farmer, P., Chatham, Kent.
Farmers Gallery, Leominster, Herefs. & Worcs.
Farmhouse Antiques, Bolton-by-Bowland, Lancs.
Farmhouse Antiques, Chester, Cheshire.
Farmhouse Antiques, Great Houghton, Yorks. South.
Farmhouse Antiques, Stoke Ferry, Norfolk.
Farnborough (Kent) Antiques, Farnborough, Kent.
Farnell, B., Dumfries, Scotland.
Farnes, C., Penzance, Cornwall.
Farnham Antique Centre, Farnham, Surrey.
Farnham, P.M., Bath, Avon.
Farnsworth, S. and V., Moreton-in-Marsh, Glos.
Farouz, P., Pelsall, West Mids.
Farr, Gloucester, Glos.
Farr, A. and J., Gloucester, Glos.
Farrelly Antiques, Tring, Herts.
Farrelly, P., Tring, Herts.
Farrelly, S., London, SW16.
Farrelly, Stephen, London, NW3.
Farrow, D.H., Hungerford, Berks.
Farrow, Liz, London, W11.
Farthings Antiques, Nantwich, Cheshire.
Faustus Fine Art Ltd, London, SW1.
Fawcett, L., London, W11.
Fawcett, P., Brasted, Kent.
Fawkes, Keith, London, NW3.
Fearfield, MissA., Budleigh Salterton, Devon.
Fears (Books), Howard, Little Walsingham, Norfolk.
Featherstone, Mrs E.A., South Cave, N. Humbs.
Featherstone-Harvey, John, London, N1.
Feely, Murray, London, W2.
Felix Gallery, Lewes, Sussex East.
Felix, R.T., Studley, Warks.
Feljoy Antiques, London, N1.
Fell Antiques, Mary, Brampton, Cumbria.
Fellowes, Edward, Warminster, Wilts.
Fellows, Maurice, Birmingham, West Mids.
Felton Park Antiques, Felton, Northumbs.
Fenlan Antiques, Turvey, Beds.
Fenwick Billiards, Wellington, Somerset.
Fenwick and Fisher Antiques, Broadway, Herefs. & Worcs.
Fenwick, M., London, SW6.
Fenwick, Nigel, Wellington, Somerset.
Ferder, S. and S., Lyndhurst, Hants.
Ferdinando, Steven, Queen Camel, Somerset.
Ferguson, H.T. and R.E., Woodbridge, Suffolk.
Ferguson, M., Birmingham, West Mids.
Fern Cottage Antique Centre, Thames Ditton, Surrey.
Fernandes and Marche, London, SW1.
Fernlea Antiques, Hollinwood, Lancs.
Ferrant Antiques, D.J., London, N1.
Ferrant, J., London, N1.
Ferraris, D. and J., Swanage, Dorset.
Ferrett, P.D., Wallasey, Merseyside.
Ferrow, David, Gt. Yarmouth, Norfolk.

Ferrow Family Antiques, The, Gt. Yarmouth, Norfolk.
Ferrow, M. and J., Gt. Yarmouth, Norfolk.
Ferry, H., Huntercombe, Oxon.
Fettes Fine Art, York, Yorks. North.
Few, Ted, London, SW17.
Ffynnon Las, Sarnau, Dyfed, Wales.
Fiddle Sticks Antiques and Decorative Items, Bath, Avon.
Fidelo, Tom, Edinburgh, Scotland.
Field, C. and G., Abinger Hammer, Surrey.
Field, P., Cheltenham, Glos.
Fielden, Brian, London, W1.
Fieldings Antiques, Haslingden, Lancs.
Fifteenth Century Bookshop, Lewes, Sussex East.
File, Mrs, Sandgate, Kent.
Fileman, David R., Steyning, Sussex West.
Filey Antiques, Filey, Yorks. North.
Fillans (Antiques) - Geoff Neary Ltd., Huddersfield, Yorks. West.
Fillibuster and Booth Ltd, Sheffield, Yorks. South.
Filsham Farmhouse Antiques, St. Leonards-on-Sea, Sussex East.
Finbow, David, Framlingham, Suffolk.
Finch, C.A., London, W11.
Finch, M. and I., Yealand Conyers, Lancs.
Finch, N., London, NW8.
Finchley Fine Art Galleries, London, N12.
Findley Antiques, Sheffield, Yorks. South.
Findley, B., Sheffield, Yorks. South.
Fine Antique Glass, Abernyte, Scotland.
Fine Art of Oakham, Oakham, Leics.
Fine Art Society plc, The, London, W1.
Fine Design, Haddington, Scotland.
Fine Oriental Rugs and Carpets of Inverness, Inverness, Scotland.
Fine Pine, Birmingham, West Mids.
Fine Pine, Southport, Merseyside.
Fine Pine Antiques, Totnes, Devon.
Fine-Lines (Fine Art), Shipston-on-Stour, Warks.
Finedon Antiques (Antiques Centre), Finedon, Northants.
Fineman, Jeffrey Lee, Glasgow, Scotland.
Finesse Fine Art, Weymouth, Dorset.
Finlay, James, Falkirk, Scotland.
Finlay Antiques, K.W., Ciliau Aeron, Dyfed, Wales.
Finlay, M.F., Eaglesham, Scotland.
Finlay, T. and M.C., Littleton, Somerset.
Finn, T., Manchester, Lancs.
Finn, V., Cheltenham, Glos.
Finnegan (Jeweller), Robin, Darlington, Durham.
Finney, G., Stow-on-the-Wold, Glos.
Finney Antique Prints and Books, Michael, London, N1.
Fire Place (Hungerford) Ltd, The, Hungerford, Berks.
Fireplace, The, London, SE9.
Firmin, Rodney, Swaffham Prior, Cambs.
Fischelis, R., London, NW2.
Fisher, R., London, SW3.
Fisher, R. and E.S., Egham, Surrey.
Fisher, Susanna, Upham, Hants.
Fisher and Sperr, London, N6.
Fisher, W.I.J., Penzance, Cornwall.
Fishers of Surrey, Egham, Surrey.
Fishlake Antiques, Fishlake, Yorks. South.
Fitch Antiques, Michael, Sandgate, Kent.
Fitchett Antiques, Alan, Brighton, Sussex East.
Fitzwilliam Antiques Centre, Peterborough, Cambs.
Fiumano, G., London, W11.
Five Five Six Antiques, London, SW6.
Five Towns Antiques, Stoke-on-Trent, Staffs.
Flame and Grate, Bristol, Avon.
Flame 'n' Grate, Barry, South Glamorgan, Wales.
Flappers, Buckingham, Bucks.
Fleamarket, The, London, N1.
Fleischer, F.J., Sedlescombe, Sussex East.
Fleming (Southsea) Ltd, A., Portsmouth, Hants.
Fleming, S. Becker, Walton-on-Thames, Surrey.
Fletcher, Mr and Mrs, Lowestoft, Suffolk.
Fletcher, H. M., London, SE1.
Fletcher, M., Preston, Lancs.
Fletcher., Mrs R.E., Stow-on-the-Wold, Glos.
Fleur de Lys Gallery, London, W11.
Flint Galleries Ltd, Sir William Russell, Wrington, Avon.
Flint, W., Weymouth, Dorset.
Flintlock Antiques, Stockport, Cheshire.

DEALERS' INDEX

Flowers Antiques, Ilford, Essex.
Floyd Ltd, George, London, SW6.
Fluck, Miss M.G., Skipton, Yorks. North.
Fluss and Charlesworth Ltd, London, W9.
Fluss, E., London, W9.
Flynn, J., Cowes, I. of Wight.
Foddy, D., Derby, Derbys.
Fogg Antiques, Epsom, Surrey.
Fogg, C.W., Stockport, Cheshire.
Fogg, R., Epsom, Surrey.
Fogg, Sam, London, W1.
Foley, C., London, W1.
Folkard, O.P., Kelvedon, Essex.
Folkes Antiques and Jewellers, Gt. Yarmouth, Norfolk.
Folkestone, Viscount, Salisbury, Wilts.
Folly, The, Longridge, Lancs.
Folly Antiques, Settle, Yorks. North.
Fomison, Mr and Mrs R., Ramsgate, Kent.
Foord Antiques, Midhurst, Sussex West.
Foord, C.G. and E.S., Midhurst, Sussex West.
Foord-Brown Antiques, David, Cuckfield, Sussex West.
For Pine, Chesham, Bucks.
Forbes, P. and L., Church Stretton, Shrops.
Ford, D., Compton, Surrey.
Ford, E. and J., Winchcombe, Glos.
Ford, I., Coltishall, Norfolk.
Ford, I., Norwich, Norfolk.
Ford, J., Tintern, Gwent, Wales.
Ford, J. and C., Bidford-on-Avon, Warks.
Ford, M.C., Burford, Oxon.
Ford, Paula, Wells-next-the-Sea, Norfolk.
Ford, Mrs R., Ledbury, Herefs. and Worcs.
Ford, Steve, Leek, Staffs.
Fordham Antiques, Fordham, Essex.
Forest Books at Magpie Antiques, Davenham, Cheshire.
Forest Books of Cheshire, Manchester, Lancs.
Forge Antiques, Synod Inn, Dyfed, Wales.
Forge Antiques, The, Coleraine, Co. Londonderry, N. Ireland.
Forge Antiques and Restorations, Sandhurst, Kent.
Forget-me-Knot Antiques, St. Albans, Herts.
Format of Birmingham Ltd, Birmingham, West Mids.
Forrer, M., Marlborough, Wilts.
Forrest and Co. Antiques, E.B., Edinburgh, Scotland.
Forrest and Co (Jewellers) Ltd, James, Glasgow, Scotland.
Forrest, M.A., Edinburgh, Scotland.
Forrest McKay, Edinburgh, Scotland.
Forrest, R., Edinburgh, Scotland.
Forrester, C., Glasgow, Scotland.
Forster, J.M.W., London, WC1.
Forster, W., London, N16.
Forsyth Antiques, Perth, Scotland.
Forsyth, A.McDonald, Perth, Scotland.
Forsyth, J.W. and L.J., Lancaster, Lancs.
Forsyth, J., Cheltenham, Glos.
Fortescue Gallery, The, Ipswich, Suffolk.
Fortescue, L., Ipswich, Suffolk.
Fortnum and Mason plc, London, W1.
Forty Nine, Manningtree, Essex.
Forum Antiques, Cirencester, Glos.
Fosse Gallery, Stow-on-the-Wold, Glos.
Fosse Way Antiques, Stow-on-the-Wold, Glos.
Foster, A. and E., Naphill, Bucks.
Foster, J., Bingley, Yorks. West.
Foster, Mrs J., Wellingborough, Northants.
Foster, J.A., Wellingborough, Northants.
Foster, Michael, London, SW3.
Foster, M.C.A., Swafield, Norfolk.
Foster, M.I., Weybridge, Surrey.
Foster, MissP.I. and K.A., Lewes, Sussex East.
Foster-Pegg, R. and S., Grundisburgh, Suffolk.
Fothergill, A., York, Yorks. North.
Foulger, Paul, Lowestoft, Suffolk.
Fountain Antiques, Honiton, Devon.
Fourteen A, Modbury, Devon.
Fowle, A. and J., London, SW16.
Fowler (Period Clocks), Robin, Aylesby, S. Humbs.
Fowler, S.G., Boughton, Kent.
Fox and Co, Yeovil, Somerset.
Fox, Judy, London, W11.
Fox, M. and P., Harrogate, Yorks. North.
Fox and Pheasant Antique Pine, White Colne, Essex.
Fox's Antique Pine and Country Furniture, Harrogate, Yorks. North.

Foye Gallery, Luton, Beds.
Foyle Ltd, W. and G., London, WC2.
Frampton, Mrs T.P.F., Beaminster, Dorset.
Franca Antiques, Tunbridge Wells, Kent.
France, Alan M., Wolverhampton, West Mids.
Frances Antiques, Sara, Alderley Edge, Cheshire.
Francis, G., Norwich, Norfolk.
Francis, Mrs P.B., Puckeridge, Herts.
Francombe, C., Eastbourne, Sussex East.
Franfam Ltd,, Grantown-on-Spey, Scotland.
Frankland, B.A., Doddington, Cambs.
Franklin, N. and I., London, SW1.
Franklin, R., London, SE5.
Franklin's Camberwell Antiques Market, London, SE5.
Franklyn, S., London, W11.
Franks, Douglas, Frensham, Surrey.
Franks , J.A.L., London, SW1.
Franks Ltd, J.A.L., London, WC1.
Franses and Sons, Robert, London, NW8.
Franses Gallery, Victor, London, SW1.
Franses Ltd, S., London, SW1.
Fraser Antiques, Coldstream, Scotland.
Fraser, Anne, St. Andrews, Scotland.
Fraser, Miss D.J., Newburgh, Scotland.
Frazer Antiques, Malcolm, Cheadle, Cheshire.
Fredericks and Son, C., London, SW3.
Fredericks, J.A. and C.J., London, W1.
Fredericks and Son, J.A., London, W1.
Fredericks, R.F., London, SW3.
Freedman, Gerald, London, SW6.
Freedman, Mrs H., London, N21.
Freeman Antiques, Roxwell, Essex.
Freeman Antiques, Carol, Monmouth, Gwent, Wales.
Freeman, G.O., St. Annes-on-Sea, Lancs.
Freeman, H., London, NW8.
Freeman, J., London, W11.
Freeman, J.G. and A., Norwich, Norfolk.
Freeman, K., Sandgate, Kent.
Freeman and Lloyd Antiques, Sandgate , Kent.
Freeman, T.A., Malmesbury, Wilts.
Freeman, Vincent, London, N1.
Freestone, F., Manningtree, Essex.
French, C., Eastbourne, Sussex East.
French Fine Arts, York, Yorks. North.
French-Greenslade, S., Tilston, Cheshire.
Frenches Farm Antiques, King's Langley, Herts.
Frere Antiques, Joan, Drumnadrochit, Scotland.
Frere, Mrs J., Drumnadrochit, Scotland.
Freuchie Antiques, Freuchie, Scotland.
Freya Antiques, Hawkedon, Suffolk.
Freya Antiques, Mildenhall, Suffolk.
Friargate Pine and Antiques Centre, Derby, Derbys.
Frid, Mrs C., Gravesend, Kent.
Friday Street Antique Centre, Henley-on-Thames, Oxon.
Frings, S., Hoby, Leics.
Frinton Antiques, Frinton-on-Sea, Essex.
Frith Antiques, Petworth, Sussex West.
Frith, H.A. and Mrs M.A., Petworth, Sussex West.
Frith, M., Hemswell Cliff, Lincs.
Frith, T. and M., London, W1.
Fritz-Denneville Fine Arts Ltd, H., London, W1.
Frocks and Tails, Bristol, Avon.
Frognal Rare Books, London, WC1.
Frost, A.P., Hampton, Middx.
Frost, C.C., Long Melford, Suffolk.
Frost, L., Eccleston, Lancs.
Frost, P.J., Iver, Bucks.
Frost and Reed Ltd, London, W1.
Frost, R.F., Martlesham, Suffolk.
Fry, A. and G., South Molton, Devon.
Fry, M., London, NW2.
Fryer, F., Ross-on-Wye, Herefs. and Worcs.
Frome Antique Centre, Frome, Somerset.
Fryer Antique Lighting, Fritz, Ross-on-Wye, Herefs. & Worcs.
Fryer, Malcolm and Sally, Southport, Merseyside.
Fulda Gallery Ltd, Manchester, Lancs.
Fulda, M.J., Manchester, Lancs.
Fulwood Antiques and The Basement Gallery, Sheffield, Yorks. South.
Fun Antiques, Sheffield, Yorks. South.
Furney Antiques and Interiors, Donaghadee, Co. Down, N. Ireland.

DEALERS' INDEX

Furney, B. and I., Donaghadee, Co. Down, N. Ireland.
Furniture Cave, The, Aberystwyth, Dyfed, Wales.
Furniture Cave, London, SW10.
Furniture Market, The , South Molton, Devon.
Furniture Mart, Margate, Kent.
Furniture Store/St. Austell Antiques Centre, The , St. Austell, Cornwall.
Furniture Vault, London, N1.
Furze, M., Much Hadham, Herts.
Fyfe's Antiques, Edinburgh, Scotland.
Fyne Antiques, Dunoon, Scotland.
Fynes, J., Easebourne, Sussex West.
Fyson Antiques, Jonathan, Burford, Oxon.
Fyson, J.R., Burford, Oxon.

G

G.B. Antiques Ltd, Lancaster, Lancs.
G.D. and S.T. Antiques, Poole, Dorset.
G. and J. Antiques, Buxton, Derbys.
G.W. Antiques, Lancaster, Lancs.
Gadsden, P., Petersfield, Hants.
Gage (Works of Art) Ltd, Deborah, London, W1.
Gage, J. and E., Topsham, Devon.
Gainsborough House Antiques, Sidmouth, Devon.
Gainsborough House Antiques, Tewkesbury, Glos.
Gair, J.A., Leigh-on-Sea, Essex.
Gale, E. and S., Portscatho, Cornwall.
Gale, P.A. and D., Warminster, Wilts.
Galerias Segui, Cowes, I. of Wight.
Galerie Antiques, Broadstone, Dorset.
Galerie Lev, Woodford Green, Essex.
Galerie Moderne Ltd, London, SW1.
Gale-Yearsley, Mrs K., Wimborne Minster, Dorset.
Galey, K.M. and R.M., Cambridge, Cambs.
Gallagher (Antiques), M., Llangollen, Clwyd, Wales.
Gallagher, M. and L., Perth, Scotland.
Galleitch, M. and H., Ardersier, Scotland.
Galleon, The, Bath, Avon.
Galleon Antiques, St. Leonards-on-Sea, Sussex East.
Galleria Fine Arts Ltd, St. Leonards-on-Sea, Sussex East.
Galleries de Fresnes, Galston, Scotland.
Gallery, Aberdeen, Scotland.
Gallery, The, Penrith, Cumbria.
Gallery, The, Portsmouth, Hants.
Gallery 6, Broseley, Shrops.
Gallery 16, Bruton, Somerset.
Gallery 23 Antiques, Chalfont St. Giles, Bucks.
Gallery '25, London, SW1.
Gallery 45, Norwich, Norfolk.
Gallery Antiques, Oakham, Leics.
Gallery Arcticus, London, SW1.
Gallery Downstairs, The, London, SW12.
Gallery Kaleidoscope, London, NW6.
Gallery Laraine Ltd.,, Eastbourne, Sussex East.
Gallery Lingard, London, SW3.
Gallery of Antique Costume and Textiles, London, NW8.
Gallery on Church Street", "The, London, NW3.
Gallery One, Perth, Scotland.
Gallery and Things, The, South Lopham, Norfolk.
Gallery Tonkin and Gallery Lyoness, Penzance, Cornwall.
Gallop, G. P., Crickhowell, Powys, Wales.
Gallop and Rivers Architectural Antiques, Crickhowell, Powys, Wales.
Galloway Antiques, Boroughbridge, Yorks. North.
Galloway and Porter Ltd, Cambridge, Cambs.
Galsworthy, A., Barry, South Glamorgan, Wales.
Game Advice, London, NW5.
Gammond, N., Fairford, Glos.
Gander, Michael, Hitchin, Herts.
Gandolfi House , Malvern Wells, Herefs. & Worcs.
Gange, C.C., Marlborough, Wilts.
Gannon, S., Settle, Yorks. North.
Gant, Elizabeth, Thames Ditton, Surrey.
Gaphar, S.A., London, SW18.
Garbett, M., Bristol, Avon.
Garden House Antiques, Tenterden, Kent.
Gardiner Antiques, Charles, Lurgan, Co. Armagh, N. Ireland.
Gardiner Antiques, John, Somerton, Somerset.
Gardiner, Mrs J., Somerton, Somerset.
Gardiner, K., Berkeley, Glos.
Gardner, A.J., London, SW3.

Gardner, G.D. and R.K.F., Kilbarchan, Scotland.
Gardner, J., Bishops Cleeve, Glos.
Gardner Antiques, Richard, Lodsworth, Sussex West.
Gardner, R. and J.A., Lodsworth, Sussex West.
Gardner's The Antique Shop, Kilbarchan, Scotland.
Gargrave Gallery, Gargrave, Yorks. North.
Garman, G., Lower Bentham, Yorks. North.
Garn House Antiques, Bow Street, Dyfed, Wales.
Garner, G., Monkton, Devon.
Garner, John, Uppingham, Leics.
Garner Antiques, P.R., Landbeach, Cambs.
Garrard & Co. Ltd (The Crown Jewellers), London, W1.
Garratt Antiques, Birmingham, West Mids.
Garratt (Fine Paintings), Stephen, London, W14.
Garrick Antiques, Philip, London, W11.
Garrow, Marilyn, London, SW13.
Garson and Co. Ltd, Manchester, Lancs.
Garth Antiques, Harrogate, Yorks. North.
Garth Antiques, Whixley, Yorks. North.
Gasson, Herbert Gordon, Rye, Sussex East.
Gasson Antiques and Interiors, Pat and Terry, Cranleigh, Surrey.
Gatehouse Antiques, Macclesfield, Cheshire.
Gates, Mrs M.A.B., Hartley Wintney, Hants.
Gates, Mrs M.A.B., London, N1.
Gateway Antiques, Burford, Oxon.
Gatland, T. and Mrs E., Ashburton, Devon.
Gauld, Maureen H., Killin, Scotland.
Gavèls, Long Preston, Yorks. North.
Gavey, Geoffrey P., Vale, Guernsey, C.I.
Gavey, G.P. and Mrs C., St. Peter Port, Guernsey, C.I.
Gavin, J.M., Penryn, Cornwall.
Gay, Bernard, Mansel Lacy, Herefs. & Worcs.
Gay, Mr and Mrs J.E., Boroughbridge, Yorks. North.
Gay, M. and B.M., Romsey, Hants.
Gaylords, Titchfield, Hants.
Gay's (Hazel Grove) Antiques Ltd, Hazel Grove, Cheshire.
Gazeley Associates Fine Art, John, Ipswich, Suffolk.
Gazelles Art Deco Interiors, Southampton, Hants.
Gealer, Mrs R., Falmouth, Cornwall.
Gear, J., Hindhead, Surrey.
Gearing, J.A., Eastbourne, Sussex East.
Geary Antiques, Leeds, Yorks. West.
Geary, J.A., Leeds, Yorks. West.
Geddes, Mrs. D., London, W11.
Gee, Colin, Tetbury, Glos.
Gem Antiques, Rochester, Kent.
Gemini Antiques, Great Missenden, Bucks.
Gemini Antiques, Wolverhampton, West Mids.
Gemini Trading, Leek, Staffs.
Gems Antiques, Chichester, Sussex West.
Geneen Ltd, Lionel, Bournemouth, Dorset.
General Trading Co Ltd, London, SW1.
Genges Farm Antiques, Limington, Somerset.
Gentle Antiques, Rupert, Milton Lilbourne, Wilts.
George, A., London, SW6.
George, D., London, SW1.
George d'Epinois, London, SW6.
George Street Antiques, Bath, Avon.
George Street Antiques Centre, Hastings, Sussex East.
George Street Gallery, The, Perth, Scotland.
Georgian Antiques, Edinburgh, Scotland.
Georgian Gems Antique Jewellers, Swanage, Dorset.
Georgian House Antiques, Bournemouth, Dorset.
Georgian House Antiques, Chipping Norton, Oxon.
Georgian House Antiques, Uckfield, Sussex East.
Georgian Village, London, N1.
Georgian Village Antiques Market, London, E17.
Georgiana's Antiques, London, E17.
Georgina Antiques, Hemel Hempstead, Herts.
Georgiou, C. and C.J., Bexhill-on-Sea, Sussex East.
Geostran Antiques, Coleshill, Warks.
Germain, Mrs M.M., Ilford, Essex.
Germain, T.C., Burnham-on-Sea, Somerset.
German, Michael C., London, W8.
Get Stuffed, London, N1.
Gewirtz, D., London, N1.
Ghassemi, F. and A., London, W1.
Ghiberti Antiques and Fine Art, Wolverhampton, West Mids.
Gholam, J. and J. M., Ringway, Cheshire.
Gibb, A., London, W14.
Gibbins Antiques, David, Woodbridge, Suffolk.

Gibbons, Derek, Cambridge, Cambs.
Gibbons, Stanley, London, WC2.
Gibbs Antiques and Decorative Arts, Paul, Conway, Gwynedd, Wales.
Gibb's Bookshop Ltd, Manchester, Lancs.
Gibbs Ltd, Christopher, London, W1.
Gibbs, C.A., Isleworth, Middx.
Gibbs, J.P. and A.M., Great Malvern, Herefs. and Worcs.
Gibbs, W.T., Kempston, Beds.
Gibson, David, Bath, Avon.
Gibson, J. and P., Reigate, Surrey.
Gibson, N., Bowdon, Cheshire.
Gibson, R., Great Wakering, Essex.
Gibson, Roderick, Nantwich, Cheshire.
Gibson, S.R. and A., Leeds, Yorks. West.
Gibson Fine Art Ltd, Thomas, London, W1.
Giddings, J.C., Wiveliscombe, Somerset.
Giffengate Antiques, Dorchester-on-Thames, Oxon.
Gilbert, B. and C., Sheffield, Yorks. South.
Gilbert, D., Canterbury, Kent.
Gilbert, D., Sutton Coldfield, West Mids.
Gilbert, H.M., Winchester, Hants.
Gilbert and Son, H.M., Southampton, Hants.
Gilbert, M., Uppingham, Leics.
Gilbert, Michael C., Altrincham, Cheshire.
Gilbert, R., Haunton, Staffs.
Gilbert, R., Limington, Somerset.
Gilbert, R.C. and A.M., Southampton, Hants.
Gilbert, R.C. and A.M., Winchester, Hants.
Gilbert and Sons, Sheffield, Yorks. South.
Gilberts of Uppingham, Uppingham, Leics.
Gilchrist and Associates, A. and C., Dorking, Surrey.
Gilham, J.E., Cawood, Yorks. North.
Gill, David, London, SW3.
Gillespie, V., Olveston, Avon.
Gillett, R. and A., Petworth, Sussex West.
Gilligan, M.T., Leek, Staffs.
Gilligans Antiques, Leek, Staffs.
Gillingham Ltd, G. and F., London, NW2.
Gillingham MPS, DBA, J.L., Mousehole, Cornwall.
Gillingham, Michael , London, SW3.
Gillman, G.W., Newton Abbot, Devon.
Gilmore Antiques, Elizabeth , Honiton, Devon.
Giltsoff, N., Warminster, Wilts.
Gilwern Antiques, Gilwern, Gwent, Wales.
Ginders, M., Ixworth, Suffolk.
Ginesi, S ., Corby Hill, Cumbria.
Ginger, G. & D., Ludlow, Shrops.
Ginnel, The, Harrogate, Yorks. North.
Ginnell, The, Manchester, Lancs.
Ginsberg, P., Prestbury, Cheshire.
Gittins, A., Sutton Bridge, Lincs.
Gittins and Son, G.J., Caerphilly, Mid. Glam., Wales.
Giuntini, Mrs G., Canterbury, Kent.
Gladrags, Edinburgh, Scotland.
Glaisyer, D. and N., Moreton-in-Marsh, Glos.
Glaisyer, D. and N., Stretton-on-Fosse, Warks.
Glaisyer, Richard and Cherry, Stow-on-the-Wold, Glos.
Glance Back Bookshop, Chepstow, Gwent, Wales.
Glance Gallery, Chepstow, Gwent, Wales.
Glanfield, R.W., Lowestoft, Suffolk.
Glasby, D.E., Leedstown, Cornwall.
Glasby and Son Antiques, A.W., Leedstown, Cornwall.
Glassdrumman Antiques, Tunbridge Wells, Kent.
Glassman, R., London, WC2.
Glencorse Antiques, Kingston-upon-Thames, Surrey.
Glendale, M. and R., London, NW3.
Glen-Doepel, Mrs D., Lincoln, Lincs.
Glenmore Interiors, King's Lynn, Norfolk.
Glenn, M.P., Dunoon, Scotland.
Glenville Antiques, Yatton, Avon.
Gliksten, M., London, NW1.
Gliksten, Malcolm, London, N1.
Gliksten, M., Malmesbury, Wilts.
Glossop Antique Centre, Glossop, Derbys.
Gloucester Antique Centre, Gloucester, Glos.
Gloucester House Antiques Ltd, Fairford, Glos.
Glover, F.D., Southport, Merseyside.
Glover (Antiques), J.K., Haslemere, Surrey.
Gluck, D., Cardiff, South Glam., Wales.
Gluck, J. and Mrs F., Llanfair Caereinion, Powys, Wales.
Glydon and Guess Ltd, Kingston-upon-Thames, Surrey.

Glynn Interiors, Knutsford, Cheshire.
Gnome Cottage Antiques, Stroud, Glos.
Goble, Paul, Brighton, Sussex East.
Goble, P., Brighton, Sussex East
Goddard, D.C., London, N1.
Goddard Antiques, Julie, Oughtibridge, Yorks. South.
Goddard, Miss J.P., Oughtibridge, Yorks. South.
Godden, Geoffrey, London, W8.
Godden, G.A., Worthing, Sussex 'Vest.
Godden, G. and J., Worthing, Sussex West.
Godden Chinaman, Geoffrey, Worthing, Sussex West.
Godden of Worthing Ltd, Worthing, Sussex West.
Godfrey Antiques Ltd, Howard, Elham, Kent.
Godfrey, Jemima, Newmarket, Suffolk.
Godsafe, B., Norwich, Norfolk.
Godsell, A.A. and C.M.J., Ridgewell, Essex.
Godson and Coles Ltd, London, SW3.
Gold Hill Antiques and Collectibles, Shaftesbury, Dorset.
Gold Shop, The, Torquay, Devon.
Gold and Silver Exchange, Exeter, Devon.
Gold and Silver Exchange, Gt. Yarmouth, Norfolk.
Gold and Silver Shop, Gorseinon, West Glam., Wales.
Gold and Silversmiths of Hove, The, Brighton, Sussex East.
Golden Cage, The, Nottingham, Notts.
Golden Goose Books, Lincoln, Lincs.
Golden Oldies, Penkridge, Staffs.
Golden Oldies, Wolverhampton, West Mids.
Golden Sovereign, Great Bardfield, Essex.
Golder, Gwendoline, Coltishall, Norfolk.
Golding, Eric, Wisbech, Cambs.
Golding, M., Stockport, Cheshire.
Golding, M.F., S.P. and N.M.J., Stow-on-the-Wold, Glos.
Golding, Pat, Arundel, Sussex West.
Golding, R.M., South Molton, Devon.
Goldmark Books, Uppingham, Leics.
Goldmark, M.M., Uppingham, Leics.
Goldsmith, A., London, W11.
Goldsmith, William, Leeds, Yorks. West.
Goldstone, Michael, Bakewell, Derbys.
Goldstraw, Mrs Y.A., Leek, Staffs.
Goldthorpe, P. and J., Godalming, Surrey.
Golebiowski, Z., London, W1.
Good Fairy Open Air Market, The, London, W11.
Good Hope Antiques, Beaminster, Dorset.
Good, Mrs K., Waddesdon, Bucks.
Goodacre Engraving Ltd, Long Eaton, Derbys.
Goodacre, K., Bournemouth, Dorset.
Goodall, Peter, Guildford, Surrey.
Gooday, Peter and Debbie, Richmond, Surrey.
Gooday, R., East Molesey, Surrey.
Gooday Shop and Studio, The, East Molesey, Surrey.
Goodbrey, B., Framlingham, Suffolk.
Goodbrey, Richard, Framlingham, Suffolk.
Goodbrey, R. and M., Framlingham, Suffolk.
Goodbreys, Framlingham, Suffolk.
Goode and Co (London) Ltd, Thomas, London, W1.
Goodfellow, Mrs A., Knaresborough, Yorks. North.
Goodinge, Mrs J.A., Henfield, Sussex West.
Goodlad, Anthony D. , Chesterfield, Derbys.
Goodland, D. and C, Spilsby, Lincs.
Goodman, A., Midhurst, Sussex West.
Goodman Gold, Grimsby, S. Humbs.
Goodman, K., Torquay, Devon.
Goodman, P. and L., Beverley, N. Humbs.
Goodman, R.J., Snodland, Kent.
Goodman, R.J., Tunbridge Wells, Kent.
Goodman, S.N., Grimsby, S. Humbs.
Goodsman, T.A., Warminster, Wilts.
Goodwin, G.A. and A.M., London, NW2.
Goodwin and Sons, John, Leamington Spa, Warks.
Goodwin and Sons, John, Warwick, Warks.
Goodwin, M., Alderley Edge, Cheshire.
Goodwin, M., Buckingham, Bucks.
Goodwin Exports, Nick, Guilsborough, Northants.
Goodwin's Antiques Ltd, Edinburgh, Scotland.
Gooley, P., London, W9.
Gordon, A. and F., London, W8.
Gordon, G. , London, NW8.
Gordon, Mr and Mrs J. F., Newton Abbot, Devon.
Gordon, Phyllis, Arundel, Sussex West.
Gordon, R., London, NW8.
Gordon, R. and J., Alford, Scotland.

DEALERS' INDEX

Gordon (Antiques), R.S., Alford, Scotland.
Gorman, Mrs J.M., Chesterfield, Derbys.
Gormley Antiques, J. and S., Broadway, Herefs. & Worcs.
Gorst Hall Restoration, Kidderminster, Herefs. & Worcs.
Goslett Gallery, Roland, Richmond, Surrey.
Gosling, C. and A., Budleigh Salterton, Devon.
Gosling, Max, Portsmouth, Hants.
Goss and Crested China Centre, Horndean, Hants.
Gossips, Otford, Kent.
Gostick Hall Antiques, Newport, Essex.
Gostling's Antique Centre, Diss, Norfolk.
Gouby, M., London, W8.
Gough, B.A., Carshalton, Surrey.
Gough Books, Simon, Holt, Norfolk.
Gough Bros. Art Shop and Gallery, Bognor Regis, Sussex West.
Gould and Sons (Antiques) Ltd, A.E., East Horsley, Surrey.
Gould and Julian Gonnermann Antiques, Betty, London, N6.
Gould, D. and P., East Horsley, Surrey.
Gould, E., Teddington, Middx.
Gould, Gillian, London, W1.
Gould and Co., Herbert, Holywood, Co. Down, N. Ireland.
Gould, Stephen, Holywood, Co. Down, N. Ireland.
Gould, S., Stratford-upon-Avon, Warks.
Goulding, G., Middleton Village, Lancs.
Gourlay, R. and I., Houndwood, Scotland.
Gowen, M., St. Leonards-on-Sea, Sussex East.
Gower, C., Burford, Oxon.
Gower, G., London, NW1.
Gower, G., Malmesbury, Wilts.
Grace, Mr and Mrs S. Staley, Ramsey, Cambs.
Grafton Country Pictures, Oakham, Leics.
Graham, A., London, W11.
Graham Antiques, Anthony, Boroughbridge, Yorks. North.
Graham, A. and M.J., Alston, Cumbria.
Graham, A.P., Newcastle-upon-Tyne, Tyne and Wear.
Graham Gallery, Burghfield Common, Berks.
Graham Gallery, The, London, N1.
Graham Gallery, Tunbridge Wells, Kent.
Graham Gallery, Gavin, London, W11.
Graham and Green, London, W11.
Graham, J., Ross-on-Wye, Herefs. and Worcs.
Graham, Miss J., Aberdour, Scotland.
Graham, Joss, London, SW1.
Graham, Joyce, Tunbridge Wells, Kent.
Graham and Oxley (Antiques) Ltd, London, W8.
Grahams of Colchester, Colchester, Essex.
Graham-Stewart, London, W11.
Graham-Stewart, M., London, W11.
Granary Galleries, The, Ash Priors, Somerset.
Grandfather Clock Shop, The, Shipston-on-Stour, Warks.
Grandma's Goodies, Cardiff, South Glam., Wales.
Grange Antiques, St. Peter Port, Guernsey, C.I.
Grange Antiques and Craft Centre, The, Tongham, Surrey.
Grange Gallery and Fine Arts Ltd, St. Helier, Jersey, C.I.
Grannie's Attic, Market Weighton, N. Humbs.
Grannie's Attic, Shottermill, Surrey.
Grannies Attic Antiques, Smethwick, West Mids.
Grannie's Parlour, Hull, N. Humbs.
Grannie's Treasures, Hull, N. Humbs.
Granny's Attic, Clare, Suffolk.
Granny's Attic, Nottingham, Notts.
Granny's Attic, Ramsgate, Kent.
Granny's Kist, Fochabers, Scotland.
Grant Antiques, Denzil, Bradfield St. George, Suffolk.
Grant Fine Art, Droitwich, Herefs. & Worcs.
Grant, J., Avening, Glos.
Grant, J., Tetbury, Glos.
Grant, Mrs P., London, SW1.
Grant, R., Boston, Lincs.
Grant, Stephanie, Barnard Castle, Durham.
Grant, Mrs V., Waddesdon, Bucks.
Grantham Clocks, Grantham, Lincs.
Grantham Furniture Emporium, Grantham, Lincs.
Grant-Zeid, Mary Jane, Broadway, Herefs. and Worcs.
Granville Antiques, Petworth, Sussex West.
Grasmere Galleries, Grasmere, Cumbria.
Grate Expectations, Camborne, Cornwall.
Grate Expectations (Fireplaces), Washington, Tyne and Wear.
Grater, S., Thundersley, Essex.
Gratton, P., Inverness, Scotland.

Gratwick, A., Hartley Wintney, Hants.
Graus Antiques, London, W1.
Graus, E. and H., London, W1.
Gravelly Bank Pine Antiques, Yeaveley, Derbys.
Gravener, Mr and Mrs, Mayfield, Sussex East.
Gravener Antiques, Wm. J., Mayfield, Sussex East.
Graves Gallery, The, Birmingham, West Mids.
Gray, Mr and Mrs A., Penrith, Cumbria.
Gray, B., London, NW8.
Gray, G.C.M., Hertford, Herts.
Gray, D. and M., Great Malvern, Herefs. and Worcs.
Gray, D. and M., Worcester, Herefs. and Worcs.
Gray, Mrs J., Cirencester, Glos.
Gray Antiques, Jay, Cirencester, Glos.
Gray, L., Kingsthorpe, Northants.
Gray, Marion, London, N4.
Gray, M., Saltaire, Yorks. West.
Gray, Mrs S., Sheffield, Yorks. South.
Grayling, David A. H., Crosby Ravensworth, Cumbria.
Graylow and Co, Bath, Avon.
Grays Antique Market, London, W1.
Gray's Antiques of Worcester, Great Malvern, Herefs. & Worcs.
Gray's Antiques of Worcester, Worcester, Herefs. & Worcs.
Grays Collectors Centre, Grays, Essex.
Grays Mews, London, W1.
Grays Portobello, London, W11.
Great Ayton Bookshop, The, Great Ayton, Yorks. North.
Great Brampton House Antiques Ltd, Hereford, Herefs. & Worcs.
Great Malvern Antiques, Great Malvern, Herefs. & Worcs.
Great Northern Architectural Antique Company Ltd, The, Tattenhall, Cheshire.
Great Western Antique Centre Ltd, Bath, Avon.
Great Western Antique Centre Ltd. - The Wednesday Market, Bath, Avon.
Great Western Pine, South Molton, Devon.
Greaves, H.J., Sheffield, Yorks. South.
Greaves, P.A., Sheffield, Yorks. South.
Green, D.S., Hartley Wintney, Hants.
Green Farm Antiques, Olveston, Avon.
Green, G.H., Sheffield, Yorks. South.
Green, J., Chichester, Sussex West.
Green, J.E., London, W11.
Green and Son, J., Queniborough, Leics.
Green, L., P. and R., Birmingham, West Mids.
Green, M., Harrogate, Yorks. North.
Green, Mrs M., Penarth, South Glam., Wales.
Green, Mr and Mrs M., Tetbury, Glos.
Green, N. and J., Coventry, West Mids.
Green Parrot, The, London, SE10.
Green, Richard, London, W1.
Green, R., Queniborough,, Leics.
Green, R., Stratford-upon-Avon, Warks.
Green, Ron, Towcester, Northants.
Green Antiques, Robert, Ross-on-Wye, Herefs. & Worcs.
Green, R.J., Colchester, Essex.
Green, Renée and Roy, Lewes, Sussex East.
Green Room, The, Bournemouth, Dorset.
Green, S., London, W8.
Green and Stone, London, SW3.
Green and Stone of Chichester, Chichester, Sussex West.
Green, T. and S., St. Gerrans, Cornwall.
Greenaway, D.L., Canterbury, Kent.
Greenaway, T., London, W1.
Greenberg, C.B. and P.R., Honiton, Devon.
Greene, I., Castle Hedingham, Essex.
Greenfield and Son, Gunmakers (Est. 1805), H.S., Canterbury, Kent.
Greenfield, T.S., Canterbury, Kent.
Greengrass Antiques, Chobham, Surrey.
Greengrass, D., Chobham, Surrey.
Greengrass, D., London, NW8.
Greenlaw Antiques, Greenlaw, Scotland.
Greenman, S., London, N12.
Green's Antique Galleries, London, W8.
Greens of Montpellier, Cheltenham, Glos.
Greenslade, C. and L., Sherborne, Dorset.
Greenwall, J., Sandgate, Kent.
Greenway Antiques, Colin, Witney, Oxon.
Greenwich Antiques and Ironware Co, London, SE10.
Greenwich Antiques Market, London, SE10.

DEALERS' INDEX

Greenwich Gallery, The, London, SE10.
Greenwood, Judy, London, SW6.
Greenwood Antiques, Simon, Burneston, Yorks. North.
Greenwood, S. and C., Burneston, Yorks. North.
Greenwood (Fine Art), W., Burneston, Yorks. North.
Greer, Robin, London, SW3.
Gregg, Mr and Mrs I.E., Ramsgate, Kent.
Gregory, Bottley and Lloyd, London, SW6.
Gregory, George, Bath, Avon.
Gregory, M., London, SW1.
Gregory Gallery, Martyn, London, SW1.
Gregory, N., Wendover, Bucks.
Gregory, Neil, Grasmere, Cumbria.
Gregory, R., Deddington, Oxon.
Gregory's Antique Pine, Helmshore, Rossendale, Lancs.
Gregson, D. and M., St. Agnes, Cornwall.
Greig, Charles, Windsor and Eton, Berks.
Gretton Old Advertising, Keith, London, SW11.
Greycroft Antiques, Errol, Scotland.
Grey-Harris and Co, Bristol, Avon.
Greystoke Antiques, Sherborne, Dorset.
Greystones Antiques, Buckden, Yorks. North.
Grice Antiques, Alan, Ormskirk, Lancs.
Grice, C.A., Shipley, Yorks. West.
Gridley, Gordon, London, N1.
Griffin Antiques, Petworth, Sussex West.
Griffin, G.E., Croydon, Surrey.
Griffin Antiques Ltd, Simon, London, W1.
Griffin, S.J., London, W1.
Griffith, J.J., Canterbury, Kent.
Griffiths, D., London, N1.
Griffiths, J., Bath, Avon.
Griffiths, M., Huddersfield, Yorks. West.
Griffiths, N.K., Weedon, Northants.
Griffiths, R. and W., Southport, Merseyside.
Griffiths, Mrs T.A., Windermere, Cumbria.
Griffiths, W. and B., Burscough, Lancs.
Griffiths, W. and S., Buckden, Yorks. North.
Griffons Court, Newbury, Berks.
Grigg, A., Norwich, Norfolk.
Grimes and Hayward,, Lewes, Sussex East.
Grimes House Antiques, Moreton-in-Marsh, Glos.
Grimes Militaria, Chris, Bristol, Avon.
Grodzinski, W., London, W1.
Gronow, R., Cardiff, South Glam., Wales.
Grosvenor Antiques, Leek, Staffs.
Grosvenor Antiques Ltd, London, W8.
Grosvenor Antiques of Chester, Chester, Cheshire.
Grosvenor House Interiors, Beaconsfield, Bucks.
Grosvenor Prints, London, WC2.
Grosvenor, R., Towcester, Northants.
Groucott, Mike, Peterborough, Cambs.
Grout, P., Moreton-in-Marsh, Gloucs.
Grove Antiques, Hazel Grove, Cheshire.
Grove Antiques, London, SW3.
Grove Collectors Centre, Harrogate, Yorks. North.
Grove Gallery, Windsor and Eton, Berks.
Grove House Antiques, Petworth, Sussex West.
Grover, D.R. and D.A., Chichester, Sussex West.
Groves, Elfyn and Elaine, Woburn, Beds.
Groves, Mrs H., Tunbridge Wells, Kent.
Groves, M.A. and A., Doveridge, Derbys.
Groves, T. and J., Holt, Norfolk.
Grozier, W.B.T., Hull, N. Humbs.
Guardroom Antiques Centre, The, Hemswell Cliff, Lincs.
Gubb, J. and A.H., Southampton, Hants.
Guest, Mrs J., St. Andrews, Scotland.
Guildhall Antique Market, Chard, Somerset.
Guildhall Fair, Chester, Cheshire.
Guildhall Gallery, Bury St. Edmunds, Suffolk.
Guildhall Street Antiques, Bury St. Edmunds, Suffolk.
Guillemot, Aldeburgh, Suffolk.
Guinevere Antiques, London, SW6.
Guiscards Miniatures and Juvenalia, Rait, Scotland.
Guiver, T., Great Malvern, Herefs. and Worcs.
Gullane Antiques, Gullane, Scotland.
Gumb, Linda, London, N1.
Gunawardena, E., Richmond, Surrey.
Gunpowder House Antiques, Faversham, Kent.
Gunnett, B.R., Brixworth, Northants.
Gunning, Mr, Todmorden, Yorks. West.
Guns and Tackle, Scunthorpe, S. Humbs.
Gunson, Mrs N., Mirfield, Yorks. West.
Gunter Fine Art, London, NW2.
Guthrie, L.W. and R.M., Shipston-on-Stour, Warks.
Guy, A.R. and D.E., Amersham, Bucks.
Guy's Antiques and Fine Furniture, Peter, Preston, Lancs.
Gwilliam, D.L., Bath, Avon.
Gwilliam, Edred A.F, Cricklade, Wilts.
Gwydir Street Antiques Centre, Cambridge, Cambs.
Gyte, P.S., Ripon, Yorks. North.

H

H.L.B. Antiques, Bournemouth, Dorset.
HRW Antiques, London, SW4.
H. and S. Collectables, Gosforth, Tyne and Wear.
Haas (A. and M. Rosenthal), Otto, London, NW3.
Hacker, P.F., Harrogate, Yorks. North.
Hackett, R. and B., Frome, Somerset.
Hackney House Antiques, Chesterfield, Derbys.
Hadfield, G.K., Shepshed, Leics.
Hadji Baba Ancient Art, London, W1.
Hadleigh Jewellers, London, W1.
Hadlow Antiques, Tunbridge Wells, Kent.
Hadwin, Mrs V., Preston, Lancs.
Hagan, K.O., Claudy, Co. Londonderry, N. Ireland.
Hagarty, Mrs M., Bow Street, Dyfed, Wales.
Hagen, Richard, Broadway, Herefs. & Worcs.
Hague Antiques, Leamington Spa, Warks.
Hague, J., Leamington Spa, Warks.
Hague, John, Pickering, Yorks. North.
Hahn, P., London, W1.
Hahn and Son Fine Art Dealers, London, W1.
Haig-Harrison, A.G., Bristol, Avon.
Haillay, Mrs C.L., Lechlade, Glos.
Haines, B., Ammanford, Dyfed, Wales.
Haines Antiques Ltd, John, London, SW14.
Haines, J. and S.D., London, SW14.
Hakeney Antiques, David K., Hull, N. Humbs.
Halabuda, Mrs I., Barry, South Glam., Wales.
Halcyon Antiques, Stockport, Cheshire.
Halcyon Days, London, EC3.
Halcyon Days, London, W1.
Halcyon Gallery, The, Birmingham, West Mids.
Haldane, J., Little Abington, Cambs.
Hale, Mrs I., Tunbridge Wells, Kent.
Hale, Mr and Mrs P., Uckfield, Sussex East.
Hales Antiques Ltd, Robert, London, W8.
Halesowen Antiques, Halesowen, West Mids.
Halewood and Sons, Preston, Lancs.
Haley, S., Halifax, Yorks. West.
Half-Door Antique Store, The, Forkhill, Co. Armagh, N. Ireland.
Haliden Oriental Rug Shop, Bath, Avon.
Halifax Antiques Centre, Halifax, Yorks. West.
Hall, Anthony C., Twickenham, Middx.
Hall, A.R. and J.M., Ash Priors, Somerset.
Hall, B.J. and H.M., Crewkerne, Somerset.
Hall, D., Hexham, Northumbs.
Hall Ltd, Douglas, Brighton, Sussex East.
Hall, Mrs G., Cheltenham, Glos.
Hall, L.M., Great Malvern, Herefs. and Worcs.
Hall, R., Ash Priors, Somerset.
Hall, Robert, London, W9.
Hall, R. and J., Llandogo, Gwent, Wales.
Hall, S., Burford, Oxon.
Hall's Antiques, Ash Priors, Somerset.
Hall's Bookshop, Tunbridge Wells, Kent.
Hallam Antiques, Michael, Norwich, Norfolk.
Hallam, M.J., Norwich, Norfolk.
Hallesy, H., Swansea, West Glam., Wales.
Hallett Antiques (Hanborough Antiques), David A., Long Hanborough, Oxon.
Halliday, F.G., Glasgow, Scotland.
Halliday's, London, SW3.
Hallidays Antiques Ltd, Dorchester-on-Thames, Oxon.
Halliwell, Sue, Knutsford, Cheshire.
Hallmarks, Brighton, Sussex East.
Hallstand, Hastings, Sussex East.
Hallstile Antiques, Hexham, Northumbs.
Halo Antiques, Altrincham, Cheshire.
Halsall, Mrs E., Preston, Lancs.
Halsall Hall Ltd, Liverpool, Merseyside.

721 DEALERS' INDEX

Halsey, M. and R., Drewsteignton, Devon.
Halstead Antiques, Halstead, Essex.
Hamblin, John, Yeovil, Somerset.
Hamblin, J. and M. A., Yeovil, Somerset.
Hamilton Antiques, Woodbridge, Suffolk.
Hamilton Antiques, Anne, Burnham Market, Norfolk.
Hamilton Antiques, Anne, East Rudham, Norfolk.
Hamilton and Co, A.D., Glasgow, Scotland.
Hamilton, D., Sherborne, Dorset.
Hamilton Fine Arts, London, NW11.
Hamilton, H., Knebworth, Herts.
Hamilton, K. and J.E., Grantham, Lincs.
Hamilton, P. and W, London, SW20.
Hamilton, Rosemary, London, SW1.
Hamilton Ltd, Ross, London, SW1.
Hamilton, Sheelagh, Fernhurst, Sussex West.
Hamilton, Sheelagh, Merrow, Surrey.
Hamilton and Tucker Billiard Co. Ltd, Knebworth, Herts.
Hamilton, V., London, NW11.
Hamilton's Corner, London, SW20.
Hamlet, E., Longridge, Lancs.
Hamlet, Miss J., Longridge, Lancs.
Hamlyn Lodge, Ollerton, Notts.
Hammer, Mrs P., Wimborne Minster, Dorset.
Hammond, D. and R., Buxton, Derbys.
Hammond, G., Chipping Campden, Glos.
Hammond, J. and E., Leominster, Herefs. and Worcs.
Hammond Antiques, Jeffery, Leominster, Herefs. & Worcs.
Hampshire Gallery, Bournemouth, Dorset.
Hampshires of Dorking, Dorking, Surrey.
Hampstead Antique Emporium, London, NW3.
Hampton Court Antiques, East Molesey, Surrey.
Hampton Court Emporium, East Molesey, Surrey.
Hampton, G., Christchurch, Dorset.
Hampton Gallery, Tetbury, Glos.
Hampton Hill Gallery, Hampton Hill, Middx.
Hampton Village Antiques Centre, Hampton, Middx.
Hampton Wick Antiques, Hampton Wick, Surrey.
Hamptons, Christchurch, Dorset.
Hanbury, Mrs D., Chobham, Surrey.
Hancock, Mark, London, SW13.
Hancock, M.L., Chichester, Sussex West.
Hancock Antiques, Peter, Chichester, Sussex West.
Hancocks and Co, London, W1.
Hancox, G. and D., Wolseley Bridge, Staffs.
Hancox, G. and R., Wansford, Cambs.
Hancox, P.E., Wansford, Cambs.
Hand in Hand, Edinburgh, Scotland.
Hand, J., Nailsworth, Glos.
Hand, K., Kidlington, Oxon.
Hand, Mr and Mrs O., Edinburgh, Scotland.
Hand Prints and Watercolours Gallery, Nailsworth, Glos.
Handbury-Madin, R. and E., Shrewsbury, Shrops.
Handcross Antiques, Handcross, Sussex West.
Handford Antiques, William, London, SW10.
Handtiques, Kidlington, Oxon.
Hanlon, W. and J., Menston, Yorks. West.
Hannant, M., Hythe, Kent.
Hannaway, Mrs M., Bloxwich, West Mids.
Hannen, L.G., London, W1.
Hannent, Jean and Donna, Fakenham, Norfolk.
Hanover Antiques, Scarborough, Yorks. North.
Hansen Chard Antiques, Pershore, Herefs. & Worcs.
Han-Shan Tang Ltd, London, SW1.
Hanson, Mrs M.E., Knaresborough, Yorks. North.
Hansord and Son, David J., Lincoln, Lincs.
Harari and Johns Ltd, London, SW1.
Harbottle, Patricia, London, W11.
Harbottle, Mrs P., London, W11.
Harcourt Antiques, London, W1.
Harcourt, P., London, W1.
Hardie Antiques, Perth, Scotland.
Hardie, S., Perth, Scotland.
Hardie, T.G., Perth, Scotland.
Hardiman, M. and G.A., Melbourn, Cambs.
Hardiman, P.N., Melbourn, Cambs.
Harding, E., Northleach, Glos.
Harding, Mrs J., Duffield, Derbys.
Harding, FBHI, K., Northleach, Glos.
Harding, N.J., Tunbridge Wells, Kent.
Harding, R., London, W1.
Harding, T., Blackmore, Essex.

Harding-Hill, M. and D., Chipping Norton, Oxon.
Harding's World of Mechanical Music, Keith, Northleach, Glos.
Hardman Antiques, Jennie, Crawley, Sussex West.
Hardwick Antiques, Streetly, West Mids.
Hardy Country, Melbury Osmond, Dorset.
Hardy, J., Bournemouth, Dorset.
Hardy Antiques, John, Oadby, Leics.
Hardy and Co, James, London, SW3.
Hardy Pine and Country Furniture, Joyce, Hacheston, Suffolk.
Hardy's Market, Bournemouth, Dorset.
Hare, Allan, Cirencester, Glos.
Hare, Allan, London, SW10.
Hares, Cirencester, Glos.
Hares Antiques, London, SW10.
Hargraves, John, Wigan, Lancs.
Harlequin Antiques, Porthcawl, Mid. Glam., Wales.
Harlequin Gallery, Lincoln, Lincs.
Harley Antiques, Christian Malford, Wilts.
Harley, G.J., Christian Malford, Wilts.
Harling, R., Lye, West Mids.
Harman Antiques, Robert, Ampthill, Beds.
Harmandian, G., Bath, Avon.
Harms, A., London, N1.
Harold's Place, London, W5.
Harp Antiques, Bradford-on-Avon, Wilts.
Harper, B. and I., Warwick, Warks.
Harper, Erica and Hugo, Chester, Cheshire.
Harper Fine Paintings, Poynton, Cheshire.
Harper, Mrs K., Leeds, Yorks. West.
Harper, M.R., Bristol, Avon.
Harper, Mrs N.C., Guildford, Surrey.
Harper, P.R., Poynton, Cheshire.
Harper Antiques, Martin and Dorothy, Bakewell, Derbys.
Harper-James, Montrose, Scotland.
Harrap, B., Sheffield, Yorks. South.
Harriman Antiques, David, Rickmansworth, Herts.
Harrington Gallery, David, London, W1.
Harrington, Mrs M., London, SW3.
Harris, A.R., Stourbridge, West Mids.
Harris Antiques, Colin, Hartley Wintney, Hants.
Harris and Sons, Antiques, Bob, Birmingham, West Mids.
Harris, B.C. and R.H., London, W1.
Harris, E.C. and D., London, EC1.
Harris, I., London, W1.
Harris, Jonathan, London, W8.
Harris (Jewellery) Ltd, Jonathan, London, EC1.
Harris, Nicholas, London, SW6.
Harris, R., Kinver, Staffs.
Harris, R.E., Birmingham, West Mids.
Harris and Son (London) Ltd, S.H., London, W1.
Harris, T.W., Northampton, Northants.
Harris, V. and H., Penryn, Cornwall.
Harrison Fine Antiques, Anna, Gosforth, Tyne and Wear.
Harrison, D., Edinburgh, Scotland.
Harrison, J., Newtonmore, Scotland.
Harrison, J.M., Leeds, Yorks. West.
Harrison, Miss P., Lewes, Sussex East.
Harrison, P., Lytham St. Annes, Lancs.
Harrison, R., London, W11.
Harrison, Ruth, Sevenoaks, Kent.
Harrison, S., Petworth, Sussex West.
Harrison Wholesale Exports, Tim, Stratford-upon-Avon, Warks.
Harrods Ltd, London, SW1.
Harrold Antique Centre, Harrold, Beds.
Harrop Fold Clocks (F. Robinson), Bolton-by-Bowland, Lancs.
Hart, Ann and Bernard, London, NW3.
Hart, E., London, N1.
Hart, Mrs Elizabeth, Ceres, Scotland.
Hart, J.A. and N., Bletchingley, Surrey.
Hart Antiques, Mitchell, Clows Top, Herefs. & Worcs.
Hart, Mr and Mrs M.B., Clows Top, Herefs. and Worcs.
Hart, Rosemary, London, N1.
Hart and Rosenberg, London, N1.
Hart, Sylvia, Bournemouth, Dorset.
Hart, Sheila, and John Giles, Aylsham, Norfolk.
Harthope House Antiques, Moffat, Scotland.
Hartley Antiques, Hartley, Kent.
Hartley Antiques Ltd, J., Ripley, Surrey.
Hartley, S.N., Wingham, Kent.
Hartnell Antiques and Victoriana, Dorothy, Sidmouth, Devon.

DEALERS' INDEX

Hartnoll, Julian, London, SW1.
Harvey Centre, The, Canterbury, Kent.
Harvey, C.S., Ludlow, Shrops.
Harvey, E., London, W11.
Harvey and Gore, London, W1.
Harvey, Mr and Mrs J.L. and L., Maentwrog, Gwynedd, Wales.
Harvey, J.M., Aylesbury, Bucks.
Harvey, Patricia, London, SW6.
Harvey, W.R. and A.D., London, W1.
Harvey & Co (Antiques) Ltd, W.R, London, W1.
Harvey-Jones, A., Woodbridge, Suffolk.
Harvey-Lee, Elizabeth, London, NW2.
Harvey-Morgan, R., Stow-on-the-Wold, Glos.
Harvey-Morgan, R., Stratford-upon-Avon, Warks.
Harvey-Owen Antiques, Maentwrog, Gwynedd, Wales.
Harwood Antiques, London, SW15.
Harwood, A. and D.B.M., Weston-Super-Mare, Avon.
Harwood, G. M., London, SW15.
Harwood, J., Grasmere, Cumbria.
Harwood, M.H., Headington, Oxon.
Harwood Tate, Market Rasen, Lincs.
Harwood Tate, J., Market Rasen, Lincs.
Harwood West End Antiques, Weston-Super-Mare, Avon.
Hasel-Britt Ltd, Radlett, Herts.
Haskell, Miriam, London, N1.
Haslam, N. and C.A., Grassmoor, Derbys.
Haslam, Mr and Mrs S., Aldeburgh, Suffolk.
Haslam and Whiteway, London, W8.
Haslam-Hopwood, R.G.G., Stow-on-the-Wold, Glos.
Haslam-Hopwood, R.G.G., Wadebridge, Cornwall.
Hastings-Spital, K., Bath, Avon.
Hassall Antiques, Geoffrey, Solihull, West Mids.
Hastie, Ian G., Salisbury, Wilts.
Hastie, Robert and Georgina, Hungerford, Berks.
Hastings Antique Centre, The, St. Leonards-on-Sea, Sussex East.
Hatch Antiques, Weybridge, Surrey.
Hatch, B.D., Weybridge, Surrey.
Hatcher, Sherry, London, N1.
Hatchwell Antiques, Simon, Brighton, Sussex East.
Hatherleigh Antiques, Hatherleigh, Devon.
Hatvany, E., Hampton, Middx.
Haugh Antiques, Roderic, Norwich, Norfolk.
Haughey Antiques, Kirkby Stephen, Cumbria.
Haughey, D.M., Kirkby Stephen, Cumbria.
Haughton Antiques, Brian, London, W1.
Havard and Havard, Cowbridge, South Glam., Wales.
Havard, Philip and Christine, Cowbridge, South Glam., Wales.
Havard, T. and P., Harpole, Northants.
Havelin Antiques, Blandford Forum, Dorset.
Haven Gallery, The, Gt. Yarmouth, Norfolk.
Havenplan's Architectural Emporium, Killamarsh, Derbys.
Haw, S., Haslemere, Surrey.
Hawkey, V., Grimsby, S. Humbs.
Hawkins Bros. Antiques, Barry, South Glam., Wales.
Hawkins Antiques, Brian, London, N1.
Hawkins Antiques, C., Kingsbridge, Devon.
Hawkins, G., Berkeley, Glos.
Hawkins, G. and J., Cambridge, Glos.
Hawkins, Mark and David, Brighton, Sussex East.
Hawkridge, Mrs M., Skipton, Yorks. North.
Hawley Antique Clocks, John and Carol, Clevedon, Avon.
Hawley Antiques, Beverley, N. Humbs.
Haworth Antiques, Harrogate, Yorks. North.
Haworth Antiques, Haworth , Yorks. West.
Haworth Antiques, Huby, Yorks. North.
Haworth Ltd - Antique Gallery, M. and N., Manchester, Lancs.
Haworth, Peter, Beetham, Cumbria.
Hawthorn, Gerard, London, W1.
Hay Antiques, Blakedown, Herefs. & Worcs.
Hay Green Antiques, Blackmore, Essex.
Hay, J.D., Glasgow, Scotland.
Hay Loft Gallery, Broadway, Herefs. & Worcs.
Hayden, B., Templecombe, Somerset.
Hayden Antiques, Shirley, Windsor and Eton, Berks.
Haydon Bridge Antiques, Haydon Bridge, Northumbs.
Haydon Gallery, Haydon Bridge, Northumbs.
Haydon House Antiques, Woburn Sands, Bucks.
Hayes, Miss M.L., North Shields, Tyne and Wear.

Hayes Gallery, Paul, Auchterarder, Scotland.
Haygate Gallery, Telford, Shrops.
Hayhurst Fine Glass, Jeanette, London, W8.
Haylett, A.P. and M.A., Outwell, Cambs.
Haynes, C., Alvechurch, West Mids.
Haynes, John, Littlehampton, Sussex West.
Haynes Fine Art, Broadway, Herefs. & Worcs.
Haynes - Antiques Finder, Roger, Leek, Staffs.
Hayter, R.W. and F.L., Ryde, I. of Wight.
Hayter's, Ryde, I. of Wight.
Hayward, D.H. and M.S., Kingsbridge, Devon.
Hazandras, J.A., London, W1.
Hazel Cottage Clocks, Eachwick, Northumbs.
Hazel of Brecon, Brecon, Powys, Wales.
Hazlitt, Gooden and Fox Ltd, London, SW1.
Head, Floydmist Ltd - P., Liss, Hants.
Head, J. and J., Salisbury, Wilts.
Head, P., St. Peter Port, Guernsey, C.I.
Heads 'n' Tails, Wiveliscombe, Somerset.
Healey, S.D. and I.J., Birmingham, West Mids.
Heaney, T., Ballyclare, Co. Antrim, N. Ireland.
Heap, Mrs M.M., Burnham-on-Sea, Somerset.
Heape's Antiques, Burnham-on-Sea, Somerset.
Hearnden, J. and S., Dorchester-on-Thames, Oxon.
Hearne, R.E.W., Beaconsfield, Bucks.
Heart of England Antiques, Haunton, Staffs.
Hearth and Home, London, NW1.
Hearth and Home, Penrith, Cumbria.
Heath Antiques, Reigate, Surrey.
Heath, A.R., Bristol, Avon.
Heath Antique Centre, Heath and Reach, Beds.
Heath, C., London, NW1.
Heath, K.W. and Y.F., Moreton-in-Marsh, Glos.
Heath Antiques, Mike, Newport, I. of Wight.
Heath, M. and B., Newport, I. of Wight.
Heath-Bullock, R.J. and M.E., Godalming, Surrey.
Heath-Bullocks, Godalming, Surrey.
Heathcote Antiques, Cross Hills, Yorks. North.
Heather Antiques, London, N1.
Heather, J.C., Woolpit, Suffolk.
Heatherlie Antiques, Selkirk, Scotland.
Hebbard, D.L., Titchfield, Hants.
Hebbard, P.E., Hay-on-Wye, Powys, Wales.
Hebbards of Hay, Hay-on-Wye, Powys, Wales.
Hebeco, Dorking, Surrey.
Hedingham Antiques, Sible Hedingham, Essex.
Hedley, Mrs E., Maldon, Essex.
Hedley, J.A. and T., Hexham, Northumbs.
Heeley, Colin, Leamington Spa, Warks.
Heelis, J., Milburn, Cumbria.
Heffer, W., Cambridge, Cambs.
Heffers Booksellers, Cambridge, Cambs.
Hefford, R. , Caldbeck, Cumbria.
Heirloom and Howard Ltd, West Yatton, Wilts.
Heirlooms, Worcester, Herefs. & Worcs.
Heirlooms (Antique Jewellers), Wareham, Dorset.
Helios & Co (Antiques), Weedon, Northants.
Helius Antiques, London, SW14.
Hellmers, P., Epping, Essex.
Hellmers, P., Epping, Essex.
Hellon, D., Chester, Cheshire.
Helm Antiques, Linda, London, N1.
Helmer, G.V., Southampton, Hants.
Helmore, Mrs W., Odiham, Hants.
Helton Antiques, Heath and Reach, Beds.
Hemswell Antiques Centres, Hemswell Cliff, Lincs.
Hemsworth, S., Portsmouth, Hants.
Henderson, Perth, Scotland.
Henderson Antiques, Coupar Angus, Scotland.
Henderson, B., Tunbridge Wells, Kent.
Henderson, F.M., Cowfold, Sussex West.
Henderson, J.G., Perth, Scotland.
Henderson, Milne, London, NW8.
Heneage Art Books, Thomas, London, SW1.
Henham (Antiques), Martin, London, N2.
Henley Antique Centre, Henley-on-Thames, Oxon.
Henley Antiques, R. and J. L., Canterbury, Kent.
Henley House Antiques, Rumford, Cornwall.
Hennell of Bond Street Ltd. Founded 1736 (incorporating Frazer and Haws (1868) and E. Lloyd Lawrence (1830), London, W1.
Hennessy, Beaminster, Dorset.

DEALERS' INDEX

Hennessy, C. and G.C., Beaminster, Dorset.
Henry's of Ash, Ash, Kent.
Henstridge, W.V., Bournemouth, Dorset.
Hepburn, T. and N., Beaconsfield, Bucks.
Hepner, R.P., Knutsford, Cheshire.
Hepworth, C.G. and I.M., Newton St. Cyres, Devon.
Hepworth Gallery, Gordon, Newton St. Cyres, Devon.
Heraldry Today, Ramsbury, Wilts.
Heraty, P., Hartley Wintney, Hants.
Heraz (David Hartwright Ltd), London, SW1.
Herbert, L., Cowbridge, South Glam., Wales.
Herbert, N.R., Newmarket, Suffolk.
Hereford Antique Centre, Hereford, Herefs. & Worcs.
Heritage Antiques, Chichester, Sussex West.
Heritage Antiques, Huddersfield, Yorks. West.
Heritage Antiques, Linlithgow, Scotland.
Heritage Antiques, London, N1.
Heritage Antiques, Oldham, Lancs.
Heritage Antiques, Paisley, Scotland.
Heritage Antiques and Stripped Pine, Cardiff, South Glam., Wales.
Heritage House Antiques, Glasgow, Scotland.
Heritage Restorations, Llanfair Caereinion, Powys, Wales.
Hermitage Antiques, London, SW1.
Hermitage Antiquities, Fishguard, Dyfed, Wales.
Heron, C., Thatcham, Berkshire.
Heron, H.N.M. and J., Yoxall, Staffs.
Heron and Son Ltd, H.W., Yoxall, Staffs.
Herrald Antiques, Edinburgh, Scotland.
Herrington, B., Gargrave, Yorks. North.
Herrington, D.M., Hungerford, Berks.
Herrington, L.R., Hungerford, Berks.
Hersheson, J., Brighton, Sussex East.
Hersheson, J.J., Brighton, Sussex East.
Hershkowitz Ltd, Robert, London, SW7.
Herts and Essex Antique Centre, The, Sawbridgeworth, Herts.
Hesketh, C., Blandford Forum, Dorset.
Heskia, London, W14.
Hesling, J. and H., Avoch, Scotland.
Heuduk, P., Hastings, Sussex East.
Hewes, P.N., Bury St. Edmunds, Suffolk.
Hewett, Mr and Mrs P., Runfold, Surrey.
Hewitt Art Deco Originals, Muir, Halifax, Yorks. West.
Hexham Antiques (Inc. Hotspur Antiques), Hexham, Northumbs.
Heyday, Saddleworth, Lancs.
Heyden, R.E.J., Cheltenham, Glos.
Heydens Antiques and Militaria, Cheltenham, Glos.
Heygate Browne Antiques, Sherborne, Dorset.
Heytesbury Antiques, Farnham, Surrey.
Heywood, D., Birmingham, West Mids.
Heywood Hill Ltd, G., London, W1.
Hezaveh, A.A., Sheffield, Yorks. South.
Hibbert Bros. Ltd, Sheffield, Yorks. South.
Hick Antiques, David, Carrefour Selous, St. Lawrence, Jersey, C.I.
Hickford, T.K. and W.E., Grundisburgh, Suffolk.
Hickmott, Mrs F., Glossop, Derbys.
Hickmott, J.R., Tunbridge Wells, Kent.
Hicks, David, London, N21.
Hicks Gallery, London, SW19.
Hicks, J., London, SW19.
Hicks, J. and M., Rudgwick, Sussex West.
Hicks, Jan, Richmond, Surrey.
Hicks, Jan, Windsor and Eton, Berks.
Hicks, M.B. and I.F., North Walsham, Norfolk.
Hicks, M.B. and I.F., Stalham, Norfolk.
Hickson CMBHI, Lewis, Seaton Ross, N. Humbs.
Hidden Gem, Macclesfield, Cheshire.
Hi-Felicity, Kidderminster, Herefs. & Worcs.
Higgins, B.R. and E.A., Brighton, Sussex East.
High Park Antiques, Broadway, Herefs. & Worcs.
High St. Antiques, Alcester, Warks.
Higham, J., Carlisle, Cumbria.
Highland Antiques, Avoch, Scotland.
Highland Antiques, Stockport, Cheshire.
Highmoor, Mrs E.M., Cambridge, Cambs.
Highway Gallery, The, Upton-upon-Severn, Herefs. & Worcs.
Higson, J. and T., Alnwick, Northumbs.
Hiley, W., London, SW14.
Hill Books, Alan , Bakewell, Derbys.

Hill Books, Sheffield, Alan, Sheffield, Yorks. South.
Hill, B.E., Pinner, Middx.
Hill, C.C., Canterbury, Kent.
Hill, D., Macclesfield, Cheshire.
Hill, David, Kirkby Stephen, Cumbria.
Hill Farm Antiques, Leckhampstead, Berks.
Hill, G.M. and J., London, SW1.
Hill, Mrs J.C.Sinclair, Horton, Berks.
Hill, J.E. and J.T., Wolverhampton, West Mids.
Hill, M., Fochabers, Scotland.
Hill, P., Oxford, Oxon.
Hill Rise Antiques, Richmond, Surrey.
Hill, R. and S., Bulkington, Warks.
Hill, Mrs S., Stratford-upon-Avon, Warks.
Hillfoot Antiques, Dollar, Scotland.
Hilliard, Mrs J., Bournemouth, Dorset.
Hillman, H., Brecon, Powys, Wales.
Hillman, L., Brecon, Powys, Wales.
Hill-Reid, J., London, SW6.
Hills Antiques, Macclesfield, Cheshire.
Hills and Partners Ltd, Richard, Plymouth, Devon.
Hillside Antiques, Halifax, Yorks. West.
Hillyers, London, SE26.
Hilmarton Manor Press, Calne, Wilts.
Hilson, A. and B., Tewkesbury, Glos.
Hilton, Simon, Dunmow, Essex.
Himsworth, Robert M., York, Yorks. North.
Hinde, P., Richmond, Surrey.
Hinde Fine Art, Sheila, Kirdford, Sussex West.
Hines, J., Costessey, Norfolk.
Hines, J., Norwich, rfolk.
Hines, Mrs W.C.M., London, SW3.
Kingstons, Cadnam, Hants.
Hinsdale Antiques, East Grinstead, Sussex West.
Hinson Fine Paintings, Sheffield, Yorks. South.
Hipkins, D.P., Birmingham, West Mids.
Hirschhorn, Robert, London, SE5.
Hirsh, A., London, EC1.
Hirsh Ltd, London, EC1.
Hirst Antiques, London, W11.
Hirst, Mrs S.M., Alnwick, Northumbs.
Hiscock & Hiscock Antiques, New Romney, Kent.
Hiscock, Erna and Paul, New Romney, Kent.
Hitchcock, E.C., Newport, Essex.
Hitchcox, P. and R., Chalgrove, Oxon.
Hitchcox Antiques, Rupert, Chalgrove, Oxon.
Hitchcox, T. and E., Stratford-upon-Avon, Warks.
Hitchin Antiques Gallery, Hitchin, Herts.
Hoare Pine Antiques, Bob, Lewes, Sussex East.
Hoare, O., London, SW1.
Hobart, A. and M., London, SW1.
Hobbs, Carlton, London, SW1.
Hobbs, Richard, Sheerness, Kent.
Hobby Horse Antiques, Bridport, Dorset.
Hobson, Platon, London, NW3.
Hobson Antiques , Claire, London, W1.
Hockin (Antiques) Ltd, Keith, Stow-on-the-Wold, Glos.
Hockley Antiques, William, Petworth, Sussex West.
Hockley Coins, Nottingham, Notts.
Hodge, Jean, Worcester, Herefs. & Worcs.
Hodge, Sarah, Worcester, Herefs. & Worcs.
Hodgkins and Co. Ltd, Ian, Slad, Glos.
Hodgkinson, B.E. and J., Newport, Essex.
Hodgkison, G.S., Brighton, Sussex East.
Hodgkiss, V.D., Maulds Meaburn, Cumbria.
Hodgson, J., Great Shefford, Berks.
Hodgson, P. and R., Birmingham, West Mids.
Hodnet Antiques, Hodnet, Shrops.
Hodsoll Ltd, Christopher, London, SW1.
Hodson, M., Parkstone, Dorset.
Hofgartner, S., Hungerford, Berks.
Hofman Antiques at the Sign of the Black Cat, George, Stockbridge, Hants.
Holder, D., London, WC1.
Holdich, R.D., London, WC2.
Hole in the Wall Antiques, Stockport, Cheshire.
Hole, S.D., Abernyte, Scotland.
Hole-in-the-Wall, The, Armagh, Co. Armagh, N. Ireland.
Holgate, Milton J., Knaresborough, Yorks. North.
Holgate Antiques, York, Yorks. North.
Hollamby, M., London, W2.
Holland and Holland Ltd, London, W1.

DEALERS' INDEX

Holland Antiques, Mary, Boston, Lincs.
Holland, Mrs M., Boston, Lincs.
Hollander Ltd, E., Dorking, Surrey.
Hollender, K., London, W1.
Hollett, R. F. G. and C. G., Sedbergh, Cumbria.
Hollett and Son, R. F. G., Sedbergh, Cumbria.
Holley, Susan M., Bath, Avon.
Holleyman and Treacher Ltd, Brighton, Sussex East.
Hollingshead and Co, London, SW6.
Hollingshead, D., London, SW6.
Hollington Antiques, Long Crendon, Bucks.
Holloway, Edward and Diana, Suckley, Herefs. and Worcs.
Holloways, Suckley, Herefs. & Worcs.
Hollywood Road Gallery, London, SW10.
Holmes Antiques, Cockermouth, Cumbria.
Holmes, C. and S., Cockermouth, Cumbria.
Holmes, D., London, W8.
Holmes House Antiques, Sedlescombe, Sussex East.
Holmes, J., Perranporth, Cornwall.
Holmes Antique Maps and Prints, Julia, South Harting, Sussex West.
Holmes Ltd, London, W1.
Holmes Field, M., Corwen, Clwyd, Wales.
Holmes, R., Cullompton, Devon.
Holmwood Antiques, Dorking, Surrey.
Holstead, M.L. and J., Fochabers, Scotland.
Holt and Co. Ltd, R., London, EC1.
Holyome, A.C., London, N1.
Home to Home, London, N6.
Homer, J.B., Bidford-on-Avon, Warks.
Homewood, R.A., Sandgate, Kent.
Homewood Antiques, Robin, Sandgate, Kent.
Hone Watercolours, Angela, Marlow, Bucks.
Honeypot Antiques, Cheadle, Cheshire.
Honiton Antique Toys, Honiton, Devon.
Honiton Clock Clinic, Honiton, Devon.
Honiton Fine Art, Honiton, Devon.
Honiton Junction, Honiton, Devon.
Honiton Lace Shop, The , Honiton, Devon.
Honiton Old Bookshop, Honiton, Devon.
Hood and Broomfield, Newcastle-under-Lyme, Staffs.
Hood, G., Easingwold, Yorks. North.
Hood and Co, Helena, Bath, Avon.
Hood, J., Newcastle-under-Lyme, Staffs.
Hood, Mrs L.M., Bath, Avon.
Hook, Anthony J., Westerham, Kent.
Hook, P., London, SW1.
Hooke, G.A., Tongham, Surrey.
Hooper Antiques, David, Leamington Spa, Warks.
Hooper, P., Worcester, Herefs. and Worcs.
Hope and Glory, London, W8.
Hope Phonographs and Gramophones, Howard, East Molesey, Surrey.
Hopkins , John, Cuckfield, Sussex West.
Hopkins, John, Petworth, Sussex West.
Hopkins, J., M. and A., Cuckfield, Sussex West.
Hopkins, John, Angela and Mona, Petworth, Sussex West.
Hopkins, M., Bath, Avon.
Hoppen Ltd, Stephanie, London, SW3.
Hoppett, D., Wolverhampton, West Mids.
Hopwell Antiques, Paul, West Haddon, Northants.
Hopwood, D. and R., Windermere, Cumbria.
Horley Antiques, Welshpool, Powys, Wales.
Horn At The Golden Past, Dorothea, Peel, I. of Man.
Horn Furniture Ltd, Simon, London, SW6.
Horncastle Antiques, Horncastle, Lincs.
Horne, Jonathan, London, W8.
Hornsey Ltd, Adrian, London, W11.
Hornsey Ltd, Adrian, London, W4.
Hornsey Ltd, Adrian, Twyford, Bucks.
Horological Workshops, Guildford, Surrey.
Horsebridge Antiques Centre, Horsebridge, Sussex East.
Horseshoe Antiques and Gallery, Burford, Oxon.
Horsman, P. and M., Long Melford, Suffolk.
Horswell, E.F., London, W1.
Horswill Antiques and Decorative Arts, Helen, West Kirby, Merseyside.
Horswill, J.O., West Kirby, Merseyside.
Horton, D. and R., Beckenham, Kent.
Horton, D. and R., Richmond, Surrey.
Horton, G.B., Henley-in-Arden, Warks.
Horton Antiques, Robert, Hertford, Herts.

Horton's, Beckenham, Kent.
Horton's, Richmond, Surrey.
Horvath-Toldi, Miss M., Wolverhampton, West Mids.
Hosains Books and Antiques, London, W2.
Hosford, Mrs.J.M., Saffron Walden, Essex.
Hoskin, Miss C., Padstow, Cornwall.
Hoskin, R., Ewhurst, Surrey.
Hoskins , Diane, Lewes, Sussex East.
Hoskins, R., Keighley, Yorks. West.
Hoskinson, P., Walsall, West Mids.
Hotspur Ltd, London, SW1.
Hotz Fine Art Ltd, Dennis, London, W1.
Houchen, B., King's Lynn, Norfolk.
Houghton Hall Antiques, Market Weighton, N. Humbs.
Houghton Antiques, Peter, Warminster, Wilts.
Houghton, P.J., Warminster, Wilts.
Houghton-Connell, D., Petworth, Sussex West.
Houndwood House Antiques, Houndwood, Scotland.
Hounslow, P., Dulverton, Somerset.
Hourston, Mrs V., Fortrose, Scotland.
House (Mitre Antiques), Bernard G., Wells, Somerset.
House of Antiques, Honiton, Devon.
House of Antiques, The, Brighton, Sussex East.
House of Antiquity, Nether Stowey, Somerset.
House of Buckingham (Antiques), London, EC1.
House of Christian Antiques, Ash Vale, Surrey.
House of Mallett, Surbiton, Surrey.
House of Mirrors, London, SW6.
House of Steel Antiques, London, N1.
House Things Antiques, Hinckley, Leics.
Houser, Mr and Mrs B.G., Newcastle Emlyn, Dyfed, Wales.
Hove Antique Clocks, Brighton, Sussex East.
How, Mrs G.E.P., London, W1.
How of Edinburgh, London, W1.
Howard Antiques, London, W1.
Howard, C., Helmsley, Yorks. North.
Howard, David, Cheltenham, Glos.
Howard, D.N., Baldock, Herts.
Howard, D.S., West Yatton, Wilts.
Howard, Jonathan, Chipping Norton, Oxon.
Howard, J., Felsted, Essex.
Howard, J.G., Chipping Norton, Oxon.
Howard, M., Bolton-by-Bowland, Lancs.
Howard, Valerie, London, W8.
Howard-Jones, H., London, W8.
Howards, Baldock, Herts.
Howards Jewellers, Stratford-upon-Avon, Warks.
Howards of Aberystwyth, Aberystwyth, Dyfed, Wales.
Howards of Broadway, Broadway, Herefs. & Worcs.
Howards of Burford, Burford, Oxon.
Howards of Stratford Ltd,, Stratford-upon-Avon, Warks.
Howe, Christopher, London, SW1.
Howell Jeweller, Charles, Oldham, Lancs.
Howell, N.G., Oldham, Lancs.
Howell, P.B., Hereford, Herefs. and Worcs.
Howells, S.A., Beaconsfield, Bucks.
Howes Bookshop, Hastings, Sussex East.
Howes, R., Horrabridge, Devon.
Howkins Antiques, John, Norwich, Norfolk.
Howkins, J.G., Norwich, Norfolk.
Howkins, Peter, Gt. Yarmouth, Norfolk.
Howse, R.S.J., Oxford, Oxon.
Hoylake Antique Centre, Hoylake, Merseyside.
Hoyle, D., York, Yorks. North.
Hoyle, D. and P., Whitby, Yorks. North.
Hoysted, Anna, Mattingley, Hants.
Hubbard Antiques, Ipswich, Suffolk.
Hubbard Antiques, Leominster, Herefs. & Worcs.
Hubbard, C.L.B., Ponterwyd,, Dyfed, Wales.
Hubbard Antiques, John, Birmingham, West Mids.
Hubbard, P., Fordham, Essex.
Hubbard's Bookshop, Doggie, Ponterwyd, Dyfed, Wales.
Huckett, A.G. and N.E., Toddington, Beds.
Huckvale, C. and G., Battle, Sussex East.
Huddersfield Antiques, Huddersfield, Yorks. West.
Huddington International Antiques Warehouse, Birmingham, West Mids.
Hudes, Eric, Braintree, Essex.
Hudes, Eric, London, W11.
Hudson, A., Burnham Market, Norfolk.
Hudson, A., East Rudham, Norfolk.
Hudson, Lady Cathleen, Stanford Dingley, Berks.

DEALERS' INDEX

Hudson, E.A., Ditchling, Sussex East.
Hudson Ltd, Felix, Dunfermline, Scotland.
Hudson, F.R., London, W11.
Hudson, J., Farnham, Surrey.
Hudson, Mrs J.B., Winyates Green, Herefs. and Worcs.
Hudson, John, Shipston-on-Stour, Warks.
Hudson, Mrs P., Emsworth, Hants.
Hudson, Thomas and Pamela, Cirencester, Glos.
Hugall, Geoffrey, Jesmond, Tyne and Wear.
Huggett and Son, L.J., Honiton, Devon.
Hughes, A., London, SW13.
Hughes, B. and M., Dumfries, Scotland.
Hughes, C., London, SW11.
Hughes Antiques, Eynon, Swansea, West Glam., Wales.
Hughes, E. and M., Swansea, West Glam., Wales.
Hughes, J. and Mrs . M.E., Bowness-on-Windermere, Cumbria.
Hughes, M., Epsom, Surrey.
Hughes, M., Mathry, Dyfed, Wales.
Hughes, P., Glasgow, Scotland.
Hughes, P., Lymington, Hants.
Hughes, Mrs S., Weybridge, Surrey.
Hughes and Smeeth Ltd, Lymington, Hants.
Huie, Duncan, Pitlochry, Scotland.
Hulbert (Antiques and Firearms), Anne and Colin, Swansea, West Glam., Wales.
Hull Gallery, Christopher, London, SW1.
Hull, Mrs P., Budleigh Salterton, Devon.
Hulme, J. Alan, Waverton, Cheshire.
Humble Antiques, Mac, Bradford-on-Avon, Wilts.
Humble, Owen, Jesmond, Tyne and Wear.
Humble, W. Mc. A. and B.J., Bradford-on-Avon, Wilts.
Hume, Dudley, Brighton, Sussex East.
Humphrey, E., Edinburgh, Scotland.
Humphrey, L.W.G. and D.E., Brighton, Sussex East.
Humphry Antiques, Petworth, Sussex West.
Humphry, J. and M., Petworth, Sussex West.
Humphrys Antiques, Brian , Penzance, Cornwall.
Hunaban, R.S. and E.A., Great Malvern, Herefs. and Worcs.
Hünersdorff Rare Books and Manuscripts, London, SW10.
Hungerford Arcade, Hungerford, Berks.
Hungerford-Boyle, Y., Dorking, Surrey.
Hunnings, P. J. M., Penn, Bucks.
Hunt and Clement, Mildenhall, Suffolk.
Hunt, Jason, Rochester, Kent.
Hunt, J.A.E., Brightling, Sussex East.
Hunt Galleries, John, Brightling, Sussex East.
Hunt, K. and Mrs M.J.A., Tenby, Dyfed, Wales.
Hunt, P.H.M., Hartley Wintney, Hants.
Hunt, Mrs S., Bolton, Lancs.
Hunt Jewellers, Stanley, Gainsborough, Lincs.
Hunt, S. and R.S., Gainsborough, Lincs.
Hunter, P.R., Barnard Castle, Durham.
Hunter Fine Art, Sally, London, SW1.
Hunter, T., London, SW1.
Huntington Antiques Ltd, Stow-on-the-Wold, Glos.
Huntley, Diana, London, N1.
Hunwick, P.F., Hungerford, Berks.
Hurdle, N., Fairford, Glos.
Hurford Antiques, Peter, London, SW6.
Hurley Antiques and Textiles, Emma, Warminster, Wilts.
Hurley, Emma and John, Warminster, Wilts.
Hursley Antiques, Hursley, Hants.
Hurst Antiques, Anthony, Woodbridge, Suffolk.
Hurst, C.G.B., Woodbridge, Suffolk.
Hurst Antiques, Edward, Salisbury, Wilts.
Hurst, E. and L., Baldock, Herts.
Hurst, G.D., Mirfield, Yorks. West.
Hutchin, D., Chesham, Bucks.
Hutchings, I.M., Tiverton, Devon.
Hutchins, E.H., Oakley, Hants.
Hutchinson, J.N., Westerham, Kent.
Hutchinson, P. and M., London, W11.
Hutchinson-Shire, N.A., Endmoor, Cumbria.
Hutchison, James, Ilminster, Somerset.
Hutton Antiques, Shrewsbury, Shrops.
Hutton, I.S., Torquay, Devon.
Hutton, Mrs P.I., Shrewsbury, Shrops.
Hutton-Clarke, Mr and Mrs J., Stow-on-the-Wold, Glos.
Hyams, M., London, W11.
Hyde Park Corner Antiques (Antiques Centre), Cambridge, Cambs.

Hyde, Shelagh, Rhos-on-Sea, Clwyd, Wales.
Hyde, W., London, NW8.
Hyland House Antiques, Ipswich, Suffolk.
Hyndford Antiques, Brighton, Sussex East.
Hyron Antiques, Sandgate , Kent.
Hythe Antique Centre, Hythe, Kent.
Hythe Galleries, Sandwich, Kent.

I

I.G.A. Old Masters Ltd, St. Lawrence, Jersey, C.I.
I. and S. Antiques, Craven Arms, Shrops.
Iconastas, London, SW1.
Idenden, R.S, London, W1.
Igel, M., Kingston-upon-Thames, Surrey.
Igel, M., London, W2.
Igel Fine Arts Ltd, Manya, London, W2.
Iglesis, D., London, SW1.
Iles, The Family, Rochester, Kent.
Iles, Francis, Rochester, Kent.
Iles, R. and C., Colchester, Essex.
Iles Gallery, Richard, Colchester, Essex.
Illingworth, V.E., London, N5.
Ilsley, R., London, NW3.
Images in Watercolour, Chalfont St. Giles, Bucks.
Images - Peter Stockham, Lichfield, Staffs.
Imperial Antiques, Hull, N. Humbs.
Imperial Antiques, Stockport, Cheshire.
Impressions and Alexandra's Antiques, St. Margaret's Bay, Kent.
Imrie Antiques, Bridge of Earn, Scotland.
Imrie, Mr and Mrs I., Bridge of Earn, Scotland.
In the Picture (The Golf Collection), Holt, Norfolk.
Incandescent Lighting Company, The, Leamington Spa, Warks.
Ingall, F., Oakham, Leics.
Ingall, I. and S., Farnham, Surrey.
Ingham, J. S., Horbury, Yorks. West.
Ingleby, Mrs E.B., Garelochhead, Scotland.
Inglenook Antiques, Harpole, Northants.
Inglenook Antiques, Ramsbury, Wilts.
Inglis, Brand, London, SW1.
Ingram, D., Edinburgh, Scotland.
Ingram, I.C., Perth, Scotland.
Ingram Hill, R., Horncastle, Lincs.
Ingrams, C., Haslemere, Surrey.
Inheritance, London, N1.
Innes Gallery, Malcolm, Edinburgh, Scotland.
Innes Gallery, Malcolm, London, SW3.
Intercoin, Newcastle-upon-Tyne, Tyne and Wear.
Intercol London, London, N1.
Iona Antiques, London, W8.
Irani, M.Z., London, SW1.
Ireland Ltd, Peter, Blackpool, Lancs.
Irena Art and Antiques, Barry, South Glam., Wales.
Ironbridge Antique Centre, Ironbridge, Shrops.
Irons, Mr and Mrs C.A., Coalville, Leics.
Irons, Lesley Ann, Wells-next-the-Sea, Norfolk.
Irwin, C. and M., Ravenstonedale, Cumbria.
Isaacs, P. and S., Leeds, Yorks. West.
Isabella Antiques, Warminster, Wilts.
Islington Antiques, London, N1.
It's About Time, Westcliff-on-Sea, Essex.
Ivanhoe Antiques, Ashby-de-la-Zouch, Leics.
Ivelet Books Ltd - Church St. Bookshop, Godalming, Surrey.
Ives Bookseller, John, Twickenham, Middx.
Ivy House Antiques, Acle, Norfolk.
Ivy House Antiques, Brasted, Kent.
Ivy House Antiques, Great Shefford, Berks.
Ixworth Antiques, Ixworth, Suffolk.

J

J.B. Antiques, Wimborne Minster, Dorset.
J. and B. Antiques, London, W11.
JBW Antiques, Holme, Cumbria.
J.H.S. Antiques, Matlock, Derbys.
J.N. Antiques, Redbourn, Herts.
J.V. Pianos and Cambridge Pianola Company, Landbeach, Cambs.
Jackdaw Antiques, Thatcham, Berks.
Jackman, F.T. and S., Jesmond,, Tyne and Wear.

DEALERS' INDEX

Jackman, Mr & Mrs J., Sayers Common, Sussex West.
Jackson, A., Hertford, Herts.
Jackson, A., Leamington Spa, Warks.
Jackson, Miss A.E., Chesham, Bucks.
Jackson, B.M., Tenterden, Kent.
Jackson, F., London, W10.
Jackson, John, Milton-under-Wychwood, Oxon.
Jackson Antiques, Jenny, Woodbridge, Suffolk.
Jackson, J.H., Milton-under-Wychwood, Oxon.
Jackson, Kenneth, Edinburgh, Scotland.
Jackson, P., Blackpool, Lancs.
Jackson, P., Windsor and Eton, Berks.
Jackson Antiques, Peter, Brackley, Northants.
Jackson, P. and V.E., London, SW3.
Jackson, R. and J., Flaxton, Yorks. North.
Jackson Antiques, S.I. , Wigton, Cumbria.
Jackson, S. and Mrs T.J., Sutton Bridge, Lincs.
Jackson, Mr and Mrs T.C., Newbury, Berks.
Jackson-Grant Antiques, Teynham, Kent.
Jackson-Grant, D.M., Teynham, Kent.
Jacksonville Antiques Warehouse, Edinburgh, Scotland.
Jacobi, Mrs P.M., Chester, Cheshire.
Jacobs Antique Centre, Cardiff, South Glam., Wales.
Jacobs, M., Norwich, Norfolk.
Jadis Ltd, Bath, Avon.
Jaffa (Antiques) Ltd, John, London, W1.
Jaffray, Alan, Melksham, Wilts.
Jakes, K.P., Worthing, Sussex West.
Jalna Antiques, Little Haywood, Staffs.
Jalna Antiques, Wolseley Bridge, Staffs.
Jamandic Ltd, Chester, Cheshire.
James and Son Ltd, Anthony, London, SW3.
James Antiques, Brian, Telford, Shrops.
James Antiques - Canalside, Birmingham, West Mids.
James, David, London, SW1.
James, D. and E., London, SW1.
James, D.R. and M.L., Montrose, Scotland.
James, G., Oldham, Lancs.
James Antiques, Joseph, Penrith, Cumbria.
James, N., Marlborough, Wilts.
James, P. and D., Birmingham, West Mids.
James, P.L., London, SW6.
James Antiques, R. A., Sileby, Leics.
James, R.M. and E., Bishops Cleeve, Glos.
James, S.N. and W., St. Albans, Herts.
James Antiques, Tim, Birmingham, West Mids.
James of St Albans, St. Albans, Herts.
Jameson and Co, A.E., Sheffield, Yorks. South.
Jameson, C., Thirsk, Yorks. North.
Jameson, P., Sheffield, Yorks. South.
Jandora, Weybridge, Surrey.
Jane, Mrs M., Wallingford, Oxon.
Jane's Fine Arts, Poynton, Cheshire.
Janes, P., Tunbridge Wells, Kent.
Janes, P. and R., Dover, Kent.
Jansons Antiques, Bwlchllan, Dyfed, Wales.
Jansons, J.C., Bwlchllan, Dyfed, Wales.
Janssens, Ben , London, W1.
Japanese Gallery, London, N1.
Japanese Gallery, London, W8.
Jarman, H., Woodbury, Devon.
Jarrett, G., Norwich, Norfolk.
Jarrett, L.S.A. and C.J., Witney, Oxon.
Jarvis, Richard, London, W1.
Jaspers Fine Arts Ltd, Maidenhead, Berks.
Jay, C.G., Looe, Cornwall.
Jay Antiques and Objets d'Art, Melvyn, London, W8.
Jay's Antique Centre, The, Harefield, Middx.
Jazz, Stratford-upon-Avon, Warks.
Jazzy Art Deco, London, NW1.
Jazzy Art Deco, London, SW3.
Jebb, T.H., Cookstown, Co. Tyrone, N. Ireland.
Jefferson, Mr and Mrs G., London, W2.
Jefferson, Patrick, London, SW6.
Jeffs at Nicholas Harris, Peter, London, SW6.
Jellinek, Tobias , London, SW3.
Jellinek, T., London, W8.
Jenkins, J., London, SE26.
Jenkins, V. and A., Bradford-on-Avon, Wilts.
Jennings, B., Brasted, Kent.
Jennings, Celia, Pratt's Bottom, Kent.
Jennings, J.R., Leominster, Herefs. and Worcs.

Jennings of Leominster, Leominster, Herefs. & Worcs.
Jennings Antiques, Paul, Angarrack, Cornwall.
Jennings, R., Bideford, Devon.
Jennings, R.J., Pulloxhill, Beds.
Jennywell Hall Antiques, Crosby Ravensworth, Cumbria.
Jeorrett, J. and A., Kiltarlity, Scotland.
Jeremiah Antiques, Llandissilio, Dyfed, Wales.
Jeremiah, S. and S., Llandissilio, Dyfed, Wales.
Jeremy Ltd, London, SW1.
Jeremy's (Oxford Stamp Centre), Oxford, Oxon.
Jesse, John, London, W8.
Jessop Classic Photographica, London, WC1.
Jewel Antiques, Cheddleton, Staffs.
Jewell, B., Evesham, Herefs. and Worcs.
Jewell Ltd, S. and H., London, WC2.
Jewett, N., Low Fell, Tyne and Wear.
Jewitt, W.H., Hexham, Northumbs.
Jewry Street Gallery Ltd, Winchester, Hants.
Jinks, G., Birmingham, West Mids.
Jobson's, Joan, Coggeshall, Essex.
Joel, Mrs J., Dorking, Surrey.
Joel, Mrs J., London, SW6 .
John Anthony Antiques, Bletchingley, Surrey.
John Antiques, Angela, Bampton, Oxon.
John (Rare Rugs) Ltd, C., London, W1.
John, P.R., London, NW8.
Johns, Patricia , London, SW7.
Johns, T., Lytchett Minster, Dorset.
Johnson, A., Colchester, Essex.
Johnson, D., Birmingham, West Mids.
Johnson, D.A., Kilmarnock, Scotland.
Johnson, E. and P.R., Burford, Oxon.
Johnson Collection, The Hugh, London, SW1.
Johnson, Mrs J.A., Cartmel, Cumbria.
Johnson, P. and Mrs J., Leek, Staffs.
Johnson, P.R., Stow-on-the-Wold, Glos.
Johnson, R., Birmingham, West Mids.
Johnson, R. and R., Birmingham, West Mids.
Johnson and Sons, Rex, Birmingham, West Mids.
Johnson, T.L., Maidenhead, Berks.
Johnson and others, Mr. and Mrs .E.M., Salisbury, Wilts.
Johnson's, Leek, Staffs.
Johnson Walker & Tolhurst Ltd, London, W1.
Johnston, D., Windsor and Eton, Berks.
Johnston, Paul, Gedney, Lincs.
Jomarc Pianos Ltd. , Walsall, West Mids.
Jones, A., Colchester, Essex.
Jones, Annabel, London, SW3.
Jones Antiques, Alan, Okehampton, Devon.
Jones Antiques, Alan, Plymouth, Devon.
Jones Antique Lighting, London, W11.
Jones, A.P., Norton, Glos.
Jones at Flore House, Christopher, Flore, Northants.
Jones, Mr and Mrs B.J., Stourbridge, West Mids.
Jones, D., Stratford-upon-Avon, Warks.
Jones, D.A., Oxford, Oxon.
Jones, D.G.M., Sidmouth, Devon.
Jones, E., Chester, Cheshire.
Jones, E.C., Birmingham, West Mids.
Jones, E.P., Liverpool, Merseyside.
Jones, G., London, SW6.
Jones, Miss G., Looe, Cornwall.
Jones, Gareth, Edinburgh, Scotland.
Jones, Howard, London, W8.
Jones Antiques, Glyn , Pembroke Dock, Dyfed, Wales.
Jones, Judy, London, W11.
Jones, J.H., Rhos-on-Sea, Clwyd, Wales.
Jones, John and Jennifer, Towcester, Northants.
Jones, J. and S., Beaumaris, Gwynedd, Wales.
Jones, L., Ludlow, Shrops.
Jones, Lionel and Angela, Chester, Cheshire.
Jones Jeweller, Michael, Northampton, Northants.
Jones, M.R.T. and E.J., Cromer, Norfolk.
Jones, M.S., Great Ayton, Yorks. North.
Jones, Mr and Mrs P., Chepstow, Gwent, Wales.
Jones, P., Watton, Norfolk.
Jones, P. and A., Nantwich, Cheshire.
Jones, P.W., Oakham, Leics.
Jones, Orlando, Bath, Avon.
Jones Antiques, Ron , Barmouth, Gwynedd, Wales.
Jones, R. and J., London, SW1.
Jones, R. and J., Rye, Sussex East.

DEALERS' INDEX

Jones, R.W., Barmouth, Gwynedd, Wales.
Jones, W., London, W11.
Jones, W.A. and E.S., Bromyard, Herefs. and Worcs.
Jones and Son (Antiques) Ltd, W., London, W11.
Jones, W.T., Ruthin, Clwyd, Wales.
Jordan, James A., Lichfield, Staffs.
Jordan, P.A. and W.E., Farnham, Surrey.
Jordan, P. and B., Farnham, Surrey.
Jordan, R.A., Barnard Castle, Durham.
Jordan (Fine Paintings), T.B. and R., Eaglescliffe, Cleveland.
Jorgen Antiques, London, SW15.
Joseph and Pearce Ltd, London, EC1.
Joseph, Booksellers, E., London, W1.
Joshua Antiques, Taunton, Somerset.
Joslin, Richard, London, W14.
Joslyn, J.H., London, SE5.
Joy, Mrs Nina, Hadlow, Kent.
Joyner, T.R.B., Newchurch, I. of Wight.
Joy's Shop, Longridge, Lancs.
Jubilee Antiques, London, SW1.
Jubilee Photographica, London, N1.
Juett, J., Walkerburn, Scotland.
Jukes, Mr and Mrs G., St. Leonards-on-Sea, Sussex East.
Julian Antiques, Hurstpierpoint, Sussex West.
Julian Antiques, London, N1.
Junk Shop, The, London, SE10.
Junktion, Stickford, Lincs.
Juno's Antiques, Brackley, Northants.
Jupiter Antiques, Rottingdean, Sussex East.
Juran and Co, Alexander, London, W1.
Jury, D., Bristol, Avon.
Just a Second, London, SW6.
Just a Second Antiques, London, SW11.
Just Desks, London, NW8.
Just the Thing, Hartley Wintney, Hants.

K

K.C. Antiques, Darwen, Lancs.
K.L.M. & Co. Antiques, Lepton, Yorks. West.
Kadwell, J.P., Malmesbury, Wilts.
Kailas, M., London, SW6.
Kaimes Smithy Antiques, Edinburgh, Scotland.
Kairis, M.V., London, N8.
Kaplan, Arne, London, NW6.
Kaplan, L.M., London, SW3.
Kaplan Associates Ltd, Lewis M., London, SW3.
Karczewski-Slowikowski, J., Manchester, Lancs.
Kasiewicz, Mr and Mrs, Auchterarder, Scotland.
Kate, Hemswell Cliff, Lincs.
Kate House, London, SW15.
Kathleen's Antiques, North Petherton, Somerset.
Katz, G. and Y., Richmond, Surrey.
Kavanagh, D., Blackpool, Lancs.
Kay, Bob and Barbara, Ashtead, Surrey.
Kaye of Lyndhurst, Lita, Lyndhurst, Hants.
Kaye, N.J., Chester, Cheshire.
Kayes of Chester, Chester, Cheshire.
Kear, P.W., Cranborne, Dorset.
Kearin, J. and J., White Colne, Essex.
Kearney & Sons, T.H., Belfast, N. Ireland.
Keddie, Mrs A.C., East Grinstead, Sussex West.
Keeble, Mrs E., Fareham, Hants.
Keegan, P., North Walsham, Norfolk.
Keen, C., Lewes, Sussex East.
Keen Antiques, Cassandra, London, N1.
Keen, Thomas, Bottesford, Leics.
Keen, T.E., Bottesford, Leics.
Keene, B.M. and J.S., Henley-on-Thames, Oxon.
Keene Gallery, The Barry M., Henley-on-Thames, Oxon.
Keens, D., Long Melford, Suffolk.
Keighley and Son, B., Keighley, Yorks. West.
Keighleys of Keighley, Keighley, Yorks. West.
Keil (Cheltenham) Ltd, H.W., Cheltenham, Glos.
Keil Ltd, H.W., Broadway, Herefs. & Worcs.
Keil Ltd, John, London, SW3.
Keil, V.M., Broadway, Herefs. and Worcs.
Kelaty Ltd, L., Wembley, Middx.
Kelford Antiques, Sutton Coldfield, West Mids.
Kellam, I., Moreton-in-Marsh, Glos.
Kelly Antiques, Rodley, Glos.
Kelly, B.D., Ayr, Scotland

Kelly, D.C., Knaresborough, Yorks. North.
Kelly, G., Rodley, Glos.
Kelly Antiques, M., Eastburn, Yorks. West.
Kelly, P., London, SE23.
Kelly Antiques, Terence, Highbridge, Somerset.
Kellys of Knaresborough, Knaresborough, Yorks. North.
Kelsall, E.S., Sutton Coldfield, West Mids.
Kelsey, P., Bramley, Surrey.
Kelvedon Antiques, Kelvedon, Essex.
Kelvedon Antiques Centre, Kelvedon, Essex.
Kelvedon Art and Antiques, Kelvedon, Essex.
Kemp, Chris and Ann, Bath, Avon.
Kemp Ltd, Melville, Nottingham, Notts.
Kemp, Peter, London, W8.
Kemp, P.M., Bristol, Avon.
Kemp, W., Newport, Essex.
Kemps, Bristol, Avon.
Kendal Antiques, London, NW3.
Kendal Studios Antiques, Kendal, Cumbria.
Kendal-Greene, R.B., Harrogate, Yorks. North.
Kendall, The English Watercolour Gallery, Beryl, London, W9.
Kendall, John, Melville, Nottingham, Notts.
Kennaugh, P. and C., London, SW10.
Kennedy Carpets and Kelims, London, W1.
Kennedy, D., Helmshore, Rossendale, Lancs.
Kennedy Fine Arts, Hythe, Kent.
Kennedy, Jane and Frank, Chipping Campden, Glos.
Kennedy, K., London, NW1.
Kennedy, M., London, W1.
Kennedy, M., Hythe, Kent.
Kennedy, Peter, London, W11.
Kennedy, Robin, London, W1.
Kennerley's, Romsley, West Mids.
Kenny, Mrs S.M., Dorking, Surrey.
Kensington Church Street Antiques Centre, London, W8.
Kensington Fine Arts, London, W8.
Kensington Sporting Paintings Ltd, London, SW20.
Kensington Tower Antiques Ltd, Liverpool, Merseyside.
Kent Cottage Antiques, Rolvenden, Kent.
Kent Antiques, David, Gloucester, Glos.
Kent, G. and P., Marlborough, Wilts.
Kent Antiques, Robert J., Frampton West, Lincs.
Kentish, B., Oxford, Oxon.
Kenulf Fine Arts, Winchcombe, Glos.
Kenworthys Ltd, Ashton-under-Lyne, Lancs.
Kenyon, R., Hemswell Cliff, Lincs.
Kenyon, R., Newark, Notts.
Kern, R.A.B. and B.S., London, SW1.
Kerr Antiques, Caroline, Glasgow, Scotland.
Kerr - Gatehouse Bookshop, Norman, Cartmel, Cumbria.
Kerr Antiques Ltd, Thomas, London, N1.
Kerridge Antiques, B. and J., Cley, Norfolk.
Kershaw, Mrs J., Orwell, Cambs.
Keshishian, London, SW1.
Kessingland Antiques, Kessingland, Suffolk.
Kestrel House Antiques and Auction Salerooms, Birmingham, West Mids.
Ketchum, B.J., Stamford, Lincs.
Ketley Antiques, Carol, London, N1.
Kettle Ltd, Thomas, London, WC2.
Keverne, Roger, London, W1.
Key Antiques, Chipping Norton, Oxon.
Keyford Antiques, Rode, Somerset.
Keymer Son & Co. Ltd, Brasted, Kent.
Keystone Antiques, Coalville, Leics.
Khan, A.K., Richmond, Surrey.
Khawaja, K., London, SW1.
Kickshaws, Southend-on-Sea, Essex.
Kihl (Wine Accessories) Ltd, Richard, London, NW1.
Kilby, Mrs M., Northfleet, Kent.
Kilim Warehouse Ltd, The, London, SW12.
Kilmacolm Antiques Ltd, Kilmacolm, Scotland.
Kimbell, Richard, Codicote, Herts.
Kimbell, Richard, Enfield, Middx.
Kimbell, Richard, Thatcham, Berks.
Kimbell Ltd, Richard, Market Harborough, Leics.
Kimbell, R. and F., Thatcham, Berks.
Kimber and Son, Malvern Link, Herefs. & Worcs.
Kime Antiques, Robert, Marlborough, Wilts.
Kindon Antiques Ltd, Terry, Melmerby, Yorks. North.
King, Wymondham, Norfolk.

DEALERS' INDEX

King, Ann, Bath, Avon.
King, B., London, SW3.
King Antique Glass, Dominic, London, SW1.
King, Edward, Cowan Bridge, Lancs.
King Antiques, Eric, London, SW6.
King, F., London, W14.
King, F., Pattishall, Northants.
King, J., London, WC2.
King, J.H., St. Leonards-on-Sea, Sussex East.
King, M., Wymondham, Norfolk.
King Antiques, Roger, Hungerford, Berks.
King, R. and G., West Peckham, Kent.
King, Mr and Mrs R.F., Hungerford, Berks.
King Street Antiques, Sandwich, Kent.
King Street Curios, Tavistock, Devon.
King Street Galleries, London, SW1.
Kingham, Mrs G., London, SE21.
King's Court Antique Centre, Glasgow, Scotland.
King's Court Galleries, Dorking, Surrey.
King's Court Galleries, London, SW6 .
King's Farm Antiques, Shapwick, Somerset.
Kings Fireplaces, Antiques and Interiors, Cardiff, South Glam., Wales.
Kings Fireplaces & Architectural Antiques, Cardiff, South Glam., Wales.
King's House Antiques, Langport, Somerset.
King-Smith, P.J., Moreton-in-Marsh, Glos.
Kingsbury Antiques, Brighton, Sussex East.
Kingsley Barn Antique Centre, Eversley, Hants.
Kingsley Gallery, Bath, Avon.
Kingston, Mrs E., London, SW19.
Kingston, Richard J., Henley-on-Thames, Oxon.
Kingswood, T., London, WC2.
Kinloch, Mrs C., Sedlescombe, Sussex East.
Kirby, Ms E., Chipping Norton, Oxon.
Kirby Antiques, R., Acrise, Kent.
Kirk, Barbara and David, Penzance, Cornwall.
Kirkby, Mrs J., Greystoke, Cumbria.
Kirkdale Pianos, London, SE26.
Kirke, Bridget, Modbury, Devon.
Kirke, Mrs M.R., Plymouth, Devon.
Kirkham, H., Tenterden, Kent.
Kirkland, G., London, SW6.
Kirkstall Antiques, Leeds, Yorks. West.
Kirsch, London , W11.
Kirsch Ltd, M., London , W11.
Kirton Antiques, Kirton, Lincs.
Kitchenalia, Longridge, Lancs.
Kitching, Robert, Horncastle, Lincs.
Klaber and Klaber, London, W8.
Klaber, Mrs B., London, W8.
Klaber, Miss P., London, W8.
Knaphill Antiques, Knaphill, Surrey.
Knicks Knacks, Sutton-on-Sea, Lincs.
Knight and Sons, B.R., St. Ives, Cambs.
Knight, D., Macclesfield, Cheshire.
Knight, Geoff and Shirley, Harrold, Beds.
Knight, J.C., Luton, Beds.
Knight, M., St. Ives, Cambs.
Knight, P., Bridport, Dorset.
Knight, Peter, Kennington, Kent.
Knights Antiques, Brassington, Derbys.
Knights Gallery, Harpenden, Herts.
Knight's Gallery, Luton, Beds.
Knights, J.C., Harpenden, Herts.
Knights, P.H., Norwich, Norfolk.
Knightsbridge Coins, London, SW1.
Knipe, D., Dorchester-on-Thames, Oxon.
Knowles, W.A. and M.A., Penkridge, Staffs.
Knowles, W.A. and M.A., Wolverhampton, West Mids.
Knox, A., Errol, Scotland.
Kojis Antique Jewellery, London, SW1.
Korn, E., London, N10.
Korn, M.E., London, N10.
Kramer, J., Elmley Lovett, Herefs. and Worcs.
Kreckovic, L. and E., London, SW6.
Krolle, Mrs D., Amersham, Bucks.
Krucker, S., Stroud, Glos.
Krüger, M.C., Northchapel, Sussex West.
Krüger Smith Fine Art, Northchapel, Sussex West.
Kruml, Richard, London, W1.
Kuhn, Nick, Bath, Avon.
Kuznierz, Mrs M., Telford, Shrops.
Kyoto House Japanese Antiques, Cheltenham, Glos.

L

L.P. Furniture (Mids) Ltd, Pelsall, West Mids.
L'Acquaforte, London, W11.
L'Antiquitès, Fochabers, Scotland.
La Barre Ltd, Leominster, Herefs. & Worcs.
La Chaise Antique, Faringdon, Oxon.
La Cloche Freres, London, W1.
La Trobe and Bigwood Restorations, Tunbridge Wells, Kent.
La Trobe, H., Brasted, Kent.
La Trobe, H., Tunbridge Wells, Kent.
La Trouvaille, Enfield, Middx.
La-di-da Interior Design, Charlecote, Warks.
Lace Basket, The, Tenterden, Kent.
Lace & Linen Shop, The , Glastonbury, Somerset.
Lace Shop, The, South Molton, Devon.
Lacewing Fine Art Gallery, Marlborough, Wilts.
Lacquer Chest, The, London, W8.
Lacy Gallery, Henley-in-Arden, Warks.
Lacy Gallery, London, W11.
Lady Newborough, The, London, W1.
Ladygate Antiques, Beverley, N. Humbs.
Lagden, J., Penzance, Cornwall.
Laila, Kingsthorpe, Northants.
Lain, H.J. and V.J., Westbourne, Sussex West.
Lain, L. and M., Bosham, Sussex West.
Lake Antiques, Lake, I. of Wight.
Lake, J. and E., Glasgow, Scotland.
Laker, I.A. and E.K., Somerton, Somerset.
Laklia, L.T., Bexley, Kent.
Laleham Antiques, Laleham, Surrey.
Lamb Arcade, The, Wallingford, Oxon.
Lamb, B., Swanage, Dorset.
Lamb Antiques, Michael, Minster, Kent.
Lamb, Malcolm C. and Rebecca, Altrincham, Cheshire.
Lamb, R. and Mrs S., Clare, Suffolk.
Lamb, S. and Mrs K., Sherborne, Dorset.
Lambden, J., Warboys, Cambs.
Lambe, Charlotte and John, Belfast, N. Ireland.
Lambert Antiques, Dorrian, Lincoln, Lincs.
Lambert, N., Woodbridge, Suffolk.
Lambert, P.M. and A.M.F.T., Halesworth, Suffolk.
Lambert, R., Lincoln, Lincs.
Lambert's Barn, Woodbridge, Suffolk.
Lamont Antiques Ltd, London, SE10.
Lamont, N., London, SE10.
Lamp Gallery, The, London, SW6.
Lampard and Sons, L.E., Horsham, Sussex West.
Lampard, Penny, Headcorn, Kent.
Lampard, Mrs P., Headcorn, Kent.
Lampard and Son Ltd, S., London, W11.
Lancaster Leisure Park Antiques Centre, Lancaster, Lancs.
Lancaster, T.J., Leek, Staffs.
Lancastrian Antiques, Lancaster, Lancs.
Lanchester, N., Debenham, Suffolk.
Landgate Antiques, Rye, Sussex East.
Lane Antiques, Stockbridge, Hants.
Lane Antiques, Barbara, Chiddingstone, Kent.
Lane, E.K., Stockbridge, Hants.
Lane Fine Art Ltd, London, W1.
Lane, Mrs N., London, W5.
Lane, R., Horsebridge, Sussex East.
Lane, R., Tewkesbury, Gloucestershire.
Lane Antiques, Russell, Warwick, Warks.
Lane, R.G.H., Warwick, Warks.
Lang Antiques, John, Dorking, Surrey.
Lang Antiques, John, St. Leonards-on-Sea, Sussex East.
Lang, J. and C., St. Leonards-on-Sea, Sussex East.
Langford, J., Shrewsbury, Shrops.
Langford, J., Telford, Shrops.
Langford, J. and R., Llangollen, Clwyd, Wales.
Langford, L.L., London, SW10.
Langford's Marine Antiques, London, SW10.
Langley Antiques, Corby Hill, Cumbria.
Langley Galleries, Rochester, Kent.
Langley's (Jewellers) Ltd, Bradford, Yorks. West.
Langmead, Mrs J., Chertsey, Surrey.
Langold Antiques, West Peckham , Kent.
Langton, M., Hull, N. Humbs.

DEALERS' INDEX

Langton, N. and V.M., Chorley, Lancs.
Lanham, Miss A., Newmarket, Suffolk.
Lankester Antiques and Books, Saffron Walden, Essex.
Lankester, J. and P., Saffron Walden, Essex.
Lankshear, M.I., Christchurch, Dorset.
Lankshear Antiques, M. & R., Christchurch, Dorset.
Lannards Gallery, Billingshurst, Sussex West.
Lansdown Antiques, Bath, Avon.
Lantern Shop, The, Sidmouth, Devon.
Lantern Shop Gallery, The, Sidmouth, Devon.
Large Gallery, George, Woburn, Beds.
Larkhall Antiques, Hebden Bridge, Yorks. West.
Larner, P., Cirencester, Glos.
Lascelles, R., London, SW6.
Lasham, L.M., Cowfold, Sussex West.
Lasher, C., London, W1.
Lassalle, Judith, London, N1.
Lasseters, Arundel, Sussex West.
Lassey, Mrs J., Settle, Yorks. North.
Last Drop Antique and Collectors Fair, Bolton, Lancs.
Latchford Antiques, Cheltenham, Glos.
Latchford, K. and R., Cheltenham, Glos.
Latham, J. and D., Hexham, Northumbs.
Latham Antiques, R.H., Blackpool, Lancs.
Latimer, E., Bicester, Oxon.
Laughton, Hugo, Edinburgh, Scotland.
Laughton, P., Buxton, Derbyshire.
Laura's Bookshop, Derby, Derbys.
Laurence Corner , London, NW1.
Laurens Antiques, Whitstable, Kent.
Laurens, G. A., Whitstable, Kent.
Laurie Antiques, Peter, London, SE10.
Laurie (Antiques) Ltd, John, London, N1.
Lavender (Antiques) Ltd, D.S., London, W1.
Lavenham Antiques, Lavenham, Suffolk.
Lavian, Joseph, London, NW5.
Law, D., Woking, Surrey.
Law, R., Worthing, Sussex West.
Law Antiques, Rathbone, Worthing, Sussex West.
Lawes, David, Harrogate, Yorks. North.
Lawlor, Timothy, Lostock Gralam, Cheshire.
Lawn and Lace, Mirfield, Yorks. West.
Lawrence, E., Westerham, Kent.
Lawrence and Sons, F.G., Redhill, Surrey.
Lawrence, R., London, SW1.
Lawrence's Warehouse Ltd.,, Worcester, Herefs. and Worcs.
Lawson, Mrs A., Glossop, Derbys.
Lawson, B. and A., Newcastle-upon-Tyne, Tyne and Wear.
Lawson and Co, E.M., East Hagbourne, Oxon.
Lawson Antiques, F. and T., Richmond, Surrey.
Lawson Gallery, The, Cambridge, Cambs.
Lawson Antique Clocks, Keith, Scratby, Norfolk.
Lawson, W.J. and K.M., East Hagbourne, Oxon.
Lawton, Ian, Folkestone, Kent.
Lawton's Antiques, Folkestone, Kent.
Layne, A.C., Carlisle, Cumbria.
Layton Antiques, Richmond, Surrey.
Layton, Lady, Richmond, Surrey.
Laywood, Anthony W., Knipton, Leics.
Lazarus Antiques, David, Hartley Wintney, Hants.
Le Bailly Antiques, Tamara , Hay-on-Wye, Powys, Wales.
le Marchant, M. and S., Bruton, Somerset.
Leach, B., Llandovery, Dyfed, Wales.
Leadenhall Gallery, Canterbury, Kent.
Leadlay Gallery, The Warwick , London, SE10.
Leamington Pine and Antique Centre, Leamington Spa, Warks.
Leaside Antiques, Luton, Beds.
Leaside Antiques, St. Albans, Herts.
Leask, M., Edinburgh, Scotland.
Leask Ward, London, NW3.
Leatherland Antiques, P.D., Reading, Berks.
Lechlade Antiques Arcade, Lechlade, Glos.
Leckhampton Antiques, Cheltenham, Glos.
Ledger, M. and A., Stockport, Cheshire.
Lee, A., Clitheroe, Lancs.
Lee, C.G., Llandudno, Gwynedd, Wales.
Lee, Mrs P., Shipley, Yorks. West.
Lee Antiques, Peter, Wiveliscombe, Somerset.
Lee, P. and A., Wiveliscombe, Somerset.
Lee, Chertsey, Surrey.
Lee (Fine Arts) Ltd, Ronald A., London, W1.

Lee, R.A. and C.B., London, W1.
Leek Antiques Centre, The, Leek, Staffs.
Leek Bookshop, The, Leek, Staffs.
Lee's Antiques, Clitheroe, Lancs.
Lees, J.A. and T.P., Glossop, Derbys.
Lees and Sons, M., Worcester, Herefs. & Worcs.
Leete, R. and B., Lubenham, Leics.
Lefevre Gallery, London, W1.
Legard, I.P., Harrogate, Yorks. North.
Leger Galleries Ltd, The, London, W1.
Legg Antiques, Michael, Dorchester, Dorset.
Legg and Son, E.C., Cirencester, Glos.
Legg, E.M.J., Dorchester, Dorset.
Legg, W. and H., Dorchester, Dorset.
Legg of Dorchester, Dorchester, Dorset.
Legge Oriental Carpets, Christopher, Oxford, Oxon.
Legge, C.T., Oxford, Oxon.
Leicestershire Sporting Gallery and Brown Jack Bookshop, Lubenham, Leics.
Leigh Coins, Antiques and Jewellery, Leigh, Lancs.
Leigh, Joan, London, W11.
Leigh Antiques, Laurie, Oxford, Oxon.
Leigh, L., D. and W., Oxford, Oxon.
Leiston Furniture Warehouses, Leiston, Suffolk.
Leiston Trading Post, Leiston, Suffolk.
Leitch, C. and W., Great Bardfield, Essex.
Leitch, C.J., Cookstown, Co. Tyrone, N. Ireland.
Leith's Brocantebury, Nan, Canterbury, Kent.
Lemington House Antiques, Moreton-in-Marsh, Glos.
Lemkow, Sara, London, N1.
Lemon, T.J. and M.C., Haddington, Scotland.
Lennard Antiques, Tingewick, Bucks.
Lennox Antiques, Bromyard, Herefs. & Worcs.
Lenson and Roy Smith, Nellie, London, NW8.
Leo, M., Bournemouth, Dorset.
Leoframes, Brighton, Sussex East.
Leominster Antiques, Leominster, Herefs. & Worcs.
Leominster Antiques Market, Leominster, Herefs. & Worcs.
Leopard, The, Brighton, Sussex East.
Leppard, A. and A., Brighton, Sussex East.
Lesley's Antiques, Hull, N. Humbs.
Leslie, I., Dingwall, Scotland.
Leslie, K.J., Southampton, Hants.
Leslie and Leslie, Haddington Scotland.
Leslie Antiques, R.K., Southampton, Hants.
Leslie, Stanley, London, SW3.
Leslie's, Portsmouth, Hants.
Lester, S., Halifax, Yorks. West.
Letham, David, Edinburgh, Scotland.
Letty's Antiques, Leicester, Leics.
Lev (Antiques) Ltd, London, W8.
Lev, Mrs , London, W8.
Levene Ltd, M.P., London, SW7.
Leveson-Gower, C.W., Standlake, Oxon.
Levine Silver Specialist, Leona, Norwich, Norfolk.
Levy, G.J., M.P.,W.Y., London, W1.
Levy, Lionel, London, W1.
Levy, M., London, W8.
Lewes Antique Centre, Lewes, Sussex East.
Lewin Antiques and Textile Arts, London, W11.
Lewin, David, London, W11.
Lewis Antiques, Buxton, Derbys.
Lewis Fine Art, Alan, Hundleby, Lincs.
Lewis, A. and M., Hundleby, Lincs.
Lewis, Arthur S., London, SW1.
Lewis, Mrs B., London, W11.
Lewis, Gerald, Montacute, Somerset.
Lewis, G. and B., Montacute, Somerset.
Lewis Antique and Fine Art Dealers, Ivor and Patricia, Peterborough, Cambs.
Lewis, J. and S., Buxton, Derbys.
Lewis, Les, Chesterfield, Derbys.
Lewis and Lloyd, London, W8.
Lewis, M. and D., London, SW1.
Lewis, M. and D., London, W11.
Lewis Antiques, Michael, London, N1.
Lewis Gallery, Michael, Bruton, Somerset.
Lewis Oriental Carpets and Rugs, Michael and Amanda, Wellington, Somerset.
Lewis, P., Four Elms, Kent.
Lewis, R.A. and E.M., Liverpool, Merseyside.
Lewzey, J.A., Woolhampton, Berks.

DEALERS' INDEX

Leyland, D.J. and C.J, Woodhall Spa, Lincs.
Lhermette, Mrs V.A., Rochester, Kent.
Li, Wan, London, N1.
Liberty, London, W1.
Libra Antiques, London, W8.
Libson, L.J., London, W1.
Liddiard, V. A., Woolhampton, Berks.
Lieber, Ian, London, W2.
Lievesley, Mrs E.E., Hartley, Kent.
Light, P. B., Stamford, Lincs.
Lighthouse Ltd, The, London, SW19.
Lightfoot, Peter, Hatton, Warks.
Lillistone, C., Ipswich, Suffolk.
Lim, T., Weston-Super-Mare, Avon.
Limb Antiques, R.R., Newark, Notts.
Limited Editions, Stockport, Cheshire.
Limpsfield Watercolours, Limpsfield, Surrey.
Lincoln Fine Art, Lincoln, Lincs.
Lincolnshire Antiques Centre, The, Horncastle, Lincs.
Linden House Antiques, Stansted, Essex.
Lindfield Galleries - David Adam, Lindfield, Sussex West.
Lindsay Antiques Ltd, London, W8.
Lindsay, Muriel, Winchcombe, Glos.
Lindsay-Stewart, G., Balcombe, Sussex West.
Lindsell Chairs, Coggeshall, Essex.
Lindsey, E.A., Gullane, Scotland.
Lindsey Fine Art Ltd, John, Stow-on-the-Wold, Glos.
Lindum Antiques, Tattershall, Lincs.
Lineham and Sons, Eric, London, W8.
Linford, Carr, Bath, Avon.
Linford, N., J. and A. Carr, Bath, Avon.
Lingard - Rope Walk Antiques, Ann, Rye, Sussex East.
Lingfield Antiques, Lingfield, Surrey.
Lingham, C., Felsted, Essex.
Linslade Antiques and Curios, Linslade, Beds.
Linsley, Mrs C.M., Gosforth, Cumbria.
Linstead, A., Tunbridge Wells, Kent.
Lintott, P., Dorking, Surrey.
Lion Antiques, Acle, Norfolk.
Lion Antiques, Richmond, Surrey.
Lion Gallery and Bookshop, Knutsford, Cheshire.
Lion and Lamb Gallery at Biggs of Farnham, Farnham, Surrey.
Lion, Witch and Lampshade, London, SW1.
Lions Den, Stratford-upon-Avon, Warks.
Lions and Unicorns, Nantwich, Cheshire.
Lipitch Ltd, J., London, W11.
Lipitch Ltd, Michael, London, SW3.
Lipitch Ltd, Peter, London, SW3.
Lipka & Son Ltd., B., London, W11.
Lis, J., London, SW5.
Lismore Gallery, Great Malvern, Herefs. & Worcs.
Lisseter, D., Bicester, Oxon.
Lisseter of Bicester, Bicester, Oxon.
Little Barrow Antiques, Lechlade, Glos.
Little Collectables, Congleton, Cheshire.
Little Curiosity Shop, The, London, N21.
Little Elms Antiques, Stow-on-the-Wold, Glos.
Little Gallery, The, Pittenweem, Scotland.
Little Gem, The, Shrewsbury, Shrops.
Little Jem's, Penzance, Cornwall.
Little, Roger, Oxford, Oxon.
Little, Dr R., Oxford, Oxon.
Little Winchester Gallery, London, W8.
Littlebury Antiques - Littlebury Restorations Ltd, Saffron Walden, Essex.
Littleton, Cilla and Ivor, Lechlade, Glos.
Littlewood, P., Witney, Oxon.
Liu, J. and Mrs . M.C., Riverhead, Kent.
Liverpool Militaria, Liverpool, Merseyside.
Livesley, W.H., Macclesfield, Cheshire.
Livingstone, N., Dundee, Scotland.
Livingstone, Neil , Dundee, Scotland.
Llandogo Antiques, Llandogo, Gwent, Wales.
Llanishen Antiques, Cardiff, South Glam., Wales.
Llewellyn, F., London, SE10.
Lloyd, A., London, W1.
Lloyd, A.S., London, W1.
Lloyd Gallery, David, Purleigh, Essex.
Lloyd, D. and E., Kew, Surrey.
Lloyd, D.S., Bournemouth, Dorset.
Lloyd Antique Textiles, Gwyneth, London, SW3.

Lloyd, Michael, Henllan, Dyfed, Wales.
Lloyd, M.R., Sandgate , Kent.
Lloyd, Philip, Barnard Castle, Durham.
Lloyd Antiques, Robin, Ross-on-Wye, Herefs. & Worcs.
Lloyd, W.M., London, W1.
Lloyd-Smith, M. and M., Kenilworth, Warks.
Lloyd's Bookshop, Wingham , Kent.
Lloyds of Kew, Kew, Surrey.
Loane, Patty, Greyabbey, Co. Down, N. Ireland.
Lock, J., Ashtead, Surrey.
Locke, M., Ashbourne, Derbys.
Lockyer, H.K., Abergavenny, Gwent, Wales.
Lockyer, S., Usk, Gwent, Wales.
Lodge, John C., Salisbury, Wilts.
Lodge-Mortimer, A., Exton, Somerset.
Loewenthal Antiques, Tillington, Sussex West.
Loftus-Potter, N., Deal, Kent.
Logan, Martin and Maureen, Wolverhampton, West Mids.
Lombard Antiques, Honiton, Devon.
Lombard, L., Honiton, Devon.
Loncraine, A.B., Marlborough, Wilts.
London Architectural Salvage and Supply Co. Ltd. (LASSCo), The, London, EC2.
London and Birmingham Properties Ltd,, Glasgow, Scotland.
London Cigarette Card Co. Ltd, The, Somerton, Somerset.
London House Antiques, Westerham, Kent.
London House Oriental Rugs and Carpets, Boston Spa, Yorks. West.
London House Oriental Rugs and Carpets, Harrogate, Yorks. North.
London Militaria Market, London, N1.
London, P. and Mrs J., Edinburgh, Scotland.
London Road Antiques, Edinburgh, Scotland.
London Silver Vaults, The, London, WC2.
London and Sussex Antiquarian Book and Print Services, Eastbourne, Sussex East.
Long, J., Manchester, Lancs.
Long, J.W.H., Aberford, Yorks. West.
Long, M.E., Herstmonceux, Sussex East.
Long Melford Antiques Centre, Long Melford, Suffolk.
Long, Stephen, London, SW10.
Longmire Ltd (Three Royal Warrants), London, SW1.
Lotinga - Dog Box/Cat Box, Heather, London, N1.
Longthorne, A.M., Brighton, Sussex East.
Lonsdale Antiques, Southend-on-Sea, Essex.
Look In" Antiques, "The, Pershore, Herefs. & Worcs.
Looking Glass of Bath, Bath, Avon.
Loomes, Brian, Pateley Bridge, Yorks. North.
Loquens Gallery, The, Stratford-upon-Avon, Warks.
Loquens, S. and J., Stratford-upon-Avon, Warks.
Lord Antiques, Alan, Folkestone, Kent.
Lord, A.G., J.A. and R.G., Folkestone, Kent.
Lord, E., Portsmouth, Hants.
Lorie, S.C. and E., London, W8.
Losh, Martin, Cheltenham, Glos.
Lostock Antiques, Lostock Gralam, Cheshire.
Lott, G.E., Faringdon, Oxon.
Lovatt Antiques Ltd, Glasgow, Scotland.
Love, David, Harrogate, Yorks. North.
Love, Mr and Mrs D.A., Harrogate, Yorks. North.
Love Lane Antiques, Nantwich, Cheshire.
Loveday, Sarah and Peter, Northleach, Glos.
Loveday, FSVA, A.K., Hertford, Herts.
Lovejoys, Wells, Somerset.
Loveland, H., Brasted, Kent.
Loveless, Clive, London, W10.
Lovett, M.J., Northampton, Northants.
Low Antiques, Michael, Forres, Scotland.
Low Mill Antiques, Lower Bentham, Yorks. North.
Low Moor Antiques, Bradford, Yorks. West.
Lowe, D., Mansfield, Notts.
Lowe, S., Instow, Devon.
Lowe, Mrs S., London, W8.
Lowe of Loughborough, Loughborough, Leics.
Lowe and Sons, Chester, Cheshire.
Lower, Graham, Flimwell, Sussex East.
Lower House Fine Antiques, Winyates Green, Herefs. & Worcs.
Lowes, Eileen and Ken, Barkham, Berks.
Lucas, N., Amersham, Bucks.
Luck, R.J., Hastings, Sussex East.
Luck, S., London, WC2.

DEALERS' INDEX

Luck, S.L., West Malling, Kent.
Luczyc-Wyhowska, J., London, SW12.
Ludby, G., Eastbourne, Sussex East.
Ludby Antiques, James, Eastbourne, Sussex East.
Luffman, J., Ludlow, Shrops.
Lukies, Pearse, Aylsham, Norfolk.
Lumb and Sons Ltd, Charles, Harrogate, Yorks. North.
Lumb, F. and A.R., Harrogate, Yorks. North.
Lummis Fine Art, Sandra, London, N8.
Lummis, Mrs. S., London, N8.
Lummis, Dr T., London, N8.
Lundie, L., London, W11.
Lunn Antiques, London, SW6.
Lunn, R.J. and Mrs . S.Y., Dorchester, Dorset.
Lunn, S., London, SW6.
Lury, R. and J., Cambridge, Cambs.
Lustre Metal Antiques Nottingham , Nottingham, Notts.
Luxon, Lyn, Sheerness, Kent.
Lyall Antiques, Alexander, Long Melford, Suffolk.
Lyall, A.J., Long Melford, Suffolk.
Lye Curios, Inc. Lye Antique Furnishings, The, Lye, West Mids.
Lymington Antiques Centre, Lymington, Hants.
Lynas, D., Easingwold, Yorks. North.
Lynch, J., Edinburgh, Scotland.
Lynch, Pamela, Wilton, Wilts.
Lynch, R.C., Feniscowles, Lancs.
Lyon, R. and J., Hurstpierpoint, Sussex West.
Lyons Gallery, John, London, NW3.
Lyons, H.S., London, W8.
Lyver & Boydell Galleries, Liverpool, Merseyside.

M

M. & A. Antique Exporters, Plymouth, Devon.
M.C. Trading Co, The, Horncastle, Lincs.
M.C.N. Antiques, London, W11.
MGJ Antiques, Wallingford, Oxon.
M.G.R. Exports, Bruton, Somerset.
M. and L. Silver Co Ltd, London, W1.
Maas Gallery, London, W1.
Maas, J.S., London, W1.
Mabey, Sarah, Kelvedon, Essex.
MacAdam, William, Edinburgh, Scotland.
Macadie, Mrs M., Crosby Ravensworth, Cumbria.
Macafee, Mrs Bea, Portstewart, Co. Londonderry, N. Ireland.
McAleer, M., London, W2.
McAleer, Mrs M., London, W2.
McAleer, M.J., London, W2.
MacAuliffe, J., Saltburn, Cleveland.
McAvoy, M., Knighton, Powys, Wales.
McBains of Exeter, Exeter, Devon.
McCabe, H. and R., Newry, Co. Down, N. Ireland.
McCabe's Antique Galleries, Newry, Co. Down, N. Ireland.
McCall, B., Aberdeen, Scotland.
McCalls (Aberdeen), Aberdeen, Scotland.
McCalls Limited, Aberdeen, Scotland.
McCamley, M., Shirley, Surrey.
McCarthy, Keith and Margot, Lavenham, Suffolk.
McCaw, S.E. , Caldbeck, Cumbria.
McClaren, J., Gosport, Hants.
McClenaghan, J., London, NW1.
McClenaghan-Gilhooly Antiques, London, NW1.
McCollum, D.C., Stockland, Devon.
MacConnal-Mason Gallery, London, SW1.
MacConnal-Mason Gallery, London, W1.
McCormack, W.B., Lancaster, Lancs.
McCormick, N., London, SW13.
McCormick, P., Harrogate, Yorks. North.
McCrudden Gallery, Rickmansworth, Herts.
McCulloch Antiques, John, Felixstowe, Suffolk.
McDermott, Mr. and Mrs J., London, E14.
McDonagh, I., Bristol, Avon.
Macdonald, A. and Mrs M., Amersham, Bucks.
MacDonald, B. and L., Stow-on-the-Wold, Glos.
MacDonald Fine Art, Gosforth, Tyne and Wear.
MacDonald, G., Inverness, Scotland.
MacDonald, Mrs I., Haddington, Scotland.
McDonald, Joy, London, SW13.
Macdonald, J., Tunbridge Wells, Kent.
MacDonald, T. and C., Gosforth, Tyne and Wear.
McDonald, W., Glasgow, Scotland.
McDonald Craig, C., Guardbridge, Scotland.
McDonell, D. and H., Reepham, Norfolk.
MacDonnell, Finbar, London, N1.
McDougall, Marjorie and Sandy, Kilbarchan, Scotland.
McEvoy, Mrs M., Comberton, Cambs.
McEwan, D. and P, Ballater, Scotland.
McEwan Gallery, The, Ballater, Scotland.
MacGillivray, G., Whitchurch, Shrops.
McGrane, I.A., Stroud, Glos.
McGrath, S., Farnham, Surrey.
McGregor, V., Halstead, Essex.
MacHenry, A., Newtownabbey, Co. Antrim, N. Ireland.
McHugo, M., Lye, West Mids.
McIan Gallery (Campbell-Gibson Fine Arts), The, Oban, Scotland.
McIlreavy, Alan and Fiona, St. Andrews, Scotland.
McIlreavy Rare and Interesting Books, A. and F., St. Andrews, Scotland.
MacInnes Antiques, Kilmarnock, Scotland.
MacInnes, Mrs M., Kilmarnock, Scotland.
Macintosh & Co, William, Edinburgh, Scotland.
McIntyre, Pat and Simon, Edinburgh, Scotland.
Mack Antiques, David, Branksome, Dorset.
McKay, R.I., London, EC1.
McKenna and Co, London, SW3.
McKenna, M., Deal, Kent.
McKenna, M., London, SW3.
McKenzie, J.W., Ewell, Surrey.
McKeown, H., London, SW1.
Mackie, E.M. and Mrs M.G., Elton, Notts.
McKillop, K.M., Pittenweem, Scotland.
McKinley, A., Wiveliscombe, Somerset.
McKinley, D., Wiveliscombe, Somerset.
McKnight, E.W., Bury St. Edmunds, Suffolk.
McLaughlin, A.J. and Mrs B., Hollinwood, Lancs.
Maclean Antiques, Llanwrda, Dyfed, Wales.
Maclean, H., Kilmacolm, Scotland.
McLean, D., Portsoy, Scotland.
McLennan, Rodd, London, SW1.
McMaster, John, Tenterden, Kent.
Macmillan, C., London, SW3.
MacMillan, W., Worcester, Herefs. and Worcs.
McMullan, C., Burnham on Crouch, Essex.
McMullan, D., Manchester, Lancs.
McNair Antiques Centre, Hugh, Westerham, Kent.
McNamara, J. and M.V., Knaresborough, Yorks. North.
McNaughtan's Bookshop, Edinburgh, Scotland.
MacNeal, D.O., Pittenweem, Scotland.
McNeilage, Mrs Cherrie, Lavenham,, Suffolk.
McPhail, R., Gourock, Scotland.
McPherson, I. and H., Coalville, Leics.
McRoberts, R.J., Carlisle, Cumbria.
Macrow, S.K., Solihull, West Mids.
McTague of Harrogate, Harrogate, Yorks. North.
McTague, P., Harrogate, Yorks. North.
McVeigh and Charpentier, London, SW10.
McWhirter, London, SW10.
McWhirter, A.J.K., London, SW10.
Maddermarket Antiques, Norwich, Norfolk.
Maddox, Mr and Mrs , Canterbury, Kent.
Made of Honour, Chester, Cheshire.
Madeira, V. and C., Flore, Northants.
Madison Gallery, The, Petworth, Sussex West.
Madoc Antiques and Art Gallery, Llandudno, Gwynedd, Wales.
Magee, D.A., Canterbury, Kent.
Magee, D.A., Sandwich, Kent.
Maggie May's, North Shields, Tyne and Wear.
Maggs Antiques Ltd, Liverpool, Merseyside.
Maggs Bros Ltd, London, W1.
Maggs, John , Falmouth, Cornwall.
Maggs, J.F., B.D. and E.F., London, W1.
Magic Lanterns, St. Albans, Herts.
Magna Gallery, Oxford, Oxon.
Magpie, St. Andrews, Scotland.
Magpie, Whitstable, Kent.
Magpie Antiques, Battle, Sussex East.
Magpie Antiques, Davenham, Cheshire.
Magpie Antiques, Long Melford, Suffolk.
Magpie Antiques, Swansea, West Glam., Wales.
Magpie House, Hockley Heath, West Mids.
Magpie Jewellers and Antiques, Evesham, Herefs. & Worcs.

DEALERS' INDEX

Magpies, London, SW6.
Magpies Nest, Morecambe, Lancs.
Magus Antiques, London, NW8.
Magus Antiques, London, W11.
Mahboubian Gallery, London, W1.
Mahboubian, H., London, W1.
Mail, S., Glasgow, Scotland.
Main, C. and K.M., Green Hammerton, Yorks. North.
Main Pine Co, The, Green Hammerton, Yorks. North.
Main Street Antiques, London, SE10.
Mainhill Gallery, Jedburgh, Scotland.
Mainline Furniture, Kesgrave, Suffolk.
Major, A.H., London, W8.
Major, A. and L., Painswick, Glos.
Major (Antiques) Ltd, C.H., London, W8.
Majors Galleries, Ipswich, Suffolk.
Maker, B.J., Penzance, Cornwall.
Maker, J.P., Camborne, Cornwall.
Malcolm Antiques, Elie, Scotland.
Maldon Antiques and Collectors Market, Maldon, Essex.
Malik and Son Ltd, David, London, NW10.
Mall Antiques Arcade, The, London, N1.
Mall Galleries, The, London, SW1.
Mall Gallery, The, Bristol, Avon.
Mall Jewellers, The, Bristol, Avon.
Mallaby, R.M., Killinghall, Yorks. North.
Mallett, K., Surbiton, Surrey.
Mallett and Son (Antiques) Ltd, London, W1.
Mallett at Bourdon House Ltd, London, W1.
Mallory and Son Ltd, E.P., Bath, Avon.
Malmed, Mrs V., London, SW1.
Malocco, Mary, Collessie, Scotland.
Maltby, C.E., Sheffield, Yorks. South.
Malthouse Antiques Centre, Alcester, Warks.
Malthouse Arcade, Hythe, Kent.
Maltings Monthly Market, Farnham, Surrey.
Malton Antique Market, Malton, Yorks. North.
Malvern Arts, Great Malvern, Herefs. & Worcs.
Malvern Bookshop, Great Malvern, Herefs. & Worcs.
Malvern Studios, Great Malvern, Herefs. & Worcs.
Mamie's Antiques Centre, Arundel, Sussex West.
Man, Margaret, London, SW7.
Manchester Antique Company, Manchester, Lancs.
Mandarin Gallery, Riverhead, Kent.
Mandell's Gallery, Norwich, Norfolk.
Mander, J.P., London, E2.
Mandrake Stephenson Antiques, Ibstock, Leics.
Mangan, P., Glasgow, Scotland.
Mangate Gallery, Laxfield, Suffolk.
Manheim (Peter Manheim) Ltd, D.M. and P., London, N6.
Manheim, P., London, N6.
Manion Antiques, Ashbourne, Derbys.
Manion, Mrs V.J., Ashbourne, Derbys.
Mankowitz, Daniel, London, W2.
Manley Antique Jewellery, Pamela, Titchfield, Hants.
Manley, J., Windsor and Eton, Berks.
Mann Antiques, Chris, Aberystwyth, Dyfed, Wales.
Mann, D., Stiffkey, Norfolk.
Mann, E., Davenham, Cheshire.
Mann, Mrs E., Manchester, Lancs.
Mann Antiques, Kathleen, Harrow, Middx.
Manners, E. and H., London, W8.
Manners Antiques, Mary, Gt. Cheverell, Wilts.
Manning, M., Darwen, Lancs.
Manor Antiques, Wilshamstead, Beds.
Manor Antiques, Wallington, Surrey.
Manor Antiques and Restorations, Woking, Surrey.
Manor Barn, Addingham, Yorks. West.
Manor Farm Antiques, Standlake, Oxon.
Manor House, Ripley, Surrey.
Manor House Antiques, Cheltenham, Glos.
Manor House Antiques, Fishguard, Dyfed, Wales.
Manor House Antiques and Furniture, Margate, Kent.
Manor House Fine Arts, Cardiff, South Glam., Wales.
Manor House Interiors, Chiddingfold, Surrey.
Mansell, William C., London, W2.
Manser and Son Ltd, F.C., Shrewsbury, Shrops.
Manser and family, G., Shrewsbury, Shrops.
Mansfield Antiques, Mansfield, Notts.
Mansfield, J. and A., Ashby-de-la-Zouch, Leics.
Mansions, Lincoln, Lincs.
Manson, Edward, Woodbridge, Suffolk.

Mansour Gallery, London, W1.
Mantoura, J.H., London, W8.
Manussis, V., London, SW1.
Manwaring, M.G., Chipping Norton, Oxon.
Map House, The, London, SW3.
Maps, Prints and Books, Brecon, Powys, Wales.
Marble Hill Gallery, Twickenham, Middx.
March Ceramics, David, Abbots Leigh, Avon.
March, D. and S., Abbots Leigh, Avon.
March, M.A., Birmingham, West Mids.
March Medals, Birmingham, West Mids.
Marchant (Antiques), Mark, Coggeshall, Essex.
Marchant, R.P., London, W8.
Marchant and Son, S., London, W8.
Marchmont Bookshop, London, WC1.
Mardall, H.H. and A.E., Gargrave, Yorks. North.
Margaret's Antique Shop, Nelson, Lancs.
Margaret's Astoria Antiques, Swansea, Mid-Glam., Wales.
Margerison, Mr and Mrs P.B., Empingham, Leics.
Margiotta, A., Brighton, Sussex East.
Marianski, N. J., Derby, Derbys.
Marie-Ange Martin Antiques, Uppingham, Leics.
Marine Gallery, The, Cowes, I. of Wight.
Mark Gallery, The, London, W2.
Mark, H., London, W2.
Market Antiques, Aberdare, Mid. Glam., Wales.
Market Antiques, Hoylake, Merseyside.
Market House, Burnham Market, Norfolk.
Market Place Antiques, Fakenham, Norfolk.
Market Square Antiques, Olney, Bucks.
Marks, A., London, W1.
Marks Antiques Ltd, London, W1.
Marks Ltd, Barrie, London, NW5.
Marks, B.J. and S., Oldham, Lancs.
Marks Antique Warehouse, Peter, Portslade, Sussex West.
Marlborough Fine Art (London) Ltd, London, W1.
Marlborough House Antiques, Yarmouth, I. of Wight.
Marlborough Parade Antique Centre, The, Marlborough, Wilts.
Marlborough Rare Books Ltd, London, W1.
Marlborough Sporting Gallery and Bookshop, Swindon, Wilts.
Marler Gallery, The Jane, Ludlow, Shrops.
Marles, M., Maidstone, Kent.
Marney, Patrick, Long Melford, Suffolk.
Marnier Antiques, Edward, Tisbury, Wilts.
Marnier, E.F., Tisbury, Wilts.
Marno, F., London, W8.
Marpole, A., Burwell, Cambs.
Marr Antiques, Iain, Beauly, Scotland.
Marr, I. and A., Beauly, Scotland.
Marrin and Sons, G. and D.I., Folkestone, Kent.
Marriott Ltd, Michael, London, SW6.
Marriott, T.I., Beaconsfield, Bucks.
Marris, N., Lincoln, Lincs.
Marryat, Richmond, Surrey.
Marryat (Richmond) Ltd., Richmond, Surrey.
Marsden, Clive, Leigh, Kent.
Marsden, Josie A., St. Albans, Herts.
Marsh and Son, A.V., London, SW15.
Marsh (Antique Clocks), Gerald E., Winchester, Hants.
Marsh, G.M., Crawley, Hants.
Marsh, Jasper, Henley-in-Arden, Warks.
Marsh, P.R.J., Henley-in-Arden, Warks.
Marsh, Roy and Jean, Hemel Hempstead, Herts.
Marsh, Simon, Bletchingley, Surrey.
Marshall, A.R., Kirton, Lincs.
Marshall, E.M., Carshalton, Surrey.
Marshall Antiques, Tim, Tingewick, Bucks.
Marston, B.F. and H.M., Hadleigh, Suffolk.
Martin, A., Sandgate, Kent.
Martin Antiques, Alan, Olney, Bucks.
Martin, A.D., Olney, Bucks.
Martin, A.R., Tavistock, Devon.
Martin, C., Windlesham, Surrey.
Martin and Co. Ltd, Cheltenham, Glos.
Martin (Coins) Ltd, C.J., London, N14.
Martin, E., London, N2.
Martin Antiques, Greg, Gravesend, Kent.
Martin House Antiques, Stow-on-the-Wold, Glos.
Martin, J., Farnborough, Hants.
Martin Antiques, John, Castle Cary, Somerset.

DEALERS' INDEX

Martin, L.M., Bournemouth, Dorset.
Martin, Mrs M.R., Hawkhurst, Kent.
Martin and Parke, Farnborough, Hants.
Martin, Peter J., Windsor and Eton, Berks.
Martin, Robin, London, W11.
Martin, R. and S., Risby, Suffolk.
Martin, Tony, Looe, Cornwall.
Martin, T.J.L. and A.M., Coggeshall, Essex.
Martin-Clifton Antiques, Otley, Yorks. West.
Martin-Quick Antiques, Wolverhampton, West Mids.
Martin-Taylor Antiques, David, London, SW6.
Martlesham Antiques, Martlesham, Suffolk.
Maryan and Daughters, Richard, London, SW19.
Ma's Antiques, Bewdley, Herefs. & Worcs.
Mascaro, R., Plymouth, Devon.
Maskell, E.J., London, N1.
Maskell, R.E and L.J., Branksome, Dorset.
Maskell, R.E. and L.J., Sturminster Newton, Dorset.
Mason, C., Brodick, Scotland.
Mason, D., South Molton, Devon.
Mason & Son, D., Harrogate, Yorks. North.
Mason, G.L. and V.L., Bath, Avon.
Mason, Harry, Brighton, Sussex East.
Mason Antique Clocks, J., Northchapel, Sussex West.
Mason Jewellers Ltd, John, Rotherham, Yorks. South.
Mason Gallery, Paul, London, SW1.
Mason-Pope, C., Woodstock, Oxon.
Massada Antiques, London, W1.
Massey and Son, D.J., Alderley Edge, Cheshire.
Massey and Son, D.J., Macclesfield, Cheshire.
Massey, J.C., Long Melford, Suffolk.
Massey, P., Debenham, Suffolk.
Massey's Antiques, Coalville, Leics.
Massingham Antiques, Roy, Brasted, Kent.
Masters, M., Stow-on-the-Wold, Glos.
Mathaf Gallery Ltd, London, SW1.
Mather, Mrs P., Corby Hill, Cumbria.
Matheson, T., Portsoy, Scotland.
Mathews, Lt. Col. and Mrs I.G., Ross-on-Wye, Herefs. and Worcs.
Mathias, R., St. Albans, Herts.
Mathieson and Co, John, Edinburgh, Scotland.
Mathon Gallery, London, SW3.
Mathon Gallery, Mathon, Herefs. & Worcs.
Matsell Antiques Ltd, Ilkeston, Derbys.
Matsell, B. and P., Ilkeston, Derbys.
Matson, J., Liverpool, Merseyside.
Matthiesen Fine Art Ltd. and Matthiesen Works of Art Ltd, London, SW1.
Matthey, P., Burford, Oxon.
Maude, Austin, Richmond, Surrey.
Maude, R.M.C., London, SW15.
Maude Tools, Richard, London, SW15.
Maufe, J., Burnham Market, Norfolk.
Maw Antiques, Matthew, Malton, Yorks. North.
Mawby, Mrs P., Northampton, Northants.
Mawer, Mr and Mrs, Penrith, Cumbria.
Mawtus, Mr P., Norwich, Norfolk.
Mawtus, Mrs P., Strachan, Scotland.
Maxtone Graham, Mr and Mrs R.M., Sandwich, Kent.
Maxtone Grahame, Mr and Mrs R.M., Hythe, Kent.
Maxwells Book Shop, Birmingham, West Mids.
May, J. and J., London, W8.
May and May Ltd, Semley, Wilts.
Maybery Antiques, Bishopston, West Glam., Wales.
Maybery, W., Bishopston, West Glam. Wales.
Maybery, W., Bishopston, West Glam. Wales.
Mayfair Antiques, Bagillt, Clwyd, Wales.
Mayfair Carpet Gallery Ltd, London, W1.
Mayfair Gallery, London, W1.
Mayfield House, Leominster, Herefs. & Worcs.
Mayflower Antiques, Harwich, Essex.
Mayflower Antiques, London, W11.
Mayflower Antiques, Padstow, Cornwall.
Maynard Antiques, Mark, London, SW6.
Mayne, R., Newhaven, Sussex East.
Mayo, J., Fairford, Glos.
Mayorcas, J.D. and L.G., London, SW1.
Mayorcas Ltd, London, SW1.
Maze of Pine and Roses, A, Mapplewell, Yorks. South.
Mazure and Co. Ltd, I.J., London, SW1.
Mazzoli, D., Eastbourne, Sussex East.

Meader, Kay, Littlehampton, Sussex West.
Meadowcroft Antiques, Stephen, Farndon, Cheshire.
Mechilli, W., Warwick, Warks.
Medalcrest Ltd, Hungerford, Berks.
Medcalf, N.K.T., Woburn Sands, Bucks.
Medcalf, Paul, Gloucester, Glos.
Medina Antiquarian Maps and Prints, Winslow, Bucks.
Medina Gallery, Bideford, Devon.
Mee, R., London, W8.
Meeks & Co, F., Birmingham, West Mids.
Meeson, J.C. and A.D., Ilford, Essex.
Megahy, Jean, Glasgow, Scotland.
Megicks, N., Lampeter, Dyfed, Wales.
Meldrum, D., Chagford, Devon.
Meldrum Walker, M. and D., London, SW6.
Melford Fine Arts, Long Melford, Suffolk.
Melliar-Smith, M.V., Honiton, Devon.
Melling, H.W. and V.I., Worthing, Sussex West.
Mellish, J., Colchester, Essex.
Mellor, C.R.J. and P.J., Lichfield, Staffs.
Mellor and A.L. Baxter, D., London, W8.
Mellor, Mrs R., Bath, Avon.
Melody, M., Chester, Cheshire.
Melody's Antique Galleries, Chester, Cheshire.
Melton Antiques, Woodbridge, Suffolk.
Melton's, London, W1.
Meltzer, L., London, W11.
Melville Watercolours, Margaret, Staines, Surrey.
Melvin, R., Edinburgh, Scotland.
Memories, Bramley, Surrey.
Memories, Rochester, Kent.
Memories Antiques, Coventry, West Mids.
Memory Lane, Sowerby Bridge, Yorks. West.
Memory Lane Antique Centre, Bolton, Lancs.
Memory Lane Antiques, Ashtead, Surrey.
Memory Lane Antiques, South Molton, Devon.
Mendez incorporating Craddock and Barnard, Christopher, London, SW1.
Mendip Pine and Antiques, Chilcompton, Somerset.
Mercat-Hughes Antiques, Glasgow, Scotland.
Mercer Antiques, Noel, Long Melford, Suffolk.
Mercury Antiques, London, W11.
Mere Antiques, Fowlmere, Cambs.
Meredith, John, Chagford, Devon.
Meredith, J. and A., Chagford, Devon.
Merkel, M.P., Dartmouth, Devon.
Merlins Antiques, Carmarthen, Dyfed, Wales.
Merola, London, SW3.
Merola, M., London, SW3.
Merrifield, Mr and Mrs B., Paisley, Scotland.
Merrill Antiques, Paul, Collingham, Notts.
Messenger, R. and D., Birmingham, West Mids.
Messum, David, Marlow, Bucks.
Metalcrafts Ltd, B.C., London, NW9.
Metcalfe, Mrs A., Helsby, Cheshire.
Metcalfe, Chris and Margaret, West Auckland, Durham.
Metro Antiques, Gateshead, Tyne and Wear.
Metropolitan Stall Markets, London, W11.
Mew Antiques, Peter and Janet, Sedlescombe, Sussex East.
Mews Antique Fireplaces and Architectural Salvage, Belfast, N. Ireland.
Mexborough, Countess of, London, SW3.
Mexborough, Lord, London, SW3.
Meyer, B.P., Dorking, Surrey.
Meyer, T., London, W8.
Meyers Gallery, Ingatestone, Essex.
Meyers, Mrs J., Ingatestone, Essex.
Meysey-Thompson Antiques, Sarah, Woodbridge, Suffolk.
Mibus, Adrian, London, W2.
Micallef Antiques, London, SE1.
Micawber Antiques, Bridgnorth, Shrops.
Micawber Antiques, Exeter, Devon .
Micawber's, Salisbury, Wilts.
Michael Coins, London, W8.
Michael's Antiques, Bristol, Avon.
Micklem Antiques, Thorne St. Margaret, Somerset.
Micklem, C.T., S.E.M. and T.J.M., Thorne St. Margaret, Somerset.
Middleton, Mr, Todmorden, Yorks. West.
Middleton Ltd, Arthur, London, WC2.
Middleton, Bobbie, Devizes, Wilts.
Middleton, T., Rushden, Northants.

Middleton's Antique Doll Shop and Dolls Hospital, Lilian, Burford, Oxon.
Midgley, N.M., Settle, Yorks. North.
Midhurst Antiques Market, Midhurst, Sussex West.
Midhurst Walk, Midhurst, Sussex West.
Midloe Grange Antiques and Design, Southoe, Cambs.
Midwinter Antiques, Richard, Newcastle-under-Lyme, Staffs.
Midwinter, Mr and Mrs R., Newcastle-under-Lyme, Staffs.
Mighell, J., London, NW1.
Mildwurf and Partners, L., Penrith, Cumbria.
Mileham, H., Brighton, Sussex East.
Miles Antiques, Kinross, Scotland.
Miles Bookshop, Archie, Gosforth, Cumbria.
Miles, David, Canterbury, Kent.
Miles, David, London, NW1.
Miles, K. and S., Kinross, Scotland.
Miles Antiques, Richard, London, SW1.
Miles Gallery, Roy, London, W1.
Miles, S., Herstmonceux, Sussex East.
Milestone Antiques, Whittington, Staffs.
Milewski, D., Richmond, Surrey.
Milford Haven Antiques, Milford Haven, Dyfed, Wales.
Military Curios, HQ84, Gloucester, Glos.
Military Parade Bookshop, The, Marlborough, Wilts.
Mill Farm Antiques, Disley, Cheshire.
Mill on the Soar Antiques Ltd, Quorn, Leics.
Millar, Miss J., Arundel, Sussex West.
Miller, B., Ross-on-Wye, Herefs. and Worcs.
Miller Fine Arts, Duncan R., London, NW3.
Miller, G.C. and P.A., Arundel, Sussex West.
Miller Antiques, H., Brighton, Sussex East.
Miller, I.E.G., Petworth, Sussex West.
Miller Antiques, James, Wooler, Northumbs.
Millers Antiques Kelvedon, Kelvedon, Essex.
Miller, Michael, Hurstpierpoint, Sussex West.
Miller, M. and V., Hurstpierpoint, Sussex West.
Miller, P., York, Yorks. North.
Miller, P.J. and A.R., Hemswell Cliff, Lincs.
Miller, R., Dorking, Surrey.
Millers of Chelsea Antiques Ltd, Ringwood, Hants.
Mill Antiques, Scunthorpe, S. Humbs.
Millgreen Antiques, Wargrave, Berks.
Millington, K.L. & J., Lepton, Yorks. West.
Millon Antiques, Windsor and Eton, Berks.
Mills Antiques, Cullompton, Devon.
Mills Antiques, Mrs, Ely, Cambs.
Mills, E.T., Ely, Cambs.
Mills, G. and J., Honiton, Devon.
Mills Architectural Antiques Ltd, Robert, Bristol, Avon.
Millward, J., Norwich, Norfolk.
Milne Henderson, S., London, NW8.
Milne and Moller, London, W11.
Milne Ltd, Nigel, London, W1.
Milne, S.A., Dollar, Scotland.
Milnthorpe, H.I., Settle, Yorks. North.
Milnthorpe and Daughters Antique Shop, Mary, Settle, Yorks. North.
Milton Antiques, Coventry, West Mids.
Milton Antiques, Fred, Wanstrow, Somerset.
Milverton Antiques, Milverton, Somerset.
Minahan, T., Newmarket, Suffolk.
Minster Gate Bookshop, York, Yorks. North.
Mirabaud, S., Lewes, Sussex East.
Miscellanea, Maidenhead, Berks.
Miscellany Antiques, Great Malvern, Herefs. & Worcs.
Miskimmin, W., Rochester, Kent.
Miss Elany, Long Eaton, Derbys.
Mister Sun Antiques, Chertsey, Surrey.
Mistral Galleries, Westerham, Kent.
Mitchell Fine Paintings, Anthony, Nottingham, Notts.
Mitchell, A. and M., Nottingham, Notts.
Mitchell, C., Totnes, Devon.
Mitchell, G., Burford, Oxon.
Mitchell and Son, John, London, W1.
Mitchell Antiques Ltd, Laurence, London, N1.
Mitchell, L. F., Hereford, Herefs. and Worcs.
Mitchell, L.P.J., London, N1.
Mitchell, Mr and Mrs M.J., Wells, Somerset.
Mitchell Ltd, Paul, London, W1.
Mitchell, R.A., Castle Douglas, Scotland.
Mitchell, R.A., Kirkcudbright, Scotland.
Mitchell Fine Art, Robert, Cirencester, Glos.
Mitchell, R.S., Norwich, Norfolk.
Mitchell, S., Blackburn, Lancs.
Mitchell Fine Arts, Sally, Askham, Notts.
Mitchell, W., Cirencester, Glos.
Mitchell-Hill, D.G., Wetherby, Yorks. West.
Mitchell-Hill Gallery, Wetherby, Yorks. West.
Mitchell's Gallery, Sally, Tuxford, Notts.
Mitchell's (Lock Antiques), Blackburn, Lancs.
Mitre House Antiques, Ludlow, Shrops.
Moate Antiques, Richard, Smeeth, Kent.
Moggach Antiques, Ian, London, SW6.
Mohamed Ltd, Bashir, London, W1.
Moira, London, W1.
Mokhtarzadeh, M., London, W1.
Mold Antiques and Interiors, Mold, Clwyd, Wales.
Mole/Antique Exports, Geoffrey, Hull, N. Humbs.
Mole Gallery, South Molton, Devon.
Mole Hall Antiques, Aldeburgh, Suffolk.
Molland Antique Mirrors, Leek, Staffs.
Molland, John and Karen, Leek, Staffs.
Moller, Mr and Mrs C., London, W11.
Molloy, P., Southport, Merseyside.
Molloy's Furnishers Ltd, Southport, Merseyside.
Mon Galerie, Amersham, Bucks.
Monaltrie Antiques, Odiham, Hants.
Monarch Antiques, Glastonbury, Somerset.
Monarch Antiques, St. Leonards-on-Sea, Sussex East.
Money (Antiques) Ltd, Lennox, London, SW1.
Money, L.B., London, SW1.
Monk and Son, D.C., London, W8.
Monkton Galleries, Hindon, Wilts.
Monro Ltd, Mrs, London, SW1.
Montacute Antiques, Montacute, Somerset.
Montague Antiques, Leicester, Leics.
Montpellier Clocks, Cheltenham, Glos.
Montpellier Gallery, The, Harrogate, Yorks. North.
Montpellier Mews Antique Market, Harrogate, Yorks. North.
Montresor, Edinburgh, Scotland.
Moody, L., Southampton, Hants.
Moolham Mill Antiques, Ilminster, Somerset.
Moon, Michael, Whitehaven, Cumbria.
Moon, M. and S., Whitehaven, Cumbria.
Mooney, Riro D., Duxford, Cambs.
Moor Antiques, Ashburton, Devon.
Moordown Antiques, Bournemouth, Dorset.
Moore, A.E., Leiston, Suffolk.
Moore, D.B., Hitchin, Herts.
Moore, D.K., Leicester, Leics.
Moore, E. and N., Tynemouth, Tyne and Wear.
Moore, Eric T., Hitchin, Herts.
Moore, Geoffrey, London, NW1.
Moore, Geoffrey, Washington, Tyne and Wear.
Moore Antiques and Stained Glass, Jack, Trawden, Lancs.
Moore, J.C., Bowness-on-Windermere, Cumbria.
Moore, L. F., Brighton, Sussex East.
Moore Antiques, Marcus, Stanton, Shrops.
Moore, M.G.J. and M.P., Stanton, Shrops.
Moore, Susan P., Hoole, Cheshire.
Moore, Thomas, Canterbury, Kent.
Moores, M.J., Sedbergh, Cumbria.
Moores, P., Leicester, Leics.
Moores and Son, Walter, Leicester, Leics.
Moorhead, F.B. and M.J., Brighton, Sussex East.
Moorhead Antiques, Patrick, Brighton, Sussex East.
Moorland Antiques, Weston-Super-Mare, Avon.
Morales Antiques, José, Deal, Kent.
Morchard Bishop Antiques, Morchard Bishop, Devon.
Moreden Prints, Yatton, Herefs. & Worcs.
Moreton (Antiques), C.S., Inchture, Scotland.
Moreton Street Gallery, London, SW1.
Morgan, C., Rochester, Kent.
Morgan, Dr and Mrs D.H., Wymondham, Norfolk.
Morgan, Glenn, Windsor and Eton, Berks.
Morgan, H., Cardiff, South Glam., Wales.
Morgan, J., Chesham, Bucks.
Morgan, M., Hitchin, Herts.
Morgan and Co, R.V., Enfield, Middx.
Morgan, Mrs S., Pateley Bridge, Yorks. North.
Morgan Stobbs, Windsor and Eton, Berks.
Morley Antiques, David, Twickenham, Middx.
Morley Antiques, Patrick and Gillian, Warwick, Warks.
Morley and Co Ltd, Robert, London, SE13.

DEALERS' INDEX

Morley Antiques, William, West Monkton, Somerset.
Morley, W.H., West Monkton, Somerset.
Morrill Ltd, W.J., Dover, Kent.
Morris, B., Leamington Spa, Warks.
Morris, G.J., St. Helier, Jersey, C.I.
Morris, Ian , Chesterfield, Derbys.
Morris and Co, James H., Northop, Clwyd, Wales.
Morris, John G., Petworth, Sussex West.
Morris, Mr and Mrs K.L., Ludlow, Shrops.
Morris, Maureen, Saffron Walden, Essex.
Morris, Pearl, Loughton, Essex.
Morris, William, Stow-on-the-Wold, Glos.
Morrish, J.S., Reigate, Surrey.
Morrison, C., York, Yorks. North.
Morrison, Guy, London, SW1.
Morrison, Mrs J., Wingham, Kent.
Morrison, M., Warwick, Warks.
Morrison, P.H., Douglas, I. of Man.
Morrison, P.H., Kirk Michael, I. of Man.
Morrison and Son, Robert, York, Yorks. North.
Morse and Son Ltd, Terence, London, W11.
Morten, Eric J., Manchester, Lancs.
Mortimer, Brian, Exeter, Devon.
Mortimer and Son, C. and J., Great Chesterford, Essex.
Mortimer, Mr and Mrs L.G., Petersfield, Hants.
Mortimer, M.C.F., North Wraxall, Wilts.
Mortlake Antiques, Kirkby Stephen, Cumbria.
Morton, Mrs Joan, Gt. Walsingham, Norfolk.
Morton, S., Bournemouth, Dorset.
Morton Harvey Antiques, Aylesbury, Bucks.
Morton Lee, J., Hayling Island, Hants.
Morton-Smith, Mrs I., Milland, Sussex West.
Moseley Antiques, Birmingham, West Mids.
Moseley, E., Romsey, Hants.
Moseley Pianos, Birmingham, West Mids.
Moss, A., London, N1.
Moss End Antique Centre, Warfield, Berks.
Moss Galleries - Rachel Moss, London, W4.
Moss, R.A. and B.A., Baldock, Herts.
Moss, Ralph and Bruce, Baldock, Herts.
Moss, S., Bath, Avon.
Moss Ltd, Sydney L., London, W1.
Mostly Boxes, Windsor and Eton, Berks.
Mostly Pine, Kingussie, Scotland.
Mott, G.W., Trent, Dorset.
Mott, J.G. and D.M., Lavenham,, Suffolk.
Mottershead, D. and Mrs, Long Eaton, Derbys.
Mottershead, Mr and Mrs J.K., Manchester, Lancs.
Motts of Lavenham, Lavenham, Suffolk.
Mouat, J.W.L., Whitchurch, Hants.
Mould Ltd, Anthony, London, W1.
Moulton, J., West Bridgford, Notts.
Moulton's Antiques, West Bridgford, Notts.
Mount, The, Woore, Shrops.
Mount Antiques, The, Whitby, Yorks. North.
Mounter, G., Dulford, Devon.
Movie Shop, The, Norwich, Norfolk.
Mowe, C. and J., Coton Clanford, Staffs.
Moxhams Antiques, Bradford-on-Avon, Wilts.
Moy, J.B. and C., London, SE10.
Moy, R.F., London, SE10.
Moyallon Antiques, Portadown, Co. Armagh, N. Ireland.
Muccio, L. and P., Bromley, Kent.
Muckle, M.A., Market Harborough, Leics.
Muddiman, A.R.T., Chesham, Bucks.
Muir, D.C., Coggeshall, Essex.
Muirhead Moffat and Co, Glasgow, Scotland.
Mulberry Bush, The, Marple Bridge, Cheshire.
Mulberry House Galleries, Pulborough, Sussex West.
Mulder, Frederick, London, NW3.
Mulherron Antiques, Edinburgh, Scotland.
Mulherron, F., A. and J., Edinburgh, Scotland.
Mulholland, H., Dumfries, Scotland.
Mullarkey, T. and N., Maidstone, Kent.
Mullarkey, T. and N., Sutton Valence, Kent.
Mulligan, Anthony J., Bovey Tracey, Devon.
Munday, G.S., Windsor and Eton, Berks.
Mundy Fine Art Ltd, Ewan, Glasgow, Scotland.
Munro, C.P., Bridgwater, Somerset.
Murdoch, P.G., Nottingham, Notts.
Murphy, I., Portsmouth, Hants.
Murphy, T.H., London, W4.

Murray, A. and I., Lowestoft, Suffolk.
Murray, D., Kilmichael Glassary, Scotland.
Murray Antique Warehouse, Ian, Perth, Scotland.
Murray-Brown, Pevensey Bay, Sussex East.
Murray-Brown, G. and J., Pevensey Bay, Sussex East.
Murren, M., Teddington, Middx.
Museum Bookshop, Woodstock, Oxon.
Museum of Childhood, Beaumaris, Gwynedd, Wales.
Mussenden and Son Antiques, Jewellery and Silver, G.B., Bournemouth, Dorset.
Mutch, A., Edinburgh, Scotland.
Myers Galleries, Gargrave, Yorks. North.
Myers, Peter, Bushey, Herts.
Myers and Son, R.N., Gargrave, Yorks. North.
Mynott, C., Warwick, Warks.
Mynott, R.H., Warwick, Warks.
Myriad Antiques, London, W11.
Mytton Antiques, Atcham, Shrops.

N

Nadin, Harold, Grantham, Lincs.
Nadin, Richard and Pamela, Bath, Avon.
Naghi, E., London, W1.
Nahum, Peter, London, SW1.
Nakota Curios, Hastings, Sussex East.
Nanbooks, Settle, Yorks. North.
Nanking Porcelain Co, London, W11.
Nantwich Art Deco and Decorative Arts, Nantwich, Cheshire.
Nanwani and Co, London, EC3.
Napier House Antiques, Sudbury, Suffolk.
Napier Ltd, Sylvia, London, SW6.
Narducci Antiques, Largs, Scotland.
Narducci Antiques, Saltcoats, Scotland.
Narducci, G., Largs, Scotland.
Narducci, G., Saltcoats, Scotland.
Nares, M.A., E.A. and J.M., Atcham, Shrops.
Nash, J., Ledbury, Herefs. and Worcs.
Nash Antiques and Interiors, John, Ledbury, Herefs. & Worcs.
Nash Antiques, Paul, Tetbury, Glos.
Nash, P. and A. Gifford, Tetbury, Glos.
Nassor, C., Hebden Bridge, Yorks. West.
Nasta, A.B., East Horsley, Surrey.
Nathan Antiques, John, Exeter, Devon.
Nathan and Co. (Birmingham) Ltd, Birmingham, West Mids.
Nautical Antique Centre, The, Weymouth, Dorset.
Neal, B.A., Branksome, Dorset.
Neal, C., London, W1.
Neal Cabinet Antiques, Isabel, Coltishall, Norfolk.
Neal, S., Bognor Regis, Sussex West.
Neale, A.N., B.J. and I.J., London, W1.
Neale, P., Rumford, Cornwall.
Neary, G., Huddersfield, Yorks. West.
Neath, P., Bournemouth, Dorset.
Nebbett, A., Exeter, Devon.
Needham, A. and A., Buxton, Derbys.
Needham, K., Cobham, Surrey.
Needham, Mrs M., Sheffield, Yorks. South.
Needham, S.R., Broughton Astley, Leics.
Neill, E.J., Southport, Merseyside.
Neill, F. and J., White Roding, Essex.
Neill Gallery, Southport, Merseyside.
Neilson, A.J., Sturminster Newton, Dorset.
Neilson, J. and A., Edinburgh, Scotland.
Neilson Ltd, T. and J. W., Edinburgh, Scotland.
Nels, P.J., London, W1.
Nels Ltd, Paul, London, W1.
Nelson, A., London, W1.
Nelson, J.M., Balcombe, Sussex West.
Nelson, John O., Edinburgh, Scotland.
Nelson, W. and L., Broughton, Lancs.
Neptune Antiques, Long Melford, Suffolk.
Nesbitt, Peggy, Warwick, Warks.
Nesfield, J., Sandhurst, Kent.
Nest Egg Antiques, Edinburgh, Scotland.
Netherley Cottage Antiques, Milburn, Cumbria.
Nettleton, S.M., Patrington, N. Humbs.
Neuman, Mrs P., Hexham, Northumbs.
Nevill Fine Paintings Ltd, Guy, London, SW3.
Neville, C. and S., Farnham, Surrey.
Neville Antiques, Howard, Tunbridge Wells, Kent.

DEALERS' INDEX

Neville, H.C.C., Tunbridge Wells, Kent.
Neville, J., Aslockton, Notts.
Neville Gallery, Jane, Aslockton, Notts.
Neville, Tony, Poole, Dorset.
Neville's Antiques, Woburn Sands, Bucks.
New Abbey Antiques, Newtownabbey, Co. Antrim, N. Ireland.
New Century, London, W8.
New Gallery, Budleigh Salterton, Devon.
New Generation Antiques Market, Penzance, Cornwall.
New Grafton Gallery, London, SW13.
New, S., Portsmouth, Hants.
New Street Antiques, Altrincham, Cheshire.
New Street Books, Penzance, Cornwall.
Newark Antique Warehouse, Newark, Notts.
Newark Antiques Centre, Newark, Notts.
Newark, G., Deddington, Oxon.
Newburgh Antiques, Newburgh, Scotland.
Newby (A.J. & M.V. Waller), H.W., London, SW8.
Newcombe, P.J., Barnstaple, Devon.
Newell-Smith, S. and D., London, N1.
Newgate Antiques Centre, York, Yorks. North.
Newhaven Flea Market, Newhaven, Sussex East.
Newhart (Pictures) Ltd, London, NW3.
Newlove, B. M., Surbiton, Surrey.
Newman Gallery, Heather, Cranham, Glos.
Newmarket Gallery, Newmarket, Suffolk.
Newnham, J. and M., Royston, Herts.
Newport Gallery, Newport, Devon.
Newsam, T.J., Salisbury, Wilts.
Newson, D. and L., Twickenham, Middx.
Newth, D.C., Pontypridd, Mid-Glam, Wales.
Newton Abbot Antiques Centre, Newton Abbot, Devon.
Newton, David, Honiton, Devon.
Newton, W.T., Coggeshall, Essex.
Newtons, Bury, Lancs.
Newtons of Bury, Bury, Lancs.
Nice Things Old and New, Glasgow, Scotland.
Nichol and Hill, Darlington, Durham.
Nicholas Antiques, East Molesey, Surrey.
Nicholas, R. and M., Towcester, Northants.
Nicholl, D. and W., South Molton, Devon.
Nicholls Jewellers and Antiques, Walsall, West Mids.
Nicholls, John, Leigh, Staffs.
Nicholls, Mrs .R., Malmesbury, Wilts.
Nicholls, R., Walsall, West Mids.
Nichols, M., Worcester, Herefs. and Worcs.
Nicholson, J.C. and A.J., Bexhill-on-Sea, Sussex East.
Nicholson, J.C. and A.J., Pevensey, Sussex East.
Nicholson, Mr and Mrs R.A, Sutton-on-Sea, Lincs.
Nicholson, Richard A., Chester, Cheshire.
Nickerson, S., London, W11.
Nicoll, Mr and Mrs D.J., Haddington, Scotland.
Nielsen Antiques, Anthony, Burford, Oxon.
Nielsen, Mrs M.K., Moreton-in-Marsh, Glos.
Nightingale, P.A., Alderney, Alderney, C.I.
Nilson, B., Ashford, Kent.
Nimbus Antiques, Whaley Bridge, Derbys.
Nimmo, G., Harrogate, Yorks. North.
Niner Antiques, Elizabeth, Cheltenham, Glos.
Niner and Hill Rare Books, Oxford, Oxon.
Niner, M., Oxford, Oxon.
Ninety-One, Norwich, Norfolk.
Ning Ltd, London, SW1.
Nithsdale Antiques, Glasgow, Scotland.
Niven, G., Edinburgh, Scotland.
No. 2 Park Street Antiques, Stow-on-the-Wold, Glos.
No. 7 Antiques, Woore, Shrops.
No.12 Queen Street, Bath, Avon.
No. 74 Antiques and Collectables, Bristol, Avon.
Noah's Ark Antique Centre, Sandwich, Kent.
Noble Antiques, Sandgate, Kent.
Noble, Avril, London, WC2.
Noble, Mrs B., Huddersfield, Yorks. West.
Noble and 4 other dealers, F.G., Sandgate, Kent.
Nolan, J., Liverpool, Merseyside.
Noller, A.M., Reigate, Surrey.
Noller (Reigate), Bertram, Reigate, Surrey.
Nook, The, Sherborne, Dorset.
Noortman, London, W1.
Noott Fine Paintings, John, Broadway, Herefs. & Worcs.
Norbury, D. and Mrs K., Leamington Spa, Warks.

Norden Antiques, Peter, Stow-on-the-Wold, Glos.
Nordens, Sandgate, Kent.
Norfolk Galleries, King's Lynn, Norfolk.
Norfolk House Galleries Antique Centre, Dorking, Surrey.
Norfolk Polyphon Centre, Bawdeswell, Norfolk.
Norgrove - Antique Clocks, P.W., Haslingden, Lancs.
Norman, B.E., London, W1.
Norman Antiques Ltd, Michael, Brighton, Sussex East.
Norman, P., Burwell, Cambs.
Norman Antiques and Restorations, Peter, Burwell, Cambs.
Norrie, Mrs E., Ceres, Scotland.
Norris, R., Biddenden, Kent.
North Bridge Antiques, Halifax, Yorks. West.
North, Desmond and Amanda, East Peckham, Kent.
North End Antiques, Lowestoft, Suffolk.
North London Clock Shop Ltd, London, N5.
North Quay Antique Centre, Weymouth, Dorset.
North Wales Antiques - Colwyn Bay, Colwyn Bay, Clwyd, Wales.
North Walsham Antique Gallery, North Walsham, Norfolk.
North Wilts Exporters, Malmesbury, Wilts.
Northam, Mrs, Long Sutton, Lincs.
Northam, E. and J., Long Sutton, Lincs.
Northcote Road Antiques Market, London, SW11.
Northern Kilim Centre, The, Knaresborough, Yorks. North.
Northfleet Hill Antiques, Northfleet, Kent.
Northgate Antiques, Bishop's Stortford, Herts.
Northleach Gallery, The, Northleach, Glos.
Northumbria Pine, Whitley Bay, Tyne and Wear.
Northwood Antiques, Northwood, Middx.
Norton Antiques, Beaconsfield, Bucks.
Norton, B.R., St. Ives, Cambs.
Norton, M.S., N.E.L., J.P. and F.E., London, W1.
Norton Galleries, Pauline, Bridgnorth, Shrops.
Nortonbury Antiques, London, WC1.
Norwich City Council,, Norwich, Norfolk.
Norwood House Antiques, Killinghall, Yorks. North.
Nostalgia, Barnstaple, Devon.
Nostalgia, Blackpool, Lancs.
Nostalgia, Dorking, Surrey.
Nostalgia Antiques, Llanishen, South Glam., Wales.
Nostalgia Antiques, Northampton, Northants.
Nostalgia Architectural Antiques, Stockport, Cheshire.
Nosworthy, Bridget and Roger, Holsworthy, Devon.
Nosworthy, G., Grampound, Cornwall.
Nosworthy, R., St. Austell, Cornwall.
Not Just Books, Uppingham, Leics.
Not Just Silver, Weybridge, Surrey.
Notions, Grantham, Lincs.
Noton Antiques, Finedon, Northants.
Nottingham Antique Centre, Nottingham, Notts.
Now and Then (Toy Centre), Edinburgh, Scotland.
Nowell, Edward A., Wells, Somerset.
Nowell, Marcus, Wells, Somerset.
Number Six Antiques, Halesworth, Suffolk.
Number Ten/Oxford Antiques, Oxford, Oxon.
Number Nineteen, London, N1.
Nunn, C.C., Falmouth, Cornwall.
Nunn, K., St. Leonards-on-Sea, Sussex East.
Nutter, Simon W., Stow-on-the-Wold, Glos.
Nutting, Mrs B.H., Brackley, Northants.
Nye, Pat, London, W11.

O

Oak Chest, Llangollen, Clwyd, Wales.
Oakes and Son, G., Bolton, Lancs.
Oakes, H. and S., Stoke-on-Trent, Staffs.
Oakham Antiques, Oakham, Leics.
Oakstar Ltd, London, W11.
Oakwood Gallery, Leeds, Yorks. West.
Oasis Antiques, Brighton, Sussex East.
Oban Antiques, Oban, Scotland.
Obelisk Antiques, Warminster, Wilts.
O'Brien and Son Antiques, R. J., Hollinwood, Lancs.
Occultique, Northampton, Northants.
Ockley Antiques, Dorking, Surrey.
Ockley Antiques, Ockley, Surrey.
O'Connor Brothers, Windsor and Eton, Berks.
Oddiquities, London, SE23.
Odeon Antiques, Leek, Staffs.
Odgers, J.W., Harwich, Essex.

DEALERS' INDEX

Odgers, J.W., London, W11.
O'Donnell, A., London, SE13.
O'Donnell, A.J., Bowdon, Cheshire.
O'Donnell, C., Wallingford, Oxon.
O'Donnell Antiques, Chris and Lin, Wallingford, Oxon.
O'Donnell, Tom, Edinburgh, Scotland.
Odiham Gallery, The, Odiham, Hants.
O'Dwyer, F., Rode, Somerset.
O'Farrell, G., Stow-on-the-Wold, Glos.
O'Flaherty, P., Belfast, N. Ireland.
Offa's Dyke Antique Centre, Knighton, Powys, Wales.
O'Flynn Antiquarian Booksellers, York, Yorks. North.
Ogden, G. and D., Alsager, Cheshire.
Ogden, J. and M., Honiton, Devon.
Ogden of Harrogate Ltd, Harrogate, Yorks. North.
Ogden Ltd, Richard, London, W1.
Ogleby, B., Thirsk, Yorks. North.
O'Grady, V., Norwich, Norfolk.
Okarma, E., Brobury, Herefs. and Worcs.
Okarma, E., Hay-on-Wye, Powys, Wales.
Okeeffe, Timothy, Prestwick, Scotland.
O'Keefe, B., Hadleigh, Suffolk.
O'Kelly, A. and J., London, E8.
Okolski, Z.J., London, W3.
Old Abbey Antiques, Auchterarder, Scotland.
Old Antique Shop, The, Budleigh Salterton, Devon.
Old Bakehouse, The, Birmingham, West Mids.
Old Bakehouse Antiques and Gallery, Broughton Astley, Leics.
Old Bakehouse Pine, Whissendine, Leics.
Old Bakery Antiques, Brasted, Kent.
Old Bakery Antiques, The, Cranbrook, Kent.
Old Bakery Antiques, Empingham, Leics.
Old Bakery Antiques, Hunstanton, Norfolk.
Old Bakery, The, Woolhampton, Berks.
Old Barley Mow Antiques, Winchfield, Hants.
Old Barn Antiques, Church Stretton, Shrops.
Old Barn Antiques Co, Trent, Dorset.
Old Barn Antiques Warehouse, Sutton Bridge, Lincs.
Old Bishop's Palace Antique Centre, The, Little Downham, Cambs.
Old Brass Kettle, The, Moretonhampstead, Devon.
Old Brigade, The, Kingsthorpe, Northants.
Old Butchery, The, Hoole, Cheshire.
Old Button Shop, The, Lytchett Minster, Dorset.
Old Cathay Fine Books and Arts, Hatfield, Herts.
Old Chapel Market, The, Tutbury, Staffs.
Old Church Galleries, London, SW3.
Old Cinema Antique Department Store, The, London, W4.
Old Coach House, Long Stratton, Norfolk.
Old Clock Shop, The, West Malling, Kent.
Old College Antiques, Wingham, Kent.
Old Copper Shop and Post House Antiques, The, South Cave, N. Humbs.
Old Corner House Antiques, Wittersham, Kent.
Old Cottage Antiques, The, Upminster, Essex.
Old Cottage Things, Romsey, Hants.
Old Cross Antiques, Greyabbey, Co. Down, N. Ireland.
Old Cross Gallery, Glossop, Derbys.
Old Curiosity Shop, The, Ayr, Scotland.
Old Curiosity Shop, Beaconsfield, Bucks.
Old Curiosity Shop, The, East Horsley, Surrey.
Old Curiosity Shop, Frome, Somerset.
Old Curiosity Shop, King's Lynn, Norfolk.
Old Curiosity Shop, The, St. Sampson, Guernsey, C.I.
Old Dairy, The, London, W4.
Old Ephemera and Newspaper Shop, The, London, SW1.
Old English Pine, Sandgate, Kent.
Old Father Time Clock Centre, London, W11.
Old Flame, Easingwold, Yorks. North.
Old Forge Antiques, Hartley Wintney, Hants.
Old George Antiques and Interiors, Tetbury, Glos.
Old George Inn Antique Galleries, Burford, Oxon.
Old Granary Antiques and Collectors Centre, The, King's Lynn, Norfolk.
Old Haberdasher, The, London, W11.
Old Hall Bookshop, The, Brackley, Northants.
Old Hall (Sphinx Gallery), Westerham, Kent.
Old Hat, Radlett, Herts.
Old Hill Auctions, Cradley Heath, West Mids.
Old House, The, Seaford, Sussex East.
Old House Antiques, Wansford, Cambs.

Old House Gallery, The, Oakham, Leics.
Old London Galleries, London, SW1.
Old Malthouse, The, Hungerford, Berks.
Old Man Antiques, The, Coniston, Cumbria.
Old Manor House Antiques, Brasted, Kent.
Old Maps and Prints, London, SW1.
Old Mill Antiques (Stirling), Bannockburn, Scotland.
Old Mill Market Shop, Tetbury, Glos.
Old Mint House, The, Bexhill-on-Sea, Sussex East.
Old Mint House, The, Pevensey, Sussex East.
Old Palace Antiques, Lostwithiel, Cornwall.
Old Passage, The, Teignmouth, Devon.
Old Pine, London, SW6.
Old Pine and Country Furniture, Boscastle, Cornwall.
Old Pine Furniture and Jouet, Kiltarlity, Scotland.
Old Pine Shop, The, London, W5.
Old Pine Shop, Ross-on-Wye, Herefs. & Worcs.
Old Post House, The, Axbridge, Somerset.
Old Post House Antiques, Playden, Sussex East.
Old Post House Antiques, Woolhampton, Berks.
Old Post Office Antiques, The, Compton, Surrey.
Old Posthouse, The, Penzance, Cornwall.
Old Ropery Antique Clocks,, The, Kilham, N. Humbs.
Old Saddlers Antiques, Goudhurst, Kent.
Old St. Andrews Gallery, St. Andrews, Scotland.
Old School Antiques, The, Dorney, Berks.
Old Smithy, Feniscowles, Lancs.
Old Smithy Antique Centre, The, Merstham, Surrey.
Old Soke Books, Peterborough, Cambs.
Old Stores, The, Christchurch, Dorset.
Old Tithe Barn, The, Horbury, Yorks. West.
Old Tool Chest, The, London, N1.
Old Town Antique Centre, The, Eastbourne, Sussex East.
Old Town Hall Antique Centre, The, Needham Market, Suffolk.
Old Treasures, Newton Abbot, Devon.
Old Troon Sporting Antiques, Troon, Scotland.
Old Tyme Antiques, Ruthin, Clwyd, Wales.
Old World Trading Co, London, SW6.
Olde Curiosity Shoppe, The, Godalming, Surrey.
Olde Forge Antiques, The, Swanage, Dorset.
Olde Red Lion, The, Bedingfield, Suffolk.
Oldfield Cottage Antiques, Southport, Merseyside.
Oldfield Gallery, Portsmouth, Hants.
Oldfield, N.E., Preston, Lancs.
Oldham, Mrs J.A., Castle Cary, Somerset.
Oldman, P. and R., Todmorden, Yorks. West.
Oldswinford Gallery, Stourbridge, West Mids.
Oldwoods, Bristol, Avon.
Olive Antiques, Alverstoke, Hants.
Olive Branch Antiques, Broadway, Herefs. & Worcs.
Olive Green Ltd, Leamington Spa, Warks.
Oliver, A., London, W8.
Oliver Antiques, West Kirby, Merseyside.
Oliver, C.A., Swansea, West Glam., Wales.
Oliver Antiques, Gerald, Haverfordwest, Dyfed, Wales.
Oliver, J., Wells, Somerset.
Oliver, Patrick, Cheltenham, Glos.
Oliver, R.A., Brighton, Sussex East.
Oliver, Tony L., Windsor and Eton, Berks.
Oliver-Sutton Antiques, London, W8.
Olney, A., Ampthill, Beds.
Olney Antique Centre, Olney, Bucks.
O'Loughlin, P.J., Glasgow, Scotland.
Omar (Harrogate) Ltd, Harrogate, Yorks. North.
Omell Galleries, London, SW1.
Omniphil Ltd, Chesham, Bucks.
Ong t/a Skoob Two, I.K., London, WC1.
O'Nians, H., London, SW1.
Onions - White Cottage Antiques, L., Tern Hill, Shrops.
Oola Boola Antiques London, London, SE1.
Oosthuizen, Jacqueline, London, N1.
Oosthuizen, Jacqueline, London, SW3.
Open Eye Gallery Ltd, Edinburgh, Scotland.
Orbell House Gallery, Castle Hedingham, Essex.
Orchard Antiques, Preston, Lancs.
Organ, G.H. and S.M., Bath, Avon.
Oriel Antiques, Hindhead, Surrey.
Oriental Carpet Centre, The, Bristol, Avon.
Oriental Art Gallery Ltd., The, London, W1.
Oriental Bronzes Ltd, London, W1.
Oriental Carpets and Decorative Arts, Dorking, Surrey.

DEALERS' INDEX 738

Oriental Gallery, Stow-on-the-Wold, Glos.
Oriental Rug Gallery Ltd, St. Albans, Herts.
Oriental Rug Shop, The, Sheffield, Yorks. South.
Original Choice, Penryn, Cornwall.
Original Choice Ltd, The, Worcester, Herefs. & Worcs.
Original Remember When , The, London, SW13.
Originals, Leeds, Yorks. West.
Ormonde, F., London, W11.
Ormonde Gallery, London, W11.
Orpin, John and Marina, Stansted, Essex.
Orssich, Paul, London, SW6.
Orton, R.J., London, N4.
Orton Antiques, Stephen, Watlington, Oxon.
Orwell Galleries, Ipswich, Suffolk.
Orwell Paint Strippers, Ipswich, Suffolk.
Osborn Baker Gallery, London, NW3.
Osborn, R.E., London, NW3.
Osborne, Kirkcudbright, Scotland.
Osborne Antiques, Sutton Coldfield, West Mids.
Osborne Art and Antiques, Jesmond, Tyne and Wear.
Osborne, C., Sutton Coldfield, West Mids.
Osborne, T.N.M., North Wraxall, Wilts.
Oscars - Antique Market, Crewkerne, Somerset.
O'Shea Gallery, London, SW1.
Osiris Antiques, Southport, Merseyside.
Ossowski, A. and M., London, SW1.
Osterley Antiques Ltd, London, SW6.
O'Sullivan, D. J. and P. M., Parkstone, Dorset.
Oswald Road Antique and Reproduction Centre, The, Oswestry, Shrops.
Other Times Antiques, Portsoy, Scotland.
O'Toole, G., Tarvin, Cheshire.
Otten, Rupert, London, SE5.
Otter Antiques, Honiton, Devon.
Ottrey Antiques, Mike, Wallingford, Oxon.
Ottrey, M.J., Wallingford, Oxon.
Oulton, P., M. C. and T., Altrincham, Cheshire.
Out of Time Antiques, Ashbourne, Derbys.
Ovell Antiques, Llandovery, Dyfed, Wales.
Overhill Antique and Old Pine Warehouse, Poole, Dorset.
Overland Antiques, John, Olney, Bucks.
Owen Antiques, Rochdale, Lancs.
Owen, Mrs A., Cambridge, Cambs.
Owen Gallery, John, Cowbridge, South Glam., Wales.
Owen, J. and P., Cowbridge, South Glam., Wales.
Owen, J. and S., Cowbridge, South Glam., Wales.
Owen, J.G.T., Rochdale, Lancs.
Owen, M., Nelson, Lancs.
Owen, T., Bolton, Lancs.
Owen's Jewellers, Newcastle-upon-Tyne, Tyne and Wear.
Owens, Mrs M., Moffat, Scotland.
Owl House, The, Dorking, Surrey.
Owls Antiques, Steeton, Yorks. West.
Oxenhams, Wellington, Somerset.
Oxford Antique Trading Co, The, Oxford, Oxon.
Oxford Antiques Centre, Oxford, Oxon.
Oxford Architectural Antiques, Oxford, Oxon.
Oxford Street Antique Centre Ltd, Leicester, Leics.
Oxfordshire Co. Council,, Woodstock, Oxon.
Oxley, L., Alresford, Hants.
Oxley Antique Clocks and Barometers, P.A., Cherhill, Wilts.

P

P.L.B. Enterprises, Hythe, Kent.
Packhouse, The, Runfold, Surrey.
Paddock Antiques, Woodhouse Eaves, Leics.
Padgett, G.R. and D.L., Hornsea, N. Humbs.
Padgett, Mrs Gioia L., Mapplewell, Yorks. South.
Padgetts Antiques, Photographic and Scientific, Hornsea, N. Humbs.
Page Antiques, Stockport, Cheshire.
Page, A. and H., London, W7.
Page Antiques, Brian, Brighton, Sussex East.
Page Antiquarian Books, Colin, Brighton, Sussex East.
Page, C.G., Brighton, Sussex East.
Page, D.R.J. and S.J., London, W11.
Page Oriental Art, Kevin, London, N1.
Page, T., Marlborough, Wilts.
Paine, D., Gorseinon, West Glam., Wales.
Painswick Antique Centre, Painswick, Glos.
Painter, R., Ludlow, Shrops.

Paisley Fine Books, Paisley, Scotland.
Palfrey, M. and L.E., Brockdish, Norfolk.
Pall Mall Antiques, Leigh-on-Sea, Essex.
Palmer, B. and J., Haverfordwest, Dyfed, Wales.
Palmer, C.D. and V.J., Richmond, Surrey.
Palmer Antiques, Dermot and Jill, Brighton, Sussex East.
Palmer, J., Honiton, Devon.
Palmer Antiques, Mary, Stradbroke, Suffolk.
Palmer, P. and G., Sarnau, Dyfed, Wales.
Palmer Galleries, Richmond, Surrey.
Palmer, M., Penzance, Cornwall.
Palmer Antiques, P.E., Ringwood, Hants.
Panormo, S.V., Gosport, Hants.
Pantelli, A., London, N1.
Pantiles Antiques, Tunbridge Wells, Kent.
Pantiles Spa Antiques, Tunbridge Wells, Kent.
Papworth, Barry, Lymington, Hants.
Parade Antiques, Hampton Hill, Middx.
Paradise, J., Nottingham, Notts.
Paragon Antiques and Collectors Market, Bath, Avon.
Paraphernalia, Harrogate, Yorks. North.
Paraphernalia, Sheffield, Yorks. South.
Paraphernalia Antiques and Collectors' Centre, Bromley, Kent.
Paravent, Twickenham, Middx.
Pardoe, S., London, W11.
Parikian, D., London, W14.
Parish, S., Barling Magna, Essex.
Park Antiques, Menston, Yorks. West.
Park Antiquities, Weymouth, Dorset.
Park Book Shop, Wellingborough, Northants.
Park Galleries, London, N3.
Park Galleries Antiques, Fine Art and Decor, Bolton, Lancs.
Park Gallery, Wellingborough, Northants.
Park House Antiques, Bladon, Oxon.
Park House Antiques, Stow-on-the-Wold, Glos.
Park, N., Tiverton, Devon.
Park Street Antiques, Berkhamsted, Herts.
Park View Antiques, Wadhurst, Sussex East.
Park Walk Gallery, London, SW10.
Parker, Elizabeth, Moreton-in-Marsh, Glos.
Parker Fine Art Ltd, Finkley, Hants.
Parker Gallery, Leeds, Yorks. West.
Parker Gallery, The, London, SW1.
Parker, L., Canterbury, Kent.
Parker, M.L., Witney, Oxon.
Parker, P.A.R., Finkley, Hants.
Parker, S., Quorn, Leics.
Parker - The Whitestocks Collections, John, Rickmansworth, Herts.
Parker-Williams Antiques, Canterbury, Kent.
Parkhouse Antiques and Jewellery, Mark, Barnstaple, Devon.
Parkhouse and Wyatt Ltd, Southampton, Hants.
Parkin, J., Derby, Derbys.
Parkin Fine Art Ltd, Michael, London, SW1.
Parkin, P.J., Bristol, Avon.
Parkinson, E. and D., Chalfont St. Giles, Bucks.
Parkinson-Large, P., Woburn, Beds.
Parks & Vinsen,, Sheringham, Norfolk.
Parmenter Antiques, Bridgnorth, Shrops.
Parmenter, J., Bridgnorth, Shrops.
Parriss, Sheringham, Norfolk.
Parriss, J.H., Sheringham, Norfolk.
Parry, H., Edinburgh, Scotland.
Parry, H., Sutton Coldfield, West Mids.
Parry Ltd, H. and R.L., Sutton Coldfield, West Mids.
Parry, R.C., Exeter, Devon.
Parsons, Mrs B.D., Tonbridge, Kent.
Partner, S.H. and M., Colchester, Essex.
Partridge Fine Arts plc, London, W1.
Partridge Antiques, Timothy, Eastbourne, Sussex East.
Partridges, Amersham, Bucks.
Partner and Puxon, Colchester, Essex.
Pass, B., London, N1.
Passell, P.A., Eastleigh, Hants.
Passers Buy (Marie Evans), Llangollen, Clwyd, Wales.
Past and Present, Blackpool, Lancs.
Past and Present, Cardiff, South Glam., Wales.
Past and Present, Leigh-on-Sea, Essex.
Past and Present, Totnes, Devon.
Past and Present, Walsall, West Mids.

DEALERS' INDEX

Pastimes Antiques, Hertford, Herts.
Pastimes (Egham) Ltd, Egham, Surrey.
Pastimes Vintage Toys, Glasgow, Scotland.
Pastorale Antiques, Lewes, Sussex East.
Pataky Antiques and Reproductions, Victoria, West Malling, Kent.
Paterson Antiques, Elizabeth, Stirling, Scotland.
Pathbrae Antiques, Newton Stewart, Scotland.
Patterson, A., Manningtree, Essex.
Patterson Co. Ltd, E.J.A., Banbury, Oxon.
Patterson Ltd, G.D., Broadway, Herefs. and Worcs.
Patterson Antiques, Jo, Crook, Durham.
Patterson Liddle, Bath, Avon.
Patterson, P., Sible Hedingham, Essex.
Patterson, W.H. and Mrs. P.M., London, W1.
Patterson Fine Arts Ltd, W.H., London, W1.
Paul, Mrs E., London, W1.
Paull Antiques, Janice, Kenilworth, Warks.
Pauw Antiques, M., London, SW6.
Pavilion, Ratcliffe-on-the-Wreake, Leics.
Pawsey and Payne, London, SW1.
Pay, D.J. and B., Dorking, Surrey.
Payman, E. and L.C., Stokesley, Yorks. North.
Payne, B.J., Alcester, Warks.
Payne and Son Ltd, Geo. A., Bournemouth, Dorset.
Payne, G.N., E.P. and J.D., Oxford, Oxon.
Payne, H.G. and N.G., Bournemouth, Dorset.
Payne Antiques, Martin, Warwick, Warks.
Payne, M.H., London, N1.
Payne, S., Grampound, Cornwall.
Payne and Son (Goldsmiths) Ltd, Oxford, Oxon.
Payton, F.B. and S., Mansfield, Notts.
Payton, Mrs M., Chagford, Devon.
Payton Antiques, Mary, Chagford, Devon.
Peacock Antiques, Chilham, Kent.
Pead, L.W., Marsham, Norfolk.
Peake, D.T., Nottingham, Notts.
Peake, N.B., Norwich, Norfolk.
Pearce, B., Ombersley, Herefs. and Worcs.
Pearl Cross Ltd, London, WC2.
Pearsey, M.E. and D.C., Holbeach, Lincs.
Pearson, J., Nantwich, Cheshire.
Pearson, J., Nottingham, Notts.
Pearson Antique Clock Restoration, John, Birstwith, Yorks. North.
Pearson Antiques, Hull, N. Humbs.
Pearson Antiques, Carol, Tisbury, Wilts.
Pearson Antiques, John A., Horton, Berks.
Pearson Antiques, Michael, Canterbury, Kent.
Pearson Paintings Prints and Works of Art, Sebastian, Cambridge, Cambs.
Pearson, Sue, Brighton, Sussex East.
Pearson - Frasco International Ltd, W.M., London, SW1.
Peasenhall Art and Antiques Gallery, Peasenhall, Suffolk.
Peckwater Antiques and Interiors, Charing, Kent.
Peco, Hampton, Middx.
Pedlar, The, Camberley, Surrey.
Pedlar's Pack, The, Hadlow, Kent.
Pedlars, Chipping Campden, Glos.
Pedler, R.S., London, SW15.
Peek, G., Gillingham, Kent.
Pegasus Antiques, Nottingham, Notts.
Pegasus Antiques and Collectables, Bournemouth, Dorset.
Pelham Galleries, London, W1.
Pelican Antiques, Greystoke, Cumbria.
Pembery, M. and L., Bakewell, Derbys.
Pembleton, Mrs A., Nottingham, Notts.
Pembleton, S., Nottingham, Notts.
Pembridge Art Gallery, London, W11.
Pembroke Antique Centre, Pembroke, Dyfed, Wales.
Pembroke Antiques, Cambridge, Cambs.
Pen Street Antiques, Boston, Lincs.
Penandrea Gallery, Redruth, Cornwall.
Pend Antiques, The, Kinghorn, Scotland.
Pendar Antiques, Tavistock, Devon.
Pendeford House Antiques, Wolverhampton, West Mids.
Pender, C., Manchester, Lancs.
Pendleton, M., Chiddingfold, Surrey.
Penfold Gallery and Antiques, Steyning, Sussex West.
Penman, V., Kingston-on-Spey, Scotland.
Penn Barn, Penn, Bucks.
Pennard House, East Pennard, Somerset.

Pennard House Antiques, Bath, Avon.
Pennies, Exwick, Devon.
Penny Farthing Antiques, London, SE1.
Penny Farthing Antiques, South Cave, N. Humbs.
Penny Post Antiques, The, Buxton, Derbys.
Penny's Antiques, Northampton, Northants.
Pennyfarthing, The, Crowmarsh Gifford, Oxon.
Penrith Coin and Stamp Centre, Penrith, Cumbria.
Penoyre Antiques, Pershore, Herefs. & Worcs.
Pepper Lane Antique Centre, Ludlow, Shrops.
Pepper, M.E., Bury St. Edmunds, Suffolk.
Pepper, T.G., Luton, Beds.
Pepper, T.G., St. Albans, Herts.
Peppers Period Pieces, Bury St. Edmunds, Suffolk.
Peppitt, Judith, Harrietsham, Kent.
Pepys Antiques, Beckenham, Kent.
Perchance Ltd, Torquay, Devon.
Percival Antiques, R. and S. M., Ruthin, Clwyd, Wales.
Perera Fine Art, Robert, Lymington, Hants.
Perera, R.J.D., Lymington, Hants.
Perez, London, SW3.
Period Brass Lights, London, SW7.
Periwinkle Press, Faversham, Kent.
Period Architectural Features and Antiques, Annahilt, Co. Down, N. Ireland.
Period Fireplaces, Bristol, Avon.
Period Furniture Showrooms, Beaconsfield, Bucks.
Perkins Antiques, Bryan, Wellingborough, Northants.
Perkins, B.H. and J., Wellingborough, Northants.
Perks, J.S., Blakedown, Herefs. and Worcs.
Perovetz Ltd, H., London, WC2.
Perrett, Mrs J., Shoreham-by-Sea, Sussex West.
Perrin, C.R., Malmesbury, Wilts.
Perry, A. and C., Woking, Surrey.
Perry, Mrs J.R., Carmarthen, Dyfed, Wales.
Perry, R.J., Hitchin, Herts.
Perry Antiques, R.J., Hitchin, Herts.
Persian Rugs, West Peckham, Kent.
Peter James Antiques, Sheffield, Yorks. South.
Peter John, St. Neots, Cambs.
Peter Pan's Bazaar, Gosport, Hants.
Peter Pan's of Gosport, Gosport, Hants.
Peters, Mrs D., Worthing, Sussex West.
Peters, D.J., Great Missenden, Bucks.
Peters, G., Ely, Cambs.
Peters, Mr and Mrs M.D., Congleton, Cheshire.
Peters Antiques, Paul M., Harrogate, Yorks. North.
Petersfield Bookshop, The, Petersfield, Hants.
Petherton Antiques, London, N5.
Pethick, K.J. and Mrs . G.M., Frinton-on-Sea, Essex.
Petre, N. and P., Hertford, Herts.
Petrou, Peter, London, W11.
Petticombe Manor Antiques, Bideford, Devon.
Pettifer Ltd, David, London, SW3.
Pettigrew, C., Glasgow, Scotland.
Pettigrew and Mail, Glasgow, Scotland.
Pettitt, J., Wolverhampton, West Mids.
Peyton-Jones, MissP., Wendover, Bucks.
Pharoah, W. and J., Eastbourne, Sussex East.
Petworth Antique Market, Petworth, Sussex West.
Pharoahs Antiques Centre, Eastbourne, Sussex East.
Phelps Antiques, Twickenham, Middx.
Phelps Antiquarian Books, Michael, London, SW15.
Phelps, R.C., Twickenham, Middx.
Philip and Sons Ltd, Trevor, London, SW1.
Phillips, E., London, NW8.
Phillips (Antiques), Edward V., Clayton-le-Moors, Lancs.
Phillips Antiques Ltd, Elaine, Harrogate, Yorks. North.
Phillips and Sons, E.S., London, W11.
Philllips, John and Veronica, London, SW12.
Phillips, Henry, London, W8.
Phillips, M., Marlborough, Wilts.
Phillips, M. and J., Hitchin, Herts.
Phillips of Hitchin (Antiques) Ltd, Hitchin, Herts.
Phillips Ltd, Ronald, London, W1.
Phillips and Sons, Cookham, Berks.
Phillips, S., Buxton, Norfolk.
Phillips Ltd, S.J., London, W1.
Phillips, S.P., Lynton, Devon.
Phillips, V., Altrincham, Cheshire.
Philp, London, W11.
Philp, R., London, W11.

DEALERS' INDEX

Philpot, P., Stoke Ferry, Norfolk.
Phipps, C., London, WC1.
Phipps and Co. Ltd, London, SW3.
Phipps and Co. Ltd,, Mathon, Herefs. and Worcs.
Phoenix Antiques, Fordham, Cambs.
Phoenix Antiques, Tunbridge Wells, Kent.
Phoenix Green Antiques, Hartley Wintney, Hants.
Piano Nobile Fine Paintings, Richmond, Surrey.
Piano Shop, The, Leeds, Yorks. West.
Pianorama (Harrogate) Ltd, Harrogate, Yorks. North.
Piccadilly Gallery, London, W1.
Piccadilly Jewellers, Birmingham, West Mids.
Pickering, P., Allonby, Cumbria.
Pickering and Chatto Ltd, London, SW1.
Pickering, Ernest, Eastbourne, Sussex East.
Pickersgill, A. and C., Barnstaple, Devon.
Pickett, D. and Mrs . J., Errol, Scotland.
Pickett, G.R., Oakham, Leicestershire.
Pickup, David, Burford, Oxon.
PIC's Bookshop, Bridport, Dorset.
Picton House Antiques, Broadway, Herefs. & Worcs.
Pictoriana, Knaresborough, Yorks. North.
Piermont Antiques Ltd, London, N21.
Pierssene, G. and K., London, N21.
Pigeon House Antiques, Hurst Green, Sussex East.
Pigney, L. and J., Stanford-le-Hope, Essex.
Pike, D., Weston-Super-Mare, Avon.
Pilbeam, R., Tunbridge Wells, Kent.
Pilbrow Antiques, Eva, London, W11.
Pilgrim Antiques, Honiton, Devon.
Pilgrims Antique Centre, Gainsborough, Lincs.
Pillory House, Nantwich, Cheshire.
Pilon, C. and D., Barnstaple, Devon.
Pine Antiques, Doveridge, Derbys.
Pine Antiques, Olney, Bucks.
Pine Antiques, St. Annes-on-Sea, Lancs.
Pine Barn, The, Pontnewynydd, Gwent, Wales.
Pine Cellars, The, Winchester, Hants.
Pine Collection, Liss, Hants.
Pine Collection, The, St. Peter Port, Guernsey, C.I.
Pine Company, Ringwood, Hants.
Pine and Country Antiques, North Petherwin, Cornwall.
Pine and Design, Balcombe, Sussex West.
Pine Design, Warwick, Warks.
Pine Design Workshop and Pine Corner Antiques, Haverfordwest, Dyfed, Wales.
Pine Dresser, The, Blackpool, Lancs.
Pine Merchants, The, Great Missenden, Bucks.
Pine Mine (Crewe-Read Antiques), The, London, SW6.
Pine, N.J., Horndean, Hants.
Pine on the Green, Sherborne, Dorset.
Pine Parlour, The, Ampthill, Beds.
Pine and Period Furniture, Grampound, Cornwall.
Pine Reflections, Hughenden Valley, Bucks.
Pine Shop, The, Merrow, Surrey.
Pine and Things, Canterbury, Kent.
Pine and Things, Shipston-on-Stour, Warks.
Pine Too, Congleton, Cheshire.
Pinecrafts, Bishops Waltham, Hants.
Pinetree Antiques, Ripon, Yorks. North.
Pinewood, Justin, Burton-on-Trent, Staffs.
Pinewood Studio, Penzance, Cornwall.
Pinfold Antiques, Ruskington, Lincs.
Pink Cottage Antiques, Widegates, Cornwall.
Pinn, K.H. and W.J., Sible Hedingham, Essex.
Pinn and Sons, W.A., Sible Hedingham, Essex.
Pinocchio, Southport, Merseyside.
Pipe, J. and W., Wrentham, Suffolk.
Pirouette, Exeter, Devon.
Pitcher Oriental Art, Nicholas S., London, W1.
Pitman, M., Darlington, Durham.
Pitminster Studio, Pitminster, Somerset.
Pitt, Mrs J.R., Broadway, Herefs. and Worcs.
Pitt, Miss S.A., Broadway, Herefs. and Worcs.
Pittaway, K., Warwick, Warks.
Pittenweem Antiques and Fine Art, Pittenweem, Scotland.
Place Antiques, Peter, London, SW6.
Plaitford House Gallery, Plaitford, Hants.
Plant, K.G., Penrith, Cumbria.
Plant, R., Bristol, Avon.
Plantenga, Pieter, Market Weighton, N. Humbs.
Platt, E., Faversham, Kent.

Pleasures of Past Times, London, WC2.
Plestor Barn Antiques, Liss, Hants.
Plough, The, Milland, Sussex West.
Plough House Interiors, Chepstow, Gwent, Wales.
Plunkett, W. and M., Newton Stewart, Scotland.
Pocock, K., North Petherton, Somerset.
Pocock, P., Weybridge, Surrey.
Pol, J., London, SW19.
Polak Gallery, London, SW1.
Poley Antiques, Alrewas, Staffs.
Poley, D.T. and A.G., Alrewas, Staffs.
Pollak, Dr. P.M., South Brent, Devon.
Pollak, P.M., South Brent, Devon.
Pollock Antiques, Jane, Penrith, Cumbria.
Pollock, Mike, Nottingham, Notts.
Pond Cottage Antiques, Stillington, Yorks. North.
Ponsford Antiques, A.J., Cirencester, Glos.
Ponsford, A.J. and R.L., Cirencester, Glos.
Ponting Antiques, Ben, Brighton, Sussex East.
Pontypridd Antiques, Pontypridd, Mid. Glam., Wales.
Poole, F.T., Landbeach, Cambs.
Poole, J., Truro, Cornwall.
Poole, J.B. and J., Bingley, Yorks. West.
Poole, M. J., Nantwich, Cheshire.
Poole, P.E., Long Sutton, Lincs.
Pope, R. and A., Croydon, Surrey.
Pople, Clive and Willow, Teignmouth, Devon.
Porcelain Collector, The, Shoreham, Kent.
Porch House Antiques, Tetbury, Glos.
Porcupines Bookroom, Instow, Devon.
Pordes Books Ltd, Henry, London, WC2.
Pordes Ltd, H., Cockfosters, Herts.
Portal Gallery, London, W1.
Portcullis Antiques, Kinross, Scotland.
Porter, Arthur, Baldock, Herts.
Porter, A.G.R., Baldock, Herts.
Porter and Son, A.W., Hartley Wintney, Hants.
Porter, D., Shoreham, Kent.
Porter, E., London, W11.
Porter Antiques, James, Sandwich, Kent.
Porter, M.A., Hartley Wintney, Hants.
Porter Prints (Broomhill), Sheffield, Yorks. South.
Porter, Fine Antique European Arms and Armour, Terence H., Steeple Claydon, Bucks.
Porter, R.E., Bournemouth, Dorset.
Porterfield, Mr and Mrs, Barrhead, Scotland.
Portique, Bournemouth, Dorset.
Portland Antiques, Newark, Notts.
Portland Gallery, London, SW1.
Portland House Antiques, Market Deeping, Lincs.
Portland Street Antiques Centre, Newark, Notts.
Portobello Antique Co, London, W11.
Portobello Antique Store, London, W11.
Portobellow Row Antiques Centre, Boston, Lincs.
Portsmouth Stamp Shop, Portsmouth, Hants.
Posnett, D.W., London, W1.
Post House Antiques, Bletchingley, Surrey.
Potashnick Antiques, David, Coulsdon, Surrey.
Pot-Pourri, Sheffield, Yorks. South.
Potter, A. and A.M., Coleshill, Warks.
Potter, B.C., Bristol, Avon.
Potter Antiques, David and Carole, Nottingham, Notts.
Potter, H. and E., Laleham, Surrey.
Potter Ltd, Jonathan, London, W1.
Potter, N.C., London, W1.
Potter and Son, W.G., Axminster, Devon.
Pottergate Antiques, Alnwick, Northumbs.
Potteries Antique Centre, The, Stoke-on-Trent, Staffs.
Potter's Antiques and Coins, Bristol, Avon.
Potterton Books, Thirsk, Yorks. North.
Potts, Mrs R., Southport, Merseyside.
Potts, Mrs R., Uppermill, Lancs.
Poulter and Son, H.W., London, SW10.
Poultney, Chriz, London, SW19.
Pout Antiques, Ian, Witney, Oxon.
Pout, I. and J., Witney, Oxon.
Powell, C., Eastbourne, Sussex East.
Powell (Hove) Ltd, J., Portslade, Sussex West.
Powell & Mathers Antiques, London, SW6.
Power, Mr and Mrs I., Ross-on-Wye, Herefs. and Worcs.
Power, Tom, London, NW8.
Powis, G.L., Hemswell Cliff, Lincs.

Powis, G.L., Newark, Notts.
Pratchett, D.C., London, WC2.
Pratt, Anita, Sandwich, Kent.
Pratt, Mrs E., Bolton, Lancs.
Pratt, J. and D., Burford, Oxon.
Pratt and Son, Leo, South Walsham, Norfolk.
Pratt, N., Acle, Norfolk.
Pratt, R., Birmingham, West Mids.
Pratt, R. and E.D., South Walsham, Norfolk.
Pratt, S.G.H., Ilkley, Yorks. West.
Precious, Roy, Settle, Yorks. North.
Preece, J., Tewkesbury, Glos.
Premier Gallery, Eastbourne, Sussex East.
Prendergast Antiques, Haverfordwest, Dyfed, Wales.
Present Bygones, Edinburgh, Scotland.
Preshaw, Arnold and Betty, Cheadle, Cheshire.
Prestbury Antiques, Prestbury, Cheshire.
Prestige Antiques, John, Brixham, Devon.
Preston and Sally Isbell, Antony, London, SW6.
Preston Antique Centre, Preston, Lancs.
Preston Antiques Ltd, Antony, Stow-on-the-Wold, Glos.
Preston Book Co, Preston, Lancs.
Preston, M. and J., Halifax, Yorks. West.
Preston, N. and I., Launceston, Cornwall.
Preston Antiques Ltd, Antony, Stow-on-the-Wold, Glos.
Prestwich Antiques Ltd, Manchester, Lancs.
Pretty Chairs, Portsmouth, Hants.
Price Antiques Ltd, Graham, Polegate, Sussex East.
Price, G.D.A., Alderley Edge, Cheshire.
Price, G.J., Tunbridge Wells, Kent.
Price, K., Sunninghill, Berks.
Price, M. and A., Harlington, Beds.
Price-Less Antiques, Shipley, Yorks. West.
Prichard Antiques, Winchcombe, Glos.
Prichard, K.H. and D.Y., Winchcombe, Glos.
Prickett, C.M., Birmingham, West Mids.
Pride Oriental Rugs, Eric, Cheltenham, Glos.
Prides of London, London, SW3.
Priest, A.C., Stow-on-the-Wold, Glos.
Priest Antiques, Michael, London, SW1.
Priestley, M., London, W8.
Priests Antiques, Stow-on-the-Wold, Glos.
Prime, M.V., Horncastle, Lincs.
Primrose Antiques, Tetbury, Glos.
Principia Arts and Sciences, Marlborough, Wilts.
Pringle Antiques, Fochabers, Scotland.
Pringle, R.S., Troon, Scotland.
Prinny's Gallery, Brighton, Sussex East.
Print Room, The, London, WC1.
Print Room Gallery, The, Deal, Kent.
Printed Page, Winchester, Hants.
Prior, R., Brighton, Sussex East.
Priory Antiques, Bridlington, N. Humbs.
Priory Antiques, Exeter, Devon.
Priory Antiques, Godalming, Surrey.
Priory Antiques, Greyabbey, Co. Down, N. Ireland.
Priory Gallery, The, Bishops Cleeve, Glos.
Probsthain, Arthur, London, WC1.
Procter, Mark, Windsor and Eton, Berks.
Proctor, C.D. and H.M., Puddletown, Dorset.
Proctor Antiques, David, St. Peter Port, Guernsey, C.I.
Proctor, E., Rye, Sussex East.
Prospect Antiques, Crawley, Hants.
Prospect Antiques, Studley, Warks.
Prothero, P. and M., Neston, Cheshire.
Pruskin Gallery, The, London, W8.
Prydal, B.S., Kingston-upon-Thames, Surrey.
Prydal, B.S., London, W2.
Pryor and Son, E., Liverpool, Merseyside.
Pugh, A., Arundel, Sussex West.
Pugh Antiques, Bernie, Telford, Shrops.
Pugh, Mrs D., Baslow, Derbys.
Pugh, J. and J., Layer de la Haye, Essex.
Pugh's Farm Antiques, Monkton, Devon.
Pugh's Porcelains, Layer de la Haye, Essex.
Pulham, L., Sproughton, Suffolk.
Pullen, D. and D., Devizes, Wilts.
Pullen, D. and D., Marlborough, Wilts.
Pullen Jeweller, Richard, Lincoln, Lincs.
Pullen, Mrs S.D.J., Guildford, Surrey.
Pulliblank, I., Cerne Abbas, Dorset.
Pulman, R.T., Swansea, West Glam., Wales.

Pulton, J.J.A. and D.A., London, SW6.
Pulton, J.J.A. and D.A., London, W8.
Punton, B. and G., Newcastle-upon-Tyne, Tyne and Wear.
Purcell, A., London, N7.
Purdon, Richard, Burford, Oxon.
Purple Shop, The, London, SW3.
Putnam, R. and M., Farnham, Surrey.
Pydar Antiques and Gallery, Truro, Cornwall.
Pye, Mrs N., Hull, N. Humbs.
Pyke - Fine British Watercolours, Beverley J., Totnes, Devon.
Pym, A.J., Tutbury, Staffs.
Pyms Gallery, London, SW1.
Pyne, D.J., St. Albans, Herts.
Pyramid, Brighton, Sussex East.
Pywell, Mrs P.C., Sleaford, Lincs.

Q

QS Antiques, Kilmarnock, Scotland.
Quadrant Antiques, Edinburgh, Scotland.
Quainton Allen, Mrs, Fakenham, Norfolk.
Quaker Lodge Antiques, Finedon, Northants.
Quaradeghini, C. and A., London, W2.
Quaradeghini, T., London, NW1.
Quaritch Ltd (Booksellers), Bernard, London, W1.
Quarter Jack Antiques, Sturminster Newton, Dorset.
Quatrefoil, Fordingbridge, Hants.
Quay Antiques, Burnham on Crouch, Essex.
Quay Antiques, Kingsbridge, Devon.
Quay Gallery Antiques Emporium, The, Exeter, Devon.
Quayles Emporium, Septimus , Hawkhurst, Kent.
Queen Adelaide Gallery, Kempston, Beds.
Queen Anne Gallery, Uppermill, Lancs.
Queen Anne House, Chesham, Bucks.
Queen of Hungary Antiques, Norwich, Norfolk.
Quentin, Paul, Manchester, Lancs.
Quest Antiques, London, W13.
Quest Antiques, Nantymoel, Mid. Glam., Wales.
Questor, Woburn, Beds.
Quiet Street Antiques, Bath, Avon.
Quigley, D., Oxted, Surrey.
Quill Antiques, Bletchingley, Surrey.
Quill Antiques, Deal, Kent.
Quilt Room, The, Dorking, Surrey.
Quilter, Michael, Amersham, Bucks.
Quinn, B., Cardiff, South Glam., Wales.
Quinn Galleries, Oundle, Northants.
Quinn, N.J., London, W4.
Quinn, T.P., Oundle, Northants.
Quinney's, Budleigh Salterton, Devon.
Quorn Pine and Decoratives, Quorn, Leics.

R

R.J.D. Fine Arts, Stroud, Glos.
R. and M. Antiques, Congleton, Cheshire.
Rabi Gallery Ltd, London, W1.
Rabilizirov, S., London, NW2.
Rabone, Mr and Mrs F., Weston, Staffs.
Rackham, D.M., J.S. and M.D., Rochester, Kent.
Rackham, Mrs P.M., Lichfield, Staffs.
Radcliffe, J., Hastings, Sussex East.
Radford Antiques, Alfriston, Sussex East.
Radford, Chris, Church Stretton, Shrops.
Radman, T. and B., Burford, Oxon.
Radio Vintage, Hythe, Kent.
Radnor House, Grampound, Cornwall.
Radosenska, Mrs E., Bath, Avon.
Rae Antiques, St. Helier, Jersey, C.I.
Rae Antiques, Lance and Marcus, St. Helier, Jersey, C.I.
Raeymaekers, F. and T., London, W1.
Rafferty, T., Ayr, Scotland.
Raffety Ltd, London, W8.
Raffles Antiques, London, NW8.
Railton, J., Chatton, Northumbs.
Raine Antiques, Harry, Consett, Durham.
Raine, P.W., Boroughbridge, Yorks. North.
Rait Village Antiques Centre, Rait, Scotland.
Rainsford, P.R., Bath, Avon.
Raleigh Antiques, Shrewsbury, Shrops.
Ramm Antiques, Haywards Heath, Sussex West.
Ramm, Mrs R.D., Haywards Heath, Sussex West.

DEALERS' INDEX

Ramm, R.E., Haywards Heath, Sussex West.
Ramsey Antiques, Alan , Darlington, Durham.
Randalls Antiques, London, SW13.
Randerson, J., London, SE10.
Randolph, Hadleigh, Suffolk.
Rankin, Alan, Edinburgh, Scotland.
Rankin Coin Co. Ltd, George, London, E2.
Ransome, B.G., Wisbech, Cambs.
Rapscallion Antiques Ltd, London, SW16.
Rare Carpets Gallery, London, SW10.
Rare Chairs, Tunbridge Wells, Kent.
Rashleigh, Brasted, Kent.
Rastro Antiques, Canterbury, Kent.
Ratcliff Ltd, G.T., Kelvedon, Essex.
Ratcliff Ltd. The Old Antique Shop, G.T., Kelvedon, Essex.
Ratcliffe, A.M., Beccles, Suffolk.
Ratcliffe, J. and R, Lincoln, Lincs.
Ratner, R., Dorking, Surrey.
Rau, H., London, SW14.
Raw, W.I., Keswick, Cumbria.
Rawes, C., Whitley Bay, Tyne and Wear.
Rawnsley, C.M., Otley, Yorks. West.
Rawson, Mrs A., Harrogate, Yorks. North.
Rawsthorne, Mrs L.B., Bishop's Stortford, Herts.
Raybould, S., Exeter, Devon.
Rayment Antiques, Derek, Barton, Cheshire.
Rayment, D.J. and K.M., Barton, Cheshire.
Rayment, D.M. and P.J., Petworth, Sussex West.
Rayner, Michael, Cheltenham, Glos.
Rea, C.J., Whitby, Yorks. North.
Read, A., Newark, Notts.
Read, John, Martlesham, Suffolk.
Read Antique Sciences, Mike, St. Ives, Cornwall.
Reading Emporium, Reading, Berks.
Real Macoy, Keighley, Yorks. West.
Reason, Mrs C., Limpsfield, Surrey.
Rebecca Antiques, Clitheroe, Lancs.
Recollect Studios, Sayers Common, Sussex West.
Recollections, Brighton, Sussex East.
Recollections, Cheadle Hulme, Cheshire.
Rectory Bungalow Workshop, Elton, Notts.
Red House Antiques, Bideford, Devon.
Red House Antiques, Yoxford, Suffolk.
Red Lion Market (Portobello Antiques Market), The, London, W11.
Red Shop, The, Wolverhampton, West Mids.
Redding, F.H., Southend-on-Sea, Essex.
Reddings Art and Antiques, Southend-on-Sea, Essex.
Redford, S. and R., Altrincham, Cheshire.
Redford, William, London, W1.
Redman, J., Much Wenlock, Shrops.
Redmile, J.W., Grantham, Lincs.
Redmile Antiques, William, Grantham, Lincs.
Reece Gallery, The Gordon, Knaresborough, Yorks. North.
Reed, Anthony, Bath, Avon.
Rees, T.G., Bristol, Avon.
Reeve, James, Warwick, Warks.
Reeve, Simon, Wisbech, Cambs.
Reeves, Paul, London, W8.
Reeves, R.J. and S.E., Cullompton, Devon.
Reeves Bookseller Ltd, William, London, SW16.
Reference Works, Swanage, Dorset.
Reflections, Knaresborough, Yorks. North.
Regal Antiques, Westerham, Kent.
Regency House Antiques, Whitchurch, Hants.
Regent Antiques, London, NW1.
Regent Antiques, Painswick, Glos.
Regent House, Northampton, Northants.
Regent House Antiques, New Mills, Derbys.
Regent House Antiques, Newtown, Cheshire.
Reid and Lefevre Ltd, Alex, London, W1.
Reid, J.C. and D.C., Edinburgh, Scotland.
Reily-Collins, E.M. and S.A., Dorchester-on-Thames, Oxon.
Reigate Galleries Ltd, Reigate, Surrey.
Reindeer Antiques Ltd, Potterspury, Northants.
Reindeer Antiques (Reindeer International Ltd.), London, W8.
Relcy Antiques, London, SE10.
Relf Antiques, Ian, Tunbridge Wells, Kent.
Relic Antiques at Brillscote Farm, Malmesbury, Wilts.
Relic Antiques at Camden Passage, London, N1.
Relic Antiques Trade Warehouse, London, NW1.

Relics, Ilfracombe, Devon.
Relics, Ross-on-Wye, Herefs. & Worcs.
Relics, Witney, Oxon.
Relics Antiques, Southampton, Hants.
Relics - Pine Furniture, Bristol, Avon.
Remington, Reg and Philip, London, WC2.
Renaissance, Solihull, West Mids.
Renaissance Antiques, Cowbridge, South Glam., Wales.
Renaissance Antiques, Tynemouth, Tyne and Wear.
Rendall Antiques, Lesley, London, SW1.
Rendezvous Gallery, The, Aberdeen, Scotland.
Rendlesham Antiques Ltd, London, SW10.
Rennie, Paul and Karen, Folkestone, Kent.
Repetto-Wright, R., Aslockton, Notts.
Resner, S. and G.R., Brighton, Sussex East.
Resners', Brighton, Sussex East.
Restall Brown and Clennell Ltd, Cosgrove, Northants.
Retro Products, Lye, West Mids.
Retrospect Antiques, Combe Martin, Devon.
Reubens, London, SE23.
Reubens, R.E., London, SE23.
Revell Antiques, Sheila, Hartley Wintney, Hants.
Rêverie, London, SW7.
Revival, Caenarfon, Gwynedd, Wales.
Revival Beds, Haydon Bridge, Northumbs.
Revival Pine Stripping, Ormskirk, Lancs.
Rex Antiques, London, W11.
Reynold, A., London, WC2.
Reynolds, C.H., Pickering, Yorks. North.
Reynolds, Mr, Aberdeen, Scotland.
Reynolds, Mrs B.A.S., Easingwold, Yorks. North.
Reynolds, Mrs C., Tonge, Leics.
Rezai Persian Carpets, A., London, W11.
Rhino Antiques, Henley-on-Thames, Oxon.
Rhudle Mill, Kilmichael Glassary, Scotland.
Rhodes Antiques, Colin, Yealmpton, Devon.
Rhodes, Isobel, Hadleigh, Suffolk.
Rhodes, Mrs J., London, SW6.
Rice, R.J., Great Malvern, Herefs. and Worcs.
Rich Designs, Stratford-upon-Avon, Warks.
Rich, S., London, SW1.
Richards, Diana, Penzance, Cornwall.
Richards and Sons, David, London, W1.
Richards and Son Antiques, G.E., Hereford, Herefs. & Worcs.
Richards, J., London, SW13.
Richards, L., London, W11.
Richards, M., H. and E., London, W1.
Richards, P.H., Bournemouth, Dorset.
Richards, S., Rhosneigr, Gwynedd, Wales.
Richardson Antiques, Nantwich, Cheshire.
Richardson, C., London, SW6.
Richardson Antiques, D., Keighley, Yorks. West.
Richardson, J., Collingham, Notts.
Richardson and Kailas Icons, London, SW6.
Richardson Antiques, Keith, Ilkley, Yorks. West.
Richardson, S. and E., Blewbury, Oxon.
Richardson, Terry, Nantwich, Cheshire.
Richardson, W.L. and M.G., Guisborough, Cleveland.
Riches, Pulloxhill, Beds.
Riches, L., Hythe, Kent.
Richmond Galleries, Chester, Cheshire.
Richmond Gallery, The, London, W1.
Richmond Traders, Richmond, Surrey.
Rickett & Co. Antiques, Shepperton, Surrey.
Ridgewell Crafts and Antiques, Ridgewell, Essex.
Ridings, I., Holmfirth, Yorks. West.
Ridler, MBHI, P.W., Pershore, Herefs. and Worcs.
Ridout, S.J., Hindhead, Surrey.
Ridsdill, Eric W. , Modbury, Devon.
Ridsdill, Marjorie, Modbury, Devon.
Ries, M.A. and Mrs I.T.H., Boston Spa, Yorks. West.
Ries, N.C., Harrogate, Yorks. North.
Rievaulx Books, Helmsley, Yorks. North.
Right Angle, Brackley, Northants.
Rignault, Mrs F., Hythe, Kent.
Riley, J.M., Chichester, Sussex West.
Riley, K., Wilmslow, Cheshire.
Riley, P. and S., Broadway, Herefs. and Worcs.
Riman Antiques, Philip, Harbury, Warks.
Rimes, R., Wansford, Cambs.
Rimington, D. and G.G., Margate, Kent.
Ringles Cross Antiques, Uckfield, Sussex East.

DEALERS' INDEX

Ripley Antiques, Ripley, Surrey.
Rippingale, S. and R., London, SW6.
Rippon Bookshop, Harrogate, Yorks. North.
Risby Barn, The, Risby, Suffolk.
Risky Business, London, NW8.
Ritchie, J., Weymouth, Dorset.
Ritchie, S., Kendal, Cumbria.
Ritchie, V., Kendal, Cumbria.
Rivers, R. A., Crickhowell, Powys, Wales.
Riverside Antiques, Bideford, Devon.
Riverside Antiques, Hungerford, Berks.
Riverside Gallery and Tearooms, Arundel, Sussex West.
Rivett Antiques and Bygones, Sue, Fakenham, Norfolk.
Rivett, Mrs S., Fakenham, Norfolk.
Rix, H., London, SW11.
Rixon, P., Shenton, Leics.
Roadside Antiques, Greystoke, Cumbria.
Roberts Antiques, Ann, Ampthill, Beds.
Roberts, Angela and Amy, Macclesfield, Cheshire.
Roberts, C., Bath, Avon.
Roberts, D., Nantwich, Cheshire.
Roberts Fine Antique Clocks, Music Boxes, Barometers, Derek, Tonbridge, Kent.
Roberts, G., Bolton, Lancs.
Roberts, I.W. and I.E., Bolton, Lancs.
Roberts Bookshop, John, Bristol, Avon.
Roberts, J. and B., Market Bosworth, Leics.
Roberts, J.T., Bristol, Avon.
Roberts, Martyn, Bristol, Avon.
Roberts Antiques, Peter, Moreton-in-Marsh, Glos.
Roberts, Mrs R., Blaenau Ffestiniog, Gwynedd, Wales.
Roberts, Mr and Mrs S.A., Beaulieu, Hants.
Roberts, T., Bletchingley, Surrey.
Roberts, T.J., Uppingham, Leics.
Robertson, A.F., Lingfield, Surrey.
Robertson and Cox Antiques, Perth, Scotland.
Robertson, D.W., Newcastle-upon-Tyne, Tyne and Wear.
Robertson, Ian A., Alnwick, Northumbs.
Robertson, Mrs I.J., Edinburgh, Scotland.
Robertson, J., Reigate, Surrey.
Robertson Antiques, Leon, Penryn, Cornwall.
Robertson, P.W., Hinckley, Leics.
Robinson, A., Bishops Waltham, Hants.
Robinson, Mrs A., Monyash, Derbys.
Robinson, C.A., Aberford, Yorks. West.
Robinson, D.A., London, NW8.
Robinson, D. and M., Chipping Norton, Oxon.
Robinson, E.J.H., Croydon, Surrey.
Robinson, F., Colwyn Bay, Clwyd, Wales.
Robinson, Mrs G., Ringwood, Hants.
Robinson, G., London, NW8.
Robinson, Jonathan, London, W1.
Robinson Antiques, John, Wigan, Lancs.
Robinson Interiors and Antiques, Glen, Ringwood, Hants.
Robinson, L., Sowerby Bridge, Yorks. West.
Robinson, M., Glasgow, Scotland.
Robinson, M.L.G., Welshpool, Powys, Wales.
Robinson, Peter, Heacham, Norfolk.
Robinson, P.H., Ash, Kent.
Robinson, R. and N., Welshpool, Powys, Wales.
Robinson, Mrs S., Brighton, Sussex East.
Robinson, Susie, Glasgow, Scotland.
Robinson, T.E., Bath, Avon.
Robinson's Bookshop Ltd, Brighton, Sussex East.
Robson Antiques, Walford, Herefs. & Worcs.
Robson, J., Walford, Herefs. and Worcs.
Roby Antiques, John, Wigan, Lancs.
Rochford, Michael, Hertford, Herts.
Rock Angus Antiques, Portaferry, Co. Down, N. Ireland.
Rocke, N., Sandwich, Kent.
Rocking Chair Antiques, The, Warrington, Cheshire.
Rocking Horse Pine, Torquay, Devon.
Rococo Antiques, Worthing, Sussex West.
Rococo Antiques and Interiors, Weedon, Northants.
Rodber, J., Bridport, Dorset.
Roderic Antiques, Richmond, Surrey.
Roderick Antique Clocks, London, W8.
Rodgers, Arthur and Ann, Ruddington, Notts.
Rodney Arthur Classics, Brighton, Sussex East.
Roe Antiques, John, Thrapston, Northants.
Roe, Mr and Mrs J., Thrapston, Northants.
Roe, P.S., London, SW1.

Roger, J., London, W8.
Roger (Antiques) Ltd, J., London, W8.
Roger's Antiques Gallery, London, W11.
Rogers Antiques and Rogers Antique Interiors, Cheam, Surrey.
Rogers Oriental Rugs, Clive, Brighton, Sussex East.
Rogers, Doreen, Hampton Hill, Middx.
Rogers, D. and G., Shapwick, Somerset.
Rogers de Rin, London, SW3.
Rogers, Eva, Kempston, Beds.
Rogers, M. and C., Cheam, Surrey.
Rogers, N.G., Radlett, Herts.
Rogers Turner Books Ltd, London, SE10.
Rogerson, P.R., Bridlington, N. Humbs.
Rogerson, T.H. and B.A., Whitegate, Cheshire.
Roland-Price, H.A. and J., Bradford-on-Avon, Wilts.
Rolleston, B.T.W., London, W8.
Romain and Sons, A.J., Wilton, Wilts.
Romantiques, Skegness, Lincs.
Romsey Medal and Collectors Centre, Romsey, Hants.
Roofe Antiques, Mary, Winchester, Hants.
Roofe, R. and M., Winchester, Hants.
Rooke, G. and A. Dyson, Tunbridge Wells, Kent.
Rookery Farm Antiques, London, N1.
Ropers Hill Antiques, Staunton Harold, Leics.
Rose Antiques, Ashbourne, Derbys.
Rose Cottage Antiques, Cambridge, Cambs.
Rose, D.H. and Mrs C., Carlton-on-Trent, Notts.
Rose Fine Art and Antiques, Ripon, Yorks. North.
Rose Ltd, Geoffrey, London, SW1.
Rose Antiques Centre, Marilyn, Newport, I. of Wight.
Rose - Source of the Unusual, Michael, London, W1.
Rose Mount, Birkenhead, Merseyside.
Rose, P.A., Cooden, Sussex East.
Rose FBHI, R.E., London, SE9.
Rose and Co, R.L., Glasgow, Scotland.
Rose, Mr and Mrs S., Ripon, Yorks. North.
Roseby, H., M. and J., Bladon, Oxon.
Rosemary Antiques and Paper Moon Books, Stow-on-the-Wold, Glos.
Rosemary and Time, Thame, Oxon.
Rosenberg, C., Heswall, Merseyside.
Rosenberg, H., London, N1.
Rosenthal Ltd, A., Oxford, Oxon.
Rosina's, Falmouth, Cornwall.
Ross, A.P., Coventry, West Mids.
Ross, B., Wadhurst, Sussex East.
Ross, Mrs C., Bushmills, Co. Antrim, N. Ireland.
Ross, D. and T., Wooler, Northumbs.
Ross Antiques and Decoration, Jane, Sevenoaks, Kent.
Ross Antiques, Marcus, London, N1.
Ross Old Book and Print Shop, Ross-on-Wye, Herefs. & Worcs.
Ross, T.C.A. and D.A.A., London, SW1.
Rosson, J., London, EC1.
Rotchell, P., Godalming, Surrey.
Rota Ltd, Bertram, London, WC2.
Rote, R. and D., London, N1.
Rothera, D., London, N1.
Rothman, London, SW1.
Rothman, J.A.F. and S.P.J., London, SW1.
Rothwell, Mrs C., Dulverton, Somerset.
Rothwell, Mrs C., Taunton, Somerset.
Rothwell, D., Eastbourne, Sussex East.
Rothwell and Dunworth, Dulverton, Somerset.
Rothwell and Dunworth, Taunton, Somerset.
Round Pond, The, Littlehampton, Sussex West.
Round, S., Brighton, Sussex East.
Rout, Mrs D., London, W13.
Rowan Antiques, Richmond, Surrey.
Rowberry, Patricia, Lincoln, Lincs.
Rowe, J., Great Bookham, Surrey.
Rowe, J.H. and J., London, SW6.
Rowland, Michael, Stow-on-the-Wold, Glos.
Rowlands, Mrs M., London, SW14.
Rowlay, J., Ripon, Yorks. North.
Rowles, C. and J., Cardiff, South Glam., Wales.
Rowlett, A.H., Lincoln, Lincs.
Rowlett, Mrs R.B., Brasted, Kent.
Rowletts of Lincoln, Lincoln, Lincs.
Rowley, J., Stoke-on-Trent, Staffs.
Roy, Patsy, London, SW19.

DEALERS' INDEX

Royal Exchange Art Gallery, London, EC3.
Royal Exchange Shopping Centre, Manchester, Lancs.
Royal Mile Curios, Edinburgh, Scotland.
Royal Victoria Arcade, Ryde, I. of Wight.
Royall Antiques, E. and C., Medbourne, Leics.
Royall Antiques, E. and C., Uppingham, Leics.
Royle, Mrs M., Beaconsfield, Bucks.
Royston Antiques, Royston, Herts.
Rubenstein Fine Art, Barbara, Cranleigh, Surrey.
Rubenstein, S.G., Manchester, Lancs.
Rubin, A. and L.J., London, W1.
Rudge Antics, Tetbury, Glos.
Rudge, T. and P., Tetbury, Glos.
Ruffell, J., Portsmouth, Hants.
Rugeley Antique Centre, Brereton, Staffs.
Ruglen, L., Balfron, Scotland.
Ruglen, L., Buchlyvie, Scotland.
Rumble, R.J. and V., Highbridge, Somerset.
Rumble Antiques, Simon and Penny, Chittering, Cambs.
Rumford, L., Worcester, Herefs. and Worcs.
Rundle, J., Stickford, Lincs.
Rupert's, London, W13.
Rush, R.D., London, W1.
Ruskin Antiques, Stow-on-the-Wold, Glos.
Russell, C., London, W1.
Russell and Son Antiques, Frank, Glasgow, Scotland.
Russell, Leonard, Newhaven, Sussex East.
Russell, M. and J., Yazor, Herefs. & Worcs.
Russell Antiques, Patricia, Tunbridge Wells, Kent.
Russell, R., Witney, Oxon.
Russell Rare Books, London, W1.
Rust Antiques, Benjamin, Cromer, Norfolk.
Rust, Mr and Mrs R.S., Kesgrave, Suffolk.
Rutherford and Son, J.T., Sandgate, Kent.
Rutland Antiques, Brighton, Sussex East.
Rutland Gallery, London, W1.
Rutter, Jon and Kate, Walsall, West Mids.
Ruttleich, P.A., Cirencester, Glos.
Ryan, Mrs J., Chertsey, Surrey.
Ryan-Wood Antiques, Liverpool, Merseyside.
Ryder, Georgina, Corfe Castle, Dorset.
Rye Antiques, Rye, Sussex East.
Ryland, B.R., Henley-on-Thames, Oxon.

S

S.A.G. Art Galleries, London, SW18.
S. and H. Antiques, London, NW8.
S.O.S. Militaria, Stourbridge, West Mids.
SPCK Bookshops, Winchester, Hants.
S.R. Furnishing and Antiques, Birmingham, West Mids.
S.W. Antiques, Pershore, Herefs. & Worcs.
Saalmans, J.A. and K.M., Grasmere, Cumbria.
Sabin Galleries Ltd, London, W8.
Sabin Ltd, Frank T., London, W1.
Sabin, John, London, W1.
Sabin, S.F, E.P. and P.G., London, W8.
Sabine Antiques, Stock, Essex.
Sabine, C.E., Stock, Essex.
Sabine, T.H., Ilminster, Somerset.
Saddle Room Antiques, The, Cookstown, Co. Tyrone, N. Ireland.
Sadler, Fenela, South Molton, Devon.
Sadler-Chapman, M., Clare, Suffolk.
Saffell, Michael and Jo, Bath, Avon.
Sagar, A.M., Harrogate, Yorks. North.
Sage Antiques and Interiors, Ripley, Surrey.
Sage, H. and C., Ripley, Surrey.
Sainsbury, Barry M., Wincanton, Somerset.
Sainsbury, Jonathan, Bournemouth, Dorset.
Salisbury, J. and J.C., Edenfield, Lancs.
Sainsbury in association with Charles Fox, Jonathan L.F., Bournemouth, Dorset.
Sainsbury, M., Bath, Avon.
Sainsbury & Mason, London, SW1.
Sainsburys of Bournemouth Ltd, Bournemouth, Dorset.
Saint Nicholas Galleries (Antiques)Ltd, Carlisle, Cumbria.
Saint Nicholas Galleries Ltd. (Antiques and Jewellery), Carlisle, Cumbria.
St. Albans Antique Market, St. Albans, Herts.
St. Andrews Fine Art, St. Andrews, Scotland.
St. Andrew's Market, Bournemouth, Dorset.

St. Breock Gallery, Stow-on-the-Wold, Glos.
St. Breock Gallery, Wadebridge, Cornwall.
St. Clair, D.V. and C.A., Upper Largo, Scotland.
St. George's Antiques, Perranporth, Cornwall.
St. George's Antiques, Stamford, Lincs.
St. Georges Antiques, Worcester, Herefs. & Worcs.
Saint George's Gallery, London, SW1.
St. Helens Antiques, St. Helens, I. of Wight.
St. Helier Galleries Ltd, St. Helier, Jersey, C.I.
St. James Antiques, Little Malvern, Herefs. & Worcs.
St. James Antiques, Manchester, Lancs.
St. James's Art Group, The, London, SW1.
St. James House Antiques, Boroughbridge, Yorks. North.
St. James's Gallery Ltd, St. Peter Port, Guernsey, C.I.
St. John Antiques, York, Yorks. North.
St. John Street Gallery, Salisbury, Wilts.
St. Leonards Antiques, Ludlow, Shrops.
St. Martin's Antiques and Craft Centre, Stamford, Lincs.
St Mary's Antique Centre, Norwich, Norfolk.
St. Mary's Galleries, Stamford, Lincs.
St. Michael at Plea Antiques Centre, Norwich, Norfolk.
St. Ouen Antiques, Puckeridge, Herts.
St. Pancras Antiques, Chichester, Sussex West.
St . Peters Art Gallery, Chester, Cheshire.
St. Peters Organ Works, London, E2.
Sakhai, E., London, W1.
Salmagundi, Maidstone, Kent.
Salisbury, R.D.N., M.E. and J.W., Sidmouth, Devon.
Salmon, L., Kingsley, Staffs.
Salt Antiques, N.P. and A., Sheffield, Yorks. South.
Salter Antiques, F.D., Clare, Suffolk.
Salter Antiques, Nicholas, Chingford, Essex.
Salter, S., London, E4.
Saltgate Antiques, Beccles, Suffolk.
Samarkand Galleries, Stow-on-the-Wold, Glos.
Sambourne House Antiques, Minety, Wilts.
Samlesbury Hall, Samlesbury, Lancs.
Samlesbury Hall Trust,, Samlesbury, Lancs.
Samne, H., London, WC2.
Samovar Antiques, Hythe, Kent.
Sampson, Anthony, Moreton-in-Marsh, Glos.
Sampson Antiques Ltd, Alistair, London, SW3.
Sampson, A.H., London, SW3.
Samuel, M., Knighton, Powys, Wales.
Samuel, W.J., Newport, Gwent, Wales.
Samuels Spencers Antiques and Decorative Arts Emporium, Winchester, Hants.
San Domenico Stringed Instruments, Cardiff, South Glam., Wales.
San Fairy Ann, London, E14.
Sanaiy Carpets, London, SW1.
Sanaiy, H., London, SW1.
Sandberg Antiques, Patrick, London, W8.
Sandberg, P.C.F., London, W8.
Sandell, M.J., Carmarthen, Dyfed, Wales.
Sanders of Oxford Ltd, Oxford, Oxon.
Sanders and Sons, Robin, London, SW6.
Sanders Penzance Gallery and Antiques, Tony, Penzance, Cornwall.
Sanderson, R.J., Leeds, Yorks. West.
Sandgate Antiques Centre, Sandgate, Kent.
Sandhill Barn Antiques (Pine and Country), Washington, Sussex West.
Sandringham Antiques, Hull, N. Humbs.
Sands, J. and M.M., Stow-on-the-Wold, Glos.
Sands, R., London, NW3.
Sandy's Antiques, Bournemouth, Dorset.
Sangster Antiques, A., Cruden Bay, Scotland.
Sangster, A.H., Cruden Bay, Scotland.
Sansom, K.W., Leicester, Leics.
Santos, A.V., London, W8.
Saracen's Lantern, The, Canterbury, Kent.
Sargeant, A.W. and K.M., Stansted, Essex.
Sargeant, Denys, Westerham, Kent.
Sarsby and Michael Pickering Fine Art, Roger, Newark, Notts.
Sarti Antiques Ltd, G., London, W11.
Sarti Gallery Ltd, London, SW1.
Satchell, S., Kendal, Cumbria.
Sattin Ltd, Gerald, London, SW1.
Sattin, G. and M., London, SW1.
Saumarez Smith, J., London, W1.

DEALERS' INDEX

Saunders Antiques, Charles, London, SW3.
Saunders, D. T. and P., Leominster, Herefs. and Worcs.
Saunders, E.A. and J.M., Weedon, Northants.
Saunders, E.S. and N., Weedon, Northants.
Saunders, J. and L., Dover, Kent.
Saunders, L. and S., Honiton, Devon.
Saunders, N., Towcester, Northants.
Saunders, R., Weybridge, Surrey.
Saunders, R.A., Bristol, Avon.
Saunderson Antiques, Elaine, Dorking, Surrey.
Saunderson, Mrs E.C., Dorking, Surrey.
Sautter Pine Furniture, Mary, Lewes, Sussex East.
Sautter, M. and M., Lewes, Sussex East.
Savage, B., Wolverhampton, West Mids.
Savage, M.J., Northampton, Northants.
Savage Antiques, Sam, Ticknall, Derbys.
Savage and Son, R.S.J., Northampton, Northants.
Savage, S. and M., Ticknall, Derbys.
Savile, Hon. C.A. and Mrs., London, SW3.
Savill, P. M., Nantwich, Cheshire.
Saville Row Gallery, The, Bath, Avon.
Sawers, Robert G., London, W1.
Saxton House Gallery, Chipping Campden, Glos.
Sayers, C. and D., Tetbury, Glos.
Saywell, I.H. and H.J., Oxford, Oxon.
Saywell Ltd. (The Oxford Stamp Shop), A.J., Oxford, Oxon.
Scales, R. and S., London, SE1.
Scallywag, Beckenham, Kent.
Scallywag, London, SW9.
Scalpay Securities Ltd,, Colchester, Essex.
Scantlebury, H. and M., Hatfield Heath, Essex.
Scaramanga Antiques, Anthony, Witney, Oxon.
Scarisbrick and Bate Ltd, London, W1.
Scarthingwell Arcades, Scarthingwell, Yorks. North.
Scarthoe Antiques, Scarthoe, S. Humbs.
Scattergood, C. and R., Burton-on-Trent, Staffs.
Schanzer, R.P., London, NW1.
Schell, Christine, London, SW3.
Schlesinger, A.R., Leicester, Leics.
Schloss, E., Edgware, Middx.
Schofield, G.M., St. Leonards-on-Sea, Sussex East.
Schofield, H. and Mrs A., Brighton, Sussex East.
Schofield, R.M., Huddersfield, Yorks. West.
Scholz, K.V., Eastbourne, Sussex East.
School House Antiques, Chipping Campden, Glos.
School House Antiques, Welshpool, Powys, Wales.
Schotten, M., Burford, Oxon.
Schotten Antiques, Manfred, Burford, Oxon.
Schrager, H.J. and G.R., London, W11.
Schredds of Portobello, London, W11.
Schryver Antiques Ltd, Michael, Dorking, Surrey.
Schuster, Thomas E., London, W1.
Schuster Gallery, The, London, W1.
Schwartz, N., London, W5.
Schwier, D.W., Wimborne Minster, Dorset.
Scientific Anglian (Bookshop), The, Norwich, Norfolk.
Scobie, W.D.L., Wallasey, Merseyside.
Scope Antiques, London, NW6.
Scott Antiques, Bath, Avon.
Scott, A.F.D., Selkirk, Scotland.
Scott House Antiques, West Malling, Kent.
Scott, Mrs J., Hodnet, Shrops.
Scott, James, Edinburgh, Scotland.
Scott, J.D., West Harptree, Avon.
Scott, P., Northampton, Northants.
Scott Antiques, Richard, Holt, Norfolk.
Scott, R.G., Margate, Kent.
Scott and Varey, Halifax, Yorks. West.
Scott, W.B., Halifax, Yorks. West.
Scott, Y., Berwick-on-Tweed, Northumbs.
Scott-Cooper Ltd, Cheltenham, Glos.
Scott-Mayfield, C.J., Leominster, Herefs. and Worcs.
Scott-Masson, Anne-Marie, Plymouth, Devon.
Scott-Moody, Christopher, Bath, Avon.
Scottish Gallery, The, Edinburgh, Scotland.
Scratchley, K.S., Sidmouth, Devon.
Scripophily Shop, The, London, W1.
Scudders Emporium, Bideford, Devon.
Scull, T. and S.E., Bristol, Avon.
Scurlock, A.K., Swansea, West Glam., Wales.
Scurlock, Kim, Swansea, West Glam., Wales.
Seabrook Antiques Ltd, Long Melford, Suffolk.

Seaby Ltd, B.A., London, W1.
Seaford's "Barn Collectors' Market" and Studio Bookshop, Seaford, Sussex East.
Seager, A.A., London, W8.
Seager Antiques Ltd, Arthur, London, W8.
Seago, London, SW1.
Seago, A.E., Cromer, Norfolk.
Seago, D.C., Cromer, Norfolk.
Seago, T.P. and L.G., London, SW1.
Seal, D., Keighley, Yorks. West.
Sealby, K. and R., Greystoke, Cumbria.
Seale Antiques, Jeremy, London, SW13.
Seals, B., Leeds, Yorks. West.
Seaman, R. and M., Axbridge, Somerset.
Searle and Co Ltd, London, EC3.
Searle, E.A., Cambridge, Cambs.
Sears, M.D., London, NW3.
Seaview Antiques, Horncastle, Lincs.
Sebley, Oswald, Norwich, Norfolk.
Seccombe, Mrs J., Charlecote, Warks.
Second Childhood, Huddersfield, Yorks. West.
Second Hand Rose, Hindhead, Surrey.
Second Sight, Carlisle, Cumbria.
Second Thoughts, Wolverhampton, West Mids.
Second Time Around, Hemswell Cliff, Lincs.
Second Time Around, Newark, Notts.
Second Time Around Antiques, Wallingford, Oxon.
Secondhand Alley, Shefford, Beds.
Secondhand and Rare Books, Manchester, Lancs.
Secondhand Rose, Plymouth, Devon.
Sedbergh Antiques and Collectables, Sedbergh, Cumbria.
Seddon, A.E. and M., Manchester, Lancs.
Sedman Antiques, Bridlington, N. Humbs.
Sedman, R.H.S. and M.A., Bridlington, N. Humbs.
Select Antiques Gallery Ltd, London, W8.
Selective Eye Gallery, The, St. Helier, Jersey, C.I.
Seligmann, M. and D., London, W8.
Sellers, M., Harrogate, Yorks. North.
Sellors, Peter, Warwick, Warks.
Selwoods, Taunton, Somerset.
Semke, B.W., Warminster, Wilts.
Semus Crafting Antiques, Peter, Portslade, Sussex West.
Senior, Mark, London, SW3.
Sensation Ltd, London, SW6.
Serendipity, Deal, Kent.
Serendipity, Ledbury, Herefs. & Worcs.
Serendipity Antiques, Arundel, Sussex West.
Serle (Antiques and Restoration), Mark A., Lechlade, Glos.
Sessacar, B., London, SE10.
Seventh Heaven, Chirk, Clwyd, Wales.
Severn, D., Truro, Cornwall.
Seville, R., Bristol, Avon.
Sewell (Antiques) Ltd, Jean, London, W8.
Sewell, R. and J., London, W8.
Sexton Antiques, Kenneth, Honiton, Devon.
Sextons, Kentisbeare, Devon.
Seyfried Antiques, David, London, SW6.
Seymour, B.A., Smethwick, West Mids.
Seymour, R.D., Coventry, West Mids.
Shabby Tiger Antiques, Stroud, Glos.
Shackleton, Daniel, Edinburgh, Scotland.
Shackleton, Mrs E.A., Snainton, Yorks. North.
Shaikh and Son (Oriental Rugs) Ltd, London, W1.
Shaikh, M., London, W1.
Shambles, The, Ashburton, Devon.
Shambles Antiques , Dorchester-on-Thames, Oxon.
Shamsa, Mr, Hemswell Cliff, Lincs.
Shamsa, M., London, SW15.
Shand, L., London, W8.
Shanklin Gallery, The, Shanklin , I. of Wight.
Shanks, Mark, Berkhamsted, Herts.
Shanly, Sally, Henley-on-Thames, Oxon.
Shapero Rare Books, Bernard T., London, W11.
Sharbooks, Upham, Hants.
Share, M., Dorking, Surrey.
Sharman, Mrs H.D., Upham, Hants.
Sharman, L.R., Clacton-on-Sea, Essex.
Shardlow Antiques Warehouse, Shardlow, Derbys.
Sharp, A. and A., Grantham, Lincs.
Sharp, Heather, St. Albans, Herts.
Sharp Antiques, Ian, Tynemouth, Tyne and Wear.
Sharrington Antiques, Sharrington, Norfolk.

DEALERS' INDEX

Shave, K.J., Cheltenham, Glos.
Shaw Antiques, Spilsby, Lincs.
Shaw Bros, Harrogate, Yorks. North.
Shaw, Charles, Knaresborough, Yorks. North.
Shaw, D., Congleton, Cheshire.
Shaw and Co, Jack, Ilkley, Yorks. West.
Shaw Antiques Ltd, John, Rotherham, Yorks. South.
Shaw, J. and C., Harrogate, Yorks. North.
Shaw, Mrs J.M, Spilsby, Lincs.
Shaw, J.M., Walsall, West Mids.
Shaw, K., Botley, Hants.
Shaw Antiques, Laurence, Horncastle, Lincs.
Shaw Antiques, Nona, Ditchling, Sussex East.
Shaw, R. and G., St. Annes-on-Sea, Lancs.
Shaw-Cooper, Susan, Ledbury, Herefs. & Worcs.
Shawforth Antiques, Shawforth, Lancs.
Sheen Gallery, London, SW14.
Sheffield Pine Centre (inc. Canterbury Place Antiques), Sheffield, Yorks. South.
Shell, Mrs L., Alnwick, Northumbs.
Shelley, A. and J., Lewes, Sussex East.
Shelron Collectors Shop, Towcester, Northants.
Shelton Arts, Brighton, Sussex East.
Shenton, Rita, Twickenham, Middx.
Shepherd, G., F. and J., Wittersham, Kent.
Shepherd, J., St. Helier, Jersey, C.I.
Shepherd Antiques, Peter, Hurst, Berks.
Shepherd's Antiques, St. Helier, Jersey, C.I.
Sheppard and Cooper Ltd, London, W1.
Sheppard, Mrs J., Balderton, Notts.
Sheppard, J., Christchurch, Dorset.
Sheppard, J. and B., Mansfield, Notts.
Sheppard, J.E., Thaxted, Essex.
Sheppard, P., Baldock, Herts.
Sheppard, S.J. and M.E., Lechlade, Glos.
Sheppards Antiques, Mansfield, Notts.
Sheppee, William, London, SW14.
Sheraton House, Torquay, Devon.
Sherborne Antique Centre, Sherborne, Dorset.
Shere Antique Centre, Shere, Surrey.
Sheridan's Bookshop Hampton, Ian, Hampton, Middx.
Sherlock Antiques, George, London, SW6.
Sherman, M., Great Wakering, Essex.
Sherman, M., Leigh-on-Sea, Essex.
Sherman and Waterman Associates Ltd, , London, WC2.
Sherston-Baker, R., Canterbury, Kent.
Sherwood Antiques Ltd, D.W., Rushden, Northants.
Shickell Antiques, Bournemouth, Dorset.
Shickell Books, Bournemouth, Dorset.
Shickell, W.J., Bournemouth, Dorset.
Shield and Allen Ltd, London, SW6.
Shield Antiques, Robin, Burford, Oxon.
Shillingford, B.C., Maidstone, Kent.
Shindler, A., Chester, Cheshire.
Shiners Architectural Reclamation, Newcastle-upon-Tyne, Tyne and Wear.
Ship Street Galleries, Brecon, Powys, Wales.
Shippey's of Boscombe, Bournemouth, Dorset.
Shire Antiques, Newby Bridge, Cumbria.
Shire Antiques, Rushden, Northants.
Shire, B. and Mrs J., Newby Bridge, Cumbria.
Shooter, J., Stickney, Lincs.
Shop of the Yellow Frog, Brighton, Sussex East.
Shorey, R.A., Weymouth, Dorset.
Shorrick, H. and Mrs S., Gosforth, Tyne and Wear.
Short, M. and K., Deal, Kent.
Short, R.J.B., Painswick, Glos.
Shortmead Antiques, Biggleswade, Beds.
Shotter, Collectors Centre, Keith, Shanklin, I. of Wight.
Shotton Antiquarian Books and Prints, J., Durham, Durham.
Showcase, Reigate, Surrey.
Shrewsbury Antique Centre, Shrewsbury, Shrops.
Shrewsbury Antique Market, Shrewsbury, Shrops.
Shrubsole, C.J., London, WC1.
Shrubsole Ltd, S.J., London, WC1.
Shuster, S., London, NW8.
Shuttleworth, L.R., Scarborough, Yorks. North.
Shuttleworths, Scarborough, Yorks. North.
Sibley (Fine Furniture), Nicholas, Whitchurch-on-Thames, Oxon.
Siden, G.T., London, NW6.

Sidmouth Antique Market, Sidmouth, Devon.
Sigma Antiques and Fine Art, Ripon, Yorks. North.
Silver, A., London, NW8.
Silver Belle, London, NW8.
Silver Mouse Trap, The, London, WC2.
Silver Thimble, The, Kendal, Cumbria.
Silver Time, Brecon, Powys, Wales.
Silverman, Michael, London, SE3.
Silverston, P. and M., Llangollen, Clwyd, Wales.
Silverstone, J., Weybridge, Surrey.
Silverton Antiques, King's Lynn, Norfolk.
Silvester, S., Burton-on-Trent, Staffs.
Silvesters, Wingham , Kent.
Sim, Michael, Chislehurst, Kent.
Sim Antiques, Roy, Blairgowrie, Scotland.
Simcox, J., Whitchurch, Shrops.
Simmonds, J. and H., Great Malvern, Herefs. and Worcs.
Simmonds, R., Cirencester, Glos.
Simmonds, R.M., Southampton, Hants.
Simmons Antiques, Christine, Barnsley, Yorks. South.
Simmons, J.C., Barnsley, Yorks. South.
Simmons, S.L., Brighton, Sussex East.
Simon, Ilkley, Yorks. West.
Simon Antiques, Grimsby, S. Humbs.
Simon Fine Art Ltd, Julian, London, SW1.
Simon, M., Nantwich, Cheshire.
Simpkin, S., Halesworth, Suffolk.
Simpkin, S., Orford, Suffolk.
Simply Capital, London, E18.
Simpson, I., Bewdley, Herefs. and Worcs.
Simpson, I., Halesowen, West Mids.
Simpson, Marianne, Fochabers, Scotland.
Simpson Ltd, Michael, London, W1.
Simpson, M.R., Fochabers, Scotland.
Simpson, Oswald, Long Melford, Suffolk.
Simpson and Sons Jewellers (Oldham)Ltd, H.C., Oldham, Lancs.
Simpsons - Bespoke Carvings, London, W14.
Sims, Mr and Mrs Derek, Billingshurst, Sussex West.
Sims, N., Stratford-upon-Avon, Warks.
Sims, Robin, London, N1.
Sims, Reed Ltd, London, SW1.
Sinai Antiques Ltd, London, W8.
Sinai, E. and M., London, W8.
Sinai, M., London, W1.
Sinclair, F.J., Stamford, Lincs.
Sinclair, G., London, NW8.
Sinclair, John, Stamford, Lincs.
Sinclair's Antique Gallery, Belfast, N. Ireland.
Sinfield Gallery, Brian, Burford, Oxon.
Sinfield, S.E., Biggleswade, Beds.
Singing Bird Antiques, Harrogate, Yorks. North.
Singleton, A., Yoxford, Suffolk.
Siodmok, Michael, Poynton, Cheshire.
Sitch and Co. Ltd., W., London, W1.
Sitch, R., London, W1.
Skeaping Gallery, Lydford, Devon.
Skeel Antique Warehouse, Keith, London, N1.
Skeel Antiques and Eccentricities, Keith, London, N1.
Skellgate Curios, Ripon, Yorks. North.
Skelson, Mrs M.C., Brighton, Sussex East.
Skiba, S., Weedon, Northants.
Skinner, Mrs M., Bristol, Avon.
Skipper, G. and K., Bungay, Suffolk.
Skipwith, W.G., Winchester, Hants.
Skoob Books Ltd, London, WC1.
Skrebowski, Justin, London, W11.
Skudder, M., Dartford, Kent.
Sladmore Gallery, The, London, W1.
Slater, C., Brighton, Sussex East.
Slater, David, London, W11.
Slater, G., Walsden, Yorks. West.
Slater, M. and Mrs P., Edinburgh, Scotland.
Slater, N., Barnt Green, Herefs. and Worcs.
Sleath, S.L., Sheffield, Yorks. South.
Sloane, E.D. and A.A., Robertsbridge, Sussex East.
Smale, B.J., Stourbridge, West Mids.
Smeeth, A.G., Leavenheath, Suffolk.
Smeeth, S., Lymington, Hants.
Smith, Mr and Mrs A., East Molesey, Surrey.
Smith, A., Leicester, Leics.
Smith, A., Ludlow, Shrops.

Smith, Angela, Cheadle Hulme, Cheshire.
Smith Antique Clocks, Allan, Swindon, Wilts.
Smith Antiques, Andrew, West Malling, Kent.
Smith, A.D., Birmingham, West Mids.
Smith, Dr A.J., Oakham, Leics.
Smith, Bryan, Leeds, Yorks. West.
Smith, B. and D.J., Cheddleton, Staffs.
Smith, B.J. and R., Tingewick, Bucks.
Smith, Mrs B.Roderick, Much Wenlock, Shrops.
Smith and Gerald Robinson Antiques, Colin, London, W11.
Smith, C. R., London, SW18.
Smith Antiques, David, Manton, Leics.
Smith, D. A. and C. R., Driffield, N. Humbs.
Smith, D.B., Chipping Campden, Glos.
Smith, D.K., Leeds, Yorks. West.
Smith, D.R. and G.B., Ringwood, Hants.
Smith, E.B. and E.M., Hungerford, Berks.
Smith (Leicester) Ltd, E., Leicester, Leics.
Smith and Sons (Peterborough)Ltd, G., Peterborough, Cambs.
Smith, Hammond, Leicester, Leics.
Smith, H.E., Northchapel, Sussex West.
Smith, H.W. and P.E., Leigh-on-Sea, Essex.
Smith, J., Haydon Bridge, Northumbs.
Smith, J., Tamworth, Staffs.
Smith, John Carlton, London, SW1.
Smith, J. and J., Haydon Bridge, Northumbs.
Smith, J.P.D., London, SW1.
Smith, J.R. and T., Eastbourne, Sussex East.
Smith, K., St. Neots, Cambs.
Smith, L. Royden, Lichfield, Staffs.
Smith, M., West Malling, Kent.
Smith, M.A., London, SW13.
Smith, M.P.W., London, NW1.
Smith, M.S. and D.J., York, Yorks. North.
Smith, N., Birmingham, West Mids.
Smith, N., Wortham, Suffolk.
Smith, Mr and Mrs P., Lye, West Mids.
Smith Antiques, Peter, Sunderland, Tyne and Wear.
Smith (Bookseller), Peter Bain, Cartmel, Cumbria.
Smith, P. and J.A., Hull, N. Humbs.
Smith, P.G. and A.E., Esh Winning, Durham.
Smith, R., Haworth, Yorks. West.
Smith, Raymond, Eastbourne, Sussex East.
Smith, R. and J., Ramsey, Cambs.
Smith, R. Morley, Rottingdean, Sussex East.
Smith, R.W., Fowlmere, Cambs.
Smith and Smith Designs, Driffield, N. Humbs.
Smith, S.A. and D.J., Ashbourne, Derbys.
Smith St. Antiques Centre, Warwick, Warks.
Smith, T., Chalfont St. Giles, Bucks.
Smith Antiques, Tom, Ipswich, Suffolk.
Smith Antiques, Tom, Lavenham, Suffolk.
Smith, V., Birmingham, West Mids.
Smith Coins and Antiques, Val, Nottingham, Notts.
Smith, V. and J., Windsor and Eton, Berks.
Smith, Vivienne and Andrew, Alderley Edge, Cheshire.
Smithfield Antiques, Lye, West Mids.
Smith's (The Rink) Ltd, Harrogate, Yorks. North.
Smithsonia, Birmingham, West Mids.
Smith-Wood, Mike, Cheltenham, Glos.
Smithy, The, Portstewart, Co. Londonderry, N. Ireland.
Smyth - Antique Textiles, Peta, London, SW1.
Snape Antiques and Collectors Centre, Snape, Suffolk.
Snell, Richard and David, Bournemouth, Dorset.
Snodin, J.H., Matlock, Derbys.
Snook, T.B. and H.J., Caversham, Berks.
Snowden Antiques, Ruby, Yarm, Cleveland.
Snowden, R.H., Yarm, Cleveland.
Snowdonia Antiques, Llanrwst, Gwynedd, Wales.
Snuff Box, Lytham St. Annes, Lancs.
Snyder, B., London, N1.
Sodbury Antiques, Chipping Sodbury, Avon.
Soleimani, R.R., London, W1.
Solent Antiques, Bembridge, I. of Wight.
Soleymani, R. and V., London, W1.
Solopark Ltd, Pampisford, Cambs.
Somerset, B. , Tonbridge, Kent.
Somervale Antiques, Midsomer Norton, Avon.
Somerville Ltd, Stephen, London, W1.
Something Old, Donyatt, Somerset.
Something Old, Something New, Redland, Avon.
Somlo Antiques, London, SW1.

Somlo, G. and S., London, SW1.
Sommers, S., Windlesham, Surrey.
Sotheran Ltd, Henry, London, W1.
Sotheran's, London, SW1.
Soucek, O., Lewes, Sussex East.
South Audley Antiques, London, W1.
South London Book Centre, London, SE10.
South Molton Antiques, South Molton, Devon.
South Yorkshire Antiques, Rotherham, Yorks. South.
Southampton Antiques Centre, Southampton, Hants.
Southdown Antiques, Lewes, Sussex East.
Southdown House Antique Galleries, Brasted, Kent.
Southgate Gallery, Moreton-in-Marsh, Glos.
Southgate, Mrs Pam, Danbury, Essex.
Southgrove Restorations, Dundee, Scotland.
Southwick Rare Art, David L.H., Kingswear, Devon.
Southworth, S. and R., Staunton Harold, Leics.
Souvenir Antiques, Carlisle, Cumbria.
Sovereign Antique Centre, The, East Molesey, Surrey.
Sovereign Antiques, Gateshead, Tyne and Wear.
Soviet Carpet and Art Centre, London, NW2.
Spa Antiques, Leamington Spa, Warks.
Spalton, A.L., Sheffield, Yorks. South.
Span Antiques, Woodstock, Oxon.
Sparth House Antiques, Clayton-le-Moors, Lancs.
Spatz, London, NW1.
Spatz, London, WC2.
Speakman, P., Rishton, Lancs.
Speakmans, Rishton, Lancs.
Spearing, B., Wrentham, Suffolk.
Speed (Maps), John, Fordcombe, Kent.
Speed, Martin, East Molesey, Surrey.
Speed Antiques, Neil, Laugharne, Dyfed, Wales.
Speelman, Alfred, London, W1.
Speelman Ltd, Edward, London, W1.
Spellman, D. and S., London, W1.
Spelman, Ken, York, Yorks. North.
Spencer, A.L., Shepperton, Surrey.
Spencer, Charles, London, W9.
Spencer Antiques, Don, Warwick, Warks.
Spencer, Michael, Heath and Reach, Beds.
Spencer, W.T. and J., Lower Bentham, Yorks. North.
Spencer-Brayn, N., Morestead, Hants.
Spencer-Brayn, N., Winchester, Hants.
Spencers Antiques, Torquay, Devon.
Spero, Simon, London, W8.
Sperr, J.R., London, N6.
Spice, London, SW6.
Spicker Jewellers, Newcastle-upon-Tyne, Tyne and Wear.
Spigard, A., London, W8.
Spilsby Antiques, Spilsby, Lincs.
Spindles, The, Tonge, Leics.
Spink, John, London, SW6.
Spink and Son Ltd, London, SW1.
Spinning Wheel, The, Beaconsfield, Bucks.
Spinning Wheel, Port Erin, I. of Man.
Spinning Wheel, The, Southport, Merseyside.
Spon End Antiques, Coventry, West Mids.
Spooner, J.G., Dorking, Surrey.
Spooner, K.L. and J.S., Leek, Staffs.
Sport and Country Gallery, Bulkington, Warks.
Sports Programmes, Coventry, West Mids.
Spratt Antiques, Jack, Newark, Notts.
Spread Eagle Antiques, London, SE10.
Spring Antiques, Ipswich, Suffolk.
Spring Park Jewellers, Shirley, Surrey.
Springett, C.M., Tunbridge Wells, Kent.
Springfield Antiques, Bexhill-on-Sea, Sussex East.
Sproughton Antiques, Sproughton, Suffolk.
Spurrier-Smith Antiques, Ashbourne, Derbys.
Spurrier-Smith, I., Ashbourne, Derbys.
Spyer and Son (Antiques) Ltd, Gerald, London, SW1.
Squires, A., Faversham, Kent.
Squires Antiques, Altrincham, Cheshire.
Squires Antiques (Faversham), Faversham, Kent.
Squires Pantry Antiques, Cowfold, Sussex West.
Squirrel Collectors Centre, Basingstoke, Hants.
Stable Antiques, Sedbergh, Cumbria.
Stablegate Antiques, Canterbury, Kent.
Stables, The , Grasmere, Cumbria.
Stables Antiques, Ombersley, Herefs. & Worcs.
Stable Antiques, Thornton le Dale, Yorks. North.

DEALERS' INDEX

Stables, K., Bath, Avon.
Stacey, D. and M., Littleton, Somerset.
Stacey and Sons, John, Leigh-on-Sea, Essex.
Stacey, Mark D., Churt, Surrey.
Stacy-Marks Ltd, E., Eastbourne, Sussex East.
Stafford Antiques, Ulla, Windsor and Eton, Berks.
Staffs Bookshop, The, Lichfield, Staffs.
Stage Door Prints, London, WC2.
Staines Antiques, Horncastle, Lincs.
Staines, Mrs M.E. , Horncastle, Lincs.
Stair and Company Ltd, London, W1.
Staithe Lodge Gallery, Swafield, Norfolk.
Stalham Antique Gallery, Stalham, Norfolk.
Stamford Antiques Centre, Stamford, Lincs.
Stamp and Sons, J., Market Harborough, Leics.
Stamp, M., Market Harborough, Leics.
Standing, Penny , Exeter, Devon .
Standley, M.E. and J.E., Wymondham, Norfolk.
Stanford, A., Coventry, West Mids.
Stanford, Miss M.A., Farnham, Surrey.
Stanforth, E.M., Whitby, Yorks. North.
Stanhope, Christina, Hampton Hill, Middx.
Staniland (Booksellers), Stamford, Lincs.
Staniland, M.G., Stamford, Lincs.
Stanley, F., Hastings, Sussex East.
Stanley and Son, K., Auchterarder, Scotland.
Stanley and Son, K., Dunkeld, Scotland.
Stanton, Louis, London, W11.
Stanton, L.R. and S.A., London, W11.
Stanwells Antiques and Jewellery, Penarth, South Glam., Wales.
Stanworth, Mr and Mrs G., Cadeby, Leics.
Stanworth (Fine Arts), P., Cadeby, Leics.
Staplegrove Lodge Antiques, Taunton, Somerset.
Stapleton, D.H., Bedford, Beds.
Stapleton, Serena, London, SW1.
Stamford Antiques, St. Annes-on-Sea, Lancs.
Stapleton's Antiques, Bedford, Beds.
Starkey Galleries, James H., Beverley, N. Humbs.
Starkie, E.S., Knaresborough, Yorks. North.
Starkie Antiques, Simon, Lancaster, Lancs.
Startime, Niton, I. of Wight.
Station Pine Antiques, Nottingham, Notts.
Stead, Geoffrey, Chastleton, Glos.
Stead, Myola, Sevenoaks, Kent.
Stead Antiques Reference Books, Graham, Tunbridge Wells, Kent.
Stebbing, Peter, Bournemouth, Dorset.
Stebbing, P.M., Bournemouth, Dorset.
Steed-Croft Antiques, Burnham Deepdale, Norfolk.
Steedman, R.D., Newcastle-upon-Tyne, Tyne and Wear.
Steeds, J., Burghfield Common, Berks.
Steel, Jeremy and Guy, London, SW1.
Steel, N., London, N1.
Steel, Mrs V., London, N2.
Steele, W.G., Stoke-on-Trent, Staffs.
Steenson, M., London, W11.
Stefani, K., London, SW19.
Steeple Antiques, Ceres, Scotland.
Stefani Antiques, Liverpool, Merseyside.
Stefani Antiques, London, SW19.
Stefani, T., Liverpool, Merseyside.
Stenlake and McCourt, Glasgow, Scotland.
Stephens, F., Corringham, Essex.
Stephens, P.M. and Mrs M., Inchture, Scotland.
Stephenson, P., Harrogate, Yorks. North.
Stephenson, Robert, London, SW3 .
Steppes Hill Farm Antiques, Stockbury, Kent
Sterling Books, Weston-Super-Mare, Avon.
Sterling Coins and Medals, Bournemouth, Dorset.
Stern Art Dealers, London, W11.
Stern and Son, M., London, W11.
Sternshine, A., Manchester, Lancs.
Stevens Antiques, St. Albans, Herts.
Stevens, A.D., Eastbourne, Sussex East.
Stevens, A.D., Lewes, Sussex East.
Stevens, Bookseller, Joan, Yoxford, Suffolk.
Stevens, J.E., St. Albans, Herts.
Stevens, Mark, Little Downham, Cambs.
Stevens and Son, Lubenham, Leics.
Stevenson, E. and W., Whissendine, Leics.
Stevenson, I. and A., Brighton, Sussex East.

Stevenson, R., Birmingham, West Mids.
Stewart, A.J., Rochester, Kent.
Stewart, F., Elgin, Scotland.
Stewart Cox, J.M., Warminster, Wilts.
Stewart - Fine Art, Lauri, London, N2.
Stewart Antiques, Michael, Coatbridge, Scotland.
Stewart Fine Art Galleries, Michael, Guildford, Surrey.
Stewart Gallery, Bexhill-on-Sea, Sussex East.
Stewart Gallery, Eastbourne, Sussex East.
Stewart, J. and D., Norham, Northumbs.
Steyne Antique Gallery, Worthing, Sussex West.
Steyne House Antiques, Seaford, Sussex East.
Stickland, W.T. and B., Tetbury, Glos.
Stiffkey Antiques, Stiffkey, Norfolk.
Stiffkey Lamp Shop, The, Stiffkey, Norfolk.
Stimpson, P.D., Hurst Green, Sussex East.
Stirling Antiques, Abinger Hammer, Surrey.
Stobo, Constance, London, W8.
Stock, Colin, Rainford, Merseyside.
Stock Exchange Antiques, Colchester, Essex.
Stockbridge Antiques, Stockbridge, Hants.
Stockbridge Antiques and Fine Art, Edinburgh, Scotland.
Stocker, C.J., Harston, Cambs.
Stocker, J., Chipping Campden, Glos.
Stockland, M., Hungerford, Berks.
Stockman, P. and D., Newton Abbot, Devon.
Stockspring Antiques, London, W8.
Stodel, Jacob, London, W8.
Stodgell Fine Art, Colin, Torquay, Devon.
Stokes, Mrs N.J., Fortrose, Scotland.
Stokes, William H., Cirencester, Glos.
Stokes, W.H., Cirencester, Glos.
Stone Antiques, Alan, London, SW15.
Stone, D.P., Basingstoke, Hants.
Stone Hall Antiques, Matching Green, Essex.
Stonehouse, D.R. and J.M., Grosmont, Yorks. North.
Stones, G.G., Stradbroke, Suffolk.
Stones Grandfather Clocks, Keith, Bessacarr, Yorks. South.
Stones, Mrs M. Palmer, Stradbroke, Suffolk.
Stoodley, Dinah, Brasted, Kent.
Stoodley, Mrs D., Brasted, Kent.
Stoppenbach and Delestre Ltd, London, W1.
Stores, The, Great Waltham, Essex.
Storey, Harold T., London, WC2.
Storey, J., Alnwick, Northumbs.
Storey, M. and J., London, SW1.
Stothert - Antiquarian Books, Chester, Cheshire.
Stothert, T. and E., Chester, Cheshire.
Stott, Miss J., Tunbridge Wells, Kent.
Stour Gallery, Blandford Forum, Dorset.
Stouts Antiques Market, London, W11.
Stove Shop", "The, London, NW2.
Stow Antiques, Stow-on-the-Wold, Glos.
Strain Antiques, David R., Tynemouth, Tyne and Wear.
Strait Antiques, The, Lincoln, Lincs.
Straiton, D., Sherborne, Dorset.
Strand Antiques, Bromsgrove, Herefs. & Worcs.
Strand Antiques, London, W4.
Strange, V., Bournemouth, Dorset.
Strange, V.H., Bampton, Devon.
Stratford Antique Centre, Stratford-upon-Avon, Warks.
Strathearn Antiques, Crieff, Scotland.
Strathspey Gallery, Grantown-on-Spey, Scotland.
Strawsons Antiques, Tunbridge Wells, Kent.
Streamer Antiques, J., Leigh-on-Sea, Essex.
Streather, Pamela, London, SW1.
Stredder, J., Atherton, Lancs.
Streeter and Daughter, Ernest, Petworth, Sussex West.
Streetwalker Antiques, Barton-on-Humber, S. Humbs.
Streetwalker Antiques Warehouse, Barton-on-Humber, S. Humbs.
Stretton Antiques , Church Stretton, Shrops.
Stretton Antiques Market, Church Stretton, Shrops.
Strickland and Dorling, Feock, Cornwall.
Strickland, P., Feock, Cornwall.
Strike One (Islington) Ltd, London, NW1.
Strip and Wax, Exeter, Devon.
Strong, C.J., Exeter, Devon.
Stroud Antiques, Peter, Chipping Norton, Oxon.
Stroud, V.N. and J., Southwell, Notts.
Strouds (of Southwell Antiques), Southwell, Notts.
Strover, Barry, Cambridge, Cambs.

DEALERS' INDEX

Strowger of Blandford, Blandford Forum, Dorset.
Stuart Antiques, D.C., Bournemouth, Dorset.
Stuart Gallery, Marlborough, Wilts.
Stuart House Antiques, Chipping Campden, Glos.
Stuart Interiors (Antiques) Ltd, Barrington, Somerset.
Stuart, J. and V., Shere, Surrey.
Stuart, T.R. and Mrs H.M., Woodford Halse, Northants.
Stubcroft Period Furnishings and Restorations, Stradbroke, Suffolk.
Stuckey, M.T., Halstead, Essex.
Studio 41, Southport, Merseyside.
Studio 101, Windsor and Eton, Berks.
Studio Arts Gallery, Lancaster, Lancs.
Studio Bookshop and Gallery, Alresford, Hants.
Stuff, Dover, Kent.
Sturgeon, J.A. and Mrs . J., Sandhurst, Berks.
Sturges, James, Totnes, Devon.
Sturman, A., M.M. and P.J., Hawes, Yorks. North.
Sturman's Antiques, Hawes, Yorks. North.
Stutchbury, Mr and Mrs D., Newark, Notts.
Style, London, N1.
Styles, P. and D., Hungerford, Berks.
Styles Silver, Hungerford, Berks.
Suffolk House Antiques, Yoxford, Suffolk.
Sugar Antiques, London, N1.
Sugarman, Elayne and Tony, London, N1.
Sugden, I., Buxton, Derbys.
Sukmano Antiques, London, W8.
Sullivan, B., Southport, Merseyside.
Summers, Davis and Son Ltd, Wallingford, Oxon.
Summers, S. and N., Nantwich, Cheshire.
Summersgill Antiques, Timothy, Easingwold, Yorks. North.
Summersons, Hatton, Warks.
Sumner, Jane, Saffron Walden, Essex.
Sumner, Mrs J., Saffron Walden, Essex.
Sumner, M.C., Uppingham, Leics.
Sumner, N.F. and M.A., Ormskirk, Lancs.
Sundial Antiques, Amersham, Bucks.
Sundridge Gallery, Sundridge, Kent.
Sunset Country Antiques, Cullompton, Devon.
Surrey Antiques Centre, Chertsey, Surrey.
Surrey Clock Centre, Haslemere, Surrey.
Surya, K., London, WC1.
Susannah, Bath, Avon.
Sussex Commemorative Ware Centre, The, Brighton, Sussex East.
Sussex Fine Art, Arundel, Sussex West.
Sussex House Antiques, Devizes, Wilts.
Sutcliffe Galleries, Harrogate, Yorks. North.
Sutcliffe, Gordon, Hadleigh, Suffolk.
Sutcliffe, R. and R., Masham, Yorks. North.
Sutcliffe Antiques, Tony and Anne, Southport, Merseyside.
Suthburgh Antiques, Long Melford, Suffolk.
Sutton, B.D., Windsor and Eton, Berks.
Sutton, G. and B., Stow-on-the-Wold, Glos.
Sutton, H., Wroughton, Wilts.
Sutton, P., London, W8.
Sutton, L., Great Malvern, Herefs. and Worcs.
Sutton and Sons, Frome, Somerset.
Sutton Valence Antiques, Maidstone, Kent.
Sutton Valence Antiques, Sutton Valence , Kent.
Swadforth House, Knaresborough, Yorks. North.
Swaffer, Spencer, Arundel, Sussex West.
Swaffham Antiques Supplies, Swaffham, Norfolk.
Swag, Preston, Lancs.
Swain, A.L., Faversham, Kent.
Swainbank, R., Liverpool, Merseyside.
Swainbanks Ltd, Liverpool, Merseyside.
Swaine, S.P., Walsall, West Midlands.
Swale, Jill and David, Wells, Somerset.
Swan Antiques, Bawtry, Yorks. South.
Swan Antiques, Chipping Campden, Glos.
Swan Antiques, Cranbrook, Kent.
Swan Antiques and Crafts Centre, The, Lechlade, Glos.
Swan Fine Art, London, N1.
Swan Gallery, Burford, Oxon.
Swan Gallery, The, Sherborne, Dorset.
Swan House Antiques and Crafts, Garboldisham, Norfolk.
Swann Galleries, Oliver, London, SW3.
Swans Antique Centre, Oakham, Leics.
Swansea Antique Centre, Swansea, West Glam., Wales.
Swanson, D., Petworth, Sussex West.

Sweet, John, Bridlington, N. Humbs.
Sweetbriar Gallery, Helsby, Cheshire.
Sweeting, K.J., Belper, Derbys.
Sweetings (Antiques 'n' Things), Belper, Derbys.
Sweet's Antiques, Bridlington, N. Humbs.
Swift, M., Camborne, Cornwall.
Swift and Sons, R.A., Bournemouth, Dorset.
Swindells, A., Rotherham, Yorks. South.
Swindells, H. and A., Bath, Avon.
Sydney House Antiques, Wansford, Cambs.
Sykes Antiques, North Kelsey Moor, Lincs.
Sykes Antiques, Christopher, Woburn, Beds.
Sykes, C. and M., Woburn, Beds.
Sykes, C.W., York, Yorks. North.
Sykes Antiques, Thomas, Kelvedon, Essex.
Sykes, T.W., Kelvedon, Essex.
Symes, B., Tetbury, Glos.
Symes, John and Sheila, Bristol, Avon.
Symes Ltd, Robin, London, SW1.
Szynowski, D., Rottingdean, Sussex East.

T

T.W. Antiques, Wimborne Minster, Dorset.
Tadema Gallery, London, N1.
Tagg, Bill, Liverpool, Merseyside.
Taikoo Books Ltd, York, Yorks. North.
Take-a-Seat, Macclesfield, Cheshire.
Talbot Court Galleries, Stow-on-the-Wold, Glos.
Talent Pastimes Ltd. (Collectors Shop), Northampton, Northants.
Talents Fine Arts Ltd, Malton, Yorks. North.
Talisman, Gillingham, Dorset.
Talisman Antiques, Horncastle, Lincs.
Talking Machine, London, NW4.
Talking Point Antiques, Sowerby Bridge, Yorks. West.
Talton, J.W., Long Sutton, Lincs.
Talton, J., W. and J.J., Long Sutton, Lincs.
Tamar Gallery (Antiques and Fine Art), Launceston, Cornwall.
Tamblyn, Alnwick, Northumbs.
Tamworth Antique Centre, The, Tamworth, Staffs.
Tanglewood, Derby, Derbys.
Tankerton Antiques, Whitstable, Kent.
Tanner, J., Clare, Suffolk.
Tanner, J., Long Melford, Suffolk.
Tanswell, P., Warminster, Wilts.
Tapley, R., Niton, I. of Wight.
Tapestry, Cheltenham, Glos.
Tappers Antiques, Eastleigh, Hants.
Tapsell Antiques, Brighton, Sussex East.
Tara Antiques, London, NW8.
Taramasco, A., London, NW8.
Tara's Hall, Hadleigh, Suffolk.
Tarran, D., Worcester, Herefs. and Worcs.
Tarrant Street Antique Centre, Arundel, Sussex West.
Tarrystone, The, Chobham, Surrey.
Tate, Andrew, Finchingfield, Essex.
Tate, J. M., Burnham Deepdale, Norfolk.
Tatters Decorative Antiques, Wolverhampton, West Mids.
Tatters of Tyseley Ltd, Birmingham, West Mids.
Tattersall, J., Uppingham, Leics.
Tattersall's, Uppingham, Leics.
Tatton Antiques, Knutsford, Cheshire.
Tauber Antiques, Laurence, Surbiton, Surrey.
Taunton Antiques Market - Silver Street, Taunton, Somerset.
Tavistock Antiques, St. Neots, Cambs.
Tay Street Gallery, Perth, Scotland.
Tayler, Mrs S.C., Lytham St. Annes, Lancs.
Taylor, B., Kingston-on-Spey, Scotland.
Taylor Antiques, Brian, Plymouth, Devon.
Taylor, B.F., Plymouth, Devon.
Taylor, C., Thatcham, Berks.
Taylor, C.D. and E.S., Hampton, Middx.
Taylor, D., Driffield, N. Humbs.
Taylor, D., Halesowen, West Mids.
Taylor, D.E., Hastings, Sussex East.
Taylor, E., Broadway, Herefs. and Worcs.
Taylor, F.W., Tewkesbury, Glos.
Taylor Gallery, The, London, W1.
Taylor, Gerald and Vera, Winforton, Herefs. & Worcs.
Taylor, I.C., Glasgow, Scotland.

DEALERS' INDEX

Taylor, Mrs J., Stockton Heath, Cheshire.
Taylor, J., London, W1.
Taylor, J., Stoke-on-Trent, Staffs.
Taylor, Mrs L., Cirencester, Glos.
Taylor, M., London, SW12.
Taylor, M., Ludlow, Shrops.
Taylor, Mark, Bournemouth, Dorset.
Taylor, M.C., Bournemouth, Dorset.
Taylor (Antiques), M. and R., Ludlow, Shrops.
Taylor, Mrs P., Henllan, Dyfed, Wales.
Taylor Antiques, Rankine, Cirencester, Glos.
Taylor, Robert, Four Oaks, West Mids.
Taylor Fine Arts, Robin, Wakefield, Yorks. West.
Taylor, R.I.G., London, SW10.
Taylor, Mrs S.M., Boston, Lincs.
Taylor Antiques, W., Lowestoft, Suffolk.
Taylor, W.D.J., Lowestoft, Suffolk.
Taylor-Halsey Antiques, Drewsteignton, Devon.
Taylor-Smith, Westerham, Kent.
Taylor-Smith, Westerham, Kent.
Tealby Pine, Wragby, Lincs.
Tebbs, Jonathan, Sawtry, Cambs.
Teger Trading and Bushe Antiques, London, N4.
Teignmouth, P., London, W8.
Teignmouth and Son, Pamela, London, W8.
Telfer-Smollett, M. and C., London, W11.
Telford Antiques Centre, Telford, Shrops.
Teltscher Ltd, F., London, W1.
Teme Valley Antiques, Ludlow, Shrops.
Temperley, D. and R.A., Birmingham, West Mids.
Temperley Fine and Antiquarian Books, David, Birmingham, West Mids.
Templar Antiques, Kelvedon, Essex.
Temple Antiques, Whitstable, Kent.
Temple Gallery, London, W11.
Temple Lighting (Jeanne Temple Antiques), Milton Keynes, Bucks.
Temple, R.C.C., London, W11.
Temptations, Ashtead, Surrey.
Tempus Fugit, Shaldon, Devon.
Tennis Bookshop, The, Ringwood, Hants.
Tenterden Antiques Centre, Tenterden, Kent.
Terrace Antiques, London, W5.
Terrett, J.S., Truro, Cornwall.
Terry, A., Mold, Clwyd, Wales.
Terry Antiques, London, W4.
Tessiers Ltd, London, W1.
Tetsworth Antiques, Tetsworth, Oxon.
Tewkesbury Antique Centre, Tewkesbury, Glos.
Textile Company, The, London, N1.
Textile Company, The, London, W11.
Thacker's Antiques, York, Yorks. North.
Thakeham Furniture, Storrington, Sussex West.
Thame Antique Galleries, Thame, Oxon.
Thames Gallery, Henley-on-Thames, Oxon.
Thames Oriental Rug Co, Henley-on-Thames, Oxon.
Thanet Antiques Trade Centre, Ramsgate, Kent.
That Little Shop, Boston, Lincs.
Thaxted Galleries, Thaxted, Essex.
Themes and Variations, London, W11.
Theobaldy, D., Cambridge, Cambs.
Thesaurus (Jersey) Ltd, St. Helier, Jersey, C.I.
Theta Gallery, Liverpool, Merseyside.
Thicke Galleries, Swansea, West Glam., Wales.
Thicke, T.G., Swansea, West Glam., Wales.
Thin (Booksellers), James, Edinburgh, Scotland.
Thirkills Antiques, Leeds, Yorks. West.
Thirty-Eight Antiques Ltd, Weedon, Northants.
This and That, Norwich, Norfolk.
This and That Antiques and Bric-a-Brac, Edinburgh, Scotland.
This and That (Furniture), London, NW1.
Thistle Antiques, Aberdeen, Scotland.
Thistle House Antiques, Woodstock, Oxon.
Thistlethwaite, E., Settle, Yorks. North.
Thom, A.W., Chapel-en-le-Frith, Derbys.
Thomas, Andrew, Stamford, Lincs.
Thomas, Mrs C., Windsor and Eton, Berks.
Thomas H. Parker Ltd, , London, SW1.
Thomas and James Antiques, Bovey Tracey, Devon.
Thomas, J.B., Fishguard, Dyfed, Wales.
Thomas, M. and V., Penn, Bucks.

Thomas, Philip, Bovey Tracey, Devon.
Thomas, R., Thornton Heath, Surrey.
Thomas, R. and D., Brasted, Kent.
Thomas, Wing Cdr.R.G., Midsomer Norton, Avon.
Thompson, B., London, N1.
Thompson, D. and Mrs S., Ipswich, Suffolk.
Thompson, J., Knaresborough, Yorks. North.
Thompson, John, Tunbridge Wells, Kent.
Thompson, J.J., Easingwold, Yorks. North.
Thompson, J. and S., Aldeburgh, Suffolk.
Thompson, N., Tunbridge Wells, Kent.
Thompson, N.F., Buxton, Derbys.
Thompson, R.E., Long Buckby, Northants.
Thompson Antiques formerly Ships and Sealing Wax, Winchester, Hants.
Thompson's, Ipswich, Suffolk.
Thompson's Gallery, Aldeburgh, Suffolk.
Thomson, A.L., St. Helier, Jersey, C.I.
Thomson - Albany Gallery, Bill, London, SW1.
Thomson, D., Ripon, Yorks. North.
Thomson Antiques, Joan, St. Helier, Jersey, C.I.
Thomson Ltd, Murray, London, W8.
Thomson, W.B., London, SW1.
Thomson's Furniture Warehouse, St Helier, Jersey, C.I.
Thorn, David J., Budleigh Salterton, Devon.
Thornber, Peter, Chester, Cheshire.
Thornbury, M., Malmesbury, Wilts.
Thorne, S., Hursley, Hants.
Thornhill Galleries Ltd, London, SW6.
Thornhill Galleries Ltd. in association with A. & R. Dockerill Ltd, London, SW15.
Thornhill Gallery Antique Centre, Thornhill, Scotland.
Thornhill, J., Shrewsbury, Shrops.
Thornley, G. and E.M., Helmsley, Yorks. North.
Thornley, J., Biddenden, Kent.
Thornton Architectural Antiques Ltd, Andy, Halifax, Yorks. West.
Thornton Gallery, Bedale, Yorks. North.
Thornton, John, London, SW10.
Through the Looking Glass Ltd, London, SW6.
Thornton Antiques, Joseph , Windermere, Cumbria.
Thornton, J.W., Ulverston, Cumbria.
Thornton, J.W., Windermere, Cumbria.
Thornton Antiques Supermarket, J.W., Bowness-on-Windermere, Cumbria.
Thornton, Sue, Winchfield, Hants.
Thornton, T. and G., York, Yorks. North.
Thorntons of Harrogate, Harrogate, Yorks. North.
Thorntons of Oxford Ltd, Oxford, Oxon.
Thorp, Thomas, St. Albans, Herts.
Thorp Bookseller, Thomas, Guildford, Surrey.
Thorpe Antiques, Finedon, Northants.
Thorpe, D.J., Llanwrda, Dyfed, Wales.
Thorpe and Foster plc, Dorking, Surrey.
Three Tuns Antiques, Stokesley, Yorks. North.
Thrie Estaits, The, Edinburgh, Scotland.
Throckmorton, Lady Isabel, Arthingworth, Northants.
Throp, R., Brasted, Kent.
Through the Looking Glass Ltd, London, W8.
Thrower, D. and V., Petworth, Sussex West.
Thuillier, William, London, W1.
Thursday Shop, The, Edinburgh, Scotland.
Thurso Antiques, Thurso, Scotland.
Thurstans, C.M. and D., Stillington, Yorks. North.
Thwaites and Co, Bushey, Herts.
Tibenham, Mrs P., Knowle, West Mids.
Tidey Antiques, Michael, Brighton, Sussex East.
Tiffany Antiques, Shrewsbury, Shrops.
Tiffins Antiques, Emsworth, Hants.
Tildesley, B. and J., Harrogate, Yorks. North.
Tilings Antiques, Brasted, Kent.
Till, M., London, N1.
Tillett, James and Ann, Norwich, Norfolk.
Tillett & Co, Thomas, Norwich, Norfolk.
Tilley, A.G.J. and A.A.J.C., Sheffield, Yorks. South.
Tilley, Mrs P., Macclesfield, Cheshire.
Tilleys Antiques, Solihull, West Mids.
Tilley's Vintage Magazine Shop, Sheffield, Yorks. South.
Tillman Ltd, William, London, SW1.
Tillou Works of Art Ltd, Peter, London, SW1.
Tilly Manor Antiques, West Harptree, Avon.
Tilly's Antiques, Leigh-on-Sea, Essex.

DEALERS' INDEX

Time in Hand, Shipston-on-Stour, Warks.
Timecraft, Greyabbey, Co. Down, N. Ireland.
Timepiece, Teignmouth, Devon.
Timewarp, Brighton, Sussex East.
Times Past, Great Wakering, Essex.
Times Past, Kelvedon, Essex.
Times Past, Portsmouth, Hants.
Times Past, Chesterfield, Derbys.
Times Past, Sheerness, Kent.
Times Past Antiques, Auchterarder, Scotland.
Times Past Antiques Ltd, Windsor and Eton, Berks.
Timms Antiques Ltd, S. and S., Ampthill, Beds.
Tina's Antiques, Codford, Wilts.
Tincknell, R.C. and L., Meare, Somerset.
Tinder Box, The, Stoke-on-Trent, Staffs.
Tindler, C., Brompton, Yorks. North.
Tingewick Antiques Centre, Tingewick, Bucks.
Tinsley, Mark, Newark, Notts.
Titchfield Antiques Ltd, Titchfield, Hants.
Titchner and Sons, John, Littleton, Cheshire.
Titchner & Sons, John, Chester, Cheshire.
Titles Old and Rare Books, Oxford, Oxon.
Titmuss, E.L., London, W8.
Titus Gallery, The, Shipley, Yorks. West.
Titus Omega, London, N1.
Tobias and The Angel, London, SW13.
Toby's Antiques, Weston-Super-Mare, Avon.
Tociapski, Igor, London, W11.
Todd and Austin Antiques of Winchester, Winchester, Hants.
Todd, A., Stockport, Cheshire.
Todd, E., Stockport, Cheshire.
Todd, M.S., Nether Stowey, Somerset.
Todd, W., Winchester, Hants.
Todmorden Fine Art, Todmorden, Yorks. West.
Token House Antiques, Ewell, Surrey.
Toll House, Sturminster Newton, Dorset.
Toll House Bookshop, The, Holmfirth, Yorks. West.
Tollett, B., Witney, Oxon.
Tolley, T.M., Worcester, Herefs. and Worcs.
Tolley's Galleries, Worcester, Herefs. & Worcs.
Tombland Bookshop, The, Norwich, Norfolk.
Tomkinson, J. and B., Clitheroe, Lancs.
Tomkinson, S., London, W11.
Tomkinson Stained Glass, London, W11.
Tomlin, D.S., London, N5.
Tomlinson and Son, F., Stockport, Cheshire.
Tomlinson (Antiques) Ltd. and Period Furniture Ltd, Raymond, Tockwith, Yorks. North.
Toms, J.A., Aberdare, Mid. Glam., Wales.
Tonkinson, J.B., Weybridge, Surrey.
Tonks, Mrs B., Wolverhampton, West Mids.
Tooke, M.D., Guildford, Surrey.
Toole, J., Liverpool, Merseyside.
Tooley Adams & Co. Ltd, London, WC2.
Tooley, CMBHI, M.V., Chesham, Bucks.
Tooley, P., Brighton, Sussex East.
Tooltique, Norwich, Norfolk.
Top Brass, Edinburgh, Scotland.
Top Hat Antiques Centre, Nottingham, Notts.
Top Hat Exhibitions Ltd,, Nottingham, Notts.
Topaz, Stourbridge, West Mids.
Torre Antique Traders, Torquay, Devon.
Torrens, R., Crieff, Scotland.
Tortoiseshell Antiques, Henllan, Dyfed, Wales.
Toth, Ferenc, London, SW6.
Toth, F. and E., London, SW6.
Totteridge Gallery, The, London, N20.
Toubian Antiques Ltd, London, W8.
Toubian, N., London, W8.
Touchwood, Herstmonceux, Sussex East.
Touchwood International, Stow-on-the-Wold, Glos.
Tourell, J., Alfriston, Sussex East.
Tower Antiques, Cranborne, Dorset.
Tower Antiques, London, W10.
Tower Bridge Antiques, London, SE1.
Tower Gallery, King's Lynn, Norfolk.
Town and Country Antiques, Bath, Avon.
Town and Country Furniture, Canterbury, Kent.
Town and Country Antiques, Tutbury, Staffs.
Town Hall Antiques, Woburn, Beds.
Town House Antiques, Barnard Castle, Durham.
Town House Antiques, Marple Bridge, Cheshire.

Townhead Antiques, Newby Bridge, Cumbria.
Townhouse Antiques, Walkerburn, Scotland.
Townley, E.M. and C.P., Newby Bridge, Cumbria.
Towns, J.M., Swansea, West Glam., Wales.
Townsend, J. and Lady Juliet, Brackley, Northants.
Townsend, John P., Cheltenham, Glos.
Townsend, M., London, NW8.
Townsends, London, NW8.
Townsford Mill Antiques Centre, Halstead, Essex.
Toynbee-Clarke, G. and D., London, W1.
Toynbee-Clarke Interiors Ltd, London, W1.
Tracy Gallery, Simon, London, NW8.
TRADA, Chipping Norton, Oxon.
Trade Antiques, Long Sutton, Lincs.
Trade Antiques - D.D. White, Manfield, Yorks. North.
Trade Wind, Rottingdean, Sussex East.
Trader Antiques, London, N13.
Trading Post, Leamington Spa, Warks.
Trading Warehouse, Rettendon, Essex.
Tradition - Military Antiques, London, W1.
Traditional Furniture, Hythe, Kent.
Traditional Interiors, Harrogate, Yorks. North.
Trafalgar Galleries, London, SW1.
Trafalgar Square Collectors Centre, London, WC2.
Tran, L., Worcester, Herefs. and Worcs.
Tran Antiques, Long, Worcester, Herefs. & Worcs.
Trash 'n' Treasure, Alsager, Cheshire.
Travers, Dr.Robert A., Richmond, Surrey.
Travis, Mrs D., St. Annes-on-Sea, Lancs.
Travis and Emery, London, WC2.
Traylen, Charles W., Guildford, Surrey.
Traylen, N.C.R. and T.A., Ventnor, I. of Wight.
Treasure Chest, Berwick-on-Tweed, Northumbs.
Treasure Chest, Birmingham, West Mids.
Treasure Chest , The, Highbridge, Somerset.
Treasure Chest, The, Weymouth, Dorset.
Treasure Chest, Whitley Bay, Tyne and Wear.
Treasure Ltd, Frederick, Preston, Lancs.
Treasure House Antiques and Collectors Market, Arundel, Sussex West.
Treasure House Antiques Centre, Bawtry, Yorks. South.
Treasure, J.F., Preston, Lancs.
Treasure, L., Exmouth, Devon.
Treasures, Exmouth, Devon.
Treasures, Oxted, Surrey.
Treasure Trove, South Molton, Devon.
Treasures, Four Elms, Kent.
Treasures of Childhood Past - Carrie Tarplett, Great Malvern, Herefs. & Worcs.
Treasures of Woodchurch, Woodchurch, Kent.
Trecilla Antiques, Ross-on-Wye, Herefs. & Worcs.
Tredant, J.C., South Molton, Devon.
Tredant, J.R., South Molton, Devon.
Tredantiques, South Molton, Devon.
Trefor Antiques, John, Rhuallt, Clwyd, Wales.
Tregenza, A., Plymouth, Devon.
Trench Puzzles, Stowmarket, Suffolk.
Trengove, Croydon, Surrey.
Trentini Antiques, West Kirby, Merseyside.
Trentini, J., West Kirby, Merseyside.
Trevers, J.P., Stow-on-the-Wold, Glos.
Trevor, Lewes, Sussex East.
Tribe and Son, Tom, Sturminster Newton, Dorset.
Trident Arms, Nottingham, Notts.
Trimbridge Galleries, Bath, Avon.
Trinder, Mr and Mrs J., Coldstream, Scotland.
Trinder, P. and R., Clare, Suffolk.
Trinders' Booksellers, Clare, Suffolk.
Trinity Antiques Centre, Colchester, Essex.
Tritec Investments Ltd,, Bristol, Avon.
Triton Gallery, Cheltenham, Glos.
Trivess, W.D., Meonstoke, Hants.
Troche, G., Washington, Sussex West.
Tron Antiques, David, London, SW3.
Trotter, J. and Mrs M., Yoxford, Suffolk.
Trove, London, SW1.
Trowbridge Gallery, London, SW6.
Trowbridge, M., London, SW6.
Truscott, Christina, London, W11.
Trueman, H., Berkeley, Glos.
Tryon, Mrs J.P., Congleton, Cheshire.
Tsar Architectural, London, N7.

DEALERS' INDEX

Tubb, Mr and Mrs C.E., Wootton Bassett, Wilts.
Tubbjoys, Wootton Bassett, Wilts.
Tucker, F.H. and S.M., Charing, Kent.
Tucker, P., Knebworth, Herts.
Tuckers Country Store and Art Gallery, Deddington, Oxon.
Tuckwell, D.K., Wakefield, Yorks. West.
Tudor Antiques, Hatfield Broad Oak, Essex.
Tudor Antiques, Long Melford, Suffolk.
Tudor Cottage Antiques, Shoreham-by-Sea, Sussex West.
Tudor House, Barnstaple, Devon.
Tudor House Antiques, Bridport, Dorset.
Tudor House Antiques, Halesowen, West Mids.
Tudor of Lichfield Antique Centre, Lichfield, Staffs.
Tudor Rose Antiques, Carlton-on-Trent, Notts.
Tuffs, C., Wraysbury, Berks.
Tulissio, David , London, SW6.
Tulissio De Beaumont, London, SW6.
Tunbridge Wells Antique Centre, Tunbridge Wells, Kent.
Tupman, D., London, NW8.
Turks Head Antiques, Windsor and Eton, Berks.
Turl, R.V. and A.M., Kimpton, Herts.
Turley, Mr and Mrs C.R., Wolverhampton, West Mids.
Turley, S.J. and N.V., Brasted, Kent.
Turn of the Century, Sheffield, Yorks. South.
Turn of the Century Antiques, Hexham, Northumbs.
Turn On Lighting Ltd, London, N1.
Turnbull, Mr and Mrs W.H., Bedale, Yorks. North.
Turner Antiques, Annmarie, Marlborough, Wilts.
Turner, C., London, N7.
Turner, Mrs D., Rye, Sussex East.
Turner, J., Cheltenham, Glos.
Turner, J., Cradley Heath, West Mids.
Turner Antiques, Joy, Cheltenham, Glos.
Turner, J.R., Berry Hill Pike, Glos.
Turner, L., Bideford, Devon.
Turner, L.C. and C., Congleton, Cheshire.
Turner, Malcolm, Norwich, Norfolk.
Turner Antiques, R. and D. , Honiton, Devon.
Turner (Antiques and Fine Art) Ltd, R. and M., Jedburgh, Scotland.
Turner Antiques, Sally, Wendover, Bucks.
Turner, W. A., London, W13.
Turner, W.G.V., Tamworth, Staffs.
Turnor Antiques, Philip, Rotherham, Yorks. South.
Turnpike Cottage Antiques and Tearooms, St. Gerrans, Cornwall.
Turpin Ltd, M., London, W1.
Turpin's Antiques, Thaxted, Essex.
Turret House, Wymondham, Norfolk.
Turtle Fine Art, Cheltenham, Glos.
Tutbury Mill Antiques, Tutbury, Staffs.
Tutt Antiques, J.C., Petworth, Sussex West.
Twentieth Century, London, SW12.
Twenty-Two Antiques, Knutsford, Cheshire.
Two Maids Antiques, Biddenden, Kent.
Twyford Antiques, Twyford, Hants.
Tyler, D., Fordham, Essex.
Tyler, T.M., Malmesbury, Wilts.
Tyndall, J., Tetbury, Glos.
Tyran, Mr , London, SW3.
Tyran, R., London, SW6.
Tyrer, T. and M., Sundridge, Kent.
Tyrrell, G. and M., Woburn Sands, Bucks.
Tyrrell, W.P. and Dr. E., Midhurst, Sussex West.
Tyson, George, Andrew and Shirley, Morecambe, Lancs.
Tyson's Antiques, Morecambe, Lancs.
Tything Antique Market, The, Worcester, Herefs. & Worcs.

U

Ullmann Ltd, A.R., London, EC1.
Ullmann, J.S., London, EC1.
Under Milkwood, London, SE24.
Under Two Flags, London, W1.
Underhill Gallery, Leigh, London, N1.
Underwood Antiques, Clive, Colsterworth, Lincs.
Underwoodhall Antiques, Woodhall Spa, Lincs.
Unicorn Antiques, Bowness-on-Windermere, Cumbria.
Unicorn Antiques, Edinburgh, Scotland.
Union Street Antique Market, St. Helier, Jersey, C.I.
Unsworth Antiques, Robin, Olney, Bucks.
Unsworth, R. and Z. M., Olney, Bucks.

Up Country, Tunbridge Wells, Kent.
Upchurch, Kenneth , Ashbourne, Derbys.
Upperbridge Antiques, Holmfirth, Yorks. West.
Uppink, Mr and Mrs M.E., Knutsford, Cheshire.
Upstairs, Downstairs, Honiton, Devon.
Upstairs Downstairs, Plymouth, Devon.
Upstairs Downstairs Antique Centre, Arundel, Sussex West.
Upton Lodge Galleries, Avening, Glos.
Upton Lodge Galleries, Tetbury, Glos.
Uriah's Heap, Ryde, I. of Wight.
Usher Antiques, Richard, Cuckfield, Sussex West.
Usher and Son Ltd, James, Lincoln, Lincs.
Utopia Antiques Ltd, Bowness-on-Windermere, Cumbria.

V

V.O.C. Antiques, Woodhall Spa, Lincs.
Valcke, Francois, London, SW6.
Vale Antiques, London, W9.
Vale Stamps and Antiques, London, SE3.
Valetta House Antiques, Somerton, Somerset.
Valley Antiques, Oldham, Lancs.
Vallis, A., Farnham, Surrey.
Valls Ltd, Rafael, London, SW1.
Valmar Antiques, Stansted, Essex.
Valtone Pine, Hampton, Middx.
van Beers Oriental Art, Jan, London, W1.
Van Daal, J. and J., Bembridge, I. of Wight.
Van Den Bussche, L., Westerham, Kent.
Van Der Breggen, F.J., London, SW3.
Van Haeften Ltd, Johnny, London, SW1.
Van Haeften, J. and S., London, SW1.
Van Hefflin, Mr, Gainsborough, Lincs.
Van Vredenburgh Ltd, Edric, London, SW1.
Van Wyngaarden, H., Little Malvern, Herefs. and Worcs.
van Zwanenberg, M., Timberscombe, Somerset.
Vanbrugh House Antiques, Stow-on-the-Wold, Glos.
Vandekar Antiques, London, W8.
Vandeleur Antiquarian Books, Epsom, Surrey.
Vandervelden, M. and Mrs G., Dunchurch, Warks.
Vane House Antiques, London, N1.
Vanity Fayre, Mousehole, Cornwall.
Varcoe, Myles, Golant, Cornwall.
Vargha, M., London, W8.
Varnham, H.J. and R.P., London, SE3.
Vaughan, London, SW6.
Vaughan, G. and J., Ruthin, Clwyd, Wales.
Vaughan, J. and J., Deddington, Oxon.
Vaughan Ltd, , London, SW6.
Vaughan, M., Frome, Somerset.
Vaughan, M.J., London, SW6.
Vaughan, Robert, Stratford-upon-Avon, Warks.
Vaughan, R. and C.M., Stratford-upon-Avon, Warks.
Vectis Fine Arts, Newchurch, I. of Wight.
Vedmore, J., Banbury, Oxon.
Vedmore Furniture and Antiques, Judy, Banbury, Oxon.
Vella, J.D. and H., Olney, Bucks.
Venables, Jeremy, Kineton, Warks.
Vendy Antiques, Lynton, Devon.
Vendy Antiques (Kibworth), Kibworth Beauchamp, Leics.
Vendy, D.R., Kibworth Beauchamp, Leics.
Vendy, T.W., Lynton, Devon.
Veness, K., Saxmundham, Suffolk.
Venn, D., Worcester, Herefs. and Worcs.
Venn, D. and G., Worcester, Herefs. and Worcs.
Venn, Edward, Williton, Somerset.
Venners Antiques, London, W1.
Ventnor Rare Books, Ventnor, I. of Wight.
Venture, The, Woking, Surrey.
Verey, Denzil, Barnsley, Glos.
Verney, J., Clare, Suffolk.
Verralls (Handcross) Ltd, Handcross, Sussex West.
Veryard, D.J., Northampton, Northants.
Vescovi, Luigino, Morecambe, Lancs.
Vicary Antiques, Lancaster, Lancs.
Vice, D., Birmingham, West Midlands.
Victoria Antiques, Alderney, Alderney, C.I.
Victoria Antiques, Holsworthy, Devon.
Victoria Antiques, Wadebridge, Cornwall.
Victoria Antiques/City Strippers, Wallasey, Merseyside.
Victoria Bookshop, Swindon, Wilts.
Victoria Cottage Antiques, West Kirby, Merseyside.

DEALERS' INDEX

Victoria and Edward Antiques Centre, Dorking, Surrey.
Victoria Gallery, Camborne, Cornwall.
Victoria Park Antiques, Caldbeck, Cumbria.
Victorian Brass Bedstead Company, The, Cocking, Sussex West.
Victorian Chairman, Bournemouth, Dorset.
Victorian Fireplace, Canterbury, Kent.
Victorian Fireplace Co, London, NW1.
Victorian House Shop, Bingley, Yorks. West.
Victorian Parlour, Bournemouth, Dorset.
Victorian Shop, The, St. Annes-on-Sea, Lancs.
Victorian Village, The, Glasgow, Scotland.
Victoriana, Sleaford, Lincs.
Victoriana Antiques, Birmingham, West Mids.
Victoriana Antiques, Stockton Heath, Cheshire.
Victoriana Antiques, Wimborne Minster, Dorset.
Victoriana Architectural, Long Clawston, Leics.
Victoriana Dolls, London, W11.
Victoria's, Atherton, Lancs.
Victoria's Bedroom, Hungerford, Berks.
Vieux-Pernon, B., London, SW1.
Vigo Carpet Gallery, London, W1.
Vigo-Sternberg Galleries, London, W1.
Village Antique Market, The, Weedon, Northants.
Village Antiques, Bexhill-on-Sea, Sussex East.
Village Antiques, Broughton, Lancs.
Village Antiques, Manchester, Lancs.
Village Clocks, Long Melford, Suffolk.
Village Green Antiques, Hertford, Herts.
Village Pine, Farnham, Surrey.
Village Studio, Brodick, Scotland.
Village Time, London, SE7.
Vince, Ian F., Rettendon, Essex.
Vince, N.B., Bawdeswell, Norfolk.
Vincent, H., Barrow-in-Furness, Cumbria.
Vine Cottage Antiques, Streatley, Berks.
Vine House Antiques, Neston, Cheshire.
Vine, M. and D., Tetsworth, Oxon.
Vines Antiques, Rochester, Kent.
Viney, Elizabeth, Stockbridge, Hants.
Viney MBE, Miss E.A., Stockbridge, Hants.
Vintage Antiques Centre, Warwick, Warks.
Vintage Cameras Ltd, London, SE26.
Vintage Toy and Train Museum, The, Sidmouth, Devon.
Vintage Wireless Co Ltd, The, Bristol, Avon.
Vintage Wireless Shop, Nottingham, Notts.
Violin Shop, The, Hexham, Northumbs.
Virginia, London, W11.
Virginia Antique Galleries, Glasgow, Scotland.
Vive Antiques, Penzance, Cornwall.
Vollaro, Mrs A., Chalfont St. Giles, Bucks.
von Dahlen, BaronessV., Long Melford, Suffolk.
von der Burg, C., London, SW1.
von Lobkowitz, I.K., London, SW19.
Von Pflugh Antiques, Johnny, London, W11.
Von Stackelberg, B., Whitstable, Kent.
von Wallwitz, Angela Gräfin, London, W1.
Von Westenholz Ltd, Piers, London, SW1.
Vosburgh, Beryl, London, N1.
Vosper, J.V., Minchinhampton, Glos.
Voss, A.G., Woodbridge, Suffolk.

W

W.13 Antiques, London, W13.
W.H.E.A.P. Antiques, Worcester, Herefs. & Worcs.
W.R.S. Architectural Antiques, Low Newton, Cumbria.
Wace Ancient Art Ltd, Rupert, London, SW1.
Wade, Mrs J., Gravesend, Kent.
Wade Antiques, Ray, Preston, Lancs.
Wade-Smith, A., Newark, Notts.
Wade-Smith and Read, Newark, Notts.
Wadge Clocks, Chris, Salisbury, Wilts.
Wadham, Peter, Exeter, Devon.
Wadley, N., Knaresborough, Yorks. North.
Waggoner, J. and J., Bath, Avon.
Wagstaff, Cara, Cheltenham, Glos.
Wagstaff, Mrs J., Oxted, Surrey.
Wain, J.I., Ripon, Yorks. North.
Wain, Peter, Woore, Shrops.
Waine, Alan and Victoria, Kelvedon, Essex.
Wainwright, David, London, W11.

Wainwright, P.J., Bridgnorth, Shrops.
Wajzner, J. and N., Southport, Merseyside.
Wakefield, Mr and Mrs A., Westcott, Surrey.
Wakefield, C.P., Freuchie, Scotland.
Wakelin and Helen Linfield, Michael, Petworth, Sussex West.
Wakeman and Taylor Antiques, Wolverhampton, West Mids.
Waknell, R.M. and Mrs F., Uppingham, Leics.
Walcot Reclamation, Bath, Avon.
Walford, G.W., London, N5.
Walker, Alan and Kym, Halfway, Berks.
Walker, C., London, SW3.
Walker, C., Witney, Oxon.
Walker, Mrs D., Ewell, Surrey.
Walker, G., Bolton, Lancs.
Walker, G.R., Penrith, Cumbria.
Walker, I., Odiham, Hants.
Walker Galleries Ltd, Harrogate, Yorks. North.
Walker Antiques, John, Dorchester, Dorset.
Walker Antiques, John, Hexham, Northumbs.
Walker Gallery, Meldrum, London, SW6.
Walker, M.W., Coleraine, Co. Londonderry, N. Ireland.
Walker, P., Burford, Oxon.
Walker, Mrs S. Kitching, Thornton le Dale, Yorks. North.
Walker and Walker, Halfway, Berks.
Walker, W.E., London, NW1.
Walker, W. and J., Jesmond, Tyne and Wear.
Walker, Zene, Burford, Oxon.
Walker-Bagshawe, London, SW3.
Walking Stick Shop, The, Arundel, Sussex West.
Walkley, R.C., Shaldon, Devon.
Wall, C.A., Ipswich, Suffolk.
Wallace Antiques Ltd, London, SE3.
Wallace, N., York, Yorks. North.
Wallbank-Fox, J.A. and M.A., Hungerford, Berks.
Wallis and Gerry Mosdell, Glenda, Bath, Avon.
Wallis, Mr and Mrs G.M.A., Wingham, Kent.
Wallis, Michael S., Gainsborough, Lincs.
Wallop, Hon N.V.B. and L.N.J., London, SW1.
Walls, C., Tenterden, Kent.
Walmsley, Anthony, Blackburn, Lancs.
Walmsley, A. and F.A., Blackburn, Lancs.
Walmsley, Shusha, Kettering, Northants.
Walne, H.S., Southport, Merseyside.
Walpole Gallery, London, W1.
Walpole, G.R., London, W11.
Walsall Antiques Centre, Walsall, West Mids.
Walsh Ltd, Bernard, Chester, Cheshire.
Walsh, M., Burwash, Sussex East.
Walters, B., Weedon, Northamptonshire.
Walters, H.J. and S.M., West Haddon, Northants.
Walters, J.D. and R.M., Rolvenden, Kent.
Walton, A., Darlington, Durham.
Walton, S.M., Bath, Avon.
Walwyn Antiques, Howard, Wootton Bassett, Wilts.
Wandle's Workshop, Mr, London, SW18.
Wansford Antiques and Oriental Pottery, Wansford, Cambs.
Warboys Antiques, Warboys, Cambs.
Warburton, E., Stockport, Cheshire.
Ward Antiques, London, SE7.
Ward, Charles H., Derby, Derbys.
Ward Antiques, C.W., Kettering, Northants.
Ward Antiques plc, Long Melford, Suffolk.
Ward and Son, L.L., Brandsby, Yorks. North.
Ward, M.G., Derby, Derbys.
Ward Antiques, Paul, Sheffield, Yorks. South.
Ward Fine Paintings, P.J., Cirencester, Glos.
Ward, R., Brandsby, Yorks. North.
Ward, S.A., Sevenoaks, Kent.
Ward, Stewart, Westerham, Kent.
Ward Properties, Stewart, Westerham, Kent.
Ward Antiques, Sheldon, Sevenoaks, Kent.
Ward, T. and M., London, SE7.
Warde, J., Farnborough, Hants.
Ward-Lee, B., Four Elms, Kent.
Ward-Smith, B.A. and F.B., Kentisbeare, Devon.
Wardle, M.S., London, SW14.
Wardle, T., Ashbourne, Derbys.
Warehouse, The, Horncastle, Lincs.
Warehouse Antiques, Honiton, Devon.
Wareside Antiques, Wareside, Herts.
Wargrave Antiques, Wargrave, Berks.
Waring, Mrs C.M., Enfield, Middx.

DEALERS' INDEX

Waring, R., Hereford, Herefs. and Worcs.
Warings of Hereford Antiques, Hereford, Herefs. & Worcs.
Warley Antique Centre, Birmingham, West Mids.
Warn, Penelope J., Ramsgate, Kent.
Warne Family, The, Tregony, Cornwall.
Warner, Christopher, Harrogate, Yorks. North.
Warner, C.C., Harrogate, Yorks. North.
Warner, Mrs C.U., Brasted, Kent.
Warner Fine Art, Newcastle-upon-Tyne, Tyne and Wear.
Warner and Son Ltd, Robert, Worthing, Sussex West.
Warner, S. and M., Newcastle-upon-Tyne, Tyne and Wear.
Warner (Antiques) Ltd, W.W., Brasted, Kent.
Waroujian, M.L., London, W6.
Warren, A.M., Ipswich, Suffolk.
Warren, B., Seaton, Devon.
Warren, C.R.H., Bristol, Avon.
Warren, Dr.D.J., Portsmouth, Hants.
Warren Antiques, Jimmy, Littlebourne, Kent.
Warren, J.R., Leiston, Suffolk.
Warren Antiques, Leigh, London, SW6.
Warren, M., London, N1.
Warren, Patricia, Rye, Sussex East.
Warren, Mrs S., Sanderstead, Surrey.
Warren, Shirley, Sanderstead, Surrey.
Warrender, F.R., Sutton, Surrey.
Warrender and Co, S., Sutton, Surrey.
Warrick, E.M. and J.K., Montacute, Somerset.
Warrington, Paul, Oakham, Leics.
Wartski Ltd, London, W1.
Warwick Antique Centre, The, Warwick, Warks.
Warwick Antiques, Warwick, Warks.
Warwick, D.C., Weymouth, Dorset.
Water Lane Antiques, Bakewell, Derbys.
Watercolour Gallery, the, Cowbridge, South Glam., Wales.
Waterfield's, Oxford, Oxon.
Waterfront Antiques Market, Falmouth, Cornwall.
Watergate Antiques, Chester, Cheshire.
Waterhouse and Dodd, London, W1.
Waterhouse, R., London, W1.
Waterloo Antiques, Cirencester, Glos.
Waterloo Antiques, Oldham, Lancs.
Waterloo Antiques, Welshpool, Powys, Wales.
Waterloo Antiques Centre, Leeds, Yorks. West.
Waterloo Trading Co., London, SE1.
Waterman Fine Art Ltd, London, SW1.
Waterman, T. and R., London, SW1.
Waters, J. and M., Penarth, South Glam., Wales.
Waterside Antiques, Ely, Cambs.
Watherington, K. and J., Leominster, Herefs. and Worcs.
Watkins Books Ltd, London, WC2.
Watkins, I., Knighton, Powys, Wales.
Watkins, Islwyn, Knighton, Powys, Wales.
Watkins, Rita and John, Devizes, Wilts.
Watkins and Stafford Ltd, Peterborough, Cambs.
Watkins, T.P.C., London, W1.
Watling Antiques, Crayford, Kent.
Watson, Mrs E., Norwich, Norfolk.
Watson, G.D., London, SW3.
Watson, Howard and Pat, Stratford-upon-Avon, Warks.
Watson, J., Shere, Surrey.
Watson, M.E., Market Weighton, N. Humbs.
Watson, Pauline, Ashtead, Surrey.
Watson FGA NAG, Pauline, Dorking, Surrey.
Watson, V., Kincardine O'Neil, Scotland.
Watt, Elizabeth, Aberdeen, Scotland.
Watt, S.M., Edinburgh, Scotland.
Watt, V., Banchory, Scotland.
Watts Antiques, Chris, Newport, I. of Wight.
Watts Oriental Rugs, Duncan, Market Harborough, Leics.
Watts, M.L., Northampton, Northants.
Watts, P.J., St. Austell, Cornwall.
Watts, R., Saltaire, Yorks. West.
Waveney Antiques Centre, Beccles, Suffolk.
Waverley Antiques, Upper Largo, Scotland.
Waverley Gallery, The, Aberdeen, Scotland.
Way, R.E. and G.B., Newmarket, Suffolk.
Waymouth, A., Milverton, Somerset.
Waymouth, J. and E., Honiton, Devon.
Wayne "The Razor Man", Neil, Belper, Derbys.
Wayside Antiques, Duffield, Derbys.
Wayside Antiques, Tattershall, Lincs.
Weald Gallery, The, Brasted, Kent.

Wearn and Son Ltd, R., London, SW3.
Weatherell's of Harrogate Antiques and Fine Arts, Harrogate, Yorks. North.
Weaver Antiques, Bernard, Cirencester, Glos.
Weaver, L., Aldeburgh, Suffolk.
Weaver, Peter, Aldeburgh, Suffolk.
Weaver, P., Hartley Wintney, Hants.
Weaver, Trude, London, W11.
Weavers Cottage Antiques, Painswick, Glos.
Web, A. M., London, W11.
Webb, D.H., Winchester, Hants.
Webb Fine Arts, Winchester, Hants.
Webb, Graham, Brighton, Sussex East.
Webb, G.P., London, E17.
Webb, M., London, N1.
Webb, M., London, N13.
Webb, M., Wallington, Surrey.
Webb Fine Art, Michael, Bodorgan, Gwynedd, Wales.
Webb, P.A., Yarmouth, I. of Wight.
Webb, Roy, Wickham Market, Suffolk.
Webber, C., Brantham, Suffolk.
Webster, A. and S., Teignmouth, Devon.
Webster, A.J., Coleshill, Warks.
Webster, E.T., Blythburgh,, Suffolk.
Webster, E.W., Bickerstaffe, Lancs.
Webster, G., Liverpool, Merseyside.
Webster, M., Cross Hills, Yorks. North.
Webster, M., Great Waltham, Essex.
Webster-Speakman, S.J., Cambridge, Cambs.
Wegner, G., London, N1.
Weidenbaum, R., Manchester, Lancs.
Weijand Fine Oriental Carpets, Karel, Farnham, Surrey.
Weiner, G., Brighton, Sussex East.
Weiner, M., Ipswich, Suffolk.
Weir, Mr and Mrs D., Bottisham, Cambs.
Weir Antiques, Gerald, Ipswich, Suffolk.
Weiss Gallery, The, London, W1.
Welbeck Gallery, The, London, W1.
Welbourne, Stephen and Sonia, Brighton, Sussex East.
Welch, K. and A., Warminster, Wilts.
Welch, R., Gateshead, Tyne and Wear.
Weldon, H.W. and N.C., Southport, Merseyside.
Weldons Jewellers and Antiques, Southport, Merseyside.
Well Cottage Antiques, Settle, Yorks. North.
Well House Antiques, Tilston, Cheshire.
Well Lane Antiques, Beverley, N. Humbs.
Wellby, C.S., Haddenham, Bucks.
Wellby Ltd, H.S., Haddenham, Bucks.
Weller, P. and R., Malvern Wells, Herefs. and Worcs.
Weller - Restoration Centre, W.H., Eastbourne, Sussex East.
Wellfield Antique Centre, Bangor, Gwynedd, Wales.
Welling Antiques, Anthony, Ripley, Surrey.
Wellington Antiques, London, W11.
Wellington Antiques, Southampton, Hants.
Wellington Gallery, London, NW8.
Wells Antique Centre, Wells-next-the-Sea, Norfolk.
Wells, G., Wallingford, Oxon.
Wells, J.H., Aberdeen, Scotland.
Wells Reclamation Company, Coxley, Somerset.
Wellstead, A.V., Woking, Surrey.
Welsh Art, Tywyn, Gwynedd, Wales.
Welsh, P., Brasted, Kent.
Welsh, R., Sandgate, Kent.
Wendover Antiques, Wendover, Bucks.
Wenlock Fine Art, Much Wenlock, Shrops.
Wentworth, J., London, N1.
Wentworth, J., London, W11.
Wertheim, Mr. and Mrs C.D., London, W8.
Wessex Medical Antiques, Portsmouth, Hants.
West, B., Canterbury, Kent.
West Borough Antiques, Fine Art, Wimborne Minster, Dorset.
West Bow Antiques, Edinburgh, Scotland.
West - Cobb Antiques Ltd, Mark J., London, N1.
West - Cobb Antiques Ltd, Mark J., London, SW19.
West End Antiques, Elgin, Scotland.
West End Antiques Market, Redruth, Cornwall.
West End Galleries, Buxton, Derbys.
West End House Antiques, Ilminster, Somerset.
West Farm Antiques, Orwell, Cambs.
West Lancs. Antiques, Burscough, Lancs.
West of Scotland Antique Centre Ltd, Glasgow, Scotland.

DEALERS' INDEX

West Park Antiques Pavilion, Harrogate, Yorks. North.
West Quay Curios, Looe, Cornwall.
West, S., Dorking, Surrey.
West-Skinn, R., Lincoln, Lincs.
West Street Antiques, Dorking, Surrey.
West Street Antiques, Midhurst, Sussex West.
West Wales Antiques, Murton, West Glam., Wales.
Westbourne Antiques, Westbourne, Sussex West.
Westbourne Grove Antique Gallery, London, W11.
Westcliffe Gallery, The, Sheringham, Norfolk.
Westcott Antiques, Westcott, Surrey.
Westcott Gallery, The, Westcott, Surrey.
Westdale Antiques, Bridport, Dorset.
Westfield Antiques, Baslow, Derbys.
Westgate Antiques, Warwick, Warks.
Westland & Company, London, EC2.
Westley-Richards, W., London, SW3.
Weston Antique Gallery, Weston, Staffs.
Weston, David, London, SW3.
Weston, D.A., London, SW3.
Weston Gallery, William, London, W1.
Weston, R. and P., Harrow, Middx.
Westover, D., Bridport, Dorset.
Westport Gallery, Dundee, Scotland.
Westrope, I., Birdbrook, Essex.
Westville House Antiques, Littleton, Somerset.
Westway Cottage Restored Pine, Helmsley, Yorks. North.
Westwood, F., Petersfield, Hants.
Westwood Antiquarian Books, Mark, Hay-on-Wye, Powys, Wales.
Wetherill, J., Northallerton, Yorks. North.
Wetherill, R., York, Yorks. North.
Weybridge Antiques, Weybridge, Surrey.
Whalley, Mrs O.M., Eye, Suffolk.
Wharton, Stuart, St. Albans, Herts.
Wharton Antiques, Tim, Redbourn, Herts.
What Not Antiques, Hindhead, Surrey.
What Now Antiques, Buxton, Derbys.
Whatnot Antiques, Wigan, Lancs.
Whatnots, Strathblane, Scotland.
Whay, K. and D., Hoylake, Merseyside.
Wheatley, R., Empingham, Leics.
Wheatleys, Gt. Yarmouth, Norfolk.
Wheeldon, Mrs D., Ellesmere, Shrops.
Wheeler Antiques: Style and Design, G. M., Bridlington, N. Humbs.
Wheeler, R.W.H. and M.J., Crewkerne, Somerset.
Wheeler-Johns, Kevin, Honiton, Devon.
Wheelwright, The, Baldock, Herts.
Wheldon and Wesley Ltd, Codicote, Herts.
Whiddons Antiques and Tearooms, Chagford, Devon.
Whillock, F., Litton Cheney, Dorset.
Whiskin, MissJ., Brighton, Sussex East.
Whitaker, J., Pickering, Yorks. North.
Whitby, C. and Mrs . B., Lane End, Bucks.
Whitby Antiques, Peter, Lechlade, Glos.
White Boar Antiques and Books, Middleham, Yorks. North.
White, B.B., London, EC1.
White, D., Ramsbury, Wilts.
White, D., Weston-Super-Mare, Avon.
White Antiques, David, Godalming, Surrey.
White, D. and Y., Godalming, Surrey.
White Elephant, The, Southport, Merseyside.
White Elephant Antiques, Bowness-on-Windermere, Cumbria.
White, E. and B., Brighton, Sussex East.
White, G., Swinton, Lancs.
White, G. and J., Harrogate, Yorks. North.
White, G. and J., Huby, Yorks. North.
White House Antiques, Princes Risborough, Bucks.
White, J., London, W1.
White House Farm Antiques, Easingwold, Yorks. North.
White, J.C., Fitzhead, Somerset.
White, Joan and David, Barnard Castle, Durham.
White, Karen, Horncastle, Lincs.
White Lion Antiques, Ellesmere, Shrops.
White, P., Cranborne, Dorset.
White Roding Antiques, White Roding, Essex.
White, R.S. and Mrs A., Cranbrook, Kent.
White, Shirley, Derby, Derbys.
White, T.E., Wimborne Minster, Dorset.
Whitehead, D. and V., Newark, Notts.

Whitehead, Joyce and Rod, Chester, Cheshire.
Whitehead, W.S.H. and Mrs M.M., Lewes, Sussex East.
Whitehouse Antique Interiors, Arundel, Sussex West.
Whiteland, K. and J., Aberaeron, Dyfed, Wales.
Whitelaw and Sons Antiques, John, Auchterarder, Scotland.
Whitelaw, Peter, Ironbridge, Shrops.
Whiteley Wright Ltd,, Addingham, Yorks. West.
Whitemoors Antiques and Fine Art, Shenton, Leics.
Whiteside, R.J., Pershore, Herefs. and Worcs.
Whitestone, S., London, NW8.
Whiteway, M., London, SW6.
Whiteway, T.M., London, W8.
Whiteway and Waldron Ltd, London, SW6.
Whiteway-Wilkinson, G.A., Maidencombe, Devon.
Whitfield, A. and S., Edinburgh, Scotland.
Whitfield, Chris, Canterbury, Kent.
Whitfield Antiques, Robert, London, SE10.
Whitford and Hughes, London, W2.
Whitgift Galleries, The, Croydon, Surrey.
Whitmore, Great Malvern, Herefs. & Worcs.
Whitney Antiques, Robert, Whitchurch, Shrops.
Whittaker, B.J., Stickney, Lincs.
Whittaker, R.A. and Mrs L.R., Angmering, Sussex West.
Whittam, C.O., St. Peter Port, Guernsey, C.I.
Whittam, P., Tetbury, Glos.
Whittingham, A., Bath, Avon.
Whitworth and O'Donnell Ltd, London, SE13.
Whyte, John, Edinburgh, Scotland.
Whyte, Philip, London, SW1.
Whytock and Reid, Edinburgh, Scotland.
Wibroe Antiques Ltd, Neil, London, W11.
Wickens, Mrs P., Sandwich, Kent.
Wickham Antiques, Honiton, Devon.
Wickins, A. and M., Peasenhall, Suffolk.
Wickins, Mrs C.J., Farnham, Surrey.
Wickstead, W., Swansea, West Glam., Wales.
Widcombe Antiques and Pine, Bath, Avon.
Widdas Fine Paintings, Roger, Bentley Heath, West Mids.
Widmerpool House Antiques, Maidenhead, Berks.
Wieliczko, J. and D., London, N6.
Wiffen, C. A., Parkstone, Dorset.
Wiffen's Antiques, Parkstone, Dorset.
Wigdor, David, Brighton, Sussex East.
Wigek, Z., London, SW6.
Wiggins and Sons Ltd, Arnold, London, SW1.
Wiggins, Peter, Chipping Norton, Oxon.
Wigington Antiques, Hay-on-Wye, Powys, Wales.
Wigington, B., Hay-on-Wye, Powys, Wales.
Wigington Antiques, James, Stratford-upon-Avon, Warks.
Wigington, R.J., Stratford-upon-Avon, Warks.
Wigram, Francis, Penn, Bucks.
Wilby, D.G. and M., Tattershall, Lincs.
Wilcox, A., Shrewsbury, Shrops.
Wilcox, S., Bristol, Avon.
Wild Goose Antiques, Modbury, Devon.
Wild Rose Antiques, Edinburgh, Scotland.
Wild, Mrs W.M., Tetbury, Glos.
Wildenstein and Co Ltd, London, W1.
Wilder, Jess, London, W1.
Wilder, M.P., Chesham, Bucks.
Wilding, Mr, Liverpool, Merseyside.
Wilding, R., Wisbech, Cambs.
Wilding-Welton, Kim, Chester, Cheshire.
Wildish., Lt. Col. V. and Mrs A., Dorney, Berks.
Wildman, K., Bushey, Herts.
Wildman, P. and M., Dalbeattie, Scotland.
Wildman's Antiques, Dalbeattie, Scotland.
Wiles, B., Witney, Oxon.
Wilkin, G.F., Honiton, Devon.
Wilkins Antiques, Brett, Wednesbury, West Mids.
Wilkins, D., Woking, Surrey.
Wilkins, Mrs J., Witney, Oxon.
Wilkins Antiques, Joan, Witney, Oxon.
Wilkins, M., London, W1.
Wilkins and Wilkins, London, W1.
Wilkinson, A., Brighton, Sussex East.
Wilkinson, A., Newhaven, Sussex East.
Wilkinson, Mrs A., Harrogate, Yorks. North.
Wilkinson, Allan and Linda, Olney, Bucks.
Wilkinson, B., Sible Hedingham, Essex.
Wilkinson, M. and P., Grantham, Lincs.
Wilkinson, M. and P., Sleaford, Lincs.

DEALERS' INDEX

Wilkinson, P.J. and Mrs J., Bowness-on-Windermere, Cumbria.
Wilkinson plc, London, SE6.
Wilkinson plc, London, W1.
Wilkinson Antiques, Rita M., Colchester, Essex.
Wilkinson, S., London, SW6.
Wilkinson, S.P. and H.S., Lancaster, Lancs.
Wilkinson Antiques Ltd, T.G., Petworth, Sussex West.
Wilkinson, T. and S., Petworth, Sussex West.
Wilkinson's, Grantham, Lincs.
Wilkinson's, Sleaford, Lincs.
Wilks-Jones, M.A., Conway, Gwynedd, Wales.
Willatt, R.F. and M., Chichester, Sussex West.
Willcox, Neil, Twickenham, Middx.
Willder, S., Birmingham, West Mids.
William, G., Winster, Derbys.
Williams, A.J., Bristol, Avon.
Williams, B., Gloucester, Glos.
Williams, Chris, Bournemouth, Dorset.
Williams Antiquarian Bookseller, Christopher, Lymington, Hants.
Williams Antiquarian Bookseller, Christopher, Parkstone, Dorset.
Williams, Betty, Tredunnock, Gwent, Wales.
Williams, Frank, Burford, Oxon.
Williams, J.R., London, W1.
Williams - Antique Anglo Am Warehouse, Lloyd, Eastbourne, Sussex East.
Williams, M., Swansea, Mid-Glam., Wales.
Williams, Nick and Sue, London, SE24.
Williams, P., Winslow, Bucks.
Williams, Paul, Synod Inn, Dyfed, Wales.
Williams, R. and Y., Coniston, Cumbria.
Williams and Son, London, W1.
Williams (Fine Art) Ltd, Thomas, London, SW1.
Williams Antiques Ltd., Thomas, Bideford, Devon.
Williamson, I.A., Lynton, Devon.
Williamson, R. and D., Newton Stewart, Scotland.
Williamson & Co, R.G., Sorbie, Scotland.
Willis, J., Norwich, Norfolk.
Willoughby, Mrs J., Northallerton, Yorks. North.
Willow Farm Pine Centre, Harlington, Beds.
Wills, Mrs H.J., Sheffield, Yorks. South.
Wilsher, Miss M., Frinton-on-Sea, Essex.
Wilson, Clive, Low Newton, Cumbria.
Wilson Antiques, Colin, Sundridge, Kent.
Wilson, F., Worthing, Sussex West.
Wilson, Frances, Boscastle, Cornwall.
Wilson, G., Eccleston, Lancs.
Wilson, G., Lamberhurst, Kent.
Wilson, Ian, London, SE1.
Wilson, J., Birmingham, West Mids.
Wilson, Mrs J., Kettering, Northants.
Wilson (Autographs) Ltd, John, Eynsham, Oxon.
Wilson, J.D., Boroughbridge, Yorks. North.
Wilson, K., Ickleton, Cambs.
Wilson, M.J., Brancaster Staithe, Norfolk.
Wilson, Nancy, Sandwich, Kent.
Wilson, O., Bideford, Devon.
Wilson Ltd, O.F., London, SW3.
Wilson, P., Kelvedon, Essex.
Wilson Ltd, Paul, Hull, N. Humbs.
Wilson, Mrs P.S., Bruton, Somerset.
Wilson, R., Petworth, Sussex West.
Wilson and Sons, R.S., Boroughbridge, Yorks. North.
Wilson, S.C., Kingsthorpe, Northants.
Wilson, Mrs S.J., Bristol, Avon.
Wilson, Timothy D., Bawtry, Yorks. South.
Wilson, T. and P., Edinburgh, Scotland.
Wilsons Antiques, Worthing, Sussex West.
Wiltshire, C.A., Twickenham, Middx.
Wiltshire, D.K. and R.M., Hurst Green, Sussex East.
Wimble, M., Rochester, Kent.
Wimsett, P., Ramsgate, Kent.
Winchmore Antiques, London, N21.
Windhill Antiquary, The, Bishop's Stortford, Herts.
Windle, Mrs W.J., Bingley, Yorks. West.
Windmill Antiques, Bembridge, I. of Wight.
Windmill Antiques, Harrogate, Yorks. North.
Windmill Antiques, Stafford, Staffs.
Windmill Gallery, The, Birmingham, West Mids.
Windrush Antiques, Witney, Oxon.

Windsor, Frank, Lynton, Devon.
Windsor Gallery, Lowestoft, Suffolk.
Windsor Gallery, David, Bangor, Gwynedd, Wales.
Windsor House Antiques Centre, Moreton-in-Marsh, Glos.
Windsor House Antiques (Leeds) Ltd., Leeds, Yorks. West.
Wingfield, Mrs M., London, SW4.
Wingfield Sporting Art, London, SW4.
Winikus, J., Sandgate, Kent.
Winkworth Antiques, Richard, Redruth, Cornwall.
Winkworth Antiques, Richard , Truro, Cornwall.
Winslow Antiques Centre, Winslow, Bucks.
Winstanley, T., Hindhead, Surrey.
Winster Arts, Winster, Derbys.
Winston Galleries, Harrow, Middx.
Winston Mac (Silversmith), Bury St. Edmunds, Suffolk.
Winter, Eveline, Rugeley, Staffs.
Winter, Mrs E., Rugeley, Staffs.
Winterflood, Mr and Mrs, Canterbury, Kent.
Winter's Antiques, Weston-Super-Mare, Avon.
Winters, R.N., E.P. and L.B., Weston-Super-Mare, Avon.
Wirth, P. and C., London, SW19.
Wisdom, M., Carshalton, Surrey.
Wisdom, M., Mitcham, Surrey.
Wise, Mary, London, W8.
Wise Owl Bookshop, The, Bristol, Avon.
Wish Ward Antiques, Rye, Sussex East.
Wiskin Antiques, Bishops Stortford, Herts.
Wiskin, K. and M., Bishops Stortford, Herts.
Wissinger, G., Chipping Norton, Oxon.
Wissinger and Antonio Mendoza, George, London, SE1.
Witch Ball, The, Brighton, Sussex East.
Witch Ball, The, London, NW9.
Witch Ball, The, London, WC2.
Witham, Norman, Beckenham, Kent.
Withers of Leicester, Hoby, Leics.
Withers - Antiques, Robert, Halesowen, West Mids.
Witney Antiques, Witney, Oxon.
Witting, Lt. Col. and Mrs D.W., Church Stretton, Shrops.
Woburn Abbey Antiques Centre, The, Woburn, Beds.
Woburn Fine Arts, Woburn, Beds.
Woda, A., London, NW8.
Wolf Antiques Ltd, H. and B., Droitwich, Herefs. & Worcs.
Wolf, H.G. and B.J., Droitwich, Herefs. and Worcs.
Wolfenden, David, Antrim, Co. Antrim, N. Ireland.
Wolfers, D., London, SW13.
Wolseley Fine Arts plc, London, SE5.
Wood, Alan, Tunbridge Wells, Kent.
Wood, Andrew S., Marazion, Cornwall.
Wood (Antiques) Ltd, Colin, Aberdeen, Scotland.
Wood Gallery, The Christopher, London, W1.
Wood, C. and P., Southport, Merseyside.
Wood, G., Aberdeen, Scotland.
Wood Fine Art, Jeremy, Petworth, Sussex West.
Wood, J. and S., Cartmel, Cumbria.
Wood Antiques, Lilian, Great Urswick, Cumbria.
Wood, Mrs M., Donyatt, Somerset.
Wood, R.M. and P.A., Hatfield Broad Oak, Essex.
Wood, S., Leeds, Yorks. West.
Wood, S., Osbournby, Lincs.
Woodall and Emery Ltd, Balcombe, Sussex West.
Woodburn, Anthony, Leigh, Kent.
Woodbury Antiques, Woodbury, Devon.
Wooden Box Antiques, Woodville, Derbys.
Wooden Chair Antiques, Cranbrook, Kent.
Wooden Fleece, Exmouth, Devon.
Woodentops Country Furniture, London, SW18.
Woodhams, W. J., Shaldon, Devon.
Woodhead, Geoffrey M. , Honiton, Devon.
Woodhouse, A., London, WC2.
Woodhouse (Antiquarian Horologist), R.C., Hunstanton, Norfolk.
Woodhouse, Mrs J.E., Hunstanton, Norfolk.
Woodland Fine Art, Alvechurch, West Mids.
Woods, B., Warrenpoint, Co. Down, N. Ireland.
Woods, G., Lancaster, Lancs.
Woods, G., Manchester, Lancs.
Wood's Wharf Antiques Bazaar, Haslemere, Surrey.
Woodstock Antiques, Woodstock, Oxon.
Woolacombe Bay Antiques, Woolacombe, Devon.
Woolf, A.D., London, N1.
Woolfsons of James Street Ltd, Glasgow, Scotland.
Woolley, David, Cocking, Sussex West.

DEALERS' INDEX

Woolman Antiques, L., Brighton, Sussex East.
Woon, Mrs D.J., Lymington, Hants.
Wooster, B.R. and P.A., Streatley, Berks.
Wooster, J.A., Twickenham, Middx.
Wootton Clocks and Watches, L.G., South Brent, Devon.
Wootton-Billingham, Northampton, Northants.
Worcester Antiques Centre, Worcester, Herefs. & Worcs.
Wordsworth, P., Manchester, Lancs.
Workman, J., Kidderminster, Herefs. and Worcs.
World Famous Portobello Market, London, W11.
Worster, M., London, W11.
Worth, G.F.E., Newport, Shrops.
Worth Antiques, Patrick, Dorking, Surrey.
Worthington, Mrs M., Edinburgh, Scotland.
Worthington, R., Bristol, Avon.
Worthington's Antiques, Edinburgh, Scotland.
Worth's, Newport, Shrops.
Wosac Ltd,, Glasgow, Scotland.
Wragg, R.G., Leek, Staffs.
Wraight, T., Weymouth, Dorset.
Wray's Lighting Emporium, Christopher, London, SW6.
Wrecclesham Antiques, Farnham, Surrey.
Wren Antiques, London, SW13.
Wren Gallery, Burford, Oxon.
Wren House Antiques, Wrentham, Suffolk.
Wren, M.J., Bath, Avon.
Wrenn Antiques, Richard, Leigh-on-Sea, Essex.
Wrentham Antiques, Wrentham, Suffolk.
Wrentham Antiques Centre, Wrentham, Suffolk.
Wrigglesworth, Linda, London, W1.
Wright Antiques Ltd, Clifford, London, SW3.
Wright, D.T.L., Alresford, Hants.
Wright, E., Bournemouth, Dorset.
Wright, F., Acle, Norfolk.
Wright - Fine Paintings, G.S., Castle Ashby, Northants.
Wright, J., London, N1.
Wright, J. and C., Winchester, Hants.
Wright, Mick and Fanny, Minchinhampton, Glos.
Wright Antiques, Peter, Great Missenden, Bucks.
Wright, Mrs R.S., King's Lynn, Norfolk.
Wright Antiques, Tim, Glasgow, Scotland.
Wright, T. and J., Glasgow, Scotland.
Wright (Booksellers), Sidney, Bournemouth, Dorset.
Wright, W., Bankfoot, Scotland.
Wrightson, J.E., Norwich, Norfolk.
Wrightson, J.E., Strachan, Scotland.
Wrigley, John R., Ecclesfield, Yorks. South.
Wroughton Antique Centre, Wroughton, Wilts.
Wyche House Antiques, Nantwich, Cheshire.
Wych House Antiques, Woking, Surrey.
Wychwood Antiques, Ascott-under-Wychwood, Oxon.
Wykeham Galleries, The, London, SW13.
Wyle Cop Antiques and Reproductions, Shrewsbury, Shrops.
Wylie, Mrs M., Hindhead, Surrey.
Wyllie Gallery, The, London, SW7.
Wyllie, J.G., London, SW7.
Wymondham Antique Centre, Wymondham, Norfolk.
Wyndham, H., London, SW1.
Wynsave Investments Ltd., Hungerford, Berks.
Wynter Ltd. Arts and Sciences, Harriet, London, SW10.
Wynyards Antiques (Lastlodge Ltd.), London, W11.
Wyrardisbury Antiques, Wraysbury, Berks.

Y

Yacobi, B. and C., London, W1.
Yale, J., Rochester, Kent.
Yandell, Mrs A., Cambridge, Cambs.
Yardy, S., London, W14.
Yarwood, Mr and Mrs G.E., Stoke-on-Trent, Staffs.
Yarwood, J.A., Settle, Yorks. North.
Yates, Mr, Nottingham, Notts.
Yates, A., Chipping Campden, Glos.
Yates Antiques, Brian , Chesterfield, Derbys.

Yates, Mrs D., York, Yorks. North.
Yates, Inez M. P., York, Yorks. North.
Yates, S., Quorn, Leics.
Ye Little Shoppe, Modbury, Devon.
Ye Olde Saddlers Shoppe, Horrabridge, Devon.
Yealland, J. M., Caversham, Berks.
Yealmantiques, Yealmpton, Devon.
Year Dot, Leeds, Yorks. West.
Yellow Lantern Antiques Ltd, Brighton, Sussex East.
Yendell, J.M., Bampton, Devon.
Yeo Antiques, Tetbury, Glos.
Yeo, G.A., Hazel Grove, Cheshire.
Yeo, W.B., Plaitford, Hants.
Yeomans, Mrs S.D., Knighton, Powys, Wales.
Yer Granny's Attic, Prestwick, Scotland.
Yesterday, Evesham, Herefs. & Worcs.
Yesterday Child, London, N1.
Yesterday Tackle and Books, Bournemouth, Dorset.
Yesterdays, Leamington Spa, Warks.
Yesterdays Antiques, Birmingham, West Mids.
Yesterday's Antiques, London, SW14.
Yesterdays Pine, Shere, Surrey.
Yesteryear, Glasgow, Scotland.
Yester-year, Iver, Bucks.
Yesteryear, Norwich, Norfolk.
Yesteryear, Ripon, Yorks. North.
Yesteryear Antiques, Ramsey, Cambs.
Yew Tree Antiques, Four Elms, Kent.
Yewman, J.S. and F. M., Abridge, Essex.
Yewtree Antiques, Templecombe, Somerset.
Yistelworth Antiques, Isleworth, Middx.
Yorath, G., Caenarfon, Gwynedd, Wales.
York Antiques Centre, York, Yorks. North.
York Arcade, London, N1.
York Cottage Antiques, Helmsley, Yorks. North.
York, G., Honiton, Devon.
York House Gallery, Bournemouth, Dorset.
York, T.O. and J., Quorn, Leics.
Yorke, J.H., St. Leonards-on-Sea, Sussex East.
Youde, Malcolm, Tarvin Sands, Cheshire.
Youll, D., Hungerford, Berks.
Youll's Antiques, Hungerford, Berks.
Young, Aldric, Edinburgh, Scotland.
Young Antiques, Edinburgh, Scotland.
Young, A.J. and A.R., Deal, Kent.
Young Antiques, Denis, Aberfeldy, Scotland.
Young, D.E. and Mrs J.M., Aberfeldy, Scotland.
Young, J., Sheffield, Yorks. South.
Young and Son (Antiques), John , Keswick, Cumbria.
Young, Leon, London, W11.
Young, M. and Mrs G., Wareham, Dorset.
Young Antiques, Robert, London, SW11.
Young and Stephen Ltd, London, W1.
Young, T.C., Edinburgh, Scotland.
Young Antiques & Fine Art, William, Aberdeen, Scotland.
Youssefian, A., London, W8.

Z

Zabell, B.L., Leigh-on-Sea, Essex.
Zacaroli, Stephen, Worcester, Herefs. and Worcs.
Zadah Gallery, London, W1.
Zebrak, London, W11.
Zebrak at Barnes Jewellers, Brighton, Sussex East.
Zebrak, T. and A., Brighton, Sussex East.
Zebrak, T. and A., London, W11.
Zeno Booksellers and Publishers, London, WC2.
Zentner, F., London, WC1.
Zippy Antiques, Stockport, Cheshire.
Zoil, S., London, SW18.
Zoulfaghari, London, NW5.
Zwan Antiques, Timberscombe, Somerset.
Zwemmer Ltd, A., London, WC2.

ANTIQUES CENTRES AND MARKETS DEALERS' INDEX

The name of the business and proprietors' names (where applicable) of that business are listed, followed by the name of the market or centre and town and county (or area of London). If the name of the market is the same as the town under which it appears, the name of the town is not shown again. The dealers in parenthesis at the end of entries are the name under which the proprietor wil be found within the appropriate market entry.

A

AG Antiques, Grays Antique Mkt, London, W1.
A. & J. Antiques, Newark Antique Warehouse, Newark, Notts.
A. M. Antiques, Newark Antique Warehouse, Newark, Notts.
A. M. W. Silverware, London Silver Vaults, London, WC2.
Aba, Preston Ant. Centre, Lancs.
Abacus, The Ginnel, Harrogate, N. Yorks.
Abacus Antiques, Grays Antique Mkt, London, W1.
Abbey Antiques, Preston Ant. Centre, Lancs.
Abe, Emmy, Bond Street Ants. Centre, London, W1.
Abramov, Eli, Bond Street Ants. Centre, London, W1.
Abstract, Kensington Church St. Ants. Centre, London, W8.
Accossato, G., Chenil Galleries, London, SW3.
Accurate Trading Co., Alfies Antique Mkt, London, NW8.
Accurate Trading Co, Bond Street Ants. Centre, London, W1.
Adamas Antiques, Royal Exchange Shopping Centre, Manchester, Lancs.
Adams, Beth, Alfies Antique Mkt, London, NW8.
Adams, M., Gt. Western Ant. Centre Ltd., Bath, Avon.
Afford, S. and J., Mall Antiques Arcade, London, N1.
Ages Ago Antiques, Preston Ant. Centre, Lancs.
Akeroyd Antiques, R., Preston Ant. Centre, Lancs.
Ala, Ryba, Hampstead Antique Emporium, London, NW3.
Aladdin's Cave, Swansea Ant. Centre, W. Glam., Wales.
Alderson, Claire, Pennard House Antiques, Bath, Avon.
Aldred, D., Preston Ant. Centre, Lancs.
Alexander Antiques, Royal Exchange Shopping Centre, Manchester, Lancs.
Alfandary, Alexandra, Mall Antiques Arcade, London, N1.
Alice Springs, Mall Antiques Arcade, London, N1.
Alicia Antiques, Lamb Arcade, Wallingford, Oxon.
Allen, Trevor, Chenil Galleries, London, SW3.
Allison, P., Preston Ant. Centre, Lancs.
Allison, Phillip and R., Furniture Cave, London, SW10.
Alloway, Nick and Sue, Antiquarius, London, SW3.
Allsops Antiques, Preston Ant. Centre, Lancs.
Alma Antiques, Mall Antiques Arcade, London, N1.
Almond, K., Preston Ant. Centre, Lancs.
Alvarino Antiques, E. A., Bath Street Antiques Galleries, Glasgow, Scotland.
Amstad, R. J., Hastings Ant. Centre, St. Leonards-on-Sea, E. Sussex.
Ancestors, Gt. Western Ant. Centre Ltd., Bath, Avon.
Anderson Antiques, Gillian, Woburn Abbey Ants. Centre, Beds.
Andretti Antiques, Paul, Westbourne Grove Antique Gallery, London, W11.
Andrews, A., Bermondsey Antique Warehouse, London, SE1.
Angeli, Patricia, Grays Mews, London, W1.
Anglo-Scandinavian, The Ginnel, Harrogate, N. Yorks.
Anne's Antiques, Victorian Village, Glasgow, Scotland.
Antics, Almshouses Arcade, Chichester, W. Sussex.
Antique and Collectables, Royal Exchange Shopping Centre, Manchester, Lancs.
Antique Clocks - Terence Plank, Mall Antiques Arcade, London, N1.
Antique Connoisseur plc, The, Grays Mews, London, W1.
Antique Fireplace, The, Royal Exchange Shopping Centre, Manchester, Lancs.
Antique Linen and Lace, Gt. Western Ant. Centre Ltd., Bath, Avon.

Antique Medical Instruments, Grays Antique Mkt, London, W1.
Antiqus, Lamb Arcade, Wallingford, Oxon.
Appleby - Jarona Antiques, Nigel, Antiquarius, London, SW3.
Applecross Antiques, Woburn Abbey Ants. Centre, Beds.
Aquarius, West Park Antiques Pavilion, Harrogate, N. Yorks.
Aramesh, Reza, Alfies Antique Mkt, London, NW8.
Arca, Grays Antique Mkt, London, W1.
Architectural Antiques, Leominster Antiques Mkt, Herefs and Worcs.
Arena, S., Antiquarius, London, SW3.
Arenski, Grays Antique Mkt, London, W1.
Argenteus Ltd, London Silver Vaults, London, WC2.
Aritaka, S., Antiquarius, London, SW3.
Armada Antiques, Grays Antique Mkt, London, W1.
Armigers, Woburn Abbey Ants. Centre, Beds.
Armstrong, R., Hastings Ant. Centre, St. Leonards-on-Sea, E. Sussex.
Armitage, Clayre, Bond Street Ants. Centre, London, W1.
Arms and Armour, Grays Mews, London, W1.
Arnold, Sean, Grays Antique Mkt, London, W1.
Art Deco, Carlisle Antique and Craft Centre, Cumbria.
Ash Brothers Antiques, McBains of Exeter, Exeter, Devon.
Assad, Elias, Grays Mews, London, W1.
Aston, Fiona, The Ginnel, Harrogate, N. Yorks.
Audley Art Ltd, Mall Antiques Arcade, London, N1.
Aurum, Grays Antique Mkt, London, W1.
Avril Antiques, Gt. Western Ant. Centre Ltd., Bath, Avon.
Aytac, Osman, Grays Antique Mkt, London, W1.

B

Bach, Mr and Mrs M., Antiquarius, London, SW3.
Baddiel, Colin, Grays Mews, London, W1.
Baddiel, Sarah Fabian, Grays Mews, London, W1.
Badir, Robert, Grays Antique Mkt, London, W1.
Baguley, Shirley, West Park Antiques Pavilion, Harrogate, N. Yorks.
Bailey, C., Grays Portobello, London, W11.
Bailey, M., Royal Exchange Shopping Centre, Manchester, Lancs.
Baker, David, Grays Mews, London, W1.
Baker, David, Grays Portobello, London, W11.
Bale, C., Gt. Western Ant. Centre Ltd., Bath, Avon.
Bamady, R., Grays Portobello, London, W11.
Bannister, Louise, Mall Antiques Arcade, London, N1.
Baptista Arts, Chenil Galleries, London, SW3.
Barbara, Hampstead Antique Emporium, London, NW3.
Barker, Bernice, Antiquarius, London, SW3.
Barkoff, B., Antiquarius, London, SW3.
Barnes, G., Clifton Antiques Mkt, Bristol, Avon.
Barnes, Jill, Grays Antique Mkt, London, W1.
Barnes, Rosemary, Grays Antique Mkt, London, W1.
Barnett, R .K., Almshouses Arcade, Chichester, W. Sussex.
Baron Antiques, Preston Ant. Centre, Lancs.
Barrington, Mrs Joan, Woburn Abbey Ants. Centre, Beds.
Bashir, M., Antiquarius, London, SW3.
Bates, Jeffrey, West Park Antiques Pavilion, Harrogate, N. Yorks.
Beard, J., Barnes House Antiques, Wimborne, Dorset.
Beaumont Antiques, David, Stouts Antique Mkt, London, W11.
Bedford and Guy Robbins, Pat, Grays Portobello, London, W11.

CENTRES & MARKETS DEALERS' INDEX

Bee, Linda, Grays Mews, London, W1.
Bees and Graves, Clifton Antiques Mkt, Bristol, Avon.
Beet, Brian, Bond Street Silver Galleries, London, W1.
Belcher and Jones, Lamb Arcade, Wallingford, Oxon.
Bell Antiques, Newton Abbot Ants. Centre, Devon.
Bellingham, Lesley, Cotswold Ants. Centre, Stow-on-the-Wold, Glos.
Benjamin, Peter, Grays Antique Mkt, London, W1.
Benjamin, R. S., Alfies Antique Mkt, London, NW8.
Benjamin Jewellery Ltd, London Silver Vaults, London, WC2.
Bennett, David, Alfies Antique Mkt, London, NW8.
Benson, B., Newark Antique Warehouse, Notts.
Berg, Barbara, Grays Antique Mkt, London, W1.
Berger, Ursula and Jurgen, Alfies Antique Mkt, London, NW8.
Bevan-Jones, A., Hastings Ant. Centre, St. Leonards-on-Sea, E. Sussex.
Bexfield Antiques, Daniel, Woburn Abbey Ants. Centre, Beds.
Bibb, Barbara, Span Antiques, Woodstock, Oxon.
Biggs, P., Clifton Antiques Mkt, Bristol, Avon.
Biggs Antiques, Newton Abbot Ants. Centre, Devon.
Billing, David, Antiquarius, London, SW3
Bird, Kit and Chizumi, Chenil Galleries, London, SW3
Black, Manley Joseph, Alfies Antique Mkt, London, NW8.
Blackburn, J., Preston Ant. Centre, Lancs.
Blanchard, Sophia, Alfies Antique Mkt, London, NW8.
Block, Lawrence, London Silver Vaults, London, WC2.
Blockley, Newton Abbot Ants. Centre, Devon.
Bloom, A., London Silver Vaults, London, WC2.
Bloomstein Ltd, A. and B., Bond Street Silver Galleries, London, W1.
Blue Lady, Swansea Ant. Centre, W. Glam., Wales.
Bodhouse Antiques, Preston Ant. Centre, Lancs.
Bolla, Alexandra, Antiquarius, London, SW3.
Bolster, Stuart, Antiquarius, London, SW3.
Bond Street Watches, Bond Street Ants. Centre, London, W1.
Boston, Nicolaus, Kensington Church St. Ants. Centre, London, W8.
Bothy, The, Rait Village Ants. Centre, Scotland.
Bottomley, Andrew, The Ginnel, Harrogate, N. Yorks.
Bottrill, Sonia, Mall Antiques Arcade, London, N1.
Bowden, David, Grays Antique Mkt, London, W1.
Bowen, Mrs S., Mall Antiques Arcade, London, N1.
Bowler, J., Preston Ant. Centre, Lancs.
Bowler, Simon, Smith St. Ants. Centre, Warwick, Warks.
Bowry, Edward, Rait Village Ants. Centre, Scotland.
Boxer, Henry, Kensington Church St. Ants. Centre, London, W8.
Boycott, B., Chenil Galleries, London, SW3
Boyd-Carpenter, Patrick, Grays Antique Mkt, London, W1.
Boyle, Sue, Gt. Western Antique Mkt Ltd., Bath, Avon.
Bracewell Antiques, David, Sandgate Ants. Centre, Kent.
Bradley, Peter, Ants. Centre, The, Guildford, Surrey.
Bradshaw and Smith, Leominster Antiques Mkt, Herefs and Worcs.
Brady, J., Antiquarius, London, SW3.
Braithwaite, Catherine, Alfies Antique Mkt, London, NW8.
Breakwell, S., Leominster Antiques Mkt, Herefs and Worcs.
Breese, Ursula, Woburn Abbey Ants. Centre, Beds.
Brewer Antiques, Anne, Lamb Arcade, Wallingford, Oxon.
Brian Antiques, Luigi, London Silver Vaults, London, WC2.
Brice, Robin, Newton Abbot Ants. Centre, Devon.
Brindle, J., Clifton Antiques Mkt, Bristol, Avon.
Brine, L., Gt. Western Ant. Centre Ltd., Bath, Avon.
Bristow, Mrs M., Chenil Galleries, London, SW3.
Britannia, Grays Antique Mkt, London, W1.
Britannia Export Antiques, Stouts Antique Mkt, London, W11.
Brixton, Sarah, Hastings Ant. Centre, St. Leonards-on-Sea, E. Sussex.
Broido, Jonathan, Grays Mews, London, W1.
Brook, Erol, Smith St. Ants. Centre, Warwick, Warks.
Brown, A., Chenil Galleries, London, SW3.
Brown, A., Gt. Western Ant. Centre Ltd., Bath, Avon.
Brown, Jean, Furniture Cave, London, SW10.
Brown, Sue, Grays Mews, London, W1.
Brown, William McLeod, Antiquarius, London, SW3.
Brown's Clocks Ltd, Bath Street Antiques Galleries, Glasgow.
Bruce, Miles, Leominster Antiques Mkt, Herefs and Worcs.
Brunel Antiques, Gt. Western Ant. Centre Ltd., Bath, Avon.
Bruno, B., Alfies Antique Mkt, London, NW8.
Brunswick, S., Alfies Antique Mkt, London, NW8.

Bryan-Peach Antiques, N., Castle Gate Ants. Centre, Newark, Notts.
Buchinger, Miss T., Antiquarius, London, SW3.
Buckle, Evelyn, Newark Antique Warehouse, Notts.
Buckle Antiques, Evelyn, Castle Gate Ants. Centre, Newark, Notts.
Buckton, M., Hastings Ant. Centre, St. Leonards-on-Sea, E. Sussex.
Bulka, S., London Silver Vaults, London, WC2.
Bunting, John, Cotswold Ants. Centre, Stow-on-the-Wold, Glos.
Burnstock, Ursula, Alfies Antique Mkt, London, NW8.
Burrows, Marcus, West Park Antiques Pavilion, Harrogate, N. Yorks.
Busato, G., Preston Ant. Centre, Lancs.
Butterworth, C., Antiquarius, London, SW3.
Bygones, The Ginnel, Harrogate, N. Yorks.

C

C. J. and K. Antiques, Preston Ant. Centre, Lancs.
Callbox, Royal Exchange Shopping Centre, Manchester, Lancs.
Cameron, Jasmin, Antiquarius, London, SW3.
Cameron, Peter, Bond Street Silver Galleries, London, W1.
Canonball, Grays Mews, London, W1.
Canonbury Antiques Ltd., Westbourne Grove Antique Gallery, London, W11.
Carey, Charles, Grays Portobello, London, W11.
Carnie, John, Mall Antiques Arcade, London, N1.
Carr, J., Newark Antique Warehouse, Notts.
Carroll, Mrs V., Antiquarius, London, SW3.
Carter, Jennifer, Ants. Centre,The, Guildford, Surrey.
Carter, Mia, The Ginnel, Harrogate, N. Yorks.
Carter, Robinson and Zeitgeist, Paul, Kensington Church St. Ants. Centre, London, W8.
Casolani, David, Alfies Antique Mkt, London, NW8.
Catherine Ann Antiques, Swansea Ant. Centre, W. Glam., Wales.
Caudwell, Doreen, Span Antiques, Woodstock, Oxon.
Caunter, Newton Abbot Ants. Centre, Devon.
Cavendish Fine Art, West Park Antiques Pavilion, Harrogate, N. Yorks.
Cavey, Christopher, Grays Antique Mkt, London, W1.
Cekay, Grays Antique Mkt, London, W1.
Chandler, Elaine, Ants. Centre, The, Guildford, Surrey.
Chandra, R., Grays Portobello, London, W11.
Chanticleer Antiques, West Park Antiques Pavilion, Harrogate, N. Yorks.
Chapman, M., Antiquarius, London, SW3.
Chapman, Michael, Newark Antique Warehouse, Notts.
Chase, Roy, Woburn Abbey Ants. Centre, Beds.
Cheeseman, Fred, Alfies Antique Mkt, London, NW8.
Chelsea Clocks, Antiquarius, London, SW3.
Chelsea Lion, Chenil Galleries, London, SW3.
Cheraghzade, A., Hampstead Antique Emporium, London, NW3.
Chew, Bryan, Barnes House Antiques, Wimborne, Dorset.
Church, Jan, Grays Antique Mkt, London, W1.
Churchstoke Booksellers, Gt. Western Ant. Centre Ltd., Bath, Avon.
City Antiques, Swansea Ant. Centre, W. Glam., Wales.
City Jewellers, Royal Exchange Shopping Centre, Manchester, Lancs.
Clapton, Nick, Cotswold Ants. Centre, Stow-on-the-Wold, Glos.
Clark, Brenda Klare Gerwat, Alfies Antique Mkt, London, NW8.
Clark, Eddie, Stouts Antique Mkt, London, W11.
Clark, Steve, Chenil Galleries, London, SW3
Clayton, Theresa, Grays Mews, London, W1.
Clements, P., Hastings Ant. Centre, St. Leonards-on-Sea, E. Sussex.
Clifton-Brown, Douglas, Grays Mews, London, W1.
Clock Studio, The, Mall Antiques Arcade (Lower Mall), London, N1.
Cloudheath, Grays Mews, London, W1.
Coach Gallery (Scorpio), Royal Exchange Shopping Centre, Manchester, Lancs.
Coakley, A., Chenil Galleries, London, SW3.
Cohen, Eli, Antiquarius, London, SW3.
Coleman Antiques, John, Woburn Abbey Ants. Centre, Beds.

CENTRES & MARKETS DEALERS' INDEX

Coleman Antiques, Robin and Jan, Pennard House Antiques, Bath, Avon.
Coles, S., Clifton Antiques Mkt, Bristol, Avon.
Collectable Costume, Gt. Western Ant. Centre Ltd., Bath, Avon.
Collection, Grays Antique Mkt, London, W1.
Collectors World, St. Georges Antiques, Worcester, Herefs. and Worcs.
Collingridge, P., Mall Antiques Arcade, London, N1.
Collins, A., Lamb Arcade, Wallingford, Oxon.
Collins Antiques, Woburn Abbey Ants. Centre, Beds.
Collins, B.L., London Silver Vaults, London, WC2.
Collins, Olivia, Grays Antique Mkt, London, W1.
Continuum, Joy, Grays Antique Mkt, London, W1.
Conynham-Hynes, Phil and Lindy, Grays Antique Mkt, London, W1.
Cook, H.P., Grays Portobello, London, W11.
Cooke, R., Preston Ant. Centre, Lancs.
Cooper Hay Rare Books, Bath Street Antiques Galleries, Glasgow.
Copeland/S. Longmead, I., Hastings Ant. Centre, St. Leonards-on-Sea, E. Sussex.
Cottage Antiques, Woburn Abbey Ants. Centre, Beds.
Country Interiors, Gt. Western Ant. Centre Ltd., Bath, Avon.
Country Life Interiors, Woburn Abbey Ants. Centre, Beds.
Coupe, J. and J., Newark Antique Warehouse, Notts.
Course, J., Antiquarius, London, SW3.
Courtier, Graham, Newton Abbot Ants. Centre, Devon.
Courtyard, The, Mamie's Ants. Centre, Arundel, W. Sussex.
Cowan, J., Antiquarius, London, SW3.
Cowdy, Mike and Kate, Span Antiques, Woodstock, Oxon.
Cox, John, Chenil Galleries, London, SW3
Cox, Mrs P., Leominster Antiques Mkt, Herefs and Worcs.
Cox, T., Clifton Antiques Mkt, Bristol, Avon.
Cozy World, Grays Antique Mkt, London, W1.
Crawford, John, Gostling's Ant. Centre, Diss, Norfolk.
Crawforth, Andrew, Span Antiques, Woodstock, Oxon.
Creed, Mrs E. W. E., Smith St. Ants. Centre, Warwick, Warks.
Crisp, R. B., Gt. Western Ant. Centre Ltd. - The Wednesday Mkt, Bath, Avon.
Crocodile Shop, Antiquarius, London, SW3.
Crocus, Royal Victoria Arcade, Ryde, I. of Wight.
Croesus, Grays Antique Mkt, London, W1.
Crofton Antiques, Gt. Western Ant. Centre Ltd., Bath, Avon.
Cromwell House Ant. Centre, Battlebridge Ant. Centre, Essex.
Cropper, Stuart, Grays Mews, London, W1.
Crowley and Mrs A. Fothergill, D., Chenil Galleries, London, SW3.
Crown Square Antiques, Preston Ant. Centre, Lancs.
Cull, Phillip, Bond Street Silver Galleries, London, W1.
Cullimore, Jill, Gt. Western Ant. Centre Ltd. - The Wednesday Mkt, Bath, Avon.
Curio Corner, Newton Abbot Ants. Centre, Devon.
Cuthbert, T., Hastings Ant. Centre, St. Leonards-on-Sea, E. Sussex.

D

D. H. Glass, Mall Antiques Arcade, London, N1.
Dahms, S., Hastings Ant. Centre, St. Leonards-on-Sea, E. Sussex.
Danby Antiques, Newgate Ants. Centre, York, N. Yorks.
Daniel, P., London Silver Vaults, London, WC2.
Darer, Alan, Grays Mews, London, W1.
Davidson, Morelle, Bond Street Ants. Centre, London, W1
Davies, Mrs, Grays Portobello, London, W11.
Davies, John, Pennard House Antiques, Bath, Avon.
Davies, M., Royal Exchange Shopping Centre, Manchester, Lancs.
Davis and Fawkes, Antiquarius, London, SW3
Davis, Ruth, Alfies Antique Mkt, London, NW8.
Dazeley, W., Hastings Ant. Centre, St. Leonards-on-Sea, E. Sussex.
de Havilland, Adele, Bond Street Ants. Centre, London, W1.
De Rooy, Guy, Grays Antique Mkt, London, W1.
de Sousa, Jo, Grays Portobello, London, W11.
Deacon, S.S., Alfies Antique Mkt, London, NW8.
Deja Vu, Gt. Western Ant. Centre Ltd., Bath, Avon.
del Grosso, Jo, Alfies Antique Mkt, London, NW8.
Delaney, Victoria, Grays Antique Mkt, London, W1.

Delmar Ant, York Arcade, London, N1.
Dench Antiques, John, Castle Gate Ants. Centre, Newark, Notts.
Dench Antiques, John, Newark Antique Warehouse, Notts.
Dewart, G., Chenil Galleries, London, SW3.
Diamond, Marie, Victorian Village, Glasgow, Scotland.
Dickinson, Sandys, Grays Mews, London, W1.
Didier Antiques, Kensington Church St. Ants. Centre, London, W8.
Dixon and Torr, Antiquarius, London, SW3.
Dog Box, York Arcade, London, N1.
Donat, B., Grays Portobello, London, W11.
Donohoe, Grays Mews, London, W1.
Donovan, J., Mall Antiques Arcade, London, N1.
Doran, Paul, Preston Ant. Centre, Lancs.
Douglas, B., London Silver Vaults, London, WC2.
Dowling, G., Clifton Antiques Mkt, Bristol, Avon.
Dowling, Paul, Chenil Galleries, London, SW3.
Downs, Andrew, Alfies Antique Mkt, London, NW8.
Downworth, M., Gt. Western Ant. Centre Ltd. - The Wednesday Mkt., Bath, Avon.
Doyle, Steve, Gostling's Ant. Centre, Diss, Norfolk.
Drake, Alfies Antique Mkt, London, NW8.
Drey, Mrs Gill, Chenil Galleries, London, SW3.
Druks, M., Alfies Antique Mkt, London, NW8.
Dubiner, M.J., London Silver Vaults, London, WC2.
Duggan, David, Bond Street Ants. Centre, London, W1.
Dukeries, The Ginnel, Harrogate, N. Yorks.
Dukeries, The, West Park Antiques Pavilion, Harrogate, N. Yorks.
Dukeries Antiques, Castle Gate Ants. Centre, Newark, Notts.
Dukeries Antiques, Newark Antique Warehouse, Notts.
Dumbrell, Mrs H., Mall Antiques Arcade, London, N1
Dunn, R., Preston Ant. Centre, Lancs.
Dunn St. James, Chris, Mall Antiques Arcade, London, N1.
Dyke, Mrs O., Leominster Antiques Mkt, Herefs and Worcs.
Dyson-Rook Antiques, Woburn Abbey Ants. Centre, Beds.

E

E. and A. Antiques, Woburn Abbey Ants. Centre, Beds.
Eames, Gary, Smith St. Ants. Centre, Warwick, Warks.
Eardisley Antiques, Leominster Antiques Mkt, Herefs and Worcs.
East Gates Antiques, Alfies Antique Mkt, London, NW8.
Ebrich, Rosemary, Grays Mews, London, W1.
Eccles, Jerome, Chenil Galleries, London, SW3.
Echoes, Royal Victoria Arcade, Ryde, I. of Wight.
Eisler, David, Grays Mews, London, W1.
Eleanor Antiques, Smith St. Ants. Centre, Warwick, Warks.
Elisabeth's Antiques, Bond Street Ants. Centre, London, W1.
Elkabas, Mr and Mrs H., Antiquarius, London, SW3.
Emerson, S., Antiquarius, London, SW3.
Emptage, P., Barnes House Antiques, Wimborne, Dorset.
English, Toby, Lamb Arcade, Wallingford, Oxon.
Enigma, Chenil Galleries, London, SW3.
Esther and Leslie, Grays Mews, London, W1.
Evans, Mrs. P., Antiquarius, London, SW3.

F

Fahimian, E., Bond Street Ants. Centre, London, W1.
Fair Finds, Rait Village Ants. Centre, Scotland.
Falloon, Ronald, Grays Antique Mkt, London, W1.
Farfalla, Smith St Ants. Centre, Warwick, Warks.
Farrow, Liz, Alfies Antique Mkt, London, NW8.
Fearon, Ricky, Victorian Village, Glasgow, Scotland.
Featherbrain, York Arcade, London, N1.
Feldman, Mrs D., Bond Street Ants. Centre, London, W1.
Feldman, M. D., London Silver Vaults, London, WC2.
Feldman Ltd, R., London Silver Vaults, London, WC2.
Feller, Sheila, Hampstead Antique Emporium, London, NW3.
Felton Park, The Ginnel, Harrogate, N. Yorks.
Fenton, P., Almshouses Arcade, Chichester, W. Sussex.
Fettes Fine Art, The Ginnel, Harrogate, N. Yorks.
Fielding, Marion, Grays Mews, London, W1.
Fiell, Peter, Chenil Galleries, London, SW3.
Fine Pine, Carlisle Antique and Craft Centre, Cumbria.
First, Jack, Grays Antique Mkt, London, W1.
First Floor, Furniture Cave, London, SW10.
Fitzgerald, York Arcade, London, N1.
Flagship (Paul Richardson), The Ginnel, Harrogate, N. Yorks.

Flight, A., Smith St. Ants. Centre, Warwick, Warks.
Flight of Fancy, Antiquarius, London, SW3.
Forbes Fine Art, James, Stouts Antique Mkt, London, W11.
Ford & Son Ltd, G. W., Woburn Abbey Ants. Centre, Beds.
Forget-me-Not, Swansea Ant. Centre, W. Glam., Wales.
Forster, Newton Abbot Ants. Centre, Devon.
Foster, Miss S., Clifton Antiques Mkt, Bristol, Avon.
Foster (Antiques), Gene and Sally, Pennard House Antiques, Bath, Avon.
Four Seasons Antiques, Span Antiques, Woodstock, Oxon.
Fox, Brenda, Hastings Ant. Centre, St. Leonards-on-Sea, E. Sussex.
Fox, Sally, Alfies Antique Mkt, London, NW8.
Frame, Ian, Victorian Village, Glasgow, Scotland.
Francis, Sylvana, Grays Antique Mkt, London, W1.
Franks Bookshop, Royal Exchange Shopping Centre, Manchester, Lancs.
Franks, I., London Silver Vaults, London, WC2.
Franks, Nicola, Grays Antique Mkt, London, W1.
Franks, Renee, Royal Exchange Shopping Centre, Manchester, Lancs.
Freeforms, Kensington Church St. Ants. Centre, London W8.
Freegard, Karen, Gt. Western Ant. Centre Ltd., Bath, Avon.
Freeman, Richard, The Ginnel, Harrogate, N. Yorks.
Freestone, Eric, Hastings Ant. Centre, St. Leonards-on-Sea, E. Sussex.
French Decorative Antiques, Grays Antique Mkt, London, W1.
French Glasshouse, Antiquarius, London, SW3.
Frydman, O., Bond Street Silver Galleries, London, W1.

G

Gallery, The, Mamie's Ants. Centre, Arundel, W. Sussex.
Gallie, F., Battlebridge Ant. Centre, Essex.
Gallie, J. F., Battlebridge Ant. Centre, Essex.
Galya Antiques (Noonstar), Antiquarius, London, SW3.
Gardiner, Robin, Alfies Antique Mkt, London, NW8.
Gardiner Antiques, Helen, Alfies Antique Mkt, London, NW8.
Gardner and Becker, Antiquarius, London, SW3
Gardner, E., Hampstead Antique Emporium, London, NW3.
Garrard, J. B., Grays Portobello, London, W11.
Garraway, William, Alfies Antique Mkt, London, NW8.
Gaunt, Peter, Grays Antique Mkt, London, W1.
Genie, Alfies Antique Mkt, London, NW8.
Georgian House, The Ginnel, Harrogate, N. Yorks.
Geris, S. A., Antiquarius, London, SW3.
German, P., Almshouses Arcade, Chichester, W. Sussex.
Gibbon, Richard, Alfies Antique Mkt, London, NW8.
Gibson, C., Antiquarius, London, SW3.
Gifford-Mead and Miles d'Agar Antiques, N. J. A., Furniture Cave, London, SW10.
Gilbert, Trevor, Grays Mews, London, W1.
Gilded Lily, The, Grays Antique Mkt, London, W1.
Gilmour, Austin, Newton Abbot Ants. Centre, Devon.
Glass, Jeffrey and Pauline, The Ginnel, Harrogate, N. Yorks.
Glenburn Antiques, Bath Street Antiques Galleries, Glasgow, Scotland.
Gmur and Ouji, Grays Mews, London, W1.
Goggin, Joan, Ants. Centre, The, Guildford, Surrey.
Gold, Mrs N., Antiquarius, London, SW3.
Golden Memories of York, Newgate Ants. Centre, York, N. Yorks.
Goldsmith and Perris, Alfies Antique Mkt, London, NW8.
Goldstrom, T. and A., Mall Antiques Arcade, London, N1.
Goode, Vyvyan, Newton Abbot Ants. Centre, Devon.
Gordon, B., Chenil Galleries, London, SW3.
Gordon, Ora, Grays Mews, London, W1.
Gordon, Phyllis, Mamie's Ant. Centre, Arundel, W. Sussex.
Gore, Teresa, Alfies Antique Mkt, London, NW8.
Gottlieb, Marie, Alfies Antique Mkt, London, NW8.
Gough, Maureen, Span Antiques, Woodstock, Oxon.
Gould, Patrick, Grays Mews, London, W1.
Grahame, Gordon, Grays Antique Mkt, London, W1.
Gramophone Workshop, Alfies Antique Mkt, London, NW8.
Grange, J., Leominster Antiques Mkt, Herefs. and Worcs.
Grant, Sylvia, Woburn Abbey Ants. Centre, Beds.
Gray, Anita, Grays Antique Mkt, London, W1.
Gray, Anthony, Grays Mews, London, W1.
Greco, Linette, Alfies Antique Mkt, London, NW8.
Green Antiques, Anthony, Bond Street Ants. Centre, London, W1.

Gt. Expectations, Lamb Arcade, Wallingford, Oxon.
Green Antiques, Ena, Alfies Antique Mkt, London, NW8.
Green Fine Art, John, Bath Street Antiques Galleries, Glasgow, Scotland.
Green, T.and A., Lamb Arcade, Wallingford, Oxon.
Greene Antiques, Richard, West Park Antiques Pavilion, Harrogate, N. Yorks.
Greenhalgh, P., Bond Street Silver Galleries, London, W1.
Greenhalgh, Syd and Dave, Preston Ant. Centre, Lancs.
Greenwall Antiques, Jonathan, Sandgate Ants. Centre, Kent.
Grenville Art Gallery, Royal Exchange Shopping Centre, Manchester, Lancs.
Gresham, R. A., Gt. Western Ant. Centre Ltd., Bath, Avon.
Greystones Antiques, West Park Antiques Pavilion, Harrogate, N. Yorks.
Griffiths, Mary, Alfies Antique Mkt, London, NW8.
Groombridge, Sarah, Grays Antique Mkt, London, W1.
Grupman, Joan, Royal Exchange Shopping Centre, Manchester, Lancs.
Guillesarian, Alice, Grays Mews, London, W1.
Guiscards, Rait Village Ants. Centre, Scotland.
Guiscards Miniatures and Juvenalia, Rait Village Ants. Centre, Scotland.
Gulley Antiques, Bernard, Woburn Abbey Ants. Centre, Beds.
Gumbrell, K., Hastings Ant. Centre, St. Leonards-on-Sea, E. Sussex.
Gunn, Mrs B., Antiquarius, London, SW3.
Gyles, D. E., Gt. Western Ant. Centre Ltd. - The Wednesday Mkt., Bath, Avon.

H

Hage, Mrs E., Bond Street Ants. Centre, London, W1
Hall, J., Alfies Antique Mkt, London, NW8.
Hall, James, Cotswold Ants. Centre, Stow-on-the-Wold, Glos.
Hall, J. and D., Cotswold Ants. Centre, Stow-on-the-Wold, Glos.
Hall-Bakker, Lis, Span Antiques, Woodstock, Oxon.
Hallmark, Grays Antique Mkt, London, W1.
Hamadani, Mrs B., Antiquarius, London, SW3.
Hamilton, London Silver Vaults, London, WC2.
Hamilton Antiques, Woburn Abbey Ants. Centre, Beds.
Hamilton Exports, Bryan, Westbourne Grove Antique Gallery, London, W11.
Hampton, Mrs S., Chenil Galleries, London, SW3.
Harby, Diana, Grays Antique Mkt, London, W1.
Harkins, Brian, Grays Antique Mkt, London, W1.
Harounoff, Ronnie, Grays Mews, London, W1.
Harrington Antiques, Preston Ant. Centre, Lancs.
Harris, A.J., Grays Portobello, London, W11.
Harris, R., Gt. Western Ant. Centre Ltd., Bath, Avon.
Harris, M. G., Stouts Antique Mkt, London, W11.
Harrison, Marguerite, Grays Portobello, London, W11.
Harvey, Declan, Grays Antique Mkt, London, W1.
Hattrell, Satoe, Grays Antique Mkt, London, W1.
Hawley, John, The Ginnel, Harrogate, N. Yorks.
Haworth Ltd, M. and N., Royal Exchange Shopping Centre, Manchester, Lancs.
Hay, Henry, Alfies Antique Mkt, London, NW8.
Haybarn and Bridgebarn Ant. Centres, Battlebridge Ant. Centre, Essex.
Hayman and Hayman, Antiquarius, London, SW3.
Haywood, Pamela, Chenil Galleries, London, SW3.
Heidarieh/A. Bagdhi, M., Alfies Antique Mkt, London, NW8.
Helmsley Antiquarian Books, The Ginnel, Harrogate, N. Yorks.
Helter Skelter, Royal Victoria Arcade, Ryde, I. of Wight.
Hendrika, Newton Abbot Ants. Centre, Devon.
Henning, Tina, Alfies Antique Mkt, London, NW8.
Henson, R., Antiquarius, London, SW3.
Hepburn, George, Alfies Antique Mkt, London, NW8.
Herbert, Peter, Alfies Antique Mkt, London, NW8.
Hickey, Messrs., Antiquarius, London, SW3.
Hicks - Bolton Galleries, Jo, Newton Abbot Ants. Centre, Devon.
Hickson, N., Preston Ant. Centre, Lancs.
Highfield Antiques, Newark Antique Warehouse, Notts.
Hill, H., Newton Abbot Ants. Centre, Devon.
Hill and L. Denney, J., Grays Portobello, London, W11.
Hislop, Gail, Gt. Western Antique Mkt Ltd., Bath, Avon.
Hobrey, A., Preston Ant. Centre, Lancs.
Hodson, B., Preston Ant. Centre, Lancs.

Hoffman Antiques, Grays Antique Mkt, London, W1.
Hoffman, Joanna, Bond Street Ants. Centre, London, W1.
Hogg, David, Grays Antique Mkt, London, W1.
Holden, E. J., Alfies Antique Mkt, London, NW8.
Hollings Antiques, Irene, Woburn Abbey Ants. Centre, Beds.
Hollis and Hollis, Bond Street Silver Galleries, London, W1.
Holmes, Lynn and Brian, Grays Antique Mkt, London, W1.
Holt, Mike, Pennard House Antiques, Bath, Avon.
Homewood Antiques, Robin, Sandgate Ants. Centre, Kent.
Houlding, Frances, Alfies Antique Mkt, London, NW8.
How, Michael, Gostling's Ant. Centre, Diss, Norfolk.
Howard, B., Gt. Western Ant. Centre Ltd., Bath, Avon.
Howe, Dudley, Alfies Antique Mkt, London, NW8.
Howe, Mick, Smith St. Ants. Centre, Warwick, Warks.
Howett, Bridget , Hastings Ant. Centre, St. Leonards-on-Sea, E. Sussex.
Hoyer-Millar, Virginia, Alfies Antique Mkt, London, NW8.
Hughes S., Almshouses Arcade, Chichester, W. Sussex.
Hunt, B., Newton Abbot Ants. Centre, Devon.
Hyder, Steven, Grays Portobello, London, W11.

I

Il Libro, Chenil Galleries, London, SW3.
Inchwood, Bond Street Ants. Centre, London, W1.
Incisioni, Alfies Antique Mkt, London, NW8.
Ind, Barbara, Leominster Antiques Mkt, Herefs and Worcs.
Inga, York Arcade, London, N1.
Inspirations, York Arcade, London, N1.
Intergrate, Preston Ant. Centre, Lancs.
Iredale, Mrs Newton Abbot Ants. Centre, Devon.
Ireland, D., Grays Portobello, London, W11.
Irving Antiques, Royal Exchange Shopping Centre, Manchester, Lancs.
It's About Time, Carlisle Antique and Craft Centre, Cumbria.
Iwona, Grays Antique Mkt, London, W1.

J

J A G, Kensington Church St. Ants. Centre, London, W8.
J. and G. Antiques, Alfies Antique Mkt, London, NW8.
Jacks, John, Bath Street Antiques Galleries, Glasgow.
Jackson Antiques, Hampstead Antique Emporium, London, NW3.
Jacques, Peter, Alfies Antique Mkt, London, NW8.
James, Chris, Smith St. Ants. Centre, Warwick, Warks.
James, Rachel, Clifton Antiques Mkt, Bristol, Avon.
James, Sandra, The Ginnel, Harrogate, N. Yorks.
Jamieson, Pauline, Bath Street Antiques Galleries, Glasgow, Scotland.
Jartelius, M., Mall Antiques Arcade, London, N1.
Jarvis, Timothy, Woburn Abbey Ants. Centre, Beds.
Jasper Antiques, Span Antiques, Woodstock, Oxon.
Jazi, Ali, Grays Mews, London, W1.
Jazy Antiques, Mall Antiques Arcade, London, N1.
Jenner, Mr, Antiquarius, London, SW3.
Jennings Antiques, P., Sandgate Ants. Centre, Kent.
Jessie's Button Box, Gt. Western Ant. Centre Ltd., Bath, Avon.
Johnson, Mr, Newton Abbot Ants. Centre, Devon.
Johnson, Pat, Cotswold Ants. Centre, Stow-on-the-Wold, Glos.
Johnson, S., Newton Abbot Ants. Centre, Devon.
Johnson-Gibbs, Ilona, Span Antiques, Woodstock, Oxon.
Jones, Mrs Gwynneth, Chenil Galleries, London, SW3.
Jones, Jenny, Royal Exchange Shopping Centre, Manchester, Lancs.
Jones, Katie, Grays Antique Mkt, London, W1.
Jones, K.P., Gt. Western Ant. Centre Ltd., Bath, Avon.
Jones, P., Clifton Antiques Mkt, Bristol, Avon.
Jones, Roderick, Alfies Antique Mkt, London, NW8.
Jones, R., Clifton Antiques Mkt, Bristol, Avon.
Jones & Son, Roy, McBains of Exeter, Exeter, Devon.
Joseph, John, Grays Antique Mkt, London, W1.
Joyce Antiques, Barry, Westbourne Grove Antique Gallery, London, W11.
Jubb, Mrs M., Clifton Antiques Mkt, Bristol, Avon.
Jupiter Antiques, Royal Exchange Shopping Centre, Manchester, Lancs.
Just In Pine, Alfies Antique Mkt, London, NW8.

K

K. and M. Antiques, Stouts Antique Mkt, London, W11.
K. & M. Antiques, Grays Antique Mkt, London, W1.
Kaae, Andre and Minoo, Grays Mews, London, W1.
Kalms, S., London Silver Vaults, London, WC2.
Kaskimo, Mrs P. A., Antiquarius, London, SW3.
Kaye, Margaret, Grays Antique Mkt, London, W1.
Keays, Mary, Alfies Antique Mkt, London, NW8.
Kelly, D., Antiquarius, London, SW3.
Kent, Rodney, West Park Antiques Pavilion, Harrogate, N. Yorks.
Kerr, Marjory, Victorian Village, Glasgow, Scotland.
Kerridge, Mrs M. T., Clifton Antiques Mkt, Bristol, Avon.
Kershaw, Jean, Woburn Abbey Ants. Centre, Beds.
Khawaja, Mrs, Alfies Antique Mkt, London, NW8.
Kikuchi Antiques, Grays Antique Mkt, London, W1.
Kilgour Antiques, Bath Street Antiques Galleries, Glasgow, Scotland.
Kilgour, Mrs C.G., Bath Street Antiques Galleries, Glasgow, Scotland.
Killinger Antiques, Sue, Woburn Abbey Ants. Centre, Beds.
Kinch, W. E., Leominster Antiques Mkt, Herefs and Worcs.
Kings Road Gallery, Furniture Cave, London, SW10.
Kingston, Dennis, Chenil Galleries, London, SW3.
Kitchen Bygones, Alfies Antique Mkt, London, NW8.
Kleanthous Antiques, Stouts Antique Mkt, London, W11.
Kleanthous, C. and C., Stouts Antique Mkt, London, W11.
Kleinman, Patricia, Mall Antiques Arcade, London, N1.
Kluth, Simon, Alfies Antique Mkt, London, NW8.
Kobako, C., Grays Portobello, London, W11.
Krell, Mrs, Chenil Galleries, London, SW3.
Kyle Antiques, Susan, London Silver Vaults, London, WC2.

L

L. and P. Antiques, West Park Antiques Pavilion, Harrogate, N. Yorks.
L. B. Antiques, Gt. Western Ant. Centre Ltd., Bath, Avon.
La Verite, Chenil Galleries, London, SW3.
Lack and Sampson, Messrs, Bond Street Ants. Centre, London, W1.
Lak, Iraj, Grays Mews, London, W1.
Lamari, Robin, Antiquarius, London, SW3.
Lamb, Jean, West Park Antiques Pavilion, Harrogate, N. Yorks.
Lamb Silverware, Alfies Antique Mkt, London, NW8.
Lambert, Adrienne, Cotswold Ants. Centre, Stow-on-the-Wold, Glos.
Lambert, J., Preston Ant. Centre, Lancs.
Lampert, B., London Silver Vaults, London, WC2.
Lancefield Antiques, David, Sandgate Ants. Centre, Kent.
Langfords, London Silver Vaults, London, WC2.
Langham Ltd, Marion, Woburn Abbey Ants. Centre, Beds.
Lankester, Barbara, Grays Antique Mkt, London, W1.
Lask, Anthony, Alfies Antique Mkt, London, NW8.
Latreville, Claude and Martine, Chenil Galleries, London, SW3.
Lawrence, John, Newton Abbot Ants. Centre, Devon.
Lawson, B., Carlisle Antique and Craft Centre, Cumbria.
Lazarell, Grays Antique Mkt, London, W1.
Lazarov, H., Antiquarius, London, SW3.
Leasingham Antiques, Castle Gate Ants. Centre, Newark, Notts.
Lee and Stacey, Hampstead Antique Emporium, London, NW3.
Lehane, Mr and Mrs, Antiquarius, London, SW3.
Lehmann, Peter, Mall Antiques Arcade (Lower Mall), London, N1.
Leigh, Hammond, Hampstead Antique Emporium, London, NW3.
Leloup, Diane, Grays Portobello, London, W11.
Lennard, Pat, Grays Antique Mkt, London, W1.
Lennie Fine Art Ltd, Barclay, Bath Street Antiques Galleries, Glasgow.
Lennox Galleries, Grays Mews, London, W1.
Leon, Stouts Antique Mkt, London, W11.
Leslie Ltd, Nat, London Silver Vaults, London, WC2.
Levine, Jenny, Grays Portobello, London, W11.
Lewis, Newton Abbot Ants. Centre, Devon.
Lewis, Sara, Alfies Antique Mkt, London, NW8.
Lewis, Sue, Grays Antique Mkt, London, W1.

CENTRES & MARKETS DEALERS' INDEX

Lexton, M., Antiquarius, London, SW3.
Liberati, L., Preston Ant. Centre, Lancs.
Libra Antiques, The Ginnel, Harrogate, N. Yorks.
Licht, Gerald, Grays Antique Mkt, London, W1.
Linden and Co. (Antiques) Ltd, London Silver Vaults, London, WC2.
Linden, H, F, H.M. and S. C., London Silver Vaults, London, WC2.
Lineham, Andrew, Mall Antiques Arcade, London, N1.
Linen and Lace, Royal Exchange Shopping Centre, Manchester, Lancs.
Lional of France, Preston Ant. Centre, Lancs.
Littlejohn, Mrs R., Clifton Antiques Mkt, Bristol, Avon.
Liv, Mrs, Grays Portobello, London, W11.
Lloyd, A., Gt. Western Ant. Centre Ltd., Bath, Avon.
Lo, Monty, Grays Antique Mkt, London, W1.
Lock, Mrs, Newton Abbot Ants. Centre, Devon.
London Antique Exporters Ltd., Westbourne Grove Antique Gallery, London, W11.
London Antique Print Room, Grays Antique Mkt, London, W1.
London, Sue, Cotswold Ants. Centre, Stow-on-the-Wold, Glos.
Long Antiques, K., Preston Ant. Centre, Lancs.
Lonsdale, C., Hastings Ant. Centre, St. Leonards-on-Sea, E. Sussex.
Loomes, Brian, The Ginnel, Harrogate, N. Yorks.
Losa Ltd, Roger, Woburn Abbey Ants. Centre, Beds.
Lovell, Mr, Newton Abbot Ants. Centre, Devon.
Lovell, Mrs, Newton Abbot Ants. Centre, Devon.
Lucas, Fay, Antiquarius, London, SW3.
Lynch, Gillian, Grays Antique Mkt, London, W1.
Lynderside Ltd, Antiquarius, London, SW3.

M

MBA, The Ginnel, Harrogate, N. Yorks.
M .S. M., Furniture Cave, London, SW10.
McAskie, Pete, Grays Mews, London, W1.
McBain, I.S., G., R. and M., McBains of Exeter, Exeter, Devon.
McBains of Exeter, McBains of Exeter, Exeter, Devon.
Macbeth, Gt. Western Ant. Centre Ltd., Bath, Avon.
McCallum, C., Rait Village Ants. Centre, Scotland.
McClean, Chenil Galleries, London, SW3.
MacDonald, Joss, Alfies Antique Mkt, London, NW8.
Macdonald, Nigel, Alfies Antique Mkt, London, NW8.
McDonald-Hobley, Mrs N., Antiquarius, London, SW3.
McDowell, M., Preston Ant. Centre, Lancs.
McHugh, Helen, Ants. Centre, The, Guildford, Surrey.
McIlroy, Murray, Bath Street Antiques Galleries, Glasgow.
Mackenzie-Smith, P., Clifton Antiques Mkt, Bristol, Avon.
McKie, N., Lamb Arcade, Wallingford, Oxon.
McLay "Saratoga Trunk", Cathy, Victorian Village, Glasgow, Scotland.
McPherson, Mrs Jeanne, Woburn Abbey Ants. Centre, Beds.
Macrae-Stewart, L., Gt. Western Ant. Centre Ltd., Bath, Avon.
Mac-Smith, Clifton Antiques Mkt, Bristol, Avon.
Mahfoot, Abdalah, Bond Street Ants. Centre, London, W1.
Mair's Antiques, Swansea Ant. Centre, W. Glam., Wales.
Malcolm, Alfies Antique Mkt, London, NW8.
Malone, Peggy, Grays Antique Mkt, London, W1.
Maltin, Elizabeth, Woburn Abbey Ants. Centre, Beds.
Mammon, C. and T., London Silver Vaults, London, WC2.
Mammon Antiques, J., London Silver Vaults, London, WC2.
Man, J., Chenil Galleries, London, SW3.
Manchester Coin and Medal Centre, Royal Exchange Shopping Centre, Manchester, Lancs.
Manor Farm Barn Antiques, Woburn Abbey Ants. Centre, Beds.
Markov, M., Antiquarius, London, SW3.
Marriott Antiques, Lamb Arcade, Wallingford, Oxon.
Martin, Mrs D., Chenil Galleries, London, SW3.
Martin, D. R. and P. E., Gt. Western Ant. Centre Ltd. - The Wednesday Mkt., Bath, Avon.
Martin, Mrs. J., Antiquarius, London, SW3.
Martin, Nigel, Alfies Antique Mkt, London, NW8.
Martire, Francesca, Alfies Antique Mkt, London, NW8.
Mary Jane, Royal Victoria Arcade, Ryde, I. of Wight.
Masquerade, Kensington Church St. Ants. Centre, London, W8.
Massey, Alison, Grays Antique Mkt, London, W1.

Mathews, Mrs, Newton Abbot Ants. Centre, Devon.
Mathews, Tony, Hastings Ant. Centre, St. Leonards-on-Sea, E. Sussex.
Maxim Antiques, Woburn Abbey Ants. Centre, Beds.
Mathias, G. S., Antiquarius, London, SW3.
Meadway Books, Hampstead Antique Emporium, London, NW3.
Mechilli, Walter, Smith St. Ants. Centre, Warwick, Warks.
Mehta, Mr, Antiquarius, London, SW3.
Mendoza, Sybil, Woburn Abbey Ants. Centre, Beds.
Mendoza, Miss S., Hampstead Antique Emporium, London, NW3.
Mennis, G., Hastings Ant. Centre, St. Leonards-on-Sea, E. Sussex.
Merchant, Nicholas, West Park Antiques Pavilion, Harrogate, N. Yorks.
Merlin Antiques, Grays Antique Mkt, London, W1.
Miall, Margaret, Alfies Antique Mkt, London, NW8.
Michaelis, George, Alfies Antique Mkt, London, NW8.
Michaels, M., Antiquarius, London, SW3.
Michelson, Mrs E., Bond Street Ants. Centre, London, W1
Middleton, Mark, The Ginnel, Harrogate, N. Yorks.
Milan, Serge, Alfies Antique Mkt, London, NW8.
Mildred, J. and S., Gt. Western Ant. Centre Ltd., Bath, Avon.
Millar, Bill, Alfies Antique Mkt, London, NW8.
Miller, David, Alfies Antique Mkt, London, NW8.
Miller, M., Alfies Antique Mkt, London, NW8.
Miller, Mrs P., Antiquarius, London, SW3.
Miscellany Antiques, McBains of Exeter, Exeter, Devon.
Mitton, B. and W., Carlisle Antique and Craft Centre, Cumbria.
Mobbs Antiques, Annette, Sandgate Ants. Centre, Kent.
Mohamed, M. O., Alfies Antique Mkt, London, NW8.
Mohammed, A., Grays Portobello, London, W11.
Molloy, Mrs T., Antiquarius, London, SW3.
Monika, Mall Antiques Arcade, London, N1.
Moonfleet, Royal Victoria Arcade, Ryde, I. of Wight.
Moorlands, West Park Antiques Pavilion, Harrogate, N. Yorks.
Morgan Antiques, Linda, Mall Antiques Arcade, London, N1.
Morland, Maureen, Carlisle Antique and Craft Centre, Cumbria.
Morrell, M., Newton Abbot Ants. Centre, Devon.
Morrison, Jan, Clifton Antiques Mkt, Bristol, Avon.
Mosdell, G., Newton Abbot Ants. Centre, Devon.
Mount Gallery, Hampstead Antique Emporium, London, NW3.
Muggeridge Farm Warehouse, Battlebridge Ant. Centre, Essex.
Muggleton, Mrs R., Chenil Galleries, London, SW3.
Murphy, D. L., Mall Antiques Arcade, London, N1.
Muston-Wise, Tricia, Woburn Abbey Ants. Centre, Beds.
Myers, Marsha, Grays Antique Mkt, London, W1.
Myra Antiques and JLA Ltd, Bond Street Ants. Centre, London, W1.

N

Naegel, Stephen, Grays Mews, London, W1.
Nagioff (Jewellery), I., London Silver Vaults, London, WC2.
Nagioff, I. and R., London Silver Vaults, London, WC2.
Namdar, Grays Antique Mkt, London, W1.
Nassar, A., Hampstead Antique Emporium, London, NW3.
Nasser, Sadi, Bond Street Ants. Centre, London, W1.
Naylor, Brian, The Ginnel, Harrogate, N. Yorks.
Necus, R .S. and S., Antiquarius, London, SW3.
Newman, T., Cotswold Ants. Centre, Stow-on-the-Wold, Glos.
Newsome, Paul, The Ginnel, Harrogate, N. Yorks.
Newton Antiques of Edinburgh, Rait Village Ants. Centre, Scotland.
Nichols, M., Cotswold Ants. Centre, Stow-on-the-Wold, Glos.
Nimmo, G., West Park Antiques Pavilion, Harrogate, N. Yorks.
Nonesuch Antiques, Bond Street Ants. Centre, London, W1.
Noorani, Mrs S., Bond Street Ants. Centre, London, W1.
Norman, George, Gostling's Ant. Centre, Diss, Norfolk.
Norman, Raymond, Gostling's Ant. Centre, Diss, Norfolk.
Norman, Sue, Antiquarius, London, SW3.
Not Cartier, Gt. Western Ant. Centre Ltd., Bath, Avon.
Notaras Antiques, Grays Mews, London, W1.
Notts Pine, Gt. Western Ant. Centre Ltd., Bath, Avon.

CENTRES & MARKETS DEALERS' INDEX

Notts Pine, Jeff and Lindy, Gt. Western Ant. Centre Ltd., Bath, Avon.
Number Ten, Swansea Ant. Centre, W. Glam., Wales.
Nunan, M. P., Gt. Western Ant. Centre Ltd., Bath, Avon.

O

Oakes, J., Clifton Antiques Mkt, Bristol, Avon.
Oakley Associates, Nik, Alfies Antique Mkt, London, NW8.
Oakwell Antiques, West Park Antiques Pavilion, Harrogate, N. Yorks.
Obelisk, Alfies Antique Mkt, London, NW8.
O'Dwyer, E., Hampstead Antique Emporium, London, NW3.
Off the Rails, Gt. Western Ant. Centre Ltd., Bath, Avon.
Old Granary Antique and Craft Centre, The, Battlebridge Ant. Centre, Essex.
Old Tyme, Preston Ant. Centre, Lancs.
Okker, Nadine, Mall Antiques Arcade, London, N1.
One of a Kind, Grays Portobello, London, W11.
Opie, Mr, Newton Abbot Ants. Centre, Devon.
Oracz, P., Preston Ant. Centre, Lancs.
Originals, The, Alfies Antique Mkt, London, NW8.
Orion, Grays Mews, London, W1.
Ortola, Maria, Alfies Antique Mkt, London, NW8.
Osman, Aytac, Antiquarius, London, SW3
Outred, Anthony, Furniture Cave, London, SW10.
Overlord, Almshouses Arcade, Chichester, W. Sussex.
Oxford Antiques, Preston Ant. Centre, Lancs.
Oxley Antique Clocks and Barometers, P.A., The Ginnel, Harrogate, N. Yorks.

P

P. & D. Antiques, Newton Abbot Ants. Centre, Devon.
P.M.R. Antiques, Bond Street Ants. Centre, London, W1.
Palmer, H. J. and Miss J., Antiquarius, London, SW3.
Parker Gallery, The Ginnel, Harrogate, N. Yorks.
Parker-Hall, Terence, York Arcade, London, N1.
Parkside Antiques, Castle Gate Ants. Centre, Newark, Notts.
Pars Antiques, Grays Mews, London, W1.
Pars Antiques, Grays Portobello, London, W11.
Partners, A. J., Alfies Antique Mkt, London, NW8.
Partt, J., Gt. Western Ant. Centre Ltd., Bath, Avon.
Pash & Son, A., Bond Street Silver Galleries, London, W1.
Passing Buy, Royal Victoria Arcade, Ryde, I. of Wight.
Past and Present, York Arcade, London, N1.
Past Reflections, The Ginnel, Harrogate, N. Yorks.
Past Times, Swansea Ant. Centre, W. Glam., Wales.
Patterson, J., Preston Ant. Centre, Lancs.
Pawle Ltd, Julian, Bond Street Silver Galleries, London, W1.
Pawle, J., Bond Street Silver Galleries, London, W1.
Payne, Michelle, Alfies Antique Mkt, London, NW8.
Peake, Geoffrey, Alfies Antique Mkt, London, NW8.
Pearman, John, Chenil Galleries, London, SW3.
Pearse, Patty, Almshouses Arcade, Chichester, Sussex West.
Peddie, Mrs, Newton Abbot Ants. Centre, Devon.
Peddler, M., Preston Ant. Centre, Lancs.
Percy's, London Silver Vaults, London, WC2.
Perez, Maria, Chenil Galleries, London, SW3.
Perez Antiques, Angelo, Castle Gate Ants. Centre, Newark, Notts.
Perkins Antiques, Bryan, Woburn Abbey Ants. Centre, Beds.
Perman, Catherine, Alfies Antique Mkt, London, NW8.
Perrin, Daniel, Alfies Antique Mkt, London, NW8.
Perry, Ron, Woburn Abbey Ants. Centre, Beds.
Perry Antiques, Christopher, Woburn Abbey Ants. Centre, Beds.
Pettitt, J. P., Battlebridge Ant. Centre, Essex.
Phillips, Bob, Alfies Antique Mkt, London, NW8.
Phillipson, M. and J., Leominster Antiques Mkt, Herefs and Worcs.
Phoenix, Alfies Antique Mkt, London, NW8.
Phoenix Antiques, Royal Exchange Shopping Centre, Manchester, Lancs.
Picasso, Matteo, Alfies Antique Mkt, London, NW8.
Pickwick Antiques, Mr, Bermondsey Antique Warehouse, London, SE1.
Pierce and M. Mara, J., Antiquarius, London, SW3.
Pillows of Bond Street, Grays Antique Mkt, London W1.
Pinchen Antiques, Newton Abbot Ants. Centre, Devon.
Pinhas, Ms O., Chenil Galleries, London, SW3.
Place Vendome, Bond Street Ants. Centre, London, W1.

Podlewski Antiques, Grays Antique Mkt, London W1.
Pollock, Miss E., Antiquarius, London, SW3.
Popper, Madeleine, Grays Mews, London, W1.
Postcard Corner, Almshouses Arcade, Chichester, Sussex West.
Powell, Mrs Sylvia, Mall Antiques Arcade, London, N1.
Preiss, Shoshi, Alfies Antique Mkt, London, NW8.
Prestwich Fine Art, The Ginnel, Harrogate, N. Yorks.
Pretty Pictures, Rait Village Ant. Centre, Scotland.
Pridham, B., Newton Abbot Ants. Centre, Devon.
Proctor, J., Antiquarius, London, SW3.
Pullan-Wells, Angela, Alfies Antique Mkt, London, NW8.
Pullen, Sylvia, Ants. Centre, The, Guildford, Surrey.
Pulley, N., Newton Abbot Ants. Centre, Devon. .
Purdy and Lloyd Antiques, Swansea Ant. Centre, W. Glam., Wales.
Purple Shop, The, Antiquarius, London, SW3.
Putting-on-the-Ritz, Victorian Village, Glasgow, Scotland.
Puzzle House Antiques, Grays Antique Mkt, London, W1.
Pye, Ross, Hampstead Antique Emporium, London, NW3.

Q

Quastel, D., Hampstead Antique Emporium, London, NW3.

R

RBR Group, Grays Antique Mkt, London, W1.
Raffaelli, G., Chenil Galleries, London, SW3.
Ralstan, J., Preston Ant. Centre, Lancs.
Ramsden, David and Karin, Royal Exchange Shopping Centre, Manchester, Lancs.
Randle, Liz, Gostling's Ant. Centre, Diss, Norfolk.
Rankin, Piers, Mall Antiques Arcade, London, N1.
Rapley Antiques, John, Woburn Abbey Ants. Centre, Beds.
Rare Art, London Silver Vaults, London WC2.
Ray, Anita, Bond Street Ants. Centre, London, W1.
Ray's, Gt. Western Ant. Centre Ltd., Bath, Avon.
Recollections, Hampstead Antique Emporium, London, NW3.
Re-Design, Alfies Antique Mkt, London, NW8.
Redmile Ltd, Anthony, Furniture Cave, London, SW10.
Reed, Graham, The Ginnel, Harrogate, N. Yorks.
Reed Fine Art, Graham, West Park Antiques Pavilion, Harrogate, N. Yorks.
Rees, Susan, Woburn Abbey Ants. Centre, Beds.
Reeves, Linda, Westbourne Grove Antique Gallery, London, W11.
Regana, Angela, Alfies Antique Mkt, London, NW8.
Reilly, K., Antiquarius, London, SW3.
Relph, S., Gt. Western Ant. Centre Ltd., Bath, Avon.
Reynolds, Celia, Alfies Antique Mkt, London, NW8.
Richards, Mrs, Newton Abbot Ants. Centre, Devon.
Richmond, Margaret, Lamb Arcade, Wallingford, Oxon.
Ridgeway Antiques, Lamb Arcade, Wallingford, Oxon.
Riley, Mrs Gwen, Antiquarius, London, SW3.
Riley, George, Mall Antiques Arcade (Lower Mall), London, N1.
Risdale, Mrs M., Clifton Antiques Mkt, Bristol, Avon.
Risoli, M., Chenil Galleries, London, SW3.
Roberts, Bobby, Swansea Ant. Centre, W. Glam., Wales.
Robertson, E., Woburn Abbey Ants. Centre, Beds.
Robertson Antiques, Leon, McBains of Exeter, Exeter, Devon.
Robinson, Christina, Alfies Antique Mkt, London, NW8.
Robinson, Jo, Alfies Antique Mkt, London, NW8.
Robinson, Wendy, Grays Antique Mkt. London, W1.
Robson, Jane, The Ginnel, Harrogate, N. Yorks.
Rocking Chair Antiques, Preston Ant. Centre, Lancs.
Rockman, Albert, Alfies Antique Mkt, London, NW8.
Rockman, B., Alfies Antique Mkt, London, NW8.
Roe Antiques, Guy, Woburn Abbey Ants. Centre, Beds.
Rolandi, Chenil Galleries, London, SW3.
Rolfe, Denise, Cotswold Ants. Centre, Stow-on-the-Wold, Glos.
Rose Fine Art, The Ginnel, Harrogate, N. Yorks.
Rosen, Peter, Bond Street Ants. Centre, London, W1.
Ross, Alvin, Alfies Antique Mkt, London, NW8.
Rosser-Rees, S., Gt. Western Ant. Centre Ltd., Bath, Avon.
Rothman, Joel and Elizabeth, Antiquarius, London, SW3.
Row, I.M., Grays Portobello, London W11.
Rowan, Mrs Michele, Antiquarius, London, SW3.
Rowe, D., Almshouses Arcade, Chichester, W. Sussex.
Rowley, Bruce, Grays Antique Market, London W1.

Rowley Antiques, J., Preston Ant. Centre, Lancs.
Ruff, J., Newton Abbot Ants. Centre, Devon.
Rutherford, Rosamund, Victorian Village, Glasgow, Scotland.
Rutterford, Paul, Ants. Centre, The, Guildford, Surrey.
Rynsard, R., Woburn Abbey Ants. Centre, Beds.

S

S. and G. Antiques, Stouts Antique Mkt, London, W11.
Salamanca, Chenil Galleries, London, SW3.
Salveson, Dick, Alfies Antique Mkt, London, NW8.
Samii, Alfies Antique Mkt, London, NW8.
Samiramis, Grays Mews, London, W1.
Sampson, Mrs M., Bond Street Ants. Centre, London, W1.
Samuels, Adam, Grays Mews, London, W1.
Sanchez-Martin, Mrs A.M., Bond Street Ants. Centre, London, W1.
Sarah, York Arcade, London, N1.
Sassower, Gad, Mall Antiques Arcade, London, N1.
Saunders, London Silver Vaults, London WC2.
Saxon, Timothy, Alfies Antique Mkt, London, NW8.
Sayers, Charlotte, Grays Antique Mkt, London, W1.
Scalpay Ltd, Antiquarius, London, SW3.
Scola, Patrick, Alfies Antique Mkt, London, NW8.
Scorpio Antiques, Hampstead Antique Emporium, London, NW3.
Scott, Miss Jerri, Antiquarius, London, SW3.
Scribes Engraving, Grays Mews, London, W1.
Scudder, Terry, Woburn Abbey Ants. Centre, Beds.
Second Time Around, Grays Antique Mkt, London, W1.
Second Time Around, Grays Antique Mkt, London, W1.
Sedler, M., Bond Street Silver Galleries, London, W1.
Sefton Antiques, Woburn Abbey Ants. Centre, Beds.
Sewell, Jeremy, Alfies Antique Mkt, London, NW8.
Shahdad Antiques, Grays Mews, London, W1.
Shams, F., Alfies Antique Mkt, London, NW8.
Shapiro, Pat and Alan, Grays Antique Mkt, London, W1.
Shapiro, Sheldon, Grays Antique Mkt, London, W1.
Share, Trudi and Bob, Alfies Antique Mkt, London, NW8.
Sharp, Mr and Mrs J., Carlisle Antique and Craft Centre, Cumbria.
Shaw & Co, J., The Ginnel, Harrogate, N. Yorks.
Shaw, N.R., Bond Street Silver Galleries, London, W1.
Shearman, P., Newton Abbot Ants. Centre, Devon.
Sheelagh's Cottage, Almshouses Arcade, Chichester, W. Sussex.
Shelagh, Hampstead Antique Emporium, London, NW3.
Shenny, D., Bond Street Ants. Centre, London, W1.
Shepherd, John, Woburn Abbey Ants. Centre, Beds.
Sherlock, Newton Abbot Ants. Centre, Devon.
Shieling Antiques, The Ginnel, Harrogate, N. Yorks.
Shieling Antiques, West Park Antiques Pavilion, Harrogate, N. Yorks.
Shine, A. and Z., Alfies Antique Mkt, London, NW8.
Shiners, Carlisle Antique and Craft Centre, Cumbria.
Shorn, D., Antiquarius, London, SW3.
Shure and Co, David S., London Silver Vaults, London, WC2.
Sidoli, Mrs C., Mall Antiques Arcade (Lower Mall), London, N1.
Silk Road Gallery, Gt. Western Ant. Centre Ltd., Bath, Avon.
Silstar, London Silver Vaults, London, WC2.
Silverman, B., London Silver Vaults, London, WC2.
Silverman, S. and R., London Silver Vaults, London, WC2.
Simons (Antiques) Ltd, Jack, London Silver Vaults, London, WC2.
Simpkiss, E., Barnes House Antiques, Wimborne, Dorset.
Simpson, M., Antiquarius, London, SW3.
Simpson, R., Grays Portobello, London, W11.
Simpsons Textiles, Grays Portobello, London, W11.
Sims, Steve and Judith, West Park Antiques Pavilion, Harrogate, N. Yorks.
Singer, A., Mall Antiques Arcade, London, N1.
Sirett Antiques Ltd, Stouts Antique Mkt, London, W11.
Sirett, Mrs A M., Stouts Antique Mkt, London, W11.
Sirett, G., Stouts Antique Mkt, London, W11.
Slater, Neil, Hastings Ant. Centre, St. Leonards-on-Sea, E. Sussex.
Sloane, Peter, Grays Mews, London, W1.
Sloane, Peter, Grays Portobello, London, W11.
Smale, Rosemary and Claire, Alfies Antique Mkt, London, NW8.
Smith, Antiquarius, London, SW3.

Smith, Michael, Bond Street Silver Galleries, London, W1.
Snodgrass Antiques, West Park Antiques Pavilion, Harrogate, N. Yorks.
Sonmez, N., Chenil Galleries, London, SW3.
Sosna, Boris, Grays Mews, London, W1.
Southern, Joan, Gt. Western Ant. Centre Ltd., Bath, Avon.
Southward Enterprises, Preston Ant. Centre, Lancs.
Southwell Antiques, Grays Mews, London, W1.
Sovereign Art, Woburn Abbey Ants. Centre, Beds.
Spa Antiques, Grays Antique Mkt, London, W1.
Spectrum, Grays Antique Mkt, London, W1.
Speight, Connie, Alfies Antique Mkt, London, NW8.
Spicer, K., Antiquarius, London, SW3.
Spooner, Kelvin, Alfies Antique Mkt, London, NW8.
SPV Antiques, Alfies Antique Mkt, London, NW8.
Stanley, Ian and Mandy, Grays Mews, London, W1.
Stanley, J., Cotswold Ants. Centre, Stow-on-the-Wold, Glos.
Stapley, Jean, Smith St. Ants. Centre, Warwick, Warks.
Stephenson, Pauline, The Ginnel, Harrogate, N. Yorks.
Stern, H., London Silver Vaults, London, WC2.
Stevens, Malcolm D., Mall Antiques Arcade (Lower Mall), London, N1.
Stewart Antiques, Michael, Leominster Antiques Mkt, Herefs and Worcs.
Stockman, Paul, Newton Abbot Ants. Centre, Devon.
Stodel, S. and J., London Silver Vaults, London, WC2.
Stone, Mrs Barbara, Antiquarius, London, SW3.
Stone, Gretel, Lamb Arcade, Wallingford, Oxon.
Strachey, Julie, Lamb Arcade, Wallingford, Oxon.
Straw, P. R., Newark Antique Warehouse, Notts.
Stroud, John, York Arcade, London, N1.
Stuart-Mobey, Alan, Span Antiques, Woodstock, Oxon.
Studio, The, Mamie's Ants. Centre, Arundel, W. Sussex.
Sturton, J., Bermondsey Antique Warehouse, London, SE1.
Sutcliffe, T., Preston Ant. Centre, Lancs.
Suttle, H. and M., The Ginnel, Harrogate, N. Yorks. .
Swallow, J., Grays Portobello, London, W11.
Swan Antiques, Royal Exchange Shopping Centre, Manchester, Lancs.
Swonnell (Silverware) Ltd, E., Bond Street Silver Galleries, London, W1.

T

Tags, Lamb Arcade, Wallingford, Oxon.
Talbot Antiques, Cotswold Ants. Centre, Stow-on-the-Wold, Glos.
Taylor, Elsie, Alfies Antique Mkt, London, NW8.
Taylor, V., Gt. Western Ant. Centre Ltd., Bath, Avon.
Templeman, Lynda, Rait Village Ant. Centre, Scotland.
Templemans, Rait Village Ants. Centre, Scotland.
Thacker's Antiques, Newgate Ants. Centre, York, N. Yorks.
Thimble Society, Grays Antique Mkt, London, W1.
Thompson Antiques, Margaret M., Castle Gate Ants. Centre, Newark, Notts.
Thompson Antiques, Michael, Castle Gate Ants. Centre, Newark, Notts.
Thompsca, Sue, Antiquarius, London, SW3.
Thorpe, S., Antiquarius, London, SW3.
Tiernan, Eugene, Alfies Antique Mkt, London, NW8.
Tiffany Antiques, Hastings Ant. Centre, St. Leonards-on-Sea, E. Sussex.
Tilleke, David, Alfies Antique Mkt, London, NW8.
Timms Antiques, S. and S., Woburn Abbey Ants. Centre, Beds.
Tina Art, Alfies Antique Mkt, London, NW8.
Tinne, G., Gt. Western Ant. Centre Ltd., Bath, Avon.
Tipping, Brian, Antiquarius, London, SW3.
Tolkien, S., Chenil Galleries, London, SW3.
Tooley and Jacqueline Statham, Christina, Woburn Abbey Ants. Centre, Beds.
Toop, Rosemary, Lamb Arcade, Wallingford, Oxon.
Toscani, G., Chenil Galleries, London, SW3.
Town and Country, West Park Antiques Pavilion, Harrogate, N. Yorks.
Trader Antiques, The, Preston Ant. Centre, Lancs.
Treadaway Antiques, Paul, Woburn Abbey Ants. Centre, Beds.
Treasures, Royal Victoria Arcade, Ryde, I. of Wight.
Treharne, Allan, Swansea Ant. Centre, W. Glam., Wales.
Trianon, Grays Antique Market, London, W1.
Trickey, S., Clifton Antiques Mkt, Bristol, Avon.

Trinity Galleries, The Ginnel, Harrogate, N. Yorks.
Trio, Grays Mews, London, W1.
Trio, Hampstead Antique Emporium, London, NW3.
Trotter and Parsons, Grays Mews, London, W1.
Turtons Antiques, Smith St Ants. Centre, Warwick, Warks.

U

Underwood Antiques, Woburn Abbey Ants. Centre, Beds.
Urbach, A., London Silver Vaults, London, WC2.
Uriah's Heap, Royal Victoria Arcade, Ryde, I. of Wight.
Urquhart, S., Gt. Western Ant. Centre Ltd. - The Wednesday Mkt., Bath, Avon.
Utopia Antiques Ltd, Preston Ant. Centre, Lancs.

V

Ventura-Pauly, Michael, Grays Antique Mkt, London, W1.
Vetro, Alfies Antique Mkt, London, NW8.
Victoria, Gt. Western Ant. Centre Ltd., Bath, Avon.
Vidich, Mr., Antiquarius, London, SW3.
Village Antiques, Newton Abbot Ants. Centre, Devon.
Vincent's, Clifton Antiques Mkt, Bristol, Avon.
Vinci Antiques, Bond Street Ants. Centre, London, W1.
Vinci, A., Bond Street Ants. Centre, London, W1.
Viventi, G., Bermondsey Antique Warehouse, London, SE1.
Vouse, Mrs, Newton Abbot Ants. Centre, Devon.

W

Wager, Almut, York Arcade, London, N1.
Wain, William, York Arcade, London, N1.
Waite Antiques, J., Preston Ant. Centre, Lancs.
Walker, Lynn, Kensington Church St. Ants. Centre, London, W8.
Wallis, Catherine, Alfies Antique Mkt, London, NW8.
Wallis, D., Alfies Antique Mkt, London, NW8.
Walter, R .W., London Silver Vaults, London, WC2.
Walter Antiques Ltd, William, London Silver Vaults, London, WC2.
Wardrope, J., Carlisle Antique and Craft Centre, Cumbria.
Warner, Marie, Alfies Antique Mkt, London, NW8.
Warham Bursey, Newton Abbot Ants. Centre, Devon.
Warwick Antiques, Carlisle Antique and Craft Centre, Cumbria.
Watch Department, The, Grays Antique Mkt, London, W1.
Waters Violins, Lamb Arcade, Wallingford, Oxon.
Watson, B., Hastings Ant. Centre, St. Leonards-on-Sea, E. Sussex.
Watson, J., Gt. Western Ant. Centre Ltd., Bath, Avon.
Watson, Steven, Alfies Antique Mkt, London, NW8.
Weedon, Mike, Mall Antiques Arcade, London, N1.
Weiss, A. and G., London Silver Vaults, London, WC2.
Weiss, Peter K., London Silver Vaults, London, WC2.
Wellard, Mary, Grays Antique Mkt, London, W1.
West Country Jewellery, Antiquarius, London, SW3.
Westminster Group, Grays Antique Mkt, London, W1.
Wharton Antiques, Tim, Woburn Abbey Ants. Centre, Beds.
Wheatley, David and Linda, Grays Antique Mkt, London, W1.
Wheeleker, Liz, Newton Abbot Ants. Centre, Devon.
Whilom, The Ginnel, Harrogate, N. Yorks.

White, Doreen, Mall Antiques Arcade, London, N1.
White, Howard, Bond Street Silver Galleries, London, W1.
White, Julian, The Ginnel, Harrogate, N. Yorks.
White, J. J., Alfies Antique Mkt, London, NW8.
Whittingham, Gt. Western Ant. Centre Ltd. - The Wednesday Mkt., Bath, Avon.
Wickersley Antiques, Newark Antique Warehouse, Notts.
Wigdor Antiques, David, Westbourne Grove Antique Gallery, London, W11.
Wigmore Interiors, Leominster Antiques Mkt, Herefs and Worcs.
Wilcocks, Norman, Alfies Antique Mkt, London, NW8.
Willcocks, C. A., Chenil Galleries, London, SW3.
Willcocks, Mrs Y. P., Chenil Galleries, London, SW3.
Williams, G., Swansea Ant. Centre, W. Glam., Wales.
Williams, Margaret, Woburn Abbey Ants. Centre, Beds.
Williamson, Aura, Grays Mews, London, W1.
Willis, Henry, Bond Street Silver Galleries, London, W1.
Willis, Simon, Chenil Galleries, London, SW3.
Wilson, Derick, Newton Abbot Ants. Centre, Devon.
Wilson, J., Bath Street Antiques Galleries, Glasgow.
Wilson, Jeff, Leominster Antiques Mkt, Herefs and Worcs.
Wimpole Antiques, Grays Antique Mkt, London, W1.
Winchester, P., Newton Abbot Ants. Centre, Devon.
Winckworth, Newton Abbot Ants. Centre, Devon.
Winkies, Swansea Ant. Centre, W. Glam., Wales.
Winstone, D., Gt. Western Ant. Centre Ltd., Bath, Avon.
Winstone Stamp Co. and S. D. Postcards, Gt. Western Ant. Centre Ltd., Bath, Avon.
Wolfe (Jewellery), London Silver Vaults, London, WC2.
Woodage, Graham, Mall Antiques Arcade (Lower Mall), London, N1.
Woodford, Mike, Gt. Western Ant. Centre Ltd., Bath, Avon.
Woodman, W., Cotswold Ants. Centre, Stow-on-the-Wold, Glos.
Wright, P., Newton Abbot Ants. Centre, Devon.
Wyncoll, Craig, Grays Antique Mkt, London, W1.

X

Xelana Antiques, Bond Street Ants. Centre, London, W1.

Y

Yates Antiques, Preston Ant. Centre, Lancs.
Yauuz, Oral, Grays Mews, London, W1.
Yesterday's Pine, Carlisle Antique and Craft Centre, Cumbria.
Yestertime Antiques, St. Georges Antiques, Worcester, Herefs. and Worcs.
Young, Denis, Woburn Abbey Ants. Centre, Beds.
Young, Mavis, Newton Abbot Ants. Centre, Devon.
Young, Michael, Mall Antiques Arcade, London, N1.

Z

Zarzycka, Basia, Chenil Galleries, London, SW3.
Zatua, Adu, Alfies Antique Mkt, London, NW8.
Zaziemski, Mrs J., Mall Antiques Arcade, London, N1.
Ziebell, J., Hastings Ant. Centre, St. Leonards-on-Sea, E. Sussex.
Zokagg, Helen, Grays Mews, London, W1.

SPECIALIST DEALERS INDEX

Most antique dealers in Britain sell a wide range of goods from furniture, through porcelain and pottery, to pictures, prints and clocks. Much of the interest in visiting antique shops comes from this diversity. However, there a a number of dealers who specialise and the following is a list of these dealers. Most of them will have in stock a representative selection of the items under their classification.

The name of the business, together with the area of London or the town and county under which the detailed entry can be found are given in the listing. Again, we would like to repeat the advice given in the intoduction that, if readers are looking for a particular item, they are advised to telephone first before making a long journey.

CLASSIFICATIONS

Antiques Centres
Antiquities
Antiquarian Books
Architectural Items
Arms and Militaria
Art Deco and Art Nouveau
Barometers
Beds
Brass - see Metalwork
Bronzes
Carriages and Cars
Carpets and Rugs
Chinese Art - see Oriental
Clocks and Watches
Coins and Medals
Dolls and Toys
Etchings and Engravings
Fire Items
Frames
Furniture
  Continental (mainly French)
  Georgian
  Oak
  Pine
  Victorian
Garden Furniture, Ornaments and Statuary
Icons - see Russian Art
Islamic Art
Japanese Art - see Oriental
Jewellery - see Silver and Jewellery
Lighting

Metalwork
Miniatures
Mirrors
Musical Boxes, Instruments and Literature
Nautical Instruments - see Scientific
Needlework - see Tapestries
Netsuke - see Oriental
Oil Paintings
Oriental Art
Photographs and Equipment
Porcelain and Pottery
Prints - see Maps
Rugs - see Carpets
Russian Art
Scientific Instruments
Sculpture
Shipping Goods and Period Furniture for
  the Trade
Sporting Items and Associated Memorabilia
Sporting Paintings and Prints
Stamps
Tapestries, Texiles and Needlework
Tools - including Needlework and Sewing
Toys - see Dolls
Trade Dealers - see Shipping Goods
Treen
Vintage Cars - see Carriages
Watercolours
Wholesale Dealers see Shipping Goods
Wine Related Items

Antiques Centres

Georgian Village Antiques Market, London, E17.
York Arcade, London, N1.
Camden Passage Antiques Centre, London, N1.
Fleamarket, The, London, N1.
London Militaria Market, London, N1.
Mall Antiques Arcade, The, London, N1.
Hampstead Antique Emporium, London, NW3.
Alfies Antique Market, London, NW8.
Antique Warehouse, London, SE1.
Bermondsey Antique Warehouse, London, SE1.
Bermondsey Antiques Hypermarket, London, SE1.
Franklin's Camberwell Antiques Market, London, SE5.
Greenwich Antiques Market, London, SE10.
Antiquarius, London, SW3.
Chelsea Antique Market, London, SW3.
Chenil Galleries, London, SW3.
Magpies, London, SW6.
Northcote Road Antiques Market, London, SW11.
Dixon's Antique Centre, London, SW14.
Bond Street Antiques Centre, London, W1.
Grays Antique Market, London, W1.
Grays Mews, London, W1.
Old Cinema Antique Department Store, The, London, W4.
Kensington Church Street Antiques Centre, London, W8.
Corner Portobello Antiques Supermarket, The, London, W11.
Dolphin Arcade, London, W11.
Good Fairy Open Air Market, The, London, W11.
Grays Portobello, London, W11.
Westbourne Grove Antique Gallery, London, W11.
World Famous Portobello Market, London, W11.
Metropolitan Stall Markets, London, W11.
Red Lion Market (Portobello Antiques Market), The, London, W11.
Roger's Antiques Gallery, London, W11.
Apple Market Stalls, London, WC2.
Covent Garden Flea Market, London, WC2.
London Silver Vaults, The, London, WC2.
Trafalgar Square Collectors Centre, London, WC2.
Bartlett Street Antique Centre, Bath, Avon.
Bath Antiques Market, Bath, Avon.
Bath Saturday Antiques Market, Bath, Avon.
Great Western Antique Centre Ltd. - The Wednesday Market, Bath, Avon.
Paragon Antiques and Collectors Market, Bath, Avon.
Bristol Antique Market, Bristol, Avon.
Clifton Antiques Market, Bristol, Avon.
Harrold Antique Centre, Harrold, Beds.
Heath Antique Centre, Heath and Reach, Beds.
Woburn Abbey Antiques Centre, The, Woburn, Beds.
Hungerford Arcade, Hungerford, Berks.
Reading Emporium, Reading, Berks.
Moss End Antique Centre, Warfield, Berks.
Amersham Antiques and Collectors Centre, Amersham, Bucks.
Olney Antique Centre, Olney, Bucks.
Bell Street Antiques Centre, Princes Risborough, Bucks.
Tingewick Antiques Centre, Tingewick, Bucks.
Antiques at Wendover, Wendover, Bucks.
Winslow Antiques Centre, Winslow, Bucks.
Collectors' Market, Cambridge, Cambs.
Gwydir Street Antiques Centre, Cambridge, Cambs.
Hyde Park Corner Antiques (Antiques Centre), Cambridge, Cambs.
Old Bishop's Palace Antique Centre, The, Little Downham, Cambs.
Fitzwilliam Antiques Centre, Peterborough, Cambs.
Guildhall Fair, Chester, Cheshire.
Davenham Antique Centre, Davenham, Cheshire.
Cutler Antique and Collectors Fairs, Stancie, Nantwich, Cheshire.
E. R. Antiques Centre, Stockport, Cheshire.
Waterfront Antiques Market, Falmouth, Cornwall.
New Generation Antiques Market, Penzance, Cornwall.
West End Antiques Market, Redruth, Cornwall.
Furniture Store/St. Austell Antiques Centre, The, St. Austell, Cornwall.
Carlisle Antique and Craft Centre, Carlisle, Cumbria.
Cockermouth Antiques Market, Cockermouth, Cumbria.
Belper Antiques Centre, Belper, Derbys.
Corry's Antiques, Derby, Derbys.
Derby Antique Centre, Derby, Derbys.
Glossop Antique Centre, Glossop, Derbys.
Shambles, The, Ashburton, Devon.
Colyton Antique Centre, Colyton, Devon.
Antique Centre on the Quay, The, Exeter, Devon.
Coombe Street Galleries, Exeter, Devon.
McBains of Exeter, Exeter, Devon.
Quay Gallery Antiques Emporium, The, Exeter, Devon.
Antique Centre Abingdon House, The, Honiton, Devon.
Newton Abbot Antiques Centre, Newton Abbot, Devon.
Barbican Antiques Centre, Plymouth, Devon.
Barbican Centre, The, Plymouth, Devon.
Courtyard Antiques and Collectors Centre, Seaton, Devon.
Devonshire House Antiques and Collectors Centre, Sidmouth, Devon.
Sidmouth Antique Market, Sidmouth, Devon.
Furniture Market, The, South Molton, Devon.
Antique Centre, The, Bournemouth, Dorset.
Hardy's Market, Bournemouth, Dorset.
St. Andrew's Market, Bournemouth, Dorset.
Bridport Antiques Centre, Bridport, Dorset.
Charmouth Antique Centre, Charmouth, Dorset.
Box of Porcelain, Dorchester, Dorset.
Colliton Antique and Craft Centre, Dorchester, Dorset.
Dorchester Antiques Market, Dorchester, Dorset.
Antique Market, Sherborne, Dorset.
Sherborne Antique Centre, Sherborne, Dorset.
North Quay Antique Centre, Weymouth, Dorset.
Barnes House Antiques, Wimborne Minster, Dorset.
Abridge Antique Centre, Abridge, Essex.
Battlesbridge Antique Centre, Battlesbridge, Essex.
Essex Antiques Centre, Colchester, Essex.
Trinity Antiques Centre, Colchester, Essex.
Epping Saturday Market, Epping, Essex.
Grays Collectors Centre, Grays, Essex.
Baddow Antique and Craft Centre, Great Baddow, Essex.
Townsford Mill Antiques Centre, Halstead, Essex.
Kelvedon Antiques Centre, Kelvedon, Essex.
Kelvedon Art and Antiques, Kelvedon, Essex.
Maldon Antiques and Collectors Market, Maldon, Essex.
Trading Warehouse, Rettendon, Essex.
Charlton Kings Antiques Centre, Cheltenham, Glos.
Cheltenham Antique Market, Cheltenham, Glos.
Cirencester Antique Market, Cirencester, Glos.
Gloucester Antique Centre, Gloucester, Glos.
Lechlade Antiques Arcade, Lechlade, Glos.
Swan Antiques and Crafts Centre, The, Lechlade, Glos.
Antique Centre, Moreton-in-Marsh, Glos.
Windsor House Antiques Centre, Moreton-in-Marsh, Glos.
Painswick Antique Centre, Painswick, Glos.
Cotswold Antiques Centre, Stow-on-the-Wold, Glos.
No. 2 Park Street Antiques, Stow-on-the-Wold, Glos.
Antiques Emporium, The, Tetbury, Glos.
Tewkesbury Antique Centre, Tewkesbury, Glos.
Lymington Antiques Centre, Lymington, Hants.
Creightons Antique Centre, Romsey, Hants.
Samuels Spencers Antiques and Decorative Arts Emporium, Winchester, Hants.
Hereford Antique Centre, Hereford, Herefs and Worcs.
Leominster Antiques Market, Leominster, Herefs and Worcs.
Antiques and Curios, Worcester, Herefs and Worcs.
St. Georges Antiques, Worcester, Herefs and Worcs.
Tything Antique Market, The, Worcester, Herefs and Worcs.
Antique and Collectors Market, Hemel Hempstead, Herts.
Hitchin Antiques Gallery, Hitchin, Herts.
Herts and Essex Antique Centre, The, Sawbridgeworth, Herts.
By George! Antiques Centre, St. Albans, Herts.
St. Albans Antique Market, St. Albans, Herts.
Grannie's Treasures, Hull, Humbs North.
Royal Victoria Arcade, Ryde, I. of Wight.
Beckenham Antique Market, Beckenham, Kent.
Bromley Antique Market, Bromley, Kent.
Paraphernalia Antiques and Collectors' Centre, Bromley, Kent.
Burgate Antique Centre, Canterbury, Kent.
Canterbury Weekly Antique Market, Canterbury, Kent.
Coach House Antiques, Canterbury, Kent.
Rastro Antiques, Canterbury, Kent.
Cranbrook Antique Centre, Cranbrook, Kent.
Hythe Antique Centre, Hythe, Kent.
Malthouse Arcade, Hythe, Kent.

SPECIALIST DEALERS

Sandgate Antiques Centre, Sandgate, Kent.
Noah's Ark Antique Centre, Sandwich, Kent.
Antiques Centre, The, Sevenoaks, Kent.
Bradbourne Gallery, Sevenoaks, Kent.
Tenterden Antiques Centre, Tenterden, Kent.
Barden House Antiques, Tonbridge, Kent.
Tunbridge Wells Antique Centre, Tunbridge Wells, Kent.
Castle Antiques Centre, Westerham, Kent.
McNair Antiques Centre, Hugh, Westerham, Kent.
Bolton Antique Centre, Bolton, Lancs.
Last Drop Antique and Collectors Fair, Bolton, Lancs.
Memory Lane Antique Centre, Bolton, Lancs.
Darwen Antique Centre, Darwen, Lancs.
Bygone Times Ltd, Eccleston, Lancs.
Assembly Rooms Market, The, Lancaster, Lancs.
G.B. Antiques Ltd, Lancaster, Lancs.
Lancaster Leisure Park Antiques Centre, Lancaster, Lancs.
Antiques Village, Manchester, Lancs.
Royal Exchange Shopping Centre, Manchester, Lancs.
Antique Centre, The, Preston, Lancs.
Preston Antique Centre, Preston, Lancs.
Aspinall Antiques, Walter, Sabden, Lancs.
Antiques Complex, The, Leicester, Leics.
Boulevard Antique and Shipping Centre, Leicester, Leics.
Oxford Street Antique Centre Ltd, Leicester, Leics.
Swans Antique Centre, Oakham, Leics.
Boston Antiques Centre, Boston, Lincs.
Portobellow Row Antiques Centre, Boston, Lincs.
Guardroom Antiques Centre, The, Hemswell Cliff, Lincs.
Hemswell Antiques Centres, Hemswell Cliff, Lincs.
Lincs Antiques Centre, The, Horncastle, Lincs.
Eastgate Antique Centre, Lincoln, Lincs.
St. Martin's Antiques and Craft Centre, Stamford, Lincs.
Stamford Antiques Centre, Stamford, Lincs.
Hoylake Antique Centre, Hoylake, Merseyside.
Hampton Village Antiques Centre, Hampton, Middx.
Jay's Antique Centre, The, Harefield, Middx.
Coltishall Antiques Centre, Coltishall, Norfolk.
Gostling's Antique Centre, Diss, Norfolk.
Fakenham Antique Centre, Fakenham, Norfolk.
Glenmore Interiors, King's Lynn, Norfolk.
Old Granary Antiques and Collectors Centre, The, King's Lynn, Norfolk.
Cloisters Antiques Fair, Norwich, Norfolk.
St Mary's Antique Centre, Norwich, Norfolk.
St. Michael at Plea Antiques Centre, Norwich, Norfolk.
Wells Antique Centre, Wells-next-the-Sea, Norfolk.
Wymondham Antique Centre, Wymondham, Norfolk.
Burnett Antiques, Jean, Finedon, Northants.
Finedon Antiques (Antiques Centre), Finedon, Northants.
Village Antique Market, The, Weedon, Northants.
Antiques and Bric-a-Brac Market, Wellingborough, Northants.
Castle Gate Antiques Centre, Newark, Notts.
Newark Antiques Centre, Newark, Notts.
Portland Street Antiques Centre, Newark, Notts.
Nottingham Antique Centre, Nottingham, Notts.
Top Hat Antiques Centre, Nottingham, Notts.
Old George Inn Antique Galleries, Burford, Oxon.
Chipping Norton Antique Centre, Chipping Norton, Oxon.
Deddington Antique Centre, The, Deddington, Oxon.
Friday Street Antique Centre, Henley-on-Thames, Oxon.
Henley Antique Centre, Henley-on-Thames, Oxon.
Oxford Antique Trading Co, The, Oxford, Oxon.
Oxford Antiques Centre, Oxford, Oxon.
Lamb Arcade, The, Wallingford, Oxon.
Span Antiques, Woodstock, Oxon.
Stretton Antiques Market, Church Stretton, Shrops.
Cleobury Mortimer Antique Centre, Cleobury Mortimer, Shrops.
Ironbridge Antique Centre, Ironbridge, Shrops.
Corve Galleries, The, Ludlow, Shrops.
Pepper Lane Antique Centre, Ludlow, Shrops.
St. Leonards Antiques, Ludlow, Shrops.
Shrewsbury Antique Centre, Shrewsbury, Shrops.
Shrewsbury Antique Market, Shrewsbury, Shrops.
Telford Antiques Centre, Telford, Shrops.
Bridgwater Antiques Market, Bridgwater, Somerset.
Guildhall Antique Market, Chard, Somerset.
Oscars - Antique Market, Crewkerne, Somerset.
Antiques Fair, Glastonbury, Somerset.
Antiques Market, Glastonbury, Somerset.

County Antiques Centre, Ilminster, Somerset.
Taunton Antiques Market - Silver Street, Taunton, Somerset.
Rugeley Antique Centre, Brereton, Staffs.
Antique Centre, The, Kinver, Staffs.
Leek Antiques Centre, The, Leek, Staffs.
Tudor of Lichfield Antique Centre, Lichfield, Staffs.
Antique Market, Newcastle-under-Lyme, Staffs.
Windmill Antiques, Stafford, Staffs.
Tamworth Antique Centre, The, Tamworth, Staffs.
Waveney Antiques Centre, Beccles, Suffolk.
Clare Antique Warehouse, Clare, Suffolk.
Debenham Antique Centre, Debenham, Suffolk.
Long Melford Antiques Centre, Long Melford, Suffolk.
Old Town Hall Antique Centre, The, Needham Market, Suffolk.
Risby Barn, The, Risby, Suffolk.
Snape Antiques and Collectors Centre, Snape, Suffolk.
Emporium Antiques and Collectors Centre, The, Southwold, Suffolk.
Memories, Bramley, Surrey.
Cambridge Parade Antiques, Carshalton, Surrey.
Surrey Antiques Centre, Chertsey, Surrey.
Antiquaries Antique Centre, Dorking, Surrey.
Dorking Antique Centre, Dorking, Surrey.
Victoria and Edward Antiques Centre, Dorking, Surrey.
Antiques Arcade, The, East Molesey, Surrey.
Sovereign Antique Centre, The, East Molesey, Surrey.
Bourne Mill Antiques, Farnham, Surrey.
Farnham Antique Centre, Farnham, Surrey.
Maltings Monthly Market, Farnham, Surrey.
Antiques Centre, The, Guildford, Surrey.
Wood's Wharf Antiques Bazaar, Haslemere, Surrey.
Old Smithy Antique Centre, The, Merstham, Surrey.
Antiques Centre, Oxted, Surrey.
Antiques Arcade, Richmond, Surrey.
Dukes Yard Market, Richmond, Surrey.
Richmond Traders, Richmond, Surrey.
Shere Antique Centre, Shere, Surrey.
Fern Cottage Antique Centre, Thames Ditton, Surrey.
Grange Antiques and Craft Centre, The, Tongham, Surrey.
Brighton Antique Wholesalers, Brighton, Sussex East.
Brighton Flea Market, Brighton, Sussex East.
Prinny's Gallery, Brighton, Sussex East.
Chateaubriand Antiques Centre, Burwash, Sussex East.
Eastbourne Antiques Market, Eastbourne, Sussex East.
Old Town Antique Centre, The, Eastbourne, Sussex East.
Pharoahs Antiques Centre, Eastbourne, Sussex East.
George Street Antiques Centre, Hastings, Sussex East.
Horsebridge Antiques Centre, Horsebridge, Sussex East.
Cliffe Antiques Centre, Lewes, Sussex East.
Cliffe Gallery Antiques , Lewes, Sussex East.
Emporium Antique Centre, The, Lewes, Sussex East.
Lewes Antique Centre, Lewes, Sussex East.
Courtyard Antiques Market, The, Seaford, Sussex East.
Seaford's "Barn Collectors' Market" and Studio Bookshop, Seaford, Sussex East.
Hastings Antique Centre, The, St. Leonards-on-Sea, Sussex East.
Antique Centre and Collectors Market, Adversane, Sussex West.
Mamie's Antiques Centre, Arundel, Sussex West.
Tarrant Street Antique Centre, Arundel, Sussex West.
Treasure House Antiques and Collectors Market, Arundel, Sussex West.
Upstairs Downstairs Antique Centre, Arundel, Sussex West.
Almshouses Arcade, Chichester, Sussex West.
Eagle House Antiques Market, Midhurst, Sussex West.
Midhurst Antiques Market, Midhurst, Sussex West.
Midhurst Walk, Midhurst, Sussex West.
Petworth Antique Market, Petworth, Sussex West.
Antiques Centre, Newcastle-upon-Tyne, Tyne and Wear.
Malthouse Antiques Centre, Alcester, Warks.
Antiques Centre, The, Bidford-on-Avon, Warks.
Country Furniture Antique Centre, Charlecote, Warks.
Dunchurch Antique Centre, Dunchurch, Warks.
Leamington Pine and Antique Centre, Leamington Spa, Warks.
Meer Street Antiques Arcade, Stratford-upon-Avon, Warks.
Stratford Antique Centre, Stratford-upon-Avon, Warks.
Smith St. Antiques Centre, Warwick, Warks.
Vintage Antiques Centre, Warwick, Warks.
Warwick Antique Centre, The, Warwick, Warks.

SPECIALIST DEALERS

City of Birmingham Antique Market, The, Birmingham, West Mids.
Warley Antique Centre, Birmingham, West Mids.
Cutler Antique and Collectors Fair, Stancie, Sutton Coldfield, West Mids.
Walsall Antiques Centre, Walsall, West Mids.
Marlborough Parade Antique Centre, The, Marlborough, Wilts.
Antique and Collectors Market, Salisbury, Wilts.
Avonbridge Antiques and Collectors Market, The, Salisbury, Wilts.
Micawber's, Salisbury, Wilts.
Wroughton Antique Centre, Wroughton, Wilts.
Ginnel, The, Harrogate, Yorks. North.
Grove Collectors Centre, Harrogate, Yorks. North.
Montpellier Mews Antique Market, Harrogate, Yorks. North.
West Park Antiques Pavilion, Harrogate, Yorks. North.
Malton Antique Market, Malton, Yorks. North.
Scarthingwell Arcades, Scarthingwell, Yorks. North.
Newgate Antiques Centre, York, Yorks. North.
York Antiques Centre, York, Yorks. North.
Treasure House Antiques Centre, Bawtry, Yorks. South.
Bingley Antiques Centre, Bingley, Yorks. West.
Halifax Antiques Centre, Halifax, Yorks. West.
Waterloo Antiques Centre, Leeds, Yorks. West.
Union Street Antique Market, St. Helier, Jersey, C. I.
Bath Street Antiques Galleries, Glasgow, Scotland.
Heritage House Antiques, Glasgow, Scotland.
King's Court Antique Centre, Glasgow, Scotland.
Victorian Village, The, Glasgow, Scotland.
Virginia Antique Galleries, Glasgow, Scotland.
West of Scotland Antique Centre Ltd, Glasgow, Scotland.
Murray Antique Warehouse, Ian, Perth, Scotland.
Rait Village Antiques Centre, Rait, Scotland.
Thornhill Gallery Antique Centre, Thornhill, Scotland.
Pembroke Antique Centre, Pembroke, Dyfed, Wales.
Jacobs Antique Centre, Cardiff, South Glam., Wales.
Swansea Antique Centre, Swansea, West Glam., Wales.
Davies Antiques Centre, Chepstow, Gwent, Wales.
Wellfield Antique Centre, Bangor, Gwynedd, Wales.
Antiques Market, Hay-on-Wye, Powys, Wales.
Offa's Dyke Antique Centre, Knighton, Powys, Wales.

Antiquities

Auld, Ian, London, N1.
Martin (Coins) Ltd, C.J., London, N14.
Faustus Fine Art Ltd, London, SW1.
Symes Ltd, Robin, London, SW1.
Wace Ancient Art Ltd, Rupert, London, SW1.
Acanthus Art Ltd, London, SW11.
Astarte Gallery, London, W1.
Ede Ltd, Charles, London, W1.
Mansour Gallery, London, W1.
Oriental Bronzes Ltd, London, W1.
Seaby Ltd, B.A., London, W1.
Sheppard and Cooper Ltd, London, W1.
Casemate, Bath, Avon.
Sainsbury, M., Bath, Avon.
Potter's Antiques and Coins, Bristol, Avon.
Bly, John, Tring, Herts.
Tamblyn, Alnwick, Northumbs.
Burton-Garbett, A., Morden, Surrey.
Alexander, Molly, Seaford, Sussex East.
Hermitage Antiquities, Fishguard, Dyfed, Wales.

Antiquarian Books (See Books)

Architectural Items

London Architectural Salvage and Supply Co. Ltd. (LASSCo), The, London, EC2.
Westland & Company, London, EC2.
Chapman Antiques, Peter, London, N1.
Townsends, London, NW8.
Lamont Antiques Ltd, London, SE10.
Edwards, Charles, London, SW6.
Old World Trading Co, London, SW6.
Thornhill Galleries Ltd, London, SW6.
Whiteway and Waldron Ltd, London, SW6.
Thornhill Galleries Ltd. in association with A. & R. Dockerill Ltd, London, SW15.
Phillips and Sons, E.S., London, W11.
Walcot Reclamation, Bath, Avon.
Mills Architectural Antiques Ltd, Robert, Bristol, Avon.
Bridgwater, David, Marshfield, Avon.
Solopark Ltd, Pampisford, Cambs.
Wilding, R., Wisbech, Cambrs.
Nostalgia Architectural Antiques, Stockport, Cheshire.
Cheshire Brick and Slate Co, Tarvin Sands, Cheshire.
Great Northern Architectural Antique Company Ltd, The, Tattenhall, Cheshire.
Antique Fireplace Centre, Hartlepool, Cleveland.
Thornton Antiques Supermarket, J.W., Bowness-on-Windermere, Cumbria.
W.R.S. Architectural Antiques, Low Newton, Cumbria.
Thornton Antiques, Joseph, Windermere, Cumbria.
Havenplan's Architectural Emporium, Killamarsh, Derbys.
Ashburton Marbles, Ashburton, Devon.
Meredith, John, Chagford, Devon.
Fagins Antiques, Exeter, Devon.
Cantabrian Antiques and Architectural Furnishing, Lynton, Devon.
Architectural Antiques, South Molton, Devon.
Bailey's Quality Antique Lighting and Accessories, Cheltenham, Glos.
Antique Pine, Norton, Glos.
Architectural Heritage, Taddington, Glos.
Burgess Farm Antiques, Morestead, Hants.
"Old Cottage Things", Romsey, Hants.
Pine Cellars, The, Winchester, Hants.
Elmley Heritage, Elmley Lovett, Herefs and Worcs.
Baileys Architectural Antiques, Ross-on-Wye, Herefs and Worcs.
Holloways, Suckley, Herefs and Worcs.
Original Choice Ltd, The, Worcester, Herefs and Worcs.
Antique Fireplaces, Manchester, Lancs.
Cowell and Sons Architectural Antiques, W.J., Broughton, Lancs.
Old Smithy, Feniscowles, Lancs.
Victoriana Architectural, Long Clawston, Leics.
Architectural Antiques, Liverpool, Merseyside.
Crowther of Syon Lodge Ltd, Isleworth, Middx.
Architectural Heritage of Northants, Weedon, Northants.
Rococo Antiques and Interiors, Weedon, Northants.
Thirty-Eight Antiques Ltd, Weedon, Northants.
Hallidays Antiques Ltd, Dorchester-on-Thames, Oxon.
Country Seat, The, Huntercombe, Oxon.
Oxford Architectural Antiques, Oxford, Oxone.
Architectural Antiques and Interiors, Ludlow, Shrops.
Wells Reclamation Company, Coxley, Somerset.
Anvil Antiques, Leek, Staffs.
Drummonds of Bramley Architectural Antiques Ltd, Bramley, Surrey.
Packhouse, The, Runfold, Surrey.
Grange Antiques and Craft Centre, The, Tongham, Surrey.
Brighton Architectural Salvage, Brighton, Sussex East.
Shiners Architectural Reclamation, Newcastle-upon-Tyne, Tyne and Wear.
Architectural Antiques of Moseley, Birmingham, West Mids.
James Antiques, Tim, Birmingham, West Mids.
Tudor House Antiques, Halesowen, West Mids.
Retro Products, Lye, West Mids.
Martin-Quick Antiques, Wolverhampton, West Mids.
Fairfax Fireplaces and General Antiques, Harriet, Langley Burrell, Wilts.
Relic Antiques at Brillscote Farm, Malmesbury, Wilts.
Coggins Antiques, Ray, Westbury, Wilts.
Old Flame, Easingwold, Yorks North.
White House Farm Antiques, Easingwold, Yorks North.
Aagaard Ltd, Robert, Knaresborough, Yorks North.
Reece Gallery, The Gordon, Knaresborough, Yorks North.
Daleside Antiques, Markington, Yorks North.
Mount Antiques, The, Whitby, Yorks North.
Thornton Architectural Antiques Ltd, Andy, Halifax, Yorks West.
Period Architectural Features and Antiques, Annahilt, Co. Down, N. Ireland.
Dunedin Antiques Ltd, Edinburgh, Scotland.
EASY - Edinburgh Architectural Salvage Yard, Edinburgh, Scotland.
Macintosh & Co, William, Edinburgh, Scotland.

Kings Fireplaces & Architectural Antiques, Cardiff, South Glam., Wales.
Annteaks, Abersoch, Gwynedd, Wales.
Gallop and Rivers Architectural Antiques, Crickhowell, Powys, Wales.

Arms and Militaria

London Militaria Market, London, N1.
Finchley Fine Art Galleries, London, N12.
Laurence Corner London, NW1.
Reubens, London, SE23.
Dale Ltd, Peter, London, SW1.
Tillou Works of Art Ltd, Peter, London, SW1.
Period Brass Lights, London, SW7.
Blunderbuss Antiques, London, W1.
Holland and Holland Ltd, London, W1.
Tradition - Military Antiques, London, W1.
German, Michael C., London, W8.
Hales Antiques Ltd, Robert, London, W8.
Grimes Militaria, Chris, Bristol, Avon.
Oliver, Tony L., Windsor and Eton, Berks.
Sundial Antiques, Amersham, Bucks.
Porter, Fine Antique European Arms and Armour, Terence H., Steeple Claydon, Bucks.
Goodlad, Anthony D., Chesterfield, Derbys.
Meredith, John, Chagford, Devon.
Blade and Bayonet, Bournemouth, Dorset.
Boscombe Militaria, Bournemouth, Dorset.
Sterling Coins and Medals, Bournemouth, Dorset.
Lankshear Antiques, M. & R., Christchurch, Dorset.
Nautical Antique Centre, The, Weymouth, Dorset.
Castle Antiques, Leigh-on-Sea, Essex.
Heydens Antiques and Militaria, Cheltenham, Glos.
Military Curios, HQ84, Gloucester, Glos.
Serle (Antiques and Restoration), Mark A., Lechlade, Glos.
Norden Antiques, Peter, Stow-on-the-Wold, Glos.
Hampton Gallery, Tetbury, Glos.
Romsey Medal and Collectors Centre, Romsey, Hants.
Trecilla Antiques, Ross-on-Wye, Herefs and Worcs.
Antique Militaria, Bridlington, Humbs North.
Guns and Tackle, Scunthorpe, Humbs South.
Greenfield and Son, Gunmakers (Est. 1805), H.S., Canterbury, Kent.
Rutherford and Son, J.T., Sandgate, Kent.
Bulldog Antiques, Manchester, Lancs.
Pinfold Antiques, Ruskington, Lincs.
Liverpool Militaria, Liverpool, Merseyside.
Old Brigade, The, Kingsthorpe, Northants.
Trident Arms, Nottingham, Notts.
Monarch Antiques, Glastonbury, Somerset.
Fox and Co, Yeovil, Somerset.
Atfield and Daughter, Ipswich, Suffolk.
West Street Antiques, Dorking, Surrey.
Casque and Gauntlet Militaria, Farnham, Surrey.
Hawkins, Mark and David, Brighton, Sussex East.
St. Pancras Antiques, Chichester, Sussex West.
Miller, Michael, Hurstpierpoint, Sussex West.
Arbour Antiques Ltd, Stratford-upon-Avon, Warks.
Wigington Antiques, James, Stratford-upon-Avon, Warks.
March Medals, Birmingham, West Mids.
S.O.S. Militaria, Stourbridge, West Mids.
Collectors' Paradise Ltd, Wolverhampton, West Mids.
Gwilliam, Edred A.F, Cricklade, Wilts.
Cairncross and Sons, Filey, Yorks North.
Hanover Antiques, Scarborough, Yorks North.
Adamson Armoury, Skipton, Yorks North.
Bottomley, Andrew Spencer, Holmfirth, Yorks West.
Dyson (Antique Weapons), D.W., Huddersfield, Yorks West.
Angus Antiques, Dundee, Scotland.
Earlshall Castle, Leuchars, Scotland.
Hermitage Antiquities, Fishguard, Dyfed, Wales.

Art Deco and Art Nouveau

Antique Trader, The, London, N1.
Haskell, Miriam, London, N1.
Style, London, N1.
Tadema Gallery, London, N1.
Titus Omega, London, N1.
Beer, John, London, N6.
Jazzy Art Deco, London, NW1.
Art Furniture (London) Ltd, London, NW1.
Lyons Gallery, John, London, NW3.
Beverley, London, NW8.
Bizarre, London, NW8.
Gallery on Church Street", "The, London, NW8.
Raffles Antiques, London, NW8.
Tracy Gallery, Simon, London, NW8.
Bloom and Son (Knightsbridge), N., London, SW1.
Cobra and Bellamy, London, SW1.
Gallery '25, London, SW1.
Butler and Wilson, London, SW3.
Jazzy Art Deco, London, SW3.
Kaplan Associates Ltd, Lewis M., London, SW3.
Purple Shop, The, London, SW3.
Walker-Bagshawe, London, SW3.
Gill, David, London, SW3.
Cavendish Designs, Rupert, London, SW6.
Jeffs at Nicholas Harris, Peter, London, SW6.
Lamp Gallery, The, London, SW6.
Twentieth Century, London, SW12.
Bloom & Son (Antiques) Ltd, N., London, W1.
Editions Graphiques Gallery, London, W1.
Liberty, London, W1.
Mayfair Gallery, London, W1.
Young and Stephen Ltd, London, W1.
Antiques 132, London, W4.
Haslam and Whiteway, London, W8.
Jesse, John, London, W8.
Cameo Gallery, The, London, W8.
Pruskin Gallery, The, London, W8.
New Century, London, W8.
Facade, The, London, W11.
Themes and Variations, London, W11.
Leigh, Joan, London, W11.
20th Century, Cambridge, Cambs.
Bizarre Decorative Arts North West, Altrincham, Cheshire.
Aldersey Hall Ltd, Chester, Cheshire.
Nantwich Art Deco and Decorative Arts, Nantwich, Cheshire.
Beaminster Antiques, Beaminster, Dorset.
Andrews Antiques, Michael, Bournemouth, Dorset.
Geneen Ltd, Lionel, Bournemouth, Dorset.
Galerie Antiques, Broadstone, Dorset.
Finesse Fine Art, Weymouth, Dorset.
Davana Original Interiors, Colchester, Essex.
Times Past, Kelvedon, Essex.
Weaver Antiques, Bernard, Cirencester, Glos.
Ruskin Antiques, Stow-on-the-Wold, Glos.
Gazelles Art Deco Interiors, Southampton, Hants.
Titchfield Antiques Ltd, Titchfield, Hants.
Vicary Antiques, Lancaster, Lancs.
Joy's Shop, Longridge, Lancs.
A.S. Antique Galleries, Manchester, Lancs.
Abstract Antiques, Manchester, Lancs.
Ginnell, The, Manchester, Lancs.
Heyday, Saddleworth, Lancs.
Birches Art Deco Shop, Leicester, Leics.
Osiris Antiques, Southport, Merseyside.
Arbiter, Wallasey, Merseyside.
Parade Antiques, Hampton Hill, Middx.
Antiques on the Square, Church Stretton, Shrops.
Expressions, Shrewsbury, Shrops.
Tara's Hall, Hadleigh, Suffolk.
Decodream, Coulsdon, Surrey.
Bits and Pieces, Farnham, Surrey.
Gooday, Peter and Debbie, Richmond, Surrey.
Cockrell Antiques, Surbiton, Surrey.
Art Deco Etc., Brighton, Sussex East.
Oasis Antiques, Brighton, Sussex East.
Page Antiques, Brian, Brighton, Sussex East.
Pyramid, Brighton, Sussex East.
Timewarp, Brighton, Sussex East.
Hancock Antiques, Peter, Chichester, Sussex West.
Art Deco Ceramics, Stratford-upon-Avon, Warks.
Jazz, Stratford-upon-Avon, Warks.
Hewitt Art Deco Originals, Muir, Halifax, Yorks West.
Rendezvous Gallery, The, Aberdeen, Scotland.
Montresor, Edinburgh, Scotland.
Gibbs Antiques and Decorative Arts, Paul, Conway, Gwynedd, Wales.

Barometers (Sere also clock dealers)

Capon, Patric, London, N1.
Strike One (Islington) Ltd, London, NW1.
Smith, John Carlton, London, SW1.
Brocklehurst, Aubrey, London, SW7.
Clock Clinic Ltd, The, London, SW15.
Fielden, Brian, London, W1.
Harvey & Co (Antiques) Ltd, W.R, London, W1.
Stair and Company Ltd, London, W1.
Raffety Ltd, London, W8.
Old Father Time Clock Centre, London, W11.
Barometer Fair, London, WC1.
Croft Antiques, John, Bath, Avon.
Gibson, David, Bath, Avon.
Barometer Shop, The, Bristol, Avon.
Clock Workshop, The, Caversham, Berks.
Medalcrest Ltd, Hungerford, Berks.
Old Malthouse, The, Hungerford, Berks.
Eton Gallery Antiques, Windsor and Eton, Berks.
Tooley, CMBHI, M.V., Chesham, Bucks.
Beazor and Sons Ltd, John, Cambridge, Cambs.
Doddington House Antiques, Doddington, Cambs.
Rayment Antiques, Derek, Barton, Cheshire.
Bosson Antiques, Peter, Wilmslow, Cheshire.
Read Antique Sciences, Mike, St. Ives, Cornwall.
Old Man Antiques, The, Coniston, Cumbria.
Honiton Clock Clinic, Honiton, Devon.
Barometer World (Barometers), Merton, Devon.
Good Hope Antiques, Beaminster, Dorset.
Taylor, M.C., Bournemouth, Dorset.
Tribe and Son, Tom, Sturminster Newton, Dorset.
Bailey Antique Clocks, John, Althorne, Essex.
Littlebury Antiques - Littlebury Restorations Ltd, Saffron Walden, Essex.
It's About Time, Westcliff-on-Sea, Essex.
Saxton House Gallery, Chipping Campden, Glos.
Preston Antiques Ltd, Antony, Stow-on-the-Wold, Glos.
Vanbrugh House Antiques, Stow-on-the-Wold, Glos.
Bristow Antiques, J. and M., Tetbury, Glos.
Evans and Evans, Alresford, Hants.
Clisby at Andwells Antiques, Bryan, Hartley Wintney, Hants.
Marsh (Antique Clocks), Gerald E., Winchester, Hants.
Todd and Austin Antiques of Winchester, Winchester, Hants.
Barometer Shop, Leominster, Herefs and Worcs.
Hansen Chard Antiques, Pershore, Herefs and Worcs.
Park Street Antiques, Berkhamsted, Herts.
Horton Antiques, Robert, Hertford, Herts.
Hickson CMBHI, Lewis, Seaton Ross, Humbs North.
Fowler (Period Clocks), Robin, Aylesby, Humbs South.
Sim, Michael, Chislehurst, Kent.
Woodburn, Anthony, Leigh, Kent.
De Tavener Antiques, Ramsgate, Kent.
Drop Dial Antiques, Bolton, Lancs.
Harrop Fold Clocks (F. Robinson), Bolton-by-Bowland, Lancs.
Bryan-Peach Antiques, N., Wymeswold, Leics.
Hansord and Son, David J., Lincoln, Lincs.
Shenton, Rita, Twickenham, Middx.
Lawson Antique Clocks, Keith, Scratby, Norfolk.
Antique Galleries, The, Paulerspury, Northants.
Wiggins, Peter, Chipping Norton, Oxon.
Rosemary and Time, Thame, Oxon.
Cave and Sons Ltd, R.G., Ludlow, Shrops.
Dodington Antiques, Whitchurch, Shrops.
House (Mitre Antiques), Bernard G., Wells, Somerset.
Nowell, Edward A., Wells, Somerset.
Jordan, James A., Lichfield, Staffs.
Antique Clocks by Simon Charles, Long Melford, Suffolk.
Marney, Patrick, Long Melford, Suffolk.
Suthburgh Antiques, Long Melford, Suffolk.
Hollander Ltd, E., Dorking, Surrey.
Gould and Sons (Antiques) Ltd, A.E., East Horsley, Surrey.
Horological Workshops, Guildford, Surrey.
Hampton Wick Antiques, Hampton Wick, Surrey.
Surrey Clock Centre, Haslemere, Surrey.
Knaphill Antiques, Knaphill, Surrey.
Saunders, R., Weybridge, Surrey.
Chattels Antiques, Woking, Surrey.
Hatchwell Antiques, Simon, Brighton, Sussex East.
Chaunt House, Burwash, Sussex East.
Cowfold Clocks, Cowfold, Sussex West.
Mason Antique Clocks, J., Northchapel, Sussex West.
Baskerville Antiques, Petworth, Sussex West.
Morris, John G., Petworth, Sussex West.
Grandfather Clock Shop, The, Shipston-on-Stour, Warks.
'Time in Hand', Shipston-on-Stour, Warks.
Collyer, R., Birmingham, West Mids.
Osborne Antiques, Sutton Coldfield, West Mids.
Oxley Antique Clocks and Barometers, P.A., Cherhill, Wilts.
Walwyn Antiques, Howard, Wootton Bassett, Wilts.
Craiglea Clocks, Edinburgh, Scotland.
Muirhead Moffat and Co, Glasgow, Scotland.

Beds

Tobias and The Angel, London, SW13.
And So To Bed Limited, London, SW6.
Horn Furniture Ltd, Simon, London, SW6.
Hirst Antiques, London, W11.
Old Dairy, The, London, W4.
Jones, Orlando , Bath, Avon.
Antique Beds, Bristol, Avon.
Victoria's Bedroom, Hungerford, Berks.
Addrison Bros, Windsor and Eton, Berks.
Country Furniture, Windsor and Eton, Berks.
Pine Merchants, The, Great Missenden, Bucks.
Barn Full of Brass Beds, A, Sawtry, Cambs.
And So To Bed, Keswick, Cumbria.
Pugh's Farm Antiques, Monkton, Devon.
Annterior Antiques, Plymouth, Devon.
Antique Metals, Coggeshall, Essex.
Antique Bed Shop, Halstead, Essex.
Roberts Antiques, Peter, Moreton-in-Marsh, Glos.
Elgin House Antiques, Tetbury, Glos.
Old Pine Shop, Ross-on-Wye, Herefs and Worcs.
Henley Antiques, R. and J. L., Canterbury, Kent.
Carrcross Gallery, Scarisbrick, Lancs.
House Things Antiques, Hinckley, Leices.
Allchin Antiques, William, Norwich, Norfolk.
Rococo Antiques and Interiors, Weedon, Northants.
Corner Cupboard, The, Woodford Halse, Northants.
Revival Beds, Haydon Bridge, Northumbs..
Lustre Metal Antiques, Nottingham, Nottingham, Notts.
Manor Farm Antiques, Standlake, Oxon.
Antiques Warehouse, Framlingham, Suffolk.
Bed Bazaar, Framlingham, Suffolk.
Country Furniture, Richmond, Surrey.
Antiques and Bedsteads, Brighton, Sussex East.
Victorian Brass Bedstead Company, The, Cocking, Sussex West.
McDougall, Marjorie and Sandy, Kilbarchan, Scotland.
Seventh Heaven, Chirk, Clwyd, Wales.
Jansons Antiques, Bwlchllan, Dyfed, Wales.
Hughes Antiques, Eynon, Swansea, West Glam., Wales.

Books (Antiquarian)

Ash Rare Books, London, EC3.
Clarke-Hall Ltd, J., London, EC4.
Finney Antique Prints and Books, Michael, London, N1.
Walford, G.W., London, N5.
Fisher and Sperr, London, N6.
Home to Home, London, N6.
Korn, M.E., London, N10.
Forster, W., London, N16.
East-Asia Co, London, NW1.
de Lotz, P.G., London, NW3.
Fawkes, Keith, London, NW3.
Glendale, M. and R., London, NW3.
Marks Ltd, Barrie, London, NW5.
Baron, H., London, NW6.
Fletcher, H. M., London, SE1.
Leadlay Gallery, The Warwick, London, SE10.
Rogers Turner Books Ltd, London, SE10.
South London Book Centre, London, SE10.
Allen & Co. (The Horseman's Bookshop) Ltd., J. A., London, SW1.
Burden Ltd, Clive A., London, SW1.
Connoisseur Gallery, The, London, SW1.
Edwards, Christopher, London, SW1.
Han-Shan Tang Ltd, London, SW1.
Heneage Art Books, Thomas, London, SW1.
O'Shea Gallery, London, SW1.

SPECIALIST DEALERS

Old Ephemera and Newspaper Shop, The, London, SW1.
Pickering and Chatto Ltd, London, SW1.
Saint George's Gallery, London, SW1.
Sims, Reed Ltd, London, SW1.
Chelsea Rare Books, London, SW3.
Greer, Robin, London, SW3.
Crawley and Asquith Ltd, London, SW4.
Constant Reader Bookshop, The, London, SW6.
Orssich, Paul, London, SW6.
Hünersdorff Rare Books and Manuscripts, London, SW10.
Thornton, John, London, SW10.
Phelps Antiquarian Books, Michael, London, SW15.
Reeves Bookseller Ltd, William, London, SW16.
Fogg, Sam, London, W1.
Heywood Hill Ltd, G., London, W1.
Joseph, Booksellers, E., London, W1.
Maggs Bros Ltd, London, W1.
Marlborough Rare Books Ltd, London, W1.
Potter Ltd, Jonathan, London, W1.
Quaritch Ltd (Booksellers), Bernard, London, W1.
Russell Rare Books, London, W1.
Sawers, Robert G., London, W1.
Schuster, Thomas E., London, W1.
Sotheran Ltd, Henry, London, W1.
Bayswater Books, London, W2.
Hosains Books and Antiques, London, W2.
Mellor and A.L. Baxter, D., London, W8.
Books & Things, London, W11.
Demetzy Books, London, W11.
Kennedy, Peter, London, W11.
Shapero Rare Books, Bernard T., London, W11.
Parikian, D., London, W14.
Atlantis Bookshop, London, WC1.
Bondy, Louis W., London, WC1.
Cinema Bookshop, London, WC1.
Frognal Rare Books, London, WC1.
Marchmont Bookshop, London, WC1.
Ong t/a Skoob Two, I.K., London, WC1.
Probsthain, Arthur, London, WC1.
Skoob Books Ltd, London, WC1.
Bell, Book and Radmall, London, WC2.
Creed Books Ltd, Ann, London, WC2.
Foyle Ltd, W. and G., London, WC2.
Pleasures of Past Times, London, WC2.
Pordes Books Ltd, Henry, London, WC2.
Remington, Reg and Philip, London, WC2.
Rota Ltd, Bertram, London, WC2.
Storey, Harold T., London, WC2.
Tooley Adams & Co. Ltd, London, WC2.
Watkins Books Ltd, London, WC2.
Zeno Booksellers and Publishers, London, WC2.
Zwemmer Ltd, A., London, WC2.
Bayntun, George, Bath, Avon.
Gregory, George, Bath, Avon.
Patterson Liddle, Bath, Avon.
Wallis ands Gerry Mosdell, Glenda, Bath, Avon.
Cotham Hill Bookshop, Bristol, Avon.
Heath, A.R., Bristol, Avon.
Roberts Bookshop, John, Bristol, Avon.
Wise Owl Bookshop, The, Bristol, Avon.
Clarke, Janet, Freshford, Avon.
Sterling Books, Weston-Super-Mare, Avon.
Flint Galleries Ltd, Sir William Russell, Wrington, Avon.
Penn Barn, Penn, Bucks.
Eaton Booksellers Ltd, Peter, Weedon, Bucks.
Bickersteth, David, Bassingbourn, Cambs.
Bookroom (Cambridge), The, Cambridge, Cambs.
David, G., Cambridge, Cambs.
Deighton Bell and Co, Cambridge, Cambs.
Galloway and Porter Ltd, Cambridge, Cambs.
Gibbons, Derek, Cambridge, Cambs.
Abington Books, Little Abington, Cambs.
Old Soke Books, Peterborough, Cambs.
Golding, Eric, Wisbech, Cambs.
Lion Gallery and Bookshop, Knutsford, Cheshire.
New Street Books, Penzance, Cornwall.
Dodd Books, Maurice, Carlisle, Cumbria.
Kerr - Gatehouse Bookshop, Norman, Cartmel, Cumbria.
Smith (Bookseller), Peter Bain, Cartmel, Cumbria.
Grayling, David A. H., Crosby Ravensworth, Cumbria.
Miles Bookshop, Archie, Gosforth, Cumbria.
Book House, The, Ravenstonedale, Cumbria.
Hollett and Son, R. F. G., Sedbergh, Cumbria.
Moon, Michael, Whitehaven, Cumbria.
Hill Books, Alan, Bakewell, Derbys.
Laura's Bookshop, Derby, Derbys.
Chantry Bookshop and Gallery, Dartmouth, Devon.
Taylor-Halsey Antiques, Drewsteignton, Devon.
Exeter Rare Books, Exeter, Devon.
Honiton Old Bookshop, Honiton, Devon.
Woodhead, Geoffrey M., Honiton, Devon.
Porcupines Bookroom, Instow, Devon.
Secondhand Rose, Plymouth, Devon.
Pollak, P.M., South Brent, Devon.
Collards Books, Totnes, Devon.
Ancient and Modern Bookshop, Blandford Forum, Dorset.
Shickell Books, Bournemouth, Dorset.
Wright (Booksellers), Sidney, Bournemouth, Dorset.
PIC's Bookshop, Bridport, Dorset.
Williams Antiquarian Bookseller, Christopher, Parkstone, Dorset.
Antique Map and Bookshop, Puddletown, Dorset.
Book in Hand (Christopher Driver), The, Shaftesbury, Dorset.
Swan Gallery, The, Sherborne, Dorset.
Reference Works, Swanage, Dorset.
Books Afloat, Weymouth, Dorset.
Shotton Antiquarian Books and Prints, J., Durham, Durham.
Bailey Antique Clocks, John, Althorne, Essex.
Elkin Mathews, Coggeshall, Essex.
Castle Bookshop, Colchester, Essex.
Beeleigh Abbey Books (W. and G. Foyle Ltd.), Maldon, Essex.
Bannister, F.R.G.S, David, Cheltenham, Glos.
Greens of Montpellier, Cheltenham, Glos.
Rayner, Michael, Cheltenham, Glos.
Hodgkins and Co. Ltd, Ian, Slad, Glos.
Rosemary Antiques and Paper Moon Books, Stow-on-the-Wold, Glos.
Studio Bookshop and Gallery, Alresford, Hants.
Hughes and Smeeth Ltd, Lymington, Hants.
Williams Antiquarian Bookseller, Christopher, Lymington, Hants.
Petersfield Bookshop, The, Petersfield, Hants.
Gilbert and Son, H.M., Southampton, Hants.
Sharbooks, Upham, Hants.
Daly PBFA, Peter M., Winchester, Hants.
Gilbert, H.M., Winchester, Hants.
SPCK Bookshops, Winchester, Hants.
Clent Books, Bewdley, Herefs and Worcs.
Broadway Old Books (formerly Stratford Trevers), Broadway, Herefs and Worcs.
Malvern Bookshop, Great Malvern, Herefs and Worcs.
Ross Old Book and Print Shop, Ross-on-Wye, Herefs and Worcs.
Antique Map and Print Gallery, Worcester, Herefs and Worcs
Boyle (Booksellers) Ltd, Andrew, Worcester, Herefs and Worcs.
Pordes Ltd, H., Cockfosters, Herts.
Wheldon and Wesley Ltd, Codicote, Herts.
Old Cathay Fine Books and Arts, Hatfield, Herts.
Moore, Eric T., Hitchin, Herts.
Burden, Clive A., Rickmansworth, Herts.
Thorp, Thomas, St. Albans, Herts.
Dickens Bookshop, Charles, Cowes, I. of Wight.
Ventnor Rare Books, Ventnor, I. of Wight.
Attic, The, Brasted, Kent.
Canterbury Bookshop, The, Canterbury, Kent.
Chaucer Bookshop, Canterbury, Kent.
Darenth Bookshop, Otford, Kent.
Baggins Book Bazaar, Rochester, Kent.
Baskerville Books, Tunbridge Wells, Kent.
Hall's Bookshop, Tunbridge Wells, Kent.
Stead Antiques Reference Books, Graham, Tunbridge Wells, Kent.
London House Antiques, Westerham, Kent.
Lloyd's Bookshop, Wingham, Kent.
McCormack, W.B., Lancaster, Lancs.
Forest Books of Cheshire, Manchester, Lancs.
Gibb's Bookshop Ltd, Manchester, Lancs.
Ginnell, The, Manchester, Lancs.
Morten, Eric J., Manchester, Lancs.
Secondhand and Rare Books, Manchester, Lancs.
Halewood and Sons, Preston, Lancs.
Preston Book Co, Preston, Lancs.
Laywood, Anthony W., Knipton, Leics.

SPECIALIST DEALERS

Hadfield, G.K., Shepshed, Leics.
Goldmark Books, Uppingham, Leics.
Not Just Books, Uppingham, Leics.
Cassidy (Books), P.J., Holbeach, Lincs.
Golden Goose Books, Lincoln, Lincs.
Harlequin Gallery, Lincoln, Lincs.
Staniland (Booksellers), Stamford, Lincs.
Broadhurst and Co Ltd, C.K., Southport, Merseyside.
Sheridan's Bookshop Hampton, Ian, Hampton, Middx.
Hall, Anthony C., Twickenham, Middx.
Ives Bookseller, John, Twickenham, Middx.
Shenton, Rita, Twickenham, Middx.
Barnard (A.B.A.), Thomas, Uxbridge, Middx.
Ferrow, David, Gt. Yarmouth, Norfolk.
Cook, R.L., Holt, Norfolk.
Gough Books, Simon, Holt, Norfolk.
Fears (Books), Howard, Little Walsingham, Norfolk.
Crowe, Antiquarian Book Seller, Peter, Norwich, Norfolk.
Scientific Anglian (Bookshop), The, Norwich, Norfolk.
Tombland Bookshop, The, Norwich, Norfolk.
Gallery and Things, The, South Lopham, Norfolk.
Turret House, Wymondham, Norfolk.
Old Hall Bookshop, The, Brackley, Northants.
Occultique, Northampton, Northants.
Wootton-Billingham, Northampton, Northants.
Park Book Shop, Wellingborough, Northants.
Book Shelf, The, Mansfield, Notts.
Doris, N.J., Nottingham, Notts.
Chipping Norton Books, Chipping Norton, Oxon.
Lawson and Co, E.M., East Hagbourne, Oxon.
Kingston, Richard J., Henley-on-Thames, Oxon.
Blackwell's Rare Books, Oxford, Oxon.
Niner and Hill Rare Books, Oxford, Oxon.
Rosenthal Ltd, A., Oxford, Oxon.
Sanders of Oxford Ltd, Oxford, Oxon.
Thorntons of Oxford Ltd, Oxford, Oxon.
Titles Old and Rare Books, Oxford, Oxon.
Waterfield's, Oxford, Oxon.
Museum Bookshop, Woodstock, Oxon.
Candle Lane Books, Shrewsbury, Shrops.
Bridgwater Antiques Market, Bridgwater, Somerset.
Rothwell and Dunworth, Dulverton, Somerset.
Old Curiosity Shop, Frome, Somerset.
Ferdinando, Steven, Queen Camel, Somerset.
Rothwell and Dunworth, Taunton, Somerset.
Leek Bookshop, The, Leek, Staffs.
Abrahams Books, Mike, Lichfield, Staffs.
Images - Peter Stockham, Lichfield, Staffs.
Smith, L. Royden, Lichfield, Staffs.
Staffs Bookshop, The, Lichfield, Staffs.
Besleys Books, Beccles, Suffolk.
Webster, E.T., Blythburgh, Suffolk.
Trinders' Booksellers, Clare, Suffolk.
Cox at College Gateway Bookshop, Claude, Ipswich, Suffolk.
Archer, R.G., Lavenham,, Suffolk.
Way, R.E. and G.B., Newmarket, Suffolk.
Stevens, Bookseller, Joan, Yoxford, Suffolk.
Vandeleur Antiquarian Books, Epsom, Surrey.
McKenzie, J.W., Ewell, Surrey.
Ivelet Books Ltd - Church St. Bookshop, Godalming, Surrey.
Stewart Fine Art Galleries, Michael, Guildford, Surrey.
Thorp Bookseller, Thomas, Guildford, Surrey.
Lloyds of Kew, Kew, Surrey.
Burton-Garbett, A., Morden, Surrey.
Reigate Galleries Ltd, Reigate, Surrey.
Gant, Elizabeth, Thames Ditton, Surrey.
Holleyman and Treacher Ltd, Brighton, Sussex East.
Page Antiquarian Books, Colin, Brighton, Sussex East.
Robinson's Bookshop Ltd, Brighton, Sussex East.
Camilla's Bookshop, Eastbourne, Sussex East.
Dew, Roderick, Eastbourne, Sussex East.
London and Sussex Antiquarian Book and Print Services, Eastbourne, Sussex East.
Premier Gallery, Eastbourne, Sussex East.
Smith, Raymond, Eastbourne, Sussex East.
Howes Bookshop, Hastings, Sussex East.
Bow Windows Book Shop, Lewes, Sussex East.
Cumming, A.J., Lewes, Sussex East.
Fifteenth Century Bookshop, Lewes, Sussex East.
Chimera Books, Hurstpierpoint, Sussex West.
Wood Fine Art, Jeremy, Petworth, Sussex West.
Steedman, R.D., Newcastle-upon-Tyne, Tyne and Wear.

Vaughan, Robert, Stratford-upon-Avon, Warks.
Allsop, Duncan M., Warwick, Warks.
Birmingham Bookshop, Birmingham, West Mids.
Maxwells Book Shop, Birmingham, West Mids.
Clent Books, Halesowen, West Mids.
Books & Prints, Bradford-on-Avon, Wilts.
Farahar and Sophie Dupré - Rare Books, Autographs and Manuscripts, Clive, Calne, Wilts.
Hilmarton Manor Press, Calne, Wilts.
Military Parade Bookshop, The, Marlborough, Wilts.
Heraldry Today, Ramsbury, Wilts.
Barn Book Supply, The, Salisbury, Wilts.
Beach, D.M, Salisbury, Wilts.
Marlborough Sporting Gallery and Bookshop, Swindon, Wilts.
Great Ayton Bookshop, The, Great Ayton, Yorks North.
Rippon Bookshop, Harrogate, Yorks North.
Rievaulx Books, Helmsley, Yorks North.
Shaw, Charles, Knaresborough, Yorks North.
White Boar Antiques and Books, Middleham, Yorks North.
Potterton Books, Thirsk, Yorks North.
Barbican Bookshop, York, Yorks North.
Minster Gate Bookshop, York, Yorks North.
O'Flynn Antiquarian Booksellers, York, Yorks North.
Spelman, Ken, York, Yorks North.
Taikoo Books Ltd, York, Yorks North.
Wrigley, John R., Ecclesfield, Yorks South.
Hill Books, Sheffield, Alan, Sheffield, Yorks South.
Brear, Jean, Halifax, Yorks West.
Toll House Bookshop, The, Holmfirth, Yorks West.
Channel Islands Galleries Ltd, St. Peter Port, Guernsey, C.I.
Gavey, Geoffrey P., Vale, Guernsey, C. I.
Blench & Son, John, St. Helier, Jersey, C. I.
Selective Eye Gallery, The, St. Helier, Jersey, C. I.
Thesaurus (Jersey) Ltd, St. Helier, Jersey, C. I.
Highland Antiques, Avoch, Scotland.
McEwan Gallery, The, Ballater, Scotland.
Anderson, I.G., Dumfries, Scotland.
McNaughtan's Bookshop, Edinburgh, Scotland.
Rankin, Alan, Edinburgh, Scotland.
Thin (Booksellers), James, Edinburgh, Scotland.
Simpson, Marianne, Fochabers, Scotland.
Amber Antiques, Kincardine, Scotland.
McIlreavy Rare and Interesting Books, A. and F., St. Andrews, Scotland.
Hubbard's Bookshop, Doggie, Ponterwyd, Dyfed, Wales.
Dylan's Bookshop, Swansea, West Glam., Wales.
Lockyer, H.K., Abergavenny, Gwent, Wales.
Glance Back Bookshop, Chepstow, Gwent, Wales.
Maps, Prints and Books, Brecon, Powys, Wales.
Booth's Bookshop, Richard, Hay-on-Wye, Powys, Wales.
Westwood Antiquarian Books, Mark, Hay-on-Wye, Powys, Wales.

Brass (See Metalwork)

Bronzes

Ferrant Antiques, D.J., London, N1.
Furniture Vault, London, N1.
Inheritance, London, N1.
Julian Antiques, London, N1.
Page Oriental Art, Kevin, London, N1.
Style, London, N1.
Finchley Fine Art Galleries, London, N12.
Lenson and Roy Smith, Nellie, London, NW8.
Church Street Antiques, London, NW8.
Magus Antiques, London, NW8.
S. and H. Antiques, London, NW8.
Tara Antiques, London, NW8.
Hamilton Fine Arts, London, NW11.
Vale Stamps and Antiques, London, SE3.
Franses Gallery, Victor, London, SW1.
Lewis, M. and D., London, SW1.
McLennan, Rodd, London, SW1.
Nahum, Peter, London, SW1.
Seago, London, SW1.
Spyer and Son (Antiques) Ltd, Gerald, London, SW1.
Trove, London, SW1.
James and Son Ltd, Anthony, London, SW3.
Cooper Fine Arts Ltd, London, SW6.

Preston and Sally Isbell, Antony, London, SW6.
Tulissio De Beaumont, London, SW6.
Bridge, Christine, London, SW13.
Kensington Sporting Paintings Ltd., London, SW20.
Redford, William, London, W1.
Sladmore Gallery, The, London, W1.
South Audley Antiques, London, W1.
Wise, Mary, London, W8.
Christie, J., London, W1.
Davies Oriental Art, Barry, London, W1.
Editions Graphiques Gallery, London, W1.
Eskenazi Ltd, London, W1.
Brower Antiques, David, London, W8.
Cameo Gallery, The, London, W8.
Deutsch Antiques, H. and W., London, W8.
Jay Antiques and Objets d'Art, Melvyn, London, W8.
Jesse, John, London, W8.
Jones, Howard, London, W8.
Pruskin Gallery, The, London, W8.
Cohen and Pearce (Oriental Porcelain), London, W11.
Garrick Antiques, Philip, London, W11.
Lewis, M. and D., London, W11.
Lipitch Ltd, J., London, W11.
M.C.N. Antiques, London, W11.
Magus Antiques, London, W11.
Petrou, Peter, London, W11.
West End Galleries, Buxton, Derbys.
Plaitford House Gallery, Plaitford, Hants.
Sim, Michael, Chislehurst, Kent.
Apollo Galleries, Westerham, Kent.
London House Antiques, Westerham, Kent.
Mistral Galleries, Westerham, Kent.
Cooper Antiques, Bruno, Long Melford, Suffolk.
Armstrong-Davis Gallery, Arundel, Sussex West.
Hinde Fine Art, Sheila, Kirdford, Sussex West.
Morris, John G., Petworth, Sussex West.

Carriages and Cars

Oliver, Tony L., Windsor and Eton, Berks.
Fieldings Antiques, Haslingden, Lancs.
Complete Automobilist, The, Greatford, Lincs.
Verralls (Handcross) Ltd, Handcross, Sussex West.
Whatnots, Strathblane, Scotland.
Andrew, Tony, Llanerchymedd, Gwynedd, Wales.

Carpets and Rugs

Soviet Carpet and Art Centre, London, NW2.
Lavian, Joseph, London, NW5.
Zoulfaghari, London, NW5.
Bolour, Y. and B., London, NW5.
Franses and Sons, Robert, London, NW8.
Belgrave Carpet Gallery Ltd, London, SW1.
Mayorcas Ltd, London, SW1.
Franses Ltd, S., London, SW1.
Franses Gallery, Victor, London, SW1.
Heraz (David Hartwright Ltd)London, SW1
Keshishian, London, SW1.
Sanaiy Carpets, London, SW1.
Perez, London, SW3.
Stephenson, Robert, London, SW3.
Antique Carpets Gallery, London, SW6.
Bookham Galleries, London, SW6.
Edwards, Charles, London, SW6.
Anglo Persian Carpet Co, London, SW7.
Rare Carpets Gallery, London, SW10.
Aaron Gallery, London, W1.
Atlantic Bay Carpets, London, W1.
Benardout and Benardout, London, W1.
John (Rare Rugs) Ltd, C., London, W1.
Juran and Co, Alexander, London, W1.
Colefax and Fowler, London, W1.
Essie Carpets, London, W1.
Hadji Baba Ancient Art, London, W1.
Kennedy Carpets and Kelims, London, W1.
Mayfair Carpet Gallery Ltd, London, W1.
Nels Ltd, Paul, London, W1.
Rabi Gallery Ltd, London, W1.
Shaikh and Son (Oriental Rugs) Ltd, London, W1.
South Audley Antiques, London, W1.
Vigo Carpet Gallery, London, W1.
Vigo-Sternberg Galleries, London, W1.
Zadah Gallery, London, W1.
Bensiglio Ltd, S., London, W5.
Waroujian, M.L., London, W6.
Coats Oriental Carpets, London, W8.
Sinai Antiques Ltd, London, W8.
Loveless, Clive, London, W10.
Black Oriental Carpets, David, London, W11.
Graham and Green, London, W11.
Fairman (Carpets) Ltd, Jack, London, W11.
Rezai Persian Carpets, A., London, W11.
Heskia, London, W14.
Haliden Oriental Rug Shop, Bath, Avon.
Oriental Carpet Centre, The, Bristol, Avon.
Norman Antiques and Restorations, Peter, Burwell, Cambs.
Copperfield, Robert, Macclesfield, Cheshire.
White Elephant Antiques, Bowness-on-Windermere, Cumbria.
Arditti, J.L., Christchurch, Dorset.
Christchurch Carpets, Christchurch, Dorset.
Hamptons, Christchurch, Dorset.
Orbell House Gallery, Castle Hedingham, Essex.
Bailey Oriental Rugs, Robert, Ongar, Essex.
Pride Oriental Rugs, Eric, Cheltenham, Glos.
Samarkand Galleries, Stow-on-the-Wold, Glos.
Odiham Gallery, The, Odiham, Hants.
Park Street Antiques, Berkhamsted, Herts.
Oriental Rug Gallery Ltd, St. Albans, Herts.
Boosey - Carpets for Country Houses, Simon, Whitwell, Herts.
North, Desmond and Amanda, East Peckham, Kent.
Samovar Antiques, Hythe, Kent.
"Persian Rugs", West Peckham, Kent.
Watts Oriental Rugs, Duncan, Market Harborough, Leics.
Tattersall's, Uppingham, Leics.
Kelaty Ltd, L., Wembley, Middx.
Country and Eastern, Norwich, Norfolk.
Quinn Galleries, Oundle, Northants.
Purdon, Richard, Burford, Oxon.
Thames Oriental Rug Co, Henley-on-Thames, Oxon.
Legge Oriental Carpets, Christopher, Oxford, Oxon.
Lewis Oriental Carpets and Rugs, Michael and Amanda, Wellington, Somerset.
Oriental Carpets and Decorative Arts, Dorking, Surrey.
Weijand Fine Oriental Carpets, Karel, Farnham, Surrey.
Rogers Oriental Rugs, Clive, Brighton, Sussex East.
De Montfort, Robertsbridge, Sussex East.
Lindfield Galleries - David Adam, Lindfield, Sussex West.
Amini - Persian Carpet Gallery, Majid, Petworth, Sussex West.
London House Oriental Rugs and Carpets, Harrogate, YorksNorth.
Omar (Harrogate) Ltd, Harrogate, Yorks North.
Northern Kilim Centre, The, Knaresborough, Yorks North.
Ellis's, Sheffield, Yorks South.
Oriental Rug Shop, The, Sheffield, Yorks South.
London House Oriental Rugs and Carpets, Boston Spa, Yorks West.
Behar Carpets, Edinburgh, Scotland.
Herrald Antiques, Edinburgh, Scotland.
Mulherron Antiques, Edinburgh, Scotland.
Whytock and Reid, Edinburgh, Scotland.
Young Antiques, Edinburgh, Scotland.
Rose and Co, R.L., Glasgow, Scotland.
Moreton (Antiques), C.S., Inchture, Scotland.
Fine Oriental Rugs and Carpets of Inverness, Inverness, Scotland.

Chinese Art (See Oriental Art)

Clocks and Watches

City Clocks, London, EC1.
Capon, Patric, London, N1.
Julian Antiques, London, N1.
Sugar Antiques, London, N1.
North London Clock Shop Ltd, London, N5.
Strike One (Islington) Ltd, London, NW1.
Brooks, Mr. Temple, London, NW6.
Bobinet Ltd, London, NW8.

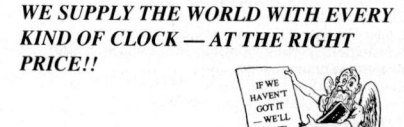

WE SUPPLY THE WORLD WITH EVERY KIND OF CLOCK — AT THE RIGHT PRICE!!

WALL
BRACKET
NOVELTY
CARRIAGE
BOOKS
AND
SPARES

Old Father Time Clock Centre
101 Portobello Road
London W11 2BQ
Tel: 081-546 6299 (24hrs.) 071-229 2796

ELECTRIC — SKELETON

Penny Farthing Antiques, London, SE1.
Village Time, London, SE7.
Rose FBHI, R.E., London, SE9.
Camerer Cuss and Co, London, SW1.
Lewis, Arthur S., London, SW1.
Rothman, London, SW1.
Smith, John Carlton, London, SW1.
Somlo Antiques, London, SW1.
Whyte, Philip, London, SW1.
Clock Clinic Ltd, The, London, SW15.
Big Ben Antique Clocks, London, SW6.
Chelsea Clocks and Antiques, London, SW6.
Brocklehurst, Aubrey, London, SW7.
Capital Clocks, London, SW8.
Carrington and Co. Ltd, London, W1.
Collingwood & Company Ltd, London, W1.
Edmonds Ltd, D.H., London, W1.
Garrard & Co. Ltd, (The Crown Jewellers), London, W1.
Graus Antiques, London, W1.
Lee (Fine Arts) Ltd, Ronald A., London, W1.
Mallett and Son (Antiques) Ltd, London, W1.
Mallett at Bourdon House Ltd, London, W1.
Rose - Source of the Unusual, Michael, London, W1.
Lampard and Son Ltd, S., London, W11.
Mayflower Antiques, London, W11.
Old Father Time Clock Centre, London, W11.
Tociapski, Igor, London, W11.
Web, A. M., London, W11.
Zebrak, London, W11.
Mansell, William C., London, W2.
Badger, The, London, W5.
Bonrose Antiques, London, W8.
Brower Antiques, David, London, W8.
Jay Antiques and Objets d'Art, Melvyn, London, W8.
Lineham and Sons, Eric, London, W8.
Raffety Ltd, London, W8.
Roderick Antique Clocks, London, W8.
Kettle Ltd, Thomas, London, WC2.
London Silver Vaults, The, London, WC2.
Pearl Cross Ltd, London, WC2.
Fiddle Sticks Antiques and Decorative Items, Bath, Avon.
Gibson, David, Bath, Avon.
Quiet Street Antiques, Bath, Avon.
Barometer Shop, The, Bristol, Avon.
Hawley Antique Clocks, John and Carol, Clevedon, Avon.
Clock Workshop, The, Caversham, Berks.
Walker and Walker, Halfway, Berks.
Hastie, Robert and Georgina, Hungerford, Berks.
Medalcrest Ltd, Hungerford, Berks.
Eton Gallery Antiques, Windsor and Eton, Berks.
Times Past Antiques Ltd, Windsor and Eton, Berks.
Wyrardisbury Antiques, Wraysbury, Berks.
Norton Antiques, Beaconsfield, Bucks.
Tooley, CMBHI, M.V., Chesham, Bucks.
Wright Antiques, Peter, Great Missenden, Bucks.
Market Square Antiques, Olney, Bucks.
Martin Antiques, Alan, Olney, Bucks.
Unsworth Antiques, Robin, Olney, Bucks.
Norman Antiques and Restorations, Peter, Burwell, Cambs.
Beazor and Sons Ltd, John, Cambridge, Cambs.
Doddington House Antiques, Doddington, Cambs.
Mere Antiques, Fowlmere, Cambs.

Firmin, Rodney, Swaffham Prior, Cambs.
Baker Antiques, Anthony, Alderley Edge, Cheshire.
Adams Antiques, Chester, Cheshire.
Boodle and Dunthorne Ltd, Chester, Cheshire.
Mill Farm Antiques, Disley, Cheshire.
Cranford Clocks, Knutsford, Cheshire.
Cheshire Antiques, Macclesfield, Cheshire.
Chapel Antiques, Nantwich, Cheshire.
Coppelia Antiques, Plumley, Cheshire.
Jane's Fine Arts, Poynton, Cheshire.
Bosson Antiques, Peter, Wilmslow, Cheshire.
Jennings Antiques, Paul, Angarrack, Cornwall.
Clocks, Art & Antiques, Bodmin, Cornwall.
Little Jem's, Penzance, Cornwall.
Layne, A.C., Carlisle, Cumbria.
Saint Nicholas Galleries Ltd. (Antiques and Jewellery), Carlisle, Cumbria.
Hill, David, Kirkby Stephen, Cumbria.
Clock House, The, Chapel-en-le-Frith, Derbys.
Derbyshire Clocks, Glossop, Derbys.
Goodacre Engraving Ltd, Long Eaton, Derbys.
Nimbus Antiques, Whaley Bridge, Derbys.
Potter and Son, W.G., Axminster, Devon.
Nathan Antiques, John, Exeter, Devon.
Honiton Clock Clinic, Honiton, Devon.
Pilgrim Antiques, Honiton, Devon.
Jones Antiques, Alan, Plymouth, Devon.
Taylor Antiques, Brian, Plymouth, Devon.
Tempus Fugit, Shaldon, Devon.
Wootton Clocks and Watches, L.G., South Brent, Devon.
Woolacombe Bay Antiques, Woolacombe, Devon.
Good Hope Antiques, Beaminster, Dorset.
Taylor, M.C., Bournemouth, Dorset.
Burgess, D.J., Parkstone, Dorset.
Tribe and Son, Tom, Sturminster Newton, Dorset.
Eden House Antiques, West Auckland, Durham.
Bailey Antique Clocks, John, Althorne, Essex.
Marchant (Antiques), Mark, Coggeshall, Essex.
Antique Clock Repair Shoppe, Gants Hill, Essex.
Pinn and Sons, W.A., Sible Hedingham, Essex.
David, Jean and John Antiques, Westcliff-on-Sea, Essex.
It's About Time, Westcliff-on-Sea, Essex.
Montpellier Clocks, Cheltenham, Glos.
Saxton House Gallery, Chipping Campden, Glos.
School House Antiques, Chipping Campden, Glos.
Beech Antique Clocks, Jonathan, Cirencester, Glos.
Blenheim Antiques, Fairford, Glos.
Farr, Gloucester, Glos.
Campbell, Gerard, Lechlade, Glos.
Wright, Mick and Fanny, Minchinhampton, Glos.
Harding's World of Mechanical Music, Keith, Northleach, Glos.
Brand Antiques, Colin, Stow-on-the-Wold, Glos.
Curiosity Shop, The, Stow-on-the-Wold, Glos.
Preston Antiques Ltd, Antony, Stow-on-the-Wold, Glos.
Vanbrugh House Antiques, Stow-on-the-Wold, Glos.
Bristow Antiques, J. and M., Tetbury, Glos.
Evans and Evans, Alresford, Hants.
Olive Antiques, Alverstoke, Hants.
Cedar Antiques, Hartley Wintney, Hants.
Clisby at Andwells Antiques, Bryan, Hartley Wintney, Hants.

SPECIALIST DEALERS

Porter and Son, A.W., Hartley Wintney, Hants.
Papworth, Barry, Lymington, Hants.
Gaylords, Titchfield, Hants.
Twyford Antiques, Twyford, Hants.
Regency House Antiques, Whitchurch, Hants.
Marsh (Antique Clocks), Gerald E., Winchester, Hants.
Chapman Antiques, Leominster, Herefs and Worcs.
Jennings of Leominster, Leominster, Herefs and Worcs.
Hansen Chard Antiques, Pershore, Herefs and Worcs.
Trecilla Antiques, Ross-on-Wye, Herefs and Worcs.
Taylor, Gerald and Vera, Winforton, Herefs and Worcs.
Howards, Baldock, Herts.
Horton Antiques, Robert, Hertford, Herts.
Harriman Antiques, David, Rickmansworth, Herts.
Clock Shop - Philip Setterfield of St. Albans, The, St. Albans, Herts.
Country Clocks, Tring, Herts.
Old Ropery Antique Clocks,The, Kilham, Humbs North.
Hickson CMBHI, Lewis, Seaton Ross, Humbs North.
Fowler (Period Clocks), Robin, Aylesby, Humbs South.
Solent Antiques, Bembridge, I. of Wight.
Startime, Niton, I. of Wight.
Chawner, John, Birchington, Kent.
Clock Shop Antiques, The, Boughton, Kent.
Keymer Son & Co. Ltd, Brasted, Kent.
Old Manor House Antiques, Brasted, Kent.
Sim, Michael, Chislehurst, Kent.
Woodburn, Anthony, Leigh, Kent.
De Tavener Antiques, Ramsgate, Kent.
Aaron Antiques, Snodland, Kent.
Roberts Fine Antique Clocks, Music Boxes, Barometers, Derek, Tonbridge, Kent.
Somerset, B., Tonbridge, Kent.
Aaron Antiques, Tunbridge Wells, Kent.
Hadlow Antiques, Tunbridge Wells, Kent.
Pantiles Spa Antiques, Tunbridge Wells, Kent.
Old Clock Shop, The, West Malling, Kent.
Regal Antiques, Westerham, Kent.
Drop Dial Antiques, Bolton, Lancs.
Harrop Fold Clocks (F. Robinson), Bolton-by-Bowland, Lancs.
Fieldings Antiques, Haslingden, Lancs.
Norgrove - Antique Clocks, P.W., Haslingden, Lancs.
Boodle and Dunthorne Ltd, Manchester, Lancs.
Bulldog Antiques, Manchester, Lancs.
Chestergate Antiques, Manchester, Lancs.
Howell Jeweller, Charles, Oldham, Lancs.
Simpson and Sons Jewellers (Oldham)Ltd, H.C., Oldham, Lancs.
Antique and Reproduction Clocks, Preston, Lancs.
Owen Antiques, Rochdale, Lancs.
Davies Antiques, Whalley, Lancs.
Lowe of Loughborough, Loughborough, Leics.
Ashley House Antiques, Measham, Leics.
Hadfield, G.K., Shepshed, Leics.
Spindles, The, Tonge, Leics.
Bryan-Peach Antiques, N., Wymeswold, Leics.
Van Hefflin, Mr, Gainsborough, Lincs.
Grantham Clocks, Grantham, Lincs.
Wilkinson's, Grantham, Lincs.
Second Time Around, Hemswell Cliff, Lincs.
Kitching, Robert, Horncastle, Lincs.
Staines Antiques, Horncastle, Lincs.
Hansord and Son, David J., Lincoln, Lincs.
Trade Antiques, Long Sutton, Lincs.
Harwood Tate, Market Rasen, Lincs.
Pinfold Antiques, Ruskington, Lincs.
Wilkinson's, Sleaford, Lincs.
Clock Shop, The, Hoylake, Merseyside.
Boodle and Dunthorne Ltd, Liverpool, Merseyside.
Theta Gallery, Liverpool, Merseyside.
Andersons, Southport, Merseyside.
Pinocchio, Southport, Merseyside.
Weldons Jewellers and Antiques, Southport, Merseyside.
Artbry's Antiques, Pinner, Middx.
Shenton, Rita, Twickenham, Middx.
As Time Goes By Antique and Tower Clocks, Buxton, Norfolk.
Woodhouse (Antiquarian Horologist), R.C., Hunstanton, Norfolk.
Clayton Jewellery, Tim, King's Lynn, Norfolk.
D'Amico Antiques Ltd, Norwich, Norfolk.
Lawson Antique Clocks, Keith, Scratby, Norfolk.

Parriss, Sheringham, Norfolk.
Chapman, M.C., Finedon, Northants.
Jones Jeweller, Michael, Northampton, Northants.
Hazel Cottage Clocks, Eachwick, Northumbs.
Caris, Gordon, Hexham, Northumbs.
Second Time Around, Newark, Notts.
Potter Antiques, David and Carole, Nottingham, Notts.
Howard, Jonathan, Chipping Norton, Oxon.
Tuckers Country Store and Art Gallery, Deddington, Oxon.
Leigh Antiques, Laurie, Oxford, Oxon.
Rosemary and Time, Thame, Oxon.
Second Time Around Antiques, Wallingford, Oxon.
Witney Antiques, Witney, Oxon.
Mytton Antiques, Atcham, Shrops.
Curiosity Shop, The, Ludlow, Shrops.
Mitre House Antiques, Ludlow, Shrops.
Dodington Antiques, Whitchurch, Shrops.
Best Antiques, Ray, Ilminster, Somerset.
Lewis, Gerald, Montacute, Somerset.
House (Mitre Antiques), Bernard G., Wells, Somerset.
Nowell, Edward A., Wells, Somerset.
Venn, Edward, Williton, Somerset.
Grosvenor Antiques, Leek, Staffs.
Jordan, James A., Lichfield, Staffs.
Midwinter Antiques, Richard, Newcastle-under-Lyme, Staffs.
Ashley Antiques, Ipswich, Suffolk.
Clock House, Leavenheath, Suffolk.
Antique Clocks by Simon Charles, Long Melford, Suffolk.
Suthburgh Antiques, Long Melford, Suffolk.
Village Clocks, Long Melford, Suffolk.
Antique Clocks by Simon Charles, Sudbury, Suffolk.
Manson, Edward, Woodbridge, Suffolk.
Voss, A.G., Woodbridge, Suffolk.
Marsh, Simon, Bletchingley, Surrey.
Hollander Ltd, E., Dorking, Surrey.
Abbott Antiques, East Molesey, Surrey.
Pastimes (Egham) Ltd, Egham, Surrey.
Davis Antiquarian Horologist, Roger A., Great Bookham, Surrey.
Horological Workshops, Guildford, Surrey.
Hampton Wick Antiques, Hampton Wick, Surrey.
Surrey Clock Centre, Haslemere, Surrey.
Knaphill Antiques, Knaphill, Surrey.
Lawson Antiques, F. and T., Richmond, Surrey.
Warrender and Co, S., Sutton, Surrey.
Clock Shop Weybridge, The, Weybridge, Surrey.
Chattels Antiques, Woking, Surrey.
Edmonds Ltd, D.H., Brighton, Sussex East.
Hatchwell Antiques, Simon, Brighton, Sussex East.
Hove Antique Clocks, Brighton, Sussex East.
Yellow Lantern Antiques Ltd, Brighton, Sussex East.
Zebrak at Barnes Jewellers, Brighton, Sussex East.
Chaunt House, Burwash, Sussex East.
Bruford and Son Ltd, Wm., Eastbourne, Sussex East.
Cowderoy Antiques, John, Eastbourne, Sussex East.
Coach House Antiques, Hastings, Sussex East.
Bruce Antiques, W.F., Herstmonceux, Sussex East.
Old Mint House, The, Pevensey, Sussex East.
Cowfold Clocks, Cowfold, Sussex West.
Clock Shop, The, Hurstpierpoint, Sussex West.
Julian Antiques, Hurstpierpoint, Sussex West.
Churchhill Clocks, Midhurst, Sussex West.
Mason Antique Clocks, J., Northchapel, Sussex West .
Baskerville Antiques, Petworth, Sussex West.
Morris, John G., Petworth, Sussex West.
Powell (Hove) Ltd, J., Portslade, Sussex West.
Smith Antiques, Peter, Sunderland, Tyne and Wear.
Summersons, Hatton, Warks.
Grandfather Clock Shop, The, Shipston-on-Stour, Warks.
'Time in Hand', Shipston-on-Stour, Warks.
Bolton, John, Warwick, Warks.
Ashleigh House Antiques, Birmingham, West Mids.
Collyer, R., Birmingham, West Mids.
Meeks & Co, F., Birmingham, West Mids.
Allen Watch and Clockmaker, M., Four Oaks, West Mids.
Osborne Antiques, Sutton Coldfield, West Mids.
France, Alan M., Wolverhampton, West Mids.
Moxhams Antiques, Bradford-on-Avon, Wilts.
Oxley Antique Clocks and Barometers, P.A., Cherhill, Wilts.
Monkton Galleries, Hindon, Wilts.
Newsam, T.J., Salisbury, Wilts.

SPECIALIST DEALERS

Wadge Clocks, Chris, Salisbury, Wilts.
Smith Antique Clocks, Allan, Swindon, Wilts.
Houghton Antiques, Peter, Warminster, Wilts.
Walwyn Antiques, Howard, Wootton Bassett, Wilts.
Pearson Antique Clock Restoration, John, Birstwith, Yorks North.
Haworth Antiques, Harrogate, Yorks North.
Mason & Son, D., Harrogate, Yorks North.
Haworth Antiques, Huby, Yorks North.
Holgate, Milton J., Knaresborough, Yorks North.
Loomes, Brian, Pateley Bridge, Yorks North.
Dodsworth, N.J. and C.S., Spennithorne, Yorks North.
Tomlinson (Antiques) Ltd. and Period Furniture Ltd, Raymond, Tockwith, Yorks North.
Stones Grandfather Clocks, Keith, Bessacarr, Yorks South.
Fishlake Antiques, Fishlake, Yorks South.
Turn of the Century, Sheffield, Yorks South.
Canterbury House, Thorne, Yorks South.
Simon, Ilkley, Yorks West.
Goldsmith, William, Leeds, Yorks West.
Park Antiques, Menston, Yorks West.
Carlton Antiques, Saltaire, Yorks West.
Antique Shop, Ballyclare, Co. Down, N. Ireland.
Rock Angus Antiques, Portaferry, Co. Down, N. Ireland.
Century Antiques, Denny, Scotland.
Hudson Ltd, Felix, Dunfermline, Scotland.
Craiglea Clocks, Edinburgh, Scotland.
Whyte, John, Edinburgh, Scotland.
West End Antiques, Elgin, Scotland.
Forrest and Co (Jewellers) Ltd, James, Glasgow, Scotland.
Muirhead Moffat and Co, Glasgow, Scotland.
D'Amico Antiques Ltd, Strachan, Scotland.
Old Tyme Antiques, Ruthin, Clwyd, Wales.
Mann Antiques, Chris, Aberystwyth, Dyfed, Wales.
Past and Present, Cardiff, South Glam., Wales.
Hughes Antiques, Eynon, Swansea, West Glam., Wales.
Madoc Antiques and Art Gallery, Llandudno, Gwynedd, Wales.
Adams Antiques, Rodney, Pwllheli, Gwynedd, Wales.
Silver Time, Brecon, Powys, Wales.

Coins and Medals

Rankin Coin Co. Ltd, George, London, E2.
Martin (Coins) Ltd, C.J., London, N14.
Eimer, Christopher, London, NW11.
Dolphin Coins, London, NW3.
Armoury of St. James's Military Antiquarians, The, London, SW1.
Knightsbridge Coins, London, SW1.
Spink and Son Ltd, London, SW1.
Beaver Coin Room, London, SW5.
Seaby Ltd, B.A., London, W1.
Michael Coins, London, W8.
Baldwin and Sons Ltd, A.H., London, WC2.
Bord (Gold Coin Exchange), M., London, WC2.
Bath Stamp and Coin Shop, Bath, Avon.
Potter's Antiques and Coins, Bristol, Avon.
Castle Coins and Chiltern International Antiques, Dunstable, Beds.
Oliver, Tony L., Windsor and Eton, Berks.
B.R.M. Coins, Knutsford, Cheshire.
Souvenir Antiques, Carlisle, Cumbria.
Penrith Coin and Stamp Centre, Penrith, Cumbria.
Gainsborough House Antiques, Sidmouth, Devon.
Sterling Coins and Medals, Bournemouth, Dorset.
Treasure Chest, The, Weymouth, Dorset.
Finnegan (Jeweller), Robin, Darlington, Durham.
Dunelme Coins and Medals, Esh Winning, Durham.
Butler and Co, Cheltenham, Glos.
Military Curios, HQ84, Gloucester, Glos.
Portsmouth Stamp Shop, Portsmouth, Hants.
Romsey Medal and Collectors Centre, Romsey, Hants.
Whitmore, Great Malvern, Herefs and Worcs.
B.B.M. Jewellery and Antiques, Kidderminster, Herefs and Worcs.
Dixon Ltd, C.J. and A.J., Bridlington, Humbs North.
Shotter, Collectors Centre, Keith, Shanklin, I. of Wight.
Coin and Jewellery Shop, The, Accrington, Lancs.
Arundel Coins Ltd, Blackpool, Lancs.
Ireland Ltd, Peter, Blackpool, Lancs.
Haworth Ltd - Antique Gallery, M. and N., Manchester, Lancs.
Rowletts of Lincoln, Lincoln, Lincs.
Gold and Silver Exchange, Gt. Yarmouth, Norfolk.
Dennett Coins, Clive, Norwich, Norfolk.
Hockley Coins, Nottingham, Notts.
Smith Coins and Antiques, Val, Nottingham, Notts.
Denver House Antiques and Collectables, Burford, Oxon.
Collectors' Gallery, Shrewsbury, Shrops.
Fox and Co, Yeovil, Somerset.
St. Pancras Antiques, Chichester, Sussex West.
Intercoin, Newcastle-upon-Tyne, Tyne and Wear.
Collectors Shop, The, Birmingham, West Mids.
Eden Coins, Birmingham, West Mids.
Format of Birmingham Ltd, Birmingham, West Mids.
Castle Galleries, Salisbury, Wilts.
Coins International and Antiques International, Leeds, Yorks West.
Cookstown Antiques, Cookstown, Co. Tyrone, N. Ireland.
Collectors Shop, The, Edinburgh, Scotland.
Edinburgh Coin Shop, Edinburgh, Scotland.
Hamilton and Co, A.D., Glasgow, Scotland.
Abbey Antiques, Stirling, Scotland.
Thurso Antiques, Thurso, Scotland.
Clwyd Coins and Stamps, Rhos-on-Sea, Clwyd, Wales.
Glance Back Bookshop, Chepstow, Gwent, Wales.

Dolls and Toys

Donay Antiques, London, N1.
Lassalle, Judith, London, N1.
Relic Antiques at Camden Passage, London, N1.
Yesterday Child, London, N1.
Dolly Land, London, N21.
Game Advice, London, NW5.
Badgers Antiques, London, SE10.
Engine 'n' Tender, London, SE25.
Under Two Flags, London, W1.
Victoriana Dolls, London, W11.
Desmonde, Kay, London, W8.
Dolls House Toys Ltd, The, London, WC2.
Dolls and Toys of Yesteryear at Bow House Antiques, Hungerford, Berks.
Armitage, Tim, Nantwich, Cheshire.
Rosina's, Falmouth, Cornwall.
Ashbourne Fine Art, Ashbourne, Derbys.
Abbey House, Derby, Derbys.
Honiton Antique Toys, Honiton, Devon.
Vintage Toy and Train Museum, The, Sidmouth, Devon.
Hobby Horse Antiques, Bridport, Dorset.
Westrope, I., Birdbrook, Essex.
Tilly's Antiques, Leigh-on-Sea, Essex.
Park House Antiques, Stow-on-the-Wold, Glos.
Peter Pan's of Gosport, Gosport, Hants.
Treasures of Childhood Past - Carrie Tarplett, Great Malvern, Herefs and Worcs.
Attic, The, Baldock, Herts.
Grannie's Parlour, Hull, Humbs North.
Hiscock & Hiscock Antiques, New Romney, Kent.
Bridge Antiques, Wingham, Kent.
Antique Dolls, Blackpool, Lancs.
Swag, Preston, Lancs.
Dring, C. and K.E., Lincoln, Lincs.
Pinocchio, Southport, Merseyside.
Stiffkey Antiques, Stiffkey, Norfolk.
Granny's Attic, Nottingham, Notts.
Middleton's Antique Doll Shop and Dolls Hospital, Lilian, Burford, Oxon.
Images - Peter Stockham, Lichfield, Staffs.
Motts of Lavenham, Lavenham, Suffolk.
Trench Puzzles, Stowmarket, Suffolk.
Collectors Corner Antiques, Croydon, Surrey.
Gant, Elizabeth, Thames Ditton, Surrey.
Bears and Friends, Brighton, Sussex East.
Goble, Paul, Brighton, Sussex East.
Pearson, Sue, Brighton, Sussex East.
Kinloch, Mrs C., Sedlescombe, Sussex East.
Hinsdale Antiques, East Grinstead, Sussex West.
Recollect Studios, Sayers Common, Sussex West.
Nesbitt, Peggy, Warwick, Warks.
Dolly Mixtures, Birmingham, West Mids.

Taylor, Robert, Four Oaks, West Mids.
Collectors Old Toy Shop and Antiques, Halifax, Yorks West.
"Second Childhood", Huddersfield, Yorks West.
Memory Lane, Sowerby Bridge, Yorks West.
Ardersier Antiques, Ardersier, Scotland.
Angus Antiques, Dundee, Scotland.
Now and Then (Toy Centre), Edinburgh, Scotland.
Stockbridge Antiques and Fine Art, Edinburgh, Scotland.
Pastimes Vintage Toys, Glasgow, Scotland.
Guiscards Miniatures and Juvenalia, Rait, Scotland.
Museum of Childhood, Beaumaris, Gwynedd, Wales.

Etching and Engravings

Royal Exchange Art Gallery, London, EC3.
Underhill Gallery, Leigh, London, N1.
Harvey-Lee, Elizabeth, London, NW2.
Moreton Street Gallery, London, SW1.
S.A.G. Art Galleries, London, SW18.
Map House, The, London, SW3.
Old Church Galleries, London, SW3.
Collino, Julie, London, SW7.
Wyllie Gallery, The, London, SW7.
Agnew's, London, W1.
Editions Graphiques Gallery, London, W1.
Harvey & Co (Antiques) Ltd, W.R, London, W1.
Welbeck Gallery, The, London, W1.
Weston Gallery, William, London, W1.
Skrebowski, Justin, London, W11.
Cartographia London, London, WC1.
Grosvenor Prints, London, WC2.
Noble, Avril, London, WC2.
Gregory, George, Bath, Avon.
Flint Galleries Ltd, Sir William Russell, Wrington, Avon.
Foye Gallery, Luton, Beds
Collectors Gallery, The, Caversham, Berks.
Mon Galerie, Amersham, Bucks.
Benet Gallery, Cambridge, Cambs.
Sweetbriar Gallery, Helsby, Cheshire.
Coleman Antiques, Polly, Chesterfield, Derbys.
A-B Gallery, Salcombe, Devon.
Lantern Shop Gallery, The, Sidmouth, Devon.
PIC's Bookshop, Bridport, Dorset.
Antique Map and Bookshop, Puddletown, Dorset.
Cannon Antiques, Elizabeth, Colchester, Essex.
Medcalf, Paul, Gloucester, Glos.
Northleach Gallery, The, Northleach, Glos.
Talbot Court Galleries, Stow-on-the-Wold, Glos.
Beaulieu Fine Arts, Beaulieu, Hants.
Oldfield Gallery, Portsmouth, Hants.
Penoyre Antiques, Pershore, Herefs and Worcs.
McCrudden Gallery, Rickmansworth, Herts.
Vectis Fine Arts, Newchurch, I. of Wight.
Shanklin Gallery, The, Shanklin, I. of Wight.
Antiquities, Chatham, Kent.
Marrin and Sons, G. and D.I., Folkestone, Kent.
London House Antiques, Westerham, Kent.
Smith, Hammond, Leicester, Leics.
Leicestershire Sporting Gallery and Brown Jack Bookshop, Lubenham, Leics.
Garner, John, Uppingham, Leics.
Cassidy (Books), P.J., Holbeach, Lincs.
Coach House, The, Costessey, Norfolk.
TRADA, Chipping Norton, Oxon.
Faringdon Gallery, Faringdon, Oxon.
Keene Gallery, The Barry M., Henley-on-Thames, Oxon.
Mount, The, Woore, Shrops.
England's Gallery, Leek, Staffs.
Weston Antique Gallery, Weston, Staffs.
Gazeley Associates Fine Art, John, Ipswich, Suffolk.
King's Court Galleries, Dorking, Surrey.
Goodall, Peter, Guildford, Surrey.
Stewart Fine Art Galleries, Michael, Guildford, Surrey.
Limpsfield Watercolours, Limpsfield, Surrey.
Reigate Galleries Ltd, Reigate, Surrey.
Palmer Galleries, Richmond, Surrey.
Boathouse Gallery, Walton-on-Thames, Surrey.
Witch Ball, The, Brighton, Sussex East.
Green and Stone of Chichester, Chichester, Sussex West.
Wood Fine Art, Jeremy, Petworth, Sussex West.
Penfold Gallery and Antiques, Steyning, Sussex West.
Osborne Art and Antiques, Jesmond, Tyne and Wear.

Warner Fine Art, Newcastle-upon-Tyne, Tyne and Wear.
Chadwick Gallery, The, Henley-in-Arden, Warks.
Allen Gallery, The, Kenilworth, Warks.
Carr, Ronald, Salisbury, Wilts.
Heirloom and Howard Ltd, West Yatton, Wilts.
Waverley Gallery, The, Aberdeen, Scotland.
McEwan Gallery, The, Ballater, Scotland.
Mundy Fine Art Ltd, Ewan, Glasgow, Scotland.
Mainhill Gallery, Jedburgh, Scotland.
George Street Gallery, The, Perth, Scotland.
Windsor Gallery, David, Bangor, Gwynedd, Wales.
Watercolour Gallery, the, Cowbridge, South Glam., Wales.

Fire Related Items

Simply Capital, London, E18.
Westland & Company, London, EC2.
House of Steel Antiques, London, N1.
Julian Antiques, London, N1.
Amazing Grates, London, N2.
Antique Shop (Valantique), The, London, N2.
Tsar Architectural, London, N7.
Acquisitions (Fireplaces) Ltd, London, NW1.
Victorian Fireplace Co, London, NW1.
Stove Shop, The, London, NW2.
Townsends, London, NW8.
Main Street Antiques, London, SE10.
Oddiquities, London, SE23.
Under Milkwood, London, SE24.
Ward Antiques, London, SE7.
Fireplace, The, London, SE9.
Poulter and Son, H.W., London, SW10.
Thornhill Galleries Ltd. in association with A. & R. Dockerill Ltd, London, SW15.
Wandle's Workshop, Mr, London, SW18.
Halliday's, London, SW3.
Wilson Ltd, O.F., London, SW3.
Crotty and Son Ltd, J., London, SW6.
Fairfax Fireplaces and Antiques, London, SW6.
Hollingshead and Co, London, SW6.
Moggach Antiques, Ian, London, SW6.
Old World Trading Co, London, SW6.
Thornhill Galleries Ltd, London, SW6.
Buckle (Antique Fireplaces), Ruby, London, W2.
Chiswick Fireplace Co., The, London, W4.
Architectural Antiques, London, W6.
Walcot Reclamation, Bath, Avon.
Au Temps Perdu, Bristol, Avon.
Flame and Grate, Bristol, Avon.
Oldwoods, Bristol, Avon.
Period Fireplaces, Bristol, Avon.
Roberts Antiques, Ann, Ampthill, Beds.
Fire Place (Hungerford) Ltd, The, Hungerford, Berks.
Sundial Antiques, Amersham, Bucks.
Grosvenor House Interiors, Beaconsfield, Bucks.
Wilding, R., Wisbech, Cambs.
Pillory House, Nantwich, Cheshire.
Nostalgia Architectural Antiques, Stockport, Cheshire.
Victoriana Antiques, Stockton Heath, Cheshire.
Antique Fireplaces and Furniture, Tarvin, Cheshire.
Antique Fireplace Centre, Hartlepool, Cleveland.
Grate Expectations, Camborne, Cornwall.
Ashburton Marbles, Ashburton, Devon.
Antique Fireplace Centre, Plymouth, Devon.
Taylor Antiques, Brian, Plymouth, Devon.
Antique Architecture and Furniture, Tiverton, Devon.
Dodge and Son, Sherborne, Dorset.
Antique Metals, Coggeshall, Essex.
Elmley Heritage, Elmley Lovett, Herefs and Worcs.
Baileys Architectural Antiques, Ross-on-Wye, Herefs and Worcs.
Original Choice Ltd, The, Worcester, Herefs and Worcs.
Victorian Fireplace Canterbury, Kent.
Old Smithy, Feniscowles, Lancs.
Antique Fireplaces, Manchester, Lancs.
Blakey Fireplaces, Colin, Nelson, Lancs.
Carrcross Gallery, Scarisbrick, Lancs.
Pine Antiques, St. Annes-on-Sea, Lancs
Britain's Heritage, Leicester, Leics.
Architectural Antiques, Liverpool, Merseyside.
Peco, Hampton, Middx.
Crowther of Syon Lodge Ltd, Isleworth, Middx.

SPECIALIST DEALERS

Marble Hill Gallery, Twickenham, Middx.
Allchin Antiques, William, Norwich, Norfolk.
Stiffkey Antiques, Stiffkey, Norfolk.
Rococo Antiques and Interiors, Weedon, Northants.
Blacksmiths Forge, Balderton, Notts.
Lustre Metal Antiques Nottingham, Nottingham, Notts.
Hallidays Antiques Ltd, Dorchester-on-Thames, Oxon.
Oxford Architectural Antiques, Oxford, Oxon
Brighton Architectural Salvage, Brighton, Sussex East.
Shiners Architectural Reclamation, Newcastle-upon-Tyne, Tyne and Wear.
Grate Expectations (Fireplaces), Washington, Tyne and Wear.
Architectural Antiques of Moseley, Birmingham, West Mids.
James Antiques, Tim, Birmingham, West Mids.
Tatters of Tyseley Ltd, Birmingham, West Mids.
Old Flame, Easingwold, Yorks North.
Aagaard Ltd, Robert, Knaresborough, Yorks North.
Chimney Piece Antique Fires, Sheffield, Yorks South.
Victorian House Shop, Bingley, Yorks West.
Chapel House Fireplaces, Holmfirth, Yorks West.
Originals, Leeds, Yorks West.
Mews Antique Fireplaces and Architectural Salvage, Belfast, N.Ireland.
Period Architectural Features and Antiques, Annahilt, Co. Down, N. Ireland.
Cinders, Edinburgh, Scotland.
EASY - Edinburgh Architectural Salvage Yard, Edinburgh, Scotland.
Macintosh & Co, William, Edinburgh, Scotland.
Neilson Ltd, T. and J. W., Edinburgh, Scotland.
Back to the Wood, Cardiff, South Glam., Wales.
Kings Fireplaces, Antiques and Interiors, Cardiff, South Glam., Wales.
Kings Fireplaces & Architectural Antiques, Cardiff, South Glam., Wales.
Flame 'n' Grate, Barry, South Glam., Wales.

Frames

Mason Gallery, Paul, London, SW1.
Wiggins and Sons Ltd, Arnold, London, SW1.
Bloom Fine Jewellery, Anne, London, W1.
Milne Ltd, Nigel, London, W1.
Mitchell Ltd, Paul, London, W1.
Bull (Antiques) Ltd, John, London, W11.
Daggett Gallery, London, W11.
Lacy Gallery, London, W11.
Looking Glass of Bath, Bath, Avon.
Mole Gallery, South Molton, Devon.
Parker Fine Art Ltd, Finkley, Hants.
Fairhurst Gallery, The, Norwich, Norfolk.
Dixon Fine Engravings, Rob, Culham, Oxon.
Lacy Gallery, Henley-in-Arden, Warks.
Allen Gallery, The, Kenilworth, Warks.
Greenwood (Fine Art), W., Burneston, Yorks North.
Coulter Galleries, York, Yorks North.

Furniture
Continental (mainly French)

Westland & Company, London, EC2.
Buck and Payne Antiques, London, N1.
Gridley, Gordon, London, N1.
Keen Antiques, Cassandra, London, N1.
Kerr Antiques Ltd, Thomas, London, N1.
Gillingham Ltd, G. and F., London, NW2.
Lenson and Roy Smith, Nellie, London, NW8.
Hirschhorn, Robert, London, SE5.
Aaron (London)Ltd, Didier, London, SW1.
Antiquités, London, SW1.
Blanchard and Alan Ltd., London, SW1.
Hermitage Antiques, London, SW1.
Hobbs, Carlton, London, SW1.
Jeremy Ltd, London, SW1.
Lewis, M. and D., London, SW1.
Sarti Gallery Ltd, London, SW1.
Rendlesham Antiques Ltd, London, SW10.
Coleman Antiques, Simon, London, SW13.
Jorgen Antiques, London, SW15.
Adams Room Antiques, London, SW19.

Bunzl, Tony, London, SW3.
Grove Antiques, London, SW3.
Wilson Ltd, O.F., London, SW3.
Armelin Antiques, Karin, London, SW6.
Brown Ltd, I. and J.L., London, SW6.
Cavendish Antiques, Rupert, London, SW6.
Hurford Antiques, Peter, London, SW6.
Jefferson, Patrick, London, SW6.
Napier Ltd, Sylvia, London, SW6.
Pauw Antiques, M., London, SW6.
Alan Ltd., Adrian, London, W1.
Alexander and Berendt Ltd, London, W1.
Bernheimer Fine Arts Ltd, London, W1.
Blairman and Sons Ltd., H., London, W1.
Cheneviere Fine Arts, Antoine, London, W1.
Howard Antiques, London, W1.
Mallett at Bourdon House Ltd, London, W1.
Partridge Fine Arts plc, London, W1.
Pelham Galleries, London, W1.
Redford, William, London, W1.
South Audley Antiques, London, W1.
Toynbee-Clarke Interiors Ltd, London, W1.
Turpin Ltd, M., London, W1.
Baillache, Serge, London, W11.
Curá Antiques, London, W11.
Di Michele Antiques, E. and A., London, W11.
Facade, The, London, W11.
Lewin Antiques and Textile Arts, London, W11.
Lewis, M. and D., London, W11.
Lipitch Ltd, J., London, W11.
Oakstar Ltd, London, W11.
Sarti Antiques Ltd, G., London, W11.
Weaver, Trude, London, W11.
Bornoff, Claude, London, W2.
Mankowitz, Daniel, London, W2.
Architectural Antiques, London, W6.
Brower Antiques, David, London, W8.
Gordon, A. and F., London, W8.
Harris, Jonathan, London, W8.
Jay Antiques and Objets d'Art, Melvyn, London, W8.
Reindeer Antiques (Reindeer International Ltd.), London, W8.
Select Antiques Gallery Ltd, London, W8.
Stodel, Jacob, London, W8.
Dryden Ltd, Peter, Bath, Avon.
Pennard House Antiques, Bath, Avon.
Stafford Antiques, Ulla, Windsor and Eton, Berks.
Phoenix Antiques, Fordham, Cambs.
Lewis Antique and Fine Art Dealers, Ivor and Patricia, Peterborough, Cambs.
Wansford Antiques and Oriental Pottery, Wansford, Cambs.
Dickinson, David H., Bramhall, Cheshire.
Adams Antiques, Chester, Cheshire.
G. and J. Antiques, Buxton, Derbys.
West End Galleries, Buxton, Derbys.
Pugh's Farm Antiques, Monkton, Devon.
Colystock Antiques, Stockland, Devon.
Hennessy, Beaminster, Dorset.
Geneen Ltd, Lionel, Bournemouth, Dorset.
Swift and Sons, R.A., Bournemouth, Dorset.
Ryder, Georgina, Corfe Castle, Dorset.
Davana Original Interiors, Colchester, Essex.
Partner and Puxon, Colchester, Essex.
Millers Antiques Kelvedon, Kelvedon, Essex.
Compton-Dando (Fine Arts) Limited, White Colne, Essex.
Stead, Geoffrey, Chastleton, Glos.
Gray Antiques, Jay, Cirencester, Glos.
Gloucester House Antiques Ltd, Fairford, Glos.
Brett, Simon, Moreton-in-Marsh, Glos.
Parker, Elizabeth, Moreton-in-Marsh, Glos.
Carrington Antiques, Craig, Painswick, Glos.
Baggott, Duncan J., Stow-on-the-Wold, Glos.
Clark Antiques, Annarella, Stow-on-the-Wold, Glos.
Preston Antiques Ltd, Antony, Stow-on-the-Wold, Glos.
Antique Interiors, Tetbury, Glos.
Cedar Antiques, Hartley Wintney, Hants.
Lazarus Antiques, David, Hartley Wintney, Hants.
Phoenix Green Antiques, Hartley Wintney, Hants.
Millers of Chelsea Antiques Ltd, Ringwood, Hants.
Brown Ltd, I. and J.L., Hereford, Herefs and Worcs.
Great Brampton House Antiques Ltd, Hereford, Herefs and Worcs.

La Barre Ltd, Leominster, Herefs and Worcs.
Lloyd Antiques, Robin, Ross-on-Wye, Herefs and Worcs.
Country Life Antiques, Bushey, Herts.
Dench Antiques, Sandgate, Kent.
Baines, Henry, Southborough, Kent.
Up Country, Tunbridge Wells, Kent.
Apollo Galleries, Westerham, Kent.
Old Hall (Sphinx Gallery), Westerham, Kent.
Bridge Antiques, Wingham, Kent.
Park Galleries Antiques, Fine Art and Decor, Bolton, Lancs.
Butterworth (Horwich), Alan, Horwich, Lancs.
Guy's Antiques and Fine Furniture, Peter, Preston, Lancs.
Green and Son, J., Queniborough, Leics.
M.C. Trading Co, The, Horncastle, Lincs.
Hansord and Son, David J., Lincoln, Lincs.
Cox Antiques, Robin, Stamford, Lincs.
Arcadia Antiques, Southport, Merseyside.
Green, Ron, Towcester, Northants.
Helios & Co (Antiques), Weedon, Northants.
Thirty-Eight Antiques Ltd, Weedon, Northants.
Ashton Gower Antiques, Burford, Oxon.
Fyson Antiques, Jonathan, Burford, Oxon.
Gateway Antiques, Burford, Oxon.
Bugle Antiques, Chipping Norton, Oxon.
Summers, Davis and Son Ltd, Wallingford, Oxon.
Doveridge House of Neachley, Albrighton, Shrops.
Civic Antiques, Whitchurch, Shrops.
Hall's Antiques, Ash Priors, Somerset.
Pennard House, East Pennard, Somerset.
Genges Farm Antiques, Limington, Somerset.
Clare Collector, The, Clare, Suffolk.
Seabrook Antiques Ltd, Long Melford, Suffolk.
Old Post Office Antiques, The, Compton, Surrey.
Heath-Bullocks, Godalming, Surrey.
Country Furniture, Richmond, Surrey.
Marryat, Richmond, Surrey.
Ripley Antiques, Ripley, Surrey.
Wych House Antiques, Woking, Surrey.
Palmer Antiques, Dermot and Jill, Brighton, Sussex East.
Delmas, Hurst Green, Sussex East.
Pigeon House Antiques, Hurst Green, Sussex East.
Cato, Lennox, Lewes, Sussex East.
Price Antiques Ltd, Graham, Polegate, Sussex East.
De Montfort, Robertsbridge, Sussex East.
Hardman Antiques, Jennie, Crawley, Sussex West.
Hopkins, John, Cuckfield, Sussex West.
Julian Antiques, Hurstpierpoint, Sussex West.
Morris, John G., Petworth, Sussex West.
Wilkinson Antiques Ltd, T.G., Petworth, Sussex West.
Apollo Antiques Ltd, Warwick, Warks.
Ghiberti Antiques and Fine Art, Wolverhampton, West Mids.
Avon Antiques, Bradford-on-Avon, Wilts.
Moxhams Antiques, Bradford-on-Avon, Wilts.
Hastie, Ian G., Salisbury, Wilts.
Marnier Antiques, Edward, Tisbury, Wilts.
Obelisk Antiques, Warminster, Wilts.
Norwood House Antiques, Killinghall, Yorks North.
Lambe, Charlotte and John, Belfast, N. Ireland.
Davidson and Begg Antiques Ltd, Edinburgh, Scotland.
Jackson, Kenneth, Edinburgh, Scotland.
Whytock and Reid, Edinburgh, Scotland.
Young, Aldric, Edinburgh, Scotland.

Furniture - Country
(For 16th-17th C furniture see also Oak)

At the Sign of the Chest of Drawers, London, N1.
Helm Antiques, Linda, London, N1.
Rookery Farm Antiques, London, N1.
This and That (Furniture), London, NW1.
Furniture Cave, London, SW10.
Christopher Antiques, London, SW11.
Young Antiques, Robert, London, SW11.
Coleman Antiques, Simon, London, SW13.
Yesterday's Antiques, London, SW14.
Sampson Antiques Ltd, Alistair, London, SW3.
Brown Ltd, I. and J.L., London, SW6.
Collins, Peter, London, SW6.
Seligmann, M. and D., London, W8.
Lansdown Antiques, Bath, Avon.
Town and Country Antiques, Bath, Avon.

Green Farm Antiques, Olveston, Avon.
Ivy House Antiques, Great Shefford, Berks.
Lennard Antiques, Tingewick, Bucks.
Strover, Barry, Cambridge, Cambs.
Rumble Antiques, Simon and Penny, Chittering, Cambs.
West Farm Antiques, Orwell, Cambs.
Haylett, A.P. and M.A., Outwell, Cambs.
Farmhouse Antiques, Chester, Cheshire.
Richmond Galleries, Chester, Cheshire.
Bunting Antiques, Peter, Hyde, Cheshire.
Old Pine and Country Furniture, Boscastle, Cornwall.
Daphne's Antiques, Penzance, Cornwall.
Langley Antiques, Corby Hill, Cumbria.
Hill, David, Kirkby Stephen, Cumbria.
Adams Antiques, Yvonne, Ashbourne, Derbys.
Yates Antiques, Brian, Chesterfield, Derbys.
Meredith, John, Chagford, Devon.
Cobweb Antiques, Cullompton, Devon.
Sunset Country Antiques, Cullompton, Devon.
Baldwin Antiques, Peter J., Drewsteignton, Devon.
Taylor-Halsey Antiques, Drewsteignton, Devon.
Mounter, G., Dulford, Devon.
Wooden Fleece, Exmouth, Devon.
Sexton Antiques, Kenneth, Honiton, Devon.
Wickham Antiques, Honiton, Devon.
Sextons, Kentisbeare, Devon.
Pugh's Farm Antiques, Monkton, Devon.
Jones Antiques, Alan, Plymouth, Devon.
Taylor Antiques, Brian, Plymouth, Devon.
Fine Pine Antiques, Totnes, Devon.
Hennessy, Beaminster, Dorset.
Bolton, Richard, Netherbury, Dorset.
Compton Antiques Ltd, Sherborne, Dorset.
Collector, The, Barnard Castle, Durham.
Dean Antiques, Margery, Colchester, Essex.
Partner and Puxon, Colchester, Essex.
Bennet (Antiques), Julia, Dunmow, Essex.
Verey, Denzil, Barnsley, Glos.
Bateman Antiques, J. and R., Chalford, Glos.
Townsend, John P., Cheltenham, Glos.
Forum Antiques, Cirencester, Glos.
Gloucester House Antiques Ltd, Fairford, Glos.
Sampson, Anthony, Moreton-in-Marsh, Glos.
Clark Antiques, Annarella, Stow-on-the-Wold, Glos.
Hockin (Antiques) Ltd, Keith, Stow-on-the-Wold, Glos.
Huntington Antiques Ltd, Stow-on-the-Wold, Glos.
Norden Antiques, Peter, Stow-on-the-Wold, Glos.
Chest of Drawers, The, Tetbury, Glos.
Day Antiques, Ann and Roger, Tetbury, Glos.
Close Antiques, Alresford, Hants.
Airdale Antiques, Hartley Wintney, Hants.
Cedar Antiques, Hartley Wintney, Hants.
Just the Thing, Hartley Wintney, Hants.
Phoenix Green Antiques, Hartley Wintney, Hants.
Hursley Antiques, Hursley, Hants.
Burgess Farm Antiques, Morestead, Hants.
Millers of Chelsea Antiques Ltd, Ringwood, Hants.
Viney, Elizabeth, Stockbridge, Hants.
Pine Cellars, The, Winchester, Hants.
Brown Ltd, I. and J.L., Hereford, Herefs and Worcs.
Stables Antiques, Ombersley, Herefs and Worcs.
Lloyd Antiques, Robin, Ross-on-Wye, Herefs and Worcs.
Russell, M. and J., Yazor, Herefs and Worcs.
Annick Antiques, Kimpton, Herts.
Barlow Antiques, Anne, Letchmore Heath, Herts.
Careless Cottage Antiques, Much Hadham, Herts.
Wharton Antiques, Tim, Redbourn, Herts.
Smith and Smith Designs, Driffield, Humbs North.
Stoodley, Dinah, Brasted, Kent.
Pearson Antiques, Michael, Canterbury, Kent.
Swan Antiques, Cranbrook, Kent.
Pedlar's Pack, The, Hadlow, Kent.
Hiscock & Hiscock Antiques, New Romney, Kent.
Baines, Henry, Southborough, Kent.
Jackson-Grant Antiques, Teynham, Kent.
Phoenix Antiques, Tunbridge Wells, Kent.
Up Country, Tunbridge Wells, Kent.
Kitchenalia, Longridge, Lancs.
Davies Antiques, Whalley, Lancs.
Johnston, Paul, Gedney, Lincs.
Doyle Antiques, Lincoln, Lincs.
Sinclair, John, Stamford, Lincs.

SPECIALIST DEALERS

Bateson Antiques, David, Bressingham, Norfolk.
Antiques, West Haddon, Northants.
Hopwell Antiques, Paul, West Haddon, Northants.
Country Pine Antiques, Chatton, Northumbs.
Wychwood Antiques, Ascott-under-Wychwood, Oxon.
Horseshoe Antiques and Gallery, Burford, Oxon.
Swan Gallery, Burford, Oxon.
Bugle Antiques, Chipping Norton, Oxon.
Key Antiques, Chipping Norton, Oxon.
Baylis Country Chairs, Chris, Cumnor, Oxon.
Shambles Antiques, Dorchester-on-Thames, Oxon.
Windrush Antiques, Witney, Oxon.
Antique Corner, Ludlow, Shrops.
Ginger, G. & D., Ludlow, Shrops.
Moore Antiques, Marcus, Stanton, Shrops.
Dodington Antiques, Whitchurch, Shrops.
Whitney Antiques, Robert, Whitchurch, Shrops.
No. 7 Antiques, Woore, Shrops.
Acorn Antiques, Dulverton, Somerset.
White, J.C., Fitzhead, Somerset.
Genges Farm Antiques, Limington, Somerset.
Milverton Antiques, Milverton, Somerset.
King's Farm Antiques, Shapwick, Somerset.
Morley Antiques, William, West Monkton, Somerset.
Johnson's, Leek, Staffs.
Guillemot, Aldeburgh, Suffolk.
Mole Hall Antiques, Aldeburgh, Suffolk.
Brantham Mill Antiques, Brantham, Suffolk.
Seabrook Antiques Ltd, Long Melford, Suffolk.
Simpson, Oswald, Long Melford, Suffolk.
Cobham Galleries, Cobham, Surrey.
Owl House, The, Dorking, Surrey.
Christopher's Antiques, Farnham, Surrey.
White Antiques, David, Godalming, Surrey.
Evans, Mollie, Richmond, Surrey.
Welling Antiques, Anthony, Ripley, Surrey.
Dycheling Antiques, Ditchling, Sussex East.
Bird Antiques, John, Lewes, Sussex East.
Pastorale Antiques, Lewes, Sussex East.
Price Antiques Ltd, Graham, Polegate, Sussex East.
Mew Antiques, Peter and Janet, Sedlescombe, Sussex East.
Georgian House Antiques, Uckfield, Sussex East.
Park View Antiques, Wadhurst, Sussex East.
Chapman Antiques, Mark, Bosham, Sussex West.
Alexander Antiques, Henfield, Sussex West.
West Street Antiques, Midhurst, Sussex West.
Frith Antiques, Petworth, Sussex West.
Griffin Antiques, Petworth, Sussex West.
Grove House Antiques, Petworth, Sussex West.
Humphry Antiques, Petworth, Sussex West.
Tutt Antiques, J.C., Petworth, Sussex West.
Wakelin and Helen Linfield, Michael, Petworth, Sussex West.
Sandhill Barn Antiques (Pine and Country), Washington, Sussex West.
Spa Antiques, Leamington Spa, Warks.
Combe Cottage Antiques, Castle Combe, Wilts.
Monkton Galleries, Hindon, Wilts.
Dovetail Antiques, Malmesbury, Wilts.
Relic Antiques at Brillscote Farm, Malmesbury, Wilts.
Turner Antiques, Annmarie, Marlborough, Wilts.
Coggins Antiques, Ray, Westbury, Wilts.
Walwyn Antiques, Howard, Wootton Bassett, Wilts.
Chapman Medd and Sons, Easingwold, Yorks North.
Bentley, Bill, Harrogate, Yorks North.
Phillips Antiques Ltd, Elaine, Harrogate, Yorks North.
York Cottage Antiques, Helmsley, Yorks North.
Crown Square Antiques, Kirkbymoorside, Yorks North.
Precious, Roy, Settle, Yorks North.
Thistlethwaite, E., Settle, Yorks North.
Coach House Antiques, Whitby, Yorks North.
Wilson, Timothy D., Bawtry, Yorks South.
Fishlake Antiques, Fishlake, Yorks South.
Clark, Robert, Micklebring, Yorks South.
Moyallon Antiques, Portadown, Co. Armagh, N. Ireland.
Jansons Antiques, Bwlchllan, Dyfed, Wales.
Cwmgwili Mill, Carmarthen, Dyfed, Wales.
Lloyd, Michael, Henllan, Dyfed, Wales.
Country Antiques, Kidwelly, Dyfed, Wales.
Ash, Jim and Pat, Llandeilo, Dyfed, Wales.
Maclean Antiques, Llanwrda, Dyfed, Wales.
Bull, Audrey, Tenby, Dyfed, Wales.
Abbey Antiques, Tintern, Gwent, Wales.

Gallop and Rivers Architectural Antiques, Crickhowell, Powys, Wales.
Heritage Restorations, Llanfair Caereinion, Powys, Wales.
Scurlock, Kim, Swansea, West Glam., Wales.

Furniture - Georgian (1714-1830)

Blake - Old Cottage Antiques, K.N. and P., London, E11.
Chapman Antiques, Peter, London, N1.
Dome Antiques (Exports) Ltd, London, N1.
Ferrant Antiques, D.J., London, N1.
Furniture Vault, London, N1.
Gridley, Gordon, London, N1.
Keen Antiques, Cassandra, London, N1.
Kerr Antiques Ltd, Thomas, London, N1.
Vane House Antiques, London, N1.
Finchley Fine Art Galleries, London, N12.
Henham (Antiques), Martin, London, N2.
Gray, Marion, London, N4.
Petherton Antiques, London, N5.
Gould and Julian Gonnermann Antiques, Betty, London, N6.
McClenaghan-Gilhooly Antiques, London, NW1.
Regent Antiques, London, NW1.
Walker, W.E., London, NW1.
Beckman, Patricia, London, NW3.
Kendal Antiques, London, NW3.
Osborn Baker Gallery, London, NW3.
Wellington Gallery, London, NW8.
Antiques Pavilion, The, London, SE1.
Euro Antiques Warehouse London SE1
Tower Bridge Antiques, London, SE1.
Relcy Antiques, London, SE10.
Hirschhorn, Robert, London, SE5.
Antique Warehouse, London, SE8.
Allsopp Antiques, John, London, SW1.
Anno Domini Antiques, London, SW1.
Bly, John, London, SW1.
Dennler Antiques, Guy, London, SW1.
Fernandes and Marche, London, SW1.
General Trading Co Ltd, London, SW1.
Harrods Ltd, London, SW1.
Hodsoll Ltd, Christopher, London, SW1.
Howe, Christopher, London, SW1.
Jeremy Ltd, London, SW1.
Jubilee Antiques, London, SW1.
Ning Ltd, London, SW1.
Priest Antiques, Michael, London, SW1.
Rendall Antiques, Lesley, London, SW1.
Rose Ltd, Geoffrey, London, SW1.
Rothman, London, SW1.
Spyer and Son (Antiques) Ltd, Gerald, London, SW1.
Streather, Pamela, London, SW1.
Tillman Ltd, William, London, SW1.
Von Westenholz Ltd, Piers, London, SW1.
Furniture Cave, London, SW10.
Hares Antiques, London, SW10.
McVeigh and Charpentier, London, SW10.
Just a Second Antiques, London, SW11.
Dining Room Shop, The, London, SW13.
McDonald, Joy, London, SW13.
Randalls Antiques, London, SW13.
Seale Antiques, Jeremy, London, SW13.
Wren Antiques, London, SW13.
Haines Antiques Ltd, John, London, SW14.
Helius Antiques, London, SW14.
Jorgen Antiques, London, SW15.
Marsh and Son, A.V., London, SW15.
Dade, Clifford and Roger, London, SW17.
Adams Room Antiques , London, SW19.
Stefani Antiques, London, SW19.
Adams Ltd, Norman, London, SW3.
Apter Fredericks Ltd, London, SW3.
Baxter and Sons, H.C, London, SW3.
Courtney Ltd, Richard, London, SW3.
Dickson Antiques Ltd, Robert, London, SW3.
Foster, Michael, London, SW3.
Fredericks and Son, C., London, SW3.
Godson and Coles Ltd, London, SW3.
James and Son Ltd, Anthony, London, SW3.
Keil Ltd, John, London, SW3.
Lipitch Ltd, Michael, London, SW3.
Lipitch Ltd, Peter, London, SW3.

SPECIALIST DEALERS

Pettifer Ltd, David, London, SW3.
Saunders Antiques, Charles, London, SW3.
Tron Antiques, David, London, SW3.
Wearn and Son Ltd, R., London, SW3.
Wright Antiques Ltd, Clifford, London, SW3.
HRW Antiques, London, SW4.
Antique and Modern Furniture Ltd, London, SW5.
Armelin Antiques, Karin, London, SW6.
Bookham Galleries, London, SW6.
Brown Antiques, Alasdair, London, SW6.
Clay, John, London, SW6.
Collins, Peter, London, SW6.
Floyd Ltd, George, London, SW6.
George d'Epinois, London, SW6.
Hurford Antiques, Peter, London, SW6.
Jefferson, Patrick, London, SW6.
King Antiques, Eric, London, SW6.
Marriott Ltd, Michael, London, SW6.
Martin-Taylor Antiques, David, London, SW6.
Moggach Antiques, Ian, London, SW6.
Osterley Antiques Ltd, London, SW6.
Pauw Antiques, M., London, SW6.
Preston and Sally Isbell, Antony, London, SW6.
Sanders and Sons, Robin, London, SW6.
Toth, Ferenc, London, SW6.
Vaughan, London, SW6.
Colefax and Fowler, London, W1.
Fielden, Brian, London, W1.
Fortnum and Mason plc, London, W1.
Harvey & Co (Antiques) Ltd, W.R, London, W1.
Mallett and Son (Antiques) Ltd, London, W1.
Scarisbrick and Bate Ltd, London, W1.
Stair and Company Ltd, London, W1.
Toynbee-Clarke Interiors Ltd, London, W1.
Turpin Ltd, M., London, W1.
B. and T. Antiques, London, W11.
Baillache, Serge, London, W11.
Briggs Ltd, F.E.A., London, W11.
Britannia Export Antiques, London, W11.
Butchoff Antiques, London, W11.
Charge Antiques, Graham, London, W11.
Davidson, Michael, London, W11.
Fox, Judy, London, W11.
Garrick Antiques, Philip, London, W11.
Lipitch Ltd, J., London, W11.
Morse and Son Ltd, Terence, London, W11.
Oakstar Ltd, London, W11.
Sarti Antiques Ltd, G., London, W11.
Stanton, Louis, London, W11.
Wellington Antiques, London, W11.
Wibroe Antiques Ltd, Neil, London, W11.
Mankowitz, Daniel, London, W2.
Terry Antiques, London, W4.
Badger, The, London, W5.
Antique Home, The, London, W8.
Bardawil, Eddy, London, W8.
Barnet Antiques, London, W8.
Coleman, Garrick D., London, W8.
Gordon, A. and F., London, W8.
Lewis and Lloyd, London, W8.
Phillips, Henry, London, W8.
Reindeer Antiques (Reindeer International Ltd.), London, W8.
Sandberg Antiques, Patrick, London, W8.
Thomson Ltd, Murray, London, W8.
Fluss and Charlesworth Ltd, London, W9.
Alderson, Bath, Avon.
Baines of Bath, G.A., Bath, Avon.
Beau Nash Antiques, Bath, Avon.
Brass and Son, Lawrence, Bath, Avon.
Breeze and Behan, Bath, Avon.
Chelsea Interiors, Bath, Avon.
Craik Ltd, Brian and Caroline, Bath, Avon.
Croft Antiques, John, Bath, Avon.
Dando, Andrew, Bath, Avon.
Dodge Interiors Ltd, Martin, Bath, Avon.
Dux Antiques, Frank, Bath, Avon.
Fiddle Sticks Antiques and Decorative Items, Bath, Avon.
Graylow and Co, Bath, Avon.
Jadis Ltd, Bath, Avon.
Linford, Carr, Bath, Avon.
Quiet Street Antiques, Bath, Avon.

Robinson, T.E., Bath, Avon.
Town and Country Antiques, Bath, Avon.
Butler, Robin, Bristol, Avon.
No. 74 Antiques and Collectables, Bristol, Avon.
Tilly Manor Antiques, West Harptree, Avon.
Harman Antiques, Robert, Ampthill, Beds.
Timms Antiques Ltd, S. and S., Ampthill, Beds.
Ball Antique and Fine Art, David, Leighton Buzzard, Beds.
Fenlan Antiques, Turvey, Beds.
Sykes Antiques, Christopher, Woburn, Beds.
Old School Antiques, The, Dorney, Berks.
Pearson Antiques, John A., Horton, Berks.
Hastie, Robert and Georgina, Hungerford, Berks.
King Antiques, Roger, Hungerford, Berks.
Medalcrest Ltd, Hungerford, Berks.
Old Malthouse, The, Hungerford, Berks.
Widmerpool House Antiques, Maidenhead, Berks.
Baker Antiques, John, Newbury, Berks.
Griffons Court, Newbury, Berks.
Millgreen Antiques, Wargrave, Berks.
Wargrave Antiques, Wargrave, Berks.
Bousfield, Guy, Windsor and Eton, Berks.
Cavendish Fine Arts - Janet Middlemiss, Windsor and Eton, Berks.
Eton Antiques Partnership, Windsor and Eton, Berks.
Eton Gallery Antiques, Windsor and Eton, Berks.
Eyre and Greig Ltd, Windsor and Eton, Berks.
Hayden Antiques, Shirley, Windsor and Eton, Berks.
Martin, Peter J., Windsor and Eton, Berks.
Millon Antiques, Windsor and Eton, Berks.
Stafford Antiques, Ulla, Windsor and Eton, Berks.
Old Post House Antiques, Woolhampton, Berks.
Cupboard Antiques, The, Amersham, Bucks.
Morton Harvey Antiques, Aylesbury, Bucks.
Elsworth - Beaconsfield Ltd, June, Beaconsfield, Bucks.
Grosvenor House Interiors, Beaconsfield, Bucks.
Norton Antiques, Beaconsfield, Bucks.
Period Furniture Showrooms, Beaconsfield, Bucks.
Spinning Wheel, The, Beaconsfield, Bucks.
Smith, T., Chalfont St. Giles, Bucks.
Overland Antiques, John, Olney, Bucks.
Country Furniture Shop, Penn, Bucks.
Bowood Antiques, Wendover, Bucks.
Wendover Antiques, Wendover, Bucks.
Haydon House Antiques, Woburn Sands, Bucks.
Neville's Antiques, Woburn Sands, Bucks.
Norman Antiques and Restorations, Peter, Burwell, Cambs.
Applin Antiques, Jess, Cambridge, Cambs.
Beazor and Sons Ltd, John, Cambridge, Cambs.
Mere Antiques, Fowlmere, Cambs.
Hardiman, P.N., Melbourn, Cambs.
Broadway Antiques, St. Ives, Cambs.
Alderley Antiques, Alderley Edge, Cheshire.
Baker Antiques, Anthony, Alderley Edge, Cheshire.
Cheyne's, Altrincham, Cheshire.
Eureka Antiques and Interiors, Bowdon, Cheshire.
Dickinson, David H., Bramhall, Cheshire.
Adams Antiques, Chester, Cheshire.
Davidson Antiques, Neil, Chester, Cheshire.
Melody's Antique Galleries, Chester, Cheshire.
Titchner & Sons, John, Chester, Cheshire.
Gay's (Hazel Grove) Antiques Ltd, Hazel Grove, Cheshire.
Bedale, David, Knutsford, Cheshire.
Glynn Interiors, Knutsford, Cheshire.
Tatton Antiques, Knutsford, Cheshire.
Titchner and Sons, John, Littleton, Cheshire.
Lostock Antiques, Lostock Gralam, Cheshire.
Edwards Antique Exports, Brian, Lower Kinnerton, Cheshire.
Cheshire Antiques, Macclesfield, Cheshire.
Copperfield, Robert, Macclesfield, Cheshire.
Mulberry Bush, The, Marple Bridge, Cheshire.
Adams Antiques, Nantwich, Cheshire.
Boyer Antiques, Rex, Nantwich, Cheshire.
Chapel Antiques, Nantwich, Cheshire.
Page Antiques, Stockport, Cheshire.
Zippy Antiques, Stockport, Cheshire.
Arden Antiques, Brenda, Tarporley, Cheshire.
Antique Fireplaces and Furniture, Tarvin, Cheshire.
Chapel Antiques, Wilmslow, Cheshire.
Snowden Antiques, Ruby, Yarm, Cleveland.
Bragg Antiques, John, Lostwithiel, Cornwall.

SPECIALIST DEALERS

Ashbrook Antiques, Ken, Penzance, Cornwall.
Pydar Antiques and Gallery, Truro, Cornwall.
Winkworth Antiques, Richard, Truro, Cornwall.
Victoria Antiques, Wadebridge, Cornwall.
Anthemion - The Antique Shop, Cartmel, Cumbria.
Jennywell Hall Antiques, Crosby Ravensworth, Cumbria.
Adamson, Alexander, Kirkby Lonsdale, Cumbria.
Haughey Antiques, Kirkby Stephen, Cumbria.
Mortlake Antiques, Kirkby Stephen, Cumbria.
Cothay Antiques, Maulds Meaburn, Cumbria.
Townhead Antiques, Newby Bridge, Cumbria.
Corney House Antiques, Penrith, Cumbria.
Elsom - Antiques, Pamela, Ashbourne, Derbys.
Chappell Antiques and Fine Art, K., Bakewell, Derbys.
Harper Antiques, Martin and Dorothy, Bakewell, Derbys.
Water Lane Antiques, Bakewell, Derbys.
Antique Exporters U.K, Brailsford, Derbys.
Knights Antiques, Brassington, Derbys.
Hackney House Antiques, Chesterfield, Derbys.
Wayside Antiques, Duffield, Derbys.
Matsell Antiques Ltd, Ilkeston, Derbys.
Shardlow Antiques Warehouse, Shardlow, Derbys.
Nimbus Antiques, Whaley Bridge, Derbys.
Wooden Box Antiques, Woodville, Derbys.
Potter and Son, W.G., Axminster, Devon.
Barnstaple Antique Centre, Barnstaple, Devon.
Collins and Son, J., Bideford, Devon.
Thomas and James Antiques, Bovey Tracey, Devon.
Prestige Antiques, John, Brixham, Devon.
Old Antique Shop, The, Budleigh Salterton, Devon.
Thorn, David J., Budleigh Salterton, Devon.
Meredith, John, Chagford, Devon.
Cullompton Old Tannery Antiques, Cullompton, Devon.
Mills Antiques, Cullompton, Devon.
Taylor-Halsey Antiques, Drewsteignton, Devon.
Priory Antiques, Exeter, Devon.
Wadham, Peter, Exeter, Devon.
Bramble Cross Antiques, Honiton, Devon.
Butler, Roderick, Honiton, Devon.
Huggett and Son, L.J., Honiton, Devon.
Lombard Antiques, Honiton, Devon.
Pilgrim Antiques, Honiton, Devon.
Turner Antiques, R. and D., Honiton, Devon.
Bagnall, W., Moretonhampstead, Devon.
Andrade, Philip, South Brent, Devon.
Tredantiques, South Molton, Devon.
Extence Antiques, Teignmouth, Devon.
Bygone Days Antiques, Tiverton, Devon.
Sheraton House, Torquay, Devon.
Past and Present, Totnes, Devon.
Woolacombe Bay Antiques, Woolacombe, Devon.
Yealmantiques, Yealmpton, Devon.
Good Hope Antiques, Beaminster, Dorset.
Strowger of Blandford, Blandford Forum, Dorset.
Geneen Ltd, Lionel, Bournemouth, Dorset.
Sainsbury in association with Charles Fox, Jonathan L.F., Bournemouth, Dorset.
Sainsburys of Bournemouth Ltd, Bournemouth, Dorset.
Stebbing, Peter, Bournemouth, Dorset.
Swift and Sons, R.A., Bournemouth, Dorset.
Mack Antiques, David, Branksome, Dorset.
Dawson Antiques, Zona, Charlton Marshall, Dorset.
Hamptons, Christchurch, Dorset.
Tower Antiques, Cranborne, Dorset.
Legg Antiques, Michael, Dorchester, Dorset.
Walker Antiques, John, Dorchester, Dorset.
Talisman, Gillingham, Dorset.
Compton Antiques Ltd, Sherborne, Dorset.
Dodge and Son, Sherborne, Dorset.
Heygate Browne Antiques, Sherborne, Dorset.
Old Barn Antiques Co, Trent, Dorset.
Antiquatat Antiques, Wimborne Minster, Dorset.
Baliol Gallery, The, Barnard Castle, Durham.
Collector, The, Barnard Castle, Durham.
Town House Antiques, Barnard Castle, Durham.
Ramsey Antiques, Alan, Darlington, Durham.
Eden House Antiques, West Auckland, Durham.
Lindsell Chairs, Coggeshall, Essex.
Dean Antiques, Margery, Colchester, Essex.
Partner and Puxon, Colchester, Essex.
Bennet (Antiques), Julia, Dunmow, Essex.
Beaumont Antiques, Michael, Hempstead, Essex.

Kelvedon Antiques, Kelvedon, Essex.
Millers Antiques Kelvedon, Kelvedon, Essex.
Ratcliff Ltd, G.T., Kelvedon, Essex.
Sykes Antiques, Thomas, Kelvedon, Essex.
Templar Antiques, Kelvedon, Essex.
Wrenn Antiques, Richard, Leigh-on-Sea, Essex.
Beardall Antiques, Clive, Maldon, Essex.
Stone Hall Antiques, Matching Green, Essex.
Brown House Antiques, Newport, Essex.
Bruschweiler (Antiques) Ltd, F.G., Rayleigh, Essex.
Dolphin Antiques, Saffron Walden, Essex.
Sumner, Jane, Saffron Walden, Essex.
Hedingham Antiques, Sible Hedingham, Essex.
Pinn and Sons, W.A., Sible Hedingham, Essex.
Barton House Antiques, Stanford-le-Hope, Essex.
Linden House Antiques, Stansted, Essex.
Thaxted Galleries, Thaxted, Essex.
Turpin's Antiques, Thaxted, Essex.
Compton-Dando (Fine Arts) Limited, White Colne, Essex.
White Roding Antiques, White Roding, Essex.
Dean Forest Antiques, Berry Hill Pike, Glos.
Keil (Cheltenham) Ltd, H.W., Cheltenham, Glos.
Latchford Antiques, Cheltenham, Glos.
Niner Antiques, Elizabeth, Cheltenham, Glos.
Cirencester Antiques Centre, Cirencester, Glos.
Forum Antiques, Cirencester, Glos.
Gray Antiques, Jay, Cirencester, Glos.
Hares, Cirencester, Glos.
Legg and Son, E.C., Cirencester, Glos.
Ponsford Antiques, A.J., Cirencester, Glos.
Taylor Antiques, Rankine, Cirencester, Glos.
Waterloo Antiques, Cirencester, Glos.
Weaver Antiques, Bernard, Cirencester, Glos.
Blenheim Antiques, Fairford, Glos.
Cirencester Antiques Ltd, Fairford, Glos.
Cook and Son Antiques, E.J., Gloucester, Glos.
Brett, Simon, Moreton-in-Marsh, Glos.
Lemington House Antiques, Moreton-in-Marsh, Glos.
Parker, Elizabeth, Moreton-in-Marsh, Glos.
Roberts Antiques, Peter, Moreton-in-Marsh, Glos.
Sampson, Anthony, Moreton-in-Marsh, Glos.
Carrington Antiques, Craig, Painswick, Glos.
Regent Antiques, Painswick, Glos.
Acorn Antiques, Stow-on-the-Wold, Glos.
Baggott, Duncan J., Stow-on-the-Wold, Glos.
Baggott Church Street Ltd, Stow-on-the-Wold, Glos.
Brand Antiques, Colin, Stow-on-the-Wold, Glos.
Bryden, D., Stow-on-the-Wold, Glos.
Clarke Antiques Ltd, Christopher, Stow-on-the-Wold, Glos.
Curiosity Shop, The, Stow-on-the-Wold, Glos.
Fosse Way Antiques, Stow-on-the-Wold, Glos.
Little Elms Antiques, Stow-on-the-Wold, Glos.
Norden Antiques, Peter, Stow-on-the-Wold, Glos.
Nutter, Simon W., Stow-on-the-Wold, Glos.
Preston Antiques Ltd, Antony, Stow-on-the-Wold, Glos.
Priests Antiques, Stow-on-the-Wold, Glos.
Stow Antiques, Stow-on-the-Wold, Glos.
Touchwood International, Stow-on-the-Wold, Glos.
Vanbrugh House Antiques, Stow-on-the-Wold, Glos.
Breakspeare Antiques, Tetbury, Glos.
Chest of Drawers, The, Tetbury, Glos.
Elgin House Antiques, Tetbury, Glos.
Nash Antiques, Paul, Tetbury, Glos.
Old George Antiques and Interiors, Tetbury, Glos.
Porch House Antiques, Tetbury, Glos.
Primrose Antiques, Tetbury, Glos.
Berkeley Antiques and Replay, Tewkesbury, Glos.
Gainsborough House Antiques, Tewkesbury, Glos.
Taylor, F.W., Tewkesbury, Glos.
Prichard Antiques, Winchcombe, Glos.
Close Antiques, Alresford, Hants.
Butterfly Pine, Botley, Hants.
Abbott, Nicholas, Hartley Wintney, Hants.
Andwells, Hartley Wintney, Hants.
Antique House, Hartley Wintney, Hants.
Deva Antiques, Hartley Wintney, Hants.
Lazarus Antiques, David, Hartley Wintney, Hants.
Phoenix Green Antiques, Hartley Wintney, Hants.
Du Cros Antiques, J., Liss, Hants.
Captain's Cabin Antiques, Lymington, Hants.
Corfield Antiques Ltd, Lymington, Hants.
Kaye of Lyndhurst, Lita, Lyndhurst, Hants.

SPECIALIST DEALERS

Monaltrie Antiques, Odiham, Hants.
Cull Antiques, Petersfield, Hants.
Millers of Chelsea Antiques Ltd, Ringwood, Hants.
Moody, L., Southampton, Hants.
Stockbridge Antiques, Stockbridge, Hants.
Viney, Elizabeth, Stockbridge, Hants.
Gaylords, Titchfield, Hants.
Regency House Antiques, Whitchurch, Hants.
Burns and Graham, Winchester, Hants.
Jewry Street Gallery Ltd, Winchester, Hants.
Roofe Antiques, Mary, Winchester, Hants.
Old Barley Mow Antiques, Winchfield, Hants.
Barnt Green Antiques, Barnt Green, Herefs and Worcs.
Fenwick and Fisher Antiques, Broadway, Herefs and Worcs.
Keil Ltd, H.W., Broadway, Herefs and Worcs.
Picton House Antiques, Broadway, Herefs and Worcs.
Hart Antiques, Mitchell, Clows Top, Herefs and Worcs.
Miscellany Antiques, Great Malvern, Herefs and Worcs.
Great Brampton House Antiques Ltd, Hereford, Herefs and Worcs.
Gorst Hall Restoration, Kidderminster, Herefs and Worcs.
Nash Antiques and Interiors, John, Ledbury, Herefs and Worcs.
Shaw-Cooper, Susan, Ledbury, Herefs and Worcs.
Chapman Antiques, Leominster, Herefs and Worcs.
Hammond Antiques, Jeffery, Leominster, Herefs and Worcs.
Jennings of Leominster, Leominster, Herefs and Worcs.
Leominster Antiques, Leominster, Herefs and Worcs.
Kimber and Son, Malvern Link, Herefs and Worcs.
Stables Antiques, Ombersley, Herefs and Worcs.
Penoyre Antiques, Pershore, Herefs and Worcs.
Green Antiques, Robert, Ross-on-Wye, Herefs and Worcs.
Robson Antiques, Walford, Herefs and Worcs.
Taylor, Gerald and Vera, Winforton, Herefs and Worcs.
Lower House Fine Antiques, Winyates Green, Herefs and Worcs.
Bygones by the Cathedral, Worcester, Herefs and Worcs.
Bygones (Worcester), Worcester, Herefs and Worcs.
Hodge, Jean, Worcester, Herefs and Worcs.
Lees and Sons, M., Worcester, Herefs and Worcs.
Butt Antiques, Anthony, Baldock, Herts.
Moss, Ralph and Bruce, Baldock, Herts.
Park Street Antiques, Berkhamsted, Herts.
Windhill Antiquary, The, Bishop's Stortford, Herts.
Gander, Michael, Hitchin, Herts.
Phillips of Hitchin (Antiques) Ltd, Hitchin, Herts.
J.N. Antiques, Redbourn, Herts.
Wharton Antiques, Tim, Redbourn, Herts.
Dolphin Antiques, St. Albans, Herts.
Bly, John, Tring, Herts.
Wareside Antiques, Wareside, Herts.
Collins Antiques (F.G. and C. Collins Ltd.), Wheathampstead, Herts.
Armson (Antiques) Ltd, Michael, Wilstone, Herts.
Priory Antiques, Bridlington, Humbs North.
Hakeney Antiques, David K., Hull, Humbs North.
Houghton Hall Antiques, Market Weighton, Humbs North.
Corrin Antiques, John, Douglas, I. of Man.
Barrington, David, Brasted, Kent.
Brooker Antiques at the Village Gallery, Elizabeth, Brasted, Kent.
Dyke, Peter, Brasted, Kent.
Keymer Son & Co. Ltd, Brasted, Kent.
Massingham Antiques, Roy, Brasted, Kent.
Tilings Antiques, Brasted, Kent.
Conquest House Antiques, Canterbury, Kent.
Parker-Williams Antiques, Canterbury, Kent.
Peacock Antiques, Chilham, Kent.
Chislehurst Antiques, Chislehurst, Kent.
Sim, Michael, Chislehurst, Kent.
Chevertons of Edenbridge Ltd, Edenbridge, Kent.
Lord Antiques, Alan, Folkestone, Kent.
Warren Antiques, Jimmy, Littlebourne, Kent.
Deo Juvante Antiques, Rochester, Kent.
Walters, J.D. and R.M., Rolvenden, Kent.
Buck Antiques, Christopher, Sandgate, Kent.
Fitch Antiques, Michael, Sandgate, Kent.
Freeman and Lloyd Antiques, Sandgate, Kent.
Porter Antiques, James, Sandwich, Kent.
Chandlers Antiques, Sevenoaks, Kent.
Stead, Myola, Sevenoaks, Kent.
Steppes Hill Farm Antiques, Stockbury, Kent.
Sutton Valence Antiques, Sutton Valence, Kent.
Garden House Antiques, Tenterden, Kent.
Jackson-Grant Antiques, Teynham, Kent.
Pantiles Spa Antiques, Tunbridge Wells, Kent.
Phoenix Antiques, Tunbridge Wells, Kent.
Strawsons Antiques, Tunbridge Wells, Kent.
Thompson, John, Tunbridge Wells, Kent.
Langold Antiques, West Peckham, Kent.
Apollo Galleries, Westerham, Kent.
Brazil Antiques Ltd, Westerham, Kent.
Hook, Anthony J., Westerham, Kent.
London House Antiques, Westerham, Kent.
Mistral Galleries, Westerham, Kent.
Laurens Antiques, Whitstable, Kent.
Tankerton Antiques, Whitstable, Kent.
Silvesters, Wingham, Kent.
Webster, E.W., Bickerstaffe, Lancs.
Park Galleries Antiques, Fine Art and Decor, Bolton, Lancs.
Brun Lea Antiques, Burnley, Lancs.
K.C. Antiques, Darwen, Lancs.
Folly, The, Longridge, Lancs.
Baron Antiques, The, Manchester, Lancs.
Bulldog Antiques, Manchester, Lancs.
Chestergate Antiques, Manchester, Lancs.
Brooks Antiques, Nelson, Lancs.
Grice Antiques, Alan, Ormskirk, Lancs.
Treasure Ltd, Frederick, Preston, Lancs.
Falk, S.C., Rochdale, Lancs.
Keen, Thomas, Bottesford, Leics.
Churchgate Antiques, Empingham, Leics.
Old Bakery Antiques, Empingham, Leics.
Withers of Leicester, Hoby, Leics.
Mandrake Stephenson Antiques, Ibstock, Leics.
Corry's, Leicester, Leics.
Montague Antiques, Leicester, Leics.
Moores and Son, Walter, Leicester, Leics.
Smith (Leicester) Ltd, E., Leicester, Leics.
Lowe of Loughborough, Loughborough, Leics.
Stamp and Sons, J., Market Harborough, Leics.
Gallery Antiques, Oakham, Leics.
Burrows, David E., Osgathorpe, Leics.
Green and Son, J., Queniborough, Leics.
Pavilion, Ratcliffe-on-the-Wreake, Leics.
Roberts, T.J., Uppingham, Leics.
Bingley Antiques, Robert, Wing, Leics.
Paddock Antiques, Woodhouse Eaves, Leics.
Underwood Antiques, Clive, Colsterworth, Lincs.
Nadin, Harold, Grantham, Lincs.
Seaview Antiques, Horncastle, Lincs.
Shaw Antiques, Laurence, Horncastle, Lincs.
Staines Antiques, Horncastle, Lincs.
Kirton Antiques, Kirton, Lincs.
Hansord and Son, David J., Lincoln, Lincs.
Ratcliffe, J. and R, Lincoln, Lincs.
Harwood Tate, Market Rasen, Lincs.
Audley House Antiques, Osbournby, Lincs.
Pinfold Antiques, Ruskington, Lincs.
Dawson of Stamford, Stamford, Lincs.
St. George's Antiques, Stamford, Lincs.
St. Mary's Galleries, Stamford, Lincs.
Underwoodhall Antiques, Woodhall Spa, Lincs.
V.O.C. Antiques, Woodhall Spa, Lincs.
Stefani Antiques, Liverpool, Merseyside.
Stock, Colin, Rainford, Merseyside.
Arcadia Antiques, Southport, Merseyside.
Decor Galleries, Southport, Merseyside.
Horswill Antiques and Decorative Arts, Helen, West Kirby, Merseyside.
Mann Antiques, Kathleen, Harrow, Middx.
Artbry's Antiques, Pinner, Middx.
Ivy House Antiques, Acle, Norfolk.
Bush and Partners, A.E., Attleborough, Norfolk.
Steed-Croft Antiques, Burnham Deepdale, Norfolk.
Cringle, M. and A., Burnham Market, Norfolk.
Hamilton Antiques, Anne, Burnham Market, Norfolk.
Market House, Burnham Market, Norfolk.
Kerridge Antiques, B. and J., Cley, Norfolk.
Bates and Sons, Eric, Coltishall, Norfolk.
Bradbury Antiques, Roger, Coltishall, Norfolk.
Rust Antiques, Benjamin, Cromer, Norfolk.
Seago, A.E., Cromer, Norfolk.
Hamilton Antiques, Anne, East Rudham, Norfolk.

SPECIALIST DEALERS

Howkins, Peter, Gt. Yarmouth, Norfolk.
Robinson, Peter, Heacham, Norfolk.
Brett and Sons Ltd, Arthur, Norwich, Norfolk.
Haugh Antiques, Roderic, Norwich, Norfolk.
Howkins Antiques, John, Norwich, Norfolk.
Cannell Antiques, M.D., Raveningham, Norfolk.
Chimes, The, Reepham, Norfolk.
Pratt and Son, Leo, South Walsham, Norfolk.
Brooke, T.C.S., Wroxham, Norfolk.
Restall Brown and Clennell Ltd, Cosgrove, Northants.
Chapman, M.C., Finedon, Northants.
Quaker Lodge Antiques, Finedon, Northants.
Jones at Flore House, Christopher, Flore, Northants.
Madeira, V. and C., Flore, Northants.
Cave, F. and C.H., Northampton, Northants.
Regent House, Northampton, Northants.
King, F., Pattishall, Northants.
Antique Galleries, The, Paulerspury, Northants.
Reindeer Antiques Ltd, Potterspury, Northants.
Robertson, Ian A., Alnwick, Northumbs.
Felton Park Antiques, Felton, Northumbs.
Boaden Antiques, Arthur, Hexham, Northumbs.
Hallstile Antiques, Hexham, Northumbs.
Miller Antiques, James, Wooler, Northumbs.
Cheshire, E.M., Bingham, Notts.
Tudor Rose Antiques, Carlton-on-Trent, Notts.
Antiques and General Trading Co, Nottingham, Notts.
Pegasus Antiques, Nottingham, Notts.
Strouds (of Southwell Antiques), Southwell, Notts.
Vedmore Furniture and Antiques, Judy, Banbury, Oxon.
Carter Antiques, Mark, Bladon, Oxon.
Park House Antiques, Bladon, Oxon.
Ashton Gower Antiques, Burford, Oxon.
Gateway Antiques, Burford, Oxon.
Nielsen Antiques, Anthony, Burford, Oxon.
Pickup, David, Burford, Oxon.
Schotten Antiques, Manfred, Burford, Oxon.
Shield Antiques, Robin, Burford, Oxon.
Swan Gallery, Burford, Oxon.
Walker, Burford, Zene, Burford, Oxon.
Hitchcox Antiques, Rupert, Chalgrove, Oxon.
Georgian House Antiques, Chipping Norton, Oxon.
Stroud Antiques, Peter, Chipping Norton, Oxon.
Giffengate Antiques, Dorchester-on-Thames, Oxon.
Hallidays Antiques Ltd, Dorchester-on-Thames, Oxon.
A. and F. Partners, Faringdon, Oxon.
La Chaise Antique, Faringdon, Oxon.
Kingston, Richard J., Henley-on-Thames, Oxon.
Country Seat, The, Huntercombe, Oxon.
Jackson, John, Milton-under-Wychwood, Oxon.
Thame Antique Galleries, Thame, Oxon.
de Albuquerque, Michael and Jane, Wallingford, Oxon.
Ottrey Antiques, Mike, Wallingford, Oxon.
Second Time Around Antiques, Wallingford, Oxon.
Summers, Davis and Son Ltd, Wallingford, Oxon.
Cross Antiques, Watlington, Oxon.
Orton Antiques, Stephen, Watlington, Oxon.
Sibley (Fine Furniture), Nicholas, Whitchurch-on-Thames, Oxon.
Greenway Antiques, Colin, Witney, Oxon.
Pout Antiques, Ian, Witney, Oxon.
Wilkins Antiques, Joan, Witney, Oxon.
Windrush Antiques, Witney, Oxon.
Witney Antiques, Witney, Oxon.
Thistle House Antiques, Woodstock, Oxon.
Woodstock Antiques, Woodstock, Oxon.
Doveridge House of Neachley, Albrighton, Shrops.
Parmenter Antiques, Bridgnorth, Shrops.
Cave and Sons Ltd, R.G., Ludlow, Shrops.
Taylor (Antiques), M. and R., Ludlow, Shrops.
Teme Valley Antiques, Ludlow, Shrops.
Brown Antiques, David, Shrewsbury, Shrops.
Manser and Son Ltd, F.C., Shrewsbury, Shrops.
Moore Antiques, Marcus, Stanton, Shrops.
James Antiques, Brian, Telford, Shrops.
Onions - White Cottage Antiques, L., Tern Hill, Shrops.
Dodington Antiques, Whitchurch, Shrops.
Granary Galleries, The, Ash Priors, Somerset.
Hall's Antiques, Ash Priors, Somerset.
M.G.R. Exports, Bruton, Somerset.
Dyte Antiques, C. and R.I., Highbridge, Somerset.
Best Antiques, Ray, Ilminster, Somerset.

Moolham Mill Antiques, Ilminster, Somerset.
West End House Antiques, Ilminster, Somerset.
Cains Antiques, Littleton, Somerset.
Lewis, Gerald, Montacute, Somerset.
Keyford Antiques, Rode, Somerset.
Nowell, Edward A., Wells, Somerset.
Nowell, Marcus, Wells, Somerset.
Venn, Edward, Williton, Somerset.
Giddings, J.C., Wiveliscombe, Somerset.
Hamblin, John, Yeovil, Somerset.
Betley Court Gallery, Betley, Staffs.
Heart of England Antiques, Haunton, Staffs.
Midwinter Antiques, Richard, Newcastle-under-Lyme, Staffs.
Browse, Stafford, Staffs.
Potteries Antique Centre, The, Stoke-on-Trent, Staffs.
Tutbury Mill Antiques, Tutbury, Staffs.
Armson's of Yoxall Antiques, Yoxall, Staffs.
Thompson's Gallery, Aldeburgh, Suffolk.
Saltgate Antiques, Beccles, Suffolk.
Grant Antiques, Denzil, Bradfield St. George, Suffolk.
Country House Antiques, Bungay, Suffolk.
Peppers Period Pieces, Bury St. Edmunds, Suffolk.
Clare Collector, The, Clare, Suffolk.
Salter Antiques, F.D., Clare, Suffolk.
Bond's Manor Antiques, Grundisburgh, Suffolk.
Randolph, Hadleigh, Suffolk.
Sutcliffe, Gordon, Hadleigh, Suffolk.
Ashley Antiques, Ipswich, Suffolk.
Hubbard Antiques, Ipswich, Suffolk.
Weir Antiques, Gerald, Ipswich, Suffolk.
Baker, J. and J., Lavenham, Suffolk.
Leiston Furniture Warehouses, Leiston, Suffolk.
Carling and Tess Sinclair, Roger, Long Melford, Suffolk.
Chater-House Gallery, Long Melford, Suffolk.
Cooper Antiques, Bruno, Long Melford, Suffolk.
Lyall Antiques, Alexander, Long Melford, Suffolk.
Neptune Antiques, Long Melford, Suffolk.
Seabrook Antiques Ltd, Long Melford, Suffolk.
Suthburgh Antiques, Long Melford, Suffolk.
Ward Antiques plc, Long Melford, Suffolk.
Martlesham Antiques, Martlesham, Suffolk.
Palmer Antiques, Mary, Stradbroke, Suffolk.
Napier House Antiques, Sudbury, Suffolk.
Antique Furniture Warehouse, Woodbridge, Suffolk.
Carter Gallery, Simon, Woodbridge, Suffolk.
Gibbins Antiques, David, Woodbridge, Suffolk.
Hamilton Antiques, Woodbridge, Suffolk.
Hurst Antiques, Anthony, Woodbridge, Suffolk.
Meysey-Thompson Antiques, Sarah, Woodbridge, Suffolk.
Voss, A.G., Woodbridge, Suffolk.
Heather, J.C., Woolpit, Suffolk.
Wrentham Antiques, Wrentham, Suffolk.
John Anthony Antiques, Bletchingley, Surrey.
Marsh, Simon, Bletchingley, Surrey.
Bramley Antiques, Bramley, Surrey.
Pedlar, The, Camberley, Surrey.
Rogers Antiques and Rogers Antique Interiors, Cheam, Surrey.
Gasson Antiques and Interiors, Pat and Terry, Cranleigh, Surrey.
Dorking Desk Shop, Dorking, Surrey.
Dorking Emporium Antiques Centre, Dorking, Surrey.
Hantss of Dorking, Dorking, Surrey.
Holmwood Antiques, Dorking, Surrey.
Norfolk House Galleries Antique Centre, Dorking, Surrey.
Saunderson Antiques, Elaine, Dorking, Surrey.
Thorpe and Foster plc, Dorking, Surrey.
West Street Antiques, Dorking, Surrey.
Worth Antiques, Patrick, Dorking, Surrey.
Gould and Sons (Antiques) Ltd, A.E., East Horsley, Surrey.
Cranleigh Antiques, Ewhurst, Surrey.
Christopher's Antiques, Farnham, Surrey.
Heytesbury Antiques, Farnham, Surrey.
Heath-Bullocks, Godalming, Surrey.
Bookham Galleries, Great Bookham, Surrey.
Bowdery, M. J., Hindhead, Surrey.
Oriel Antiques, Hindhead, Surrey.
Glencorse Antiques, Kingston-upon-Thames, Surrey.
Knaphill Antiques, Knaphill, Surrey.
Andrews Antiques, Michael, Milford, Surrey.
Addison Antiques, Michael, Purley, Surrey.
Lawrence and Sons, F.G., Redhill, Surrey.

SPECIALIST DEALERS

Antique Mart, Richmond, Surrey.
Hill Rise Antiques, Richmond, Surrey.
Lawson Antiques, F. and T., Richmond, Surrey.
Layton Antiques, Richmond, Surrey.
Marryat, Richmond, Surrey.
Rowan Antiques, Richmond, Surrey.
Hartley Antiques Ltd, J., Ripley, Surrey.
Ripley Antiques, Ripley, Surrey.
Sage Antiques and Interiors, Ripley, Surrey.
Cockrell Antiques, Surbiton, Surrey.
Newlove, B. M., Surbiton, Surrey.
Caldwell, Ian, Walton-on-the-Hill and Tadworth, Surrey.
Westcott Antiques, Westcott, Surrey.
Church House Antiques, Weybridge, Surrey.
Hatch Antiques, Weybridge, Surrey.
Saunders, R., Weybridge, Surrey.
Country Antiques, Windlesham, Surrey.
Alexandria Antiques, Brighton, Sussex East.
Brighton Antique Wholesalers, Brighton, Sussex East.
Carmichael, P., Brighton, Sussex East.
Cowen Antiques, Christopher G., Brighton, Sussex East.
Fitchett Antiques, Alan, Brighton, Sussex East.
Hume, Dudley, Brighton, Sussex East.
Norman Antiques Ltd, Michael, Brighton, Sussex East.
Ponting Antiques, Ben, Brighton, Sussex East.
Yellow Lantern Antiques Ltd, Brighton, Sussex East.
Dycheling Antiques, Ditchling, Sussex East.
Botting Antiques, John, Horam, Sussex East.
Pigeon House Antiques, Hurst Green, Sussex East.
Cato, Lennox, Lewes, Sussex East.
Charleston Antiques, Lewes, Sussex East.
Dennison and Son, H.P., Lewes, Sussex East.
Green, Renée and Roy, Lewes, Sussex East.
Trevor, Lewes, Sussex East.
De Montfort, Robertsbridge, Sussex East.
Trade Wind, Rottingdean, Sussex East.
Bragge and Sons, Rye, Sussex East.
Gasson, Herbert Gordon, Rye, Sussex East.
Rye Antiques, Rye, Sussex East.
Old House, The, Seaford, Sussex East.
Aarquebus Antiques, St. Leonards-on-Sea, Sussex East.
Ringles Cross Antiques, Uckfield, Sussex East.
Bygones, Angmering, Sussex West.
Country Life by Bursig, Arundel, Sussex West.
Gordon, Phyllis, Arundel, Sussex West.
Antique Shop, Chichester, Sussex West.
Foord-Brown Antiques, David, Cuckfield, Sussex West.
Hopkins, John, Cuckfield, Sussex West.
Usher Antiques, Richard, Cuckfield, Sussex West.
Hinsdale Antiques, East Grinstead, Sussex West.
Callingham Antiques, N. and S., Northchapel, Sussex West.
Baskerville Antiques, Petworth, Sussex West.
Cooper Antiques, Philip, Petworth, Sussex West.
Cracknell (Antiques) Ltd, Nigel, Petworth, Sussex West.
Granville Antiques, Petworth, Sussex West.
Hockley Antiques, William, Petworth, Sussex West.
Hopkins, John, Petworth, Sussex West.
Madison Gallery, The, Petworth, Sussex West.
Morris, John G., Petworth, Sussex West.
Tutt Antiques, J.C., Petworth, Sussex West.
Wakelin and Helen Linfield, Michael, Petworth, Sussex West.
Wilkinson Antiques Ltd, T.G., Petworth, Sussex West.
Powell (Hove) Ltd, J., Portslade, Sussex West.
Thakeham Furniture, Storrington, Sussex West.
Loewenthal Antiques, Tillington, Sussex West.
Cheriton Antiques, Worthing, Sussex West.
Wilsons Antiques, Worthing, Sussex West.
Crown Antiques, Bidford-on-Avon, Warks.
Marsh, Jasper, Henley-in-Arden, Warks.
Venables, Jeremy, Kineton, Warks.
Olive Green Ltd, Leamington Spa, Warks.
Apollo Antiques Ltd, Warwick, Warks.
Bolton, John, Warwick, Warks.
Morley Antiques, Patrick and Gillian, Warwick, Warks.
Reeve, James, Warwick, Warks.
Westgate Antiques, Warwick, Warks.
Ashleigh House Antiques, Birmingham, West Mids.
Clark Antiques, Peter, Birmingham, West Mids.
Harris and Sons, Antiques, Bob, Birmingham, West Mids.
Hubbard Antiques, John, Birmingham, West Mids.
Old Bakehouse, The, Birmingham, West Mids.
Hassall Antiques, Geoffrey, Solihull, West Mids.
Coulborn and Sons, Thomas, Sutton Coldfield, West Mids.
Ghiberti Antiques and Fine Art, Wolverhampton, West Mids.
Martin-Quick Antiques, Wolverhampton, West Mids.
Wakeman and Taylor Antiques, Wolverhampton, West Mids.
Avon Antiques, Bradford-on-Avon, Wilts.
Harp Antiques, Bradford-on-Avon, Wilts.
Moxhams Antiques, Bradford-on-Avon, Wilts.
Harley Antiques, Christian Malford, Wilts.
Eden, Matthew, Corsham, Wilts.
Britten Antiques, Andrew, Malmesbury, Wilts.
Cross Hayes Antiques, Malmesbury, Wilts.
Dovetail Antiques, Malmesbury, Wilts.
Antique and Book Collector, The, Marlborough, Wilts.
Cracknell (Antiques) Ltd, Nigel, Marlborough, Wilts.
Kime Antiques, Robert, Marlborough, Wilts.
Jaffray, Alan, Melksham, Wilts.
Gentle Antiques, Rupert, Milton Lilbourne, Wilts.
Bradley, Robert, Salisbury, Wilts.
Hastie, Ian G., Salisbury, Wilts.
Hurst Antiques, Edward, Salisbury, Wilts.
St. John Street Gallery, Salisbury, Wilts.
Marnier Antiques, Edward, Tisbury, Wilts.
Pearson Antiques, Carol, Tisbury, Wilts.
Bishopstrow Antiques, Warminster, Wilts.
Houghton Antiques, Peter, Warminster, Wilts.
Romain and Sons, A.J., Wilton, Wilts.
Galloway Antiques, Boroughbridge, Yorks North.
Graham Antiques, Anthony, Boroughbridge, Yorks North .
St. James House Antiques, Boroughbridge, Yorks North.
Wilson and Sons, R.S., Boroughbridge, Yorks North.
Greenwood Antiques, Simon, Burneston, Yorks North.
Bow Antiques, Easingwold, Yorks North.
Elm Tree Antiques, Flaxton, Yorks North.
Dickinson, Bernard, Gargrave, Yorks North.
Myers Galleries, Gargrave, Yorks North.
Armstrong, Harrogate, Yorks North.
Daffern Antiques, John, Harrogate, Yorks North.
Derbys Antiques Ltd, Harrogate, Yorks North.
Garth Antiques, Harrogate, Yorks North.
Haworth Antiques, Harrogate, Yorks North.
Love, David, Harrogate, Yorks North.
Lumb and Sons Ltd, Charles, Harrogate, Yorks North.
Thorntons of Harrogate, Harrogate, Yorks North.
Walker Galleries Ltd, Harrogate, Yorks North.
Windmill Antiques, Harrogate, Yorks North.
Holgate, Milton J., Knaresborough, Yorks North.
Trade Antiques - D.D. White, Manfield, Yorks North.
Daleside Antiques, Markington, Yorks North.
Aura Antiques, Masham, Yorks North.
White Boar Antiques and Books, Middleham, Yorks North.
Brown's Antiques, Richmond, Yorks North.
Sigma Antiques and Fine Art, Ripon, Yorks North.
Browns Antiques, Scarborough, Yorks North.
Folly Antiques, Settle, Yorks North.
Milnthorpe, H.I., Settle, Yorks North.
Dodsworth, N.J. and C.S., Spennithorne, Yorks North.
Ogleby, B., Thirsk, Yorks North.
Tomlinson (Antiques) Ltd. and Period Furniture Ltd, Raymond, Tockwith, Yorks North.
Mount Antiques, The, Whitby, Yorks North.
Garth Antiques, Whixley, Yorks North.
Morrison and Son, Robert, York, Yorks North.
Goddard Antiques, Julie, Oughtibridge, Yorks South.
Jameson and Co, A.E., Sheffield, Yorks South.
Peter James Antiques, Sheffield, Yorks South.
Turn of the Century, Sheffield, Yorks South.
Berry Antiques, Peter, Huddersfield, Yorks West.
Burrows and Raper, Ilkley, Yorks West.
Cooper and Son (Ilkley) Ltd, J.H., Ilkley, Yorks West.
Simon, Ilkley, Yorks West.
Barleycote Hall Antiques, Keighley, Yorks West.
Geary Antiques, Leeds, Yorks West.
Windsor House Antiques (Leeds) Ltd., Leeds, Yorks West.
Park Antiques, Menston, Yorks West.
Carlton Antiques, Saltaire, Yorks West.
Victoria Antiques, Alderney, C. I.
Blower Antiques, Mark, St. Martin, Guernsey, C. I.
Grange Antiques, St. Peter Port, Guernsey, C. I.
Proctor Antiques, David, St. Peter Port, Guernsey, C. I.
St. James's Gallery Ltd, St. Peter Port, Guernsey, C.I.
Drury Antiques, Anne, Vale, Guernsey, C. I.
Antique Shop, Ballyclare, Co. Antrim, N. Ireland.

SPECIALIST DEALERS

Dunluce Antiques, Bushmills, Co. Antrim, N. Ireland.
Furney Antiques and Interiors, Donaghadee, Co. Down, N. Ireland.
Downshire House Antiques, Newry, Co. Down, N. Ireland.
Antiques and Fine Art Gallery, Warrenpoint, Co. Down, N. Ireland.
Hagan, K.O., Claudy, Co. Londonderry, N. Ireland.
Wood (Antiques) Ltd, Colin, Aberdeen, Scotland.
Young Antiques & Fine Art, William, Aberdeen, Scotland.
Bell of Aberdeen Ltd, John, Banchory, Scotland.
Beaty, T.W., Beattock, Scotland.
Stewart Antiques, Michael, Coatbridge, Scotland.
Coldstream Antiques, Coldstream, Scotland.
Sangster Antiques, A., Cruden Bay, Scotland.
Hillfoot Antiques, Dollar, Scotland.
Antiquarian, The, Dumfries, Scotland.
Dunkeld Interiors, Dunkeld, Scotland.
Black Ltd, Laurance, Edinburgh, Scotland.
Davidson and Begg Antiques Ltd, Edinburgh, Scotland.
Dunedin Antiques Ltd, Edinburgh, Scotland.
Georgian Antiques, Edinburgh Scotland.
Jackson, Kenneth, Edinburgh, Scotland.
Mulherron Antiques, Edinburgh, Scotland.
Stockbridge Antiques and Fine Art, Edinburgh, Scotland.
Whytock and Reid, Edinburgh, Scotland.
Worthington's Antiques, Edinburgh, Scotland.
Young, Aldric, Edinburgh, Scotland.
Errol Antiques, Errol, Scotland.
Greycroft Antiques, Errol, Scotland.
Albany Antiques, Glasgow, Scotland.
Butler's Furniture Galleries Ltd, Glasgow, Scotland.
Muirhead Moffat and Co, Glasgow, Scotland.
Houndwood House Antiques, Houndwood, Scotland.
Moreton (Antiques), C.S., Inchture, Scotland.
Kilmacolm Antiques Ltd, Kilmacolm, Scotland.
Rhudle Mill, Kilmichael Glassary, Scotland.
Harper-James, Montrose, Scotland.
Crossroads Antiques, Prestwick, Scotland.
Ainslie Antiques, Robert, Scone, Scotland.
Magpie, St. Andrews, Scotland.
Waverley Antiques, Upper Largo, Scotland.
Davies, Norman, Holt, Clwyd, Wales.
Langford, J. and R., Llangollen, Clwyd, Wales.
Finlay Antiques, K.W., Ciliau Aeron, Dyfed, Wales.
Country Antiques, Kidwelly, Dyfed, Wales.
Barn Court Antiques, Narberth, Dyfed, Wales.
Castle Antiques, Newcastle Emlyn, Dyfed, Wales.
Clareston Antiques, Tenby, Dyfed, Wales.
Renaissance Antiques, Cowbridge, South Glam., Wales.
Aspley Antiques and Reproductions Ltd., Barmouth, Gwynedd, Wales.
Madoc Antiques and Art Gallery, Llandudno, Gwynedd, Wales.
Wigington Antiques, Hay-on-Wye, Powys, Wales.
Anderson and Son, F.E., Welshpool, Powys, Wales.
School House Antiques, Welshpool, Powys, Wales.

Furniture - Oak (Prior to 1700)

Helm Antiques, Linda, London, N1.
Csaky's Antiques, London, SW1.
Furniture Cave, London, SW10.
Christopher Antiques, London, SW11.
Young Antiques, Robert, London, SW11.
McDonald, Joy, London, SW13.
Apter Fredericks Ltd, London, SW3.
Booth, Joanna, London, SW3.
Sampson Antiques Ltd, Alistair, London, SW3.
Tron Antiques, David, London, SW3.
Sanders and Sons, Robin, London, SW6.
Stanton, Louis, London, W11.
Seager Antiques Ltd, Arthur, London, W8.
Dux Antiques, Frank, Bath, Avon.
Green Farm Antiques, Olveston, Avon.
Bently Antiques, Pat, Ampthill, Beds.
Stapleton's Antiques, Bedford, Beds.
Fenlan Antiques, Turvey, Beds.
Baker Antiques, John, Newbury, Berks.
Csaky's Antiques, Sonning-on-Thames, Berks.
Bartram, Albert, Chesham, Bucks.
Overland Antiques, John, Olney, Bucks.
Lennard Antiques, Tingewick, Bucks.

Rumble Antiques, Simon and Penny, Chittering, Cambs.
Davidson Antiques, Neil, Chester, Cheshire.
Melody's Antique Galleries, Chester, Cheshire.
Bunting Antiques, Peter, Hyde, Cheshire.
Boyer Antiques, Rex, Nantwich, Cheshire.
Pillory House, Nantwich, Cheshire.
Arden Antiques, Brenda, Tarporley, Cheshire.
Langley Antiques, Corby Hill, Cumbria.
Jennywell Hall Antiques, Crosby Ravensworth, Cumbria.
Kendal Studios Antiques, Kendal, Cumbria.
Cothay Antiques, Maulds Meaburn, Cumbria.
Shire Antiques, Newby Bridge, Cumbria.
Antiques of Penrith, Penrith, Cumbria.
Adams Antiques, Yvonne, Ashbourne, Derbys.
Beedham Antiques Ltd, Bakewell, Derbys.
Goldstone, Michael, Bakewell, Derbys.
Dean Antiques, G.L., Glossop, Derbys.
Byles, Robert, Bampton, Devon.
Collins and Son, J., Bideford, Devon.
Thomas and James Antiques, Bovey Tracey, Devon.
Meredith, John, Chagford, Devon.
Cullompton Old Tannery Antiques, Cullompton, Devon.
Taylor-Halsey Antiques, Drewsteignton, Devon.
Priory Antiques, Exeter, Devon.
Gilmore Antiques, Elizabeth, Honiton, Devon.
Warehouse Antiques, Honiton, Devon.
Wickham Antiques, Honiton, Devon.
Bagnall, W., Moretonhampstead, Devon.
Colystock Antiques, Stockland, Devon.
Chancery Antiques, Tiverton, Devon.
Hennessy, Beaminster, Dorset.
Collector, The, Barnard Castle, Durham.
Bennet (Antiques), Julia, Dunmow, Essex.
Mortimer and Son, C. and J., Great Chesterford, Essex.
Millers Antiques Kelvedon, Kelvedon, Essex.
Freeman Antiques, Roxwell, Essex.
Sumner, Jane, Saffron Walden, Essex.
Thaxted Galleries, Thaxted, Essex.
Turpin's Antiques, Thaxted, Essex.
Bateman Antiques, J. and R., Chalford, Glos.
School House Antiques, Chipping Campden, Glos.
Forum Antiques, Cirencester, Glos.
Stokes, William H., Cirencester, Glos.
Gloucester House Antiques Ltd, Fairford, Glos.
Baggott, Duncan J., Stow-on-the-Wold, Glos.
Caspall Antiques, J. and J., Stow-on-the-Wold, Glos.
Hockin (Antiques) Ltd, Keith, Stow-on-the-Wold, Glos.
Norden Antiques, Peter, Stow-on-the-Wold, Glos.
Priests Antiques, Stow-on-the-Wold, Glos.
Touchwood International, Stow-on-the-Wold, Glos.
Day Antiques, Ann and Roger, Tetbury, Glos.
Close Antiques, Alresford, Hants.
Quatrefoil, Fordingbridge, Hants.
Cedar Antiques, Hartley Wintney, Hants.
Viney, Elizabeth, Stockbridge, Hants.
Regency House Antiques, Whitchurch, Hants.
Keil Ltd, H.W., Broadway, Herefs and Worcs.
Eddy, P. and S.N., Leominster, Herefs and Worcs.
Hubbard Antiques, Leominster, Herefs and Worcs.
La Barre Ltd, Leominster, Herefs and Worcs.
Lloyd Antiques, Robin, Ross-on-Wye, Herefs and Worcs.
Russell, M. and J., Yazor, Herefs and Worcs.
Dobson's Antiques, Abbots Langley, Herts.
Phillips of Hitchin (Antiques) Ltd, Hitchin, Herts.
Wharton Antiques, Tim, Redbourn, Herts.
Collins Antiques (F.G. and C. Collins Ltd.), Wheathampstead, Herts.
Kirby Antiques, R., Acrise, Kent.
Stoodley, Dinah, Brasted, Kent.
Pearson Antiques, Michael, Canterbury, Kent.
Old Bakery Antiques, The, Cranbrook, Kent.
Swan Antiques, Cranbrook, Kent.
Farnborough (Kent) Antiques, Farnborough, Kent.
Warren Antiques, Jimmy, Littlebourne, Kent.
Baines, Henry, Southborough, Kent.
Jackson-Grant Antiques, Teynham, Kent.
Cowden Antiques, Tunbridge Wells, Kent.
Old Hall (Sphinx Gallery), Westerham, Kent.
Starkie Antiques, Simon, Lancaster, Lancs.
Baron Antiques, The, Manchester, Lancs.
Lowe of Loughborough, Loughborough, Leics.
Johnston, Paul, Gedney, Lincs.

Cox Antiques, Robin, Stamford, Lincs.
Sinclair, John, Stamford, Lincs.
St. Mary's Galleries, Stamford, Lincs.
Lukies, Pearse, Aylsham, Norfolk.
Brett and Sons Ltd, Arthur, Norwich, Norfolk.
Queen of Hungary Antiques, Norwich, Norfolk.
Hopwell Antiques, Paul, West Haddon, Northants.
Cheshire, E.M., Bingham, Notts.
Antiques and General Trading Co, Nottingham, Notts.
Carter Antiques, Mark, Bladon, Oxon.
Horseshoe Antiques and Gallery, Burford, Oxon.
Swan Gallery, Burford, Oxon.
Bugle Antiques, Chipping Norton, Oxon.
Key Antiques, Chipping Norton, Oxon.
Stroud Antiques, Peter, Chipping Norton, Oxon.
Windrush Antiques, Witney, Oxon.
Witney Antiques, Witney, Oxon.
Moore Antiques, Marcus, Stanton, Shrops.
Onions - White Cottage Antiques, L., Tern Hill, Shrops.
Whitney Antiques, Robert, Whitchurch, Shrops.
Stuart Interiors (Antiques) Ltd, Barrington, Somerset.
Moolham Mill Antiques, Ilminster, Somerset.
Genges Farm Antiques, Limington, Somerset.
Milverton Antiques, Milverton, Somerset.
King's Farm Antiques, Shapwick, Somerset.
Morley Antiques, William, West Monkton, Somerset.
Sainsbury, Barry M., Wincanton, Somerset.
Nicholls, John, Leigh, Staffs.
Midwinter Antiques, Richard, Newcastle-under-Lyme, Staffs.
Peppers Period Pieces, Bury St. Edmunds, Suffolk.
Agnus, Clare, Suffolk.
Clare Collector, The, Clare, Suffolk.
Salter Antiques, F.D., Clare, Suffolk.
Baker, J. and J., Lavenham, Suffolk.
Mercer Antiques, Noel, Long Melford, Suffolk.
Seabrook Antiques Ltd, Long Melford, Suffolk.
Simpson, Oswald, Long Melford, Suffolk.
Suthburgh Antiques, Long Melford, Suffolk.
Carter Gallery, Simon, Woodbridge, Suffolk.
Hurst Antiques, Anthony, Woodbridge, Suffolk.
Lang Antiques, John, Dorking, Surrey.
Sage Antiques and Interiors, Ripley, Surrey.
Welling Antiques, Anthony, Ripley, Surrey.
Newlove, B. M., Surbiton, Surrey.
Saunders, R., Weybridge, Surrey.
Westcott Antiques, Westcott, Surrey.
White, E. and B., Brighton, Sussex East.
Lower, Graham, Flimwell, Sussex East.
Gasson, Herbert Gordon, Rye, Sussex East.
Georgian House Antiques, Uckfield, Sussex East.
Park View Antiques, Wadhurst, Sussex East.
Country Life by Bursig, Arundel, Sussex West.
Chapman Antiques, Mark, Bosham, Sussex West.
Cooper Antiques, Philip, Petworth, Sussex West.
Cracknell (Antiques) Ltd, Nigel, Petworth, Sussex West.
Frith Antiques, Petworth, Sussex West.
Griffin Antiques, Petworth, Sussex West.
Humphry Antiques, Petworth, Sussex West.
Marsh, Jasper, Henley-in-Arden, Warks.
Spa Antiques, Leamington Spa, Warks.
Reeve, James, Warwick, Warks.
Monkton Galleries, Hindon, Wilts.
Dovetail Antiques, Malmesbury, Wilts.
Walwyn Antiques, Howard, Wootton Bassett, Wilts.
Chapman Medd and Sons, Easingwold, Yorks North.
Dickinson, Bernard, Gargrave, Yorks North.
Myers Galleries, Gargrave, Yorks North.
Bentley, Bill, Harrogate, Yorks North.
Derbyshire Antiques Ltd, Harrogate, Yorks North.
Phillips Antiques Ltd, Elaine, Harrogate, Yorks North.
York Cottage Antiques, Helmsley, Yorks North.
Crown Square Antiques, Kirkbymoorside, Yorks North.
Folly Antiques, Settle, Yorks North.
Precious, Roy, Settle, Yorks North.
Coach House Antiques, Whitby, Yorks North.
Mount Antiques, The, Whitby, Yorks North.
Wilson, Timothy D., Bawtry, Yorks South.
Clark, Robert, Micklebring, Yorks South.
Batty's Antiques, Leeds, Yorks West.
Frere Antiques, Joan, Drumnadrochit, Scotland.
Strathspey Gallery, Grantown-on-Spey, Scotland.
Trefor Antiques, John, Rhuallt, Clwyd, Wales.

Jansons Antiques, Bwlchllan, Dyfed, Wales.
Cwmgwili Mill, Carmarthen, Dyfed, Wales.

Furniture - Pine

Simply Capital, London, E18.
At the Sign of the Chest of Drawers, London, N1.
Islington Antiques, London, N1.
Lewis Antiques, Michael, London, N1.
Rookery Farm Antiques, London, N1.
Trader Antiques, London, N13.
Adams Antiques, London, NW1.
Hearth and Home, London, NW1.
This and That (Furniture), London, NW1.
Barewood Company, The, London, NW6.
Main Street Antiques, London, SE10.
Under Milkwood, London, SE24.
Abbott Antiques and Country Pine (formerly Olwen Carthew), London, SE26.
Ning Ltd, London, SW1.
Furniture Cave, London, SW10.
Original Remember When, The, London, SW13.
Yesterday's Antiques, London, SW14.
Woodentops Country Furniture, London, SW18.
Antique Mews, The, London, SW19.
Bishops Park Antiques, London, SW6.
Old Pine, London, SW6.
Pine Mine (Crewe-Read Antiques), The, London, SW6.
Beech, Nicholas, London, SW8.
Scallywag, London, SW9.
Andy's All Pine, London, W14.
Old Dairy, The, London, W4.
Old Pine Shop, The, London, W5.
Terrace Antiques, London, W5.
Lansdown Antiques, Bath, Avon.
Pennard House Antiques, Bath, Avon.
Widcombe Antiques and Pine, Bath, Avon.
Oldwoods, Bristol, Avon.
Relics - Pine Furniture, Bristol, Avon.
Bay Tree House Antiques, Weston-Super-Mare, Avon.
Pine Parlour, The, Ampthill, Beds.
Willow Farm Pine Centre, Harlington, Beds.
Ivy House Antiques, Great Shefford, Berks.
Bye Antiques, Ann, Reading, Berks.
Kimbell, Richard, Thatcham, Berks.
Flappers, Buckingham, Bucks.
For Pine, Chesham, Bucks.
Pine Merchants, The, Great Missenden, Bucks.
Pine Reflections, Hughenden Valley, Bucks.
Bach Antiques, Lane End, Bucks.
Pine Antiques, Olney, Bucks.
Cambridge Pine, Bottisham, Cambs.
Strover, Barry, Cambridge, Cambs.
Abbey Antiques, Ramsey, Cambs.
Midloe Grange Antiques and Design, Southoe, Cambs.
Wilding, R., Wisbech, Cambs.
Brook Lane Antiques, Alderley Edge, Cheshire.
City Strippers, Chester, Cheshire.
Richmond Galleries, Chester, Cheshire.
Pine Too, Congleton, Cheshire.
Blackhurst, Steven, Crewe, Cheshire.
Take-a-Seat, Macclesfield, Cheshire.
Chapel Antiques, Nantwich, Cheshire.
Pine and Period Furniture, Grampound, Cornwall.
Pine and Country Antiques, North Petherwin, Cornwall.
Pinewood Studio, Penzance, Cornwall.
Blackwater Pine Antiques, Truro, Cornwall.
Pydar Antiques and Gallery, Truro, Cornwall.
Utopia Antiques Ltd, Bowness-on-Windermere, Cumbria.
Corney House Antiques, Penrith, Cumbria.
Friargate Pine and Antiques Centre, Derby, Derbys.
Tanglewood, Derby, Derbys.
Pine Antiques, Doveridge, Derbys.
Allcroft Antiques, Michael, Hayfield, Derbys.
Gravelly Bank Pine Antiques, Yeaveley, Derbys.
Byles, Robert, Bampton, Devon.
Barnstaple Antique Centre, Barnstaple, Devon.
Petticombe Manor Antiques, Bideford, Devon.
Brookfield Gallery, Colyton, Devon.
Cobweb Antiques, Cullompton, Devon.
Cullompton Old Tannery Antiques, Cullompton, Devon.
Sunset Country Antiques, Cullompton, Devon.

SPECIALIST DEALERS

Baldwin Antiques, Peter J., Drewsteignton, Devon.
Mounter, G., Dulford, Devon.
Wooden Fleece, Exmouth, Devon.
Warehouse Antiques, Honiton, Devon.
Sextons, Kentisbeare, Devon.
Annterior Antiques, Plymouth, Devon.
M. & A. Antique Exporters, Plymouth, Devon.
Great Western Pine, South Molton, Devon.
South Molton Antiques, South Molton, Devon.
Colystock Antiques, Stockland, Devon.
King Street Curios, Tavistock, Devon.
Chancery Antiques, Tiverton, Devon.
Rocking Horse Pine, Torquay, Devon.
Fine Pine Antiques, Totnes, Devon.
Hennessy, Beaminster, Dorset.
Antiques and Furnishings, Bournemouth, Dorset.
Westdale Antiques, Bridport, Dorset.
Hardy Country, Melbury Osmond, Dorset.
Overhill Antique and Old Pine Warehouse, Poole, Dorset.
Castleton Country Furniture, Sherborne, Dorset.
Pine on the Green, Sherborne, Dorset.
Hay Green Antiques, Blackmore, Essex.
Antique Pine, Coggeshall, Essex.
Dean Antiques, Margery, Colchester, Essex.
Tate, Andrew, Finchingfield, Essex.
Stores, The, Great Waltham, Essex.
Churchgate Antiques, Sible Hedingham, Essex.
Fox and Pheasant Antique Pine, White Colne, Essex.
Verey, Denzil, Barnsley, Glos.
Bed of Roses, Cheltenham, Glos.
Townsend, John P., Cheltenham, Glos.
Campden Country Pine, Chipping Campden, Glos.
Waterloo Antiques, Cirencester, Glos.
Antique Pine, Norton, Glos.
Country Living, Painswick, Glos.
Kelly Antiques, Rodley, Glos.
Country Homes, Tetbury, Glos.
Elgin House Antiques, Tetbury, Glos.
Rudge Antics, Tetbury, Glos.
Pinecrafts, Bishops Waltham, Hants.
Butterfly Pine, Botley, Hants.
Buckingham, C.W., Cadnam, Hants.
Prospect Antiques, Crawley, Hants.
Airdale Antiques, Hartley Wintney, Hants.
Pine Collection, Liss, Hants.
Burgess Farm Antiques, Morestead, Hants.
Pine Company, Ringwood, Hants.
Pine Cellars, The, Winchester, Hants.
Hi-Felicity, Kidderminster, Herefs and Worcs.
La Barre Ltd, Leominster, Herefs and Worcs.
St. James Antiques, Little Malvern, Herefs and Worcs.
S.W. Antiques, Pershore, Herefs and Worcs.
Old Pine Shop, Ross-on-Wye, Herefs and Worcs.
Antique Warehouse, Worcester, Herefs and Worcs.
Dobson's Antiques, Abbots Langley, Herts.
Porter, Arthur, Baldock, Herts.
Wiskin Antiques, Bishops Stortford, Herts.
Country Life Antiques, Bushey, Herts.
Kimbell, Richard, Codicote, Herts.
Frenches Farm Antiques, King's Langley, Herts.
Smith and Smith Designs, Driffield, Humbs North.
Boothferry Antiques, Hull, Humbs North.
Imperial Antiques, Hull, Humbs North.
Wilson Ltd, Paul, Hull, Humbs North.
Plantenga, Pieter, Market Weighton, Humbs North.
Bell Antiques, Grimsby, Humbs South.
Galerias Segui, Cowes, I. of Wight.
Scallywag, Beckenham, Kent.
Antique and Design, Canterbury, Kent.
Pine and Things, Canterbury, Kent.
Swan Antiques, Cranbrook, Kent.
Country Pine Antiques Co, The, Cuxton, Kent.
Lampard, Penny, Headcorn, Kent.
Traditional Furniture, Hythe, Kent.
Ash House, Ramsgate, Kent.
Old English Pine, Sandgate, Kent.
Empire Antiques, Sandwich, Kent.
Moate Antiques, Richard, Smeeth, Kent.
Antique Pine Shop, The, Tunbridge Wells, Kent.
Treasures of Woodchurch, Woodchurch, Kent.
Blackpool Antiques Centre, Blackpool, Lancs.
Christian, Ann and Peter, Blackpool, Lancs.

Pine Dresser, The, Blackpool, Lancs.
Phillips (Antiques), Edward V., Clayton-le-Moors, Lancs.
Enloc Antiques, Colne, Lancs.
Gregory's Antique Pine, Helmshore, Rossendale, Lancs.
G.W. Antiques, Lancaster, Lancs.
Starkie Antiques, Simon, Lancaster, Lancs.
Kitchenalia, Longridge, Lancs.
Clifton Antiques, Lytham, Lancs.
Revival Pine Stripping, Ormskirk, Lancs.
Pine Antiques, St. Annes-on-Sea, Lancs.
Burley Workshop, Burley-oh-the-Hill, Leics.
House Things Antiques, Hinckley, Leics.
Victoriana Architectural, Long Clawston, Leics.
Country Antiques, Market Bosworth, Leics.
Kimbell Ltd, Richard, Market Harborough, Leics.
Burrows, David E., Osgathorpe, Leics.
Quorn Pine and Decoratives, Quorn, Leics.
James Antiques, R. A., Sileby, Leics.
Old Bakehouse Pine, Whissendine, Leics.
Kent Antiques, Robert J., Frampton West, Lincs.
Kate, Hemswell Cliff, Lincs.
Talisman Antiques, Horncastle, Lincs.
Warehouse, The, Horncastle, Lincs.
Designs on Pine, Lincoln, Lincs.
Sykes Antiques, North Kelsey Moor, Lincs.
Thomas, Andrew, Stamford, Lincs.
Allens Antiques, Stapleford, Lincs.
Tealby Pine, Wragby, Lincs.
Delta Antiques, Liverpool, Merseyside.
Fine Pine, Southport, Merseyside.
Pinocchio, Southport, Merseyside.
Kimbell, Richard, Enfield, Middx.
Valtone Pine, Hampton, Middx.
Earsham Hall Pine, Earsham, Norfolk.
Ninety-One, Norwich, Norfolk.
Queen of Hungary Antiques, Norwich, Norfolk.
Goodwin Exports, Nick, Guilsborough, Northants.
Laila, Kingsthorpe, Northants.
Country Pine Shop, The, West Haddon, Northants.
Corner Cupboard, The, Woodford Halse, Northants.
Country Pine Antiques, Alnwick, Northumbs.
Country Pine Antiques, Chatton, Northumbs.
Haydon Bridge Antiques, Haydon Bridge, Northumbs.
Adamson Antique Stripped Pine, Joyce, Ministeracres, Northumbs.
Spratt Antiques, Jack, Newark, Notts.
Station Pine Antiques, Nottingham, Notts.
Tuckers Country Store and Art Gallery, Deddington, Oxon.
Country Pine Antiques, Witney, Oxon.
Civic Antiques, Whitchurch, Shrops.
Mendip Pine and Antiques, Chilcompton, Somerset.
Antique and Country Pine, Crewkerne, Somerset.
Pennard House, East Pennard, Somerset.
Chalon U.K. Ltd, Hambridge, Somerset.
Genges Farm Antiques, Limington, Somerset.
Westville House Antiques, Littleton, Somerset.
Baytree House Antiques, Lympsham, Somerset.
Milverton Antiques, Milverton, Somerset.
Burton Antiques, Burton-on-Trent, Staffs.
Pinewood, Justin, Burton-on-Trent, Staffs.
Country Cottage Interiors, Kingsley, Staffs.
Anvil Antiques, Leek, Staffs.
Aspleys Antiques and Reproductions Ltd, Leek, Staffs.
Directmoor Ltd, Leek, Staffs.
Gemini Trading, Leek, Staffs.
Haynes - Antiques Finder, Roger, Leek, Staffs.
Johnson's, Leek, Staffs.
Town and Country Antiques, Tutbury, Staffs.
Guillemot, Aldeburgh, Suffolk.
Brantham Mill Antiques, Brantham, Suffolk.
Hardy Pine and Country Furniture, Joyce, Hacheston, Suffolk.
Blyth Bygones, Halesworth, Suffolk.
Orwell Galleries, Ipswich, Suffolk.
Orwell Paint Strippers, Ipswich, Suffolk.
Carlton Road Antiques, Lowestoft, Suffolk.
Hunt and Clement, Mildenhall, Suffolk.
House of Christian Antiques, Ash Vale, Surrey.
Cherub Antiques, Carshalton, Surrey.
Antics, Cobham, Surrey.
Ockley Antiques, Dorking, Surrey.
Owl House, The, Dorking, Surrey.

Fogg Antiques, Epsom, Surrey.
Putnam, R. and M., Farnham, Surrey.
Village Pine, Farnham, Surrey.
Wrecclesham Antiques, Farnham, Surrey.
Pine Shop, The, Merrow, Surrey.
Cherub Antiques, Mitcham, Surrey.
Ockley Antiques, Ockley, Surrey.
Country Furniture, Richmond, Surrey.
Packhouse, The, Runfold, Surrey.
Yesterdays Pine, Shere, Surrey.
Venture, The, Woking, Surrey.
Touchwood, Herstmonceux, Sussex East.
Bird Antiques, John, Lewes, Sussex East.
Hoare Pine Antiques, Bob, Lewes, Sussex East.
Pastorale Antiques, Lewes, Sussex East.
Sautter Pine Furniture, Mary, Lewes, Sussex East.
Price Antiques Ltd, Graham, Polegate, Sussex East.
Lingard - Rope Walk Antiques, Ann, Rye, Sussex East.
Park View Antiques, Wadhurst, Sussex East.
Pine and Design, Balcombe, Sussex West.
Squires Pantry Antiques, Cowfold, Sussex West.
Hamilton, Sheelagh, Fernhurst, Sussex West.
Grove House Antiques, Petworth, Sussex West.
Brocante, Rudgwick, Sussex West.
Northumbria Pine, Whitley Bay, Tyne and Wear.
Hague Antiques, Leamington Spa, Warks.
Pine and Things, Shipston-on-Stour, Warks.
Pine Design, Warwick, Warks.
Fine Pine, Birmingham, West Mids.
Old Bakehouse, The, Birmingham, West Mids.
L.P. Furniture (Mids) Ltd, Pelsall, West Mids.
Sambourne House Antiques, Minety, Wilts.
Coggins Antiques, Ray, Westbury, Wilts.
Ward and Son, L.L., Brandsby, Yorks North.
Country Pine Antiques, Brompton, Yorks North.
Heathcote Antiques, Cross Hills, Yorks North.
Main Pine Co, The, Green Hammerton, Yorks North.
Fox's Antique Pine and Country Furniture, Harrogate, Yorks North.
Traditional Interiors, Harrogate, Yorks North.
Westway Cottage Restored Pine, Helmsley, Yorks North.
Emporium, The, Knaresborough, Yorks North.
Pictoriana, Knaresborough, Yorks North.
Low Mill Antiques, Lower Bentham, Yorks North.
Spencer, W.T. and J., Lower Bentham, Yorks North.
Daleside Antiques, Markington, Yorks North.
Kindon Antiques Ltd, Terry, Melmerby, Yorks North.
Pinetree Antiques, Ripon, Yorks North.
St. John Antiques, York, Yorks North.
Fishlake Antiques, Fishlake, Yorks South.
Maze of Pine and Roses, A, Mapplewell, Yorks South.
Peter James Antiques, Sheffield, Yorks South.
Sheffield Pine Centre (inc. Canterbury Place Antiques), Sheffield, Yorks South.
Aberford Antiques Ltd, Aberford, Yorks West.
Manor Barn, Addingham, Yorks West.
Kelly Antiques, M., Eastburn, Yorks West.
Batty's Antiques, Leeds, Yorks West.
Boston Pine Co., Leeds, Yorks West.
Kirkstall Antiques, Leeds, Yorks West.
K.L.M. & Co. Antiques, Lepton, Yorks West.
Memory Lane, Sowerby Bridge, Yorks West.
Cottage Antiques (1984) Ltd, Walsden, Yorks West.
Pine Collection, The, St. Peter Port, Guernsey, C. I.
Moyallon Antiques, Portadown, Co. Armagh, N. Ireland.
Gould and Co., Herbert, Holywood, Co. Down, N. Ireland.
Hagan, K.O., Claudy, Co. Londonderry, N. Ireland.
Times Past Antiques, Auchterarder, Scotland.
Southgrove Restorations, Dundee, Scotland.
London Road Antiques, Edinburgh, Scotland.
West of Scotland Antique Centre Ltd, Glasgow, Scotland.
QS Antiques, Kilmarnock, Scotland.
Old Pine Furniture and Jouet, Kiltarlity, Scotland.
Mostly Pine, Kingussie, Scotland.
Abbey Antiques, Stirling, Scotland.
Paterson Antiques, Elizabeth, Stirling, Scotland.
Percival Antiques, R. and S. M., Ruthin, Clwyd, Wales.
Furniture Cave, The, Aberystwyth, Dyfed, Wales.
Jansons Antiques, Bwlchllan, Dyfed, Wales.
Pine Design Workshop and Pine Corner Antiques, Haverfordwest, Dyfed, Wales.
Barn Antiques, Lampeter, Dyfed, Wales.

Ash, Jim and Pat, Llandeilo, Dyfed, Wales.
Maclean Antiques, Llanwrda, Dyfed, Wales.
Jones Antiques, Glyn, Pembroke Dock, Dyfed, Wales.
Back to the Wood, Cardiff, South Glam., Wales.
Heritage Antiques and Stripped Pine, Cardiff, South Glam., Wales.
Scurlock, Kim, Swansea, West Glam., Wales.
Pine Barn, The, Pontnewynydd, Gwent, Wales.
Abbey Antiques, Tintern, Gwent, Wales.
Aspley Antiques and Reproductions Ltd., Barmouth, Gwynedd, Wales.
Heritage Restorations, Llanfair Caereinion, Powys, Wales.

Furniture - Victorian (1830-1901)

Georgiana's Antiques, London, E17.
After Noah, London, N1
Bushwood Antiques, London, N1.
Furniture Vault, London, N1.
Graham Gallery, The, London, N1.
Hawkins Antiques, Brian, London, N1.
Ross Antiques, Marcus, London, N1.
Finchley Fine Art Galleries, London, N12.
Petherton Antiques, London, N5.
Gould and Julian Gonnermann Antiques, Betty, London, N6.
Home to Home, London, N6.
Regent Antiques, London, NW1.
Gillingham Ltd, G. and F., London, NW2.
Kendal Antiques, London, NW3.
Church Street Antiques, London, NW8.
Just Desks, London, NW8.
Witch Ball, The, London, NW9.
Antiques Pavilion, The, London, SE1.
Euro Antiques Warehouse, London, SE1
Oola Boola Antiques London, London, SE1.
Tower Bridge Antiques, London, SE1.
Badgers Antiques, London, SE10.
Whitfield Antiques, Robert, London, SE10.
Allen Antiques Ltd. World Wide Antique Exporters, Peter, London, SE15.
Abbott Antiques and Country Pine (formerly Olwen Carthew), London, SE26.
Ward Antiques, London, SE7.
Harrods Ltd, London, SW1.
Lewis, M. and D., London, SW1.
Just a Second Antiques, London, SW11.
Wren Antiques, London, SW13.
Fowle, A. and J., London, SW16.
Chelsea Bric-a-Brac Shop Ltd, London, SW19.
Stefani Antiques, London, SW19.
Kreckovic, L. and E., London, SW6.
Alan Ltd, Adrian, London, W1.
Barham, P.R., London, W11.
Barham Antiques, London, W11.
Briggs Ltd, F.E.A., London, W11.
Graham and Green, London, W11.
Jones and Son (Antiques) Ltd, W., London, W11.
Lewis, M. and D., London, W11.
Rex Antiques, London, W11.
Craven Gallery, London, W2.
Terrace Antiques, London, W5.
Coleman, Garrick D., London, W8.
Haslam and Whiteway, London, W8.
Lewis and Lloyd, London, W8.
No. 74 Antiques and Collectables, Bristol, Avon.
Tilly Manor Antiques, West Harptree, Avon.
Ampthill Emporium, Ampthill, Beds.
Riches, Pulloxhill, Beds.
Manor Antiques, Wilshamstead, Beds.
Bow House Antiques, Hungerford, Berks.
Hill Farm Antiques, Leckhampstead, Berks.
Baker Antiques, John, Newbury, Berks.
Addrison Bros, Windsor and Eton, Berks.
Martin, Peter J., Windsor and Eton, Berks.
Cupboard Antiques, The, Amersham, Bucks.
Morton Harvey Antiques, Aylesbury, Bucks.
A Thing of Beauty, Farnham Common, Bucks.
Unsworth Antiques, Robin, Olney, Bucks.
Country Furniture Shop, Penn, Bucks.
Sydney House Antiques, Wansford, Cambs.
City Strippers, Chester, Cheshire.
Buckley Antiques Exports, W., Congleton, Cheshire.

SPECIALIST DEALERS

Glynn Interiors, Knutsford, Cheshire.
Tatton Antiques, Knutsford, Cheshire.
Edwards Antique Exports, Brian, Lower Kinnerton, Cheshire.
Mulberry Bush, The, Marple Bridge, Cheshire.
Chapel Antiques, Nantwich, Cheshire.
Limited Editions, Stockport, Cheshire.
Page Antiques, Stockport, Cheshire.
Zippy Antiques, Stockport, Cheshire.
Victoriana Antiques, Stockton Heath, Cheshire.
Antique Fireplaces and Furniture, Tarvin, Cheshire.
Bradley's Antiques and Jewellery, Middlesbrough, Cleveland.
Old Pine and Country Furniture, Boscastle, Cornwall.
Bragg Antiques, John, Lostwithiel, Cornwall.
Pydar Antiques and Gallery, Truro, Cornwall.
Winkworth Antiques, Richard, Truro, Cornwall.
Pink Cottage Antiques, Widegates, Cornwall.
Fell Antiques, Mary, Brampton, Cumbria.
Charm Antiques, Carlisle, Cumbria.
Haughey Antiques, Kirkby Stephen, Cumbria.
Mortlake Antiques, Kirkby Stephen, Cumbria.
Cothay Antiques, Maulds Meaburn, Cumbria.
Corney House Antiques, Penrith, Cumbria.
Sedbergh Antiques and Collectables, Sedbergh, Cumbria.
Aquarius Antiques, Buxton, Derbys.
G. and J. Antiques, Buxton, Derbys.
Dean Antiques, G.L., Glossop, Derbys.
Wooden Box Antiques, Woodville, Derbys.
Petticombe Manor Antiques, Bideford, Devon.
Prestige Antiques, John, Brixham, Devon.
Old Antique Shop, The, Budleigh Salterton, Devon.
Mills Antiques, Cullompton, Devon.
Strip and Wax, Exeter, Devon.
Pennies, Exwick, Devon.
House of Antiques, Honiton, Devon.
Turner Antiques, R. and D., Honiton, Devon.
Secondhand Rose, Plymouth, Devon.
South Molton Antiques, South Molton, Devon.
Tredantiques, South Molton, Devon.
Pendar Antiques, Tavistock, Devon.
Bygone Days Antiques, Tiverton, Devon.
Woodbury Antiques, Woodbury, Devon.
Yealmantiques, Yealmpton, Devon.
Dunton Antiques, Richard, Bournemouth, Dorset.
Victorian Parlour, Bournemouth, Dorset.
Tower Antiques, Cranborne, Dorset.
Baliol Gallery, The, Barnard Castle, Durham.
Town House Antiques, Barnard Castle, Durham.
Bygones, Darlington, Durham.
Nichol and Hill, Darlington, Durham.
Ramsey Antiques, Alan, Darlington, Durham.
Eden House Antiques, West Auckland, Durham.
Hay Green Antiques, Blackmore, Essex.
Salter Antiques, Nicholas, Chingford, Essex.
Lindsell Chairs, Coggeshall, Essex.
Wilkinson Antiques, Rita M., Colchester, Essex.
Argyll House Antiques, Felsted, Essex.
Tilly's Antiques, Leigh-on-Sea, Essex.
Abacus Antiques, Maldon, Essex.
Beardall Antiques, Clive, Maldon, Essex.
Brown House Antiques, Newport, Essex.
Bruschweiler (Antiques) Ltd, F.G., Rayleigh, Essex.
Bush Antiques, Saffron Walden, Essex.
Hedingham Antiques, Sible Hedingham, Essex.
It's About Time, Westcliff-on-Sea, Essex.
White Roding Antiques, White Roding, Essex.
Dean Forest Antiques, Berry Hill Pike, Glos.
Latchford Antiques, Cheltenham, Glos.
Niner Antiques, Elizabeth, Cheltenham, Glos.
Acorn Antiques, Stow-on-the-Wold, Glos.
Bryden, D., Stow-on-the-Wold, Glos.
Park House Antiques, Stow-on-the-Wold, Glos.
Rosemary Antiques and Paper Moon Books, Stow-on-the-Wold, Glos.
Balmuir House Antiques, Tetbury, Glos.
Chest of Drawers, The, Tetbury, Glos.
Berkeley Antiques and Replay, Tewkesbury, Glos.
Antique House, Hartley Wintney, Hants.
Plestor Barn Antiques, Liss, Hants.
Corfield Antiques Ltd, Lymington, Hants.
Affordable Antiques, Portsmouth, Hants.
Gallery, The, Portsmouth, Hants.

Pretty Chairs, Portsmouth, Hants.
Robinson Interiors and Antiques, Glen, Ringwood, Hants.
Moody, L., Southampton, Hants.
Gaylords, Titchfield, Hants.
Thompson Antiques formerly Ships and Sealing Wax, Winchester, Hants.
Webb Fine Arts, Winchester, Hants.
Old Barley Mow Antiques, Winchfield, Hants.
Hay Antiques, Blakedown, Herefs and Worcs.
Hart Antiques, Mitchell, Clows Top, Herefs and Worcs.
Carlton Antiques, Great Malvern, Herefs and Worcs.
Miscellany Antiques, Great Malvern, Herefs and Worcs.
Warings of Hereford Antiques, Hereford, Herefs and Worcs.
Gorst Hall Restoration, Kidderminster, Herefs and Worcs.
Nash Antiques and Interiors, John, Ledbury, Herefs and Worcs.
Shaw-Cooper, Susan, Ledbury, Herefs and Worcs.
Chapman Antiques, Leominster, Herefs and Worcs.
Hammond Antiques, Jeffery, Leominster, Herefs and Worcs.
Lower House Fine Antiques, Winyates Green, Herefs and Worcs.
Antiques and Interiors (Victoriana), Worcester, Herefs and Worcs.
Country Life Antiques, Bushey, Herts.
Annick Antiques, Kimpton, Herts.
Careless Cottage Antiques, Much Hadham, Herts.
J.N. Antiques, Redbourn, Herts.
Wareside Antiques, Wareside, Herts.
Collins Antiques (F.G. and C. Collins Ltd.), Wheathampstead, Herts.
Priory Antiques, Bridlington, Humbs North.
Hakeney Antiques, David K., Hull, Humbs North.
Mole/Antique Exports, Geoffrey, Hull, Humbs North.
Penny Farthing Antiques, South Cave, Humbs North.
Solent Antiques, Bembridge, I. of Wight.
Courtyard Antiques, Brasted, Kent.
Dyke, Peter, Brasted, Kent.
Keymer Son & Co. Ltd, Brasted, Kent.
Harvey Centre, The, Canterbury, Kent.
Chislehurst Antiques, Chislehurst, Kent.
Chevertons of Edenbridge Ltd, Edenbridge, Kent.
Eden Antiques, Edenbridge, Kent.
Lawton's Antiques, Folkestone, Kent.
Lord Antiques, Alan, Folkestone, Kent.
Charles International Antiques, Maidstone, Kent.
Northfleet Hill Antiques, Northfleet, Kent.
Deo Juvante Antiques, Rochester, Kent.
Fitch Antiques, Michael, Sandgate, Kent.
Wilson Antiques, Colin, Sundridge, Kent.
La Trobe and Bigwood Restorations, Tunbridge Wells, Kent.
Phoenix Antiques, Tunbridge Wells, Kent.
Stead Antiques Reference Books, Graham, Tunbridge Wells, Kent.
Langold Antiques, West Peckham, Kent.
Brazil Antiques Ltd, Westerham, Kent.
Hook, Anthony J., Westerham, Kent.
Mistral Galleries, Westerham, Kent.
Laurens Antiques, Whitstable, Kent.
Tankerton Antiques, Whitstable, Kent.
Silvesters, Wingham, Kent.
Brun Lea Antiques, Burnley, Lancs.
Phillips (Antiques), Edward V., Clayton-le-Moors, Lancs.
Rebecca Antiques, Clitheroe, Lancs.
K.C. Antiques, Darwen, Lancs.
Booth Antiques and Reproductions, L., Freckleton, Lancs.
O'Brien and Son Antiques, R. J., Hollinwood, Lancs.
Folly, The, Longridge, Lancs.
Baron Antiques, The, Manchester, Lancs.
Bulldog Antiques, Manchester, Lancs.
Chestergate Antiques, Manchester, Lancs.
Prestwich Antiques Ltd, Manchester, Lancs.
Brooks Antiques, Nelson, Lancs.
Treasure Ltd, Frederick, Preston, Lancs.
Carrcross Gallery, Scarisbrick, Lancs.
Ivanhoe Antiques, Ashby-de-la-Zouch, Leics.
Old Bakery Antiques, Empingham, Leics.
House Things Antiques, Hinckley, Leics.
Withers of Leicester, Hoby, Leics.
Mandrake Stephenson Antiques, Ibstock, Leics.
Corry's, Leicester, Leics.
Montague Antiques, Leicester, Leics.
Moores and Son, Walter, Leicester, Leics.

SPECIALIST DEALERS

Smith (Leicester) Ltd, E., Leicester, Leics.
Stamp and Sons, J., Market Harborough, Leics.
Ashley House Antiques, Measham, Leics.
Underwood Antiques, Clive, Colsterworth, Lincs.
Pilgrims Antique Centre, Gainsborough, Lincs.
Grantham Furniture Emporium, Grantham, Lincs.
Nadin, Harold, Grantham, Lincs.
M.C. Trading Co, The, Horncastle, Lincs.
Seaview Antiques, Horncastle, Lincs.
Shaw Antiques, Laurence, Horncastle, Lincs.
Staines Antiques, Horncastle, Lincs.
Dring, C. and K.E., Lincoln, Lincs.
Audley House Antiques, Osbournby, Lincs.
Sinclair, John, Stamford, Lincs.
St. George's Antiques, Stamford, Lincs.
Underwoodhall Antiques, Woodhall Spa, Lincs.
V.O.C. Antiques, Woodhall Spa, Lincs.
Stefani Antiques, Liverpool, Merseyside.
Stock, Colin, Rainford, Merseyside.
Decor Galleries, Southport, Merseyside.
Sutcliffe Antiques, Tony and Anne, Southport, Merseyside.
Northwood Antiques, Northwood, Middx.
Phelps Antiques, Twickenham, Middx.
Ivy House Antiques, Acle, Norfolk.
Brancaster Staithe Antiques, Brancaster Staithe, Norfolk.
Bates and Sons, Eric, Coltishall, Norfolk.
Rust Antiques, Benjamin, Cromer, Norfolk.
Seago, A.E., Cromer, Norfolk.
Howkins, Peter, Gt. Yarmouth, Norfolk.
Robinson, Peter, Heacham, Norfolk.
Norfolk Galleries, King's Lynn, Norfolk.
Old Coach House, Long Stratton, Norfolk.
Anglia Antique Exporters, North Walsham, Norfolk.
Bates and Sons, Eric, North Walsham, Norfolk.
Haugh Antiques, Roderic, Norwich, Norfolk.
Howkins Antiques, John, Norwich, Norfolk.
Cannell Antiques, M.D., Raveningham, Norfolk.
Chimes, The, Reepham, Norfolk.
Pratt and Son, Leo, South Walsham, Norfolk.
Stalham Antique Gallery, Stalham, Norfolk.
Standley, M.E. and J.E., Wymondham, Norfolk.
Brackley Antiques, Brackley, Northants.
Restall Brown and Clennell Ltd, Cosgrove, Northants.
Quaker Lodge Antiques, Finedon, Northants.
Thorpe Antiques, Finedon, Northants.
Cave, F. and C.H., Northampton, Northants.
Regent House, Northampton, Northants.
King, F., Pattishall, Northants.
Corner Cupboard, The, Woodford Halse, Northants.
Haydon Bridge Antiques, Haydon Bridge, Northumbs.
Boaden Antiques, Arthur, Hexham, Northumbs.
Miller Antiques, James, Wooler, Northumbs.
Blacksmiths Forge, Balderton, Notts.
Tudor Rose Antiques, Carlton-on-Trent, Notts.
Antiques Warehouse, Mansfield, Notts.
Fair Deal Antiques, Mansfield, Notts.
Sheppards Antiques, Mansfield, Notts.
D. and G. Antiques, Newark, Notts.
D. and V. Antiques, Newark, Notts.
Nielsen Antiques, Anthony, Burford, Oxon.
Pickup, David, Burford, Oxon.
Shield Antiques, Robin, Burford, Oxon.
Hitchcox Antiques, Rupert, Chalgrove, Oxon.
Ryland, B.R., Henley-on-Thames, Oxon.
Country Seat, The, Huntercombe, Oxon.
Second Time Around Antiques, Wallingford, Oxon.
Summers, Davis and Son Ltd, Wallingford, Oxon.
Cross Antiques, Watlington, Oxon.
Orton Antiques, Stephen, Watlington, Oxon.
Sibley (Fine Furniture), Nicholas, Whitchurch-on-Thames, Oxon.
Greenway Antiques, Colin, Witney, Oxon.
Pout Antiques, Ian, Witney, Oxon.
Wilkins Antiques, Joan, Witney, Oxon.
Parmenter Antiques, Bridgnorth, Shrops.
Hodnet Antiques, Hodnet, Shrops.
Brown Antiques, David, Shrewsbury, Shrops.
Manser and Son Ltd, F.C., Shrewsbury, Shrops.
James Antiques, Brian, Telford, Shrops.
M.G.R. Exports, Bruton, Somerset.
Cary Antiques Ltd, Castle Cary, Somerset.
Dyte Antiques, C. and R.I., Highbridge, Somerset.

Cains Antiques, Littleton, Somerset.
Westville House Antiques, Littleton, Somerset.
Keyford Antiques, Rode, Somerset.
Selwoods, Taunton, Somerset.
Milton Antiques, Fred, Wanstrow, Somerset.
Lovejoys, Wells, Somerset.
Hamblin, John, Yeovil, Somerset.
Betley Court Gallery, Betley, Staffs.
Aspleys Antiques and Reproductions Ltd, Leek, Staffs.
Gilligans Antiques, Leek, Staffs.
Browse, Stafford, Staffs.
Castle Antiques, Stoke-on-Trent, Staffs.
Potteries Antique Centre, The, Stoke-on-Trent, Staffs.
Tutbury Mill Antiques, Tutbury, Staffs.
Saltgate Antiques, Beccles, Suffolk.
Country House Antiques, Bungay, Suffolk.
Abbott Antiques, A., Ipswich, Suffolk.
Weir Antiques, Gerald, Ipswich, Suffolk.
Ixworth Antiques, Ixworth, Suffolk.
Mainline Furniture, Kesgrave, Suffolk.
Kessingland Antiques, Kessingland, Suffolk.
Motts of Lavenham, Lavenham, Suffolk.
Leiston Furniture Warehouses, Leiston, Suffolk.
Bell, Raine, Long Melford, Suffolk.
Carling and Tess Sinclair, Roger, Long Melford, Suffolk.
Chater-House Gallery, Long Melford, Suffolk.
Carlton Road Antiques, Lowestoft, Suffolk.
Hunt and Clement, Mildenhall, Suffolk.
Palmer Antiques, Mary, Stradbroke, Suffolk.
Napier House Antiques, Sudbury, Suffolk.
Hamilton Antiques, Woodbridge, Suffolk.
Hurst Antiques, Anthony, Woodbridge, Suffolk.
Lambert's Barn, Woodbridge, Suffolk.
Wrentham Antiques, Wrentham, Suffolk.
House of Christian Antiques, Ash Vale, Surrey.
Pedlar, The, Camberley, Surrey.
Gasson Antiques and Interiors, Pat and Terry, Cranleigh, Surrey.
Holmwood Antiques, Dorking, Surrey.
Norfolk House Galleries Antique Centre, Dorking, Surrey.
Gould and Sons (Antiques) Ltd, A.E., East Horsley, Surrey.
Bowdery, M. J., Hindhead, Surrey.
Oriel Antiques, Hindhead, Surrey.
Glencorse Antiques, Kingston-upon-Thames, Surrey.
Knaphill Antiques, Knaphill, Surrey.
Addison Antiques, Michael, Purley, Surrey.
Lawrence and Sons, F.G., Redhill, Surrey.
Antique Mart, Richmond, Surrey.
Rowan Antiques, Richmond, Surrey.
Sage Antiques and Interiors, Ripley, Surrey.
Cockrell Antiques, Surbiton, Surrey.
Hatch Antiques, Weybridge, Surrey.
Country Antiques, Windlesham, Surrey.
Old Mint House, The, Bexhill-on-Sea, Sussex East.
Alexandria Antiques, Brighton, Sussex East.
Ashton's Antiques, Brighton, Sussex East.
Cowen Antiques, Christopher G., Brighton, Sussex East.
Fitchett Antiques, Alan, Brighton, Sussex East.
Hume, Dudley, Brighton, Sussex East.
Rodney Arthur Classics, Brighton, Sussex East.
Dycheling Antiques, Ditchling, Sussex East.
Partridge Antiques, Timothy, Eastbourne, Sussex East.
Abbey Antiques, Hastings, Sussex East.
Botting Antiques, John, Horam, Sussex East.
Charleston Antiques, Lewes, Sussex East.
Old Mint House, The, Pevensey, Sussex East.
Price Antiques Ltd, Graham, Polegate, Sussex East.
Rye Antiques, Rye, Sussex East.
Aarquebus Antiques, St. Leonards-on-Sea, Sussex East.
Monarch Antiques, St. Leonards-on-Sea, Sussex East.
Bygones, Angmering, Sussex West.
Gordon, Phyllis, Arundel, Sussex West.
Usher Antiques, Richard, Cuckfield, Sussex West.
Hinsdale Antiques, East Grinstead, Sussex West.
Callingham Antiques, N. and S., Northchapel, Sussex West.
Powell (Hove) Ltd, J., Portslade, Sussex West.
Cheriton Antiques, Worthing, Sussex West.
Wilsons Antiques, Worthing, Sussex West.
Walker, W. and J., Jesmond, Tyne and Wear.
Renaissance Antiques, Tynemouth, Tyne and Wear.
Strain Antiques, David R., Tynemouth, Tyne and Wear.
Venables, Jeremy, Kineton, Warks.

SPECIALIST DEALERS

Goodwin and Sons, John, Leamington Spa, Warks.
Harrison Wholesale Exports, Tim, Stratford-upon-Avon, Warks.
Apollo Antiques Ltd, Warwick, Warks.
Goodwin and Sons, John, Warwick, Warks.
Reeve, James, Warwick, Warks.
Spencer Antiques, Don, Warwick, Warks.
Always Antiques, Birmingham, West Mids.
Archives, Birmingham, West Mids.
Clark Antiques, Peter, Birmingham, West Mids.
Harris and Sons, Antiques, Bob, Birmingham, West Mids.
Hubbard Antiques, John, Birmingham, West Mids.
Old Bakehouse, The, Birmingham, West Mids.
Memories Antiques, Coventry, West Mids.
Retro Products, Lye, West Mids.
L.P. Furniture (Mids) Ltd, Pelsall, West Mids.
Wilkins Antiques, Brett, Wednesbury, West Mids.
Golden Oldies, Wolverhampton, West Mids.
Wakeman and Taylor Antiques, Wolverhampton, West Mids.
Cross Hayes Antiques, Malmesbury, Wilts.
Antique and Book Collector, The, Marlborough, Wilts.
Cracknell (Antiques) Ltd, Nigel, Marlborough, Wilts.
Amos Antiques, Joan, Salisbury, Wilts.
Pearson Antiques, Carol, Tisbury, Wilts.
Isabella Antiques, Warminster, Wilts.
Welch, K. and A., Warminster, Wilts.
Galloway Antiques, Boroughbridge, Yorks North.
Graham Antiques, Anthony, Boroughbridge, Yorks North
St. James House Antiques, Boroughbridge, Yorks North.
Wilson and Sons, R.S., Boroughbridge, Yorks North.
Greenwood Antiques, Simon, Burneston, Yorks North.
Bow Antiques, Easingwold, Yorks North.
Elm Tree Antiques, Flaxton, Yorks North.
Haworth Antiques, Harrogate, Yorks North.
Love, David, Harrogate, Yorks North.
Sturman's Antiques, Hawes, Yorks North.
Norwood House Antiques, Killinghall, Yorks North.
Reflections, Knaresborough, Yorks North.
Trade Antiques - D.D. White, Manfield, Yorks North.
White Boar Antiques and Books, Middleham, Yorks North.
Brown's Antiques, Richmond, Yorks North.
Sigma Antiques and Fine Art, Ripon, Yorks North.
Browns Antiques, Scarborough, Yorks North.
Corn Mill Antiques, Skipton, Yorks North.
Goddard Antiques, Julie, Oughtibridge, Yorks South.
Salt Antiques, N.P. and A., Sheffield, Yorks South.
Ward Antiques, Paul, Sheffield, Yorks South.
Berry Antiques, Peter, Huddersfield, Yorks West.
Berry Brow Antiques, Huddersfield, Yorks West.
Barleycote Hall Antiques, Keighley, Yorks West.
Antique Exchange, The, Leeds, Yorks West.
Geary Antiques, Leeds, Yorks West.
Kirkstall Antiques, Leeds, Yorks West.
Windsor House Antiques (Leeds) Ltd., Leeds, Yorks West.
Park Antiques, Menston, Yorks West.
Carlton Antiques, Saltaire, Yorks West.
Victoria Antiques, Alderney, C. I.
Proctor Antiques, David, St. Peter Port, Guernsey, C. I.
Lambe, Charlotte and John, Belfast, N. Ireland.
Country Antiques, The, Antrim, Co. Antrim, N. Ireland.
Dunluce Antiques, Bushmills, Co. Antrim, N. Ireland.
Downshire House Antiques, Newry, Co. Down, N. Ireland.
Antiques and Fine Art Gallery, Warrenpoint, Co. Down, N. Ireland.
Hagan, K.O., Claudy, Co. Londonderry, N. Ireland.
Wood (Antiques) Ltd, Colin, Aberdeen, Scotland.
Old Abbey Antiques, Auchterarder, Scotland.
Highland Antiques, Avoch, Scotland.
Old Curiosity Shop, The, Ayr, Scotland.
C.P.R. Antiques and Services, Barrhead, Scotland.
Beaty, T.W., Beattock, Scotland.
Stewart Antiques, Michael, Coatbridge, Scotland.
Sangster Antiques, A., Cruden Bay, Scotland.
Hillfoot Antiques, Dollar, Scotland.
Antiquarian, The, Dumfries, Scotland.
Dunkeld Interiors, Dunkeld, Scotland.
Black Ltd, Laurance, Edinburgh, Scotland.
Cabbies Antiques, Edinburgh, Scotland.
Davidson and Begg Antiques Ltd, Edinburgh, Scotland.
Day Antiques, Alan, Edinburgh, Scotland.
Georgian Antiques, Edinburgh, Scotland.
Worthington's Antiques, Edinburgh, Scotland.

Young Antiques, Edinburgh, Scotland.
Errol Antiques, Errol, Scotland.
Pringle Antiques, Fochabers, Scotland.
Dene Hard Antiques, Garelochhead, Scotland.
Albany Antiques, Glasgow, Scotland.
Butler's Furniture Galleries Ltd, Glasgow, Scotland.
Fine Design, Haddington, Scotland.
Houndwood House Antiques, Houndwood, Scotland.
Miles Antiques, Kinross, Scotland.
C.S. Antiques, Leslie By Insch, Scotland.
Heritage Antiques, Paisley, Scotland.
Deuchar and Son, A.S., Perth, Scotland.
Crossroads Antiques, Prestwick, Scotland.
Ainslie Antiques, Robert, Scone, Scotland.
Magpie, St. Andrews, Scotland.
North Wales Antiques - Colwyn Bay, Colwyn Bay, Clwyd, Wales.
Mold Antiques and Interiors, Mold, Clwyd, Wales.
Furniture Cave, The, Aberystwyth, Dyfed, Wales.
Country Antiques, Kidwelly, Dyfed, Wales.
Barn Court Antiques, Narberth, Dyfed, Wales.
Castle Antiques, Newcastle Emlyn, Dyfed, Wales.
Clareston Antiques, Tenby, Dyfed, Wales.
Evans Antiques, Steven, Treherbert, Mid. Glam., Wales.
Evans Antiques, Steven, Treorchy, Mid. Glam., Wales.
Irena Art and Antiques, Barry, South Glam., Wales.
Renaissance Antiques, Cowbridge, South Glam., Wales.
Plough House Interiors, Chepstow, Gwent, Wales.
Collinge Antiques, Llandudno, Gwynedd, Wales.
Madoc Antiques and Art Gallery, Llandudno, Gwynedd, Wales.
Collinge Antiques, Llandudno Junction, Gwynedd, Wales.

See also Shipping Goods and Period Furniture for the Trade

Garden Furniture, Ornaments and Statuary

London Architectural Salvage and Supply Co. Ltd. (LASSCo), The, London, EC2.
Westland & Company, London, EC2.
House of Steel Antiques, London, N1.
Number Nineteen, London, N1.
Teger Trading and Bushe Antiques, London, N4.
Hearth and Home, London, NW1.
Tara Antiques, London, NW8.
Greenwich Antiques and Ironware Co, London, SE10.
Seago, London, SW1.
Edwards, Charles, London, SW6.
Napier Ltd, Sylvia, London, SW6.
Gibbs Ltd, Christopher, London, W1.
Mallett at Bourdon House Ltd, London, W1.
Walcot Reclamation, Bath, Avon.
Bridgwater, David, Marshfield, Avon.
Cheshire Brick and Slate Co, Tarvin Sands, Cheshire.
Great Northern Architectural Antique Company Ltd, The, Tattenhall, Cheshire.
Haughey Antiques, Kirkby Stephen, Cumbria.
Townhead Antiques, Newby Bridge, Cumbria.
Warehouse Antiques, Honiton, Devon.
Talisman, Gillingham, Dorset.
Wiffen's Antiques, Parkstone, Dorset.
Westrope, I., Birdbrook, Essex.
Bennet (Antiques), Julia, Dunmow, Essex.
Roberts Antiques, Peter, Moreton-in-Marsh, Glos.
Antique Pine, Norton, Glos.
Baggott, Duncan J., Stow-on-the-Wold, Glos.
Architectural Heritage, Taddington, Glos.
Holloways, Suckley, Herefs and Worcs.
Warren Antiques, Jimmy, Littlebourne, Kent.
Rebecca Antiques, Clitheroe, Lancs.
Garner, John, Uppingham, Leics.
Crowther of Syon Lodge Ltd, Isleworth, Middx.
Reindeer Antiques Ltd, Potterspury, Northants.
Merrill Antiques, Paul, Collingham, Notts.
Country Seat, The, Huntercombe, Oxon.
Cross Antiques, Watlington, Oxon.
Heath-Bullocks, Godalming, Surrey.
Packhouse, The, Runfold, Surrey.

Brighton Architectural Salvage, Brighton, Sussex East.
Palmer Antiques, Dermot and Jill, Brighton, Sussex East.
Bird Antiques, John, Lewes, Sussex East.
Cato, Lennox, Lewes, Sussex East.
Charleston Antiques, Lewes, Sussex East.
Old Bakehouse, The, Birmingham, West Mids.
Eden, Matthew, Corsham, Wilts.
Relic Antiques at Brillscote Farm, Malmesbury, Wilts.
White House Farm Antiques, Easingwold, Yorks North.
Annteaks, Abersoch, Gwynedd, Wales.

Glass

Huntley, Diana, London, N1.
Ketley Antiques, Carol, London, N1.
West - Cobb Antiques Ltd, Mark J., London, N1.
Kihl (Wine Accessories) Ltd, Richard, London, NW1.
Ashcroft, Nan S., London, NW3.
Magus Antiques, London, NW8.
Wellington Gallery, London, NW8.
Wilkinson plc, London, SE6.
Antiquus, London, SW1.
Galerie Moderne Ltd, London, SW1.
King Antique Glass, Dominic, London, SW1.
Sattin Ltd, Gerald, London, SW1.
Bridge , Christine, London, SW13.
Brook Antiques, Beverley, London, SW13.
Dining Room Shop, The, London, SW13.
West - Cobb Antiques Ltd, Mark J., London, SW19.
Burne (Antique Glass) Ltd, W.G.T., London, SW3.
Newby (A.J. & M.V. Waller), H.W., London, SW8.
Douch, A., London, W1.
Goode and Co (London) Ltd, Thomas, London, W1.
Sheppard and Cooper Ltd, London, W1.
Wilkinson plc, London, W1.
Harbottle, Patricia, London, W11.
Mercury Antiques, London, W11.
Phillips and Sons, E.S., London, W11.
Tomkinson Stained Glass, London, W11.
Craven Gallery, London, W2.
Coleman, Garrick D., London, W8.
Crick, Mrs. M.E., London, W8.
Denton Antiques, London, W8.
Hayhurst Fine Glass, Jeanette, London, W8.
Hope and Glory, London, W8.
Lineham and Sons, Eric, London, W8.
Dux Antiques, Frank, Bath, Avon.
Robinson, T.E., Bath, Avon.
Carnival Antiques, Bristol, Avon.
Cotham Galleries, Bristol, Avon.
Potter's Antiques and Coins, Bristol, Avon.
Somervale Antiques, Midsomer Norton, Avon.
Shepherd Antiques, Peter, Hurst, Berks.
Cavendish Fine Arts - Janet Middlemiss, Windsor and Eton, Berks.
Eyre and Greig Ltd, Windsor and Eton, Berks.
A Thing of Beauty, Farnham Common, Bucks.
Sweetbriar Gallery, Helsby, Cheshire.
Zippy Antiques, Stockport, Cheshire.
Antiques, Marazion, Cornwall.
Brownside Coach House, Alston, Cumbria.
Adamson, Alexander, Kirkby Lonsdale, Cumbria.
Elizabeth and Son, Ulverston, Cumbria.
Harper Antiques, Martin and Dorothy, Bakewell, Derbys.
Payton Antiques, Mary, Chagford, Devon.
Allnutt Antiques, Topsham, Devon.
Bogan House Antiques, Totnes, Devon.
A & D Antiques, Blandford Forum, Dorset.
Stebbing, Peter, Bournemouth, Dorset.
Quarter Jack Antiques, Sturminster Newton, Dorset.
Templar Antiques, Kelvedon, Essex.
Wrenn Antiques, Richard, Leigh-on-Sea, Essex.
Latchford Antiques, Cheltenham, Glos.
Taylor Antiques, Rankine, Cirencester, Glos.
Grimes House Antiques, Moreton-in-Marsh, Glos.
Acorn Antiques, Stow-on-the-Wold, Glos.
Bell Passage Antiques, Wotton-under-Edge, Glos.
Burnham-Slipper Antiques, Jane, Botley, Hants.
Stockbridge Antiques, Stockbridge, Hants.
Todd and Austin Antiques of Winchester, Winchester, Hants.
Wolf Antiques Ltd, H. and B., Droitwich, Herefs and Worcs.
Chandlers Antiques, Sevenoaks, Kent.

Sargeant, Denys, Westerham, Kent.
Ethos Gallery, Clitheroe, Lancs.
Moore Antiques and Stained Glass, Jack, Trawden, Lancs.
Keystone Antiques, Coalville, Leics.
Artbry's Antiques, Pinner, Middx.
Allport-Lomax, Liz, Coltishall, Norfolk.
Dorothy's Antiques, Sheringham, Norfolk.
Wilkins Antiques, Joan, Witney, Oxon.
Abbey Antiques, Glastonbury, Somerset.
Best Antiques, Ray, Ilminster, Somerset.
Palmer Antiques, Mary, Stradbroke, Suffolk.
Warren, Shirley, Sanderstead, Surrey.
Circus Antiques, Brighton, Sussex East.
Golding, Pat, Arundel, Sussex West.
Fileman, David R., Steyning, Sussex West.
High St. Antiques, Alcester, Warks.
Delomosne and Son Ltd, North Wraxall, Wilts.
Dragon Antiques, Harrogate, Yorks North.
York Cottage Antiques, Helmsley, Yorks North.
Balme Antiques, Ken, Halifax, Yorks West.
Dunluce Antiques, Bushmills, Co. Antrim, N. Ireland.
Young Antiques, Denis, Aberfeldy, Scotland.
Fine Antique Glass, Abernyte, Scotland.
MacAdam, William, Edinburgh, Scotland.
Forsyth Antiques, Perth, Scotland.
Gallery One, Perth, Scotland.
David Charles, Pontypridd, Mid-Glam, Wales.

Icons (See Russsian Art)

Islamic Art

Ahuan (UK) Ltd, London, SW1.
Connoisseur Gallery, The, London, SW1.
Spink and Son Ltd, London, SW1.
Aaron Gallery, London, W1.
Emanouel Antiques Ltd, London, W1.
Hadji Baba Ancient Art, London, W1.
Mansour Gallery, London, W1.
Mohamed Ltd, Bashir, London, W1.
Rabi Gallery Ltd, London, W1.
Axia Art Consultants Ltd, London, W11.
Hosains Books and Antiques, London, W2.
Al Mashreq Galleries, London, W8.
Little, Roger, Oxford, Oxon
Rogers Oriental Rugs, Clive, Brighton, Sussex East.
De Montfort, Robertsbridge, Sussex East.

Japanese Art (See Oriental)

Jewellery (see Silver and Jewellery)

Lighting

Lemkow, Sara, London, N1.
Turn On Lighting Ltd, London, N1.
Antique Shop (Valantique), The, London, N2.
Winchmore Antiques, London, N21.
McClenaghan-Gilhooly Antiques, London, NW1.
Malik and Son Ltd, David, London, NW10.
Metalcrafts Ltd, B.C., London, NW9.
Oddiquities, London, SE23.
Wilkinson plc, London, SE6.
Blanchard and Alan Ltd., London, SW1.
Hobbs, Carlton, London, SW1.
Howe, Christopher, London, SW1.
Jeremy Ltd, London, SW1.
Lion, Witch and Lampshade, London, SW1.
Money (Antiques) Ltd, Lennox, London, SW1.
Lighthouse Ltd, The, London, SW19.
Burne (Antique Glass) Ltd, W.G.T., London, SW3.
Cochrane Antiques, Fergus, London, SW6.
Crotty and Son Ltd, J., London, SW6.
Hollingshead and Co, London, SW6.
Lamp Gallery, The, London, SW6.
Pauw Antiques, M., London, SW6.
Preston and Sally Isbell, Antony, London, SW6.
Tulissio De Beaumont, London, SW6.
Vaughan, London, SW6.
Wray's Lighting Emporium, Christopher, London, SW6.

SPECIALIST DEALERS

Period Brass Lights, London, SW7.
Sitch and Co. Ltd., W., London, W1.
Stair and Company Ltd, London, W1.
Turpin Ltd, M., London, W1.
Wilkinson plc, London, W1.
Facade, The, London, W11.
Jones Antique Lighting, London, W11.
Davighi, N., London, W6.
Crick, Mrs. M.E., London, W8.
Cohn, George and Peter, London, WC1.
McCarthy, Ian and Dianne, Clutton, Avon.
Manor Antiques, Wilshamstead, Beds.
Temple Lighting (Jeanne Temple Antiques), Milton Keynes, Bucks.
White House Antiques, Princes Risborough, Bucks.
Old House Antiques, Wansford, Cambs.
Edge Antiques, The, Alderley Edge, Cheshire.
Victoriana Antiques, Stockton Heath, Cheshire.
Lantern Shop, The, Sidmouth, Devon.
Green Room, The, Bournemouth, Dorset.
Bailey's Quality Antique Lighting and Accessories, Cheltenham, Glos.
Keil (Cheltenham) Ltd, H.W., Cheltenham, Glos.
Caspall Antiques, J. and J., Stow-on-the-Wold, Glos.
St. James Antiques, Little Malvern, Herefs and Worcs.
Penoyre Antiques, Pershore, Herefs and Worcs.
Fryer Antique Lighting, Fritz, Ross-on-Wye, Herefs and Worcs.
Lower House Fine Antiques, Winyates Green, Herefs and Worcs.
Magic Lanterns, St. Albans, Herts.
Antiquities, Chatham, Kent.
Sargeant, Denys, Westerham, Kent.
Finch, M. and I., Yealand Conyers, Lancs.
Arcadia Antiques, Southport, Merseyside.
Allchin Antiques, William, Norwich, Norfolk.
Stiffkey Lamp Shop, The, Stiffkey, Norfolk.
Barclay Antiques, Headington, Oxon.
Cains Antiques, Littleton, Somerset.
Tinder Box, The, Stoke-on-Trent, Staffs.
Antiques, Carshalton, Surrey.
Timewarp, Brighton, Sussex East.
Hopkins, John, Cuckfield, Sussex West.
Hopkins, John, Petworth, Sussex West.
Fileman, David R., Steyning, Sussex West.
Incandescent Lighting Company, The, Leamington Spa, Warks.
Delomosne and Son Ltd, North Wraxall, Wilts.
Inglenook Antiques, Ramsbury, Wilts.
Old Flame, Easingwold, Yorks North.
Kellys of Knaresborough, Knaresborough, Yorks North.
'Bobbins' Wool Craft Antiques, Whitby, Yorks North.
Fine Antique Glass, Abernyte, Scotland.
Antiques & Bygones, Bankfoot, Scotland.
Berlands of Edinburgh, Edinburgh, Scotland.
Macintosh & Co, William, Edinburgh, Scotland.
Nest Egg Antiques, Edinburgh, Scotland.

Maps and Prints

Ash Rare Books, London, EC3.
Clarke-Hall Ltd, J., London, EC4.
Boutique Fantasque, London, N1.
Finney Antique Prints and Books, Michael, London, N1.
Lassalle, Judith, London, N1.
MacDonnell, Finbar, London, N1.
Totteridge Gallery, The, London, N20.
Park Galleries, London, N3.
Centaur Gallery, London, N6.
Harvey-Lee, Elizabeth, London, NW2.
Mulder, Frederick, London, NW3.
Denham Gallery, John, London, NW6.
Gallery Kaleidoscope, London, NW6.
Leadlay Gallery, The Warwick, London, SE10.
Addison-Ross Gallery, London, SW1.
Artemis Fine Arts Limited, London, SW1.
Burden Ltd, Clive A., London, SW1.
Douwes Fine Art Ltd, London, SW1.
Faustus Fine Art Ltd, London, SW1.
Franks, J.A.L., London, SW1.
Hartnoll, Julian, London, SW1.
Mason Gallery, Paul, London, SW1.
Mendez incorporating Craddock and Barnard, Christopher, London, SW1.
O'Shea Gallery, London, SW1.
Old London Galleries, London, SW1.
Old Maps and Prints, London, SW1.
Parker Gallery, The, London, SW1.
Parkin Fine Art Ltd, Michael, London, SW1.
Sotheran's, London, SW1.
Gallery Downstairs, The, London, SW12.
Sheen Gallery, London, SW14.
S.A.G. Art Galleries, London, SW18.
Chelsea Rare Books, London, SW3.
Map House, The, London, SW3.
Old Church Galleries, London, SW3.
Crawley and Asquith Ltd, London, SW4.
Wingfield Sporting Art, London, SW4.
20th Century Gallery, London, SW6.
Armelin Antiques, Karin, London, SW6.
Barclay Samson Ltd, London, SW6.
King's Court Galleries, London, SW6.
Marriott Ltd, Michael, London, SW6.
Orssich, Paul, London, SW6.
Trowbridge Gallery, London, SW6.
Valcke, Francois, London, SW6.
Burlington Gallery Ltd, London, W1.
Cazalet Ltd, Lumley, London, W1.
Day Ltd, Richard, London, W1.
Edmunds, Andrew, London, W1.
Fritz-Denneville Fine Arts Ltd, H., London, W1.
Potter Ltd, Jonathan, London, W1.
Schuster Gallery, The, London, W1.
Somerville Ltd, Stephen, London, W1.
Sotheran Ltd, Henry, London, W1.
Welbeck Gallery, The, London, W1.
Blackburn, Norman, London, W11.
Kennedy, Peter, London, W11.
L'Acquaforte, London, W11.
Skrebowski, Justin, London, W11.
Albion Art (UK) Ltd, London, W2.
Bayswater Books, London, W2.
Connaught Galleries, London, W2.
Campbell Gallery, The Lucy B., London, W8.
Graham and Oxley (Antiques) Ltd, London, W8.
Spencer, Charles, London, W9.
Austin/Desmond & Phipps, London, WC1.
Cartographia London, London, WC1.
Franks Ltd, J.A.L., London, WC1.
Print Room, The, London, WC1.
Noble, Avril, London, WC2.
Stage Door Prints, London, WC2.
Storey, Harold T., London, WC2.
Tooley Adams & Co. Ltd, London, WC2.
Witch Ball, The, London, WC2.
Patterson Liddle, Bath, Avon.
Trimbridge Galleries, Bath, Avon.
Alexander Gallery, Bristol, Avon.
Cotham Hill Bookshop, Bristol, Avon.
Roberts Bookshop, John, Bristol, Avon.
Clevedon Fine Arts (with Clevedon Books), Clevedon, Avon.
Flint Galleries Ltd, Sir William Russell, Wrington, Avon.
Graham Gallery, Burghfield Common, Berks.
Jaspers Fine Arts Ltd, Maidenhead, Berks.
Grove Gallery, Windsor and Eton, Berks.
"Mon Galerie", Amersham, Bucks.
Omniphil Ltd, Chesham, Bucks.
Penn Barn, Penn, Bucks.
Medina Antiquarian Maps and Prints, Winslow, Bucks.
Benet Gallery, Cambridge, Cambs.
Lawson Gallery, The, Cambridge, Cambs.
Nicholson, Richard A., Chester, Cheshire.
Lion Gallery and Bookshop, Knutsford, Cheshire.
Brooks, Philip, Macclesfield, Cheshire.
Harper Fine Paintings, Poynton, Cheshire.
Hulme, J. Alan, Waverton, Cheshire.
Maggs, John, Falmouth, Cornwall.
Broad Street Gallery, Penryn, Cornwall.
Gallery Tonkin and Gallery Lyonesse, Penzance, Cornwall.
Miles Bookshop, Archie, Gosforth, Cumbria.
Kendal Studios Antiques, Kendal, Cumbria.
Hollett and Son, R. F. G., Sedbergh, Cumbria.
Hill Books, Alan, Bakewell, Derbys.
Coleman Antiques, Polly, Chesterfield, Derbys.

SPECIALIST DEALERS

Laura's Bookshop, Derby, Derbys.
Artavia Gallery, Barnstaple, Devon.
Medina Gallery, Bideford, Devon.
New Gallery, Budleigh Salterton, Devon.
Payton Antiques, Mary, Chagford, Devon.
Chantry Bookshop and Gallery, Dartmouth, Devon.
A-B Gallery, Salcombe, Devon.
Lantern Shop Gallery, The, Sidmouth, Devon.
Mole Gallery, South Molton, Devon.
Birbeck Gallery, Torquay, Devon.
Artist Gallery, The, Bournemouth, Dorset.
PIC's Bookshop, Bridport, Dorset.
Whillock, F., Litton Cheney, Dorset.
Antique Map and Bookshop, Puddletown, Dorset.
Swan Gallery, The, Sherborne, Dorset.
Treasure Chest, The, Weymouth, Dorset.
Shotton Antiquarian Books and Prints, J., Durham, Durham.
Castle Bookshop, Colchester, Essex.
Hilton, Simon, Dunmow, Essex.
Newport Gallery, Newport, Essex.
Cleeve Picture Framing, Bishops Cleeve, Glos.
Bannister, F.R.G.S, David, Cheltenham, Glos.
Turtle Fine Art, Cheltenham, Glos.
Bartrick, Steven D., Gloucester, Glos.
Avon Gallery, The, Moreton-in-Marsh, Glos.
Hand Prints and Watercolours Gallery, Nailsworth, Glos.
Northleach Gallery, The, Northleach, Glos.
Talbot Court Galleries, Stow-on-the-Wold, Glos.
Vanbrugh House Antiques, Stow-on-the-Wold, Glos.
Kenulf Fine Arts, Winchcombe, Glos.
Bell Passage Antiques, Wotton-under-Edge, Glos.
Studio Bookshop and Gallery, Alresford, Hants.
Hughes and Smeeth Ltd, Lymington, Hants.
Trivess, W.D., Meonstoke, Hants.
Petersfield Bookshop, The, Petersfield, Hants.
Oldfield Gallery, Portsmouth, Hants.
Evelyn , Hugh , Steepmarsh, Hants.
Bell Fine Art, Winchester, Hants.
Printed Page, Winchester, Hants.
Skipwith, W.G., Winchester, Hants.
Bracebridge Gallery, Astwood Bank, Herefs and Worcs.
Broadway Old Books (formerly Stratford Trevers), Broadway, Herefs and Worcs.
Brobury House Gallery, Brobury, Herefs and Worcs.
Coltsfoot Gallery, Leominster, Herefs and Worcs.
Farmers Gallery, Leominster, Herefs and Worcs.
Ross Old Book and Print Shop, Ross-on-Wye, Herefs and Worcs.
Antique Map and Print Gallery, Worcester, Herefs and Worcs.
Moreden Prints, Yatton, Herefs and Worcs.
Knights Gallery, Harpenden, Herts.
Old Cathay Fine Books and Arts, Hatfield, Herts.
Moore, Eric T., Hitchin, Herts.
Burden, Clive A., Rickmansworth, Herts.
McCrudden Gallery, Rickmansworth, Herts.
James of St Albans, St. Albans, Herts.
Thorp, Thomas, St. Albans, Herts.
Houghton Hall Antiques, Market Weighton, Humbs North.
Cameron Gallery, Julia Margaret, Cowes, I. of Wight.
Galerias Segui, Cowes, I. of Wight.
Shanklin Gallery, The, Shanklin , I. of Wight.
Ventnor Rare Books, Ventnor, I. of Wight.
Marlborough House Antiques, Yarmouth, I. of Wight.
Canterbury Bookshop, The, Canterbury, Kent.
Chaucer Bookshop, Canterbury, Kent.
Leadenhall Gallery, Canterbury, Kent.
Cranbrook Gallery, Cranbrook, Kent.
Print Room Gallery, The, Deal, Kent.
Periwinkle Press, Faversham, Kent.
Marrin and Sons, G. and D.I., Folkestone, Kent.
China Locker, The, Lamberhurst, Kent.
Darenth Bookshop, Otford, Kent.
Langley Galleries, Rochester, Kent.
Buck Antiques, Christopher, Sandgate, Kent.
Hythe Galleries, Sandwich, Kent.
Franca Antiques, Tunbridge Wells, Kent.
London House Antiques, Westerham, Kent.
Lloyd's Bookshop, Wingham, Kent.
Studio Arts Gallery, Lancaster, Lancs.
Browzers, Manchester, Lancs.
Forest Books of Cheshire, Manchester, Lancs.

Halewood and Sons, Preston, Lancs.
Churchgate Antiques, Empingham, Leics.
Leicestershire Sporting Gallery and Brown Jack Bookshop, Lubenham, Leics.
Grafton Country Pictures, Oakham, Leics.
Old House Gallery, The, Oakham, Leics.
Cassidy (Books), P.J., Holbeach, Lincs.
Castle Gallery, Lincoln, Lincs.
Harlequin Gallery, Lincoln, Lincs.
Lyver & Boydell Galleries, Liverpool, Merseyside.
Hampton Hill Gallery s, Hampton Hill, Middx.
Barnard (A.B.A.), Thomas, Uxbridge, Middx.
Coach House, The, Costessey, Norfolk.
Ferrow, David, Gt. Yarmouth, Norfolk.
Haven Gallery, The, Gt. Yarmouth, Norfolk.
In the Picture (The Golf Collection), Holt, Norfolk.
Cathedral Gallery, Norwich, Norfolk.
Crome Gallery and Frame Shop, Norwich, Norfolk.
Crowe, Antiquarian Book Seller, Peter, Norwich, Norfolk.
Tombland Bookshop, The, Norwich, Norfolk.
Right Angle, Brackley, Northants.
Savage and Son, R.S.J., Northampton, Northants.
Park Book Shop, Wellingborough, Northants.
Park Gallery, Wellingborough, Northants.
Neville Gallery, Jane, Aslockton, Notts.
Rodgers, Arthur and Ann, Ruddington, Notts.
TRADA, Chipping Norton, Oxon.
Dixon Fine Engravings, Rob, Culham, Oxon.
Dorchester Galleries, Dorchester-on-Thames, Oxon.
Keene Gallery, The Barry M., Henley-on-Thames, Oxon.
Magna Gallery, Oxford, Oxon.
Sanders of Oxford Ltd, Oxford, Oxon.
Marler Gallery, The Jane, Ludlow, Shrops.
Mount, The, Woore, Shrops.
Lewis Gallery, Michael, Bruton, Somerset.
Armytage, Julian, Crewkerne, Somerset.
House of Antiquity, Nether Stowey, Somerset.
Barrett Antiques and Prints, Philip, Taunton, Somerset.
Betley Court Gallery, Betley, Staffs.
Broadway Studios, Burton-on-Trent, Staffs.
Bournemouth Gallery Ltd, The, Lichfield, Staffs.
Weston Antique Gallery, Weston, Staffs.
Besleys Books, Beccles, Suffolk.
Guildhall Gallery, Bury St. Edmunds, Suffolk.
Suthburgh Antiques, Long Melford, Suffolk.
King's Court Galleries, Dorking, Surrey.
Vandeleur Antiquarian Books, Epsom, Surrey.
Stewart Fine Art Galleries, Michael, Guildford, Surrey.
Reigate Galleries Ltd, Reigate, Surrey.
Palmer Galleries, Richmond, Surrey.
Leoframes, Brighton, Sussex East.
Shelton Arts, Brighton, Sussex East.
Witch Ball, The, Brighton, Sussex East.
Smith, Raymond, Eastbourne, Sussex East.
Deverall, Ivan R., Uckfield, Sussex East.
Baynton-Williams, Arundel, Sussex West.
Serendipity Antiques, Arundel, Sussex West.
Antique Atlas, The, East Grinstead, Sussex West.
Antique Print Shop, The, East Grinstead, Sussex West.
Holmes Antique Maps and Prints, Julia, South Harting, Sussex West.
Osborne Art and Antiques, Jesmond, Tyne and Wear.
Warner Fine Art, Newcastle-upon-Tyne, Tyne and Wear.
Lacy Gallery, Henley-in-Arden, Warks.
Paull Antiques, Janice, Kenilworth, Warks.
Vaughan, Robert, Stratford-upon-Avon, Warks.
Eastgate Fine Arts, Warwick, Warks.
Woodland Fine Art, Alvechurch, West Mids.
Carleton Gallery, Birmingham, West Mids.
Broad Street Gallery, Wolverhampton, West Mids.
Beach, D.M. Salisbury, Wilts.
Booth Gallery and Titanic Signals Archive, Westbury, Wilts.
Great Ayton Bookshop, The, Great Ayton, Yorks North.
Country Connections (Esk House Arts), Grosmont, Yorks North.
McTague of Harrogate, Harrogate, Yorks North.
O'Flynn Antiquarian Booksellers, York, Yorks North.
Hill Books, Sheffield, Alan, Sheffield, Yorks South.
Porter Prints (Broomhill), Sheffield, Yorks South.
Brear, Jean, Halifax, Yorks West.
Oakwood Gallery, Leeds, Yorks West.
Channel Islands Galleries Ltd, St. Peter Port, Guernsey, C.I.

SPECIALIST DEALERS

Gavey, Geoffrey P., Vale, Guernsey, C. I.
Blench & Son, John, St. Helier, Jersey, C.I.
Grange Gallery and Fine Arts Ltd, St. Helier, Jersey, C. I.
Selective Eye Gallery, The, St. Helier, Jersey, C. I.
St. Helier Galleries Ltd, St. Helier, Jersey, C. I.
Thesaurus (Jersey) Ltd, St. Helier, Jersey, C. I.
Arnold Gallery Antiques, Phyllis, Greyabbey, Co. Down, N. Ireland.
Waverley Gallery, The, Aberdeen, Scotland.
McEwan Gallery, The, Ballater, Scotland.
Calton Gallery, Edinburgh, Scotland.
Clark Gallery. Scotia Maps - Mapsellers, The Carson, Edinburgh, Scotland.
Nelson, John O., Edinburgh, Scotland.
Rankin, Alan, Edinburgh, Scotland.
Ovell Antiques, Llandovery, Dyfed, Wales.
Manor House Fine Arts, Cardiff, South Glam., Wales.
Davies, Philip, Swansea, West Glam., Wales.
Lockyer, H.K., Abergavenny, Gwent, Wales.
Glance Back Bookshop, Chepstow, Gwent, Wales.
Glance Gallery, Chepstow, Gwent, Wales.
Windsor Gallery, David, Bangor, Gwynedd, Wales.
Andrew, Tony, Llanerchymedd, Gwynedd, Wales.
Maps, Prints and Books, Brecon, Powys, Wales.

Metalwork

Heritage Antiques, London, N1.
House of Steel Antiques, London, N1.
Lemkow, Sara, London, N1.
Bangs, Christopher, London, SW11.
Christopher Antiques, London, SW11.
Young Antiques, Robert, London, SW11.
Chelsea Bric-a-Brac Shop Ltd, London, SW19.
Fairfax Fireplaces and Antiques, London, SW6.
Place Antiques, Peter, London, SW6.
Casimir Ltd, Jack, London, W11.
Magus Antiques, London, W11.
Von Pflugh Antiques, Johnny, London, W11.
Seager Antiques Ltd, Arthur, London, W8.
Craik Ltd, Brian and Caroline, Bath, Avon.
Town and Country Antiques, Bath, Avon.
McCarthy, Ian and Dianne, Clutton, Avon.
Bridgwater, David, Marshfield, Avon.
Tilly Manor Antiques, West Harptree, Avon.
Roberts Antiques, Ann, Ampthill, Beds.
Manor Antiques, Wilshamstead, Beds.
Sykes Antiques, Christopher, Woburn, Beds.
Fire Place (Hungerford) Ltd, The, Hungerford, Berks.
Berkshire Metal Finishers Ltd, Sandhurst, Berks.
Martin, Peter J., Windsor and Eton, Berks.
Sundial Antiques, Amersham, Bucks.
Smith, T., Chalfont St. Giles, Bucks.
Bartram, Albert, Chesham, Bucks.
Haydon House Antiques, Woburn Sands, Bucks.
Phoenix Antiques, Fordham, Cambs.
Antique Shop, The, Chester, Cheshire.
Tatton Antiques, Knutsford, Cheshire.
Victoriana Antiques, Stockton Heath, Cheshire.
Arden Antiques, Brenda, Tarporley, Cheshire.
Shire Antiques, Newby Bridge, Cumbria.
Elsom - Antiques, Pamela, Ashbourne, Derbys.
Water Lane Antiques, Bakewell, Derbys.
Butler, Roderick, Honiton, Devon.
Morchard Bishop Antiques, Morchard Bishop, Devon.
Andrade, Philip, South Brent, Devon.
Stebbing, Peter, Bournemouth, Dorset.
J.B. Antiques, Wimborne Minster, Dorset.
Antique Metals, Coggeshall, Essex.
Partner and Puxon, Colchester, Essex.
Wrenn Antiques, Richard, Leigh-on-Sea, Essex.
Dolphin Antiques, Saffron Walden, Essex.
Turpin's Antiques, Thaxted, Essex.
Stokes, William H., Cirencester, Glos.
Caspall Antiques, J. and J., Stow-on-the-Wold, Glos.
Clarke Antiques Ltd, Christopher, Stow-on-the-Wold, Glos.
Hockin (Antiques) Ltd, Keith, Stow-on-the-Wold, Glos.
Primrose Antiques, Tetbury, Glos.
Prichard Antiques, Winchcombe, Glos.
Close Antiques, Alresford, Hants.
Cedar Antiques, Hartley Wintney, Hants.
Hursley Antiques, Hursley, Hants.

Du Cros Antiques, J., Liss, Hants.
Monaltrie Antiques, Odiham, Hants.
Cull Antiques, Petersfield, Hants.
Viney, Elizabeth, Stockbridge, Hants.
Regency House Antiques, Whitchurch, Hants.
Shaw-Cooper, Susan, Ledbury, Herefs and Worcs.
Hubbard Antiques, Leominster, Herefs and Worcs.
Gander, Michael, Hitchin, Herts.
Perry Antiques, R.J., Hitchin, Herts.
Two Maids Antiques, Biddenden, Kent.
Stoodley, Dinah, Brasted, Kent.
Peacock Antiques, Chilham, Kent.
Webster, E.W., Bickerstaffe, Lancs.
Keen, Thomas, Bottesford, Leics.
Burley Workshop, Burley-on-the-Hill, Leics.
House Things Antiques, Hinckley, Leics.
Robinson, Peter, Heacham, Norfolk.
Brett and Sons Ltd, Arthur, Norwich, Norfolk.
Cannell Antiques, M.D., Raveningham, Norfolk.
Madeira, V. and C., Flore, Northants.
Rococo Antiques and Interiors, Weedon, Northants.
Antiques, West Haddon, Northants.
Cheshire, E.M., Bingham, Notts.
Lustre Metal Antiques Nottingham, Nottingham, Notts.
Fyson Antiques, Jonathan, Burford, Oxon.
Horseshoe Antiques and Gallery, Burford, Oxon.
Nielsen Antiques, Anthony, Burford, Oxon.
Key Antiques, Chipping Norton, Oxon.
Ottrey Antiques, Mike, Wallingford, Oxon.
Wilkins Antiques, Joan, Witney, Oxon.
Best Antiques, Ray, Ilminster, Somerset.
Micklem Antiques, Thorne St. Margaret, Somerset.
House (Mitre Antiques), Bernard G., Wells, Somerset.
Morley Antiques, William, West Monkton, Somerset.
Peppers Period Pieces, Bury St. Edmunds, Suffolk.
Baker, J. and J., Lavenham, Suffolk.
Welling Antiques, Anthony, Ripley, Surrey.
Rickett & Co. Antiques, Shepperton, Surrey.
Weller - Restoration Centre, W.H., Eastbourne, Sussex East.
Rye Antiques, Rye, Sussex East.
Mew Antiques, Peter and Janet, Sedlescombe, Sussex East.
Park View Antiques, Wadhurst, Sussex East.
Frith Antiques, Petworth, Sussex West.
Griffin Antiques, Petworth, Sussex West.
Wakelin and Helen Linfield, Michael, Petworth, Sussex West.
Retro Products, Lye, West Mids.
Combe Cottage Antiques, Castle Combe, Wilts.
Monkton Galleries, Hindon, Wilts.
Fairfax Fireplaces and General Antiques, Harriet, Langley Burrell, Wilts.
Cracknell (Antiques) Ltd, Nigel, Marlborough, Wilts.
Gentle Antiques, Rupert, Milton Lilbourne, Wilts.
St. James House Antiques, Boroughbridge, Yorks North.
Bentley, Bill, Harrogate, Yorks North.
Garth Antiques, Harrogate, Yorks North.
Lumb and Sons Ltd, Charles, Harrogate, Yorks North.
Phillips Antiques Ltd, Elaine, Harrogate, Yorks North.
York Cottage Antiques, Helmsley, Yorks North.
Aura Antiques, Masham, Yorks North.
Thistlethwaite, E., Settle, Yorks North.
Garth Antiques, Whixley, Yorks North.
Geary Antiques, Leeds, Yorks West.
Park Antiques, Menston, Yorks West.
C.P.R. Antiques and Services, Barrhead, Scotland.
Top Brass, Edinburgh, Scotland.
Wright Antiques, Tim, Glasgow, Scotland.
Maclean Antiques, Llanwrda, Dyfed, Wales.

Miniatures

Asprey Ltd, Maurice, London, SW1.
Lavender (Antiques) Ltd, D.S., London, W1.
Phillips Ltd, S.J., London, W1.
Deutsch Antiques, H. and W., London, W8.
Wendover Antiques, Wendover, Bucks.
Brett, Simon, Moreton-in-Marsh, Glos
Sim, Michael, Chislehurst, Kent.
Regal Antiques, Westerham, Kent.
Gough Bros. Art Shop and Gallery, Bognor Regis, Sussex West.
Arden Gallery, Henley-in-Arden, Warks.

Mirrors

Julian Antiques, London, N1.
Relic Antiques Trade Warehouse, London, NW1.
Anno Domini Antiques, London, SW1.
Fernandes and Marche, London, SW1.
Ossowski, A. and M., London, SW1.
Rothman, London, SW1.
Spyer and Son (Antiques) Ltd, Gerald, London, SW1.
McDonald, Joy, London, SW13.
Adams Ltd, Norman, London, SW3.
James and Son Ltd, Anthony, London, SW3.
Lipitch Ltd, Peter, London, SW3.
Wright Antiques Ltd, Clifford, London, SW3.
House of Mirrors, London, SW6.
Hurford Antiques, Peter, London, SW6.
James, P.L., London, SW6.
Through the Looking Glass Ltd, London, SW6.
Toth, Ferenc, London, SW6.
Bloom Fine Jewellery, Anne, London, W1.
Fielden, Brian, London, W1.
Harvey & Co (Antiques) Ltd, W.R, London, W1.
Stair and Company Ltd, London, W1.
Turpin Ltd, M., London, W1.
Simpsons - Bespoke Carvings, London, W14.
Bardawil, Eddy, London, W8.
Howard, Valerie, London, W8.
Through the Looking Glass Ltd, London, W8.
Looking Glass of Bath, Bath, Avon.
Quiet Street Antiques, Bath, Avon.
Doddington House Antiques, Doddington, Cambs.
Baliol Gallery, The, Barnard Castle, Durham.
Roberts Antiques, Peter, Moreton-in-Marsh, Glos.
Curiosity Shop, The, Stow-on-the-Wold, Glos.
Stow Antiques, Stow-on-the-Wold, Glos.
Balmuir House Antiques, Tetbury, Glos.
Penoyre Antiques, Pershore, Herefs and Worcs.
Windhill Antiquary, The, Bishop's Stortford, Herts.
Garson and Co. Ltd, Manchester, Lancs.
Finch, M. and I., Yealand Conyers, Lancs.
Tattersall's, Uppingham, Leics.
Castle Gallery, Lincoln, Lincs.
Haugh Antiques, Roderic, Norwich, Norfolk.
Ashton Gower Antiques, Burford, Oxon.
Molland Antique Mirrors, Leek, Staffs.
Antique Warehouse, Marlesford, Suffolk.
Cashin Gallery, Sheila, Brighton, Sussex East.
Palmer Antiques, Dermot and Jill, Brighton, Sussex East.
Cato, Lennox, Lewes, Sussex East.
Julian Antiques, Hurstpierpoint, Sussex West.
Riman Antiques, Philip, Harbury, Warks.
Woodland Fine Art, Alvechurch, West Mids.
Marnier Antiques, Edward, Tisbury, Wilts.
Greenwood (Fine Art), W., Burneston, Yorks North.

Music Boxes, Instruments and Literature

Curious Grannies, London, E8.
Freeman, Vincent, London, N1.
Miles, David, London, NW1.
Bingham, Tony, London, NW3.
Haas (A. and M. Rosenthal), Otto, London, NW3.
Talking Machine, London, NW4.
Baron, H., London, NW6.
Lewis, Arthur S., London, SW1.
Reeves Bookseller Ltd, William, London, SW16.
Acanthus Antiques, London, SW19.
Beare, John and Arthur, London, W1.
Biddulph, Peter, London, W1.
Pelham Galleries, London, W1.
Mayflower Antiques, London, W11.
Tociapski, Igor, London, W11.
Web, A. M., London, W11.
Travis and Emery, London, WC2.
Aspidistra, Bath, Avon.
Dollin and Daines, Bath, Avon.
Gibson, David, Bath, Avon.
Wise Owl Bookshop, The, Bristol, Avon.
J.V. Pianos and Cambridge Pianola Company, Landbeach, Cambs.
Mill Farm Antiques, Disley, Cheshire.
Miss Elany, Long Eaton, Derbys.
Taylor, M.C., Bournemouth, Dorset.
Mayflower Antiques, Harwich, Essex.
Harding's World of Mechanical Music, Keith, Northleach, Glos.
Vanbrugh House Antiques, Stow-on-the-Wold, Glos.
Evans and Evans, Alresford, Hants.
Thwaites and Co, Bushey, Herts.
Roberts Fine Antique Clocks, Music Boxes, Barometers, Derek, Tonbridge, Kent.
Hadlow Antiques, Tunbridge Wells, Kent.
Pantiles Spa Antiques, Tunbridge Wells, Kent.
Old Smithy, Feniscowles, Lancs.
O'Brien and Son Antiques, R. J., Hollinwood, Lancs.
Norfolk Polyphon Centre, Bawdeswell, Norfolk.
Violin Shop, The, Hexham, Northumbs.
Limb Antiques, R.R., Newark, Notts.
Leigh Antiques, Laurie, Oxford, Oxon.
Treasure Chest, The, Highbridge, Somerset.
Berryman Music Boxes, Shelagh, Wells, Somerset.
Chater-House Gallery, Long Melford, Suffolk.
Hope Phonographs and Gramophones, Howard, East Molesey, Surrey.
Holleyman and Treacher Ltd, Brighton, Sussex East.
Webb, Graham, Brighton, Sussex East.
Cowderoy Antiques, John, Eastbourne, Sussex East.
Blaydon Antique Centre, Blaydon, Tyne and Wear.
Moseley Pianos, Birmingham, West Mids.
Jomarc Pianos Ltd., Walsall, West Mids.
May and May Ltd, Semley, Wilts.
Pianorama (Harrogate) Ltd, Harrogate, Yorks North.
Piano Shop, The, Leeds, Yorks West.
Thirkills Antiques, Leeds, Yorks West.
K.L.M. & Co. Antiques, Lepton, Yorks West.
Talking Point Antiques, Sowerby Bridge, Yorks West.
Thurso Antiques, Thurso, Scotland.
Carpenter, John, Llanelli, Dyfed, Wales.
San Domenico Stringed Instruments, Cardiff, South Glam., Wales.
Chugg Antiques, Keith, Swansea, West Glam., Wales.

Nautical Instruments (See Scientific Instruments)

Needlework (see Tapestries)

Netsuke (See Oriental Art)

Oil Paintings

Royal Exchange Art Gallery, London, EC3.
Chapman Antiques, Peter, London, N1.
Graham Gallery, The, London, N1.
Swan Fine Art, London, N1.
Underhill Gallery, Leigh, London, N1.
Finchley Fine Art Galleries, London, N12.
Henham (Antiques), Martin, London, N2.
Stewart - Fine Art, Lauri, London, N2.
Totteridge Gallery, The, London, N20.
Park Galleries, London, N3.
Centaur Gallery, London, N6.
Lummis Fine Art, Sandra, London, N8.
Barkes and Barkes, London, NW1.
Hamilton Fine Arts, London, NW11.
Gunter Fine Art, London, NW2.
Leask Ward, London, NW3.
Miller Fine Arts, Duncan R., London, NW3.
Newhart (Pictures) Ltd, London, NW3.
Denham Gallery, John, London, NW6.
Gallery Kaleidoscope, London, NW6.
Camden Art Gallery, London, NW8.
Drummond/Wrawby Moor Art Gallery Ltd, Nicholas, London, NW8.
Greenwich Gallery, The, London, SE10.
Relcy Antiques, London, SE10.
Aaron (London)Ltd, Didier, London, SW1.
Ackermann & Johnson , London, SW1.
Addison-Ross Gallery, London, SW1.
Amell Ltd, Verner, London, SW1.
Antiquus, London, SW1.

SPECIALIST DEALERS

Belgrave Gallery, London, SW1.
Brisigotti Antiques Ltd, London, SW1.
Carritt Limited, David, London, SW1.
Chaucer Fine Arts, London, SW1.
Cohen, Edward, London, SW1.
Cox and Company, London, SW1.
Douwes Fine Art Ltd, London, SW1.
Eaton Gallery, London, SW1.
Gregory Gallery, Martyn, London, SW1.
Hamilton Ltd, Ross, London, SW1.
Harari and Johns Ltd, London, SW1.
Hartnoll, Julian, London, SW1.
Hazlitt, Gooden and Fox Ltd, London, SW1.
Hermitage Antiques, London, SW1.
Hull Gallery, Christopher, London, SW1.
Jones, R. and J., London, SW1.
King Street Galleries, London, SW1.
MacConnal-Mason Gallery, London, SW1.
Mall Galleries, The, London, SW1.
Mason Gallery, Paul, London, SW1.
Mathaf Gallery Ltd, London, SW1.
Matthiesen Fine Art Ltd. and Matthiesen Works of Art Ltd, London, SW1.
Moreton Street Gallery, London, SW1.
Morrison, Guy, London, SW1.
Nahum, Peter, London, SW1.
Old Maps and Prints, London, SW1.
Omell Galleries, London, SW1.
Parker Gallery, The, London, SW1.
Parkin Fine Art Ltd, Michael, London, SW1.
Pawsey and Payne, London, SW1.
Polak Gallery, London, SW1.
Portland Gallery, London, SW1.
Priest Antiques, Michael, London, SW1.
Pyms Gallery, London, SW1.
Sarti Gallery Ltd, London, SW1.
Simon Fine Art Ltd, Julian, London, SW1.
Spink and Son Ltd, London, SW1.
St. James's Art Group, The, London, SW1.
Streather, Pamela, London, SW1.
Thomson - Albany Gallery, Bill, London, SW1.
Tillou Works of Art Ltd, Peter, London, SW1.
Trafalgar Galleries, London, SW1.
Valls Ltd, Rafael, London, SW1.
Van Haeften Ltd, Johnny, London, SW1.
Waterman Fine Art Ltd, London, SW1.
Clark Ltd, Jonathan, London, SW10.
Hollywood Road Gallery, London, SW10.
Park Walk Gallery, London, SW10.
Hancock, Mark, London, SW13.
New Grafton Gallery, London, SW13.
Wykeham Galleries, The, London, SW13.
Sheen Gallery, London, SW14.
Few, Ted, London, SW17.
S.A.G. Art Galleries, London, SW18.
Hicks Gallery, London, SW19.
Kensington Sporting Paintings Ltd, London, SW20.
Campbell Picture Frames Ltd, John, London, SW3.
Century Gallery, London, SW3.
Daggett Gallery, Charles, London, SW3.
Hoppen Ltd, Stephanie, London, SW3.
Innes Gallery, Malcolm, London, SW3.
Mathon Gallery, London, SW3.
Pettifer Ltd, David, London, SW3.
Swann Galleries, Oliver, London, SW3.
Walker-Bagshawe, London, SW3.
Crawley and Asquith Ltd, London, SW4.
Wingfield Sporting Art, London, SW4.
20th Century Gallery, London, SW6.
Barclay Samson Ltd, London, SW6.
Bowmoore Gallery, London, SW6.
Cavendish Antiques, Rupert, London, SW6.
Cooper Fine Arts Ltd, London, SW6.
Edwards, Charles, London, SW6.
Valcke, Francois, London, SW6.
Walker Gallery, Meldrum, London, SW6.
Collino, Julie, London, SW7.
Wyllie Gallery, The, London, SW7.
Agnew's, London, W1.
Browse and Darby Ltd, London, W1.
Burlington Paintings Ltd, London, W1.
Colnaghi & Co Ltd, P. and D., London, W1.

D'Offay, Anthony, London, W1.
Editions Graphiques Gallery, London, W1.
Fine Art Society plc, The, London, W1.
Fritz-Denneville Fine Arts Ltd, H., London, W1.
Frost and Reed Ltd, London, W1.
Gage (Works of Art) Ltd, Deborah, London, W1.
Gibbs Ltd, Christopher, London, W1.
Gibson Fine Art Ltd, Thomas, London, W1.
Green, Richard, London, W1.
Hahn and Son Fine Art Dealers, London, W1.
Harrington Gallery, David, London, W1.
Harvey & Co (Antiques) Ltd, W.R, London, W1.
Lane Fine Art Ltd, London, W1.
Lefevre Gallery, London, W1.
Leger Galleries Ltd, The, London, W1.
Maas Gallery, London, W1.
MacConnal-Mason Gallery, London, W1.
Miles Gallery, Roy, London, W1.
Mitchell and Son, John, London, W1.
Mould Ltd, Anthony, London, W1.
Noortman, London, W1.
Partridge Fine Arts plc, London, W1.
Richmond Gallery, The, London, W1.
Rutland Gallery, London, W1.
Simpson Ltd, Michael, London, W1.
Somerville Ltd, Stephen, London, W1.
South Audley Antiques, London, W1.
Speelman Ltd, Edward, London, W1.
Stoppenbach and Delestre Ltd, London, W1.
Taylor Gallery, The, London, W1.
Teltscher Ltd, F., London, W1.
Thuillier, William, London, W1.
Walpole Gallery, London, W1.
Waterhouse and Dodd, London, W1.
Wildenstein and Co Ltd, London, W1.
Wilkins and Wilkins, London, W1.
Williams and Son, London, W1.
Wood Gallery, The Christopher, London, W1.
Addison Fine Art, London, W11.
Butchoff Antiques, London, W11.
Caelt Gallery, London, W11.
Collectors' Fine Art at Rostrum, London, W11.
Curá Antiques, London, W11.
Daggett Gallery, London, W11.
Fleur de Lys Gallery, London, W11.
Graham Gallery, Gavin, London, W11.
Graham-Stewart, London, W11.
Lacy Gallery, London, W11.
Milne and Moller, London, W11.
Philp, London, W11.
Skrebowski, Justin, London, W11.
Stern Art Dealers, London, W11.
Von Pflugh Antiques, Johnny, London, W11.
Garratt (Fine Paintings), Stephen, London, W14.
Joslin, Richard, London, W14.
Albion Art (UK) Ltd, London, W2.
Bonham, Murray Feely Fine Art, John, London, W2.
Igel Fine Arts Ltd, Manya, London, W2.
Whitford and Hughes, London, W2.
Okolski, Z.J., London, W3.
Coats, Dick, London, W4.
Ealing Gallery, London, W5.
Baumkotter Gallery, London, W8.
Dare, George, London, W8.
Iona Antiques, London, W8.
Kensington Fine Arts, London, W8.
Little Winchester Gallery, London, W8.
Sabin Galleries Ltd, London, W8.
Spencer, Charles, London, W9.
Austin/Desmond & Phipps, London, WC1.
Adam Gallery, Bath, Avon.
Beau Nash Antiques, Bath, Avon.
Dodge Interiors Ltd, Martin , Bath, Avon.
Saville Row Gallery, The, Bath, Avon.
Trimbridge Galleries, Bath, Avon.
Alexander Gallery, Bristol, Avon.
Cross (Fine Art), David , Bristol, Avon.
Mall Gallery, The, Bristol, Avon.
Brindleys, Heath and Reach, Beds.
Charterhouse Gallery Ltd, Heath and Reach, Beds.
Queen Adelaide Gallery, Kempston, Beds.
Foye Gallery, Luton, Beds.

SPECIALIST DEALERS

Sykes Antiques, Christopher, Woburn, Beds.
Woburn Fine Arts, Woburn, Beds.
Graham Gallery, Burghfield Common, Berks.
Collectors Gallery, The, Caversham, Berks.
Phillips and Sons, Cookham, Berks.
Alway Fine Art, Marian and John, Datchet, Berks.
Pearson Antiques, John A., Horton, Berks.
Jaspers Fine Arts Ltd, Maidenhead, Berks.
Eyre and Greig Ltd, Windsor and Eton, Berks.
Grove Gallery, Windsor and Eton, Berks.
Cole (Fine Paintings) Ltd, Christopher, Beaconsfield, Bucks.
Norton Antiques, Beaconsfield, Bucks.
Wellby Ltd, H.S., Haddenham, Bucks.
Baroq Antiques, Little Brickhill, Bucks.
Messum, David, Marlow, Bucks.
Penn Barn, Penn, Bucks.
Cambridge Fine Art Ltd, Cambridge, Cambs.
Pearson Paintings Prints and Works of Art, Sebastian, Cambridge, Cambs.
Alderley Antiques, Alderley Edge, Cheshire.
Baron Fine Art, Chester, Cheshire.
St. Peters Art Gallery, Chester, Cheshire.
Brooks, Philip , Macclesfield, Cheshire.
Harper Fine Paintings, Poynton, Cheshire.
Jordan (Fine Paintings), T.B. and R., Eaglescliffe, Cleveland.
Charlton Fine Art and Porcelain, E. and N.R., Marton, Cleveland.
Varcoe, Myles, Golant, Cornwall.
Copperhouse Gallery - W. Dyer & Sons, Hayle, Cornwall.
Broad Street Gallery, Penryn, Cornwall.
Gallery Tonkin and Gallery Lyonesse, Penzance, Cornwall.
Sanders Penzance Gallery and Antiques, Tony, Penzance, Cornwall.
Gallery, The, Penrith, Cumbria.
Hollett and Son, R. F. G., Sedbergh, Cumbria.
Ashbourne Fine Art, Ashbourne, Derbys.
Cavendish House Gallery, Ashbourne, Derbys.
Upchurch, Kenneth , Ashbourne, Derbys.
Ward, Charles H., Derby, Derbys.
Collins and Son, J., Bideford, Devon.
Medina Gallery, Bideford, Devon.
New Gallery, Budleigh Salterton, Devon.
Honiton Fine Art, Honiton, Devon.
Skeaping Gallery, Lydford, Devon.
Hepworth Gallery, Gordon, Newton St. Cyres, Devon.
Armada Gallery, Plymouth, Devon.
A-B Gallery, Salcombe, Devon.
Lantern Shop, The, Sidmouth, Devon.
Bygone Days Antiques, Tiverton, Devon.
Birbeck Gallery, Torquay, Devon.
Stodgell Fine Art, Colin, Torquay, Devon.
Stour Gallery, Blandford Forum, Dorset.
Hants Gallery, Bournemouth, Dorset.
York House Gallery, Bournemouth, Dorset.
Baliol Gallery, The, Barnard Castle, Durham.
Brandler Galleries, Brentwood, Essex.
Bond and Son, S., Colchester, Essex.
Hilton, Simon, Dunmow, Essex.
Mortimer and Son, C. and J., Great Chesterford, Essex.
Barn Gallery, Hatfield Heath, Essex.
Meyers Gallery, Ingatestone, Essex.
Sykes Antiques, Thomas, Kelvedon, Essex.
Newport Gallery, Newport, Essex.
Lloyd Gallery, David, Purleigh, Essex.
Reddings Art and Antiques, Southend-on-Sea, Essex.
Galerie Lev, Woodford Green, Essex.
Upton Lodge Galleries, Avening, Glos.
Cleeve Picture Framing, Bishops Cleeve, Glos.
Priory Gallery, The, Bishops Cleeve, Glos.
Howard, David, Cheltenham, Glos.
Keil (Cheltenham) Ltd, H.W., Cheltenham, Glos.
Turtle Fine Art, Cheltenham, Glos.
School House Antiques, Chipping Campden, Glos.
Mitchell Fine Art, Robert, Cirencester, Glos.
Ward Fine Paintings, P.J., Cirencester, Glos.
Cook and Son Antiques, E.J., Gloucester, Glos.
Medcalf, Paul, Gloucester, Glos.
Bell Fine Arts, Lechlade, Glos.
Campbell, Gerard, Lechlade, Glos.
Astley House - Fine Art, Moreton-in-Marsh, Glos.
Southgate Gallery, Moreton-in-Marsh, Glos.
Baggott, Duncan J., Stow-on-the-Wold, Glos.

Baggott Church Street Ltd, Stow-on-the-Wold, Glos.
Cotswold Galleries, Stow-on-the-Wold, Glos.
Davies Fine Paintings, John, Stow-on-the-Wold, Glos.
Fosse Gallery, Stow-on-the-Wold, Glos.
Park House Antiques, Stow-on-the-Wold, Glos.
Balmuir House Antiques, Tetbury, Glos.
Old George Antiques and Interiors, Tetbury, Glos.
Upton Lodge Galleries, Tetbury, Glos.
Kenulf Fine Arts, Winchcombe, Glos.
Bell Passage Antiques, Wotton-under-Edge, Glos.
Parker Fine Art Ltd, Finkley, Hants.
Corfield Antiques Ltd, Lymington, Hants.
Perera Fine Art, Robert, Lymington, Hants.
Petersfield Bookshop, The, Petersfield, Hants.
Plaitford House Gallery, Plaitford, Hants.
Bell Fine Art, Winchester, Hants.
Webb Fine Arts, Winchester, Hants.
Bracebridge Gallery, Astwood Bank, Herefs and Worcs.
Hagen, Richard, Broadway, Herefs and Worcs.
Hay Loft Gallery, Broadway, Herefs and Worcs.
Haynes Fine Art, Broadway, Herefs and Worcs.
Noott Fine Paintings, John, Broadway, Herefs and Worcs.
Malvern Arts, Great Malvern, Herefs and Worcs.
Farmers Gallery, Leominster, Herefs and Worcs.
Jennings of Leominster, Leominster, Herefs and Worcs.
Gandolfi House , Malvern Wells, Herefs and Worcs.
Mathon Gallery, Mathon, Herefs and Worcs.
Highway Gallery, The, Upton-upon-Severn, Herefs and Worcs.
Knights Gallery, Harpenden, Herts.
Countrylife Gallery, Hitchin, Herts.
McCrudden Gallery, Rickmansworth, Herts.
Starkey Galleries, James H., Beverley, Humbs North.
Dews Fine Art, Steven, Hull, Humbs North.
Houghton Hall Antiques, Market Weighton, Humbs North.
Marine Gallery, The, Cowes, I. of Wight.
Shanklin Gallery, The, Shanklin, I. of Wight.
Dyke, Peter, Brasted, Kent.
Morrill Ltd, W.J., Dover, Kent.
Kennedy Fine Arts, Hythe, Kent.
Iles, Francis, Rochester, Kent.
Langley Galleries, Rochester, Kent.
Impressions and Alexandra's Antiques, St. Margaret's Bay, Kent.
Sundridge Gallery, Sundridge, Kent.
Clare Gallery, Tunbridge Wells, Kent.
Graham Gallery, Tunbridge Wells, Kent.
Apollo Galleries, Westerham, Kent.
London House Antiques, Westerham, Kent.
Mistral Galleries, Westerham, Kent.
Ethos Gallery, Clitheroe, Lancs.
King, Edward, Cowan Bridge, Lancs.
Studio Arts Gallery, Lancaster, Lancs.
Charnley Fine Arts, Longridge, Lancs.
Fulda Gallery Ltd, Manchester, Lancs.
Garson and Co. Ltd, Manchester, Lancs.
St. James Antiques, Manchester, Lancs.
Owen Antiques, Rochdale, Lancs.
Donn Gallery, Henry, Whitefield, Lancs.
Stanworth (Fine Arts), P., Cadeby, Leics.
Churchgate Antiques, Empingham, Leics.
Corry's, Leicester, Leics.
Leics Sporting Gallery and Brown Jack Bookshop, Lubenham, Leics.
Fine Art of Oakham, Oakham, Leics.
Old House Gallery, The, Oakham, Leics.
Garner, John, Uppingham, Leics.
Lewis Fine Art, Alan, Hundleby, Lincs.
Castle Gallery, Lincoln, Lincs.
Lincoln Fine Art, Lincoln, Lincs.
Lyver & Boydell Galleries, Liverpool, Merseyside.
Neill Gallery, Southport, Merseyside.
Studio 41, Southport, Merseyside.
Artbry's Antiques, Pinner, Middx.
Ailsa Gallery, Twickenham, Middx.
Coach House, The, Costessey, Norfolk.
Deacon and Blyth Fine Art, Great Bircham, Norfolk.
Haven Gallery, The, Gt. Yarmouth, Norfolk.
Bank House Gallery, The, Norwich, Norfolk.
Crome Gallery and Frame Shop, Norwich, Norfolk.
Fairhurst Gallery, The, Norwich, Norfolk.
Mandell's Gallery, Norwich, Norfolk.

SPECIALIST DEALERS

Westcliffe Gallery, The, Sheringham, Norfolk.
Staithe Lodge Gallery, Swafield, Norfolk.
Coughton Galleries Ltd, Arthingworth, Northants.
Right Angle, Brackley, Northants.
Castle Ashby Gallery, Castle Ashby, Northants.
Dragon Antiques, Kettering, Northants.
Savage and Son, R.S.J., Northampton, Northants.
King, F., Pattishall, Northants.
Clark Galleries, Towcester, Northants.
Green, Ron, Towcester, Northants.
Perkins Antiques, Bryan, Wellingborough, Northants.
Haydon Bridge Antiques, Haydon Bridge, Northumbs.
Haydon Gallery, Haydon Bridge, Northumbs.
Boaden Antiques, Arthur, Hexham, Northumbs.
Border Sporting Gallery, Wooler, Northumbs.
Mitchell Fine Arts, Sally, Askham, Notts.
Neville Gallery, Jane, Aslockton, Notts.
Mitchell Fine Paintings, Anthony, Nottingham, Notts.
Dickins, H.C., Bloxham, Oxon.
Horseshoe Antiques and Gallery, Burford, Oxon.
Shield Antiques, Robin, Burford, Oxon.
Sinfield Gallery, Brian, Burford, Oxon.
Swan Gallery, Burford, Oxon.
Georgian House Antiques, Chipping Norton, Oxon.
Tuckers Country Store and Art Gallery, Deddington, Oxon.
Dorchester Galleries, Dorchester-on-Thames, Oxon.
Hallidays Antiques Ltd, Dorchester-on-Thames, Oxon.
Faringdon Gallery, Faringdon, Oxon.
Keene Gallery, The Barry M., Henley-on-Thames, Oxon.
Thames Gallery, Henley-on-Thames, Oxon.
Thame Antique Galleries, Thame, Oxon.
Norton Galleries, Pauline, Bridgnorth, Shrops.
Gallery 6, Broseley, Shrops.
Marler Gallery, The Jane, Ludlow, Shrops.
Teme Valley Antiques, Ludlow, Shrops.
Wenlock Fine Art, Much Wenlock, Shrops.
Haygate Gallery, Telford, Shrops.
Mount, The, Woore, Shrops.
Hall's Antiques, Ash Priors, Somerset.
Bruton Gallery, Bruton, Somerset.
Gallery 16, Bruton, Somerset.
Pitminster Studio, Pitminster, Somerset.
Cotton Antiques and Fine Art, Nick, Watchet, Somerset.
Lovejoys, Wells, Somerset.
Betley Court Gallery, Betley, Staffs.
Broadway Studios, Burton-on-Trent, Staffs.
Heart of England Antiques, Haunton, Staffs.
England's Gallery, Leek, Staffs.
Hood and Broomfield, Newcastle-under-Lyme, Staffs.
Midwinter Antiques, Richard, Newcastle-under-Lyme, Staffs.
Thompson's Gallery, Aldeburgh, Suffolk.
Guildhall Gallery, Bury St. Edmunds, Suffolk.
Fortescue Gallery, The, Ipswich, Suffolk.
Gazeley Associates Fine Art, John, Ipswich, Suffolk.
Baker, J. and J., Lavenham, Suffolk.
Mangate Gallery, Laxfield, Suffolk.
Ashley Gallery, Long Melford, Suffolk.
Bell, Raine, Long Melford, Suffolk.
Cooper Antiques, Bruno, Long Melford, Suffolk.
Windsor Gallery, Lowestoft, Suffolk.
Equus Art Gallery, Newmarket, Suffolk.
Peasenhall Art and Antiques Gallery, Peasenhall, Suffolk.
Carter Gallery, Simon, Woodbridge, Suffolk.
Falcon Gallery, The, Wortham, Suffolk.
Cider House Galleries Ltd, Bletchingley, Surrey.
Cobham Galleries, Cobham, Surrey.
Whitgift Galleries, The, Croydon, Surrey.
Court Gallery, The, East Molesey, Surrey.
Pastimes (Egham) Ltd, Egham, Surrey.
Asplund Fine Art, Jenny, Esher, Surrey.
Heytesbury Antiques, Farnham, Surrey.
Lion and Lamb Gallery at Biggs of Farnham, Farnham, Surrey.
Goldthorpe, P. and J., Godalming, Surrey.
Glencorse Antiques, Kingston-upon-Thames, Surrey.
Bourne Gallery Ltd, Reigate, Surrey.
Goslett Gallery, Roland, Richmond, Surrey.
Horton's, Richmond, Surrey.
Lawson Antiques, F. and T., Richmond, Surrey.
Marryat, Richmond, Surrey.
Piano Nobile Fine Paintings, Richmond, Surrey.
Cedar House Gallery, Ripley, Surrey.

Sage Antiques and Interiors, Ripley, Surrey.
Newlove, B. M., Surbiton, Surrey.
Curzon Gallery, The David, Thames Ditton, Surrey.
Boathouse Gallery, Walton-on-Thames, Surrey.
Westcott Gallery, The, Westcott, Surrey.
Cross - Fine Paintings, Edward, Weybridge, Surrey.
Weybridge Antiques, Weybridge, Surrey.
Barclay Antiques, Bexhill-on-Sea, Sussex East.
Stewart Gallery, Bexhill-on-Sea, Sussex East.
Hunt Galleries, John, Brightling, Sussex East.
Welbourne, Stephen and Sonia, Brighton, Sussex East.
Day of Eastbourne Fine Art, John, Eastbourne, Sussex East.
Premier Gallery, Eastbourne, Sussex East.
Stacy-Marks Ltd, E., Eastbourne, Sussex East.
Stewart Gallery, Eastbourne, Sussex East.
Ewhurst Gallery, Ewhurst Green, Sussex East.
Delmas, Hurst Green, Sussex East.
Murray-Brown, Pevensey Bay, Sussex East.
Old Post House Antiques, Playden, Sussex East.
Alexander, Molly, Seaford, Sussex East.
Alexander, Richard, Seaford, Sussex East.
Holmes House Antiques, Sedlescombe, Sussex East.
Barnes Gallery, Uckfield, Sussex East.
Bowlby, Nicholas, Uckfield, Sussex East.
Serendipity Antiques, Arundel, Sussex West.
Lannards Gallery, Billingshurst, Sussex West.
Gough Bros. Art Shop and Gallery, Bognor Regis, Sussex West.
Canon Gallery, The, Chichester, Sussex West.
Botting, Susan and Robert, Felpham, Sussex West.
Hinde Fine Art, Sheila, Kirdford, Sussex West.
Krüger Smith Fine Art, Northchapel, Sussex West.
Wilkinson Antiques Ltd, T.G., Petworth, Sussex West.
Wood Fine Art, Jeremy, Petworth, Sussex West.
Mulberry House Galleries, Pulborough, Sussex West.
Penfold Gallery and Antiques, Steyning, Sussex West.
Wilsons Antiques, Worthing, Sussex West.
Harrison Fine Antiques, Anna, Gosforth, Tyne and Wear.
MacDonald Fine Art, Gosforth, Tyne and Wear.
Osborne Art and Antiques, Jesmond, Tyne and Wear.
Dean Gallery, The, Newcastle-upon-Tyne, Tyne and Wear.
Warner Fine Art, Newcastle-upon-Tyne, Tyne and Wear.
Sport and Country Gallery, Bulkington, Warks.
Arden Gallery, Henley-in-Arden, Warks.
Colmore Galleries Ltd, Henley-in-Arden, Warks.
Lacy Gallery, Henley-in-Arden, Warks.
Allen Gallery, The, Kenilworth, Warks.
Olive Green Ltd, Leamington Spa, Warks.
Fine-Lines (Fine Art), Shipston-on-Stour, Warks.
Astley House - Fine Art, Stretton-on-Fosse, Warks.
Woodland Fine Art, Alvechurch, West Mids.
Widdas Fine Paintings, Roger, Bentley Heath, West Mids.
Ashleigh House Antiques, Birmingham, West Mids.
Edgbaston Gallery, Birmingham, West Mids.
Graves Gallery, The, Birmingham, West Mids.
Halcyon Gallery, The, Birmingham, West Mids.
Hubbard Antiques, John, Birmingham, West Mids.
Kestrel House Antiques and Auction Salerooms, Birmingham, West Mids.
Withers - Antiques, Robert, Halesowen, West Mids.
Oldswinford Gallery, Stourbridge, West Mids.
Driffold Gallery, Sutton Coldfield, West Mids.
Broad Street Gallery, Wolverhampton, West Mids.
Lacewing Fine Art Gallery, Marlborough, Wilts.
St. John Street Gallery, Salisbury, Wilts.
Pearson Antiques, Carol, Tisbury, Wilts.
Fellowes, Edward, Warminster, Wilts.
Brook, Antiques and Picture Gallery, Ian J., Wilton, Wilts.
Thornton Gallery, Bedale, Yorks North.
Galloway Antiques, Boroughbridge, Yorks North.
Graham Antiques, Anthony, Boroughbridge, Yorks North.
Greenwood (Fine Art), W., Burneston, Yorks North.
Country Connections (Esk House Arts), Grosmont, Yorks North.
Garth Antiques, Harrogate, Yorks North.
Sutcliffe Galleries, Harrogate, Yorks North.
Walker Galleries Ltd, Harrogate, Yorks North.
Reflections, Knaresborough, Yorks North.
Gavèls, Long Preston, Yorks North.
Talents Fine Arts Ltd, Malton, Yorks North.
Rose Fine Art and Antiques, Ripon, Yorks North.
Precious, Roy, Settle, Yorks North.

Bennett, Richard, Thirsk, Yorks North.
Garth Antiques, Whixley, Yorks North.
Coulter Galleries, York, Yorks North.
Fettes Fine Art, York, Yorks North.
French Fine Arts, York, Yorks North.
Fulwood Antiques and The Basement Gallery, Sheffield, Yorks South.
Hibbert Bros. Ltd, Sheffield, Yorks South.
Hinson Fine Paintings, Sheffield, Yorks South.
Carrol, E., Bingley, Yorks West.
Oakwood Gallery, Leeds, Yorks West.
Parker Gallery, Leeds, Yorks West.
Thirkills Antiques, Leeds, Yorks West.
Carlton Antiques, Saltaire, Yorks West.
Titus Gallery, The, Shipley, Yorks West.
Todmorden Fine Art, Todmorden, Yorks West.
Taylor Fine Arts, Robin, Wakefield, Yorks West.
Mitchell-Hill Gallery, Wetherby, Yorks West.
Channel Islands Galleries Ltd, St. Peter Port, Guernsey, C.I.
Gavey, Geoffrey P., Vale, Guernsey, C. I.
Grange Gallery and Fine Arts Ltd, St. Helier, Jersey, C.I.
Selective Eye Gallery, The, St. Helier, Jersey, C. I.
St. Helier Galleries Ltd, St. Helier, Jersey, C. I.
I.G.A. Old Masters Ltd, St. Lawrence, Jersey, C. I.
Bell Gallery, The, Belfast, N. Ireland.
Dunluce Antiques, Bushmills, Co. Antrim, N. Ireland.
Antiques and Fine Art Gallery, Warrenpoint, Co. Down, N.Ireland.
Atholl Antiques, Aberdeen, Scotland.
Rendezvous Gallery, The, Aberdeen, Scotland.
Waverley Gallery, The, Aberdeen, Scotland.
Wood (Antiques) Ltd, Colin, Aberdeen, Scotland.
Young Antiques & Fine Art, William, Aberdeen, Scotland.
Ardersier Antiques, Ardersier, Scotland.
Hayes Gallery, Paul, Auchterarder, Scotland.
Highland Antiques, Avoch, Scotland.
Old Curiosity Shop, The, Ayr, Scotland.
McEwan Gallery, The, Ballater, Scotland.
Black Ltd, Laurance, Edinburgh, Scotland.
Bourne Fine Art Ltd, Edinburgh, Scotland.
Calton Gallery, Edinburgh, Scotland.
Fidelo, Tom, Edinburgh, Scotland.
Forrest McKay, Edinburgh, Scotland.
Innes Gallery, Malcolm, Edinburgh, Scotland.
Mathieson and Co, John, Edinburgh, Scotland.
Shackleton, Daniel, Edinburgh, Scotland.
Stockbridge Antiques and Fine Art, Edinburgh, Scotland.
Young Antiques, Edinburgh, Scotland.
Errol Antiques, Errol, Scotland.
Billcliffe Fine Art, The Roger, Glasgow , Scotland.
Mundy Fine Art Ltd, Ewan, Glasgow, Scotland.
Pettigrew and Mail, Glasgow, Scotland.
Houndwood House Antiques, Houndwood, Scotland.
Mainhill Gallery, Jedburgh Scotland.
Kilmacolm Antiques Ltd, Kilmacolm, Scotland.
Newburgh Antiques, Newburgh, Scotland.
McIan Gallery (Campbell-Gibson Fine Arts), The, Oban, Scotland.
Gallery One, Perth, Scotland.
George Street Gallery, The, Perth, Scotland.
Pittenweem Antiques and Fine Art, Pittenweem, Scotland.
St. Andrews Fine Art, St. Andrews, Scotland.
Abbey Antiques, Stirling, Scotland.
Barn Court Antiques, Narberth, Dyfed, Wales.
Manor House Fine Arts, Cardiff, South Glam., Wales.
Owen Gallery, John, Cowbridge, South Glam., Wales.
Davies, Philip, Swansea, West Glam., Wales.
Thicke Galleries, Swansea, West Glam., Wales.
Windsor Gallery, David, Bangor, Gwynedd, Wales.
Webb Fine Art, Michael, Bodorgan, (Anglesey), Gwynedd, Wales.
Welsh Art, Tywyn, Gwynedd, Wales.
Corner Shop, The, Hay-on-Wye, Powys, Wales.
School House Antiques, Welshpool, Powys, Wales.

Oriental Art

Holt and Co. Ltd, R., London, EC1.
Nanwani and Co, London, EC2.
Chancery Antiques Ltd, London, N1.
Hart and Rosenberg, London, N1.
Inheritance, London, N1.
Japanese Gallery, London, N1.
Li, Wan, London, N1.
Mitchell Antiques Ltd, Laurence, London, N1.
Page Oriental Art, Kevin, London, N1.
Ross Antiques, Marcus, London, N1.
East-Asia Co, London, NW1.
Henderson, Milne, London, NW8.
Magus Antiques, London, NW8.
Metalcrafts Ltd, B.C., London, NW9.
Barbagallo, Sebastiano, London, SE1.
Cavendish, Odile, London, SW1.
Ciancimino Ltd, London, SW1.
Connoisseur Gallery, The, London, SW1.
Day Ltd, Shirley, London, SW1.
Miles Antiques, Richard, London, SW1.
Sainsbury & Mason, London, SW1.
Spink and Son Ltd, London, SW1.
Van Vredenburgh Ltd, Edric, London, SW1.
Sampson Antiques Ltd, Alistair, London, SW3.
Brandt Oriental Antiques, London, SW6.
Freedman, Gerald, London, SW6.
Napier Ltd, Sylvia, London, SW6.
Baker Oriental Art, Gregg, London, W1.
Bernheimer Fine Arts Ltd, London, W1.
Davies Oriental Art, Barry, London, W1.
de Biolley Oriental Art, Jehanne, London, W1.
Eskenazi Ltd, London, W1.
Kennedy, Robin, London, W1.
Kruml, Richard, London, W1.
Moss Ltd, Sydney L., London, W1.
Oriental Art Gallery Ltd., The, London, W1.
Oriental Bronzes Ltd, London, W1.
Pitcher Oriental Art, Nicholas S., London, W1.
Robinson, Jonathan, London, W1.
Speelman, Alfred, London, W1.
Toynbee-Clarke Interiors Ltd, London, W1.
van Beers Oriental Art, Jan, London, W1.
Wrigglesworth, Linda, London, W1.
Cohen and Pearce (Oriental Porcelain), London, W11.
Hudes, Eric, London, W11.
M.C.N. Antiques, London, W11.
Nanking Porcelain Co, London, W11.
Ormonde Gallery, London, W11.
Telfer-Smollett, M. and C., London, W11.
Truscott, Christina, London, W11.
Brower Antiques, David, London, W8.
Coats Oriental Carpets, London, W8.
Deutsch Antiques, H. and W., London, W8.
Japanese Gallery, London, W8.
Kemp, Peter, London, W8.
Manners, E. and H., London, W8.
Marchant and Son, S., London, W8.
Monk and Son, D.C., London, W8.
Santos, A.V., London, W8.
Sinai Antiques Ltd, London, W8.
Sukmano Antiques, London, W8.
Vandekar Antiques, London, W8.
Wise, Mary, London, W8.
Hall, Robert, London, W9.
Haliden Oriental Rug Shop, Bath, Avon.
Cossa Antiques, Gabor, Cambridge, Cambs.
Pearson Paintings Prints and Works of Art, Sebastian, Cambridge, Cambs.
Highland Antiques, Stockport, Cheshire.
Southwick Rare Art, David L.H., Kingswear, Devon.
Taylor Antiques, Brian, Plymouth, Devon.
Sandy's Antiques, Bournemouth, Dorset.
Hudes, Eric, Braintree, Essex.
Kyoto House Japanese Antiques, Cheltenham, Glos.
Oriental Gallery, Stow-on-the-Wold, Glos.
Art-Tique, Tetbury, Glos.
Artemesia, Alresford, Hants.
Tolley's Galleries, Worcester, Herefs and Worcs.
Georgina Antiques, Hemel Hempstead, Herts.
Oriental Rug Gallery Ltd, St. Albans, Herts.
Sim, Michael, Chislehurst, Kent.
Mandarin Gallery, Riverhead, Kent.
Country Seat, The, Huntercombe, Oxon.
Jackson, John, Milton-under-Wychwood, Oxon.
Manser and Son Ltd, F.C., Shrewsbury, Shrops.
Wain, Peter, Woore, Shrops.
Hyndford Antiques, Brighton, Sussex East.

SPECIALIST DEALERS

Page Antiques, Brian, Brighton, Sussex East.
Rogers Oriental Rugs, Clive, Brighton, Sussex East.
Alexander, Richard, Seaford, Sussex East.
Galleon Antiques, St. Leonards-on-Sea, Sussex East.
Ringles Cross Antiques, Uckfield, Sussex East.
Marsh, Jasper, Henley-in-Arden, Warks.
Heirloom and Howard Ltd, West Yatton, Wilts.
Peters Antiques, Paul M., Harrogate, Yorks North.
Young Antiques, Denis, Aberfeldy, Scotland.
Another World, Edinburgh, Scotland.
Albany Antiques, Glasgow, Scotland.
Megahy, Jean, Glasgow, Scotland.
Amber Antiques, Kincardine O'Neil, Scotland.
Paterson Antiques, Elizabeth, Stirling, Scotland.

Photographs and Equipment

Jubilee Photographica, London, N1.
Laurie Antiques, Peter, London, SE8.
Vintage Cameras Ltd, London, SE26.
Hershkowitz Ltd, Robert, London, SW7.
Bayswater Books, London, W2.
Classic Collection, London, WC1.
Jessop Classic Photographica, London, WC1.
Artavia Gallery, Barnstaple, Devon.
Medina Gallery, Bideford, Devon.
Peter Pan's Bazaar, Gosport, Hants.
Padgetts Antiques, Photographic and Scientific, Hornsea, Humbs North.
Adams Bygones Shop, Tony, Ipswich, Suffolk.

Pottery and Porcelain

"Commemoratives", London, N1.
Hart and Rosenberg, London, N1.
Huntley, Diana, London, N1.
Inheritance, London, N1.
Ketley Antiques, Carol, London, N1.
Mitchell Antiques Ltd, Laurence, London, N1.
Oosthuizen, Jacqueline, London, N1.
Page Oriental Art, Kevin, London, N1.
Finchley Fine Art Galleries, London, N12.
Henham (Antiques), Martin, London, N2.
Manheim (Peter Manheim) Ltd, D.M. and P., London, N6.
Clark Antiques, Gerald, London, NW7.
Collector, The, London, NW8.
Magus Antiques, London, NW8.
S. and H. Antiques, London, NW8.
Wellington Gallery, London, NW8.
Vale Stamps and Antiques, London, SE3.
Amor Ltd, Albert, London, SW1.
Galerie Moderne Ltd, London, SW1.
Hamilton Ltd, Ross, London, SW1.
Jones, R. and J., London, SW1.
Lewis, M. and D., London, SW1.
Ning Ltd, London, SW1.
Sattin Ltd, Gerald, London, SW1.
Long, Stephen, London, SW10.
Acanthus Art Ltd, London, SW11.
Young Antiques, Robert, London, SW11.
Brook Antiques, Beverley, London, SW13.
Barnes Antiques, R.A., London, SW15.
Oosthuizen, Jacqueline, London, SW3.
Rogers de Rin, London, SW3.
Sampson Antiques Ltd, Alistair, London, SW3.
Freedman, Gerald, London, SW6.
Sanders and Sons, Robin, London, SW6.
Newby (A.J. & M.V. Waller), H.W., London, SW8.
Goode and Co (London) Ltd, Thomas, London, W1.
Harcourt Antiques, London, W1.
Haughton Antiques, Brian, London, W1.
Hobson Antiques, Claire, London, W1.
South Audley Antiques, London, W1.
Venners Antiques, London, W1.
von Wallwitz, Angela Gräfin, London, W1.
Fox, Judy, London, W11.
Hudes, Eric, London, W11.
J. and B. Antiques, London, W11.
Lewis, M. and D., London, W11.
Mercury Antiques, London, W11.
Nye, Pat, London, W11.

Schredds of Portobello, London, W11.
Badger, The, London, W5.
Harold's Place, London, W5.
Atkins, Garry, London, W8.
Brower Antiques, David, London, W8.
Davies Antiques, London, W8.
Dennis, Richard, London, W8.
Deutsch Antiques, H. and W., London, W8.
Godden, Geoffrey, London, W8.
Graham and Oxley (Antiques) Ltd, London, W8.
Grosvenor Antiques Ltd, London, W8.
Hope and Glory, London, W8.
Horne, Jonathan, London, W8.
Howard, Valerie, London, W8.
Jones, Howard, London, W8.
Kemp, Peter, London, W8.
Klaber and Klaber, London, W8.
Libra Antiques, London, W8.
Lindsay Antiques Ltd, London, W8.
Lineham and Sons, Eric, London, W8.
Manners, E. and H., London, W8.
May, J. and J., London, W8.
Oliver-Sutton Antiques, London, W8.
Seager Antiques Ltd, Arthur, London, W8.
Seligmann, M. and D., London, W8.
Sewell (Antiques) Ltd, Jean, London, W8.
Spero, Simon, London, W8.
Stobo, Constance, London, W8.
Stockspring Antiques, London, W8.
Wise, Mary, London, W8.
Anchor Antiques Ltd, London, WC2.
March Ceramics, David, Abbots Leigh, Avon.
Dando, Andrew, Bath, Avon.
Quiet Street Antiques, Bath, Avon.
No. 74 Antiques and Collectables, Bristol, Avon.
Tilly Manor Antiques, West Harptree, Avon.
Brindleys, Heath and Reach, Beds.
Cobblers Hall Antiques, Toddington, Beds.
Sykes Antiques, Christopher, Woburn, Beds.
Old School Antiques, The, Dorney, Berks.
Old Malthouse, The, Hungerford, Berks.
Cavendish Fine Arts - Janet Middlemiss, Windsor and Eton, Berks.
Compton Gallery, The, Windsor and Eton, Berks.
Baroq Antiques, Little Brickhill, Bucks.
Cossa Antiques, Gabor, Cambridge, Cambs.
Cottage Antiques, Cambridge, Cambs.
Abbey Antiques, Ramsey, Cambs.
Sydney House Antiques, Wansford, Cambs.
Wansford Antiques and Oriental Pottery, Wansford, Cambs.
Cheyne's, Altrincham, Cheshire.
Eureka Antiques and Interiors, Bowdon, Cheshire.
Honeypot Antiques, Cheadle, Cheshire.
Aldersey Hall Ltd, Chester, Cheshire.
Antique Shop, The, Chester, Cheshire.
Davidson Antiques, Neil, Chester, Cheshire.
Made of Honour, Chester, Cheshire.
Watergate Antiques, Chester, Cheshire.
Sweetbriar Gallery, Helsby, Cheshire.
Lostock Antiques, Lostock Gralam, Cheshire.
Mulberry Bush, The, Marple Bridge, Cheshire.
Jane's Fine Arts, Poynton, Cheshire.
Imperial Antiques, Stockport, Cheshire.
Zippy Antiques, Stockport, Cheshire.
Charlton Fine Art and Porcelain, E. and N.R., Marton, Cleveland.
Endeavour Antiques, Saltburn, Cleveland.
Tamar Gallery (Antiques and Fine Art), Launceston, Cornwall.
Antiques, Marazion, Cornwall.
St. George's Antiques, Perranporth, Cornwall.
Ages Ago Antiques, St. Agnes, Cornwall.
Clock Tower Antiques, Tregony, Cornwall.
Bennett, Alan, Truro, Cornwall.
Victoria Park Antiques, Caldbeck, Cumbria.
Saint Nicholas Galleries Ltd. (Antiques and Jewellery), Carlisle, Cumbria.
Souvenir Antiques, Carlisle, Cumbria.
Blakemore - Dower House Antiques, Brian, Kendal, Cumbria.
Kendal Studios Antiques, Kendal, Cumbria.
Adamson, Alexander, Kirkby Lonsdale, Cumbria.
Netherley Cottage Antiques, Milburn, Cumbria.

SPECIALIST DEALERS

Corney House Antiques, Penrith, Cumbria.
Westfield Antiques, Baslow, Derbys.
Riverside Antiques, Bideford, Devon.
Thomas and James Antiques, Bovey Tracey, Devon.
Old Antique Shop, The, Budleigh Salterton, Devon.
Thorn, David J., Budleigh Salterton, Devon.
Payton Antiques, Mary, Chagford, Devon.
Old Brass Kettle, The, Moretonhampstead, Devon.
Gainsborough House Antiques, Sidmouth, Devon.
Lantern Shop, The, Sidmouth, Devon.
Andrade, Philip, South Brent, Devon.
Charterhouse Antiques, Teignmouth, Devon.
Allnutt Antiques, Topsham, Devon.
Boscombe Antiques, Bournemouth, Dorset.
Dunton Antiques, Richard, Bournemouth, Dorset.
Galerie Antiques, Broadstone, Dorset.
Heygate Browne Antiques, Sherborne, Dorset.
Reference Works, Swanage, Dorset.
West Borough Antiques, Fine Art, Wimborne Minster, Dorset.
Domino Antiques, Barling Magna, Essex.
Hudes, Eric, Braintree, Essex.
Partner and Puxon, Colchester, Essex.
Bush House, Corringham, Essex.
Argyll House Antiques, Felsted, Essex.
Pugh's Porcelains, Layer de la Haye, Essex.
Castle Antiques, Leigh-on-Sea, Essex.
Wrenn Antiques, Richard, Leigh-on-Sea, Essex.
Morris, Pearl, Loughton, Essex.
Bush Antiques, Saffron Walden, Essex.
Barton House Antiques, Stanford-le-Hope, Essex.
Stuart House Antiques, Chipping Campden, Glos.
Swan Antiques, Chipping Campden, Glos.
Gray Antiques, Jay, Cirencester, Glos.
Chandlers Antiques, Moreton-in-Marsh, Glos.
Nielsen, Mrs M.K., Moreton-in-Marsh, Glos.
Acorn Antiques, Stow-on-the-Wold, Glos.
Brand Antiques, Colin, Stow-on-the-Wold, Glos.
Martin House Antiques, Stow-on-the-Wold, Glos.
Dolphin Antiques, Tetbury, Glos.
Lindsay, Muriel, Winchcombe, Glos.
Bell Passage Antiques, Wotton-under-Edge, Glos.
Close Antiques, Alresford, Hants.
Goss and Crested China Centre, Horndean, Hants.
Kaye of Lyndhurst, Lita, Lyndhurst, Hants.
Davies Antiques, Barbara, Ringwood, Hants.
Gazelles Art Deco Interiors, Southampton, Hants.
Lane Antiques, Stockbridge, Hants.
Court Antiques, Broadway, Herefs and Worcs.
Wolf Antiques Ltd, H. and B., Droitwich, Herefs and Worcs.
Stables Antiques, Ombersley, Herefs and Worcs.
Bygones by the Cathedral, Worcester, Herefs and Worcs.
Bygones (Worcester), Worcester, Herefs and Worcs.
Edwards Antiques, John, Worcester, Herefs and Worcs.
Lees and Sons, M., Worcester, Herefs and Worcs.
Tran Antiques, Long, Worcester, Herefs and Worcs.
Worcester Antiques Centre, Worcester, Herefs and Worcs.
Barlow Antiques, Anne, Letchmore Heath, Herts.
Dolphin Antiques, St. Albans, Herts.
Crested China Co, The, Driffield, Humbs North.
Houghton Hall Antiques, Market Weighton, Humbs North.
Tilings Antiques, Brasted, Kent.
Warner (Antiques) Ltd, W.W., Brasted, Kent.
Den of Antiquity, The, Hythe, Kent.
Amherst Antiques, Riverhead, Kent.
Kent Cottage Antiques, Rolvenden, Kent.
Beaubush House Antiques, Sandgate, Kent.
Delf Stream Gallery, Sandwich, Kent.
Chandlers Antiques, Sevenoaks, Kent.
Porcelain Collector, The, Shoreham, Kent.
Steppes Hill Farm Antiques, Stockbury, Kent.
Annexe Antiques, Tunbridge Wells, Kent.
Pantiles Spa Antiques, Tunbridge Wells, Kent.
Wood, Alan, Tunbridge Wells, Kent.
Mistral Galleries, Westerham, Kent.
Old Corner House Antiques, Wittersham, Kent.
Bunn, Roy W., Barnoldswick, Lancs.
Park Galleries Antiques, Fine Art and Decor, Bolton, Lancs.
Falik, Mrs S., Burnley, Lancs.
Cottage Antiques, Darwen, Lancs.
Clare's Antiques and Auction Galleries, Garstang, Lancs.
Village Antiques, Manchester, Lancs.
Ivanhoe Antiques, Ashby-de-la-Zouch, Leics.
Montague Antiques, Leicester, Leics.
Ashley House Antiques, Measham, Leics.
Gallery Antiques, Oakham, Leics.
Old House Gallery, The, Oakham, Leics.
Roberts, T.J., Uppingham, Leics.
Paddock Antiques, Woodhouse Eaves, Leics.
Staines Antiques, Horncastle, Lincs.
Strait Antiques, The, Lincoln, Lincs.
Lindum Antiques, Tattershall, Lincs.
Underwoodhall Antiques, Woodhall Spa, Lincs.
Victoria Cottage Antiques, West Kirby, Merseyside.
Ivy House Antiques, Acle, Norfolk.
Allport-Lomax, Liz, Coltishall, Norfolk.
Bradbury Antiques, Roger, Coltishall, Norfolk.
Neal Cabinet Antiques, Isabel, Coltishall, Norfolk.
Robinson, Peter, Heacham, Norfolk.
Scott Antiques, Richard, Holt, Norfolk.
Turner, Malcolm, Norwich, Norfolk.
Dorothy's Antiques, Sheringham, Norfolk.
Pratt and Son, Leo, South Walsham, Norfolk.
Brooke, T.C.S., Wroxham, Norfolk.
Jackson Antiques, Peter, Brackley, Northants.
Nicholas, R. and M., Towcester, Northants.
Felton Park Antiques, Felton, Northumbs.
Kemp Ltd, Melville, Nottingham, Notts.
Potter Antiques, David and Carole, Nottingham, Notts.
Swan Gallery, Burford, Oxon.
Walker, Burford, Zene, Burford, Oxon.
Giffengate Antiques, Dorchester-on-Thames, Oxon.
Little, Roger, Oxford, Oxon.
Number Ten/Oxford Antiques, Oxford, Oxon.
Scaramanga Antiques, Anthony, Witney, Oxon.
Woodstock Antiques, Woodstock, Oxon.
Micawber Antiques, Bridgnorth, Shrops.
Dickenson, Bill, Ironbridge, Shrops.
Whitelaw, Peter, Ironbridge, Shrops.
Teme Valley Antiques, Ludlow, Shrops.
Wain, Peter, Woore, Shrops.
Something Old, Donyatt, Somerset.
Dowlish Wake Antiques, Dowlish Wake, Somerset.
Lodge-Mortimer, A., Exton, Somerset.
Best Antiques, Ray, Ilminster, Somerset.
West End House Antiques, Ilminster, Somerset.
Cains Antiques, Littleton, Somerset.
Micklem Antiques, Thorne St. Margaret, Somerset.
Zwan Antiques, Timberscombe, Somerset.
Betley Court Gallery, Betley, Staffs.
Chapman Antiques, Sylvia, Leek, Staffs.
Winter, Eveline, Rugeley, Staffs.
Five Towns Antiques, Stoke-on-Trent, Staffs.
Potteries Antique Centre, The, Stoke-on-Trent, Staffs.
Weston Antique Gallery, Weston, Staffs.
Sutcliffe, Gordon, Hadleigh, Suffolk.
Baker, J. and J., Lavenham, Suffolk.
Motts of Lavenham, Lavenham, Suffolk.
Read, John, Martlesham, Suffolk.
Gibbins Antiques, David, Woodbridge, Suffolk.
Red House Antiques, Yoxford, Suffolk.
Churt Curiosity Shop, Churt, Surrey.
Decodream, Coulsdon, Surrey.
Burton and Rod Johnston, Tom, Dorking, Surrey.
Court Gallery, The, East Molesey, Surrey.
Church Street Antiques, Godalming, Surrey.
Heath Antiques, Reigate, Surrey.
Becker, Susan, Walton-on-Thames, Surrey.
Not Just Silver, Weybridge, Surrey.
Barclay Antiques, Bexhill-on-Sea, Sussex East.
Camelot Antiques, Boreham Street, Sussex East.
Circus Antiques, Brighton, Sussex East.
Sussex Commemorative Ware Centre, The, Brighton, Sussex East.
Woolman Antiques, L., Brighton, Sussex East.
Yellow Lantern Antiques Ltd, Brighton, Sussex East.
Stewart Gallery, Eastbourne, Sussex East.
Southdown Antiques, Lewes, Sussex East.
Russell, Leonard, Newhaven, Sussex East.
Jupiter Antiques, Rottingdean, Sussex East.
Curiosity Antiques, Rye, Sussex East.
Gasson, Herbert Gordon, Rye, Sussex East.
Steyne House Antiques, Seaford, Sussex East.
Golding, Pat, Arundel, Sussex West.

SPECIALIST DEALERS

Foord-Brown Antiques, David, Cuckfield, Sussex West.
Hockley Antiques, William, Petworth, Sussex West.
Godden Chinaman, Geoffrey, Worthing, Sussex West.
Godden of Worthing Ltd, Worthing, Sussex West.
High St. Antiques, Alcester, Warks.
Riman Antiques, Philip, Harbury, Warks.
Marsh, Jasper, Henley-in-Arden, Warks.
Paull Antiques, Janice, Kenilworth, Warks.
Bow Cottage Antiques, Stratford-upon-Avon, Warks.
Burman Antiques, Stratford-upon-Avon, Warks.
Lions Den, Stratford-upon-Avon, Warks.
Rich Designs, Stratford-upon-Avon, Warks.
Pendeford House Antiques, Wolverhampton, West Mids.
Tatters Decorative Antiques, Wolverhampton, West Mids.
Harp Antiques, Bradford-on-Avon, Wilts.
Moxhams Antiques, Bradford-on-Avon, Wilts.
Manners Antiques, Mary, Gt. Cheverell, Wilts.
Antiques - Rene Nicholls, Malmesbury, Wilts.
Amos Antiques, Joan, Salisbury, Wilts.
Fellowes, Edward, Warminster, Wilts.
Heirloom and Howard Ltd, West Yatton, Wilts.
Bow Antiques, Easingwold, Yorks North.
Daffern Antiques, John, Harrogate, Yorks North.
Love, David, Harrogate, Yorks North.
Shaw Bros, Harrogate, Yorks North.
York Cottage Antiques, Helmsley, Yorks North.
Milnthorpe, H.I., Settle, Yorks North.
Nanbooks, Settle, Yorks North.
Well Cottage Antiques, Settle, Yorks North.
Caedmon House, Whitby, Yorks North.
Bennion, Peter, Halifax, Yorks West.
Hewitt Art Deco Originals, Muir, Halifax, Yorks West.
Hillside Antiques, Halifax, Yorks West.
Berry Antiques, Peter, Huddersfield, Yorks West.
Grange Antiques, St. Peter Port, Guernsey, C.I
Drury Antiques, Anne, Vale, Guernsey, C. I.
Dunluce Antiques, Bushmills, Co. Antrim, N. Ireland.
Half-Door Antique Store, The, Forkhill, Co. Armagh, N.Ireland.
Old Cross Antiques, Greyabbey, Co. Down, N. Ireland.
Downshire House Antiques, Newry, Co. Down, N. Ireland.
Young Antiques, Denis, Aberfeldy, Scotland.
Steeple Antiques, Ceres, Scotland.
Collessie Antiques, Collessie, Scotland.
Black Ltd, Laurance, Edinburgh, Scotland.
Present Bygones, Edinburgh, Scotland.
Scottish Gallery, The, Edinburgh, Scotland.
Worthington's Antiques, Edinburgh, Scotland.
Young Antiques, Edinburgh, Scotland.
Wright Antiques, Tim, Glasgow, Scotland.
Strathspey Gallery, Grantown-on-Spey, Scotland.
Elm House Antiques, Haddington, Scotland.
Fine Design, Haddington, Scotland.
Miles Antiques, Kinross, Scotland.
Harper-James, Montrose, Scotland.
Newburgh Antiques, Newburgh, Scotland.
Pathbrae Antiques, Newton Stewart, Scotland.
Thurso Antiques, Thurso, Scotland.
Waverley Antiques, Upper Largo, Scotland.
Old Tyme Antiques, Ruthin, Clwyd, Wales.
Howards of Aberystwyth, Aberystwyth, Dyfed, Wales.
Manor House Antiques, Fishguard, Dyfed, Wales.
Clareston Antiques, Tenby, Dyfed, Wales.
West Wales Antiques, Murton, West Glam., Wales.
Castle Antiques, Usk, Gwent, Wales.
Gibbs Antiques and Decorative Arts, Paul, Conway, Gwynedd, Wales.
Hebbards of Hay, Hay-on-Wye, Powys, Wales.
Watkins, Islwyn, Knighton, Powys, Wales.

Prints (See Maps)

Rugs (See Carpets)

Russian Art

Soviet Carpet and Art Centre, London, NW2.
Asprey Ltd, Maurice, London, SW1.
Iconastas, London, SW1.
Mazure and Co. Ltd, I.J., London, SW1.
Andipa Icon Gallery, Maria, London, SW3.

Century Gallery, London, SW3.
Asprey plc, London, W1.
Bentley & Co Ltd, London, W1.
Ermitage Ltd, London, W1.
Harrington Gallery, David, London, W1.
Miles Gallery, Roy, London, W1.
Wartski Ltd, London, W1.
Temple Gallery, London, W11.
Mark Gallery, The, London, W2.

Scientific Instruments

Gridley, Gordon, London, N1.
Finchley Fine Art Galleries, London, N12.
Bobinet Ltd, London, NW8.
Burness Antiques and Scientific Instruments, Victor, London, SE1.
Laurie Antiques, Peter, London, SE10.
Relcy Antiques, London, SE10.
Reubens, London, SE23.
Vintage Cameras Ltd, London, SE26.
Philip and Sons Ltd, Trevor, London, SW1.
Wynter Ltd. Arts and Sciences, Harriet, London, SW10.
Maude Tools, Richard, London, SW15.
Weston , David, London, SW3.
Gould, Gillian, London, W1.
Delehar, Peter, London, W1.
Mayflower Antiques, London, W11.
Tociapski, Igor, London, W11.
Von Pflugh Antiques, Johnny, London, W11.
Barometer Fair, London, WC1.
Middleton Ltd, Arthur, London, WC2.
Barometer Shop, The, Bristol, Avon.
Grimes Militaria, Chris, Bristol, Avon.
Sykes Antiques, Christopher, Woburn, Beds.
Cremyll Antiques, Cremyll, Cornwall.
Read Antique Sciences, Mike, St. Ives, Cornwall.
Jones Antiques, Alan, Plymouth, Devon.
Branksome Antiques, Branksome, Dorset.
Toll House, Sturminster Newton, Dorset.
Nautical Antique Centre, The, Weymouth, Dorset.
Mayflower Antiques, Harwich, Essex.
Chart House, The, Shenfield, Essex.
Wessex Medical Antiques, Portsmouth, Hants.
Barometer Shop, Leominster, Herefs and Worcs.
Padgetts Antiques, Photographic and Scientific, Hornsea, Humbs North.
Sim, Michael, Chislehurst, Kent.
Hadlow Antiques, Tunbridge Wells, Kent.
Hansord and Son, David J., Lincoln, Lincs.
Chimes, The, Reepham, Norfolk.
Turret House, Wymondham, Norfolk.
House (Mitre Antiques), Bernard G., Wells, Somerset.
Marney, Patrick, Long Melford, Suffolk.
Arnold, Roy, Needham Market, Suffolk.
Meeks & Co, F., Birmingham, West Mids.
Relic Antiques at Brillscote Farm, Malmesbury, Wilts.
Principia Arts and Sciences, Marlborough, Wilts.
Rock Angus Antiques, Portaferry, Co. Down, N. Ireland.
Quadrant Antiques, Edinburgh, Scotland.

Sculpture

Haskell, Miriam, London, N1.
Tadema Gallery, London, N1.
Underhill Gallery, Leigh, London, N1.
Centaur Gallery, London, N6.
Miller Fine Arts, Duncan R., London, NW3.
Wolseley Fine Arts plc, London, SE5.
Belgrave Gallery, London, SW1.
Chaucer Fine Arts, London, SW1.
Hazlitt, Gooden and Fox Ltd, London, SW1.
Seago, London, SW1.
Van Vredenburgh Ltd, Edric, London, SW1.
Clark Ltd, Jonathan, London, SW10.
Wykeham Galleries, The, London, SW13.
Few, Ted, London, SW17.
Mathon Gallery, London, SW3.
Tulissio De Beaumont, London, SW6.
Agnew's, London, W1.
Browse and Darby Ltd, London, W1.

SPECIALIST DEALERS

Cazalet Ltd, Lumley, London, W1.
Christie, J., London, W1.
Colnaghi & Co Ltd, P. and D., London, W1.
D'Offay, Anthony, London, W1.
Editions Graphiques Gallery, London, W1.
Eskenazi Ltd, London, W1.
Fine Art Society plc, The, London, W1.
Hotz Fine Art Ltd, Dennis, London, W1.
Sladmore Gallery, The, London, W1.
Stoppenbach and Delestre Ltd, London, W1.
van Beers Oriental Art, Jan, London, W1.
Wood Gallery, The Christopher, London, W1.
Curá Antiques, London, W11.
Milne and Moller, London, W11.
Philp, London, W11.
Stanton, Louis, London, W11.
Bonham, Murray Feely Fine Art, John, London, W2.
Whitford and Hughes, London, W2.
Coats, Dick, London, W4.
Hilton, Simon, Dunmow, Essex.
Quatrefoil, Fordingbridge, Hants.
Mathon Gallery, Mathon, Herefs and Worcs.
Farnborough (Kent) Antiques, Farnborough, Kent.
London House Antiques, Westerham, Kent.
Cox Antiques, Robin, Stamford, Lincs.
Neill Gallery, Southport, Merseyside.
Lukies, Pearse, Aylsham, Norfolk.
Brett and Sons Ltd, Arthur, Norwich, Norfolk.
Keene Gallery, The Barry M., Henley-on-Thames, Oxon.
Bruton Gallery, Bruton, Somerset.
Pitminster Studio, Pitminster, Somerset.
Equus Art Gallery, Newmarket, Suffolk.
Hunt Galleries, John, Brightling, Sussex East.
Armstrong-Davis Gallery, Arundel, Sussex West.
Humphry Antiques, Petworth, Sussex West.
Apollo Antiques Ltd, Warwick, Warks.
Morley Antiques, Patrick and Gillian, Warwick, Warks.
Calton Gallery, Edinburgh, Scotland.
Billcliffe Fine Art, The Roger, Glasgow, Scotland.

Shipping Goods and Period Furniture for the Trade

Skeel Antique Warehouse, Keith, London, N1.
Crispin Antiques, Ian, London, NW1.
Regent Antiques, London, NW1.
Dade, Clifford and Roger, London, SW17.
Fredericks and Son, J.A., London, W1.
Mankowitz, Daniel, London, W2.
Bristol Trade Antiques, Bristol, Avon.
Tavistock Antiques, St. Neots, Cambs.
Gay's (Hazel Grove) Antiques Ltd, Hazel Grove, Cheshire.
Edwards Antique Exports, Brian, Lower Kinnerton, Cheshire.
Evans, Stewart, Malpas, Cheshire.
Jennings Antiques, Paul, Angarrack, Cornwall.
Antique Exporters U.K, Brailsford, Derbys.
Mounter, G., Dulford, Devon.
McBains of Exeter, Exeter, Devon.
Sextons, Kentisbeare, Devon.
Dunton Antiques, Richard, Bournemouth, Dorset.
Bolton, Richard, Netherbury, Dorset.
Wiffen's Antiques, Parkstone, Dorset.
Toll House, Sturminster Newton, Dorset.
Patterson Antiques, Jo, Crook, Durham.
Ramsey Antiques, Alan, Darlington, Durham.
Jobson's, Joan, Coggeshall, Essex.
Stone Hall Antiques, Matching Green, Essex.
Barton House Antiques, Stanford-le-Hope, Essex.
Regent Antiques, Painswick, Glos.
Breakspeare Antiques, Tetbury, Glos.
Thompson Antiques formerly Ships and Sealing Wax, Winchester, Hants.
Mole/Antique Exports, Geoffrey, Hull, Humbs North.
Streetwalker Antiques Warehouse, Barton-on-Humber, Humbs South.
Charles International Antiques, Maidstone, Kent.
Sutton Valence Antiques, Maidstone, Kent.
Times Past, Sheerness, Kent.
Sutton Valence Antiques, Sutton Valence, Kent.
Curiosity Shop, Bolton, Lancs.

Brun Lea Antiques (J. Waite Ltd), Burnley, Lancs.
West Lancs. Antiques, Burscough, Lancs.
Castle Antiques, Clitheroe, Lancs.
Antique Shop, The, Edenfield, Lancs.
Brown Antiques, P.J., Haslingden, Lancs.
O'Brien and Son Antiques, R. J., Hollinwood, Lancs.
Butterworth (Horwich), Alan, Horwich, Lancs.
Exports, G.G., Middleton Village, Lancs.
Tyson's Antiques, Morecambe, Lancs.
Robinson Antiques, John, Wigan, Lancs.
M.C. Trading Co, The, Horncastle, Lincs.
Seaview Antiques, Horncastle, Lincs.
Kirton Antiques, Kirton, Lincs.
Brewer, Michael, Lincoln, Lincs.
Dring, C. and K.E., Lincoln, Lincs.
Trade Antiques, Long Sutton, Lincs.
Crowson, G.H., Skegness, Lincs.
Bridge Antiques, Sutton Bridge, Lincs.
Old Barn Antiques Warehouse, Sutton Bridge, Lincs.
Halsall Hall Ltd, Liverpool, Merseyside.
Kensington Tower Antiques Ltd, Liverpool, Merseyside.
Swainbanks Ltd, Liverpool, Merseyside.
Theta Gallery, Liverpool, Merseyside.
Molloy's Furnishers Ltd, Southport, Merseyside.
Sutcliffe Antiques, Tony and Anne, Southport, Merseyside.
Phelps Antiques, Twickenham, Middx.
Hart and John Giles, Sheila, Aylsham, Norfolk.
Lukies, Pearse, Aylsham, Norfolk.
Bates and Sons, Eric, Coltishall, Norfolk.
Old Coach House, Long Stratton, Norfolk.
Bates and Sons, Eric, North Walsham, Norfolk.
Madeira, V. and C., Flore, Northants.
Thompson, R.E., Long Buckby, Northants.
Roe Antiques, John, Thrapston, Northants.
Perkins Antiques, Bryan, Wellingborough, Northants.
Miller Antiques, James, Wooler, Northumbs.
Baker, T., Langford, Notts.
Antiques Warehouse, Mansfield, Notts.
Fair Deal Antiques, Mansfield, Notts.
Newark Antique Warehouse, Newark, Notts.
M.G.R. Exports, Bruton, Somerset.
Pennard House, East Pennard, Somerset.
Dyte Antiques, T.M., Highbridge, Somerset.
Treasure Chest, The, Highbridge, Somerset.
Keyford Antiques, Rode, Somerset.
Giddings, J.C., Wiveliscombe, Somerset.
Mowe, C. and J., Coton Clanford, Staffs.
Cordelia and Perdy's Antique Junk Shop, Lichfield, Staffs.
Armson's of Yoxall Antiques, Yoxall, Staffs.
Goodbreys, Framlingham, Suffolk.
Abbott Antiques, A., Ipswich, Suffolk.
Antique Furniture Warehouse, Woodbridge, Suffolk.
Antics, Cobham, Surrey.
Ashton's Antiques, Brighton, Sussex East.
Attic Antiques, Brighton, Sussex East.
Rodney Arthur Classics, Brighton, Sussex East.
Woolman Antiques, L., Brighton, Sussex East.
Williams - Antique Anglo Am Warehouse, Lloyd, Eastbourne, Sussex East.
Abbey Antiques, Hastings, Sussex East.
Atkinson Antiques, Keith, East Grinstead, Sussex West.
Powell (Hove) Ltd, J., Portslade, Sussex West.
Smith Antiques, Peter, Sunderland, Tyne and Wear.
Renaissance Antiques, Tynemouth, Tyne and Wear.
Venables, Jeremy, Kineton, Warks.
Harrison Wholesale Exports, Tim, Stratford-upon-Avon, Warks.
Milton Antiques, Coventry, West Mids.
Magpie House, Hockley Heath, West Mids.
L.P. Furniture (Mids) Ltd, Pelsall, West Mids.
Grannies Attic Antiques, Smethwick, West Mids.
Wilkins Antiques, Brett, Wednesbury, West Mids.
Wakeman and Taylor Antiques, Wolverhampton, West Mids.
Harley Antiques, Christian Malford, Wilts.
Sambourne House Antiques, Minety, Wilts.
Welch, K. and A., Warminster, Wilts.
Kendal-Greene, R.B., Harrogate, Yorks North.
Maw Antiques, Matthew, Malton, Yorks North.
Trade Antiques - D.D. White, Manfield, Yorks North.
Ogleby, B., Thirsk, Yorks North.
Tomlinson (Antiques) Ltd. and Period Furniture Ltd, Raymond, Tockwith, Yorks North.

SPECIALIST DEALERS

Appleyard Ltd, Roger, Rotherham, Yorks South.
Turnor Antiques, Philip, Rotherham, Yorks South.
Dronfield Antiques, Sheffield, Yorks South.
Gilbert and Sons, Sheffield, Yorks South.
Salt Antiques, N.P. and A., Sheffield, Yorks South.
North Bridge Antiques, Halifax, Yorks West.
Haworth Antiques, Haworth, Yorks West.
Finlay Antiques, K.W., Ciliau Aeron, Dyfed, Wales.
Times Past Antiques, Auchterarder, Scotland.
Imrie Antiques, Bridge of Earn, Scotland.
Livingstone, Neil, Dundee, Scotland.
Duff Antiques, George, Edinburgh, Scotland.
Georgian Antiques, Edinburgh, Scotland.
Quadrant Antiques, Edinburgh, Scotland.
Galleries de Fresnes, Galston, Scotland.
Narducci Antiques, Largs, Scotland.
Heritage Antiques, Paisley, Scotland.
Deuchar and Son, A.S., Perth, Scotland.
Narducci Antiques, Saltcoats, Scotland.
Lloyd, Michael, Henllan, Dyfed, Wales.
Douglas, W.H., Cardiff, South Glam., Wales.
Hulbert (Antiques and Firearms), Anne and Colin, Swansea, West Glam., Wales.

Silver and Jewellery

Rankin Coin Co. Ltd, George, London, E2.
Harris (Jewellery) Ltd, Jonathan, London, EC1.
Hirsh Ltd, London, EC1.
Joseph and Pearce Ltd, London, EC1.
McKay, R.I., London, EC1.
Ullmann Ltd, A.R., London, EC1.
Nanwani and Co, London, EC3.
Searle and Co Ltd, London, EC3.
Graham Gallery, The, London, N1.
Hart, Rosemary, London, N1.
Hatcher, Sherry, London, N1.
Heather Antiques, London, N1.
Inheritance, London, N1.
Laurie (Antiques) Ltd, John, London, N1.
Lotinga - Dog Box/Cat Box, Heather, London, N1.
Oosthuizen, Jacqueline, London, N1.
Little Curiosity Shop, The, London, N21.
Delieb Antiques, London, NW11.
Corner Cupboard, The, London, NW2.
Osborn Baker Gallery, London, NW3.
Silver Belle, London, NW8.
Wellington Gallery, London, NW8.
Whitworth and O'Donnell Ltd, London, SE13.
Vale Stamps and Antiques, London, SE3.
Village Time, London, SE7.
Asprey Ltd, Maurice, London, SW1.
Bloom and Son (Knightsbridge), N., London, SW1.
Bourdon-Smith Ltd, J.H., London, SW1.
Cornucopia, London, SW1.
Davis (Works of Art) Ltd, Kenneth, London, SW1.
Franklin, N. and I., London, SW1.
Inglis, Brand, London, SW1.
Kojis Antique Jewellery, London, SW1.
Longmire Ltd (Three Royal Warrants), London, SW1.
Sattin Ltd, Gerald, London, SW1.
Spink and Son Ltd, London, SW1.
Steel, Jeremy and Guy, London, SW1.
Brook Antiques, Beverley, London, SW13.
Stefani Antiques, London, SW19.
Boodle and Dunthorne Ltd, London, SW3.
Hardy and Co, James, London, SW3.
Jones, Annabel, London, SW3.
Leslie, Stanley, London, SW3.
McKenna and Co, London, SW3.
Merola, London, SW3.
Oosthuizen, Jacqueline, London, SW3.
Schell, Christine, London, SW3.
Harris, Nicholas, London, SW6.
Levene Ltd, M.P., London, SW7.
Page, A. and H., London, SW7.
A.D.C. Heritage Ltd, London, W1.
Antrobus Ltd, Philip, London, W1.
Armour-Winston Ltd, London, W1.
Asprey plc, London, W1.
Bennett, Paul, London, W1.
Bentley & Co Ltd, London, W1.
Bloom Fine Jewellery, Anne, London, W1.
Bloom & Son (Antiques) Ltd, N., London, W1.
Bond Street Silver Galleries, London, W1.
Bruford and Heming Ltd, London, W1.
Bull (Antiques) Ltd, John, London, W1.
Carrington and Co. Ltd, London, W1.
Christie, J., London, W1.
Collingwood & Company Ltd, London, W1.
Cronan Ltd, Sandra, London, W1.
Davies Ltd, A. B., London, W1.
Demas, London, W1.
Douch, A., London, W1.
Editions Graphiques Gallery, London, W1.
Edmonds Ltd, D.H., London, W1.
Ermitage Ltd, London, W1.
Flowerdew at Trianon, Liliane, London, W1.
Garrard & Co. Ltd (The Crown Jewellers), London, W1.
Graus Antiques, London, W1.
Grays Mews, London, W1.
Griffin Antiques Ltd, Simon, London, W1.
Hadleigh Jewellers, London, W1.
Hancocks and Co, London, W1.
Harris and Son (London) Ltd, S.H., London, W1.
Harvey and Gore, London, W1.
Hennell of Bond Street Ltd. Founded 1736 (incorporating Frazer and Haws (1868) and E. Lloyd Lawrence (1830)), London, W1.
Holmes Ltd, London, W1.
How of Edinburgh, London, W1.
Jaffa (Antiques) Ltd, John, London, W1.
Johnson Walker & Tolhurst Ltd, London, W1.
Lady Newborough, The, London, W1.
Lavender (Antiques) Ltd, D.S., London, W1.
M. and L. Silver Co Ltd, London, W1.
Marks Antiques Ltd, London, W1.
Massada Antiques, London, W1.
Milne Ltd, Nigel, London, W1.
Moira, London, W1.
Newborough, The Lady, London, W1.
Ogden Ltd, Richard, London, W1.
Phillips Ltd, S.J., London, W1.
Richards and Sons, David, London, W1.
Rose - Source of the Unusual, Michael, London, W1.
Tessiers Ltd, London, W1.
Wartski Ltd, London, W1.
Young and Stephen Ltd, London, W1.
Britannia Export Antiques, London, W11.
Bull (Antiques) Ltd, John, London, W11.
Freeman, J., London, W11.
Lampard and Son Ltd, S., London, W11.
Portobello Antique Store, London, W11.
Schredds of Portobello, London, W11.
Stouts Antiques Market, London, W11.
Zebrak, London, W11.
Albion Art (UK) Ltd, London, W2.
Craven Gallery, London, W2.
Mansell, William C., London, W2.
McAleer, M., London, W2.
Cooke Antiques Ltd, Mary, London, W8.
Deutsch Antiques, H. and W., London, W8.
Green's Antique Galleries, London, W8.
Jay Antiques and Objets d'art, Melvyn, London, W8.
Jesse, John, London, W8.
Jones, Howard, London, W8.
Lev (Antiques) Ltd, London, W8.
Sinai Antiques Ltd, London, W8.
Nortonbury Antiques, London, WC1.
Shrubsole Ltd, S.J., London, WC1.
Kettle Ltd, Thomas, London, WC2.
London Silver Vaults, The, London, WC2.
Pearl Cross Ltd, London, WC2.
Perovetz Ltd, H., London, WC2.
Silver Mouse Trap, The, London, WC2.
Abbey Galleries, Bath, Avon.
Bladud House Antiques, Bath, Avon.
Dickinson, D. and B., Bath, Avon.
Mallory and Son Ltd, E.P., Bath, Avon.
Grey-Harris and Co, Bristol, Avon.
Kemps, Bristol, Avon.
Mall Jewellers, The, Bristol, Avon.
Beach Antiques, Clevedon, Avon.
Brindleys, Heath and Reach, Beds.

SPECIALIST DEALERS

Styles Silver, Hungerford, Berks.
Turks Head Antiques, Windsor and Eton, Berks.
Elsworth - Beaconsfield Ltd, June, Beaconsfield, Bucks.
Collectors' Corner, Waddesdon, Bucks.
Buckies, Cambridge, Cambs.
Pembroke Antiques, Cambridge, Cambs.
Peter John, St. Neots, Cambs.
Attic Gallery, Wisbech, Cambs.
Massey and Son, D.J., Alderley Edge, Cheshire.
Cheyne's, Altrincham, Cheshire.
Honeypot Antiques, Cheadle, Cheshire.
Boodle and Dunthorne Ltd, Chester, Cheshire.
Grosvenor Antiques of Chester, Chester, Cheshire.
Kayes of Chester, Chester, Cheshire.
Lowe and Sons, Chester, Cheshire.
Walsh Ltd, Bernard, Chester, Cheshire.
Watergate Antiques, Chester, Cheshire.
Bolton Antiques, Paula, Macclesfield, Cheshire.
Massey and Son, D.J., Macclesfield, Cheshire.
Imperial Antiques, Stockport, Cheshire.
Baker and Sons, A., Warrington, Cheshire.
Endeavour Antiques, Saltburn, Cleveland.
Humphrys Antiques, Brian, Penzance, Cornwall.
Little Jem's, Penzance, Cornwall.
Bennett, Alan, Truro, Cornwall.
Saint Nicholas Galleries Ltd. (Antiques and Jewellery), Carlisle, Cumbria.
Silver Thimble, The, Kendal, Cumbria.
Arcade Antiques and Jewellery, Penrith, Cumbria.
Pollock Antiques, Jane, Penrith, Cumbria.
Elizabeth and Son, Ulverston, Cumbria.
Clock House, The, Chapel-en-le-Frith, Derbys.
Parkhouse Antiques and Jewellery, Mark, Barnstaple, Devon.
Coward Fine Silver, Timothy, Braunton, Devon.
Thorn, David J., Budleigh Salterton, Devon.
Bruford and Son Ltd, Wm., Exeter, Devon.
Gold and Silver Exchange, Exeter, Devon.
Mortimer, Brian, Exeter, Devon.
Nathan Antiques, John, Exeter, Devon.
Boase and Vaughan Antiques and Jewellery, Exmouth, Devon.
Barrymore and Co, J., Honiton, Devon.
Otter Antiques, Honiton, Devon.
Old Treasures, Newton Abbot, Devon.
Charterhouse Antiques, Teignmouth, Devon.
Extence Antiques, Teignmouth, Devon.
Allnutt Antiques, Topsham, Devon.
Gold Shop, The, Torquay, Devon.
Bogan House Antiques, Totnes, Devon.
Beaminster Antiques, Beaminster, Dorset.
Mussenden and Son Antiques, Jewellery and Silver, G.B., Bournemouth, Dorset.
Payne and Son Ltd, Geo. A., Bournemouth, Dorset.
Porter, R.E., Bournemouth, Dorset.
Portique, Bournemouth, Dorset.
Shippey's of Boscombe, Bournemouth, Dorset.
Stebbing, Peter, Bournemouth, Dorset.
Batten's Jewellers, Bridport, Dorset.
D. J. Jewellery, Parkstone, Dorset.
Greystoke Antiques, Sherborne, Dorset.
Georgian Gems Antique Jewellers, Swanage, Dorset.
Heirlooms (Antique Jewellers), Wareham, Dorset.
Finnegan (Jeweller), Robin, Darlington, Durham.
Cannon Antiques, Elizabeth, Colchester, Essex.
Grahams of Colchester, Colchester, Essex.
Streamer Antiques, J., Leigh-on-Sea, Essex.
Wrenn Antiques, Richard, Leigh-on-Sea, Essex.
Abacus Antiques, Maldon, Essex.
Gostick Hall Antiques, Newport, Essex.
Greens of Montpellier, Cheltenham, Glos.
Martin and Co. Ltd, Cheltenham, Glos.
Scott-Cooper Ltd, Cheltenham, Glos.
Swan Antiques, Chipping Campden, Glos.
Bull and Son (Cirencester) Ltd, Walter, Cirencester, Glos.
Cirencester Antiques Centre, Cirencester, Glos.
Taylor Antiques, Rankine, Cirencester, Glos.
Waterloo Antiques, Cirencester, Glos.
Farr, Gloucester, Glos.
Wright, Mick and Fanny, Minchinhampton, Glos.
Bryden, D., Stow-on-the-Wold, Glos.
Olive Antiques, Alverstoke, Hants.

Squirrel Collectors Centre, Basingstoke, Hants.
Burnham-Slipper Antiques, Jane, Botley, Hants.
Porter and Son, A.W., Hartley Wintney, Hants.
Papworth, Barry, Lymington, Hants.
Leslie's, Portsmouth, Hants.
Campbell, Meg, Southampton, Hants.
Leslie Antiques, R.K., Southampton, Hants.
Parkhouse and Wyatt Ltd, Southampton, Hants.
Manley Antique Jewellery, Pamela, Titchfield, Hants.
Ewart, Gavina, Broadway, Herefs and Worcs.
Howards of Broadway, Broadway, Herefs and Worcs.
Magpie Jewellers and Antiques, Evesham, Herefs and Worcs.
Warings of Hereford Antiques, Hereford, Herefs and Worcs.
B.B.M. Jewellery and Antiques, Kidderminster, Herefs and Worcs.
Lower House Fine Antiques, Winyates Green, Herefs and Worcs.
Bygones by the Cathedral, Worcester, Herefs and Worcs.
Bygones (Worcester), Worcester, Herefs and Worcs.
Abbey Antiques and Fine Art, Hemel Hempstead, Herts.
Bexfield Antiques, Hitchin, Herts.
Forget-me-Knot Antiques, St. Albans, Herts.
Wharton, Stuart, St. Albans, Herts.
Berry Antiques, Lesley, Flamborough, Humbs North.
Bell Antiques, J. and H., Castletown, I. of Man.
Allom and Co. Ltd, P.G., Ramsey, I. of Man.
Shotter, Collectors Centre, Keith, Shanklin, I.of Wight.
Horton's, Beckenham, Kent.
Baker, R. J., Canterbury, Kent.
Peacock Antiques, Chilham, Kent.
Amherst Antiques, Riverhead, Kent.
Hythe Galleries, Sandwich, Kent.
Steppes Hill Farm Antiques, Stockbury, Kent.
Glassdrumman Antiques, Tunbridge Wells, Kent.
Pantiles Spa Antiques, Tunbridge Wells, Kent.
Russell Antiques, Patricia, Tunbridge Wells, Kent.
Strawsons Antiques, Tunbridge Wells, Kent.
Smith Antiques, Andrew, West Malling, Kent.
Brittons Jewellers and Antiques, Accrington, Lancs.
Coin and Jewellery Shop, The, Accrington, Lancs.
Kenworthys Ltd, Ashton-under-Lyne, Lancs.
Ancient and Modern, Blackburn, Lancs.
Edwards Group, Charles, Blackburn, Lancs.
Mitchell's (Lock Antiques), Blackburn, Lancs.
Arundel Coins Ltd, Blackpool, Lancs.
Leigh Coins, Antiques and Jewellery, Leigh, Lancs.
Snuff Box, Lytham St. Annes, Lancs.
Boodle and Dunthorne Ltd, Manchester, Lancs.
Cathedral Jewellers, Manchester, Lancs.
St. James Antiques, Manchester, Lancs.
Brittons Jewellers and Antiques, Nelson, Lancs.
Howell Jeweller, Charles, Oldham, Lancs.
Simpson and Sons Jewellers (Oldham)Ltd, H.C., Oldham, Lancs.
Keystone Antiques, Coalville, Leics.
Churchgate Antiques, Empingham, Leics.
Corry's, Leicester, Leics.
Letty's Antiques, Leicester, Leics.
Gallery Antiques, Oakham, Leics.
That Little Shop, Boston, Lincs.
Hunt Jewellers, Stanley, Gainsborough, Lincs.
Pilgrims Antique Centre, Gainsborough, Lincs.
Van Hefflin, Mr, Gainsborough, Lincs.
Wilkinson's, Grantham, Lincs.
Pullen Jeweller, Richard, Lincoln, Lincs.
Rowletts of Lincoln, Lincoln, Lincs.
Usher and Son Ltd, James, Lincoln, Lincs.
Crowson, G.H., Skegness, Lincs.
Wilkinson's, Sleaford, Lincs.
Spilsby Antiques, Spilsby, Lincs.
Dawson of Stamford, Stamford, Lincs.
St. Mary's Galleries, Stamford, Lincs.
Rosenberg, C., Heswall, Merseyside.
Clock Shop, The, Hoylake, Merseyside.
Boodle and Dunthorne Ltd, Liverpool, Merseyside.
Edward's Jewellers, Liverpool, Merseyside.
Stefani Antiques, Liverpool, Merseyside.
Walne, H.S., Southport, Merseyside.
Weldons Jewellers and Antiques, Southport, Merseyside.
Bond Street Antiques (inc. Jas. J. Briggs Est. 1820), Cromer, Norfolk.
Market Place Antiques, Fakenham, Norfolk.

SPECIALIST DEALERS

Barry's Antiques, Gt. Yarmouth, Norfolk.
Folkes Antiques and Jewellers, Gt. Yarmouth, Norfolk.
Gold and Silver Exchange, Gt. Yarmouth, Norfolk.
Howkins, Peter, Gt. Yarmouth, Norfolk.
Wheatleys, Gt. Yarmouth, Norfolk.
Clayton Jewellery, Tim, King's Lynn, Norfolk.
Albrow and Sons, Norwich, Norfolk.
Dennett Coins, Clive, Norwich, Norfolk.
Levine Silver Specialist, Leona, Norwich, Norfolk.
Maddermarket Antiques, Norwich, Norfolk.
Sebley, Oswald, Norwich, Norfolk.
Tillett, James and Ann, Norwich, Norfolk.
Tillett & Co, Thomas, Norwich, Norfolk.
Denis, Rose, Sheringham, Norfolk.
Parriss, Sheringham, Norfolk.
Jones Jeweller, Michael, Northampton, Northants.
Boaden Antiques, Arthur, Hexham, Northumbs.
Kemp Ltd, Melville, Nottingham, Notts.
Howards of Burford, Burford, Oxon.
Barclay Antiques, Headington, Oxon.
Thames Gallery, Henley-on-Thames, Oxon.
Davis Ltd, Reginald, Oxford, Oxon.
Payne and Son (Goldsmiths) Ltd, Oxford, Oxon.
MGJ Antiques, Wallingford, Oxon.
English Heritage, Bridgnorth, Shrops.
Teme Valley Antiques, Ludlow, Shrops.
Cruck House Antiques, Much Wenlock, Shrops.
Hutton Antiques, Shrewsbury, Shrops.
Little Gem, The, Shrewsbury, Shrops.
Manser and Son Ltd, F.C., Shrewsbury, Shrops.
Castle Antiques, Burnham-on-Sea, Somerset.
Abbots House, Glastonbury, Somerset.
Zwan Antiques, Timberscombe, Somerset.
Heart of England Antiques, Haunton, Staffs.
Steele, W.G., Stoke-on-Trent, Staffs.
Aldeburgh Galleries, Aldeburgh, Suffolk.
Winston Mac (Silversmith), Bury St. Edmunds, Suffolk.
Agnus, Clare, Suffolk.
Abbott Antiques, A., Ipswich, Suffolk.
Cordell Antiques, Sonia, Ipswich, Suffolk.
Croydon and Sons Ltd, Ipswich, Suffolk.
Antiques, Lavenham, Suffolk.
Collins, Noel, Dorking, Surrey.
Collins, T. M., Dorking, Surrey.
Hebeco, Dorking, Surrey.
Hollander Ltd, E., Dorking, Surrey.
Watson FGA NAG, Pauline, Dorking, Surrey.
Cry for the Moon, Godalming, Surrey.
Bijoux Jewellers, Guildford, Surrey.
Glydon and Guess Ltd, Kingston-upon-Thames, Surrey.
Horton's, Richmond, Surrey.
Lion Antiques, Richmond, Surrey.
Spring Park Jewellers, Shirley, Surrey.
Warrender and Co, S., Sutton, Surrey.
Church House Antiques, Weybridge, Surrey.
Not Just Silver, Weybridge, Surrey.
Diamond and Son, Harry, Brighton, Sussex East.
Doyle Antiques, James, Brighton, Sussex East.
Edmonds Ltd, D.H., Brighton, Sussex East.
Fitchett Antiques, Alan, Brighton, Sussex East.
Goble, Paul, Brighton, Sussex East.
Gold and Silversmiths of Hove, The, Brighton, Sussex East.
Hall Ltd, Douglas, Brighton, Sussex East.
Hallmarks, Brighton, Sussex East.
House of Antiques, The, Brighton, Sussex East.
Kingsbury Antiques, Brighton, Sussex East.
Mason, Harry, Brighton, Sussex East.
Miller Antiques, H., Brighton, Sussex East.
Resners', Brighton, Sussex East.
Shop of the Yellow Frog, Brighton, Sussex East.
Simmons, S.L., Brighton, Sussex East.
Zebrak at Barnes Jewellers, Brighton, Sussex East.
Bruford and Son Ltd, Wm., Eastbourne, Sussex East.
Trade Wind, Rottingdean, Sussex East.
Rye Antiques, Rye, Sussex East.
Aarquebus Antiques, St. Leonards-on-Sea, Sussex East.
Lasseters, Arundel, Sussex West.
Hancock Antiques, Peter, Chichester, Sussex West.
Streeter and Daughter, Ernest, Petworth, Sussex West.
Westbourne Antiques, Westbourne, Sussex West.
Law Antiques, Rathbone, Worthing, Sussex West.
Sovereign Antiques, Gateshead, Tyne and Wear.

Davidson's The Jewellers Ltd, Newcastle-upon-Tyne, Tyne and Wear.
Intercoin, Newcastle-upon-Tyne, Tyne and Wear.
Owen's Jewellers, Newcastle-upon-Tyne, Tyne and Wear.
Spicker Jewellers, Newcastle-upon-Tyne, Tyne and Wear.
Bateman, Jean A., Stratford-upon-Avon, Warks.
Howards Jewellers, Stratford-upon-Avon, Warks.
Bray Ltd, H.H., Warwick, Warks.
Lane Antiques, Russell, Warwick, Warks.
Payne Antiques, Martin, Warwick, Warks.
Westgate Antiques, Warwick, Warks.
Clark Antiques, Peter, Birmingham, West Mids.
Collectors Shop, The, Birmingham, West Mids.
Fellows, Maurice, Birmingham, West Mids.
Johnson and Sons, Rex, Birmingham, West Mids.
Johnson and Sons, Rex, Birmingham, West Mids.
Nathan and Co. (Birmingham) Ltd, Birmingham, West Mids.
Piccadilly Jewellers, Birmingham, West Mids.
Smithsonia, Birmingham, West Mids.
Hardwick Antiques, Streetly, West Mids.
Parry Ltd, H. and R.L., Sutton Coldfield, West Mids.
Nicholls Jewellers and Antiques, Walsall, West Mids.
Cross Keys Jewellers, Devizes, Wilts.
Cross Keys Jewellers, Marlborough, Wilts.
Country Antiques, Boroughbridge, Yorks North.
Mason & Son, D., Harrogate, Yorks North.
Ogden of Harrogate Ltd, Harrogate, Yorks North.
Shaw Bros, Harrogate, Yorks North.
Warner, Christopher, Harrogate, Yorks North.
Milnthorpe and Daughters Antique Shop, Mary, Settle, Yorks North.
Cattle, Barbara, York, Yorks North.
Himsworth, Robert M., York, Yorks North.
Mason Jewellers Ltd, John, Rotherham, Yorks South.
Pot-Pourri, Sheffield, Yorks South.
Fillans (Antiques) - Geoff Neary Ltd., Huddersfield, Yorks West.
Burrows and Raper, Ilkley, Yorks West.
Shaw and Co, Jack, Ilkley, Yorks West.
Keigheys of Keighley, Keighley, Yorks West.
Aladdin's Cave, Leeds, Yorks West.
Coins International and Antiques International, Leeds, Yorks West.
Goldsmith, William, Leeds, Yorks West.
Sinclair's Antique Gallery, Belfast, N. Ireland.
Dunluce Antiques, Bushmills, Co. Antrim, N. Ireland.
Bolt Antiques, Brian R., Portballintrae, Co. Antrim, N.Ireland.
Old Cross Antiques, Greyabbey, Co. Down, N. Ireland.
Priory Antiques, Greyabbey, Co. Down, N. Ireland.
Timecraft, Greyabbey, Co. Down, N.Ireland.
Cookstown Antiques, Cookstown, Co. Tyrone, N. Ireland.
McCalls (Aberdeen), Aberdeen, Scotland.
McCalls Limited, Aberdeen, Scotland.
Young Antiques & Fine Art, William, Aberdeen Scotland.
Wildman's Antiques, Dalbeattie, Scotland.
Hudson Ltd, Felix, Dunfermline, Scotland.
Bonnar, Jewellers, Joseph, Edinburgh, Scotland.
Cabbies Antiques, Edinburgh, Scotland.
Goodwin's Antiques Ltd, Edinburgh, Scotland.
Montresor, Edinburgh, Scotland.
Royal Mile Curios, Edinburgh, Scotland.
Scottish Gallery, The, Edinburgh, Scotland.
Whyte, John, Edinburgh, Scotland.
West End Antiques, Elgin, Scotland.
Fairlie Antique Shop, Fairlie, Scotland.
Dene Hard Antiques, Garelochhead, Scotland.
Forrest and Co (Jewellers) Ltd, James, Glasgow, Scotland.
Hamilton and Co, A.D., Glasgow, Scotland.
Wright Antiques, Tim, Glasgow, Scotland.
Fine Design, Haddington, Scotland.
Kilmacolm Antiques Ltd, Kilmacolm, Scotland.
Amber Antiques, Kincardine O'Neil, Scotland.
Harthope House Antiques, Moffat, Scotland.
Harper-James, Montrose, Scotland.
Pathbrae Antiques, Newton Stewart, Scotland.
Forsyth Antiques, Perth, Scotland.
Gallery One, Perth, Scotland.
Hardie Antiques, Perth, Scotland.
Magpie, St. Andrews, Scotland.
Old St. Andrews Gallery, St. Andrews, Scotland.
Abbey Antiques, Stirling, Scotland.

Thurso Antiques, Thurso, Scotland.
Oak Chest, Llangollen, Clwyd, Wales.
Margaret's Astoria Antiques, Swansea, Mid-Glam., Wales.
Alexander Antiques, Cardiff, South Glam., Wales.
Cronin Antiques, Cardiff, South Glam., Wales.
Gold and Silver Shop, Gorseinon, West Glam., Wales.
Allan, James, Swansea, West Glam., Wales.
Elizabeth Antiques, Swansea, West Glam., Wales.
Hazel of Brecon, Brecon, Powys, Wales.
Silver Time, Brecon, Powys, Wales.
School House Antiques, Welshpool, Powys, Wales.

Sporting Items and Associated Memorabilia

Risky Business, London, NW8.
Arnold, Sean, London, W1.
World Famous Portobello Market, London, W11.
Bentley Billiards (Antique Billiard Table Specialist Company), William, Hungerford, Berks.
Warboys Antiques, Warboys, Cambs.
Yesterday Tackle and Books, Bournemouth, Dorset.
Burton Natural Craft Taxidermy, John, Ebrington, Glos.
Brett, Simon, Moreton-in-Marsh, Glos.
Tennis Bookshop, The, Ringwood, Hants.
Grant Fine Art, Droitwich, Herefs and Worcs.
Hamilton and Tucker Billiard Co. Ltd, Knebworth, Herts.
Garden House Antiques, Tenterden, Kent.
Schotten Antiques, Manfred, Burford, Oxon.
Zwan Antiques, Timberscombe, Somerset.
Fenwick Billiards, Wellington, Somerset.
Academy Billiard Antiques, West Byfleet, Surrey.
Frith Antiques, Petworth, Sussex West.
Burman Antiques, Stratford-upon-Avon, Warks.
Wigington Antiques, James, Stratford-upon-Avon, Warks.
Sports Programmes, Coventry, West Mids.
Fun Antiques, Sheffield, Yorks South.
Old St. Andrews Gallery, St. Andrews, Scotland.
Old Troon Sporting Antiques, Troon, Scotland.

Sporting Paintings and Prints

Swan Fine Art, London, N1.
Relcy Antiques, London, SE10.
Ackermann & Johnson , London, SW1.
Addison-Ross Gallery, London, SW1.
Mason Gallery, Paul, London, SW1.
O'Shea Gallery, London, SW1.
Old Maps and Prints, London, SW1.
Trove, London, SW1.
Kensington Sporting Paintings Ltd, London, SW20.
Innes Gallery, Malcolm, London, SW3.
Nevill Fine Paintings Ltd, Guy, London, SW3.
Old Church Galleries, London, SW3.
Wingfield Sporting Art, London, SW4.
King's Court Galleries, London, SW6.
Arnold, Sean, London, W1.
Burlington Gallery Ltd, London, W1.
Frost and Reed Ltd, London, W1.
Green, Richard, London, W1.
Holland and Holland Ltd, London, W1.
Lane Fine Art Ltd, London, W1.
Sabin Ltd, Frank T., London, W1.
Blackburn, Norman, London, W11.
Lacy Gallery, London, W11.
Connaught Galleries, London, W2.
Iona Antiques, London, W8.
Avon Gallery, The, Moreton-in-Marsh, Glos.
Priests Antiques, Stow-on-the-Wold, Glos.
Bracebridge Gallery, Astwood Bank, Herefs and Worcs.
Coltsfoot Gallery, Leominster, Herefs and Worcs.
Marrin and Sons, G. and D.I., Folkestone, Kent.
Leicestershire Sporting Gallery and Brown Jack Bookshop, Lubenham, Leics.
Grafton Country Pictures, Oakham, Leics.
Garner, John, Uppingham, Leics.
In the Picture (The Golf Collection), Holt, Norfolk.
Hopwell Antiques, Paul, West Haddon, Northants.
Border Sporting Gallery, Wooler, Northumbs.
Mitchell Fine Arts, Sally, Askham, Notts.
Neville Gallery, Jane, Aslockton, Notts.

Mitchell's Gallery, Sally, Tuxford, Notts.
Dickins, H.C., Bloxham, Oxon.
Marler Gallery, The Jane, Ludlow, Shrops.
Armytage, Julian, Crewkerne, Somerset.
Barrett Antiques and Prints, Philip, Taunton, Somerset.
Zwan Antiques, Timberscombe, Somerset.
Guildhall Gallery, Bury St. Edmunds, Suffolk.
Equus Art Gallery, Newmarket, Suffolk.
Newmarket Gallery, Newmarket, Suffolk.
Lion and Lamb Gallery at Biggs of Farnham, Farnham, Surrey.
Holmes Antique Maps and Prints, Julia, South Harting, Sussex West.
Lacy Gallery, Henley-in-Arden, Warks.
Burman Antiques, Stratford-upon-Avon, Warks.
Marlborough Sporting Gallery and Bookshop, Swindon, Wilts.
Shaw, Charles, Knaresborough, Yorks North.
Hayes Gallery, Paul, Auchterarder, Scotland.
Innes Gallery, Malcolm, Edinburgh, Scotland.
Strathspey Gallery, Grantown-on-Spey, Scotland.

Stamps

Franks, J.A.L., London, SW1.
Argyll Etkin Gallery, London, W1.
Michael Coins, London, W8.
Franks Ltd, J.A.L., London, WC1.
Gibbons, Stanley, London, WC2.
Bath Stamp and Coin Shop, Bath, Avon.
Corridor Stamp Shop, Bath, Avon.
Avalon Post Card and Stamp Shop, Chester, Cheshire.
Penrith Coin and Stamp Centre, Penrith, Cumbria.
Portsmouth Stamp Shop, Portsmouth, Hants.
Franca Antiques, Tunbridge Wells, Kent.
Haworth Ltd - Antique Gallery, M. and N., Manchester, Lancs.
Talent Pastimes Ltd. (Collectors Shop), Northampton, Northants.
Denver House Antiques and Collectables, Burford, Oxon.
Jeremy's (Oxford Stamp Centre), Oxford, Oxon.
Saywell Ltd. (The Oxford Stamp Shop), A.J., Oxford, Oxon.
Collectors' Gallery, Shrewsbury, Shrops.
Pastimes (Egham) Ltd, Egham, Surrey.
Lawes, David, Harrogate, Yorks North.
Edinburgh Coin Shop, Edinburgh, Scotland.
Clwyd Coins and Stamps, Rhos-on-Sea, Clwyd, Wales.
Glance Back Bookshop, Chepstow, Gwent, Wales.

Tapestries, Textiles and Needlework

Gumb, Linda, London, N1.
Textile Company, The, London, N1.
Hobson, Platon, London, NW3.
Bolour, Y. and B., London, NW5.
Lavian, Joseph, London, NW5.
Franses and Sons, Robert, London, NW8.
Gallery of Antique Costume and Textiles, London, NW8.
Franses Ltd, S., London, SW1.
Graham, Joss, London, SW1.
Heraz (David Hartwright Ltd), London, SW1.
Keshishian, London, SW1.
Mayorcas Ltd, London, SW1.
Sanaiy Carpets, London, SW1.
Smyth - Antique Textiles, Peta, London, SW1.
Rare Carpets Gallery, London, SW10.
Acanthus Art Ltd, London, SW11.
Antiques and Things, London, SW11.
Kilim Warehouse Ltd, The, London, SW12.
Garrow, Marilyn, London, SW13.
Tobias and The Angel, London, SW13.
Booth, Joanna, London, SW3.
Lloyd Antique Textiles, Gwyneth, London, SW3.
Stephenson, Robert, London, SW3.
Antique Carpets Gallery, London, SW6.
Five Five Six Antiques, London, SW6.
Greenwood, Judy, London, SW6.
Lunn Antiques, London, SW6.
Atlantic Bay Carpets, London, SW7.
Benardout and Benardout, London, W1.
John (Rare Rugs) Ltd, C., London, W1.

SPECIALIST DEALERS

Juran and Co, Alexander, London, W1.
Nels Ltd, Paul, London, W1.
Pelham Galleries, London, W1.
Vigo Carpet Gallery, London, W1.
Vigo-Sternberg Galleries, London, W1.
Wrigglesworth, Linda, London, W1.
Zadah Gallery, London, W1.
Loveless, Clive, London, W10.
Briggs Ltd, F.E.A., London, W11.
Cook, Sheila, London, W11.
Fairman (Carpets) Ltd, Jack, London, W11.
Nye, Pat, London, W11.
Old Haberdasher, The, London, W11.
Pilbrow Antiques, Eva, London, W11.
Textile Company, The, London, W11.
Burdon, Alyson, London, W14.
Charleville Gallery, London, W14.
Heskia, London, W14.
Mankowitz, Daniel, London, W2.
Coats Oriental Carpets, London, W8.
Coote Tapestries, Belinda, London, W8.
Horne, Jonathan, London, W8.
Antique Linens and Lace, Bath, Avon.
Cooper t/a Sheila Smith Antiques, Sheila, Bath, Avon.
No.12 Queen Street, Bath, Avon.
Susannah, Bath, Avon.
Hastie, Robert and Georgina, Hungerford, Berks.
Pearson Paintings Prints and Works of Art, Sebastian, Cambridge, Cambs.
Made of Honour, Chester, Cheshire.
Whitehead, Joyce and Rod, Chester, Cheshire.
Catherine and Mary Antiques, Penzance, Cornwall.
Victoria Park Antiques, Caldbeck, Cumbria.
Cothay Antiques, Maulds Meaburn, Cumbria.
Harper Antiques, Martin and Dorothy, Bakewell, Derbys.
Cooper Antiques, Eileen, Braunton, Devon.
Honiton Lace Shop, The, Honiton, Devon.
Lace Shop, The, South Molton, Devon.
Pegasus Antiques and Collectables, Bournemouth, Dorset.
Ryder, Georgina, Corfe Castle, Dorset.
Morris, Maureen, Saffron Walden, Essex.
Huntington Antiques Ltd, Stow-on-the-Wold, Glos.
Andrews, Meg, Harpenden, Herts.
Penny Farthing Antiques, South Cave, Humbs North.
Two Maids Antiques, Biddenden, Kent.
Hiscock & Hiscock Antiques, New Romney, Kent.
Lace Basket, The, Tenterden, Kent.
Farmhouse Antiques, Bolton-by-Bowland, Lancs.
Clutter, Uppingham, Leics.
Mansions, Lincoln, Lincs.
Country and Eastern, Norwich, Norfolk.
Burnett Antiques, Jean, Finedon, Northants.
Barn, The, Collingham, Notts.
Scaramanga Antiques, Anthony, Witney, Oxon.
Faded Elegance, Dulverton, Somerset.
Lace & Linen Shop, The, Glastonbury, Somerset.
Moolham Mill Antiques, Ilminster, Somerset.
Johnson's, Leek, Staffs.
Midwinter Antiques, Richard, Newcastle-under-Lyme, Staffs.
Tara's Hall, Hadleigh, Suffolk.
Antiques, Lavenham, Suffolk.
Simpson, Oswald, Long Melford, Suffolk.
Meysey-Thompson Antiques, Sarah, Woodbridge, Suffolk.
Nostalgia, Dorking, Surrey.
Heytesbury Antiques, Farnham, Surrey.
Leopard, The, Brighton, Sussex East.
Bird Antiques, John, Lewes, Sussex East.
De Montfort, Robertsbridge, Sussex East.
Curiosity Antiques, Rye, Sussex East.
Morley Antiques, Patrick and Gillian, Warwick, Warks.
Tatters Decorative Antiques, Wolverhampton, West Mids.
Hurley Antiques and Textiles, Emma, Warminster, Wilts.
Greystones Antiques, Buckden, Yorks North.
Greenwood Antiques, Simon, Burneston, Yorks North.
Bloomers, Harrogate, Yorks North.
Reece Gallery, The Gordon, Knaresborough, Yorks North.
London House Oriental Rugs and Carpets, Boston Spa, YorksWest.
Real Macoy, Keighley, Yorks West.
Lawn and Lace, Mirfield, Yorks West.
Echoes, Todmorden, Yorks West.
Another Time, Another Place, Edinburgh, Scotland.
Barrass, Paddy, Edinburgh, Scotland.
Present Bygones, Edinburgh, Scotland.
McDougall, Marjorie and Sandy, Kilbarchan, Scotland.
Townhouse Antiques, Walkerburn, Scotland.
Tortoiseshell Antiques, Henllan, Dyfed, Wales.

Tools (including Needlework and Sewing)

Old Tool Chest, The, London, N1.
Maude Tools, Richard, London, SW15.
Cooper t/a Sheila Smith Antiques, Sheila, Bath, Avon.
Norton Antiques, Beaconsfield, Bucks.
Ye Little Shoppe, Modbury, Devon.
Hudson, Thomas and Pamela, Cirencester, Glos.
Serle (Antiques and Restoration), Mark A., Lechlade, Glos.
All Our Yesterdays Rural Bygones, Holbeach, Lincs.
St. Mary's Galleries, Stamford, Lincs.
Tooltique, Norwich, Norfolk.
Burnett Antiques, Jean, Finedon, Northants.
Peppers Period Pieces, Bury St. Edmunds, Suffolk.
Arnold, Roy, Needham Market, Suffolk.
Plough, The, Milland, Sussex West.
Fishlake Antiques, Fishlake, Yorks South.
Tortoiseshell Antiques, Henllan, Dyfed, Wales.

Toys (See Dolls)

Trade Dealers (See Shipping Goods)

Treen

Halcyon Days, London, EC3.
Young Antiques, Robert, London, SW11.
Sheppee, William, London, SW14.
Halcyon Days, London, W1.
Wynyards Antiques (Lastlodge Ltd.), London, W11.
Seager Antiques Ltd, Arthur, London, W8.
Seligmann, M. and D., London, W8.
Cobblers Hall Antiques, Toddington, Beds.
Foster, A. and E., Naphill, Bucks.
Rumble Antiques, Simon and Penny, Chittering, Cambs.
Phoenix Antiques, Fordham, Cambs.
Haylett, A.P. and M.A., Outwell, Cambs.
Broadway Antiques, St. Ives, Cambs.
Shire Antiques, Newby Bridge, Cumbria.
Morchard Bishop Antiques, Morchard Bishop, Devon.
Verey, Denzil, Barnsley, Glos.
Baggott Church Street Ltd, Stow-on-the-Wold, Glos.
Huntington Antiques Ltd, Stow-on-the-Wold, Glos.
Touchwood International, Stow-on-the-Wold, Glos.
Country Homes, Tetbury, Glos.
Day Antiques, Ann and Roger, Tetbury, Glos.
Prichard Antiques, Winchcombe, Glos.
Close Antiques, Alresford, Hants.
Du Cros Antiques, J., Liss, Hants.
Millers of Chelsea Antiques Ltd, Ringwood, Hants.
Viney, Elizabeth, Stockbridge, Hants.
de Courcy-Ireland, Polly, Winchester, Hants.
Roofe Antiques, Mary, Winchester, Hants.
Fenwick and Fisher Antiques, Broadway, Herefs and Worcs.
Two Maids Antiques, Biddenden, Kent.
Swan Antiques, Cranbrook, Kent.
Annexe Antiques, Tunbridge Wells, Kent.
Webster, E.W., Bickerstaffe, Lancs.
All Our Yesterdays Rural Bygones, Holbeach, Lincs.
Audley House Antiques, Osbournby, Lincs.
St. Mary's Galleries, Stamford, Lincs.
Castle, Simon, Twickenham, Middx.
Antiques, West Haddon, Northants.
Barn, The, Collingham, Notts.
Guillemot, Aldeburgh, Suffolk.
Peppers Period Pieces, Bury St. Edmunds, Suffolk.
Agnus, Clare, Suffolk.
Cordell Antiques, Sonia, Ipswich, Suffolk.
Barclay Antiques, Bexhill-on-Sea, Sussex East.
Foord Antiques, Midhurst, Sussex West.
Moxhams Antiques, Bradford-on-Avon, Wilts.
Combe Cottage Antiques, Castle Combe, Wilts.
Dovetail Antiques, Malmesbury, Wilts.
Turner Antiques, Annmarie, Marlborough, Wilts.

SPECIALIST DEALERS

Bentley, Bill, Harrogate, Yorks North.
Traditional Interiors, Harrogate, Yorks North.
Bolt Antiques, Brian R., Portballintrae, Co. Antrim, N. Ireland.
Maclean Antiques, Llanwrda, Dyfed, Wales.
Watkins, Islwyn, Knighton, Powys, Wales.

Vintage Cars (See Carriages and Cars)

Watercolours

Royal Exchange Art Gallery, London, EC3.
Boutique Fantasque, London, N1.
Finney Antique Prints and Books, Michael, London, N1.
Helm Antiques, Linda, London, N1.
Finchley Fine Art Galleries, London, N12.
Stewart - Fine Art, Lauri, London, N2.
Totteridge Gallery, The, London, N20.
Park Galleries, London, N3.
Centaur Gallery, London, N6.
Lummis Fine Art, Sandra, London, N8.
Barkes and Barkes, London, NW1.
Hamilton Fine Arts, London, NW11.
Gunter Fine Art, London, NW2.
Newhart (Pictures) Ltd, London, NW3.
Osborn Baker Gallery, London, NW3.
Gallery Kaleidoscope, London, NW6.
Greenwich Gallery, The, London, SE10.
Beetles Ltd Watercolours and Paintings, Chris, London, SW1.
Belgrave Gallery, London, SW1.
Douwes Fine Art Ltd, London, SW1.
Gregory Gallery, Martyn, London, SW1.
James, David, London, SW1.
King Street Galleries, London, SW1.
Moreton Street Gallery, London, SW1.
Old Maps and Prints, London, SW1.
Parkin Fine Art Ltd, Michael, London, SW1.
Pawsey and Payne, London, SW1.
Polak Gallery, London, SW1.
Spink and Son Ltd, London, SW1.
Thomson - Albany Gallery, Bill, London, SW1.
Waterman Fine Art Ltd, London, SW1.
Hollywood Road Gallery, London, SW10.
Park Walk Gallery, London, SW10.
Gallery Downstairs, The, London, SW12.
Sheen Gallery, London, SW14.
S.A.G. Art Galleries, London, SW18.
Hicks Gallery, London, SW19.
Campbell Picture Frames Ltd, John, London, SW3.
Gallery Lingard, London, SW3.
Green and Stone, London, SW3.
Hoppen Ltd, Stephanie, London, SW3.
Mathon Gallery, London, SW3.
Nevill Fine Paintings Ltd, Guy, London, SW3.
Pettifer Ltd, David, London, SW3.
Senior, Mark, London, SW3.
Walker-Bagshawe, London, SW3.
Crawley and Asquith Ltd, London, SW4.
20th Century Gallery, London, SW6.
Barclay Samson Ltd, London, SW6.
Bowmoore Gallery, London, SW6.
Cooper Fine Arts Ltd, London, SW6.
Spink, John, London, SW6.
Walker Gallery, Meldrum, London, SW6.
Collino, Julie, London, SW7.
Agnew's, London, W1.
Burlington Paintings Ltd, London, W1.
Editions Graphiques Gallery, London, W1.
Fine Art Society plc, The, London, W1.
Frost and Reed Ltd, London, W1.
Leger Galleries Ltd, The, London, W1.
Maas Gallery, London, W1.
Mitchell and Son, John, London, W1.
Piccadilly Gallery, London, W1.
Rutland Gallery, London, W1.
Somerville Ltd, Stephen, London, W1.
Waterhouse and Dodd, London, W1.
Wood Gallery, The Christopher, London, W1.
Collectors' Fine Art at Rostrum, London, W11.
L'Acquaforte, London, W11.
Milne and Moller, London, W11.
Skrebowski, Justin, London, W11.
Garratt (Fine Paintings), Stephen, London, W14.
Joslin, Richard, London, W14.
Bonham, Murray Feely Fine Art, John, London, W2.
Moss Galleries - Rachel Moss, London, W4.
Ealing Gallery, London, W5.
Dare, George, London, W8.
Spero, Simon, London, W8.
Kendall, The English Watercolour Gallery, Beryl, London, W9.
Abbott and Holder, London, WC1.
D'Orsai Ltd, Sebastian, London, WC1.
Adam Gallery, Bath, Avon.
Dodge Interiors Ltd, Martin, Bath, Avon.
Trimbridge Galleries, Bath, Avon.
Alexander Gallery, Bristol, Avon.
Cross (Fine Art), David, Bristol, Avon.
Mall Gallery, The, Bristol, Avon.
Flint Galleries Ltd, Sir William Russell, Wrington, Avon.
Brindleys, Heath and Reach, Beds.
Charterhouse Gallery Ltd, Heath and Reach, Beds.
Queen Adelaide Gallery, Kempston, Beds.
Ball Antique and Fine Art, David, Leighton Buzzard, Beds.
Foye Gallery, Luton, Beds.
Knight's Gallery, Luton, Beds.
Graham Gallery, Burghfield Common, Berks.
Collectors Gallery, The, Caversham, Berks.
Alway Fine Art, Marian and John, Datchet, Berks.
Jaspers Fine Arts Ltd, Maidenhead, Berks.
Eyre and Greig Ltd, Windsor and Eton, Berks.
Grove Gallery, Windsor and Eton, Berks.
Manley, J., Windsor and Eton, Berks.
Mon Galerie, Amersham, Bucks.
Morton Harvey Antiques, Aylesbury, Bucks.
Norton Antiques, Beaconsfield, Bucks.
Images in Watercolour, Chalfont St. Giles, Bucks.
Baroq Antiques, Little Brickhill, Bucks.
Hone Watercolours, Angela, Marlow, Bucks.
Messum, David, Marlow, Bucks.
Penn Barn, Penn, Bucks.
Medina Antiquarian Maps and Prints, Winslow, Bucks.
Pearson Paintings Prints and Works of Art, Sebastian, Cambridge, Cambs.
Baron Fine Art, Chester, Cheshire.
Davidson Antiques, Neil, Chester, Cheshire.
Nicholson, Richard A., Chester, Cheshire.
St. Peters Art Gallery, Chester, Cheshire.
Brooks, Philip, Macclesfield, Cheshire.
Harper Fine Paintings, Poynton, Cheshire.
Jordan (Fine Paintings), T.B. and R., Eaglescliffe, Cleveland.
Charlton Fine Art and Porcelain, E. and N.R., Marton, Cleveland.
Varcoe, Myles, Golant, Cornwall.
Copperhouse Gallery - W. Dyer & Sons, Hayle, Cornwall.
Tamar Gallery (Antiques and Fine Art), Launceston, Cornwall.
Broad Street Gallery, Penryn, Cornwall.
Sanders Penzance Gallery and Antiques, Tony, Penzance, Cornwall.
Penandrea Gallery, Redruth, Cornwall.
St. Breock Gallery, Wadebridge, Cornwall.
Gallery, The, Penrith, Cumbria.
Ashbourne Fine Art, Ashbourne, Derbys.
Cavendish House Gallery, Ashbourne, Derbys.
Upchurch, Kenneth, Ashbourne, Derbys.
Ward, Charles H., Derby, Derbys.
Collins and Son, J., Bideford, Devon.
Medina Gallery, Bideford, Devon.
Honiton Fine Art, Honiton, Devon.
Skeaping Gallery, Lydford, Devon.
Armada Gallery, Plymouth, Devon.
A-B Gallery, Salcombe, Devon.
Lantern Shop, The, Sidmouth, Devon.
Bygone Days Antiques, Tiverton, Devon.
Pyke - Fine British Watercolours, Beverley J., Totnes, Devon.
Stour Gallery, Blandford Forum, Dorset.
Hants Gallery, Bournemouth, Dorset.
York House Gallery, Bournemouth, Dorset.
Swan Gallery, The, Sherborne, Dorset.
Baliol Gallery, The, Barnard Castle, Durham.
Domino Antiques, Barling Magna, Essex.
Brandler Galleries, Brentwood, Essex.

SPECIALIST DEALERS

Bond and Son, S., Colchester, Essex.
Iles Gallery, Richard, Colchester, Essex.
Hilton, Simon, Dunmow, Essex.
Barn Gallery, Hatfield Heath, Essex.
Meyers Gallery, Ingatestone, Essex.
Newport Gallery, Newport, Essex.
Lloyd Gallery, David, Purleigh, Essex.
Reddings Art and Antiques, Southend-on-Sea, Essex.
Galerie Lev, Woodford Green, Essex.
Upton Lodge Galleries, Avening, Glos.
Cleeve Picture Framing, Bishops Cleeve, Glos.
Priory Gallery, The, Bishops Cleeve, Glos.
Howard, David, Cheltenham, Glos.
Turtle Fine Art, Cheltenham, Glos.
School House Antiques, Chipping Campden, Glos.
Mitchell Fine Art, Robert, Cirencester, Glos.
Newman Gallery, Heather, Cranham, Glos.
Cook and Son Antiques, E.J., Gloucester, Glos.
Medcalf, Paul, Gloucester, Glos.
Bell Fine Arts, Lechlade, Glos.
Astley House - Fine Art, Moreton-in-Marsh, Glos.
Hand Prints and Watercolours Gallery, Nailsworth, Glos.
Davies Fine Paintings, John, Stow-on-the-Wold, Glos.
Fosse Gallery, Stow-on-the-Wold, Glos.
Park House Antiques, Stow-on-the-Wold, Glos.
St. Breock Gallery, Stow-on-the-Wold, Glos.
Upton Lodge Galleries, Tetbury, Glos.
Kenulf Fine Arts, Winchcombe, Glos.
Bell Passage Antiques, Wotton-under-Edge, Glos.
Beaulieu Fine Arts, Beaulieu, Hants.
Antique House, Hartley Wintney, Hants.
Morton Lee, J., Hayling Island, Hants.
Corfield Antiques Ltd, Lymington, Hants.
Perera Fine Art, Robert, Lymington, Hants.
Hoysted, Anna, Mattingley, Hants.
Petersfield Bookshop, The, Petersfield, Hants.
Plaitford House Gallery, Plaitford, Hants.
Evelyn, Hugh, Steepmarsh, Hants.
Bell Fine Art, Winchester, Hants.
Hagen, Richard, Broadway, Herefs and Worcs.
Hay Loft Gallery, Broadway, Herefs and Worcs.
Haynes Fine Art, Broadway, Herefs and Worcs.
Noott Fine Paintings, John, Broadway, Herefs and Worcs.
Brobury House Gallery, Brobury, Herefs and Worcs.
Lismore Gallery, Great Malvern, Herefs and Worcs.
Malvern Arts, Great Malvern, Herefs and Worcs.
Coltsfoot Gallery, Leominster, Herefs and Worcs.
Gandolfi House, Malvern Wells, Herefs and Worcs.
Mathon Gallery, Mathon, Herefs and Worcs.
Highway Gallery, The, Upton-upon-Severn, Herefs and Worcs.
Knights Gallery, Harpenden, Herts.
Abbey Antiques and Fine Art, Hemel Hempstead, Herts.
Countrylife Gallery, Hitchin, Herts.
McCrudden Gallery, Rickmansworth, Herts.
Starkey Galleries, James H., Beverley, Humbs North.
Galerias Segui, Cowes, I. of Wight.
Marine Gallery, The, Cowes, I. of Wight.
Vectis Fine Arts, Newchurch, I. of Wight.
Shanklin Gallery, The, Shanklin, I. of Wight.
Weald Gallery, The, Brasted, Kent.
Cranbrook Gallery, Cranbrook, Kent.
Peppitt, Judith, Harrietsham, Kent.
Kennedy Fine Arts, Hythe, Kent.
Iles, Francis, Rochester, Kent.
Langley Galleries, Rochester, Kent.
Sundridge Gallery, Sundridge, Kent.
Graham Gallery, Tunbridge Wells, Kent.
Apollo Galleries, Westerham, Kent.
Old Corner House Antiques, Wittersham, Kent.
Ethos Gallery, Clitheroe, Lancs.
King, Edward, Cowan Bridge, Lancs.
Studio Arts Gallery, Lancaster, Lancs.
Fulda Gallery Ltd, Manchester, Lancs.
Garson and Co. Ltd, Manchester, Lancs.
Barronfield Gallery, Preston, Lancs.
Smith, Hammond, Leicester, Leics.
Fine Art of Oakham, Oakham, Leics.
Old House Gallery, The, Oakham, Leics.
Lewis Fine Art, Alan, Hundleby, Lincs.
Castle Gallery, Lincoln, Lincs.
Lincoln Fine Art, Lincoln, Lincs.

Lyver & Boydell Galleries, Liverpool, Merseyside.
Neill Gallery, Southport, Merseyside.
Studio 41, Southport, Merseyside.
Hampton Hill Gallery, Hampton Hill, Middx.
Marble Hill Gallery, Twickenham, Middx.
Coach House, The, Costessey, Norfolk.
Deacon and Blyth Fine Art, Great Bircham, Norfolk.
Morton, Mrs Joan, Gt. Walsingham, Norfolk.
Haven Gallery, The, Gt. Yarmouth, Norfolk.
Crome Gallery and Frame Shop, Norwich, Norfolk.
Fairhurst Gallery, The, Norwich, Norfolk.
Mandell's Gallery, Norwich, Norfolk.
Westcliffe Gallery, The, Sheringham, Norfolk.
Gallery and Things, The, South Lopham, Norfolk.
Staithe Lodge Gallery, Swafield, Norfolk.
Coughton Galleries Ltd, Arthingworth, Northants.
Right Angle, Brackley, Northants.
Dragon Antiques, Kettering, Northants.
Savage and Son, R.S.J., Northampton, Northants.
Haydon Bridge Antiques, Haydon Bridge, Northumbs.
Haydon Gallery, Haydon Bridge, Northumbs.
Sarsby and Michael Pickering Fine Art, Roger, Newark, Notts.
Mitchell Fine Paintings, Anthony, Nottingham, Notts.
Dickins, H.C., Bloxham, Oxon.
Burford Gallery, The, Burford, Oxon.
Horseshoe Antiques and Gallery, Burford, Oxon.
Sinfield Gallery, Brian, Burford, Oxon.
Wren Gallery, Burford, Oxon.
Tuckers Country Store and Art Gallery, Deddington, Oxon.
Faringdon Gallery, Faringdon, Oxon.
Keene Gallery, The Barry M., Henley-on-Thames, Oxon.
Jackson, John, Milton-under-Wychwood, Oxon.
Thame Antique Galleries, Thame, Oxon.
Norton Galleries, Pauline, Bridgnorth, Shrops.
Gallery 6, Broseley, Shrops.
Marler Gallery, The Jane, Ludlow, Shrops.
Teme Valley Antiques, Ludlow, Shrops.
Cruck House Antiques, Much Wenlock, Shrops.
Haygate Gallery, Telford, Shrops.
Mount, The, Woore, Shrops.
Hall's Antiques, Ash Priors, Somerset.
Gallery 16, Bruton, Somerset.
Coach House Gallery, Wedmore, Somerset.
Swale, Jill and David, Wells, Somerset.
Betley Court Gallery, Betley, Staffs.
Broadway Studios, Burton-on-Trent, Staffs.
England's Gallery, Leek, Staffs.
Hood and Broomfield, Newcastle-under-Lyme, Staffs.
Midwinter Antiques, Richard, Newcastle-under-Lyme, Staffs.
Weston Antique Gallery, Weston, Staffs.
Thompson's Gallery, Aldeburgh, Suffolk.
Guildhall Gallery, Bury St. Edmunds, Suffolk.
Fortescue Gallery, The, Ipswich, Suffolk.
Gazeley Associates Fine Art, John, Ipswich, Suffolk.
Baker, J. and J., Lavenham, Suffolk.
Mangate Gallery, Laxfield, Suffolk.
Equus Art Gallery, Newmarket, Suffolk.
Peasenhall Art and Antiques Gallery, Peasenhall, Suffolk.
Carter Gallery, Simon, Woodbridge, Suffolk.
Falcon Gallery, The, Wortham, Suffolk.
Red House Antiques, Yoxford, Suffolk.
Cobham Galleries, Cobham, Surrey.
Rubenstein Fine Art, Barbara, Cranleigh, Surrey.
Court Gallery, The, East Molesey, Surrey.
Pastimes (Egham) Ltd, Egham, Surrey.
Asplund Fine Art, Jenny, Esher, Surrey.
Glencorse Antiques, Kingston-upon-Thames, Surrey.
Limpsfield Watercolours, Limpsfield, Surrey.
Bourne Gallery Ltd, Reigate, Surrey.
Goslett Gallery, Roland, Richmond, Surrey.
Lawson Antiques, F. and T., Richmond, Surrey.
Marryat, Richmond, Surrey.
Palmer Galleries, Richmond, Surrey.
Cedar House Gallery, Ripley, Surrey.
Sage Antiques and Interiors, Ripley, Surrey.
Melville Watercolours, Margaret, Staines, Surrey.
Curzon Gallery, The David, Thames Ditton, Surrey.
Boathouse Gallery, Walton-on-Thames, Surrey.
Westcott Gallery, The, Westcott, Surrey.
Cross - Fine Paintings, Edward, Weybridge, Surrey.
Weybridge Antiques, Weybridge, Surrey.

SPECIALIST DEALERS

Barclay Antiques, Bexhill-on-Sea, Sussex East.
Hunt Galleries, John, Brightling, Sussex East.
Welbourne, Stephen and Sonia, Brighton, Sussex East.
Day of Eastbourne Fine Art, John, Eastbourne, Sussex East.
Premier Gallery, Eastbourne, Sussex East.
Ewhurst Gallery, Ewhurst Green, Sussex East.
Alexander, Molly, Seaford, Sussex East.
Alexander, Richard, Seaford, Sussex East.
Holmes House Antiques, Sedlescombe, Sussex East.
Barnes Gallery, Uckfield, Sussex East.
Bowlby, Nicholas, Uckfield, Sussex East.
Serendipity Antiques, Arundel, Sussex West.
Sussex Fine Art, Arundel, Sussex West.
Lannards Gallery, Billingshurst, Sussex West.
Gough Bros. Art Shop and Gallery, Bognor Regis, Sussex West.
Canon Gallery, The, Chichester, Sussex West.
Green and Stone of Chichester, Chichester, Sussex West.
Hopkins, John, Cuckfield, Sussex West.
Antique Print Shop, The, East Grinstead, Sussex West.
Botting, Susan and Robert, Felpham, Sussex West.
Hinde Fine Art, Sheila, Kirdford, Sussex West.
Krüger Smith Fine Art, Northchapel, Sussex West.
Wood Fine Art, Jeremy, Petworth, Sussex West.
Mulberry House Galleries, Pulborough, Sussex West.
Penfold Gallery and Antiques, Steyning, Sussex West.
Wilsons Antiques, Worthing, Sussex West.
Harrison Fine Antiques, Anna, Gosforth, Tyne and Wear.
MacDonald Fine Art, Gosforth, Tyne and Wear.
Osborne Art and Antiques, Jesmond, Tyne and Wear.
Dean Gallery, The, Newcastle-upon-Tyne, Tyne and Wear.
Warner Fine Art, Newcastle-upon-Tyne, Tyne and Wear.
Sport and Country Gallery, Bulkington, Warks.
Arden Gallery, Henley-in-Arden, Warks.
Chadwick Gallery, The, Henley-in-Arden, Warks.
Colmore Galleries Ltd, Henley-in-Arden, Warks.
Lacy Gallery, Henley-in-Arden, Warks.
Allen Gallery, The, Kenilworth, Warks.
Castle Gallery, Kenilworth, Warks.
Fine-Lines (Fine Art), Shipston-on-Stour, Warks.
Loquens Gallery, The, Stratford-upon-Avon, Warks.
Woodland Fine Art, Alvechurch, West Mids.
Widdas Fine Paintings, Roger, Bentley Heath, West Mids.
Ashleigh House Antiques, Birmingham, West Mids.
Edgbaston Gallery, Birmingham, West Mids.
Graves Gallery, The, Birmingham, West Mids.
Halcyon Gallery, The, Birmingham, West Mids.
Hubbard Antiques, John, Birmingham, West Mids.
Windmill Gallery, The, Birmingham, West Mids.
Withers - Antiques, Robert, Halesowen, West Mids.
Oldswinford Gallery, Stourbridge, West Mids.
Driffold Gallery, Sutton Coldfield, West Mids.
Broad Street Gallery, Wolverhampton, West Mids.
Lacewing Fine Art Gallery, Marlborough, Wilts.
St. John Street Gallery, Salisbury, Wilts.
Marlborough Sporting Gallery and Bookshop, Swindon, Wilts.
Fellowes, Edward, Warminster, Wilts.
Houghton Antiques, Peter, Warminster, Wilts.
Brook, Antiques and Picture Gallery, Ian J., Wilton, Wilts.
Thornton Gallery, Bedale, Yorks North.
Graham Antiques, Anthony, Boroughbridge, Yorks North .
Greenwood (Fine Art), W., Burneston, Yorks North.
Garth Antiques, Harrogate, Yorks North.
McTague of Harrogate, Harrogate, Yorks North.
Walker Galleries Ltd, Harrogate, Yorks North.
Gavèls, Long Preston, Yorks North.
Talents Fine Arts Ltd, Malton, Yorks North.

Rose Fine Art and Antiques, Ripon, Yorks North.
Bennett, Richard, Thirsk, Yorks North.
Garth Antiques, Whixley, Yorks North.
Coulter Galleries, York, Yorks North.
Fulwood Antiques and The Basement Gallery, Sheffield, Yorks South.
Hibbert Bros. Ltd, Sheffield, Yorks South.
Hinson Fine Paintings, Sheffield, Yorks South.
Carrol, E., Bingley, Yorks West.
Carlton Antiques, Saltaire, Yorks West.
Titus Gallery, The, Shipley, Yorks West.
Todmorden Fine Art, Todmorden, Yorks West.
Taylor Fine Arts, Robin, Wakefield, Yorks West.
Mitchell-Hill Gallery, Wetherby, Yorks West.
Channel Islands Galleries Ltd, St. Peter Port, Guernsey, C. I.
Gavey, Geoffrey P., Vale, Guernsey, C. I.
St. Helier Galleries Ltd, St. Helier, Jersey, C.I.
Bell Gallery, The, Belfast, N. Ireland.
Arnold Gallery Antiques, Phyllis, Greyabbey, Co. Down, N.Ireland.
Rendezvous Gallery, The, Aberdeen, Scotland.
Waverley Gallery, The, Aberdeen, Scotland.
McEwan Gallery, The, Ballater, Scotland.
Calton Gallery, Edinburgh, Scotland.
Forrest McKay, Edinburgh, Scotland.
Innes Gallery, Malcolm, Edinburgh, Scotland.
Mathieson and Co, John, Edinburgh, Scotland.
Nelson, John O., Edinburgh, Scotland.
Shackleton, Daniel, Edinburgh, Scotland.
Young Antiques, Edinburgh, Scotland.
Billcliffe Fine Art, The Roger, Glasgow, Scotland.
Mundy Fine Art Ltd, Ewan, Glasgow, Scotland.
Mainhill Gallery, Jedburgh, Scotland.
Newburgh Antiques, Newburgh, Scotland.
George Street Gallery, The, Perth, Scotland.
St. Andrews Fine Art, St. Andrews, Scotland.
Barn Court Antiques, Narberth, Dyfed, Wales.
Manor House Fine Arts, Cardiff, South Glam., Wales.
Owen Gallery, John, Cowbridge, South Glam., Wales.
Watercolour Gallery, the, Cowbridge, South Glam., Wales.
Davies, Philip, Swansea, West Glam., Wales.
Thicke Galleries, Swansea, West Glam., Wales.
Williams, Betty, Tredunnock, Gwent, Wales.
Windsor Gallery, David, Bangor, Gwynedd, Wales.
Webb Fine Art, Michael, Bodorgan, (Anglesey) Gwynedd, Wales.
Madoc Antiques and Art Gallery, Llandudno, Gwynedd, Wales.
Corner Shop, The, Hay-on-Wye, Powys, Wales.
School House Antiques, Welshpool, Powys, Wales.

Wholesale Dealers (See Shipping Goods)

Wine Related Items

Kihl (Wine Accessories) Ltd, Richard, London, NW1.
Ashcroft, Nan S., London, NW3.
Johnson Collection, The Hugh, London, SW1.
King Antique Glass, Dominic, London, SW1.
Harbottle, Patricia, London, W11.
Butler, Robin, Bristol, Avon.
Sykes Antiques, Christopher, Woburn, Beds.
Bacchus Antiques -In the Service of Wine, Cartmel, Cumbria.
Bacchus, Douglas, I. of Man.
Willcox, Neil, Twickenham, Middx.
Bacchus Gallery, The, Petworth, Sussex West.

STOP PRESS AND AMENDMENTS

London W.11

June and Tony Stone Fine Antique Boxes
Abras Gallery, 292 Westbourne Grove, Portobello Rd. Open Wed. 7-3, Sat. 8-4. SIZE: Small. STOCK: Fine antique boxes, 18th-19th C, £300-£1,000. TEL: Home - 0273 822866 or 0836 279191. FAIRS: Heritage (Sun.) and Decorative, Chelsea Harbour. VAT: Stan/Spec.

London S.W.1

Simon Dickinson Ltd.
58 Jermyn St. (Simon Dickinson and David Ker). SLAD. Open Mon.-Thurs. 10-5.30, Fri. 10-4.30. CL: Sat. SIZE: Large. STOCK: Important Old Master and Modern Master paintings. LOC: 2 mins. from Piccadilly. TEL: 071 493 0340. SER: Valuations; restorations; buys at auction. VAT: Spec.

London N.1

June and Tony Stone Fine Antique Boxes
12 Pierrepont Row, Camden Passage. Open Wed. 7-3, Sat. 8-4. SIZE: Small. STOCK: Fine antique boxes, 18th-19th C, £300-£1,000. TEL: Home - 0273 822866 or 0836 279191. FAIRS: Heritage (Sun.) and Decorative, Chelsea Harbour. VAT: Stan/Spec.

Berkshire

CAVERSHAM, Nr. Reading

Pat Howard Antiques
35 Prospect St. (Mrs. P.A. Howard and M.G. Howard). Est. 1978. Open 9.30-5. CL: Wed. SIZE: Medium. STOCK: China, glass and linen, 17th-20th C, £5-£25; furniture, 18th-19th C, £50-£100; gold and silver, 19th C, £50-£100. TEL: 0734 483744. LOC: North of Reading, over Caversham bridge. PARK: Nearby. SER: Restorations (clocks and furniture).

Cheshire

DUTTON, Nr. Warrington

R.W. Hayward
Dutton Hall Workshop, Northwich Rd. STOCK: Furniture including pine, shipping goods and woodworking tools. TEL: 0928 701354. SER: Restorations.

KNUTSFORD

The Knutsford Antique Centre
16 King St. Open Mon. to Sat. CL: Wed. p.m. SIZE: 5 dealers. STOCK: General antiques. LOC: Main street. PARK: Easy. TEL: 0565 755334.

Derbyshire

BAKEWELL

Lewis Antiques
King St. (Les Lewis). Est. 1977. Open 10-5, Sun. 11-5. CL: Wed. and Thurs. SIZE: Small. STOCK: Town and country furniture, clocks, barometers, pictures and porcelain, 18th-19th C, £50-£5,000. TEL: 0629 813141. LOC: Follow Youlgreave road from town centre. PARK: Nearby. SER: Buys at auction (as stock). VAT: Stan/Spec.

CHESTERFIELD

Times Past Antiques
13 Chatsworth Rd. Business closed.

Hampshire

BISHOPS WALTHAM, Nr. Southampton

The Victorian Country Kitchen
The Still Room, High St. (Mrs. I. Jenkinson). Est. 1973. Open 9-5.30, Wed. 9-2, Sat. 9-4. SIZE: Small. STOCK: Victoriana, £5-£250. TEL: 0489 894567; home - 0489 894893. LOC: Just off A333. PARK: Public, at rear. SER: Valuations; restorations (china); buys at auction.

Hertfordshire

BUSHEY, Nr. Watford

Bushey Antique Centre
39 High St. (Graham Lindsay). Est. 1983. Open 9.30-5.30, Sun. 10-4.30. SIZE: 30 dealers. STOCK: Furniture, 18th-20th C, £5-£500; smalls, collectables, clocks, dolls and jewellery, £5-£250; fireplaces and chimney pieces, 18th-19th C, £160-£800. TEL: 081 950 5040; home - same. LOC: Between Harrow and Watford. PARK: At rear. SER: Valuations; restorations (woodwork and furniture); buys at auction (furniture and fires). VAT: Spec.

Kent

SANDGATE, Nr. Folkstone

Hole in the Wall Antiques
30b High St. (R.J. and S.A. Finch). Est. 1978. Open 9.30-6, Sun. 11-5. SIZE: Medium. STOCK: Furniture, 1800-1920, £150-£3,500; silver plate, 1860-1930, £5-£250; writing items, £25-£400. TEL: 0303 240725. LOC: No shop front, down a side entrance. PARK: Easy. SER: Restorations (furniture, French polishing).

TUNBRIDGE WELLS

Harlequin Antiques
109 St. John's Rd. (Clare Anvar). Est. 1983. Open Sat., other days by appointment. SIZE: Small. STOCK: Islamic and Oriental items, 17th-19th C, £50-£5,000; furniture, 19th C, £500-£5,000; curios and decorative items including typewriters, medical and scientific, corkscrews and chess sets, 18th-19th C, £100-£2,000. TEL: 0892 543414; home - same. LOC: A26 Tonbridge road. PARK: Easy. SER: Valuations; restorations (china, terracotta, papier mâché). FAIRS: IACF, Ardingly.

Lancashire
MANCHESTER

Premiere Antiques
373 Bury New Rd., Prestwich. (S. Harris). GADAR. STOCK: Furniture, mainly Victorian and Edwardian inlaid. TEL: 061 773 0500; fax - 061 792 0232. SER: Restorations (furniture).

Leicestershire
LEICESTER

The Rug Gallery
50 Montague Rd., Clarendon Park. (Dr. Roy Short). Est. 1987. Open Sat. 10-4 or by appointment. SIZE: Medium. STOCK: Oriental rugs and kilims, early 19th to 20th C, £100-£2,000; Swat and Afghan furniture, 18th-19th C, £50-£1,000; tribal embroidery and jewellery, 19th-20th C, £10-£1,000. TEL: 0533 700085; home - 0533 737087. LOC: From London A6, take Victoria Park Rd., to Queens Rd., then Montague Rd. PARK: Easy.

Somerset
TAUNTON

Taunton Antique Village
57 East Reach. Open Mon., Fri. and Sat. 9-5 (later by appt.). CL: Tues., Wed. and Thurs. SIZE: Large - 17 units. STOCK: China and porcelain, 19th C, £10-£3,000; furniture, 18th-19th C, £50-£2,000; watercolours and oils, 19th and early 20th C, £20-£1,500. LOC: 1 mile from Junction 25 (M5) towards town centre. PARK: Easy (30 mins.) TEL: 0823 322757. SER: Valuations; restorations (china and furniture); buys at auction (china, furniture, fireplaces). VAT: Stan/Spec.

Suffolk
STOKE BY NAYLAND, Nr. Colchester

Suffolk Antique Connection
Scotland Place. (Julia and Matthew Pike). STOCK: 17th-18th C oak and walnut. TEL: 0206 262098;

Stoke by Nayland continued
mobile - 0850 825144; fax - 0206 263339. SER: Search for home and office.

Wiltshire
MELKSHAM

King Street Curios
8 King St. (Girven, Wilson and Crittenden). Est. 1991. SIZE: Medium. STOCK: Porcelain and furniture, late 18th C. TEL: 0225 790623; home - 0249 812425. LOC: A350. PARK: Own at rear. SER: Valuations. FAIRS: Oasis, Swindon; Neeld Hall, Chippenham; Templemeads (Brunel), Bristol. VAT: Stan.

Yorkshire North
BRADLEY

Ryefield House Antiques
Ryefield House, Skipton Rd. (Mr. and Mrs. I.C. Roberts). Est. 1976. Open Mon., Thurs. and Fri. 8.30-5, other times by appointment. SIZE: Small. STOCK: Pottery and porcelain, 18th-19th C, £5-£1,500; bronzes, spelter and metalware, 19th C, £5-£500; small furniture, 19th C to Edwardian, £50-£1,500. TEL: 0535 633192; home - same. LOC: Village 2 miles from Skipton, off A629. From village centre, turn left, premises on right, lions on gateway. PARK: Easy. SER: Valuations; restorations (furniture); buys at auction (pottery and porcelain). VAT: Stan/Spec.

Yorkshire West
BRADFORD

Heaton Antiques
278 Keighley Rd. (T. Steward). Est. 1991. Open 10-5. CL: Mon. SIZE: Medium. STOCK: Furniture, silver plate and bric-a-brac, pre 1930, £10-£1,000. TEL: 0274 480630; home - 0274 635887. LOC: Near A650. PARK: Easy. SER: Valuations. FAIRS: NEC; Yorkshire Showground, Harrogate; Newark.

HUDDERSFIELD

Heritage Antiques
The above named business is no longer trading.

Services
ANTIQUE RESTORATION

Roland Haycraft
The Lamb Arcade, Wallingford, Oxon. GADAR. TEL: 0491 839622. *All aspects of antique restorations; one-off reproductions and copying. Stringed instrument maker and restorer/repairer.*

FOR A NEW OR SUBSTANTIALLY ALTERED ENTRY USE THIS FORM

Please complete and return this form; there is no charge

NAME OF SHOP ....

ADDRESS OF SHOP ....

....
full address including actual county (not postal area)

Name (or names) and initials of proprietor(s) ....
(Mr/Mrs/Miss/or title)

Previous trading address (if applicable) ....

....

State whether 'Trade Only' (Yes or No) ....

BADA (Yes or No) .... LAPADA (Yes or No) ....

Year Established .... Resident on premises (Yes or No) ....

OPENING HOURS: (One entry, e.g. '9.30—5.30' if open all day or part day. Two entries, e.g. '9.30—1.00, 2,00—5.30' if closed for lunch)

Please put 'CLOSED' and 'BY APPT.' where applicable

	Morning	Afternoon
Sunday	....	....
Monday	....	....
Tuesday	....	....
Wednesday	....	....
Thursday	....	....
Friday	....	....
Saturday	....	....

SIZE OF SHOWROOM
- Small (up to 600 sq.ft.) ....
- Medium (600 to 1,500 sq.ft.) ....
- Large (over 1,500 sq.ft.) ....

HOW TO GET TO YOUR SHOP (BUSINESS)

Brief helpful details from the nearest well-known road:

....
....
....
....

OF WHAT DOES YOUR STOCK CHIEFLY CONSIST?

(A) Please list in order of importance	(B) Approximate period or date of stock	(C) Indication of price range of stock eg £50 – £100 or £5 – £25
1. (Principal stock)		
2.		
3.		

IS PARKING *OUTSIDE* **YOUR SHOP (BUSINESS)** Easy (Yes or No) ....

TELEPHONE NUMBER: Business ....
Home ....
(only if customers can ring for appointments outside business hours)

V.A.T. scheme operated — Standard/Special/Both ....

SERVICES OFFERED:

Valuations (Yes or No) ....

Restorations (Yes or No) ....

Type of work ....

Buying specific items at auction for a commission (Yes or No) ....

Type of item ....

FAIRS:
At which fairs (if any) do you normally exhibit? ....
....
....

CERTIFICATION:
The information given above is accurate and you may publish it in the Guide.
I understand that this entry is entirely free.

Signed..

Date..

NOTES

NOTES

ENGLISH COUNTY BOUNDARIES

Map showing county boundaries of England. For county boundary details of Northern Ireland, Scotland and Wales see maps at start of relevant sections.

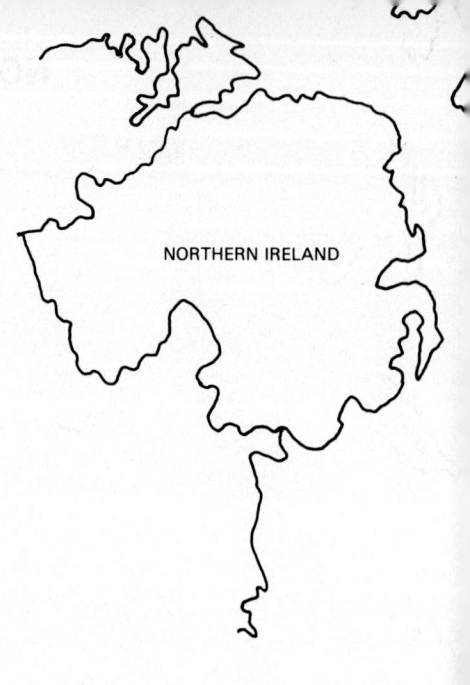

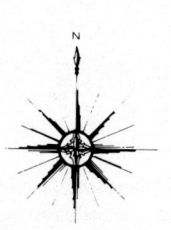

NORTHERN IRELAND

CORNWALL

DEV